175   367
       166
       167
       168 169   777
                         779
                         662
                         366
E J N Fine   178
   June 30/1908   179
        Mishawaka Ind   180
                         181
539 Spring 2/14/09 Sunday

Page 430 - Village Smithy
                    150 Ships that pass
                         in the night
May 1/1909

   Friday   646 Is of the same
                   opinion still

CYCLOPEDIA

OF

PRACTICAL QUOTATIONS

THE
CYCLOPEDIA OF
PRACTICAL
QUOTATIONS

English, Latin, and
Modern Foreign ..
Languages . . . . .

Names, Dates, and Nationality of . . .
Quoted Authors, with Copious Indexes

By J. K. HOYT

A NEW EDITION, REVISED, CORRECTED, AND ENLARGED

FUNK & WAGNALLS COMPANY
NEW YORK and LONDON

A book which hath been culled from the flowers of all books.

—GEORGE ELIOT.

They have been at a great feast of languages, and stolen the scraps.

—SHAKESPEARE.

The art of quotation requires more delicacy in the practice than those conceive who can see nothing more in a quotation than an extract.

—ISAAC DISRAELI.

PREFACE.

THIS work is the first thorough revision of the Cyclopedia of Practical Quotations issued over twelve years ago, and the labor begun five years ago has been steadily pursued, most of the time with a large corps of assistants. The plan of the work has been considerably altered. Hundreds of new quotations have been added with new headings, and it has been the aim of the compiler to bring this work down to date and to include every familiar phrase and sentence that has currency in the English language.

The concordance will be found the most complete of any ever compiled for a work of this kind, and by its assistance it will be easy to find whatever may be sought for. Even the English translations of the foreign selections are included in this index.

Shortly after the first edition was published, a letter was received asking why the line was not given, as well as the act and scene in the quotations from Shakespeare. There were several reasons why this was not done originally, but, acting on the principle that what interests one may interest many, the work was undertaken, and the labor on this alone may be understood when it is stated that there are at least two thousand quotations from that author, and that some scenes in the plays contain over 800 lines. Then there came a demand for another and obviously needed work, covering the whole volume— the verification of every quotation in the book, and a large number of talented ladies were engaged on this for many months, putting under tribute every large library in New York, and others outside. Thus it is hoped that all errors have been found and corrected, and if a few books have not been found by the compiler and his corps of assistants, it will be useless for the reader to look for them. Here and there a rare book wanted can be found in the library of the British Museum alone.

Some of the departments in the first edition were found not to be appropriate to a work of this kind, and have been omitted, while others have been transferred to the body of the work, but the proverbs and foreign quotations and mottoes have been retained, being, however, all brought into two departments— English and Foreign. Many new topical headings have been given, and the chapter of epigrams presents a collection of the best and cleanest sayings of the poet Martial taken from an expurgated edition, which fact will account for differences in the location of some of the epigrams.

The compiler begs to call particular attention to the "Guide to the Use of this Book," which will much facilitate its employment.

As the first edition of the Cyclopedia owed much of its value to the fostering care and intelligence of a woman, the compiler but performs an agreeable duty in saying that this edition has been watched with tender care and devotion from the first line to the last by Miss Kate Louise Roberts, of Newark, N. J., a lady singularly gifted with the native and acquired ability to superintend a work of this kind.

Thanking the great discriminating public for its past favorable reception of this work he commends this volume to their critical examination.

NEWARK, JAN. 1ST, 1895.   J. K. H.

Mr. Hoyt did not live to see the completion of the work which had been the object of his absorbing interest and solicitude for so many years. He passed into the other life in February, 1895.

Jan. 1st, 1896.   K. L. ROBERTS.

GUIDE TO THE USE OF THIS BOOK.

THOSE who consult the Cyclopedia of Practical Quotations will do well to notice the following explanations:

The Cyclopedia claims to be a novelty in the abundance of its matter and in that it combines the features of the arrangement of other books of the kind, namely: The quotations are grouped as accurately as possible under *subjects* or *headings*. The *authority* for each quotation is given as *fully and accurately* as possible, and there is virtually a grouping according to *authors*, since in the Biographies, after each author's name will be found the number of the pages whereon he is quoted.

The object of the book is not to treat exhaustively of any subject, but to glean whatever is useful and well known upon that subject. Not one line has been added merely to expand the book, but in a few instances quotations have been purposely retained under more than one heading where they might be of actual service.

There are some subdivisions of the book, but practically there are but two parts: the ENGLISH and the FOREIGN. Among the English quotations will be found a chapter of Proverbs, and at the end of the Foreign department a chapter of mottoes from the Latin and French. Translations of the foreign quotations are put in the English concordance, which, when properly consulted, is a sure guide to every phrase of prominence. The Foreign department is divided into Latin and the modern tongues, and is believed to be unusually rich in the verbal treasures of each language. All the foreign quotations and mottoes are included in a new concordance which is as complete as the best efforts of the compiler could make it.

As many lovers of the several poets have expressed a desire to know on which pages the quotations of their favorite poets can be found, and as in some names, such as Shakespeare, Tennyson, Byron, etc., a mere list of pages would convey no information whatever, the plan has been adopted of marking those who are largely quoted with a special sign in the index, the same as was done with Shakespeare in the first edition whose * marks 2,000 extracts. The sign for each is designated at the foot of each page of the concordance. The pages where may be found the quotations from authors not so designated will be given after the author's name in the biographical list. We feel assured that this feature will be appreciated.

A great improvement in this work over the previous edition is the tracing of every Shakespearian quotation, and all others in fact, where possible, to its line in the scene or poem from which it is taken. This involved great labor, but as it included also a verification of each quotation and the rectification of many errors, it was labor well spent. It may not, however, occur to every one that in counting the lines no two editions of Shakespeare will exactly agree, especially in plays in which prose is a dominant feature, as there are no two editions in which the length of the lines is the same. The figures given are at least approximately correct and will prove of great assistance in finding the context. The number of the line applies to the first in each quotation. The Globe Edition has been the general authority for the text. As far as possible each author's peculiarities of spelling or composition have been respected.

All the Latin quotations have been traced to the exact book and place in the author quoted from. This department would make a volume of itself equal in size and value to any other of like character, and is believed to include all the noted sayings of the classic writers in that language.

Special attention is called to the quotations under collective headings, a new feature which much simplifies the work of those seeking quotations in those subjects. They are as follows:

Animals.	Flowers.	Rivers.
Birds.	Insects.	Seasons.
Cities.	Months.	Trees.
Countries.	Occupations.	

In consulting this volume it is supposed that each reader has one of two objects: either to find a quotation applicable to some topic under consideration, or to find one of which he has not a clear remembrance and of which he desires to know the exact reading. In the first case he will be naturally assisted by the division of the book into chapters under topical headings (see the index of the headings with *cross references*). If he is writing, for instance, about life or death, love or marriage, he will naturally turn to those headings, but if he is looking for a definite quotation which he partly remembers he will turn to the index, and searching for any prominent word he will be sure to find it; or if he cannot remember the reading of the line but knows the author, a reference to the biographies and the pages where that author may be found will give him the line. Bear in mind that the italic letter in the index corresponds with the same letter in the page, thus enabling the searcher to put his finger upon it at once.

It is not to be supposed that all the beauties of every author are to be found in any book of quotations. All those that make up the current quotations of the day are supposed to be here and such others as, in the judgment of the compiler, are appropriate to the several headings. Shakespeare's name does not appear in the body of the book, the names of the plays being sufficient to indicate the author.

The book is alphabetically arranged throughout. The authors follow each other alphabetically under each heading and the quotations under each author, save in the proverbs, where the arrangement is according to alphabetical order of lines, and in the modern languages, where the quotations are grouped in the various tongues, the order being French, German, Italian, and Spanish. Everything possible has been done to facilitate search.

There are no quotations from the Bible in this volume, the editor believing that book to be amply provided for by the many works devoted entirely to it.

Table of Contents.

NOTE.—Readers who merely seek for quotations of a general character will find them best under one of the topical heads. Those in search of a special verse or line should look for it in the Concordance guided by some prominent or special word.

TOPICAL INDEX,

WITH CROSS-REFERENCES.

THE CYCLOPEDIA

OF

PRACTICAL QUOTATIONS.

A.

ABDICATION.

He was utterly without ambition [Chas. II.].
He detested business, and would sooner have
abdicated his crown than have undergone the
trouble of really directing the administration.
a.　　Macaulay—*History of England.*
(*Character of Charles II.*).
Vol. I. Ch. II.

To see her abdicate this majesty to play at
precedence with her next door neighbor.
b.　　Ruskin—*Sesame and Lilies. Of Queen's
Gardens.* P. 92. (J. B. A., '85.)

I give this heavy weight from off my head,
And this unwieldy sceptre from my hand,
The pride of kingly sway from out my heart;
With mine own tears I wash away my value,
With mine own hands I give away my crown,
With mine own tongue deny my sacred state,
With mine own breath release all duteous
　oaths.
c.　　*Richard II.* Act IV. Sc. 1. L. 204.

ABHORRENCE.

The self-same thing they will abhor
One way, and long another for.
d.　　Butler—*Hudibras.* Pt. I. Canto I.
L. 219.

I find no abhorring in my appetite.
e.　　Donne—*Devotion.*

Nature abhors the old.
f.　　Emerson—*Essays. Circles.*

The arts of pleasure in despotic courts
I spurn abhorrent.
g.　　Glover—*Leonidas.* Bk. X.

　　　　　Justly thou abhorr'st
That son, who on the quiet state of men
Such trouble brought, affecting to subdue
Rational liberty ; yet know withal,
Since thy original lapse, true liberty
Is lost.
h.　　Milton—*Paradise Lost.* Bk. XII.
L. 79.

　　　　　Boils and plagues
Plaster you o'er, that you may be abhorr'd
Further than seen.
i.　　*Coriolanus.* Act I. Sc. 4. L. 37.

* * * few things loves better
Than to abhor himself,
j.　　*Timon of Athens.* Act I. Sc. 1. L. 60.

How abhorred in my imagination it is !
k.　　*Hamlet.* Act V. Sc. 1. L. 206.

It doth abhor me now I speak the word.
l.　　*Othello.* Act IV. Sc. 2. L. 162.

* * * more abhorr'd
Than spotted livers in the sacrifice.
m.　　*Troilus and Cressida.* Act V. Sc. 3.
L. 18.

Though thou abhorr'dst in us our human
　griefs.
n.　　*Timon of Athens.* Act V. Sc. 5. L. 11.

Whom my very soul abhors.
o.　　*Two Gentlemen of Verona.* Act IV.
Sc. 3. L. 17.

* * * make the abhorrent eye
Roll back and close.
p.　　Southey—*Curse of Kehama.* VIII. 9.

　　　　　For, if the worlds
In worlds enclosed should on his senses
　burst * * *
He would abhorrent turn.
q.　　Thomson—*Seasons. Summer.* L. 313.

When it was become an abhorring even to
them that had loved it best.
r.　　Trench—*Miracles.* XXIX. 414.

ABILITY.

Men who undertake considerable things,
even in a regular way, ought to give us ground
to presume ability.

 a. BURKE—*Reflections on the Revolution in
France.*

He could raise scruples dark and nice,
And after solve 'em in a trice;
As if Divinity had catch'd
The itch, on purpose to be scratch'd.

 b. BUTLER—*Hudibras.* Pt. I. Canto I.
L. 163.

You are a devil at everything, and there is
no kind of thing in the 'versal world but what
you can turn your hand to.

 c. CERVANTES—*Don Quixote.* Pt. I.
Bk. III. Ch. XI.

The dwarf sees farther than the giant, when
he has the giant's shoulders to mount on.

 d. COLERIDGE—*The Friend.* Sect. I.
Essay VIII.

Could swell the soul to rage, or kindle soft
desire.

 e. DRYDEN—*Alexander's Feast.* L. 160.

As we advance in life, we learn the limits of
our abilities.

 f. FROUDE—*Short Studies on Great
Subjects. Education.*

Every person is responsible for all the good
within the scope of his abilities, and for no
more, and none can tell whose sphere is the
largest.

 g. GAIL HAMILTON—*Country Living and
Country Thinking. Men and Women.*

To the very last, he [Napoleon] had a kind
of idea; that, namely, of *la carrière ouverte
aux talent*—the tools to him that can handle
them.

 h. LOCKHART—*Sir Walter Scott.* London
and Westminster Review, 1838.

A Traveller at Sparta, standing long upon
one leg, said to a Lacedæmonian, "I do not
believe you can do as much." "True," said
he, "but every goose can."

 i. PLUTARCH—*Laconic Apothegms.
Remarkable Speeches of Some Obscure
Men.*

Read my little fable:
 He that runs may read.
Most can raise the flowers now,
 For all have got the seed.

 j. TENNYSON—*The Flowers.*

Who does the best his circumstance allows,
Does well, acts nobly; angels could no more.

 k. YOUNG—*Night Thoughts.* Night II.
L. 91.

ABSENCE.

Absence makes the heart grow fonder.

 l. THOMAS HAYNES BAYLY—*Isle of
Beauty.*

Wives in their husband's absences grow sub-
tler,
And daughters sometimes run off with the
butler.

 m. BYRON—*Don Juan.* Canto III. St. 22.

Where'er I roam, whatever realms to see,
My heart untravelled, fondly turns to thee;
Still to my brother turns, with ceaseless pain,
And drags at each remove a lengthening chain.

 n. GOLDSMITH—*Traveller.* L. 7.

Achilles absent, was Achilles still.

 o. HOMER—*The Iliad.* Bk. 22. L. 415.
Pope's trans.

   In the hope to meet
Shortly again, and make our absence sweet.

 p. BEN JONSON—*Underwoods.
Miscellaneous Poems, LIX.*

Ever absent, ever near;
Still I see thee, still I hear;
Yet I cannot reach thee, dear!

 q. FRANCIS KAZINCZY—*Separation.*

What shall I do with all the days and hours
 That must be counted ere I see thy face?
How shall I charm the interval that lowers
 Between this time and that sweet time of
  grace?

 r. FRANCES ANNE KEMBLE—*Absence.*

For with G. D., to be absent from the body
is sometimes (not to speak it profanely) to be
present with the Lord.

 s. CHARLES LAMB—*Oxford in the Vacation.*

Your absence of mind we have borne, till
your presence of body came to be called in
question by it.

 t. CHARLES LAMB—*Amicus Redivivus.*

Oft in the tranquil hour of night,
 When stars illume the sky,
I gaze upon each orb of light,
 And wish that thou wert by.

 u. GEORGE LINLEY—*Song.*

Thou art gone from my gaze like a beautiful
 dream,
And I seek thee in vain by the meadow and
 stream.

 v. GEORGE LINLEY—*Thou Art Gone.*

There's little pleasure in the house
When our gudeman's awa.

 w. W. J. MICKLE—*There's Nae Luck Aboot
the House.*

With what a deep devotedness of woe
I wept thy absence—o'er and o'er again
Thinking of thee, still thee, till thought grew
    pain,
And memory, like a drop that, night and
    day,
Falls cold and ceaseless, wore my heart
    away !
  a.   Moore—*Lalla Rookh.   The Veiled
               Prophet of Khorassin.*

Condemned whole years in absence to deplore,
And image charms he must behold no more.
  b.   Pope—*Eloise to Abelard.*   L. 361.

Days of absence, sad and dreary,
  Clothed in sorrow's dark array,—
Days of absence, I am weary ;
  She I love is far away.
  c.   Rousseau—*Days of Absence.*

Conspicuous by his absence.
  d.   Lord John Russell—*Quoted from
             Tacitus.   Annals,* III., 76.

All days are nights to see till I see thee,
And nights bright days when dreams do show
    thee me.
  e.   *Sonnet XLIII.*

How like a winter hath my absence been
  From thee, the pleasure of the fleeting year !
What freezings have I felt, what dark days
    seen !
What old December's bareness everywhere.
  f.   *Sonnet XCVII.*

I dote on his very absence, and I wish them
a fair departure.
  g.   *Merchant of Venice.*   Act I.   Sc. 2.
                       L. 120.

'Tis said that absence conquers love ;
  But oh ! believe it not.
I've tried, alas ! its power to prove,
  But thou art not forgot.
  h.   Frederick W. Thomas—*Absence
                    Conquers Love.*

Since you have waned from us,
  Fairest of women !
I am a darkened cage
  Songs cannot hymn in.
My songs have followed you,
  Like birds the summer ;
Ah ! bring them back to me,
  Swiftly, dear comer !
    *Seraphim,
    Her to hymn,
    Might leave their portals ;
    And at my feet learn
    The harping of mortals !*
  i.   Francis Thompson—*A Carrier Song.*

ACCIDENT.

Chapter of accidents.
  j.   Burke—*Notes for Speeches* (edition
             1852).   Vol. II.   P. 426.

Chapter of accidents.
  k.   Earl of Chesterfield—*Letter,*
               February 16, 1753.

To what happy accident is it that we owe
so unexpected a visit?
  l.   Goldsmith—*Vicar of Wakefield.*
                      Ch. XIX.

Our wanton accidents take root, and grow
To vaunt themselves God's laws.
  m.   Charles Kingsley—*Saint's Tragedy.*
                   Act II.   Sc. 4.

At first laying down, as a fact fundamental,
That nothing with God can be accidental.
  n.   Longfellow—*Christus.   The Golden
                  Legend.*   Pt. VI.

By many a happy accident.
  o.   Thomas Middleton—*No Wit, no Help,
           like a Woman's.*   Act IV.   Sc. 1.

I have shot mine arrow o'er the house
And hurt my brother.
  p.   *Hamlet.*   Act V.   Sc. 2.   L. 254.

Moving accidents by flood and field.
  q.   *Othello.*   Act 1.   Sc. 3.   L. 135.

The chapter of accidents is the longest
chapter in the book.
  r.   *Attributed to* John Wilkes *by*
        Southey—*The Doctor.*   Ch. CXVIII.

The accident of an accident.
  s.   Lord Thurlow—*Speech in reply to
                   Lord Grafton.*

ACTING (*See* Occupations).

ACTION.

Let's meet and either do or die.
  t.   Beaumont and Fletcher.—*The Island
             Princess.*   Act II.   Sc. 2.

Of every noble action the intent
Is to give worth reward, vice punishment.
  u.   Beaumont and Fletcher.
            The Captain.   Act V.   Sc. 5.

Think that day lost whose (low) descending
    Sun
Views from thy hand no noble action done.
  v.   Jacob Bobart—*In David Krieg's
             Album in British Museum.*
  See also Staniford—*Art of Reading.*

That low man seeks a little thing to do,
  Sees it and does it;
This high man, with a great thing to pursue,
  Dies ere he knows it.
  a.   ROBERT BROWNING—*A Grammarian's
                              Funeral.*

What's done we partly may compute,
But know not what's resisted.
  b.   BURNS—*Address to the Unco Guid.*

Put his shoulder to the wheel.
  c.   BURTON—*Anatomy of Melancholy.*
                  Pt. II. Sect 1. Memb. 2.

To-morrow let us do or die.
  d.   CAMPBELL—*Gertrude of Wyoming.*
                            Pt. III. St. 37.

  Our grand business undoubtedly is, not to
see what lies dimly at a distance, but to *do*
what lies clearly at hand.
  e.   CARLYLE—*Essays. Signs of the Times.*

  The best way to keep good acts in memory
is to refresh them with new.
  f.   *Attributed to* CATO *by* BACON—
                        Apothegms. No. 247.

He is at no end of his actions blest
Whose ends will make him greatest and not
  best.
  g.   GEORGE CHAPMAN—*Tragedy of Charles,
            Duke of Byron.* Act V. Sc. 1.

It is better to wear out than to rust out.
  h.   BISHOP CUMBERLAND. See Horne's
            *Sermon—On the Duty of Contending
                            for the Truth.*

  Actions of the last age are like almanacs of
the last year.
  i.   SIR JOHN DENHAM—*The Sophy.
                                A Tragedy.*

                      For strong souls
Live like fire-hearted suns; to spend their
  strength
In furthest striving action.
  j.   GEORGE ELIOT—*Spanish Gypsy.* Bk. 4.

A great mind is a good sailor, as a great
heart is.
  k.   EMERSON—*English Traits. Voyage to
                        England.* Chap. II.

  The manly part is to do with might and
main what you can do.
  l.   EMERSON—*The Conduct of Life.
                                    Wealth.*

Our acts, our angels are, or good or ill,
Our fatal shadows that walk by us still.
  m.   JOHN FLETCHER—*Upon an Honest
                        Man's Fortune.* L. 37.

A fiery chariot, borne on buoyant pinions,
Sweeps near me now! I soon shall ready be
To pierce the ether's high, unknown
  dominions,
To reach new spheres of pure activity!
  n.   GOETHE—*Faust.* Bk. 1. Sc. 1.

Do well and right, and let the world sink.
  o.   HERBERT—*Country Parson.* Ch. XXIX.

Let thy mind still be bent, still plotting, where,
And when, and how thy business may be
  done.
Slackness breeds worms; but the sure traveller,
Though he alights sometimes, still goeth on.
  p.   HERBERT—*Temple. Church Porch.*
                                    St. 57.

Attempt the end, and never stand to doubt;
Nothing's so hard but search will find it out.
  q.   HERRICK—*Seek and Find.*

A man that's fond precociously of *stirring*
Must be a spoon.
  r.   HOOD—*Morning Meditations.*

  That action which appears most conducive
to the happiness and virtue of mankind.
  s.   FRANCES HUTCHESON—*A System of
            Moral Philosophy. The General No-
            tions of Rights, and Laws Explained.*
                        Bk. II. Ch. III.

  Attack is the reaction; I never think I have
hit hard unless it rebounds.
  t.   SAM'L JOHNSON—*Boswell's Life of
                        Johnson.* 1775.

When desperate ills demand a speedy cure,
Distrust is cowardice, and prudence folly.
  u.   SAM'L JOHNSON—*Irene.* Act IV.
                                Sc. 1. L. 87.

  I have always thought the actions of men
the best interpreters of their thoughts.
  v.   LOCKE—*Human Understanding.* Bk. I.
                                    Ch. 3.

Let us then be up and doing,
  With a heart for any fate;
Still achieving, still pursuing,
  Learn to labour and to wait.
  w.   LONGFELLOW—*Psalm of Life.*

The good one, after every action, closes
His volume, and ascends with it to God.
The other keeps his dreadful day-book open
Till sunset, that we may repent; which doing,
The record of the action fades away,
And leaves a line of white across the page,
Now if my act be good, as I believe,
It cannot be recalled. It is already
Sealed up in heaven, as a good deed accom-
  plished.
The rest is yours.
  x.   LONGFELLOW—*Christus, The Golden
                        Legend.* Pt. VI.

Trust no future, howe'er pleasant !
  Let the dead past bury its dead !
Act,—act in the living present !
  Heart within and God o'erhead.
  a.   Longfellow—*Psalm of Life.*

With useless endeavour,
Forever, forever,
Is Sisyphus rolling
His stone up the mountain !
  b.   Longfellow—*The Masque of Pandora.*
             Chorus of the Eumenides.

Every man feels instinctively that all the
beautiful sentiments in the world weigh less
than a single lovely action.
  c.   Lowell—*Among my Books. Rousseau*
             and the Sentimentalists.

He nothing common did, or mean,
Upon that memorable scene.
  d.   Andrew Marvell—*A Horatian Ode.*
        Upon Cromwell's Return from Ireland.

So much one man can do,
That does both act and know.
  e.   Andrew Marvell—*A Horatian Ode.*
        Upon Cromwell's Return from Ireland.

Awake, arise, or be forever fall'n !
  f.   Milton—*Paradise Lost.*   Bk. I.
                      L. 330.

Execute their aery purposes.
  g.   Milton—*Paradise Lost.*   Book I.
                      L. 430.

          Those graceful acts,
Those thousand decencies that daily flow
From all her words and actions.
  h.   Milton—*Paradise Lost.*   Bk. VIII.
                      L. 600.

Push on,—keep moving.
  i.   Thomas Morton—*A Cure for the*
        Heartache.   Act II.   Sc. 1.

What the Puritans gave the world was not
thought, but *action.*
  j.   Wendell Phillips—*Speech. The*
        Pilgrims.   Dec. 21, 1855.

Not always actions show the man ; we find
Who does a kindness is not therefore kind.
  k.   Pope—*Moral Essays.*   Epistle I.
                      L. 109.

          But I remember now
I am in this earthly world ; where, to do
  harm,
Is often laudable ; to do good, sometime,
Accounted dangerous folly.
  l.   *Macbeth.* Act IV. Sc. 2. L. 74.

          From this moment,
The very firstlings of my heart shall be
The firstlings of my hand.   And even now,
To crown my thoughts with acts, be it
    thought and done.
  m.   *Macbeth.*   Act IV.   Sc. 1.   L. 146.

How my achievements mock me !
I will go meet them.
  n.   *Troilus and Cressida.*   Act IV.   Sc. 2.
                      L. 71.

If it were done, when 'tis done, then 'twere
  well
It were done quickly.
  o.   *Macbeth.*   Act I.   Sc. 7.   L. 1.

          In such business
Action is eloquence, and the eyes of the ignorant
More learned than the ears.
  p.   *Coriolanus.* Act III.   Sc. 2.   L. 75.

I profess not talking : only this,
Let each man do his best.
  q.   *Henry IV.*   Pt. I.   Act V.   Sc. 2.
                      L. 92.

So smile the Heavens upon this holy act
That after hours with sorrow chide us not !
  r.   *Romeo and Juliet.*   Act II.   Sc. 6.
                      L. 1.

Suit the action to the word, the word to the
action, with this special observance, that you
o'erstep not the modesty of nature.
  s.   *Hamlet.*   Act III.   Sc. 2.   L. 19.

* * * the blood more stirs
To rouse a lion, than to start a hare.
  t.   *Henry IV.*   Pt. I.   Act I.   Sc. 3.
                      L. 197.

          Things done well,
And with a care, exempt themselves from fear ;
Things done without example, in their issue
Are to be fear'd.
  u.   *Henry VIII.*   Act I.   Sc. 2.   L. 88.

          We must not stint
Our necessary actions, in the fear
To cope malicious censurers.
  v.   *Henry VIII.*   Act I.   Sc. 2.   L. 76.

Only the actions of the just
Smell sweet and blossom in the dust.
  w.   Shirley—*Death's Final Conquest.*

Heaven ne'er helps the men who will not act.
  x.   Sophocles—*Fragment 288.*

Rightness expresses of actions, what *straight-
ness* does of lines ; and there can no more be
two kinds of right action than there can be
two kinds of straight line.
  y.   Herbert Spencer—*Social Statics.*
                   Ch. XXXII.   Par. 4.

Theirs not to make reply,
Theirs not to reason why,
Theirs but to do and die.
> *a.* TENNYSON—*The Charge of the Light
> Brigade.* St. 2.

A slender acquaintance with the world must convince every man that actions, not words, are the true criterion of the attachment of friends; and that the most liberal professions of good-will are very far from being the surest marks of it.
> *b.* GEORGE WASHINGTON—*Social Maxims.
> Friendship.*

Action is transitory, a step, a blow,
The motion of a muscle—this way or that.
> *c.* WORDSWORTH—*The Borderers.* Act III.

And all may do what has by man been done.
> *d.* YOUNG—*Night Thoughts.* Night VI.
> L. 611.

ADMIRATION.

No nobler feeling than this, of admiration for one higher than himself, dwells in the breast of man. It is to this hour, and at all hours, the vivifying influence in man's life.
> *e.* CARLYLE—*Heroes and Hero Worship.*
> Lecture I.

Let others hail the rising sun:
I bow to that whose course is run.
> *f.* GARRICK—*On the Death of Mr. Pelham.*

The king himself has follow'd her
When she has walk'd before.
> *g.* GOLDSMITH—*Elegy on Mrs. Mary Blaize.*

We always love those who admire us, and we do not always love those whom we admire.
> *h.* LA ROCHEFOUCAULD—*Maxim* 305.

Few men are admired by their servants.
> *i.* MONTAIGNE—*Essays. Of Repentance.*
> Bk. III. Ch. 2.

For fools admire, but men of sense approve.
> *j.* POPE—*Essay on Criticism.* L. 391.

Season your admiration for awhile.
> *k.* *Hamlet.* Act I. Sc. 2. L. 192.

How his eyes languish! how his thoughts adore
That painted coat, which Joseph never wore!
He shows, on holidays, a sacred pin,
That touch'd the ruff, that touched Queen Bess' chin.
> *l.* YOUNG—*Love of Fame.* Satire IV.
> L. 119.

ADVENTURE.

Some bold adventurers disdain
The limits of their little reign,
And unknown regions dare descry.
> *m.* GRAY—*Ode on a Distant Prospect of
> Eton College.*

* * * and now expecting
Each hour their great adventurer, from the search
Of foreign worlds.
> *n.* MILTON—*Paradise Lost.* Bk. X.
> L. 439.

ADVERSITY.

And these vicissitudes come best in youth;
For when they happen at a riper age,
People are apt to blame the Fates, forsooth,
And wonder Providence is not more sage.
Adversity is the first path to truth:
He who hath proved war, storm or woman's rage,
Whether his winters be eighteen or eighty,
Has won the experience which is deem'd so weighty.
> *o.* BYRON—*Don Juan.* Canto XII. St. 50.

Adversity is sometimes hard upon a man; but for one man who can stand prosperity, there are a hundred that will stand adversity.
> *p.* CARLYLE—*Heroes and Hero Worship.*
> Lecture V.

Aromatic plants bestow
No spicy fragrance while they grow;
But crush'd or trodden to the ground,
Diffuse their balmy sweets around.
> *q.* GOLDSMITH—*The Captivity.* Act I.

Thou tamer of the human breast,
Whose iron scourge and tort'ring hour
The bad affright, afflict the best!
> *r.* GRAY—*Hymn to Adversity.* St. 1.

In the adversity of our best friends we often find something which does not displease us.
> *s.* LA ROCHEFOUCAULD—*Maxim* 245.

The Good are better made by Ill,
As odours crushed are sweeter still.
> *t.* SAM'L ROGERS—*Jacqueline.* St. 3.

A wretched soul, bruis'd with adversity,
We bid be quiet when we hear it cry;
But were we burthen'd with like weight of pain,
As much, or more, we should ourselves complain.
> *u.* *Comedy of Errors.* Act II. Sc. 1. L. 34.

Bold adversity
Cries out for noble York and Somerset,
To beat assailing death from his weak legions.
And whiles the honourable captain there
Drops bloody sweat from his war-wearied limbs.
> *v.* *Henry VI.* Pt. I. Act IV. Sc. 4.
> L. 14.

His overthrow heap'd happiness upon him;
For then, and not till then, he felt himself,
And found the blessedness of being little.
> *w.* *Henry VIII.* Act IV. Sc. 2. L. 64.

Sweet are the uses of adversity;
Which, like the toad, ugly and venómous,
Wears yet a precious jewel in his head.
    a.   *As You Like It.* Act II. Sc. I. L. 12.

Then know, that I have little wealth to lose;
A man I am cross'd with adversity.
    b.   *Two Gentlemen of Verona.* Act IV.
                        Sc. 1. L. 11.

ADVICE.

The worst men often give the best advice.
Our deeds are sometimes better than our
    thoughts.
    c.   BAILEY—*Festus.* Sc. *A Village Feast.*
                      Evening. L. 917.

Ah, gentle dames! it gars me greet,
To think how mony counsels sweet,
How mony lengthened, sage advices,
The husband frae the wife despises.
    d.   BURNS—*Tam o' Shanter.* L. 33.

And may you better reck the rede,
Than ever did th' adviser.
    e.   BURNS—*Epistle to a Young Friend.*

She had a good opinion of advice,
Like all who give and eke receive it gratis,
For which small thanks are still the market
    price,
Even where the article at highest rate is.
    f.   BYRON—*Don Juan.* Canto XV. St. 29.

Let no man value at a little price
A virtuous woman's counsel; her wing'd spirit
Is feather'd oftentimes with heavenly words.
    g.   GEORGE CHAPMAN—*The Gentleman*
                    Usher. Act IV. Sc. 1.

'Twas good advice, and meant,
"My son, be good."
    h.   GEORGE CRABBE—*The Learned Boy.*
                    Vol. V. Tale XXI.

For women with a mischief to their kind,
Pervert with bad advice our better mind.
    i.   DRYDEN—*Cock and Fox.* Line 555.

Know when to speake; for many times it brings
Danger to give the best advice to kings.
    j.   HERRICK—*Caution in Councell.*

We give advice, but we do not inspire conduct.
    k.   LA ROCHEFOUCAULD—*Maxim* 403.

Be niggards of advice on no pretense;
For the worst avarice is that of sense.
    l.   POPE—*Essay on Criticism.* L. 578.

             Bosom up my counsel,
You'll find it wholesome.
    m.   *Henry VIII.* Act I. Sc. 1. L. 112.

Direct not him, whose way himself will
    choose;
'Tis breath thou lack'st, and that breath wilt
    thou lose.
    n.   *Richard II.* Act II. Sc. 1. L. 29.

Here comes a man of comfort, whose advice
Hath often still'd my brawling discontent.
    o.   *Measure for Measure.* Act IV. Sc. 1.
                            L. 8.

I pray thee cease thy counsel,
Which falls into mine ears as profitless
As water in a sieve.
    p.   *Much Ado About Nothing.* Act V.
                      Sc. 1. L. 3.

When a wise man gives thee better counsel,
give me mine again.
    q.   *King Lear.* Act II. Sc. 4. L. 76.

Many receive advice, only the wise profit by it.
    r.   PUBLIUS SYRUS—*Maxim* 152.

AFFECTATION.

Affectation is an awkward and forced Imitation of what should be genuine and easy,
wanting the Beauty that accompanies what is
natural.
    s.   LOCKE—*On Education.* Sec. 66.
                       Affectation.

There Affectation, with a sickly mien,
Shows in her cheek the roses of eighteen.
    t.   POPE—*The Rape of the Lock.* Canto 4.

AFFECTION.

Affection is the broadest basis of good in life.
    u.   GEORGE ELIOT—*Daniel Deronda.*
                    Bk. V. Ch. 35.

Even children follow'd with endearing wile,
And pluck'd his gown, to share the good
    man's smile.
    v.   GOLDSMITH—*The Deserted Village.*
                      L. 183.

Dear as the light that visits these sad eyes;
Dear as the ruddy drops that warm my heart.
    w.   GRAY—*The Bard.* I. 3. L. 12.

The objects that we have known in better
days are the main props that sustain the
weight of our affections, and give us strength
to await our future lot.
    x.   WM. HAZLITT—*Table Talk. On the*
                       Past and Future.

I may not to the world impart
    The secret of its power,
But treasured in my inmost heart
    I keep my faded flower.
    y.   ELLEN C. HOWARTH—*'Tis but a Little*
                       Faded Flower.

Who hath not saved some trifling thing
  More prized than jewels rare,
A faded flower, a broken ring,
  A tress of golden hair.
a.   ELLEN C. HOWARTH—'*Tis but a Little*
                       Faded Flower.

Talk not of wasted affection, affection never
    was wasted ;
If it enrich not the heart of another, its waters,
    returning
Back to their springs, like the rain, shall fill
    them full of refreshment ;
That which the fountain sends forth returns
    again to the fountain.
b.   LONGFELLOW—*Evangeline.* Pt. II. St. 1.

Affection is a coal that must be cool'd';
Else, suffer'd, it will set the heart on fire.
c.   *Venus and Adonis.*   Line 387.

Of such affection and unbroken faith
As temper life's worst bitterness.
d.   SHELLEY—*The Cenci.* Act III. Sc. 1.

AFFLICTION.

Now let us thank th' eternal power, convinc'd
That Heaven but tries our virtue by affliction:
That oft the cloud which wraps the present
    hour,
Serves but to brighten all our future days !
e.   JOHN BROWN—*Barbarossa.*   Act V.
                             Sc. 3.

Affliction's sons are brothers in distress ;
A brother to relieve, how exquisite the bliss !
f.   BURNS—*A Winter Night.*

Affliction is enamour'd of thy parts,
And thou art wedded to calamity.
g.   *Romeo and Juliet.* Act III. Sc. 3.
                             L. 2.

       Henceforth I'll bear
Affliction till it do cry out itself,
Enough, enough, and die.
h.   *King Lear.* Act IV. Sc. 6.   L. 75.

Thou art a soul in bliss ; but I am bound
Upon a wheel of fire ; that mine own tears
Do scald like molten lead.
i.   *King Lear.* Act IV. Sc. 7. L. 46.

     Affliction is not sent in vain, young man,
From that good God, who chastens whom he
    loves.
j.   SOUTHEY—*Madoc in Wales.* III.
                             L. 176.

     The Lord gets his best soldiers out of the
highlands of affliction.
k.   SPURGEON—*Gleanings Among the*
              Sheaves. Sorrow's Discipline.

With silence only as their benediction,
    God's angels come
Where in the shadow of a great affliction,
    The soul sits dumb !
l.   WHITTIER—*To my Friend on the Death*
                         of his Sister.

Affliction is the good man's shining scene ;
Prosperity conceals his brightest ray ;
As night to stars, woe lustre gives to man.
m.   YOUNG—*Night Thoughts.*   Night IX.
                             L. 415.

AGE (OLD).

Backward, flow backward, O tide of the years !
I am so weary of toil and of tears,—
Toil without recompense, tears all in vain—
Take them and give me my childhood again !
n.   ELIZABETH AKERS ALLEN—*Rock Me*
                         to Sleep.

Weak withering age no rigid law forbids,
With frugal nectar, smooth and slow with
    balm,
The sapless habit daily to bedew,
And give the hesitating wheels of life
Gliblier to play.
o.   JOHN ARMSTRONG—*Art of Preserving*
                 Health. Bk. II. L. 484.

What is it to grow old ?
Is it to lose the glory of the form,
    The lustre of the eye ?
Is it for Beauty to forego her wreath ?
Yes ; but not this alone.
p.   MATTHEW ARNOLD—*Growing Old.*

     Men of age object too much, consult too
long, adventure too little, repent too soon,
and seldom drive business home to the full
period, but content themselves with a mediocrity of success.
q.   BACON—*Essay XLII. Of Youth and Age.*

     Old wood best to burn, old wine to drink,
old friends to trust, and old authors to read.
r.   Quoted by BACON—*Apothegm* 97.

Old age comes on apace to ravage all the
    clime.
s.   BEATTIE—*The Minstrel.* Bk. I. St. 25.

Old age doth in sharp pains abound ;
  We are belabored by the gout,
Our blindness is a dark profound,
  Our deafness each one laughs about.
Then reason's light with falling ray
  Doth but a trembling flicker cast.
Honor to age, ye children pay !
  Alas ! my fifty years are past !
t.   BERANGER—*Cinquante Ans. Translated*
                       by C. L. Betts.

To resist with success the frigidity of old age, one must combine the body, the mind, and the heart; to keep these in parallel vigor one must exercise, study and love.

a.　BONSTETTEN—*In Abel Stevens' Madame de Staël.*　Ch. XXVI.

Age shakes Athena's tower, but spares gray Marathon.

b.　BYRON—*Childe Harold.*　Canto II.
St. 88.

He has grown aged in this world of woe,
In deeds, not years, piercing the depths of life.
So that no wonder waits him.

c.　BYRON—*Childe Harold.*　Canto III.
St. 5.

Just as old age is creeping on apace,
And clouds come o'er the sunset of our day,
They kindly leave us, though not quite alone,
But in good company—the gout or stone.

d.　BYRON—*Don Juan.*　Canto III.
St. 59.

My days are in the yellow leaf;
The flowers and fruits of love are gone;
The worm, the canker, and the grief
　Are mine alone!

e.　BYRON—*On this day I complete my Thirty-sixth Year.*

Oh, for one hour of blind old Dandolo,
Th' octogenarian chief, Byzantium's conquering foe!

f.　BYRON—*Childe Harold.*　Canto IV.
St. 12.

What is the worst of woes that wait on age?
　What stamps the wrinkle deeper on the brow?
To view each loved one blotted from life's page,
　And be alone on earth as I am now.

g.　BYRON—*Childe Harold.*　Canto II.
Sc. 98.

　　* * * Years steal
Fire from the mind, as vigor from the limb;
And life's enchanted cup but sparkles near the brim.

h.　BYRON—*Childe Harold.*　Canto III.
St. 8.

For oute of olde feldys, as men sey,
　Comyth al this newe corn from yere to yere;
And out of olde bokis, in good fey,
　Comyth al this newe science that men lere.

i.　CHAUCER—*The Parlement of Fowles.*
L. 21.

The spring, like youth, fresh blossoms doth produce,
But autumn makes them ripe and fit for use:
So Age a mature mellowness doth set
On the green promises of youthful heat.

j.　SIR JOHN DENHAM—*Cato Major.*
Pt. IV. L. 47.

The Disappointment of Manhood succeeds to the delusion of Youth; let us hope that the heritage of Old Age is not Despair.

k.　DISRAELI (Earl Beaconsfield)—
Vivian Grey.　Bk. VIII.　Ch. IV.

Youth is a blunder; Manhood a struggle; Old Age a regret.

l.　DISRAELI (Earl Beaconsfield)—
Coningsby.　Bk. III.　Ch. I.

Fate seem'd to wind him up for fourscore years;
Yet freshly ran he on ten winters more;
Till like a clock worn out with eating time,
The wheels of weary life at last stood still.

m.　DRYDEN—*Œdipus.*　Act IV.　Sc. I.

　　His hair just grizzled
As in a green old age.

n.　DRYDEN—*Œdipus.*　Act III.　Sc. I.

We do not count a man's years, until he has nothing else to count.

o.　EMERSON—*Society and Solitude.*
Old Age.

Remote from cities liv'd a Swain,
Unvex'd with all the cares of gain;
His head was silver'd o'er with age,
And long experience made him sage.

p.　GAY—*Fables.*　Part I.
The Shepherd and the Philosopher.

Old age is courteous—no one more:
For time after time he knocks at the door,
But nobody says. "Walk in, sir, pray!"
Yet turns he not from the door away,
But lifts the latch, and enters with speed,
And then they cry, "A cool one, indeed."

q.　GOETHE—*Old Age.*

Alike all ages: dames of ancient days
Have led their children thro' the mirthful maze.
And the gay grandsire, skill'd in gestic lore,
Has frisk'd beneath the burthen of threescore.

r.　GOLDSMITH—*The Traveller.*　L. 251.

I love everything that's old: old friends, old times, old manners, old books, old wine.

s.　GOLDSMITH—*She Stoops to Conquer.*
Act I.　Sc. I.

O blest retirement! friend to life's decline—
Retreats from care, that never must be mine
How blest is he who crowns, in shades like these,
A youth of labour with an age of ease!

t.　GOLDSMITH—*The Deserted Village.*
L. 97.

They say women and music should never be dated.

u.　GOLDSMITH—*She Stoops to Conquer.*
Act III.

Slow-consuming age.
> *a.*   GRAY—*Ode on a Distant Prospect of
> Eton College.* St. 9.

To be seventy years young is sometimes far more cheerful and hopeful than to be forty years old.
> *b.*   O. W. HOLMES—*On the seventieth birth-
> day of Julia Ward Howe,* May 27, 1889.

A green old age, unconscious of decays,
That proves the hero born in better days.
> *c.*   HOMER—*Iliad.* Bk. 23. L. 925.
> Pope's trans.

When he's forsaken,
Wither'd and shaken,
What can an old man do but die?
> *d.*   HOOD—*Ballad.*

Boys must not have th' ambitious care of men,
Nor men the weak anxieties of age.
> *e.*   HORACE—*Of the Art of Poetry.* Trans.
> by Wentworth Dillon. L. 212.

Superfluous lags the veteran on the stage,
Till pitying Nature signs the last release,
And bids afflicted worth retire to peace.
> *f.*   SAM'L JOHNSON—*Vanity of Human
> Wishes.* L. 308.

Few people know how to be old.
> *g.*   LA ROCHEFOUCAULD—*Maxims and
> Moral Sentences.* No. 448.

And the bright faces of my young companions
Are wrinkled like my own, or are no more.
> *h.*   LONGFELLOW—*Spanish Student.*
> Act III. Sc. 3.

For age is opportunity no less
Than youth itself, though in another dress,
And as the evening twilight fades away
The sky is filled with stars, invisible by day.
> *i.*   LONGFELLOW—*Morituri Salutamus.*
> L. 281.

How far the gulf-stream of our youth may
flow
Into the arctic regions of our lives,
Where little else than life itself survives.
> *j.*   LONGFELLOW—*Morituri Salutamus.*
> L. 250.

The course of my long life hath reached at
last,
In fragile bark o'er a tempestuous sea,
The common harbor, where must rendered
be,
Account of all the actions of the past.
> *k.*   LONGFELLOW—*Old Age.*

The sunshine fails, the shadows grow more
dreary,
And I am near to fall, infirm and weary.
> *l.*   LONGFELLOW—*Canzone.*

Whatever poet, orator, or sage
May say of it, old age is still old age.
> *m.*   LONGFELLOW—*Morituri Salutamus.*
> L. 264.

Age is not all decay; it is the ripening, the swelling, of the fresh life within, that withers and bursts the husk.
> *n.*   GEORGE MACDONALD—*The Marquis of
> Lossie.* Ch. XL.

What find you better or more honorable than age? * * * Take the preheminence of it in everything;—in an old friend, in old wine, in an old pedigree.
> *o.*   SHAKERLEY MARMION—*Antiquary.*
> Act II. Sc. 1.

Set is the sun of my years;
And over a few poor ashes,
I sit in my darkness and tears.
> *p.*   GERALD MASSEY—*A Wail.*

Old wood to burn! Old wine to drink! Old friends to trust! Old authors to read!—Alon-so of Aragon was wont to say in commenda-tion of age, that age appeared to be best in these four things.
> *q.*   MELCHIOR—*Floresta Española de
> Apothegmas o Sentencias,* etc. II.
> 1. 20.

The ages roll
Forward; and forward with them, draw my
soul
Into time's infinite sea.
And to be glad, or sad, I care no more:
But to have done, and to have been, before
I cease to do and be.
> *r.*   OWEN MEREDITH (Lord Lytton)—*The
> Wanderer.* Bk. IV. *A Confession
> and Apology.* St. 9. [P.P. '93].

So may'st thou live, till like ripe fruit thou
drop
Into thy mother's lap, or be with ease
Gather'd, not harshly pluck'd, for death mature.
> *s.*   MILTON—*Paradise Lost.* Bk. XI.
> L. 535.

So Life's year begins and closes;
Days, though short'ning, still can shine;
What though youth gave love and roses,
Age still leaves us friends and wine.
> *t.*   MOORE—*Spring and Autumn.*

Thyself no more deceive, thy youth hath fled.
> *u.*   PETRARCH—*To Laura in Death.*
> Sonnet LXXXII.

Learn to live well, or fairly make your will;
You've played, and loved, and ate, and drank
your fill.
Walk sober off, before a sprightlier age
Comes tittering on, and shoves you from the
stage.
> *v.*   POPE—*Imitations of Horace.* Bk. II.
> Ep. 2. L. 322.

Me let the tender office long engage
To rock the cradle of reposing age;
With lenient arts extend a mother's breath,
Make languor smile, and smooth the bed of
     death;
Explore the thought, explain the asking eye!
And keep awhile one parent from the sky.
    a.   POPE—*Prologue to the Satires.*   L. 408.

Why will you break the Sabbath of my days?
Now sick alike of Envy and of Praise.
    b.   POPE—*First Book of Horace.*   Ep. I.
                           L. 3.

Through the sequester'd vale of rural life,
The venerable patriarch guileless held
The tenor of his way.
    c.   PORTEUS—*Death.*   L. 109.

O, roses for the flush of youth,
And laurel for the perfect prime;
But pluck an ivy branch for me
Grown old before my time.
    d.   CHRISTINA G. ROSSETTI—*Song.*   St. 1.

I'm growing fonder of my staff;
I'm growing dimmer in the eyes;
I'm growing fainter in my laugh;
I'm growing deeper in my sighs;
I'm growing careless of my dress;
I'm growing frugal of my gold;
I'm growing wise; I'm growing,—yes,—
I'm growing old.
    e.   SAXE—*I'm Growing Old.*

On his bold visage middle age
Had slightly press'd its signet sage.
    f.   SCOTT—*Lady of the Lake.*   Canto I.
                          Pt. XXI.

Thus aged men, full loth and slow,
The vanities of life forego,
And count their youthful follies o'er,
Till Memory lends her light no more.
    g.   SCOTT—*Rokeby.*   Canto V. St. 1.

Thus pleasures fade away;
Youth, talents, beauty, thus decay,
And leave us dark, forlorn, and gray;
    h.   SCOTT—*Marmion.*   Introduction to
                       Canto II. St. 7.

Old friends are best. King James us'd to
call for his Old Shoes, they were easiest for
his Feet.
    i.   SELDEN—*Table Talk.*   *Friends.*

               And his big manly voice,
Turning again toward childish treble, pipes
And whistles in his sound.
    j.   *As You Like It.*   Act II.   Sc. 7.
                          L. 161.

An old man is twice a child.
    k.   *Hamlet.*   Act II.   Sc. 2.   L. 404.

As you are old and reverend, you should be
     wise.
    l.   *King Lear.*   Act I.   Sc. 4.   L. 261.

                         At your age,
The hey-day in the blood is tame, it's humble,
And waits upon the judgment.
    m.   *Hamlet.*   Act III.   Sc. 4.   L. 68.

Begin to patch up thine old body for heaven.
    n.   *Henry IV.*   Pt. II.   Act II.   Sc. 4.
                          L. 193.

For we are old, and on our quick'st decrees
The inaudible and noiseless foot of Time
Steals ere we can effect them.
    o.   *All's Well that Ends Well.*   Act V.
                         Sc. 3.   L. 40.

Give me a staff of honor for mine age,
But not a sceptre to control the world.
    p.   *Titus Andronicus.*   Act I.   Sc. 1.
                          L. 198.

Men shut their doors against a setting sun.
    q.   *Timon of Athens.*   Act I.   Sc. 2.
                          L. 129.

                 My way of life
Is fallen into the sear, the yellow leaf,
And that which should accompany old age,
As honor, love, obedience, troops of friends,
I must not look to have; but, in their stead,
Curses not loud, but deep, mouth-honor,
     breath,
Which the poor heart would fain deny, and
     dare not.
    r.   *Macbeth.*   Act V.   Sc. 3.   L. 22.

Nor age so eat up my invention.
    s.   *Much Ado About Nothing.*   Act IV.
                       Sc. 1.   L. 192.

                 O, father Abbot,
An old man, broken with the storms of State,
Is come to lay his weary bones among ye;
Give him a little earth for charity!
    t.   *Henry VIII.*   Act IV.   Sc. 2.   L. 20.

                 O, heavens,
If you do love old men, if your sweet sway
Allow obedience, if yourselves are old,
Make it your cause.
    u.   *King Lear.*   Act II.   Sc. 4.   L. 193.

Pray, do not mock me:
I am a very foolish fond old man,
Fourscore and upward; not an hour more nor
     less,
And, to deal plainly,
I fear I am not in my perfect mind.
    v.   *King Lear.*   Act IV.   Sc. 7.   L. 59.

Some smack of age in you, some relish of
the saltness of time.
    w.   *King Henry IV.*   Pt. II.   Act I.
                       Sc. 2.   L. 91.

Superfluity comes sooner by white hairs,
but competency lives longer.
    x.   *Merchant of Venice.*   Act I.   Sc. 2.
                          L. 8.

Though I look old, yet I am strong and lusty;
For in my youth I never did apply
Hot and rebellious liquors in my blood;
Nor did not with unbashful forehead woo
The means of weakness and debility;
Therefore my age is as a lusty winter,
Frosty, but kindly.
   a.   *As You Like It.* Act II. Sc. 3. L. 47.

Though now this grained face of mine be hid
In sap-consuming winter's drizzled snow,
And all the conduits of my blood froze up,
Yet hath my night of life some memory.
   b.   *Comedy of Errors.* Act V. Sc. 1.
                         L. 311.

          What should we speak of
When we are old as you? When we shall hear
The rain and wind beat dark December.
   c.   *Cymbeline.* Act III. Sc. 3. L. 36.

              You are old;
Nature in you stands on the very verge
Of her confine.
   d.   *King Lear.* Act II. Sc. 4. L. 148.

"You are old, Father William," the young
      man cried,
"The few locks which are left you are gray;
You are hale, Father William,—a hearty old
      man:
Now tell me the reason, I pray."
   e.   Southey—*The Old Man's Comforts, and*
             how he Gained Them.

Every man desires to live long; but no man
would be old.
   f.   Swift—*Thoughts on Various Subjects,*
             Moral and Diverting.

I swear she's no chicken; she's on the
wrong side of thirty, if she be a day.
   g.   Swift—*Polite Conversation.* Dialogue I.

O good gray head which all men knew.
   h.   Tennyson—*On the Death of the Duke of*
                Wellington. St. 4.

Age too shines out: and, garrulous, recounts
The feats of youth.
   i.   Thomson—*The Seasons.* *Autumn.*
                       L. 1231.

Venerable men! you have come down to us
from a former generation. Heaven has bounteously lengthened out your lives, that you
might behold this joyous day.
   j.   Daniel Webster—*Address at Laying*
         the Corner-Stone of the Bunker Hill
         Monument, June 17, 1825.

Is not old wine wholesomest, old pippins
toothsomest, old wood burn brightest, old
linen wash whitest? Old soldiers, sweetheart,
are surest, and old lovers are soundest.
   k.   John Webster—*Westward Ho.* Act II.
                         Sc. 1.

But an old age serene and bright,
And lovely as a Lapland night,
Shall lead thee to thy grave.
   l.   Wordsworth—*To a Young Lady.*

The monumental pomp of age
Was with this goodly Personage;
A stature undepressed in size,
Unbent, which rather seemed to rise
In open victory o'er the weight
Of seventy years, to loftier height.
   m.   Wordsworth—*The White Doe of*
                   Rylstone. Canto III.

Thus fares it still in our decay,
   And yet the wiser mind
Mourns less for what age takes away
   Than what it leaves behind.
   n.   Wordsworth—*The Fountain.* St. 9.

AGRICULTURE (*See* Occupations).

ALCHEMY (*See* Occupations).

AMBITION.

To take a soldier without ambition is to pull
off his spurs.
   o.   Bacon—*Essays.* *Of Ambition.*

No man is born without ambitious worldly
desires.
   p.   Carlyle—*Essays.* *Schiller.*

The noblest spirit is most strongly attracted
by the love of glory.
   q.   Cicero.

I've reared a monument alone
More durable than brass or stone;
Whose cloudy summit is more hid
Than regal height of pyramid.
   r.   Abraham Coles—*Memorial Tributes :*
         P. 130. Trans. of Horace. Lib.
                   III. Car. XXX.

I had a soul above buttons.
   s.   George Colman (the Younger)—*Syl-*
        vester Daggerwood, or New Hay at the
                     Old Market. Sc. 1.

By low ambition and the thirst of praise.
   t.   Cowper—*Table Talk.* L. 591.

            On the summit see,
The seals of office glitter in his eyes;
He climbs, he pants, he grasps them! At his
      heels,
Close at his heels, a demagogue ascends,
And with a dexterous jerk soon twists him
      down,
And wins them, but to lose them in his turn.
   u.   Cowper—*Task.* Bk. IV. L. 58.

But wild Ambition loves to slide, not stand,
And Fortune's ice prefers to Virtue's land.
   a.   DRYDEN—*Absalom and Achitophel.*
            Pt. I.   L. 198.

They please, are pleas'd, they give to get es-
      teem
Till, seeming blest, they grow to what they
      seem.
   b.   GOLDSMITH—*The Traveller.*   L. 266.

           For all may have,
If they dare try, a glorious life, or grave.
   c.   HERBERT—*The Temple. The*
                    Church-Porch.

Unmoved though Witlings sneer and Rivals
      rail ;
Studious to please, yet not ashamed to fail.
   d.   SAM'L JOHNSON—*Prologue to Tragedy of*
                           Irene.

I see, but cannot reach, the height
That lies forever in the light.
   e.   LONGFELLOW—*Christus. The Golden*
            Legend. Pt. II. A Village Church.

Most people would succeed in small things
if they were not troubled with great ambitions.
   f.   LONGFELLOW—*Drift-Wood. Table-Talk.*

Ambition has no rest !
   g.   BULWER-LYTTON—*Richelieu.*   Act III.
                            Sc. 1.

The man who seeks one thing in life, and but
      one,
May hope to achieve it before life be done ;
But he who seeks all things, wherever he goes,
Only reaps from the hopes which around him
      he sows
A harvest of barren regrets.
   h.   OWEN MEREDITH (Lord Lytton)—
           Lucile. Pt. I. Canto II. St. 8.

Better to reign in hell than serve in heaven.
   i.   MILTON—*Paradise Lost.*   Bk. I.
                         L. 263.

But what will not ambition and revenge
Descend to ? who aspires must down as low
As high he soar'd, obnoxious first or last
To basest things.
   j.   MILTON—*Paradise Lost.*   Bk. IX.
                         L. 168.

Here may we reign secure, and in my choice
To reign is worth ambition, though in Hell.
   k.   MILTON—*Paradise Lost.*   Bk. I.
                         L. 261.

If at great things thou would'st arrive,
Get riches first, get wealth, and treasure heap,
Not difficult, if thou hearken to me ;
Riches are mine, fortune is in my hand,
They whom I favor thrive in wealth amain,
While virtue, valor, wisdom, sit in want.
   l.   MILTON—*Paradise Regained.*   Bk. II.
                         L. 426.

Such joy ambition finds.
   m.   MILTON—*Paradise Lost.*   Bk. IV.
                         L. 92.

I'll make thee glorious by my pen,
And famous by my sword.
   n.   MARQUIS OF MONTROSE (Jas. Graham)—
                My Dear and Only Love.

But see how oft ambition's aims are cross'd,
And chiefs contend 'til all the prize is lost !
   o.   POPE—*Rape of the Lock.*   Canto V.
                         L. 108.

Men would be angels, angels would be gods.
   p.   POPE—*Essay on Man.*   Ep. I.   L. 126.

Oh, sons of earth ! attempt ye still to rise,
By mountains pil'd on mountains to the skies ?
Heav'n still with laughter the vain toil sur-
      veys,
And buries madmen in the heaps they raise.
   q.   POPE—*Essay on Man.*   Ep. IV.   L. 74.

Who knows but He, whose hand the lightning
      forms,
Who heaves old ocean, and who wings the
      storms,
Pours fierce ambition in a Cæsar's mind.
   r.   POPE—*Essay on Man.*   Ep. I.   L. 157.

Be always displeased at what thou art, if
thou desire to attain to what thou art not ; for
where thou hast pleased thyself, there thou
abidest.
   s.   QUARLES—*Emblems.*   Bk. IV.
                         Emblem 3.

Ambition is no cure for love !
   t.   SCOTT—*Lay of the Last Minstrel.*
                        Canto I.   St. 27.

O fading honours of the dead !
O high ambition, lowly laid !
   u.   SCOTT—*Lay of the Last Minstrel.*
                        Canto II.   St. 10.

Ambition's debt is paid.
   v.   *Julius Cæsar.*   Act III.   Sc. 1.   L. 83.

           I have no spur
To prick the sides of my intent, but only
Vaulting ambition, which o'erleaps itself,
And falls on the other.
   w.   *Macbeth.*   Act I.   Sc. 7.   L. 25.

Ill-weav'd ambition, how much art thou
      shrunk !
When that this body did contain a spirit,
A kingdom for it was too small a bound ;
But now, two paces of the vilest earth
Is room enough.
   x.   *Henry IV.*   Pt. I.   Act V.   Sc. 4.
                         L. 88.

Mark but my fall, and that that ruin'd me.
Cromwell, I charge thee, fling away ambition.
By that sin fell the angels; how can man then,
The image of his Maker, hope to win by it?
a.   *Henry VIII.*   Act III.   Sc. 2.   L. 437.

        The noble Brutus
Hath told you Cæsar was ambitious:
If it were so, it was a grievous fault;
And grievously hath Cæsar answered it.
b.   *Julius Cæsar.*   Act III.   Sc. 2.   L. 75.

The very substance of the ambitious is merely
    the shadow of a dream.
c.   *Hamlet.*   Act II.   Sc. 2.   L. 264.

      'Tis a common proof,
That lowliness is young ambition's ladder,
Whereto the climber upward turns his face;
But when he once attains the upmost round,
He then unto the ladder turns his back,
Looks in the clouds, scorning the base degrees
By which he did ascend.
d.   *Julius Cæsar.*   Act II.   Sc. 1.   L. 21.

Virtue is chok'd with foul ambition.
e.   *Henry VI.*   Pt. II.   Act III.   Sc. 1.
                        L. 143.

Ambition is our idol, on whose wings
Great minds are carry'd only to extreme;
To be sublimely great, or to be nothing.
f.   Thos. Southerne—*The Loyal Brother.*
                        Act I.   Sc. 1.

And mad ambition trumpeteth to all.
g.   Willis—*From a Poem delivered at the
    Departure of the Senior Class of Yale
                College* (1827).

How like a mounting devil in the heart
Rules the unreined ambition!
h.   Willis—*Parrhasius.*

Ambition has but one reward for all:
A little power, a little transient fame,
A grave to rest in, and a fading name!
i.   William Winter—*The Queen's
                Domain.*   L. 90.

      Talents angel-bright,
If wanting worth are shining instruments
In false ambition's hand, to finish faults
Illustrious, and give infamy renown.
j.   Young—*Night Thoughts.*   Night VI.
                        L. 276.

Too low they build who build beneath the
    stars.
k.   Young—*Night Thoughts.*   Night VIII.
                        L. 225.

AMUSEMENTS.

Diverse men have diverse recreations and
exercises.
l.   Burton—*Anatomy of Melancholy.*
                Pt. 2.   Sec. 2.   Mem. 4.

Every palace, every city almost hath his
peculiar walks, cloisters, terraces, groves,
theatres, pageants, games, and several recreations; every country, some professed gymnics
to exhilarate their minds and exercise their
bodies.
m.   Burton.   *Anatomy of Melancholy.*
                Pt. 2.   Sec. 2.   Mem. 4.

Let them freely feast, sing and dance, have
their puppet-plays, hobby-horses, tabors,
crowds, bag-pipes, etc., play at ball, and
barley-breaks, and what sports and recreations they like best.
n.   Burton—*Anatomy of Melancholy.*
                Pt. 2.   Sec. 2.   Mem. 4.

So good things may be abused, and that
which was first invented to refresh men's
weary spirits.
o.   Burton—*Anatomy of Melancholy.*
                Pt. 2.   Sec. 2.   Mem. 4.

With spots quadrangular of diamond form,
Ensanguined hearts, clubs typical of strife,
And spades, the emblems of untimely graves.
p.   Cowper—*The Task.*   Bk. IV.   *The
             Winter Evening.*   L. 217.

Cards were at first for benefits designed,
Sent to amuse, not to enslave the mind.
q.   Garrick—*Epilogue to Ed. Moore's
                Gamester.*

The pictures placed for ornament and use,
The twelve good rules, the royal game of
    goose.
r.   Goldsmith—*Deserted Village.*   L. 231.

By sports like these are all their cares be-
    guil'd,
The sports of children satisfy the child.
s.   Goldsmith—*The Traveller.*   L. 153.

It is a poor sport that is not worth the candle.
t.   Herbert—*Jacula Prudentum.*

I am a great friend to public amusements;
for they keep people from vice.
u.   Sam'l Johnson—*Boswell's Life of
                Johnson.*   1772.

A clear fire, a clean hearth, and the rigour
of the game.
v.   Charles Lamb—*Mrs. Battle's Opinions
                on Whist.*

When I play with my cat, who knows
whether I do not make her more sport, than
she makes me?
w.   Montaigne—*Apology for Raimond
                de Sebonde.*

Hail, blest Confusion! here are met
  All tongues, and times, and faces;
The Lancers flirt with Juliet,
  The Brahmin talks of races;
   a.   PRAED—*Fancy Ball.* St. 6.

* * * let's to billiards. Come, Charmian,
My arm is sore: best play with Mardian.
   b.   *Antony and Cleopatra.* Act II.
                           Sc. V. L. 3.

Where is our usual manager of mirth?
What revels are in hand? Is there no play,
To ease the anguish of a torturing hour?
   c.   *Midsummer Night's Dream.* Act V.
                           Sc. I. L. 35.

We cry for mercy to the next amusement,
The next amusement mortgages our fields.
   d.   YOUNG—*Night Thoughts.* Night II.
                                L. 131.

ANCESTRY.

The wisdom of our ancestors.
   e.   BACON—(*According to Lord*
                             Brougham.)

People will not look forward to posterity,
who never look backward to their ancestors.
   f.   BURKE—*Reflections on the Revolution in*
                      France. Page 48.

Some decent regulated pre-eminence, some
preference (not exclusive appropriation) given
to birth, is neither unnatural, nor unjust, nor
impolitic.
   g.   BURKE—*Reflections on the Revolution in*
                France—1790. Vol. III. P. 299.

The power of perpetuating our property in
our families is one of the most valuable and
interesting circumstances belonging to it, and
that which tends the most to the perpetuation
of society itself. It makes our weakness subservient to our virtue; it grafts benevolence
even upon avarice. The possession of family
wealth and of the distinction which attends
hereditary possessions (as most concerned in
it,) are the natural securities for this trans-
mission.
   h.   BURKE—*Reflections on the Revolution in*
                France—1790. Vol. III. P. 298.

Great families of yesterday we show,
And lords whose parents were the Lord knows
   who.
   i.   DANIEL DEFOE—*The True-Born*
              Englishman. Part I. L. 372.

Few sons attain the praise of their great
sires, and most their sires disgrace.
   j.   HOMER—*Odyssey.* Bk. II. L. 315.
                           Pope's trans.

"My nobility," said he, "begins in me, but
yours ends in you."
   k.   IPHICRATES. *See Plutarch's Morals.*
                Apothegms of Kings and Great
                     Commanders. Iphicrates.

I know nothing about it; I am my own
ancestor.
   l.   JUNOT, *Duc d' Abrantes* (when asked
                      as to his ancestry).

The man who has not anything to boast of
but his illustrious ancestors is like a potato,—
the only good belonging to him is under
ground.
   m.   SIR THOMAS OVERBURY—*Characters.*

If there be no nobility of descent, all the
more indispensable is it that there should be
nobility of ascent,—a character in them that
bear rule so fine and high and pure that as
men come within the circle of its influence
they involuntarily pay homage to that which
is the one pre-eminent distinction,—the royalty
of virtue.
   n.   BISHOP HENRY C. POTTER—*Address at*
           the Washington Centennial Service in
               St. Paul's Chapel, New York.
                       Apr. 30, 1889.

Our ancestors are very good kind of folks;
but they are the last people I should choose
to have a visiting acquaintance with.
   o.   SHERIDAN—*The Rivals.* Act IV.
                               Sc. 1.

I make little account of genealogical trees.
Mere family never made a man great. Thought
and deed, not pedigree, are the passports to
enduring fate.
   p.   GENERAL SKOBELEFF—*Fortnightly*
                   Review. Oct., 1882.

'Tis happy for him that his father was born
before him.
   q.   SWIFT—*Polite Conversation.*
                         Dialogue III.

From yon blue heavens above us bent,
The gardener Adam and his wife
Smile at the claims of long descent.
   r.   TENNYSON—*Lady Clara Vere de Vere.*
                            St. 7.

He seems to be a man sprung from himself.
   s.   TIBERIUS—*See Annals of Tacitus.*
                      Bk. XI. Sc. 21.

As though there were a tie,
And obligation to posterity!
We get them, bear them, breed and nurse.
What has posterity done for us,
That we, lest they their rights should lose,
Should trust our necks to gripe of noose?
   t.   JOHN TRUMBULL—*McFingal.*
                    Canto II. L. 121.

Bishop Warburton is reported to have said that high birth was a thing which he never knew any one disparage except those who had it not, and he never knew any one make a boast of it who had anything else to be proud of.

    a.   WHATELY—*Annot. on Bacon's Essay, Of Nobility.*

Rank is a farce: if people Fools will be
A Scavenger and King's the same to *me*.

    b.   JOHN WOLCOTT—(*Peter Pindar*).
                 Title Page. Peter's Prophecy.

They that on glorious ancestors enlarge,
Produce their debt, instead of their discharge.

    c.   YOUNG—*Love of Fame.* Satire I.
                             L. 147.

ANGELS.

Like those of angels, short and far between.
    d.   BLAIR—*The Grave.* L. 582.

As the moths around a taper,
  As the bees around a rose,
As the gnats around a vapour,
  So the spirits group and close
Round about a holy childhood, as if drinking
    its repose.

    e.   E. B. BROWNING—*A Child Asleep.*

But sad as angels for the good man's sin,
Weep to record, and blush to give it in.

    f.   CAMPBELL—*Pleasures of Hope.* Pt. II.
                             L. 357.

Like angel visits, few and far between.
    g.   CAMPBELL—*Pleasures of Hope.* Pt. II.
                             L. 378.

Hold the fleet angel fast until he bless thee.
    h.   NATHANIEL COTTON—*To-morrow.* L. 36.

When one that holds communion with the
    skies
Has fill'd his urn where these pure waters
    rise,
And once more mingles with us meaner things,
'Tis e'en as if an angel shook his wings.

    i.   COWPER—*Charity.* L. 439.

In merest prudence men should teach
    *   *   *   *   *   *
That science ranks as monstrous things
Two pairs of upper limbs; so wings—
E'en Angel's wings!—are fictions.

    j.   AUSTIN DOBSON—*A Fairy Tale.*

Let old Timotheus yield the prize
  Or both divide the crown;
He rais'd a mortal to the skies
  She drew an angel down.

    k.   DRYDEN—*Alexander's Feast.* Last St.

Unbless'd thy hand!—if in this low disguise
Wander, perhaps, some inmate of the skies.

    l.   HOMER—*Odyssey.* Bk. 17. L. 570.
                           Pope's trans.

O, though oft depressed and lonely,
  All my fears are laid aside,
If I but remember only
  Such as these have lived and died!

    m.   LONGFELLOW—*Footsteps of Angels.*
                            St. 10.

But all God's angels come to us disguised:
Sorrow and sickness, poverty and death,
One after other lift their frowning masks,
And we behold the Seraph's face beneath,
All radiant with the glory and the calm
Of having looked upon the front of God.

    n.   LOWELL—*On the Death of a Friend's
                            Child.* L. 21.

In this dim world of clouding cares,
  We rarely know, till 'wildered eyes
  See white wings lessening up the skies,
The Angels with us unawares.

    o.   GERALD MASSEY—*The Ballad of Babe
                           Christabel.*

As far as angel's ken.
    p.   MILTON—*Paradise Lost.* Bk. I. L. 59.

              For God will deign
To visit oft the dwellings of just men
Delighted, and with frequent intercourse
Thither will send his winged messengers
On errands of supernal grace.

    q.   MILTON—*Paradise Lost.* Bk. VII.
                             L. 569.

How sweetly did they float upon the wings
Of silence through the empty-vaulted night,
At every fall smoothing the raven down
Of darkness till it smiled!

    r.   MILTON—*Comus.* L. 249.

  The helmed Cherubim,
  And sworded Seraphim,
Are seen in glittering ranks with wings dis-
    play'd.

    s.   MILTON—*Hymn on the Nativity.*
                            L. 112.

Then too when angel voices sung
The mercy of their God, and strung
Their harps to hail, with welcome sweet,
That moment watched for by all eyes.

    t.   MOORE—*Loves of the Angels. Third
                           Angel's Story.*

A guardian angel o'er his life presiding,
Doubling his pleasures, and his cares divid-
    ing.

    u.   SAM'L ROGERS—*Human Life.* L. 353.

And flights of angels sing thee to thy rest!
    v.   *Hamlet.* Act V. Sc. 2. L. 371.

Angels are bright still, though the brightest
    fell.

    w.   *Macbeth.* Act IV. Sc. 3. L. 22.

How oft do they their silver bowers leave
To come to succour us that succour want!
   a.   SPENSER—*Faerie Queene.* Bk. II.
                     Canto VIII. St. 2.

Around our pillows golden ladders rise,
  And up and down the skies,
  With winged sandals shod,
The angels come, and go, the Messengers of
  God!
Nor, though they fade from us, do they de-
  part—
It is the childly heart:
We walk as heretofore,
Adown their shining ranks, but see them
  nevermore.
   b.   R. H. STODDARD—*Hymn to the
                   Beautiful.* St. 3.

Sweet souls around us watch us still,
  Press nearer to our side;
Into our thoughts, into our prayers,
  With gentle helpings glide.
   c.   HARRIET BEECHER STOWE—*The Other
                         World.*

I have no angels left
  Now, Sweet, to pray to:
Where you have made your shrine
  They are away to.
They have struck Heaven's tent,
  And gone to cover you:
Whereso you keep your state
  Heaven is pitched over you.
   d.   FRANCIS THOMPSON—*A Carrier Song.*
                         St. 4.

ANGER.

I was angry with my friend:
I told my wrath, my wrath did end.
I was angry with my foe;
I told it not, my wrath did grow.
   e.   WM. BLAKE—*Christian Forbearance.*

Nursing her wrath to keep it warm.
   f.   BURNS—*Tam o' Shanter.* L. 12.

Alas! they had been friends in youth;
But whispering tongues can poison truth,
And constancy lives in realms above;
And life is thorny, and youth is vain;
And to be wroth with one we love
Doth work like madness in the brain.
   g.   COLERIDGE—*Christabel.* Pt. II.

Fill'd with fury, rapt, inspired.
   h.   WILLIAM COLLINS—*The Passions.*
                         L. 10.

Beware the fury of a patient man.
   i.   DRYDEN—*Absalom and Achitophel.*
                    Pt. I. L. 1002.

A man deep-wounded may feel too much pain
To feel much anger.
   j.   GEORGE ELIOT—*Spanish Gypsy.* Bk. I.
   2

             Anger seeks its prey,—
Something to tear with sharp-edged tooth
  and claw,
Likes not to go off hungry, leaving Love
To feast on milk and honeycomb at will.
   k.   GEORGE ELIOT—*Spanish Gypsy.* Bk. I.

Anger is one of the sinews of the soul.
   l.   FULLER—*The Holy and Profane States.
                           Anger.*

Anger wishes that all mankind had only
one neck; love, that it had only one heart:
grief, two tear-glands; and pride, two bent
knees.
   m.   RICHTER—*Flower, Fruit and Thorn
                      Pieces.* Ch. VI.

No pale gradations quench his ray,
No twilight dews his wrath allay.
   n.   SCOTT—*Rokeby.* Canto VI. St. 21.

             Anger is like
A full-hot horse; who being allowed his way,
Self-mettle tires him.
   o.   *Henry VIII.* Act I. Sc. 1. L. 132.

Anger's my meat; I sup upon myself,
And so shall starve with feeding.
   p.   *Coriolanus.* Act IV. Sc. 2. L. 50.

          Being once chaf'd, he cannot
Be rein'd again to temperance; then he speaks
What 's in his heart.
   q.   *Coriolanus.* Act III. Sc. 3. L. 27.

Come not within the measure of my wrath.
   r.   *Two Gentlemen of Verona.* Act V.
                      Sc. 4. L. 127.

If I had a thunderbolt in mine eye,
I can tell who should down.
   s.   *As You Like It.* Act I. Sc. 2. L. 226.

It engenders choler, planteth anger;
And better 'twere that both of us did fast,
Since, of ourselves, ourselves are choleric,
Than feed it with such over-roasted flesh.
   t.   *Taming of the Shrew.* Act IV. Sc. 1.
                      L. 175.

Never anger made good guard for itself.
   u.   *Antony and Cleopatra.* Act IV. Sc. 1.
                      L. 9.

        Touch me with noble anger!
And let not women's weapons, water drops,
Stain my man's cheeks.
   v.   *King Lear.* Act II. Sc. 4. L. 279.

What, drunk with choler?
   w.   *Henry IV.* Pt. I. Act I. Sc. 3.
                      L. 129.

What sudden anger's this? How have I
    reap'd it?
He parted frowning from me, as if ruin
Leap'd from his eyes: So looks the chafed
    lion
Upon the daring huntsman that has gall'd
    him;
Then makes him nothing.
    a.   *Henry VIII.* Act III. Sc. 2. L. 204.

        You are yoked with a lamb,
That carries anger as the flint bears fire;
Who, much enforced, shows a hasty spark,
And straight is cold again.
    b.   *Julius Cæsar.* Act IV. Sc. 3. L. 109.

Not die here in a rage, like a poisoned rat
in a hole.
    c.   Swift—*Letter to Bolingbroke*, March 21,
        1729.

        Senseless, and deformed,
Convulsive Anger storms at large; or pale,
And silent, settles into fell revenge.
    d.   Thomson—*The Seasons. Spring.*
        L. 28.

ANGLING.

A rod twelve feet long and a ring of wire,
A winder and barrel, will help thy desire
In killing a Pike; but the forked stick,
With a slit and a bladder,—and that other
    fine trick,
Which our artists call snap, with a goose or a
    duck,—
Will kill two for one, if you have any luck;
The gentry of Shropshire do merrily smile,
To see a goose and a belt the fish to beguile;
When a Pike suns himselfe and a-frogging
    doth go,
The two-inched hook is better, I know,
Than the ord'nary snaring: but still I must
    cry,
When the Pike is at home, minde the cookery.
    e.   Barker—*The Art of Angling* (Reprint
        of 1820 of the 1657 edition).

For angling-rod he took a sturdy oak;
For line, a cable that in storm ne'er broke;
His hook was such as heads the end of pole
To pluck down house ere fire consumes it
    whole;
This hook was bated with a dragon's tail,—
And then on rock he stood to bob for whale.
    f.   Sir William Davenant—*Britannia
        Triumphans.* P. 15.

To fish in troubled waters.
    g.   Mathew Henry—*Commentaries.*
        Psalm LX.

In genial spring, beneath the quivering shade,
Where cooling vapors breathe along the mead,
The patient fisher takes his silent stand,
Intent, his angle trembling in his hand;
With looks unmov'd, he hopes the scaly breed,
And eyes the dancing cork, and bending reed.
    h.   Pope—*Windsor Forest.* L. 135.

Give me mine angle, we'll to the river; there,
My music playing far off, I will betray
Tawny-finn'd fishes; my bended hook shall
    pierce
Their slimy jaws.
    i.   *Antony and Cleopatra.* Act II. Sc. 5.
        L. 10.

The pleasant'st angling is to see the fish
Cut with her golden oars the silver stream,
And greedily devour the treacherous bait.
    j.   *Much Ado About Nothing.* Act III.
        Sc. 1. L. 26.

Shrimps and the delicate periwinkle
    Such are the sea-fruits lasses love:
Ho! to your nets till the blue stars twinkle,
    And the shutterless cottages gleam above!
    k.   Bayard Taylor—*The Shrimp-Gatherers*
        (Parody of Jean Ingelow).

        But should you lure
From his dark haunt, beneath the tangled
    roots
Of pendent trees, the Monarch of the brook,
Behoves you then to ply your finest art.
    l.   Thomson—*The Seasons. Spring.*
        L. 420.

And upon all that are lovers of virtue; and
dare trust in his providence; and be quiet;
and go a-angling.
    m.   Izaak Walton—*The Complete Angler.*
        Pt. I. Ch. XXI.

An excellent angler, and now with God.
    n.   Izaak Walton—*The Complete Angler.*
        Pt. I. Ch. IV.

Angling is somewhat like Poetry, men are
to be born so.
    o.   Izaak Walton—*The Complete Angler.*
        Pt. I. Ch. I.

Angling may be said to be so like the mathematics that it can never be fully learnt.
    p.   Izaak Walton—*The Complete Angler.*
        Author's Preface.

As no man is born an artist, so no man is
born an angler.
    q.   Izaak Walton—*The Complete Angler.*
        Author's Preface.

Doubt not but angling will prove to be so
pleasant, that it will prove to be, like virtue,
a reward to itself.
    r.   Izaak Walton—*The Complete Angler.*
        Pt. I. Ch. I.

I am, Sir, a brother of the angle.
    s.   Izaak Walton—*The Complete Angler.*
        Pt. I. Ch. I.

I shall stay him no longer than to wish * * * that if he be an honest angler, the east wind may never blow when he goes a fishing.

a.   IZAAK WALTON—*The Complete Angler.*
The Author's Preface.

It [angling] deserves commendations; * * * it is an art worthy the knowledge and practice of a wise man.

b.   IZAAK WALTON—*The Complete Angler.*
Pt. I. Ch. I.

Of recreation there is none
So free as fishing is, alone;
All other pastimes do not less
Than mind and body, both possess:
  My hand alone my work can do;
  So I can fish and study too.

c.   IZAAK WALTON—*The Complete Angler.*
The Angler's Song.

O! the gallant fisher's life,
It is the best of any;
'Tis full of pleasure, void of strife,
And 'tis beloved by many.
    Other joys
    Are but toys;
    Only this,
    Lawful is;
    For our skill
    Breeds no ill,
But content and pleasure.

d.   IZAAK WALTON—*The Complete Angler.*
Ch. XVI.

The first men that our Saviour dear
Did choose to wait upon Him here,
Blest fishers were; and fish the last
Food was, that He on earth did taste:
I therefore strive to follow those,
Whom He to follow Him hath chose.

e.   IZAAK WALTON—*The Complete Angler.*
The Angler's Song.

Thus use your frog: * * * put your hook, I mean the arming wire, through his mouth, and out at his gills, and then with a fine needle and silk sow the upper part of his leg with only one stitch to the arming wire of your hook, or tie the frog's leg above the upper joint to the armed wire; and in so doing use him as though you loved him.

f.   IZAAK WALTON—*The Complete Angler.*
Pt. I. Ch. VIII.

We may say of angling as Dr. Boteler said of strawberries: "Doubtless God could have made a better berry, but doubtless God never did;" and so, (if I might be judge,) God never did make a more calm, quiet, innocent recreation than angling.

g.   IZAAK WALTON—*The Complete Angler.*
Pt. I. Ch. V.

ANIMALS.

Ass.

John Trott was desired by two witty peers
To tell them the reason why asses had ears.
"An't please you," quoth John, "I'm not
  given to letters;
Nor dare I pretend to know more than my
  betters:
Howe'er, from this time I shall ne'er see your
  graces,
As I hope to be saved! without thinking on
  asses."

h.   GOLDSMITH—*The Clown's Reply.*

Bear.

The fur that warms a monarch, warm'd a bear.

i.   POPE—*Essay on Man.* Ep. III. L. 44.

Cat.

Lauk! what a monstrous tail our cat has got!

j.   HENRY CAREY—*The Dragon of Wantley.*
Act II. Sc. 1.

Mrs. Crupp had indignantly assured him that there wasn't room to swing a cat there; but as Mr. Dick justly observed to me, sitting down on the foot of the bed, nursing his leg, "You know, Trotwood, I don't want to swing a cat. I never do swing a cat. Therefore what does that signify to *me!*"

k.   DICKENS—*David Copperfield.* Vol. II.
Ch. VI.

Confound the cats! All cats—alway—
Cats of all colours, black, white, grey;
By night a nuisance and by day—
      Confound the cats!

l.   ORLANDO THOS. DOBBIN—*A Dithyramb*
on Cats.

If 'twere not for my cat and dog,
  I think I could not live.

m.   EBENEZER ELLIOTT—*Poor Andrew.*
St. 1.

It has been the providence of nature to give this creature nine lives instead of one.

n.   PILPAY—*Fable III.*

Cow.

A cow is a very good animal in the field; but we turn her out of a garden.

o.   SAM'L JOHNSON—*Boswell's Life of*
Johnson, 1772.

Dog.

His faithful dog salutes the smiling guest.

p.   CAMPBELL—*Pleasures of Hope.*
Pt. I. L. 86.

And in that town a dog was found,
  As many dogs there be,
Both mongrel, puppy, whelp and hound,
  And curs of low degree.

q.   GOLDSMITH—*Elegy on the Death of a*
Mad Dog.

The man recover'd of the bite,
  The dog it was that died.
  a.   GOLDSMITH—*Elegy on the Death of a
                              Mad Dog.*

But thinks, admitted to that equal sky,
His faithful dog shall bear him company.
  b.   POPE—*Essay on Man.* Ep. I. L. 111.

I am his Highness' dog at Kew;
Pray tell me, sir, whose dog are you?
  c.   POPE—*Epigrams. On the Collar of a Dog.*

I have a dog of Blenheim birth,
With fine long ears and full of mirth;
And sometimes, running o'er the plain,
  He tumbles on his nose:
But quickly jumping up again,
  Like lightning on he goes!
  d.   RUSKIN—*My Dog Dash.*

            The little dogs and all,
Tray, Blanche, and Sweetheart, see, they bark
    at me.
  e.   *King Lear.* Act III. Sc. 6. L. 65.

Thou hast seen a farmer's dog bark at a
beggar?
  f.   *King Lear.* Act IV. Sc. 6. L. 159.

We are two travellers, Roger and I.
Roger's my dog—come here, you scamp!
Jump for the gentleman—mind your eye!
Over the table,—look out for the lamp!
The rogue is growing a little old;
Five years we've tramped through wind and
    weather,
And slept out-doors when nights were cold,
And ate and drank and starved together.
  g.   JOHN T. TROWBRIDGE—*The Vagabonds.*

Donkey.

Janet! Donkeys!
  h.   DICKENS—*David Copperfield.* Vol. I.
                                      Ch. XIII.

Elephant.

            Th' unwieldy elephant,
To make them mirth, us'd all his might, and
    wreathed
His lithe proboscis.
  i.   MILTON—*Paradise Lost.* Bk. IV.
                                      L. 345.

The elephant hath joints, but none for
courtesy: his legs are legs for necessity, not
for flexure.
  j.   *Troilus and Cressida.* Act II. Sc. 3.
                                      L. 97.

Gazelle.

The gazelles so gentle and clever
  Skip lightly in frolicsome mood.
  k.   HEINE—*Book of Songs, Lyrical.*
                              Interlude No. 9.

I never nurs'd a dear gazelle,
  To glad me with its soft black eye,
But when it came to know me well
  And love me, it was sure to die.
  l.   MOORE—*The Fire Worshippers.*

Horse.

Then I cast loose my buff coat, each halter let
    fall,
Shook off both my jack-boots, let go belt and
    all,
Stood up in the stirrup, leaned, patted his ear,
Called my Roland his pet name, my horse
    without peer;
Clapped my hands, laughed and sang, any
    noise bad or good,
'Til at length into Aix Roland galloped and
    stood.
  m.   ROBERT BROWNING—*How they Brought
                              the News from Ghent.*

Gamaun is a dainty steed,
Strong, black, and of a noble breed,
Full of fire, and full of bone,
With all his line of fathers known;
Fine his nose, his nostrils thin,
But blown abroad by the pride within;
His mane is like a river flowing,
And his eyes like embers glowing
In the darkness of the night,
And his pace as swift as light.
  n.   BARRY CORNWALL—*The Blood Horse.*

All the ten-to-oners were in the rear, and a
dark horse, which had never been thought of,
and which the careless St. James had never
even observed in the list, rushed past the
grand stand in sweeping triumph.
  o.   BENJ. DISRAELI (Earl Beaconsfield)—
                              The Young Duke.
                              Bk. II. Ch. V.

The courser paw'd the ground with restless
    feet,
And snorting foam'd, and champ'd the golden
    bit.
  p.   DRYDEN—*Palamon and Arcite.*
                              Pt. III. L. 1733.

Morgan!—She ain't nothing else, and I've got
    the papers to prove it.
Sired by Chippewa Chief, and twelve hundred
    dollars won't buy her.
Briggs of Turlumne owned her. Did you
    know Briggs of Turlumne?—
Busted hisself in White Pine and blew out his
    brains down in Frisco?
  q.   BRET HARTE—*Chiquita.*

I saw them go; one horse was blind,
The tails of both hung down behind,
Their shoes were on their feet.
  r.   Horace and James Smith's
                              *Rejected Addresses. The Baby's
                              Début.*

Villain, a horse—Villain, I say, give me a
horse to fly,
To swim the river, villain, and to fly.
   a.   GEORGE PEELE—*Battle of Alcazar.*
Act V. L. 104.

A horse! a horse! my kingdom for a horse!
   b.   *Richard III.* Act V. Sc. 4. L. 7.

Give me another horse: bind up my wounds.
   c.   *Richard III.* Act V. Sc. 3. L. 177.

Round-hoof'd, short-jointed, fetlocks shag
and long,
Broad breast, full eye, small head and nostril
wide,
High crest, short ears, straight legs and passing strong,
Thin mane, thick tail, broad buttock, tender
hide:
Look, what a horse should have he did not
lack,
Save a proud rider on so proud a back.
   d.   *Venus and Adonis.* L. 295.

Steed threatens steed, in high and boastful
neighs,
Piercing the night's dull ear.
   e.   *Henry V.* Chorus to Act IV. L. 10.

Jackal.

The jackal's troop, in gather'd cry,
Bay'd from afar complainingly,
With a mix'd and mournful sound,
Like crying babe, and beaten hound.
   f.   BYRON—*Siege of Corinth.* Pt. XXXIII.

Lion.

They rejoice
Each with their kind, lion with lioness,
So fitly them in pairs thou hast combined.
   g.   MILTON—*Paradise Lost.* Bk. VII.
L. 392.

Wouldst thou view the lion's den?
Search afar from haunts of men,—
Where the reed-encircled rill,
Oozes from the rocky hill,
By its verdure far descried
'Mid the desert brown and wide.
   h.   THOS. PRINGLE—*The Lion and Giraffe.*

Rouse the lion from his lair.
   i.   SCOTT—*The Talisman.*
Heading of Ch. VI.

The man that once did sell the lion's skin
While the beast lived, was killed with hunting
him.
   j.   *Henry V.* Act IV. Sc. 3. L. 93.

Mouse.

I holde a mouses herte nat worth a leek.
That hath but oon hole for to sterte to.
   k.   CHAUCER—*Preamble of The Wyves Tale
of Bath.* L. 572.

"Once on a time there was a mouse," quoth
she,
"Who sick of worldly tears and laughter,
grew
Enamoured of a sainted privacy;
To all terrestrial things he bade adieu,
And entered, far from mouse, or cat, or man,
A thick-walled cheese, the best of Parmesan."
   l.   LORENZO PIGNOTTI—*The Mouse Turned
Hermit.*

The mouse that always trusts to one poor
hole,
Can never be a mouse of any soul.
   m.   POPE—*The Wife of Bath. Her Prologue.*
L. 298.

The mouse ne'er shunn'd the cat as they did
budge
From rascals worse than they.
   n.   *Coriolanus.* Act I. Sc. 6. L. 44.

Ox.

And the plain ox,
That harmless, honest, guileless animal,
In what has he offended? he whose toil,
Patient and ever ready, clothes the land
With all the pomp of harvest.
   o.   THOMSON—*The Seasons.*

Serpent.

Spit on a serpent, and his vigor flies.
He straight devours himself, and quickly
dies.
   p.   LUCRETIUS—Bk. 4. V. 642, 643.
See VOLTAIRE—*A Philosophical
Dictionary. Serpents.*

Sheep.

A leap year
Is never a good sheep year.
   q.   *Old English Saying.*

The mountain sheep are sweeter,
But the valley sheep are fatter.
   r.   THOS. L. PEACOCK—*The Misfortunes of
Elphin. The War-Song of Dinas
Vawr.*

Stag.

The swift stag from underground
Bore up his branching head.
   s.   MILTON—*Paradise Lost.* Bk. VII.
L. 469.

Swine.

The fattest hog in Epicurus' sty.
   t.   WILLIAM MASON—*Heroic Epistle.*

How Instinct varies in the grov'ling swine.
   u.   POPE—*Essay on Man.* Ep. I. L. 221.

The hog that ploughs not, nor obeys thy call,
Lives on the labours of this lord of all.
   v.   POPE—*Essay on Man.* Ep. III. L. 41.

Tiger.

Tiger, tiger, burning bright
In the forests of the night,
What immortal hand or eye,
Could frame thy fearful symmetry?
   a.   WILLIAM BLAKE—*The Tiger.*

ANTICIPATION.

Drawing near her death, she sent most pious thoughts as harbingers to heaven ; and her soul saw a glimpse of happiness through the chinks of her sickness-broken body.
   b.   THOMAS FULLER—*Life of Monica.*

Far off his coming shone.
   c.   MILTON—*Paradise Lost.* Bk. VI.
                          L. 768.

I would not anticipate the relish of any happiness, nor feel the weight of any misery, before it actually arrives.
   d.   *Spectator*—No. 7.

ANTIQUITY.

How pure the joy, when first my hands unfold
The small, rare volume, black with tarnished gold !
   e.   JOHN FERRIAR—*Illustrations of Sterne.*
          Bibliomania. L. 139.

Now cheaply bought for thrice their weight in gold.
   f.   JOHN FERRIAR—*Illustrations of Sterne.*
          Bibliomania. L. 69.

Antiquity, what is it else (God only excepted) but man's authority born some ages before us? Now for the truth of things time makes no alteration; things are still the same they are, let the time be past, present, or to come.
Those things which we reverence for antiquity what were they at their first birth? Were they false?—time cannot make them true. Were they true?—time cannot make them more true. The circumstances therefore of time in respect of truth and error is merely impertinent.
   g.   JOHN HALES (The Ever Memorable)—
          Of Inquiry and Private Judgment in
                    Religion.

Damn the age; I will write for Antiquity.
   h.   CHARLES LAMB—*Bon Mots by Charles*
          Lamb and Douglas Jerrold. Ed. by
                    Walter Jerrold.

With sharpen'd sight pale Antiquaries pore,
Th' inscription value, but the rust adore.
This the blue varnish, that the green endears ;
The sacred rust of twice ten hundred years.
   i.   POPE—*Epistle to Mr. Addison.* L. 35.

My copper-lamps, at any rate,
For being true antique, I bought ;
Yet wisely melted down my plate,
On modern models to be wrought ;
And trifles I alike pursue,
Because they're old, because they're new.
   j.   PRIOR—*Alma.* Canto III.

Nor rough, nor barren, are the winding ways
Of hoar Antiquity, but strewn with flowers.
   k.   THOMAS WARTON—*Written in a blank*
            Leaf of Dugdale's Monasticon.

APPAREL.

Thy clothes are all the soul thou hast.
   l.   BEAUMONT AND FLETCHER—*Honest*
          Man's Fortune. Act V. Sc. 3.
                        L. 170.

A painted vest Prince Voltiger had on,
Which from a naked Pict his grandsire won.
   m.   *Ascribed to Blackmore.*

To treat a poor wretch with a bottle of Burgundy, and fill his snuff-box, is like giving a pair of laced ruffles to a man that has never a shirt on his back.
   n.   TOM BROWN—*Laconics.*

Gars auld claes look amaist as weel's the new.
   o.   BURNS—*The Cotter's Saturday Night.*

His locked, lettered, braw brass collar,
Shewed him the gentleman and scholar.
   p.   BURNS—*The Twa Dogs.*

And said to myself, as I lit my cigar,
"Supposing a man had the wealth of the Czar
Of the Russias to boot, for the rest of his days,
On the whole do you think he would have
         much to spare
If he married a woman with nothing to
         wear?"
   q.   WM. ALLEN BUTLER—*Nothing to Wear.*

But I do mean to say, I have heard her declare,
When at the same moment she had on a dress
Which cost five hundred dollars, and not a
         cent less,
And jewelry worth ten times more, I should
         guess,
That she had not a thing in the wide world to
         wear !
   r.   WM. ALLEN BUTLER—*Nothing to Wear.*

Dresses for breakfasts, and dinners, and balls;
Dresses to sit in, and stand in, and walk in ;
Dresses to dance in, and flirt in, and talk in,
Dresses in which to do nothing at all ;
Dresses for Winter, Spring, Summer, and Fall ;
All of them different in color and shape,
Silk, muslin, and lace, velvet, satin, and crape,
Brocade and broadcloth, and other material,
Quite as expensive and much more ethereal.
   s.   WM. ALLEN BUTLER—*Nothing to Wear.*

Miss Flora McFlimsey of Madison Square,
　Has made three separate journeys to Paris,
And her father assures me each time she was
　　　there
　That she and her friend Mrs. Harris

　　*　　*　　*　　*　　*

Spent six consecutive weeks, without stopping
In one continuous round of shopping,—

　　*　　*　　*　　*　　*　　*

And yet, though scarce three months have
　　　passed since the day
　This merchandise went on twelve carts, up
　　　Broadway,
This same Miss McFlimsey of Madison Square
The last time we met was in utter despair
Because she had nothing whatever to wear.
　　a.　　WM. ALLEN BUTLER—*Nothing to Wear.*

Around his form his loose long robe was
　　　thrown,
And wrapt a breast bestowed on heaven
　　　alone.
　　b.　　BYRON—*Corsair.*　Canto II.　St. 3.

Dress drains our cellar dry,
And keeps our larder lean ; puts out our fires.
And introduces hunger, frost, and woe,
Where peace and hospitality might reign.
　　c.　　COWPER—*The Task.*　Bk. II.　L. 614.

　He that is proud of the russling of his silks,
like a madman, laughs at the ratling of his
fetters.　For indeed, Clothes ought to be our
remembrancers of our lost innocency.
　　d.　　FULLER—*The Holy and Profane States.*
　　　　　　　　　　　　　　　　Apparel.

A night-cap deck'd his brows instead of
　　　bay,
A cap by night,—a stocking all the day.
　　e.　　GOLDSMITH—*Description of an Author's
　　　　　　　　　　　　Bed-chamber.*

It's like sending them ruffles, when wanting a
　　　shirt.
　　f.　　GOLDSMITH—*The Haunch of Venison.*

Old Grimes is dead, that good old man,
　We ne'er shall see him more ;
He used to wear a long black coat
　All button'd down before.
　　g.　　ALBERT G. GREENE—*Old Grimes.*

Old Abram Brown is dead and gone,—
　You'll never see him more ;
He used to wear a long brown coat
　That buttoned down before.
　　h.　　HALLIWELL—*Nursery Rhymes of
　　　　　　　　　　England.　Tales.*

A sweet disorder in the dresse
Kindles in cloathes a wantonnesse.
　　i.　　HERRICK—*Delight in Disorder.*

A winning wave, (deserving note,)
In the tempestuous petticote
A carelesse shoe-string, in whose tye
I see a wilde civility,—
Doe more bewitch me then when art
Is too precise in every part.
　　j.　　HERRICK—*Delight in Disorder.*

It is not linen you're wearing out,
But human creatures' lives.
　　k.　　HOOD—*Song of the Shirt.*

　After all there is something about a wedding-
gown prettier than in any other gown in the
world.
　　l.　　DOUGLAS JERROLD—*A Wedding-Gown.
　　　　　　　　　　　　　　　Jerrold's Wit.*

Still to be neat, still to be drest,
As you were going to a feast,
Still to be powder'd, still perfum'd.
　　m.　　BEN JONSON—*Epicoene ; or, The Silent
　　　　　　　　　　　Woman.*　Act 1.　Sc. 1 (Song).

Each Bond-street buck conceits, unhappy elf;
He shows his clothes ! alas ! he shows him-
　　　self.
O that they knew, these overdrest self-lovers,
What hides the body oft the mind discovers.
　　n.　　KEATS—*Epigrams.　Clothes.*

John Lee is dead, that good old man,—
　We ne'er shall see him more :
He used to wear an old drab coat
　All buttoned down before.
　　o.　　*To the memory of John Lee, who died
　　　　　　　May 21, 1823.*　An inscription in
　　　　　　　　　Matherne Church-yard.

Dwellers in huts and in marble halls—
　From Shepherdess up to Queen—
Cared little for bonnets, and less for shawls,
　And nothing for crinoline.
But now simplicity's *not* the rage,
　And it's funny to think how cold
The dress they wore in the Golden Age
　Would seem in the Age of Gold.
　　p.　　HENRY S. LEIGH—*The Two Ages.*　St. 4.

Let thy attyre bee comely, but not costly.
　　q.　　LYLY—*Euphues.*　1579.　P. 39.

Be plain in dress, and sober in your diet ;
In short, my deary, kiss me ! and be quiet.
　　r.　　LADY M. W. MONTAGUE—*Summary of
　　　　　　　　　　　Lord Littelton's Advice.*

He was a wight of high renowne,
And thosne but of a low degree :
Itt's pride that putts the countrye downe,
Man, take thine old cloake about thee.
　　s.　　THOMAS PERCY—*Take thy Old Cloake
　　　　　　　　　　　　　about Thee.*

My galligaskins, that have long withstood
The winter's fury, and encroaching frosts,
By time subdued (what will not time subdue!)
An horrid chasm disclosed.
 a. JOHN PHILIPS—*The Splendid Shilling.*
           L. 121.

A vest as admired Voltiger had on,
Which from this Island's foes his grandsire
 won,
Whose artful colour pass'd the Tyrian dye,
Obliged to triumph in this legacy.
 b. *The British Princes.* 1669. P. 96.

Costly thy habit as thy purse can buy,
But not express'd in fancy; rich, not gaudy;
For the apparel oft proclaims the man.
 c. *Hamlet.* Act I. Sc. 3. Line 70.

Give me your gloves, I'll wear them for your
 sake.
 d. *Merchant of Venice.* Act IV. Sc. 1.
           L. 426.

He will come to her in yellow stockings,
and 'tis a color she abhors; and cross-gartered,
a fashion she detests.
 e. *Twelfth Night.* Act II. Sc. 5. L. 216.

   So tedious is this day,
As is the night before some festival
To an impatient child, that hath new robes,
And may not wear them.
 f. *Romeo and Juliet.* Act III. Sc. 2.
           L. 28.

The soul of this man is his clothes.
 g. *All's Well That Ends Well.* Act II.
        Sc. 5. L. 45.

   Thou villain base,
Know'st me not by my clothes?
 h. *Cymbeline.* Act IV. Sc. 2. L. 80.

With silken coats, and caps, and golden rings,
With ruffs, and cuffs, and farthingales, and
 things;
With scarfs, and fans, and double change of
 bravery,
With amber bracelets, beads, and all this
 knavery.
 i. *Taming of the Shrew.* Act IV. Sc. 3.
           L. 55.

Her cap, far whiter than the driven snow,
Emblem right meet of decency does yield.
 j. SHENSTONE—*The Schoolmistress.*
           St. 6.

She wears her clothes as if they were thrown
on her with a pitchfork.
 k. SWIFT—*Polite Conversation.* Dialogue I.

Attired to please herself: no gems of any kind
She wore, nor aught of borrowed gloss in
 Nature's stead;
And, then her long, loose hair flung deftly
 round her head
Fell carelessly behind.
 l. TERENCE—*The Self-Tormentor.* Act II.
   Sc. 2. Translated by F. W. Ricord.

So for thy spirit did devise
Its Maker seemly garniture,
Of its own essence parcel pure,—
From grave simplicities a dress,
And reticent demureness,
And love encinctured with reserve;
Which the woven vesture would subserve.
For outward robes in their ostents
Should show the soul's habiliments.
Therefore I say,—Thou'rt fair even so,
But better Fair I use to know.
 m. FRANCIS THOMPSON—*Gilded Gold.* St. **2.**

   Her polish'd limbs,
Veil'd in a simple robe, their best attire;
Beyond the pomp of dress; for Loveliness
Needs not the foreign aid of ornament,
But is, when unadorn'd, adorn'd the most.
 n. THOMSON—*Seasons. Autumn.* L. 202.

O fair undress, best dress! it checks no vein,
But every flowing limb in pleasure drowns,
And heightens ease with grace.
 o. THOMSON—*Castle of Indolence.*
        Canto I. St. 26.

   She's adorned
Amply, that in her husband's eye looks
 lovely,—
The truest mirror that an honest wife
Can see her beauty in!
 p. JOHN TOBIN—*The Honeymoon.* Act III.
           Sc. 4.

Their feet through faithless leather met the
 dirt,
And oftener chang'd their principles than
 shirt.
 q. YOUNG. *To Mr. Pope.* Epistle I.
           L. 283.

APPARITIONS.

Great Pompey's shade complains that we are
 slow,
And Scipio's ghost walks unavenged amongst
 us!
 r. ADDISON—*Cato.* Act II. Sc. 1.

Who gather round, and wonder at the tale
Of horrid apparition, tall and ghastly,
That walks at dead of night, or takes his stand
O'er some new-open'd grave; and, (strange to
 tell!)
Evanishes at crowing of the cock.
 s. BLAIR—*The Grave.* L. 67.

Where entity and quiddity,
The ghosts of defunct bodies, fly.
    a.   BUTLER—*Hudibras.* Pt. I. Canto I.
                       L. 145.

The Nightmare Life-in-Death was she.
    b.   COLERIDGE—*The Ancient Mariner.*
                       Pt. III.

Thin, airy shoals of visionary ghosts.
    c.   HOMER—*Odyssey.* Bk. XI. L. 48.
                     Pope's trans.

So many ghosts, and forms of fright,
Have started from their graves to-night,
They have driven sleep from mine eyes away;
I will go down to the chapel and pray.
    d.   LONGFELLOW—*The Golden Legend.*
                     Pt. IV.

Whence and what art thou, execrable shape?
    e.   MILTON—*Paradise Lost.* Bk. II.
                     L. 681.

What beck'ning ghost along the moonlight
    shade
Invites my steps, and points to yonder glade?
    f.   POPE—*Elegy to the Memory of an*
                 Unfortunate Lady. L. 1.

A dagger of the mind, a false creation,
Proceeding from the heat-oppressed brain?
    g.   *Macbeth.* Act II. Sc. 1. L. 38.

Is this a dagger which I see before me,
The handle toward my hand?
    h.   *Macbeth.* Act II. Sc. 1. L. 33.

Now it is the time of night,
That the graves, all gaping wide,
Every one lets forth his sprite,
In the church-way paths to glide.
    i.   *Midsummer Night's Dream.* Act V.
                  Sc. 1. L. 386.

There needs no ghost, my lord, come from the
    grave
To tell us this.
    j.   *Hamlet.* Act I. Sc. 5. L. 126.

            What are these,
So wither'd, and so wild in their attire;
That look not like the inhabitants o' th'
    earth,
And yet are on 't?
    k.   *Macbeth.* Act I. Sc. 3. L. 39.

My people too were scared with eerie sounds,
A footstep, a low throbbing in the walls,
A noise of falling weights that never fell,
Weird whispers, bells that rang without a
    hand,
Door-handles turn'd when none was at the
    door,
And bolted doors that open'd of themselves;
And one betwixt the dark and light had seen
Her, bending by the cradle of her babe.
    l.   TENNYSON—*The Ring.*

I look for ghosts; but none will force
    Their way to me; 'tis falsely said
That even there was intercourse
    Between the living and the dead.
    m.   WORDSWORTH—*Affliction of Margaret.*

APPEARANCE.

            We understood
Her by her sight; her pure and eloquent blood
Spoke in her cheeks, and so distinctly wrought.
That one might almost say her body thought.
    n.   DONNE—*Funeral Elegies. Of the*
          Progress of the Soul. By occasion of
              Religious Death of Mistress
                   Elizabeth Drury.

Gloomy as night he stands.
    o.   HOMER—*Odyssey.* Bk. XI. L. 744.
                     Pope's trans.

He had a head which statuaries loved to
copy, and a foot the deformity of which the
beggars in the streets mimicked.
    p.   MACAULAY—*On Moore's Life of Lord*
                   Byron, 1831.

A sweet attractive kinde of grace,
A full assurance given by lookes,
Continuall comfort in a face
The lineaments of Gospell bookes.
    q.   MATTHEW ROYDEN. *Lament for*
             Astrophel (Sir Philip Sidney).

    Looked as if she had walked straight out of
the Ark.
    r.   SYDNEY SMITH—*Memoir.* Vol. I.
                     Ch. 7.

She looks as if butter wouldn't melt in her
mouth.
    s.   SWIFT—*Polite Conversation.*
                     Dialogue I.

A man of sense can *artifice* disdain,
As men of wealth may venture to go *plain.*
        *   *   *   *
I find the *fool* when I behold the *screen,*
For 'tis the wise man's interest to be seen.
    t.   YOUNG—*Love of Fame.* Satire II.
                     L. 193.

APPETITE.

And gazed around them to the left and right
With the prophetic eye of appetite.
    u.   BYRON—*Don Juan.* Canto V. St. 50.

His thirst he slakes at some pure neighboring
    brook,
Nor seeks for sauce where Appetite stands
    cook.
    v.   CHURCHILL—*Gotham III.* L. 133.

Govern well thy appetite, lest Sin
Surprise thee, and her black attendant Death,
    w.   MILTON—*Paradise Lost.* Bk. VII.
                     L. 546.

Appetite comes with eating, says Angeston.
a.   RABELAIS—*Works*. Bk. I. Ch. V.

Doth not the appetite alter? A man loves the meat in his youth, that he cannot endure in his age.
b.   *Much Ado About Nothing*. Act II.
Sc. 3. L. 250.

Epicurean cooks
Sharpen with cloyless sauce his appetite.
c.   *Antony and Cleopatra*. Act II. Sc. 1.
L. 24.

Now good digestion wait on appetite,
And health on both!
d.   *Macbeth*. Act III. Sc. 4. L. 38.

Read o'er this;
And after, this; and then to breakfast, with
What appetite you have.
e.   *Henry VIII*. Act III. Sc. 2. L. 201.

The sweetest honey
Is loathsome in his own deliciousness,
And in the taste confounds the appetite.
f.   *Romeo and Juliet*. Act II. Sc. 6.
L. 11.

Or cloy the hungry edge of appetite?
g.   *Richard II*. Act I. Sc. 3. L. 296.

And through the hall there walked to and fro,
A jolly yeoman, marshall of the same,
Whose name was Appetite; he did bestow
Both guestes and meate, whenever in they
came,
And knew them how to order without blame.
h.   SPENSER—*Faerie Queene*. Bk. II.
Canto IX. St. 28.

APPLAUSE.

Applause is the spur of noble minds, the end and aim of weak ones.
i.   C. C. COLTON—*Lacon*. P. 205.

O Popular Applause! what heart of man
Is proof against thy sweet, seducing charms?
j.   COWPER—*Task*. Bk. II. L. 431.

The silence that accepts merit as the most natural thing in the world, is the highest applause.
k.   EMERSON—*An Address*. July 15, 1838.

The applause of a single human being is of great consequence.
l.   SAM'L JOHNSON—*Boswell's Life of
Johnson*, 1780.

Like Cato, give his little senate laws,
And sit attentive to his own applause.
m.   POPE—*Prologue to the Satires*. L. 207.

I love the people,
But do not like to stage me to their eyes;
Though it do well, I do not relish well
Their loud applause, and Aves vehement;
Nor do I think the man of safe discretion,
That does affect it.
n.   *Measure for Measure*. Act I. Sc. 1.
L. 68.

I would applaud thee to the very echo,
That should applaud again.
o.   *Macbeth*. Act V. Sc. 3. L. 53.

They threw their caps
As they would hang them on the horns o' the
moon,
Shouting their emulation.
p.   *Coriolanus*. Act I. Sc. 1. L. 216.

APRIL (*See* MONTHS).

ARCHITECTURE (*See* OCCUPATIONS).

ARGUMENT.

Much might be said on both sides.
q.   ADDISON—*Spectator*. No. 122.

Where we desire to be informed 'tis good to contest with men above ourselves; but to confirm and establish our opinions, 'tis best to argue with judgments below our own, that the frequent spoils and victories over their reasons may settle in ourselves an esteem and confirmed opinion of our own.
r.   SIR THOS. BROWNE—*Religio Medici*.
Pt. I. VI.

And there began a lang digression
About the lords o' the creation.
s.   BURNS—*The Twa Dogs*.

He'd undertake to prove, by force
Of argument, a man's no horse.
He'd prove a buzzard is no fowl,
And that a Lord may be an owl,
A calf an Alderman, a goose a Justice,
And rooks, Committee-men or Trustees.
t.   BUTLER—*Hudibras*. Pt. I. Canto I.
L. 71.

I've heard old cunning stagers
Say, fools for arguments use wagers.
u.   BUTLER—*Hudibras*. Pt. II. Canto I.
L. 297.

Whatever Sceptic could inquire for,
For every why he had a wherefore.
v.   BUTLER—*Hudibras*. Pt. I. Canto I.
L. 131.

'Twas blow for blow, disputing inch by inch,
For one would not retreat, nor t'other flinch.
w.   BYRON—*Don Juan*. Canto VIII.
St. 77.

When Bishop Berkeley said, "there was no matter,"
And proved it—'twas no matter what he said.
   a.   BYRON—*Don Juan.* Canto XI. St. I.

The noble lord is the Rupert of debate.
   b.   BENJ. DISRAELI—*Speech.* April, 1844.

A knock-down argument; 'tis but a word and a blow.
   c.   DRYDEN—*Amphitryon.* Act I. Sc. 1.

Reproachful speech from either side
The want of argument supplied;
They rail, reviled; as often ends
The contests of disputing friends.
   d.   GAY—*Fables. Ravens. Sexton and Earth Worm.* Pt. II. L. 117.

His conduct still right with his argument wrong.
   e.   GOLDSMITH—*Retaliation.* L. 46.

In arguing, too, the parson own'd his skill,
For even though vanquished he could argue still.
   f.   GOLDSMITH—*The Deserted Village.*
                           L. 211.

Be calm in arguing; for fierceness makes
Error a fault, and truth discourtesy.
   g.   HERBERT—*Temple. Church Porch.* St. 52.

I have found you an argument; but I am not obliged to find you an understanding.
   h.   SAM'L JOHNSON—*Boswell's Life of Johnson.* 1784.

Nay, if he take you in hand, sir, with an argument,
He'll bray you in a mortar.
   i.   BEN JONSON—*The Alchemist.* Act II. Sc. 1.

There is no good in arguing with the inevitable. The only argument available with an east wind is to put on your overcoat.
   j.   LOWELL—*Democracy and Other Addresses. Democracy.*

The brilliant chief, irregularly great,
Frank, haughty, rash,—the Rupert of debate.
   k.   BULWER LYTTON—*The New Timon.* Pt. 1. 1846.

In argument with men a woman ever
Goes by the worse, whatever be her cause.
   l.   MILTON—*Samson Agonistes.* L. 903.

Like doctors thus, when much dispute has past,
We find our tenets just the same at last.
   m.   POPE—*Moral Essays.* Epis. III. L. 15.

In argument
Similes are like songs in love:
They must describe; they nothing prove.
   n.   PRIOR—*Alma.* Canto III.

One single positive weighs more,
You know, than negatives a score.
   o.   PRIOR—*Epistle to Fleetwood Shepherd.*

Soon their crude notions with each other fought;
The adverse sect denied what this had taught;
And he at length the amplest triumph gain'd,
Who contradicted what the last maintain'd.
   p.   PRIOR—*Solomon.* Bk. I. L. 717.

And sheath'd their swords for lack of argument.
   q.   *Henry V.* Act III. Sc. 1. L. 21.

For they are yet but ear-kissing arguments.
   r.   *King Lear.* Act II. Sc. 1. L. 9.

Leave this keen encounter of our wits,
And fall somewhat into a slower method.
   s.   *Richard III.* Act I. Sc. 2. L. 115.

                 She hath prosperous art
When she will play with reason and discourse,
And well she can persuade.
   t.   *Measure for Measure.* Act I. Sc. 2. L. 189.

There is occasions and causes why and wherefore in all things.
   u.   *Henry V.* Act V. Sc. 1. L. 3.

The first the Retort Courteous; the second the Quip Modest; the third the Reply Churlish; the fourth the Reproof Valiant; the fifth the Countercheck Quarrelsome; the sixth the Lie with Circumstance; the seventh the Lie Direct.
   v.   *As You Like It.* Act V. Sc. 4. L. 96.

If thou continuest to take delight in idle argumentation thou mayest be qualified to combat with the sophists, but never know how to love with men.
   w.   SOCRATES.

ART.

Now nature is not at variance with art, nor art with nature; they being both the servants of his providence. Art is the perfection of nature. Were the world now as it was the sixth day, there were yet a chaos. Nature hath made one world, and art another. In brief, all things are artificial; for nature is the art of God.
   x.   SIR THOMAS BROWNE—*Religio Medici.* Sec. 16.

It is the glory and good of Art,
That Art remains the one way possible
Of speaking truth, to mouths like mine at least.
   y.   ROBERT BROWNING—*The Ring and the Book. The Book and the Ring.* L. 842.

There is an art of reading, as well as an art of thinking, and an art of writing.

a.   ISAAC DISRAELI—*Literary Character.*
Ch. XI.

The conscious utterance of thought, by speech or action, to any end, is art.

b.   EMERSON—*Society and Solitude. Art.*

The hand that rounded Peter's dome,
And groined the aisles of Christian Rome,
Wrought in a sad sincerity;
Himself from God he could not free;
He builded better than he knew;—
The conscious stone to beauty grew.

c.   EMERSON—*The Problem.* L. 19.

His pencil was striking, resistless, and grand;
His manners were gentle, complying, and bland;
Still born to improve us in every part,
His pencil our faces, his manners our heart.

d.   GOLDSMITH—*Retaliation.* L. 139.

The canvas glow'd beyond ev'n nature warm;
The pregnant quarry teem'd with human form.

e.   GOLDSMITH—*The Traveller.* L. 137.

The perfection of an art consists in the employment of a comprehensive system of laws, commensurate to every purpose within its scope, but concealed from the eye of the spectator; and in the production of effects that seem to flow forth spontaneously, as though uncontrolled by their influence, and which are equally excellent, whether regarded individually, or in reference to the proposed result.

f.   JOHN MASON GOOD—*The Book of Nature.* Series 1. Lecture IX.

There are two kinds of artists in this world; those that work because the spirit is in them, and they cannot be silent if they would, and those that speak from a conscientious desire to make apparent to others the beauty that has awakened their own admiration.

g.   ANNA KATHARINE GREEN—*The Sword of Damocles.* Bk. I. Ch. V.

The temple of art is built of words. Painting and sculpture and music are but the blazon of its windows, borrowing all their significance from the light, and suggestive only of the temple's uses.

h.   J. G. HOLLAND—*Plain Talks on Familiar Subjects. Art and Life.*

The one thing that marks the true artist is a clear perception and a firm, bold hand, in distinction from that imperfect mental vision and uncertain touch which give us the feeble pictures and the lumpy statues of the mere artisans on canvas or in stone.

i.   O. W. HOLMES—*The Professor at the Breakfast Table.* Ch. IX.

It is not strength, but art, obtains the prize,
And to be swift is less than to be wise.
'Tis more by art, than force of numerous strokes.

j.   HOMER—*Iliad.* Bk. 23. L. 382.
Pope's trans.

Piety in art—poetry in art—Puseyism in art—let us be careful how we confound them.

k.   MRS. JAMESON—*Memoirs and Essays. The House of Titian.*

We have learned to whittle the Eden Tree to the shape of a surplice peg,
We have learned to bottle our parents twain in the yelk of an addled egg,
We know that the tail must wag the dog, for the horse is drawn by the cart,
But the devil whoops, as he whooped of old; It's clever, but is it art?

l.   RUDYARD KIPLING—*The Conundrum of the Workshops.*

Art is Power.

m.   LONGFELLOW—*Hyperion.* Bk. 3. Ch. V.

Art is the child of Nature; yes,
Her darling child in whom we trace
The features of the mother's face,
Her aspect and her attitude.

n.   LONGFELLOW—*Keramos.* L. 382.

Dead he is not, but departed,—for the artist never dies.

o.   LONGFELLOW—*Nuremburg.* St. 13.

The counterfeit and counterpart
Of Nature reproduced in art.

p.   LONGFELLOW—*Keramos.* L. 380.

Art, in fact, is the effort of man to express the ideas which Nature suggests to him of a power above Nature, whether that power be within the recesses of his own being, or in the Great First Cause of which Nature, like himself, is but the effect.

q.   BULWER LYTTON—*Caxtoniana. On the Moral Effect of Writers.*

Artists may produce excellent designs, but they will avail little, unless the taste of the public is sufficiently cultivated to appreciate them.

r.   GEORGE C. MASON—*Art Manufactures.*
Ch. XIX.

One of the first principles of decorative art is, that in all manufactures, ornament must hold a place subordinate to that of utility; and when, by its exuberance, ornament interferes with utility, it is misplaced and vulgar.

s.   GEORGE C. MASON—*Art Manufactures.*
Ch. XIX.

For Art is Nature made by Man
To Man the interpreter of God.
   a.   OWEN MEREDITH (Lord Lytton)—*The Artist.* St. 26.

The perfection of art is to conceal art.
   b.   QUINTILIAN.

Greater completion marks the progress of art, absolute completion usually its decline.
   c.   RUSKIN—*The Seven Lamps of Architecture.* Ch. IV. Pt. XXX. *The Lamp of Beauty.*

Seraphs share with thee
Knowledge; But Art, O Man, is thine alone!
   d.   SCHILLER—*The Artists.* St. 2.

His art with nature's workmanship at strife,
As if the dead the living should exceed.
   e.   *Venus and Adonis.* L. 291.

In framing an artist, art hath thus decreed,
To make some good, but others to exceed.
   f.   *Pericles.* Act II. Sc. 3. L. 15.

To gild refined gold, to paint the lily,
To throw a perfume on the violet,
To smooth the ice, or add another hue
Unto the rainbow.
   g.   *King John.* Act IV. Sc. 2. L. 11.

It was Homer who gave laws to the artist.
   h.   FRANCIS WAYLAND—*The Iliad and the Bible.*

Around the mighty master came
  The marvels which his pencil wrought,
Those miracles of power whose fame
Is wide as human thought.
   i.   WHITTIER—*Raphael.* St. 8.

ASTRONOMY (See OCCUPATIONS).

AUGUST (See MONTHS).

AURORA.

Aurora had but newly chased the night,
And purpled o'er the sky with blushing light.
   j.   DRYDEN—*Palamon and Arcite.* Bk. I. L. 186.

But when Aurora, daughter of the dawn,
With rosy lustre purpled o'er the lawn.
   k.   HOMER—*Odyssey.* Bk. III. L. 621. Pope's trans.

Night's son was driving
His golden-haired horses up;
Over the eastern firths
High flashed their manes.
   l.   CHARLES KINGSLEY—*The Longbeards' Saga.*

Zephyr, with Aurora playing,
As he met her once a-Maying.
   m.   MILTON—*L'Allegro.* L. 19.

See now, that radiant bow of pillared fires
Spanning the hills like dawn, until they lie
  In soft tranquillity,
And all night's ghastly glooms asunder roll.
   n.   D. M. MULOCK—*The Aurora on the Clyde.*

For night's swift dragons cut the clouds full fast,
And yonder shines Aurora's harbinger;
At whose approach ghosts, wandering here and there,
Troop home to churchyards:
   o.   *Midsummer Night's Dream.* Act III. Sc. 2. L. 379.

The wolves have prey'd: and look, the gentle day,
Before the wheels of Phœbus, round about,
Dapples the drowsy east with spots of grey.
   p.   *Much Ado About Nothing.* Act V. Sc. 3. L. 25.

At last, the golden orientall gate
Of greatest heaven gan to open fayre,
And Phœbus, fresh as brydegrome to his mate,
Came dauncing forth, shaking his dewie hayre;
And hurls his glistring beams through gloomy ayre.
   q.   SPENSER—*Faerie Queene.* Bk. I. Canto V. St. 2.

AUTHORITY.

All authority must be out of a man's self, turned * * * either upon an art, or upon a man.
   r.   BACON—*Natural History. Century X. Touching emission of immateriate virtues, etc.*

Authority intoxicates,
And makes mere sots of magistrates;
The fumes of it invade the brain,
And make men giddy, proud, and vain.
   s.   BUTLER—*Miscellaneous Thoughts.* L. 283.

And though authority be a stubborn bear, yet he is oft led by the nose with gold.
   t.   *A Winter's Tale.* Act IV. Sc. 4, L. 831.

                   Shall remain!
Hear you this Triton of the minnows? mark you
His absolute "shall"?
   u.   *Coriolanus.* Act III. Sc. 1. L. 88.

There is no fettering of authority.
   v.   *All's Well That Ends Well.* Act II. Sc. 3. L. 248.

Those he commands, move only in command,
Nothing in love: now does he feel his title
Hang loose about him, like a giant's robe
Upon a dwarfish thief.
   a.   *Macbeth.*   Act V.   Sc. 2.   L. 19.

Thou hast seen a farmer's dog bark at a beg-
    gar,
And the creature run from the cur: There.
There, thou might'st behold the great image
   of authority;
A dog's obeyed in office.
   b.   *King Lear.*   Act IV.   Sc. 6.   L. 159.

Thus can the demi-god Authority
Make us pay down for our offense by weight.
   c.   *Measure for Measure.*   Act I.   Sc. 2.
                             L. 124.

All people said she had authority.
   d.   Tennyson—*The Princess.*   Pt. VI.
                             L. 221.

Authority forgets a dying king,
Laid widow'd of the power in his eye
That bow'd the will.
   e.   Tennyson—*Morte d'Arthur.*   L. 121.

But see that some one with authority
Be near her still.
   f.   Tennyson—*The Princess.*   Pt. VI.
                             L. 219.

AUTHORSHIP (*See* Occupations).

AUTUMN (*See* Seasons).

AVARICE.

So for a good old-gentlemanly vice,
I think I must take up with avarice.
   g.   Byron—*Don Juan.*   Canto I.   St. 216.

               That disease
Of which all old men sicken, avarice.
   h.   Thomas Middleton—*The Roaring Girl.*
                          Act I.   Sc. 1.

Be niggards of advice on no pretence;
For the worst avarice is that of sense.
   i.   Pope—*Essay on Criticism.*   L. 578.

                    There grows,
In my most ill-compos'd affection such
A stanchless avarice, that, were I king,
I should cut off the nobles for their lands.
   j.   *Macbeth.*   Act IV.   Sc. 3.   L. 76.

There is thy gold; worse poison to men's souls.
   k.   *Romeo and Juliet.*   Act V.   Sc. 1.   L. 79.

                  This avarice
Strikes deeper, grows with more pernicious
   root.
   l.   *Macbeth.*   Act IV.   Sc. 3.   L. 84.

Poverty is in want of much, but avarice of
everything.
   m.   Publius Syrus—*Maxims.*   441.

AWKWARDNESS.

Awkward, embarrassed, stiff, without the
   skill
Of moving gracefully or standing still,
One leg, as if suspicious of his brother,
Desirous seems to run away from t'other.
   n.   Churchill—*Rosciad.*   L. 438.

What's a fine person, or a beauteous face,
Unless deportment gives them decent grace?
Blessed with all other requisites to please,
Some want the striking elegance of ease;
The curious eye their awkward movement
   tires:
They seem like puppets led about by wires.
   o.   Churchill—*Rosciad.*   L. 741.

B.

BABYHOOD.

Oh those little, those little blue shoes!
Those shoes that no little feet use.
     Oh, the price were high
That those shoes would buy,
Those little blue unused shoes!
   p.   William C. Bennett—*Baby's Shoes.*

Sweet babe, in thy face
Soft desires I can trace,
Secret joys and secret smiles,
Little pretty infant wiles.
   q.   William Blake—*A Cradle Song.*

Sweet sleep, with soft down
Weave thy brows an infant crown!
Sweet sleep, angel mild,
Hover o'er my happy child.
   r.   William Blake—*A Cradle Song.*

He smiles, and sleeps!—sleep on
And smile, thou little, young inheritor
Of a world scarce less young: sleep on and
   smile!
Thine are the hours and days when both are
   cheering
And innocent!
   s.   Byron—*Cain.*   Act III.   Sc. 1.   L. 24.

How lovely he appears! his little cheeks
In their pure incarnation, vying with
The rose leaves strewn beneath them.
And his lips, too,
How beautifully parted! No; you shall not
Kiss him; at least not now; he will wake
   soon—
His hour of midday rest is nearly over.
   t.   Byron—*Cain.*   Act III.   Sc. 1.   L. 14.

Look ! how he laughs and stretches out his
    arms,
And opens wide his blue eyes upon thine,
To hail his father ; while his little form
Flutters as winged with joy. Talk not of pain !
The childless cherubs well might envy thee
The pleasures of a parent.
    a.   BYRON—*Cain.* Act III. Sc. 1. L. 171.

Lo ! at the couch where infant beauty sleeps ;
Her silent watch the mournful mother keeps ;
She, while the lovely baby unconscious lies,
Smiles on her slumbering child with pensive
    eyes.
    b.   CAMPBELL—*Pleasures of Hope.* Pt. I.
               L. 225.

When you fold your hands, Baby Louise !
Your hands like a fairy's, so tiny and fair,
With a pretty, innocent, saintlike air,
Are you trying to think of some angel-taught
    prayer
    You learned above, Baby Louise ?
    c.   MARGARET EYTINGE—*Baby Louise.*

Baloo, baloo, my wee, wee thing.
    d.   RICHARD GALL—*Cradle Song.*

What is the little one thinking about ?
Very wonderful things, no doubt ;
    Unwritten history !
    Unfathomed mystery !
Yet he laughs and cries, and eats and drinks,
And chuckles and crows, and nods and winks,
As if his head were as full of kinks
And curious riddles as any sphinx !
    e.   J. G. HOLLAND—*Bitter-Sweet. First
               Movement.* L. 6.

When the baby died,
    On every side
Rose stranger's voices, hard and harsh and
    loud.
The baby was not wrapped in any shroud.
The mother made no sound. Her head was
    bowed
That men's eyes might not see
    Her misery.
    f.   HELEN HUNT—*When the Baby Died.*

Sweet is the infant's waking smile,
    And sweet the old man's rest—
But middle age by no fond wile,
    No soothing calm is blest.
    g.   KEBLE—*The Christian Year. St. Philip
               and St. James.* St. 3.

Suck, baby ! suck ! mother's love grows by
    giving :
Drain the sweet founts that only thrive by
    wasting !
Black manhood comes when riotous guilty
    living
Hands thee the cup that shall be death in
    tasting.
    h.   CHARLES LAMB—*The Gypsy's Malison.
           Sonnet in Letter to Mrs. Procter*, Jan.
                    29, 1829.

A tight little bundle of wailing and flannel,
Perplex'd with the newly found fardel of life.
    i.   FRED. LOCKER—*The Old Cradle.*

The hair she means to have is gold,
Her eyes are blue, she 's twelve weeks old,
    Plump are her fists and pinky.
She fluttered down in lucky hour
From some blue deep in yon sky bower—
    I call her " Little Dinky."
    j.   FRED. LOCKER—*Little Dinky.*

O child ! O new-born denizen
Of life's great city ! on thy head
The glory of the morn is shed,
Like a celestial benison !
Here at the portal thou dost stand,
And with thy little hand
Thou openest the mysterious gate
Into the future's undiscovered land.
    k.   LONGFELLOW—*To a Child.*

A baby was sleeping,
Its mother was weeping.
    l.   SAMUEL LOVER—*The Angel's Whisper.*

    Her beads while she numbered,
    The baby still slumbered,
And smiled in her face, as she bended her
    knee ;
    Oh ! bless'd be that warning,
    My child, thy sleep adorning,
For I know that the angels are whispering
    with thee.
    m.   SAMUEL LOVER—*The Angel's Whisper.*

He seemed a cherub who had lost his way
And wandered hither, so his stay
With us was short, and 'twas most meet
That he should be no delver in earth's clod,
Nor need to pause and cleanse his feet
To stand before his God :
O blest word—Evermore !
    n.   LOWELL—*Threnodia.*

How did they all just come to be you?
God thought about me and so I grew.
    o.   GEO. MACDONALD—*Song in " At The
           Back of The North Wind."* Ch. 33.

Where did you come from, baby dear?
Out of the Everywhere into here.
    p.   GEO. MACDONALD—*Song in " At The
           Back of The North Wind."* Ch. 33

And thou hast stolen a jewel, Death !
Shall light thy dark up like a Star.
A Beacon kindling from afar
Our light of love and fainting faith.
    q.   GERALD MASSEY—*Babe Christabel.*

A sweet, new blossom of Humanity,
Fresh fallen from God's own home to flower
    on earth.
    r.   GERALD MASSEY—*Wooed and Won.*

You scarce could think so small a thing
  Could leave a loss so large;
Her little light such shadow fling
  From dawn to sunset's marge.
In other springs our life may be
  In bannered bloom unfurled,
But never, never match our wee
  White Rose of all the world.
  a.   GERALD MASSEY—*Our Wee White Rose.*

Wee Willie Winkie rins through the toun,
Up stairs and doon stairs in his nicht-goun,
Tirlin' at the window, cryin' at the lock,
"Are the weans in their bed? for it's now
    ten o'clock."
  b.   WILLIAM MILLER—*Willie Winkie.*

When the baby died we said,
With a sudden secret dread;
"Death be merciful and pass;-
Leave the other!"—but alas!
While we watched he waited there,
One foot on the golden stair,
One hand beckoning at the gate,
Till the home was desolate.
  c.   NORA PERRY—*Loss and Gain.*

As living jewels dropped unstained from
    heaven.
  d.   POLLOCK—*Course of Time.* Bk. V.
                         L. 158.

  A daughter and a goodly babe,
Lusty and like to live: the queen receives
Much comfort in 't.
  e.   *Winter's Tale.* Act II. Sc. 2. L. 27.

Fie, fie, how wayward is this foolish love
That, like a testy babe, will scratch the nurse
And presently all humbled kiss the rod!
  f.   *Two Gentlemen of Verona.* Act I.
                    Sc. 2. L. 57.

      God mark thee to his grace!
Thou wast the prettiest babe that e'er I nursed:
An I might live to see thee married once,
I have my wish.
  g.   *Romeo and Juliet.* Act I. Sc. 3. L. 59.

Sleep, little baby! sleep!
  h.   CAROLINE SOUTHEY—*In Vol. Entitled*
        Solitary Hours. *To a Dying Infant.*

A little soul scarce fledged for earth
  Takes wing with heaven again for goal,
Even while we hailed as fresh from birth
  A little soul.
  i.   SWINBURNE—*A Baby's Death.*

Beat upon mine, little heart! beat, beat!
Beat upon mine! you are mine, my sweet!
All mine from your pretty blue eyes to your
    feet,
  My sweet!
  j.   TENNYSON—*Song from Romney's*
                      Remorse.

      But what am I?
An infant crying in the night:
An infant crying for the light:
And with no language but a cry.
  k.   TENNYSON—*In Memoriam.* Pt. LIV.
                          St. 5.

Baby smiled, mother wailed,
Earthward while the sweetling sailed;
Mother smiled, baby wailed,
  When to earth came Viola.
  l.   FRANCIS THOMPSON—*The Making of*
                      Viola. St. 9.

Smile, sweet baby, smile,
For you will have weeping-while;
Native in Heaven is your smile,—
  But your weeping, Viola?
  m.   FRANCIS THOMPSON—*The Making of*
                      Viola. St. 10.

A babe in a house is a well-spring of pleasure.
  n.   TUPPER—*Of Education.*

Hush, my dear, lie still and slumber,
  Holy angels guard thy bed!
Heavenly blessings without number
  Gently falling on thy head.
  o.   WATTS—*A Cradle Hymn.*

BALLADS.

I've now got the music book ready,
Do sit up and sing like a lady
A recitative from Tancredi,
And something about "Palpiti!"
Sing forte when first you begin it,
Piano the very next minute,
They'll cry "What expression there's in it!"
Don't sing English ballads to me!
  p.   THOMAS HAYNES BAYLY—*Don't Sing*
                    English Ballads to Me.

Thespis, the first professor of our art,
At country wakes sung ballads from a cart.
  q.   DRYDEN—*Prologue to Sophonisba.*

I knew a very wise man that believed that
* * * if a man were permitted to make all
the ballads, he need not care who should make
the laws of a nation.
  r.   ANDREW FLETCHER—*Letter to the*
        Marquis of Montrose, the Earl of
                          Rothes.

Some people resemble ballads which are
only sung for a certain time.
  s.   LA ROCHEFOUCAULD—*Maxims and*
                Moral Sentences. No. 220.

I have a passion for ballads. * * * They
are the gypsy children of song, born under
green hedgerows in the leafy lanes and by-
paths of literature,—in the genial Summer-
time.
  t.   LONGFELLOW—*Hyperion.* Bk. II.
                          Ch. II.

For a ballad's a thing you expect to find
    lies in.
   a.   SAMUEL LOVER—*Paddy Blake's Echo.*

I had rather be a kitten, and cry mew!
Than one of these same metre ballad-mongers.
   b.   *Henry IV.* Pt. I. Act III. Sc. 1
                        L. 129.

I love a ballad but even too well; if it be
doleful matter, merrily set down, or a very
pleasant thing indeed, and sung lamentably.
   c.   *Winter's Tale.* Act IV. Sc. 4. L. 187.

A famous man is Robin Hood,
The English ballad-singer's joy.
   d.   WORDSWORTH—*Rob Roy's Grave.*

BANISHMENT.

The world was all before them, where to
    choose
Their place of rest, and Providence their guide;
They, hand in hand, with wandering steps
    and slow,
Through Eden took their solitary way.
   e.   MILTON—*Paradise Lost.* Bk. XII.
                        L. 646.

                Banished?
O friar, the damned use that word in hell;
Howlings attend it: How hast thou the heart,
Being a divine, a ghostly confessor,
A sin-absolver, and my friend profess'd,
To mangle me with that word—banished?
   f.   *Romeo and Juliet.* Act III. Sc. 3.
                        L. 47.

Had we no other quarrel else to Rome, but
    that
Thou art thence banish'd, we would muster all
From twelve to seventy; and pouring war
Into the bowels of ungrateful Rome,
Like a bold flood o'erbear.
   g.   *Coriolanus.* Act IV. Sc. 5. L. 133.

Have stooped my neck under your injuries
And sighed my English breath in foreign
    clouds,
Eating the bitter bread of banishment.
   h.   *Richard II.* Act III. Sc. 1. L. 19.

No, my good lord: banish Peto, banish Bar-
dolph, banish Poins; but for sweet Jack Falstaff, kind Jack Falstaff, true Jack Falstaff,
valiant Jack Falstaff, and therefore more
valiant, being as he is, old Jack Falstaff,
banish not him thy Harry's company: banish
plump Jack and banish all the world.
   i.   *Henry IV.* Pt. I. Act II. Sc. 4.
                        L. 520.

   3

BEAUTY.

Beauty soon grows familiar to the lover,
Fades in his eye, and palls upon the sense.
   j.   ADDISON—*Cato.* Act I. Sc. 4.

I must not say that she was true,
   Yet let me say that she was fair;
And they, that lovely face who view,
   They should not ask if truth be there.
   k.   MATTHEW ARNOLD—*Euphrosyne.*

The beautiful are never desolate;
But some one alway loves them—God or man.
If man abandons, God himself takes them.
   l.   BAILEY—*Festus.* Sc. *Water and Wood.*
                        Midnight. L. 370.

There's nothing that allays an angry mind
So soon as a sweet beauty.
   m.   BEAUMONT AND FLETCHER—*The Elder*
                  Brother. Act III. Sc. 5.

Ye gods! but she is wondrous fair!
   For me her constant flame appears;
The garland she hath culled, I wear
   On brows bald since my thirty years.
Ye veils that deck my loved one rare,
   Fall, for the crowning triumph's nigh.
Ye Gods! but she is wondrous fair!
   And I, so plain a man am I!
   n.   BERANGER—*Qu'elle est jolie.*
              Translated by C. L. Betts.

          The beautiful seems right
By force of beauty, and the feeble wrong
Because of weakness.
   o.   E. B. BROWNING—*Aurora Leigh.* Bk. I.

The essence of all beauty, I call love,
The attribute, the evidence, and end,
The consummation to the inward sense
Of beauty apprehended from without,
I still call love.
   p.   E. B. BROWNING—*Sword Glare.*

   And behold there was a very stately palace
before him, the name of which was Beautiful.
   q.   BUNYAN—*Pilgrim's Progress.* Pt. I.

A lovely being, scarcely formed or moulded,
A rose with all its sweetest leaves yet folded.
   r.   BYRON—*Don Juan.* Canto 15. St. 43.

Her glossy hair was cluster'd o'er a brow
Bright with intelligence, and fair and smooth;
Her eyebrow's shape was like the aërial bow,
Her cheek all purple with the beam of youth,
Mounting, at times, to a transparent glow,
As if her veins ran lightning.
   s.   BYRON—*Don Juan.* Canto I. St. 61.

She walks in beauty like the night
Of cloudless chimes and starry skies;
And all that's best of dark and bright
Meet in her aspect and her eyes:
Thus mellowed to that tender light
Which heaven to gaudy day denies.
   t.   BYRON—*She Walks in Beauty.*

The light of love, the purity of grace,
The mind, the Music breathing from her face,
The heart whose softness harmonized the
 whole,
And, oh! the eye was in itself a Soul!
 a. Byron—*The Bride of Abydos.* Canto I.
         St. 6.

  Thou who hast
The fatal gift of beauty
 b. Byron—*Childe Harold.* Canto IV.
         St. 42.

Who doth not feel, until his failing sight
Faints into dimness with its own delight,
His changing cheek, his sinking heart confess,
The might—the majesty of Loveliness?
 c. Byron—*The Bride of Abydos.* Canto I.
         St. 6.

Exceeding fair she was not; and yet fair
In that she never studied to be fairer
Than Nature made her; beauty cost her noth-
 ing,
Her virtues were so rare.
 d. George Chapman—*All Fools.* Act I.
         Sc. I.

  We do love beauty at first sight; and we do
cease to love it, if it is not accompanied by
amiable qualities.
 e. Lydia Maria Child—*Beauty.*

She is not fair to outward view
 As many maidens be;
Her loveliness I never knew
 Until she smiled on me:
Oh! then I saw her eye was bright,
A well of love, a spring of light.
 f. Hartley Coleridge—*Song.*

Her gentle limbs did she undress,
And lay down in her loveliness.
 g. Coleridge—*Christabel.* Pt. I. St. 24.

'Twas not the fading charms of face
 That riveted Love's golden chain;
It was the high celestial grace
 Of goodness, that doth never wane—
Whose are the sweets that never pall,
Delicious, pure, and crowning all.
 h. Abraham Coles—*The Microcosm and
       other Poems.* P. 244.

Old as I am, for ladies' love unfit,
The power of beauty I remember yet,
Which once inflam'd my soul, and still inspires my wit.
 i. Dryden—*Cymon and Iphigenia.* L. 1.

She, though in full-blown flower of glorious
 beauty,
Grows cold, even in the summer of her age.
 j. Dryden—*Œdipus.* Act IV. Sc. 1.

When beauty fires the blood, how love exalts the mind!
 k. Dryden—*Cymon and Iphigenia.* L. 41.

  If eyes were made for seeing,
Then beauty is its own excuse for being.
 l. Emerson—*The Rhodora.*

  The beautiful rests on the foundations of
the necessary.
 m. Emerson—*Essay. On the Poet.*

Who gave thee, O Beauty,
 The keys of this breast,—
Too credulous lover
 Of blest and unblest?
Say, when in lapsed ages
 Thee knew I of old?
Or what was the service
 For which I was sold?
 n. Emerson—*Ode to Beauty.* St. 1.

In beauty, faults conspicuous grow;
The smallest speck is seen on snow.
 o. Gay—*Fable. The Peacock, Turkey
        and Goose.* L. 1.

'Tis impious pleasure to delight in harm,
And beauty should be kind, as well as charm.
 p. Geo. Granville (Lord Lansdowne)—
        To Myra. L. 21.

The dimple that thy chin contains has beauty
 in its round,
That never has been fathomed yet by myriad
 thoughts profound.
 q. Hafiz—*Odes.* CXLIII.

Beauty was lent to nature as the type
Of heaven's unspeakable and holy joy,
Where all perfection makes the sum of bliss.
 r. S. J. Hale—*Beauty. In Dict. of
       Poetical Quotations.*

There's beauty all around our paths, if but
 our watchful eyes
Can trace it 'midst familiar things, and
 through their lowly guise.
 s. Mrs. Hemans—*Our Daily Paths.*

  Beauty is the index of a larger fact than
wisdom.
 t. O. W. Holmes—*The Professor at the
       Breakfast Table.* II.

A heaven of charms divine Nausicaa lay.
 u. Homer—*Odyssey.* Bk. VI. L. 22.
         Pope's trans.

A queen devoid of beauty is not queen;
She needs the royalty of beauty's mien.
 v. Victor Hugo—*Eviradnus.* V.

A thing of beauty is a joy forever;
Its loveliness increases; it will never
Pass into nothingness; but still will keep
A bower quiet for us, and a sleep
Full of sweet dreams, and health, and quiet
 breathing.
 w. Keats—*Endymion.* Bk. I. L. 1.

Beauty is truth, truth beauty.
   a.   KEATS—*Ode on a Grecian Urn.*

'Tis beauty calls, and glory shows the way.
   b.   NATHANIEL LEE—*Alexander the Great;*
        or, The Rival Queens. Act IV. Sc. 2.

Beautiful in form and feature,
   Lovely as the day,
Can there be so fair a creature
   Formed of common clay?
   c.   LONGFELLOW—*Masque of Pandora.*
        The Workshop of Hephæstus.
        Chorus of the Graces.

Blue were her eyes as the fairy-flax,
   Her cheeks like the dawn of day,
And her bosom white as the hawthorn buds,
   That ope in the month of May.
   d.   LONGFELLOW—*The Wreck of the*
                 Hesperus. St. 2.

Oh, could you view the melodie
Of ev'ry grace,
And musick of her face,
You'd drop a teare,
Seeing more harmonie
In her bright eye,
Then now you heare.
   e.   LOVELACE—*Orpheus to Beasts.*

Beauty, like wit, to judges should be shown;
Both most are valued where they best are
   known.
   f.   LORD LYTTLETON—*Soliloquy of a*
        Beauty in the Country. L. 13.

Where none admire, 'tis useless to excel;
Where none are beaux, 'tis vain to be a belle.
   g.   LORD LYTTLETON—*Soliloquy of a*
        Beauty in the Country. L. 11.

Beauty and sadness always go together.
Nature thought beauty too rich to go forth
Upon the earth without a meet alloy.
   h.   GEORGE MACDONALD— *Within and*
        Without. Pt. IV. Sc. 3.

O, thou art fairer than the evening air
Clad in the beauty of a thousand stars.
   i.   MARLOWE—*Faustus.*

Was this the face that launch'd a thousand
   ships,
And burnt the topless towers of Ilium?
Sweet Helen, make me immortal with a
   kiss.—
Her lips suck forth my soul; see, where it
   flies!—
   j.   MARLOWE—*Faustus.*

Too fair to worship, too divine to love.
   k.   HENRY HART MILMAN—*The Belvidere*
                 Apollo.

And ladies of the Hesperides, that seemed
Fairer than feign'd of old.
   l.   MILTON—*Paradise Regained.* Bk. II.
                 L. 357.

Beauty is nature's brag, and must be shown
In courts, at feasts, and high solemnities,
Where most may wonder at the workmanship.
   m.   MILTON—*Comus.* L. 745.

Beauty is Nature's coin, must not be hoarded,
But must be current, and the good thereof
Consists in mutual and partaken bliss.
   n.   MILTON—*Comus.* L. 739.

* * * for beauty stands
In the admiration only of weak minds
Led captive. Cease to admire, and all her
   plumes
Fall flat and shrink into a trivial toy,
At every sudden slighting quite abash'd.
   o.   MILTON—*Paradise Regained.* Bk. II.
                 L. 220.

Hung over her enamour'd, and beheld
Beauty, which, whether waking or asleep,
Shot forth peculiar graces.
   p.   MILTON—*Paradise Lost.* Bk. V. L. 13.

* * * in naked beauty more adorn'd,
More lovely than Pandora.
   q.   MILTON—*Paradise Lost.* Bk. IV.
                 L. 713.

Yet beauty, tho' injurious, hath strange power,
After offence returning, to regain
Love once possess'd.
   r.   MILTON—*Samson Agonistes.* L. 1003.

The maid who modestly conceals
Her beauties, while she hides, reveals:
Gives but a glimpse, and fancy draws
Whate'er the Grecian Venus was.
   s.   EDWARD MOORE—*The Spider and the*
                 Bee. Fable X.

Not more the rose, the queen of flowers,
Outblushes all the bloom of bower,
Than she unrivall'd grace discloses;
The sweetest rose, where all are roses.
   t.   MOORE—*Odes of Anacreon.* Ode LXVI.

To weave a garland for the rose,
   And think thus crown'd 'twould lovelier be,
Were far less vain than to suppose
   That silks and gems add grace to thee.
   u.   MOORE—*Songs from the Greek Anthology.*
                 To Weave a Garland.

An' fair as was her sweet bodie,
   Yet fairer was her mind:—
Menie's the queen among the flowers,
   The wale o' womankind.
   v.   ROBERT NICOLL—*Menie.*

Hast thou left thy blue course in heaven,
golden-haired son of the sky! The west has
opened its gates; the bed of thy repose is there.
The waves come, to behold thy beauty. They
lift their trembling heads. They see thee lovely in thy sleep; they shrink away with fear.
Rest, in thy shadowy cave, O sun! let thy
return be in joy.
    a.   Ossian—*Carric-Thura.* St. 1.

And all the carnal beauty of my wife
Is but skin-deep.
    b.   Sir Thos. Overbury—*A Wife.*

Beauties in vain their pretty eyes may roll;
Charms strike the sight, but merit wins the
        soul.
    c.   Pope—*Rape of the Lock.* Canto V.
                      L. 33.

'Tis not a lip, or eye, we beauty call,
But the joint force and full result of all.
    d.   Pope—*Essay. On Criticism.* Pt. II.
                      L. 45.

For, when with beauty we can virtue join,
We paint the semblance of a form divine.
    e.   Prior—*To the Countess of Oxford.*

No longer shall the bodice aptly lac'd
From thy full bosom to thy slender waist,
That air and harmony of shape express,
Fine by degrees, and beautifully less.
    f.   Prior—*Henry and Emma.* L. 429.

Is she not more than painting can express,
Or youthful poets fancy, when they love?
    g.   Nicholas Rowe—*The Fair Penitent.*
                    Act III. Sc. 1.

Remember that the most beautiful things in
the world are the most useless; peacocks and
lilies, for instance.
    h.   Ruskin.

The beauty that addresses itself to the eyes
is only the spell of the moment; the eye of
the body is not always that of the soul.
    i.   Georges Sand—*Handsome Lawrence.*
                    Ch. I.

All things of beauty are not theirs alone
  Who hold the fee; but unto him no less
Who can enjoy, than unto them who own,
  Are sweetest uses given to possess.
    j.   J. G. Saxe—*The Beautiful.*

And ne'er did Grecian chisel trace
A Nymph, a Naiad, or a Grace,
Of finer form, or lovelier face!
    k.   Scott—*Lady of the Lake.* Canto I.
                    St. 18.

There was a soft and pensive grace,
A cast of thought upon her face,
That suited well the forehead high,
The eyelash dark, and downcast eye;
    l.   Scott—*Rokeby.* Canto IV. St. 5.

Why thus longing, thus forever sighing
For the far-off, unattain'd, and dim,
While the beautiful all round thee lying
Offers up its low, perpetual hymn?
    m.   Harriet W. Sewall—*Why Thus*
                           Longing.

Beauty comes, we scarce know how, as an
emanation from sources deeper than itself.
    n.   Shairp—*Studies in Poetry and*
                Philosophy. Moral Motive Power.

Beauty doth varnish age.
    o.   *Love's Labour's Lost.* Act IV. Sc. 3.
                    L. 244.

                Beauty is a witch,
Against whose charms faith melteth into blood.
    p.   *Much Ado About Nothing.* Act II.
                    Sc. 1. L. 186.

Beauty is bought by judgment of the eye,
Not utter'd by base sale of chapmen's tongues.
    q.   *Love's Labour's Lost.* Act II. Sc.1.
                    L. 15.

Beauty is but a vain and doubtful good;
A shining gloss that vadeth suddenly;
A flower that dies when first it 'gins to bud;
A brittle glass that's broken presently;
    A doubtful good, a gloss, a glass, a flower,
    Lost, vaded, broken, dead within an hour.
    r.   *The Passionate Pilgrim.* St. 13.

Beauty provoketh thieves sooner than gold.
    s.   *As You Like It.* Act I. Sc. 3. L. 112.

                Beauty's ensign yet
Is crimson in thy lips, and in thy cheeks,
And death's pale flag is not advanced there.
    t.   *Romeo and Juliet.* Act V. Sc. 3.
                    L. 94.

              For her own person,
It beggar'd all description.
    u.   *Antony and Cleopatra.* Act II. Sc. 2.
                    L. 202.

              Heaven bless thee!
Thou hast the sweetest face I ever looked on;
Sir, as I have a soul, she is an angel.
    v.   *Henry VIII.* Act IV. Sc. 1. L. 43.

                Her beauty makes
This vault a feasting presence full of light.
    w.   *Romeo and Juliet.* Act V. Sc. 3.
                    L. 85.

I'll not shed her blood;
Nor scar that whiter skin of hers than snow,
And smooth as monumental alabaster.
    x.   *Othello.* Act V. Sc. 2. L. 3.

Of Nature's gifts thou may'st with lilies boast
And with the half-blown rose.
    y.   *King John.* Act III. Sc. 1. L. 53.

O, she doth teach the torches to burn bright!
It seems she hangs upon the cheek of night,
Like a rich jewel in an Ethiope's ear:
Beauty too rich for use, for earth too dear!
　　a.　　*Romeo and Juliet.* Act I. Sc. 5. L. 46.

Say that she frown; I'll say she looks as clear
As morning roses newly wash'd with dew.
　　b.　　*Taming of the Shrew.* Act II. Sc. 1.
　　　　　　　　　　　　　　　　L. 173.

See where she comes, apparell'd like the
　　spring.
　　c.　　*Pericles.* Act I. Sc. 1. L. 12.

There's nothing ill can dwell in such a temple:
If the ill spirit have so fair a house,
Good things will strive to dwell with't.
　　d.　　*Tempest.* Act I. Sc. 2. L. 458.

'Tis beauty truly blent, whose red and white
Nature's own sweet and cunning hand laid on.
　　e.　　*Twelfth Night.* Act I. Sc. 5. L. 257.

A lovely lady, garmented in light
From her own beauty.
　　f.　　SHELLEY—*The Witch of Atlas.* St. 5.

O beloved Pan, and all ye other gods of this
place, grant me to become beautiful in the
inner man.
　　g.　　SOCRATES—*in Plato's Phædrus.* End.

For all that faire is, is by nature good;
That is a signe to know the gentle blood.
　　h.　　SPENSER—*An Hymne in Honour of
　　　　　　　　　　　Beauty.* L. 139.

Her face so faire, as flesh it seemed not,
But heavenly pourtraict of bright angels' hew,
Cleare as the skye withouten blame or blot,
Through goodly mixture of complexion's dew.
　　i.　　SPENSER—*Faerie Queene.* Canto III.
　　　　　　　　　　　　　　　　St. 22.

They seemed to whisper: "How handsome
　　she is!
What wavy tresses! what sweet perfume!
Under her mantle she hides her wings;
Her flower of a bonnet is just in bloom."
　　j.　　E. C. STEDMAN—*Translation. Jean
　　　　　　Prouvaire's Song at the Barricade.*

She wears a rose in her hair,
　　At the twilight's dreamy close:
Her face is fair,—how fair
　　Under the rose!
　　k.　　R. H. STODDARD—*Under the Rose.*

A daughter of the gods, divinely tall,
And most divinely fair.
　　l.　　TENNYSON—*A Dream of Fair Women.*
　　　　　　　　　　　　　　　　St. 22.

How should I gauge what beauty is her dole,
Who cannot see her countenance for her soul,
As birds see not the casement for the sky?
And as 'tis check they prove its presence by,
I know not of her body till I find
My flight debarred the heaven of her mind.
　　m.　　FRANCIS THOMPSON—*Her Portrait.* St. 9.

Whose body other ladies well might bear
As soul,—yea, which it profanation were
For all but you to take as fleshly woof,
Being spirit truest proof.
　　n.　　FRANCIS THOMPSON—*"Manus Animam
　　　　　　　　　　　　Pinxit."* St. 3.

Whose form is as a grove
Hushed with the cooing of an unseen dove.
　　o.　　FRANCIS THOMPSON—*"Manus Animam
　　　　　　　　　　　　Pinxit."* St. 3.

Loveliness
Needs not the foreign aid of ornament,
But is when unadorn'd adorn'd the most.
　　p.　　THOMSON—*The Seasons. Autumn.*
　　　　　　　　　　　　　　　　L. 204.

Thoughtless of beauty, she was Beauty's self.
　　q.　　THOMSON—*The Seasons. Autumn.*
　　　　　　　　　　　　　　　　L. 209.

All the beauty of the world, 'tis but skin deep.
　　r.　　RALPH VENNING—*Orthodoxe Paradoxes*
　　　　　　(Third Edition, 1650). *The Triumph
　　　　　　　　　　　of Assurance.* P. 41.

The yielding marble of her snowy breast.
　　s.　　EDMUND WALLER—*On a Lady Passing
　　　　　　　　through a Crowd of People.*

Be she fairer than the day,
Or the flowery meads in May,
If she be not so to me,
What care I how fair she be?
　　t.　　GEORGE WITHER—*The Shepherd's
　　　　　　　　　　　　　Resolution.*

Alas! how little can a moment show
　　Of an eye where feeling plays
　　In ten thousand dewy rays;
A face o'er which a thousand shadows go!
　　u.　　WORDSWORTH—*The Triad.*

And beauty born of murmuring sound.
　　v.　　WORDSWORTH—*Three Years She Grew in
　　　　　　　　　　　　Sun and Shower.*

Elysian beauty, melancholy grace,
Brought from a pensive, though a happy
　　place.
　　w.　　WORDSWORTH—*Laodamia.*

Her eyes as stars of Twilight fair,
Like Twilight's, too, her dusky hair,
But all things else about her drawn
From May-time and the cheerful Dawn.
　　x.　　WORDSWORTH—*She was a Phantom of
　　　　　　　　　　　　　Delight.*

True beauty dwells in deep retreats,
    Whose veil is unremoved
Till heart with heart in concord beats,
    And the lover is beloved.
a.   WORDSWORTH—*To* ———. *Let Other*
                        Bards of Angels Sing.

What's female beauty, but an air divine,
Through which the mind's all-gentle graces
        shine?
They, like the Sun, irradiate all between;
The body *charms*, because the soul is *seen.*
b.   YOUNG—*Love of Fame.* Satire VI.
                                L. 151.

BED.

Matthew, Mark, Luke and John,
The bed be blest that I lye on.
c.   THOMAS ADY—*A Cradle in the Dark.*
                    P. 58 (London, 1656).

In bed we laugh, in bed we cry;
And born in bed, in bed we die;
The near approach a bed may show
Of human bliss to human woe.
d.   ISAAC DE BENSERADE—*Translated by*
                            Dr. Johnson.

    To rise with the lark, and go to bed with
the lamb.
e.   NICHOLAS BRETON—*Court and County.*
                (1618: reprint.) P. 183.

Like feather-bed betwixt a wall
And heavy brunt of cannon ball.
f.   BUTLER—*Hudibras.* Pt. I. Canto II.
                                L. 871.

O bed! O bed! delicious bed!
That heaven upon earth to the weary head.
g.   HOOD—*Miss Kilmansegg. Her Dream.*

Night is the time for rest;
    How sweet, when labors close,
To gather round an aching breast
    The curtain of repose.
Stretch the tir'd limbs and lay the head
Down on our own delightful bed!
h.   JAMES MONTGOMERY—*Night.*

    The bed has become a place of luxury to
me! I would not exchange it for all the
thrones in the world.
i.   NAPOLEON I.

BEGGARY.

Beggars must be no choosers.
j.   BEAUMONT AND FLETCHER—*Scornful*
                    Lady. Act V. Sc. 3.

    Homer himself must beg if he want means,
and as by report sometimes he did "go from
door to door and sing ballads, with a company
of boys about him."
k.   BURTON—*Anatomy of Melancholy.*
            Pt. I. Sec. II. Mem. 4.
                        Subsec. VI.

His house was known to all the vagrant train,
He chid their wanderings but reliev'd their
        pain;
The long remembered beggar was his guest,
Whose beard descending swept his aged breast.
l.   GOLDSMITH—*Deserted Village.* L. 149.

To get thine ends, lay bashfulnesse aside;
Who feares to aske, doth teach to be deny'd.
m.   HERRICK—*No Bashfulnesse in Begging.*

A beggar through the world am I,
From place to place I wander by.
Fill up my pilgrim's scrip for me,
For Christ's sweet sake and charity.
n.   LOWELL—*The Beggar.*

A beggar that is dumb, you know,
May challenge double pity.
o.   SIR WALTER RALEIGH—*The Silent*
                            Lover. St. 9.

Beggar that I am, I am even poor in thanks.
p.   *Hamlet.* Act II. Sc. 2. L. 281.

I see, Sir, you are liberal in offers:
You taught me first to beg; and now, me-
        thinks,
You teach me how a beggar should be an-
        swer'd.
q.   *Merchant of Venice.* Act IV. Sc. 1.
                                L. 437.

Speak with me, pity me, open the door:
A beggar begs that never begg'd before.
r.   *Richard II.* Act V. Sc. 3. L. 77.

Unless the old adage must be verified,
That beggars mounted, run their horse to
        death.
s.   *Henry VI.* Pt. III. Act I. Sc. 4.
                                L. 126.

Well, whiles I am a beggar I will rail
And say, there is no sin but to be rich;
And being rich, my virtue then shall be
To say, there is no vice but beggary.
t.   *King John.* Act II. Sc. 1. L. 593.

BELIEF.

    They that deny a God destroy man's nobil-
ity; for certainly man is of kin to the beasts
by his body; and, if he be not of kin to God
by his spirit, he is a base and ignoble creature.
u.   BACON—*Essays. Of Atheism.*

For fools are stubborn in their way,
As coins are harden'd by th' allay;
And obstinacy's ne'er so stiff
As when 'tis in a wrong belief.
v.   BUTLER—*Hudibras.* Pt. III.
                    Canto II. L. 481.

    Belief consists in accepting the affirmations
of the soul; unbelief, in denying them.
w.   EMERSON—*Montaigne.*

The practical effect of a belief is the real test of its soundness.
a.   FROUDE—*Short Studies on Great Subjects. Calvinism.*

When in God thou believest, near God thou wilt certainly be!
b.   LELAND—*The Return of the Gods.*
       L. 150.

O thou, whose days are yet all spring,
   Faith, blighted once, is past retrieving;
Experience is a dumb, dead thing;
   The victory's in believing.
c.   LOWELL—*To ——.*

They believed—faith, I'm puzzled—I think I may call
Their belief a believing in nothing at all,
Or something of that sort; I know they all went
For a general union of total dissent.
d.   LOWELL—*A Fable for Critics.* L. 851.

A man may be a heretic in the truth; and if he believe things only because his pastor says so, or the assembly so determines, without knowing other reason, though his belief be true, yet the very truth he holds becomes his heresy.
e.   MILTON—*Areopagitica.*

Nothing is so firmly believed as what we least know.
f.   MONTAIGNE—*Essays. Of Divine Ordinances.* Bk. I. Ch. XXXI.

And when religious sects ran mad,
   He held, in spite of all his learning,
That if a man's belief is bad,
   It will not be improved by burning.
g.   PRAED—*Poems of Life and Manners.*
       Pt. II. *The Vicar.* St. 9.

Till their own dreams at length deceive 'em,
And oft repeating, they believe 'em.
h.   PRIOR—*Alma.* Canto III. L. 13.

Do not believe what I tell you here any more than if it were some tale of a tub.
i.   RABELAIS—*Works.* Bk. IV.
       Ch. XXXVIII.

           My circumstances
Being so near the truth as I will make them,
Must first induce you to believe.
j.   *Cymbeline.* Act II. Sc. 4. L. 62.

Stands not within the prospect of belief.
k.   *Macbeth.* Act. I. Sc. 3. L. 74.

And to add greater honours to his age
Than man could give him, he died fearing
   God.
l.   *Henry VIII.* Act IV. Sc. 2. L. 67.

When my love swears that she is made of truth,
I do believe her, though I know she lies.
m.   *Sonnet.* CXXXVIII.

There littleness was not; the least of things
Seemed infinite; and there his spirit shaped
Her prospects, nor did he believe,—he *saw*.
n.   WORDSWORTH—*The Excursion.* Bk. I.
       St. 12.

What ardently we wish, we soon believe.
o.   YOUNG—*Night Thoughts.* Night VII.
       Pt. II. L. 1311.

BELLS.

How sweet the tuneful bells' responsive peal!
p.   REV. WM. LISLE BOWLES—*Fourteen Sonnets. Ostend. On Hearing the Bells at Sea.*

That all-softening, overpowering knell,
The tocsin of the soul—the dinner bell.
q.   BYRON—*Don Juan.* Canto V. St. 49.

How soft the music of those village bells,
Falling at intervals upon the ear
In cadence sweet; now dying all away,
Now pealing loud again, and louder still,
Clear and sonorous, as the gale comes on!
With easy force it opens all the cells
Where Memory slept.
r.   COWPER—*Task.* Bk. VI. L. 6.

The church-going bell.
s.   COWPER—*Verses supposed to be written by Alexander Selkirk.*

Your voices break and falter in the darkness,—
Break, falter, and are still.
t.   BRET HARTE—*The Angelus.*

While the steeples are loud in their joy,
To the tune of the bells' ring-a-ding,
Let us chime in a peal, one and all,
For we all should be able to sing Hullah baloo.
u.   HOOD—*Song for the Million.*

The old mayor climbed the belfry tower,
   The ringers ran by two, by three;
" Pull, if ye never pulled before;
   Good ringers, pull your best," quoth he.
" Play uppe, play uppe, O Boston bells!
Ply all your changes, all your swells,
   Play uppe The Brides of Enderby."
v.   JEAN INGELOW—*High Tide on the Coast of Lincolnshire.*

I call the Living—I mourn the Dead—
I break the Lightning.
    a.   *Inscribed on the Great Bell of the Minster*
        of Schaffhausen—also on that of the
        Church of Art, near Lucerne.

The cheerful Sabbath bells, wherever heard,
Strike pleasant on the sense, most like the
    voice
Of one, who from the far-off hills proclaims
Tidings of good to Zion.
    b.   CHARLES LAMB—*The Sabbath Bells.*

Bell, thou soundest merrily,
When the bridal party
    To the church doth hie!
Bell, thou soundest solemnly,
When, on Sabbath morning,
    Fields deserted lie!
    c.   LONGFELLOW (quoted)—*Hyperion.*
                 Bk. III. Ch. 3.

For bells are the voice of the church;
They have tones that touch and search
    The hearts of young and old.
    d.   LONGFELLOW—*The Bells of San Blas.*

He heard the convent bell,
Suddenly in the silence ringing
For the service of noonday.
    e.   LONGFELLOW—*Christus.   The Golden*
                  Legend.   Pt. II.

It cometh into court and pleads the cause
Of creatures dumb and unknown to the laws;
And this shall make, in every Christian clime,
The bell of Atri famous for all time.
    f.   LONGFELLOW—*Tales of a Wayside Inn.*
        The Sicilian's Tale.   The Bell of Atri.

Seize the loud, vociferous bells, and
Clashing, clanging to the pavement
Hurl them from their windy tower!
    g.   LONGFELLOW—*Christus.   The Golden*
                  Legend.   Prologue.

The bells themselves are the best of preachers,
Their brazen lips are learned teachers,
From their pulpits of stone, in the upper air,
Sounding aloft, without crack or flaw,
Shriller than trumpets under the Law,
Now a sermon and now a prayer.
    h.   LONGFELLOW—*Christus.   The Golden*
                  Legend.   Pt. III.

These bells have been anointed,
And baptized with holy water!
    i.   LONGFELLOW—*Christus.   The Golden*
                  Legend.   Prologue.

Those evening bells! those evening bells!
How many a tale their music tells!
    j.   MOORE—*Those Evening Bells.*

Hear the mellow wedding bells,
    Golden bells!
What a world of happiness their harmony
    foretells
    Through the balmy air of night
    How they ring out their delight!
    From the molten golden notes,
        And all in tune
    What a liquid ditty floats
To the turtle-dove that listens while she gloats
        On the moon!
    k.   POE—*The Bells. St. 2.*

With deep affection
And recollection
I often think of
    Those Shandon bells,
Whose sounds so wild would,
In the days of childhood,
Fling round my cradle
    Their magic spells.
    l.   FATHER PROUT (Francis Mahony).
                 The Bells of Shandon.

        And the Sabbath bell,
That over wood and wild and mountain dell
Wanders so far, chasing all thoughts unholy
With sounds most musical, most melancholy.
    m.   SAMUEL ROGERS—*Human Life. L. 517.*

And this be the vocation fit,
For which the founder fashioned it:
High, high above earth's life, earth's labor
E'en to the heaven's blue vault to soar.
To hover as the thunder's neighbor,
The very firmament explore.
To be a voice as from above
Like yonder stars so bright and clear,
That praise their Maker as they move,
And usher in the circling year.
Tun'd be its metal mouth alone
To things eternal and sublime.
And as the swift wing'd hours speed on
May it record the flight of time!
    n.   SCHILLER—*Song of the Bell.*
                E. A. Bowring's trans.

        Around, around,
Companions all, take your ground,
And name the bell with joy profound!
CONCORDIA is the word we've found
Most meet to express the harmonious sound,
That calls to those in friendship bound.
    o.   SCHILLER—*Song of the Bell.*

Through the bride's fair locks so dear
    Twines the virgin chaplet bright,
When the church bells ringing clear
    To the joyous feast invite.
    p.   SCHILLER—*Song of the Bell.*
                E. A. Bowring's Trans.

Like sweet bells jangled, out of tune and harsh
    q.   *Hamlet. Act III. Sc. 1. L. 166.*

Then get thee gone and dig my grave thyself,
And bid the merry bells ring to thine ear
That thou art crowned, not that I am dead.
    a.   *Henry IV.* Pt. II. Act IV. Sc. 5.
                        L. 111.

Hark, how chimes the passing bell!
There's no music to a knell ;
All the other sounds we hear,
Flatter, and but cheat our ear.
This doth put us still in mind
That our flesh must be resigned,
And, a general silence made,
The world be muffled in a shade.
[Orpheus' lute, as poets tell,
Was but moral of this bell,
And the captive soul was she,
Which they called Eurydice,
Rescued by our holy groan,
A loud echo to this tone.]
    b.   SHIRLEY—*The Passing Bell.*

Ring in the valiant man and free,
  The larger heart, the kindlier hand ;
  Ring out the darkness of the land ;
Ring in the Christ that is to be.
    c.   TENNYSON—*In Memoriam.* Pt. CVI.

Ring out old shapes of foul disease ;
  Ring out the narrowing lust of gold ;
  Ring out the thousand wars of old,
Ring in the thousand years of peace.
    d.   TENNYSON—*In Memoriam.* Pt. CVI.

Ring out the old, ring in the new,
Ring, happy bells, across the snow.
    e.   TENNYSON—*In Memoriam.* Pt. CVI.

Ring out, wild bells, to the wild sky,
The flying cloud, the frosty light.
    f.   TENNYSON—*In Memoriam.* Pt. CVI.

Hark ! the loud-voiced bells
  Stream on the world around
With the full wind, as it swells,
  Seas of sound !
    g.   FREDERICK TENNYSON—*The Bridal.*

Softly the loud peal dies,
  In passing winds it drowns,
But breathes, like perfect joys,
  Tender tones,
    h.   FREDERICK TENNYSON—*The Bridal.*

How like the leper, with his own sad cry
Enforcing his own solitude, it tolls !
That lonely bell set in the rushing shoals,
To warn us from the place of jeopardy !
    i.   CHARLES TENNYSON TURNER—*The*
                      Buoy Bell.

BENEVOLENCE.

A kind and gentle heart he had,
  To comfort friends and foes ;
The naked every day he clad
  When he put on his clothes.
    j.   GOLDSMITH—*Elegy on the Death of a*
                           Mad Dog.

Thus to relieve the wretched was his pride,
And e'en his failings lean'd to virtue's side.
    k.   GOLDSMITH—*The Deserted Village.*
                        L. 163.

Large was his bounty, and his soul sincere,
Heaven did a recompense as largely send ;
He gave to misery (all he had) a tear,
He gain'd from Heaven ('twas all he wish'd)
  a friend.
    l.   GRAY—*Elegy. The Epitaph.*

Scatter plenty o'er a smiling land.
    m.   GRAY—*Elegy in a Country Churchyard.*
                        St. 16.

By Jove the stranger and the poor are sent,
And what to those we give, to Jove is lent.
    n.   HOMER—*Odyssey.* Bk. 6. L. 247.
                      Pope's trans.

In every sorrowing soul I pour'd delight,
And poverty stood smiling in my sight.
    o.   HOMER—*Odyssey.* Bk. 17. L. 505.
                      Pope's trans.

          It never was our guise
To slight the poor, or aught humane despise.
    p.   HOMER—*Odyssey.* Bk. 14. L. 65.
                      Pope's trans.

In misery's darkest cavern known,
  His useful care was ever nigh,
Where hopeless anguish pour'd his groan,
  And lonely want retir'd to die.
    q.   SAM'L JOHNSON—*On the Death of*
                Mr. Robert Levet. St. 5.

Who gives himself with his alms feeds three,
Himself, his hungering neighbor, and me.
    r.   LOWELL—*The Vision of Sir Launfal.*
                    Pt. II. VIII.

          For his bounty
There was no winter in't ; an autumn 'twas
That grew the more by reaping : his delights
Were dolphin-like.
    s.   *Antony and Cleopatra.* Act V. Sc. 2.
                      L. 87.

  The poor must be wisely visited and liberally
cared for, so that mendicity shall not be
tempted into mendacity, nor want exasperated
into crime.
    t.   ROBERT C. WINTHROP—*Yorktown*
                    Oration in 1881.

BIRDS.

Come, all ye feathery people of mid-air,
Who sleep 'midst rocks, or on the mountain
        summits
Lie down with the wild winds ; and ye who
        build
Your homes amidst green leaves by grottoes
        cool ;
And ye who on the flat sands hoard your eggs
For suns to ripen, come !
    a.   BARRY CORNWALL—*An Invocation to*
                    Birds.

When the swallows homeward fly,
When the roses scattered lie,
When from neither hill or dale,
Chants the silvery nightingale :
In these words my bleeding heart
Would to thee its grief impart ;
When I thus thy image lose
Can I, ah ! can I, e'er know repose ?
    b.   KARL HERRLOSSOHN—*When the*
                Swallows Homeward Fly.

I was always a lover of soft-winged things.
    c.   VICTOR HUGO—*I Was Always a Lover.*

Do you ne'er think what wondrous beings
        these ?
Do you ne'er think who made them, and who
        taught
The dialect they speak, where melodies
    Alone are the interpreters of thought ?
Whose household words are songs in many
        keys,
Sweeter than instrument of man e'er caught !
    d.   LONGFELLOW—*Tales of a Wayside Inn.*
            The Poet's Tale. The Birds of
                      Killingworth.

Hear how the birds, on ev'ry blooming spray,
With joyous musick wake the dawning day !
    e.   POPE—*Pastorals. Spring. L. 23.*

Albatross.

And a good south wind sprung up behind,
    The Albatross did follow,
And every day, for food or play,
    Came to the mariner's hollo !

In mist or cloud, on mast or shroud,
    It perched for vespers nine ;
Whiles all the night, through fog-smoke white,
    Glimmered the white moonshine.

" God save thee, ancient Mariner !
    From the fiends that plague thee thus !—
Why look'st thou so ?"—" With my cross-bow
    I shot the Albatross."
    f.   COLERIDGE—*Ancient Mariner.* Pt. I.
                             St. 18.

Great albatross !—the meanest birds
    Spring up and flit away,
While thou must toil to gain a flight,
    And spread those pinions grey ;
But when they once are fairly poised,
    Far o'er each chirping thing
Thou sailest wide to other lands,
    E'en sleeping on the wing.
    g.   CHAS. G. LELAND—*Perseverando.*

Bat.

The sun was set ; the night came on apace,
And falling dews bewet around the place ;
The bat takes airy rounds on leathern wings,
And the hoarse owl his woeful dirges sings.
    h.   GAY—*Shepherd's Week. Wednesday ;*
                        or, The Dumps.

Far different there from all that charm'd
        before,
The various terrors of that horrid shore ;
    *   *   *   *   *   *
Those matted woods where birds forget to sing,
But silent bats in drowsy clusters cling.
    i.   GOLDSMITH—*The Deserted Village.*
                                L. 345.

                Ere the bat hath flown
His cloister'd flight.
    j.   *Macbeth.* Act III. Sc. 2. L. 40.

On the bat's back I do fly
After summer merrily.
    k.   *Tempest.* Act V. Sc. 1. L. 91.

Beach Bird.

Thou little bird, thou dweller by the sea,
Why takest thou its melancholy voice,
    And with that boding cry
Along the waves dost thou fly ?
Oh ! rather, bird, with me
    Through this fair land rejoice !
    l.   R. H. DANA—*The Little Beach Bird.*

Blackbird.

The birds have ceased their songs,
All save the blackbird, that from yon tall ash,
'Mid Pinkie's greenery, from his mellow
        throat,
In adoration of the setting sun,
Chants forth his evening hymn.
    m.   MOIR—*An Evening Sketch.*

Golden Bill ! Golden Bill !
    Lo, the peep of day ;
All the air is cool and still,
From the elm-tree on the hill,
    Chant away :
    *   *   *   *   *   *
Let thy loud and welcome lay
Pour alway
Few notes but strong.
    n.   MONTGOMERY—*The Blackbird.*

A slender young Blackbird built in a thorn-
   tree :
A spruce little fellow as ever could be ;
His bill was so yellow, his feathers so black,
So long was his tail, and so glossy his back,
That good Mrs. B., who sat hatching her eggs,
And only just left them to stretch her poor
   legs,
And pick for a minute the worm she preferred,
Thought there never was seen such a beautiful
   bird.
   a.   D. M. Mulock—*The Blackbird and the*
                      Rooks.

O Blackbird ! sing me something well :
   While all the neighbors shoot thee round,
I keep smooth plats of fruitful ground,
   Where thou may'st warble, eat and dwell.
   b.   Tennyson—*The Blackbird.*

How sweet the harmonies of the afternoon !
   The Blackbird sings along the sunny breeze
His ancient song of leaves, and summer boon ;
   Rich breath of hayfields streams thro' whis-
      pering trees ;
And birds of morning trim their bustling
      wings,
And listen fondly—while the Blackbird sings.
   c.   Frederick Tennyson—*The Blackbird.*

Bluebird.

" So the Bluebirds have contracted, have they,
   for a house?
   And a nest is under way for little Mr.
      Wren ? "
"Hush, dear, hush ! Be quiet, dear ! quiet as a
   mouse.
   These are weighty secrets, and we must
      whisper them."
   d.   Susan Coolidge—*Secrets.*

In the thickets and the meadows
Piped the bluebird, the Owaissa.
On the summit of the lodges
Sang the robin, the Opechee.
   e.   Longfellow—*Hiawatha.* **Pt. XXI.**

   Whither away, Bluebird,
      Whither away?
The blast is chill, yet in the upper sky
   Thou still canst find the color of thy wing,
      The hue of May.
Warbler, why speed thy southern flight? ah,
   why,
   Thou too, whose song first told us of the
      Spring?
      Whither away?
   f.   E. C. Stedman—*The Flight of the Birds.*

Bobolink.

Modest and shy as a nun is she ;
   One weak chirp is her only note ;
Braggarts and prince of braggarts is he,
   Pouring boasts from his little throat.
   g.   Bryant—*Robert of Lincoln.*

Robert of Lincoln is gayly drest,
   Wearing a bright black wedding-coat :
White are his shoulders and white his crest.
   h.   Bryant—*Robert of Lincoln.*

Robert of Lincoln's Quaker wife,
   Pretty and quiet, with plain brown wings,
Passing at home a patient life,
   Broods in the grass while her husband sings.
   i.   Bryant—*Robert of Lincoln.*

One day in the bluest of summer weather,
   Sketching under a whispering oak,
I heard five bobolinks laughing together,
   Over some ornithological joke.
   j.   C. P. Cranch—*Bird Language.*

When Nature had made all her birds,
   With no more cares to think on,
She gave a rippling laugh and out
   There flew a Bobolinkon.
   k.   C. P. Cranch—*The Bobolinks.*

Bobolink ! that in the meadow,
   Or beneath the orchard's shadow,
Keepest up a constant rattle
Joyous as my children's prattle,
Welcome to the north again.
   l.   Thos. Hill—*The Bobolink.*

The crack-brained bobolink courts his crazy
      mate,
Poised on a bulrush tipsy with his weight.
   m.   O. W. Holmes—*Spring.*

Out of the fragrant heart of bloom,
   The bobolinks are singing ;
Out of the fragrant heart of bloom
The apple-tree whispers to the room,
" Why art thou but a nest of gloom
While the bobolinks are singing ? "
   n.   W. D. Howells—*The Bobolinks are*
                      Singing.

The broad blue mountains lift their brows
   Barely to bathe them in the blaze ;
The bobolinks from silence rouse
   And flash along melodious ways !
   o.   Harriet Prescott Spofford—
                      Daybreak.

Canary.

Thou should'st be carolling thy Maker's praise,
Poor bird ! now fetter'd, and here set to draw,
With graceless toil of beak and added claw,
The meagre food that scarce thy want allays !
And this—to gratify the gloating gaze
Of fools, who value Nature not a straw,
But know to prize the infraction of her law
And hard perversion of her creatures' ways !
Thee the wild woods await, in leaves attired,
Where notes of liquid utterance should engage
Thy bill, that now with pain scant forage earns.
   p.   Julian Fane—*Poems. Second Edition,*
               with Additional Poems. To a
               Canary Bird.

Sing away, ay, sing away,
    Merry little bird
Always gayest of the gay,
    Though a woodland roundelay
    You ne'er sung nor heard ;
Though your life from youth to age
Passes in a narrow cage.
    a.   D. M. Mulock—*The Canary in his Cage.*

Bird of the amber beak,
Bird of the golden wing !
Thy dower is thy carolling ;
Thou hast not far to seek
Thy bread, nor needest wine
To make thy utterance divine ;
Thou art canopied and clothed
And unto Song betrothed.
    b.   E. C. Stedman—*The Songster.*   St. 2.

Cock.

Good-morrow to thy sable beak,
And glossy plumage, dark and sleek,
Thy crimson moon and azure eye,
Cock of the heath, so wildly shy !
    c.   Joanna Baillie—*The Black Cock.*
                                        St. 1.

While the cock with lively din
Scatters the rear of darkness thin,
And to the stack or the barn door
Stoutly struts his dames before.
    d.   Milton—*L'Allegro.*

Hark, hark ! I hear
The strain of strutting chanticleer
Cry, cock-a-diddle-dow.
    e.   *Tempest.*   Act I.   Sc. 2.   L. 384.

The cock, that is the trumpet to the morn,
Doth with his lofty and shrill-sounding throat
Awake the god of day.
    f.   *Hamlet.*   Act I.   Sc. 1.   L. 150.

            The early village cock
Hath twice done salutation to the morn.
    g.   *Richard III.*   Act V.   Sc. 3.   L. 209.

            The morning cock crew loud,
And at the sound it shrunk in haste away,
And vanish'd from our sight.
    h.   *Hamlet.*   Act I.   Sc. 2.   L. 217.

Crow.

To shoot at crows is powder flung away.
    i.   Gay.   Ep. IV.   Last line.

Only last night he felt deadly sick, and, after
a great deal of pain, two black crows flew out
of his mouth and took wing from the room.
    j.   *Gesta Romanorum*—Tale XLV.

Even the blackest of them all, the crow,
Renders good service as your man-at-arms,
Crushing the beetle in his coat of mail,
And crying havoc on the slug and snail.
    k.   Longfellow—*Tales of a Wayside Inn.
                The Poet's Tale.   Birds of
                Killingworth.*   St. 19.

        Light thickens ; and the crow
Makes wing to the rooky wood.
    l.   *Macbeth.*   Act III.   Sc. 2.   L. 49.

The crow doth sing as sweetly as the lark
When neither is attended.
    m.   *Merchant of Venice.*   Act V.   Sc. 1.
                                        L. 102.

As the many-winter'd crow that leads the
        clanging rookery home.
    n.   Tennyson—*Locksley Hall.*   St. 34.

Cuckoo.

The Attic warbler pours her throat
Responsive to the cuckoo's note.
    o.   Gray—*Ode on the Spring.*

And now I hear its voice again,
    And still its message is of peace,
    It sings of love that will not cease,
For me it never sings in vain.
    p.   Fred'k Locker—*The Cuckoo.*

Oh, could I fly, I'd fly with thee !
    We'd make, with joyful wing,
Our annual visit o'er the globe,
    Companions of the spring.
    q.   John Logan—*To the Cuckoo.*

Sweet bird ! thy bower is ever green,
    Thy sky is ever clear ;
Thou hast no sorrow in thy song,
    No winter in thy year !
    r.   John Logan—*To the Cuckoo.*

And being fed by us you used us so
As that ungentle gull, the cuckoo's bird,
Useth the sparrow.
    s.   *Henry IV.*   Pt. I.   Act V.   Sc. 1.
                                        L. 59.
The cuckoo builds not for himself.
    t.   *Antony and Cleopatra.*   Act II.   Sc. 6.
                                        L. 28.

The cuckoo then on every tree,
Mocks married men ; for thus sings he,
                Cuckoo !
Cuckoo ! Cuckoo ! O word of fear,
Unpleasing to a married ear.
    u.   *Love's Labour's Lost.*   Act V.   Sc. 2.
                                        L. 908.

The merry cuckow, messenger of Spring,
His trumpet shrill hath thrice already sounded
    v.   Spenser—*Sonnet 19.*

               While I deduce,
From the first note the hollow cuckoo sings,
The symphony of spring.
   a.   THOMSON—*The Seasons.* *Spring.*
                      L. 576.

List—'twas the cuckoo—O, with what delight
Heard I that voice! and catch it now, though
     faint,
Far off and faint, and melting into air,
Yet not to be mistaken. Hark again !
Those louder cries give notice that the bird,
Although invisible as Echo's self,
Is wheeling hitherward.
   b.   WORDSWORTH—*The Cuckoo at Laverna.*

O blithe New-comer ! I have heard,
I hear thee and rejoice ;
O Cuckoo ! shall I call thee Bird,
Or but a wandering Voice ?
   c.   WORDSWORTH—*To the Cuckoo*

Cygnet.

Their cygnets following through the foamy
     wake,
Picking the leaves of plants, pursuing insects.
   d.   MONTGOMERY—*Pelican Island.*
                Canto IV. L. 236.

A golden chariot in the midst is set,
And silver signets seem to feel its weight.
   e.   PRIOR—*Solomon.* Bk. II. *Pleasure.*
                      L. 643.

I am the cygnet to this pale faint swan,
Who chants a doleful hymn to his own death ;
And, from the organ-pipe of frailty, sings
His soul and body to their lasting rest.
   f.   *King John.* Act V. Sc. 7. L. 21.

So doth the swan her downy cygnets save,
Keeping them prisoner underneath her wings.
   g.   *Henry VI.* Pt. I. Act V. Sc. 3.
                      L. 56.

Dove.

Oh ! when 'tis summer weather,
And the yellow bee, with fairy sound,
The waters clear is humming round,
And the cuckoo sings unseen,
And the leaves are waving green—
     Oh ; then 'tis sweet,
     In come retreat,
To hear the murmuring dove,
With those whom on earth alone we love,
And to wind through the greenwood together.
   h.   REV. WM. LISLE BOWLES—*The*
                             Greenwood.

And there my little doves did sit
   With feathers softly brown
And glittering eyes that showed their right
To general Nature's deep delight.
   i.   E. B. BROWNING—*My Doves.*

The thrustelcok made eek hir lay,
The wode dove upon the spray
She sang ful loude and cleere.
   j.   CHAUCER—*The Rime of Sir Thopas.*

As when the dove returning bore the mark
Of earth restored to the long labouring ark ;
The relics of mankind, secure of rest,
Oped every window to receive the guest,
And the fair bearer of the message bless'd.
   k.   DRYDEN—*To Her Grace of Ormond.*
                      L. 70.

Shatter'd and torn, before the flag they fly
Like doves, that the exalted eagle spy
Ready to stoop and seize them from on high.
   l.   DUKE—*On the Death of Charles II.*

   Listen, sweet Dove, unto my song,
And spread thy golden wings in me ;
   Hatching my tender heart so long,
Till it get wing, and flie away with Thee.
   m.   HERBERT—*The Church.* *Whitsunday.*

See how that pair of billing doves
With open murmurs own their loves
And, heedless of censorious eyes,
Pursue their unpolluted joys :
No fears of future want molest
The downy quiet of their nest.
   n.   LADY MONTAGU—*Verses.* *Written in a*
                     Garden. St. 1.

                The Dove,
On silver pinions, winged her peaceful way.
   o.   MONTGOMERY—*Pelican Island.*
                Canto I. L. 173.

Not half so swift the trembling doves can fly,
When the fierce eagle cleaves the liquid sky ;
Not half so swiftly the fierce eagle moves,
When thro' the clouds he drives the trem-
     bling doves.
   p.   POPE—*Windsor Forest.* L. 185.

Anon, as patient as the female dove,
When that her golden couplets are disclosed,
His silence will sit drooping.
   q.   *Hamlet.* Act V. Sc. 1. L. 309.

   But I will aggravate my voice so that I will
roar you as gently as any sucking dove.
   r.   *A Midsummer Night's Dream.* Act I.
                     Sc. 2. L. 83.

So shows a snowy dove trooping with crows.
   s.   *Romeo and Juliet.* Act I. Sc. 5.
                      L. 50.

The dove and very blessed spirit of peace.
   t.   *Henry IV.* Pt. II. Act IV. Sc. 1.
                      L. 46.

And oft I heard the tender dove
In firry woodlands making moan.
   u.   TENNYSON—*Miller's Daughter.*

I heard a Stock-dove sing or say
His homely tale, this very day;
His voice was buried among trees,
Yet to be come at by the breeze:
He did not cease; but cooed—and cooed;
And somewhat pensively he wooed:
He sang of love, with quiet blending,
Slow to begin, and never ending;
Of serious faith, and inward glee;
That was the song,—the song for me!
 a. WORDSWORTH—*O Nightingale! Thou
     Surely Art.*

Eagle.

So the struck eagle, stretched upon the plain,
No more through rolling clouds to soar again,
Viewed his own feather on the fatal dart,
And wing'd the shaft that quivered in his
 heart.
 b. BYRON—*English Bards and Scotch
     Reviewers.* L. 826.

    Tho' he inherit
Nor the pride, nor ample pinion,
 That the Theban eagle bear,
Sailing with supreme dominion
 Thro' the azure deep of air,
 c. GRAY—*The Progress of Poesy.*

King of the peak and glacier,
 King of the cold, white scalps,
He lifts his head at that close tread,
 The eagle of the Alps.
 d. VICTOR HUGO—*The Swiss Mercenaries.*

The bird of Jove, stoop'd from his aery tour,
Two birds of gayest plume before him drove.
 e. MILTON—*Paradise Lost.* Bk. XI.
         L. 184.

Bird of the broad and sweeping wing,
 Thy home is high in heaven,
Where wide the storms their banners fling,
 And the tempest clouds are driven.
 f. PERCIVAL—*To the Eagle.*

So, in the Libyan fable it is told
That once an eagle, stricken with a dart,
Said, when he saw the fashion of the shaft,
"With our own feathers, not by others' hands,
 Are we now smitten."
 g. ED. H. PLUMPTRES—*Æschylus.*
        Fragm. 123.

And little eagles wave their wings in gold.
 h. POPE—*Moral Essays.* *Ep. to Addison.*
          L. 30.

But flies an eagle flight, bold and forth on,
Leaving no track behind.
 i. *Timon of Athens.* Act I. Sc. 1.
          L. 49.

I saw Jove's bird, the Roman eagle, wing'd
From the spungy south to this part of the
 west,
There vanish'd in the sunbeams.
 j. *Cymbeline.* Act IV. Sc. 2. L. 348.

The eagle suffers little birds to sing,
And is not careful what they mean thereby.
 k. *Titus Andronicus.* Act IV. Sc. 4.
          L. 83.

Around, around, in ceaseless circles wheeling
With clangs of wings and scream, the Eagle
 sailed
Incessantly.
 l. SHELLEY—*Revolt of Islam.* Canto I.
          St. 10.

He clasps the crag with hooked hands;
Close to the sun in lonely lands,
Ring'd with the azure world, he stands.
The wrinkled sea beneath him crawls:
He watches from his mountain walls,
And like a thunderbolt he falls.
 m. TENNYSON—*The Eagle.*

Shall eagles not be eagles? wrens be wrens?
If all the world were falcons, what of that?
The wonder of the eagle were the less,
But he not less the eagle.
 n. TENNYSON—*The Golden Year.* L. 37.

Estridge.

Prince Edward all in gold, as he great Jove
 had been,
The Mountfords all in plumes, like estridges
 were seen.
 o. DRAYTON—*Poly-Olbion.* St. 22.

    All furnish'd, all in arms;
All plum'd, like estridges that with the wind
Baited, like eagles having lately bath'd.
 p. *Henry IV.* Pt. I. Act IV. Sc. 1.
          L. 97.

Falcon.

The falcon and the dove sit there together,
And th' one of them doth prune the other's
 feather.
 q. DRAYTON—*Noah's Flood.*

I know a falcon swift and peerless
 As e'er was cradled in the pine;
No bird had ever eye so fearless,
 Or wing so strong as this of mine.
 r. LOWELL—*The Falcon.*

Say, will the falcon, stooping from above,
Smit with her varying plumage, spare the
 dove?
Admires the jay the insect's gilded wings?
Or hears the hawk when Philomela sings?
 s. POPE—*Essay on Man.* Ep. III. L. 53.

A falcon, tow'ring in her pride of place,
Was by a mousing owl hawk'd at and kill'd.
    a.   *Macbeth.* Act II. Sc. 4. L. 12.

My falcon now is sharp, and passing empty ;
And till she stoop, she must not be full-gorg'd,
For then she never looks upon her lure.
    b.   *Taming of the Shrew.* Act IV. Sc. 1.
                              L. 193.

So, when a falcon skims the airy way,
Stoops from the clouds, and pounces on his
    prey,
Dash'd on the earth the feather'd victim lies,
Expands its feeble wings, and, flutt'ring, dies.
    c.   P. WHITEHEAD—*The Gymnasiad.*
                              Bk. III.

Fowl, Wild.

The wildfowl nestled in the brake
And sedges, brooding in their liquid bed.
    d.   BYRON—*Don Juan.* Canto XIII.
                              St. 57.

Goldfinch.

Two goldfinches, whose sprightly song
Had been their mutual solace long,
Lived happy prisoners there.
    e.   COWPER—*Faithful Bird.*

A goldfinch there I saw, with gawdy pride
Of painted plumes, that hopped from side to
    side.
    f.   DRYDEN—*The Flower and the Leaf.*
                              L. 106.

Goose.

I dare not hope to please a Cinna's ear.
Or sing what Varus might vouchsafe to hear ;
Harsh are the sweetest lays that I can bring,
So screams a goose where swans melodious
    sing.
    g.   BEATTIE—*Virgil.* Pastoral 9.

Shall I, like Curtius, desperate in my zeal,
O'er head and ears plunge for the common
    weal?
Or rob Rome's ancient geese of all their
    glories,
And cackling save the monarchy of Tories?
    h.   POPE—*Dunciad.* Bk. I. L. 209.

As wild geese that the creeping fowler eye,
Or russet-pated choughs, many in sort,
Rising and cawing at the gun's report,
Sever themselves, and madly sweep the sky,
    i.   *Midsummer Night's Dream.* Act III.
                        Sc. 2. L. 20.

Gull, Sea.

Lack-lustre eye, and idle wing,
And smirched breast that skims no more,
White as the foam itself, the wave—
Hast thou not even a grave
Upon the dreary shore,
Forlorn, forsaken thing?
    j.   D. M. MULOCK—*A Dead Sea-Gull.*

And being fed by us you used us so
As that ungentle gull, the cuckoo's bird,
Useth the sparrow.
    k.   *Henry IV.* Pt. I. Act V. Sc. I.
                              L. 59.

Hawk.

The winds are pillow'd on the waveless deep,
And from the curtain'd sky the midnight
    moon
Looks sombred o'er the forest depths, that
    sleep
Unstirring, while a soft, melodious tune,
Nature's own voice, the lapsing stream, is
    heard,
And ever and anon th'unseen, night-wander-
    ing bird.
    l.   MOIR—*The Night Hawk.*

Between two hawks, which flies the higher
    pitch.
    m.   *Henry VI.* Pt. I. Act II. Sc. 4.
                              L. 11.

Dost thou love hawking? thou hast hawks
    will soar
Above the morning lark.
    n.   *Taming of the Shrew.* Induction. Sc. 2.
                              L. 45.

I am but mad north-north-west : when the
wind is southerly, I know a hawk from a
handsaw.
    o.   *Hamlet.* Act II. Sc. 2. L. 395.

No marvel, an it like your majesty,
My lord protector's hawks do tower so well ;
They know their master loves to be aloft
And bears his thoughts above his falcon's
    pitch.
    p.   *Henry VI.* Pt. II. Act II. Sc. 1.
                              L. 9.

When I bestride him I soar, I am a hawk.
    q.   *Henry V.* Act III. Sc. 7. L. 14.

The wild hawk stood with the down on his
    beak
And stared with his foot on the prey.
    r.   TENNYSON—*The Poet's Song.*

Humming-bird.

And the humming-bird that hung
    Like a jewel up among
The tilted honeysuckle horns
    They mesmerized and swung
In the palpitating air,
    Drowsed with odors strange and rare,
And, with whispered laughter, slipped away
    And left him hanging there.
    s.   JAMES WHITCOMB RILEY—*The South
                            Wind and the Sun.*

Jackdaw.

The Jackdaw sat in the Cardinal's chair!
Bishop and Abbot and Prior were there,
  Many a monk and many a friar,
  Many a knight and many a squire,
With a great many more of lesser degree,—
In sooth a goodly company ;
And they served the Lord Primate on bended
    knee.
          Never, I ween,
          Was a prouder seen,
Read of in books or dreamt of in dreams,
Than the Cardinal Lord Archbishop of
    Rheims.
  a.   R. H. BARHAM—*Ingoldsby Legends.*
                The Jackdaw of Rheims.

An old miser kept a tame jackdaw, that
used to steal pieces of money, and hide them
in a hole, which a cat observing, asked, "Why
he would hoard up those round shining things
that he could make no use of?" "Why," said
the jackdaw, "my master has a whole chest-
full, and makes no more use of them than I
do."
  b.   SWIFT—*Thoughts on Various Subjects.*

Jay.

What, is the jay more precious than the lark,
Because his feathers are more beautiful?
  c.   *Taming of the Shrew.*   Act IV.   Sc. 3.
                          L. 177.

And startle from his ashen spray,
Across the glen, the screaming jay.
  d.   WARTON—*The Hamlet.*   Ode 2.

Kingfisher.

  I can tell you what that bird was—a king-
fisher, the celebrated halcyon of the ancients
about which so many tales are told.   It lives
on fish which it catches in the manner you
saw.   It builds in holes in the banks, is a
shy retiring bird, never to be seen far from
the stream where it inhabits.
  e.   JOHN AIKEN—*Eyes and Eyes.*

She rears her young on yonder tree ;
She leaves her faithful mate to mind 'em ;
Like us, for fish she sails to sea,
And, plunging, shows us where to find 'em.
Yo, ho, my hearts! let's seek the deep,
Ply every oar, and cheerly wish her,
While slow the bending net we sweep,
God bless the fish-hawk and the fisher.
  f.   ALEXANDER WILSON—*The Fisherman's
                          Hymn.*

Lapwing.

Changed to a lapwing by th' avenging god,
He made the barren waste his lone abode,
And oft on soaring pinions hover'd o'er
The lofty palace then his own no more.
  g.   BEATTIE—*Virgil.*   Pastoral 6.

The false lapwynge, full of trecherye.
  h.   CHAUCER—*The Parlement of Fowles.*
                          L. 47.

Amid thy desert-walks the lapwing flies,
And tires their echoes with unvaried cries.
  i.   GOLDSMITH—*Deserted Village.*   L. 44.

For look where Beatrice, like a lapwing, runs
Close by the ground, to hear our conference.
  j.   *Much Ado About Nothing.*   Act III.
                          Sc. 1.   L. 25.

Lark.

The music soars within the little lark,
And the lark soars.
  k.   E. B. BROWNING—*Aurora Leigh.*
                    Bk. III.   L. 155.

Oh, stay, sweet warbling woodlark, stay,
Nor quit for me the trembling spray,
A hapless lover courts thy lay,
  Thy soothing, fond complaining.
        *   *   *   *   *   *

Thou tells o' never-ending care,
O' speechless grief, and dark despair ;
For pity's sake, sweet bird, nae mair !
  Or my poor heart is broken !
  l.   BURNS—*Address to the Woodlark.*
                    Sts. 1 and 4

The merry lark he soars on high,
  No worldly thought o'ertakes him.
He sings aloud to the clear blue sky,
  And the daylight that awakes him.
  m.   HARTLEY COLERIDGE—*Song.*

The lark now leaves his watery nest,
  And climbing, shakes his dewy wings.
He takes your window for the East
  And to implore your light he sings.
  n.   SIR WILLIAM DAVENANT—*The Lark
              now Leaves his Watery Nest.*

Musical cherub, soar, singing, away !
  Then, when the gloaming comes,
  Low in the heather blooms
Sweet will thy welcome and bed of love be !
  Emblem of happiness,
  Blest is thy dwelling-place—
O, to abide in the desert with thee !
  o.   HOGG—*The Skylark.*

Rise with the lark, and with the lark to bed.
  p.   HURDIS—*The Village Curate.*   L. 276.

None but the lark so shrill and clear ;
Now at heaven's gate she claps her wings,
The morn not waking till she sings.
  q.   LYLY—*The Songs of Birds.*

          And now the herald lark
Left his ground-nest, high tow'ring to descry
The morn's approach, and greet her with his
    song.
  r.   MILTON—*Paradise Regained.*   Bk. II.
                          L. 279

To hear the lark begin his flight,
And singing startle the dull Night,
From his watch-tower in the skies,
Till the dappled dawn doth rise.
    a.   MILTON—*L'Allegro.* L. 41.

The bird that soars on highest wing,
  Builds on the ground her lowly nest;
And she that doth most sweetly sing,
  Sings in the shade when all things rest :
In lark and nightingale we see
What honor hath humility.
    b.   MONTGOMERY—*Humility.*

I said to the sky-poised Lark :
  " Hark—hark !
Thy note is more loud and free
Because there lies safe for thee
  A little nest on the ground."
    c.   D. M. MULOCK—*A Rhyme About Birds.*

No more the mounting larks, while Daphne
    sings,
Shall, list'ning, in mid-air suspend their wings.
    d.   POPE—*Pastorals. Winter.* L. 53.

O earliest singer ! O care-charming bird !
Married to morning, by a sweeter hymn
Than priest e'er chanted from his cloister dim
At midnight,—or veiled virgin's holier word
At sunrise or the paler evening heard.
    e.   ADELAIDE PROCTER—*The Flood of*
                          Thessaly.

O happy skylark springing
  Up to the broad, blue sky,
Too fearless in thy winging,
Too gladsome in thy singing,
  Thou also soon shalt lie
Where no sweet notes are ringing.
    f.   CHRISTINA G. ROSSETTI—*Gone Forever.*
                            St. 2.

The sunrise wakes the lark to sing.
    g.   CHRISTINA G. ROSSETTI—*Bird Raptures.*
                            L. 1.

Hark ! hark ! the lark at heaven's gate sings,
  And Phoebus 'gins arise,
His steeds to water at those springs
  On chalic'd flowers that lies.
    h.   *Cymbeline*—Act II. Sc. 3. *Song.*
                            L. 21.

It is the lark that sings so out of tune,
Straining harsh discords and unpleasing
    sharps.
    i.   *Romeo and Juliet*—Act III. Sc. 5.
                            L. 27.

It was the lark, the herald of the morn.
    j.   *Romeo and Juliet*—Act III. Sc. 5.
                            L. 6.

Lo ! here the gentle lark, weary of rest,
From his moist cabinet mounts up on high,
And wakes the morning. from whose silver
    breast
The sun ariseth in his majesty.
    k.   *Venus and Adonis*—L. 853.

4

Some say, that ever 'gainst that season comes
Wherein our Saviour's birth is celebrated,
The bird of dawning singeth all night long :
And then, they say, no spirit dare stir
    abroad ;
The nights are wholesome ; then no planets
    strike,
No fairy takes, nor witch hath power to
    charm,
So hallow'd and so gracious is the time.
    l.   *Hamlet*—Act I. Sc. 1. L. 158.

Then my dial goes not true ; I took this lark
    for a bunting.
    m.   *All's Well That Ends Well*—Act II.
                        Sc. 5. L. 5.

Better than all measures
  Of delightful sound,
Better than all treasures
  That in books are found,
Thy skill to poet were, thou scorner of the
    ground !
    n.   SHELLEY—*To a Skylark.*

Sound of vernal showers
  On the twinkling grass,
Rain-awakened flowers,
  All that ever was
Joyous, and clear, and fresh, thy music doth
    surpass.
    o.   SHELLEY—*To a Skylark.*

                        Up springs the lark,
Shrill-voiced, and loud, the messenger of
    morn ;
Ere yet the shadows fly, he mounted sings.
Amid the dawning clouds, and from their
    haunts
Calls up the tuneful nations.
    p.   THOMSON—*The Seasons. Spring.*
                            L. 587.

The lark sung loud ; the music at his heart
Had called him early ; upward straight he
    went,
And bore in nature's quire the merriest part,
As to the lake's broad shore my steps I bent.
    q.   CHARLES TENNYSON TURNER—*Sonnet.*
                         An April Day.

The lark that shuns on lofty boughs to build
Her humble nest, lies silent in the field.
    r.   EDMUND WALLER—*Of the Queen.*

Ethereal minstrel ! pilgrim of the sky !
Dost thou despise the earth where cares
    abound ?
Or, while the wings aspire, are heart and eye
Both with thy nest upon the dewy ground ?
Thy nest which thou canst drop into at will,
Those quivering wings composed, that music
    still !
    s.   WORDSWORTH—*Poems of the*
               Imagination. To a Skylark.

Leave to the nightingale her shady wood;
A privacy of glorious light is thine:
Whence thou dost pour upon the world a
   flood
Of harmony, with instinct more divine:
Type of the wise who soar, but never roam:
True to the kindred points of Heaven and
   Home!
  a.   WORDSWORTH—*Poems of the
                Imagination. To a Skylark.*

Linnet.

Is it for thee the linnet pours his throat?
Loves of his own, and raptures swell the note.
  b.   POPE—*Essay on Man.* Ep. III. L. 33.

Perch'd on the cedar's topmost bough,
  And gay with gilded wings,
Perchance the patron of his vow,
  Some artless linnet sings.
  c.   SHENSTONE—*Valentine's Day.*

I do but sing because I must,
And pipe but as the linnets sing.
  d.   TENNYSON—*In Memoriam.* Pt. XXI.
                        St. 6.

          Linnets * * * sit
On the dead tree, a dull despondent flock.
  e.   THOMSON—*The Seasons. Autumn.*
                        L. 974.

Hail to thee, far above the rest
  In joy of voice and pinion!
Thou, linnet! in thy green array,
Presiding spirit here to-day,
  Dost lead the revels of the May;
  And this is thy dominion.
  f.   WORDSWORTH—*The Green Linnet.*

Martlet.

          The martlet
Builds in the weather on the outward wall,
Even in the force and road of casualty.
  g.   *Merchant of Venice.* Act II. Sc. 9.
                        L. 28.

        This guest of summer,
The temple-haunting martlet, does approve,
By his lov'd mansionry, that the heaven's
   breath
Smells wooingly here; no jutty, frieze,
Buttress, nor coign of vantage, but this bird
Hath made its pendent bed, and procreant
   cradle:
Where they most breed and haunt, I have
   observ'd,
The air is delicate.
  h.   *Macbeth.* Act I. Sc. 6. L. 3.

Mocking-bird.

Then from the neighboring thicket the mocking-bird, wildest of singers,
Swinging aloft on a willow spray that hung
   o'er the water,
Shook from his little throat such floods of
   delirious music,
That the whole air and the woods and the
   waves seemed silent to listen.
  i.   LONGFELLOW—*Evangeline.* Pt. II.
                        St. 2.

Living echo, bird of eve,
Hush thy wailing, cease to grieve;
Pretty warbler, wake the grove
To notes of joy, to songs of love.
  j.   THOMAS MORTON—*Pretty Mocking-Bird.*

Winged mimic of the woods! thou motley fool!
Who shall thy gay buffoonery describe?
Thine ever-ready notes of ridicule
Pursue thy fellows still with jest and jibe:
Wit, sophist, songster, Yorick of thy tribe
Thou sportive satirist of Nature's school;
To thee the palm of scoffing we ascribe,
Arch-mocker and mad abbot of misrule!
  k.   ROBERT WILDE, D.D.—*Sonnet. To
                     the Mocking-Bird.*

Nightingale.

Hark! ah, the nightingale—
The tawny-throated!
Hark from that moonlit cedar what a burst!
What triumph! hark!—what pain!
     * * * * *
Listen, Eugenia—
How thick the bursts come crowding through
   the leaves!
Again—thou hearest?
Eternal passion!
Eternal pain!
  l.   MATTHEW ARNOLD—*Philomela.* L. 32.

For as nightingales do upon glow-worms feed,
So poets live upon the living light.
  m.   BAILEY—*Festus.* Sc. *Home.*

As it fell upon a day
In the merry month of May,
Sitting in a pleasant shade
Which a grove of myrtles made.
  n.   RICHARD BARNFIELD—*Address to the
                     Nightingale.*

It is the hour when from the boughs
  The nightingale's high note is heard;
It is the hour when lovers' vows
  Seem sweet in every whisper'd word.
  o.   BYRON—*Parisina.* St. 1.

  "Most musical, most melancholy" bird!
A melancholy bird! Oh! idle thought!
  In nature there is nothing melancholy.
  p.   COLERIDGE—*The Nightingale.* L. 13.

'Tis the merry nightingale
That crowds, and hurries, and precipitates
With fast thick warble his delicious notes,
As he were fearful that an April night
Would be too short for him to utter forth
His love-chant, and disburthen his full soul
Of all its music!
a.　COLERIDGE—*The Nightingale.*　L. 43.

Sweet bird, that sing'st away the early hours,
Of winter's past or coming void of care,
Well pleaséd with delights which present
　are,
Fair seasons, budding sprays, sweet-smelling
　flowers.
b.　DRUMMOND—*Sonnet.　To a Nightingale.*

Like a wedding-song all-melting
Sings the nightingale, the dear one.
c.　HEINE—*Book of Songs.　Donna Clara.*

The nightingale appear'd the first,
　And as her melody she sang,
The apple into blossom burst,
　To life the grass and violets sprang.
d.　HEINE—*Book of Songs.　New Spring.*
　　　　　　　　　　　　　　　No. 9.

And the nightingale's sweet music
Fills the air and leafy bowers.
e.　HEINE—*Book of Songs.　New Spring.*
　　　　　　　　　　　　　　　No. 31.

Adieu! adieu! thy plaintive anthem fades
Past the near meadows, over the still stream,
Up the hill-side; and now 'tis buried deep
In the next valley-glades:
Was it a vision, or a waking dream?
Fled is that music:—do I wake or sleep?
f.　KEATS—*To a Nightingale.*

Thou wast not born for death, immortal bird!
No hungry generations tread thee down;
The voice I hear this passing night was heard
In ancient days by emperor and clown.
g.　KEATS—*To a Nightingale.*

Where the nightingale doth sing
Not a senseless, tranced thing,
But divine melodious truth.
h.　KEATS—*Ode, " Bards of Passion and of
　　　　　　　　　　　　　Mirth."*

Soft as Memnon's harp at morning,
　To the inward ear devout,
Touched by light, with heavenly warning
　Your transporting chords ring out.
Every leaf in every nook
Every wave in every brook,
Chanting with a solemn voice
Minds us of our better choice.
i.　JOHN KEBLE—*The Nightingale.*

To the red rising moon, and loud and deep
The nightingale is singing from the steep.
j.　LONGFELLOW—*Keats.*

What bird so sings, yet does so wail?
O, 'tis the ravish'd nightingale—
Jug, jug, jug, jug—tereu—she cries,
And still her woes at midnight rise.
k.　LYLY—*The Songs of Birds.*

O nightingale, that on yon bloomy spray
　Warblest at eve, when all the woods are
　　still;
　Thou with fresh hope the lover's heart
　　dost fill
While the jolly hours lead on propitious May.
l.　MILTON—*Sonnet.　To the Nightingale.*

Sweet bird that shunn'st the noise of folly,
Most musical, most melancholy!
Thee, chauntress, oft, the woods among,
I woo, to hear thy even-song.
m.　MILTON—*Il Penseroso.*　L. 61.

Thy liquid notes that close the eye of day;
　First heard before the shallow cuckoo's
　　bill,
　Portend success in love;
n.　MILTON—*Sonnet.　To the Nightingale.*

I said to the Nightingale;
　" Hail, all hail!
Pierce with thy trill the dark,
Like a glittering music-spark,
　When the earth grows pale and dumb."
o.　D. M. MULOCK—*A Rhyme About Birds*

Yon nightingale, whose strain so sweetly
　flows,
Mourning her ravish'd young or much-loved
　mate,
A soothing charm o'er all the valleys throws
And skies, with notes well tuned to her sad
　state.
p.　PETRARCH—*To Laura in Death.*
　　　　　　　　　　　　　Sonnet XLIII.

Hark! that's the nightingale,
　Telling the self-same tale
Her song told when this ancient earth was
　young:
So echoes answered when her song was sung
　In the first wooded vale.
q.　CHRISTINA G. ROSSETTI—*Twilight Calm.*
　　　　　　　　　　　　　St. 7.

The sunrise wakes the lark to sing,
　The moonrise wakes the nightingale.
Come, darkness, moonrise, everything
　That is so silent, sweet, and pale:
Come, so ye wake the nightingale.
r.　CHRISTINA G. ROSSETTI—*Bird Raptures.*
　　　　　　　　　　　　　St. 1.

The angel of spring, the mellow-throated
　nightingale.
s.　*Sappho.　Fragm. 39.*

The nightingale, if she should sing by day,
When every goose is cackling, would be
    thought
No better a musician than the wren.
How many things by season season'd are
To their right praise, and true perfection!
   a.   *Merchant of Venice.* Act V. Sc. 1.
                           L. 104.

Wilt thou be gone? it is not yet near day:
It was the nightingale, and not the lark,
That pierc'd the fearful hollow of thine ear;
Nightly she sings on yon pomegranate tree:
Believe me, love, it was the nightingale.
   b.   *Romeo and Juliet.* Act III. Sc. 5.
                           L. 1.

Wilt thou have music? hark, Apollo plays,
And twenty caged nightingales do sing.
   c.   *Taming of the Shrew.* Induction.
                      Sc. 2.   L. 37.

One nightingale in an interfluous wood
Satiate the hungry dark with melody.
   d.   SHELLEY—*The Woodman and the*
                         Nightingale.

        O Nightingale,
Cease from thy enamoured tale.
   e.   SHELLEY—*Scenes from*
                " *Magico Prodigioso.*" Sc. 3.

The nightingale as soon as April bringeth
  Unto her rested sense a perfect waking,
While late bare earth, proud of new clothing,
    springeth,
Sings out her woes, a thorn her song-book
    making.
And mournfully bewailing,
  Her throat in tunes expresseth
What grief her breast oppresseth.
   f.   SIR PHILIP SIDNEY—*O Philomela Fair.*

Lend me your song, ye Nightingales!   O,
    pour
The mazy-running soul of melody
Into my varied verse.
   g.   THOMSON—*The Seasons. Spring.*
                           L. 574.

O honey-throated warbler of the grove!
That in the glooming woodland art so proud
Of answering thy sweet mates in soft or loud,
Thou dost not own a note we do not love.
   h.   CHARLES TENNYSON TURNER—
               Sonnets and Fugitive Pieces.
                     To the Nightingale.

The rose looks out in the valley,
  And thither will I go,
To the rosy vale, where the nightingale
  Sings his song of woe.
   i.   GIL VICENTE—*The Nightingale.*
                     Bowring's trans.

  —Under the linden,
    On the meadow,
Where our bed arranged was,
  —There now you may find e'en
    In the shadow
Broken flowers and crushed grass.
  —Near the woods, down in the vale,
    Tandaradi!
Sweetly sang the nightingale.
   j.   WALTER VON DER VOGELWEIDE—
         Trans. in The Minnesinger of
         Germany. Under the Linden.

Owl.

The large white owl that with eye is blind,
That hath sate for years in the old tree hollow.
Is carried away in a gust of wind.
   k.   E. B. BROWNING—*Isobel's Child.*
                           St. 19.

The Roman senate, when within
The city walls an owl was seen,
Did cause their clergy, with lustrations
    *   *   *   *   *   *
The round-fac'd prodigy t' avert,
From doing town or country hurt.
   l.   BUTLER—*Hudibras.* Pt. II.
                Canto III.   L. 709.

In the hollow tree, in the old gray tower,
  The spectral Owl doth dwell;
Dull, hated, despised, in the sunshine hour,
  But at dusk—he's abroad and well!
Not a bird of the forest e'er mates with him—
  All mock him outright, by day:
But at night, when the woods grow still and
    dim,
  The boldest will shrink away!
O, when the night falls, and roosts the fowl,
Then, then, is the reign of the Horned Owl!
   m.   BARRY CORNWALL—*The Owl.*

The startled bats flew out—bird after bird—
  The screech owl overhead began to flutter,
And seem'd to mock the cry that she had
    heard
  Some dying victim utter.
   n.   HOOD—*The Haunted House.* Pt. II.
                         St. 11.

St. Agnes' Eve—Ah, bitter chill it was!
The owl, for all his feathers, was a-cold.
   o.   KEATS—*The Eve of St. Agnes.*

The screech-owl, with ill-boding cry,
  Portends strange things, old women say;
Stops every fool that passes by,
  And frights the school-boy from his play.
   p.   LADY MONTAGU—*The Politicians.*
                           St. 4.

It was the owl that shriek'd, the fatal bell-
    man,
Which gives the stern'st good night.
   q.   *Macbeth.* Act II. Sc. 2. L. 3.

Then nightly sings the staring owl,
          Tu-whit;
Tu-who, a merry note.
    a.   *Love's Labour's Lost.*   Act V.   Sc. 2.
                                          L. 928.

The clamorous owl, that nightly hoots and
          wonders
At our quaint spirits.
    b.   *Midsummer Night's Dream.*   Act II.
                                          Sc. 2.   L. 6.

          O you virtuous owle,
The wise Minerva's only fowle.
    c.   SIR PHILIP SIDNEY—*A Remedy for
                                          Love.*   L. 77.

When cats run home and light is come,
    And dew is cold upon the ground,
And the far-off stream is dumb,
    And the whirring sail goes round,
    And the whirring sail goes round;
          Alone and warming his five wits,
          The white owl in the belfry sits.
    d.   TENNYSON—*Song.   The Owl.*

Then lady Cynthia, mistress of the shade,
Goes, with the fashionable owls, to bed.
    e.   YOUNG—*Love of Fame.*   Satire V.
                                          L. 209.

Bird of Paradise.

Those golden birds that, in the spice-time,
          drop
About the gardens, drunk with that sweet
          food
Whose scent hath lur'd them o'er the summer
          flood;
And those that under Araby's soft sun
Build their high nests of budding cinnamon.
    f.   MOORE—*Lalla Rookh.   The Veiled
                                          Prophet of Khorassan.*

Partridge.

Ah, nut-brown partridges! Ah, brilliant
          pheasants!
And ah, ye poachers!—'Tis no sport for
          peasants.
    g.   BYRON—*Don Juan.*   Canto XIII.
                                          St. 75.

Or have you mark'd a partridge quake,
    Viewing the towering falcon nigh?
She cuddles low behind the brake:
    Nor would she stay; nor dares she fly.
    h.   PRIOR—*The Dove.*   St. 14.

Who finds the partridge in the puttock's nest,
But may imagine how the bird was dead,
Although the kite soar with unbloodied beak?
    i.   *Henry VI.*   Pt. II.   Act III.   Sc. 2.
                                          L. 191.

Like as a feareful partridge, that is fledd
From the sharpe hauke which her attacked
          neare,
And falls to ground to seeke for succor theare,
Whereas the hungry spaniells she does spye,
With greedy jawes her ready for to teare.
    j.   SPENSER—*Faerie Queene.*   Bk. III.
                                          Canto VIII.   St. 33.

Peacock.

For everything seemed resting on his nod,
    As they could read in all eyes. Now to
          them,
Who were accustomed, as a sort of god,
    To see the sultan, rich in many a gem,
Like an imperial peacock stalk abroad
    (That royal bird, whose tail's a diadem,)
With all the pomp of power, it was a doubt
How power could condescend to do without.
    k.   BYRON—*Don Juan.*   Canto VII.
                                          St. 74.

To frame the little animal, provide
All the gay hues that wait on female pride:
Let Nature guide thee; sometimes golden wire
The shining bellies of the fly require;
The peacock's plumes thy tackle must not
          fail,
Nor the dear purchase of the sable's tail.
    l.   GAY—*Rural Sports.*   Canto I.
                                          L. 177.

To Paradise, the Arabs say,
Satan could never find the way
    Until the peacock led him in.
    m.   LELAND—*The Peacock.*

"Fly pride," says the peacock.
    n.   *The Comedy of Errors.*   Act IV.   Sc. 3.
                                          L. 81.

Let frantic Talbot triumph for a while
And like a peacock sweep along his tail.
    o.   *Henry VI.*   Pt. I.   Act III.   Sc. 3.
                                          L. 5.

Why, he stalks up and down like a peacock,
—a stride and a stand.
    p.   *Troilus and Cressida.*   Act III.   Sc. 3.
                                          L. 251.

And there they placed a peacock in his pride,
Before the damsel.
    q.   TENNYSON—*Gareth and Lynette.*

Pelican.

What, wouldst thou have me turn pelican,
and feed thee out of my own vitals?
    r.   CONGREVE—*Love for Love.*   Act II.
                                          Sc. 1.

By them there sat the loving pelican,
Whose young ones, poison'd by the serpent's
          sting,
With her own blood to life again doth bring.
    s.   DRAYTON—*Noah's Flood.*

Nature's prime favourites were the Pelicans;
High-fed, long-lived, and sociable and free.
    a.   MONTGOMERY—*Pelican Island.*
                    Canto V.   L. 144.

Nimbly they seized and secreted their prey,
Alive and wriggling in the elastic net,
Which Nature hung beneath their grasping
    beaks;
Till, swoln with captures, the unwieldy bur-
    den
Clogg'd their slow flight, as heavily to land,
These mighty hunters of the deep return'd.
There on the cragged cliffs they perch'd at
    ease,
Gorging their hapless victims one by one;
Then full and weary, side by side, they slept,
Till evening roused them to the chase again.
    b.   MONTGOMERY—*Pelican Island.*
                    Canto IV.   L. 141.

The nursery of brooding Pelicans,
The dormitory of their dead, had vanish'd,
And all the minor spots of rock and verdure,
The abodes of happy millions, were no more.
    c.   MONTGOMERY—*Pelican Island.*
                    Canto VI.   L. 74.

Petrel.

The petrel's wing, though frail,
Is set against the gale
Which rounds the mariner's sail;
And his it is to fly
In a vortex of the sky.
    d.   RICHARD EDWIN DAY—*The Petrel.*

Pheasant.

Fesaunt excedeth all fowles in sweetnesse
and holsomnesse, and is equall to capon in
nourishynge.
    e.   SIR T. ELYOT—*The Castle of Helth.*
                            Ch. 8.

The fesant hens of Colchis, which have two
ears as it were consisting of feathers, which
they will set up and lay down as they list.
    f.   PLINY—*Natural History.* Bk. X.
                  Ch. 48.   Holland's trans.

See! from the brake the whirring pheasant
    springs,
And mounts exulting on triumphant wings:
Short is his joy; he feels the fiery wound,
Flutters in blood, and panting beats the
    ground.
    g.   POPE—*Windsor Forest.* L. 111.

Pigeon.

Wood-pigeons cooed there, stock-doves nestled
    there;
My trees were full of songs and flowers and
    fruit,
Their branches spread a city to the air.
    h.   CHRISTINA G. ROSSETTI—*From House to*
                          Home. St. 7.

This fellow pecks up wit as pigeons pease.
    i.   *Love's Labour's Lost.* Act V. Sc. 2.
                                L. 315.

Thou pigeon-egg of discretion.
    j.   *Love's Labour's Lost.* Act V. Sc. 1.
                                L. 75.

With his mouth full of news
Which he will put on us, as pigeons feed their
    young.
    k.   *As You Like It.* Act I. Sc. 2. L. 98.

On the cross-beam under the Old South bell
The nest of a pigeon is builded well.
In summer and winter that bird is there,
Out and in with the morning air.
    l.   WILLIS—*The Belfry Pigeon.*

'Tis a bird I love, with its brooding note,
And the trembling throb in its mottled throat;
There's a human look in its swelling breast,
And the gentle curve of its lowly crest;
And I often stop with the fear I feel—
He runs so close to the rapid wheel.
    m.   WILLIS—*The Belfry Pigeon.*

Quail.

In jalousie I rede eek thou hym bynde
And thou shalt make him couche as doeth
    a quaille.
    n.   CHAUCER—*The Clerke's Tale.*
                             L. 13,541.

The song-birds leave us at the summer's close,
Only the empty nests are left behind,
And pipings of the quail among the sheaves.
    o.   LONGFELLOW—*The Harvest Moon.*

An honest fellow enough, and one that
loves quails.
    p.   *Troilus and Cressida.* Act V. Sc. 1.
                              L. 58.

Raven.

The raven once in snowy plumes was drest,
White as the whitest dove's unsullied breast,
Fair as the guardian of the Capitol,
Soft as the swan; a large and lovely fowl;
His tongue, his prating tongue had changed
    him quite
To sooty blackness from the purest white.
    q.   ADDISON—*Translations, Ovid's*
                  Metamorphoses. *Story of Coronis.*

The raven was screeching, the leaves fast fell,
The sun gazed cheerlessly down on the sight.
    r.   HEINE—*Book of Songs.* *Lyrical*
                    Interludes. No. 26.

That Raven on yon left-hand oak
(Curse on his ill-betiding croak)
Bodes me no good.
    s.   GAY—*Fables.* *The Farmer's Wife and*
                      the Raven.

The Raven's house is built with reeds,—
  Sing woe, and alas is me!
And the Raven's couch is spread with weeds,
  High on the hollow tree;
And the Raven himself, telling his beads
In penance for his past misdeeds,
  Upon the top I see.
  a.   THOS. DARCY McGEE—*The Penitent
                                  Raven.*

And the Raven, never flitting,
  Still is sitting, still is sitting
On the pallid bust of Pallas
  Just above my chamber door;
  And his eyes have all the seeming
  Of a demon's that is dreaming,
  And the lamplight o'er him streaming
  Throws his shadow on the floor,
And my soul from out that shadow,
  That lies floating on the floor,
      Shall be lifted—nevermore.
  b.   POE—*The Raven.* St. 18.

Did ever raven sing so like a lark,
That gives sweet tidings of the sun's uprise?
  c.   *Titus Andronicus.* Act III. Sc. 1.
                                        L. 158.

        O, it comes o'er my memory,
As doth the raven o'er the infected house,
Boding to all.
  d.   *Othello.* Act IV. Sc. 1. L. 20.

The croaking raven doth bellow for revenge.
  e.   *Hamlet.* Act III. Sc. 2. L. 264.

        The raven himself is hoarse
That croaks the fatal entrance of Duncan
Under my battlements.
  f.   *Macbeth.* Act I. Sc. 5. L. 40.

Robin.

Poor Robin sits and sings alone,
  When showers of driving sleet.
By the cold winds of winter blown.
  The cottage casement beat.
  g.   REV. WM. LISLE BOWLES—*Winter.
                                  Redbreast.*

The wood-robin sings at my door,
  And her song is the sweetest I hear
From all the sweet birds that incessantly
    pour
  Their notes through the noon of the year.
  h.   JAMES G. CLARKE—*The Wood Robin.*

The redbreast oft, at evening hours,
  Shall kindly lend his little aid,
With hoary moss, and gathered flowers,
  To deck the ground where thou art laid.
  i.   WILLIAM COLLINS—*Odes. Dirge in
                                  Cymbeline.*

There scatter'd oft, the earliest of the year,
  By hands unseen are showers of violets
    found;
The Redbreast loves to build and warble
    there,
And light footsteps lightly print the ground.
  j.   GRAY—*Elegy.* Last St. (*Early
                                  Edition.*)

Bearing His cross, while Christ passed forth
    forlorn,
His God-like forehead by the mock crown
    torn,
A little bird took from that crown one thorn.
To soothe the dear Redeemer's throbbing
    head,
That bird did what she could; His blood, 'tis
    said,
Down dropping, dyed her tender bosom red.
Since then no wanton boy disturbs her nest;
Weasel nor wild cat will her young molest;
All sacred deem the bird of ruddy breast.
  k.   HOSKYNS-ABRAHALL—*The Redbreast.
                A Bréton Legend. In English
                                      Lyrics.*

The sobered robin, hunger-silent now,
Seeks cedar-berries blue, his autumn cheer.
  l.   LOWELL—*An Indian Summer Reverie.*
                                        St. 6.

Poor robin, driven in by rain-storms wild
To lie submissive under household hands
With beating heart that no love understands
And scared eye, like a child
Who only knows that he is all alone
And summer's gone.
  m.   D. M. MULOCK—*Summer Gone.* St. 2.

On fair Britannia's isle, bright bird,
  A legend strange is told of thee,—
'Tis said thy blithesome song was hushed
  While Christ toiled up Mount Calvary,
    Bowed 'neath the sins of all mankind;
    And humbled to the very dust
By the vile cross, while viler man
  Mocked with a crown of thorns the Just.
Pierced by our sorrows, and weighed down
  By our transgressions,—faint and weak,
Crushed by an angry Judge's frown,
  And agonies no word can speak,—
'Twas then, dear bird, the legend says
  That thou, from out His crown, didst tear
The thorns, to lighten the distress,
  And ease the pain that he must bear,
While pendant from thy tiny beak
  The gory points thy bosom pressed,
And crimsoned with thy Saviour's blood
  The sober brownness of thy breast!
Since which proud hour for thee and thine,
  As an especial sign of grace
God pours like sacramental wine
  Red signs of favor o'er thy race!
  n.   DELLE W. NORTON—*To the Robin
                                  Redbreast.*

The robin redbreast till of late had rest,
And children sacred held a martin's nest. •
   a.   Pope—*Second Book of Horace.*
                  Satire II.   L. 37.

You have learned, like Sir Proteus, to wreathe
your arms, like a malcontent; to relish a
love-song, like a robin redbreast.
   b.   *Two Gentlemen of Verona.*   Act II.
                    Sc. 1.   L. 16.

Whither away, Robin,
    Whither away?
Is it through envy of the maple leaf,
Whose blushes mock the crimson of thy breast,
    Thou wilt not stay?
The summer days now long, yet all too brief
The happy season thou hast been our guest:
    Whither away?
   c.   E. C. Stedman—*The Flight of the Birds.*

The Redbreast, sacred to the household gods,
Wisely regardful of the embroiling sky,
In joyless fields and thorny thickets leaves
His shivering mates, and pays to trusted Man
His annual visit.
   d.   Thomson—*The Seasons.   Winter.*
                        L. 246.

Call for the robin-red-breast, and the wren,
Since o'er shady groves they hover,
And with leaves and flowers do cover
The friendless bodies of unburied men.
   e.   John Webster—*The White Devil, or,*
             Vittoria Corombona.   A Dirge.

Each morning, when my waking eyes first
    see,
Through the wreathed lattice, golden day
    appear,
There sits a robin on the old elm-tree,
And with such stirring music fills my ear,
I might forget that life had pain or fear,
And feel again as I was wont to do,
When hope was young, and life itself were
    new.
   f.   Anna Maria Wells—*The Old Elm*
                        Tree.

Art thou the bird whom Man loves best,
The pious bird with the scarlet breast,
    Our little English Robin;
The bird that comes about our doors
When autumn winds are sobbing?
   g.   Wordsworth—*The Redbreast Chasing*
                   the Butterfly.

Now when the primrose makes a splendid
    show,
And lilies face the March-winds in full blow,
And humbler growths as moved with one
    desire
Put on, to welcome spring, their best attire,
Poor Robin is yet flowerless; but how gay
With his red stalks upon this sunny day!
   h.   Wordsworth—*Poor Robin.*

Stay, little cheerful Robin! stay,
    And at my casement sing,
Though it should prove a farewell lay
    And this our parting spring.
     * * * * * *
Then, little Bird, this boon confer,
    Come, and my requiem sing,
Nor fail to be the harbinger
    Of everlasting spring.
   i.   Wordsworth—*To a Redbreast.*
                      In Sickness.

Rook.

Those Rooks, dear, from morning till night
They seem to do nothing but quarrel and
    fight,
And wrangle and jangle, and plunder.
   j.   D. M. Mulock—*Thirty Years.   The*
             Blackbird and the Rooks.

The building rook'll caw from the windy
    tall elm-tree.
   k.   Tennyson—*The May Queen.   New*
                Year's Eve.   St. 5.

Invite the rook who high amid the boughs,
In early spring, his airy city builds,
And ceaseless caws amusive.
   l.   Thomson—*The Seasons.   Spring.*
                        L. 756.

Where in venerable rows
Widely waving oaks enclose
The moat of yonder antique hall,
Swarm the rooks with clamorous call;
And, to the toils of nature true,
Wreath their capacious nests anew.
   m.   Warton—*Ode* 10.

Sand-Piper.

Across the narrow beach we flit,
    One little sand-piper and I;
And fast I gather, bit by bit,
    The scattered drift-wood, bleached and dry.
The wild waves reach their hands for it,
    The wild wind raves, the tide runs high,
As up and down the beach we flit,
    One little sand-piper and I.
   n.   Celia Thaxter—*The Sand-Piper.*

Sea Bird.

How joyously the young sea-mew
Lay dreaming on the waters blue,
Whereon our little bark had thrown
A little shade, the only one;
But shadows ever man pursue.
   o.   E. B. Browning—*The Sea-Mew.*

Vainly the fowler's eye
Might mark thy distant flight to do thee wrong.
As, darkly painted on the crimson sky,
    Thy figure floats along.
   p.   Bryant—*To a Water Fowl.*

Up and down! Up and down!
From the base of the wave to the billow's
　　crown;
And amidst the flashing and feathery foam
The Stormy Petrel finds a home,—
A home, if such a place may be,
For her who lives on the wide, wide sea,
On the craggy ice, in the frozen air,
And only seeketh her rocky lair
To warm her young and to teach them spring
At once o'er the waves on their stormy wing!
　　a.　　BARRY CORNWALL—*The Stormy Petrel.*

Between two seas the sea-bird's wing makes
　　halt,
Wind-weary; while with lifting head he waits
For breath to reinspire him from the gates
That open still toward sunrise on the vault
High-domed of morning.
　　b.　　SWINBURNE—*Songs of the Spring Tides.*
　　　　　　Introductory lines to Birthday Ode
　　　　　　　　　　to Victor Hugo.

Sedge-Bird.

Fixed in a white-thorn bush, its summer guest,
So low, e'en grass o'er-topped its tallest twig,
A sedge-bird built its little benty nest,
Close by the meadow pool and wooden brig.
　　c.　　CLARE—*The Rural Muse. Poems. The*
　　　　　　　　Sedge-Bird's Nest.

Sparrow.

Blithe wanderer of the wintry air,
Now here, now there, now everywhere,
　　Quick drifting to and fro,
A cheerful life devoid of care,
　　A shadow on the snow.
　　d.　　GEORGE W. BUNGAY—*The English*
　　　　　　　　　　　　Sparrow.

Tell me not of joy: there's none
Now my little sparrow's gone;
　　He, just as you,
　　Would toy and woo,
He would chirp and flatter me,
　　He would hang the wing awhile,
　　Till at length he saw me smile,
Lord! how sullen he would be!
　　e.　　WM. CARTWRIGHT—*Lesbia and the*
　　　　　　　　　　　　Sparrow.

The sparrows chirped as if they still were
　　proud
Their race in Holy Writ should mentioned be.
　　f.　　LONGFELLOW—*Tales of a Wayside Inn.*
　　　　　　The Poet's Tale. The Birds of
　　　　　　　　Killingworth. St. 2.

And in thy own sermon, thou
That the sparrow falls dost allow,
It shall not cause me any alarm;
For neither so comes the bird to harm,
Seeing our Father, thou hast said,
Is by the sparrow's dying bed;
Therefore it is a blessed place,
And the sparrow in high grace.
　　g.　　GEORGE MACDONALD—*Paul Faber.*
　　　　　　Consider the Ravens. Ch. XXI.

The hedge-sparrow fed the cuckoo so long,
That it had it head bit off by it young.
　　h.　　*King Lear.* Act I. Sc. 4. Line 235.

Behold, within the leafy shade,
Those bright blue eggs together laid!
On me the chance-discovered sight
Gleamed like a vision of delight.
　　i.　　WORDSWORTH—*The Sparrow's Nest.*

Swallow.

Down comes rain drop, bubble follows;
　　On the house-top one by one
Flock the synagogue of swallows,
　　Met to vote that autumn's gone.
　　j.　　THEOPHILE GAUTIER—*Life, a Bubble.*
　　　　　　　　A Bird's-Eye View Thereof.

But, as old Swedish legends say,
Of all the birds upon that day,
The swallow felt the deepest grief,
And longed to give her Lord relief,
And chirped when any near would come,
'*Hugswala swal swal honom!*'
Meaning, as they who tell it deem,
Oh, cool, oh, cool and comfort Him!
　　k.　　LELAND—*The Swallow.*

The swallow is come!
The swallow is come!
O, fair are the seasons, and light
　　Are the days that she brings,
　　With her dusky wings,
And her bosom snowy white!
　　l.　　LONGFELLOW—*Hyperion.* Bk. II.
　　　　　　　　　　　　　　Ch. 1.

It's surely summer, for there's a swallow:
Come one swallow, his mate will follow,
The bird race quicken and wheel and thicken.
　　m.　　CHRISTINA G. ROSSETTI—*A Bird Song.*
　　　　　　　　　　　　St. 2.

　　There goes the swallow,—
　　Could we but follow!
　　　Hasty swallow, stay,
　　Point us out the way;
Look back swallow, turn back swallow, stop
　　swallow.
　　n.　　CHRISTINA G. ROSSETTI—*Songs in a*
　　　　　　　　　　Cornfield. St. 7.

Now to the Goths as swift as swallow flies.
　　o.　　*Titus Andronicus.* Act IV. Sc. 2.
　　　　　　　　　　　　L. 172.

　　The swallow follows not summer more willing than we your lordship.
　　p.　　*Timon of Athens.* Act III. Sc. 6.
　　　　　　　　　　　　L. 31.

True hope is swift, and flies with swallow's
　　wings;
Kings it makes gods, and meaner creatures
　　kings.
　　q.　　*Richard III.* Act V. Sc. 2. L. 23.

The swallow twitters about the eaves;
  Blithely she sings, and sweet, and clear;
Around her climb the woodbine leaves
  In a golden atmosphere.
a.   CELIA THAXTER—*The Swallow.* St. 1.

          The swallow sweeps
The slimy pool, to build his hanging house.
b.   THOMSON—*The Seasons. Spring.*
                              L. 651.

When autumn scatters his departing gleams,
Warn'd of approaching winter, gather'd, play
The swallow-people; and toss'd wide around,
O'er the calm sky, in convolution swift,
The feather'd eddy floats; rejoicing once,
Ere to their wintry slumbers they retire.
c.   THOMSON—*Seasons. Autumn.* L. 836.

Swan.

The jelous swan, agens hire deth that syngith.
d.   CHAUCER—*Parlement of Fowles.*
                              L. 342.

And over the pond are sailing
  Two swans all white as snow;
Sweet voices mysteriously wailing
  Pierce through me as onward they go.
They sail along, and a ringing
  Sweet melody rises on high;
And when the swans begin singing,
  They presently must die.
e.   HEINE—*Early Poems. Evening Songs.*
                              No. 2.

The swan in the pool is singing,
  And up and down doth he steer,
And, singing gently ever,
  Dips under the water clear.
f.   HEINE—*Book of Songs. Lyrical
                    Interlude.* No. 64.

The swan, like the soul of the poet,
By the dull world is ill understood.
g.   HEINE—*Early Poems. Evening Songs.*
                              No. 3.

The swan murmurs sweet strains with a
faltering tongue, itself the singer of its own
dirge.
h.   MARTIAL—*Epigrams.* Bk. XIII.
                              Ep. LXXVII.

          The swan, with arched neck
Between her white wings mantling proudly,
          rows
Her state with oary feet.
i.   MILTON—*Paradise Lost.* Bk. VII.
                              L. 438.

Thus does the white swan, as he lies on the
          wet grass, when the
Fates summon him, sing at the fords of
          Mæander.
j.   OVID—Ep. VII. Riley's trans.

          As I have seen a swan
With bootless labour swim against the tide
And spend her strength with over-matching
          waves.
k.   *Henry VI.* Pt. III. Act I. Sc. 4.
                              L. 19.

For all the water in the ocean,
Can never turn the swan's black legs to white,
Although she lave them hourly in the flood.
l.   *Titus Andronicus.* Act IV. Sc. 2.
                              L. 101.

          The swan's down-feather,
That stands upon the swell at full of tide,
And neither way inclines.
m.   *Antony and Cleopatra.* Act III. Sc. 2.
                              L. 48.

          A melody loud and sweet
That made the wild-swan pause in her cloud.
n.   TENNYSON—*The Poet's Song.*

          The stately-sailing swan
Gives out his snowy plumage to the gale;
And, arching proud his neck, with oary feet
Bears forward fierce, and guards his osier isle,
Protective of his young.
o.   THOMSON—*The Seasons. Spring.*
                              L. 775.

Throstle.

In the gloamin' o' the wood
The throssil whusslit sweet.
p.   WM. MOTHERWELL—*Jeanie Morrison.*

The throstle with his note so true,
The wren with little quill.
q.   *Midsummer Night's Dream.* Act III.
                              Sc. 1. L. 130.

And hark! how blithe the throstle sings!
  He, too, is no mean preacher:
Come forth into the light of things,
  Let Nature be your teacher.
r.   WORDSWORTH—*The Tables Turned.*

Thrush.

Within a thick and spreading hawthorn bush
  That overhung a molehill large and round,
I heard from morn to morn a merry thrush
  Sing hymns of rapture, while I drank the
          sound
With joy—and oft an unintruding guest,
  I watch'd her secret toils from day to day;
How true she warp'd the moss to form her
          nest,
  And modell'd it within with wood and clay.
s.   CLARE—*The Thrush's Nest.*

Across the noisy street
I hear him careless throw
One warning utterance sweet;
Then faint at first, and low,
  The full notes closer grow;
  Hark what a torrent gush!
They pour, they overflow—
Sing on, sing on, O thrush!
t.   AUSTIN DOBSON—*Ballad of the Thrush.*

O thrush, your song is passing sweet,
But never a song that you have sung
Is half so sweet as thrushes sang
When my dear love and I were young.
    a.   WM. MORRIS—*Other Days.*

I said to the brown, brown thrush :
     " Hush—hush !
Through the wood's full strains I hear
Thy monotone deep and clear,
     Like a sound amid sounds most fine."
    b.   D. M. MULOCK—*A Rhyme About Birds.*

       There the thrushes
Sing till latest sunlight flushes
In the west.
    c.   CHRISTINA G. ROSSETTI—*Sound Sleep.*
                                        St. 2.

Sing, sweet thrushes, forth and sing !
   Meet the moon upon the lea ;
Are the emeralds of the spring
   On the angler's trysting-tree ?
Tell, sweet thrushes, tell to me,
   Are there buds on our willow-tree ?
Buds and birds on our trysting-tree ?
    d.   THOMAS TOD STODDART—*The Angler's*
                                   Trysting-Tree.

When rosy plumelets tuft the larch,
And rarely pipes the mounted thrush.
    e.   TENNYSON—*In Memoriam.*   Pt. XCI.

At the corner of Wood Street, when daylight
     appears,
Hangs a thrush that sings loud, it has sung
     for three years.
    f.   WORDSWORTH—*Reverie of Poor Susan.*

Whip-poor-will.

Where deep and misty shadows float
In forest's depths is heard thy note.
Like a lost spirit, earthbound still,
Art thou, mysterious whip-poor-will.
    g.   MARIE LE BARON—*The Whip-Poor-*
                                        Will.

But the whip-poor-will wails on the moor,
   And day has deserted the west :
The moon glimmers down thro' the vines at
     my door
And the robin has flown to her nest.
    h.   JAMES G. CLARKE—*The Wood-Robin.*

     The moan of the whip-poor-will from the
hillside ; the boding cry of the tree-toad, that
harbinger of storm ; the dreary hooting of the
screechowi.
    i.   IRVING—*Sketch Book.   The Legend of*
                                   Sleepy Hollow.

White-Throat.

The happy white-throat on the swaying bough,
Rocked by the impulse of the gadding wind
That ushers in the showers of April, now
Carols right joyously ; and now reclined,
Crouching, she clings close to her moving
     seat,
To keep her hold.
    j.   CLARE—*The Rural Muse.   Poems.*
                                  The Happy Bird.

Wren.

But then as little wrens, but newly fledge,
First by their nests hop up and down the
     hedge ;
Then one from bough to bough gets up a tree.
    k.   BROWNE—*Britannia's Pastorals.*   Bk. 1.
                                       Sc. 4.

And then the wren gan scippen and to daunce.
    l.   CHAUCER—*Court of Love.*   L. 1372.

I took the wren's nest ;—
Heaven forgive me !
Its merry architects so small
Had scarcely finished their wee hall,
That, empty still, and neat and fair,
Hung idly in the summer air.
    m.   D. M. MULOCK—*The Wren's Nest.*

            For the poor wren,
The most diminutive of birds, will fight,
Her young ones in her nest, against the owl.
    n.   *Macbeth.*   Act IV.   Sc. 2.   L. 9.

     Thus the fable tells us, that the wren
mounted as high as the eagle, by getting upon
his back.
    o.   *Tatler.*   No. 224.

Among the dwellings framed by birds
   In field or forest with nice care,
Is none that with the little wren's
   In snugness may compare.
    p.   WORDSWORTH—*A Wren's Nest.*

Yellow-Bird.

Yellow-bird, where did you learn that song,
   Perched on the trellis where grape-vines
     clamber,
In and out fluttering, all day long,
   With your golden breast bedropped with
     amber ?
    q.   CELIA THAXTER—*Yellow-Bird.*

BIRTHDAY.

My birthday !—" How many years ago ?
   Twenty or thirty ? "   Don't ask me !
" Forty or fifty ? "—How can I tell ?
   I do not remember my birth, you see !
    r.   JULIA C. R. DORR—*My Birthday.*

A birthday :—and now a day that rose
  With much of hope, with meaning rife—
A thoughtful day from dawn to close :
  The middle day of human life.
  a.   JEAN INGELOW—*A Birthday Walk.*

And show me your nest with the young ones
    in it,
  I will not steal them away ;
I am old ! you may trust me, linnet, linnet—
I am seven times one to-day.
  b.   JEAN INGELOW—*Songs of Seven.*
                    Seven Times One.

As this auspicious day began the race
Of ev'ry virtue join'd with ev'ry grace ;
May you, who own them, welcome its return,
Till excellence, like yours, again is born.
The years we wish, will half your charms
    impair ;
The years we wish, the better half will spare ;
The victims of your eyes will bleed no more,
But all the beauties of your mind adore.
  c.   JEFFREY—*Miscellanies.   To a Lady on
                    her Birthday.*

  This is my birthday, and a happier one
was never mine.
  d.   LONGFELLOW—*The Divine Tragedy.
          The Second Passover.   Pt. II.*

Believing hear, what you deserve to hear :
Your birthday as my own to me is dear.
Blest and distinguish'd days ! which we
    should prize
The first, the kindest bounty of the skies.
But yours gives most ; for mine did only lend
Me to the world ; yours gave to me a friend.
  e.   MARTIAL—*Epigrams.* Bk. IX. Ep. 53.

My birthday !—what a different sound
  That word had in my youthful ears ;
And how each time the day comes round,
  Less and less white its mark appears.
  f.   MOORE—*My Birthday.*

Is that a birthday ? 'tis, alas ! too clear ;
'Tis but the funeral of the former year.
  g.   POPE—*To Mrs. M. B.* L. 9.

BLACKSMITHING (*See* OCCUPATIONS).

BLASPHEMY.

And each blasphemer quite escape the rod,
Because the insult's not on man, but God ?
  h.   POPE—*Epilogue to Satires.* Dialogue II.
                    L. 199.

That in the captain's but a choleric word,
Which in the soldier is flat blasphemy.
  i.   *Measure for Measure.* Act II.   Sc. 2.
                    L. 130.

BLESSINGS.

'Tis not for mortals always to be blest.
  j.   ARMSTRONG—*Art of Preserving Health.*
                    Bk. IV.   L. 260.

Prosperity is the blessing of the Old Testa-
    ment ;
Adversity is the blessing of the New.
  k.   BACON—*Of Adversity.*

Blessings star forth forever ; but a curse
Is like a cloud—it passes.
  l.   BAILEY—*Festus.* Sc. *Hades.*

                    Blest
Is he whose heart is the home of the great
    dead,
And their great thoughts.
  m.   BAILEY—*Festus.* Sc. *A Village Feast.*

A spring of love gushed from my heart,
And I bless'd them unaware.
  n.   COLERIDGE—*The Ancient Mariner.*
                    Pt. IV.

For blessings ever wait on virtuous deeds,
And though a late, a sure reward succeeds.
  o.   CONGREVE—*The Mourning Bride.*
                    Act V.   Sc. 3.

Bless the hand that gave the blow.
  p.   DRYDEN—*The Spanish Friar.* Act II.
                    Sc. 1.

To heal divisions, to relieve the oppress'd,
In virtue rich ; in blessing others, bless'd.
  q.   HOMER—*Odyssey.* Bk. VII. L. 95.
                    Pope's trans.

A man's best things are nearest him,
Lie close about his feet.
  r.   RICH. MONCKTON MILNES—*The Men of
                    Old.* St. 7.

The blest to-day is as completely so,
As who began a thousand years ago.
  s.   POPE—*Essay on Man.* Ep. I. L. 75.

Jove bless thee, master Parson.
  t.   *Twelfth Night.* Act IV.   Sc. 2. L. 14.

The benediction of these covering heavens
Fall on their heads like dew !
  u.   *Cymbeline.* Act V.   Sc. 5.   L. 350.

Amid my list of blessings infinite,
Stands this the foremost, " That my heart
    has bled."
  v.   YOUNG—*Night Thoughts.* Night IX.
                    L. 497.

Like birds, whose beauties languish half con-
    cealed,
Till, mounted on the wing, their glossy
    plumes
Expanded, shine with azure, green and gold ·
How blessings brighten as they take their
    flight.
  w.   YOUNG—*Night Thoughts.* Night II.
                    L. 589.

BLINDNESS.

Oh, say ! what is that thing call'd light,
   Which I must ne'er enjoy ?
What are the blessings of the sight ?
   Oh, tell your poor blind boy !
   a.   Colley Cibber—*The Blind Boy.*

None so blind as those that will not see.
   b.   Mathew Henry—*Commentaries.*
                    Jeremiah XX.

Dispel this cloud, the light of heaven restore ;
Give me to see, and Ajax asks no more.
   c.   Homer—*Iliad.* Bk. 17. L. 730.
                    Pope's trans.

O dark, dark, dark, amid the blaze of noon,
Irrecoverably dark ! total eclipse,
Without all hope of day.
   d.   Milton—*Samson Agonistes.* L. 80.

O loss of sight, of thee I most complain !
Blind among enemies, O worse than chains,
Dungeon, or beggary, or decrepit age !
   e.   Milton—*Samson Agonistes.* L. 67.

        These eyes, tho' clear
To outward view of blemish or of spot,
Bereft of light, their seeing have forgot,
Nor to their idle orbs doth sight appear
Of sun, or moon, or star, throughout the year,
Or man, or woman. Yet I argue not
Against Heaven's hand or will, nor bate a jot
Of heart or hope ; but still bear up and steer
Right onward.
   f.   Milton—*Sonnet XXII.* L. 1.

But love is blind, and lovers cannot see
The pretty follies that themselves commit ;
   g.   *Merchant of Venice.* Act II. Sc. VI.
                    L. 36.

He that is strucken blind cannot forget
The precious treasure of his eyesight lost.
   h.   *Romeo and Juliet.* Act I. Sc. 1.
                    L. 238.

There's none so blind as they that won't see.
   i.   Swift—*Polite Conversation.*
                    Dialogue III.

        And when a damp
Fell round the path of Milton, in his hand
The Thing became a trumpet ; whence he
   blew
Soul-animating strains—alas ! too few.
   j.   Wordsworth—*Scorn Not the Sonnet ;*
             Critic, You Have Frowned.

BLISS.

What though my winged hours of bliss have
   been,
Like angel-visits, few and far between.
   k.   Campbell—*The Pleasures of Hope.*
                Pt. II. L. 375.

        Unending is this bliss.
The pillared firmament and all the spheres
May sink, perchance, in the long lapse of
   years,
      Swallowed in Night's abyss—
But to the dwellers in Eternity
A thousand years shall as a moment be.
   l.   Abraham Coles—*The Microcosm and*
             Other Poems. P. 289.

Domestic Happiness, thou only bliss
Of Paradise, that has survived the fall !
   m.   Cowper—*The Task.* Bk. III. L .41.

Vain, very vain, my weary search to find
That bliss which only centres in the mind.
   n.   Goldsmith—*The Traveller.* L. 423.

The hues of bliss more brightly glow,
Chastis'd by sabler tints of woe.
   o.   Gray—*Ode on the Pleasure arising*
              from Vicissitude. L. 45.

And for our country 'tis a bliss to die.
   p.   Homer—*Iliad.* Bk. XV. L. 583.
                    Pope's trans.

Alas ! by some degree of woe
   We every bliss must gain ;
The heart can ne'er a transport know,
   That never feels a pain.
   q.   Lord Lyttleton—*Song.*

But such a sacred and home-felt delight,
Such sober certainty of waking bliss,
I never heard till now.
   r.   Milton—*Comus.* L. 262.

Bliss in possession will not last ;
Remember'd joys are never past ;
At once the fountain, stream, and sea,
They were,—they are,—they yet shall be.
   s.   Montgomery—*The Little Cloud.*

Condition, circumstance, is not the thing ;
Bliss is the same in subject or in king.
   t.   Pope—*Essay on Man.* Ep. IV. L. 57.

Some place the bliss in action, some in ease,
Those call it pleasure, and contentment these.
   u.   Pope—*Essay on Man.* Ep. IV. L. 21.

The way to bliss lies not on beds of down,
And he that had no cross deserves no crown.
   v.   Quarles—*Esther.*

I know I am—that simplest bliss
The millions of my brothers miss.
I know the fortune to be born,
Even to the meanest wretch they scorn.
   w.   Bayard Taylor—*Prince Deukalion.*
                    Act IV.

Health is the vital principle of bliss,
And exercise of health.
   x.   Thomson—*The Castle of Indolence.*
                Canto II. St. 55.

We thinke no greater blisse then such
To be as be we would,
When blessed none but such as be
The same as be they should.

  a.   WILLIAM WARNER—*Albion's England.*
           Bk. X. Ch. LIX. St. 68.

Bliss was it in that dawn to be alive,
But to be young was very Heaven!

  b.   WORDSWORTH—*The Prelude.* Bk. XI.

          That inward eye
Which is the bliss of solitude.

  c.   WORDSWORTH—*I Wandered Lonely.*

The spider's most attenuated thread
Is cord, is cable, to man's tender tie
On earthly bliss; it breaks at every breeze.

  d.   YOUNG—*Night Thoughts.* Night 1.
                               L. 178.

BLUSHES.

An Arab, by his earnest gaze,
  Has clothed a lovely maid with blushes;
A smile within his eyelids plays
  And into words his longing gushes.

  e.   WM. R. ALGER—*Oriental Poetry. Love
            Sowing and Reaping Roses.*

Girls blush, sometimes, because they are alive,
Half wishing they were dead to save the
    shame.
The sudden blush devours them, neck and
    brow;
They have drawn too near the fire of life, like
    gnats,
And flare up bodily, wings and all.

  f.   E. B. BROWNING—*Aurora Leigh.*
                          Bk. II. L. 732.

Blushed like the waves of hell.

  g.   BYRON—*The Devil's Drive.* St. 5.

Pure friendship's well-feigned blush.

  h.   BYRON—*Stanzas to Her who can Best
                    Understand Them.* St. 12.

So sweet the blush of bashfulness,
E'en pity scarce can wish it less!

  i.   BYRON—*Bride of Abydos.* Canto 1.
                                St. 8.

'Tis not on youth's smooth cheek the blush
    alone, which fades so fast,
But the tender bloom of heart is gone, ere
    youth itself be past.

  j.   BYRON—*Stanzas for Music.*

Who has not seen that feeling born of flame
Crimson the cheek at mention of a name?
The rapturous touch of some divine surprise
Flash deep suffusion of celestial dyes:
When hands clasped hands, and lips to lips
    were pressed,
And the heart's secret was at once confessed?

  k.   ABRAHAM COLES—*Man, the Microcosm.*
                                P. 25.

I pity bashful men, who feel the pain
Of fancied scorn and undeserved disdain,
And bear the marks upon a blushing face,
Of needless shame, and self-impos'd disgrace.

  l.   COWPER—*Conversation.* L. 347.

Once he saw a youth blushing, and addressed
him, "Courage, my boy; that is the complexion
of virtue."

  m.   DIOGENES LAERTIUS—*Diogenes.* VI.

A blush is no language: only a dubious flag-
signal which may mean either of two con-
tradictories.

  n.   GEORGE ELIOT—*Daniel Deronda.*
                        Bk. V. Ch. XXXV.

The rising blushes, which her cheek o'er-
    spread,
Are opening roses in the lily's bed.

  o.   GAY—*Dione.* Act II. Sc. 3.

Blushing is the colour of virtue.

  p.   MATTHEW HENRY—*Commentaries.*
                          Jeremiah III.

          Such a blush
In the midst of brown was born,
Like red poppies grown with corn.

  q.   HOOD—*Ruth.*

While mantling on the maiden's cheek
Young roses kindled into thought.

  r.   MOORE—*Evenings in Greece.*
                        Evening II. *Song.*

From every blush that kindles in thy cheeks,
Ten thousand little loves and graces spring
To revel in the roses.

  s.   NICHOLAS ROWE—*Tamerlane.* Act I.
                                Sc. 1.

And bid the cheek be ready with a blush
Modest as morning when she coldly eyes
The youthful Phœbus.

  t.   *Troilus and Cressida.* Act I. Sc. 3.
                                L. 228.

          By noting of the lady I have mark'd
A thousand blushing apparitions
To start into her face, a thousand innocent
    shames.
In angel whiteness beat away those blushes.

  u.   *Much Ado About Nothing.* Act IV.
                          Sc. 1. L. 160.

Come, quench your blushes and present
    yourself
That which you are, mistress o' the feast.

  v.   *The Winter's Tale.* Act IV. Sc. 4.
                                L. 67.

Where now I have no one to blush with me,
To cross their arms and hang their heads with
    mine.

  w.   *The Rape of Lucrece.* L. 792.

          I will go wash;
And when my face is fair, you shall perceive
Whether I blush or no.
a.   *Coriolanus.* Act I. Sc. 9. L. 68.

Lay by all nicety and prolixious blushes,
That banish what they sue for.
b.   *Measure for Measure.* Act II. Sc. 4.
                            L. 162.

Two red fires in both their faces blazed;
She thought he blush'd,   *   *   *
And, blushing with him, wistly on him gazed.
c.   *The Rape of Lucrece.* Line 1,353.

Yet will she blush, here be it said,
To hear her secrets so bewrayed.
d.   *The Passionate Pilgrim.* Pt. XIX.
                            L. 351.

          How pretty
Her blushing was, and how she blush'd
     again.
e.   TENNYSON—*The Princess.* Pt. III.
                            L. 83.

The man that blushes is not quite a brute.
f.   YOUNG—*Night Thoughts.* Night VII.
                            L. 496.

BOATING.

Oh, swiftly glides the bonnie boat,
   Just parted from the shore,
And to the fisher's chorus-note,
   Soft moves the dipping oar!
g.   JOANNA BAILLIE—*Song. Oh, Swiftly
                 glides the Bonnie Boat.*

           On the ear
Drops the light drip of the suspended oar.
h.   BYRON—*Childe Harold.* Canto III.
                            St. 86.

But oars alone can ne'er prevail
   To reach the distant coast;
The breath of Heaven must swell the sail,
   Or all the toil is lost.
i.   COWPER—*Human Frailty.* St. 6.

We lie and listen to the hissing waves,
   Wherein our boat seems sharpening its keel,
Which on the sea's face all unthankful graves
   An arrowed scratch as with a tool of steel.
j.   JOHN DAVIDSON—*In a Music-Hall and
               Other Poems. For Lovers.* L. 17.

And all the way, to guide their chime,
With falling oars they kept the time.
k.   ANDREW MARVELL—*Bermudas.*

   Like the watermen who advance forward
while they look backward.
l.   MONTAIGNE—Bk. II. Ch. XXIX.
                 Of Profit and Honesty.

Faintly as tolls the evening chime,
Our voices keep tune and our oars keep time,
Soon as the woods on shore look dim,
We'll sing at St. Ann's our parting hymn;
Row, brothers, row, the stream runs fast,
The rapids are near and the daylight's past!
m.   MOORE—*A Canadian Boat Song.*

Gracefully, gracefully glides our bark
   On the bosom of Father Thames,
And before her bows the wavelets dark
   Break into a thousand gems.
n.   THOS. NOEL—*A Thames Voyage.*

Learn of the little nautilus to sail,
Spread the thin oar, and catch the driving
     gale.
o.   POPE—*Essay on Man.* Ep. III. L. 177.

         The oars were silver:
Which to the tune of flutes kept stroke.
p.   *Antony and Cleopatra.* Act II. Sc. 2.
                            L. 199.

BOOKS.

Books are the legacies that a great genius
leaves to mankind, which are delivered down
from generation to generation, as presents to
the posterity of those who are yet unborn.
q.   ADDISON—*The Spectator.* No. 166.

That is a good book which is opened with
expectation and closed with profit.
r.   ALCOTT—*Table Talk.* Bk. I.
                      Learning-Books.

The books that charmed us in youth recall
the delight ever afterwards; we are hardly
persuaded there are any like them, any deserving equally our affections. Fortunate if
the best fall in our way during this susceptible and forming periods of our lives.
s.   ALCOTT—*Table Talk.* Bk. I.
                      Learning-Books.

Books are delightful when prosperity happily smiles; when adversity threatens, they
are inseparable comforters. They give
strength to human compacts, nor are grave
opinions brought forward without books.
Arts and sciences, the benefits of which no
mind can calculate, depend upon books.
t.   RICHARD AUNGERVYLE (Richard De
              Bury)—*Philobiblon.* Ch. I.

You, O Books, are the golden vessels of the
temple, the arms of the clerical militia with
which the missiles of the most wicked are destroyed; fruitful olives, vines of Engaddi, fig-
trees knowing no sterility; burning lamps to
be ever held in the hand.
u.   RICHARD AUNGERVYLE (Richard De
              Bury)—*Philobiblon.* Ch. XV.

Books must follow sciences, and not sciences books.

  a.　　BACON—*Proposition touching*
  　　　　　　Amendment of Laws.

But the images of men's wits and knowledges remain in books, exempted from the wrong of time, and capable of perpetual renovation.

  b.　　BACON—*Advancement of Learning.*
  　　　　　Bk. I.　*Advantages of Learning.*

Some books are to be tasted, others to be swallowed, and some few to be chewed and digested.

  c.　　BACON—*Essay. Of Studies.*

  　　　　　　　　Worthy books
  Are not companions—they are solitudes :
  We lose ourselves in them and all our cares.

  d.　　BAILEY—*Festus.* Sc. *A Village Feast.*
  　　　　　　　　　　　　Evening.

  　　　　　That place that does contain
  My books, the best companions, is to me
  A glorious court, where hourly I converse
  With the old sages and philosophers ;
  And sometimes, for variety, I confer
  With kings and emperors, and weigh their
  　　　counsels.

  e.　　BEAUMONT AND FLETCHER—*The Elder*
  　　　　　　Brother. Act I. Sc. 2.

  　　　　　Books, books, books !
  I had found the secret of a garret room
  Piled high with cases in my father's name ;
  Piled high, packed large,—where, creeping in
  　　　and out
  Among the giant fossils of my past,
  Like some small nimble mouse between the
  　　　ribs
  Of a mastodon, I nibbled here and there
  At this or that box, pulling through the gap,
  In heats of terror, haste, victorious joy,
  The first book first.　And how I felt it beat
  Under my pillow, in the morning's dark,
  An hour before the sun would let me read !
  My books !
  　　At last, because the time was ripe,
  I chanced upon the poets.

  f.　　E. B. BROWNING—*Aurora Leigh.*
  　　　　　　　　　Bk. I.　L. 830.

  　　　　　We get no good
  By being ungenerous, even to a book,
  And calculating profits—so much help
  By so much reading.　It is rather when
  We gloriously forget ourselves, and plunge
  Soul-forward, headlong, into a book's pro-
  　　　found,
  Impassioned for its beauty, and salt of truth—
  'Tis then we get the right good from a book.

  g.　　E. B. BROWNING—*Aurora Leigh.*
  　　　　　　　　　Bk. I.　L. 700.

Some said, John, print it, others said, Not so;
Some said, It might do good, others said, No.

  h.　　BUNYAN—*Apology for his Book.*　L. 39.

Some books are lies frae end to end.

  i.　　BURNS—*Death and Dr. Hornbook.*

'Tis pleasant, sure, to see one's name in print ;
A book's a book, although there's nothing in't.

  j.　　BYRON—*English Bards and Scotch*
  　　　　　　　　Reviewers.　L. 51.

All that Mankind has done, thought, gained or been it is lying as in magic preservation in the pages of Books.　They are the chosen possession of men.

  k.　　CARLYLE—*Heroes and Hero Worship.*
  　　　　　　　　　　　　Lecture V.

If a book come from the heart, it will contrive to reach other hearts ; all art and authorcraft are of small amount to that.

  l.　　CARLYLE—*Heroes and Hero Worship.*
  　　　　　　　　　　　　Lecture II.

If time is precious, no book that will not improve by repeated readings deserves to be read at all.

  m.　　CARLYLE—*Essays. Goethe's Helena.*

In books lies the soul of the whole Past Time ; the articulate audible voice of the Past, when the body and material substance of it has altogether vanished like a dream.

  n.　　CARLYLE—*Heroes and Hero Worship.*
  　　　　　　The Hero as a Man of Letters.

In the poorest cottage are Books : is one Book, wherein for several thousands of years the spirit of man has found light, and nourishment, and an interpreting response to whatever is Deepest in him.

  o.　　CARLYLE—*Essays. Corn-Law Rhymes.*

The true University of these days is a collection of Books.

  p.　　CARLYLE—*Heroes and Hero-Worship.*
  　　　　　　The Hero as a Man of Letters.

" There is no book so bad," said the bachelor, " but something good may be found in it."

  q.　　CERVANTES—*Don Quixote.* Pt. II.
  　　　　　　　　　　　　Ch. III.

It is chiefly through books that we enjoy intercourse with superior minds, and these invaluable means of communication are in the reach of all.　In the best books, great men talk to us, give us their most precious thoughts, and pour their souls into ours.

  r.　　CHANNING—*On Self-Culture.*

And as for me, though than I konne but lyte,
On bokes for to rede I me delyte,
And to hem yeve I feyth and ful credence,
And in myn herte have hem in reverence
So hertely, that ther is game noon,
That fro my bokes maketh me to goon,
But yt be seldome on the holy day.
Save, certeynly, when that the monthe of May
Is comen, and that I here the foules synge,
And that the floures gynnen for to sprynge,
Farwel my boke, and my devocion.

　　a.　　CHAUCER—*Legende of Goode Women.*
　　　　　　　　　　Prologue.　L. 29.

Go, litel boke ! go litel myn tregedie !

　　b.　　CHAUCER—*Canterbury Tales. Troilus
　　　　　　and Creseide.*　Book V.　L. 1,800.

O little booke, thou art so unconning,
How darst thou put thyself in prees for dred ?

　　c.　　CHAUCER—*The Flower and the Leaf.*
　　　　　　　　　　　　L. 591.

It is saying less than the truth to affirm
that an excellent book (and the remark holds
almost equally good of a Raphael as of a Milton) is like a well-chosen and well-tended
fruit tree.　Its fruits are not of one season
only.　With the due and natural intervals,
we may recur to it year after year, and it will
supply the same nourishment and the same
gratification, if only we ourselves return to it
with the same healthful appetite.

　　d.　　COLERIDGE—*Literary Remains.
　　　　　　Prospectus of Lectures.*

Books should, not Business, entertain the
　　Light;
And Sleep, as undisturb'd as Death, the Night.

　　e.　　COWLEY—*Of Myself.*

Books cannot always please, however good ;
Minds are not ever craving for their food.

　　f.　　CRABBE—*The Borough.　Letter XXIV.
　　　　　　Schools.　L. 402.*

The monument of vanished mindes.

　　g.　　SIR WM. DAVENANT—*Gondibert.*
　　　　　　　　　Bk. II.　Canto V.

Books should to one of these four ends con-
　　duce,
For wisdom, piety, delight, or use.

　　h.　　SIR JOHN DENHAM—*Of Prudence.*

He ate and drank the precious words,
　　His spirit grew robust ;
He knew no more that he was poor,
　　Nor that his frame was dust.
He danced along the dingy days,
　　And this bequest of wings
Was but a book.　What liberty
　　A loosened spirit brings !

　　i.　　EMILY DICKINSON—*A Book.*
　　　　　　　　　　　(Ed. 1891).

Golden volumes ! richest treasures,
Objects of delicious pleasures !
You my eyes rejoicing please,
You my hands in rapture seize !
Brilliant wits and musing sages,
Lights who beam'd through many ages !
Left to your conscious leaves their story,
And dared to trust you with their glory ;
And now their hope of fame achiev'd,
Dear volumes ! you have not deceived !

　　j.　　ISAAC DISRAELI—*Curiosities of
　　　　　　　　　Literature.　Libraries.*

The spectacles of books.

　　k.　　DRYDEN—*Essay on Dramatic Poetry.*

Books are the best things, well used : abused,
among the worst.

　　l.　　EMERSON—*The American Scholar.*

In every man's memory, with the hours
when life culminated are usually associated
certain books which met his views.

　　m.　　EMERSON—*Letters and Social Aims.
　　　　　　Quotation and Originality.*

There are many virtues in books, but the
essential value is the adding of knowledge to
our stock by the record of new facts, and,
better, by the record of intuitions which dis-
tribute facts, and are the formulas which
supersede all histories.

　　n.　　EMERSON—*Letters and Social Aims.
　　　　　　Persian Poetry.*

We prize books, and they prize them most
who are themselves wise.

　　o.　　EMERSON—*Letters and Social Aims.
　　　　　　Quotation and Originality.*

Learning hath gained most by those books
by which the Printers have lost.

　　p.　　FULLER—*The Holy and the Profane
　　　　　　State.　Of Books.*

Some Books are onely cursorily to be tasted
of.

　　q.　　FULLER—*The Holy and the Profane
　　　　　　State.　Of Books.*

Books are necessary to correct the vices of
the polite ; but those vices are ever changing,
and the antidote should be changed accord-
ingly—should still be new.

　　r.　　GOLDSMITH—*The Citizen of the World.*
　　　　　　　　　　Letter LXXII.

I armed her against the censures of the
world ; showed her that books were sweet un-
reproaching companions to the miserable, and
that if they could not bring us to enjoy life,
they would at least teach us to endure it.

　　s.　　GOLDSMITH—*Vicar of Wakefield.*
　　　　　　　　　　Ch. XXII.

In proportion as society refines, new books must ever become more necessary.

> *a.*   GOLDSMITH—*The Citizen of the World.*
> Letter LXXII.

I have ever gained the most profit, and the most pleasure also, from the books which have made me think the most: and, when the difficulties have once been overcome, these are the books which have struck the deepest root, not only in my memory and understanding, but likewise in my affections.

> *b.*   J. C. and A. W. HARE—*Guesses at Truth.* P. 458.

Thou art a plant sprung up to wither never,
But, like a laurell, to grow green forever.

> *c.*   HERRICK—*Hesperides.* To His Booke.

The foolishest book is a kind of leaky boat on a sea of wisdom; some of the wisdom will get in anyhow.

> *d.*   O. W. HOLMES—*The Poet at the Breakfast-Table.* **XI.**

Medicine for the soul.

> *e.*   *Inscription over the door of the Library at Thebes. Diodorus Siculus.* I. 49, 3.

A man will turn over half a library to make one book.

> *f.*   SAM'L JOHNSON—*Boswell's Life of Johnson.* 1775.

Books have always a secret influence on the understanding; we cannot at pleasure obliterate ideas: he that reads books of science, though without any desire fixed of improvement, will grow more knowing; he that entertains himself with moral or religious treatises, will imperceptibly advance in goodness; the ideas which are often offered to the mind, will at last find a lucky moment when it is disposed to receive them.

> *g.*   SAM'L JOHNSON—*The Adventurer.* No. 137.

Pray thee, take care, that tak'st my book in hand,
To read it well; that is to understand.

> *h.*   BEN JONSON—*Epigram* 1.

When I would know thee * * * my thought looks
Upon thy well-made choice of friends and books;
Then do I love thee, and behold thy ends
In making thy friends books, and thy books friends.

> *i.*   BEN JONSON—*Epigram* 86.

Books which are no books.

> *j.*   CHARLES LAMB—*Last Essay of Elia. Detached Thoughts on Books.*

I love to lose myself in other men's minds. When I am not walking, I am reading; I cannot sit and think. Books think for me.

> *k.*   CHARLES LAMB—*Last Essays of Elia. Detached Thoughts on Books and Reading.*

A book is a friend whose face is constantly changing. If you read it when you are recovering from an illness, and return to it years after, it is changed surely, with the change in yourself.

> *l.*   ANDREW LANG—*The Library.* Ch. I.

As friends and companions, as teachers and consolers, as recreators and amusers, books are always with us, and always ready to respond to our wants. We can take them with us in our wanderings, or gather them around us at our firesides. In the lonely wilderness, and the crowded city, their spirit will be with us, giving a meaning to the seemingly confused movements of humanity, and peopling the desert with their own bright creations.

> *m.*   LANGFORD—*The Praise of Books. Preliminary Essay.*

A wise man will select his books, for he would not wish to class them all under the sacred name of friends. Some can be accepted only as acquaintances. The best books of all kinds are taken to the heart, and cherished as his most precious possessions. Others to be chatted with for a time, to spend a few pleasant hours with, and laid aside, but not forgotten.

> *n.*   LANGFORD—*The Praise of Books. Preliminary Essay.*

No matter what his rank or position may be, the lover of books is the richest and the happiest of the children of men.

> *o.*   LANGFORD—*The Praise of Books. Preliminary Essay.*

The love of books is a love which requires neither justification, apology, nor defence.

> *p.*   LANGFORD—*The Praise of Books. Preliminary Essay.*

Books are sepulchres of thought.

> *q.*   LONGFELLOW—*The Wind Over the Chimney.* St. 8.

Leaving us heirs to amplest heritages
Of all the best thoughts of the greatest sages,
And giving tongues unto the silent dead!

> *r.*   LONGFELLOW—*Sonnet on Mrs. Kemble's Reading from Shakespeare.*

The pleasant books, that silently among
Our household treasures take familiar places,
And are to us as if a living tongue
Spake from the printed leaves or pictured faces!

> *s.*   LONGFELLOW—*Seaside and Fireside. Dedication.*

If I were asked what book is better than a cheap book, I would answer that there is one book better than a cheap book, and that is a book honestly come by.

   a.   LOWELL—*Before the U. S. Senate Committee on Patents*, Jan. 29, 1886.

What a sense of security in an old book which Time has criticised for us!

   b.   LOWELL—*My Study Windows. Library of Old Authors.*

Gentlemen use books as Gentlewomen handle their flowers, who in the morning stick them in their heads, and at night strawe them at their heeles.

   c.   LYLY—*Euphues. To the Gentlemen Readers.*

All books grow homilies by time; they are Temples, at once, and Landmarks.

   d.   BULWER-LYTTON—*The Souls of Books.* St. 4. L. 1.

> Hark, the world so loud,
> And they, the movers of the world, so still!

   e.   BULWER-LYTTON—*The Souls of Books.* St. 3. L. 14.

> In you are sent
> The types of Truths whose life is THE TO COME;
> In you soars up the Adam from the fall;
> In you the FUTURE as the PAST is given—
> Ev'n in our death ye bid us hail our birth;—
> Unfold these pages, and behold the Heaven,
> Without one grave-stone left upon the Earth.

   f.   BULWER-LYTTON—*The Souls of Books.* St. 5. L. 11.

Laws die, Books never.

   g.   BULWER-LYTTON—*Richelieu.* Act. I. Sc. 2.

There is no Past, so long as Books shall live!

   h.   BULWER-LYTTON—*The Souls of Books.* St. 4. L. 9.

> The Wise
> (Minstrel or Sage,) *out* of their books are clay;
> But *in* their books, as from their graves they
>   rise.
> Angels—that, side by side, upon our way,
> Walk with and warn us!

   i.   BULWER-LYTTON—*The Souls of Books.* St. 3. L. 9.

We call some books immortal! *Do they live?* If so, believe me, TIME hath made them pure. In Books, the veriest wicked rest in peace.

   j.   BULWER-LYTTON—*The Souls of Books.* St. 3. L. 22.

That wonderful book, while it obtains admiration from the most fastidious critics, is loved by those who are too simple to admire it.

   k.   MACAULAY—*On Bunyan's Pilgrim's Progress.* 1831

As you grow ready for it, somewhere or other you will find what is needful for you in a book.

   l.   GEORGE MacDONALD—*The Marquis of Lossie.* Ch. XLII.

A good book is the precious life-blood of a master-spirit imbalmed and treasured up on purpose to a life beyond life.

   m.   MILTON—*Areopagitica.*

As good almost kill a man as kill a good book; who kills a man kills a reasonable creature, God's image; but he who destroys a good book kills reason itself, kills the image of God, as it were, in the eye.

   n.   MILTON—*Areopagitica.*

Books are not absolutely dead things, but do contain a progeny of life in them to be as active as that soul was whose progeny they are; nay, they do preserve as in a vial the purest efficacy and extraction of that living intellect that bred them.

   o.   MILTON—*Areopagitica.*

Deep vers'd in books, and shallow in himself.

   p.   MILTON—*Paradise Regained.* Bk. IV. L. 327.

For books are as meats and viands are; some of good, some of evil substance.

   q.   MILTON—*Areopagitica.*

> Silent companions of the lonely hour,
>   Friends, who can alter or forsake,
> Who for inconstant roving have no power,
>   And all neglect, perforce, must calmly take.

   r.   Mrs. NORTON—*Sonnet. To My Books.*

> Next o'er his books his eyes began to roll,
> In pleasing memory of all he stole.

   s.   POPE—*Dunciad.* Bk. I. L. 127.

> Chiefs of elder Art!
> Teachers of wisdom! who would once beguile
> My tedious hours, and lighten every toil,
> I now resign you.

   t.   WILLIAM ROSCOE—*Poetical Works. To my Books on Parting with Them.*

> Within that awful volume lies
> The mystery of mysteries!

   u.   SCOTT—*The Monastery.* Vol. I. Ch. XII.

> And deeper than did ever plummet sound,
> I'll drown my book.

   v.   *The Tempest.* Act. V. Sc. 1. L. 56.

I had rather than forty shillings, I had my Book of Songs and Sonnets here.

   w.   *The Merry Wives of Windsor.* Act I. Sc. 1. L. 204.

> Keep * * * thy pen from lenders' books,
>   and defy the foul fiend.

   x.   *King Lear.* Act III. Sc. 4. L. 100.

Knowing I lov'd my books, he furnished me
From mine own library with volumes that
I prize above my dukedom.
   a.   *The Tempest.*   Act I.   Sc. 2.   L. 165.

O, let my books be then the eloquence
And dumb presagers of my speaking breast;
Who plead for love and look for recompense
More than that tongue that more hath more
         express'd.
   b.   *Sonnet XXIII.*

O, sir, we quarrel in print, by the book; as
you have books for good manners:
   c.   *As You Like It.*   Act V.   Sc. 4.   L. 94.

Sir, he hath never fed of the dainties that are
bred in a book.
   d.   *Love's Labour's Lost.*   Act IV.   Sc. 2.
                                            L. 24.

That book in many's eyes doth share the
      glory,
That in gold clasps locks in the golden story;
   e.   *Romeo and Juliet.*   Act I.   Sc. 3.   L. 91.

We turn'd o'er many books together:
   f.   *Merchant of Venice.*   Act IV.   Sc. 1.
                                            L. 156.

Their books of stature small they take in hand,
Which with pellucid horn secured are;
To save from finger wet the letters fair.
   g.   Shenstone—*The Schoolmistress.*   St. 18.

You shall see them on a beautiful quarto
page, where a neat rivulet of text shall meander through a meadow of margin.
   h.   Sheridan—*School for Scandal.*   Act I.
                                            Sc. 1.

Some books are drenched sands,
On which a great soul's wealth lies all in
      heaps,
Like a wrecked argosy.
   i.   Alexander Smith—*A Life Drama.*
                                            Sc. 2.

Books, the children of the brain.
   j.   Swift—*Tale of a Tub.*   Sec. I.

Books, like proverbs, receive their chief value
from the stamp and esteem of ages through
which they have passed.
   k.   Sir Wm. Temple—*Ancient and
                                Modern Learning.*

But every page having an ample marge,
And every marge enclosing in the midst
A square of text that looks a little blot.
   l.   Tennyson—*Idylls of the King. Merlin
                                and Vivien.*   L. 669.

Thee will I sing in comely wainscot bound
And golden verge enclosing thee around;
The faithful horn before, from age to age
Preserving thy invulnerable page.
Behind thy patron saint in armor shines
With sword and lance to guard the sacred
      lines;
Th' instructive handle's at the bottom fixed
Lest wrangling critics should pervert the text.
   m.   Tickell—*The Hornbook.*

A small number of choice books are sufficient.
   n.   Voltaire—*A Philosophical Dictionary.
                                Books.*   Vol. II.   Sec. III.

They are for company the best friends, in
Doubts Counsellors, in Damps Comforters,
Time's Prospective, the Home Traveller's Ship
or Horse, the busie Man's best Recreation, the
Opiate of idle Weariness, the Mindes best
Ordinary, Nature's Garden and Seed-plot of
Immortality.
   o.   Bulstrode Whitelock—*Zootamia.*
                                            1654.

                                Books, we know,
Are a substantial world, both pure and good:
Round these, with tendrils strong as flesh and
      blood,
Our pastime and our happiness will grow.
   p.   Wordsworth—*Poetical Works.*
                                            Personal Talk.

Some future strain, in which the muse shall
      tell
How science dwindles, and how volumes
      swell.
How commentators each dark passage shun,
And hold their farthing candle to the sun.
   q.   Young—*Love of Fame.*   Satire VII.
                                            L. 95.

Unlearned men of books assume the care,
As eunuchs are the guardians of the fair.
   r.   Young—*Love of Fame.*   Satire II.
                                            L. 83.

BORES.

Society is now one polished horde,
Formed of two mighty tribes, the *Bores* and
      Bored.
   s.   Byron—*Don Juan.*   Canto XIII.
                                            St. 95.

The bore is usually considered a harmless
creature, or of that class of irrational bipeds
who hurt only themselves.
   t.   Maria Edgeworth—*Thoughts on Bores.*

Got the ill name of augurs, because they
were bores.
   u.   Lowell—*A Fable for Critics.*   L. 55.

That old hereditary bore,
The steward.
  a. ROGERS—*Italy. A Character.* L. 13.

Again I hear that creaking step!—
  He's rapping at the door!
Too well I know the boding sound
  That ushers in a bore.
  b. J. G. SAXE—*My Familiar.*

He says a thousand pleasant things,—
  But never says "Adieu.'
  c. J. G. SAXE—*My Familiar.*

          O, he's as tedious
As is a tir'd horse, a railing wife;
Worse than a smoky house; I had rather live
With cheese and garlic in a windmill, far,
Than feed on cates, and have him talk to me,
In any summer-house in Christendom.
  d. *Henry IV.* Pt. I. Act III. Sc. I.
                                      L. 159.

BORROWING.

Great collections of books are subject to
certain accidents besides the damp, the worms,
and the rats; one not less common is that of
the *borrowers*, not to say a word of the *pur-
loiners*.
  e. ISAAC DISRAELI—*Curiosities of
                Literature. The Bibliomania.*

Neither a borrower nor a lender be:
For loan oft loses both itself and friend,
And borrowing dulls the edge of husbandry.
  f. *Hamlet.* Act I. Sc. 3. L. 75.

What question can be here? Your own true
      heart
Must needs advise you of the only part:
That may be claim'd again which was but
      lent,
And should be yielded with no discontent,
Nor surely can we find herein a wrong,
That it was left us to enjoy it long.
  g. RICHARD CHENEVIX TRENCH—*The
                            Lent Jewels.*

Who goeth a-borrowing,
Goeth a-sorrowing.
  h. TUSSER—*Five Hundred Points of Good
                Husbandry. June's Abstract.*

Who borrow much, then fairly make it
      known,
And damn it with improvements of their own.
  i. YOUNG—*Love of Fame.* Satire III.
                                      L. 23.

BRAVERY.

Brave men were living before Agamemnon.
  j. BYRON—*Don Juan.* Canto I. St. 5.

          The truly brave,
When they behold the brave oppressed with
      odds,
Are touched with a desire to shield and save:—
  A mixture of wild beasts and demi-gods
Are they—now furious as the sweeping wave,
  Now moved with pity; even as sometimes
      nods
The rugged tree unto the summer wind,
Compassion breathes along the savage mind.
  k. BYRON—*Don Juan.* Canto VIII.
                                    St. 106.

How sleep the brave, who sink to rest,
By all their country's wishes blest!
  l. COLLINS—*Ode written in 1746.*

Toll for the brave!
The brave that are no more.
  m. COWPER—*On the Loss of the Royal
                                George.*

General Taylor never surrenders.
  n. THOS. L. CRITTENDEN—*Reply to Gen.
                Santa Anna. Buena Vista.*
                          Feb. 22, 1847.

The brave man seeks not popular applause,
Nor, overpower'd with arms, deserts his cause;
Unsham'd, though foil'd, he does the best he
      can,
Force is of brutes, but honor is of man.
  o. DRYDEN—*Palamon and Arcite.* Bk. III.
                                    L. 2,015.

          The god-like hero sate
          On his imperial throne:
          His valiant peers were placed around,
Their brows with roses and with myrtles
          bound
      (So should desert in arms be crowned).
The lovely Thais, by his side,
Sate like a blooming Eastern bride
In flower of youth and beauty's pride.
      Happy, happy, happy pair!
        None but the brave,
        None but the brave,
      None but the brave deserve the fair.
  p. DRYDEN—*Alexander's Feast.* St. 1.

Then rush'd to meet the insulting foe:
They took the spear, but left the shield.
  q. PHILIP FRENEAU—*To the Memory of the
            Brave Americans (who fell at Eutaw
                                    Springs).*

          The brave
Love mercy, and delight to save.
  r. GAY—*Fable. The Lion, Tiger and
                            Traveller.* L. 33.

O friends, be men; so act that none may feel
Ashamed to meet the eyes of other men.
Think each one of his children and his wife,
His home, his parents, living yet or dead.
For them, the absent ones, I supplicate,
And bid you rally here, and scorn to fly.
  s. HOMER—*Iliad.* Bk. XV. L. 843.
                              Bryant's trans

Without a sign his sword the brave man draws,
And asks no omen but his country's cause.
   a.   Homer—*Iliad.* Bk. XII. L. 283.
                     Pope's trans.

True bravery is shown by performing without witness what one might be capable of doing before all the world.
   b.   La Rochefoucauld. *Maxims.* 216.

There's a brave fellow! There's a man of pluck!
A man who's not afraid to say his say,
Though a whole town's against him.
   c.   Longfellow—*Christus.* Pt. III.
           John Endicott. Act II. Sc. 2.

How well Horatius kept the bridge
In the brave days of old.
   d.   Macaulay—*Lays of Ancient Rome.*
                  Horatius. 70.

In adversity it is easy to despise life; the truly brave man is he who can endure to be miserable.
   e.   Martial. Bk. XI. Ep. LVI.

'Tis more brave
To live, than to die.
   f.   Owen Meredith (Lord Lytton)
        Lucile. Pt. II. Canto VI. St. 11.

Who combats bravely is not therefore brave:
He dreads a death-bed like the meanest slave.
   g.   Pope—*Moral Essays.* Epistle I. L. 115.

Come one, come all! this rock shall fly
From its firm base as soon as I.
   h.   Scott—*Lady of the Lake.* Canto V.
                     St. 10.

He did look far
Into the service of the time, and was
Discipled of the bravest; he lasted long;
But on us both did haggish age steal on
And wore us out of act.
   i.   *All's Well That Ends Well.* Act I.
                  Sc. 2. L. 26.

What art thou? Have not I
An arm as big as thine? a heart as big?
Thy words, I grant, are bigger, for I wear not
My dagger in my mouth.
   j.   *Cymbeline.* Act IV. Sc. 2. L. 76.

What's brave, what's noble,
Let's do it after the high Roman fashion,
And make death proud to take us.
   k.   *Antony and Cleopatra.* Act IV.
                  Sc. 15. L. 86.

A brave soul is a thing which all things serve.
   l.   Alex. Smith—*A Life Drama.* Sc. 4.

It is besides necessary that whoever is brave, should be a man of great soul.
   m.   Cicero—*The Tusculan Disputations.*
        Bk. III. Ch. VII. Yonge's trans.

BRIBERY.

And ye sall walk in silk attire,
  And siller hae to spare,
Gin ye'll consent to be his bride,
  Nor think o' Donald mair.
   n.   Susanna Blamire—*The Siller Crown.*

'Tis pleasant purchasing our fellow-creatures;
  And all are to be sold, if you consider
Their passions, and are dext'rous; some by features
Are bought up, others by a warlike leader;
Some by a place—as tend their years or natures;
The most by ready cash—but all have prices,
From crowns to kicks, according to their vices.
   o.   Byron—*Don Juan.* Canto V. St. 27.

Too poor for a bribe, and too proud to importune,
He had not the method of making a fortune.
   p.   Gray—*On His Own Character.*

But here more slow, where all are slaves to gold,
Where looks are merchandise, and smiles are sold.
   q.   Sam'l Johnson—*London.* L. 177.

Our supple tribes repress their patriot throats,
And ask no questions but the price of votes.
   r.   Sam'l Johnson—*Vanity of Human
                 Wishes.* L. 95.

What, shall one of us,
That struck the foremost man of all this world
But for supporting robbers, shall we now
Contaminate our fingers with base bribes?
   s.   *Julius Cæsar.* Act IV. Sc. 3. L. 22.

All men have their price.
   t.   *Ascribed to* Walpole.

BROOKS.

The streams, rejoiced that winter's work is done,
Talk of to-morrow's cowslips as they run.
   u.   Ebezener Elliott—*The Village
         Patriarch. Love and Other Poems.
                    Spring.*

From Helicon's harmonious springs
A thousand rills their mazy progress take.
   v.   Gray—*The Progress of Poesy.* I. 1.
                     L. 3

Sweet are the little brooks that run
O'er pebbles glancing in the sun,
  Singing in soothing tones.
   w.   Hood—*Town and Country.* St. 9.

Thou hastenest down between the hills to
  meet me at the road,
The secret scarcely lisping of thy beautiful
  abode
Among the pines and mosses of yonder
  shadowy height,
Where thou dost sparkle into song, and fill
  the woods with light.
  a.   LUCY LARCOM—*Friend Brook.* St. 1.

See, how the stream has overflowed
Its banks, and o'er the meadow road
  Is spreading far and wide!
  b.   LONGFELLOW—*Christus. The Golden
          Legend.* Pt. III. Sc. VII. *The
                              Nativity.*

The music of the brook silenced all conversation.
  c.   LONGFELLOW—*Kavanagh.* Ch. XXI.

I wandered by the brook-side,
  I wandered by the mill;
I could not hear the brook flow,
  The noisy wheel was still.
  d.   RICHARD MONCKTON MILNES (Lord
                  Houghton)—*The Brookside.*

I chatter, chatter, as I flow
  To join the brimming river,
For men may come and men may go,
  But I go on for ever.
  e.   TENNYSON—*The Brook.*

Brook! whose society the poet seeks,
Intent his wasted spirits to renew;
And whom the curious painter doth pursue
Through rocky passes, among flowery creeks,
And tracks thee dancing down thy water-
  breaks.
  f.   WORDSWORTH—*Brook! Whose Society
                        the Poet Seeks.*

BUTCHERING (*See* OCCUPATIONS).

C.

CABINET-MAKING (*See* OCCUPATIONS).

CALMNESS.

How calm, how beautiful comes on
The stilly hour, when storms are gone!
When warring winds have died away,
And clouds, beneath the glancing ray,
Melt off, and leave the land and sea
Sleeping in bright tranquillity!
  g.   MOORE—*Lalla Rookh. Fire
                    Worshippers.* St. 52.

'Tis Noon;—a calm, unbroken sleep
Is on the blue waves of the deep;
A soft haze, like a fairy dream,
Is floating over wood and stream;
And many a broad magnolia flower,
Within its shadowy woodland bower,
Is gleaming like a lovely star.
  h.   GEO. D. PRENTICE—*To an Absent Wife.*
                                  St. 2.

The noonday quiet holds the hill.
  i.   TENNYSON—*Œnone.* L. 2.

Pure was the temperate Air, an even Calm
Perpetual reign'd, save what the Zephyrs
  bland
Breath'd o'er the blue expanse.
  j.   THOMSON—*Seasons. Spring.* L. 323.

CALUMNY.

Calumny is only the noise of madmen.
  k.   DIOGENES.

A nickname a man may chance to wear out;
but a system of calumny, pursued by a faction, may descend even to posterity. This
principle has taken full effect on this state favorite.
  l.   ISAAC DISRAELI—*Amenities of
              Literature. The First Jesuits in
                                  England.*

There are calumnies against which even innocence loses courage.
  m.   NAPOLEON I.

Be thou as chaste as ice, as pure as snow,
thou shalt not escape calumny.
  n.   *Hamlet.* Act II. Sc. 1. L. 138.

                        Calumny will sear
Virtue itself;—these shrugs, these hums, and
  ha's.
  o.   *Winter's Tale.* Act II. Sc. 1. L. 73.

No might nor greatness in mortality
Can censure 'scape; back-wounding calumny
The whitest virtue strikes. What king so
  strong,
Can tie the gall up in the slanderous tongue?
  p.   *Measure for Measure.* Act III.
                              Sc. 2. L. 146.

Virtue itself 'scapes not calumnious strokes:
  q.   *Hamlet.* Act I. Sc. 3. L. 38.

CANDOR.

Candor is the seal of a noble mind, the ornament and pride of man, the sweetest charm
of woman, the scorn of rascals, and the rarest
virtue of sociability.
  r.   BENTZEL-STERNAŨ.

           As frank as rain
On cherry blossoms.
> a.   E. B. Browning—*Aurora Leigh.*
>   Bk. III.   L. 957.

Give me the avowed, the erect ,the manly foe ;
Bold I can meet—perhaps may turn his blow ;
But of all plagues, good Heaven, thy wrath
    can send,
Save, save, oh ! save me from the candid
    friend.
> b.   George Canning—*New Morality.*

CARE.

When one is past, another care we have ;
Thus woe succeeds a woe, as wave a wave.
> c.   Herrick—*Sorrows Succeed.*

Care that is entered once into the breast
Will have the whole possession ere it rest.
> d.   Ben Jonson—*Tale of a Tub.*   Act I.
>   Sc. 4.

And ever, against eating cares,
Lap me in soft Lydian airs.
> e.   Milton—*L'Allegro.*   L. 135.

Begone, old Care, and I prithee begone from
    me ;
For i' faith, old Care, thee and I shall never
    agree.
> f.   Playford's *Musical Companion.*
>   Catch 13.

    Eat not thy heart ; which forbids to afflict
our souls, and waste them with vexatious
cares.
> g.   Plutarch—*Morals. Of the Training*
>   *of Children.*

Old Care has a mortgage on every estate,
And that's what you pay for the wealth that
    you get.
> h.   J. G. Saxe—*Gifts of the Gods.*

Care is no cure, but rather a corrosive,
For things that are not to be remedied.
> i.   *Henry VI.* Pt. I. Act III.   Sc. 3.
>   L. 3.

Care keeps his watch in every old man's eye,
And where care lodges, sleep will never lie ;
But where unbruised youth with unstuff'd
    brain
Doth couch his limbs, there golden sleep doth
    reign.
> j.   *Romeo and Juliet.*   Act II.   Sc. 3.
>   L. 34.

For some must watch, while some must sleep :
So runs the world away.
> k.   *Hamlet.* Act III. Sc. 2. L. 284.

I am sure, care's an enemy to life.
> l.   *Twelfth Night.* Act I. Sc. 3. L. 2.

No, no, he cannot long hold out these pangs ;
The incessant care and labour of his mind
Hath wrought the mure, that should confine
    it in,
So thin that life looks through and will
    break out.
> m.   *Henry IV.* Pt. II. Act IV.
>   Sc. 4.   L. 117.

O polished perturbation ! golden care !
That keep'st the ports of slumber open wide
To many a watchful night !
> n.   *Henry IV.* Pt. II. Act IV. Sc. 5.
>   L. 23.

I could lie down like a tired child,
And weep away the life of care
Which I have borne, and yet must bear.
> o.   Shelley—*Stanzas written in*
>   *Dejection, near Naples.*

Care to our coffin adds a nail, no doubt ;
And every Grin, so merry, draws one out
> p.   John Wolcott (Peter Pindar)—
>   *Expostulatory Odes.* Ode 15.

And care, whom not the gayest can outbrave,
Pursues its feeble victim to the grave.
> q.   Henry Kirke White—*Childhood.*
>   Pt. II.   L. 17.

CARPENTRY (*See* Occupations.)

CAUSE.

To legislate each duty, were to count
Drops of a stream that issue from one fount.
God gives, since all effects are in their cause,
For narrow prescripts universal laws.
> r.   Abraham Coles—*The Evangel.* P. 215.

         To all facts there are laws,
The effect has its cause, and I mount to the
    cause.
> s.   Owen Meredith (Lord Lytton)—
>   *Lucile.* Pt. II. Canto III. St. 8.

Ask you what provocation I have had ?
The strong antipathy of good to bad.
> t.   Pope—*Epilogue to Satires.* Dia. 2.
>   L. 205.

    Find out the cause of this effect,
Or rather say, the cause of this defect,
For this effect defective comes by cause.
> u.   *Hamlet.* Act II. Sc. 2. L. 101.

God befriend us, as our cause is just !
> v.   *Henry IV.* Pt. I. Act V. Sc. 1. L. 120.

Mine's not an idle cause.
> w.   *Othello.* Act I. Sc. 2. L. 95.

Your cause doth strike my heart.
> x.   *Cymbeline.* Act I. Sc. 6. L. 118.

CEREMONY.

Papa, potatoes, poultry, prunes and prism, are all very good words for the lips,—especially prunes and prism.
    a.   DICKENS—*Little Dorrit.* Bk. II.
                           Ch. V.

Ceremony was but devis'd at first
To set a gloss on faint deeds, hollow welcomes,
Recanting goodness, sorry ere 'tis shown.
    b.   *Timon of Athens.* Act I. Sc. 2. L. 16.

O ceremony, show me but thy worth!
What is thy soul of adoration?
Art thou aught else but place, degree, and form,
Creating awe and fear in other men?
    c.   *Henry V.* Act IV. Sc. 1. L. 261.

                 To feed were best at home;
From thence the sauce to meat is ceremony;
Meeting were bare without it.
    d.   *Macbeth.* Act III. Sc. 4. L. 36.

              What art thou, thou idol ceremony?
What kind of god art thou, that suffer'st more
Of mortal griefs than do thy worshippers?
    e.   *Henry V.* Act IV. Sc. 1. L. 257.

              What infinite heart's ease
Must kings neglect, that private men enjoy?
And what have kings that privates have not too,
Save ceremony, save general ceremony?
    f.   *Henry V.* Act IV. Sc. 1. L. 253.

When love begins to sicken and decay,
It useth an enforced ceremony,
There are no tricks in plain and simple faith.
    g.   *Julius Cæsar.* Act IV. Sc. 2. L. 20.

CHALLENGE.

Life, that dares send
A challenge to his end,
And when it comes, say, " Welcome, friend!"
    h.   RICHARD CRASHAW— *Wishes to his*
                    (Supposed) Mistress. St. 29.

An I thought he had been valiant and so cunning in fence, I'ld have seen him damned ere I'ld have challenged him.
    i.   *Twelfth Night.* Act III. Sc. 4. L. 311.

But thou liest in thy throat; that is not the matter I challenge thee for.
    j.   *Twelfth Night.* Act III. Sc. 4. L. 172.

               I never in my life
Did hear a challenge urg'd more modestly,
Unless a brother should a brother dare
To gentle exercise and proof of arms.
    k.   *Henry IV.* Pt. I. Act V. Sc. 2. L. 52.

              There I throw my gage,
To prove it on thee to the extremest point
Of mortal breathing.
    l.   *Richard II.* Act IV. Sc. 1. L. 46.

CHANCE.

How slight a chance may raise or sink a soul!
    m.   BAILEY—*Festus. A Country Town.*

Perhaps it may turn out a sang,
Perhaps turn out a sermon.
    n.   BURNS—*Epistle to a Young Friend.*

           Next him high arbiter
Chance governs all.
    o.   MILTON—*Paradise Lost.* Bk. II.
                           L. 909.

             Or that power
Which erring men call chance.
    p.   MILTON—*Comus.* L. 587.

Chance is blind and is the sole author of creation.
    q.   J. X. B. SAINTINE—*Picciola.* Ch. III.

Discouragement seizes us only when we can no longer count on chance.
    r.   GEORGES SAND—*Handsome Lawrence.*
                           Ch. II.

Chance will not do the work—Chance sends the breeze;
But if the pilot slumber at the helm,
The very wind that wafts us towards the port
May dash us on the shelves.—The steersman's part is vigilance,
Blow it or rough or smooth.
    s.   SCOTT—*Fortunes of Nigel.* Ch. XXII.

Against ill chances men are ever merry;
But heaviness foreruns the good event.
    t.   *Henry IV.* Pt. II. Act IV. Sc. 2.
                           L. 82.

But as the unthought-on accident is guilty
To what we wildly do, so we profess
Ourselves to be the slaves of chance, and flies
Of every wind that blows.
    u.   *Winter's Tale.* Act IV. Sc. 4. L. 549.

I shall show the cinders of my spirits
Through the ashes of my chance.
    v.   *Antony and Cleopatra.* Act V. Sc. 2.
                           L. 173.

And grasps the skirts of happy chance,
And breasts the blows of circumstance.
    w.   TENNYSON—*In Memoriam.* Pt. LXIV.

A lucky chance, that oft decides the fate
Of mighty monarchs.
    x.   THOMSON—*The Seasons. Summer.*
                          L. 1,285.

Chance is a word void of sense; nothing can exist without a cause.
    y.   VOLTAIRE—*A Philosophical Dictionary.*

CHANGE.

Joy comes and goes, hope ebbs and flows
    Like the wave;
Change doth unknit the tranquil strength of
    men.
      Love lends life a little grace,
      A few sad smiles ; and then,
      Both are laid in one cold place,
        In the grave .
  a.   MATTHEW ARNOLD—*A Question.* St. 1.

Will change the Pebbles of our puddly
    thought
To *Orient* Pearls.
  b.   DU BARTAS—*Divine Weekes and Workes,*
          Second Week, Third Day. Pt. 1.

Earth changes, but thy soul and God stand
sure.
  c.   ROBERT BROWNING—*Rabbi Ben Ezra.*
                        St. 27.

Weep not that the world changes—did it keep
A stable, changeless state, it were cause indeed
    to weep.
  d.   BRYANT—*Mutation.*

A change came o'er the spirit of my dream.
  e.   BYRON—*The Dream.* St. 3.

And one by one in turn, some grand mistake
Casts off its bright skin yearly like the snake.
  f.   BYRON—*Don Juan.* Canto V. St. 21.

Full from the fount of Joy's delicious springs
Some bitter o'er the flowers its bubbling venom
    flings.
  g.   BYRON—*Childe Harold.* Canto I. St. 82.

How chang'd since last her speaking eye
Glanc'd gladness round the glitt'ring room,
Where high-born men were proud to wait—
Where Beauty watched to imitate.
  h.   BYRON—*Parisina.* St. 10.

      I am not now
That which I have been.
  i.   BYRON—*Childe Harold.* Canto IV.
                        St. 185.

Shrine of the mighty! can it be,
That this is all remains of thee?
  j.   BYRON—*The Giaour.* L. 106.

    To-day is not yesterday : we ourselves
change ; how can our Works and Thoughts,
if they are always to be the fittest, continue
always the same? Change, indeed, is painful ;
yet ever needful ; and if Memory have its force
and worth, so also has Hope.
  k.   CARLYLE—*Essays. Characteristics.*

Sancho Panza by name is my own self, if I was
    not changed in my cradle.
  l.   CERVANTES—*Don Quixote.* Pt. II.
                        Ch. XXX.

So many great nobles, things, administrations,
So many high chieftains, so many brave
    nations,
So many proud princes, and power so splendid,
In a moment, a twinkling, all utterly ended.
  m.   ABRAHAM COLES—Trans. of Jacopone
          (XIII. Century) *De Contemptu*
          Mundi," *Old Gems in New*
                    Settings." P. 75.

Still ending, and beginning still.
  n.   COWPER—*The Task.* Bk. III. L. 627.

Heaven gave him all at once ; then snatched
    away,
Ere mortals all his beauties could survey ;
Just like the flower that buds and withers in a
    day.
  o.   DRYDEN—*On the Death of Amyntas.*

"Passing away" is written on the world,
and all the world contains.
  p.   MRS. HEMANS—*Passing Away.*

Gather ye rose-buds while ye may,
    Old Time is still a flying,
And this same flower that smiles to-day,
    To-morrow will be dying.
  q.   HERRICK—*To the Virgins to make much*
                        of Time.

Thus times do shift ; each thing his turne does
    hold ;
New things succeed, as former things grow
    old.
  r.   HERRICK—*Ceremonies for Candlemas*
                        Eve.

Good to the heels the well-worn slipper feels
    When the tired player shuffles off the buskin ;
A page of Hood may do a fellow good
    After a scolding from Carlyle or Ruskin.
  s.   O. W. HOLMES—*How not to Settle It.*

Nor can one word be chang'd but for a worse.
  t.   HOMER—*Odyssey.* Bk. 8. L. 192.
                    Pope's trans.

    As the rolling stone gathers no moss, so the
roving heart gathers no affections.
  u.   MRS. JAMESON—*Studies. Detached*
          Thoughts. Sternberg's Novels.

He is no wise man that will quit a certainty
for an uncertainty.
  v.   SAM'L JOHNSON—*The Idler.* No. 57.

The world goes up and the world goes down,
    And the sunshine follows the rain ;
And yesterday's sneer and yesterday's frown
    Can never come over again.
  w.   CHARLES KINGSLEY—*Songs.* II.

Time fleeth on,
Youth soon is gone,
  Naught earthly may abide;
Life seemeth fast,
But may not last—
  It runs as runs the tide.
    a.   LELAND—*Many in One.* Pt. II. St. 21.

          All things must change
To something new, to something strange.
    b.   LONGFELLOW—*Kéramos.* L. 32.

But the nearer the dawn the darker the night,
And by going wrong all things come right;
Things have been mended that were worse,
And the worse, the nearer they are to mend.
    c.   LONGFELLOW—*Tales of a Wayside Inn.*
         The Baron of St. Castine. L. 265.

'Tis well to be merry and wise,
  'Tis well to be honest and true;
'Tis well to be off with the old love
  Before you are on with the new.
    d.   *Lines used by* MATURIN, *as the motto to
        "Bertram," produced at Drury
        Lane, 1816.*

Do not think that years leave us and find us
  the same!
    e.   OWEN MEREDITH (Lord Lytton)—
        Lucile. Pt. II. Canto II. St. 3.

Weary the cloud falleth out of the sky,
  Dreary the leaf lieth low.
All things must come to the earth by and by,
  Out of which all things grow.
    f.   OWEN MEREDITH (Lord Lytton)—
        The Wanderer. Earth's Havings.
        Bk. III.

In dim eclipse, disastrous twilight sheds
On half the nations, and with fear of change
Perplexes monarchs.
    g.   MILTON—*Paradise Lost.* Bk. I. L. 597.

To-morrow to fresh woods, and pastures new.
    h.   MILTON—*Lycidas.* L. 193.

Saturninus said, "Comrades, you have lost
a good captain to make him an ill general."
    i.   MONTAIGNE—*Of Vanity.* Bk. III.
        Ch. IX.

All that's bright must fade,—
  The brightest still the fleetest;
All that's sweet was made
  But to be lost when sweetest.
    j.   MOORE—*National Airs. All That's
        Bright Must Fade.*

          Alack, this world
Is full of change, change, change—nothing
  but change!
    k.   D. M. MULOCK—*Immutable.*

    The sublime and ridiculous are often so
nearly related that it is difficult to class them
separately. One step below the sublime makes
the ridiculous, and one step above the ridiculous makes the sublime again.
    l.   THOMAS PAINE—*Theological Works.
        The Age of Reason.* Pt. II.

    If the nose of Cleopatra had been shorter,
the whole face of the earth would have been
changed.
    m.   PASCAL—*Thoughts.* Ch. VIII. 29.

My merry, merry, merry roundelay
  Concludes with Cupid's curse,
They that do change old love for new,
  Pray gods, they change for worse!
    n.   GEORGE PEELE—*Cupid's Curse; From
        the Arraignment of Paris.*

  Revolutions are not made; they come.
    o.   WENDELL PHILLIPS—*Speech. Public
        Opinion,* Jan. 28, 1852.

  Revolutions never go backward.
    p.   WENDELL PHILLIPS—*Speech.
        Progress,* Feb. 17, 1861.

Alas! in truth, the man but chang'd his mind,
Perhaps was sick, in love, or had not dined.
    q.   POPE—*Moral Essays.* Ep. I. Pt. II.

Manners with Fortunes, Humours turn with
  Climes,
Tenets with Books, and Principles with
  Times.
    r.   POPE—*Moral Essays.* Ep. I. Pt. II.

See dying vegetables life sustain,
See life dissolving vegetate again;
All forms that perish other forms supply;
(By turns we catch the vital breath and die.)
    s.   POPE—*Essay on Man.* Ep. III. L. 15.

Till Peter's keys some christen'd Jove adorn,
And Pan to Moses lends his Pagan horn.
    t.   POPE—*The Dunciad.* Bk. 3. L. 109.

As hope and fear alternate chase
Our course through life's uncertain race.
    u.   SCOTT—*Rokeby.* Canto VI. St. 2.

With every change his features play'd,
As aspens show the light and shade.
    v.   SCOTT—*Rokeby.* Canto III. St. 5.

When change itself can give no more,
  'Tis easy to be true.
    w.   Sir CHAS. SEDLEY—*Reasons for
        Constancy.*

    All things that we ordained festival,
Turn from their office to black funeral;
Our instruments to melancholy bells,
Our wedding cheer to a sad burial feast,
Our solemn hymns to sullen dirges change,
Our bridal flowers serve for a buried corse,
And all things change them to the contrary.
    x.   *Romeo and Juliet.* Act IV. Sc. 5.
        L. 84.

Full fathom five thy father lies;
  Of his bones are coral made;
Those are pearls that were his eyes:
  Nothing of him that doth fade,
But doth suffer a sea-change
Into something rich and strange.
   a.   *Tempest.* Act. 1. Sc. 2. L. 396.

                  I am not so nice,
To change true rules for old inventions.
   b.   *Taming of the Shrew.* Act III. Sc. 1.
                                 L. 80.

Now, the melancholy god protect thee; and
the tailor make thy doublet of changeable taf-
feta, for thy mind is a very opal.
   c.   *Twelfth Night.* Act II. Sc. 4. L. 74.

                  That we would do,
We should do when we would; for this
  "would" changes
And hath abatements and delays as many
As there are tongues, are hands, are accidents;
And then this "should" is like a spendthrift
  sigh,
That hurts by easing.
   d.   *Hamlet.* Act IV. Sc. 7. L. 119.

The love of wicked men converts to fear;
That fear to hate, and hate turns one or both
To worthy danger and deserved death.
   e.   *Richard II.* Act V. Sc. 1. L. 65.

This is the state of man: to-day he puts forth
  The tender leaves of hope; to-morrow blos-
    soms,
And bears his blushing honours thick upon
  him:
The third day comes a frost, a killing frost,
And, when he thinks, good easy man, full
  surely
His greatness is a-ripening, nips his root,
And then he falls, as I do.
   f.   *Henry VIII.* Act III. Sc. 2. L. 352.

This world is not for aye, nor 'tis not strange
That even our loves should with our fortunes
  change.
   g.   *Hamlet.* Act III. Sc. 2. L. 210.

When we were happy we had other names.
   h.   *King John.* Act V. Sc. 4. L. 7.

Life may change, but it may fly not;
Hope may vanish, but can die not;
Truth be veiled, but still it burneth;
Love repulsed,—but it returneth.
   i.   SHELLEY—*Hellas.* Semi-chorus.

Men must reap the things they sow,
Force from force must ever flow,
Or worse; but 'tis a bitter woe
That love or reason cannot change.
   j.   SHELLEY—*Lines Written among the*
                          Euganean Hills. L. 232.

Nought may endure but Mutability.
   k.   SHELLEY—*Mutability.*

This sad vicissitude of things.
   l.   LAURENCE STERNE—*Sermons.* XVI.
                       The Character of Shimel.

   The life of any one can by no means be
changed after death; an evil life can in no
wise be converted into a good life, or an infernal into an angelic life: because every spirit,
from head to foot, is of the character of his
love, and, therefore, of his life; and to convert
this life into its opposite, would be to destroy
the spirit utterly.
   m.   SWEDENBORG—*Heaven and Hell.* 527.

White rose in red rose-garden
  Is not so white;
Snowdrops, that plead for pardon
  And pine for fright
Because the hard East blows
Over their maiden vows,
  Grow not as this face grows from pale to
    bright.
   n.   SWINBURNE—*Before the Mirror.*

Not in vain the distance beacons. Forward,
  forward let us range.
Let the great world spin forever down the
  ringing grooves of change.
   o.   TENNYSON—*Locksley Hall.* St. 91.

The stone that is rolling, can gather no moss.
Who often removeth is suer of loss.
   p.   TUSSER—*Five Hundred Points of Good*
                   Husbandry. Lessons. St. 46.

Life is arched with changing skies:
  Rarely are they what they seem:
Children we of smiles and sighs—
  Much we know, but more we dream.
   q.   WILLIAM WINTER—*Light and Shadow.*

"A jolly place," said he, "in times of old!
But something ails it now; the spot is curst."
   r.   WORDSWORTH—*Hart-leap Well.* Pt. II.

As high as we have mounted in delight
In our dejection do we sink as low.
   s.   WORDSWORTH—*Resolution and*
                      Independence. St. 4.

CHAOS.

Temple and tower went down, nor left a
  site:—
Chaos of ruins!
   t.   BYRON—*Childe Harold.* Canto IV.
                                St. 80.

The chaos of events.
   u.   BYRON—*The Prophecy of Dante.*
                      Canto II. L. 6.

                  The world was void,
The populous and the powerful was a lump,
Seasonless, herbless, treeless, manless, life-
  less—
A lump of death—a chaos of hard clay.
   v.   BYRON—*Darkness.* L. 69.

Chaos, that reigns here
In double night of darkness and of shades.
a.   MILTON—*Comus.* L. 334.

Fate shall yield
To fickle Chance, and Chaos judge the strife.
b.   MILTON—*Paradise Lost.* Bk. II.
L. 232.

Where eldest Night
And Chaos, ancestors of nature, hold
Eternal anarchy, amidst the noise
Of endless wars, and by confusion stand.
c.   MILTON—*Paradise Lost.* Bk. II.
L. 894.

Lo: thy dread empire, Chaos, is restored;
Light dies before thy uncreating word:
Thy hand, great Anarch! lets the curtain fall;
And universal darkness buries all.
d.   POPE—*Dunciad.* Bk. IV. L. 649.

Then rose the seed of Chaos, and of Night,
To blot out order and extinguish light.
e.   POPE—*The Dunciad.* Bk. IV. L. 13.

For he being dead, with him is beauty slain,
And, beauty dead, black chaos comes again.
f.   *Venus and Adonis.* L. 1,019.

Nay, had I power, I should
Pour the sweet milk of concord into hell,
Uproar the universal peace, confound
All unity on earth.
g.   *Macbeth.* Act IV. Sc. 3. L. 97.

CHARACTER.

Young men soon give, and soon forget affronts;
Old age is slow in both.
h.   ADDISON—*Cato.* Act II. Sc. 5.

No great genius was ever without some mixture of madness, nor can anything grand or
superior to the voice of common mortals be
spoken except by the agitated soul.
i.   ARISTOTLE.

Both man and womankind belie their nature
When they are not kind.
j.   BAILEY—*Festus.* Sc. *Home.*

Zealous, yet modest; innocent, though free;
Patient of toil; serene amidst alarms;
Inflexible in faith; invincible in arms.
k.   BEATTIE—*The Minstrel.* Bk. I. St. 11.

See! There is Jackson standing like a stone
wall.
l.   BERNARD E. BEE—*Battle of Manassas*
(*Bull Run*). July 21, 1861.

Many men are mere warehouses full of merchandise—the head, the heart, are stuffed with
goods. * * * There are apartments in their
souls which were once tenanted by taste, and
love, and joy, and worship, but they are all
deserted now, and the rooms are filled with
earthy and material things.
m.   HENRY WARD BEECHER—*Life
Thoughts.*

Many men build as cathedrals were built,
the part nearest the ground finished; but that
part which soars toward heaven, the turrets
and the spires, forever incomplete.
n.   HENRY WARD BEECHER—*Life
Thoughts.*

No, when the fight begins within himself,
A man's worth something.
o.   ROBERT BROWNING—*Men and Women.*
Bishop Blougram's Apology.

Incivility is not a Vice of the Soul, but the
effect of several Vices; of Vanity, Ignorance
of Duty, Laziness, Stupidity, Distraction, Contempt of others, and Jealousy.
p.   DE LA BRUYÈRE—*The Characters or
Manners of the Present Age.*
Vol. II. Ch. XI.

All men that are ruined, are ruined on the
side of their natural propensities.
q.   BURKE—*Letters.* Letter 1. On a
Regicide Peace.

He was not merely a chip of the old Block,
but the old Block itself.
r.   BURKE—*About Wm. Pitt—Wraxall's
Memoirs.* Vol. II. P. 342.

Hannibal, as he had mighty virtues, so had
he many vices; * * * he had two distinct
persons in him.
s.   BURTON—*Anatomy of Melancholy.*
Democritus to the Reader.

Heroic, stoic Cato, the sententious,
Who lent his lady to his friend Hortensius.
t.   BYRON—*Don Juan.* Canto VI. St. 7.

So well she acted all and every part
By turns—with that vivacious versatility,
Which many people take for want of heart.
They err—'tis merely what is call'd mobility,
A thing of temperament and not of art,
Though seeming so, from its supposed fa-
cility;
And false—though true; for surely they're
sincerest
Who are strongly acted on by what is nearest.
u.   BYRON—*Don Juan.* Canto XVI.
St. 97.

With more capacity for love than earth
Bestows on most of mortal mould and birth,
His early dreams of good out-stripp'd the
    truth,
And troubled manhood follow'd baffled youth.
    a.   Byron—*Lara.* Canto I. St. 18.

Genteel in personage,
Conduct, and equipage;
Noble by heritage,
Generous and free.
    b.   Henry Carey—*The Contrivances.*
        Act I. Sc. 2. L. 22.

Clever men are good, but they are not the
best.
    c.   Carlyle—*Goethe. Edinburgh
        Review,* 1828.

It can be said of him, When he departed
he took a Man's life with him. No sounder
piece of British manhood was put together in
that eighteenth century of Time.
    d.   Carlyle—*Sir Walter Scott. London
        and Westminster Review.* 1838.

It is in general more profitable to reckon up
our defects than to boast of our attainments.
    e.   Carlyle—*Essays. Signs of the Times.*

We are firm believers in the maxim that,
for all right judgment of any man or thing, it
is useful, nay, essential, to see his good qualities before pronouncing on his bad.
    f.   Carlyle—*Essays. Goethe.*

Every one is the son of his own works.
    g.   Cervantes—*Don Quixote.* Pt. I.
        Bk. IV. Ch. XX.

I can look sharp as well as another, and let
me alone to keep the cobwebs out of my eyes.
    h.   Cervantes—*Don Quixote.* Pt. II.
        Ch. XXXIII.

Thou art a cat, and rat, and a coward to boot.
    i.   Cervantes—*Don Quixote.* Pt. I.
        Bk. III. Ch. VIII.

He was a verray perfight gentil knight.
    j.   Chaucer—*Canterbury Tales.* Prologue.
        L. 72.

The nation looked upon him as a deserter,
and he shrunk into insignificancy and an
Earldom.
    k.   Earl of Chesterfield—*Character of
        Pulteney.* 1763.

He (Hampden) had a head to contrive, a
tongue to persuade, and a hand to execute,
any mischief.
    l.   Ed. Hyde Clarendon—*History of the
        Rebellion.* Vol. III. Bk. VII.

In numbers warmly pure, and sweetly
strong.
    m.   Collins—*Ode to Simplicity.*

There is the love of knowing without the
love of learning; the beclouding here leads
to extravagant conduct.
    n.   Confucius—*Analects.* Bk. XVII.
        Ch. VIII.

An honest man, close-button'd to the chin,
Broadcloth without, and a warm heart within.
    o.   Cowper—*Epistle to Joseph Hill.*

Elegant as simplicity, and warm
As ecstasy.
    p.   Cowper—*Table Talk.* Line 588.

He cannot drink five bottles, bilk the score,
Then kill a constable, and drink five more;
But he can draw a pattern, make a tart,
And has the ladies' etiquette by heart.
    q.   Cowper—*Progress of Error.* L. 191.

His mind his kingdom, and his will his law.
    r.   Cowper—*Truth.* Line 405.

The Frenchman, easy, debonair and brisk,
Give him his lass, his fiddle, and his frisk,
Is always happy, reign whoever may,
And laughs the sense of mis'ry far away.
    s.   Cowper—*Table Talk.* L. 237.

Virtue and vice had boundaries in old time,
Not to be pass'd.
    t.   Cowper—*The Task.* Bk. III. L. 75.

O could I flow like thee! and make thy stream
My great example, as it is my theme:
Though deep, yet clear; though gentle, yet
    not dull;
Strong without rage, without o'erflowing full.
    u.   Sir John Denham—*Cooper's Hill.*
        L. 189.

Did you ever hear of Captain Wattle?
He was all for love and a little for the bottle.
    v.   Chas. Dibdin—*Captain Wattle and
        Miss Rol.*

He's tough, ma'am,—tough is J. B.; tough
and de-vilish sly.
    w.   Dickens—*Dombey and Son.* Ch. VII.

A man so various, that he seem'd to be
Not one, but all mankind's epitome;
Stiff in opinions, always in the wrong,
Was everything by starts, and nothing long;
But in the course of one revolving moon,
Was chymist, fiddler, statesman, and buffoon.
    x.   Dryden—*Absalom and Achitophel.*
        Pt. I. L. 545.

For every inch that is not fool, is rogue.
    y.   Dryden—*Absalom and Achitophel.*
        Pt. II. L. 463.

Her wit was more than man, her innocence
a child.
    z.   Dryden—*Elegy on Mrs. Killigrew.*
        L. 70.

Plain without pomp, and rich without a show.
    a.   DRYDEN—*The Flower and the Leaf.*
                  L. 187.

           So over violent, or over civil,
That every man with him was God or Devil.
    b.   DRYDEN—*Absalom and Achitophel.*
                Pt. I. L. 557.

    Thus all below is strength, and all above is grace.
    c.   DRYDEN—*Epistle to Congreve.* L. 19.

    There is a great deal of unmapped country within us which would have to be taken into account in an explanation of our gusts and storms.
    d.   GEORGE ELIOT—*Daniel Deronda.*
              Bk. III. Ch. XXIV.

    Character is higher than intellect. * * * A great soul will be strong to live, as well as to think.
    e.   EMERSON—*The American Scholar.*

    No change of circumstances can repair a defect of character.
    f.   EMERSON—*Essay. On Character.*

    A great character, founded on the living rock of principle, is, in fact, not a solitary phenomenon, to be at once perceived, limited, and described. It is a dispensation of Providence, designed to have not merely an immediate, but a continuous, progressive, and never-ending agency. It survives the man who possessed it; survives his age,—perhaps his country, his language.
    g.   ED. EVERETT—*Speech.* July 4, 1835.
              The Youth of Washington.

    Every one of us, whatever our speculative opinions, knows better than he practices, and recognizes a better law than he obeys.
    h.   FROUDE—*Short Studies on Great*
           Subjects. On Progress. Pt. II.

    Human improvement is from within outwards.
    i.   FROUDE—*Short Studies on Great*
             Subjects. Divus Cæsar.

    Our thoughts and our conduct are our own.
    j.   FROUDE—*Short Studies on Great*
             Subjects. Education.

Hearts of oak are our ships,
Gallant tars are our men.
    k.   GARRICK—*Hearts of Oak.*

    In every deed of mischief, he had a heart to resolve, a head to contrive, and a hand to execute.
    l.   GIBBON—*Decline and Fall of the Roman*
        Empire. Ch. XLVIII. A. D. 1180.
                  Sept. 24.

That man may last, but never lives,
Who much receives, but nothing gives;
Whom none can love, whom none can thank,—
Creation's blot, creation's blank.
    m.   THOMAS GIBBONS—*When Jesus Dwelt.*

A man not perfect, but of heart
    So high, of such heroic rage,
That even his hopes became a part
    Of earth's eternal heritage.
    n.   R. W. GILDER—*At the President's Grave.*
                    Epitaph.

    To be engaged in opposing wrong affords, under the conditions of our mental constitution, but a slender guarantee for being right.
    o.   GLADSTONE—*Time and Place of Homer.*
                  Introduction.

Here lies David Garrick—describe me, who can,
An abridgment of all that was pleasant in man.
As an actor, confess'd without rival to shine;
As a wit, if not first, in the very first line.
    p.   GOLDSMITH—*Retaliation.* L. 93.

Our Garrick's a salad; for in him we see
Oil, vinegar, sugar, and saltness agree.
    q.   GOLDSMITH—*Retaliation.* L. 11.

Though equal to all things, for all things unfit;
Too nice for a statesman, too proud for a wit.
    r.   GOLDSMITH—*Retaliation.* L. 37.

Hands, that the rod of empire might have swayed,
Or waked to ecstasy the living lyre.
    s.   GRAY—*Elegy in a Country Churchyard.*
                    St. 12.

Rugged strength and radiant beauty—
    These were one in Nature's plan;
Humble toil and heavenward duty—
    These will form the perfect man.
    t.   SARAH J. HALE—*Iron.* St. VI.

Green be the turf above thee,
    Friend of my better days!
None knew thee but to love thee,
    Nor named thee but to praise.
    u.   FITZ-GREENE HALLECK—*On the death*
                 of Joseph R. Drake

    Thought is the wind, knowledge the sail, and mankind the vessel.
    v.   J. C. and A. W. HARE—*Guesses at*
                    Truth.

    Any one must be mainly ignorant or thoughtless, who is surprised at everything he sees; or wonderfully conceited who expects everything to conform to his standard of propriety.
    w.   WM. HAZLITT—*Lectures on the English*
        Comic Writers. On Wit and Humour.

Only a sweet and virtuous soul,
Like season'd timber, never gives;
But though the whole world turn to coal,
Then chiefly lives.
> a. HERBERT—*The Church. Vertue.*

'Tis the *same* with *common* natures;
Use 'em *kindly*, they rebel:
But, be *rough* as *Nutmeg-graters*,
And the rogues obey you well.
> b. AARON HILL—*Verses Written on a
> Window, In a Journey to Scotland.*

O Douglas, O Douglas!
Tendir and trewe.
> c. SIR RICHARD HOLLAND—*The Buke of
> Howlat.* St. XXXI.

We must have a weak spot or two in a character before we can love it much. People that do not laugh or cry, or take more of anything than is good for them, or use anything but dictionary-words, are admirable subjects for biographies. But we don't care most for those flat pattern flowers that press best in the herbarium.
> d. O. W. HOLMES—*The Professor at the
> Breakfast Table.* Ch. III. *Iris.*

Whatever comes from the brain carries the hue of the place it came from, and whatever comes from the heart carries the heat and color of its birthplace.
> e. O. W. HOLMES—*The Professor at the
> Breakfast Table.* Ch. VI.

But he whose inborn worth his acts commend,
Of gentle soul, to human race a friend.
> f. HOMER—*Odyssey.* Bk. 19. L. 383.
> Pope's trans.

Gentle of speech, beneficent of mind.
> g. HOMER—*Odyssey.* Bk. IV. L. 917.
> Pope's trans.

In death a hero, as in life a friend!
> h. HOMER—*Iliad.* Bk. 17. L. 758.
> Pope's trans.

Wise to resolve, and patient to perform.
> i. HOMER—*Odyssey.* Bk. IV. L. 372.
> Pope's trans.

The love of moral beauty, and that retention of the spirit of youth, which is implied by the indulgence of a poetical taste, are evidences of good disposition in any man, and argue well for the largeness of his mind in other respects.
> j. LEIGH HUNT—*Men, Women and Books.
> Of Statesmen Who Have Written
> Verses.*

A Soul of power, a well of lofty Thought
A chastened Hope that ever points to Heaven.
> k. JOHN HUNTER—*Sonnet. A Replication
> of Rhymes.*

He was worse than provincial—he was parochial.
> l. HENRY JAMES, JR.—*Of Thoreau. A
> Critical Life of Hawthorne.*

Where the vivacity of the intellect and the strength of the passions, exceed the development of the moral faculties, the character is likely to be embittered or corrupted by extremes, either of adversity or prosperity.
> m. MRS. JAMESON—*Studies. On the Female
> Character.*

A very unclubable man.
> n. SAM'L JOHNSON—*Boswell's Life of
> Johnson.* 1764. Note.

If he does really think that there is no distinction between virtue and vice, why, Sir, when he leaves our houses let us count our spoons.
> o. SAM'L JOHNSON—*Boswell's Life of
> Johnson.* 1763.

Officious, innocent, sincere,
Of every friendless name the friend.
> p. SAM'L JOHNSON—*Verses on the Death
> of Mr. Robert Levet.* St. 2.

The heart to conceive, the understanding to direct, or the hand to execute.
> q. JUNIUS—*City Address and the King's
> Answer.* Letter XXXVII.

He is truly great that is little in himself, and that maketh no account of any height of honors.
> r. THOMAS À KEMPIS—*Imitation of
> Christ.* Bk. I. Ch. III.

When a man dies they who survive him ask what property he has left behind. The angel who bends over the dying man asks what good deeds he has sent before him.
> s. *The Koran.*

First in war, first in peace, first in the hearts of his countrymen.
> t. Gen. HENRY LEE—*Funeral Oration
> on Washington.*

First in war, first in peace, first in the hearts of his fellow citizens.
> u. *Resolution on Washington's Death.
> Prepared by* GENERAL HENRY LEE *and
> offered in the House of Representatives
> by* JOHN MARSHALL.

They eat, and drink, and scheme, and plod,
They go to church on Sunday;
And many are afraid of God,—
And more of *Mrs. Grundy.*
> v. FREDERICK LOCKER—*The Jester's Plea.*

A tender heart; a will inflexible.

    a.   LONGFELLOW—*Christus.* Pt. III. *The New England Tragedies. John Endicott.* Act III. Sc. 2.

In this world a man must either be anvil or hammer.

    b.   LONGFELLOW—*Hyperion.* Bk. IV. Ch. VI.

Not in the clamor of the crowded street,
Not in the shouts and plaudits of the throng,
But in ourselves, are triumph and defeat.

    c.   LONGFELLOW—*The Poets.*

Sensitive, swift to resent, but as swift in atoning for error.

    d.   LONGFELLOW—*Courtship of Miles Standish.* Pt. IX. *The Wedding Day.*

So mild, so merciful, so strong, so good,
So patient, peaceful, loyal, loving, pure.

    e.   LONGFELLOW—*Christus. The Golden Legend.* Pt. V. L. 319.

Thou hast the patience and the faith of Saints.

    f.   LONGFELLOW—*Christus.* Pt. III. *The New England Tragedies. John Endicott.* Act III. Sc. 3.

All that hath been majestical
  In life or death, since time began,
Is native in the simple heart of all,
  The angel heart of man.

    g.   LOWELL—*An Incident in a Railroad Car.* St. 10.

A nature wise
With finding in itself the types of all,—
With watching from the dim verge of the time
What things to be are visible in the gleams
Thrown forward on them from the luminous past,—
Wise with the history of its own frail heart,
With reverence and sorrow, and with love,
Broad as the world, for freedom and for man.

    h.   LOWELL—*Prometheus.* L. 216 .

Endurance is the crowning quality,
And patience all the passion of great hearts.

    i.   LOWELL—*Columbus.* L. 237.

For me Fate gave, whate'er she else denied,
A nature sloping to the southern side:
I thank her for it, though when clouds arise
Such natures double-darken gloomy skies.

    j.   LOWELL—*An Epistle to George William Curtis.* Postscript 1887. L. 53.

For she was jes' the quiet kind
Whose naturs never vary,
Like streams that keep a summer mind
Snowhid in Jenooary.

    k.   LOWELL—*The Courtin'.* St. 22.

6

It is by presence of mind in untried emergencies that the native metal of a man is tested.

    l.   LOWELL—*My Study Windows. Abraham Lincoln.*

Our Pilgrim stock wuz pethed with hardihood.

    m.   LOWELL—*Biglow Papers.* Second Series. No. 6. L. 38.

Soft-heartedness, in times like these,
Shows sof'ness in the upper story.

    n.   LOWELL—*Biglow Papers.* Second Series. No. 7. L. 119.

To judge human character rightly, a man may sometimes have very small experience, provided he has a very large heart.

    o.   BULWER-LYTTON—*What Will He Do With It?* Bk. V. Ch. IV.

And the chief-justice was rich, quiet, and infamous.

    p.   MACAULAY—*On Warren Hastings.* 1841.

We hardly know any instance of the strength and weakness of human nature so striking and so grotesque as the character of this haughty, vigilant, resolute, sagacious blue-stocking, half Mithridates and half Trissotin, bearing up against a world in arms, with an ounce of poison in one pocket and a quire of bad verses in the other.

    q.   MACAULAY—*On Frederick the Great.* 1842.

Now will I show myself to have more of the serpent than the dove; that is—more knave than fool.

    r.   MARLOWE—*The Jew of Malta.* Act II. Sc. 3.

Who knows nothing base,
Fears nothing known.

    s.   OWEN MEREDITH (Lord Lytton)— *A Great Man.* St. 8.

Sae true his heart, sae smooth his speech,
  His breath like cauler air,
His very foot has music in 't,
  As he comes up the stair.

    t.   MICKLE—*There's nae Luck About the House.* (Attributed also to Jean Adam.)

Great thoughts, great feelings, came to them,
Like instincts, unawares.

    u.   RICH. MONCKTON MILNES.—*The Men of Old.*

Adam the goodliest man of men since born
His sons, the fairest of her daughters, Eve.

    v.   MILTON—*Paradise Lost.* Bk. IV. L. 323.

For contemplation he and valor formed,
For softness she and sweet attractive grace.
  a.   MILTON—*Paradise Lost.* Bk. IV.
                                        L. 297.

Her virtue and the conscience of her worth,
That would be wooed, and not unsought be
      won.
  b.   MILTON—*Paradise Lost.* Bk. VIII.
                                        L. 502.

He that has light within his own clear breast
May sit i' the centre, and enjoy bright day :
But he that hides a dark soul and foul
      thoughts
Benighted walks under the mid-day sun ;
Himself is his own dungeon.
  c.   MILTON—*Comus.* L. 381.

Ofttimes nothing profits more
Than self-esteem, grounded on just and right
Well manag'd.
  d.   MILTON—*Paradise Lost.* Bk. VIII.
                                        L. 571.

Quips and Cranks and wanton Wiles,
Nods and Becks and wreathèd Smiles.
  e.   MILTON—*L' Allegro.* L. 27.

Sufficient to have stood, though free to fall.
  f.   MILTON—*Paradise Lost.* Bk. III.
                                        L. 99.

Unrespited, unpitied, unreprieved.
  g.   MILTON—*Paradise Lost.* Bk. II.
                                        L. 185.

Yet, where an equal poise of hope and fear
Does arbitrate the event, my nature is
That I incline to hope rather than fear,
And gladly banish squint suspicion.
  h.   MILTON—*Comus.* L. 410.

Good at a fight, but better at a play ;
Godlike in giving, but the devil to pay.
  i.   MOORE—*On a Cast of Sheridan's Hand.*

To those who know thee not, no words can
      paint ;
And those who know thee, know all words are
      faint !
  j.   HANNAH MORE—*Sensibility.*

I see the right, and I approve it too,
Condemn the wrong, and yet the wrong
      pursue.
  k.   OVID—*Metamorphoses.* VII.

Every man has at times in his mind the
ideal of what he should be, but is not. This
ideal may be high and complete, or it may be
quite low and insufficient ; yet in all men
that really seek to improve, it is better than
the actual character. * * * Man never falls
so low that he can see nothing higher than
himself.
  l.   THEODORE PARKER—*Critical and
          Miscellaneous Writings.* Essay I. *A
                        Lesson for the Day.*

Yet, if he would, man cannot live all to this
world. If not religious, he will be superstitious. If he worship not the true God, he will
have his idols.
  m.   THEODORE PARKER—*Critical and
          Miscellaneous Writings.* Essay I. *A
                        Lesson for the Day.*

Studious of ease, and fond of humble things.
  n.   AMBROSE PHILIPS—*From Holland to
                        a Friend in England.*

Grand, gloomy and peculiar, he sat upon
the throne, a sceptred hermit, wrapped in the
solitude of his awful originality.
  o.   CHARLES PHILLIPS—*Character of
                        Napoleon I.* Historical.

Beauty that shocks you, parts that none will
      trust,
Wit that can creep, and pride that licks the
      dust.
  p.   POPE—*Prologue to Satires.* L. 332.

Charms strike the sight, but merit wins the
soul.
  q.   POPE—*Rape of the Lock.* Canto V.
                                        L. 34.

Fine by defect and delicately weak.
  r.   POPE—*Moral Essays.* Ep. II. L. 43.

From loveless youth to unrespected age,
No passion gratified, except her rage,
So much the fury still outran the wit,
That pleasure miss'd her, and the scandal hit.
  s.   POPE—*Moral Essays.* Ep. II. L. 125.

Good-humor only teaches charms to last,
Still makes new conquests and maintains the
      past.
  t.   POPE—*Epistle to Mrs. Blount.* *With the
                        Works of Voiture.*

Heav'n forming each on other to depend,
A master, or a servant, or a friend,
Bids each on other for assistance call,
Till one man's weakness grows the strength of
      all.
  u.   POPE—*Essay on Man.* Ep. II. L. 250.

In men we various ruling passions find ;
In women two almost divide the kind ;
Those only fixed, they first or last obey,
The love of pleasure, and the love of sway.
  v.   POPE—*Moral Essays.* Ep. II. L. 207.

'Tis from high Life high Characters are
      drawn ;
A Saint in Crape is twice a Saint in Lawn :
A Judge is just, a Chanc'llor juster still ;
A Gownman learn'd ; a Bishop what you
      will ;
Wise if a minister ; but if a King,
More wise, more learn'd, more just, more
      ev'rything.
  w.   POPE—*Moral Essays.* Ep. I. Pt. II.

What then remains, but well our power to
    use,
And keep good-humor still whate'er we lose?
And trust me, dear, good-humor can prevail,
When airs, and flights, and screams, and
    scolding fail.
    a.   Pope—*Rape of the Lock.*   Canto V.
                            L. 29.

Who ne'er knew joy but friendship might
    divide,
Or gave his father grief but when he died.
    b.   Pope—*Epitaph on the Hon. S. Harcourt.*

With too much Quickness ever to be taught;
With too much Thinking to have common
    Thought.
    c.   Pope—*Moral Essays.*   Ep. II.   L. 97.

No man's defects sought they to know;
So never made themselves a foe.
No man's good deeds did they commend;
So never rais'd themselves a friend.
    d.   Prior—*An Epitaph.*

So much his courage and his mercy strive,
He wounds to cure, and conquers to forgive.
    e.   Prior—*Ode in Imitation of Horace.*
                       Bk. III.   Ode II.

He that sweareth
Till no man trust him,
He that lieth
Till no man believe him;
He that borroweth
Till no man will lend him;
Let him go where
No man knoweth him.
    f.   Hugh Rhodes—*Cautions.*

The Good are better made by Ill,
As odours crushed are sweeter still!
    g.   Sam'l Rogers—*Jacqueline.*   St. 3.

Was never eie did see that face,
    Was never eare did heare that tong,
Was never minde did minde his grace,
    That ever thought the travell long,
But eies and eares and ev'ry thought
Were with his sweete perfections caught.
    h.   Mathew Royden—*An Elegie. On the
                    Death of Sir Philip Sidney.*

It is of the utmost importance that a nation
should have a correct standard by which to
weigh the character of its rulers.
    i.   Lord John Russell—*Introduction to
            the 3rd Vol. of the Correspondence of
            the Duke of Bedford.*

Be thou familiar, but by no means vulgar.
    j.   *Hamlet.*   Act I.   Sc. 3.   L. 61.

But I have that within which passeth show;
These, but the trappings and the suits of woe.
    k.   *Hamlet.*   Act I.   Sc. 2.   L. 84.

Good name in man and woman, dear my
    lord,
Is the immediate jewel of their souls:
Who steals my purse steals trash; 'tis some-
    thing, nothing.
    l.   *Othello.*   Act III.   Sc. 3.   L. 156.

      *   *   *   *   *   *
He hath a daily beauty in his life
That makes me ugly.
    m.   *Othello.*   Act V.   Sc. 1.   L. 19.

He is deformed, crooked, old, and sere,
Ill-faced, worse-bodied, shapeless everywhere;
Vicious, ungentle, foolish, blunt, unkind,
Stigmatical in making, worse in mind.
    n.   *Comedy of Errors.*   Act IV.   Sc. 2.
                            L. 19.

He wants wit that wants resolved will.
    o.   *Two Gentlemen of Verona.*   Act II.
                         Sc. 6. L. 12.

His words are bonds, his oaths are oracles;
His love sincere, his thoughts immaculate;
      *   *   *   *   *   *
His heart as far from fraud as heaven from
    earth.
    p.   *Two Gentlemen of Verona.*   Act II.
                         Sc. 7. L. 75.

                     How this grace
Speaks his own standing! what a mental
    power
This eye shoots forth! How big imagination
Moves in this lip! to the dumbness of the ges-
    ture
One might interpret.
    q.   *Timon of Athens.*   Act I.   Sc. 1.   L. 30.

I am no proud Jack, like Falstaff; but a
Corinthian, a lad of mettle, a good boy.
    r.   *Henry IV.*   Pt. I.   Act II.   Sc. 4.
                           L. 12.

    I do profess to be no less than I seem; to
serve him truly that will put me in trust; to
love him that is honest; to converse with him
that is wise, and says little; to fear judgment;
to fight when I cannot choose; and to eat no
fish.
    s.   *King Lear.*   Act I.   Sc. 4.   L. 14.

             I grant him bloody,
Luxurious, avaricious, false, deceitful,
Sudden, malicious, smacking of every sin
That has a name.
    t.   *Macbeth.*   Act IV.   Sc. 3.   L. 57.

           I know him a notorious liar,
Think him a great way fool, solely a coward;
Yet these fix'd evils sit so fit in him,
That they take place, when virtue's steely
    bones
Look bleak i' the cold wind.
    u.   *All's Well That Ends Well.*   Act I.
                         Sc. 1. L. 111.

Long is it since I saw him,
But time hath nothing blur'd those lines of
    favour
Which then he wore.
   a.   *Cymbeline.* Act IV. Sc. 2. L. 104.

Look, as I blow this feather from my face,
And as the air blows it to me again,
Obeying with my wind when I do blow,
And yielding to another when it blows,
Commanded always by the greater gust;
Such is the lightness of you common men.
   b.   *Henry VI.* Pt. III. Act III. Sc. 1.
                        L. 85.

Men's evil manners live in brass; their virtues
We write in water.
   c.   *Henry VIII.* Act IV. Sc. 2. L. 46.

Nature hath fram'd strange fellows in her
    time:
Some that will evermore peep through their
    eyes,
And laugh, like parrots, at a bagpiper:
And other of such vinegar aspect
That they'll not show their teeth in way of
    smile,
Though Nestor swear the jest be laughable.
   d.   *Merchant of Venice.* Act 1. Sc. 1.
                        L. 51.

        Now do I play the touch,
To try if thou be current gold indeed.
   e.   *Richard III.* Act IV. Sc. 2. L. 9.

O do not slander him, for he is kind;
Right
As snow in harvest.
   f.   *Richard III.* Act 1. Sc. 4. L. 247.

O, he sits high in all the people's hearts:
And that which would appear offence in us,
His countenance, like richest alchemy,
Will change to virtue and to worthiness.
   g.   *Julius Cæsar.* Act 1. Sc. 3. L. 157.

There is a kind of character in thy life,
That to the observer doth thy history
Fully unfold.
   h.   *Measure for Measure.* Act I. Sc. 1.
                        L. 28.

There's neither honesty, manhood, nor good
fellowship in thee.
   i.   *Henry IV.* Pt. I. Act I. Sc. 2. L. 154.

The trick of singularity.
   j.   *Twelfth Night.* Act II. Sc. 5. L. 164.

       Thou art most rich, being poor;
Most choice, forsaken; and most lov'd, de-
    spis'd!
Thee and thy virtues here I seize upon:
   k.   *King Lear.* Act I. Sc. 1. L. 252.

Though I am not splenitive and rash,
Yet have I something in me dangerous.
   l.   *Hamlet.* Act V. Sc. 1. L. 285.

What a frosty-spirited rogue is this!
   m.   *Henry IV.* Pt. I. Act II. Sc. 3.
                        L. 21.

        What thou wouldst highly,
That wouldst thou holily; wouldst not play
    false,
And yet wouldst wrongly win.
   n.   *Macbeth.* Act 1. Sc. 5. L. 21.

When he is best, he is a little worse than a
man, and when he is worst, he is little better
than a beast.
   o.   *Merchant of Venice.* Act I. Sc. 2.
                        L. 94.

Why, now I see there's mettle in thee, and
even from this instant do build on thee a better opinion than ever before.
   p.   *Othello.* Act IV. Sc. 2. L. 205.

You are thought here to be the most senseless and fit man for the constable of the watch;
therefore bear you the lantern.
   q.   *Much Ado About Nothing.* Act III.
                   Sc. 3. L. 20.

I'm called away by particular business,
But I leave my character behind me.
   r.   SHERIDAN—*School for Scandal.* Act II.
                        Sc. 2.

Lax in their gaiters, laxer in their gait.
   s.   JAMES SMITH—*The Theatre.*

Daniel Webster struck me much like a steam
engine in trousers.
   t.   SYDNEY SMITH—*Lady Holland's
                  Memoir.* Vol. I. P. 267.

A bold bad man!
   u.   SPENSER—*Faerie Queene.* Bk. I.
                   Canto I. St. 37.

Worth, courage, honor, these indeed
Your sustenance and birthright are.
   v.   E. C. STEDMAN—*Beyond the Portals.*
                      Pt. 10.

Yet though her mien carries much more invitation than command, to behold her is an
immediate check to loose behaviour; and to
love her is a liberal education.
   w.   STEELE—*Tatler.* No. 49.

High characters (cries one), and he would see
Things that ne'er were, nor are, nor e'er will
    be.
   x.   SIR JOHN SUCKLING—*The Goblin's
                     Epilogue.*

The true greatness of nations is in those
qualities which constitute the greatness of the
individual.
   y.   CHARLES SUMNER—*Oration on the True
                  Grandeur of Nations*

With every man there are good spirits and
evil spirits ; by good spirits, man has conjunction with heaven, and by evil spirits with hell.

   a.   Swedenborg—*Heaven and Hell.*
                              Par. 292.

His own character is the arbiter of every one's
    fortune.

   b.   Publius Syrus—*Maxims.*　286.

Fame is what you have taken,
    Character's what you give ;
When to this truth you waken,
    Then you begin to live.

   c.   Bayard Taylor—*Improvisations.*
                              St. XI.

The hearts that dare are quick to feel ;
The hands that wound are soft to heal.

   d.   Bayard Taylor—*Soldiers of Peace.*

                 Such souls,
Whose sudden visitations daze the world,
Vanish like lightning, but they leave behind
A voice that in the distance far away
Wakens the slumbering ages.

   e.   Henry Taylor—*Philip Van Artevelde.*
                Pt. I.　Act I.　Sc. 7.

He makes no friend who never made a foe.

   f.   Tennyson—*Idylls of the King.*
         Launcelot and Elaine.　L. 1109.

His honor rooted in dishonor stood,
And faith unfaithful kept him falsely true.

   g.   Tennyson—*Idylls of the King.*
         Launcelot and Elaine.　L. 885.

She with all the charm of woman,
She with all the breadth of man.

   h.   Tennyson—*Locksley Hall Sixty*
              Years After.　L. 48.

None but himself can be his parallel.

   i.   Lewis Theobald—*The Double*
                   Falsehood.

          Whoe'er amidst the sons
Of reason, valor, liberty and virtue,
Displays distinguished merit, is a noble
Of Nature's own creating.

   j.   Thomson—*Coriolanus.*　Act III.　Sc. 3.

Just men, by whom impartial laws were given,
And saints, who taught and led the way to
    heaven !

   k.   Tickell—*On the Death of Mr. Addison.*
                        L. 41.

Nor e'er was to the bowers of bliss conveyed
A fairer spirit, or more welcome shade.

   l.   Tickell—*On the Death of Mr. Addison.*
                        L. 45.

Though lone the way as that already trod,
Cling to thine own integrity and God !

   m.   H. T. Tuckerman—*Sonnet.　To One*
                      Deceived.

I hope I shall always possess firmness and
virtue enough to maintain what I consider
the most enviable of all titles, the character
of an " Honest Man."

   n.   George Washington—*Moral Maxims.*

Lord of the golden tongue and smiting eyes ;
Great out of season and untimely wise :
A man whose virtue, genius, grandeur, worth,
Wrought deadlier ill than ages can undo.

   o.   Wm. Watson—*The Political Luminary.*

Charity and personal force are the only
investments worth anything.

   p.   Walt Whitman—*Leaves of Grass.*
        Manhattan's Streets I Sauntered,
                  Pondering. St. 6.

         Formed on the good old plan,
A true and brave and downright honest man !
He blew no trumpet in the market-place,
Nor in the church with hypocritic face
Supplied with cant the lack of Christian
    grace ;
Loathing pretence, he did with cheerful will
What others talked of while their hands were
    still.

   q.   Whittier—*Daniel Neall.*　II.

And through the heat of conflict keeps the law
In calmness made, and sees what he foresaw.

   r.   Wordsworth—*Character of a Happy*
                Warrior.　L. 53.

But who, if he be called upon to face
Some awful moment to which Heaven has
    joined
Great issues, good or bad for humankind,
Is happy as a lover.

   s.   Wordsworth—*Character of a Happy*
                Warrior.　L. 48.

One that would peep and botanize
Upon his mother's grave.

   t.   Wordsworth—*A Poet's Epitaph.*　St. 5.

The reason firm, the temperate will,
Endurance, foresight, strength and skill.

   u.   Wordsworth—*She was a Phantom of*
                    Delight.

Whom neither shape of danger can dismay,
Nor thought of tender happiness betray.

   v.   Wordsworth—*Character of a Happy*
                Warrior.　L. 72.

The man that makes a character, makes foes.

   w.   Young—*Epistles to Mr. Pope.*　Ep. 1.
                        L. 28.

       The man who consecrates his hours
By vig'rous effort and an honest aim,
At once he draws the sting of life and death ;
He walks with nature and her paths are peace.

   x.   Young—*Night Thoughts.*　Night II.
                        L. 187.

CHARITY.

In charity to all mankind, bearing no malice or ill-will to any human being, and even compassionating those who hold in bondage their fellow-men, not knowing what they do.

a.   JOHN QUINCY ADAMS—*Letter to A. Bronson.* July 30, 1838.

Charity is a virtue of the heart, and not of the hands.

b.   ADDISON—*The Guardian.* No. 166.

Gifts and alms are the expressions, not the essence, of this virtue.

c.   ADDISON—*The Guardian.* No. 166.

The desire of power in excess caused the angels to fall; the desire of knowledge in excess caused man to fall; but in charity there is no excess, neither can angel or man come in danger by it.

d.   BACON—*Essay. On Goodness.*

No sound ought to be heard in the church but the healing voice of Christian charity.

e.   BURKE—*Reflections on the Revolution in France.* 1790.

True Charity, a plant divinely nurs'd.

f.   COWPER—*Charity.* L. 573.

No farther seek his merits to disclose,
  Or draw his frailties from their dread abode
(There they alike in trembling hope repose),
  The bosom of his Father and his God.

g.   GRAY—*Elegy in a Country Churchyard. Epitaph.*

Alas! for the rarity
Of Christian charity
Under the sun.

h.   HOOD—*The Bridge of Sighs.*

Meek and lowly, pure and holy,
Chief among the "blessed three."

i.   CHARLES JEFFERYS—*Charity.*

In silence, * * *
Steals on soft-handed Charity,
Tempering her gifts, that seem so free,
      By time and place,
Till not a woe the bleak world see,
      But finds her grace.

j.   KEBLE—*The Christian Year. The Sunday After Ascension Day.* St. 6.

He is truly great who hath a great charity.

k.   THOMAS À KEMPIS—*Imitation of Christ.* Bk. I. Ch. III. (Trans. by Dibdin).

Act a charity sometimes.

l.   CHARLES LAMB—*Complaint of the Decay of Beggars in the Metropolis.*

Shut not thy purse-strings always against painted distress.

m.   CHARLES LAMB—*Complaint of the Decay of Beggars in the Metropolis.*

With malice toward none, with charity for all, with firmness in the right, as God gives us to see the right.

n.   ABRAHAM LINCOLN—*Second Inaugural Address,* March 4th, 1865.

A beggar through the world am I,—
From place to place I wander by.
Fill up my pilgrim's scrip for me,
For Christ's sweet sake and charity.

o.   LOWELL—*The Beggar.* St. 1.

O chime of sweet Saint Charity,
  Peal soon that Easter morn
When Christ for all shall risen be,
  And in all hearts new-born!
That Pentecost when utterance clear
  To all men shall be given,
When all shall say *My Brother* here,
  And hear *My Son* in heaven!

p.   LOWELL—*Godminster Chimes.* St. 7.

To pity distress is but human; to relieve it is Godlike.

q.   HORACE MANN—*Lectures on Education.* Lecture VI.

All crush'd and stone-cast in behaviour,
  She stood as a marble would stand,
Then the Saviour bent down, and the Saviour
  In silence wrote on in the sand.

r.   JOAQUIN MILLER—*Charity.*

In Faith and Hope the world will disagree,
But all mankind's concern is charity.

s.   POPE—*Essay on Man.* Ep. III. L. 307.

Soft peace she brings, wherever she arrives:
She builds our quiet, as she forms our lives:
Lays the rough paths of peevish Nature even,
And opens in each heart a little Heaven.

t.   PRIOR—*Charity.*

An old man, broken with the storms of state,
Is come to lay his weary bones among ye;
Give him a little earth for charity!

u.   *Henry VIII.* Act. IV. Sc. 2. L. 21.

A tear for pity and a hand
Open as day for melting charity.

v.   *Henry IV.* Pt. II. Act. IV. Sc. 4. L. 31.

Charity itself fulfils the law,
And who can sever love from charity?

w.   *Love's Labour's Lost.* Act IV. Sc. 3. L. 364.

Charity,
Which renders good for bad, blessings for curses.

x.   *Richard III.* Act. I. Sc. 2. L. 68.

For this relief, much thanks: 'tis bitter cold,
And I am sick at heart.

y.   *Hamlet.* Act I. Sc. 1. L. 8.

So may he rest; his faults lie gently on him!
a.   *Henry VIII.* Act IV. Sc. 2. L. 31.

We are born to do benefits: * * * O, what a precious comfort 'tis to have so many, like brothers, commanding one another's fortunes!
b.   *Timon of Athens.* Act. I. Sc. 2.
L. 105.

You find people ready enough to do the Samaritan, without the oil and twopence.
c.   SYDNEY SMITH—*Lady Holland's Memoir.* Vol. I. P. 261.

Charity itself consists in acting justly and faithfully in whatever office, business and employment a person is engaged in.
d.   SWEDENBORG—*True Christian Religion.*
Par. 422.

'Tis a little thing
To give a cup of water; yet its draught
Of cool refreshment, drain'd by fever'd lips,
May give a shock of pleasure to the frame
More exquisite than when nectarean juice
Renews the life of joy in happiest hours.
e.   THOS. NOON TALFOURD—*Ion.* Act I.
Sc. 2.

CHASE, THE.

Ay, and when huntsmen wind the merry horn,
And from its covert starts the fearful prey;
Who, warm'd with youth's blood in his swelling veins,
Would, like a lifeless clod, outstretched lie,
Shut up from all the fair creation offers?
f.   JOANNA BAILLIE—*Ethwald.* Pt. I.
Act 1. Sc. 1.

Broad are these streams—my steed obeys,
Plunges, and bears me through the tide.
Wide are these woods—I tread the maze
Of giant stems, nor ask a guide.
I hunt till day's last glimmer dies
O'er woody vale and glassy height;
And kind the voice, and glad the eyes
That welcome my return at night.
g.   BRYANT—*The Hunter of the Prairies.*

He thought at heart like courtly Chesterfield,
Who, after a long chase o'er hills, dales, bushes,
And what not, though he rode beyond all price,
Ask'd next day, "if men ever hunted *twice?*"
h.   BYRON—*Don Juan.* Canto XIV.
St. 35.

Archers ever
Have two strings to a bow; and shall great Cupid
(Archer of archers both in men and women),
Be worse provided than a common archer?
i.   CHAPMAN—*Bussy D'Ambois.* Act II.
Sc. 1.

The dusky night rides down the sky
And ushers in the morn:
The hounds all join in glorious cry,
The huntsman winds his horn;
And a-hunting we will go.
j.   HENRY FIELDING—*And a-Hunting We Will Go.*

Soon as Aurora drives away the night,
And edges eastern clouds with rosy light,
The healthy huntsman, with the cheerful horn,
Summons the dogs, and greets the dappled morn.
k.   GAY.—*Rural Sports.* Canto II. L. 93.

Love's torments made me seek the chase;
Rifle in hand, I roam'd apace.
Down from the tree, with hollow scoff,
The raven cried: 'Head-off! head-off!'
l.   HEINE—*Book of Songs. Youthful Sorrows.* No. 8.

Of horn and morn, and hark and bark,
And echo's answering sounds,
All poets' wit hath ever writ
In dog-rel verse of hounds.
m.   HOOD—*Epping Hunt.* St. 10.

It (hunting) was the labour of the savages of North America, but the amusement of the gentlemen of England.
n.   SAM'L JOHNSON—*Johnsoniana.*

Proud Nimrod first the bloody chase began,
A mighty hunter, and his prey was man.
o.   POPE—*Windsor Forest.* L. 61.

Together let us beat this ample field,
Try what the open, what the covert yield.
p.   POPE—*Essay on Man.* Ep. I. L. 9.

Come, shall we go and kill us venison?
q.   *As You Like It.* Act. II. Sc. 1. L. 21.

CHASTITY.

There's a woman like a dew-drop,
She's so purer than the purest.
r.   ROBERT BROWNING—*A Blot in the 'Scutcheon.* Act I. Sc. 3.

That chastity of honour which felt a stain like a wound.
s.   BURKE—*Reflections on the Revolution in France.*

As pure as a pearl,
And as perfect: a noble and innocent girl.
t.   OWEN MEREDITH (Lord Lytton)—*Lucile.* Pt. II. Canto VI. St. 16.

So dear to Heaven is saintly chastity,
That, when a soul is found sincerely so,
A thousand liveried angels lacky her,
Driving far off each thing of sin and guilt.
u.   MILTON—*Comus.* L. 453

'Tis chastity, my brother, chastity;
She that is clad in complete steel,
And, like a quiver'd nymph with arrows keen,
May trace huge forests, and unharbour'd
　　heaths,
Infamous hills, and sandy perilous wilds;
Where, through the sacred rays of chastity,
No savage fierce, bandite, or mountaineer,
Will dare to soil her virgin purity.
　　a.　　MILTON—Comus. L. 420.

Like the stain'd web that whitens in the sun,
Grow pure by being purely shone upon.
　　b.　　MOORE—Lalla Rookh.　The Veiled
　　　　　　　　　　Prophet of Khorassan.

If she seem not chaste to me,
What care I how chaste she be?
　　c.　　SIR WALTER RALEIGH—Written the
　　　　　　　　night before his death.

As chaste as unsunn'd snow.
　　d.　　Cymbeline. Act II. Sc. 5. L. 14.

　　　　　　　　Chaste as the icicle
That's curded by the frost from purest snow
And hangs on Dian's temple.
　　e.　　Coriolanus. Act V. Sc. 3. L. 66.

My chastity's the jewel of our house,
Bequeathed down from many ancestors.
　　f.　　All's Well That Ends Well. Act IV.
　　　　　　　　　　　　Sc. 2. L. 46.

The very ice of chastity is in them.
　　g.　　As You Like It. Act III. Sc. 4. L. 18.

Whiter than new snow on a raven's back.
　　h.　　Romeo and Juliet. Act III. Sc. 2.
　　　　　　　　　　　　　　　L. 19.

A nice man is a man of nasty ideas.
　　i.　　SWIFT—Thoughts on Various Subjects,
　　　　　　Moral and Diverting. Oct., 1706.

Then she rode forth, clothed on with chastity:
The deep air listen'd round her as she rode,
And all the low wind hardly breathed for fear.
　　j.　　TENNYSON—Godiva. L. 53.

Even from the body's purity, the mind
Receives a secret sympathetic aid.
　　k.　　THOMSON—Season. Summer. L. 1,269.

CHEERFULNESS.

A cheerful temper joined with innocence
will make beauty attractive, knowledge delightful, and wit good-natured.
　　l.　　ADDISON—The Tatler. No. 192.

Cheered up himself with ends of verse
And sayings of philosophers.
　　m.　　BUTLER—Hudibras. Pt. I. Canto III.
　　　　　　　　　　　　　　L. 1,011.

Cheerful at morn he wakes from short repose,
Breathes the keen air, and carols as he goes.
　　n.　　GOLDSMITH—The Traveller. L. 1853.

　　　　　　　　　It is good
To lengthen to the last a sunny mood.
　　o.　　LOWELL—Legend of Brittany. Pt. 1.
　　　　　　　　　　　　　　St. 35.

A merry heart goes all the day,
Your sad tires in a mile-a.
　　p.　　A Winter's Tale. Act IV. Sc. 3.
　　　　　　　　　　　　　　L. 134.

　　　　　Had she been light, like you,
Of such a merry, nimble, stirring spirit,
She might ha' been a grandam ere she died;
And so may you; for a light heart lives long.
　　q.　　Love's Labour's Lost. Act V. Sc. 2.
　　　　　　　　　　　　　　L. 15.

He makes a July's day short as December,
And with his varying childness cures in me
Thoughts that would thick my blood.
　　r.　　A Winter's Tale. Act I. Sc. 2. L. 169.

　　　　　Look cheerfully upon me.
Here, love; thou seest how diligent I am.
　　s.　　Taming of the Shrew. Act IV.
　　　　　　　　　　　　Sc. 3. L. 38.

CHILDHOOD.

　　　　　　My lovely living Boy,
My hope, my hap, my Love, my life, my joy.
　　t.　　DU BARTAS—Divine Weekes and Workes.
　　　　　　Second Week, Fourth Day. Bk. II.

　　　　　　　'Tis not a life,
'Tis but a piece of childhood thrown away.
　　u.　　BEAUMONT AND FLETCHER—Philaster.
　　　　　　　　　Act V. Sc. 2. L. 15.

Do ye hear the children weeping, O my
　　brothers,
Ere the sorrow comes with years?
They are leaning their young heads against
　　their mothers,
And that cannot stop their tears.
　　v.　　E. B. BROWNING—The Cry of the
　　　　　　　　　　　　　　Children.

　　　　　　　　Women know
The way to rear up children (to be just);
They know a simple, merry, tender knack
Of tying sashes, fitting baby-shoes,
And stringing pretty words that make no
　　sense,
And kissing full sense into empty words;
Which things are corals to cut life upon,
Although such trifles.
　　w.　　E. B. BROWNING—Aurora Leigh.
　　　　　　　　　　　　Bk. I. L. 48.

Your father used to come home to my mother, and why may not I be a chippe of the same block out of which you two were cutte?

a.   BULLEN's *Old Plays.* II. 60. *Dick of Devonshire.*

Diogenes struck the father when the son swore.

b.   BURTON—*Anatomy of Melancholy.*
                    Pt. III. Sect. II. Memb. 6.
                                        Subsect. 5.

[Witches] steal young children out of their cradles, *ministerio dæmonum,* and put deformed in their rooms, which we call changelings.

c.   BURTON—*Anatomy of Melancholy.*
                    Pt. I. Sect. II. Memb. 1.
                                        Subsect. 3.

A little curly-headed, good-for-nothing,
And mischief-making monkey from his birth.

d.   BYRON—*Don Juan.* Canto I. St. 25.

Besides, they always smell of bread and butter.

e.   BYRON—*Beppo.* St. 39.

Better to be driven out from among men than to be disliked of children.

f.   R. H. DANA—*The Idle Man. Domestic Life.*

They are idols of hearts and of households;
    They are angels of God in disguise ;
His sunlight still sleeps in their tresses,
    His glory still gleams in their eyes ;
Those truants from home and from Heaven
    They have made me more manly and mild ;
And I know now how Jesus could liken
    The kingdom of God to a child.

g.   CHAS. M. DICKINSON—*The Children.*

When the lessons and tasks are all ended,
    And the school for the day is dismissed,
The little ones gather around me,
    To bid me good-night and be kissed ;
Oh, the little white arms that encircle
    My neck in their tender embrace
Oh, the smiles that are halos of heaven,
    Shedding sunshine of love on my face.

h.   CHAS. M. DICKINSON—*The Children.*

Childhood has no forebodings; but then, it is soothed by no memories of outlived sorrow.

i.   GEORGE ELIOT—*The Mill on the Floss.*
                                    Bk. I. Ch. IX.

Teach your child to hold his tongue,
He'll learn fast enough to speak.

j.   BENJ. FRANKLIN—*Poor Richard Maxims,* 1734.

Alike all ages, dames of ancient days
Have led their children thro' the mirthful maze ;
And the gay grandsire, skill'd in gestic lore,
Has frisk'd beneath the burden of threescore.

k.   GOLDSMITH—*The Traveller.* L. 251.

By sports like these are all their cares beguil'd,
The sports of children satisfy the child.

l.   GOLDSMITH—*The Traveller.* L. 153.

Alas ! regardless of their doom,
    The little victims play ;
No sense have they of ills to come,
    Nor care beyond to-day.

m.   GRAY—*On a Distant Prospect of Eton College.* St. 6.

But still when the mists of doubt prevail,
    And we lie becalmed by the shores of age,
We hear from the misty troubled shore
The voice of the children gone before.
    Drawing the soul to its anchorage.

n.   BRET HARTE—*A Greyport Legend.*
                                                St. 6.

You hear that boy laughing ? You think he's all fun ;
But the angels laugh, too, at the good he has done.
The children laugh loud as they troop to his call,
And the poor man that knows him laughs loudest of all !

o.   O. W. HOLMES—*The Boys.* St. 9.

                        Few sons attain the praise
Of their great sires and most their sires' disgrace.

p.   HOMER—*Odyssey.* Bk. II. L. 315.
                                        Pope's trans.

Another tumble ! that's his precious nose !

q.   HOOD—*Parental Ode to My Son.*

Oh, when I was a tiny boy
My days and nights were full of joy.
    My mates were blithe and kind !
No wonder that I sometimes sigh
And dash the tear drop from my eye
    To cast a look behind !

r.   HOOD—*A Retrospective Review.*

                        Children, ay, forsooth,
They bring their own love with them when they come,
But if they come not there is peace and rest ;
The pretty lambs ! and yet she cries for more:
Why, the world's full of them, and so is heaven—
They are not rare.

s.   JEAN INGELOW—*Supper at the Mill.*

Oh, would I were a boy again,
When life seemed formed of sunny years,
And all the heart then knew of pain
Was wept away in transient tears!
   a.   MARK LEMON—*Oh, Would I Were a
Boy Again.*

Ah! what would the world be to us
If the children were no more?
We should dread the desert behind us
Worse than the dark before.
   b.   LONGFELLOW—*Children.* St. 4.

Perhaps there lives some dreamy boy, untaught
In schools, some graduate of the field or street,
Who shall become a master of the art,
An admiral sailing the high seas of thought
Fearless and first, and steering with his fleet
For lands not yet laid down in any chart.
   c.   LONGFELLOW—*Possibilities.*

Who wer as lyke as one pease is to another.
   d.   JOHN LYLY—*Euphues.* P. 215.

Who can foretell for what high cause
This darling of the gods was born?
   e.   ANDREW MARVELL—*Picture of T. C.
in a Prospect of Flowers.*

Ay, these young things lie safe in our hearts
   just so long
As their wings are in growing; and when
   these are strong
They break it, and farewell! the bird flies!
   f.   OWEN MEREDITH (Lord Lytton)—
Lucile. Canto VI. Pt. II. St. 29.

As children gath'ring pebbles on the shore.
   g.   MILTON—*Paradise Regained.* Bk. IV.
L. 330.

The childhood shows the man,
As morning shows the day.
   h.   MILTON—*Paradise Regained.* Bk. IV.
L. 220.

Ah! there are no longer any children!
   i.   MOLIERE—*Le Malade Imaginaire.*
Act II. Sc. 11.

And when with envy Time transported
Shall think to rob us of our joys,
You'll in your girls again be courted,
And I'll go wooing in my boys.
   j.   THOMAS PERCY—*Winifreda.* 1720.

Behold the child, by Nature's kindly law,
Pleas'd with a rattle, tickled with a straw.
   k.   POPE—*Essay on Man.* Ep. II. L. 275.

Pointing to such, well might Cornelia say,
When the rich casket shone in bright array,
"These are *my* Jewels!" Well of such as he,
When Jesus spake, well might the language
   be,
"Suffer these little ones to come to me!"
   l.   SAM'L ROGERS—*Human Life.* L. 202.

And children know,
Instinctive taught, the friend and foe.
   m.   SCOTT—*Lady of the Lake.* Canto II.
St. 14.

Behold, my lords,
Although the print be little, the whole
   matter
And copy of the father, eye, nose, lip,
The trick of 's frown, his forehead, nay, the
   valley,
The pretty dimples of his chin and cheek; his
   smiles;
The very mould and frame of hand, nail,
   finger.
   n.   *Winter's Tale.* Act II. Sc. 3. L. 98.

O lord! my boy, my Arthur, my fair son!
My life, my joy, my food, my all the world!
My widow-comfort, and my sorrow's cure!
   o.   *King John.* Act III. Sc. 4. L. 103.

Oh, 'tis a parlous boy;
Bold, quick, ingenious, forward, capable;
He's all the mother's from the top to toe.
   p.   *Richard III.* Act III. Sc. 1. L. 154.

We have no such daughter, nor shall ever see
That face of hers again. Therefore begone
Without our grace, our love, our benizon.
   q.   *King Lear.* Act I. Sc. 1. L. 266.

Your children were vexation to your youth,
But mine shall be a comfort to your age.
   r.   *Richard III.* Act IV. Sc. 4. L. 305.

A truthful page is childhood's lovely face,
   Whereon sweet Innocence has record
   made,—
An outward semblance of the young heart's
   grace,
   Where truth, and love, and trust are all portrayed.
   s.   SHILLABER—*On a Picture of Lillie.*

In winter I get up at night
And dress by yellow candle-light.
In summer, quite the other way,
I have to go to bed by day.
   t.   ROBERT LOUIS STEVENSON—*A Child's
Garden of Verses. Bed in Summer.*

While here at home, in shining day,
We round the sunny garden play,
Each little Indian sleepy-head
Is being kissed and put to bed.
   u.   ROBERT LOUIS STEVENSON—*A Child's
Garden of Verses. The Sun's Travels.*

Children are the keys of Paradise;
They alone are good and wise,
   Because their thoughts, their very lives, are
   prayer.
   v.   R. H. STODDARD—*The Children's
Prayer.* L. 43.

If there is anything that will endure
The eye of God, because it still is pure,
It is the spirit of a little child,
Fresh from his hand, and therefore undefiled.
   a.   R. H. STODDARD—*The Children's*
                              Prayer.

"Not a child : I call myself a boy,"
Says my king, with accent stern yet mild;
Now nine years have brought him change of
    joy—
  "Not a child."
   b.   SWINBURNE—*Not a Child.* St. 1.

But still I dream that somewhere there must
    be
The spirit of a child that waits for me.
   c.   BAYARD TAYLOR—*The Poet's Journal.*
                            Third Evening.

Oh, for boyhood's time of June,
Crowding years in one brief moon,
When all things I heard or saw,
Me, their master, waited for.
   d.   WHITTIER—*The Barefoot Boy.* St. 3.

       A simple child,
That lightly draws its breath,
And feels its life in every limb,
What should it know of death?
   e.   WORDSWORTH—*We Are Seven.*

Sweet childish days, that were as long
As twenty days are now.
   f.   WORDSWORTH—*To a Butterfly.*

The child is father of the man.
   g.   WORDSWORTH—*My Heart Leaps Up.*

The booby father craves a booby **son,**
And by heaven's blessing thinks himself un-
    done.
   h.   YOUNG—*Love of Fame.* Satire II.
                                L. 1.

CHOICE.

Both Regiments or none.
   i.   SAMUEL ADAMS—(*For the Boston Town*
            Meeting.) *To Gov. Hutchinson,*
            demanding the withdrawal of
            the British troops from
            Boston after March
            5th, 1776.

Be ignorance thy choice where knowledge
leads to woe.
   j.   BEATTIE—*The Minstrel.* Bk. II.
                            St. 30.

He that will not when he may,
When he will he shall have nay.
   k.   BURTON—*Quoted in Anat. of Mel.*
        Pt. III. Sect. 2. Mem. 5. Subs. 5.

Better to sink beneath the shock
Than moulder piecemeal on the rock!
   l.   BYRON—*The Giaour.* L. 969.

What voice did on my spirit fall,
  Peschiera, when thy bridge I crost?
  'Tis better to have fought and lost
Than never to have fought at all!
   m.   ARTHUR HUGH CLOUGH—*Peschiera.*

Life often presents us with a choice of evils,
rather than of goods.
   n.   C. C. COLTON—*Lacon.* P. 362.

The strongest principle of growth lies in human choice.
   o.   GEORGE ELIOT—*Daniel Deronda.*
                     Bk. VI. Ch. XLII.

God offers to every mind its choice between
truth and repose.
   p.   EMERSON—*Essay. Intellect.*

Give house-room to the best; 'tis never
    known
Vertue and pleasure both to dwell in one.
   q.   HERRICK—*Hesperides. Choose for the*
                              Best.

More dear is meadow breath than stormy
    wind,
And when my mind for meditation's meant,
The seaweed is preferred to the shore's ex-
    tent,
The swallow to the main it leaves behind.
   r.   VICTOR HUGO—*The Humble Home.*

Where passion leads or prudence points the
way.
   s.   ROBERT LOWTH—*The Choice of*
                       Hercules. 1.

       Rather than be less
Car'd not to be at all.
   t.   MILTON—*Paradise Lost.* Bk. II. L. 47.

Who would not, finding way, break loose
    from hell,
  *   *   *   *   *   *
And boldly venture to whatever place
Farthest from pain?
   u.   MILTON—*Paradise Lost.* Bk. IV.
                           L. 889.

Choose always the way that seems the best,
however rough it may be. Custom will render it easy and agreeable.
   v.   PYTHAGORAS—*Ethical Sentences from*
                            Stobæus.

I had rather crack my sinews, break my back,
Than you should such dishonour undergo.
   w.   *Tempest.* Act. III. Sc. 1. L. 26.

I will not choose what many men desire,
Because I will not jump with common spirits,
And rank me with the barbarous multitudes.
   x.   *Merchant of Venice.* Act II. Sc. 9.
                            L. 31.

Preferment goes by letter and affection.
a.   *Othello.* Act I.   Sc. 1.   L. 36.

         Which of them shall I take?
Both? one? or neither? Neither can be enjoy'd,
If both remain alive.
b.   *King Lear.* Act V.   Sc. 1.   L. 57.

"Thy royal will be done—'tis just,"
Replied the wretch, and kissed the dust;
"Since, my last moments to assuage,
Your Majesty's humane decree
Has deigned to leave the choice to me,
   I'll die, so please you, of old age."
c.   Horace Smith—*The Jester Condemned*
                     to Death.

When to elect there is but one,
'Tis Hobson's *Choice; take that or none.*
d.   Thos. Ward—*England's Reformation.*
                     Canto IV. L. 896.

         Great God! I'd rather be
A Pagan, suckled in a creed outworn;
So might I, standing on this pleasant lea,
   Have glimpses that would make me less for-
       lorn;
Have sight of Proteus rising from the sea,
   Or hear old Triton blow his wreathed horn.
e.   Wordsworth—*Miscellaneous Sonnets.*
              Pt. I.   Sonnet XXXIII.

A strange alternative   *   *   *
Must women have a doctor or a dance?
f.   Young—*Love of Fame.* Satire V.
                         L. 189.

CHRIST.

Star unto star speaks light, and world to
     world
Repeats the passage of the universe
To God; the name of Christ—the one great
     word
Well worth all languages in earth or Heaven.
g.   Bailey—*Festus.* 1st Sc.   *Heaven.*

           Lovely was the death
Of Him whose life was Love! Holy with
     power,
He on the thought-benighted Skeptic beamed
Manifest Godhead.
h.   Coleridge—*Religious Musings.* L. 29.

Hail, O bleeding Head and wounded,
With a crown of thorns surrounded,
Buffeted, and bruised and battered,
Smote with reed by striking shattered,
   Face with spittle vilely smeared!
Hail, whose visage sweet and comely,
Marred by fouling stains and homely,
Changed as to its blooming color,
All now turned to deathly pallor,
   Making heavenly hosts affeared!
i.   Abraham Coles—*In Literature and*
           Poetry by Philip Schaff. P. 250.
           Translation of Passion Hymn of
           St. Bernard of Clairvaux.

He was the word that spake it,
He took the bread and brake it;
And what that word did make it,
I do believe and take it.
j.   Donne—*Divine Poems. On the*
           Sacrament. (In Chalmer's English
                         Poets.)

In darkness there is no choice. It is light
that enables us to see the differences between
things; and it is Christ that gives us light.
k.   J. C. and A. W. Hare—*Guesses at*
                         Truth.

Who did leave His Father's throne,
To assume thy flesh and bone?
Had He life, or had He none?
If He had not liv'd for thee,
Thou hadst died most wretchedly
And two deaths had been thy fee.
l.   Herbert—*The Church. Business.*

One Name above all glorious names
   With its ten thousand tongues
The everlasting sea proclaims,
   Echoing angelic songs.
m.   Keble—*The Christian Year.*
           Septuagesima Sunday. St. 9.

All His glory and beauty come from within,
and there He delights to dwell, His visits there
are frequent, His conversation sweet, His comforts refreshing; and His peace passing all
understanding.
n.   Thomas à Kempis—*Imitation of Christ.*
           Bk. II.   Ch. I.   Dibdin's trans.

God never gave man a thing to do concerning which it were irreverent to ponder
how the Son of God would have done it.
o.   George Macdonald—*The Marquis of*
           Lossie. Vol. II.   Ch. XVII.

The Pilot of the Galilean Lake.
p.   Milton—*Lycidas.* L. 109.

           But chiefly Thou,
Whom soft-eyed Pity once led down from
     Heaven
To bleed for man, to teach him how to live,
And, oh! still harder lesson! how to die
q.   Bishop Porteus—*Death.* L. 316.

           In those holy fields.
Over whose acres walk'd those blessed feet
Which, fourteen hundred years ago, were
     nail'd
For our advantage on the bitter cross.
r.   *Henry IV.* Pt. I.   Act I.   Sc. 1.
                         L. 24

And so the Word had breath, and wrought
   With human hands the creed of creeds
   In loveliness of perfect deeds,
More strong than all poetic thought;

Which he may read that binds the sheaf,
   Or builds the house, or digs the grave,
   And those wild eyes that watch the waves
In roarings round the coral reef.
s.   Tennyson—*In Memoriam.* Pt. XXXVI.

His love at once and dread instruct our
    thought;
As man He suffer'd and as God He taught.
    a.   EDMUND WALLER—*Of Divine Love.*
                    Canto III.   L. 41.

CHRISTIAN.

Christians have burnt each other, quite
    persuaded
That all the Apostles would have done as they
    did.
    b.   BYRON—*Don Juan.* Canto I. St. 83.

His Christianity was muscular.
    c.   BENJ. DISRAELI—*Endymion.* Ch. XIV.

A Christian is God Almighty's gentleman.
    d.   J. C. and A. W. HARE—*Guesses at
                                Truth.*

Look in, and see Christ's chosen saint
    In triumph wear his Christ-like chain;
No fear lest he should swerve or faint;
    "His life is Christ, his death is gain."
    e.   KEBLE—*The Christian Year.* St. Luke.
                            The Evangelist.

Servant of God, well done, well hast thou
    fought
The better fight.
    f.   MILTON—*Paradise Lost.* Bk. VI.
                            L. 29.

Persons of mean understandings, not so inquisitive, nor so well instructed, are made
good Christians, and by reverence and obedience, implicitly believe, and abide by their
belief.
    g.   MONTAIGNE—*Essays.* Of Vain
                            Subtleties.

Yes,—rather plunge me back in pagan night,
And take my chance with Socrates for bliss,
Than be the Christian of a faith like this,
Which builds on heavenly cant its earthly
    sway,
And in a convert mourns to lose a prey.
    h.   MOORE—*Intolerance.* L. 68.

Yet still a sad, good Christian at the heart.
    i.   POPE—*Moral Essay.* Ep. II. L. 68.

You are Christians of the best edition, all
picked and culled.
    j.   RABELAIS—*Works.* Bk. IV. Ch. L.

A virtuous and a Christian-like conclusion,
To pray for them that have done scathe to
    us.
    k.   *Richard III.* Act I. Sc. 3. L. 316.

For in converting Jews to Christians, you
raise the price of pork.
    l.   *Merchant of Venice.* Act III. Sc. 5.
                            L. 38.

If thou keep promise, I shall end this strife,
Become a Christian and thy loving wife.
    m.   *Merchant of Venice.* Act II. Sc. 3.
                            L. 20.

I hate him for he is a Christian.
    n.   *Merchant of Venice.* Act I. Sc. 3.
                            L. 43.

It is spoke as Christians ought to speak.
    o.   *Merry Wives of Windsor.* Act I. Sc. 1.
                            L. 103.

    Methinks sometimes I have no more wit
than a Christian or an ordinary man has.
    p.   *Twelfth Night.* Act I. Sc. 3. L. 88.

My daughter! O, my ducats! O, my daughter!
Fled with a Christian! O my Christian
    ducats.
    q.   *Merchant of Venice.* Act II. Sc. 8.
                            L. 15.

O father Abram, what these Christians are,
Whose own hard dealings teaches them
    suspect
The thoughts of others.
    r.   *Merchant of Venice.* Act I. Sc. 3.
                            L. 162.

Plant neighborhood and Christian-like accord
In their sweet bosoms.
    s.   *Henry V.* Act 5. Sc. 2. L. 381.

The Hebrew will turn Christian: he grows
    kind.
    t.   *Merchant of Venice.* Act I. Sc. 3.
                            L. 179.

    This making of Christians will raise the
price of hogs: if we grow all to be pork-eaters,
we shall not shortly have a rasher on the coals
for money.
    u.   *Merchant of Venice.* Act III. Sc. 5.
                            L. 24.

I thank the goodness and the grace
Which on my birth have smiled,
And made me, in these Christian days
A happy Christian child.
    v.   JANE TAYLOR—*A Child's Hymn of
                            Praise.*

    Whatever makes men good Christians,
makes them good citizens.
    w   DANIEL WEBSTER—*Speech at Plymouth.*
                Dec. 22, 1820. Vol. I. P. 44.

A Christian is the highest style of man.
    x.   YOUNG—*Night Thoughts.* Night IV.
                            L. 788.

CHRISTMAS.

The mistletoe hung in the castle hall,
The holly branch shone on the old oak wall.
    a.   THOS. HAYNES BAYLY—*The Mistletoe*
                      Bough.

No trumpet-blast profaned
    The hour in which the Prince of Peace was
      born;
No bloody streamlet stained
    Earth's silver rivers on that sacred morn.
    b.   BRYANT—*Christmas in 1875.*

For little children everywhere
    A joyous season still we make;
We bring our precious gifts to them,
    Even for the dear child Jesus' sake.
    c.   PHEBE CARY—*Christmas.*

O most illustrious of the days of time!
Day full of joy and benison to earth
When Thou wast born, sweet Babe of
    Bethlehem!
With dazzling pomp descending angels sung
Good will and peace to men, to God due praise,
Who on the errand of salvation sent
Thee, Son Beloved! of plural Unity
Essential part, made flesh that mad'st all
    worlds.
    d.   ABRAHAM COLES—*The Microcosm and*
                 Other Poems. P. 118.

We ring the bells and we raise the strain,
We hang up garlands everywhere
And bid the tapers twinkle fair,
    And feast and frolic—and then we go
    Back to the same old lives again.
    e.   SUSAN COOLIDGE—*Christmas.*

How bless'd, how envied, were our life,
Could we but scape the poulterer's knife!
But man, curs'd man, on Turkeys preys,
And Christmas shortens all our days:
Sometimes with oysters we combine,
Sometimes assist the savory chine;
From the low peasant to the lord,
The Turkey smokes on every board.
    f.   GAY—*Fables.* Pt. 1. Fable 39.

What babe new born is this that in a manger
    cries?
Near on her lowly bed his happy mother lies.
Oh, see the air is shaken with white and
    heavenly wings—
This is the Lord of all the earth, this is the
    King of Kings.
    g.   R. W. GILDER—*A Christmas Hymn.*
                           St. 4.

Hail to the King of Bethlehem,
Who weareth in his diadem
The yellow crocus for the gem
Of his authority!
    h.   LONGFELLOW—*Christus. Golden Legend.*
                          Pt. III.

I heard the bells on Christmas Day
Their old, familiar carols play,
    And wild and sweet
    The words repeat
Of peace on earth, good-will to men!
    i.   LONGFELLOW—*Christmas Bells.* St. 1.

Shepherds at the grange,
    Where the Babe was born,
Sang with many a change,
    Christmas carols until morn.
    j.   LONGFELLOW—*By the Fireside.*
               A Christmas Carol. St. 3.

Ring out, ye crystal spheres!
Once bless our human ears,
    If ye have power to touch our senses so;
And let your silver chime
Move in melodious time,
    And let the bass of Heaven's deep organ
      blow;
And with your ninefold harmony
Make up full consort to the angelic symphony.
    k.   MILTON—*Hymn. On the Morning of*
                 Christ's Nativity. St. 13.

This is the month, and this the happy morn,
Wherein the Son of Heaven's eternal King,
Of wedded maid and virgin mother born,
Our great redemption from above did bring,
For so the holy sages once did sing,
That He our deadly forfeit should release,
And with His Father work us a perpetual
    peace.
    l.   MILTON—*Hymn. On the Morning of*
                      Christ's Nativity.

'Twas the night before Christmas, when all
    through the house
Not a creature was stirring,—not even a mouse:
The stockings were hung by the chimney with
    care,
In hopes that St. Nicholas soon would be
    there.
    m.   CLEMENT C. MOORE—*A Visit from St.*
                        Nicholas.

God rest ye, little children; let nothing you
    affright,
For Jesus Christ, your Saviour, was born this
    happy night;
Along the hills of Galilee the white flocks
    sleeping lay,
When Christ, the Child of Nazareth, was born
    on Christmas day.
    n.   D. M. MULOCK—*A Christmas Carol.*
                           St. 2.

It is the Christmas time:
And up and down 'twixt heaven and earth,
In glorious grief and solemn mirth,
The shining angels climb.
    o.   D. M. MULOCK—*A Hymn for Christmas*
                         Morning.

At Christmas-tide the open hand
Scatters its bounty o'er sea and land,
And none are left to grieve alone,
For Love is heaven and claims its own.
    a.   MARGARET E. SANGSTER—*The Christmas
                   Tide.*

As many mince pies as you taste at Christmas, so many happy months will you have.
    b.   *Old English Saying.*

England was merry England, when
Old Christmas brought his sports again.
'Twas Christmas broach'd the mightiest ale ;
'Twas Christmas told the merriest tale ;
A Christmas gambol oft could cheer
The poor man's heart through half the year.
    c.   SCOTT—*Marmion.*   Canto VI.
                       Introduction.

At Christmas I no more desire a rose,
Than wish a snow in May's new-fangled
    mirth.
    d.   *Love's Labour's Lost.*   Act. I.   Sc. 1.
                          L. 107.

Be merry all, be merry all,
With holly dress the festive hall ;
Prepare the song, the feast, the ball,
      To welcome merry Christmas.
    e.   W. R. SPENCER—*The Joys of Christmas.*

The time draws near the birth of Christ :
    The moon is hid ; the night is still ;
    The Christmas bells from hill to hill
Answer each other in the mist.
    f.   TENNYSON—*In Memoriam.*
                     Pt. XXVIII.

With trembling fingers did we weave
    The holly round the Christmas hearth ;
    A rainy cloud possess'd the earth,
And sadly fell our Christmas-eve.
    g.   TENNYSON—*In Memoriam.*   Pt. XXX.

At Christmas play, and make good cheer,
For Christmas comes but once a year.
    h.   TUSSER—*Five Hundred Points of Good
               Husbandry.*   Ch. XII.

         The sun doth shake
Light from his locks, and, all the way
Breathing perfumes, doth spice the day.
    i.   HENRY VAUGHAN—*Christ's Nativity.*

Blow, bugles of battle, the marches of peace ;
East, west, north, and south let the long
        quarrel cease ;
Sing the song of great joy that the angels
        began,
Sing of glory to God and of good-will to man !
    j.   WHITTIER—*A Christmas Carmen.*
                         St. 3.

CHURCHES.

Oh ! St. Patrick was a gentleman
    Who came of decent people ;
He built a church in Dublin town,
    And on it put a steeple.
    k.   HENRY BENNETT—*St. Patrick Was a
                       Gentleman.*

An instinctive taste teaches men to build
their churches in flat countries with spire
steeples, which, as they cannot be referred to
any other object, point as with silent finger to
the sky and stars.
    l.   COLERIDGE—*The Friend.*

" What is a church ? "   Let Truth and reason
       speak,
They would reply, " The faithful, pure and
       meek,
From Christian folds, the one selected race,
Of all professions, and in every place."
    m.   CRABBE—*The Borough.*   Letter II.   L. 1.

What is a church ?—Our honest sexton tells,
'Tis a tall building, with a tower and bells.
    n.   CRABBE—*The Borough.*   Letter II.
                       L. 11.

Whenever God erects a house of prayer
The devil always builds a chapel there ;
And 'twill be found, upon examination,
The latter has the largest congregation.
    o.   DEFOE—*True Born Englishman.*
                     Pt. I.   L. 1.

God never had a church but there, men say,
The devil a chapel hath raised by some wiles,
I doubted of this saw, till on a day
I westward spied great Edinburgh's Saint
    Giles.
    p.   DRUMMOND—*Posthumous Poems.*
                     A Proverb.

It is common for those that are *farthest from
God*, to boast themselves most of their *being
near to the Church.*
    q.   MATHEW HENRY—*Commentaries.*
                     Jeremiah VII.

And she (the Roman Catholic Church) may
still exist in undiminished vigor, when some
traveller from New Zealand shall, in the
midst of a vast solitude, take his stand on a
broken arch of London Bridge to sketch the
ruins of St. Paul's.
    r.   MACAULAY—*Review of Ranke's History
                     of the Popes.*

No silver saints, by dying misers giv'n,
Here brib'd the rage of ill-requited heav'n :
But such plain roofs as Piety could raise,
And only vocal with the Maker's praise.
    s.   POPE—*Eloisa to Abelard.*   L. 137.

Who builds a church to God, and not to Fame,
Will never mark the marble with his Name.
    a.   POPE—*Moral Essays.* Ep. III. L. 285.

Spires whose " silent finger points to heaven."
    b.   WORDSWORTH—*The Excursion.*
       Bk. VI.   Quoted from Coleridge—
                The Friend.

An itch of disputing will prove the scab of
    churches.
    c.   SIR HENRY WOTTON—*A Panegyric to*
                King Charles.

CIRCLES.

Circles and right lines limit and close all
bodies, and the mortal right-lined circle must
conclude and shut up all.
    d.   SIR THOMAS BROWNE—*Hydriotaphia.*
                Ch. V.

 The eye is the first circle; the horizon
which it forms is the second; and throughout
nature this primary figure is repeated without
end. It is the highest emblem in the cipher
of the world.
    e.   EMERSON—*Essays. Circles.*

As the small pebble stirs the peaceful lake;
The centre mov'd, a circle straight succeeds,
Another still, and still another spreads.
    f.   POPE—*Essay on Man.* Ep. IV.
                L. 364

I'm up and down and round about,
Yet all the world can't find me out;
Though hundreds have employed their leisure,
They never yet could find my measure.
    g.   SWIFT—*On a Circle.*

I watch'd the little circles die;
They past into the level flood.
    h.   TENNYSON—*The Miller's Daughter.*
                St. 10.

          On the lecture slate
The circle rounded under female hands
With flawless demonstration.
    i.   TENNYSON—*The Princess.* II. L. 349.

Circles are praised, not that abound
In largeness, but the exactly round.
    j.   EDMUND WALLER—*Long and Short Life.*

CIRCUMSTANCE.

The fortuitous or casual concourse of atoms.
    k.   RICHARD BENTLEY—*Sermons*, VII.
          Works, Vol. III., p. 147. 1692.
          See also SIR ROBERT PEEL's *Address.*
          Quarterly Review. Vol. LIII.
          p. 270. 1835.

I am the very slave of circumstance
And impulse—borne away with every breath!
    l.   BYRON—*Sardanapalus.* Act IV. Sc. 1.

Men are the sport of circumstances, when
The circumstances seem the sport of men.
    m.   BYRON—*Don Juan.* Canto V. St. 17.

Thus neither the praise nor the blame is our
own.
    n.   COWPER—*Letter to Mr. Newton.*

Man is not the creature of circumstances,
Circumstances are the creatures of men.
    o.   BENJ. DISRAELI—*Vivian Grey.* Vol. II.
                Bk. VI. Ch. 7.

It is circumstances (difficulties) which show
what men are.
    p.   EPICTETUS—Ch. XXIV. Quoted
          from Ovid—*Tristia.* IV. 3. 79.
          Sc. 1. Long's trans.

To what fortuitous occurrence do we not
owe every pleasure and convenience of our
lives.
    q.   GOLDSMITH—*The Vicar of Wakefield.*
                Ch. XXI.

Circumstances alter cases.
    r.   HALIBURTON—*The Old Judge.* Ch. XV.

Thus we see, too, in the world that some
persons assimilate only what is ugly and evil
from the same moral circumstances which
supply good and beautiful results—the fragrance of celestial flowers—to the daily life of
others.
    s.   NATH. HAWTHORNE—*Mosses from an*
                Old Manse. The Old Manse.

For these attacks do not contribute to make
us frail but rather show us to be what we are.
    t.   THOS. à KEMPIS—*Imitation of Christ.*
          Dibdin's trans. Bk. I. Ch. XVI.

Condition, circumstance is not the thing.
    u.   POPE—*Essay on Man.* Ep. IV. L. 57.

The happy combination of fortuitous circumstances.
    v.   SCOTT—*Answer of the Author of Waverly*
          to the Letter of Captain Clutterbuck.
                The Monastery.

Leave frivolous circumstances.
    w.   *Taming of the Shrew.* Act V. Sc. 1.
                L. 27.

          My circumstances
Being so near the truth as I will make them,
Must first induce you to believe.
    x.   *Cymbeline.* Act II. Sc. 4. L. 62.

The Lie with Circumstance.
    y.   *As You Like It.* Act V. Sc. 4. L. 100.

And grasps the skirts of happy chance,
And breasts the blows of circumstance.
    z.   TENNYSON—*In Memoriam.* Pt. LXIII.
                St. 2.

So runs the round of life from hour to hour.
    aa.   TENNYSON—*Circumstance.*

This fearful concatenation of circumstances.
   a.   DAN'L WEBSTER—*Argument. The
      Murder of Captain Joseph White.*
      1830. Vol. VI. P. 88.

Circumstances over which I have no control.
   b.   WELLINGTON (Duke of)—*Letters.*
      About 1839 or 1840.

Who does the best that circumstance allows,
Does well, acts nobly, angels could no more.
   c.   YOUNG—*Night Thoughts.* Night II.
      L. 90.

CITIES.

Seven cities vied for Homer's birth with emulation pious :
Salamis, Samos, Calophon, Rhodes, Argos,
   Athens, Chios,
   d.   *Greek Anthology.*

I live not in myself, but I become
Portion of that around me ; and to me
High mountains are a feeling, but the hum
Of human cities torture.
   e.   BYRON—*Childe Harold.* Canto III.
      St. 72.

In the busy haunts of men.
   f.   MRS. HEMANS—*Tale of the Secret
      Tribunal.* Pt. 1. L. 2.

The axis of the earth sticks out visibly
through the centre of each and every town or
city.
   g.   O. W. HOLMES—*The Autocrat of the
      Breakfast Table.* VI.

Far from gay cities, and the ways of men.
   h.   HOMER—*The Odyssey.* Bk. 14. L. 410.
      Pope's trans.

Even cities have their graves !
   i.   LONGFELLOW—*Amalfi.* St. 6.

Towered cities please us then,
And the busy hum of men.
   j.   MILTON—*L'Allegro.* L. 117.

The people are the city.
   k.   *Coriolanus.* Act III. Sc. 1. L. 200.

The city of dreadful night.
   l.   JAMES THOMSON—*Current Literature for*
      1889. P. 492.

Athens.

Ancient of days ! august Athena ! where,
Where are thy men of might? thy grand in
   soul?
Gone—glimmering through the dream of
   things that were ;
First in the race that led to glory's goal,
They won, and pass'd away—Is this the whole?
   m.   BYRON—*Childe Harold.* Canto II.
      St. 2.

Athens, the eye of Greece, mother of arts
And eloquence.
   n.   MILTON—*Paradise Regained.* Bk. IV.
      L. 240.

Boston.

The sea returning day by day
   Restores the world-wide mart.
So let each dweller on the Bay
   Fold Boston in his heart
Till these echoes be choked with snows
Or over the town blue ocean flows.
   o.   EMERSON—*Boston.* St. 20.

Boston State-house is the hub of the solar
system. You couldn't pry that out of a Boston
man if you had the tire of all creation straight-
ened out for a crow-bar.
   p.   O. W. HOLMES—*The Autocrat of the
      Breakfast Table.* VI.

A solid man of Boston
A comfortable man with dividends,
And the first salmon and the first green peas.
   q.   LONGFELLOW—*New England Tragedies.
      John Endicott.* Act IV.

Carcassonne.

How old I am ! I'm eighty years !
I've worked both hard and long,
Yet patient as my life has been,
One dearest sight I have not seen—
   It almost seems a wrong ;
A dream I had when life was new,
Alas our dreams ! they come not true ;
I thought to see fair Carcassonne,
That lovely city—Carcassonne !
   r.   GUSTAVE NADAUD—Quoted in Marvin
      R. Vincent's *In the Shadow of the
      Pyrenees.* Ch. XVII.

Cologne.

In Köln, a town of monks and bones,
And pavement fang'd with murderous stones.
And rags and hags, and hideous wenches,
I counted two-and-seventy stenches,
All well defined, and several stinks !
Ye nymphs that reign o'er sewers and sinks,
The River Rhine, it is well known,
Doth wash your city of Cologne ;
But tell me, nymphs ! what power divine
Shall henceforth wash the river Rhine?
   s.   COLERIDGE—*Cologne.*

Delft.

What land is this? Yon pretty town
   Is Delft, with all its wares displayed :
The pride, the market-place, the crown
   And centre of the Potter's trade,
   t.   LONGFELLOW—*Keramos.* L. 66.

Dresden.

At Dresden on the Elbe, that handsome city,
  Where straw hats, verses, and cigars are
    made,
They've built (it well may make us feel
    afraid,)
A music club and music warehouse pretty.
   a.   HEINE—*Book of Songs. Sonnets.*
                   Dresden Poetry.

Florence.

Ungrateful Florence! Dante sleeps afar,
Like Scipio, buried by the upbraiding shore.
   b.   BYRON—*Childe Harold.*
                 Canto IV. St. 57.

London.

A mighty mass of brick, and smoke, and
    shipping,
  Dirty and dusty, but as wide as eye
Could reach, with here and there a sail just
    skipping
  In sight, then lost amidst the forestry
Of masts; a wilderness of steeples peeping
  On tiptoe through their sea-coal canopy;
A huge, dun cupola, like a foolscap crown
On a fool's head—and there is London Town,
   c.   BYRON—*Don Juan.* Canto X. St. 82.

London! the needy villain's general home,
The common sewer of Paris and of Rome!
With eager thirst, by folly or by fate,
Sucks in the dregs of each corrupted state.
   d.   SAM'L JOHNSON—*London.* L. 93.

Naples.

Naples sitteth by the sea, keystone of an arch
  of azure.
   e.   TUPPER—*Proverbial Philosophy.*
                   Of Death. L. 53.

Nuremburg.

In the valley of the Pegnitz, where,
  Across broad meadow-lands,
Rise the blue Franconian mountains,
Nuremburg, the ancient, stands.
   f.   LONGFELLOW—*Nuremburg.*

Paris.

Good Americans when they die go to Paris.
   g.   THOS. APPLETON—See also O. W.
        Holmes. *Autocrat of the Breakfast
                  Table.* VI.

When you've walked up the Rue la Paix at
    Paris,
  Been to the Louvre and the Tuileries,
And to Versailles, although to go so far is
  A thing not quite consistent with your ease,
And—but the mass of objects quite a bar is
  To my describing what the traveller sees.
You who have ever been to Paris, know;
And you who have not been to Paris—go!
   h.   RUSKIN—*A Tour Through France.*
                     St. 12.

Philadelphia.

Hail! Philadelphia, tho' Quaker thou be,
The birth-day of medical honors to thee
In this country belongs; 'twas thou caught
    the flame,
That crossing the ocean from Englishmen
    came,
And kindled the fires of Wisdom and Knowl-
    edge,
Inspired the student, erected a college,
First held a commencement with suitable
    state,
In the year of our Lord, seventeen sixty-eight.
   i.   WM. TODD HELMUTH—*The Story of a
                       City Doctor.*

Rome.

O Rome! my country! city of the soul!
   j.   BYRON—*Childe Harold.* Canto IV.
                       St. 78.

When falls the Coliseum, Rome shall fall;
And when Rome falls—the World.
   k.   BYRON—*Childe Harold.* Canto IV.
                       St. 145.

It was the calm and silent night!
  Seven hundred years and fifty-three
Had Rome been growing up to might
  And now was queen of land and sea.
No sound was heard of clashing wars,
  Peace brooded o'er the hushed domain;
Apollo, Pallas, Jove and Mars,
  Held undisturbed their ancient reign,
In the solemn midnight,
  Centuries ago.
   l.   ALFRED DOMETT—*Christmas Hymn.*

Rome, Rome, thou art no more
  As thou hast been!
On thy seven hills of yore
  Thou sat'st a queen.
   m.   MRS. HEMANS—*Roman Girl's Song.*

See the wild Waste of all-devouring years!
How Rome her own sad Sepulchre appears,
With nodding arches, broken temples spread!
The very Tombs now vanish'd like their dead!
   n.   POPE—*Moral Essays.* Ep. to Addison.

I am in Rome! Oft as the morning ray
Visits these eyes, waking at once I cry,
Whence this excess of joy? What has befallen
    me?
And from within a thrilling voice replies,
Thou art in Rome! A thousand busy thoughts
Rush on my mind, a thousand images;
And I spring up as girt to run a race!
   o.   SAM'L ROGERS—*Rome.*

Venice.

In Venice, Tasso's echoes are no more,
  And silent rows the songless gondolier;
Her palaces are crumbling to the shore,
  And music meets not always now the ear,
   p.   BYRON—*Childe Harold.* Canto IV.
                       St. 3.

I stood in Venice, on the Bridge of Sighs;
　A palace and a prison on each hand;
I saw from out the wave her structure rise
　As from the stroke of the enchanter's wand:
A thousand years their cloudy wings expand
Around me, and a dying Glory smiles
O'er the far times, when many a subject land
Look'd to the wingèd Lion's marble piles,
Where Venice sate [in state, throned on her
　　hundred isles.
　　a.　　Byron—*Childe Harold.* Canto IV.
　　　　　　　　　　　　　　　　　St. 1.

　　　　　　Venice once was dear,
The pleasant place of all festivity,
The revel of the earth, the masque of Italy.
　　b.　　Byron—*Childe Harold.* Canto IV.
　　　　　　　　　　　　　　　　　St. 3.

White swan of cities, slumbering in thy nest
So wonderfully built among the reeds
　Of the lagoon, that fences thee and feeds,
As sayeth thy old historian and thy guest!
　　c.　　Longfellow—*Venice.*

The sylphs and ondines
And the sea-kings and queens
Long ago, long ago, on the waves built a city,
　As lovely as seems
　To some bard in his dreams,
The soul of his latest love-ditty.
　　d.　　Owen Meredith—*Venice.*

CLEANLINESS.

　For cleanness of body was ever esteemed
to proceed from a due reverence to God, to
society, and to ourselves.
　　e.　　Bacon—*Advancement of Learning.*
　　　　　　　　　　　　　　　　　Bk. II.

If dirt was trumps, what hands you would
hold!
　　f.　　Charles Lamb—*Lamb's Suppers.*
　　　　　　　　　　Vol. II. Last Chapter.

I'll purge and leave sack and live cleanly.
　　g.　　*Henry IV.* Pt. 1. Act V. Sc. 4.
　　　　　　　　　　　　　　　　　L. 168.

Then bless thy secret growth, nor catch
　At noise, but thrive unseen and dumb;
Keep clean, be as fruit, earn life, and watch,
　Till the white-winged reapers come.
　　h.　　Henry Vaughan—*The Seed Growing
　　　　　　　　　　　　　　　　Secretly.*

　Certainly this is a duty, not a sin. "Cleanliness is indeed next to godliness."
　　i.　　John Wesley—*Sermon XCII.*
　　　　　　　　　　　　　　　On Dress.

CLOUDS.

I saw two clouds at morning
　Tinged by the rising sun,
And in the dawn they floated on
　And mingled into one.
　　j.　　John G. C. Brainard—*I Saw Two
　　　　　　　　　　　　　Clouds at Morning.*

O, it is pleasant, with a heart at ease,
Just after sunset, or by moonlight skies,
To make the shifting clouds be what you
　　please,
Or let the easily persuaded eyes
Own each quaint likeness issuing from the
　　mould
Of a friend's fancy.
　　k.　　Coleridge—*Fancy in Nubibus.*

　The sky is filled with rolling, fleecy clouds,
whose flat receding bases seem to float upon
a transparent amber sea.
　　l.　　W. H. Gibson—*Pastoral Days.*
　　　　　　　　　　　　　　　　Autumn.

Die down, O dismal day! * * *
And come, blue deeps! magnificently strewn
With colored clouds—large, light, and fugi-
　　tive—
By upper winds through pompous motions
　　blown.
　　m.　　David Gray—*In the Shadows.* St. 11.

The cloudlets are lazily sailing
　O'er the blue Atlantic sea.
　　n.　　Heine—*Early Poems. Evening Songs.*
　　　　　　　　　　　　　　　　No. 4.

The clouds,—the only birds that never sleep.
　　o.　　Victor Hugo—*The Vanished City.*

By unseen hands uplifted in the light
Of sunset, yonder solitary cloud
Floats, with its white apparel blown abroad,
And wafted up to heaven.
　　p.　　Longfellow—*Michael Angelo.*
　　　　　　　　　　　　　　　Pt. II. 2.

See yonder little cloud, that, borne aloft
So tenderly by the wind, floats fast away
Over the snowy peaks!
　　q.　　Longfellow—*Christus. The Golden
　　　　　　　　　　　　Legend.* Pt. V. L. 145.

　　　　　The low'ring element
Scowls o'er the darken'd landscape
　　r.　　Milton—*Paradise Lost.* Bk. II.
　　　　　　　　　　　　　　　　L. 490.

　　　　There does a sable cloud
Turn forth her silver lining on the night,
And casts a gleam over this tufted grove.
　　s.　　Milton—*Comus.* L. 223.

If woolly fleeces spread the heavenly way
No rain, be sure, disturbs the summer's day.
　　t.　　*Old Weather Rhyme.*

When clouds appear like rocks and towers,
The earth's refreshed by frequent showers.
　　u.　　*Old Weather Rhyme.*

Clouds on clouds, in volumes driven,
Curtain round the vault of heaven.
　　v.　　Thomas Love Peacock—*Rhododaphne.*
　　　　　　　　　　　　Canto V. L. 257.

Choose a firm cloud before it fall, and in it
Catch, ere she change, the Cynthia of this
          minute.
   a.   Pope—*Moral Essays.* Epistle 2. L. 19.

            Clouds on the western side
Grow gray and grayer, hiding the warm sun.
   b.   Christina G. Rossetti—*Twilight Calm.*

We often praise the evening clouds,
   And tints so gay and bold,
But seldom think upon our God,
   Who tinged these clouds with gold.
   c.   Scott—*The Setting Sun.*

Yon towers, whose wanton tops do buss the
   clouds.
   d.   *Troilus and Cressida.* Act IV. Sc. 5.
                               L. 220.

I bring fresh showers for the thirsting
   flowers,
       From the seas and the streams;
I bear light shade for the leaves when laid
       In their noonday dreams.

From my wings are shaken the dews that
   waken
       The sweet buds every one,
When rocked to rest on their mother's breast,
       As she dances about the sun.
I wield the flail of the lashing hail,
       And whiten the green plains under,
And then again I dissolve it in rain,
       And laugh as I pass in thunder.
   e.   Shelley—*The Cloud.*

Bathed in the tenderest purple of distance,
Tinted and shadowed by pencils of air,
Thy battlements hang o'er the slopes and the
   forests,
Seats of the gods in the limitless ether,
Looming sublimely aloft and afar.
   f.   Bayard Taylor—*Kilimandjaro.*

           Yonder cloud
That rises upward always higher,
·And onward drags a laboring breast,
And topples round the dreary west,
A looming bastion fringed with fire.
   g.   Tennyson—*In Memoriam.* Pt. XV.

A cloud lay cradled near the setting sun;
A gleam of crimson tinged its braided snow;
   *   *   *   *   *   *
Tranquil its spirit seemed and floated slow;
Even in its very motion there was rest;
While every breath of eve that chanced to
   blow
Wafted the traveller to the beauteous west.
   h.   John Wilson—*Isle of Palms and other
             Poems. The Evening Cloud.*

The clouds that gather round the setting sun
Do take a sober coloring from an eye
That hath kept watch o'er man's mortality.
   i.   Wordsworth—*Ode. Intimations of
                  Immortality.* St. 11.

COMFORT.

They have most satisfaction in themselves,
and consequently the sweetest relish of their
creature comforts.
   j.   Mathew Henry—*Commentaries.*
                      Psalm XXXVII.

From out the throng and stress of lies,
From out the painful noise of sighs,
One voice of comfort seems to rise:
" It is the meaner part that dies."
   k.   Wm. Morris—*Comfort.*

          And He that doth the ravens feed,
Yea, providently caters for the sparrow,
Be comfort to my age!
   l.   *As You Like It.* Act II. Sc. 3. L. 43.

                         Men
Can counsel and speak comfort to that grief
Which they themselves not feel.
   m.   *Much Ado About Nothing.* Act V.
                          Sc. 1. L. 21.

That comfort comes too late;
'Tis like a pardon after execution;
That gentle physic, given in time, had cur'd
   me;
But now I am past all comforts here, but
   Prayers.
   n.   *Henry VIII.* Act IV. Sc. 2. L. 119.

COMPANIONSHIP.

His ancient, trusty, drouthy crony,
Tam lo'ed him like a vera brither—
They had been fou for weeks thegither!
   o.   Burns—*Tam o' Shanter.*

We twa hae run about the braes,
And pu'd the gowans fine.
   p.   Burns—*Auld Lang Syne.*

Say, shall my little bark attendant sail,
Pursue the triumph, and partake the gale?
   q.   Pope—*Essay on Man.* Ep. 4. L. 385.

No man can be provident of his time that is
not prudent in the choice of his company.
   r.   Jeremy Taylor—*Holy Living and
                Dying.* Ch. I. Sec. I.

COMPARISONS.

Defining night by darkness, death by dust.
   s.   Bailey—*Festus.* Sc. *Water and Wood.*

Tis light translateth night; 'tis inspiration
Expounds experience; 'tis the west explains
The east; 'tis time unfolds Eternity.
   t.   Bailey—*Festus.* Sc. *A Ruined Temple.*

Glass antique! 'twixt thee and Nell
Draw us here a parallel!
She, like thee, was forced to bear
All reflections, foul or fair.
　　Thou art deep and bright within,
　　Depths as bright belong'd to Gwynne;
　　Thou art very frail as well,
　　Frail as flesh is,—so was Nell.
a.　　L. Blanchard—*Nell Gwynne's
　　　　　　Looking Glass*. St. 1.

It's wiser being good than bad;
　It's safer being meek than fierce:
It's fitter being sane than mad.
　My own hope is, a sun will pierce
The thickest cloud earth ever stretched;
　That, after Last, returns the First,
Though a wide compass round be fetched;
　That what began best, can't end worst,
Nor what God blessed once, prove accurst.
b.　　Robert Browning—*Apparent Failure*.
　　　　　　　　　　　VII.

It has all the contortions of the sibyl without the inspiration.
c.　　Burke—*Prior's Life of Burke*.

There's some are fou o' love divine,
There's some are fou o' brandy.
d.　　Burns—*The Holy Fair*. St. 30.

To liken them to your auld-warld squad,
I must needs say comparisons are odd.
e.　　Burns—*Brigs of Ayr*. L. 177.

There's but the twinkling of a star
Between a man of peace and war.
f.　　Butler—*Hudibras*. Pt. II. Canto III.
　　　　　　　　　　L. 957.

I've read in many a novel, that unless they've
　souls that grovel—
Folks *prefer* in fact a hovel to your dreary
　marble halls.
g.　　Calverley—*In the Gloaming*.

Is it possible your pragmatical worship
should not know that the comparisons made
between wit and wit, courage and courage,
beauty and beauty, birth and birth, are always odious and ill taken?
h.　　Cervantes—*Don Quixote*. Pt. II.
　　　　　　　　　　　Ch. I.

At whose sight, like the sun,
All others with diminish'd lustre shone.
i.　　Cicero—*Tusculan Disp*. Bk. III.
　　　　　　　Div. 18. Yonge's trans.

Right is more beautiful than private affection; and love is compatible with universal
wisdom.
j.　　Emerson—*Essays*. *On Shakespeare*.

Expression is action; beauty is repose.
k.　　J. C. and A. W. Hare—*Guesses at
　　　　　　　　　　　Truth*.

Everything *is* twice as large, measured on
a three-year-old's three-foot scale as on a
thirty-year-old's six-foot scale.
l.　　O. W. Holmes—*The Poet at the
　　　　　　　Breakfast Table*. I.

Too great refinement is false delicacy, and
true delicacy is solid refinement.
m.　　La Rochefoucauld—*Maxims and
　　　　　　Moral Sentences*. No. 131.

The country is lyric,—the town dramatic.
When mingled, they make the most perfect
musical drama.
n.　　Longfellow—*Kavanagh*. Ch. XIII.

And but two ways are offered to our will,
Toil with rare triumph, ease with safe disgrace,
The problem still for us and all of human
　race.
o.　　Lowell—*Under the Old Elm*.
　　　　　　　　Pt. VII. St. 3.

Comparisons do ofttime great grievance.
p.　　John Lydgate—*Bochas*. Bk. III.
　　　　　　　　　　Ch. VIII.

And in the lowest deep a lower deep
Still threatening to devour me opens wide;
To which the hell I suffer seems a heaven.
q.　　Milton—*Paradise Lost*. Bk. IV. L. 76.

A man must either imitate the vicious or
hate them.
r.　　Montaigne—*Of Solitude*.

The souls of emperors and cobblers are cast
in the same mould. * * * The same reason
that makes us wrangle with a neighbour causes
a war betwixt princes.
s.　　Montaigne—*Apology for Raimond de
　　　　　　Sebond*. Bk. II. Ch. XII.

We are nearer neighbours to ourselves than
whiteness to snow, or weight to stones.
t.　　Montaigne—*Essays*. Bk. II. Ch. XII.

The magnificent and the ridiculous are so
near neighbours that they touch each other.
u.　　Edward Lord Oxford—*Ms. Common
　　　　　　　Place Book*.

Everye white will have its blacke,
And everye sweet its soure.
v.　　Thos. Percy—*Reliques*. *Sir Curline*.

Another yet the same.
w.　　Pope—*The Dunciad*. Bk. III. L. 90.

The rose and thorn, the treasure and dragon,
joy and sorrow, all mingle into one.
x.　　Saadi—*The Gulistan*. Ch. VII.
　　　　　　Apologue 21. Ross' trans.

　　　　　　As false
As air, as water, wind, or sandy earth,
As fox to lamb, as wolf to heifer's calf,
Pard to the hind, or stepdame to her son.
y.　　*Troilus and Cressida*. Act III. Sc. 2.
　　　　　　　　　　L. 198.

Crabbed age and youth cannot live together.
>   *a.   Passionate Pilgrim.   Pt. XII.*

Hyperion to a satyr.
>   *b.   Hamlet.   Act I.   Sc. 2.   L. 140.*

Nature hath meal and bran, contempt and grace.
>   *c.   Cymbeline.   Act IV.   Sc. 2.   L. 27.*

>   No more like my father
> Than I to Hercules.
>   *d.   Hamlet.   Act I.   Sc. 2.   L. 152.*

>   O, the more angel she,
> And you the blacker devil !
>   *e.   Othello.   Act V.   Sc. 2.   L. 130.*

Those that are good manners at the court are as ridiculous in the country as the behaviour of the country is most mockable at the court.
>   *f.   As You Like It.   Act III.   Sc. 2.   L. 46.*

> What, is the jay more precious than the lark,
> Because his feathers are more beautiful?
> Or is the adder better than the eel,
> Because his painted skin contents the eye?
>   *g.   Taming of the Shrew.   Act IV.   Sc. 3.
>   L. 177.*

> Here and there a cotter's babe is royal—born
>   by right divine ;
> Here and there my lord is lower than his oxen
>   or his swine.
>   *h.   TENNYSON—Locksley Hall.   Sixty Years
>   After.   St. 63.*

The little may contrast with the great, in painting, but cannot be said to be contrary to it. Oppositions of colors contrast ; but there are also colors contrary to each other, that is, which produce an ill effect because they shock the eye when brought very near it.
>   *i.   VOLTAIRE—A Philosophical Dictionary.
>   Essay.   Contrast.*

The happy married man dies in good stile at home, surrounded by his weeping wife and children. The old bachelor don't die at all— he sort of rots away, like a pollywog's tail.
>   *j.   ARTEMUS WARD—The Draft in
>   Baldinsville.*

> And homeless near a thousand homes I stood,
> And near a thousand tables pined and wanted
>   food.
>   *k.   WORDSWORTH—Guilt and Sorrow.
>   St. 41.*

> The time for Pen and Sword was when
>   "My ladye fayre," for pity,
> Could tend her wounded knight, and then
>   Grow tender at his ditty.
> Some ladies now make pretty songs,
>   And some make pretty nurses :
> Some men are good for righting wrongs,
>   And some for writing verses.
>   *l.   FREDERICK LOCKER—The Jester's Plea.*

COMPENSATION.

I called the New World into existence to redress the balance of the Old.
>   *m.   GEORGE CANNING—The King's
>   Message.   Dec. 12, 1826.*

Honors come by diligence ; riches spring from economy.
>   *n.   JOHN FRANCIS DAVIS—Chinese Moral
>   Maxims.*

> What we gave, we have :
> What we spent, we had :
> What we left, we lost.
>   *o.   Epitaph of Edward, Earl of Devon.*

> 'Tis toil's reward, that sweetens industry,
> As love inspires with strength the enraptur'd
>   thrush.
>   *p.   EBENEZER ELLIOT—Corn Law
>   Rhymes.   No. 7.*

> As some tall cliff that lifts its awful form,
> Swells from the vale, and midway leaves the
>   storm,
> Though round its breast the rolling clouds are
>   spread,
> Eternal sunshine settles on its head.
>   *q.   GOLDSMITH—The Deserted Village.
>   L. 189.*

'Tis always morning somewhere in the world.
>   *r.   RICHARD HENGEST HORNE—Orion.
>   Bk. III.   Canto II.*

> O weary hearts ! O slumbering eyes !
> O drooping souls, whose destinies
> Are fraught with fear and pain,
> Ye shall be loved again.
>   *s.   LONGFELLOW—Endymion.   St. 7.*

'Tis always morn somewhere.
>   *t.   LONGFELLOW—Tales of a Wayside Inn.
>   Birds of Killingworth.   St. 16.*

> Earth gets its price for what Earth gives us,
>   The beggar is taxed for a corner to die in,
> The priest hath his fee who comes and
>   shrives us,
>   We bargain for the graves we lie in ;
> At the devil's booth are all things sold,
> Each ounce of dross costs its ounce of gold ;
>   For a cap and bells our lives we pay,
> Bubbles we buy with a whole soul's tasking,
>   'Tis heaven alone that is given away,
> 'Tis only God may be had for the asking,
> No price is set on the lavish summer ;
> June may be had by the poorest comer.
>   *u.   LOWELL—The Vision of Sir Launfal.
>   Prelude to Pt. I.*

> Merciful Father, I will not complain.
> I know that the sunshine shall follow the rain.
>   *v.   JOAQUIN MILLER—For Princess Maud.*

What though the field be lost?
All is not lost; th' unconquerable will,
And study of revenge, immortal hate,
And courage never to submit or yield.
   a.   MILTON—*Paradise Lost.* Bk. I. L. 105.

Long pains are light ones,
Cruel ones are brief!
   b.   J. G. SAXE—*Compensation.*

That not a moth with vain desire
Is shrivel'd in a fruitless fire,
Or but subserves another's gain.
   c.   TENNYSON—*In Memoriam.* Pt. LIV.

And light is mingled with the gloom,
  And joy with grief;
Divinest compensations come,
Through thorns of judgment mercies bloom
  In sweet relief.
   d.   WHITTIER—*Anniversary Poem.* St. 15.

COMPLIMENTS.

A compliment is usually accompanied with
a bow, as if to beg pardon for paying it.
   e.   J. C. and A. W. HARE—*Guesses at Truth.*

        What honour that,
But tedious waste of time, to sit and hear
So many hollow compliments and lies.
   f.   MILTON—*Paradise Regained.* Bk. IV.
                     L. 122.

        'Twas never merry world
Since lowly feigning was called compliment.
   g.   *Twelfth Night.* Act III. Sc. 1. L. 109.

A woman * * * always feels herself
complimented by love, though it may be from
a man incapable of winning her heart, or
perhaps even her esteem.
   h.   ABEL STEVENS—*Life of Madame de
                   Staël.* Ch. III.

        Current among men,
Like coin, the tinsel clink of compliment.
   i.   TENNYSON—*The Princess.* Pt. II.
                     L. 40.

CONCEIT.

I've never any pity for conceited people,
because I think they carry their comfort
about with them.
   j.   GEORGE ELIOT—*The Mill on the Floss.*
                   Bk. V. Ch. IV.

For what are they all in their high conceit,
When man in the bush with God may meet?
   k.   EMERSON—*Good-Bye.* St. 4.

The world knows only two, that's Rome
and I.
   l.   BEN JONSON—*Sejanus.* Act V. Sc. 1.

In men this blunder still you find,
All think their little set mankind.
   m.   HANNAH MORE—*Florio.* Pt. I.

We think our fathers fools, so wise we grow;
Our wiser sons, no doubt, will think us so.
   n.   POPE—*Essay on Criticism.* Pt. II.
                     L. 438.

If she undervalue me,
What care I how fair she be?
   o.   Sir WALTER RALEIGH—*Bayley's Life of
                   Raleigh.*

  Conceit may puff a man up, but never prop
him up.
   p.   RUSKIN—*True and Beautiful. Morals
             and Religion. Function of the Artist.*

Conceit in weakest bodies strongest works.
   q.   *Hamlet.* Act III. Sc. 4. L. 114.

Conceit, more rich in matter than in words,
Brags of his substance, not of ornament:
They are but beggars that can count their
    worth.
   r.   *Romeo and Juliet.* Act II. Sc. 6.
                     L. 29.

I am not in the roll of common men.
   s.   *Henry IV.* Pt. I. Act III. Sc. 1.
                     L. 43.

Whoe'er imagines prudence all his own,
Or deems that he hath powers to speak and
    judge
Such as none other hath, when they are
    known,
They are found shallow.
   t.   SOPHOCLES—*Antig.* 707.

Faith, that's as well said as if I had said it
myself.
   u.   SWIFT—*Polite Conversation.*
                   Dialogue II.

CONFESSION.

Confess thee freely of thy sin;
For to deny each article with oath
Cannot remove nor choke the strong concep-
    tion
That I do groan withal.
   v.   *Othello.* Act V. Sc. 2. L. 54.

        Confess yourself to heaven;
Repent what's past; avoid what is to come.
   w.   *Hamlet.* Act III. Sc. 4. L. 149.

Nor do we find him forward to be sounded
But, with a crafty madness, keeps aloof,
When we would bring him on to some con-
    fession
Of his true state.
   x.   *Hamlet.* Act III. Sc. 1. L. 7.

I own the soft impeachment.
   y.   SHERIDAN—*The Rivals.* Act V. Sc. 3.

CONFIDENCE.

He who does not respect confidence, will never find happiness in his path. The belief in virtue vanishes from his heart, the source of nobler actions becomes extinct in him.

a.   AUFFENBURG.

He who has lost confidence can lose nothing more.

b.   BOISTE.

Confidence is that feeling by which the mind embarks in great and honourable courses with a sure hope and trust in itself.

c.   CICERO—*Rhetorical Invention.*

I see before me the statue of a celebrated minister, who said that confidence was a plant of slow growth. But I believe, however gradual may be the growth of confidence, that of credit requires still more time to arrive at maturity.

d.   BENJ. DISRAELI—*Speech.* Nov. 9, 1867.

Self-trust is the essence of heroism.

e.   EMERSON—*Essay. Heroism.*

The hearing ear is always found close to the speaking tongue; and no genius can long or often utter anything which is not invited and gladly entertained by men around him.

f.   EMERSON—*Race.*

He knows little who will tell his wife all he knows.

g.   THOMAS FULLER—*Holy and Profane State.* Maxim VII. *The Good Husband.*

Though wisdom wake, suspicion sleeps
At wisdom's gate, and to simplicity
Resigns her charge, while goodness thinks no ill
Where no ill seems.

h.   MILTON—*Paradise Lost.* Bk. III. L. 686.

He that wold not when he might,
He shall not when he wold-a.

i.   THOS. PERCY—*Reliques. The Baffled Knight.* St. 14.

Confidence is a plant of slow growth in an aged bosom.

j.   WILLIAM PITT (Earl of Chatham)— *Speech.* Jan. 14, 1766.

Be as just and gracious unto me,
As I am confident and kind to thee.

k.   *Titus Andronicus.* Act I. Sc. 1. L. 60.

I renounce all confidence.

l.   *Henry VI.* Pt I. Act I. Sc. 2. L. 97.

I would have some confidence with you that decerns you nearly.

m.   *Much Ado About Nothing.* Act III. Sc. 5. L. 3.

Trust not him that hath once broken faith.

n.   *Henry VI.* Pt. III. Act IV. Sc. 4. L. 30

Your wisdom is consum'd in confidence.
Do not go forth to-day.

o.   *Julius Cæsar.* Act II. Sc. 2. L. 49.

Confidence is conqueror of men; victorious both over them and in them;
The iron will of one stout heart shall make a thousand quail:
A feeble dwarf, dauntlessly resolved, will turn the tide of battle,
And rally to a nobler strife the giants that had fled.

p.   TUPPER—*Proverbial Philosophy. Of Faith.* L. 11.

CONQUEST.

Great things thro' greatest hazards are achiev'd,
And then they shine.

q.   BEAUMONT AND FLETCHER—*Loyal Subject.* Act I. Sc. 5.

He who surpasses or subdues mankind,
Must look down on the hate of those below.

r.   BYRON—*Childe Harold.* Canto III. St. 45.

Then fly betimes, for only they
Conquer love that run away.

s.   THOMAS CAREW—*Song. Conquest by Flight.*

And though mine **arm** should conquer twenty worlds,
There's a lean fellow beats all conquerors.

t.   THOS. DEKKER—*The Comedie of Old Fortunatus.* Act I. Sc. 1.

Like Douglas conquer, or like Douglas die.

u.   JOHN HOME—*Douglas.* Act V. Sc. 1. L. 100.

Self conquest is the greatest of victories.

v.   PLATO.

Brave conquerors! for so you are
That war against your own affections,
And the huge army of the world's desires.

w.   *Love's Labour's Lost.* Act I. Sc. 1. L. 8.

Shall they hoist me up,
And show me to the shouting varletry
Of censuring Rome? Rather a ditch in Egypt
Be gentle grave unto me, rather on Nilus' mud
Lay me stark naked, and let the water-flies
Blow me into abhorring!

x.   *Antony and Cleopatra.* Act V. Sc. 2. L. 55.

CONSCIENCE.

Oh! think what anxious moments pass between
The birth of plots, and their last fatal periods,
Oh! 'tis a dreadful interval of time,
Filled up with horror all, and big with death!
    a.   ADDISON—*Cato.* Act I. Sc. 3.

They have cheveril consciences that will
stretch.
    b.   BURTON—*Anatomy of Melancholy.*
           Pt. III. Sec. IV. Memb. 2.
                   Subsect. 3.

Why should not Conscience have vacation
As well as other Courts o' th' nation?
Have equal power to adjourn,
Appoint appearance and return?
    c.   BUTLER—*Hudibras.* Pt. II. Canto II.
                      L. 317.

A quiet conscience makes one so serene!
Christians have burnt each other, quite persuaded
That all the Apostles would have done as they
   did.
    d.   BYRON—*Don Juan.* Canto I. St. 83.

But at sixteen the conscience rarely gnaws
So much, as when we call our old debts in
At sixty years, and draw the accounts of evil,
And find a deuced balance with the devil.
    e.   BYRON—*Don Juan.* Canto I. St. 167.

But quiet to quick bosoms is a hell,
And there hath been thy bane.
    f.   BYRON—*Childe Harold.* Canto III.
                      St. 42.

Nor ear can hear nor tongue can tell
The tortures of that inward hell!
    g.   BYRON—*The Giaour.* L. 748.

            There is no future pang
Can deal that justice on the self condemn'd
He deals on his own soul.
    h.   BYRON—*Manfred.* Act III. Sc. 1.

Yet still there whispers the small voice within,
Heard through Gain's silence, and o'er Glory's
   din;
Whatever creed be taught or land be trod,
Man's conscience is the oracle of God.
    i.   BYRON—*The Island.* Canto I. St. 6.

The great theatre for virtue is conscience.
    j.   CICERO.

            The Past lives o'er again
In its effects, and to the guilty spirit
The ever-frowning Present is its image.
    k.   COLERIDGE—*Remorse.* Act I. Sc. 2.

When Conscience wakens who can with her
   strive?
Terrors and troubles from a sick soul drive?
Naught so unpitying as the ire of sin,
The inappeas'ble Nemesis within.
    l.   ABRAHAM COLES—*The Light of the
                   World.* P. 314.

The still small voice is wanted.
    m.   COWPER—*The Task.* Bk. V. L. 687.

Oh, Conscience! Conscience! man's most
   faithful friend,
Him canst thou comfort, ease, relieve, defend;
But if he will thy friendly checks forego,
Thou art, oh! woe for me, his deadliest foe!
    n.   CRABBE—*Struggles of Conscience.* Last
                      Lines.

Conscience is harder than our enemies,
Knows more, accuses with more nicety.
    o.   GEORGE ELIOT—*Spanish Gypsy.* Bk. I.

Conscience is a coward, and those faults it
has not strength to prevent, it seldom has
justice enough to accuse.
    p.   GOLDSMITH—*Vicar of Wakefield.*
                      Ch. XIII.

Man, wretched man, whene'er he stoops to
   sin,
Feels, with the act, a strong remorse within.
    q.   JUVENAL—*Satires. Satire XIII.* L. 1.
                   Wm. Gifford's trans.

He that has light within his own clear breast,
May sit i' the centre, and enjoy bright day;
But he that hides a dark soul, and foul
   thoughts,
Benighted walks under the mid-day sun;
Himself is his own dungeon.
    r.   MILTON—*Comus.* L. 381.

Let his tormentor conscience find him out.
    s.   MILTON—*Paradise Regained.* Bk. IV.
                      L. 130.

          Now conscience wakes despair
That slumber'd, wakes the bitter memory
Of what he was, what is, and what must be
Worse; of worse deeds worse sufferings must
   ensue!
    t.   MILTON—*Paradise Lost.* Bk. IV.
                      L. 23.

O Conscience, into what abyss of fears
And horrors hast thou driven me, out of
   which
I find no way, from deep to deeper plunged.
    u.   MILTON—*Paradise Lost.* Bk. X.
                      L. 842.

          Whom conscience, ne'er asleep,
Wounds with incessant strokes, not loud, but
   deep.
    v.   MONTAIGNE—*Essays.* Bk. II. Ch. V.
                     Of Conscience.

As the mind of each man is conscious of
good or evil, so does he conceive within his
breast hope or fear, according to his actions.
    w.   OVID—*Fasti.* Bk. I. 476–501.
                     Riley's trans.

Let Joy or Ease, let Affluence or Content,
And the gay Conscience of a life well spent,
Calm ev'ry thought, inspirit ev'ry grace,
Glow in thy heart, and smile upon thy face.
   a.   Pope—*To Mrs. M. B., on her Birthday.*

One self-approving hour whole years out-
     weighs
Of stupid starers and of loud huzzas.
   b.   Pope—*Essay on Man.* Ep. IV.
                                L. 255.

Some scruple rose, but thus he eas'd his
     thought,
" I'll now give sixpence where I gave a groat ;
Where once I went to church, I'll now go
     twice—
And am so clear too of all other vice."
   c.   Pope—*Moral Essays.* Ep. III. L. 365.

True, conscious Honour is to feel no sin,
He's arm'd without that's innocent within ;
Be this thy screen, and this thy wall of Brass.
   d.   Pope—*First Book of Horace.*
                            Ep. I. L. 93.

What Conscience dictates to be done,
   Or warns me not to do ;
This teach me more than Hell to shun,
   That more than Heav'n pursue.
   e.   Pope—*Universal Prayer.*

But there is a higher law than the Constitution.
   f.   Wm. H. Seward—*Speech.* March 11,
                                  1850.

Ah, what a sign it is of evil life,
Where death's approach is seen so terrible !
   g.   *Henry VI.* Pt. II. Act III. Sc. 3.
                                  L. 5.

                   Better be with the dead,
Whom we, to gain our peace, have sent to
     peace,
Than on the torture of the mind to lie
In restless ecstasy.
   h.   *Macbeth.* Act III. Sc. 2. L. 19.

Conscience is but a word that cowards use,
Devised at first to keep the strong in awe.
   i.   *Richard III.* Act V. Sc. 3. L. 309.

I hate the murderer, love him murdered.
The guilt of conscience take thou for thy
     labour,
But neither my good word nor princely
     favour :
With Cain go wander through shades of night,
And never show thy head by day nor light.
   j.   *Richard II.* Act V. Sc. 6. L. 40.

I know myself now ; and I feel within me
A peace above all earthly dignities ;
A still and quiet conscience.
   k.   *Henry VIII.* Act III. Sc. 2. L. 377.

                 I know thou art religious,
And hast a thing within thee called con-
     science,
With twenty popish tricks and ceremonies,
Which I have seen thee careful to observe.
   l.   *Titus Andronicus.* Act V. Sc. 1.
                                  L. 75.

My conscience hath a thousand several
     tongues,
And every tongue brings in a several tale,
And every tale condemns me for a villain.
   m.   *Richard III.* Act V. Sc. 3. L. 193.

Now, if you can blush and cry " guilty," car-
     dinal,
You'll show a little honesty.
   n.   *Henry VIII.* Act III. Sc. 2. L. 306.

                   Soft, I did but dream.
O coward conscience, how dost thou afflict
     me !
   o.   *Richard III.* Act V. Sc. 3. L. 179.

The worm of conscience still begnaw thy
     soul !
Thy friends suspect for traitors while thou
     liv'st,
And take deep traitors for thy dearest friends !
   p.   *Richard III.* Act I. Sc. 3. L. 222.

Thus conscience does make cowards of us all ;
And thus the native hue of resolution
Is sicklied o'er with the pale cast of thought.
   q.   *Hamlet.* Act III. Sc. 1. L. 83.

'Tis a blushing shamefast spirit that muti-
nies in a man's bosom ; it fills one full of obstacles.
   r.   *Richard III.* Act I. Sc. 4. L. 141.

                   Unnatural deeds
Do breed unnatural troubles : infected minds
To their deaf pillows will discharge their
     secrets.
   s.   *Macbeth.* Act V. Sc. 1. L. 79.

Trust that man in nothing who has not a
Conscience in everything.
   t.   Sterne—*Tristram Shandy.* Bk. II.
                               Ch. XVII.

Labor to keep alive in your breast that little
spark of celestial fire, called Conscience.
   u.   George Washington—*Moral Maxims.*
                Virtue and Vice. Conscience.

Men who can hear the Decalogue and feel
No self-reproach.
   v.   Wordsworth—*The Old Cumberland*
                          Beggar. L. 136.

CONSIDERATION.

A stirring dwarf we do allowance give
Before a sleeping giant.
a. *Troilus and Cressida.* Act II. Sc. 3.
     L. 146.

Consideration, like an angel came
And whipp'd the offending Adam out of him,
Leaving his body as a paradise,
To envelope and contain celestial spirits.
b. *Henry V.* Act I. Sc. 1. L. 28.

Fathers that wear rags
 Do make their children blind;
But fathers that bear bags
 Shall see their children kind.
c. *King Lear.* Act II. Sc. 4. L. 48.

Let me have audience for a word or two.
d. *As You Like It.* Act V. Sc. 4. L. 157.

The lustre in your eye, heaven in your cheek,
Pleads your fair usage.
e. *Troilus and Cressida.* Act IV. Sc. 4.
     L. 120.

    What you have said
I will consider; what you have to say
I will with patience hear, and find a time
Both meet to hear and answer such high
 things.
f. *Julius Cæsar.* Act I. Sc. 2. L. 168.

CONSISTENCY.

Of right and wrong he taught
Truths as refin'd as ever Athens heard;
And (strange to tell) he practis'd what he
 preach'd.
g. JOHN ARMSTRONG—*Art of Preserving
    Health.* Bk. IV. L. 302.

Tush! tush! my lassie, such thoughts resigne,
Comparisons are cruele:
Fine pictures suit in frames as fine,
Consistencie's a jewell.
For thee and me coarse cloathes are best,
Rude folks in homelye raiment drest,
Wife Joan and goodman Robin.
h. *Jolly Robyn-Roughhead.* Author
       unknown.

A foolish consistency is the hobgoblin of
little minds, adored by little statesmen and
philosophers and divines.
i. EMERSON—*Essays. Self-Reliance.*

With consistency a great soul has simply
nothing to do. * * * Speak what you think
to-day in words as hard as cannon balls, and
to-morrow speak what to-morrow thinks in
hard words again, though it contradict everything you said to-day.
j. EMERSON—*Essays. Self-Reliance.*

Gineral C. is a dreffle smart man:
 He's been on all sides that give places or
  pelf;
But consistency still wuz a part of his plan;
He's been true to *one* party, and that is, him-
 self;—
 So John P.
 Robinson, he
Sez he shall vote for Gineral C.
k. LOWELL—*The Biglow Papers.*
     Series I. No. 3.

CONSOLATION.

Prosperity is not without many fears and
distastes, and Adversity is not without comforts and hopes.
l. BACON—*Of Adversity.*

All are not taken! there are left behind
Living Beloveds, tender looks to bring,
And make the daylight still a happy thing,
And tender voices, to make soft the wind.
m. E. B. BROWNING—*Consolation.*

The drying up a single tear has more
Of honest fame, than shedding seas of gore.
n. BYRON—*Don Juan.* Canto VIII. St. 3.

God has commanded time to console the afflicted.
o. JOSEPH JOUBERT—*Thoughts.* Ch. V.

Sprinkled along the waste of years
Full many a soft green isle appears:
Pause where we may upon the desert road,
Some shelter is in sight, some sacred safe
 abode.
p. KEBLE—*The Christian Year. The First
    Sunday in Advent.* St. 8.

And empty heads console with empty sound.
q. POPE—*The Dunciad.* Bk. IV. L. 542.

For grief is crowned with consolation;
r. *Antony and Cleopatra.* Act I. Sc. 2.
     L. 173.

     I will be gone:
That pitiful rumour may report my flight,
To consolate thine ear.
s. *All's Well That Ends Well.* Act III.
     Sc. 2. L. 129.

For all things are less dreadful than they
 seem.
t. WORDSWORTH—*Ecclesiastical Sonnets.*
      Recovery.

CONSPIRACY.

Conspiracies no sooner should be formed
Than executed.
u. ADDISON—*Cato.* Act I. Sc. 2.

I had forgot that foul conspiracy
Of the beast Caliban, and his confederates
Against my life.
  a.   *Tempest.* Act IV. Sc. 1. L. 139.

                    O conspiracy,
Sham'st thou to show thy dang'rous brow by
    night,
When evils are most free?
  b.   *Julius Cæsar.* Act II. Sc. 1. L. 76.

Open-eye conspiracy
  His time doth take.
  c.   *Tempest.* Act II. Sc. 1. *Song.*
                                      L. 301.

                    Take no care
Who chafes, who frets; and where conspirers
    are:
Macbeth shall never vanquish'd be.
  d.   *Macbeth.* Act IV. Sc. 1. L. 89.

Thou dost conspire against thy friend, Iago,
If thou but think'st him wrong'd and mak'st
    his ear
A stranger to thy thoughts.
  e.   *Othello.* Act III. Sc. 3. L. 142.

CONSTANCY.

Through perils both of wind and limb,
Through thick and thin she follow'd him.
  f.   BUTLER—*Hudibras.* Pt. I. Canto II.
                                      L. 369.

True as the dial to the sun,
Although it be not shined upon.
  g.   BUTLER—*Hudibras.* Pt. III. Canto II.
                                      L. 175.

Only a sweet and virtuous soul,
Like seasoned timber, never gives.
  h.   HERBERT—*Virtue.*

'Tis often constancy to change the mind.
  i.   HOOLE—*Metastasio. Sieves.*

Changeless march the stars above,
Changeless morn succeeds to even;
And the everlasting hills,
Changeless watch the changeless heaven.
  j.   CHARLES KINGSLEY—*Saint's Tragedy.*
                                   Act II. Sc. 2.

Be true to your word and your work and
your friend.
  k.   JOHN BOYLE O'REILLY—*Rules of the
                                      Road.*

Abra was ready ere I call'd her name;
And, though I call'd another, Abra came.
  l.   PRIOR—*Solomon on the Vanity of the
                             World.* Bk. II. L. 364.

He that parts us shall bring a brand from
    heaven,
And fire us hence like foxes.
  m.   *King Lear.* Act V. Sc. 3. L. 22.

I could be well moved if I were as you;
If I could pray to move, prayers would move
    me;
But I am constant as the northern star,
Of whose true fix'd and resting quality
There is no fellow in the firmament.
  n.   *Julius Cæsar.* Act III. Sc. 1. L. 58.

          If ever thou shalt love,
In the sweet pangs of it remember me;
For such as I am all true lovers are,
Unstaid and skittish in all motions else,
Save in the constant image of the creature
That is belov'd.
  o.   *Twelfth Night.* Act II. Sc. 4. L. 15.

I would have men of such constancy put
to sea, that their business might be everything and their intent everywhere; for that's
it that always makes a good voyage of nothing.
  p.   *Twelfth Night.* Act II. Sc. 4. L. 77.

                    Now from head to foot
I am marble-constant: now the fleeting moon
No planet is of mine.
  q.   *Antony and Cleopatra.* Act V. Sc. 2.
                                      L. 238.

O constancy, be strong upon my side,
Set a huge mountain 'tween my heart and
    tongue!
I have a man's mind, but a woman's might.
  r.   *Julius Cæsar.* Act II. Sc. 4. L. 7.

                    O heaven! were man
But constant, he were perfect. That one error
Fills him with faults; makes him run through
    all the sins:
Inconstancy falls off ere it begins.
  s.   *Two Gentlemen of Verona.* Act V.
                                   Sc. 4. L. 109.

Whose worth's unknown, although his height
    be taken.
Love's not Time's fool, though rosy lips and
    cheeks
  Within his bending sickle's compass come;
Love alters not with his brief hours and weeks,
  But bears it out even to the edge of doom.
  t.   *Sonnet CXVI.*

Out upon it! I have lov'd
  Three whole days together;
And am like to love three more,
  If it prove fair weather.
  u.   SIR JOHN SUCKLING—*Constancy.*

CONTEMPLATION.

The act of contemplation then creates the
thing contemplated.
  v.   ISAAC DISRAELI—*Literary Character.*
                                      Ch. XII.

But first and chiefest, with thee bring
Him that yon soars on golden wing,
Guiding the fiery-wheeled throne,
The Cherub Contemplation.
　　a.　　MILTON—*Il Penseroso.*　L. 51.

In discourse more sweet,
(For Eloquence the Soul, Song charms the
　　sense,)
Others apart sat on a hill retir'd,
In thoughts more elevate, and reasoned high
Of Providence, Foreknowledge, Will and Fate,
Fixed fate, free will, foreknowledge absolute;
And found no end, in wand'ring mazes lost.
　　b.　　MILTON—*Paradise Lost.*　Bk. II.
　　　　　　　　　　　　　　　L. 555.

Contemplation makes a rare turkey-cock of
him : how he jets under his advanced plumes.
　　c.　　*Twelfth Night.*　Act II.　Sc. 5.　L. 35.

When holy and devout religious men
Are at their beads, 'tis hard to draw them
　　thence ;
So sweet is zealous contemplation.
　　d.　　*Richard III.*　Act III.　Sc. 7.　L. 92.

CONTEMPT.

Go—let thy less than woman's hand
Assume the distaff—not the brand.
　　e.　　BYRON—*Bride of Abydos.*　Canto I.
　　　　　　　　　　　　　　　St. 4.

So let him stand, through ages yet unborn,
Fix'd statue on the pedestal of Scorn.
　　f.　　BYRON—*Curse of Minerva.*　L. 206.

There was a laughing Devil in his sneer,
That raised emotions both of rage and fear.
　　g.　　BYRON—*The Corsair.*　Canto I.　St. 9.

I find my familiarity with thee has bred con-
　　tempt.
　　h.　　CERVANTES—*Don Quixote.*　Pt. I.
　　　　　　　　　　　　　　　Bk. III.　Ch. VI.

We shall find no fiend in hell can match the
fury of a disappointed woman,—scorn'd!
slighted! dismiss'd without a parting pang.
　　i.　　COLLEY CIBBER—*Love's Last Shift.*
　　　　　　　　　　　　　　　Act IV.　Sc. 1.

When they talk'd of their Raphaels, Cor-
　　reggios, and stuff,
He shifted his trumpet, and only took snuff.
　　j.　　GOLDSMITH—*Retaliation.*　L. 145.

He hears
On all sides, from innumerable tongues
A dismal universal hiss, the sound
Of public scorn.
　　k.　　MILTON—*Paradise Lost.*　Bk. X.
　　　　　　　　　　　　　　　L. 506.

Who can refute a sneer?
　　l.　　PALEY—*Moral Philosophy.* Of
　　　　　Reverencing the Deity.　Bk. V.
　　　　　　　　　　　　　　　Ch. IX.

Grown all to all, from no one vice exempt,
And most contemptible to shun contempt.
　　m.　　POPE—*Moral Essays.*　Pt. III.　L. 21.

Becomes it thee to taunt his valiant age
And twit with cowardice a man half dead?
　　n.　　*Henry VI.*　Pt. I.　Act III.　Sc. 2.
　　　　　　　　　　　　　　　L. 55.

But, alas! to make me
A fixed figure for the time of scorn
To point his slow unmoving finger at!
　　o.　　*Othello.*　Act IV.　Sc. 2.　L. 53.

Call me what instrument you will, though
you can fret me, yet you cannot play upon me.
　　p.　　*Hamlet.*　Act III.　Sc. 2.　L. 378.

He talks to me that never had a son.
　　q.　　*King John.*　Act III.　Sc. 4.　L. 91.

I had rather be a dog, and bay the moon,
Than such a Roman.
　　r.　　*Julius Cæsar.*　Act IV.　Sc. 3.　L. 27.

I had rather chop this hand off at a blow,
And with the other fling it at thy face,
Than bear so low a sail, to strike to thee.
　　s.　　*Henry VI.*　Pt. III.　Act V.　Sc. 1.
　　　　　　　　　　　　　　　L. 49.

O, what a deal of scorn looks beautiful
In the contempt and anger of his lip!
　　t.　　*Twelfth Night.*　Act III.　Sc. 1.　L. 156.

CONTENT.

Content thyself to be obscurely good.
When vice prevails and impious men bear
　　sway,
The post of honor is a private station.
　　u.　　ADDISON—*Cato.*　Act IV.　Sc. 4.

Ten poor men sleep in peace on one straw
　　heap, as Saadi sings,
But the immensest empire is too narrow for
　　two kings.
　　v.　　WM. R. ALGER—*Oriental Poetry.*
　　　　　　　　　　　　　　　Elbow Room.

Ah, sweet Content, where doth thine harbour
　　hold?
　　w.　　BARNABE BARNES—*Parthenophil and
　　　　　　　　　　　　　　　Parthenophe.*

Happy am I; from care I'm free!
Why aren't they all contented like me?
　　x.　　*Opera of La Bayadère.*

From labour health, from health contentment
　　spring ;
Contentment opes the source of every joy.
　　y.　　JAMES BEATTIE—*The Minstrel.*　Bk. 1.
　　　　　　　　　　　　　　　St. 13.

In Paris a queer little man you may see,
  A little man all in gray;
Rosy and round as an apple is he,
Content with the present whate'er it may be,
While from care and from cash he is equally
    free,
  And merry both night and day!
"Ma foi! I laugh at the world," says he,
" I laugh at the world, and the world laughs
    at me!"
What a gay little man in gray.
  a.   BERANGER—*The Little Man all in Gray.*
           Trans. by Amelia B. Edwards.

There was a jolly miller once,
  Lived on the River Dee;
He worked and sang, from morn to night;
  No lark so blithe as he.
And this the burden of his song,
  Forever used to be,—
" I care for nobody, not I,
  If no one cares for me."
  b.   BICKERSTAFF—*Love in a Village.*
                    Act I. Sc. 5.

Some things are of that nature as to make
One's fancy chuckle, while his heart doth ache.
  c.   BUNYAN—*The Author's Way of Sending
         Forth his Second Part of the Pilgrim.*
                     L. 126.

Contented wi' little, and cantie wi' mair
  d.   BURNS—*Contented wi' Little.*

I'll be merry and free,
  I'll be sad for nae-body;
If nae-body cares for me,
  I'll care for nae-body.
  e.   BURNS—*Nae-body.*

With more of thanks and less of thought,
  I strive to make my matters meet;
To seek what ancient sages sought,
  Physic and food in sour and sweet,
To take what passes in good part,
And keep the hiccups from the heart.
  f.   JOHN BYROM—*Careless Content.*

I would do what I pleased, and doing what
I pleased, I should have my will, and having
my will, I should be contented; and when one
is contented, there is no more to be desired;
and when there is no more to be desired, there
is an end of it.
  g.   CERVANTES—*Don Quixote.*   Pt. I.
                   Bk. IV.   Ch. XXIII.

Therefore all seasons shall be sweet to thee,
Whether the summer clothe the general earth
With greenness, or the redbreast sit and sing
Betwixt the tufts of snow on the bare branch
Of mossy apple-tree, while the nigh thatch
Smokes in the sunthaw; whether the eve-
    drops fall,
Heard only in the trances of the blast,
Or if the secret ministry of frost
Shall hang them up in silent icicles,
Quietly shining to the quiet moon.
  h.   COLERIDGE—*Frost at Midnight.*

We'll therefore relish with content,
Whate'er kind Providence has sent,
  Nor aim beyond our pow'r;
For, if our stock be very small,
'Tis prudent to enjoy it all,
  Nor lose the present hour.
  i.   NATHANIEL COTTON—*The Fireside.*
                      St. 10.

Enjoy the present hour, be thankful for the
    past,
And neither fear nor wish th' approaches of
    the last.
  j.   COWLEY—*Imitations. Martial.* Lib. X.
                      Ep. XLVII.

'Tis pleasant, through the loopholes of retreat,
To peep at such a world; to see the stir
Of the Great Babel, and not feel the crowd.
  k.   COWPER—*The Task.* Bk. IV. L. 88.

Content with poverty, my soul I arm;
And virtue, though in rags, will keep me
    warm.
  l.   DRYDEN—*Third Book of Horace.* Ode 29.

He trudged along, unknowing what he sought,
And whistled as he went, for want of thought.
  m.   DRYDEN—*Cymon and Iphigenia.* L. 84.

Since every man who lives is born to die,
And none can boast sincere felicity,
With equal mind, what happens let us bear,
Nor joy nor grieve too much for things beyond
    our care.
Like pilgrims, to th' appointed place we tend;
The world's an inn, and death the journey's
    end.
  n.   DRYDEN—*Palamon and Arcite.* Bk. III.
                      L. 2,159.

Map me no maps, sir; my head is a map, a
    map of the whole world.
  o.   FIELDING—*Rape upon Rape.* Act I.
                      Sc. 5.

Give me, kind Heaven, a private station,
A mind serene for contemplation:
Title and profit I resign;
The post of honour shall be mine.
  p.   GAY—*Fables.* Pt. II. *The Vulture,
                 the Sparrow and other Birds.*

What happiness the rural maid attends,
In cheerful labour while each day she spends!
She gratefully receives what Heav'n has sent,
And, rich in poverty, enjoys content.
  q.   GAY—*Rural Sports.* Canto II. L. 148.

Man wants but little here below,
Nor wants that little long.
  r.   GOLDSMITH—*The Hermit.* St. 8.

Their wants but few, their wishes all confin'd.
  s.   GOLDSMITH—*The Traveller.* L. 210.

Where wealth and freedom reign, contentment
    fails,
And honour sinks where commerce long pre-
    vails.
    a.   GOLDSMITH—*The Traveller.* L. 91.

Happy the man, of mortals happiest he,
Whose quiet mind from vain desires is free ;
Whom neither hopes deceive, nor fears tor-
    ment,
But lives at peace, within himself content ;
In thought, or act, accountable to none
But to himself, and to the gods alone.
    b.   GEO. GRANVILLE (Lord Lansdowne)—
        Epistle to Mrs. Higgons, 1690. L. 79.

Sweet are the thoughts that savour of content ;
The quiet mind is richer than a crown ;
Sweet are the nights in careless slumber spent ;
The poor estate scorns fortune's angry frown :
Such sweet content, such minds, such sleep,
    such bliss,
Beggars enjoy, when princes oft do miss.
    c.   ROBERT GREENE—*Song.* *Farewell to*
                            Folly.

Let's live with that small pittance which we
    have ;
Who covets more is evermore a slave.
    d.   HERRICK—*The Covetous Still Captive.*

Praise they that will times past, I joy to see
My selfe now live : this age best pleaseth mee.
    e.   HERRICK—*The Present Time Best*
                            Pleaseth.

Let the world slide, let the world go ;
A fig for care and a fig for woe !
If I can't pay, why I can owe,
And death makes equal the high and low.
    f.   JOHN HEYWOOD—*Be Merry Friends.*

Little I ask ; my wants are few ;
    I only wish a hut of stone,
(A *very plain* brown stone will do),
    That I may call my own ;—
And close at hand is such a one
In yonder street that fronts the sun.
    g.   O. W. HOLMES—*Contentment.*

Yes ! in the poor man's garden grow,
    Far more than herbs and flowers,
Kind thoughts, contentment, peace of mind,
    And joy for weary hours.
    h.   MARY HOWITT—*The Poor Man's Garden.*

Contentment furnishes constant joy. Much
covetousness, constant grief. To the contented, even poverty is joy. To the discontented, even wealth is a vexation.
    i.   MING SUM PAOU KEËN—*In Chinese*
        Repository. Trans. by Dr. Milne.

O what a glory doth this world put on
For him who, with a fervent heart, goes **forth**
Under the bright and glorious sky, and looks
On duties well performed, and days well spent !
    j.   LONGFELLOW—*Autumn.*

Stone walls doe not a prison make,
    Nor iron bars a cage,
Minds innocent and quiet take
    That for an hermitage.
    k.   LOVELACE—*To Althea from Prison.*
                Percy's Reliques. 343.

I rest content ; I kiss your eyes,
I kiss your hair in my delight :
I kiss my hand and say " Good-night."
    l.   JOAQUIN MILLER—*Songs of the Sun-*
        Lands. *Isles of the Amazons.* Pt. V.
                Introductory Stanzas.

            So well to know
Her own, that what she wills to do or say
Seems wisest, virtuousest, discreetest, best.
    m.   MILTON—*Paradise Lost.* Bk. VIII.
                            L. 548.

No eye to watch, and no tongue to wound us,
All earth forgot, and all heaven around us !
    n.   MOORE—*Come O'er the Sea.*

The eagle nestles near the sun ;
    The dove's low nest for me !—
The eagle's on the crag ; sweet one,
    The dove's in our green tree !
For hearts that beat like thine and mine
    Heaven blesses humble earth ;—
The angels of our Heaven shall shine
    The angels of our Hearth !
    o.   J. J. PIATT—*A Song of Content.*

Whate'er the passion, knowledge, fame, or
    pelf,
Not one will change his neighbor with him-
    self.
    p.   POPE—*Essay on Man.* Ep. II. L. 261.

For mine own part, I could be well content
To entertain the lag-end of my life
With quiet hours.
    q.   *Henry IV.* Pt. I. Act V. Sc. 1.
                            L. 23.

He is well paid that is well satisfied.
    r.   *Merchant of Venice.* Act IV. Sc. 1.
                            L. 415.

He that commends me to mine own content
Commends me to the thing I cannot get.
    s.   *Comedy of Errors.* Act I. Sc. 2.
                            L. 33.

I earn that I eat, get that I wear, owe no
man hate, envy no man's happiness ; glad of
other men's good, content with my harm.
    t.   *As You Like It.* Act III. Sc. 2.
                            L. 77.

            If it were now to die,
'Twere now to be most happy ; for I fear
My soul hath her content so absolute
That not another comfort like to this
Succeeds in unknown fate.
    u.   *Othello.* Act II. Sc. 1. L. 191.

My crown is in my heart, not on my head ;
Not deck'd with diamonds and Indian stones,
Nor to be seen : my crown is called content ;
A crown it is that seldom kings enjoy.
    a.   *Henry VI.* Pt. III. Act III. Sc. 1.
                       L. 63.

My more-having would be as a sauce
To make me hunger more.
    b.   *Macbeth.* Act IV. Sc. 3. L. 81.

           Our content
Is our best having.
    c.   *Henry VIII.* Act II. Sc. 3. L. 23.

           Shut up
In measureless content.
    d.   *Macbeth.* Act II. Sc. 1. L. 17.

          The shepherd's homely curds,
His cold thin drink out of his leathern bottle,
His wonted sleep under a fresh tree's shade,
All which secure and sweetly he enjoys,
Is far beyond a prince's delicates,
His viands sparkling in a golden cup,
His body couched in a curious bed,
When care, mistrust, and treason wait on
    him.
    e.   *Henry VI.* Pt. III. Act II. Sc. 5.
                       L. 47.

'Tis better to be lowly born,
And range with humble livers in content,
Than to be perk'd up in a glistering grief,
And wear a golden sorrow.
    f.   *Henry VIII.* Act II. Sc. 3. L. 19.

  'Tis not so deep as a well, nor so wide as a
church door ; but 'tis enough, 'twill serve.
    g.   *Romeo and Juliet.* Act III. Sc. 1.
                     L. 102.

The noblest mind the best contentment has.
    h.   SPENSER—*Faerie Queene.* Bk. I.
                   Canto I. St. 35.

Dear little head, that lies in calm content
  Within the gracious hollow that God made
In every human shoulder, where He meant
  Some tired head for comfort should be laid.
    i.   CELIA THAXTER—*Song.*

An elegant Sufficiency, Content,
Retirement, rural Quiet, Friendship, Books,
Ease and alternate Labor, useful Life,
Progressive Virtue, and approving Heaven !
    j.   THOMSON—*The Seasons. Spring.*
                     L. 1,159.

This is the charm, by sages often told,
Converting all it touches into gold :
Content can soothe, where'er by fortune
    placed,
Can rear a garden in the desert waste.
    k.   HENRY KIRK WHITE—*Clifton Grove.*
                     L. 130.

There is a jewel which no Indian mines can
    buy,
  No chymic art can counterfeit ;
It makes men rich in greatest poverty,
  Makes water wine ; turns wooden cups to
    gold ;
  The homely whistle to sweet music's strain,
Seldom it comes ;—to few from Heaven sent,
That much in little, all in naught, *Content.*
    l.   JOHN WILBYE—*Madrigales. There Is a*
                         Jewel.

A Man he seems of cheerful yesterdays
And confident to-morrows.
    m.   WORDSWORTH—*The Excursion.*
                       Bk. VII.

Lord of himself, though not of lands ;
And having nothing, yet hath all.
    n.   SIR HENRY WOTTON—*The Character of*
                      a Happy Life.

Give me, indulgent gods ! with mind serene,
And guiltless heart, to range the sylvan scene;
No splendid poverty, no smiling care,
No well-bred hate, or servile grandeur, there.
    o.   YOUNG—*Love of Fame.* Satire I.
                       L. 235.

CONTENTION.

  Did thrust (as now) in others' corn his
sickle.
    p.   DU BARTAS—*Divine Weekes and*
            Workes. Second Week, Second Day.
                      Pt. II.

He that wrestles with us strengthens our
nerves, and sharpens our skill. Our antagonist is our helper.
    q.   BURKE—*Reflections on the Revolution in*
               France. Vol. III. P. 195.

'Tis a hydra's head contention ; the more
they strive the more they may : and as Praxiteles did by his glass, when he saw a scurvy
face in it, brake it in pieces ; but for that one
he saw many more as bad in a moment.
    r.   BURTON—*Anat. of Mel.* Pt. II. Sc. 3.
                      Mem. 7.

Some say, compared to Bononcini,
That Mynheer Handel's but a ninny ;
Others aver,—that he to Handel
Is scarcely fit to hold a candle :
Strange all this difference should be,
'Twixt tweedle-dum and tweedle-dee !
    s.   JOHN BYROM—*Epigram on the Feuds*
              between Handel and Bononcini.

Great contest follows, and much learned dust
Involves the combatants ; each claiming truth,
And truth disclaiming both.
    t.   COWPER—*Task.* Bk. III. L. 161.

So when two dogs are fighting in the streets,
When a third dog one of the two dogs meets:
With angry teeth he bites him to the bone,
And this dog smarts for what that dog has
    done.
   a.   HENRY FIELDING—*Tom Thumb the
           Great.* Act I. Sc. 5. L. 55.

Not hate, but glory, made these chiefs con-
    tend;
And each brave foe was in his soul a friend.
   b.   HOMER—*The Iliad.* Bk. VII. L. 364.
                    Pope's trans.

                  Contentions fierce,
Ardent, and dire, spring from no petty cause.
   c.   SCOTT—*Peveril of the Peak.* Ch. XL.

It is an irrepressible conflict between opposing and enduring forces.
   d.   WILLIAM H. SEWARD—*Speech. The
           Irrepressible Conflict.* Oct. 25, 1858.

Thus when a barber and collier fight,
The barber beats the luckless collier—white;
The dusty collier heaves his ponderous sack,
And, big with vengeance, beats the barber—
    black.
In comes the brick-dust man, with grime
    o'erspread,
And beats the collier and the barber—red;
Black, red, and white, in various clouds are
    toss'd,
And in the dust they raise the combatants are
    lost.
   e.   CHRISTOPHER SMART—*Soliloquy of the
        Princess Periwinkle in " A Trip to
        Cambridge." See " Campbell's
        Specimens of the British
        Poets."* Vol. VI.
                       P. 185.

Birds in their little nests agree:
And 'tis a shameful sight,
When children of one family
Fall out, and chide, and fight.
   f.   ISAAC WATTS—*Divine Songs.* XVII.

CONVERSATION.

Method is not less requisite in ordinary
conversation than in writing, provided a man
would talk to make himself understood.
   g.   ADDISON—*The Spectator.* No. 476.

With good and gentle-humored hearts
I choose to chat where'er I come
Whate'er the subject be that starts.
But if I get among the glum
I hold my tongue to tell the truth
And keep my breath to cool my broth.
   h.   JOHN BYROM—*Careless Content.*

In conversation avoid the extremes of for-
wardness and reserve.
   i.   CATO.
8

But conversation, choose what theme we may,
And chiefly when religion leads the way,
Should flow, like waters after summer show'rs,
Not as if raised by mere mechanic powers.
   j.   COWPER—*Conversation.* L. 703.

Conversation is a game of circles.
   k.   EMERSON—*Essays. Circles.*

Conversation is the laboratory and workshop of the student.
   l.   EMERSON—*Society and Solitude. Clubs.*

I never, with important air,
In conversation overbear.
     *   *   *   *   *   *
My tongue within my lips I rein;
For who talks much must talk in vain.
   m.   GAY—*Fables.* Pt. I. Introduction.
                           L. 53.

With thee conversing I forget the way.
   n.   GAY—*Trivia.* Bk. II. L. 480.

They would talk of nothing but high life
and high-lived company, with other fashionable topics, such as pictures, taste, Shakespeare,
and the musical glasses.
   o.   GOLDSMITH—*Vicar of Wakefield.*
                           Ch. IX.

And when you stick on conversation's burs,
Don't strew your pathway with those dreadful
    urs.
   p.   O. W. HOLMES—*A Rhymed Lesson.
                          Urania.*

Discourse, the sweeter banquet of the mind.
   q.   HOMER—*The Odyssey.* Bk. 15. L. 433.
                       Pope's trans.

His conversation does not show the *minute*
hand; but he strikes the hour very correctly.
   r.   SAM'L JOHNSON—*Johnsoniana.*
                      Kearsley. L. 604.

Questioning is not the mode of conversation
among gentlemen.
   s.   SAM'L JOHNSON—*Boswell's Life of
        Johnson.* Vol. VI. Ch. IV. 1776.

Tom Birch is as brisk as a bee in conversation; but no sooner does he take a pen in his
hand, than it becomes a torpedo to him, and
benumbs all his faculties.
   t.   SAM'L JOHNSON—*Boswell's Life of
                    Johnson.* 1743.

A single conversation across the table with
a wise man is better than ten years' study of
books.
   u.   LONGFELLOW—*Quoted from the Chinese
                 in Hyperion.* Ch. VII.

Men of great conversational powers almost universally practise a sort of lively sophistry and exaggeration which deceives for the moment both themselves and their auditors.

   a.   MACAULAY—*Essay. On the Athenian Orators.*

With thee conversing I forget all time:
All seasons and their change, all please alike.

   b.   MILTON—*Paradise Lost.* Bk. IV.
                    L. 639.

Form'd by thy converse, happily to steer
From grave to gay, from lively to severe.

   c.   POPE—*Essay on Man.* Ep. IV. L. 379.

A dearth of words a woman need not fear;
But 'tis a task indeed to learn *to hear :*
In that the skill of conversation lies;
That *shows* or *makes* you both polite and wise.

   d.   YOUNG—*Love of Fame.* Satire V.
                    L. 57.

COQUETRY.

Or light or dark, or short or tall,
She sets a springe to snare them all :
All's one to her—above her fan
She'd make sweet eyes at Caliban.

   e.   T. B. ALDRICH—*Quatrains. Coquette.*

Like a lovely tree
She grew to womanhood, and between whiles
Rejected several suitors, just to learn
How to accept a better in his turn.

   f.   BYRON—*Don Juan.* Canto II. St. 128.

Such is your cold coquette, who can't say " No,"
And won't say " Yes," and keeps you on and off-ing
On a lee-shore, till it begins to blow,
Then sees your heart wreck'd, with an inward scoffing.

   g.   BYRON—*Don Juan.* Canto XII. St. 63.

In the School of Coquettes
  Madam Rose is a scholar ;—
O, they fish with all nets
In the School of Coquettes !
When her brooch she forgets
'Tis to show her new collar ;
In the School of Coquettes
Madam Rose is a scholar !

   h.   AUSTIN DOBSON—*Rose-Leaves. Circe.*

How happy could I be with either,
  Were t'other dear charmer away !
But while ye thus tease me together,
  To neither a word will I say.

   i.   GAY—*Beggar's Opera.* Act II. Sc. 2.

Coquetry is the essential characteristic, and the prevalent humor of women ; but they do not all practise it, because the coquetry of some is restrained by fear or by reason.

   j.   LA ROCHEFOUCAULD—*Maxims and Moral Sentences.* No. 252.

It is a species of coquetry to make a parade of never practising it.

   k.   LA ROCHEFOUCAULD—*Maxims and Moral Sentences.* No. 110.

The greatest miracle of love is the cure of coquetry.

   l.   LA ROCHEFOUCAULD—*Maxims and Moral Sentences.* No. 359.

Women know not the whole of their coquetry.

   m.   LA ROCHEFOUCAULD—*Maxims and Moral Sentences.* No. 342.

Coquetry whets the appetite ; flirtation depraves it. Coquetry is the thorn that guards the rose—easily trimmed off when once plucked. Flirtation is like the slime on water-plants, making them hard to handle, and when caught, only to be cherished in slimy waters.

   n.   IK MARVEL—*Reveries of a Bachelor.*
                  Sea Coal. I.

Ye belles, and ye flirts, and ye pert little things,
  Who trip in this frolicsome round,
Pray tell me from whence this impertinence springs,
  The sexes at once to confound ?

   o.   WHITEHEAD—*Song for Ranelagh.*

CORRUPTION.

Corruption is a tree, whose branches are
Of an immeasurable length : they spread
Ev'rywhere ; and the dew that drops from thence
Hath infected some chairs and stools of authority.

   p.   BEAUMONT AND FLETCHER—*Honest Man's Fortune.* Act III. Sc. 3.

* * * thieves at home must hang ; but he that puts
Into his overgorged and bloated purse
The wealth of Indian provinces, escapes.

   q.   COWPER—*Task.* Bk. I. L. 736.

When rogues like these (a sparrow cries)
To honours and employments rise,
I court no favor, ask no place,
For such preferment is disgrace.

   r.   GAY—*Fables.* Pt. II. Fable 2.

Like a young eagle, who has lent his plume,
To fledge the shaft by which he meets his doom,
See their own feathers pluck'd, to wing the dart,
Which rank corruption destines for their heart !

   s.   MOORE—*Corruption.*

At length corruption, like a general flood
(So long by watchful ministers withstood),
Shall deluge all ; and avarice, creeping on,
Spread like a low-born mist, and blot the sun.

   t.   POPE—*Moral Essays.* Ep. III. L. 135.

Blest paper credit ! last and best supply !
That lends corruption lighter wings to fly.

   u.   POPE—*Moral Essays.* Ep. III. L. 39.

COUNTRIES.

America.

America! half brother of the world!
With something good and bad of every land.
   a.   BAILEY—*Festus.* Sc. *The Surface.*
                                 L. 340.

A people who are still, as it were, but in the
gristle, and not yet hardened into the bone of
manhood.
   b.   BURKE—*Speech on Conciliation with*
               America. Works. Vol. II.

Young man, there is America—which at
this day serves for little more than to amuse
you with stories of savage men and uncouth
manners; yet shall, before you taste of death,
show itself equal to the whole of that commerce
which now attracts the envy of the world.
   c.   BURKE—*Speech on Conciliation with*
               America. Works. Vol. II.

Columbia, Columbia, to glory arise,
The queen of the world and the child of the
    skies!
Thy genius commands thee; with rapture
    behold,
While ages on ages thy splendors unfold.
   d.   TIMOTHY DWIGHT—*Columbia.*

Down to the Plymouth Rock, that had been
    to their feet as a doorstep
Into a world unknown,—the corner-stone of
    a nation!
   e.   LONGFELLOW—*Courtship of Miles*
              Standish. Pt. V. St. 2.

Earth's biggest Country's gut her soul
An' risen up Earth's Greatest Nation.
   f.   LOWELL—*The Biglow Papers.* Second
              Series. No. 7. St. 21.

In the four quarters of the globe, who reads
an American book? or goes to an American
play? or looks at an American picture or
statue?
   g.   SYDNEY SMITH—*Works. Vol. II.*
        America. (*Edinburgh Review, 1820.*)

America has furnished to the world the
character of Washington! And if our American institutions had done nothing else, that
alone would have entitled them to the respect
of mankind.
   h.   DANIEL WEBSTER—*Completion of*
        Bunker Hill Monument. June 17,
        1843. Vol. I. P. 105.

Lo! body and soul!—this land!
Mighty Manhattan, with spires, and
The sparkling and hurrying tides, and the
    ships;
The varied and ample land,—the South
And the North in the light—Ohio's shores,
    and flashing Missouri,
And ever the far-spreading prairies, covered
    with grass and corn.
   i.   WALT WHITMAN—*Sequel to Drum-Taps.*
        When Lilacs Last in the Door-Yard
                Bloom'd. St. 12.

Egypt.

Egypt! from whose all dateless tombs arose
Forgotten Pharaohs from their long repose,
And shook within their pyramids to hear
A new Cambyses thundering in their ear;
While the dark shades of forty ages stood
Like startled giants by Nile's famous flood.
   j.   BYRON—*The Age of Bronze.* V.

England.

England! my country, great and free!
Heart of the world, I leap to thee!
   k.   BAILEY—*Festus.* Sc. *The Surface.*
                                   L. 376.

        Be England what she will,
With all her faults, she is my country still.
   l.   CHURCHILL—*The Farewell.*

England, a happy land we know,
Where follies naturally grow,
Where, without culture they arise,
And tow'r above the common size.
   m.   CHURCHILL—*Ghost.* Bk. I. L. 111.

The land of scholars, and the nurse of arms.
   n.   GOLDSMITH—*The Traveller.* L. 356.

His home!—the Western giant smiles,
    And turns the spotty globe to find it;—
This little speck the British Isles?
'Tis but a freckle,—never mind it.
   o.   O. W. HOLMES—*A Good Time Going.*

The noblest prospect which a Scotchman
ever sees is the high-road that leads him to
England.
   p.   SAM'L JOHNSON—*Boswell's Life of*
        Johnson. Vol. II. Ch. V. 1763.

Oh, when shall Britain, conscious of her claim,
Stand emulous of Greek and Roman fame?
In living medals see her wars enroll'd,
And vanquished realms supply recording
    gold?
   q.   POPE—*Moral Essays. Epistle to*
                Addison. L. 53.

O England! model to thy inward greatness,
Like little body with a mighty heart,
What might'st thou do, that honour would
    thee do,
Were all thy children kind and natural!
But see thy fault!
  a.   *Henry V.* Act II. Chorus. L. 16.

This royal throne of kings, this scepter'd isle,
This earth of majesty, this seat of Mars,
This other Eden, demi-paradise,
This fortress built by nature for herself
Against infection and the hand of war;
This happy breed of men, this little world,
This precious stone set in the silver sea.
  b.   *Richard II.* Act II. Sc. 1. L. 40.

There is no land like England,
  Whate'er the light of day be;
There are no hearts like English hearts,
  Such hearts of oak as they be;
There is no land like England,
  Whate'er the light of day be:
There are no men like Englishmen,
  So tall and bold as they be!
And these will strike for England,
  And man and maid be free
To foil and spoil the tyrant
  Beneath the greenwood tree.
  c.   TENNYSON—*The Foresters. Song.*

Rule, Britannia, rule the waves;
Britons never will be slaves.
  d.   THOMSON—*Songs from " Alfred."*
            Rule Britannia.

A power which has dotted over the surface
of the whole globe with her possessions and
military posts, whose morning drum-beat,
following the sun, and keeping company with
the hours, circles the earth with one continuous and unbroken strain of the martial airs
of England.
  e.   DANIEL WEBSTER—*Speech. The*
      Presidential Protest. May 7, 1834.
            Vol. IV. P. 110.

Set in this stormy Northern sea,
  Queen of these restless fields of tide,
England! what shall men say of thee,
  Before whose feet the worlds divide?
  f.   OSCAR WILDE—*Ave Imperatrix.*

Greece.

Fair Greece! sad relic of departed worth!
Immortal, though no more; though fallen,
  great!
  g.   BYRON—*Childe Harold.* Canto II.
                  St. 73.

Such is the aspect of this shore;
'Tis Greece, but living Greece no more!
So coldly sweet, so deadly fair,
We start, for soul is wanting there.
  h.   BYRON—*The Giaour.* L. 90.

The mountains look on Marathon—
  And Marathon looks on the sea;
And musing there an hour alone,
  I dreamed that Greece might still be free.
  i.   BYRON.—*Don Juan.* Canto III.
                  St. 86.

Ireland.

Arm of Erin, prove strong, but be gentle as
  brave,
And, uplifted to strike, still be ready to save;
Nor one feeling of vengeance presume to defile
The cause or the men of the Emerald Isle.
  j.   DR. WILLIAM DRENNAN—*Erin.*

Italy.

Italy, my Italy!
Queen Mary's saying serves for me—
(When fortune's malice
Lost her Calais)—
Open my heart and you will see
Graved inside of it, " Italy."
  k.   ROBERT BROWNING—*Men and Women.*
               " De Gustibus." 2

Italia! O Italia! thou who hast
  The fatal gift of beauty, which became
A funeral dower of present woes and past,
  On thy sweet brow is sorrow plough'd by
    shame,
And annals graved in characters of flame.
  l.   BYRON—*Childe Harold.* Canto IV.
                  St. 42.

Scotland.

Give me but one hour of Scotland,
Let me see it ere I die.
  m.   WM. E. AYTOUN—*Lays of the Scottish*
        Cavaliers—Charles Edward at
             Versailles. L. 111.

Hear, Land o' Cakes and brither Scots
Frae Maiden Kirk to Johnny Groat's.
  n.   BURNS—*On Capt. Grose's Peregrinations*
             Thro' Scotland.

O Scotia! my dear, my native soil!
For whom my warmest wish to heaven is sent;
Long may thy hardy sons of rustic toil
Be blest with health, and peace, and sweet
  content!
  o.   BURNS—*Cotter's Saturday Night.*
                 St. 20.

The Scots are poor, cries surly English pride;
True is the charge, nor by themselves denied.
Are they not then in strictest reason clear,
Who wisely come to mend their fortunes here?
  p.   CHURCHILL—*Prophecy of Famine.*
                L. 195.

O Caledonia! stern and wild,
Meet nurse for a poetic child!
Land of brown heath and shaggy wood,
Land of the mountain and the flood,
Land of my sires! what mortal hand
Can e'er untie the filial band,
That knits me to thy rugged strand!
  q.   SCOTT—*Lay of the Last Minstrel.*
             Canto VI. St. 2.

Spain.

Fair land! of chivalry the old domain,
Land of the vine and olive, lovely Spain!
Though not for thee with classic shores to vie
In charms that fix th' enthusiast's pensive eye;
Yet hast thou scenes of beauty richly fraught
With all that wakes the glow of lofty thought.
   a.   Mrs. Hemans—*Abencerrage.* Canto II.
                              L. 1.

COUNTRY LIFE.

God Almighty first planted a Garden.
   b.   Bacon—*Essays. Of Gardens.*

Nor rural sights alone, but rural sounds
Exhilarate the spirit, and restore
The tone of languid Nature.
   c.   Cowper—*The Task.* Bk. I. L. 181.

They love the country, and none else, who
    seek
For their own sake its silence and its shade.
Delights which who would leave, that has a
    heart
Susceptible of pity, or a mind
Cultured and capable of sober thought.
   d.   Cowper—*The Task.* Bk. III. L. 320.

I hate the countrie's dirt and manners, yet
I love the silence; I embrace the wit
A courtship, flowing here in full tide.
But loathe the expense, the vanity and pride.
No place each way is happy.
   e.   William Habington—*To my Noblest
                    Friend, I. C. Esquire.*

Far from the gay cities, and the ways of men.
   f.   Homer—*Odyssey.* Bk. XIV. L. 410.
                          Pope's trans.

To one who has been long in city pent,
'Tis very sweet to look into the fair
And open face of heaven,—to breathe a prayer
Full in the smile of the blue firmament.
   g.   Keats—*Sonnet XIV.* L. 1.

              And as I read
I hear the crowing cock, I hear the note
Of lark and linnet, and from every page
Rise odors of ploughed field or flowery mead.
   h.   Longfellow—*Chaucer.*

Somewhat back from the village street
Stands the old-fashion'd country seat.
Across its antique portico
Tall poplar-trees their shadows throw;
And from its station in the hall
An ancient time-piece says to all,—
         " Forever! never!
           Never—forever!"
   i.   Longfellow—*The Old Clock on the
                   Stairs.* St. 1.

Mine be a cot beside the hill;
  A beehive's hum shall soothe my ear;
A willowy brook, that turns a mill,
  With many a fall, shall linger near.
   j.   Sam'l Rogers—*A Wish.*

Now the summer's in prime
  Wi' the flowers richly blooming,
And the wild mountain thyme
  A' the moorlands perfuming.
To own dear native scenes
  Let us journey together,
Where glad innocence reigns
  'Mang the braes o' Balquhither.
   k.   Robert Tannahill—*The Braes o'
                       Balquhither.*

COUNTRY, LOVE OF.

There ought to be a system of manners in
every nation which a well-formed mind would
be disposed to relish. To make us love our
country, our country ought to be lovely.
   l.   Burke—*Reflections on the Revolution
                  in France.* Vol. III. P. 100.

               My dear, my native soil!
For whom my warmest wish to Heav'n is
    sent,
Long may thy hardy sons of rustic toil
Be blest with health, and peace, and sweet
    content!
   m.   Burns—*Cotter's Saturday Night.*
                          St. 20.

I can't but say it is an awkward sight
  To see one's native land receding through
The growing waters; it unman's one quite,
  Especially when life is rather new.
   n.   Byron—*Don Juan.* Canto II. St. 12.

Oh, Christ! it is a goodly sight to see
What Heaven hath done for this delicious
    land!
   o.   Byron—*Childe Harold.* Canto I.
                          St. 15.

Yon Sun that sets upon the sea
  We follow in his flight;
Farewell awhile to him and thee,
  My native land—Good Night!
   p.   Byron—*Childe Harold.* Canto I.
                          St. 13.

There came to the beach a poor Exile of Erin,
  The dew on his thin robe was heavy and
    chill;
For his country he sigh'd, when at twilight
    repairing,
  To wander alone by the wind-beaten hill.
   q.   Campbell—*The Exile of Erin.*

O beautiful and grand,
My own, my Native Land
  Of thee I boast:
Great Empire of the West,
The dearest and the best,
Made up of all the rest,
   I love thee most.
   r.   Abraham Coles—*My Native Land.*

England, with all thy faults, I love thee still—
My Country! and, while yet a nook is left
Where English minds and manners may be
    found,
Shall be constrained to love thee.
   a.   COWPER—*The Task.* Bk. II. L. 206.

Without one friend, above all foes,
Britannia gives the world repose.
   b.   COWPER—*To Sir Joshua Reynolds.*

    And nobler is a limited command,
Given by the love of all your native land,
Than a successive title, long and dark,
Drawn from the mouldy rolls of Noah's Ark.
   c.   DRYDEN—*Absalom and Achitophel.*
                      Pt. I. L. 299.

So the loud torrent, and the whirlwind's roar,
But bind him to his native mountains more.
   d.   GOLDSMITH—*The Traveller.* L. 207.

They love their land, because it is their own,
   And scorn to give aught other reason why;
Would shake hands with a king upon his
    throne,
   And think it kindness to his majesty.
   e.   FITZ-GREENE HALLECK—*Connecticut.*

Our hearts, our hopes, are all with thee,
Our hearts, our hopes, our prayers, our tears,
Our faith triumphant o'er our fears,
Are all with thee,—are all with thee!
   f.   LONGFELLOW—*The Building of the Ship.*

Sweet the memory is to me
Of a land beyond the sea,
Where the waves and mountains meet.
   g.   LONGFELLOW—*Amalfi.* St. 1.

Who dare to love their country, and be poor.
   h.   POPE—*On his Grotto at Twickenham.*

Farewell, my dear country, so savage and
    hoar!
I shall range on thy heath-covered Sinnburgh
    no more;
For lo! I am snatched to a far distant shore,
   To wish for my country in vain.
   i.   RUSKIN—*Shagram's Farewell to
                            Shetland.*

Breathes there the man with soul so dead,
Who never to himself hath said,
This is my own, my native land!
Whose heart hath ne'er within him burn'd,
As home his footsteps he hath turn'd,
From wandering on a foreign strand!
   j.   SCOTT—*Lay of the Last Minstrel.*
                     Canto VI. St. 1.

Land of my sires! what mortal hand
Can e'er untie the filial band
That knits me to thy rugged strand!
   k.   SCOTT—*Lay of the Last Minstrel.*
                     Canto VI. St. 2.

My foot is on my native heath, and my name
   is MacGregor.
   l.   SCOTT—*Rob Roy.* Ch. XXXIV.

COURAGE.

The soul, secured in her existence, smiles
At the drawn dagger, and defies its point.
   m.   ADDISON—*Cato.* Act V. Sc. 1.

The schoolboy, with his satchel in his hand,
Whistling aloud to bear his courage up.
   n.   BLAIR—*The Grave.* Pt. I. L. 58.

A man of courage is also full of faith.
   o.   CICERO—*The Tusculan Disputations.*
        Bk. III. Ch. VIII. Yonge's trans.

   None of the prophets old,
     So lofty or so bold!
No form of danger shakes his dauntless breast;
    In loneliness sublime
   He dares confront the time,
And speak the truth, and give the world no
   rest:
No kingly threat can cowardize his breath,
He with majestic step goes forth to meet his
   death.
   p.   ABRAHAM COLES—*John the Baptist.*
               "The Light of the World."
                   Pp. 107–108.

For be sure our hearts would lose
   Future years of woe,
If our courage could refuse
   The present hour with " No."
   q.   ELIZA COOK—*Journal.* *"No."*
                   Vol. II. St. 2.

    The charm of the best courages is that they
are inventions, inspirations, flashes of genius.
   r.   EMERSON—*Society and Solitude.*
                      Courage.

Courage, the highest gift, that scorns to bend
To mean devices for a sordid end.
Courage—an independent spark from Heav-
   en's bright throne,
By which the soul stands raised, triumphant,
   high, alone.
Great in itself, not praises of the crowd,
Above all vice, it stoops not to be proud.
Courage, the mighty attribute of powers above,
By which those great in war, are great in love.
The spring of all brave acts is seated here,
As falsehoods draw their sordid birth from
   fear.
   s.   FARQUHAR—*Love and a Bottle.* *Part
          of dedication to the Lord Marquis
                    of Carmarthen.*

Courage is, on all hands, considered as an
essential of high character.
   t.   FROUDE—*Representative Men.*

Few persons have courage enough to appear
as good as they really are.
   u.   J. C. and A. W. HARE—*Guesses at
                           Truth.*

Tender handed stroke a nettle,
  And it stings you for your pains ;
Grasp it like a man of mettle,
  And it soft as silk remains.
  a.   AARON HILL—*Verses Written on a
                              Window.*

O friends, be men, and let your hearts be
    strong,
And let no warrior in the heat of fight
Do what may bring him shame in others'
    eyes ;
For more of those who shrink from shame are
    safe
Than fall in battle, while with those who flee
Is neither glory nor reprieve from death.
  b.   HOMER—*Iliad.* Bk. V. L. 663.
                              Bryant's trans.

" Be bold ! " *first gate;* " Be bold, be bold,
and evermore be bold," *second gate ;* " Be not
too bold ! " *third gate.*
  c.   *Inscription on the Gates of Busyrane.*

Write on your doors the saying wise and old,
" Be bold ! be. bold ! " and everywhere—" Be
    bold ;
Be not too bold ! " Yet better the excess
Than the defect ; better the more than less ;
Better like Hector in the field to die,
Than like a perfumed Paris turn and fly.
  d.   LONGFELLOW—*Morituri Salutamus.*
                              L. 100.

What ! shall one monk, scarce known beyond
    his cell,
Front Rome's far-reaching bolts, and scorn
    her frown?
Brave Luther answered, "Yes" ; that thunder's
    swell
Rocked Europe, and discharmed the triple
    crown.
  e.   LOWELL—*To W. L. Garrison.* St. 5.

                              I argue not
Against Heaven's hand or will, nor bate a jot
Of heart or hope ; but still bear up and steer
Right onward.
  f.   MILTON—*Sonnet. To Cyriack Skinner.*

Stand fast * * *
And all temptation to transgress repel.
  g.   MILTON—*Paradise Lost.* Bk. VIII.
                              L. 640.

Cowards may fear to die ; but courage stout,
Rather than live in snuff, will be put out.
  h.   SIR WALTER RALEIGH—*The night before
              he died. Bayley's Life of Raleigh.*
                              P. 157.

Come one, come all ! this rock shall fly
From its firm base, as soon as I.
  i.   SCOTT—*Lady of the Lake.* Canto V.
                              St. 10.

And fearless minds climb soonest unto crowns.
  j.   *Henry VI.* Pt. III. Act IV. Sc. 7.
                              L. 63.

By how much unexpected, by so much
We must awake endeavour for defence ;
For courage mounteth with occasion :
  k.   *King John.* Act II. Sc. 1. L. 80.

Come, let us take a muster speedily :
Doomsday is near ; die all, die merrily.
  l.   *Henry IV.* Pt. I. Act IV. Sc. 1.
                              L. 133.

He hath borne himself beyond the promise
of his age, doing, in the figure of a lamb, the
feats of a lion.
  m.   *Much Ado About Nothing.* Act I.
                              Sc. 1. L. 13.

I dare do all that may become a man :
Who dares do more, is none.
  n.   *Macbeth.* Act I. Sc. 7. L. 47.

Muster your wits : stand in your own defence ;
Or hide your heads like cowards, and fly
    hence.
  o.   *Love's Labour's Lost.* Act V. Sc. 2.
                              L. 85.

          O, the blood more stirs
To rouse a lion than to start a hare !
  p.   *Henry IV.* Pt. I. Act I. Sc. 3.
                              L. 198.

The smallest worm will turn being trodden
    on,
And doves will peck in safeguard of their
    brood.
  q.   *Henry VI.* Pt. III. Act II. Sc. 2.
                              L. 17.

                      The thing of courage
As rous'd with rage with rage doth sympa-
    thise,
And, with an accent tun'd in self-same key,
Retorts to chiding fortune.
  r.   *Troilus and Cressida.* Act I. Sc. 3.
                              L. 51.

Think you a little din can daunt mine ears ?
Have I not in my time heard lions roar ?
      *   *   *   *   *   *
Have I not heard great ordnance in the field,
And heaven's artillery thunder in the skies ?
      *   *   *   *   *   *
And do you tell me of a woman's tongue,
That gives not half so great a blow to hear
As will a chestnut in a farmer's fire ?
  s.   *Taming of the Shrew.* Act I. Sc. 2.
                              L. 200.

                              We fail !
But screw your courage to the sticking-place,
And we'll not fail.
  t.   *Macbeth.* Act I. Sc. 7. L. 59.

Why, courage then ! what cannot be avoided
'Twere childish weakness to lament or fear.
  u.   *Henry VI.* Pt. III. Act V. Sc. 4.
                              L. 37.

You must not think
That we are made of stuff so fat and dull
That we can let our beard be shook with
    danger
And think it pastime.
  a.   *Hamlet.* Act IV. Sc. 7. L. 29.

Hold the Fort! I am coming.
  b.   Gen. W. T. Sherman—*Signalled to Gen.*
                            Corse. Oct. 5, 1864.

Who stemm'd the torrent of a downward age.
  c.   Thomson—*The Seasons. Summer.*
                                    L. 1,516.

COURTESY.

A moral, sensible, and well-bred man
Will not affront me, and no other can.
  d.   Cowper—*Conversation.* L. 193.

Life is not so short but that there is always
time enough for courtesy.
  e.   Emerson—*Social Aims.*

How sweet and gracious, even in common
    speech,
Is that fine sense which men call Courtesy!
Wholesome as air and genial as the light,
Welcome in every clime as breath of flowers,
It transmutes aliens into trusting friends,
And gives its owner passport round the globe.
  f.   James T. Fields—*Courtesy.*

Their accents firm and loud in conversation
    Their eyes and gestures eager, sharp and
    quick
Showed them prepared on proper provocation
    To give the lie, pull noses, stab and kick!
And for that very reason it is said
They were so very courteous and well-bred.
  g.   John Hookham Frere—*Prospectus*
                and Specimen of an Intended National
                                    Work.

When the king was horsed thore,
Launcelot lookys he upon,
How courtesy was in him more
Than ever was in any mon.
  h.   Morte Arthur—*Harleian Library*
                (British Museum). MS. 2,252.

In thy discourse, if thou desire to please;
All such is courteous, useful, new, or wittie:
Usefulness comes by labour, wit by ease;
Courtesie grows in court; news in the citie.
  i.   Herbert—*The Church. Church Porch.*
                                    St. 49.

Shepherd, I take thy word,
And trust thy honest offer'd courtesy,
Which oft is sooner found in lowly sheds
With smoky rafters, than in tap'stry halls,
And courts of princes.
  j.   Milton—*Comus.* L. 322.

Dissembling courtesy! How fine this tyrant
Can tickle where she wounds!
  k.   *Cymbeline.* Act I. Sc. 1. L. 84.

I am the very pink of courtesy.
  l.   *Romeo and Juliet.* Act II. Sc. 4.
                                        L. 61.

The mirror of all courtesy.
  m.   *Henry VIII.* Act II. Sc. 1. L. 53.

The Retort Courteous.
  n.   *As You Like It.* Act V. Sc. 4. L. 76.

                        The thorny point
Of bare distress hath ta'en from me the show
Of smooth civility.
  o.   *As You Like It.* Act II. Sc. 7. L. 94.

That's too civil by half.
  p.   Sheridan—*The Rivals.* Act III. Sc. 4.

High erected thoughts seated in a heart of
courtesy.
  q.   Sir Philip Sidney—*The Arcadia.*
                            Bk. I. Par. II.

COURTIERS.

                    A mere court butterfly,
That flutters in the pageant of a monarch.
  r.   Byron—*Sardanapalus.* Act V. Sc. 1.

To shake with laughter ere the jest they hear,
To pour at will the counterfeited tear;
And, as their patron hints the cold or heat,
To shake in dog-days, in December sweat.
  s.   Sam'l Johnson—*London.* L. 140.

At the throng'd levee bends the venal tribe:
With fair but faithless smiles each varnish'd
    o'er,
Each smooth as those that mutually deceive,
And for their falsehood each despising each.
  t.   Thomson—*Liberty.* Pt. V. L. 190.

COVETOUSNESS.

Excess of wealth is cause of covetousness.
  u.   Marlowe—*The Jew of Malta.* Act I.
                                        Sc. 2.

            I am not covetous for gold,
Nor care I who doth feed upon my cost;
It yearns me not if men my garments wear;
Such outward things dwell not in my desires:
But if it be a sin to covet honor
I am the most offending soul alive.
  v.   *Henry V.* Act IV. Sec. 3. L. 24.

When workmen strive to do better than well,
They do confound their skill in covetousness.
  w.   *King John.* Act IV. Sc. 2. L. 28.

COWARDICE—COWARDS.

For those that run away and fly,
Take place at least o' th' enemy.
　　a.　　BUTLER—*Hudibras.* Pt. I. Canto III.
　　　　　　　　　　　　　L. 609.

To see what is right and not to do it is want
of courage.
　　b.　　CONFUCIUS—*Analects.* Bk. II.
　　　　　　　　　　　　Ch. XXIV.

Grac'd with a sword, and worthier of a fan.
　　c.　　COWPER—*Task.* Bk. I. L. 771.

That all men would be cowards if they dare,
Some men we know have courage to declare.
　　d.　　CRABBE—*Tale I. The Dumb Orators.*
　　　　　　　　　　　　　L. 11.

The coward never on himself relies,
But to an equal for assistance flies.
　　e.　　CRABBE—*Tale III. The Gentleman*
　　　　　　　　　　Farmer. L. 84.

That same man, that rennith awaie,
Maie again fight, an other daie.
　　f.　　ERASMUS—*Apophthegmes.* Bk. II.
　　　　　　　Demonsthenes. Trans. by Udall.

Cowards are cruel, but the brave
Love mercy, and delight to save.
　　g.　　GAY—*Fables.* Pt. I. Fable 1.

He who fights and runs away
May live to fight another day.
But he who is in battle slain,
Can never rise to fight again.
　　h.　　GOLDSMITH—*The Art of Poetry on a*
　　　　　　　　New Plan. Vol. II. P. 147.

When desp'rate ills demand a speedy cure,
Distrust is cowardice, and prudence folly.
　　i.　　SAM'L JOHNSON—*Irene.* Act IV.
　　　　　　　　　　　　　　Sc. 1.

　　　　　　　　　　　　　　　He
That kills himself to avoid misery, fears it,
And, at the best, shows but a bastard valour.
This life's a fort committed to my trust,
Which I must not yield up, till it be forced :
Nor will I. He's not valiant that dares die,
But he that boldly bears calamity.
　　j.　　MASSINGER—*Maid of Honour.* Act IV.
　　　　　　　　　　　　　　Sc. 3.

Men lie, who lack courage to tell truth—the
cowards!
　　k.　　JOAQUIN MILLER—*Ina.* Sc. 3.

He that fights and runs away
May turn and fight another day ;
But he that is in battle slain
Will never rise to fight again.
　　l.　　RAY—*History of the Rebellion.* Bristol,
　　　　　　　　　　　　　　1752.

Where's the coward that would not dare
To fight for such a land !
　　m.　　SCOTT—*Marmion.* Canto IV. St. 30.

When all the blandishments of life are gone,
The coward sneaks to death, the brave live on.
　　n.　　DR. SEWELL—*The Suicide.*

A coward, a most devout coward, religious
in it.
　　o.　　*Twelfth Night.* Act III. Sc. 4.
　　　　　　　　　　　　　　L. 427.

By this good light, this is a very shallow
monster !—I afear'd of him !—A very weak
monster !—The man i' the moon !—A most
poor, credulous monster !—Well drawn, monster, in good sooth !
　　p.　　*Tempest.* Act II. Sc. 2. L. 144.

Cowards die many times before their deaths ;
The valiant never taste of death but once.
Of all the wonders that I yet have heard,
It seems to me most strange that men should
　　　　fear ;
Seeing that death, a necessary end,
Will come when it will come.
　　q.　　*Julius Cæsar.* Act II. Sc. 2. L. 33.

Dost thou now fall over to my foes?
Thou wear a lion's hide ! doff it for shame,
And hang a calf's skin on those recreant
　　limbs.
　　r.　　*King John.* Act III. Sc. 1. L. 127.

How many cowards, whose hearts are all as
　　false
As stairs of sand, wear yet upon their chins
The beards of Hercules and frowning Mars,
Who, inward search'd, have livers white as
　　milk.
　　s.　　*Merchant of Venice.* Act III. Sc. 2,
　　　　　　　　　　　　　　L. 83.

　　　　　　　I hold it cowardice
To rest mistrustful where a noble heart
Hath pawn'd an open hand in sign of love.
　　t.　　*Henry VI.* Pt. III. Act IV. Sc. 2.
　　　　　　　　　　　　　　L. 6.

　　　　　　I may speak it to my shame,
I have a truant been to chivalry.
　　u.　　*Henry IV.* Pt. I. Act V. Sc. I.
　　　　　　　　　　　　　　L. 93.

　　　　　It was great pity, so it was,
That villanous saltpetre should be digg'd
Out of the bowels of the harmless earth,
Which many a good tall fellow had destroy'd
So cowardly ; and but for these vile guns
He would himself have been a soldier.
　　v.　　*Henry IV.* Pt. I. Act I. Sc. 3.
　　　　　　　　　　　　　　L. 59.

　　　I would give all my fame for a pot of ale
and safety.
　　w.　　*Henry V.* Act III. Sc. 2. L. 13.

Milk-liver'd man!
That bear'st a cheek for blows, a head for
        wrongs,
Who hast not in thy brows an eye discerning
Thine honor from thy suffering.
   a.   *King Lear.* Act IV. Sc. 2. L. 50.

Plague on't; an I thought he had been valiant, and so cunning in fence, I'ld have seen
him damned ere I'ld have challenged him.
   b.   *Twelfth Night.* Act III. Sc. 4.
                                        L. 311.

So bees with smoke and doves with noisome
        stench
Are from their hives and houses driven away.
They call'd us for our fierceness English dogs;
Now, like whelps, we crying run away.
   c.   *Henry VI.* Pt. I. Act I. Sc. 5.
                                        L. 23.

So cowards fight when they can fly no
        further;
As doves do peck the falcon's piercing talons;
So desperate thieves, all hopeless of their lives,
Breathe out invectives 'gainst the officers.
   d.   *Henry VI.* Pt. III. Act I. Sc. 4.
                                        L. 39.

That which in mean men we entitle patience
Is pale cold cowardice in noble breasts.
   e.   *Richard II.* Act I. Sc. 2. L. 33.

Thou slave, thou wretch, thou coward!
Thou little valiant, great in villany!
Thou ever strong upon the stronger side!
Thou Fortune's champion, that dost never
        fight
But when her humorous ladyship is by
To teach thee safety!
   f.   *King John.* Act III. Sc. 1. L. 116.

What a slave art thou, to hack thy sword
as thou hast done, and then say it was in
fight!
   g.   *Henry IV.* Pt. I. Act II. Sc. 4.
                                        L. 286.

Who knows himself a braggart,
Let him fear this, for it will come to pass
That every braggart shall be found an ass.
   h.   *All's Well That Ends Well.* Act IV.
                                    Sc. 3. L. 369.

Wouldst thou have that
Which thou esteem'st the ornament of life,
And live a coward in thine own esteem,
Letting 'I dare not' wait upon, 'I would';
Like the poor cat i' the adage?
   i.   *Macbeth.* Act I. Sc. 7. L. 41.

You are the hare of whom the proverb goes,
Whose valor plucks dead lions by the beard.
   j.   *King John.* Act II. Sc. 1. L. 137.

You souls of geese,
That bear the shapes of men, how have you
        run
From slaves that apes would beat!
   k.   *Coriolanus.* Act I. Sc. 4. L. 35.

My valor is certainly going!—it is sneaking
off!—I feel it oozing out, as it were, at the
palms of my hands.
   l.   Sheridan—*The Rivals.* Act V. Sc. 3.

Ah, Foole! faint heart faire lady n'ere could
win.
   m.   Spenser—*Britain's Ida.* Canto V.
                                        St. I.

The man that lays his hand on woman,
Save in the way of kindness, is a wretch
Whom 'twere gross flattery to name a coward.
   n.   Tobin—*The Honeymoon.* Act II.
                                        Sc. 1.

CREATION.

Had I been present at the creation, I would
have given some useful hints for the better
ordering of the universe.
   o.   Alphonso the Wise.

Creation is great, and cannot be understood.
   p.   Carlyle—*Essays. Characteristics.*

Silently as a dream the fabric rose;
No sound of hammer or of saw was there.
   q.   Cowper—*The Task.* Bk. V. L. 144.

From harmony, from heavenly harmony,
   This universal frame began:
From harmony, to harmony
   Through all the compass of the notes it ran,
   The diapason closing full in man.
   r.   Dryden—*A Song for St. Cecilia's Day.*
                                        L. 11.
Then tower'd the palace, then in awful state
The temple rear'd its everlasting gate.
No workman steel, no ponderous axes rung.
Like some tall palm the noiseless fabric
        sprung.
   s.   Bishop Heber—*Palestine.* L. 197.

Two urns by Jove's high throne have ever
        stood,
The source of evil, one, and one of good.
   t.   Homer—*The Iliad.* Bk. 24. L. 663.
                                    Pope's trans.
Nature they say, doth dote,
And cannot make a man
Save on some worn-out plan,
Repeating us by rote.
   u.   Lowell—*Ode at the Harvard
                Commemoration, July 21, 1865.* VI.

Open, ye heavens, your living doors; let in
The great Creator from his work return'd
Magnificent, his six days' work, a world!
   v.   Milton—*Paradise Lost.* Bk. VII.
                                        L. 566.

Though to recount almighty works
What words of tongue or seraph can suffice,
Or heart of man suffice to comprehend?
　a.　　Milton—*Paradise Lost.*　Bk. VII.
　　　　　　　　　　　　　　　　　L. 112.

What cause
Moved the Creator in his holy rest
Through all eternity so late to build
In chaos, and, the work begun, how soon
Absolved.
　b.　　Milton—*Paradise Lost.*　Bk. VII.
　　　　　　　　　　　　　　　　　L. 90.

All are but parts of one stupendous whole,
Whose body Nature is, and God the soul.
　c.　　Pope—*Essay on Man.*　Ep. I.　L. 267.

No man saw the building of the New Jerusalem, the workmen crowded together, the
unfinished walls and unpaved streets; no man
heard the clink of trowel and pickaxe; it
descended *out of heaven from God.*
　d.　　Seeley—*Ecce Homo.*　Ch. XXIV.

Through knowledge we behold the world's
　　　creation,
How in his cradle first he fostered was;
And judge of Nature's cunning operation,
How things she formed of a formeless mass.
　e.　　Spenser—*Tears of the Muses.　Urania.*
　　　　　　　　　　　　　　　　　L. 499.

One God, one law, one element,
And one far-off divine event,
To which the whole creation moves.
　f.　　Tennyson—*In Memoriam.　Conclusion.*
　　　　　　　　　　　　　　　　Last Stanza.

The chain that's fixed to the throne of Jove,
On which the fabric of our world depends,
One link dissolved, the whole creation ends.
　g.　　Edmund Waller—*Of the Danger His
　　　　　　　　Majesty Escaped.*　L. 68.

CREDIT.

Private credit is wealth; public honor is
security; the feather that adorns the royal
bird supports its flight; strip him of his
plumage, and you fix him to the earth.
　h.　　Junius—*Affair of the Falkland Islands.*
　　　　　　　　　　　Vol. I.　Letter XLII.

Blest paper-credit! last and best supply!
That lends corruption lighter wings to fly.
　i.　　Pope—*Moral Essays.*　Ep. 3.　L. 39.

He smote the rock of the national resources,
and abundant streams of revenue gushed forth.
He touched the dead corpse of Public Credit,
and it sprung upon its feet.
　j.　　Daniel Webster—*Speech on Hamilton,
　　　　　　March 10, 1831.*　Vol. I.　P. 200.

CRIME.

Nor all that heralds rake from coffin'd clay,
Nor florid prose, nor honied lies of rhyme,
Can blazon evil deeds, or consecrate a crime.
　k.　　Byron—*Childe Harold.*　Canto I. St. 3.

But many a crime deemed innocent on earth
Is registered in Heaven; and these no doubt
Have each their record, with a curse annex'd.
　l.　　Cowper—*The Task.*　Bk. VI.　L. 439.

Crime is not punished as an offense against
God, but as prejudicial to society.
　m.　　Froude—*Short Studies on Great Sub-
　　　　　jects.　Reciprocal Duties of State and
　　　　　　　　　　　　　　　　Subjects.*

Every crime destroys more Edens than our
own.
　n.　　Nath. Hawthorne—*Marble Faun.*
　　　　　　　　　　　　　Vol. I.　Ch. XXIII.

'Tis no sin love's fruits to steal;
But the sweet thefts to reveal;
To be taken, to be seen,
These have crimes accounted been.
　o.　　Ben Jonson—*Volpone.*　Act III.　Sc. 6.

A man who has no excuse for crime, is indeed defenceless!
　p.　　Bulwer-Lytton—*The Lady of Lyons.*
　　　　　　　　　　　　　Act IV.　Sc. 1.

Between the acting of a dreadful thing
And the first motion, all the interim is
Like a phantasma, or a hideous dream.
　q.　　*Julius Cæsar.*　Act II.　Sc. 1.　L. 63.

Beyond the infinite and boundless reach
Of mercy, if thou didst this deed of death,
Art thou damn'd, Hubert.
　r.　　*King John.*　Act IV.　Sc. 3.　L. 117.

　　　　　　　　　　　Foul deeds will rise,
Though all the earth o'erwhelm them, to
　　　men's eyes.
　s.　　*Hamlet.*　Act I.　Sc. 2.　L. 257.

If little faults, proceeding on distemper,
Shall not be wink'd at, how shall we stretch
　　　our eye
When capital crimes, chew'd, swallow'd, and
　　　digested,
Appear before us?
　t.　　*Henry V.*　Act II.　Sc. 2.　L. 54.

　　　　　O, would the deed were good!
For now the devil, that told me I did well,
Says that this deed is chronicled in hell.
　u.　　*Richard II.*　Act V.　Sc. 5.　L. 115.

　　　　　　　There shall be done
A deed of dreadful note.
　v.　　*Macbeth.*　Act III.　Sc. 2.　L. 43.

The time has been
That, when the brains were out, the man would die,
And there an end; but now they rise again,
With twenty mortal murders on their crowns,
And push us from our stools.
a.   *Macbeth*.   Act III.   Sc. 4.   L. 77.

Tremble, thou wretch,
That has within thee undivulged crimes,
Unwhipp'd of justice.
b.   *King Lear*.   Act III.   Sc. 2.   L. 51.

Unnatural deeds
Do breed unnatural troubles: infected minds
To their deaf pillows will discharge their secrets.
c.   *Macbeth*.   Act V.   Sc. 1.   L. 79.

CRITICISM.

When I read rules of criticism, I immediately inquire after the works of the author who has written them, and by that means discover what it is he likes in a composition.
d.   ADDISON—*Guardian*.   No. 115.

He was in Logic, a great critic,
Profoundly skill'd in Analytic;
He could distinguish, and divide
A hair 'twixt south and south-west side.
e.   BUTLER—*Hudibras*.   Pt. I.   Canto I.
               L. 65.

A man must serve his time to every trade
Save censure—critics all are ready made.
Take hackney'd jokes from Miller, got by rote,
With just enough of learning to misquote;
A mind well skill'd to find or forge a fault;
A turn for punning, call it Attic salt;
To Jeffrey go, be silent and discreet,
His pay is just ten sterling pounds per sheet;
Fear not to lie, 'twill seem a lucky hit;
Shrink not from blasphemy, 'twill pass for wit;
Care not for feeling—pass your proper jest,
And stand a critic, hated yet caress'd.
f.   BYRON—*English Bards and Scotch*
               Reviewers.   L. 63.

As soon
Seek roses in December—ice in June,
Hope, constancy in wind, or corn in chaff;
Believe a woman or an epitaph,
Or any other thing that's false, before
You trust in critics.
g.   BYRON—*English Bards and Scotch*
               Reviewers.   L. 75.

A servile race
Who, in mere want of fault, all merit place;
Who blind obedience pay to ancient schools,
Bigots to Greece, and slaves to musty rules.
h.   CHURCHILL—*The Rosciad*.   L. 183.

But spite of all the criticizing elves,
Those who would make us feel—must feel themselves.
i.   CHURCHILL—*The Rosciad*.   L. 961.

Though by whim, envy, or resentment led,
They damn those authors whom they never read.
j.   CHURCHILL—*The Candidate*.   L. 57.

Who shall dispute what the Reviewers say?
Their word's sufficient; and to ask a reason,
In such a state as theirs, is downright treason.
k.   CHURCHILL—*Apology*.   L. 94.

Reviewers are usually people who would have been poets, historians, biographers, etc., if they could: they have tried their talents at one or the other, and have failed; therefore they turn critics.
l.   COLERIDGE—*Lectures on Shakespeare and*
               Milton.   P. 36.

Too nicely Jonson knew the critic's part,
Nature in him was almost lost in art.
m.   COLLINS—*Epistle to Sir Thomas Hanmer*
               on his Edition of Shakspere.

There are some Critics so with Spleen diseased,
They scarcely come inclining to be pleased:
And sure he must have more than mortal Skill,
Who pleases one against his Will.
n.   CONGREVE—*The Way of the World*.
               Epilogue.

The press, the pulpit, and the stage,
Conspire to censure and expose our age.
o.   WENTWORTH DILLON—*Essay on*
               Translated Verse.   L. 7.

It is much easier to be critical than to be correct.
p.   BENJ. DISRAELI—*Speech in the House*
               of Commons.   Jan'y 24, 1860.

You know who critics are?—the men who have failed in literature and art.
q.   BENJ. DISRAELI—*Lothair*.   Ch. XXXV.

The most noble criticism is that in which the critic is not the antagonist so much as the rival of the author.
r.   ISAAC DISRAELI—*Curiosities of*
               Literature.   *Literary Journals*.

Those who do not read criticism will rarely merit to be criticised.
s.   ISAAC DISRAELI—*Literary Character of*
               Men of Genius.   Ch. VI.

Blame where you must, be candid where you can,
And be each critic the Good-natured Man.
t.   GOLDSMITH—*The Good-Natured Man*.
               Epilogue.

Reviewers are forever telling authors they can't understand them. The author might often reply: Is that my fault?

    a.   J. C. and A. W. HARE—*Guesses at Truth.*

The readers and the hearers like my books,
But yet some writers cannot them digest;
But what care I? for when I make a feast,
I would my guests should praise it, not the cooks.

    b.   SIR JOHN HARRINGTON—*Against Writers that Carp at other Men's Books.*

'Tis not the wholesome sharp morality,
Or modest anger of a satiric spirit,
That hurts or wounds the body of a state,
But the sinister application
Of the malicious, ignorant, and base
Interpreter; who will distort and strain
The general scope and purpose of an author
To his particular and private spleen.

    c.   BEN JONSON—*Poetaster.* Act V. Sc. 1.

Critics are sentinels in the grand army of letters, stationed at the corners of newspapers and reviews, to challenge every new author.

    d.   LONGFELLOW—*Kavanagh.* Ch. XIII.

A wise scepticism is the first attribute of a good critic.

    e.   LOWELL—*Among My Books. Shakespeare Once More.*

Nature fits all her children with something to do,
He who would write and can't write, can surely review;
Can set up a small booth as critic and sell us his
Petty conceit and his pettier jealousies.

    f.   LOWELL—*A Fable for Critics.*

In truth it may be laid down as an almost universal rule that good poets are bad critics.

    g.   MACAULAY—*Criticisms on the Principal Italian Writers. Dante.*

The opinion of the great body of the reading public is very materially influenced even by the unsupported assertions of those who assume a right to criticise.

    h.   MACAULAY—*Mr. Robert Montgomery's Poems.*

To check young Genius' proud career,
  The slaves who now his throne invaded,
Made Criticism his prime Vizier,
  And from that hour his glories faded.

    i.   MOORE—*Genius and Criticism.* St. 4.

Ah, ne'er so dire a thirst of glory boast,
Nor in the Critic let the Man be lost.

    j.   POPE—*Essay on Criticism.* L. 522.
                            Pt. II.

And you, my Critics! in the chequer'd shade,
Admire new light thro' holes yourselves have made.

    k.   POPE—*Dunciad.* Bk. IV. L. 125.

A perfect Judge will read each work of Wit
With the same spirit that its author writ:
Survey the Whole, nor seek slight faults to find
Where nature moves, and rapture warms the mind.

    l.   POPE—*Essay on Criticism.* Pt. II.
                            L. 235.

Be not the first by whom the new are tried,
Nor yet the last to lay the old aside.

    m.   POPE—*Essay on Criticism.* Pt. II.
                            L. 336.

But you with pleasure own your errors past,
And make each day a critic on the last.

    n.   POPE—*Essay on Criticism.* Pt. III.
                            L. 571.

I lose my patience, and I own it too,
When works are censur'd, not as bad but new;
While if our Elders break all reason's laws,
These fools demand not pardon but Applause.

    o.   POPE—*Second Book of Horace.* Ep. I.
                            L. 115.

In every work regard the writer's End,
Since none can compass more than they intend;
And if the means be just, the conduct true,
Applause, in spite of trivial faults, is due.

    p.   POPE—*Essay on Criticism.* Pt. II.
                            L. 255.

Ten censure wrong for one who writes amiss.

    q.   POPE—*Essay on Criticism.* Pt. I. L. 6.

The generous Critic fann'd the Poet's fire,
And taught the world with reason to admire.

    r.   POPE—*Essay on Criticism.* Pt. I.
                            L. 100.

The line too labours, and the words move slow.

    s.   POPE—*Essay on Criticism.* Pt. II.
                            L. 171.

For I am nothing, if not critical.

    t.   *Othello.* Act II. Sc. 1. L. 120.

    For 'tis a physic
That's bitter to sweet end.

    u.   *Measure for Measure.* Act IV. Sc. 6.
                            L. 7.

In such a time as this it is not meet
That every nice offence should bear his comment.

    v.   *Julius Cæsar.* Act IV. Sc. 3. L. 7.

Of all the cants which are canted in this canting world—though the cant of hypocrites may be the worst—the cant of criticism is the most tormenting.

    w.   LAURENCE STERNE—*Life and Opinions of Tristram Shandy.* (Orig. ed.)
                      Vol. III. Ch. XII.

For, poems read without a name,
We justly praise, or justly blame ;
And critics have no partial views,
Except they know whom they abuse.
And since you ne'er provoke their spite,
Depend upon't their judgment's right.
   a.   Swift—*On Poetry.* L. 129.

For since he would sit on a Prophet's seat,
  As a lord of the Human soul,
We needs must scan him from head to feet,
  Were it but for a wart or a mole.
   b.   Tennyson—*The Dead Prophet.*
                       St. XIV.

Critics are like brushers of noblemen's clothes.
   c.   *Attributed to* Sir Henry Wotton *by*
        Bacon. *Apothegms.* No. 64.

How commentators each dark passage shun,
And hold their farthing candle to the sun.
   d.   Young—*Love of Fame.* Satire VII.
                       L. 97.

CRUELTY.

Man's inhumanity to man
Makes countless thousands mourn !
   e.   Burns—*Man Was Made to Mourn.*

               Detested sport,
That owes its pleasures to another's pain.
   f.   Cowper—*The Task.* Bk. III. L. 326.

It is not linen you're wearing out,
But human creatures' lives.
   g.   Hood—*Song of the Shirt.*

An angel with a trumpet said,
" Forever more, forever more,
The reign of violence is o'er ! "
   h.   Longfellow—*The Occultation of Orion.*
                       St. 6.

   The Puritan hated bear-baiting, not because
it gave pain to the bear, but because it gave
pleasure to the spectators.
   i.   Macaulay—*History of England.*
                 Vol. I. Ch. II.

         If ever henceforth thou
These rural latches to his entrance open,
Or hoop his body more with thy embraces,
I will devise a death as cruel for thee
As thou art tender to't.
   j.   *Winter's Tale.* Act IV. Sc. 4. L. 448.

I must be cruel, only to be kind.
   k.   *Hamlet.* Act III. Sc. 4. L. 178.

            Men so noble,
However faulty, yet should find respect
For what they have been ; 'tis a cruelty
To load a falling man.
   l.   *Henry VIII.* Act V. Sc. 3. L. 74.

See what a rent the envious Casca made.
   m.   *Julius Cæsar.* Act III. Sc. 2. L. 179.

You are the cruell'st she alive,
If you will lead these graces to the grave
And leave the world no copy.
   n.   *Twelfth Night.* Act I. Sc. 5. L. 259.

Inhumanity is caught from man,
From smiling man.
   o.   Young—*Night Thoughts.* Night V.
                       L. 158.

CULINARY (*See* Occupations).

CURIOSITY.

Each window like a pill'ry appears,
With heads thrust through nail'd by the ears.
   p.   Butler—*Hudibras.* Pt. II.
                 Canto III. L. 391.

I loathe that low vice—curiosity.
   q.   Byron—*Don Juan.* Canto I. St. 23.

The poorest of the sex have still an itch
To know their fortunes, equal to the rich.
The dairy-maid inquires, if she shall take
The trusty tailor, and the cook forsake.
   r.   Dryden—*Sixth Satire of Juvenal.*
                       L. 762.

   Ask me no questions, and I'll tell you no
fibs.
   s.   Goldsmith—*She Stoops to Conquer.*
                     Act III.

   Talk to him of Jacob's ladder, and he would
ask the number of steps.
   t.   Douglas Jerrold—*A Matter-of-Fact*
                Man. Jerrold's Wit.

Rise up, rise up, Xarifa ! lay your golden
  cushion down ;
Rise up ! come to the window, and gaze with
  all the town !
   u.   John G. Lockhart—*The Bridal of*
                      Andella.

Zaccheus, he
Did climb the tree,
His Lord to see.
   v.   *From the New England Primer.* 1814.

   I saw and heard, for we sometimes,
Who dwell this wild, constrained by want,
  come forth
To town or village nigh, nighest is far,
Where aught we hear, and curious are to hear,
What happens new ; fame also finds us out.
   w.   Milton—*Paradise Regained.* Bk. I.
                       L. 330.

   I have perceived a most faint neglect of
late, which I have rather blamed as mine own
jealous curiosity than as a very pretence and
purpose of unkindness.
   x.   *King Lear.* Act I. Sc. 4. L. 73.

O, Romeo, Romeo! wherefore art thou,
Romeo?
   a.   *Romeo and Juliet.* Act II. Sc. 2.
                            L. 33.

They mocked thee for too much curiosity.
   b.   *Timon of Athens.* Act IV. Sc. 3.
                           L. 302.

What, will the line stretch out to the crack
   of doom?
   c.   *Macbeth.* Act IV. Sc. 1. L. 117.

                I have seen
A curious child, who dwelt upon a tract
Of inlaid ground, applying to his ear
The convolutions of a smooth-lipped shell;
To which, in silence hushed, his very soul
Listened intensely.
   d.   WORDSWORTH—*The Excursion.* Bk. 4.

CUSTOM.

Only that he may conform
To (Tyrant) customs.
   e.   DU BARTAS—*Divine Weekes and Workes.*
          Second Week. Third Day. Pt. II.

   Great things astonish us, and small dishearten us. Custom makes both familiar.
   f.   DE LA BRUYÈRE—*The Characters or*
        Manners of the Present Age. Vol. II.
                  Ch. I. *On Judgments.*

Such dupes are men to custom, and so prone
To rev'rence what is ancient, and can plead
A course of long observance for its use,
That even servitude, the worst of ills,
Because deliver'd down from sire to son,
Is kept and guarded as a sacred thing!
   g.   COWPER—*Task.* Bk. V. L. 298.

The slaves of custom and established mode,
With pack-horse constancy we keep the road
Crooked or straight, through quags or thorny
   dells,
True to the jingling of our leader's bells.
   h.   COWPER—*Tirocinium.* L. 251.

Man yields to custom, as he bows to fate,
In all things ruled—mind, body, and estate;
In pain, in sickness, we for cure apply
To them we know not, and we know not why.
   i.   CRABBE—*Tale III. The Gentleman*
                      Farmer. L. 86.

   The laws of conscience, which we pretend
to be derived from nature, proceed from
custom.
   j.   MONTAIGNE—*Of Custom and Law.*
                      Ch. XXII.

   Montaigne is wrong in declaring that custom ought to be followed simply because it is
custom, and not because it is reasonable or
just.
   k.   PASCAL—*Thoughts.* Ch. IV. 6.

But to my mind, though I am native here,
And to the manner born, it is a custom
More honor'd in the breach than the observance.
   l.   *Hamlet.* Act I. Sc. 4. L. 15.

                 Custom calls me to 't:
What custom wills, in all things should we
   do't,
The dust on antique time would lie unswept,
And mountainous error be too highly heap't
For truth to o'erpeer.
   m.   *Coriolanus.* Act II. Sc. 3. L. 124.

               New customs,
Though they be never so ridiculous,
Nay, let 'em be unmanly, yet are followed.
   n.   *Henry VIII.* Act I. Sc. 3. L. 3.

That monster, custom, * * * is angel yet
   in this,
That to the use of actions fair and good
He likewise gives a frock or livery,
That aptly is put on.
   o.   *Hamlet.* Act III. Sc. 4. L. 161.

The tyrant custom, most grave senators,
Hath made the flinty and steel couch of war
My thrice-driven bed of down.
   p.   *Othello.* Act I. Sc. 3. L. 230.

D.

DANCING.

O give me new figures! I can't go on dancing
The same that were taught me ten seasons ago;
The schoolmaster over the land is advancing,
Then why is the master of dancing so slow?
It is such a bore to be always caught tripping
In dull uniformity year after year;
Invent something new, and you'll set me a
   skipping:
I want a new figure to dance with my Dear!
   q.   THOMAS HAYNES BAYLY—*Quadrille*
                      a la Mode.

And then he danced;—all foreigners excel
The serious Angles in the eloquence
Of pantomime;—he danced, I say, right
   well,
With emphasis, and also with good sense—
A thing in footing indispensable:
He danced without theatrical pretence,
Not like a ballet-master in the van
Of his drill'd nymphs, but like a gentle-
   man.
   r.   BYRON—*Don Juan.* Canto XIV.
                      St. 38.

A thousand hearts beat happily ; and when
Music arose with its voluptuous swell,
Soft eyes look'd love to eyes which spake
    again,
And all went merry as a marriage bell.
   a.   Byron—*Childe Harold.* Canto III.
                           St. 21.

Endearing Waltz—to thy more melting tune
Bow Irish jig, and ancient rigadoon.
Scotch reels, avaunt! and country-dance
    forego
Your future claims to each fantastic toe !
Waltz—Waltz alone—both legs and arms
    demands,
Liberal of feet, and lavish of her hands.
   b.   Byron—*The Waltz.* L. 109.

Hot from the hands promiscuously applied,
Round the slight waist, or down the glowing
    side.
   c.   Byron—*The Waltz.* L. 234.

Imperial Waltz ! imported from the Rhine
(Famed for the growth of pedigrees and wine),
Long be thine import from all duty free,
And hock itself be less esteem'd than thee.
   d.   Byron—*The Waltz.* L. 29.

On with the dance ! let joy be unconfin'd ;
No sleep till morn, when Youth and Pleasure
    meet.
   e.   Byron—*Childe Harold.* Canto III.
                           St. 22.

The rout is Folly's circle, which she draws
With magic wand. So potent is the spell,
That none decoy'd into that fatal ring,
Unless by Heaven's peculiar grace, escape.
There we grow early gray, but never wise.
   f.   Cowper—*Task.* Bk. II. L. 627.

Such pains, such pleasures now alike are o'er,
And beaus and etiquette shall soon exist no
    more
  At their speed behold advancing
  Modern men and women dancing ;
Step and dress alike express
Above, below from heel to toe,
Male and female awkwardness.
Without a hoop, without a ruffle,
One eternal jig and shuffle,
Where's the air and where's the gait?
Where's the feather in the hat ?
Where the frizzed toupee? and where
Oh ! where's the powder for the hair ?
   g.   Catherine Fanshawe—*The Abrogation*
              of the Birth-Night Ball.

    To brisk notes in cadence beating
Glance their many-twinkling feet.
   h.   Gray—*Progress of Poesy.* Pt. I.
                   St. 3. L. 10.

Alike all ages : dames of ancient days
Have led their children through the mirthful
    maze ;
And the gay grandsire, skill'd in gestic lore,
Has frisk'd beneath the burden of threescore.
   i.   Goldsmith—*Traveller.* L. 251.

And the dancing has begun now,
And the dancers whirl round gaily
In the waltz's giddy mazes,
And the ground beneath them trembles.
   j.   Heine—*Book of Songs. Don Ramiro.*
                          St. 23.

Twelve dancers are dancing, and taking no
    rest,
And closely their hands together are press'd ;
And soon as a dance has come to a close,
Another begins, and each merrily goes.
   k.   Heine—*Dream and Life.*

Merrily, merrily whirled the wheels of the
    dizzying dances
Under the orchard-trees and down the path to
    the meadows ;
Old folk and young together, and children
    mingled among them.
   l.   Longfellow—*Evangeline.* Pt. I. IV.

        He who esteems the Virginia reel
A bait to draw saints from their spiritual weal,
And regards the quadrille as a far greater
    knavery
Than crushing His African children with
    slavery,
Since all who take part in a waltz or cotillon
Are mounted for hell on the devil's own pillion,
Who, as every true orthodox Christian well
    knows,
Approaches the heart through the door of the
    toes.
   m.   Lowell—*A Fable for Critics.* L. 492.

Come and trip it as ye go,
On the light fantastic toe.
   n.   Milton—*L'Allegro.* L. 33.

Come, knit hands, and beat the ground
In a light fantastic round.
   o.   Milton—*Comus.* L. 143.

Dancing in the chequer'd shade.
   p.   Milton—*L'Allegro.* L. 96.

        Dear creature !—you'd swear
When her delicate feet in the dance twinkle
    round,
That her steps are of light, that her home is
    the air,
And she only *par complaisance* touches the
    ground.
   q.   Moore—*The Fudge Family in Paris.*
                   Letter V. L. 50.

Oh ! if to dance all night, and dress all day,
Charm'd the small-pox, or chas'd old age
   away ;

*   *   *   *   *   *

To patch, nay ogle, might become a saint,
Nor could it sure be such a sin to paint.
> a.   POPE—*Rape of the Lock.* Canto V.
> L. 19.

Others import yet nobler arts from France,
Teach kings to fiddle, and make senates dance.
> b.   POPE—*Dunciad.* Bk. IV. L. 597.

I know the romance, since it's over,
  'Twere idle, or worse, to recall ;—
I know you're a terrible rover ;
  But, Clarence, you'll come to our ball.
> c.   PRAED—*Our Ball.*

I saw her at a country ball ;
  There when the sound of flute and fiddle
Gave signal sweet in that old hall,
  Of hands across and down the middle,
Hers was the subtlest spell by far
  Of all that sets young hearts romancing :
She was our queen, our rose, our star ;
  And when she danced—oh, heaven, her
    dancing !
> d.   PRAED—*The Belle of the Ball.*

He, perfect dancer, climbs the rope,
And balances your fear and hope.
> e.   PRIOR—*Alma, or the Progress of the
> Mind.* Canto II. L. 9.

Once on a time, the wight Stupidity
For his throne trembled,
When he discovered in the brains of men
Something like thoughts assembled,
And so he searched for a plausible plan-
One of validity,—
And racked his brains, if rack his brains he can
None having, or a very few !
At last he hit upon a way
For putting to rout,
And driving out
From our dull clay
These same intruders new—
This Sense, these Thoughts, these Speculative
  ills—
What could he do? He introduced quadrilles.
> f.   RUSKIN—*The Invention of Quadrilles.*

   They have measured many a mile,
To tread a measure with you on this grass.
> g.   *Love's Labour's Lost.* Act V. Sc. 2.
> L. 186.

   When you do dance, I wish you
A wave o' th' sea, that you might ever do
Nothing but that.
> h.   *Winter's Tale.* Act IV. Sc. 4. L. 140.

While his off-heel, insidiously aside,
Provokes the caper which he seems to chide.
> i.   SHERIDAN—*Pizarro.* *The Prologue.*

9

But O, she dances such a way !
No sun upon an Easter-day,
Is half so fine a sight.
> j.   SIR JOHN SUCKLING—*A Ballad Upon a
> Wedding.* St. 8.

And beautiful maidens moved down in the
  dance,
With the magic of motion and sunshine of
  glance ;
And white arms wreathed lightly, and tresses
  fell free
As the plumage of birds in some tropical tree.
> k.   WHITTIER—*Cities of the Plain.* St. 4.

DANGER.

I have not quailed to danger's brow
When high and happy—need I now ?
> l.   BYRON—*Giaour.* L. 1,035.

A daring pilot in extremity ;
Pleas'd with the danger, when the waves
  went high
He sought the storms.
> m.   DRYDEN—*Absalom and Achitophel.*
> Pt. I. L. 159.

   When the judges shall be obliged to go
armed, it will be time for the courts to be
closed.
> n.   S. J. FIELD—(*When advised to arm
> himself. California.* 1889).

We are dancing on a volcano.
> o.   COMTE DE SALVANDY—*At a fête given to
> the King of Naples.* 1830.

For though I am not splenitive and rash,
Yet have I something in me dangerous.
> p.   *Hamlet.* Act V. Sc. 1. L. 285.

Out of this nettle, danger, we pluck this
  flower, safety.
> q.   *Henry IV.* Pt. I. Act II. Sc. 3.
> L. 10.

Some of us will smart for it.
> r.   *Much Ado About Nothing.* Act V.
> Sc. 1. L. 109.

There is, betwixt that smile we would aspire
  to,
That sweet aspect of princes, and their ruin,
More pangs and fears than war or women
  have.
> s.   *Henry VIII.* Act III. Sc. 2. L. 368.

   Upon this hint I spake ;
She loved me for the dangers I had passed
And I loved her that she did pity them.
> t.   *Othello.* Act I. Sc. 3. L. 166.

We have scotched the snake, not killed it :
She'll close and be herself, whilst our poor
  malice
Remains in danger of our former tooth.
> u.   *Macbeth.* Act III. Sc. 2. L. 13.

Too much wit makes the world rotten.
   a.   Tennyson—*Idylls of the King. The Last Tournament.*

Time flies, Death urges, knells call, Heaven
   invites,
Hell threatens.
   b.   Young—*Night Thoughts.* Night II.
   L. 291.

DARING.

A decent boldness ever meets with friends.
   c.   Homer—*The Odyssey.* Pope's trans.
   Bk. 7. L. 67.

And what he greatly thought, he nobly dared.
   d.   Homer—*The Odyssey.* Pope's trans.
   Bk. II. L. 312.

And what they dare to dream of, dare to do.
   e.   Lowell—*Ode Recited at the Harvard Commemoration.* July 21, 1865.
   St. 3.

He either fears his fate too much,
   Or his deserts are small,
That dares not put it to the touch
   To gain or lose it all.
   f.   Marquis of Montrose—*My Dear and Only Love.*

Who dares this pair of boots displace,
Must meet Bombastes face to face.
   g.   William B. Rhodes—*Bombastes Furioso.* Act I. Sc. 4.

   And dar'st thou then
To beard the lion in his den,
The Douglas in his hall?
   h.   Scott—*Marmion.* Canto VI. St. 14.

He that climbs the tall tree has won right to
   the fruit,
He that leaps the wide gulf should prevail in
   his suit.
   i.   Scott—*The Bloody Vest.* See *Talisman.*
   Ch. XXVI.

   What man dare, I dare :
Approach thou like the rugged Russian bear,
The arm'd rhinoceros, or the Hyrcan tiger;
Take any shape but that, and my firm nerves
Shall never tremble.
   j.   *Macbeth.* Act III. Sc. IV. L. 99.

Be bolde, be bolde, and everywhere, be bolde.
   k.   Spenser—*Faerie Queene.* Bk. III.
   Canto XI. St. 54.

DARKNESS.

The waves were dead ; the tides were in their
   grave,
The Moon, their Mistress, had expired before ;
The winds were wither'd in the stagnant air,
And the clouds perish'd ; darkness had no
   need
Of aid from them—she was the Universe.
   l.   Byron—*Darkness.*

Darkness of slumber and death, forever sinking and sinking.
   m.   Longfellow—*Evangeline.* Pt. II.
   V. L. 108.

The prayer of Ajax was for light;
Through all that dark and desperate fight,
The blackness of that noonday night.
   n.   Longfellow—*The Goblet of Life.*

Lo ! darkness bends down like a mother of
   grief
On the limitless plain, and the fall of her hair
It has mantled a world.
   o.   Joaquin Miller—*From Sea to Sea.*
   St. 4.

   Yet from those flames
No light, but rather darkness visible.
   p.   Milton—*Paradise Lost.* Bk. I. L. 62.

Brief as the lightning in the collied night,
That, in a spleen, unfolds both heaven and
   earth,
And ere a man had power to say, Behold !
The jaws of darkness do devour it up.
   q.   *Midsummer Night's Dream.* Act I.
   Sc. 1. L. 144.

I charge thee, Satan, hous'd within this man,
To yield possession to my holy prayers,
And to thy state of darkness hie thee straight ;
I conjure thee by all the saints in heaven!
   r.   *Comedy of Errors.* Act IV. Sc. 4.
   L. 57.

   The charm dissolves apace,
And as the morning steals upon the night,
Melting the darkness, so their rising senses
Begin to chase the ignorant fumes that mantle
Their clearer reason.
   s.   *Tempest.* Act V. Sc. 1. L. 64.

DAY.

Day is a snow-white Dove of heaven
   That from the East glad message brings :
Night is a stealthy, evil Raven,
   Wrapt to the eyes in his black wings.
   t.   T. B. Aldrich—*Day and Night.*

The long days are no happier than the short
   ones.
   u.   Bailey—*Festus.* Sc. *A Village Feast. Evening.*

Day !
Faster and more fast,
O'er night's brim, day boils at last;
Boils, pure gold, o'er the cloud-cup's brim.
   v.   Robert Browning—*Introduction to Pippa Passes*

Days, that need borrow
No part of their good morrow
From a fore-spent night of sorrow.
   w.   Richard Crashaw—*Wishes to His (Supposed) Mistress.*

Sweet day, so cool, so calm, so bright,
  The bridal of the earth and sky,
The dew shall weep thy fall to-night;
  For thou must die.
  a.   HERBERT—*The Temple. Virtue.*

O sweet, delusive Noon,
  Which the morning climbs to find,
O moment sped too soon,
  And morning left behind.
  b.   HELEN HUNT—*Verses. Noon.*

O summer day beside the joyous sea!
O summer day so wonderful and white,
So full of gladness and so full of pain!
Forever and forever shalt thou be
To some the gravestone of a dead delight,
To some the landmark of a new domain.
  c.   LONGFELLOW—*Summer Day by the Sea.*

Hide me from day's garish eye.
  d.   MILTON—*Il Penseroso. L. 141.*

Blest power of sunshine!—genial day,
What balm, what life is in thy ray!
To feel there is such real bliss,
That had the world no joy but this,
To sit in sunshine calm and sweet,—
It were a world too exquisite
For man to leave it for the gloom,
The deep, cold shadow, of the tomb.
  e.   MOORE—*Lalla Rookh.   The Fire
                                    Worshippers.*

O, how glorious is Noon-day!
With the cool large shadows lying
Underneath the giant forest,
The far hill-tops towering dimly
    O'er the conquered plains below.
  f.   D. M. MULOCK—*A Stream's Singing.*

The evening red, the morning gray
Are certain signs of a fair day.
  g.   *Old Weather Rhyme.*

How troublesome is day!
It calls us from our sleep away;
It bids us from our pleasant dreams awake,
And sends us forth to keep or break
    Our promises to pay.
How troublesome is day!
  h.   THOMAS LOVE PEACOCK—*Fly-By-Night.*
            (Paper Money Lyrics.)

Sweet Phosphor, bring the day!
Light will repay
The wrongs of night; sweet Phosphor, bring
    the day!
  i.   QUARLES—*Emblems.   Bk. 1.   Em. 14.
                                        St. 5.*

Sweet Phosphor, bring the day
Whose conquering ray
May chase these fogs; sweet Phosphor, bring
    the day!
  j.   QUARLES—*Emblems.   Bk. I.   Em. 14.
                                        St. 1.*

          O, such a day,
So fought, so follow'd and so fairly won.
  k.   *Henry IV.   Pt. II.   Act I.   Sc. 1.
                                        L. 20.*

The sun is in the heaven, and the proud day,
Attended with the pleasures of the world,
Is all too wanton.
  l.   *King John.   Act III.   Sc. 3.   L. 34.*

What hath this day deserv'd? what hath it
    done,
That it in golden letters should be set
Among the high tides in the calendar?
  m.   *King John.   Act III.   Sc. 1.   L. 84.*

Day is the Child of Time,
And Day must cease to be:
But Night is without a sire,
And cannot expire,
One with Eternity.
  n.   R. H. STODDARD—*Day and Night.*

" A day for Gods to stoop," * * * ay,
And men to soar.
  o.   TENNYSON—*The Lover's Tale.   L. 304.*

One of those heavenly days that cannot die.
  p.   WORDSWORTH—*Nutting.*

"I've lost a day"—the prince who nobly
    cried,
Had been an emperor without his crown.
  q.   YOUNG—*Night Thoughts.   Night II.
                                        L. 99.*

The spirit walks of every day deceased.
  r.   YOUNG—*Night Thoughts.   Night II.
                                        L. 180.*

DEATH.

Death is a black camel, which kneels at the
gates of all.
  s.   ABD-EL-KADER.

This is the last of earth! I am content.
  t.   JOHN QUINCY ADAMS—*His Last Words.*
            (*Memoirs of Life of John Quincy
                Adams by Josiah Quincy.*)

But when the sun in all his state,
  Illumed the eastern skies,
She passed through glory's morning gate,
  And walked in Paradise.
  u.   JAMES ALDRICH—*A Death Bed.*

He who died at Azan sends
This to comfort all his friends:

Faithful friends! It lies I know
Pale and white and cold as snow;
And ye say, "Abdallah's dead!"
Weeping at the feet and head.
I can see your falling tears,
I can hear your sighs and prayers;
Yet I smile and whisper this:
I am not the thing you kiss.
Cease your tears and let it lie;
It was mine—it is not I.
  v.   EDWIN ARNOLD—*He Who Died at Azan.*

It is as natural to die as to be born; and to a little infant, perhaps, the one is as painful as the other.

a.   BACON—*Essays. Of Death.*

Men fear Death, as children fear to go in the dark; and as that natural fear in children is increased with tales, so is the other.

b.   BACON—*Essays. Of Death.*

What then remains, but that we still should cry
Not to be born, or being born to die.

c.   *Ascribed to* BACON. (*Pharaphrase of a Greek Epigram.*)

Death is the universal salt of states;
Blood is the base of all things—law and war.

d.   BAILEY—*Festus. Sc. A Country Town.*

The death-change comes.
Death is another life. We bow our heads
At going out, we think, and enter straight
Another golden chamber of the king's,
Larger than this we leave, and lovelier.
And then in shadowy glimpses, disconnect,
The story, flower-like, closes thus its leaves.
The will of God is all in all. He makes,
Destroys, remakes, for His own pleasure, all.

e.   BAILEY—*Festus. Sc. Home.*

So fades a summer cloud away;
So sinks the gale when storms are o'er;
So gently shuts the eye of day;
So dies a wave along the shore.

f.   MRS. BARBAULD—*The Death of the Virtuous.*

It is only the dead who do not return.

g.   BERTRAND BARÈRE—*Speech.* 1794.

But whether on the scaffold high,
Or in the battle's van,
The fittest place where man can die
Is where he dies for man.

h.   MICHAEL J. BARRY—*The Dublin Nation.*
        Sept. 28, 1844. Vol. II. P. 809.

Death hath so many doors to let out life.

i.   BEAUMONT AND FLETCHER—*The Custom of the Country.* Act II. Sc. 2.

We must all die!
All leave ourselves, it matters not where, when,
Nor how, so we die well; and can that man that does so
Need lamentation for him?

j.   BEAUMONT AND FLETCHER—*Valentinian.* Act IV. Sc. 4.

How shocking must thy summons be, O Death!
To him that is at ease in his possessions:
Who, counting on long years of pleasure here,
Is quite unfurnish'd for that world to come!

k.   BLAIR—*The Grave.* L. 350.

Sure 'tis a serious thing to die! My soul!
What a strange moment must it be, when, near
Thy journey's end, thou hast the gulf in view!
That awful gulf, no mortal e'er repass'd
To tell what's doing on the other side.

l.   BLAIR—*The Grave.* L. 369.

'Tis long since Death had the majority.

m.   BLAIR—*The Grave.* L. 451.

The thousand doors that lead to death.

n.   SIR THOMAS BROWNE—*Religio Medici.*
        Pt. I. Sec. XLIV.

For I say, this is death and the sole death,
When a man's loss comes to him from his gain,
Darkness from light, from knowledge ignorance,
And lack of love from love made manifest.

o.   ROBERT BROWNING—*A Death in the Desert.*

But, oh! fell Death's untimely frost,
That nipt my flower sae early.

p.   BURNS—*Highland Mary.*

Friend Ralph! thou hast
Outrun the constable at last!

q.   BUTLER—*Hudibras.* Pt. I. Canto III.
        L. 1,367.

All that tread
The globe are but a handful to the tribes
That slumber in its bosom.

r.   BRYANT—*Thanatopsis.*

Ah! surely nothing dies but something mourns!

s.   BYRON—*Don Juan.* Canto III.
        St. 108.

Death, so called, is a thing which makes men weep,
And yet a third of life is pass'd in sleep.

t.   BYRON—*Don Juan.* Canto XIV.
        St. 3.

Down to the dust!—and, as thou rott'st away,
Even worms shall perish on thy poisonous clay.

u.   BYRON—*A Sketch.*

Heaven gives its favourites—early death.

v.   BYRON—*Childe Harold.* Canto IV.
        St. 102. *Also Don Juan.* Canto IV.
        St. 12.

He who hath bent him o'er the dead
Ere the first day of death is fled,
The first dark day of nothingness,
The last of danger and distress,
(Before Decay's effacing fingers
Have swept the lines where beauty lingers)
And mark'd the mild angelic air,
The rapture of repose that's there.

w.   BYRON—*The Giaour.* L. 68.

Oh, God! it is a fearful thing
To see the human soul take wing
In any shape, in any mood!

a.   BYRON—*Prisoner of Chillon.* St. 8.

Without a grave, unknell'd, uncoffin'd, and
  unknown.

b.   BYRON—*Childe Harold.* Canto IV.
St. 179.

Brougham delivered a very warm panegyric
upon the ex-Chancellor, and expressed a hope
that he would make a good end, although to
an expiring Chancellor death was now armed
with a new terror.

c.   CAMPBELL—*Lives of the Chancellors.*
Vol. VII. P. 163.

At length, fatigued with life, he bravely fell,
And health with Boerhaave bade the world
  farewell.

d.   BENJ. CHURCH—*The Choice.* 1754.

Some men make a womanish complaint
that it is a great misfortune to die before our
time. I would ask what time? Is it that of
Nature? But she, indeed, has lent us life, as
we do a sum or money, only no certain day
is fixed for payment. What reason then to
complain if she demands it at pleasure, since
it was on this condition that you received it.

e.   CICERO.

Let us not doubt that God has a father's
pity towards us, and that in the removal of
that which is dearest to us He is still loving
and kind. Death separates, but it also unites.
It reunites whom it separates.

f.   ABRAHAM COLES—*Memorial Volume.*

Thank God for death: bright thing with
  dreary name,
We wrong with mournful flowers her pure,
  still brow.

g.   SUSAN COOLIDGE—*Benedicam Domino.*

All flesh is grass, and all its glory fades
Like the fair flower dishevell'd in the wind;
Riches have wings, and grandeur is a dream;
The man we celebrate must find a tomb,
And we that worship him, ignoble graves.

h.   COWPER—*Task.* Bk. III. L. 261.

Round, round the cypress bier
  Where she lies sleeping,
On every turf a tear,
  Let us go weeping!
          Wail!

i.   GEORGE DARLEY—*Dirge.*

And though mine arm should conquer
  twenty worlds,
There's a lean fellow beats all conquerors.

j.   THOMAS DEKKER—*Old Fortunatus.*
Act I. Sc. 1.

Death, be not proud, though some have called
  thee
Mighty and dreadful, for thou art not so:
For those, whom thou think'st thou dost
  overthrow,
Die not, poor Death.

k.   DONNE—*Divine Poems.* *Holy Sonnets.*
No. 17.

Death in itself is nothing; but we fear
To be we know not what, we know not where.

l.   DRYDEN—*Aurengzebe.* Act IV. Sc. 1.

He was exhal'd; his great Creator drew
His spirit, as the sun the morning dew.

m.   DRYDEN—*On the Death of a Very Young
Gentleman.*

Like a led victim, to my death I'll go,
And, dying, bless the hand that gave the
  blow.

n.   DRYDEN—*The Spanish Friar.* Act II.
Sc. 1. L. 64.

Of no distemper, of no blast he died,
But fell like autumn fruit that mellow'd long.

o.   DRYDEN—*Œdipus.* Act IV. Sc. 1.
L. 265.

Xerxes the great did die;
And so must you and I.

p.   From the New England Primer. 1814.

Death is the king of this world: 'tis his park
Where he breeds life to feed him. Cries of
  pain
Are music for his banquet.

q.   GEORGE ELIOT—*Spanish Gypsy.*
Bk. II.

Good-bye, proud world! I'm going home:
Thou art not my friend, and I'm not thine.

r.   EMERSON—*Good-Bye.*

He thought it happier to be dead,
To die for Beauty, than live for bread.

s.   EMERSON—*Beauty.* L. 25.

Drawing near her death, she sent most pious
thoughts as harbingers to heaven; and her
soul saw a glimpse of happiness through the
chinks of her sicknesse broken body.

t.   FULLER—*The Holy and the Profane
State.* Bk. I. Ch. II.

To die is landing on some silent shore,
Where billows never break nor tempests roar;
Ere well we feel the friendly stroke 'tis o'er.

u.   SIR SAMUEL GARTH—*The Dispensary.*
Canto III. L. 225.

The prince who kept the world in awe,
The judge whose dictate fix'd the law;
The rich, the poor, the great, the small,
Are levell'd; death confounds 'em all.

v.   GAY—*Fables.* Pt. II. Fable 16.

Where the brass knocker, wrapt in flannel
        band,
Forbids the thunder of the footman's hand,
Th' upholder, rueful harbinger of death,
Waits with impatience for the dying breath.
   a.   GAY—*Trivia.* Bk. II L. 467.

None who e'er knew her can believe her dead;
Though, should she die, they deem it well
        might be
Her spirit took its everlasting flight
In summer's glory, by the sunset sea,
That onward through the Golden Gate is fled.
Ah, where that bright soul is cannot be night.
   b.   R. W. GILDER—"*H. H.*"

What if thou be saint or sinner,
Crooked gray-beard, straight beginner,—
Empty paunch, or jolly dinner,
   When Death thee shall call.
All alike are rich and richer,
King with crown, and cross-legged stitcher,
   When the grave hides all.
   c.   R. W. GILDER—*Drinking Song.*

Ye living soldiers of the mighty war,
   Once more from roaring cannon and the
        drums
   And bugles blown at morn, the summons
        comes;
Forget the halting limb, each wound and
        scar:
   Once more your Captain calls to you;
   Come to his last review!
   d.   R. W. GILDER—*The Burial of Grant.*

Can storied urn or animated bust
   Back to its mansion call the fleeting breath?
Can honour's voice provoke the silent dust,
   Or flattery soothe the dull cold ear of death?
   e.   GRAY—*Elegy.* St. 11.

The living throne, the sapphire blaze,
Where angels tremble while they gaze,
He saw; but blasted with excess of light,
Closed his eyes in endless night.
   f.   GRAY—*Progress of Poesy.* III. 2.
                       L. 99.

Fling but a stone, the giant dies.
   g.   MATTHEW GREEN—*The Spleen.* L. 93.

Death borders upon our birth; and our
cradle stands in our grave.
   h.   BISHOP HALL—*Epistles.* Decade III.
                      Ep. II.

Come to the bridal-chamber, Death!
   Come to the mother's, when she feels,
For the first time, her first-born's breath!
   Come when the blessed seals
That close the pestilence are broke,
And crowded cities wail its stroke!
   i.   FITZ-GREENE HALLECK—*Marco*
                      Bozzaris.

Come when the heart beats high and warm,
   With banquet-song, and dance and wine;
And thou art terrible,—the tear,
   The groan, the knell, the pall, the bier;
And all we know, or dream, or fear
   Of agony, are thine.
   j.   FITZ-GREENE HALLECK—*Marco*
                      Bozzaris.

                Ere the dolphin dies
Its hues are brightest. Like an infant's
        breath
Are tropic winds before the voice of death.
   k.   FITZ-GREENE HALLECK—*Fortune.*

The ancients dreaded death: the Christian
can only fear dying.
   l.   J. C. and A. W. HARE—*Guesses at*
                      Truth.

On a lone barren isle, where the wild roaring
        billows
   Assail the stern rock, and the loud tempests
        rave,
The hero lies still, while the dew-drooping
        willows,
   Like fond weeping mourners, lean over his
        grave.
The lightnings may flash and the loud thun-
        ders rattle;
   He heeds not, he hears not; he's free from
        all pain.
He sleeps his last sleep, he has fought his last
        battle;
   No sound can awake him to glory again!
   m.   LEONARD HEATH—*The Grave of*
                      Bonaparte.

Death rides on every passing breeze,
He lurks in every flower.
   n.   BISHOP HEBER—*At a Funeral.* St. 3.

Dust, to its narrow house beneath!
   Soul, to its place on high!
They that have seen thy look in death,
   No more may fear to die.
   o.   MRS. HEMANS—*A Dirge. Calm on the*
                Bosom of thy God.

Leaves have their time to fall,
And flowers to wither at the north wind's
        breath,
   And stars to set—but all.
Thou hast all seasons for thine own, O Death.
   p.   MRS. HEMANS—*The Hour of Death.*

The mossy marbles rest
On the lips that he has pressed
   In their bloom;
And the names he loved to hear
Have been carved for many a year
   On the tomb.
   q.   O. W. HOLMES—*The Last Leaf.*

And they die
An equal death,—the idler and the man
Of mighty deeds.
    a.   Homer—*The Iliad.* Bk. IX. L. 396.
                     Bryant's trans.

He slept an iron sleep,—
Slain fighting for his country.
    b.   Homer—*The Iliad.* Bk. XI. L. 285.
                     Bryant's trans.

Then Sleep and Death, two twins of winged
    race,
Of matchless swiftness, but of silent pace.
    c.   Homer—*The Iliad.* Bk. XVI. L. 831.
                     Pope's trans.

One more unfortunate
    Weary of breath,
Rashly importunate,
    Gone to her death!
    d.   Hood—*Bridge of Sighs.*

We watch'd her breathing thro' the night,
    Her breathing soft and low,
As in her breast the wave of life
    Kept heaving to and fro.
    *   *   *   *   *   *
Our very hopes belied our fears,
    Our fears our hopes belied;
We thought her dying when she slept,
    And sleeping when she died.
    e.   Hood—*The Death-bed.*

Then with no fiery throbbing pain,
    No cold gradations of decay,
Death broke at once the vital chain,
    And freed his soul the nearest way.
    f.   Sam'l Johnson—*Verses on the Death of*
                 Mr. Robert Levet. St. 9.

Strange—is it not?—that of the myriads who
Before us passed the door of Darkness through,
Not one returns to tell us of the road
Which to discover we must travel too.
    g.   Omar Khayyam—*Rubaiyat.* St. 68.

The world will turn when we are earth
    As though we had not come nor gone;
There was no lack before our birth,
    When we are gone there will be none.
    h.   Omar Khayyam. Bodenstedt's trans.

The merry, merry lark was up and singing,
    And the hare was out and feeding on the
        lea;
And the merry, merry bells below were
        ringing,
    When my child's laugh rang through me.
Now the hare is snared and dead beside the
        snow-yard,
    And the lark beside the dreary winter sea;
And the baby in his cradle in the churchyard
    Sleeps sound till the bell brings me.
    i.   Charles Kingsley—*A Lament.*

Gone before
To that unknown and silent shore.
    j.   Charles Lamb—*Hester.* St. 1.

One destin'd period men in common have,
The great, the base, the coward, and the
    brave,
All food alike for worms, companions in the
    grave.
    k.   Lord Lansdowne—*Meditation on*
                          Death.

And, as she looked around, she saw how
    Death, the consoler,
Laying his hand upon many a heart, had
    healed it forever.
    l.   Longfellow—*Evangeline.* Pt. II. V.

Death never takes one alone, but two!
Whenever he enters in at a door,
Under roof of gold or roof of thatch,
He always leaves it upon the latch,
And comes again ere the year is o'er,
Never one of a household only.
    m.   Longfellow—*Christus.* *The Golden*
               Legend. Pt. VI. *The Farm-House*
                     in the Odenwald.

Oh, what hadst thou to do with cruel Death,
Who wast so full of life, or Death with thee,
That thou shouldst die before thou hadst
    grown old!
    n.   Longfellow—*Three Friends of Mine.*
                          Pt. II.

Then fell upon the house a sudden gloom,
    A shadow on those features fair and thin;
And softly, from that hushed and darkened
    room,
    Two angels issued, where but one went in.
    o.   Longfellow—*The Two Angels.* St. 9.

There is a Reaper whose name is Death,
    And with his sickle keen,
He reaps the bearded grain at a breath,
    And the flowers that grow between.
    p.   Longfellow—*The Reaper and the*
                        Flowers.

There is no confessor like unto Death!
    Thou canst not see him, but he is near:
Thou needest not whisper above thy breath,
    And he will hear;
He will answer the questions,
    The vague surmises and suggestions,
    That fill thy soul with doubt and fear.
    q.   Longfellow—*Christus.* *The Golden*
               Legend. Pt. V. *The Inn at Genoa.*

There is no Death! What seems so is transi-
    tion;
    This life of mortal breath
Is but a suburb of the life elysian,
    Whose portal we call Death.
    r.   Longfellow—*Resignation.*

There is no flock, however watched and
    tended,
    But one dead lamb is there!
There is no fireside howsoe'er defended,
    But has one vacant chair.
  a.   LONGFELLOW—*Resignation.*

The young may die, but the old must!
  b.   LONGFELLOW—*Christus. The Golden*
                  Legend. Pt. IV. The Cloisters.

But life is sweet, though all that makes it
    sweet
Lessen like sound of friends' departing feet;
And Death is beautiful as feet of friend
Coming with welcome at our journey's end.
  c.   LOWELL—*An Epistle to George William*
                           Curtis.

Though in midst of life we be
Snares of death surround us.
  d.   MARTIN LUTHER—*Hymn XVIII.*

To every man upon this earth
    Death cometh soon or late,
And how can man die better
    Than facing fearful odds,
For the ashes of his fathers
    And the temples of his gods?
  e.   MACAULAY—*Lays of Ancient Rome.*
                     Horatius. XXVII.

I want to meet my God awake.
  f.   CARLYLE *attributes the saying to* MARIA
        THERESA, *who refused to take*
        morphine.

She thought our good-night kiss was given,
    And like a lily her life did close;
    Angels uncurtain'd that repose,
And the next waking dawn'd in heaven.
  g.   GERALD MASSEY—*The Ballad of Babe*
                      Christabel.

Death hath a thousand doors to let out life.
I shall find one.
  h.   MASSINGER—*A Very Woman. Act V.*
                         Sc. 4.

There's nothing certain in man's life but this:
That he must lose it.
  i.   OWEN MEREDITH (Lord Lytton)—
           Clytemnestra. Pt. XX.

Death is delightful. Death is dawn,
The waking from a weary night
Of fevers unto truth and light.
  j.   JOAQUIN MILLER—*Even So. St. 35.*

           They are fair resting-places
For the dear, weary dead on their way up to
    heaven.
  k.   JOAQUIN MILLER—*Ina. Sc. 1.*

And over them triumphant Death his dart
Shook, but delay'd to strike, though oft
    invoked.
  l.   MILTON—*Paradise Lost. Bk. XI.*
                         L. 491.

Before mine eyes in opposition sits
Grim Death, my son and foe.
  m.   MILTON—*Paradise Lost. Bk. II.*
                         L. 803.

           Behind her Death
Close following pace for pace, not mounted
    yet
On his pale horse.
  n.   MILTON—*Paradise Lost. Bk. X.*
                         L. 588.

               Death
Grinned horrible a ghastly smile, to hear
His famine should be filled.
  o.   MILTON—*Paradise Lost. Bk. II.*
                         L. 845.

            Eas'd the putting off
These troublesome disguises which we wear.
  p.   MILTON—*Paradise Lost. Bk. IV.*
                         L. 739.

          I fled, and cried out Death;
Hell trembled at the hideous name, and
    sigh'd
From all her caves, and back resounded
    Death.
  q.   MILTON—*Paradise Lost. Bk. II.*
                         L. 787.

O fairest flower; no sooner blown but blasted,
Soft, silken primrose fading timelessly.
  r.   MILTON—*Ode on the Death of a Fair*
                Infant Dying of a Cough.

So spake the grisly Terror.
  s.   MILTON—*Paradise Lost. Bk. II.*
                         L. 704.

           That golden key
That opes the palace of eternity.
  t.   MILTON—*Comus. L. 13.*

There's nothing terrible in death;
    'Tis but to cast our robes away,
And sleep at night, without a breath
    To break repose till dawn of day.
  u.   MONTGOMERY—*In Memory of E. G.*

Weep not for those whom the veil of the
    tomb
    In life's happy morning hath hid from our
      eyes,
Ere sin threw a blight o'er the spirit's young
    bloom,
    Or earth had profaned what was born for the
      skies.
  v.   MOORE—*Song. Weep not for Those.*

But since, howe'er protracted, death will come
Why fondly study, with ingenious pains,
To put it off?—To breathe a little longer
Is to defer our fate, but not to shun it.
  w.   HANNAH MORE—*David and Goliath.*

How short is human life! the very breath,
Which frames my words, accelerates my
    death.
   a.   HANNAH MORE—*King Hezekiah.*

Two hands upon the breast,
   And labor's done;
Two pale feet cross'd in rest,
   The race is won.
   b.   D. M. MULOCK—*Now and Afterwards.*

And die with decency.
   c.   THOMAS OTWAY—*Venice Preserved.*
                    Act V. Sc. 3.

Death's but a path that must be trod,
If man would ever pass to God.
   d.   PARNELL—*A Night-Piece on Death.*
                       L. 67.

What shall we do now, Mary being dead,
   Or say, or write, that shall express the half?
What can we do but pillow that fair head,
   And let the springtime write her epitaph?
   e.   THOMAS WM. PARSONS—*Dirge.*

Death comes to all. His cold and sapless
    hand
Waves o'er the world, and beckons us away.
Who shall resist the summons?
   f.   THOMAS LOVE PEACOCK—*Time.*

O lady, he is dead and gone!
   Lady, he's dead and gone!
And at his head a green grass turfe,
   And at his heels a stone.
   g.   THOS. PERCY—*Reliques. The Friar of*
                          Orders Gray.

For death betimes is comfort, not dismay,
And who can rightly die needs no delay.
   h.   PETRARCH—*To Laura in Death.*
                      Canzone V. St. 6.

Come! let the burial rite be read—
   The funeral song be sung!—
An anthem for the queenliest dead
   That ever died so young—
A dirge for her, the doubly dead
   In that she died so young.
   i.   POE—*Lenore.* St. 1.

Out—out are the lights—out all!
 , And, over each quivering form,
The curtain, a funeral pall,
   Comes down with the rush of a storm,
And the angels, all pallid and wan,
   Uprising, unveiling, affirm
That the play is the tragedy, "Man,"
   And its hero the Conqueror Worm.
   j.   POE—*The Conqueror Worm.* St. 5.

A heap of dust alone remains of thee;
'Tis all thou art, and all the proud shall be!
   k.   POPE—*Elegy to the Memory of an*
                Unfortunate Lady. L. 73.

But thousands die without or this or that,
Die, and endow a college or a cat.
   l.   POPE—*Moral Essays.* Ep. III. L. 95.

By foreign hands thy dying eyes were clos'd,
By foreign hands thy decent limbs| compos'd,
By foreign hands thy humble grave adorn'd,
By strangers honour'd, and by strangers
   mourn'd.
   m.   POPE—*Elegy to the Memory of an*
                  Unfortunate Lady. L. 51.

O Death, all eloquent! you only prove
What dust we dote on, when 'tis man we
   love.
   n.   POPE—*Eloisa to Abelard.* L. 355.

See my lips tremble and my eyeballs roll,
Suck my last breath, and catch my flying
   soul!
   o.   POPE—*Eloisa to Abelard.* L. 323.

Tell me, my soul! can this be death?
   p.   POPE—*The Dying Christian to His Soul.*
                Paraphrased from Hadrian.

The world recedes; it disappears;
Heav'n opens on my eyes; my ears
   With sounds seraphic ring:
Lend, lend your wings! I mount! I fly!
O Grave! where is thy victory?
   O Death! where is thy sting?
   q.   POPE—*The Dying Christian to His Soul.*
                Paraphrased from Hadrian.

Till tired, he sleeps, and life's poor play is
o'er.
   r.   POPE—*Essay on Man.* Ep. II. L. 282.

              Teach him how to live,
And, oh! still harder lesson! how to die.
   s.   BISHOP PORTEUS—*Death.* L. 316.

Death aims with fouler spite
At fairer marks.
   t.   QUARLES—*Divine Poems.* Ed. 1669.

O eloquent, just, and mighty Death! whom
none could advise, thou hast persuaded;
what none hath dared, thou hast done; and
whom all the world hath flattered, thou only
hast cast out of the world and despised: thou
hast drawn together all the far stretchèd
greatness, all the pride, cruelty and ambition
of man, and covered it all over with these two
narrow words, Hic jacet!
   u.   SIR WALTER RALEIGH—*Historie of the*
             World. Bk. V. Pt. I. Ch. 6.

Not dead, but gone before.
   v.   SAM'L ROGERS—*Human Life.*

Sleep that no pain shall wake,
Night that no morn shall break,
Till joy shall overtake
   Her perfect peace.
  a.   Christina G. Rossetti—*Dream-Land.*
                St. 4.

There is no music more for him :
  His lights are out, his feast is done ;
His bowl that sparkled to the brim
  Is drained, is broken, cannot hold.
  b.   Christina G. Rossetti—*A Peal of*
                  Bells.

When I am dead, my dearest,
  Sing no sad songs for me ;
Plant thou no roses at my head,
  No shady cypress tree.
  c.   Christina G. Rossetti—*Song.*

Death is the privilege of human nature,
And life without it were not worth our
    taking :
Thither the poor, the pris'ner, and the
    mourner
Fly for relief, and lay their burthens down.
  d.   Nicholas Rowe—*The Fair Penitent.*
             Act V. Sc. 1. L. 138.

Oh, stanch thy bootlesse teares, thy weeping
    is in vaine ;
I am not lost, for we in heaven shall one day
    meet againe.
  e.   *Roxburghe Ballads. The Bride's*
        Buriall. Edited by Chas. Hindley.

Day's lustrous eyes grow heavy in sweet
    death.
  f.   Schiller—*The Assignation.* St. 4.
             Lord Lytton's trans.

Haste thee, haste thee, to be gone !
Earth flits fast and time draws on :
Gasp thy gasp, and groan thy groan !
Day is near the breaking.
  g.   Scott—*Death Chant.*

Like the dew on the mountain,
  Like the foam on the river,
Like the bubble on the fountain,
  Thou art gone, and for ever !
  h.   Scott—*Lady of the Lake.* Canto III.
                    St. 16.

Soon the shroud shall lap thee fast,
And the sleep be on thee cast
That shall ne'er know waking.
  i.   Scott—*Guy Mannering.* Ch. XXVII.

He whom we thought dead, is only gone be-
    fore us.
  j.   Seneca—*Consolatory, on the Death*
        of a Son. Ep. XCVII.

After life's fitful fever, he sleeps well ;
Treason has done his worst: nor steel, nor
    poison,
Malice domestic, foreign levy, nothing,
Can touch him further.
  k.   *Macbeth.* Act III. Sc. 2. L. 23.

A'made a finer end and went away an it
had been any christom child ; a' parted even
just between twelve and one, e'en at the turning o' th' tide : for after I saw him fumble
with the sheets, and play with flowers,
and smile upon his fingers' ends, I knew
there was but one way ; for his nose was as
sharp as a pen, and a' babbled of green fields.
"How now, Sir John ?" quoth I : "what,
man ! be o' good cheer." So a' cried out
"God, God, God !" three or four times. Now
I, to comfort him, bid him a' should not think
of God ; I hoped there was no need to trouble
himself with any such thoughts yet.
  l.   *Henry V.* Act II. Sc. 3. L. 12.

A man can die but once ; we owe God a
    death.
  m.   *Henry IV.* Pt. II. Act III. Sc. 2.
                    L. 250.

        And there at Venice gave
His body to that pleasant country's earth,
And his pure soul unto his captain Christ,
Under whose colours he had fought so long.
  n.   *Richard II.* Act IV. Sc. 1. L. 97.

And we shall feed like oxen at a stall,
The better cherish'd, still the nearer death.
  o.   *Henry IV.* Pt. I. Act V. Sc. 2.
                    L. 14.

Come away, come away, death,
  And in sad cypress let me be laid ;
Fly away, fly away, breath :
  I am slain by a fair cruel maid.
My shroud of white, stuck all with yew,
  Oh, prepare it !
My part of death no one so true
  Did share it.
  p.   *Twelfth Night.* Act II. Sc. 4. L. 52.

Cut off even in the blossoms of my sin,
Unhousel'd, disappointed, unanel'd ;
No reckoning made, but sent to my account
With all my imperfections on my head.
  q.   *Hamlet.* Act I. Sc. 5. L. 76.

              Dar'st thou die ?
The sense of death is most in apprehension ;
And the poor beetle that we tread upon,
In corporal sufferance feels a pang as great
As when a giant dies.
  r.   *Measure for Measure.* Act III. Sc. 1.
                    L. 77.

Death, a necessary end,
Will come when it will come.
  a.   *Julius Cæsar.* Act II. Sc. 2. L. 36.

Death, as the Psalmist saith, is certain to
all ; all shall die.
  b.   *Henry IV.* Pt. II. Act III. Sc. 2.
                                L. 41.

Death, death'; oh, amiable, lovely death !
     *   *   *   *   *   *
Come, grin on me, and I will think thou
    smilest.
  c.   *King John.* Act III. Sc. 4. D. 34.

Death lies on her, like an untimely frost
Upon the sweetest flower of all the field.
  d.   *Romeo and Juliet.* Act IV. Sc. 5. L. 28.

Death, that hath suck'd the honey of thy
    breath,
Hath had no power yet upon thy beauty ;
Thou art not conquer'd ; beauty's ensign yet
Is crimson in thy lips, and in thy cheeks,
And death's pale flag is not advanced there.
  e.   *Romeo and Juliet.* Act V. Sc. 3.
                                  L. 92.

                  Eyes, look your last !
Arms, take your last embrace ! and lips, O
    you
The doors of breath, seal with a righteous kiss
A dateless bargain to engrossing death.
  f.   *Romeo and Juliet.* Act V. Sc. 3.
                                 L. 112.

For he being dead, with him is beauty slain,
And, beauty dead, black chaos comes again.
  g.   *Venus and Adonis.* L. 1,019.

Golden lads and girls all must,
As chimney-sweepers, come to dust.
  h.   *Cymbeline.* Act IV. Sc. 2. *Song.*
                                 L. 262.

For in that sleep of death what dreams may
    come.
  i.   *Hamlet.* Act III. Sc. 1. L. 66.

Go thou, and fill another room in hell.
That hand shall burn in never-quenching fire,
That staggers thus my person. Exton, thy
    fierce hand
Hath with thy king's blood stain'd the
    king's own land.
Mount, mount, my soul ! thy seat is up on
    high ;
Whilst my gross flesh sinks downward, here
    to die.
  j.   *Richard II.* Act V. Sc. 5. L. 107.

Have I not hideous death within my view,
Retaining but a quantity of life
Which bleeds away, even as a form of wax
Resolveth from its figure 'gainst the fire ?
  k.   *King John.* Act V. Sc. 4. L. 22.

He dies, and makes no sign.
  l.   *Henry VI.* Pt. II. Act III. Sc. 3.
                                  L. 28.

He gave his honours to the world again,
His blessed part to heaven, and slept in peace.
  m.   *Henry VIII.* Act IV. Sc. 2. L. 29.

Here is my journey's end, here is my butt,
And very sea-mark of my utmost sail.
  n.   *Othello.* Act V. Sc. 2. L. 267.

He that cuts off twenty years of life
Cuts off so many years of fearing death.
  o.   *Julius Cæsar.* Act III. Sc. 1. L. 101.

He that dies pays all debts.
  p.   *Tempest.* Act III. Sc. 2. L. 140.

How oft, when men are at the point of death,
Have they been merry ! which their keepers
    call
A lightning before death.
  q.   *Romeo and Juliet.* Act V. Sc. 3. L. 88.

I do not set my life at a pin's fee ;
And, for my soul, what can it do to that,
Being a thing immortal as itself ?
  r.   *Hamlet.* Act I. Sc. 4. L. 67.

                  If I must die
I will encounter darkness as a bride,
And hug it in mine arms.
  s.   *Measure for Measure.* Act III. Sc. 1.
                                  L. 83

Let's choose executors and talk of wills :
And yet not so, for what can we bequeath,
Save our desposed bodies to the ground ?
  t.   *Richard II.* Act III. Sc. 2. L. 148.

                My sick heart shows
That I must yield my body to the earth,
And, by my fall, the conquest to my foe.
Thus yields the cedar to the axe's edge,
Whose arms gave shelter to the princely eagle ;
Under whose shade the ramping lion slept :
Whose top-branch overpeer'd Jove's spreading
    tree,
And kept low shrubs from winter's powerful
    wind.
  u.   *Henry VI.* Pt. III. Act V. Sc. 2.
                                  L. 8.

Nothing can we call our own but death
And that small model of the barren earth
Which serves as paste and cover to our bones.
  v.   *Richard II.* Act III. Sc. 2. L. 152.

                Nothing in his life
Became him like the leaving it.
  w.   *Macbeth.* Act I. Sc. 4. L. 7.

                   O, our lives' sweetness !
That we the pain of death would hourly die
Rather than die at once !
  x.   *King Lear.* Act V. Sc. 3. L. 184.

O proud death,
What feast is toward in thine eternal cell,
That thou so many princes at a shot
So bloodily hast struck?
　　a.　　*Hamlet.*　Act V.　Sc. 2.　L. 375.

Safe in a ditch he bides,
With twenty trenched gashes on his head;
The least a death to nature.
　　b.　　*Macbeth.*　Act III.　Sc. 4.　L. 26.

That we shall die we know; 'tis but the time
And drawing days out, that men stand upon.
　　c.　　*Julius Cæsar.*　Act III.　Sc. 1.　L. 99.

The graves stood tenantless, and the sheeted
　　dead
Did squeak and gibber in the Roman streets.
　　d.　　*Hamlet.*　Act I.　Sc. 1.　L. 115.

The weariest and most loathed worldly life
That age, ache, penury and imprisonment
Can lay on nature, is a paradise
To what we fear of death.
　　e.　　*Measure for Measure.*　Act III.　Sc. 1.
　　　　　　　　　　　　　　　　　　L. 129.

The wills above be done! but I would fain
die a dry death.
　　f.　　*Tempest.*　Act I.　Sc. 1.　L. 70.

Thou know'st 'tis common; all that lives must
　　die,
Passing through nature to eternity.
　　g.　　*Hamlet.*　Act I.　Sc. 2.　L. 72.

'Tis a vile thing to die, my gracious lord,
When men are unprepared and look not for
　　it.
　　h.　　*Richard III.*　Act III.　Sc. 2.　L. 64.

To be imprison'd in the viewless winds,
And blown with restless violence roundabout
The pendent world; or to be worse than
　　worst
Of those, that lawless and incertain thought
Imagine howling; 'tis too horrible!
　　i.　　*Measure for Measure.*　Act III.　Sc. 1.
　　　　　　　　　　　　　　　　　　L. 124.

To die:—to sleep:
No more; and, by a sleep to say we end
The heart-ache and the thousand natural
　　shocks
That flesh is heir to, 'tis a consummation
Devoutly to be wished.
　　j.　　*Hamlet.*　Act III.　Sc. 1.　L. 60.

We cannot hold mortality's strong hand.
　　k.　　*King John.*　Act IV.　Sc. 2.　L. 82.

We must die, Messala:
With meditating that she must die once,
I have the patience to endure it now.
　　l.　　*Julius Cæsar.*　Act IV.　Sc. 3.　L. 190.

We should profane the service of the dead,
To sing a requiem and such rest to her
As to peace-parted souls.
　　m.　　*Hamlet.*　Act V.　Sc. 1.　L. 259.

What, is the old king dead?
As nail in door.
　　n.　　*Henry IV.*　Pt. II.　Act V.　Sc. 3.
　　　　　　　　　　　　　　　　　　L. 126.

What's yet in this,
That bears the name of life? Yet in this life
Lie hid more thousand deaths: yet death we
　　fear,
That makes these odds all even.
　　o.　　*Measure for Measure.*　Act III.　Sc. 1.
　　　　　　　　　　　　　　　　　　L. 38.

When beggars die, there are no comets seen;
The heavens themselves blaze forth the death
　　of princes.
　　p.　　*Julius Cæsar.*　Act II.　Sc. 2.　L. 30.

Who pass'd, methought, the melancholy flood
With that grim ferryman which poets write
　　of,
Unto the kingdom of perpetual night.
　　q.　　*Richard III.*　Act. I.　Sc. 4.　L. 45.

Why, what is pomp, rule, reign, but earth and
　　dust?
And, live we how we can, yet die we must.
　　r.　　*Henry VI.*　Pt. III.　Act V.　Sc. 2.
　　　　　　　　　　　　　　　　　　L. 27.

Within the hollow crown
That rounds the mortal temples of a king,
Keeps Death his court; and there the antic
　　sits,
Scoffing his state and grinning at his pomp.
　　s.　　*Richard II.*　Act III.　Sc. 2.　L. 161.

Woe, destruction, ruin, and decay;
The worst is death, and death will have his
　　day.
　　t.　　*Richard II.*　Act. III.　Sc. 2.　L. 102.

First our pleasures die—and then
Our hopes, and then our fears—and when
These are dead, the debt is due,
Dust claims dust—and we die too.
　　u.　　Shelley—*Death.*　(1820).

How wonderful is Death, Death and his
　　brother Sleep!
　　v.　　Shelley—*Queen Mab.*　L. 1.

All buildings are but monuments of death,
All clothes but winding-sheets for our last
　　. knell,
All dainty fattings for the worms beneath,
All curious music but our passing bell:
Thus death is nobly waited on, for why?
All that we have is but death's livery.
　　w.　　Shirley.

Death calls ye to the crowd of common men.
　　x.　　Shirley—*Cupid and Death.*

He that on his pillow lies,
Fear-embalmed before he dies
Carries, like a sheep, his life,
To meet the sacrificer's knife,
And for eternity is prest,
Sad bell-wether to the rest.
    a.   SHIRLEY—*The Passing Bell.*

The glories of our blood and state
Are shadows, not substantial things;
There is no armour against fate,
Death lays his icy hand on kings.
      Scepter and crown
      Must tumble down,
And, in the dust, be equal made
With the poor crooked scythe and spade.
    b.   SHIRLEY—*Contention of Ajax and*
                Ulysses. Sc. 3.

Yet 'twill only be a sleep:
When, with songs and dewy light,
Morning blossoms out of Night,
She will open her blue eyes
'Neath the palms of Paradise,
While we foolish ones shall weep.
    c.   EDWARD ROWLAND SILL—*Sleeping.*

We count it death to falter, not to die.
    d.   SIMONIDES—*Jacobs I.* 63, 20.

         To our graves we walk
In the thick footprints of departed men.
    e.   ALEX. SMITH—*Horton.* L. 570.

Death! to the happy thou art terrible;
But how the wretched love to think of thee,
O thou true comforter! the friend of all
Who have no friend beside!
    f.   SOUTHEY—*Joan of Arc.* Bk. I. L. 318.

A man after death is not a natural but a spiritual man; nevertheless he still appears in all respects like himself.
    g.   SWEDENBORG—*Conjugal Love.* Par. 31.

And hands that wist not though they dug a
      grave,
Undid the hasps of gold, and drank, and gave,
And he drank after, a deep glad kingly
      draught:
And all their life changed in them, for they
      quaffed
Death; if it be death so to drink, and fare
As men who change and are what these twain
      were.
    h.   SWINBURNE—*Tristram of Lyonesse.*
         The Sailing of the Swallow. L. 789.

Death, if thou wilt, fain would I plead with
      thee:
Canst thou not spare, of all our hopes have
      built,
One shelter where our spirits fain would be,
Death, if thou wilt?
    i.   SWINBURNE—*A Dialogue.* St. 1.

For thee, O now a silent soul, my brother,
   Take at my hands this garland and farewell.
Thin is the leaf, and chill the wintry smell,
And chill the solemn earth, a fatal mother.
    j.   SWINBURNE—*Ave Atque Vale.* St. 18.

Death is not rare, alas! nor burials few,
And soon the grassy coverlet of God
Spreads equal green above their ashes pale.
    k.   BAYARD TAYLOR—*The Picture of St.*
             John. Bk. III. St. 84.

He that would die well must always look
for death, every day knocking at the gates of
the grave; and then the gates of the grave
shall never prevail upon him to do him
mischief.
    l.   JEREMY TAYLOR—*Holy Dying.* Ch. II.
                        Pt. I.

         Death has made
His darkness beautiful with thee.
    m.   TENNYSON—*In Memoriam.* LXXIV.

God's finger touched him, and he slept.
    n.   TENNYSON—*In Memoriam.* LXXXV.

The night comes on that knows not morn,
When I shall cease to be all alone,
To live forgotten, and love forlorn.
    o.   TENNYSON—*Mariana in the South.*
                      Last stanza.

Whatever crazy sorrow saith,
No life that breathes with human breath
Has ever truly long'd for death.
    p.   TENNYSON—*Two Voices.* St. 132.

I hear a voice you cannot hear,
   Which says, I must not stay;
I see a hand you cannot see,
   Which beckons me away.
    q.   TICKELL—*Colin and Lucy.*

Boatman, come, thy fare receive;
Thrice thy fare I gladly give,
For unknown, unseen by thee,
Spirits twain have crossed with me.
    r.   UHLAND—*The Ferry Boat.* Skeat's
                        trans.

But God, who is able to prevail, wrestled
with him, as the angel did with Jacob, and
marked him; marked him for his own.
    s.   IZAAK WALTON—*Life of Donne.*

The tall, the wise, the reverend head,
Must lie as low as ours.
    t.   ISAAC WATTS—*Hymns and Spiritual*
                Songs. Bk. II. Hymn 63.

I know death hath ten thousand several doors
For men to take their exits.
    u.   JOHN WEBSTER—*Duchess of Malfi.*
                      Act IV. Sc. 2.

How beautiful it is for a man to die
Upon the walls of Zion! to be called
Like a watch-worn and weary sentinel,
To put his armour off, and rest in heaven!
 a. Willis—*On the Death of a Missionary.*

For I know that Death is a guest divine,
Who shall drink my blood as I drink this
 wine;
And he cares for nothing! a king is he—
Come on, old fellow, and drink with me!
With you I will drink to the solemn past,
Though the cup that I drain should be my last.
 b. William Winter—*Orgia. The Song
          of a Ruined Man.*

But he lay like a warrior taking his rest,
With his martial cloak around him.
 c. Chas. Wolfe—*The Burial of Sir John
            Moore.*

If I had thought thou couldst have died
 I might not weep for thee;
But I forgot, when by thy side,
 That thou couldst mortal be;
It never through my mind had passed,
 That time would e'er be o'er
When I on thee should look my last,
 And thou shouldst smile no more!
 d. Chas. Wolfe—*Song. The Death of
             Mary.*

      O, sir! the good die first,
And they whose hearts are dry as summer
  dust
Burn to the socket.
 e. Wordsworth—*The Excursion.* Bk. I.

He first deceased: she for a little tried
To live without him, lik'd it not, and died.
 f. Sir Henry Wotton—*On the Death of
         Sir Albert Morton's Wife.*

A death-bed's a detector of the heart.
 g. Young—*Night Thoughts.* Night II.
              L. 641.

And feels a thousand deaths, in fearing one.
 h. Young—*Night Thoughts.* Night IV.
              L. 17.

      Death is the crown of life;
Were death denyed, poor man would live in
  vain;
Were death denyed, to live would not be life;
Were death denyed, ev'n fools would wish to
  die.
 i. Young—*Night Thoughts.* Night III.
              L. 523.

Death loves a shining mark, a signal blow.
 j. Young—*Night Thoughts.* Night V.
              L. 1,011.

Early, bright, transient, chaste, as morning
 dew,
She sparkled, was exhal'd, and went to
 heaven.
 k. Young—*Night Thoughts.* Night V.
              L. 600.
Insatiate archer! could not one suffice?
Thy shaft flew thrice; and thrice my peace
 was slain!
 l. Young—*Night Thoughts.* Night I.
              L. 212.
Lovely in death the beauteous ruin lay;
And if in death still lovely, lovelier there;
Far lovelier! pity swells the tide of love.
 m. Young—*Night Thoughts.* Night III.
              L. 104.
Men drop so fast, ere life's mid stage we tread,
Few know so many friends alive, as dead.
 n. Young—*Love of Fame.* L. 97.

The chamber where the good man meets his
 fate
Is privileged beyond the common walk
Of virtuous life, quite in the verge of heaven.
 o. Young—*Night Thoughts.* Night II.
              L. 633.
The knell, the shroud, the mattock and the
 grave,
The deep, damp vault, the darkness, and the
 worm.
 p. Young—*Night Thoughts.* Night IV.
              L. 10.
       Who can take
Death's portrait? The tyrant never sat.
 q. Young—*Night Thoughts.* Night II.
              L. 52.

DEBT.

I hold every man a debtor to his profession.
 r. Bacon—*Maxims of the Law.* Preface.

Anticipated rents, and bills unpaid,
Force many a shining youth into the shade,
Not to redeem his time, but his estate,
And play the fool, but at the cheaper rate.
 s. Cowper—*Retirement.* L. 559.

Wilt thou seal up the avenues of ill?
Pay every debt as if God wrote the bill!
 t. Emerson—*Suum Cuique.*

A national debt, if it is not excessive, will
be to us a national blessing.
 u. Alex. Hamilton—*Letter to Robert
         Morris.* April 30, 1781.

At the time we were funding our national
debt, we heard much about "a public debt
being a public blessing;" that the stock rep-
resenting it was a creation of active capital
for the aliment of commerce, manufactures
and agriculture.
 v. Thomas Jefferson—*On Public Debts.*
    Letter to John W. Epps. Nov. 6,
              1813.

The slender debt to Nature's quickly paid,
Discharged, perchance, with greater ease than
    made.
  a.   QUARLES—*Emblems.* Bk. II.
                          Emblem 13.

DECAY.

The unbought grace of life, the cheap defence of nations, the nurse of manly sentiment
and heroic enterprise, is gone!
  b.   BURKE—*Reflections on the Revolution in*
                    France. Vol. III.
                            P. 331.

A gilded halo hovering round decay.
  c.   BYRON—*Giaour.* L. 100.

You have the Pyrrhic dance as yet,
Where is the Pyrrhic phalanx gone?
Of two such lessons, why forget
The nobler and the manlier one?
You have the letters Cadmus gave—
Think ye he meant them for a slave?
  d.   BYRON—*Don Juan.* Canto III.
                        St. 86. 10.

He that loves a rosy cheek,
Or a coral lip admires,
Or from star-like eyes doth seek
  Fuel to maintain his fires;—
As old Time makes these decay,
So his flames must waste away.
  e.   THOMAS CAREW—*Disdain Returned.*

A worm is in the bud of youth,
And at the root of age.
  f.   COWPER—*Stanzas Subjoined to a Bill of*
                           Mortality.

Ill fares the land, to hastening ills a prey,
Where wealth accumulates, and men decay;
Princes and Lords may flourish, or may fade—
A breath can make them, as a breath has
    made—
But a bold peasantry, their country's pride,
When once destroy'd can never be supplied.
  g.   GOLDSMITH—*Deserted Village.* L. 51.

  History fades into fable; fact becomes
clouded with doubt and controversy; the inscription moulders from the tablet: the statue
falls from the pedestal. Columns, arches,
pyramids, what are they but heaps of sand;
and their epitaphs, but characters written in
the dust?
  h.   IRVING—*The Sketch Book.* *Westminster*
                            Abbey.

An age that melts with unperceiv'd decay,
And glides in modest innocence away.
  i.   SAM'L JOHNSON—*Vanity of Human*
                      Wishes. L. 293.

  There seems to be a constant decay of all
our ideas; even of those which are struck
deepest, and in minds the most retentive, so
that if they be not sometimes renewed by repeated exercises of the senses, or reflection
on those kinds of objects which at first occasioned them, the print wears out, and at last
there remains nothing to be seen.
  j.   LOCKE—*Human Understanding.*
                        Bk. II. Ch. 10.

All that's bright must fade,—
  The brightest still the fleetest;
All that's sweet was made
  But to be lost when sweetest.
  k.   MOORE—*National Airs.* *Indian Air.*

        In the sweetest bud
The eating canker dwells.
  l.   *Two Gentlemen of Verona.* Act I.
                      Sc. 1. L. 42.

The ripest fruit first falls, and so doth he;
His time is spent.
  m.   *Richard II.* Act II. Sc. 1. L. 153.

I shall be like that tree,—I shall die at the top.
  n.   SWIFT—*Scott's Life of Swift.*

Fires that shook me once, but now to silent
    ashes fall'n away.
Cold upon the dead volcano sleeps the gleam
    of dying day.
  o.   TENNYSON—*Locksley Hall.* *Sixty Years*
                      After. St. 21.

DECEIT.

God is not averse to deceit in a holy cause.
  p.   ÆSCHYLUS—*Frag. Incert.* II.

Think'st thou there are no serpents in the
    world
But those who slide along the grassy sod,
And sting the luckless foot that presses them?
There are who in the path of social life
Do bask their spotted skins in Fortune's sun,
And sting the soul.
  q.   JOANNA BAILLIE—*De Montfort.* Act I.
                            Sc. 2.

  What song the Syrens sang, or what name
Achilles assumed when he hid himself among
women.
  r.   SIR THOMAS BROWNE—*Urn-Burial.*
                           Ch. V.

If the world will be gulled, let it be gulled.
  s.   BURTON—*Anatomy of Melancholy.*
             Pt. III. Sec. IV. Memb. 1.
                        Subsec. 2

  Quoth Hudibras, I smell a rat;
Ralpho, thou dost prevaricate.
  t.   BUTLER—*Hudibras.* Pt. I. Canto I.
                        L. 821.

Think not I am what I appear.
    a.   BYRON—*The Bride of Abydos.*
                  Canto I. Sc. 12.

But every thyng which schyneth as the gold,
Nis nat gold, as that I have herd it told.
    b.   CHAUCER—*Canterbury Tales.*
           Chanounes Yemanne's Tale.
              Preamble. L. 17,362.

Appearances to save, his only care;
So things seem right, no matter what they are.
    c.   CHURCHILL—*Rosciad.* L. 299.

Yet still we hug the dear deceit.
    d.   NATHANIEL COTTON—*Visions in Verse.*
              Content. Vision IV.

Stamps God's own name upon a lie just made,
To turn a penny in the way of trade.
    e.   COWPER—*Table Talk.* L. 421.

          Transforms old print
To zigzag manuscript, and cheats the eyes
Of gallery critics by a thousand arts.
    f.   COWPER—*The Task.* Bk. II. *The*
              Time Piece. L. 363.

Nothing is more easy than to deceive one's
self, as our affections are subtle persuaders.
    g.   DEMOSTHENES.

Of all the evil spirits abroad at this hour in
the world, insincerity is the most dangerous.
    h.   FROUDE—*Short Studies on Great*
              Subjects. *Education.*

By outward show let's not be cheated;
An ass should like an ass be treated.
    i.   GAY—*Fables.* Pt. II. *The Pack-Horse*
              and the Carrier.

Roy's wife of Aldivalloch,
Wat ye how she cheated me,
As I came o'er the braes of Balloch?
    j.   ANNE GRANT—*Roy's Wife.*

Not all that tempts your wandering eyes
And heedless hearts is lawful prize,
Nor all that glisters gold.
    k.   GRAY—*Ode on a Favorite Cat.*

That for ways that are dark
  And for tricks that are vain,
The heathen Chinee is peculiar.
    l.   BRET HARTE—*Plain Language from*
              Truthful James.

The angel answer'd, "Nay, sad soul; go
  higher!
To be deceived in your true heart's desire
Was bitterer than a thousand years of fire!"
    m.   JOHN HAY—*A Woman's Love.*

Judas had given them the slip.
    n.   MATHEW HENRY—*Commentaries.*
              Matthew XXII.

Hateful to me as are the gates of hell,
Is he who, hiding one thing in his heart,
Utters another.
    o.   HOMER—*The Iliad.* Bk. IX. L. 386.
                  Bryant's trans.

Perhaps it was right to dissemble your love,
But why did you kick me down stairs?
    p.   J. P. KEMBLE—*The Panel.* Act I.
                      Sc. 1.

Trust him not with your secrets, who, when
left alone in your room, turns over your
papers.
    q.   LAVATER—*Aphorisms.* No. 439.

It is in vain to find fault with those arts of
deceiving, wherein men find pleasure to be
deceived.
    r.   LOCKE—*Human Understanding.*
              Bk. III. Ch. X. 34.

              He seemed
For dignity compos'd and high exploit:
But all was false and hollow.
    s.   MILTON—*Paradise Lost.* Bk. II.
                  L. 110.

Perfidious Albion.
    t.   NAPOLEON—*Exclamation on leaving*
              England for St. Helena.

    With one hand he put
A penny in the urn of poverty,
And with the other took a shilling out.
    u.   POLLOK—*Course of Time.* Bk. VIII.
                  L. 632.

Shut, shut the door, good John! fatigu'd I
  said;
Tie up the knocker, say I'm sick, I'm dead.
    v.   POPE—*Prologue to the Satires.* L. 1.

Of Adam's first wife, Lilith, it is told
  (The witch he loved before the gift of Eve)
  That ere the snakes, her sweet tongue could
    deceive
And her enchanted hair was the first gold—
And still she sits, young while the earth is old
And, subtly of herself contemplative,
  Draws men to watch the bright net she can
    weave,
Till heart and body and life are in its hold.
    w.   DANTE GABRIEL ROSSETTI—*Lilith.*

O, what a tangled web we weave,
When first we practise to deceive.
    x.   SCOTT—*Marmion.* Canto VI. St. 17.

    And here we wander in illusions;
Some blessed power deliver us from hence!
    y.   *Comedy of Errors.* Act IV. Sc. 3.
                  L. 42.

All that glisters is not gold;
Often have you heard that told;
Many a man his life hath sold
But my outside to behold.
　a.　　*Merchant of Venice.*　Act II.　Sc. 7.
　　　　　　　　　　　　　　　　L. 65.

An evil soul producing holy witness
Is like a villain with a smiling cheek;
A goodly apple rotten at the heart:
O, what a goodly outside falsehood hath!
　b.　　*Merchant of Venice.*　Act I.　Sc. 3.
　　　　　　　　　　　　　　　　L. 100.

A quicksand of deceit.
　c.　　*Henry VI.*　Pt. III.　Act V.　Sc. 4.
　　　　　　　　　　　　　　　　L. 26.

Make the Moor thank me, love me and re-
　　　ward me,
For making him egregiously an ass.
　d.　　*Othello.*　Act II.　Sc. 1.　L. 317.

Oh, that deceit should steal such gentle
　　　shapes,
And with a virtuous vizard hide foul guile.
　e.　　*Richard III.*　Act II.　Sc. 2.　L. 27.

　　　　　　O, that deceit should dwell
In such a gorgeous palace!
　f.　　*Romeo and Juliet.*　Act III.　Sc. 2.
　　　　　　　　　　　　　　　　L. 84.

The instruments of darkness tell us truths,
Win us with honest trifles, to betray us
In deepest consequence.
　g.　　*Macbeth.*　Act I.　Sc. 3.　L. 124.

The world is still deceiv'd with ornament,
In law, what plea so tainted and corrupt,
But, being season'd with a gracious voice,
Obscures the show of evil? In religion,
What damned error, but some sober brow
Will bless it and approve it with a text,
Hiding the grossness with fair ornament?
　h.　　*Merchant of Venice.*　Act III.　Sc. 2.
　　　　　　　　　　　　　　　　L. 74.

They fool me to the top of my bent. I will
　　　come by and by.
　i.　　*Hamlet.*　Act III.　Sc. 2.　L. 401.

When I was stamp'd, some coiner with his
　　　tools
Made me a counterfeit.
　j.　　*Cymbeline.*　Act II.　Sc. 5.　L. 5.

　Who makes the fairest show means most
deceit.
　k.　　*Pericles.*　Act I.　Sc. 4.　L. 75.

Why, I can smile, and murder whiles I smile,
And cry, "Content" to that which grieves my
　　　heart;
And wet my cheeks with artificial tears,
And frame my face to all occasions.
　l.　　*Henry VI.*　Pt. III.　Act III.　Sc. 2.
　　　　　　　　　　　　　　　　L. 182.

10

With an auspicious and a dropping eye,
With mirth in funeral, and with dirge in
　　　marriage,
In equal scale weighing delight and dole.
　m.　　*Hamlet.*　Act I.　Sc. 2.　L. 12.

DECEMBER (*See* Months).

DECISION.

And her *yes*, once said to you,
　Shall be Yes for evermore.
　n.　　E. B. Browning—*The Lady's Yes.*

　He only is a well-made man who has a good
determination.
　o.　　Emerson—*Essay. Culture.*

Decide not rashly. The decision made
Can never be recalled. The gods implore not,
Plead not, solicit not; they only offer
Choice and occasion, which once being passed
Return no more. Dost thou accept the gift?
　p.　　Longfellow—*Masque of Pandora.*
　　　　　　　Tower of Prometheus on Mount
　　　　　　　　　　　　　　　　Caucasus.

Once to every man and nation come the
　　　moment to decide,
In the strife of Truth with Falsehood, for the
　　　good or evil side.
　q.　　Lowell—*The Present Crisis.*

I am here; I shall remain here.
　r.　　Marshal MacMahon—*In the*
　　　　　　　Trenches before the Malakoff.

Men must be decided on what they will
NOT do, and then they are able to act with
vigor *in what they ought to do.*
　s.　　Mencius—*Works.* Bk. IV. Pt. II.
　　　　　　　　　　　　　　　Ch. VIII.

Joking decides great things,
Stronger and better oft than earnest can.
　t.　　Milton—*Horace.*

Who shall decide when doctors disagree,
And soundest casuists doubt, like you and me?
　u.　　Pope—*Moral Essays.* Ep. III.

Be absolute for death; either death or life
Shall thereby be the sweeter.
　v.　　*Measure for Measure.* Act III. Sc. 1.
　　　　　　　　　　　　　　　　L. 4.

　　　　　　Determine on some course,
More than a wild exposure to each chance
That starts i' the way before thee.
　w.　　*Coriolanus.* Act IV. Sc. 1. L. 35.

For what I will, I will, and there an end.
　x.　　*Two Gentlemen of Verona.* Act I.
　　　　　　　　　　　　　　Sc. 3. L. 65.

Pleasure and revenge
Have ears more deaf than adders to the voice
Of any true decision.
a.　　　*Troilus and Cressida.*　Act II.　Sc. 2.
L. 171.

There is no mistake; there has been no
mistake; and there shall be no mistake.
b.　　　DUKE OF WELLINGTON—*Letter to Mr.*
Huskisson.

DEEDS.

Who doth right deeds
Is twice born, and who doeth ill deeds vile.
c.　　　EDWIN ARNOLD—*Light of Asia.*
Bk. VI.　L. 78.

All your better deeds
Shall be in water writ, but this in marble.
d.　　　BEAUMONT and FLETCHER—*Philaster.*
Act V.　Sc. 3.

'Tis not what man Does which exalts him,
but what man Would do.
e.　　　ROBERT BROWNING—*Saul. XVIII.*

For now the field is not far off
Where we must give the world a proof
Of deeds, not words.
f.　　　BUTLER—*Hudibras.*　Pt. I.　Canto I.
L. 867.

His deedes inimitable, like the Sea
That shuts still as it opes, and leaves no tracts
Nor prints of Precedent for poore men's facts.
g.　　　GEORGE CHAPMAN—*Bussy D'Ambois.*
Act I.　Sc. 1.

So our lives
In acts exemplarie, not only winne
Ourselves good Names, but doth to others
give
Matter for virtuous Deedes, by which wee live.
h.　　　GEORGE CHAPMAN—*Bussy D'Ambois.*
Act I.　Sc. 1.

This is the Thing that I was born to do.
i.　　　SAMUEL DANIEL—*Musophilus.*　St. 100.

Our deeds determine us, as much as we
determine our deeds.
j.　　　GEORGE ELIOT—*Adam Bede.*
Ch. XXIX.

Things of to-day?
Deeds which are harvest for Eternity!
k.　　　EBENEZER ELLIOTT—*Hymn.*　L. 22.

Go put your creed into your deed,
Nor speak with double tongue.
l.　　　EMERSON—*Ode. Concord.* July 4, 1857.

For as one star another far exceeds,
So souls in heaven are placèd by their deeds.
m.　　　ROBERT GREENE—*A Maiden's Dream.*

My hour at last has come;
Yet not ingloriously or passively
I die, but first will do some valiant deed,
Of which mankind shall hear in after time.
n.　　　HOMER—*The Iliad.*　Bk. XXII.
Bryant's trans.

Oh! 'tis easy
To beget great deeds; but in the rearing of
them—
The threading in cold blood each mean detail,
And furze brake of half-pertinent circum-
stance—
There lies the self-denial.
o.　　　CHARLES KINGSLEY—*Saint's Tragedy.*
Act IV.　Sc. 3.

We are our own fates.　Our own deeds
Are our doomsmen.　Man's life was made
Not for men's creeds,
But men's actions.
p.　　　OWEN MEREDITH (Lord Lytton)—
Lucile.　Pt. II.　Canto V.　St. 8.

I on the other side
Us'd no ambition to commend my deeds;
The deeds themselves, though mute, spoke
loud the doer.
q.　　　MILTON—*Samson Agonistes.*　L. 246.

Nor think thou with wind
Of aery threats to awe whom yet with deeds
Thou canst not.
r.　　　MILTON—*Paradise Lost.*　Bk. VI.
L. 282.

See golden days, fruitful of golden deeds,
With joy and love triumphing.
s.　　　MILTON—*Paradise Lost.*　Bk. III.
L. 336.

You do the deeds,
And your ungodly deeds find me the words.
t.　　　MILTON's trans. of Sophocles.
Electra.　L. 624.

Little deeds of kindness, little words of love,
Make our earth an Eden like the heaven above.
u.　　　**JULIA A. CARNEY**—*Little Things.*

The deed I intend is great,
But what, as yet, I know not.
v.　　　OVID—*Metamorphoses.*　Sandy's trans.

A mighty deed is like the Heaven's thunder,
That wakes the nation's slumberers from
their rest.
w.　　　RAUPACH.

Your deeds are known,
In words that kindle glory from the stone.
x.　　　SCHILLER—*The Walk.*

A deed without a name.
y.　　　*Macbeth.*　Act IV.　Sc. 1.　L. 49.

From lowest place when virtuous things pro-
ceed,
The place is dignified by the doer's deed:
Where great additions swell's and virtue none,
It is a dropsied honour.   Good alone
Is good without a name.

   a.   *All's Well That Ends Well.*   Act II.
                    Sc. 3.   L. 132.

Go in, and cheer the town: we'll forth and
fight;
Do deeds worth praise and tell you them at
night.

   b.   *Troilus and Cressida.*   Act V.   Sc. 3.
                          L. 92.

                He covets less
Than misery itself would give; rewards
His deeds with doing them, and is content
To spend the time to end it.

   c.   *Coriolanus.*   Act II.   Sc. 2.   L. 130.

How far that little candle throws his beams!
So shines a good deed in a naughty world.

   d.   *Merchant of Venice.*   Act V.   Sc. 1.
                          L. 90.

I am in this earthly world; where to do harm,
Is often laudable, to do good sometime
Accounted dangerous folly.

   e.   *Macbeth.*   Act IV.   Sc. 2.   L. 75.

I give thee thanks in part of thy deserts,
And will with deeds requite thy gentleness.

   f.   *Titus Andronicus.*   Act I.   Sc. 1,
                          L. 236.

                I never saw
Such noble fury in so poor a thing;
Such precious deeds in one that promis'd
nought
But beggary and poor looks.

   g.   *Cymbeline.*   Act V.   Sc. 5.   L. 7.

          One good deed dying tongueless
Slaughters a thousand waiting upon that.
Our praises are our wages.

   h.   *Winter's Tale.*   Act I.   Sc. 2.   L. 92.

The flighty purpose never is o'ertook,
Unless the deed go with it.

   i.   *Macbeth.*   Act IV.   Sc. 1.   L. 146.

They look into the beauty of thy mind,
And that, in guess, they measure by thy deeds.

   j.   *Sonnet LXIX.*

DELAY.

All delays are dangerous in war.

   k.   Dryden—*Tyrannic Love.*   Act I.   Sc. 1.

Ah! nothing is too late
Till the tired heart shall cease to palpitate.

   l.   Longfellow—*Morituri Salutamus.*
                          St. 25.

          Do not delay,
Do not delay: the golden moments fly!

   m.   Longfellow—*Masque of Pandora.*
                        Pt. VII.

Delay leads impotent and snail-paced beggary.

   n.   *Richard III.*   Act IV.   Sc. 3.   L. 53.

Late, late, so late! but we can enter still.
Too late, too late! ye cannot enter now.

   o.   Tennyson—*Idylls of the King.*
                  Guinevere.   L. 169.

And Mecca saddens at the long delay.

   p.   Thomson—*The Seasons.*   *Summer.*
                        L. 979.

Be wise to-day; 'tis madness to defer;
Next day the fatal precedent will plead;
Thus on, till wisdom is push'd out of life.

   q.   Young—*Night Thoughts.*   Night I.
                        L. 390.

DELIGHT.

I am convinced that we have a degree of
delight, and that no small one, in the real
misfortunes and pains of others.

   r.   Burke—*The Sublime and Beautiful.*
                     Pt. I.   Sec. 14.

In this fool's paradise he drank delight.

   s.   Crabbe—*The Borough Payers.*
                      Letter XII.

Man delights not me: no, nor woman neither,
though, by your smiling, you seem to say so.

   t.   *Hamlet.*   Act II.   Sc. 2.   L. 321.

Their tables were stor'd full, to glad the sight,
And not so much to feed on as delight:
All poverty was scorn'd, and pride so great,
The name of help grew odious to repeat.

   u.   *Pericles.*   Act I.   Sc. 4.   L. 28.

These violent delights have violent ends
And in their triumph die, like fire and
powder,
Which as they kiss consume.

   v.   *Romeo and Juliet.*   Act II.   Sc. 6.
                         L. 9.

Why, all delights are vain; and that most
vain,
Which with pain purchas'd, doth inherit pain.

   w.   *Love's Labour's Lost.*   Act I.   Sc. 1.
                        L. 72.

A voice of greeting from the wind was sent;
   The mists enfolded me with soft white arms;
The birds did sing to lap me in content,
   The rivers wove their charms,—
And every little daisy in the grass
Did look up in my face, and smile to see me
   pass!

   x.   R. H. Stoddard—*Hymn to the*
                      Beautiful.   St. 4.

DENTISTRY (*See* Occupations).

DESIRE.

The thing we long for, that we are
For one transcendent moment.
   a.   Lowell—*Longing.*

Oh! could I throw aside these earthly bands
That tie me down where wretched mortals
   sigh—
To join blest spirits in celestial lands!
   b.   Petrarch—*To Laura in Death.*
                   Sonnet XLV.

Can one desire too much of a good thing?
   c.   *As You Like It.* Act IV. Sc. 1.
                     L. 123.

Had doting Priam checked his son's desire,
Troy had been bright with fame and not with
   fire.
   d.   *Rape of Lucrece.* L. 1,490.

I do desire we may be better strangers.
   e.   *As You Like It.* Act III. Sc. 2.
                     L. 274.

           I have
Immortal longings in me.
   f.   *Antony and Cleopatra.* Act V. Sc. 2.
                     L. 282.

Methinks I have a great desire to a bottle
of hay: good hay, sweet hay, hath no fellow.
   g.   *Midsummer Night's Dream.* Act IV.
                     Sc. 1. L. 36.

No more of that, Hal, an thou lovest me.
   h.   *Henry IV.* Pt. I. Act II. Sc. 4. L. 312.

Speak but one rhyme, and I am satisfied;
Cry but—"Ay me!" pronounce but "love"
   and "dove."
   i.   *Romeo and Juliet.* Act II. Sc. 1.
                     L. 9.

The desire of the moth for the star,
Of the night for the morrow,
The devotion to something afar
   From the sphere of our sorrow.
   j.   Shelley—*To ——. One Word is too
                  Often Profaned.*

We grow like flowers, and bear desire,
The odor of the human flowers.
   k.   R. H. Stoddard—*The Squire of Low
         Degree. The Princess Answers.* I. **L. 13.**

But O! for the touch of a vanish'd hand,
And the sound of a voice that is still!
   l.   Tennyson—*Break, Break, Break.*

Father of light and life! Thou Good Supreme!
     *   *   *   *   *   *
Save me from folly, vanity, and vice,
From every low pursuit! and feed my Soul
With knowledge, conscious peace, and virtue
   pure—
Sacred, substantial, never-fading bliss!
   m.   Thomson—*The Seasons. Winter.*
                     L. 217.

Give unto me, made lowly wise,
The spirit of self-sacrifice;
The confidence of reason give;
And in the light of truth thy
Bondman let me live!
   n.   Wordsworth—*Ode to Duty.*

DESOLATION.

On rolls the stream with a perpetual sigh;
The rocks moan wildly as it passes by;
Hyssop and wormwood border all the strand,
And not a flower adorns the dreary land.
   o.   Bryant—Trans. *The Paradise of Tears.*

None are so desolate but something dear,
Dearer than self, possesses or possess'd
A thought, and claims the homage of a tear.
   p.   Byron—*Childe Harold.* Canto II.
                     St. 24.

Desolate—Life is so dreary and desolate—
Women and men in the crowd meet and
   mingle,
Yet with itself every soul standeth single,
Deep out of sympathy moaning its moan—
Holding and having its brief exultation—
Making its lonesome and low lamentation—
Fighting its terrible conflicts alone.
   q.   Alice Cary—*Life.*

No soul is desolate as long as there is a
human being for whom it can feel trust and
reverence.
   r.   George Eliot—*Romola.* Ch. XLIV.

No one is so accursed by fate,
No one so utterly desolate,
   But some heart, though unknown,
   Responds unto his own.
   s.   Longfellow—*Endymion.*

My desolation does begin to make
A better life.
   t.   *Antony and Cleopatra.* Act V. Sc. 2.
                     L. 1.

There is no creature loves me;
And if I die, no soul shall pity me.
   u.   *Richard III.* Act V. Sc. 3. L. 200.

                  Gone—flitted away,
Taken the stars from the night and the sun
   From the day!
Gone, and a cloud in my heart.
   v.   Tennyson—*The Window. Gone.*

DESPAIR.

I will indulge my sorrows, and give way
To all the pangs and fury of despair.
   a.   ADDISON—*Cato.* Act IV. Sc. 3.

Despair of ever being saved, "except thou
be born again," or of seeing God "without
holiness," or of having part in Christ except
thou "love him above father, mother, or thy
own life." This kind of despair is one of the
first steps to heaven.
   b.   BAXTER—*Saint's Rest.* Ch. VI.

The world goes whispering to its own,
"This anguish pierces to the bone;"
And tender friends go sighing round,
"What love can ever cure this wound?"
My days go on, my days go on.
   c.   E. B. BROWNING—*De Profundis.* St. 5.

The name of the slough was Despond.
   d.   BUNYAN—*Pilgrim's Progress.* Pt. I.
                                    Ch. II.

Hark! to the hurried question of Despair:
"Where is my child?"—an Echo answers—
      "Where?"
   e.   BYRON—*The Bride of Abydos.*
                            Canto II. St. 27.

Hope, withering, fled—and Mercy sighed farewell.
   f.   BYRON—*The Corsair.* Canto I. St. 9.

Beware of desperate steps. The darkest day,
Live till to-morrow, will have pass'd away.
   g.   COWPER—*Needless Alarm.* L. 132.

To tell men that they cannot help themselves is to fling them into recklessness and
despair.
   h.   FROUDE—*Short Studies on Great
                          Subjects. Calvinism.*

How gladly would I meet
Mortality my sentence, and be earth
Insensible! how glad would lay me down
As in my mother's lap!
   i.   MILTON—*Paradise Lost.* Bk. X.
                                  L. 775.

So farewell hope, and with hope farewell fear,
Farewell remorse: all good to me is lost;
Evil, be thou my good.
   j.   MILTON—*Paradise Lost.* Bk. IV.
                                  L. 108.

Stood up, the strongest and the fiercest spirit
That fought in heaven, now fiercer by despair.
   k.   MILTON—*Paradise Lost.* Bk. II.
                                  L. 44.

           Thus repuls'd, our final hope
Is flat despair.
   l.   MILTON—*Paradise Lost.* Bk. II.
                                  L. 141.

           Thus with the year
Seasons return, but not to me returns
Day, or the sweet approach of even or morn,
Or sight of vernal bloom, or summer's rose,
Or flocks, or herds, or human face divine;
But cloud instead, and ever-during dark
Surrounds me, from the cheerful ways of men
Cut off, and for the book of knowledge fair
Presented with a universal blank
Of Nature's works to me expunged and rased,
And wisdom at one entrance quite shut out.
   m.   MILTON—*Paradise Lost.* Bk. III.
                                  L. 40.

         Discomfort guides my tongue
And bids me speak of nothing but despair.
   n.   *Richard II.* Act III. Sc. 2. L. 65.

For nothing canst thou to damnation add
Greater than that.
   o.   *Othello.* Act III. Sc. 3. L. 372.

I am a tainted wether of the flock,
Meetest for death; the weakest kind of fruit
Drops earliest to the ground; and so let me.
   p.   *Merchant of Venice.* Act IV. Sc. 1.
                                  L. 114.

           Let me have
A dram of poison, such soon-speeding gear
As will disperse itself through all the veins
That the life-weary taker may fall dead
And that the trunk may be discharg'd of
    breath
As violently as hasty powder fir'd
Doth hurry from the fatal cannon's womb.
   q.   *Romeo and Juliet.* Act V. Sc. 1.
                                  L. 59.

Oh, break, my heart! poor bankrupt, break
    at once!
To prison, eyes, ne'er look on liberty!
Vile earth, to earth resign; end motion here;
And thou and Romeo press one heavy bier!
   r.   *Romeo and Juliet.* Act III. Sc. 2.
                                  L. 57.

O, that this too too solid flesh would melt,
Thaw and resolve itself into a dew!
   s.   *Hamlet.* Act I. Sc. 2. L. 129.

         That it should come to this!
But two months dead: nay, not so much,
    not two!
   t.   *Hamlet.* Act I. Sc. 2. L. 137.

They have tied me to a stake; I cannot fly,
But, bear-like, I must fight the course.
   u.   *Macbeth.* Act V. Sc. 7. L. 1.

           Thou tyrant!
Do not repent these things, for they are
    heavier
Than all thy woes can stir: therefore, betake
    thee
To nothing but despair.
   v.   *Winter's Tale.* Act III. Sc. 2. L. 208.

Would I were dead! if God's good will were
　　so:
For what is in this world but grief and woe?
　a.　　*Henry VI*. Pt. III. Act II. Sc. 5.
　　　　　　　　　　　　　　　L. 19.

You take my house when you do take the
　　prop
That doth sustain my house; you take my
　　life
When you do take the means whereby I live.
　b.　　*Merchant of Venice*. Act IV. Sc. 1.
　　　　　　　　　　　　　　　L. 375.

No change, no pause, no hope! Yet I endure.
　c.　　SHELLEY—*Prometheus Unbound*.
　　　　　　　　　　　　　Act I. L. 24.

　　　　* * * then black despair,
The shadow of a starless night, was thrown
Over the world in which I moved alone.
　d.　　SHELLEY—*Revolt of Islam*. *Dedication*.
　　　　　　　　　　　　　　　St. 6.

Inconsolable to the minuet in Ariadne!
　e.　　SHERIDAN—*The Critic*. Act II.
　　　　　　　　　　　　　　　Sc. 2.

Alas for him who never sees
The stars shine through his cypress-trees!
Who, hopeless, lays his dead away,
Nor looks to see the breaking day
Across the mournful marbles play!
　f.　　WHITTIER—*Snow-Bound*. L. 204.

　　　　　The fear that kills;
And hope that is unwilling to be fed.
　g.　　WORDSWORTH—*Resolution and
　　　　　　　　　　　　　Independence*.

When pain can't bless, heaven quits us in
despair.
　h.　　YOUNG—*Night Thoughts*. Night IX.
　　　　　　　　　　　　　　　L. 500.

DESTINY.

　　　　　My death and life,
My bane and antidote, are both before me.
　i.　　ADDISON—*Cato*. Act V. Sc. 1.

Life treads on life, and heart on heart;
We press too close in church and mart
To keep a dream or grave apart.
　j.　　E. B. BROWNING—*A Vision of Poets*.
　　　　　　　　　　　　　Conclusion.

Born in the garret, in the kitchen bred.
　k.　　BYRON—*A Sketch*. L. 1.

　　　　　For I am a weed,
Flung from the rock, on Ocean's foam, to sail,
Where'er the surge may sweep, the tempest's
　　breath prevail.
　l.　　BYRON—*Childe Harold*. Canto III.
　　　　　　　　　　　　　　　St. 2.

　　　　　　　There comes
For ever something between us and what
We deem our happiness.
　m.　　BYRON—*Sardanapalus*. Act I. Sc. 2.

"Whom the gods love die young," was said
　　of yore.
　n.　　BYRON—*Don Juan*. Canto IV. St. 12.

All has its date below; the fatal hour
Was register'd in Heav'n ere time began.
We turn to dust, and all our mightiest works
Die too.
　o.　　COWPER—*The Task*. Bk. V. *The
　　　　　　　　　Winter Morning Walk*. L. 540.

Not heaven itself upon the past has power;
But what has been, has been, and I have had
　　my hour.
　p.　　DRYDEN—*Imitation of Horace*. Bk. I.
　　　　　　　　　　　　Ode XXIX. L. 71.

Art and power will go on as they have
done,—will make day out of night, time out
of space, and space out of time.
　q.　　EMERSON—*Society and Solitude*.
　　　　　　　　　　　　Work and Days.

Take life too seriously, and what is it
worth? If the morning wake us to no new
joys, if the evening bring us not the hope of
new pleasures, is it worth while to dress and
undress? Does the sun shine on me to-day
that I may reflect on yesterday? That I may
endeavour to foresee and to control what can
neither be foreseen nor controlled—the destiny of to-morrow?
　r.　　GOETHE—*Egmont*. *Lewes' Life of
　　　　　　　　　　　　　Goethe*.

That each thing, both in small and in great,
fulfilleth the task which destiny hath set
down.
　s.　　HIPPOCRATES.

All, soon or late, are doom'd that path to
　　tread.
　t.　　HOMER—*The Odyssey*. Bk. XII. L. 31.
　　　　　　　　　　　　Pope's trans.

No living man can send me to the shades
Before my time; no man of woman born,
Coward or brave, can shun his destiny.
　u.　　HOMER—*The Iliad*. Bk. VI. L. 623.
　　　　　　　　　　　　Bryant's trans.

Ships that pass in the night, and speak each
　　other in passing,
Only a signal shown and a distant voice in
　　the darkness:
So on the ocean of life we pass and speak
　　one another,
Only a look and a voice, then darkness again
　　and a silence.
　v.　　LONGFELLOW—*Tales of a Wayside Inn*.
　　　　　The Theologian's Tale. *Elizabeth*.
　　　　　　　　　　　　　　Pt. IV.

What a glorious thing human life is, * * *
and how glorious man's destiny !
> *a.*   LONGFELLOW—*Hyperion.*   Bk. II.
> Ch. VI.

The future works out great men's destinies :
The present is enough for common souls,
Who, never looking forward, are indeed
Mere clay wherein the footprints of their age
Are petrified forever.
> *b.*   LOWELL—*Act for Truth.*

There are certain events which to each
man's life are as comets to the earth, seemingly strange and erratic portents ; distinct
from the ordinary lights which guide our
course and mark our seasons, yet true to their
own laws, potent in their own influences.
> *c.*   BULWER-LYTTON— *What Will He Do*
> *with It ?*   Bk. II.   Ch. XIV.

Alas ! how easily things go wrong !
A sigh too deep, or a kiss too long,
And then comes a mist and a weeping rain,
And life is never the same again.
> *d.*   GEORGE MACDONALD—*Phantastes. A*
> *Fairy Story.*

Our days and nights
Have sorrows woven with delights.
> *e.*   MALHERBE—*To Cardinal Richelieu.*
> Longfellow's trans.

They only fall, that strive to move,
Or lose, that care to keep.
> *f.*   OWEN MEREDITH (Lord Lytton)—*The*
> *Wanderer.*   Bk. III.   *Futility.*   St. 6.

Unseen hands delay
The coming of what oft seems close in ken,
And, contrary, the moment, when we say
"'Twill never come!" comes on us even then.
> *g.*   OWEN MEREDITH (Lord Lytton)—
> *Thomas Muntzer to Martin Luther.*
> L. 382.

We are but as the instrument of Heaven.
Our work is not design, but destiny.
> *h.*   OWEN MEREDITH (Lord Lytton)—
> *Clytemnestra.*   Pt. XIX.

We are what we must
And not what we would be.   I know that one
hour
Assures not another. The will and the
power
Are diverse.
> *i.*   OWEN MEREDITH (Lord Lytton)—
> *Lucile.*   Pt. I.   Canto III.   St. 19.

The irrevocable Hand
That opes the year's fair gate, doth ope and
shut
The portals of our earthly destinies ;
We walk through blindfold, and the noiseless
doors
Close after us, forever.
> *j.*   D. M. MULOCK—*April.*

Every man meets his Waterloo at last.
> *k.*   WENDELL PHILLIPS—*Speech.*
> Nov. 1, 1859.

He whom the gods love dies young, while
he is in health, has his senses and his judgment sound.
> *l.*   PLAUTUS—*Bacchid.*   IV.   7, 18.

Alive ridiculous, and dead forgot !
> *m.*   POPE—*Moral Essays.*   Ep. II.   L. 248.

Oh blindness to the future ! kindly given,
That each may fill the circle mark'd by heav'n ;
Who sees with equal eye, as God of all,
A hero perish, or a sparrow fall.
> *n.*   POPE—*Essay on Man.*   Ep. I.   L. 85.

We met, hand to hand,
We clasped hands close and fast,
As close as oak and ivy stand ;
But it is past :
Come day, come night, day comes at last.
> *o.*   CHRISTINA G. ROSSETTI—*Twilight.*
> *Night.*   I.   St. 1.

A man may fish with the worm that hath
eat of a king, and eat of the fish that hath
fed of that worm.
> *p.*   *Hamlet.*   Act IV.   Sc. 3.   L. 28.

A man whom both the waters and the wind,
In that vast tennis-court, hath made the ball
For them to play upon.
> *q.*   *Pericles.*   Act II.   Sc. 1.   L. 63.

Farewell ! a long farewell, to all my greatness !
This is the state of man : to-day he puts forth
The tender leaves of hope ; to-morrow
blossoms,
And bears his blushing honours thick upon
him :
The third day comes a frost, a killing frost,
And, when he thinks, good easy man, full
surely
His greatness is a-ripening, nips his root,
And then he falls, as I do.
> *r.*   *Henry VIII.*   Act III.   Sc. 2.   L. 351.

For it is a knell
That summons thee to heaven or to hell.
> *s.*   *Macbeth.*   Act II.   Sc. 1.   L. 63.

For some must watch, while some must sleep ;
So runs the world away.
> *t.*   *Hamlet.*   Act III.   Sc. 2.   L. 284.

Here burns my candle out ; ay, here it dies,
Which, whiles it lasted, gave King Henry
light.
> *u.*   *Henry VI.*   Pt. III.   Act II.   Sc. 6.
> L. 1.

If he had been as you and you as he,
You would have slipt like him.
> *v.*   *Measure for Measure.*   Act II.   Sc. 2.
> L. 64.

I have touched the highest point of all my
    greatness :
And, from that full meridian of my glory,
I haste now to my setting.
    a.   *Henry VIII.* Act III. Sc. 2. L. 223.

Imperious Cæsar, dead and turn'd to clay,
Might stop a hole to keep the wind away :
O, that that earth, which kept the world in
    awe,
Should patch a wall to expel the winter's
    flaw !
    b.   *Hamlet.* Act V. Sc. 1. L. 234.

Let Hercules himself do what he may,
The cat will mew and dog will have his day.
    c.   *Hamlet.* Act V. Sc. 1. L. 315.

    There is divinity in odd numbers, either in
nativity, chance or death.
    d.   *Merry Wives of Windsor.* Act V.
        Sc. 1. L. 3.

They that stand high have many blasts to
    shake them ;
And if they fall, they dash themselves to
    pieces.
    e.   *Richard III.* Act I. Sc. 3. L. 259.

Things at the worst will cease, or else climb
    upward
To what they were before.
    f.   *Macbeth.* Act IV. Sc. 2. L. 24.

Think you I bear the shears of destiny?
Have I commandment on the pulse of life?
    g.   *King John.* Act IV. Sc. 2. L. 91.

We shall be winnow'd with so rough a wind
That even our corn shall seem as light as
    chaff,
And good from bad find no partition.
    h.   *Henry IV.* Pt. II. Act. IV. Sc. 1.
        L. 194.

What a falling-off was there !
    i.   *Hamlet.* Act I. Sc. 5. L. 47.

What is done cannot be now amended.
    j.   *Richard III.* Act IV. Sc. 4. L. 291.

When I shun Scylla, your father, I fall into
    Charybdis, your mother.
    k.   *Merchant of Venice.* Act III. Sc. 5.
        L. 18.

The seed ye sow, another reaps ;
The wealth ye find, another keeps ;
The robes ye weave, another wears ;
The arms ye forge, another bears.
    l.   SHELLEY—*Song. To Men of England.*

We rest—A dream has power to poison sleep ;
We rise—One wandering thought pollutes the
    day.
    m.   SHELLEY—*Mutability.*

    And all the bustle of departure—sometimes
sad, sometimes intoxicating—just as fear or
hope may be inspired by the new chances of
coming destiny.
    n.   MADAME DE STAËL—*Corinne.* Bk. X.
        Ch. VI.

And from his ashes may be made
The violet of his native land.
    o.   TENNYSON—*In Memoriam.* XVIII.
        St. 1.

Pluck one thread, and the web ye mar ;
    Break but one
Of a thousand keys, and the paining jar
Through all will run.
    p.   WHITTIER—*My Soul and I.* St. 38.

To be a Prodigal's favourite,—then, worse
    truth,
A Miser's Pensioner,—behold our lot !
    q.   WORDSWORTH—*The Small Celandine.*

DEVIL, THE.

    The Devil himself, which is the author of
confusion and lies.
    r.   BURTON—*Anatomy of Melancholy.*
        Pt. III. Sec. IV. Memb. I.
        Subsect. 3.

And bid the devil take the hin'most.
    s.   BUTLER—*Hudibras.* Pt. I. Canto II.
        L. 633.

Nick Machiavel had ne'er a trick
(Though he gave his name to our Old Nick).
    t.   BUTLER—*Hudibras.* Pt. III. Canto I.
        L. 1,313.

I call'd the devil, and he came,
    And with wonder his form did I closely
        scan ;
He is not ugly, and is not lame,
    But really a handsome and charming man.
A man in the prime of life is the devil,
Obliging, a man of the world, and civil ;
A diplomatist too, well skill'd in debate,
He talks quite glibly of church and state.
    u.   HEINE—*Pictures of Travels. The*
        Return Home. No. 37.

The Devil is an ass, I do acknowledge it.
    v.   BEN JONSON—*The Devil is an Ass.*
        Act IV. Sc. 1.

    It is Lucifer,
The son of mystery ;
And since God suffers him to be,
He, too, is God's minister,
And labors for some good
By us not understood.
    w.   LONGFELLOW—*Christus. The Golden*
        Legend. Epilogue. Last stanza.

The Devil, my friends, is a woman just now.
'Tis a woman that reigns in Hell.
  a.   Owen Meredith (Lord Lytton)—
                              News.

        Black it stood as night,
Fierce as ten furies, terrible as hell,
And shook a dreadful dart; what seem'd his
    head
The likeness of a kingly crown had on.
Satan was now at hand.
  b.   Milton—*Paradise Lost.* Bk. II.
                          L. 670.

          From morn
To noon he fell, from noon to dewy eve,
A summer's day; and with the setting sun
Dropt from the zenith like a falling star.
  c.   Milton—*Paradise Lost.* Bk. I.
                          L. 742.

      His form had yet not lost
All his original brightness, nor appear'd
Less than arch-angel ruined, and th' excess
Of glory obscured.
  d.   Milton—*Paradise Lost.* Bk. I.
                          L. 591.

Incens'd with indignation Satan stood
Unterrified, and like a comet burn'd,
That fires the length of Ophiucus huge
In th' arctic sky, and from his horrid hair
Shakes pestilence and war.
  e.   Milton—*Paradise Lost.* Bk. II.
                          L. 707.

Satan exalted sat, by merit raised
To that bad eminence.
  f.   Milton—*Paradise Lost.* Bk. II. L. 5.

Satan; so call him now, his former name
Is heard no more in heaven.
  g.   Milton—*Paradise Lost.* Bk. V.
                          L. 658.

Swinges the scaly horror of his folded tail.
  h.   Milton—*Hymn on Christ's Nativity.*
                          L. 172.

The infernal serpent; he it was whose guile,
Stirr'd up with envy and revenge, deceived
The mother of mankind.
  i.   Milton—*Paradise Lost.* Bk. I. L. 34.

        With grave
Aspect he rose, and in his rising seem'd
A pillar of state; deep on his front engraven
Deliberation sat and public care;
And princely counsel in his face yet shone,
Majestic though in ruin.
  j.   Milton—*Paradise Lost.* Bk. II.
                          L. 300.

The Devil was sick, the Devil a monk would
    be;
The Devil was well, the Devil a monk was he.
  k.   Rabelais—*Works.* Bk. IV.
                        Ch. XXIV.

Let me say "amen" betimes, lest the devil
cross my prayer.
  l.   *Merchant of Venice.* Act III. Sc. 1.
                          L. 22.

Nay, then, let the devil wear black, for I'll
have a suit of sables.
  m.   *Hamlet.* Act III. Sc. 2. L. 136.

The lunatic, the lover and the poet,
Are of imagination all compact:
One sees more devils than vast hell can hold.
  n.   *Midsummer Night's Dream.* Act V.
                      Sc. 1. L. 7.

The prince of darkness is a gentleman.
  o.   *King Lear.* Act III. Sc. 4. L. 147.

This is a devil, and no monster; I will
leave him; I have no long spoon.
  p.   *The Tempest.* Act II. Sc. 2. L. 101.

What, man! defy the devil: consider, he's
an enemy to mankind.
  q.   *Twelfth Night.* Act III. Sc. 4. L. 107.

From his brimstone bed, at break of day,
    A-walking the Devil is gone,
To look at his little snug farm of the world,
    And see how his stock went on.
  r.   Southey—*The Devil's Walk.* St. 1.

The Satanic school.
  s.   Southey—*Vision of Judgment.*
                  Original Preface. III.

The prince of darkness is a gentleman.
  t.   Sir John Suckling—*The Goblins.*
                      Song. Act III.

The bane of all that dread the Devil!
  u.   Wordsworth—*The Idiot Boy.* St. 67.

DEW.

The Dewdrop slips into the shining sea!
  v.   Edwin Arnold—*Light of Asia.*
                  Bk. VIII. Last Line.

    Dewdrops, Nature's tears, which she
Sheds in her own breast for the fair which
    die.
The sun insists on gladness; but at night,
When he is gone, poor Nature loves to weep.
  w.   Bailey—*Festus.* Sc. *Water and Wood.*
                        Midnight.

          The dew,
'Tis of the tears which stars weep, sweet with
    joy.
  x.   Bailey—*Festus.* Sc. *Another and a*
                      Better World.

Within the rose I found a trembling tear,
Close curtained in a gloom of crimson night
By tender petals from the outer light.
  y.   Boyesen—*Within the Rose I Found a*
                      Trembling Tear.

The dews of the evening most carefully shun;
Those tears of the sky for the loss of the sun.
   a.   Earl of Chesterfield—*Advice to a
                       Lady in Autumn.*

Dew-drops are the gems of morning,
But the tears of mournful eve!
   b.   Coleridge—*Youth and Age.*

        The dew-bead
Gem of earth and sky begotten.
   c.   George Eliot—*The Spanish Gypsy.*
                     Song. Bk. I.

Every dew-drop and rain-drop had a whole
heaven within it.
   d.   Longfellow—*Hyperion.* Bk. III.
                         Ch. VII.

Or stars of morning, dew-drops which the sun
Impearls on every leaf and every flower.
   e.   Milton—*Paradise Lost.* Bk. V. L. 746.

The dew-drops in the breeze of morn,
Trembling and sparkling on the thorn,
Falls to the ground, escapes the eye,
Yet mounts on sunbeams to the sky.
   f.   Montgomery—*A Recollection of
                       Mary F.*

I must go seek some dewdrops here,
And hang a pearl in every cowslip's ear.
   g.   *Midsummer-Night's Dream.* Act II.
                      Sc. 1. L. 14.

And every dew-drop paints a bow.
   h.   Tennyson—*In Memoriam.* Pt. CXXII.

DIFFICULTIES.

Pursuit of knowledge under difficulties.
   i.   Lord Brougham—*Title given to a Book.*

Many things difficult to design prove easy
to performance.
   j.   Sam'l Johnson—*Rasselas.* Ch. XIII.

So he with difficulty and labor hard
Mov'd on, with difficulty and labor he.
   k.   Milton—*Paradise Lost.* Bk. II.
                         L. 1021.

It is as hard to come as for a camel
To thread the postern of a small needle's eye.
   l.   *Richard II.* Act V. Sc. 5. L. 16.

There is such a choice of difficulties, that I
own myself at a loss how to determine.
   m.   James Wolfe—*Dispatch to Pitt.*
                      Sept. 2, 1759.

DIGNITY.

Remember this,—that there is a proper dignity and proportion to be observed in the
performance of every act of life.
   n.   Marcus Aurelius—*Meditations.*
                      IV. 32.

        The dignity of truth is lost
With much protesting.
   o.   Ben Jonson—*Catiline.* Act III. Sc. 2.

       * * * With grave
Aspect he rose, and in his rising seem'd
A pillar of state; deep on his front engraven
Deliberation sat, and public care;
And princely counsel in his face yet shone
Majestic, though in ruin: sage he stood,
With Atlantéan shoulders, fit to bear
The weight of mightiest monarchies; his look
Drew audience and attention still as night
Or summer's noontide air.
   p.   Milton—*Paradise Lost.* Bk. II. L. 300.

Virtue, I grant you, is an empty boast;
But shall the dignity of vice be lost?
   q.   Pope—*Epilogue to Satires.* Dialogue I.

We have exchanged the Washingtonian
dignity for the Jeffersonian simplicity, which
was in truth only another name for the Jeffersonian vulgarity.
   r.   Bishop Henry C. Potter—*Address at
                  the Washington Centennial Service.*
                 New York, April 30, 1889.

But clay and clay differs in dignity,
Whose dust is both alike.
   s.   *Cymbeline.* Act IV. Sc. 2. L. 6.

        Let none presume
To wear an undeserved dignity.
   t.   *Merchant of Venice.* Act II. Sc. 9.
                         L. 39.

DIMPLES.

Then did she lift her hands unto his chin,
And praised the pretty dimpling of his skin.
   u.   Beaumont—*Salmacis and
                   Hermaphroditus.* L. 661.

   In each cheek appears a pretty dimple;
Love made those hollows; if himself were
     slain,
He might be buried in a tomb so simple;
Foreknowing well, if there he came to lie,
Why, there Love lived and there he could
     not die.
   v.   *Venus and Adonis.* L. 242.

DISAPPOINTMENT.

A thousand years a poor man watched
   Before the gate of Paradise:
But while one little nap he snatched,
   It oped and shut. Ah! was he wise?
   w.   Wm. R. Alger—*Oriental Poetry.*
                    Swift Opportunity.

The best-laid schemes o' mice an' men,
   Gang aft a-gley,
And leave us nought but grief and pain,
   For promised joy.
   x.   Burns—*To a Mouse.* St. 7.

Like to the apples on the Dead Sea's shore,
All ashes to the taste.
   a.   Byron—*Childe Harold.* III. 34.

Defend me, therefore, common sense, say I,
From reveries so airy, from the toil
Of dropping buckets into empty wells,
And growing old in drawing nothing up.
   b.   Cowper—*Task.* Bk. III. L. 187.

As distant prospects please us, but when near
We find but desert rocks and fleeting air.
   c.   Sir Sam'l Garth—*The Dispensary.*
                 Canto III. L. 27.

Lightly I sped when hope was high
  And youth beguiled the chase,—
I follow, follow still : But I
  Shall never see her face.
   d.   Fred'k Locker—*The Unrealized Ideal.*

But O ! as to embrace me she inclin'd,
I wak'd, she fled, and day brought back my
    night.
   e.   Milton—*On His Deceased Wife.*

Oh ! ever thus, from childhood's hour,
  I've seen my fondest hopes decay ;
I never loved a tree or flower,
  But 'twas the first to fade away.
I never nursed a dear gazelle,
  To glad me with its soft black eye,
But when it came to know me well,
  And love me, it was sure to die !
   f.   Moore—*Lalla Rookh. The Fire*
               Worshippers. L. 278.

Oh ! that a dream so sweet, so long enjoy'd,
Should be so sadly, cruelly destroy'd !
   g.   Moore—*Lalla Rookh. Veiled Prophet*
              of Khorassan. St. 62.

All is but toys ; renown and grace is dead ;
The wine of life is drawn, and the mere lees
Is left this vault to brag of.
   h.   *Macbeth.* Act II. Sc. 3. L. 99.

Full little knowest thou that hast not tried,
What hell it is in suing long to bide :
To loose good dayes, that might be better
    spent ;
To waste long nights in pensive discontent ;
To speed to-day, to be put back to-morrow ;
To feed on hope, to pine with feare and sor-
    row.
   i.   Spenser—*Mother Hubberd's Tale.*
                     L. 895.

DISCONTENT.

In such a strait the wisest may well be perplexed, and the boldest staggered.
   j.   Burke—*Thoughts on the Cause of the*
           Present Discontents. Vol. I. P. 516.

Whoe'er was edified, themselves were not.
   k.   Cowper—*The Task.* Bk. II. *The*
                 Time Piece. L. 444.

The best of things beyond their measure cloy.
   l.   Homer—*The Iliad.* Bk. XIII. L. 795.
                     Pope's trans.

It happens as with cages ; the birds without
despair to get in, and those within despair of
getting out.
   m.   Montaigne—*Upon some Verses of Virgil.*
                    Bk. III. Ch. V.

To sigh, yet feel no pain,
  To weep, yet scarce know why ;
To sport an hour with Beauty's chain,
  Then throw it idly by.
   n.   Moore—*The Blue Stocking.*

I know a discontented gentleman,
Whose humble means match not his haughty
    mind.
   o.   *Richard III.* Act IV. Sc. 2. L. 36.

I see your brows are full of discontent,
Your hearts of sorrow and your eyes of tears.
   p.   *Richard II.* Act IV. Sc. I. L. 331.

Past and to come seem best ; things present
    worst.
   q.   *Henry IV.* Pt. II. Act I. Sc. 3.
                     L. 108.

Seldom he smiles and smiles in such a sort
As if he mocked himself and scorned his
    spirit
That could be moved to smile at anything.
   r.   *Julius Cæsar.* Act I. Sc. 2. L. 205.

No great thought, no great object, satisfies
the mind at first view—nor at the last.
   s.   Abel Stevens—*Madame de Staël.*
                    Ch. XXXVIII.

We love in others what we lack ourselves,
and would be everything but what we are.
   t.   R. H. Stoddard—*Arcadian Idyl.* L. 30.

I was *born* to other things.
   u.   Tennyson—*In Memoriam.* CXX.

Poor in abundance, famish'd at a feast.
   v.   Young—*Night Thoughts.* Night VII.
                     L. 44.

DISCRETION.

It shew'd discretion, the best part of valor.
   w.   Beaumont and Fletcher—*A King*
               and No King. Act IV. Sc. 3.

Covering discretion with a coat of folly.
   x.   *Henry V.* Act II. Sc. 4. L. 38.

For 'tis not good that children should know
any wickedness : old folks, you know, have
discretion, as they say, and know the world.
   y.   *Merry Wives of Windsor.* Act II.
                    Sc. 2. L. 131.

I have seen the day of wrong through the little hole of discretion.

    a.   *Love's Labour's Lost.* Act V. Sc. 2.
                          L. 733.

Let's teach ourselves that honourable stop,
Not to outsport discretion.

    b.   *Othello.* Act II. Sc. 3. L. 2.

Let your own discretion be your tutor: suit the action to the word, the word to the action.

    c.   *Hamlet.* Act III. Sc. 2. L. 18.

The better part of valour is discretion; in the which better part I have saved my life.

    d.   *Henry IV.* Pt. I. Act V. Sc. 4.
                          L. 121.

DISEASE.

Apoplexie, and *Lethargie,*
As forlorn hope, assault the enemy.

    e.   Du Bartas—*Divine Weekes and Workes.*
        Second Week. First Day. Pt. III.
                      The Furies.

[Diseases] crucify the soul of man, attenuate our bodies, dry them, wither them, shrivel them up like old apples, make them as so many anatomies.

    f.   Burton—*Anatomy of Melancholy.*
             Pt. I. Sc. 2. Memb. 3.
                      Subsect. 10.

That dire disease, whose ruthless power
Withers the beauty's transient flower.

    g.   Goldsmith—*Double Transformation.*
                          L. 75.

A bodily disease which we look upon as whole and entire within itself, may, after all, be but a symptom of some ailment in the spiritual part.

    h.   Nath. Hawthorne—*Scarlet Letter.*
                          Ch. X.

Against diseases here the strongest fence,
Is the defensive virtue, abstinence.

    i.   Herrick—*Abstinence.*

As man, perhaps, the moment of his breath,
Receives the lurking principle of death,
The young disease, that must subdue at
    length,
Grows with his growth, and strengthens with
    his strength.

    j.   Pope—*Essay on Man.* Ep. II.
                          L. 133.

But just disease to luxury succeeds,
And ev'ry death its own avenger breeds.

    k.   Pope—*Essay on Man.* Ep. III.
                          L. 165.

Diseases desperate grown
By desperate appliance are reliev'd,
Or not at all.

    l.   *Hamlet.* Act IV. Sc. 3. L. 9.

                        I'll forbear;
And am fallen out with my more headier will,
To take the indispos'd and sickly fit
For the sound man.

    m.   *King Lear.* Act II. Sc. 4. L. 110.

O, he's a limb, that has but a disease;
Mortal, to cut it off; to cure it, easy.

    n.   *Coriolanus.* Act III. Sc. 1. L. 296.

Therefore the moon, the governess of floods,
Pale in her anger, washes all the air,
That rheumatic diseases do abound.

    o.   *Midsummer Night's Dream.* Act II.
                      Sc. 1. L. 103.

This apoplexy is, as I take it, a kind of lethargy, an't please your lordship; a kind of sleeping in the blood, a whoreson tingling.

    p.   *Henry IV.* Pt. II. Act I. Sc. 2.
                          L. 125.

        This sickness doth infect
The very life-blood of our enterprise.

    q.   *Henry IV.* Pt. I. Act IV. Sc. 1.
                          L. 28.

So when a raging fever burns,
We shift from side to side by turns;
And 'tis a poor relief we gain,
To change the place but keep the pain.

    r.   Watts—*Hymns and Spiritual Songs.*
                    Bk. II. Hymn 146.

DISGRACE.

The unbought grace of life, the cheap defence of nations, the nurse of manly sentiment and heroic enterprise, is gone !

    s.   Burke—*Reflections on the Revolution in*
                            France.

Could he with reason murmur at his case,
Himself sole author of his own disgrace?

    t.   Cowper—*Hope.* L. 316.

Come, Death, and snatch me from disgrace.

    u.   Bulwer-Lytton—*Richelieu.* Act IV.
                          Sc. 1.

And wilt thou still be hammering treachery,
To tumble down thy husband and thyself
From top of honour to disgrace's feet?

    v.   *Henry VI.* Pt. II. Act I. Sc. 2.
                          L. 47.

DISSENSION.

Have always been at daggers-drawing,
And one another clapper-clawing.

    w.   Butler—*Hudibras.* Pt. II. Canto II.
                          L. 79.

And Doubt and Discord step 'twixt thine and
    thee.

    x.   Byron—*The Prophecy of Dante.*
                    Canto II. L. 140.

That each pull'd different ways with many an
    oath,
" Arcades ambo," *id est*—blackguards both.
   a.   Byron—*Don Juan.* Canto IV. St. 93.

Dissensions, like small streams, are first be-
    gun,
Scarce seen they rise, but gather as they run :
So lines that from their parallel decline,
More they proceed the more they still disjoin.
   b.   Sir Sam'l Garth—*The Dispensary.*
                   Canto III. L. 184.

And bitter waxed the fray ;
Brother with brother spake no word
  When they met in the way.
   c.   Jean Ingelow—*Poems. Strife and
                        Peace.*

An old affront will stir the heart
Through years of rankling pain.
   d.   Jean Ingelow—*Poems. Strife and
                        Peace.*

Alas ! how light a cause may move
Dissension between hearts that love !
Hearts that the world in vain had tried,
And sorrow but more closely tied ;
That stood the storm when waves were rough.
Yet in a sunny hour fall off.
   e.   Moore—*Lalla Rookh. The Light of
                  the Harem.* L. 183.

Believe me, lords, my tender years can tell
Civil dissension is a viperous worm
That gnaws the bowels of the commonwealth.
   f.   *Henry VI.* Pt. I. Act III. Sc. 1.
                        L. 71.

If they perceive dissension in our looks
And that within ourselves we disagree,
How will their grudging stomachs be pro-
    voked
To wilful disobedience and rebel !
   g.   *Henry VI.* Pt. I. Act IV. Sc. 1.
                        L. 139.

Now join your hands, and with your hands
    your hearts,
That no dissension hinder government.
   h.   *Henry VI.* Pt. III. Act IV. Sc. 6.
                        L. 39.

Let dogs delight to bark and bite,
For God hath made them so ;
Let bears and lions growl and fight,
For 'tis their nature to.
   i.   Watts—*Divine Songs. Song XVI.*

Discord, a sleepless hag who never dies,
With Snipe-like nose, and Ferret-glowing eyes,
Lean sallow cheeks, long chin with beard
    supplied,
Poor crackling joints, and wither'd parchment
    hide,
As if old Drums, worn out with martial din,
Had clubb'd their yellow Heads to form her
    Skin.
   j.   John Wolcott (Peter Pindar)—*The
             Louisad.* Canto III. L. 121.

DISTRUST.

Self-distrust is the cause of most of our
failures. In the assurance of strength there
is strength, and they are the weakest, however strong, who have no faith in themselves
or their powers.
   k.   Bovee—*Summaries of Thought.
                    Self-Reliance.*

What loneliness is more lonely than distrust?
   l.   George Eliot—*Middlemarch.* Bk. V.
                      Ch. XLIV.

A certain amount of distrust is wholesome,
but not so much of others as of ourselves ;
neither vanity nor conceit can exist in the
same atmosphere with it.
   m.   Madame Necker.

Three things a wise man will not trust,
The wind, the sunshine of an April day,
And woman's plighted faith.
   n.   Southey—*Madac in Azthan.*
                  Pt. XXIII.   L. 51.

DOCTRINE.

For his religion, it was fit
To match his learning and his wit;
'Twas Presbyterian true blue ;
For he was of that stubborn crew
Of errant saints, whom all men grant
To be the true Church Militant;
Such as do build their faith upon
The holy text of pike and gun ;
Decide all controversies by
Infallible artillery ;
And prove their doctrine orthodox,
By Apostolic blows and knocks.
   o.   Butler—*Hudibras.* Pt. I.   Canto I.
                      L. 189.

What makes all doctrines plain and clear?—
About two hundred pounds a year.
And that which was prov'd true before
Prove false again? Two hundred more.
   p.   Butler—*Hudibras.* Pt. III. Canto I.
                      L. 1,277.

Sapping a solemn creed with a solemn sneer.
   q.   Byron—*Childe Harold.* Canto III.
                      St. 107.

Forth from his dark and lonely hiding-place,
(Portentous sight) the owlet Atheism,
Sailing on obscene wings athwart the noon,
Drops his blue-fringed lids, and holds them
    close,
And hooting at the glorious sun in Heaven,
Cries out, " Where is it?"
   r.   Coleridge—*Fears in Solitude.* L. 81.

O how far remov'd,
Predestination! is thy foot from such
As see not the First Cause entire: and ye,
O mortal men! be wary how ye judge:
For we, who see the Maker, know not yet
The number of the chosen; and esteem
Such scantiness of knowledge our delight:
For all our good is, in that primal good,
Concentrate; and God's will and ours are one.
  a.   DANTE—*Vision of Paradise.*
                                    Canto XX. L. 122.

The Athanasian Creed is the most splendid
ecclesiastical lyric ever poured forth by the
genius of man.
  b.   BENJ. DISRAELI—*Endymion.* Ch. LIV.

You can and you can't,
You will and you won't;
You'll be damn'd if you do,
You'll be damn'd if you don't.
  c.   LORENZO DOW—*Chain (Definition of
                                    Calvinism).*

And after hearing what our Church can say,
If still our reason runs another way,
That private reason 'tis more just to curb,
Than by disputes the public peace disturb;
For points obscure are of small use to learn,
But common quiet is mankind's concern.
  d.   DRYDEN—*Religio Laici.* L. 445.

Go put your creed into your deed
Nor speak with double tongue.
  e.   EMERSON—*Ode. Concord. July 4, 1857.*

Shall I ask the brave soldier, who fights by
    my side
  In the cause of mankind, if our creeds agree?
Shall I give up the friend I have valued and
    tried,
  If he kneel not before the same altar with
    me?
From the heretic girl of my soul should I fly,
  To seek somewhere else a more orthodox
    kiss?
No! perish the hearts, and the laws that try
  Truth, valour, or love, by a standard like
    this!
  f.   MOORE—*Irish Melodies.   Come Send
                                    Round the Wine.*

  "Get Money, money still!
And then let virtue follow, if she will."
This, this the saving doctrine preach'd to all,
From low St. James' up to high St. Paul.
  g.   POPE—*First Book of Horace.* Ep. I.
                                    L. 79.

Slave to no sect, who takes no private road,
But looks through nature up to nature's God.
  h.   POPE—*Essay on Man.* Ep. IV. L. 330.

  "Orthodoxy, my Lord," said Bishop Warburton, in a whisper,—"orthodoxy is my
doxy,—heterodoxy is another man's doxy."
  i.   JOSEPH PRIESTLY—*Memoirs.* Vol. I.
                                    P. 572.

Live to explain thy doctrine by thy life.
  j.   PRIOR—*To Dr. Sherlock.   On his
                            Practical Discourse Concerning
                                    Death.*

As thou these ashes, little brook! will bear
Into the Avon, Avon to the tide
Of Severn, Severn to the narrow seas,
Into main ocean they, this deed accurst,
An emblem yields to friends and enemies
How the bold teacher's doctrine, sanctified
By truth, shall spread throughout the world
    dispersed.
  k.   WORDSWORTH—*Ecclesiastical Sketches.*
                            Pt. II.   *Wicliffe.*

DOUBT.

Who never doubted, never half believed.
Where doubt there truth is—'tis her shadow.
  l.   BAILEY—*Festus.* Sc. *A Country Town.*

He would not, with a peremptory tone,
Assert the nose upon his face his own.
  m.   COWPER—*Conversation.* L. 121.

        Uncertain ways unsafest are,
And doubt a greater mischief than despair.
  n.   SIR JOHN DENHAM—*Cooper's Hill.*
                                    L. 399.

Doubt indulged soon becomes doubt realized.
  o.   F. R. HAVERGAL—*Royal Bounty.   The
                        Imagination of the Thoughts of the
                                    Heart.*

The doubtful beam long nods from side to side.
  p.   POPE—*Rape of the Lock.* Canto V.
                                    L. 73.

Fain would I but I dare not; I dare, and yet
    I may not;
I may, although I care not for pleasure when
    I play not.
  q.   SIR WALTER RALEIGH—*A Lover's
                                    Verses.*

        But the gods are dead—
Ay, Zeus is dead, and all the gods but Doubt,
And Doubt is brother devil to Despair!
  r.   JOHN BOYLE O'REILLY—*Prometheus.
                                    Christ.*

But now I am cabin'd, cribb'd, confin'd,
    bound in
To saucy doubts and fears.
  s.   *Macbeth.* Act III. Sc. 4. L. 24.

But yet, madam—
I do not like "But yet," it does allay
The good precedence; fie upon "But yet;"
"But yet" is as a gaoler to bring forth
Some monstrous malefactor.
  t.   *Antony and Cleopatra.* Act II. Sc. 5.
                                    L. 49.

He that is more than a youth, is not for
me, and he that is less than man, I am not
for him.

   a.   *Much Ado About Nothing.* Act II.
                        Sc. 1. L. 40.

          Modest doubt is call'd
The beacon of the wise.

   b.   *Troilus and Cressida.* Act II. Sc. 2.
                                L. 15.

            No hinge nor loop,
To hang a doubt on; or woe upon thy life!

   c.   *Othello.* Act III. Sc. 3. L. 366.

Our doubts are traitors
And make us lose the good we oft might win
By fearing to attempt.

   d.   *Measure for Measure.* Act I. Sc. 4.
                                L. 77.

          To be once in doubt
Is once to be resolv'd.

   e.   *Othello.* Act III. Sc. 3. L. 179.

To be, or not to be, that is the question :
Whether 'tis nobler in the mind to suffer
The slings and arrows of outrageous fortune ;
Or to take arms against a sea of troubles,
And by opposing end them ?

   f.   *Hamlet.* Act III. Sc. 1. L. 56.

To believe with certainty we must begin with
     doubting.

   g.   STANISLAUS (King of Poland)—*Maxims
            and Moral Sentences.* No. 61.

There lives more faith in honest doubt,
Believe me, than in half the creeds.

   h.   TENNYSON—*In Memoriam.* Pt. XCV.
                              St. 3.

Of the terrible doubt of appearances,
Of the uncertainty after all, that we may-be
     deluded,
That may-be reliance and hope are but specu-
     lations after all,
That may-be identity beyond the grave is a
     beautiful fable only,
May-be the things I perceive, the animals,
     plants, men, hills, shining and flowing
     waters,
The skies of day and night, colors, densities,
     forms, may-be these are (as doubtless
     they are) only apparitions, and the real
     something has yet to be known.

   i.   WALT. WHITMAN—*Of the Terrible
                      Doubt of Appearances.*

DREAMS.

When to soft Sleep we give ourselves away,
   And in a dream as in a fairy bark
   Drift on and on through the enchanted dark
To purple daybreak—little thought we pay
To that sweet bitter world we know by day.

   j.   T. B. ALDRICH—*Sonnet. Sleep.*

Sweet sleep be with us, one and all!
And if upon its stillness fall
The visions of a busy brain,
We'll have our pleasure o'er again,
To warm the heart, to charm the sight,
Gay dreams to all! good night, good night.

   k.   JOANNA BAILLIE—*The Phantom. Song.*

Sleep brings dreams; and dreams are often
most vivid and fantastical, before we have yet
been wholly lost in slumber.

   l.   ROBERT MONTGOMERY BIRD—*Calavar.*
                             Ch. XXXI.

A change came o'er the spirit of my dream.

   m.   BYRON—*The Dream.* St. 3.

And dreams in their development have breath,
And tears, and tortures, and the touch of joy ;
They have a weight upon our waking
     thoughts,
They take a weight from off our waking toils,
They do divide our being.

   n.   BYRON—*The Dream.* St. 1.

I had a dream, which was not all a dream.

   o.   BYRON—*Darkness.*

The fisher droppeth his net in the stream,
   And a hundred streams are the same as one ;
And the maiden dreameth her love-lit dream ;
   And what is it all, when all is done?
The net of the fisher the burden breaks,
And always the dreaming the dreamer wakes.

   p.   ALICE CARY—*Lover's Diary.*

          Like the dreams,
Children of night, of indigestion bred.

   q.   CHURCHILL—*The Candidate.* L. 784.

And so, his senses gradually wrapt
In a half sleep, he dreams of better worlds,
And dreaming hears thee still, O singing lark:
That singest like an angel in the clouds.

   r.   COLERIDGE—*Fears in Solitude.* L. 25.

My eyes make pictures, when they are shut.

   s.   COLERIDGE—*A Day Dream.*

          Dream after dream ensues ;
And still they dream that they shall still suc-
     ceed ;
And still are disappointed.

   t.   COWPER—*The Task.* Bk. III. L. 127.

Dreams are but interludes, which fancy
     makes ;
When monarch reason sleeps, this mimic
     wakes.

   u.   DRYDEN—*Fables. The Cock and the Fox.*
                                L. 325.

In blissful dream, in silent night,
There came to me, with magic might,
With magic might, my own sweet love,
Into my little room above.

   v.   HEINE—*Youthful Sorrows.* Pt. VI.
                              St. 1.

Fly, dotard, fly!
With thy wise dreams and fables of the sky.
   a.   Homer—*The Odyssey.* Bk. 2. L. 207.
                          Pope's trans.

Some dreams we have are nothing else but
    dreams,
Unnatural and full of contradictions;
Yet others of our most romantic schemes
Are something more than fictions.
   b.   Hood—*The Haunted House.* Pt. I.

And the dream that our mind had sketched in
    haste
Shall others continue, but never complete.
For none upon earth can achieve his scheme;
    The best as the worst are futile here:
We wake at the self-same point of the dream,—
    All is here begun, and finished elsewhere.
   c.   Victor Hugo—*Early Love Revisited.*

Abou Ben Adhem (may his tribe increase!)
Awoke one night from a deep dream of peace.
   d.   Leigh Hunt—*Abou Ben Adhem.*

Ever of thee I'm fondly dreaming,
Thy gentle voice my spirit can cheer.
   e.   George Linley—*Ever of Thee.*

Is this a dream? O, if it be a dream,
Let me sleep on, and do not wake me yet!
   f.   Longfellow—*Spanish Student.*
                       Act III. Sc. 5.

'Twas but a dream,—let it pass,—let it vanish
    like so many others!
What I thought was a flower is only a weed,
    and is worthless.
   g.   Longfellow—*Courtship of Miles
             Standish.* Pt. VII.

For dhrames always go by conthraries, my
    dear.
   h.   Samuel Lover—*Rory O'More.*

Ground not upon dreams, you know they are
    ever contrary.
   i.   Thos. Middleton—*The Family of Love.*
                       Act IV. Sc. 3.

I believe it to be true that Dreams are the
true Interpreters of our Inclinations; but
there is Art required to sort and understand
them.
   j.   Montaigne—*Essays.* Bk. III.
                       Ch. XIII.

One of those passing rainbow dreams,
Half light, half shade, which fancy's beams
Paint on the fleeting mists that roll,
In trance or slumber, round the soul!
   k.   Moore—*Lalla Rookh. Fire
             Worshippers.* St. 54.

Friday night's dreams on Saturday told
Are sure to come true—be they never so old.
   l.   *Old Sayings.*

Dreams, which, beneath the hov'ring shades
    of night,
Sport with the ever-restless minds of men,
Descend not from the gods. Each busy brain
Creates its own.
   m.   Thomas Love Peacock—*Dreams.*
                      From Petronius Arbiter.

What was your dream?
   It seemed to me that a woman in white
raiment, graceful and fair to look upon, came
towards me and calling me by name said:
   On the third day, Socrates, thou shalt reach
the coast of fertile Phthia.
   n.   Plato—*Crito.*

That holy dream—that holy dream,
   While all the world were chiding,
Hath cheered me as a lovely beam
   A lonely spirit guiding.
   o.   Poe—*A Dream.* St. 3.

Yet eat in dreams, the custard of the day.
   p.   Pope—*The Dunciad.* Bk. I. L. 92.

O Brethren, weep to-day,
The silent God hath quenched my Torch's
    ray,
And the vain dream hath flown.
   q.   Schiller—*Resignation.* Bowring's
                          trans.

I'll dream no more—by manly mind
Not even in sleep is well resigned.
My midnight orisons said o'er,
I'll turn to rest and dream no more.
   r.   Scott—*Lady of the Lake.* Canto I.
                          St. 35.

For never yet one hour in his bed
Have I enjoyed the golden dew of sleep,
But have been waked by his timorous dreams.
   s.   *Richard III.* Act IV. Sc. 1. L. 83.

If I may trust the flattering truth of sleep,
My dreams presage some joyful news at hand:
My bosom's lord sits lightly in his throne;
And all this day an unaccustom'd spirit
Lifts me above the ground with cheerful
    thoughts.
   t.   *Romeo and Juliet.* Act V. Sc. 1.
                          L. 1.

I have had a most rare vision. I have had
a dream, past the wit of man to say what
dream it was.
   u.   *Midsummer-Night's Dream.* Act IV.
                    Sc. 1. L. 211.

I talk of dreams,
Which are the children of an idle brain,
Begot of nothing but vain fantasy,
Which is as thin of substance as the air
And more inconstant than the wind.
   v.   *Romeo and Juliet.* Act I. Sc. 4.
                          L. 96.

Oh! I have pass'd a miserable night,
So full of ugly sights, of ghastly dreams,
That, as I am a Christian faithful man,
I would not spend another such a night,
Though 'twere to buy a world of happy days.
   a.   *Richard III.* Act I. Sc. 4. L. 2.

Sometime she driveth o'er a soldier's neck,
And then dreams he of cutting foreign throats,
Of breaches, ambuscadoes, Spanish blades,
Of healths five-fathom deep.
   b.   *Romeo and Juliet.* Act 1. Sc. 4.
                             L. 82.

There is some ill a-brewing towards my rest,
For I did dream of money-bags to-night.
   c.   *Merchant of Venice.* Act II. Sc. 5.
                             L. 17.

This is the rarest dream that e'er dull sleep
Did mock sad fools withal.
   d.   *Pericles.* Act V. Sc. 1. L. 164.

              Thou hast beat me out
Twelve several times, and I have nightly
   since
Dreamt of encounters 'twixt thyself and me.
   e.   *Coriolanus.* Act IV. Sc. 5. L. 127.

              We are such stuff
As dreams are made on, and our little life
Is rounded with a sleep.
   f.   *Tempest.* Act IV. Sc. 1. L. 156.

In an ocean of dreams without a sound.
   g.   SHELLEY—*The Sensitive Plant.* Pt. I.
                             St. 26.

Those dreams, that on the silent night
   intrude,
And with false flitting shades our minds
   delude,
Jove never sends us downward from the
   skies;
Nor can they from infernal mansions rise;
But are all mere productions of the brain,
And fools consult interpreters in vain.
   h.   SWIFT—*On Dreams.*

In the world of dreams, I have chosen my
   part.
   To sleep for a season and hear no word
Of true love's truth or of light love's art,
   Only the song of a secret bird.
   i.   SWINBURNE—*A Ballad of Dreamland.*
                             Envoi.

Like glimpses of forgotten dreams.
   j.   TENNYSON—*The Two Voices.*
                       St. CXXVII.

Seeing, I saw not, hearing not, I heard.
Tho', if I saw not, yet they told me all
So often that I spake as having seen.
   k.   TENNYSON—*The Princess.* VI. L. 3.
   11

                   The dream
Dreamed by a happy man, when the dark
   East,
Unseen, is brightening to his bridal morn.
   l.   TENNYSON—*The Gardener's Daughter.*
                             L. 71.

The chambers in the house of dreams
   Are fed with so divine an air,
That Time's hoar wings grow young therein,
   And they who walk there are most fair.
   m.   FRANCIS THOMPSON—*Dream Tryst.*
                             St. 3.

And yet, as angels in some brighter dreams
Call to the soul when man doth sleep,
So some strange thoughts transcend our
   wonted dreams,
And into glory peep.
   n.   VAUGHAN—*Ascension Hymn.*

Hunt half a day for a forgotten dream.
   o.   WORDSWORTH—*Hart-Leap Well.*
                        Pt. II. St. 9.

DRINKING.

Fill up the goblet and reach to me some!
Drinking makes wise, but dry fasting makes
   glum.
   p.   WM. R. ALGER—*Oriental Poetry.*
                      Wine Song of Kaitmas.

Here
With my beer
I sit,
While golden moments flit:
Alas!
They pass
Unheeded by:
And as they fly,
I,
Being dry,
Sit, idly sipping here
My beer.
   q.   GEORGE ARNOLD—*Beer.*

Or merry swains, who quaff the nut-brown ale,
And sing enamour'd of the nut-brown maid.
   r.   BEATTIE—*The Minstrel.* Bk. I. St. 44.

Drink to-day, and drown all sorrow;
You shall perhaps not do it to-morrow.
   s.   BEAUMONT AND FLETCHER—*The Bloody
              Brother. Song.* Act II. Sc. 2.

What harm in drinking can there be,
Since punch and life so well agree?
   t.   BLACKLOCK—*An Epigram on Punch.*
                             L. 15.

When the liquor's out, why clink the
   cannikin?
   u.   ROBERT BROWNING—*The Flight of the
                      Duchess.* XVI.

Fill full! Why this is as it should be : here
Is my true realm, amidst bright eyes and
    faces
Happy as fair! Here sorrow cannot reach.
  a.   BYRON—*Sardanapalus.*   Act III.
                                 Sc. 1.

I drink when I have occasion, and sometimes when I have no occasion.
  b.   CERVANTES—*Don Quixote.*   Pt. II.
                             Ch. XXXIII.

And broughte of mighty ale a large quart.
  c.   CHAUCER—*Canterbury Tales.*   The
                    Milleres Tale.   L. 3,497.

If you are invited to drink at any man's
house more than you think is wholesome,
you may say "you wish you could, but so
little makes you both drunk and sick ; that
you should only be bad company by doing
so."
  d.   LORD CHESTERFIELD—*Principles of
      Politeness and of Knowing the World.
      Sec.   Sundry Little Accomplishments.*

Mynheer Vandunck, though he never was
    drunk,
Sipped brandy and water gayly.
  e.   GEORGE COLMAN (" The Younger.")—
                  Mynheer Vandunck.

Nothing in Nature's sober found,
But an eternal Health goes round.
Fill up the Bowl then, fill it high—
Fill all the Glasses there ; for why
Should every Creature Drink but I?
Why, Man of Morals, tell me why?
  f.   COWLEY—*Anacreon II.   Drinking.*

The thirsty Earth soaks up the Rain,
And drinks, and gapes for Drink again ;
The Plants suck in the Earth and are
With constant Drinking fresh and fair.
  g.   COWLEY—*Anacreon II.   Drinking.*

When I got up to the Peacock—where I
found everybody drinking hot punch in self-
preservation.
  h.   DICKENS—*The Holly Tree Inn.*

Inebriate of air am I,
And debauchee of dew,
Reeling, through endless summer days,
From inns of molten blue.
  i.   EMILY DICKINSON—*Poems.*   XX.
                         (Ed. 1891.)

And pines with thirst amidst a sea of waves.
  j.   HOMER—*The Odyssey.*   Bk. XI.   L. 722.
                         Pope's trans.

If you'd dip in such joys, come—the better,
    the quicker !—
But remember the fee—for it suits not my
    ends
To let you make havoc, scot free, with my
    liquor,
As though I were one of your heavy-pursed
    friends.
  k.   HORACE.   Bk. IV.   Ode XII.   *To
          Virgil.*   Trans. by Theo. Martin.

Nor shall our cups make any guilty men ;
But at our parting, we will be, as when
We innocently met.
  l.   BEN JONSON—*Epigram CI.*

Well, as he brews, so shall he drink.
  m.   BEN JONSON—*Every Man in His
             Humour.*   Act II.   Sc. 1.

Now to rivulets from the mountains
  Point the rods of fortune-tellers ;
Youth perpetual dwells in fountains,
  Not in flasks, and casks, and cellars.
  n.   LONGFELLOW—*Drinking Song.*   St. 8.

                      One sip of this
Will bathe the drooping spirits in delight,
Beyond the bliss of dreams.
  o.   MILTON—*Comus.*   L. 811.

Then to the spicy nut-brown ale.
  p.   MILTON—*L'Allegro.*   L. 100.

When treading London's well-known ground,
  If e'er I feel my spirits tire,
I haul my sail, look up around,
  In search of Whitbread's best entire.
  q.   From " The Myrtle and the Vine."   A
          Complete Vocal Library.   A Pot of
                        Porter, Ho !

They never taste who always drink.
  r.   PRIOR—*On a Passage in the
                      Scaligerana*

I drink no more than a sponge.
  s.   RABELAIS—*Works.*   Bk. I.   Ch. V.

Drink down all unkindness.
  t.   *Merry Wives of Windsor.*   Act I.   Sc. 1.
                            L. 203.

This bottle's the sun of our table,
His beams are rosy wine ;
We planets that are not able
Without his help to shine.
  u.   R. B. SHERIDAN—*The Duenna.*
                     Act III.   Sc. 5.

Back and side go bare, go bare,
Both foot and hand go cold ;
But belly, God send thee good ale enough,
Whether it be new or old.
  v.   BISHOP STILL—*Gammer Gurton's
                  Needle.*   Act II.

I cannot eat but little meat,
My stomach is not good ;
But sure I think that I can drink
With him that wears a hood.
> a.   BISHOP STILL—*Gammer Gurton's*
>   *Needle.*   Act II.

While briskly to each patriot lip
Walks eager round the inspiring flip ;
Delicious draught, whose pow'rs inherit
The quintessence of public spirit!
> b.   JOHN TRUMBULL—*McFingal.*
>   Canto III.   L. 21.

Drink, pretty creature, drink !
> c.   WORDSWORTH—*The Pet Lamb.*

For drink, there was beer which was very
strong when not mingled with water, but was
agreeable to those who were used to it. They
drank this with a reed, out of the vessel that
held the beer, upon which they saw the
barley swim.
> d.   XENOPHON—*Anabasis.*   Bk. IV.
>   Ch. V.

DUELLING.

It has a strange, quick jar upon the ear,
   That cocking of a pistol, when you know
A moment more will bring the sight to bear
Upon your person, twelve yards off or so.
> e.   BYRON—*Don Juan.*   Canto IV.   St. 41.

Some fiery fop, with new commission vain,
Who sleeps on brambles till he kills his man ;
Some frolic drunkard, reeling from a feast,
Provokes a broil, and stabs you for a jest.
> f.   SAM'L JOHNSON—*London.*   L. 226.

DUTY.

Thanks to the gods ! my boy has done his
   duty.
> g.   ADDISON—*Cato.*   Act IV.   Sc. 4.

In doing what we ought we deserve no praise,
because it is our duty.
> h.   ST. AUGUSTINE.

He who is false to present duty breaks a
thread in the loom, and will find the flaw
when he may have forgotten its cause.
> i.   HENRY WARD BEECHER—*Life*
>   *Thoughts.*

Maintain your post : That's all the fame you
   need ;
For 'tis impossible you should proceed.
> j.   DRYDEN—*To Mr. Congreve, on his*
>   *Comedy " The Double Dealer."*

Not aw'd to duty by superior sway.
> k.   DRYDEN—*Eleonora.*   L. 178.

And rank for her meant duty, various,
Yet equal in its worth, done worthily.
Command was service ; humblest service done
By willing and discerning souls was glory.
> l.   GEORGE ELIOT—*Agatha.*

The reward of one duty is the power to fulfil another.
> m.   GEORGE ELIOT—*Daniel Deronda.*
>   Bk. VI.   Ch. XLVI.

So nigh is grandeur to our dust,
   So near is God to man.
When Duty whispers low, *Thou must,*
   The youth replies, *I can.*
> n.   EMERSON—*Voluntaries.*   St. 3.   L. 13.

When I'm not thank'd at all, I'm thank'd
   enough :
I've done my duty, and I've done no more.
> o.   FIELDING—*Tom Thumb.*   Act I.   Sc. 3.

In common things the law of sacrifice takes
the form of positive duty.
> p.   FROUDE—*Short Studies on Great*
>   *Subjects.   Sea Studies.*

Let no guilty man escape, if it can be avoided.
No personal consideration should stand in
the way of performing a public duty.
> q.   ULYSSES S. GRANT—*Indorsement of a*
>   *Letter relating to the Whiskey Ring,*
>   July 29, 1875.

Hath the spirit of all beauty
Kissed you in the path of duty ?
> r.   ANNA KATHARINE GREEN—*On the*
>   *Threshold.*

Then on ! then on ! where duty leads,
   My course be onward still.
> s.   BISHOP HEBER—*Journal.*

I slept and dreamed that life was Beauty ;
I woke, and found that life was Duty :—
Was thy dream then a shadowy lie ?
> t.   ELLEN STURGIS HOOPER—*Duty.*

Let us have faith that right makes might,
and in that faith let us, to the end, dare to do
our duty as we understand it.
> u.   ABRAHAM LINCOLN—*Address.*   Feb.
>   21, 1859.

New occasions teach new duties.
> v.   LOWELL—*The Present Crisis.*   St. 18.

Thet tells the story ! Thet's wut we shall git
By tryin' squirtguns on the burnin' Pit ;
For the day never comes when it'll du
To kick off dooty like a worn-out shoe.
> w.   LOWELL—*The Biglow Papers.*   No. 11.

Every mission constitutes a pledge of duty.
Every man is bound to consecrate his every
faculty to its fulfilment. He will derive his
rule of action from the profound conviction
of that duty.
> x.   MAZZINI—*Life and Writings.   Young*
>   *Europe.   General Principles.*

The things which must be, must be for the
　　best,
God helps us do our duty and not shrink,
And trust His mercy humbly for the rest.
　　a.　　Owen Meredith (Lord Lytton)—
　　　　　　　　　　　　Imperfection.

　　　　Zeal and duty are not slow ;
But on occasion's forelock watchful wait.
　　b.　　Milton—*Paradise Regained.*　Bk. III.
　　　　　　　　　　　　　　L. 172.

Knowledge is the hill which few may wish to
　　climb ;
Duty is the path that all may tread.
　　c.　　Lewis Morris—*Epic of Hades.*
　　　　　　Quoted by John Bright at Unveiling
　　　　　　　　　of Cobden Statue.

England expects every man will do his duty.
　　d.　　Horatio Nelson—*Southey's Life of
　　　　　　Nelson.*　(See description of his
　　　　　　　　　　　　last battle.)

Thy sum of duty let two words contain,
(O may they graven in thy heart remain !)
Be humble and be just.
　　e.　　Prior—*Solomon on the Vanity of the
　　　　　　　　　　　　World.*　Bk. III.

And I read the moral—A brave endeavour
　　To do thy duty, whate'er its worth,
Is better than life with love forever,
　　And love is the sweetest thing on earth.
　　f.　　James J. Roche—*Sir Hugo's Choice.*

We require from buildings, as from men,
two kinds of goodness : first, the doing their
practical duty well : then that they be graceful and pleasing in doing it ; which last is
itself another form of duty.
　　g.　　Ruskin—*The Stones of Venice.*　Vol. I.
　　　　　　　　　　　　Ch. II.

Alas ! when duty grows thy law, enjoyment
　　fades away.
　　h.　　Schiller—*The Playing Infant.*

　　　　Blow wind ! come, wrack !
At least we'll die with the harness on our
　　back.
　　i.　　*Macbeth.*　Act V.　Sc. 5.　L. 51.

I do perceive here a divided duty.
　　j.　　*Othello.*　Act I.　Sc. 3.　L. 181.

　　　　I thought the remnant of mine age
Should have been cherish'd by her child-like
　　duty.
　　k.　　*Two Gentlemen of Verona.*　Act III.
　　　　　　　　　　　　Sc. 1.　L. 74.

Such duty as the subject owes the prince,
Even such a woman oweth to her husband.
　　l.　　*Taming of the Shrew.*　Act V.　Sc. 2.
　　　　　　　　　　　　　　L. 155.

Not once or twice in our rough island story,
The path of duty was the way to glory.
　　m.　　Tennyson—*Ode on the Death of the
　　　　　　　　Duke of Wellington.*　St. 8.

Simple duty hath no place for fear.
　　n.　　Whittier—*Tent on the Beach.
　　　　　　Abraham Davenport.*　Last Line.

Stern Daughter of the Voice of God.
　　o.　　Wordsworth—*Ode to Duty.*

The primal duties shine aloft, like stars ;
The charities that soothe, and heal, and bless
Are scattered at the feet of Man, like flowers.
　　p.　　Wordsworth—*The Excursion.* Bk. IX.

Who art a light to guide, a rod
To check the erring, and reprove.
　　q.　　Wordsworth—*Ode to Duty.*

E.

EASTER.

Awake, thou wintry earth—
　　Fling off thy sadness !
Fair vernal flowers, laugh forth
　　Your ancient gladness !
　　　　Christ is risen.
　　r.　　Thomas Blackburn—*An Easter Hymn.*

Yes, He is ris'n who is the First and Last ;
　　Who was and is ; who liveth and was dead ;
Beyond the reach of death He now has pass'd,
　　Of the one glorious Church the glorious
　　Head.
　　s.　　Horatius Bonar, D.D.—*He is Risen.*

O Risen Christ ! O Easter Flower !
　　How dear Thy Grace has grown !
From East to West, with loving power,
　　Make all the world Thine own.
　　t.　　Phillips Brooks—*The Easter Flower.*

Tomb, thou shalt not hold Him longer ;
Death is strong, but Life is stronger ;
Stronger than the dark, the light ;
Stronger than the wrong, the right ;
Faith and Hope triumphant say
Christ will rise on Easter Day.
　　u.　　Phillips Brooks—*An Easter Carol.*

Ye Heavens, how sang they in your courts,
  How sang the angelic choir that day,
When from his tomb the imprisoned God,
  Like the strong sunrise, broke away?
  a.   FREDERICK WILLIAM FABER, D.D.—
                           Jesus Risen.

Hail, Day of days! in peals of praise
  Throughout all ages owned,
When Christ, our God, hell's empire trod,
  And high o'er heaven was throned.
  b.   FORTUNATUS (Bishop of Poictiers)—
                Hail, Day of Days! in Peals
                            of Praise.

Jesus lives, to Him the Throne
  Over all the world is given,
May we go where He is gone,
  Rest and reign with Him in Heaven.
      Alleluia!
  c.   C. F. GILLERT—*Jesus Lives.*

Christ hath arisen! O mountain peaks, attest—
Witness, resounding glen and torrent wave!
The immortal courage in the human breast
Sprung from that victory—tell how oft the
    brave
    To camp 'midst rock and cave,
Nerved by those words, their struggling faith
    have borne,
Planting the cross on high above the clouds
    of morn!
  d.   MRS. HEMANS—*Easter Day in a*
                    Mountain Churchyard.

Rise, heart! thy Lord is risen. Sing His praise
    Without delays
Who takes thee by the hand, that thou like-
    wise
    With Him mayst rise—
That as His death condemned thee to dust,
His life may make thee gold, and much more
    just.
  e.   HERBERT—*Easter.*

Come, ye saints, look here and wonder,
  See the place where Jesus lay;
He has burst His bands asunder;
  He has borne our sins away;
    Joyful tidings,
  Yes, the Lord has risen to-day.
  f.   THOMAS KELLY—*Come, Ye Saints, Look*
                  Here and Wonder.

'Twas Easter-Sunday. The full-blossomed
    trees
Filled all the air with fragrance and with joy.
  g.   LONGFELLOW—*Spanish Student.* Act I.
                        Sc. 3.

In the bonds of Death He lay
  Who for our offence was slain;
But the Lord is risen to-day,
  Christ hath brought us life again,
Wherefore let us all rejoice,
Singing loud, with cheerful voice,
    Hallelujah!
  h.   MARTIN LUTHER—*In the Bonds of*
                  Death He Lay.

Hallelujah! Hallelujah!
On the third morning He arose,
Bright with victory o'er his foes.
    Sing we lauding,
    And applauding,
    Hallelujah!
  i.   *Hallelujah! Hallelujah! From the*
      Latin of the 12th Century. Trans. by
                    J. M. NEALE.

I think of the garden after the rain;
  And hope to my heart comes singing,
" At morn the cherry-blooms will be white,
  And the Easter bells be ringing!"
  j.   EDNA DEAN PROCTER—*Easter Bells.*

The fasts are done; the Aves said;
  The moon has filled her horn;
And in the solemn night I watch
  Before the Easter morn.
So pure, so still the starry heaven,
  So hushed the brooding air,
I could hear the sweep of an angel's wings
  If one should earthward fare.
  k.   EDNA DEAN PROCTER—*Easter Morning.*

Spring bursts to-day,
For Christ is risen and all the earth's at play.
  l.   CHRISTINA G. ROSSETTI—*An Easter*
                            Carol.

God expects from men something more than
at such times, and that it were much to be
wished for the credit of their religion as well
as the satisfaction of their conscience that
their Easter devotions would in some measure
come up to their Easter dress.
  m.   SOUTH—*Sermons.* Vol. II. Ser. 8.

Ring, snow-white bells, your purest praise
To glorify this Easter day,
And let our risen Saviour's joy
Your voiceless, fragrant breath employ:—
Fill every valley with perfume
And lighten death's appalling gloom,
Teach ye our troubled hearts the way
To trust our Saviour every day.
  n.   W. J. R. TAYLOR—*Easter Lilies.*

Sing aloud, children! sing to the glorious
    King
Of Redemption, who sits on the throne,
For the seraphim high veil their faces, and
    cry,
And the angels are praising the Son.

With His raiment blood-dyed, and with
    wounds in His side,
He returns like a chief from the war,
When His champion blow hath laid death
    and hell low,
And hath driven destruction afar.
  o.   A. R. THOMPSON, D.D.—*Sing Aloud,*
                    Children.

Christ is our Passover!
And we will keep the feast
  With the new leaven,
  The bread of heaven:
All welcome, even the least!
  a.   A. R. THOMPSON, D.D.—*We Keep The*
              Festival. From the Roman
              Breviary.

"Christ the Lord is risen to-day,"
Sons of men and angels say.
Raise your joys and triumphs high;
Sing, ye heavens, and earth reply.
  b.   CHARLES WESLEY—"*Christ the Lord is*
              Risen To-day."

Jesus Christ is risen to-day,
Our triumphant holy day;
Who did once upon the cross
Suffer to redeem our loss.
          Hallelujah!
  c.   *Jesus Christ is Risen To-day. From a*
              Latin Hymn of the 15th Century—
              Translator unknown.

EATING.

The poor man will praise it so hath he good
    cause,
  That all the year eats neither partridge nor
    quail,
But sets up his rest and makes up his feast,
  With a crust of brown bread and a pot of
    good ale.
  d.   *An old English Song, from "An*
              Antidote Against Melancholy."
                          (1661.)

When the Sultan Shah-Zaman
Goes to the city Ispahan,
Even before he gets so far
As the place where the clustered palm-trees
    are,
At the last of the thirty palace-gates,
The pet of the harem, Rose-in-Bloom,
Orders a feast in his favorite room—
Glittering square of colored ice,
Sweetened with syrup, tinctured with spice,
Creams, and cordials, and sugared dates,
Syrian apples, Othmanee quinces,
Limes and citrons and apricots,
And wines that are known to Eastern princes.
  e.   T. B. ALDRICH—*When the Sultan Goes*
                          to Ispahan.

I sing the sweets I know, the charms I feel,
My morning incense, and my evening meal,
The sweets of Hasty-Pudding.
  f.   JOEL BARLOW—*The Hasty Pudding.*
                          Canto I.

Some hae meat and canna eat,
And some wad eat that want it;
But we hae meat, and we can eat;
Sae let the Lord be thankit.
  g.   BURNS—*Grace Before Meat.*

              All human history attests
That happiness for man,—the hungry
    sinner!—
Since Eve ate apples, much depends on
    dinner.
  h.   BYRON—*Don Juan.* Canto XIII.
                              St. 99.

Man is a carnivorous production,
  And must have meals, at least one meal a
    day;
He cannot live, like woodcocks, upon suction,
  But, like the shark and tiger, must have
    prey;
Although his anatomical construction
  Bears vegetables, in a grumbling way,
Your laboring people think beyond all
    question,
Beef, veal, and mutton better for digestion.
  i.   BYRON—*Don Juan.* Canto II. St. 67.

That famish'd people must be slowly nurst,
And fed by spoonfuls, else they always burst.
  j.   BYRON—*Don Juan.* Canto II. St. 158.

A loaf of bread, the Walrus said,
  Is what we chiefly need:
Pepper and vinegar besides
  Are very good indeed—
Now if you're ready, Oysters, dear,
  We can begin to feed!
  k.   LEWIS CARROLL—*The Walrus and the*
              Carpenter. From " Alice in The
                          Looking-Glass."

The proof of the pudding is in the eating.
  l.   CERVANTES—*Don Quixote.* Ch. XXIV.

For he on honey-dew hath fed,
And drunk the milk of Paradise.
  m.   COLERIDGE—*Kubla Khan.*

              Oh, dainty and delicious!
Food for the gods! Ambrosia for Apicius!
Worthy to thrill the soul of sea-born Venus,
Or titillate the palate of Silenus!
  n.   W. A. CROFFUT—*Clam Soup.*

"Here, dearest Eve," he exclaims, " here is
food." " Well," answered she, with the germ
of a housewife stirring within her, "we have
been so busy to-day that a picked-up dinner
must serve."
  o.   NATH. HAWTHORNE—*Mosses from an*
              Old Manse. The New Adam and Eve.

"Good well-dress'd turtle beats them hollow,—
It almost makes me wish, I vow,
To have *two* stomachs, like a cow!"
And lo! as with the cud, an inward thrill
Upheaved his waistcoat and disturb'd his
    frill,
His mouth was oozing, and he work'd his
    jaw—
"I almost think that I could eat one raw."
  p.   HOOD—*The Turtles.*

The consummate pleasure (in eating) is not in the costly flavour, but in yourself. Do you seek for sauce by sweating?
a.   HORACE—*Satires* II. 2.

For a man seldom thinks with more earnestness of anything than he does of his dinner.
b.   SAM'L JOHNSON—*Piozzi's Anecdotes
of Johnson.*

For I look upon it, that he who does not mind his belly will hardly mind anything else.
c.   SAM'L JOHNSON—*Boswell's Life of
Johnson.*

Digestive cheese, and fruit there sure will be.
d.   BEN JONSON—*Epigram CI.*

Yet shall you have to rectify your palate,
An olive, capers, or some better salad
Ushering the mutton; with a short-legged hen,
If we can get her, full of eggs, and then,
Limons, and wine for sauce: to these a coney
Is not to be despaired of for our money;
And though fowl now be scarce, yet there are clerks,
The sky not falling, think we may have larks.
e.   BEN JONSON—*Epigram CI.*

And lucent syrops, tinct with cinnamon.
f.   KEATS—*The Eve of St. Agnes.* St. 30.

What baron or squire
Or knight of the shire
Lives half so well as a holy friar.
g.   JOHN O'KEEFE—*I am a Friar of Orders
Gray.*

A woman asked a coachman, "Are you full inside?" Upon which Lamb put his head through the window and said: "I am quite full inside; that last piece of pudding at Mr. Gillman's did the business for me."
h.   CHARLES LAMB—*Autobiographical
Recollections*, by Chas. R. Leslie.

Your supper is like the Hidalgo's dinner; very little meat, and a great deal of table-cloth.
i.   LONGFELLOW—*The Spanish Student.*
Act I. Sc. 4.

Oh, better no doubt is a dinner of herbs,
When season'd by love, which no rancour disturbs
And sweeten'd by all that is sweetest in life
Than turbot, bisque, ortolans, eaten in strife!
But if, out of humour, and hungry, alone
A man should sit down to dinner, each one
Of the dishes of which the cook chooses to spoil
With a horrible mixture of garlic and oil,
The chances are ten against one, I must own,
He gets up as ill-tempered as when he sat down.
j.   OWEN MEREDITH (Lord Lytton)—
Lucile. Pt. I. Canto II. St. 27.

O hour, of all hours, the most bless'd upon earth,
The blessèd hour of our dinners!
k.   OWEN MEREDITH (Lord Lytton)—
Lucile. Pt. I. Canto II. St. 23.

We may live without poetry, music and art;
We may live without conscience, and live without heart;
We may live without friends; we may live without books;
But civilized man cannot live without cooks.
He may live without books,—what is knowledge but grieving?
He may live without hope,—what is hope but deceiving?
He may live without love,—what is passion but pining?
But where is the man that can live without dining?
l.   OWEN MEREDITH (Lord Lytton)—
Lucile. Pt. I. Canto II. St. 24.

Their best and most wholesome feeding is upon one dish and no more and the same plaine and simple: for surely this hudling of many meats one upon another of divers tastes is pestiferous. But sundrie sauces are more dangerous than that.
m.   PLINY—*Natural History.* Bk. XI.
Ch. LIII. Holland's trans.

What, did you not know, then, that to-day Lucullus dines with Lucullus?
n.   PLUTARCH—*Lives. Life of Lucullus.*
Vol. III. P. 280.

And solid pudding against empty praise.
o.   POPE—*The Dunciad.* Bk. I. L. 54.

"An't it please your Honour," quoth the Peasant,
"This same Dessert is not so pleasant:
Give me again my hollow Tree,
A crust of Bread, and Liberty."
p.   POPE—*Second Book of Horace.*
Last lines.

"Live like yourself," was soon my lady's word,
And lo! two puddings smok'd upon the board.
q.   POPE—*Moral Essays.* Ep. III. L. 461.

One solid dish his week-day meal affords,
An added pudding solemniz'd the Lord's.
r.   POPE—*Moral Essays.* Ep. III. L. 447.

"Pray take them, Sir,—Enough's a Feast;
Eat some, and pocket up the rest."
s.   POPE—*First Book of Horace.* Ep. VII.
L. 24.

And men sit down to that nourishment which is called supper.
t.   *Love's Labour's Lost.* Act I. Sc. 1.
L. 239.

A surfeit of the sweetest things
The deepest loathing to the stomach brings.
a.   *Midsummer Night's Dream.*   Act II.
Sc. 2.   L. 137.

At dinner-time,
I pray you, have in mind where we must meet.
b.   *Merchant of Venice.*   Act I.   Sc. 1.
L. 70.

Come, we have a hot venison pasty to dinner; come, gentlemen, I hope we shall drink
down all unkindness.
c.   *Merry Wives of Windsor.*   Act I.   Sc. 1.
L. 202.

He hath eaten me out of house and home.
d.   *Henry IV.*   Pt. II.   Act II.   Sc. 1.
L. 81.

I fear it is too choleric a meat.
How say you to a fat tripe finely broil'd?
e.   *Taming of the Shrew.*   Act IV.   Sc. 3.
L. 19.

If you do, expect spoon-meat; or bespeak
a long spoon.
f.   *Comedy of Errors.*   Act IV.   Sc. 3.
L. 61.

I will make an end of my dinner; there's
pippins and cheese to come.
g.   *Merry Wives of Windsor.*   Act I.   Sc. 2.
L. 12.

I wished your venison better; it was ill
kill'd.
h.   *Merry Wives of Windsor.*   Act I.   Sc. 1.
L. 83.

Let me not stay a jot for dinner; go get it
ready.
i.   *King Lear.*   Act I.   Sc. 4.   L. 8.

Perhaps some merchant hath invited him
And from the mart he's somewhere gone to
dinner.
Good sister, let us dine and never fret.
j.   *Comedy of Errors.*   Act II.   Sc. 1.   L. 4.

Sit down and feed, and welcome to our
table.
k.   *As You Like It.*   Act II.   Sc. 7.
L. 106.

Strive mightily, but eat and drink as friends.
l.   *Taming of the Shrew.*   Act I.   Sc. 2.
L. 279.

They are as sick that surfeit with too much,
as they that starve with nothing.
m.   *Merchant of Venice.*   Act I.   Sc. 2.
L. 5.

What say you to a piece of beef and mus-
tard?
n.   *Taming of the Shrew.*   Act IV.   Sc. 3.
L. 23.

Will you go with me? We'll mend our
dinner here.
o.   *Comedy of Errors.*   Act IV.   Sc. 3.
L. 60.

With eager feeding food doth choke the
feeder.
p.   *Richard II.*   Act II.   Sc. 1.   L. 37.

You would eat chickens i' the shell.
q.   *Troilus and Cressida.*   Act I.   Sc. 2.
L. 147.

Though we eat little flesh and drink no wine,
Yet let's be merry; we'll have tea and toast;
Custards for supper, and an endless host
Of syllabubs and jellies and mince-pies,
And other such ladylike luxuries.
r.   SHELLEY—*Letter to Maria Gisborne.*

An oyster may be crossed in love! Who says
A whale's a bird?—Ha! did you call my
love?—
He's here! he's there! he's everywhere!
Ah me! he's nowhere!
s.   R. B. SHERIDAN—*The Critic. A
Tragedy Rehearsed.*   Act III.   Sc. 1.

Oh, herbaceous treat!
'Twould tempt the dying anchorite to eat;
Back to the world he'd turn his fleeting soul,
And plunge his fingers in the salad bowl;
Serenely full the epicure would say,
"Fate cannot harm me,—I have dined
to-day."
t.   SYDNEY SMITH—*A Receipt for a Salad.*

Bad men live that they may eat and drink,
whereas good men eat and drink that they
may live.
u.   *Attributed to* SOCRATES *by* PLUTARCH—
*Morals. How a Young Man
Ought to Hear Poems.*

He was a bold man that first eat an oyster.
v.   SWIFT—*Polite Conversation.*
Dialogue II.

Lord, Madame, I have fed like a farmer; I
shall grow as fat as a porpoise.
w.   SWIFT—*Polite Conversation.*
Dialogue II.

They say fingers were made before forks,
and hands before knives.
x.   SWIFT—*Polite Conversation.*
Dialogue II.

This dish of meat is too good for any but
anglers, or very honest men.
y.   IZAAK WALTON—*The Complete Angler.*
Pt. I.   Ch. VIII.

"Very astonishing indeed ! strange thing !"
(Turning the Dumpling round, rejoined the
    King),
" 'Tis most extraordinary, then, all this is ;
It beats Penetti's conjuring all to pieces ;
Strange I should never of a Dumpling dream !
But, Goody, tell me where, where, where's
    the Seam ?"
" Sire, there's no Seam," quoth she ; " I never
    knew
That folks did Apple-Dumplings sew."
" No !" cried the staring Monarch with a grin ;
" How, how the devil got the Apple in ?"
    a.   JOHN WOLCOTT (Peter Pindar)—*The*
        Apple Dumplings and a King.

ECHO.

Let echo, too, perform her part,
Prolonging every note with art ;
And in a low expiring strain,
Play all the comfort o'er again.
    b.   ADDISON—*Ode for St. Cecilia's Day.*

Pursuing echoes calling 'mong the rocks.
    c.   ABRAHAM COLES—*The Microcosm.*
        Hearing. Powers of Sound.

Even Echo speaks not on these radiant moors.
    d.   BARRY CORNWALL—*English Songs and*
        Other Small Poems. The Sea
        in Calm. Pt. III.

Mysterious haunts of echoes old and far,
The voice divine of human loyalty.
    e.   GEORGE ELIOT—*The Spanish Gypsy.*
        Bk. IV. L. 149.

Echo waits with art and care
And will the faults of song repair.
    f.   EMERSON—*May-day.* L. 439.

Multitudinous echoes awoke and died in the
    distance.
    *   *   *   *   *   *
And, when the echoes had ceased, like a sense
    of pain was the silence.
    g.   LONGFELLOW—*Evangeline.* Pt. II.
        L. 56.

Sweetest Echo, sweetest nymph, that liv'st
    unseen
  Within thy airy shell,
By slow Meander's margent green,
  And in the violet-embroidered vale.
    h.   MILTON—*Comus. Song.*

How sweet the answer Echo makes
    To music at night,
When, roused by lute or horn, she wakes,
And far away, o'er lawns and lakes,
    Goes answering light.
    i.   MOORE—*Echo.*

And more than echoes talk along the walls.
    j.   POPE—*Eloisa to Abelard.* L. 306.

But her voice is still living immortal,
  The same you have frequently heard,
In your rambles in valleys and forests.
  Repeating your ultimate word.
    k.   J. G. SAXE—*The Story of Echo.*

The babbling echo mocks the hounds,
Replying shrilly to the well-tun'd horns,
As if a double hunt were heard at once.
    l.   *Titus Andronicus.* Act II. Sc. 3.
        L. 17.

Lost Echo sits amid the voiceless mountains,
And feeds her grief.
    m.   SHELLEY—*Adonais.* St. 15.

Never sleeping, still awake,
Pleasing most when most I speak ;
The delight of old and young,
Though I speak without a tongue.
Nought but one thing can confound me,
Many voices joining round me,
Then I fret, and rave, and gabble,
Like the labourers of Babel.
    n.   SWIFT—*An Echo.*

And a million horrible bellowing echoes
    broke
From the red-ribb'd hollow behind the wood,
And thunder'd up into Heaven.
    o.   TENNYSON—*Maud.* Pt. XXIII.

    I heard * * *
* * * the great echo flap
And buffet round the hills from bluff to bluff.
    p.   TENNYSON—*The Golden Year.* L. 75.

Our echoes roll from soul to soul,
  And grow for ever and for ever.
Blow, bugle, blow, set the wild echoes flying,
And answer, echoes, answer, dying, dying,
    dying.
    q.   TENNYSON—*Princess.* IV. *Bugle Song.*

Like—but oh ! how different !
    r.   WORDSWORTH—*Yes, it Was the*
        Mountain Echo.

ECONOMY.

There are but two ways of paying debt :
increase of industry in raising income, increase of thrift in laying out.
    s.   CARLYLE—*Past and Present.*
        Government. Ch. X.

I knew once a very covetous, sordid fellow,
who used to say : "Take care of the pence ;
for the pounds will take care of themselves."
    t.   EARL OF CHESTERFIELD—*Letter.*
        To his Son, on Education.
        Nov. 6, 1747.

A penny saved is two pence clear,
A pin a day's a groat a year.
    u.   BENJ. FRANKLIN—*Necessary Hints to*
        those that would be Rich.

To balance Fortune by a just expense,
Join with Economy, Magnificence.
   a.   Pope—*Moral Essays.* Ep. III. L. 223.

Economy, the poor man's mint.
   b.   Tupper—*Proverbial Philosophy. Of
                    Society.* L. 191.

EDUCATION.

Histories make men wise; poets, witty; the
mathematics, subtile; natural philosophy,
deep; morals, grave; logic and rhetoric, able
to contend.
   c.   Bacon—*Essays. Of Studies.*

Education commences at the mother's knee,
and every word spoken within the hearsay of
little children tends towards the formation of
character.
   d.   Hosea Ballou—*MS. Sermons.*

But to go to school in a summer morn,
Oh, it drives all joy away !
Under a cruel eye outworn,
The little ones spend the day—
In sighing and dismay.
   e.   Wm. Blake—*The Schoolboy.* St. 2.

Let the soldier be abroad if he will, he can
do nothing in this age. There is another
personage,—a personage less imposing in the
eyes of some, perhaps insignificant. The
schoolmaster is abroad, and I trust to him,
armed with his primer, against the soldier in
full military array.
   f.   Lord Brougham—*Speech.* Jan. 29, 1828.

How much a dunce that has been sent to
     roam
Excels a dunce that has been kept at home.
   g.   Cowper—*Progress of Error.* L. 410.

The Self-Educated are marked by stubborn
peculiarities.
   h.   Isaac Disraeli—*Literary Character.
                    Ch. VI.*

By education most have been misled.
   i.   Dryden—*Hind and Panther.* Pt. III.
                          L. 389.

A boy is better unborn than untaught.
   j.   Gascoigne.

Impartially their talents scan,
Just education forms the man.
   k.   Gay—*The Owl, Swan, Cock, Spider, Ass,
          and the Farmer. To a Mother.* L. 9.

Of course everybody likes and respects self-
made men. It is a great deal better to be
made in that way than not to be made at all.
   l.   O. W. Holmes—*The Autocrat of the
                 Breakfast Table.* L. 1.

The true purpose of education is to cherish
and unfold the seed of immortality already
sown within us; to develop, to their fullest
extent, the capacities of every kind with
which the God who made us has endowed us.
   m.   Mrs. Jameson—*Education. Winter
              Studies and Summer Rambles.*

Much may be made of a Scotchman if he be
    caught young.
   n.   Sam'l Johnson—*Boswell's Life of
                Johnson.* 1772.

But it was in making education not only
common to all, but in some sense compulsory
on all, that the destiny of the free republics
of America was practically settled.
   o.   Lowell—*Among my Books. New
            England Two Centuries Ago.*

Finally, education alone can conduct us to
that enjoyment which is, at once, best in
quality and infinite in quantity.
   p.   Horace Mann—*Lectures and Reports
            on Education.* Lecture I.

Enflamed with the study of learning, and
the admiration of virtue; stirred up with high
hopes of living to be brave men, and worthy
patriots, dear to God, and famous to all ages.
   q.   Milton—*Tract on Education.*

Education is the only interest worthy the
deep, controlling anxiety of the thoughtful
man.
   r.   Wendell Phillips—*Speeches. Idols.*

'Tis education forms the common mind ;
Just as the twig is bent the tree's inclined.
   s.   Pope—*Moral Essays.* Ep. I. L. 149.

God hath blessed you with a good name:
to be a well-favored man is the gift of fortune,
but to write and read comes by nature.
   t.   *Much Ado About Nothing.* Act III.
                       Sc. 3. L. 13.

He can write and read and cast accompt.
O monstrous !
We took him setting of boys' copies.
Here's a villain !
   u.   *Henry VI.* Pt. II. Act IV. Sc. 2.
                        L. 92.

Only the refined and delicate pleasures that
spring from research and education can build
up barriers between different ranks.
   v.   Madame de Staël—*Corinne.* Bk. IX.
                        Ch. I.

Slavery is but half abolished, emancipation
is but half completed, while millions of freemen with votes in their hands are left without
education.
   w.   Robert C. Winthrop—*Yorktown
               Oration.* Oct. 19, 1881.

EFFECTS.

As on the smooth expanse of crystal lakes
The sinking stone at first a circle makes;
The trembling surface by the motion stirr'd,
Spreads in a second circle, then a third;
Wide, and more wide, the floating rings advance,
Fill all the watery plain, and to the margin dance.

a.   Pope—*Temple of Fame.* L. 436.

What dire offence from amorous causes springs,
What mighty contests rise from trivial things.

b.   Pope—*Rape of the Lock.* Canto I.
                        L. 1.

ELECTRICITY.

For the poplars showed
The white of their leaves, the amber grain
Shrunk in the wind—and the lightning now
Is tangled in tremulous skeins of rain.

c.   T. B. Aldrich—*Before the Rain.*

The earth is rocking, the skies are riven—
Jove in a passion, in god-like fashion,
Is breaking the crystal urns of heaven.

d.   Robert Buchanan—*Horatius*
                     Cogitandibus. St. 16.

Stretches, for leagues and leagues, the Wire,
A hidden path for a Child of Fire—
Over its silent spaces sent,
Swifter than Ariel ever went,
From continent to continent.

e.   Wm. Henry Burleigh—*The Rhyme*
                        of the Cable.

Striking the electric chain wherewith we are darkly bound.

f.   Byron—*Childe Harold.* Canto IV.
                        St. 23.

Is it a fact—or have I dreamt it—that by means of electricity, the world of matter has become a great nerve, vibrating thousands of miles in a breathless point of time? Rather, the round globe is a vast head, a brain, instinct with intelligence: or shall we say it is itself a thought, nothing but thought, and no longer the substance which we dreamed it.

g.   Nathaniel Hawthorne—*The House*
        of the Seven Gables. The Flight of
                        Two Owls.

Swift as a shadow, short as any dream;
Brief as the lightning in the collied night,
That, in a spleen, unfolds both heaven and earth,
And ere a man hath power to say "Behold!"
The jaws of darkness do devour it up.

h.   *Midsummer Night's Dream.* Act I.
                     Sc. 1. L. 144.

Too like the lightning, which doth cease to be
Ere one can say "It lightens."

i.   *Romeo and Juliet.* Act II. Sc. 2.
                        L. 119.

ELOQUENCE.

Eloquence is to the sublime what the whole is to its part.

j.   De La Bruyère—*The Characters or*
        Manners of the Present Age. Ch. I.

Eloquence may be found in conversations and in all kinds of writings; it is rarely found when looked for, and sometimes discovered where it is least expected.

k.   De La Bruyère—*The Characters.*
                        Ch. I. 55.

Profane eloquence is transferred from the bar, where Le Maître, Pucelle, and Fourcroy formerly practised it, and where it has become obsolete, to the Pulpit, where it is out of place.

l.   De La Bruyère—*The Characters.*
                        Ch. XVI. 2.

Discourse may want an animated "No"
To brush the surface, and to make it flow;
But still remember, if you mean to please,
To press your point with modesty and ease.

m.   Cowper—*Conversation.* L. 101.

* * * as that dishonest victory
At Chæronea, fatal to liberty,
Killed with report that old man eloquent.*

n.   Milton—*Sonnet X.*

Pour the full tide of eloquence along,
Serenely pure, and yet divinely strong.

o.   Pope—*Imitation of Horace.* Bk. II.
                      Ep. II. L. 171.

There is as much eloquence in the tone of voice, in the eyes, and in the air of a speaker as in his choice of words.

p.   La Rochefoucauld—*Maxims and*
           Moral Sentences. No. 261.

True eloquence consists in saying all that is necessary, and nothing but what is necessary.

q.   La Rochefoucauld—*Maxims and*
           Moral Sentences. No. 262.

Action is eloquence.

r.   *Coriolanus.* Act III. Sc. 2. L. 76.

A man in all the world's new fashion planted,
That hath a mint of phrases in his brain.

s.   *Love's Labour's Lost.* Act I. Sc. 1.
                        L. 165.

              Every tongue that speaks
But Romeo's name speaks heavenly eloquence.

t.   *Romeo and Juliet.* Act III. Sc. 2.
                        L. 32.

Say she be mute and will not speak a word;
Then I'll commend her volubility,
And say she uttereth piercing eloquence.

u.   *Taming of the Shrew.* Act II. Sc. 1.
                        L. 175.

---

* Isocrates, the celebrated Orator of Greece.

That aged ears play truant at his tales
And younger hearings are quite ravished;
So sweet and voluble is his discourse.
  a.   Love's Labour's Lost.   Act II.   Sc. 1.
                                    L. 74.

To try thy eloquence, now 'tis time.
  b.   Antony and Cleopatra.   Act III.   Sc. 12.
                                    L. 26.

            When he speaks,
The air, a charter'd libertine, is still,
And the mute wonder lurketh in men's ears,
To steal his sweet and honey'd sentences.
  c.   Henry V.   Act I.   Sc. 1.   L. 47.

But while listening Senates hang upon thy
        tongue,
Devolving through the maze of eloquence
A roll of periods, sweeter than her song.
  d.   Thomson—The Seasons.   Autumn.
                                    L. 15.

EMIGRATION.

Beheld the duteous son, the sire decayed,
The modest matron, and the blushing maid,
Forc'd from their homes, a melancholy train,
To traverse climes beyond the Western main.
  e.   Goldsmith—Traveller.   L. 407.

Down where yon anch'ring vessel spreads the
        sail,
That, idly waiting, flaps with every gale,
Downward they move, a melancholy band,
Pass from the shore and darken all the strand.
  f.   Goldsmith—Deserted Village.   L. 399.

ENEMY.

It is better to decide a difference between
enemies than friends, for one of our friends
will certainly become an enemy and one of
our enemies a friend.
  g.   Bias.

You and I were long friends; you are now
my enemy, and I am yours.
  *h.   Benj. Franklin—Letter to William
              Strahan.   July 5, 1775.*

None but yourself who are your greatest foe.
  i.   Longfellow—Michael Angelo.
                                    Pt. II.   3.

Whatever the number of a man's friends,
there will be times in his life when he has one
too few; but if he has only one enemy, he is
lucky indeed if he has not one too many.
  *j.   Bulwer-Lytton—What Will He Do
              With It?   Bk. IX.   Ch. III.*
                                    Introduction.

            My nearest
And dearest enemy.
  *k.   Thomas Middleton—Anything for a
              Quiet Life.   Act V.   Sc. 1.*

What boots it at one gate to make defence,
And at another to let in the foe?
  l.   Milton—Samson Agonistes.   L. 560.

The world is large when its weary leagues two
        loving hearts divide;
But the world is small when your enemy is
        loose on the other side.
  m.   John Boyle O'Reilly—Distance.

A merely fallen enemy may rise again, but
the reconciled one is truly vanquished.
  n.   Schiller.

Heat not a furnace for your foe so hot
That it do singe yourself.
  o.   Henry VIII.   Act I.   Sc. 1.   L. 140.

            I do believe,
Induced by potent circumstances, that
You are mine enemy, and make my challenge
You shall not be my judge.
  p.   Henry VIII.   Act II.   Sc. 4.   L. 76.

I do defy him, and I spit at him;
Call him a slanderous coward and a villain:
Which to maintain I would allow him odds,
And meet him, were I tied to run afoot
Even to the frozen ridges of the Alps.
  q.   Richard II.   Act I.   Sc. 1.   L. 60.

In cases of defence 'tis best to weigh
The enemy more mighty than he seems;
So the proportions of defence are fill'd;
Which of a weak and niggardly projection
Doth, like a miser, spoil his coat with scanting
A little cloth.
  r.   Henry V.   Act II.   Sc. 4.   L. 43.

It will let in and out the enemy
With bag and baggage.
  s.   Winter's Tale.   Act I.   Sc. 2.   L. 205.

O cunning enemy, that, to catch a saint,
With saints dost bait thy hook!
  t.   Measure for Measure.   Act II.   Sc. 2.
                                    L. 180.

That you have many enemies, that know not
Why they are so, but, like to village-curs,
Bark when their fellows do.
  u.   Henry VIII.   Act II.   Sc. 4.   L. 158.

They are our outward consciences.
  v.   Henry V.   Act IV.   Sc. 1   L. 8.

ENJOYMENT.

How small of all that human hearts endure,
That part which laws or kings can cause or
        cure!
Still to ourselves in every place consigned,
Our own felicity we make or find.
With secret course, which no loud storms
        annoy,
Glides the smooth current of domestic joy.
  w.   Goldsmith—The Traveller.   L. 423.

For Solomon, he lived at ease, and full
Of honour, wealth, high fare, aimed not be-
    yond
Higher design than to enjoy his state.
   a.   MILTON—*Paradise Regained.* Bk. II.
                           L. 201.

Though throned in highest bliss
Equal to God, and equally enjoying
God-like fruition.
   b.   MILTON—*Paradise Lost.* Bk. III.
                           L. 305.

        Who can enjoy alone?
Or all enjoying what contentment find?
   c.   MILTON—*Paradise Lost.* Bk. VIII.
                           L. 365.

  Heaven forbids, it is true, certain gratifica-
tions, but there are ways and means of com-
pounding such matters.
   d.   MOLIÈRE—*Tartuffe.* Act IV. Sc. 5.

Whether with Reason, or with Instinct blest,
Know, all enjoy that pow'r which suits them
    best.
   e.   POPE—*Essay on Man.* Ep. III. L. 79.

  Sleep, riches, and health, to be truly enjoyed, must be interrupted.
   f.   RICHTER—*Flour, Fruit, and Thorn*
                       Pieces. Ch. VIII.

  You were made for enjoyment, and the
world was filled with things which you will
enjoy, unless you are too proud to be pleased
by them, or too grasping to care for what you
cannot turn to other account than mere delight.
   g.   RUSKIN—*Stones of Venice.* Vol. I.
                          Ch. II. 2.

And 'tis my faith that every flower
Enjoys the air it breathes.
   h.   WORDSWORTH—*Lines Written in Early*
                             Spring.

Nature's old felicities.
   i.   WORDSWORTH—*The Trosachs.*

They most the world enjoy who least admire.
   j.   YOUNG—*Night Thoughts.* Night VIII.
                          L. 1,173.

ENTHUSIASM.

However, 'tis expedient to be wary:
Indifference certes don't produce distress;
And rash enthusiasm in good society
Were nothing but a moral inebriety.
   k.   BYRON—*Don Juan.* Canto XIII.
                           St. 35.

No wild enthusiast ever yet could rest,
Till half mankind were like himself pos-
    sess'd.
   l.   COWPER—*Progress of Error.* L. 470.

  Enthusiasm is that secret and harmonious
spirit which hovers over the production of
genius, throwing the reader of a book, or the
spectator of a statue, into the very ideal presence whence these works have really originated. A great work always leaves us in a
state of musing.
   m.   ISAAC DISRAELI—*Literary Character.*
                    Ch. XII. Last lines.

  Nothing great was ever achieved without
enthusiasm.
   n.   EMERSON—*Essay. On Circles.* Last
                           Par.

His rash fierce blaze of riot cannot last,
For violent fires soon burn out themselves;
Small showers last long, but sudden storms
    are short.
   o.   *Richard II.* Act II. Sc. 1. L. 33.

  Enthusiasm is grave, inward, self-controlled;
mere excitement outward, fantastic, hysteri-
cal, and passing in a moment from tears to
laughter.
   p.   JOHN STERLING—*Essays and Tales.*
                    Crystals from a Cavern.

  Enthusiasm is that temper of the mind in
which the imagination has got the better of
the judgment.
   q.   BISHOP WARBURTON—*Divine Legation.*
                      Bk. V. App.

ENVY.

With that malignant envy which turns pale,
And sickens, even if a friend prevail.
   r.   CHURCHILL—*The Rosciad.* L. 127.

Envy's a sharper spur than pay:
No author ever spar'd a brother.
   s.   GAY—*Fables.* Pt. I. Fable 10.

Fools may our scorn, not envy, raise.
For envy is a kind of praise.
   t.   GAY—*The Hound and the Huntsman.*

But, oh! what mighty magician can assuage
A woman's envy?
   u.   GEO. GRANVILLE (Lord Lansdowne)
                     —*Progress of Beauty.*

Envy not greatness: for thou mak'st thereby
Thyself the worse, and so the distance greater.
   v.   HERBERT—*The Church. Church Porch.*
                         St. 44.

The artist envies what the artist gains,
The bard the rival bard's successful strains.
   w.   HESIOD—*Works and Days.* Bk. I.
                           L. 43.

I envy them, those monks of old;
Their books they read, and their beads they
    told.
   x.   G. P. R. JAMES—*The Monks of Old.*

Envy, to which th' ignoble mind's a slave,
Is emulation in the learn'd or brave.
a.   Pope—*Essay on Man.* Ep. II. L. 191.

Envy will merit as its shade pursue,
But like a shadow proves the substance true.
b.   Pope—*Essay on Criticism.* Pt. II.
L. 266.

It is the practice of the multitude to bark at
eminent men, as little dogs do at strangers.
c.   Seneca—*Of a Happy Life.* Ch. XIX.

Arise, fair sun, and kill the envious moon,
Who is already sick and pale with grief,
That thou her maid art far more fair than
she :
Be not her maid, since she is envious.
d.   *Romeo and Juliet.* Act II. Sc. 2. L. 4.

In seeking tales and informations
Against this man, whose honesty the devil
And his disciples only envy at,
Ye blew the fire that burns ye.
e.   *Henry VIII.* Act V. Sc. 3. L. 110.

No metal can,
No, not the hangman's axe, bear half the
keenness
Of thy sharp envy.
f.   *Merchant of Venice.* Act IV. Sc. 1.
L. 124.

Such men as he be never at heart's ease
Whiles they behold a greater than themselves:
And therefore are they very dangerous.
g.   *Julius Cæsar.* Act I. Sc. 2. L. 208.

The general's disdain'd
By him one step below ; he by the next ;
That next by him beneath ; so every step,
Exampled by the first pace that is sick
Of his superior, grows to an envious fever
Of pale and bloodless emulation.
h.   *Troilus and Cressida.* Act I. Sc. 3.
L. 129.

We make ourselves fools, to disport ourselves ;
And spend our flatteries, to drink those men
Upon whose age we void it up again,
With poisonous spite and envy.
i.   *Timon of Athens.* Act I. Sc. 2. L. 141.

Base Envy withers at another's joy,
And hates that excellence it cannot reach.
j.   Thomson—*The Seasons. Spring.*
L. 28.

EPIGRAMS
From Martial.

While the daring Leander was seeking the
sweet object of his love, and exhausted, was
just being ingulfed by the swelling waves, the
unfortunate adventurer is said to have thus
addressed the menacing surges : "Spare me
on my way ; drown me on my return."
k.   Martial—*On the Public Shows.*
Introduction. Ep. 25.

If I remember right, Ælia, you had four
teeth ; a cough displaced two, another two
more. You can now cough without anxiety
all the day long. A third cough can find
nothing to do in your mouth.
l.   Martial—*Epigrams.* Bk. I. Ep. 19.

Whoever believes it is of yesterday's wine
that Acerra smells, is mistaken : Acerra always drinks till morning.
m.   Martial—*Epigrams.* Bk. I. Ep. 28.

Report says that you, Fidentinus, recite my
compositions in public as if they were your
own. If you allow them to be called mine,
I will send you my verses gratis ; if you wish
them to be called yours, pray buy them, that
they may be mine no longer.
n.   Martial—*Epigrams.* Bk. I. Ep. 29.

I do not love thee, Sabidius, nor can I say
why ; I can only say this, I do not love thee.
o.   Martial—*Epigrams.* Bk. I. Ep. 32.

The book which you are reading aloud is
mine, Fidentinus ; but, while you read it so
badly, it begins to be yours.
p.   Martial—*Epigrams.* Bk. I. Ep. 38.

When Portia had heard the fate of her consort, Brutus, and her grief was seeking the
weapon, which had been carefully removed
from her, "Ye know not yet," she cried,
"that death cannot be denied : I had supposed
that my father had taught you this lesson by
his fate." She spoke, and with eager mouth
swallowed the blazing coals. "Go now, officious attendants, and refuse me a sword, if
you will."
q.   Martial—*Epigrams.* Bk. I. Ep. 42.

Diaulus, lately a doctor, is now an undertaker ; what he does as an undertaker, he
used to do also as a doctor.
r.   Martial—*Epigrams.* Bk. I. Ep. 47.

My books need no one to accuse or judge
you : the page which is yours stands up
against you and says, "You are a thief."
s.   Martial—*Epigrams.* Bk. I. Ep. 53.

Do you ask what sort of maid I desire or
dislike, Flaccus ? I dislike one too easy and
one too coy. The just mean, which lies between the two extremes, is what I approve ;
I like neither that which tortures nor that
which cloys.
t.   Martial—*Epigrams.* Bk. I. Ep. 57.

You are pretty,—we know it ; and young,—
it is true ; and rich,—who can deny it ? But
when you praise yourself extravagantly,
Fabulla, you appear neither rich, nor pretty,
nor young.
u.   Martial—*Epigrams.* Bk. I. Ep. 64.

" You are too free spoken," is your constant remark to me, Chœrilus. He who speaks against you, Chœrilus, is indeed a free speaker.

　　a.　Martial—*Epigrams.* Bk. I. Ep. 67.

He who prefers to give Linus the half of what he wishes to borrow, rather than to lend him the whole, prefers to lose only the half.

　　b.　Martial—*Epigrams.* Bk. I. Ep. 75.

You do not publish your own verses, Lælius; you criticise mine. Pray cease to criticise mine, or else publish your own.

　　c.　Martial—*Epigrams.* Bk. I. Ep. 91.

You complain, Velox, that the epigrams which I write are long. You yourself write nothing; your attempts are shorter.

　　d.　Martial—*Epigrams.* Bk. I. Ep. 110.

Since your reputation for wisdom, and the care which you bestow on your labors, are equal, and since your piety is not inferior to your genius, he who is surprised that a book and incense are presented to you, Regulus, is ignorant how to adapt presents to deserts.

　　e.　Martial—*Epigrams.* Bk. I. Ep. 111.

A certain damsel, envious Procillus, is desperately in love with me,—a nymph more white than the spotless swan, than silver, than snow, than lily, than privet : already you will be thinking of hanging yourself. But I long for one darker than night, than the ant, than pitch, than the jack-daw, than the cricket. If I know you well, Procillus, you will spare your life.

　　f.　Martial—*Epigrams.* Bk. I. Ep. 115.

I commend you, Postumus, for kissing me with only half your lip : you may, however, if you please, withhold even the half of this half. Are you inclined to grant me a boon still greater, and even inexpressible? Keep this whole half entirely to yourself, Postumus.

　　g.　Martial—*Epigrams.* Bk. II. Ep. 10.

What's this that myrrh doth still smell in
　　thy kiss,
And that with thee no other odour is?
'Tis doubt, my Postumus, he that doth smell
So sweetly always, smells not very well.

　　h.　Martial—*Epigrams.* Bk. II. Ep. 12.

In what have I offended you, Apollo, and ye nine Sisters? For, behold, the Muse of gayety brings ill to her poet. Postumus before used to kiss me with half a lip. Now he has begun to kiss me with both lips.

　　i.　Martial—*Epigrams.* Bk. II. Ep. 22.

Why do I not kiss you, Philænis? you are bald. Why do I not kiss you, Philænis? you are carrotty. Why do I not kiss you, Philænis? you are one-eyed. He who kisses you, Philænis, sins against nature.

　　j.　Martial—*Epigrams.* Bk. II. Ep. 33.

Since your legs, Phœbus, resemble the horns of the moon, you might bathe your feet in a cornucopia.

　　k.　Martial—*Epigrams.* Bk. II. Ep. 35.

In whatever place you meet me, Postumus, you cry out immediately, and your very first words are, " How do you do?" You say this, even if you meet me ten times in one single hour : you, Postumus, have nothing, I suppose, to do.

　　l.　Martial—*Epigrams.* Bk. II. Ep. 67.

Fannius, as he was fleeing from the enemy, put himself to death. Is not this, I ask, madness,—to die for fear of dying?

　　m.　Martial—*Epigrams.* Bk. II. Ep. 80.

Jack writes severe lampoons on me, 'tis said—
But he writes nothing, who is never read.

　　n.　Martial—*Epigrams.* Bk. III. Ep. 9.

A slave, branded on the forehead by his master, saved him when proscribed. Thus, while the life of the master was preserved, his infamy was perpetuated.

　　o.　Martial—*Epigrams.* Bk. III. Ep. 21.

If you wish, Faustinus, a bath of boiling water to be reduced in temperature,—a bath, such as scarcely Julianus could enter,—ask the rhetorician Sabinæus to bathe himself in it. He would freeze the warm baths of Nero.

　　p.　Martial—*Epigrams.* Bk. III. Ep. 25.

You wonder that Marius' ear smells unpleasantly. You are the cause of this, Nestor; you whisper into it.

　　q.　Martial—*Epigrams.* Bk. III. Ep. 28.

I prefer a lady; but if such is denied me, my next choice would be a freed-woman. A slave is the last resource; but if her beauty indemnifies the want of birth, I shall prefer her to either.

　　r.　Martial—*Epigrams.* Bk. III. Ep. 33.

You see those fish before you, a beautiful example of the sculpture of Phidias; give them water, and they will swim.

　　s.　Martial—*Epigrams.* Bk. III. Ep. 35.

My rich friends, you know nothing save how to put yourselves into a passion. It is not a nice thing for you to do, but it suits your purpose. Do it.

　　t.　Martial—*Epigrams.* Bk. III. Ep. 37.

The lizard, wrought upon this vessel by the hand of Mentor, is so lifelike that the silver becomes an object of terror.

　　u.　Martial—*Epigrams.* Bk. III. Ep. 41.

When you try to conceal your wrinkles, Polla, with paste made from beans, you deceive yourself, not me. Let a defect, which is possibly but small, appear undisguised. A fault concealed is presumed to be great.

　　v.　Martial—*Epigrams.* Bk. III. Ep. 42.

I could do without your face, and your neck, and your hands, and your limbs, and your bosom, and other of your charms. Indeed, not to fatigue myself with enumerating each of them, I could do without you, Chloe, altogether.

a. MARTIAL—*Epigrams.* Bk. III. Ep. 53.

A crafty innkeeper at Ravenna lately cheated me. I asked him for wine and water; he sold me pure wine.

b. MARTIAL—*Epigrams.* Bk. III. Ep. 57.

Lycoris has buried all the female friends she had, Fabianus: would she were the friend of my wife!

c. MARTIAL—*Epigrams.* Bk. IV. Ep. 24.

The bee is enclosed, and shines preserved, in a tear of the sisters of Phæton, so that it seems enshrined in its own nectar. It has obtained a worthy reward for its great toils; we may suppose that the bee itself would have desired such a death.

d. MARTIAL—*Epigrams.* Bk. IV. Ep. 32.

Your beard is white, Olus, your hair is black. The reason is, that you cannot dye your beard, though you can dye your hair.

e. MARTIAL—*Epigrams.* Bk. IV. Ep. 36.

Galla, say "No:" love is soon sated, unless our pleasures are mixed with some pain; but do not continue, Galla, to say "No" too long.

f. MARTIAL—*Epigrams.* Bk. IV. Ep. 38.

Why, Thais, are you constantly saying that I am old? One is never too old, Thais, for what you require.

g. MARTIAL—*Epigrams.* Bk. IV. Ep. 50.

You were constantly, Matho, a guest at my villa at Tivoli. Now you buy it—I have deceived you; I have merely sold you what was already your own.

h. MARTIAL—*Epigrams.* Bk. IV. Ep. 79.

Myrtale often smells of wine, but, wise,
With eating bay-leaves thinks it to disguise:
So nott with water tempers the wine's heate,
But covers it. Henceforth if her you meete
With red face and swell'd veynes, modestly
    say,
"Sure Myrtale hath drunk o' th' bayes to-
    day?"

i. MARTIAL—*Epigrams.* Bk. V. Ep. 4.
    Trans. in a MS. 16th century.

My friend Stella, Severus, wears on his fingers sardonyxes, emeralds, diamonds, jaspers. Though there are many gems on his fingers, there are more in his verses, whence, I conclude, his hand is so decorated.

j. MARTIAL—*Epigrams.* Bk. V. Ep. 11.

Thirty times in this one year, Charinus, while you have been arranging to make your will, have I sent you cheese cakes dripping with Hyblæan thyme. I am ruined: have pity on me at length, Charinus. Make your will less often, or do that once for all, for which your cough is ever falsely leading us to hope. I have emptied my coffers and my purse. Had I been richer than Crœsus, Charinus, I should become poorer than Irus, if you so frequently devoured my poor repast.

k. MARTIAL—*Epigrams.* Bk. V. Ep. 39.

Thais has black, Læcania white teeth; what is the reason? Thais has her own, Læcania bought ones.

l. MARTIAL—*Epigrams.* Bk. V. Ep. 43.

Philo swears that he has never dined at home, and it is so; he does not dine at all, except when invited out.

m. MARTIAL—*Epigrams.* Bk. V. Ep .47.

Though I often salute you, you never salute me first; I shall therefore, Pontilianus, salute you with an eternal farewell.

n. MARTIAL—*Epigrams.* Bk. V. Ep. 66.

Do you wonder for what reason, Theodorus, notwithstanding your frequent requests and importunities, I have never presented you with my works? I have an excellent reason; it is lest you should present me with yours.

o. MARTIAL—*Epigrams.* Bk. V. Ep. 73.

Mithridates, by frequently drinking poison, rendered it impossible for any poison to hurt him. You, Cinna, by always dining on next to nothing, have taken due precaution against ever perishing from hunger.

p. MARTIAL—*Epigrams.* Bk. V. Ep. 76.

If you are poor now, Æmilianus, you will always be poor. Riches are now given to none but the rich.

q. MARTIAL—*Epigrams.* Bk. V. Ep. 81.

You pursue, I fly; you fly, I pursue; such is my humor. What you wish, Dondymus, I do not wish; what you do not wish, I do.

r. MARTIAL—*Epigrams.* Bk. V. Ep. 83.

While an ant was wandering under the shade of the tree of Phæton, a drop of amber enveloped the tiny insect; thus she, who in life was disregarded, became precious by death.

s. MARTIAL—*Epigrams.* Bk. VI. Ep. 15.

My suit has nothing to do with the assault, or battery, or poisoning, but is about three goats, which, I complain, have been stolen by my neighbor. This the judge desires to have proved to him; but you, with swelling words and extravagant gestures, dilate on the Battle of Cannæ, the Mithridatic war, and the perjuries of the insensate Carthaginians, the Syllæ, the Marii, and the Mucii. It is time, Postumus, to say something about my three goats.

t. MARTIAL—*Epigrams.* Bk. VI. Ep. 19.

You imagine, Calliodorus, that your jesting is witty, and that you, above all others, overflow with an abundance of Attic salt. You smile at all, you utter pleasantries upon all, and you think that by so doing you will please at the dinner table. But I will tell you something, not very nice, but very true. No one will invite you, Calliodorus, to drink out of his glass.

a.   MARTIAL—*Epigrams.* Bk. VI. Ep. 44.

When your crowd of attendants so loudly applaud you, Pomponius, it is not you, but your banquet, that is eloquent.

b.   MARTIAL—*Epigrams.* Bk. VI. Ep. 48.

You manufacture, with the aid of unguents, a false head of hair, and your bald and dirty skull is covered with dyed locks. There is no need to have a hairdresser for your head. A sponge, Phœbus, would do the business better.

c.   MARTIAL—*Epigrams.* Bk. VI. Ep. 57.

You know, Marianus, that you are obsequiously courted; you know that he who courts you is a covetous fellow; you know what his attentions mean; and yet you name him in your will, foolish man, as your heir, and destine him, as if you were out of your mind, to take your place. " But he has sent me," you say, "large presents." True, but they are a baited hook; and can the fish ever love the fisherman? Will this pretender bewail your death with real sorrow? If you desire him to weep, Marianus, give him nothing.

d.   MARTIAL—*Epigrams.* Bk. VI. Ep. 63.

"You write epigrams in hexameters," is what Tucca, I know, is saying. There are, Tucca, precedents for it; in a word, Tucca, it is allowable. " But this one," you say, "is very long." There are precedents for its length also, Tucca, and it is allowable. If you approve of the shorter ones, read only my distichs. Let us agree, Tucca, that I shall be at liberty to write long epigrams, and you be at liberty not to read them.

e.   MARTIAL—*Epigrams.* Bk. VI. Ep. 65.

He who thinks that the lives of Priam and of Nestor were long is much deceived and mistaken. Life consists not in living, but in enjoying health.

f.   MARTIAL—*Epigrams.* Bk. VI. Ep. 70.

You are sad in the midst of every blessing. Take care that Fortune does not observe, or she will call you ungrateful.

g.   MARTIAL—*Epigrams.* Bk. VI. Ep. 79.

O wine of Setia! O excellent snow! O goblets constantly refilled! when am I to drink you with no doctor to prevent me? He is a fool, and ungrateful, and unworthy of so great a boon, who would rather be heir to the rich Midas than enjoy you. May he who is envious of me possess the harvests of Libya, and the Hermus, and the Tagus, and drink warm water.

h.   MARTIAL—*Epigrams.* Bk. VI. Ep. 86.

Cascellius numbers sixty years, and is a man of talent. When will he be a man of eloquence?

i.   MARTIAL—*Epigrams.* Bk. VII. Ep. 9.

I have not a farthing in the house; one thing only remains for me to do, Regulus, and that is, to sell the presents which I have received from you; are you inclined to buy them?

j.   MARTIAL—*Epigrams.* Bk. VII. Ep. 16.

A wild boar, a devourer of Tuscan acorns, and heavy with the fruit of many an oak, second in fame only to the monster of Ætolia, a boar which my friend Dexter pierced with glittering spear, lies an envied prey for my kitchen fire. Let my Penates fatten and exude with the pleasing steam, and my kitchen, festally adorned, blaze with a whole mountain of felled wood. But, ah! my cook will consume a vast heap of pepper, and will have to add Falernian wine to the mysterious sauce. No, return to your master, ruinous wild-boar: my kitchen fire is not for such as you; I hunger for less costly delicacies.

k.   MARTIAL—*Epigrams.* Bk. VII. Ep. 27.

Cælius, unable any longer to endure with patience the constant running from place to place, the morning calls, and the pride and cold salutations of the great, began to pretend that he had the gout. But, while he was over-eager to prove his disease real, and was plastering and bandaging his sound feet, and walking with laboured step (such is the efficacy of care and art in feigned pain) he ceased to feign.

l.   MARTIAL—*Epigrams.* Bk. VII. Ep. 39.

Annius has some two hundred tables, and servants for every table. Dishes run hither and thither, and plates fly about. Such entertainments as these keep to yourselves, ye pompous; I am ill pleased with a supper that walks.

m.   MARTIAL—*Epigrams.* Bk. VII. Ep. 48.

You importune me, Tucca, to present you with my books. I shall not do so; for you want to sell, not to read, them.

n.   MARTIAL—*Epigrams.* Bk. VII. Ep. 77.

I have drunk some consular wine. You ask how old and how generous? It was bottled in the consul's own year; and he who gave it me, Severus, was that consul himself.

o.   MARTIAL—*Epigrams.* Bk. VII. Ep. 79.

Whilst the barber Eutrapelus is going the round of Lupercus's face, and carefully smoothing his cheeks, another beard springs up.

p.   MARTIAL—*Epigrams.* Bk. VII. Ep. 83.

For sometimes writing quatrains which are not devoid of humour, Sabellus, and for composing a few distichs prettily, I commend you; but I am not astonished at you. It is easy to write a few epigrams prettily; but to write a book of them is difficult.

a.   MARTIAL—*Epigrams.* Bk. VII. Ep. 85.

What the small onyx box contained was perfume; Papilus smelt it, and it is become a mass of corruption.

b.   MARTIAL—*Epigrams.* Bk. VII. Ep. 94.

Is this pleading causes, Cinna? Is this speaking eloquently, to say nine words in ten hours? Just now you asked with a loud voice for four more clepsydræ. What a long time you take to say nothing, Cinna!

c.   MARTIAL—*Epigrams.* Bk. VIII. Ep. 7.

Hylas, the blear-eyed, lately offered to pay you three-quarters of his debt; now that he has lost one eye he offers you half. Hasten to take it; the opportunity for getting it may soon pass, for if Hylas should become blind, he would pay you nothing.

d.   MARTIAL—*Epigrams.* Bk. VIII. Ep. 9.

Do you ask why I am unwilling to marry a rich wife? It is because I am unwilling to be taken to husband by my wife. The mistress of the house should be subordinate to her husband, for in no other way, Priscus, will the wife and husband be on an equality.

e.   MARTIAL—*Epigrams.* Bk. VIII. Ep. 12.

I bought what you called a fool for twenty thousand sesterces. Return me my money, Gargilianus; he is no fool at all.

f.   MARTIAL—*Epigrams.* Bk. VIII. Ep. 13.

I pleaded your cause, Sextus, having agreed to do so for two thousand sesterces. How is it that you have sent me only a thousand? "You said nothing," you tell me; "and this cause was lost through you." You ought to give me so much the more, Sextus, as I had to blush for you.

g.   MARTIAL—*Epigrams.* Bk. VIII. Ep. 18.

I seem to you cruel and too much addicted to gluttony, when I beat my cook for sending up a bad dinner. If that appears to you too trifling a cause, say for what cause you would have a cook flogged.

h.   MARTIAL—*Epigrams.* Bk. VIII.
                                   Ep. 23.

He who makes presents to you, Gaurus, rich and old as you are, says plainly, if you have but sense and can understand him, "Die!"

i.   MARTIAL—*Epigrams.* Bk. VIII. Ep. 27.

He who writes distichs, wishes, I suppose, to please by brevity. But, tell me, of what avail is their brevity, when there is a whole book full of them?

j.   MARTIAL—*Epigrams.* Bk. VIII. Ep. 29.

You make a pretty confession about yourself, Dento, when, after taking a wife, you petition for the rights of the father of three children. But cease to importune the emperor, and return, though a little behind time, to your own country; for, after so long seeking three children far away from your deserted wife, you will find four at home.

k.   MARTIAL—*Epigrams.* Bk. VIII. Ep. 31.

Fabius buries his wives, Chrestilla her husbands; each shakes a funeral torch over the nuptial couch. Unite these conquerors, Venus, and the result will then be that Libitina will carry them both off together.

l.   MARTIAL—*Epigrams.* Bk. VIII. Ep. 43.

Part of your face is clipped, part shaven, part has the hair pulled out. Who would think that you have but one head?

m.   MARTIAL—*Epigrams.* Bk. VIII. Ep. 47.

You admire, Vacerra, only the poets of old, and praise only those who are dead. Pardon me, I beseech you, Vacerra, if I think death too high a price to pay for your praise.

n.   MARTIAL—*Epigrams.* Bk. VIII. Ep. 49.

Cædicianus, I lent my barber (a young man, but skilled in his art even beyond Nero's Thalamus, whose lot it was to clip the beards of the Drusi) to Rufus, at his request, to make his cheeks smooth for once. But, at Rufus' orders, he was so long occupied in going over the same hairs again and again, consulting the mirror that guided his hand, cleaning the skin, and making a tedious second attack on the locks previously shorn, that my barber at last returned to me with his own beard full grown.

o.   MARTIAL—*Epigrams.* Bk. VIII. Ep. 52.

All your female friends are either old or ugly; nay, more ugly than old women usually are. These you lead about in your train, and drag with you to feasts, porticos, and theaters. Thus, Fabulla, you seem handsome, thus you seem young.

p.   MARTIAL—*Epigrams.* Bk. VIII. Ep. 79.

You wish, Paula, to marry Priscus. I am not surprised; you are wise: Priscus will not marry you and he is wise.

q.   MARTIAL—*Epigrams.* Bk. IX. Ep. 5.

I have been desirous for five whole days, Afer, to greet you on your return from among the people of Africa. "He is engaged," or "he is asleep," is the answer I have received on calling two or three times. It is enough, Afer; you do not wish me to say, "How do you do?" so I'll say, "Good-by."

r.   MARTIAL—*Epigrams.* Bk. IX. Ep. 7.

Fabius has bequeathed you nothing, Bithynicus; although you used to present him yearly, if I remember right, with six thousand sesterces. He has bequeathed nothing more to any one; so do not complain, Bithynicus; he has at least saved you six thousand sesterces a year.

a.   MARTIAL—*Epigrams.* Bk. IX. Ep. 9.

Though you willingly dine at other people's houses, Cantharus, you indulge yourself there in clamour, and complaints, and threats. Lay aside this fierce humour, I advise you. A man cannot be both independent and a glutton.

b.   MARTIAL—*Epigrams.* Bk. IX. Ep. 10.

The shameless Chloe placed on the tombs of her seven husbands the inscription, "The work of Chloe." How could she have expressed herself more plainly?

c.   MARTIAL—*Epigrams.* Bk. IX. Ep. 15.

You praise, in three hundred verses, Sabellus, the baths of Ponticus, who gives such excellent dinners. You wish to dine, Sabellus, not to bathe.

d.   MARTIAL—*Epigrams.* Bk. IX. Ep. 19.

On your birthday, Quintus, I wished to make you a small present: you forbade me; you are imperious. I must obey your injunction: let that be done which we both desire, and which will please us both. Do you, Quintus, make me a present.

e.   MARTIAL—*Epigrams.* Bk. IX. Ep. 53.

O Liber, whose brows are adorned with the Spartan crown, and whose Roman hand strikes blows worthy of Greece, when you send me a dinner, why does the wicker basket, in which it is conveyed, contain no wine-flask as an accompaniment? If you mean to make presents worthy of your name, you are aware, I suppose, that you ought to have sent me.

f.   MARTIAL—*Epigrams.* Bk. IX. Ep. 72.

An astrologer declared, Munna, that you would soon come to an end; and I believe he spoke the truth. For, through fear of leaving anything behind you, you have squandered your inheritance in luxuries; your two millions have dwindled away in less than a year. Tell me, Munna, is not this coming soon to an end?

g.   MARTIAL—*Epigrams.* Bk. IX. Ep. 82.

While you were trying to catch me, Rufus, you used to send me presents; since you have caught me, you have given me nothing. To keep me when caught, send presents to me now as you did before, lest the boar, being badly fed, escape from his cage.

h.   MARTIAL—*Epigrams.* Bk. IX. Ep. 88.

The doctor Herodes had filched a cup belonging to his patients. Being detected, he exclaimed: "Fool! what need have you of drink?"

i.   MARTIAL—*Epigrams.* Bk. IX. Ep. 96.

The produce of the vineyards has not failed everywhere, Ovidius. The heavy rains have been productive. Coranus made up a hundred jars by means of the water.

j.   MARTIAL—*Epigrams.* Bk. IX. Ep. 98.

You give me back, Phœbus, my bond for four hundred thousand sesterces; lend me rather a hundred thousand morè. Seek some one else to whom you may vaunt your empty present: what I cannot pay you, Phœbus, is my own.

k.   MARTIAL—*Epigrams.* Bk. IX. Ep. 102.

Marius neither asks any one to dinner, nor sends presents, nor becomes security for any one, nor is willing to lend; indeed, he has nothing to lend. Nevertheless, a crowd is found to court his barren friendship. Alas! how besotted, Rome, are the wearers of thy toga!

l.   MARTIAL—*Epigrams.* Bk. X. Ep. 18.

Do you ask, Philænis, why I often come abroad with plaister on my chin, or with my lips covered with salve when nothing ails them? I do not wish to kiss you.

m.   MARTIAL—*Epigrams.* Bk. X. Ep. 22.

The happy Antonius Primus now numbers fifteen Olympiads (60 years) passed in tranquillity; he looks back upon the days that are gone, and the whole of his past years, without fearing the waters of Lethe, to which he daily draws nearer. Not one day of his brings remorse or an unpleasant reflection; there is none which he would be unwilling to recall. A good man lengthens his term of existence; to be able to enjoy our past life is to live twice.

n.   MARTIAL—*Epigrams.* Bk. X. Ep. 23.

Why do you swear, Lesbia, that you were born in the consulship of Brutus? You say falsely, Lesbia; you were born in the reign of Numa. Should you even admit that, you would seem to say falsely; for, judging by your decrepitude, you must have been formed by the hand of Prometheus.

o.   MARTIAL—*Epigrams.* Bk. X. Ep. 39.

Your seventh wife, Phileros, is now being buried in your field. No man's field brings him greater profit than yours, Phileros.

p.   MARTIAL—*Epigrams.* Bk. X. Ep. 43.

You are always wishing, Matho, to speak finely; speak sometimes merely well; sometimes neither well or ill; sometimes even ill.

q.   MARTIAL—*Epigrams.* Bk. X. Ep. 46.

You put fine dishes on your table, Olus, but you alway put them on covered. This is ridiculous; in the same way I could put fine dishes on my table.

a.   MARTIAL—*Epigrams*. Bk. X. Ep. 54.

You collect your straggling hairs on each side, Marinus, endeavoring to conceal the vast expanse of your shining bald pate by the locks which still grow on your temples. But the hairs disperse, and return to their own place with every gust of wind; flanking your bare poll on either side with crude tufts. We might imagine we saw Hermeros of Cydas standing between Speudophorus and Telesphorus. Why not confess yourself an old man? Be content to seem what you really are, and let the barber shave off the rest of your hair. There is nothing more contemptible than a bald man who pretends to have hair.

b.   MARTIAL—*Epigrams*. Bk. X.   Ep. 83.

This Juno, Polycletus, your happy workmanship and masterpiece, which would do honor to the hand of Phidias, displays such beauty that, had she thus appeared on Mount Ida, the Judge would have felt no hesitation in preferring her to the other goddesses. If Jupiter had not loved his sister Juno, he might, Polycletus, have fallen in love with your Juno.

c.   MARTIAL—*Epigrams*. Bk. X. Ep. 89.

While the lightly-piled funeral pyre was being supplied with paper to kindle it; while the desolate wife was buying myrrh and lavender; when the grave, the bier, the corpse-anointer, were all ready, Numa made me his heir, and forthwith recovered.

d.   MARTIAL—*Epigrams*. Bk. X. Ep. 97.

Why, simpleton, do you mix your verses with mine? What have you to do, foolish man, with writings that convict you of theft? Why do you attempt to associate foxes with lions, and make owls pass for eagles? Though you had one of Ladas's legs, you would not be able, blockhead, to run with the other leg of wood.

e.   MARTIAL—*Epigrams*. Bk. X. Ep. 100.

Charm of my life, Telesphorus, sweet object of my cares, whose like never before lay in my arms, give me, fair one, kisses redolent of the fragrance of old Falernian, give me goblets of which thy lips have first partaken. If, in addition to this, you grant me the pleasure of true affection, I shall say that Jove is not more happy at the side of Ganymede.

f.   MARTIAL—*Epigrams*. Bk. XI. Ep. 26.

You invite some three hundred guests, all unknown to me, and then wonder that I do not accept your invitation, and complain, and are ready to quarrel with me. Fabullus, I do not like to dine alone.

g.   MARTIAL—*Epigrams*. Bk. XI. Ep. 35.

You ask for lively epigrams, and propose lifeless subjects. What can I do, Cæcilianus? You expect Hyblæn or Hymethian honey to be produced, and yet offer the Attic bee nothing but Corsican thyme?

h.   MARTIAL—*Epigrams*. Bk. XI. Ep. 42.

To relieve your throat, Parthenopæus, which is incessantly inflamed by a severe cough, your doctor prescribes honey, and nuts, and sweet cakes, and everything that is given to children to prevent them from being unruly. But you do not give over coughing all day long. A cough is not your malady, Parthenopæus; it is gluttony.

i.   MARTIAL—*Epigrams*. Bk. XI. Ep. 86.

And have you been able, Flaccus, to see the slender Thais? Then, Flaccus, I suspect you can see what is invisible.

j.   MARTIAL—*Epigrams*. Bk. XI. Ep. 101.

You utter all sorts of falsehoods, Pontilianus; I assent to them. You recite bad verses; I praise them. You sing; I do the same. You drink, Pontilianus; I drink also. You are rude; I pretend not to perceive it. You wish to play at chess; I allow myself to be beaten. There is one thing only which you do without me, and I hold my tongue on the subject. Yet you never make me the slightest present. "When I die," say you, "I shall remember you handsomely." I do not look for anything; but die.

k.   MARTIAL—*Epigrams*. Bk. XII. Ep. 40.

When to secure your bald pate from the
        weather,
You lately wore a cap of black neats' leather;
He was a very wag, who to you said,
"Why do you wear your slippers on your
        head?"

l.   MARTIAL—*Epigrams*. Bk. XII. Ep. 45.
            Trans. by Hay.

In all thy humours, whether grave or mellow,
Thou'rt such a touchy, testy, pleasant fellow;
Hast so much wit, and mirth, and spleen
        about thee,
That there's no living with thee, or without
        thee.

m.   MARTIAL—*Epigrams*. Bk. XII. Ep. 47.
        Trans. by Addison. Spectator. No. 68.

Tom had a lad lame with a broken thigh;
And an old housekeeper with but one eye:
On greasy steaks from chop-house did regale;
And against drunkards most devoutly rail.
Did you for bottles after dinner call;
He damn'd the bottles, glasses, wine and all.
Now an estate is from an uncle come;
He from the tavern ne'er goes sober home;
Such the effect of plate and lacqueys five!
When poor, Tom was the soberest man alive.

n.   MARTIAL—*Epigrams*. Bk. XII. Ep. 70.
            Trans. by Hay.

I have granted you much that you asked: and yet you never cease to ask of me. He who refuses nothing, Atticilla, will soon have nothing to refuse.

a.   MARTIAL—*Epigrams.* Bk. XII. Ep. 79.

You often ask me, Priscus, what sort of person I should be, if I were to become suddenly rich and powerful. Who can determine what would be his future conduct? Tell me, if you were to become a lion, what sort of a lion would you be?

b.   MARTIAL—*Epigrams.* Bk. XII. Ep. 92.

Lettuce, which closed the suppers of our
    sires,
Tell me, why our commencing feast admires?

c.   MARTIAL—*Epigrams.* Bk. XIII.
                Ep. 14. Trans. by Elphinston.

The duck decoys you. Pick the neck and
    breast.
And to the worthy cook return the rest.

d.   MARTIAL—*Epigrams.* Bk. XIII.
                Ep. 52. Trans. by Elphinston.

As long as I have fat turtle-doves, a fig for your lettuce, my friend, and you may keep your shell-fish to yourself. I have no wish to waste my appetite.

e.   MARTIAL—*Epigrams.* Bk. XIII.
                Ep. 53.

See, how the liver is swollen larger than a fat goose! In amazement you will exclaim: Where could this possibly grow?

f.   MARTIAL—*Epigrams.* Bk. XIII.
                Ep. 58.

Whether woodcock or partridge, what does it signify, if the taste is the same? But the partridge is dearer, and therefore thought preferable.

g.   MARTIAL—*Epigrams.* Bk. XIII.
                Ep. 76.

However great the dish that holds the turbot, the turbot is still greater than the dish.

h.   MARTIAL—*Epigrams.* Bk. XIII.
                Ep. 81.

I am a shell-fish just come from being saturated with the waters of the Lucrine lake, near Baiæ; but now I luxuriously thirst for noble pickle.

i.   MARTIAL—*Epigrams.* Bk. XIII.
                Ep. 82.

If my opinion is of any worth, the fieldfare is the greatest delicacy among birds, the hare among quadrupeds.

j.   MARTIAL—*Epigrams.* Bk. XIII.
                Ep. 92.

See how the mountain goat hangs from the summit of the cliff; you would expect it to fall; it is merely showing its contempt for the dogs.

k.   MARTIAL—*Epigrams.* Bk. XIII.
                Ep. 99.

Attic honey thickens the nectar-like Falernian. Such drink deserves to be mixed by Ganymede.

l.   MARTIAL—*Epigrams.* Bk. XIII.
                Ep. 108.

Let Nepos place Cæretan wine on table, and you will deem it Setine. But he does not give it to all the world; he drinks it only with a trio of friends.

m.   MARTIAL—*Epigrams.* Bk. XIII.
                Ep. 124.

Never think of leaving perfumes or wine to your heir. Administer these yourself, and let him have your money.

n.   MARTIAL—*Epigrams.* Bk. XIII.
                Ep. 126.

Why do strong arms fatigue themselves with frivolous dumb-bells? To dig a vineyard is a worthier exercise for men.

o.   MARTIAL—*Epigrams.* Bk. XIV.
                Ep. 49.

That which prevents disagreeable flies from feeding on your repast, was once the proud tail of a splendid bird.

p.   MARTIAL—*Epigrams.* Bk. XIV.
                Ep. 67.

If your slave commits a fault, do not smash his teeth with your fists; give him some of the (hard) biscuit which famous Rhodes has sent you.

q.   MARTIAL—*Epigrams.* Bk. XIV.
                Ep. 68.

I, a parrot, am taught by you the names of others; I have learned of myself to say, "Hail! Cæsar!"

r.   MARTIAL—*Epigrams.* Bk. XIV.
                Ep. 73.

This hand will protect your shoulders from the bite of the troublesome flea, or from other things more offensive than a flea.

s.   MARTIAL—*Epigrams.* Bk. XIV.
                Ep. 83.

You crystal break, for fear of breaking it:
Careless and careful hands like faults commit.

t.   MARTIAL—*Epigrams.* Bk. XIV.
                Ep. 111. Trans. by Wright.

I'm what I seem; not any dyer gave,
But nature dyed this colour that I have.

u.   MARTIAL—*Epigrams.* Bk. XIV.
                Ep. 133. Trans. by Wright.

(On a shorthand writer.)

The swifter hand doth the swift words outrun :
Before the tongue hath spoke the hand hath
done.

a.   MARTIAL—*Epigrams.* Bk. XIV.
              Ep. 208. Trans. by Wright.

A cook should double one sense have : for he
Should taster for himself and master be.

b.   MARTIAL—*Epigrams.* Bk. XIV.
                              Ep. 220.

EPITAPH.

Here lie the remains of James Pady, Brick-
maker, in hope that his clay will be remoulded
in a workmanlike manner, far superior to his
former perishable materials.

c.   *Epitaphs from Addiscombe Church-yard,*
                             Devonshire.

Here lies Anne Mann ; she lived an
Old maid and died an old Mann.

d.   *Bath Abbey.*

And the voice of men shall call,
" He is fallen like us all,
   Though the weapon of the Lord was in his
     hand : "
And thine epitaph shall be—
" He was wretched ev'n as we ;"
   And thy tomb may be unhonoured in the
     land.

e.   ROBERT BUCHANAN—*The Modern*
                        Warrior. St. 7.

Kind reader ! take your choice to cry or laugh ;
Here HAROLD lies—but where's his Epitaph ?
If such you seek, try Westminster, and view
Ten thousand, just as fit for him as you.

f.   BYRON—*Substitute for an Epitaph.*

Shrine of the mighty ! can it be,
That this is all remains of thee ?

g.   BYRON—*Giaour.* L. 106.

And here the precious dust is laid ;
Whose purely temper'd clay was made
So fine that it the guest betray'd.
Else the soule grew so fast within,
It broke the outward shell of sinne
And so was hatch'd a cherubin.

h.   THOS. CAREW—*Inscription on Tomb of*
                    Lady Mary Wentworth.

It is so soon that I am done for,
I wonder what I was begun for !

i.   *Epitaph in Cheltenham Church-yard.*

Ere sin could blight or sorrow fade,
Death came with friendly care ;
The opening bud to Heaven conveyed,
And bade it blossom there.

j.   COLERIDGE—*Epitaph on an Infant.*

Peas to his Hashes.

k.   *Epitaph on a London Cook.*

Underneath this crust
Lies the mouldering dust
  Of Eleanor Batchelor Shoven,
Well versed in the arts
Of pies, custards and tarts,
  And the lucrative trade of the oven.
When she lived long enough,
She made her last puff,
  A puff by her husband much praised,
And now she doth lie
And make a dirt pie,
  In hopes that her crust may be raised.

l.   *Epitaph on a Yorkshire Cook.*

In Memory of GEORGE PHILLPOT,
Who died March 22nd, 1850, aged 74 years.

    Full many a life he saved
      With his undaunted crew ;
    He put his trust in Providence,
      AND CARED NOT HOW IT BLEW.

m.   *Epitaph in Deal Churchyard.*

He was exhal'd ; his great Creator drew
His spirit, as the sun the morning dew.

n.   DRYDEN—*On the Death of a Very Young*
                           Gentleman.

If e'er she knew an evil thought
  She spoke no evil word :
Peace to the gentle ! She hath sought
  The bosom of her Lord.

o.   EBENEZER ELLIOT—*Hannah Ratcliff.*

Let there be no inscription upon my tomb ;
let no man write my epitaph ; no man can
write my epitaph.

p.   ROBERT EMMET—*Speech on his Trial*
            and Conviction for High Treason.
                       September, 1803.

The body of Benjamin Franklin, Printer,
(Like the cover of an old book, its contents
torn out and stript of its lettering and gilding),
Lies here, food for worms ; But the work shall
not be lost, for it will (as he believed) appear
once more in a new and more elegant edition,
revised and corrected by the author.

q.   BENJAMIN FRANKLIN—*Epitaph on*
               Himself. Written in 1728.

" Fuller's earth."

r.   THOMAS FULLER—*Epitaph written by*
                          Himself.

Here lies Nolly Goldsmith, for shortness
    called Noll,
Who wrote like an angel, and talked like
    poor Poll.

s.   DAVID GARRICK.

Life is a jest, and all things show it,
I thought so once, but now I know it.

t.   GAY—*My Own Epitaph.*

And many a holy text around she strews
  That teach the rustic moralist to die.
  a.   GRAY—*Elegy in a Country Churchyard.*
                                          St. 21.

Beneath these green trees rising to the skies,
The planter of them, Isaac Greentrees, lies;
The time shall come when these green trees
    shall fall,
And Isaac Greentrees rise above them all.
  b.   *Epitaph at Harrow.*

Man's life is like unto a winter's day,
Some break their fast and so depart away,
Others stay dinner then depart full fed;
The longest age but sups and goes to bed.
Oh, reader, then behold and see,
As we are now so must you be.
  c.   BISHOP HENSHAW—*Horæ Succisivæ.*

Here she lies a pretty bud,
Lately made of flesh and blood;
Who, as soone fell fast asleep,
As her little eyes did peep.
Give her strewings, but not stir
The earth that lightly covers her.
  d.   HERRICK—*Upon a Child that Dyed.*

He touched nothing that he did not adorn.
  e.   *Quoted by Sam'l Johnson in his Epitaph*
                                  on Goldsmith.

The hand of him here torpid lies,
  That drew th' essential form of grace,
Here closed in death th' attentive eyes
  That saw the manners in the face.
  f.   SAM'L JOHNSON—*Epitaph for Hogarth.*

Underneath this stone doth lie
As much beauty as could die;
Which in life did harbor give
To more virtue than doth live.
If at all she had a fault,
Leave it buried in this vault.
  g.   BEN JONSON—*Epigram CXXIV.*

Here lies one whose name was writ in water.
  h.   *Engraved on Keats' tombstone at his own*
                                          desire.

I conceive disgust at these impertinent and
misbecoming familiarities inscribed upon your
ordinary tombstone.
  i.   CHARLES LAMB.

Satire does not look pretty upon a tombstone.
  j.   CHARLES LAMB.

Emigravit, is the inscription on the tombstone
    where he lies;
Dead he is not, but departed,—for the artist
    never dies.
  k.   LONGFELLOW—*Nuremberg.*

Calmly he looked on either Life, and here
Saw nothing to regret, or there to fear:
From Nature's temp'rate feast rose satisfy'd,
Thank'd Heaven that he had lived, and that
    he died.
  l.   POPE—*Epitaph X.*

Nature and Nature's laws lay hid in night.
God said " *Let Newton be !* " and all was light.
  m.   POPE—*Epitaph XIII.*

Of Manners gentle, of Affections mild ;
In Wit a man ; Simplicity, a child.
  n.   POPE—*Epitaph XI.*

To this sad shrine, whoe'er thou art! draw
    near!
Here lies the friend most lov'd, the son most
    dear;
Who ne'er knew joy but friendship might
    divide,
Or gave his father grief but when he died.
  o.   POPE—*Epitaph on Harcourt.*

Under this marble, or under this sill,
Or under this turf, or e'en what they will,
Whatever an heir, or a friend in his stead,
Or any good creature shall lay o'er my head,
Lies one who ne'er car'd, and still cares not a
    pin
What they said or may say of the mortal
    within ;
But who, living and dying, serene, still and
    free,
Trusts in God that as well as he was he
    shall be.
  p.   POPE—*Epitaph.*

Nobles and heralds, by your leave,
  Here lies what once was Matthew Prior;
The son of Adam and of Eve;
  Can Bourbon or Nassau claim higher?
  q.   PRIOR—*Epitaph. Extempore.*

I came at morn—'twas spring, I smiled,
  The fields with green were clad ;
I walked abroad at noon,—and lo !
  'Twas summer,—I was glad ;
I sate me down ; 'twas autumn eve,
  And I with sadness wept ;
I laid me down at night, and then
  'Twas winter,—and I slept.
  r.   MARY PYPER—*Epitaph. A Life.*

Johnny Carnegie lies here
  Descendit of Adam and Eve,
Gif only can gang hieher,
  I'se willing give him leve.
  s.   *Epitaph in an old Scottish Churchyard.*

GOOD FREND FOR JESVS SAKE FOR-
    BEARE,
TO DIGG THE DVST ENCLOASED HEARE.
BLESE BE Y̐ MAN Y̐ SPARES THES
    STONES,
AND CVRST BE HE Y̐ MOVES MY BONES.
  t.   *Epitaph on Shakespeare's Tombstone*
                    at Stratford-on-Avou.

Traveller, let your step be light,
  So that sleep these eyes may close,
For poor Scarron, till to-night,
  Ne'er was able e'en to doze.
  a.   Scarron—*Epitaph written by himself.*

After your death you were better have a
bad epitaph than their ill report while you
live.
  b.   *Hamlet.* Act II. Sc. 2. L. 548.

          And if your love
Can labour aught in sad invention,
Hang her an epitaph upon her tomb
And sing it to her bones, sing it to-night.
  c.   *Much Ado About Nothing.* Act V.
                            Sc. 1. L. 291.

Either our history shall with full mouth
Speak freely of our acts, or else our grave,
Like Turkish mute, shall have a tongueless
      mouth,
Not worshipp'd with a waxen epitaph.
  d.   *Henry V.* Act I. Sc. 2. L. 230.

          Of comfort no man speak :
Let's talk of graves, of worms and epitaphs.
  e.   *Richard II.* Act III. Sc. 2. L. 144.

On your family's old monument
Hang mournful epitaphs.
  f.   *Much Ado About Nothing.* Act IV.
                            Sc. 1. L. 208.

You cannot better be employ'd, Bassanio,
Than to live still and write mine epitaph.
  g.   *Merchant of Venice.* Act IV. Sc. 1.
                            L. 117.

These are two friends whose lives were un-
      divided :
So let their memory be, now they have glided
Under the grave ; let not their bones be
      parted,
For their two hearts in life were single-
      hearted.
  h.   Shelley—*Epitaph.*

The turf has drank a
  Widow's tear ;
Three of her husbands
  Slumber here.
  i.   *Epitaph at Staffordshire.*

Thou third great Canning, stand among our
      best
And noblest, now thy long day's work hath
      ceased,
Here silent in our minster of the West
Who wert the voice of England in the East.
  j.   Tennyson—*Epitaph on Lord Stratford
                            De Redcliffe.*

He directed the stone over his grave to be
thus inscribed :
  Hic jacet hujus Sententiæ primus Author :
  Disputandi pruritus ecclesiarum scabies.
    Nomen alias quære.
  Here lies the first author of this sentence ;
" The itch of disputation will prove the scab of
the Church." Inquire his name elsewhere.
  k.   Izaak Walton—*Life of Wotton.*

He first deceas'd ; she for a little tri'd
To live without him, lik'd it not, and died.
  l.   Sir Henry Wotton—*Upon the Death
              of Sir Albertus Morton's Wife.*

Si monumentum requiris circumspice.
(If you would see his monument look around.)
  m.   *Inscription on the tomb of Sir
              Christopher Wren in St. Paul's,
                            London.*

EQUALITY.

Men are made by nature unequal. It is
vain, therefore, to treat them as if they were
equal.
  n.   Froude—*Short Studies on Great
                Subjects. Party Politics.*

The equal right of all men to the use of land
is as clear as their equal right to breathe the
air—it is a right proclaimed by the fact of
their existence. For we cannot suppose that
some men have a right to be in this world,
and others no right.
  o.   Henry George—*Progress and Poverty.*
                            Bk. VII. Ch. I.

Sir, your levellers wish to level *down* as far
as themselves : but they cannot bear levelling
up to themselves.
  p.   Sam'l Johnson—*Boswell's Life of
                            Johnson,* 1763.

For some must follow, and some command,
Though all are made of clay !
  q.   Longfellow—*Keramos.* L. 6.

Among unequals what society
Can sort, what harmony, or true delight?
  r.   Milton—*Paradise Lost.* Bk. VIII.
                            L. 383.

Equality of two domestic powers
Breeds scrupulous faction.
  s.   *Antony and Cleopatra.* Act I. Sc. 3.
                            L. 47.

Heralds, from off our towers we might behold,
From first to last, the onset and retire
Of both your armies ; whose equality
By our best eyes cannot be censured :
Blood hath bought blood and blows have
      answer'd blows ;
Strength match'd with strength, and power
      confronted power :
Both are alike ; and both alike we like.
  t.   *King John.* Act II. Sc. 1. L. 325.

Mean and mighty, rotting
Together, have one dust.
　　a.　　*Cymbeline.*　Act IV.　Sc. 2.　L. 246.

　　She in beauty, education, blood,
Holds hand with any princess of the world.
　　b.　　*King John.*　Act II.　Sc. 1.　L. 493.

The trickling rain doth fall
Upon us one and all;
The south-wind kisses
The saucy milkmaid's cheek,
The nun's, demure and meek,
Nor any misses.
　　c.　　E. C. STEDMAN—*A Madrigal.*　St. 3.

Equality is the life of conversation; and he
is as much out who assumes to himself any
part above another, as he who considers himself below the rest of the society.
　　d.　　STEELE—*Tatler.*　No. 225.

The tall, the wise, the reverend head,
Must be as low as ours.
　　e.　　WATTS—*Hymns and Spiritual Songs,*
　　　　　　　　　　　Bk. II.　*Hymn* 63.

ERROR.

The truth is perilous never to the true,
Nor knowledge to the wise; and to the fool,
And to the false, error and truth alike,
Error is worse than ignorance.
　　f.　　BAILEY—*Festus.*　Sc. *A Mountain
　　　　　　　　　　　　　　　Sunrise.*

Have too rashly charged the troops of error
and remain as trophies unto the enemies of
truth.
　　g.　　SIR THOMAS BROWNE—*Religio Medici.*
　　　　　　　　　　　P I. I.　Sec. VI.

Mistake, error, is the discipline through
which we advance.
　　h.　　CHANNING—*Address on The Present Age.*

The cautious seldom err.
　　i.　　CONFUCIUS—*Analects.*　Bk. IV.
　　　　　　　　　　　　　　Ch. XXIII.

Man on the dubious waves of error toss'd.
　　j.　　COWPER—*Poem on Truth.*　L. 1.

Errors, like straws, upon the surface flow;
He who would search for pearls, must dive
　　below.
　　k.　　DRYDEN—*All for Love.*　Prologue.

For Art may err, but Nature cannot miss.
　　l.　　DRYDEN—*Fables.*　*The Cock and the
　　　　　　　　　　　　　　Fox.*　L. 452.

Brother, brother; we are both in the wrong.
　　m.　　GAY—*Beggar's Opera.*　Act II.　Sc. 2.

Dark Error's other hidden side is truth.
　　n.　　VICTOR HUGO—*La Légende des Siècles.*

Knowledge being to be had only of visible
and certain truth, error is not a fault of our
knowledge, but a mistake of our judgment,
giving assent to that which is not true.
　　o.　　LOCKE—*Essay Concerning Human
　　　　　　　　Understanding.*　Bk. IV.　*Of Wrong
　　　　　　　　　　　Assent or Error.*　Ch. XX.

Sometimes we may learn more from a man's
errors than from his virtues.
　　p.　　LONGFELLOW—*Hyperion.*　Bk. IV.
　　　　　　　　　　　　　　Ch. III.

For to err in opinion, though it be not the
part of wise men, is at least human.
　　q.　　PLUTARCH—*Morals.*　*Against Colotes the
　　　　　　　　　　　　　　Epicurean.*

Some positive persisting fops we know,
Who, if once wrong, will needs be always so;
But you with pleasure own your errors past,
And make each day a critique on the last.
　　r.　　POPE—*Essay on Criticism.*　Pt. III.
　　　　　　　　　　　　　　L. 9.

When people once are in the wrong,
Each line they add is much too long;
Who fastest walks, but walks astray,
Is only furthest from his way.
　　s.　　PRIOR—*Alma.*　Canto III.　L. 194.

How far your eyes may pierce, I cannot tell;
Striving to better, oft we mar what's well.
　　t.　　*King Lear.*　Act I.　Sc. 4.　L. 368.

It may be right; but you are i' the wrong
To speak before your time.
　　u.　　*Measure for Measure.*　Act V.　Sc. 1.
　　　　　　　　　　　　　　L. 86.

Omission to do what is necessary
Seals a commission to a blank of danger.
　　v.　　*Troilus and Cressida.*　Act III.　Sc. 3.
　　　　　　　　　　　　　　L. 230.

　　　　Purposes mistook
Fall'n on the inventors' heads.
　　w.　　*Hamlet.*　Act V.　Sc. 2.　L. 395.

The error of our eye directs our mind:
What error leads must err.
　　x.　　*Troilus and Cressida.*　Act V.　Sc. 2.
　　　　　　　　　　　　　　L. 110.

　　Shall error in the round of time
Still father Truth?
　　y.　　TENNYSON—*Love and Duty.*

The progress of rivers to the ocean is not so
rapid as that of man to error.
　　z.　　VOLTAIRE—*A Philosophical Dictionary.*
　　　　　　　　　　　　　　Rivers.

ETERNITY.

Eternity! thou pleasing dreadful thought!
Through what variety of untried being,
Through what new scenes and changes must
　　we pass!
　　aa.　　ADDISON—*Cato.*　Act. V.　Sc. 1.

'Tis the divinity that stirs within us ;
'Tis heaven itself, that points out an hereafter,
And indicates eternity to man.
  a.   ADDISON—*Cato.* Act V. Sc. 1.

Then gazing up 'mid the dim pillars high,
The foliaged marble forest where ye lie,
Hush, ye will say, it is eternity !
This is the glimmering verge of heaven, and
    there
The columns of the heavenly palaces.
  b.   MATTHEW ARNOLD—*The Tomb.*

Eternity forbids thee to forget.
  c.   BYRON—*Lara.* Canto I. St. 23.

Eternity ! How know we but we stand
On the precipitous and crumbling verge
Of Time e'en now, Eternity below ?
  d.   ABRAHAM COLES—*The Microcosm and*
                Other Poems, 1841. P. 125.

Nothing is there to come, and nothing past,
But an eternal Now does always last.
  e.   COWLEY—*Davideis.* Bk. I. L. 360.

        That golden key,
That opes the palace of eternity.
  f.   MILTON—*Comus.* L. 13.

This speck of life in time's great wilderness
This narrow isthmus 'twixt two boundless
    seas,
The past, the future, two eternities !
  g.   MOORE—*Lalla Rookh. The Veiled*
             Prophet of Khorassan. St. 42.

The time will come when every change shall
    cease,
This quick revolving wheel shall rest in peace:
No summer then shall glow, nor winter freeze;
Nothing shall be to come, and nothing past,
But an eternal now shall ever last.
  h.   PETRARCH—*The Triumph of Eternity.*
                      L. 117.

Those spacious regions where our fancies
    roam,
Pain'd by the past, expecting ills to come,
In some dread moment, by the fates assign'd,
Shall pass away, nor leave a rack behind ;
And Time's revolving wheels shall lose at
    last
The speed that spins the future and the past :
And, sovereign of an undisputed throne,
Awful eternity shall reign alone.
  i.   PETRARCH—*The Triumph of Eternity.*
                      L. 102.

The Pilgrim of Eternity, whose fame
Over his living head like Heaven is bent,
  An early but enduring monument,
Came, veiling all the lightnings of his song
  In sorrow.
  j.   SHELLEY—*Adonais.* XXX.

In time there is no present,
In eternity no future,
In eternity no past.
  k.   TENNYSON—*The " How " and " Why."*

But felt through all this fleshly dresse
Bright shootes of everlastingnesse.
  l.   HENRY VAUGHAN—*The Retreate.*

And can eternity belong to me,
Poor pensioner on the bounties of an hour?
  m.   YOUNG—*Night Thoughts.* Night I.
                      L. 66.

EVENING.

To me at least was never evening yet
But seemed far beautifuller than its day.
  n.   ROBERT BROWNING—*The Ring and the*
                 Book. Pompilia. L. 357.

Hath not thy heart within thee burned,
At evening's calm and holy hour ?
  o.   S. G. BULFINCH—*Meditation.*

It is the hour when from the boughs
  The nightingale's high note is heard ;
It is the hour when lovers' vows
  Seem sweet in every whispered word ;
And gentle winds, and waters near,
Make music to the lonely ear.
Each flower the dews have lightly wet,
And in the sky the stars are met,
And on the wave is deeper blue,
And on the leaf a browner hue,
And in the heaven that clear obscure,
So softly dark, and darkly pure.
Which follows the decline of day,
As twilight melts beneath the moon away.
  p.   BYRON—*Parisina.* St. 1.

Now stir the fire, and close the shutters fast,
Let fall the curtains, wheel the sofa round,
And while the bubbling and loud-hissing urn
Throws up a steamy column, and the cups,
That cheer but not inebriate, wait on each,
So let us welcome peaceful evening in.
  q.   COWPER—*Task.* Bk. IV. L. 36.

When day is done, and clouds are low,
  And flowers are honey-dew,
And Hesper's lamp begins to glow
  Along the western blue ;
And homeward wing the turtle-doves,
Then comes the hour the poet loves.
  r.   GEORGE CROLY—*The Poet's Hour.*

The curfew tolls the knell of parting day,
  The lowing herd winds slowly o'er the lea,
The ploughman homeward plods his weary
    way,
  And leaves the world to darkness and to me.
  s.   GRAY—*Elegy in a Country Churchyard.*

How gently rock yon poplars high
Against the reach of primrose sky
  With heaven's pale candles stored.
  t.   JEAN INGELOW—*Supper at the Mill.*
                      Song.

But when eve's silent footfall steals
  Along the eastern sky,
And one by one to earth reveals
  Those purer fires on high.
  a.   KEBLE—*The Christian Year. Fourth*
                Sunday After Trinity.

Day, like a weary pilgrim, had reached the
western gate of heaven, and Evening stooped
down to unloose the latchets of his sandal
shoon.
  b.   LONGFELLOW—*Hyperion.* Bk. IV.
                        Ch. V.

O precious evenings! all too swiftly sped !
  c.   LONGFELLOW—*Sonnet. On Mrs. Kem-*
          ble's Readings from Shakespeare.

Just then return'd at shut of evening flowers.
  d.   MILTON—*Paradise Lost.* Bk. IX.
                       L. 278.

Now came still evening on; and twilight gray
Had in her sober livery all things clad :
Silence accompanied; for beast and bird,
They to their grassy couch, these to their
    nests,
Were slunk, all but the wakeful nightingale.
  e.   MILTON—*Paradise Lost.* Bk. IV.
                       L. 598.

Fly not yet, 'tis just the hour
When pleasure, like the midnight flower
That scorns the eye of vulgar light,
Begins to bloom for sons of night,
  And maids who love the moon.
  f.   MOORE—*Fly Not Yet.*

O how grandly cometh Even,
Sitting on the mountain summit,
Purple-vestured, grave, and silent,
Watching o'er the dewy valleys,
  Like a good king near his end.
  g.   D. M. MULOCK—*A Stream's Singing.*

One by one the flowers close,
Lily and dewy rose
Shutting their tender petals from the moon.
  h.   CHRISTINA G. ROSSETTI—*Twilight Calm.*

The pale child, Eve, leading her mother,
  Night.
  i.   ALEXANDER SMITH—*A Life Drama.*
                       Sc. 8.

The lights begin to twinkle from the rocks :
The long day wanes: the slow moon climbs:
    the deep
Moans round with many voices.
  j.   TENNYSON—*Ulysses.* L. 54.

I was heavy with the even,
When she lit her glimmering tapers
Round the day's dead sanctities.
I laughed in the morning's eyes.
  k.   FRANCIS THOMPSON—*The Hound of*
                   Heaven. L. 84.

The holy time is quiet as a Nun
Breathless with adoration.
  l.   WORDSWORTH—*It is a Beauteous*
                      Evening.

EVIL.

Evil events from evil causes spring.
  m.   ARISTOPHANES.

Evil beginning houres may end in good.
  n.   BEAUMONT AND FLETCHER—*The Knight*
            of Malta. Act II. Sc. 5.

It is some compensation for great evils that
they enforce great lessons.
  o.   BOVEE—*Summaries of Thought.*
                      Compensation.

None are all evil.
  p.   BYRON—*The Corsair.* Canto I. St. 12.

He who does evil that good may come,
pays a toll to the devil to let him into heaven.
  q.   J. C. and A. W. HARE—*Guesses at*
                  Truth. P. 444.

But evil is wrought by want of Thought,
As well as want of Heart!
  r.   HOOD—*The Lady's Dream.* St. 16.

Evil springs up, and flowers, and bears no
    seed,
And feeds the green earth with its swift
    decay,
Leaving it richer for the growth of truth.
  s.   LOWELL—*Prometheus.* L. 263.

I have wrought great use out of evil tools.
  t.   BULWER-LYTTON—*Richelieu.* Act III.
                     Sc. 1. L. 49.

And out of good still to find means of evil.
  u.   MILTON—*Paradise Lost.* Bk. I. L. 165.

Timely advis'd, the coming evil shun :
Better not do the deed, than weep it done.
  v.   PRIOR—*Henry and Emma.* L. 308.

Multitudes think they like to do evil; yet
no man ever really enjoyed doing evil since
God made the world.
  w.   RUSKIN—*Stones of Venice.* Vol. I.
                         Ch. II.

But then I sigh; and, with a piece of Scripture,
Tell them that God bids us do good for evil,
  x.   *Richard III.* Act I. Sc. 3. L. 334.

The evil that men do lives after them;
The good is oft interred with their bones.
  y.   *Julius Cæsar.* Act III. Sc. 2. L. 80.

    The world is grown so bad
That wrens make prey where eagles dare not
    perch.
  z.   *Richard III.* Act I. Sc. 3. L. 69.

So far as any one shuns evils, so far he does
good.
  aa.   SWEDENBORG—*Doctrine of Life.* 21.

EVOLUTION.

Observe constantly that all things take place by change, and accustom thyself to consider that the nature of the Universe loves nothing so much as to change the things which are, and to make new things like them.

a.   MARCUS AURELIUS—*Meditations.*

Ch. IV. 36.

The expression often used by Mr. Herbert Spencer of the Survival of the Fittest is more accurate, and is sometimes equally convenient.

b.   CHARLES DARWIN—*The Origin of Species.* Chap. III.

Till o'er the wreck, emerging from the storm, Immortal NATURE lifts her changeful form : Mounts from her funeral pyre on wings of flame,
And soars and shines, another and the same.

c.   ERASMUS DARWIN—*Botanic Garden.*

Pt. I. Canto IV. L. 389.

This survival of the fittest, which I have here sought to express in mechanical terms, is that which Mr. Darwin has called " natural selection, or the preservation of favoured races in the struggle for life."

d.   HERBERT SPENCER—*Principles of Biology. Indirect Equilibration.*

Evolution ever climbing after some ideal good And Reversion ever dragging Evolution in the mud.

e.   TENNYSON—*Locksley Hall Sixty Years After.* L. 200.

Is there evil but on earth ? Or pain in every peopled sphere ?
Well, be grateful for the sounding watchword " Evolution " here.

f.   TENNYSON—*Locksley Hall Sixty Years After.* L. 198

Let the great world spin forever down the ringing grooves of change.

g.   TENNYSON—*Locksley Hall.* L. 182.

The Lord let the house of a brute to the soul of a man,
And the man said, " Am I your debtor ? "
And the Lord—" Not yet : but make it as clean as you can,
And then I will let you a better."

h.   TENNYSON—*By an Evolutionist.*

EXAMPLE.

Example is the school of mankind, and they will learn at no other.

i.   BURKE—*Letter I. On a Regicide Peace.* Vol. 5. P. 331.

Why doth one man's yawning make another yawn ?

j.   BURTON—*Anatomy of Melancholy.*

Pt. I. Sec. II. Memb. 3. Subsect. 2.

This noble ensample to his sheepe he gaf,— That firste he wroughte and afterward he taughte.

k.   CHAUCER—*Canterbury Tales. Prologue.* L. 496.

O, could I flow like thee ! and make thy stream My great example, as it is my theme ; Though deep yet clear, though gentle yet not dull ;
Strong without rage, without o'erflowing full.

l.   SIR JOHN DENHAM—*Cooper's Hill.*

L. 189.

The character, the counsels, and example of our Washington * * * they will guide us through the doubts and difficulties that beset us ; they will guide our children and our children's children in the paths of prosperity and peace, while America shall hold her place in the family of nations.

m.   ED. EVERETT—*Speech.* July 5, 1858. *Washington Abroad and at Home.*

Allured to brighter worlds, and led the way.

n.   GOLDSMITH—*Deserted Village.* L. 170.

Since truth and constancy are vain, Since neither love, nor sense of pain, Nor force of reason, can persuade, Then let example be obey'd.

o.   GEO. GRANVILLE (Lord Lansdowne)— *To Myra.*

Tarquin and Cæsar had each his Brutus— Charles the First, his Cromwell—and George the Third—(" Treason !" shouted the Speaker) —may profit by their example. If this be treason, make the most of it.

p.   PATRICK HENRY—*Speech.* 1765.

Content to follow when we lead the way.

q.   HOMER—*The Iliad.* Bk. X. L. 141. Pope's trans.

I do not give you to posterity as a pattern to imitate, but as an example to deter.

r.   JUNIUS—Letter XII. *To the Duke of Grafton.*

Lives of great men all remind us We can make our lives sublime, And, departing, leave behind us Footprints on the sands of time.

s.   LONGFELLOW—*A Psalm of Life.*

He who should teach men to die, would at the same time teach them to live.

t.   MONTAIGNE—*Essays.* Bk. I.

Ch. XIX.

He was indeed the glass Wherein the noble youth did dress themselves.

u.   *Henry IV.* Pt. II. Act II. Sc. 3.

L. 21.

Thieves for their robbery have authority
When judges steal themselves.

a.　*Measure for Measure.*　Act II.　Sc. 2.
L. 176.

These taught us how to live; and (oh, too high
The price for knowledge!) taught us how to die.

b.　THOMAS TICKELL—*On the Death of Mr. Addison.*　L. 81.　See also BISHOP PORTEUS—*Death.*　L. 316.

EXPECTATION.

"Yet doth he live!" exclaims th' impatient heir,
And sighs for sables which he must not wear.

c.　BYRON—*Lara.*　Canto I.　St. 3.

Everything comes if a man will only wait.

d.　BENJ. DISRAELI—*Tancred.*　Bk. IV.
Ch. VIII.　1847.

They that marry ancient people merely in expectation to bury them, hang themselves in hope that one will come and cut the halter.

e.　FULLER—*Holy and Profane State. Of Marriage.*

Since yesterday I have been in Alcalá.
Erelong the time will come, sweet Preciosa,
When that dull distance shall no more divide us;
And I no more shall scale thy wall by night
To steal a kiss from thee, as I do now.

f.　LONGFELLOW—*The Spanish Student.*
Act I.　Sc. 3.

What else remains for me?
Youth, hope and love;
To build a new life on a ruined life.

g.　LONGFELLOW—*Masque of Pandora.*
In the Garden.　Pt. VIII.

To-day what is there in the air
　That makes December seem sweet May?
There are no swallows anywhere,
　Nor crocuses to crown your hair
　And hail you down my garden way.
Last night the full moon's frozen stare
　Struck me, perhaps; or did you say
Really—you'd come, sweet Friend and fair!
　To-Day?

h.　THEOPHILE MARZIALS—*Rondel.*

Expectation whirls me round.
The imaginary relish is so sweet
That it enchants my sense.

i.　*Troilus and Cressida.*　Act III.　Sc. 2.
L. 19.

He hath indeed better bettered expectation than you must expect of me to tell you how.

j.　*Much Ado About Nothing.*　Act I.
Sc. 1.　L. 15.

Oft expectation fails and most oft there
Where most it promises, and oft it hits
Where hope is coldest and despair most fits.

k.　*All's Well That Ends Well.*　Act II.
Sc. 1.　L. 145.

Promising is the very air o' the time; it opens the eyes of expectation: performance is ever the duller for his act; and, but in the plainer and simpler kind of people, the deed of saying is quite out of use.

l.　*Timon of Athens.*　Act V.　Sc. 1.　L. 24.

There have sat
The live-long day, with patient expectation,
To see great Pompey pass the streets of Rome.

m.　*Julius Cæsar.*　Act I.　Sc. 1.　L. 45.

When clouds appear, wise men put on their cloaks;
When great leaves fall, then winter is at hand;
When the sun sets, who doth not look for night?
Untimely storms make men expect a dearth.

n.　*Richard III.*　Act II.　Sc. 3.　L. 32.

'Tis expectation makes a blessing dear;
Heaven were not Heaven, if we knew what it were.

o.　SIR JOHN SUCKLING—*Against Fruition.*

Although I enter not,
Yet round about the spot
　Ofttimes I hover;
And near the sacred gate,
With longing eyes I wait,
　Expectant of her.

p.　THACKERAY—*Pendennis.*　*At the Church Gate.*　St. 1.

The gratitude of place expectants is a lively sense of future favours.

q.　SIR ROBERT WALPOLE.

EXPERIENCE.

Behold, we live through all things,—famine, thirst,
　Bereavement, pain; all grief and misery,
All woe and sorrow; life inflicts its worst
　On soul and body,—but we cannot die,
Though we be sick, and tired, and faint, and worn,—
Lo, all things can be borne!

r.　ELIZABETH AKERS ALLEN—
Endurance.

Making all futures fruits of all the pasts.

s.　EDWIN ARNOLD—*The Light of Asia.*
Bk. V.　L. 432.

Oh, who can tell, save he whose heart hath tried?

t.　BYRON—*The Corsair.*　Canto I.　St. 1.

A sadder and a wiser man,
He rose the morrow morn.
>   *a.*   COLERIDGE—*The Ancient Mariner.*
>   Pt. VII. Last St.

In her experience all her friends relied,
Heaven was her help and nature was her
    guide.
>   *b.*   CRABBE—*Parish Register.* Pt. III.

To show the world what long experience
    gains,
Requires not courage, though it calls for
    pains;
But at life's outset to inform mankind
Is a bold effort of a valiant mind.
>   *c.*   CRABBE—*The Borough.* Letter VII.
>   L. 47.

I think there are stores laid up in our human
nature that our understandings can make no
complete inventory of.
>   *d.*   GEORGE ELIOT—*The Mill on the Floss.*
>   Bk. V. Ch. I.

Only so much do I know, as I have lived.
>   *e.*   EMERSON—*Oration. The American
>   Scholar.*

Experience is no more transferable in morals
than in art.
>   *f.*   FROUDE—*Short Studies on Great
>   Subjects. Education.*

Experience teaches slowly, and at the cost
of mistakes.
>   *g.*   FROUDE—*Short Studies on Great
>   Subjects. Party Politics.*

We read the past by the light of the present,
and the forms vary as the shadows fall, or as
the point of vision alters.
>   *h.*   FROUDE—*Short Studies on Great
>   Subjects. Society in Italy in the
>   Last Days of the Roman Republic.*

For just experience tells, in every soil,
That those who think must govern those that
    toil.
>   *i.*   GOLDSMITH—*The Traveller.* L. 372.

Experience join'd with common sense,
To mortals is a providence.
>   *j.*   MATTHEW GREEN—*The Spleen.* L. 312.

I have but one lamp by which my feet are
guided, and that is the lamp of experience.
>   *k.*   PATRICK HENRY—*Speech at Virginia
>   Convention.* March 23, 1775.

Nor deem the irrevocable Past,
    As wholly wasted, wholly vain,
If, rising on its wrecks, at last
    To something nobler we attain.
>   *l.*   LONGFELLOW—*The Ladder of St.
>   Augustine.*

One thorn of experience is worth a whole
wilderness of warning.
>   *m.*   LOWELL—*Among my Books.
>   Shakespeare Once More.*

                            We gain
Justice, judgment, with years, or else years
    are in vain.
>   *n.*   OWEN MEREDITH (Lord Lytton)—
>   *Lucile.* Pt. I. Canto III. St. 16.

        Experience, next, to thee I owe,
Best guide; not following thee, I had remain'd
In ignorance; thou open'st wisdom's way,
And giv'st access, though secret she retire.
>   *o.*   MILTON—*Paradise Lost.* Bk. IX.
>   L. 807.

What man would be wise, let him drink of
        the river
    That bears on his bosom the record of time;
A message to him every wave can deliver
    To teach him to creep till he knows how to
        climb.
>   *p.*   JOHN BOYLE O'REILLY—*Rules of the
>   Road.*

Who heeds not experience, trust him not.
>   *q.*   JOHN BOYLE O'REILLY—*Rules of the
>   Road.*

Like bubbles on the sea of matter borne,
They rise, they break, and to that sea return.
>   *r.*   POPE—*Essay on Man.* Ep. III. L. 19.

I shall the effect of this good lesson keep,
As watchman to my heart.
>   *s.*   *Hamlet.* Act I. Sc. 3. L. 45.

My grief lies onward, and my joy behind.
>   *t.*   *Sonnet. L.*

                            I know
The past and thence I will essay to glean
A warning for the future, so that man
May profit by his errors, and derive
Experience from his folly;
For, when the power of imparting joy
Is equal to the will, the human soul
            Requires no other heaven.
>   *u.*   SHELLEY—*Queen Mab.* III. L. 6.

Learn the lesson of your own pain—learn to
seek God, not in any single event of past
history, but in your own soul—in the constant
verifications of experience, in the life of Christian love.
>   *v.*   MRS. HUMPHRY WARD—*Robert
>   Elsmere.* Ch. XXVII.

EXPRESSION.

Preserving the sweetness of proportion and
expressing itself beyond expression.
>   *w.*   BEN JONSON—*The Masque of Hymen.*

                    Patience and sorrow strove
Who should express her goodliest. You have
        seen
Sunshine and rain at once: her smile and
        tears
Were like a better way.
>   *x.*   *King Lear.* Act IV. Sc. 3. L. 18.

EXTREMES.

Extremes are faulty and proceed from men : compensation is just, and proceeds from God.

a.   DE LA BRUYÈRE—*The Characters or Manners of the Present Age.* Ch. XVII.

Thus each extreme to equal danger tends, Plenty, as well as Want, can separate friends.

b.   COWLEY—*Davideis.* Bk. III. L. 205.

Extremes meet.

c.   MERCIER—*Tableaux de Paris.* (1782.) Vol. IV. Title of Ch. 348.

He that had never seen a river imagined the first he met with to be the sea; and the greatest things that have fallen within our knowledge we conclude the extremes that nature makes of the kind.

d.   MONTAIGNE—*Essays.* Bk. I. Ch. XXVI.

Avoid Extremes ; and shun the fault of such Who still are pleas'd too little or too much.

e.   POPE—*Essay on Criticism.* L. 385.

Extremes in nature equal good produce ; Extremes in man concur to general use.

f.   POPE—*Moral Essays.* Ep. III. L. 161.

And where two raging fires meet together, They do consume the thing that feeds their fury :
Though little fire grows great with little wind, Yet extreme gusts will blow out fire and all.

g.   *Taming of the Shrew.* Act II. Sc. 1. L. 133.

Like to the time o' the year between the extremes
Of hot and cold, he was nor sad nor merry.

h.   *Antony and Cleopatra.* Act I. Sc. 5. L. 51.

Not fearing death, nor shrinking for distress, But always resolute in most extremes.

i.   *Henry VI.* Pt. I. Act IV. Sc. 1. L. 37.

Who can be patient in such extremes ?

j.   *Henry VI.* Pt. III. Act I. Sc. 1. L. 215.

EYES.

In her eyes a thought
Grew sweeter and sweeter, deepening like the dawn,
A mystical forewarning.

k.   T. B. ALDRICH—*Pythagoras.*

A gray eye is a sly eye,
    And roguish is a brown one ;
Turn full upon me thy eye,—
    Ah, how its wavelets drown one !
A blue eye is a true eye ;
    Mysterious is a dark one,
Which flashes like a spark-sun !
    A black eye is the best one.

l.   W. R. ALGER—*Oriental Poetry.* *Mirtsa Schaffy on Eyes.*

There are whole veins of diamonds in thine eyes,
Might furnish crowns for all the Queens of earth.

m.   BAILEY—*Festus.* Sc. *A Drawing Room.*

These lovely lamps, these windows of the soul.

n.   DU BARTAS—*Divine Weekes and Workes.* First Week. Sixth Day.

Eyes of gentianellas azure,
Staring, winking at the skies.

o.   E. B. BROWNING—*Hector in the Garden.*

Thine eyes are springs in whose serene
And silent waters heaven is seen.
Their lashes are the herbs that look
On their young figures in the brook.

p.   BRYANT—*Oh, Fairest of the Rural Maids.*

Her eye (I'm very fond of handsome eyes)
    Was large and dark, suppressing half its fire
Until she spoke, then through its soft disguise
    Flash'd an expression more of pride than ire,
And love than either ; and there would arise,
    A something in them which was not desire,
But would have been, perhaps, but for the soul,
Which struggled through and chasten'd down the whole.

q.   BYRON—*Don Juan.* Canto I. St. 60.

With eyes that look'd into the very soul—
*   *   *   *   *   *
Bright—and as black and burning as a coal.

r.   BYRON—*Don Juan.* Canto IV. St. 94.

There are eyes half defiant,
Half meek and compliant ;
Black eyes, with a wondrous, witching charm
To bring us good or to work us harm.

s.   PHEBE CARY—*Dove's Eyes.*

My eyes make pictures, when they are shut.

t.   COLERIDGE—*A Day-Dream.*

Eyes, that displaces
The neighbor diamond, and out-faces
That sun-shine by their own sweet graces.

u.   RICHARD CRASHAW—*Wishes. To his (Supposed) Mistress.*

Not in mine eyes alone is Paradise.

v.   DANTE—*Paradise.* XVIII. 21.

A suppressed resolve will betray itself in the eyes.

w.   GEORGE ELIOT—*The Mill on the Floss.* Bk. V. Ch. XIV.

An eye can threaten like a loaded and levelled gun, or can insult like hissing or kicking ; or, in its altered mood, by beams of kindness, it can make the heart dance with joy.

x.   EMERSON—*Conduct of Life. Behavior.*

Eyes are bold as lions,—roving, running, leaping, here and there, far and near. They speak all languages. They wait for no introduction; they are no Englishmen; ask no leave of age or rank; they respect neither poverty nor riches, neither learning nor power, nor virtue, nor sex, but intrude, and come again, and go through and through you in a moment of time. What inundation of life and thought is discharged from one soul into another through them!

   a.   EMERSON—*Conduct of Life. Behavior.*

To sun myself in Huncamunca's eyes.

   b.   HENRY FIELDING—*The Life and Death of Tom Thumb the Great.* Act I. Sc. 3.

Eyes so transparent,
That through them one sees the soul.

   c.   THEOPHILE GAUTIER—*The Two Beautiful Eyes.*

Tell me, eyes, what 'tis ye're seeking;
  For ye're saying something sweet,
  Fit the ravish'd ear to greet.
Eloquently, softly speaking.

   d.   GOETHE—*April.*

On woman Nature did bestow two eyes,
Like Hemian's bright lamps, in matchless beauty shining,
Whose beams do soonest captivate the wise
And wary heads, made rare by art's refining.

   e.   ROBERT GREENE—*Philomela.* Sonnet.

I everywhere am thinking
  Of thy blue eyes' sweet smile;
A sea of blue thoughts is spreading
  Over my heart the while.

   f.   HEINE—*New Spring.* Pt. XVIII. St. 2.

Her eyes the glow-worme lend thee,
The shooting starres attend thee;
And the elves also,
Whose little eyes glow
Like the sparks of fire, befriend thee.

   g.   HERRICK—*The Night Piece to Julia.*

We credit most our sight; one eye doth please
Our trust farre more than ten eare-witnesses.

   h.   HERRICK—*Hesperides. The Eyes Before the Ears.*

Thine eye was on the censer,
And not the hand that bore it.

   i.   O. W. HOLMES—*Lines by a Clerk.*

The eyes of a man are of no use without the observing power.

   j.   E. PAXTON HOOD.

Blue! Gentle cousin of the forest-green,
  Married to green in all the sweetest flowers—
Forget-me-not,—the blue bell,—and, that queen
  Of secrecy, the violet: what strange powers
Hast thou, as a mere shadow! But how great,
When in an Eye thou art alive with fate!

   k.   KEATS—*Answer to a Sonnet by J. H. Reynolds.*

Dark eyes—eternal soul of pride!
  Deep life in all that's true!
    *   *   *   *   *   *
Away, away to other skies!
  Away o'er seas and sands!
Such eyes as those were never made
  To shine in other lands.

   l.   LELAND—*Callirhoe.*

And thy deep eyes, amid the gloom,
Shine like jewels in a shroud.

   m.   LONGFELLOW—*Christus. The Golden Legend.* Pt. IV.

I dislike an eye that twinkles like a star. Those only are beautiful which, like the planets, have a steady, lambent light,—are luminous, but not sparkling.

   n.   LONGFELLOW—*Hyperion.* Bk. III. Ch. IV.

O lovely eyes of azure,
Clear as the waters of a brook that run
Limpid and laughing in the summer sun!

   o.   LONGFELLOW—*The Masque of Pandora.* Pt. I.

The flash of his keen, black eyes
Forerunning the thunder.

   p.   LONGFELLOW—*Christus. The Golden Legend.* Pt. IV.

             Within her tender eye
The heaven of April, with its changing light.

   q.   LONGFELLOW—*The Spirit of Poetry.* L. 45.

Since your eyes are so sharpe, that you cannot onely looke through a milstone, but cleane through the minde.

   r.   LYLY—*Euphues and his England.* P. 289.

The learned compute that seven hundred and seven millions of millions of vibrations have penetrated the eye before the eye can distinguish the tints of a violet.

   s.   BULWER-LYTTON—*What Will He Do With It?* Bk. VIII. Ch. II.

Where did you get your eyes so blue?
Out of the sky as I came through.

   t.   GEO. MACDONALD—*Song in " At the Back of the North Wind."* Ch. 33.

             Those true eyes
Too pure and too honest in aught to disguise
The sweet soul shining through them.

   u.   OWEN MEREDITH (Lord Lytton)— *Lucile.* Pt. II. Canto II. St. 3.

And looks commercing with the skies,
Thy rapt soul sitting in thine eyes.

   v.   MILTON—*Il Penseroso.* L. 39.

           Ladies, whose bright eyes
Rain influence.

   w.   MILTON—*L'Allegro.* L. 121.

And the world's so rich in resplendent eyes,
'Twere a pity to limit one's love to a pair.
  a.   MOORE—'*Tis Sweet to Think.*

And violets, transform'd to eyes,
Inshrined a soul within their blue.
  b.   MOORE—*Evenings in Greece.   Second
                                        Evening.*
Eyes of most unholy blue!
  c.   MOORE—*Irish Melodies.   By that Lake
                            whose Gloomy Shore.*

Those eyes, whose light seem'd rather given
  To be ador'd than to adore—
Such eyes as may have looked *from* heaven,
  But ne'er were raised to it before!
  d.   MOORE—*Loves of the Angels.   Third
                            Angel's Story.   St. 7.*

Bright as the sun her eyes the gazers strike,
And, like the sun, they shine on all alike.
  e.   POPE—*Rape of the Lock.   Canto II.
                                        L. 13.*

Why has not man a microscopic eye?
For this plain reason, Man is not a Fly.
Say, what the use, were finer optics giv'n,
T' inspect a mite, not comprehend the heav'n?
  f.   POPE—*Essay on Man.   Ep. I.   L. 193.*

            Dark eyes are dearer far
Than those that mock the hyacinthine bell.
  g.   J. H. REYNOLDS—*Sonnet.*

Alack, there lies more peril in thine eye
Than twenty of their swords.
  h.   *Romeo and Juliet—Act II.   Sc. 2.
                                        L. 71.*

A lover's eyes will gaze an eagle blind.
  i.   *Love's Labour's Lost.   Act IV.   Sc. 3.
                                        L. 334.*

An eye like Mars, to threaten and command.
  j.   *Hamlet.   Act III.   Sc. 4.   L. 57.*

But hers, which through the crystal tears
      gave light,
Shone like the moon in water seen by night.
  k.   *Venus and Adonis.   L. 491.*

Disdain and scorn ride sparkling in her eyes.
  l.   *Much Ado About Nothing.   Act III.
                                        Sc. 1.   L. 51.*

            Faster than his tongue
Did make offence his eye did heal it up.
  m.   *As You Like It.   Act III.   Sc. 5.
                                        L. 116.*

For where is any author in the world
Teaches such beauty as a woman's eye?
  n.   *Love's Labour's Lost.   Act IV.   Sc. 3.
                                        L. 312.*

            Her eyes in heaven
Would through the airy region stream so
      bright,
That birds would sing and think it were not
      night.
  o.   *Romeo and Juliet.   Act II.   Sc. 2.
                                        L. 20.*

13

Her eyes, like marigolds, had sheath'd their
      light;
And, canopied in darkness, sweetly lay,
Till they might open to adorn the day.
  p.   *Rape of Lucrece.   L. 397.*

Her two blue windows faintly she up-heaveth,
Like the fair sun, when in his fresh array
He cheers the morn, and all the earth re-
      lieveth;
And as the bright sun glorifies the sky,
So is her face illumin'd with her eye.
  q.   *Venus and Adonis.   L. 482.*

If I could write the beauty of your eyes,
And in fresh numbers number all your graces,
The age to come would say, " This poet lies;
Such heavenly touches ne'er touch'd earthly
      faces."
  r.   *Sonnet XVII.*

I have a good eye, uncle; I can see a church
by daylight.
  s.   *Much Ado About Nothing.   Act II.
                                        Sc. 1.   L. 85.*

I see how thine eye would emulate the diamond: thou hast the right archèd beauty
of the brow.
  t.   *Merry Wives of Windsor.   Act III.
                                        Sc. 3.   L. 58.*

            Sometimes from her eyes
I did receive fair speechless messages.
  u.   *Merchant of Venice.   Act I.   Sc. 1.
                                        L. 163.*

The fringed curtains of thine eye advance,
And say what thou seest yond.
  v.   *Tempest.   Act I.   Sc. 2.   L. 407.*

The image of a wicked heinous fault
Lives in his eye: that close aspect of his
Does show the mood of a much troubled breast.
  w.   *King John.   Act IV.   Sc. 2.   L. 71.*

Thou tell'st me there is murder in mine eye;
'Tis pretty, sure, and very probable,
That eyes, that are the frail'st and softest
      things,
Who shut their coward gates on atomies,
Should be call'd tyrants, butchers, mur-
      derers!
  x.   *As You Like It.   Act III.   Sc. 5.   L. 10.*

            You have seen
Sunshine and rain at once. * * * those
      happy smilets,
That play'd on her ripe lip, seem'd not to
      know
What guests were in her eyes; which parted
      thence,
As pearls from diamonds dropp'd.
  y.   *King Lear.   Act IV.   Sc. 3.   L. 19.*

Thine eyes are like the deep, blue, boundless
    heaven
Contracted to two circles underneath
Their long, fine lashes; dark, far, measureless,
Orb within orb, and line through line in-
    woven.
  a.   Shelley—*Prometheus Unbound.*
                      Act II.   Sc. 1.

Think ye by gazing on each other's eyes
To multiply your lovely selves?
  b.   Shelley—*Prometheus Unbound.*
                      Act VI.   Sc. 4.

Her eyes are homes of silent prayer.
  c.   Tennyson—*In Memoriam.* XXXII.

The Father of Heaven.
    Scoop, young Jesus, for her eyes,
    Wood-browned pools of Paradise—
    Young Jesus, for the eyes,
    For the eyes of Viola.
Angels.
    Tint, Prince Jesus, a
    Duskèd eye for Viola!
  d.   Francis Thompson—*The Making of*
                         Viola. St. 2.

But optics sharp it needs, I ween,
To see what is not to be seen.
  e.   John Trumbull—*McFingal.*   Canto I.
                                L. 67.

How blue were Ariadne's eyes
    When, from the sea's horizon line,
At eve, she raised them on the skies!
My Psyche, bluer far are thine.
  f.   Aubrey De Vere—*Psyche.*

Blue eyes shimmer with angel glances,
Like spring violets over the lea.
  g.   Constance F. Woolson—*October's*
                               Song.

Deep brown eyes running over with glee;
    Blue eyes are pale, and gray eyes are sober;
Bonnie brown eyes are the eyes for me.
  h.   Constance F. Woolson—*October's*
                               Song.

The harvest of a quiet eye,
That broods and sleeps on his own heart.
  i.   Wordsworth—*A Poet's Epitaph.*
                                St. 13.

F.

FACE.

There is a garden in her face,
    Where roses and white lilies blow;
A heavenly paradise is that place,
    Wherein all pleasant fruits do grow.
There cherries grow that none may buy,
Till cherry ripe themselves do cry.
  j.   From An Howres Recreation in Musike.
         1606.   Set to music by Richard
         Alison.   Oliphant's *La Messa*
         Madrigalesca. P. 229.

It is the common wonder of all men, how
among so many millions of faces there should
be none alike.
  k.   Sir Thomas Browne—*Religio Medici.*
                     Pt. II.   Sec. II.

             And her face so fair
Stirr'd with her dream, as rose-leaves with the
    air.
  l.   Byron—*Don Juan.*   Canto IV.   St. 29.

             And to his eye
There was but one beloved face on earth,
And that was shining on him.
  m.   Byron—*The Dream.* St. 2.

The mind, the Music breathing from her face.
  n.   Byron—*Bride of Abydos.*   Canto I.
                                  St. 6.

Yet even her tyranny had such a grace,
The women pardoned all, except her face.
  o.   Byron—*Don Juan.*   Canto V.   St. 113.

The magic of a face.
  p.   Thomas Carew—*Epitaph on the*
                           Lady S——.

He had a face like a benediction.
  q.   Cervantes—*Don Quixote.*   Bk. II.
                        Pt. I.   Ch. IV.

Contending Passions jostle and displace
And tilt and tourney mostly in the Face:
    *   *   *   *   *   *
Unmatched by Art, upon this wondrous scroll
Portrayed are all the secrets of the soul.
  r.   Abraham Coles—*Man, the Microcosm.*
                           Pp. 26-27.

The face the index of a feeling mind.
  s.   Crabbe—*Tales of the Hall.*

Well had the boding tremblers learn'd to
    trace
The day's disasters in his morning face.
  t.   Goldsmith—*The Deserted Village.*
                                L. 199.

Some asked me where the rubies grew,
    And nothing I did say,
But with my finger pointed to
    The lips of Julia.
  u.   Herrick—*The Rock of Rubies, and the*
                           Quarrie of Pearls.

Her face betokened all things dear and good,
The light of somewhat yet to come was there
Asleep, and waiting for the opening day,
When childish thoughts, like flowers, would
    drift away.
  a.   JEAN INGELOW—*Margaret in the Xebec.*
St. 57.

How some they have died, and some they
    have left me,
And some are taken from me; all are de-
    parted;
All, all are gone, the old familiar faces.
  b.   CHARLES LAMB—*The Old Familiar
Faces.*

A face that had a story to tell. How different faces are in this particular! Some of
them speak not. They are books in which
not a line is written, save perhaps a date.
  c.   LONGFELLOW—*Hyperion.* Bk. I.
Ch. IV.

The light upon her face
Shines from the windows of another world.
Saints only have such faces.
  d.   LONGFELLOW—*Michael Angelo.*
Pt. II. 6.

These faces in the mirrors
Are but the shadows and phantoms of myself.
  e.   LONGFELLOW—*The Masque of Pandora.*
Pt. II. *The House of Epimetheus.*
L. 72.

Oh! could you view the melody
Of every grace,
And music of her face.
  f.   LOVELACE—*Orpheus to Beasts.* St. 2.

Showing that if a good face is a letter of
recommendation, a good heart is a letter of
credit.
  g.   BULWER-LYTTON—*What Will He Do
With It?* Bk. II. Title of Ch. XI.

Dusk faces with white silken turbans wreath'd.
  h.   MILTON—*Paradise Regained.* Bk. IV.
L. 76.

Human face divine.
  i.   MILTON—*Paradise Lost.* Bk. III. L. 44.

In her face excuse
Came prologue, and apology too prompt.
  j.   MILTON—*Paradise Lost.* Bk. IX.
L. 853.

Cheek * * *
Flushing white and mellow'd red;
Gradual tints, as when there glows
In snowy milk the bashful rose.
  k.   MOORE—*Odes of Anacreon.* Ode XV.
L. 27.

With faces like dead lovers who died true.
  l.   D. M. MULOCK—*Indian Summer.*

If to her share some female errors fall
Look on her face, and you'll forget 'em all.
  m.   POPE—*Rape of the Lock.* Canto II.
L. 17.

Nose, nose, nose, nose!
And who gave thee that jolly red nose?
Sinament and Ginger, Nutmegs and Cloves,
And that gave me my jolly red nose.
  n.   RAVENSCROFT—*Deuteromela.* Song.
No. 7. 1609.

On his bold visage middle age
Had slightly press'd its signet sage,
Yet had not quenched the open truth
And fiery vehemence of youth;
Forward and frolic glee was there,
The will to do, the soul to dare.
  o.   SCOTT—*Lady of The Lake.* Canto I.
St. 21.

Sea of upturned faces.
  p.   SCOTT—*Rob Roy.* Vol. II. Ch. XX.
Quoted by Daniel Webster. *Speech.*
Sept. 30, 1842.

A countenance more in sorrow than in anger.
  q.   *Hamlet.* Act I. Sc. 2. L. 232.

All men's faces are true, whatsome'er their
    hands are.
  r.   *Antony and Cleopatra.* Act II. Sc 6.
L. 102.

Black brows they say
Become some women best, so that there be not
Too much hair there, but in a semicircle
Or a half-moon made with a pen.
  s.   *Winter's Tale.* Act II. Sc. 1. L. 8.

Compare her face with some that I shall show;
And I will make thee think thy swan a crow.
  t.   *Romeo and Juliet.* Act I. Sc. 2. L. 91.

I have seen better faces in my time
Than stands on any shoulder that I see.
  u.   *King Lear.* Act II. Sc. 2. L. 99.

In thy face
I see thy fury: if I longer stay
We shall begin our ancient bickerings.
  v.   *Henry VI.* Pt. II. Act I. Sc. 1. L. 142.

There is a fellow somewhat near the door;
he should be a brazier by his face.
  w.   *Henry VIII.* Act V. Sc. 4. L. 41.

There's no art
To find the mind's construction in the face.
  x.   *Macbeth.* Act I. Sc. 4. L. 11.

Thou hast a grim appearance, and thy face
Bears a command in 't: though thy tackle's
    torn,
Thou show'st a noble vessel.
  y.   *Coriolanus.* Act IV. Sc. 5. L. 66.

Thus is his cheek the map of days outworn.
  z.   *Sonnet LXVIII.*

You have such a February face,
So full of frost, of storm, of cloudiness.
   a.   *Much Ado About Nothing.* Act. V.
                        Sc. 4. L. 41.

Your face, my thane, is a book where men
May read strange matters. To beguile the
   time,
Look like the time.
   b.   *Macbeth.* Act I. Sc. 5. L. 63.

An unforgiving eye, and a damned disin-
heriting countenance.
   c.   R. B. SHERIDAN—*School for Scandal.*
                      Act IV. Sc. 1.

              Her angel's face,
As the great eye of heaven, shyned bright,
And made a sunshine in the shady place.
   d.   SPENSER—*Faerie Queene.* Bk. I.
                  Canto III. St. 4.

Her cheeks so rare a white was on,
No daisy makes comparison;
   (Who sees them is undone) ;
For streaks of red were mingled there,
Such as are on a Cath'rine pear,
   (The side that's next the Sun).
   e.   SIR JOHN SUCKLING—*A Ballad Upon a*
                  Wedding. St. 10.

Her face is like the Milky Way i' the sky,—
A meeting of gentle lights without a name.
   f.   SIR JOHN SUCKLING—*Brennoralt.*
                      Act III.

Her lips were red, and one was thin,
Compared to that was next her chin,
   (Some bee had stung it newly).
   g.   SIR JOHN SUCKLING—*A Ballad Upon a*
                  Wedding. St. 11.

For my soul prays, Sweet,
Still to your face in Heaven,
   Heaven in your face, Sweet.
   h.   FRANCIS THOMPSON—*A Carrier Song.*
                      St. 7.

With that she dasht her on the lippes,
So dyed double red ;
Hard was the heart that gave the blow,
Soft were those lippes that bled.
   i.   WILLIAM WARNER—*Albion's England.*
              Bk. VIII. Ch. XLI. St. 53.

As a pomegranate, cut in twain,
White-seeded is her crimson mouth.
   j.   OSCAR WILDE—*La Bella Donna*
                  Della Mia Mente.

A face with gladness overspread !
Soft smiles, by human kindness bred !
   k.   WORDSWORTH—*To a Highland Girl.*

FAILURE.

Now a' is done that men can do,
And a' is done in vain.
   l.   BURNS—*It Was a' for our Rightfu' King.*

Failed the bright promise of your early day ?
   m.   BISHOP HEBER—*Palestine.* L. 113.

In the lexicon of youth, which
Fate reserves for a bright manhood, there is
   no such word
As—*fail !*
   n.   BULWER-LYTTON—*Richelieu.* Act II.
                         Sc. 2.

             If this fail,
The pillar'd firmament is rottenness
And earth's base built on stubble.
   o.   MILTON—*Comus.* L. 597.

FAIRIES.

Up the airy mountain,
   Down the rushy glen,
We daren't go a-hunting
   For fear of little men;
Wee folk, good folk,
   Trooping all together,
Green jacket, red cap,
   And white owl's feather !
   p.   WILLIAM ALLINGHAM—*The Fairies.*

Bright Eyes, Light Eyes ! Daughter of a Fay !
I had not been a married wife a twelvemonth
   and a day,
I had not nursed my little one a month upon
   my knee,
When down among the blue bell banks rose
   elfins three times three :
They griped me by the raven hair, I could
   not cry for fear,
They put a hempen rope around my waist
   and dragged me here ;
They made me sit and give thee suck as mortal
   mothers can,
Bright Eyes, Light Eyes ! strange and weak
   and wan !
   q.   ROBERT BUCHANAN—*The Fairy Foster*
                      Mother.

Then take me on your knee, mother;
   And listen, mother of mine.
A hundred fairies danced last night,
   And the harpers they were nine.
   r.   MARY HOWITT—*The Fairies of the*
                 Caldon Low. St. 5.

         * * * Or fairy elves,
Whose midnight revels by a forest side
Or fountain, some belated peasant sees,
Or dreams he sees, while overhead the **Moon**
Sits arbitress, and nearer to the Earth
Wheels her pale course; they, on their mirth
   and dance
Intent, with jocund music charm his ear;
At once with joy and fear his heart rebounds.
   s.   MILTON—*Paradise Lost.* Bk. I. L. 781.

The dances ended, all the fairy train
For pinks and daisies search'd the flow'ry
   plain.
   t.   POPE—*January and May.* L. 624.

Fairies, black, grey, green, and white,
You moonshine revellers, and shades of night.
  a.   *Merry Wives of Windsor.*   Act V.
                                Sc. 5. L. 41.

        In silence sad,
Trip we after night's shade:
We the globe can compass soon,
Swifter than the wand'ring moon.
  b.   *Midsummer Night's Dream.*   Act IV.
                                Sc. 1. L. 100.

O, then, I see Queen Mab hath been with you.
She is the fairies' midwife, and she comes
In shape no bigger than an agate-stone
On the forefinger of an alderman.
  e.   *Romeo and Juliet.*   Act I. Sc. 4.
                                        L. 54.

        Set your heart at rest:
The fairyland buys not the child of me.
  d.   *Midsummer Night's Dream.*   Act II.
                                Sc. 1. L. 121.

The honey-bags steal from the humble-bees,
And for night-tapers crop their waxen thighs
And light them at the fiery glow-worm's eyes.
  e.   *Midsummer Night's Dream.*   Act III.
                                Sc. 1. L. 171.

They are fairies; he that speaks to them shall
    die:
I'll wink and couch: no man their works
    must eye.
  f.   *Merry Wives of Windsor.*   Act V.
                                Sc. 5. L. 51.

This is the fairy-land; O spite of spites!
We talk with goblins, owls and sprites.
  g.   *Comedy of Errors.*   Act II. Sc. 2.
                                        L. 191.

Where the bee sucks, there suck I;
In a cowslip's bell I lie;
There I couch when owls do cry.
On the bat's back I do fly.
  h.   *Tempest.* Act V. Sc. 1. L. 88. Song.

Her berth was of the wombe of morning dew
And her conception of the joyous prime.
  i.   SPENSER—*Faerie Queene.*   Bk. III.
                                Canto VI. St. 3.

But light as any wind that blows
  So fleetly did she stir,
The flower, she touch'd on, dipt and rose,
  And turned to look at her.
  j.   TENNYSON—*The Talking Oak.*   St. 33.

FAITH.

Mahomet made the people believe that he
would call a hill to him, and from the top of
it offer up his prayers for the observers of his
law. The people assembled; Mahomet called
the hill to come to him, again and again, and
when the hill stood still, he was never a whit
abashed, but said, if the hill will not come to
Mahomet, Mahomet will go to the hill.
  k.   BACON—*Of Boldness*

Faith is a higher faculty than reason.
  l.   BAILEY—*Festus.* *Prœm.* L. 84.

There is one inevitable criterion of judgment touching religious faith in doctrinal
matters. Can you reduce it to practice? If
not, have none of it.
  m.   HOSEA BALLOU—*MS. Sermons.*

His faith, perhaps, in some nice tenets might
Be wrong; his life, I'm sure, was in the right.
  n.   COWLEY—*On the Death of Crashaw.*
                                        L. 55.

Faith is a fine invention
  For gentlemen who see;
But Microscopes are prudent
  In an emergency.
  o.   EMILY DICKINSON—*Poems.* *Second
                                Series.* XXX.

To take up half on trust, and half to try,
Name it not faith but bungling bigotry.
  p.   DRYDEN—*The Hind and the Panther.*
                                Pt. I. L. 141.

We lean on Faith; and some less wise have
    cried,
"Behold the butterfly, the seed that's cast!"
Vain hopes that fall like flowers before the
    blast!
What man can look on Death unterrified?
  q.   R. W. GILDER—*Love and Death.* St. 2.

What sought they thus afar?
  Bright jewels of the mine?
The wealth of seas, the spoils of war?—
  They sought a faith's pure shrine!
  r.   Mrs. HEMANS—*Landing of the Pilgrim
                                Fathers.*

Mirror of constant faith, revered and mourn'd!
  s.   HOMER—*Odyssey.* Bk. IV. L. 229.
                                Pope's trans.

And we shall be made truly wise if we be
made content; content, too, not only with
what we can understand, but content with
what we do not understand—the habit of
mind which theologians call—and rightly—
faith in God.
  t.   CHARLES KINGSLEY—*Health and
                    Education.* *On Bio-Geology.*

"Patience!" * * * "have faith and thy
prayer will be answered!"
  u.   LONGFELLOW—*Evangeline.* Pt. II.
                                St. 4. L. 139.

The only faith that wears well and holds its
color in all weathers is that which is woven
of conviction and set with the sharp mordant
of experience.
  v.   LOWELL—*My Study Windows.*
                                Abraham Lincoln. 1864.

O welcome pure-ey'd Faith, white-handed
    Hope,
Thou hovering angel, girt with golden wings!
a.   MILTON—*Comus.* L. 213.

        That in such righteousness
To them by faith imputed they may find
Justification towards God, and peace
Of conscience.
b.   MILTON—*Paradise Lost.* Bk. XII.
                      L. 294.

        Yet I argue not
Again Heaven's hand or will, nor bate a jot
Of right or hope; but still bear up and steer
Right onward.
c.   MILTON—*To Cyriac Skinner.*

But Faith, fanatic Faith, once wedded fast
To some dear falsehood, hugs it to the last.
d.   MOORE—*Lalla Rookh. The Veiled
                  Prophet of Khorassan.*

If faith produce no works, I see
That faith is not a living tree.
Thus faith and works together grow;
No separate life they e'er can know:
They're soul and body, hand and heart:
What God hath joined, let no man part.
e.   HANNAH MORE—*Dan and Jane.*

For modes of faith let graceless zealots fight;
His can't be wrong whose life is in the right.
f.   POPE—*Essay on Man.* Ep. III.
                      L. 305.

The enormous faith of many made for one.
g.   POPE—*Essay on Man.* Ep. III.
                      L. 242.

        Set on your foot,
And with a heart new-fir'd I follow you,
To do I know not what: but it sufficeth
That Brutus leads me on.
h.   *Julius Cæsar.* Act II. Sc. 1. L. 331.

Thou almost makest me waver in my faith
To hold opinion with Pythagoras,
That souls of animals infuse themselves
Into the trunks of men.
i.   *Merchant of Venice.* Act IV. Sc. 1.
                      L. 130.

The saddest thing that can befall a soul
Is when it loses faith in God and woman.
j.   ALEXANDER SMITH—*A Life Drama.*
                      Sc. 12.

Faith is the subtle chain
Which binds us to the infinite; the voice
Of a deep life within, that will remain
Until we crowd it thence.
k.   ELIZABETH OAKES SMITH—*Atheism in
                Three Sonnets. Faith.*

It is always right that a man should be able
to render a reason for the faith that is within
him.
l.   SYDNEY SMITH—*Lady Holland's
                Memoir.* Vol. I. P. 53.

Faith and unfaith can ne'er be equal powers;
Unfaith in aught is want of faith in all.
m.   TENNYSON—*Idylls of the King. Merlin
                and Vivien.* L. 388.

There lives more faith in honest doubt,
Believe me, than in half the creeds.
n.   TENNYSON—*In Memoriam.* XCVI.

Whose faith has centre everywhere,
Nor cares to fix itself to form.
o.   TENNYSON—*In Memoriam.* XXXIII.

From seeming evil still educing good.
p.   THOMSON—*Hymn.* L. 114.

A bending staff I would not break,
A feeble faith I would not shake,
Nor even rashly pluck away
The error which some truth may stay,
Whose loss might leave the soul without
A shield against the shafts of doubt.
q.   WHITTIER—*Questions of Life.* St. 1.

Through this dark and stormy night
Faith beholds a feeble light
    Up the blackness streaking;
Knowing God's own time is best,
In a patient hope I rest
    For the full day-breaking!
r.   WHITTIER—*Barclay of Ury.* St. 16.

"But they are dead; those two are dead!
    Their spirits are in Heaven!"
'Twas throwing words away; for still
The little Maid would have her will,
And said, "Nay, we are seven!"
s.   WORDSWORTH—*We Are Seven.*

Of one in whom persuasion and belief
Had ripened into faith, and faith become
A passionate intuition.
t.   WORDSWORTH—*The Excursion.* Bk. IV.

'Tis hers to pluck the amaranthine flower
    Of Faith, and round the sufferer's temples
        bind
Wreaths that endure affliction's heaviest
        shower,
And do not shrink from sorrow's keenest
        wind.
u.   WORDSWORTH—*Weak is the Will of
                Man.*

Faith builds a bridge across the gulf of Death,
To break the shock blind nature cannot shun,
And lands Thought smoothly on the further
    shore.
v.   YOUNG—*Night Thoughts.* Night IV.
                      L. 721.

One eye on death, and one full fix'd on
    heaven.
w.   YOUNG—*Night Thoughts.* Night V.
                      L. 838.

FALSEHOOD.

Falsehood is cowardice,—truth is courage.
a.   HOSEA BALLOU—*MS. Sermons.*

And none speaks false, when there is none to
  hear.
b.   BEATTIE—*The Minstrel.* Bk. II.
St. 24.

And, after all, what is a lie? 'Tis but
The truth in masquerade.
c.   BYRON—*Don Juan.* Canto XI. St. 37.

Some truth there was, but dash'd and brew'd
  with lies,
To please the fools, and puzzle all the wise.
d.   DRYDEN—*Absalom and Achitophel.*

Sin has many tools, but a lie is the handle
which fits them all.
e.   O. W. HOLMES—*The Autocrat of the
Breakfast Table.* VI.

Urge him with truth to frame his fair replies;
And sure he will; for wisdom never lies.
f.   HOMER—*Odyssey.* Bk. III. L. 25.
Pope's trans.

Who dares think one thing, and another tell,
My heart detests him as the gates of hell.
g.   HOMER—*Iliad.* Bk. IX. L. 412.
Pope's trans.

For my part getting up seems not so easy
By half as lying.
h.   HOOD—*Morning Meditations.*

Round numbers are always false.
i.   SAM'L JOHNSON—*Johnsoniana.*
Apothegms, Sentiment, etc. From
Hawkins' Collective Edition.

For no falsehood can endure
Touch of celestial temper.
j.   MILTON—*Paradise Lost.* Bk. IV.
L. 811.

It is not without good reason said, that he
who has not a good memory should never
take upon him the trade of lying.
k.   MONTAIGNE—*Of Liars.* Bk. I. Ch. IX.

Some lie beneath the churchyard stone,
And some before the Speaker.
l.   PRAED—*School and School Fellows.*

For my part, if a lie may do thee grace,
I'll gild it with the happiest terms I have.
m.   *Henry IV.* Pt. I. Act V. Sc. 4.
L. 161.

He will lie, sir, with such volubility, that
you would think truth were a fool.
n.   *All's Well That Ends Well.* Act IV.
Sc. 3. L. 283.

Lord, Lord, how subject we old men are to
this vice of lying!
o.   *Henry IV.* Pt. II. Act III. Sc. 2.
L. 325.

Lord, Lord, how this world is given to lying!
I grant you I was down and out of breath;
and so was he: but we rose both at an instant
and fought a long hour by Shrewsbury clock.
p.   *Henry IV.* Pt. I. Act V. Sc. 4.
L. 149.

Oh, what a goodly outside falsehood hath!
q.   *Merchant of Venice.* Act I. Sc. 3.
L. 103.

These lies are like the father that begets
them; gross as a mountain, open, palpable.
r.   *Henry IV.* Pt. I. Act II. Sc. 4.
L. 249.

'Tis as easy as lying.
s.   *Hamlet.* Act III. Sc. 2. L. 372.

To lapse in fulness
Is sorer than to lie for need, and falsehood
Is worse in kings than beggars.
t.   *Cymbeline.* Act III. Sc. 6. L. 12.

Whose tongue soe'er speaks false,
Not truly speaks; who speaks not truly, lies.
u.   *King John.* Act IV. Sc. 3. L. 91.

Your bait of falsehood takes this carp of truth.
v.   *Hamlet.* Act II. Sc. 1. L. 63.

You lie—under a mistake—
For this is the most civil sort of lie
That can be given to a man's face, I now
Say what I think.
w.   SHELLEY—*Trans. of Calderon's Magico
Prodigioso.* Sc. 1.

Had I a heart for falsehood framed.
I ne'er could injure you.
x.   R. B. SHERIDAN—*The Duenna.* Act. 1.
Sc. 5.

This shows that liars ought to have good
memories.
y.   ALGERNON SIDNEY—*Discourses on
Government.* Ch. II. Sec. XV.

A lie never lives to be old.
z.   SOPHOCLES—*Acrisius.* Frag. 59.

I mean you lie—under a mistake.
aa.   SWIFT—*Polite Conversation.* Dialogue 1.

That a lie which is half a truth is ever the
  blackest of lies;
That a lie which is all a lie may be met and
  fought with outright—
But a lie which is part a truth is a harder
  matter to fight.
bb.   TENNYSON—*The Grandmother.* St. 8.

And he that does one fault at first,
And lies to hide it, makes it two.
   a.   WATTS—*Song XV.*

I give him joy that's awkward at a lie.
   b.   YOUNG—*Night Thoughts.* Night VIII.
                     L. 361.

FAME.

Were not this desire of fame very strong,
the difficulty of obtaining it, and the danger
of losing it when obtained, would be sufficient
to deter a man from so vain a pursuit.
   c.   ADDISON—*The Spectator.* No. 255.

Ah! who can tell how hard it is to climb
The steep where Fame's proud temple shines
    afar!
   d.   BEATTIE—*The Minstrel.* St. 1.

Nothing can cover his high fame but Heaven:
No pyramids set off his memories
But the eternal substance of his greatness;
To which I leave him.
   e.   BEAUMONT AND FLETCHER—*The False
              One.* Act II. Sc. 1. L. 169.

The best-concerted schemes men lay for fame.
Die fast away: only themselves die faster.
The far-fam'd sculptor, and the laurell'd bard,
Those bold insurancers of deathless fame,
Supply their little feeble aids in vain.
   f.   BLAIR—*The Grave.* L. 185.

Herostratus lives that burnt the temple of
Diana; he is almost lost that built it.
   g.   SIR THOMAS BROWNE—*Hydriotaphia.*
                      Ch. V.

Folly loves the martyrdom of fame.
   h.   BYRON—*Monody on the Death of
             Sheridan.* L. 68.

I awoke one morning and found myself
    famous.
   i.   BYRON—*From his Life by Moore.*

O Fame!—if I e'er took delight in thy praises,
'Twas less for the sake of thy high-sounding
    phrases,
Than to see the bright eyes of the dear one
    discover
She thought that I was not unworthy to love
    her.
   j.   BYRON—*Stanzas Written on the Road
            Between Florence and Pisa.*

What is the end of Fame? 'tis but to fill
   A certain portion of uncertain paper:
Some liken it to climbing up a hill,
   Whose summit, like all hills, is lost in
    vapour:
For this men write, speak, preach, and heroes
    kill,
   And bards burn what they call their "mid-
    night taper,"
To have, when the original is dust,
A name, a wretched picture, and worse bust.
   k.   BYRON—*Don Juan.* Canto I. St. 218.

Who hath not owned, with rapture-smitten
    frame,
The power of grace, the magic of a name?
   l.   CAMPBELL—*Pleasures of Hope.* Pt. II.
                      L. 5.

Fame, we may understand, is no sure test
of merit, but only a probability of such: it is
an accident, not a property of a man.
   m.   CARLYLE—*Essay. Goethe.*

Scarcely two hundred years back can Fame
recollect articulately at all; and there she but
maunders and mumbles.
   n.   CARLYLE—*Past and Present.* Ch. XVII.

Men the most infamous are fond of fame,
And those who fear not guilt, yet start at
    shame.
   o.   CHURCHILL—*The Author.* L. 233.

The aspiring youth that fired the *Ephesian*
    dome
Outlives, in fame, the pious fool that rais'd it.
   p.   COLLEY CIBBER—*Richard III.*
             (Altered.) Act III. Sc. 1.

Where's Cæsar gone now, in command high
    and able?
Or Xerxes the splendid, complete in his table?
Or Tully, with powers of eloquence ample?
Or Aristotle, of genius the highest example?
   q.   ABRAHAM COLES—Trans. of
             De Contemptu Mundi (*Jacopone,
             XIII. Century*) "*Old Gems
             in New Settings.*" P. 75.

I am not the rose, but I have lived near the
    rose.
   r.   H. B. CONSTANT—*See Hayward's
             Introduction to The Autobiography
             and Letters of Mrs. Piozzi.*

What shall I do to be forever known,
And make the age to come my own?
   s.   COWLEY—*The Motto.* L. 1.

Who fears not to do ill yet fears the name,
And free from conscience, is a slave to fame.
   t.   SIR JOHN DENHAM—*Cooper's Hill.*
                      L. 129.

The Duke of Wellington brought to the
post of first minister immortal fame; a quality
of success which would almost seem to include all others.
   u.   BENJ. DISRAELI—*Sybil.* Bk. I.
                      Ch. III.

Fame then was cheap, and the first courier
    sped;
And they have kept it since, by being dead.
   v.   DRYDEN—*The Conquest of Grenada.*
                    Epilogue.

Then Naldo: "'Tis a petty kind of fame
At best, that comes of making violins;
And saves no masses, either. Thou wilt go
To purgatory none the less."
   w.   GEORGE ELIOT—*Stradivarius.* L. 85.

Here once the embattl'd farmers stood
And fired the shot heard round the world.
   a.   EMERSON—*Hymn. Concord Fight.*

Fame is the echo of actions, resounding them to the world, save that the echo repeats only the last part, but fame relates all, and often more than all.
   b.   FULLER—*The Holy and Profane States.*
                  Of Fame.

From kings to cobblers 'tis the same;
Bad servants wound their master's fame.
   c.   GAY—*Fables. The Squire and his Cur.*
                  Pt. II.

Some village Hampden, that, with dauntless
   breast,
The little tyrant of his fields withstood,
Some mute inglorious Milton here may rest,
  Some Cromwell guiltless of his country's
   blood.
   d.   GRAY—*Elegy in a Country Churchyard.*
                  St. 15.

One of the few, the immortal names,
That were not born to die.
   e.   FITZ-GREENE HALLECK—*Marco*
                  Bozzaris.

The temple of fame stands upon the grave: the flame that burns upon its altars is kindled from the ashes of dead men.
   f.   HAZLITT—*Lectures on The English*
             Poets. Lecture VIII.

Thou hast a charmed cup, O Fame!
  A draught that mantles high,
And seems to lift this earthly frame
  Above mortality.
Away! to me—a woman—bring
Sweet water from affection's spring.
   g.   MRS. HEMANS—*Woman and Fame.*

If that thy fame with ev'ry toy be pos'd,
'Tis a thin web, which poysonous fancies
  make;
But the great souldier's honour was compos'd
Of thicker stuf, which would endure a shake.
  Wisdom picks friends; civility playes the
   rest;
  A toy shunn'd cleanly passeth with the
   best.
   h.   HERBERT—*The Temple. The Church*
             Porch. St. 38.

Seven cities warr'd for Homer being dead,
Who living had no roofe to shroud his head.
   i.   THOS. HEYWOOD—*Hierarchie of the*
             Blessed Angells.

But sure the eye of time beholds no name,
So blest as thine in all the rolls of fame.
   j.   HOMER—*Odyssey.* Bk. XI. L. 591.
                  Pope's trans.

Earth sounds my wisdom, and high heaven
  my fame.
   k.   HOMER—*Odyssey.* Bk. IX. L. 20.
                  Pope's trans.

Short is my date, but deathless my renown.
   l.   HOMER—*Iliad.* Bk. IX. L. 535.
                  Pope's trans.

The life, which others pay, let us bestow,
And give to fame what we to nature owe.
   m.   HOMER—*Iliad.* Bk. XII. L. 393.
                  Pope's trans.

The rest were vulgar deaths unknown to fame.
   n.   HOMER—*Iliad.* Bk. XI. L. 394.
                  Pope's trans.

Under the shadow of a leafy bough
  That leaned toward a singing rivulet,
One pure white stone, whereon, like crown on
   brow,
  The image of the vanished star was set;
And this was graven on the pure white stone
In golden letters—"WHILE SHE LIVED SHE
  SHONE."
   o.   JEAN INGELOW—*The Star's Monument.*
                  St. 47.

Fame has no necessary conjunction with praise: it may exist without the breath of a word: it is a *recognition of excellence* which *must be felt* but need not be *spoken.* Even the envious must feel it: feel it, and hate it in silence.
   p.   MRS. JAMESON—*Memoirs and Essays.*
             Washington Allston.

Reputation being essentially contemporaneous, is always at the mercy of the Envious and the Ignorant. But Fame, whose very birth is *posthumous*, and which is only *known to exist by the echo of its footsteps through congenial minds*, can neither be increased nor diminished by any degree of wilfulness.
   q.   MRS. JAMESON—*Memoirs and Essays.*
             Washington Allston.

He left the name, at which the world grew
  pale,
To point a moral, or adorn a tale.
   r.   SAM'L JOHNSON—*Vanity of Human*
               Wishes. L. 221.

I never have sought the world; the world was not to seek me.
   s.   SAM'L JOHNSON—*Boswell's Life of*
             Johnson. 1783.

Building nests in Fame's great temple,
As in spouts the swallows build.
   t.   LONGFELLOW—*Nuremberg.* St. 16.

Fame comes only when deserved, and then is as inevitable as destiny, for it is destiny.
   u.   LONGFELLOW—*Hyperion.* Bk. I.
                  Ch. VIII.

His fame was great in all the land.
   v.   LONGFELLOW—*Tales of a Wayside Inn.*
        The Student's Tale. Emma and
             Eginhard. L. 50.

Fame lulls the fever of the soul, and makes
Us feel that we have grasp'd an immortality.
   a.   JOAQUIN MILLER—*Ina.* Sc. 4. L. 273.

Fame, if not double fac'd, is doubled mouth'd,
And with contrary blast proclaims most
   deeds ;
On both his wings, one black, the other white,
Bears greatest names in his wild aery flight.
   b.   MILTON—*Samson Agonistes.* L. 971.

Fame is no plant that grows on mortal soil.
   c.   MILTON—*Lycidas.* L. 78.

Fame is the spur that the clear spirit doth
   raise,
(That last infirmity of noble mind)
To scorn delights, and live laborious days ;
  But the fair guerdon when we hope to find,
And think to burst out into sudden blaze,
Comes the blind Fury with th' abhorred
   shears,
And slits the thin-spun life.
   d.   MILTON—*Lycidas.* L. 70.

I'll make thee glorious by my pen
And famous by my sword.
   e.   MARQUIS OF MONTROSE—*My Dear and
                Only Love.* (See also Scott—
                Legend of Montrose.
                Ch. XV.)
Go where glory waits thee ;
But while fame elates thee,
Oh ! still remember me.
   f.   MOORE—*Go Where Glory Waits Thee.*

        Who grasp'd at earthly fame,
Grasped wind : nay, worse, a serpent grasped
   that through
His hand slid smoothly, and was gone ; but
   left
A sting behind which wrought him endless
   pain.
   g.   POLLOK—*Course of Time.* Bk. III.
                          L. 533.

Above all Greek, above all Roman fame.
   h.   POPE—*Epistles of Horace.* Ep. I.
                      Bk. II. L. 26.

All crowd, who foremost shall be damn'd to
   fame.
   i.   POPE—*The Dunciad.* Bk. III. L. 158.

And what is Fame? the Meanest have their
   Day,
The Greatest can but blaze, and pass away.
   j.   POPE—*First Book of Horace.* Ep. VI.
                      L. 46.

If parts allure thee, think how Bacon shin'd,
The wisest, brightest, meanest of mankind :
Or, ravish'd with the whistling of a name,
See Cromwell, damn'd to everlasting fame.
   k.   POPE—*Essay on Man.* Ep. IV. L. 281.

Let humble Allen, with an awkward shame,
Do good by stealth, and blush to find it Fame.
   l.   POPE—*Epilogue to Satire.* Dialogue I.
                          L. 135.

Nor fame I slight, nor for her favors call ;
She comes unlooked for, if she comes at all.
   m.   POPE—*Temple of Fame.* L. 513.

Unblemish'd let me live or die unknown ;
Oh, grant an honest fame, or grant me none!
   n.   POPE—*Temple of Fame.* L. 523.

What's fame ? a fancy'd life in others' breath.
A thing beyond us, e'en before our death.
   o.   POPE—*Essay on Man.* Ep. IV. L. 237.

Sound, sound the clarion, fill the fife !
  To all the sensual world proclaim,
One crowded hour of glorious life
  Is worth an age without a name.
   p.   SCOTT—*Old Mortality.* Ch. XXXIV.

Great Homer's birthplace seven rival cities
   claim,
Too mighty such monopoly of Fame.
   q.   THOMAS SEWARD—*On Shakespeare's
                Monument at Stratford-upon-Avon.*

Better to leave undone, than by our deed
Acquire too high a fame, when him we serve's
   away.
   r.   *Antony and Cleopatra.* Act III. Sc. 1.
                        L. 14.

Death makes no conquest of this conqueror :
For now he lives in fame, though not in life.
   s.   *Richard III.* Act III. Sc. 1. L. 87.

He lives in fame, that died in virtue's cause.
   t.   *Titus Andronicus.* Act I. Sc. 1. L. 390.

Let fame, that all hunt after in their lives,
Live register'd upon our brazen tombs.
   u.   *Love's Labour's Lost.* Act I. Sc. 1.
                          L. 1.

Sloth views the towers of fame with envious
   eyes,
Desirous still, still impotent to rise.
   v.   SHENSTONE—*Moral Pieces. The
                Judgment of Hercules.* L. 436.

No true and permanent Fame can be founded
except in labors which promote the happiness
of mankind.
   w.   CHARLES SUMNER—*Fame and Glory.*
                An Address before the Literary
                Societies of Amherst College.
                      Aug. 11, 1847.

Censure is the tax a man pays to the public
for being eminent.
   x.   SWIFT—*Thoughts on Various Subjects.*

Give lettered pomp to teeth of Time,
So "Bonnie Doon" but tarry:
Blot out the epic's stately rhyme,
But spare his Highland Mary!
   a.   WHITTIER—*Burns.* Last Stanza.

What rage for fame attends both great and
     small!
Better be d—n'd than mentioned *not at all.*
   b.   JOHN WOLCOTT (Peter Pindar)—*To the*
               Royal Academicians. Lyric Odes for
               the Year. 1783. Ode IX.

Fame is the shade of immortality,
And in itself a shadow. Soon as caught,
Contemn'd; it shrinks to nothing in the grasp.
   c.   YOUNG—*Night Thoughts.* Night VII.
                            L. 363.

He stands for fame on his forefather's feet,
By heraldry, proved valiant or discreet!
   d.   YOUNG—*Love of Fame.* Satire I.
                            L. 123.

Men should press forward, in fame's glorious
     chase;
Nobles look backward, and so lose the race.
   e.   YOUNG—*Love of Fame.* Satire I.
                            L. 129.

Narcissus is the glory of his race:
For who does nothing with a better grace?
   f.   YOUNG—*Love of Fame.* Satire IV.
                            L. 85.

With fame, in just proportion, envy grows.
   g.   YOUNG—*Epistle to Mr. Pope.* Ep. I.
                            L. 27.

Wouldst thou be famed? have those high
     acts in view,
Brave men would act though scandal would
     ensue.
   h.   YOUNG—*Love of Fame.* Satire VII.
                            L. 175.

FAMILIARITY.

I hold he loves me best that calls me Tom.
   i.   THOMAS HEYWOOD—*Hierarchie of the*
                        Blessed Angells.

And sweets grown common lose their dear
     delight.
   j.   *Sonnet CII.*

Staled by frequence, shrunk by usage into
     commonest commonplace!
   k.   TENNYSON—*Locksley Hall Sixty Years*
                      After. St. 38.

And friend received with thumps upon the
     back.
   l.   YOUNG—*Love of Fame.* Satire I.

FANCY.

Some things are of that nature as to make
One's fancy chuckle, while his heart doth
     ache.
   m.   BUNYAN—*Pilgrim's Progress. The*
               Author's Way of Sending Forth his
                    Second Part of the Pilgrim.
                            Pt. II.

While fancy, like the finger of a clock,
Runs the great circuit, and is still at home.
   n.   COWPER—*The Task.* Bk. IV. L. 118.

Ever let the Fancy roam,
Pleasure never is at home.
   o.   KEATS—*Fancy.*

Sentiment is intellectualized emotion, emotion precipitated, as it were, in pretty crystals
by the fancy.
   p.   LOWELL—*Among My Books. Rousseau*
                    and the Sentimentalists.

Two meanings have our lightest fantasies,
One of the flesh, and of the spirit one.
   q.   LOWELL—*Sonnet XXXIV.* Ed. 1844.

And my heart rocked its babe of bliss,
     And soothed its child of air,
With something 'twixt a song and kiss,
     To keep it nestling there.
   r.   GERALD MASSEY—*On a Wedding Day.*
                            St. 3.

She's all my fancy painted her,
She's lovely, she's divine.
   s.   WM. MEE—*Alice Gray.*

The difference is as great between
The optics seeing as the objects seen.
All manners take a tincture from our own;
Or come discolor'd through our passions
     shown;
Or fancy's beam enlarges, multiplies,
Contracts, inverts, and gives ten thousand
     dyes.
   t.   POPE—*Moral Essays.* Ep. 1. L. 31.

When at the close of each sad, sorrowing day,
Fancy restores what vengeance snatch'd away.
   u.   POPE—*Eloisa to Abelard.* L. 225.

Woe to the youth whom Fancy gains,
Winning from Reason's hand the reins,
Pity and woe! for such a mind
Is soft, contemplative, and kind.
   v.   SCOTT—*Rokeby.* Canto I. St. 31.

But were it to my fancy given
To rate her charms, I'd call them heaven;
For though a mortal made of clay,
Angels must love Ann Hathaway;
She hath a way so to control,
To rapture the imprisoned soul,
And sweetest heaven on earth display,
That to be heaven Ann hath a way;
     She hath a way,
        Ann Hathaway,—
To be heaven's self Ann hath a way.
   w.   *Attributed to* SHAKESPEARE.

Let fancy still my sense in Lethe steep;
If it be thus to dream, still let me sleep!
  a.   *Twelfth Night.* Act IV. Sc. 1. L. 66.

Pacing through the forest,
Chewing the food of sweet and bitter fancy.
  b.   *As You Like It.* Act IV. Sc. 3.
          L. 101.

So full of shapes is fancy,
That it alone is high fantastical.
  c.   *Twelfth Night.* Act I. Sc. 1. L. 14.

Tell me where is fancy bred,
Or in the heart or in the head?
How begot, how nourished?
    Reply, reply.
It is engender'd in the eyes,
With gazing fed; and fancy dies
In the cradle where it lies.
  d.   *Merchant of Venice.* Act III. Sc. 2.
          L. 63.

We figure to ourselves
The thing we like, and then we build it up
As chance will have it, on the rock or sand:
For Thought is tired of wandering o'er the
    world,
And homebound Fancy runs her bark ashore.
  e.   Sir Henry Taylor—*Philip Van*
         Artevelde. Pt. I. Act I. Sc. 5.

Fancy light from Fancy caught.
  f.   Tennyson—*In Memoriam.* Pt. XXIII.

Sad fancies do we then affect,
In luxury of disrespect
To our own prodigal excess
Of too familiar happiness.
  g.   Wordsworth—*Ode to Lycoris.*

FAREWELL.

He turn'd him right and round about
  Upon the Irish shore,
And gae his bridle reins a shake,
  With Adieu for evermore,
    My dear,
  With Adieu for evermore.
  h.   Burns—*It Was a' for our Rightfu'*
         King.

Farewell! a word that must be, and hath
    been—
A sound which makes us linger;—yet—fare-
    well!
  i.   Byron—*Childe Harold.* Canto IV.
         St. 186.

"Farewell!"
For in that word—that fatal word—howe'er
We promise—hope—believe—there breathes
    despair.
  j.   Byron—*The Corsair.* Canto I. St. 15.

One kind kiss before we part,
  Drop a tear, and bid adieu;
Though we sever, my fond heart
  Till we meet shall pant for you.
  k.   Robert Dodsley—*Colin's Kisses.*
        The Parting Kiss. Song VI. St. 1.

"Adieu," she cries, and waved her lily hand.
  l.   Gay—*Sweet William's Farewell to*
         Black-eyed Susan.

Friend, ahoy! Farewell! farewell!
  Grief unto grief, joy unto joy,
Greeting and help the echoes tell
  Faint, but eternal—Friend, ahoy!
  m.   Helen Hunt—*Verses.* *Friend, Ahoy!*

Farewell, happy fields,
Where joy forever dwells; hail, horrors!
  n.   Milton—*Paradise Lost.* Bk. I. L. 249.

Gude nicht, and joy be wi' you a'.
  o.   Lady Nairne—*Gude Nicht, etc.*

Farewell to Lochaber, and farewell, my Jean,
Where heartsome wi' thee I hae mony day
    been:
For Lochaber no more, Lochaber no more,
We'll maybe return to Lochaber no more.
  p.   Allan Ramsay—*Farewell to Lochaber.*

To all, to each, a fair good-night,
And pleasing dreams, and slumbers light.
  q.   Scott—*Marmion.* *L'Envoy.* To the
         Reader.

Fare thee well;
The elements be kind to thee, and make
Thy spirits all of comfort!
  r.   *Antony and Cleopatra.* Act III. Sc. 2.
         L. 39.

Farewell, and stand fast.
  s.   *Henry IV.* Pt. I. Act II. Sc. 2.
         L. 75.

Farewell the plumed troop, and the big wars,
That make ambition virtue! O, farewell!
Farewell the neighing steed, and the shrill
    trump,
The spirit-stirring drum, the ear-piercing fife.
  t.   *Othello.* Act III. Sc. 3. L. 349.

Here's my hand.
And mine, with my heart in't: and now fare-
    well,
Till half an hour hence.
  u.   *Tempest.* Act III. Sc. 1. L. 89.

Sweets to the sweet; farewell!
  v.   *Hamlet.* Act V. Sc. 1. L. 266.

Then westward ho! Grace and good disposi-
    tion
Attend your ladyship!
  w.   *Twelfth Night.* Act III. Sc. 1. L. 146.

So sweetly she bade me adieu,
I thought that she bade me return.
a.   SHENSTONE—*A Pastoral Ballad.* Pt. I.
Absence. St. 5.

FASHION.

Squinting upon the lustre
Of the rich Rings which on his fingers glistre;
And, snuffing with a wrythed nose the Amber,
The Musk and Civet that perfum'd the
chamber.
b.   DU BARTAS—*Divine Weekes and Workes.*
Second Week. Third Day. Pt. III.

Nothing is thought rare
Which is not new, and follow'd; yet we know
That what was worn some twenty years ago
Comes into grace again.
c.   BEAUMONT AND FLETCHER—*Prologue
to the Noble Gentleman.* L. 4.

He is only fantastical that is not in fashion.
d.   BURTON—*Anatomy of Melancholy.*
Pt. III. Sec. II. Memb. 2.
Subsec. 3.

And as the French we conquer'd once,
Now give us laws for pantaloons,
The length of breeches and the gathers,
Port-cannons, periwigs, and feathers.
e.   BUTLER—*Hudibras.* Pt. I. Canto III.
L. 923.

Fashion—a word which knaves and fools may
use,
Their knavery and folly to excuse.
f.   CHURCHILL—*Rosciad.* L. 455.

As good be out of the World as out of the
Fashion.
g.   COLLEY CIBBER—*Love's Last Shift.*
Act II.

I'll be at charges for a looking-glass,
And entertain some score or two of tailors,
To study fashions to adorn my body:
Since I am crept in favour with myself,
I will maintain it with some little cost.
h.   *Richard III.* Act I. Sc. 2. L. 256.

I see that the fashion wears out more apparel
than the man.
i.   *Much Ado About Nothing.* Act III.
Sc. 3. L. 148.

The glass of fashion and the mould of form,
The observ'd of all observers.
j.   *Hamlet.* Act III. Sc. 1. L. 161.

Their clothes are after such a pagan cut too,
That, sure, they've worn out Christendom.
k.   *Henry VIII.* Act I. Sc. 3. L. 14.

You, sir, I entertain for one of my hundred; only I do not like the fashion of your
garments.
l.   *King Lear.* Act III. Sc. 6. L. 88.

At present there is no distinction among
the upper ten thousand of the city.
m.   N. P. WILLIS—*Necessity for a
Promenade Drive.*

FATE.

The dawn is overcast, the morning lowers,
And heavily in clouds brings on the day,
The great, the important day, big with the
fate
Of Cato, and of Rome.
n.   ADDISON—*Cato.* Act I. Sc. 1.

So in the Libyan fable it is told
That once an eagle stricken with a dart,
Said, when he saw the fashion of the shaft,
"With our own feathers, not by other's
hands,
Are we now smitten."
o.   ÆSCHYLUS—*Fragm. 123.* Plumptre's
trans.

The bow is bent, the arrow flies,
The wingéd shaft of fate.
p.   IRA ALDRIDGE—*On William Tell.*
St. 12.

Yet who shall shut out Fate?
q.   EDWIN ARNOLD—*Light of Asia.*
Bk. III. L. 336.

The heart is its own Fate.
r.   BAILEY—*Festus.* Sc. *Wood and Water.
Sunset.*

Let those deplore their doom,
Whose hope still grovels in this dark sojourn:
But lofty souls, who look beyond the tomb,
Can smile at Fate, and wonder how they
mourn.
s.   BEATTIE—*The Minstrel.* Bk. I.

Success, the mark no mortal wit,
Or surest hand, can always hit:
For whatsoe'er we perpetrate,
We do but row, we're steer'd by Fate,
Which in success oft disinherits,
For spurious causes, noblest merits.
t.   BUTLER—*Hudibras.* Pt. I. Canto I.
L. 879.

So the struck eagle, stretch'd upon the plain,
No more through rolling clouds to soar again,
View'd his own feather on the fatal dart,
And wing'd the shaft that quiver'd in his
heart.
u.   BYRON—*English Bards and Scotch
Reviewers.* L. 841.

To bear is to conquer our fate.
v.   CAMPBELL—*On Visiting a Scene in
Argyleshire.*

Fate steals along with silent tread,
Found oftenest in what least we dread;
Frowns in the storm with angry brow,
But in the sunshine strikes the blow.
  a.   COWPER—*A Fable. Moral.*

All human things are subject to decay,
And when fate summons, monarchs must
    obey.
  b.   DRYDEN—*Mac Flecknoe.* L. 1.

For those whom God to ruin has design'd,
He fits for fate, and first destroys their mind.
  c.   DRYDEN—*Hind and Panther.* L. 1,092.

                Fate has carried me
'Mid the thick arrows: I will keep my
    stand.—
Not shrink and let the shaft pass by my
    breast
To pierce another.
  d.   GEORGE ELIOT—*The Spanish Gypsy.*
                                Bk. III.

                Stern fate and time
Will have their victims; and the best die first,
Leaving the bad still strong, though past their
    prime,
To curse the hopeless world they ever curs'd,
Vaunting vile deeds, and vainest of the worst.
  e.   EBENEZER ELLIOTT—*The Village
                    Patriarch.* Bk. IV. Pt. IV.

One common fate we both must prove;
You die with envy, I with love.
  f.   GAY—*Fable. The Poet and Rose.*
                                L. 29.

All is created and goes after order; yet o'er
mankind's life time, the precious gift, rules
an uncertain fate.
  g.   GOETHE.

Each curs'd his fate that thus their project
    cross'd;
How hard their lot who neither won nor lost.
  h.   GRAVES—*An Incident in High Life.*

Yet, ah! why should they know their fate,
Since sorrow never comes too late,
And happiness too swiftly flies?
Thought would destroy their paradise.
  i.   GRAY—*On a Distant Prospect of Eton
                                College.*

'Tis writ on Paradise's gate,
"Woe to the dupe that yields to Fate!"
  j.   HAFIZ.

Toil is the lot of all, and bitter woe
The fate of many.
  k.   HOMER—*Iliad.* Bk. XXI. L. 646.
                            Bryant's trans.

And not a man appears to tell their fate.
  l.   HOMER—*Odyssey.* Bk. X. L. 308.
                            Pope's trans.

Jove lifts the golden balances that show
The fates of mortal men, and things below.
  m.   HOMER—*Iliad.* Bk. XXII. L. 271.
                            Pope's trans.

With equal pace, impartial Fate
Knocks at the palace, as the cottage gate.
  n.   HORACE—Bk. I. *Ode IV.* L. 17.
                            Francis' trans.

Must helpless man, in ignorance sedate,
Roll darkling down the torrent of his fate?
  o.   SAM'L JOHNSON—*Vanity of Human
                                Wishes.* L. 345.

Fate holds the strings, and Men like children
    move
But as they're led: Success is from above.
  p.   LORD LANSDOWNE—*Heroic Love.*
                                Act V. Sc. 1.

All are architects of Fate,
  Working in these walls of Time;
Some with massive deeds and great,
  Some with ornaments of rhyme.
  q.   LONGFELLOW—*The Builders.* St. 1.

No one is so accursed by fate,
No one so utterly desolate,
  But some heart, though unknown,
  Responds unto his own.
  r.   LONGFELLOW—*Endymion.* St. 8.

It lies not in our power to love or hate,
For will in us is over-rul'd by fate.
  s.   MARLOWE—*Hero and Leander. First
                                Sestiad.* L. 167.

And sing to those that hold the vital shears;
And turn the adamantine spindle round,
On which the fate of gods and men is wound.
  t.   MILTON—*Arcades.*

Fixed fate, free will, foreknowledge absolute.
  u.   MILTON—*Paradise Lost.* Bk. II.
                                L. 560.

                Necessity and chance
Approach not me, and what I will is fate.
  v.   MILTON—*Paradise Lost.* Bk. VII.
                                L. 72.

A brave man struggling in the storms of fate.
  w.   POPE—*Prologue to Addison's Cato.*

But blind to former as to future fate,
What mortal knows his pre-existent state?
  x.   POPE—*Dunciad.* Bk. III. L. 47.

Heaven from all creatures hides the book of
    fate.
  y.   POPE—*Essay on Man.* Ep. I. L. 77.

Fate sits on these dark battlements, and
    frowns;
And as the portals open to receive me,
Her voice, in sullen echoes, through the courts,
Tells of a nameless deed.
  z.   ANN RADCLIFFE—*The Motto to "The
                    Mysteries of Udolpho."*

But, O vain boast!
Who can control his fate?
  a.   *Othello.* Act V. Sc. 2. L. 264.

But yet I'll make assurance double sure,
And take a bond of fate: thou shalt not live.
  b.   *Macbeth.* Act IV. Sc. 1. L. 83.

Eat, speak, and move, under the influence
of the most received star; and though the
devil lead the measure such are to be followed.
  c.   *All's Well That Ends Well.* Act II.
                    Sc. 1. L. 56.

Fate, show thy force; ourselves we do not
  owe;
What is decreed must be, and be this so.
  d.   *Twelfth Night.* Act I. Sc. 5. L. 329.

Fates, we will know your pleasures:
That we shall die we know; 'tis but the time
And drawing days out, that men stand upon.
  e.   *Julius Cæsar.* Act III. Sc. 1. L. 98.

If thou read this, O Cæsar, thou mayst live;
If not, the Fates with traitors do contrive.
  f.   *Julius Cæsar.* Act II. Sc. 3. L. 15.

It boots not to resist both wind and tide.
  g.   *Henry VI.* Pt. III. Act IV. Sc. 3.
                          L. 59.

        My fate cries out,
And makes each petty artery in this body
As hardy as the Numean lion's nerve.
  h.   *Hamlet.* Act I. Sc. 4. L. 81.

O God! that one might read the book of fate,
And see the revolutions of the times
Make mountains level, and the continent
Weary of solid firmness, melt itself
Into the sea!
  i.   *Henry IV.* Pt. II. Act III. Sc. 1.
                          L. 45.

Our wills and fates do so contrary run
That our devices still are overthrown;
Our thoughts are ours, their ends none of our
  own.
  j.   *Hamlet.* Act III. Sc. 2. L. 221.

What fates impose, that men must needs
  abide;
It boots not to resist both wind and tide.
  k.   *Henry VI.* Pt. III. Act IV. Sc. 3.
                          L. 58.

What should be spoken here, where our fate,
Hid within an auger-hole, may rush, and seize
  us?
  l.   *Macbeth.* Act II. Sc. 3. L. 127.

    You fools! I and my fellows
Are ministers of Fate; the elements
Of whom your swords are temper'd, may as
  well
Wound the loud winds, or with bemock'd-at
  stabs
Kill the still-closing waters, as diminish
One dowle that's in my plume.
  m.   *Tempest.* Act III. Sc. 3. L. 60.

The glories of our blood and state
  Are shadows, not substantial things;
There is no armour against fate;
  Death lays his icy hand on kings.
  n.   Shirley—*Contention of Ajax and*
                    Ulysses. Sc. 3.

Alas, by what rude fate
Our lives, like ships at sea, an instant meet,
Then part forever on their courses fleet.
  o.   E. C. Stedman—*Blameless Prince.*
                          St. 51.

When fate has allowed to any man more
than one great gift, accident or necessity
seems usually to contrive that one shall en-
cumber and impede the other.
  p.   Swinburne—*Essays and Studies. The*
                Poems of Dante Gabriel Rossetti.

Sometimes an hour of Fate's serenest weather
  Strikes through our changeful sky its com-
    ing beams;
Somewhere above us, in elusive ether,
  Waits the fulfilment of our dearest dreams.
  q.   Bayard Taylor—*Ad Amicos.*

And out of darkness came the hands
That reach thro' nature, moulding men.
  r. . Tennyson—*In Memoriam.* CXXIV.

That eagle's fate and mine are one,
  Which, on the shaft that made him die,
Espied a feather of his own,
  Wherewith he wont to soar so high.
  s.   Edmund Waller—*To a Lady Singing*
            a Song of his Composing. Ep. XIV.

I saw him even now going the way of all
  flesh.
  t.   John Webster—*Westward Ho.*
                      Act II. Sc. 2.

This day we fashion Destiny, our web of Fate
  we spin.
  u.   Whittier—*The Crisis.* St. 10.

FAULTS.

Then farewell, Horace; whom I hated so,
Not for thy faults, but mine.
  v.   Byron—*Childe Harold.* Canto IV.
                          St. 77.

    The greatest of faults, I should say, is to be
conscious of none.
  w.   Carlyle—*Heroes and Hero-Worship.*
                         Ch. II.

Men still had faults, and men will have them
  still;
He that hath none, and lives as angels do,
Must be an angel.
  x.   Wentworth Dillon—*Miscellanies.*
        On Mr. Dryden's Religio Laici.
                          L. 8.

Who mix'd reason with pleasure, and wisdom
with mirth;
If he had any faults, he has left us in doubt.
    a.   GOLDSMITH—*Retaliation.* L. 24.

Do you wish to find out a person's weak
points? Note the failings he has the quickest
eye for in others. They may not be the very
failings he is himself conscious of; but they
will be their next-door neighbors. No man
keeps such a jealous lookout as a rival.
    b.   J. C. and A. W. HARE—*Guesses at
                          Truth.*

Bad men excuse their faults, good men will
leave them.
    c.   BEN JONSON—*Catiline.* Act III. Sc. 2.

Her new bark is worse than ten times her
old bite.
    d.   LOWELL—*A Fable for Critics.* L. 28.

The glorious fault of angels and of gods.
    e.   POPE—*To the Memory of an Unfortunate
                         Lady.* L. 14.

        And oftentimes, excusing of a fault
Doth make the fault the worse by the excuse,
As patches set upon a little breach,
Discredit more in hiding of the fault,
Than did the fault before it was so patched.
    f.   *King John.* Act IV. Sc. 2. L. 30.

Condemn the fault, and not the actor of it?
Why, every fault's condemn'd ere it be done;
Mine were the very cipher of a function,
To fine the faults whose fine stands in record,
And let go by the actor.
    g.   *Measure for Measure.* Act II. Sc. 2.
                          L. 37.

Every one fault seeming monstrous till his
fellow-fault came to match it.
    h.   *As You Like It.* Act III. Sc. 2.
                          L. 372.

Faults that are rich are fair.
    i.   *Timon of Athens.* Act I. Sc. 2. L. 13.

                Go to your bosom;
Knock there, and ask your heart what it
    doth know
That's like my brother's fault.
    j.   *Measure for Measure.* Act II. Sc. 2.
                          L. 136.

Her only fault, and that is faults enough,
Is that she is intolerable curst
And shrewd and froward, so beyond all
    measure
That, were my state far worser than it is,
I would not wed her for a mine of gold.
    k.   *Taming of the Shrew.* Act I. Sc. 2.
                          L. 88.

Roses have thorns, and silver fountains mud;
Clouds and eclipses stain both moon and sun,
And loathsome canker lives in sweetest bud.
All men make faults.
    l.   *Sonnet XXXV.*

FEAR.

No one loves the man whom he fears.
    m.   ARISTOTLE.

The brave man is not he who feels no fear,
For that were stupid and irrational;
But he, whose noble soul its fear subdues,
And bravely dares the danger nature shrinks
    from.
    n.   JOANNA BAILLIE—*Basil.* Act III.
                         Sc. 1. L. 151.

The fear o' hell's the hangman's whip
    To haud the wretch in order;
But where ye feel your honor grip,
    Let that aye be your border.
    o.   BURNS—*Epistle to a Young Friend.*

Fear is an ague, that forsakes
And haunts, by fits, those whom it takes;
And they'll opine they feel the pain
And blows they felt, to-day, again.
    p.   BUTLER—*Hudibras.* Pt. I. Canto III.
                          L. 471.

His fear was greater than his haste:
For fear, though fleeter than the wind,
Believes 'tis always left behind.
    q.   BUTLER—*Hudibras.* Pt. III. Canto III.
                          L. 64.

Like one, that on a lonesome road
    Doth walk in fear and dread,
And having once turned round, walks on,
    And turns no more his head;
Because he knows a frightful fiend
    Doth close behind him tread.
    r.   COLERIDGE—*The Ancient Mariner.*
                         Pt. VI.

His frown was full of terror, and his voice
Shook the delinquent with such fits of awe
As left him not, till penitence had won
Lost favor back again, and clos'd the breach.
    s.   COWPER—*The Task.* Bk. II. L. 659.

The clouds dispell'd, the sky resum'd her
    light,
And Nature stood recover'd of her fright.
But fear, the last of ills, remain'd behind,
And horror heavy sat on every mind.
    t.   DRYDEN—*Theodore and Honoria.*
                         L. 336.

Whistling to keep myself from being afraid.
    u.   DRYDEN—*Amphitryon.* Act III. Sc. 1.

    We are not apt to fear for the fearless, when
we are companions in their danger.
    v.   GEORGE ELIOT—*The Mill on the Floss.*
                        Bk. VII. Ch. V.

Fear always springs from ignorance.
    w.   EMERSON—*The American Scholar.*

Fear is cruel and mean.
    x.   EMERSON—*Society and Solitude.*
                        Courage.

Fear is the parent of cruelty.

　　a.　　Froude—*Short Studies on Great
　　　　　　Subjects. Party Politics.*

You are uneasy, * * * you never sailed
with *me* before, I see.

　　b.　　Andrew Jackson—*Parton's Life of
　　　　　　Jackson.* Vol. III. P. 493.

Oh, fear not in a world like this,
　　And thou shalt know ere long,—
Know how sublime a thing it is
　　To suffer and be strong.

　　c.　　Longfellow—*The Light of Stars.* St. 9.

They are slaves who fear to speak
For the fallen and the weak.

　　d.　　Lowell—*Stanzas on Freedom.* Last
　　　　　　　　　　　　　　　　　　Stanza.

The direst foe of courage is the fear itself,
not the object of it; and the man who can
overcome his own terror is a hero and more.

　　e.　　George MacDonald—*Sir Gibbie.*
　　　　　　　　　　　　　　　　　Ch. XX.

The thing in the world I am most afraid of
is fear, and with good reason; that passion
alone, in the trouble of it, exceeding all other
accidents.

　　f.　　Montaigne—*Essays. Fear.*

Imagination frames events unknown,
In wild, fantastic shapes of hideous ruin,
And what it fears creates.

　　g.　　Hannah More—*Belshazzar.* Pt. II.

Then flash'd the living lightning from her
　　eyes,
And screams of horror rend th' affrighted
　　skies,
Not louder shrieks to pitying Heaven are cast,
When husbands, or when lap dogs, breathe
　　their last;
Or when rich China vessels fallen, from high,
In glittering dust and painted fragments lie.

　　h.　　Pope—*Rape of the Lock.* Canto III.
　　　　　　　　　　　　　　　　　　L. 155.

A lamb appears a lion, and we fear
Each bush we see's a bear.

　　i.　　Quarles—*Emblems.* Bk. I.
　　　　　　　　　　　Emblem XIII. L. 19.

Fain would I climb, yet fear I to fall.

　　j.　　Sir Walter Raleigh—*Written in a
　　　　　　　　　　　　　　　　　Window.*

A man should always allow his fears to rise
to their highest possible pitch, and then some
consolation or other will suddenly fall, like a
warm rain-drop, upon his heart.

　　k.　　Richter—*Flower, Fruit and Thorn
　　　　　　　　　　Pieces.* Bk. II. Ch. VI.

And being thus frighted swears a prayer or
　　two,
And sleeps again.

　　l.　　*Romeo and Juliet.* Act I. Sc. 4. L. 87.

14

And make my seated heart knock at my ribs.

　　m.　　*Macbeth.* Act I. Sc. 3. L. 136.

Ere we will eat our meal in fear, and sleep
In the affliction of these terrible dreams
That shake us nightly.

　　n.　　*Macbeth.* Act III. Sc. 2. L. 17.

　　　　　　For I am sick and capable of fears,
Opress'd with wrongs, and therefore full of
　　fears,
A widow, husbandless, subject to fears,
A woman, naturally born to fears.

　　o.　　*King John.* Act III. Sc. 1. L. 12.

His flight was madness: when our actions do
　　not,
Our fears do make us traitors.

　　p.　　*Macbeth.* Act IV. Sc. 2. L. 3.

I could a tale unfold whose lightest word
Would harrow up thy soul, freeze thy young
　　blood,
Make thy two eyes, like stars, start from their
　　spheres,
Thy knotted and combined locks to part
And each particular hair to stand on end,
Like quills upon the fretful porpentine.

　　q.　　*Hamlet.* Act I. Sc. 5. L. 15.

　　　　　　　　If ever fearful
To do a thing, where I the issue doubted,
Whereof the execution did cry out
Against the non-performance, 'twas a fear
Which oft infects the wisest.

　　r.　　*Winter's Tale.* Act I. Sc. 2. L. 258.

I have a faint cold fear thrills through my
　　veins,
That almost freezes up the heat of life.

　　s.　　*Romeo and Juliet.* Act IV. Sc. 3.
　　　　　　　　　　　　　　　　　　L. 15.

I thought upon one pair of English legs
Did march three Frenchmen.

　　t.　　*Henry V.* Act III. Sc. 6. L. 158.

It is a basilisk unto mine eye,
Kills me to look on't.

　　u.　　*Cymbeline.* Act II. Sc. 4. L. 107.

It is the part of men to fear and tremble,
When the most mighty gods by tokens send
Such dreadful heralds to astonish us.

　　v.　　*Julius Cæsar.* Act I. Sc. 3. L. 54.

Or in the night, imagining some fear,
How easy is a bush suppos'd a bear!

　　w.　　*Midsummer Night's Dream.* Act V.
　　　　　　　　　　　　　　　　　Sc. 1. L. 21.

　　　　　　　Present fears
Are less than horrible imaginings.

　　x.　　*Macbeth.* Act I. Sc. 3. L. 137.

　　　　　　There is not such a word
Spoke of in Scotland as this term of fear.

　　y.　　*Henry IV.* Pt. I. Act IV. Sc. I.
　　　　　　　　　　　　　　　　　　L. 84.

They spake not a word;
But, like dumb statues or breathing stones,
Gazed each on other, and look'd deadly pale.
a.   *Richard III.* Act III. Sc. 7. L. 24.

Things done well,
And with a care, exempt themselves from
     fear;
Things done without example, in their issue
Are to be feared.
b.   *Henry VIII.* Act I. Sc. 2. L. 88.

Thou can'st not say I did it; never shake
Thy gory locks at me.
c.   *Macbeth.* Act III. Sc. 4. L. 49.

Thou tremblest; and the whiteness in thy
     cheek
Is apter than thy tongue to tell thy errand.
d.   *Henry IV.* Pt. II. Act I. Sc. 1.
                                          L. 68.

'Tis time to fear when tyrants seem to kiss.
e.   *Pericles.* Act I. Sc. 2. L. 79.

To fear the foe, since fear oppresseth strength,
Gives in your weakness strength unto your
     foe.
f.   *Richard II.* Act III. Sc. 2. L. 180.

Truly the souls of men are full of dread :
Ye cannot reason almost with a man
That looks not heavily and full of fear.
g.   *Richard III.* Act II. Sc. 3. L. 39.

You can behold such sights,
And keep the natural ruby of your cheeks,
When mine is blanch'd with fear.
h.   *Macbeth.* Act III. Sc. 4. L. 114.

Fear
Stared in her eyes, and chalk'd her face.
i.   Tennyson—*The Princess.* IV. L. 357.

Desponding Fear, of feeble fancies full,
Weak and unmanly, loosens every power.
j.   Thomson—*The Seasons. Spring.*
                                          L. 286.

Full twenty times was Peter feared,
For once that Peter was respected.
k.   Wordsworth—*Peter Bell.* Pt. 1. St. 3.

Less base the fear of death than fear of life.
l.   Young—*Night Thoughts.* Night V.
                                          L. 441.

FEBRUARY (*See* Months).

FEELING.

He thought as a sage, though he felt as a man.
m.   Beattie—*The Hermit.* L. 8.

But, spite of all the criticising elves,
Those who would make us feel, must feel
     themselves.
n.   Churchill—*Rosciad.* L. 961.

Thought is deeper than all speech,
Feeling deeper than all thought;
Souls to souls can never teach
What unto themselves was taught.
o.   C. P. Cranch—*Thought.*

The moment of finding a fellow-creature is
often as full of mingled doubt and exultation,
as the moment of finding an idea.
p.   George Eliot—*Daniel Deronda.*
                              Bk. II. Ch. XVII.

If the man who turnip cries
Cry not when his father dies,
'Tis a proof that he had rather,
Have a turnip than his father.
q.   Sam'l Johnson—*Johnsoniana.*
                        Anecdotes by Mrs. Piozzi.

Feeling is deep and still; and the word that
     floats on the surface
Is as the tossing buoy, that betrays where the
     anchor is hidden.
r.   Longfellow—*Evangeline.* Pt. II.
                              Sc. 2. L. 212.

For there are moments in life, when the heart
     is so full of emotion,
That if by chance it be shaken, or into its
     depths like a pebble
Drops some careless word, it overflows, and
     its secret,
Spilt on the ground like water, can never be
     gathered together.
s.   Longfellow—*Courtship of Miles
          Standish.* Pt. VI. *Priscilla.* L. 12.

The wealth of rich feelings—the deep—the
     pure;
With strength to meet sorrow, and faith to
     endure.
t.   Frances S. Osgood—*To F. D. Maurice.*

The soul of music slumbers in the shell,
Till wak'd and kindled by the master's spell,
And feeling hearts touch them but lightly—
     pour
A thousand melodies unheard before!
u.   Sam'l Rogers—*Human Life.* L. 359.

Some feelings are to mortals given,
With less of earth in them than heaven.
v.   Scott—*Lady of the Lake.* Canto II.
                                          St. 22.

Sensations sweet,
Felt in the blood, and felt along the heart.
w.   Wordsworth—*Lines Composed a Few
               Miles Above Tintern Abbey.*

FESTIVITIES.

Some men are born to feast, and not to fight;
Whose sluggish minds, e'en in fair honor's
     field,
Still on their dinner turn—
Let such pot-boiling varlets stay at home,
And wield a flesh-hook rather than a sword.
x.   Joanna Baillie—*Basil.* Act I. Sc. 1.

As much valour is to be found in feasting as
in fighting, and some of our city captains and
carpet knights will make this good, and prove
it.
    a.   Burton—*Anatomy of Melancholy.*
                Pt. I.   Sec. 2.   Memb. 2.
                           Subsect. 2.

The music, and the banquet, and the wine—
The garlands, the rose odors, and the flowers,
The sparkling eyes, and flashing ornaments—
The white arms and the raven hair—the
     braids,
And bracelets; swan-like bosoms, and the
     necklace,
An India in itself, yet dazzling not.
    b.   Byron—*Marino Faliero.*   Act IV.
                       Sc. 1.   L. 51.

There was a sound of revelry by night,
    And Belgium's capital had gather'd then
Her Beauty and her Chivalry, and bright
The lamps shone o'er fair women and brave
     men.
    c.   Byron—*Childe Harold.*   Canto III.
                           St. 21.

        Venice once was dear,
The pleasant place of all festivity,
The rival of the earth, the masque of Italy.
    d.   Byron—*Childe Harold.*   Canto IV.
                           St. 3.

Blest be those feasts, with simple plenty
     crowned,
Where all the ruddy family around
Laugh at the jests or pranks that never fail
Or sigh with pity at some mournful tale.
    e.   Goldsmith—*The Traveller.*   L. 17.

The service was of great array,
That they were served with that day.
Thus they ate, and made them glad,
With such service as they had—
When they had dined, as I you say,
Lordis and ladies yede to play ;
Some to tables and some to chess,
With other games more and less.
    f.   *The Life of Ipomydon.*   *Harleian*
                Library.   (British Museum).
                     MS. No. 2,252.

Out did the meate, out did the frolick wine.
    g.   Herrick—*Ode for Ben Jonson.*

Born but to banquet, and to drain the bowl.
    h.   Homer—*Odyssey.*   Bk. X.   L. 622.
                      Pope's trans.

They eat, they drink, and in communion
     sweet
Quaff immortality and joy.
    i.   Milton—*Paradise Lost.*   Bk. V.
                           L. 637.

The feast of reason and the flow of soul.
    j.   Pope—*First Satire.*   *Horace.*   Bk. II.
                           L. 131.

                But, first
Or last, your fine Egyptian cookery
Shall have the fame.   I have heard that
     Julius Cæsar
Grew fat with feasting there.
    k.   *Antony and Cleopatra.*   Act II.   Sc. 6.
                           L. 63.

Each man to his stool, with that spur as he
would to the lip of his mistress; your diet
shall be in all places alike.   Make not a city
feast of it, to let the meat cool ere we can
agree upon the first place.
    l.   *Timon of Athens.*   Act III.   Sc. 6.
                           L. 73.

Fat paunches have lean pates, and dainty
     bits
Make rich the ribs, but bankrupt quite the
     wits.
    m.   *Love's Labour's Lost.*   Act I.   Sc. 1.
                           L. 26.

I charge thee, invite them all; let in the tide
Of knaves once more: my cook and I'll pro-
     vide.
    n.   *Timon of Athens.*   Act III.   Sc. 4.
                           L. 118.

My cake is dough : but I'll in among the rest,
Out of hope of all, but my share of the feast.
    o.   *Taming of the Shrew.*   Act V.   Sc. 1.
                           L. 143.

                Our feasts
In every mess have folly, and the feeders
Digest with it a custom, I should blush
To see you so attir'd.
    p.   *Winter's Tale.*   Act IV.   Sc. 4.   L. 10.

This night I hold an old accustom'd feast,
Whereto I have invited many a guest,
Such as I love ; and you among the store,
One more, most welcome, makes my number
     more.
    q.   *Romeo and Juliet.*   Act I.   Sc. 2.   L. 20.

             Who riseth from a feast
With that keen appetite that he sits down?
    r.   *Merchant of Venice.*   Act II.   Sc. 6.
                           L. 8.

We keep the day.   With festal cheer,
    With books and music, surely we
    Will drink to him, whate'er he be,
And sing the songs he loved to hear.
    s.   Tennyson—*In Memorian.*   CVII.

Oh, leave the gay and festive scenes,
The halls of dazzling light.
    t.   H. S. Vandyke—*The Light Guitar.*

FICKLENESS.

A man so various that he seem'd to be,
Not one, but all mankind's epitome.
Stiff in opinions, always in the wrong;
Was everything by starts, and nothing long;
But, in the course of one revolving moon,
Was chymist, fiddler, statesman and buffoon.

a.   DRYDEN—*Absalom and Achitophel.*
                    Pt. I. L. 545.

He cast off his friends, as a huntsman his
    pack,
For he knew when he pleased he could
    whistle them back.

b.   GOLDSMITH—*Retaliation.* L. 107.

Ladies, like variegated tulips, show
'Tis to their changes half their charms we owe.

c.   POPE—*Moral Essays.* Ep. II. L. 41.

Who o'er the herd would wish to reign,
Fantastic, fickle, fierce, and vain?
Vain as the leaf upon the stream,
And fickle as a changeful dream;
Fantastic as a woman's mood,
And fierce as Frenzy's fever'd blood—
Thou many-headed monster thing,
Oh, who would wish to be thy king?

d.   SCOTT—*Lady of the Lake.* Canto V.
                          St. 30.

Sigh no more, ladies, sigh no more,
  Men were deceivers ever,
One foot in sea and one on shore;
  To one thing constant never.

e.   *Much Ado About Nothing.* Act II.
        Sc. 3. L. 64. See also THOS. PERCY,
                The Friar of Orders Gray.

Was ever feather so lightly blown to and
fro as this multitude?

f.   *Henry VI.* Pt. II. Act IV. Sc. 8.
                          L. 57.

FIDELITY.

True as the needle to the pole,
Or as the dial to the sun.

g.   BARTON BOOTH—*Song.*

No man can mortgage his injustice as a
pawn for his fidelity.

h.   BURKE—*Reflections on the Revolution in*
                      France.

Then come the wild weather, come sleet or
    come snow,
We will stand by each other, however it blow.

i.   SIMON DACH—*Annie of Tharaw.*
             Longfellow's trans. L. 7.

                He who, being bold
For life to come, is false to the past sweet
Of mortal life, hath killed the world above.
For why to live again if not to meet?
And why to meet if not to meet in love?
And why in love if not in that dear love of
    old?

j.   SYDNEY DOBELL—*Sonnet.* *To a Friend*
                    in Bereavement.

But faithfulness can feed on suffering,
And knows no disappointment.

k.   GEORGE ELIOT—*Spanish Gypsy.*
                          Bk. III.

Thou givest life and love for Greece and
    Right:
I will stand by thee lest thou shouldst be
    weak
Not weak of soul.—I will but hold in sight,
Thy marvelous beauty.—Here is
        She you seek!

l.   W. J. LINTON—*Iphigenia at Aulis.*

So spake the seraph Abdiel, faithful found,
Among the faithless faithful only he.

m.   MILTON—*Paradise Lost.* Bk. V.
                          L. 896.

Be not the first by whom the new are tried,
Nor yet the last to lay the old aside.

n.   POPE—*Essay on Criticism.* L. 336.

When change itself can give no more,
'Tis easy to be true.

o.   CHARLES SEDLEY—*Reasons for*
                      Constancy.

You draw me, you hard-hearted adamant;
But yet you draw not iron, for my heart
Is true as steel.

p.   *Midsummer Night's Dream.* Act II.
                    Sc. 1. L. 195.

To be true to each other, let 'appen what maäy
    Till the end o' the daäy
    An the last loäd hoäm.

q.   TENNYSON—*The Promise of May.*
                 Song. Act II.

To God, thy countrie, and thy friend be true.

r.   VAUGHAN—*Rules and Lessons.* St. 8.

FIRE.

Yet in oure asshen olde is fyr yreke.

s.   CHAUCER—*Canterbury Tales.* *The*
                Reves Prologue. L. 3,881.

Be of good comfort, Master Ridley, play the
man! We shall this day light such a candle,
by God's grace, in England, as I trust shall
never be put out.

t.   LATIMER—*The Martyrdom.* P. 523.

Whirlwinds of tempestuous fire.

u.   MILTON—*Paradise Lost.* Bk. I. L. 77.

Divert her eyes with pictures in the fire.
  a.   POPE—*Epistle to Mrs. Teresa Blount, on
            her leaving the Town after the
                   Coronation.*

A little fire is quickly trodden out ;
Which, being suffer'd, rivers cannot quench.
  b.   *Henry VI.* Pt. III. Act IV. Sc. 8.
                       L. 6.

Fire that's closest kept burns most of all.
  c.   *Two Gentlemen of Verona.* Act I.
                  Sc. 2. L. 30.

The fire i' the flint
Shows not till it be struck.
  d.   *Timon of Athens.* Act I. Sc. 1. L. 22.

FISH.

It is unseasonable and unwholesome in all
months that have not an R in their names to
eat an oyster.
  e.   BUTLER—*Dyet's Dry Dinner.* 1599.

"Will you walk a little faster ? " said a whiting
    to a snail,
"There's a porpoise close behind us, and he's
    treading on my tail !
See how eagerly the lobsters and the turtles
    all advance :
They are waiting on the shingle—will you
    come and join the dance ?"
  f.   LEWIS CARROLL—*Song in " Alice in
                  Wonderland."*

Here when the labouring fish does at the foot
    arrive,
And finds that by his strength but vainly he
    doth strive ;
His tail takes in his teeth, and bending like a
    bow,
That's to the compass drawn, aloft himself
    doth throw :
Then springing at his height, as doth a little
    wand,
That, bended end to end, and flerted from the
    hand,
Far off itself doth cast, so does the salmon
    vaut.
And if at first he fail, his second summersaut
He instantly assays· and from his nimble
    ring,
Still yarking never leaves, until himself he
    fling
Above the streamful top of the surrounded
    heap.
  g.   DRAYTON—*Poly-Olbion.* Sixth Song.
                       L. 45.

When if or chance or hunger's powerful sway
Directs the roving trout this fatal way,
He greedily sucks in the twining bait,
And tugs and nibbles the fallacious meat.
  h.   GAY—*Rural Sports.* Canto I. L. 150.

O scaly, slippery, wet, swift, staring wights,
What is 't ye do ? what life lead ? eh, dull
    goggles ?
How do ye vary your vile days and nights ?
How pass your Sundays ? Are ye still but
    joggles
In ceaseless wash ? Still nought but gapes
    and bites,
And drinks, and stares, diversified with
    boggles.
  i.   LEIGH HUNT—*Sonnets. The Fish, the
                  Man, and the Spirit.*

Fishes that tipple in the deepe,
Know no such liberty.
  j.   LOVELACE—*To Althea from Prison.*
                       St. 2.

Cut off my head, and singular I am,
Cut off my tail, and plural I appear ;
Although my middle's left, there's nothing
    there !
What is my head cut off ? A sounding sea ;
What is my tail cut off ? A rushing river ;
And in their mingling depths I fearless
    play,
Parent of sweetest sounds, yet mute forever.
  k.   MACAULAY—*Enigma. On the Codfish.*

Our plenteous streams a various race supply,
The bright-eyed perch with fins of Tyrian
    dye,
The silver eel, in shining volumes roll'd,
The yellow carp, in scales bedropp'd with
    gold,
Swift trouts, diversified with crimson stains,
And pikes, the tyrants of the wat'ry plains.
  l.   POPE—*Windsor Forest.* L. 141.

'Tis true, no turbots dignify my boards,
But gudgeons, flounders, what my Thames
    affords.
  m.   POPE—*Second Book of Horace.*
                 Satire II. L. 141.

It's no fish ye're buying—its men's lives.
  n.   SCOTT—*The Antiquary.* Ch. XI.

    Master, I marvel how the fishes live in
the sea.
    Why, as men do a-land : the great ones eat
up the little ones.
  o.   *Pericles.* Act II. Sc. 1. L. 29.

    They say fish should swim thrice * * *
first it should swim in the sea (do you mind
me ?) then it should swim in butter, and at
last, sirrah, it should swim in good claret.
  p.   SWIFT—*Polite Conversation.*
                     Dialogue II.

FLAGS.

The meteor flag of England.
  a.   Campbell—*Ye Mariners of England.*

Ye mariners of England !
  That guard our native seas ;
Whose flag has braved a thousand years,
  The battle and the breeze !
  b.   Campbell—*Ye Mariners of England.*

Fling out, fling out, with cheer and shout,
  To all the winds Our Country's Banner !
Be every bar, and every star,
  Displayed in full and glorious manner !
Blow, zephyrs, blow, keep the dear ensign
    flying !
Blow, zephyrs, sweetly mournful, sighing,
    sighing, sighing !
  c.   Abraham Coles—*The Microcosm and
              other Poems.* P. 191.

If any one attempts to haul down the American flag, shoot him on the spot.
  d.   John A. Dix—*Speeches and Addresses.*
              Vol. II. P. 440. *An Official
              Dispatch.* Jan. 29, 1861.

Flag of the free heart's hope and home !
By angel hands to valour given,
Thy stars have lit the welkin dome,
And all thy hues were born in heaven.
  e.   Joseph Rodman Drake—*The Croakers.
              The American Flag.* St. 6.

When Freedom from her mountain height
Unfurled her standard to the air.
  f.   Joseph Rodman Drake—*The Croakers.
              The American Flag.* St. 1.

Ay, tear her tattered ensign down !
Long has it waved on high,
And many an eye has danced to see
  That banner in the sky.
  g.   O. W. Holmes—*A Metrical Essay.*

Nail to the mast her holy flag,
  Set every threadbare sail,
And give her to the God of storms,
  The lightning and the gale.
  h.   O. W. Holmes—*A Metrical Essay.*

Praise the Power that hath made and pre-
    served us a nation !
Then conquer we must when our cause it is
    just.
And this be our motto, " In God is our trust !"
And the star-spangled banner in triumph
    shall wave
O'er the land of the free and the home of the
    brave.
  i.   F. S. Key—*The Star-Spangled Banner.*

Under spread ensigns moving nigh, in slow
But firm battalion.
  j.   Milton—*Paradise Lost.* Bk. VI.
                                  L. 533.

Under the sooty flag of Acheron,
Harpies and Hydras.
  k.   Milton—*Comus.* L. 604.

              Bastard Freedom waves
Her fustian flag in mockery over slaves.
  l.   Moore—*To the Lord Viscount Forbes.*

" A song for our banner?"—The watchword
    recall
Which gave the Republic her station ;
" United we stand—divided we fall !"
It made and preserves us a nation !
  m.   George P. Morris—*The Flag of Our
                                  Union.*

The flag of our Union forever !
  n.   George P. Morris—*The Flag of Our
                                  Union.*

              A garish flag,
To be the aim of every dangerous shot.
  o.   *Richard III.* Act IV. Sc. 4. L. 89.

This token serveth for a flag of truce
Betwixt ourselves and all our followers.
  p.   *Henry VI.* Pt. I. Act III. Sc. 1.
                                  L. 138.

Banner of England, not for a season,
  O banner of Britain, hast thou
Floated in conquering battle or flapt to the
    battle-cry !
Never with mightier glory than when we had
    rear'd thee on high,
  Flying at top of the roofs in the ghastly
    siege of Lucknow—
Shot thro' the staff or the halyard, but ever
    we raised thee anew,
And ever upon the topmost roof our banner
    of England blew.
  q.   Tennyson—*The Defence of Lucknow.*

Let it rise ! let it rise, till it meet the sun in
his coming ; let the earliest light of the morning gild it, and the parting day linger and
play on its summit.
  r.   Daniel Webster—*Address on Laying
              the Corner Stone of the Bunker Hill
              Monument.* Works. Vol. I.
                                  P. 62.

A star for every State, and a State for every
star.
  s.   Robert C. Winthrop—*Address on
              Boston Common.* 1862.

FLATTERY.

And wrinkles, the d—d democrats, won't
flatter.
    a.   Byron—*Don Juan.* Canto X.
St. XXIV.

Greatly his foes he dreads, but more his
friends,
He hurts me most who lavishly commends.
    b.   Churchill—*The Apology.* L. 19.

Of praise a mere glutton, he swallow'd what
came,
And the puff of a dunce, he mistook it for fame;
Till his relish grown callous, almost to dis-
please,
Who pepper'd the highest was surest to please.
    c.   Goldsmith—*Retaliation.* L. 109.

Gallantry of mind consists in saying flattering things in an agreeable manner.
    d.   La Rochefoucauld—*Maxims and
Moral Sentences.* No. 103.

No adulation; 'tis the death of virtue;
Who flatters, is of all mankind the lowest
Save he who courts the flattery.
    e.   Hannah More—*Daniel.*

By flatterers besieged
And so obliging that he ne'er obliged;
Like Cato, give his little senate laws,
And sit attentive to his own applause.
    f.   Pope—*Prologue to Satires.* L. 207.

* * * for ne'er
Was flattery lost on Poet's ear;
A simple race! they waste their toil
For the vain tribute of a smile.
    g.   Scott—*Lay of the Last Minstrel.*
Canto IV. Last Stanza.

But when I tell him he hates flatterers,
He says he does, being then most flattered.
    h.   *Julius Cæsar.* Act II. Sc. 1. L. 208.

By God, I cannot flatter: I do defy
The tongues of soothers; but a braver place
In my heart's love, hath no man than your-
self;
Nay, task me to my word; approve me, lord.
    i.   *Henry IV.* Pt. 1. Act IV. Sc. 1.
L. 6.

Faith, there have been many great men
that have flattered the people, who ne'er loved
them; and there be many that they have loved,
they know not wherefore; so that, if they love
they know not why, they hate upon no better
a ground.
    j.   *Coriolanus.* Act II. Sc. 2. L. 7.

Lay not that flattering unction to your soul.
    k.   *Hamlet.* Act III. Sc. 4. L. 145.

Mine eyes
Were not in fault, for she was beautiful;
Mine ears, that heard her flattery; nor my
heart,
That thought her like her seeming; it had
been vicious
To have mistrusted her.
    l.   *Cymbeline.* Act V. Sc. 5. L. 63.

O, that men's ears should be
To counsel deaf, but not to flattery!
    m.   *Timon of Athens.* Act I. Sc. 2.
L. 256.

Take no repulse, whatever she doth say;
For, "get you gone," she doth not mean,
"away."
Flatter and praise, commend, extol their
graces;
Though ne'er so black, say they have angels'
faces.
That man that hath a tongue, I say, is no man,
If with his tongue he cannot win a woman.
    n.   *Two Gentlemen of Verona.* Act III.
Sc. 1. L. 100.

They do abuse the king that flatter him:
For flattery is the bellows blows up sin.
    o.   *Pericles.* Act I. Sc. 2. L. 38.

What drink'st thou oft, instead of homage
sweet,
But poison'd flattery?
    p.   *Henry V.* Act IV. Sc. 1. L. 267.

Why should the poor be flatter'd?
No, let the candied tongue lick absurd pomp,
And crook the pregnant hinges of the knee,
Where thrift may follow fawning.
    q.   *Hamlet.* Act III. Sc. 2. L. 65.

'Tis an old maxim in the schools,
That flattery's the food of fools;
Yet now and then your men of wit
Will condescend to take a bit.
    r.   Swift—*Cadenus and Vanessa.* L. 769.

Where Young must torture his invention
To flatter knaves, or lose his pension.
    s.   Swift—*Poetry, a Rhapsody.* L. 279.

FLIRTING.

I assisted at the birth of that most significant
word flirtation, which dropped from the most
beautiful mouth in the world, and which has
since received the sanction of our most accurate Laureate in one of his comedies.
    t.   Chesterfield—*The World.* No. 101.

From a grave thinking mouser, she was grown
The gayest flirt that coach'd it round the
town.
    u.   Pitt—*Fable. The Young Man and
His Cat.*

FLOWERS.

Part I.—Unclassified Flora.

A wilderness of sweets.
    a.   Milton—*Paradise Lost.* Bk. V. L. 294.

The breath of flowers is far sweeter in the air (where it comes and goes like the warbling of music) than in the hand.
    b.   Bacon—*Essay. Of Gardening.*

Sweet letters of the angel tongue,
  I've loved ye long and well,
And never have failed in your fragrance sweet
  To find some secret spell,—
A charm that has bound me with witching power,
  For mine is the old belief,
That midst your sweets and midst your bloom,
  There's a soul in every leaf!
    c.   M. M. Ballou—*Flowers.*

As for marigolds, poppies, hollyhocks, and valorous sunflowers, we shall never have a garden without them, both for their own sake, and for the sake of old-fashioned folks, who used to love them.
    d.   Henry Ward Beecher—*Star Papers. A Discourse of Flowers.*

Flowers have an expression of countenance as much as men or animals. Some seem to smile; some have a sad expression; some are pensive and diffident; others again are plain, honest and upright, like the broad-faced sunflower and the hollyhock.
    e.   Henry Ward Beecher—*Star Papers. A Discourse of Flowers.*

Flowers are Love's truest language; they betray,
  Like the divining rods of Magi old,
Where precious wealth lies buried, not of gold,
But love—strong love, that never can decay!
    f.   Park Benjamin—*Sonnet. Flowers Love's Truest Language.*

And sleepy *poppies* nod upon their stems;
The humble *violet* and the dulcet *rose*,
The stately *lily* then, and *tulip* blows.
    g.   Anne E. Bleecker—*Return to Tomhanick.*

Another rose may bloom as sweet,
  Other magnolias ope in whiteness.
    h.   Maria Brooks—*Written on Seeing Pharamond.*

Ah, ah, Cytherea! Adonis is dead.
She wept tear after tear, with the blood which was shed,—
And both turned into flowers for the earth's garden-close;
Her tears, to the wind-flower,—his blood, to the rose.
    i.   E. B. Browning—*A Lament for Adonis.* St. 6.

The flower-girl's prayer to buy roses and pinks,
Held out in the smoke, like stars by day.
    j.   E. B. Browning—*The Soul's Travelling.*

It was roses, roses, all the way,
  With myrtle mixed in my path like mad.
    k.   Robert Browning—*The Patriot.*

The windflower and the violet, they perished long ago,
And the brier-rose and the orchis died amid the summer glow;
But on the hills the golden-rod, and the aster in the wood,
And the yellow sunflower by the brook, in autumn beauty stood,
Till fell the frost from the clear cold heaven, as falls the plague on men,
And the brightness of their smile was gone, from upland glade and glen.
    l.   Bryant—*The Death of the Flowers.*

Where fall the tears of love the rose appears,
And where the ground is bright with friendship's tears,
Forget-me-not, and violets, heavenly blue,
Spring glittering with the cheerful drops like dew.
    m.   Bryant—*Trans. of N. Müller's. The Paradise of Tears.*

Mourn, little harebells o'er the lea;
Ye stately foxgloves fair to see!
Ye woodbines, hanging bonnilie
    In scented bowers!
Ye roses on your thorny tree
    The first o' flow'rs.
    n.   Burns—*Elegy on Capt. Matthew Henderson.*

Now blooms the lily by the bank,
  The primrose down the brae;
The hawthorn's budding in the glen,
  And milkwhite is the slae.
    o.   Burns—*Lament of Mary, Queen of Scots.*

The snowdrop and primrose our woodlands
    adorn,
And violets bathe in the wet o' the morn.
  a.   Burns—*My Nannie's Awa.*

Yet all beneath the unrivalled rose,
The lovely daisy sweetly blows.
  b.   Burns—*The Vision. Duan Second.*
                    St. 21.

Rose, what is become of thy delicate hue?
And where is the violet's beautiful blue?
Does aught of its sweetness the blossom
    beguile?
That meadow, those daisies, why do they not
    smile?
  c.   John Byrom—*A Pastoral.* St. 8.

Ye field flowers! the gardens eclipse you 'tis
    true:
Yet wildings of nature, I dote upon you,
    For ye waft me to summers of old,
When the earth teem'd around me with fairy
    delight,
And when daisies and buttercups gladden'd
    my sight,
    Like treasures of silver and gold.
  d.   Campbell—*Field Flowers.*

The berries of the brier rose
  Have lost their rounded pride:
The bitter-sweet chrysanthemums
  Are drooping heavy-eyed.
  e.   Alice Cary—*Faded Leaves.*

I know not which I love the most,
  Nor which the comeliest shows,
The timid, bashful violet,
  Or the royal-hearted rose:

The pansy in her purple dress,
  The pink with cheek of red,
Or the faint, fair heliotrope, who hangs,
  Like a bashful maid her head.
  f.   Phebe Cary—*Spring Flowers.*

The anemone in snowy hood,
The sweet arbutus in the wood.
And to the smiling skies above
I say, "Bend brightly o'er my love."
  g.   Mary Clemmer—*Good-By, Sweetheart.*

Ye living flowers that skirt the eternal frost!
  h.   Coleridge—*Hymn Before Sunrise in*
              the Vale of Chamouni.

There spring the wild-flowers—fair as can be.
  i.   Eliza Cook—*Journal. My Grave.*
                  Vol. V. St. 7.

Who does not recollect the hours
  When burning words and praises
Were lavished on those shining flowers,
  Buttercups and daisies?
  j.   Eliza Cook—*Journal. Buttercups and*
          Daisies. Vol. IV. St. 4.

They know the time to go!
  The fairy clocks strike their inaudible hour
  In field and woodland, and each punctual
    flower
Bows at the signal an obedient head
           And hastes to bed.
  k.   Susan Coolidge—*Time to Go.*

                 Not a flower
But shows some touch, in freckle, streak or
    stain,
Of his unrivall'd pencil.
  l.   Cowper—*The Task.* Bk. VI. L. 241.

Who loves a garden loves a greenhouse too.
  m.   Cowper—*The Task.* Bk. III. L. 576.

          Flowers are words
Which even a babe may understand.
  n.   Bishop Coxe—*The Singing of Birds.*

And all the meadows, wide unrolled,
Were green and silver, green and gold,
Where buttercups and daisies spun
Their shining tissues in the sun.
  o.   Julia C. R. Dorr—*Unanswered.*

The harebells nod as she passes by,
The violet lifts its tender eye,
The ferns bend her steps to greet,
And the mosses creep to her dancing feet.
  p.   Julia C. R. Dorr—*Over the Wall.*

Up from the gardens floated the perfume
Of roses and myrtle, in their perfect bloom.
  q.   Julia C. R. Dorr—*Vashti's Scroll.*
                    L. 91.

The rose is fragrant, but it fades in time:
The violet sweet, but quickly past the prime:
White lilies hang their heads, and soon decay,
And white snow in minutes melts away.
  r.   Dryden—*Trans. from Theocritus. The*
              Despairing Lover. L. 57.

The flowers of the forest are a' wede away.
  s.   Jane Elliott—*The Flowers of the*
                  Forest.

Why does the rose her grateful fragrance
    yield,
And yellow cowslips paint the smiling field?
  t.   Gay—*Panthea.* L. 71.

They speak of hope to the fainting heart,
With a voice of promise they come and part,
They sleep in dust through the wintry hours,
They break forth in glory—bring flowers,
    bright flowers!
  u.   Mrs. Hemans—*Bring Flowers.*

Through the laburnum's dropping gold
Rose the light shaft of orient mould,
And Europe's violets, faintly sweet,
Purpled the moss-beds at its feet.
  v.   Mrs. Hemans—*The Palm-Tree.*

Faire pledges of a fruitful tree
   Why do yee fall so fast?
   Your date is not so past
But you may stay yet here awhile
   To blush and gently smile
   And go at last.
  a.   HERRICK—*To Blossoms.*

The daisy is fair, the day-lily rare,
The bud o' the rose as sweet as it's bonnie.
  b.   HOGG—*Auld Joe Nicolson's Nannie.*

What are the flowers of Scotland,
   All others that excel?
The lovely flowers of Scotland,
   All others that excel!
The thistle's purple bonnet,
   And bonny heather bell,
Oh, they're the flowers of Scotland
   All others that excel!
  c.   HOGG—*The Flowers of Scotland.*

Yellow japanned buttercups and star-disked
dandelions,—just as we see them lying in the
grass, like sparks that have leaped from the
kindling sun of summer.
  d.   O. W. HOLMES—*The Professor at the
           Breakfast-Table.* X.

I remember, I remember
   The roses, red and white,
The violets, and the lily-cups,
   Those flowers made of light!
The lilacs, where the robin built,
   And where my brother set
The laburnum on his birthday,—
   The tree is living yet.
  e.   HOOD—*I Remember, I Remember.*

           At the roots
Of peony bushes lay in rose-red heaps,
Or snowy, fallen bloom.
  f.   JEAN INGELOW—*Songs with Preludes.
           Wedlock.*

I have brought a budding world,
   Of orchis spires and daisies rank,
And ferny plumes but half uncurled,
   From yonder bank.
  g.   JEAN INGELOW—*The Letter L. Absent.*

           Above his head
Four lily stalks did their white honours wed
To make a coronal; and round him grew
All tendrils green, of every bloom and hue,
Together intertwined and trammell'd fresh;
The vine of glossy sprout; the ivy mesh,
Shading its Ethiop berries.
  h.   KEATS—*Endymion.* Bk. II. L. 413.

   And O and O,
     The daisies blow,
And the primroses are waken'd;
   And the violets white
     Sit in silver plight,
And the green bud's as long as the spike end.
  i.   KEATS—*In a Letter to Haydon.*

But the rose leaves herself upon the brier,
For winds to kiss and grateful bees to feed.
  j.   KEATS—*On Fame.*

Of primroses by shelter'd rills,
And daisies on the aguish hills.
  k.   KEATS—*The Eve of St. Mark.*

Roses, and pinks, and violets, to adorn
The shrine of Flora in her early May.
  l.   KEATS—*Dedication to Leigh Hunt.*

          * * * the rose
Blendeth its odor with the violet,—
Solution sweet.
  m.   KEATS—*The Eve of St. Agnes.* St. 36.

Underneath large blue-bells tented
Where the daisies are rose-scented,
And the rose herself has got
Perfume which on earth is not.
  n.   KEATS—*Ode. Bards of Passion and of
           Mirth.*

Young playmates of the rose and daffodil,
Be careful ere ye enter in, to fill
   Your baskets high
With fennel green, and balm, and golden
   pines
Savory latter-mint, and columbines.
  o.   KEATS—*Endymion.* Bk. IV. L. 575.

The loveliest flowers the closest cling to earth,
And they first feel the sun: so violets blue;
So the soft star-like primrose—drenched in
   dew—
The happiest of Spring's happy, fragrant
   birth.
  p.   KEBLE—*Miscellaneous Poems. Spring
           Showers.*

Gorgeous flowerets in the sunlight shining,
   Blossoms flaunting in the eye of day,
Tremulous leaves, with soft and silver lining,
   Buds that open only to decay.
  q.   LONGFELLOW—*Flowers.* St. 6.

Spake full well, in language quaint and
   olden,
One who dwelleth by the castled Rhine,
When he called the flowers, so blue and
   golden,
   Stars, that in the earth's firmament do shine.
  r.   LONGFELLOW—*Flowers.* St. 1.

Who that has loved knows not the tender tale
Which flowers reveal, when lips are coy to
   tell?
  s.   BULWER-LYTTON—*Corn Flowers. The
           First Violets.* Bk. I. St. 1.

And I will make thee beds of roses,
And a thousand fragrant posies.
  t.   MARLOWE—*The Passionate Shepherd
           to his Love.*

And throw sweet garland wreaths into her
    stream,
Of pansies, pinks, and gaudy daffodils.
   a.   MILTON—*Comus.* L. 850.

And touched by her fair tendance, gladlier
    grew.
   b.   MILTON—*Paradise Lost.* Bk. VIII.
                             L. 47.

       * * * at shut of evening flowers.
   c.   MILTON—*Paradise Lost.* Bk. IX.
                             L. 278.

Flowers of all hue, and without thorn the
    rose.
   d.   MILTON—*Paradise Lost.* Bk. IV.
                             L. 256.

The bright consummate flower.
   e.   MILTON—*Paradise Lost.* Bk. V.
                             L. 481.

The foxglove, with its stately bells
Of purple, shall adorn thy dells;
The wallflower, on each rifted rock,
From liberal blossoms shall breathe down,
(Gold blossoms frecked with iron-brown,)
Its fragrance; while the hollyhock,
The pink, and the carnation vie
With lupin and with lavender,
To decorate the fading year;
And larkspurs, many-hued, shall drive
Gloom from the groves, where red leaves lie,
And Nature seems but half alive.
   f.   D. M. MOIR—*The Birth of the Flowers.*
                             St. 14.

Crocus-cups of gold and blue,
Snowdrops drooping early.
   g.   MONTGOMERY—*The Valentine Wreath.*

The purple heath and golden broom
   On moory mountains catch the gale,
O'er lawns the lily sheds perfume,
   The violet in the vale.
   h.   MONTGOMERY—*A Field Flower.*

How the rose, of orient glow,
Mingles with the lily's snow.
   i.   MOORE—*Odes of Anacreon.* Ode LI.

The Wreath's of brightest myrtle wove
With brilliant tears of bliss among it,
And many a rose leaf cull'd by Love
To heal his lips when bees have stung it.
   j.   MOORE—*The Wreath and the Chain.*

Yet, no—not words, for they
   But half can tell love's feeling;
Sweet flowers alone can say
   What passion fears revealing:
A once bright rose's wither'd leaf,
   A tow'ring lily broken,—
Oh, these may paint a grief
   No words could e'er have spoken.
   k.   MOORE—*The Language of Flowers.*

He bore a simple wild-flower wreath:
   Narcissus, and the sweet brier rose;
Vervain, and flexile thyme, that breathe
   Rich fragrance; modest heath, that glows
With purple bells; the amaranth bright,
   That no decay, nor fading knows,
Like true love's holiest, rarest light;
   And every purest flower, that blows
In that sweet time, which Love most blesses,
   When spring on summer's confines presses.
   l.   THOMAS LOVE PEACOCK—*Rhododaphne.*
                       Canto I. L. 107.

In Eastern lands they talk in flowers,
   And they tell in a garland their loves and
     cares;
Each blossom that blooms in their garden
    bowers,
   On its leaves a mystic language bears.
   m.   PERCIVAL—*The Language of Flowers.*

Nay, tell me first, in what more happy fields,
The Thistle springs, to which the Lily yields.
   n.   POPE—*Spring.* L. 89.

Flowers preach to us if we will hear.
   o.   CHRISTINA G. ROSSETTI—*Consider the
                         Lilies of the Field.*

The lily, snowdrop, and the violet fair,
And queenly rose, that blossoms for a day.
   p.   MRS. C. M. SAWYER—*The Blind Girl.*

Here eglantine embalm'd the air,
Hawthorne and hazel mingled there;
The primrose pale, and violet flower,
Found in each cliff a narrow bower;
Fox-glove and nightshade, side by side,
Emblems of punishment and pride,
Group'd their dark hues with every stain
The weather-beaten crags retain.
   q.   SCOTT—*The Lady of the Lake.* Canto I.
                             St. 12.

The rose is fairest when 'tis budding new,
And hope is brightest when it dawns from
    fears;
The rose is sweetest wash'd with morning
    dew,
And love is loveliest when embalm'd in tears.
   r.   SCOTT—*The Lady of the Lake.*
                        Canto IV. St. 1.

                    Daffodils,
That come before the swallow dares, and take
The winds of March with beauty; violets dim,
But sweeter than the lids of Juno's eyes,
Or Cytherea's breath; pale primroses,
That die unmarried ere they can behold
Bright Phœbus in his strength—a malady
Most incident to maids; bold oxlips and
The crown-imperial; lilies of all kinds,
The flower-de-luce being one!
   s.   *Winter's Tale.* Act IV. Sc. 4. L. 118.

In emerald tufts, flowers purple, blue, and
      white;
Like sapphire, pearl and rich embroidery.
  a.   *Merry Wives of Windsor.* Act V.
                          Sc. 5. L. 74.

Quite over-canopied with luscious woodbine,
With sweet musk-roses and with eglantine.
  b.   *Midsummer-Night's Dream.* Act II.
                          Sc. 1. L. 251.

            The fairest flowers o' the season
Are our carnations and streak'd gillyvors.
  c.   *Winter's Tale.* Act IV. Sc. 4. L. 81.

    These flowers are like the pleasures of the
world.
  d.   *Cymbeline.* Act. IV. Sc. 2. L. 296.

To strew thy green with flowers; the yellows,
      blues,
The purple violets, and marigolds.
  e.   *Pericles.* Act. IV. Sc. 1. L. 15.

Faint oxlips; tender bluebells at whose birth
The sod scarce heaved.
  f.   SHELLEY—*The Question.*

There grew pied wind-flowers and violets,
    Daisies, those pearled Arcturi of the earth,
The constellated flower that never sets.
  g.   SHELLEY—*The Question.*

Day stars! that ope your frownless eyes to
      twinkle
From rainbow galaxies of earth's creation,
And dew-drops on her lonely altars sprinkle
      As a libation.
  h.   HORACE SMITH—*Hymn to the Flowers.*

Ye bright Mosaics! that with storied beauty,
    The floor of Nature's temple tesselate,
What numerous emblems of instructive duty
        Your forms create!
  i.   HORACE SMITH—*Hymn to the Flowers.*

Those few pale Autumn flowers!
    How beautiful they are!
Than all that went before,
Than all the Summer store,
    How lovelier far!
  j.   CAROLINE SOUTHEY—*Solitary Hours.*
                      Autumn Flowers.

            Roses red and violets blew,
And all the sweetest flowres that in the forrest
      grew.
  k.   SPENSER—*Faerie Queene.* Bk. III.
                          Canto VI. St. 6.

Strowe me the ground with daffadowndillies,
And cowslips, and kingcups and loved lillies.
  l.   SPENSER—*The Shepherd's Calender.*
                          Song. St. 12.

Sweet is the rose, but grows upon a brere;
Sweet is the juniper, but sharp his bough;
Sweet is the eglantine, but sticketh nere;
Sweet is the firbloome, but its braunches
      rough;
Sweet is the cypress, but its rynd is tough;
Sweet is the nut, but bitter is his pill;
Sweet is the broome-flowre, but yet sowre
      enough;
And sweet is moly, but his root is ill.
  m.   SPENSER—*Amoretti. Sonnet XXVI.*

For here the violet in the wood
    Thrills with the sweetness you shall take,
And wrapped away from life and love
    The wild rose dreams, and fain would wake.
  n.   HARRIET PRESCOTT SPOFFORD—*O Soft
                      Spring Airs!* St. 4.

The violets ope their purple heads;
The roses blow, the cowslip springs.
  o.   SWIFT—*Answer to a Scandalous Poem.*
                          L. 150.

Primrose-eyes each morning ope
In their cool, deep beds of grass;
Violets make the air that pass
Tell-tales of their fragrant slope.
  p.   BAYARD TAYLOR—*Home and Travel.*
                Ariel in the Cloven Pine. L. 57.

The amorous odors of the moveless air, —
Jasmine and tuberose and gillyflower,
Carnation, heliotrope, and purpling shower
Of Persian roses.
  q.   BAYARD TAYLOR—*The Picture of
                St. John.* Bk. II. St. 18.

With roses musky-breathed,
    And drooping daffodilly,
    And silver-leaved lily.
And ivy darkly-wreathed,
I wove a crown before her,
For her I love so dearly.
  r.   TENNYSON—*Anacreontics.*

And buttercups are coming,
    And scarlet columbine,
And in the sunny meadows
    The dandelions shine.
  s.   CELIA THAXTER—*Spring.* St. 4.

The daisy, primrose, violet darkly blue;
And polyanthus of unnumbered dyes.
  t.   THOMSON—*The Seasons. Spring.*
                          L. 529.

A love-tint flushes the wind-flower's cheek,
Rich melodies gush from the violet's beak,
On the rifts of the rock, the wild columbines
      grow,
Their heavy honey-cups bending low.
  u.   SARAH HELEN WHITMAN—
                Wood-Walks in Spring. L. 37.

But when they had unloosed the linen band,
  Which swathed the Egyptian's body,—lo!
    was found,
Closed in the wasted hollow of her hand,
  A little seed, which, sown in English ground,
Did wondrous snow of starry blossoms bear,
And spread rich odours through our spring-
    tide air.
  a.   Oscar Wilde—*Athanasia.* St. 2.

Hope smiled when your nativity was cast,
Children of Summer!
  b.   Wordsworth—*Staffa Sonnets.*
          *Flowers on the Top of the Pillars at
              the Entrance of the Cave.*

Pansies, lilies, kingcups, daisies,
Let them live upon their praises.
  c.   Wordsworth—*To the Small Celandine.*

The flower of sweetest smell is shy and lowly.
  d.   Wordsworth—*Sonnet. Not Love,
                        Not War, Nor, etc.*

There bloomed the strawberry of the wilder-
    ness;
The trembling eyebright showed her sapphire
    blue,
The thyme her purple, like the blush of Even;
And if the breath of some to no caress
Invited, forth they peeped so fair to view,
All kinds alike seemed favourites of Heaven.
  e.   Wordsworth—*The River Duddon.
                        Flowers.* VI.

To me the meanest flower that blows can give
Thoughts that do often lie too deep for tears.
  f.   Wordsworth—*Intimations of
                        Immortality.*

Part II.—Classified Flora.

Hast thou the flower there?
  g.   *Midsummer-Night's Dream.* Act II. Sc. 1. L. 247.

Amaranth.
Amarantus.

Nosegays! leave them for the waking,
Throw them earthward where they grew
Dim are such, beside the breaking
Amaranths he looks unto.
Folded eyes see brighter colors than the open
    ever do.
  h.   E. B. Browning—*A Child Asleep.*

Bid amaranthus all his beauty shed,
And daffodillies fill their cups with tears,
To strew the laureate hearse where Lycid
    lies.
  i.   Milton—*Lycidas.* L. 149.

Immortal amaranth, a flower which once
In Paradise, fast by the Tree of Life,
Began to bloom, but soon for Man's offence,
To heav'n remov'd, where first it grew, there
    grows,
And flow'rs aloft shading the fount of life.
  j.   Milton—*Paradise Lost.* Bk. III.
                                    L. 353.

Amaranths such as crown the maids
That wander through Zamara's shades.
  k.   Moore—*Lalla Rookh. Light of the
                        Harem.* L. 318.

Amaryllis.
Amaryllis.

Where, here and there, on sandy beaches
A milky-bell'd amaryllis blew.
  l.   Tennyson—*The Daisy.* St. 4.

Anemone.

                    Within the woods,
Whose young and half transparent leaves
    scarce cast
A shade, gray circles of anemones
Danced on their stalks.
  m.   Bryant—*The Old Man's Counsel.*

Thy subtle charm is strangely given,
  My fancy will not let thee be,—
Then poise not thus 'twixt earth and heaven,
  O white anemone!
  n.   Elaine Goodale—*Anemone.*

Anemone, so well
Named of the wind, to which thou art all free.
  o.   George MacDonald—*Wild Flowers.*
                                        L. 9.
Anemones and seas of gold,
  And new-blown lilies of the river,
And those sweet flow'rets that unfold
  Their buds on Camadera's quiver.
  p.   Moore—*Lalla Rookh. Light of the
                                    Harem.*

A spring upon whose brink the anemones
And hooded violets and shrinking ferns
And tremulous woodland things crowd un-
    afraid,
Sure of the refreshing that they always find.
  q.   Margaret J. Preston—*Unvisited.*

From the soft wing of vernal breezes shed,
Anemones, auriculas, enriched
With shining meal o'er all their velvet leaves.
  r.   Thomson—*The Seasons. Spring.*
                                    L. 533.

Apple Blossoms.

Underneath an apple-tree
Sat a maiden and her lover;
And the thoughts within her he
Yearned, in silence, to discover.
Round them danced the sunbeams bright,
Green the grass-lawn stretched before them,
While the apple blossoms white
Hung in rich profusion o'er them.

　a.　WILL CARLETON—*Apple Blossoms.*

Of all the months that fill the year,
　Give April's month to me,
For earth and sky are then so filled
　With sweet variety.

The apple blossoms' shower of pearl,
　Though blent with rosier hue,
As beautiful as woman's blush,
　As evanescent too.

　b.　L. E. LANDON—*Apple Blossoms.*

All day in the green, sunny orchard,
　When May was a marvel of bloom,
I followed the busy bee-lovers
Down paths that were sweet with perfume.

　c.　MARGARET E. SANGSTER—*Apple
　　　　　　　　　　　　Blossoms.*

Aquilegia.

Aquilegia Canadensis.

The aquilegia sprinkled on the rocks
　A scarlet rain; the yellow violet
Sat in the chariot of its leaves; the phlox
　Held spikes of purple flame in meadows
　　　　wet,
And all the streams with vernal-scented reed
Were fringed, and streaky bells of miskodeed.

　d.　BAYARD TAYLOR—*Home and Travel.*
　　　　　　　　　Mon-Da-Min. St. 17.

Arbutus, Trailing.

Epigea repens.

Darlings of the forest!
　Blossoming alone
When Earth's grief is sorest
　For her jewels gone—
Ere the last snow-drift melts your tender
　buds have blown.

　e.　ROSE T. COOKE—*Trailing Arbutus.*

The Mayflowers bloomed and perished,
　And the sweet June roses died!
　f.　JULIA C. R. DORR—*Margery Grey.*
　　　　　　　　　　　　　St. 18.

Now the tender, sweet arbutus
　Trails her blossom-clustered vines,
And the many-fingered cinquefoil
　In the shadow hollow twines.

　g.　DORA READ GOODALE—*May.*

Pure and perfect, sweet arbutus
Twines her rosy-tinted wreath.

　h.　ELAINE GOODALE—*The First Flowers.*

The shy little Mayflower weaves her nest,
But the south wind sighs o'er the fragrant
　　loam,
And betrays the path to her woodland home.

　i.　SARAH HELEN WHITMAN—*The Waking
　　　　　　　　　　　　of the Heart.*

Asphodel.

Asphodelus.

With her ankles sunken in asphodel
She wept for the roses of earth which fell.

　j.　E. B. BROWNING—*Calls on the Heart.*

By the streams that ever flow,
By the fragrant winds that blow
　O'er the Elysian flow'rs;
By those happy souls who dwell
In yellow mead of asphodel.

　k.　POPE—*Ode on St. Cecilia's Day.*

Aster.

Aster.

Chide me not, laborious band!
　For the idle flowers I brought;
Every aster in my hand
　Goes home loaded with a thought.

　l.　EMERSON—*The Apology.*

The Autumn wood the aster knows,
　The empty nest, the wind that grieves,
The sunlight breaking thro' the shade,
The squirrel chattering overhead,
The timid rabbits lighter tread
　Among the rustling leaves.

　m.　DORA READ GOODALE—*Asters.*

The purple asters bloom in crowds
　In every shady nook,
And ladies' eardrops deck the banks
　Of many a babbling brook.

　n.　ELAINE GOODALE—*Autumn.*

The aster greets us as we pass
With her faint smile.

　o.　SARAH HELEN WHITMAN—*A Day of
　　　　　　　　　　the Indian Summer.* L. 35.

Along the river's summer walk,
　The withered tufts of asters nod;
And trembles on its arid stalk
　The hoar plume of the golden-rod.
And on a ground of sombre fir,
And azure-studded juniper,
The silver birch its buds of purple shows,
And scarlet berries tell where bloomed the
　　sweet wild-rose!

　p.　WHITTIER—*The Last Walk in Autumn.*

Azalea.

Rhododendron.

And in the woods a fragrance rare
Of wild azaleas fills the air,
And richly tangled overhead
We see their blossoms sweet and red.

　q.　DORA READ GOODALE—*Spring Scatters
　　　　　　　　　　　　Far and Wide.*

The fair azalea bows
Beneath its snowy crest.
  a.   Sarah Helen Whitman—*She Blooms*
no More.

Baldursbra.
Anthemis Cotula.

Purer than snow in its purity,
White as the foam-crested waves of the sea,
Bloometh alone in the twilight gray,
A flower, the gods call Baldursbra.
  b.   C. C. Baldur—*Family Herald.*
Vol. XXVII. P. 260.

Basil.
Pycnanthemum.

The basil tuft, that waves
Its fragrant blossom over graves.
  c.   Moore—*Lalla Rookh. Light of the*
Harem.

Bean.
Faba.

I know the scent of bean-fields.
  d.   Jean Ingelow—*Gladys and Her*
Island. L. 231.

Bloodroot.
Sanguinaria Canadensis.

Sanguinaria from whose brittle stem
The red drops fell like blood.
  e.   Bryant—*The Fountain.*

A pure large flower of simple mold,
  And touched with soft peculiar bloom,
  Its petals faint with strange perfume,
And in their midst a disk of gold!
  f.   Elaine Goodale—*Bloodroot.*

Within the infant rind of this small flower
Poison hath residence, and medicine power:
For this, being smelt, with that part cheers
  each part:
Being tasted, slays all senses with the heart.
  g.   *Romeo and Juliet.* Act II. Sc. 3.
L. 23.

Bluebell.
Campanula rotundifolia.

Hang-head Bluebell,
Bending like Moses' sister over Moses,
Full of a secret that thou dar'st not tell!
  h.   George MacDonald— *Wild Flowers.*

Oh! roses and lilies are fair to see;
But the wild bluebell is the flower for me.
  i.   Louisa A. Meredith—*The Bluebell.*

Borage.
Borago officinalis.

The flaming rose gloomed swarthy red;
  The borage gleams more blue;
And low white flowers, with starry head,
  Glimmer the rich dusk through.
  j.   George MacDonald—*Songs of the*
Summer Night. Pt. III.

Bramble.
Rubus.

And sweete as is the brembul flour
That bereth the rede hepe.
  k.   Chaucer—*The Tale of Sir Thopas.*
L. 35.

Thy fruit full well the schoolboy knows,
  Wild bramble of the brake!
So, put thou forth thy small white rose;
  I love it for his sake.
  l.   Ebenezer Elliott—*To the Bramble*
Flower.

Buttercup.
Ranunculus.

He likes the poor things of the world the best,
I would not, therefore, if I could be rich.
It pleases him to stoop for buttercups.
  m.   E. B. Browning—*Aurora Leigh.*
Bk. IV.

All will be gay when noontide wakes anew
The buttercups, the little children's dower.
  n.   Robert Browning—*Home Thoughts*
From Abroad.

The buttercups, bright-eyed and bold,
Held up their chalices of gold
To catch the sunshine and the dew.
  o.   Julia C. R. Dorr—*Centennial Poem.*
L. 165.

Against her ankles as she trod
The lucky buttercups did nod.
  p.   Jean Ingelow—*Reflections.*

And O the buttercups! that field
  O' the cloth of gold, where pennons swam—
Where France set up his lilied shield,
  His oriflamb,
And Henry's lion-standard rolled:
  What was it to their matchless sheen,
Their million million drops of gold
  Among the green!
  q.   Jean Ingelow—*The Letter L Present.*
St. 3.

The buttercups across the field
Made sunshine rifts of splendor.
  r.   D. M. Mulock—*A Silly Song.*

When buttercups are blossoming,
  The poets sang, 'tis best to wed:
So all for love we paired in Spring—
  Blanche and I—ere youth had sped.
  s.   E. C. Stedman—*Bohemia.*

Cactus.
Cactus.

And cactuses, a queen might don,
If weary of a golden crown
And still appear as royal.
  t.   E. B. Browning—*A Flower in a Letter.*

Camomile.

Anthemis nobilis.

For though the camomile, the more it is
trodden on the faster it grows.

a.   *Henry IV.* Pt. I. Act II. Sc. 4.
L. 441.

Cardinal-flower.

Lobelia Cardinalis.

Whence is yonder flower so strangely bright?
  Would the sunset's last reflected shine
Flame so red from that dead flush of light?
  Dark with passion is its lifted line,
Hot, alive, amid the falling night.

b.   Dora Read Goodale—*Cardinal Flower.*

Carnation.

Dianthus Caryophyllus.

Carnation, purple, azure, or speck'd with gold.

c.   Milton—*Paradise Lost.* Bk. IX.
L. 429.

Cassia.

Cassia.

While cassias blossom in the zone of calms.

d.   Jean Ingelow—*Sand Martins.*

Catalpa.

Catalpa.

                  The catalpa's blossoms flew,
Light blossoms, dropping on the grass like
  snow.

e.   Bryant—*The Winds.*

Celandine.

Chelidonium.

Eyes of some men travel far
For the finding of a star;
Up and down the heavens they go,
  Men that keep a mighty rout!
I'm as great as they, I trow,
  Since the day I found thee out,
Little Flower!—I'll make a stir,
Like a sage astronomer.

f.   Wordsworth—*To the Small Celandine.*

Long as there's a sun that sets,
  Primroses will have their glory;
Long as there are violets,
  They will have a place in story:
There's a flower that shall be mine,
'Tis the little Celandine.

g.   Wordsworth—*To the Small Celandine.*

Pleasures newly found are sweet
When they lie about our feet:
February last, my heart
  First at sight of thee was glad;
All unheard of as thou art,
  Thou must needs, I think, have had,
Celandine! and long ago,
Praise of which I nothing know.

h.   Wordsworth—*To the Same Flower.*

Champac.

Michelia Champaca.

The maid of India, blessed again to hold
In her full lap the Champac's leaves of gold.

i.   Moore—*Lalla Rookh. The Veiled
Prophet of Khorassan.*

Chrysanthemum.

Chrysanthemum.

Fair gift of Friendship! and her ever bright
  And faultless image! welcome now thou
  art,
In thy pure loveliness—thy robes of white,
  Speaking a moral to the feeling heart;
Unscattered by heats—by wintry blasts un-
  moved—
Thy strength thus tested—and thy charms
  improved.

j.   Anna Peyre Dinnies—*To a White
Chrysanthemum.*

Chrysanthemums from gilded argosy
Unload their gaudy scentless merchandise.

k.   Oscar Wilde—*Humanitad.* St. 11.

Clematis.

Clematis.

Where the woodland streamlets flow,
  Gushing down a rocky bed,
Where the tasselled alders grow,
  Lightly meeting overhead,
When the fullest August days
  Give the richness that they know,
    Then the wild clematis comes,
    With her wealth of tangled blooms,
Reaching up and drooping low.
        *   *   *   *   *   *
But when Autumn days are here,
  And the woods of Autumn burn,
Then her leaves are black and sere,
  Quick with early frosts to turn!
As the golden Summer dies,
  So her silky green has fled,
    And the smoky clusters rise
    As from fires of sacrifice,—
Sacred incense to the dead!

l.   Dora Read Goodale—*Wild Clematis.*

Clover.

Trifolium.

Where the wind-rows are spread for the butterfly's bed,
And the clover-bloom falleth around.

m.   Eliza Cook—*Journal.* Vol. VII.
St. 2. *Song of the Haymakers.*

Crimson clover I discover
  By the garden gate,
And the bees about her hover,
  But the robins wait.
    Sing, robins, sing,
    Sing a roundelay,—
  'Tis the latest flower of Spring
    Coming with the May!

n.   Dora Read Goodale—*Red Clover.*

The fields have lost their lingering light,
The path is dusky thro' the night,—
The clover is too sweet to lose
Her fragrance with the gathering dews,—
The skies are warm above her.
a.   DORA READ GOODALE—*White Clover.*

Flocks thick-nibbling through the clovered
vale.
b.   THOMSON—*The Seasons. Summer.*
L. 1,235.

What airs outblown from ferny dells
And clover-bloom and sweet brier smells.
c.   WHITTIER—*The Last Walk in Autumn.*
St. 6.

Columbine.
Aquilegia Canadensis.
Or columbines, in purple dressed
Nod o'er the ground-bird's hidden nest.
d.   BRYANT—*To the Fringed Gentian.*

Skirting the rocks at the forest edge
With a running flame from ledge to ledge,
Or swaying deeper in shadowy glooms,
A smoldering fire in her dusky blooms;
Bronzed and molded by wind and sun,
Maddening, gladdening every one
With a gypsy beauty full and fine,—
A health to the crimson columbine!
e.   ELAINE GOODALE—*Columbine.*

O columbine, open your folded wrapper,
Where two twin turtle-doves dwell!
O cuckoopint, toll me the purple clapper
That hangs in your clear green bell!
f.   JEAN INGELOW—*Songs of Seven. Seven
Times One.*

Columbine, Golden.
Aquilegia Chrysantha.
Sweet flower of the golden horn,
Thy beauty passeth praise!
But why should spring thy gold adorn
Most meet for summer days?
Well may the mighty sycamore
His shelter o'er thee throw,
And spring-time winds, which elsewhere roar,
Breathe gently as they go.
g.   HENRY H. RUSBY—*To the Golden
Columbine.*

Compass-plant.
Silphium laciniatum.
Look at this vigorous plant that lifts its head
from the meadow,
See how its leaves are turned to the north, as
true as the magnet;
This is the compass-flower, that the finger of
God has planted
Here in the houseless wild, to direct the
traveller's journey
Over the sea-like, pathless, limitless waste of
the desert,
Such in the soul of man is faith.
h.   LONGFELLOW—*Evangeline. Pt. II.*
St. 4. L. 140.

15

Convolvulus.
Convolvulus.
There is an herb named in Latine Convol-
vulus (*i. e.* with wind), growing among shrubs
and bushes, which carrieth a flower not unlike to this Lilly, save that it yeeldeth no
smell nor hath those chives within; for white-
nesse they resemble one another very much,
as if Nature in making this floure were a
learning and trying her skill how to frame
the Lilly indeed.
i.   PLINY—*Natural History.* Bk. XXI.
Ch. X. Holland's trans.

Coral-tree.
Erythrina.
The crimson blossoms of the coral-tree
In the warm isles of India's sunny sea.
j.   MOORE—*Lalla Rookh.   The Veiled
Prophet of Khorassan.*

Cowslip.
Primula.
Smiled like yon knot of cowslips on a cliff.
k.   BLAIR—*The Grave.* L. 520.

Yet soon fair Spring shall give another scene,
And yellow cowslips gild the level green.
l.   ANNE E. BLEECKER—*Return to
Tomhanick.*

Methinks I hear his faint reply—
When cowslips deck the plain.
m.   WM. LISLE BOWLES—*Winter Redbreast.*

And wild-scatter'd cowslips bedeck the green
dale.
n.   BURNS—*The Chevalier's Lament.*

Ilk cowslip cup shall kep a tear.
o.   BURNS—*Elegy on Capt. Matthew
Henderson.*

The nesh yonge coweslipe bendethe wyth the
dewe.
p.   THOMAS CHATTERTON—*Rowley Poems.
Ælla.*

The cowslip is a country wench.
q.   HOOD—*Flowers.*

I sometimes wonder how I can be glad,
Even in cowslip time when hedges sprout.
r.   JEAN INGELOW—*Songs With Preludes.
Regret.*

The first wan cowslip, wet
With tears of the first morn.
s.   OWEN MEREDITH (Lord Lytton)—*Ode
to a Starling.*

Through tall cowslips nodding near you,
Just to touch you as you pass.
t.   OWEN MEREDITH (Lord Lytton)—*Song.*

Thus I set my printless feet
O'er the cowslip's velvet head,
That bends not as I tread.
   a.   MILTON—*Comus. Song.*

The cowslips tall her pensioners be;
In their gold coats spots you see:
Those be rubies, fairy favours;
In those freckles live their savours.
   b.   *Midsummer-Night's Dream.* Act II.
               Sc. 1. L. 10.

The even mead, that erst brought sweetly
   forth
The freckled cowslip, burnet and green clover.
   c.   *Henry V.* Act V. Sc. 2. L. 48.

And by the meadow-trenches blow the faint
   sweet cuckoo-flowers.
   d.   TENNYSON—*The May Queen.* St. 8.

And ye talk together still,
In the language wherewith Spring
Letters cowslips on the hill.
   e.   TENNYSON—*Adeline.* St. 5.

Crocus.
Crocus.

Welcome, wild harbinger of spring!
  To this small nook of earth;
Feeling and fancy fondly cling
  Round thoughts which owe their birth
To thee, and to the humble spot
Where chance has fixed thy lowly lot.
   f.   BERNARD BARTON—*To a Crocus.*

Hail to the King of Bethlehem,
Who weareth in his diadem
The yellow crocus for the gem
  Of his authority!
   g.   LONGFELLOW—*Christus.* Pt. II. *The
               Golden Legend.* IX.

Daffodil.
Narcissus Pseudo-Narcissus.

Brazen helm of daffodillies,
  With a glitter toward the light.
Purple violets for the mouth,
  Breathing perfumes west and south;
And a sword of flashing lilies,
  Holden ready for the fight.
   h.   E. B. BROWNING—*Hector in the Garden.*

The daffodil is our doorside queen;
She pushes upward the sword already,
  To spot with sunshine the early green.
   i.   BRYANT—*An Invitation to the Country.*

What ye have been ye still shall be
When we are dust the dust among,
   O yellow flowers!
   j.   AUSTIN DOBSON—*To Daffodils.*

Fair daffadills, we weep to see
  You haste away so soone;
As yet the early-rising sun
  Has not attained its noone.
      *   *   *   *   *
We have short time to stay as you,
  We have as short a spring;
As quick a growth to meet decay
  As you or anything.
   k.   HERRICK—*Daffadills.*

When a daffadill I see,
Hanging down his head t'wards me,
Guesse I may, what I must be:
First, I shall decline my head;
Secondly, I shall be dead:
Lastly, safely buryed.
   l.   HERRICK—*Hesperides. Divination by a
               Daffadill.*

" O fateful flower beside the rill—
The daffodil, the daffodil! "
   m.   JEAN INGELOW—*Persephone.* St. 16.

                     Daffodils,
That come before the swallow dares, and take
The winds of March with beauty.
   n.   *Winter's Tale.* Act IV. Sc. 3. L. 118.

When the face of night is fair in the dewy
   downs
And the shining daffodil dies.
   o.   TENNYSON—*Maud.* Pt. III. St. 1.

O Love-star of the unbeloved March,
  When cold and shrill,
Forth flows beneath a low, dim-lighted arch
  The wind that beats sharp crag and barren
    hill,
  And keeps unfilmed the lately torpid rill!
   p.   AUBREY DE VERE—*Ode to the Daffodil.*

Daffy-down-dilly came up in the cold,
       Through the brown mould
Although the March breezes blew keen on her
    face,
Although the white snow lay in many a place.
   q.   ANNA WARNER—*Daffy-Down-Dilly.*

There is a tiny yellow daffodil,
The butterfly can see it from afar,
Although one summer evening's dew could fill
Its little cup twice over, ere the star
Had called the lazy shepherd to his fold,
And be no prodigal.
   r.   OSCAR WILDE—*The Burden of Stys.*

A host of golden daffodils;
Beside the lake, beneath the trees,
Fluttering and dancing in the breeze.
   s.   WORDSWORTH—*I Wandered Lonely as a
               Cloud.*

Dahlia.

Dahlia.

The garden glows with dahlias large and new.
a. EBENEZER ELLIOTT—*The Vicarage.*

Daisy.

Bellis.

And a breastplate made of daisies,
  Closely fitting, leaf on leaf,
Periwinkles interlaced
  Drawn for belt about the waist;
While the brown bees, humming praises,
  Shot their arrows round the chief.
b. E. B. BROWNING—*Hector in the
                Garden.*

And open pastures, where you scarcely tell
White daisies from white dew.
c. E. B. BROWNING—*Aurora Leigh.* Bk. I.

Even thou who mournst the daisy's fate,
That fate is thine—no distant date;
Stern Ruin's ploughshare drives, elate,
          Full on thy bloom,
Till crushed beneath the furrow's weight
          Shall be thy doom!
d. BURNS—*To a Mountain Daisy.*

The daisy's for simplicity and unaffected air.
e. BURNS—*O Luve Will Venture In.*

You may wear your virtues as a crown,
  As you walk through life serenely,
And grace your simple rustic gown
  With a beauty more than queenly.
Though only one for you shall care,
  One only speak your praises;
And you never wear in your shining hair,
  A richer flower than daisies.
f. PHEBE CARY—*The Fortune in the Daisy.*

Yun daiseyd mantels ys the mountayne
  dyghte.
g. THOMAS CHATTERTON—*Rowley Poems.
                Ælla.*

That men by reason well it calle may
The daisie or elles the eye of day
The emperice, and floure of floures alle.
h. CHAUCER—*Canterbury Tales. The
          Legend of Good Women.* L. 184.

That of all the floures in the mede,
Thanne love I most these floures white and
  rede,
Suche as men callen daysyes in her toune.
i. CHAUCER—*Canterbury Tales. The
          Legend of Good Women.* L. 41.

And still at every close she would repeat
The burden of the song. The daisy is so
  sweet.
j. DRYDEN—*The Flower and the Leaf.*
                L. 366.

A tuft of daisies on a flowery lay
They saw, and thitherward they bent their
          way.
k. DRYDEN—*The Flower and the Leaf.*
                L. 360.

Ah! Bring childhood's flower!
The half-blown daisy bring.
l. EBENEZER ELLIOTT—*Flowers for the
                Heart.* L. 23.

Daisies infinite
Uplift in praise their little glowing hands,
O'er every hill that under heaven expands.
m. EBENEZER ELLIOTT—*Miscellaneous
                Poems. Spring.* L. 13.

Stoop where thou wilt, thy careless hand
  Some random bud will meet;
Thou canst not tread, but thou wilt find
  The daisy at thy feet.
n. HOOD—*Song.*

All summer she scattered the daisy leaves;
  They only mocked her as they fell.
She said: "The daisy but deceives;
  'He loves me not', 'he loves me well,'
One story no two daisies tell."
Ah foolish heart, which waits and grieves
  Under the daisy's mocking spell.
o. HELEN HUNT JACKSON—*The Sign of
                the Daisy.*

There is a flower, a little flower
  With silver crest and golden eye,
That welcomes every changing hour,
  And weathers every sky.
p. MONTGOMERY—*A Field Flower.*

The Rose has but a Summer reign,
The daisy never dies.
q. MONTGOMERY—*The Daisy. On Finding
          One in Bloom on Christmas Day.*

Bright flowers, whose home is everywhere
Bold in maternal nature's care
And all the long year through the heir
  Of joy and sorrow,
Methinks that there abides in thee
Some concord with humanity,
Given to no other flower I see
  The forest through.
r. WORDSWORTH—*To the Daisy.*

The poet's darling.
s. WORDSWORTH—*To the Daisy.*

Thou unassuming Commonplace
Of Nature.
t. WORDSWORTH—*To the Same Flower.*

We meet thee, like a pleasant thought,
When such are wanted.
    a.   WORDSWORTH—*To the Daisy.*

Daisy, Ox-eye.
Chrysanthemum Leucanthemum.

Clear and simple in white and gold,
  Meadow blossom, of sunlit spaces,—
The field is full as it well can hold
  And white with the drift of the ox-eye
    daisies!
    b.   DORA READ GOODALE—*Daisies.*

Dandelion.
Taraxacum Dens-leonis.

You cannot forget if you would those golden
kisses all over the cheeks of the meadow,
queerly called *dandelions.*
    c.   HENRY WARD BEECHER—*Star Papers.*
                      A Discourse of Flowers.

Upon a showery night and still,
  Without a sound of warning,
A trooper band surprised the hill,
  And held it in the morning.
We were not waked by bugle notes,
  No cheer our dreams invaded,
And yet at dawn, their yellow coats
  On the green slopes paraded.
    d.   HELEN GRAY CONE—*The Dandelions.*

Dear common flower, that grow'st beside the
    way,
  Fringing the dusty road with harmless gold,
First pledge of blithesome May,
  Which children pluck, and, full of pride,
    uphold,
High-hearted buccaneers, o'erjoyed that they
  An Eldorado in the grass have found,
  Which not the rich earth's ample round
May match in wealth, thou art more dear
    to me
Than all the prouder summer-blooms may be.
    e.   LOWELL—*To the Dandelion.*

Young Dandelion
  On a hedge-side,
Said young Dandelion,
  Who'll be my bride?

Said young Dandelion
  With a sweet air,
I have my eye on
  Miss Daisy fair.
    f.   D. M. MULOCK—*Young Dandelion.*

Dittany.
Cunila Mariana.

There blossomed suddenly a magic bed
Of sacred dittany.
    g.   KEATS—*Endymion.* Bk. I. L. 561.

Dodder.
Cuscuta.

In the roadside thicket hiding,
  Sing, robin, sing!
See the yellow dodder, gliding,
  Ring, bluebells, ring!
Like a living skein inlacing,
Coiling, climbing, turning, chasing,
Through the fragrant sweet-fern racing—
  Laugh, O murmuring Spring!
    h.   SARAH F. DAVIS—*Summer Song.*

Flag.
Iris.

The yellow flags * * * would stand
Up to their chins in water.
    i.   JEAN INGELOW—*Song of the Night*
                    Watches. Watch I.

And nearer to the river's trembling edge
  There grew broad flag-flowers, purple,
    prankt with white;
And starry river buds among the sedge;
  And floating water-lilies, broad and bright.
    j.   SHELLEY—*The Question.*

Flower-de-Luce.
Iris.

Born in the purple, born to joy and pleasance,
  Thou dost not toil nor spin,
But makest glad and radiant with thy pres-
    ence
  The meadow and the lin.
    k.   LONGFELLOW—*Flower-de-Luce.* St. 3.

O flower-de-luce, bloom on, and let the river
  Linger to kiss thy feet!
O flower of song, bloom on, and make for-
    ever
  The world more fair and sweet.
    l.   LONGFELLOW—*Flower-de-Luce.* St. 8.

    Lilies of all kinds,
The flower-de-luce being one!
    m.   *Winters' Tale.* Act IV. Sc. 4. L. 126.

Forget-me-not.
Myosotis.

That blue and bright-eyed floweret of the
    brook,
Hope's gentle gem, the sweet Forget-me-not.
    n.   COLERIDGE—*The Keepsake.*

And rose with aspect almost calm,
  And filled her hand
With cherry-bloom, and moved away
  To gather wild forget-me-not.
    o.   JEAN INGELOW—*The Letter L Absent.*
                              St. 22.

Forget-me-not, and violets, heavenly blue,
Spring, glittering with the cheerful drops
  like dew.
    p.   N. MÜLLER—*The Paradise of Tears.*
                        Trans. by Bryant.

The sweet forget-me-nots,
That grow for happy lovers.
   a.   TENNYSON—*The Brook.* L. 172.

Foxglove.
Digitalis.
An empty sky, a world of heather,
  Purple of foxglove, yellow of broom;
We two among them wading together,
  Shaking out honey, treading perfume.
   b.   JEAN INGELOW—*Divided.* Pt. I.

Furze.
Ulex.
With blossom'd furze unprofitably gay.
   c.   GOLDSMITH—*The Deserted Village.*
                       L. 194.

Gentian.
Gentiana.
And the blue gentian-flower, that, in the
  breeze,
Nods lonely, of her beauteous race the last.
   d.   BRYANT—*November.*

Thou blossom! bright with autumn dew,
And colour'd with the heaven's own blue,
That openest when the quiet light
Succeeds the keen and frosty night.
   e.   BRYANT—*To the Fringed Gentian.*

Along this quiet wood road, winding slow,
  When free October ranged its sylvan ways,
And, vaulting up the terraced steep below,
  Chased laughing sunbeams thro' the golden
    days,
In matchless beauty, tender and serene,
The gentian reigned, an undisputed queen.
   f.   ELAINE GOODALE—*Fringed Gentian.*

Blue thou art, intensely blue;
Flower, whence came thy dazzling hue?
   g.   MONTGOMERY—*The Gentianella.*

Beside the brook and on the umbered meadow,
  Where yellow fern-tufts fleck the faded
    ground,
With folded lids beneath their palmy shadow
  The gentian nods in dewy slumbers bound.
   h.   SARAH HELEN WHITMAN—*A Still Day
                 in Autumn.* St. 6.

Near where yon rocks the stream inurn
The lonely gentian blossoms still.
   i.   SARAH HELEN WHITMAN—*Evening on
    the Banks of the Moshassuck.* St. 3.

Gillyflower.
Matthiola.
  The fairest flowers o'the season
Are our carnations and streak'd gillyvors,
Which some call nature's bastards.
       *   *   *   *   *
Then make your garden rich in gillyvors,
And do not call them bastards.
   j.   *Winter's Tale.* Act IV. Sc. 3. L. 81.

Bring hether the pincke and purple cullambine,
With gelliflowres.
   k.   SPENSER—*The Shepherd's Calendar.*
                   Song. St. 12.

Goldenrod.
Solidago.
Still the Goldenrod of the roadside clod
  Is of all, the best!
   l.   SIMEON TUCKER CLARK—*Goldenrod.*

I lie amid the Goldenrod,
I love to see it lean and nod;
I love to feel the grassy sod
Whose kindly breast will hold me last,
Whose patient arms will fold me fast!—
Fold me from sunshine and from song,
Fold me from sorrow and from wrong:
Through gleaming gates of Goldenrod
I'll pass into the rest of God.
   m.   MARY CLEMMER—*Goldenrod.*
                   Last stanza.

Nature lies disheveled, pale,
  With her feverish lips apart,—
Day by day the pulses fail,
  Nearer to her bounding heart;
Yet that slackened grasp doth hold
Store of pure and genuine gold;
Quick thou comest, strong and free,
Type of all the wealth to be,—
    Goldenrod!
   n.   ELAINE GOODALE—*Goldenrod.*

    I know the lands are lit
With all the autumn blaze of Goldenrod.
   o.   HELEN HUNT JACKSON—*Asters and
                   Goldenrod.*

Because its myriad glimmering plumes
  Like a great army's stir and wave;
Because its golden billows blooms,
  The poor man's barren walks to lave:
Because its sun-shaped blossoms show
  How souls receive the light of God,
And unto earth give back that glow—
  I thank Him for the Goldenrod.
   p.   LUCY LARCOM—*Goldenrod.*

Welcome, dear Goldenrod, once more,
  Thou mimic, flowering elm!
I always think that Summer's store
  Hangs from thy laden stem.
   q.   HORACE H. SCUDDER—*To the Goldenrod
                 at Midsummer.*

The hollows are heavy and dank
  With the steam of the Goldenrods.
   r.   BAYARD TAYLOR—*The Guests of Night.*

Graceful, tossing plume of glowing gold,
  Waving lonely on the rocky ledge;
Leaning seaward, lovely to behold,
  Clinging to the high cliff's ragged edge.
   s.   CELIA THAXTER—*Seaside Goldenrod.*

Gorse.
Ulex.

Mountain gorses, do ye teach us

* * * * * *

That the wisest word man reaches
Is the humblest he can speak?
  a.   E. B. BROWNING—*Lessons from the
                        Gorse.*

Mountain gorses, ever-golden.
Cankered not the whole year long!
Do ye teach us to be strong,
Howsoever pricked and holden
Like your thorny blooms and so
Trodden on by rain and snow,
Up the hillside of this life, as bleak as where
  ye grow?
  b.   E. B. BROWNING—*Lessons from the
                        Gorse.*

Love you not, then, to list and hear
The crackling of the gorse-flower near,
Pouring an orange-scented tide
Of fragrance o'er the desert wide?
  c.   WM. HOWITT—*A June Day.*

                But I have seen
The gay gorse bushes in their flowering time.
  d.   JEAN INGELOW—*Gladys and her Island.*
                        L. 240.

Harebell.
Campanula rotundifolia.

In the hemlock's fragrant shadow
Harebells nod by the drowsy pool.
  e.   JULIA C. R. DORR—*The Ghost.*

The harebell trembled on its stem
Down where the rushing waters gleam.
  f.   JULIA C. R. DORR—*Centennial Poem.*
                        L. 161.

I love the fair lilies and roses so gay,
They are rich in their pride and their splen-
    dor;
But still more do I love to wander away
    To the meadow so sweet,
    Where down at my feet,
The harebell blooms modest and tender.
  g.   DORA READ GOODALE—*Queen Harebell.*

With drooping bells of clearest blue
Thou didst attract my childish view,
    Almost resembling
The azure butterflies that flew
Where on the heath thy blossoms grew
    So lightly trembling.
  h.   BISHOP HEBER—*The Harebell.*

Simplest of blossoms! To mine eye
Thou bring'st the summer's painted sky;
The May-thorn greening in the nook;
The minnows sporting in the brook;
The bleat of flocks; the breath of flowers;
The song of birds amid the bowers;
The crystal of the azure seas;
The music of the southern breeze;
And, over all, the blessed sun,
Telling of halcyon days begun.
  i.   MOIR—*The Harebell.*

High in the clefts of the rock 'mid the cedars
Hangeth the harebell the waterfall nigh;
Blue are its petals, deep-blue tinged with
    purple,
Mystical tintings that mirror the sky.
  j.   L. D. PYCHOWSKA—*Harebells.*

                Thou shalt not lack
The flower that's like thy face, pale primrose,
    nor
The azur'd harebell, like thy veins.
  k.   *Cymbeline.* Act IV. Sc. 2. L. 220.

Heath.
Erica.

E'en wild heath displays her purple dyes,
And 'midst the desert fruitful fields arise.
  l.   POPE—*Windsor Forest.* L. 25.

And oft, with bolder wing, they, soaring, dare
The purple heath.
  m.   THOMSON—*The Seasons. Spring.*
                        L. 511.

Heliotrope.
Heliotropium.

While heliotropes with meekly lifted brow,
Say to me: "Go not yet."
  n.   JULIA C. R. DORR—*Without and Within.*

I drink deep draughts of its nectar.
  o.   E. C. STEDMAN—*Heliotrope.*

O sweetest of all the flowrets
    That bloom where angels tread!
But never such marvelous odor,
    From heliotrope was shed.
  p.   E. C. STEDMAN—*Heliotrope.*

Hepatica.
Hepatica.

All the woodland path is broken
    By warm tints along the way,
    And the low and sunny slope
    Is alive with sudden hope
When there comes the silent token
    Of an April day,—
        Blue hepatica!
  q.   DORA READ GOODALE—*Hepatica.*

Hollyhock.
Althea Rosea.

And Queen hollyhocks,
With butterflies for crowns.
  r.   JEAN INGELOW—*Honors.* Pt. I.

Honeysuckle.
Lonicera.

Around in silent grandeur stood
The stately children of the wood;
Maple and elm and towering pine
Mantled in folds of dark woodbine.
  s.   JULIA C. R. DORR—*At the Gate.*

A honeysuckle link'd
Around, with its red tendrils and pink
  flowers.
a.   L. E. Landon—*The Oak.* L. 15.

I sat me down to watch upon a bank
With ivy canopied and interwove
With flaunting honeysuckle.
b.   Milton—*Comus.* L. 543.

I plucked a honeysuckle where
  The hedge on high is quick with thorn,
  And climbing for the prize, was torn,
And fouled my feet in quag-water;
  And by the thorns and by the wind
  The blossom that I took was thinn'd,
And yet I found it sweet and fair.
c.   D. G. Rossetti—*The Honeysuckle.*

And honeysuckle loved to crawl
Up the low crag and ruin'd wall.
d.   Scott—*Marmion.* Canto III.
                  Introduction.

And bid her steal into the pleached bower,
Where honeysuckles, ripen'd by the sun,
Forbid the sun to enter, like favorites,
Made proud by princes, that advance their
    pride
Against that power that bred it.
e.   *Much Ado About Nothing.* Act III.
                Sc. 1. L. 7.

The honeysuckle round the porch has woven
  its wavy bowers.
f.   Tennyson—*The May Queen.* St. 8.

Hyacinth.
Hyacinthus.

The hyacinth for constancy wi' its unchanging blue.
g.   Burns—*O Luve Will Venture In.*

Come, evening gale! the crimsonne rose
  Is drooping for thy sighe of dewe;
The hyacinthe wooes thy kisse to close
  In slumberre sweete its eye of blue.
h.   George Croly—*Inscription for a*
                     Grotto.

By field and by fell, and by mountain gorge,
Shone Hyacinths blue and clear.
i.   Lucy Hooper—*Legends of Flowers.*
                      St. 3.

Here hyacinths of heavenly blue
Shook their rich tresses to the morn.
j.   Montgomery—*The Adventure of a Star.*

And the hyacinth purple, and white, and blue,
Which flung from its bells a sweet peal anew
Of music so delicate, soft, and intense,
It was felt like an odour within the sense.
k.   Shelley—*The Sensitive Plant.* Pt. I.

Indian Pipe.
Monotropa Uniflora.

Pale, mournful flower, that hidest in shade
Mid dewy damps and murky glade,
With moss and mould,
Why dost thou hang thy ghastly head,
So sad and cold?
l.   Catherine E. Beecher—*To the*
          Monotropa, or Ghost Flower.

Where the long, slant rays are beaming,
Where the shadows cool lie dreaming,
Pale the Indian pipes are gleaming—
  Laugh, O murmuring Spring!
m.   Sarah F. Davis—*Summer Song.*

      I hear, I hear
The twang of harps, the leap
Of fairy feet and know the revel's ripe,
While like a coral stripe
The lizard cool doth creep,
Monster, but monarch there, up the pale In-
  dian Pipe.
n.   Charles De Kay—*Arcana Sylvarum.*

    Death in the wood,—
In the death-pale lips apart;
  Death in a whiteness that curdled the
    blood,
Now black to the very heart:
  The wonder by her was formed
Who stands supreme in power;
  To show that life by the spirit comes
She gave us a soulless flower!
o.   Elaine Goodale—*Indian Pipe.* St. 4.

Iris.
Iris.

Iris all hues, roses and jessamin.
p.   Milton—*Paradise Lost.* Bk. IV.
                      L. 698.

Ivy.
Hedera Helix.

For ivy climbs the crumbling hall
To decorate decay.
q.   Bailey—*Festus.* Sc. *A Large Party*
                 and Entertainment.

That headlong ivy! not a leaf will grow
But thinking of a wreath, * * *
I like such ivy; bold to leap a height
'Twas strong to climb! as good to grow on
    graves
As twist about a thyrsus; pretty too
(And that's not ill) when twisted round a
    comb.
r.   E. B. Browning—*Aurora Leigh.*
                    Bk. II.

Walls must get the weather stain
Before they grow the ivy.
s.   E. B. Browning—*Aurora Leigh.*
                  Bk. VIII.

The rugged trees are mingling
Their flowery sprays in love;
The ivy climbs the laurel
To clasp the boughs above.
  a.   BRYANT—*The Serenade.*

As creeping ivy clings to wood or stone,
And hides the ruin that it feeds upon.
  b.   COWPER—*The Progress of Error.*
                     L. 285.

Oh, a dainty plant is the ivy green,
That creepeth o'er ruins old!
Of right choice food are his meals I ween,
In his cell so lone and cold.
     *   *   *   *   *   *
Creeping where no life is seen,
A rare old plant is the ivy green.
  c.   DICKENS—*Pickwick.* Ch. VI.

                    Direct
The clasping ivy where to climb.
  d.   MILTON—*Paradise Lost.* Bk. IX.
                     L. 216.

On my velvet couch reclining
Ivy leaves my brow entwining,
While my soul expands with glee,
What are kings and crowns to me?
  e.   MOORE—*Odes of Anacreon.*
                  Ode *XLVIII.*

Bring, bring the madding Bay, the drunken
  vine;
The creeping, dirty, courtly Ivy join.
  f.   POPE—*The Dunciad.* Bk. I. L. 303.

Round broken columns clasping ivy twin'd.
  g.   POPE—*Windsor Forest.* L. 69.

Where round some mould'ring tow'r pale ivy
  creeps,
And low-brow'd rocks hang nodding o'er the
  deeps.
  h.   POPE—*Eloisa to Abelard.* L. 243.

Jasmine.
Jasminum.

And at my silent window-sill
The jessamine peeps in.
  i.   BRYANT—*The Hunter's Serenade.*

         And across the porch
Thick jasmins twined.
  j.   COLERIDGE—*Reflections on Leaving a
               Place of Retirement.*

Where the golden stars of the jasmine glow,
And the roses bloom alway!
  k.   JULIA C. R. DORR—*My Mocking Bird.*

Jasmine is sweet, and has many loves.
  l.   HOOD—*Flowers.*

It was a jasmine bower, all bestrown
With golden moss.
  m.   KEATS—*Endymion.* Bk. II. L. 686.

Jas in the Arab language is despair,
And *Min* the darkest meaning of a lie.
Thus cried the Jessamine among the flowers,
    How justly doth a lie
    Draw on its head despair!
Among the fragrant spirits of the bowers
The boldest and the strongest still was I.
    Although so fair,
    Therefore from Heaven
A stronger perfume unto me was given
Than any blossom of the summer hours.
   *   *   *   *   *   *
Among the flowers no perfume is like mine;
  That which is best in me comes from
    within.
So those who in this world would rise and
  shine
Should seek internal excellence to win.
And though 'tis true that falsehood and
  despair
Meet in my name, yet bear it still in mind
That where they meet they perish. All is fair
When they are gone and nought remains
  behind.
  n.   LELAND—*Jessamine.*

And the jasmine flower in her fair young
  breast,
  (O the faint, sweet smell of that jasmine
    flower!)
And the one bird singing alone to his nest.
  And the one star over the tower.
  o.   OWEN MEREDITH (Lord Lytton)—
               Aux Italiens. St. 13.

It smelt so faint, and it smelt so sweet
  It made me creep and it made me cold.
Like the scent that steals from the crumbling
  sheet
  Where a mummy is half unroll'd.
  p.   OWEN MEREDITH (Lord Lytton)—
                  Aux Italiens.

Out in the lonely woods the jasmine burns
Its fragrant lamps, and turns
Into a royal court with green festoons
The banks of dark lagoons.
  q.   HENRY TIMROD—*Spring.*

Kingcup (Buttercup).
Ranunculus.

The royal kingcup bold
Dares not don his coat of gold.
  r.   EDWIN ARNOLD—*Almond Blossoms.*

With kingcups and daisies, that all the year
  please,
Sprays, petals, and leaflets, that nod in the
  breeze.
  s.   COLERIDGE—*Morning Invitation to a
                   Child.*

Fair is the kingcup that in meadow blows,
Fair is the daisy that beside her grows.
  t.   GAY—*Shepherd's Week. Monday.*
                      L. 43.

The gold-eyed kingcups fine,
The frail bluebell peereth over
Rare broidery of the purple clover.
　a.　TENNYSON—*A Dirge.* St. VI.

Laurel.
Laurus.

Wait till the laurel bursts its buds,
　And creeping ivy flings its graces
About the lichen'd rocks, and floods
　Of sunshine fill the shady places.
　b.　MARGARET J. PRESTON—*Through the Pass.*

This flower that smells of honey and the sea,
White laurustine, seems in my hand to be
　A white star made of memory long ago
Lit in the heaven of dear times dead to me.
　c.　SWINBURNE—*Relics.*

Lily.
Lilium.

I like not lady-slippers,
Nor yet the sweet-pea blossoms,
Nor yet the flaky roses,
　Red or white as snow;
I like the chaliced lilies,
The heavy Eastern lilies,
The gorgeous tiger-lilies,
　That in our garden grow.
　d.　T. B. ALDRICH—*Tiger Lilies.* St. 1.

Blossoms, all around me sighing,
Fragrance, from the lilies straying.
　e.　MARIA BROOKS—*Song of Egla.*

　　　And lilies are still lilies, pulled
By smutty hands, though spotted from their
　white.
　f.　E. B. BROWNING—*Aurora Leigh.*
　　　　　　　　　　　Bk. III.

And lilies white, prepared to touch
The whitest thought, nor soil it much,
Of dreamer turned to lover.
　g.　E. B. BROWNING—*A Flower in a Letter.*

* * * purple lilies Dante blew
To a larger bubble with his prophet breath.
　h.　E. B. BROWNING—*Aurora Leigh.*
　　　　　　　　　　　Bk. VII.

　　　Very whitely still
The lilies of our lives may reassure
Their blossoms from their roots, accessible
Alone to heavenly dews that drop not fewer;
Growing straight out of man's reach, on the
　hill
God only, who made us rich, can make us
　poor.
　i.　E. B. BROWNING—*Sonnets from the Portuguese.* XXIV.

　　　The milk-white lilies,
That lean from the fragrant ledge.
　j.　ALICE CARY—*Pictures of Memory.*

The citron-tree or spicy grove for me would
　never yield
A perfume half so grateful as the lilies of the
　field.
　k.　ELIZA COOK—*Journal. England.*
　　　　　　　　　　　Vol. IV. St. 2.

Darlings of June, and brides of summer sun,
　Chill pipes the stormy wind, the skies are
　drear;
Dull and despoiled the gardens every one:
　What do you here?
　l.　SUSAN COOLIDGE—*Easter Lilies.*

I wish I were the lily's leaf
　To fade upon that bosom warm,
Content to wither, pale and brief,
　The trophy of thy paler form.
　m.　DIONYSIUS.

And the stately lilies stand
　Fair in the silvery light,
Like saintly vestals, pale in prayer;
　Their pure breath sanctifies the air,
As its fragrance fills the night.
　n.　JULIA C. R. DORR—*A Red Rose.*

Yet, the great ocean hath no tone of power
Mightier to reach the soul, in thought's
　hushed hour,
Than yours, ye Lilies! chosen thus and
　graced!
　o.　MRS. HEMANS—*Sonnet. The Lilies of the Field.*

The lily is all in white, like a saint,
And so is no mate for me.
　p.　HOOD—*Flowers.*

We are Lilies fair,
　The flower of virgin light;
Nature held us forth, and said,
　"Lo! my thoughts of white."
　q.　LEIGH HUNT—*Songs and Chorus of the Flowers. Lilies.*

And round about them grows a fringe of
　reeds,
And then a floating crown of lily-flowers.
　r.　JEAN INGELOW—*The Four Bridges.*

The hallowed lilies of the field
　In glory are arrayed,
And timid, blue-eyed violets yield
　Their fragrance to the shade.
　s.　E. C. KINNEY—*The Spirit of Song.*
　　　　　　　　　　　St. 4.

"Look to the lilies how they grow!"
'Twas thus the Saviour said, that we,
Even in the simplest flowers that blow,
　God's ever-watchful care might see.
　t.　MOIR—*Lilies.*

For her, the lilies hang their heads and die.
a.   POPE—*Pastorals. Autumn.* L. 26.

Gracious as sunshine, sweet as dew
  Shut in a lily's golden core.
b.   MARGARET J. PRESTON—*Agnes.*

The creamy leaf the pasture lily shows.
c.   MARGARET J. PRESTON—*Fra Angelico.*
                              St. 10.

  Is not this lily pure?
  What fuller can procure
A white so perfect, spotless clear
As in this flower doth appear?
d.   QUARLES—*The School of the Heart.*
                         Ode XXX. St. 4.

                   ow bravely thou becomest thy bed, fresh lily.
e.   *Cymbeline*—Act II. Sc. 2. L. 15.

                         Like the lily,
That once was mistress of the field and
      flourish'd,
I'll hang my head and perish.
f.   *Henry VIII.* Act III. Sc. 1. L. 151.

And the wand-like lily which lifted up,
As a Mænad, its moonlight-coloured cup,
Till the fiery star, which is its eye,
Gazed through clear dew on the tender sky.
g.   SHELLEY—*The Sensitive Plant.* Pt. I.

"Thou wert not, Solomon! in all thy glory,
Array'd," the lilies cry, "in robes like ours;
How vain your grandeur! Ah, how transitory
Are human flowers!"
h.   HORACE SMITH—*Hymn to the Flowers.*
                              St. 10.

A pure, cool lily, bending
Near the rose all flushed and warm.
i.   ELIZA L. SPROAT—*Guonare.*

But who will watch my lilies,
  When their blossoms open white?
By day the sun shall be sentry,
  And the moon and the stars by night!
j.   BAYARD TAYLOR—*The Poet's Journal.*
                The Garden of Roses. St. 14.

But lilies, stolen from grassy mold,
No more curlèd state unfold,
Translated to a vase of gold;
In burning throne though they keep still
Serenities unthawed and chill.
k.   FRANCIS THOMPSON—*Gilded Gold.* St. 1.

Yet in that bulb, those sapless scales,
  The lily wraps her silver vest,
Till vernal suns and vernal gales
  Shall kiss once more her fragrant breast.
l.   MARY TIGHE—*The Lily.*

Lily-of-the-valley.
Convallaria Majalis.

The lily of the vale, of flowers the queen,
Puts on the robe she neither sew'd nor spun.
m.   MICHAEL BRUCE—*Elegy.*

White bud! that in meek beauty dost lean
  Thy cloistered cheek as pale as moonlight
      snow,
Thou seem'st, beneath thy huge, high leaf of
      green,
  An Eremite beneath his mountain's brow.
n.   GEORGE CROLY—*The Lily of the Valley.*

            And in his left he held a basket full
Of all sweet herbs that searching eye could
      cull
Wild thyme, and valley-lilies whiter still
Than Leda's love, and cresses from the rill.
o.   KEATS—*Endymion.* Bk. I. L. 155.

And the Naiad-like lily of the vale,
  Whom youth makes so fair and passion so
      pale,
That the light of its tremulous bells is seen,
Through their pavilions of tender green.
p.   SHELLEY—*The Sensitive Plant.* Pt. I.

The broad-leaf'd lily of the vale,
And the meek forget-me-not.
q.   LYDIA SIGOURNEY—*Farewell to a Rural
                              Residence.*

Where scattered wild the Lily of the Vale
Its balmy essence breathes.
r.   THOMSON—*The Seasons. Spring.*
                              L. 445.

            And leaves of that shy plant,
(Her flowers were shed) the lily of the vale.
That loves the ground, and from the sun
      withholds
Her pensive beauty, from the breeze her
      sweets.
s.   WORDSWORTH—*The Excursion.*
                         Bk. IX. L. 540

Lotus.
Nymphæa Lotus.

The lotus flower is troubled
  At the sun's resplendent light;
With sunken head and sadly
  She dreamily waits for the night.
t.   HEINE—*Book of Songs. Lyrical
                         Interlude.* No. 10.

Lotos, the name; divine, nectareous juice!
u.   HOMER—*Odyssey.* Bk. 9. L. 106.
                         Pope's trans.

Stone lotus cups, with petals dipped in sand.
v.   JEAN INGELOW—*Gladys and her Island.*
                              L. 460.

The Lotos blooms below the barren peak :
The Lotos blooms by every winding creek :
All day the wind breathes low with mellower
    tone :
Thro' every hollow cave and alley lone,
Round and round the spicy downs the yellow
    Lotos-dust is blown.
  a.   TENNYSON—*The Lotos-Eaters. Choric
                Song. St. 8.*

In that dusk land of mystic dream
  Where dark Osiris sprung,
It bloomed beside his sacred stream
  While yet the world was young ;
And every secret Nature told,
  Of golden wisdom's power,
Is nestled still in every fold,
  Within the Lotos flower.
  b.   WM. WINTER—*A Lotos Flower.*

Love Lies Bleeding.
Amarantus Caudatus.
Love lies bleeding in the bed whereover
  Roses lean with smiling mouths or pleading :
Earth lies laughing where the sun's dart clove
  her :
  Love lies bleeding.
  c.   SWINBURNE—*Love Lies Bleeding.*

This flower that first appeared as summer's
  guest
Preserves her beauty 'mid autumnal leaves
And to her mournful habits fondly cleaves.
  d.   WORDSWORTH—*Love Lies Bleeding.*
                (Companion Poem.)

Magnolia Grandiflora.
Magnolia.
Majestic flower ! How purely beautiful
  Thou art, as rising from thy bower of green,
Those dark and glossy leaves so thick and full,
  Thou standest like a high-born forest queen
Among thy maidens clustering round so fair;—
  I love to watch thy sculptured form un-
  folding,
And look into thy depths, to image there
  A fairy cavern, and while thus beholding,
And while thy breeze floats o'er thee, match-
  less flower,
  I breathe the perfume, delicate and strong,
That comes like incense from thy petal-bower;
  My fancy roams those southern woods
  along,
Beneath that glorious tree, where deep among
  The unsunned leaves thy large white flower-
  cups hung !
  e.   C. P. CRANCH—*Poem to the
              Magnolia Grandiflora.*

Mallow.
Malva.
Alas ! alas ! when in a garden fair
Mallows, crisp dill, or parsley yields to fate,
These with another year regerminate.
  f.   MOSCHUS—*Idyll III.*

Marigold.
Tagetes.
The marigold, whose courtier's face
Echoes the sun, and doth unlace
Her at his rise, at his full stop
Packs and shuts up her gaudy shop.
  g.   JOHN CLEVELAND—*On Phillis Walking
                       Before Sunrise.*

The marigold abroad her leaves doth spread,
Because the sun's and her power is the same.
  h.   HENRY CONSTABLE—*Diana.*

No marigolds yet closed are,
No shadowes great appeare.
  i.   HERRICK—*Hesperides. To Daisies.
               Not to Shut so Soone.*

Open afresh your round of starry folds,
Ye ardent marigolds !
Dry up the moisture from your golden lips.
  j.   KEATS—*I Stood Tiptoe Upon a Little
                        Hill.*

The sun-observing marigold.
  k.   QUARLES—*The School of the Heart.
               Ode XXX. St. 5.*

Nor shall the marigold unmentioned die,
Which Acis once found out in Sicily ;
She Phœbus loves, and from him draws his
  hue,
And ever keeps his golden beams in view.
  l.   RAPIN—*In His Latin Poem on Gardens.
           Trans. by Gardiner in 1706.*

And winking Mary-buds begin
To ope their golden eyes.
  m.   *Cymbeline.* Act II. Sc. 3. *Song.*
                        L. 25.

        Here's flowers for you :
Hot lavender, mints, savory, marjoram :
The marigold, that goes to bed wi' the sun,
And with him rises weeping.
  n.   *Winter's Tale.* Act IV. Sc. 4. L. 103.

When with a serious musing I behold
The graceful and obsequious marigold,
How duly every morning she displays
Her open breast, when Titan spreads his rays.
  o.   GEORGE WITHER—*The Marigold.*

Marsh Marigold.
Caltha Palustris.
And in yonder marshes burns
The fiery-flaming marigold.
  p.   DORA READ GOODALE—*May.*

The seal and guerdon of wealth untold
We clasp in the wild marsh marigold.
  q.   ELAINE GOODALE—*Nature's Coinage.*

Fair is the marigold, for pottage meet.
  r.   GAY—*Shepherd's Week. Monday.*
                        L. 46.

A little marsh-plant, yellow green,
  And prick'd at lip with tender red.
  Tread close, and either way you tread,
Some faint black water jets between
  Lest you should bruise the curious head.
  a.   SWINBURNE—*The Sundew.*

Meadow Rue.
Thalictrum.

When emerald slopes are drowned in song,
  When weary grows the unclouded blue,
When warm winds sink in billowy bloom,
And flood you with a faint perfume,
One moment leave the rapturous throng
  To seek the haunts of meadow rue !
  b.   ELAINE GOODALE—*Meadow Rue.*

Mignonette.
Reseda Odorata.

Here bloom red roses, dewy wet,
And beds of fragrant mignonette.
  c.   ELAINE GOODALE—*Thistles and Roses.*

Moccasin Flower.
Cypripedium.

With careless joy we thread the woodland
    ways
    And reach her broad domain.
Thro' sense of strength and beauty, free as air.
    We feel our savage kin,—
And thus alone with conscious meaning wear
    The Indian's moccasin !
  d.   ELAINE GOODALE—*Moccasin Flower.*

Morning-Glory.
Ipomœa.

                Wondrous interlacement !
Holding fast to threads by green and silky
    rings,
With the dawn it spreads its white and pur-
    ple wings ;
Generous in its bloom, and sheltering while it
    clings,
    Sturdy morning-glory.
  e.   HELEN HUNT—*Verses. Morning-Glory.*

The morning-glory's blossoming
  Will soon be coming round ;
We see their rows of heart-shaped leaves
  Upspringing from the ground.
  f.   MARIA WHITE LOWELL—*The Morning-
                                Glory.*

Myrtle.
Myrtus Communis.

Nor myrtle—which means chiefly love : and
    love
Is something awful which one dare not touch
So early o' mornings.
  g.   E. B. BROWNING—*Aurora Leigh.*
                                Bk. II.

          In the open air
Our myrtles blossomed.
  h.   COLERIDGE—*Reflections on Leaving a
                        Place of Retirement.*

The myrtle (ensign of supreme command,
Consigned by Venus to Melissa's hand)
Not less capricious than a reigning fair,
Oft favors, oft rejects a lover's prayer ;
In myrtle shades oft sings the happy swain
In myrtle shades despairing ghosts complain.
  i.   SAM'L JOHNSON—*Written at the Request
                        of a Gentleman.* L. 3.

Dark-green and gemm'd with flowers of snow,
  With close uncrowded branches spread
Not proudly high, nor meanly low,
  A graceful myrtle rear'd its head.
  j.   MONTGOMERY—*The Myrtle.*

While the myrtle, now idly entwin'd with his
    crown.
Like the wreath of Harmodius, shall cover his
    sword.
  k.   MOORE—*O, Blame Not The Bard.*

Orchid.
Orchis.

In the marsh pink orchid's faces,
  With their coy and dainty graces,
  Lure us to their hiding places—
    Laugh, O murmuring Spring !
  l.   SARAH F. DAVIS—*Summer Song.*

Purple orchis lasteth long,
  m.   JEAN INGELOW—*Brothers, and a Sermon.
                                Song.*

Around the pillars of the palm-tree bower
  The orchids cling, in rose and purple
    spheres ;
Shield-broad the lily floats ; the aloe flower
  Foredates its hundred years.
  n.   BAYARD TAYLOR—*Canopus.*

Painted Cup.
Castilleia.

                Scarlet tufts
Are glowing in the green, like flakes of fire ;
The wanderers of the prairie know them well,
And call that brilliant flower the Painted Cup.
  o.   BRYANT—*The Painted Cup.*

Pansy.
Viola Tricolor.

Of all the bonny buds that blow
  In bright or cloudy weather,
Of all the flowers that come and go
  The whole twelve moons together,
The little purple pansy brings
Thoughts of the sweetest, saddest things,
  p.   MARY E. BRADLEY—*Heart's Ease.*

Deep violets you liken to
The kindest eyes that look on you,
Without a thought disloyal.
    a.   E. B. BROWNING—*A Flower in a Letter.*

    For summer has a close,
And pansies bloom not in the snows.
    b.   E. B. BROWNING—*Wisdom Unapplied.*

Pansies for ladies all—(I wis
That none who wear such brooches miss
    A jewel in the mirror).
    c.   E. B. BROWNING—*A Flower in a Letter.*

Pansies? You praise the ones that grow to-
    day
Here in the garden; had you seen the place
When Sutherland was living!
Here they grew,
From blue to deeper blue, in midst of each
A golden dazzle like a glimmering star,
Each broader, bigger than a silver crown;
While here the weaver sat, his labor done,
Watching his azure pets and rearing them,
Until they seem'd to know his step and touch,
And stir beneath his smile like living things:
The very sunshine loved them, and would lie
Here happy, coming early, lingering late,
Because they were so fair.
    d.   ROBERT BUCHANAN—*Hugh Sutherland's
    Pansies.*

I pray, what flowers are these?
The pansy this,
O, that's for lover's thoughts.
    e.   GEO. CHAPMAN—*All Fools.* Act II.
    Sc. 1. L. 248.

I send thee pansies while the year is young,
    Yellow as sunshine, purple as the night;
Flowers of remembrance, ever fondly sung
    By all the chiefest of the Sons of Light;
And if in recollection lives regret
    For wasted days and dreams that were not
    true,
I tell thee that the " pansy freak'd with jet"
    Is still the heart's ease that the poets knew.
Take all the sweetness of a gift unsought,
And for the pansies send me back a thought.
    f.   SARAH DOWDNEY—*Pansies.*

By scattered rocks and turbid waters shining,
    By furrowed glade and dell,
To feverish men thy calm, sweet face uplifting,
    Thou stayest them to tell.

The delicate thought, that cannot find ex-
    pression,
    For ruder speech too fair,
That, like thy petals, trembles in possession,
    And scatters on the air.
    g.   BRET HARTE—*The Mountain
    Heart's Ease.*

Heart's ease! one could look for half a day
Upon this flower, and shape in fancy out
Full twenty different tales of love and sorrow,
That gave this gentle name.
    h.   MARY HOWITT—*Heart's Ease.*

They are all in the lily-bed, cuddled close
    together—
Purple, Yellow-cap, and little Baby-blue;
How they ever got there you must ask the
    April weather,
The morning and the evening winds, the
    sunshine and the dew.
    i.   NELLIE M. HUTCHINSON—*Vagrant
    Pansies.*

The pansy freaked with jet.
    j.   MILTON—*Lycidas.* L. 144.

The beauteous pansies rise
    In purple, gold, and blue,
    With tints of rainbow hue
Mocking the sunset skies.
    k.   THOMAS J. OUSELEY—*The Angel of the
    Flowers.*

    Pray, love, remember: and there is pansies,
that's for thoughts.
    l.   *Hamlet.* Act IV. Sc. 5. L. 176.

    The bolt of Cupid fell:
* * * upon a little western flower,
Before milk-white, now purple with love's
    wound,
And maidens call it love-in-idleness.
    m.   *Midsummer-Night's Dream.* Act II.
    Sc. 1. L. 165.

Heart's ease or pansy, pleasure or thought,
Which would the picture give us of these?
Surely the heart that conceived it sought
Heart's ease.
    n.   SWINBURNE—*A Flower Piece by Fanten.*

Pansies in soft April rains
Fill their stalks with honeyed sap
Drawn from Earth's prolific lap.
    o.   BAYARD TAYLOR—*Home and Travel.
    Ariel in the Cloven Pine.* L. 37.

Darker than darkest pansies.
    p.   TENNYSON—*Gardener's Daughter.*

Early pansies, one by one,
Opening the violet eye.
    q.   SARAH HELEN WHITMAN—*She Blooms
    no More.*

Passion Flower.
Passiflora.

Art thou a type of beauty, or of power,
    Of sweet enjoyment, or disastrous sin?
For each thy name denoteth, Passion flower!
    O no! thy pure corolla's depth within
We trace a holier symbol; yea, a sign
    'Twixt God and man; a record of that hour
When the expiatory act divine
    Cancelled that curse which was our mortal
    dower.
It is the Cross!
    r.   SIR AUBREY DE VERE—*A Song of Faith,
    Devout Exercises and Sonnets. The
    Passion Flower.*

Papaw.

Asimina.

And brown is the papaw's shade-blossoming
    cup,
In the wood, near the sun-loving maize.
   a.   WILLIAM FOSDICK—*The Maize.*

Pea, Sweet.

Lathyrus Odoratus.

The pea is but a wanton witch
In too much haste to wed,
And clasps her rings on every hand.
   b.   HOOD—*Flowers.*

Here are sweet peas, on tiptoe for a flight;
With wings of gentle flush o'er delicate white,
And taper fingers catching at all things,
To bind them all about with tiny rings.
   c.   KEATS—*I Stood Tiptoe Upon a Little
Hill.*

Pimpernel.

Anagallis Arvensis.

The turf is warm beneath her feet,
  Bordering the beach of stone and shell,
And thick about her path the sweet
  Red blossoms of the pimpernel.
   d.   CELIA THAXTER—*The Pimpernel.*

Pink.

Dianthus.

You take a pink,
You dig about its roots and water it,
And so improve it to a garden-pink,
But will not change it to a heliotrope.
   e.   E. B. BROWNING—*Aurora Leigh.*
Bk. VI.

And I will pu' the pink, the emblem o' my
    dear,
For she's the pink o' womankind, and blooms
    without a peer.
   f.   BURNS—*O Luve Will Venture In.*

The beauteous pink I would not slight,
Pride of the gardener's leisure.
   g.   GOETHE—*The Floweret Wondrous Fair.*
St. 8. John S. Dwight's trans.

The wild pink crowns the garden wall,
And with the flowers are intermingled stones
Sparry and bright, rough scatterings of the
    hills.
   h.   WORDSWORTH—*The Excursion.* Bk. VI.
L. 1,166.

Poppy.

Papaver.

I sing the Poppy! The frail snowy weed!
  The flower of Mercy! that within its heart
Doth keep "a drop serene" for human need,
  A drowsy balm for every bitter smart.
For happy hours the Rose will idly blow—
The Poppy hath a charm for pain and woe.
   i.   MARY A. BARR—*White Poppies.*

A Poppy grows upon the shore
Bursts her twin cup in summer late:
Her leaves are glaucous green and hoar,
Her petals yellow, delicate.
   j.   ROBERT BRIDGES—*The Sea Poppy.*

But pleasures are like poppies spread,
You seize the flow'r its bloom is shed.
   k.   BURNS—*Tam o' Shanter.*

Till gold flashed out from the wheat-ear brown,
And flame from the poppy's leaf.
   l.   ELIZA COOK—*Journal. Stanzas.*
Vol. IV. St. 3.

We are slumberous poppies,
  Lords of Lethe downs,
Some awake, and some asleep,
  Sleeping in our crowns.
What perchance our dreams may know,
Let our serious beauty show.
   m.   LEIGH HUNT—*Songs and Chorus of the
Flowers. Poppies.*

On one side is a field of drooping oats,
Through which the poppies show their scarlet
    coats.
   n.   KEATS—*Epistle to My Brother George.*

The poppies hung
Dew-dabbled on their stalks.
   o.   KEATS—*Endymion.* Bk. I. L. 681.

Through the dancing poppies stole
A breeze most softly lulling to my soul.
   p.   KEATS—*Endymion.* Bk. I. L. 565.

Find me next a Poppy posy,
Type of his harangues so dozy.
   q.   MOORE—*Wreaths for the Ministers.*

Let but my scarlet head appear
And I am held in scorn;
Yet juice of subtile virtue lies
Within my cup of curious dyes,
   r.   CHRISTINA G. ROSSETTI—"*Consider the
Lilies of the Field.*"

Gentle sleep!
Scatter thy drowsiest poppies from above;
And in new dreams not soon to vanish, bless
My senses with the sight of her I love.
   s.   HORACE SMITH—*Poppies and Sleep.*

No odors sweet proclaim the spot
Where its soft leaves unfold;
Nor mingled hues of beauty-bright
Charm and allure the captive sight
With forms and tints untold.
   t.   CYNTHIA TAGGART—*Ode to the Poppy.*
St. 4.

One simple hue the plant portrays
Of glowing radiance rare,
Fresh as the roseate morn displays,
And seeming sweet and fair.
   u.   CYNTHIA TAGGART—*Ode to the Poppy.*
St. 5.

And far and wide, in a scarlet tide,
The poppy's bonfire spread.

> a.   BAYARD TAYLOR—*Poems of the Orient.*
> *The Poet in the East.* St. 4.

Summer set lip to earth's bosom bare,
And left the flushed print in a poppy there :
Like a yawn of fire from the grass it came,
And the fanning wind puffed it to flapping
    flame.
With burnt mouth red like a lion's it drank
The blood of the sun as he slaughtered sank,
And dipped its cup in the purpurate shine
When the eastern conduits ran with wine.

> b.   FRANCIS THOMPSON—*The Poppy.*

Bring poppies for a weary mind
That saddens in a senseless din.

> c.   WM. WINTER—*The White Flag.*

Primrose.

Primula.

Ring-ting ! I wish I were a primrose,
   A bright yellow primrose blowing in the
      spring !
     The stooping boughs above me,
     The wandering bee to love me,
The fern and moss to creep across,
   And the elm-tree for our king !

> d.   WM. ALLINGHAM— *Wishing.*   *A Child's*
> *Song.* St. 1.

'Tis the first primrose ! see how meek,
Yet beautiful it looks ;
As just a lesson it may speak
As that which is in books.

> e.   REV. WM. LISLE BOWLES—*Primrose.*

The primrose banks how fair !

> f.   BURNS—*My Chloris, Mark How Green*
> *the Groves.*

Welcome, pale primrose ! starting up between
   Dead matted leaves of ash and oak that
     strew
   The every lawn, the wood, and spinney
     through.
'Mid creeping moss and ivy's darker green ;
   How much thy presence beautifies the
     ground !
How sweet thy modest unaffected pride
Glows on the sunny bank and wood's warm
     side

> g.   JOHN CLARE—*The Primrose.*   *A Sonnet.*

I see the bright primroses burst where I stand,
And I laugh like a child as they drip in my
     hand.

> h.   ELIZA COOK—*Journal. Summer Is*
> *Nigh.* Vol. VIII. St. 4.

Music, sweet music, sounds over the earth ;
One glad choral song greets the primrose's
     birth.

> i.   ELIZA COOK—*Journal. Spring.*
> Vol. IV. St. 2.

The primrose opes its eye,
And the young moth flutters by.

> j.   ELIZA COOK—*Christmas Tide.*

" Three bunches a penny, primroses ! "
   Oh, dear is the greeting of Spring,
When she offers her dew-spangled posies,
   The fairest creation can bring.

> k.   ELIZA COOK—*Journal. Old Cries.*
> Vol. VIII. St. 11.

" I could have brought you some primroses,
but I do not like to mix violets with anything."
   "They say primroses make a capital salad,"
said Lord St. Jerome.

> l.   BENJ. DISRAELI—*Lothair.*   Ch. XIII.

Her modest looks the cottage might adorn,
Sweet as the primrose peeps beneath the
     thorn.

> m.   GOLDSMITH—*The Deserted Village.*
> L. 329.

Why doe ye weep, sweet babes ?   Can tears
     Speak griefe in you,
      Who were but borne
      Just as the modest morne
     Teemed her refreshing dew ?

> n.   HERRICK—*To Primroses.*

Bountiful Primroses,
   With outspread heart that needs the rough
     leaves' care.

> o.   GEORGE MACDONALD— *Wild Flowers.*

Mild offspring of a dark and sullen sire !
Whose modest form, so delicately fine,
     Was nursed in whirling storms,
     And cradled in the winds.
Thee when young spring first question'd
     winter's sway,
And dared the sturdy blusterer to the fight,
   Thee on his bank he threw
   To mark his victory.

> p.   HENRY KIRKE WHITE—*To an Early*
> *Primrose.*

A primrose by a river's brim,
A yellow primrose was to him,
And it was nothing more.

> q.   WORDSWORTH—*Peter Bell.*   Pt. I.
> St. 12.

Primroses, the Spring may love them ;
Summer knows but little of them.

> r.   WORDSWORTH—*Foresight.*

The Primrose for a veil had spread
   The largest of her upright leaves ;
And thus for purposes benign,
   A simple flower deceives.

> s.   WORDSWORTH—*A Wren's Nest.*

Primrose, Evening.

Œnothera.

A tuft of evening primroses,
O'er which the mind may hover till it dozes ;
O'er which it well might take a pleasant sleep,
But that 'tis ever startled by the leap
Of buds into ripe flowers.

a. KEATS—*I Stood Tiptoe Upon a Little Hill.*

Reed.

Phragmites.

Those tall flowering-reeds which stand,
In Arno like a sheaf of sceptres, left
By some remote dynasty of dead gods.

b. E. B. BROWNING—*Aurora Leigh.*
Bk. VII.

Rhodora.

Rhodora.

In May, when sea-winds pierced our solitudes,
I found the fresh Rhodora in the woods,
Spreading its leafless blooms in a damp nook,
To please the desert and the sluggish brook.
The purple petals, fallen in the pool,
Made the black water with their beauty gay ;
Here might the red-bird come his plumes to cool,
And court the flower that cheapens his array.
Rhodora ! if the sages ask thee why
This charm is wasted on the earth and sky,
Tell them, dear, that if eyes were made for seeing,
Then Beauty is its own excuse for being :
Why thou wert there, O rival of the rose !
I never thought to ask, I never knew ;
But, in my simple ignorance, suppose
The self-same power that brought me there brought you.

c. EMERSON—*The Rhodora.*

Rose.

Rosa.

She wore a wreath of roses,
The night that first we met.

d. THOS. HAYNES BAYLY—*She Wore a Wreath of Roses.*

The rose that all are praising
Is not the rose for me.

e. THOS. HAYNES BAYLY—*The Rose That all are Praising.*

Thus to the Rose, the Thistle :
Why art thou not of thistle-breed ?
Of use thou'dst, then, be truly,
For asses might upon thee feed.

f. F. N. BODENSTEDT—*The Rose and Thistle.* Trans. from the German by Frederick Ricord.

The full-blown rose, mid dewy sweets
Most perfect dies.

g. MARIA BROOKS—*Written on Seeing Pharamond.*

A rose as fair as ever saw the North,
Grew in a little garden all alone :
A sweeter flower did Nature ne'er put forth,
Nor fairer garden yet was never known.

h. WILLIAM BROWNE—*Visions. Sonnet V.*

And thus, what can we do,
Poor rose and poet too,
Who both antedate our mission
In an unprepared season ?

i. E. B. BROWNING—*A Lay of the Early Rose.*

A white rosebud for a guerdon.

j. E. B. BROWNING—*Romance of the Swan's Nest.*

" For if I wait," said she,
" Till time for roses be,—
For the moss-rose and the musk-rose,
Maiden-blush and royal-dusk rose,—

" What glory then for me
In such a company ?—
Roses plenty, roses plenty
And one nightingale for twenty ? "

k. E. B. BROWNING—*A Lay of the Early Rose.*

O rose, who dares to name thee ?
No longer roseate now, nor soft, nor sweet,
But pale, and hard, and dry, as stubble-wheat,—
Kept seven years in a drawer, thy titles shame thee.

l. E. B. BROWNING—*A Dead Rose.*

This guelder rose, at far too slight a beck
Of the wind, will toss about her flower-apples,

m. E. B. BROWNING—*Aurora Leigh.*
Bk. II.

'Twas a yellow rose,
By that south window of the little house,
My cousin Romney gathered with his hand
On all my birthdays, for me, save the last ;
And then I shook the tree too rough, too rough,
For roses to stay after,

n. E. B. BROWNING—*Aurora Leigh.*
Bk. VI.

You smell a rose through a fence :
If two should smell it, what matter ?

o. E. B. BROWNING—*Lord Walter's Wife.*

All June I bound the rose in sheaves.
Now, rose by rose, I strip the leaves.

p. ROBERT BROWNING—*One Way of Love.*

Loveliest of lovely things are they
On earth that soonest pass away.
The rose that lives its little hour
Is prized beyond the sculptured flower.

q. BRYANT—*A Scene on the Banks of the Hudson.*

I'll pu' the budding rose, when Phœbus peeps
    in view,
For its like a baumy kiss o' her sweet bonnie
    mou' !
   a.   Burns—*The Posie.*

Yon rose-buds in the morning dew,
    How pure amang the leaves sae green !
   b.   Burns—*To Chloris.*

When love came first to earth, the Spring
Spread rose-beds to receive him.
   c.   Campbell—*Song. When Love Came*
                  First To Earth.

For those roses bright, oh, those roses bright !
    I have twined them in my sister's locks
That are hid in the dust from sight.
   d.   Phebe Cary—*Our Homestead.*

Roses were sette of swete savour,
With many roses that thei bere.
   e.   Chaucer—*The Romaunt of the Rose.*

Till the rose's lips grow pale
With her sighs.
   f.   Rose Terry Cooke—*Rêve Du Midi.*

I wish I might a rose-bud grow
    And thou wouldst cull me from the bower,
To place me on that breast of snow
    Where I should bloom a wintry flower
   g.   Dionysius.

O beautiful, royal Rose,
    O Rose, so fair and sweet !
Queen of the garden art thou,
    And I—the Clay at thy feet !
   *   *   *   *   *   *
Yet, O thou beautiful Rose !
    Queen rose, so fair and sweet,
What were lover or crown to thee
    Without the Clay at thy feet ?
   h.   Julia C. R. Dorr—*The Clay to the*
                        Rose.

It never will rain roses : when we want
To have more roses we must plant more trees.
   i.   George Eliot—*Spanish Gypsy.*
                        Bk. III.

The gathered rose and the stolen heart
Can charm but for a day.
   j.   Emma Embury—*Ballad.*

In Heaven's happy bowers
There blossom two flowers,
One with fiery glow
And one as white as snow ;
While lo ! before them stands,
With pale and trembling hands,
A spirit who must choose
One, and one refuse.
   k.   R. W. Gilder—*The White and Red*
                        Rose.

16

It is written on the rose
    In its glory's full array :
Read what those buds disclose—
    " Passing away "
   l.   Mrs. Hemans—*Passing Away.*

Sweet rose, whose hue, angry and brave,
    Bids the rash gazer wipe his eye,
Thy root is even in the grave,
    And thou must die.
   m.   Herbert—*Vertue.* St. 2.

Gather ye rose-buds while ye may,
    Old time is still a flying,
And this same flower that smiles to-day,
    To-morrow will be dying.
   n.   Herrick—*To the Virgins to Make Much*
                    of Time.

It was not in the winter
    Our loving lot was cast :
It was the time of roses ;
    We pluck'd them as we pass'd.
   o.   Hood—*Ballad. It was not in the*
                    Winter.

Poor Peggy hawks nosegays from street to
    street
Till—think of that who find life so sweet !—
    She hates the smell of roses.
   p.   Hood—*Miss Kilmansegg.*

We are blushing Roses,
    Bending with our fulness,
'Midst our close-capp'd sister buds,
    Warming the green coolness.
   q.   Leigh Hunt—*Songs and Chorus of the*
                    Flowers. Roses.

             And the guelder rose
In a great stillness dropped, and ever dropped,
Her wealth about her feet.
   r.   Jean Ingelow—*Laurance.* Pt. III.

The roses that in yonder hedge appear
Outdo our garden-buds which bloom within ;
But since the hand may pluck them every
    day,
Unmarked they bud, bloom, drop, and drift
    away.
   s.   Jean Ingelow—*The Four Bridges.*
                        St. 61.

             The vermeil rose had blown
In frightful scarlet, and its thorns outgrown
Like spiked aloe.
   t.   Keats—*Endymion.* Bk. I. L. 694.

But when, O Wells ! thy roses came to me,
    My sense with their deliciousness was
    spell'd :
Soft voices had they, that with tender plea
    Whisper'd of peace, and truth, and friendli-
    ness unquell'd.
   u.   Keats—*To a Friend who Sent me Some*
                    Roses.

Woo on, with odour wooing me,
 Faint rose with fading core;
For God's rose-thought, that blooms in thee,
 Will bloom forevermore.
 a. GEORGE MacDONALD—*Songs of the*
       Summer Night. Pt. III.

And I will make thee beds of roses,
And a thousand fragrant posies.
 b. MARLOWE—*The Passionate Shepherd to*
       his Love. St. 3.

Flowers of all hue, and without thorn the
 rose.
 c. MILTON—*Paradise Lost.* Bk. IV.
           L. 256.

Rose of the desert! thou art to me
An emblem of stainless purity,—
Of those who, keeping their garments white,
Walk on through life with steps aright.
 d. D. M. MOIR—*The White Rose.*

While rose-buds scarcely show'd their hue,
But coyly linger'd on the thorn.
 e. MONTGOMERY—*The Adventures of a*
           Star.

Two roses on one slender spray
 In sweet communion grew,
Together hailed the morning ray
 And drank the evening dew.
 f. MONTGOMERY—*The Roses.*

Long, long be my heart with such memories
 fill'd!
Like the vase, in which roses have once been
 distill'd—
You may break, you may shatter the vase if
 you will,
But the scent of the roses will hang round it
 still.
 g. MOORE—*Farewell! but Whenever you*
         Welcome the Hour.

No flower of her kindred,
 No rosebud is nigh,
To reflect back her blushes,
 Or give sigh for sigh.
 h. MOORE—*Last Rose of Summer.*

Rose of the Desert! thus should woman be
Shining uncourted, lone and safe, like thee.
 i. MOORE—*Rose of the Desert.*

Rose of the Garden! such is woman's lot—
Worshipp'd while blooming—when she fades,
 forgot.
 j. MOORE—*Rose of the Desert.*

Rose! thou art the sweetest flower,
That ever drank the amber shower;
Rose! thou art the fondest child
Of dimpled Spring, the wood-nymph wild.
 k. MOORE—*Odes of Anacreon. Ode XLIV.*

Sometimes, when on the Alpine rose
 The golden sunset leaves its ray,
So like a gem the flow'ret glows,
 We thither bend our headlong way;
And though we find no treasure there,
We bless the rose that shines so fair.
 l. MOORE—*The Crystal-Hunters.*

Why do we shed the rose's bloom
Upon the cold, insensate tomb?
Can flowery breeze, or odor's breath,
Afflict the slumbering chill of death?
 m. MOORE—*Odes of Anacreon.*
          Ode XXXII.

There's a bower of roses by Bendemeer's
 stream,
 And the nightingale sings round it all the
  day long,
In the time of my childhood 'twas like a
 sweet dream,
 To sit in the roses and hear the bird's
  song.
 n. MOORE—*Lalla Rookh. The Veiled*
       Prophet of Khorassan.

Oh! there is naught in nature bright
Whose roses do not shed their light;
When morning paints the Orient skies,
Her fingers burn with roseate dyes.
 o. MOORE—*Odes of Anacreon. Ode LV.*

The rose distils a healing balm
The beating pulse of pain to calm.
 p. MOORE—*Odes of Anacreon. Ode LV.*

'Tis the last rose of summer,
 Left blooming alone.
 q. MOORE—*Last Rose of Summer.*

What would the rose with all her pride be
 worth,
Were there no sun to call her brightness
 forth?
 r. MOORE—*Love Alone.*

O rose! the sweetest blossom,
Of spring the fairest flower,
O rose! the joy of heaven.
The god of love, with roses
His yellow locks adorning,
Dances with the hours and graces.
 s. J. G. PERCIVAL—*Anacreontic.* St. 2.

Die of a rose in aromatic pain.
 t. POPE—*Essay on Man.* Ep. I. L. 200.

Let opening roses knotted oaks adorn,
And liquid amber drop from every thorn.
 u. POPE—*Autumn.* L. 36.

Like roses, that in deserts bloom and die.
 v. POPE—*Rape of the Lock.* Canto IV.
           L. 158.

And when the parent-rose decays and dies,
With a resembling face the daughter-buds
 arise.
 w. PRIOR—*Celia to Damon.*

The rose
Propt at the cottage door with careful hands,
Bursts its green bud, and looks abroad for
May.
a.   Thos. Buchanan Read—*The New
Pastoral.* Bk. VI. L. 150.

We bring roses, beautiful fresh roses,
   Dewy as the morning and coloured like the
dawn;
Little tents of odour, where the bee reposes,
   Swooning in sweetness of the bed he dreams
upon.
b.   Thos. Buchanan Read—*The New
Pastoral.* Bk. VII. L. 51.

I watched a rose-bud very long
   Brought on by dew and sun and shower,
Waiting to see the perfect flower:
Then when I thought it should be strong
   It opened at the matin hour
And fell at even-song.
c.   Christina G. Rossetti—*Symbols.*

The rose saith in the dewy morn,
   I am most fair;
Yet all my loveliness is born
Upon a thorn.
d.   Christina G. Rossetti—*Consider the
Lilies of the Field.*

The rose is fairest when 'tis budding new,
   And hope is brightest when it dawns from
fears;
The rose is sweetest wash'd with morning dew,
   And love is loveliest when embalm'd in
tears.
e.   Scott—*Lady of the Lake.* Canto IV.

From off this brier pluck a white rose with me.
f.   *Henry VI.* Pt. I. Act II. Sc 4.
L. 30.

Hoary-headed frosts
Fall in the fresh lap of the crimson rose.
g.   *Midsummer-Night's Dream.* Act II.
Sc.1. L. 107.

Then will I raise aloft the milk-white rose,
With whose sweet smell the air shall be perfumed.
h.   *Henry VI.* Pt. II. Act I. Sc. 1.
L. 254.

The red rose on triumphant brier.
i.   *Midsummer-Night's Dream.* Act III.
Sc. 1. L. 96.

There will we make our peds of roses,
And a thousand fragrant posies.
j.   *Merry Wives of Windsor.* Act III.
Sc. 1. L. 19. *Song.*

And the rose like a nymph to the bath ad-
drest,
Which unveiled the depth of her glowing
breast,
Till, fold after fold, to the fainting air,
The soul of her beauty and love lay bare.
k.   Shelley—*The Sensitive Plant.* Pt. I.

I am the one rich thing that morn
   Leaves for the ardent noon to win;
Grasp me not, I have a thorn,
   But bend and take my being in.
l.   Harriet Prescott Spofford—*Flower
Songs. The Rose.*

It was nothing but a rose I gave her,—
     Nothing but a rose
Any wind might rob of half its savor,
     Any wind that blows.

   *   *   *   *   *   *

Withered, faded, pressed between these pages,
     Crumpled, fold on fold,—
Once it lay upon her breast, and ages
     Cannot make it old!
m.   Harriet Prescott Spofford—*A Sigh.*

The year of the rose is brief;
From the first blade blown to the sheaf,
   From the thin green leaf to the gold,
   It has time to be sweet and grow old,
To triumph and leave not a leaf.
n.   Swinburne—*The Year of the Rose.*

And half in shade and half in sun;
   The Rose sat in her bower,
With a passionate thrill in her crimson heart.
o.   Bayard Taylor—*Poems of the Orient.
The Poet in the East.* St. 5.

And is there any moral shut
   Within the bosom of the rose?
p.   Tennyson—*The Day-Dream. Moral.*

The fairest things have fleetest end:
   Their scent survives their close,
But the rose's scent is bitterness
   To him that loved the rose!
q.   Francis Thompson—*Daisy.* St. 10.

I saw the rose-grove blushing in pride,
I gathered the blushing rose—and sigh'd—
I come from the rose-grove, mother,
I come from the grove of roses.
r.   Gil Vicente—*I Come from the
Rose-grove, Mother.* Trans. by
John Bowring.

Go, lovely Rose!
   Tell her that wastes her time and me
That now she knows,
   When I resemble her to thee,
How sweet and fair she seems to be.
s.   Edmund Waller—*The Rose.*

How fair is the Rose! what a beautiful flower.
   The glory of April and May!
But the leaves are beginning to fade in an
hour,
   And they wither and die in a day.
Yet the Rose has one powerful virtue to boast,
   Above all the flowers of the field;
When its leaves are all dead, and fine colours
are lost,
   Still how sweet a perfume it will yield!
t.   Isaac Watts—*The Rose.*

The rosebuds lay their crimson lips together.
a.   AMELIA B. WELBY—*Hopeless Love.*
         St. 5.

The budding rose above the rose full blown.
b.   WORDSWORTH—*The Prelude.*   Bk. XI.

Rose, Musk-.
Rosa Moschata.

I saw the sweetest flower wild nature yields,
   A fresh-blown musk-rose; 'twas the first
     that threw
Its sweets upon the summer.
c.   KEATS—*To a Friend who Sent some*
         Roses.

     And mid-May's eldest child,
The coming musk-rose, full of dewy wine,
The murmurous haunt of flies on summer
   eves.
d.   KEATS—*Ode to a Nightingale.*

Rose, Sweetbrier.
(*Eglantine*), *Rosa Rubiginosa.*

     Yet here's eglantine,
Here's ivy!—take them as I used to do
Thy flowers, and keep them where they shall
   not pine.
Instruct thine eyes to keep their colours true,
And tell thy soul their roots are left in mine.
e.   E. B. BROWNING—*Trans. from the*
         Portuguese.   XLIV.

Sometimes I choose the lily, without stain;
   The royal rose sometimes the best I call;
Then the low daisy, dancing with the rain,
   Doth seem to me the finest flower of all;
And yet if only one could bloom for me—
I know right well what flower that one would
   be!
f.   ALICE CARY—*The Field Sweetbrier.*

The sweetbrier, under the window-sill,
   Which the early birds made glad,
And the damask rose by the garden-fence,
   Were all the flowers we had.
g.   PHEBE CARY—*Our Homestead.*

For sycamores with eglantine were spread,
A hedge about the sides, a covering overhead.
h.   DRYDEN—*The Flower and the Leaf.*
         L. 72.

The fresh eglantine exhaled a breath,
Whose odours were of power to raise from
   death.
i.   DRYDEN—*The Flower and the Leaf.*
         L. 96.

The sweetbrier rose—the wayside rose,
   Still spreads its fragrant arms,
Where graciously to passing eyes
   It gave its simple charms.
j.   CAROLINE GILMAN—*Return to*
         Massachusetts.

Wild-rose, Sweetbriar, Eglantine,
All these pretty names are mine,
And scent in every leaf is mine,
And a leaf for all is mine,
And the scent—Oh, that's divine!
Happy-sweet and pungent fine,
Pure as dew, and pick'd as wine.
k.   LEIGH HUNT—*Songs and Chorus of*
         the Flowers.   Sweetbriar.

It's sides I'll plant with dew-sweet eglantine.
l.   KEATS—*Endymion.*   Bk. IV.   L. 700.

         Rain-scented eglantine
Gave temperate sweets to that well-wooing
   sun.
m.   KEATS—*Endymion.*   Bk. I.   L. 100.

         As through the verdant maze
Of sweetbriar hedges I pursue my walk;
Or taste the smell of dairy.
n.   THOMSON—*The Seasons.   Spring.*
         L. 105.

The garden rose may richly bloom
   In cultured soil and genial air,
To cloud the light of Fashion's room
   Or droop in Beauty's midnight hair,
In lonelier grace, to sun and dew
   The sweetbrier on the hillside shows
Its single leaf and fainter hue,
   Untrained and wildly free, yet still a sister
     rose!
o.   WHITTIER—*The Bride of Pennacook.*
         Pt. III.   *The Daughter.*

Rose, Wild.
Rosa Lucida.

A wild rose roofs the ruined shed,
   And that and summer well agree.
p.   COLERIDGE—*A Day Dream.*

         A brier rose, whose buds
Yield fragrant harvest for the honey bee.
q.   L. E. LANDON—*The Oak.*   L. 17.

A waft from the roadside bank
   Tells where the wild rose nods.
r.   BAYARD TAYLOR—*The Guests of Night.*

Rosemary.
Rosmarinus.

     Dreary rosmarye
That always mourns the dead.
s.   HOOD—*Flowers.*

     The humble rosemary
Whose sweets so thanklessly are shed
To scent the desert and the dead.
t.   MOORE—*Lalla Rookh.   Light of the*
         Harem.

There's rosemary, that's for remembrance.
u.   *Hamlet.*   Act IV.   Sc. 5.   L. 175.

Safflower.

Carthamus.

And the saffron flower
Clear as a flame of sacrifice breaks out.
a.   JEAN INGELOW—*The Doom.* Bk. II.

Sensitive Plant.

Mimosa Pudica.

A Sensitive Plant in a garden grew,
And the young winds fed it with silver dew,
And it opened its fan-like leaves to the light,
And clothed them beneath the kisses of night.
b.   SHELLEY—*The Sensitive Plant.* Pt. I.

For the Sensitive Plant has no bright flower;
Radiance and odour are not its dower;
It loves, even like Love, its deep heart is full,
It desires what it has not, the beautiful.
c.   SHELLEY—*The Sensitive Plant.* Pt. I.

Shamrock.

Trifolium Repens.

I'll seek a four-leaved shamrock in all the
   fairy dells,
And if I find the charmèd leaves, oh, how I'll
   weave my spells!
d.   SAMUEL LOVER—*The Four-Leaved
                              Shamrock.*

O, the Shamrock, the green, immortal Sham-
   rock!
Chosen leaf
Of Bard and Chief,
Old Erin's native Shamrock.
e.   MOORE—*Oh, the Shamrock.*

Snow-Drop.

Galanthus Nivalis.

At the head of Flora's dance;
Simple Snow-drop, then in thee
All thy sister-train I see;
Every brilliant bud that blows,
From the blue-bell to the rose;
All the beauties that appear,
On the bosom of the Year,
All that wreathe the locks of Spring,
Summer's ardent breath perfume,
Or on the lap of Autumn bloom,
All to thee their tribute bring.
f.   MONTGOMERY—*The Snow-Drop.*

The morning star of flowers.
g.   MONTGOMERY—*The Snow-Drop.*

Winter's gloomy night withdrawn
Lo! the young romantic Hours,
Search the hill, the dale, the lawn
To behold the snow-drop white, start to light.
h.   MONTGOMERY—*The Snow-Drop.*

Lone Flower, hemmed in with snows and
   white as they
But hardier far, once more I see thee bend
Thy forehead, as if fearful to offend,
Like an unbidden guest. Though day by day,
Storms, sallying from the mountain tops,
   waylay
The rising sun, and on the plains descend;
Yet art thou welcome, welcome as a friend
Whose zeal outruns his promise!
i.   WORDSWORTH—*To a Snow-Drop.*

Nor will I then thy modest grace forget,
Chaste Snow-drop, venturous harbinger of
   Spring,
And pensive monitor of fleeting years!
j.   WORDSWORTH—*To a Snow-Drop.*

Spiræa.

Spiræa.

And yet she follows every turn
With spires of closely clustered bloom,
   And all the wildness of the place,
   The narrow pass, the rugged ways,
But give her larger room.

And near the unfrequented road,
By waysides scorched with barren heat,
   In clouded pink or softer white
She holds the Summer's generous light,—
Our native meadow sweet!
k.   DORA READ GOODALE—*Spiræa.*

Strawberry.

Fragaria.

When the fields are sweet with clover,
   And the woods are glad with song,
When the brooks are running over,
   And the days are bright and long,
Then, from every nook and bower,
Peeps the dainty strawberry flower.
l.   DORA READ GOODALE—*Strawberries.*

Fill your lap and fill your bosom;
Only spare the strawberry-blossom.
m.   WORDSWORTH—*Foresight.*

Sunflower.

Helianthus.

Ah, Sunflower, weary of time,
Who countest the steps of the sun;
Seeking after that sweet golden clime,
Where the traveller's journey is done;

Where the youth pined away with desire,
And the pale virgin shrouded in snow,
Arise from their graves, and aspire
Where my Sunflower wishes to go!
n.   WILLIAM BLAKE—*The Sunflower.*

Miles and miles of golden green
    Where the sunflowers blow
    In a solid glow.
    a.   ROBERT BROWNING—*A Lover's Quarrel.*
            St. 6.

And the yellow sunflower by the brook, in
    autumn beauty stood.
    b.   BRYANT—*The Death of the Flowers.*

Light-enchanted sunflower, thou
Who gazest ever true and tender
On the sun's revolving splendour.
    c.   CALDERON—*Magico Prodigioso.*
          Sc. 3. Shelley's Trans.

Restless sunflower; cease to move.
    d.   CALDERON—*Magico Prodigioso.*
          Sc. 3. Shelley's Trans.

The Sunflow'r, thinking 'twas for him foul
    shame
To nap by daylight, strove t' excuse the blame;
It was not sleep that made him nod, he said,
But too great weight and largeness of his head.
    e.   COWLEY—*Of Plants.* Bk. IV.
         Of Flowers. *The Poppy.* L. 102.

With zealous step he climbs the upland lawn,
And bows in homage to the rising dawn;
Imbibes with eagle eye the golden ray,
And watches, as it moves, the orb of day.
    f.   ERASMUS DARWIN—*Loves of the Plants.*
          . Canto I. L. 225.

Space for the sunflower, bright with yellow
    glow,
    To court the sky.
    g.   CAROLINE GILMAN—*To the Ursulines.*

And here the sunflower of the spring
Burns bright in morning's beam.
    h.   EBENEZER ELLIOTT—*The Wonders of*
         the Lane. L. 77.

Eagle of flowers! I see thee stand,
    And on the sun's noon-glory gaze;
With eye like his, thy lids expand,
    And fringe their disk with golden rays:
Though fix'd on earth, in darkness rooted
    there,
Light is thy element, thy dwelling air,
    Thy prospect heaven.
    i.   MONTGOMERY—*The Sunflower.*

Like sunflowers by the sides of brooks,
Turn'd to the sun.
    j.   MOORE—*The Summer Fête.*

As the sunflower turns on her god when he
    sets,
The same look which she turn'd when he rose.
    k.   MOORE—*Believe Me, if all Those*
         Endearing Young Charms.

Unloved, the sunflower, shining fair,
    Ray round with flames her disk of seed,
    And many a rose-carnation feed
With summer spice the humming air.
    l.   TENNYSON—*In Memoriam.* CI.

But one, the lofty follower of the Sun,
Sad when he sets, shuts up her yellow
    leaves
Drooping all night; and, when he warm re-
    turns,
Points her enamoured bosom to his ray.
    m.   THOMSON—*The Seasons.* *Summer.*
             L. 216.

Sweet Basil.

Ocymum Basilicum.

I pray your Highness mark this curious
    herb :
Touch it but lightly, stroke it softly, Sir,
And it gives forth an odor sweet and rare ;
But crush it harshly and you'll make a
    scent
Most disagreeable.
    n.   LELAND—*Sweet Basil.*

Thistle.

Cnicus.

Up wi' the flowers o' Scotland,
    The emblems o' the free,
Their guardians for a thousand years,
    Their guardians still we'll be.
A foe had better brave the de'il
    Within his reeky cell,
Than our thistle's purple bonnet,
    Or bonny heather bell.
    o.   HOGG—*The Flowers of Scotland.*

When on the breath of Autumn's breeze,
    From pastures dry and brown,
Goes floating, like an idle thought,
    The fair, white thistle-down ;
O, then what joy to walk at will,
Upon the golden harvest-hill !
    p.   MARY HOWITT—*Corn-Fields.*

Thorn.

Cratægus.

There is a Thorn,—it looks so old,
In truth, you'd find it hard to say
How it could ever have been young,
It looks so old and gray.
Not higher than a two years child
It stands erect, this aged Thorn ;
No leaves it has, no prickly points ;
It is a mass of knotted joints,
A wretched thing forlorn.
It stands erect, and like a stone
With lichens is it overgrown.
    q.   WORDSWORTH—*The Thorn.*

Thyme.

Thymus.

I know a bank where the wild thyme
　　blows.

　a.　　*Midsummer-Night's Dream.*　Act II.
　　　　　　　　　　　　Sc. I.　L. 249.

Trillium, Birth-Root.

Trillium.

Now about the rugged places
　　And along the ruined way,
Light and free in sudden graces
　　Comes the careless tread of May,—
Born of tempest, wrought in power,
　　Stirred by sudden hope and fear,
You may find a mystic flower
　　In the spring-time of the year!

　b.　　Dora Read Goodale—*Trillium.*

Tuberose.

Polianthes Tuberosa.

The tuberose, with her silvery light,
　　That in the gardens of Malay
Is call'd the Mistress of the Night,
So like a bride, scented and bright;
　　She comes out when the sun's away.

　c.　　Moore—*Lalla Rookh.　Light of the
　　　　　　　　　　　　　　　　Harem.*

Tulip.

Tulipa.

And tulips, children love to stretch
Their fingers down, to feel in each
Its beauty's secret nearer.

　d.　　E. B. Browning—*A Flower in a Letter.*

　　　　　　　　　　　　You believe
In God, for your part?—ay? that He who
　　makes,
Can make good things from ill things, best
　　from worst,
As men plant tulips upon dunghills when
They wish them finest.

　e.　　E. B. Browning—*Aurora Leigh.*
　　　　　　　　　　　　　　　　Bk. II.

'Mid the sharp, short emerald wheat, scarce
　　risen three fingers well,
The wild tulip at end of its tube, blows out
　　its great red bell,
Like a thin clear bubble of blood, for the
　　children to pick and sell.

　f.　　Robert Browning—*Up at a Villa.
　　　　　　　　　　Down in the City.*　St. 6.

Bring the tulip and the rose,
While their brilliant beauty glows.

　g.　　Eliza Cook—*Journal.*　Vol. IV.
　　　　　　　　　　St. 2.　*The Heart That's True.*

The tulip is a courtly quean,
Whom, therefore, I will shun.

　h.　　Hood—*Flowers.*

Dutch tulips from their beds
Flaunted their stately heads.

　i.　　Montgomery—*The Adventure of a Star.*

Not one of Flora's brilliant race
　　A form more perfect can display ;
Art could not feign more simple grace
　　Nor Nature take a line away.

　j.　　Montgomery—*On Planting a
　　　　　　　　　　　　　　Tulip-Root.*

The tulip's petals shine in dew,
All beautiful, but none alike.

　k.　　Montgomery—*On Planting a
　　　　　　　　　　　　　　Tulip-Root.*

Like tulip-beds of different shape and dyes,
Bending beneath the invisible west-wind's
　　sighs.

　l.　　Moore—*Lalla Rookh.　The Veiled
　　　　　　　　　　　　Prophet of Khorassan.*

Verbena.

Verbena.

Sweet verbena, which, being brushed against
Will hold you three hours after by the
　　smell,
In spite of long walks on the windy hills.

　m.　　E. B. Browning—*Aurora Leigh.*
　　　　　　　　　　　　　　　　Bk. VIII.

Violet.

Viola.

Early violets blue and white
Dying for their love of light.

　n.　　Edwin Arnold—*Almond Blossoms.*

Down in the valley under the hill,
Droppeth the snow-flake white and still,
Wrapping the violet, near my feet,
Cold and stiff in its winding sheet.

　o.　　J. N. Barker—*Under the Snow.*

Deep violets, you liken to
The kindest eyes that look on you,
Without a thought disloyal.

　p.　　E. B. Browning—*A Flower in a Letter.*

I know where the young May violet grows,
In its lone and lowly nook.

　q.　　Bryant—*An Indian Story.*　St. 2.

The country ever has a lagging Spring,
Waiting for May to call its violets forth.

　r.　　Bryant—*Spring in Town.*

Thou comest not when violets lean
O'er wandering brooks and springs unseen.
   a.   Bryant—*To the Fringed Gentian.*

Violets spring in the soft May shower.
   b.   Bryant—*The Maiden's Sorrow.*

When beechen buds begin to swell,
  And woods the blue-bird's warble know,
The yellow violet's modest bell
  Peeps from the last year's leaves below.
   c.   Bryant—*The Yellow Violet.*

    The violets golden
That sprinkle the vale below.
   d.   Alice Cary—*Pictures of Memory.*

Stars will blossom in the darkness,
  Violets bloom beneath the snow.
   e.   Julia C. R. Dorr—*For a Silver
                        Wedding.*

Yet there upon that upland height
The darlings of the early spring—
Blue violets—were blossoming.
   f.   Julia C. R. Dorr—*Unanswered.*

Again the violet of our early days
Drinks beauteous azure from the golden sun,
And kindles into fragrance at his blaze.
   g.   Ebenezer Elliott—*Miscellaneous
                    Poems. Spring.*

Cold blows the wind against the hill,
  And cold upon the plain ;
I sit me by the bank, until
  The violets come again.
   h.   Richard Garnett—*Violets.*

A vi'let on the meadow grew,
That no one saw, that no one knew,
It was a modest flower.
A shepherdess pass'd by that way—
Light-footed, pretty and so gay ;
That way she came,
Softly warbling forth her lay.
   i.   Goethe—*The Violet.* Frederick
                  Ricord's Trans.

A blossom of returning light,
  An April flower of sun and dew ;
The earth and sky, the day and night
  Are melted in her depth of blue !
   j.   Dora Read Goodale—*Blue Violets.*

The modest, lowly violet
In leaves of tender green is set ;
So rich she cannot hide from view,
But covers all the bank with blue.
   k.   Dora Read Goodale—*Spring Scatters
                Far and Wide.*

The eyes of spring, so azure,
  Are peeping from the ground ;
They are the darling violets,
  That I in nosegays bound.
   l.   Heine—*Book of Songs. New Spring.
                  No. 13. St. 1.*

The violets prattle and titter,
  And gaze on the stars high above.
   m.   Heine—*Book of Songs. Lyrical
             Interlude. No. 9. St. 3.*

Welcome, maids of honor,
    You doe bring
      In the spring,
And wait upon her.
   n.   Herrick—*To Violets.*

The violet is a nun.
   o.   Hood—*Flowers.*

We are violets blue,
  For our sweetness found
Careless in the mossy shades,
  Looking on the ground.
Love's dropp'd eyelids and a kiss,—
Such our breath and blueness is.
   p.   Leigh Hunt—*Songs and Chorus of the
                Flowers. Violets.*

              And shade the violets,
That they may bind the moss in leafy nets.
   q.   Keats—*I Stood Tiptoe Upon a Little
                    Hill.*

Violets !—deep-blue violets !
April's loveliest coronets !
There are no flowers grow in the vale,
Kiss'd by the dew, woo'd by the gale,—
None by the dew of the twilight wet,
So sweet as the deep-blue violet.
   r.   L. E. Landon—*The Violet.*

Violet ! sweet violet !
Thine eyes are full of tears ;
    Are they wet
    Even yet
With the thought of other years ?
   s.   Lowell—*Song.*

Winds wander, and dews drip earthward ;
  Rains fall, suns rise and set ;
Earth whirls, and all but to prosper
  A poor little violet.
   t.   Lowell—*The Changeling.*

The violets were past their prime,
Yet their departing breath
Was sweeter, in the blast of death,
Than all the lavish fragrance of the time.
   u.   Montgomery—*The Adventure of a Star.*

Hath the pearl less whiteness
　Because of its birth?
Hath the violet less brightness
　For growing near earth?
　a.　　MOORE—*Desmond's Song.*

　　　　Steals timidly away,
Shrinking as violets do in summer's ray.
　b.　　MOORE—*Lalla Rookh. Veiled Prophet
　　　　　　　　of Khorassan.*

Surely as cometh the Winter, I know
There are Spring violets under the snow.
　c.　　R. H. NEWELL (Orpheus C. Kerr)—
　　　　　　Spring Violets under the Snow.

The violet thinks, with her timid blue eye,
To pass for a blossom enchantingly shy.
　d.　　FRANCIS S. OSGOOD—*Garden Gossip.
　　　　　　　　　St. 3.*

In the Spring time: April violets glow
In wayside nooks, close clustering into
　　groups,
Like shy elves hiding from the traveller's
　　eye.
　e.　　THOS. BUCHANAN READ—*The New
　　　　　　Pastoral.* Bk. I. L. 73.

The violets whisper from the shade
Which their own leaves have made:
Men scent our fragrance on the air,
Yet take no heed
Of humble lessons we would read.
　f.　　CHRISTINA G. ROSSETTI—" *Consider the
　　　　　　Lilies of the Field.*" L. 13.

　　　　　The sweet sound,
That breathes upon a bank of violets,
Stealing and giving odour!
　g.　　*Twelfth Night.* Act I. Sc. 1. L. 5.

　　　　　Violets dim,
But sweeter than the lids of Juno's eyes.
Or Cytherea's breath.
　h.　　*Winter's Tale.* Act IV. Sc. 4. L. 120.

　　　　Who are the violets now
That strew the green lap of the new come
　　spring.
　i.　　*Richard II.* Act V. Sc. 2. L. 46.

And the violet lay dead while the odour
　flew
On the wings of the wind o'er the waters
　blue.
　j.　　SHELLEY—*Music.*

The tender violet bent in smiles
　To elves that sported nigh,
Tossing the drops of fragrant dew
　To scent the evening sky.
　k.　　ELIZABETH OAKES SMITH—*Field Elves.*

Oh! faint delicious spring-time violet,
　Thine odor like a key,
Turns noiselessly in memory's wards to let
　A thought of sorrow free.
　l.　　W. W. STORY—*The Violet.*

And from his ashes may be made
The violet of his native land.
　m.　　TENNYSON—*In Memoriam.* XVIII.

　　　　　And in my breast
Spring wakens too; and my regret
　Becomes an April violet,
And buds and blossoms like the rest.
　n.　　TENNYSON—*In Memoriam.* CXV.

The smell of violets, hidden in the green,
　Pour'd back into my empty soul and frame
The times when I remembered to have been
　Joyful and free from blame.
　o.　　TENNYSON—*A Dream of Fair Women.
　　　　　　　　　St. 20.*

A humble flower long time I pined
　Upon the solitary plain,
And trembled at the angry wind,
　And shrunk before the bitter rain.
And oh! 'twas in a blessed hour
　A passing wanderer chanced to see,
And, pitying the lonely flower,
　To stoop and gather me.
　p.　　THACKERAY—*Song of the Violet.*

The violet would thy dusk hair deck
With graces like thine own unsought.
Ah! but such place would daze and wreck
Its simple, lowly rustic thought.
For so advancèd, dear, to thee,
It would unlearn humility!
　q.　　FRANCIS THOMPSON—*Gilded Gold.
　　　　　　　　　St. 3.*

Banks that slope to the southern sky
Where languid violets love to lie.
　r.　　SARAH HELEN WHITMAN—*Wood Walks
　　　　　　　　in Spring.* L. 11.

Here oft we sought the violet, as it lay
Buried in beds of moss and lichens gray.
　s.　　SARAH HELEN WHITMAN—*A Day of
　　　　　　the Indian Summer.* L. 33.

In kindly showers and sunshine bud
The branches of the dull gray wood;
Out from its sunned and sheltered nooks
The blue eye of the violet looks.
　t.　　WHITTIER—*Mogg Megone.* Pt. III.

A violet by a mossy stone
　Half hidden from the eye!
Fair as a star when only one
　Is shining in the sky.
　u.　　WORDSWORTH—*She Dwelt Among the
　　　　　　Untrodden Ways.*

The violets of five seasons reappear
And fade, unseen by any human eye.
    a.   WORDSWORTH—*Nutting.*

You violets that first appear,
  By your pure purple mantles known,
Like the proud virgins of the year,
  As if the spring were all your own—
What are you when the rose is blown?
    b.   SIR HENRY WOTTON—*To his Mistress
        the Queen of Bohemia.*

Wallflower.
Cheiranthus Cheiri.

The Wall-flower—the Wall-flower,
  How beautiful it blooms!
It gleams above the ruined tower,
  Like sunlight over tombs;
It sheds a halo of repose
  Around the wrecks of time.
To beauty give the flaunting rose,
  The Wall-flower is sublime.
    c.   D. M. MOIR—*The Wall-Flower.*

Water-lily.
Nymphæa.

What loved little islands, twice seen in their
    lakes,
  Can the wild water-lily restore.
    d.   CAMPBELL—*Field Flowers.*

The slender water-lily
  Peeps dreamingly out of the lake;
The moon, oppress'd with love's sorrow,
  Looks tenderly down for her sake.
    e.   HEINE—*Book of Songs. New Spring.
        No. 15. St. 1.*

Those virgin lilies, all the night
  Bathing their beauties in the lake,
That they may rise more fresh and bright,
  When their beloved sun's awake.
    f.   MOORE—*Lalla Rookh. Paradise and
        the Peri.*

Broad water-lilies lay tremulously,
And starry river-buds glimmered by,
And around them the soft stream did glide
    and dance
With a motion of sweet sound and radiance.
    g.   SHELLEY—*The Sensitive Plant. Pt. I.*

She saw the river onward glide,
The lilies nodding on the tide.
    h.   SUSAN A. TALLEY—*Ennerslie.*

Now folds the lily all her sweetness up,
And slips into the bosom of the lake;
So fold thyself, my dearest, thou, and slip
Into my bosom, and be lost in me.
    i.   TENNYSON—*The Princess. VII. L. 171.*

The water-lily starts and slides
Upon the level in little puffs of wind,
Tho' anchor'd to the bottom.
    j.   TENNYSON—*The Princess. IV. L. 236.*

Swan flocks of lilies shoreward lying,
In sweetness, not in music, dying,—
  Hardhack, and virgin's-bower,
  And white-spiked clethra-flower.
    k.   WHITTIER—*The Maids of Attitash.*

Rapaciously we gathered flowery spoils
From land and water; lilies of each hue,—
Golden and white, that float upon the
    waves,
And court the wind.
    l.   WORDSWORTH—*The Excursion. Bk. IX.
        L. 540.*

Windflower.
Anemone.

Or, bide thou where the poppy blows
With windflowers frail and fair.
    m.   BRYANT—*The Arctic Lover.*

The little windflower, whose just opened
    eye
Is blue as the spring heaven it gazes at.
    n.   BRYANT—*A Winter Piece.*

The starry, fragile windflower,
  Poised above in airy grace,
Virgin white, suffused with blushes,
  Shyly droops her lovely face.
    o.   ELAINE GOODALE—*The First Flowers.*

Thou lookest up with meek, confiding eye
  Upon the clouded smile of April's face,
Unharmed though Winter stands uncertain by,
  Eyeing with jealous glance each opening
    grace.
    p.   JONES VERY—*The Windflower.*

Woodbine.
Lonicera.

       And stroke with listless hand'
The woodbine through the window, till at
    last
I came to do it with a sort of love.
    q.   E. B. BROWNING—*Aurora Leigh. Bk. I.*

A filbert-hedge with wild-briar overtwined,
And clumps of woodbine taking the soft
    wind
Upon their summer thrones.
    r.   KEATS—*I Stood Tiptoe Upon a Little
        Hill.*

And the woodbine spices are wafted abroad,
And the musk of the rose is blown.
    s.   TENNYSON—*Maud. Pt. XXII. St. I.*

FOLLY.

The picture placed the busts between
Adds to the thought much strength :
Wisdom and Wit are little seen,
But Folly's at full length.
　　a.　　JANE BRERETON—*On Beau Nash's*
　　　　　　Picture at full length between the Busts
　　　　　　of Sir Isaac Newton and Mr. Pope.

For blocks are better cleft with wedges,
Than tools of sharp or subtle edges,
And dullest nonsense has been found
By some to be the most profound.
　　b.　　BUTLER—*Pindaric Ode.　IV.　*L. 82.

He made an instrument to know
If the moon shine at full or no.
　　*　　*　　*　　*　　*
And prove that she's not made of green
　　cheese.
　　c.　　BUTLER—*Hudibras.　*Pt. II.
　　　　　　　　　　Canto III.　L. 261.

To swallow gudgeons ere they're catch'd.
And count their chickens ere they're hatch'd.
　　d.　　BUTLER—*Hudibras.　*Pt. II.
　　　　　　　　　　Canto III.　L. 923.

Folly loves the martyrdom of Fame.
　　e.　　BYRON—*Monody on the Death of the*
　　　　　　*Right Hon. R. B. Sheridan.　*L. 68.

Fools are my theme, let satire be my song.
　　f.　　BYRON—*English Bards and Scotch*
　　　　　　　　　　*Reviewers.　*L. 6.

Young men think old men are fools ; but
old men know young men are fools.
　　g.　　GEO. CHAPMAN—*All Fools.　*Act V.
　　　　　　　　　　Sc. 1.　L. 292.

Fool beckons fool, and dunce awakens dunce.
　　h.　　CHURCHILL—*Apology.　*L. 42.

A fool must now and then be right by chance.
　　i.　　COWPER—*Conversation.　*L. 96.

The solemn fop ; significant and budge ;
A fool with judges, amongst fools a judge.
　　j.　　COWPER—*Conversation.　*L. 299.

Swear, fool, or starve ; for the dilemma's
　　even ;
A tradesman thou ! and hope to go to heaven ?
　　k.　　DRYDEN—*Persius.　*Satire V.　L. 204.

Like his that lights a candle to the sun.
　　l.　　FLETCHER—*Letter to Sir Walter Aston.*

He has paid dear, very dear, for his whistle.
　　m.　　BENJ. FRANKLIN—*The Whistle.*

A fool and a wise man are alike both in
the starting-place—their birth, and at the
post—their death ; only they differ in the
race of their lives.
　　n.　　FULLER—*The Holy and Profane States.*
　　　　　　*Of Natural Fools.　*Maxim IV.

By outward show let's not be cheated ;
An ass should like an ass be treated.
　　o.　　GAY—*Fables.　The Packhorse and*
　　　　　　　　　　*Carrier.　*Pt. II.　L. 99.

A rational reaction against irrational ex-
cesses and vagaries of skepticism may * * *
readily degenerate into the rival folly of
credulity.
　　p.　　GLADSTONE—*Time and Place of Homer.*
　　　　　　　　　　Introductory.

　　　　　　　　He is a fool
Who only sees the mischiefs that are past.
　　q.　　HOMER—*Iliad.　*Bk. XVII.　L. 39.
　　　　　　　　　　Bryant's Trans.

A man may be as much a fool from the
want of sensibility as the want of sense.
　　r.　　MRS. JAMESON—*Studies.　Detached*
　　　　　　　　　　*Thoughts.　*P. 122.

He is one of those wise philanthropists who,
in a time of famine, would vote for nothing
but a supply of toothpicks.
　　s.　　DOUGLAS JERROLD—*Douglas Jerrold's*
　　　　　　　　　　Wit.

The right to be a cussed fool
　　Is safe from all devices human,
It's common (ez a gin'l rule)
　　To every critter born of woman.
　　t.　　LOWELL—*The Biglow Papers.　*Second
　　　　　　　　　　Series.　No. 7.　St. 16.

I have play'd the fool, the gross fool, to be-
　　lieve
The bosom of a friend will hold a secret
Mine own could not contain.
　　u.　　MASSINGER—*Unnatural Combat.*
　　　　　　　　　　Act V.　Sc. 2.

Young men think old men fools, and old
men know young men to be so.
　　v.　　*Quoted by* CAMDEN *as a saying of*
　　　　　　　　　　DR. METCALF.

In a bowl to sea went wise men three,
　　On a brilliant night in June :
They carried a net, and their hearts were set
　　On fishing up the moon.
　　w.　　THOMAS LOVE PEACOCK—*The Wise*
　　　　　　　　　Men of Gotham.　Paper Money
　　　　　　　　　　*Lyrics.　*St. 1.

Die and endow a college or a cat.
　　x.　　POPE—*Moral Essays.　*Ep. III.
　　　　　　　　　　*To Bathurst.　*L. 96.

Fire in each eye, and papers in each hand,
They rave, recite, and madden round the land.
　　y.　　POPE—*Prologue to Satires.　*L. 5.

For fools rush in where angels fear to tread.
　　z.　　POPE—*Essay on Criticism.　*Pt. III.
　　　　　　　　　　L. 66.

Just as a blockhead rubs his thoughtless skull,
And thanks his stars he was not born a fool.
　　aa.　　POPE—*Epilogue of Jane Shore.　*L. 7.

Leave such to trifle with more grace and ease,
Whom Folly pleases, and whose Follies please.
> *a.*   POPE—*Second Book of Horace.*   Ep. II.
> L. 326.

No creature smarts so little as a fool.
> *b.*   POPE—*Prologue to Satires.*   L. 84.

So by false learning is good sense defac'd;
Some are bewilder'd in the maze of schools,
And some made coxcombs Nature meant but
fools.
> *c.*   POPE—*Essay on Criticism.*   Pt. I.
> L. 25.

The fool is happy that he knows no more.
> *d.*   POPE—*Essay on Man.*   Ep. II.   L. 264.

The rest on outside merit but presume,
Or serve (like other fools) to fill a room.
> *e.*   POPE—*The Dunciad.*   Bk. I.   L. 136.

Whether the charmer sinner it, or saint it,
If folly grow romantic, I must paint it.
> *f.*   POPE—*Moral Essays.*   Ep. 2.   L. 15.

By robbing Peter he paid Paul, he kept the
moon from the wolves, and was ready to catch
larks if ever the heavens should fall.
> *g.*   RABELAIS—*Works.*   Bk. I.   Ch. XI.

After a man has sown his wild oats in the
years of his youth, he has still every year to
get over a few weeks and days of folly.
> *h.*   RICHTER—*Flower, Fruit, and Thorn*
> *Pieces.*   Bk. II.   Ch. V.

Where lives the man that has not tried,
How mirth can into folly glide,
And folly into sin!
> *i.*   SCOTT—*Bridal of Triermain.*   Canto I.
> St. 21.

Thou little thinkest what a little foolery
governs the whole world.
> *j.*   JOHN SELDEN—*Table Talk.*   *Pope.*

A fool, a fool! I met a fool i' the forest,
A motley fool; a miserable world!
As I do live by food, I met a fool;
Who laid him down and bask'd him in the
sun.
> *k.*   *As You Like It.*   Act II.   Sc. 7.
> L. 12.

A fool's bolt is soon shot.
> *l.*   *Henry V.*   Act III.   Sc. 7.   L. 132.

Fools are not mad folks.
> *m.*   *Cymbeline.*   Act II.   Sc. 3.   L. 105.

He capers nimbly in a lady's chamber
To the lascivious pleasing of a lute.
> *n.*   *Richard III.*   Act I.   Sc. 1.   L. 12.

I had rather have a fool to make me merry
than experience to make me sad: and to
travel for it too!
> *o.*   *As You Like It.*   Act IV.   Sc. 1.
> L. 26.

I hold him but a fool that will endanger
His body for a girl that loves him not.
> *p.*   *Two Gentlemen of Verona.*   Act V.
> Sc. 4.   L. 133.

Let the doors be shut upon him, that he
may play the fool nowhere but in 's own
house.
> *q.*   *Hamlet.*   Act III.   Sc. 1.   L. 134.

Marry, sir, they praise me and make an
ass of me; now my foes tell me plainly I am
an ass; so that by my foes, sir, I profit in the
knowledge of myself.
> *r.*   *Twelfth Night.*   Act V.   Sc. 1.   L. 19.

O murderous coxcomb! what should such a
fool
Do with so good a woman?
> *s.*   *Othello.*   Act V.   Sc. 2.   L. 233.

O noble fool!
A worthy fool! Motley's the only wear.
> *t.*   *As You Like It.*   Act II.   Sc. 7.   L. 33.

Sir, for a *quart d'écu* he will sell the fee-
simple of his salvation, the inheritance of it;
and cut the entail from all remainders.
> *u.*   *All's Well That Ends Well.*   Act IV.
> Sc. 3.   L. 311.

The fool doth think he is wise, but the wise
man knows himself to be a fool.
> *v.*   *As You Like It.*   Act V.   Sc. 1.   L. 34.

The fool hath planted in his memory
An army of good words; and I do know
A many fools, that stand in better place,
Garnish'd like him, that for a tricksy word
Defy the matter.
> *w.*   *Merchant of Venice.*   Act III.   Sc. 5.
> L. 71.

This fellow is wise enough to play the fool;
And to do that well craves a kind of wit.
> *x.*   *Twelfth Night.*   Act III.   Sc. 1.   L. 67.

To gild refined gold, to paint the lily,
To throw a perfume on the violet,
To smooth the ice, or add another hue
Unto the rainbow, or with taper-light
To seek the beauteous eye of heaven to garnish,
Is wasteful and ridiculous excess.
> *y.*   *King John.*   Act IV.   Sc. 2.   L. 11.

To wisdom he's a fool that will not yield.
> *z.*   *Pericles.*   Act II.   Sc. 4.   L. 54.

Well, thus we play the fools with the time,
and the spirits of the wise sit in the clouds
and mock us.

   a.   *Henry IV.*   Pt. II.   Act II.   Sc. 2.
                                 L. 154.

             You may as well
Forbid the sea for to obey the moon
As or by oath remove or counsel shake
The fabric of his folly.

   b.   *Winter's Tale.*   Act I.   Sc. 2.   L. 426.

'Tis not by guilt the onward sweep
Of truth and right, O Lord, we stay;
'Tis by our follies that so long
We hold the earth from heaven away.

   c.   E. R. SILL—*The Fool's Prayer.*

He has spent all his life in letting down
empty buckets into empty wells, and he is
frittering away his age in trying to draw them
up again.

   d.   SYDNEY SMITH—*Lady Holland's*
                    Memoir. Vol. I.   P. 259.

For take thy ballaunce if thou be so wise,
And weigh the winde that under heaven doth
     blow;
Or weigh the light that in the east doth rise;
Or weigh the thought that from man's mind
     doth flow.

   e.   SPENSER—*Faerie Queen.*   Bk. V.
                         Canto II.   St. 43.

He had been eight years upon a project for
extracting sunbeams out of cucumbers, which
were to be put in phials hermetically sealed,
and let out to warm the air in raw, inclement
summers.

   f.   SWIFT—*Gulliver's Travels.*   Pt. III.
                  Ch. V.   *Voyage to Laputa.*

'Tis my maxim, he's a fool that marries;
but he's a greater that does not marry a fool.

   g.   WYCHERLY—*The Country Wife.*   Act I.
                         Sc. 1.   L. 502.

And hold their farthing candle to the sun.

   h.   YOUNG—*Satire VII.*   L. 56.

At thirty man suspects himself a fool;
Knows it at forty, and reforms his plan.

   i.   YOUNG—*Night Thoughts.*   Night I.
                               L. 417.

Men may live fools, but fools they cannot die.

   j.   YOUNG—*Night Thoughts.*   Night IV.
                           Last line.

We bleed, we tremble; we forget, we smile—
The mind turns fool, before the cheek is dry.

   k.   YOUNG—*Night Thoughts.*   Night V.
                               L. 511.

What folly can be ranker? Like our shadows,
Our wishes lengthen as our sun declines.

   l.   YOUNG—*Night Thoughts.*   Night V.
                               L. 661.

FOOT.

To one commending an orator for his skill
in amplifying petty matters, Agesilaus said;
"I do not think that shoemaker a good workman that makes a great shoe for a little foot."

   m.   AGESILAUS THE GREAT—*Laconic*
                            Apophthegmns.

And the prettiest foot! Oh, if a man could
but fasten his eyes to her feet, as they steal in
and out, and play at bo-peep under her petti-
coats!

   n.   CONGREVE—*Love for Love.*   Act I.
                                 Sc. 1.

Her pretty feet
Like snails did creep
     A little out, and then,
As if they played at bo-peep
     Did soon draw in agen.

   o.   HERRICK—*Upon her Feet.*

Feet that run on willing errands!

   p.   LONGFELLOW—*Hiawatha.*   Pt. X.
                    Hiawatha's Wooing.   L. 33.

An old doting fool, with one foot already in
the grave.

   q.   PLUTARCH—*Morals.*   *On the Training*
                              of Children.

'Tis all one as if they should make the
Standard for the measure, we call a Foot, a
Chancellor's Foot; what an uncertain Meas-
ure would this be! one Chancellor has a long
Foot, another a short Foot, a Third an indif-
ferent Foot. 'Tis the same thing in the
Chancellor's Conscience.

   r.   JOHN SELDEN—*Table Talk.*   *Equity.*

Nay, her foot speaks.

   s.   *Troilus and Cressida.*   Act IV.   Sc. 5.
                                 L. 56.

          O, so light a foot
Will ne'er wear out the everlasting flint.

   t.   *Romeo and Juliet.*   Act II.   Sc. 6.
                                 L. 16.

          O happy earth,
Whereon thy innocent feet doe ever tread!

   u.   SPENSER—*Faerie Queene.*   Bk. I.
                         Canto X.   St. 9.

Her feet beneath her petticoat,
Like little mice, stole in and out,
     As if they feared the light:
But oh! she dances such a way!
No sun upon an Easter day
     Is half so fine a sight.

   v.   SIR JOHN SUCKLING—*Ballad Upon a*
                          Wedding.   St. 8.

And feet like sunny gems on an English green.

   w.   TENNYSON—*Maud.*   Pt. V.   St. 2.

FOOTSTEPS.

              The tread
Of coming footsteps cheats the midnight
    watcher
Who holds her heart and waits to hear them
    pause,
And hears them never pause, but pass and
    die.
    a.   George Eliot—*The Spanish Gypsy.*
                    Bk. III.

          And so to tread
As if the wind, not she, did walk ;
Nor prest a flower, nor bow'd a stalk.
    b.   Ben Jonson—*Masques. The Vision of*
                    Delight.

Her treading would not bend a blade of
    grass,
Or shake the downy blow-ball from his
    stalk !
    c.   Ben Jonson—*The Sad Shepherd.*

I heard him walking across the floor,
And he always does, with a heavy tread.
    d.   Longfellow—*Christus.* Pt. II. *The*
                    Golden Legend. II.

A foot more light, a step more true,
Ne'er from the heath-flower dashed the
    dew.
    e.   Scott—*Lady of the Lake.* Canto I.
                    St. 18.

The grass stoops not, she treads on it so light.
    f.   *Venus and Adonis.* L. 1,028.

Steps with a tender foot, light as on air,
The lovely, lordly creature floated on.
    g.   Tennyson—*The Princess.* VI. L. 72.

Methought I saw the footsteps of a throne.
    h.   Wordsworth—*Miscellaneous Sonnets.*
                Methought I Saw the Footsteps of a
                    Throne.

FOPPERY.

'Tis mean for empty praise of wit to write,
As fopplings grin to show their teeth are
    white.
    i.   Brown—*Essay on Satire.* St. 2.

I marched the lobby, twirled my stick,
    *   *   *   *   *   *
The girls all cried, " He's quite the kick."
    j.   Geo. Colman (The Younger)—*Broad*
                Grins. Song. St. 1.

Of all the fools that pride can boast,
A Coxcomb claims distinction most.
    k.   Gay—*Fables.* Pt. II. *Fable 5.*

    A beau is one who arranges his curled
locks gracefully, who ever smells of balm, and
cinnamon ; who hums the songs of the Nile,
and Cadiz ; who throws his sleek arms into
various attitudes ; who idles away the whole
day among the chairs of the ladies, and is ever
whispering into some one's ear ; who reads
little billets-doux from this quarter and that,
and writes them in return ; who avoids ruffling his dress by contact with his neighbour's
sleeve, who knows with whom everybody is
in love ; who flutters from feast to feast, who
can recount exactly the pedigree of Hirpinus.
What do you tell me ? is this a beau, Cotilus ?
Then a beau, Cotilus, is a very trifling thing.
    l.   Martial—*Epigrams.* Bk. III. Ep. 6.

Nature made every fop to plague his brother,
Just as one beauty mortifies another.
    m.   Pope—*Satire IV.* L. 258.

A lofty cane, a sword with silver hilt,
A ring, two watches, and a snuff box gilt.
    n.   Recipe " *To Make a Modern Fop.*"
                    About 1770.

A fop ? In this brave, licentious age
To bring his musty morals on the stage ?
Rhime us to reason ? and our lives redress
In metre, as Druids did the savages.
    o.   Tuke—*The Adventures of Five Hours.*
                    Act V.

Has death his fopperies ?
    p.   Young—*Night Thoughts.* Night II.
                    L. 231.

FORGETFULNESS.

    There is nothing new except what is for-
gotten.
    q.   Attributed to Mlle. Bertin, *Milliner to*
                Marie Antoinette.

But my thoughts ran a wool-gathering ; and
I did like the countryman, who looked for
his ass while he was mounted on his back.
    r.   Cervantes—*Don Quixote.* Pt. II.
                    Ch. LVII.

The pyramids themselves, doting with age,
have forgotten the names of their founders.
    s.   Fuller—*Holy and Profane States. Of*
                Tombs. Maxim VI.

Some men treat the God of their fathers as
they treat their father's friend. They do not
deny him ; by no means : they only deny
themselves to him, when he is good enough
to call upon them.
    t.   J. C. and A. W. Hare—*Guesses at*
                    Truth.

Forgotten? No, we never do forget:
We let the years go; wash them clean with
    tears,
Leave them to bleach out in the open day,
Or lock them careful by, like dead friends'
    clothes,
Till we shall dare unfold them without pain,—
But we forget not, never can forget.
    a.   D. M. Mulock—*A Flower of a Day.*

Mistakes remember'd are not faults forgot.
    b.   R. H. Newell—*The Orpheus C. Kerr
        Papers. Second Series. Columbia's
        Agony.* St. 9.

        We bury love,
Forgetfulness grows over it like grass;
That is a thing to weep for, not the dead.
    c.   Alexander Smith—*City Poems.
        A Boy's Poem.* Pt. III.

One day I wrote her name upon the strand,
    But came the waves and washed it away;
Agayne I wrote it with a second hand,
    But came the tyde and made my paynes his
        prey.
    d.   Spenser—*Sonnet LXXV.*

Go, forget me—why should sorrow
    O'er that brow a shadow fling?
Go, forget me—and to-morrow
    Brightly smile and sweetly sing.
Smile—though I shall not be near thee;
Sing—though I shall never hear thee.
    e.   Charles Wolfe—*Song. Go, Forget Me!*

FORGIVENESS.

Good, to forgive;
Best to forget.
    f.   Robert Browning—*La Saisiaz.*
        Prologue.

The fairest action of our human life
    Is scorning to revenge an injury;
For who forgives without a further strife,
    His adversary's heart to him doth tie:
And 'tis a firmer conquest, truly said,
To win the heart than overthrow the head.
    g.   Lady Elizabeth Carew—*Chorus from
        " Mariam."*

We read that we ought to forgive our enemies; but we do not read that we ought to
forgive our friends.
    h.   *Attributed to* Cosmus, *Duke of Florence,
        by* Bacon. *Apothegms.* No. 206.

Thou whom avenging pow'rs obey,
Cancel my debt (too great to pay)
Before the sad accounting day.
    i.   Wentworth Dillon—*On the Day of
        Judgment.* St. 11.

Forgiveness to the injured does belong,
But they ne'er pardon who have done the
    wrong.
    j.   Dryden—*Conquest of Granada.*
        Pt. II. Act I. Sc. 2.

She hugged the offender, and forgave the
    offense,
Sex to the last.
    k.   Dryden—*Cymon and Iphigenia.*
        L. 367.

His heart was as great as the world, but
there was no room in it to hold the memory
of a wrong.
    l.   Emerson—*Letters and Social Aims.
        Greatness.*

The offender never pardons.
    m.   Herbert—*Jacula Prudentum.*
        No. 563.

    For 'tis sweet to stammer one letter
Of the Eternal's language;—on earth it is callèd
    Forgiveness!
    n.   Longfellow—*The Children of the Lord's
        Supper.* L. 214.

    These evils I deserve, and more
    *   *
Justly, yet despair not of his final pardon,
Whose ear is ever open, and his eye
Gracious to re-admit the suppliant.
    o.   Milton—*Samson Agonistes.* L. 1170.

Good-nature and good-sense must ever join;
To err is human, to forgive, divine.
    p.   Pope—*Essay on Criticism.* L. 522.

I pardon him, as God shall pardon me.
    q.   *Richard II.* Act V. Sc. 3. L. 131.

        What if this cursed hand
Were thicker than itself with brother's blood?
Is there not rain enough in the sweet heavens
To wash it white as snow?
    r.   *Hamlet.* Act III. Sc. 3. L. 43.

The more we know, the better we forgive;
Whoe'er feels deeply, feels for all who live.
    s.   Madame de Staël—*Corinne.*
        Bk. XVIII. Ch. V.

Pardon, not wrath, is God's best attribute.
    t.   Bayard Taylor—*Poems of the Orient.
        Temptation of Hassan Ben Khaled.*
        St. 11. L. 31.

        The sin
That neither God nor man can well forgive.
    u.   Tennyson—*Sea Dreams.*

FORTUNE.

But chiefly, the mould of a man's fortune is
in his own hands.
    v.   Bacon—*Essays. Of Fortune.*

Therefore if a man look sharply and atten-
tively, he shall see Fortune: for though she
be blind, yet she is not invisible.
    w.   Bacon—*Essays. Of Fortune.*

Fortune, now see, now proudly
Pluck off thy veil, and view thy triumph ; look,
Look what thou hast brought this land to !—
   a.   BEAUMONT AND FLETCHER—*The*
          Tragedy of Bonduca. Act V. Sc. 5.

Just for a handful of silver he left us,
   Just for a ribbon to stick in his coat ;
Found the one gift of which Fortune bereft
     us,
   Lost all the others she lets us devote.
   b.   ROBERT BROWNING—*The Lost Leader.*

Fortune, the great commandress of the world,
Hath divers ways to advance her followers :
To some she gives honor without deserving ;
To other some, deserving without honor ;
Some wit, some wealth,—and some, wit with-
     out wealth ;
Some wealth without wit ; some nor wit nor
     wealth.
   c.   GEO. CHAPMAN—*All Fools.* Act V.
                             Sc. 1.

Ill fortune seldom comes alone.
   d.   DRYDEN—*Cymon and Iphigenia.*
                           L. 592.

Let fortune empty her whole quiver on me.
I have a soul that, like an ample shield,
Can take in all, and verge enough for more.
   e.   DRYDEN—*Don Sebastian.* Act I. Sc. 1.

Neuer thinke you fortune can beare the sway,
Where Virtue's force, can cause her to obay.
   f.   QUEEN ELIZABETH—*Preserved by*
         Geo. Puttenham in his "Art of Poesie."
         Bk. III. *Of Ornament, "which"*
         (*he says*) *" our soueraigne Lady*
                wrote in defiance of
                      Fortune."

Vicissitudes of fortune, which spares neither
man nor the proudest of his works, which
buries empires and cities in a common grave.
   g.   GIBBON—*Decline and Fall of the*
          Roman Empire. Ch. LXXI.

Too poor for a bribe, and too proud to im-
     portune ;
He had not the method of making a fortune.
   h.   GRAY—*On his own Character.*

Fortune, men say, doth give too much to
     many,
But yet she never gave enough to any.
   i.   SIR JOHN HARRINGTON—*Epigram. Of*
                           Fortune.

The bitter dregs of Fortune's cup to drain.
   j.   HOMER—*Iliad.* Bk. XX. L. 85.
                         Pope's trans.

Fortune comes well to all that comes not
     late.
   k.   LONGFELLOW—*Spanish Student.*
               Act III. Sc. 5. L. 281.

I wish thy lot, now bad, still worse, my
     friend,
For when at worst, they say, things always
     mend.
   l.   OWEN—*To a Friend in Distress.*
                      Cowper's trans.

Fortune in men has some small diff'rence
     made,
One flaunts in rags, one flutters in brocade ;
The cobbler apron'd, and the parson gown'd,
The friar hooded, and the monarch crown'd.
   m.   POPE—*Essay on Man.* Ep. IV. L. 195.

Who thinks that fortune cannot change her
     mind,
Prepares a dreadful jest for all mankind.
And who stands safest ? Tell me, is it he
That spreads and swells in puff'd prosperity,
Or bless'd with little, whose preventing care
In peace provides fit arms against a war ?
   n.   POPE—*Second Book of Horace.*
                Satire II. L. 123.

Every one is the architect of his own fortune.
   o.   PSEUDO-SALLUST—*Ep. de Rep. Ordin.*
                  Ep. II. St. 1.

A good man's fortune may grow out at heels.
   p.   *King Lear.* Act II. Sc. 2. L. 164.

And rail'd on Lady Fortune in good terms.
   q.   *As You Like It.* Act II. Sc. 7. L. 16.

Fortune brings in some boats, that are not
     steer'd.
   r.   *Cymbeline.* Act IV. Sc. 3. L. 46.

                   Fortune is merry,
And in this mood will give us anything.
   s.   *Julius Cæsar.* Act III. Sc. 2. L. 271.

                   Fortune knows,
We scorn her most, when most she offers
     blows.
   t.   *Antony and Cleopatra.* Act III. Sc. 11.
                         L. 73.

Fortune, that arrant whore,
Ne'er turns the key to the poor.
   u.   *King Lear.* Act II. Sc. 4. L. 52.

How some men creep in skittish Fortune's
     hall,
While others play the idiots in her eyes !
   v.   *Troilus and Cressida.* Act III. Sc. 3.
                         L. 134.

I find my zenith doth depend upon
A most auspicious star ; whose influence
If now I court not, but omit, my fortunes
Will ever after droop.
   w.   *Tempest.* Act I. Sc. 2. L. 181.

O fortune, fortune ! all men call thee fickle.
   x.   *Romeo and Juliet.* Act III. Sc. 5.
                         L. 60.

The great man down, you mark his favorite
    flies,
The poor advanced makes friends of enemies.
   a.   *Hamlet.* Act III. Sc. 2. L. 214.

That they are not a pipe for fortune's finger
To sound what stop she please.
   b.   *Hamlet.* Act III. Sc. 2. L. 75.

When Fortune means to men most good,
She looks upon them with a threatening eye.
   c.   *King John.* Act III. Sc. 4. L. 119.

Will Fortune never come with both hands full,
But write her fair words still in foulest letters ?
She either gives a stomach, and no food ;
Such are the poor, in health ; or else a feast,
And takes away the stomach ; such are the
    rich,
That have abundance, and enjoy it not.
   d.   *Henry IV.* Pt. II. Act IV. Sc. 4.
                      L. 103.

     Ye gods, it doth amaze me,
A man of such a feeble temper should
So get the start of the majestic world,
And bear the palm alone.
   e.   *Julius Cæsar.* Act I. Sc. 2. L. 128.

            So is Hope
Changed for Despair—one laid upon the shelf,
We take the other. Under heaven's high cope
Fortune is god—all you endure and do
Depends on circumstance as much as you.
   f.   Shelley—*Epigrams. From the Greek.*

Fortune, my friend, I've often thought,
Is weak, if Art assist her not :
So equally all Arts are vain,
If Fortune help them not again.
   g.   Sheridan—*Love Epistles of*
                    Aristænetus. Ep. XIII.

   Fortune is like glass—the brighter the glitter, the more easily broken.
   h.   Publius Syrus. *Maxims.* 283.

Forever, Fortune, wilt thou prove
An unrelenting foe to love,
And, when we meet a mutual heart,
Come in between, and bid us part ?
   i.   Thomson—*Song. To Fortune.*

For fortune's wheel is on the turn,
And some go up and some go down.
   j.   Mary F. Tucker—*Going Up and*
                    Coming Down.

FRAILTY.

Glass antique ! 'twixt thee and Nell
Draw we here a parallel.
She, like thee, was forced to bear
All reflections, foul or fair.
   Thou art deep and bright within,—
   Depths as bright belong'd to Gwynne ;
   Thou art very frail as well,
   Frail as flesh is,—so was Nell.
   k.   L. Blanchard—*Nell Gwynne's Looking*
                    Glass. St. 1.

This is the porcelain clay of human kind.
   l.   Dryden—*Don Sebastian.* Act I.
                        Sc. 1.

Unthought-of Frailties cheat us in the Wise.
   m.   Pope—*Moral Essays.* Ep. *To Temple.*
                      L. 69.

Alas ! our frailty is the cause, not we ;
For, such as we are made of, such we be.
   n.   *Twelfth Night.* Act II. Sc. 2. L. 32.

Frailty, thy name is woman !
   o.   *Hamlet.* Act I. Sc. 2. L. 146.

   Sometimes we are devils to ourselves,
When we will tempt the frailty of our powers,
Presuming on their changeful potency.
   p.   *Troilus and Cressida.* Act IV. Sc. 4.
                      L. 96.

FRAUD.

   The first and worst of all frauds is to cheat
One's self.
   q.   Bailey—*Festus.* Sc. *Anywhere.*

Perplexed and troubled at his bad success
The Tempter stood, nor had what to reply,
Discovered in his fraud, thrown from his
   hope.
   r.   Milton—*Paradise Regained.* Bk. IV.
                      L. 1.

So glistered the dire Snake, and into fraud
Led Eve, our credulous mother, to the Tree
Of Prohibition, root of all our woe.
   s.   Milton—*Paradise Lost.* Bk. IX.
                      L. 643.

            Some cursed fraud
Of enemy hath beguiled thee, yet unknown,
And me with thee hath ruined.
   t.   Milton—*Paradise Lost.* Bk. IX.
                      L. 904.

   His heart as far from fraud as heaven from
earth.
   u.   *Two Gentlemen of Verona.* Act II.
                    Sc. 7. L. 78.

FREEDOM.

Here the free spirit of mankind, at length,
   Throws its last fetters off ; and who shall
      place
A limit to the giant's unchained strength,
   Or curb his swiftness in the forward race ?
   v.   Bryant—*The Ages.* XXXIII.

For Freedom's battle once begun,
Bequeath'd by bleeding sire to son,
Though baffled oft is ever won.
   w.   Byron—*The Giaour.* L. 123.

Hereditary bondsmen ! Know ye not
Who would be free themselves must strike the
   blow ?
   x.   Byron—*Childe Harold.* Canto II.
                    St. 76.

17

The mountains look on Marathon,
  And Marathon looks on the sea;
And musing there an hour alone
  I dream'd that Greece might still be free.
For standing on the Persians' grave
I could not deem myself a slave.
  a.   BYRON—*The Isles of Greece.*

Yet, Freedom! yet thy banner, torn, but flying,
Streams like the thunder-storm *against* the
  wind.
  b.   BYRON—*Childe Harold.*
                          Canto IV. St. 98.

Hope for a season bade the world farewell,
And Freedom shrieked as Kosciusko fell!
  *   *   *   *   *   *
O'er Prague's proud arch the fires of ruin glow.
  c.   CAMPBELL—*Pleasures of Hope.* L. 381.

England may as well dam up the waters of
the Nile with bulrushes to fetter the step of
Freedom, more proud and firm in this youthful land than where she treads the sequestered
glens of Scotland, or couches herself among
the magnificent mountains of Switzerland.
  d.   LYDIA MARIA CHILD—*Supposititious
          Speech of James Otis.   The Rebels.*
                                Ch. IV.

We hail the return of the day of thy birth,
  Fair Columbia! washed by the waves of
    two oceans—
Where men from the farthest dominions of
    earth
  Rear altars to Freedom, and pay their de-
    votions;
Where our fathers in fight, nobly strove for
    the Right,
Struck down their fierce foemen or put them
    to flight;
Through the long lapse of ages, that so there
    might be
An asylum for all in the Land of the Free.
  e.   ABRAHAM COLES—*The Microcosm,
          and Other Poems.   National Lyrics,*
                                P. 213.

He is the freeman whom the truth makes
    free,
And all are slaves besides.
  f.   COWPER—*The Task.* Bk. V. L. 733.

No, Freedom has a thousand charms to show
That slaves, howe'er contented, never know.
  g.   COWPER—*Table Talk.* L. 260.

When Freedom from her mountain height
  Unfurled her standard to the air,
She tore the azure robe of night,
  And set the stars of glory there.
  h.   JOSEPH RODMAN DRAKE—*The Croakers.
          The American Flag.* St. 1.

I am as free as nature first made man,
Ere the base laws of servitude began,
When wild in woods the noble savage ran.
  i.   DRYDEN—*Conquest of Granada.*
                          Act. I.   Sc. 1.

My angel,—his name is Freedom,—
Choose him to be your king;
He shall cut pathways east and west,
And fend you with his wing.
  j.   EMERSON—*Boston Hymn.*

We grant no dukedoms to the few,
  We hold like rights and shall;
Equal on Sunday in the pew,
  On Monday in the mall.
For what avail the plough or sail,
Or land, or life, if freedom fail?
  k.   EMERSON—*Boston.* St. 5.

Yes! to this thought I hold with firm per-
    sistence;
  The last result of wisdom stamps it true;
He only earns his freedom and existence
  Who daily conquers them anew.
  l.   GOETHE—*Faust.* Act V. Sc. 6.

Ay, call it holy ground,
  The soil where first they trod,
They have left unstained, what there they
    found,—
  Freedom to worship God.
  m.   MRS. HEMANS—*Landing of the Pilgrim
                                Fathers.*

In the beauty of the lilies Christ was born
    across the sea,
With a glory in his bosom that transfigures
    you and me;
As he died to make men holy, let us die to
    make men free,
While God is marching on.
  n.   JULIA WARD HOWE—*Later Lyrics.
          Battle Hymn of the Republic.*

Know ye why the Cypress tree as freedom's
    tree is known?
Know ye why the Lily fair as freedom's
    flower is shown?
Hundred arms the Cypress has, yet never
    plunder seeks;
With ten well-developed tongues, the Lily
    never speaks!
  o.   OMAR KHAYYAM. Trans. by
                          Frederich Bodenstedt.

I intend no modification of my oft-expressed
wish that all men everywhere could be free.
  p.   ABRAHAM LINCOLN—*Letter to Horace
          Greeley.* Aug. 22, 1862. See Ray-
          mond's "*History of Lincoln's
                          Administration.*"

Freedom needs all her poets; it is they
  Who give her aspirations wings,
And to the wiser law of music sway
  Her wild imaginings.
  q.   LOWELL—*Memorial Verses. To the
                          Memory of Hood.* St. 4.

Sufficient to have stood, though free to fall.
a.   MILTON—*Paradise Lost.*   Bk. III.
                 L. 99.

Oh! let me live my own, and die so too!
(To live and die is all I have to do :)
Maintain a poet's dignity and ease,
And see what friends, and read what books I
    please.
b.   POPE—*Prologue to Satires.*   L. 261.

Blandishments will not fascinate us, nor
will threats of a "halter" intimidate. For,
under God, we are determined that wheresoever, whensoever, or howsoever we shall be
called to make our exit, we will die free men.
c.   JOSIAH QUINCY—*Observations on the*
               Boston Port Bill, 1774.

Free soil, free men, free speech, Fremont.
d.   *Republican Rallying Cry,* 1856.

Freedom is only in the land of Dreams :
e.   SCHILLER—*Commencement of the New*
               Century.   Last line.

When the mind's free,
The body's delicate.
f.   *King Lear.*   Act III.   Sc. 4.   L. 11.

The last link is broken
    That bound me to thee,
And the words thou hast spoken
    Have render'd me free.
g.   FANNY STEERS—*Song.*

The nations lift their right hands up and
    swear
Their oath of freedom.
h.   WHITTIER—*Garibaldi.*

How does the Meadow flower its bloom
    unfold ?
Because the lovely little flower is free
Down to its root, and in that freedom, bold.
i.   WORDSWORTH—*A Poet! He hath put*
               his Heart to School.

We must be free or die, who speak the tongue
That Shakespeare spake; the faith and morals
    hold
Which Milton held.
j.   WORDSWORTH—*Sonnets to National*
           Independence and Liberty.   Pt. XVI.

FRIENDS.

In all thy humours, whether grave or mellow,
Thou'rt such a touchy, testy, pleasant fellow,
Hast so much wit and mirth, and spleen
    about thee,
That there's no living with thee, nor without
    thee.
k.   ADDISON—*Spectator.*   No. 68.

No friend's a friend till [he shall] prove a
friend.
l.   BEAUMONT AND FLETCHER—*The*
           Faithful Friends.   Act III.   Sc. 3.
                 L. 50.

I have loved my friends as I do virtue, my
soul, my God.
m.   SIR THOMAS BROWNE—*Religio Medici.*
               Pt. II.   Sec. V.

Now with my friend I desire not to share or
participate, but to engross his sorrows, that,
by making them mine own, I may more easily
discuss them ; for in mine own reason, and
within myself, I can command that which I
cannot entreat without myself, and within
the circle of another.
n.   SIR THOMAS BROWNE—*Religio Medici.*
               Pt. II.   Sec. V.

                  Let my hand,
This hand, lie in your own—my own true
    friend ;
Aprile! Hand-in-hand with you, Aprile!
o.   ROBERT BROWNING—*Paracelsus.*   Sc. 5.

One faithful Friend is enough for a man's
self; 'tis much to meet with such an one, yet
we can't have too many for the sake of others.
p.   DE LA BRUYÈRE—*The Characters or*
           Manners of the Present Age.   Ch. V.

Ah! were I sever'd from thy side,
Where were thy friend and who my guide?
Years have not seen, Time shall not see
The hour that tears my soul from thee.
q.   BYRON—*The Bride of Abydos.*   Canto I.
                 St. 11.

Heroic, stoic Cato, the sententious,
Who lent his lady to his friend Hortensius.
r.   BYRON—*Don Juan.*   Canto VI.   St. 7.

'Twas sung, how they were lovely in their
    lives,
And in their deaths had not divided been.
s.   CAMPBELL—*Gertrude of Wyoming.*
               Pt. III.   St. 33.

Friends I have made, whom Envy must com-
    mend,
But not one foe whom I would wish a friend.
t.   CHURCHILL—*Conference.*   L. 297.

You must therefore love me, myself, and
not my circumstances, if we are to be real
friends.
u.   CICERO—*De Finibus.*   Yonge's trans.

Our very best friends have a tincture of
jealousy even in their friendship ; and when
they hear us praised by others, will ascribe it
to sinister and interested motives if they can.
v.   C. C. COLTON—*Lacon.*   P. 80.

I would not enter on my list of friends
(Though graced with polish'd manners and
    fine sense,
Yet wanting sensibility) the man
Who needlessly sets foot upon a worm.
    a.   Cowper—*The Task.* Bk. VI. L. 560.

                      She that asks
Her dear five hundred friends, contemns them
    all,
And hates their coming.
    b.   Cowper—*The Task.* Bk. II. L. 642.

The man that hails you Tom or Jack,
And proves by thumps upon your back
    How he esteems your merit,
Is such a friend, that one had need
Be very much his friend indeed
    To pardon or to bear it.
    c.   Cowper—*On Friendship.*

"Wal'r, my boy," replied the captain; "in
the Proverbs of Solomon you will find the following words: 'May we never want a friend
in need, nor a bottle to give him!' When
found, make a note of."
    d.   Dickens—*Dombey and Son.* Vol. I.
                              Ch. XV.

Be kind to my remains; and O defend,
Against your judgment, your departed friend.
    e.   Dryden—*Epistle to Congreve.* L. 72.

The poor make no new friends;
  But oh, they love the better still
The few our Father sends.
    f.   Lady Dufferin—*Lament of the Irish
                         Emigrant.*

The fallying out of faithful frends is the
reunyng of love.
    g.   Richard Edwards—*The Paradise of
                Dainty Devices.* No. 42. St. 1.

Animals are such agreeable friends—they
ask no questions, they pass no criticisms.
    h.   George Eliot—*Mr. Gilfil's Love-
                        Story.* Ch. VII.

Best friend, my well-spring in the wilderness!
    i.   George Eliot—*The Spanish Gypsy.*
                                Bk. III.

Friend more divine than all divinities.
    j.   George Eliot—*The Spanish Gypsy.*
                                Bk. IV.

Where you have friends you should not go
to inns.
    k.   George Eliot—*Agatha.*

To act the part of a true friend requires more
conscientious feeling than to fill with credit
and complacency any other station or capacity
in social life.
    l.   Mrs. Ellis—*Pictures of Private Life.
             Second Series. The Pains of
             Pleasing.* Ch. IV.

A day for toil, an hour for sport,
But for a friend is life too short.
    m.   Emerson—*Considerations by the Way.*

Our friends early appear to us as represen-
tatives of certain ideas, which they never pass
or exceed. They stand on the brink of the
ocean of thought and power, but they never
take a single step that would bring them
there.
    n.   Emerson—*Essays.* *Of Experience.*

The only way to have a friend is to be one.
    o.   Emerson—*Essays.* *Of Friendship.*

'Tis thus that on the choice of friends
Our good or evil name depends.
    p.   Gay—*The Old Woman and Her Cats.*
                                  Pt. I.

He cast off his friends, as a huntsman his pack;
For he knew, when he pleas'd, he could whistle
    them back.
    q.   Goldsmith—*Retaliation.* L. 107.

A favourite has no friend.
    r.   Gray—*On a Favourite Cat Drowned.*
                                St. 6.

Dear lost companions of my tuneful art,
  Dear as the light that visits these sad eyes,
Dear as the ruddy drops that warm my heart.
    s.   Gray—*The Bard.* St. 3.

Of all the heavenly gifts that mortal men
    commend,
What trusty treasure in the world can coun-
    tervail a friend?
    t.   Grimoald—*Of Friendship.* L. 1.

We never know the true value of friends.
While they live, we are too sensitive of their
faults; when we have lost them, we only see
their virtues.
    u.   J. C. and A. W. Hare—*Guesses at
                               Truth.*

For my boyhood's friend hath fallen, the
    pillar of my trust,
The true, the wise, the beautiful, is sleeping
    in the dust.
    v.   Hillard—*On Death of Motley.*

Two friends, two bodies with one soul
inspir'd.
    w.   Homer—*Iliad.* Bk. 16. L. 267.
                             Pope's trans.

True friends appear less mov'd than counterfeit.
    x.   Horace—*Of the Art of Poetry.* L. 486.
              Wentworth Dillon's trans.

        The new is older than the old;
And newest friend is oldest friend in this:
That, waiting him, we longest grieved to miss
One thing we sought.
    y.   Helen Hunt—*My New Friend.*

True happiness
Consists not in the multitude of friends,
But in the worth and choice. Nor would I
  have
Virtue a popular regard pursue:
Let them be good that love me, though but
  few.
    a.   BEN JONSON—*Cynthia's Revels.*
                        Act III. Sc. 2.

'Tis sweet, as year by year we lose
Friends out of sight, in faith to muse
How grows in Paradise our store.
    b.   KEBLE—*Burial of the Dead.* St. 11.

Friend of my bosom, thou more than a
  brother,
Why wert not thou born in my father's
  dwelling?
    c.   CHARLES LAMB—*The Old Familiar
                       Faces.*

Ah, how good it feels!
The hand of an old friend.
    d.   LONGFELLOW—*The New England
          Tragedies. John Endicott.* Act IV.
                            Sc. 1.

Alas! to-day I would give everything
To see a friend's face, or hear a voice
That had the slightest tone of comfort in it.
    e.   LONGFELLOW—*Judas Maccabæus.*
                 Act IV. Sc. 3. L. 32.

My designs and labors
And aspirations are my only friends.
    f.   LONGFELLOW—*The Masque of Pandora.
          Tower of Prometheus on Mount
          Caucasus.* Pt. III. L. 74.

O friend! O best of friends! Thy absence
  more
Than the impending night darkens the landscape o'er!
    g.   LONGFELLOW—*Christus.* Pt. II. *The
                     Golden Legend.* I.

Yes, we must ever be friends; and of all who
  offer you friendship
Let me be ever the first, the truest, the nearest and dearest!
    h.   LONGFELLOW—*The Courtship of Miles
          Standish.* Pt. VI. *Priscilla.* L. 72.

Women, like princes, find few real friends.
    i.   LORD LYTTLETON—*Advice to a Lady.*
                            St. 2.

There is no man so friendless but what he
can find a friend sincere enough to tell him
disagreeable truths.
    j.   BULWER-LYTTON—*What Will He Do
          With It?* Bk. II. Ch. XIV.

A true friend is forever a friend.
    k.   GEORGE MACDONALD—*The Marquis of
                     Lossie.* Ch. LXXI.

Friends are like melons. Shall I tell you
  why?
To find one good, you must a hundred try.
    l.   CLAUDE MERMET—*Epigram on Friends.*

As we sail through life towards death,
Bound unto the same port—heaven,—
Friend, what years could us divide?
    m.   D. M. MULOCK—*Thirty Years. A
                      Christmas Blessing.*

We have been friends together
In sunshine and in shade.
    n.   CAROLINE E. S. NORTON—*We Have
                         Been Friends.*

But oh! if grief thy steps attend,
  If want, if sickness be thy lot,
And thou require a soothing friend,
  Forget me not! forget me not!
    o.   MRS. OPIE—*Song.*

But sweeter none than voice of faithful friend;
Sweet always, sweetest heard in loudest storm.
Some I remember, and will ne'er forget.
    p.   POLLOK—*Course of Time.* Bk. V.
                           L. 310.

For all are friends in heaven, all faithful
  friends;
And many friendships in the days of time
Begun, are lasting here, and growing still.
    q.   POLLOK—*Course of Time.* Bk. V.
                           L. 336.

Friends given by God in mercy and in love;
My counsellors, my comforters, and guides;
My joy in grief, my second bliss in joy;
Companions of my young desires; in doubt
My oracles; my wings in high pursuit.
Oh! I remember, and will ne'er forget
Our meeting spots, our chosen sacred hours;
Our burning words, that utter'd all the soul,
Our faces beaming with unearthly love;—
Sorrow with sorrow sighing, hope with hope
Exulting, heart embracing heart entire.
    r.   POLLOK—*Course of Time.* Bk. V.
                           L. 315.

Ah, friend! to dazzle let the vain design;
To raise the thought and touch the heart be
  thine.
    s.   POPE—*Moral Essays.* Ep. II. L. 248.

Be not the first by whom the new are tried;
Nor yet the last to lay the old aside.
    t.   POPE—*Essay on Criticism.* L. 336.

Trust not yourself; but your defects to know,
Make use of ev'ry friend—and ev'ry foe.
    u.   POPE—*Essay on Criticism.* L. 214.

There is no treasure the which may be com-
　pared unto a faithful friend ;
Gold soone decayeth, and worldly wealth
　consumeth, and wasteth in the winde ;
But love once planted in a perfect and pure
　minde indureth weale and woe ;
The frownes of fortune, come they never so
　unkinde, cannot the same overthrowe.
　a.　　Roxburghe Ballads.　The Bride's Good-
　　　　　　Morrow.　Ed. by John Payne
　　　　　　　　　　　　　　Collier.

Dear is my friend—yet from my foe, as from
　my friend, comes good :
My friend shows what I can do, and my foe
　what I should.
　b.　Schiller—Votive Tablets.　Friend
　　　　　　　　　　　　　　and Foe.

A friend should bear his friend's infirmities,
But Brutus makes mine greater than they are.
　c.　　Julius Cæsar.　Act IV.　Sc. 3.　L. 86.

　　　　　　　　　　　　　For by these
Shall I try friends : you shall perceive how
　you
Mistake my fortunes ; I am wealthy in my
　friends.
　d.　　Timon of Athens.　Act II.　Sc. 2.
　　　　　　　　　　　　　　　L. 191.

For who not needs shall never lack a friend,
And who in want a hollow friend doth try,
Directly seasons him his enemy.
　e.　　Hamlet.　Act III.　Sc. 2.　L. 217.

I am not of that feather to shake off
My friend when he must need me.
　f.　　Timon of Athens.　Act I.　Sc. 1.
　　　　　　　　　　　　　　　L. 100.

I would be friends with you and have your
love.
　g.　　Merchant of Venice.　Act. I.　Sc. 3.
　　　　　　　　　　　　　　　L. 139.

　　　　Keep thy friend
Under thy own life's key.
　h.　　All's Well That Ends Well.　Act I.
　　　　　　　　　　　　Sc. 1.　L. 75.

Those friends thou hast, and their adoption
　tried,
Grapple them to thy soul with hoops of steel ;
But do not dull thy palm with entertainment
Of each new-hatch'd, unfledg'd comrade.
　i.　　Hamlet.　Act I.　Sc. 3.　L. 59.

　　　　To wail friends lost
Is not by much so wholesome—profitable,
As to rejoice at friends but newly found.
　j.　　Love's Labour's Lost.　Act V.　Sc. 2.
　　　　　　　　　　　　　　　L. 759.

Two lovely berries moulded on one stem :
So, with two seeming bodies, but one heart.
　k.　　Midsummer-Night's Dream.　Act III.
　　　　　　　　　　　　Sc. 2.　L. 211.

　　　　We still have slept together,
Rose at an instant, learn'd, play'd, eat to-
　gether ;
And wheresoe'er we went, like Juno's swans,
Still we went coupled and inseparable.
　l.　　As You Like It.　Act I.　Sc. 3.　L. 75.

Where you are liberal of your loves and
　counsels,
Be sure you be not loose ; for those you make
　friends
And give your hearts to, when they once
　perceive
The least rub in your fortunes, fall away
Like water from ye, never found again
But where they mean to sink ye.
　m.　　Henry VIII.　Act II.　Sc. 1.　L. 126.

We twain have met like the ships upon the
　sea,
Who hold an hour's converse, so short, so
　sweet ;
One little hour ! and then, away they speed
On lonely paths, through mist, and cloud,
　and foam,
To meet no more.
　n.　　Alexander Smith—Life Drama.
　　　　　　　　　　　　　　　Sc. IV.

　For to cast away a virtuous friend, I call as
bad as to cast away one's own life, which one
loves best.
　o.　　Sophocles—Œdipus Tyrannis.
　　　　　　　Oxford trans.　Revised by Buckley.

　For whoever knows how to return a kindness he has received must be a friend above
all price.
　p.　　Sophocles—Philoctetes.　Oxford trans.
　　　　　　　　　　　Revised by Buckley.

'Tis something to be willing to commend ;
But my best praise is, that I am your friend.
　q.　　Southerne—To Mr. Congreve on the
　　　　　　　　　　Old Bachelor.　Last line.

It's an owercome sooth fo' age an' youth,
　And it brooks wi' nae denial,
That the dearest friends are the auldest friends,
　And the young are just on trial.
　r.　　Robt. Louis Stevenson—Underwoods.
　　　　　　　　　　It's an Owercome Sooth.

He who has a thousand friends has not a
　friend to spare,
And he who has one enemy shall meet him
　everywhere.
　s.　　Ali Ben Abu Taleb.

　A good man is the best friend, and therefore soonest to be chosen, longer to be retained ; and indeed, never to be parted with,
unless he cease to be that for which he was
chosen.
　t.　　Jeremy Taylor—A Discourse of the
　　　　　　Nature, Measures, and Offices of
　　　　　　　　　　　　　　　Friendship.

Choose for your friend him that is wise and good, and secret and just, ingenious and honest, and in those things which have a latitude, use your own liberty.

   a.   Jeremy Taylor—*A Discourse of the Nature, Measures, and Offices of Friendship.*

When I choose my friend, I will not stay till I have received a kindness; but I will choose such a one that can do me many if I need them; but I mean such kindnesses which make me wiser, and which make me better.

   b.   Jeremy Taylor—*A Discourse of the Nature, Measures, and Offices of Friendship.*

Then came your new friend: you began to change—
I saw it and grieved.

   c.   Tennyson—*The Princess.* IV. L. 279.

Defend me from my friends; I can defend myself from my enemies.

   d.   *The French Ana. Assigned to* Marshal Villars *taking leave of* Louis XIV.

A slender acquaintance with the world must convince every man, that actions, not words, are the true criterion of the attachment of friends; and that the most liberal professions of good-will are very far from being the surest marks of it.

   e.   George Washington—*Social Maxims. Friendship. Actions, not Words.*

I have *friends* in Spirit Land,—
Not shadows in a shadowy band,
Not *others* but *themselves* are they,
And still I think of them the same
As when the Master's summons came.

   f.   Whittier—*Lucy Hooper.*

Poets, like friends to whom you are in debt, you hate.

   g.   Wycherley—*The Plain Dealer.*
                        Prologue.

A foe to God was ne'er true friend to man,
Some sinister intent taints all he does.

   h.   Young—*Night Thoughts.* Night VIII.
                        L. 704.

A friend is worth all hazards we can run.

   i.   Young—*Night Thoughts.* Night II.
                        L. 571.

FRIENDSHIP.

Great souls by instinct to each other turn,
Demand alliance, and in friendship burn.

   j.   Addison—*The Campaign.* L. 102.

The friendships of the world are oft
Confederacies in vice, or leagues of pleasure;
Ours has severest virtue for its basis,
And such a friendship ends not but with life.

   k.   Addison—*Cato.* Act III. Sc. 1.

The friendship between me and you I will not compare to a chain; for that the rains might rust, or the falling tree might break.

   l.   Bancroft—*History of the United States. Wm. Penn's Treaty with the Indians.*

Friendship! mysterious cement of the soul,
Sweet'ner of life, and solder of society.

   m.   Blair—*The Grave.* L. 87.

                         Hand
Grasps at hand, eye lights eye in good friendship,
And great hearts expand
And grow one in the sense of this world's life.

   n.   Robert Browning—*Saul.* St. VII.

In Friendship we only see those faults which may be prejudicial to our friends. In love we see no faults but those by which we suffer ourselves.

   o.   De La Bruyère—*The Characters or Manners of the Present Age.* Ch. V.

Love and friendship exclude each other.

   p.   De La Bruyère—*The Characters or Manners of the Present Age.* Ch. V.

Pure friendship is something which men of an inferior intellect can never taste.

   q.   De La Bruyère—*The Characters or Manners of the Present Age.* Ch. V.

Should auld acquaintance be forgot,
  And never brought to mind?
Should auld acquaintance be forgot,
  And days o' lang syne?

   r.   Burns—*Auld Lang Syne.*

Friendship is Love without his wings!

   s.   Byron—*L'Amitié est l' Amour sans Ailes.* St. 1.

In friendship I early was taught to believe;
   *   *   *   *   *
I have found that a friend may profess, yet deceive.

   t.   Byron—*Lines addressed to the Rev. J. T. Becher.* St. 7.

Oh, how you wrong our friendship, valiant youth.
With friends there is not such a word as debt:
Where amity is ty'd with band of truth,
All benefits are there in common set.

   u.   Lady Carew—*Marian.*

Friendship is a sheltering tree.

   v.   Coleridge—*Youth and Age.*

Literary friendship is a sympathy not of manners, but of feelings.

   w.   Isaac Disraeli—*Literary Characters.*
                        Ch. XIX.

For friendship, of itself a holy tie,
Is made more sacred by adversity.
> *a.*   DRYDEN—*The Hind and the Panther.*
> Pt. III.   L. 47.

Friendships begin with liking or gratitude—
roots that can be pulled up.
> *b.*   GEORGE ELIOT—*Daniel Deronda.*
> Bk. IV.   Ch. XXXII.

So, if I live or die to serve my friend,
'Tis for my love—'tis for my friend alone,
And not for any rate that friendship bears
In heaven or on earth.
> *c.*   GEORGE ELIOT—*Spanish Gypsy.*

Friendship should be surrounded with
ceremonies and respects, and not crushed into
corners.   Friendship requires more time than
poor, busy men can usually command.
> *d.*   EMERSON—*Essays. Behavior.*

I hate the prostitution of the name of
friendship to signify modish and worldly
alliances.
> *e.*   EMERSON—*Essays. Of Friendship.*

The condition which high friendship demands is ability to do without it.
> *f.*   EMERSON—*Essays. Of Friendship.*

The highest compact we can make with our
fellow is,—Let there be truth between us two
forevermore. * * * It is sublime to feel
and say of another, I need never meet, or
speak, or write to him ; we need not reinforce
ourselves or send tokens of remembrance ; I
rely on him as on myself ; if he did thus or
thus, I know it was right.
> *g.*   EMERSON—*Essays. Behavior.*

There can never be deep peace between two
spirits, never mutual respect, until, in their
dialogue, each stands for the whole world.
> *h.*   EMERSON—*Essays. Of Friendship.*

A sudden thought strikes me—Let us swear
an eternal friendship.
> *i.*   JOHN H. FRERE—*The Rovers.*   Act I.
> Sc. 1.

Friendship, like love, is but a name,
Unless to one you stint the flame.
> *j.*   GAY—*The Hare with Many Friends.*

To friendship every burden's light.
> *k.*   GAY—*The Hare with Many Friends.*

Who friendship with a knave hath made,
Is judg'd a partner in the trade.
> *l.*   GAY—*The Old Woman and Her Cats.*

And what is friendship but a name,
A charm that lulls to sleep ;
A shade that follows wealth or fame,
And leaves the wretch to weep?
> *m.*   GOLDSMITH—*Edwin and Angelina, or
> The Hermit.* St. 19.

O Friendship, flavor of flowers! O lively
sprite of life !
O sacred bond of blissful peace, the stalworth
staunch of strife.
> *n.*   GRIMOALD—*Of Friendship.*   L. 21.

Friendship closes its eye, rather than see
the moon eclipst ; while malice denies that it
is ever at the full.
> *o.*   J. C. and A. W. HARE—*Guesses at
> Truth.*

Friendship is Love, without either flowers
or veil.
> *p.*   J. C. and A. W. HARE—*Guesses at
> Truth.*

Fast as the rolling seasons bring
The hour of fate to those we love,
Each pearl that leaves the broken string
Is set in Friendship's crown above.
As narrower grows the earthly chain,
The circle widens in the sky ;
These are our treasures that remain,
But those are stars that beam on high.
> *q.*   O. W. HOLMES—*Songs of Many Seasons.
> Our Classmate, F. W. C.,* 1864.

A generous friendship no cold medium knows,
Burns with one love, with one resentment
glows ;
One should our interests and our passions be,
My friend must hate the man that injures me.
> *r.*   HOMER—*Iliad.* Bk. IX.   L. 725.
> Pope's trans.

True friendship's laws are by this rule express'd,
Welcome the coming, speed the parting guest.
> *s.*   HOMER—*Odyssey.* Bk. XV. L. 83.
> Pope's trans.

If a man does not make new acquaintances,
as he advances through life, he will soon find
himself left alone. A man, Sir, should keep
his friendship in constant repair.
> *t.*   SAM'L JOHNSON—*Boswell's Life of
> Johnson,* 1755.

Friendship, peculiar boon of Heaven,
The noble mind's delight and pride,
To men and angels only given,
To all the lower world denied.
> *u.*   SAM'L JOHNSON—*Friendship. An Ode.*

The endearing elegance of female friendship.
> *v.*   SAM'L JOHNSON—*Rasselas.*   Ch. XLVI.

Come back ! ye friendships long departed !
That like o'erflowing streamlets started,
And now are dwindled, one by one,
To stony channels in the sun !
Come back ! ye friends, whose lives are ended,
Come back, with all that light attended,
Which seemed to darken and decay
When ye arose and went away !
> *w.*   LONGFELLOW—*Christus.* Pt. II.   *The
> Golden Legend.   I.*

" You will forgive me, I hope, for the sake of
    the friendship between us,
Which is too true and too sacred to be so
    easily broken !"
   a.   LONGFELLOW—*The Courtship of Miles
       Standish. Priscilla. Pt. VI. L. 22.*

Oh, call it by some better name,
For Friendship sounds too cold.
   b.   MOORE—*Oh, call it by some better Name.*

" There is nothing that is meritorious but
virtue and friendship ; and indeed friendship
itself is only a part of virtue."
   c.   POPE—*Dr. Johnson's Lives of the Poets ;
       Life of Pope.*

           What ill-starr'd rage
Divides a friendship long confirm'd by age?
   d.   POPE—*The Dunciad.* Bk. III. L. 173.

Call you that backing of your friends? A
plague upon such backing ! give me them
that will face me.
   e.   *Henry IV.* Pt. I. Act II. Sc. 4.
                     L. 165.

        Ceremony was but devised at first
To set a gloss on faint deeds, hollow welcomes,
Recanting goodness, sorry ere 'tis shown ;
But where there is true friendship, there needs
    none.
   f.   *Timon of Athens.* Act I. Sc. 2. L. 15.

Friendship is constant in all other things,
Save in the office and affairs of love :
Therefore, all hearts in love use their own
    tongues ;
Let every eye negotiate for itself,
And trust no agent.
   g.   *Much Ado About Nothing.* Act II.
                  Sc. 1. L. 182.

Friendship's full of dregs.
   h.   *Timon of Athens.* Act I. Sc. 2.
                     L. 240.

Most friendship is feigning.
   i.   *As You Like It. Song.* Act II. Sc. 7.
                     L. 181.

Out upon this half-fac'd fellowship !
   j.   *Henry IV.* Pt. I. Act I. Sc. 3.
                     L. 208.

The amity that wisdom knits not, folly may
    easily untie.
   k.   *Troilus and Cressida.* Act II. Sc. 3.
                     L. 110.

       When did friendship take
A breed for barren metal of his friend?
   l.   *Merchant of Venice.* Act I. Sc. 3.
                     L. 134.

Life is to be fortified by many friendships.
To love, and to be loved, is the greatest happiness of existence.
   m.   SYDNEY SMITH—*Of Friendship. Lady
       Holland's Memoir.*

I thought you and he were hand-in-glove.
   n.   SWIFT—*Polite Conversation.*
                     Dialogue II.

Friendship is like rivers, and the strand of
seas, and the air, common to all the world ;
but tyrants, and evil customs, wars, and want
of love, have made them proper and peculiar.
   o.   JEREMY TAYLOR—*A Discourse of the
       Nature, Measures, and Offices of
                  Friendship.*

Nature and religion are the bands of friendship, excellence and usefulness are its great
endearments.
   p.   JEREMY TAYLOR—*A Discourse of the
       Nature, Measures, and Offices of
                  Friendship.*

Some friendships are made by nature, some
by contract, some by interest, and some by
souls.
   q.   JEREMY TAYLOR—*A Discourse of the
       Nature, Measures, and Offices of
                  Friendship.*

For tho' the faults were thick as dust
In vacant chambers, I could trust
    Your kindness.
   r.   TENNYSON—*To the Queen.* St. 5.

O friendship, equal-poised control,
O heart, with kindliest motion warm,
O sacred essence, other form,
O solemn ghost, O crowned soul !
   s.   TENNYSON—*In Memoriam.* LXXXV.

True friendship is a plant of slow growth,
and must undergo and withstand the shocks
of adversity, before it is entitled to the ap-
pellation.
   t.   GEORGE WASHINGTON—*Social Maxims.
                   Friendship.*

Friendship's the wine of life : but friendship
    new
   * * * is neither strong nor pure.
   u.   YOUNG—*Night Thoughts.* Night II.
                     L. 582.

FRUITS.

Like strawberry wives, that laid two or
three great strawberries at the mouth of their
pot, and all the rest were little ones.
   v.   BACON—*Apothegms.* No. 54.

Like to the apples on the Dead Sea's shore,
All ashes to the taste.
   w.   BYRON—*Childe Harold.* Canto III.
                     St. 34.

" Now, Sire," quod she, " for aught that may
    bityde,
I moste haue of the peres that I see,
Or I moote dye, so soore longeth me
To eten of the smalle peres grene."
   x.   CHAUCER—*Canterbury Tales. The
       Merchantes Tale.* L. 14,669.

Nay, in death's hand, the grape-stone proves
As strong as thunder is in Jove's.
a.　　ABRAHAM COWLEY—*Elegy upon
　　　　　　　　　Anacreon.*　L. 106.

Nothing great is produced suddenly, since
not even the grape or the fig is.　If you say to
me now that you want a fig, I will answer to
you that it requires time: let it flower first,
then put forth fruit, and then ripen.
b.　　EPICTETUS—*Discourses.　What
　　　　Philosophy Promises.*　Ch. XV.
　　　　　　　　Geo. Long's trans.

"Very well," cried I, "that's a good girl; I
find you are perfectly qualified for making
converts, and so go help your mother to make
the gooseberry pye."
c.　　GOLDSMITH—*Vicar of Wakefield.*
　　　　　　　　　　　Ch. VII.

The muse might tell what culture will entice
The ripen'd melon to perfume each month.
d.　　GRAINGER—*The Sugar Cane.*　Bk. IV.

All the heart was full of feeling: love had
　　　ripened into speech,
Like the sap that turns to nectar, in the velvet
　　　of the peach.
e.　　WM. WALLACE HARNEY—*Adonais.*

Oh! happy are the apples when the south
　　　winds blow.
f.　　WM. WALLACE HARNEY—*Adonais.*

To satisfy the sharp desire I had
Of tasting those fair apples, I resolv'd
Not to defer; hunger and thirst at once
Powerful persuaders, quicken'd at the scent
Of that alluring fruit, urged me so keen.
g.　　MILTON—*Paradise Lost.*　Bk. IX.
　　　　　　　　　　　L. 584.

But the fruit that can fall without shaking,
　　　Indeed is too mellow for me.
h.　　LADY MONTAGU—*Answered for
　　　　　　　　Lord Wm. Hamilton.*

Like Dead Sea fruit that tempts the eye,
But turns to ashes on the lips!
i.　　MOORE—*Lalla Rookh.　The Fire
　　　　　　　Worshippers.*　L. 1,018.

Thus do I live, from pleasure quite debarred,
Nor taste the fruits that the sun's genial rays
Mature, john-apple, nor the downy peach.
j.　　JOHN PHILIPS—*The Splendid Shilling.*
　　　　　　　　　　　L. 115.

As touching peaches in general, the very
name in Latine whereby they are called Per-
sica, doth evidently show that they were
brought out of Persia first.
k.　　PLINY— *Natural History.*　Bk. XV.
　　　　　　　Ch. 13.　Holland's trans.

The ripest peach is highest on the tree.
l.　　JAMES WHITCOMB RILEY—*The Ripest
　　　　　　　　　　　Peach.*

All the other gifts appertinent to man, as
the malice of this age shapes them, are not
worth a gooseberry.
m.　　*Henry IV.*　Part II.　Act 1.　Sc. 2.
　　　　　　　　　　　L. 194.

Before thee stands this fair Hesperides,
With golden fruit, but dangerous to be
　　　touched.
n.　　*Pericles.*　Act I.　Sc. 1.　L. 27.

Fruits that blossom first will first be ripe.
o.　　*Othello.*　Act II.　Sc. 3.　L. 383.

　　　　　　　　　Superfluous branches
We lop away, that bearing boughs may live.
p.　　*Richard II.*　Act III.　Sc. 4.　L. 63.

The ripest fruit first falls.
q.　　*Richard II.*　Act II.　Sc. I.　L. 153.

The strawberry grows underneath the nettle
And wholesome berries thrive and ripen best
Neighbour'd by fruit of baser quality.
r.　　*Henry V.*　Act. I.　Sc. 1.　L. 60.

My living in Yorkshire was so far out of
the way, that it was actually twelve miles
from a lemon.
s.　　SYDNEY SMITH—*Lady Holland's
　　　　　　　Memoir.*　Vol. I.　P. 262.

The barberry and currant must escape
Though her small clusters imitate the grape.
t.　　TATE—*Cowley.*

After the conquest of Afric, Greece, the
lesser Asia, and Syria were brought into Italy
all the sorts of their Mala, which we inter-
prete apples, and might signify no more at
first; but were afterwards applied to many
other foreign fruits.
u.　　SIR WM. TEMPLE—*On Gardening.*

　　　　　　　　　The juicy pear
Lies, in a soft profusion, scattered round.
v.　　THOMSON—*The Seasons.　Autumn.*
　　　　　　　　　　　L. 632.

And the Creole of Cuba laughs out to behold,
Through orange leaves shining the broad
　　　spheres of gold.
w.　　WHITTIER—*The Pumpkin.*

Let other lands, exulting, glean
　　　The apple from the pine,
The orange from its glossy green,
　　　The cluster from the vine.
x.　　WHITTIER—*The Corn Song.*

O,—fruit loved of boyhood!—the old days re-
  calling,
When wood-grapes were purpling and brown
  nuts were falling!
When wild, ugly faces we carved in its skin,
Glaring out through the dark with a candle
  within!
When we laughed round the corn-heap, with
  hearts all in tune,
Our chair a broad pumpkin,—our lantern the
  moon,
Telling tales of the fairy who travelled like
  steam
In a pumpkin-shell coach, with two rats for
  her team!
  a.   WHITTIER—*The Pumpkin.*

What does the good ship bear so well?
The cocoa-nut with its stony shell,
And the milky sap of its inner cell.
  b.   WHITTIER—*The Palm Tree.*

FUTURITY.

That what will come, and must come, shall
  come well.
  c.   EDWIN ARNOLD—*Light of Asia.*
                       Bk. VI. L. 274.

Some day Love shall claim his own
Some day Right ascend his throne,
Some day hidden Truth be known;
  Some day—some sweet day.
  d.   LEWIS J. BATES—*Some Sweet Day.*

The year goes wrong, and tares grow strong,
  Hope starves without a crumb;
But God's time is our harvest time,
  And that is sure to come.
  e.   LEWIS J. BATES—*Our Better Day.*

            God keeps a niche
In Heaven, to hold our idols; and albeit
He brake them to our faces, and denied
That our close kisses should impair their
  white,—
I know we shall behold them raised, complete,
The dust swept from their beauty, glorified,
New Memnons singing in the great God-light.
  f.   E. B. BROWNING—*Sonnet. Futurity*
                       with the Departed.

You can never plan the future by the past.
  g.   BURKE—*Letter to a Member of the*
                National Assembly. Vol. IV. P. 55.

With mortal crisis doth portend,
My days to appropinque an end.
  h.   BUTLER—*Hudibras.* Pt. I. Canto III.
                       L. 589.

But ask not bodies (doomed to die),
  To what abode they go;
Since knowledge is but sorrow's spy,
  It is not safe to know.
  i.   DAVENANT—*The Just Italian.* Act. V.
                       Sc. 1. *Song.*

What cities, as great as this, have * * *
promised themselves immortality! posterity
can hardly trace the situation of some. The
sorrowful traveller wanders over the awful
ruins of others.
  j.   GOLDSMITH—*The Bee.* No. IV. 1759.
                       A City Night Piece.

You'll see that, since our fate is ruled by
  chance,
  Each man, unknowing, great,
Should frame life so that at some future hour
Fact and his dreamings meet.
  k.   VICTOR HUGO—*To His Orphan*
                       Grandchildren.

Trust no Future, howe'er pleasant!
Let the dead Past bury its dead!
  l.   LONGFELLOW—*A Psalm of Life.*

Dear Land to which Desire forever flees;
  Time doth no present to our grasp allow,
Say in the fixed Eternal shall we seize
  At last the fleeting Now?
  m.   BULWER-LYTTON—*Corn Flowers.* Bk. I.
                       The First Violets.

She (the R. C. Church) may still exist in undiminished vigour when some traveller from
New Zealand shall, in the midst of a vast solitude, take his stand on a broken arch of London Bridge to sketch the ruins of St. Paul's.
  n.   MACAULAY—*On von Ranke's History of*
                       the Popes. 1840.

There's a good time coming, boys;
  A good time coming:
We may not live to see the day,
  But earth shall glisten in the ray
    Of the good time coming.
Cannon-balls may aid the truth,
  But thought's a weapon stronger;
We'll win our battle by its aid,
  Wait a little longer.
  o.   CHAS. MACKAY—*The Good Time*
                       Coming.

    When the world dissolves,
And every creature shall be purified,
All places shall be hell that are not heaven.
  p.   MARLOWE—*Faustus.* L. 543.

        The never-ending flight
Of future days.
  q.   MILTON—*Paradise Lost.* Bk. II.
                       L. 221.

Beyond this vale of tears
  There is a life above,
Unmeasured by the flight of years;
  And all that life is love.
  r.   MONTGOMERY—*The Issues of Life and*
                       Death. Hymn CCXIV.

There's nae sorrow there, John,
There's neither cauld nor care, John,
The day is aye fair,
In the land o' the leal.
   a.   Lady Nairne—*The Land o' the Leal.*

In adamantine chains shall Death be bound,
And Hell's grim tyrant feel th' eternal wound.
   b.   Pope—*Messiah.* L. 47.

Oh, blindness to the future! kindly giv'n,
That each may fill the circle mark'd by
   heaven.
   c.   Pope—*Essay on Man.* Ep. I. L. 85.

But there's a gude time coming.
   d.   Scott—*Rob Roy.* Ch. XXXII.

And, father cardinal, I have heard you say
That we shall see and know our friends in
   heaven :
If that be true, I shall see my boy again;
For since the birth of Cain, the first male
   child,
To him that did but yesterday suspire,
There was not such a gracious creature born.
   e.   *King John.* Act III. Sc. 4. L. 76.

Ay, but to die, and go we know not where;
To lie in cold obstruction and to rot.
   f.   *Measure for Measure.* Act III. Sc. 1.
                               L. 118.

               God, if Thy will be so,
Enrich the time to come with smooth-faced
   peace,
With smiling plenty and fair prosperous
   days !
   g.   *Richard III.* Act V. Sc. 5. L. 32.

           Who would fardels bear,
To grunt and sweat under a weary life;
But that the dread of something after death,
The undiscover'd country from whose bourn
No traveller returns, puzzles the will
And makes us rather bear those ills we have
Than fly to others that we know not of?
   h.   *Hamlet.* Act III. Sc. 1. L. 76.

          What a world were this
How unendurable its weight, if they
Whom Death hath sundered did not meet
   again !
   i.   Southey—*Inscription XVII. Epitaph.*

For tho' from out our bourne of Time and
   Place
   The flood may bear me far,
I hope to see my Pilot face to face
   When I have crossed the bar.
   j.   Tennyson—*Crossing the Bar.* St. 4.

It may be we shall touch the Happy Isles,
And see the great Achilles, whom we knew.
   k.   Tennyson—*Ulysses.* L. 65.

         The great world's altar-stairs
That slope thro' darkness up to God.
   l.   Tennyson—*In Memoriam.* Pt. LV.

Who knows but he will sit down solitary amid
silent ruins, and weep a people inurned,
and their greatness changed into an empty
name?
   m.   Volney—*Ruins. Meditations.* Ch. II.

At last some curious traveller from Lima
will visit England, and give a description of
the ruins of St. Paul's, like the editions of
Balbec and Palmyra.
   n.   Horace Walpole—*Letter to Sir
               Horace Mann.* Nov. 24, 1774.

Where now is Britain?
   *   *   *   *   *   *
Even as the savage sits upon the stone
That marks where stood her capitols, and
   hears
The bittern booming in the weeds, he shrinks
From the dismaying solitude.
   o.   Henry Kirke White—*Time.*

Happy he whose inward ear
Angel comfortings can hear,
   O'er the rabble's laughter;
And, while Hatred's fagots burn,
Glimpses through the smoke discern
   Of the good hereafter.
   p.   Whittier—*Barclay of Ury.*

G.

GAIN.

Everywhere in life, the true question is not
what we *gain,* but what we *do.*
   q.   Carlyle—*Essays. Goethe's Helena.*

Keep thy shop, and thy shop will keep thee.
Light gains make heavy purses. 'Tis good to
be merry and wise.
   r.   George Chapman—*Eastward Ho.*
                         Act I. Sc. 1.

And if you mean to profit, learn to please.
   s.   Churchill—*Gotham.* Bk. II. L. 88.

The sweet simplicity of the three per cents.
   t.   Benj. Disraeli—*Endymion.*
                          Ch. XCVI.

The elegant simplicity of the three per cents.
   u.   Lord Eldon. See Campbell's *Lives
             of the Lord Chancellors.* Vol. X.
             Ch. CCXII. P. 218.

Counts his sure gains, and hurries back for more.

a.   MONTGOMERY—*The West Indies.*
Pt. III.

Little pains
In a due hour employ'd great profit yields.

b.   JOHN PHILIPS—*Cider.* Bk. I. L. 126.

Men that hazard all
Do it in hope of fair advantages:
A golden mind stoops not to shows of dross.

c.   *Merchant of Venice.* Act II. Sc. 7.
L. 18.

No profit grows where is no pleasure ta'en;
In brief, sir, study what you most affect.

d.   *Taming of the Shrew.* Act I. Sc. 1.
L. 39.

Share the advice betwixt you: if both gain, all
The gift doth stretch itself as 'tis receiv'd,
And is enough for both.

e.   *All Well That's Ends Well.* Act II.
Sc. 1. L. 3.

As to pay, Sir, I beg leave to assure the Congress that as no pecuniary consideration could have tempted me to accept this arduous employment at the expense of my domestic ease and happiness, I do not wish to make any profit from it.

f.   GEORGE WASHINGTON—*In Congress on his Appointment as Commander-in-Chief,* June 16, 1775.

GAMBLING.

Whose game was empires, and whose stakes
   were thrones;
Whose table earth, whose dice were human
   bones.

g.   BYRON—*The Age of Bronze.* St. 3.

The gamester, if he die a martyr to his profession, is doubly ruined. He adds his soul to every other loss, and by the act of suicide, renounces earth to forfeit Heaven.

h.   C. C. COLTON—*Lacon. Reflection.*

Cards were at first for benefits designed,
Sent to amuse, not to enslave the mind.

i.   DAVID GARRICK—*Prologue to Ed.
Moore's Gamester.*

Our Quixote bard sets out a monster taming.
Arm'd at all points to fight that hydra, gaming.

j.   DAVID GARRICK—*Prologue to Ed.
Moore's Gamester.*

Shake off the shackles of this tyrant vice;
Hear other calls than those of cards and dice:
Be learn'd in nobler arts than arts of play;
And other debts than those of honour pay.

k.   DAVID GARRICK—*Prologue to Ed.
Moore's Gamester.*

Look round, the wrecks of play behold;
Estates dismember'd, mortgag'd, sold!
Their owners now to jails confin'd,
Show equal poverty of mind.

l.   GAY—*Fables.* Pt. II. Fables 12.

Ay, rail at gaming—'tis a rich topic, and affords noble declamation. Go, preach against it in the city—you'll find a congregation in every tavern.

m.   ED. MOORE—*The Gamester.* Act IV.
Sc. 1.

I'll tell thee what it says; it calls me villain, a treacherous husband, a cruel father, a false brother; one lost to nature and her charities; or to say all in one short word, it calls me—gamester.

n.   ED. MOORE—*The Gamester.* Act II.
Sc. 1.

Oh, this pernicious vice of gaming!

o.   ED. MOORE—*The Gamester.* Act I.
Sc. 1.

How, sir! not damn the sharper, but the dice?

p.   POPE—*Epilogue to the Satires.*
Dialogue II. L. 13.

It [gaming] is the child of avarice, the brother of inquity, and the father of mischief.

q.   GEORGE WASHINGTON—*Letter to
Bushrod Washington.* Jan. 15,
1783.

GARDEN.

God Almighty first planted a garden.

r.   BACON—*Of Gardens.*

God the first garden made, and the first city Cain.

s.   ABRAHAM COWLEY—*The Garden.*
Essay V.

My garden is a forest ledge
   Which older forests bound;
The banks slope down to the blue lake-edge,
   Then plunge to depths profound!

t.   EMERSON—*My Garden.* St. 3.

An album is a garden, not for show
Planted, but use; where wholesome herbs
   should grow.

u.   CHARLES LAMB—*In an Album to a
Clergyman's Lady.*

And add to these retired Leisure,
That in trim gardens takes his pleasure.

v.   MILTON—*Il Penseroso.* L. 49.

Grove nods at grove, each alley has a brother,
And half the platform just reflects the other.
The suff'ring eye inverted nature sees,
Trees cut in statues, statues thick as trees;
With here a fountain never to be play'd,
And there a summer-house that knows no
   shade.

w.   POPE—*Moral Essays.* Ep. IV. L. 117.

A little garden square and wall'd ;
And in it throve an ancient evergreen,
A yew-tree, and all round it ran a walk
Of shingle, and a walk divided it.
a.　Tennyson—*Enoch Arden.* L. 731.

The garden lies,
A league of grass, wash'd by a slow broad
　stream.
b.　Tennyson—*The Gardener's Daughter.*
L. 40.

The splash and stir
Of fountains spouted up and showering down
In meshes of the jasmine and the rose :
And all about us peal'd the nightingale,
Rapt in her song, and careless of the snare.
c.　Tennyson—*The Princess.* Pt. I.
L. 214.

GENIUS.

As diamond cuts diamond, and one hone
smooths a second, all the parts of intellect
are whetstones to each other; and genius,
which is but the result of their mutual sharpening, is character too.
d.　C. A. Bartol—*Radical Problems.*
Individualism.

Intelligence is to genius as the whole is in
proportion to its part.
e.　De La Bruyère—*The Characters or
Manners of the Present Age.
Opinions.*

Every work of Genius is tinctured by the
feelings, and often originates in the events of
times.
f.　Isaac Disraeli—*Literary Character of
Men of Genius.* Ch. XXV.

Fortune has rarely condescended to be the
companion of genius.
g.　Isaac Disraeli—*Curiosities of Literature. Poverty of the Learned.*

Many men of genius must arise before a
particular man of genius can appear.
h.　Isaac Disraeli—*Literary Character of
Men of Genius.*

Philosophy becomes poetry, and science
imagination, in the enthusiasm of genius.
i.　Isaac Disraeli—*Literary Character of
Men of Genius.* Ch. XII.

To think, and to feel, constitute the two
grand divisions of men of genius—the men of
reasoning and the men of imagination.
j.　Isaac Disraeli—*Literary Character of
Men of Genius.* Ch. II.

But genius must be born, and never can be
taught.
k.　Dryden—*Epistle X. To Congreve.*
L. 60.

Genius and its rewards are briefly told :
A liberal nature and a niggard doom,
A difficult journey to a splendid tomb.
l.　Forster—*Dedication of the Life and
Adventures of Oliver Goldsmith.*

Here lies our good Edmund, whose genius
　was such
We scarcely can praise it or blame it too much;
Who, born for the universe, narrow'd his
　mind,
And to party gave up what was meant for
　mankind.
m.　Goldsmith—*Retaliation.* L. 29.

Perhaps, moreover, he whose genius appears
deepest and truest excels his fellows in nothing save the knack of expression ; he throws
out occasionally a lucky hint at truths of
which every human soul is profoundly though
unutterably conscious.
n.　Nath. Hawthorne—*Mosses from an
Old Manse. The Procession of Life.*

Genius, like humanity, rusts for want of use.
o.　Hazlitt—*Table Talk. On Application
to Study.*

Nature is the master of talent; genius is the
master of nature.
p.　J. G. Holland—*Plain Talk on Familiar
Subjects. Art and Life.*

We declare to you that the earth has exhausted its contingent of master-spirits. Now
for decadence and general closing. We must
make up our minds to it. We shall have no
more men of genius.
q.　Victor Hugo—*Wm. Shakespeare.*
Bk. V. Ch. I.

Not oft near home does genius brightly shine,
No more than precious stones while in the
　mine.
r.　Omar Khayyam. Bodenstedt's trans.

Many a genius has been slow of growth.
Oaks that flourish for a thousand years do not
spring up into beauty like a reed.
s.　Geo. Henry Lewes—*The Spanish
Drama. Life of Lope De Vega.*
Ch. II.

All the means of action—
The shapeless masses, the materials—
Lie everywhere about us. What we need
Is the celestial fire to change the flint
Into transparent crystal, bright and clear.
That fire is genius !
t.　Longfellow—*The Spanish Student.*
Act I. Sc. 5.

There is no work of genius which has not
been the delight of mankind, no word of
genius to which the human heart and soul
have not, sooner or later, responded.
u.　Lowell—*Among my Books. Rousseau
and the Sentimentalists.*

There is none but he
Whose being I do fear; and, under him,
My Genius is rebuk'd: as, it is said,
Mark Antony's was by Cæsar.
  a.   *Macbeth.*   Act III.   Sc. 1.   L. 54.

Genius inspires this thirst for fame: there
is no blessing undesired by those to whom
Heaven gave the means of winning it.
  b.   MADAME DE STAËL—*Corinne.*   Bk. XVI.
                       Ch. I.

Genius is essentially creative; it bears the
stamp of the individual who possesses it.
  c.   MADAME DE STAËL—*Corinne.*   Bk. VII.
                       Ch. I.

Genius can never despise labour.
  d.   ABEL STEVENS—*Life of Madame de
             Staël.*   Ch. XXXVIII.

GENTLEMEN.

Oh! St. Patrick was a gentleman,
Who came of decent people.
  e.   HENRY BENNETT—*St. Patrick was a
                    Gentleman.*

Tho' modest, on his unembarrass'd brow
Nature had written—"Gentleman."
  f.   BYRON—*Don Juan.*   Canto IX.   St. 83.

I was ne'er so thrummed since I was a gentleman.
  g.   THOMAS DEKKER—*The Honest Whore.*
                Pt. I.   Act IV.   Sc. 2.

                  The best of men
That e'er wore earth about him was a suf-
   ferer;
A soft, meek, patient, humble, tranquil spirit,
The first true gentleman that ever breathed.
  h.   THOMAS DEKKER—*The Honest Whore.*
                Pt. I.   Act I.   Sc. 2.

His tribe were God Almighty's gentlemen.
  i.   DRYDEN—*Absalom and Achitophel.*
                      Pt. I.   L. 645.

A gentleman born, master parson; who
writes himself 'Armigero;' in any bill, warrant, quittance, or obligation, 'Armigero.'
  j.   *Merry Wives of Windsor.*   Act I.   Sc. 1.
                         L. 9.

An affable and courteous gentleman.
  k.   *Taming of the Shrew.*   Act I.   Sc. 2.
                         L. 98.

"I am a gentleman." I'll be sworn thou art;
Thy tongue, thy face, thy limbs, actions and
   spirit,
Do give thee five-fold blazon.
  l.   *Twelfth Night.*   Act I.   Sc. 5.   L. 310.

I freely told you, all the wealth I had
Ran in my veins, I was a gentleman.
  m.   *Merchant of Venice.*   Act III.   Sc. 2.
                         L. 257.

My master hath been an honourable gentleman; tricks he hath had in him, which
gentlemen have.
  n.   *All's Well That Ends Well.*   Act V.
                      Sc. 3.   L. 238.

Since every Jack became a gentleman,
There's many a gentle person made a Jack.
  o.   *Richard III.*   Act I.   Sc. 3.   L. 72.

You are not like Cerberus, three gentlemen
at once, are you?
  p.   R. B. SHERIDAN—*The Rivals.*   Act IV.
                         Sc. 2.

The gentle minde by gentle deeds is knowne;
For a man by nothing is so well bewrayed
As by his manners.
  q.   SPENSER—*Faerie Queene.*
              Bk. VI.   Canto III.   St. 1.

And thus he bore without abuse
The grand old name of gentleman,
Defamed by every charlatan
And soiled with all ignoble use.
  r.   TENNYSON—*In Memoriam.*   CX.   St. 6.

GENTLENESS.

He is gentil that doth gentil dedis.
  s.   CHAUCER—*Canterbury Tales.   The Wyf
                 of Bathes Tale.*   L. 6695.

The mildest manners and the gentlest heart.
  t.   HOMER—*Iliad.*   Bk. 17.   L. 756.
                     Pope's trans.

Let gentleness my strong enforcement be.
  u.   *As You Like It.*   Act II.   Sc. 7.   L. 113.

                 They are as gentle
As zephyrs blowing below the violet.
  v.   *Cymbeline.*   Act IV.   Sc. 2.   L. 171.

      Those that do teach young babes
Do it with gentle means and easy tasks:
  w.   *Othello.*   Act IV.   Sc. 2.   L. 111.

What would you have? your gentleness shall
   force
More than your force move us to gentleness.
  x.   *As You Like It.*   Act II.   Sc. 7.   L. 102.

Let mildness ever attend thy tongue.
  y.   THEOGIUS—*Maxims.*   L. 368.

GIFTS.

Of gifts, there seems none more becoming
to offer a friend than a beautiful book.
  z.   AMOS BRONSON ALCOTT—*Concord Days.
                       June Books.*

The landlady and Tam grew gracious
Wi' favours secret, sweet and precious.
  aa.   BURNS—*Tam o' Shanter.*   St. 7.

He ne'er consider'd it as loth
To look a gift-horse in the mouth,
And very wisely would lay forth
No more upon it than 'twas worth;
But as he got it freely, so
He spent it frank and freely too:
For saints themselves will sometimes be,
Of gifts that cost them nothing, free.

a.   BUTLER—*Hudibras.* Pt. I. Canto I.
L. 489.

The gift, to be true, must be the flowing of the giver unto me, correspondent to my flowing unto him.

b.   EMERSON—*Essays. Of Gifts.*

Rare gift! but oh, what gift to fools avails !

c.   HOMER—*Odyssey.* Bk. 10. L. 29.
Pope's trans.

" Presents," I often say, " endear Absents."

d.   CHARLES LAMB—*A Dissertation upon
Roast Pig.*

Not what we give, but what we share,—
For the gift without the giver is bare.

e.   LOWELL—*The Vision of Sir Launfal.*
Pt. II. St. 8.

In giving, a man receives more than he gives, and the more is in proportion to the worth of the thing given.

f.   GEORGE MACDONALD—*Mary Marston.*
Ch. V.

Take gifts with a sigh : most men give to be paid.

g.   JOHN BOYLE O'REILLY—*Rules of the
Road.*

Let us sit and mock the good housewife Fortune from her wheel, that her gifts may henceforth be bestowed equally.
I would we could do so, for her benefits are mightily misplaced, and the bountiful blind woman doth most mistake in her gifts to women.

h.   *As You Like It.* Act I. Sc. 2. L. 34.

Rich gifts wax poor when givers prove un-kind.

i.   *Hamlet.* Act III. Sc. 1. L. 101.

Win her with gifts, if she respect not words;
Dumb jewels often in their silent kind
More than quick words do move a woman's mind.

j.   *Two Gentlemen of Verona.* Act III.
Sc. 1. L. 89.

She gave me eyes, she gave me ears;
And humble cares, and delicate fears;
A heart, the fountain of sweet tears;
And love, and thought, and joy.

k.   WORDSWORTH—*The Sparrow's Nest.*

That every gift of noble origin
Is breathed upon by Hope's perpetual breath.

l.   WORDSWORTH—*These Times Strike
Monied Worldlings.*

GLORY.

So may a glory from defect arise.

m.   ROBERT BROWNING—*Deaf and Dumb.*

The glory dies not, and the grief is past.

n.   BRYDGES—*On the Death of
Sir Walter Scott.*

Who track the steps of Glory to the grave.

o.   BYRON—*Monody on the Death of the
Right Hon. R. B. Sheridan.*

* * * glory built
On selfish principles is shame and guilt.

p.   COWPER—*Table Talk.* L. 1.

The paths of glory lead but to the grave.

q.   GRAY—*Elegy in a Country Churchyard.*
St. 9.

Visions of glory, spare my aching sight !
Ye unborn ages, crowd not on my soul !

r.   GRAY—*The Bard.* III. I. L. 107.

The first in glory, as the first in place.

s.   HOMER—*Odyssey.* Bk. XI.
L. 441. Pope's trans.

Ye sons of France, awake to glory !
Hark ! Hark ! what myriads bid you rise !
Your children, wives, and grandsires hoary,
Behold their tears and hear their cries !

t.   ROUGET DE L'ISLE—*The Marseilles
Hymn.* 1792. A translation.

The glory of Him who
Hung His masonry pendant on naught, when
the world He created.

u.   LONGFELLOW—*The Children of the
Lord's Supper.* L. 177.

This goin' ware glory waits ye haint one agree-able feetur.

v.   LOWELL—*The Biglow Papers.* First
Series. No. II.

The muffled drum's sad roll has beat
The soldier's last tattoo ;
No more on Life's parade shall meet
The brave and fallen few.
On Fame's eternal camping-ground
Their silent tents are spread,
And Glory guards, with solemn round
The bivouac of the dead.

w.   THEODORE O'HARA—*The Bivouac of the
Dead.* St. 1.

Who pants for glory, finds but short repose;
A breath revives him, or a breath o'erthrows.

x.   POPE—*Second Book of Horace.* Ep. I.
L. 300.

May see thee now, though late, redeem thy
    name,
And glorify what else is damn'd to fame.
    a.   RICHARD SAVAGE—*Character of Foster.*

Sound, sound the clarion, fill the fife!
    To all the sensual world proclaim,
One crowded hour of glorious life
    Is worth an age without a name.
    b.   SCOTT—*Old Mortality.* Ch. XXXIV.
                Introductory Stanza.

Glory is like a circle in the water,
Which never ceaseth to enlarge itself
Till, by broad spreading it disperse to nought.
    c.   *Henry VI.* Pt. I. Act I. Sc. 2.
                          L. 133.

              I have ventur'd,
Like little wanton boys that swim on bladders,
This many summers in a sea of glory,
But far beyond my depth: my high-blown
    pride
At length broke under me.
    d.   *Henry VIII.* Act III. Sc. 2. L. 358.

Like madness is the glory of this life.
    e.   *Timon of Athens.* Act I. Sc. 2. L. 139.

Some glory in their birth, some in their skill,
Some in their wealth, some in their bodies'
    force,
Some in their garments, though new-fangled
    ill;
Some in their hawks and hounds, some in
    their horse;
And every humor hath his adjunct pleasure,
Wherein it finds a joy above the rest.
    f.   *Sonnet XCI.*

When the moon shone, we did not see the
    candle;
So doth the greater glory dim the less.
    g.   *Merchant of Venice.* Act V. Sc. 1.
                          L. 92.

Who would be so mock'd with glory?
    h.   *Timon of Athens.* Act IV. Sc. 2.
                          L. 33.

    Avoid shame, but do not seek glory,—noth-
ing so expensive as glory.
    i.   SYDNEY SMITH—*Lady Holland's
                 Memoir.* Vol. I. P. 86.

'Twas glory once to be a Roman;
She makes it glory, now, to be a man.
    j.   BAYARD TAYLOR—*The National Ode.*

Glories, like glow-worms, afar off shine bright,
But look'd to near have neither heat nor light.
    k.   JOHN WEBSTER—*The White Devil.*
                      Act V. Sc. 1.

Great is the glory, for the strife is hard!
    l.   WORDSWORTH—*To B. R. Haydon.* L. 14.
    18

We rise in glory, as we sink in pride:
Where boasting ends, there dignity begins.
    m.   YOUNG—*Night Thoughts.* Night VIII.
                          L. 508.

GOD.

God's wisdom and God's goodness!—Ay, but
    fools
Mis-define thee, till God knows them no more.
Wisdom and goodness they are God!—what
    schools
Have yet so much as heard this simpler lore.
This no Saint preaches, and this no Church
    rules:
'Tis in the desert, now and heretofore.
    n.   MATTHEW ARNOLD—*The Divinity.*
                          St. 3.

Let us think less of men and more of God.
    o.   BAILEY—*Festus.* Sc. *Wood and Water.*

        Naught but God
Can satisfy the soul.
    p.   BAILEY—*Festus.* Sc. *Heaven.*

He made little, too little of sacraments and
priests, because God was so intensely real to
him. What should he do with lenses who
stood thus full in the torrent of the sunshine.
    q.   PHILLIPS BROOKS—*Sermons. The
                     Seriousness of Life.*

It never frightened a Puritan when you
bade him stand still and listen to the speech
of God. His closet and his church were full
of the reverberations of the awful, gracious,
beautiful voice for which he listened.
    r.   PHILLIPS BROOKS—*Sermons. The
                     Seriousness of Life.*

All service is the same with God,
With God, whose puppets, best and worst,
Are we: there is no last nor first.
    s.   ROBERT BROWNING—*Pippa Passes.*
                          Pt. IV.

         God is the perfect poet,
Who in his person acts his own creations.
    t.   ROBERT BROWNING—*Paracelsus.*
                          Pt. II.

God's in His Heaven—
All's right with the world!
    u.   ROBERT BROWNING—*Pippa Passes.*
                          Pt. I.

    Of what I call God,
And fools call Nature.
    v.   ROBERT BROWNING—*The Ring and the
                 Book. The Pope.* L. 1,073.

That we devote ourselves to God is seen
In living just as though no God there were.
    w.   ROBERT BROWNING—*Paracelsus.* Pt. I.

"There is no god but God!—to prayer—lo!
    God is great!"
   a.   Byron—*Childe Harold.*   Canto II.
                            St. 59.

God! sing, ye meadow-streams, with glad-
    some voice!
Ye pine-groves, with your soft and soul-like
    sounds!
And they too have a voice, yon piles of snow,
And in their perilous fall shall thunder, God!
   b.   Coleridge—*Hymn before Sunrise in the
                        Vale of Chamouni.*

Acquaint thyself with God, if thou would'st
    taste
His works.   Admitted once to his embrace,
Thou shalt perceive that thou wast blind be-
    fore:
Thine eye shall be instructed; and thine
    heart
Made pure shall relish with divine delight
Till then unfelt, what hands divine have
    wrought.
   c.   Cowper—*The Task.* Bk. V. L. 782.

But who with filial confidence inspired,
Can lift to Heaven an unpresumptuous eye,
And smiling say, My Father made them all.
   d.   Cowper—*The Task.* Bk. V. *The
              Winter Morning Walk.* L. 745.

God moves in a mysterious way
    His wonders to perform;
He plants his footsteps in the sea
    And rides upon the storm.
   e.   Cowper—*Hymn. Light Shining out of
                          Darkness.*

God never meant that man should scale the
    Heavens
By strides of human wisdom.   In his works,
Though wondrous, he commands us in his
    word
To seek him rather where his mercy shines.
   f.   Cowper—*The Task.* Bk. III. L. 217.

There is a God! the sky his presence shares,
    His hand upheaves the billows in their
        mirth,
Destroys the mighty, yet the humble spares
And with contentment crowns the thought
    of worth.
   g.   Charlotte Cushman—*There is a God.*

My God, my Father, and my Friend,
Do not forsake me in the end.
   h.   Wentworth Dillon—*Translation of
                         Dies Iræ.*

'Twas much, that man was made like God
    before:
But, that God should be made like man, much
    more.
   i.   Donne—*Holy Sonnets.* Sonnet XXII.

By tracing Heaven his footsteps may be found:
Behold! how awfully he walks the round!
God is abroad, and wondrous in his ways
The rise of empires, and their fall surveys.
   j.   Dryden—*Britannia Rediviva.* L. 75.

                      He who loves
God and his law must hate the foes of God.
   k.   George Eliot—*Spanish Gypsy.* Bk. I.

God enters by a private door into every individual.
   l.   Emerson—*Essays. Of Intellect.*

When the Master of the universe has points
to carry in his government he impresses his
will in the structure of minds.
   m.   Emerson—*Letters and Social Aims.
                          Immortality.*

                          I know
My God commands, whose power no power
    resists.
   n.   Robert Greene—*Looking-Glass for
                    London and England.*

Restore to God His due in tithe and time;
A tithe purloin'd cankers the whole estate.
   o.   Herbert—*The Temple. The Church
                      Porch.* St. 65.

I askt the seas and all the deeps below
          My God to know,
I askt the reptiles, and whatever is
          In the abyss;
Even from the shrimps to the leviathan
          Enquiry ran;
But in those deserts that no line can sound
The God I sought for was not to be found.
   p.   Thos. Heywood—*Searching after God.*

Forgetful youth! but know, the Power above
With ease can save each object of his love;
Wide as his will, extends his boundless grace.
   q.   Homer—*Odyssey.* Bk. 3. L. 285.
                      Pope's trans.

O thou, whose certain eye foresees
The fix'd event of fate's remote decrees.
   r.   Homer—*Odyssey.* Bk. IV. L. 627.
                      Pope's trans.

From thee, great God, we spring, to thee we
    tend,—
Path, motive, guide, original, and end.
   s.   Sam'l Johnson—*Motto to The Rambler.*
                      No. 7.

The sun and every vassal star,
    All space, beyond the soar of angel's wings,
Wait on His word: and yet He stays His car
    For every sigh a contrite suppliant brings.
   t.   Keble—*The Christian Year. Ascension
                          Day.*

All but God is changing day by day.
   u.   Charles Kingsley—*The Saints'
                    Tragedy. Prometheus.*

God! there is no God but he, the living, the
self-subsisting.
    a.   *The Koran.*   Ch. II.   Pt. III.

God had sifted three kingdoms to find the
wheat for this planting.
    b.   LONGFELLOW—*The Courtship of Miles
Standish.*   IV.

An' you've gut to git up airly
Ef you want to take in God.
    c.   LOWELL—*The Biglow Papers.*   First
Series.   No. 1.   St. 5.

'Tis heaven alone that is given away,
'Tis only God may be had for the asking.
    d.   LOWELL—*The Vision of Sir Launfal.*
Prelude to Pt. I.   L. 29.

A voice is in the wind I do not know;
A meaning on the face of the high hills
Whose utterance I cannot comprehend.
A something is behind them : that is God.
    e.   GEORGE MACDONALD—*Within and
Without.*   Pt. I.   Sc. 1.

One sole God ;
One sole ruler,—his Law ;
One sole interpreter of that law—Humanity.
    f.   MAZZINI—*Life and Writings. Young
Europe. General Principles.*   No. 1.

And justify the ways of God to men.
    g.   MILTON—*Paradise Lost.*   Bk. I.   L. 26.

These are thy glorious works, Parent of good.
    h.   MILTON—*Paradise Lost.*   Bk. V.   L. 153.

                 Who best
Bear his mild yoke, they serve him best : his
state
Is kingly ; thousands at his bidding speed,
And post o'er land and ocean without rest.
    i.   MILTON—*Sonnet. On His Blindness.*

One on God's side is a majority.
    j.   WENDELL PHILLIPS—*Speech.*   Harper's
Ferry.   Nov. 1, 1859.

God is truth and light his shadow.
    k.   PLATO.

He mounts the storm, and walks upon the
wind.
    l.   POPE—*Essay on Man.*   Ep. II.   L. 110.

Laugh where we must, be candid where we
can,
But vindicate the ways of God to man.
    m.   POPE—*Essay on Man.*   Ep. I.   L. 15.

Lo, the poor Indian ! whose untutored mind
Sees God in clouds, or hears him in the wind.
    n.   POPE—*Essay on Man.*   Ep. I.   L. 99.

Thou Great First Cause, least understood.
    o.   POPE—*Universal Prayer.*

To Him no high, no low, no great, no small ;
He fills, He bounds, connects and equals all !
    p.   POPE—*Essay on Man.*   Ep. I.   L. 277.

Give us a God—a living God,
   One to wake the sleeping soul,
One to cleanse the tainted blood
   Whose pulses in our bosoms roll.
    q.   C. G. ROSENBERG—*The Winged Horn.*
St. 7.

God is our fortress, in whose conquering
name
Let us resolve to scale their flinty bulwarks.
    r.   *Henry VI.*   Pt. I.   Act II.   Sc. 1.
L. 26.

              God shall be my hope,
My stay, my guide and lantern to my feet.
    s.   *Henry VI.*   Pt. II.   Act II.   Sc. 3.
L. 24.

The divine essence itself is love and wisdom.
    t.   SWEDENBORG—*Divine Love and
Wisdom.*   Par. 28.

At last I heard a voice upon the slope
Cry to the summit, " Is there any hope ?"
To which an answer pealed from that high
land,
But in a tongue no man could understand ;
And on the glimmering limit far withdrawn,
God made himself an awful rose of dawn.
    u.   TENNYSON—*Vision of Sin.*   V.

              But I lose
Myself in Him, in Light ineffable !
Come then, expressive Silence, muse His
praise.
These, as they change, Almighty Father, these
Are but the varied God.   The rolling Year
Is full of Thee.
    v.   THOMSON—*Hymn.*   L. 116.

             What, but God ?
Inspiring God ! who boundless Spirit all,
And unremitting Energy, pervades,
Adjusts, sustains, and agitates the whole.
    w.   THOMSON—*The Seasons. Spring.*
L. 849.

God, from a beautiful necessity, is Love.
    x.   TUPPER—*Of Immortality.*

If there were no God, it would be necessary
to invent him.
    y.   VOLTAIRE—*Epitre à l' Auteur du Livre
des Trois Imposteurs.*   CXI.

The Somewhat which we name but cannot
know.
Ev'n as we name a star and only see
Its quenchless flashings forth, which ever
show
And ever hide him, and which are not he.
    z.   WILLIAM WATSON—*Wordsworth's
Grave.*   I.   St. 6.

I know not where His islands lift
  Their fronded palms in air;
I only know I cannot drift
  Beyond His love and care.
  a.   WHITTIER—*The Eternal Goodness.*
                              St. 20.

A Deity believed, is joy begun;
A Deity adored, is joy advanced;
A Deity beloved, is joy matured.
Each branch of piety delight inspires.
  b.   YOUNG. *Night Thoughts.* Night VIII.
                              L. 720.

A God all mercy is a God unjust.
  c.   YOUNG—*Night Thoughts.* Night IV.
                              L. 234.

A God alone can comprehend a God.
  d.   YOUNG—*Night Thoughts.* Night IX.
                              L. 835.

By night an atheist half believes a God.
  e.   YOUNG—*Night Thoughts.* Night V.
                              L. 177.

Though man sits still, and takes his ease,
  God is at work on man;
No means, no moment unemploy'd,
  To bless him, if he can.
  f.   YOUNG—*Resignation.* Pt. I. St. 119.

                          Thou, my all!
My theme! my inspiration! and my crown!
My strength in age! my rise in low estate!
My soul's ambition, pleasure, wealth!—my
    world!
My light in darkness! and my life in death!
My boast through time! bliss through eternity!
Eternity, too short to speak thy praise!
Or fathom thy profound of love to man!
  g.   YOUNG—*Night Thoughts.* Night IV.
                              L. 586.

GODS (THE).

Speak of the gods as they are.
  h.   BIAS.

And that dismal cry rose slowly
  And sank slowly through the air,
Full of spirit's melancholy
  And eternity's despair!
And they heard the words it said—
Pan is dead! great Pan is dead!
  Pan, Pan is dead!
  i.   E. B. BROWNING—*The Dead Pan.*

Never, believe me,
Appear the Immortals,
Never alone.
  j.   COLERIDGE—*The Visit of the Gods.*
                     Imitated from Schiller.

Nature's self's thy Ganymede.
  k.   ABRAHAM COWLEY—*Anacreontics. The*
                       Grasshopper. L. 8.

Creator Venus, genial power of love,
The bliss of men below, and gods above!
Beneath the sliding sun thou runn'st thy race,
Dost fairest shine, and best become thy place;
For thee the winds their eastern blasts forbear,
Thy mouth reveals the spring, and opens all
    the year;
Thee, goddess, thee, the storms of winter fly,
Earth smiles with flowers renewing, laughs
    the sky.
  l.   DRYDEN—*Palamon and Arcite.*
                     Bk. III. L. 1405.

With ravish'd ears
The monarch hears,
Assumes the god,
Affects to nod,
And seems to shake the spheres.
  m.   DRYDEN—*Alexander's Feast.* L. 37.

Cupid is a casuist, a mystic, and a cabalist,—
Can your lurking thought surprise,
And interpret your device,
     *   *   *   *   *
All things wait for and divine him,—
How shall I dare to malign him?
  n.   EMERSON—*Initial Dæmonic and*
                         Celestial Love. Pt. I.

Either Zeus came to earth to shew his form
    to thee,
Phidias, or thou to heaven hast gone the god
    to see.
  o.   *Greek Anthology.*

I, Phœbus, sang those songs that gained so
    much renown
I, Phœbus, sang them; Homer only wrote
    them down.
  p.   *Greek Anthology.*

Say, Bacchus, why so placid? What can
    there be
In commune held by Pallas and by thee?
Her pleasure is in darts and battles; thine
In joyous feasts and draughts of rosy wine.
  q.   *Greek Anthology.*

Some thoughtlessly proclaim the Muses nine:
A tenth is Sappho, maid divine.
  r.   *Greek Anthology.*

In saffron-colored mantle from the tides
Of Ocean rose the Morning to bring light
To gods and men.
  s.   HOMER—*Iliad.* Bk. XIX. L. 1.
                           Bryant's trans.

                  The son of Saturn gave
The nod with his dark brows. The ambrosial
    curls
Upon the Sovereign One's immortal head
Were shaken, and with them the mighty
    mount,
Olympus trembled.
  t.   HOMER—*Iliad.* Bk. I. L. 666.
                           Bryant's trans.

Who hearkens to the gods, the gods give ear.
a.   HOMER—*Iliad.* Bk. I. L. 280.
                     Bryant's trans.

Jove weighs affairs of earth in dubious scales,
And the good suffers while the bad prevails.
b.   HOMER—*Odyssey.* Bk. VI. L. 229.
                     Pope's trans.

Shakes his ambrosial curls, and gives the nod,
The stamp of fate, and sanction of the god.
c.   HOMER—*Iliad.* Bk. I. L. 684.
                     Pope's trans.

The matchless Ganymede, divinely fair.
d.   HOMER—*Iliad.* Bk. 20. L. 278.
                     Pope's trans.

Where'er he moves, the goddess shone before.
e.   HOMER—*Iliad.* Bk. 20. L. 127.
                     Pope's trans.

Of Pan we sing, the best of leaders Pan,
  That leads the Naiads and the Dryads forth;
And to their dances more than Hermes can,
  Hear, O you groves, and hills resound his
    worth.
f.   BEN JONSON—*Pan's Anniversary
                     Hymn.* I.

                    The gods
Grow angry with your patience. 'Tis their
  care,
And must be yours, that guilty men escape
  not:
As crimes do grow, justice should rouse
  itself.
g.   BEN JONSON—*Catiline.* Act III.
                     Sc. 5.

To that large utterance of the early gods!
h.   KEATS—*Hyperion.* Bk. I.

High in the home of the summers, the seats
  of the happy immortals,
Shrouded in knee-deep blaze, unapproachable;
  there ever youthful
Hebé, Harmonié, and the daughter of Jove,
  Aphrodité,
Whirled in the white-linked dance, with the
  gold-crowned Hours and Graces.
i.   CHARLES KINGSLEY—*Andromeda.*

Hoeder, the blind old god
Whose feet are shod with silence.
j.   LONGFELLOW—*Tegner's Drapa.* St. 6.

In the elder days of Art,
  Builders wrought with greatest care
Each minute and unseen part;
  For the gods see everywhere.
k.   LONGFELLOW—*The Builders.* St. 5.

Janus am I; oldest of potentates!
Forward I look and backward and below
I count—as god of avenues and gates—
The years that through my portals come and
  go.
I block the roads and drift the fields with
  snow,
I chase the wild-fowl from the frozen fen;
My frosts congeal the rivers in their flow,
My fires light up the hearths and hearts of
  men.
l.   LONGFELLOW—*Written for the
                    Children's Almanac.*

A boy of five years old serene and gay,
Unpitying Hades hurried me away.
Yet weep not for Callimachus: if few
The days I lived, few were my sorrows too.
m.   LUCIAN—*Greek Anthology.*

No wonder Cupid is a murderous boy;
A fiery archer making pain his joy.
His dam, while fond of Mars, is Vulcan's
  wife,
And thus 'twixt fire and sword divides her
  life.
n.   MELEAGER—*Greek Anthology.*

                    That moly
That Hermes once to wise Ulysses gave.
o.   MILTON—*Comus.* L. 637.

                Who knows not Circe,
The daughter of the Sun, whose charmed cup
Whoever tasted, lost his upright shape,
And downward fell into a groveling swine?
p.   MILTON—*Comus.* L. 50.

Man is certainly stark mad; he cannot
make a flea, and yet he will be making gods
by dozens.
q.   MONTAIGNE—*Apology for Raimond
               Sebond.* Bk. II. Ch. XII.

The god we now behold with opened eyes,
A herd of spotted panthers round him lies
In glaring forms; the grapy clusters spread
On his fair brows, and dangle on his head.
r.   OVID—*Metamorphoses.* Bk. III. L. 789.
                     Addison's trans.

The Graces sought some holy ground,
  Whose sight should ever please;
And in their search the soul they found
  Of Aristophanes.
s.   PLATO—*Greek Anthology.*

Or ask of yonder argent fields above
Why Jove's satellites are less than Jove
t.   POPE—*Essay on Man.* I. 42.

As flies to wanton boys, are we to the gods;
They kill us for their sport.
u.   *King Lear.* Act IV. Sc. 1. L. 38.

As sweet and musical
As bright Apollo's lute, strung with his hair;
And when Love speaks, the voice of all the gods
Makes heaven drowsy with the harmony.
　a.　　*Love's Labour's Lost.*　Act IV.　Sc. 3.
　　　　　　　　　　　　L. 342.

Cupid is a knavish lad,
Thus to make poor females mad.
　b.　　*Midsummer-Night's Dream.*　Act III.
　　　　　　　　　　　Sc. 2.　L. 440.

I would the gods had made thee poetical.
　c.　　*As You Like It.*　Act III.　Sc. 3.
　　　　　　　　　　　　　L. 15.

　　The basest horn of his hoof is more musical
than the pipe of Hermes.
　d.　　*Henry V.*　Act III.　Sc. 7.　L. 17.

The gods are just, and of our pleasant vices
Make instruments to plague us.
　e.　　*King Lear.*　Act V.　Sc. 3.　L. 170.

This senior-junior, giant-dwarf, Dan Cupid:
Regent of love-rhymes, lord of folded arms,
The anointed sovereign of sighs and groans,
Liege of all loiterers and malcontents.
　f.　　*Love's Labour's Lost.*　Act III.　Sc. 1.
　　　　　　　　　　　　　L. 182.

Wilt thou draw near the nature of the gods?
Draw near them then in being merciful;
Sweet mercy is nobility's true badge.
　g.　　*Titus Andronicus.*　Act I.　Sc. 1.
　　　　　　　　　　　　　L. 117.

Me goatfoot Pan of Arcady—the Median fear,
The Athenian's friend, Miltiades placed here.
　h.　　SIMONIDES—*Greek Anthology.*

A glimpse of Breidablick, whose walls are light
As e'en the silver on the cliff it shone;
Of dark blue steel its columns azure height
And the big altar was one agate stone.
It seemed as if the air upheld alone
Its dome, unless supporting spirits bore it,
Studded with stars Odin's spangled throne,
A light inscrutable burned fiercely o'er it;
In sky-blue mantles,
Sat the gold-crowned gods before it.
　i.　　TEGNER—*Fridthjof's Saga.*
　　　　　　　　　Canto XXIII.　St. 13.

But a bevy of Eroses apple-cheeked
In a shallop of crystal ivory-beaked.
　j.　　TENNYSON—*The Islet.*

　　　　　　Here comes to-day
Pallas and Aphrodite, claiming each
This meed of fairest.
　k.　　TENNYSON—*Œnone.*　St. 9.

Or else flushed Ganymede, his rosy thigh
Half buried in the Eagle's down,
Sole as a flying star, shot thro' the sky,
Above the pillared town.
　l.　　TENNYSON—*Palace of Art.*　St. 31.

Or sweet Europa's mantle blew unclasped
From off her shoulder backward borne;
From one hand drooped a crocus: one hand
　grasped
The mild bull's golden horn.
　m.　　TENNYSON—*The Palace of Art.*　St. 30.

Oh, meet is the reverence unto Bacchus paid!
We will praise him still in the songs of our
　fatherland,
We will pour the sacred wine, the chargers
　lade,
And the victim kid shall unresisting stand,
Led by his horns to the altar, where we turn
The hazel spits while the dripping entrails
　burn.
　n.　　VERGIL—*Georgics.*　Bk. II.　St. 17.
　　　　　　　L. 31.　H. W. Preston's trans.

GOLD.

　　　　　　　　A thirst for gold,
The beggar's vice, which can but overwhelm
The meanest hearts.
　o.　　BYRON—*The Vision of Judgment.*　St. 43.

And yet he hadde "a thombe of gold" pardee.
　p.　　CHAUCER—*Canterbury Tales.*
　　　　　　　　　　　Prologue.　L. 563.

For gold in phisik is a cordial;
Therefore he lovede gold in special.
　q.　　CHAUCER—*Canterbury Tales.*
　　　　　　　　　　　Prologue.　L. 443.

Gold begets in brethren hate;
Gold in families debate;
Gold does friendship separate;
Gold does civil wars create.
　r.　　ABRAHAM COWLEY—*Anacreontics.*
　　　　　　　　　　　　　Gold.　L. 17.

What female heart can gold despise?
What cat's averse to fish?
　s.　　GRAY—*On the Death of a Favourite Cat.*

Gold! Gold! Gold! Gold!
Bright and yellow, hard and cold.
　t.　　HOOD—*Miss Kilmansegg.*　*Her Moral.*

Stronger than thunder's winged force
All-powerful gold can speed its course;
Through watchful guards its passage make,
And loves through solid walls to break.
　u.　　HORACE—*Ode XVI.*　Bk. III.　L. 12.
　　　　　　　　　　　　Francis' trans.

The lust of gold succeeds the rage of conquest;
The lust of gold, unfeeling and remorseless!
The last corruption of degenerate man.
　v.　　SAM'L JOHNSON—*Irene.*　Act I.　Sc. 1.

Judges and senates have been bought for gold;
Esteem and love were never to be sold.
    a.   POPE—*Essay on Man.* Ep. IV. L. 187.

What nature wants, commodious gold bestows;
'Tis thus we cut the bread another sows.
    b.   POPE—*Moral Essay.* Ep. III. L. 21.

How quickly nature falls into revolt
When gold becomes her object!
For this the foolish over-careful fathers
Have broke their sleep with thoughts, their
    brains with care,
Their bones with industry :
For this they have engrossed and pil'd up
The canker'd heaps of strange-achieved gold;
For this they have been thoughtful to invest
Their sons with arts and martial exercises.
    c.   *Henry IV.* Pt. II. Act IV. Sc. 5.
                        L. 66.

        There is gold for you.
Sell me your good report.
    d.   *Cymbeline.* Act II. Sc. 3. L. 87.

There is thy gold, worse poison to men's souls,
Doing more murders in this loathsome world,
Than these poor compounds that thou mayst
    not sell.
I sell thee poison, thou hast sold me none.
    e.   *Romeo and Juliet.* Act V. Sc. 1. L. 80.

Thou that so stoutly hast resisted me,
Give me thy gold, if thou hast any gold ;
For I have bought it with an hundred blows.
    f.   *Henry VI.* Pt. III. Act II. Sc. 5. L. 79.

                 'Tis gold
Which buys admittance; oft it doth ; yea, and
    makes
Diana's rangers false themselves, yield up
Their deer to the stand o' the stealer : and 'tis
    gold
Which makes the true man kill'd and saves
    the thief;
Nay, sometime hangs both thief and true man.
    g.   *Cymbeline.* Act II. Sc. 3. L. 72.

Commerce has set the mark of selfishness,
The signet of its all-enslaving power
Upon a shining ore, and called it gold ;
Before whose image bow the vulgar great,
The vainly rich, the miserable proud,
The mob of peasants, nobles, priests, and
    kings,
And with blind feelings reverence the power
That grinds them to the dust of misery.
But in the temple of their hireling hearts
Gold is a living god, and rules in scorn
All earthly things but virtue.
    h.   SHELLEY—*Queen Mab.* Pt. V. St. 4.

No, let the monarch's bags and coffers hold
The flattering, mighty, nay, *all*-mighty gold.
    i.   JOHN WOLCOTT—*To Kieu Long.* Ode IV.

GOODNESS.

Whatever any one does or says, I must be
good.
    j.   AURELIUS ANTONINUS—*Meditations.*
                        Ch. VII.

What good I see humbly I seek to do,
And live obedient to the law, in trust
That what will come, and must come, shall
    come well.
    k.   EDWIN ARNOLD—*The Light of Asia.*
                    Bk. VI. L. 273.

Because indeed there was never law, or sect,
or opinion, did so much magnify goodness, as
the Christian religion doth.
    l.   BACON—*Essays. Of Goodness and*
                    Goodness of Nature.
           The good he scorned
Stalked off reluctant, like an ill-used ghost,
Not to return ; or if it did, in visits
Like those of angels, short and far between.
    m.   BLAIR—*The Grave.* Pt. 2. L. 586.

There shall never be one lost good ! What
    was shall live as before;
The evil is null, is nought, is silence imply-
    ing sound ;
What was good shall be good, with, for evil,
    so much good more;
On the earth the broken arcs; in the heaven
    a perfect round.
    n.   ROBERT BROWNING—*Abt Vogler.* IX.

No good Book, or good thing of any sort,
shows its best face at first.
    o.   CARLYLE—*Essays. Novalis.*

                Doing good,
Disinterested good, is not our trade.
    p.   COWPER—*The Task.* Bk. I. *The Sofa.*
                        L. 673.

That good diffused may more abundant grow.
    q.   COWPER—*Conversation.* L. 441.

Now, at a certain time, in pleasant mood,
He tried the luxury of doing good.
    r.   CRABBE—*Tales of the Hall.* Bk. III.

Who soweth good seed shall surely reap;
The year grows rich as it groweth old,
And life's latest sands are its sands of gold !
    s.   JULIA C. R. DORR—*To the " Bouquet*
                        Club."

Look around the habitable world, how few
Know their own good, or knowing it, pursue.
    t.   DRYDEN—*Juvenal.* Satire X.

If e'er she knew an evil thought,
    She spoke no evil word :
Peace to the gentle! She hath sought
    The bosom of her Lord.
    u.   EBENEZER ELLIOT—*Hannah Ratcliff.*

If you wish to be good, first believe that
you are bad.
    a.   EPICTETUS—*Fragments.* Long's trans.

And learn the luxury of doing good.
    b.   GOLDSMITH—*The Traveller.* L. 22.

Impell'd with steps unceasing to pursue
Some fleeting good, that mocks me with the
       view,
That, like the circle bounding earth and skies,
Allures from far, yet, as I follow, flies.
    c.   GOLDSMITH—*The Traveller.* L. 25.

If goodness leade him not, yet wearinesse
May tosse him to my breast.
    d.   HERBERT—*The Pulley.* St. 4.

God whose gifts in gracious flood
    Unto all who seek are sent,
Only asks you to be good
    And is content.
    e.   VICTOR HUGO—*God whose Gifts in
                              Gracious Flood.*

He was so good he would pour rose-water
on a toad.
    f.   DOUGLAS JERROLD—*Jerrold's Wit.
                            A Charitable Man.*

How near to good is what is fair !
    g.   BEN JONSON—*Love Freed from
                          Ignorance and Folly.*

Be good, sweet maid, and let who will be
     clever ;
    Do noble things, not dream them all day
     long ;
And so make life, death, and that vast forever
One grand, sweet song.
    h.   CHARLES KINGSLEY—*A Farewell.*

The soil out of which such men as he are
made is good to be born on, good to live on,
good to die for and to be buried in.
    i.   LOWELL—*Among my Books. Second
                       Series. Garfield.*

                          None
But such as are good men can give good
     things,
And that which is not good, is not delicious
To a well-governed and wise appetite.
    j.   MILTON—*Comus.* L. 702.

               Since good, the more
Communicated, more abundant grows.
    k.   MILTON—*Paradise Lost.* Bk. V. L. 71.

A glass is good, and a lass is good,
    And a pipe to smoke in cold weather ;
The world is good, and the people are good,
    And we're all good fellows together.
    l.   JOHN O'KEEFE—*Sprigs of Laurel.*
                         Act II. Sc. 1.

You're good for Madge or good for Cis
    Or good for Kate, maybe :
But what's to me the good of this
    While you're not good for me ?
    m.   CHRISTINA ROSSETTI—*Jessie Cameron.*
                                         St. 3.

What is beautiful is good, and who is good
will soon also be beautiful.
    n.   SAPPHO—*Fragment.* 101.

My meaning in saying he is a good man
is to have you understand me that he is
sufficient.
    o.   *Merchant of Venice.* Act I. Sc. 3.
                                     L. 14.

There is some soul of goodness in things evil,
Would men observingly distil it out.
    p.   *Henry V.* Act IV. Sc. 1. L. 4.

There lives within the very flame of love
A kind of wick or snuff that will abate it ;
And nothing is at a like goodness still ;
For goodness, growing to a pleurisy,
Dies in his own too much.
    q.   *Hamlet.* Act IV. Sc. 7. L. 115.

Your great goodness, out of holy pity,
Absolv'd him with an axe.
    r.   *Henry VIII.* Act III. Sc. 2. L. 263.

Only the actions of the just
Smell sweet, and blossom in their dust.
    s.   SHIRLEY—*The Contention of Ajax and
                         Ulysses.* Sc. 3. L. 23.

She has more goodness in her little finger
than he has in his whole body.
    t.   SWIFT—*Polite Conversation.*
                               Dialogue II.

Man should be ever better than he seems.
    u.   SIR AUBREY DE VERE—*A Song of Faith.*

GOSSIP.

Whoever keeps an open ear
For tattlers will be sure to hear
The trumpet of contention.
    v.   COWPER—*Friendship.* St. 17.

Gossip is a sort of smoke that comes from
the dirty tobacco-pipes of those who diffuse
it ; it proves nothing but the bad taste of the
smoker.
    w.   GEORGE ELIOT—*Daniel Deronda.*
                               Bk. II. Ch. XIII.

He's gone, and who knows how may he re-
     port
Thy words by adding fuel to the flame ?
    x.   MILTON—*Samson Agonistes.* L. 1350.

Foul whisperings are abroad.
    y.   *Macbeth.* Act V. Sc. 1. L. 79.

If my gossip Report be an honest woman of
her word.
a.　　*Merchant of Venice.* Act III. Sc. 1.
L. 7.

This act is as an ancient tale new told;
And, in the last repeating, troublesome,
Being urged at a time unseasonable.
b.　　*King John.* Act IV. Sc. 2. L. 18.

GOVERNMENT.

* * * The manners of women are the surest
criterion by which to determine whether a
republican government is practicable in a nation or not.
c.　　JOHN ADAMS—*Diary, June 2, 1778.*
Charles Francis Adams' Life of
Adams. Vol. III. P. 171.

Not stones, nor wood, nor the art of artisans
make a state; but where men are who know
how to take care of themselves, these are
cities and walls.
d.　　*Attributed to* ALCÆUS *by* ARISTIDES—
Orations. Vol. II. (Jebb's edition).
Austin's trans.

States are great engines moving slowly.
e.　　BACON—*Advancement of Learning.*
Bk. II.

For where's the State beneath the Firmament,
That doth excell the Bees for Government?
f.　　DU BARTAS—*Divine Weekes and Workes.*
First Week. Fifth Day. Pt. I.

"Whatever is, is not," is the maxim of the
anarchist, as often as anything comes across
him in the shape of a law which he happens
not to like.
g.　　RICHARD BENTLEY—*Declaration of*
Rights.

Well, will anybody deny now that the
Government at Washington, as regards its
own people, is the strongest government in
the world at this hour? And for this simple
reason, that it is based on the will, and the
good will, of an instructed people.
h.　　JOHN BRIGHT—*Speech at Rochdale.*
Nov. 24, 1863.

And having looked to Government for
bread, on the very first scarcity they will
turn and bite the hand that fed them.
i.　　BURKE—*Thoughts and Details on*
Scarcity. Vol. V. P. 156.

So then because some towns in England
are not represented, America is to have no
representative at all. They are "our children;" but when children ask for bread we
are not to give a stone.
j.　　BURKE—*Speech on American Taxation.*
Vol. II. P. 74.

Nothing's more dull and negligent
Than an old, lazy government,
That knows no interest of state,
But such as serves a present strait.
k.　　BUTLER—*Miscellaneous Thoughts.*
L. 159.

A thousand years scarce serve to form a state;
An hour may lay it in the dust.
l.　　BYRON—*Childe Harold.* Canto II.
St. 84.

A power has arisen up in the Government
greater than the people themselves, consisting
of many and various and powerful interests,
combined into one mass, and held together
by the cohesive power of the vast surplus in
the banks.
m.　　JOHN C. CALHOUN—*In the U. S. Senate.*
May 28, 1836.

And the first thing I would do in my
government, I would have nobody to control
me, I would be absolute; and who but I:
now, he that is absolute, can do what he
likes; he that can do what he likes, can take
his pleasure; he that can take his pleasure,
can be content; and he that can be content,
has no more to desire; so the matter's over.
n.　　CERVANTES—*Don Quixote.* Pt. I.
Bk. IV. Ch. XXIII.

There was a State without kings or nobles;
there was a church without a bishop; there
was a people governed by grave magistrates
which it had elected, and equal laws which it
had framed.
o.　　RUFUS CHOATE—*Speech before the New*
England Society. December 22, 1843.

Who's in or out, who moves this grand ma-
chine,
Nor stirs my curiosity nor spleen:
Secrets of state no more I wish to know
Than secret movements of a puppet show:
Let but the puppets move, I've my desire,
Unseen the hand which guides the master
wire.
p.　　CHURCHILL—*Night.* L. 257.

Government is a trust, and the officers of
the government are trustees; and both the
trust and the trustees are created for the benefit of the people.
q.　　HENRY CLAY—*Speech at Lexington.*
May 16, 1829.

I have considered the pension list of the
republic a roll of honor.
r.　　GROVER CLEVELAND—*Veto of Mary Ann*
Dougherty's Pension, July 5, 1888.

Though the people support the government
the government should not support the people.
s.　　GROVER CLEVELAND—*Veto of Texas*
Seed-bill, Feb 16, 1887.

I am the State.

    a.   Dulaure *attributes this saying to* Louis XIV. *in his History of Paris*, 1863. P. 387.

Whatever was required to be done, the Circumlocution Office was beforehand with all the public departments in the art of perceiving how not to do it.

    b.   Dickens—*Little Dorrit.* Bk. III. Ch. X.

A Conservative Government is an organized hypocrisy.

    c.   Benj. Disraeli—*Speech.* March 17, 1845.

Free trade is not a principle, it is an expedient.

    d.   Benj. Disraeli—*On Import Duties.* April 25, 1843.

Resolv'd to ruin or to rule the state.

    e.   Dryden—*Absalom and Achitophel.* Pt. I. L. 174.

That those who think must govern those that toil.

    f.   Goldsmith—*The Traveller.* L. 372.

Unnecessary taxation is unjust taxation.

    g.   Abram S. Hewitt—*Democratic Platform.* 1884.

The trappings of a monarchy would set up an ordinary commonwealth.

    h.   Sam'l Johnson—*Life of Milton.*

The congress of Vienna does not walk, but it dances.

    i.   Prince de Ligne.

A house divided against itself cannot stand. I believe this government cannot endure permanently half-slave and half-free.

    j.   Abraham Lincoln—*Speech*, June 17, 1858. See W. O. Stoddard's Life of Lincoln.

That this nation, under God, shall have a new birth of freedom, and that government of the people, by the people, for the people, shall not perish from the earth.

    k.   Abraham Lincoln—*Speech at Gettysburg*, Nov. 19, 1863.

All your strength is in your union,
All your danger is in discord.

    l.   Longfellow—*The Song of Hiawatha.* I. L. 112.

That is the best government which desires to make the people happy, and knows how to make them happy.

    m.   Macaulay—*On Mitford's History of Greece*, 1824.

The Commons, faithful to their system, remained in a wise and masterly inactivity.

    n.   Sir James Mackintosh—*Vindiciæ Gallicæ.* Sec. I.

Let wealth and commerce, laws and learning, die,
But leave us still our old nobility.

    o.   Lord John Manners—*England's Trust.* Pt. III. L. 227.

To make a bank, was a great plot of state;
Invent a shovel, and be a magistrate.

    p.   Andrew Marvell—*The Character of Holland.*

Hope nothing from foreign governments. They will never be really willing to aid you until you have shown that you are strong enough to conquer without them.

    q.   Mazzini—*Life and Writings. Young Italy.*

If the prince of a State love benevolence, he will have no opponent in all the empire.

    r.   Mencius—*Works.* Bk. IV. Pt. I. Ch. 7.

There is what I call the American idea. * * * This idea demands, as the proximate organization thereof, a democracy,—that is, a government of all the people, by all the people, for all the people; of course, a government of the principles of eternal justice, the unchanging law of God; for shortness' sake I will call it the idea of Freedom.

    s.   Theodore Parker—*Speech at the N. E. Anti-Slavery Convention, Boston*, 1850. May 29.

Better a hundred times an honest and capable administration of an erroneous policy than a corrupt and incapable administration of a good one.

    t.   E. J. Phelps—*At Dinner of the N. Y. Chamber of Commerce*, Nov. 19, 1889.

The government will take the fairest of names, but the worst of realities—mob rule.

    u.   Polybius. VI. 57.

The right divine of kings to govern wrong.

    v.   Pope—*The Dunciad.* Bk. IV. L. 188.

Say to the seceded States—*Wayward sisters, depart in peace!*

    w.   Winfield Scott—*Letter to W. H. Seward*, March 3, 1861.

For government, through high and low and lower,
Put into parts, doth keep in one consent,
Congreeing in a full and natural close,
Like music.

    x.   *Henry V.* Act I. Sc. 2. L. 180.

How, in one house,
Should many people, under two commands,
Hold amity? 'Tis hard; almost impossible.

    y.   *King Lear.* Act II. Sc. 4. L. 243.

Why, this it is, when men are rul'd by women.

    z.   *Richard III.* Act I. Sc. 1. L. 62.

Men who prefer any load of infamy, however great, to any pressure of taxation, however light.

    a.   SYDNEY SMITH—*On American Debts.*

The schoolboy whips his taxed top, the beardless youth manages his taxed horse, with a taxed bridle, on a taxed road; and the dying Englishman, pouring his medicine, which has paid seven per cent., flings himself back on his chintz bed, which has paid twenty-two per cent., and expires in the arms of an apothecary who has paid a license of a hundred pounds for the privilege of putting him to death.

    b.   SYDNEY SMITH—*Review of Seybert's Annals. United States.*

Ill can he rule the great that cannot reach the small.

    c.   SPENSER—*Faerie Queene.* Bk. V. Canto II. St. 51.

The people's government made for the people, made by the people, and answerable to the people.

    d.   DANIEL WEBSTER—*Second Speech on Foot's Resolution,* Jan. 26, 1830.

When my eyes shall be turned to behold, for the last time, the sun in heaven, may I not see him shining on the broken and dishonored fragments of a once glorious Union; on States dissevered, discordant, belligerent; on a land rent with civil feuds, or drenched, it may be, in fraternal blood!

    e.   DANIEL WEBSTER—*Second Speech on Foot's Resolution,* Jan. 26, 1830.

Wherever magistrates were appointed from among those who complied with the injunctions of the laws, he (Socrates) considered the government to be an aristocracy.

    f.   XENOPHON—*Memorabilia of Socrates.* Bk. IV. Ch. 6.

GRACE.

Take time enough—all other graces
Will soon fill up their proper places.

    g.   BYRON—*Advice to the Messrs. H——
and H—— to preach slow.* St. 8.

Who hath not own'd, with rapture-smitten frame,
The power of grace, the magic of a name?

    h.   CAMPBELL—*Pleasures of Hope.* Pt. II. L. 5.

Whatever he did, was done with so much ease,
In him alone 'twas natural to please.

    i.   DRYDEN—*Absalom and Achitophel.* Pt. I. L. 27.

Stately and tall he moves in the hall,
The chief of a thousand for grace.

    j.   KATE FRANKLIN—*Life at Olympus.* *Godey's Lady's Book.* Vol. XXIII. P. 33.

And grace that won who saw to wish her stay.

    k.   MILTON—*Paradise Lost.* Bk. VIII. L. 43.

From vulgar bounds with brave disorder part,
And snatch a grace beyond the reach of art.

    l.   POPE—*Essay on Criticism.* L. 152.

        For several virtues
Have I lik'd several women; never any
With so full soul, but some defect in her
Did quarrel with the noblest grace she ow'd,
And put it to the foil.

    m.   *Tempest.* Act III. Sc. 1. L. 42.

God give him grace to groan!

    n.   *Love's Labour's Lost.* Act IV. Sc. 3. L. 21.

Hail to thee, lady! and the grace of heaven,
Before, behind thee and on every hand,
Enwheel thee round!

    o.   *Othello.* Act II. Sc. 1. L. 85.

He does it with a better grace, but I do it more natural.

    p.   *Twelfth Night.* Act II. Sc. 3. L. 88.

O, then, what graces in my love do dwell,
That he hath turn'd a heaven unto a hell!

    q.   *Midsummer-Night's Dream.* Act I. Sc. 1. L. 206.

But the tender grace of a day that is dead
Will never come back to me.

    r.   TENNYSON—*Break, Break, Break.*

GRATITUDE.

Gratitude is the fairest blossom which springs from the soul; and the heart of man knoweth none more fragrant.

    s.   HOSEA BALLOU—*MS. Sermons.*

Gratitude is expensive.

    t.   GIBBON—*Decline and Fall of the Roman Empire.*

The still small voice of gratitude.

    u.   GRAY—*For Music.* St. 5.

        A grateful mind
By owing owes not, but still pays, at once
Indebted and discharg'd.

    v.   MILTON—*Paradise Lost.* Bk. IV. L. 55.

Th' unwilling gratitude of base mankind!

    w.   POPE—*Second Book of Horace.* Ep. I. L. 14.

Let but the commons hear this testament—
Which, pardon me, I do not mean to read—
And they would go and kiss dead Cæsar's
    wounds
And dip their napkins in his sacred blood,
Yea, beg a hair of him for memory,
And, dying, mention it within their wills,
Bequeathing it as a rich legacy
Unto their issue.
    a.   *Julius Cæsar.* Act III. Sc. 2. L. 135.

             Now the good gods forbid
That our renowned Rome, whose gratitude
Towards her deserved children is enroll'd
In Jove's own book, like an unnatural dam
Should now eat up her own!
    b.   *Coriolanus.* Act III. Sc. 1. L. 290.

I've heard of hearts unkind, kind deeds
    With coldness still returning;
Alas! the gratitude of men
    Hath often left me mourning.
    c.   WORDSWORTH—*Simon Lee.*

GRAVE (THE).

Mine be the breezy hill that skirts the down;
    Where a green grassy turf is all I crave,
With here and there a violet bestrown,
    Fast by a brook or fountain's murmuring
        wave;
And many an evening sun shine sweetly on
    my grave!
    d.   BEATTIE—*The Minstrel.* Bk. II.
                        St. 17.

Lie lightly on my ashes, gentle earth!
    e.   BEAUMONT AND FLETCHER—*Bonduca.*
                     Act IV. Sc. 3.

            The grave, dread thing!
Men shiver when thou'rt named: Nature
    appalled,
Shakes off her wonted firmness.
    f.   BLAIR—*The Grave.*

The grave is Heaven's golden gate,
And rich and poor around it wait;
O Shepherdess of England's fold,
Behold this gate of pearl and gold!
    g.   WM. BLAKE—*Dedication of the Designs
        to Blair's "Grave."*   To Queen
                       Charlotte.

Build me a shrine, and I could kneel
    To rural Gods, or prostrate fall;
Did I not see, did I not feel.
    That one GREAT SPIRIT governs all.
O Heaven, permit that I may lie
    Where o'er my corse green branches wave;
And those who from life's tumults fly
    With kindred feelings press my grave.
    h.   BLOOMFIELD—*Love of the Country.*
                        St. 4.

Gravestones tell truth scarce forty years.
    i.   SIR THOMAS BROWNE—*Hydriotaphia.*
                        Ch. V.

I gazed upon the glorious sky
    And the green mountains round,
And thought that when I came to lie
    At rest within the ground,
'Twere pleasant that in flowery June
When brooks send up a cheerful tune,
    And groves a joyous sound,
The sexton's hand, my grave to make,
The rich, green mountain turf should break.
    j.   BRYANT—*June.*

I would rather sleep in the southern corner
of a little country churchyard, than in the
tombs of the Capulets.
    k.   BURKE—*Letter to Matthew Smith.*

                        Of all
The fools who flock'd to swell or see the
    show,
Who car'd about the corpse? The funeral
Made the attraction, and the black the woe;
    There throbb'd not there a thought which
        pierc'd the pall.
    l.   BYRON—*Vision of Judgment.* St. 10.

                Perhaps the early grave
Which men weep over may be meant to save.
    m.   BYRON—*Don Juan.* Canto IV. St. 12.

What's hallow'd ground? Has earth a clod
Its Maker mean'd not should be trod
By man, the image of his God,
    Erect and free,
Unscourged by Superstition's rod
    To bow the knee.
    n.   CAMPBELL—*Hallowed Ground.*

But an untimely grave.
    o.   CAREW—*On the Duke of Buckingham.*

The grave, where sets the orb of being, sets
To rise, ascend, and culminate above
Eternity's horizon evermore.
    p.   ABRAHAM COLES—*The Microcosm and
                   Other Poems.* P. 125.

In yonder grave a Druid lies.
    q.   COLLINS—*Ode on the Death of Thomson.*

The solitary, silent, solemn scene,
Where Cæsars, heroes, peasants, hermits lie,
Blended in dust together; where the slave
Rests from his labors; where th' insulting
    proud
Resigns his powers; the miser drops his
    hoard:
Where human folly sleeps.
    r.   DYER—*Ruins of Rome.* L. 540.

Some mute inglorious Milton here may rest,
Some Cromwell guiltless of his country's
    blood.
    s.   GRAY—*Elegy in a Country Churchyard.*
                        St. 15.

Such graves as his are pilgrim shrines,
  Shrines to no code or creed confined,—
The Delphian vales, the Palestines,
  The Meccas of the mind.
  a.   FITZ-GREENE HALLECK—*Burns.* St. 32.

Graves they say are warm'd by glory;
Foolish words and empty story.
  b.   HEINE—*Latest Poems.* Epilogue.
                                       L. 1.

Where shall we make her grave?
Oh! where the wild flowers wave
  In the free air!
When shower and singing-bird
'Midst the young leaves are heard,
  There—lay her there!
  c.   MRS. HEMANS—*Dirge. Where Shall
                         we Make her Grave?*

Then to the grave I turned me to see what
    therein lay;
'Twas the garment of the Christian, worn out
    and thrown away.
  d.   KRUMMACHER—*Death and the Christian.*

I see their scattered gravestones gleaming
    white
Through the pale dusk of the impending
    night.
O'er all alike the imperial sunset throws
Its golden lilies mingled with the rose;
We give to each a tender thought and pass
Out of the graveyards with their tangled
    grass.
  e.   LONGFELLOW—*Morituri Salutamus.*
                                       L. 120.

This is the field and Acre of our God,
  This is the place where human harvests
    grow!
  f.   LONGFELLOW—*God's Acre.*

There are slave-drivers quietly whipped under-
    ground,
There bookbinders, done up in boards, are
    fast bound,
There card-players wait till the last trump be
    played,
There all the choice spirits get finally laid,
There the babe that's unborn is supplied with
    a berth,
There men without legs get their six feet of
    earth,
There lawyers repose, each wrapped up in
    his case,
There seekers of office are sure of a place,
There defendant and plaintiff get equally
    cast,
There shoemakers quietly stick to the last.
  g.   LOWELL—*Fables for Critics.* L. 1,656.

And so sepulchred in such pomp dost lie;
That kings for such a tomb would wish to die.
  h.   MILTON—*Epitaph on Shakespeare.*

There is a calm for those who weep,
  A rest for weary pilgrims found,
They softly lie and sweetly sleep
  Low in the ground.
  i.   MONTGOMERY—*The Grave.*

I stood beside the grave, and I gazed upon the
    stone:
And the name of Robert Burns was engraven
    thereupon.
  j.   ROBERT NICOLL—*The Grave of Burns.*

The grave unites; where e'en the great find
    rest,
And blended lie th' oppressor and th' op-
    pressed!
  k.   POPE—*Windsor Forest.* L. 317.

Yet shall thy grave with rising flow'rs be
    dressed,
And the green turf lie lightly on thy breast;
There shall the morn her earliest tears bestow,
There the first roses of the year shall blow.
  l.   POPE—*Elegy on an Unfortunate Lady.*
                                       L. 65.

Never the grave gives back what it has won!
  m.   SCHILLER—*A Funeral Fantasy.*
                                 Last line.

To that dark inn, the Grave!
  n.   SCOTT—*The Lord of the Isles.* VI.
                                       L. 26.

                   Bear from hence his body;
And mourn you for him: let him be regarded
As the most noble corse that ever herald
Did follow to his urn.
  o.   *Coriolanus.* Act V. Sc. 6. L. 143.

Gilded tombs do worms infold.
  p.   *Merchant of Venice.* Act II. Sc. 7.
                                       L. 69.

                   Lay her i' the earth;
And from her fair and unpolluted flesh
May violets spring!
  q.   *Hamlet.* Act V. Sc. 1. L. 261.

Let's choose executors and talk of wills:
And yet not so, for what can we bequeath
Save our deposed bodies to the ground?
  r.   *Richard II.* Act III. Sc. 2. L. 148.

Taking the measure of an unmade grave.
  s.   *Romeo and Juliet.* Act III. Sc. 3.
                                       L. 70.

                   The sepulchre,
Wherein we saw thee quietly inurn'd,
Hath op'd his ponderous and marble jaws.
  t.   *Hamlet.* Act I. Sc. 4. L. 48.

They bore him barefac'd on the bier;
    *   *   *   *   *   *   *
And in his grave rain'd many a tear.
  u.   *Hamlet.* Act IV. Sc. 5. L. 164.

Within their chiefest temple I'll erect
A tomb, wherein his corpse shall be interr'd.
  a.   *Henry VI.* Pt. I. Act II. Sc. 2.
                        L. 12.

O heart, and mind, and thoughts! what thing do you
Hope to inherit in the grave below?
  b.   SHELLEY—*Sonnet. Ye Hasten to the Dead!*

The lone couch of his everlasting sleep.
  c.   SHELLEY—*Alastor.* L. 57.

Kings have no such couch as thine,
As the green that folds thy grave.
  d.   TENNYSON—*A Dirge.* St. 6.

Our father's dust is left alone
And silent under other snows.
  e.   TENNYSON—*In Memoriam.* Pt. CV.

Hark! from the tombs a doleful sound.
  f.   WATTS—*Hymns and Spiritual Songs. Funeral Thoughts.* Bk. II. Vol. IX. Hymn 63.

Ah, the grave's a quiet bed:
  She shall sleep a pleasant sleep,
And the tears that you may shed
  Will not wake her—therefore weep!
  g.   WM. WINTER—*The Last Scene.* St. 2.

But the grandsire's chair is empty,
  The cottage is dark and still;
There's a nameless grave on the battle-field,
  And a new one under the hill.
  h.   WM. WINTER—*After All.*

GREATNESS.

                   Burn to be great,
Pay not thy praise to lofty things alone.
The plains are everlasting as the hills,
The bard cannot have two pursuits; aught else
Comes on the mind with the like shock as though
Two worlds had gone to war, and met in air.
  i.   BAILEY—*Festus.* Sc. *Home.*

Nothing can cover his high fame but heaven;
No pyramids set off his memories,
But the eternal substance of his greatness,—
To which I leave him.
  j.   BEAUMONT AND FLETCHER—*The False One.* Act II. Sc. I.

Man's Unhappiness, as I construe, comes of his Greatness; it is because there is an Infinite in him, which with all his cunning he cannot quite bury under the Finite.
  k.   CARLYLE—*Sartor Resartus. The Everlasting Yea.* Bk. II. Ch. IX.

We have not the love of greatness, but the love of the love of greatness.
  l.   CARLYLE—*Essays. Characteristics.* Vol. III.

The great man who thinks greatly of himself, is not diminishing that greatness in heaping fuel on his fire.
  m.   ISAAC DISRAELI—*Literary Character of Men of Genius.* Ch. XV.

So let his name through Europe ring!
  A man of mean estate,
Who died as firm as Sparta's king,
  Because his soul was great.
  n.   SIR FRANCIS HASTINGS DOYLE—*The Private of the Buffs.*

       No great deed is done
By falterers who ask for certainty.
  o.   GEORGE ELIOT—*The Spanish Gypsy.* Bk. I. 56th line from end.

He is great who is what he is from Nature, and who never reminds us of others.
  p.   EMERSON—*Essays. Second Series. Uses of Great Men.*

Nature never sends a great man into the planet, without confiding the secret to another soul.
  q.   EMERSON—*Uses of Great Men.*

He who comes up to his own idea of greatness, must always have had a very low standard of it in his mind.
  r.   HAZLITT—*Table Talk. Whether Genius is Conscious of its own Power.*

No really great man ever thought himself so.
  s.   HAZLITT—*Table Talk. Whether Genius is Conscious of its own Power.*

Ajax the great * * *
Himself a host.
  t.   HOMER—*Iliad.* Bk. III. L. 293. Pope's trans.

For he that once is good, is ever great.
  u.   BEN JONSON—*The Forest. To Lady Aubigny.*

Greatness on goodness loves to slide, not stand,
And leaves, for fortune's ice, vertue's firm land.
  v.   RICHARD KNOLLES—*Turkish History.* Under a portrait of Mustapha I. L. 13.

Great men stand like solitary towers in the city of God.
  w.   LONGFELLOW—*Kavanagh.* Ch. I.

A great man is made up of qualities that meet or make great occasions.
  x.   LOWELL—*My Study Windows. Garfield.*

The great man is he who does not lose his child's heart.
  y.   MENCIUS—*Works.* Bk. IV. Pt. II. Ch. XII.

Are not great
Men the models of nations?

   a.   OWEN MEREDITH (Lord Lytton)—
             Lucile.   Pt. II.   Canto VI.
                              St. 29.

That man is great, and he alone,
Who serves a greatness not his own,
  For neither praise nor pelf:
Content to know and be unknown:
  Whole in himself.

   b.   OWEN MEREDITH (Lord Lytton)—
                     A Great Man.

Are yet two Romans living such as these?
The last of all the Romans, fare thee well!

   c.   *Julius Cæsar.* Act V. Sc. 3. L. 98.

But thou art fair, and at thy birth, dear boy,
Nature and Fortune join'd to make thee great.

   d.   *King John.* Act III. Sc. 1. L. 54.

Greatness knows itself.

   e.   *Henry IV.* Pt. I. Act IV. Sc. 3. L. 74.

Some are born great, some achieve greatness,
and some have greatness thrust upon 'em.

   f.   *Twelfth Night.* Act II. Sc. 5. L. 157.

They that stand high have many blasts to
   shake them;
And if they fall, they dash themselves to pieces.

   g.   *Richard III.* Act I. Sc. 3. L. 259.

Why, man, he doth bestride the narrow world
Like a Colossus, and we petty men
Walk under his huge legs and peep about
To find ourselves dishonorable graves.

   h.   *Julius Cæsar.* Act I. Sc. 2. L. 135.

      Your name is great
In mouths of wisest censure.

   i.   *Othello.* Act II. Sc. 3. L. 192.

Not that the heavens the little can make great,
But many a man has lived an age too late.

   j.   R. H. STODDARD—*To Edmund Clarence*
                        Stedman.

   Censure is the tax a man pays to the public
for being eminent.

   k.   SWIFT—*Thoughts on Various Subjects.*

   The world knows nothing of its greatest
men.

   l.   HENRY TAYLOR—*Philip Van Artevelde.*
                        Act I. Sc. 5.

He fought a thousand glorious wars,
  And more than half the world was his,
And somewhere, now, in yonder stars,
  Can tell, mayhap, what greatness is.

   m.   THACKERAY—*The Chronicle of the*
                    Drum. Last verse.

O, happy they that never saw the court,
Nor ever knew great men but by report!

   n.   JOHN WEBSTER—*The White Devil; or,*
                Vittoria Corombona. Act V. Sc. VI.

Great is Youth—equally great is Old Age—
  great are Day and Night.
Great is Wealth—great is Poverty—great is
  Expression—great is Silence.

   o.   WALT WHITMAN—*Leaves of Grass.*
                Great are the Myths. St. 3.

Great let me call him, for he conquered me.

   p.   YOUNG—*The Revenge.* Act I. Sc. 1.

High stations, tumult, but not bliss, create;
None think the great unhappy, but the great.

   q.   YOUNG—*Love of Fame.* Satire I.
                           L. 237.

GRIEF.

Why wilt thou add to all the griefs I suffer
Imaginary ills, and fancy'd tortures?

   r.   ADDISON—*Cato.* Act IV. Sc. 1.

O, brothers! let us leave the shame and sin
Of taking vainly in a plaintive mood,
The holy name of *Grief*—holy herein,
That, by the grief of One, came all our good.

   s.   E. B. BROWNING—*Sonnets.*
                     Exaggeration.

Thank God, bless God, all ye who suffer not
More grief than ye can weep for. That is
  well—
That is light grieving!

   t.   E. B. BROWNING—*Tears.*

No greater grief than to remember days
Of joy, when misery is at hand.

   u.   DANTE—*Hell.* Canto V. L. 121.

In all the silent manliness of grief.

   v.   GOLDSMITH—*Deserted Village.* L. 384.

Oh! call my brother back to me!
  I cannot play alone;
The summer comes with flower and bee,—
  Where is my brother gone?

   w.   MRS. HEMANS—*The Child's First Grief.*

Grief tears his heart, and drives him to and
  fro,
In all the raging impotence of woe.

   x.   HOMER—*Iliad.* Bk. 22. L. 526.
                       Pope's trans.

        On me, on me
Time and change can heap no more!
  The painful past with blighting grief
  Hath left my heart a withered leaf.
Time and change can do no more.

   y.   RICHARD HENGIST HORNE—*Dirge.*

The only cure for grief is action.

   z.   GEO. HENRY LEWES—*The Spanish*
            Drama. Life of Lope De Vega.
                           Ch. II.

Oh, well has it been said, that there is no
grief like the grief which does not speak!

   aa.   LONGFELLOW—*Hyperion.* Bk. II.
                           Ch. II.

There is a solemn luxury in grief.
  a.   WM. MASON—*The English Garden*.

What need a man forestall his date of grief,
And run to meet what he would most avoid?
  b.   MILTON—*Comus*. L. 362.

Alas, poor man! grief has so wrought on him,
He takes false shadows for true substances.
  c.   *Titus Andronicus*. Act III. Sc. 2.
                                    L. 79.

                        But I have
That honourable grief lodg'd here which
      burns
Worse than tears drown.
  d.   *Winter's Tale*. Act II. Sc. 1. L. 110.

But I have that within which passeth show;
These but the trappings and the suits of woe.
  e.   *Hamlet*. Act I. Sc. 2. L. 85.

But then the mind much sufferance doth
      o'er-skip,
When grief hath mates.
  f.   *King Lear*. Act III. Sc. 6. L. 113.

Each substance of a grief hath twenty
      shadows,
Which shows like grief itself, but is not so;
For sorrow's eye, glazed with blinding tears,
Divides one thing entire to many objects.
  g.   *Richard II*. Act II. Sc. 2. L. 14.

Every one can master a grief but he that has
      it.
  h.   *Much Ado About Nothing*. Act III.
                              Sc. 2. L. 29.

For grief is proud and makes his owner stoop.
  i.   *King John*. Act III. Sc. 1. L. 69.

Great griefs, I see, medicine the less.
  j.   *Cymbeline*. Act IV. Sc. 2. L. 243.

Grief fills the room up of my absent child,
Lies in his bed, walks up and down with me,
Puts on his pretty looks, repeats his words,
Remembers me of all his gracious parts,
Stuffs out his vacant garments with his form;
Then, have I reason to be fond of grief?
  k.   *King John*. Act III. Sc. 4. L. 93.

Griefs of mine own lie heavy in my breast,
Which thou wilt propagate, to have it prest
With more of thine.
  l.   *Romeo and Juliet*. Act I. Sc. 1.
                                    L. 193.

I am not mad; I would to heaven I were!
For then, 'tis like I should forget myself:
O, if I could, what grief should I forget!
  m.   *King John*. Act III. Sc. 4. L. 48.

If thou engrossest all the griefs are thine,
Thou robb'st me of a moiety.
  n.   *All's Well That Ends Well*. Act III.
                              Sc. 2. L. 68.

                              Men
Can counsel and speak comfort to that grief
Which they themselves not feel; but, tasting it,
Their counsel turns to passion, which before
Would give preceptial medicine to rage,
Fetter strong madness in a silken thread,
Charm ache with air and agony with words.
  o.   *Much Ado About Nothing*. Act V.
                              Sc. 1. L. 20.

            My grief lies all within;
And these external manners of laments
Are merely shadows to the unseen grief
That swells with silence in the tortur'd soul.
  p.   *Richard II*. Act IV. Sc. 1. L. 295.

My grief lies onward and my joy behind.
  q.   *Sonnet L*.

            Nor doth the general care
Take hold on me, for my particular grief
Is of so flood-gate and o'erbearing nature
That it engluts and swallows other sorrows
And it is still itself.
  r.   *Othello*. Act I. Sc. 3. L. 54.

Oft have I heard that grief softens the mind
And makes it fearful and degenerate.
  s.   *Henry VI*. Pt. II. Act IV. Sc. 4.
                                    L. 1.

O, grief hath chang'd me since you saw me
      last,
And careful hours with time's deform'd
      hand
Have written strange defeatures in my face.
  t.   *Comedy of Errors*. Act V. Sc. 1.
                                    L. 297.

            Some grief shows much of love;
But much of grief shows still some want of wit.
  u.   *Romeo and Juliet*. Act III. Sc. 5.
                                    L. 73.

That we two are asunder; let that grieve him;
Some griefs are medicinable.
  v.   *Cymbeline*. Act III. Sc. 2. L. 32.

            The grief that does not speak
Whispers the o'er-fraught heart and bids it
      break.
  w.   *Macbeth*. Act IV. Sc. 3. L. 209.

What private griefs they have, alas, I know
      not,
That made them do it.
  x.   *Julius Cæsar*. Act III. Sc. 2. L. 216.

You may my glories and my state depose,
But not my griefs; still am I king of those.
  y.   *Richard II*. Act IV. Sc. 1. L. 192.

Dark is the realm of grief: but human things
Those may not know of who cannot weep for
      them.
  z.   SHELLEY—*Otho*. (A projected poem.)

Winter is come and gone,
But grief returns with the revolving year.
> *a.* 　SHELLEY—*Adonais.* St. 18.

"Oh, but," quoth she, "great griefe will not
be tould,
And can more easily be thought than said."
> *b.* 　SPENSER—*Faerie Queene.* Bk. I.
> Canto VII. St. 41.

He gave a deep sigh; I saw the iron enter
into his soul.
> *c.* 　STERNE—*Sentimental Journey.* The
> Captive.

Never morning wore
To evening, but some heart did break.
> *d.* 　TENNYSON—*In Memoriam.* Pt. VI.

Men are we, and must grieve when even the
Shade
Of that which once was great is passed away.
> *e.* 　WORDSWORTH—*On the Extinction of
> the Venetian Republic.*

GROWTH.

What? Was man made a wheel-work to
wind up,
And be discharged, and straight wound up
anew?
No! grown, his growth lasts; taught, he ne'er
forgets;
May learn a thousand things, not twice the
same.
> *f.* 　ROBERT BROWNING—*A Death in the
> Desert.* L. 447.

The lofty oak from a small acorn grows.
> *g.* 　LEWIS DUNCOMBE—*Translation of
> De Minimis Maxima.*

He builded better than he knew;—
The conscious stone to beauty grew.
> *h.* 　EMERSON—*The Problem.* L. 23.

Man seems the only growth that dwindles
here.
> *i.* 　GOLDSMITH—*The Traveller.* L. 126.

It is not growing like a tree
In bulk, doth make man better be;
Or standing long an oak, three hundred year,
To fall a log at last, dry, bald, and sere:
A lily of a day
Is fairer far in May,
Although it fall and die that night—
It was the plant and flower of Light.
> *j.* 　BEN JONSON—*The Noble Nature.*

Our pleasures and our discontents,
Are rounds by which we may ascend.
> *k.* 　LONGFELLOW—*The Ladder of St.
> Augustine.* St. 2.

And so all growth that is not towards God
Is growing to decay.
> *l.* 　GEORGE MACDONALD—*Within and
> Without.* Pt. I. Sc. 3.

Arts and sciences are not cast in a mould,
but are found and perfected by degrees, by
often handling and polishing, as bears leisurely
lick their cubs into shape.
> *m.* 　MONTAIGNE—*Apology for Raimond
> Sebond.* Bk. II. Ch. XII.

Grows with his growth, and strengthens with
his strength.
> *n.* 　POPE—*Essay on Man.* Ep. II. L. 136.

'Tis thus the mercury of man is fix'd,
Strong grows the virtue with his nature mix'd.
> *o.* 　POPE—*Essay on Man.* Ep. II. L. 178.

Jock, when ye hae naething else to do, ye
may be aye sticking in a tree; it will be growing, Jock, when ye're sleeping.
> *p.* 　SCOTT—*The Heart of Midlothian.*
> Ch. VIII.

"Ay," quoth my uncle Gloucester,
"Small herbs have grace, great weeds do grow
apace:"
And since, methinks, I would not grow so fast,
Because sweet flowers are slow and weeds
make haste.
> *q.* 　*Richard III.* Act II. Sc. 4. L. 12.

Gardener, for telling me these news of woe,
Pray God the plants thou graft'st may never
grow.
> *r.* 　*Richard II.* Act III. Sc. 4. L. 100.

O, my lord,
You said that idle weeds are fast in growth:
The prince my brother hath outgrown me far.
> *s.* 　*Richard III.* Act III. Sc. 1. L. 102.

Then bless thy secret growth, nor catch
At noise, but thrive unseen and dumb;
Keep clean, be as fruit, earn life, and watch
Till the white-wing'd reapers come.
> *t.* 　HENRY VAUGHAN—*The Seed Growing
> Secretly.*

GUESTS.

For whom he means to make an often guest,
One dish shall serve; and welcome make the
rest.
> *u.* 　JOSEPH HALL—*Come Dine with Me.*

For I, who holds sage Homer's rule the best,
Welcome the coming, speed the going guest.
> *v.* 　POPE—*Satire II.* Bk. II. L. 159.
> See also HOMER—*Odyssey.* Bk. XV.
> L. 83. Pope's trans.

Be bright and jovial among your guests to-
night.
> *w.* 　*Macbeth.* Act III. Sc. 2. L. 28.

Here's our chief guest.
If he had been forgotten,
It had been as a gap in our great feast.
    a.   *Macbeth.* Act III. Sc. 1. L. 11.

Methinks a father
Is at the nuptial of his son a guest
That best becomes the table.
    b.   *Winter's Tale.* Act IV. Sc. 4. L. 405.

          See, your guests approach :
Address yourself to entertain them sprightly,
And let's be red with mirth.
    c.   *Winter's Tale.* Act IV. Sc. 4. L. 52.

          Unbidden guests
Are often welcomest when they are gone.
    d.   *Henry VI.* Pt. I. Act II. Sc. 2. L. 55.

You must come home with me and be my
    guest ;
You will give joy to me, and I will do
All that is in my power to honour you.
    e.   SHELLEY—*Hymn to Mercury.* St. 5.

GUILT.

    What we call real estate—the solid ground
to build a house on—is the broad foundation
on which nearly all the guilt of this world
rests.
    f.   NATH. HAWTHORNE—*The House of the*
        Seven Gables. The Flight of Two Owls.

How guilt once harbour'd in the conscious
    breast,
Intimidates the brave, degrades the great.
    g.   SAM'L JOHNSON—*Irene.* Act IV. Sc. 8.

Guilt's a terrible thing.
    h.   BEN JONSON—*Bartholomew Fair.*
                    Act IV. Sc. 1.

These false pretexts and varnished colours
    failing,
Rare in thy guilt how foul must thou appear.
    i.   MILTON—*Samson Agonistes.* L. 901.

How glowing guilt exalts the keen delight !
    j.   POPE—*Eloisa to Abelard.* L. 230.

          Haste, holy Friar,
Haste, ere the sinner shall expire !
Of all his guilt let him be shriven,
And smooth his path from earth to heaven !
    k.   SCOTT—*Lay of the Last Minstrel.*
                   Canto 5. St. 22.

And then it started like a guilty thing
Upon a fearful summons.
    l.   *Hamlet.* Act I. Sc. 1. L. 148.

          O, she is fallen
Into a pit of ink, that the wide sea
Hath drops too few to wash her clean again.
    m.   *Much Ado About Nothing.* Act IV.
                    Sc. 1. L. 141.

Let guilty men remember, their black deeds
Do lean on crutches made of slender reeds.
    n.   JOHN WEBSTER—*The White Devil ; or,*
        Vittoria Corombona. Act V. Sc. 6.

A land of levity is a land of guilt.
    o.   YOUNG—*Night Thoughts.* Night VII.
                        Preface.

H.

HABIT.

    A civil habit
Oft covers a good man.
    p.   BEAUMONT AND FLETCHER—*Beggar's*
        Bush. Act II. Sc. 3. L. 210.

Habit with him was all the test of truth ;
"It must be right : I've done it from my
    youth."
    q.   CRABBE—*The Borough.* Letter III.

A man used to vicissitudes is not easily de-
    jected.
    r.   SAM'L JOHNSON—*Rasselas.* Ch. XII.

Small habits, well pursued betimes,
May reach the dignity of crimes.
    s.   HANNAH MORE—*Florio.* Pt. I.

Ill habits gather by unseen degrees,
As brooks make rivers, rivers run to seas.
    t.   OVID—*Metamorphoses.* Bk. XV.
              L. 155. Dryden's trans.

How use doth breed a habit in a man !
This shadowy desert, unfrequented woods,
I better brook than flourishing peopled towns.
    u.   *Two Gentlemen of Verona.* Act V.
                     Sc. 4. L. 1.

HAIR.

Dear, dead women, with such hair, too—
    what's become of all the gold
Used to hang and brush their bosoms?
    v.   ROBERT BROWNING—*Men and Women.*
        A Toccata of Galuppi's. St. 15.

Those curious locks so aptly twin'd,
Whose every hair a soul doth bind.
    w.   CAREW—*To A. L. Persuasions to Love.*
                        L. 37.

An harmless flaming meteor shone for hair,
And fell adown his shoulders with loose care.
    x.   ABRAHAM COWLEY—*Davideis.* Bk. II.
                        L. 803.

His head,
Not yet by time completely silver'd o'er,
Bespoke him past the bounds of freakish
    youth,
But strong for service still, and unimpair'd.
    a.   Cowper—*The Task.* Bk. II. *The
          Timepiece.* L. 702.

Tresses, that wear
Jewels, but to declare
How much themselves more precious are.
    b.   Richard Crashaw—*Wishes to his
          (supposed) Mistress.*

    When you see fair hair
Be pitiful.
    c.   George Eliot—*The Spanish Gypsy.*
          Bk. IV.

Beware of her fair hair, for she excels
All women in the magic of her locks ;
And when she winds them round a young
    man's neck,
She will not ever set him free again.
    d.   Goethe—*Scenes from Faust.* Sc. *The
          Hartz Mountain.* L. 335.
          Shelley's trans.

Loose his beard, and hoary hair
Stream'd, like a meteor, to the troubled air.
    e.   Gray—*The Bard.* I. 2. L. 5.

It was brown with a golden gloss, Janette,
It was finer than silk of the floss, my pet ;
'Twas a beautiful mist falling down to your
    wrist,
'Twas a thing to be braided, and jewelled, and
    kissed—
'Twas the loveliest hair in the world, my pet.
    f.   Chas. G. Halpine (Miles O'Reilly)
          —*Janette's Hair.*

And yonder sits a maiden,
    The fairest of the fair,
With gold in her garment glittering,
    And she combs her golden hair.
    g.   Heine—*The Lorelei.* St. 3.

I pray thee let me and my fellow have
A hair of the dog that bit us last night.
    h.   John Heywood—*Proverbs.* Pt. I.
          Ch. XI. L. 424.

The little wind that hardly shook
The silver of the sleeping brook
Blew the gold hair about her eyes,—
    A mystery of mysteries.
So he must often pause, and stoop,
And all the wanton ringlets loop
Behind her dainty ear—emprise
    Of slow event and many sighs.
    i.   W. D. Howells—*Through the Meadow.*

Her cap of velvet could not hold
The tresses of her hair of gold,
That flowed and floated like the stream,
And fell in masses down her neck.
    j.   Longfellow—*Christus. The Golden
          Legend.* Pt. VI. L. 375.

Though time has touched it in his flight,
And changed the auburn hair to white.
    k.   Longfellow—*Christus. The Golden
          Legend.* Pt. IV. L. 388.

Fair tresses man's imperial race insnare,
And beauty draws us with a single hair.
    l.   Pope—*Rape of the Lock.* Canto II.
          L. 27.

Then cease, bright nymph ! to mourn thy
    ravish'd hair
Which adds new glory to the shining sphere ;
Not all the tresses that fair head can boast
Shall draw such envy as the lock you lost,
For after all the murders of your eye,
When, after millions slain, yourself shall die ;
When those fair suns shall set, as set they
    must,
And all those tresses shall be laid in dust,
This Lock the Muse shall consecrate to fame,
And 'midst the stars inscribe Belinda's name.
    m.   Pope—*Rape of the Lock.* Canto V.
          Last lines.

Golden hair, like sunlight streaming
On the marble of her shoulder.
    n.   J. G. Saxe—*The Lover's Vision.* St. 3.

Alas, poor chin ! many a wart is richer.
    o.   *Troilus and Cressida.* Act I. Sc. 2.
          L. 154.

    And her sunny locks
Hang on her temples like a golden fleece.
    p.   *Merchant of Venice.* Act I. Sc. 1.
          L. 169.

Bind up those tresses. O, what love I note.
In the fair multitude of those her hairs !
Where but by chance a silver drop hath
    fallen,
Even to that drop ten thousand wiry friends
Do glue themselves in sociable grief,
Like true, inseparable, faithful loves,
Sticking together in calamity.
    q.   *King John.* Act III. Sc. 4. L. 61.

Comb down his hair; look, look ! it stands
    upright.
    r.   *Henry VI.* Pt. II. Act III. Sc. 3.
          L. 15.

Her hair is auburn, mine is perfect yellow :
If that be all the difference in his love,
I'll get me such a colour'd periwig.
    s.   *Two Gentlemen of Verona.* Act IV.
          Sc. 4. L. 194.

His hair is of a good colour.
An excellent colour ; your chestnut was ever
    the only colour.
    t.   *As You Like It.* Act III. Sc. 4. L. 11.

How ill white hairs become a fool and jester !
    u.   *Henry IV.* Pt. II. Act V. Sc. 5.
          L. 52.

Thy fair hair my heart enchained.
    a.   Sir Philip Sidney—*Neapolitan*
                            Villanell.

Her long loose yellow locks lyke golden wyre,
Sprinckled with perle, and perling flowres
    atweene,
Doe lyke a golden mantle her attyre.
    b.   Spenser—*Epithalamion.* St. 9.

Ah, thy beautiful hair! so was it once braided
    for me, for me;
Now for death is it crowned, only for death,
    lover and lord of thee.
    c.   Swinburne—*Choriambics.* St. 5.

The Father of Heaven.
    Spin, daughter Mary, spin,
    Twirl your wheel with silver din;
    Spin, daughter Mary, spin,
    Spin a tress for Viola.
    d.   Francis Thompson—*The Making of*
                            Viola. St. 1.

Come let me pluck that silver hair
    Which 'mid thy clustering curls I see;
The withering type of time or care
    Has nothing, sure, to do with thee.
    e.   Alaric Alex Watts—*The Grey Hair.*

Her hair is bound with myrtle leaves,
    (Green leaves upon her golden hair!)
Green grasses through the yellow sheaves
    Of Autumn corn are not more fair.
    f.   Oscar Wilde—*La Bella Donna della*
                            mia Mente.

HAND.

Even to the delicacy of their hand
    There was resemblance such as true blood
    wears.
    g.   Byron—*Don Juan.* Canto IV. St. 45.

For through the South the custom still com-
    mands
The gentleman to kiss the lady's hands.
    h.   Byron—*Don Juan.* Canto V. St. 105.

                'Twas a hand
White, delicate, dimpled, warm, languid, and
    bland.
The hand of a woman is often, in youth,
Somewhat rough, somewhat red, somewhat
    graceless, in truth;
Does its beauty refine, as its pulses grow calm,
Or as sorrow has crossed the life line in the
    palm?
    i.   Owen Meredith (Lord Lytton)—
              Lucile. Pt. I. Canto III. St. 18.

His red right hand.
    j.   Milton—*Paradise Lost.* Bk. II.
                            L. 174.

All the perfumes of Arabia will not sweeten
this little hand.
    k.   *Macbeth.* Act V. Sc. 1. L. 57.

                O, that her hand,
In whose comparison all whites are ink,
Writing their own reproach, to whose soft
    seizure
The cygnet's down is harsh and spirit of sense
Hard as the palm of ploughman.
    l.   *Troilus and Cressida.* Act I. Sc. 1.
                            L. 55.

                They may seize
On the white wonder of dear Juliet's hand.
    m.   *Romeo and Juliet.* Act III. Sc. 3.
                            L. 35.

Without the bed her other fair hand was,
    On the green coverlet; whose perfect white
Show'd like an April daisy on the grass,
    With pearly sweat, resembling dew of night.
    n.   *Lucrece.* L. 393.

HAPPINESS.

'Twas a jolly old pedagogue, long ago,
    Tall and slender, and sallow and dry;
His form was bent, and his gait was slow,
His long thin hair was white as snow,
    But a wonderful twinkle shone in his eye.
And he sang every night as he went to bed,
    "Let us be happy down here below;
The living should live, though the dead be
    dead,"
    Said the jolly old pedagogue long ago.
    o.   George Arnold—*The Jolly Old*
                            Pedagogue.

Real happiness is cheap enough, yet how
dearly we pay for its counterfeit.
    p.   Hosea Ballou—*MS. Sermons.*

To have been happy, madame, adds to calamity.
    q.   Beaumont and Fletcher—*The Fair*
              Maid of the Inn. Act I. Sc. 1.
                            L. 250.

Priestly was the first (unless it was Beccaria)
who taught my lips to pronounce this sacred
truth—that the greatest happiness of the greatest number is the foundation of morals and
legislation.
    r.   Bentham—Vol. X. P. 142. See also
             Beccaria's introduction to *Essay on*
             Crimes and Punishments.

       * * * all who joy would win
Must share it,—Happiness was born a twin.
    s.   Byron—*Don Juan.* Canto II. St. 172.

Oh, Mirth and Innocence! Oh, Milk and
    Water!
Ye happy mixtures of more happy days!
    t.   Byron—*Beppo.* St. 80.

O, why has happiness so short a day.
    u.   Barry Cornwall—*A Sicilian Story.*
                        Dedicatory Sonnet.

If solid happiness we prize,
Within our breast this jewel lies,
   And they are fools who roam;
The world has nothing to bestow,
From our own selves our bliss must flow,
   And that dear hut,—our home.
  a.   NATHANIEL COTTON—*The Fireside.*

Domestic Happiness, thou only bliss
Of Paradise that hast survived the Fall!
  b.   COWPER—*Task.* Bk. III. L. 41.

Thus happiness depends, as Nature shows,
Less on exterior things than most suppose.
  c.   COWPER—*Table Talk.* L. 246.

Who is the happiest of men? He who values
   the merits of others,
And in their pleasure takes joy, even as
   though 'twere his own.
  d.   GOETHE—*Distichs.*

Still to ourselves in every place consign'd,
Our own felicity we make or find.
  e.   GOLDSMITH—*The Traveller.* L. 431.

Now happiness consists in activity: such is
the constitution of our nature: it is a running
stream, and not a stagnant pool.
  f.   GOOD—*The Book of Nature.* Series III.
                     Lecture VII.

The loss of wealth is loss of dirt,
As sages in all times assert;
The happy man's without a shirt.
  g.   JOHN HEYWOOD—*Be Merry Friends.*

And there is ev'n a happiness
That makes the heart afraid.
  h.   HOOD—*Ode to Melancholy.*

A sound Mind in a sound Body, is a short
but full description of a happy State in this
World.
  i.   LOCKE—*Thoughts Concerning Education.*

The rays of happiness, like those of light,
are colorless when unbroken.
  j.   LONGFELLOW—*Kavanagh.* Ch. XIII.

   To be strong
Is to be happy!
  k.   LONGFELLOW—*Christus. The Golden
                Legend.* Pt. II. L. 731.

Now the heart is so full that a drop overfills it,
We are happy now because God wills it.
  l.   LOWELL—*The Vision of Sir Launfal.*
                 Prelude to Pt. I. L. 61.

And feel that I am happier than I know.
  m.   MILTON—*Paradise Lost.* Bk. VIII.
                           L. 282.

No eye to watch and no tongue to wound us,
All earth forgot, and all heaven around us.
  n.   MOORE—*Come o'er the Sea.*

Thus we never live, but we hope to live; and
always disposing ourselves to be happy, it is
inevitable that we never become so.
  o.   BLAISE PASCAL—*Thoughts.* Ch. V.
                           Sec. I.

   Said Scopas of Thessaly, "But we rich men
count our felicity and happiness to lie in
these superfluities, and not in those necessary
things."
  p.   PLUTARCH—*Morals.* Vol. II. *Of the
                         Love of Wealth.*

Fix'd to no spot is Happiness sincere;
'Tis nowhere to be found, or ev'rywhere;
'Tis never to be bought, but always free.
  q.   POPE—*Essay on Man.* Ep. IV. L. 15.

Heaven to mankind impartial we confess,
If all are equal in their happiness;
But mutual wants this happiness increase,
All nature's difference keeps all nature's peace.
  r.   POPE—*Essay on Man.* Ep. IV. L. 53.

Oh happiness! our being's end and aim!
Good, Pleasure, Ease, Content! whate'er thy
   name;
That something still which prompts th' eternal
   sigh,
For which we bear to live, or dare to die.
  s.   POPE—*Essay on Man.* Ep. IV. L. 1.

To happy convents, bosom'd deep in vines,
Where slumber abbots purple as their wines.
  t.   POPE—*The Dunciad.* Bk. IV. L. 301.

Ye gods, annihilate but space and time,
And make two lovers happy.
  u.   POPE—*Martinus Scriblerus on the Art of
                   Sinking in Poetry.* Ch. XI.

   Happiness lies in the consciousness we have
of it, and by no means in the way the future
keeps its promises.
  v.   GEORGES SAND—*Handsome Lawrence.*
                           Ch. III.

But earthlier happy is the rose distill'd,
Than that which withering on the virgin
   thorn
Grows, lives and dies in single blessedness.
  w.   *Midsummer-Night's Dream.* Act I.
                         Sc. 1. L. 76.

But, O, how bitter a thing it is to look into
happiness through another man's eyes!
  x.   *As You Like It.* Act V. Sc. 2. L. 47.

Ye seek for happiness—alas, the day!
Ye find it not in luxury nor in gold,
Nor in the fame, nor in the envied sway
For which, O willing slaves to Custom old,
Severe taskmistress! ye your hearts have sold.
  y.   SHELLEY—*Revolt of Islam.* Canto XI.
                           St. 17.

Magnificent spectacle of human happiness.
>a.   SYDNEY SMITH—*America.*   Edinburgh
Review, July, 1824.

Mankind are always happier for having
been happy; so that if you make them happy
now, you make them happy twenty years
hence by the memory of it.
>b.   SYDNEY SMITH—*Lecture on Benevolent
Affections.*

Be happy, but be happy through piety.
>c.   MADAME DE STAËL—*Corinne.* Bk. XX.
Ch. III.

For it stirs the blood in an old man's heart;
And makes his pulses fly,
To catch the thrill of a happy voice,
And the light of a pleasant eye.
>d.   N. P. WILLIS—*Saturday Afternoon.*
St. 1.

We're charm'd with distant views of happi-
ness,
But near approaches make the prospect less.
>e.   THOS. YALDEN—*Against Enjoyment.*
L. 23.

True happiness ne'er entered at an eye;
True happiness resides in things unseen.
>f.   YOUNG—*Night Thoughts.* Night VIII.
L. 1,021.

HARVEST.

For now, the corn house filled, the harvest
home,
Th' invited neighbors to the husking come;
A frolic scene, where work and mirth and
play
Unite their charms to cheer the hours away.
>g.   JOEL BARLOW—*The Hasty Pudding.*

To glean the broken ears after the man
That the main harvest reaps.
>h.   *As You Like It.* . Act III. Sc. 5. L. 102.

And thus of all my harvest-hope I have
Nought reaped but a weedye crop of care.
>i.   SPENSER—*The Shepherd's Calender.*
December. L. 121.

Think, oh, grateful think!
How good the God of Harvest is to you;
Who pours abundance o'er your flowing fields,
While those unhappy partners of your kind
Wide-hover round you, like the fowls of
heaven,
And ask their humble dole.
>j.   THOMSON—*Autumn.* L. 169.

Fancy with prophetic glance
Sees the teeming months advance;
The field, the forest, green and gay;
The dappled slope, the tedded hay;
Sees the reddening orchard blow,
The Harvest wave, the vintage flow.
>k.   WARTON—*Ode. The First of April.*
L. 97.

HASTE.

Then horn for horn they stretch and strive;
Deil tak the hindmost, on they drive.
>l.   BURNS—*To a Haggis.*

Haste is of the Devil.
>m.   *The Koran.*

Stay awhile that we may make an end the
sooner.
>n.   *Attributed to* SIR AMICE PAWLET *by*
BACON. *Apothegms.* No. 76.

On wings of winds came flying all abroad.
>o.   POPE—*Prologue to the Satires.* L. 208.

Celerity is never more admired
Than by the negligent.
>p.   *Antony and Cleopatra.* Act III. Sc. 7.
L. 25.

He tires betimes that spurs too fast betimes;
With eager feeding food doth choke the
feeder.
>q.   *Richard II.* Act II. Sc. 1. L. 36.

It is too rash, too unadvis'd, too sudden;
Too like the lightning, which doth cease to be
Ere one can say "It lightens."
>r.   *Romeo and Juliet.* Act II. Sc. 2.
L. 118.

Nay, but make haste; the better foot before.
>s.   *King John.* Act IV. Sc. 2. L. 170.

Stand not upon the order of your going,
But go at once.
>t.   *Macbeth.* Act III. Sc. 4. L. 119.

Swifter than arrow from the Tartar's bow.
>u.   *Midsummer-Night's Dream.* Act III.
Sc. 2. L. 101.

Wisely, and slow; they stumble that run fast.
>v.   *Romeo and Juliet.* Act II. Sc. 3.
L. 94.

HATRED.

Hatred is self-punishment.
>w.   HOSEA BALLOU—*MS. Sermons.*

Now hatred is by far the longest pleasure;
Men love in haste, but they detest at leisure.
>x.   BYRON—*Don Juan.* Canto XIII. St. 6.

These two hated with a hate
Found only on the stage.
>y.   BYRON—*Don Juan.* Canto IV. St. 93.

Heaven has no rage like love to hatred turned.
>z.   CONGREVE—*The Mourning Bride.*
Act III. Sc. 2.

There are glances of hatred that stab and
raise no cry of murder.
>aa.   GEORGE ELIOT—*Felix Holt.*
Introduction.

Then let him know that hatred without end
Or intermission is between us two.
  a.   HOMER—*Iliad*. Bk. XV. L. 270.
                              Bryant's trans.

"He was a very good *hater*."
  b.   SAM'L JOHNSON—*Mrs. Piozzi's
                      Anecdotes of Johnson*. P. 38.

I like a good hater.
  c.   SAM'L JOHNSON—*Mrs. Piozzi's
                      Anecdotes of Johnson*. P. 89.

But I do hate him as I hate the devil.
  d.   BEN JONSON—*Every Man Out of his
                    Humour*. Act I. Sc. 1.

    For never can true reconcilement grow,
Where wounds of deadly hate have pierced so
    deep.
  e.   MILTON—*Paradise Lost*. Bk. IV.
                                      L. 98.

How like a fawning publican he looks!
I hate him for he is a Christian,
But more for that in low simplicity
He lends out money gratis and brings down
The rate of usance here with us in Venice.
  f.   *Merchant of Venice*. Act I. Sc. 3.
                                      L. 42.

In time we hate that which we often fear.
  g.   *Antony and Cleopatra*. Act I. Sc. 3.
                                      L. 12.

Though I do hate him as I do hell-pains.
  h.   *Othello*. Act I. Sc. 1. L. 155.

              Yet 'tis greater skill
In a true hate, to pray they have their will.
  i.   *Cymbeline*. Act II. Sc. 5. L. 33.

HATTERS (*See* OCCUPATIONS).

HEALTH.

    Health and cheerfulness mutually beget
each other.
  j.   ADDISON—*The Spectator*. No. 387.

When health, affrighted, spreads her rosy
      wing,
And flies with every changing gale of spring.
  k.   BYRON—*Childish Recollections*. L. 3.

Nor love, nor honour, wealth nor pow'r,
Can give the heart a cheerful hour
When health is lost. Be timely wise;
With health all taste of pleasure flies.
  l.   GAY—*Fables*. Pt. I. Fable 31.

Health that snuffs the morning air.
  m.   JAMES GRAINGER—*Solitude*. An Ode.
                                      L. 35.

    There are three wicks you know to the
lamp of a man's life: brain, blood, and breath.
Press the brain a little, its light goes out,
followed by both the others. Stop the heart
a minute, and out go all three of the wicks.
Choke the air out of the lungs, and presently
the fluid ceases to supply the other centres of
flame, and all is soon stagnation, cold, and
darkness.
  n.   O. W. HOLMES—*Professor at the
                          Breakfast-Table*. XI.

Preserving the health by too strict a regimen
is a wearisome malady.
  o.   LA ROCHEFOUCAULD—*Maxims*. No. 285.

Health consists with Temperance alone.
  p.   POPE—*Essay on Man*. Ep. IV. L. 81.

              May be he is not well:
Infirmity doth still neglect all office
Whereto our health is bound.
  q.   *King Lear*. Act II. Sc. 4. L. 107.

Now, good digestion wait on appetite,
And health on both!
  r.   *Macbeth*. Act III. Sc. 4. L. 38.

Ah! what avail the largest gifts of Heaven,
   When drooping health and spirits go amiss?
How tasteless then whatever can be given!
   Health is the vital principle of bliss,
And exercise of health.
  s.   THOMSON—*Castle of Indolence*.
                              Canto II. St. 55.

    Health is the second blessing that we
mortals are capable of: a blessing that money
cannot buy.
  t.   IZAAK WALTON—*The Complete Angler*.
                              Pt. I. Ch. XXI.

Gold that buys health can never be ill spent,
Nor hours laid out in harmless merriment.
  u.   JOHN WEBSTER—*Westward Ho*.
                          Act V. Sc. 3. L. 345.

HEARING.

He ne'er presumed to make an error clearer;—
In short, there never was a better hearer.
  v.   BYRON—*Don Juan*. Canto XIV.
                                      St. 37.

Within a bony labyrinthean cave,
Reached by the pulse of the aërial wave,
This sibyl, sweet, and Mystic Sense is found,
Muse, that presides o'er all the Powers of
      Sound.
  w.   ABRAHAM COLES—*Man, the Microcosm;
                          and the Cosmos*. P. 51.

None so deaf as those that will not hear.
  x.   MATHEW HENRY—*Commentaries*.
                              Psalm LVIII.

Hear ye not the hum
Of mighty workings?
   a.   Keats—*Addressed to Haydon.*
                     Sonnet X.

Where did you get that pearly ear?
God spoke and it came out to hear.
   b.   George Macdonald—*Song. At The
                  Back of the North Wind.
                     Ch. XXXIII.*

                 Heard so oft
In worst extremes, and on the perilous edge
Of battle.
   c.   Milton—*Paradise Lost.* Bk. I.
                     L. 275.

                 I was all ear,
And took in strains that might create a soul
Under the ribs of death.
   d.   Milton—*Comus.* L. 560.

Where more is meant than meets the ear.
   e.   Milton—*Il Penseroso.* L. 120.

Friends, Romans, countrymen, lend me your
     ears.
   f.   *Julius Cæsar.* Act III. Sc. 2. L. 78.

Hear me for my cause, and be silent, that you
     may hear.
   g.   *Julius Cæsar.* Act III. Sc. 2. L. 13.

Such an exploit have I in hand, Ligarius,
Had you a healthful ear to hear of it.
   h.   *Julius Cæsar.* Act II. Sc. 1. L. 318.

   They never would hear,
   But turn the deaf ear,
As a matter they had no concern in.
   i.   Swift—*Dingley and Brent.*

Strike, but hear me.
   j.   Themistocles—*Rollin's Ancient
               History.* Bk. VI. Ch. II.
                     Sect. VIII.

HEART.

A man's first care should be to avoid the
     reproaches of his own heart.
   k.   Addison—*Sir Roger on the Bench.*

I have a heart with room for every joy.
   l.   Bailey—*Festus.* Sc. *A Mountain.*

   The heart of man is the place the devil
dwells in; I feel sometimes a hell dwells
within myself.
   m.   Sir Thomas Browne—*Religio Medici.*
                     Pt. I. Sec. LI.

My heart's in the Highlands, my heart is not
     here;
My heart's in the Highlands a-chasing the
     deer.
   n.   Burns—*My Heart's in the Highlands.*

His heart was one of those which most enam-
     our us,
Wax to receive, and marble to retain.
   o.   Byron—*Beppo.* St. 34.

Maid of Athens, ere we part,
Give, oh, give me back my heart!
   p.   Byron—*Maid of Athens.* St. 1.

Make room, my heart! that pour'st thyself
     abroad
Deep, central, awful mystery of God!
Lord of my bosom! wonder of the breast!
"Welcome the coming, speed the parting
     guest."
   q.   Abraham Coles—*Man, the Microcosm.*
                     P. 67.

   Some hearts are hidden, some have not a
heart.
   r.   Crabbe—*The Borough.* Letter XVII.

The heart asks pleasure first,
And then, excuse from pain;
And then, those little anodynes
That deaden suffering;

And then, to go to sleep;
And then, if it should be
The will of its Inquisitor,
The liberty to die.
   s.   Emily Dickinson—*Poems.*
                IX. (Ed. 1891.)

There is an evening twilight of the heart,
When its wild passion-waves are lulled to rest.
   t.   Fitz-Greene Halleck—*Twilight.*

For his heart was in his work, and the heart
Giveth grace unto every Art.
   u.   Longfellow—*The Building of the
                   Ship.* L. 7.

Something the heart must have to cherish,
   Must love, and joy, and sorrow learn;
Something with passion clasp, or perish,
   And in itself to ashes burn.
   v.   Longfellow—*Hyperion.* Bk. II.
                   Introduction.

Better to have the poet's heart than brain,
Feeling than song.
   w.   George MacDonald—*Within and
             Without.* Pt. III. Sc. 9. L. 30.

The heart is like an instrument whose strings
Steal nobler music from Life's many frets:
The golden threads are spun thro' Suffering's
     fire,
Wherewith the marriage-robes for heaven are
     woven:
And all the rarest hues of human life
Take radiance, and are rainbow'd out in tears.
   x.   Gerald Massey—*Wedded Love.*

But the beating of my own heart
Was all the sound I heard.
   y.   Richard Monckton Milnes (Lord
            Houghton)—*The Brookside.*

And when once the young heart of a maiden
  is stolen,
The maiden herself will steal after it soon.
  a.   MOORE—*Ill Omens.*

Oh, the heart is a free and a fetterless thing,—
A wave of the ocean, a bird on the wing.
  b.   JULIA PARDOE—*The Captive Greek Girl.*

The incense of the heart may rise.
  c.   PIERPONT—*Every Place a Temple.*

The heart is a small thing, but desireth
great matters. It is not sufficient for a kite's
dinner, yet the whole world is not sufficient
for it.
  d.   QUARLES—*Emblems.*   Bk. I.
                        Hugo de Anima.

This house is to be let for life or years,
Her rent is sorrow, and her income tears;
Cupid, 't has long stood void; her bills make
  known,
She must be dearly let, or let alone.
  e.   QUARLES—*Emblems.*   Bk. II.
                        Epigram X.

                        Even at this sight
My heart is turn'd to stone: and while 'tis
  mine,
It shall be stony.
  f.   *Henry VI.* Pt. II. Act V. Sc. 2.
                        L. 49.

The very firstlings of my heart shall be
The firstlings of my hand.
  g.   *Macbeth.* Act IV. Sc. I. L. 147.

Worse than a bloody hand is a hard heart.
  h.   SHELLEY—*The Cenci.* Act V. Sc. 2.

Heaven's Sovereign saves all beings but himself,
That hideous sight, a naked human heart.
  i.   YOUNG—*Night Thoughts.* Night III.
                        L. 226.

Who, for the poor renown of being smart,
Would leave a sting within a brother's heart?
  j.   YOUNG—*Love of Fame.* Satire II.
                        L. 113.

HEAVEN.

Love lent me wings; my path was like a stair;
A lamp unto my feet, that sun was given;
And death was safety and great joy to find;
But dying now, I shall not climb to Heaven.
  k.   MICHAEL ANGELO—*Sonnet LXIII,*
                        After Sunset.

In hope to merit Heaven by making earth a
  Hell.
  l.   BYRON—*Childe Harold.* Canto I.
                        St. 20.

Heaven means to be one with God.
  m.   CONFUCIUS, *quoted by* CANON FARRAR.
          *Sermons. Eternal Hopes. What
                    Heaven Is.* Last Line.

And so upon this wise I prayed,—
  Great Spirit, give to me
A heaven not so large as yours
  But large enough for me.
  n.   EMILY DICKINSON—*A Prayer.*

Nor can his blessed soul look down from
  heaven,
Or break the eternal sabbath of his rest.
  o.   DRYDEN—*The Spanish Friar.* Act V.
                        Sc. 2.

Since heaven's eternal year is thine.
  p.   DRYDEN—*Elegy on Mrs. Killegrew.*
                        L. 15.

'Twas whispered in Heaven, 'twas muttered
  in hell
And echo caught faintly the sound as it fell.
On the confines of earth 'twas permitted to
  rest,
And the depths of the ocean its presence confessed.
  q.   CATHERINE M. FANSHAWE—*Enigma.*
                        (*The letter H.*)

While resignation gently slopes the way;
And, all his prospects brightening to the last,
His heaven commences ere the world be past.
  r.   GOLDSMITH—*The Deserted Village.*
                        L. 110.

They had finished her own crown in glory,
and she couldn't stay away from the coronation.
  s.   GRAY—*Enigmas of Life.*

Eye hath not seen it, my gentle boy!
Ear hath not heard its deep songs of joy;
Dreams cannot picture a world so fair—
Sorrow and death may not enter there;
Time doth not breathe on its fadeless bloom,
For beyond the clouds, and beyond the tomb,
  It is there, it is there, my child!
  t.   MRS. HEMANS—*The Better Land.*

All this, and Heaven too!
  u.   PHILIP HENRY—*Mathew Henry's Life
                    of Philip Henry.* P. 70.

Just are the ways of heaven; from Heaven
  proceed
The woes of man; Heaven doom'd the Greeks
  to bleed.
  v.   HOMER—*Odyssey.* Bk. VIII. L. 128.
                        Pope's trans.

Heav'n but the Vision of fulfill'd Desire.
And Hell the Shadow from a Soul on fire.
  w.   OMAR KHAYYÁM—*Rubáiyat.* St. 67.

There is another, and a better world.
a.   August Von Kotzebue—*The Stranger.*
              Act I. Sc. I. L. 193.

The heaven of poetry and romance still lies
around us and within us.
b.   Longfellow—*Drift-Wood. Twice-
                          Told Tales.*

We see but dimly through the mists and
        vapors ;
  Amid these earthly damps
What seem to us but sad, funereal tapers
  May be heaven's distant lamps.
c.   Longfellow—*Resignation.* St. 4.

A heaven on earth.
d.   Milton—*Paradise Lost.* Bk. IV.
                                  L. 208.

              Heaven open'd wide
Her ever-during gates, harmonious sound
On golden hinges moving.
e.   Milton—*Paradise Lost.* Bk. VII.
                                  L. 205.

It were a journey like the path to heaven,
To help you find them.
f.   Milton—*Comus.* L. 302.

              The hasty multitude
Admiring enter'd, and the work some praise,
And some the architect : his hand was known
In heaven by many a tower'd structure high,
Where scepter'd angels held their residence,
And sat as princes.
g.   Milton—*Paradise Lost.* Bk. I.
                                  L. 730.

              The starry cope
Of heaven.
h.   Milton—*Paradise Lost.* Bk. IV.
                                  L. 992.

        Though in heav'n the trees
Of life ambrosial fruitage bear, and vines
Yield nectar.
i.   Milton—*Paradise Lost.* Bk. V.
                                  L. 426.

There is a world above,
  Where parting is unknown ;
A whole eternity of love,
  Form'd for the good alone ;
And faith beholds the dying here
  Translated to that happier sphere.
j.   Montgomery—*Friends.*

A Persian's Heaven is eas'ly made,
'Tis but black eyes and lemonade.
k.   Moore—*Intercepted Letters.* Letter VI.

      A sea before
The Throne is spread ;—its pure still glass
Pictures all earth-scenes as they pass.
  We, on its shore,
Share, in the bosom of our rest,
God's knowledge, and are blest.
l.   Cardinal Newman—*A Voice from Afar.*

It was the rampart of God's house
  That she was standing on ;
By God built over the sheer depth,
  The which is Space begun ;
So high, that looking downward thence,
  She scarce could see the sun.
m.   Dante Gabriel Rossetti—*The Blessed
                                    Damozel.*

All places that the eye of heaven visits,
Are to a wise man ports and happy havens.
n.   *Richard II.* Act I. Sc. 3. L. 275.

        For the selfsame heaven
That frowns on me looks sadly upon him.
o.   *Richard III.* Act V. Sc. 3. L. 285.

Heaven's face doth glow.
p.   *Hamlet.* Act III. Sc. 4. L. 48.

        There's husbandry in heaven ;
Their candles are all out.
q.   *Macbeth.* Act II. Sc. 1. L. 5.

Well, God's above all ; and there be souls
must be saved, and there be souls must not
be saved.
r.   *Othello.* Act II. Sc. 3. L. 105.

Were it not good your grace could fly to
        heaven ?
The treasury of everlasting joy.
s.   *Henry VI.* Pt. II. Act II. Sc. 1. L. 17.

For all we know
Of what the blessed do above
Is, that they sing, and that they love.
t.   Edmund Waller—*Song. While I
                    Listen to Thy Voice.* St. 2.

I have been there, and still would go ;
'Tis like a little heaven below.
u.   Isaac Watts—*Divine Songs.* Song
                                  XXVIII.

HELL.

Hell is more bearable than nothingness.
v.   Bailey—*Festus.* Sc. *Heaven.*

Hell is the wrath of God—His hate of sin.
w.   Bailey—*Festus.* Sc. *Hell.* L. 194.

There is in hell a place stone-built through-
        out,
Called Malebolge, of an iron hue,
Like to the wall that circles it about.
x.   Dante—*Inferno.* Canto XVIII. L. 1.

        We spirits have just such natures
We had for all the world, when human crea-
        tures ;
And, therefore, I, that was an actress here,
Play all my tricks in hell, a goblin there.
y.   Dryden—*Tyrannick Love.* Epilogue.

Hell is full of good meanings and wishings.
z.   Herbert—*Jacula Prudentum.*
                                  No. 176

Hell is no other but a soundlesse pit,
Where no one beame of comfort peeps in it.
  a.   HERRICK—*Noble Numbers. Hell.*

And, bid him go to hell, to hell he goes.
  b.   SAM'L JOHNSON—*London.* L. 116.

Hell is paved with good intentions.
  c.   SAM'L JOHNSON—(*Quoted*) *Boswell's*
                  Life of Johnson. 1775.

Look where he goes! but see he comes again
Because I stay! Techelles, let us march
And weary death with bearing souls to hell.
  d.   MARLOWE—*Tamburlane the Great.*
              Act 5. Sc. III. L. 75.

A dungeon horrible, on all sides round,
As one great furnace, flamed; yet from those
    flames
No light, but rather darkness visible
Serv'd only to discover sights of woe,
Regions of sorrow, doleful shades, where peace
And rest can never dwell, hope never comes
That comes to all; but torture without end.
  e.   MILTON—*Paradise Lost.* Bk. 1. L. 61.

All hell broke loose.
  f.   MILTON—*Paradise Lost.* Bk. IV.
                        L. 918.

Hail, horrors, hail,
Infernal world! and thou profoundest hell,
Receive thy new possessor.
  g.   MILTON—*Paradise Lost.* Bk. I. L. 251.

            Hell
Grew darker at their frown.
  h.   MILTON—*Paradise Lost.* Bk. II. L. 719.

            Long is the way
And hard, that out of hell leads up to light.
  i.   MILTON—*Paradise Lost.* Bk. II. L. 432.

            Myself am hell;
And in the lowest deep a lower deep,
Still threat'ning to devour me, opens wide;
To which the hell I suffer seems a heaven.
  j.   MILTON—*Paradise Lost.* Bk. IV. L. 75.

            Nor from hell
One step no more than from himself can fly
By change of place.
  k.   MILTON—*Paradise Lost.* Bk. IV. L. 21.

            On a sudden open fly
With impetuous recoil and jarring sound
Th' infernal doors, and on their hinges grate
Harsh thunder.
  l.   MILTON—*Paradise Lost.* Bk. II.
                        L. 879.

            The gates that now
Stood open wide, belching outrageous flame
Far into Chaos, since the fiend pass'd through.
  m.   MILTON—*Paradise Lost.* Bk. X. L. 232.

To rest, the cushion and soft dean invite,
Who never mentions hell to ears polite.
  n.   POPE—*Moral Essays.* Ep. IV. L. 149.

Do not be troubled by Saint Bernard's saying that hell is full of good intentions and
wills.
  o.   FRANCIS DE SALES—*Spiritual Letters.*
                        Letter XII.

      Black is the badge of hell,
The hue of dungeons and the suit of night.
  p.   *Love's Labour's Lost.* Act IV. Sc. 3.
                        L. 254.

       Hell is empty,
And all the devils are here.
  q.   *Tempest.* Act I. Sc. 2. L. 214.

I think the devil will not have me damned,
lest the oil that's in me should set hell on fire.
  r.   *Merry Wives of Windsor.* Act V.
                      Sc. 5. L. 38.

Self-love and the love of the world constitute hell.
  s.   SWEDENBORG—*Apocalypse Explained.*
                      Par. 1,144.

Nay, then, what flames are these that leap and
    swell
As 'twere to show, where earth's foundations
    crack,
The secrets of the sepulchres of hell
    On Dante's track?
  t.   SWINBURNE—*In Guernsey.* Pt. IV.
                        St. 3.

        In the throat
Of Hell, before the very vestibule
Of opening Orcus, sit Remorse and Grief,
And pale Disease, and sad Old Age and Fear,
And Hunger that persuades to crime, and
    Want:
Forms terrible to see. Suffering and Death
Inhabit here, and Death's own brother Sleep;
And the mind's evil lusts and deadly War,
Lie at the threshold, and the iron beds
Of the Eumenides; and Discord wild
Her viper-locks with bloody fillets bound.
  u.   VIRGIL—*Æneid.* Bk. VI. L. 336.
                  C. P. Cranch's trans.

That's the greatest torture souls feel in hell,
In hell, that they must live, and cannot die.
  v.   JOHN WEBSTER—*Duchess of Malfi.*
                Act IV. Sc. I. L. 84.

HELP.

    The foolish ofttimes teach the wise:
I strain too much this string of life, belike,
Meaning to make such music as shall save.
Mine eyes are dim now that they see the truth,
My strength is waned now that my need is
    most;
Would that I had such help as man must have,
For I shall die, whose life was all men's hope.
  w.   EDWIN ARNOLD—*Light of Asia.*
                Bk. VI. L. 109.

Heaven's help is better than early rising.
a.   CERVANTES—*Don Quixote.* Vol. III.
Pt. II. Ch. XXXIV.

He that wrestles with us strengthens our
nerves, and sharpens our skill. Our antagonist is our helper.
b.   BURKE—*Reflections on the Revolution in
France.*

I would help others out of a fellow-feeling.
c·   BURTON—*Anatomy of Melancholy.
Democritus to the Reader.*

The careful pilot of my proper woe.
d.   BYRON—*Epistle to Augusta.* No. 3.
St. 3.

Turn, gentle Hermit of the Dale,
And guide my lonely way
To where yon taper cheers the vale
With hospitable ray.
e.   GOLDSMITH—*Vicar of Wakefield. The
Hermit.* Ch. VIII.

Light is the task when many share the toil.
f.   HOMER—*Iliad.* Bk. XII. L. 493.
Bryant's trans.

Is not a patron, my lord, one who looks
with unconcern on a man struggling for life
in the water, and when he has reached ground
encumbers him with help?
g.   SAM'L JOHNSON—*Boswell's Life of
Johnson.* 1754.

So *we're* all right, an' I, for one,
Don't think our cause'll lose in vally
By rammin' Scriptur' in our gun,
An' gittin' Natur' for an ally.
h.   LOWELL—*The Biglow Papers.* Second
Series. No. 7. St. 17.

I want to help you to grow as beautiful as
God meant you to be when he thought of you
first.
i.   GEORGE MACDONALD—*The Marquis of
Lossie.* Ch. XXII.

Aid the dawning, tongue and pen :
Aid it, hopes of honest men !
j.   CHARLES MACKAY—*Clear the Way.*

Truths would you teach, or save a sinking
land ?
All fear, none aid you, and few understand.
k.   POPE—*Essay on Man.* Ep. IV. L. 264.

In man's most dark extremity
Oft succour dawns from Heaven.
l.   SCOTT—*Lord of the Isles.* Canto I.
St. 20.

Help me, Cassius, or I sink !
m.   *Julius Cæsar*—Act I. Sc. 2. L. 111.

Now, ye familiar spirits, that are cull'd
Out of the powerful regions under earth,
Help me this once.
n.   *Henry VI.* Pt. I. Act V. Sc. 3.
L. 10.

'Tis not enough to help the feeble up,
But to support him after.
o.   *Timon of Athens.* Act I. Sc. 1. L. 107.

God helps those who help themselves.
p.   ALGERNON SIDNEY—*Discourse
Concerning Government.* Ch. II.
Pt. XXIII.

HERBAGE.

Grass grows at last above all graves.
q.   JULIA C. R. DORR—*Grass-Grown.*

A blade of grass is always a blade of grass,
whether in one country or another.
r.   SAM'L JOHNSON—*Mrs. Piozzi's Anecdotes
of Johnson.* P. 100.

The green grass floweth like a stream
Into the ocean's blue.
s.   LOWELL—*The Sirens.* L. 87.

The gadding vine.
t.   MILTON—*Lycidas.* L. 40.

A barren detested vale, you see it is ;
The trees, though summer, yet forlorn and
lean,
O'ercome with moss and baleful mistletoe.
u.   *Titus Andronicus.* Act II. Sc. 3.
L. 93.

How lush and lusty the grass looks! how
green !
v.   *Tempest.* Act II. Sc. 1. L. 52.

If aught possess thee from me, it is dross,
Usurping ivy, brier, or idle moss ;
Who, all for want of pruning, with intrusion
Infect thy sap and live on thy confusion.
w.   *Comedy of Errors.* Act II. Sc. 2.
L. 179.

Pun-provoking thyme.
x.   SHENSTONE—*The Schoolmistress.* St. 11.

HEROES.

The hero is the world-man, in whose heart
One passion stands for all, the most indulged.
y·   BAILEY—*Festus. Proem.* L. 114.

I want a hero : an uncommon want,
When every year and month sends forth a
new one.
z.   BYRON—*Don Juan.* Canto I. St. 1.

Hero-worship exists, has existed, and will
forever exist, universally among Mankind.
aa.   CARLYLE—*Sartor Resartus. Organic
Filaments.*

If Hero mean *sincere man*, why may not every one of us be a Hero?

   a.   CARLYLE—*Heroes and Hero-Worship*.
                        Lecture IV.

Worship of a hero is transcendent admiration of a Great Man.

   b.   CARLYLE—*Heroes and Hero-Worship*.
                        Lecture I.

He's of stature somewhat low—
Your hero always should be tall, you know.

   c.   CHURCHILL—*The Rosciad*. L. 1,029.

Each man is a hero and an oracle to somebody, and to that person whatever he says has an enhanced value.

   d.   EMERSON—*Letters and Social Aims*.
               Quotation and Originality.

The hero is not fed on sweets,
Daily his own heart he eats;
Chambers of the great are jails,
And head-winds right for royal sails.

   e.   EMERSON—*Essays. Heroism*.
                     Introduction.

But to the hero, when his sword
  Has won the battle for the free,
Thy voice sounds like a prophet's word,
And in its hollow tones are heard
  The thanks of millions yet to be.

   f.   FITZ-GREENE HALLECK—*Marco*
                      Bozzaris.

It hath been an antient custom among them [Hungarians] that none should wear a fether but he who had killed a Turk, to whom onlie yt was lawful to shew the number of his slaine enemys by the number of fethers in his cappe.

   g.   RICHARD HANSARD—*Description of*
         Hungary, Anno 1599. Lansdowne
         MS. 775. Vol. 149. *British*
                   Museum.

The boy stood on the burning deck
  Whence all but he had fled;
The flame that lit the battle's wreck,
  Shone round him o'er the dead.

    *   *   *   *   *   *

The flames roll'd on—he would not go
  Without his Father's word;
That Father, faint in death below,
  His voice no longer heard.

   h.   MRS. HEMANS—*Casabianca*.

Heroes as great have died, and yet shall fall.

   i.   HOMER—*Iliad*. Bk. XV. L. 157.
                   Pope's trans.

Hail, Columbia! happy land!
Hail, ye heroes! heaven-born band!
Who fought and bled in Freedom's cause.

   j.   JOSEPH HOPKINSON—*Hail, Columbia!*

The idol of to-day pushes the hero of yesterday out of our recollection; and will, in turn, be supplanted by his successor of to-morrow.

   k.   WASHINGTON IRVING—*The Sketch Book*.
                Westminster Abbey.

There are heroes in evil as well as in good.

   l.   LA ROCHEFOUCAULD—*Maxims*. No. 194.

Dost thou know what a hero is? Why, a hero is as much as one should say,— a hero.

   m.   LONGFELLOW—*Hyperion*. Bk. I. Ch. 1.

'Tis as easy to be heroes as to sit the idle
  slaves
Of a legendary virtue carved upon our father's
  graves.

   n.   LOWELL—*The Present Crisis*. St. 15.

See the conquering hero comes.

   o.   DR. THOS. MORELL—Words used by
         HANDEL in *Joshua*, and *Judas Macca-*
         bæus (introduced in late versions
              of LEE's *Rival Queens*).

HISTORY.

I have read somewhere or other, in Dionysius of Halicarnassus, I think, that history is philosophy teaching by examples.

   p.   LORD BOLINGBROKE (Henry St. John)
         —*On the Study and Use of History*.
         Letter 2. Also quoted by
             CARLYLE—*Essays.*
                    History.

The dignity of history.

   q.   LORD BOLINGBROKE (Henry St. John)
         —*On the Study and Use of History*.
         Letter V. See also FIELDING
          —*Tom Jones*. Bk. XI.
                    Ch. II.

And history with all her volumes vast,
Hath but *one* page.

   r.   BYRON—*Childe Harold*. Canto IV.
                     St. 108.

What want these outlaws conquerors should
  have
But History's purchased page to call them
  great?

   s.   BYRON—*Childe Harold*. Canto III.
                     St. 48.

Happy the People whose Annals are blank in History-Books.

   t.   CARLYLE—*Life of Frederick the Great*.
                Bk. XVI. Ch. I.

Histories are as perfect as the Historian is wise, and is gifted with an eye and a soul.

   u.   CARLYLE—*Cromwell's Letters and*
         Speeches. Introduction. Ch. I.

History, as it lies at the root of all science, is also the first distinct product of man's spiritual nature; his earliest expression of what can be called Thought.

   v.   CARLYLE—*Essays. On History*.

History is the essence of innumerable Biographies.

    a.   CARLYLE—*Essays. On History.*

In a certain sense all men are historians.

    b.   CARLYLE—*Essays. On History.*

Assassination has never changed the history of the world.

    c.   BENJ. DISRAELI—*Speech.* May, 1865.

And read their history in a nation's eyes.

    d.   GRAY—*Elegy in a Country Churchyard.*
                  St. 16.

The long historian of my country's woes.

    e.   HOMER—*Odyssey.* Bk. 3. L. 142.
                  Pope's trans.

History casts its shadow far into the land of song.

    f.   LONGFELLOW—*Outre-Mer. Ancient*
                  Spanish Ballads.

They who live in history only seemed to walk the earth again.

    g.   LONGFELLOW—*The Belfry of Bruges.*
                  St. 9.

I shall cheerfully bear the reproach of having descended below the dignity of history.

    h.   MACAULAY—*History of England.*
                Vol. I. Ch. I.

[History] hath triumphed over Time, which besides it, nothing but Eternity hath triumphed over.

    i.   SIR WALTER RALEIGH—*The History of*
                the World. Preface.

In a word, we may gather out of history a policy no less wise than eternal; by the comparison and application of other men's forepassed miseries with our own like errors and ill deservings.

    j.   SIR WALTER RALEIGH—*History of the*
              World. Preface. Par. 9.

History is little else than a picture of human crimes and misfortunes.

    k.   VOLTAIRE—*L' Ingenu.* Ch. X. 1767.

Anything but history, for history must be false.

    l.   HORACE WALPOLE—*Walpoliana.*
                No. CXLI.

Those old credulities, to nature dear,
Shall they no longer bloom upon the stock
Of History.

    m.   WORDSWORTH—*Memorials of a Tour in*
              Italy. 1V. At Rome.

HOLIDAYS.

The second day of July, 1776, will be the most memorable epoch in the history of America. I am apt to believe that it will be celebrated by succeeding generations as the great anniversary festival. It ought to be commemorated as the day of deliverance, by solemn acts of devotion to God Almighty. It ought to be solemnized with pomp and parade, with shows, games, sports, guns, bells, bonfires, and illuminations, from one end of this continent to the other, from this time forward forevermore.

    n.   JOHN ADAMS—*Letter to Mrs. Adams.*
                July 3, 1776.

There were his young barbarians all at play
There was their Dacian mother—he, their sire,
Butcher'd to make a Roman holiday.

    o.   BYRON—*Childe Harold.* Canto IV.
                St. 141.

And that was the way
The deuce was to pay
As it always is, at the close of the day
That gave us—
    Hurray! Hurray! Hurray!
(With some restrictions, the fault-finders say)
That which, please God, we will keep for aye,
Our National Independence!

    p.   WILL CARLETON—*How We Kept the Day.*

The holiest of all holidays are those
    Kept by ourselves in silence and apart;
    The secret anniversaries of the heart,
When the full river of feeling overflows;—
The happy days unclouded to their close;
    The sudden joys that out of darkness start
    As flames from ashes; swift desires that dart
Like swallows singing down each wind that
    blows!

    q.   LONGFELLOW—*Holidays.* L. 1.

Being holiday, the beggar's shop is shut.

    r.   *Romeo and Juliet.* Act V. Sc. 1. L. 56.

For now I am in a holiday humour.

    s.   *As You Like It.* Act 4. Sc. 1. L. 69.

If all the year were playing holidays,
To sport would be as tedious as to work.

    t.   *Henry IV.* Pt. I. Act I. Sc. 2. L. 228.

You sunburnt sicklemen, of August weary,
Come hither from the furrow and be merry:
Make holiday; your rye-straw hats put on
And these fresh nymphs encounter every one
In country footing.

    u.   *Tempest.* Act IV. Sc. 1. L. 134.

             Time for work,—yet take
Much holiday for art's and friendship's sake.

    v.   GEORGE JAMES DE WILDE—*Sonnet.*
              On the Arrival of Spring.

HOLINESS.

Might make a saintship of an anchorite.
   a.   BYRON—*Childe Harold.* Canto I. St. 11.

Where'er we tread 'tis haunted, holy ground.
   b.   BYRON—*Childe Harold.* Canto II.
                               St. 88.

          God attributes to place
No sanctity, if none be thither brought
By men who there frequent.
   c.   MILTON—*Paradise Lost.* Bk. XI.
                               L. 836.

Whoso lives the holiest life
Is fittest far to die.
   d.   MARGARET J. PRESTON—*Ready.*

But all his mind is bent to holiness,
To number Ave-Maries on his beads;
His champions are the prophets and apostles,
His weapons holy saws of sacred writ,
His study is his tilt-yard, and his loves
Are brazen images of canonized saints.
   e.   *Henry VI.* Pt. II. Act I. Sc. 3.
                               L. 58.

He who the sword of heaven will bear
Should be as holy as severe;
Pattern in himself to know,
Grace to stand, and virtue go;
More nor less to others paying
Than by self-offences weighing.
Shame to him whose cruel striking
Kills for faults of his own liking!
   f.   *Measure for Measure.* Act III. Sc. 2.
                               L. 275.

Our holy lives must win a new world's crown.
   g.   *Richard II.* Act V. Sc. 1. L. 24.

Holiness is the architectural plan upon
which God buildeth up His living temple.
   h.   SPURGEON—*Gleanings Among the
                   Sheaves. Holiness.*

HOME.

At length his lonely cot appears in view,
   Beneath the shelter of an aged tree;
Th' expectant *wee-things*, toddlin, stacher thro'
To meet their Dad, wi' flichterin noise an'
   glee.
   i.   BURNS—*The Cotter's Saturday Night.*
                               St. 3.

To make a happy fireside clime
     To weans and wife,
That's the true pathos and sublime
     Of human life.
   j.   BURNS—*Epistle to Dr. Blacklock.*

Home is home, though it be never so homely.
   k.   JOHN CLARKE—*Paroemiologia.* P. 101.

For a man's house is his castle.
   l.   SIR EDWARD COKE—*Institutes.* Pt. III.
                 *Against Going, or Riding
                      Armed.* P. 162.

The house of every one is to him as his
castle and fortress, as well for his defence
against injury and violence, as for his repose.
   m.   SIR EDWARD COKE—*Reports. Semaynes'
               Case.* Vol. III. Pt. V. P. 185.

For the whole world, without a native home,
Is nothing but a prison of larger room.
   n.   ABRAHAM COWLEY—*To the Bishop of
                       Lincoln.* L. 27.

I am far frae my hame, an' I'm weary aften
   whiles,
For the longed-for hame-bringing an' my
   Father's welcome smiles.
   o.   ERASTUS ELLSWORTH—*My Ain Countrie.*
                  See MOODY and SANKEY'S
                       Hymns, No. 5.

          Come home!
Would I could send my spirit o'er the deep!
Would I could wing it like a bird to thee,
To commune with thy thoughts, to fill thy
   sleep
With these unwearying words of melody
       Brother, come home!
   p.   CATHERINE H. W. ESLING—*Brother,
                       Come Home.*

At night returning, every labour sped,
He sits him down, the monarch of a shed;
Smiles by his cheerful fire, and round surveys
His children's looks, that brighten at the
   blaze;
While his lov'd partner, boastful of her
   hoard,
Displays her cleanly platter on the board.
   q.   GOLDSMITH—*The Traveller.* L. 191.

The whitewash'd wall, the nicely sanded
   floor,
The varnish'd clock that click'd behind the
   door;
The chest contriv'd a double debt to pay,
A bed by night, a chest of drawers by day.
   r.   GOLDSMITH—*The Deserted Village.*
                             L. 227.

The stately Homes of England,
   How beautiful they stand!
Amidst their tall ancestral trees,
   O'er all the pleasant land.
   s.   MRS. HEMANS—*Homes of England.*

My house, my house, though thou art small,
Thou art to me the Escurial.
   t.   HERBERT—*Jacula Prudentum.*
                             No. 416.

His native home deep imag'd in his soul.
   u.   HOMER—*Odyssey.* Bk. XIII. L. 38.
                         Pope's trans.

Peace and rest at length have come
   All the day's long toil is past;
And each heart is whispering, "Home,
   Home at last!"
   v.   HOOD—*Home At Last.*

Who hath not met with home-made bread,
A heavy compound of putty and lead—
And home-made wines that rack the head,
  And home-made liquors and waters?
Home-made pop that will not foam,
And home-made dishes that drive one from
  home—
     *   *   *   *   *   *
  Home-made by the homely daughters.
  a.   HOOD—*Miss Kilmansegg.*

Cling to thy home! If there the meanest
  shed
Yield thee a hearth and shelter for thy head,
And some poor plot, with vegetables stored,
Be all that Heaven allots thee for thy board,
Unsavory bread, and herbs that scatter'd
  grow
Wild on the river-brink or mountain-brow;
Yet e'en this cheerless mansion shall provide
More heart's repose than all the world beside.
  b.   LEONIDAS—*Home.*

Stay, stay at home, my heart, and rest;
Home-keeping hearts are happiest,
For those that wander they know not where
Are full of trouble and full of care;
  To stay at home is best.
  c.   LONGFELLOW—*Song.* St. 1.

Far from all resort of mirth,
Save the cricket on the hearth.
  d.   MILTON—*Il Penseroso.* L. 81.

It is for homely features to keep home,
They had their name thence.
  e.   MILTON—*Comus.* L. 748.

His home, the spot of earth supremely blest,
A dearer, sweeter spot than all the rest.
  f.   MONTGOMERY—*West Indies.* Pt. III.
                         L. 67.

Who has not felt how sadly sweet
  The dream of home, the dream of home,
Steals o'er the heart, too soon to fleet,
  When far o'er sea or land we roam?
  g.   MOORE—*The Dream of Home.* St. 1.

Subduing and subdued, the petty strife,
Which clouds the colour of domestic life;
The sober comfort, all the peace which springs
From the large aggregate of little things;
On these small cares of daughter, wife or
  friend,
The almost sacred joys of home depend.
  h.   HANNAH MORE—*Sensibility.*

By the fireside still the light is shining,
The children's arms round the parents twining.
From love so sweet, O who would roam?
Be it ever so homely, home is home.
  i.   D. M. MULOCK—*A Shetland Fairy
                     Tale.* Sc. 4.

Ye gentlemen of England,
  That live at home at ease,
Ah! little do you think upon
  The dangers of the seas.
  j.   MARTYN PARKER—*Song.*

'Mid pleasures and palaces though we may
  roam,
Be it ever so humble, there's no place like
  Home.
  k.   J. HOWARD PAYNE—*Home, Sweet Home.*

The poorest man may in his cottage bid defiance to all the force of the Crown. It may
be frail, its roof may shake; the wind may
blow through it; the storms may enter,—the
rain may enter,—but the King of England
cannot enter; all his forces dare not cross the
threshold of the ruined tenement!
  l.   WILLIAM PITT (*Earl of Chatham*)—
               Speech on the Excise Bill.

Just the wee cot—the cricket's chirr—
Love and the smiling face of her.
  m.   JAMES WHITCOMB RILEY—*Ike Walton's
                       Prayer.*

To fireside happiness, to hours of ease
Blest with that charm, the certainty to please.
  n.   SAM'L ROGERS—*Human Life.* L. 347.

And I'll still stay, to have thee still forget,
Forgetting any other home but this.
  o.   *Romeo and Juliet.* Act II. Sc. 2.
                        L. 175.

Home-keeping youth have ever homely wits.
  p.   *Two Gentlemen of Verona.* Act I.
                      Sc. 1. L. 2.

That is my home of love.
  q.   *Sonnet CIX.*

                 Home is the resort
Of love, of joy, of peace, and plenty; where
Supporting and supported, polished friends
And dear relations mingle into bliss.
  r.   THOMSON—*The Seasons. Autumn.*
                        L. 65.

They dreamt not of a perishable home.
  s.   WORDSWORTH—*Inside of King's College
                      Chapel, Cambridge.*

The man who builds, and wants wherewith
  to pay,
Provides a home from which to run away.
  t.   YOUNG—*Love of Fame.* Satire I.
                        L. 171.

HONESTY.

A prince can mak a belted knight,
  A marquis, duke, and a' that;
But an honest man's aboon his might,
  Guid faith, he maunna fa' that.
  u.   BURNS—*For a' That and a' That.*

A honest man's word is as good as his bond.
    a.   Cervantes—*Don Quixote.* Vol. III.
             Pt. II. Ch. XXXIV.

Honesty is the best policy.
    b.   Cervantes—*Don Quixote.* Pt. II.
             Ch. XXXIII.

He is one that will not plead that cause
wherein his tongue must be confuted by his
conscience.
    c.   Fuller—*Holy and Profane States.*
        The Good Advocate. Bk. II. Ch. I.

He that departs with his own honesty
For vulgar praise, doth it too dearly buy.
    d.   Ben Jonson—*Epigram II.*

The measure of life is not length, but
honestie.
    e.   Lyly—*Euphues. The Anatomy of Wit.*
        Letters of Euphues. Euphues and
                    Eubulus.

Friends, if we be honest with ourselves, we
shall be honest with each other.
    f.   George MacDonald—*The Marquis*
               of Lossie. Ch. LXXI.

An honest man's the noblest work of God.
    g.   Pope—*Essay on Man.* Ep. IV. L. 247.

Yet Heav'n, that made me honest, made me
    more
Than ever king did, when he made a lord.
    h.   Nicholas Rowe—*Jane Shore.* Act II.
                  Sc. 1. L. 261.

An honest tale speeds best being plainly told.
    i.   *Richard III.* Act IV. Sc. 4. L. 358.

At many times I brought in my accounts,
Laid them before you; you would throw
    them off,
And say, you found them in mine honesty.
    j.   *Timon of Athens.* Act II. Sc. 2. L. 142.

Ay, sir; to be honest, as this world goes, is
to be one man picked out of ten thousand.
    k.   *Hamlet.* Act II. Sc. 2. L. 178.

There is no terror, Cassius, in your threats,
For I am arm'd so strong in honesty
That they pass by me as the idle wind,
Which I respect not.
    l.   *Julius Cæsar.* Act IV. Sc. 3. L. 66.

                    What's the news?
None, my lord, but that the world's grown
    honest.
    Then is doomsday near.
    m.   *Hamlet.* Act II. Sc. 2. L. 240.

Were there no heaven nor hell
I should be honest.
    n.   John Webster—*Duchess of Malfi.*
                    Act I. Sc. I.

  20

"Honesty is the best policy," but he who
acts on that principle is not an honest man.
    o.   Archbishop Whately—*Thoughts and*
        Apothegms. Pt. II. Ch. XVIII.
                    Pious Frauds.

An Ambassador is an honest man sent to
lie abroad for the commonwealth.
    p.   Sir Henry Wotton—*A Panegyric to*
                    King Charles.

How happy is he born and taught
  That serveth not another's will;
Whose armour is his honest thought,
  And simple truth his utmost skill.
    q.   Sir Henry Wotton—*The Character of*
                    a Happy Life.

HONOR.

Better to die ten thousand deaths,
Than wound my honour.
    r.   Addison—*Cato.* Act I. Sc. 4.

The sense of honour is of so fine and delicate
a nature, that it is only to be met with in
minds which are naturally noble, or in such
as have been cultivated by good examples, or
a refined education.
    s.   Addison—*The Guardian.* No. 161.

As quick as lightning, in the breach
Just in the place where honour's lodged,
As wise philosophers have judged,
Because a kick in that place more
Hurts honour than deep wounds before.
    t.   Butler—*Hudibras.* Pt. II. Canto III.
                  L. 1,066.

If he that in the field is slain
Be in the bed of honour lain,
He that is beaten may be said
To lie in Honour's truckle-bed.
    u.   Butler—*Hudibras.* Pt. I. Canto III.
                  L. 1,047.

Now, while the honour thou hast got
Is spick and span new.
    v.   Butler—*Hudibras.* Pt. I. Canto III.
                  L. 397.

Honor lies in honest toil.
    w.   Grover Cleveland—*Letter Accepting*
        Nomination for President. Aug. 18,
        1884. Wm. O. Stoddard. *Life of*
            Grover Cleveland. Ch. XV.

   *   *   * Therefore I am wel pleased to
take any coulor to defend your honour and
hope you wyl remember that who seaketh two
strings to one bowe, he may shute strong but
neuer strait.
    x.   Queen Elizabeth to James VI.—
        Letter X. Edited by John Bruce.

Titles of honour add not to his worth,
Who is himself an honour to his titles.
    y.   John Ford—*The Lady's Trial.* Act 1.
                  Sc. 3. L. 30.

Title and profit I resign;
The post of honour shall be mine.

> a.　GAY—*Fables. The Vulture, the Sparrow,*
> *and other Birds.* L. 71.

Your word is as good as the Bank, sir.

> b.　HOLCROFT—*The Road to Ruin.* Act I.
> Sc. 3.　L. 235.

Great honours are great burdens, but on whom
They are cast with envy, he doth bear two loads.
His cares must still be double to his joys,
In any dignity.

> c.　BEN JONSON—*Catiline. His Conspiracy.*
> Act III.　Sc. 1.　L. 1.

Dead on the field of honour.

> d.　*Answer given in the roll-call of* LA TOUR
> D' AUVERGNE'S *regiment after his*
> *death.*

Honour is purchas'd by the deeds we do;
* * * honour is not won,
Until some honourable deed be done.

> e.　MARLOWE—*Hero and Leander. First*
> *Sistiad.* L. 276.

When honor comes to you be ready to take it;
But reach not to seize it before it is near.

> f.　JOHN BOYLE O'REILLY—*Rules of the*
> *Road.*

Honour, the spur that pricks the princely mind,
To follow rule and climb the stately chair.

> g.　GEORGE PEELE—*The Battle of Alcazar.*
> Act I.

We'll shine in more substantial honours,
And to be noble, we'll be good.

> h.　THOS. PERCY—*Reliques. Winifreda.*

Honour and shame from no condition rise;
Act well your part, there all the honour lies.

> i.　POPE—*Essay on Man.* Ep. IV. L. 193.

And as the sun breaks through the darkest clouds,
So honour peereth in the meanest habit.

> j.　*Taming of the Shrew.* Act IV. Sc. 3.
> L. 175.

And if his name be George, I'll call him Peter;
For new-made honour doth forget men's names.

> k.　*King John.* Act I. Sc. 1. L. 186.

And pluck up drowned honour by the locks.

> l.　*Henry IV.* Pt. I. Act I. Sc. 3. L. 205.

A scar nobly got, or a noble scar, is a good livery of honour.

> m.　*All's Well That Ends Well.* Act IV.
> Sc. 5. L. 105.

But if it be a sin to covet honour,
I am the most offending soul alive.

> n.　*Henry V.* Act IV. Sc. 3. L. 28.

For Brutus is an honourable man;
So are they all, all honourable men.

> o.　*Julius Cæsar.* Act III. Sc. 2. L. 87.

For he's honourable
And doubling that, most holy.

> p.　*Cymbeline.* Act III. Sc. 4. L. 179.

For honour travels in a strait so narrow,
Where one but goes abreast.

> q.　*Troilus and Cressida.* Act III. Sc. 3.
> L. 154.

Honours thrive,
When rather from our acts we them derive
Than our foregoers.

> r.　*All's Well That Ends Well.* Act II.
> Sc. 3. L. 142.

If I lose mine honour,
I lose myself; better I were not yours
Than yours so branchless.

> s.　*Antony and Cleopatra.* Act III. Sc. 4.
> L. 22.

Let none presume
To wear an undeserv'd dignity.
O, that estates, degrees and offices
Were not deriv'd corruptly, and that clear honour
Were purchas'd by the merit of the wearer!

> t.　*Merchant of Venice.* Act II. Sc. 9.
> L. 39.

Methinks it were an easy leap,
To pluck bright honour from the pale-fac'd moon.

> u.　*Henry IV.* Pt. I. Act I. Sc. 3. L. 201.

Mine honour let me try;
In that I live, and for that will I die.

> v.　*Richard II.* Act I. Sc. I. L. 184.

See that you come
Not to woo honour, but to wed it.

> w.　*All's Well That Ends Well.* Act II.
> Sc. 1. L. 14.

Thou art a fellow of a good respect;
Thy life hath had some smatch of honour in it.

> x.　*Julius Cæsar.* Act V. Sc. 5. L. 45.

Well, 'tis no matter; honour pricks me on.
Yea, but how if honour prick me off, when I
come on? how then? Can honour set to a leg?
no: or an arm? no: or take away the grief
of a wound? no: Honour hath no skill in
surgery, then? no. What is honour? a word.
What is in that word honour? What is that
honour? air. A trim reckoning! Who hath
it? he that died o' Wednesday. Doth he
feel it? no. Doth he hear it? no. 'Tis insensible, then. Yea, to the dead. But will it
not live with the living? no. Why? detraction will not suffer it. Therefore, I'll none of
it. Honour is a mere scutcheon; and so **ends**
my catechism.

> y.　*Henry IV.* Pt. I. Act V. Sc. 1.
> L. 129.

Honour sits smiling at the sale of truth.
   a.   Shelley—*Queen Mab.* Canto IV.
                          L. 218.

His honor rooted in dishonor stood,
And faith unfaithful kept him falsely true.
   b.   Tennyson—*Idyls of the King.*
               Lancelot and Elaine. L. 886.

HOPE.

Know then, whatever cheerful and serene
Supports the mind, supports the body too :
Hence, the most vital movement mortals feel
Is hope, the balm and lifeblood of the soul.
   c.   John Armstrong—*Art of Preserving*
             Health. Bk. IV. L. 310.

Our greatest good, and what we least can
    spare,
Is hope : the last of all our evils, fear.
   d.   John Armstrong—*Art of Preserving*
             Health. Bk. IV. L. 318.

It is to hope, though hope were lost.
   e.   Mrs. Barbauld—*Come here, Fond*
                        Youth.

Hope ! thou nurse of young desire.
   f.   Bickerstaff—*Love in a Village.*
              Act I. Sc. 1. L. 1.

Hope springs exulting on triumphant wing.
   g.   Burns—*The Cotter's Saturday Night.*
                        St. 16.

                But still there clung
One hope, like a keen sword on starting
    threads uphung.
   h.   Byron—*Revolt of Islam.*

Auspicious Hope ! in thy sweet garden grow
Wreaths for each toil, a charm for every woe.
   i.   Campbell—*Pleasures of Hope.* Pt. I.
                        L. 45.

Cease, every joy, to glimmer in my mind,
But leave,—oh ! leave the light of Hope be-
    hind !
What though my winged hours of bliss have
    been,
Like angel-visits, few and far between.
   j.   Campbell—*Pleasures of Hope.* Pt. II.
                        L. 375.

I laugh, for hope hath happy place with me,
If my bark sinks, 'tis to another sea.
   k.   Wm. Ellery Channing—*A Poet's*
                    Hope. St. 13.

Work without hope draws nectar in a sieve,
And hope without an object cannot live.
   l.   Coleridge—*Work Without Hope.* St. 2.

   And Hope enchanted smiled, and waved her
golden hair.
   m.   Collins—*Ode on the Passions.* L. 3.

But thou, O Hope, with eyes so fair,
What was thy delighted measure ?
Still it whisper'd promised pleasure,
And bade the lovely scenes at distance hail !
   n.   Collins—*Ode on the Passions.* L. 29.

Hope ! of all ills that men endure,
The only cheap and universal cure.
   o.   Abraham Cowley—*The Mistress.* *For*
                                Hope.

All hope abandon, ye who enter here.
   p.   Dante—*Hell.* Canto III. S. 9.

                Hopes have precarious life.
They are oft blighted, withered, snapped sheer
    off
In vigorous growth and turned to rottenness.
   q.   George Eliot—*The Spanish Gypsy.*
                         Bk. III.

While there is life there's hope, (he cried,)
Then why such haste ?—so groan'd and died.
   r.   Gay—*The Sick Man and The Angel.*

Hope, like the gleaming taper's light,
    Adorns and cheers our way ;
And still, as darker grows the night,
    Emits a brighter ray.
   s.   Goldsmith—*The Captivity.* Act II.
                           Sc. 1.

In all my wanderings round this world of care,
In all my griefs—and God has given my share—
I still had hopes my latest hours to crown,
Amidst these humble bowers to lay me down.
   t.   Goldsmith—*The Deserted Village.*
                          L. 81.

The wretch condemn'd with life to part,
    Still, still on hope relies ;
And every pang that rends the heart
    Bids expectation rise.
   u.   Goldsmith—*Captivity.* *Song.*

Gay hope is theirs by fancy fed,
    Less pleasing when possest ;
The tear forgot as soon as shed,
    The sunshine of the breast.
   v.   Gray—*On a Distant Prospect of Eton*
                       College. St. 5.

Thus heavenly hope is all serene,
    But earthly hope, how bright so e'er,
Still fluctuates o'er this changing scene,
    As false and fleeting as 'tis fair.
   w.   Bishop Heber—*Lines.* St. 2.

Youth fades ; love droops ; the leaves of
    friendship fall ;
A mother's secret hope outlives them all.
   x.   O. W. Holmes—*A Mother's Secret.*

   In all the wedding cake, hope is the sweetest of the plums.
   y.   Douglas Jerrold—*Jerrold's Wit.*
                         The Catspaw.

Where there is no hope, there can be no endeavour.

　　a.　　SAM'L JOHNSON—*The Rambler.*
　　　　　　　　　　　　　　　　　　No. 110.

So, when dark thoughts my boding spirit
　　shroud,
Sweet Hope! celestial influence round me
　　shed,
Waving thy silver pinions o'er my head.

　　b.　　KEATS—*Hope.* St. 8.

One only hope my heart can cheer,—
The hope to meet again.

　　c.　　GEO. LINLEY—*Song.*

Races, better than we, have leaned on her
　　wavering promise,
Having naught else but Hope.

　　d.　　LONGFELLOW—*The Children of the
　　　　　　　　　　Lord's Supper.* L. 230.

The setting of a great hope is like the setting
of the sun. The brightness of our life is gone.

　　e.　　LONGFELLOW—*Hyperion.* Bk. I. Ch. I.

Who bids me Hope, and in that charming
　　word
Has peace and transport to my soul restor'd.

　　f.　　LORD LYTTLETON—*The Progress of Love.
　　　　　　　　Hope.* Eclogue II. L. 41.

Hope elevates, and joy
Brightens his crest.

　　g.　　MILTON—*Paradise Lost.* Bk. IX.
　　　　　　　　　　　　　　　　　　L. 633.

What reinforcement we may gain from hope;
If not, what resolution from despair.

　　h.　　MILTON—*Paradise Lost.* Bk. I. L. 190.

　　　　　　　　　　　　　　Where peace
And rest can never dwell, hope never comes,
That comes to all.

　　i.　　MILTON—*Paradise Lost.* Bk. I. L. 65.

Hope against hope, and ask till ye receive.

　　j.　　MONTGOMERY—*The World before the
　　　　　　　　　　　Flood.* Canto V.

Things which you don't hope happen more
frequently than things which you do hope.

　　k.　　PLAUTUS—*Mostellaria.* Act I. Sc. 3.
　　　　　　　　　　　　　　　　　　L. 71.

Hope springs eternal in the human breast;
Man never *is*, but always *to be* blest.

　　l.　　POPE—*Essay on Man.* Ep. I. L. 95.

Hope travels through, nor quits us when
we die.

　　m.　　POPE—*Essay on Man.* Ep. II. L. 273.

For hope is but the dream of those that wake!

　　n.　　PRIOR—*Solomon on the Vanity of the
　　　　　　　　　World.* Bk. III. L. 102.

Our hopes, like tow'ring falcons, aim
　　At objects in an airy height;
The little pleasure of the game
　　Is from afar to view the flight.

　　o.　　PRIOR—*To Hon. Chas. Montague.*

Hope dead lives nevermore,
　　No, not in heaven.

　　p.　　CHRISTINA G. ROSSETTI—*Dead Hope.*

Who in Life's battle firm doth stand
Shall bear Hope's tender blossoms
Into the Silent Land.

　　q.　　J. G. VAN SALIS—*Song of the Silent
　　　　　　　　　　　　　　　　　Land.*

Hope is brightest when it dawns from fears.

　　r.　　SCOTT—*Lady of the Lake.* Canto IV.
　　　　　　　　　　　　　　　　　　St. 1.

The sickening pang of hope deferr'd.

　　s.　　SCOTT—*Lady of the Lake.* Canto III.
　　　　　　　　　　　　　　　　　　St. 22.

　　　　　　　　　　　　　　　　Farewell
The hopes of court! my hopes in heaven do
　　dwell.

　　t.　　*Henry VIII.* Act III. Sc. 2. L. 458.

Hope is a lover's staff; walk hence with that
And manage it against despairing thoughts.

　　u.　　*Two Gentlemen of Verona.* Act III.
　　　　　　　　　　　　　　Sc. 1. L. 246.

The miserable have no other medicine
But only hope:
I 've hope to live, and am prepar'd to die.

　　v.　　*Measure for Measure.* Act III. Sc. 1.
　　　　　　　　　　　　　　　　　　L. 2.

True hope is swift, and flies with swallow's
　　wings:
Kings it makes gods, and meaner creatures
　　kings.

　　w.　　*Richard III.* Act V. Sc. 2. L. 23.

But hope will make thee young, for Hope and
　　Youth
Are children of one mother, even Love.

　　x.　　SHELLEY—*Revolt of Islam.* Canto VIII.
　　　　　　　　　　　　　　　　　　St. 27.

Through the sunset of hope,
　　Like the shapes of a dream,
What paradise islands of glory gleam!

　　y.　　SHELLEY—*Hellas.* Semi-chorus I.

　　　　　　　　　　　　To hope till hope creates
From its own wreck the thing it contemplates.

　　z.　　SHELLEY—*Prometheus.* Act IV.
　　　　　　　　　　　　　　　　Last stanza.

　　　　　　　　　　　　Worse than despair,
Worse than the bitterness of death, is hope.

　　aa.　　SHELLEY—*The Cenci.* Act V. Sc. 4.

Through thick and thin, both over banck and
    bush,
In hope her to attaine by hooke or crooke.
   a.   Spenser—*Faerie Queene.* Bk. III.
                  Canto I. St. 17.

Behold, we know not anything;
  I can but trust that good shall fall
  At last—far off—at last, to all,
And every winter change to spring.
   b.   Tennyson—*In Memoriam.* LIV.

The mighty hopes that make us men.
   c.   Tennyson—*In Memoriam.* LXXXV.

Behind the cloud the starlight lurks,
  Through showers the sunbeams fall;
For God, who loveth all his works,
  Has left his Hope with all.
   d.   Whittier—*Dream of Summer.*

Hopes, what are they?—Beads of morning
  Strung on slender blades of grass;
Or a spider's web adorning
  In a straight and treacherous pass.
   e.   Wordsworth—*Hopes, What are They?*

                Is Man
A child of hope? Do generations press
On generations, without progress made?
Halts the individual, ere his hairs be gray,
Perforce?
   f.   Wordsworth—*The Excursion.* Bk. V.

Hope tells a flattering tale,
  Delusive, vain and hollow.
Ah! let not hope prevail,
  Lest disappointment follow.
   g.   Miss Wrother—*The Universal
                Songster.* Vol. II. P. 86.

Hope, like a cordial, innocent, though strong,
Man's heart, at once, inspirits, and serenes;
Nor makes him pay his wisdom for his joys.
   h.   Young—*Night Thoughts.* Night VII.
                      L. 1,514.

HOSPITALITY.

He kept no Christmas-house for once a yeere,
Each day his boards were fild with Lordly
    fare:
He fed a rout of yeoman with his cheer,
Nor was his bread and beefe kept in with
    care;
His wine and beere to strangers were not spare,
And yet beside to all that hunger greved,
His gates were ope, and they were there relived.
   i.   Robert Greene—*A Maiden's Dream.*
                        L. 232.

Hospitality sitting with gladness.
   j.   Longfellow—*Translation from
                Frithiof's Saga.*

So saying, with despatchful looks in haste
She turns, on hospitable thoughts intent.
   k.   Milton—*Paradise Lost.* Bk. V.
                        L. 331.

                    I am your host;
With robbers' hands my hospitable favours
You should not ruffle thus.
   l.   *King Lear.* Act III. Sc. 7. L. 39.

I charge thee, invite them all: let in the tide
Of knaves once more; my cook and I'll
    provide.
   m.   *Timon of Athens.* Act III. Sc. 4.
                        L. 118.

My master is of churlish disposition
And little recks to find the way to heaven
By doing deeds of hospitality.
   n.   *As You Like It.* Act II. Sc. 4. L. 80.

HUMANITY.

                Yet should one,
A single sufferer from the field escaped,
Panting and pale, and bleeding at his feet,
Lift his imploring eyes,—the hero weeps;
He is grown human, and capricious Pity,
Which would not stir for thousands, melts
    for one
With sympathy spontaneous:—'Tis not Virtue,
Yet 'tis the weakness of a virtuous mind.
   o.   Anna Lætitia Barbauld—*The
                  Caterpillar.* L. 35.

Love, hope, fear, faith—these make humanity;
These are its sign and note and character.
   p.   Robert Browning—*Paracelsus.* Sc. 3.

Fra Lippo, we have learned from thee
A lesson of humanity:
To every mother's heart forlorn,
In every house the Christ is born.
   q.   R. W. Gilder—*A Madonna of Fra
                Lippo Lippi.*

He held his seat; a friend to human race.
   r.   Homer—*Iliad.* Bk. 6. L. 18.
                    Pope's trans.

Respect us, human, and relieve us, poor.
   s.   Homer—*Odyssey.* Bk. 9. L. 338.
                    Pope's trans.

For He, who gave this vast machine to roll,
Breathed *Life* in them, in us a *Reasoning Soul;*
That kindred feelings might our state improve,
And mutual wants conduct to mutual love.
   t.   Juvenal—*Satire XV.* L. 203.

Every human heart is human.
   u.   Longfellow—*Hiawatha.*
                Introduction. L. 91.

Laborin' man an' laborin' woman
  Hev one glory an' one shame;
Ev'ythin' thet's done inhuman
  Injers all on 'em the same.
   v.   Lowell—*The Biglow Papers.* First
                Series. No. 1. St. 10.

But hearing oftentimes
The still, sad music of humanity.
    a.   WORDSWORTH—*Tintern Abbey.*

Never to blend our pleasure or our pride
With sorrow of the meanest thing that feels.
    b.   WORDSWORTH—*Hart-leap Well.* Pt. II.

HUMILITY.

Lowliness is the base of every virtue,
And he who goes the lowest builds the safest.
    c.   BAILEY—*Festus.* Sc. *Home.*

My favored temple is an humble heart.
    d.   BAILEY—*Festus.* Sc. *Colonnade and
Lawn.*

To be nameless in worthy deeds, exceeds an infamous history.
    e.   SIR THOMAS BROWNE—*Hydriotaphia.*
Ch. V.

O wad some power the giftie gie us
To see oursel's as ithers see us!
It wad frae monie a blunder free us.
    And foolish notion;
What airs in dress and gait wad lea'e us,
    And ev'n devotion!
    f.   BURNS—*To a Louse.*

And be the Spartan's epitaph on me—
"Sparta hath many a worthier son than he."
    g.   BYRON—*Childe Harold.* Canto IV.
St. 10.

He saw a cottage with a double coach-house,
    A cottage of gentility!
And the Devil did grin, for his darling sin
    Is pride that apes humility.
    h.   COLERIDGE—*Devil's Thoughts.* (See
SOUTHEY's *Devil's Walk.*)

I am well aware that I am the 'umblest person going * * * let the other be where he may.
    i.   DICKENS—*David Copperfield.* Vol. I.
Ch. XVI.

'Umble we are, 'umble we have been, 'umble we shall ever be.
    j.   DICKENS—*David Copperfield.* Vol. I.
Ch. XVII.

Extremes meet, and there is no better example than the haughtiness of humility.
    k.   EMERSON—*Letters and Social Aims.
Greatness.*

God hath sworn to lift on high
Who sinks himself by true humility.
    l.   KEBLE—*Miscellaneous Poems.* At
Hooker's Tomb.

O be very sure
That no man will learn anything at all,
Unless he first will learn humility.
    m.   OWEN MEREDITH (Lord Lytton)—
Vanini. L. 327.

At whose sight all the stars
Hide their diminish'd heads.
    n.   MILTON—*Paradise Lost.* Bk. IV.
L. 34.

One may be humble out of pride.
    o.   MONTAIGNE—*Of Presumption.* Bk. II.
Ch. XVII.

Fairest and best adorned is she
Whose clothing is humility.
    p.   MONTGOMERY—*Humility.*

Nearest the throne itself must be
The footstool of humility.
    q.   MONTGOMERY—*Humility.*

Humility, that low, sweet root,
From which all heavenly virtues shoot.
    r.   MOORE—*Loves of the Angels.* Third
Angel's Story. St. 11.

I was not born for Courts or great affairs;
pay my debts, believe, and say my pray'rs.
    s.   POPE—*Prologue to Satires.* L. 268.

Who, noteless as the race from which he
    sprung,
Saved others' names, but left his own unsung.
    t.   SCOTT—*Waverley.* Ch. XIII.

It is the witness still of excellency
To put a strange face on his own perfection.
    u.   *Much Ado About Nothing.* Act II.
Sc. 3. L. 48.

Humility is to make a right estimate of one's self. It is no humility for a man to think less of himself than he ought, though it might rather puzzle him to do that.
    v.   SPURGEON—*Gleanings Among the
Sheaves. Humility.*

The higher a man is in grace, the lower he will be in his own esteem.
    w.   SPURGEON—*Gleanings Among the
Sheaves. The Right Estimate.*

HUMOR.

Humor has justly been regarded as the finest perfection of poetic genius.
    x.   CARLYLE—*Essays. Schiller.*

I never dare to write
As funny as I can.
    y.   O. W. HOLMES—*The Height of the
Ridiculous.*

Now I perceive the devil understands Welsh;
And 'tis no marvel he is so humorous.
    z.   *Henry IV.* Pt. I. Act III. Sc. 1.
L. 233.

A little nonsense now and then
Is relished by the wisest men.
    aa.   ANONYMOUS.

HUNGER.

Hunger is sharper than the sword.
  a.   BEAUMONT AND FLETCHER—*The Honest*
        Man's Fortune. Act II. Sc. 2.
                L. 1.

Bone and Skin, two millers thin,
  Would starve us all, or near it;
But be it known to Skin and Bone
  That Flesh and Blood can't bear it.
  b.   JOHN BYROM—*Epigram on Two*
                Monopolists.

But man is a carnivorous production,
  And must have meals, at least one meal a
    day;
He cannot live, like woodcocks, upon suction,
  But, like the shark and tiger, must have
    prey.
  c.   BYRON—*Don Juan.* Canto II. St. 67.

Famished people must be slowly nursed,
And fed by spoonfuls, else they always burst.
  d.   BYRON—*Don Juan.* Canto II. St. 158.

Hunger was the best seasoning for meat.
  e   CICERO—*De Finibus.* Bk. II.
          Pt. XXVIII. Yonge's trans.

They that die by famine die by inches.
  f.   MATHEW HENRY—*Commentaries.*
                Psalm LIX.

      Our stomachs
Will make what's homely savoury.
  g.   *Cymbeline.* Act III. Sc. 6. L. 32.

They said they were an-hungry; sigh'd forth
  proverbs,
That hunger broke stone walls, that dogs must
  eat,
That meat was made for mouths, that the
  gods sent not
Corn for the rich men only: with these
  shreds
They vented their complainings.
  h.   *Coriolanus.* Act I. Sc. 1. L. 209.

Yond Cassius has a lean and hungry look.
  i.   *Julius Cæsar.* Act I. Sc. 2. L. 194.

Cruel as death, and hungry as the grave.
  j.   THOMSON—*The Seasons. Winter.*
                L. 393.

HUSBAND.

And truant husband should return, and say,
"My dear, I was the first who came away."
  k.   BYRON—*Don Juan.* Canto I. St. 141.

The lover in the husband may be lost.
  l.   LORD LYTTLETON—*Advice to a Lady.*
                L. 112.

        And to thy husband's will
Thine shall submit; he over thee shall rule.
  m.   MILTON—*Paradise Lost.* Bk. X.
                L. 195.

God is thy law, thou mine.
  n.   MILTON—*Paradise Lost.* Bk. IV.
                L. 637.

The wife, where danger or dishonour lurks,
Safest and seemliest by her husband stays,
Who guards her, or with her the worst
  endures.
  o.   MILTON—*Paradise Lost.* Bk. IX.
                L. 267.

        With thee goes
Thy husband, him to follow thou art bound;
Where he abides, think there thy native soil.
  p.   MILTON—*Paradise Lost.* Bk. XI.
                L. 290.

The stoic husband was the glorious thing.
The man had courage, was a sage, 'tis true,
And lov'd his country.
  q.   POPE—*Epilogue to Rowe's Jane Shore.*

Well, if our author in the wife offends
He has a husband that will make amends;
He draws him gentle, tender, and forgiving,
And sure such kind good creatures may be
  living.
  r.   POPE—*Epilogue to Rowe's Jane Shore.*

A very man—not one of nature's clods—
  With human failings, whether saint or
    sinner:
Endowed perhaps with genius from the gods
  But apt to take his temper from his dinner.
  s.   J. G. SAXE—*About Husbands.*

If I should marry him, I should marry twenty
  husbands.
  t.   *Merchant of Venice.* Act I. Sc. 2.
                L. 67.

I will attend my husband, be his nurse,
Diet his sickness, for it is my office.
  u.   *Comedy of Errors.* Act V. Sc. 1.
                L. 98.

No worse a husband than the best of men.
  v.   *Antony and Cleopatra.* Act II. Sc. 2.
                L. 131.

That lord whose hand must take my plight
  shall carry
Half my love with him, half my care and
  duty.
  w.   *King Lear.* Act I. Sc. 1. L. 103.

Thy husband is thy lord, thy life, thy keeper,
Thy head, thy sovereign; one that cares for
  thee,
And for thy maintenance.
  x.   *Taming of the Shrew.* Act V. Sc. 2.
                L. 146.

HYPOCRISY.

　　　　　　　　　　　　And the veil
Spun from the cobweb fashion of the times,
To hide the feeling heart?
　　a.　　AKENSIDE—*Pleasures of Imagination.*
　　　　　　　　　　　Bk. II.　L. 147.

When a man puts on a Character he is a
stranger to, there's as much difference between
what he appears, and what he is really in
himself, as there is between a Vizor and a Face.
　　b.　　DE LA BRUYÈRE—*The Characters or
　　　　　Manners of the Present Age. Of Men.
　　　　　　　　　　　　　　Ch. XI.*

Saint abroad, and a devil at home.
　　c.　　BUNYAN—*Pilgrim's Progress.* Pt. I.

Be hypocritical, be cautious, be
Not what you *seem* but always what you *see.*
　　d.　　BYRON—*Don Juan.* Canto XI. St. 86.

Oh, for a *forty-parson power* to chant
　Thy praise, Hypocrisy! Oh, for a hymn
Loud as the virtues thou dost loudly vaunt,
　Not practise!
　　e.　　BYRON—*Don Juan.* Canto X. St. 34.

And prate and preach about what others prove,
As if the world and they were hand and glove.
　　f.　　COWPER—*Table Talk.* L. 173.

A hypocrite is in himself both the archer and
the mark, in all actions shooting at his own
praise or profit.
　　g.　　FULLER—*The Holy and Profane States.
　　　　　The Hypocrite.* Maxim 1. Bk. V.
　　　　　　　　　　　　　　Ch. VIII.

An open foe may prove a curse,
But a pretended friend is worse.
　　h.　　GAY—*The Shepherd's Dog and the Wolf.*
　　　　　　　　　　　　　　L. 33.

Thus 'tis with all; their chief and constant
　　care
Is to seem everything but what they are.
　　i.　　GOLDSMITH—*Epilogue to The Sisters.*
　　　　　　　　　　　　　　L. 25.

Some hypocrites and seeming mortified men,
that held down their heads, were like the
little images that they place in the very bowing of the vaults of churches, that look as if
they held up the church, but are but puppets.
　　j.　　*Attributed to* DR. LAND *by* BACON—
　　　　　　　　　　Apothegms. No. 273.

But all was false and hollow; though his
　　tongue
Dropped manna, and could make the worse
　　appear
The better reason, to perplex and dash
Maturest counsels.
　　k.　　MILTON—*Paradise Lost.* Bk. II. L. 112.

For neither man nor angel can discern
Hypocrisy, the only evil that walks
Invisible, except to God alone,
By his permissive will, through heav'n and
　　earth.
　　l.　　MILTON—*Paradise Lost.* Bk. III.
　　　　　　　　　　　　　　L. 682.

　　　　　　　　　　He was a man
Who stole the livery of the court of Heaven
To serve the Devil in.
　　m.　　POLLOK—*Course of Time.* Bk. VIII.
　　　　　　　　　　　　　　L. 616.

Constant at Church and 'Change; his gains
　　were sure;
His givings rare, save farthings to the poor.
　　n.　　POPE—*Moral Essays.* Ep. III. L. 347.

Thou hast prevaricated with thy friend,
By underhand contrivances undone me:
And while my open nature trusted in thee,
Thou hast stept in between me and my hopes,
And ravish'd from me all my soul held dear.
Thou hast betray'd me.
　　o.　　NICHOLAS ROWE—*Lady Jane Grey.*
　　　　　　　　　　　Act II. Sc. 1. L. 235.

Not he who scorns the Saviour's yoke
Should wear his cross upon the heart.
　　p.　　SCHILLER—*The Fight with the Dragon.*
　　　　　　　　　　　　　　St. 24.

Away, and mock the time with fairest show;
False face must hide what the false heart doth
　　know.
　　q.　　*Macbeth.* Act I. Sc. 7. L. 81.

God has given you one face, and you make
yourselves another.
　　r.　　*Hamlet.* Act III. Sc. 1. L. 149.

I will speak daggers to her, but use none;
My tongue and soul in this be hypocrites.
　　s.　　*Hamlet.* Act III. Sc. 2. L. 414.

My tables,—meet it is I set it down,
That one may smile, and smile, and be a
　　villain;
At least I'm sure it may be so in Denmark.
　　t.　　*Hamlet.* Act I. Sc. 5. L. 107.

O serpent heart, hid with a flowering face!
Did ever a dragon keep so fair a cave?
　　u.　　*Romeo and Juliet.* Act III. Sc. 2.
　　　　　　　　　　　　　　L. 73.

O, what may man within him hide,
Though angel on the outward side!
　　v.　　*Measure for Measure.* Act III. Sc. 2.
　　　　　　　　　　　　　　L. 285.

So smooth he daub'd his vice with show of
　　virtue,

* 　 * 　 * 　 * 　 * 　 *

He liv'd from all attainder of suspect.
　a.　　*Richard III.*　Act III.　Sc. 5.　L. 29.

'Tis too much proved—that with devotion's
　　visage
And pious action we do sugar o'er
The devil himself.
　b.　　*Hamlet.*　Act III.　Sc. 1.　L. 47.

How inexpressible is the meanness of being
a hypocrite! how horrible is it to be a mis-
chievous and malignant hypocrite.
　c.　　Voltaire—*A Philosophical Dictionary.*
　　　　　　　　　　　　Philosopher.　Sec. 1.

A man I knew who lived upon a smile,
And well it fed him; he look'd plump and fair,
While rankest venom foam'd through every
　　vein.
　d.　　Young—*Night Thoughts.*　Night VIII.
　　　　　　　　　　　　　　　L. 336.

I.

IDLENESS.

Idleness is emptiness; the tree in which the
sap is stagnant, remains fruitless.
　e.　　Hosea Ballou—*MS. Sermons.*

For idleness is an appendix to nobility.
　f.　　Burton—*Anatomy of Melancholy.*
　　　　　　　　　Pt. I.　Sec. II.　Memb. 2.
　　　　　　　　　　　　　　Subsec. 6.

An idler is a watch that wants both hands;
As useless if it goes as when it stands.
　g.　　Cowper—*Retirement.*

How various his employments whom the
　　world
Calls idle; and who justly in return
Esteems that busy world an idler too!
　h.　　Cowper—*The Task.*　Bk. III.　*The*
　　　　　　　　　　　　Garden.　L. 342.

Thus idly busy rolls their world away.
　i.　　Goldsmith—*The Traveller.*　L. 256.

What heart can think, or tongue express,
The harm that groweth of idleness?
　j.　　John Heywood—*Idleness.*

I live an idle burden to the ground.
　k.　　Homer—*Iliad.*　Bk. XVIII.　L. 134.
　　　　　　　　　　　　　Pope's trans.

Gloomy calm of idle vacancy.
　l.　　Sam'l Johnson—*Boswell's Life of*
　　　　　　　　　　Johnson.　Dec. 8, 1763.

Thee too, my Paridel! she mark'd thee there,
Stretch'd on the rack of a too easy chair,
And heard thy everlasting yawn confess
The Pains and Penalties of Idleness.
　m.　　Pope—*Dunciad.*　Bk. IV.　L. 341.

I rather would entreat thy company,
To see the wonders of the world abroad
Than living, dully sluggardized at home,
Wear out thy youth with shapeless idleness.
　n.　　*Two Gentlemen of Verona.*　Act I.
　　　　　　　　　　　　　　Sc. 1.　L. 5.

Their only labour was to kill the time;
And labour dire it is, and weary woe,
They sit, they loll, turn o'er some idle rhyme,
Then, rising sudden, to the glass they go,
Or saunter forth, with tottering steps and
　　slow.
　o.　　Thomson—*Castle of Indolence.*
　　　　　　　　　　　　Canto I.　LXXII.

There is no remedy for time misspent;
No healing for the waste of idleness,
Whose very languor is a punishment
Heavier than active souls can feel or guess.
　p.　　Sir Aubrey de Vere—*A Song of Faith,*
　　　　　　　　Devout Exercises, and Sonnets.

But how can he expect that others should
Build for him, sow for him, and at his call
Love him, who for himself will take no heed
　　at all?
　q.　　Wordsworth—*Resolution and*
　　　　　　　　　　Independence.　St. 6.

IGNORANCE.

Be ignorance thy choice, where knowledge
leads to woe.
　r.　　Beattie—*The Minstrel.*　Bk. II.
　　　　　　　　　　　　　　St. 30.

The truest characters of ignorance
Are vanity, and pride, and annoyance.
　s.　　Butler—*Hudibras.*

Ignorance seldom vaults into knowledge,
but passes into it through an intermediate
state of obscurity, even as night into day
through twilight.
　t.　　Coleridge—*Essay XVI.*

Ignorance never settles a question.
　u.　　Benj. Disraeli—*Speech in House of*
　　　　　　　　Commons, May 14, 1866.

Mr. Kremlin himself was distinguished for
ignorance, for he had only one idea, and that
was wrong.
　v.　　Benj. Disraeli—*Sybil.*　Bk. IV.
　　　　　　　　　　　　　　Ch. V.

For your ignorance is the mother of your devotion to me.

a.   DRYDEN—*The Maiden Queen.* Act I.
Sc. 2.

He trudg'd along, unknowing what he sought,
And whistled as he went, for want of thought.
b.   DRYDEN—*Cymon and Iphigenia.* L. 84.

Ignorance gives one a large range of probabilities.
c.   GEORGE ELIOT—*Daniel Deronda.*
Bk. II. Ch. XIII.

Ignorance is the dominion of absurdity.
d.   FROUDE—*Short Studies on Great
Subjects. Party Politics.*

Often the cock-loft is empty, in those whom nature hath built many stories high.
e.   FULLER—*Andronicus.* Sect. VI.
Par. 18. 1.

Nothing is more terrible than active ignorance.
f.   GOETHE—*Opinions.*

And his best riches, ignorance of wealth.
g.   GOLDSMITH—*Deserted Village.* L. 61.

Where ignorance is bliss,
'Tis folly to be wise.
h.   GRAY—*On a Distant Prospect of Eton
College.* St. 10.

Who ne'er knew salt, or heard the billows roar.
i.   HOMER—*Odyssey.* Bk. XI. L. 153.
Pope's trans.

It was a childish ignorance,
But now 'tis little joy
To know I'm further off from heaven
Than when I was a boy.
j.   HOOD—*I Remember, I Remember.*

The living man who does not learn, is dark, dark, like one walking in the night.
k.   MING LUM PAOU KEËN—Trans. for
Chinese Repository by Dr. Wm. Milne.

A man may live long, and die at last in ignorance of many truths, which his mind was capable of knowing, and that with certainty.
l.   LOCKE—*Human Understanding.*
Bk. I. Ch. II.

But let a man know that there are things to be known, of which he is ignorant, and it is so much carved out of his domain of universal knowledge.
m.   HORACE MANN—*Lectures on Education.*
Lecture VI.

Not to know me argues yourselves unknown,
The lowest of your throng.
n.   MILTON—*Paradise Lost.* Bk. IV.
L. 830.

It is better to be unborn than untaught: for ignorance is the root of misfortune.
o.   PLATO.

From ignorance our comfort flows,
The only wretched are the wise.
p.   PRIOR—*To the Hon. Chas. Montague.*
1692.

And seeing ignorance is the curse of God,
Knowledge the wing wherewith we fly to heaven.
q.   *Henry VI.* Pt. II. Act IV. Sc. 7.
L. 78.

Madam, thou errest: I say, there is no darkness, but ignorance; in which thou art more puzzled, than the Egyptians in their fog.
r.   *Twelfth Night.* Act IV. Sc. 2. L. 44.

O thou monster, Ignorance, how deformed dost thou look!
s.   *Love's Labour's Lost.* Act IV. Sc. 2.
L. 21.

Ignorance is the mother of devotion.
t.   JEREMY TAYLOR—*To a Person newly
Converted to the Church of England.*
1657.

* * * Where blind and naked Ignorance
Delivers brawling judgments, unashamed,
On all things all day long.
u.   TENNYSON—*Idylls of the King.* *Vivien.*
L. 515.

IMAGINATION.

Imagination is the air of mind.
v.   BAILEY—*Festus.* Sc. *Another and a
Better World.*

Seem'd washing his hands with invisible soap
In imperceptible water.
w.   HOOD—*Miss Kilmansegg.* *Her
Christening.*

To those who see only with their eyes, the distant is always indistinct and little, becoming less and less as it recedes, till utterly lost; but to the imagination, which thus reverses the perspective of the senses, the far off is great and imposing, the magnitude increasing with the distance.
x.   MRS. JAMESON—*Studies. Detached
Thoughts.*

These are the gloomy companions of a disturbed imagination; the melancholy madness of poetry, without the inspiration.
y.   JUNIUS—*Letter VIII. To Sir W.
Draper.*

When I could not sleep for cold
  I had fire enough in my brain,
And builded with roofs of gold
  My beautiful castles in Spain!
   a.   Lowell—*Aladdin.* St. 1.

His imagination resembled the wings of an
ostrich. It enabled him to run, though not
to soar.
   b.   Macaulay—*On John Dryden.* 1828.

Imagination rules the world.
   c.   Napoleon I.

And as imagination bodies forth
The forms of things unknown, the poet's pen
Turns them to shapes and gives to airy
    nothing
A local habitation and a name.
   d.   *Midsummer-Night's Dream.* Act V.
                        Sc. 1. L. 14.

In my mind's eye, Horatio.
   e.   *Hamlet.* Act I. Sc. 2. L. 186.

Look, what thy soul holds dear, imagine it
To lie that way thou go'st, not whence thou
    com'st:
Suppose the singing birds musicians;
The grass whereon thou tread'st the presence
    strew'd;
The flowers fair ladies, and thy steps no more
Than a delightful measure or a dance.
   f.   *Richard II.* Act I. Sc. 3. L. 286.

The best in this kind are but shadows; and
the worst are no worse, if imagination amend
them.
   g.   *Midsummer-Night's Dream.* Act V.
                        Sc. 1. L. 213.

The lunatic, the lover and the poet
Are of imagination all compact.
   h.   *Midsummer-Night's Dream.* Act V.
                        Sc. 1. L. 7.

This is a gift that I have, simple, simple;
a foolish extravagant spirit, full of forms,
figures, shapes, objects, ideas, apprehensions,
motions, revolutions; these are begot in the
ventricle of memory, nourished in the womb
of *pia mater*, and delivered upon the mellow-
ing of occasion.
   i.   *Love's Labour's Lost.* Act IV. Sc. 2.
                        L. 67.

This is the very coinage of your brain:
This bodiless creation ecstasy.
   j.   *Hamlet.* Act III. Sc. 4. L. 137.

But thou, that did'st appear so fair
  To fond imagination,
Dost rival in the light of day
  Her delicate creation.
   k.   Wordsworth—*Yarrow Visited.*

IMMORTALITY.

It must be so—Plato, thou reasonest well!—
Else whence this pleasing hope, this fond
    desire,
This longing after immortality?
Or whence this secret dread, and inward
    horror,
Of falling into nought? Why shrinks the
    soul
Back on herself, and startles at destruction?
'Tis the divinity that stirs within us;
'Tis heaven itself, that points out an hereafter,
And intimates eternity to man.
   l.   Addison—*Cato.* Act V. Sc. 1.

The stars shall fade away, the sun himself
Grow dim with age, and nature sink in years,
But thou shall flourish in immortal youth,
Unhurt amidst the wars of elements,
The wrecks of matter, and the crush of worlds.
   m.   Addison—*Cato.* Act V. Sc. 1.

No, no! The energy of life may be
Kept on after the grave, but not begun;
And he who flagg'd not in the earthly strife,

From strength to strength advancing—only he
His soul well-knit, and all his battles won,
Mounts, and that hardly, to eternal life.
   n.   Matthew Arnold—*Sonnet.*
                         Immortality.

On the cold cheek of Death smiles and roses
    are blending,
And beauty immortal awakes from the tomb.
   o.   James Beattie—*The Hermit.* St. 6.
                        Last lines.

There is nothing strictly immortal, but
immortality. Whatever hath no beginning
may be confident of no end.
   p.   Sir Thomas Browne—*Hydriotaphia.*
                        Ch. V.

I have been dying for twenty years, now I
am going to live.
   q.   Jas. Drummond Burns—*His Last*
                        Words.

A good man never dies.
   r.   Callimachus—*Epigrams.* X.

Immortality is the glorious discovery of
Christianity.
   s.   Wm. Ellery Channing—*Immortality.*

'Tis immortality to die aspiring,
As if a man were taken quick to heaven.
   t.   Geo. Chapman—*Byron's Conspiracy.*
               Act I. Sc. 1. L. 254.

There is, I know not how, in the minds of
men, a certain presage, as it were, of a future
existence! and this takes the deepest root,
and is most discoverable, in the greatest
geniuses and most exalted souls.
   u.   Cicero.

One short sleep past, we wake eternally,
And Death shall be no more; Death, thou
　　shalt die.
　　a.　　DONNE—*Sonnet.*

Yet spirit immortal, the tomb cannot bind
　　thee,
　　But like thine own eagle that soars to the
　　　　sun
Thou springest from bondage and leavest be-
　　hind thee
A name which before thee no mortal hath
　　won.
　　b.　　LEONARD HEATH—*The Grave of
　　　　　　　　　　　　　　　Bonaparte.*

'Tis true; 'tis certain; man though dead
　　retains
Part of himself; the immortal mind remains.
　　c.　　HOMER—*Iliad.* Bk. XXIII. L. 122.
　　　　　　　　　　　　　Pope's trans.

But all lost things are in the angels' keeping,
　　Love;
No past is dead for us, but only sleeping,
　　Love;
The years of Heaven with all earth's little
　　pain
　　　　Make good,
Together there we can begin again
　　　　In babyhood.
　　d.　　HELEN HUNT—*At Last.* St. 6.

He ne'er is crowned with immortality
Who fears to follow where airy voices lead.
　　e.　　KEATS—*Endymion.* Bk. II.

I long to believe in immortality. * * *
If I am destined to be happy with you here—
how short is the longest life. I wish to believe
in immortality—I wish to live with you
forever.
　　f.　　KEATS—*Letters to Fanny Brawne.*
　　　　　　　　　　　　　　　　XXXVI.

No, no, I'm sure,
My restless spirit never could endure
To brood so long upon one luxury,
Unless it did, though fearfully, espy
A hope beyond the shadow of a dream.
　　g.　　KEATS—*Endymion.* Bk. I.

And in the wreck of noble lives
Something immortal still survives.
　　h.　　LONGFELLOW—*The Building of the Ship.*
　　　　　　　　　　　　　　　　L. 375.

Safe from temptation, safe from sin's pollu-
　　tion,
She lives, whom we call dead.
　　i.　　LONGFELLOW—*Resignation.* St. 7.

I came from God, and I'm going back to
God, and I won't have any gaps of death in
the middle of my life.
　　j.　　GEORGE MACDONALD—*Mary Marston.*
　　　　　　　　　　　　　　　　Ch. LVII.

For spirits that live throughout
Vital in every part, not as frail man,
In entrails, heart or head, liver or reins,
Cannot but by annihilating die.
　　k.　　MILTON—*Paradise Lost.* Bk. VI.
　　　　　　　　　　　　　　　　L. 345.

　　　　　　　For who would lose,
Though full of pain, this intellectual being,
Those thoughts that wander through eternity,
To perish rather, swallow'd up and lost
In the wide womb of uncreated night,
Devoid of sense and motion?
　　l.　　MILTON—*Paradise Lost.* Bk. II.
　　　　　　　　　　　　　　　　L. 146.

They eat, they drink, and in communion
　　sweet
Quaff immortality and joy.
　　m.　　MILTON—*Paradise Lost.* Bk. V.
　　　　　　　　　　　　　　　　L. 637.

When the good man yields his breath
(For the good man never dies).
　　n.　　MONTGOMERY—*The Wanderer of
　　　　　　　　　　　　Switzerland.* Pt. V.

　　　　　　　Immortality
Alone could teach this mortal how to die.
　　o.　　D. M. MULOCK—*Looking Death in the
　　　　　　　　　　　　　Face.* L. 77.

All men desire to be immortal.
　　p.　　THEODORE PARKER—*A Sermon on
　　　　　　　Immortal Life.* Sept. 20, 1846.

　　　　　　　　I hold it ever,
Virtue and cunning were endowments greater
Than nobleness and riches: careless heirs
May the two latter darken and expend;
But immortality attends the former,
Making a man a god.
　　q.　　*Pericles.* Act III. Sc. 2. L. 26.

Look, here's the warrant, Claudio, for thy
　　death:
'Tis now dead midnight, and by eight to-
　　morrow
Thou must be made immortal.
　　r.　　*Measure for Measure.* Act IV. Sc. 2.
　　　　　　　　　　　　　　　　L. 66.

Thy lord shall never die, the whiles this verse
Shall live, and surely it shall live for ever:
For ever it shall live, and shall rehearse
His worthy praise, and vertues dying never,
Though death his soule do from his bodie
　　sever;
And thou thyselfe herein shalt also live;
Such grace the heavens doe to my verses give.
　　s.　　SPENSER—*The Ruines of Time.* L. 253.

Man is so created that as to his internal he
cannot die; for he is capable of believing in
God, and thus of being conjoined to God by
faith and love, and to be conjoined to God is
to live to eternity.
　　t.　　SWEDENBORG—*The New Jerusalem and
　　　　　　　Its Heavenly Doctrine.* Par. 223.

Ah, Christ, that it were possible,
For one short hour to see
The souls we loved, that they might tell us
What and where they be.
a.   TENNYSON—*Maud.*   Pt. XXVI.

Though inland far we be,
Our souls have sight of that immortal sea
Which brought us hither.
b.   WORDSWORTH—*Ode. Intimations of
              Immortality.* St. 9.

'Tis immortality, 'tis that alone,
Amid life's pains, abasements, emptiness,
The soul can comfort, elevate, and fill.
That only, and that amply this performs.
c.   YOUNG—*Night Thoughts.* Night VI.
                        L. 573.

IMPATIENCE.

Impatient straight to flesh his virgin sword.
d.   HOMER—*Odyssey.* Bk. 20.
              L. 381.   Pope's trans.

I wish, and I wish that the spring would go
    faster,
Nor long summer bide so late;
And I could grow on like the foxglove and
    aster,
For some things are ill to wait.
e.   JEAN INGELOW—*Song of Seven. Seven
                     Times Two.*

         I am on fire
To hear this rich reprisal is so nigh
And yet not ours.
f.   *Henry IV.* Pt. I. Act IV. Sc. 1.
                       L. 117.

IMPOSSIBILITY.

A poet without love were a physical and
metaphysical impossibility.
g.   CARLYLE—*Burns. Edinburgh Review.*
                        1828.

It is not a lucky word, this same *impossible;*
no good comes of those that have it so often in
their mouth.
h.   CARLYLE—*French Revolution.* Pt. III.
                     Bk. III. Ch X.

And what's impossible, can't be,
And never, never comes to pass.
i.   GEO. COLMAN (The Younger)—*Broad
             Grins. The Maid of the Moor.*

Hope not for impossibilities.
j.   FULLER—*The Holy and Profane States.
          Of Expecting Preferment.* Maxim 1.

Few things are impossible to diligence and
skill.
k.   SAM'L JOHNSON—*Rasselas.* Ch. XII.

Certainly nothing is unnatural that is not
physically impossible.
l.   R. B. SHERIDAN—*The Critic.* Act II.
                        Sc. 1.

The fact is certain because it is impossible.
m.   TERTULLIAN—*On the Flesh of Christ.*
                    Ch. V.   Pt. II.

INCONSTANCY.

I hate inconstancy—I loathe, detest,
   Abhor, condemn, abjure the mortal made
Of such quicksilver clay that in his breast
   No permanent foundation can be laid.
n.   BYRON—*Don Juan.* Canto II. St. 209.

         Love is not love
Which alters when it alteration finds,
   Or bends with the remover to remove;
O, no! it is an ever-fixed mark
   That looks on tempests and is never shaken;
It is the star to every wandering bark,
   Whose worth's unknown, although his
     height be taken.
o.   *Sonnet CXVI.*

Or as one nail by strength drives out another,
So the remembrance of my former love
Is by a newer object quite forgotten.
p.   *Two Gentlemen of Verona.* Act II.
                     Sc. 4. L. 193.

O, swear not by the moon, the inconstant
         moon,
That monthly changes in her circled orb,
Lest that thy love prove likewise variable.
q.   *Romeo and Juliet.* Act II. Sc. 2.
                       L. 109.

They are not constant, but are changing still.
r.   *Cymbeline.* Act II. Sc. i   L. 30.

INDEPENDENCE.

I have not loved the world, nor the world me;
I have not flatter'd its rank breath, nor bow'd
To its idolatries a patient knee.
s.   BYRON—*Childe Harold.* Canto III.
                        St. 113.

I never thrust my nose into other men's
porridge. It is no bread and butter of mine:
Every man for himself and God for us all.
t.   CERVANTES—*Don Quixote.* Pt. I.
                     Bk. III. Ch. XI.

All we ask is to be let alone.
u.   JEFFERSON DAVIS—*First Message to the
           Confederate Congress,* April 29, 1861.

The whole trouble is that we won't let God
help us.
v.   GEORGE MACDONALD—*The Marquis of
                    Lossie.* Ch. XXVII.

I'll never
Be such a gosling to obey instinct, but stand,
As if a man were author of himself
And knew no other kin.
   a.   *Coriolanus.* Act V. Sc. 3. L. 34.

Speak then to me, who neither beg nor fear
Your favours nor your hate.
   b.   *Macbeth.* Act I. Sc. 3. L. 60.

Thy spirit, Independence, let me share!
   Lord of the lion-heart and eagle-eye,
Thy steps I follow with my bosom bare,
   Nor heed the storm that howls along the sky.
   c.   SMOLLETT—*Ode to Independence.* L. 1.

               * * *   but while
I breathe Heaven's air, and Heaven looks
      down on me,
And smiles at my best meanings, I remain
Mistress of mine own self and mine own soul.
   d.   TENNYSON—*The Foresters.* Act IV.
                                     Sc. 1.

Hail! Independence, hail! Heaven's next
      best gift,
To that of life and an immortal soul!
   e.   THOMSON—*Liberty.* Pt. V. L. 124.

Independence *now;* and INDEPENDENCE FOR-
EVER.
   f.   DANIEL WEBSTER—*Eulogy on Adams
                  and Jefferson,* Aug. 2, 1826.

INDIFFERENCE.

I care for nobody, no, not I,
   If no one cares for me.
   g.   BICKERSTAFF—*Love in a Village.*
                        Act I. Sc. 3. *Song.*

Let the world slide, let the world go:
A fig for care, and a fig for woe!
If I can't pay, why I can owe,
And death makes equal the high and low.
   h.   JOHN HEYWOOD—*Be Merry, Friends.*

And still care not a pin
What they said, or may say.
   i.   POPE—*Epitaph on One who would not
                  be Buried in Westminster.*

At length the morn and cold indifference
came.
   j.   NICHOLAS ROWE—*The Fair Penitent.*
                        Act I. Sc. 1. L. 169.

Set honour in one eye and death i' the other,
And I will look on both indifferently.
   k.   *Julius Cæsar.* Act I. Sc. 2. L. 86.

INFLUENCE.

For witnesses, like watches, go
Just as they're set, too fast or slow;
And, where in Conscience they're strait-lac'd,
'Tis ten to one that side is cast.
   l.   BUTLER—*Hudibras.* Pt. II. Canto III.
                                     L. 361.

For no Act of a man, no Thing (how much
less the man himself!) is extinguished when
it disappears: through considerable time it
still visibly works, though done and vanished.
   m.   CARLYLE—*Essays. The Diamond
                        Necklace.* Ch. XIV.

The work an unknown good man has done
is like a vein of water flowing hidden underground, secretly making the ground green.
   n.   CARLYLE—*Essays. Varnhagen von
                        Ense's Memoirs.*

Be a pattern to others, and then all will go
well; for as a whole city is affected by the
licentious passions and vices of great men, so
it is likewise reformed by their moderation.
   o.   CICERO.

He raised a mortal to the skies;
She drew an angel down.
   p.   DRYDEN—*Alexander's Feast.* L. 169.

Blessed influence of one true loving human
soul on another.
   q.   GEORGE ELIOT—*Janet's Repentance.*
                                     Ch. XIX.

O may I join the choir invisible
Of those immortal dead who live again
In minds made better by their presence; live
In pulses stirred to generosity,
In deeds of daring rectitude, in scorn
For miserable aims that end with self.
In thoughts sublime that pierce the night like
      stars,
And with their mild persistence urge man's
      search
To vaster issues.
   r.   GEORGE ELIOT—*O May I Join the Choir
                                     Invisible.*

Nor knowest thou what argument
Thy life to thy neighbor's creed has lent,
All are needed by each one;
Nothing is fair or good alone.
   s.   EMERSON—*Each and All.*

'Tis Lilith.
         Who?
Adam's first wife is she.
Beware the lure within her lovely tresses,
The splendid sole adornment of her hair;
When she succeeds therewith a youth to snare,
Not soon again she frees him from her jesses.
   t.   GOETHE—*Faust.* Sc. XXI. *Walpurgis
                  Night.* Bayard Taylor's trans.

He spake, and into every heart his words
Carried new strength and courage.
   u.   HOMER—*Iliad.* Bk. V. L. 586.
                              Bryant's trans.

No action, whether foul or fair,
Is ever done, but it leaves somewhere
A record, written by fingers ghostly,
As a blessing or a curse, and mostly
In the greater weakness or greater strength
Of the acts which follow it.
   v.   LONGFELLOW—*Christus. The Golden
                  Legend.* Pt. II. *A Village Church.*

So when a great man dies,
  For years beyond our ken,
The light he leaves behind him lies
  Upon the paths of men.
  a.   LONGFELLOW—*Charles Sumner.* St. 9.

The very room, coz she was in,
Seemed warm f'om floor to ceilin'.
  b.   LOWELL—*The Biglow Papers.* Second
              Series. *The Courtin'.* St. 6.

You've got to save your own soul first, and
then the souls of your neighbors if they will
let you; and for that reason you must cultivate, not a spirit of criticism, but the talents
that attract people to the hearing of the Word.
  c.   GEO. MACDONALD— *The Marquis of
              Lossie.* Ch. XXVII.

                                No life
Can be pure in its purpose or strong in its
    strife
And all life not be purer and stronger thereby.
  d.   OWEN MEREDITH (Lord Lytton)—
              Lucile. Pt. II. Canto VI. St. 40.

Thou wert my guide, philosopher, and
friend.
  e.   POPE—*Essay on Man.* Ep. IV. L. 390.

                              Such souls,
Whose sudden visitations daze the world,
Vanish like lightning, but they leave behind
A voice that in the distance far away
Wakens the slumbering ages.
  f.   SIR HENRY TAYLOR—*Philip Van
              Artevelde.* Pt. I. Act 1. Sc. 7.

I am a part of all that I have met.
  g.   TENNYSON—*Ulysses.* L. 18.

I thank God that if I am gifted with little
of the spirit which is said to be able to raise
mortals to the skies, I have yet none, as I trust,
of that other spirit, which would drag angels
down.
  h.   DANIEL WEBSTER—*Second Speech on
              Foot's Resolution,* Jan. 26, 1830.

It is very true that I have said that I considered Napoleon's presence in the field equal
to forty thousand men in the balance. This
is a very loose way of talking; but the idea
is a very different one from that of his presence at a battle being equal to a reinforcement
of forty thousand men.
  i.   DUKE OF WELLINGTON—*Memorandum.*
              Sept. 18, 1836.

Controls them and subdues, transmutes, be-
    reaves
Of their bad influence, and their good receives.
  j.   WORDSWORTH—*Character of the Happy
              Warrior.*

Whose powers shed round him in the com-
    mon strife,
Or mild concerns of ordinary life,
A constant influence, a peculiar grace.
  k.   WORDSWORTH—*Character of the Happy
              Warrior.*

INGRATITUDE.

Deserted, at his utmost need,
By those his former bounty fed;
On the bare earth exposed he lies,
With not a friend to close his eyes.
  l.   DRYDEN—*Alexander's Feast.* St. 4.

Ingratitude's a weed of every clime,
It thrives too fast at first, but fades in time.
  m.   SIR SAM'L GARTH—*Epistle to the Earl
              of Godolphin.* L. 27.

That man may last, but never lives,
Who much receives, but nothing gives;
Whom none can love, whom none can thank,
Creation's blot, creation's blank.
  n.   THOMAS GIBBONS— *When Jesus Dwelt.*

A man is very apt to complain of the ingratitude of those who have risen far above
him.
  o.   SAM'L JOHNSON—*Boswell's Life of
              Johnson.* 1776.

All the stor'd vengeances of heaven fall
On her ungrateful top.
  p.   *King Lear.* Act II. Sc. 4. L. 164.

Blow, blow, thou winter wind,
Thou art not so unkind
  As man's ingratitude:
Thy tooth is not so keen,
Because thou art not seen,
  Although thy breath be rude.
  q.   *As You Like It.* Act II. Sc. 7. L. 174.

He hath eaten me out of house and home.
  r.   *Henry IV.* Pt. II. Act II. Sc. 1.
                                        L. 79.

    How sharper than a serpent's tooth it is
To have a thankless child.
  s.   *King Lear.* Act I. Sc. 4. L. 310.

I hate ingratitude more in a man,
Than lying, vainness, babbling, drunkenness,
Or any taint of vice.
  t.   *Twelfth Night.* Act III. Sc. 4. L. 388.

Ingratitude is monstrous; and for the multitude to be ingrateful, were to make a
monster of the multitude.
  u.   *Coriolanus.* Act II. Sc. 3. L. 8.

Ingratitude! thou marble-hearted fiend,
More hideous, when thou show'st thee in a
    child,
Than the sea-monster!
  v.   *King Lear.* Act I. Sc. 4. L. 28.

This was the most unkindest cut of all;
For when the noble Cæsar saw him sta℧
Ingratitude, more strong than traitor's arms,
Quite vanquish'd him; then burst his mighty
      heart;
And, in his mantle muffling up his face,
Even at the base of Pompey's statue,
Which all the while ran blood, great Cæsar fell.
  a.   *Julius Cæsar.* Act III. Sc. 2. L. 187.

What, would'st thou have a serpent sting
thee twice?
  b.   *Merchant of Venice.* Act IV. Sc. 1.
                              L. 69.

He that's ungrateful, has no guilt but one;
All other crimes may pass for virtues in him.
  c.   Young—*Busiris.*

INHERITANCE.

And all to leave what with his toil he won,
To that unfeather'd two-legged thing, a son.
  d.   Dryden—*Absalom and Achitophel.*
                      Pt. I. L. 169.

He lives to build, not boast, a generous race;
No tenth transmitter of a foolish face.
  e.   Richard Savage—*The Bastard.* L. 7.

INJUSTICE.

Injustice swift, erect and unconfin'd,
Sweeps the wide earth, and tramples o'er
      mankind.
  f.   Homer—*Iliad.* Bk. IX. L. 576.
                      Pope's trans.

Ah, how unjust to Nature and himself
Is thoughtless, thankless, inconsistent man!
  g.   Young—*Night Thoughts.* Night II.
                      L. 112.

INN-KEEPING (*See* Occupations).

INNOCENCE.

E'en drunken Andrew felt the blow
  That innocence can give,
When its resistless accents flow
  To bid affection live.
  h.   Bloomfield—*The Drunken Father.*
                      St. 18.

What can innocence hope for,
When such as sit her judges are corrupted!
  i.   Massinger—*Maid of Honor.* Act V.
                      Sc. 2.

Oh, keep me innocent, make others great!
  j.   *Written on a window by* Caroline
          Matilda, *Queen of Denmark.*

He's armed without that's innocent within.
  k.   Pope—*Epistles of Horace.* Ep. I. Bk. I.
                      L. 94.

Hence, bashful cunning!
And prompt me, plain and holy innocence!
  l.   *Tempest.* Act III. Sc. I. L. 81.

I doubt not then but innocence shall make
False accusation blush, and tyranny
Tremble at patience.
  m.   *Winter's Tale.* Act III. Sc. 2. L. 31.

O, take the sense, sweet, of my innocence,
Love takes the meaning in love's conference.
  n.   *Midsummer-Night's Dream.* Act II.
                  Sc. 2. L. 45.

We were as twinn'd lambs that did frisk i' the
      sun,
And bleat the one at the other; what we
      chang'd
Was innocence for innocence; we knew not
The doctrine of ill-doing, nor dream'd
That any did.
  o.   *Winter's Tale.* Act I. Sc. 2. L. 67.

O, white innocence,
That thou shouldst wear the mask of guilt to
      hide
Thine awful and serenest countenance
From those who know thee not!
  p.   Shelley—*The Cenci.* Act V. Sc. 3.
                      L. 24.

INSANITY.

No excellent soul is exempt from a mixture
of madness.
  q.   Aristotle—*Problem.* Sect. 30.

A mere madness, to live like a wretch, and
die rich.
  r.   Burton—*Anatomy of Melancholy.*
             Pt. I. Sect. 2. Memb. 3.
                    Subsect. 13.

Much madness is divinest sense
  To a discerning eye;
Much sense the starkest madness.
  'Tis the majority
In this, as all, prevails.
  Assent, and you are sane;
Demur,—you're straightway dangerous,
  And handled with a chain.
  s.   Emily Dickinson—*Poems.* XI.
                    (Ed. 1891).

For those whom God to ruin has designed
He fits for fate, and first destroys their mind.
  t.   Dryden—*Fables.* *The Hind and the
          Panther.* Pt. III. L. 2,387.

There is a pleasure, sure,
In being mad, which none but madmen know!
  u.   Dryden—*Spanish Friar.* Act II.
                    St. 1.

The alleged power to charm down insanity,
or ferocity in beasts, is a power behind the eye.
  v.   Emerson—*Essays.* *Conduct of Life.
                  Of Behaviour.*

O, hark! what mean those yells and cries?
  His chain some furious madman breaks;
He comes—I see his glaring eyes;
  Now, now, my dungeon grate he shakes.
Help! Help! He's gone!—O fearful woe,
  Such screams to hear, such sights to see!
My brain, my brain,—I know, I know
  I am *not* mad but soon *shall be.*
    a.   MATTHEW GREGORY LEWIS (" Monk
           Lewis ")—*The Maniac.*

My dear Sir, take any road, you can't go
amiss. The whole State is one vast insane
asylum.
    b.   JAMES L. PETIGRU—*On being asked the
         way to the Charleston, S. C., Insane
         Asylum.* 1860.

Fetter strong madness in a silken thread.
    c.   *Much Ado About Nothing.* Act V.
                   Sc. 1. L. 25.

I am not mad; I would to heaven I were!
For then, 'tis like I should forget myself.
    d.   *King John.* Act III. Sc. 4. L. 48.

                 It shall be so:
Madness in great ones must not unwatch'd go.
    e.   *Hamlet.* Act III. Sc. 1. L. 196.

Madam, I swear I use no art at all.
That he is mad, 'tis true, 'tis true 'tis pity;
And pity 'tis 'tis true.
    f.   *Hamlet.* Act II. Sc. 2. L. 96.

  Though this be madness, yet there is
method in 't.
    g.   *Hamlet.* Act II. Sc. 2. L. 208.

You will never run mad, niece;
No, not till a hot January.
    h.   *Much Ado About Nothing.* Act I.
                   Sc. 1. L. 93.

           We are not ourselves
When nature, being oppress'd, commands
  the mind
To suffer with the body.
    i.   *King Lear.* Act II. Sc. 4. L. 109.

Were such things here as we do speak about?
Or have we eaten on the insane root
That takes the reason prisoner?
    j.   *Macbeth.* Act I. Sc. 3. L. 83.

INSECTS.
Ant.

Ants never sleep.
    k.   EMERSON—*Nature.* Ch. IV.

Bacillus.

Oh, powerful bacillus,
With wonder how you fill us,
    Every day!
While medical detectives,
With powerful objectives,
    Watch your play.
    l.   WM. TOD HELMUTH—*Ode to the
                    Bacillus.*

21

Bee.

The honey-bee that wanders all day long
The field, the woodland, and the garden o'er,
To gather in his fragrant winter store,
Humming in calm content his winter song,
Seeks not alone the rose's glowing breast,
The lily's dainty cup, the violet's lips,
But from all rank and noxious weeds he sips
The single drop of sweetness closely pressed
Within the poison chalice.
    m.   ANNE C. LYNCH BOTTA—*The Lesson of
                    the Bee.*

His labor is a chant,
  His idleness a tune;
Oh, for a bee's experience
  Of clovers and of noon!
    n.   EMILY DICKINSON—*Poems.* XV.
                    The Bee.

The pedigree of honey
  Does not concern the bee;
A clover, any time, to him
  Is aristocracy.
    o.   EMILY DICKINSON—*Poems.* V.
                  (Ed. 1891).

Burly, dozing humblebee,
Where thou art is clime for me.
Let them sail for Porto Rique,
Far-off heats through seas to seek.
I will follow thee alone,
Thou animated torrid-zone!
    p.   EMERSON—*The Humble-Bee.*

Seeing only what is fair,
Sipping only what is sweet,
    *   *   *   *   *   *
Leave the chaff, and take the wheat.
    q.   EMERSON—*The Humble-Bee.*

The careful insect 'midst his works I view,
Now from the flowers exhaust the fragrant
    dew,
With golden treasures load his little thighs,
And steer his distant journey through the
    skies.
    r.   GAY—*Rural Sports.* Canto I. L. 82.

Bees work for man, and yet they never bruise
  Their Master's flower, but leave it having
    done,
As fair as ever and as fit to use;
  So both the flower doth stay and honey run.
    s.   HERBERT—*The Church. Providence.*

"O bees, sweet bees!" I said; "that nearest
    field
Is shining white with fragrant immortelles.
Fly swiftly there and drain those honey
    wells."
    t.   HELEN HUNT—*My Bees.*

          Listen! O, listen!
Here ever hum the golden bees
Underneath full-blossomed trees,
At once with glowing fruit and flowers
    crowned.
    u.   LOWELL—*The Sirens.* L. 94.

The bee is enclosed, and shines preserved, in a tear of the sisters of Phaëton, so that it seems enshrined in its own nectar.   It has obtained a worthy reward for its great toils; we may suppose that the bee itself would have desired such a death.

   a.   Martial—*Epigrams.* Bk. IV.
Ep. 32.

For so work the honey-bees,
Creatures that by a rule in nature teach
The act of order to a peopled kingdom.
They have a king and officers of sorts,
Where some, like magistrates, correct at home,
Others, like merchants, venture trade abroad,
Others like soldiers, armed in their stings,
Make boot upon the summer's velvet buds,
Which pillage they with merry march bring
    home.

   b.   *Henry V.* Act I. Sc. 2. L. 188.

My banks they are furnish'd with bees,
Whose murmur invites one to sleep.

   c.   Shenstone—*A Pastoral Ballad.*
Pt. II. *Hope.*

The solitary Bee
Whose buzzing was the only sound of life,
    Flew there on restless wing,
Seeking in vain one blossom where to fix.

   d.   Southey—*Thalaba.* Bk. VI. St. 13.

The little bee returns with evening's gloom,
   To join her comrades in the braided hive,
Where, housed beside their mighty honey-
    comb,
They dream their polity shall long survive.

   e.   Charles (Tennyson) Turner—*A
Summer Night in the Bee Hive.*

How doth the little busy bee
   Improve each shining hour,
And gather honey all the day
   From every opening flower.

   f.   Watts—*Song.* 20.

The wild Bee reels from bough to bough
   With his furry coat and his gauzy wing,
Now in a lily cup, and now
   Setting a jacinth bell a-swing,
    In his wandering.

   g.   Oscar Wilde—*Her Voice.*

Beetle.

O'er folded blooms
   On swirls of musk,
The beetle booms adown the glooms
   And bumps along the dusk.

   h.   James Whitcomb Riley—*The Beetle.*

And often, to our comfort, shall we find
The sharded beetle in a safer hold
Than is the full-winged eagle.

   i.   *Cymbeline.* Act III. Sc. 3. L. 19.

And the poor beetle that we tread upon,
In corporal sufferance finds a pang as great
As when a giant dies.

   j.   *Measure for Measure.* Act III. Sc. 1.
L. 79.

Butterfly.

I'd be a butterfly, born in a bower,
Where roses and lilies and violets meet.

   k.   Thomas Haynes Bayly—*I'd be a
Buttevfly, Born in a Bower.*

With the rose the butterfly's deep in love,
   A thousand times hovering round;
But round himself, all tender like gold,
   The sun's sweet ray is hovering found.

   l.   Heine—*Book of Songs. New Spring.*
No. 7. St. 1.

Far out at sea,—the sun was high,
   While veer'd the wind and flapped the sail,
We saw a snow-white butterfly
   Dancing before the fitful gale,
    Far out at sea.

   m.   Richard Hengist Horne—*Genius.*

The gold-barr'd butterflies to and fro
   And over the waterside wander'd and wove
As heedless and idle as clouds that rove
And drift by the peaks of perpetual snow.

   n.   Joaquin Miller—*Songs of the
Sun-Lands. Isles of the Amazons.*
Pt. III. St. 41.

Much converse do I find in thee,
Historian of my infancy!
Float near me; do not yet depart!
Dead times revive in thee:
Thou bring'st, gay creature as thou art!
A solemn image to my heart.

   o.   Wordsworth—*To a Butterfly.*

Dragonfly.

The beauteous dragonfly's dancing
By the waves of the rivulet glancing;
She dances here and she dances there,
The glimmering, glittering flutterer fair.

   p.   Heine—*Latest Poems. The Dragonfly.*

Firefly.

The fireflies o'er the meadow
   In pulses come and go.

   q.   Lowell—*Midnight.* St. 3.

Flea.

" I cannot raise my worth too high ;
Of what vast consequence am I ! "
" Not of the importance you suppose,"
Replies a Flea upon his nose ;
" Be humble, learn thyself to scan ;
Know, pride was never made for man."

   r.   Gay—*The Man and the Flea.*

A blockhead, bit by fleas, put out the light,
And chuckling cried, "Now you can't see
    to bite."

   s.   *Greek Anthology.*

It was many and many a year ago,
  In a District styled E. C.,
That a monster dwelt whom I came to know
  By the name of Cannibal Flea,
And the brute was possessed with no other
    thought
Than to live—and to live on me.
   a.   THOS. HOOD, JR.—*The Cannibal Flea.*
               Parody on POE's *Annabel Lee.*

So, naturalists observe, a flea
Has smaller fleas that on him prey;
And these have smaller still to bite 'em,
And so proceed *ad infinitum.*
   b.   SWIFT—*Poetry. A Rhapsody.*

Fly.

We see how flies, and spiders, and the like,
get a sepulchre in amber, more durable than
the monument and embalming of the body of
any king.
   c.   BACON—*Sylvia Sylvarum.* Century I.
                      Experiment 100.

The fly that sips treacle is lost in the sweets.
   d.   GAY—*The Beggar's Opera.* Act II.
                      Sc. 2. L. 35.

Busy, curious, thirsty fly,
Drink with me and drink as I!
Freely welcome to my cup,
Could'st thou sip and sip it up;
Make the most of life you may;
Life is short and wears away.
   e.   WILLIAM OLDYS—*The Fly.*

Oh! that the memories which survive us here
Were half so lovely as these wings of thine!
Pure relics of a blameless life, that shine
Now thou art gone.
   f.   CHARLES (TENNYSON) TURNER—*On
              Finding a Small Fly Crushed in a
                       Book.*

Glow-worm.

Glow-worms on the ground are moving,
As if in the torch-dance circling.
   g.   HEINE—*Book of Songs. Donna Clara.*
                       St. 17.

Ye living lamps, by whose dear light
  The nightingale does sit so late;
And studying all the summer night,
  Her matchless songs does meditate.
   h.   ANDREW MARVELL—*The Mower to the
                         Glow-worm.*

Here's a health to the glow-worm, Death's
sober lamplighter.
   i.   OWEN MEREDITH (Lord Lytton)—
                    Au Café. XXXIX.

When evening closes Nature's eye,
  The glow-worm lights her little spark
To captivate her favorite fly
  And tempt the rover through the dark.
   j.   MONTGOMERY—*The Glow-worm.*

Among the crooked lanes, on every hedge,
The glow-worm lights his gem; and through
    the dark,
A moving radiance twinkles.
   k.   THOMSON—*The Seasons. Summer.*
                       L. 1,682.

Gnat.

A work of skill, surpassing sense,
A labor of Omnipotence;
Though frail as dust it meet thine eye,
He form'd this gnat who built the sky.
   l.   MONTGOMERY—*The Gnat.*

Grasshopper.

Happy insect! what can be
In happiness compared to thee?
Fed with nourishment divine,
The dewy morning's gentle wine!
Nature waits upon thee still,
And thy verdant cup does fill;
'Tis fill'd wherever thou dost tread,
Nature's self's thy Ganymede.
   m.   ABRAHAM COWLEY—*Anacreontiques.*
              No. 10.   *The Grasshopper.*

Green little vaulter, in the sunny grass,
  Catching your heart up at the feel of June;
  Sole noise that's heard amidst the lazy noon,
When ev'n the bees lag at the summoning
    brass.
   n.   LEIGH HUNT—*To the Grasshopper and
                      the Cricket.*

When all the birds are faint with the hot sun,
And hide in cooling trees, a voice will run
From hedge to hedge about the new-mown
    mead;
That is the grasshopper's—he takes the lead
  In summer luxury—he has never done
  With his delights, for when tired out with
    fun,
He rests at ease beneath some pleasant weed.
   o.   KEATS—*On the Grasshopper and Cricket.*

Katydid.

Thou art a female, Katydid!
  I know it by the trill
That quivers through thy piercing notes
  So petulant and shrill.
I think there is a knot of you
  Beneath the hollow tree,
A knot of spinster Katydids,—
  Do Katydids drink tea?
   p.   O. W. HOLMES—*To an Insect.*

Where the katydid works her chromatic reed
  on the walnut-tree over the well.
   q.   WALT WHITMAN—*Leaves of Grass.*
               Pt. XXXIII. St. 196.

Louse.

Ha! Whare ye gaun, ye crawlin' ferlie?
Your impudence protects you sairly;
I canna say but ye strunt rarely
  Owre gauze an' lace;
Though faith! I fear ye dine but sparely
On sic a place.
  a.   BURNS—*To a Louse.*

Midge.

Meanwhile, there is dancing in yonder green
    bower,
  A swarm of young midges, they dance high
    and low;
'Tis a sweet little species that lives but one
    hour,
  And the eldest was born half an hour ago.
  b.   OWEN MEREDITH (Lord Lytton)—
                                Midges.

The midge's wing beats to and fro
A thousand times ere one can utter " O."
  c.   COVENTRY PATMORE—*The Cry at
                                Midnight.*

Mosquito.

Fair insect! that, with threadlike legs spread
    out,
  And blood-extracting bill and filmy wing,
Dost murmur, as thou slowly sail'st about,
  In pitiless ears full many a plaintive thing,
And tell how little our large veins would bleed,
Would we but yield them to thy bitter need.
  d.   BRYANT—*To a Mosquito.*

Mote.

The gay motes that people the sunbeams.
  e.   MILTON—*Il Penseroso.* L. 8.

Moth.

What gained we, little moth? Thy ashes,
  Thy one brief parting pang may show:
And withering thoughts for soul that dashes,
  From deep to deep, are but a death more
    slow.
  f.   CARLYLE—*Tragedy of the Night Moth.*
                                St. 14.

Spider.

We see spiders, flies, or ants entombed and
preserved forever in amber, a more than royal
tomb.
  g.   BACON—*Historia Vitæ et Mortis.*

Or (almost) like a Spider, who, confin'd
In her Web's centre, shakt with every winde;
Moves in an instant, if the buzzing Flie
Stir but a string of her Lawn Canopie.
  h.   DU BARTAS—*Divine Weekes and Workes.
        First Week. Sixth Day.* L. 998.

I've lately had two spiders
Crawling upon my startled hopes—
Now though thy friendly hand has brushed
    'em from me,
Yet still they crawl offensive to mine eyes:
I would have some kind friend to tread upon
    'em.
  i.   COLLEY CIBBER—*Richard III.* (altered).
                        Act IV. Sc. 2. L. 15.

Much like a subtle spider, which doth sit
  In middle of her web, which spreadeth wide:
If aught do touch the utmost thread of it,
  She feels it instantly on every side.
  j.   SIR JOHN DAVIES—*The Immortality of
            the Soul.* Sec. XVIII. *Feeling.*

" Will you walk into my parlour?"
  Said a spider to a fly;
" 'Tis the prettiest little parlour
  That ever you did spy."
  k.   MARY HOWITT—*The Spider and the Fly.*

The spider's touch, how exquisitely fine!
Feels at each thread, and lives along the line.
  l.   POPE—*Essay on Man.* Ep. I. L. 217.

INSTINCT.

But honest instinct comes a volunteer;
Sure never to o'er-shoot, but just to hit,
While still too wide or short in human wit.
  m.   POPE—*Essay on Man.* Ep. III. L. 85.

How instinct varies in the grov'lling swine,
Compar'd, half-reasoning elephant, with
    thine!
'Twixt that and reason what a nice barrier!
Forever sep'rate, yet forever near!
  n.   POPE—*Essay on Man.* Ep. I. L. 221.

Instinct and reason how can we divide?
'Tis the fool's ignorance, and the pedant's
    pride.
  o.   PRIOR—*Solomon on the Vices of the
                World.* Bk. I. L. 231.

Instinct is a great matter; I was a coward
on instinct.
  p.   *Henry IV.* Pt. I. Act II. Sc. 4.
                                L. 299.

A few strong instincts and a few plain rules.
  q.   WORDSWORTH—*Alas! What Boots the
                Long Laborious Quest?*

INSTRUCTION.

We must not contradict, but instruct him
that contradicts us; for a madman is not
cured by another running mad also.
  r.   ANTISTHENES.

He is wise who can instruct us and assist us
in the business of daily virtuous living.
  s.   CARLYLE—*Essays. Schiller.*

Seek to delight, that they may mend mankind.
And, while they captivate, inform the mind.
 a.   COWPER—*Hope.* L. 770.

Instruction does not prevent waste of time
or mistakes; and mistakes themselves are
often the best teachers of all.
 b.   FROUDE—*Short Studies on Great
                    Subjects. Education.*

Men must be taught as if you taught them
    not,
And things unknown propos'd as things
    forgot.
 c.   POPE—*Essay on Criticism.* Pt. III.
                                    L. 15.

            To dazzle let the vain design,
To raise the thought and touch the heart, be
    thine!
 d.   POPE—*Moral Essays.* Ep. II. L. 249.

INTELLECT.

The hand that follows intellect can achieve.
 e.   MICHAEL ANGELO—*The Artist.*
                            Longfellow's trans.

The growth of the intellect is spontaneous
in every expansion. The mind that grows
could not predict the times, the means, the
mode of that spontaneity. God enters by a
private door into every individual.
 f.   EMERSON—*Essays. Intellect.*

'Tis good-will makes intelligence.
 g.   EMERSON—*The Titmouse.* L. 65.

Works of the intellect are great only by
comparison with each other.
 h.   EMERSON—*Literary Ethics.*

Thou living ray of intellectual fire.
 i.   FALCONER—*The Shipwreck.* Canto I.
                                    L. 104.

Glorious indeed is the world of God around
us, but more glorious the world of God within
us. There lies the Land of Song; there lies
the poet's native land.
 j.   LONGFELLOW—*Hyperion.* Bk. I.
                                    Ch. VIII.

A man is not a wall, whose stones are
crushed upon the road; or a pipe, whose
fragments are thrown away at a street corner.
The fragments of an intellect are always good.
 k.   GEORGES SAND—*Handsome Lawrence.*
                                    Ch. II.

The march of intellect.
 l.   SOUTHEY—*Sir Thos. More; or, Colloquies
                on the Progress and Prospects of
                Society.* Vol. II. P. 361.

Mind is the great lever of all things; human
thought is the process by which human ends
are alternately answered.
 m.   DANIEL WEBSTER—*Address at the
                Laying of the Corner Stone of the
                Bunker Hill Monument.*

INTEMPERANCE.

Inspiring bold John Barleycorn,
What dangers thou canst make us scorn!
Wi' tippenny, we fear nae evil;
Wi' usquebae, we'll face the devil!
 n.   BURNS—*Tam o' Shanter.* L. 105.

Man, being reasonable, must get drunk;
    The best of life is but intoxication:
Glory, the grape, love, gold, in these are sunk
    The hopes of all men and of every nation;
Without their sap, how branchless were the
        trunk
Of life's strange tree, so fruitful on occasion:
But to return,—Get very drunk; and when
You wake with headache, you shall see what
        then.
 o.   BYRON—*Don Juan.* Canto II. St. 179.

Ha! see where the wild-blazing Grog-Shop
        appears,
    As the red waves of wretchedness swell,
How it burns on the edge of tempestuous
        years
    The horrible Light-House of Hell!
 p.   M'DONALD CLARKE—*The Rum Hole.*

We blame the drunkard and despise him,
but why? He cannot help the thirst that
dominates over him; but he could have
helped that rash tampering with the causes
that produced it, for this he is responsible.
The folly and the guilt lie in the tampering,
all the rest is law.
 q.   ABRAHAM COLES—*The Evangel.*
                            P. 219. *Note.*

All learned, and all drunk!
 r.   COWPER—*The Task.* Bk. IV. L. 478.

Gloriously drunk, obey the important call.
 s.   COWPER—*The Task.* Bk. IV. L. 510.

He calls drunkenness an expression identi-
cal with ruin.
 t.   DIOGENES LAERTIUS—*Lives of the
                Philosophers. Pythagoras.* VI.

Then hasten to be drunk, the business of the
        day.
 u.   DRYDEN—*Cymon and Iphigenia.* L. 407.

Petition me no petitions, Sir, to-day;
Let other hours be set apart for business,
To-day it is our pleasure to be drunk;
And this our queen shall be as drunk as we.
 v.   HENRY FIELDING—*Tom Thumb the
                            Great.* Act I. Sc. 2.

        He that is drunken * * *
Is outlawed by himself; all kind of ill
Did with his liquor slide into his veins.
 w.   HERBERT—*The Temple. The Church
                                    Porch.* St. 6.

Shall I, to please another wine-sprung minde,
　Lose all mine own? God hath giv'n me a
　　measure
Short of His can and body; must I find
A pain in that, wherein he finds a pleasure?
　　a.　　Herbert—*The Temple.   The Church
　　　　　　　　　　　Porch.   St.* 7.

Touch the goblet no more !
It will make thy heart sore
To its very core !
　　b.　　Longfellow—*Christus.   The Golden
　　　　　　　　　　　Legend.   Pt.* 1.

　　　　　　　　And when night
Darkens the streets, then wander forth the
　　sons
Of Belial, flown with insolence and wine.
　　c.　　Milton—*Paradise Lost.   L.* 507.

Soon as the potion works, their human count'-
　　nance,
Th' express resemblance of the gods, is
　　chang'd
Into some bruitish form of wolf or bear,
Or ounce or tiger, hog, or bearded goat,
All other parts remaining as they were;
And they, so perfect in their misery,
Not once perceive their foul disfigurement.
　　d.　　Milton—*Comus.   L.* 64.

In vain I trusted that the flowing bowl
Would banish sorrow, and enlarge the soul.
To the late revel, and protracted feast,
Wild dreams succeeded, and disorder'd rest.
　　e.　　Prior—*Solomon.   Bk.* II.   *L.* 106.

　　　　　　　And now, in madness,
Being full of supper and distempering
　　draughts,
Upon malicious bravery, dost thou come
To start my quiet.
　　f.　　*Othello.*   Act I.   Sc. I.   L. 98.

　　　　　Boundless intemperance
In nature is a tyranny, it hath been
Th' untimely emptying of the happy throne,
And fall of many kings.
　　g.　　*Macbeth.*   Act IV.   Sc. 3.   L. 66.

Every inordinate cup is unblessed and the in-
　　gredient is a devil.
　　h.　　*Othello.*   Act II.   Sc. 3.   L. 309.

I have very poor and unhappy brains for
drinking: I could wish courtesy would invent some other custom of entertainment.
　　i.　　*Othello.*   Act II.   Sc. 3.   L. 35.

I told you, sir, they were red-hot with drink-
　　ing;
So full of valour that they smote the air
For breathing in their faces; beat the ground
For kissing of their feet.
　　j.　　*Tempest.*   Act IV.   Sc. 1.   L. 171.

I will ask him for my place again; he shall
tell me, I am a drunkard! Had I as many
mouths as Hydra, such an answer would stop
them all. To be now a sensible man, by and
by a fool, and presently a beast !
　　k.　　*Othello.*   Act II.   Sc. 3.   L. 305.

O monstrous ! but one half-penny-worth of
bread to this intolerable deal of sack !
　　l.　　*Henry IV.*   Pt. I.   Act II.   Sc. 4.   L. 591.

O God, that men should put an enemy in
their mouths to steal away their brains ! that
we should, with joy, pleasance, revel, and applause, transform ourselves into beasts !
　　m.　　*Othello.*   Act II.   Sc. 3.   L. 293.

　　　　　Sweet fellowship in shame !
One drunkard loves another of the name.
　　n.　　*Love's Labour's Lost.*   Act IV.   Sc. 3.
　　　　　　　　　　　　　　　　　L. 48.
What's a drunken man like, fool?
Like a drowned man, a fool and a madman :
one draught above heat makes him a fool; the
second mads him; and a third drowns him.
　　o.　　*Twelfth Night.*   Act I.   Sc. 5.   L. 136.

Drunkenness is an immoderate affection and
use of drink. That I call immoderation that
is besides or beyond that order of good things
for which God hath given us the use of drink.
　　p.　　Jeremy Taylor—*Holy Living.   Of
　　　　　　　　　　　Drunkenness.   Ch.* II.   Pt. 2.

A drunkard clasp his teeth and not undo 'em,
To suffer wet damnation to run through 'em.
　　q.　　Cyril Tourneur—*The Revenger's
　　　　　　　　　　　Tragedy.   Act* III.   Sc. I.

INVESTIGATION.

Nothing has such power to broaden the
mind as the ability to investigate systemati-
cally and truly all that comes under thy ob-
servation in life.
　　r.　　Marcus Aurelius—*Meditations.*
　　　　　　　　　　　　　　　　　Ch. II.
Attempt the end and never stand to doubt;
Nothing's so hard but search will find it out.
　　s.　　Herrick--*Hesperides.   Seeke and
　　　　　　　　　　　　　　　　Finde.*
Hail, fellow, well met,
All dirty and wet :
Find out, if you can,
Who's master, who's man.
　　t.　　Swift—*My Lady's Lamentation.*

INVENTION.

The golden hour of invention must terminate like other hours, and when the man of
genius returns to the cares, the duties, the
vexations, and the amusements of life, his
companions behold him as one of themselves
—the creature of habits and infirmities.
　　u.　　Isaac Disraeli—*Literary Character of
　　　　　　　　　　　Men of Genius.   Ch.* XVI.

Only an inventor knows how to borrow,
and every man is or should be an inventor.

a.　　EMERSON—*Letters and Social Aims.*
Quotation and Originality.

Take the advice of a faithful friend, and
submit thy inventions to his censure.

b.　　FULLER—*The Holy and Profane States.*
Bk. III.　*Of Fancy.*

Electric telegraphs, printing, gas,
　Tobacco, balloons, and steam,
Are little events that have come to pass
　Since the days of the old *régime.*
And, spite of Lemprière's dazzling page,
　I'd give—though it might seem bold—
A hundred years of the Golden Age
　For a year of the Age of Gold.

c.　　HENRY S. LEIGH—*The Two Ages.*

This is a man's invention and his hand.

d.　　*As You Like It.*　Act IV.　Sc. 3.　L. 29.

ISLANDS.

From the sprinkled isles,
Lily on lily, that o'erlace the sea.

e.　　ROBERT BROWNING—*Cleon.*

Fast-anchor'd isle.

f.　　COWPER—*The Task.*　Bk. II.　*The*
Timepiece.　L. 151.

O, it's a snug little island !
A right little, tight little island !

g.　　THOS. DIBDIN—*The Snug Little Island.*

An island salt and bare,
The haunt of seals, and orcs, and sea-mews'
　clang.

h.　　MILTON—*Paradise Lost.*　Bk. XI.
L. 834.

The isle is full of noises,
Sounds, and sweet airs, that give delight and
　hurt not.

i.　　*Tempest.*　Act III.　Sc. 2.　L. 144.

Your isle, which stands
As Neptune's park, ribbed and paled in
With rocks unscalable, and roaring waters.

j.　　*Cymbeline.*　Act III.　Sc. 1.　L. 18.

Ay, many flowering islands lie
In the waters of wide Agony.

k.　　SHELLEY—*Lines written among the*
Enganean Hills.　L. 66.

Sark, fairer than aught in the world that the
　lit skies cover,
Laughs inly behind her cliffs, and the sea-
　farers mark
As a shrine where the sunlight serves, though
　the blown clouds hover, Sark.

l.　　SWINBURNE—*Insularum Ocelle.*

Island of bliss ! amid the subject Seas,
That thunder round thy rocky coasts, set up,
At once the wonder, terror, and delight
Of distant nations ; whose remotest shore
Can soon be shaken by thy naval arm ;
Not to be shook thyself, but all assaults
Baffling, like thy hoar cliffs the loud sea-wave.

m.　　THOMSON—*Seasons.*　*Summer.*　L. 1,597.

J.

JANUARY (*See* MONTHS).

JEALOUSY.

Yet he was jealous, though he did not show it,
For jealousy dislikes the world to know it.

n.　　BYRON—*Don Juan.*　Canto I.　St. 65.

Anger and jealousy can no more bear to
lose sight of their objects than love.

o.　　GEORGE ELIOT—*The Mill on the Floss.*
Bk. I.　Ch. X.

Jealousy is never satisfied with anything
short of an omniscience that would detect the
subtlest fold of the heart.

p.　　GEORGE ELIOT—*The Mill on the Floss.*
Bk. VI.　Ch. X.

Then grew a wrinkle on fair Venus' brow,
The amber sweet of love is turn'd to gall !
Gloomy was Heaven ; bright Phœbus did
　avow
He would be coy, and would not love at all ;
Swearing no greater mischief could be
　wrought,
Than love united to a jealous thought.

q.　　ROBERT GREENE—*Jealousy.*

Jealousy is said to be the offspring of Love.
Yet, unless the parent makes haste to strangle
the child, the child will not rest till it has
poisoned the parent.

r.　　J. C. and A. W. HARE—*Guesses at*
Truth.

In jealousy there is more self-love than love.

s.　　LA ROCHEFOUCAULD—*Maxims.*　No. 334.

O jealousy,
Thou ugliest fiend of hell ! thy deadly venom
Preys on my vitals, turns the healthful hue
Of my fresh cheek to haggard sallowness,
And drinks my spirit up !

t.　　HANNAH MORE—*David and Goliath.*
Pt. V.

No true love there can be without
Its dread penalty—jealousy.

u.　　OWEN MEREDITH (Lord Lytton)—
Lucile.　Pt. II.　Canto I.　St. 24.　L. 8.

Nor jealousy
Was understood, the injur'd lover's hell.

v.　　MILTON—*Paradise Lost.*　Bk. V.
L. 449.

Can't I another's face commend,
Or to her virtues be a friend,
But instantly your forehead louers,
As if her merit lessen'd yours?
   a.   EDWARD MOORE—*The Farmer, the
         Spaniel, and the Cat.* Fable 9. L. 5.

Bear, like the Turk, no brother near the
    throne.
   b.   POPE—*Prologue to the Satires.* L. 197.

But jealous souls will not be answer'd so;
They are not ever jealous for the cause,
But jealous for they are jealous.
   c.   *Othello.* Act III. Sc. 4. L. 158.

          If I shall be condemn'd
Upon surmises, all proofs sleeping else
But what your jealousies awake, I tell you,
'Tis rigour, and not law.
   d.   *Winter's Tale.* Act III. Sc. 2. L. 112.

O, beware, my lord of jealousy;
It is the green-eyed monster which doth
    mock
The meat it feeds on; that cuckold lives in
    bliss
Who, certain of his fate, loves not his wronger;
But, O, what damned minutes tells he o'er
Who dotes, yet doubts, suspects, yet strongly
    loves!
   e.   *Othello.* Act III. Sc. 3. L. 166.

So full of artless jealousy is guilt,
It spills itself in fearing to be spilt!
   f.   *Hamlet.* Act IV. Sc. 5. L. 19.

Though I perchance am vicious in my guess,
As, I confess, it is my nature's plague
To spy into abuses, and oft my jealousy
Shapes faults that are not.
   g.   *Othello.* Act III. Sc. 3. L. 146.

         Trifles light as air
Are to the jealous confirmations strong
As proofs of holy writ.
   h.   *Othello.* Act III. Sc. 3. L. 322.

Entire affection hateth nicer hands.
   i.   SPENSER—*Faerie Queene.* Bk. I.
          Canto VIII. St. 40.

        But through the heart
Should Jealousy its venom once diffuse,
'Tis then delightful misery no more,
  But agony unmixed, incessant gall,
  Corroding every thought, and blasting all
Love's paradise.
   j.   THOMSON—*The Seasons.* *Spring.*
          L. 1,073.

JESTING.

  A man who could make so vile a pun would
not scruple to pick a pocket.
   k.   JOHN DENNIS—*The Gentleman's
         Magazine.* Vol. LI. P. 324.

  He that will lose his friend for a jest, deserves to die a beggar by the bargain.
   l.   FULLER—*The Holy and Profane States.
         Of Jesting.* Maxim VII.

Jest not with the two-edged sword of God's
word.
   m.   FULLER—*The Holy and Profane States.
         Of Jesting.* Maxim II.

  No time to break jests when the heartstrings
are about to be broken.
   n.   FULLER—*The Holy and Profane States.
         Of Jesting.* Maxim VIII.

Less at thine own things laugh; lest in the
    jest
Thy person share, and the conceit advance,
Make not thy sport abuses: for the fly
That feeds on dung is colored thereby.
   o.   HERBERT—*Temple.* *Church Porch.*
         St. 39.

  People that make puns are like wanton
boys that put coppers on the railroad tracks.
   p.   O. W. HOLMES—*The Autocrat of the
         Breakfast Table.* I.

Of all the griefs that harass the distress'd,
Sure the most bitter is a scornful jest;
Fate never wounds more deep the generous
    heart,
Than when a blockhead's insult points the
    dart.
   q.   SAM'L JOHNSON—*London.* L. 165.

A jest's prosperity lies in the ear
Of him that hears it, never in the tongue
Of him that makes it.
   r.   *Love's Labour's Lost.* Act V. Sc. 2.
         L. 871.

How ill white hairs become a fool and jester!
   s.   *Henry IV.* Pt. II. Act V. Sc. 5. L. 52.

I do not like this fooling.
   t.   *Troilus and Cressida.* Act V. Sc. 2.
         L. 102.

Jesters do often prove prophets.
   u.   *King Lear.* Act V. Sc. 3. L. 71.

  It requires a surgical operation to get a joke
well into a Scotch understanding.
   v.   SYDNEY SMITH—*Lady Holland's
         Memoir.* Vol. I. P. 15.

A college joke to cure the dumps.
   w.   SWIFT—*Cassinus and Peter.*

JEWELER (See OCCUPATIONS).

JEWS.

The Jews are among the aristocracy of every land; if a literature is called rich in the possession of a few classic tragedies, what shall we say to a national tragedy lasting for fifteen hundred years, in which the poets and the actors were also the heroes.

a.   GEORGE ELIOT—*Daniel Deronda.*
Bk. VI. Ch. XLII.

The Jews spend at Easter.

b.   HERBERT—*Jacula Prudentum.* No. 244.

A Hebrew knelt in the dying light,
  His eye was dim and cold ;
The hairs on his brow were silver white,
  And his blood was thin and old.

c.   THOMAS K. HERVEY—*The Devil's
Progress.*

To undo a Jew is charity, and not sin.

d.   MARLOWE—*The Jew of Malta.* Act IV.
Sc. 6.

Who hateth me but for my happiness?
Or who is honored now but for his wealth?
Rather had I, a Jew, be hated thus,
Than pitied in a Christian poverty.

e.   MARLOWE—*The Jew of Malta.* Act I.
Sc. 1.

This is the Jew
That Shakespeare drew.

f.   *Attributed to* POPE. *See Biographia
Dramatica.* Vol. I. P. 469.

I am a Jew: Hath not a Jew eyes? hath not a Jew hands, organs, dimensions, senses, affections, passions? fed with the same food, hurt with the same weapons, subject to the same diseases, healed by the same means, warmed and cooled by the same winter and summer, as a Christian is?

g.   *Merchant of Venice.* Act III. Sc. 1.
L. 60.

JOURNALISM (*See* OCCUPATIONS).

JOY.

And these are joys, like beauty, but skin deep.

h.   BAILEY—*Festus.* Sc. *A Village Feast.*
L. 26.

                                        Joys
Are bubble-like—what makes them bursts them too.

i.   BAILEY—*Festus.* Sc. *A Library and
Balcony. A Summer Night.* L. 62.

The joy late coming late departs.

j.   LEWIS J. BATES—*Some Sweet Day.*

Capacity for joy
Admits temptation.

k.   E. B. BROWNING—*Aurora Leigh.* Bk. I.
L. 703.

An infant when it gazes on a light,
  A child the moment when it drains the
    breast,
A devotee when soars the Host in sight,
  An Arab with a stranger for a guest,
A sailor when the prize has struck in fight,
  A miser filling his most hoarded chest,
Feel rapture ; but not such true joy are reaping
As they who watch o'er what they love
    while sleeping.

l.   BYRON—*Don Juan.* Canto II. St. 196.

There's not a joy the world can give like that
    it takes away.

m.   BYRON—*Stanzas for Music.* *There's not
a joy, etc.*

Joy rul'd the day, and Love the night.

n.   DRYDEN—*The Secular Masque.* L. 82.

Our joy is dead, and only smiles on us.

o.   GEORGE ELIOT—*Spanish Gypsy.* Bk. III.

And, e'en while fashion's brightest arts decoy,
The heart, distrusting, asks if this be joy.

p.   GOLDSMITH—*The Deserted Village.*
L. 263.

They hear a voice in every wind,
And snatch a fearful joy.

q.   GRAY—*On a Distant Prospect of Eton
College.* St. 4.

But were there ever any
Writhed not at passed joy?

r.   KEATS—*Stanzas.* *In Drear Nighted
December.*

    Joys too exquisite to last,
And yet more exquisite when past.

s.   MONTGOMERY—*The Little Cloud.*

How fading are the joys we dote upon !
  Like apparitions seen and gone;
But those which soonest take their flight
  Are the most exquisite and strong ;
Like angel's visits short and bright,
  Mortality's too weak to bear them long.

t.   JOHN NORRIS—*The Parting.* St. 4.

Joy, in Nature's wide dominion,
  Mightiest cause of all is found ;
And 'tis Joy that moves the pinion.
  When the wheel of time goes round.

u.   SCHILLER—*Hymn to Joy.* Bowring's
trans.

For bonny sweet Robin is all my joy.

v.   *Hamlet.* Act IV. Sc. 5. L. 186.

I wish you all the joy that you can wish.

w.   *Merchant of Venice.* Act III. Sc. 2.
L. 192.

                        My plenteous joys,
Wanton in fulness, seek to hide themselves
In drops of sorrow.

x.   *Macbeth.* Act I. Sc. 4. L. 35.

Sweets with sweets war not, joy delights in
    joy.
  a.   *Sonnet VIII.*

I have drunken deep of joy,
And I will taste no other wine to-night.
  b.   Shelley—*The Cenci.* Act I. Sc. 3.
                    L. 92.

There is a sweet joy which comes to us
through sorrow.
  c.   Spurgeon—*Gleanings Among the
             Sheaves. Sweetness in Sorrow.*

Beauty for Ashes, and oil of joy!
  d.   Whittier—*The Preacher.* St. 26.

And often, glad no more,
  We wear a face of joy, because
We have been glad of yore.
  e.   Wordsworth—*The Fountain.*

Joys season'd high, and tasting strong of guilt.
  f.   Young—*Night Thoughts.* Night VIII.
                    L. 835.

JUDGES.

Judges ought to be more learned than witty,
more reverend than plausible, and more advised than confident. Above all things, integrity is their portion and proper virtue.
  g.   Bacon—*Essays. Of Judicature.*

The cold neutrality of an impartial judge.
  h.   Burke—*Preface to Brissot's Address.*
                Vol. V. P. 67.

The hungry judges soon the sentence sign,
And wretches hang that jurymen may dine.
  i.   Pope—*Rape of the Lock.* Canto III.
                    L. 21.

Heaven is above all yet; there sits a judge,
That no king can corrupt.
  j.   *Henry VIII.* Act III. Sc. 1. L. 100.

He who the sword of heaven will bear
Should be as holy as severe;
Pattern in himself to know,
Grace to stand, and virtue go;
More nor less to others paying
Than by self-offenses weighing.
Shame to him, whose cruel striking
Kills for faults of his own liking!
  k.   *Measure for Measure.* Act III. Sc. 2.
                L. 275.

It doth appear you are a worthy judge;
You know the law; your exposition
Hath been most sound.
  l.   *Merchant of Venice.* Act IV. Sc. 1.
                L. 236.

Therefore I say again,
I utterly abhor, yea from my soul
Refuse you for my judge; whom, yet once
    more,
I hold my most malicious foe, and think not
At all a friend to truth.
  m.   *Henry VIII.* Act II. Sc. 4. L. 80.

To offend, and judge, are distinct offices
And of opposed natures.
  n.   *Merchant of Venice.* Act II. Sc. 9.
                L. 61.

What is my offence?
Where are the evidence that do accuse me?
What lawful quest have given their verdict up
Unto the frowning judge?
  o.   *Richard III.* Act I. Sc. 4. L. 187.

Four things belong to a judge : to hear cour-
teously, to answer wisely, to consider soberly,
and to decide impartially.
  p.   Socrates.

JUDGMENT.

On you, my lord, with anxious fear I wait,
And from your judgment must expect my
    fate.
  q.   Addison—*A Poem to His Majesty.*
                L. 21.

Cruel and cold is the judgment of man,
  Cruel as winter, and cold as the snow;
But by-and-by will the deed and the plan
  Be judged by the motive that lieth below.
  r.   Lewis J. Bates—*By-and-By.*

Mortal vision is a grievous bar
To weigh true worth.
  s.   Geo. H. Boker—*To the Memory of
                M. A. R.* L. 8.

Next to sound Judgment, Diamonds and
Pearls are the rarest things to be met with.
  t.   De La Bruyère—*The Characters or
             Manners of the Present Age. Of
                      Judgments.*

My friend, judge not me,
Thou seest I judge not thee;
Betwixt the stirrup and the ground,
Mercy I askt, mercy I found.
  u.   Camden—*Remaines Concerning
             Britaine.* 1637. P. 392.

Woe to him, * * * who has no court of
appeal against the world's judgment.
  v.   Carlyle—*Essays. Mirabeau.*

Be kind to my remains; and O, defend,
Against your judgment, your departed friend!
  w.   Dryden—*Epistle to Congreve.* L. 72.

We judge others according to results; how
else?—not knowing the process by which results are arrived at.
  x.   George Eliot—*The Mill on the Floss.*
               Bk. VII. Ch. II.

In other men we faults can spy,
And blame the mote that dims their eye;
Each little speck and blemish find,
To our own stronger errors blind.
  y.   Gay—*The Turkey and the Ant.* Pt. I.
                L. 1.

So comes a reck'ning when the banquet's o'er,
The dreadful reck'ning, and men smile no
  more.
  a.   GAY—*The What D'ye Call It.*   Act II.
                                            Sc. 9.

I know of no way of judging the future but
by the past.
  b.   PATRICK HENRY—*Speech on the Virginia
                                Convention.*   1775.

He that judges without informing himself
to the utmost that he is capable, cannot acquit
himself of judging amiss.
  c.   LOCKE—*Human Understanding.*
                            Bk. II.   Ch. XXI.

We judge ourselves by what we feel capable
of doing, while others judge us by what we
have already done.
  d.   LONGFELLOW—*Kavanagh.*   Ch. I.

When thou attended gloriously from heaven,
Shalt in the sky appear, and from thee send
Thy summoning archangels to proclaim
Thy dread tribunal.
  e.   MILTON—*Paradise Lost.*   Bk. III.
                                         L. 323.

          There written all
Black as the damning drops that fall
From the denouncing Angel's pen,
Ere Mercy weeps them out again.
  f.   MOORE—*Lalla Rookh. Paradise and
                                the Peri.*   St. 28.

'Tis with our judgments as our watches, none
Go just alike, yet each believes his own.
  g.   POPE—*Essay on Criticism.*   L. 9.

For twelve honest men have decided the cause,
Who are judges alike of the facts and the laws.
  h.   WILLIAM PULTENEY—*The Honest Jury.*

Commonly we say a Judgment falls upon a
Man for something in him we cannot abide.
  i.   JOHN SELDEN—*Table Talk. Judgments.*

For I do not distinguish by the eye, but by
the mind, which is the proper judge of the
man.
  j.   SENECA—*On a Happy Life.*   Ch. I.

We shall be judged, not by what we might
have been, but what we have been.
  k.   SEWELL—*Passing Thoughts on Religion.
                        Sympathy in Gladness.*

A Daniel come to judgment! yea, a Daniel.
  l.   *Merchant of Venice.*   Act IV.   Sc. 1.
                                            L. 223.

Forbear to judge, for we are sinners all.
  m.   *Henry VI.*   Pt. II.   Act III.   Sc. 3.
                                            L. 31.

Give every man thy ear, but few thy voice;
Take each man's censure, but reserve thy
  judgment.
  n.   *Hamlet.*   Act I.   Sc. 3.   L. 68.

He that of greatest works is finisher
Oft does them by the weakest minister :
So holy writ in babes hath judgment shown,
When judges have been babes.
  o.   *All's Well That Ends Well.*   Act II.
                                         Sc. 1.   L. 139.

              How would you be,
If He, which is the top of judgment, should
But judge you as you are?
  p.   *Measure for Measure.*   Act II.   Sc. 2.
                                            L. 76.

          I charge you by the law,
Whereof you are a well deserving pillar,
Proceed to judgment.
  q.   *Merchant of Venice.*   Act IV.   Sc. 1.
                                            L. 238.

          I see men's judgments are
A parcel of their fortunes; and things out-
  ward
Do draw the inward quality after them,
To suffer all alike.
  r.   *Antony and Cleopatra.*   Act III.
                                         Sc. 13.   L. 31.

I stand for judgment: answer: shall I have
  it?
  s.   *Merchant of Venice.*   Act IV.   Sc. 1.
                                            L. 103.

O judgment! thou art fled to **brutish beasts,**
And men have lost their reason!
  t.   *Julius Cæsar.*   Act III.   Sc. 2.   L. 109.

The jury, passing on the prisoner's life,
May in the sworn twelve have a thief or two
Guiltier than him they try.
  u.   *Measure for Measure.*   Act II.   Sc. 1.
                                            L. 19.

The urging of that word, judgment, hath
bred a kind of remorse in me.
  v.   *Richard III.*   Act I.   Sc. 4.   L. 109.

              What we oft do best,
By sick interpreters, once weak ones, is
Not ours, or not allow'd; what worst, as oft,
Hitting a grosser quality, is cried up
For our best act.
  w.   *Henry VIII.*   Act I.   Sc. 2.   L. 81.

But as when an authentic watch is shown,
Each man winds up and rectifies his own,
  So in our very judgments.
  x.   SIR JOHN SUCKLING—*Aglaura.*
                                    Epilogue.

JULY (*See* MONTHS).

JUNE (*See* MONTHS).

JUSTICE.

Justice discards party, friendship, kindred, and is therefore always represented as blind.
a.   ADDISON—*The Guardian.* No. 99.

There is no virtue so truly great and godlike as justice.
b.   ADDISON—*The Guardian.* No. 99.

Justice is that virtue of the soul which is distributive according to desert.
c.   ARISTOTLE—*Metaphysics. On the Virtues and Vices. Justice.*

God's justice, tardy though it prove perchance,
Rests never on the track until it reach
Delinquency.
d.   ROBERT BROWNING—*Ceuciaja.*

It looks to me to be narrow and pedantic to apply the ordinary ideas of criminal justice to this great public contest. I do not know the method of drawing up an indictment against a whole people.
e.   BURKE—*Speech on Conciliation with America.* Works. Vol. II. P. 136.

Justice is itself the great standing policy of civil society; and any eminent departure from it, under any circumstances, lies under the suspicion of being no policy at all.
f.   BURKE—*Reflections on the Revolution in France.*

So justice while she winks at crimes,
Stumbles on innocence sometimes.
g.   BUTLER—*Hudibras.* Canto II. Pt. I.
L. 1177.

Amongst the sons of men how few are known
Who dare be just to merit not their own.
h.   CHURCHILL—*Epistle to Hogarth.* L. 1.

Whoever fights, whoever falls,
Justice conquers evermore.
i.   EMERSON—*Voluntaries.*

Justice without wisdom is impossible.
j.   FROUDE—*Short Studies on Great Subjects. Party Politics.*

That which is unjust can really profit no one; that which is just can really harm no one.
k.   HENRY GEORGE—*The Land Question.*
Ch. XIV.

I have loved justice and hated iniquity; and therefore I die in exile.
l.   POPE GREGORY VII. (HILDEBRAND).
Bowden's Life of Gregory VII. Vol. II.
Bk. III. Ch. XX.

Man is unjust, but God is just; and finally justice
Triumphs.
m.   LONGFELLOW—*Evangeline.* Pt. I. III.
L. 34.

But the sunshine aye shall light the sky.
As round and round we run ;
And the Truth shall ever come uppermost,
And Justice shall be done.
n.   CHARLES MACKAY—*Eternal Justice.*
St. 4.

Just are the ways of God,
And justifiable to men.
o.   MILTON—*Samson Agonistes.* L. 293.

Yet I shall temper so
Justice with mercy, as may illustrate most
Them fully satisfied, and thee appease.
p.   MILTON—*Paradise Lost.* Bk. X.
L. 77.

He shall have merely justice and his bond.
q.   *Merchant of Venice.* Act IV. Sc. 1.
L. 339.

I have done the state some service, and they know 't;
No more of that, I pray you, in your letters,
When you shall these unlucky deeds relate,
Speak of me as I am ; nothing extenuate,
Nor set down aught in malice.
r.   *Othello.* Act V. Sc. 2. L. 339.

I show it most of all when I show justice;
For then I pity those I do not know,
Which a dismiss'd offence would after gall ;
And do him right that, answering one foul wrong,
Lives not to act another.
s.   *Measure for Measure.* Act II. Sc. 2.
L. 99.

O, I were damn'd beneath all depth in hell,
But that I did proceed upon just grounds
To this extremity.
t.   *Othello.* Act V. Sc. 2. L. 137.

There is more owing her than is paid; and more shall be paid her than she'll demand.
u.   *All's Well That Ends Well.* Act I.
Sc. 3. L. 107.

This bond is forfeit;
And lawfully by this the Jew may claim
A pound of flesh.
v.   *Merchant of Venice.* Act IV. Sc. 1.
L. 230.

This even-handed justice
Commends the ingredients of our poison'd chalice
To our own lips.
w.   *Macbeth.* Act I. Sc. 7. L. 9.

This shows you are above
Your justicers; that these our nether crimes
So speedily can venge!
x.   *King Lear.* Act IV. Sc. 2. L. 78.

Thrice is he arm'd that hath his quarrel just,
And he but naked, though lock'd up in steel,
Whose conscience with injustice is corrupted.
   a.   *Henry VI.* Pt. II. Act III. Sc. 2.
                       L. 232.

      Thyself shalt see the act:
For, as thou urgest justice, be assur'd
Thou shalt have justice more than thou desir'st.
   b.   *Merchant of Venice.* Act IV. Sc. 1.
                       L. 315.

Use every man after his desert, and who
   should
'Scape whipping !
   c.   *Hamlet.* Act II. Sc. 2. L. 554.

Truth is its [justice's] handmaid, freedom
is its child, peace is its companion, safety
walks in its steps, victory follows in its train ;
it is the brightest emanation from the gospel ;
it is the attribute of God.
   d.   Sydney Smith—*Lady Holland's
             Memoir.* Vol. I. P. 29.

A sense of justice is a noble fancy.
   e.   Tegner—*Frithjof's Saga.* Canto VIII.

Justice, sir, is the great interest of man on
earth.
   f.   Daniel Webster—*On Mr. Justice
             Story, 1845.*

K.

KINDNESS.

Kindness is wisdom. There is none in life
But needs it and may learn.
   g.   Bailey—*Festus.* Sc. *Home.*

Their cause I plead—plead it in heart and
   mind ;
A fellow-feeling makes one wondrous kind.
   h.   David Garrick—*Epilogue on Quitting
           the Stage. June,* 1776.

And Heaven, that every virtue bears in mind,
E'en to the ashes of the just is kind.
   i.   Homer—*Iliad.* Bk. XXIV. L. 523.
                   Pope's trans.

Though he was rough, he was kindly.
   j.   Longfellow—*Courtship of Miles
             Standish.* Pt. III.

There's no dearth of kindness
  In this world of ours ;
Only in our blindness
  We gather thorns for flowers.
   k.   Gerald Massey—*There's no Dearth of
              Kindness.*

      When your head did but ache,
I knit my handkerchief about your brows,
The best I had, a princess wrought it me,
And I did never ask it you again ;
And with my hand at midnight held your
   head,
And, like the watchful minutes to the hour,
Still and anon cheer'd up the heavy time,
Saying, "What lack you?" and, "Where
   lies your grief?"
   l.   *King John.* Act IV. Sc. 1. L. 41.

      Yet do I fear thy nature ;
It is too full o' the milk of human kindness.
   m.   *Macbeth.* Act I. Sc. 5. L. 14.

On that best portion of a good man's life,
His little, nameless, unremembered acts
Of kindness and of love.
   n.   Wordsworth—*Lines Composed Above
             Tintern Abbey.*

KISSES.

Blush, happy maiden, when you feel
The lips which press love's glowing seal ;
But as the slow years darklier roll,
Grown wiser, the experienced soul
Will own as dearer far than they
The lips which kiss the tears away.
   o.   Elizabeth Akers Allen—*Kisses.*

            But is there nothing else,
That we may do but only walk? Methinks,
Brothers and sisters lawfully may kiss.
   p.   Beaumont and Fletcher—*A King
           and No King.* Act IV. Sc. 4.

Kiss till the cows come home.
   q.   Beaumont and Fletcher—*Scornful
           Lady.* Act II. Sc. 2.

Remember the Viper:—'twas close at your
   feet,
  How you started and threw yourself into
   my arms ;
Not a strawberry there was so ripe nor so
   sweet
  As the lips which I kiss'd to subdue your
   alarms.
   r.   Bloomfield—*Nancy.* St. 4.

* * * And when my lips meet thine
Thy very soul is wedded unto mine.
   s.   H. H. Boyesen—*Thy Gracious Face
          I Greet with Glad Surprise.*

First time he kiss'd me, he but only kiss'd
The fingers of this hand wherewith I write ;
And ever since it grew more clean and white.
   t.   E. B. Browning—*Sonnets from the
          Portuguese.* Sonnet XXXVIII.

I was betrothed that day ;
I wore a troth kiss on my lips I could not
    give away.
    a.   E. B. BROWNING—*The Lay of the*
                      Brown Rosary.   Pt. II.

Thy lips which spake wrong counsel, I kiss
close.
    b.   E. B. BROWNING—*Drama of Exile.*
              Sc. *Farther on, etc.*   L. 992.

A long, long kiss, a kiss of youth, and love.
    c.   BYRON—*Don Juan.*   Canto II.   St. 186.

Come, lay thy head upon my breast,
And I will kiss thee into rest.
    d.   BYRON—*The Bride of Abydos.*
                      Canto I.   St. 11.

When age chills the blood, when our pleas-
    ures are past—
For years fleet away with the wings of the
    dove—
The dearest remembrance will still be the
    last,
Our sweetest memorial the first kiss of love.
    e.   BYRON—*The First Kiss of Love.*   St. 7.

One kind kiss before we part,
    Drop a tear and bid adieu ;
Though we sever, my fond heart
    Till we meet shall pant for you.
    f.   ROBERT DODSLEY—*Colin's Kisses.*
              The Parting Kiss.   Song VI.

Since there's no help, come let us kiss and
    part.
    g.   DRAYTON—*Sonnet.*

Kisses honeyed by oblivion.
    h.   GEORGE ELIOT—*The Spanish Gypsy.*
              Bk. III.   L. 251 from end of Bk.

The kiss you take is paid by that you give :
The joy is mutual, and I'm still in debt.
    i.   GEO. GRANVILLE (Lord Lansdowne)—
              Heroic Love.   Act V.   Sc. 1.

Tell me who first did kisses suggest ?
It was a mouth all glowing and blest ;
It kissed and it thought of nothing beside.
The fair month of May was then in its pride,
The flowers were all from the earth fast
    springing,
The sun was laughing, the birds were singing.
    j.   HEINE—*Book of Songs.*   *New Spring.*
              Prologue.   No. 25.   St. 2.

Give me a kisse, and to that kisse a score ;
Then to that twenty, adde a hundred more ;
A thousand to that hundred ; so kiss on,
To make that thousand up a million ;
Treble that million, and when that is done,
Let's kisse afresh, as when we first begun.
    k.   HERRICK—*Hesperides.*   *To Anthea.*

What is a kisse ? Why this, as some approve :
The sure sweet sement, glue, and lime of love.
    l.   HERRICK—*Hesperides.*   *A Kiss.*

Then press my lips, where plays a flame of
    bliss,—
A pure and holy love-light,—and forsake
The angel for the woman in a kiss,
          At once I wis,
          My soul will wake !
    m.   VICTOR HUGO—*Come When I Sleep.*

                 A soft lip,
Would tempt you to eternity of kissing !
    n.   BEN JONSON—*Volpone ; or, the Fox.*
                        Act I.   Sc. I.

Or leave a kiss but in the cup,
And I'll not look for wine.
    o.   BEN JONSON—*The Forest.*   *To Celia.*

When she kissed me once in play,
Rubies were less bright than they ;
And less bright were those which shone
In the palace of the Sun.
Will they be as bright again ?
Not if kiss'd by other men.
    p.   WALTER SAVAGE LANDOR—*Rubies.*

What is a kiss ? Alacke ! at worst,
A single Dropp to quenche a Thirst,
Tho' oft it prooves, in happie Hour,
The first swete Dropp of our long Showre.
    q.   LELAND—*In the Old Time.*

Says he—" I'd better call agin ;"
Says she—" Think likely, Mister ! "
Thet last word pricked him like a pin,
An'—Wal, he up an' kist her.
    r.   LOWELL—*The Courtin.*

The kiss, in which he half forgets even such
    a yoke as yours.
    s.   MACAULAY—*Lays of Ancient Rome.*
                     Virginia.   L. 138.

I throw a kiss across the sea,
    I drink the winds as drinking wine,
And dream they all are blown from thee,
    I catch the whisper'd kiss of thine.
    t.   JOAQUIN MILLER—*England.*   1871.
                         Introduction.

One kiss the maiden gives, one last,
Long kiss, which she expires in giving.
    u.   MOORE—*Lalla Rookh.*   *Paradise and*
                        the Peri.   L. 200.

How should great Jove himself do else than
    miss
To win the woman he forgets to kiss.
    v.   COVENTRY PATMORE—*De Natura*
                            Deorum.

Give me kisses! Nay, 'tis true
I am just as rich as you;
And for every kiss I owe,
I can pay you back, you know.
Kiss me, then,
Every moment—and again.
> *a.*   J. G. Saxe—*To Lesbia.*

Thou knowest the maiden who ventures to kiss a sleeping man, wins of him a pair of gloves.
> *b.*   Scott—*Fair Maid of Perth.* Ch. V.

Yet whoop, Jack! kiss Gillian the quicker,
Till she bloom like a rose, and a fig for the vicar!
> *c.*   Scott—*Lady of the Lake.* VI. 5.

And his kissing is as full of sanctity as the touch of holy bread.
> *d.*   *As You Like It.* Act III. Sc. 4. L. 17.

And steal immortal blessing from her lips;
Who, even in pure and vestal modesty,
Still blush, as thinking their own kisses sin.
> *e.*   *Romeo and Juliet.* Act III. Sc. 3. L. 36.

But, thou know'st this,
'Tis time to fear when tyrants seem to kiss.
> *f.*   *Pericles.* Act I. Sc. 2. L. 78.

By my troth I kiss thee with a most constant heart.
> *g.*   *Henry IV.* Pt. II. Act II. Sc. 4. L. 292.

I can express no kinder sign of love,
Than this kind kiss.
> *h.*   *Henry VI.* Pt. II. Act I. Sc. 1. L. 18.

I'll take that winter from your lips.
> *i.*   *Troilus and Cressida.* Act IV. Sc. 5. L. 23.

It is not a fashion for the maids in France to kiss before they are married.
> *j.*   *Henry V.* Act V. Sc. 2. L. 286.

I understand thy kisses, and thou mine,
And that's a feeling disputation.
> *k.*   *Henry IV.* Pt. I. Act III. Sc. 1. L. 205.

Kissing with inside lip? stopping the career
Of laughter with a sigh?
> *l.*   *Winter's Tale.* Act I. Sc. 2. L. 287.

O, a kiss,
Long as my exile, sweet as my revenge!
Now, by the jealous queen of heaven, that kiss
I carried from thee, dear.
> *m.*   *Coriolanus.* Act V. Sc. 3. L. 44.

Or ere I could
Give him that parting kiss, which I had set
Betwixt two charming words, comes in my father
And like the tyrannous breathing of the north
Shakes all our buds from growing.
> *n.*   *Cymbeline.* Act I. Sc. 3. L. 33.

Strangers and foes do sunder, and not kiss.
> *o.*   *All's Well That Ends Well.* Act II. Sc. 5. L. 91.

Take, O take those lips away,
That so sweetly were foresworn;
And those eyes, the break of day,
Lights that do mislead the morn;
But my kisses bring again,
Seals of love, but sealed in vain.
> *p.*   *Measure for Measure.* Act IV. Sc. 1. L. 1.

Teach not thy lips such scorn; for they were made
For kissing, lady, not for such contempt.
> *q.*   *Richard III.* Act I. Sc. 2. L. 172.

Their lips were four red roses on a stalk,
Which in their summer beauty kiss'd each other.
> *r.*   *Richard III.* Act IV. Sc. 3. L. 12.

This done, he took the bride about the neck
And kiss'd her lips with such a clamorous smack
That at the parting, all the church did echo.
> *s.*   *Taming of the Shrew.* Act III. Sc. 2. L. 179.

Upon thy cheek lay I this zealous kiss,
As seal to this indenture of my love.
> *t.*   *King John.* Act II. Sc. 1. L. 19.

We have kiss'd away
Kingdoms and provinces.
> *u.*   *Antony and Cleopatra.* Act III. Sc. 10. L. 5.

Why, then we'll make exchange; here, take you this,
And seal the bargain with a holy kiss.
> *v.*   *Two Gentlemen of Verona.* Act II. Sc. 2. L. 6.

As in the soft and sweet eclipse,
When soul meets soul on lover's lips.
> *w.*   Shelley—*Prometheus Unbound.* Act IV.

Kiss me, so long but as a kiss may live;
And in my heartless breast and burning brain
That word, that kiss shall all thoughts else survive,
With food of saddest memory kept alive.
> *x.*   Shelley—*Adonais.* St. 26.

My lips till then had only known
The kiss of mother and of sister,
But somehow, full upon her own
Sweet, rosy, darling mouth,—I kissed her.
> *y.*   E. C. Stedman—*The Door-Step.*

Lord! I wonder what fool it was that first invented kissing.
a. SWIFT—*Polite Conversation.*
        Dialogue II.

And our spirits rushed together at the touching of the lips.
b. TENNYSON—*Locksley Hall.* St. 19.

       Once he drew
With one long kiss my whole soul thro'
My lips, as sunlight drinketh dew.
c. TENNYSON—*Fatima.* St. 3.

A kiss from my mother made me a painter.
d. BENJAMIN WEST.

KNAVERY.

Now I will show myself
To have more of the serpent than the dove;
That is—more knave than fool.
e. MARLOWE—*The Jew of Malta.* Act II.
           Sc. 3.

Zeno first started that doctrine, that knavery is the best defence against a knave.
f. PLUTARCH—*Morals.* Vol. I. *Of*
          Bashfulness.

A knave; a rascal; an eater of broken meats.
g. *King Lear.* Act II. Sc. 2. L. 14.

There's ne'er a villain dwelling in all Denmark But he's an arrant knave.
h. *Hamlet.* Act I. Sc. 5. L. 124.

Whip me such honest knaves.
i. *Othello.* Act I. Sc. 1. L. 49.

KNOWLEDGE.

Knowledge is, indeed, that which, next to virtue, truly and essentially raises one man above another.
j. ADDISON—*The Guardian. Letter of*
   Alexander to Aristotle. No. 111.

For all knowledge and wonder (which is the seed of knowledge) is an impression of pleasure in itself.
k. BACON—*Advancement of Learning.*
            Bk. I.

Knowledge bloweth up, but charity buildeth up.
l. BACON—*Rendering of I Cor. VIII.* I.

Knowledge is power.
m. BACON—*Meditationes Sacræ.*

Pursuit of knowledge under difficulties.
n. *Title given by* LORD BROUGHAM *to a book*
  published under the superintendence
  of the Society for the Diffusion of
  Useful Knowledge. 1830.

Knowledge by suffering entereth,
And Life is perfected by Death.
o. E. B. BROWNING—*A Vision of Poets.*
       Conclusion. St. 37.

What's done we partly may compute,
But know not what's resisted.
p. BURNS—*Address to Unco Guid.* St. 8.

Deep sighted in intelligences,
Ideas, atoms, influences.
q. BUTLER—*Hudibras.* Pt. I. Canto I.
           L. 533.

He knew whats'ever 's to be known,
But much more than he knew would own.
r. BUTLER—*Hudibras.* Pt. II.
       Canto III. L. 297.

He knew what's what, and that's as high
As metaphysic wit can fly.
s. BUTLER—*Hudibras.* Pt. 1. Canto I.
           L. 149.

Nor do I know what is become
Of him, more than the Pope of Rome.
t. BUTLER—*Hudibras.* Pt. 1. Canto 3.
           L. 263.

Knowledge is not happiness, and science
But an exchange of ignorance for that
Which is another kind of ignorance.
u. BYRON—*Manfred.* Act II. Sc. 4.

Know ye the land where the cypress and myrtle
Are emblems of deeds that are done in their clime,
Where the rage of the vulture, the love of the turtle,
Now melt into sorrow, now madden to crime?
v. BYRON—*Bride of Abydos.* Canto I.

For love is ever the beginning of Knowledge, as fire is of light.
w. CARLYLE—*Essays. Death of Goethe.*

What is all Knowledge too but recorded Experience, and a product of History; of which, therefore, Reasoning and Belief, no less than Action and Passion, are essential materials?
x. CARLYLE—*Essays. On History.*

When you know a thing, to hold that you know it; and when you do not know a thing, to allow that you do not know it; this is knowledge.
y. CONFUCIUS—*Analects.* Bk. II.
          Ch. XVII.

Knowledge and Wisdom, far from being one,
Have oft-times no connexion. Knowledge dwells
In heads replete with thoughts of other men,
Wisdom in minds attentive to their own.
z. COWPER—*The Task.* Bk. VI. L. 88.

Knowledge is proud that he has learn'd so
   much;
Wisdom is humble that he knows no more.
   a.   COWPER—*The Task.* Bk. VI. L. 96.

              Knowledge comes
Of learning well retain'd, unfruitful else.
   b.   DANTE—*Vision of Paradise.* Canto V.
                                      L. 41.

Since knowledge is but sorrow's spy,
It is not safe to know.
   c.   WM. DAVENANT—*The Just Italian.*
                          Act V. Sc. 1.

  To be conscious that you are ignorant is a
great step to knowledge.
   d.   BENJ. DISRAELI—*Sybil.* Bk. I.
                                Chap. V.

Knowledge is the antidote to fear,—
Knowledge, Use and Reason, with its higher
   aids.
   e.   EMERSON—*Society and Solitude.*
                             Courage.

  Our knowledge is the amassed thought and
experience of innumerable minds.
   f.   EMERSON—*Letters and Social Aims.*
                  Quotation and Originality.

There is no knowledge that is not power.
   g.   EMERSON—*Society and Solitude.* *Old*
                                  Age.

Who can direct, when all pretend to know?
   h.   GOLDSMITH—*The Traveller.* L. 64.

  The first step to self-knowledge is self-distrust. Nor can we attain to any kind of
knowledge, except by a like process.
   i.   J. C. and A. W. HARE—*Guesses at*
                      Truth. P. 454.

  A desire of knowledge is the natural feeling
of mankind; and every human being whose
mind is not debauched, will be willing to give
all that he has to get knowledge.
   j.   SAM'L JOHNSON—*Boswell's Life of*
             Johnson. Conversation on
             Saturday, July 30, 1763.

Knowledge is more than equivalent to force.
   k.   SAM'L JOHNSON—*Rasselas.*
                          Chap. XIII.

  Knowledge is of two kinds. We know a
subject ourselves, or we know where we can
find information upon it.
   l.   SAM'L JOHNSON—*Boswell's Life of*
                  Johnson. 1775.

  The improvement of the understanding is
for two ends: first, for our own increase of
knowledge; secondly, to enable us to deliver
and make out that knowledge to others.
   m.   LOCKE—*Some Thoughts Concerning*
           Reading and Study. *Appendix B.*

22

  A kind of semi-Solomon, half-knowing
everything, from the cedar to the hyssop.
   n.   MACAULAY—(*About Brougham*). *Life*
             and Letters. Vol. I. P. 175.

Diffused knowledge immortalizes itself.
   o.   SIR JAMES MACKINTOSH—*Vindiciœ*
                          Gallicœ.

  Every addition to true knowledge is an addition to human power.
   p.   HORACE MANN—*Lectures and Reports*
             on Education. Lecture I.

  Only by knowledge of that which is not
Thyself, shall thyself be learned.
   q.   OWEN MEREDITH (Lord Lytton)—
                          Know Thyself.

I went into the temple, there to hear
The teachers of our law, and to propose
What might improve my knowledge or their
   own.
   r.   MILTON—*Paradise Regained.* Bk. I.
                                L. 211.

All things I thought I knew; but now confess
The more I know I know, I know the less.
   s.   OWEN—*Works.* Bk. VI. 39.

In vain sedate reflections we would make
When half our knowledge we must snatch,
   not take.
   t.   POPE—*Moral Essays.* Ep. I. L. 39.

That virtue only makes our bliss below,
And all our knowledge is ourselves to know.
   u.   POPE—*Essay on Man.* Ep. IV. L. 397.

  Then I began to think, that it is very true
which is commonly said, that the one-half of
the world knoweth not how the other half
liveth.
   v.   RABELAIS—*Works.* Bk. II.
                               Ch. XXXII.

Far must thy researches go
Wouldst thou learn the world to know;
Thou must tempt the dark abyss
Wouldst thou prove what *Being* is;
Naught but firmness gains the prize,
Naught but fullness makes us wise,
Buried deep truth e'er lies.
   w.   SCHILLER—*Proverbs of Confucius.*
                        Bowring's trans.

Wouldst thou know thyself, observe the
   actions of others.
Wouldst thou other men know, look thou
   within thine own heart.
   x.   SCHILLER—*Votive Tablets.* *The Key.*

And seeing ignorance is the curse of God,
Knowledge the wing wherewith we fly to
   heaven.
   y.   *Henry VI.* Pt. II. Act IV. Sc. 7.
                                  L. 78.

If you can look into the seeds of time,
And say which grain will grow and which
     will not;
Speak then to me.
   a.   *Macbeth.* Act I. Sc. 3. L. 58.

I know a hawk from a handsaw.
   b.   *Hamlet.* Act II. Sc. 2. L. 394.

           But the full sum of me * * *
Is an unlesson'd girl, unschool'd, unpractis'd;
Happy in this, she is not yet so old
  But she may learn.
   c.   *Merchant of Venice.* Act III. Sc. 2.
                                L. 159.

Too much to know is to know naught but
     fame.
   d.   *Love's Labour's Lost.* Act I. Sc. 1.
                                L. 92.

We know what we are, but know not what
     we may be.
   e.   *Hamlet.* Act IV. Sc. 5. L. 42.

And thou my minde aspire to higher things;
Grow rich in that which never taketh rust.
   f.   Sir Philip Sidney—*Sonnet. Leave
                          me, O Love.*

Sweet food of sweetly uttered knowledge.
   g.   Sir Philip Sidney—*Defence of Poesy.*

A life of knowledge is not often a life of
injury and crime.
   h.   Sydney Smith—*Pleasures of Knowledge.*

Knowledge alone is the being of Nature,
Giving a soul to her manifold features,
Lighting through paths of the primitive dark-
     ness,
The footsteps of Truth and the vision of Song.
   i.   Bayard Taylor—*Kilimandjaro.* St. 2.

Knowledge comes, but wisdom lingers.
   j.   Tennyson—*Locksley Hall.* St. 71.

Who loves not Knowledge? Who shall rail
  Against her beauty? May she mix
  With men and prosper! Who shall fix
Her pillars? Let her work prevail.
   k.   Tennyson—*In Memoriam.* CXIV.

Knowledge, in truth, is the great sun in the
firmament. Life and power are scattered with
all its beams.
   l.   Daniel Webster—*Address delivered at
          the Laying of the Corner-Stone of
          Bunker Hill Monument,* 1825.

Knowledge is the only fountain, both of the
love and the principles of human liberty.
   m.   Daniel Webster—*Address Delivered on
          Bunker Hill,* June 17, 1843.

Yet all that I have learn'd (hugh toyles now
     past)
By long experience, and in famous schooles,
Is but to know my ignorance at last,
Who think themselves most wise are greatest
     fools.
   n.   William, Earl of Stirling—
          Recreations with the Muses. London.
                      Fol. 1637. P. 7.

                  He who binds
His soul to knowledge, steals the key of heaven.
   o.   N. P. Willis—*The Scholar of Thibèt
                Ben Khorat.* II.

             Oh, be wise, Thou!
Instructed that true knowledge leads to love.
   p.   Wordsworth—*Lines left upon a Seat
                in a Yew-tree.*

L.

LABOR.

Such hath it been—shall be—beneath the sun
The many still must labour for the one.
   q.   Byron—*The Corsair.* Canto I. St. 8.

And yet without labour there were no ease,
no rest, so much as conceivable.
   r.   Carlyle—*Essays. Characteristics.*

Labor is discovered to be the grand conqueror, enriching and building up nations
more surely than the proudest battles.
   s.   Wm. Ellery Channing—*War.*

Honest labour bears a lovely face.
   t.   Thos. Dekker—*Patient Grissell.* Act I.
                           Sc. 1.

Labour itself is but a sorrowful song,
The protest of the weak against the strong.
   u.   F. W. Faber—*The Sorrowful World.*

For as labor cannot produce without the
use of land, the denial of the equal right to
the use of land is necessarily the denial of the
right of labor to its own produce.
   v.   Henry George—*Progress and Poverty.*
                    Bk. VII. Ch. I.

How blest is he who crowns in shades like
  these,
A youth of labour with an age of ease.
   w.   Goldsmith—*The Deserted Village.* L. 99.

If little labour, little are our gaines:
Man's fortunes are according to his paines.
   x.   Herrick—*Hesperides. No Paines,
                     No Gaines.*

Our fruitless labours mourn,
And only rich in barren fame return.
  a. HOMER—*Odyssey.* Bk. X. L. 46.
                              Pope's trans.

To labour is the lot of man below ;
And when Jove gave us life, he gave us woe.
  b. HOMER—*Iliad.* Bk. X. L. 78.
                              Pope's trans.

With fingers weary and worn,
  With eyelids heavy and red,
A woman sat in unwomanly rags,
  Plying her needle and thread.
  c. HOOD—*Song of the Shirt.*

For men must work and women must weep.
  d. CHARLES KINGSLEY—*The Three Fishers.*

From labor there shall come forth rest.
  e. LONGFELLOW—*To a Child.* L. 162.

            Taste the joy
That springs from labor.
  f. LONGFELLOW—*Masque of Pandora.*
                      Pt. VI. *In the Garden.*

The heights by great men reached and kept
  Were not attained by sudden flight,
But they, while their companions slept,
  Were toiling upward in the night.
  g. LONGFELLOW—*Birds of Passage. The
              Ladder of St. Augustine.* St. 10.

But now my task is smoothly done,
I can fly, or I can run.
  h. MILTON—*Comus.* L. 1,012.

Labor is life ! 'Tis the still water faileth ;
Idleness ever despaireth, bewaileth ;
Keep the watch wound, for the dark rust
        assaileth.
  i. FRANCES S. OSGOOD—*To Labor is to
                                    Pray.*

Labor is rest—from the sorrows that greet us ;
Rest from all petty vexations that meet us,
Rest from sin-promptings that ever entreat us,
  Rest from world-sirens that hire us to ill.
Work—and pure slumbers shall wait on thy
        pillow ;
Work—thou shalt ride over Care's coming
        billow ;
Lie not down wearied 'neath Woe's weeping
        willow !
  Work with a stout heart and resolute will !
  j. FRANCES S. OSGOOD—*To Labor is to
                                    Pray.*

The man who by his labour gets
  His bread, in independent state,
Who never begs, and seldom eats,
  Himself can fix or change his fate.
  k. PRIOR—*The Old Gentry.*

And many strokes, though with a little axe,
Hew down and fell the hardest-timber'd oak.
  l. *Henry VI.* Pt. III. Act II. Sc. 1.
                                    L. 54.

I have had my labour for my travail.
  m. *Troilus and Cressida.* Act I. Sc. 1.
                                    L. 72.

The labour we delight in physics pain.
  n. *Macbeth.* Act II. Sc. 3. L. 55.

Why, Hal, 'tis my vocation. Hal : 'tis no
sin for a man to labour in his vocation.
  o. *Henry IV.* Pt. I. Act I. Sc. 2.
                                    L. 116.

Labor in this country is independent and
proud. It has not to ask the patronage of
capital, but capital solicits the aid of labor.
  p. DANIEL WEBSTER—*Speech,* April, 1824.

LANGUAGE.

Well languag'd Danyel.
  q. WILLIAM BROWNE—*Britannia's
              Pastorals.* Bk. II. Song 2. L. 303.

A Babylonish dialect
Which learned pedants much affect.
  r. BUTLER—*Hudibras.* Pt. I. Canto I.
                                    L. 93.

Pedantry consists in the use of words unsuitable to the time, place, and company.
  s. COLERIDGE—*Biographia Literaria.*
                                    Ch. 10.

        * * * Philologists, who chase
A panting syllable through time and space,
Start it at home, and hunt it in the dark,
To Gaul, to Greece, and into Noah's Ark.
  t. COWPER—*Retirement.* L. 691.

Language is a city to the building of which
every human being brought a stone.
  u. EMERSON—*Letters and Social Aims.*
                      Quotation and Originality.

Language is fossil poetry.
  v. EMERSON—*Essays. The Poet.*

And don't confound the language of the
        nation
With long-tailed words in *osity* and *ation.*
  w. J. HOOKHAM FRERE—*King Arthur and
              his Round Table.* Introduction.
                                    St. 6.

Language is only the instrument of science,
and words are but the signs of ideas.
  x. SAM'L JOHNSON—*Preface to his
                          English Dictionary.*

Syllables govern the world.
  y. JOHN SELDEN—*Table Talk. Power.*

                Fie, fie upon her !
There's language in her eye, her cheek, her
        lip,
Nay, her foot speaks ; her wanton spirits look
        out
At every joint and motive of her body.
  z. *Troilus and Cressida.* Act IV. Sc. 5.
                                    L. 55.

He has strangled
His language in his tears.
a.   *Henry VIII.* Act V. Sc. 1. L. 158.

O, but they say the tongues of dying men
Enforce attention like deep harmony:
Where words are scarce, they are seldom spent
in vain,
For they breathe truth that breathe their
words in pain.
He that no more must say is listen'd more.
b.   *Richard II.* Act II. Sc. 1. L. 5.

Sweet smoke of rhetoric!
c.   *Love's Labour's Lost.* Act III. Sc. 1.
L. 65.

There was speech in their dumbness, language in their very gesture.
d.   *Winter's Tale.* Act V. Sc. 2. L. 12.

Thou whoreson Zed! thou unnecessary letter!
e.   *King Lear.* Act II. Sc. 2. L. 66.

You taught me language; and my profit on't
Is, I know how to curse. The red plague rid
you
For learning me your language!
f.   *Tempest.* Act I. Sc. 2. L. 363.

Language is the expression of ideas, and if
the people of one country cannot preserve an
identity of ideas they cannot retain an identity of language.
g.   Noah Webster—*Preface to Dictionary.*
Edition of 1828.

From purest wells of English undefiled
None deeper drank than he, the New World's
Child,
Who in the language of their farm field spoke
The wit and wisdom of New England folk.
h.   Whittier—*James Russell Lowell.*

Where nature's end of language is declined,
And men talk only to conceal the mind.
i.   Young—*Love of Fame.* Satire II.
L. 207.

LAUGHTER.

We must laugh before we are happy, for
fear we die before we laugh at all.
j.   De La Bruyère—*The Characters or
Manners of the Present Age.*
Ch. IV.

The landlord's laugh was ready chorus.
k.   Burns—*Tam o' Shanter.*

And if I laugh at any mortal thing,
'Tis that I may not weep.
l.   Byron—*Don Juan.* Canto IV. St. 4.

How much lies in Laughter: the cipher-
key, wherewith we decipher the whole man.
m.   Carlyle—*Sartor Resartus.* Bk. I.
Ch. IV.

And the loud laugh that spoke the vacant
mind.
n.   Goldsmith—*The Deserted Village.*
L. 121.

Low gurgling laughter, as sweet
As the swallow's song i' the South,
And a ripple of dimples that, dancing, meet
By the curves of a perfect mouth.
o.   Paul Hamilton Hayne—*Ariel.*

Laugh not too much; the witty man laughs
least:
For wit is news only to ignorance.
Lesse at thine own things laugh; lest in the
jest
Thy person share, and the conceit advance.
p.   Herbert—*The Temple. Church Porch.*
St. 39.

You hear that boy laughing?—you think he's
all fun;
But the angels laugh, too, at the good he has
done;
The children laugh loud as they troop to his
call,
And the poor man that knows him laughs
loudest of all.
q.   O. W. Holmes—*The Boys.*

And unextinguish'd laughter shakes the skies.
r.   Homer—*Iliad.* Bk. I. L. 771.
Pope's trans.

Laugh, and be fat, sir, your penance is known.
They that love mirth, let them heartily drink,
'Tis the only receipt to make sorrow sink.
s.   Ben Jonson—*Entertainments. The
Penates.*

Sport, that wrinkled Care derides,
And Laughter holding both his sides.
t.   Milton—*L'Allegro.* L. 31.

To laugh, if but for an instant only, has
never been granted to man before the fortieth
day from his birth, and then it is looked upon
as a miracle of precocity.
u.   Pliny the Elder—*Natural History.*
Bk. VII. Ch. I. Holland's trans.

Laugh at your friends, and if your friends are
sore
So much the better, you may laugh the more.
v.   Pope—*Epilogue to Satire.* Dialogue I.
L. 55.

The man that loves and laughs must sure
do well.
w.   Pope—*Imitations of Horace.* Ep. VI.
Bk. I. L. 129.

To laugh were want of goodness and of grace;
And to be grave, exceeds all pow'r of face.
x.   Pope—*Prologue to Satires.* L. 35.

One inch of joy surmounts of grief a span,
Because to laugh is proper to the man.
y.   Rabelais—*To the Readers.*

O, I am stabb'd with laughter.
  a.   *Love's Labour's Lost.* Act V. Sc. 2.
                     L. 79.

O, you shall see him laugh till his face be
like a wet cloak ill laid up.
  b.   *Henry IV.* Pt. II. Act V. Sc. 1.
                     L. 88.

The brain of this foolish-compounded clay,
man, is not able to invent anything that tends
to laughter, more than I invent or is invented
on me.
  c.   *Henry IV.* Pt. II. Act I. Sc. 2.
                     L. 6.

They laugh that win.
  d.   *Othello.* Act IV. Sc. 1. L. 124.

With his eyes in flood with laughter.
  e.   *Cymbeline.* Act I. Sc. 6. L. 74.

Laughter almost ever cometh of things
most disproportioned to ourselves and nature:
delight hath a joy in it either permanent or
present; laughter hath only a scornful tickling.
  f.   SIR PHILIP SIDNEY—*The Defence of
                          Poesy.*

For still the World prevail'd, and its dread
     laugh,
Which scarce the firm Philosopher can scorn.
  g.   THOMSON—*The Seasons. Autumn.*
                     L. 233.

Fight Virtue's cause, stand up in Wit's defence,
Win us from vice and laugh us into sense.
  h.   TICKELL—*On the Prospect of Peace.*
                     St. 38.

Laugh and the world laughs with you.
  i.   ELLA WHEELER WILCOX—*Solitude.*

Care to our coffin adds a nail, no doubt;
And every Grin, so merry, draws one out.
  j.   JOHN WOLCOTT (Peter Pindar)—
                 Expostulatory Odes. Ode 15.

The house of laughter makes a house of woe.
  k.   YOUNG—*Night Thoughts.* Night VIII.
                     L. 757.

LAW (*See* OCCUPATIONS).

LEARNING.

The green retreats
Of Academus.
  l.   AKENSIDE—*Pleasures of the
               Imagination.* Canto I. L. 591.

Learning hath his infancy, when it is but
beginning and almost childish; then his
youth, when it is luxuriant and juvenile;
then his strength of years, when it is solid
and reduced; and lastly his old age, when it
waxeth dry and exhaust.
  m.   BACON—*Essays Civil and Moral.
               Of Vicissitude of Things.*

Reading maketh a full man; conference a
ready man; and writing an exact man.
  n.   BACON—*Essays. Of Studies.*

Learning will be cast into the mire and
trodden down under the hoofs of a swinish
multitude.
  o.   BURKE—*Reflections on the Revolution in
                         France.*

Out of too much learning become mad.
  p.   BURTON—*Anatomy of Melancholy.*
               Pt. III. Sec. 4. Memb. 1.
                     Subsec. 2.

And wisely tell what hour o' th' day
The clock does strike by Algebra.
  q.   BUTLER—*Hudibras.* Pt. I. Canto I.
                     L. 125.

In mathematics he was greater
Than Tycho Brahe, or Erra Pater;
For he, by geometric scale,
Could take the size of pots of ale.
  r.   BUTLER—*Hudibras.* Pt. I. Canto I.
                     L. 119.

The languages, especially the dead,
     The sciences, and most of all the abstruse,
The arts, at least all such as could be said
     To be the most remote from common use,
In all these he was much and deeply read.
  s.   BYRON—*Don Juan.* Canto I. St. 40.

And gladly wolde he lerne and gladly teche.
  t.   CHAUCER—*Canterbury Tales.*
                 Prologue. L. 308.

Learning without thought is labor lost;
thought without learning is perilous.
  u.   CONFUCIUS—*Analects.* Bk. II. Ch. XV.

There is the love of knowing without the
love of learning; the beclouding here leads to
dissipation of mind.
  v.   CONFUCIUS—*Analects.* Bk. XVII.
                     Ch. VIII.

Here the heart
May give a useful lesson to the head,
And learning wiser grow without his books.
  w.   COWPER—*The Task.* Bk. VI. *Winter
                   Walk at Noon,* L. 85.

There is no other Royal path which leads
to geometry.
  x.   EUCLID TO PTOLEMY I. *See Proclus'
              Commentaries on Euclid's Elements.*
                   Bk. II. Ch. IV.

Learning by study must be won;
'Twas ne'er entail'd from son to son.
  y.   GAY—*The Pack Horse and Carrier.*
                     L. 41.

Whence is thy learning? Hath thy toil
O'er books consum'd the midnight oil?
  z.   GAY—*Shepherd and Philosopher.* L. 15.

I've studied now Philosophy
And Jurisprudence, Medicine
And even, alas, Theology
From end to end with labor keen;
And here, poor fool; with all my lore
I stand no wiser than before.
   a.   Goethe—*Faust.* I. *Night.* Bayard
                Taylor's trans.

And still they gazed, and still the wonder
   grew,
That one small head should carry all he
   knew.
   b.   Goldsmith—*The Deserted Village.*
                        L. 215.

While words of learned length and thundering sound
Amaz'd the gazing rustics rang'd around.
   c.   Goldsmith—*The Deserted Village.*
                        L. 211.

Yet, he was kind, or, if severe in aught,
The love he bore to learning was in fault;
The village all declar'd how much he knew,
'Twas certain he could write and cipher too.
   d.   Goldsmith—*The Deserted Village.*
                        L. 205.

Men of polite learning and a liberal education.
   e.   Mathew Henry—*Commentaries.*
                    The Acts. Ch. X.

There mark what ills the scholar's life assail,
Toil, envy, want, the patron, and the jail.
   f.   Sam'l Johnson—*Vanity of Human
                Wishes.* L. 159.

The Lord of Learning who upraised mankind
From being silent brutes to singing men.
   g.   Leland—*The Music-lesson of Confucius.*

Thou art an heyre to fayre lyving, that is
nothing, if thou be disherited of learning, for
better were it to thee to inherite righteousnesse
then riches, and far more seemly were it for
thee to haue thy Studie full of bookes, then thy
pursse full of mony.
   h.   Lyly—*Euphues. Letters to a Young
                Gentleman in Naples named Alcius.*

A little learning is a dangerous thing;
Drink deep, or taste not the Pierian spring;
Their shallow draughts intoxicate the brain,
And drinking largely sobers us again.
   i.   Pope—*Essays on Criticism.* L. 215.

Ask of the Learn'd the way? The Learn'd
   are blind;
This bids to serve, and that to shun mankind;
Some place the bliss in action, some in ease,
Those call it Pleasure, and Contentment these.
   j.   Pope—*Essay on Man.* Ep. IV. L. 19.

Learn from the birds what food the thickets
   yield;
Learn from the beasts the physic of the field;
The arts of building from the bee receive;
Learn of the mole to plough, the worm to
   weave.
   k.   Pope—*Essay on Man.* Ep. III. L. 173.

Few men make themselves Masters of the
things they write or speak.
   l.   John Selden—*Table Talk. Learning.*

No man is the wiser for his Learning * * *
Wit and Wisdom are born with a man.
   m.   John Selden—*Table Talk. Learning.*

Learning is but an adjunct to ourself
And where we are our learning likewise is.
   n.   *Love's Labour's Lost.* Act IV. Sc. 3.
                        L. 314.

O this learning, what a thing it is!
   o.   *Taming of the Shrew.* Act I. Sc. 2.
                        L. 160.

Well, for your favour, sir, why, give God
thanks, and make no boast of it; and for
your writing and reading, let that appear
when there is no need of such vanity.
   p.   *Much Ado About Nothing.* Act III.
                    Sc. 3. L. 17.

I would by no means wish a daughter of
mine to be a progeny of learning.
   q.   R. B. Sheridan—*The Rivals.* Act I.
                        Sc. 2.

Learn to live, and live to learn,
Ignorance like a fire doth burn,
Little tasks make large return.
   r.   Bayard Taylor—*To My Daughter.*

Much learning shows how little mortals know;
Much wealth, how little worldings can enjoy.
   s.   Young—*Night Thoughts.* Night VI.
                        L. 519.

Were man to live coeval with the sun,
The patriarch-pupil would be learning still.
   t.   Young—*Night Thoughts.* Night VII.
                        L. 86.

LEISURE.

And leave us leisure to be good.
   u.   Gray—*Hymn. Adversity.* Sc. 3.

No blessed leisure for Love or Hope,
But only time for Grief.
   v.   Hood—*The Song of the Shirt.*

                Retired Leisure,
That in trim gardens takes his pleasure.
   w.   Milton—*Il Penseroso.* L. 49.

Mend when thou canst; be better at thy
   leisure.
   x.   *King Lear.* Act II. Sc. 4. L. 232.

Leisure is pain; take off our chariot wheels,
How heavily we drag the load of life!
Blest leisure is our curse; like that of Cain,
It makes us wander, wander earth around
To fly that tyrant, thought.
    a.   YOUNG—*Night Thoughts.*   Night II.
                                L. 125.

LETTERS (*See* OCCUPATIONS—Post).

LIBERALITY.

                    He that's liberal
To all alike, may do a good by chance,
But never out of judgment.
    b.   BEAUMONT AND FLETCHER—*The Spanish
                        Curate.* Act I.   Sc. 1.

Then gently scan your brother man,
   Still gentler sister woman ;
Tho' they may gang a kennin' wrang,
   To step aside is human.
    c.   BURNS—*Address to the Unco Guid.*

It is better to believe that a man does possess good qualities than to assert that he does not.
    d.   *Chinese Moral Maxims.*   Compiled by
                John Francis Davis, F. R. S.
                          China, 1823.

To hide the fault I see :
That mercy I to others show,
     That mercy show to me.
    e.   POPE—*Universal Prayer.*

              Shall I say to Cæsar
What you require of him? for he partly begs
To be desir'd to give. It much would please
   him,
That of his fortunes you should make a staff
To lean upon.
    f.   *Antony and Cleopatra.*   Act III.
                         Sc. 13.   L. 67.

'Tis pity bounty had not eyes behind,
That man might ne'er be wretched for his
   mind.
    g.   *Timon of Athens.*   Act I.   Sc. 2.   L. 170.

But, by all thy nature's weakness,
   Hidden faults and follies known,
Be thou, in rebuking evil,
   Conscious of thine own.
    h.   WHITTIER—*What the Voice Said.* St. 15.

LIBERTY.

A day, an hour, of virtuous liberty
Is worth a whole eternity in bondage.
    i.   ADDISON—*Cato.*   Act II.   Sc. 1.

But what is liberty without wisdom, and without virtue? It is the greatest of all possible evils; for it is folly, vice, and madness, without tuition or restraint.
    j.   BURKE—*Reflections on the Revolution in
                             France.*

My vigour relents. I pardon something to
the spirit of liberty.
    k.   BURKE—*Speech on the Conciliation of
                    America.*   Vol. II.   P. 118.

The people never give up their liberties but
under some delusion.
    l.   BURKE—*Speech at a County Meeting at
                        Bucks.*   1784.

Liberty's in every blow !
Let us do or die.
    m.   BURNS—*Bruce to His Men at
                         Bannockburn.*

Yes, while I stood and gazed, my temples bare,
And shot my being through earth, sea, and air,
Possessing all things with intensest love,
O Liberty ! my spirit felt thee there.
    n.   COLERIDGE—*France.*   *An Ode.*   V.

Then liberty, like day,
Breaks on the soul, and by a flash from
     Heaven
Fires all the faculties with glorious joy.
    o.   COWPER—*The Task.*   Bk. V.   L. 882.

'Tis liberty alone that gives the flower
Of fleeting life its lustre and perfume ;
And we are weeds without it.
    p.   COWPER—*The Task.*   Bk. V.   L. 446.

Eternal vigilance is the price of liberty.
    q.   JOHN PHILPOT CURRAN—*Speech.*
                              Dublin.   1808.

The condition upon which God hath given
liberty to man is eternal vigilance.
    r.   JOHN PHILPOT CURRAN—*Speech.*
                           July 10, 1790.

The love of liberty with life is given,
And life itself the inferior gift of Heaven.
    s.   DRYDEN—*Palamon and Arcite.*   Bk. II.
                                L. 291.

Those who would give up essential liberty
to purchase a little temporary safety deserve
neither liberty nor safety.
    t.   BENJ. FRANKLIN—*Motto to Historical
                      Review of Pennsylvania.*

Where liberty dwells, there is my country.
    u.   BENJ. FRANKLIN.

Give me liberty, or give me death.
    v.   PATRICK HENRY—*Speech.* March, 1775.

The God who gave us life, gave us liberty at
the same time.
    w.   THOMAS JEFFERSON—*Summary View
                   of the Rights of British America.*

License they mean when they cry, Liberty !
For who loves that, must first be wise and
   good.
    x.   MILTON—*On the Detraction which
                followed upon my Writing Certain
                        Treatises.*

Oh! if there be, on this earthly sphere,
A boon, an offering Heaven holds dear,
'Tis the last libation Liberty draws
From the heart that bleeds and breaks in her
    cause!
a.   Moore—*Lalla Rookh. Paradise and
    the Peri.* St. 11.

Give me again my hollow tree
A crust of bread, and liberty!
b.   Pope—*Imitations of Horace.* Bk. II.
    Satire VI. L. 220.

O liberty! liberty! how many crimes are
committed in thy name!
c.   Madame Roland—*Macaulay.*
    Mirabeau.

        I must have liberty
Withal, as large a charter as the wind,
To blow on whom I please.
d.   *As You Like It.* Act II. Sc. 7. L. 47.

So every bondman in his own hand bears
The power to cancel his captivity.
e.   *Julius Cæsar.* Act I. Sc. 3. L. 101.

Why, headstrong liberty is lash'd with woe;
There's nothing, situate under heaven's eye
But hath his bound, in earth, in sea, in sky.
f.   *Comedy of Errors.* Act II. Sc. 1.
    L. 15.

Deep in the frozen regions of the north,
A goddess violated brought thee forth,
Immortal Liberty!
g.   Smollett—*Ode to Independence.* L. 5.

Behold! in Liberty's unclouded blaze
We lift our heads, a race of other days.
h.   Charles Sprague—*Centennial Ode.*
    St. 22.

  God grants liberty only to those who love it,
and are always ready to guard and defend it.
i.   Daniel Webster—*Speech.* June 3,
    1834.

Liberty exists in proportion to wholesome
restraint.
j.   Daniel Webster—*Speech at the
    Charleston Bar Dinner.* May 10, 1847.

On the light of Liberty you saw arise the
light of Peace, like
        "another morn,
        Risen on mid-noon;"
and the sky on which you closed your eye was
cloudless.
k.   Daniel Webster—*Speeches. The
    Bunker Hill Monument.* 1825.

LIBRARIES.

The richest minds need not large libraries.
l.   Amos Bronson Alcott—*Table Talk.*
    Bk. I. *Learning-Books.*

    Libraries are as the shrines where all the
relics of the ancient saints, full of true virtue,
and that without delusion or imposture, are
preserved and reposed.
m.   Bacon—*Libraries.*

      That place that does contain
My books, the best companions, is to me
A glorious court, where hourly I converse
With the old sages and philosophers;
And sometimes, for variety, I confer
With kings and emperors, and weigh their
    counsels;
Calling their victories, if unjustly got,
Unto a strict account, and, in my fancy,
Deface their ill-placed statues.
n.   Beaumont and Fletcher—*The Elder
    Brother.* Act I. Sc. 2. L. 177.

A library is but the soul's burial-ground.
It is the land of shadows.
o.   Henry Ward Beecher—*Star Papers.
    Oxford. Bodleian Library.*

    The true University of these days is a col-
lection of Books.
p.   Carlyle—*Heroes and Hero Worship.
    The Hero as a Man of Letters.*

All round the room my silent servants wait,
My friends in every season, bright and dim.
q.   Barry Cornwall—*My Books.*

A great library contains the diary of the
human race.
r.   Dawson—*Address on Opening the
    Birmingham Free Library.*

    It is a vanity to persuade the world one
hath much learning, by getting a great library.
s.   Fuller—*The Holy and Profane States.
    Of Books.* Maxim 1.

    Every library should try to be complete on
something, if it were only the history of pin-
heads.
t.   O. W. Holmes—*The Poet at the
    Breakfast Table.* VIII.

    The first thing naturally when one enters
a scholar's study or library, is to look at his
books. One gets a notion very speedily of
his tastes and the range of his pursuits by a
glance round his book-shelves.
u.   O. W. Holmes—*The Poet at the
    Breakfast Table.* VIII.

    What a place to be in is an old library! It
seems as though all the souls of all the writers
that have bequeathed their labours to these
Bodleians were reposing here as in some
dormitory, or middle state. I do not want to
handle, to profane the leaves, their winding-
sheets. I could as soon dislodge a shade. I
seem to inhale learning, walking amid their
foliage; and the odor of their old moth-
scented coverings is fragrant as the first bloom
of those sciential apples which grew amid the
happy orchard.
v.   Charles Lamb—*Essays of Elia. Oxford
    in the Vacation.*

I love vast libraries; yet there is a doubt,
If one be better with them or without,—
Unless he use them wisely, and, indeed,
Knows the high art of what and how to read.
   a.   J. G. SAXE—*The Library.*

'Tis well to borrow from the good and great;
'Tis wise to learn; 'tis God-like to create!
   b.   J. G. SAXE—*The Library.*

Come, and take choice of all my library,
And so beguile thy sorrow.
   c.   *Titus Andronicus.* Act IV. Sc. 1.
                         L. 34.

                He furnish'd me
From mine own library with volumes that
I prize above my dukedom.
   d.   *Tempest.* Act I. Sc. 2. L. 166.

A circulating library in a town is as an
evergreen tree of diabolical knowledge.
   e.   R. B. SHERIDAN—*The Rivals.* Act I.
                         Sc. 2.

         Shelved around us lie
The mummied authors.
   f.   BAYARD TAYLOR—*The Poet's Journal.*
                     Third Evening.

LIFE.

Every man's life is a fairy-tale written by
God's fingers.
   g.   HANS CHRISTIAN ANDERSEN—*Preface*
                      to Works.

Life, which all creatures love and strive to
   keep,
Wonderful, dear and pleasant unto each,
Even to the meanest; yea, a boon to all
Where pity is, for pity makes the world
Soft to the weak and noble for the strong.
   h.   EDWIN ARNOLD—*Light of Asia.* Bk. V.
                        L. 401.

With aching hands and bleeding feet
  We dig and heap, lay stone on stone;
We bear the burden and the heat
  Of the long day, and wish 'twere done.
Not till the hours of light return
All we have built do we discern.
   i.   MATTHEW ARNOLD—*Morality.* St. 2.

The World's a bubble, and the Life of Man
  less than a span:
In his conception wretched, from the womb
  so to the tomb;
Curst from his cradle, and brought up to years
  with cares and fears.
Who then to frail mortality shall trust,
But limns the water, or but writes in dust.
   j.   BACON—*Life. Preface to the*
              Translation of Certain Psalms.

It matters not how long we live, but how.
   k.   BAILEY—*Festus.* Sc. *Wood and Water.*

Life hath more awe than death.
   l.   BAILEY—*Festus.* Sc. *Wood and Water.*

We live in deeds, not years: in thoughts, not
  breaths;
In feelings, not in figures on a dial.
We should count time by heart-throbs. He
  most lives
Who thinks most, feels the noblest, acts the
  best.
   m.   BAILEY—*Festus.* Sc. *A Country Town.*

   Life! we've been long together
Through pleasant and through cloudy
  weather:
  'Tis hard to part when friends are dear:
  Perhaps 'twill cost a sigh, a tear;
  Then steal away, give little warning,
    Choose thine own time,
Say not Good-night,—but in some brighter
  clime
    Bid me Good-morning.
   n.   ANNA LETITIA BARBAULD—*Life.*

Our lives are but our marches to the grave.
   o.   BEAUMONT AND FLETCHER—*The*
             Humorous Lieutenant. Act III.
                        Sc. 5. L. 76.

We sleep, but the loom of life never stops;
and the pattern which was weaving when the
sun went down is weaving when it comes up
to-morrow.
   p.   HENRY WARD BEECHER—*Life*
                    Thoughts. P. 12.

Life, believe, is not a dream,
  So dark as sages say;
Oft a little morning rain
  Foretells a pleasant day!
   q.   CHARLOTTE BRONTË—*Life.*

Life is a pure flame, and we live by an invisible sun within us.
   r.   SIR THOMAS BROWNE—*Hydriotaphia.*
                         Ch. V.

Whose life is a bubble, and in length a span.
   s.   WM. BROWNE—*Britannia Pastorals.*
                     Bk. I. Song II.

I know—is all the mourner saith,
Knowledge by suffering entereth;
And Life is perfected by Death.
   t.   E. B. BROWNING—*Vision of Poets.*
                       St. 321.

Have you found your life distasteful?
  My life did, and does, smack sweet.
Was your youth of pleasure wasteful?
  Mine I saved and hold complete.
Do your joys with age diminish?
  When mine fail me, I'll complain.
Must in death your daylight finish?
  My sun sets to rise again.
   u.   ROBERT BROWNING—*At the "Mermaid."*
                       St. 10.

I count life just a stuff
To try the soul's strength on.
   a.   ROBERT BROWNING—*In a Balcony.*

No! let me taste the whole of it, fare like my
    peers
  The heroes of old,
Bear the brunt, in a minute pay glad life's
    arrears
  Of pain, darkness and cold.
   b.   ROBERT BROWNING—*Prospice.*

Life is a kind of Sleep: old Men sleep longest,
nor begin to wake but when they are to die.
   c.   DE LA BRUYÈRE—*The Characters or*
                   Manners of the Present Age.
                       On Men.   Ch. XI.

Life is but a day at most.
   d.   BURNS—*Friars' Carse Hermitage.*

O, Life! how pleasant is thy morning,
Young Fancy's rays the hills adorning!
Cold pausing Caution's lesson scorning,
  We frisk away,
Like schoolboys, at the expected warning,
  To joy and play.
   e.   BURNS—*Epistle to James Smith.*

O Life! thou art a galling load,
Along a rough, a weary road,
  To wretches such as I!
   f.   BURNS—*Despondency.*

All is concentred in a life intense,
Where not a beam, nor air, nor leaf is lost,
But hath a part of being.
   g.   BYRON—*Childe Harold.   Canto III.*
                            St. 89.

           Did man compute
Existence by enjoyment, and count o'er
Such hours 'gainst years of life, say, would he
  name threescore?
   h.   BYRON—*Childe Harold.   Canto III.*
                            St. 34.

Our life is two-fold; sleep hath its own world,
A boundary between the things misnamed
Death and existence.
   i.   BYRON—*The Dream.   St. 1.   L. 1.*

The dust we tread upon was once alive.
   j.   BYRON—*Sardanapalus.   Act IV.*
                         Sc. 1.   L. 66.

Heaven gives our years of fading strength
  Indemnifying fleetness;
And those of Youth a seeming length,
  Proportioned to their sweetness.
   k.   CAMPBELL—*A Thought Suggested by*
                         the New Year.

A well-written life is almost as rare as a
well-spent one.
   l.   CARLYLE—*Essays.   Jean Paul Fried-*
                         rich Richter.

One life;—a little gleam of Time between two
  Eternities.
   m.   CARLYLE—*Heroes and Hero Worship.*
                 The Hero as a Man of Letters.

There is no life of a man, faithfully recorded,
but is a heroic poem of its sort, rhymed or
unrhymed.
   n.   CARLYLE—*Essays.   Memoirs on the*
                         Life of Scott.

How many lives we live in one,
And how much less than one, in all.
   o.   ALICE CARY—*Life's Mysteries.*

Life is but thought.
   p.   COLERIDGE—*Youth and Age.*

To know, to esteem, to love,—and then to
  part,
Makes up life's tale to many a feeling heart.
   q.   COLERIDGE—*On Taking Leave of ——.*

His faith, perhaps, in some nice tenets might
Be wrong; his life, I'm sure, was in the right.
   r.   ABRAHAM COWLEY—*On the Death of Mr.*
                         Crashaw.   L. 56.

Life for delays and doubts no time does give,
None ever yet made haste enough to live.
   s.   ABRAHAM COWLEY—*Martial.   Lib. II.*
                            XC.

Men deal with life as children with their play,
Who first misuse, then cast their toys away.
   t.   COWPER—*Hope.   L. 127.*

Oh, that those lips had language! Life has
  pass'd
With me but roughly since I heard thee last.
   u.   COWPER—*On the Receipt of my Mother's*
                         Picture.

Our wasted oil unprofitably burns,
Like hidden lamps in old sepulchral urns.
   v.   COWPER—*Conversation.   L. 357.*

What is it but a map of busy life,
Its fluctuations, and its vast concerns?
   w.   COWPER—*The Task.   Bk. IV.   L. 55.*

Let's learn to live, for we must die alone.
   x.   CRABBE—*The Borough.   Letter X.*

Life is not measured by the time we live.
   y.   CRABBE—*The Village.   Bk. II.*

Shall he who soars, inspired by loftier views,
Life's little cares and little pains refuse?
Shall he not rather feel a double share
Of mortal woe, when doubly arm'd to bear?
   z.   CRABBE—*The Library.*

Learn to live well, that thou may'st die so too;
To live and die is all we have to do.
   aa.   SIR JOHN DENHAM—*Of Prudence.   L. 93.*

My life is one demd horrid grind.
   a.   DICKENS—*Nicholas Nickleby.* Vol. II.
                            Ch. XXXII.

" Live, while you live," the epicure would say,
" And seize the pleasures of the present day ; "
" Live, while you live," the sacred *preacher*
    cries,
" And give to God each moment as it flies."
" Lord, in my views let both united be ;
I live in *pleasure,* when I live to *Thee."*
   b.   PHILIP DODDRIDGE—" *Dum vivimus*
          vivamus." Lines written under
          Motto of his Family Arms.

My life lies in those eyes which have me slain.
   c.   DRUMMOND—*Sonnet XXIX.* L. 14.

So that my life be brave, what though not
    long?
   d.   DRUMMOND—*Sonnet.*

Bankrupt of life, yet prodigal of ease.
   e.   DRYDEN—*Absalom and Achitophel.*
                            L. 168.

Take not away the life you cannot give :
For all things have an equal right to live.
   f.   DRYDEN—*Pythagorean Phil.* L. 705.

'Tis not for nothing that we life pursue ;
It pays our hopes with something still that's
    new.
   g.   DRYDEN—*Aureng-Zebe.* Act IV. Sc. 1.

When I consider life, 'tis all a cheat ;
Yet, fooled with hope, men favour the deceit.
   h.   DRYDEN—*Aureng-Zebe.* Act IV. Sc. 1.

A little rule, a little sway,
A sunbeam in a winter's day,
Is all the proud and mighty have
Between the cradle and the grave.
   i.   JOHN DYER—*Grongar Hill.* L. 89.

A man's ingress into the world is naked and
    bare,
His progress through the world is trouble and
    care ;
And lastly, his egress out of the world, is no-
    body knows where.
If we do well here, we shall do well there ;
I can tell you no more if I preach a whole
    year.
   j.   JOHN EDWIN—*The Eccentricities of*
        John Edwin (second edition). Vol. I.
                            P. 74.

            Life's a vast sea
That does its mighty errand without fail,
Painting in unchanged strength though
    waves are changing.
   k.   GEORGE ELIOT—*Spanish Gypsy.*
                            Bk. III.

Life is short, and time is swift ;
Roses fade, and shadows shift.
   l.   EBENEZER ELLIOT—*Epigram.*

Sooner or later that which is now life shall
be poetry, and every fair and manly trait
shall add a richer strain to the song.
   m.   EMERSON—*Letters and Social Aims.*
                 Poetry and Imagination.

When life is true to the poles of nature, the
streams of truth will roll through us in song.
   n.   EMERSON—*Letters and Social Aims.*
                 Poetry and Imagination.

Born in a Cellar, * * * and living in a
Garret.
   o.   FOOTE—*The Author.* Act II. Sc. 1.
                            L. 375.

Dost thou love life? Then do not squander
time, for that is the stuff life is made of.
   p.   BENJ. FRANKLIN—*Poor Richard.*

We live merely on the crust or rind of
things.
   q.   FROUDE—*Short Studies on Great*
                      Subjects. Lucian.

How short is life ! how frail is human trust !
   r.   GAY—*Trivia.* Bk. III. L. 235.

The pregnant quarry teem'd with human
    form.
   s.   GOLDSMITH—*The Traveller.* L. 138.

Along the cool sequestered vale of life,
They kept the noiseless tenour of their way.
   t.   GRAY—*Elegy in a Country Churchyard.*
                           St. 19.

I made a posy, while the day ran by :
Here will I smell my remnant out, and tie
       My life within this band.
But time did beckon to the flowers, and they
By noon most cunningly did steal away,
       And wither'd in my hand.
   u.   HERBERT—*Life.*

Life is short, art long.
   v.   HIPPOCRATES—*Aphorisms.* Sec. 1.

No arts ; no letters ; no society ; and which
is worst of all, continual fear, and danger of
violent death ; and the life of man, solitary,
poor, nasty, brutish, and short.
   w.   THOMAS HOBBES—*Leviathan.* Pt. I.
             Of Man. Ch. XVIII.

For Fate has wove the thread of life with
    pain,
And twins ev'n from the birth are Misery and
    Man !
   x.   HOMER—*Odyssey.* Bk. VII. L. 263.
                        Pope's trans.

Life is not to be bought with heaps of gold ;
Not all Apollo's Pythian treasures hold,
Or Troy once held, in peace and pride of sway,
Can bribe the poor possession of the day.
   y.   HOMER—*Iliad.* Bk. IX. L. 524.
                        Pope's trans.

There is but halting for the wearied foot;
The better way is hidden.   Faith hath failed;
One stronger far than reason mastered her.
It is not reason makes faith hard, but life.
a. . JEAN INGELOW—*A Pastor's Letter to a*
　　　　　Young Poet. Pt. II. L. 231.

Catch, then, oh! catch the transient hour,
　Improve each moment as it flies;
Life's a short summer—man a flower;
　He dies—alas! how soon he dies!
b.　SAM'L JOHNSON—*Winter.* *An Ode.*
　　　　　　　　　　　　　　　　L. 33.

"Enlarge my life with multitude of days!"
In health, in sickness, thus the suppliant
　prays:
Hides from himself its state, and shuns to
　know,
That life protracted is protracted woe.
c.　SAM'L JOHNSON—*Vanity of Human*
　　　　　　　　　　Wishes. L. 255.

In life's last scene what prodigies surprise,
Fears of the brave, and follies of the wise!
From Marlborough's eyes the streams of
　dotage flow,
And Swift expires a driveller and a show.
d.　SAM'L JOHNSON—*Vanity of Human*
　　　　　　　　　　Wishes. L. 315.

Learn that the present hour alone is man's.
e.　SAM'L JOHNSON—*Irene.* Act III.
　　　　　　　　　　　　Sc. 2. L. 33.

Reflect that life, like every other blessing,
Derives its value from its use alone.
f.　SAM'L JOHNSON—*Irene.* Act III.
　　　　　　　　　　　　Sc. 8. L. 28.

Our whole life is like a play.
g.　BEN JONSON—*Discoveries de Vita*
　　　　　　　　　　　　Humana.

A sacred burden is this life ye bear,
Look on it, lift it, bear it solemnly,
Stand up and walk beneath it steadfastly;
Fail not for sorrow, falter not for sin,
But onward, upward, till the goal ye win.
h.　FRANCIS ANNE KEMBLE—*Lines to the*
　　　　　Young Gentlemen leaving the Lennox
　　　　　　　　　　Academy, Mass.

But helpless Pieces of the Game He plays
Upon this Checker-board of Nights and Days;
Hither and thither moves, and checks, and
　slays,
And one by one back in the Closet lays.
i.　OMAR KHAYYÁM—*Rubáiyát.* LXIX.
　　　　　　　　　　Fitzgerald's trans.

Life will be lengthened while growing, for
Thought is the measure of life.
j.　LELAND—*The Return of the Gods.*
　　　　　　　　　　　　　　　　L. 85.

Art is long, and Time is fleeting,
　And our hearts, though stout and brave,
Still, like muffled drums, are beating
　Funeral marches to the grave.
k.　LONGFELLOW—*A Psalm of Life.* St. 4.

Life hath quicksands, Life hath snares!
l.　LONGFELLOW—*Maidenhood.* St. 9.

Love is sunshine, hate is shadow,
Life is checkered shade and sunshine.
m.　LONGFELLOW—*Hiawatha.* Pt. X.
　　　　　　　Hiawatha's Wooing. L. 265.

Tell me not, in mournful numbers,
　Life is but an empty dream!
n.　LONGFELLOW—*A Psalm of Life.* St. 1.

This life of ours is a wild æolian harp of many
　a joyous strain,
But under them all there runs a loud per-
　petual wail, as of souls in pain.
o.　LONGFELLOW—*Christus.* *The Golden*
　　　　　　　　　Legend. Pt. IV. St. 2.

Thus at the flaming forge of life
　Our fortunes must be wrought;
Thus on its sounding anvil shaped
　Each burning deed and thought!
p.　LONGFELLOW—*The Village Blacksmith.*
　　　　　　　　　　　　　　　　St. 8.

Truly there is a tide in the affairs of men;
but there is no gulf-stream setting forever in
one direction.
q.　LOWELL—*Among my Books.* *First*
　　　　　　　Series. New England
　　　　　　　Two Centuries Ago.

Life is a mission. Every other definition of
life is false, and leads all who accept it astray.
Religion, science, philosophy, though still at
variance upon many points, all agree in this,
that every existence is an aim.
r.　MAZZINI—*Life and Writings.* Ch. V.

　　　　　　Life hath set
No landmarks before us.
s.　OWEN MEREDITH (Lord Lytton)—
　　　　Lucile. Pt. II. Canto V. St. 14.

When life leaps in the veins, when it beats in
　the heart,
When it thrills as it fills every animate part,
Where lurks it? how works it? * * * we
　scarcely detect it.
t.　OWEN MEREDITH (Lord Lytton)—
　　　　Lucile. Pt. II. Canto I. St. 5.

A man's best things are nearest him,
Lie close about his feet.
u.　RICHARD MONCKTON MILNES (Lord
　　　　Houghton)—*The Men of Old.*
　　　　　　　　　　　　　　St. 7.

For men to tell how human life began
Is hard; for who himself beginning knew?

    a.   Milton—*Paradise Lost.*   Bk. VIII.
                                    L. 250.

Nor love thy life, nor hate; but what thou
    liv'st
Live well; how long or short permit to
    heav'n.

    b.   Milton—*Paradise Lost.*   Bk. XI.
                                    L. 553.

So may'st thou live, till like ripe fruit thou
    drop
Into thy mother's lap.

    c.   Milton—*Paradise Lost.*   Bk. XI.
                                    L. 535.

'Tis not the whole of life to live;
Nor all of death to die.

    d.   Montgomery—*The Issues of Life and*
                                       Death.

Life is a waste of wearisome hours,
    Which seldom the rose of enjoyment adorns,
And the heart that is soonest awake to the
    flowers,
    Is always the first to be touch'd by the
    thorns.

    e.   Moore—*Oh! Think not My Spirits are*
                               always as Light.

I would not live alway; I ask not to stay
Where storm after storm rises dark o'er the
    way.

    f.   William A. Muhlenberg—*I would*
                           not Live Alway.

A mighty maze, but not without a plan.

    g.   Pope—*Essay on Man.*   Ep. I.   **L. 6.**

Fix'd like a plant on his peculiar spot,
To draw nutrition, propagate and rot.

    h.   Pope—*Essay on Man.*   Ep. II.   L. 63.

For forms of government let fools contest;
Whate'er is best administer'd is best;
For modes of faith let graceless zealots fight;
His can't be wrong whose life is in the right.

    i.   Pope—*Essay on Man.*   Ep. III.   L. 303.

Learn to live well, or fairly make your will;
You've play'd, and lov'd, and ate, and drank
    your fill:
Walk sober off, before a sprightlier age
Comes titt'ring on, and shoves you from the
    stage.

    j.   Pope—*Second Book of Horace.*   Ep. II.
                                      L. 322.

        Life can little more supply,
Then just to look about us and to die.

    k.   Pope—*Essay on Man.*   Ep. I.   L. 3.

Like following life through creatures you dis-
    sect,
You lose it in the moment you detect.

    l.   Pope—*Moral Essays.*   Ep. I.   L. 29.

On life's vast ocean diversely we sail,
Reason the card, but passion is the gale.

    m.   Pope—*Essay on Man.*   Ep. II.   L. 107.

See how the World its Veterans rewards!
A Youth of Frolics, an old Age of Cards;
Fair to no purpose, artful to no end,
Young without Lovers, old without a Friend;
A Fop their Passion, but their Prize a Sot;
Alive ridiculous, and dead forgot.

    n.   Pope—*Moral Essays.*   Ep. II.   L. 243.

She went from opera, park, assembly, play,
To morning walks, and prayers three hours a
    day.
To part her time 'twixt reading and bohea,
To muse, and spill her solitary tea,
Or o'er cold coffee trifle with the spoon,
Count the slow clock, and dine exact at noon.

    o.   Pope—*Ep. to Miss Blount on Leaving*
                               Town.   L. 13.

To be, contents his natural desire,
He asks no angel's wing, no seraph's fire;
But thinks, admitted to that equal sky,
His faithful dog shall bear him company.

    p.   Pope—*Essay on Man.*   Ep. I.   L. 109.

Our days begin with trouble here, our life is
    but a span,
And cruel death is always near, so frail a
    thing is man.

    q.   *New England Primer.*   1777.

So vanishes our state; so pass our days;
So life but opens now, and now decays;
The cradle and the tomb, alas! so nigh,
To live is scarce distinguish'd from to die.

    r.   Prior—*Solomon on the Vanity of the*
                         World.   Bk. III.   L. 527.

Who breathes must suffer; and who thinks,
    must mourn;
And he alone is bless'd who ne'er was born.

    s.   Prior—*Solomon on the Vanity of the*
                         World.   Bk. III.   L. 240.

Half my life is full of sorrow,
    Half of joy, still fresh and new;
One of these lives is a fancy,
    But the other one is true.

    t.   Adelaide A. Procter—*Dream-Life.*

This life is but the passage of a day,
This life is but a pang and all is over;
But in the life to come which fades not away
Every love shall abide and every lover.

    u.   Christina G. Rossetti—*Saints and*
                                 Angels.

Life's but a span, or a tale, or a word,
That in a trice, or suddaine, is rehearsèd.

    v.   *The Roxburghe Ballads.*   *A Friend's*
                              Advice.   Pt. II.   Edited by
                                  Wm. Chappell.

Say, what is life? 'Tis to be born,
    A helpless Babe, to greet the light
With a sharp wail, as if the morn
    Foretold a cloudy noon and night;
To weep, to sleep, and weep again,
    With sunny smiles between; and then?

    w.   J. G. Saxe—*The Story of Life.*

I've lived and loved.
　　a.　　Schiller—*Wallenstein*. Pt. I.
　　　　　(*Piccolomini*.) Song in Act II. Sc. 6.
　　　　　　　　　　Coleridge's trans.

O'er Ocean, with a thousand masts, sails forth
　　the stripling bold—
One boat, hard rescued from the deep, draws
　　into port the old!
　　b.　　Schiller—*Votive Tablets*. *Expectation
　　　　　　　　　　　and Fulfilment*.

Sound, sound the clarion, fill the fife!
　　To all the sensual world proclaim,
One crowded hour of glorious life
　　Is worth an age without a name.
　　c.　　Scott—*Old Mortality*. Ch. XXXIV.
　　　　　　　　　　Head of Chapter.

And a man's life's no more than to say
　　"One."
　　d.　　*Hamlet*. Act V. Sc. 2. L. 74.

And so, from hour to hour, we ripe and ripe,
And then, from hour to hour, we rot and rot;
And thereby hangs a tale.
　　e.　　*As You Like It*. Act II. Sc. 7. L. 26.

And this our life, exempt from public haunt,
Finds tongues in trees, books in the running
　　brooks,
Sermons in stones, and good in everything.
　　f.　　*As You Like It*. Act II. Sc. 1. L. 15.

Had I but died an hour before this chance,
I had liv'd a blessed time; for, from this in-
　　stant,
There's nothing serious in mortality: .
All is but toys; renown, and grace is dead;
The wine of life is drawn, and the mere lees
Is left this vault to brag of.
　　g.　　*Macbeth*. Act II. Sc. 3. L. 96.

Her father lov'd me; oft invited me;
Still question'd me the story of my life,
From year to year, the battles, sieges, for-
　　tunes,
That I have pass'd.
　　h.　　*Othello*. Act I. Sc. 3. L. 128.

I bear a charmed life.
　　i.　　*Macbeth*. Act V. Sc. 8. L. 12.

I cannot tell what you and other men
Think of this life; but, for my single self,
I had as lief not be as live to be
In awe of such a thing as I myself.
　　j.　　*Julius Cæsar*. Act I. Sc. 2. L. 93.

It is silliness to live when to live is torment;
and then have we a prescription to die when
death is our physician.
　　k.　　*Othello*. Act I. Sc. 3. L. 309.

Let life be short; else shame will be too long.
　　l.　　*Henry V*. Act IV. Sc. 5. L. 23.

Life is a shuttle.
　　m.　　*Merry Wives of Windsor*. Act V.
　　　　　　　　　　Sc. 1. L. 20.

Life is as tedious as a twice-told tale
Vexing the dull ear of a drowsy man.
　　n.　　*King John*. Act III. Sc. 4. L. 108.

Nor stony tower, nor walls of beaten brass,
Nor airless dungeon, nor strong links of iron,
Can be retentive to the strength of spirit;
But life, being weary of these worldly bars,
Never lacks power to dismiss itself.
　　o.　　*Julius Cæsar*. Act I. Sc. 3. L. 93.

O excellent! I love long life better than figs.
　　p.　　*Antony and Cleopatra*. Act I. Sc. 2.
　　　　　　　　　　L. 32.

O gentlemen, the time of life is short!
To spend that shortness basely were too long,
If life did ride upon a dial's point,
Still ending at the arrival of an hour.
　　q.　　*Henry IV*. Pt. I. Act V. Sc. 2. L. 82

　　Out, out, brief candle!
Life's but a walking shadow.
　　r.　　*Macbeth*. Act V. Sc. 5. L. 23.

　　Reason thus with life:
If I do lose thee, I do lose a thing
That none but fools would keep.
　　s.　　*Measure for Measure*. Act III. Sc. 1.
　　　　　　　　　　L. 6.

So weary with disasters tugg'd with fortune,
That I would set my life on any chance,
To mend, or be rid on't.
　　t.　　*Macbeth*. Act III. Sc. I. L. 113.

　　　　　　　That but this blow
Might be the be-all and the end-all here,
But here, upon this bank and shoal of time,
We'd jump the life to come.
　　u.　　*Macbeth*. Act I. Sc. 7. L. 4.

The sands are number'd that make up my life;
Here must I stay, and here my life must end.
　　v.　　*Henry VI*. Pt. III. Act I. Sc. 4.
　　　　　　　　　　L. 25.

　　The web of our life is of a mingled yarn, good
and ill together.
　　w.　　*All's Well That Ends Well*. Act IV.
　　　　　　　　　　Sc. 3. L. 80.

This day I breathed first: time is come round,
And where I did begin there shall I end;
My life is run his compass.
　　x.　　*Julius Cæsar*. Act V. Sc. 3. L. 23.

Thy life's a miracle.
　　y.　　*King Lear*. Act IV. Sc. 6. L. 55.

When we are born, we cry, that we are come
To this great stage of fools.
　　z.　　*King Lear*. Act IV. Sc. 6. L. 186.

Why, what should be the fear?
I do not set my life at a pin's fee.
  a.   *Hamlet.* Act I. Sc. 4. L. 66.

Life, like a dome of many-coloured glass,
Stains the white radiance of Eternity.
  b.   Shelley—*Adonais.* St. 52.

              We have two lives;
The soul of man is like the rolling world,
One half in day, the other dipt in night;
The one has music and the flying cloud,
The other, silence and the wakeful stars.
  c.   Alex. Smith—*Horton.* L. 76.

Yes, this is life; and everywhere we meet,
Not victor crowns, but wailings of defeat.
  d.   Elizabeth Oakes Smith—*Sonnet.*
                     The Unattained.

"Life is not lost," said she, "for which is
    bought
Endlesse renowne."
  e.   Spenser—*Faerie Queene.* Bk. III.
                 Canto XI. St. 19.

Man is an organ of life, and God alone is life.
  f.   Swedenborg—*True Christian Religion.*
                     Par. 504.

What ought to be more dear to a man than
his life to eternity?
  g.   Swedenborg—*Arcana.* Par. 794.

May you live all the days of your life.
  h.   Swift—*Polite Conversation.*
                   Dialogue II.

           So his life has flowed
From its mysterious urn a sacred stream,
In whose calm depth the beautiful and pure
Alone are mirrored; which, though shapes
    of ill
May hover round its surface, glides in light,
And takes no shadow from them.
  i.   Thomas Noon Talfourd—*Ion.* Act I.
              Sc. 1. L. 138.

For life lives only in success.
  j.   Bayard Taylor—*Amran's Wooing.*
                   St. 5.

Our life is scarce the twinkle of a star
In God's eternal day.
  k.   Bayard Taylor—*Autumnal Vespers.*

I cannot rest from travel: I will drink
Life to the lees.
  l.   Tennyson—*Ulysses.* L. 6.

Life is not as idle ore,
But iron dug from central gloom,
    And heated hot with burning fears,
    And dipt in baths of hissing tears,
And batter'd with the shocks of doom,
    To shape and use.
  m.   Tennyson—*In Memoriam.* Pt. CXVIII.
                   St. 5.

The white flower of a blameless life.
  n.   Tennyson—*Dedication to Idylls of the*
                           King.

My life is like a stroll upon the beach,
  o.   Thoreau—*A Week on the Concord and*
                    Merrimack Rivers.

The tree of deepest root is found
Least willing still to quit the ground;
'Twas therefore said by ancient sages,
    That love of life increased with years
So much, that in our latter stages,
When pain grows sharp, and sickness rages,
    The greatest love of life appears.
  p.   Hester L. Thrale—*Three Warnings.*

We live not in our moments or our years:
The present we fling from us like the rind
Of some sweet future, which we after find
Bitter to taste.
  q.   Richard Chenevix Trench—*To ——.*

Life let us cherish, while yet the taper glows,
And the fresh flow'ret pluck ere it close;
Why are we fond of toil and care?
Why choose the rankling thorn to wear?
  r.   J. M. Usteri—*Life let us Cherish.*

Our life contains a thousand springs,
    And dies if one be gone.
Strange! that a harp of thousand strings
    Should keep in tune so long.
  s.   Watts—*Hymns and Spiritual Songs.*
               Bk. II. Hymn XIX.

Our lives are albums written through
With good or ill, with false or true;
And as the blessed angels turn
    The pages of our years,
God grant they read the good with smiles,
    And blot the ill with tears!
  t.   Whittier—*Written in a Lady's Album.*

Ah! somehow life is bigger after all
Than any painted angel could we see
The God that is within us!
  u.   Oscar Wilde—*Humanitad.* St. 60.

My life is like the summer rose,
    That opens to the morning sky;
But ere the shades of evening close,
    Is scattered on the ground—to die.
  v.   R. H. Wilde—*Summer Rose.* *Lament*
                  of the Captive. St. 1.

We live by Admiration, Hope, and Love;
And, even as these are well and wisely fixed,
In dignity of being we ascend.
  w.   Wordsworth—*The Excursion.* Bk. IV.

And cradles rock us nearer to the tomb:
Our birth is nothing but our death begun.
  x.   Young—*Night Thoughts.* Night V.
                   L. 718.

For what are men who grasp at praise sub-
    lime,
But bubbles on the rapid stream of time,
That rise, and fall, that swell, and are no
    more,
Born, and forgot, ten thousand in an hour?
    a.   YOUNG—*Love of Fame.* Satire II. L. 285.

Still seems it strange, that thou shouldst live
    forever?
Is it less strange, that thou shouldst live at all?
This is a miracle; and that no more.
    b.   YOUNG—*Night Thoughts.* Night VII.
                            L. 1,396.

That life is long, which answers life's great
    end.
    c.   YOUNG—*Night Thoughts.* Night V.
                            L. 773.

LIGHT.

Corruption springs from light: 'tis one same
    power
Creates, preserves, destroys; matter whereon
It works, one e'er self-transmutative form,
Common to now the living, now the dead.
    d.   BAILEY—*Festus.* Sc. *Water and Wood.*

For I light my candle from their torches.
    e.   BURTON—*Anatomy of Melancholy.*
             Pt. III. Sec. 2. Memb. 5. Subsec. 1.

Light is the first of painters. There is no
object so foul that intense light will not make
it beautiful.
    f.   EMERSON—*Nature.* Ch. III.

Light (God's eldest daughter!).
    g.   FULLER—*The Holy and Profane States.*
                  Bk. III. *Of Building.*

Against the darkness outer
    God's light his likeness takes,
And he from the mighty doubter
    The great believer makes.
    h.   R. W. GILDER—*The New Day.* Pt. IV.
                          Song XV.

And this I know; whether the one True
    Light
Kindle to Love, or Wrath consume me quite,
One Flash of It within the Tavern caught
Better than in the Temple lost outright.
    i.   OMAR KHAYYÁM—*Rubáiyát.* St. 77.
                      Fitzgerald's trans.

The prayer of Ajax was for light.
    j.   LONGFELLOW—*The Goblet of Life.* St. 8.

          And from her native east
To journey through the aery gloom began,
Spher'd in a radiant cloud, for yet the sun
Was not.
    k.   MILTON—*Paradise Lost.* Bk. VII.
                        L. 245.

But let my due feet never fail
To walk the studious cloisters pale,
And love the high embowed roof,
With antique pillars massy proof,
And storied windows richly dight;
Casting a dim religious light.
    l.   MILTON—*Il Penseroso.* L. 155.

Dark with excessive bright.
    m.   MILTON—*Paradise Lost.* Bk. III.
                            L. 380.

Hail, holy light! offspring of heaven first-
    born!
Or of th' eternal coeternal beam,
May I express thee unblam'd? since God is
    light
And never but in unapproached light
Dwelt from eternity, dwelt then in thee,
Bright effluence of bright essence increate!
    n.   MILTON—*Paradise Lost.* Bk. III. L. 1.

He that has light within his own clear breast
May sit i' th' centre and enjoy bright day;
But he that hides a dark soul and foul thoughts
Benighted walks under the mid-day sun.
    o.   MILTON—*Comus.* L. 381.

        There swift return
Diurnal, merely to officiate light
Round this opacous earth, this punctual spot.
    p.   MILTON—*Paradise Lost.* Bk. VIII.
                          L. 21.

Where glowing embers through the room
Teach light to counterfeit a gloom.
    q.   MILTON—*Il Penseroso.* L. 79.

With thy long levell'd rule of streaming light.
    r.   MILTON—*Comus.* L. 340.

Nature and Nature's laws lay hid in night:
God said, "Let Newton be!" and all was
    light.
    s.   POPE—*Epitaph Intended for Sir Isaac
                          Newton.*

Light seeking light doth light of light beguile:
So, ere you find where light in darkness lies,
Your light grows dark by losing of your eyes.
    t.   *Love's Labour's Lost.* Act I. Sc. 1.
                          L. 77.

But it is not necessary to light a candle to
the sun.
    u.   ALGERNON SIDNEY—*Discourses on
                Government.* Ch. II. Sec. 23.

        'Twas a light that made
Darkness itself appear
A thing of comfort.
    v.   SOUTHEY—*The Curse of Kehama.
                      Padalon.* St. 2.

An unreflected light did never yet
Dazzle the vision feminine.
    w.   SIR HENRY TAYLOR—*Philip Van
             Artevelde.* Pt. I. Act I. Sc. 5. L. 88.

Where God and Nature met in light.
a.   TENNYSON—*In Memoriam.*   Pt. CXI.
St. 5.

A remnant of uneasy light.
b.   WORDSWORTH—*The Matron of*
Jedborough, and Her Husband.

LINGUISTS.

Languages are no more than the keys of Sciences. He who despises one, slights the other.
c.   DE LA BRUYÈRE—*The Characters or*
Manners of the Present Age.
Ch. XII.

Besides 't is known he could speak Greek
As naturally as pigs squeak;
That Latin was no more difficile
Than to a blackbird 't is to whistle.
d.   BUTLER—*Hudibras.*   Pt. I.   Canto I.
L. 51.

I love the language, that soft bastard Latin,
Which melts like kisses from a female mouth.
e.   BYRON—*Beppo.*   St. 44.

He Greek and Latin speaks with greater ease
Than hogs eat acorns, and tame pigeons peas.
f.   CRANFIELD—*Panegyric on Tom Coriate.*

Lash'd into Latin by the tingling rod.
g.   GAY—*The Birth of the Squire.*   L. 46.

Small Latin, and less Greek.
h.   BEN JONSON—*To the Memory of*
Shakespeare.

Away with him, away with him! he speaks Latin.
i.   *Henry VI.*   Pt. II.   Act IV.   Sc. 7.
L. 62.

By your own report
A linguist.
j.   *Two Gentlemen of Verona.*   Act IV.
Sc. 1.   L. 56.

O! good my lord, no Latin;
I'm not such a truant since my coming,
As not to know the language I have liy'd in.
k.   *Henry VIII.*   Act III.   Sc. 1.   L. 42.

Speaks three or four languages word for word without a book.
l.   *Twelfth Night.*   Act I.   Sc. 3.   L. 28.

This is your devoted friend, sir, the manifold linguist.
m.   *All's Well that Ends Well.*   Act IV.
Sc. 3.   L. 262.

Egad, I think the interpreter is the hardest to be understood of the two!
n.   R. B. SHERIDAN—*The Critic.*   Act I.
Sc. 2.

LISTENING.

But yet she listen'd—'tis enough—
Who listens once will listen twice;
Her heart, be sure, is not of ice,
And one refusal no rebuff.
o.   BYRON—*Mazeppa.*   St. 6.

He holds him with his glittering eye—
   *   *   *   *   *   *
And listens like a three years' child.
p.   COLERIDGE—*The Ancient Mariner*
Pt. I.   St. 4.

He ceas'd; but left so pleasing on their ear
His voice, that list'ning still they seem'd to hear.
q.   HOMER—*Odyssey.*   Bk. XIII.   L. 1.
Pope's trans.

Listen, every one
That listen may, unto a tale
That's merrier than the nightingale.
r.   LONGFELLOW—*Tales of a Wayside Inn.*
Pt. III.   *The Sicilian's Tale.*
Interlude Before the Monk of
Casal-Maggiore.

In listening mood she seemed to stand,
The guardian Naiad of the strand.
s.   SCOTT—*The Lady of the Lake.*   Canto I.
St. 17.

And this cuff was but to knock at your ear, and beseech listening.
t.   *Taming of the Shrew.*   Act IV.   Sc. 1.
L. 66.

I have seen
A curious child, who dwelt upon a tract
Of inland ground, applying to his ear
The convolutions of a smooth-lipped shell;
To which, in silence hushed, his very soul
Listened intensely; and his countenance soon
Brightened with joy; for from within were heard
Murmurings, whereby the monitor expressed
Mysterious union with its native sea.
u.   WORDSWORTH—*The Excursion.*   Bk. IV.

LITERATURE.

Literary Men are * * * a perpetual priesthood.
v.   CARLYLE—*Essays.*   State of German
Literature.

Literature is the thought of thinking Souls.
w.   CARLYLE—*Essays.*   Memoirs of the Life
of Scott.

But, indeed, we prefer books to pounds; and we love manuscripts better than florins; and we prefer small *pamphlets* to war horses.
x.   ISAAC DISRAELI—*Curiosities of*
Literature. Pamphlets.

23

Literature is an avenue to glory, ever open for those ingenious men who are deprived of honours or of wealth.
a.   Isaac Disraeli—*Literary Character.*
            Ch. XXIV.

Time the great destroyer of other men's happiness, only enlarges the patrimony of literature to its possessor.
b.   Isaac Disraeli—*Literary Character of Men of Genius.*   Ch. XXII.

Republic of letters.
c.   Henry Fielding—*Tom Jones.*
            Bk. XIV.   Ch. I.

Our poetry in the eighteenth century was prose; our prose in the seventeenth, poetry.
d.   J. C. and A. W. Hare—*Guesses at Truth.*

The leader, mingling with the vulgar host,
Is with the common mass of matter lost!
e.   Homer—*Odyssey.* Bk. IV. L. 397.
            Pope's trans.

* * * A man of the world amongst men of letters, a man of letters amongst men of the world.
f.   Macaulay—*On Sir William Temple.*

There is first the literature of *knowledge,* and secondly, the literature of *power.* The function of the first is—to *teach ;* the function of the second is—to *move ;* the first is a rudder, the second an oar or a sail. The first speaks to the *mere* discursive understanding; the second speaks ultimately, it may happen, to the higher understanding or reason, but always *through* affections of pleasure and sympathy.
g.   Thomas De Quincey—*Essays on the Poets. Alexander Pope.*

We cultivate literature on a little oat-meal.
h.   Sydney Smith—*Lady Holland's Memoir.*   Vol. I.   P. 23.

LIVERY (*See* Occupations).

LOSS.

Losers must have leave to speak.
i.   Colley Cibber—*The Rival Fools.*
            Act I.   L. 17.

For 'tis a truth well known to most,
That whatsoever thing is lost,
We seek it, ere it come to light,
In every cranny but the right.
j.   Cowper—*The Retired Cat.*   L. 95.

What's saved affords
No indication of what's lost.
k.   Owen Meredith (Lord Lytton)—*The Scroll.*

Abashed the Devil stood,
And felt how awful goodness is, and saw
Virtue in her own shape how lovely ; saw
And pined his loss.
l.   Milton—*Paradise Lost.*   Bk. IV.
            L. 846.

A wise man loses nothing, if he but save himself.
m.   Montaigne—*Essays. Of Solitude.*

When wealth is lost, nothing is lost;
When health is lost, something is lost;
When character is lost, all is lost!
n.   *Motto Over the Walls of a School in Germany.*

That puts it not unto the touch
To win or lose it all.
o.   Napier—*Montrose and the Covenanters. Montrose's Poems.* No. 1. Vol. II.
            P. 566.

Like the dew on the mountain,
   Like the foam on the river,
Like the bubble on the fountain,
   Thou art gone, and forever !
p.   Scott—*Lady of the Lake.*   Canto III.
            St. 16.

Wise men ne'er sit and wail their loss,
But cheerly seek how to redress their harms.
q.   *Henry VI.* Pt. III. Act V. Sc. 4. L. 1.

But over all things brooding slept
The quiet sense of something lost.
r.   Tennyson—*In Memoriam.*
            Pt. LXXVIII.   St. 2.

That loss is common would not make
   My own less bitter, rather more:
   Too common! Never morning wore
To evening, but some heart did break.
s.   Tennyson—*In Memoriam.*   Pt. VI.
            St. 2.

No man can lose what he never had.
t.   Izaak Walton—*The Complete Angler.*
            Pt. I.   Ch. V.

On all important time, thro' ev'ry age,
Tho' much, and warm, the wise have urged;
       the man
Is yet unborn, who duly weighs an hour,
" I've lost a day "—the prince who nobly cried
Had been an emperor without his crown;
Of Rome? say rather, lord of human race.
u.   Young—*Night Thoughts.*   Night II.
            L. 97.

LOVE.

Mysterious love, uncertain treasure,
Hast thou more of pain or pleasure!
   *   *   *   *   *
Endless torments dwell about thee:
Yet who would live, and live without thee!
v.   Addison—*Rosamond.*   Act III.   Sc. 2.

When love once pleads admission to our
    hearts,
(In spite of all the virtue we can boast),
The woman that deliberates is lost.
   a.   ADDISON—*Cato.* Act IV. Sc. 1.

When love's well-timed 'tis not a fault to love;
The strong, the brave, the virtuous, and the
    wise,
Sink in the soft captivity together.
   b.   ADDISON—*Cato.* Act III. Sc. 1.

Ask not of me, love, what is love?
Ask what is good of God above;
Ask of the great sun what is light;
Ask what is darkness of the night;
Ask sin of what may be forgiven;
Ask what is happiness of heaven;
Ask what is folly of the crowd;
Ask what is fashion of the shroud;
Ask what is sweetness of thy kiss;
Ask of thyself what beauty is.
   c.   BAILEY—*Festus.* Sc. *A Party and*
                                Entertainment.

Could I love less, I should be happier now.
   d.   BAILEY—*Festus.* Sc. *Garden and*
                                Bower by the Sea.

I cannot love as I have loved,
   And yet I know not why;
It is the one great woe of life
   To feel all feeling die.
   e.   BAILEY—*Festus.* Sc. *A Party and*
                                Entertainment.

Love spends his all, and still hath store.
   f.   BAILEY—*Festus.* Sc. *A Party and*
                                Entertainment.

The sweetest joy, the wildest woe is love.
   g.   BAILEY—*Festus.* Sc. *Alcove and*
                                Garden.

The truth of truths is love.
   h.   BAILEY—*Festus.* Sc. *Another and a*
                                Better World.

How many times do I love, again?
Tell me how many beads there are
    In a silver chain
    Of evening rain
Unravelled from the trembling main
And threading the eye of a yellow star:—
So many times do I love again.
   i.   THOS. LOVELL BEDDOES—*How Many*
                                Times.

To Chloe's breast young Cupid slily stole,
But he crept in at Myra's pocket-hole.
   j.   WILLIAM BLAKE—*Couplets and*
                                Fragments. IV.

I am young—so is she—and how fair!
   Then love shall my moments employ;
I am caught by her berry brown hair,
   And the rose on her cheek is my joy!
   k.   BLOOMFIELD—*Hazelwood Hall.* Act I.
                                    Sc. 1.

Love in a shower safe shelter took,
In a rosy bower beside a brook,
And winked and nodded with conscious pride
To his votaries drenched on the other side.
Come hither, sweet maids, there's a bridge
    below,
The toll-keeper, Hymen, will let you through.
Come over the stream to me.
   l.   BLOOMFIELD—*Glee.* St. 1.

Love is that orbit of the restless soul
   Whose circle grazes the confines of space,
Bounding within the limits of its race
Utmost extremes.
   m.   GEO. H. BOKER—*Sonnet. Love is*
                                that Orbit.

Love is like fire. * * * Wounds of fire
are hard to bear; harder still are those of love.
   n.   HJALMAR HJORTH BOYESEN—*Gunnar.*
                                Ch. IV.

Much ado there was, God wot;
He woold love, and she woold not,
She sayd, "Never man was trewe;"
He sayes, "None was false to you."
   o.   NICHOLAS BRETON—*Phillida and*
                                Corydon.

   There is musick, even in the beauty and the
silent note which Cupid strikes, far sweeter
than the sound of an instrument.
   p.   SIR THOS. BROWNE—*Religio Medici.*
                            Pt. II. Sec. IX.

       Behold me! I am worthy
Of thy loving, for I love thee!
   q.   E. B. BROWNING—*Lady Geraldine's*
                            Courtship. St. 79.

       But I love you, sir:
And when a woman says she loves a man,
The man must hear her, though he love her
    not.
   r.   E. B. BROWNING—*Aurora Leigh.*
                                Bk. IX.

For none can express thee, though all should
   approve thee.
I love thee so, Dear, that I only can love thee.
   s.   E. B. BROWNING—*Insufficiency.*

I would not be a rose upon the wall
A queen might stop at, near the palace-door,
To say to a courtier, "Pluck that rose for me,
It's prettier than the rest." O Romney Leigh!
I'd rather far be trodden by his foot,
Than lie in a great queen's bosom.
   t.   E. B. BROWNING—*Aurora Leigh.*
                                Bk. IV.

        Who can fear
Too many stars, though each in heaven shall
    roll?
   Too many flowers, though each shall crown
    the year?
Say thou dost love me, love me, love me—toll
   The silver iterance!—only minding, Dear,
To love me also in silence, with thy soul.
   u.   E. B. BROWNING—*Sonnets from the*
                        Portuguese. Sonnet XXI.

Whoever lives true life, will love true love.
　a.　　E. B. Browning—*Aurora Leigh.*
　　　　　　　　　　　　　　　Bk. I.　L. 1096.

I think, am sure, a brother's love exceeds
All the world's loves in its unworldliness.
　b.　　Robert Browning—*Blot in the
　　　　　　　　　　'Scutcheon.*　Act II.　Sc. 1.

Love begins with love.
　c.　　De La Bruyère—*The Characters and
　　　　　　Manners of the Present Age.*　Ch. IV.

What, know you not, old man (quoth he)—
Your hair is white, your face is wise—
That Love must kiss that Mortal's eyes
Who hopes to see fair Arcady?
No gold can buy you entrance there;
But beggared Love may go all bare—
No wisdom won with weariness;
But love goes in with Folly's dress—
No fame that wit could ever win;
But only Love may lead Love in.
To Arcady, to Arcady.
　d.　　H. C. Bunner—*The Way to Arcady.*

But to see her was to love her,
Love but her, and love forever.
　e.　　Burns—*Song.　Ae Fond Kiss.*

Oh my luve's like a red, red rose,
　That's newly sprung in June;
Oh my luve's like the melodie
　That's sweetly played in tune.
　f.　　Burns—*A Red, Red Rose.*

The golden hours on angel wings
　Flew o'er me and my dearie,
For dear to me as light and life
　Was my sweet Highland Mary.
　g.　　Burns—*Highland Mary.*

And this is that Homer's golden chain,
which reacheth down from heaven to earth,
by which every creature is annexed, and depends on his Creator.
　h.　　Burton—*Anatomy of Melancholy.*
　　　　　　　　　　Pt. III.　Sec. 1.　Memb. 1.
　　　　　　　　　　　　　　　Subsec. 7.

No cord nor cable can so forcibly draw, or
hold so fast, as love can do with a twined
thread.
　i.　　Burton—*Anatomy of Melancholy.*
　　　　　　　　　　Pt. III.　Sec. 2.　Memb. 1.
　　　　　　　　　　　　　　　Subsec. 2.

Love is a boy by poets styl'd:
Then spare the rod and spoil the child.
　j.　　Butler—*Hudibras.*　Pt. II.　Canto I.
　　　　　　　　　　　　　　　L. 843.

　What mad lover ever dy'd,
To gain a soft and gentle bride?
Or for a lady tender-hearted,
In purling streams or hemp departed?
　k.　　Butler—*Hudibras.*　Pt. III.　Canto I.

I love my neighbor as myself,
　Myself like him too, by his leave,
Nor to his pleasure, power or pelf
　Came I to crouch, as I conceive.
Dame Nature doubtless has designed
A man the monarch of his mind.
　l.　　John Byrom—*Careless Content.*

When things were as fine as could possibly be
I thought 'twas the spring; but alas it was
　she.
　m.　　John Byrom—*A Pastoral.*

Alas! the love of women! it is known
To be a lovely and a fearful thing.
　n.　　Byron—*Don Juan.*　Canto II.　St. 199.

　　　　　　　　　　And to his eye
There was but one beloved face on earth,
And that was shining on him.
　o.　　Byron—*The Dream.*　St. 2.

In her first passion woman loves her lover;
In all the others, all she loves is love.
　p.　　Byron—*Don Juan.*　Canto III.　St. 3.
　　　　　See also La Rochefoucauld.
　　　　　　　　　　　　　Maxims, No. 497.

Man's love is of man's life a thing apart,
　'Tis woman's whole existence: man may
　　range
The court, camp, church, the vessel, and the
　mart,
　Sword, gown, gain, glory, offer in exchange
Pride, fame, ambition, to fill up his heart,
　And few there are whom these cannot es-
　　trange;
Men have all these resources, we but one,
To love again, and be again undone.
　q.　　Byron—*Don Juan.*　Canto I.　St. 194.

Oh Love! young Love! bound in thy rosy
　band,
Let sage or cynic prattle as he will,
These hours, and only these, redeem Life's
　years of ill.
　r.　　Byron—*Childe Harold.*　Canto II.
　　　　　　　　　　　　　　　St. 81.

O! that the Desert were my dwelling-place,
With one fair Spirit for my minister,
That I might all forget the human race,
And, hating no one, love but only her!
　s.　　Byron—*Childe Harold.*　Canto IV.
　　　　　　　　　　　　　　　St. 177.

She knew she was by him beloved,—she knew
For quickly comes such knowledge, that his
　heart
Was darken'd with her shadow.
　t.　　Byron—*The Dream.*　St. 3.

The cold in clime are cold in blood,
Their love can scarce deserve the name.
　u.　　Byron—*The Giaour.*　L. 1,099.

Who loves, raves—'tis youth's frenzy—but
　　the cure
Is bitterer still.
　　a.　　BYRON—*Childe Harold.*　Canto IV.
　　　　　　　　　　　　　　　S. 123.

Why did she love him? Curious fool!—be
　　still—
Is human love the growth of human will?
　　b.　　BYRON—*Lara.*　Canto II.　St. 22.

Yes, Love indeed is light from heaven;
　　A spark of that immortal fire
With angels shared, by Allah given
　　To lift from earth our low desire.
　　c.　　BYRON—*The Giaour.*　L. 1,131.

I'll bid the hyacinth to blow,
　　I'll teach my grotto green to be;
And sing my true love, all below
　　The holly bower and myrtle tree.
　　d.　　CAMPBELL—*Caroline.*　Pt. I.

My love lies bleeding.
　　e.　　CAMPBELL—*O'Connor's Child.*　St. 5.

Then fly betimes, for only they
Conquer love, that run away.
　　f.　　THOS. CAREW—*Song.　Conquest by*
　　　　　　　　　　　　　　　　Flight.

Let Time and Chance combine, combine!
Let Time and Chance combine!
The fairest love from heaven above,
　　That love of yours was mine,
　　　　　　　　My Dear!
　　That love of yours was mine.
　　g.　　CARLYLE—*Adieu.*

　　I have eaten his bread—I love him well, and
there is no love lost between us.
　　h.　　CERVANTES—*Don Quixote.*　Pt. II.
　　　　　　　　　　　　　　　　Ch. 33.

I tell thee Love is Nature's second sun,
Causing a spring of virtues where he shines.
　　i.　　GEORGE CHAPMAN—*All Fools.*　Act I.
　　　　　　　　　　　　　　　Sc. 1.　L. 98.

None ever loved, but at first sight they loved.
　　j.　　GEORGE CHAPMAN—*The Blind Beggar*
　　　　　　　　　　　　　　of Alexandria.

Banish that fear; my flame can never waste,
For love sincere refines upon the taste.
　　k.　　COLLEY CIBBER—*The Double Gallant.*
　　　　　　　　　　　　　　Act V.　Sc. 1.

Her very frowns are fairer far
Than smiles of other maidens are.
　　l.　　HARTLEY COLERIDGE—*Song.　She is*
　　　　　　　　　　　　　　　　not Fair.

All thoughts, all passions, all delights,
　　Whatever stirs this mortal frame,
All are but ministers of Love,
　　And feed his sacred flame.
　　m.　　COLERIDGE—*Love.*　St. 1.

And to be wroth with one we love
Doth work like madness in the brain.
　　n.　　COLERIDGE—*Christabel.*　Pt. II.　L. 81.

I have heard of reasons manifold
　　Why Love must needs be blind,
But this is the best of all I hold—
　　His eyes are in his mind.
　　o.　　COLERIDGE—*To a Lady.*　St. 2.

Heaven has no rage like love to hatred turned.
　　p.　　CONGREVE—*The Mourning Bride.*
　　　　　　　　　　　　　　Act III.　Sc. 2.

If there's delight in love, 'tis when I see
The heart, which others bleed for, bleed for
　　me.
　　q.　　CONGREVE—*Way of the World.*
　　　　　　　　　　　　　　Act III.　Sc. 3.

A mighty pain to love it is,
And 'tis a pain that pain to miss;
But, of all pains, the greatest pain
Is to love, but love in vain.
　　r.　　ABRAHAM COWLEY—*Anacreontiques.*
　　　　　　　　　　　　　　　VII.　Gold.

Our love is principle, and has its root
In reason, is judicious, manly, free.
　　s.　　COWPER—*The Task.*　Bk. V.　L. 353.

　　When a man loves a woman, it is of nature:
when a woman loves a woman, it is of grace—
of the grace that woman makes by her loveliness.
　　t.　　CHARLES F. DEEMS—*Address at Funeral*
　　　　　　　　　　　　　　of Alice Cary.

　　We are all born for love. ＊ ＊ ＊ It is the
principle of existence and its only end.
　　u.　　BENJ. DISRAELI—*Sybil.*　Bk. V.　Ch. IV.

Fool, not to know that love endures no tie,
And Jove but laughs at lovers' perjury.
　　v.　　DRYDEN—*Palamon and Arcite.*　Bk. II.
　　　　　　　　　　　　　　　　L. 75.

　　　　　　　Give, you gods,
Give to your boy, your Cæsar,
The rattle of a globe to play withal,
This gewgaw world, and put him cheaply off;
I'll not be pleased with less than Cleopatra.
　　w.　　DRYDEN—*All for Love.*　Act II.　Sc. 1.

Pains of love be sweeter far
Than all other pleasures are.
　　x.　　DRYDEN—*Tyrannic Love.*　Act IV.　Sc. I.

I'm sitting on the stile, Mary,
Where we sat side by side.
　　y.　　LADY DUFFERIN—*Lament of the Irish*
　　　　　　　　　　　　　　　Emigrant.

But is it what we love, or how we love,
That makes true good?
　　z.　　GEORGE ELIOT—*The Spanish Gypsy.*
　　　　　　　　　　　　　　　Bk. I.

I think we had the chief of all love's joys
Only in knowing that we love each other.
   a.   GEORGE ELIOT—*The Spanish Gypsy.*
                     Bk. III.

'Tis what I love determines how I love.
   b.   GEORGE ELIOT—*The Spanish Gypsy.*
                     Bk. I.

      Women know no perfect love:
Loving the strong, they can forsake the strong;
Man clings because the being whom he loves
Is weak and needs him.
   c.   GEORGE ELIOT—*The Spanish Gypsy.*
                     Bk. III.

All mankind love a lover.
   d.   EMERSON—*Essays. Of Love.*

A ruddy drop of manly blood
   The surging sea outweighs;
The world uncertain comes and goes,
   The lover rooted stays.
   e.   EMERSON—*Essays. First Series.*
                 Epigraph to Friendship.

Love, which is the essence of God, is not for
levity, but for the total worth of man.
   f.   EMERSON—*Essays. Of Friendship.*

The solid, solid universe
   Is pervious to Love;
With bandaged eyes he never errs,
   Around, below, above.
      His blinding light
      He flingeth white
On God's and Satan's brood,
      And reconciles
      By mystic wiles
The evil and the good.
   g.   EMERSON—*Cupido.*

Venus, when her son was lost,
Cried him up and down the coast,
In hamlets, palaces, and parks,
And told the truant by his marks,—
Golden curls, and quiver, and bow.
   h.   EMERSON—*Initial, Demoniac and*
                 Celestial Love. St. 1.

Venus, thy eternal sway
All the race of men obey.
   i.   EURIPIDES—*Austice.*

Love is the tyrant of the heart; it darkens
Reason, confounds discretion; deaf to Counsel
It runs a headlong course to desperate madness.
   j.   JOHN FORD—*The Lover's Melancholy.*
                Act III. Sc. 3. L. 105.

Love, then, hath every bliss in store;
'Tis friendship, and 'tis something more.
Each other every wish they give;
Not to know love is not to live.
   k.   GAY—*Plutus, Cupid and Time.* L. 135.

I saw and loved.
   l.   GIBBON—*Autobiographic Memoirs.*
                     P. 48.

I love her doubting and anguish;
   I love the love she withholds,
I love my love that loveth her,
   And anew her being moulds.
   m.   R. W. GILDER—*The New Day.* Pt. III.
                    Song XV.

Love, Love, my Love.
   The best things are the truest!
When the earth lies shadowy dark below
   Oh, then the heavens are bluest!
   n.   R. W. GILDER—*The New Day.* Pt. IV
                    Song 1

As for murmurs, mother, we grumble a little
now and then, to be sure; but there's no love
lost between us.
   o.   GOLDSMITH—*She Stoops to Conquer.*
                 Act IV. L. 255.

The bashful virgin's sidelong looks of love.
   p.   GOLDSMITH—*The Deserted Village.*
                     L. 29.

Thus let me hold thee to my heart,
   And every care resign:
And we shall never, never part,
   My life—my all that's mine!
   q.   GOLDSMITH—*The Hermit.* St. 39.

Dear as the light that visits these sad eyes,
Dear as the ruddy drops that warm my heart.
   r.   GRAY—*The Bard.* I. 3. L. 12.

O'er her warm cheek, and rising bosom, move
The bloom of young Desire and purple light
   of love.
   s.   GRAY—*The Progress of Poesy.* I. 3.
                     L. 16.

Love is a lock that linketh noble minds,
Faith is the key that shuts the spring of love.
   t.   ROBERT GREENE—*Alcida. Verses*
              Written under a Carving of Cupid
               Blowing Bladders in the Air.

The chemist of love
   Will this perishing mould,
Were it made out of mire,
   Transmute into gold.
   u.   HAFIZ—*Divan.*

Love understands love; it needs no talk.
   v.   F. R. HAVERGAL—*Royal*
             Commandments. Loving Allegiance.

And once again we plighted our troth,
And titter'd, caress'd, kiss'd so dearly.
   w.   HEINE—*Book of Songs. Youthful*
              Sorrows. No. 57. St. 2.

Alas! for love, if thou art all,
And nought beyond, O earth.
   x.   MRS. HEMANS—*The Graves of a*
                     Household.

No, not Jove
Himselfe, at one time, can be wise and love.
　　a.　　HERRICK—*Hesperides.　To Silvia.*

You say to me-wards your affection's strong;
Pray love me little, so you love me long.
　　b.　　HERRICK—*Love me Little, Love me
　　　　　　　　　　　　　　　　　　Long.*

O, love, love, love!
　Love is like a dizziness;
It winna let a poor body
　Gang about his biziness!
　　c.　　HOGG—*Love is like a Dizziness.　L. 9.*

Soft is the breath of a maiden's Yes:
Not the light gossamer stirs with less;
But never a cable that holds so fast
Through all the battles of wave and blast.
　　d.　　O. W. HOLMES—*Songs of Many Seasons.
　　　　　　　　　　Dorothy.　II.　St. 7.*

For love deceives the best of woman kind.
　　e.　　HOMER—*Odyssey.　Bk. 15.　L. 463.
　　　　　　　　　　　　Pope's trans.*

Who love too much, hate in the like extreme.
　　f.　　HOMER—*Odyssey.　Bk. XV.　L. 79.
　　　　　　　　　　　　Pope's trans.*

What's our baggage?　Only vows,
　Happiness, and all our care,
And the flower that sweetly shows
　Nestling lightly in your hair.
　　g.　　VICTOR HUGO—*Eviradnus.　XI.*

But great loves, to the last, have pulses red;
All great loves that have ever died dropped
　　　dead.
　　h.　　HELEN HUNT—*Dropped Dead.*

Love has a tide!
　　i.　　HELEN HUNT—*Verses.　Tides.*

When love is at its best, one loves
So much that he cannot forget.
　　j.　　HELEN HUNT—*Two Truths.*

If you become a Nun, dear,
　The bishop Love will be;
The Cupids every one, dear!
　Will chant—'We trust in thee!'
　　k.　　LEIGH HUNT—*The Nun.*

From henceforth thou shalt learn that there
　　　is love
To long for, pureness to desire, a mount
Of consecration it were good to scale.
　　l.　　JEAN INGELOW—*A Parson's Letter to a
　　　　　　Young Poet.　Pt. II.　L. 55.*

Love's like the flies, and, drawing-room or
garret, goes all over a house.
　　m.　　DOUGLAS JERROLD—*Jerrold's Wit.　Love.*

I wish you could invent some means to
make me at all happy without you.　Every
hour I am more and more concentrated in
you; everything else tastes like chaff in my
mouth.
　　n.　　KEATS—*Letters.　No. XXXVII.*

Love in a hut, with water and a crust,
Is—Love, forgive us!—cinders, ashes, dust.
　　o.　　KEATS—*Lamia.　Pt. II.*

The more we love a mistress, the nearer we
are to hating her.
　　p.　　LA ROCHEFOUCAULD—*Maxims.　114.*

The pleasure of love is in loving.　We are
happier in the passion we feel than in what
we excite.
　　q.　　LA ROCHEFOUCAULD—*Maxims.　78.*

Love leads to present rapture,—then to pain;
But all through Love in time is healed again.
　　r.　　LELAND—*Sweet Marjoram.*

A warrior so bold, and a virgin so bright
Conversed as they sat on the green.
They gazed on each other with tender delight,
Alonzo the Brave was the name of the knight—
The maiden's the Fair Imogene.
　　s.　　M. G. LEWIS—*Alonzo the Brave and
　　　　　　　　　　the Fair Imogene.*

Does not all the blood within me
Leap to meet thee, leap to meet thee,
As the springs to meet the sunshine.
　　t.　　LONGFELLOW—*Hiawatha.　Wedding
　　　　　　　　　　Feast.　L. 153.*

How can I tell the signals and the signs
By which one heart another heart divines?
How can I tell the many thousand ways
By which it keeps the secret it betrays?
　　u.　　LONGFELLOW—*Tales of a Wayside Inn.
　　　　　Pt. III.　The Student's Tale.
　　　　　Emma and Eginhard.　L. 75.*

I do not love thee less for what is done,
And cannot be undone.　Thy very weakness
Hath brought thee nearer to me, and hence-
　　　forth
My love will have a sense of pity in it,
Making it less a worship than before.
　　v.　　LONGFELLOW—*Masque of Pandora.
　　　　　　Pt. VIII.　In the Garden.　L. 39.*

I love thee, as the good love heaven.
　　w.　　LONGFELLOW—*The Spanish Student.
　　　　　　　　　　Act I.　Sc. 3.　L. 146.*

It is difficult to know at what moment love
begins; it is less difficult to know that it has
begun.
　　x.　　LONGFELLOW—*Kavanagh.　Ch. XXI.*

Like Dian's kiss, unask'd, unsought,
Love gives itself, but is not bought.
　　y.　　LONGFELLOW—*Endymion.　St. 4.*

Love contending with friendship, and self
　　　with each generous impulse.
To and fro in his breast his thoughts were
　　　heaving and dashing,
As in a foundering ship.
　　z.　　LONGFELLOW—*Courtship of Miles
　　　　　　　　　　Standish.　Pt. III.　L. 7.*

Love keeps the cold out better than a cloak.
     It serves for food and raiment.
　　a.　　Longfellow—*The Spanish Student.*
　　　　　　　　Act I. Sc. 5. L. 52.

O, there is nothing holier, in this life of
ours, than the first consciousness of love,—
the first fluttering of its silken wings.
　b.　　Longfellow—*Hyperion.* Bk. III.
　　　　　　　　　　　　　　Ch. VI.

That was the first sound in the song of love!
Scarce more than silence is, and yet a sound.
Hands of invisible spirits touch the strings
Of that mysterious instrument, the soul,
And play the prelude of our fate. We hear
The voice prophetic, and are not alone.
　　c.　　Longfellow—*The Spanish Student.*
　　　　　　　　Act I. Sc. 3. L. 109.

I could not love thee, dear, so much,
Loved I not honor more.
　　d.　　Lovelace—*To Lucasta, Going to the
　　　　　　　　Warres.* St. 3.

Not as all other women are
　Is she that to my soul is dear;
Her glorious fancies come from far,
　Beneath the silver evening star,
　　And yet her heart is ever near.
　　e.　　Lowell—*My Love.* St. 1.

True love is but a humble, low born thing,
And hath its food served up in earthenware;
It is a thing to walk with, hand in hand,
Through the every-dayness of this workday
　　world.
　　f.　　Lowell—*Love.* L. 1.

As love knoweth no lawes, so it regardeth
no conditions.
　　g.　　Lyly—*Euphues.* P. 84.

Cupid and my Campaspe play'd
At cards for kisses ; Cupid paid ;
He stakes his quiver, bow and arrows,
His mother's doves, and team of sparrows;
Loses them too ; then down he throws
The coral of his lip,—the rose
Growing on's cheek (but none knows how)
With these, the crystal on his brow,
And then the dimple of his chin ;
All these did my Campaspe win.
At last he set her both his eyes,
She won, and Cupid blind did rise.
O Love ! hath she done this to thee?
What shall, alas ! become of me?
　　h.　　Lyly—*Alexander and Campaspe.*
　　　　　　　　Act III. Sc. V. *Song.*

None without hope e'er lov'd the brightest
　　fair :
But Love can hope where Reason would
　　despair.
　　i.　　Lord Lyttleton—*Epigram.*

The lover in the husband may be lost.
　　j.　　Lord Lyttleton—*Advice to a Lady.*
　　　　　　　　　　　　　　St. 13.

Love has no thought of self!
Love buys not with the ruthless usurer's
　　gold
The loathsome prostitution of a hand
Without a heart ! Love sacrifices all things
To bless the thing it loves !
　　k.　　Bulwer-Lytton—*The Lady of Lyons.*
　　　　　　　　Act V. Sc. 2. L. 23.

Love thou, and if thy love be deep as mine,
Thou wilt not laugh at poets.
　　l.　　Bulwer-Lytton—*Richelieu.* Act I.
　　　　　　　　　　　Sc. 1. L. 177.

But thou, through good and evil, praise and
　　blame,
　Wilt not thou love me for myself alone?
Yes, thou wilt love me with exceeding love,
　And I will tenfold all that love repay ;
Still smiling, though the tender may reprove,
　Still faithful, though the trusted may be-
　　tray.
　　m.　　Macaulay—*Lines Written July 30,*
　　　　　　　　　　　　　　　　1847.

Come live with me, and be my love,
And we will all the pleasures prove,
That valleys, groves, or hills, or fields,
Or woods and steepy mountains, yield.
　　n.　　Marlowe—*The Passionate Shepherd to
　　　　　　　　his Love.* St. 1.

Love me little, love me long.
　　o.　　Marlowe—*The Jew of Malta.* Act IV.
　　　　　　　　　　　　　　Sc. 6.

Who ever lov'd, that lov'd not at first sight?
　　p.　　Marlowe—*Hero and Leander.* *First
　　　　　　　　Sestiad.* L. 176.

'Tis well to be off with the old love
　Before you are on with the new.
　　q.　　Maturin—*Motto to the Play of Bertram.*

I loved you ere I knew you ; know you now,
And having known you, love you better still.
　　r.　　Owen Meredith (Lord Lytton)—
　　　　　　　　　　　　　　Vanini.

Love is all in fire, and yet is ever freezing;
Love is much in winning, yet is more in
　　leesing :
Love is ever sick, and yet is never dying ;
Love is ever true, and yet is ever lying ;
Love does doat in liking, and is mad in
　　loathing ;
Love indeed is anything, yet indeed is nothing.
　　s.　　Thos. Middleton—*Blurt, Master
　　　　　　　　Constable.* Act II. Sc. 2.

Imparadis'd in one another's arms.
　　t.　　Milton—*Paradise Lost.* Bk. IV. L. 50.

It is not virtue, wisdom, valour, wit,
Strength, comeliness of shape, or amplest
　　merit
That woman's love can win, or long inherit.
But what it is, hard is to say,
Harder to hit.
　　u.　　Milton—*Samson Agonistes.* L. 1,010.

So dear I love him, that with him all deaths
I could endure, without him live no life.
   a.   Milton—*Paradise Lost.* Bk. IX.
                                      L. 832.

If a man should importune me to give a
reason why I loved him, I find it could no
otherwise be expressed than by making answer, Because it was he; because it was I.
There is beyond all that I am able to say, I
know not what inexplicable and fated power
that brought on this union.
   b.   Montaigne—*Essays.* Bk. I.
                                  Ch. XXVII.

But there's nothing half so sweet in life
As love's young dream.
   c.   Moore—*Love's Young Dream.* St. 1.

I know not, I ask not, if guilt's in that heart,
I but know that I love thee, whatever thou
art.
   d.   Moore—*Come, Rest in This Bosom.*
                                      St. 2.

Love on through all ills, and love on till they
die!
   e.   Moore—*Lalla Rookh.*   *The Light of
                          the Harem.* L. 653.

No, the heart that has truly loved never
   forgets,
   But as truly loves on to the close,
As the sunflower turns on her god, when he
   sets,
   The same look which she turn'd when he
   rose.
   f.   Moore—*Believe Me, If All Those
                Endearing Young Charms.* St. 2.

" Tell me, what's Love;" said Youth, one day,
To drooping Age, who crost his way.—
" It is a sunny hour of play ;
For which repentance dear doth pay ;
   Repentance! Repentance!
And this is Love, as wise men say."
   g.   Moore—*Youth and Age.*

   Duty's a slave that keeps the keys,
But Love, the master goes in and out
Of his goodly chambers with song and shout,
   Just as he please—just as he please.
   h.   D. M. Mulock—*Plighted.*

Let those love now who never lov'd before,
Let those who always loved now love the more.
   i.   Thos. Parnell—*Trans. of the
                Pervigilium Veneris.* Ascribed
                             to Catullus.

The moods of love are like the wind ;
And none knows whence or why they rise.
   j.   Coventry Patmore—*The Angel in the
                 House. Sarum Plain.*

What thing is love?—for (well I wot) love is
   a thing.
It is a prick, it is a sting,
It is a pretty, pretty thing ;
It is a fire, it is a coal,
Whose flame creeps in at every hole!
   k.   George Peele—*Miscellaneous Poems.
                    The Hunting of Cupid.*

Love will make men dare to die for their
beloved—love alone; and women as well as
men.
   l.   Plato—*The Symposium.*

Ah ! what avails it me the flocks to keep,
Who lost my heart while I preserv'd my
   sheep.
   m.   Pope—*Autumn.* L. 79.

Is it, in Heav'n, a crime to love too well?
To bear too tender or too firm a heart,
To act a lover's or a Roman's part?
Is there no bright reversion in the sky
For those who greatly think, or bravely die?
   n.   Pope—*Elegy on an Unfortunate Lady.*

Love, free as air, at sight of human ties,
Spreads his light wings, and in a moment flies.
   o.   Pope—*Epistle to Eloisa.* *Last Line.*

Of all affliction taught a lover yet,
'Tis sure the hardest science to forget.
   p.   Pope—*Eloisa to Abelard.* L. 189.

O Love ! for Sylvia let me gain the prize,
And make my tongue victorious as her eyes.
   q.   Pope—*Spring.* L. 49.

One thought of thee puts all the pomp to
   flight;
Priests, tapers, temples, swim before my sight.
   r.   Pope—*Eloisa to Abelard.* L. 273.

Divine is Love and scorneth worldly pelf,
And can be bought with nothing but with
   self.
   s.   Sir Walter Raleigh—*Love the Only
                       Price of Love.*

If all the world and love were young,
And truth in every shepherd's tongue,
These pretty pleasures might me move
To live with thee, and be thy love.
   t.   Sir Walter Raleigh—*The Nymph's
                Reply to the Passionate Shepherd.*

Oh ! she was good as she was fair.
   None—none on earth above her !
As pure in thought as angels are,
   To know her was to love her.
   u.   Sam'l Rogers—*Jacqueline.* Pt. I.
                                    L. 68.

Those that he loved so long and sees no more,
Loved and still loves—not dead, but gone
   before,
He gathers round him.
   v.   Sam'l Rogers—*Human Life.* L. 739.

Time is short, life is short. * * *
 Life is sweet, love is sweet, use to-day while
  you may;
Love is sweet, and to-morrow may fail;
 Love is sweet, use to-day.
 a. CHRISTINA G. ROSSETTI—*The Prince's*
        Progress. St. 7.

A pressing lover seldom wants success,
Whilst the respectful, like the Greek, sits
 down
And wastes a ten years' siege before one town.
 b. NICHOLAS ROWE—*To the Inconstant.*
        Epilogue. L. 18.

Ah, to that far distant strand
 Bridge there was not to convey,
Not a bark was near at hand,
 Yet true love soon found the way.
 c. SCHILLER—*Hero and Leander.*
        Bowring's trans.

Love illumes the realms of night!
 d. SCHILLER—*The Triumph of Love.*
         St. 21.

And love is loveliest when embalm'd in tears.
 e. SCOTT—*Lady of the Lake.* Canto IV.
         St. 1.

Her blue eyes sought the west afar,
For lovers love the western star.
 f. SCOTT—*The Lay of the Last Minstrel.*
      Canto III. St. 24.

In peace, Love tunes the shepherd's reed;
In war, he mounts the warrior's steed;
In halls, in gay attire is seen;
In hamlets, dances on the green.
Love rules the court, the camp, the grove,
And men below, and saints above;
For love is heaven, and heaven is love.
 g. SCOTT—*The Lay of the Last Minstrel.*
      Canto III. St. 2.

True love's the gift which God has given
To man alone beneath the heaven.
  * * * * * *
It is the secret sympathy,
The silver link, the silken tie,
Which heart to heart, and mind to mind,
In body and in soul can bind.
 h. SCOTT—*The Lay of the Last Minstrel.*
      Canto V. St. 13.

Where shall the lover rest,
 Whom the fates sever
From his true maiden's breast,
 Parted for ever?
Where, through groves deep and high,
 Sounds the far billow,
Where early violets die,
 Under the willow.
 i. SCOTT—*Marmion.* Canto III. St. 10.

A lover's eyes will gaze an eagle blind.
A lover's ear will hear the lowest sound.
 j. *Love's Labour's Lost.* Act IV. Sc. 3.
         L. 334.

And swearing till my very roof was dry
With oaths of love.
 k. *Merchant of Venice.* Act III. Sc. 2.
         L. 206.

And when Love speaks, the voice of all the
 gods
Makes heaven drowsy with the harmony.
 l. *Love's Labour's Lost.* Act IV. Sc. 3.
         L. 344.

And writers say, As the most forward bud
Is eaten by the canker ere it blow,
Even so by love the young and tender wit
Is turn'd to folly, blasting in the bud,
Losing his verdure even in the prime.
 m. *Two Gentlemen of Verona.* Act I.
       Sc. 1. L. 45.

   At lovers' perjuries,
They say, Jove laughs.
 n. *Romeo and Juliet.* Act II. Sc. 2.
         L. 92.

Ay me! for aught that I ever could read,
Could ever hear by tale or history,
The course of true love never did run smooth.
 o. *Midsummer-Night's Dream.* Act I.
       Sc. 1. L. 132.

But are you so much in love as your rhymes
speak?
 Neither rhyme nor reason can express how
much.
 p. *As You Like It.* Act III. Sc. 2.
         L. 418.

But love is blind, and lovers cannot see
The pretty follies that themselves commit.
 q. *Merchant of Venice.* Act II. Sc. 6.
         L. 36.

   But love that comes too late,
Like a remorseful pardon slowly carried,
To the great sender turns a sour offence.
 r. *All's Well That Ends Well.* Act V.
       Sc. 3. L. 57.

By heaven, I do love: and it hath taught
me to rhyme, and to be melancholy.
 s. *Love's Labour's Lost.* Act IV. Sc. 3.
         L. 10.

Didst thou but know the inly touch of love,
Thou wouldst as soon go kindle fire with
 snow,
As seek to quench the fire of love with words.
 t. *Two Gentlemen of Verona.* Act II.
       Sc. 7. L. 18.

Except I be by Sylvia in the night,
There is no music in the nightingale.
 u. *Two Gentlemen of Verona.* Act III.
       Sc. 1. L. 178.

For he was more than over shoes in love.
 v. *Two Gentlemen of Verona.* Act I.
       Sc. 1. L. 23.

For stony limits cannot hold love out,
And what love can do that dares love attempt.

  a.   *Romeo and Juliet.*   Act II. Sc. 2.
                           L. 67.

              For to be wise, and love
Exceeds man's might; that dwells with gods
    above.

  b.   *Troilus and Cressida.* Act III. Sc. 2.
                         L. 163.

            Forty thousand brothers
Could not, with all their quantity of love,
Make up my sum.

  c.   *Hamlet.* Act V. Sc. 1. L. 292.

Friendship is constant in all other things
Save in the office and affairs of love:
Therefore, all hearts in love use their own
    tongues;
Let every eye negotiate for itself
And trust no agent.

  d.   *Much Ado About Nothing.* Act II.
                       Sc. 1. L. 182.

Give me my Romeo; and, when he shall die,
Take him, and cut him out in little stars,
And he will make the face of heaven so fine,
That all the world will be in love with night,
And pay no worship to the garish sun.

  e.   *Romeo and Juliet.* Act III. Sc. 2.
                         L. 21.

Good shepherd, tell this youth what 'tis to
    love.
It is to be all made of sighs and tears;—
   *   *   *   *   *   *
It is to be all made of faith and service;—
   *   *   *   *   *   *
It is to be all made of fantasy.

  f.   *As You Like It.* Act V. Sc. 2. L. 89.

He is far gone, far gone: and truly in my
youth I suffered much extremity for love;
very near this.

  g.   *Hamlet.* Act II. Sc. 2. L. 188.

How wayward is this foolish love,
That, like a testy babe, will scratch the nurse
And presently, all humbled, kiss the rod.

  h.   *Two Gentlemen of Verona.* Act I.
                         Sc. 2. L. 57.

I do not seek to quench your love's hot fire,
But qualify the fire's extreme rage,
Lest it should burn above the bounds of
    reason.

  i.   *Two Gentlemen of Verona.* Act II.
                         Sc. 7. L. 21.

If heaven would make me such another world
Of one entire and perfect chrysolite,
I'ld not have sold her for it.

  j.   *Othello.* Act V. Sc. 2. L. 144.

If thou remember'st not the slightest folly
That ever love did make thee run into,
Thou hast not lov'd.

  k.   *As You Like It.* Act II. Sc. 4. L. 34.

                   I know not why
I love this youth; and I have heard you say,
Love's reason's without reason.

  l.   *Cymbeline.* Act IV. Sc. 2. L. 20.

It is as easy to count atomies as to resolve
the propositions of a lover.

  m.   *As You Like It.* Act III. Sc. 2.
                         L. 245.

It is my soul that calls upon my name;
How silver-sweet sound lovers' tongues by
    night,
Like softest music to attending ears.

  n.   *Romeo and Juliet.* Act II. Sc. 2.
                         L. 165.

I will not be sworn but love may transform
me to an oyster; but I'll take my oath on it,
till he have made an oyster of me, he shall
never make me such a fool.

  o.   *Much Ado About Nothing.* Act II.
                     Sc. 3. L. 20.

                Let me twine
Mine arms about that body, where against
My grained ash an hundred times hath broke,
And scarr'd the moon with splinters.

  p.   *Coriolanus.* Act IV. Sc. 5. L. 112.

Love goes toward love as school-boys from
    their books,
But love from love, toward school with heavy
    looks.

  q.   *Romeo and Juliet.* Act II. Sc. 2.
                         L. 157.

Love is a smoke rais'd with the fume of sighs;
Being purg'd, a fire sparkling in a lover's
    eyes;
Being vex'd, a sea nourish'd with lovers'
    tears:
What is it else? a madness most discreet,
A choking gall and a preserving sweet.

  r.   *Romeo and Juliet.* Act I. Sc. 1.
                         L. 196.

Love is your master, for he masters you;
And he that is so yoked by a fool,
Methinks, should not be chronicled for wise.

  s.   *Two Gentlemen of Verona.* Act I.
                         Sc. 1. L. 39.

Love keeps his revels where there are but
    twain.

  t.   *Venus and Adonis.* L. 123.

Love like a shadow flies when substance love
    pursues;
Pursuing that that flies, and flying what pur-
    sues.

  u.   *Merry Wives of Windsor.* Act II.
                     Sc. 2. L. 217.

Love looks not with the eyes, but with the
    mind;
And therefore is winged Cupid painted blind.

  v.   *Midsummer-Night's Dream.* Act I.
                     Sc. 1. L. 234.

Love's heralds should be thoughts,
Which ten times faster glide than the sun's
   beams,
Driving back shadows over louring hills;
Therefore do nimble-pinion'd doves draw
   love,
And therefore hath the wind-swift Cupid
   wings.
   a.   *Romeo and Juliet.* Act II. Sc. 5. L. 4.

Love's not Time's fool.
   b.   *Sonnet CXVI.*

Love sought is good, but given unsought is
   better.
   c.   *Twelfth Night.* Act III. Sc. 1. L. 167.

Love's tongue proves dainty Bacchus gross in
   taste :
For valour, is not Love a Hercules,
Still climbing trees in the Hesperides?
   d.   *Love's Labour's Lost.* Act IV. Sc. 3.
   L. 339.

Love, therefore, and tongue-tied simplicity
In least speak most, to my capacity.
   e.   *Midsummer-Night's Dream.* Act V.
   Sc. 1. L. 104.

Love thyself last: cherish those hearts that
   hate thee.
   f.   *Henry VIII.* Act III. Sc. 2. L. 444.

Love, whose month is ever May,
Spied a blossom passing fair
Playing in the wanton air :
Through the velvet leaves the wind,
All unseen can passage find;
That the lover, sick to death,
Wish himself the heaven's breath.
   g.   *Love's Labour's Lost.* Act IV. Sc. 3.
   Song.

My bounty is as boundless as the sea,
My love as deep; the more I give to thee
The more I have, for both are infinite.
   h.   *Romeo and Juliet.* Act II. Sc. 2.
   L. 133.

No sooner met but they looked, no sooner
looked but they loved, no sooner loved but
they sighed, no sooner sighed but they asked
one another the reason.
   i.   *As You Like It.* Act V. Sc. 2. L. 36.

O coz, coz, coz, my pretty little coz, that
thou didst know how many fathom deep I
am in love! But it cannot be sounded; my
affection hath an unknown bottom, like the
bay of Portugal.
   j.   *As You Like It.* Act IV. Sc. 1. L. 208.

O, how this spring of love resembleth
   Th' uncertain glory of an April day,
Which now shows all the beauty of the sun,
   And by and by a cloud takes all away!
   k.   *Two Gentlemen of Verona.* Act I.
   Sc. 3. L. 84.

O spirit of love! how quick and fresh art thou,
That notwithstanding thy capacity
Receiveth as the sea, nought enters there,
Of what validity and pitch soe'er,
But falls into abatement and low price,
Even in a minute!
   l.   *Twelfth Night.* Act I. Sc. 1. L. 9.

Perdition catch my soul,
But I do love thee! and when I love thee not,
Chaos is come again.
   m.   *Othello.* Act III. Sc. 3. L. 89.

See, how she leans her cheek upon her hand!
O, that I were a glove upon that hand,
That I might touch that cheek!
   n.   *Romeo and Juliet.* Act II. Sc. 2.
   L. 23.

So loving to my mother
That he might not beteem the winds of heaven
Visit her face too roughly.
   o.   *Hamlet.* Act I. Sc. 2. L. 140.

Some Cupid kills with arrows, some with
   traps.
   p.   *Much Ado About Nothing.* Act III.
   Sc. 1. L. 106.

Speak low, if you speak love.
   q.   *Much Ado About Nothing.* Act II.
   Sc. 1. L. 102.

Then let thy love be younger than thyself,
Or thy affection cannot hold the bent.
   r.   *Twelfth Night.* Act II. Sc. 4. L. 37.

Therefore love moderately; long love doth so;
Too swift arrives as tardy as too slow.
   s.   *Romeo and Juliet.* Act II. Sc. 6.
   L. 14.

There's beggary in the love that can be
reckoned.
   t.   *Antony and Cleopatra.* Act I. Sc. 1.
   L. 15.

They say all lovers swear more performance
than they are able, and yet reserve an ability
that they never perform.
   u.   *Troilus and Cressida.* Act III. Sc. 2.
   L. 91.

This is the very ecstasy of love,
Whose violent property foredoes itself,
And leads the will to desperate undertakings.
   v.   *Hamlet.* Act II. Sc. 1. L. 102.

Though last, not least in love!
   w.   *Julius Cæsar.* Act III. Sc. 1. L. 189.

'Tis almost morning; I would have thee gone:
And yet no further than a wanton's bird;
Who lets it hop a little from her hand,
Like a poor prisoner in his twisted gyves,
And with a silk thread plucks it back again.
So loving-jealous of his liberty.
   x.   *Romeo and Juliet.* Act II. Sc. 2.
   L. 177.

Upon this hint I spake;
She lov'd me for the dangers I had pass'd,
And I lov'd her, that she did pity them.
This only is the witchcraft I have us'd:
Here comes the lady; let her witness it.
   a.   *Othello.* Act I. Sc. 3. L. 166.

What! keep a week away? seven days and
   nights?
Eight score eight hours? and lovers' absent
   hours,
More tedious than the dial eight score times?
Oh, weary reckoning!
   b.   *Othello.* Act III. Sc. 4. L. 173.

What 'tis to love? how want of love tormenteth?
   c.   *Venus and Adonis.* L. 202.

Where love is great, the littlest doubts are fear;
When little fears grow great, great love grows
   there.
   d.   *Hamlet.* Act III. Sc. 2. L. 181.

Which of you shall we say doth love us most?
That we our largest bounty may extend
Where nature doth with merit challenge.
   e.   *King Lear.* Act I. Sc. 1. L. 52.

Yet I have not seen
So likely an ambassador of love;
A day in April never came so sweet,
To show how costly summer was at hand,
As this fore-spurrer comes before his lord.
   f.   *Merchant of Venice.* Act II. Sc. 9.
                           L. 91.

You would for paradise break faith and troth,
And Jove, for your love, would infringe an
   oath.
   g.   *Love's Labour's Lost.* Act IV. Sc. 3.
                           L. 143.

Love's Pestilence, and her slow dogs of war.
   h.   SHELLEY—*Hellas.* L. 321.

Yet all love is sweet
Given or returned. Common as light is love,
And its familiar voice wearies not ever
   *   *   *   *   *   *
They who inspire it most are fortunate,
As I am now: but those who feel it most
Are happier still after long sufferings
As I shall soon become.
   i.   SHELLEY—*Prometheus Unbound.* Act II.
                           Sc. 5.

My true-love hath my heart, and I have his,
   By just exchange, one for the other given;
I hold his dear, and mine he cannot miss,
   There never was a better bargain driven.
   j.   SIR PHILIP SIDNEY—*My True Love
                        Hath my Heart.*

They love indeed who quake to say they love.
   k.   SIR PHILIP SIDNEY—*Astrophel and
                        Stella.* LIV.

Thy fatal shafts unerring move;
I bow before thine altar, Love!
   l.   SMOLLETT—*Roderick Random.* Ch. XL.
                           St. 1.

And when my own Mark Antony
   Against young Cæsar strove,
And Rome's whole world was set in arms.
   The cause was,—all for love.
   m.   SOUTHEY—*All for Love.* Pt. II. St. 26.

They sin who tell us Love can die:
With life all other passions fly,
All others are but vanity.
In Heaven Ambition cannot dwell,
Nor Avarice in the vaults of Hell.
   n.   SOUTHEY—*Curse of Kehama.* Mount
                        Meru. St. 10.

Gather the rose of love whilst yet is time.
   o.   SPENSER—*The Faerie Queene.* Bk. III.
                    Canto XII. St. 75.

Love is the emblem of eternity: it confounds all notion of time: effaces all memory of a beginning, all fear of an end.
   p.   MADAME DE STAËL—*Corinne.* Bk. VIII.
                          Ch. II.

Where we really love, we often dread more
than we desire the solemn moment that exchanges hope for certainty.
   q.   MADAME DE STAËL—*Corinne.* Bk. VIII.
                          Ch. IV.

Why so pale and wan, fond lover,
   Prithee, why so pale?
Will, when looking well can't move her,
   Looking ill prevail?
   Prithee why so pale?
   r.   SIR JOHN SUCKLING—*Song.* St. 1.

Conjugial love is celestial, spiritual, and
holy, because it corresponds to the celestial,
spiritual, and holy marriage of the Lord and
the Church.
   s.   SWEDENBORG—*Conjugial Love.* Par. 62.

Love in its essence is spiritual fire.
   t.   SWEDENBORG—*True Christian Religion.*
                           Par. 31.

Love is the life of man.
   u.   SWEDENBORG—*Divine Love and Wisdom.*
                           Par. 1.

The love that reigns in the celestial kingdom is love to the Lord, and the light of truth
thence derived is wisdom.
   v.   SWEDENBORG—*Heaven and Hell.*
                          Par. 148.

In all I wish, how happy should I be,
Thou grand Deluder, were it not for thee?
So weak thou art that fools thy power despise;
And yet so strong, thou triumph'st o'er the
   wise.
   w.   SWIFT—*To Love.*

Love laid his sleepless head
On a thorny rose bed :
And his eyes with tears were red,
And pale his lips as the dead.
  a.   SWINBURNE—*Love Laid his Sleepless*
                                     Head.

O Love, O great god Love, what have I done,
That thou shouldst hunger so after my death ?
My heart is harmless as my life's first day :
Seek out some false fair woman, and plague
    her
Till her tears even as my tears fill her bed.
  b.   SWINBURNE—*The Complaint of Lisa.*

When gloaming treads the heels of day
And birds sit cowering on the spray,
Along the flowery hedge I stray,
To meet mine ain dear somebody.
  c.   ROBERT TANNAHILL—*Love's Fear.*

For love's humility is Love's true pride.
  d.   BAYARD TAYLOR—*The Poet's Journal.*
                     Third Evening.   The Mother.

I love thee, I love but thee,
With a love that shall not die
    Till the sun grows cold,
    And the stars are old,
And the leaves of the Judgment Book unfold !
  e.   BAYARD TAYLOR—*Bedouin Song.*

Love better is than Fame.
  f.   BAYARD TAYLOR—*Christmas Sonnets.*
                     Lyrics.   To J. L. G.

Love's history, as Life's, is ended not
By marriage.
  g.   BAYARD TAYLOR—*Lars.*   Bk. III.

And on her lover's arm she leant,
    And round her waist she felt it fold,
And far across the hills they went
    In that new world which is the old.
  h.   TENNYSON—*The Day Dream.   The
                                     Departure.*   I.

For love reflects the thing beloved.
  i.   TENNYSON—*In Memoriam.*   Pt. LII.

I loved you, and my love had no return,
And therefore my true love has been my death.
  j.   TENNYSON—*Lancelot and Elaine.*
                                     L. 1,298.

Love is hurt with jar and fret ;
Love is made a vague regret.
  k.   TENNYSON—*The Miller's Daughter.*
                                     St. 28.

Love lieth deep ; Love dwells not in lip-depths.
  l.   TENNYSON—*The Lover's Tale.*   L. 466.

Where love could walk with banish'd Hope
    no more.
  m.   TENNYSON—*The Lover's Tale.*   L. 813.

Love's arms were wreathed about the neck of
    Hope,
And Hope kiss'd Love, and Love drew in her
    breath
In that close kiss and drank her whisper'd
    tales.
They say that Love would die when Hope
    was gone.
And Love mourn'd long, and sorrow'd after
    Hope ;
At last she sought out Memory, and they trod
The same old paths where Love had walked
    with Hope,
And Memory fed the soul of Love with tears.
  n.   TENNYSON—*The Lover's Tale.*   L. 815.

Love's too precious to be lost,
A little grain shall not be spilt.
  o.   TENNYSON—*In Memoriam.*   Pt. LXV.

Shall it not be scorn to me to harp on such **a**
    moulder'd string ?
I am shamed through all my nature to have
    lov'd so slight a thing.
  p.   TENNYSON—*Locksley Hall.*   St. 74.

She is coming, my own, my sweet ;
    Were it ever so airy a tread,
My heart would hear her and beat,
    Were it earth in an earthy bed ;
My dust would hear her and beat,
    Had I lain for a century dead ;
Would start and tremble under her feet,
    And blossom in purple and red.
  q.   TENNYSON—*Maud.*   Pt. XXII.   St. **11.**

There has fallen a splendid tear
    From the passion-flower at the gate.
She is coming, my dove, my dear ;
    She is coming, my life, my fate ;
The red rose cries, " She is near, she is near ; "
    And the white rose weeps, " She is late ; "
The larkspur listens, " I hear ; I hear ; "
    And the lily whispers, " I wait."
  r.   TENNYSON—*Maud.*   Pt. XXII.   St. 10.

'Tis better to have loved and lost,
Than never to have loved at all.
  s.   TENNYSON—*In Memoriam.*   Pt. XXVII.
                                     St. 4.

It is best to love wisely, no doubt ; but to
love foolishly is better than not to be able to
love at all.
  t.   THACKERAY—*Pendennis.*   Ch. VI.

Werther had a love for Charlotte,
    Such as words could never utter ;
Would you know how first he met her ?
    She was cutting bread and butter.
  u.   THACKERAY—*The Sorrows of Werther.*

Like to a wind-blown sapling grow I from
The cliff, Sweet, of your skyward-jetting
    soul,—
Shook by all gusts that sweep it, overcome
By all its clouds incumbent ; O be true
To your soul, dearest, as my life to you !
For if that soil grow sterile, then the whole
Of me must shrivel, from the topmost shoot
Of climbing poesy, and my life, killed through,
Dry down and perish to the foodless root.
    a.   Francis Thompson—*Manus Animam
                    Pinxit.* St. 1.

And let th' aspiring Youth beware of Love,
Of the smooth glance beware ; for 'tis too
    late,
When on his heart the torrent-softness pours,
Then Wisdom prostrate lies, and fading Fame
Dissolves in air away.
    b.   Thomson—*The Seasons. Spring.*
                              L. 981.

O, what are you waiting for here? young
    man !
What are you looking for over the bridge ?—
A little straw hat with the streaming blue
    ribbons
Is soon to come dancing over the bridge.
    c.   Thomson—*Waiting.*

Why should we kill the best of passions, love?
It aids the hero, bids ambition rise
To nobler heights, inspires immortal deeds,
Even softens brutes, and adds a grace to
    virtue.
    d.   Thomson—*Sophonisba.* Act V. Sc. 2.

For Truth makes holy Love's illusive dreams,
And their best promise constantly redeems.
    e.   Tuckerman—*Sonnets.* XXII.

The warrior for the True, the Right,
    Fights in Love's name ;
The love that lures thee from that fight
    Lures thee to shame :
That love which lifts the heart, yet leaves
    The spirit free,—
That love, or none, is fit for one
    Man-shaped like thee.
    f.   Aubrey Thos. De Vere—
                Miscellaneous Poems. Song.

Could we forbear dispute, and practise love,
We should agree as angels do above.
    g.   Edmund Waller—*Divine Poems.
        Divine Love.* Canto III. L. 25.

To love is to believe, to hope, to know ;
'Tis an essay, a taste of Heaven below !
    h.   Edmund Waller—*Divine Poems.
        Divine Love.* Canto III. L. 17.

" I'm sorry that I spell'd the word ;
    I hate to go above you,
Because "—the brown eyes lower fell,—
    ``Because, you see, I love you ! "
    i.   Whittier—*In School-Days.* St. 4.

O, rank is good, and gold is fair,
    And high and low mate ill ;
But love has never known a law
    Beyond its own sweet will !
    j.   Whittier—*Amy Wentworth.* St. 18.

Your love in a cottage is hungry,
    Your vine is a nest for flies—
Your milkmaid shocks the Graces,
    And simplicity talks of pies !
You lie down to your shady slumber
    And wake with a bug in your ear,
And your damsel that walks in the morning
    Is shod like a mountaineer.
    k.   N. P. Willis—*Love in a Cottage.* St. 3.

He loves not well whose love is bold !
    I would not have thee come too nigh.
The sun's gold would not seem pure gold
    Unless the sun were in the sky :
To take him thence and chain him near
Would make his beauty disappear.
    l.   William Winter—*Love's Queen.*

                      For mightier far
Than strength of nerve or sinew, or the sway
Of magic potent over sun and star,
Is love, though oft to agony distrest,
And though his favourite seat be feeble wom-
    an's breast.
    m.   Wordsworth—*Laodamia.* St. 15.

Farewell, Love, and all thy lawes for ever.
    n.   Sir Thomas Wyatt—*Songs and Sonnets.
                A Renouncing of Love.*

LOYALTY.

It's guid to be merry and wise,
    It's guid to be honest and true,
It's guid to support Caledonia's cause,
    And bide by the buff and the blue !
    o.   Burns—*Here's a Health to Them that's
                         Awa'.*

God save our gracious king,
Long live our noble king,
    God save the king.
    p.   Henry Carey—*God Save the King.*

Now let us sing, long live the king.
    q.   Cowper—*History of John Gilpin.*

The first great work (a task performed by few)
Is that yourself may to yourself be true.
    r.   Wentworth Dillon—*An Essay on
                  Translated Verse.* L. 71.

Over the hills, and over the main,
To Flanders, Portugal, or Spain ;
The Queen commands, and we'll obey,
Over the hills and far away.
    s.   George Farquhar—*The Recruiting
        Officer.* Act II. Sc. 2. (Quoted by
                        Swift and Gay.)

Wake in our breast the living fires,
The holy faith that warmed our sires;
Thy hand hath made our Nation free;
To die for her is serving Thee.
    a.   O. W. HOLMES—*Army Hymn.* St. 2.

Master, go on, and I will follow thee,
To the last gasp, with truth and loyalty.
    b.   *As You Like It.* Act II. Sc. 3. L. 69.

Not that I loved Cæsar less, but that I loved
Rome more.
    c.   *Julius Cæsar.* Act III. Sc. 2. L. 22.

O, where is loyalty?
If it be banish'd from the frosty head,
Where shall it find a harbour in the earth?
    d.   *Henry VI.* Pt. II. Act V. Sc. 1.
            L. 166.

The swallow follows not summer more
willing than we your lordship.
    e.   *Timon of Athens.* Act III. Sc. 6.
            L. 31.

To thine own self be true,
And it must follow, as the night the day,
Thou canst not then be false to any man.
    f.   *Hamlet.* Act I. Sc. 3. L. 78.

LUCK.

O, once in each man's life, at least,
  Good luck knocks at his door;
And wit to seize the flitting guest
  Need never hunger more.
But while the loitering idler waits
  Good luck beside his fire,
The bold heart storms at fortune's gates,
  And conquers its desire.
    g.   LEWIS J. BATES—*Good Luck.*

As they who make
Good luck a god count all unlucky men.
    h.   GEORGE ELIOT—*The Spanish Gypsy.*
            Bk. I.

A farmer travelling with his load
Picked up a horseshoe on the road,
And nailed it fast to his barn door,
That luck might down upon him pour;
That every blessing known in life
Might crown his homestead and his wife,
And never any kind of harm
Descend upon his growing farm.
    i.   JAMES T. FIELDS—*The Lucky Horseshoe.*

Some people are so fond of ill-luck that they
run half-way to meet it.
    j.   DOUGLAS JERROLD—*Jerrold's Wit.*
            Meeting Trouble Half-Way.

Happy art thou, as if every day thou hadst
  picked up a horseshoe.
    k.   LONGFELLOW—*Evangeline.* Pt. I.
            St. 2.

"Then here goes another," says he, "to make
  sure,
For there's luck in odd numbers," says Rory
  O'More.
    l.   SAMUEL LOVER—*Rory O'More.*

Good luck befriend thee, Son; for at thy birth
The fairy ladies danced upon the hearth.
    m.   MILTON—*At a Vacation Exercise in the
            College.*

And good luck go with thee.
    n.   *Henry V.* Act IV. Sc. 3. L. 11.

As good luck would have it.
    o.   *Merry Wives of Windsor.* Act III.
            Sc. 5. L. 83.

By the luckiest stars.
    p.   *All's Well That Ends Well.* Act I.
            Sc. 3. L. 252.

Good luck lies in odd numbers * * *
They say there is divinity in odd numbers,
either in nativity, chance, or death.
    q.   *Merry Wives of Windsor.* Act V. Sc. 1.
            L. 2.

When mine hours were nice and lucky.
    r.   *Antony and Cleopatra.* Act III.
            Sc. 13. L. 179.

And wheresoe'er thou move, good luck
Shall fling her old shoe after.
    s.   TENNYSON—*Will Waterproof's Lyrical
            Monologue.* St. 27.

LUXURY.

Blesses his stars, and thinks it luxury.
    t.   ADDISON—*Cato.* Act I. Sc. 4.

Sofas 'twas half a sin to sit upon,
So costly were they; carpets, every stitch
Of workmanship so rare, they make you wish
You could glide o'er them like a golden fish.
    u.   BYRON—*Don Juan.* Canto V. St. 65.

Blest hour! It was a luxury—to be!
    v.   COLERIDGE—*Reflections on having left
            a Place of Retirement.* L. 43.

What will not luxury taste? Earth, sea, and
  air,
Are daily ransack'd for the bill of fare.
Blood stuffed in skins is British Christians'
  food,
And France robs marshes of the croaking
  brood.
    w.   GAY—*Trivia.* Bk. III. L. 199.

O Luxury! thou curst by Heaven's decree.
    x.   GOLDSMITH—*The Deserted Village.*
            L. 385.

Such dainties to them, their health it might
    hurt:
It's like sending them ruffles, when wanting
    a shirt.
   a.   GOLDSMITH—*The Haunch of Venison.*

Fell luxury! more perilous to youth
Than storms or quicksands, poverty or
    chains.
   b.   HANNAH MORE—*Belshazzar.*

Luxury and dissipation, soft and gentle as
their approaches are, and silently as they
throw their silken chains about the heart, enslave it more than the most active and turbu-
lent vices.
   c.   HANNAH MORE—*Essays. Dissipation.*

              On his weary couch
Fat Luxury, sick of the night's debauch,
Lay groaning, fretful at the obtrusive beam
That through his lattice peeped derisively.
   d.   POLLOK—*Course of Time.* Bk. VII. L. 69.

Luxury is an enticing pleasure, a bastard
mirth, which hath honey in her mouth, gall
in her heart, and a sting in her tail.
   e.   QUARLES—*Emblems.* Bk. I. *Hugo.*

      Rings put upon his fingers,
A most delicious banquet by his bed,
And brave attendants near him when he
    wakes,
Would not the beggar then forget himself?
   f.   *Taming of the Shrew.* Induction.
                           Sc. 1. L. 38.
Falsely luxurious, will not man awake?
   g.   THOMSON—*The Seasons. Summer.* L. 67.

M.

MAMMON.

I rose up at the dawn of day,—
"Get thee away! get thee away!
Pray'st thou for riches? Away, away!
This is the throne of Mammon grey."
   h.   WILLIAM BLAKE—*Mammon.*

Maidens, like moths, are ever caught by glare,
And Mammon wins his way where seraphs
    might despair.
   i.   BYRON—*Childe Harold.* Canto I. St. 9.

Cursed Mammon be, when he with treasures
    To restless action spurs our fate!
Cursed when for soft, indulgent leisures,
    He lays for us the pillows straight.
   j.   GOETHE—*Faust.*

           Mammon led them on—
Mammon, the least erected Spirit that fell
From Heaven: for even in Heaven his looks
    and thoughts
Were always downward bent, admiring more
The riches of Heaven's pavement, trodden
    gold,
Than aught divine or holy else enjoyed
In vision beatific.
   k.   MILTON—*Paradise Lost.* Bk. I. L. 678.

Who sees pale Mammon pine amidst his store,
Sees but a backward steward for the poor.
   l.   POPE—*Moral Essays.* Ep. III. L. 171.

What treasures here do Mammon's sons be-
    hold!
Yet know that all that which glitters is not
    gold.
   m.   QUARLES—*Emblems.* Bk. II.
                                Emblem V.

MAN.

The man forget not, though in rags he lies,
And know the mortal through a crown's dis-
    guise.
   n.   AKENSIDE—*Epistle to Curio.*

Man only,—rash, refined, presumptuous
    Man—
Starts from his rank, and mars Creation's
    plan!
Born the free heir of nature's wide domain,
To art's strict limits bounds his narrow'd
    reign;
Resigns his native rights for meaner things,
For Faith and Fetters, Laws and Priests and
    Kings.
   o.   *Poetry of the Anti-Jacobin. The*
                      Progress of Man. L. 55.

My Lord St. Albans said that wise nature
did never put her precious jewels into a garret
four stories high; and therefore that exceeding tall men had ever very empty heads.
   p.   BACON—*Apothegms.* No. 17. *From*
                   Rawley's Common Place Book.

Let each man think himself an act of God,
His mind a thought, his life a breath of God.
   q.   BAILEY—*Festus. Proem.* L. 162.

Man is the nobler growth our realms supply,
And souls are ripened in our northern sky.
   r.   ANNA LETITIA BARBAULD—*The*
                            Invitation.

There is no Theam more plentifull to scan,
Then is the glorious goodly Frame of Man.
   s.   DU BARTAS—*Divine Weekes and Workes.*
                First Week, Sixth Day. L. 421.

Thou wilt scarce be a man before thy mother.
   a.   BEAUMONT AND FLETCHER—*Love's Cure.*
                        Act II. Sc. 2.

Man is a noble animal, splendid in ashes
and pompous in the grave.
   b.   SIR THOMAS BROWNE—*Urn Burial.*
                                 Ch. V.

A man's a man for a' that!
   c.   BURNS—*For A' That and A' That.*

A prince can mak a belted knight,
 A marquis, duke, and a' that;
But an honest man's aboon his might:
 Guid faith, he maunna fa' that.
   d.   BURNS—*For A' That and A' That.*

Man,—whose heaven-erected face
 The smiles of love adorn,—
Man's inhumanity to man
 Makes countless thousands mourn!
   e.   BURNS—*Man Was Made to Mourn.*

But we, who name ourselves its sovereigns, we,
Half dust, half deity, alike unfit
To sink or soar.
   f.   BYRON—*Manfred.* Act I. Sc. 2. L. 39.

Lord of himself;—that heritage of woe!
   g.   BYRON—*Lara.* Canto I. St. 2.

The precious porcelain of human clay.
   h.   BYRON—*Don Juan.* Canto IV. St. 11.

                        Man!
Thou pendulum betwixt a smile and tear.
   i.   BYRON—*Childe Harold.* Canto IV.
                              St. 109.

Where the virgins are soft as the roses they
    twine,
And all, save the spirit of man, is divine?
   j.   BYRON—*The Bride of Abydos.* Canto I.
                              St. 1.

Without our hopes, without our fears,
Without the home that plighted love endears,
Without the smile from partial beauty won,
Oh! what were man?—a world without a sun.
   k.   CAMPBELL—*Pleasures of Hope.* Pt. II.
                              L. 21.

No sadder proof can be given by a man of
his own littleness than disbelief in great men.
   l.   CARLYLE—*Heroes and Hero Worship.*
                          Lecture I.

The proper Science and Subject for Man's
Contemplation is *Man* himself.
   m.   CHARRON—*Of Wisdom.* Bk. I. Ch. I.
                        Stanhope's trans.

Men the most infamous are fond of fame:
And those who fear not guilt, yet start at
    shame.
   n.   CHURCHILL—*The Author.* L. 233.

A self-made man? Yes—and worships his
creator.
   o.   HENRY CLAPP. Said also by JOHN
                    BRIGHT of DISRAELI.
There was an ape in the days that were earlier,
Centuries passed and his hair became curlier;
Centuries more gave a thumb to his wrist—
Then he was a MAN and a Positivist.
   p.   MORTIMER COLLINS—*The British Birds.*
                              St. 5.

Vain, weak-built isthmus, which dost proudly
    rise
Up between two eternities!
   q.   ABRAHAM COWLEY—*Ode on Life and
                           Fame.* L. 18.

An honest man, close-buttoned to the chin,
Broadcloth without, and a warm heart within.
   r.   COWPER—*Epistle to Joseph Hill.*

But strive still to be a man before your
    mother.
   s.   COWPER—*Motto of No. 111. Connoisseur.*

So man, the moth, is not afraid, it seems,
To span Omnipotence, and measure might
That knows no measure, by the scanty rule
And standard of his own, that is to-day,
And is not ere to-morrow's sun go down.
   t.   COWPER—*The Task.* Bk. VI. L. 211.

         Unless above himself he can
Erect himself, how poor a thing is man!
   u.   SAM'L DANIEL—*Epistle to the Countess
                       of Cumberland.* St. 12.

A sacred spark created by his breath,
 The immortal mind of man his image bears;
A spirit living 'midst the forms of death,
 Oppressed, but not subdued, by mortal cares.
   v.   SIR H. DAVY—*Written After Recovery
                      from a Dangerous Illness.*

His tribe were God Almighty's men.
   w.   DRYDEN—*Absalom and Achitophel.*
                        Pt. I. L. 645.

This is the porcelain clay of humankind.
   x.   DRYDEN—*Don Sebastian.* Act I. Sc. 1.

A man is the whole encyclopedia of facts.
The creation of a thousand forests is in one
acorn, and Egypt, Greece, Rome, Gaul, Britain, America, lie folded already in the first
man.
   y.   EMERSON—*Essays. History.*

Man is his own star, and the soul that can
Render an honest and a perfect man,
Commands all light.
   z.   JOHN FLETCHER—*Upon an Honest
                      Man's Fortune.* L. 33.

Stood I, O Nature! man alone in thee,
Then were it worth one's while a man to be.
   aa.   GOETHE—*Faust.*

Lords of humankind.
a.   GOLDSMITH—*The Traveller.* L. 327.

Man is all symmetrie,
Full of proportions, one limbe to another,
And all to all the world besides:
Each part may call the farthest, brother:
For head with foot hath privite amitie,
And both with moons and tides.
b.   HERBERT—*The Temple.   The Church.*
Man.

Man is one world, and hath
Another to attend him.
c.   HERBERT—*The Temple.   The Church.*
Man.

Forget the brother and resume the man.
d.   HOMER—*Odyssey.* Bk. IV. L. 732.
Pope's trans.

Like leaves on trees the race of man is found,—
Now green in youth, now withering on the
ground;
Another race the following spring supplies;
They fall successive; and successive rise.
e.   HOMER—*Iliad.* Bk. 6. L. 181.
Pope's trans.

The fool of fate, thy manufacture, man.
f.   HOMER—*Odyssey.* Bk. 20. L. 254.
Pope's trans.

Man dwells apart, though not alone,
He walks among his peers unread;
The best of thoughts which he hath known
For lack of listeners are not said.
g.   JEAN INGELOW—*Afternoon at a
Parsonage.   Afterthought.*

Man passes away; his name perishes from
record and recollection; his history is as a
tale that is told, and his very monument becomes a ruin.
h.   WASHINGTON IRVING—*The Sketch
Book.   Westminster Abbey.*

The only competition worthy a wise man
is with himself.
i.   MRS. JAMESON—*Memoirs and Essays.
Washington Allston.*

Where soil is, men grow,
Whether to weeds or flowers.
j.   KEATS—*Endymion.* Bk. II.

Limited in his nature, infinite in his desires,
man is a fallen god who remembers the
heavens.
k.   LAMARTINE—*Second Meditations.*

As man; false man, smiling destructive man.
l.   NATHANIEL LEE—*Theodosius.* Act III.
Sc. 2. L. 50.

A man of mark.
m.   LONGFELLOW—*Tales of a Wayside Inn.*
Pt. I.   *The Musician's Tale.   Saga
of King Olaf.* Pt. IX. St. 2.

Before man made us citizens, great Nature
made us men.
n.   LOWELL—*The Capture of Fugitive Slaves
Near Washington.*

Three-fifths of him genius and two-fifths sheer
fudge.
o.   LOWELL—*Fable for Critics.* L. 1,296.

The hearts of men are their books; events
are their tutors; great actions are their eloquence.
p.   MACAULAY—*Essays.   Conversation
Touching the Great Civil War.*

Pouter, tumbler, and fantail are from the
same source;
The racer and hack may be traced to one
Horse;
So men were developed from monkeys of
course,
Which nobody can deny.
q.   LORD NEAVES—*The Origin of Species.*

What a chimera, then, is man! what a
novelty, what a monster, what a chaos, what
a subject of contradiction, what a prodigy!
A judge of all things, feeble worm of the
earth, depositary of the truth, *eloaca* of uncertainty and error, the glory and the shame
of the universe!
r.   PASCAL—*Thoughts.* Ch. X.

Fields and trees are not willing to teach me
anything; but this can be effected by men
residing in the city.
s.   PLATO—*Works.* Vol. III.
The Phædrus.

A minister, but still a man.
t.   POPE—*Epistle to James Craggs.*

An honest man's the noblest work of God.
u.   POPE—*Essay on Man.* Ep. IV. L. 248.

Chaos of thought and passion, all confused;
Still by himself abused and disabused;
Created half to rise, and half to fall;
Great lord of all things, yet a prey to all;
Sole judge of truth, in endless error hurled;
The glory, jest and riddle of the world!
v.   POPE—*Essay on Man.* Ep. 2. L. 13.

Let us (since life can little more supply
Than just to look about us and to die)
Expatiate free o'er all this scene of man;
A mighty maze! but not without a plan.
w.   POPE—*Essay on Man.* Ep. I. L. 1.

Know then thyself, presume not God to scan;
The proper study of mankind is man.
x.   POPE—*Essay on Man.* Ep. II. L. 1.

So man, who here seems principal alone,
Perhaps acts second to some sphere unknown,
Touches some wheel, or verges to some goal;
'Tis but a part we see, and not a whole.
y.   POPE—*Essay on Man.* Ep. I. L. 57.

Virtuous and vicious every man must be,
Few in the extreme, but all in the degree.
   a.   POPE—*Essay on Man.* Ep. II. L. 231.

Why has not man a microscopic eye?
For this plain reason, man is not a fly.
   b.   POPE—*Essay on Man.* Ep. I. L. 193.

So, if unprejudiced you scan
The goings of this clock-work, man,
You find a hundred movements made
By fine devices in his head ;
But 'tis the stomach's solid stroke
That tells his being what's o'clock.
   c.   PRIOR—*Alma; or, the Progress of the
                  Mind.* Pt. III. L. 272.

" How poor a thing is man !" alas 'tis true
I'd half forgot it when I chanced on you.
   d.   SCHILLER—*The Moral Poet.*

A proper man as one shall see in a summer's
    day.
   e.   *Midsummer-Night's Dream.* Act I.
                  Sc. 2. L. 89.

Are you good men and true?
   f.   *Much Ado About Nothing.* Act III.
                  Sc. 3. L. 1.

            For men, like butterflies,
Show not their mealy wings but to the sum-
    mer.
   g.   *Troilus and Cressida.* Act III. Sc. 3.
                  L. 78.

            Give me that man
That is not passion's slave, and I will wear
    him
In my heart's core, ay, in my heart of heart,
As I do thee.
   h.   *Hamlet.* Act III. Sc. 2. L. 76.

God made him, and therefore let him pass
    for a man.
   i.   *Merchant of Venice.* Act I. Sc. 2.
                  L. 60.

He was a man, take him for all in all,
I shall not look upon his like again.
   j.   *Hamlet.* Act I. Sc. 2. L. 187.

His life was gentle, and the elements
So mix'd in him that Nature might stand up,
And say to all the world, This was a man !
   k.   *Julius Cæsar.* Act V. Sc. 5. L. 73.

   I have thought some of Nature's journeymen had made men and not made them well,
they imitated humanity so abominably.
   l.   *Hamlet.* Act III. Sc. 2. L. 37.

I wonder men dare trust themselves with
    men.
   m.   *Timon of Athens.* Act I. Sc. 2. L. 42.

Men at some time are masters of their fates :
The fault, dear Brutus, is not in our stars,
But in ourselves, that we are underlings.
   n.   *Julius Cæsar.* Act I. Sc. 2. L. 139.

Men have died from time to time and worms
have eaten them, but not for love.
   o.   *As You Like It.* Act IV. Sc. 1.
                  L. 105.

            Men that make
Envy and crooked malice nourishment,
Dare bite the best.
   p.   *Henry VIII.* Act V. Sc. 3. L. 43.

The foremost man of all this world.
   q.   *Julius Cæsar.* Act IV. Sc. 3. L. 22.

   What a piece of work is a man ! How noble
in reason ! how infinite in faculty ! in form
and moving how express and admirable ! in
action how like an angel ! in apprehension
how like a god ! the beauty of the world ! the
paragon of animals ! And yet, to me, what
is this quintessence of dust ? man delights not
me : no, nor women neither, though by your
smiling, you seem to say so.
   r.   *Hamlet.* Act II. Sc. 2. L. 313.

            What is a man,
If his chief good and market of his time
Be but to sleep and feed ?
   s.   *Hamlet.* Act IV. Sc. 4. L. 33.

Why, he's a man of wax.
   t.   *Romeo and Juliet.* Act I. Sc. 3.
                  L. 76.

Man is of soul and body, formed for deeds
Of high resolve; on fancy's boldest wing.
   u.   SHELLEY—*Queen Mab.* Canto IV.
                  L. 160.

Of the king's creation you may be; but he
who makes a count, ne'er made a man.
   v.   THOMAS SOUTHERNE—*Sir Anthony Love.*
                  Act II. Sc. 1.

* * * Man's wretched state,
That floures so fresh at morne, and fades at
    evening late.
   w.   SPENSER—*Faerie Queene.* Bk. III.
                  Canto IX. St. 39.

A man's body and his mind, with the utmost reverence to both I speak it, are exactly
like a jerkin and a jerkin's lining ;—rumple
the one,—you rumple the other.
   x.   STERNE—*Tristram Shandy.* Bk. III.
                  Ch. IV.

When I beheld this I sighed, and said within
myself, Surely man is a Broomstick !
   y.   SWIFT—*A Meditation upon a Broomstick.*

            But what am I?
An infant crying in the night :
An infant crying for the light,
And with no language but a cry.
   z.   TENNYSON—*In Memoriam.* LIV.
                  St. 5.

I am a part of all that I have met.
  a.   TENNYSON—*Ulysses.* L. 18.

Man is man, and master of his fate.
  b.   TENNYSON—*Enid. Song of Fortune and
                                  Her Wheel.*

That men may rise on stepping-stones
Of their dead selves to higher things.
  c.   TENNYSON—*In Memoriam.* Pt. I.

I am a man, nothing that is human do I think
    unbecoming in me.
  d.   TERENCE—*Heauton-Timoroumenos.*
              Act I. Sc. 1. F. W. Ricord's trans.

The mind's the standard of the man.
  e.   WATTS—*Horæ Lyricæ.* Bk. II. *False
                                        Greatness.*

When faith is lost, when honor dies,
        The man is dead !
  f.   WHITTIER—*Ichabod.* St. 8.

I weigh the man, not his title; 'tis not the
king's stamp can make the metal better or
heavier.
  g.   WYCHERLY—*The Plaindealer.* Act I.
                                        Sc. 1.

Ah ! how unjust to nature, and himself,
Is thoughtless, thankless, inconsistent man.
  h.   YOUNG—*Night Thoughts.* Night II.
                                        L. 112.

How poor, how rich, how abject, how august,
How complicate, how wonderful, is man !
How passing wonder He, who made him
    such !
  i.   YOUNG—*Night Thoughts.* Night I.
                                        L. 68.

The man of wisdom is the man of years.
  j.   YOUNG—*Night Thoughts.* Night V.
                                        L. 775.

MANNERS.

He was the mildest manner'd man
That ever scuttled ship or cut a throat.
  k.   BYRON—*Don Juan.* Canto III. St. 41.

Manners must adorn knowledge, and smooth
its way through the world. Like a great
rough diamond, it may do very well in a closet
by way of curiosity, and also for its intrinsic
value; but it will never be worn, nor shine,
if it is not polished.
  l.   CHESTERFIELD—*Letters. July 1, 1748.*

A moral, sensible, and well-bred man
Will not affront me, and no other can.
  m.   COWPER—*Conversation.* L. 193.

Nobody ought to have been able to resist
her coaxing manner; and nobody had any
business to try. Yet she never seemed to
know it was her manner at all. That was the
best of it.
  n.   DICKENS—*Martin Chuzzlewit.* Vol. II.
                                        Ch. XIV.

Fine manners need the support of fine man-
    ners in others.
  o.   EMERSON—*The Conduct of Life.
                                        Behavior.*

Good manners are made up of petty sacrifices.
  p.   EMERSON—*Letters and Social Aims.*

The mildest manners with the bravest mind.
  q.   HOMER—*Iliad.* Bk. 24. L. 963.
                                    Pope's trans.

He was so generally civil, that nobody
thanked him for it.
  r.   SAM'L JOHNSON—*Boswell's Life of
                                        Johnson, 1777.*

We call it only pretty Fanny's way.
  s.   THOMAS PARNELL—*An Elegy to an Old
                                        Beauty.*

Eye nature's walks, shoot folly as it flies,
And catch the manners, living as they rise;
Laugh where we must, be candid where we
    can,
But vindicate the ways of God to man.
  t.   POPE—*Essay on Man.* Ep. I. L. 13.

Manners with fortunes, humors turn with
    climes,
Tenets with books, and principles with times.
  u.   POPE—*Moral Essays.* Ep. I. L. 172.

Fit for the mountains and the barb'rous caves,
Where manners ne'er were preach'd.
  v.   *Twelfth Night.* Act IV. Sc. 1. L. 52.

Her manners had not that repose
Which stamps the caste of Vere de Vere.
  w.   TENNYSON—*Lady Clara Vere de Vere.*
                                        St. 5.

MARCH (*See* MONTHS).

MARTYRDOM.

Christians have burnt each other, quite per-
    suaded
That all the Apostles would have done as they
    did.
  x.   BYRON—*Don Juan.* Canto I. St. 83.

Who falls for love of God, shall rise a star.
  y.   BEN JONSON—*Underwoods. An Epistle
                                        to a Friend.*

He strove among God's suffering poor
    One gleam of brotherhood to send ;
The dungeon oped its hungry door
To give the truth one martyr more,
    Then shut,—and here behold the end !
  z.   LOWELL—*On the Death of C. T. Torrey.*

Martyrs! who left for our reaping
　Truths you had sown in your blood—
Sinners! whom long years of weeping
　Chasten'd from evil to good—

　　*　　*　　*　　*　　*　　*

Say, through what region enchanted
　Walk ye, in Heaven's sweet air?
Say, to what spirits 'tis granted,
　Bright souls, to dwell with you there?
　a.　　Moore—*Where is Your Dwelling, Ye
　　　　　　　　　　　　　　　Sainted?*

It is the cause, and not the death, that makes
the martyr.
　b.　　Napoleon I.

His wife and children, being eleven in
number, ten able to walk, and one sucking on
her breast, met him by the way as he went
towards Smithfield: this sorrowful sight of
his own flesh and blood, dear as they were to
him, could yet nothing move him, but that
he constantly and cheerfully took his death
with wonderful patience, in the defence and
support of Christ's Gospel.
　c.　　*Martyrdom of* John Rogers.　See
　　　　*Richmond's Selection from the Writings
　　　　　of the Reformers and Early
　　　　　Protestant Divines of the
　　　　　Church of England.*

Like a pale martyr in his shirt of fire.
　d.　　Alex. Smith—*A Life Drama.*　Sc. 2.
　　　　　　　　　　　　　　　　　　L. 225.

MASONS (*See* Occupations).

MATRIMONY.

He that hath a wife and children hath given
hostages to fortune; for they are impediments
to great enterprises, either of virtue or mischief.
　e.　　Bacon—*Essays.　Of Marriage and
　　　　　　　　　　　　　　　　Single Life.*

Now voe me I can zing on my business abrode:
Though the storm do beat down on my poll,
There's a wife brighten'd vire at the end of
　my road,
An' her love, voe the jaÿ o' my soul.
　f.　　William Barnes—*Don't Ceare.*　St. 5.

My fond affection thou hast seen,
　Then judge of my regret
To think more happy thou hadst been
　If we had never met!

And has that thought been shared by thee?
　Ah, no! that smiling cheek
Proves more unchanging love for me
　Than labor'd words could speak.
　g.　　Thos. Haynes Bayly—*To My Wife.*

No jealousy their dawn of love o'ercast,
　Nor blasted were their wedded days with
　　strife;
Each season looked delightful as it past,
　To the fond husband and the faithful wife.
　h.　　James Beattie—*The Minstrel.*　Bk. I.
　　　　　　　　　　　　　　　　　　St. 14.

He that said it was not good for man to be
alone, placed the celibate amongst the inferior
states of perfection.
　i.　　Boyle—*Works.*　Vol. VI.　P. 292.
　　　　　　　　　　Letter from Mr. Evelyn.

Cursed be the man, the poorest wretch in life,
The crouching vassal to the tyrant wife,
Who has no will but by her high permission;
Who has not sixpence but in her possession;
Who must to her his dear friend's secret tell;
Who dreads a curtain lecture worse than hell.
Were such the wife had fallen to my part,
I'd break her spirit or I'd break her heart.
　j.　　Burns—*The Henpecked Husband.*

Women wear the breeches.
　k.　　Burton—*Anatomy of Melancholy.*
　　　　　　　　　　Democritus to the Reader.

'Cause grace and virtue are within
Prohibited degrees of kin;
And therefore no true Saint allows,
They shall be suffer'd to espouse.
　l.　　Butler—*Hudibras.*　Pt. 3.　Canto I.
　　　　　　　　　　　　　　　　　L. 1,293.

For talk six times with the same single lady,
And you may get the wedding dresses ready.
　m.　　Byron—*Don Juan.*　Canto XII.　St. 59.

There was no great disparity of years,
　Though much in temper; but they never
　　clash'd,
They moved like stars united in their spheres,
　Or like the Rhône by Leman's waters
　　wash'd,
Where mingled and yet separate appears
　The river from the lake, all bluely dash'd
Through the serene and placid glassy deep,
Which fain would lull its river-child to sleep.
　n.　　Byron—*Don Juan.*　Canto XIV.
　　　　　　　　　　　　　　　　　St. 87.

To sit, happy married lovers; Phillis trifling
　with a plover's
Egg, while Corydon uncovers with a grace the
　Sally Lunn,
Or dissects the lucky pheasant—that, I think,
　were passing pleasant
As I sit alone at present, dreaming darkly of
　a dun.
　o.　　Calverley—*In the Gloaming.*　(*Parody
　　　　　　　　　　　　　on Mrs. Browning.*)

　　　　　　　　Man and wife,
Coupled together for the sake of strife.
　p.　　Churchill—*The Rosciad.*　L. 1,005.

Oh! how many torments lie in the small
circle of a wedding ring.
    a.   COLLEY CIBBER.

Thus grief still treads upon the heels of
    pleasure,
Marry'd in haste, we may repent at leisure.
    b.   CONGREVE—*The Old Bachelor.* Act V.
                       Sc. 1.

Misses! the tale that I relate
This lesson seems to carry—
Choose not alone a proper mate,
   But proper time to marry.
    c.   COWPER—*Pairing Time Anticipated.*
                       (*Moral.*)

Wedlock, indeed, hath oft compared been
To public feasts, where meet a public rout,
Where they that are without would fain go in,
And they that are within would fain go out.
    d.   SIR JOHN DAVIES—*Contention Betwixt*
                       a Wife, etc.

At length cried she, I'll marry :
       What should I tarry for?
I may lead apes in hell forever.
    e.   DIBDIN—*Tack and Tack.*

Is not marriage an open question, when it
is alleged, from the beginning of the world,
that such as are in the institution wish to get
out, and such as are out wish to get in.
    f.   EMERSON—*Representative Men.*
                       Montaigne.

           A bachelor
May thrive by observation on a little,
A single life's no burthen : but to draw
In yokes is chargeable, and will require
A double maintenance.
    g.   JOHN FORD—*The Fancies Chaste and*
                 Noble. Act I. Sc. 3. L. 82.

The joys of marriage are the heaven on earth,
Life's paradise, great princess, the soul's quiet,
Sinews of concord, earthly immortality,
Eternity of pleasures.
    h.   JOHN FORD—*The Broken Heart.* Act II.
                     Sc. 2. L. 102.

They that marry ancient people, merely in
expectation to bury them, hang themselves,
in hope that one will come and cut the halter.
    i.   FULLER—*Holy and Profane States.*
                 Bk. III. *Of Marriage.*

The husband's sullen, dogged, shy,
The wife grows flippant in reply ;
He loves command and due restriction,
And she as well likes contradiction.
She never slavishly submits ;
She'll have her way, or have her fits.
He his way tugs, she t'other draws ;
The man grows jealous and with cause.
    j.   GAY—*Cupid, Hymen, and Plutus.*

So, with decorum all things carry'd ;
Miss frown'd, and blush'd, and then was—
    married.
    k.   GOLDSMITH—*The Double*
                 Transformation. St. 3.

An unhappy gentleman, resolving to wed
nothing short of perfection, keeps his heart
and hand till both get so old and withered
that no tolerable woman will accept them.
    l.   NATH. HAWTHORNE—*Mosses from an*
                 Old Manse. Mrs. Bullfrog.

Andromache! my soul's far better part.
    m.   HOMER—*Iliad.* Bk. VI. L. 624.
                     Pope's trans.

Yet while my Hector still survives, I see
My father, mother, brethren, all in thee.
    n.   HOMER—*Iliad.* Bk. VI. L. 544.
                     Pope's trans.

I have met with women whom I really
think would like to be married to a Poem,
and to be given away by a Novel.
    o.   KEATS—*Letters to Fanny Brawne.*
                     Letter II.

Ay, marriage is the life-long miracle,
The self-begetting wonder, daily fresh.
    p.   CHARLES KINGSLEY—*Saint's Tragedy.*
                     Act II. Sc. 9.
As unto the bow the cord is,
So unto the man is woman ;
Though she bends him she obeys him
Though she draws him, yet she follows,
Useless each without the other !
    q.   LONGFELLOW—*Hiawatha.* Pt. X. L. 1.

Sure the shovel and tongs
To each other belongs.
    r.   SAMUEL LOVER—*Widow Machree.*

Cling closer, closer, life to life,
    Cling closer, heart to heart ;
The time will come, my own wed Wife,
    When you and I must part !
Let nothing break our band but Death,
    For in the world above
'Tis the breaker Death that soldereth
    Our ring of Wedded Love.
    s.   GERALD MASSEY—*On a Wedding Day.*
                     St. 11.

And, to all married men, be this a caution,
Which they should duly tender as their life,
Neither to doat too much, nor doubt a wife.
    t.   MASSINGER—*Picture.* Act V. Sc. 3.

The sum of all that makes a just man happy
Consists in the well choosing of his wife :
And there, well to discharge it, does require
Equality of years, of birth, of fortune ;
For beauty being poor, and not cried up
By birth or wealth, can truly mix with neither.
And wealth, when there's such difference in
    years,
And fair descent, must make the yoke uneasy.
    u.   MASSINGER—*New Way to Pay Old*
                 Debts. Act IV. Sc. 1.

For what thou art is mine :
Our state cannot be sever'd ; we are one,
One flesh ; to lose thee were to lose myself.
  a.   MILTON—*Paradise Lost.* Bk. IX.
                                   L. 957.

Hail, wedded love, mysterious law; true
        source
Of human offspring.
  b.   MILTON—*Paradise Lost.* Bk. IV.
                                   L. 750.

Therefore God's universal law
Gave to the man despotic power
Over his female in due awe,
Not from that right to part an hour,
Smile she or lour.
  c.   MILTON—*Samson Agonistes.* L. 1,053.

                    To the nuptial bower
I led her, blushing like the morn ; all Heaven,
And happy constellations on that hour
Shed their selectest influence; the earth
Gave sign of gratulation, and each hill ;
Joyous the birds ; fresh gales and gentle airs
Whisper'd it to the woods, and from their
        wings
Flung rose, flung odours from the spicy shrub.
  d.   MILTON—*Paradise Lost.* Bk. VIII.
                                   L. 510.

It happens, as with cages, the birds without
despair to get in, and those within despair of
getting out.
  e.   MONTAIGNE—*Upon some Verses of Virgil.*
                                   Bk. III. Ch. V.

There's a bliss beyond all that the minstrel
        has told,
    When two, that are link'd in one heavenly
        tie,
With heart never changing, and brow never
        cold,
    Love on thro' all ills, and love on till they
        die.
  f.   MOORE—*Lalla Rookh. Light of the
                           Harem.* St. 42.

Drink, my jolly lads, drink with discerning,
Wedlock's a lane where there is no turning ;
Never was owl more blind than a lover,
Drink and be merry, lads, half seas over.
  g.   D. M. MULOCK—*Magnus and Morna.*
                                   Sc. 3.

Grave authors say, and witty poets sing,
That honest wedlock is a glorious thing.
  h.   POPE—*January and May.* L. 21.

The garlands fade, the vows are worn away ;
So dies her love, and so my hopes decay.
  i.   POPE—*Autumn.* L. 70.

There swims no goose so gray, but soon or late
She finds some honest gander for her mate.
  j.   POPE—*Wife of Bath. Her Prologue.*
                           From Chaucer. L. 98.

Before I trust my Fate to thee,
    Or place my hand in thine,
Before I let thy Future give
    Color and form to mine,
Before I peril all for thee,
Question thy soul to-night for me.
  k.   ADELAIDE ANN PROCTER—*A Woman's
                                   Question.*

Widowed wife and wedded maid.
  l.   SCOTT—*The Betrothed.* Ch. XV.

Marriage is a desperate thing.
  m.   JOHN SELDEN—*Table Talk. Marriage.*

As are those dulcet sounds in break of day
That creep into the dreaming bridegroom's
        ear
And summon him to marriage.
  n.   *Merchant of Venice.* Act III. Sc. 2.
                                   L. 51.

A world-without-end bargain.
  o.   *Love's Labour's Lost.* Act V. Sc. 2.
                                   L. 799.

But earthlier happy is the rose distill'd,
Than that which with'ring on the virgin
        thorn
Grows, lives and dies in single blessedness.
  p.   *Midsummer-Night's Dream.* Act I.
                                   Sc. 1. L. 76.

Ere yet the salt of most unrighteous tears
Had left the flushing in her galled eyes,
She married.
  q.   *Hamlet.* Act I. Sc. 2. L. 154.

God, the best maker of all marriages,
Combine your hearts in one.
  r.   *Henry V.* Act I. Sc. 2. L. 387.

Happiest of all, is, that her gentle spirit
Commits itself to yours to be directed,
As from her lord, her governor, her king.
  s.   *Merchant of Venice.* Act III. Sc. 2.
                                   L. 162.

He is the half part of a blessed man,
Left to be finished by such as she ;
And she a fair divided excellence,
Whose fulness of perfection lies in him.
  t.   *King John.* Act II. Sc. 1. L. 437.

If she deny to wed, I'll crave the day
When I shall ask the banns and when be
        married.
  u .   *Taming of the Shrew.* Act II. Sc. 1.
                                   L. 180.

                    If you shall marry,
You give away this hand, and that is mine ;
You give away heaven's vows, and those are
        mine ;
You give away myself, which is known mine.
  v.   *All's Well That Ends Well.* Act V.
                                   Sc. 3. L. 169.

I will fasten on this sleeve of thine:
Thou art an elm, my husband, I, a vine.
    a.   *Comedy of Errors.* Act II. Sc. 2. L. 175.

I will marry her, sir, at your request; but
if there be no great love in the beginning, yet
heaven may decrease it upon better acquaintance * * * I hope, upon familiarity will
grow more contempt: I will marry her; that
I am freely dissolved, and dissolutely.
    b.   *Merry Wives of Windsor.* Act I. Sc. 1.
    L. 253.

I would not marry her, though she were
endowed with all that Adam had left him
before he transgressed: she would have made
Hercules have turned spit, yea, and have cleft
his club to make the fire too. * * * I
would to God some scholar would conjure
her; for certainly, while she is here, a man
may live as quiet in hell as in a sanctuary.
    c.   *Much Ado About Nothing.* Act II.
    Sc. 1. L. 258.

        Let husbands know,
Their wives have sense like them: they see,
    and smell,
And have their palates both for sweet and
    sour,
As husbands have.
    d.   *Othello.* Act IV. Sc. 3. L. 94.

        Let still the woman take
An elder than herself: so wears she to him
So sways she level in her husband's heart:
For, boy, however we do praise ourselves,
Our fancies are more giddy and unfirm,
More longing, wavering, sooner lost and worn
Than women's are.
    e.   *Twelfth Night.* Act II. Sc. 4. L. 29.

Men are April when they woo, December
when they wed; maids are May when they
are maids, but the sky changes when they are
wives.
    f.   *As You Like It.* Act IV. Sc. 1. L. 147.

Men's vows are women's traitors! All good
    seeming,
By thy revolt, O husband, shall be thought
Put on for villany; not born where 't grows,
But worn a bait for ladies.
    g.   *Cymbeline.* Act III. Sc. 4. L. 55.

No, the world must be peopled. When I
said, I would die a bachelor, I did not think
I should live till I were married.
    h.   *Much Ado About Nothing.* Act II.
    Sc. 1. L. 253.

Now go with me and with this holy man
Into the chantry by: there, before him,
And underneath that consecrated roof,
Plight me the full assurance of your faith.
    i.   *Twelfth Night.* Act IV. Sc. 3. L. 23.

        O ye gods,
Render me worthy of this noble wife!
    j.   *Julius Cæsar.* Act II. Sc. 1. L. 303.

        She is mine own,
And I as rich in having such a jewel
As twenty seas, if all their sand were pearl,
The water nectar and the rocks pure gold.
    k.   *Two Gentlemen of Verona.* Act II.
    Sc. 4. L. 168.

She is your treasure, she must have a husband;
I must dance barefoot on her wedding day
And for your love to her lead apes in hell.
    l.   *Taming of the Shrew.* Act II. Sc. 1.
    L. 32.

        She shall watch all night:
And if she chance to nod I'll rail and brawl
And with the clamour keep her still awake.
This is the way to kill a wife with kindness.
    m.   *Taming of the Shrew.* Act IV. Sc. 1.
    L. 218.

She is not well married that lives married long;
But she's best married that dies married young.
    n.   *Romeo and Juliet.* Act IV. Sc. 5.
    L. 77.

The instances that second marriage move
Are base respects of thrift, but none of love.
    o.   *Hamlet.* Act III. Sc. 2. L. 192.

Thy husband * * * commits his body
To painful labour, both by sea and land,
    *   *   *   *   *   *
And craves no other tribute at thy hands,
But love, fair looks, and true obedience;
Too little payment for so great a debt.
    p.   *Taming of the Shrew.* Act V. Sc. 2.
    L. 152.

Thou art mine, thou hast given thy word,
    Close, close in my arms thou art clinging;
    Alone for my ear thou art singing
A song which no stranger hath heard:
But afar from me yet, like a bird,
Thy soul in some region unstirr'd
    On its mystical circuit is winging.
    q.   E. C. STEDMAN—*Stanzas for Music.*

The reason why so few marriages are happy
is because young ladies spend their time in
making nets, not in making cages.
    r.   SWIFT—*Thoughts on Various Subjects.*

Under this window in stormy weather
I marry this man and woman together;
Let none but Him who rules the thunder
Put this man and woman asunder.
    s.   SWIFT—*Marriage Service from his
    Chamber Window.*

As the husband is the wife is; thou art mated
    with a clown,
And the grossness of his nature will have
    weight to drag thee down.
    t.   TENNYSON—*Locksley Hall.* St. 24.

Marriages are made in Heaven.
  a.   TENNYSON—*Aylmer's Field.* L. 188.

But happy they, the happiest of their kind !
Whom gentler stars unite, and in one fate
Their Hearts, their Fortunes, and their Beings
      blend.
  b.   THOMSON—*Seasons. Spring.* L. 1,111.

Thrice happy is that humble pair,
Beneath the level of all care !
Over whose heads those arrows fly
Of sad distrust and jealousy.
  c.   EDMUND WALLER—*Of the Marriage of
                  the Dwarfs.* L. 7.

'Tis just like a summer bird cage in a garden ; the birds that are without despair to get
in, and the birds that are within despair, and
are in a consumption, for fear they shall never
get out.
  d.   JOHN WEBSTER—*The White Devil.*
                  Act I. Sc. 2.

Why do not words, and kiss, and solemn
      pledge,
And nature that is kind in woman's breast,
And reason that in man is wise and good,
And fear of Him who is a righteous Judge,—
Why do not these prevail for human life,
To keep two hearts together, that began
Their spring-time with one love.
  e.   WORDSWORTH—*The Excursion.* Bk. VI.

Body and soul, like peevish man and wife,
United jar, and yet are loth to part.
  f.   YOUNG—*Night Thoughts.* Night II.
                  L. 175.

MAY (*See* MONTHS).

MEDICINE (*See* OCCUPATIONS).

MEDITATION.

Thy thoughts to nobler meditations give,
And study how to die, not how to live.
  g.   GEO. GRANVILLE (Lord Lansdowne)—
                  Meditation on Death. St. 1.

Happy the heart that keeps its twilight hour,
And, in the depths of heavenly peace reclined,
Loves to commune with thoughts of tender
      power,—
Thoughts that ascend, like angels beautiful,
A shining Jacob's-ladder of the mind !
  h.   PAUL H. HAYNE—*Sonnet IX.*

Divinely bent to meditation ;
And in no worldly suits would he be mov'd,
To draw him from his holy exercise.
  i.   *Richard III.* Act III. Sc. 7. L. 61.

In maiden meditation, fancy-free.
  j.   *Midsummer-Night's Dream.* Act II.
                  Sc. 1. L. 164.

MEETING.

As two floating planks meet and part on the
      sea,
O friend ! so I met and then drifted from thee.
  k.   WM. R. ALGER—*Oriental Poetry. The
                  Brief Chance Encounter.*

We met—'twas in a crowd.
  l.   THOMAS HAYNES BAYLY—*We Met.*

Ships that pass in the night, and speak each
      other in passing,
Only a signal shown and a distant voice in
      the darkness :
So on the ocean of life, we pass and speak one
      another,
Only a look and a voice, then darkness again
      and a silence.
  m.   LONGFELLOW—*Tales of a Wayside Inn.
                  The Theologian's Tale. Elizabeth.*
                  Pt. IV.

The joy of meeting not unmixed with pain.
  n.   LONGFELLOW—*Morituri Salutamus.*
                  L. 113.

In life there are meetings which seem
Like a fate.
  o.   OWEN MEREDITH (Lord Lytton)—
                  Lucile. Pt. II. Canto III. St. 8.

Some day, some day of days, threading the
      street
    With idle, heedless pace,
    Unlooking for such grace,
    I shall behold your face !
Some day, some day of days, thus may we
      meet.
  p.   NORA PERRY—*Some Day of Days.*

And so he'll die ; and, rising so again,
When I shall meet him in the court of heaven
I shall not know him.
  q.   *King John.* Act III. Sc. 4. L. 86.

When shall we three meet again
In thunder, lightning, or in rain ?
  r.   *Macbeth.* Act I. Sc. 1. L. 1.

MELANCHOLY.

All my griefs to this are jolly,
Naught so damn'd as melancholy.
  s.   BURTON—*Abstract to Anatomy of
                  Melancholy.*

All my joys to this are folly,
Naught so sweet as melancholy.
  t.   BURTON—*Abstract to Anatomy of
                  Melancholy.*

As melancholy as an unbraced drum.
  u.   CENTLIVRE—*Wonder.* Act II. Sc. 1.

With eyes upraised, as one inspired,
Pale Melancholy sate retired ;
And, from her wild, sequester'd seat,
In notes by distance made more sweet,
Pour'd through the mellow horn her pensive
      soul.
  v.   COLLINS—*The Passions.* L. 57.

Melancholy
Is not, as you conceive, indisposition
Of body, but the mind's disease.
    a.   JOHN FORD—*The Lover's Melancholy.*
                     Act III.   Sc. 1.   L. 111.

Tell us, pray, what devil
This melancholy is, which can transform
Men into monsters.
    b.   JOHN FORD—*The Lover's Melancholy.*
                     Act III.   Sc. 1.   L. 107.

Here rests his head upon the lap of earth,
  A youth, to fortune and to fame unknown ;
Fair Science frowned not on his humble birth,
  And Melancholy marked him for his own.
    c.   GRAY—*Elegy in a Country Churchyard.*
                           The Epitaph.

Employment, sir, and hardships, prevent
melancholy.
    d.   SAM'L JOHNSON—*Boswell's Life of*
                      Johnson.   1777.

Moping melancholy,
And moon-struck madness.
    e.   MILTON—*Paradise Lost.*   Bk. XI.
                               L. 485.

Go—you may call it madness, folly,
  You shall not chase my gloom away.
There's such a charm in melancholy,
  I would not, if I could, be gay !
    f.   SAM'L ROGERS—*To* ——.   St. 1.

Oh, if you knew the pensive pleasure
  That fills my bosom when I sigh,
You would not rob me of a treasure
  Monarchs are too poor to buy.
    g.   SAM'L ROGERS—*To* ——.   St. 2.

And melancholy is the nurse of frenzy.
    h.   *Taming of the Shrew.*   Induction.
                         Sc. 2.   L. 135.

I can suck melancholy out of a song.
    i.   *As You Like It.*   Act II.   Sc. 5.   L. 12.

O melancholy !
Who ever yet could sound thy bottom ? find
The ooze, to show what coast thy sluggish
  crare
Might easiliest harbour in?
    j.   *Cymbeline.* Act IV.   Sc. 2.   L. 205.

The greatest note of it is his melancholy.
    k.   *Much Ado About Nothing.*   Act III.
                        Sc. 2.   L. 53.

MEMORY.

Friends depart, and memory takes them
To her caverns, pure and deep.
    l.   THOMAS HAYNES BAYLY—*Teach Me to*
                         Forget.

Oh, I have roamed o'er many lands,
  And many friends I've met ;
Not one fair scene or kindly smile
  Can this fond heart forget.
    m.   THOMAS HAYNES BAYLY—*O, Steer my*
                     Bark to Erin's Isle.

Tell me the tales that to me were so dear,
  Long, long ago, long, long ago.
    n.   THOMAS HAYNES BAYLY—*Long, Long*
                           Ago.

The mother may forget the child
  That smiles sae sweetly on her knee ;
But I'll remember thee, Glencairn,
  And all that thou hast done for me !
    o.   BURNS—*Lament for Glencairn.*

To live in hearts we leave behind,
Is not to die.
    p.   CAMPBELL—*Hallowed Ground.*   St. 6.

Oh, how cruelly sweet are the echoes that
  start
When Memory plays an old tune on the
  heart !
    q.   ELIZA COOK—*Journal.*   Vol. IV.   *Old*
                         Dobbin. St. 16.

What peaceful hours I once enjoy'd !
  How sweet their memory still !
But they have left an aching void
  The world can never fill.
    r.   COWPER—*Walking with God.*

Don't you remember sweet Alice, Ben Bolt?
  Sweet Alice, whose hair was so brown ;
Who wept with delight when you gave her
  a smile,
  And trembl'd with fear at your frown !
    s.   THOMAS DUNN ENGLISH—*Ben Bolt.*

Memory [is] like a purse,—if it be over-full
that it cannot shut, all will drop out of it.
Take heed of a gluttonous curiosity to feed
on many things, lest the greediness of the
appetite of thy memory spoil the digestion
thereof.
    t.   FULLER—*Holy and Profane States.*
                   Bk. III.   *Of Memory.*

Remembrance wakes with all her busy train,
Swells at my breast, and turns the past to
  pain.
    u.   GOLDSMITH—*The Deserted Village.*
                             L. 81.

Where'er I roam, whatever realms to see,
My heart untravell'd fondly turns to thee ;
Still to my brother turns, with ceaseless pain,
And drags at each remove a lengthening
  chain.
    v.   GOLDSMITH—*The Traveller.*   L. 7.

A place in thy memory, Dearest !
  Is all that I claim :
To pause and look back when thou hearest
  The sound of my name.
    w.   GERALD GRIFFIN—*A Place in Thy*
                      Memory, Dearest.

It is a suggestive idea to track those worn feet backward through all the paths they have trodden ever since they were the tender and rosy little feet of a baby, and (cold as they now are) were kept warm in his mother's hand.

a.   NATH. HAWTHORNE—*The Marble Faun.*
Vol. I. Ch. XXI.

I remember, I remember,
　The house where I was born,
The little window where the sun
　Came peeping in at morn;
He never came a wink too soon,
　Nor brought too long a day,
But now, I often wish the night
　Had borne my breath away!

b.   HOOD—*I Remember, I Remember.*

'Tis but a little faded flower,
　But oh, how fondly dear!
'Twill bring me back one golden hour,
　Through many a weary year.

c.   ELLEN C. HOWARTH—*'Tis but a Little*
Faded Flower.

Where is the heart that doth not keep,
　Within its inmost core,
Some fond remembrance hidden deep,
　Of days that are no more?

d.   ELLEN C. HOWARTH—*'Tis but a Little*
Faded Flower.

Badness of memory every one complains of, but nobody of the want of judgment.

e.   LA ROCHEFOUCAULD—*Reflections and*
Moral Maxims. No. 463.

Tho' lost to sight to mem'ry dear
Thou ever wilt remain.

f.   GEO. LINLEY—*Though Lost to Sight.*

I recollect a nurse called Ann,
Who carried me about the grass,
And one fine day a fine young man
Came up and kissed the pretty lass.
　She did not make the least objection.
　　　Thinks I, " *Aha,*
When I can talk I'll tell Mama,"
And that's my earliest recollection.

g.   FRED. LOCKER—*A Terrible Infant.*

　　　Nothing now is left
But a majestic memory.

h.   LONGFELLOW—*Three Friends of Mine.*
L. 10.

The heart hath its own memory, like the
　mind,
　And in it are enshrined
The precious keepsakes, into which is wrought
　The giver's loving thought.

i.   LONGFELLOW—*From My Arm-Chair.*
St. 12.

The leaves of memory seemed to make
A mournful rustling in the dark.

j.   LONGFELLOW—*The Fire of Drift-Wood.*

There comes to me out of the Past
A voice, whose tones are sweet and wild,
Singing a song almost divine,
And with a tear in every line.

k.   LONGFELLOW—*Tales of a Wayside Inn.*
Pt. III.   *Interlude before " The*
Mother's Ghost."

This memory brightens o'er the past,
　As when the sun concealed
Behind some cloud that near us hangs,
　Shines on a distant field.

l.   LONGFELLOW—*A Gleam of Sunshine.*

　　　　Wakes the bitter memory
Of what he was, what is, and what must be
Worse.

m.   MILTON—*Paradise Lost.* Bk. IV.
L. 24.

Oft in the stilly night
　E'er slumber's chain has bound me,
Fond memory brings the light
　Of other days around me.

n.   MOORE—*Oft in the Stilly Night.*

To live with them is far less sweet
　Than to remember thee!

o.   MOORE—*I Saw Thy Form in Youthful*
Prime.

When I remember all
　The friends so link'd together,
I've seen around me fall,
　Like leaves in wintry weather
I feel like one who treads alone
　Some banquet hall deserted,
Whose lights are fled, whose garlands dead,
　And all but he departed.

p.   MOORE—*Oft in the Stilly Night.*

When time who steals our years away
　Shall steal our pleasures too,
The mem'ry of the past will stay
　And half our joys renew.

q.   MOORE—*Song. From Juvenile Poems.*

I've wandered east, I've wandered west,
　I've bourne a weary lot;
But in my wanderings far or near
　Ye never were forgot.
The fount that first burst frae this heart
　Still travels on its way
And channels deeper as it rins
　The luve o' life's young day.

r.   WM. MOTHERWELL—*Jeanie Morrison.*

I remember, I remember
　How my childhood fleeted by,—
The mirth of its December,
　And the warmth of its July.

s.   PRAED—*I Remember, I Remember.*

Hail, memory, hail! in thy exhaustless mine
From age to age unnumbered treasures shine!
Thought and her shadowy brood thy call obey,
And Place and Time are subject to thy sway!
   a.   Sam'l Rogers—*Pleasures of Memory.*
                       Pt. II.   L. 428.

I have a room whereinto no one enters
      Save I myself alone:
There sits a blessed memory on a throne,
      There my life centres.
   b.   Christina G. Rossetti—*Memory.*
                       Pt. II.

I wept for memory.
   c.   Christina G. Rossetti—*Song. She
              Sat and Sang Always.*

Still are the thoughts to memory dear.
   d.   Scott—*Rokeby.* Canto I. St. 32.

Though varying wishes, hopes, and fears,
Fever'd the progress of these years,
Yet now, days, weeks, and months but seem
The recollection of a dream.
   e.   Scott—*Marmion.*   Introduction to
                       Canto IV.

Still so gently o'er me stealing,
Mem'ry will bring back the feeling,
Spite of all my grief revealing
That I love thee,—that I dearly love thee still.
   f.   Scribe—*Opera of La Sonnambula.*

Be in their flowing cups freshly remembered.
   g.   *Henry V.* Act IV. Sc. 3. L. 55.

Briefly thyself remember.
   h.   *King Lear.* Act IV. Sc. 6. L. 233.

Die two months ago, and not forgotten yet?
Then there's hope a great man's memory may
outlive his life half a year.
   i.   *Hamlet.* Act III. Sc. 2. L. 137.

How sharp the point of this remembrance is!
   j.   *Tempest.* Act V. Sc. 1. L. 137.

I cannot but remember such things were,
That were most precious to me.
   k.   *Macbeth.* Act IV. Sc. 3. L. 222.

I count myself in nothing else so happy
As in a soul rememb'ring my good friends;
And, as my fortune ripens with thy love,
It shall be still thy true love's recompense.
   l.   *Richard II.* Act II. Sc. 3. L. 46.

If a man do not erect in this age his own
tomb ere he dies, he shall live no longer in
monument than the bell rings, and the
widow weeps. * * * An hour in clamour
and a quarter in rheum.
   m.   *Much Ado About Nothing.* Act V.
                       Sc. 2. L. 76.

          Looking on the lines
Of my boy's face, my thoughts I did recoil
Twenty-three years; and saw myself un-
     breech'd,
In my green velvet coat, my dagger muzzled,
Lest it should bite its master, and so prove,
As ornaments oft do, too dangerous.
   n.   *Winter's Tale.* Act I. Sc. 2. L. 153.

        Remember thee!
Yea, from the table of my memory
I'll wipe away all trivial fond records.
   o.   *Hamlet.* Act I. Sc. 5. L. 97.

That memory, the warder of the brain,
Shall be a fume.
   p.   *Macbeth.* Act I. Sc. 7. L. 65.

Thou comest as the memory of a dream,
Which now is sad because it hath been sweet.
   q.   Shelley—*Prometheus Unbound.*
                       Act II. Sc. 1.

   The Right Honorable gentleman is indebted
to his memory for his jests and to his imagination for his facts.
   r.   R. B. Sheridan—*Speech in Reply to
                       Mr. Dundas.*

Where Washington hath left
His awful memory
A light for after times!
   s.   Southey—*Ode Written during the War
                  with America. 1814.*

   In vain does Memory renew
The hours once tinged in transport's dye:
The sad reverse soon starts to view
And turns the past to agony.
   t.   Mrs. Dugald Stewart—*The Tear I
                       Shed.*

The sweet remembrance of the just
Shall flourish when he sleeps in dust.
   u.   Tate and Brady—*Psalm CXII.* St. 6.

A land of promise, a land of memory,
A land of promise flowing with the milk
And honey of delicious memories!
   v.   Tennyson—*The Lover's Tale.* L. 333.

   Memory, in widow's weeds, with naked feet
stands on a tombstone.
   w.   Aubrey De Vere—*Widowhood.*

As the dew to the blossom, the bud to the bee,
As the scent to the rose, are those memories
     to me.
   x.   Amelia B. Welby—*Pulpit Eloquence.*

Ah! memories of sweet summer eves,
Of moonlit wave and willowy way,
Of stars and flowers, and dewy leaves,
   And smiles and tones more dear than they!
   y.   Whittier—*Memories.* St. 4.

The dust is old upon my " sandal-shoon,"
And still I am a pilgrim ; I have roved
From wild America to Bosphor's waters,
And worshipp'd at innumerable shrines
Of beauty ; and the painter's art, to me,
And sculpture, speak as with a living tongue,
And of dead kingdoms I recall the soul,
Sitting amid their ruins.
> *a.*   N. P. WILLIS—*Florence Gray.* L. 46.

>   And when the stream
Which overflowed the soul was passed away,
A consciousness remained that it had left,
Deposited upon the silent shore
Of memory, images and precious thoughts,
That shall not die, and cannot be destroyed.
> *b.*   WORDSWORTH—*The Excursion.*
>   Bk. VII.

The vapours linger round the Heights,
> They melt, and soon must vanish ;
One hour is theirs, nor more is mine,—
> Sad thought, which I would banish,
But that I know, where'er I go,
> Thy genuine image, Yarrow !
Will dwell with me,—to heighten joy,
> And cheer my mind in sorrow.
> *c.*   WORDSWORTH—*Yarrow Visited.*

MERCANTILE (*See* OCCUPATIONS).

MERCY.

When all thy mercies, O my God,
> My rising soul surveys,
Transported with the view I'm lost,
> In wonder, love and praise.
> *d.*   ADDISON—*Hymn.*

Mercy to him that shows it, is the rule.
> *e.*   COWPER—*The Task.* Bk. VI. L. 595.

And shut the gates of mercy on mankind.
> *f.*   GRAY—*Elegy in a Country Churchyard.*
>   St. 17.

A sentinel angel sitting high in glory
Heard this shrill wail ring out from Purgatory:
" Have mercy, mighty angel, hear my story ! "
> *g.*   JOHN HAY—*A Woman's Love.*

Being all fashioned of the self-same dust,
Let us be merciful as well as just.
> *h.*   LONGFELLOW—*Tales of a Wayside Inn.*
>   Pt. III.   *The Student's Tale. Emma
>   and Eginhard.* L. 177.

Mercy stood in the cloud, with eye that wept
Essential love.
> *i.*   POLLOK—*The Course of Time.* Bk. III.
>   L. 658.

'Tis vain to flee ; till gentle Mercy show
Her better eye, the farther off we go,
The swing of Justice deals the mightier blow.
> *j.*   QUARLES—*Emblems.* Bk. III.
>   Emblem XVI.

>   Think not the good,
The gentle deeds of mercy thou hast done,
Shall die forgotten all ; the poor, the prisoner,
The fatherless, the friendless, and the widow,
Who daily owe the bounty of thy hand,
Shall cry to Heaven, and pull a blessing on
> thee.
> *k.*   NICHOLAS ROWE—*Jane Shore.* Act I.
>   Sc. 2. L. 173.

Mercy but murders, pardoning those that kill.
> *l.*   *Romeo and Juliet.* Act III. Sc. 1.
>   L. 202.

Mercy is not itself, that oft looks so ;
Pardon is still the nurse of second woe.
> *m.*   *Measure for Measure.* Act II. Sc. 1.
>   L. 297.

Open thy gate of mercy, gracious God !
My soul flies through these wounds to seek
> out thee.
> *n.*   *Henry VI.* Pt. III. Act 1. Sc. 4.
>   L. 177.

Straight in her heart did mercy come.
> *o.*   *Sonnet CXLV.*

The quality of mercy is not strain'd ;
It droppeth as the gentle rain from heaven
Upon the place beneath : it is twice blest ;
It blesseth him that gives and him that takes ;
'Tis mightiest in the mightiest ; it becomes
The throned monarch better than his crown ;
His sceptre shows the force of temporal power,
The attribute to awe and majesty,
Wherein doth sit the dread and fear of kings ;
But mercy is above this sceptred sway ;
It is enthroned in the hearts of kings,
It is an attribute to God himself ;
And earthly power doth then show likest
> God's
When mercy seasons justice.
> *p.*   *Merchant of Venice.* Act IV. Sc. 1.
>   L. 184.

>   We do pray for mercy ;
And that same prayer doth teach us all to
> render
The deeds of mercy.
> *q.*   *Merchant of Venice.* Act IV. Sc. 1.
>   L. 198.

>   Whereto serves mercy,
But to confront the visage of offence ?
> *r.*   *Hamlet.* Act III. Sc. 3. L. 46.

You must not dare, for shame, to talk of
> mercy ;
For your own reasons turn into your bosoms,
As dogs upon their masters, worrying you.
> *s.*   *Henry V.* Act II. Sc. 2. L. 81.

Who will not mercie unto others show,
How can he mercie ever hope to have ?
> *t.*   SPENSER—*Faerie Queene.* Bk. VI.
>   Canto I. St. 42.

Sweet Mercy! to the gates of Heaven
This Minstrel lead, his sins forgiven;
The rueful conflict, the heart riven
　With vain endeavour,
And memory of earth's bitter leaven
Effaced forever.
　a.　　WORDSWORTH—*Thoughts Suggested on*
　　　　　　　　　　　　the Banks of the Nith.

MERIT.

Thy father's merit sets thee up to view,
And shows thee in the fairest point of light,
To make thy virtues, or thy faults, conspicu-
　ous.
　b.　　ADDISON—*Cato.*　Act I.　Sc. 2.

View the whole scene, with critic judgment
　scan,
And then deny him merit if you can.
Where he falls short, 'tis Nature's fault alone;
Where he succeeds, the merit's all his own.
　c.　　CHURCHILL—*The Rosciad.*　L. 1,023.

It sounds like stories from the land of spirits,
If any man obtain that which he merits,
Or any merit that which he obtains.
　d.　　COLERIDGE—*Complaint.*

On their own merits modest men are dumb.
　e.　　GEORGE COLMAN (The Younger)—
　　　　　　　　Epilogue to The Heir-at-Law.

　　　　By merit raised
To that bad eminence.
　f.　　MILTON—*Paradise Lost.*　Bk. II.　L. 5.

The sufficiency of merit is to know that my
merit is not sufficient.
　g.　　QUARLES—*Emblems.*　Bk. II.　Em. I.

　　　O, that estates, degrees and offices
Were not deriv'd corruptly, and that clear
　honour
Were purchas'd by the merit of the wearer.
　h.　　*Merchant of Venice.*　Act II.　Sc. 9.
　　　　　　　　　　　　　　　　L. 41.

MERMAIDS.

O, train me not, sweet mermaid, with thy
　note,
To drown me in thy sister's flood of tears.
　i.　　*Comedy of Errors.*　Act III.　Sc. 2.
　　　　　　　　　　　　　　　　L. 45.

　　　Since once I sat upon a promontory,
And heard a mermaid on a dolphin's back
Uttering such dulcet and harmonious breath,
That the rude sea grew civil at her song:
And certain stars shot madly from their
　spheres,
To hear the sea-maid's music.
　j.　　*Midsummer-Night's Dream.*　Act II.
　　　　　　　　　　　　Sc. 1.　L. 149.

Slow sail'd the weary mariners and saw,
Betwixt the green brink and the running
　　foam,
Sweet faces, rounded arms, and bosoms prest
To little harps of gold ; and while they mused
Whispering to each other half in fear,
Shrill music reach'd them on the middle sea.
　k.　　TENNYSON—*The Sea Fairies.*

　　　　Who would be
　　　　A mermaid fair,
　　　　Singing alone,
　　　　Combing her hair
　　　　Under the sea,
　　　　In a golden curl
　　　　With a comb of pearl,
　　　　On a throne?
　　I would be a mermaid fair;
I would sing to myself the whole of the day;
With a comb of pearl I would comb my hair;
And still as I comb I would sing and say,
"Who is it loves me? who loves not me?"
　l.　　TENNYSON—*The Mermaid.*

MERRIMENT.

As Tammie glow'red, amazed and curious,
The mirth and fun grew fast and furious.
　m.　　BURNS—*Tam o' Shanter.*

Go then merrily to Heaven.
　n.　　BURTON—*Anatomy of Melancholy.*
　　　　　　　Pt. II.　Sec. 3.　Memb. 1.

　The country hath his recreations, the city
his several gymnics and exercises, May games,
feasts, wakes and merry meetings to solace
themselves.
　o.　　BURTON—*Anatomy of Melancholy.*
　　　　　　　Pt. II.　Sec. 2.　Memb. 4.

A very merry, dancing, drinking,
Laughing, quaffing, and unthinking time.
　p.　　DRYDEN—*The Secular Masque.*　L. 40.

There's not a string attuned to mirth
But has its chord in melancholy.
　q.　　HOOD—*Ode to Melancholy.*

Haste thee, Nymph, and bring with thee
Jest, and youthful Jollity,
Quips, and Cranks, and wanton Wiles,
Nods, and Becks, and wreathed Smiles,
Such as hang on Hebe's cheek,
And love to live in dimple sleek ;
Sport that wrinkled Care derides,
And Laughter holding both his sides.
　r.　　MILTON—*L'Allegro.*　L. 25.

Mirth, admit me of thy crew,
To live with her, and live with thee,
In unreprov'd pleasures free.
　s.　　MILTON—*L'Allegro.*　L. 38.

Forward and frolic glee was there,
The will to do, the soul to dare.
　t.　　SCOTT—*Lady of the Lake.*　Canto I.
　　　　　　　　　　　　　　　St. 21.

Where lives the man that has not tried,
How mirth can into folly glide,
And folly into sin!
  a.   Scott—*Bridal of Trierman.*   Canto I.
                                          St. 21.

And frame your mind to mirth and mer-
    riment,
Which bars a thousand harms and lengthens
    life.
  b.   *Taming of the Shrew.*   Induction.
                                  Sc. 2. L. 137.

And, if you can be merry then, I'll say
A man may weep upon his wedding day.
  c.   *Henry VIII.*   Prologue.   L. 31.

And let's be red with mirth.
  d.   *Winter's Tale.*   Act IV.   Sc. 4.   L. 54.

As merry as the day is long.
  e.   *Much Ado About Nothing.*   Act II.
                                      Sc. 1.   L. 45.

                        As 'tis ever common
That men are merriest when they are from
    home.
  f.   *Henry V.*   Act I.   Sc. 2.   L. 271.

Be large in mirth; anon we'll drink a measure
The table round.
  g.   *Macbeth.*   Act III.   Sc. 4.   L. 11.

                        But a merrier man,
Within the limit of becoming mirth,
I never spent an hour's talk withal.
  h.   *Love's Labour's Lost.*   Act II.   Sc. 1.
                                              L. 66.

Hostess, clap to the doors; watch to-night,
pray to-morrow. Gallants, lads, boys, hearts
of gold, all the titles of good fellowship come
to you! What, shall we be merry? Shall
we have a play extempore?
  i.   *Henry IV.*   Pt. I.   Act II.   Sc. 4.
                                           L. 305.

I am not merry; but I do beguile
The thing I am by seeming otherwise.
  j.   *Othello.*   Act II.   Sc. 1.   L. 123.

I had rather have a fool to make me merry,
than experience to make me sad.
  k.   *As You Like It.*   Act IV.   Sc. 1.
                                        L. 28.

Jog on, jog on, the foot-path way,
  And merrily hent the stile-a:
A merry heart goes all the day,
  Your sad tires in a mile-a.
  l.   *Winter's Tale.*   Act IV.   Sc. 3.   L. 132.

Merrily, merrily, shall I live now
Under the blossom that hangs on the bough.
  m.   *Tempest.*   Act V.   Sc. 1.   L. 93.

What should a man do but be merry?
  n.   *Hamlet.*   Act III.   Sc. 2.   L. 131.

                        When every room
Hath blaz'd with lights and brayed with
    minstrelsy.
  o.   *Timon of Athens.*   Act II.   Sc. 2.
                                          L. 169.

With mirth and laughter let old wrinkles
    come,
And let my liver rather heat with wine
Than my heart cool with mortifying groans.
  p.   *Merchant of Venice.*   Act I.   Sc. 1.
                                           L. 80.

The glad circle round them yield their souls
To festive mirth, and wit that knows no gall.
  q.   Thomson—*The Seasons.*   *Summer.*
                                          L. 403.

MIDNIGHT.

                        Is there not
A tongue in every star that talks with man,
And wooes him to be wise? nor wooes in
    vain;
This dead of midnight is the noon of thought,
And wisdom mounts her zenith with the
    stars.
  r.   Anna Letitia Barbauld—*A Summer
                        Evening's Meditation.*   L. 48.

That hour o' night's black arch the keystane.
  s.   Burns—*Tam o' Shanter.*

It is the hour when from the boughs
  The nightingale's high note is heard;
It is the hour when lovers' vows
  Seem sweet in every whisper'd word.
  t.   Byron—*Parisina.*   St. 1.

                        It was evening here,
But upon earth the very noon of night.
  u.   Dante—*Purgatorio.*   Canto XV.   L. 5.

Midnight! the outpost of advancing day!
  The frontier town and citadel of night!
  v.   Longfellow—*The Two Rivers.*   Pt. I.

O wild and wondrous midnight,
  There is a might in thee
To make the charmed body
  Almost like spirit be,
And give it some faint glimpses
  Of immortality!
  w.   Lowell—*Midnight.*

'Tis midnight now. The bent and broken
    moon,
Batter'd and black, as from a thousand battles,
Hangs silent on the purple walls of Heaven.
  x.   Joaquin Miller—*Ina.*   Sc. 2.

Soon as midnight brought on the dusky hour
Friendliest to sleep and silence.
  y.   Milton—*Paradise Lost.*   Bk. V.
                                          L. 667.

The iron tongue of midnight hath told twelve;
Lovers, to bed; 'tis almost fairy time.
  z.   *Midsummer-Night's Dream.*   Act V.
                                        Sc. 1.   L. 370.

MILITARY (*See* OCCUPATIONS).

MIND.

I had rather believe all the fables in the Legends and the Talmud and the Alcoran, than that this universal frame is without a mind.
a.   BACON—*Essays. Of Atheism.*

That last infirmity of noble mind.
b.   *The Tragedy of* SIR JOHN VAN OLDEN BARNEVELT (1622). See also MILTON—*Lycidas.* L. 71.

Measure your mind's height by the shade it casts.
c.   ROBERT BROWNING—*Paracelsus.* II.

The march of the human mind is slow.
d.   BURKE—*Speech on the Conciliation of America.*

Such as take lodgings in a head
That's to be let unfurnished.
e.   BUTLER—*Hudibras.* Pt. I.   Canto I.
L. 161.

My mind to me a kingdom is;
  Such perfect joy therein I find,
That it excels all other bliss
  That God or Nature hath assign'd,
Though much I want that most would have,
Yet still my mind forbids to crave.
f.   WM. BYRD—*My Mind to Me a Kingdom Is.* See also SIR EDWARD DYER— *My Mind to Me a Kingdom Is* (T. H. WARD's *English Poets*).

The mind, the Music breathing from her face.
g.   BYRON—*Bride of Abydos.* Canto I.
St. 6.

'Tis strange the mind, that very fiery particle,
Should let itself be snuff'd out by an article.
h.   BYRON—*Don Juan.* Canto XI. St. 60.

When Bishop Berkeley said "there was no matter,"
And proved it,—'Twas no matter what he said.
i.   BYRON—*Don Juan.* Canto XI. St. 1.

Constant attention wears the active mind,
Blots out our pow'rs, and leaves a blank behind.
j.   CHURCHILL—*Epistle to Hogarth.* L. 647.

How fleet is a glance of the mind!
  Compared with the speed of its flight,
The tempest itself lags behind,
  And the swift-winged arrows of light.
k.   COWPER—*Verses supposed to be written by* ALEXANDER SELKIRK.

As that the walls worn thin, permit the mind
To look out through, and his Frailty find.
l.   SAMUEL DANIEL—*History of the Civil War.* Bk. IV. St. 84.

Babylon in all its desolation is a sight not so awful as that of the human mind in ruins.
m.   SCROPE DAVIES—*Letter to Thomas Raikes,* May 25, 1835.

Each mind has its own method.
n.   EMERSON—*Essays. Intellect.*

A noble mind disdains to hide his head,
And let his foes triumph in his overthrow.
o.   ROBERT GREENE—*Alphonso, King of Arragon.* Act I.

The mind is like a sheet of white paper in this, that the impressions it receives the oftenest, and retains the longest, are black ones.
p.   J. C. and A. W. HARE—*Guesses at Truth.*

A faultless body and a blameless mind.
q.   HOMER—*Odyssey.* Bk. III. L. 138.
Pope's trans.

And bear unmov'd the wrongs of base mankind,
The last, and hardest, conquest of the mind.
r.   HOMER—*Odyssey.* Bk. XIII. L. 353.
Pope's trans.

The glory of a firm capacious mind.
s.   HOMER—*Odyssey.* Bk. IV. L. 262.
Pope's trans.

Whose little body lodged a mighty mind,
t.   HOMER—*Iliad.* Bk. V. L. 999.
Pope's trans.

The true, strong, and sound mind is the mind that can embrace equally great things and small.
u.   SAM'L JOHNSON—*Boswell's Life of Johnson.* 1778.

What is mind? No matter. What is matter? Never mind.
v.   T. H. KEY (*once Head Master of University School*)—*On the authority of F. J. Furnivall.*

Nobody, I believe, will deny, that we are to form our judgment of the true nature of the human mind, not from sloth and stupidity of the most degenerate and vilest of men, but from the sentiments and fervent desires of the best and wisest of the species.
w.   ARCHBISHOP LEIGHTON—*Theological Lectures.* No. 5. *Of the Immortality of the Soul.*

Stern men with empires in their brains.
x.   LOWELL—*The Biglow Papers.* Second Series. No. 2.

The conformation of his mind was such, that whatever was little seemed to him great, and whatever was great seemed to him little.
y.   MACAULAY—*On Horace Walpole.*

25

The mind is its own place, and in itself
Can make a heaven of hell, a hell of heaven.
   a.   MILTON—*Paradise Lost.* Bk. I. L. 254.

Love, Hope, and Joy, fair pleasure's smiling
     train,
Hate, Fear, and Grief, the family of pain,
These mix'd with art, and to due bounds
     confin'd
Make and maintain the balance of the mind.
   b.   POPE—*Essay on Man.* Ep. II. L. 117.

Strength of mind is exercise, not rest.
   c.   POPE—*Essay on Man.* Ep. II. L. 104.

Whose cockloft is unfurnished.
   d.   RABELAIS—*The Author's Prologue to
             the Fifth Book.*

For I do not distinguish them by the eve,
but by the mind, which is the proper judge
of the man.
   e.   SENECA—*Of a Happy Life.* Ch. I.
               (*L'Estrange's Abstract.*)

And when the mind is quicken'd, out of doubt,
The organs, though defunct and dead before,
Break up their drowsy grave and newly move
With casted slough and fresh legerity.
   f.   *Henry V.* Act IV. Sc. 1. L. 20.

For 'tis the mind that makes the body rich.
   g.   *Taming of the Shrew.* Act IV. Sc. 3.
                      L. 174.

O, what a noble mind is here o'erthrown!
The courtier's, soldier's, scholar's, eye, tongue,
     sword!
   h.   *Hamlet.* Act III. Sc. 1. L. 158.

                There's no art
To find the mind's construction in the face.
   i.   *Macbeth.* Act I. Sc. 4. L. 11.

'Tis but a base, ignoble mind
That mounts no higher than a bird can soar.
   j.   *Henry VI.* Pt. II. Act II. Sc. 1.
                      L. 13.

Not body enough to cover his mind decently
with; his intellect is improperly exposed.
   k.   SYDNEY SMITH—*Lady Holland's
             Memoir.* Vol. I. P. 258.

Man's mind a mirror is of heavenly sights,
A brief wherein all marvels summèd lie,
Of fairest forms and sweetest shapes the store,
Most graceful all, yet thought may grace
     them more.
   l.   ROBT. SOUTHWELL—*Look Home.*

Were I so tall to reach the pole,
   Or grasp the ocean with my span,
I must be measur'd by my soul:
   The mind's the standard of the man.
   m.   WATTS—*False Greatness. Horæ Lyricæ.*
                      Bk. II.

In years that bring the philosophic mind.
   n.   WORDSWORTH—*Ode. Intimations of
             Immortality.* St. 10.

Minds that have nothing to confer
Find little to perceive.
   o.   WORDSWORTH—*Yes! Thou Art Fair.*

MIRACLE.

Every believer is God's miracle.
   p.   BAILEY—*Festus.* Sc. *Home.*

Thou water turn'st to wine, fair friend of life;
Thy foe, to cross the sweet arts of Thy reign,
Distils from thence the tears of wrath and
     strife,
And so turns wine to water back again.
   q.   CRASHAW—*Steps to the Temple. To Our
           Lord upon the Water Made Wine.*

Man is the miracle in nature. God
Is the One Miracle to man. Behold,
"There is a God," thou sayest. Thou sayest
     well:
In that thou sayest all. To Be is more
Of wonderful, than being, to have wrought,
Or reigned, or rested.
   r.   JEAN INGELOW—*Story of Doom.*
                   Bk. VII. L. 271.

                Great floods have flown
From simple sources, and great seas have
     dried
When miracles have by the greatest been
     denied.
   s.   *All's Well That Ends Well.* Act II.
                    Sc. 1. L. 142.

It must be so; for miracles are ceased;
And therefore we must needs admit the means
How things are perfected.
   t.   *Henry V.* Act I. Sc. 1. L. 67.

Accept a miracle instead of wit,—
See two dull lines with Stanhope's pencil writ.
   u.   YOUNG—*Lines written with the Diamond
           Pencil of Lord Chesterfield.*

What is a miracle?—'Tis a reproach,
'Tis an implicit satire on mankind;
And while it satisfies, it censures too.
   v.   YOUNG—*Night Thoughts.* Night IX.
                      L. 1,245.

MISCHIEF.

What plaguy mischief and mishaps
Do dog him still with after claps!
   w.   BUTLER—*Hudibras.* Pt. I. Canto III.
                      L. 3.

             Let them call it mischief:
When it is past and prospered 'twill be virtue.
   x.   BEN JONSON—*Catiline.* Act III. Sc. 3.

In life it is difficult to say who do you the
most mischief, enemies with the worst intentions, or friends with the best.

a.   BULWER LYTTON— *What Will He Do
          With It?* Bk. III. Heading to
                              Ch. XVII.

When to mischief mortals bend their will,
How soon they find fit instruments of ill.

b.   POPE—*Rape of the Lock.* Canto III.
                                    St. 125.

Now let it work: Mischief, thou art afoot,
Take thou what course thou wilt.

c.   *Julius Cæsar.* Act III. Sc. 2. L. 265.

O mischief, thou art swift
To enter in the thoughts of desperate men!

d.   *Romeo and Juliet.* Act V. Sc. 1.
                                    L. 35.

To mourn a mischief that is past and gone
Is the next way to draw new mischief on.

e.   *Othello.* Act I. Sc. 3. L. 204.

MISERS.

And were it not that they are loath to lay
out money on a rope, they would be hanged
forthwith, and sometimes die to save charges.

f.   BURTON—*Anatomy of Melancholy.*
          Pt. I. Sec. 2. Memb. 3. Subsec. 12.

If I knew a miser, who gave up every kind
of comfortable living, all the pleasure of doing
good to others, all the esteem of his fellow-
citizens, and the joys of benevolent friendship,
for the sake of accumulating wealth, Poor
man, said I, you pay too much for your whistle.

g.   BENJ. FRANKLIN—*The Whistle.*

Hoards after hoards his rising raptures fill;
Yet still he sighs, for hoards are wanting still.

h.   GOLDSMITH—*The Traveller.*

The unsunn'd heaps
Of miser's treasures.

i.   MILTON—*Comus.* L. 398.

He sat among his bags, and, with a look
Which hell might be ashamed of, drove the
          poor
Away unalmsed; and midst abundance died—
Sorest of evils!—died of utter want.

j.   POLLOK—*Course of Time.* Bk. III.
                                    L. 276.

'Tis strange the miser should his cares employ
To gain those riches he can ne'er enjoy;
Is it less strange the prodigal should waste
His wealth to purchase what he ne'er can taste?

k.   POPE—*Moral Essays.* Ep. IV. L. 1.

Decrepit miser; base, ignoble wretch;
I am descended of a gentler blood.

l.   *Henry VI.* Pt. I. Act V. Sc. 4. L. 7.

MISERY.

The Niobe of nations! there she stands,
Childless and crownless, in her voiceless woe.

m.   BYRON—*Childe Harold.* Canto IV.
                                    St. 79.

The worst of misery
Is when a nature framed for noblest things
Condemns itself in youth to petty joys,
And, sore athirst for air, breathes scanty life
Gasping from out the shallows.

n.   GEORGE ELIOT—*The Spanish Gypsy.*
                                    Bk. III.

There are a good many real miseries in life
that we cannot help smiling at, but they are
the smiles that make wrinkles and not dimples.

o.   O. W. HOLMES—*The Poet at the
                    Breakfast-Table.* III.

This, this is misery! the last, the worst,
That man can feel.

p.   HOMER—*Iliad.* Bk. XXII. L. 106.
                              Pope's trans.

That to live by one man's will became the
cause of all men's misery.

q.   RICHARD HOOKER—*Ecclesiastical Polity.*
                    Bk. I. Chap. X. 5.

The child of misery, baptized in tears!

r.   LANGHORNE—*The Country Justice.*
                              Pt. 1. L. 166.

But O yet more miserable!
Myself my sepulchre, a moving grave.

s.   MILTON—*Samson Agonistes.* L. 101.

And bear about the mockery of woe
To midnight dances and the public show.

t.   POPE—*To the Memory of an Unfortunate
                          Lady.* L. 57.

Meagre were his looks,
Sharp misery had worn him to the bones.

u.   *Romeo and Juliet.* Act V. Sc. 1. L. 40.

Misery acquaints a man with strange bed-
fellows.

v.   *Tempest.* Act II. Sc. 2. L. 40.

Misery makes sport to mock itself.

w.   *Richard II.* Act II. Sc. 1. L. 85.

MISFORTUNE.

Calamity is man's true touch-stone.

x.   BEAUMONT AND FLETCHER—*Four Plays
          in One. The Triumph of Honour.*
                              Sc. 1. L. 67.

For of Fortune's sharpe adversite,
   The worste kynde of infortune is this,
A man to hav bent in prosperite,
   And it remembren whan it passed is.

y.   CHAUCER—*Canterbury Tales. Troylus
          and Crysseyde.* Bk. III. L. 1,625.

He went like one that hath been stunn'd,
  And is of sense forlorn :
A sadder and a wiser man,
  He rose the morrow morn.
  a.   COLERIDGE—*Ancient Mariner.* Pt. VII.
                                      Last stanza.

Most of our misfortunes are more supportable than the comments of our friends upon
them.
  b.   C. C. COLTON—*Lacon.* P. 238.

I was a stricken deer that left the herd
Long since.
  c.   COWPER—*The Task.* Bk. III. L. 108.

Fallen, fallen, fallen, fallen,
Fallen from his high estate,
  And welt'ring in his blood ;
Deserted at his utmost need,
By those his former bounty fed ;
On the bare earth expos'd he lies,
With not a friend to close his eyes.
  d.   DRYDEN—*Alexander's Feast.* L. 77.

              But strong of limb
And swift of foot misfortune is, and, far
Outstripping all, comes first to every land,
And there wreaks evil on mankind, which
      prayers
Do afterwards redress.
  e.   HOMER—*Iliad.* Bk. IX. L. 625.
                                Bryant's trans.

One more unfortunate
  Weary of breath,
Rashly importunate,
  Gone to her death.
  f.   HOOD—*Bridge of Sighs.*

Let us be of good cheer, however, remembering that the misfortunes hardest to bear are
those which never come.
  g.   LOWELL—*Democracy and Addresses.*
                                      Democracy.

Rocks whereon greatest men have oftest
      wreck'd.
  h.   MILTON—*Paradise Regained.* Bk. II.
                                      L. 228.

I never knew any man in my life, who could
not bear another's misfortunes perfectly like
a Christian.
  i.   POPE—See SWIFT'S *Thoughts on
                            Various Subjects.*

Sometimes virtue starves, while vice is fed.
  j.   POPE—*Essay on Man.* Ep. IV. L. 149.

As if Misfortune made the Throne her Seat,
And none could be unhappy but the Great.
  k.   NICHOLAS ROWE—*The Fair Penitent.*
                              Prologue. L. 3.

              O, give me thy hand,
One writ with me in sour misfortune's book.
  l.   *Romeo and Juliet.* Act V. Sc. 3
                                      L. 81.

              Such a house broke !
So noble a master fallen ! All gone ! and not
One friend to take his fortune by the arm,
And go along with him.
  m.   *Timon of Athens.* Act IV. Sc. 2. L. 5.

              The worst is not
So long as we can say " This is the worst."
  n.   *King Lear.* Act IV. Sc. 1. L. 29.

We have seen better days.
  o.   *Timon of Athens.* Act IV. Sc. 2. L. 27.

From good to bad, and from bad to worse,
From worse unto that is worst of all,
And then return to his former fall.
  p.   SPENSER—*The Shepherd's Calendar.*
                                Feb. L. 12.

Misfortune had conquered her, how true it
is, that sooner or later the most rebellious
must bow beneath the same yoke.
  q.   MADAME DE STAËL—*Corinne.*
                              Bk. XVII. Ch. II

So fallen ! so lost ! the light withdrawn
  Which once he wore ;
The glory from his gray hairs gone
  For evermore !
  r.   WHITTIER—*Ichabod.*

Wrongs unredressed, or insults unavenged.
  s.   WORDSWORTH—*The Excursion.* Bk. III.

Woes cluster ; rare are solitary woes ;
They love a train, they tread each other's
      heel.
  t.   YOUNG—*Night Thoughts.* Night III.
                                      L. 63.

MODERATION.

Moderation is the silken string running
through the pearl-chain of all virtues.
  u.   FULLER—*Holy and Profane States.*
                  Bk. III. *Of Moderation.* See
                  also BISHOP HALL—*Christian
                  Moderation.* Introduction.

The moderation of fortunate people comes
from the calm which good fortune gives to
their tempers.
  v.   LA ROCHEFOUCAULD—*Maxims.* No. 18.

Take this at least, this last advice, my son :
Keep a stiff rein, and move but gently on :
The coursers of themselves will run too fast,
Your art must be to moderate their haste.
  w.   OVID—*Metamorphoses. Story of Phaeton.*
                  Bk. II. L. 147. Addison's trans.

He knows to live who keeps the middle state,
And neither leans on this side nor on that.
  x.   POPE—Bk. II. Satire II. L. 61.

Be moderate, be moderate.
Why tell you me of moderation?
The grief is fine, full, perfect, that I taste,
And violenteth in a sense as strong
As that which causeth it: how can I mod-
erate it?
a.   *Troilus and Cressida.* Act IV. Sc. 4.
L. 1.

There is a limit to enjoyment, though the
sources of wealth be boundless,
And the choicest pleasures of life lie within
the ring of moderation.
b.   TUPPER—*Proverbial Philosophy.* *Of
Compensation.* L. 15.

MODESTY.

Modesty is to merit, what shade is to figures
in a picture; it gives it strength and makes it
stand out.
c.   DE LA BRUYÈRE—*The Characters or
Manners of the Present Age.* Ch. II.
Sec. 17.

Modesty is that feeling by which honorable shame acquires a valuable and lasting
authority.
d.   CICERO—*Rhetorical Invention.* Bk. II.
Sec. LVI.

Immodest words admit of no defence;
For want of decency is want of sense.
e.   WENTWORTH DILLON—*Essay on
Translated Verse.* L. 113.

Thy modesty's a candle to thy merit.
f.   HENRY FIELDING—*Tom Thumb the
Great.* Act I. Sc. 3. L. 8.

Her modest looks the cottage might adorn,
Sweet as the primrose peeps beneath the thorn.
g.   GOLDSMITH—*The Deserted Village.*
L. 329.

Can it be
That modesty may more betray our sense
Than woman's lightness? Having waste
ground enough,
Shall we desire to raze the sanctuary
And pitch our evils there?
h.   *Measure for Measure.* Act 2. Sc. 2.
L. 167.

Not stepping o'er the bounds of modesty.
i.   *Romeo and Juliet.* Act IV. Sc. 2.
L. 27.

He saw her charming, but he saw not half
The charms her downcast modesty conceal'd.
j.   THOMSON—*The Seasons. Autumn.*
L. 229.

MONEY.

Still amorous, and fond, and billing,
Like Philip and Mary on a shilling.
k.   BUTLER—*Hudibras.* Pt. III. Canto I.
L. 687.

How beauteous are rouleaus! how charming
chests
Containing ingots, bags of dollars, coins
(Not of old victors, all whose heads and crests
Weigh not the thin ore where their visage
shines,
But) of fine unclipt gold, where dully rests
Some likeness, which the glittering cirque
confines,
Of modern, reigning, sterling, stupid stamp;—
Yes! ready money is Aladdin's lamp.
l.   BYRON—*Don Juan.* Canto XII. St. 12.

The way to resumption is to resume.
m.   SALMON P. CHASE—*Letter to Horace
Greeley.* May 17, 1866.

As I sat at the Café I said to myself,
They may talk as they please about what they
call pelf,
They may sneer as they like about eating and
drinking,
But help it I cannot, I cannot help thinking
How pleasant it is to have money, heigh-ho;
How pleasant it is to have money!
n.   ARTHUR HUGH CLOUGH—*Spectator
Ab Extra.*

Money was made, not to command our will,
But all our lawful pleasures to fulfil.
Shame and woe to us, if we our wealth obey;
The horse doth with the horseman run away.
o.   ABRAHAM COWLEY—*Imitations. Tenth
Epistle of Horace.* Bk. I. L. 75.

This bank-note world.
p.   FITZ-GREENE HALLECK—*Alnwick
Castle.*

Get to live;
Then live, and use it; else, it is not true
That thou hast gotten. Surely use alone
Makes money not a contemptible stone.
q.   HERBERT—*The Temple. The Church
Porch.* St. 26.

Fight thou with shafts of silver, and o'ercome
When no force else can get the masterdome.
r.   HERRICK—*Money Gets the Mastery.*

The almighty dollar, that great object of
universal devotion throughout our land, seems
to have no genuine devotees in these peculiar
villages.
s.   WASHINGTON IRVING—*The Creole
Village.*

Get money; still get money, boy;
No matter by what means.
t.   BEN JONSON—*Every Man in His
Humour.* Act II. Sc. 3.

Whilst that for which all virtue now is sold,
And almost every vice, almighty gold.
u.   BEN JONSON—*Epistle to Elizabeth,
Countess of Rutland.*

Money brings honor, friends, conquest, and realms.
> a.   MILTON—*Paradise Regained*. Bk. II.
> L. 422.

Trade it may help, society extend,
But lures the Pirate, and corrupts the friend :
It raises armies in a nation's aid,
But bribes a senate, and the land's betray'd.
> b.   POPE—*Moral Essays*. Ep. III. L. 29.

Subject to a kind of disease, which at that time they called lack of money.
> c.   RABELAIS—*Works*. Bk. II. Ch. XVI.

But, by the Lord, lads, I am glad you have the money.
> d.   *Henry IV*. Pt. I. Act II. Sc. 4.
> L. 298.

For they say, if money go before, all ways do lie open.
> e.   *Merry Wives of Windsor*. Act II.
> Sc. 2. L. 173.

Money is a good soldier, sir, and will on.
> f.   *Merry Wives of Windsor*. Act II.
> Sc. 2. L. 175.

Why, give him gold enough and marry him to a puppet or an aglet-baby ; or an old trot with ne'er a tooth in her head, though she have as many diseases as two-and-fifty horses ; why, nothing comes amiss, so money comes withal.
> g.   *Taming of the Shrew*. Act I. Sc. 2.
> L. 78.

But the jingling of the guinea helps the hurt that Honor feels.
> h.   TENNYSON—*Locksley Hall*. St. 53.

MONTHS.

Fourth, eleventh, ninth, and sixth,
Thirty days to each affix ;
Every other thirty-one,
Except the second month alone.
> i.   *Common in Chester Co., Pa., among the
> Friends.*

Thirty days hath September,
April, June, and November ;
All the rest have thirty-one
Excepting February alone :
Which hath but twenty-eight, in fine,
Till leap year gives it twenty-nine.
> j.   *Common in New England States.*

Thirty dayes hath November,
April, June, and September,
February hath xxviii alone,
And all the rest have xxxi.
> k.   RICHARD GRAFTON—*Abridgement of the
> Chronicles of Englande*. 1570. 8vo.
> " *A rule to knowe how many dayes
> every moneth in the yeare hath.*"

Thirty days hath September,
April, June, and November ;
February eight-and-twenty all alone,
And all the rest have thirty-one :
Unless that leap-year doth combine,
And give to February twenty-nine.
> l.   *Return from Parnassus.* (London. 1606.)

January.

Janus was invoked at the commencement of most actions ; even in the worship of the other gods the votary began by offering wine and incense to Janus. The first month in the year was named from him ; and under the title of Matutinus he was regarded as the opener of the day. Hence he had charge of the gates of Heaven, and hence, too, all gates, *Januæ*, were called after him, and supposed to be under his care. Hence, perhaps, it was, that he was represented with a staff and key, and that he was named the Opener (*Patulcius*), and the Shutter (*Clusius*).
> m.   M. A. DWIGHT—*Grecian and Roman
> Mythology. Janus.*

That blasts of January
Would blow you through and through.
> n.   *Winter's Tale*. Act IV. Sc. 4. L. 111.

February.

Come when the rains
Have glazed the snow and clothed the trees
    with ice,
While the slant sun of February pours
Into the bowers a flood of light. Approach !
The incrusted surface shall upbear thy steps
And the broad arching portals of the grove
Welcome thy entering.
> o.   BRYANT—*A Winter Piece*. L. 60.

The February sunshine steeps your boughs
And tints the buds and swells the leaves
    within.
> p.   BRYANT—*Among the Trees*. L. 53.

February makes a bridge, and
March breaks it.
> q.   HERBERT—*Jacula Prudentum*.

March.

March. Its tree, Juniper. Its stone, Bloodstone. Its motto, "Courage and strength in
times of danger."
   a.　　*Old Saying.*

Ah, passing few are they who speak,
  Wild, stormy month! in praise of thee:
Yet though thy winds are loud and bleak,
  Thou art a welcome month to me.

For thou, to northern lands, again
  The glad and glorious sun dost bring,
And thou hast joined the gentle train
  And wear'st the gentle name of Spring.
   b.　　BRYANT—*March.*

The stormy March is come at last,
  With wind, and cloud, and changing skies;
I hear the rushing of the blast,
  That through the snowy valley flies.
   c.　　BRYANT—*March.*

The hazel-blooms, in threads of crimson hue,
  Peep through the swelling buds, foretelling
    Spring,
Ere yet a white-thorn leaf appears in view,
  Or March finds throstles pleased enough to
    sing.
   d.　　CLARE—*The Rural Muse. First Sight*
                    of Spring.

March! A cloudy stream is flowing,
And a hard, steel blast is blowing;
  Bitterer now than I remember
Ever to have felt or seen,
  In the depths of drear December,
When the white doth hide the green.
   e.　　BARRY CORNWALL—*March, April, May.*

      Ah, March! we know thou art
Kind-hearted, spite of ugly looks and threats,
And, out of sight, art nursing April's violets!
   f.　　HELEN HUNT JACKSON—*Verses.*
                     March.

Slayer of the winter, art thou here again?
  O welcome, thou that bring'st the summer
    nigh!
The bitter wind makes not the victory vain,
  Nor will we mock thee for thy faint blue
    sky.
   g.　　WILLIAM MORRIS—*March.* St. 1.

The ides of March are come.
   h.　　*Julius Cæsar.* Act III. Sc. 1. L. 1.

In fierce March weather
White waves break tether,
And whirled together
  At either hand,
Like weeds uplifted,
The tree-trunks rifted
In spars are drifted,
  Like foam or sand,
   i.　　SWINBURNE—*Four Songs of Four*
                  Seasons. St. 11.

With rushing winds and gloomy skies
The dark and stubborn Winter dies:
Far-off, unseen, Spring faintly cries,
Bidding her earliest child arise;
       March!
   j.　　BAYARD TAYLOR—*March.*

All in the wild March-morning I heard the
    angels call;
It was when the moon was setting, and the
    dark was over all;
The trees began to whisper, and the wind
    began to roll,
And in the wild March-morning I heard them
    call my soul.
   k.　　TENNYSON—*The May Queen.*
               Conclusion. St. 7.

Up from the sea, the wild north wind is blow-
    ing
  Under the sky's gray arch;
Smiling I watch the shaken elm boughs,
    knowing
  It is the wind of March.
   l.　　WHITTIER—*March.*

Like an army defeated
The snow hath retreated,
And now doth fare ill
On the top of the bare hill;
The Ploughboy is whooping—anon—anon!
  There's joy in the mountains:
  There's life in the fountains;
  Small clouds are sailing,
  Blue sky prevailing;
The rain is over and gone.
   m.　　WORDSWORTH—*Written in March.*

April.

There is no glory in star or blossom
  Till looked upon by a loving eye;
There is no fragrance in April breezes
  Till breathed with joy as they wander by.
   n.　　BRYANT—*An Invitation to the Country.*

      When April winds
Grew soft, the maple burst into a flush
Of scarlet flowers. The tulip tree, high up,
Opened in airs of June her multitude
Of golden chalices to humming birds
And silken-wing'd insects of the sky.
   o.　　BRYANT—*The Fountain.*

Old April wanes, and her last dewy morn
  Her death-bed steeps in tears; to hail the
    May
New blooming blossoms 'neath the sun are
    born,
  And all poor April's charms are swept away.
   p.　　CLARE—*The Village Minstrel and Other*
            Poems. The Last of April.

Every tear is answered by a blossom,
  Every sigh with songs and laughter blent,
Apple-blooms upon the breezes toss them.
  April knows her own, and is content.
   q.　　SUSAN COOLIDGE—*April.*

Now the noisy winds are still;
April's coming up the hill!
All the spring is in her train,
Led by shining ranks of rain;
 Pit, pat, patter, clatter,
 Sudden sun and clatter patter!
 * * * * * *
All things ready with a will,
April's coming up the hill!
 a. MARY MAPES DODGE—*Now the Noisy*
         Winds are Still.

The April winds are magical,
 And thrill our tuneful frames;
The garden-walks are passional
 To bachelors and dames.
 b. EMERSON—*April.*

Oh, the lovely fickleness of an April day!
 c. W. H. GIBSON—*Pastoral Days. Spring.*

Golden and snowy and red the flowers,
 Golden, snowy and red in vain;
Robins call robins through sad showers;
 The white dove's feet are wet with rain.
 * * * * * *
For April sobs while these are so glad
 April weeps while these are so gay,—
Weeps like a tired child who had,
 Playing with flowers, lost its way.
 d. HELEN HUNT JACKSON—*Verses. April.*

The children with the streamlets sing,
 When April stops at last her weeping;
And every happy growing thing
 Laughs like a babe just roused from sleeping.
 e. LUCY LARCOM—*The Sister Months.*

     I love the season well
When forest glades are teeming with bright
   forms,
Nor dark and many-folded clouds foretell
 The coming on of storms.
 f. LONGFELLOW—*An April Day.* L. 6.

Sweet April! many a thought
 Is wedded unto thee, as hearts are wed;
Nor shall they fail, till, to its autumn brought,
 Life's golden fruit is shed.
 g. LONGFELLOW—*An April Day.* St. 8.

Sweet April-time—O cruel April-time!
Year after year returning, with a brow
Of promise, and red lips with longing paled,
And backward-hidden hands that clutch the
   joys
Of vanished springs, like flowers.
 h. D. M. MULOCK—*April.*

The first of April, some do say,
Is set apart for All Fools' day;
But why the people call it so,
Nor I, nor they themselves, do know.
 i. *Poor Robin's Almanac.* 1760. *All*
         Fools' Day.
Spongy April.
 j. *Tempest.* Act IV. Sc. 1. L. 65.

When proud-pied April dress'd in all his trim
Hath put a spirit of youth in everything.
 k. *Sonnet XCVIII.*

When well apparell'd April on the heel
Of limping winter treads.
 l. *Romeo and Juliet.* Act I. Sc. 2. L. 27.

Sweet April's tears,
Dead on the hem of May.
 m. ALEX. SMITH—*A Life Drama.* Sc. 8.
            L. 308.

A gush of bird-song, a patter of dew,
 A cloud, and a rainbow's warning,
Suddenly sunshine and perfect blue—
 An April day in the morning.
 n. HARRIET PRESCOTT SPOFFORD—*April.*

Sweet April showers
Do bring May flowers.
 o. TUSSER—*Five Hundred Points of Good*
        Husbandry. Ch. XXXIX.

Again the blackbirds sing; the streams
Wake, laughing, from their winter dreams,
And tremble in the April showers
The tassels of the maple flowers.
 p. WHITTIER—*The Singer.* St. 20.

May.

Hebe's here, May is here!
 The air is fresh and sunny;
And the miser-bees are busy
 Hoarding golden honey.
 q. T. B. ALDRICH—*May.*

As it fell upon a day
In the merry month of May,
Sitting in a pleasant shade
Which a grove of myrtles made.
 r. RICHARD BARNFIELD—*Address to the*
          Nightingale.

Spring's last-born darling, clear-eyed, sweet,
Pauses a moment, with white twinkling feet,
 And golden locks in breezy play,
Half teasing and half tender, to repeat
 Her song of " May."
 s. SUSAN COOLIDGE—*May.*

But winter lingering chills the lap of May.
 t. GOLDSMITH—*The Traveller.* L. 172.

Sweet May hath come to love us,
 Flowers, trees, their blossoms don;
And through the blue heavens above us
 The very clouds move on.
 u. HEINE—*Book of Songs. New Spring.*
           No. 5.

O month when they who love must love and
   wed.
 v. HELEN HUNT JACKSON—*Verses. May.*

The voice of one who goes before to make
The paths of June more beautiful, is thine,
Sweet May!

    *   *   *   *   *

O May, sweet-voiced one, going thus before,
Forever June may pour her warm red wine
Of life and passion,—sweeter days are thine!
   a.   HELEN HUNT JACKSON—*Verses. May.*

When April steps aside for May,
  Like diamonds all the rain-drops glisten;
Fresh violets open every day:
  To some new bird each hour we listen.
   b.   LUCY LARCOM—*The Sister Months.*

It was a pleasure to live on that bright and
    happy May morning!
   c.   LONGFELLOW—*Tales of a Wayside Inn.*
         Pt. III.   *The Theologian's Tale.*
                   Elizabeth.

Ah! my heart is weary waiting,
    Waiting for the May:
Waiting for the pleasant rambles
Where the fragrant hawthorn brambles,
With the woodbine alternating,
    Scent the dewy way;
Ah! my heart is weary, waiting,
    Waiting for the May.
   d.   DENIS FLORENCE MCCARTHY—*Summer
                       Longings.*

Now the bright morning star, day's harbinger,
Comes dancing from the east, and leads with
    her
The flowery May, who from her green lap
    throws
The yellow cowslip, and the pale primrose.
Hail, bounteous May, that doth inspire
Mirth, and youth, and warm desire;
Woods and groves are of thy dressing,
Hill and dale doth boast thy blessing,
Thus we salute thee with our early song,
And welcome thee, and wish thee long.
   e.   MILTON—*Song. On May Morning.*

As full of spirit as the month of May.
   f.   *King Henry IV.*   Pt. I.   Act IV.
                       Sc. 1.   L. 101.

In beauty as the first of May.
   g.   *Much Ado About Nothing.*   Act I.
                       Sc. 1.   L. 194.

No doubt they rose up early to observe
The rite of May.
   h.   *Midsummer-Night's Dream.*   Act IV.
                       Sc. 1.   L. 137.

Rough winds do shake the darling buds of
    May.
   i.   *Sonnet XVIII.*

Another May new buds and flowers shall
    bring:
Ah! why has happiness no second Spring?
   j.   CHARLOTTE SMITH—*Elegiac Sonnets,
             and Other Poems.*   Sonnet II.

When May, with cowslip-braided locks,
  Walks through the land in green attire,
And burns in meadow-grass the phlox
  His torch of purple fire:

    *   *   *   *   *

And when the punctual May arrives,
  With cowslip-garland on her brow,
We know what once she gave our lives,
  And cannot give us now!
   k.   BAYARD TAYLOR—*The Lost May.*

For I'm to be Queen o' the May, mother, I'm
  to be Queen o' the May.
   l.   TENNYSON—*The May Queen.*   St. 1.

Among the changing months, May stands
    confest
The sweetest, and in fairest colors dressed.
   m.   THOMSON—*On May.*

May, queen of blossoms,
  And fulfilling flowers,
With what pretty music
  Shall we charm the hours?
Wilt thou have pipe and reed,
Blown in the open mead?
Or to the lute give heed
  In the green bowers?
   n.   LORD THURLOW—*To May.*

June.

I gazed upon the glorious sky
  And the green mountains round,
And thought that when I came to lie
  At rest within the ground,
'Twere pleasant, that in flowery June,
When brooks send up a cheerful tune,
  And groves a joyous sound,
The sexton's hand, my grave to make,
The rich, green mountain-turf should break.
   o.   BRYANT—*June.*

June falls asleep upon her bier of flowers;
In vain are dewdrops sprinkled o'er her,
In vain would fond winds fan her back to life,
Her hours are numbered on the floral dial.
   p.   LUCY LARCOM—*Death of June.*   L. 1.

And what is so rare as a day in June?
  Then, if ever, come perfect days;
Then Heaven tries earth if it be in tune,
  And over it softly her warm ear lays.
   q.   LOWELL—*The Vision of Sir Launfal.*

So sweet, so sweet the roses in their blowing,
  So sweet the daffodils, so fair to see;
So blithe and gay the humming-bird a-going
  From flower to flower, a-hunting with the
    bee.
   r.   NORA PERRY—*In June.*

It is the month of June,
  The month of leaves and roses,
When pleasant sights salute the eyes
  And pleasant scents the noses.
   s.   N. P. WILLIS—*The Month of June.*

July.

The linden, in the fervors of July,
Hums with a louder concert. When the wind
Sweeps the broad forest in its summer prime,
As when some master-hand exulting sweeps
The keys of some great organ, ye give forth
The music of the woodland depths, a hymn
Of gladness and of thanks.
   a.   Bryant—*Among the Trees.* L. 62.

Loud is the summer's busy song
The smallest breeze can find a tongue,
While insects of each tiny size
Grow teasing with their melodies,
Till noon burns with its blistering breath
Around, and day lies still as death.
   b.   Clare—*July.*

The Summer looks out from her brazen tower,
  Through the flashing bars of July.
   c.   Francis Thompson—*A Corymbus for
                     Autumn.* St. 3.

August.

The August cloud * * * suddenly
Melts into streams of rain.
   d.   Bryant—*Sella.*

In the parching August wind,
  Cornfields bow the head,
Sheltered in round valley depths,
  On low hills outspread.
   e.   Christina G. Rossetti—*A Year's
                    Windfalls.* St. 8.

Dead is the air, and still! the leaves of the
  locust and walnut
Lazily hang from the boughs, inlaying their
  intricate outlines
Rather on space than the sky,—on a tideless
  expansion of slumber.
   f.   Bayard Taylor—*Home Pastorals.
                      August.* I.

September.

O sweet September, thy first breezes bring
  The dry leaf's rustle and the squirrel's
    laughter,
The cool fresh air whence health and vigor
  spring
  And promise of exceeding joy hereafter.
   g.   George Arnold—*September Days.*

The morrow was a bright September morn;
The earth was beautiful as if new-born;
There was that nameless splendor everywhere,
That wild exhilaration in the air,
Which makes the passers in the city street
Congratulate each other as they meet.
   h.   Longfellow—*Tales of a Wayside Inn.*
              Pt. I. *The Student's Tale. The
              Falcon of Sir Federigo.* L. 135.

October.

October turned my maple's leaves to gold;
The most are gone now; here and there one
    lingers;
Soon these will slip from out the twig's weak
    hold,
Like coins between a dying miser's fingers.
   i.   T. B. Aldrich—*Maple Leaves.*

O'er hill and field October's glories fade;
O'er hill and field the blackbirds southward
    fly;
The brown leaves rustle down the forest glade,
Where naked branches make a fitful shade,
And the lost blooms of Autumn withered lie.
   j.   George Arnold—*October.*

And suns grow meek, and the meek suns
    grow brief,
And the year smiles as it draws near its death.
   k.   Bryant—*October.*

The sweet calm sunshine of October, now
  Warms the low spot; upon its grassy mould
The purple oak-leaf falls; the birchen bough
  Drops its bright spoil like arrow-heads of
    gold.
   l.   Bryant—*October, 1866.*

October's tinted days have fled;
Both welcomes and farewells been said;
Make glad our threshold with your tread,
     Sweet Friends, once more!
"Salve!" is writ, beneath, o'erhead,
     An open door.
   m.   Abraham Coles—*The Microcosm and
                     other Poems.* P. 167.

October's gold is dim—the forests rot,
The weary rain falls ceaseless, while the day
Is wrapped in damp.
   n.   David Gray—*In the Shadows.*
                         Sonnet XIX.

Is it the shrewd October wind
  Brings the tears into her eyes?
Does it blow so strong that she must fetch
  Her breath in sudden sighs?
   o.   W. D. Howells—*Gone.*

Yellow leaves, how fast they flutter—woodland hollows thickly strewing,
Where the wan October sunbeams scantly in
  the mid-day win,
While the dim gray clouds are drifting, and
  in saddened hues imbuing
All without and all within!
   p.   Jean Ingelow—*On the Deaths of Three
                         Children.*

Bending above the spicy woods which blaze,
Arch skies so blue they flash, and hold the
    sun
Immeasurably far; the waters run
Too slow, so freighted are the river-ways
With gold of elms and birches from the maze
Of forests.
   q.   Helen Hunt Jackson—*Verses.*
                         October.

October's foliage yellows with his cold.
  a.   RUSKIN—*The Months.*

No clouds are in the morning sky,
  The vapors hug the stream,
Who says that life and love can die
  In all this northern gleam?
At every turn the maples burn,
  The quail is whistling free,
The partridge whirs, and the frosted burs
  Are dropping for you and me.
      Ho! hillyho! heigh O!
        Hillyho!
In the clear October morning.
  b.   E. C. STEDMAN—*Autumn Song.*

And close at hand, the basket stood
With nuts from brown October's wood.
  c.   WHITTIER—*Snow-bound.*

November.

On my cornice linger the ripe black grapes
  ungathered;
Children fill the groves with the echoes of
  their glee,
Gathering tawny chestnuts, and shouting
  when beside them
Drops the heavy fruit of the tall black-walnut
  tree.
  d.   BRYANT—*The Third of November. 1861.*

                    When shrieked
The bleak November winds, and smote the
  woods,
And the brown fields were herbless, and the
  shades
That met above the merry rivulet
Were spoiled, I sought, I loved them still;
  they seemed
Like old companions in adversity.
  e.   BRYANT—*A Winter Piece. L. 22.*

The dusky waters shudder as they shine,
The russet leaves obstruct the straggling way
Of oozy brooks, which no deep banks define,
And the gaunt woods, in ragged scant array,
Wrap their old limbs with sombre ivy twine.
  f.   HARTLEY COLERIDGE—*November.*

Dry leaves upon the wall,
  Which flap like rustling wings and seek
    escape,
  A single frosted cluster on the grape
Still hangs—and that is all.
  g.   SUSAN COOLIDGE—*November.*

Fie upon thee, November! thou dost ape
The airs of thy young sisters, * * * thou
    hast stolen
The witching smile of May to grace thy lip,
And April's rare capricious loveliness
Thou 'rt trying to put on!
  h.   JULIA C. R. DORR—*November.*

No park—no ring—no afternoon gentility—
No company—no nobility—
No warmth, no cheerfulness, no healthful ease,
No comfortable feel in any member—
No shade, no shine, no butterflies, no bees,
No fruits, no flowers, no leaves, no birds,
  November!
  i.   HOOD—*November.*

November woods are bare and still;
November days are clear and bright;
Each noon burns up the morning's chill,
The morning's snow is gone by night;
Each day my steps grow slow, grow light,
As through the woods I reverent creep
Watching all things lie "down to sleep."
  j.   HELEN HUNT JACKSON—*Down to Sleep.*

The dead leaves their rich mosaics
  Of olive and gold and brown
Had laid on the rain-wet pavements,
  Through all the embowered town.
  k.   SAMUEL LONGFELLOW—*November.*

Now Neptune's sullen month appears,
The angry night cloud swells with tears,
And savage storms infuriate driven,
Fly howling in the face of heaven!
Now, now, my friends, the gathering gloom
With roseate rays of wine illume:
And while our wreaths of parsley spread
Their fadeless foliage round our head,
We'll hymn th' almighty power of wine,
And shed libations on his shrine!
  l.   MOORE—*Odes of Anacreon.*
                            Ode LXVIII.

All brilliant flowers are pale and dead
  And sadly droop to earth,
While pansies chill in velvet robes
  Count life but little worth;
But in these dark November days
  That wander wild and wet,
Our thoughts are winged to summer hours
  On breath of mignonette.
  m.   ELIZA O. PIERSON—*Mignonette.*

In rattling showers dark November's rain,
From every stormy cloud, descends amain.
  n.   RUSKIN—*The Months.*

The wild November come at last
  Beneath a veil of rain;
The night wind blows its folds aside,
  Her face is full of pain.

The latest of her race, she takes
  The Autumn's vacant throne:
She has but one short moon to live,
  And she must live alone.
  o.   R. H. STODDARD—*November.*

Wrapped in his sad-colored cloak, the Day,
    like·a Puritan, standeth
Stern in the joyless fields, rebuking the linger-
    ing color,—
Dying hectic of leaves and the chilly blue of
    the asters,—
Hearing, perchance, the croak of a crow on
    the desolate tree-top.
    a.   BAYARD TAYLOR—*Home Pastorals.*
                         November. I.

December.

Only the sea intoning,
  Only the wainscot-mouse,
Only the wild wind moaning
  Over the lonely house.
    b.   T. B. ALDRICH—*December, 1863.*

Wild was the day; the wintry sea
  Moaned sadly on New England's strand,
When first the thoughtful and the free,
  Our fathers, trod the desert land.
    c.   BRYANT—*The Twenty-second of*
                           December.

December drops no weak, relenting tear,
  By our fond Summer sympathies ensnared,
Nor from the perfect circle of the year
  Can even Winter's crystal gems be spared.
    d.   C. P. CRANCH—*December.*

Shout now! The months with loud acclaim,
  Take up the cry and send it forth;
May breathing sweet her Spring perfumes,
  November thundering from the North.
With hands upraised, as with one voice,
  They join their notes in grand accord:
Hail to December! say they all,
  It gave to Earth our Christ the Lord!
    e.   J. K. HOYT—*The Meeting of the Months.*

In a drear-nighted December,
  Too happy, happy brook,
Thy bubblings ne'er remember
  Apollo's summer look;
But with a sweet forgetting,
They stay their crystal fretting,
Never, never petting
  About the frozen time.
    f.   KEATS—*Stanzas.*

  In December ring
  Every day the chimes;
  Loud the gleemen sing
In the streets their merry rhymes.
  Let us by the fire
  Ever higher
Sing them till the night expire!
    g.   LONGFELLOW—*By the Fireside.*
                          A Christmas Carol.

In cold December fragrant chaplets blow,
And heavy harvests nod beneath the snow.
    h.   POPE—*Dunciad.* Bk. I. L. 77.

                      When we shall hear
The rain and wind beat dark December, how,
In this our pinching cave, shall we discourse
The freezing hours away?
    i.   *Cymbeline.* Act III. Sc. 3. L. 36.

The sun that brief December day
Rose cheerless over hills of gray,
And, darkly circled, gave at noon
A sadder light than waning moon.
    j.   WHITTIER—*Snow-Bound.*

MONUMENTS.

The tap'ring pyramid, the Egyptian's pride,
And wonder of the world, whose spiky top
Has wounded the thick cloud.
    k.   BLAIR—*The Grave.* L. 190.

Gold once out of the earth is no more due
unto it; what was unreasonably committed
to the ground, is reasonably resumed from it;
let monuments and rich fabricks, not riches,
adorn men's ashes.
    l.   SIR THOMAS BROWNE—*Hydriotaphia.*
                            Ch. III.

To extend our memories by monuments,
whose death we daily pray for, and whose
duration we cannot hope, without injury to
our expectations in the advent of the last day,
were a contradiction to our belief.
    m.   SIR THOMAS BROWNE—*Hydriotaphia.*
                            Ch. V.

But monuments themselves memorials need.
    n.   CRABBE—*The Borough.* Letter II.

You shall not pile, with servile toil,
Your monuments upon my breast,
Nor yet within the common soil
Lay down the wreck of power to rest,
Where man can boast that he has trod
On him that was "the scourge of God."
    o.   EDWARD EVERETT—*Alaric the Visigoth.*

Tombs are the clothes of the dead. A grave
is but a plain suit, and a rich monument is
one embroidered.
    p.   FULLER—*The Holy and Profane States.*
                      Bk. III. *Of Tombs.*

I have completed a monument more lasting
than brass, and more sublime than the regal
elevation of pyramids, which neither the
wasting shower, the unavailing north-wind,
or an innumerable succession of years, and
the flight of seasons, shall be able to demolish.
    q.   HORACE—Bk. III. *Ode XXX.*
                          Smart's trans.

Thou, in our wonder and astonishment
Hast built thyself a live-long monument.
    r.   MILTON—*Epitaph. On Shakespeare.*

Where London's column, pointing at the
    skies,
Like a tall bully, lifts the head and lies.
    a.   Pope—*Moral Essays.* Ep. III. L. 339.

She sat, like patience on a monument,
Smiling at grief.
    b.   *Twelfth Night.* Act II. Sc. 4. L. 117.

This grave shall have a living monument.
    c.   *Hamlet.* Act V. Sc. 1. L. 320.

MOON (THE).

Soon as the evening shades prevail,
The moon takes up the wondrous tale,
And nightly to the listening earth
Repeats the story of her birth.
    d.   Addison—*Spectator.* No. 465. *Ode.*

The moon is a silver pin-head vast,
That holds the heaven's tent-hangings fast.
    e.   Wm. R. Alger—*Oriental Poetry. The
        Use of the Moon.*

The moon is at her full, and riding high,
    Floods the calm fields with light.
The airs that hover in the summer sky
    Are all asleep to-night.
    f.   Bryant—*The Tides.*

Doth the moon care for the barking of a
dog?
    g.   Burton—*Anatomy of Melancholy.*
        Pt. II. Sec. III. Mem. 7.

He made an instrument to know
If the moon shine at full or no;
That would, as soon as e'er she shone straight,
Whether 'twere day or night demonstrate;
Tell what her d'ameter to an inch is,
And prove that she's not made of green cheese.
    h.   Butler—*Hudibras.* Pt. II. Canto III.
        L. 261.

The moon pull'd off her veil of light,
That hides her face by day from sight
(Mysterious veil, of brightness made,
That's both her lustre and her shade,)
And in the lantern of the night,
With shining horns hung out her light,
    i.   Butler—*Hudibras.* Pt. II. Canto I.
        L. 905.

The devil's in the moon for mischief; they
Who call'd her chaste, methinks, began too
    soon
    Their nomenclature; there is not a day,
The longest, not the twenty-first of June,
    Sees half the business in a wicked way,
On which three single hours of moonshine
    smile—
And then she looks so modest all the while!
    j.   Byron—*Don Juan.* Canto I. St. 113.

The sun had sunk and the summer skies
    Were dotted with specks of light
That melted soon in the deep moon-rise
    That flowed over Groton Height.
    k.   McDonald Clarke—*The Graveyard.*

The moving moon went up the sky,
    And nowhere did abide;
Softly she was going up,
    And a star or two beside.
    l.   Coleridge—*The Ancient Mariner.*
        Pt. IV.

How like a queen comes forth the lonely
    Moon
From the slow opening curtains of the clouds;
Walking in beauty to her midnight throne!
    m.   George Croly—*Diana.*

As the moon's fair image quaketh
    In the raging waves of ocean,
Whilst she, in the vault of heaven,
    Moves with silent peaceful motion.
    n.   Heine—*Book of Songs. New Spring.*
        Prologue. No. 23.

Mother of light! how fairly dost thou go
    Over those hoary crests, divinely led!
Art thou that huntress of the silver bow
    Fabled of old? Or rather dost thou tread
Those cloudy summits thence to gaze below,
Like the wild chamois from her Alpine snow,
Where hunters never climbed—secure from
    dread?
    o.   Hood—*Ode to the Moon.*

The moon, the moon, so silver and cold,
Her fickle temper has oft been told,
Now shady—now bright and sunny—
But of all the lunar things that change,
The one that shows most fickle and strange,
And takes the most eccentric range,
Is the moon—so called—of honey!
    p.   Hood—*Miss Kilmansegg. Her
        Honeymoon.*

The stars were glittering in the heaven's dusk
    meadows,
Far west, among those flowers of the shadows,
The thin, clear crescent lustrous over her,
Made Ruth raise question, looking through
    the bars
Of heaven, with eyes half-oped, what God,
    what comer
Unto the harvest of the eternal summer,
Had flung his golden hook down on the field
    of stars.
    q.   Victor Hugo—*Boaz Asleep.*

Such a slender moon, going up and up,
Waxing so fast from night to night,
And swelling like an orange flower-bud,
    bright,
Fated, methought, to round as to a golden
    cup,
And hold to my two lips life's best of wine.
    r.   Jean Ingelow—*Songs of the Night
        Watches. The First Watch.* Pt. II.

Queen and huntress, chaste and fair,
  Now the sun is laid to sleep,
Seated in thy silver car,
  State in wonted manner keep.
Hesperus entreats thy light,
Goddess, excellently bright!
  a.   BEN JONSON—*Hymn.   To Cynthia.*

The moon put forth a little diamond peak
No bigger than an unobserved star,
Or tiny point of fairy cimetar.
  b.   KEATS—*Endymion. Bk. IV. L. 499.*

Sweet through the green leaves shines the
    moon.
  c.   LELAND—*The Swan.*

It is the Harvest Moon! On gilded vanes
  And roofs of villages, on woodland crests
  And their aerial neighborhoods of nests
Deserted, on the curtained window-panes
Of rooms where children sleep, on country
    lanes
  And harvest-fields, its mystic splendor rests.
  d.   LONGFELLOW—*The Harvest Moon.*

See yonder fire! It is the moon
Slow rising o'er the eastern hill.
It glimmers on the forest tips,
And through the dewy foliage drips
In little rivulets of light,
And makes the heart in love with night.
  e.   LONGFELLOW—*Christus.   The Golden
            Legend.   Pt. VI.   L. 462.*

The dews of summer night did fall;
  The moon (sweet regent of the sky)
Silver'd the walls of Cumnor Hall,
  And many an oak that grew thereby.
  f.   WM. J. MICKLE—*Cumnor Hall.*

Let the air strike our tune,
Whilst we show reverence to yond peeping
    moon.
  g.   THOMAS MIDDLETON—*The Witch.*
            Act V. Sc. 2.

* * * now glow'd the firmament
With living sapphires; Hesperus, that led
The starry host rode brightest, till the Moon,
Rising in clouded majesty, at length,
Apparent queen, unveil'd her peerless light,
And o'er the dark her silver mantle threw.
  h.   MILTON—*Paradise Lost. Bk. IV.*
            L. 604.
      The moon looks
      On many brooks,
The brook can see no moon but this.
  i.   MOORE—*Irish Melodies.   While Gazing
            on the Moon's Light.*

      Hail, pallid crescent, hail!
Let me look on thee where thou sitt'st for
    aye
Like memory—ghastly in the glare of day,
But in the evening, light.
  j.   D. M. MULOCK—*The Moon in the
                        Morning.*

      No rest—no dark.
Hour after hour that passionless bright face
Climbs up the desolate blue.
  k.   D. M. MULOCK—*Moon-Struck.*

Late, late yestreen I saw the new moone,
Wi' the auld moon in hir arme.
  l.   THOMAS PERCY—*Reliques.   Sir Patrick
            Spens.   See also SCOTT—Minstrelsy
                        of the Scottish Border.*

He * * * thought the moon was made
of green cheese.
  m.   RABELAIS—*Works. Bk. I. Ch. XI.*

Day glimmer'd in the east, and the white
    Moon
Hung like a vapor in the cloudless sky.
  n.   SAM'L ROGERS—*Italy.   The Lake of
                        Geneva.*

Again thou reignest in thy golden hall,
Rejoicing in thy sway, fair queen of night!
The ruddy reapers hail thee with delight:
Theirs is the harvest, theirs the joyous call
For tasks well ended ere the season's fall.
  o.   ROSCOE—*Sonnet.   To the Harvest Moon.*

The sun was gone now; the curled moon was
    like a little feather
Fluttering far down the gulf.
  p.   D. G. ROSSETTI—*The Blessed Damozel.*
                        St. 10.

Good even, good fair moon, good even to thee;
I prithee, dear moon, now show to me
The form and the features, the speech and
    degree,
Of the man that true lover of mine shall be.
  q.   SCOTT—*Heart of Mid-Lothian.*
                        Ch. XVII.

If thou would'st view fair Melrose aright,
Go visit it by the pale moonlight;
For the gay beams of lightsome day
Gild, but to flout, the ruins gray.
  r.   SCOTT—*Lay of the Last Minstrel.*
                        Canto II. St. 1.
      How slow
This old moon wanes! she lingers my desires,
Like to a step-dame or a dowager
Long withering out a young man's revenue.
  s.   *Midsummer-Night's Dream.   Act I.
                        Sc. 1. L. 3.*

How sweet the moonlight sleeps upon this
    bank.
  t.   *Merchant of Venice. Act V. Sc. 1.
                        L. 54.*

It is the very error of the moon:
She comes more nearer earth than she was
    wont,
And makes men mad.
  u.   *Othello. Act V. Sc. 2. L. 109.*

The moon of Rome, chaste as the icicle
That's curded by the frost from purest snow.
  v.   *Coriolanus. Act V. Sc. 3. L. 65.*

Therefore the moon, the governess of floods,
Pale in her anger, washes all the air,
That rheumatic diseases do abound :
And through this distemperature we see
The seasons alter.
   a.   *Midsummer-Night's Dream.* Act II.
                    Sc. 1. L. 103.

   Art thou pale for weariness
Of climbing heaven, and gazing on the earth,
   Wandering companionless
Among the stars that have a different birth,—
And ever changing, like a joyless eye
That finds no object worth its constancy?
   b.   SHELLEY—*To the Moon.*

That orbed maiden, with white fire laden,
Whom mortals call the moon.
   c.   SHELLEY—*The Cloud.* IV.

The young moon has fed
   Her exhausted horn
     With the sunset's fire.
   d.   SHELLEY—*Hellas.* *Semi-Chorus II.*

With how sad steps, O moon, thou climb'st
   the skies !
How silently, and with how wan a face !
   e.   SIR PHILIP SIDNEY—*Astrophel and*
               Stella. *Sonnet XXXI.*

The Moon arose : she shone upon the lake,
Which lay one smooth expanse of silver light ;
She shone upon the hills and rocks, and cast
Upon their hollows and their hidden glens
A blacker depth of shade.
   f.   SOUTHEY—*Madoc.* Pt. II. *The Close*
                  of the Century.

I with borrow'd silver shine,
What you see is none of mine.
First I show you but a quarter,
Like the bow that guards the Tartar :
Then the half, and then the whole,
Ever dancing round the pole.
   g.   SWIFT—*On the Moon.*

As like the sacred queen of night,
Who pours a lovely, gentle light
Wide o'er the dark, by wanderers blest,
Conducting them to peace and rest.
   h.   THOMSON—*Ode to Seraphina.*

The crimson Moon, uprising from the sea,
With large delight, foretells the harvest near.
   i.   LORD THURLOW—*Select Poems. The*
                 Harvest Moon.

And suddenly the moon withdraws
   Her sickle from the lightening skies,
   And to her sombre cavern flies,
Wrapped in a veil of yellow gauze.
   j.   OSCAR WILDE—*La Fuite de la Lune.*

MORALITY.

Morality, when vigorously alive, sees farther
than intellect, and provides unconsciously for
intellectual difficulties.
   k.   FROUDE—*Short Studies on Great*
               Subjects. Divus Cæsar.

The moral system of the universe is like a
document written in alternate ciphers, which
change from line to line.
   l.   FROUDE—*Short Studies on Great*
               Subjects. Calvinism.

Morality without religion is only a kind of
dead reckoning,—an endeavor to find our
place on a cloudy sea by measuring the distance we have run, but without any observation of the heavenly bodies.
   m.   LONGFELLOW—*Kavanagh.* Ch. XIII.

We know no spectacle so ridiculous as the
British public in one of its periodical fits of
morality.
   n.   MACAULAY—*On Moore's Life of Lord*
               Byron. 1830.

I find the doctors and the sages
Have differ'd in all climes and ages,
And two in fifty scarce agree
On what is pure morality.
   o.   MOORE—*Morality.*

MORNING.

The summer morn is bright and fresh, the
   birds are darting by
As if they loved to breast the breeze that
   sweeps the cool clear sky.
   p.   BRYANT—*The Strange Lady.*

The morn is up again, the dewy morn,
With breath all incense, and with cheek all
   bloom,
Laughing the clouds away with playful scorn,
And living as if earth contained no tomb,—
And glowing into day.
   q.   BYRON—*Childe Harold.* Canto III.
                      St. 98.

Slow buds the pink dawn like a rose
   From out night's gray and cloudy sheath ;
Softly and still it grows and grows,
   Petal by petal, leaf by leaf.
   r.   SUSAN COOLIDGE—*The Morning Comes*
               Before the Sun.

Awake thee, my Lady-Love !
   Wake thee, and rise !
The sun through the bower peeps
   Into thine eyes.
   s.   GEORGE DARLEY—*Sylvia ; or, The May*
              Queen. Act IV. Sc. 1.

I saw myself the lambent easy light
Gild the brown horror, and dispel the night.
   t.   DRYDEN—*Hind and Panther.* Pt. I.
                 L. 1,230.

The breezy call of incense-breathing morn.
 a. Gray—*Elegy in a Country Churchyard.*
           St. 5.

Now from the smooth deep ocean-stream the
  sun
Began to climb the heavens, and with new
  rays
Smote the surrounding fields.
 b. Homer—*Iliad.* Bk. VII. L. 525.
          Bryant's trans.

The Morn! she is the source of sighs,
The very face to make us sad ;
If but to think in other times
The same calm quiet look she had.
 c. Hood—*Ode to Melancholy.*

The blessed morn has come again ;
  The early gray
Taps at the slumberer's window pane,
  And seems to say,
Break, break from the enchanter's chain,
  Away, away !
 d. Ralph Hoyt—*Snow. A Winter Sketch.*

I have heard the mavis singing
 Its love-song to the morn ;
I've seen the dew-drop clinging
 To the rose just newly born.
 e. Charles Jeffreys—*Mary of Argyle.*

Hues of the rich unfolding morn,
That, ere the glorious sun be born,
By some soft touch invisible
Around his path are taught to swell.
 f. Keble—*The Christian Year. Morning.*

Behold how brightly breaks the morning!
Though bleak our lot, our hearts are warm.
 g. James Kenney—*Behold How Brightly
            Breaks.*

      A fine morning,
Nothing's the matter with it that I know of.
I have seen better and I have seen worse.
 h. Longfellow—*Christus.* Pt. III.
     John Endicott. Act V. Sc. 2.

Far off I hear the crowing of the cocks,
And through the opening door that time unlocks
Feel the fresh breathing of To-morrow creep.
 i. Longfellow—*To-morrow.*

Flames in the forehead of the morning sky.
 j. Milton—*Lycidas.* L. 171.
          Morn,
Wak'd by the circling hours, with rosy hand
Unbarr'd the gates of light.
 k. Milton—*Paradise Lost.* Bk. VI. L. 2.

Now morn, her rosy steps in th' eastern clime
Advancing, sow'd the earth with Orient pearl.
 l. Milton—*Paradise Lost.* Bk. V. L. 1.

Sweet is the breath of morn, her rising sweet,
With charm of earliest birds.
 m. Milton—*Paradise Lost.* Bk. IV.
           L. 641.
      Till morning fair
Came forth with pilgrim steps in amice gray.
 n. Milton—*Paradise Regained.* Bk. IV.
           L. 426.
Under the opening eyelids of the morn.
 o. Milton—*Lycidas.* L. 26.

When did morning ever break,
And find such beaming eyes awake ?
 p. Moore—*Fly not Yet.*

O how beautiful is morning !
How the sunbeams strike the daisies
And the kingcups fill the meadow
Like a golden-shielded army
Marching to the uplands fair.
 q. D. M. Mulock—*A Stream's Singing.*

The eastern hanging crescent climbeth higher ;
See, purple on the azure softly steals,
And Morning, faintly touched with quivering
  fire,
Leans on the frosty summits of the hills,
Like a young girl over her hoary sire.
 r. Roscoe—*Poems and Essays.*

Clothing the palpable and familiar
With golden exhalations of the dawn.
 s. Schiller—*The Death of Wallenstein.*
    Act V. Sc. 1. Coleridge's trans.

   An hour before the worshipp'd sun
Peer'd forth the golden window of the east.
 t. *Romeo and Juliet.* Act I. Sc. 1.
           L. 125.
As when the golden sun salutes the morn,
And, having gilt the ocean with his beams,
Gallops the zodiac in his glistering coach.
 u. *Titus Andronicus.* Act II. Sc. 1. L. 5.

But, look, the morn, in russet mantle clad,
Walks o'er the dew of yon high eastern hill.
 v. *Hamlet.* Act I. Sc. 1. L. 166.

Night's candles are burnt out, and jocund day
Stands tiptoe on the misty mountain tops.
 w. *Romeo and Juliet.* Act III. Sc. 5. L. 9.

See how the morning opes her golden gates,
And takes her farewell of the glorious sun !
How well resembles it the prime of youth,
Trimm'd like a younker prancing to his love.
 x. *Henry VI.* Pt. III. Act II. Sc. 1.
           L. 21.
       The busy day,
Wak'd by the lark, hath rous'd the ribald
  crows,
And dreaming night will hide our joys no
  longer.
 y. *Troilus and Cressida.* Act IV. Sc. 2.
           L. 8.

The day begins to break, and night is fled,
Whose pitchy mantle over-veil'd the earth.
   a.   *Henry VI.* Pt. I. Act II. Sc. 2. L. 1.

The grey-ey'd morn smiles on the frowning
     night,
Chequering the eastern clouds with streaks
     of light.
   b.   *Romeo and Juliet.* Act II. Sc. 3. L. 1.

                     Darkness is fled.
Now, flowers unfold their beauties to the sun,
And, blushing, kiss the beam he sends to
     wake them.
   c.   R. B. Sheridan—*The Critic.* Act II.
                           Sc. 2.

Hail, gentle Dawn! mild blushing goddess,
     hail!
Rejoic'd I see thy purple mantle spread
O'er half the skies, gems pave thy radiant way,
And orient pearls from ev'ry shrub depend.
   d.   Wm. Somerville—*The Chase.* Bk. II.
                           L. 79.

And yonder fly his scattered golden arrows,
And smite the hills with day.
   e.   Bayard Taylor—*The Poet's Journal.*
                Third Evening. Morning.

Now the frosty stars are gone:
I have watched them one by one,
Fading on the shores of Dawn.
Round and full the glorious sun
Walks with level step the spray,
Through his vestibule of Day.
   f.   Bayard Taylor—*Ariel in the Cloven*
                            Pine.

Morn in the white wake of the morning star
Came furrowing all the orient into gold.
   g.   Tennyson—*The Princess.* Pt. III.
                            L. 1.

Rise, happy morn, rise, holy morn,
Draw forth the cheerful day from night;
  O Father, touch the east, and light
The light that shone when Hope was born.
   h.   Tennyson—*In Memoriam.* Pt. XXX.

The meek-eyed Morn appears, mother of
     Dews.
   i.   Thomson—*The Seasons. Summer.*
                           L. 47.

The yellow fog came creeping down
The bridges, till the houses' walls
Seemed changed to shadows, and St. Paul's
Loomed like a bubble o'er the town.
   j.   Oscar Wilde—*Impression du Matin.*

MORTALITY.

Lo! as the wind is so is mortal life,
A moan, a sigh, a sob, a storm, a strife.
   k.   Edwin Arnold—*The Light of Asia.*
                        Bk. III. L. 25.

26

To smell to a turf of fresh earth is wholesome for the body; no less are thoughts of
mortality cordial to the soul.
   l.   Fuller—*Holy and Profane States.*
                 Bk. IV. *The Court Lady.*

That flesh is but the glasse, which holds the
     dust
That measures all our time; which also shall
Be crumbled into dust.
   m.   Herbert—*The Temple. Church*
                           Monuments.

                         Consider
The lilies of the field whose bloom is brief:—
     We are as they;
     Like them we fade away
As doth a leaf.
   n.   Christina G. Rossetti—*Consider.*

The immortal could we cease to contemplate,
The mortal part suggests its every trait.
God laid His fingers on the ivories
Of her pure members as on smoothèd keys,
And there out-breathed her spirit's harmonies.
   o.   Francis Thompson—*Her Portrait.*
                           St. 7.

At thirty, man suspects himself a fool,
Knows it at forty, and reforms his plan;
At fifty, chides his infamous delay,
Pushes his prudent purpose to resolve,
In all the magnanimity of thought;
Resolves, and re-resolves, then dies the same.
And why? because he thinks himself im-
     mortal,
All men think all men mortal but themselves.
   p.   Young—*Night Thoughts.* Night I.
                           L. 417

Man wants but little, nor that little long;
How soon must he resign his very dust,
Which frugal nature lent him for an hour!
   q.   Young—*Night Thoughts.* Night IV.
                           L. 118

MOTHERHOOD.

A mother is a mother still,
   The holiest thing alive.
   r.   Coleridge—*The Three Graves.* St. 10.

                        There is none,
In all this cold and hollow world, no fount
Of deep, strong, deathless love, save that
     within
A mother's heart.
   s.   Mrs. Hemans—*Siege of Valencia.* Sc.
          Room in a Palace of Valencia.

The mother said to her daughter, "Daughter, bid thy daughter tell her daughter that
her daughter's daughter hath a daughter."
   t.   George Hokewell—*Apology.* Bk. III.
                       Ch. V. Sec. 9.

When the rose of thine own being
  Shall reveal its central fold,
Thou shalt look within and marvel,
  Fearing what thine eyes behold ;
What it shows and what it teaches
  Are not things wherewith to part ;
Thorny rose ! that always costeth
  Beatings at the heart.
> *a.*   JEAN INGELOW—*A Mother Showing the*
> *Portrait of Her Child.*

There was a place in childhood that I remember well,
And there a voice of sweetest tone bright fairy
  tales did tell.
> *b.*   SAMUEL LOVER—*My Mother Dear.*

A woman's love
Is mighty, but a mother's heart is weak,
And by its weakness overcomes.
> *c.*   LOWELL—*Legend of Brittany.*   Pt. II.
> St. 43.

And all my mother came into mine eyes
And gave me up to tears.
> *d.*   *Henry V.* Act IV. Sc. 6. L. 32.

And say to mothers what a holy charge
Is theirs—with what a kingly power their love
Might rule the fountains of the new-born
  mind.
> *e.*   MRS. SIGOURNEY—*The Mother of*
> *Washington.* L. 33.

Who ran to help me when I fell,
And would some pretty story tell,
Or kiss the place to make it well ?
  My mother.
> *f.*   JANE TAYLOR—*My Mother.* St. 6.

Happy he
With such a mother ! faith in womankind
Beats with his blood, and trust in all things
  high
Comes easy to him, and though he trip and
  fall,
He shall not blind his soul with clay.
> *g.*   TENNYSON—*The Princess.* Canto VII.
> L. 308.

The bearing and the training of a child
Is woman's wisdom.
> *h.*   TENNYSON—*The Princess.* Canto V.
> L. 456.

They say that man is mighty,
  He governs land and sea,
He wields a mighty scepter
  O'er lesser powers that be ;
But a mightier power and stronger
  Man from his throne has hurled,
For the hand that rocks the cradle
  Is the hand that rules the world.
> *i.*   WM. ROSS WALLACE—*What Rules the*
> *World.*

MOTIVE.

Iago's soliloquy—the motive-hunting of a
motiveless malignity—how awful it is !
> *j.*   COLERIDGE—*Shakespeare. Notes on*
> *Othello.*

What makes life dreary is the want of
motive.
> *k.*   GEORGE ELIOT—*Daniel Deronda.*
> Bk. VIII. Ch. LXV.

A good intention clothes itself with sudden
power.
> *l.*   EMERSON—*Essays. Fate.*

For there's nothing we read of in torture's
  inventions,
Like a well-meaning dunce, with the best of
  intentions.
> *m.*   LOWELL—*A Fable for Critics.* L. 250.

Men's minds are as variant as their faces.
Where the motives of their actions are pure,
the operation of the former is no more to be
imputed to them as a crime, than the appearance of the latter ; for both, being the work
of nature, are alike unavoidable.
> *n.*   GEO. WASHINGTON—*Social Maxims.*
> *Difference of Opinion no Crime.*

MOUNTAINS.

Mont Blanc is the monarch of mountains ;
  They crown'd him long ago
On a throne of rocks, in a robe of clouds,
  With a diadem of snow.
> *o.*   BYRON—*Manfred.* Act I. Sc. 1. L. 62.

'Tis distance lends enchantment to the view,
And robes the mountain in its azure hue.
> *p.*   CAMPBELL—*Pleasures of Hope.* Pt. I.
> L. 7.

Whose sun-bright summit mingles with the
  sky.
> *q.*   CAMPBELL—*Pleasures of Hope.* L. 4.

Mountains interposed
Make enemies of nations, who had else
Like kindred drops been mingled into one.
> *r.*   COWPER—*The Task.* Bk. II. L. 17.

Round its breast the rolling clouds are spread,
Eternal sunshine settles on its head.
> *s.*   GOLDSMITH—*The Deserted Village.*
> L. 192.

Heav'd on Olympus tottering Ossa stood ;
On Ossa, Pelion nods with all his wood.
> *t.*   HOMER—*Odyssey.* Bk. XI. L. 387.
> Pope's trans.

Hills peep o'er hills, and Alps on Alps arise.
> *u.*   POPE—*Essay on Criticism.* Pt. II. L. 32.

Mountains are the beginning and the end of all natural scenery.

a.   RUSKIN—*True and Beautiful.   Nature.*
Mountains.   P. 91.

See the mountains kiss high heaven,
And the waves clasp one another.
b.   SHELLEY—*Love's Philosophy.*

MOURNING.

He had kept
The whiteness of his soul, and thus men o'er
him wept.
c.   BYRON—*Childe Harold.   Canto III.*
St. 57.

O! sing unto my roundelay,
O! drop the briny tear with me.
Dance no more at holiday,
Like a running river be;
    My love is dead,
    Gone to his death bed
All under the willow tree.
d.   THOS. CHATTERTON—*Ælla.   Minstrel's*
Songs.

Each lonely scene shall thee restore;
For thee the tear be duly shed;
Belov'd till life can charm no more,
And mourn'd till Pity's self be dead.
e.   COLLINS—*Dirge in Cymbeline.*

When I am dead, no pageant train
Shall waste their sorrows at my bier,
Nor worthless pomp of homage vain
Stain it with hypocritic tear.
f.   EDWARD EVERETT—*Alaric the Visigoth.*

Forever honour'd, and forever mourn'd.
g.   HOMER—*Iliad.   Bk. 22.   L. 422.*
Pope's trans.

His death eclipsed the gayety of nations, and impoverished the public stock of harmless pleasure.
h.   SAM'L JOHNSON—*Life of Edmund*
Smith (on the Death of Garrick).

He that lacks time to mourn, lacks time to mend.
Eternity mourns that.   'Tis an ill cure
For life's worst ills to have no time to feel them.
i.   SIR HENRY TAYLOR—*Philip Van*
Artevelde.   Pt. I.   Act I.   Sc. 5.

Let us weep in our darkness—but weep not for him!
Not for him—who, departing, leaves millions in tears!
Not for him—who has died full of honor and years!
Not for him—who ascended Fame's ladder so high.
From the round at the top he has stepped to the sky.
j.   N. P. WILLIS—*The Death of Harrison.*
St. 6.

He mourns the dead who lives as they desire.
k.   YOUNG—*Night Thoughts.   Night II.*
L. 24.

MURDER.

Carcasses bleed at the sight of the murderer.
l.   BURTON—*Anatomy of Melancholy.*
Pt. I.   Sec. I.   Memb. II.   Subsec. V.

Blood, though it sleep a time, yet never dies.
The gods on murtherers fix revengeful eyes.
m.   GEO. CHAPMAN—*The Widow's Tears.*
Act V.   Sc. IV.

Murder may pass unpunish'd for a time,
But tardy justice will o'ertake the crime.
n.   DRYDEN—*The Cock and the Fox.   L. 285.*

Murder, like talent, seems occasionally to run in families.
o.   GEORGE HENRY LEWES—*Physiology of*
Common Life.   Ch. XII.

One murder made a villain,
Millions a hero.—Princes were privileg'd
To kill, and numbers sanctified the crime.
Ah! why will kings forget that they are men,
And men that they are brethren?
p.   BISHOP PORTEUS—*Death.   L. 154.*

Blood hath been shed ere now, i' the olden time,
Ere humane statute purg'd the gentle weal;
Ay, and since too, murders have been performe'd
Too terrible for the ear: the time has been,
That, when the brains were out, the man would die,
And there an end; but now they rise again,
With twenty mortal murders on their crowns,
And push us from our stools: this is more strange
Than such a murder is.
q.   *Macbeth.   Act III.   Sc. 4.   L. 76.*

For murder, though it have no tongue, will speak
With most miraculous organ.
r.   *Hamlet.   Act II.   Sc. 2.   L. 622.*

He took my father grossly, full of bread;
With all his crimes broad blown, as flush as May;
And how his audit stands who knows save heaven?
s.   *Hamlet.   Act III.   Sc. 3.   L. 80.*

Murder most foul, as in the best it is;
But this most foul, strange and unnatural.
t.   *Hamlet.   Act I.   Sc. 5.   L. 27.*

No place, indeed, should murder sanctuarize.
u.   *Hamlet.   Act IV.   Sc. 7.   L. 128.*

O, pardon me, thou bleeding piece of earth,
That I am meek and gentle with these
      butchers!
Thou art the ruins of the noblest man
That ever lived in the tide of times.
Woe to the hand that shed this costly blood
Over thy wounds now do I prophesy.
  a.   *Julius Cæsar.* Act III. Sc. 1. L. 254.

      The great King of kings
Hath in the table of his law commanded
That thou shalt do no murder: and wilt thou,
      then,
Spurn at his edict and fulfill a man's?
  b.   *Richard III.* Act I. Sc. 4. L. 200.

Will all great Neptune's ocean wash this blood
Clean from my hand? No, this my hand
      will rather
The multitudinous seas incarnadine,
Making the green one red.
  c.   *Macbeth.* Act II. Sc. 2. L. 60.

Cast not the clouded gem away,
Quench not the dim but living ray,—
  My brother man, Beware!
With that deep voice which from the skies
Forbade the Patriarch's sacrifice,
  God's angel cries, Forbear!
  d.   WHITTIER—*Human Sacrifice.* Pt. VII.

One to destroy is murder by the law,
And gibbets keep the lifted hand in awe;
To murder thousands takes a specious name,
War's glorious art, and gives immortal fame.
  e.   YOUNG—*Love of Fame.* Satire VII.
                          L. 55.

MUSIC.

Music religious heat inspires,
  It wakes the soul, and lifts it high,
And wings it with sublime desires,
  And fits it to bespeak the Deity.
  f.   ADDISON—*A Song for St. Cecilia's Day.*
                        St. 4.

Music exalts each joy, allays each grief,
Expels diseases, softens every pain,
Subdues the rage of poison, and the plague.
  g.   JOHN ARMSTRONG—*Art of Preserving
                Health.* Bk. IV. L. 512.

That rich celestial music thrilled the air
From hosts on hosts of shining ones, who
      thronged
Eastward and westward, making bright the
      night.
  h.   EDWIN ARNOLD—*Light of Asia.*
                    Bk. IV. L. 418.

Music tells no truths.
  i.   BAILEY—*Festus.* Sc. *A Village Feast.*

Gayly the troubadour
Touched his guitar.
  j.   THOMAS HAYNES BAYLY—*Welcome Me
                          Home.*

God is its author, and not man; he laid
The key-note of all harmonies; he planned
All perfect combinations, and he made
Us so that we could hear and understand.
  k.   J. G. BRAINARD—*Music.*

The rustle of the leaves in summer's hush
When wandering breezes touch them, and
      the sigh
That filters through the forest, or the gush
That swells and sinks amid the branches
      high,—
'Tis all the music of the wind, and we
Let fancy float on this æolian breath.
  l.   J. G. BRAINARD—*Music.*

  And sure there is music even in the beauty,
and the silent note which Cupid strikes, far
sweeter than the sound of an instrument; for
there is music wherever there is harmony,
order, or proportion; and thus far we may
maintain the music of the spheres.
  m.   SIR THOMAS BROWNE—*Religio Medici.*
                     Pt. II. Sec. IX.

For discords make the sweetest airs.
  n.   BUTLER—*Hudibras.* Pt. III. Canto I.
                        L. 919.

Music arose with its voluptuous swell,
Soft eyes look'd love to eyes which spake
      again,
And all went merry as a marriage bell.
  o.   BYRON—*Childe Harold.* Canto III.
                        St. 21.

Soprano, basso, even the contra-alto
Wished him five fathom under the Rialto.
  p.   BYRON—*Beppo.* St. 32.

There's music in the sighing of a reed;
  There's music in the gushing of a rill;
There's music in all things, if men had ears:
Their earth is but an echo of the spheres.
  q.   BYRON—*Don Juan.* Canto XV. St. 5.

And hears thy stormy music in the drum!
  r.   CAMPBELL—*Pleasures of Hope.* Pt. I.

Music is well said to be the speech of angels.
  s.   CARLYLE—*Essays. The Opera.*

In hollow murmurs died away.
  t.   COLLINS—*The Passions.* L. 68.

In notes by distance made more sweet.
  u.   COLLINS—*The Passions.* L. 60.

When Music, heavenly maid, was young,
While yet in early Greece she sung,
The Passions oft, to hear her shell,
Throng'd around her magic cell.
  v.   COLLINS—*The Passions.* L. 1.

Music has charms to sooth a savage breast,
To soften rocks, or bend a knotted oak.
I've read that things inanimate have moved,
And, as with living souls, have been inform'd,
By magic numbers and persuasive sound.
   a.   CONGREVE—*The Mourning Bride.*
                       Act I. Sc. 1.

With melting airs, or martial, brisk, or grave ;
Some chord in unison with what we hear
Is touch'd within us, and the heart replies.
   b.   COWPER—*The Task.* Bk. VI. *Winter
                     Walk at Noon.* L. 3.

The soft complaining flute
  In dying notes discovers
  The woes of hopeless lovers,
Whose dirge is whisper'd by the warbling
  lute.
   c.   DRYDEN—*A Song for St. Cecilia's Day.*

For there is no feeling, perhaps, except the
extremes of fear and grief, that does not find
relief in music—that does not make a man
sing or play the better.
   d.   GEORGE ELIOT—*The Mill on the Floss.*
                     Bk. VI. Ch. VII.

Music sweeps by me as a messenger
Carrying a message that is not for me.
   e.   GEORGE ELIOT—*Spanish Gypsy.*
                     Bk. III.

         'Tis God gives skill,
But not without men's hands : He could not
  make
Antonio Stradivari's violins
Without Antonio.
   f.   GEORGE ELIOT—*Stradivarius.* L. 151.

The silent organ loudest chants
The master's requiem.
   g.   EMERSON—*Dirge.*

Where through the long-drawn aisle and
    fretted vault
The pealing anthem swells the note of praise.
   h.   GRAY—*Elegy in a Country Church Yard.*
                      St. 10.

He stood beside a cottage lone,
  And listened to a lute,
One summer's eve, when the breeze was gone,
  And the nightingale was mute.
   i.   THOS. HERVEY—*The Devil's Progress.*

Why should the devil have all the good tunes ?
   j.   ROWLAND HILL—*Sermons.*

  Music was a thing of the soul—a rose-lipped
shell that murmured of the eternal sea—a
strange bird singing the songs of another
shore.
   k.   J. G. HOLLAND—*Plain Talks on
            Familiar Subjects. Art and Life.*

     Ere music's golden tongue
Flattered to tears this aged man and poor.
   l.   KEATS—*The Eve of St. Agnes.* St. 3.

Heard melodies are sweet, but those unheard
  Are sweeter ; therefore, ye soft pipes, play
  on ;
Not to the sensual ear, but, more endear'd,
  Pipe to the spirit ditties of no tone.
   m.   KEATS—*Ode on a Grecian Urn.*

The silver, snarling trumpets 'gan to chide.
   n.   KEATS—*The Eve of St. Agnes.* St. 4.

  I even think that, sentimentally, I am disposed to harmony. But organically I am incapable of a tune.
   o.   CHARLES LAMB—*A Chapter on Ears.*

A velvet flute-note fell down pleasantly,
Upon the bosom of that harmony,
And sailed and sailed incessantly,
As if a petal from a wild-rose blown
Had fluttered down upon that pool of tone,
And boatwise dropped o' the convex side
And floated down the glassy tide
And clarified and glorified
The solemn spaces where the shadows bide.
From the warm concave of that fluted note
Somewhat, half song, half odour forth did
  float
As if a rose might somehow be a throat.
   p.   SIDNEY LANIER—*The Symphony.*

Music is in all growing things ;
And underneath the silky wings
  Of smallest insects there is stirred
  A pulse of air that must be heard ;
Earth's silence lives, and throbs, and sings.
   q.   LATHROP—*Music of Growth.*

Of all the arts, great music is the art
To raise the soul above all earthly storms.
   r.   LELAND—*The Music Lesson of
                          Confucius.*

He is dead, the sweet musician !
     *   *   *   *   *
He has moved a little nearer
To the Master of all music.
   s.   LONGFELLOW—*Hiawatha.* Pt. XV.
                      L. 56.

Music is the universal language of mankind.
   t.   LONGFELLOW—*Outre-Mer. Ancient
                  Spanish Ballads.*

  When she had passed, it seemed like the
ceasing of exquisite music.
   u.   LONGFELLOW—*Evangeline.* Pt. I. 1.

Who, through long days of labor,
  And nights devoid of ease,
Still heard in his soul the music
  Of wonderful melodies.
   v.   LONGFELLOW—*The Day is Done.* St. 8.

Writ in the climate of heaven, in the language
    spoken by angels.
   w.   LONGFELLOW—*The Children of the
                 Lord's Supper.* L. 262.

Yea, music is the Prophet's art;
Among the gifts that God hath sent,
One of the most magnificent!
   a.   Longfellow—*Christus.* Pt. III.
           Second Interlude. St. 5.

As in an organ from one blast of wind
To many a row of pipes the soundboard
    breathes.
   b.   Milton—*Paradise Lost.* Bk. I. L. 708.

Can any mortal mixture of earth's mould
Breathe such divine enchanting ravishment?
   c.   Milton—*Comus.* L. 244.

Lap me in soft Lydian airs,
Married to immortal verse,
Such as the meeting soul may pierce,
In notes, with many a winding bout
Of linked sweetness long drawn out.
   d.   Milton—*L'Allegro.* L. 136.

      Ring out ye crystal spheres!
      Once bless our human ears,
If ye have power to touch our senses so;
    And let your silver chime
    Move in melodious time;
And let the base of Heaven's deep organ blow,
And with your ninefold harmony,
Make up full consort to the angelic symphony.
   e.   Milton—*Hymn on the Nativity.* St. 13.

Such sweet compulsion doth in music lie.
   f.   Milton—*Arcades.* L. 68.

There let the pealing organ blow,
To the full voiced quire below,
In service high, and anthems clear,
As may with sweetness, through mine ear,
Dissolve me into ecstasies,
And bring all heaven before mine eyes.
   g.   Milton—*Il Penseroso.* L. 161.

  Untwisting all the chains that tie the hidden
soul of harmony.
   h.   Milton—*L'Allegro.* L. 143.

  Who shall silence all the airs and madrigals
that whisper softness in chambers?
   i.   Milton—*Areopagitica.*

And music too—dear music! that can touch
Beyond all else the soul that loves it much—
Now heard far off, so far as but to seem
Like the faint, exquisite music of a dream.
   j.   Moore—*Lalla Rookh.* *The Veiled*
               Prophet of Khorassan.

If the pulse of the patriot, soldier, or lover,
Have throbb'd at our lay, 'tis thy glory alone;
I was but as the wind, passing heedlessly over,
And all the wild sweetness I wak'd was thy
    own.
   k.   Moore—*Dear Harp of My Country.*
                       St. 2.

If thou would'st have me sing and play
  As once I play'd and sung,
First take this time-worn lute away,
  And bring one freshly strung.
   l.   Moore—*If Thou Would'st Have Me Sing*
                       and Play.

The harp that once through Tara's halls
  The soul of music shed,
Now hangs as mute on Tara's walls,
  As if that soul were fled.
   m.   Moore—*The Harp That Once.*

"This *must* be music," said he, "of the *spears*,
For I am cursed if each note of it doesn't run
    through one!"
   n.   Moore—*The Fudge Family in Paris.*
                  Letter V. L. 28.

'Tis believ'd that this harp which I wake now
    for thee
Was a siren of old who sung under the sea.
   o.   Moore—*The Origin of the Harp.*

And wheresoever, in his rich creation,
  Sweet music breathes—in wave, or bird, or
    soul—
'Tis but the faint and far reverberation
  Of that great tune to which the planets roll!
   p.   Frances S. Osgood—*Music.*

How light the touches are that kiss
The music from the chords of life!
   q.   Coventry Patmore—*By the Sea.*

He touched his harp, and nations heard, en-
    tranced,
As some vast river of unfailing source,
Rapid, exhaustless, deep, his numbers flowed,
And opened new fountains in the human
    heart.
   r.   Pollok—*Course of Time.* Bk. IV.
                       L. 674.

        As some to Church repair,
Not for the doctrine, but the music there.
   s.   Pope—*Essay on Criticism.* L. 343.

By music minds an equal temper know,
Nor swell too high, nor sink too low.
    *   *   *   *   *   *
Warriors she fires with animated sounds,
Pours balm into the bleeding lover's wounds.
   t.   Pope—*Ode on St. Cecilia's Day.*

Hark! the numbers soft and clear,
Gently steal upon the ear;
Now louder, and yet louder rise
And fill with spreading sounds the skies.
   u.   Pope—*Ode on St. Cecilia's Day.*

In a sadly pleasing strain
Let the warbling lute complain.
   v.   Pope—*Ode on St. Cecilia's Day.*

Light quirks of music, broken and uneven,
Make the soul dance upon a jig to Heav'n.
   w.   Pope—*Moral Essays.* Ep. IV. L. 143.

Music resembles poetry : in each
Are nameless graces which no methods teach,
And which a master-hand alone can reach.
    a.   POPE—*Essay on Criticism.* L. 143.

What woful stuff this madrigal would be
In some starv'd hackney sonnetteer, or me!
But let a Lord once own the happy lines,
How the wit brightens ! how the style refines !
    b.   POPE—*Essay on Criticism.* L. 418.

Above the pitch, out of tune, and off the
hinges.
    c.   RABELAIS—*Works.* Bk. IV. Ch. XIX.

The soul of music slumbers in the shell,
Till waked and kindled by the Master's spell ;
And feeling hearts—touch them but lightly—
    pour
A thousand melodies unheard before !
    d.   SAM'L ROGERS—*Human Life.* L. 363.

And it will discourse most eloquent music.
    e.   *Hamlet.* Act III. Sc. 2. L. 374.

Everything that heard him play,
Even the billows of the sea,
Hung their heads, and then lay by ;
In sweet music is such art :
Killing care and grief of heart
Fall asleep, or, hearing, die.
    f.   *Henry VIII.* Act III. Sc. 1. L. 9.

Give me some music ; music, moody food
Of us that trade in love.
    g.   *Antony and Cleopatra.* Act II. Sc. 5.
    L. 1.

How irksome is this music to my heart !
When such strings jar, what hope of harmony?
    h.   *Henry VI.* Pt. II. Act II. Sc. 1.
    L. 56.

How sweet the moonlight sleeps upon this
    bank !
Here will we sit and let the sounds of music
Creep in our ears : soft stillness, and the night
Become the touches of sweet harmony.
    i.   *Merchant of Venice.* Act V. Sc. 1.
    L. 54.

I am advised to give her music o' mornings ;
they say it will penetrate.
    j.   *Cymbeline.* Act II. Sc. 3. L. 12.

If music be the food of love, play on ;
Give me excess of it, that, surfeiting,
The appetite may sicken, and so die.
That strain again ! it had a dying fall :
O, it came o'er my ear like the sweet sound
That breathes upon a bank of violets,
Stealing and giving odour.
    k.   *Twelfth Night.* Act I. Sc. 1. L. 1.

Let music sound while he doth make his
    choice ;
Then, if he lose, he makes a swan-like end,
Fading in music.
    l.   *Merchant of Venice.* Act III. Sc. 2.
    L. 43.

    Music do I hear?
Ha ! ha ! keep time : how sour sweet music is,
When time is broke and no proportion kept !
    m.   *Richard II.* Act V. Sc. 5. L. 41.

One whom the music of his own vain tongue
Doth ravish like enchanting harmony.
    n.   *Love's Labour's Lost.* Act I. Sc. 1.
    L. 167.

Orpheus with his lute made trees,
And the mountain-tops that freeze,
    Bow themselves, when he did sing :
To his music, plants and flowers
Ever sprung ; as sun and showers,
    There had made a lasting spring.
    o.   *Henry VIII.* Act III. Sc. 1. L. 3.

Preposterous ass, that never read so far
To know the cause why music was ordain'd !
Was it not to refresh the mind of man,
After his studies or his usual pain?
    p.   *Taming of the Shrew.* Act III. Sc. 1.
    L. 9.

Take but degree away, untune that string,
And, hark, what discord follows !
    q.   *Troilus and Cressida.* Act I. Sc. 3.
    L. 109.

    The choir,
With all the choicest music of the kingdom,
Together sung *Te Deum.*
    r.   *Henry VIII.* Act IV. Sc. 1. L. 90.

The man that hath no music in himself,
Nor is not moved with concord of sweet
    sounds,
Is fit for treasons, stratagems and spoils.
    s.   *Merchant of Venice.* Act V. Sc. 1.
    L. 83.

This music crept by me upon the waters,
Allaying both their fury and my passion
With its sweet air.
    t.   *Tempest.* Act I. Sc. 2. L. 391.

    Though music oft hath such a charm
To make bad good, and good provoke to harm.
    u.   *Measure for Measure.* Act IV. Sc. 1.
    L. 14.

Wilt thou have music ? hark ! Apollo plays
And twenty caged nightingales do sing.
    v.   *Taming of the Shrew.* Induction.
    Sc. 2. L. 37.

Musick ! soft charm of heav'n and earth,
Whence didst thou borrow thy auspicious
    birth?
Or art thou of eternal date,
Sire to thyself, thyself as old as Fate.
    w.   EDMUND SMITH—*Ode in Praise of*
    Musick.

See to their desks Apollo's sons repair,
Swift rides the rosin o'er the horse's hair!
In unison their various tones to tune,
Murmurs the hautboy, growls the hoarse bas-
    soon;
In soft vibration sighs the whispering lute,
Tang goes the harpsichord, too-too the flute,
Brays the loud trumpet, squeaks the fiddle
    sharp,
Winds the French-horn, and twangs the
    tingling harp;
Till, like great Jove, the leader, figuring in,
Attunes to order the chaotic din.
   a.   HORACE and JAMES SMITH—*Rejected
        Addresses. The Theatre.* L. 20.

So dischord ofte in musick makes the sweeter
    lay.
   b.   SPENSER—*Faerie Queene.* Bk. III.
        Canto II. St. 15.

Music revives the recollections it would ap-
    pease.
   c.   MADAME DE STAËL—*Corinne.* Bk. IX.
        Ch. II.

The gauger walked with willing foot,
And aye the gauger played the flute;
And what should Master Gauger play
But *Over the Hills and Far Away.*
   d.   ROBT. LOUIS STEVENSON—*Underwoods.
        A Song of the Road.*

How her fingers went when they moved by
    note
Through measures fine, as she marched them
    o'er
The yielding plank of the ivory floor.
   e.   BENJ. F. TAYLOR—*Songs of Yesterday.
        How the Brook Went to Mill.* St. 3.

It is the little rift within the lute
That by and by will make the music mute,
And ever widening slowly silence all.
   f.   TENNYSON—*Idylls of the King. Merlin
        and Vivien.* L. 393.

Music that brings sweet sleep down from the
    blissful skies.
   g.   TENNYSON—*The Lotos Eaters. Choric
        Song.* St. 1.

Music that gentlier on the spirit lies
Than tir'd eyelids upon tir'd eyes.
   h.   TENNYSON—*The Lotos Eaters. Choric
        Song.* St. 1.

       And with a secret pain,
And smiles that seem akin to tears,
We hear the wild refrain.
   i.   WHITTIER—*At Port Royal.*

Her ivory hands on the ivory keys
    Strayed in a fitful fantasy,
Like the silver gleam when the poplar trees
    Rustle their pale leaves listlessly
Or the drifting foam of a restless sea
When the waves show their teeth in the flying
    breeze.
   j.   OSCAR WILDE—*In the Gold Room.
        A Harmony.*

What fairy-like music steals over the sea,
Entrancing our senses with charmed melody?
   k.   MRS. M. C. B. WILSON—*What Fairy-like
        Music.*

Bright gem instinct with music, vocal spark.
   l.   WORDSWORTH—*A Morning Exercise.*

Soft is the music that would charm forever:
The flower of sweetest smell is shy and lowly.
   m.   WORDSWORTH—*Not Love, Not War.*

         Sweetest melodies
Are those that are by distance made more
    sweet.
   n.   WORDSWORTH—*Personal Talk.* St. 2.

The music in my heart I bore,
Long after it was heard no more.
   o.   WORDSWORTH—*The Solitary Reaper.*

         Where music dwells
Lingering, and wandering on as loth to die;
Like thoughts whose very sweetness yieldeth
    proof
That they were born for immortality.
   p.   WORDSWORTH—*Ecclesiastical Sonnets.*
        Pt. III. 63. *Inside of King's Chapel,
            Cambridge.*

N.

NAME.

Oh! no! we never mention her,
Her name is never heard;
My lips are now forbid to speak
That once familiar word.
   q.   THOMAS HAYNES BAYLY—*Melodies of
        Various Nations. Oh! No! We
            Never Mention Her.*

He left a Corsair's name to other times,
Linked with one virtue, and a thousand crimes.
   r.   BYRON—*The Corsair.* Canto III. St. 24.

I have a passion for the name of "Mary,"
    For once it was a magic sound to me,
And still it half calls up the realms of fairy,
    Where I beheld what never was to be.
   s.   BYRON—*Don Juan.* Canto V. St. 4.

Oh, Amos Cottle!—Phœbus! what a name!
a.   BYRON—*English Bards and Scotch*
                          Reviewers. L. 399.

Who hath not own'd, with rapture-smitten
    frame,
The power of grace, the magic of a name.
b.   CAMPBELL—*Pleasures of Hope.* Pt. II.
                          L. 5.

Some to the fascination of a name
Surrender judgment hoodwinked.
c.   COWPER—*Task.* Bk. VI. L. 101.

He lives who dies to win a lasting name.
d.   DRUMMOND—*Sonnet.* 12.

"Whose name was writ in water!" What
    large laughter
Among the immortals when that word was
    brought!
Then when his fiery spirit rose flaming after,
    High toward the topmost heaven of heavens
    up-caught!
"All hail! our younger brother!" Shakespeare
    said,
And Dante nodded his imperial head.
e.   R. W. GILDER—*Keats.*

My name is Norval; on the Grampian hills
My father feeds his flocks; a frugal swain,
Whose constant cares were to increase his
    store,
And keep his only son, myself, at home.
f.   JOHN HOME—*Douglas.* Act II. Sc. 1.
                          L. 42.

And, lo! Ben Adhem's name led all the rest.
g.   LEIGH HUNT—*Abou Ben Adhem.*

Have heard her sigh and soften out the name.
h.   WALTER SAVAGE LANDOR—*Gebir.*
                          Bk. V. L. 145.

Out of his surname they have coined an
epithet for a knave, and out of his Christian
name a synonyme for the Devil.
i.   MACAULAY—*On Machiavelli.* 1825.

The name that dwells on every tongue,
No minstrel needs.
j.   DON JORGE MANRIQUE—*Coplas de
              Manrique.* St. 54. Longfellow's
                          trans.

"What is thy name, faire maid?" quoth he.
"Penelophon, O King," quoth she.
k.   THOS. PERCY—*Reliques.* *King
              Cophetua and the Beggar-Maid.*

O name forever sad! forever dear!
Still breath'd in sighs, still usher'd with a
    tear.
l.   POPE—*Eloisa to Abelard.* L. 31.

May see thee now, though late, redeem thy
    name,
And glorify what else is damn'd to fame.
m.   RICHARD SAVAGE—*Character of the Rev.
                          James Foster.* L. 43.

My foot is on my native heath, and my name
    is MacGregor!
n.   SCOTT—*Rob Roy.* Ch. XXXIV.

I cannot tell what the dickens his name is.
o.   *Merry Wives of Windsor.* Act III.
                          Sc. 2. L. 17.

              I do beseech you—
Chiefly, that I might set it in my prayers—
What is your name?
p.   *Tempest.* Act III. Sc. 1. L. 32.

              Then shall our names,
Familiar in his mouth as household words—
        *   *   *   *   *   *
Be in their flowing cups freshly remembered.
q.   *Henry V.* Act IV. Sc. 3. L. 51.

              The one so like the other
As could not be distinguish'd but by names.
r.   *Comedy of Errors.* Act I. Sc. 1. L. 52.

What's in a name? that which we call a rose
By any other name would smell as sweet.
s.   *Romeo and Juliet.* Act II. Sc. 2.
                          L. 43.

And last of all an Admiral came,
A terrible man with a terrible name,—
A name which you all know by sight very
    well;
But which no one can speak, and no one can
    spell.
t.   SOUTHEY—*The March to Moscow.* St. 8.

I'll give you leave to call me anything, if
you don't call me spade.
u.   SWIFT—*Polite Conversation.*
                          Dialogue II.

Charmed with the foolish whistling of a
name.
v.   VIRGIL—*Georgics.* Bk. II. L. 72.
                          Cowley's trans.

NATURE.

If there's a power above us, (and that there
    is all nature cries aloud
Through all her works) he must delight in
    virtue.
w.   ADDISON—*Cato.* Act V. Sc. 1.

Nature's great law, and law of all men's
    minds?—
To its own impulse every creature stirs;
Live by thy light, and earth will live by hers!
x.   MATTHEW ARNOLD—*Religious Isolation.*
                          St. 4.

Nature means Necessity.
y.   BAILEY—*Festus.* *Dedication.*

The course of Nature seems a course of Death,
And nothingness the whole substantial thing.
z.   BAILEY—*Festus.* Sc. *Water and Wood.*

Out of the book of Nature's learned breast.
  a.   Du Bartas—*Divine Weekes and Workes.*
        Second Week.   Fourth Day.
                        Bk. II.   L. 566.

At the close of the day, when the hamlet is
    still,
  And mortals the sweets of forgetfulness
    prove,
When nought but the torrent is heard on the
    hill,
  And nought but the nightingale's song in
    the grove.
  b.   Beattie—*The Hermit.*

Nature too unkind ;
That made no medicine for a troubled mind !
  c.   Beaumont and Fletcher—*Philaster.*
                        Act III.   Sc. 1.

Now nature is not at variance with art, nor
art with nature, they being both servants of
his providence : art is the perfection of nature ;
were the world now as it was the sixth day,
there were yet a chaos ; nature hath made one
world, and art another.   In brief, all things
are artificial ; for nature is the art of God.
  d.   Sir Thomas Browne—*Religio Medici.*
                        Pt. XVI.

Rich with the spoils of nature.
  e.   Sir Thomas Browne—*Religio Medici.*
                        Pt. XIII.

There are no grotesques in nature; not
anything framed to fill up empty cantons,
and unnecessary spaces.
  f.   Sir Thomas Browne—*Religio Medici.*
                        Pt. XV.

"There is no God," the foolish saith,
  But none, "There is no sorrow,"
And nature oft the cry of faith
  In bitter need will borrow.
  g.   E. B. Browning—*The Cry of the
                        Human.*

I trust in Nature for the stable laws
Of beauty and utility.   Spring shall plant
And Autumn garner to the end of time.
I trust in God—the right shall be the right
And other than the wrong, while he endures ;
I trust in my own soul, that can perceive
The outward and the inward, Nature's good
And God's.
  h.   Robert Browning—*A Soul's Tragedy.*
                        Act I.

Go forth under the open sky, and list
To Nature's teachings.
  i.   Bryant—*Thanatopsis.*

To him who in the love of Nature holds
Communion with her visible forms. she
    speaks
A various language.
  j.   Bryant—*Thanatopsis.*

See one promontory (said Socrates of old),
one mountain, one sea, one river, and see all.
  k.   Burton—*Anatomy of Melancholy.*
        Pt. I.   Sec. 2.   Memb. 4.   Subsec. 7.

Nature vicarye of the Almighty Lord.
  l.   Chaucer—*Parlement of Foules.*   L. 379.

Not without art, but yet to Nature true.
  m.   Churchill—*The Rosciad.*   L. 699.

Nature, exerting an unwearied power,
Forms, opens, and gives scent to every flower ;
Spreads the fresh verdure of the field, and
    leads
The dancing Naiads through the dewy meads.
  n.   Cowper—*Table Talk.*   L. 690.

Nor rural sights alone, but rural sounds,
Exhilarate the spirit, and restore
The tone of languid Nature.
  o.   Cowper—*The Task.*   Bk. I.   *The Sofa.*
                        L. 187.

I have called this principle, by which each
slight variation, if useful, is preserved, by the
term of Natural Selection.
  p.   Charles Darwin—*The Origin of
                        Species.*   Ch. III.

By viewing nature, nature's handmaid, art,
Makes mighty things from small beginnings
    grow ;
Thus fishes first to shipping did impart,
Their tail the rudder, and their head the prow.
  q.   Dryden—*Annus Mirabilis.*   St. 155.

Whate'er he did, was done with so much ease,
In him alone 't was natural to please.
  r.   Dryden—*Absalom and Achitophel.*
                        Pt. I.   L. 27.

Ever charming, ever new,
When will the landscape tire the view?
  s.   John Dyer—*Grongar Hill.*   L. 102.

By fate, not option, frugal Nature gave
One scent to hyson and to wall-flower,
One sound to pine-groves and to water-falls,
One aspect to the desert and the lake.
It was her stern necessity : all things
Are of one pattern made ; bird, beast, and
    flower,
Song, picture, form, space, thought, and char-
    acter
Deceive us, seeming to be many things,
And are but one.
  t.   Emerson—*Xenophones.*

Nature is a mutable cloud which is always
and never the same.
  u.   Emerson—*Essays.   First Series.*
                        History.

Nature seems to wear one universal grin.
  v.   Henry Fielding—*Tom Thumb the
                        Great.*   Act I.   Sc. 1.

As distant prospects please us, but when near
We find but desert rocks and fleeting air.
   a.   Sir Sam'l Garth—*The Dispensary.*
                     Canto III. L. 27.

Over the hills and far away.
   b.   Gay—*The Beggar's Opera.* Act I.
                     Sc. 1. (Air.)

To me more dear, congenial to my heart,
One native charm, than all the gloss of art.
   c.   Goldsmith—*Deserted Village.* L. 253.

E'en from the tomb the voice of nature cries,
E'en in our ashes live their wonted fires.
   d.   Gray—*Elegy in a Country Churchyard.*
                     St. 23.

That undefined and mingled hum,
Voice of the desert never dumb !
   e.   Hogg—*Verses to Lady Anne Scott.*

        No stir of air was there,
Not so much life as on a summer's day
Robs not one light seed from the feather'd
     grass,
But where the dead leaf fell, there did it rest.
   f.   Keats—*Hyperion.* Bk. I. L. 7.

Nature with folded hands seemed there,
Kneeling at her evening prayer !
   g.   Longfellow—*Voices of the Night.*
                     Prelude. St. 11.

        No tears
Dim the sweet look that Nature wears.
   h.   Longfellow—*Sunrise on the Hills.*
                     L. 35.

O what a glory doth this world put on
For him who, with a fervent heart, goes forth
Under the bright and glorious sky, and looks
On duties well performed, and days well
     spent !
For him the wind, ay, and the yellow leaves,
Shall have a voice, and give him eloquent
     teachings.
   i.   Longfellow—*Autumn.* L. 30.

So Nature deals with us, and takes away
  Our playthings one by one, and by the hand
  Leads us to rest so gently, that we go,
Scarce knowing if we wish to go or stay,
  Being too full of sleep to understand
How far the unknown transcends the what
  we know.
   j.   Longfellow—*Nature.* L. 9.

The natural alone is permanent.
   k.   Longfellow—*Kavanagh.* Ch. XIII.

His Nature's a glass of champagne with the
     foam on 't,
As tender as Fletcher, as witty as Beaumont;
So his best things are done in the flash of the
     moment.
   l.   Lowell—*A Fable for Critics.* L. 834.

But on and up, where Nature's heart
Beats strong amid the hills.
   m.   Richard Monckton Milnes (Lord
          Houghton)—*Tragedy of the Lac de
                     Gaube.* St. 2.

Accuse not Nature, she hath done her part;
Do thou but thine !
   n.   Milton—*Paradise Lost.* Bk. VIII.
                     L. 561.

And liquid lapse of murmuring streams.
   o.   Milton—*Paradise Lost.* Bk. VIII.
                     L. 263.

And live like Nature's bastards, not her sons.
   p.   Milton—*Comus.* L. 727.

                Into this wild abyss,
The womb of Nature and perhaps her grave.
   q.   Milton—*Paradise Lost.* Bk. II.
                     L. 910.

Let us a little permit Nature to take her own
way ; she better understands her own affairs
than we.
   r.   Montaigne—*Essays. Experience.*

And not from Nature up to Nature's God,
But down from Nature's God look Nature
     through.
   s.   Robert Montgomery—*Luther.*
             A Landscape of Domestic Life.

There is not in the wide world a valley so sweet
As that vale in whose bosom the bright waters
     meet.
   t.   Moore—*The Meeting of the Waters.*

And we, with Nature's heart in tune,
Concerted harmonies.
   u.   Wm. Motherwell—*Jeannie Morrison.*

All are but parts of one stupendous whole,
Whose body Nature is, and God the soul ;
That chang'd thro' all, and yet in all the same,
Great in the earth as in th' ethereal frame ;
Warms in the sun, refreshes in the breeze,
Glows in the stars, and blossoms in the trees ;
Lives thro' all life, extends thro' all extent,
Spreads undivided, operates unspent ;
Breathes in our soul, informs our mortal part,
As full, as perfect, in a hair as heart.
   v.   Pope—*Essay on Man.* Ep. I. L. 267.

All Nature is but art unknown to thee ;
All chance direction, which thou canst not see.
   w.   Pope—*Essay on Man.* Ep. I. L. 289.

Eye Nature's walks, shoot folly as it flies,
And catch the manners living as they rise.
   x.   Pope—*Essay on Man.* Ep. I. L. 13.

Seas roll to waft me, suns to light me rise;
My footstool Earth, my canopy the skies.
  a.   POPE—*Essay on Man.* Ep. I. L. 139.

See plastic Nature working to this end,
The single atoms each to other tend,
Attract, attracted to, the next in place
Form'd and impell'd its neighbor to embrace.
  b.   POPE—*Essay on Man.* Ep. III. L. 9.

Slave to no sect, who takes no private road,
But looks through Nature up to Nature's God.
  c.   POPE—*Essay on Man.* Ep. IV. L. 331.

Oh, Brignall banks are wild and fair,
  And Greta woods are green,
And you may gather garlands there
  Would grace a summer queen.
  d.   SCOTT—*Rokeby.* Canto III. St. 16.

Some touch of Nature's genial glow.
  e.   SCOTT—*Lord of the Isles.* Canto III.
                                        St. 14.

              And Nature does require
Her times of preservation, which perforce
I, her frail son, amongst my brethren mortal,
Must give my tendance to.
  f.   *Henry VIII.* Act III. Sc. 2. L. 147.

Diseased Nature oftentimes breaks forth
In strange eruptions.
  g.   *Henry IV.* Pt. I. Act III. Sc. 1.
                                        L. 27.

How hard it is to hide the sparks of Nature!
  h.   *Cymbeline.* Act III. Sc. 3. L. 79.

How sometimes Nature will betray its folly,
Its tenderness, and make itself a pastime
To harder bosoms!
  i.   *Winter's Tale.* Act I. Sc. 2. L. 151.

In Nature's infinite book of secrecy
A little I can read.
  j.   *Antony and Cleopatra.* Act I. Sc. 2.
                                        L. 9.

One touch of nature makes the whole world
    kin.
  k.   *Troilus and Cressida.* Act III. Sc. 3.
                                        L. 175.

  To hold, as 'twere, the mirror up to Nature;
to shew virtue her own feature, scorn her own
image, and the very age and body of the time
his form and pressure.
  l.   *Hamlet.* Act III. Sc. 2. L. 24.

      Yet nature is made better by no mean
But nature makes that mean: so, over that art
Which, you say, adds to nature, is an art
That nature makes.
  m.   *Winter's Tale.* Act IV. Sc. 4. L. 89.

My banks they are furnish'd with bees,
  Whose murmur invites one to sleep;
My grottoes are shaded with trees,
  And my hills are white over with sheep.
  n.   SHENSTONE—*A Pastoral Ballad.*
                              Pt. II. *Hope.*

  Certainly nothing is unnatural that is not
physically impossible.
  o.   R. B. SHERIDAN—*The Critic.* Act II.
                                        Sc. 1.

For all that Nature by her mother-wit
Could frame in earth.
  p.   SPENSER—*Faerie Queene.* Bk. IV.
                              Canto X. St. 21.

What more felicitie can fall to creature
Than to enjoy delight with libertie,
And to be lord of all the workes of Nature,
To raine in th' aire from earth to highest skie,
To feed on flowres and weeds of glorious
    feature.
  q.   SPENSER—*The Fate of the Butterfly.*
                                        L. 209.

Yet neither spinnes, nor cards, ne cares nor
    fretts,
But to her mother Nature all her care she letts.
  r.   SPENSER—*Faerie Queene.* Bk. II.
                                  Canto VI.

Once, when the days were ages,
  And the old Earth was young,
The high gods and the sages
From Nature's golden pages
  Her open secrets wrung.
  s.   R. H. STODDARD—*Brahma's Answer.*

Here are cool mosses deep,
And thro' the moss the ivies creep,
And in the stream the long-leaved flowers
    weep,
And from the craggy ledge the poppy hangs
    in sleep.
  t.   TENNYSON—*The Lotos-Eaters.*
                          Choric Song. Pt. I.

Myriads of rivulets hurrying through the
    lawn,
The moan of doves in immemorial elms,
And murmuring of innumerable bees.
  u.   TENNYSON—*The Princess.* Canto VII.
                                        L. 205.

Nothing in Nature is unbeautiful.
  v.   TENNYSON—*The Lover's Tale.* L. 348.

              But who can paint
Like Nature? Can imagination boast,
Amid its gay creation, hues like hers?
Or can it mix them with that matchless skill,
And lose them in each other, as appears
In every bud that blows?
  w.   THOMSON—*The Seasons.* *Spring.*
                                        L. 465.

I care not, Fortune, what you me deny;
　You cannot rob me of free Nature's grace,
You cannot shut the windows of the sky,
　Through which Aurora shows her brighten-
　　ing face;
You cannot bar my constant feet to trace
The woods and lawns, by living stream, at
　eve.
　　a.　　THOMSON—*The Castle of Indolence.*
　　　　　　　　　　　Canto II.　St. 3.

O Nature! * * *
Enrich me with the knowledge of thy works;
Snatch me to Heaven.
　　b.　　THOMSON—*The Seasons. Autumn.*
　　　　　　　　　　　　　　　L. 1,352.

Rocks rich in gems, and Mountains big with
　mines,
That on the high Equator, ridgy, rise,
Whence many a bursting Stream auriferous
　plays.
　　c.　　THOMSON—*The Seasons. Summer.*
　　　　　　　　　　　　　　　L. 646.

Nature is always wise in every part.
　　d.　　LORD THURLOW—*Select Poems. The
　　　　　　　　　　　　　Harvest Moon.*

Divine Nature gave the fields, human art
　built the cities.
　　e.　　VARRO—*De re Rustica.* III. 1.

Talk not of temples, there is one
　Built without hands, to mankind given;
Its lamps are the meridian sun
　And all the stars of heaven,
Its walls are the cerulean sky,
　Its floor the earth so green and fair,
The dome its vast immensity;
　All Nature worships there!
　　f.　　DAVID VEDDER—*The Temple of Nature.*

In such green palaces the first kings reign'd,
Slept in their shades, and angels entertain'd;
With such old counsellors they did advise,
And by frequenting sacred groves grew wise.
　　g.　　EDMUND WALLER—*On St. James' Park.*
　　　　　　　　　　　　　　　L. 71.

Ah, what a warning for a thoughtless man,
Could field or grove, could any spot of earth,
Show to his eye an image of the pangs
Which it hath witnessed; render back an
　echo
Of the sad steps by which it hath been trod!
　　h.　　WORDSWORTH—*The Excursion.* Bk. VI.

And recognizes ever and anon
The breeze of Nature stirring in his soul.
　　i.　　WORDSWORTH—*The Excursion.* Bk. IV.

As in the eye of Nature he has lived,
So in the eye of Nature let him die!
　　j.　　WORDSWORTH—*The Old Cumberland
　　　　　　　　　　Beggar.*　Last Lines.

　　　　　　　　Nature never did betray
The heart that loved her.
　　k.　　WORDSWORTH—*Lines Composed Above
　　　　　　　　　　　　Tintern Abbey.*

One impulse from a vernal wood
　May teach you more of man,
Of moral evil and of good,
　Than all the sages can.
　　l.　　WORDSWORTH—*The Tables Turned.*

The stars of midnight shall be dear
To her; and she shall lean her ear
　In many a secret place
Where rivulets dance their wayward round,
And beauty born of murmuring sound
　Shall pass into her face.
　　m.　　WORDSWORTH—*Three Years She Grew
　　　　　　　　　　　in Sun and Shower.*

The streams with softest sound are flowing,
The grass you almost hear it growing,
You hear it now, if e'er you can.
　　n.　　WORDSWORTH—*The Idiot Boy.*　St. 57.

　　　　　　　　　To the solid ground
Of Nature trusts the Mind that builds for aye.
　　o.　　WORDSWORTH—*A Volant Tribe of
　　　　　　　　　　　Bards on Earth.*

Two Voices are there: one is of the sea,
One of the mountains; each a mighty Voice.
　　p.　　WORDSWORTH—*Thought of a Briton on
　　　　　　　　　the Subjugation of Switzerland.*

In distant wilds, by human eyes unseen,
She rears her flowers, and spreads her velvet
　　green;
Pure gurgling rills the lonely desert trace
And waste their music on the savage race.
　　q.　　YOUNG—*Love of Fame.*　Satire V.
　　　　　　　　　　　　　　　L. 232.

Nothing in Nature, much less conscious being,
Was e'er created solely for itself.
　　r.　　YOUNG—*Night Thoughts.*　Night IX.
　　　　　　　　　　　　　　　L. 711.

　　　　　　Such blessings Nature pours,
O'erstock'd mankind enjoy but half her stores.
　　s.　　YOUNG—*Love of Fame.*　Satire V.
　　　　　　　　　　　　　　　L. 230.

The course of Nature is the art of God.
　　t.　　YOUNG—*Night Thoughts.*　Night IX.
　　　　　　　　　　　　　　　L. 1,280.

NAVIGATION (*See* OCCUPATIONS).

NECESSITY.

Necessity is stronger far than art.
　　u.　　ÆSCHYLUS—*Prometheus Chained.*
　　　　　　　　　　　　　　　L. 513.

Thanne is it wysdom, as thynketh me,
To maken vertu of necessité,
And take it weel, that we may not eschu,
And namely that that to us alle is due.
　　v.　　CHAUCER—*Canterbury Tales. The
　　　　　　　　　Knighte's Tale.*　L. 2,182.

Then 'tis our best, since thus ordained to die,
To make a virtue of necessity.
　　a.　　DRYDEN—*Palamon and Arcite.*
　　　　　　　　　　Bk. III.　L. 1,084.

　　　　　　　　Not mine
This saying, but the sentence of the sage,
Nothing is stronger than necessity.
　　b.　　EURIPIDES—*Helena.*　L. 560.

Art imitates nature, and necessity is the
mother of invention.
　　c.　　RICHARD FRANCK—*Northern Memoirs.*
　　　　　　Written in 1658, printed in 1696.
　　　　　　　　　　　　　　P. 52.

So spake the Fiend, and with necessity,
The tyrant's plea, excused his devilish deeds.
　　d.　　MILTON—*Paradise Lost.*　Bk. IV.
　　　　　　　　　　　　　　L. 393.

My steps have pressed the flowers,
That to the Muses' bowers
The eternal dews of Helicon have given:
And trod the mountain height,
Where Science, young and bright,
Scans with poetic gaze the midnight-heaven.
Yet have I found no power to vie
With thine, severe necessity!
　　e.　　THOMAS LOVE PEACOCK—*Necessity.*

Necessity was the argument of tyrants; it
was the creed of slaves.
　　f.　　WM. PITT—*Speech on the India Bill.*
　　　　　　　　　　Nov. 18, 1783.

Obliged by hunger and request of friends.
　　g.　　POPE—*Epistle to Dr. Arbuthnot.*
　　　　　　Prologue to the Satires.　L. 44.

Necessity—thou best of peacemakers,
As well as surest prompter of invention.
　　h.　　SCOTT—*Peveril of the Peak.*　Heading
　　　　　　　　　　　of Ch. XXVI.

Necessity's sharp pinch!
　　i.　　*King Lear.*　Act II.　Sc. 4.　L. 214.

Now sit we close about this taper here,
And call in question our necessities.
　　j.　　*Julius Cæsar.*　Act IV.　Sc. 3.　L. 165.

Teach thy necessity to reason thus:
There is no virtue like necessity.
　　k.　　*Richard II.*　Act I.　Sc. 3.　L. 277.

Spirit of Nature! all-sufficing Power!
Necessity, thou mother of the world!
　　l.　　SHELLEY—*Queen Mab.*　Pt. VI.

Necessity, the mother of invention.
　　m.　　WYCHERLY—*Love in a Wood.*　Act III.
　　　　　　　　　　　　　　Sc. 3.

NEGLECT.

A wise and salutary neglect.
　　n.　　BURKE—*Speech on the Conciliation of
　　　　　　　　America.*　Vol. II.　P. 117.

Give me a look, give me a face,
That makes simplicity a grace:
Robes loosely flowing, hair as free;
Such sweet neglect more taketh me
Than all the adulteries of art;
They strike mine eyes, but not my heart.
　　o.　　BEN JONSON—*The Silent Woman.*
　　　　　　　　　　Act I.　Sc. 1.

His noble negligences teach
What others' toils despair to reach.
　　p.　　PRIOR—*Alma.*　Canto II.　L. 7.

NEWS.

There is nothing new except what is forgotten.
　　q.　　MADEMOISELLE BERTIN (*Milliner to
　　　　　　　　　　Marie Antoinette.*)

It is good news, *worthy of all acceptation;*
and yet not too good to be true.
　　r.　　MATHEW HENRY—*Commentaries.*
　　　　　　　　　　I. Timothy i. 15.

News, news, news, my gossiping friends,
I have wonderful news to tell,
A lady by me her compliments sends;
And this is the news from Hell!
　　s.　　OWEN MEREDITH (Lord Lytton)—*News.*

Here comes Monsieur le Beau
With his mouth full of news,
Which he will put on us, as pigeons feed their
　　　　　　young.
Then shall we be news-crammed.
　　t.　　*As You Like It.*　Act I.　Sc. 2.　L. 96.

How goes it now, sir? this news which is
called true is so like an old tale, that the
verity of it is in strong suspicion.
　　u.　　*Winter's Tale.*　Act V.　Sc. 2.　L. 25.

I drown'd these news in tears.
　　v.　　*Henry VI.*　Pt. III.　Act II.　Sc. 1.
　　　　　　　　　　　　　　L. 104.

　　　　　　If it be summer news,
Smile to 't before: if winterly, thou need'st
But keep that countenance still.
　　w.　　*Cymbeline.*　Act III.　Sc. 4.　L. 12.

My heart hath one poor string to stay it by,
Which holds but till thy news be uttered.
　　x.　　*King John.*　Act V.　Sc. 7.　L. 55.

There's villainous news abroad.
　　y.　　*Henry IV.*　Pt. I.　Act II.　Sc. 4.
　　　　　　　　　　　　　　L. 365.

Though it be honest, it is never good
To bring bad news; give to a gracious mes-
　　　sage
An host of tongues; but let ill tidings tell
Themselves when they be felt.
　　a.　　*Antony and Cleopatra.*　Act II.　Sc. 5.
　　　　　　　　　　　　　　　　L. 85.

Yet the first bringer of unwelcome news
Hath but a losing office; and his tongue
Sounds ever after as a sullen bell,
Remember'd tolling a departed friend.
　　b.　　*Henry IV.*　Pt. II.　Act I.　Sc. 1.
　　　　　　　　　　　　　　　　L. 100.

NIGHT.

Day is a snow-white Dove of heaven.
　　That from the East glad message brings:
Night is a stealthy, evil Raven,
　　Wrapt to the eyes in his black wings.
　　c.　　T. B. ALDRICH—*Day and Night.*

I love night more than day—she is so lovely;
But I love night the most because she brings
My love to me in dreams which scarcely lie.
　　d.　　BAILEY—*Festus.*　Sc. *Water and Wood.*
　　　　　　　　　　　　　　　　Midnight.

Night comes, world-jewelled,　＊　＊　＊
The stars rush forth in myriads as to wage
War with the lines of Darkness; and the moon,
Pale ghost of Night, comes haunting the cold
　　earth
After the sun's red sea-death—quietless.
　　e.　　BAILEY—*Festus.*　Sc. *Garden and*
　　　　　　　　　　　　　　Bower by the Sea.

Night's black Mantle covers all alike.
　　f.　　DU BARTAS—*Divine Weekes and Workes.*
　　　　　　　First Week.　*First Day.*　L. 562.

When it draws near to witching time of night.
　　g.　　BLAIR—*The Grave.*　L. 55.

　　　　　　　　For the night
Shows stars and women in a better light.
　　h.　　BYRON—*Don Juan.*　Canto II.　St. 152.

　　　　Most glorious night!
Thou wert not sent for slumber!
　　i.　　BYRON—*Childe Harold.*　Canto III.
　　　　　　　　　　　　　　　　St. 93.

The stars are forth, the moon above the tops
Of the snow-shining mountains—Beautiful!
I linger yet with Nature, for the night
Hath been to me a more familiar face
Than that of man; and in her starry shade
Of dim and solitary loveliness,
I learn'd the language of another world.
　　j.　　BYRON—*Manfred.*　Act III.　Sc. 4.

The crackling embers on the hearth are dead;
The indoor note of industry is still;
The latch is fast; upon the window-sill
The small birds wait not for their daily bread;
The voiceless flowers—how quietly they shed
Their nightly odours;—and the household rill
Murmurs continuous dulcet sounds that fill
The vacant expectation, and the dread
Of listening night.
　　k.　　HARTLEY COLERIDGE—*Miscellaneous*
　　　　　　　　　　　Sonnets. XVIII.　Night.

Dark the Night, with breath all flowers,
And tender broken voice that fills
With ravishment the listening hours,—
Whisperings, wooings,
Liquid ripples, and soft ring-dove cooings
In low-toned rhythm that love's aching stills!
Dark the night
Yet is she bright,
For in her dark she brings the mystic star,
Trembling yet strong, as is the voice of love,
From some unknown afar.
　　l.　　GEORGE ELIOT—*Spanish Gypsy.　Song.*
　　　　　　　　　　　　　　　　Bk. I.

O radiant Dark! O darkly fostered ray!
Thou hast a joy too deep for shallow Day.
　　m.　　GEORGE ELIOT—*The Spanish Gypsy.*
　　　　　　　　　　　　　　　　Bk. 1.

The watch-dog's voice that bay'd the whisper-
　　ing wind,
And the loud laugh that spoke the vacant
　　mind:
These all in sweet confusion sought the shade,
And fill'd each pause the nightingale had
　　made.
　　n.　　GOLDSMITH—*The Deserted Village.*
　　　　　　　　　　　　　　　　L. 121.

He pass'd the flaming bounds of place and
　　time:
The living throne, the sapphire blaze,
Where angels tremble while they gaze,
He saw; but, blasted with excess of light,
Closed his eyes in endless night.
　　o.　　GRAY—*The Progress of Poesy.*　III.　2.

Now deep in ocean sunk the lamp of light,
And drew behind the cloudy vale of night.
　　p.　　HOMER—*Iliad.*　Bk. VIII.　L. 605.
　　　　　　　　　　　　　　　Pope's trans.

'Tis the witching hour of night,
Orbed is the moon and bright,
And the stars they glisten, glisten,
Seeming with bright eyes to listen—
　　For what listen they?
　　q.　　KEATS—*A Prophecy.*　L. 1.

And the night shall be filled with music,
　　And the cares, that infest the day,
Shall fold their tents, like the Arabs,
　　And as silently steal away.
　　r.　　LONGFELLOW—*The Day is Done.*

I heard the trailing garments of the Night
Sweep through her marble halls.
  a.   LONGFELLOW—*Hymn to the Night.*

O holy Night! from thee I learn to bear
  What man has borne before!
Thou layest thy finger on the lips of Care,
  And they complain no more.
  b.   LONGFELLOW—*Hymn to the Night.*

The night is calm and cloudless,
  And still as still can be,
And the stars come forth to listen
  To the music of the sea.
They gather, and gather, and gather,
  Until they crowd the sky,
And listen, in breathless silence,
  To the solemn litany.
  c.   LONGFELLOW—*Christus. The Golden
                           Legend. Pt. 5.*

The night is come, but not too soon;
  And sinking silently,
All silently, the little moon
  Drops down behind the sky.

There is no light in earth or heaven
  But the cold light of stars;
And the first watch of night is given
  To the red planet Mars.
  d.   LONGFELLOW—*The Light of Stars.*

Then stars arise, and the night is holy.
  e.   LONGFELLOW—*Hyperion. Bk. I. Ch. I.*

God makes sech nights, all white an' still
  Fur'z you can look or listen,
Moonshine an' snow on field an' hill,
  All silence an' all glisten.
  f.   LOWELL—*The Courtin.*

        Quiet night, that brings
Rest to the labourer, is the outlaw's day,
In which he rises early to do wrong,
And when his work is ended dares not sleep.
  g.   MASSINGER—*The Guardian. Act II.
                             Sc. 4.*

A night of tears! for the gusty rain
  Had ceased, but the eaves were dripping
    yet;
And the moon look'd forth, as tho' in pain,
  With her face all white and wet.
  h.   OWEN MEREDITH (Lord Lytton)—
         The Wanderer. Bk. II. The Portrait.

       * * * and when night
Darkens the streets, then wander forth the
    sons
Of Belial, flown with insolence and wine.
  i.   MILTON—*Paradise Lost. Bk. I. L. 500.*

           Darkness now rose,
As daylight sunk, and brought in low'ring
  Night,
Her shadowy offspring.
  j.   MILTON—*Paradise Regained. Bk. IV.
                            L. 397.*

            Eldest Night
And Chaos, ancestors of Nature.
  k.   MILTON—*Paradise Lost. Bk. II.*
                              L. 894.

        * * * for now began
Night with her sullen wings to double-shade
The desert; fowls in their clay nests were
  couch'd,
And now wild beasts came forth, the woods
  to roam.
  l.   MILTON—*Paradise Regained. Bk. I.*
                              L. 499.

     * * * now glowed the firmament
With living sapphires; Hesperus, that led
The starry host, rode brightest, till the Moon,
Rising in clouded majesty, at length
Apparent queen, unveiled her peerless light,
And o'er the dark her silver mantle threw.
  m.   MILTON—*Paradise Lost. Bk. IV.*
                              L. 604.

            O thievish Night,
Why shouldst thou, but for some felonious
  end,
In thy dark lantern thus close up the stars,
That nature hung in heaven, and filled their
  lamps
With everlasting oil, to give due light
To the misled and lonely traveller?
  n.   MILTON—*Comus. L. 195.*

Sable-vested Night, eldest of things.
  o.   MILTON—*Paradise Lost. Bk. 2. L. 962.*

Hey, now the day's dawning,
The jolly cock's crowing,
The eastern sky's glowing,
    Stars fade one by one.
The thistle cock's crying
On lovers long lying,
Cease vowing and sighing,
    The night is nigh gone.
  p.   ALEXANDER MONTGOMERY—*Night
                              is Nigh Gone.*

Night is the time for rest;
  How sweet, when labours close,
To gather round an aching breast
  The curtain of repose,
Stretch the tired limbs, and lay the head
Down on our own delightful bed!
  q.   MONTGOMERY—*Night. St. 1.*

  And the best of all ways
    To lengthen our days
Is to steal a few hours from the night, my
  dear.
  r.   MOORE—*The Young May Moon.*

There never was night that had no morn.
  s.   D. M. MULOCK—*The Golden Gate.*

Day is ended, Darkness shrouds
The shoreless seas and lowering clouds.
  t.   THOMAS LOVE PEACOCK—*Rhododaphne.
                            Canto V. L. 264.*

Ghastly, grim, and ancient Raven, wandering
　　from the Nightly shore,—
Tell me what thy lordly name is on the Night's
　　Plutonian shore!
　　Quoth the Raven " Nevermore!"
　　a.　　Poe—*The Raven.*　St. 8.

O Night, most beautiful and rare!
　　Thou giv'st the heavens their holiest hue,
And through the azure fields of air
　　Bring'st down the gentle dew.
　　b.　　Thomas Buchanan Read—*Night.*

On dreary night let lusty sunshine fall.
　　c.　　Schiller—*Pompeii and Herculaneum.*

To all, to each, a fair good night,
And pleasing dreams, and slumbers light.
　　d.　　Scott—*Marmion.*　Canto VI.　Last
　　　　　　　　　　　　　　　　　　　　Lines.

　　　　　　And night is fled,
Whose pitchy mantle overveil'd the earth.
　　e.　　*Henry VI.*　Pt. I.　Act II.　Sc. 2.　L. 1.

Come, gentle night, come, loving, blackbrow'd
　　night.
　　f.　　*Romeo and Juliet.*　Act III.　Sc. 2.
　　　　　　　　　　　　　　　　　　　　L. 20.

　　　　　　Come, seeling night,
Skarf up the tender eye of pitiful day;
And with thy bloody and invisible hand
Cancel and tear to pieces that great bond
Which keeps me pale!
　　g.　　*Macbeth.*　Act III.　Sc. 2.　L. 46.

I must become a borrower of the night
For a dark hour or twain.
　　h.　　*Macbeth.*　Act III.　Sc. 1.　L. 27.

In the dead vast and middle of the night.
　　i.　　*Hamlet.*　Act I.　Sc. 2.　L. 198.

　　　　　Light thickens; and the crow
Makes wing to the rooky wood:
Good things of the day begin to droop and
　　drowse;
Whiles night's black agents to their preys do
　　rouse.
　　j.　　*Macbeth.*　Act III.　Sc. 2.　L. 50.

Making night hideous.
　　k.　　*Hamlet.*　Act I.　Sc. 4.　L. 54.

Now the hungry lion roars,
　　And the wolf behowls the moon;
Whilst the heavy ploughman snores,
　　All with weary task foredone.
　　l.　　*Midsummer-Night's Dream.*　Act V.
　　　　　　　　　　　　　　　　　Sc. 1.　L. 378.

The night is long that never finds the day.
　　m.　　*Macbeth.*　Act IV.　Sc. 3.　L. 240.

　　　　　　This is the night
That either makes me or fordoes me quite.
　　n.　　*Othello.*　Act V.　Sc. 1.　L. 128.

27

'Tis now the very witching time of night,
When churchyards yawn and hell itself
　　breathes out
Contagion to this world.
　　o.　　*Hamlet.*　Act III.　Sc. 2.　L. 404.

How beautiful this night! the balmiest sigh
Which Vernal Zephyrs breathe in evening's
　　ear
Were discord to the speaking quietude
That wraps this moveless scene.　Heaven's
　　ebon vault,
Studded with stars, unutterably bright,
Through which the moon's unclouded gran-
　　deur rolls,
Seems like a canopy which love has spread
To curtain her sleeping world.
　　p.　　Shelley—*Queen Mab.*　**Pt. IV.**

Swiftly walk over the western wave,
　　Spirit of Night!
　　q.　　Shelley—*To Night.*

How beautiful is night!
A dewy freshness fills the silent air;
No mist obscures, nor cloud nor speck nor
　　stain
Breaks the serene of heaven.
　　r.　　Southey—*Thalaba.*　Bk. 1.

Dead sounds at night come from the inmost
　　hills,
Like footsteps upon wool.
　　s.　　Tennyson—*Ænone.*　St. 20.

Now black and deep the Night begins to fall,
A shade immense! Sunk in the quenching
　　Gloom,
Magnificent and vast, are heaven and earth.
Order confounded lies; all beauty void,
Distinction lost, and gay variety
One universal blot: such the fair power
Of light, to kindle and create the whole.
　　t.　　Thomson—*The Seasons.　Autumn.*
　　　　　　　　　　　　　　　　　　　　L. 113.

Curfew must not ring to-night.
　　u.　　Rosa H. Thorpe—*Title of Poem.*

How is night's sable mantle labor'd o'er,
How richly wrought with attributes divine!
What wisdom shines! what love! this mid-
　　night pomp,
This gorgeous arch, with golden worlds inlaid
Built with divine ambition!
　　v.　　Young—*Night Thoughts.*　Night IV.
　　　　　　　　　　　　　　　　　　　　L. 385.

Mine is the night, with all her stars.
　　w.　　Young—*Paraphrase on Job.*　**L. 147.**

Night, sable goddess! from her ebon throne,
In rayless majesty, now stretches forth
Her leaden sceptre o'er a slumbering world.
Silence, how dead! and darkness, how pro-
    found!
Nor eye, nor list'ning ear, an object finds;
Creation sleeps. 'Tis as the general pulse
Of life stood still, and nature made a pause;
An awful pause! prophetic of her end.
    a.   YOUNG—*Night Thoughts.* Night I. L. 18.

NOBILITY.

Ay, these look like the workmanship of
    heaven;
This is the porcelain clay of human kind,
And therefore cast into these noble moulds.
    b.   DRYDEN—*Don Sebastian.* Act I. Sc. 1.

O lady, nobility is thine, and thy form is
the reflection of thy nature!
    c.   EURIPIDES—*Ion.* 238.

There are epidemics of nobleness as well as
epidemics of disease.
    d.   FROUDE—*Short Studies on Great
            Subjects. Calvinism.*

Fond man! though all the heroes of your line
Bedeck your halls, and round your galleries
    shine
In proud display; yet take this truth from
    me—
Virtue alone is true nobility!
    e.   JUVENAL—*Satire VIII.* L. 29.
                            Gifford's trans.
Be noble in every thought
And in every deed!
    f.   LONGFELLOW—*Christus. The Golden
            Legend.* Pt. II.

Noble by birth, yet nobler by great deeds.
    g.   LONGFELLOW—*Tales of a Wayside Inn.*
            Pt. III. *The Student's Tale. Emma
            and Eginhard.* L. 82.

Be noble! and the nobleness that lies
In other men, sleeping, but never dead,
Will rise in majesty to meet thine own.
    h.   LOWELL—*Sonnet IV.*

Let wealth and commerce, laws and learning
    die,
But leave us still our old nobility.
    i.   LORD JOHN MANNERS—*England's
                    Trust.* Pt. III. L. 227.

We'll shine in more substantial honours,
And to be noble we'll be good.
    j.   THOMAS PERCY—*Reliques. Winifreda.*

His nature is too noble for the world:
He would not flatter Neptune for his trident,
Or Jove for 's power to thunder.
    k.   *Coriolanus.* Act III. Sc. 1. L. 255.

This was the noblest Roman of them all:
All the conspirators save only he
Did that they did in envy of great Cæsar;
He only, in a general honest thought
And common good to all, made one of them.
    l.   *Julius Cæsar.* Act V. Sc. 5. L. 68.

The two noblest of things, which are sweetness and light.
    m.   SWIFT—*Battle of the Books.*

Better not to be at all
Than not be noble.
    n.   TENNYSON—*The Princess.* Pt. II.
                            L. 79.
From yon blue heavens above us bent
The gardener Adam and his wife
Smile at the claims of long descent.
    o.   TENNYSON—*Lady Clara Vere de Vere.*
                            St. 7.

Howe'er it be, it seems to me,
'Tis only noble to be good.
Kind hearts are more than coronets,
    And simple faith than Norman blood.
    p.   TENNYSON—*Lady Clara Vere de Vere.*
                            St. 7.

Whoe'er amidst the sons
Of reason, valor, liberty, and virtue
Displays distinguished merit, is a noble
Of Nature's own creating.
    q.   THOMSON—*Coriolanus.* Act III. Sc. 3.

Titles are marks of *honest* men, and *wise:*
The fool or knave that wears a title *lies.*
    r.   YOUNG—*Love of Fame.* Satire I. L. 145.

NOVEMBER (*See* MONTHS).

O.

OATHS.

He that imposes an Oath makes it,
Not he that for Convenience takes it.
    s.   BUTLER—*Hudibras.* Pt. II. Canto II.
                            L. 377.
Oaths were not purpos'd, more than law,
To keep the Good and Just in awe,
But to confine the Bad and Sinful,
Like mortal cattle in a penfold.
    t.   BUTLER—*Hudibras.* Pt. II. Canto II.
                            L. 197.

Then how can any man be said
To break an oath he never made?
    u.   BUTLER—*Hudibras.* Pt. II. Canto II.
                            L. 379.

Jack was embarrassed—never hero more,
And as he knew not what to say, he swore.
    v.   BYRON—*The Island.* Canto III. St. 5.

I will take my corporal oath on it.
    w.   CERVANTES—*Don Quixote.* Pt. I.
                            Bk. IV. Ch. X.

And hast thou sworn on every slight pretence,
Till perjuries are common as bad pence,
While thousands, careless of the damning sin,
Kiss the book's outside, who ne'er look'd
    within ?
a.   Cowper—*Expostulation.*   L. 384.

They fix attention, heedless of your pain,
With oaths like rivets forced into the brain;
And e'en when sober truth prevails through-
    out,
They swear it, till affirmance breeds a doubt.
b.   Cowper—*Conversation.*   L. 63.

Take not His name, who made thy mouth,
    in vain ;
It gets thee nothing, and hath no excuse.
c.   Herbert—*Temple.   Church Porch.*
                      St. 10.

And for the support of this declaration, we
mutually pledge to each other our lives, our
fortunes, and our sacred honor.
d.   Thomas Jefferson—*Declaration of
                          Independence.*

In lapidary inscriptions a man is not upon
oath.
e.   Sam'l Johnson—*Boswell's Life of
                         Johnson.*   1775.

Vows with so much passion, swears with so
    much grace,
That 't is a kind of Heaven to be deluded by
    him.
f.   Nathaniel Lee—*The Rival Queens ;
    or, Alexander the Great.*   Act I.   Sc. 1.

I take the official oath to-day with no mental
reservations and with no purpose to construe
the Constitution by any hypercritical rules.
g.   Abraham Lincoln—*First Inaugural
               Address.*   March 4, 1861.

You can have no oath registered in heaven
to destroy the Government ; while I shall have
the most solemn one to " preserve, protect,
and defend " it.
h.   Abraham Lincoln—*First Inaugural
               Address.*   March 4, 1861.

Ease would recant
Vows made in pain, as violent and void.
i.   Milton—*Paradise Lost.*   Bk. IV.
                          L. 96.

Let us embrace, and from this very moment
Vow an eternal misery together.
j.   Thomas Otway—*The Orphan.*   Act IV.
                          Sc. 1

And then a whoreson jackanapes must take
me up for swearing ; as if I borrowed mine
oaths of him and might not spend them at
my pleasure.
k.   *Cymbeline.*   Act II.   Sc. 1.   L. 3.

An oath, an oath, I have an oath in heaven :
Shall I lay perjury upon my soul?
No, not for Venice.
l.   *Merchant of Venice.*   Act IV.   Sc. 1.
                          L. 228.

Do not swear at all ;
Or, if thou wilt, swear by thy gracious self,
Which is the god of my idolatry,
And I'll believe thee.
m.   *Romeo and Juliet.*   Act II.   Sc. 2.   L. 112.

For it comes to pass oft that a terrible oath,
with a swaggering accent sharply twanged
off, gives manhood more approbation than
ever proof itself would have earned him.
n.   *Twelfth Night.*   Act III.   Sc. 4.   L. 196.

I'll be damned for never a king's son in
    Christendom.
o.   *Henry IV.*   Pt. I.   Act I.   Sc. 2.   L. 109

I'll take thy word for faith, not ask thine
    oath ;
Who shuns not to break one will sure crack
    both.
p.   *Pericles.*   Act I.   Sc. 2.   L. 120.

It is a great sin to swear unto a sin,
But greater sin to keep a sinful oath.
q.   *Henry VI.*   Pt. II.   Act V.   Sc. 1.
                          L. 182.

Or, having sworn too hard a keeping oath,
Study to break it and not break my troth.
r.   *Love's Labour's Lost.*   Act I.   Sc. 1.
                          L. 65.

'Tis not the many oaths that makes the truth,
But the plain single vow that is vow'd true.
s.   *All's Well That Ends Well.*   Act IV.
                      Sc. 2.   L. 21.

What fool is not so wise
To lose an oath to win a paradise?
t.   *Love's Labour's Lost.*   Act IV.   Sc. 3.
                          L. 72.

When a gentleman is disposed to swear, it
is not for any standers-by to curtail his oaths.
u.   *Cymbeline.*   Act II.   Sc. 1.   L. 11.

" He shall not die, by God," cried my
uncle Toby.
    The Accusing Spirit which flew up to
heaven's chancery with the oath, blushed as
he gave it in : and the Recording Angel as he
wrote it down, dropped a tear upon the word
and blotted it out forever.
v.   Sterne—*Tristram Shandy.*   Bk. VI.
                         Ch. VIII.

OBEDIENCE.

The fear of some divine and supreme powers
keeps men in obedience.
a.   BURTON—*Anatomy of Melancholy.*
            Pt. III. Sec. 4. Memb. 1. Subsec. 2.

He who obeys with modesty appears worthy
of some day or other being allowed to command.
b.   CICERO—*On the Laws.* Bk. III. Pt. III.

'Tis the *same*, with *common* natures,
Use 'em *kindly*, they *rebel*,
But, be *rough* as *nutmeg graters*,
And the rogues *obey* you well.
c.   AARON HILL—*Verses written on a
            Window in a Journey to Scotland.*

I find the doing of the will of God, leaves
me no time for disputing about His plans.
d.   GEORGE MACDONALD—*The Marquis of
            Lossie.* Ch. LXXII.

Obedience is the key to every door.
e.   GEORGE MACDONALD—*The Marquis of
            Lossie.* Ch. LIII.

Ascend, I follow thee, safe guide, the path
Thou lead'st me, and to the hand of heav'n
    submit.
f.   MILTON—*Paradise Lost.* Bk. XI.
                                        L. 371.

                    Son of Heav'n and Earth,
Attend! That thou art happy, owe to God;
That thou continuest such, owe to thyself,
That is, to thy obedience; therein stand.
g.   MILTON—*Paradise Lost.* Bk. V. L. 519.

Obedience decks the Christian most.
h.   SCHILLER—*Fight with the Dragon.*
                                        Bowring's trans.

It fits thee not to ask the reason why,
Because we bid it.
i.   *Pericles.* Act I. Sc. 1. L. 157.

Let them obey that know not how to rule.
j.   *Henry VI.* Pt. II. Act V. Sc. 1.
                                        L. 6.

                    One so small
Who knowing nothing knows but to obey.
k.   TENNYSON—*Idylls of the King.*
                                        Guinevere. L. 183.

OBLIVION.

Oblivion is not to be hired.
l.   SIR THOMAS BROWNE—*Hydriotaphia.*
                                        Ch. V.

* * * For those sacred powers
Tread on oblivion: no desert of ours
Can be entombed in their celestial breasts.
m.   WM. BROWNE—*Britannia's Pastorals.*
            Bk. III. Song II. St. 23.

It is not in the storm nor in the strife
    We feel benumb'd, and wish to be no more,
    But in the after-silence on the shore,
When all is lost, except a little life.
n.   BYRON—*Lines on Hearing that Lady
                            Byron was Ill.* L. 9.

Without oblivion, there is no remembrance
possible. When both oblivion and memory
are wise, when the general soul of man is
clear, melodious, true, there may come a
modern Iliad as memorial of the Past.
o.   CARLYLE—*Cromwell's Letters and
                        Speeches.* Introduction. Ch. I.

And o'er the past oblivion stretch her wing.
p.   HOMER—*Odyssey.* Bk. XXIV. L. 557.
                                        Pope's trans.

What's past and what's to come is strew'd
    with husks
And formless ruin of oblivion.
q.   *Troilus and Cressida.* Act IV. Sc. 5.
                                        L. 166.

But from your mind's chilled sky
It needs must drop, and lie with stiffened
    wings
Among your soul's forlornest things;
A speck upon your memory, alack!
A dead fly in a dusty window-crack.
r.   FRANCIS THOMPSON—"*Manus Animam
                            Pinxit.*" St. 2.

OBSCURITY.

Content thyself to be obscurely good.
s.   ADDISON—*Cato.* Act IV. Sc. 4.

I give the fight up; let there be an end,
A privacy, an obscure nook for me,
I want to be forgotten even by God.
t.   ROBERT BROWNING—*Paracelsus.* Pt. V.

As night the life-inclining stars best shows,
So lives obscure the starriest souls disclose.
u.   GEORGE CHAPMAN—*Hymns and
                Epigrams of Homer. The Translator's
                            Epilogue.* L. 74.

Our wasted oil unprofitably burns,
Like hidden lamps in old sepulchral urns.
v.   COWPER—*Conversation.* L. 357.

Full many a flower is born to blush unseen,
And waste its sweetness on the desert air.
w.   GRAY—*Elegy in a Country Churchyard.*
                                        St. 14.

Some write their wrongs in marble: he more
    just,
Stoop'd down serene and wrote them in the
    dust,
Trod under foot, the sport of every wind,
Swept from the earth and blotted from his
    mind.
There, secret in the grave, he bade them lie,
And grieved they could not 'scape the
    Almighty eye.
x.   SAMUEL MADDEN—*Boulter's Monument.*

The palpable obscure.
  a.   MILTON—*Paradise Lost.* Bk. II. L. 406.

How happy is the blameless vestal's lot!
The world forgetting, by the world forgot.
  b.   POPE—*Eloisa to Abelard.* L. 207.

Thus let me live, unseen, unknown,
  Thus unlamented let me die;
Steal from the world, and not a stone
  Tell where I lie.
  c.   POPE—*Ode on Solitude.*

Yet was he but a squire of low degree.
  d.   SPENSER—*Faerie Queene.* Bk. IV.
                                Canto VII. St. 15.

The world knows nothing of its greatest men.
  e.   SIR HENRY TAYLOR—*Philip Van
            Artevelde.* Pt. I. Act I. Sc. 5.

She dwelt among the untrodden ways
Beside the springs of Dove,
A maid whom there were none to praise
And very few to love.
  f.   WORDSWORTH—*She Dwelt Among the
                                Untrodden Ways.*

She lived unknown, and few could know
When Lucy ceased to be;
But she is in her grave, and oh!
The difference to me!
  g.   WORDSWORTH—*She Dwelt Among the
                                Untrodden Ways.*

OBSERVATION.

Oh, wad some power the giftie gie us
To see oursel's as ithers see us!
It wad frae monie a blunder free us,
  And foolish notion.
  h.   BURNS—*To a Louse.*

Let Observation, with extensive view,
Survey mankind from China to Peru.
  i.   SAM'L JOHNSON—*The Vanity of Human
                                Wishes.*

And in his brain,
Which is as dry as the remainder biscuit
After a voyage, he hath strange places cramm'd
With observation, the which he vents
In mangled forms.
  j.   *As You Like It.* Act II. Sc. 7. L. 38.

OCCUPATIONS.

I hold every man a debtor to his profession;
from the which as men of course do seek to
receive countenance and profit, so ought they
of duty to endeavor themselves, by way of
amends, to be a help and ornament there-
unto.
  k.   BACON—*Maxims of the Law.* Preface.

The ugliest of trades have their moments of
pleasure. Now, if I were a grave-digger, or
even a hangman, there are some people I
could work for with a great deal of enjoyment.
  l.   DOUGLAS JERROLD—*Jerrold's Wit.
                                Ugly Trades.*

And sure the Eternal Master found
The single talent well employ'd.
  m.   SAM'L JOHNSON—*On the Death of
                                Robert Levet.* St. 7.

The hand of little employment hath the
daintier sense.
  n.   *Hamlet.* Act V. Sc. 1. L. 77.

Thus Nero went up and down Greece and
challenged the fiddlers at their trade. Æropus,
a Macedonian king, made lanterns; Har-
catius, the king of Parthia, was a mole-
catcher; and Biantes, the Lydian, filed needles.
  o.   JEREMY TAYLOR—*Holy Living.* Ch. I.
            Sec. 1.   *Rules for Employing Our Time.*

Acting—The Stage.

Farce follow'd Comedy, and reach'd her prime,
In ever-laughing Foote's fantastic time;
Mad wag! who pardon'd none, nor spared
        the best,
And turn'd some very serious things to jest.
Nor church nor state escaped his public sneers,
Arms nor the gown, priests, lawyers, volun-
        teers;
"Alas, poor Yorick!" now forever mute!
Whoever loves a laugh must sigh for Foote.

We smile, perforce, when histrionic scenes
Ape the swoln dialogue of kings and queens,
When "Chrononhotonthologos must die,"
And Arthur struts in mimic majesty.
  p.   BYRON—*Hints from Horace.* L. 329.

I think I love and reverence all arts equally, only putting my own just above the
others; because in it I recognize the union
and culmination of my own. To me it seems
as if when God conceived the world, that was
Poetry; He formed it, and that was Sculpture; He colored it, and that was Painting;
He peopled it with living beings, and that
was the grand, divine, eternal Drama.
  q.   CHARLOTTE CUSHMAN.

See, how these rascals use me! They will
not let my play run; and yet they steal my
thunder.
  r.   JOHN DENNIS—See *Biographia
                                Britannica.* Vol. V. P. 103.

Like hungry guests, a sitting audience looks:
Plays are like suppers; poets are the cooks.
The founder's you: the table is this place:
The carvers we: the prologue is the grace.
Each act, a course, each scene, a different dish,
Though we're in Lent, I doubt you're still for
   flesh.
Satire's the sauce, high-season'd, sharp and
   rough.
Kind masks and beaux, I hope you're pepper-
   proof?
Wit is the wine; but 'tis so scarce the true
Poets, like vintners, balderdash and brew.
Your surly scenes, where rant and bloodshed
   join,
Are butcher's meat, a battle's a sirloin:
Your scenes of love, so flowing, soft and
   chaste,
Are water-gruel without salt or taste.
   a.   GEORGE FARQUHAR—*The Inconstant;*
       or, The Way to Win Him. Prologue.

Prologues like compliments are loss of time;
'Tis penning bows and making legs in rhyme.
   b.   DAVID GARRICK—*Prologue to Crisp's*
       Tragedy of Virginia.

Prologues precede the piece in mournful verse,
As undertakers walk before the hearse.
   c.   DAVID GARRICK—*Apprentice.*
                     Prologue.

On the stage he was natural, simple, affecting,
'Twas only that when he was off, he was acting.
   d.   GOLDSMITH—*Retaliation.* L. 101.

Everybody has his own theatre, in which
he is manager, actor, prompter, playwright,
sceneshifter, boxkeeper, doorkeeper, all in
one, and audience into the bargain.
   e.   J. C. AND A. W. HARE—*Guesses at*
                          Truth.

The world's a theatre, the earth a stage,
Which God and Nature do with actors fill.
   f.   THOMAS HEYWOOD—*An Apology for*
       Actors. The Author to His Booke.

It's very hard! Oh, Dick, my boy,
It's very hard one can't enjoy
   A little private spouting;
But sure as Lear or Hamlet lives,
Up comes our master, Bounce! and gives
   The tragic Muse a routing.
   g.   HOOD—*The Stage-Struck Hero.*

And Tragedy should blush as much to stoop
To the low mimic follies of a farce,
As a grave matron would to dance with girls.
   h.   HORACE—*Of the Art of Poetry.* L. 272.
               Wentworth Dillon's trans.

The drama's laws, the drama's patrons give.
For we that live to please, must please to live.
   i.   SAM'L JOHNSON—*Prologue Spoken by*
       Mr. Garrick on Opening Drury Lane
           Theatre. 1747. L. 53.

Who teach the mind its proper face to scan,
And hold the faithful mirror up to man.
   j.   ROBERT LLOYD—*The Actor.* L. 265.

Is it not a noble farce wherein kings, republics, and emperors have for so many ages
played their parts, and to which the vast
universe serves for a theatre?
   k.   MONTAIGNE—*Of the Most Excellent Men.*

A long, exact, and serious comedy;
In every scene some moral let it teach,
And, if it can, at once both please and preach.
   l.   POPE—*Epistle to Mrs. Blount. With*
             the Works of Voiture. L. 22.

There still remains to mortify a wit
The many-headed monster of the pit.
   m.   POPE—*Horace.* Ep. I. Bk. II. L. 304.

To wake the soul by tender strokes of art,
To raise the genius, and to mend the heart;
To make mankind, in conscious virtue bold,
Live o'er each scene, and be what they be-
   hold—
For this the tragic Muse first trod the stage.
   n.   POPE—*Prologue to Addison's Cato.*
                          L. 1.

Your scene precariously subsists too long
On French translation and Italian song.
Dare to have sense yourselves; assert the
   stage;
Be justly warm'd with your own native rage.
   o.   POPE—*Prologue to Addison's Cato.*
                        L. 42.

Tom Goodwin was an actor-man,
   Old Drury's pride and boast,
In all the light and spritely parts,
   Especially the ghost.
   p.   J. G. SAXE—*The Ghost Player.*

The play bill which is said to have announced the tragedy of Hamlet, the character
of the Prince of Denmark being left out.
   q.   SCOTT—*The Talisman.* Introduction.

A beggarly account of empty boxes.
   r.   *Romeo and Juliet.* Act V. Sc. 1.
                        L. 45.

A hit, a very palpable hit.
   s.   *Hamlet.* Act V. Sc. 2. L. 294.

And, like a strutting player, whose conceit
Lies in his hamstring, and doth think it rich
To hear the wooden dialogue and sound
'Twixt his stretch'd footing and the scaf-
   foldage.
   t.   *Troilus and Cressida.* Act I. Sc. 3.
                       L. 153.

A play there is, my lord, some ten words long,
Which is as brief as I have known a play;
But by ten words, my lord, it is too long,
Which makes it tedious.
   u.   *Midsummer-Night's Dream.* Act V.
                     Sc. 1. L. 61.

As in a theatre, the eyes of men,
After a well-grac'd actor leaves the stage,
Are idly bent on him that enters next,
Thinking his prattle to be tedious.
a.　　*Richard II.* Act V. Sc. 2. L. 23.

Come, sit down, every mother's son, and rehearse your parts.
b.　　*Midsummer-Night's Dream.* Act III.
Sc. I. L. 74.

Good, my lord, will you see the players well
bestowed? Do you hear, let them be well
used; for they are the abstract and brief
chronicles of the time: after your death you
were better have a bad epitaph than their ill
report while you live.
c.　　*Hamlet.* Act II. Sc. 2. L. 545.

I can counterfeit the deep tragedian;
Speak and look back, and pry on every side,
Tremble and start at wagging of a straw,
Intending deep suspicion.
d.　　*Richard III.* Act III. Sc. 5. L. 5.

If it be true that good wine needs no bush,
'tis true that a good play needs no epilogue.
e.　　*As You Like It.* Epilogue. L. 3.

I have heard
That guilty creatures sitting at a play,
Have, by the very cunning of the scene,
Been struck so to the soul that presently
They have proclaim'd their malefactions;
For murder, though it have no tongue, will
speak
With most miraculous organ.
f.　　*Hamlet.* Act II. Sc. 2. L. 617.

Is it not monstrous that this player here,
But in a fiction, in a dream of passion,
Could force his soul so to his own conceit
That from her working all his visage wann'd.
g.　　*Hamlet.* Act II. Sc. 2. L. 577.

Is there no play,
To ease the anguish of a torturing hour?
h.　　*Midsummer-Night's Dream.* Act V.
Sc. 1. L. 36.

Like a dull actor now,
I have forgot my part, and I am out,
Even to a full disgrace.
i.　　*Coriolanus.* Act V. Sc. 3. L. 40.

O, there be players that I have seen play,
and heard others praise, and that highly, not
to speak it profanely, that, neither having the
accent of Christians nor the gait of Christian,
pagan, nor man, have so strutted and bellowed that I have thought some of nature's
journeymen had made men and not made
them well, they imitated humanity so abominably.
j.　　*Hamlet.* Act III. Sc. 2. L. 32.

Speak the speech, I pray you, as I pro-
nounced it to you, trippingly on the tongue;
but if you mouth it, as many of your players
do, I had as lief the town-crier spoke my
lines. Nor do not saw the air too much with
your hand, thus, but use all gently; for in
the very torrent, tempest, and, as I may say,
the whirlwind of passion, you must acquire
and beget a temperance that may give it
smoothness.
k.　　*Hamlet.* Act III. Sc. 2. L. 1.

The play's the thing
Wherein I'll catch the conscience of the king.
l.　　*Hamlet.* Act II. Sc. 2. L. 633.

What's Hecuba to him, or he to Hecuba,
That he should weep for her? What would
he do,
Had he the motive and the cue for passion
That I have? He would drown the stage with
tears.
m.　　*Hamlet.* Act II. Sc. 2. L. 585.

Lo, where the Stage, the poor, degraded Stage,
Holds its warped mirror to a gaping age!
n.　　CHARLES SPRAGUE—*Curiosity.*

The play is done; the curtain drops,
Slow falling to the prompter's bell:
A moment yet the actor stops,
And looks around, to say farewell.
It is an irksome word and task:
And, when he's laughed and said his say,
He shows, as he removes the mask,
A face that's anything but gay.
o.　　THACKERAY—*The End of the Play.*

In other things the knowing artist may
Judge better than the people; but a play,
(Made for delight, and for no other use)
If you approve it not, has no excuse.
p.　　EDMUND WALLER—*Prologue to the
Maid's Tragedy.* L. 35.

Agriculture.

Look up! the wide extended plain
Is billowy with its ripened grain,
And on the summer winds are rolled
Its waves of emerald and gold.
q.　　WM. HENRY BURLEIGH—*The Harvest-
Call.* St. 5.

The first farmer was the first man, and all
historic nobility rests on possession and use
of land.
r.　　EMERSON—*Society and Solitude.
Farming.*

Oft did the harvest to their sickle yield:
Their furrow oft the stubborn glebe has
broke:
How jocund did they drive their team a-field!
How bow'd the woods beneath their sturdy
stroke!
s.　　GRAY—*Elegy in a Country Churchyard.*
St. 7.

Ye rigid Ploughmen! bear in mind
  Your labor is for future hours.
Advance! spare not! nor look behind!
  Plough deep and straight with all your
    powers!
   a.   RICHARD HENGIST HORNE—*The Plough.*

Earth is here so kind, that just tickle her
with a hoe and she laughs with a harvest.
   b.   DOUGLAS JERROLD—*A Land of Plenty.*
            (Australia.)
The life of the husbandman,—a life fed by
the bounty of earth and sweetened by the airs
of heaven.
   c.   DOUGLAS JERROLD—*Jerrold's Wit. The
            Husbandman's Life.*
And the maize-field grew and ripened,
Till it stood in all the splendor
Of its garments green and yellow.
   d.   LONGFELLOW—*Hiawatha.* Pt. XIII.
                      L. 175.
Adam, well may we labour, still to dress
This garden, still to tend plant, herb, and
    flower.
   e.   MILTON—*Paradise Lost.* Bk. IX.
                      L. 205.
                  Each tree
Laden with fairest fruit, that hung to th' eye
Tempting, stirr'd in me sudden appetite
To pluck and eat.
   f.   MILTON—*Paradise Lost.* Bk. VIII.
                      L. 306.
Here Ceres' gifts in waving prospect stand,
And nodding tempt the joyful reaper's hand.
   g.   POPE—*Windsor Forest.* L. 39.

Our rural ancestors, with little blest,
Patient of labour when the end was rest,
Indulg'd the day that hous'd their annual
    grain,
With feasts, and off'rings, and a thankful strain.
   h.   POPE—*Second Book of Horace.* Ep. I.
                      L. 241.
When weary reapers quit the sultry field,
And, crown'd with corn, their thanks to Ceres
    yield.
   i.   POPE—*Summer.* L. 65.

Where grows?—where grows it not? If vain
    our toil,
We ought to blame the culture, not the soil.
   j.   POPE—*Essay on Man.* Ep. IV. L. 13.

In ancient times, the sacred Plough employ'd
The Kings and awful Fathers of mankind :
And some, with whom compared your insect-
    tribes
Are but the beings of a summer's day,
Have held the Scale of Empire, ruled the
    Storm
Of mighty War; then, with victorious hand,
Disdaining little delicacies, seized
The Plough, and, greatly independent, scorned
All the vile stores corruption can bestow.
   k.   THOMSON—*The Seasons. Spring.*
                      L. 58.

Ill husbandry braggeth
  To go with the best:
Good husbandry baggeth
  Up gold in his chest.
   l.   TUSSER—*Five Hundred Points
           of Good Husbandry.* Ch. LII.
           Comparing Good Husbandry.

Ill husbandry lieth
  In prison for debt:
Good husbandry spieth
  Where profit to get.
   m.   TUSSER—*Five Hundred Points
           of Good Husbandry.* Ch. LII.
           Comparing Good Husbandry.

E'en in mid-harvest, while the jocund swain
Pluck'd from the brittle stalk the golden grain,
Oft have I seen the war of winds contend,
And prone on earth th' infuriate storm de-
    scend,
Waste far and wide, and by the roots uptorn,
The heavy harvest sweep through ether borne,
As the light straw and rapid stubble fly
In dark'ning whirlwinds round the wintry
    sky.
   n.   VIRGIL—*Georgics I.* L. 351.
                    Sotheby's trans.

Blessed be agriculture! if one does not have
too much of it.
   o.   CHAS. DUDLEY WARNER—*My Summer
           in a Garden.* Preliminary.

When tillage begins, other arts follow. The
farmers, therefore, are the founders of human
civilization.
   p.   DANIEL WEBSTER—*Remarks on
           Agriculture, Jan. 13, 1840.* P. 457.

But let the good old corn adorn
  The hills our fathers trod;
Still let us, for his golden corn,
  Send up our thanks to God!
   q.   WHITTIER—*The Corn-Song.*

Heap high the farmer's wintry hoard!
  Heap high the golden corn!
No richer gift has Autumn poured
  From out her lavish horn!
   r.   WHITTIER—*The Corn-Song.*

The cattle are grazing,
Their heads never raising:
There are forty feeding like one!
   s.   WORDSWORTH—*The Cock is Crowing.*
      (*Written in March while on the bridge.*

Alchemy.

               If by fire
Of sooty coal th' empiric alchymist
Can turn, or holds it possible to turn,
Metals of drossiest ore to perfect gold.
   t.   MILTON—*Paradise Lost.* Bk. V.
                    L. 439.

The starving chemist in his golden views
Supremely blest.
  a. POPE—*Essay on Man.* Ep. II. L. 269.

          The glorious sun
Stays in his course and plays the alchemist,
Turning with splendour of his precious eye
The meager cloddy earth to glittering gold.
  b. *King John.* Act III. Sc. 1. L. 77.

You are an alchemist; make gold of that.
  c. *Timon of Athens.* Act V. Sc. 1.
                                      L. 117.

Architecture.

Houses are built to live in, not to look on;
therefore, let use be preferred before uniformity, except where both may be had.
  d. BACON—*Essays. Of Building.*

There was King Bradmond's palace,
Was never none richer, the story says:
For all the windows and the walls
Were painted with gold, both towers and
  halls;
Pillars and doors all were of brass;
Windows of latten were set with glass;
It was so rich in many wise,
That it was like a paradise.
  e. SIR BEVIS OF HAMPTOUN—*MS. in Caius
                                      College.*

Old houses mended,
Cost little less than new, before they're ended.
  f. COLLEY CIBBER—*Prologue to the Double
                              Gallant.* L. 15.

A man who could build a church, as one
may say, by squinting at a sheet of paper.
  g. DICKENS—*Martin Chuzzelwit.* Vol. II.
                                      Ch. VI.

Earth proudly wears the Parthenon
As the best gem upon her zone.
  h. EMERSON—*The Problem.*

The Gothic cathedral is a blossoming in
stone subdued by the insatiable demand of
harmony in man. The mountain of granite
blooms into an eternal flower, with the lightness and delicate finish, as well as the ærial
proportions and perspective of vegetable
beauty.
  i. EMERSON—*Essays. Of History.*

The hand that rounded Peter's dome
And groined the aisles of Christian Rome,
Wrought in a sad sincerity:
Himself from God he could not free;
He builded better than he knew;
The conscious stone to beauty grew.
  j. EMERSON—*The Problem.*

Rich windows that exclude the light,
And passages that lead to nothing.
  k. GRAY—*A Long Story.*

No workman steel, no pond'rous axes rung:
Like some tall palm the noiseless fabric sprung.
  l. BISHOP HEBER—*Palestine.* L. 163.

Grandeur * * * consists in form, and
not in size: and to the eye of the philosopher,
the curve drawn on a paper two inches long,
is just as magnificent, just as symbolic of
divine mysteries and melodies, as when embodied in the span of some cathedral roof.
  m. CHARLES KINGSLEY—*Prose Idylls.
                              My Winter Garden.*

          The architect
Built his great heart into these sculptured
  stones,
And with him toiled his children, and their
  lives
Were builded, with his own, into the walls,
As offerings unto God.
  n. LONGFELLOW—*Christus. The Golden
              Legend.* Pt. III. *In the Cathedral.*

    A fabric huge
Rose, like an exhalation.
  o. MILTON—*Paradise Lost.* Bk. I. L. 710.

          A pillar'd shade
High over-arch'd, and echoing walks between.
  p. MILTON—*Paradise Lost.* Bk. IX.
                                      L. 1,106.

          Nor did there want
Cornice or frieze with bossy sculpture graven.
  q. MILTON—*Paradise Lost.* Bk. I. L. 715.

          The hasty multitude
Admiring enter'd, and the work some praise,
And some the architect: his hand was known
In heaven by many a tower'd structure high,
Where scepter'd angels held their residence,
And sat as princes.
  r. MILTON—*Paradise Lost.* Bk. I. L. 730.

Thus when we view some well-proportion'd
  dome,
      *   *   *   *   *   *
No single parts unequally surprise,
All comes united to th' admiring eyes.
  s. POPE—*Essay on Criticism.* Pt. II.
                                      L. 47.

Architecture is the work of nations.
  t. RUSKIN—*True and Beautiful.
                              Sculpture.*

Better the rudest work that tells a story or
records a fact, than the richest without meaning. There should not be a single ornament
put upon great civic buildings, without some
intellectual intention.
  u. RUSKIN—*Seven Lamps of Architecture.
                      The Lamp of Memory.*

It was stated, * * * that the value of
architecture depended on two distinct characters:—the one, the impression it receives
from human power; the other, the image it
bears of the natural creation.
  v. RUSKIN—*Seven Lamps of Architecture.
                      The Lamp of Beauty.*

I would have, then, our ordinary dwelling-houses built to last, and built to be lovely ; as rich and full of pleasantness as may be within and without : * * * with such differences as might suit and express each man's character and occupation, and partly his history.

> *a.* RUSKIN—*Seven Lamps of Architecture.*
> *The Lamp of Memory.*

No person who is not a great sculptor or painter, *can* be an architect. If he is not a sculptor or painter, he can only be a *builder.*

> *b.* RUSKIN—*True and Beautiful.*
> *Sculpture.*

Ornamentation is the principal part of architecture, considered as a subject of fine art.

> *c.* RUSKIN—*True and Beautiful.*
> *Sculpture.*

Therefore when we build, let us think that we build (public edifices) forever. Let it not be for present delight, nor for present use alone, let it be such work as our descendants will thank us for, and let us think, as we lay stone on stone, that a time is to come when those stones will be held sacred because our hands have touched them, and that men will say as they look upon the labor and wrought substance of them, " See ! this our fathers did for us."

> *d.* RUSKIN—*Seven Lamps of Architecture.*
> *The Lamp of Memory.*

Architecture is frozen music.

> *e.* SCHELLING—*Philosophie der Kunst.*
> P. 576.

'Fore God, you have here a goodly dwelling and a rich.

> *f.* *Henry IV.* Pt. II. Act V. Sc. 3.
> L. 6.

He that has a house to put 's head in has a good head-piece.

> *g.* *King Lear.* Act III. Sc. 2. L. 25.

> When we mean to build,
> We first survey the plot, then draw the model ;
> And when we see the figure of the house,
> Then must we rate the cost of the erection.
> *h.* *Henry IV.* Pt. II. Act I. Sc. 3. L. 41.

Astronomy.

It does at first appear that an astronomer rapt in abstraction, while he gazes on a star, must feel more exquisite delight than a farmer who is conducting his team.

> *i.* ISAAC DISRAELI—*Literary Character of
> Men of Genius. On Habituating
> Ourselves to an Individual Pursuit.*

> And God made two great lights, great for their use
> To man, the greater to have rule by day,
> The less by night, altern.
> *j.* MILTON—*Paradise Lost.* Bk. VII.
> L. 346.

At night astronomers agree.

> *k.* PRIOR—*Phillis's Age.* St. 3.

> And teach me how
> To name the bigger light, and how the less,
> That burn by day and night.
> *l.* *Tempest.* Act I. Sc. 2. L. 334.

> My lord, they say five moons were seen to-night :
> Four fixed, and the fifth did whirl about
> The other four in wondrous motion.
> *m.* *King John.* Act IV. Sc. 2. L. 182.

> These earthly godfathers of heaven's lights
> That give a name to every fixed star
> Have no more profit of their shining nights
> Than those that walk, and wot not what they are.
> *n.* *Love's Labour's Lost.* Act I. Sc. 1.
> L. 88.

> " But," quoth his neighbor, " when the sun
> From East to West his course has run,
> How comes it that he shows his face
> Next morning in his former place?"
> " Ho ! there's a pretty question, truly !"
> Replied our wight, with an unruly
> Burst of laughter and delight,
> So much his triumph seemed to please him :
> " Why, blockhead ! he goes back at night,
> And that's the reason no one sees him !"
> *o.* HORACE SMITH—*The Astronomical
> Alderman.* St. 5.

> O how loud
> It calls devotion ! genuine growth of night !
> Devotion ! daughter of Astronomy !
> An undevout Astronomer is mad.
> *p.* YOUNG—*Night Thoughts.* Night IX.
> L. 774.

Authorship.

The circumstance which gives authors an advantage above all these great masters, is this, that they can multiply their originals; or rather, can make copies of their works, to what number they please, which shall be as valuable as the originals themselves.

> *q.* ADDISON—*The Spectator.* No. 166.

> Write to the mind and heart, and let the ear
> Glean after what it can.
> *r.* BAILEY—*Festus.* Sc. *Home.*

Indeed, unless a man can link his written thoughts with the everlasting wants of men, so that they shall draw from them as from wells, there is no more immortality to the thoughts and feelings of the soul than to the muscles and the bones.

> *s.* HENRY WARD BEECHER—*Star Papers.*
> *Oxford. Bodleian Library.*

There is probably no hell for authors in the next world—they suffer so much from critics and publishers in this.

    a.   Bovee—*Summaries of Thought.*
                            Authors.

A man of moderate Understanding, thinks he writes divinely : A man of good Understanding, thinks he writes reasonably.

    b.   De La Bruyère—*The Characters or
             Manners of the Present Age.* Ch. I.

A man starts upon a sudden, takes Pen, Ink, and Paper, and without ever having had a thought of it before, resolves within himself he will write a Book ; he has no Talent at Writing, but he wants fifty Guineas.

    c.   De La Bruyère—*The Characters or
             Manners of the Present Age.* Ch. XV.

         And so I penned
It down, until at last it came to be,
For length and breadth, the bigness which
     you see.

    d.   Bunyan—*Pilgrim's Progress. Apology
                          for his Book.*

Writers, especially when they act in a body and with one direction, have great influence on the public mind.

    e.   Burke—*Reflections on the Revolution in
                              France.*

The book that he has made renders its author this service in return, that so long as the book survives, its author remains immortal and cannot die.

    f.   Richard de Bury—*Philobiblon.*
            Ch. I. 21. E. C. Thomas' trans.

And force them, though it was in spite
Of Nature and their stars, to write.

    g.   Butler—*Hudibras.* Pt. I. Canto I.
                              L. 647.

But every fool describes, in these bright days,
His wondrous journey to some foreign court,
And spawns his quarto, and demands your
     praise,—
Death to his publisher, to him 'tis sport.

    h.   Byron—*Don Juan.* Canto V. St. 52.

But words are things, and a small drop of
     ink,
Falling, like dew, upon a thought produces
That which makes thousands, perhaps millions think.

    i.   Byron—*Don Juan.* Canto III. St. 88.

Dear authors! suit your topics to your
     strength,
And ponder well your subject, and its length ;
Nor lift your load, before you're quite aware
What weight your shoulders will, or will not,
     bear.

    j.   Byron—*Hints from Horace.* L. 59.

Apt Alliteration's artful aid.

    k.   Churchill—*The Prophecy of Famine.*
                              L. 86.

That writer does the most, who gives his reader the *most* knowledge, and takes from him the *least* time.

    l.   C. C. Colton—*Lacon.* Preface.

Habits of close attention, thinking heads,
Become more rare as dissipation spreads,
Till authors hear at length one general cry
Tickle and entertain us, or we die !

    m.   Cowper—*Retirement.* L. 707.

None but an author knows an author's cares,
Or Fancy's fondness for the child she bears.

    n.   Cowper—*The Progress of Error.* L. 518.

    So that the jest is clearly to be seen,
Not in the words—but in the gap between ;
Manner is all in all, whate'er is writ,
The substitute for genius, sense, and wit.

    o.   Cowper—*Table Talk.* L. 540.

Oh ! rather give me commentators plain,
Who with no deep researches vex the brain ;
Who from the dark and doubtful love to run,
And hold their glimmering tapers to the sun.

    p.   Crabbe—*The Parish Register.* Pt. I.
                          Introduction.

"Gracious heavens ! " he cries out, leaping up and catching hold of his hair, "what's this? Print ! "

    q.   Dickens—*Christmas Stories. Somebody's
                      Luggage.* Ch. III.

And choose an author as you choose a friend.

    r.   Wentworth Dillon—*Essay on
                      Translated Verse.* L. 96.

The men, who labour and digest things most,
Will be much apter to despond than boast ;
For if your author be profoundly good,
'Twill cost you dear before he's understood.

    s.   Wentworth Dillon—*Essay on
                      Translated Verse.* L. 163.

The author who speaks about his own books is almost as bad as a mother who talks about her own children.

    t.   Benj. Disraeli—*Speech.* Nov. 19, 1870.

And, after all, it is style alone by which posterity will judge of a great work, for an author can have nothing truly his own but his style.

    u.   Isaac Disraeli—*Literary Miscellanies.
                              Style.*

The unhappy man, who once has trail'd a
     pen,
Lives not to please himself, but other men ;
Is always drudging, wastes his life and blood,
Yet only eats and drinks what you think
     good.

    v.   Dryden—*Prologue to Lee's Cæsar
                             Borgia.*

All writing comes by the grace of God, and all doing and having.
> *a.* EMERSON—*Essays. Of Experience.*

For no man can write anything who does not think that what he writes is, for the time, the history of the world.
> *b.* EMERSON—*Essays. Of Nature.*

The lover of letters loves power too.
> *c.* EMERSON—*Society and Solitude. Clubs.*

The writer, like a priest, must be exempted from secular labor. His work needs a frolic health ; he must be at the top of his condition.
> *d.* EMERSON—*Poetry and Imagination.*
> *Creation.*

Envy's a sharper spur than pay :
No author ever spar'd a brother ;
Wits are gamecocks to one another.
> *e.* GAY—*The Elephant and the Bookseller.*
> L. 74.

Every author, in some degree, portrays himself in his works even be it against his will.
> *f.* GOETHE—*The Poet's Year.*

The most original modern authors are not so because they advance what is new, but simply because they know how to put what they have to say, as if it had never been said before.
> *g.* GOETHE.

One writer, for instance, excels at a plan, or a title-page, another works away the body of the book, and a third is a dab at an index.
> *h.* GOLDSMITH—*The Bee.* No. 1.
> Oct. 6, 1759.

His [Burke's] imperial fancy has laid all nature under tribute, and has collected riches from every scene of the creation and every walk of art.
> *i.* ROBERT HALL—*Apology for the*
> *Freedom of the Press.* Sec. IV.

Whatever an author puts between the two covers of his book is public property ; whatever of himself he does not put there is his private property, as much as if he had never written a word.
> *j.* GAIL HAMILTON—*Country Living and*
> *Country Thinking.* Preface.

To be really cosmopolitan a man must be at home even in his own country.
> *k.* T. W. HIGGINSON—*Short Studies of*
> *American Authors. Henry James, Jr.*

But every little busy scribbler now
Swells with the praises which he gives himself;
And, taking sanctuary in the crowd,
Brags of his impudence, and scorns to mend.
> *l.* HORACE—*Of the Art of Poetry.* L. 475.
> Wentworth Dillon's trans.

Let your literary compositions be kept from the public eye for nine years at least.
> *m.* HORACE—*An Introduction to the Art of*
> *Poetry.*

A man may write at any time if he set himself doggedly to it.
> *n.* SAM'L JOHNSON—*Boswell's Life of*
> *Johnson.* 1773.

Each change of many-coloured life he drew,
Exhausted worlds and then imagined new :
Existence saw him spurn her bounded reign,
And panting Time toil'd after him in vain.
> *o.* SAM'L JOHNSON—*Prologue on the*
> *Opening of the Drury Lane Theatre.*

No man but a blockhead ever wrote except for money.
> *p.* SAM'L JOHNSON—*Boswell's Life of*
> *Johnson.* 1776.

The chief glory of every people arises from its authors.
> *q.* SAM'L JOHNSON—*Preface to Dictionary.*

There are two things which I am confident I can do very well ; one is an introduction to any literary work, stating what it is to contain, and how it should be executed in the most perfect manner.
> *r.* SAM'L JOHNSON—*Boswell's Life of*
> *Johnson.* 1755.

To write much, and to write rapidly, are empty boasts. The world desires to know *what* you have done, and not *how* you did it.
> *s.* GEORGE HENRY LEWES—*The Spanish*
> *Drama.* Ch. III.

If you once understand an author's character, the comprehension of his writings becomes easy.
> *t.* LONGFELLOW—*Hyperion.* Bk. I.
> Ch. V.

Look, then, into thine heart and write !
> *u.* LONGFELLOW—*Voices of the Night.*
> Prelude. St. 19.

Perhaps the greatest lesson which the lives of literary men teach us is told in a single word : Wait !
> *v.* LONGFELLOW—*Hyperion.* Bk. I.
> Ch. VIII.

Whatever hath been written shall remain,
Nor be erased nor written o'er again ;
The unwritten only still belongs to thee :
Take heed, and ponder well what that shall be.
> *w.* LONGFELLOW—*Morituri Salutamus.*
> L. 168.

It may be glorious to write
Thoughts that shall glad the two or three
High souls, like those far stars that come in sight
Once in a century.
> *x.* LOWELL—*An Incident in a Railroad*
> *Car.*

He that commeth in print because he woulde be knowen, is like the foole that commeth into the Market because he woulde be seen.

a.   LYLY—*Euphues.   The Anatomy of Wit.
To the Gentlemen Readers.*

He who writes prose builds his temple to Fame in rubble; he who writes verses builds it in granite.

b.   BULWER-LYTTON—*Caxtoniana.
Essay XXVII.   The Spirit of
Conservatism.*

No author ever drew a character, consistent to human nature, but what he was forced to ascribe to it many inconsistencies.

c.   BULWER-LYTTON—*What Will He Do
With It?* Bk. IV. Ch. XIV.
Heading.

The ink of the scholar is more sacred than the blood of the martyr.

d.   MOHAMMED—*Tribute to Reason.*

Authors are partial to their wit, 'tis true, But are not critics to their judgment too?

e.   POPE—*Essay on Criticism.* L. 17.

Authors, like coins, grow dear as they grow old.

f.   POPE—*Satires. Epistles. Odes of
Horace.* Ep. I. Bk. II. L. 35.

E'en copious Dryden wanted, or forgot, The last and greatest art—the art to blot.

g.   POPE—*Second Book of Horace.*
Ep. I. L. 280.

In every work regard the writer's end, Since none can compass more than they intend.

h.   POPE—*Essay on Criticism.* Pt. II.
L. 55.

'Tis hard to say if greater want of skill Appear in writing or in judging ill; But, of the two less dang'rous is th' offence To tire our patience than mislead our sense.

i.   POPE—*Essay on Criticism.* L. 1.

True ease in writing comes from art, not chance, As those move easiest who have learn'd to dance.

j.   POPE—*Essay on Criticism.* L. 362.

Whether the darken'd room to muse invite, Or whiten'd wall provoke the skew'r to write; In durance, exile, Bedlam, or the Mint, Like Lee or Budgel I will rhyme and print.

k.   POPE—*Second Book of Horace.*
Satire I. L. 97.

Why did I write? what sin to me unknown Dipt me in ink, my parents', or my own? As yet a child, nor yet a fool to fame, I lisp'd in numbers, for the numbers came.

l.   POPE—*Prologue to Satires.* L. 125.

With him most authors steal their works, or buy; Garth did not write his own Dispensary.

m.   POPE—*Essay on Criticism.* L. 618.

Let him be kept from paper, pen, and ink; So may he cease to write, and learn to think.

n.   PRIOR—*To a Person who Wrote Ill.
On Same Person.*

'Tis not how well an author says, But 'tis how much, that gathers praise.

o.   PRIOR—*Epistle to Fleetwood Shepherd.*

As though I lived to write, and wrote to live.

p.   SAM'L ROGERS—*Italy. A Character.*
L. 16.

Devise, wit; write, pen; for I am for whole volumes in folio.

q.   *Love's Labour's Lost.* Act I. Sc. 2.
L. 190.

Write till your ink be dry, and with your tears Moist it again, and frame some feeling line That may discover such integrity.

r.   *Two Gentlemen of Verona.* Act III.
Sc. 2. L. 74.

Of all those arts in which the wise excel, Nature's chief masterpiece is writing well.

s.   JOHN SHEFFIELD (Duke of
Buckinghamshire)—*Essay on Poetry.*

Look in thy heart and write.

t.   SIR PHILIP SIDNEY—*Wm. Gray's Life
of Sir Philip Sidney.*

The great and good do not die even in this world. Embalmed in books, their spirits walk abroad. The book is a living voice. It is an intellect to which one still listens.

u.   SAM'L SMILES—*Character.* Ch. X.

In every author let us distinguish the man from his works.

v.   VOLTAIRE—*A Philosophical Dictionary.
Poets.*

So must the writer, whose productions should Take with the vulgar, be of vulgar mould.

w.   EDMUND WALLER—*Epistle to Mr.
Killegrew.*

This dull product of a scoffer's pen.

x.   WORDSWORTH—*The Excursion.* Bk. II.

An author! 'tis a venerable name! How few deserve it, and what numbers claim! Unbless'd with sense above their peers re-fined, Who stand up dictators to mankind? Nay, who dare shine, if not in virtue's cause? That sole proprietor of just applause.

y.   YOUNG—*Epistles to Mr. Pope.* Ep. II.
From Oxford. L. 15.

For who can write so fast as men run mad?
  a.   YOUNG—*Love of Fame.* Satire I.
                          L. 286.

Some write, confin'd by physic; some, by debt;
Some, for 'tis Sunday; some, because 'tis wet;
    *   *   *   *   *   *
Another writes because his father writ,
And proves himself a bastard by his wit.
  b.   YOUNG—*Epistle to Pope.* Bk. I. L. 75.

Blacksmithing.

And him who, with the steady sledge,
Smites the shrill anvil all day long.
  c.   BRYANT—*The Song of the Sower.* St. 4.

Curs'd be that wretch (Death's factor sure)
    who brought
Dire swords into the peaceful world, and
    taught
Smiths (who before could only make
The spade, the plough-share, and the rake)
Arts, in most cruel wise
Man's left to epitomize!
  d.   ABRAHAM COWLEY—*In Commendation
           of the Time we live under, the Reign
           of our gracious King, Charles II.*

Come, see the Dolphin's anchor forged; 'tis
    at a white heat now:
The billows ceased, the flames decreased;
    though on the forge's brow
The little flames still fitfully play through
    the sable mound;
And fitfully you still may see the grim smiths
    ranking round,
All clad in leathern panoply, their broad
    hands only bare;
Some rest upon their sledges here, some work
    the windlass there.
  e.   SAM'L FERGUSON—*The Forging of the
                  Anchor.* St. 1.

And the smith his iron measures hammered
    to the anvil's chime;
Thanking God, whose boundless wisdom
    makes the flowers of poesy bloom
In the forge's dust and cinders, in the tissues
    of the loom.
  f.   LONGFELLOW—*Nuremberg.* L. 34.

As great Pythagoras of yore,
Standing beside the blacksmith's door,
And hearing the hammers, as they smote
The anvils with a different note,
Stole from the varying tones, that hung
Vibrant on every iron tongue,
The secret of the sounding wire,
And formed the seven-chorded lyre.
  g.   LONGFELLOW—*To a Child.* L. 175.

Under a spreading chestnut tree
  The village smithy stands;
The smith, a mighty man is he,
  With large and sinewy hands;
And the muscles of his brawny arms
  Are strong as iron bands.
  h.   LONGFELLOW—*The Village Blacksmith.*

And he sang: "Hurra for my handiwork!"
  And the red sparks lit the air;
Not alone for the blade was the bright steel
    made;
  And he fashioned the first ploughshare.
  i.   CHAS. MACKAY—*Tubal Cain.* St. 4.

In other part stood one who, at the forge
Labouring, two massy clods of iron and brass
Had melted.
  j.   MILTON—*Paradise Lost.* Bk. XI.
                          L. 564.

I saw a smith stand with his hammer, thus,
The whilst his iron did on the anvil cool.
  k.   *King John.* Act IV. Sc. 2. L. 193.

The paynefull smith, with force of fervent
    heat,
The hardest yron soone doth mollify,
That with his heavy sledge he can it beat,
And fashion it to what he it list apply.
  l.   SPENSER—*Sonnet XXXII.*

Butchering.

Whoe'er has gone thro' London street,
Has seen a butcher gazing at his meat,
    And how he keeps
    Gloating upon a sheep's
Or bullock's personals, as if his own;
    How he admires his halves
    And quarters—and his calves,
As if in truth upon his own legs grown.
  m.   HOOD—*A Butcher.*

Who finds the heifer dead and bleeding fresh
And sees fast by a butcher with an axe,
But will suspect 'twas he that made the
    slaughter?
  n.   *Henry VI.* Pt. II. Act III. Sc. 2.
                          L. 188.

Why, that's spoken like an honest drovier;
    so they sell bullocks.
  o.   *Much Ado About Nothing.* Act II.
                      Sc. 1. L. 201.

The butcher in his killing clothes.
  p.   WALT WHITMAN—*The Workingmen.*
                      Pt. VI. St. 32.

Cabinet-Making.

Carved with figures strange and sweet,
All made out of the carver's brain.
  q.   COLERIDGE—*Christabel.* Pt. I.

Ingenious Fancy, never better pleased
Than when employ'd t' accommodate the
    fair,
Heard the sweet moan of pity, and devised
The soft settee; one elbow at each end,
And in the midst an elbow it received,
United yet divided, twain at once.
  r.   COWPER—*The Task.* Bk. I. L. 71.

[Handwritten note at bottom of page:] * the "smithy" is the blacksmith shop not the blacksmith GWV 3/21/51

Joint-stools were then created ; on three legs
Upborne they stood. Three legs upholding
    firm
A massy slab, in fashion square or round.
On such a stool immortal Alfred sat.
   a.   Cowper—*The Sofa.* Bk. I. L. 19.

           Necessity invented stools,
Convenience next suggested elbow-chairs,
And Luxury the accomplish'd Sofa last.
   b.   Cowper—*The Task.* Bk. I. L. 86.

A three-legg'd table, O ye fates !
   c.   Horace.

When on my three-foot stool I sit.
   d.   *Cymbeline.* Act III. Sc. 3. L. 89.

Carpentry.

Are the tools without, which the carpenter
puts forth his hands to, or are they and all
the carpentry within himself; and would he
not smile at the notion that chest or house is
more than he?
   e.   Cyrus A. Bartol—*The Rising Faith.*
                                 Personality.

In the elder days of Art,
  Builders wrought with greatest care
Each minute and unseen part ;
  For the Gods see everywhere.
   f.   Longfellow—*The Builders.* St. 5.

Sure if they cannot cut, it may be said
His saws are toothless, and his hatchets lead.
   g.   Pope—*Epilogue to Satires.* Dialogue II.
                                  L. 151.

He talks of wood : it is some carpenter.
   h.   *Henry VI.* Pt. I. Act V. Sc. 3.
                                  L. 90.

Speak, what trade art thou?
Why, sir, a carpenter.
  Where is thy leather apron and thy rule?
What dost thou with thy best apparel on?
   i.   *Julius Cæsar.* Act I. Sc. 1. L. 5.

The carpenter dresses his plank—the tongue
of his fore-plane whistles its wild ascending
lisp.
   j.   Walt Whitman—*Leaves of Grass.*
             Walt Whitman. Pt. XV. St. 77.

The house-builder at work in cities or any-
    where,
The preparatory jointing, squaring, sawing,
    mortising,
The hoist-up of beams, the push of them in
    their places, laying them regular,
Setting the studs by their tenons in the mor-
    tises, according as they were prepared,
The blows of the mallets and hammers.
   k.   Walt Whitman—*Song of the
             Broad-Axe.* Pt. III. St. 4.

Culinary.

Great pity were it if this beneficence of
Providence should be marr'd in the ordering,
so as to justly merit the Reflection of the old
proverb, that though God sends us meat, yet
the D— does cooks.
   l.   *The Cooks' and Confectioners' Dictionary,
        or the Accomplished Housewife's
        Companions.* London. 1724.

Cookery is become an art, a noble science ;
cooks are gentlemen.
   m.   Burton—*Anatomy of Melancholy.*
        Pt. I. Sec. II. Memb. 2. Subsec. II.

And nearer as they came, a genial savour
Of certain stews, and roast-meats, and pilaus,
Things which in hungry mortals' eyes find
    favour.
   n.   Byron—*Don Juan.* Canto V. St. 47.

Yet smelt roast meat, beheld a huge fire shine,
And cooks in motion with their clean arms
    bared.
   o.   Byron—*Don Juan.* Canto V. St. 50.

Ever a glutton, at another's cost,
But in whose kitchen dwells perpetual frost.
   p.   Dryden—*Fourth Satire of Persius.*
                                  L. 58.

Heaven sends us good meat, but the devil
sends us cooks.
   q.   David Garrick—*Epigram on
             Goldsmith's Retaliation.*

Here is *bread, which strengthens man's heart,*
and therefore is called *the staff of Life.*
   r.   Mathew Henry—*Commentaries.*
                   Psalm CIV. Verse 15.

Of herbs, and other country messes,
Which the neat-handed Phillis dresses.
   s.   Milton—*L'Allegro.* L. 85.

The vulgar boil, the learned roast, an egg.
   t.   Pope—*Satires. Horace. Epistle II.*
                           Bk. II. L. 85.

He that will have a cake out of the wheat
must needs tarry the grinding.
  Have I not tarried ?
  Ay, the grinding : but you must tarry the
bolting.
  Have I not tarried ?
  Ay, the bolting : but you must tarry the
leavening.
  Still have I tarried.
  Ay, to the leavening : but here's yet in the
word "hereafter" the kneading, the making
of the cake, the heating of the oven and the
baking : nay, you must stay the cooling too,
or you may chance to burn your lips.
   u.   *Troilus and Cressida.* Act I. Sc. 1.
                                  L. 15.

Hire me twenty cunning cooks.

   a.   *Romeo and Juliet.* Act IV. Sc. 2.
                               L. 2.

Let housewives make a skillet of my helm.

   b.   *Othello.* Act I. Sc. 3. L. 273.

She would have made Hercules have turned spit.

   c.   *Much Ado About Nothing.* Act II.
                            Sc. 1. L. 260.

The capon burns, the pig falls from the spit,
The clock hath strucken twelve.

   d.   *Comedy of Errors.* Act I. Sc. 2. L. 44.

        'Tis burnt; and so is all the meat.
What dogs are these! Where is the rascal
    cook?
How durst you, villains, bring it from the
    dresser,
And serve it thus to me that love it not?

   e.   *Taming of the Shrew.* Act IV. Sc. 1.
                              L. 164.

Weke, weke! so cries a pig prepared to the spit.

   f.   *Titus Andronicus.* Act IV. Sc. 2.
                              L. 146.

Were not I a little pot and soon hot, my very
lips might freeze to my teeth.

   g.   *Taming of the Shrew.* Act IV. Sc. 1.
                              L. 5.

What's there?
Things for the cook, sir: but I know not
what.

   h.   *Romeo and Juliet.* Act IV. Sc. 4.
                              L. 14.

Where's the cook? is supper ready, the
house trimmed, rushes strewed, cobwebs
swept?

   i.   *Taming of the Shrew.* Act IV. Sc. 1.
                              L. 47.

Would the cook were of my mind!

   j.   *Much Ado About Nothing.* Act I.
                          Sc. 3. L. 74.

The waste of many good materials, the vexation that frequently attends such mismanagements, and the curses not unfrequently bestowed on cooks with the usual reflection, that whereas God sends good meat, the devil sends cooks.

   k.   E. SMITH—*The Compleat Housewife.*
                              1727.

Dentistry.

Those cherries fairly do enclose
  Of orient pearl a double row,
Which, when her lovely laughter shows,
  They look like rosebuds fill'd with snow.

   l.   *Set to music by* RICHARD ALISON—*An
        Howre's Recreation in Musike.* (See
        Oliphant's *La Messa Madrigalesca.*
                        P. 229.)

My curse upon thy venom'd stang,
That shoots my tortured gums alang;
And through my lugs gies monie a twang,
  Wi' gnawing vengeance,
Tearing my nerves wi' bitter pang,
  Like racking engines!

   m.   BURNS—*Address to the Toothache.*

One said a tooth drawer was a kind of unconscionable trade, because his trade was nothing else but to take away those things whereby every man gets his living.

   n.   HAZLITT—*Shakespeare Jest Books.
              Conceits, Clinches, Flashes and
                      Whimzies.* No. 84.

For there was never yet philosopher
That could endure the toothache patiently.

   o.   *Much Ado About Nothing.* Act V.
                          Sc. 1. L. 35.

        I have the toothache.
      *   *   *   *   *
What! sigh for the toothache?

   p.   *Much Ado About Nothing.* Act III.
                          Sc. 2. L. 21.

Hatters.

"Sye," he seyd, "be the same hatte
I can knowe yf my wyfe be badde
To me by eny other man;
If my floures ouver fade or falle,
Then doth my wyfe me wrong wyth alle
As many a woman can."

   q.   ADAM (*of Cobsham*)—*The Wright's
                      Chaste Wife.* L. 265.

So Britain's monarch once uncovered sat,
While Bradshaw bullied in a broad-brimmed
    hat.

   r.   JAMES BRAMSTON—*Man of Taste.*

A hat not much the worse for wear.

   s.   COWPER—*History of John Gilpin.*

My new straw hat that's trimly lin'd with
    green,
Let Peggy wear.

   t.   GAY—*Shepherd's Week. Friday.* L. 125.

I know it is a sin
For me to sit and grin
  At him here;
But the old three-cornered hat
And the breeches and all that
  Are so queer.

   u.   O. W. HOLMES—*The Last Leaf.*

The hat is the *ultimum moriens* of respectability.

   v.   O. W. HOLMES—*The Autocrat of the
                      Breakfast Table.* VIII.

The Quaker loves an ample brim,
A hat that bows to no Salaam;
And dear the beaver is to him
As if it never made a dam.

   w.   HOOD—*All Round my Hat.*

A sermon on a hat: "'The hat, my boy, the hat, whatever it may be, is in itself nothing—makes nothing, goes for nothing; but, be sure of it, everything in life depends upon the cock of the hat.' For how many men—we put it to your own experience, reader—have made their way through the thronging crowds that beset fortune, not by the innate worth and excellence of their hats, but simply, as Sampson Piebald has it, by 'the cock of their hats'? The cock's all."

a.　Douglas Jerrold—*The Romance of a Keyhole*. Ch. III.

He wears his faith but as the fashion of his hat; it ever changes with the next block.

b.　*Much Ado About Nothing*. Act I. Sc. 1. L. 75.

I never saw so many shocking bad hats in my life.

c.　Attributed to Duke of Wellington, upon seeing the first Reformed Parliament.

Inn-Keeping.

He who has not been at a tavern knows not what a paradise it is. O holy tavern! O miraculous tavern!—holy, because no carking cares are there, nor weariness, nor pain; and miraculous, because of the spits, which of themselves turn round and round!

d.　Aretino—Quoted by Longfellow in *Hyperion*. Bk. III. Ch. II.

Now musing o'er the changing scene
Farmers behind the tavern screen
Collect; with elbows idly press'd
On hob, reclines the corner's guest,
Reading the news to mark again
The bankrupt lists or price of grain.
Puffing the while his red-tipt pipe
He dreams o'er troubles nearly ripe,
Yet, winter's leisure to regale,
Hopes better times, and sips his ale.

e.　Clare—*Shepherd's Calendar*.

There is nothing which has yet been contrived by man, by which so much happiness is produced as by a good tavern or inn.

f.　Sam'l Johnson—*Boswell's Life of Johnson*. 1776.

Souls of poets dead and gone,
What Elysium have ye known,
Happy field or mossy cavern,
Choicer than the Mermaid Tavern?

g.　Keats—*Mermaid Tavern*.

In the worst inn's worst room, with mat half hung.

h.　Pope—*Moral Essays*. Ep. 3. L. 299.

Now spurs the lated traveler apace
To gain the timely inn.

i.　*Macbeth*. Act III. Sc. 3. L. 7.

28

Shall I not take mine ease in mine inn?

j.　*Henry IV*. Pt. I. Act III. Sc. 3. L. 92.

Whoe'er has travel'd life's dull round,
　Where'er his stages may have been,
May sigh to think he still has found
　The warmest welcome, at an inn.

k.　Shenstone—*Written at an Inn at Henley*.

　　　　We left the shade:
And, ere the stars were visible, had reached
A village inn,—our evening resting-place.

l.　Wordsworth—*The Excursion*. Bk. I. Last lines.

Jeweler.

JANUARY.

By her who in this month is born,
No gems save *Garnets* should be worn;
They will insure her constancy,
True friendship and fidelity.

FEBRUARY.

The February born will find
Sincerity and peace of mind;
Freedom from passion and from care,
If they the *Pearl* will wear.

MARCH.

Who in this world of ours their eyes
In March first open shall be wise:
In days of peril firm and brave,
And wear a *Bloodstone* to their grave.

APRIL.

She who from April dates her years,
Diamonds should wear, lest bitter tears
For vain repentance flow; this stone,
Emblem of innocence is known.

MAY.

Who first beholds the light of day
In Spring's sweet flowery month of May
And wears an *Emerald* all her life,
Shall be a loved and happy wife.

JUNE.

Who comes with Summer to this earth
And owes to June her day of birth,
With ring of *Agate* on her hand,
Can health, wealth, and long life command.

JULY.

The glowing *Ruby* should adorn
Those who in warm July are born
Then will they be exempt and free
From love's doubt and anxiety.

AUGUST.

Wear a *Sardonyx* or for thee
No conjugal felicity.
The August-born without this stone
'Tis said must live unloved and lone.

SEPTEMBER.

A maiden born when Autumn leaves
Are rustling in September's breeze,
A *Sapphire* on her brow should bind,
'Twill cure diseases of the mind.

OCTOBER.

October's child is born for woe,
And life's vicissitudes must know;
But lay an *Opal* on her breast,
And hope will lull those woes to rest.

NOVEMBER.

Who first comes to this world below
With drear November's fog and snow
Should prize the *Topaz*' amber hue—
Emblem of friends and lovers true.

DECEMBER.

If cold December gave you birth,
The month of snow and ice and mirth,
Place on your hand a *Turquoise* blue,
Success will bless whate'er you do.

If that a pearl may in a toad's head dwell,
And may be found too in an oyster shell.
  a.   BUNYAN—*Apology for his Book.* L. 89.

Black is a pearl in a woman's eye.
  b.   GEORGE CHAPMAN—*An Humorous*
                       Day's Mirth.

Stones of small worth may lie unseen by day,
But night itself does the rich gem betray.
  c.   ABRAHAM COWLEY—*Davideis.* Bk. III.
                             L. 37.

These gems have life in them: their colors
  speak,
Say what words fail of.
  d.   GEORGE ELIOT—*The Spanish Gypsy.*
                           Bk. I.

Full many a gem of purest ray serene
  The dark unfathom'd caves of ocean bear.
  e.   GRAY—*Elegy in a Country Churchyard.*
                           St. 14.

There is many a rich stone laid up in the
bowels of the earth, many a fair pearl laid up
in the bosom of the sea, that never was seen
nor never shall be.
  f.   BISHOP HALL—*Contemplations.*
              Bk. VI.   *The Veil of Moses.*

Some ask'd how pearls did grow, and where,
  Then spoke I to my girle,
To part her lips, and showed them there
  The quarelets of pearl.
  g.   HERRICK—*The Rock of Rubies, and the*
                        Quarrie of Pearls.

And I had lent my watch last night to one
That dines to-day at the sheriff's.
  h.   BEN JONSON—*Alchemist.* Act I. Sc. 1.

It strikes! one, two,
Three, four, five, six. Enough, enough, dear
  watch,
Thy pulse hath beat enough. Now sleep and
  rest;
Would thou could'st make the time to do so
  too;
I'll wind thee up no more.
  i.   BEN JONSON—*Staple of News.* Act I.
                              Sc. 1.

Rich and rare were the gems she wore,
And a bright gold ring on her wand she bore.
  j.   MOORE—*Irish Melodies.* *Rich and Rare*
                       were the Gems She Wore.

On her white breast a sparkling cross she
  wore,
Which Jews might kiss and Infidels adore.
  k.   POPE—*Rape of the Lock.* Canto II.
                             L. 7.

Nay, tarry a moment, my charming girl;
Here is a jewel of gold and pearl;
A beautiful cross it is I ween
As ever on beauty's breast was seen;
There's nothing at all but love to pay;
Take it and wear it, but only stay!
Ah! Sir Hunter, what excellent taste!
I'm not—in such—particular—haste.
  l.   J. G. SAXE—*The Hunter and the*
                      Milkmaid. Trans.

And jewels, two stones, two rich and precious
  stones,
Stol'n by my daughter!
  m.   *Merchant of Venice.* Act II. Sc. 8.
                            L. 20.

A quarrel * * *
About a hoop of gold, a paltry ring.
  n.   *Merchant of Venice.* Act V. Sc. 1.
                            L. 146.

Ever out of frame,
And never going aright, being a watch,
But being watch'd that it may still go right!
  o.   *Love's Labour's Lost.* Act III. Sc. 1.
                            L. 193.
I'll give my jewels for a set of beads.
  p.   *Richard II.* Act III. Sc. 3. L. 147.

I see the jewel best enameled
Will lose his beauty; and the gold 'bides still,
That others touch, and often touching will
Wear gold.
  q.   *Comedy of Errors.* Act II. Sc. 1.
                            L. 109.

The clock upbraids me with the waste of time.
  r.   *Twelfth Night.* Act III. Sc. 1. L. 141.

'Tis plate of rare device, and jewels
Of rich and exquisite form; their value's
  great;
And I am something curious, being strange,
To have them in safe stowage.
  s.   *Cymbeline.* Act I. Sc. 6. L. 189.

Your ring first ;
And here the bracelet of the truest princess
That ever swore her faith.
a.   *Cymbeline.* Act V. Sc. 5. L. 416.

The tip no jewel needs to wear:
The tip is jewel of the ear.
b.   SIR PHILIP SIDNEY—*Sonnet. What
Tongue can Her Perfection Tell?*

Jewels five-words-long,
That on the stretch'd forefinger of all Time
Sparkle for ever.
c.   TENNYSON—*The Princess.* Pt. II.
L. 355.

The lively Diamond drinks thy purest rays,
Collected light, compact.
d.   THOMSON—*The Seasons. Summer.*
L. 142.

Journalism.

Advertisements are of great use to the vulgar.
First of all, as they are instruments of ambition. A man that is by no means big
enough for the Gazette, may easily creep into
the advertisements ; by which means we often
see an apothecary in the same paper of news
with a plenipotentiary, or a running footman
with an ambassador.
e.   ADDISON—*Tatler.* No. 224.

I would * * * earnestly advise them
for their good to order this paper to be punc-
tually served up, and to be looked upon as a
part of the tea equipage.
f.   ADDISON—*Spectator.* No. 10.

The great art in writing advertisements is
the finding out a proper method to catch the
reader's eye ; without which a good thing
may pass over unobserved, or be lost among
commissions of bankrupt.
g.   ADDISON—*The Tatler.* No. 224.

They consume a considerable quantity of
our paper manufacture, employ our artisans
in printing, and find business for great numbers of indigent persons.
h.   ADDISON—*Spectator.* No. 367.

The highest reach of a news-writer is an
empty Reasoning on Policy, and vain Conjectures on the public Management.
i.   DE LA BRUYÈRE—*The Characters or
Manners of the Present Age.* Ch. I.

The News-writer lies down at Night in
great Tranquillity, upon a piece of News
which corrupts before Morning, and which
he is obliged to throw away as soon as he
awakes.
j.   DE LA BRUYÈRE—*The Characters or
Manners of the Present Age.* Ch. I.

Hear, land o' cakes, and brither Scots,
Frae Maidenkirk to Johnny Groat's ;
If there's a hole in a' your coats,
    I rede you tent it :
A chiel's amang you taking notes,
    And, faith, he'll prent it.
k.   BURNS—*On Capt. Grose's
Peregrinations Through Scotland.*

A would-be satirist, a hired buffoon,
A monthly scribbler of some low lampoon,
Condemn'd to drudge, the meanest of the
    mean,
And furbish falsehoods for a magazine.
l.   BYRON—*English Bards and Scotch
Reviewers.* L. 975.

The editor sat in his sanctum, his counte-
    nance furrowed with care,
His mind at the bottom of business, his feet
    at the top of a chair,
His chair-arm an elbow supporting, his right
    hand upholding his head,
His eyes on his dusty old table, with different
    documents spread.
m.   WILL CARLETON—*Farm Ballads.
The Editor's Guests.*

The press is the fourth estate of the realm.
n.   CARLYLE—*Heroes and Hero-Worship.*
Sec. V.

Only a newspaper! Quick read, quick lost,
Who sums the treasure that it carries hence?
Torn, trampled under feet, who counts thy
    cost,
Star-eyed intelligence?
o.   MARY CLEMMER—*The Journalist.* St. 9.

To serve thy generation, this thy fate :
" Written in water," swiftly fades thy name;
But he who loves his kind does, first and late,
A work too great for fame.
p.   MARY CLEMMER—*The Journalist.*
Last Stanza.

Did Charity prevail, the press would prove
A vehicle of virtue, truth, and love.
q.   COWPER—*Charity.* L. 624.

He comes, the herald of a noisy world,
With spatter'd boots, strapp'd waist, and
    frozen locks ;
News from all nations lumbering at his back.
r.   COWPER—*The Task.* Bk. IV. L. 5.

Miscellanists are the most popular writers
among every people ; for it is they who form
a communication between the learned and
the unlearned, and, as it were, throw a bridge
between those two great divisions of the
public.
s.   ISAAC DISRAELI—*Literary Character of
Men of Genius. Miscellanists.*

Newspapers always excite curiosity.   No
one ever lays one down without a feeling of
disappointment.
a.   CHARLES LAMB—*Essays of Elia.*
                    *Detached Thoughts on Books and
                                    Reading.*

For evil news rides post, while good news
baits.
b.   MILTON—*Samson Agonistes.*   L. 1538.

He's gone, and who knows how he may
report
Thy words by adding fuel to the flame?
c.   MILTON—*Samson Agonistes.*   L. 1,350.

Four hostile newspapers are more to be
feared than a thousand bayonets.
d.   NAPOLEON I.

The mob of gentlemen who wrote with ease.
e.   POPE—*Epistles of Horace.*   Ep. I.
                                    Bk. II.   L. 108.
Bring me no more reports.
f.   *Macbeth.*   Act V.   Sc. 3.   L. 1.

Master, master! news, old news, and such
news as you never heard of!
g.   *Taming of the Shrew.*   Act III.   Sc. 2.
                                    L. 30.

            News fitting to the night,
Black, fearful, comfortless and horrible.
h.   *King John.*   Act V.   Sc. 6.   L. 19.

            Prithee, friend,
Pour out the pack of matter to mine ear,
The good and bad together.
i.   *Antony and Cleopatra.*   Act II.   Sc. 5.
                                    L. 53.
Ram thou thy fruitful tidings in mine ears,
That long time have been barren.
j.   *Antony and Cleopatra.*   Act II.   Sc. 5.
                                    L. 24.

            Report me and my cause aright
To the unsatisfied.
k.   *Hamlet.*   Act V.   Sc. 2.   L. 350.

The newspapers! Sir, they are the most
villanous—licentious—abominable—infernal
—not that I ever read them—no—I make it a
rule never to look into a newspaper.
l.   R. B. SHERIDAN—*The Critic.*   Act I.
                                    Sc. 1.
Trade hardly deems the busy day begun
Till his keen eye along the sheet has run ;
The blooming daughter throws her needle by,
And reads her schoolmate's marriage with a
    sigh ;
While the grave mother puts her glasses on,
And gives a tear to some old crony gone.
The preacher, too, his Sunday theme lays
    down,
To know what last new folly fills the town ;
Lively or sad, life's meanest, mightiest things,
The fate of fighting cocks, or fighting kings.
m.   SPRAGUE—*Curiosity.*

Here shall the Press the People's right
    maintain,
Unawed by influence and unbribed by gain ;
Here Patriot Truth her glorious precepts
    draw,
Pledged to Religion, Liberty, and Law.
n.   JOSEPH STORY—*Motto of the Salem
            Register.*   Adopted 1802.   WM. W.
            STORY's *Life of Joseph Story.*
                                    Vol. I.   Ch. VI.

Law.

One of the Seven was wont to say : " That
laws were like cobwebs ; where the small flies
were caught, and the great brake through."
o.   BACON—*Apothegms.*   No. 181.

I do not know the method of drawing up
an indictment against an whole people.
p.   BURKE—*Speech on the Conciliation of
                                    America.*

Our wrangling lawyers * * * are so litigious and busy here on earth, that I think
they will plead their clients' causes hereafter,
some of them, in hell.
q.   BURTON—*Anatomy of Melancholy.
                    Democritus to the Reader.*

Is not the winding up witnesses,
And nicking, more than half the bus'ness?
For witnesses, like watches, go
Just as they're set, too fast or slow ;
And where in Conscience they're strait-lac'd,
'Tis ten to one that side is cast.
r.   BUTLER—*Hudibras.*   Pt. II.   Canto II.
                                    L. 359.
Your pettifoggers damn their souls,
To share with knaves in cheating fools.
s.   BUTLER—*Hudibras.*   Pt. II.   Canto I.
                                    L. 515.

The law of heaven and earth is life for life.
t.   BYRON—*The Curse of Minerva.*   St. 15.

Who to himself is law, no law doth need,
Offends no law, and is a king indeed.
u.   GEORGE CHAPMAN—*Bussy D'Ambois.*
                                    Act II.   Sc. 1.

Possession is eleven points in the law.
v.   COLLEY CIBBER—*Woman's Wit.*   Act I.

For as the law is set over the magistrate,
even so are the magistrates set over the people.
And therefore, it may be truly said, "that the
magistrate is a speaking law, and the law is a
silent magistrate."
w.   CICERO—*On the Laws.*   Bk. III.   I.

After an existence of nearly twenty years of
almost innocuous desuetude these laws are
brought forth.
x.   GROVER CLEVELAND—*Message.*
                                    March 1, 1886.

Magna Charta is such a fellow that he will have no sovereign.

a.   SIR EDWARD COKE—*Debate in the Commons.* May 17, 1628.

Reason is the life of the law; nay, the common law itself is nothing else but reason. * * * The law which is perfection of reason.

b.   SIR EDWARD COKE—*First Institute.*

The gladsome light of jurisprudence.

c.   SIR EDWARD COKE—*First Institute.*

If it's near dinner time, the foreman takes out his watch when the jury have retired and says: "Dear me, gentlemen, ten minutes to five, I declare! I dine at five, gentlemen." "So do I," says everybody else except two men who ought to have dined at three, and seem more than half disposed to stand out in consequence. The foreman smiles, and puts up his watch: "Well, gentlemen, what do we say? Plaintiff, defendant, gentlemen? I rather think so far as I am concerned, gentlemen—I say I rather think—but don't let that influence you—I rather think the plaintiff's the man." Upon this two or three other men are sure to say they think so too—as of course they do; and then they get on very unanimously and comfortably.

d.   DICKENS—*Pickwick Papers.* Vol. II. Ch. VI.

I know'd what 'ud come o' this here mode o' doin' business. Oh Sammy, Sammy, vy worn't there a alleybi!

e.   DICKENS—*Pickwick Papers.* Vol. II. Ch. VI.

Just laws are no restraint upon the freedom of the good, for the good man desires nothing which a just law will interfere with.

f.   FROUDE—*Short Studies on Great Subjects. Reciprocal Duties of State and Subject.*

Our human laws are but the copies, more or less imperfect, of the eternal laws so far as we can read them.

g.   FROUDE—*Short Studies on Great Subjects. Calvinism.*

A justice with grave justices shall sit; He praise their wisdom, they admire his wit.

h.   GAY—*The Birth of the Squire.* L. 77.

Whenever the offence inspires less horror than the punishment, the rigour of penal law is obliged to give way to the common feelings of mankind.

i.   GIBBON—*The Decline and Fall of the Roman Empire.* Ch. XIV. Vol. I.

Laws grind the poor, and rich men rule the law.

j.   GOLDSMITH—*The Traveller.* L. 386.

I know no method to secure the repeal of bad or obnoxious laws so effective as their stringent execution.

k.   U. S. GRANT—*Inaugural Address,* March 4, 1869.

Art thou a magistrate? then be severe:
If studious, copy fair what time hath blurr'd,
Redeem truth from his jaws: if soldier,
Chase brave employments with a naked sword
Throughout the world.   Fool not, for all may have
If they dare try, a glorious life, or grave.

l.   HERBERT—*The Church Porch.* St. 15.

The law is the last result of human wisdom acting upon human experience for the benefit of the public.

m.   SAM'L JOHNSON—*Johnsoniana.* Piozzi's Anecdotes, 58.

So wise, so grave, of so perplex'd a tongue,
And loud withal, that would not wag, nor scarce
Lie still without a fee.

n.   BEN JONSON—*Volpone.* Act I. Sc. 1.

We must never assume that which is incapable of proof.

o.   GEO. HENRY LEWES—*The Physiology of Common Life.* Ch. XIII.

And folks are beginning to think it looks odd,
To choke a poor scamp for the glory of God.

p.   LOWELL—*A Fable for Critics.* L. 492.

The law is a sort of hocus-pocus science, that smiles in yeer face while it picks yeer pocket: and the glorious uncertainty of it is of mair use to the professors than the justice of it.

q.   MACKLIN—*Love à la Mode.* Act II. Sc. 1.

Litigious terms, fat contentions, and flowing fees.

r.   MILTON—*Prose Works.* Vol. I. *Of Education.*

There is no man so good, who, were he to submit all his thoughts and actions to the laws, would not deserve hanging ten times in his life.

s.   MONTAIGNE—*Essays. Of Vanity.*

Where law ends, there tyranny begins.

t.   WILLIAM PITT (Earl of Chatham)— *Case of Wilkes. Speech.* Jan. 9, 1770. Last line.

Alas! the small discredit of a bribe
Scarce hurts the lawyer, but undoes the scribe.

u.   POPE—*Epilogue to Satire.* Dialogue II. L. 46.

All, all look up with reverential awe,
At crimes that 'scape, or triumph o'er the law.

v.   POPE—*Epilogue to Satire.* Dialogue I. L. 167.

Curse on all laws but those which love has made.

   a.   POPE—*Eloisa to Abelard.* L. 74.

Once (says an Author; where, I need not say)
Two Trav'lers found an Oyster in their way;
Both fierce, both hungry; the dispute grew strong,
While Scale in hand Dame Justice pass'd along.
Before her each with clamour pleads the Laws.
Explain'd the matter, and would win the cause,
Dame Justice weighing long the doubtful Right,
Takes, opens, swallows it, before their sight.
The cause of strife remov'd so rarely well,
"There take" (says Justice), "take ye each a shell."
We thrive at Westminster on Fools like you:
'Twas a fat oyster—live in peace—Adieu."

   b.   POPE—*Verbatim from Boileau.*

Piecemeal they win this acre first, then that,
Glean on, and gather up the whole estate.

   c.   POPE—*Satires of Dr. Donne.* Satire II. L. 91.

Let us consider the reasons of the case. For nothing is law that is not reason.

   d.   SIR JOHN POWELL—*Coggs vs. Bernard.* 2 Ld. Raym., 911.

There is a higher law than the Constitution.

   e.   W. H. SEWARD—*Speech.* March 11, 1850.

Before I be convict by course of law,
To threaten me with death is most unlawful.

   f.   *Richard III.* Act I. Sc. 4. L. 192.

Bold of your worthiness, we single you
As our best-moving fair solicitor.

   g.   *Love's Labour's Lost.* Act II. Sc. 1. L. 28.

But in these nice sharp quillets of the law,
Good faith, I am no wiser than a daw.

   h.   *Henry VI.* Pt. I. Act II. Sc. 4. L. 11.

But, I prithee, sweet wag, shall there be gallows standing in England when thou art king? and resolution thus fobbed as it is with the rusty curb of old father antic the law?

   i.   *Henry IV.* Pt. I. Act I. Sc. 2. L. 65.

But is this law?
Ay, marry is't; crowner's quest law.

   j.   *Hamlet.* Act V. Sc. 1. L. 23.

Do as adversaries do in law,
Strive mightily, but eat and drink as friends.

   k.   *Taming of the Shrew.* Act I. Sc. 2. L. 278.

Faith, I have been a truant in the law,
And never yet could frame my will to it;
And therefore frame the law unto my will.

   l.   *Henry VI.* Pt. I. Act II. Sc. 4. L. 7.

He hath resisted law,
And therefore law shall scorn him further trial
Than the severity of the public power.

   m.   *Coriolanus.* Act III. Sc. 1. L. 267.

              I am a subject,
And I challenge law: attorneys are denied me;
And therefore personally I lay my claim
To my inheritance of free descent.

   n.   *Richard II.* Act II. Sc. 3. L. 133.

In law, what plea so tainted and corrupt
But, being season'd with a gracious voice,
Obscures the show of evil?

   o.   *Merchant of Venice.* Act III. Sc. 2. L. 75.

In the corrupted currents of this world
Offence's gilded hand may shove by justice,
And oft 'tis seen the wicked prize itself
Buys out the law: but 'tis not so above;
There is no shuffling, there the action lies
In his true nature; and we ourselves compell'd,
Even to the teeth and forehead of our faults,
To give in evidence.

   p.   *Hamlet.* Act III. Sc. 3. L. 57.

It must not be; there is no power in Venice
Can alter a decree established:
'Twill be recorded for a precedent;
And many an error by the same example
Will rush into the state.

   q.   *Merchant of Venice.* Act IV. Sc. 1. L. 218.

Press not a falling man too far! 'tis virtue:
His faults lie open to the laws; let them,
Not you, correct him.

   r.   *Henry VIII.* Act III. Sc. 2. L. 333.

Still you keep o' the windy side of the law.

   s.   *Twelfth Night.* Act III. Sc. 4. L. 181.

        The bloody book of law
You shall yourself read in the bitter letter
After your own sense.

   t.   *Othello.* Act I. Sc. 3. L. 67.

The first thing we do, let's kill all the lawyers.

   u.   *Henry VI.* Pt. II. Act IV. Sc. 2. L. 84.

They have been grand-jurymen since before Noah was a sailor.

   v.   *Twelfth Night.* Act III. Sc. 2. L. 16.

'Tis like the breath of an unfee'd lawyer;
you gave me nothing for 't.

   w.   *King Lear.* Act I. Sc. 4. L. 142.

To offend, and judge, are distinct offices
And of opposed natures.

   x.   *Merchant of Venice.* Act II. Sc. 9. L. 61.

We are for law; he dies.

   y.   *Timon of Athens.* Act III. Sc. 5. L. 86.

We have strict statutes and most biting laws.
a.   *Measure for Measure.* Act I. Sc. 3.
             L. 19.

We must not make a scarecrow of the law,
Setting it up to fear the birds of prey,
And let it keep one shape, till custom make it
Their perch and not their terror.
b.   *Measure for Measure.* Act II. Sc. 1.
             L. 1.

       When law can do no right,
Let it be lawful that law bar no wrong.
c.   *King John.* Act III. Sc. 1. L. 185.

You wear out a good wholesome forenoon
in hearing a cause between an orange-wife and
a fosset-seller; and then rejourn the controversy of three pence to a second day of
audience.
d.   *Coriolanus.* Act II. Sc. 1. L. 77.

Corruption abounding in the commonwealth, the commonwealth abounded in laws.
e.   Tacitus—*Annals.* Bk. III. P. 160.
            Thos. Gordon's trans.

No man e'er felt the halter draw,
With good opinion of the law.
f.   John Trumbull—*McFingal.*
            Canto III. L. 489.

The Law: It has honored us, may we honor it.
g.   Daniel Webster—*Toast at the*
       Charleston Bar Dinner. May 10, 1847.

And he that gives us in these days
New Lords may give us new laws.
h.   George Wither—*Contented Man's*
            Morrice.

Livery.

Go, call a coach, and let a coach be called;
And let the man who calleth be the caller;
And in his calling, let him nothing call,
But coach! coach! coach! O for a coach, ye
    gods!
i.   Henry Carey—*Chrononhotonthologos.*
            Act II. Sc. 4. L. 46.

Come, my coach! Good-night, ladies.
j.   *Hamlet.* Act IV. Sc. 5. L. 72.

Many carriages he hath dispatched.
k.   *King John.* Act V. Sc. 7. L. 90.

Our chariots and our horsemen be in readiness.
l.   *Cymbeline.* Act III. Sc. 5. L. 23.

When I am in my coach, which stays for us
At the park gate.
m.   *Merchant of Venice.* Act III. Sc. 4.
            L. 82.

Masons.

Sir, he made a chimney in my father's
house, and the bricks are alive at this day to
testify it.
n.   *Henry VI.* Pt. II. Act IV. Sc. 2.
            L. 156.

The elder of them, being put to nurse,
Was by a beggar-woman stolen away;
And, ignorant of his birth and parentage,
Became a bricklayer when he came to age.
o.   *Henry VI.* Pt. II. Act IV. Sc. 2.
            L. 150.

The crowded line of masons with trowels in
       their right hands, rapidly laying the
       long side-wall,
The flexible rise and fall of backs, the con-
       tinual click of the trowels striking the
       bricks,
The bricks, one after another, each laid so
       workmanlike in its place, and set with
       a knock of the trowel-handle.
p.   Walt Whitman—*Song of the Broad-*
            Axe. Pt. III. St. 4.

Medicine.

A man's own observation, what he finds
good of, and what he finds hurt of, is the best
physic to preserve health.
q.   Bacon—*Essays. Of Regimen of*
            Health.

Even as a Surgeon, minding off to cut
Some cureless limb, before in use he put
His violent Engins on the vicious member,
Bringeth his Patient in a senseless slumber,
And grief-less then (guided by use and art),
To save the whole, sawes off th' infected part.
r.   Du Bartas—*Divine Weekes and Workes.*
            First Week. Sixth Day. L. 1,018.

Learn'd he was in medic'nal lore,
For by his side a pouch he wore,
Replete with strange hermetic powder
That wounds nine miles point-blank would
       solder.
s.   Butler—*Hudibras.* Pt. I. Canto II.
            L. 223.

'Tis not amiss, ere ye're giv'n o'er,
To try one desp'rate med'cine more;
For where your case can be no worse,
The desp'rat'st is the wisest course.
t.   Butler—*Epistle of Hudibras to*
            Sidrophel. L. 5.

This is the way that physicians mend or end
       us,
Secundum artem: but although we sneer
In health—when ill, we call them to attend
       us,
Without the least propensity to jeer.
u.   Byron—*Don Juan.* Canto X. St. 42.

When taken
To be well shaken.
v.   George Colman (the Younger)—*Broad*
       Grins. The Newcastle Apothecary.
            St. 12.

Take a little rum
  The less you take the better,
Pour it in the lakes
  Of Wener or of Wetter.

Dip a spoonful out
  And mind you don't get groggy,
Pour it in the lake
  Of Winnipissiogie.

Stir the mixture well
  Lest it prove inferior,
Then put half a drop
  Into Lake Superior.

Every other day
  Take a drop in water,
You'll be better soon
  Or at least you oughter.
> *a.*   Rt. Rev. Bishop G. W. Doane—*Lines on Homeopathy.*

Better to hunt in fields for health unbought,
Than fee the doctor for a nauseous draught.
The wise for cure on exercise depend ;
God never made his work for man to mend.
> *b.*   Dryden—*Epistle to John Dryden of Chesterton.* L. 92.

So liv'd our sires, ere doctors learn'd to kill,
And multiplied with theirs the weekly bill.
> *c.*   Dryden—*To John Dryden, Esq.* L. 71.

See one physician, like a sculler plies,
The patient lingers, and by inches dies ;
But two physicians, like a pair of oars,
Waft him more swiftly to the Stygian shores.
> *d.*   "D." (Probably John Dunscombe)— *A Note in Nichols' Select Collection of Poems.*

"Is there no hope?" the sick man said,
The silent doctor shook his head,
And took his leave with signs of sorrow,
Despairing of his fee to-morrow.
> *e.*   Gay—*The Sick Man and the Angel.*

She sent for me in haste to come and see,
What her condition for a cure might be.
Dear me ! a patient—what a happy tone,
To have a patient and one all my own—
To have a patient and myself be feed,
Raised expectations very high indeed—
I saw a practice growing from the seed.
> *f.*   Wm. Tod Helmuth—*My First Patient.*

Extreme remedies are very appropriate for
extreme diseases.
> *g.*   Hippocrates—*Aphorisms.* 6.

I firmly believe that if the whole *materia
medica* could be sunk to the bottom of the sea,
it would be all the better for mankind and all
the worse for the fishes.
> *h.*   O. W. Holmes—*Lecture before the Harvard Medical School.*

A pill that at the present moment is daily
bread to thousands.
> *i.*   Douglas Jerrold—*The Catspaw.* Act I. Sc. 1.

  You behold in me
Only a travelling Physician ;
One of the few who have a mission
To cure incurable diseases,
Or those that are called so.
> *j.*   Longfellow—*Christus. The Golden Legend.* Pt. I.

And in requital ope his leathern scrip,
And show me simples of a thousand names,
Telling their strange and vigorous faculties.
> *k.*   Milton—*Comus.* L. 626.

How the Doctor's brow should smile
Crown'd with wreaths of **camomile.**
> *l.*   Moore—*Wreaths for Ministers.*

Time is generally the best doctor.
> *m.*   Ovid.

Banished the doctor, and expell'd the friend.
> *n.*   Pope—*Moral Essays.* Ep. III. L. 330.

Learn from the beasts the physic of the field.
> *o.*   Pope—*Essay on Man.* Ep. III. L. 174.

So modern 'pothecaries, taught the art
By doctor's bills to play the doctor's part,
Bold in the practice of mistaken rules,
Prescribe, apply, and call their masters fools.
> *p.*   Pope—*Essay on Criticism.* L. 108.

But, when the wit began to wheeze,
  And wine had warm'd the politician,
Cur'd yesterday of my disease,
  I died last night of my physician.
> *q.*   Prior—*The Remedy Worse than the Disease.*

You tell your doctor, that y' are ill ;
And what does he, but write a bill,
Of which you need not read one letter ;
The worse the scrawl, the dose the better.
For if you knew but what you take,
Though you recover, he must break.
> *r.*   Prior—*Alma.* Canto III. L. 97.

Physicians, of all men, are most happy :
whatever good success soever they have, the
world proclaimeth ; and what faults they commit, the earth covereth.
> *s.*   Quarles—*Hieroglyphics of the Life of Man.*

Use three Physicians,
Still-first Dr. Quiet,
Next Dr. Merry-man
And Dr. Dyet.
> *t.*   From *Regimen Sanitatis Salernitanum.* Edition 1607.

Before the curing of a strong disease,
Even in the instant of repair and health,
The fit is strongest ; evils that take leave,
On their departure most of all show evil.
   a.   *King John.*   Act III.   Sc. 4.   L. 112.

By medicine life may be prolonged, yet death
Will seize the doctor too.
   b.   *Cymbeline.*   Act V.   Sc. 5.   L. 29.

Canst thou not minister to a mind diseas'd,
Pluck from the memory a rooted sorrow,
Raze out the written troubles of the brain,
And with some sweet oblivious antidote
Cleanse the stuff'd bosom of that perilous
   stuff
Which weighs upon the heart?
                Therein the patient
Must minister to himself.
      Throw physic to the dogs ; I'll none of it.
   c.   *Macbeth.*   Act V.   Sc. 3.   L. 40.

How does your patient, doctor?
Not so sick, my lord,
As she is troubled with thick-coming fancies.
   d   *Macbeth.*   Act V.   Sc. 3.   L. 37.

I do remember an apothecary,—
And hereabouts he dwells,—whom late I noted
In tatter'd weeds, with overwhelming brows,
Culling of simples ; meagre were his looks,
Sharp misery had worn him to the bones :
And in his needy shop a tortoise hung,
An alligator stuff'd, and other skins
Of ill-shaped fishes ; and about his shelves
A beggarly account of empty boxes,
Green earthen pots, bladders and musty seeds,
Remnants of packthread and old cakes of
   roses,
Were thinly scatter'd to make up a show.
   e   *Romeo and Juliet.*   Act V.   Sc. 1.   L. 37.

      If thou couldst, doctor, cast
The water of my land, find her disease,
And purge it to a sound and pristine health,
I would applaud thee to the very echo,
That should applaud again.
   f.   *Macbeth.*   Act V.   Sc. 3.   L. 50.

In poison there is physic ; and these news,
Having been well, that would have made me
   sick ;
Being sick, have in some measure made me
   well.
   g.   *Henry IV.*   Pt. II.   Act I.   Sc. 1.
                           L. 137.

          In such a night
Medea gather'd the enchanted herbs
That did renew old Æson.
   h.   *Merchant of Venice.*   Act V.   Sc. 1.
                           L. 12.

          In this point
All his tricks founder, and he brings his
   physic
After his patient's death.
   i.   *Henry VIII.*   Act III.   Sc. 2.   L. 39.

          No cataplasm so rare,
Collected from all simples that have virtue
Under the moon, can save the thing from
   death.
   j.   *Hamlet.*   Act IV.   Sc. 7.   L. 144.

          Take physic, pomp ;
Expose thyself to feel what wretches feel.
   k.   *King Lear.*   Act III.   Sc. 4.   L. 33.

'Tis time to give 'em physic, their diseases
Are grown so catching.
   l.   *Henry VIII.*   Act I.   Sc. 3.   L. 36.

          Trust not the physician ;
His antidotes are poison, and he slays
More than you rob.
   m.   *Timon of Athens.*   Act IV.   Sc. 3.
                           L. 434.

When I was sick, you gave me bitter pills.
   n.   *Two Gentlemen of Verona.*   Act II.
                      Sc. IV.   L. 149.

          You rub the sore,
When you should bring the plaster.
   o.   *Tempest.*   Act II.   Sc. 1.   L. 138.

But nothing is more estimable than a physician who, having studied nature from his
youth, knows the properties of the human
body, the diseases which assail it, the remedies
which will benefit it, exercises his art with
caution, and pays equal attention to the rich
and the poor.
   p.   Voltaire—*A Philosophical Dictionary.*
                           Physicians.

Mercantile.

The soul's Rialto hath its merchandise,
I barter curl for curl upon that mart.
   q.   E. B. Browning—*Sonnets from the
                         Portuguese.* XIX.

When we speak of the commerce with our
colonies, fiction lags after truth, invention is
unfruitful, and imagination cold and barren.
   r.   Burke—*Speech on the Conciliation of
                          America.*

Despatch is the soul of business.
   s.   Earl of Chesterfield—*Letters.*
                          Feb. 5, 1750.

This business will never hold water.
   t.   Colley Cibber—*She Wou'd and She
                      Wou'd Not.* Act IV.

They (corporations) cannot commit treason,
nor be outlawed, nor excommunicated, for
they have no souls.
   u.   Sir Edward Coke—*Reports.* Vol. V.
                   The Case of Sutton's Hospital.

A business with an income at its heels.
   v.   Cowper—*Retirement.* L. 614.

In every age and clime we see,
Two of a trade can ne'er agree.
> a.   GAY—*Fables. Rat-Catcher and Cats.*
> L. 43.

A manufacturing district * * * sends out,
as it were, suckers into all its neighborhood.
> b.   HALLAM—*View of the State of Europe during the Middle Ages.* Ch. IX.

Lord Stafford mines for coal and salt,
The Duke of Norfolk deals in malt,
The Douglas in red herrings.
> c.   FITZ-GREENE HALLECK—*Alnwick Castle.*

Those that are above business.
> d.   MATHEW HENRY—*Commentaries. Matthew XX.*

Trade's proud empire hastes to swift decay.
> e.   SAM'L JOHNSON—*Line added to Goldsmith's Deserted Village.*

There is no better ballast for keeping the
mind steady on its keel, and saving it from
all risk of *crankiness*, than business.
> f.   LOWELL—*Among My Books. New England Two Centuries Ago.*

Business dispatched is business well done,
but business hurried is business ill done.
> g.   BULWER-LYTTON—*Caxtoniana.* Essay
> XXVI. *Readers and Writers.*

The merchant, to secure his treasure,
Conveys it in a borrow'd name.
> h.   PRIOR—*An Ode. The Merchant, to Secure his Treasure.*

No mortal thing can bear so high a price,
But that with mortal thing it may be bought.
> i.   SIR WALTER RALEIGH—*Love the Only Price of Love.*

A merchant of great traffic through the world.
> j.   *Taming of the Shrew.* Act I. Sc. 1.
> L. 12.

Bad is the trade that must play fool to sorrow.
> k.   *King Lear.* Act IV. Sc. 1. L. 40.

I'll give thrice so much land
To any well-deserving friend ;
But in the way of bargain, mark ye me,
I'll cavil on the ninth part of a hair.
> l.   *Henry IV.* Pt. I. Act III. Sc. 1.
> L. 137.

Losses,
That have of late so huddled on his back,
Enow to press a royal merchant down
And pluck commiseration of his state
From brassy bosoms and rough hearts of flint.
> m.   *Merchant of Venice.* Act IV. Sc. 1.
> L. 27.

To business that we love we rise betime,
And go to 't with delight.
> n.   *Antony and Cleopatra.* Act IV. Sc. 4.
> L. 20.

To things of sale a seller's praise belongs.
> o.   *Love's Labour's Lost.* Act IV. Sc. 3.
> L. 240.

Traffic's thy god; and thy god confound
thee!
> p.   *Timon of Athens.* Act I. Sc. I. L. 246.

To found a great empire for the sole purpose
of raising up a people of customers, may at
first sight appear a project fit only for a
nation of shopkeepers.
> q.   ADAM SMITH—*Wealth of Nations.*
> Vol. II. Bk. IV. Ch. VII. Pt. III.

And what is true of a shopkeeper, is true of
a shopkeeping nation.
> r.   TUCKER (Dean of Gloucester)—
> Tract, 1766.

That which is everybody's business, is nobody's business.
> s.   IZAAK WALTON—*Compleat Angler.*
> Pt. I. Ch. II.

Military.

An Austrian army awfully arrayed.
> t.   ANONYMOUS—Quoted in *Wheeler's Magazine.* Winchester, Eng. 1828.

All quiet along the Potomac they say
Except now and then a stray picket
Is shot as he walks on his beat, to and fro,
By a rifleman hid in the thicket.
> u.   ETHEL LYNN BEERS—*The Picket Guard.*

Ay me! what perils do environ
The man that meddles with cold iron!
> v.   BUTLER—*Hudibras.* Pt. I. Canto III.
> L. 1.

Earth! render back from out thy breast
A remnant of our Spartan dead!
Of the three hundred grant but three,
To make a new Thermopylæ!
> w.   BYRON—*Don Juan.* Canto III.
> St. 86.

His breast with wounds unnumber'd riven,
His back to earth, his face to heaven.
> x.   BYRON—*The Giaour.* L. 675.

For the army is a school in which the miser
becomes generous, and the generous prodigal ;
miserly soldiers are like monsters, but very
rarely seen.
> y.   CERVANTES—*Don Quixote.*
> Ch. XXXIX.

O Chryste, it is a grief for me to telle,
How manie a noble erle and valrous knyghte
In fyghtynge for Kynge Harrold noblie fell,
Al sleyne on Hastyng's field in bloudie fyghte.
> z.   CHATTERTON—*Battle of Hastings.*

He stands erect; his slouch becomes a walk;
He steps right onward, martial in his air,
His form and movement.
  a.　　Cowper—*The Task*. Bk. IV. L. 638.

Terrible he rode alone,
With his yemen sword for aid;
Ornament it carried none
But the notches on the blade.
  b.　　*The Death Feud. An Arab War Song*.
　　　　St. 14. *Tait's Edinburgh Magazine*.
　　　　　　　　　　　　　　　July, 1850.

Mouths without hands; maintained at vast
　　expense,
In peace a charge, in war a weak defense:
Stout once a month they march, a blustering
　　band,
And ever, but in times of need, at hand.
  c.　　Dryden—*Cymon and Iphigenia*. L. 401.

The broken soldier, kindly bade to stay;
Sat by his fire, and talked the night away,
Wept o'er his wounds, or tales of sorrow done,
Shoulder'd his crutch, and show'd how fields
　　were won.
  d.　　Goldsmith—*The Deserted Village*.
　　　　　　　　　　　　　　　L. 155.

Wake, soldier wake, thy war-horse waits
　　To bear thee to the battle back ;—
Thou slumberest at a foeman's gates,—
　　Thy dog would break thy bivouac;
Thy plume is trailing in the dust,
And thy red falchion gathering rust.
  e.　　T. K. Hervey—*The Dead Trumpeter*.

He slept an iron sleep,—
Slain fighting for his country.
  f.　　Homer—*Iliad*. Bk. XI. L. 285.
　　　　　　　　　　　　　Bryant's trans.

Take thou thy arms and come with me,
For we must quit ourselves like men, and
　　strive
To aid our cause, although we be but two.
Great is the strength of feeble arms combined,
And we can combat even with the brave.
  g.　　Homer—*Iliad*. Bk. XIII. L. 289.
　　　　　　　　　　　　　Bryant's trans.

The sex is ever to a soldier kind.
  h.　　Homer—*Odyssey*. Bk. XIV. L. 246.
　　　　　　　　　　　　　Pope's trans.

Ben Battle was a soldier bold,
　　And used to war's alarms;
But a cannon-ball took off his legs,
　　So he laid down his arms.
  i.　　Hood—*Faithless Nellie Gray*.

As we pledge the health of our general, who
　　fares as rough as we,
What can daunt us, what can turn us, led to
　　death by such as he?
  j.　　Charles Kingsley—*A March*.

"What are the bugles blowin' for?" said
　　Files-on-Parade.
"To turn you out, to turn you out," the Colour
　　Sergeant said.
"What makes you look so white, so white?"
　　said Files-on-Parade.
"I'm dreadin' what I've got to watch," the
　　Colour-Sergeant said.
　　"For they're hangin' Danny Deever, you
　　can hear the dead march play.
　　The regiment's in 'ollow square—They're
　　hangin' him to-day;
　　They're taken of his buttons off an' cut
　　his stripes away.
　　And they're hangin' Danny Deever in the
　　morning."
  k.　　Rudyard Kipling—*Danny Deever*.

And, though the warrior's sun has set,
Its light shall linger round us yet,
Bright, radiant, blest.
  l.　　Don Jorge Manrique—*Coplas De
　　　　Manrique*. Last Lines. Trans. by
　　　　　　　　　　　　　Longfellow.

"Companions," said he [Saturninus], "you
have lost a good captain, to make of him a
bad general."
  m.　　Montaigne—*Essays. Of Vanity*.

He came and spoke to Ossian. "King of
spears!" he said, "my son has not fallen
without his fame. The young warrior did
not fly; but met death as he went forward in
his strength. Happy are they who die in
youth, when their renown is heard!"
  n.　　Ossian—*Croma*. Last Stanza.

Although too much of a soldier among
sovereigns, no one could claim with better
right to be a sovereign among soldiers.
  o.　　Scott—*Life of Napoleon*.

And the stern joy which warriors feel
In foemen worthy of their steel.
  p.　　Scott—*Lady of the Lake*. Canto V.
　　　　　　　　　　　　　St. 10.

Hail to the chief who in triumph advances.
  q.　　Scott—*Lady of the Lake*. Canto II.
　　　　　　　　　　　　　St. 19.

Soldier, rest! thy warfare o'er,
Dream of fighting fields no more:
Sleep the sleep that knows not breaking,
Morn of toil, nor night of waking.
  r.　　Scott—*Lady of the Lake*. Canto I.
　　　　　　　　　　　　　St. 31.

Warriors!—and where are warriors found,
If not on martial Britain's ground?
And who, when waked with note of fire,
Love more than they the British lyre?
  s.　　Scott—*Lord of the Isles*. Canto IV.
　　　　　　　　　　　　　St. 20.

Yet what can they see in the longest kingly
line in Europe, save that it runs back to a
successful soldier?
   a.   Scott—*Woodstock.* Ch. XXXVII.

A braver soldier never couched lance,
A gentler heart did never sway in court.
   b.   *Henry VI.* Pt. I. Act III. Sc. 2.
                              L. 134.

Drummer, strike up, and let us march away.
   c.   *Henry VI.* Pt. III. Act IV. Sc. 7.
                              L. 50.

Fie, my Lord, fie! a soldier, and afear'd?
   d.   *Macbeth.* Act V. Sc. 1. L. 41.

Give them great meals of beef and iron and
steel, they will eat like wolves and fight like
devils.
   e.   *Henry V.* Act III. Sc. 7. L. 161.

             God's soldier be he!
Had I as many sons as I have hairs,
I would not wish them to a fairer death:
And so his knell is knoll'd.
   f.   *Macbeth.* Act V. Sc. 8. L. 47.

He is a soldier fit to stand by Cæsar
And give direction.
   g.   *Othello.* Act II. Sc. 3. L. 127.

I am a soldier and unapt to weep
Or to exclaim on fortune's fickleness.
   h.   *Henry VI.* Pt. I. Act V. Sc. 3. L. 134.

I said an elder soldier, not a better.
Did I say, **better?**
   i.   *Julius Cæsar.* Act IV. Sc. 3. L. 56.

May that soldier a mere recreant prove
That means not, hath not, or is not in love!
   j.   *Troilus and Cressida.* Act I. Sc. 3.
                              L. 287.

             Then a soldier,
Full of strange oaths and bearded like the pard,
Jealous in honour, sudden and quick in
    quarrel,
Seeking the bubble reputation
Even in the cannon's mouth.
   k.   *As You Like It.* Act II. Sc. 7. L. 149.

The painful warrior famoused for fight,
After a thousand victories once foiled,
Is from the book of honour razed quite,
And all the rest forgot for which he toiled.
   l.   *Sonnet XXV.*

            'Tis the soldier's life
To have their balmy slumbers wak'd with
    strife.
   m.   *Othello.* Act II. Sc. 3. L. 257.

Worthy fellows; and like to prove most sinewy
    sword-men.
   n.   *All's Well That Ends Well.* Act II.
                          Sc. 1. L. 61.

You may relish him more in the soldier than
    in the scholar.
   o.   *Othello.* Act II. Sc. 1. L. 166.

Sleep, soldiers! still in honored rest
   Your truth and valor wearing:
The bravest are the tenderest,—
   The loving are the daring.
   p.   Bayard Taylor—*The Song of the Camp.*

For this is England's greatest son,
   He that gain'd a hundred fights,
And never lost an English gun.
   q.   Tennyson—*Ode on the Death of the*
                    Duke of Wellington. St. 6.

Not a drum was heard, not a funeral note,
As his corse to the rampart we hurried.
   r.   Chas. Wolfe—*The Burial of Sir John*
                  Moore at Carunna. St. 1.

No useless coffin enclosed his breast,
   Not in sheet nor in shroud we wound him;
But he lay like a warrior taking his rest
   With his martial cloak around him.
   s.   Chas. Wolfe—*The Burial of Sir John*
                  Moore at Carunna. St. 3.

Some for hard masters, broken under arms,
In battle lopt away, with half their limbs,
Beg bitter bread thro' realms their valour
    saved.
   t.   Young—*Night Thoughts.* Night I.
                              L. 250.

Navigation.

O pilot! 'tis a fearful night,
There's danger on the deep.
   u.   Thomas Haynes Bayly—*The Pilot.*

The royal navy of England has ever been its
greatest defence and ornament; it is its ancient
and natural strength; the floating bulwark of
the island.
   v.   Sir Wm. Blackstone—*Commentaries.*
                Vol. I. Bk. I. Ch. XIII.

Cooped in their winged sea-girt citadel.
   w.   Byron—*Childe Harold.* Canto II.
                            St. 28.

O'er the glad waters of the dark blue sea,
Our thoughts as boundless, and our souls as
    free,
Far as the breeze can bear, the billows foam,
Survey our empire, and behold our home!
   x.   Byron—*The Corsair.* Canto I. St. 1.

Ye Mariners of England!
   That guard our native seas;
Whose flag has braved a thousand years
   The battle and the breeze!
   y.   Campbell—*Ode. Ye Mariners of*
                              England.

Here's to the pilot that weathered the storm.
   z.   Canning—*The Pilot that Weathered the*
                             Storm.

And as great seamen, using all their wealth
And skills in Neptune's deep invisible paths,
In tall ships richly built and ribbed with brass,
To put a girdle round about the world.
  a.   GEO. CHAPMAN—*Bussy D'Ambois.*
                Act I.   Sc. 1.   L. 20.

A wet sheet and a flowing sea,
  A wind that follows fast
And fills the white and rustling sails,
  And bends the gallant mast!
And bends the gallant mast, my boys,
  While, like the eagle free,
Away the good ship flies, and leaves
  Old England in the lee.
  b.   ALLAN CUNNINGHAM—*Songs of Scotland.*
          A Wet Sheet and a Flowing Sea.

Skill'd in the globe and sphere, he gravely
    stands,
And, with his compass, measures seas and
    lands.
  c.   DRYDEN—*Sixth Satire of Juvenal.*
                    L. 760.

All in the Downs the fleet was moor'd.
  d.   GAY—*Sweet William's Farewell to*
               Black-Eyed Susan.

The winds and waves are always on the
side of the ablest navigators.
  e.   GIBBON—*Decline and Fall of the Roman*
            Empire.   Ch. LXVIII.

Though pleas'd to see the dolphins play,
I mind my compass and my way.
  f.   MATTHEW GREEN—*The Spleen.*   L. 826.

Thus, I steer my bark, and sail
On even keel, with gentle gale.
  g.   MATTHEW GREEN—*The Spleen.*   L. 814.

What though the sea be calm? trust to the
    shore,
Ships have been drown'd, where late they
    danc'd before.
  h.   HERRICK—*Safety on the Shore.*

Yet the best pilots have need of mariners,
besides sails, anchor and other tackle.
  i.   BEN JONSON—*Discoveries. Illiteratus*
                    Princeps.

There were gentlemen and there were seamen in the navy of Charles the Second.
But the seamen were not gentlemen; and the
gentlemen were not seamen.
  j.   MACAULAY—*History of England.*
         Vol. I.   Ch. III.   Pt. XXXII.

Some love to roam o'er the dark sea's foam,
Where the shrill winds whistle free.
  k.   CHARLES MACKAY—*Some Love to Roam.*

Thus far we run before the wind.
  l.   ARTHUR MURPHY—*The Apprentice.*
         Act I.   Sc. 1.   L. 344.

Ye gentlemen of England
  That live at home at ease,
Ah! little do you think upon
  The dangers of the seas.
  m.   MARTYN PARKER—*Ye Gentlemen*
                  of England.

A strong nor'wester's blowing, Bill!
  Hark! don't ye hear it roar now?
Lord help 'em, how I pities them
  Unhappy folks on shore now!
  n.   WILLIAM PITT—*The Sailor's*
                  Consolation.

And that all seas are made calme and still
with oile; and therefore the Divers under the
water doe spirt and sprinkle it abroad with
their mouthes because it dulceth and allaieth
the unpleasant nature thereof, and carrieth a
light with it.
  o.   PLINY—*Natural History.*   Bk. II.
           Ch. CIII.   Holland's trans.

Why does pouring Oil on the Sea make it
Clear and Calm?   Is it for that the winds,
slipping the smooth oil, have no force, nor
cause any waves?
  p.   PLUTARCH—*Morals. Natural Questions.*
                      XII.

Through the black night and driving rain
A ship is struggling, all in vain,
To live upon the stormy main;—
    Miserere Domine!
  q.   ADELAIDE A. PROCTER—*The Storm.*

Merrily, merrily goes the bark
  On a breeze from the northward free,
So shoots through the morning sky the lark,
  Or the swan through the summer sea.
  r.   SCOTT—*Lord of the Isles.*   Canto IV.
                    St. 10.

Upon the gale she stoop'd her side,
And bounded o'er the swelling tide,
  As she were dancing home;
The merry seamen laugh'd to see
Their gallant ship so lustily
  Furrow the green sea-foam.
  s.   SCOTT—*Marmion.*   Canto II.   St. 1.

Well, then—our course is chosen—spread the
    sail—
Heave oft the lead, and mark the soundings
    well—
Look to the helm, good master—many a shoal
Marks this stern coast, and rocks, where sits
    the Siren
Who, like ambition, lures men to their ruin.
  t.   SCOTT—*Kenilworth.*   Ch. XVII. Verses
               at head of Chapter.

    Behold the threaden sails,
Borne with the invisible and creeping wind,
Draw the huge bottoms through the furrow'd
    sea,
Breasting the lofty surge.
  u.   *Henry V.* Act III. Chorus. L. 10.

She comes majestic with her swelling sails,
  The gallant Ship : along her watery way,
Homeward she drives before the favouring
    gales ;
  Now flirting at their length the streamers
    play,
And now they ripple with the ruffling breeze.
  a.   SOUTHEY—*Sonnet XIX.*

Cease, rude Boreas, blustering railer !
  List, ye landsmen all, to me :
Messmates, hear a brother sailor
  Sing the dangers of the sea.
  b.   GEORGE A. STEVENS—*The Storm.*

And the stately ships go on
  To their haven under the hill.
  c.   TENNYSON—*Break, Break, Break.* St. 3.

Thou bringest the sailor to his wife,
  And travell'd men from foreign lands,
  And letters unto trembling hands ;
And, thy dark freight, a vanish'd life.
  d.   TENNYSON—*In Memoriam.* Pt. X.

On deck beneath the awning,
I dozing lay and yawning ;
It was the gray of dawning,
  Ere yet the Sun arose ;
And above the funnel's roaring,
And the fitful wind's deploring,
I heard the cabin snoring
  With universal noise.
  e.   THACKERAY—*The White Squall.*

Speed on the ship ;—But let her bear
  No merchandise of sin,
No groaning cargo of despair
  Her roomy hold within ;
No Lethean drug for Eastern lands,
  Nor poison-draught for ours ;
But honest fruits of toiling hands
  And Nature's sun and showers.
  f.   WHITTIER—*The Ship-Builders.*

Painting.

And those who paint 'em truest praise 'em
most.
  g.   ADDISON—*The Campaign.* Last line.

From the mingled strength of shade and light
A new creation rises to my sight
Such heav'nly figures from his pencil flow,
So warm with light his blended colors glow.
    *   *   *   *   *   *
The glowing portraits, fresh from life, that
    bring
Home to our hearts the truth from which
    they spring.
  h.   BYRON—*Monody on the death of the Rt.
          Hon. R. B. Sheridan.* St. 3.

A picture is a poem without words.
  i.   CORNIFICUS—*Anet. ad Her.* 4. 28.

Here, take my likeness with you, whilst 'tis so ;
For, when from hence you go,
The next sun's rising will behold
Me pale, and lean, and old.
The man who did this picture draw
Will swear next day my face he never saw.
  j.   ABRAHAM COWLEY—*The Mistress. My
                                        Picture.*

Hard features every bungler can command :
To draw true beauty shows a master's hand.
  k.   DRYDEN—*To Mr. Lee, on his Alexander.*
                                        L. 53.

Pictures must not be too picturesque.
  l.   EMERSON—*Essays. Of Art.*

A flattering painter, who made it his care
To draw men as they ought to be, not as they
    are
  m.   GOLDSMITH—*Retaliation.* L. 63.

The fellow mixes blood with his colors.
  n.   Said by GUIDO RENI of RUBENS.

One picture in ten thousand, perhaps, ought
to live in the applause of mankind, from
generation to generation until the colors fade
and blacken out of sight or the canvas rot
entirely away.
  o.   NATH. HAWTHORNE—*Marble Faun.*
                                Bk. II. Ch. XII.

Well, something must be done for May,
  The time is drawing nigh—
To figure in the Catalogue,
  And woo the public eye.

Something I must invent and paint ;
  But oh my wit is not
Like one of those kind substantives
  That answer Who and What ?
  p.   HOOD—*The Painter Puzzled.*

He that seeks popularity in art closes the
door on his own genius : as he must needs
paint for other minds, and not for his own.
  q.   MRS. JAMESON—*Memoirs and Essays.
                                Washington Allston.*

The only good copies are those which
exhibit the defects of bad originals.
  r.   LA ROCHEFOUCAULD—*Maxims.* No. 136.

The picture that approaches sculpture nearest
Is the best picture.
  s.   LONGFELLOW—*Michael Angelo.*
                                        Pt. II. 4.

Vain is the hope by colouring to display
The bright effulgence of the noontide ray
Or paint the full-orb'd ruler of the skies
With pencils dipt in dull terrestrial dyes.
  t.   MASON—*Fresnoy's Art of Painting.*

He best can paint them who shall feel them
    most.
  u.   POPE—*Eloisa and Abelard.* Last line.

Lely on animated canvas stole
The sleepy eye, that spoke the melting soul.
a.　Pope—*Second Book of Horace.* Ep. I.
L. 149.

If it is the love of that which your work
represents—if, being a landscape painter, it is
love of hills and trees that moves you—if,
being a figure painter, it is love of human
beauty, and human soul that moves you—if,
being a flower or animal painter, it is love, and
wonder, and delight in petal and in limb that
move you, then the Spirit is upon you, and
the earth is yours, and the fullness thereof.
b.　Ruskin—*The Two Paths.* Lect. I.

Painting with all its technicalities, difficulties, and peculiar ends, is nothing but a
noble and expressive language, invaluable as
the vehicle of thought, but by itself nothing.
c.　Ruskin—*True and Beautiful.*
Painting. Introduction.

I will say of it,
It tutors nature : artificial strife
Lives in these touches, livelier than life.
d.　*Timon of Athens.* Act I. Sc. 1. L. 36.

Look here, upon this picture, and on this.
e.　*Hamlet.* Act III. Sc. 4. L. 53.

The painting is almost the natural man :
For since dishonour traffics with man's na-
ture,
He is but outside; pencill'd figures are
Ev'n such as they give out.
f.　*Timon of Athens.* Act I. Sc. 1. L. 157.

What demi-god
Hath come so near creation?
g.　*Merchant of Venice.* Act III. Sc. 2.
L. 116.

Wrought he not well that painted it?
He wrought better that made the painter;
and yet he's but a filthy piece of work.
h.　*Timon of Athens.* Act I. Sc. 1. L. 200.

With hue like that when some great painter
dips
His pencil in the gloom of earthquake and
eclipse.
i.　Shelley—*The Revolt of Islam.*
Canto V. St. 23.

There is no such thing as a dumb poet or a
handless painter. The essence of an artist is
that he should be articulate.
j.　Swinburne—*Essays and Studies.*
Matthew Arnold's New Poems.

They dropped into the yolk of an egg the
milk that flows from the leaf of a young fig-
tree, with which, instead of water, gum or
gumdragant, they mixed their last layer of
colours.
k.　Walpole—*Anecdotes of Painting.*
Vol. I. Ch. 2.

I would I were a painter, for the sake
Of a sweet picture, and of her who led,
A fitting guide, with reverential tread,
Into that mountain mystery.
l.　Whittier—*Mountain Pictures.* No. 2.

Perfumery.

In virtue, nothing earthly could surpass her,
Save thine "incomparable oil," Macassar !
m.　Byron—*Don Juan.* Canto I. St. 17.

And the ripe harvest of the new-mown hay
Gives it a sweet and wholesome odour.
n.　Colley Cibber—*Richard III.*
(*Altered.*) Act V. Sc. 3. L. 44.

I cannot talk with civet in the room,
A fine puss gentleman that's all perfume.
o.　Cowper—*Conversation.* L. 283.

An amber scent of odorous perfume
Her harbinger.
p.　Milton—*Samson Agonistes.* L. 720.

A stream of rich distill'd perfumes.
q.　Milton—*Comus.* 556.

Sabean odours from the spicy shore
Of Arabie the blest.
r.　Milton—*Paradise Lost.* Bk. IV. L. 162.

And all Arabia breathes from yonder box.
s.　Pope—*The Rape of the Lock.* Canto I.
L. 134.

And all your courtly civet cats can vent
Perfume to you, to me is excrement.
t.　Pope—*Epilogue to the Satires.*
Dialogue II. L. 188.

Die of a rose in aromatic pain.
u.　Pope—*Essay on Man.* L. 200.

From the barge
A strange invisible perfume hits the sense
Of the adjacent wharfs.
v.　*Antony and Cleopatra.* Act II. Sc. 2.
L. 216.

Hast thou not learn'd me how
To make perfumes? distil? preserve? yea, so
That our great king himself doth woo me oft
For my confections?
w.　*Cymbeline.* Act I. Sc. 5. L. 12.

Perfume for a lady's chamber.
x.　*Winter's Tale.* Act IV. Sc. 4. L. 225.

So perfumed that
The winds were love-sick.
y.　*Antony and Cleopatra.* Act II. Sc. 2.
L. 198.

Take your paper, too,
And let me have them very well perfumed,
For she is sweeter than perfume itself
To whom they go to.
z.　*Taming of the Shrew.* Act I. Sc. 2.
L. 151.

The perfumed tincture of the roses.
aa.　*Sonnet LIV.*

Post (Letters).

Belshazzar had a letter,—
 He never had but one;
Belshazzar's correspondent
 Concluded and begun
In that immortal copy
 The conscience of us all
Can read without its glasses
 On revelation's wall.
> *a.*   EMILY DICKINSON—*Poems.* XXV.
> (Ed. 1891.) *Belshazzar had a Letter.*

The welcome news is in the letter found;
The carrier's not commission'd to expound;
It speaks itself, and what it does contain,
In all things needful to be known, is plain.
> *b.*   DRYDEN—*Religio Laici.* L. 366.

Every day brings a ship,
Every ship brings a word;
Well for those who have no fear,
Looking seaward well assured
That the word the vessel brings
Is the word they wish to hear.
> *c.*   EMERSON—*Letters.*

Thy letter sent to prove me,
 Inflicts no sense of wrong;
No longer wilt thou love me,—
 Thy letter, though, is long.
> *d.* · HEINE—*Book of Songs.   New Spring.*
> No. 34.

Letters, from *absent* friends, extinguish *fear,*
Unite *division,* and draw distance *near;*
Their *magic* force each *silent* wish conveys,
And wafts *embodied* thought, a thousand
 ways:
Could *souls* to *bodies* write, *death's* pow'r were
 mean
For minds could then *meet* minds with heav'n
 between.
> *e.*   AARON HILL—*Verses Written on a
> Window in a Journey to Scotland.*

An exquisite invention this,
Worthy of Love's most honeyed kiss,—
This art of writing billet-doux—
In buds, and odors, and bright hues!
In saying all one feels and thinks
In clever daffodils and pinks;
In puns of tulips; and in phrases,
Charming for their truth, of daisies.
> *f.*   LEIGH HUNT—*Love-Letters Made of
> Flowers.*

Growing one's own choice words and fancies
In orange tubs, and beds of pansies;
One's sighs and passionate declarations,
In odorous rhetoric of carnations.
> *g.*   LEIGH HUNT—*Love-Letters Made of
> Flowers.*

A piece of simple goodness—a letter gushing
from the heart; a beautiful unstudied vindication of the worth and untiring sweetness of
human nature—a record of the invulner-
ability of man, armed with high purpose,
sanctified by truth.
> *h.*   DOUGLAS JERROLD—*Specimens of
> Jerrold's Wit. The Postman's Budget.*

A strange volume of real life in the daily
packet of the postman. Eternal love and
instant payment!
> *i.*   DOUGLAS JERROLD—*Specimens of
> Jerrold's Wit. The Postman's Budget.*

Kind messages, that pass from land to land;
 Kind letters, that betray the heart's deep
 history,
In which we feel the pressure of a hand,—
 One touch of fire,—and all the rest is
 mystery!
> *j.*   LONGFELLOW—*The Seaside and Fireside.
> Dedication.* St. 5.

Good-bye—my paper's out so nearly,
I've only room for, Yours sincerely.
> *k.*   MOORE—*The Fudge Family in Paris.*
> Letter VI.

Heav'n first taught letters for some wretch's
 aid,
Some banish'd lover, or some captive maid.
> *l.*   POPE—*Eloisa to Abelard.* L. 51.

Line after line my gushing eyes o'erflow,
Led thro' a sad variety of woe:
Now warm in love, now with'ring in my
 bloom,
Lost in a convent's solitary gloom!
> *m.*   POPE—*Eloisa to Abelard.* L. 35.

Soon as thy letters trembling I unclose,
That well-known name awakens all my woes.
> *n.*   POPE—*Eloisa to Abelard.* L. 29.

And oft the pangs of absence to remove
By letters, soft interpreters of love.
> *o.*   PRIOR—*Henry and Emma.* L. 147.

Ev'n so, with all submission, I
　　*   *   *   *   *   *
Send you each year a homely letter,
Who may return me much a better.
> *p.*   PRIOR—*Epistle to Fleetwood Shepherd.*
> L. 23.

I will touch
My mouth unto the leaves, caressingly;
And so wilt thou. Thus, from these lips of
 mine
My message will go kissingly to thine,
With more than Fancy's load of luxury,
And prove a true love-letter.
> *q.*   J. G. SAXE—*Sonnet. (With a Letter.)*

Here are a few of the unpleasant'st words
That ever blotted paper!
> *r.*   *Merchant of Venice.* Act III. Sc. 2.
> L. 254.

If this letter move him not, his legs cannot.
I'll give 't him.
   a.   *Twelfth Night.* Act III. Sc. 4. L. 188.

          I have a letter from her
Of such contents as you will wonder at:
The mirth whereof so larded with my matter,
That neither singly can be manifested,
Without the show of both.
   b.   *Merry Wives of Windsor.* Act IV.
                 Sc. 6. L. 12.

Jove and my stars be praised! Here is yet
a postscript.
   c.   *Twelfth Night.* Act II. Sc. 5. L. 187.

Let me hear from thee by letters.
   d.   *Two Gentlemen of Verona.* Act I.
                 Sc. 1. L. 57.

Tell him there's a post come from my
master, with his horn full of good news.
   e.   *Merchant of Venice.* Act V. Sc. 1.
                     L. 46.

The letter is too long by half a mile.
   f.   *Love's Labour's Lost.* Act V. Sc. 2.
                     L. 54.

What! have I 'scaped love-letters in the
holiday-time of my beauty, and am I now a
subject for them?
   g.   *Merry Wives of Windsor.* Act II.
                 Sc. 1. L. 1.

Go, little letter, apace, apace,
      Fly;
Fly to the light in the valley below—
Tell my wish to her dewy blue eye.
   h.   Tennyson—*The Letter.* St. 2.

             I read
Of that glad year that once had been,
In those fall'n leaves which kept their green,
The noble letters of the dead:
And strangely on the silence broke
The silent-speaking words.
   i.   Tennyson—*In Memoriam.* **Pt. XCV.**

Thou bringest * * *
* * * letters unto trembling hands.
   j.   Tennyson—*In Memoriam.* **Pt. X.**

Pottery.

Thou spring'st a leak already in thy crown,
A flaw is in thy ill-bak'd vessel found;
'Tis hollow, and returns a jarring sound,
Yet thy moist clay is pliant to command,
Unwrought, and easy to the potter's hand:
Now take the mould; now bend thy mind to
    feel
The first sharp motions of the forming wheel.
   k.   Dryden—*Third Satire of Persius.*
                     L. 35.

A potter near his modest cot
Was shaping many an urn and pot;
He took the clay for the earthen things
From beggars' feet and heads of kings.
   l.   Omar Khayyám—*Bodenstedt.* Trans.

29

And yonder by Nankin, behold!
The Tower of Porcelain, strange and old,
Uplifting to the astonished skies
Its ninefold painted balconies,
With balustrades of twining leaves,
And roofs of tile, beneath whose eaves
Hang porcelain bells that all the time
Ring with a soft, melodious chime;
While the whole fabric is ablaze
With varied tints, all fused in one
Great mass of color, like a maze
Of flowers illumined by the sun.
   m.   Longfellow—*Keramos.* L. 336.

Figures that almost move and speak.
   n.   Longfellow—*Keramos.* L. 236.

Turn, turn, my wheel! Turn round and round
Without a pause, without a sound:
  So spins the flying world away!
This clay, well mixed with marl and sand,
Follows the motion of my hand;
For some must follow, and some command,
    Though all are made of clay!
   o.   Longfellow—*Keramos.* L. 1.

Preaching.

      Of right and wrong he taught
Truths as refined as ever Athens heard;
And (strange to tell) he practis'd what he
    preach'd.
   p.   John Armstrong—*The Art of Preserving
             Health.* Bk. IV. L. 301.

I met a preacher there I knew, and said,
Ill and overworked, how fare you in this scene?
Bravely! said he; for I of late have been
Much cheered with thoughts of Christ, the
    living bread.
   q.   Matthew Arnold—*East London.*

I preached as never sure to preach again,
And as a dying man to dying men.
   r.   Richard Baxter—*Love Breathing
           Thanks and Praise.* Pt. 2. St. 29.

Man resolves in himself he will preach; and
    he preaches.
   s.   De La Bruyère—*The Characters or
        Manners of the Present Age.* Ch. XV.

Hear how he clears the points o' Faith
Wi' rattlin' an' thumpin'!
Now meekly calm, now wild in wrath,
He's stampin', an' he's jumpin'!
   t.   Burns—*Holy Fair.* St. 13.

And pulpit, drum ecclesiastic,
Was beat with fist instead of a stick.
   u.   Butler—*Hudibras.* Pt. I. Canto I.
                     L. 11.

Oh for a forty-parson power!
   v.   Byron—*Don Juan.* Canto X. St. 34.

But Cristes loore, and his Apostles twelve,
He taughte, but first he folowed it hymselfe.
   w.   Chaucer—*Canterbury Tales.* Prologue.
                     L. 52.

A kick that scarce would move a horse,
May kill a sound divine.
   a.   Cowper—*The Yearly Distress.* St. 16.

He that negotiates between God and man,
As God's ambassador, the grand concerns
Of judgment and of mercy, should beware
Of lightness in his speech.
   b.   Cowper—*The Task.* Bk. II. L. 463.

I venerate the man whose heart is warm,
Whose hands are pure, whose doctrine and
    whose life,
Coincident, exhibit lucid proof
That he is honest in the sacred cause.
   c.   Cowper—*The Task.* Bk. II. L. 372.

There goes the parson, oh illustrious spark!
And there, scarce less illustrious, goes the
    clerk.
   d.   Cowper—*On Observing Some Names of
    Little Note.*

The things that mount the rostrum with a
    skip,
And then skip down again, pronounce a text,
Cry hem ; and reading what they never wrote
Just fifteen minutes, huddle up their work,
And with a well-bred whisper close the scene !
   e.   Cowper—*The Task.* Bk. II. L. 408.

This priest he merry is, and blithe
Three-quarters of a year,
But oh ! it cuts him like a scythe
When tithing time draws near.
   f.   Cowper—*The Yearly Distress.* St. 2.

Would I describe a preacher,
   *   *   *   *   *   *
I would express him simple, grave, sincere;
In doctrine uncorrupt; in language plain,
And plain in manner ; decent, solemn, chaste,
And natural in gesture ; much impress'd
Himself, as conscious of his awful charge,
And anxious mainly that the flock he feeds
May feel it too ; affectionate in look,
And tender in address, as well becomes
A messenger of grace to guilty men.
   g.   Cowper—*The Task.* Bk. II. L. 394.

Go forth and preach impostures to the world,
But give them truth to build on.
   h.   Dante—*Vision of Paradise.*
    Canto XXIX. L. 116.

God preaches, a noted clergyman,
And the sermon is never long ;
So instead of getting to heaven at last,
I'm going all along.
   i.   Emily Dickinson—*Poems.* VI. *A
    Service of Song.*

The proud he tam'd, the penitent he cheer'd :
Nor to rebuke the rich offender fear'd.
His preaching much, but more his practice
    wrought ;
(A living sermon of the truths he taught ;)
For this by rules severe his life he squar'd :
That all might see the doctrines which they
    heard.
   j.   Dryden—*Character of a Good Parson.*
    L. 75.

Alas for the unhappy man that is called to
stand in the pulpit, and *not* give the bread of
life.
   k.   Emerson—*An Address to the Senior
    Class in Divinity College, Cambridge,
    July 15, 1838.*

And, as a bird each fond endearment tries
To tempt its new-fledg'd offspring to the skies,
He tried each art, reprov'd each dull delay,
Allur'd to brighter worlds, and led the way.
   l.   Goldsmith—*The Deserted Village.*
    L. 167.

At church, with meek and unaffected grace,
His looks adorn'd the venerable place ;
Truth from his lips prevailed with double
    sway,
And fools, who came to scoff, remain'd to pray.
   m.   Goldsmith—*The Deserted Village.*
    L. 177.

But in his duty prompt at every call,
He watch'd and wept, he pray'd and felt for
    all.
   n.   Goldsmith—*The Deserted Village.*
    L. 165.

Judge not the preacher ; for he is thy judge :
If thou mislike him, thou conceiv'st him not.
God calleth preaching folly. Do not grudge
To pick out treasures from an earthen pot.
The worst speaks something good.
   o.   Herbert—*The Temple. The Church
    Porch.* St. 72.

Sir, a woman preaching is like a dog's walking on his hind legs. It is not done well : but
you are surprised to find it done at all.
   p.   Sam'l Johnson—*Boswell's Life of
    Johnson.* 1763.

As pleasant songs, at morning sung,
The words that dropped from his sweet tongue
Strengthened our hearts ; or, heard at night,
Made all our slumbers soft and light.
   q.   Longfellow—*Christus. The Golden
    Legend.* Pt. I.

It is by the Vicar's skirts that the
Devil climbs into the Belfry.
   r.   Longfellow—*The Spanish Student.*
    Act I. Sc. 2.

Skilful alike with tongue and pen,
He preached to all men everywhere
The Gospel of the Golden Rule,
The New Commandment given to men,
Thinking the deed, and not the creed,
Would help us in our utmost need.
    a.   LONGFELLOW—*Prelude to Tales of a*
                           Wayside Inn.   L. 217.

He of their wicked ways
Shall them admonish, and before them set
The paths of righteousness.
    b.   MILTON—*Paradise Lost.*   Bk. XI.
                               L. 812.

So clomb the first grand thief into God's fold ;
So since into his church lewd hirelings climb.
    c.   MILTON—*Paradise Lost.*   Bk. IV.
                               L. 192.

And truths divine came mended from that
    tongue.
    d.   POPE—*Eloisa to Abelard.*   L. 66.

The gracious Dew of Pulpit Eloquence,
And all the well-whip'd Cream of Courtly
    Sense.
    e.   POPE—*Epilogue to the Satires.*
                       Dialogue I.   L. 70.

He was a shrewd and sound divine
    Of loud Dissent the mortal terror ;
And when, by dint of page and line,
He 'stablished Truth, or startled Error,
The Baptist found him far too deep,
    The Deist sighed with saving sorrow,
And the lean Levite went to sleep
    And dreamt of eating pork to-morrow.
    f.   PRAED—*The Vicar.*

His sermon never said or showed
    That Earth is foul, that Heaven is gracious,
Without refreshment on the road
    From Jerome, or from Athanasius.
And sure a righteous zeal inspired,
    The hand and head that penned and planned
        them,
For all who understood, admired—
    And some who did not understand them.
    g.   PRAED—*The Vicar.*

The lilies say : Behold how we
Preach without words of purity.
    h.   CHRISTINA G. ROSSETTI—*Consider the*
                            Lilies of the Field.

I have taught you, my dear flock, for above
thirty years how to live ; and I will show you
in a very short time how to die.
    i.   SANDYS—*Anglorum Speculum.*   P. 903.

Do not, as some ungracious pastors do,
Show me the steep and thorny way to heaven ;
Whiles, like a puff'd and reckless libertine,
Himself the primrose path of dalliance treads,
And recks not his own rede.
    j   *Hamlet.*   Act I.   Sc. 3.   L. 47.

He who the sword of heaven will **bear**
Should be as holy as severe ;
Pattern in himself to know,
Grace to stand, and virtue go.
    k.   *Measure for Measure.*   Act III.   Sc. 2.
                               L. 275.

It is a good divine that follows his own instructions ; I can easier teach twenty what
were good to be done, than be one of the twenty
to follow mine own teaching.
    l.   *Merchant of Venice.*   Act I.   Sc. 2.
                               L. 15.

Sermons in stones and good in every thing.
    m.   *As You Like It.*   Act II.   Sc. 1.   L. **17.**

Who should be pitiful, if you be not?
Or who should study to prefer a peace,
If holy churchmen take delight in broils?
    n.   *Henry VI.*   Pt. I.   Act III.   Sc. 1.
                               L. 109.

Perhaps thou wert a priest,—if so, my struggles
Are vain, for priestcraft never owns its juggles.
    o.   HORACE SMITH—*Address to a Mummy.*
                               St. 4.

He taught them how to live and how to die.
    p.   WM. SOMERVILLE—*In Memory of the*
                          Rev. Mr. Moore.   L. 21.

With a little hoard of maxims preaching down
    a daughter's heart.
    q.   TENNYSON—*Locksley Hall.*   L. 94.

A little, round, fat, oily man of God.
    r.   THOMSON—*Castle of Indolence.*   Canto I.
                               St. 69.

" Dear sinners all," the fool began, "man's
    life is but a jest,
A dream, a shadow, bubble, air, a vapour at
    the best.
In a thousand pounds of law I find not a single
    ounce of love,
A blind man killed the parson's cow in shoot-
    ing at the dove ;
The fool that eats till he is sick must fast till
    he is well,
The wooer who can flatter most will bear
    away the belle."
     *   *   *   *   *   *
And then again the women screamed, and
    every staghound bayed ;
And why? because the motley fool so wise a
    sermon made.
    s.   GEORGE W. THORNBURY—*The Jester's*
                               Sermon.

Printing.

Every school boy and school girl who has
arrived at the age of reflection ought to know
something about the history of the art of
printing.
    t.   HORACE MANN—*The Common School*
                Journal. February, 1843. *Printing*
                       and Paper Making.

Though an angel should write, still 'tis *devils* must print.

a.　　Moore—*The Fudge Family in England.*
　　　　　　　　　　　　　　Letter III.

　　　　　　　I'll print it,
And shame the fools.

b.　　Pope—*Prologue to Satires.* L. 61.

Thou hast most traitorously corrupted the youth of the realm in erecting a grammar school: and whereas, before, our forefathers had no other books but the score and the tally, thou hast caused printing to be used, and, contrary to the king, his crown and dignity, thou hast built a paper-mill.

c.　　*Henry VI.* Pt. II. Act IV. Sc. 7.
　　　　　　　　　　　　　　L. 35.

The jour printer with gray head and gaunt jaws works at his case,
He turns his quid of tobacco, while his eyes blurr with the manuscript.

d.　　Walt Whitman—*Leaves of Grass.*
　　　　　　Walt Whitman. Pt. XV. St. 77.

Publishing.

But I account the use that a man should seek of the publishing of his own writings before his death, to be but an untimely anticipation of that which is proper to follow a man, and not to go along with him.

e.　　Bacon—*An Advertisement Touching a*
　　　　　　　　　Holy War. Epistle Dedicatory.

Yon second-hand bookseller is second to none in the worth of the treasures which he dispenses.

f.　　Leigh Hunt—*On the Beneficence of*
　　　　　　　　　　　　　　Book-stalls.

If I publish this poem for you, speaking as a trader, I shall be a considerable loser. Did I publish all I admire, out of sympathy with the author, I should be a ruined man.

g.　　Bulwer-Lytton—*My Novel.* Bk. VI.
　　　　　　　　　　　　　　Ch. XIV.

If the bookseller happens to desire a privilege for his merchandize, whether he is selling Rabelais or the Fathers of the Church, the magistrate grants the privilege without answering for the contents of the book.

h.　　Voltaire—*A Philosophical Dictionary.*
　　　　　　　　　　　　Books. Sec. 1.

Sculpture.

The stone unhewn and cold
Becomes a living mould,
The more the marble wastes
The more the statue grows.

i.　　Michael Angelo—*Sonnet.* Mrs.
　　　　　　　　　　Henry Roscoe's trans.

　　　　　　　A sculptor wields
The chisel, and the stricken marble grows
To beauty.

j.　　Bryant—*The Flood of Years.*

In sculpture did ever anybody call the Apollo a fancy piece? Or say of the Laocoön how it might be made different? A masterpiece of art has in the mind a fixed place in the chain of being, as much as a plant or a crystal.

k.　　Emerson—*Society and Solitude. Art.*

Sculpture is more divine, and more like Nature,
That fashions all her works in high relief,
And that is Sculpture. This vast ball, the
　　　Earth,
Was moulded out of clay, and baked in fire;
Men, women, and all animals that breathe
Are statues, and not paintings.

l.　　Longfellow—*Michael Angelo.*
　　　　　　　　　　　　Pt. III.　5.

Sculpture is more than painting. It is greater
To raise the dead to life than to create
Phantoms that seem to live.

m.　　Longfellow—*Michael Angelo.*
　　　　　　　　　　　　Pt. III.　5.

And the cold marble leapt to life a God.

n.　　H. H. Milman—*The Belvedere Apollo.*

The Paphian Queen to Cnidos made repair
Across the tide to see her image there:
Then looking up and round the prospect wide,
When did Praxiteles see me thus? she cried.

o.　　Plato—*Greek Anthology.*

Then marble, soften'd into life, grew warm.

p.　　Pope—*Second Book of Horace.* Ep. I.
　　　　　　　　　　　　　　L. 146.

The sculptor does not work for the anatomist, but for the common observer of life and nature.

q.　　Ruskin—*True and Beautiful.*
　　　　　　　　　　　　　　Sculpture.

So stands the statue that enchants the world,
So bending tries to veil the matchless boast,
The mingled beauties of exulting Greece.

r.　　Thomson—*The Seasons. Summer.*
　　　　　　　　　　　　　　L. 1,346.

The marble index of a mind forever
Voyaging through strange seas of thought,
　　　alone.

s.　　Wordsworth—*The Prelude.* Bk. III.

Shoemaking.

A cobbler, * * * produced several new grins of his own invention, having been used to cut faces for many years together over his last.

t.　　Addison—*Spectator.* No. 173.

Ye tuneful cobblers! still your notes prolong,
Compose at once a slipper and a song;
So shall the fair your handiwork peruse,
Your sonnets sure shall please—perhaps your
　　　shoes.

u.　　Byron—*English Bards and Scotch*
　　　　　　　　　　Reviewers. L. 751.

The shoemaker makes a good shoe because he makes nothing else.

a.   EMERSON—*Letters and Social Aims.*
Greatness.

Let firm, well hammer'd soles protect thy feet
Through freezing snows, and rains, and soak-
ing sleet;
Should the big last extend the shoe too wide,
Each stone will wrench the unwary step
aside;
The sudden turn may stretch the swelling
vein,
The cracking joint unhinge, or ankle sprain;
And when too short the modish shoes are
worn,
You'll judge the seasons by your shooting
corn.

b.   GAY—*Trivia.* Bk. I. L. 33.

I was not made of common calf,
Nor ever meant for country loon;
If with an axe I seem cut out,
The workman was no cobbling clown;
A good jack boot with double sole he made,
To roam the woods, or through the rivers
wade.

c.   GIUSEPPE GIUSTI—*The Chronicle of the*
Boot.

Marry because you have drank with the king,
And the king hath so graciously pledged you,
You shall no more be called shoemakers,
But you and yours to the world's end
Shall be called the trade of the gentle craft.

d.   *Probably a play of* GEORGE A. GREENE.
Time of Edward IV.

As he cobbled and hammered from morning
till dark,
With the footgear to mend on his knees,
Stitching patches, or pegging on soles as he
sang,
Out of tune, ancient catches and glees.

e.   OSCAR H. HARPEL—*The Haunted*
Cobbler.

One said he wondered that leather was not
dearer than any other thing. Being demanded
a reason: because, saith he, it is more stood
upon than any other thing in the world.

f.   HAZLITT—*Shakespeare Jest Books.*
Conceits, Clinches, Flashes and
Whimzies. No. 86.

A careless shoe string, in whose tie
I see a wilde civility.

g.   HERRICK—*Delight in Disorder.*

Cinderella's *lefts and rights*
To Geraldine's were frights,
And I trow
The damsel, deftly shod,
Has dutifully trod
Until now.

h.   FREDERICK LOCKER—*To My Mistress's*
Boots.

Oh, where did hunter win
So delicate a skin
For her feet?
You lucky little kid,
You perished, so you did,
For my sweet.

i.   FREDERICK LOCKER—*To My Mistress's*
Boots.

The fairy stitching gleams
On the sides and in the seams,
And it shows
That Pixies were the wags
Who tipped these funny tags
And these toes.

j.   FREDERICK LOCKER—*To My Mistress's*
Boots.

But from the hoop's bewitching round,
Her very shoe has power to wound.

k.   EDWARD MOORE—*The Spider and the*
Bee. Fable X. L. 29.

* * * And holding out his shoe, asked
them whether it was not new and well made.
"Yet," added he, "none of you can tell
where it pinches me."

l.   PLUTARCH—*Lives.* Vol. II. *Life of*
Æmilius Paulus.

Hans Grovendraad, an honest clown,
By cobbling in his native town,
Had earned a living ever.
His work was strong and clean and fine,
And none who served at Crispin's shrine
Was at his trade more clever.

m.   JAN VAN RYSWICK—*Hans Grovendraad.*
Translated from the French by
F. W. Ricord.

Thou art a cobbler, art thou?
Truly, sir, all that I live by is with the awl:
* * * I am, indeed, sir, a surgeon to old
shoes.

n.   *Julius Cæsar.* Act I. Sc. 1. L. 23.

What trade are you?
Truly, sir, in respect of a fine workman, I am
but, as you would say, a cobbler.

o.   *Julius Cæsar.* Act I. Sc. 1. L. 9.

What trade art thou? answer me directly.
A trade, sir, that, I hope, I may use with a
safe conscience; which is, indeed, sir, a mender of bad soles.

p.   *Julius Cæsar.* Act I. Sc. 1. L. 12.

Wherefore art not in thy shop to-day?
Why dost thou lead these men about the
streets?
Truly, sir, to wear out their shoes, to get
myself into more work.

q.   *Julius Cæsar.* Act I. Sc. 1. L. 31.

When bootes and shoes are torne up to the
    lefts,
Coblers must thrust their awles up to the
    hefts.
  a.   NATHANIEL WARD—*The Simple Cobler*
        of Aggavvam in America.
        Title Page.

Rap, rap! upon the well-worn stone,
  How falls the polished hammer!
Rap, rap! the measured sound has grown
  A quick and merry clamor.
Now shape the sole! now deftly curl
  The glassy vamp around it,
And bless the while the bright-eyed girl
  Whose gentle fingers bound it!
  b.   WHITTIER—*The Shoemakers.*

Statesmanship.

A disposition to preserve, and an ability to
improve, taken together, would be my standard of a statesman.
  c.   BURKE—*Reflections on the Revolution in*
        France.

No statesman e'er will find it worth his pains
To tax our labours and excise our brains.
  d.   CHURCHILL—*Night.* L. 271.

It is strange so great a statesman should
Be so sublime a poet.
  e.   BULWER-LYTTON—*Richelieu.* Act I.
        Sc. 2.

Who would not praise Patricio's high desert,
His hand unstain'd, his uncorrupted heart,
His comprehensive head? all interests
  weigh'd,
All Europe sav'd, yet Britain not betray'd.
  f.   POPE—*Moral Essays.* Ep. I. L. 82.

Statesman, yet friend to truth; of soul sincere,
In action faithful, and in honour clear;
Who broke no promise, serv'd no private end,
Who gain'd no title, and who lost no friend;
Ennobled by himself, by all approv'd,
And prais'd, unenvy'd, by the Muse he lov'd.
  g.   POPE—*Epistle to Addison.* L. 67.

And lives to clutch the golden keys,
To mould a mighty state's decrees,
And shape the whisper of the throne.
  h.   TENNYSON—*In Memoriam.* Pt. LXIII.

And statesmen at her council met
  Who knew the seasons when to take
Occasion by the hand, and make
The bounds of freedom wider yet.
  i.   TENNYSON—*To the Queen.* St. 8.

Why don't you show us a statesman who
can rise up to the emergency, and cave in the
emergency's head.
  j.   ARTEMUS WARD—*Things in New York.*

Tailoring.

Thy clothes are all the soul thou hast.
  k.   BEAUMONT AND FLETCHER—*Honest*
        Man's Fortune. Act V. Sc. 3.
        L. 170.

May Moorland weavers boast Pindaric skill,
And tailors' lays be longer than their bill!
While punctual beaux reward the grateful
  notes,
And pay for poems—when they pay for coats.
  l.   BYRON—*English Bards and Scotch*
        Reviewers. L. 781.

Great is the Tailor, but not the greatest.
  m.   CARLYLE—*Essays. Goethe's Works.*

Sister, look ye,
How, by a new creation of my tailor's
I've shook off old mortality.
  n.   JOHN FORD—*The Fancies Chaste and*
        Noble. Act I. Sc. 3.

A tailor, though a man of upright dealing,—
True but for lying,—honest but for stealing,—
Did fall one day extremely sick by chance
And on the sudden was in wondrous trance.
  o.   SIR JOHN HARRINGTON—*Of a Precise*
        Tailor.

One commending a Tayler for his dexteritie
in his profession, another standing by ratified
his opinion, saying tailors had their business
at their fingers' ends.
  p.   HAZLITT—*Shakespeare Jest Books.*
        Conceits, Clinches, Flashes and
        Whimzies. No. 93.

      As if thou e'er wert angry
But with thy tailor! and yet that poor shred
Can bring more to the making up of a man,
Than can be hoped from thee; thou art his
  creature;
And did he not, each morning, new create
  thee,
Thou'dst stink and be forgotten.
  q.   MASSINGER—*Fatal Dowry.* Act III.
        Sc. 1.

      What a fine man
Hath your tailor made you!
  r.   MASSINGER—*City Madam.* Act I. Sc. 2.

Yes, if they would thank their maker,
And seek no further; but they have new
  creators,
God tailor and god mercer.
  s.   MASSINGER—*A Very Woman.* Act III.
        Sc. 1. L. 161.

King Stephen was a worthy peere,
  His breeches cost him but a crowne;
He held them sixpence all too deere,
  Therefore he call'd the taylor lowne.
  t.   THOMAS PERCY—*Reliques. Take Thy*
        Old Cloak About Thee. St. 7.

Th' embroider'd suit at least he deem'd his
    prey ;
That suit an unpaid tailor snatch'd away.
   a.   POPE—*The Dunciad.* Bk. II. L. 117.

Thou art a strange fellow : a tailor make a
man?
   Ay, a tailor, sir ; a stone-cutter or a painter
could not have made him so ill, though he
had been but two hours at the trade.
   b.   *King Lear.* Act II. Sc. 2. L. 61.

       Thou villain base,
Know'st me not by my clothes?
   No, nor thy tailor, rascal,
Who is thy grandfather : he made those
   clothes,
Which, as it seems, make thee.
   c.   *Cymbeline.* Act IV. Sc. 2. L. 80.

Thy gown? why, ay ;—come, tailor, let us
   see't.
O mercy, God ! what masquing stuff is here?
What's this ? a sleeve ? 'tis like a demi-cannon :
What, up and down, carv'd like an apple-
   tart ?
Here's snip and nip and cut and slish and
   slash,
Like to a censer in a barber's shop :
Why, what i' devil's name, tailor, call'st
   thou this !
   d.   *Taming of the Shrew.* Act IV. Sc. 3.
                            L. 86.

Teaching.

O ye ! who teach the ingenious youth of na-
   tions,
   Holland, France, England, Germany or
   Spain,
I pray ye flog them upon all occasions,
   It mends their morals, never mind the pain.
   e.   BYRON—*Don Juan.* Canto II. St. 1.

'Tis pleasing to be school'd in a strange tongue
   By female lips and eyes—that is, I mean,
When both the teacher and the taught are
   young,
   As was the case, at least, where I have been ;
They smile so when one's right; and when
   one's wrong
They smile still more.
   f.   BYRON—*Don Juan.* Canto II. St. 164.

The sounding jargon of the schools.
   g.   COWPER—*Truth.* L. 367.

   There is no teaching until the pupil is
brought into the same state or principle in
which you are ; a transfusion takes place; he
is you, and you are he ; there is a teaching;
and by no unfriendly chance or bad company
can he ever quite lose the benefit.
   h.   EMERSON—*Essays. Of Spiritual Laws.*

Full well they laughed, with counterfeited
   glee,
At all his jokes, for many a joke had he :
Full well the busy whisper, circling round,
Convey'd the dismal tidings when he frown'd.
   i.   GOLDSMITH—*Deserted Village.* L. 201.

Grave is the Master's look ; his forehead wears
Thick rows of wrinkles, prints of worrying
   cares :
Uneasy lies the heads of all that rule,
His worst of all whose kingdom is a school.
Supreme he sits ; before the awful frown
That binds his brows the boldest eye goes
   down ;
Not more submissive Israel heard and saw
At Sinai's foot the Giver of the Law.
   j.   O. W. HOLMES—*The School Boy.*

   Whilst that the childe is young, let him be
instructed in vertue and lytterature.
   k.   LYLY—*Euphues. The Anatomy of Wit.*
                  Of the Education of Youth.

What's all the noisy jargon of the schools?
   l.   POMFRET—*Reason. A Poem written in*
                      1700. L. 57.

All jargon of the schools.
   m.   PRIOR—*An Ode on Exodus III. 14.* " *I
                      am that I am.*"

I do present you with a man of mine,
Cunning in music and the mathematics,
To instruct her fully in those sciences.
   n.   *Taming of the Shrew.* Act II. Sc. 1.
                            L. 55.

Schoolmasters will I keep within my house,
Fit to instruct her youth. ✻ ✻ ✻
      ✻ ✻ ✻ To cunning men
I will be very kind, and liberal
To mine own children in good bringing up,
   o.   *Taming of the Shrew.* Act I. Sc. 1.
                            L. 94.

We'll set thee to school to an ant, to teach
thee there's no labouring i' the winter.
   p.   *King Lear.* Act II. Sc. 4. L. 67.

When I am forgotten, as I shall be,
And sleep in dull cold marble,
   ✻   ✻   ✻   ✻   ✻
       Say, I taught thee.
   q.   *Henry VIII.* Act III. Sc. 2. L. 433.

A little bench of heedless bishops here,
And there a chancellor in embryo.
   r.   SHENSTONE—*The School Mistress.* St. 28.

Whoe'er excels in what we prize,
Appears a hero in our eyes ;
Each girl, when pleased with what is taught,
Will have the teacher in her thought.
   ✻   ✻   ✻   ✻   ✻
A blockhead with melodious voice,
In boarding-schools may have his choice.
   s.   SWIFT—*Cadenus and Vanessa.* L. 733.

Delightful task! to rear the tender Thought,
To teach the young Idea how to shoot,
To pour the fresh Instruction o'er the Mind,
To breathe the enlivening Spirit, and to fix
The generous Purpose in the glowing breast.
<blockquote>a.   THOMSON—The Seasons. Spring.
L. 1,150.</blockquote>

Tobacconists.

Am I not—a smoker and a brother?
<blockquote>b.   A VETERAN OF SMOKEDOM—The
Smoker's Guide.</i> Ch. IV. Last line.</blockquote>

Look at me—follow me—smell me! The
"stunning" cigar I am smoking is one of a
sample intended for the Captain General of
Cuba, and the King of Spain, and positively
cost a shilling! Oh! * * * I have some
dearer at home. Yes, the expense is frightful,
but —— it! who can smoke the monstrous rubbish of the shops?
<blockquote>c.   A VETERAN OF SMOKEDOM—The
Smoker's Guide.</i> Ch. IV.</blockquote>

To smoke a cigar through a mouthpiece is
equivalent to kissing a lady through a res-
pirator.
<blockquote>d.   A VETERAN OF SMOKEDOM—The
Smoker's Guide.</i> Ch. V.</blockquote>

After he had administer'd a dose
Of snuff mundungus to his nose;
And powder'd th' inside of his skull,
Instead of th' outward jobbernol,
He shook it with a scornful look
On th' adversary, and thus he spoke.
<blockquote>e.   BUTLER—Hudibras. Pt. III. Canto II.
L. 1,005.</blockquote>

Sublime tobacco! which from east to west,
Cheers the tar's labour or the Turkman's rest;
Which on the Moslem's ottoman divides
His hours, and rivals opium and his brides;
Magnificent in Stamboul, but less grand,
Though not less loved, in Wapping or the
    Strand:
Divine in hookas, glorious in a pipe,
When tipp'd with amber, mellow, rich, and
    ripe;
Like other charmers, wooing the caress
More dazzlingly when daring in full dress;
Yet thy true lovers more admire by far
Thy naked beauties—Give me a cigar!
<blockquote>f.   BYRON—The Island. Canto II. St. 19.</blockquote>

Pernicious weed! whose scent the fair annoys,
Unfriendly to society's chief joys,
Thy worst effect is banishing for hours
The sex whose presence civilizes ours.
<blockquote>g.   COWPER—Conversation. L. 251.</blockquote>

The pipe, with solemn interposing puff,
Makes half a sentence at a time enough;
The dozing sages drop the drowsy strain,
Then pause, and puff—and speak, and pause
    again.
<blockquote>h.   COWPER—Conversation. L. 245.</blockquote>

Tobacco, an outlandish weed,
Doth in the land strange wonders breed;
It taints the breath, the blood it dries,
It burns the head, it blinds the eyes;
It dries the lungs, scourgeth the lights,
It 'numbs the soul, it dulls the sprites;
It brings a man into a maze,
And makes him sit for others' gaze;
It mars a man, it mars a purse,
A lean one fat, a fat one worse;
A white man black, a black man white,
A night a day, a day a night;
It turns the brain like cat in pan,
And makes a Jack a gentleman.
<blockquote>i.   FAIRHOLT—J. Payne Collier's MS.</blockquote>

Tobacco is a traveler,
  Come from the Indies hither;
    It passed sea and land
    Ere it came to my hand,
And 'scaped the wind and weather.
Tobacco's a musician,
  And in a pipe delighteth;
    It descends in a close,
    Through the organ of the nose,
With a relish that inviteth.
<blockquote>j.   BARTEN HOLIDAY—Song in Play of
Technogamia.</blockquote>

Some sigh for this and that;
  My wishes don't go far;
The world may wag at will,
  So I have my cigar.
<blockquote>k.   HOOD—The Cigar.</blockquote>

Ods me I marle what pleasure or felicity
they have in taking their roguish tobacco. It
is good for nothing but to choke a man, and
fill him full of smoke and embers.
<blockquote>l.   BEN JONSON—Every Man in His
Humour.</i> Act III. Sc. 2.</blockquote>

For Maggie has written a letter to give me my
    choice between
The wee little whimpering Love and the great
    god Nick O'Teen.

And I have been servant of Love for barely a
    twelvemonth clear,
But I have been priest of Portagas a matter
    of seven year.

And the gloom of my bachelor days is flecked
    with the cherry light
Of stumps that I burned to friendship, and
    pleasure and work and fight.
<blockquote>m.   RUDYARD KIPLING—The Betrothed.</blockquote>

For I hate, yet love thee, so,
That, whichever thing I show,
The plain truth will seem to be
A constrained hyperbole,
And the passion to proceed
More from a mistress than a weed.
<blockquote>n.   CHARLES LAMB—A Farewell to Tobacco.</blockquote>

For thy sake, tobacco, I
Would do anything but die.
   a.   CHARLES LAMB—*A Farewell to Tobacco.*

            Nay, rather,
Plant divine, of rarest virtue;
Blisters on the tongue would hurt you.
   b.   CHARLES LAMB—*A Farewell to Tobacco.*

Thou in such a cloud dost bind us,
That our worst foes cannot find us,
And ill fortune, that would thwart us,
Shoots at rovers, shooting at us;
While each man, through thy height'ning
   steam,
Does like a smoking Etna seem.
   c.   CHARLES LAMB—*A Farewell to Tobacco.*

Thou through such a mist dost show us,
That our best friends do not know us.
   d.   CHARLES LAMB—*A Farewell to Tobacco.*

He who doth not smoke hath either known
no great griefs, or refuseth himself the softest
consolation, next to that which comes from
heaven.
   e.   BULWER-LYTTON—*What Will He Do
             With It?* Bk. I. Ch. VI.

The man who smokes, thinks like a sage and
acts like a *Samaritan!*
   f.   BULWER-LYTTON—*Night and Morning.*
                 Bk. I. Ch. VI.

Woman in this scale, the weed in that,
Jupiter, hang out thy balance, and weigh
them both; and if thou give the preference
to woman, all I can say is, the next time Juno
ruffles thee—O Jupiter, try the weed.
   g.   BULWER-LYTTON—*What Will He Do
             With It?* Bk. I. Ch. VI.

I would I were a cigarette
   Between my Lady's lithe sad lips,
Where Death like Love, divinely set,
   With exquisite sighs and sips
      Feeds and is fed.
   *   *   *   *   *   *
For life is Love and Love is death,
It was my hap, a well-a-day!
To burn my little hour away.
   h.   H. A. PAGE—*Vers de Société.*
                 Madonna Mia.

Old man, God bless you, does your pipe taste
   sweetly?
A beauty, by my soul!
A ruddy flower-pot, rimmed with gold so
   neatly,
What ask you for the bowl?
O sir, that bowl for worlds I would not part
   with;
A brave man gave it me,
Who won it—now what think you—of a
   bashaw?
At Belgrade's victory.
   i.   GOTTFRIED KONRAD PFEFFEL—*The
                   Tobacco Pipe.*

Just where the breath of life his nostrils drew,
A charge of snuff the wily virgin threw;
The gnomes direct, to every atom just,
The pungent grains of titillating dust,
Sudden, with starting tears each eye o'erflows,
And the high dome re-echoes to his nose.
   j.   POPE—*Rape of the Lock.* Canto V.
                        L. 81.

Sir Plume, of amber snuff-box justly vain,
And the nice conduct of a clouded cane.
   k.   POPE—*Rape of the Lock.* Canto IV.
                       L. 122.

Divine Tobacco.
   l.   SPENSER—*Faerie Queene.* Bk. III.
                  Canto V. St. 32.

Yes, social friend, I love thee well,
   In learned doctors' spite;
Thy clouds all other clouds dispel
   And lap me in delight.
   m.   CHARLES SPRAGUE—*To My Cigar.*

Dick Stoype
Was a dear friend and lover of the pipe.
He used to say one pipe of Wishart's best
Gave life a zest.
To him 'twas meat and drink and physic,
To see the friendly vapor
Curl round his midnight taper,
And the black fume
Clothe all the room,
In clouds as dark as sciences metaphysic.
   n.   CHARLES WESTMACOTT—*Points of
                        Misery.*

Tonsorial.

With odorous oil thy head and hair are sleek;
And then thou kemb'st the tuzzes on thy
   cheek:
Of these, my barbers take a costly care.
   o.   DRYDEN—*Fourth Satire of Persius.*
                        L. 89.

Of a thousand shavers, two do not shave so
much alike as not to be distinguished.
   p.   SAM'L JOHNSON—*Boswell's Life of
                    Johnson.* 1777.

But he shaved with a shell when he chose,
'Twas the manner of primitive man.
   q.   ANDREW LANG—*Double Ballad of
                   Primitive Man.*

Thy boist'rous locks, no worthy match
For valour to assail, nor by the sword
   *   *   *   *   *
But by the barber's razor best subdued.
   r.   MILTON—*Samson Agonistes.* L. 1,167.

The first (barbers) that entered Italy came
out of Sicily and it was in the 454 yeare after
the foundation of Rome. Brought in they
were by P. Ticinius Mena as Varra doth report
for before that time they never cut their hair.
The first that was shaven every day was Scipio
Africanus, and after him cometh Augustus the
Emperor who evermore used the rasor.
   s.   PLINY—*Natural History.* Bk. VII.
               Ch. LIX. Holland's trans.

Hoary whiskers and a forky beard.
   a.   POPE—*Rape of the Lock.*   Canto III.
             L. 37.

Ere on thy chin the springing beard began
To spread a doubtful down, and promise man.
   b.   PRIOR—*An Ode to the Memory of the*
           Honourable Colonel George Villiers.
             L. 5.

          And his chin new reap'd,
Show'd like a stubble-land at harvest-home.
   c.   *Henry IV.*   Pt. I.   Act I.   Sc. 3.   L. 34.

I must to the barber's; * * * for methinks I am marvellous hairy about the face.
   d.   *Midsummer-Night's Dream.*   Act IV.
             Sc. 1. L. 23.

          Our courteous Antony,
    *   *   *   *   *
Being barber'd ten times o'er, goes to the feast.
   e.   *Antony and Cleopatra.*   Act II.   Sc. 2.
             L. 227.

The barber's man hath been seen with him,
and the old ornament of his cheek hath already stuffed tennis-balls.
   f.   *Much Ado About Nothing.*   Act III.
             Sc. 2. L. 45.

What a beard hast thou got! thou hast got
more hair on thy chin than Dobbin my fill-
horse has on his tail.
   g.   *Merchant of Venice.*   Act II.   Sc. 2.
             L. 99.

Whose beard they have sing'd off with brands
    of fire ;
And ever, as it blaz'd, they threw on him
Great pails of puddled mire to quench the
    hair :
My master preaches patience to him and the
    while
His man with scissors nicks him like a fool.
   h.   *Comedy of Errors.* Act V. Sc. 1. L. 171.

A Fellow in a market town,
Most musical, cried Razors up and down.
   i.   JOHN WOLCOTT—*Farewell Odes.*   Ode 3.

Umbrella-Making.

And like umbrellas, with their feathers
Shield you in all sorts of weathers.
   j.   MICHAEL DRAYTON—*Davis.*

Good housewives all the winter's rage despise,
Defended by the riding-hood's disguise ;
Or, underneath the umbrella's oily shade,
Safe through the wet on clinking pattens
    tread,
Let Persian dames the umbrella's ribs display,
To guard their beauties from the sunny ray ;
Or sweating slaves support the shady load,
When eastern monarchs show their state
    abroad ;
Britain in winter only knows its aid,
To guard from chilling showers the walking
    maid.
   k.   GAY—*Trivia.*   Bk. I.   L. 209.

When my water-proof umbrella proved a
    sieve, sieve, sieve,
When my shiny new umbrella proved a sieve.
   l.   ROSSITER JOHNSON—*A Rhyme of the*
             Rain.

The inseparable gold umbrella which in
that country [Burma] as much denotes the
grandee as the star or garter does in England.
   m.   J. W. PALMER—*Up and Down the*
             Irrawadde.

The tucked-up sempstress walks with hasty
    strides,
While streams run down her oil'd umbrella's
    sides.
   n.   SWIFT—*Description of a City Shower.*

Undertakers.

Nigh to a grave that was newly made,
Leaned a sexton old on his earth-worn spade.
   o.   PARK BENJAMIN—*The Old Sexton.*

See yonder maker of the dead man's bed,
The sexton, hoary-headed chronicle,
Of hard, unmeaning face, down which ne'er
    stole
A gentle tear.
   p.   BLAIR—*The Grave.*   L. 451.

          Ye undertakers, tell us,
'Midst all the gorgeous figures you exhibit,
Why is the principal conceal'd, for which
You make this mighty stir ?
   q.   BLAIR—*The Grave.*   L. 170.

There was a man bespake a thing,
Which when the owner home did bring,
He that made it did refuse it :
And he that brought it would not use it,
And he that hath it doth not know
Whether he hath it yea or no.
   r.   SIR JOHN DAVIES—*A Riddle upon a*
             Coffin.

Alas, poor Tom ! how oft, with merry heart,
Have we beheld thee play the Sexton's part ;
Each comic heart must now be grieved to see
The Sexton's dreary part performed on thee.
   s.   ROBERT FERGUSSON—*Epigram on the*
             Death of Mr. Thomas Lancashire,
             Comedian.

Why is the hearse with scutcheons blazon'd
    round,
And with the nodding plume of ostrich
    crown'd ?
No ; the dead know it not, nor profit gain ;
It only serves to prove the living vain.
   t.   GAY—*Trivia.*   Bk. III.   L. 231.

Has this fellow no feeling of his business
that he sings at grave-making ?
Custom hath made it in him a property of
easiness.
   u.   *Hamlet.*   Act V.   Sc. 1.   L. 73.

The houses that he makes last till doomsday.
   v.   *Hamlet.*   Act V.   Sc. 1.   L. 66.

OCEAN.

Ye waves
That o'er th' interminable ocean wreathe
Your crisped smiles.

a.   ÆSCHYLUS—*Prometheus Chained.*
           L. 95.

The sea heaves up, hangs loaded o'er the land,
Breaks there, and buries its tumultuous
    strength.

b.   ROBERT BROWNING—*Luria.*   Act I.

Old Ocean's gray and melancholy waste
Are but the solemn decorations all
Of the great tomb of man.

c.   BRYANT—*Thanatopsis.*   L. 43.

And I have loved thee, Ocean! and my joy
Of youthful sports was on thy breast to be
Borne, like thy bubbles, onward; from a boy
I wanton'd with thy breakers.

d.   BYRON—*Childe Harold.*   Canto IV.
           St. 184.

Once more upon the waters! yet once more!
And the waves bound beneath me as a steed
That knows his rider.

e.   BYRON—*Childe Harold.*   Canto III.
           St. 2.

Roll on, thou deep and dark blue Ocean—roll!
Ten thousand fleets sweep over thee in vain;
Man marks the earth with ruin—his control
Stops with the shore.

f.   BYRON—*Childe Harold.*   Canto IV.
           St. 179.

The image of Eternity—the throne
    Of the Invisible; even from out thy slime
The monsters of the deep are made; each
    zone
Obeys thee; thou goest forth, dread, fathom-
    less, alone.

g.   BYRON—*Childe Harold.*   Canto IV.
           St. 183.

There's not a sea the passenger e'er pukes in,
Turns up more dangerous breakers than the
    Euxine.

h.   BYRON—*Don Juan.*   Canto V.   St. 5.

What are the wild waves saying,
    Sister, the whole day long,
That ever amid our playing
    I hear but their low, lone song?

i.   JOSEPH E. CARPENTER—*What are the
           Wild Waves Saying?*

I never was on the dull, tame shore,
But I loved the great sea more and more.

j.   BARRY CORNWALL—*The Sea.*

The sea! the sea! the open sea!
The blue, the fresh, the ever free!
Without a mark, without a bound,
It runneth the earth's wide regions round;
It plays with the clouds; it mocks the skies;
Or like a cradled creature lies.

k.   BARRY CORNWALL—*The Sea.*

Rushes lean over the water,
    Shells lie on the shore,
And thou, the blue Ocean's daughter,
    Sleep'st soft in the song of its roar.

l.   GEO. WM. CURTIS—*Song.*

Behold the Sea,
The opaline, the plentiful and strong,
Yet beautiful as is the rose in June,
Fresh as the trickling rainbow of July;
Sea full of food, the nourisher of kinds,
Purger of earth, and medicine of men;
Creating a sweet climate by my breath,
Washing out harms and griefs from memory,
And, in my mathematic ebb and flow,
Giving a hint of that which changes not.

m.   EMERSON—*Sea Shore.*

The sea is flowing ever,
The land retains it never.

n.   GOETHE—*Hikmet Nameh.*   *Book of
           Proverbs.*

Alone I walked the ocean strand,
A pearly shell was in my hand;
I stooped, and wrote upon the sand
    My name, the year, the day.
As onward from the spot I passed,
One lingering look behind I cast,
A wave came rolling high and fast,
    And washed my lines away.

o.   HANNAH FLAGG GOULD—*A Name in
           the Sand.*

The sea appears all golden
    Beneath the sun-lit sky.

p.   HEINE—*Book of Songs.*   *New Poems.*
           Seraphina.   No. 15.

The breaking waves dashed high
    On a stern and rock-bound coast,
And the woods against a stormy sky,
    Their giant branches toss'd.

q.   MRS. HEMANS—*The Landing of the
           Pilgrim Fathers in New England.*

Whilst breezy waves toss up their silvery
    spray.

r.   HOOD—*Ode to the Moon.*

Quoth the Ocean, "Dawn! O fairest, clearest,
    Touch me with thy golden fingers bland;
For I have no smile till thou appearest
    For the lovely land."

s.   JEAN INGELOW—*Winstanley.*   *The
           Apology.*

Come o'er the moonlit sea,
The waves are brightly glowing.

t.   CHARLES JEFFERYS—*The Moonlit Sea.*

Love the sea? I dote upon it—from the
beach.

u.   DOUGLAS JERROLD—*Specimen of
           Jerrold's Wit.*   *Love of the Sea.*

Tut! the best thing I know between France and England is the sea.

a.   DOUGLAS JERROLD—*Jerrold's Wit. The Anglo-French Alliance.*

Past are three summers since she first beheld
The ocean; all around the child await
Some exclamation of amazement here:
She coldly said, her long-lasht eyes abased,
Is this the mighty ocean? is this all?

b.   WALTER SAVAGE LANDOR—*Gebir.*
Bk. V.

The land is dearer for the sea,
The ocean for the shore.

c.   LUCY LARCOM—*On the Beach.* St. 11.

"Would'st thou,"—so the helmsman answered,
"Learn the secret of the sea?
Only those who brave its dangers
Comprehend its mystery!"

d.   LONGFELLOW—*The Secret of the Sea.*
Verse 8.

Distinct as the billows, yet one as the sea.

e.   MONTGOMERY—*The Ocean.* St. 6.

And Thou, vast Ocean! on whose awful face
Time's iron feet can print no ruin trace.

f.   ROBERT MONTGOMERY—*The Omnipresence of the Deity.* Pt. I.
St. 20.

He laid his hand upon "the Ocean's mane,"
And played familiar with his hoary locks.

g.   POLLOK—*Course of Time.* Bk. IV.
L. 689.

Why does the sea moan evermore?
Shut out from heaven it makes its moan,
It frets against the boundary shore;
All earth's full rivers cannot fill
The sea, that drinking thirsteth still.

h.   CHRISTINA G. ROSSETTI—*By the Sea.*
St. 1.

A life on the ocean wave!
A home on the rolling deep;
Where the scattered waters rave,
And the winds their revels keep!

i.   EPES SARGENT—*Life on the Ocean Wave.*

The always wind-obeying deep.

j.   *Comedy of Errors.* Act I. Sc. 1. L. 64.

See the mountains kiss high heaven,
And the waves clasp one another.

k.   SHELLEY—*Love's Philosophy.*

There the sea I found
Calm as a cradled child in dreamless slumber bound.

l.   SHELLEY—*The Revolt of Islam.*
Canto I. St. 15.

Blue, darkly, deeply, beautifully blue.

m.   SOUTHEY—*Madoc in Wales.* Pt. V.

Ye who dwell at home,
Ye do not know the terrors of the main.

n.   SOUTHEY—*Madoc in Wales.* Pt. IV.

I loved the Sea.
Whether in calm it glassed the gracious day
With all its light, the night with all its fires;
Whether in storm it lashed its sullen spray,
Wild as the heart when passionate youth expires;
Or lay, as now, a torture to my mind,
In yonder land-locked bay, unwrinkled by the wind.

o.   R. H. STODDARD—*Carmen Naturæ Triumphale.* L. 192.

Thou wert before the Continents, before
The hollow heavens, which like another sea
Encircles them and thee, but whence thou wert,
And when thou wast created, is not known,
Antiquity was young when thou wast old.

p.   R. H. STODDARD—*Hymn to the Sea.*
L. 104.

We follow and race
In shifting chase,
Over the boundless ocean-space!
Who hath beheld when the race begun?
Who shall behold it run?

q.   BAYARD TAYLOR—*The Waves.*

Rocked in the cradle of the deep,
I lay me down in peace to sleep.

r.   EMMA WILLARD—*The Cradle of the Deep.*

Ocean into tempest wrought,
To waft a feather, or to drown a fly.

s.   YOUNG—*Night Thoughts.* Night I.
L. 153.

OCTOBER (*See* MONTHS).

OPINION.

Sure 'tis an orthodox opinion,
That grace is founded in dominion.

t.   BUTLER—*Hudibras.* Pt. I. Canto III.
L. 1,173.

With books and money plac'd, for show
Like nest eggs, to make clients lay,
And for his false opinion pay.

u.   BUTLER—*Hudibras.* Pt. III.
Canto III. L. 624.

For most men (till by losing rendered sager)
Will back their own opinions by a wager.

v.   BYRON—*Beppo.* St. 27.

Monuments of the safety with which errors of opinion may be tolerated where reason is left free to combat it.

w.   THOMAS JEFFERSON—*First Inaugural Address.* March 4, 1801.

Even opinion is of force enough to make
itself to be espoused at the expense of life.
a.   MONTAIGNE—*Of Good and Evil.*
Ch. XL.

There never was in the world two opinions
alike, no more than two hairs, or two grains;
the most universal quality is diversity.
b.   MONTAIGNE—*Essays. Of the*
Resemblance of Children to their
Fathers.

What will Mrs. Grundy say!
c.   THOS. MORTON—*Speed the Plough.*
Act I. Sc. 1.

Some praise at morning what they blame at
night,
But always think the last opinion right.
d.   POPE—*Essay on Criticism.* Pt. II.
L. 230.

I have bought
Golden opinions from all sorts of people,
Which would be worn now in their newest
gloss,
Not cast aside so soon.
e.   *Macbeth.* Act I. Sc. 7. L. 32.

Opinion's but a fool, that makes us scan
The outward habit by the inward man.
f.   *Pericles.* Act II. Sc. 2. L. 56.

OPPORTUNITY.

There is an hour in each man's life appointed
To make his happiness, if then he seize it.
g.   BEAUMONT AND FLETCHER—*Custom of*
the Country. Act II. Sc. 3. L. 85.

This could but have happened once,
And we missed it, lost it forever.
h.   ROBERT BROWNING—*Youth and Art.*
XVII.

He that will not when he may,
When he will he shall have nay.
i.   BURTON—*Quoted in Anatomy of*
Melancholy. Pt. III. Sec. 2.
Memb. 5. Subsec. 5.

Danger will wink on opportunity.
j.   MILTON—*Comus.* L. 401.

Zeal and duty are not slow
But on occasion's forelock watchful wait.
k.   MILTON—*Paradise Regained.* Bk. III.
L. 172.

He that would not when he might,
He shall not when he wolda.
l.   THOS. PERCY—*Reliques. The Baffled*
Knight.

A staff is quickly found to beat a dog.
m.   *Henry VI.* Pt. II. Act III. Sc. 1.
L. 471.

O opportunity, thy guilt is great!
'Tis thou that executest the traitor's treason;
Thou set'st the wolf where he the lamb may
get;
Whoever plots the sin, thou 'point'st the
season;
'Tis thou that spurn'st at right, at law, at
reason.
n.   *The Rape of Lucrece.* L. 876.

There is a tide in the affairs of men,
Which, taken at the flood, leads on to fortune;
Omitted, all the voyage of their life
Is bound in shallows and in miseries.
o.   *Julius Cæsar.* Act IV. Sc. 3. L. 218.

There's place and means for every man alive.
p.   *All's Well That Ends Well.* Act IV.
Sc. 3. L. 375.

Urge them while their souls
Are capable of this ambition,
Lest zeal, now melted by the windy breath
Of soft petitions, pity and remorse,
Cool and congeal again to what it was.
q.   *King John.* Act II. Sc. 2. L. 475.

Who seeks, and will not take when once 'tis
offer'd,
Shall never find it more.
r.   *Antony and Cleopatra.* Act II. Sc. 7.
L. 89.

Turning for them who pass, the common dust
Of servile opportunity to gold.
s.   WORDSWORTH—*Desultory Stanzas.*

ORACLE.

The oracles are dumb,
No voice or hideous hum
Runs thro' the arched roof in words deceiving.
t.   MILTON—*Hymn on Christ's Nativity.*
L. 173.

I am Sir Oracle,
And when I ope my lips let no dog bark!
u.   *Merchant of Venice.* Act I. Sc. 1. L. 93.

ORATORY.

For rhetoric, he could not ope
His mouth, but out there flew a trope.
v.   BUTLER—*Hudibras.* Pt. I. Canto I.
L. 81.

The Orator persuades and carries all with
him, he knows not how; the Rhetorician can
prove that he ought to have persuaded and
carried all with him.
w.   CARLYLE—*Essays. Characteristics.*

He mouths a sentence as curs mouth a bone.
x.   CHURCHILL—*The Rosciad.* L. 322.

I asked of my dear friend Orator Prig:
"What's the first part of oratory?" He said,
   "A great wig."
"And what is the second?" Then, dancing a
   jig
And bowing profoundly, he said, "A great
   wig."
"And what is the third?" Then he snored
   like a pig,
And puffing his cheeks out, he replied, "A
   great wig."
   a.   GEO. COLMAN (the Younger)—*Orator*
                     Prig.

We fear that the glittering generalities of
the speaker have left an impression more
delightful than permanent.
   b.   F. J. DICKMAN—*Review of Lecture by*
                     Rufus Choate.

There is no true orator who is not a hero.
   c.   EMERSON—*Letters and Social Aims.*
                     Eloquence.

You'd scarce expect one of my age
To speak in public on the stage;
And if I chance to fall below
Demosthenes or Cicero,
Don't view me with a critic's eye,
But pass my imperfections by.
Large streams from little fountains flow,
Tall oaks from little acorns grow.
   d.   DAVID EVERETT—*Lines Written for a*
                     School Declamation.

The passions are the only orators that always persuade: they are, as it were, a natural
art, the rules of which are infallible; and the
simplest man with passion is more persuasive
than the most eloquent without it.
   e.   LA ROCHEFOUCAULD—*Maxims.* No. 9.

The object of oratory alone is not truth, but
persuasion.
   f.   MACAULAY—*Essay on Athenian Orators.*

Thence to the famous orators repair,
Those ancient, whose resistless eloquence
Wielded at will that fierce democratie,
Shook the Arsenal, and fulmined over Greece,
To Macedon, and Artaxerxes' throne.
   g.   MILTON—*Paradise Regained.* Bk. IV.
                     L. 267.

The capital of the orator is in the bank of
the highest sentimentalities and the purest
enthusiasms.
   h.   EDW. G. PARKER—*The Golden Age of*
                 American Oratory. Ch. I.

When Demosthenes was asked what was
the first part of Oratory, he answered,
"Action," and which was the second, he replied, "Action," and which was the third, he
still answered "Action."
   i.   PLUTARCH—*Morals. Lives of the Ten*
                     Orators.
Be not thy tongue thy own shame's orator.
   j.   *Comedy of Errors.* Act III. Sc. 2.
                     L. 10.

Bid me discourse, I will enchant thine ear,
Or, like a fairy, trip upon the green.
   k.   *Venus and Adonis.* L. 145.

Fear not, my lord, I'll play the orator
As if the golden fee for which I plead
Were for myself.
   l.   *Richard III.* Act III. Sc. 5. L. 95.

I come not, friends, to steal away your hearts;
I am no orator, as Brutus is;
* * * I only speak right on.
   m.   *Julius Cæsar.* Act III. Sc. 2. L. 220.

List his discourse of war, and you shall hear
A fearful battle render'd you in music.
   n.   *Henry V.* Act I. Sc. 1. L. 43.

What means this passionate discourse,
This peroration with such circumstance?
   o.   *Henry VI.* Pt. II. Act I. Sc. 1. L. 104.

ORDER.

For the world was built in order
   And the atoms march in tune;
Rhyme the pipe, and Time the warder,
   The sun obeys them, and the moon.
   p.   EMERSON—*Monadnock.* St. 12.

Can any man have a higher notion of the
rule of right and the eternal fitness of things?
   q.   HENRY FIELDING—*Tom Jones.* Bk. IV.
                     Ch. IV.
Still to be neat, still to be drest,
As you were going to a feast.
   r.   BEN JONSON—*The Silent Woman.*
                 Act I. Sc. 1.
Confusion heard his voice, and wild uproar
Stood ruled, stood vast infinitude confined;
Till at his second bidding darkness fled,
Light shone, and order from disorder sprung.
   s.   MILTON—*Paradise Lost.* Bk. III.
                     L. 710.
Mark what unvary'd laws preserve each state,
Laws wise as Nature, and as fixed as Fate.
   t.   POPE—*Essay on Man.* Ep. III. L. 189.

Not chaos-like together crush'd and bruis'd,
But, as the world, harmoniously confused:
Where order in variety we see,
And where, tho' all things differ, all agree.
   u.   POPE—*Windsor Forest.* L. 13.

Order is Heaven's first law; and this confest,
Some are and must be greater than the rest.
   v.   POPE—*Essay on Man.* Ep. IV. L. 49.
             Not a mouse
Shall disturb this hallow'd house:
I am sent with broom before,
To sweep the dust behind the door.
   w.   *Midsummer-Night's Dream.* Act V.
                  Sc. 1. L. 394.
The heavens themselves, the planets and this
   centre
Observe degree, priority and place,
Insisture, course, proportion, season, form,
Office and custom, in all line of order.
   x.   *Troilus and Cressida.* Act I. Sc. 3. L. 85.

P.

PAIN.

World's use is cold, world's love is vain,
World's cruelty is bitter bane
But pain is not the fruit of pain.
 a. E. B. BROWNING—*A Vision of Poets.*
          St. 146.

 Rich the treasure,
  Sweet the pleasure,
Sweet is pleasure after pain.
 b. DRYDEN—*Alexander's Feast.* L. 58.

Nature knows best, and she says, *roar!*
 c. MARIA EDGEWORTH—*Ormond.* Ch. V.
    King Corny in a Paroxysm of the Gout.

So great was the extremity of his pain and
anguish, that he did not only sigh but roar.
 d. MATHEW HENRY—*Commentaries.*
        Job III. V. 24.

There is purpose in pain,
Otherwise it were devilish.
 e. OWEN MEREDITH (Lord Lytton)—
    Lucile. Pt. II. Canto V. St. 8.

You purchase pain with all that joy can give,
And die of nothing but a rage to live.
 f. POPE—*Moral Essays.* Ep. II. L. 99.

Pain is no longer pain when it is past.
 g. MARGARET J. PRESTON—*Old Songs and
    New. Nature's Lesson.*

Why, all delights are vain; but that most vain,
Which, with pain purchas'd, doth inherit pain.
 h. *Love's Labour's Lost.* Act I. Sc. 1.
          L. 72.

The scourge of life, and death's extreme disgrace,
The smoke of hell,—that monster callèd Paine.
 i. SIR PHILIP SIDNEY—*Sidera. Paine.*

Nothing begins, and nothing ends,
 That is not paid with moan;
For we are born in others' pain,
 And perish in our own.
 j. FRANCIS THOMPSON—*Daisy.* St. 15.

A man of pleasure is a man of pains.
 k. YOUNG—*Night Thoughts.* Night VIII.
          L. 793.

PAINTING (*See* OCCUPATIONS).

PARADISE.

But when the sun in all his state
 Illumed the eastern skies,
She passed through Glory's morning-gate,
 And walked in Paradise.
 l. JAMES ALDRICH—*A Death Bed.*

In the nine heavens are eight Paradises;
Where is the ninth one? In the human
  breast.
Only the blessed dwell in th' Paradises,
But blessedness dwells in the human breast.
 m. WM. R. ALGER—*Oriental Poetry.*
       The Ninth Paradise.

In this fool's paradise, he drank delight.
 n. CRABBE—*The Borough Players.*
         Letter XII.

The meanest floweret of the vale,
The simplest note that swells the gale,
The common sun, the air, the skies,
To him are open paradise.
 o. GRAY—*Ode on the Pleasure Arising
      from Vicissitudes.* L. 53.

Mahomet was taking his afternoon nap in
his Paradise. An houri had rolled a cloud
under his head, and he was snoring serenely
near the fountain of Salsabil.
 p. EARNEST L'EPINE—*Croquemitaine.*
    Bk. II. Ch. IX. Hood's trans.

A limbo large and broad since call'd
The Paradise of fools to few unknown.
 q. MILTON—*Paradise Lost.* Bk. III.
          L. 495.

So on he fares, and to the border comes,
Of Eden, where delicious Paradise,
Now nearer, crowns with her enclosure
  green,
As with a rural mound, the champain head
Of a steep wilderness.
 r. MILTON—*Paradise Lost.* Bk. IV.
          L. 131.

One morn a Peri at the gate
Of Eden stood disconsolate.
 s. MOORE—*Lalla Rookh. Paradise and
         the Peri.*

The loves that meet in Paradise shall cast out
  fear,
And Paradise hath room for you and me and
  all.
 t. CHRISTINA G. ROSSETTI—*Saints and
        Angels.* St. 10.

There is no expeditious road
To pack and label men for God,
And save them by the barrel-load.
Some may perchance, with strange surprise,
Have blundered into Paradise.
 u. FRANCIS THOMPSON—*Epilogue.* St. 2.

PARADOX.

For thence,—a paradox
Which comforts while it mocks,—
Shall life succeed in that it seems to fail:
What I aspired to be,
And was not, comforts me:
A brute I might have been, but would not
   sink i' the scale.
  a.   Robert Browning—*Rabbi-Ben-Ezra*.
                        St. 7.

Then there is that glorious Epicurean paradox, uttered by my friend, the Historian, in
one of his flashing moments: "Give us the
luxuries of life, and we will dispense with its
necessaries."
  b.   O. W. Holmes—*The Autocrat of the
                Breakfast Table*. VI.

These are old fond paradoxes to make fools
   laugh i' the alehouse.
  c.   *Othello*. Act II. Sc. 1. L. 139.

You undergo too strict a paradox,
Striving to make an ugly deed look fair.
  d.   *Timon of Athens*. Act III. Sc. 5. L. 24.

The mind begins to boggle at unnatural
substances as things paradoxical and incom-
prehensible.
  e.   Bishop South—*Sermons*.

PARTING.

           Till then, good-night!
You wish the time were now? And I.
You do not blush to wish it so?
You would have blush'd yourself to death
To own so much a year ago.
What! both these snowy hands? ah, then
I'll have to say, Good-night again.
  f.   T. B. Aldrich—*Palabras Cariñosas*.

Fare thee well! and if for ever,
Still for ever, fare thee well.
  g.   Byron—*Fare Thee Well*.

Let's not unman each other—part at once;
All farewells should be sudden, when forever,
Else they make an eternity of moments,
And clog the last sad sands of life with tears.
  h.   Byron—*Sardanapalus*. Act V. Sc. 1.

Such partings break the heart they fondly
   hope to heal.
  i.   Byron—*Childe Harold*. Canto I.
                        St. 10.

We two parted
  In silence and tears,
Half broken-hearted
  To sever for years.
  j.   Byron—*When We Two Parted*.

One kind kiss before we part,
  Drop a tear, and bid adieu;
Though we sever, my fond heart
  Till we meet shall pant for you.
  k.   Dodsley—*Colin's Kisses*. *The Parting
                             Kiss*.
In every parting there is an image of death.
  l.   George Eliot—*Amos Barton*. Ch. X.

Excuse me, then! you know my heart;
But dearest friends, alas! must part.
  m.   Gay—*The Hare and Many Friends*.
                              L. 61.
We only part to meet again.
  n.   Gay—*Black-eyed Susan*. St. 4.

Good-night! good-night! as we so oft have
   said
  Beneath this roof at midnight, in the days
  That are no more, and shall no more return.
Thou hast but taken up thy lamp and gone to
  bed;
  I stay a little longer, as one stays
  To cover up the embers that still burn.
  o.   Longfellow—*Three Friends of Mine*.
                            Pt. IV.

Two lives that once part, are as ships that
   divide
When, moment on moment, there rushes between
  The one and the other, a sea;—
Ah, never can fall from the days that have
   been
  A gleam on the years that shall be!
  p.   Bulwer-Lytton—*A Lament*. L. 10.

           If we must part forever,
Give me but one kind word to think upon,
And please myself with, while my heart's
   breaking.
  q.   Thos. Otway—*The Orphan*. Act III.
                            Sc. 1.

Shall I bid her goe? what and if I doe?
Shall I bid her goe and spare not?
Oh no, no, no, I dare not.
  r.   Thomas Percy—*Reliques*. *Corydon's
                       Farewell to Phillis*.

My Book and *Heart*
Shall never part.
  s.   *From the New England Primer*. 1814.

Now fitted the halter, now travers'd the cart,
And often took leave; but was loth to part.
  t.   Prior—*The Thief and the Cordelier*.

But in vain she did conjure him,
  To depart her presence so,
Having a thousand tongues t' allure him
  And but one to bid him go.
    When lips invite,
    And eyes delight,
And cheeks as fresh as rose in June,
    Persuade delay,—
    What boots to say
Forego me now, come to me soon.
  u.   Sir Walter Raleigh—*Dulcina*. See
      Cayley's *Life of Raleigh*. Vol. I.
                           Ch. III.

Good-night, good-night! parting is such sweet
   sorrow,
That I shall say good-night till it be morrow.
  v.   *Romeo and Juliet*. Act II. Sc. 2.
                            L. 185.
If we do meet again, we'll smile indeed;
If not, 'tis true this parting was well made.
  w.   *Julius Cæsar*. Act V. Sc. 1. L. 121.

They say he parted well, and paid his score;
And so, God be with him!
   a.   *Macbeth.*   Act V.   Sc. 8.   L. 52.

So sweetly she bade me adieu,
I thought that she bade me return.
   b.   SHENSTONE—*A Pastoral Ballad.*
                        Absence.   Pt. I.

             And must we part?
Well, if—we must—we must—and in that case
The less is said the better.
   c.   R. B. SHERIDAN—*The Critic.*   Act II.
                                Sc. 2.

Twilight and evening bell,
   And after that the dark!
And may there be no sadness of farewell
   When I embark.
   d.   TENNYSON—*Crossing the Bar.*

She went her unremembering way,
   She went and left in me
The pang of all the partings gone,
   And partings yet to be.
   e.   FRANCIS THOMPSON—*Daisy.*   St. 12.

But fate ordains that dearest friends must
     part.
   f.   YOUNG—*Love of Fame.*   Satire II.
                                L. 232.

PASSION.

Fountain-heads and pathless groves,
Places which pale passion loves!
   g.   BEAUMONT AND FLETCHER—*The Nice*
        Valour. Song.   Act III.   Sc. **3.**

       Only I discern
Infinite passion, and the pain
Of finite hearts that yearn.
   h.   ROBERT BROWNING—*Two in the*
                     Campagna.   St. 12.

Misled by Fancy's meteor-ray,
   By passion driven;
But yet the light that led astray,
   Was light from Heaven.
   i.   BURNS—*The Vision.*

For one heat, all know, doth drive out another,
One passion doth expel another still.
   j.   GEORGE CHAPMAN—*Monsieur D'Olive.*
                    Act V.   Sc. 1.   L. 8.

Filled with fury, rapt, inspir'd.
   k.   COLLINS—*The Passions.*   L. 10.

We are ne'er like angels till our passion dies.
   l.   THOMAS DEKKER—*The Honest Whore.*
                      Pt. II.   Act I.   Sc. 2.

Bee to the blossom, moth to the flame;
Each to his passion; what's in a name?
   m.   HELEN HUNT JACKSON—*Vanity of*
                              Vanities.

If we resist our passions it is more from
their weakness than from our strength.
   n.   LA ROCHEFOUCAULD—*Maxims.*   No. 125.

30

Where passion leads or prudence points the
    way.
   o.   ROBERT LOWTH—*Choice of Hercules.*

            Take heed lest passion sway
Thy judgment to do aught, which else free
        will
Would not admit.
   p.   MILTON—*Paradise Lost.*   Bk. VIII.
                                L. 634.

And you, brave Cobham! to the latest breath
Shall feel your ruling passion strong in death.
   q.   POPE—*Moral Essays.*   Ep. I.   L. 262.

In men, we various ruling passions find;
In women two almost divide the kind;
Those only fix'd, they first or last obey,
The love of pleasure, and the love of sway.
   r.   POPE—*Moral Essays.*   Ep. II.   L. 207.

Search then the ruling passion; there alone,
The wild are constant, and the cunning
         known;
The fool consistent, and the false sincere;
Priests, princes, women, no dissemblers here.
   s.   POPE—*Moral Essays.*   Ep. I.   L. 174.

The ruling passion, be it what it will,
The ruling passion conquers reason still.
   t.   POPE—*Moral Essays.*   Ep. III.   L. 153.

May I govern my passions with absolute sway,
And grow wiser and better as my strength
        wears away.
   u.   WALTER POPE—*The Old Man's Wish.*

Passions are likened best to floods and streams,
The shallow murmur, but the deep are dumb.
   v.   SIR WALTER RALEIGH—*The Silent*
        Lover.   See CAYLEY's *Life of Raleigh.*
                      Vol. I.   Ch. III.

Alas, why gnaw you so your nether lip?
Some bloody passion shakes your very frame;
These are portents; but yet I hope, I hope,
They do not point on me.
   w.   *Othello.*   Act V.   Sc. 2.   L. 43.

A little fire is quickly trodden out;
Which, being suffer'd, rivers cannot quench.
   x.   *Henry VI.*   Pt. III.   Act IV.   Sc. 8.
                                L. 7.

          Give me that man
That is not passion's slave.
   y.   *Hamlet.*   Act III.   Sc. 2.   L. 75.

O, that my tongue were in the thunder's
    mouth!
Then with a passion would I shake the world.
   z.   *King John.*   Act III.   Sc. 4.   L. 38.

What to ourselves in passion we propose,
The passion ending, doth the purpose lose.
   aa.   *Hamlet.*   Act III.   Sc. 2.   L. 204.

He will hold thee, when his passion shall
　　have spent its novel force,
Something better than his dog, a little dearer
　　than his horse.
　　a.　　TENNYSON—*Locksley Hall.* St. 25.

The seas are quiet when the winds give o'er;
So calm are we when passions are no more!
　　b.　　EDMUND WALLER—*On Divine Poems.*
　　　　　　　　　　　　　　　　　　L. 7.

But, children, you should never let
　　Such angry passions rise;
Your little hands were never made
　　To tear each other's eyes.
　　c.　　ISAAC WATTS—*Divine Songs.*
　　　　　　　　　　　　　　Song XVI.

And beauty, for confiding youth,
Those shocks of passion can prepare
That kill the bloom before its time,
And blanch, without the owner's crime,
The most resplendent hair.
　　d.　　WORDSWORTH—*Lament of Mary, Queen
　　　　　　　　　　　　　　　　　of Scots.*

PAST (THE).

Therefore Agathon rightly says: "Of this
alone even God is deprived, the power of making things that are past never to have been."
　　e.　　ARISTOTLE—*Ethics.* Bk. VI. Ch. II.
　　　　　　　　　　　　　R. W. Browne's trans.

But how carve way i' the life that lies before,
If bent on groaning ever for the past?
　　f.　　ROBERT BROWNING—*Balaustion's
　　　　　　　　　　　　　　　　Adventure.*

John Anderson, my jo, John,
　　When we were first acquent,
Your locks were like the raven,
　　Your bonny brow was brent.
　　g.　　BURNS—*John Anderson.*

Gone—glimmering through the dream of
things that were.
　　h.　　BYRON—*Childe Harold.* Canto II.
　　　　　　　　　　　　　　　　St. 2.

The best of prophets of the future is the past.
　　i.　　BYRON—*Letter.* Jan. 28, 1821.

Not heaven itself upon the past has power;
But what has been, has been, and I have had
　　my hour.
　　j.　　DRYDEN—*Imitation of Horace.* Bk. III.
　　　　　　　　　　　　　Ode XXIX. L. 71.

　　　　　　We remain
Safe in the hallowed quiets of the past.
　　k.　　LOWELL—*The Cathedral.* L. 234.

Weep no more, lady, weep no more,
　　Thy sorrowe is in vaine,
For violets pluckt, the sweetest showers
　　Will ne'er make grow againe.
　　l.　　THOS. PERCY—*Reliques. The Friar of
　　　　　　　　Orders Gray.* See FLETCHER—*The
　　　　　　　　Queen of Corinth.* Act III. Sc. 2.

O there are Voices of the Past,
　　Links of a broken chain,
Wings that can bear me back to Times
　　Which cannot come again;
Yet God forbid that I should lose
　　The echoes that remain!
　　m.　　ADELAIDE A. PROCTER—*Voices of the
　　　　　　　　　　　　　　　　　　Past.*

What's past is prologue.
　　n.　　*Tempest.* Act II. Sc. 1. L. 253.

The past Hours weak and gray
With the spoil which their toil
　　Raked together
From the conquest but One could foil.
　　o.　　SHELLEY—*Prometheus Unbound.*
　　　　　　　　　　　　　　Act IV. Sc. 1.

The eternal landscape of the past.
　　p.　　TENNYSON—*In Memoriam.* Pt. XLVI.

For old, unhappy, far-off things,
And battles long ago.
　　q.　　WORDSWORTH—*The Solitary Reaper.*

Though nothing can bring back the hour
Of splendour in the grass, of glory in the
　　flower.
　　r.　　WORDSWORTH—*Ode. Intimations of
　　　　　　　　　　　　Immortality.* St. 10.

That awful independent on to-morrow!
Whose work is done; who triumphs in the
　　past;
Whose yesterdays look backward with a smile
Nor, like the Parthian, wound him as they
　　fly.
　　s.　　YOUNG—*Night Thoughts.* Night II.
　　　　　　　　　　　　　　　　L. 322.

PATIENCE.

With strength and patience all his grievous
　　loads are borne,
And from the world's rose-bed he only asks a
　　thorn.
　　t.　　WM. R. ALGER—*Oriental Poetry.
　　　　　　　　　Mussud's Praise of the Camel.*

　　　　　　And I must bear
What is ordained with patience, being aware
Necessity doth front the universe
With an invincible gesture.
　　u.　　E. B. BROWNING—*Prometheus Bound.*

I worked with patience which means almost
　　power.
　　v.　　E. B. BROWNING—*Aurora Leigh.*
　　　　　　　　　　　　　　Bk. III. L. 205.

But there are times when patience proves at
fault.
　　w.　　ROBERT BROWNING—*Paracelsus.* Sc. 3.

There is however a limit at which forbearance ceases to be a virtue.
　　x.　　BURKE—*Observations on a Late
　　　　　　　Publication on the Present State of
　　　　　　　　　　　　　　　the Nation.*

To bear is to conquer our fate.
  a.   CAMPBELL—*Lines Written on Visiting a Scene in Argyleshire.*

Patience and shuffle the cards.
  b.   CERVANTES—*Don Quixote.* Pt. II. Bk. I. Ch. VI.

Thus with hir fader for a certeyn space
Dwelleth this flour of wyfly pacience,
That neither by hir wordes ne hir face
Biforn the folk, ne eek in her absence,
Ne shewed she that hir was doon offence.
  c.   CHAUCER—*The Clerkes Tale.* V. L. 13,254.

Patience is sorrow's salve.
  d.   CHURCHILL—*Prophecy of Famine.* L. 363.

His patient soul endures what Heav'n ordains,
But neither feels nor fears ideal pains.
  e.   CRABBE—*The Borough.* Letter XVII.

Patience is a necessary ingredient of genius.
  f.   BENJ. DISRAELI—*Contarini Fleming.* Pt. IV. Ch. V.

The worst speak something good; if all want sense,
God takes a text, and preacheth patience.
  g.   HERBERT—*The Church Porch.* St. 72.

For patience, sov'reign o'er transmuted ill.
  h.   SAM'L JOHNSON—*The Vanity of Human Wishes.* L. 352.

All things come round to him who will but wait.
  i.   LONGFELLOW—*Tales of a Wayside Inn. The Student's Tale.* Pt. I.

Rule by patience, Laughing Water!
  j.   LONGFELLOW—*Hiawatha.* Pt. X. *Hiawatha's Wooing.*

Still achieving, still pursuing,
  Learn to labor and to wait.
  k.   LONGFELLOW—*A Psalm of Life* St. 9.

Endurance is the crowning quality,
And patience all the passion of great hearts.
  l.   LOWELL—*Columbus.* L. 241.

Or arm th' obdured breast
With stubborn patience as with triple steel.
  m.   MILTON—*Paradise Lost.* Bk. II. L. 568.

A high hope for a low heaven: God grant us patience!
  n.   *Love's Labour's Lost.* Act I. Sc. 1. L. 195.

And makes us rather bear those ills we have
Than fly to others that we know not of?
  o.   *Hamlet.* Act III. Sc. 1. L. 81.

Had it pleas'd heaven
To try me with affliction * * *
I should have found in some place of my soul
A drop of patience.
  p.   *Othello.* Act IV. Sc. 2. L. 47.

How poor are they that have not patience!
What wound did ever heal but by degrees?
  q.   *Othello.* Act II. Sc. 3. L. 376.

I do oppose
My patience to his fury, and am arm'd
To suffer, with a quietness of spirit,
The very tyranny and rage of his.
  r.   *Merchant of Venice.* Act IV. Sc. 1. L. 10.

I will with patience hear, and find a time
Both meet to hear and answer such high things.
Till then, my noble friend, chew upon this.
  s.   *Julius Cæsar.* Act I. Sc. 2. L. 169.

Like Patience gazing on kings' graves, and smiling
Extremity out of act.
  t.   *Pericles.* Act V. Sc. 1. L. 139.

She never told her love,
But let concealment, like a worm i' the bud,
Feed on her damask cheek; she pin'd in thought,
And with a green and yellow melancholy
She sat like patience on a monument,
Smiling at grief.
  u.   *Twelfth Night.* Act II. Sc. 4. L. 114.

Since you will buckle fortune on my back,
To bear her burthen, whether I will or no,
I must have patience to endure the load.
  v.   *Richard III.* Act III. Sc. 7. L. 228.

Sufferance is the badge of all our tribe.
  w.   *Merchant of Venice.* Act I. Sc. 3. L. 111.

That which in mean men we entitle patience
Is pale cold cowardice in noble breasts.
  x.   *Richard II.* Act I. Sc. 2. L. 33.

There's some ill planet reigns;
I must be patient till the heavens look
With an aspect more favorable.
  y.   *Winter's Tale.* Act II. Sc. 1. L. 105.

'Tis all men's office to speak patience
To those that ring under the load of sorrow,
But no man's virtue nor sufficiency
To be so moral when he shall endure
The like himself.
  z.   *Much Ado About Nothing.* Act V. Sc. 1. L. 27.

PATRIOTISM.

Who would not be that youth? What pity
    is it
That we can die but once to save our country!
    a.   ADDISON—*Cato.* Act IV. Sc. 4.

Our ships were British oak,
And hearts of oak our men.
    b.   S. J. ARNOLD—*Death of Nelson.*

True patriots all; for be it understood
We left our country for our country's good.
    c.   GEORGE BARRINGTON—*New South
        Wales. Prologue for the Opening of
        the Playhouse at New South Wales,*
                    Jan. 16, 1796.

Be Briton still to Britain true,
  Among oursel's united;
For never but by British hands
  Maun British wrangs be righted.
    .d.   BURNS—*Dumfries Volunteers.*

While Washington's a watchword, such as
  ne'er
Shall sink while there's an echo left to air.
    e.   BYRON—*Age of Bronze.* St. 5.

Again to the battle, Achaians!
Our hearts bid the tyrants defiance!
Our land, the first garden of liberty's tree—
It has been, and shall yet be, the land of the
  free.
    f.   CAMPBELL—*Song of the Greeks.*

We join ourselves to no party that does not
carry the flag and keep step to the music of
the Union.
    g.   RUFUS CHOATE—*Letter to a Worcester
        Whig Convention.* Oct. 1, 1855.

I have heard something said about allegiance
to the South; I know no South, no North,
no East, no West, to which I owe any allegiance.
    h.   HENRY CLAY—*In the U. S. Senate.* 1848.

How sleep the brave, who sink to rest,
By all their country's wishes blest!
     *   *   *   *   *   *
By fairy hands their knell is rung,
By forms unseen their dirge is sung.
    i.   COLLINS—*Ode Written in* 1746.

Our country! In her intercourse with
foreign nations, may she always be in the
right; but our country, right or wrong.
    j.   STEPHEN DECATUR—*Toast given at
        Norfolk, April,* 1816. See
        MACKENZIE's *Life of
        Stephen Decatur.*
        Ch. XIV.

'Twas for the good of my country that
I should be abroad.
    k.   GEO. FARQUHAR—*The Beaux' Stratagem.*
        Act III. Sc. 2. L. 89.

O Washington! thrice glorious name,
  What due rewards can man decree—
Empires are far below thy aim,
  And scepters have no charms for thee;
Virtue alone has your regards,
And she must be your great reward.
    l.   PHILIP FRENEAU—*Washington's
              Arrival in Philadelphia.*

Our country is the world—our countrymen
are all mankind.
    m.   WILLIAM LLOYD GARRISON—*Motto of
        the Liberator,* 1837—1839.

Such is the patriot's boast, where'er we roam,
His first best country ever is at home.
    n.   GOLDSMITH—*The Traveller.* L. 73.

I only regret that I have but one life to lose
for my country.
    o.   NATHAN HALE—(His Last Words,
        Sept. 22, 1776.) STEWART's *Life of
        Capt. Nathan Hale.* Ch. VII.

Strike—for your altars and your fires;
Strike—for the green graves of your sires;
  God—and your native land!
    p.   FITZ-GREENE HALLECK—*Marco
                 Bozzaris.*

I am not a Virginian but an American.
    q.   PATRICK HENRY—*In the Continental
        Congress.* Sept. 5, 1774.

One flag, one land, one heart, one hand,
One Nation evermore!
    r.   O. W. HOLMES—*Voyage of the Good
        Ship Union. Poems of the Class of '29.*

Old England is our home and Englishmen
  are we,
Our tongue is known in every clime, our flag
  on every sea.
    s.   MARY HOWITT—*Old England is Our
                Home.*

Who fears to speak of Ninety-eight?
  Who blushes at the name?
When cowards mock the patriot's fate,
  Who hangs his head for shame?
    t.   JOHN K. INGRAM—*The Dublin Nation.*
        April 1, 1843. Vol. II. P. 339.

Our federal Union: it must be preserved.
    u.   ANDREW JACKSON—*Toast given at the
        Jefferson Birthday Celebration in* 1830.
        See W. J. SUMNER's *Life of Jackson.*

Patriotism is the last refuge of a scoundrel.
    v.   SAM'L JOHNSON—*Boswell's Life of
        Johnson.* 1775.

That man is little to be envied, whose
patriotism would not gain force upon the
plain of *Marathon,* or whose piety would not
grow warmer among the ruins of *Iona.*
    w.   SAM'L JOHNSON—*A Journey to the
        Western Islands. Inch Kenneth.*

The mystic chords of memory, stretching from every battlefield and patriot grave to every living heart and hearthstone all over this broad land, will yet swell the chorus of the Union, when again touched, as surely they will be, by the better angels of our nature.

   a.   ABRAHAM LINCOLN—*Inaugural Address.* March 4, 1861.

This nation, under God, shall have a new birth of freedom, and that government of the people, by the people, for the people, shall not perish from the earth.

   b.   ABRAHAM LINCOLN—*Speech at Gettysburg.* Nov. 19, 1863.

Thou, too, sail on, O Ship of State!
Sail on, O Union, strong and great!
Humanity with all its fears,
With all the hopes of future years,
Is hanging breathless on thy fate!

   c.   LONGFELLOW—*The Building of the Ship.* L. 367.

And how can man die better
  Than facing fearful odds,
For the ashes of his fathers
  And the temple of his gods?

   d.   MACAULAY—*Horatius keeps the Bridge.*

To Greece we give our shining blades.

   e.   MOORE—*Evenings in Greece. First Evening.*

Life, for my country and the cause of freedom,
Is but a trifle for a worm to part with;
And, if preservèd in so great a contest,
  Life is redoubled.

   f.   NILES—*The American Hero.*

My country is the world, and my religion is to do good.

   g,   THOS. PAINE—*Rights of Man.* Ch. V.

Millions for defence, but not one cent for tribute.

   h.   CHAS. C. PINCKNEY—*When Ambassador to the French Republic.* 1796.

If I were an American, as I am an Englishman, while a foreign troop was landed in my country I never would lay down my arms, never! never! never!

   i.   WILLIAM PITT (Earl of Chatham)—*Speech.* Nov. 18, 1777.

When asked what State he hails from,
  Our sole reply shall be,
He comes from Appomattox
  And its famous apple tree.

   j.   MILES O'REILLY—*Poem quoted by Roscoe Conkling.* June, 1880.

Where's the coward that would not dare
To fight for such a land?

   k.   SCOTT—*Marmion.* Canto IV. St. 30.

Had I a dozen sons,—each in my love alike,
* * * I had rather have eleven die nobly for their country, than one voluptuously surfeit out of action.

   l.   *Coriolanus.* Act I. Sc. 3. L. 24.

                I do love
My country's good with a respect more tender,
More holy and profound, than mine own life.

   m.   *Coriolanus.* Act III. Sc. 3. L. 111.

My country, 'tis of thee,
Sweet land of liberty,—
  Of thee I sing:
Land where my fathers died,
Land of the Pilgrim's pride,
From every mountain side
  Let freedom ring.

   n.   SAM'L F. SMITH—*National Hymn.*

O saviour of the silver-coasted isle.

   o.   TENNYSON—*Ode on Death of Duke of Wellington.* Pt. VI.

I was born an American; I live an American; I shall die an American!

   p.   DANIEL WEBSTER—*Speech.* July 17, 1850.

Let our object be, our country, our whole country, and nothing but our country.

   q.   DANIEL WEBSTER—*Address at the Laying of the Corner-Stone of the Bunker Hill Monument.* June 17, 1825.

Sink or swim, live or die, survive or perish, I give my hand and heart to this vote.

   r.   DANIEL WEBSTER—*Eulogy on Adams and Jefferson.*

Thank God, I—I also—am an American!

   s.   DANIEL WEBSTER—*Completion of Bunker Hill Monument.* June 17, 1843.

"Shoot, if you must, this old gray head,
But spare your country's flag," she said.

   t.   WHITTIER—*Barbara Frietchie.*

Our country—whether bounded by the St. John's and the Sabine, or however otherwise bounded or described, and be the measurements more or less;—still our country, to be cherished in all our hearts, and to be defended by all our hands.

   u.   ROBT. C. WINTHROP—*Toast at Faneuil Hall.* July 4, 1845.

There are no points of the compass on the chart of true patriotism.

   v.   ROBT. C. WINTHROP—*Letter to Boston Commercial Club.* June 12, 1879.

PEACE.

This hand, to tyrants ever sworn the foe,
For freedom only deals the deadly blow ;
Then sheathes in calm repose the vengeful
    blade,
For gentle peace in freedom's hallowed shade.
a.   JOHN QUINCY ADAMS—*Written in an
    Album.*

The fiercest agonies have shortest reign ;
And after dreams of horror, comes again
The welcome morning with its rays of peace.
b.   BRYANT—*Mutation.* L. 4.

The trenchant blade Toledo trusty,
For want of fighting was grown rusty,
And ate into itself for lack
Of somebody to hew and hack.
c.   BUTLER—*Hudibras.* Pt. I. Canto I.
    L. 359.

Mark ! where his carnage and his conquests
    cease,
He makes a solitude and calls it—peace !
d.   BYRON—*Bride of Abydos.* Canto II.
    St. 20.

The gentleman [Josiah Quincy] cannot
have forgotten his own sentiment, uttered
even on the floor of this House, " Peaceably if
we can, forcibly if we must."
e.   HENRY CLAY—*Speech. On the New
    Army Bill.* 1813.

Peace rules the day, where reason rules the
mind.
f.   COLLINS—*Eclogue II. Hassan.* L. 68.

O for a lodge in some vast wilderness,
Some boundless contiguity of shade ;
Where rumor of oppression and deceit,
Of unsuccessful or successful war,
Might never reach me more.
g.   COWPER—*The Task.* Bk. II. L. 1.

Nothing can bring you peace but yourself.
Nothing can bring you peace but the triumph
of principles.
h.   EMERSON—*Essays. Of Self-Reliance.*

Breathe soft, ye winds ! ye waves, in silence
sleep !
i.   GAY—*To a Lady.* Ep. I. L. 17.

Let us have peace.
j.   U. S. GRANT—*Accepting Nomination.*
    May 20, 1868.

So peaceful shalt thou end thy blissful days,
And steal thyself from life by slow decays.
k.   HOMER—*Odyssey.* Bk. XI. L. 164.
    Pope's trans.

O for a seat in some poetic nook,
Just hid with trees, and sparkling with a
brook.
l.   LEIGH HUNT—*Politics and Poetics.*

We love peace as we abhor pusillanimity ;
but not peace at any price. There is a peace
more destructive of the manhood of living
man than war is destructive of his material
body. Chains are worse than bayonets.
m.   DOUGLAS JERROLD—*Jerrold's Wit.
    Peace.*

The days of peace and slumberous calm are
    fled.
n.   KEATS—*Hyperion.* Bk. II.

Buried was the bloody hatchet ;
Buried was the dreadful war-club ;
Buried were all warlike weapons,
And the war-cry was forgotten.
Then was peace among the nations.
o.   LONGFELLOW—*Hiawatha.* Pt. XIII.
    L. 7.

Peace ! and no longer from its brazen portals
    The blast of War's great organ shakes the
    skies !
But beautiful as songs of the immortals,
    The holy melodies of love arise.
p.   LONGFELLOW—*The Arsenal at
    Springfield.*

In the inglorious arts of peace.
q.   ANDREW MARVELL—*Upon Cromwell's
    Return from Ireland.*

    Peace hath her victories,
No less renowned than war.
r.   MILTON—*Sonnet. To the Lord General
    Cromwell.*

How calm, how beautiful comes on
The stilly hour, when storms are gone.
s.   MOORE—*Lalla Rookh. The Fire
    Worshippers.* Pt. III. St. 7.

I knew by the smoke that so gracefully curled
    Above the green elms, that a cottage was
    near,
And I said, " If there's peace to be found in
    the world,
    A heart that was humble might hope for it
    here."
t.   MOORE—*Ballad Stanzas.*

The Empire means peace.
u.   LOUIS NAPOLEON—*Speech to the
    Chamber of Commerce in Bordeaux,*
    Oct. 9, 1852. See B. JERROLD'S
    Life of Louis Napoleon.

For peace do not hope ; to be just you must
    break it.
Still work for the minute and not for the year.
v.   JOHN BOYLE O'REILLY—*Rules of the
    Road.*

His helmet now shall make a hive for bees,
    And lover's sonnets turn'd to holy psalms ;
A man at arms must now serve on his knees,
    And feed on prayers, which are his age's
    alms.
w.   GEO. PEELE—*Sonnet ad fin.
    Polyhymnia.*

An equal doom clipp'd Time's blest wings of
　　peace.
　　a.　　Petrarch—*To Laura in Death.*
　　　　　　　　　　Sonnet XLVIII.　L. 18.

People are always expecting to get peace in
heaven: but you know whatever peace they
get there will be ready-made.　Whatever making of peace *they* can be blest for, must be on
the earth here.
　　b.　　Ruskin—*The Eagle's Nest.*　Lecture IX.

And for the peace of you I hold such strife
As 'twixt a miser and his wealth is found.
　　c.　　*Sonnet LXXV.*

A peace is of the nature of a conquest;
For then both parties nobly are subdued,
And neither party loser.
　　d.　　*Henry IV.*　Pt. II.　Act IV.　Sc. 2.
　　　　　　　　　　　　　　L. 89.

In peace there's nothing so becomes a man
As modest stillness and humility.
　　e.　　*Henry V.*　Act III.　Sc. 1.　L. 3.

　　　　　　　　　　　　　　　Peace,
Dear nurse of arts, plenties and joyful births.
　　f.　　*Henry V.*　Act V.　Sc. 2.　L. 34.

Still in thy right hand carry gentle peace,
To silence envious tongues.
　　g.　　*Henry VIII.*　Act III.　Sc. 2.　L. 445.

To reap the harvest of perpetual peace,
By this one bloody trial of sharp war.
　　h.　　*Richard III.*　Act V.　Sc. 2.　L. 15.

Let the bugles sound the *Truce of God* to the
whole world forever.
　　i.　　Charles Sumner—*Oration on the
　　　　　　　　　　True Grandeur of Nations.*

Peace the offspring is of Power.
　　j.　　Bayard Taylor—*A Thousand Years.*

　　　　　No more shall ＊ ＊ ＊ Peace
Pipe on her pastoral hillock a languid note,
And watch her harvest ripen.
　　k.　　Tennyson—*Maud.*　St. 28.

As on the Sea of Galilee,
The Christ is whispering " Peace."
　　l.　　Whittier—*The Tent on the Beach.
　　　　　　　　　　Kallundborg Church.*

Ne'er to meet, or ne'er to part, is peace.
　　m.　　Young—*Night Thoughts.*　Night V.
　　　　　　　　　　　　　　L. 1,058.

PEN (THE).

Art thou a pen, whose task shall be
　　To drown in ink
　　What writers think?
　　Oh, wisely write,
　　That pages white
Be not the worse for ink and thee.
　　n.　　Ethel Lynn Beers—*The Gold Nugget.*

　　　　　　　　Whose noble praise
Deserves a quill pluckt from an angel's wing.
　　o.　　Dorothy Berry—*Sonnet.*

Oh! nature's noblest gift—my gray-goose
　　quill!
Slave of my thoughts, obedient to my will,
Torn from thy parent-bird to form a pen,
That mighty instrument of little men!
　　p.　　Byron—*English Bards and Scotch
　　　　　　　　　　Reviewers.*　L. 7.

The pen wherewith thou dost so heavenly
　　sing
Made of a quill from an angel's wing.
　　q.　　Henry Constable—*Sonnet.*

The pen became a clarion.
　　r.　　Longfellow—*Monte Cassino.*　St. 13.

Beneath the rule of men entirely great
The pen is mightier than the sword.
　　s.　　Bulwer-Lytton—*Richelieu.*　Act II.
　　　　　　　　　　　　　　Sc. 2.

Let there be gall enough in thy ink, though
thou write with a goose-pen, no matter.
　　t.　　*Twelfth Night.*　Act III.　Sc. 2.　L. 52.

" You write with ease, to show your breeding,
But easy writing's curst hard reading."
　　u.　　R. B. Sheridan—*Clio's Protest.*　See
　　　　　Moore's *Life of Sheridan.*　Vol. I.
　　　　　　　　　　　　　　P. 55.

　　　　　The feather, whence the pen
Was shaped that traced the lives of these good
　　men,
Dropped from an Angel's wing.
　　v.　　Wordsworth—*Ecclesiastical Sonnets.*
　　　　　Pt. III.　V.　*Walton's Book of Lives.*

PERCEPTION.

As men of inward light are wont
To turn their optics in upon't.
　　w.　　Butler—*Hudibras.*　Pt. III.　Canto I.
　　　　　　　　　　　　　　L. 481.

For the eye of the intellect "sees in all objects what it brought with it the means of
seeing."
　　x.　　Carlyle—*Varnhagen Von Ense's
　　　　　Memoirs.*　London and Westminster
　　　　　　　　　　Review.*　1838.

He gives us the very quintessence of perception.
　　y.　　Lowell—*My Study Windows.*
　　　　　　　　　　　　Coleridge.

Minds that have nothing to confer
　　Find little to perceive.
　　z.　　Wordsworth—*Yes, Thou art Fair.*

PERFECTION.

What's come to perfection perishes,
Things learned on earth we shall practise in
    heaven;
Works done least rapidly Art most cherishes.
a.   ROBERT BROWNING—*Old Pictures in
                        Florence.* St. 17.

Thou hast no faults, or I no faults can spy;
Thou art all beauty, or all blindness I.
b.   CHRISTOPHER CODRINGTON—*On Garth's
                        Dispensary.*

The very pink of perfection.
c.   GOLDSMITH—*She Stoops to Conquer.*
                        Act I. Sc. 1.

Whoever thinks a faultless piece to see,
Thinks what ne'er was, nor is, nor e'er shall be.
d.   POPE—*Essay on Criticism.* Pt. II.
                        L. 53.

How many things by season season'd are
To their right praise and true perfection!
e.   *Merchant of Venice.* Act V. Sc. 1.
                        L. 107.

Whose dear perfection hearts that scorn'd to
    serve
Humbly call'd mistress.
f.   *All's Well That Ends Well.* Act V.
                        Sc. 3. L. 16.

A man cannot have an idea of perfection in
another, which he was never sensible of in
himself.
g.   STEELE—*The Tatler.* No. 227.

In this broad earth of ours,
Amid the measureless grossness and the slag,
Enclosed and safe within its central heart,
Nestles the seed perfection.
h.   WALT. WHITMAN—*Song of the
                        Universal.*

PERFUMERY (*See* OCCUPATIONS).

PERILS.

Ay me! what perils do environ
The man that meddles with cold iron!
i.   BUTLER—*Hudibras.* Pt. I. Canto III.
                        L. 1.
Ay me, how many perils doe enfold
The righteous man to make him daily fall!
j.   SPENSER—*Faerie Queene.* Bk. I.
                        Canto VIII. St. 1.

PERSEVERANCE.

Attempt the end and never stand to doubt;
Nothing's so hard, but search will find it out.
k.   HERRICK—*Seeke and Finde.*

For thine own purpose, thou hast sent
The strife and the discouragement!
l.   LONGFELLOW—*Christus.* The Golden
                        Legend. Pt. II.

So Satan, whom repulse upon repulse
Met ever, and to shameful silence brought,
Yet gives not o'er, though desperate of success.
m.   MILTON—*Paradise Regained.* Bk. IV.
                        L. 21.

Hope against hope, and ask till ye receive.
n.   MONTGOMERY—*The World Before the
                        Flood.* Canto V.

We shall escape the uphill by never turning
    back.
o.   CHRISTINA G. ROSSETTI—*Amor Mundi.*

        Perseverance, dear my lord,
Keeps honour bright: to have done is to hang
Quite out of fashion, like a rusty mail
In monumental mockery.
p.   *Troilus and Cressida.* Act III. Sc. 3.
                        L. 150.

Neither to change, nor falter, nor repent;
This, like thy glory, Titan! is to be
Good, great, and joyous, beautiful and free;
This is alone Life, Joy, Empire and Victory.
q.   SHELLEY—*Prometheus.* Act IV.

PERSUASION.

Persuasion tips his tongue whene'er he talks.
r.   COLLEY CIBBER—*Parody on Pope's lines.*

He, from whose lips divine persuasion flows.
s.   HOMER—*Iliad.* Bk. 7. L. 143.
                        Pope's trans.

Persuasive speech, and more persuasive sighs,
Silence that spoke, and eloquence of eyes.
t.   HOMER—*Iliad.* Bk. XIV. L. 251.
                        Pope's trans.

        Though his tongue
Dropp'd manna, and could make the worse
    appear
The better reason, to perplex and dasb
Maturest counsels.
u.   MILTON—*Paradise Lost.* Bk. II. L. 112.

Yet hold it more humane, more heav'nly, first,
By winning words to conquer willing hearts,
And make persuasion do the work of fear.
v.   MILTON—*Paradise Regained.* Bk. I.
                        L. 221.

Persuade me not; I will make a Star-chamber
    matter of it.
w.   *Merry Wives of Windsor.* Act I. Sc. 1.
                        L. 1.

PHILOSOPHY.

A little philosophy inclineth man's mind
to atheism; but depth in philosophy bringeth
men's minds about to religion.
x.   BACON—*Essays.* Atheism.

Beside, he was a shrewd philosopher,
And had read ev'ry text and gloss over;
Whate'er the crabbed'st author hath,
He understood b' implicit faith.
   a.   Butler—*Hudibras.* Pt. I. Canto I.
                     L. 127.

Before Philosophy can teach by Experience,
the Philosophy has to be in readiness, the
Experience must be gathered and intelligibly
recorded.
   b.   Carlyle—*Essays. On History.*

The Beginning of Philosophy * * * is a
Consciousness of your own Weakness and
inability in necessary things.
   c.   Epictetus—*Discourses.* Bk. II.
                   Ch. XI. St. 1.

Philosophy goes no further than probabilities, and in every assertion keeps a doubt in
reserve.
   d.   Froude—*Short Studies on Great*
              Subjects. Calvinism.

This same philosophy is a good horse in the
stable, but an arrant jade on a journey.
   e.   Goldsmith—*The Good-Natured Man.*
                     Act I.

I strove with none, for none was worth my
    strife;
   Nature I loved; and next to Nature, art.
I warm'd both hands against the fire of life;
   It sinks, and I am ready to depart.
   f.   Walter Savage Landor—*Dying*
           Speech of an Old Philosopher.

              Sublime Philosophy!
Thou art the patriarch's ladder, reaching
    heaven,
And bright with beckoning angels;—but alas!
We see thee, like the patriarch, but in dreams,
By the first step,—dull slumbering on the
    earth.
   g.   Bulwer-Lytton—*Richelieu.* Act III.
                  Sc. 1. L. 4.

How charming is divine philosophy!
Not harsh, and crabbed, as dull fools suppose,
But musical as is Apollo's lute,
And a perpetual feast of nectar'd sweets,
Where no crude surfeit reigns.
   h.   Milton—*Mask of Comus.* L. 476.

That stone, * * *
Philosophers in vain so long have sought.
   i.   Milton—*Paradise Lost.* Bk. III.
                     L. 600.

Philosophy is nothing but Discretion.
   j.   John Selden—*Table Talk. Philosophy.*

Adversity's sweet milk, philosophy.
   k.   *Romeo and Juliet.* Act III. Sc. 3.
                     L. 55.

There are more things in heaven and earth,
    Horatio,
Than are dreamt of in your philosophy.
   l.   *Hamlet.* Act I. Sc. 5. L. 166.

The bosom-weight, your stubborn gift,
That no philosophy can lift.
   m.   Wordsworth—*Presentiments.*

Why should not grave Philosophy be styled,
Herself, a dreamer of a kindred stock,
A dreamer, yet more spiritless and dull?
   n.   Wordsworth—*The Excursion.* Bk. III.

PHRENOLOGY.

'Tis strange how like a very dunce,
Man, with his bumps upon his sconce,
Has lived so long, and yet no knowledge he
Has had, till lately, of Phrenology—
A science that by simple dint of
Head-combing he should find a hint of,
When scratching o'er those little pole-hills
The faculties throw up like mole hills.
   o.   Hood—*Craniology.*

PITY.

Of all the paths that lead to a woman's love
Pity's the straightest.
   p.   Beaumont and Fletcher—*The Knight*
            of Malta. Act I. Sc. 1. L. 73.

He scorn'd his own, who felt another's woe.
   q.   Campbell—*Gertrude of Wyoming.*
                  Pt. I. St. 24.

          Pity speaks to grief
More sweetly than a band of instruments.
   r.   Barry Cornwall—*The Florentine*
                   Party.

For pity melts the mind to love.
Softly sweet, in Lydian measures,
Soon he sooth'd his soul to pleasures.
War, he sung, is toil and trouble;
Honour but an empty bubble.
   s.   Dryden—*Alexander's Feast.* L. 96.

More helpful than all wisdom is one draught
of simple human pity that will not forsake us.
   t.   George Eliot—*The Mill on the Floss.*
                Bk. VII. Ch. I.

Careless their merits or their faults to scan,
His pity gave ere charity began.
   u.   Goldsmith—*The Deserted Village.*
                     L. 161.

Taught by that Power that pities me,
   I learn to pity them.
   v.   Goldsmith—*The Hermit.* St. 6.

Pity the sorrows of a poor old man,
Whose trembling limbs have brought him to
    your door.
   w.   Thos. Moss—*The Beggar.*

At length some pity warm'd the master's
    breast
('Twas then, his threshold first receiv'd a
    guest),
Slow creaking turns the door with jealous
    care,
And half he welcomes in the shivering pair.
    a.   PARNELL—*The Hermit.* L. 97.

O God, show compassion on the wicked.
The virtuous have already been blessed by
    Thee in being virtuous.
    b.   *Prayer of a Persian Dervish.*

                But, I perceive,
Men must learn now with pity to dispense;
For policy sits above conscience.
    c.   *Timon of Athens.* Act III. Sc. 2. L. 92.

I shall despair. There is no creature loves me;
And if I die, no soul shall pity me :
Nay, wherefore should they, since that I my-
    self
Find in myself no pity to myself?
    d.   *Richard III.* Act V. Sc, 3. L. 200.

Is there no pity sitting in the clouds,
That sees into the bottom of my grief?
    e.   *Romeo and Juliet.* Act III. Sc. 5.
                              L. 198.

My friend, I spy some pity in thy looks;
O, if thine eye be not a flatterer,
Come thou on my side, and entreat for me,
As you would beg, were you in my distress :
A begging prince what beggar pities not?
    f.   *Richard III.* Act I. Sc. 4. L. 270.

My pity hath been balm to heal their wounds,
My mildness hath allay'd their swelling griefs.
    g.   *Henry VI.* Pt. III. Act IV. Sc. 8.
                              L. 41.
Pity is the virtue of the law,
And none but tyrants use it cruelly.
    h.   *Timon of Athens.* Act III. Sc. 5. L. 8.

Tear-falling pity dwells not in this eye.
    i.   *Richard III.* Act IV. Sc. 2. L. 66.

Soft pity never leaves the gentle breast
Where love has been received a welcome guest.
    j.   R. B. SHERIDAN—*The Duenna.* Act II.
                          Sc. 3. Last trio.

Pity's akin to love; and every thought
Of that soft kind is welcome to my soul.
    k.   THOS. SOUTHERNE—*Oroonoko.* Act II.
                          Sc. 2. L. 64.

PLAGIARISM.

They lard their lean books with the fat of
others' works.
    l.   BURTON—*Anatomy of Melancholy.*
                Democritus to the Reader.

We can say nothing but what hath been said,
* * * Our poets steal from Homer * * *
Our storydressers do as much; he that comes
last is commonly best.
    m.   BURTON—*Anatomy of Melancholy.*
                Democritus to the Reader.

The Plagiarism of orators is the art, or an
ingenious and easy mode, which some adroitly
employ to change, or disguise, all sorts of
speeches of their own composition, or that of
other authors, for their pleasure, or their
utility; in such a manner that it becomes
impossible even for the author himself to
recognise his own work, his own genius, and
his own style, so skilfully shall the whole be
disguised.
    n.   ISAAC DISRAELI—*Curiosities of
         Literature. Professors of Plagiarism
                         and Obscurity.*

It has come to be practically a sort of rule
in literature, that a man, having once shown
himself capable of original writing, is entitled
thenceforth to steal from the writings of
others at discretion.
    o.   EMERSON—*Shakespeare.*

For such kind of borrowing as this, if it be
not bettered by the borrower, among good
authors is accounted plagiary.
    p.   MILTON—*Iconoclastes.* XXIII.

Amongst so many borrowed things, am
glad if I can steal one, disguising and altering
it for some new service.
    q.   MONTAIGNE—*Essays. Of Physiognomy.*

Next o'er his books his eyes began to roll,
In pleasing memory of all he stole;
How here he sipp'd, how there he plunder'd
    snug,
And suck'd all o'er like an industrious bug.
    r.   POPE—*Dunciad.* Bk. I. L. 127.

Steal!—to be sure they may; and egad,
serve your best thoughts as gypsies do stolen
children, disfigure them to make 'em pass for
their own.
    s.   R. B. SHERIDAN—*The Critic.* Act I.
                              Sc. 1.

Call them if you please bookmakers, not
authors; range them rather among second-
hand dealers than plagiarists.
    t.   VOLTAIRE—*A Philosophical Dictionary.
                            Plagiarism.*

I am but a gatherer and disposer of other
men's stuff.
    u.   SIR HENRY WOTTON—*Preface to the
                          Elements of Architecture.*

PLEASURE.

Pleasures lie thickest where no pleasures seem ;
  There's not a leaf that falls upon the ground
  But holds some joy of silence or of sound,
Some sprite begotten of a summer dream.
  a.   BLANCHARD—*Sonnet VII. Hidden*
                         Joys.

Every age has its pleasures, its style of wit,
and its own ways.
  b.   NICHOLAS BOILEAU-DESPREAUX—*The*
      Art of Poetry. Canto III. L. 374.

But pleasures are like poppies spread ;
You seize the flower, its bloom is shed.
  c.   BURNS—*Tam o' Shanter.* L. 59.

The rule of my life is to make business a
pleasure, and pleasure my business.
  d.   AARON BURR.

Doubtless the pleasure is as great
Of being cheated as to cheat.
  e.   BUTLER—*Hudibras.* Pt. II. Canto III.
                              L. 1.

There is a pleasure in the pathless woods,
  There is a rapture on the lonely shore,
There is society where none intrudes
  By the deep Sea, and music in its roar.
  f.   BYRON—*Childe Harold.* Canto IV.
                            St. 178.

Who pleases one against his will.
  g.   CONGREVE—*The Way of the World.*
                          Epilogue.

Pleasure admitted in undue degree
Enslaves the will, nor leaves the judgment
  free.
  h.   COWPER—*Progress of Error.* L. 267.

That, though on pleasure she was bent,
  She had a frugal mind.
  i.   COWPER—*History of John Gilpin.* St. 8.

  Rich the treasure,
  Sweet the pleasure,
Sweet is pleasure after **pain**
  j.   DRYDEN—*Alexander's Feast.* L. 58.

I fly from pleasure, because pleasure has
ceased to please : I am lonely because I am
miserable.
  k.   SAM'L JOHNSON—*Rasselas.* Ch. III.

Pleasure the servant, Virtue looking on.
  l.   BEN JONSON—*Pleasure Reconciled to*
                        Virtue.

Ever let the Fancy roam,
Pleasure never is at home.
  m.   KEATS—*Fancy.*

There is a pleasure which is born of pain.
  n.   OWEN MEREDITH (Lord Lytton)—
      The Wanderer. Bk. I. Prologue.
                           Pt. I.

Take all the pleasures of all the spheres,
And multiply each through endless years,
One minute of Heaven is worth them all.
  o.   MOORE—*Lalla Rookh. Paradise and*
                           the Peri.

The roses of pleasure seldom last long
enough to adorn the brow of him who plucks
them ; for they are the only roses which do
not retain their sweetness after they have lost
their beauty.
  p.   HANNAH MORE—*Essays on Various*
              Subjects. On Dissipation.

God made all pleasures innocent.
  q.   MRS. NORTON—*Lady of La Garaye.*
                            Pt. I.

Pleas'd to the last he crops the flowery food,
And licks the hand just rais'd to shed his
  blood.
  r.   POPE—*Essay on Man.* Ep. I. L. 83.

Pleasures are ever in our hands or eyes ;
And when in act they cease, in prospect rise.
  s.   POPE—*Essay on Man.* Ep. II. L. 123.

Reason's whole pleasure, all the joys of sense,
Lie in three words,—health, peace, and com-
  petence.
  t.   POPE—*Essay on Man.* Ep. IV. L. 79.

In the days when we went gypsying
  A long time ago.
  u.   EDWIN RANSFORD—*In the Days when*
                  We Went Gypsying.

Spangling the wave with lights as vain
As pleasures in this vale of pain,
That dazzle as they fade.
  v.   SCOTT—*Lord of the Isles.* Canto I.
                          St. 23.

Boys who, being mature in knowledge,
Pawn their experience to their present pleasure.
  w.   *Antony and Cleopatra.* Act I. Sc. 4.
                              L. 31.

And painefull pleasure turnes to pleasing
  paine.
  x.   SPENSER—*Faerie Queene.* Bk. III.
                    Canto X. St. 60.

I built my soul a lordly pleasure-house,
Wherein at ease for aye to dwell.
  y.   TENNYSON—*The Palace of Art.* St. 1.

They who are pleased themselves must always
  please.
  z.   THOMSON—*The Castle of Indolence.*
                      Canto I. St. 15.

All human race from China to Peru,
Pleasure, howe'er disguis'd by art, pursue.
  aa.   THOMAS WARTON—*The Universal Love*
                         of Pleasure.

Sure as night follows day,
Death treads in Pleasure's footsteps round the
world,
When Pleasure treads the paths which Reason
shuns.
  a.   YOUNG—*Night Thoughts.* Night V.
                                    L. 863.

To frown at pleasure, and to smile in pain.
  b.   YOUNG—*Night Thoughts.* Night VIII.
                                    L. 1,045.

POETRY.

Poetry is itself a thing of God;
He made his prophets poets; and the more
We feel of poesie do we become
Like God in love and power,—under-makers.
  c.   BAILEY—*Festus.* Proem. L. 5.

For rhyme the rudder is of verses,
With which, like ships, they steer their
courses.
  d.   BUTLER—*Hudibras.* Pt. I. Canto I.
                                    L. 463.

Some force whole regions, in despite
O' geography, to change their site;
Make former times shake hands with latter,
And that which was before come after;
But those that write in rhyme still make
The one verse for the other's sake;
For one for sense, and one for rhyme,
I think's sufficient at one time.
  e.   BUTLER—*Hudibras.* Pt. II. Canto I.
                                    L. 23.

Nor florid prose, nor honied lies of rhyme,
Can blazon evil deeds, or consecrate a crime.
  f.   BYRON—*Childe Harold.* Canto I. St. 3.

The fatal facility of the octosyllabic verse.
  g.   BYRON—*The Corsair.* Preface.

For there is no heroic poem in the world
but is at bottom a biography, the life of a
man; also, it may be said, there is no life of
a man, faithfully recorded, but is a heroic
poem of its sort, rhymed or unrhymed.
  h.   CARLYLE—*Sir Walter Scott. London
            and Westminster Review.* 1838.

In the hexameter rises the fountain's silvery
column:
In the pentameter aye falling in melody back.
  i.   COLERIDGE—*The Ovidian Elegiac Metre.*

Prose—words in their best order;—poetry—
the best words in their best order.
  j.   COLERIDGE—*Table Talk.* July 12, 1827.

That passage is what I call the sublime
dashed to pieces by cutting too close with the
fiery four-in-hand round the corner of nonsense.
  k.   COLERIDGE—*Table Talk.* Jan. 20, 1834.

Made poetry a mere mechanic art.
  l.   COWPER—*Table Talk.* L. 654.

Feel you the barren flattery of a rhyme?
Can poets soothe you, when you pine for
bread,
By winding myrtle round your ruin'd shed?
  m.   CRABBE—*The Village.* Bk. I.

When the brain gets as dry as an empty nut,
When the reason stands on its squarest toes,
When the mind (like a beard) has a " formal
cut,"—
There is a place and enough for the pains of
prose;
But whenever the May-blood stirs and glows,
And the young year draws to the "golden
prime,"
And Sir Romeo sticks in his ear a rose,—
Then hey! for the ripple of laughing rhyme!
  n.   AUSTIN DOBSON—*The Ballad of Prose
                        and Rhyme.*

Doeg, though without knowing how or why,
Made still a blundering kind of melody;
Spurr'd boldly on, and dash'd through thick
and thin,
Through sense and nonsense, never out nor in;
Free from all meaning whether good or bad,
And in one word, heroically mad.
  o.   DRYDEN—*Absalom and Achitophel.*
                            Pt. II. L. 412.

Happy who in his verse can gently steer
From grave to light, from pleasant to severe.
  p.   DRYDEN—*The Art of Poetry.* Canto I.
                                    L. 75.

For it is not metres, but a metre-making
argument that makes a poem.
  q.   EMERSON—*Essays. The Poet.*

It does not need that a poem should be long.
Every word was once a poem.
  r.   EMERSON—*Essays. The Poet.*

The finest poetry was first experience.
  s.   EMERSON—*Shakespeare.*

The true poem is the poet's mind.
  t.   EMERSON—*Essays. Of History.*

Verse sweetens toil, however rude the sound;
All at her work the village maiden sings,
Nor while she turns the giddy wheel around,
Revolves the sad vicissitudes of things.
  u.   GIFFORD—*Contemplation.*

What is a Sonnet? 'Tis the pearly shell
That murmurs of the far-off, murmuring sea;
A precious jewel carved most curiously;
It is a little picture painted well.
What is a Sonnet? 'Tis the tear that fell
From a great poet's hidden ecstacy;
A two-edged sword, a star, a song—ah me!
Sometimes a heavy tolling funeral bell.
  v.   R. W. GILDER—*The Sonnet.*

A verse may finde him who a sermon flies,
And turn delight into a sacrifice.
  w.   HERBERT—*The Temple. The Church
                                    Porch.*

To write a verse or two, is all the praise
That I can raise.
　　a.　　HERBERT—*The Church.* *Praise.*

For dear to gods and men is sacred song.
Self-taught I sing; by Heaven and Heaven
　　alone,
The genuine seeds of poesy are sown.
　　b.　　HOMER—*Odyssey.* Bk. XXII. L. 382.
　　　　　　　　　　　　Pope's trans.

The essence of poetry is invention; such
invention as, by producing something unexpected, surprises and delights.
　　c.　　SAM'L JOHNSON—*The Lives of the
　　　　　　　English Poets. Life of Waller.*

Still may syllables jar with time,
Still may reason war with rhyme,
　　　　Resting never!
　　d.　　BEN JONSON—*Underwoods. Fit of
　　　　　　　Rhyme Against Rhyme.*

These are the gloomy comparisons of a disturbed imagination; the melancholy madness
of poetry, without the inspiration.
　　e.　　JUNIUS—*Letter No. VII. To Sir W.
　　　　　　　　　　　　Draper.*

A drainless shower
Of light is poesy: 'tis the supreme of power;
'Tis might half slumbering on its own right
　　arm.
　　f.　　KEATS—*Sleep and Poetry.* L. 237.

The poetry of earth is never dead;
　　*　　*　　*　　*　　*　　*
The poetry of earth is ceasing never.
　　g.　　KEATS—*On the Grasshopper and Cricket.*

For, of all compositions, he thought that the
　　sonnet
Best repaid all the toil you expended upon it.
　　h.　　LOWELL—*A Fable for Critics.* L. 368.

It ["The Ancient Mariner"] is marvellous
in its mastery over that delightfully fortuitous
inconsequence that is the adamantine logic of
dreamland.
　　i.　　LOWELL—*Among My Books. Coleridge.*

Never did Poesy appear
　　So full of heaven to me, as when
I saw how it would pierce through pride and
　　fear
　　To the lives of coarsest men.
　　j.　　LOWELL—*An Incident in a Railroad
　　　　　　　　　　　Car.* St. 18.

These pearls of thought in Persian gulfs were
　　bred,
Each softly lucent as a rounded moon;
The diver Omar plucked them from their bed,
Fitzgerald strung them on an English thread.
　　k.　　LOWELL—*In a Copy of Omar Khayyám.*

　　　　You speak
As one who fed on poetry.
　　l.　　BULWER-LYTTON—*Richelieu.* Act I.
　　　　　　　　　　　　　　　Sc. 1.

The merit of poetry, in its wildest forms,
still consists in its truth—truth conveyed to
the understanding, not directly by the words,
but circuitously by means of imaginative
associations, which serve as its conductors.
　　m.　　MACAULAY—*Essays. On the Athenian
　　　　　　　　　　　　　　Orators.*

We hold that the most wonderful and
splendid proof of genius is a great poem produced in a civilized age.
　　n.　　MACAULAY—*On Milton.* 1825.

My unpremeditated verse.
　　o.　　MILTON—*Paradise Lost.* Bk. IX. L. 24.

A needless Alexandrine ends the song,
That, like a wounded snake, drags its slow
　　　length along.
　　p.　　POPE—*Essay on Criticism.* Pt. II.
　　　　　　　　　　　　　　　L. 156.

Curst be the verse, how well soe'er it flow,
That tends to make one worthy man my foe,
Give virtue scandal, innocence a fear,
Or from the soft-eyed virgin steal a tear!
　　q.　　POPE—*Prologue to Satires.* L. 283.

The varying verse, the full resounding line,
The long majestic march, and energy divine.
　　r.　　POPE—*Horace.* Bk. II. Ep. I. L. 267.

What woful stuff this madrigal would be,
In some starv'd hackney sonneteer or me!
But let a lord once own the happy lines,
How the wit brightens! how the style refines.
　　s.　　POPE—*Essay on Criticism.* L. 418.

O for a Muse of fire, that would ascend
The brightest heaven of invention.
　　t.　　*Henry V.* Chorus. L. 1.

The elegancy, facility, and golden cadence
of poesy.
　　u.　　*Love's Labour's Lost.* Act IV. Sc. 2.
　　　　　　　　　　　　　　　L. 126.

I consider poetry very subordinate to moral
and political science.
　　v.　　SHELLEY—*Letter to Thomas L. Peacock.*
　　　　　　　　　　Naples. Jan. 26, 1819.

A poem round and perfect as a star.
　　w.　　ALEX. SMITH—*A Life Drama.* Sc. 2.

I was promised on a time,
To have reason for my rhyme;
From that time unto this season,
I received nor rhyme nor reason.
　　x.　　SPENSER—*Lines on His Promised
　　　　　　　Pension.* See *Fuller's Worthies,* by
　　　　　　　NUTTALL. Vol. II. P. 379.

One merit of poetry few persons will deny:
it says more and in fewer words than prose.
  a.   Voltaire—*A Philosophical Dictionary.*
                          Poets.

Old-fashioned poetry, but choicely good.
  b.   Izaak Walton—*The Compleat Angler.*
                       Pt. I. Ch. IV.

The vision and the faculty divine;
Yet wanting the accomplishment of verse.
  c.   Wordsworth—*The Excursion.* Bk. I.

Wisdom married to immortal verse.
  d.   Wordsworth—*The Excursion.*
                          Bk. VII.

        There is in Poesy a decent pride,
Which well becomes her when she speaks to
    Prose,
Her younger sister.
  e.   Young—*Night Thoughts.* Night V.
                         L. 64.

POETS.

A poet not in love is out at sea;
He must have a lay-figure.
  f.   Bailey—*Festus.* Sc. *Home.*

Poets are all who love,—who feel great truths,
And tell them.
  g.   Bailey—*Festus.* Sc. *Another and a*
                       Better World.

God's prophets of the Beautiful,
These Poets were.
  h.   E. B. Browning—*Vision of Poets.*
                        St. 98.

O brave poets, keep back nothing;
Nor mix falsehood with the whole!
Look up Godward! speak the truth in
Worthy song from earnest soul!
Hold, in high poetic duty,
Truest Truth the fairest Beauty.
  i.   E. B. Browning—*The Dead Pan.*
                        St. 39.

        One fine day,
Says Mister Mucklewraith to me, says he,
"So! you've a poet in your house," and
    smiled;
"A poet? God forbid," I cried; and then
It all came out: how Andrew slyly sent
Verse to the paper; how they printed it
In Poets' Corner.
  j.   Robert Buchanan—*Poet Andrew.*
                        L. 161.

And poets by their sufferings grow,—
As if there were no more to do,
To make a poet excellent,
But only want and discontent.
  k.   Butler—*Miscellaneous Thoughts.*

Ovid's a rake, as half his verses show him,
  Anacreon's morals are a still worse sample,
Catullus scarcely has a decent poem,
  I don't think Sappho's Ode a good example,
Although Longinus tells us there is no hymn
  Where the sublime soars forth on wings
    more ample;
But Virgil's songs are pure, except that horrid
  one
Beginning with "Formosum Pastor Cory-
  don."
  l.   Byron—*Don Juan.* Canto I. St. 42.

A Poet without Love were a physical and
metaphysical impossibility.
  m.   Carlyle—*Essays. Burns.*

Most joyful let the Poet be;
It is through him that all men see.
  n.   William E. Channing—*The Poet of*
                   the Old and New Times.

He koude songes make and wel endite.
  o.   Chaucer—*Canterbury Tales.*
                    Prologue. L. 95.

Who all in raptures their own works rehearse,
And drawl out measur'd prose, which they
    call verse.
  p.   Churchill—*Independence.* L. 295.

Poets by Death are conquer'd; but the wit
Of poets triumphs over it.
  q.   Abraham Cowley—*On the Praise of*
                  Poetry. Ode I. L. 13.

And spare the poet for his subject's sake.
  r.   Cowper—*Charity.* Last line.

There is a pleasure in poetic pains,
Which only poets know.
  s.   Cowper—*The Task.* Bk. II. L. 285.

They best can judge a poet's worth,
  Who oft themselves have known
The pangs of a poetic birth
  By labours of their own.
  t.   Cowper—*To Dr. Darwin.* St. 2.

I can no more believe old Homer blind,
Than those who say the sun hath never
    shined;
The age wherein he lived was dark, but he
Could not want sight who taught the world to
    see.
  u.   Sir John Denham—*Progress of*
                  Learning. L. 61.

Sure there are poets which did never dream
Upon Parnassus, nor did taste the stream
Of Helicon; we therefore may suppose
Those made not poets, but the poets those.
  v.   Sir John Denham—*Cooper's Hill.*

  The poet must be alike polished by an intercourse with the world as with the studies
of taste; one to whom labour is negligence,
refinement a science, and art a nature.
  w.   Isaac Disraeli—*Literary Character of*
              Men of Genius. Vers de Société.

For that fine madness still he did retain,
Which rightly should possess a poet's brain.
 a. DRAYTON—*To Henry Reynolds. Of Poets and Poesy.* L. 109.

Three poets in three distant ages born,
Greece, Italy, and England did adorn.
The first in loftiness of thought surpass'd;
The next, in majesty; in both, the last.
The force of nature could no further go;
To make a third, she join'd the former two.
 b. DRYDEN—*Under Mr. Milton's Picture.*

All men are poets at heart.
 c. EMERSON—*Literary Ethics.*

Poets should be law-givers; that is, the boldest lyric inspiration should not chide and insult, but should announce and lead the civil code, and the day's work.
 d. EMERSON—*Essays. Of Prudence.*

"Give me a theme," the little poet cried,
 "And I will do my part,"
"'Tis not a theme you need," the world replied;
 "You need a heart."
 e. R. W. GILDER—*Wanted, a Theme.*

Thou best-humour'd man with the worst-humour'd muse.
 f. GOLDSMITH—*Retaliation.* Postscript.

Singing and rejoicing,
As aye since time began,
The dying earth's last poet
Shall be the earth's last man.
 g. ANASTASIUS GRÜN—*The Last Poet.*

His virtues formed the magic of his song.
 h. *Inscription on the Tomb of Cowper.*
 L. 10. See HAYLEY's *Life of Cowper.*
 Vol. IV. P. 189.

Lo! there he lies, our Patriarch Poet, dead!
 The solemn angel of eternal peace
Has waved a wand of mystery o'er his head,
 Touched his strong heart, and bade his pulses cease.
 i. PAUL H. HAYNE—*To Bryant, Dead.*

In his own verse the poet still we find,
In his own page his memory lives enshrined,
As in their amber sweets the smothered bees,—
As the fair cedar, fallen before the breeze,
Lies self-embalmed amidst the mouldering trees.
 j. O. W. HOLMES—*Songs of Many Seasons. Bryant's Seventieth Birthday.* St. 17 and 18.

We call those poets who are first to mark
 Through earth's dull mist the coming of the dawn,—
Who see in twilight's gloom the first pale spark,
 While others only note that day is gone.
 k. O. W. HOLMES—*Memorial Verses. Shakespeare.* St. 4.

Where go the poet's lines?—
Answer, ye evening tapers!
Ye auburn locks, ye golden curls,
Speak from your folded papers!
 l. O. W. HOLMES—*The Poet's Lot.* St. 3.

Poets, the first instructors of mankind,
Brought all things to their proper native use.
 m. HORACE—*Of the Art of Poetry.* L. 449. Wentworth Dillon's trans.

Was ever poet so trusted before!
 n. SAM'L JOHNSON—*Boswell's Life of Johnson.* 1774.

For a good poet's made, as well as born.
 o. BEN JONSON—*To the Memory of Shakespeare.*

O 'tis a very sin
For one so weak to venture his poor verse
In such a place as this.
 p. KEATS—*Endymion.* Bk. III. L. 965.

For his chaste Muse employed her heaven-taught lyre
None but the noblest passions to inspire,
Not one immortal, one corrupted thought,
One line, which dying he could wish to blot.
 q. LORD LYTTLETON—*Prologue to Thomson's Coriolanus.*

All that is best in the great poets of all countries is not what is national in them, but what is universal.
 r. LONGFELLOW—*Kavanagh.* Ch. XX.

For next to being a great poet is the power of understanding one.
 s. LONGFELLOW—*Hyperion.* Bk. II. Ch. III.

For voices pursue him by day,
 And haunt him by night,—
And he listens, and needs must obey,
 When the Angel says: "Write!"
 t. LONGFELLOW—*L'Envoi. The Poet and His Songs.* St. 7.

Like the river, swift and clear,
Flows his song through many a heart.
 u. LONGFELLOW—*Oliver Basselin.* St. 11.

O ye dead Poets, who are living still
Immortal in your verse, though life be fled,
And ye, O living Poets, who are dead
Though ye are living, if neglect can kill,
Tell me if in the darkest hours of ill,
With drops of anguish falling fast and red
From the sharp crown of thorns upon your head,
Ye were not glad your errand to fulfill?
 v. LONGFELLOW—*The Poets.*

A terrible thing to be pestered with poets!
But, alas, she is dumb, and the proverb holds good,
She never will cry till she's out of the wood!
 w. LOWELL—*A Fable for Critics.* L. 73.

The clear, sweet singer with the crown of snow
Not whiter than the thoughts that housed
    below !
  a.   Lowell—*An Epistle to George William
            Curtis.* L. 43. Postscript.

Poets alone are sure of immortality; they
are the truest diviners of nature.
  b.   Bulwer-Lytton—*Caxtoniana.*
                  Essay XXVII.

Poets are sultans, if they had their will :
For every author would his brother kill.
  c.   Orrery—*Prologues (according to
                 Johnson).*

Poets utter great and wise things which they
do not themselves understand.
  d.   Plato—*The Republic.* Bk. II. Sec. V.

And he whose fustian's so sublimely bad,
It is not poetry, but prose run mad.
  e.   Pope—*Prologue to Satires.* L. 185.

Dulness ! whose good old cause I yet defend,
With whom my muse began, with whom shall
    end.
  f.   Pope—*The Dunciad.* Bk. I. L. 165.

Poets like painters, thus unskill'd to trace
The naked nature and the living grace,
With gold and jewels cover every part,
And hide with ornaments their want of art.
  g.   Pope—*Essay on Criticism.* L. 293.

The bard whom pilfer'd pastorals renown,
Who turns a Persian tale for half a crown,
Just writes to make his barrenness appear,
And strains from hard-bound brains eight
    lines a year.
  h.   Pope—*Prologue to Satires.* L. 179.

Then from the Mint walks forth the man of
    rhyme,
Happy to catch me, just at dinner-time.
  i.   Pope—*Prologue to Satires.* L. 13.

Vain was the chief's, the sage's pride !
They had no poet, and they died.
  j.   Pope—*Odes of Horace.* Bk. IV.
                       Ode 9.

While pensive poets painful vigils keep,
Sleepless themselves to give their readers sleep.
  k.   Pope—*The Dunciad.* Bk. I. L. 93.

Call it not vain :—they do not err,
Who say that, when the Poet dies,
Mute Nature mourns her worshipper,
And celebrates his obsequies.
  l.   Scott—*The Lay of the Last Minstrel.*
                   Canto V. St. 1.

Never durst poet touch a pen to write
Until his ink were temper'd with Love's sighs.
  m.   *Love's Labour's Lost.* Act IV. Sc. 3.
                       L. 346.

The poet's eye, in a fine frenzy rolling,
Doth glance from heaven to earth, from earth
    to heaven ;
And as imagination bodies forth
The forms of things unknown, the poet's pen
Turns them to shapes and gives to airy nothing
A local habitation and a name.
  n.   *Midsummer-Night's Dream.* Act V.
                  Sc. 1. L. 12.

           Most wretched men
Are cradled into poetry by wrong;
They learn in suffering what they teach in
    song.
  o.   Shelley—*Julian and Maddalo.* L. 556.

Dan Chaucer, well of English undefyled,
On Fame's eternall beadroll worthie to be
    fyled.
  p.   Spenser—*Faerie Queene.* Bk. IV.
                 Canto II. St. 32.

I learnt life from the poets.
  q.   Madame de Staël—*Corinne.*
                Bk. XVIII. Ch. V.

With no companion but the constant Muse,
Who sought me when I needed her—ah, when
Did I not need her, solitary else ?
  r.   R. H. Stoddard—*Proem.* L. 87.

                The Poet in his Art
Must imitate the whole, and say the smallest
    part.
  s.   W. W. Story—*The Unexpressed.*

Then, rising with Aurora's light,
The Muse invoked, sit down to write;
Blot out, correct, insert, refine,
Enlarge, diminish, interline.
  t.   Swift—*On Poetry.*

Unjustly poets we asperse :
Truth shines the brighter clad in verse,
And all the fictions they pursue
Do but insinuate what is true.
  u.   Swift—*To Stella.*

To have read the greatest works of any great
poet, to have beheld or heard the greatest
works of any great painter or musician, is a
possession added to the best things of life.
  v.   Swinburne—*Essays and Studies.*
              Victor Hugo. *L'Année Terrible.*

The Poet's leaves are gathered one by one,
In the slow process of the doubtful years.
  w.   Bayard Taylor—*The Poet's Journal.*
                   Third Evening.

For now the Poet cannot die,
  Nor leave his music as of old,
  But round him ere he scarce be cold
Begins the scandal and the cry.
  x.   Tennyson—*To ——, after Reading a
             Life and Letters.* St. 4.

The poet in a golden clime was born,
  With golden stars above;
Dower'd with the hate of hate, the scorn of
  scorn,
The love of love.
  a.   TENNYSON—*The Poet.*

A bard here dwelt, more fat than bard
beseems.
  b.   THOMSON—*The Castle of Indolence.*
                          Canto I. St. 68.

Poets lose half the praise they should have got,
Could it be known what they discreetly blot.
  c.   EDMUND WALLER—*Miscellanies. Upon
              the Earl of Roscommon's Translation
              of Horace, De Arte Poetica.* L. 41.

It was Homer who inspired the poet.
  d.   WAYLAND—*The Iliad and the Bible.*

In Spring the Poet is glad,
  And in Summer the Poet is gay;
But in Autumn the Poet is sad,
  And has something sad to say.
  e.   BYRON FORCEYTHE WILLSON—
                          Autumn Song.

                  And, when a damp
Fell round the path of Milton, in his hand
The Thing became a trumpet; whence he
  blew
Soul-animating strains,—alas! too few.
  f.   WORDSWORTH—*Miscellaneous Sonnets.*
                  Pt. II.   *Scorn not the Sonnet.*

Blessings be with them, and eternal praise,
  Who gave us nobler loves, and nobler
    cares,—
The Poets, who on earth have made us heirs
Of truth and pure delight by heavenly lays!
  g.   WORDSWORTH—*Personal Talk.*

I thought of Chatterton, the marvellous Boy,
  The sleepless Soul that perished in his pride;
Of him who walked in glory and in joy,
  Following his plough, along the mountain
    side.
  h.   WORDSWORTH—*Resolution and
                          Independence.* St. 7.

    That mighty orb of song,
The divine Milton.
  i.   WORDSWORTH—*The Excursion.* Bk. I.
                          L. 252.

POISON.

While Fell was reposing himself in the hay,
A reptile concealed bit his leg as he lay;
But, all venom himself, of the wound he made
  light,
And got well, while the scorpion died of the
  bite.
  j.   LESSING—*Paraphrase of a Greek
                  Epigram by Demodocus.*

All men carry about them that which is
poyson to serpents: for if it be true that is
reported, they will no better abide the touching with man's spittle than scalding water
cast upon them: but if it happen to light
within their chawes or mouth, especially if it
come from a man that is fasting, it is present
death.
  k.   PLINY—*Natural History.* Bk. VII.
                  Chap. II. Holland's trans.

POLICY.

When I am at Rome I fast as the Romans
do; when I am at Milan I do not fast. So
likewise you, whatever church you come to,
observe the custom of the place, if you would
neither give offence to others, nor take offence
from them.
  l.   ST. AMBROSE—*Advice to St. Austin on
                          Sabbath Keeping.*

Mahomet made the people believe that he
would call a hill to him, and from the top of
it offer up his prayers for the observers of his
law. The people assembled; Mahomet called
the hill to come to him, again and again; and
when the hill stood still, he was never a whit
abashed, but said, "If the hill will not come
to Mahomet, Mahomet will go to the hill."
  m.   BACON—*Essays. Of Boldness.*

Kings will be tyrants from policy, when
subjects are rebels from principle.
  n.   BURKE—*Reflections on the Revolution in
                          France.*

Of this stamp is the cant of, not men, but
measures.
  o.   BURKE—*Thoughts on the Cause of the
                          Present Discontents.*

Like Æsop's fox, when he had lost his tail,
would have all his fellow foxes cut off theirs.
  p.   BURTON—*Anatomy of Melancholy.*
                  Democritus to the Reader.

They had best not stir the rice, though it
sticks to the pot.
  q.   CERVANTES—*Don Quixote.* Pt. II.
                          Ch. XXXVII.

Measures, not men, have always been my
  mark.
  r.   GOLDSMITH—*The Good-Natured Man.*
                          Act II.

Factions among yourselves; preferring such
To offices and honors, as ne'er read
The elements of saving policy;
But deeply skilled in all the principles
That usher to destruction.
  s.   MASSINGER—*The Bondman.* Act I.
                          Sc. 3. L. 210.

When I see a merchant over-polite to his customers, begging them to taste a little brandy and throwing half his goods on the counter,— thinks I, that man has an axe to grind.
  a.   CHARLES MINER—*Who'll turn*
                                    Grindstones?

The publick weal requires that a man should betray, and lye, and massacre.
  b.   MONTAIGNE—*Essays. Of Profit and*
                                    Honesty.

                        To beguile the time,
Look like the time; bear welcome in your eye,
Your hand, your tongue: look like the inno-
    cent flower,
But be the serpent under 't.
  c.   *Macbeth.* Act I. Sc. 5. L. 65.

Turn him to any cause of policy,
The Gordian knot of it he will unloose,
Familiar as his garter: that, when he speaks,
The air, a charter'd libertine, is still.
  d.   *Henry V.* Act I. Sc. 1. L. 45.

In this country [England] it is found requi-
site, now and then, to put one admiral to death in order to spirit up the others to fight.
  e.   VOLTAIRE—*Candide.* Ch. XXIII.

POLITICS.

I consider biennial elections as a security that the sober, second thought of the people shall be law.
  f.   FISHER AMES—*Speech.* Jan., 1788.

Listen! John A. Logan is the Head Centre, the Hub, the King Pin, the Main Spring, Mogul, and Mugwump of the final plot by which partisanship was installed in the Commission.
  g.   ISAAC H. BROMLEY—*Editorial in the*
        New York Tribune. Feb. 16, 1877.

We are Republicans, and don't propose to leave our party and identify ourselves with the party whose antecedents have been Rum, Romanism, and Rebellion.
  h.   SAMUEL D. BURCHARD—*One of the*
        deputation visiting Mr. Blaine.
                                    Oct. 29, 1884.

Protection and patriotism are reciprocal.
  i.   CALHOUN—*Speech delivered in the House*
        of Representatives in 1812.

It is a *condition* which confronts us—not a theory.
  j.   GROVER CLEVELAND—*Annual Message.*
                                    1887.

Party honesty is party expediency.
  k.   GROVER CLEVELAND—*Interview in New*
        York Commercial Advertiser.
                                    Sept. 19, 1889.

What is a Communist? One who has **yearn-**
    ings
For equal division of unequal earnings.
  l.   EBENEZER ELLIOT—*Epigram.*

It is more than a crime; it is a political fault.
  m.   FOUCHÉ—*Memoirs of Fouché.*

Give 'em Jessie.
  n.   FREMONT'S *Supporters in the Presidential*
        Campaign of 1856.

Who, born for the universe, narrow'd his
    mind,
And to party gave up what was meant for
    mankind.
  o.   GOLDSMITH—*Retaliation.* L. 31.

I accept your nomination in the confident trust that the masses of our countrymen, North and South, are eager to clasp hands across the bloody chasm which has so long divided them.
  p.   HORACE GREELEY—*Acceptance of the*
        Liberal Republican Nomination.
                                    May 20, 1872.

He serves his party best who serves the country best.
  q.   RUTHERFORD B. HAYES—*Inaugural*
                    Address. March 5, 1877.

The freeman casting, with unpurchased
    hand,
The vote that shakes the turrets of the land.
  r.   O. W. HOLMES—*Poetry. A Metrical*
                                    Essay. L. 83.

Free trade, one of the greatest blessings which a government can confer on a people, is in almost every country unpopular.
  s.   MACAULAY—*On Mitford's History of*
                                    Greece.

A weapon that comes down as still
    As snowflakes fall upon the sod;
But executes a freeman's will,
    As lightning does the will of God;
And from its force, nor doors nor locks
Can shield you; 'tis the ballot-box.
  t.   PIERPONT—*A Word from a Petitioner.*

Old politicians chew on wisdom past,
And totter on in business to the last.
  u.   POPE—*Moral Essays.* Ep. I. L. 228.

A mugwump is a person educated beyond his intellect.
  v.   HORACE PORTER—*A Bon-Mot in the*
        Cleveland–Blaine Campaign of 1884.

                        Get thee glass eyes;
And, like a scurvy politician, seem
To see the things thou dost not.
  w.   *King Lear.* Act IV. Sc. 6. L. 174.

O, that estates, degrees, and offices
Were not deriv'd corruptly, and that clear
    honour
Were purchased by the merit of the wearer!
  a.   *Merchant of Venice.* Act II. Sc. 9.
                                L. 41.

Something is rotten in the state of Denmark.
  b.   *Hamlet.* Act I. Sc. 4. L. 90.

As long as I count the votes what are you
going to do about it? Say.
  c.   WM. M. TWEED—*The Ballot in* 1871.

POPULARITY.

Their poet, a sad trimmer, but no less
In company a very pleasant fellow,
Had been the favorite of full many a mess
Of men, and made them speeches when
    half mellow;
And though his meaning they could rarely
    guess,
Yet still they deign'd to hiccup or to bellow
The glorious meed of popular applause,
Of which the first ne'er knows the second
    cause.
  d.   BYRON—*Don Juan.* Canto III. St. 82.

Some shout him, and some hang upon his car,
To gaze in his eyes, and bless him. Maidens
    wave
Their 'kerchiefs, and old women weep for joy;
While others, not so satisfied, unhorse
The gilded equipage, and turning loose
His steeds, usurp a place they well deserve.
  e.   COWPER—*The Task.* Bk. VI. L. 708.

And to some men popularity is always suspicious. Enjoying none themselves, they are
prone to suspect the validity of those attainments which command it.
  f.   GEO. HENRY LEWES—*The Spanish
                    Drama.* Ch. III.

I have seen the dumb men throng to see him,
    and
The blind to hear him speak: matrons flung
    gloves,
Ladies and maids their scarfs and handker-
    chers
Upon him as he passed; the nobles bended,
As to Jove's statue, and the commons made
A shower and thunder with their caps and
    shouts.
  g.   *Coriolanus.* Act II. Sc. 1. L. 278.

          The ladies call him sweet;
The stairs, as he treads on them, kiss his feet.
  h.   *Love's Labour's Lost.* Act V. Sc. 2.
                              L. 329.

POSSESSION.

When I behold what pleasure is pursuit,
    What life, what glorious eagerness it is,
    Then mark how full possession falls from
        this,
How fairer seems the blossom than the fruit,—
I am perplext, and often stricken mute,
    Wondering which attained the higher bliss,
    The winged insect, or the chrysalis
It thrust aside with unreluctant foot.
  i.   T. B. ALDRICH—*Sonnet. Pursuit and
                      Possession.*

I die,—but first I have possess'd,
And come what may, I *have been* bless'd.
  j.   BYRON—*The Giaour.* L. 1,114.

Providence has given to the French the
empire of the land, to the English that of the
sea, to the Germans that of—the air!
  k.   CARLYLE—*Essays. Richter.*

Of a rich man who was mean and niggardly,
he said, "That man does not possess his estate,
but his estate possesses him."
  l.   DIOGENES LAERTIUS—*Lives of Eminent
                    Philosophers.* Bion. III.

Property has its duties as well as its rights.
  m.   THOMAS DRUMMOND—*Letter to the
                Tipperary Magistrates.* May 22, 1838.

It may be said of them [the Hollanders],
as of the Spaniards, that the sun never sets
upon their Dominions.
  n.   THOS. GAGE—*New Survey of the West
             Indies. Epistle Dedicatory.*
                (London, 1648.)

The proud daughter of that monarch to
whom when it grows dark [elsewhere] the
sun never sets.
  o.   GUARINI—*Pastor Fido* (1590). *On the
            Marriage of the Duke of Savoy with
                Catherine of Austria.*

Aspiration sees only one side of every question; possession, many.
  p.   LOWELL—*Among my Books. New
            England Two Centuries Ago.*

Cleon hath ten thousand acres,—
    Ne'er a one have I;
Cleon dwelleth in a palace,—
    In a cottage I.
  q.   CHARLES MACKAY—*Cleon and I.*

The sun never sets on the immense empire
of Charles V.
  r.   SCOTT—*Life of Napoleon.* Ch. LIX.

That what we have we prize not to the worth
Whiles we enjoy it, but being lack'd and lost,
Why, then we rack the value, then we find
The virtue that possession would not show us
While it was ours.
  s.   *Much Ado About Nothing.* Act IV.
                      Sc. 1. L. 220.

I ne'er could any lustre see
In eyes that would not look on me;
I ne'er saw nectar on a lip
But where my own did hope to sip.
a.   R. B. SHERIDAN—*Duenna. Air.* Act I.
Sc. 2.

Why should the brave Spanish soldiers
brag, The sunne never sets in the Spanish dominions, but ever shineth on one part or other
we have conquered for our king.
b.   CAPTAIN JOHN SMITH—*Advertisements*
for the Unexperienced, etc. Mass.
Hist. Soc. Coll. Third Series.
Vol. III. P. 49.

People may have *too much* of a good *thing :*
Full as an egg of wisdom thus I sing.
c.   JOHN WOLCOTT (Peter Pindar)—
Subjects for Painters. The Gentleman
and his Wife.

Lord of himselfe, though not of lands,
And having nothing, yet hath all.
d.   SIR HENRY WOTTON—*The Character of*
a Happy Life. St. 6.

POST (*See* OCCUPATIONS).

POSTERITY.

Think of your forefathers! Think of your
posterity!
e.   JOHN Q. ADAMS—*Speech at Plymouth.*
Dec. 22, 1802.

People will not look forward to posterity
who never look backward to their ancestors.
f.   BURKE—*Reflections on the Revolution in*
France. Vol. III. P. 274.

Here you would know, and enjoy, what posterity will say of Washington. For a thousand leagues have nearly the same effect with
a thousand years.
g.   BENJ. FRANKLIN—*Letter to Washington.*
March 5, 1780.

What has poster'ty done for us,
That we, lest they their rights should lose,
Should trust our necks to gripe of noose?
h.   JOHN TRUMBULL—*McFingal.* Canto II.
L. 121.

A foreign nation is a kind of contemporaneous posterity.
i.   H. B. WALLACE—*Stanly.* Vol. II.
P. 89.

POTTERY (*See* OCCUPATIONS).

POVERTY.

Leave the poor
Some time for self-improvement. Let them
not
Be forced to grind the bones out of their arms
For bread, but have some space to think and
feel
Like moral and immortal creatures.
j.   BAILEY—*Festus.* Sc. *A Country Town.*

Needy knife-grinder! whither are ye going?
Rough is the road, your wheel is out of order;
Bleak blows the blast—your hat has got a
hole in it.
So have your breeches.
k.   CANNING—*The Friend of Humanity and*
the Knife-Grinder.

The beggarly last doit.
l.   COWPER—*The Task.* Bk. V. *The*
Winter Morning Walk. L. 316.

And plenty makes us poor.
m.   DRYDEN—*The Medal.* L. 126.

Thou source of all my bliss and all my woe,
That found'st me poor at first, and keep'st
me so.
n.   GOLDSMITH—*Deserted Village.* L. 413.

Chill penury repress'd their noble rage,
And froze the genial current of the soul.
o.   GRAY—*Elegy in a Country Churchyard.*
St. 13.

Yes, child of suffering, thou may'st well be
sure
He who ordained the Sabbath loves the poor!
p.   O. W. HOLMES—*Urania; or, A*
Rhymed Lesson. L. 325.

O God! that bread should be so dear,
And flesh and blood so cheap!
q.   HOOD—*The Song of the Shirt.*

Stitch! stitch! stitch!
In poverty, hunger, and dirt,
And still with a voice of dolorous pitch,
Would that its tone could reach the Rich,
She sang this "Song of the Shirt!"
r.   HOOD—*Song of the Shirt.* St. 11.

All this [wealth] excludes but one evil,—
poverty.
s.   SAM'L JOHNSON—*Boswell's Life of*
Johnson. 1777.

O Poverty, thy thousand ills combined
Sink not so deep into the generous mind,
As the contempt and laughter of mankind.
t.   JUVENAL—*Satire III.* L. 226.
Gifford's trans.

Rattle his bones over the stones!
He's only a pauper whom nobody owns!
u.   THOMAS NOEL—*The Pauper's Drive.*

But to the world no bugbear is so great,
As want of figure and a small estate.
v.   POPE—*First Book of Horace.* Ep. I.
L. 67.

Where are those troops of poor, that throng'd
of yore
The good old landlord's hospitable door?
w.   POPE—*Satires of Dr. Donne.* Satire II.
L. 113.

I am as poor as Job, my lord, but not so
    patient.
a.   *Henry IV.* Pt. II. Act I. Sc. 2.
                                    L. 144.

                    It is still her use
To let the wretched man outlive his wealth,
To view with hollow eye and wrinkled brow
An age of poverty.
b.   *Merchant of Venice.* Act IV. Sc. 1.
                                    L. 268.

No, madam, 'tis not so well that I am poor,
though many of the rich are damned.
c.   *All's Well That Ends Well.* Act I.
                            Sc. 3. L. 17.

Poor and content is rich and rich enough,
But riches fineless is as poor as winter
To him that ever fears he shall be poor.
d.   *Othello.* Act III. Sc. 3. L. 172.

Steep'd me in poverty to the very lips.
e.   *Othello.* Act IV. Sc. 2. L. 50.

The world affords no law to make thee rich;
Then be not poor, but break it, and take this.
My poverty, but not my will, consents.
I pay thy poverty, and not thy will.
f.   *Romeo and Juliet.* Act V. Sc. 1. L. 73.

His rawbone cheekes, through penurie and
    pine,
Were shronke into his jawes, as he did never
    dyne.
g.   Spenser—*Faerie Queene.* Bk. I.
                            Canto IX. St. 35.

Whose plenty made him pore.
h.   Spenser—*Faerie Queene.* Bk. I.
                            Canto IV. St. 29.

POWER.

Give me a lever long enough
And a prop strong enough,
I can single handed move the world.
i.   Archimedes.

Odin, thou whirlwind, what a threat is this
Thou threatenest what transcends thy might,
    even thine,
For of all powers the mightiest far art thou,
Lord over men on earth, and Gods in Heaven;
Yet even from thee thyself hath been withheld
One thing—to undo what thou thyself hast
    ruled.
j.   Matthew Arnold—*Balder Dead.* *The
                                    Funeral.*

He hath no power that hath not power to use.
k.   Bailey—*Festus.* Sc. *A Visit.*

Then, everlasting Love, restrain thy will;
'Tis god-like to have power, but not to kill.
l.   Beaumont and Fletcher—*The
                    Chances.* Act II. Sc. 2. *Song.*

'Tis true no lover has that pow'r
T' enforce a desperate amour,
As he that has two strings t' his bow,
And burns for love and money too.
m.   Butler—*Hudibras.* Pt. III. Canto I.
                                    L. 1.

Dim with the mist of years, gray flits the
shade of power.
n.   Byron—*Childe Harold.* Canto II.
                                    St. 2.

Men are never very wise and select in the
exercise of a new power.
o.   Wm. Ellery Channing—*The Present
                    Age. An Address.* 1841.

To know the pains of power, we must go to
those who have it; to know its pleasures, we
must go to those who are seeking it: the
pains of power are real, its pleasures imaginary.
p.   C. C. Colton—*Lacon.* P. 255.

So mightiest powers by deepest calms are fed,
And sleep, how oft, in things that gentlest be!
q.   Barry Cornwall—*Songs. The Sea
                            in Calm.* L. 13.

For what can power give more than food and
    drink,
To live at ease, and not be bound to think?
r.   Dryden—*Medal.* L. 235.

She knows her man, and when you rant and
    swear,
Can draw you to her with a single hair.
s.   Dryden—*Persius.* Satire V. L. 246.

Patience and Gentleness is Power.
t.   Leigh Hunt—*Sonnet. On a Lock of
                            Milton's Hair.*

                Without his rod revers'd,
And backward mutters of dissevering power.
u.   Milton—*Comus.* L. 816.

And deal damnation round the land.
v.   Pope—*The Universal Prayer.* St. 7.

No pent-up Utica contracts your powers,
But the whole boundless continent is yours.
w.   Jonathon Sewall—*Epilogue to
                            Addison's Cato.*

            The devil hath power
To assume a pleasing shape.
x.   *Hamlet.* Act II. Sc. 2. L. 628.

Power, like a desolating pestilence,
Pollutes whate'er it touches; and obedience,
Bane of all genius, virtue, freedom, truth,
Makes slaves of men, and of the human frame
A mechanized automaton.
y.   Shelley—*Queen Mab.* Pt. III.

The awful shadow of some unseen Power
Floats, tho' unseen, amongst us.
z.   Shelley—*Hymn to Intellectual Beauty.*

The omnipotence of God shines forth from the universe.

   a.   SWEDENBORG—*Apocalypse Explained.*
                  Par. 726.

The balance of power.

   b.   SIR ROBT. WALPOLE—*Speech.* 1741.

Because the good old rule
Sufficeth them, the simple plan,
That they should take who have the power,
And they should keep who can.

   c.   WORDSWORTH—*Rob Roy's Grave.*

The intellectual power, though words and things,
Went sounding on, a dim and perilous way!

   d.   WORDSWORTH—*The Excursion.* Bk. III.

Who murders Time, he crushes in the birth
a power ethereal.

   e.   YOUNG—*Night Thoughts.* Night II.
                  L. 110.

PRAISE.

Earth, with her thousand voices, praises God.

   f.   COLERIDGE—*Hymn Before Sunrise in the Vale of Chamouni.* Last line.

Praise enough
To fill the ambition of a private man,
That Chatham's language was his mother-tongue.

   g.   COWPER—*The Task.* Bk. II. L. 235.

When needs he must, yet faintly then he praises;
Somewhat the deed, much more the means he raises:
So marreth what he makes, and praising most, dispraises.

   h.   PHINEAS FLETCHER—*The Purple Island.* Canto VII. St. 67.

Long open panegyric drags at best,
And praise is only praise when well address'd.

   i.   GAY—*Ep.* I. L. 29.

Good people all, with one accord,
Lament for Madame Blaize,
Who never wanted a good word—
From those who spoke her praise.

   j.   GOLDSMITH—*Elegy on Mrs. Mary Blaize.*

Praise from a friend, or censure from a foe,
Are lost on hearers that our merits know.

   k.   HOMER—*Iliad.* Bk. X. L. 293.
                  Pope's trans.

Praise me not too much,
Nor blame me, for thou speakest to the Greeks
Who know me.

   l.   HOMER—*Iliad.* Bk. X. L. 289.
                  Bryant's trans.

A refusal of praise is a desire to be praised twice.

   m.   LA ROCHEFOUCAULD—*Maxims.* No. 152.

The sweeter sound of woman's praise.

   n.   MACAULAY—*Lines Written on the Night of 30th of July, 1847.*

And touch'd their golden harps, and hymning praised
God and his works.

   o.   MILTON—*Paradise Lost.* Bk. VII.
                  L. 258.

Join voices, all ye living souls: ye birds,
That singing up to heaven-gate ascend,
Bear on your wings and in your notes his praise.

   p.   MILTON—*Paradise Lost.* Bk. V. L. 197.

Of whom to be disprais'd were no small praise.

   q.   MILTON—*Paradise Regained.* Bk. 3.
                  L. 56.

Damn with faint praise, assent with civil leer,
And without sneering, teach the rest to sneer.

   r.   POPE—*Prologue to Satires.* L. 201.

Solid pudding against empty praise.

   s.   POPE—*Dunciad.* Bk. I. L. 54.

To what base ends, and by what abject ways,
Are mortals urg'd through sacred lust of praise!

   t.   POPE—*Essay on Criticism.* L. 520.

Delightful praise!—like summer rose,
That brighter in the dew-drop glows,
The bashful maiden's cheek appear'd,
For Douglas spoke, and Malcolm heard.

   u.   SCOTT—*Lady of the Lake.* Canto II.
                  St. 24.

All tongues speak of him, and the bleared sights
Are spectacled to see him.

   v.   *Coriolanus.* Act II. Sc. 1. L. 221.

Our praises are our wages.

   w.   *Winter's Tale.* Act I. Sc. 2. L. 94.

Praising what is lost
Makes the remembrance dear.

   x.   *All's Well That Ends Well.* Act V.
                  Sc. 3. L. 19.

Thou wilt say anon he is some kin to thee,
Thou spend'st such high-day wit in praising him.

   y.   *Merchant of Venice.* Act II. Sc. 9.
                  L. 97.

We bow our heads before Thee, and we laud
And magnify Thy name, Almighty God!
But Man is Thy most awful instrument,
In working out a pure intent.

   z.   WORDSWORTH—*Ode. Imagination ne'er before Content.*

I grant the man is vain who writes for praise.
Praise no man e'er deserved who sought no more.

   aa.   YOUNG—*Night Thoughts.* Night V.
                  L. 3.

The love of praise, howe'er conceal'd by art,
Reigns more or less, and glows, in ev'ry heart.
    a.   YOUNG—*The Love of Fame.* Satire I.
                       L. 51.

The most pleasing of all sounds that of your
    own praise.
    b.   XENOPHON—*Hiero.* I. 14. Watson's
                       trans.

PRAYER.

Nearer, my God, to Thee—
    Nearer to Thee!
E'en though it be a cross
    That raiseth me;
Still all my song shall be
Nearer, my God, to Thee,
    Nearer to Thee!
    c.   SARAH FLOWER ADAMS—*Nearer, my*
                       God, to Thee!

Yet then from all my grief, O Lord,
    Thy mercy set me free,
Whilst in the confidence of pray'r
    My soul took hold on thee.
    d.   ADDISON—*Miscellaneous Poems.*
           Divine Ode, made by a Gentleman on
           the Conclusion of his Travels.
                       Verse 6.

My favoured temple is an humble heart.
    e.   BAILEY—*Festus.* Sc. *Colonnade and*
                       Lawn.

Prayer is the spirit speaking truth to Truth.
    f.   BAILEY—*Festus.* Sc. *Elsewhere.*

And from the prayer of Want, and plaint of
    Woe,
O never, never turn away thine ear!
Forlorn, in this bleak wilderness below,
Ah! what were man, should Heaven refuse
    to hear!
    g.   BEATTIE—*Minstrel.* Bk. I. St. 29.

God answers sharp and sudden on some
    prayers,
And thrusts the thing we have prayed for in
    our face,
A gauntlet with a gift in 't.
    h.   E. B. BROWNING—*Aurora Leigh.*
                       Bk. II.

                  Hope, he called, belief
In God,—work, worship * * * therefore
    let us pray!
    i.   E. B. BROWNING—*Aurora Leigh.*
                       Bk. III.

Just my vengeance complete,
The man sprang to his feet,
Stood erect, caught at God's skirts, and
    prayed!
So, I was afraid!
    j.   ROBERT BROWNING—*Instans Tyrannus.*
                       VII.

They never sought in vain that sought the
    Lord aright!
    k.   BURNS—*The Cotter's Saturday Night.*
                       St. 6.

Father! no prophet's laws I seek,—
    Thy laws in Nature's works appear ;—
I own myself corrupt and weak,
    Yet will I pray, for thou wilt hear.
    l.   BYRON—*The Prayer of Nature.*

Father of Light! great God of Heaven!
    Hear'st thou the accents of despair?
Can guilt like man's be e'er forgiven?
    Can vice atone for crimes by prayer?
    m.   BYRON—*The Prayer of Nature.*

Be not afraid to pray—to pray is right.
Pray, if thou canst, with hope; but ever pray,
Though hope be weak or sick with long delay;
Pray in the darkness, if there be no light.
    n.   HARTLEY COLERIDGE—*Poems.*
               (*Posthumous.*)   *Prayer.*

Pray to be perfect, though material leaven
Forbid the spirit so on earth to be;
But if for any wish thou darest not pray,
Then pray to God to cast that wish away.
    o.   HARTLEY COLERIDGE—*Poems.*
               (*Posthumous.*)   *Prayer.*

He prayeth best who loveth best
All things, both great and small.
    p.   COLERIDGE—*The Ancient Mariner.*
                       Pt. VII.

He prayeth well who loveth well
Both man and bird and beast.
    q.   COLERIDGE—*The Ancient Mariner.*
                       Pt. VII.

The saints will aid if men will call:
For the blue sky bends over all.
    r.   COLERIDGE—*Christabel.* Conclusion to
                       Pt. I.

And Satan trembles when he sees
The weakest saint upon his knees.
    s.   COWPER—*Hymns. Exhortation to*
                       Prayer.

I ask not a life for the dear ones,
    All radiant, as others have done,
But that life may have just enough shadow
    To temper the glare of the sun;
I would pray God to guard them from evil,
    But my prayer would bound back to myself;
Ah! a seraph may pray for a sinner,
    But a sinner must pray for himself.
    t.   CHARLES M. DICKINSON—*The Children.*

Our vows are heard betimes! and Heaven
    takes care
To grant, before we can conclude the prayer.
    u.   DRYDEN—*Britannia Rediviva.* L. 1.

Grant folly's prayers that hinder folly's wish,
And serve the ends of wisdom.
    v.   GEORGE ELIOT—*The Spanish Gypsy.*
                       Bk. IV.

Almighty Father! let thy lowly child,
  Strong in his love of truth, be wisely bold,—
A patriot bard, by sycophants reviled,
  Let him live usefully, and not die old!
a.   EBENEZER ELLIOTT—*Corn Law Rhymes.*
                     A Poet's Prayer.

Though I am weak, yet God, when prayed,
Cannot withhold his conquering aid.
b.   EMERSON—*The Nun's Aspiration.*

To pray, * * * is to desire; but it is to
  desire what God would have us desire.
He who desires not from the bottom of his
  heart, offers a deceitful prayer.
c.   FÉNELON—*Pious Thoughts. Advice
        Concerning Prayer.* Mrs. Mant's
                       trans.

Ejaculations are short prayers darted up to
God on emergent occasions.
d.   FULLER—*Good Thoughts in Bad Times.
        Meditations on all Kinds of Prayers.
        Ejaculations, their Use.* V.

So a good prayer, though often used, is still
fresh and fair in the ears and eyes of Heaven.
e.   FULLER—*Good Thoughts in Bad Times.
        Meditations on all Kinds of Prayers.*
                      XII.

And fools who came to scoff, remain'd to pray.
f.   GOLDSMITH—*The Deserted Village.*
                     L. 179.

He that will learn to pray, let him go to Sea.
g.   HERBERT—*Jacula Prudentum.* No. 89.

Who goes to bed, and doth not pray,
Maketh two nights to every day!
h.   HERBERT—*The Temple. The Church.
        Charms and Knots.* St. 4.

In prayer the lips ne'er act the winning part
Without the sweet concurrence of the heart.
i.   HERRICK—*Hesperides. The Heart.*

        The prayer of Noah,
He cried out in the darkness, Hear, O God,
Hear HIM: hear this one; through the gates
  of death,
If life be all past praying for, O give
To Thy great multitude a way to peace;
Give them to HIM.
j.   JEAN INGELOW—*A Story of Doom.*
                 Bk. IX. St. 6.

Let one unceasing, earnest prayer
Be, too, for light,—for strength to bear
Our portion of the weight of care,
That crushes into dumb despair
  One half the human race.
k.   LONGFELLOW—*The Goblet of Life.*
                     St. 10.

Like one in prayer I stood.
l.   LONGFELLOW—*Voices of the Night.*
                Prelude. St. 11.

Not what we wish, but what we want,
  Oh! let thy grace supply,
The good unask'd, in mercy grant;
  The ill, though ask'd, deny.
m.   MERRICK—*Hymn.*

            And if by prayer
Incessant I could hope to change the will
Of Him who all things can, I would not cease
To weary Him with my assiduous cries.
n.   MILTON—*Paradise Lost.* Bk. XI.
                     L. 307.

But that from us aught should ascend to
  heav'n
So prevalent as to concern the mind
Of God high-bless'd, or to incline his will,
Hard to belief may seem, yet this will prayer.
o.   MILTON—*Paradise Lost.* Bk. XI.
                     L. 143.

          Hear his sighs though mute;
Unskilful with what words to pray, let me
Interpret for him.
p.   MILTON—*Paradise Lost.* Bk. XI.
                     L. 31.

Prayer is the soul's sincere desire,
  Uttered or unexpressed,
The motion of a hidden fire
  That trembles in the breast.
q.   MONTGOMERY—*Original Hymns.*
                  What is Prayer?

As down in the sunless retreats of the ocean
  Sweet flowers are springing no mortal can
    see,
So deep in my soul the still prayer of de-
  votion
  Unheard by the world, rises silent to Thee.
r.   MOORE—*Song. As Down in the Sunless
                      Retreats.*

             O sad estate
Of human wretchedness; so weak is man,
So ignorant and blind, that did not God
Sometimes withhold in mercy what we ask,
We should be ruined at our own request.
s.   HANNAH MORE—*Moses in the Bulrushes.*
                     Pt. I.

Lo! all life this truth declares,
Laborare est orare;
And the whole earth rings with prayers.
t.   D. M. MULOCK—*Labour is Prayer.* St. 4.

Whose very looks are prayers.
u.   D. M. MULOCK—*An Evening Hymn.
                A Sketch.* St. 3.

Now I lay me down to take my sleep,
I pray thee, Lord, my soul to keep;
If I should die before I wake,
I pray thee, Lord, my soul to take.
v.   *From the New England Primer.* 1814.

He pray'd by quantity,
And with his repetitions, long and loud,
All knees were weary.
w.   POLLOK—*Course of Time.* Pt. VIII.
                     L. 628.

Father of All! in every age,
  In every clime ador'd,
By saint, by savage, and by sage,
  Jehovah, Jove, or Lord!
  a.   POPE—*Universal Prayer.*

If I am right, Thy grace impart,
  Still in the right to stay;
If I am wrong, O teach my heart
  To find that better way!
  b.   POPE—*Universal Prayer.*

In all thou dost first let thy Prayers ascend,
And to the Gods thy Labours first commend,
From them implore Success, and hope a prosperous End.
  c.   PYTHAGORAS—*Golden Verses.* L. 49.
      See M. DACIER'S *Life of Pythagoras.*

The first petition that we are to make to
Almighty God is for a good *conscience*, the
next for *health of mind*, and then of *body.*
  d.   SENECA—*Epistle XIV.*

All his mind is bent to holiness,
To number Ave-Maries on his beads.
  e.   *Henry VI.* Pt. II. Act I. Sc. 3. L. 58.

        "Amen"
Stuck in my throat.
  f.   *Macbeth.* Act II. Sc. 2. L. 32.

Bow, stubborn knees! and heart with strings
  of steel
Be soft as sinews of the new-born babe.
  g.   *Hamlet.* Act III. Sc. 3. L. 70.

Go with me, like good angels, to my end;
And, as the long divorce of steel falls on me,
Make of your prayers one sweet sacrifice,
And lift my soul to heaven.
  h.   *Henry VIII.* Act II. Sc. 1. L. 75.

His worst fault is, that he is given to
prayer; he is something peevish that way;
but nobody but has his fault; but let that
pass.
  i.   *Merry Wives of Windsor.* Act I. Sc. 4.
                              L. 13.

If you bethink yourself of any crime
Unreconcil'd as yet to heaven and grace,
Solicit for it straight.
  j.   *Othello.* Act V. Sc. 2. L. 26.

                    My prayers
Are not words duly hallow'd nor my wishes
More worth than empty vanities; yet prayers
  and wishes
Are all I can return.
  k.   *Henry VIII.* Act II. Sc. 3. L. 67.

                  Rather let my head
Stoop to the block than these knees bow to any
Save to the God of heaven and to my king.
  l.   *Henry VI.* Pt. II. Act IV. Sc. 1.
                              L. 124.

Well, if my wind were but long enough to
say my prayers, I would repent.
  m.   *Merry Wives of Windsor.* Act IV.
                              Sc. 5. L. 104.

When I would pray and think, I think and
  pray
To several subjects; Heaven hath my empty
  words.
  n.   *Measure for Measure.* Act II. Sc. 4.
                              L. 1.

Earth bears no balsams for mistakes;
  Men crown the knave, and scourge the tool
That did his will: but thou, O Lord,
  Be merciful to me, a fool.
  o.   EDWARD ROWLAND SILL—*The Fool's
                              Prayer.*

Four things which are not in thy treasury,
I lay before thee, Lord, with this petition:—
  My nothingness, my wants,
  My sins, and my contrition.
  p.   SOUTHEY—*Occasional Pieces.* XIX.
              Imitated from the Persian.

Prayers are heard in heaven very much in
proportion to our faith. Little faith will get
very great mercies, but great faith still greater.
  q.   SPURGEON—*Gleanings Among the
                    Sheaves. Believing Prayer.*

To pray together, in whatever tongue or
ritual, is the most tender brotherhood of hope
and sympathy that men can contract in this
life.
  r.   MADAME DE STAËL—*Corinne.* Bk. X.
                              Ch. V.

Labor, you know, is Prayer.
  s.   BAYARD TAYLOR—*Improvisations.* 11.

Battering the gates of heaven with storms of
  prayer.
  t.   TENNYSON—*St. Simeon Stylites.* L. 7.

        More things are wrought by prayer
Than this world dreams of. Wherefore, let
  thy voice
Rise like a fountain for me night and day.
For what are men better than sheep or goats
That nourish a blind life within the brain,
If, knowing God, they lift not hands of prayer
Both for themselves and those who call them
  friend?
  u.   TENNYSON—*Morte D'Arthur.* L. 247.

"'Twas then belike," Honorious cried,
"When you the public fast defied,
Refused to heav'n to raise a prayer,
Because you'd no connections there."
  v.   JOHN TRUMBULL—*McFingal.* Canto I.
                              L. 541.

        Prayer is
The world in tune,
A spirit-voyce,
And vocall joyes,
Whose Eccho is heaven's blisse.
  w.   HENRY VAUGHAN—*The Morning Watch.*

Prayer moves the Hand which moves the world.

   a.   JOHN AIKMAN WALLACE—*There is an Eye that Never Sleeps.* L. 19.

Who is this before whose presence idols tumble to the sod?
While he cries out—"Allah Akbar! and there is no god but God!"

   b.   WM. ROSS WALLACE—*El Amin. The Faithful.*

Making their lives a prayer.

   c.   WHITTIER—*To A. K. on Receiving a Basket of Sea Mosses.*

The bells of Rylstone seemed to say,
While she sat listening in the shade,
With vocal music, "God us ayde!"
And all the hills were glad to bear
Their part in this effectual prayer.

   d.   WORDSWORTH—*The White Doe of Rylstone.* Canto VII. St. 11.

The imperfect offices of prayer and praise.

   e.   WORDSWORTH—*The Excursion.* Bk. I.

"What is good for a bootless bene?"
With these dark words begins my Tale;
And their meaning is, whence can comfort spring
When Prayer is of no avail?

   f.   WORDSWORTH—*Force of Prayer.*

Prayer ardent opens heaven.

   g.   YOUNG—*Night Thoughts.* Night VIII. L. 721.

PREACHING (*See* OCCUPATIONS).

PREJUDICE.

He hears but half who hears one party only.
   h.   ÆSCHYLUS—*Eum.* 428.

Prejudice renders a man's virtue his habit, and not a series of unconnected acts. Through just prejudice, his duty becomes a part of his nature.

   i.   BURKE—*Reflections on the Revolution in France.*

Much of our ignorance is of ourselves. Our eyes are full of dust. Prejudice blinds us.

   j.   ABRAHAM COLES—*The Light of the World.* P. 200.

Remember, when the judgment's weak,
The prejudice is strong.

   k.   KANE O'HARA—*Midas. Air.* Act I. Sc. 3.

PRESUMPTION.

Presume to lay their hand upon the ark
Of her magnificent and awful cause.

   l.   COWPER—*The Task.* Bk. II. *The Timepiece.* L. 231.

         Who dares
To say that he alone has found the truth?

   m.   LONGFELLOW—*Christus.* Pt. III. *John Endicott.* Act II. Sc. 3.

He will steal himself into a man's favour and for a week escape a great deal of discoveries; but when you find him out, you have him ever after.

   n.   *All's Well That Ends Well.* Act III. Sc. 6. L. 97.

How dare the plants look up to heaven, from whence
They have their nourishment?

   o.   *Pericles.* Act I. Sc. 2. L. 55.

It is not so with Him that all things knows
As 'tis with us that square our guess by shows:
But most it is presumption in us when
The help of heaven we count the act of men.

   p.   *All's Well That Ends Well.* Act II. Sc. 1. L. 152.

PRIDE.

As proud as Lucifer.

   q.   BAILEY—*Festus.* Sc. *A Country Town.*

Ay, do despise me, I'm the prouder for it;
I like to be despised.

   r.   BICKERSTAFF—*The Hypocrite.* Act V. Sc. 1.

They are proud in humility, proud in that they are not proud.

   s.   BURTON—*Anatomy of Melancholy.* Pt. I. Sec. II. Memb. 3. Subsec. XIV.

Pride (of all others the most dang'rous fault)
Proceeds from want of sense, or want of thought.

   t.   WENTWORTH DILLON—*Essay on Translated Verse.* L. 161.

Soothed with the sound, the king grew vain;
Fought all his battles o'er again;
And thrice he routed all his foes; and thrice he slew the slain.

   u.   DRYDEN—*Alexander's Feast.* L. 66.

Pride in their port, defiance in their eye,
I see the lords of humankind pass by.

   v.   GOLDSMITH—*The Traveller.* L. 327.

Oh! Why should the spirit of mortal be proud?
Like a swift-fleeting meteor, a fast flying cloud,
A flash of the lightning, a break of the wave
Man passes from life to his rest in the grave.

   w.   WM. KNOX—*Oh! Why Should the Spirit of Mortal be Proud?*

And, but herself, admits no parallel.

   x.   MASSINGER—*Duke of Milan.* Act IV. Sc. 3.

In pride, in reas'ning pride, our error lies ;
All quit their sphere and rush into the skies.
Pride still is aiming at the bless'd abodes,
Men would be angels, angels would be gods.

   a.   POPE—*Essay on Man.* Ep. I. L. 124.

Thus unlamented pass the proud away,
The gaze of fools and pageant of a day ;
So perish all, whose breast ne'er learn'd to
    glow
For others' good, or melt at others' woe.

   b.   POPE—*Memory of an Unfortunate Lady.*
                  L. 4.

What the weak head with strongest bias rules,
Is pride, the never-failing vice of fools.

   c.   POPE—*Essay on Criticism.* L. 203.

When Adam dalfe and Eve spane
   To spire of thou may spede,
Whare was then the pride of man,
   That now merres his meed ?

   d.   RICHARD ROLLE DE HAMPOLE—*Early
         English Text Society Reprints.* No.
         26. P. 79.

Is this that haughty, gallant, gay Lothario ?

   e.   NICHOLAS ROWE—*The Fair Penitent.*
          Act V. Sc. 1. L. 37.

In general, pride is at the bottom of all
great mistakes.

   f.   RUSKIN—*True and Beautiful. Morals
         and Religion. Conception of God.*
         P. 426.

      But man, proud man,
Drest in a little brief authority,
Most ignorant of what he's most assur'd,
His glassy essence, like an angry ape,
Plays such fantastic tricks before high heaven,
As make the angels weep.

   g.   *Measure for Measure.* Act II. Sc. 2.
               L. 117.

He is so plaguy proud that the death tokens
   of it
Cry " No recovery."

   h.   *Troilus and Cressida.* Act II. Sc. 3.
               L. 187.

He that is proud eats up himself : pride is
his own glass, his own trumpet, his own
chronicle ; and whatever praises itself but in
the deed, devours the deed in the praise.

   i.   *Troilus and Cressida.* Act II. Sc. 3.
               L. 164.

I do hate a proud man, as I hate the engendering of toads.

   j.   *Troilus and Cressida.* Act II. Sc. 3.
               L. 169.

               I have ventur'd,
Like little wanton boys that swim on bladders,
This many summers in a sea of glory,
But far beyond my depth : my high-blown
   pride
At length broke under me.

   k.   *Henry VIII.* Act III. Sc. 2. L. 358.

O world, how apt the poor are to be proud !

   l.   *Twelfth Night.* Act III. Sc. 1. L. 138.

         Pride hath no other glass
To show itself but pride, for supple knees
Feed arrogance and are the proud man's fees.

   m.   *Troilus and Cressida.* Act III. Sc. 3.
               L. 47.

Prouder than rustling in unpaid-for silk.

   n.   *Cymbeline.* Act III. Sc. 3. L. 24.

She bears a duke's revenues on her back,
And in her heart she scorns our poverty.

   o.   *Henry VI.* Pt. II. Act I. Sc. 3. L. 83.

      Why, who cries out on pride,
That can therein tax any private party?
Doth it not flow as hugely as the sea.

   p.   *As You Like It.* Act II. Sc. 7. L. 70.

PRINCIPLE.

Principle is ever my motto, no expediency.

   q.   BENJ. DISRAELI—*Sybil.* Bk. II. Ch. II.

Ez to my princerples, I glory
In hevin' nothin' o' the sort.

   r.   LOWELL—*The Biglow Papers.* First
         Series. No. VII. St. 10.

I *don't* believe in princerple,
But, oh, I *du* in interest.

   s.   LOWELL—*The Biglow Papers.* First
         Series. No. VI. St. 9.

PRINTING (*See* OCCUPATIONS).

PRISON.

Eternal Spirit of the chainless Mind !
  Brightest in dungeons, Liberty ! thou art,
  For there thy habitation is the heart—
The heart which love of thee alone can bind ;
And when thy sons to fetters are consign'd—
  To fetters and the damp vault's dayless
    gloom,
  Their country conquers with their martyr-
    dom.

   t.   BYRON—*Sonnet. On Chillon.
        Introductory to Prisoner of Chillon.*

Whene'er with haggard eyes I view
  This dungeon that I'm rotting in,
I think of those companions true
Who studied with me at the U-
    Niversity of Göttingen.

   u.   CANNING—*Song. Of One Eleven
             Years in Prison.*

Stone walls do not a prison make,
  Nor iron bars a cage ;
Minds innocent and quiet take
  That for an hermitage.

   v.   LOVELACE—*To Althea, from Prison.* IV.

I have been studying how I may compare
This prison where I live unto the world :
And for because the world is populous
And here is not a creature but myself,
I cannot do it ; yet I'll hammer it out.

   w.   *Richard II.* Act V. Sc. 5. L. 1.

PROGRESSION.

Westward the star of empire takes its way.
a.   Epigraph to BANCROFT'S *History of United States.*

Laws and institutions are constantly tending to gravitate. Like clocks, they must be occasionally cleansed, and wound up, and set to true time.
b.   HENRY WARD BEECHER—*Life Thoughts.*

Westward the course of empire takes its way;
The four first Acts already past,
A fifth shall close the Drama with the day;
Time's noblest offspring is the last.
c.   BISHOP BERKELEY—*Verses, on the Prospect of Planting Arts and Learning in America.*

Finds progress, man's distinctive mark alone,
Not God's, and not the beast's;
God is, they are,
Man partly is, and wholly hopes to be.
d.   ROBERT BROWNING—*A Death in the Desert.*

Progress is
The law of life, man is not
Man as yet.
e.   ROBERT BROWNING—*Paracelsus.* Pt. V.

All things journey : sun and moon,
Morning, noon, and afternoon,
Night and all her stars;
'Twixt the east and western bars
Round they journey,
Come and go!
We go with them!
f.   GEORGE ELIOT—*Spanish Gypsy.*
Bk. III. *Song.*

So long as all the increased wealth which modern progress brings, goes but to build up great fortunes, to increase luxury, and make sharper the contrast between the House of Have and the House of Want, progress is not real and cannot be permanent.
g.   HENRY GEORGE—*Progress and Poverty. Introductory. The Problem.*

To look up and not down,
To look forward and not back,
To look out and not in—and
To lend a hand.
h.   EDWARD EVERETT HALE—*Rule of the "Harry Wadsworth Club"* (*from "Ten Times One is Ten."* 1870).
Ch. IV.

We are swinging round the circle.
i.   ANDREW JOHNSON—*Of the Presidential "Reconstruction,"* August, 1866.

From lower to the higher next,
Not to the top, is Nature's text;
And embryo good, to reach full stature,
Absorbs the evil in its nature.
j.   LOWELL—*Festina Lente. Moral.*

Beneath this starry arch,
Naught resteth or is still;
But all things hold their march
As if by one great will.
Move one, move all :
Hark to the footfall!
On, on, forever.
k.   HARRIET MARTINEAU—*Stanzas.*

That in our proper motion we ascend
Up to our native seat; descent and fall
To us is adverse.
l.   MILTON—*Paradise Lost.* Bk. II. L. 75.

The march of intellect.
m.   ROBERT SOUTHEY— *Sir T. More, or Colloquies on the Progress and Prospects of Society.* Vol. II. P. 361.

Press on !—" for in the grave there is no work
And no device"—Press on ! while yet ye may !
n.   N. P. WILLIS—*From a Poem Delivered at Yale College,* 1827. L. 45.

PROMISES.

Promise is most given when the least is said.
o.   GEORGE CHAPMAN—*Musæus of Hero and Leander.* L. 234.

You never bade me hope, 'tis true;
I asked you not to swear :
But I looked in those eyes of blue,
And read a promise there.
p.   GERALD GRIFFIN—*You Never Bade Me Hope, 'Tis True.*

We promise according to our hopes, and perform according to our fears.
q.   LA ROCHEFOUCAULD—*Maxims.* No. 39.

And be these juggling fiends no more believ'd,
That palter with us in a double sense :
That keep the word of promise to our ear,
And break it to our hope.
r.   *Macbeth.* Act V. Sc. 8. L. 19.

His promises were, as he then was, mighty;
But his performance, as he is now, nothing.
s.   *Henry VIII.* Act IV. Sc. 2. L. 41.

Thy promises are like Adonis' gardens
That one day bloomed and fruitful were the next.
t.   *Henry VI.* Pt. I. Act I. Sc. 6. L. 6.

There buds the promise of celestial worth.
u.   YOUNG—*The Last Day.* Bk. III. L. 317.

PROPHECY.

Be thou the rainbow to the storms of life !
The evening beam that smiles the clouds away,
And tints to-morrow with prophetic ray !
v.   BYRON—*Bride of Abydos.* Canto II.
St. 20.

Of all the horrid, hideous notes of woe,
Sadder than owl-songs or the midnight blast;
Is that portentous phrase, "I told you so."
    a.   BYRON—*Don Juan.* Canto XIV. St. 50.

The prophet's mantle, ere his flight began,
Dropt on the world—a sacred gift to man.
    b.   CAMPBELL—*Pleasures of Hope.* Pt. I.
                            L. 43.

Ancestral voices prophesying war.
    c.   COLERIDGE— *Kubla Khan.*

Thy voice sounds like a prophet's word;
And in its hollow tones are heard
The thanks of millions yet to be.
    d.   FITZ-GREENE HALLECK—*Marco*
                              Bozzaris.

Prophet of evil! never hadst thou yet
A cheerful word for me. •To mark the signs
Of coming mischief is thy great delight,
Good dost thou ne'er foretell nor bring to pass.
    e.   HOMER—*Iliad.* Bk. I. L. 138.
                          Bryant's trans.

No mighty trance, or breathed spell
Inspires the pale-eyed priest from the pro-
    phetic cell.
    f.   MILTON—*Hymn on Christ's Nativity.*
                            L. 173.

In nature's infinite book of secrecy
A little I can read.
    g.   *Antony and Cleopatra.* Act I. Sc. 2.
                            L. 9.

O my prophetic soul!
My uncle!
    h.   *Hamlet.* Act I. Sc. 5. L. 40.

There is a history in all men's lives,
Figuring the nature of the times deceas'd,
The which observed, a man may prophesy
With a near aim, of the main chance of things
As yet not come to life, which in their seeds
And weak beginnings lie intreasured.
    i.   *Henry IV.* Pt. II. Act III. Sc. 1.
                            L. 80.

PROSPERITY.

I wish you every kind of prosperity, with a
little more taste.
    j.   ALAIN RENÉ LE SAGE—*Gil Blas.*
              Bk. VII. Ch. IV. Henri Van
                        Laun's trans.

Surer to prosper than prosperity could have
assur'd us.
    k.   MILTON—*Paradise Lost.* Bk. II. L. 39.

Prosperity's the very bond of love.
    l.   *Winter's Tale.* Act IV. Sc. 4. L. 584.

There shall be in England seven halfpenny
loaves sold for a penny: the three-hooped
pot shall have ten hoops; and I will make it
felony to drink small beer.
    m.   *Henry VI.* Pt. II. Act IV. Sc. 2.
                            L. 70.

Prosperity doth bewitch men, seeming clear;
As seas do laugh, show white, when rocks
    are near.
    n.   JOHN WEBSTER—*White Devil.* Act V.
                           Sc. 6.

Oh, how portentous is prosperity!
How comet-like, it threatens while it shines.
    o.   YOUNG—*Night Thoughts.* Night V.
                          L. 915.

PROVERBS.

Well-known Sayings and Expressions.

As Love and I late harbour'd in one inn,
With proverbs thus each other entertain:
"In love there is no lack," thus I begin;
"Fair words make fools," replieth he again;
"Who spares to speak doth spare to speed,"
    quoth I;
"As well," saith he, "too forward as too
    slow;"
"Fortune assists the boldest," I reply;
"A hasty man," quoth he, "ne'er wanted
    woe;"
"Labour is light where love," quoth I, "doth
    pay;"
Saith he, "Light burden's heavy, if far
    borne;"
Quoth I, "The main lost, cast the by away;"
"Y'have spun a fair thread," he replies in
    scorn.
    And having thus awhile each other
        thwarted
Fools as we met, so fools again we parted.
    p.   MICHAEL DRAYTON—*Proverbs.*

The genius, wit, and spirit of a nation are
discovered in its proverbs.
    q.   BACON.

This formal fool, your man, speaks naught
    but proverbs,
And speak men what they can to him he'll
    answer
With some rhyme, rotten sentence, or old
    saying,
Such spokes as ye ancient of ye parish use.
    r.   HENRY PORTER—*The Proverb Monger.*
           From *Two Angry Women of Abindon.*

A proverb is one man's wit and all men's
wisdom.
    s.   LORD JOHN RUSSELL—Quoted in
          Memoirs of Mackintosh. Vol. II.
                          P. 473.

I can tell thee where that saying was born.
    t.   *Twelfth Night.* Act I. Sc. 5. L. 9.

A baker's dozen.
   a.   RABELAIS—*Works.* Bk. V. Ch. XXII.

A beggarly people,
A church and no steeple.
   b.   Attributed to MALONE by SWIFT. See
            Prior's Life. 1860. 381. Of St.
            Ann's Church, Dublin.

A bird in the hand is worth two in the bush.
   c.   CERVANTES—*Don Quixote.* Pt. I.
            Ch. IV.

A black sheep is a biting beast.
   d.   BASTARD'S CHRESTOLEROS. 1598. P. 90.

A blind bargain.
   e.   *Merrie Tales of the Madmen of Gottam.*
            1630. No. 13.

Abstain from beans.
   f.   PYTHAGORAS *to his Followers.* See also
            PLUTARCH. *Of the Training of
            Children.*

A carpenter's known by his chips.
   g.   SWIFT—*Polite Conversation.*
            Dialogue II.

A cat may look at a king.
   h.   *Title of a Pamphlet* (published 1652).

A cheerful look makes a dish a feast.
   i.   HERBERT—*Jacula Prudentum.*

A cleere conscience is a sure carde.
   j.   LYLY—*Euphues.* P. 207. Arbor's
            reprint. 1579.

A cool mouth, and warm feet, live long.
   k.   HERBERT—*Jacula Prudentum.*

A crier of green sauce.
   l.   RABELAIS—*Works.* Bk. II.
            Ch. XXXI.

A crooked log makes a straight fire.
   m.   HERBERT—*Jacula Prudentum.*

A curst cow hath short horns.
   n.   HERBERT—*Jacula Prudentum.*

A dead father's counsel, a wise son heedeth.
   o.   TEGNER—*Fridthjof's Saga.* Canto VIII.

A delusion, a mockery, and a snare.
   p.   LORD DENMAN—*O'Connell vs. The
            Queen. Clark and Finnelly Reports.*

A Dwarf on a Giant's shoulder sees farther
of the two.
   q.   HERBERT—*Jacula Prudentum.*

A fair exterior is a silent recommendation.
   r.   PUBLIUS SYRUS—*Maxims.*

A feather in hand is better than a bird in
the air.
   s.   HERBERT—*Jacula Prudentum.*

A fishmonger's wife may feed of a conger;
but a serving-man's wife may starve for
hunger.
   t.   *A Health to the Gentlemanly Profession
            of Serving-men.* 1598.

A flea in one's ear.
   u.   SIMON FORMAN—*Notes to Marriage of
            Wit and Wisdom.*

A god out of a machine.
   v.   SOCRATES—*See* PLATO'S *Cratylus.* 425.

A great ship asks deep waters.
   w.   HERBERT—*Jacula Prudentum.*

Agreed to differ.
   x.   SOUTHEY—*Life of Wesley.*

A happy accident.
   y.   MADAME DE STAËL—*L'Allemagne.*
            Ch. XVI.

A heavy heart bears not a humble tongue.
   z.   *Love's Labour's Lost.* Act V. Sc. 2.
            L. 747.

A knock-down argument.
   aa.   DRYDEN—*Amphytrion.* Act I. Sc. 1.

A little house well fill'd, a little field well
till'd, and a little wife well will'd, are great
riches.
   bb.   *Written in a copy of the Grete Herbell,*
            1561.

A little more than kin, and less than kind.
   cc.   *Hamlet.* Act I. Sc. 2. L. 65.

A little snow, tumbled about, anon becomes
a mountain.
   dd.   *King John.* Act III. Sc. 4. L. 176.

A little too wise they say do ne'er live long.
   ee.   THOS. MIDDLETON—*The Phenix.* Act I.
            Sc. 1.

A little wind kindles, much puts out the fire.
   ff.   HERBERT—*Jacula Prudentum.*

All concord's born of contraries.
   gg.   BEN JONSON—*Cynthia's Revels.* Act V.
            Sc. 2.

All flesh is grass, and all its glory fades.
   hh.   COWPER—*Task.* Bk. III. L. 259.

All hoods make not monks.
   ii.   *Henry VIII.* Act III. Sc. 1. L. 23.

All is not gold that glistereth in bed.
       FREIRE DENISE CORDELIER—*Sayings.*
            1300.
   jj.   THOS. MIDDLETON—*A Fair Quarrel.*
            Act V. Sc. 1.

All our geese are swans.
   kk.   BURTON—*Anatomy of Melancholy.*
            Pt. I. Sec. II. Memb. 3. Subsec. 14.

All places are distant from heaven alike.
a.   BURTON—*Anatomy of Melancholy.*
                Pt. II. Sec. III. Memb. 4.

All quiet along the Potomac.
b.   Proverbial in 1861–62. *Supposed to have originated with* GEN. McCLELLAN. *See* ETHEL LYNN BEERS—*The Picket Guard.*

All's not offence that indiscretion finds.
c.   *King Lear.* Act II. Sc. 4. L. 198.

All's well that ends well.
d.   *All's Well That Ends Well.* Act V.
                Sc. 1. L. 28.

All that glisters is not gold.
      CERVANTES—*Don Quixote.* Pt. II.
                Ch. XXXIII.
      HERBERT—*Jacula Prudentum.*
      ALANUS DE INSULIS—*Parabolæ.*
      Merchant of Venice. Act II. Sc. 7. L. 67.
e.   UDALL—*Ralph Royster Doyster.* 1566.

All the fatt's in the fire.
f.   MARSTON—*What You Will.* 1607.

All this for a song.
g.   BURLEIGH—*To Queen Elizabeth* (when ordered to give £100 to Spenser).

All truths are not to be told.
h.   HERBERT—*Jacula Prudentum.*

A lover's soul lives in the body of his mistress.
i.   PLUTARCH.

Although the last, not least.
j.   *King Lear.* Act I. Sc. 1. L. 85.

A morning Sun, and a Wine-bred child, and a Latin-bred woman seldom end well.
k.   HERBERT—*Jacula Prudentum.*

An animal without feathers and walking on two legs.
l.   PLATO—*Definition of a Man.*

And all labor without any play, boys, Makes Jack a dull boy in the end.
m.   H. A. PAGE—*Vers de Société.*

And he that stands upon a slippery place Makes nice of no vile hold to stay him up.
n.   *King John.* Act III. Sc. 4. L. 138.

An undutiful Daughter will prove an unmanageable Wife.
o.   BENJ. FRANKLIN—*Poor Richard.* 1752.

A penny for your thought.
p.   SWIFT—*Polite Conversation.*
                Introduction.

A piece of a Churchyard fits everybody.
q.   HERBERT—*Jacula Prudentum.*

Arm'd at point exactly, cap-à-pie.
r.   *Hamlet.* Act I. Sc. 2. L. 200.

A rolling stone gathers no moss.
s.   PUBLIUS SYRUS—*Maxims.* No. 524.

Art may err, but nature cannot miss.
t.   DRYDEN—*The Cock and Fox.* L. 452.

As busie as a Bee.
u.   LYLY—*Euphues and his England.*
                P. 252.

As clear and as manifest as the nose in a man's face.
v.   BURTON—*Anatomy of Melancholy.*
                Pt. III. Sec. III. Memb. 4.
                Subsec. I.

As clear as a whistle.
w.   JOHN BYROM—*Epistle to Lloyd.* I.

As cold as cucumbers.
x.   BEAUMONT AND FLETCHER—*Cupid's Revenge.* Act I. Sc. 1.

As high as Heaven, as deep as Hell.
y.   BEAUMONT AND FLETCHER—*The Honest Man's Fortune.* Act IV. Sc. 1.

As sure as a gun.
z.   DRYDEN—*The Spanish Friar.* Act III.
                Sc. 2.

As the case stands.
aa.   THOS. MIDDLETON—*The Old Law.*
                Act II. Sc. 1.

As you sow, y' are like to reap.
bb.   BUTLER—*Hudibras.* Pt. II. Canto II.
                L. 504.

At our wittes end.
cc.   HEYWOOD—*Proverbs.* Pt. I. Ch VIII.

A weak Invention of the Enemy.
dd.   COLLEY CIBBER—*Richard III.* (altered).
                Act V. Sc. 3.

Barkis is willin'!
ee.   DICKENS—*David Copperfield.* Ch. I.

Beat all your feathers as flat down as pancakes.
ff.   THOS MIDDLETON—*The Roaring Girl.*
                Act II. Sc. 1.

Beauty draws more than oxen.
gg.   HERBERT—*Jacula Prudentum.*

Before you could say Jack Robinson.
hh.   HUDSON—*Song.*

Before you make a friend eat a bushel of salt with him.
ii.   HERBERT—*Jacula Prudentum.*

Bells call others, but themselves enter not into the Church.
jj.   HERBERT—*Jacula Prudentum.*

Best safety lies in fear.
kk.   *Hamlet.* Act I. Sc. 3. L. 43.

Be sure you are right, then go ahead
ll.   DAVID CROCKETT—*Motto.*

Better a bad excuse, than none at all.
a. CAMDEN—*Remaines. Proverbs.* P. 293.

Better a barefoot than none.
b. HERBERT—*Jacula Prudentum.*

Better a witty fool than a foolish wit.
c. *Twelfth Night.* Act I. Sc. 5. L. 40.
(Quoted.)

Better fifty years of Europe than a cycle of Cathay.
d. TENNYSON—*Locksley Hall.* St. 92.

Better halfe a loafe than no bread.
e. CAMDEN—*Remaines. Proverbs.* P. 293.

Better is to bow than breake.
f. HEYWOOD—*Proverbs.* Pt. I. Ch. IX.

Better late than never.
g. DIONYSIUS—*Halicarnassus.* IX. 9.

Better one byrde in hand than ten in the wood.
h. HEYWOOD—*Proverbs.* Pt. I. Ch. XI.

Better the feet slip than the tongue.
i. HERBERT—*Jacula Prudentum.*

Better your room than your company.
j. SIMON FORMAN—*Marriage of Wit and Wisdom.* About 1570.

Be wisely worldly, but not worldly wise.
k. QUARLES—*Emblems.* Bk. II. Em. 2.

Birds of a feather will gather together.
l. BURTON—*Anatomy of Melancholy.* Pt. III. Sec. I. Memb. 1. Subsec. II.

Blood is thicker than water.
m. SCOTT—*Guy Mannering.* Ch. XXXVIII.

Bread is the staff of life.
n. SWIFT—*Tale of a Tub.*

Brevity is the soul of wit.
o. *Hamlet.* Act II. Sc. 2. L. 90.

Build castles in Spain.
p. HERBERT—*Jacula Prudentum.*

Build castles in the air.
q. BURTON—*Anatomy of Melancholy.* Pt. I. Sec. II. Memb. 1. Subsec. III.

But me no buts.
HENRY FIELDING—*Rape upon Rape.* Act II. Sc. 2.
r. AARON HILL—*Snake in the Grass.* Sc. 1.

But ne'er the rose without the thorn.
s. HERRICK—*The Rose.*

But when the fox hath once got in his nose,
He'll soon find means to make the body follow.
t. *Henry VI.* Pt. III. Act IV. Sc. 7. L. 25.

By all that's good and glorious.
u. BYRON—*Sardanapalus.* Act I. Sc. 2.

By hooke or crooke.
v. HEYWOOD—*Proverbs.* Pt. I. Ch. XI.

Can one desire too much of a good thing?
CERVANTES—*Don Quixote.* Pt. I. Bk. I. Ch. VI.
w. *As You Like It.* Act IV. Sc. 1. L. 123.

Clean your Finger before you point at my Spots.
x. BENJ. FRANKLIN—*Poor Richard.* 1750.

Come home to men's business and bosoms.
y. BACON—*Essays. Dedication.* Ed. 1625.

Comparisons are odious.
BURTON—*Anatomy of Melancholy.* Pt. III. Sec. III. Memb. 1. Subsec. II.
CERVANTES—*Don Quixote.* Pt. II. Ch. I.
FORTESCUE—*De Laudibus Leg. Angliæ.* Ch. 19.
HERBERT—*Jacula Prudentum.*
HEYWOOD—*A Woman Killed with Kindness.* Act I. Sc. 2.
LE ROUX DE LINCY—*Le Livre des Proverbes Français.*
z. *Much Ado About Nothing.* Act III. Sc. 5. L. 19.

Corne, which is the staffe of life.
aa. WINSLOW—*Good News from New England.*

Couldst thou both eat thy cake and have it?
bb. HERBERT—*The Church. The Size.*

Curses are like young chickens,
And still come home to roost!
cc. *Arabian Proverb* quoted by BULWER-LYTTON—*The Lady of Lyons.* Act V. Sc. 2.

Cut and come again.
dd. CRABBE—*Tales VII.* L. 26.

Dark as pitch.
ee. BUNYAN—*Pilgrim's Progress.* Pt. I.

Deceive not thy Physician, Confessor, nor Lawyer.
ff. HERBERT—*Jacula Prudentum.*

Deed are males, words females are.
gg. DAVIES—*Scene of Folly.* P. 147.

Deeds, not words.
hh. BEAUMONT AND FLETCHER—*The Lover's Progress.* Act III. Sc. 6.

Delay always heeds danger.
ii. CERVANTES—*Don Quixote.* Bk. IV. Ch. III.

Delays have dangerous ends.
jj. *Henry VI.* Pt. I. Act III. Sc. 2. L. 33.

Diamonds cut diamonds.
a.   JOHN FORD—*The Lover's Melancholy.*
Act I. Sc. 3.

Don't cross the bridge till you come to it,
Is a proverb old, and of excellent wit.
b.   LONGFELLOW—*Christus. The Golden
Legend.* Pt. VI.

Doubtless the pleasure is as great
Of being cheated as to cheat.
c.   BUTLER—*Hudibras.* Pt. II. Canto 3.
L. 1.

Do you think I was born in a wood to be
afraid of an owl?
d.   SWIFT—*Polite Conversation.* Dialogue I.

England is a paradise for women, and hell
for horses: Italy is a paradise for horses, hell
for women.
e.   BURTON—*Anatomy of Melancholy.*
Pt. III. Sec. III. Memb. 1.
Subsec. II.

Enough is as good as a feast.
f.   GEORGE CHAPMAN—*Eastward Ho!*
Act III. Sc. 2.

Eureka! Eureka!
g.   ARCHIMEDES.

Every fat must stand upon his bottom.
h.   BUNYAN—*Pilgrim's Progress.* Pt. I.

Every honest miller has a golden thumb.
i.   CHAUCER—*Canterbury Tales. The
Knight's Tale.* L. 2,408.

Every man for himself, his own ends, the
devil for all.
j.   BURTON—*Anatomy of Melancholy.*
Pt. III. Sec. I. Memb. 3.

Every man is odd.
k.   *Troilus and Cressida.* Act IV. Sc. 5.
L. 42.

Every man is the architect of his own fortunes.
l.   PSEUDO SALLUST—*Epistle de Rep.
Ordin.* II. 1.

Every one stretcheth his legs according to his
coverlet.
m.   HERBERT—*Jacula Prudentum.*

Everything that is unknown is taken to be
grand.
n.   TACITUS—*Agricola.* 30.

Every why hath a wherefore.
o.   *Comedy of Errors.* Act II. Sc. 2.
L. 44.

Facts are stubborn things.
p.   LE SAGE—*Gil Blas.* Bk. X. Ch. I.
Smollet's trans.

Faint harts faire ladies never win.
q.   *A Proper New Ballad in Praise of My
Lady Marques.* 1569. Reprint
Philobiblian So. 1867. P. 22.

32

Faint heart ne'er won fair lady.
r.   PHINEAS FLETCHER—*Brittain's Ida.*
Canto V. I. St. 1. *Ballad of*
W. ELDERTON. 1569.

Fame is the perfume of heroic deeds.
s.   SOCRATES.

Familiarity breeds contempt.
t.   PUBLIUS SYRUS—*Maxims.* 640.

Fast bind, fast find;
A proverb never stale in thrifty mind.
Merchant of Venice. Act II. Sc. 5.
L. 54.
u.   HEYWOOD—*Proverb.* Pt. I. Ch. III.

Fat, fair, and forty.
v.   SCOTT—*St. Ronan's Well.* Ch. VII.

Fer from eye, fer from herte.
w.   HENDYING—*Proverbs.* MSS. About
1320.

Fingers were made before forks and hands before knives.
x.   SWIFT—*Polite Conversation.*
Dialogue II.

Fitted him to a T.
y.   SAM'L JOHNSON—*Boswell's Life of
Johnson.* 1784.

Follow pleasure, and then will pleasure flee;
Flee pleasure, and pleasure will follow thee.
z.   HEYWOOD—*Proverbs.* Pt. I. Ch. XI.

Fools make feasts, and wise men eat them.
aa.   BENJ. FRANKLIN—*Poor Richard.* 1733.

Forgiveness is better than revenge.
bb.   PITTACUS—*Quoted by Heraclitus.*

For Satan finds some mischief still
For idle hands to do.
cc.   WATTS—*Divine Songs.* Song XX.

Fortune befriends the bold.
CICERO—*De Finibus.* Bk. III. Div. 4.
dd.   VIRGIL—*Æneid.* X. 284.

For want of a nail the shoe is lost, for want
of a shoe the horse is lost, for want of a horse
the rider is lost.
ee.   HERBERT—*Jacula Prudentum.*

For where God built a church, there the
devil would also build a chapel.
ff.   MARTIN LUTHER—*Table Talk.* LXVII.

For young hot colts being rag'd, do rage the
more.
gg.   *Richard II.* Act II. Sc. I. L. 70.

Frieth in her own grease.
hh.   HEYWOOD—*Proverbs.* Pt. I. Ch. XI.

From the crown of our head to the sole of our
foot.
    BEAUMONT AND FLETCHER—*The Honest
        Man's Fortune.* Act II. Sc. 2.
a. THOS. MIDDLETON—*A Mad World, My
        Masters.* Act I. Sc. 3.

Give an inch, he'll take an ell.
    HOBBES—*Liberty and Necessity.* No. 111.
b. JOHN WEBSTER—*Sir Thomas Wyatt.*

Give not Saint *Peter* so much, to leave Saint
Paul nothing.
c. HERBERT—*Jacula Prudentum.*

Give the devil his due.
d. DRYDEN—*Epilogue to the Duke of Guise.*

Glass, China, and Reputation, are easily
crack'd and never well mended.
e. BENJ. FRANKLIN—*Poor Richard.* 1750.

Gluttony kills more than the sword.
f. HERBERT—*Jacula Prudentum.*

God defend the right.
g. *Richard II.* Act I. Sc. 3. L. 101.

God made the country, and man made the
town.
h. COWPER—*The Task.* Bk. I. L. 749.

God never sendeth mouth but he sendeth
meat.
i. HEYWOOD—*Proverbs.* Pt. I. Ch. IV.

God save the mark!
j. *Henry IV.* Pt. I. Act I. Sc. 3. L. 57.

God sends cold according to clothes.
k. HERBERT—*Jacula Prudentum.*

God's Mills grind slow but sure.
l. HERBERT—*Jacula Prudentum.*

God's mills grind slow,
But they grind woe.
m. WM. R. ALGER—*Oriental Poetry.*
        Delayed Retribution.

Going as if he trod upon eggs.
n. BURTON—*Anatomy of Melancholy.*
        Pt. III. Sect. II. Memb. 3.

Gold all is not that doth golden seem.
o. SPENSER—*Faerie Queene.* Bk. II.
        Canto VIII. St. 14.

Good company in a journey makes the
way to seem the shorter.
p. IZAAK WALTON—*The Compleat Angler.*
        Pt. I. Ch. I.
Go West, young man! Go West.
q. JOHN L. B. SOULE—*In the Terre Haute
        Express.* 1851.

Great Estates may venture more. Little
Boats must keep near Shore.
r. BENJ. FRANKLIN—*Poor Richard.* 1751.

Greatest happiness of the greatest number.
s. HUTCHESON—*Moral Good and Evil.*
        Sec. III.

Hail, fellow, well met.
t. SWIFT—*My Lady's Lamentation.*

Half as sober as a judge.
u. CHARLES LAMB—*Letter to Mr. and Mrs.
        Moxon.* August, 1833.

Half the world knows not how the other half
lies.
v. HERBERT—*Jacula Prudentum.*

Handsome is that handsome does.
w. GOLDSMITH—*The Vicar of Wakefield.*
        Ch. I.

Hanging and wiving goes by destiny.
x. *Merchant of Venice.* Act II. Sc. 9.
        L. 83.

Hanging was the worst use a man could be
put to.
y. SIR HENRY WOTTON—*The Disparity
        between Buckingham and Essex.*

Harp not on that string.
z. *Richard III.* Act IV. Sc. 4. L. 366.

Have yee him on the hip?
aa. HEYWOOD—*Proverbs.* Pt. II. Ch. V.

Have you summoned your wits from wool-
gathering?
bb. THOS. MIDDLETON—*The Family of Love.*
        Act V. Sc. 3.

He always looked a given horse in the mouth.
cc. RABELAIS—*Works.* Bk. I. Ch. XI.

He can give little to his servant that licks his
knife.
dd. HERBERT—*Jacula Prudentum.*

He comes not in my books.
ee. BEAUMONT AND FLETCHER—*The Widow.*
        Act I. Sc. 1.

He did not care a button for it.
ff. RABELAIS—*Works.* Bk. II. Ch. XVI.

He is a fool who lets slip a bird in the hand
for a bird in the bush.
gg. PLUTARCH—*Of Garrulity.*

He jests at scars that never felt a wound.
hh. *Romeo and Juliet.* Act II. Sc. 2. L. 1.

He knew what is what.
ii. SKELTON—*Why Come Ye nat to Courte?*
        L. 1,106.

He must have a long spoon that must eat
with the devil.
jj. *Comedy of Errors.* Act IV. Sc. 3.
        L. 64.

He must needes go that the dyvell dryveth.
　　In " *Johan the Husbande, Tyb His Wyfe
　　and Syr Jhan the Priest* "—printed by
　　　　　　　　　　Rastall. 1533.
a.　*All's Well That Ends Well.*　Act I.
　　　　　　　　　　Sc. 3.　L. 31.

He pares his apple that will cleanly feed.
b.　Herbert—*Church Porch.*　St. 2.

Here is the devil-and-all to pay.
c.　Cervantes—*Don Quixote.*　Bk. IV.
　　　　　　　　　　　　Ch. X.

Here's metal more attractive.
d.　*Hamlet.*　Act III.　Sc. 2.　L. 115.

He rolls it under his tongue as a sweet morsel.
e.　Mathew Henry—*Commentaries.*
　　　　　　　　　Psalm XXXVI.

Her that ruled the rost in the kitchen.
f.　Thos. Heywood—*History of Women.*
　　　　　　　　　(Ed. 1624.)　P. 286.

He ruleth all the roste.
g.　Skelton—*Why Come Ye nat to Courte ?*
　　　　　　　　　　　L. 198.

He's a sure card.
h.　Dryden—*The Spanish Friar.*　Act II.
　　　　　　　　　　　　Sc. 2.

He that can't live upon love deserves to die
　　in a ditch.
i.　Congreve.

He that goes to bed thirsty rises healthy.
j.　Herbert—*Jacula Prudentum.*

He that has two strings t' his bow.
k.　Butler—*Hudibras.*　Pt. III.　Canto I.
　　　　　　　　　　　　L. 3.

He that is down can fall no lower.
l.　Butler—*Hudibras.*　Pt. I.　Canto III.
　　　　　　　　　　　　L. 878.

He that is down needs fear no fall.
m.　Bunyan—*Pilgrim's Progress.*　Pt. II.

He that keeps nor crust nor crum,
Weary of all, shall want some.
n.　*King Lear.*　Act I.　Sc. 4.　L. 216.

He that runs may read.
o.　Cowper—*Tirocinium.*　L. 80.

He was born within the sound of Bow-bell.
p.　Fuller—*Gnomologia.*

He went away with a flea in 's ear.
q.　Beaumont and Fletcher—*Love's Cure.*
　　　　　　　　　Act III.　Sc. 3.

　He who lives after nature, shall never be
poor ; after opinion, shall never be rich.
r.　Seneca.

He who moves not forward goes backward !
　　A capital saying !
s.　Goethe—*Herman and Dorothea.*
　　　　　　　　　Canto III.　L. 66.

He will give the devil his due.
t.　*Henry IV.*　Pt. I.　Act I.　Sc. 2.
　　　　　　　　　　　　L. 132.

Hide their diminished heads.
u.　Milton—*Paradise Lost.*　Bk. IV.　L. 35.

Hier lies that should fetch a perfect woman
　　over the coles.
v.　Sir Gyles Goosecappe.　1606.

Him that makes shoes go barefoot himself.
w.　Burton—*Anatomy of Melancholy.*
　　　　Democritus to the Reader.　P. 34.
　　　　　　　　　　　Ed. 1887.

His bark is worse than his bite.
x.　Herbert—*Country Parson.*　Ch. XXIX.

　* * * his master was in a manner always
in a wrong Boxe and building castels in the
ayre or catching Hares with Tabers.
y.　*Letter by F. A. to L. B.* 1575-76.　Repr.
　　　　　　in *Miscell. Antiq. Anglic.*

His time is forever, everywhere his place.
z.　Abraham Cowley—*Friendship in
　　　　　　　　　　　　Absence.*

Hit the nail on the head.
aa.　Beaumont and Fletcher—*Love's
　　　　　　　Cure.*　Act II.　Sc. 1.

　Hold one another's noses to the grindstone
hard.
bb.　Burton—*Anatomy of Melancholy.*
　　　　　　Pt. III.　Sect. 1.　Memb. 3.

Hold their noses to the grindstone.
cc.　Thos. Middleton—*Blurt, Master
　　　　　　Constable.*　Act III.　Sc. 3.

Home is where the heart is.
dd.　Pliny.

Homo proponit et Deus disponit
And governeth alle goode virtues.
ee.　*Piers Ploughman.*　L. 13,994.

How we apples swim.
ff.　Swift—*Brother Protestants.*

How well I feathered my nest.
gg.　Rabelais—*Works.*　Bk. II.　Ch. XVII.

Huzzaed out of my seven senses.
hh.　*Spectator.*　No. 616.　Nov. 5, 1774.

　I am almost frightened out of my seven
senses.
ii.　Cervantes—*Don Quixote.*　Pt. I.
　　　　　　　　　　Bk. III.　Ch. 9.

　I am glad that my *Adonis* hath a sweete
tooth in his head.
jj.　Lyly—*Euphues and his England.*
　　　　　　　　　　　　P. 308.

I am just going to leap into the dark.
kk.　Rabelais—*From Motteux's Life.*

I can tell where my own shoe pinches me.
   a.   CERVANTES—*Don Quixote.* Pt. I.
                    Ch. IV.

If a man could half his wishes he would
double his Troubles.
   b.   BENJ. FRANKLIN—*Poor Richard.* 1752.

I find the medicine worse than the malady.
   c.   BEAUMONT AND FLETCHER—*Love's Cure.*
                Act III. Sc. 2.

If your Riches are yours, why don't you
take them with you to the t'other world?
   d.   BENJ. FRANKLIN—*Poor Richard.* 1751.

If you would be loved, love and be lovable.
   e.   BENJ. FRANKLIN—*Poor Richard.* 1755.

I have other fish to fry.
   f.   CERVANTES—*Don Quixote.* Pt. II.
                 Ch. XXXV.

I have you on the hip.
   g.   *Merchant of Venice.* Act IV. Sc. 1.
                 L. 334.

I'll be with you in the squeezing of a lemon.
   h.   GOLDSMITH—*She Stoops to Conquer.*
                Act I. Sc. 2.

Ill blows the wind that profits nobody.
   i.   *Henry VI.* Pt. III. Act II. Sc. 5.
                 L. 55.

         I'll make the fur
Fly 'bout the ears of the old cur.
   j.   BUTLER—*Hudibras.* Pt. I. Canto III.
                 L. 278.

Ill news is wing'd with fate, and flies apace.
   k.   DRYDEN—*Threnodia Augustalis.* L. 49.

Illustrious Predecessor.
   l.   BURKE—*Thoughts on the Cause of the
            Present Discontents.* Edition 1775.
                 P. 26.

Ill ware is never cheap.
   m.   HERBERT—*Jacula Prudentum.*

Ill wind which blows no man to good.
   n.   *Henry IV.* Pt. II. Act V. Sc. 3.
                 L. 90.

I look upon you as a gem of the old rock.
   o.   SIR THOMAS BROWNE—*Dedication to
                  Urn Burial.*

Imitation is the sincerest of flattery.
   p.   C. C. COLTON—*Lacon.* P. 127.

In hope her to attain by hook or crook.
   q.   SPENSER—*Faerie Queene.* Bk. III.
                Canto I. St. 17.

In the great right of an excessive wrong.
   r.   ROBERT BROWNING—*The Ring and the
            Book. The other Half—Rome.*
                 L. 1,055.

In the name of the Prophet—figs.
   s.   HORACE SMITH—*Johnson's Ghost.*

In the spyght of his tethe.
   t.   SKELTON—*Why Come Ye nat to Courte.*
                 L. 939.

I owe you one.
   u.   GEORGE COLMAN (the Younger)—*The
            Poor Gentleman.* Act I. Sc. 2.

I shall tread in the footsteps of my illustrious
predecessor.
   v.   MARTIN VAN BUREN—*Inaugural
            Address.* March 4, 1837.

I smell a device.
   w.   *Twelfth Night.* Act II. Sc. 3. L. 176.

                It had need to bee
A wylie mouse that should breed in the cat's
   eare.
   x.   HEYWOOD—*Proverbs.* Pt. II. Ch. V.

              It is always good
When a man has two irons in the fire.
   y.   BEAUMONT AND FLETCHER—*The
            Faithful Friends.* Act I. Sc. 2.

It is a poor sport that is not worth the candle.
   z.   HERBERT—*Jacula Prudentum.*

It is a wise father that knows his own child.
   aa.   *Merchant of Venice.* Act II. Sc. 2.
                 L. 80.

It is better to wear out than to rust out.
   bb.   BISHOP CUMBERLAND.
       See BISHOP HORNE'S *Sermon on the
            Duty of Contending for the Truth.*

It is good to have a hatch before the durre.
   cc.   HEYWOOD—*Proverbs.* Pt. I. Ch. XI.

It is no jesting with edge tools.
   dd.   *The True Tragedy of Richard III.* 1594.

It is the lot of man but once to die.
   ee.   QUARLES—*Emblems.* Bk. V. Em. 7.

It is well to moor your bark with two anchors.
   ff.   PUBLIUS SYRUS—*Maxims.* 119.

I will die in the last ditch.
   gg.   WILLIAM OF ORANGE—*Hume's England.*
                 Ch. LXV.

I won't quarrel with my bread and butter.
   hh.   SWIFT—*Polite Conversation.*
                Dialogue I.

Jack shall pipe, and Jill shall dance.
   ii.   GEORGE WITHER—*Poem on Christmas.*

Keep what goods the Gods provide you.
   jj.   PLAUTUS—*Rudens.* Act IV. Sc. 8.
                Riley's trans.

Laugh and be fat.
   kk.   JOHN TAYLOR—*Title of a Tract.* 1615.

Leap out of the frying pan into the fire.
   ll.   CERVANTES—*Don Quixote.* Pt. I.
                Bk. III. Ch. IV.

Let all live as they would die.
   mm.   HERBERT—*Jacula Prudentum.*

Let pride go afore, shame will follow after.
a.   GEORGE CHAPMAN—*Eastward Ho.*
Act IV. Sc. 1.

Lette mee stande to thee maine chaunce.
b.   LYLY—*Euphues.* Arbor's Reprint.
1579. P. 104.

Let the world slide.
BEAUMONT AND FLETCHER—*Wit
Without Money.* Act V. Sc. 2.
c.   *Taming of the Shrew.* Induction.
Sc. 1. L. 5.

Let the world slip.
d.   *Taming of the Shrew.* Induction.
Sc. 2. L. 146.

Let the worst come to the worst.
e.   CERVANTES—*Don Quixote.* Bk. III.
Ch. V.

Let us do or die.
f.   BURNS—*Bannockburn.*

Life is short, yet sweet.
g.   EURIPIDES.

Light burdens, long borne, grow heavy.
h.   HERBERT—*Jacula Prudentum.*

Light cares speak, great ones are dumb.
i.   SENECA.

Like sending owls to Athens, as the proverb is.
j.   DIOGENES LAERTIUS—*Lives of Eminent
Philosophers. Plato.* XXXII.

Like to like.
k.   GASCOIGNE—*Complaynt of Philomene.*

Little pitchers have wide ears.
l.   HERBERT—*Jacula Prudentum.*

Little said is soonest mended.
m.   GEORGE WITHER—*The Shepherd's
Hunting.*

Live and think.
n.   SAMUEL LOVER—*Father Roach.*

Living from hand to mouth.
o.   DU BARTAS—*Divine Weekes and Workes.*
Second Week. First Day. Pt. IV.

Long ailments wear out pain, and long
hopes joy.
p.   STANISLAUS (King of Poland)—*Maxims
and Moral Sentences.* No. 8.

Look before you ere you leap.
q.   BUTLER—*Hudibras.* Pt. II. Canto II.
L. 503.

Looked unutterable things.
r.   THOMSON—*Seasons. Summer.* L. 1,188.

Look ere thou leap.
HEYWOOD—*Proverbs.* Pt. I. Ch. II.
s.   TOTTEL—*Miscellany.* 1557.

Look not for musk in a dog's kennel.
t.   HERBERT—*Jacula Prudentum.*

Lord, what fools these mortals be!
u.   *Midsummer-Night's Dream.* Act III.
Sc. 2. L. 115.

Love all, trust a few,
Do wrong to none.
v.   *All's Well That Ends Well.* Act I.
Sc. I. L. 73.

Love, and a Cough, cannot be hid.
w.   HERBERT—*Jacula Prudentum.*

Love your neighbor, yet pull not down your
hedge.
x.   HERBERT—*Jacula Prudentum.*

Mad as a March hare.
HALLIWELL—*Archaic Diet.* Vol. II.
Art. "*March Hare.*"
y.   HEYWOOD—*Proverbs.* Pt. II. Ch. V.

Madde March hare.
z.   SKELTON—*Replycacion Agaynst
Certayne Yong Scolers, etc.* L. 35.

Made no more bones.
aa.   DU BARTAS—*The Maiden Blush.*

Make a virtue of necessity.
bb.   BURTON—*Anatomy of Melancholy.*
Pt. III. Sec. III. Memb. 4.
Subsec. I.

Make ducks and drakes with shillings.
cc.   GEORGE CHAPMAN—*Eastward Ho.*
Sc. 1. Act I.

Make three bites of a cherry.
dd.   RABELAIS—*Works.* Bk. V.
Ch. XXVIII.

Man proposes, but God disposes.
ee.   THOS. À KEMPIS—*Imitation of Christ.*
Bk. I. Ch. XIX. Thos. Dibdin's
trans.

Many a smale maketh a grate.
ff.   CHAUCER—*Persones Tale.*

Many go out for wool, and come home shorn
themselves.
gg.   CERVANTES—*Don Quixote.* Pt. II.
Ch. XXXVII.

Many-headed multitude.
hh.   SIR PHILIP SIDNEY—*Arcadia.* Bk. II.

Matches are made in heaven.
ii.   BURTON—*Anatomy of Melancholy.*
Pt. III. Sec. II. Memb. 5.
Subsec. V.

Men are but children of a larger growth.
jj.   DRYDEN—*All for Love.* Act IV. Sc. I.

Men are neither suddenly rich nor suddenly
good.
kk.   LIBANIUS.

Midnight Oil.
ll.   Used by COWPER, LLOYD, QUARLES,
SHENSTONE, and others.

Moche Crye and no Wull.

a.   FORTESCUE—*De Laudibus Leg. Angliæ.*
       Ch. X.

Mordre wol out, that see we day by day.

b.   CHAUCER—*Canterbury Tales. The Nonnes Preestes Tale.* L. 15,058.

More knave than fool.

c.   CERVANTES—*Don Quixote.* Pt. I.
       Bk. IV. Ch. 2.

Much of a muchness.

d.   VANBRUGH—*The Provoked Husband.*
       Act I. Sc. 1.

My appetite comes to me while eating.

e.   MONTAIGNE—*Essays. Of Vanity.*
       Bk. III. Ch. IX.

My man's as true as steel.

f.   *Romeo and Juliet.* Act II. Sc. 4.
       L. 209.

My thoughts ran a wool-gathering.

g.   CERVANTES—*Don Quixote.* Pt. II.
       Ch. LVII.

Neat, not gaudy.

h.   CHARLES LAMB—*Letter to Wordsworth.*
       June 11, 1806.

Necessity knows no law except to conquer.

i.   PUBLIUS SYRUS—*Maxims.* 553.

Nede hath no lawe.

j.   SKELTON—*Colyn Cloute.* L. 865.

Needle in a bottle of hay.

k.   FIELD—*A Woman's a Weathercock.*
       Reprint 1612. P. 20.

Never leave that till to-morrow which you can do to-day.

l.   BENJ. FRANKLIN—*Poor Richard.*

Never look for birds of this year in the nests of the last.

m.   CERVANTES—*Don Quixote.* Pt. II.
       Ch. LXXIV.

Never say
" *Fail*" again.

n.   BULWER-LYTTON—*Richelieu.* Act II.
       Sc. 2.

Nick of Time!

o.   SIR JOHN SUCKLING—*The Goblins.*
       Act V.

No better than you should be.

p.   BEAUMONT AND FLETCHER—*The Coxcomb.* Act IV. Sc. 3.

No cross, no crown.

q.   ST. PAULINUS (Bishop of Nola).

No man is a hero to his valet-de-chambre.
       Attributed to MARSHAL CATINAT.
       Also to MME. CORNULL (by Mme.
       Aisse).

r.   MONTAIGNE—*Essays.* Bk. III. Ch. II.

No rule is so general, which admits not some exception.

s.   BURTON—*Anatomy of Melancholy.*
       Pt. I. Sec. II. Memb. 2. Subsec. III.

Nothing is certain but death and taxes.

t.   BENJ. FRANKLIN—*Letter to M. Leroy.*
       1789.

Not if I know myself at all.

u.   CHARLES LAMB—*Essays of Elia. The Old and the New Schoolmaster.*

Not lost, but gone before.
       MATHEW HENRY—*Commentaries.*
       Matthew II.

v.   SENECA—*Epistolæ* 63. 16.

Not to know me argues yourselves unknown,
The lowest of your throng.

w.   MILTON—*Paradise Lost.* Bk. IV.
       L. 830.

Nought venter nought have.
       HEYWOOD—*Proverbs.* Pt. I. Ch. XI.

x.   THOS. TUSSER—*Five Hundred Points of Good Husbandry. October's Extract.*

Now for good lucke, cast an old shooe after mee.

y.   HEYWOOD—*Proverbs.* Pt. I. Ch. IX.

Of harmes two the lesse is for to chese.

z.   CHAUCER—*Troilus and Criseyde.* Bk. II.
       L. 470.

Oft times many things fall out between the cup and the lip.

aa.   GREENE—*Perimedes.* 1588.

Of two evils I have chose the least.

bb.   PRIOR—*Imitation of Horace.* Bk. I.
       Ep. IX.

Of two evils the least should be chosen.

cc.   ERASMUS—*Cicero de Officiis.* III. 1.

Of two
Evils we take the less.

dd.   HOOKER—*Laws of Ecclesiastical Polity.*
       Bk. V. Ch. LXXXI.

Oil on troubled waters.
       BEDE—*Ecclesiastical History.* Bk. III.
       Ch. XV. Written about 716–731,
       describes the use of oil for
       calming the sea.

ee.   See DAVID M. STONE—*Journal of Commerce,* March 31, 1882.

One foot in the grave.

ff.   BEAUMONT AND FLETCHER—*The Little French Lawyer.* Act I. Sc. 1.

One hour's sleep before midnight is worth three after.

gg.   HERBERT—*Jacula Prudentum.*

On his last legs.

hh.   THOS. MIDDLETON—*The Old Law.*
       Act V. Sc. 1.

Originality provokes originality.

ii.   GOETHE.

Or shear swine, all cry and no wool.

jj.   BUTLER—*Hudibras.* Pt. I. Canto I.
       L. 852.

Ossa on Pelion.
   a.   OVID—*Metamorphosis I.*

Others set carts before the horses.
   b.   RABELAIS—*Works.* Bk. V. Ch. XXII.

Out of mind as soon as out of sight.
   c.   LORD BROOKE—*Sonnet.* 56.

Out of syght, out of mynd.
   d.   GOOGE—*Title of Eclog.*

Penny wise, pound foolish.
   e.   BURTON—*Anatomy of Melancholy.*
                Democritus to the Reader. P. 35.
                             Ed. 1887.

Performed to a T.
   f.   RABELAIS—*Works.* Bk. IV. Ch. LI.

Pigmies placed on the shoulders of giants
see more than the giants themselves.
   g.   DIDACUS STELLA—*Lucan* 10. Tome II.

Pity's akin to love.
   h.   THOS. SOUTHERNE—*Oroonoko.* Act II.
                               Sc. 2.

Plain as a nose in a man's face.
   i.   RABELAIS—*Works. The Author's*
               Prologue to the Fifth Book.

Pleasing ware is half sold.
   j.   HERBERT—*Jacula Prudentum.*

Poverty is no sin.
   k.   HERBERT—*Jacula Prudentum.*

Poverty is the mother of health.
   l.   HERBERT—*Jacula Prudentum.*

Praise the bridge that carried you over.
   m.   GEO. COLMAN (the Younger)—*Heir-at-*
               Law. Act I. Sc. 1.

Praise the sea, but keep on land.
   n.   HERBERT—*Jacula Prudentum.*

Prosperity engenders sloth.
   o.   LIVY.

Prosperity lets go the bridle.
   p.   HERBERT—*Jacula Prudentum.*

Prosperity makes friends and adversity tries
them.
   q.   PACUVIUS.

Push on—keep moving.
   r.   THOS. MORTON—*A Cure for the*
             Heartache. Act III. Sc. 1.

Put himself upon his good behaviour.
   s.   BYRON—*Don Juan.* Canto V. St. 47.

Put your toong in your purse.
   t.   HEYWOOD—*Dialogue of Wit and Folly.*
                        Pt. II. L. 263.

Rather to bowe than breke is profitable.
   u.   CHRISTYNE—*Morale Proverbs.*
              Translated from the French by Earl
                                 Rivers.

Right as a trivet.
   v.   R. H. BARHAM—*The Ingoldsby Legends.*
                             Auto-da-fé.

Rise with the lark and with the lark to bed.
   w.   JAMES HURDIS—*The Village Curate.*

Robbe Peter and pay Paule.
   x.   HEYWOOD—*Proverbs.* Pt. I. Ch. XI.

Rome was not built in one day.
   y.   HEYWOOD—*Proverbs.* Pt. I. Ch. XI.

Rouse the lion from his lair.
   z.   SCOTT—*The Talisman.* Ch. VI.

Safe bind, safe find.
   aa.   TUSSER—*Five Hundred Points of Good*
                     Husbandry. Washing.

Scared out of his seven senses.
   bb.   SCOTT—*Rob Roy.* Ch. XXIV.

Scoundrel maxim.
   cc.   THOMSON—*The Castle of Indolence.*
                      Canto I. St. 50.
See and to be seen.
        BEN JONSON—*Epithalamion.* St. 3. L. 4.
   dd.   GOLDSMITH—*Citizen of the World.*
                         Letter 71.

Seize time by the forelock.
   ee.   PITTACUS, of Mytilene.

Set a beggar on horseback, and he will ride a
     gallop.
   ff.   BURTON—*Anatomy of Melancholy.*
               Pt. II. Sect. III. Memb. 2.

Set all at sixe and seven.
   gg.   HEYWOOD—*Proverbs.* Pt. I. Ch. XI.

Set the cart before the horse.
   hh.   HEYWOOD—*Proverbs.* Pt. II. Ch. VII.

Sharp's the word with her.
   ii.   SWIFT—*Polite Conversation.* Dialogue
                                  III.
She is no better than she should be.
   jj.   HENRY FIELDING—*The Temple Beau.*
                      Act IV. Sc. 3.

She watches him as a cat would watch a
     mouse.
   kk.   SWIFT—*Polite Conversation.* Dialogue
                                  III.

Show me a liar, and I will show thee a thief.
   ll.   HERBERT—*Jacula Prudentum.*

Silence gives consent.
        FULLER—*Wise Sentences.*
   mm.   GOLDSMITH—*The Good-Natured Man.*
                           Act II.

Smell a rat.
     CERVANTES—*Don Quixote.* Pt. I.
                           Bk. IV. Ch. X.
     BEN JONSON—*Tale of a Tub.* Act IV.
                                   Sc. 3.
a.   THOS. MIDDLETON—*Blurt, Master*
              Constable. Act III. Sc. 3.

Smooth runs the water where the brook is deep.
b.   *Henry VI.* Pt. II. Act III. Sc. 1.
                                  L. 53.

Snug as a bug in a rug.
c.   *The Stratford Jubilee.* II. 1. 1779.

Some are weather-wise, some are otherwise.
d.   BENJ. FRANKLIN—*Poor Richard.* 1735.

Some people are more nice than wise.
e.   COWPER—*Mutual Forbearance.*

Something given that way.
f.   BEAUMONT AND FLETCHER—*The*
             Lovers' Progress. Act I. Sc. 1.

So obliging that he ne'er oblig'd.
g.   POPE—*Prologue to Satires.* L. 207.

So was hir jolly whistel wel y-wette.
h.   CHAUCER—*Canterbury Tales.* The
             Reeve's Tale. L. 4,155.

Spare your breath to cool your porridge.
     CERVANTES—*Don Quixote.* Pt. II.
                               Ch. V.
i.   RABELAIS—*Works.* Bk. V.
                           Ch. XXVIII.

Speak boldly, and speak truly, shame the devil.
j.   BEAUMONT AND FLETCHER—*Wit*
             Without Money. Act IV. Sc. 4.

Speech is silver, silence is golden.
k.   CARLYLE—*A Swiss Inscription.*
             Quoted in *Sartor Resartus.* Bk. III.
                               Ch. III.

Spick and span new.
     CERVANTES—*Don Quixote.* Pt. II.
                               Ch. LVIII.
l.   THOS. MIDDLETON—*The Family of Love.*
                           Act IV. Sc. 3.

Stay a little, and news will find you.
m.   HERBERT—*Jacula Prudentum.*

Steal the hog, and give the feet for alms.
n.   HERBERT—*Jacula Prudentum.*

Strike the iron whilst it is hot.
o.   RABELAIS—*Works.* Bk II. Ch. XXXI.

Strike while the iron is hot.
     FARQUHAR—*The Beaux' Stratagem.*
                             Act IV. Sc. 2.
p.   SCOTT—*The Fair Maid of Perth.* Ch. V.

Take heed of still waters, they quick pass away.
q.   HERBERT—*Jacula Prudentum.*

Take Time by the forelock.
r.   THALES (of Miletus).

Tall oaks from little acorns grow.
s.   DAVID EVERETT—*Lines for a School*
                                 Declamation.

Tell me thy company and I will tell thee what thou art.
t.   CERVANTES—Quoted in *Don Quixote.*
             Vol. III. Pt. II. Ch. XXIII.

Tell tales out of schoole.
u.   HEYWOOD—*Proverbs.* Pt. I. Ch. X.

Thank you for nothing.
v.   CERVANTES—*Don Quixote.* Pt. I.
                           Bk. III. Ch. VIII.

That byrd ys nat honest
That fylythe hys owne nest.
w.   SKELTON—*Poems against Garnesche.*
                                 III.

That felde hath eyen, and wode hath eres.
x.   CHAUCER—*Canterbury Tales.* The
                     Knight's Tale. L. 1,522.

That is gold which is worth gold.
y.   HERBERT—*Jacula Prudentum.*

That was laid on with a trowel.
z.   *As You Like It.* Act I. Sc. 2. L. 112.

That which is everybody's business is nobody's business.
aa.   IZAAK WALTON—Quoted in *The*
             Compleat Angler. Pt. I. Ch. II.

The age of chivalry is gone.
bb.   BURKE—*Reflections on the Revolution in*
                                 France.

The belly is the commanding part of the body.
cc.   HOMER.

The better day the better deed.
     SIR JOHN HOLT—*Sir Wm. Moore's Case.*
dd.   THOS. MIDDLETON—*The Phœnix.*
                           Act III. Sc. 1.

The better day, the worse deed.
ee.   MATHEW HENRY—*Commentaries.*
                           Genesis III.

The bow too tensely strung is easily broken.
ff.   PUBLIUS SYRUS—*Maxims.* 388.

The burnt child dreads the fire.
gg.   BEN JONSON—*The Devil is an Ass.*
                             Act I. Sc. 2.

The Cat in Gloves catches no Mice.
hh.   BENJ. FRANKLIN—*Poor Richard.* 1754.

The cat would eat fish, and would not wet her feet.
ii.   HEYWOOD—*Proverbs.* Pt. I. Ch. XI.

The coast was clear.
jj.   MICHAEL DRAYTON—*Nymphia.*

The end must justify the means.
   a.   PRIOR—*Hans Carvel.* L. 67.

The eyes have one language everywhere.
   b.   HERBERT—*Jacula Prudentum.*

The fat is in the fire.
   c.   HEYWOOD—*Proverbs.* Pt. I. Ch. III.

The finest edge is made with the blunt whetstone.
   d.   LYLY—*Euphues.* Arber's Reprint.
                           1579. P. 47.

The foule Toade hath a faire stone in his head.
   e.   LYLY—*Euphues.* Arber's Reprint.
                           1679. P. 53.

The Friar preached against stealing, and had a goose in his sleeve.
   f.   HERBERT—*Jacula Prudentum.*

The frivolous work of polished idleness.
   g.   SIR JAMES MACKINTOSH—*Dissertation on Ethical Philosophy.* *Remarks on Thomas Brown.*

The game is up.
   h.   *Cymbeline.* Act III. Sc. 3. L. 108.

The gray mare will prove the better horse.
   i.   PRIOR—*Epilogue to Lucius.* Last line.

The head is always the dupe of the heart.
   j.   LA ROCHEFOUCAULD—*Maxims.* No. 105.

The honey of Hybla.
   k.   *Henry IV.* Pt. I. Act I. Sc. 2. L. 47.

The King is dead! Long live the King!
   l.   PARDOE—*Life of Louis XIV.* Vol. III.
                           P. 457.

The lion is not so fierce as they paint him.
   m.   HERBERT—*Jacula Prudentum.*

The man that heweth over high,
Some chip falleth in his eye.
   n.   *Story of Sir Eglamour of Artoys.* MSS. in *Garrick Collection.*

The many still must labor for the one.
   o.   BYRON—*Corsair.* Canto I. St. 8.

The miller sees not all the water that goes by his mill.
   p.   BURTON—*Anatomy of Melancholy.*
          Pt. III. Sec. III. Memb. 4. Subsec. I.

The mill will never grind with the water that is past.
        SARAH DOWDNEY—*The Watermill.*
   q.   HERBERT—*Jacula Prudentum.*

The more the merrier.
   r.   HEYWOOD—*Proverbs.* Pt. II. Ch. VII.

The more haste, ever the worst speed.
   s   CHURCHILL—*The Ghost.* Bk. IV.
                        L. 1,162.

The more thou stir it the worse it will be.
   t.   CERVANTES—*Don Quixote.* Bk. III.
                        Ch. VIII.

The most delightful pleasures cloy without variety.
   u.   PUBLIUS SYRUS.

The mouse that hath but one hole is quickly taken.
   v.   HERBERT—*Jacula Prudentum.*

The next way home's the farthest way about.
   w.   QUARLES—*Emblems.* Bk. IV.
                      Em. 2. Ep. 2.

The palpable obscure.
   x.   MILTON—*Paradise Lost.* Bk. II. L. 406.

The point is plain as a pike staff.
   y.   JOHN BYROM—*Epistle to a Friend.*

There are some remedies worse than the disease.
   z.   PUBLIUS SYRUS—*Maxims.* 301.

There can be no affinity nearer than our country.
   aa.   PLATO.

There can no great smoke arise, but there must be some fire.
   bb.   LYLY—*Euphues and his Emphœbus.*
                        P. 153.

Therefore it behooveth hire a ful long spoon
That shal ete with a feend.
   cc.   CHAUCER—*The Squire's Tale.* L. 15,378.

There is no gathering the rose without being pricked by the thorns.
   dd.   PILPAY—*The Two Travellers.* Ch. II.
                      Fable VI.

There is no jesting with edge tools.
   ee.   BEAUMONT AND FLETCHER—*The Little French Lawyer.* Act IV. Sc. 7.

The remedy is worse than the disease.
        BACON—*Of Seditions.*
   ff.   DRYDEN—*Juvenal.* Satire XVI. L. 31.

There's a time for all things.
   gg.   *Comedy of Errors.* Act II. Sc. 2.
                      L. 66.

There shall be no love lost.
   hh.   BEN JONSON—*Every Man out of his Humour.* Act II. Sc. 1.

There's luck in odd numbers.
   ii.   SAMUEL LOVER—*Rory O' More.* St. 3.

There's no hate lost between us.
   jj.   THOS. MIDDLETON—*The Witch.*
                      Act IV. Sc. 3.

There's small choice in rotten apples.
   kk.   *Taming of the Shrew.* Act I. Sc. 1.
                      L. 138.

There's two words to that bargain.
   ll.   SWIFT—*Polite Conversation.*
                      Dialogue III.

There thou beholdest the walls of Sparta and every man a brick.
a. PLUTARCH.

There, though last, not least.
b. SPENSER—*Colin Clout.* L. 444.

The Royal Crown cures not the headache.
c. HERBERT—*Jacula Prudentum.*

The scalded dog fears cold water.
d. HERBERT—*Jacula Prudentum.*

The short and the long of it.
e. *Merry Wives of Windsor.* Act II. Sc. 2. L. 60.

The shortest answer is doing.
f. HERBERT—*Jacula Prudentum.*

The sight of you is good for sore eyes.
g. SWIFT—*Polite Conversation.* Dialogue I.

The sign brings customers.
h. LA FONTAINE—*Fables. The Fortune-Tellers.* Bk. VII. Fable 15.

The smith and his penny both are black.
i. HERBERT—*Jacula Prudentum.*

The stone that is rolling, can gather no moss.
j. TUSSER—*Five Hundred Points of Good Husbandry. Huswifely Admonitions.*

The sum of earthly bliss.
k. MILTON—*Paradise Lost.* Bk. VIII. L. 522.

The time is out of joint.
l. *Hamlet.* Act I. Sc. 5. L. 189.

The total depravity of inanimate things.
m. KATHERINE K. C. WALKER—*Title of an Essay in the Atlantic Monthly.* Sept., 1864.

The true Amphitryon.
n. DRYDEN—*Amphitryon.* Act IV. Sc. 1.

The true beginning of our end.
o. *Midsummer-Night's Dream.* Act V. Sc. 1. L. 111.

The very pink of perfection.
p. GOLDSMITH—*She Stoops to Conquer.* Act I. Sc. 1.

The wearer knows where the shoe wrings.
q. HERBERT—*Jacula Prudentum.*

The will for the deed.
r. COLLEY CIBBER—*The Rival Fools.* Act III.

The wine in the bottle does not quench thirst.
s. HERBERT—*Jacula Prudentum.*

The wolf must die in his own skin.
t. HERBERT—*Jacula Prudentum.*

The word impossible is not in my dictionary.
u. NAPOLEON I.

They do not love that do not show their love.
v. HEYWOOD—*Proverbs.* Pt. II. Ch. IX.

They're only truly great who are truly good.
w. GEO. CHAPMAN—*Revenge for Honour.* Act V. Sc. 2.

They that touch pitch will be defiled.
x. *Much Ado About Nothing.* Act III. Sc. 3. L. 60.

Things bad begun make strong themselves by ill.
y. *Macbeth.* Act III. Sc. 2. L. 56.

Things past redress are now with me past care.
z. *Richard II.* Act II. Sc. 3. L. 171.

Things sweet to taste prove in digestion sour.
aa. *Richard II.* Act I. Sc. 3. L. 237.

Things that are not at all, are never lost.
bb. MARLOWE—*Hero and Leander. First Sestiad.* L. 276.

This flea which I have in my ear.
cc. RABELAIS—*Works.* Bk. III. Ch. XXXI.

This many-headed monster.
dd. MASSINGER—*The Roman Actor.* Act III. Sc. 2.

This peck of troubles.
ee. CERVANTES—*Don Quixote.* Pt. II. Ch. LIII.

This whole universe is one city.
ff. EPICTETUS.

Those that God loves, do not live long.
gg. HERBERT—*Jacula Prudentum.*

Though I say 't that should not say 't.
hh. BEAUMONT AND FLETCHER—*Wit at Several Weapons.* Act II. Sc. 2.

Though men determine, the gods do dispose.
ii. GREENE—*Perimedes.* 1588.

Though this may be play to you,
'Tis death to us.
jj. ROGER L'ESTRANGE—*Fables.* 398.

Thou will scarce be a man before thy mother.
kk. BEAUMONT AND FLETCHER—*Love's Cure.* Act II. Sc. 2.

Three can hold their peace if two be away.
ll. HERBERT—*Jacula Prudentum.*

Three may keep a secret if two of them are dead.
mm. BENJ. FRANKLIN—*Poor Richard.* 1735.

Three things are men most likely to be cheated in, a horse, a wig, and a wife.
nn. BENJ. FRANKLIN—*Poor Richard.* 1736.

Through thick and thin, both over bank and bush.
a.　　Spenser—*Faerie Queene*.　Bk. III.
　　　　　　　　　　　　　Canto I.　St. 17.

Through thick and thin, both over Hill and Plain.
b.　　Du Bartas—*Divine Weekes and Workes*.
　　　Second Week.　Fourth Day.　Bk. IV.

Thursday come, and the week is gone.
c.　　Herbert—*Jacula Prudentum*.

Thy Will for Deed I do accept.
d.　　Du Bartas—*Divine Weekes and Workes*.
　　　Second Week.　Third Day.　Pt. II.

Time is money.
e.　　Bulwer-Lytton—*Money*.　Act III.
　　　　　　　　　　　　　　　　Sc. 3.

Times change and we change with them.
f.　　*Altered from a poem of* Matthias
　　　　　　　　　　　　　　Borbonius.

'Tis as cheap sitting as standing.
g.　　Swift—*Polite Conversation*.
　　　　　　　　　　　　　Dialogue I.

'Tis a stinger.
h.　　Thos. Middleton—*More Dissemblers
　　　Besides Women*.　Act III.　Sc. II.

'Tis good in every case, you know,
To have two strings unto our bow.
i.　　Churchill—*The Ghost*.　Bk. IV.
　　　　　　　　　　　　　　L. 1,295.

'Tis in grain, sir; 'twill endure wind and weather.
j.　　*Twelfth Night*.　Act I.　Sc. 5.　L. 253.

'Tis more noble to forgive, and more manly to despise, than to revenge an Injury.
k.　　Benj. Franklin—*Poor Richard*.　1752.

'Tis neither here nor there.
l.　　*Othello*.　Act IV.　Sc. 3.　L. 58.

'Tis nothing when you are used to it.
m.　　Swift—*Polite Conversation*.　Dialogue
　　　　　　　　　　　　　　　　III.

'Tis safer to be that which we destroy
Than by destruction dwell in doubtful joy.
n.　　*Macbeth*.　Act III.　Sc. 2.　L. 9.

To a boiling pot flies come not.
o.　　Herbert—*Jacula Prudentum*.

To a close shorn sheep, God gives wind by measure.
p.　　Herbert—*Jacula Prudentum*.

To a crazy ship all winds are contrary.
q.　　Herbert—*Jacula Prudentum*.

To add to golden numbers golden numbers.
r.　　Thos. Dekker—*Patient Grissell*.
　　　　　　　　　　　　　Act I.　Sc. 1.

To blow and swallow at the same moment isn't easy to be done.
s.　　Plautus—*Mostellaria*.　Act III.　Sc. 2.
　　　　　　　　　　　　　Riley's trans.

To make a mountain of a mole-hill.
t.　　Henry Ellis—*Original Letters*.
　　　　　　　　　　Second Series.　P. 312.

To make a virtue of necessity.
u.　　*Two Gentlemen of Verona*.　Act IV.
　　　　　　　　　　　　　　Sc. 1.　L. 62.

To put a girdle round about the world.
v.　　Geo. Chapman—*Bussy D'Ambois*.
　　　　　　　　　　　　　Act I.　Sc. 1.

To rise with the lark, and go to bed with the lamb.
w.　　Breton—*Court and Country*.　1618.

To take the nuts from the fire with the dog's foot.
x.　　Herbert—*Jacula Prudentum*.

Turn over a new leaf.
　　　Thos. Dekker—*The Honest Whore*.
　　　　　　　　　Pt. II.　Act II.　Sc. 1
y.　　Also *A Health to the Gentlemanly
　　　Profession of Serving-Men*.　1598,

Two heads are better then one.
z.　　Heywood—*Proverbs*.　Pt. I.　Ch. IX.

Two of a trade can ne'er agree.
aa.　　Gay—*The Ratcatcher and Cats*.　L. 44.

Unquiet meals make ill digestions.
bb.　　*Comedy of Errors*.　Act V.　Sc. I.　L. 75.

Virtue is her own reward.
　　　Dryden—*Tyrannic Love*.　Act II.
　　　　　　　　　　　　　　Sc. III.
cc.　　Prior—*Ode in Imitation of Horace*. III.
　　　　　　　　　　　　Ode 2.　L. 146,

Virtue is its own reward.
　　　Gay—*Epistle to Methuen*.　L. 42.
dd.　　Home—*Douglas*.　Act III.　Sc. 1.
　　　　　　　　　　　　　　L. 294

Virtue is to herself the best reward.
ee.　　Henry Moore—*Cupid's Conflict*.

Walls have tongues, and hedges ears.
ff.　　Swift—*Pastoral Dialogue*.　L. 7.

Waste brings woe, and sorrow hates despair.
gg.　　Robert Greene—*Sonnet*.

Weakness of mind is the only fault incapable of correction.
hh.　　La Rochefoucauld—*Maxims*.　No. 133.

We are never so happy, or so unhappy, as we imagine.
ii.　　La Rochefoucauld—*Maxims*.　No. 50.

We cannot all be masters, nor all masters cannot be truly followed.
jj.　　*Othello*.　Act I.　Sc. 1.　L. 43.

We have here other fish to fry.
a.   RABELAIS—*Works.* Bk. V. Ch. XII.

We have scotch'd the snake, not killed it.
b.   *Macbeth.* Act III. Sc. 2. L. 14.

Well may he smell fire, whose gown burns.
c.   HERBERT—*Jacula Prudentum.*

We'll take the good-will for the deed.
d.   RABELAIS—*Works.* Bk. IV.
Ch. XLIX.

Went in at the one eare and out at the other.
e.   HEYWOOD—*Proverbs.* Pt. II. Ch. IX.

We should never remember the benefits we have conferred, nor forget the favours received.
f.   CHILO.

Westward-ho!
g.   *Twelfth Night.* Act III. Sc. 1. L. 146.

We that live to please must please to live.
h.   SAM'L JOHNSON—*Prologue on Opening the Drury Lane Theatre.*

Whatever is worth doing at all is worth doing well.
i.   EARL OF CHESTERFIELD—*Letters.*
March 10, 1746.

What is got over the devil's back is spent under his belly.
j.   Attributed to ISOCRATES by ALAIN RENÉ LE SAGE—*Gil Blas.* Bk. VIII. Ch. IX.

What is not in a man cannot come out of him surely.
k.   GOETHE—*Herman and Dorothea.*
Canto III. L. 3.

What is sauce for the goose is sauce for a gander.
l.   TOM BROWN—*New Maxims.* P. 123.

What is valuable is not new, and what is new is not valuable.
m.   DAN'L WEBSTER—*Quoted by him in a Speech.* Sept. 1, 1848.

What is yours is mine, and all mine is yours.
n.   PLAUTUS—*Trinummus.* Act II. Sc. 2.
Riley's trans.

What mare's nest hast thou found?
o.   BEAUMONT AND FLETCHER—*Bonduca.*
Act V. Sc. 2.

What's done cannot be undone.
p.   *Macbeth.* Act V. Sc. 1. L. 75.

What's one man's poison, signior,
Is another's meat or drink.
q.   BEAUMONT AND FLETCHER—*Love's Cure.* Act III. Sc. 2.

What will Mrs. Grundy say?
r.   THOS. MORTON—*Speed the Plough.*
Act I. Sc. 1. Ed. 1808.

What you would not have done to yourselves, never do unto others.
s.   ALEXANDER SEVERUS.

When a building is about to fall down all the mice desert it.
t.   PLINY THE ELDER—*Natural History.*
Bk. VIII. Sec. CIII.

When a dog is drowning, every one offers him drink.
u.   HERBERT—*Jacula Prudentum.*

When men speak ill of thee, live so as nobody may believe them.
v.   PLATO.

When once removed from sight, soon perishes from remembrance.
w.   THOS. À KEMPIS—*Imitation of Christ.*
Bk. I. Ch. XXIII. Thos. Dibdin's trans.

When remedies are past, the griefs are ended By seeing the worst, which late on hopes depended.
x.   *Othello.* Act I. Sc. 3. L. 202.

When the age is in, the wit is out.
y.   *Much Ado About Nothing.* Act III.
Sc. 5. L. 37.

When the candles are out all women are fair.
z.   PLUTARCH—*Conjugal Precepts.*

When the lion's skin cannot prevail, a little of the fox's must be used.
aa.   LYSANDER—*Laconic Apophthegms.*

Where God hath a temple, the devil will have a chapel.
bb.   BURTON—*Anatomy of Melancholy.*
Pt. III. Sec. IV. Memb. 1.
Subsec. I.

Where McGregor sits, there is the head of the table.
cc.   EMERSON—Quoted in *American Scholar.*

Where the drink goes in, there the wit goes out.
dd.   HERBERT—*Jacula Prudentum.*

Where there's marriage without love, there will be love without marriage.
ee.   BENJ. FRANKLIN—*Poor Richard.* 1734.

Where the streame runneth smoothest, the water is deepest.
ff.   LYLY—*Euphues and His England.*
P. 287.

Which he by hook or crook has gather'd And by his own inventions father'd.
gg.   BUTLER—*Hudibras.* Pt. III. Canto I.
L. 109.

While you seek to avoid Charybdis you fall upon Scylla.
hh.   HOMER—*Odyssey.* Bk. XII. L. 85.

Whistle, and I'll come to you, my lad.
a.   BURNS—*Whistle, and I'll Come to You, My Lad.*

Whistle, and she'll come to you.
b.   BEAUMONT AND FLETCHER—*Wit Without Money.* Act IV. Sc. 4.

Who are a little wise, the best fools be.
c.   DONNE—*The Triple Fool.*

Who can refute a sneer?
d.   WILLIAM PALEY—*Moral Philosophy.* Vol. II. Bk. V. Ch. IX.

Who digs hills because they do aspire,
Throws down one mountain to cast up a higher.
e.   *Pericles.* Act I. Sc. 4. L. 6.

Who does not love wine, women, and song
Remains a fool his whole life long.
f.   *Attributed to* LUTHER, *probably a saying of* J. H. Voss.

Who drives fat oxen should himself be fat.
g.   SAM'L JOHNSON—*Boswell's Life of Johnson.* 1784.

Who is so deaf as he that will not hear?
h.   HERBERT—*Jacula Prudentum.*

Whose house is of glass, must not throw stones at another.
i.   HERBERT—*Jacula Prudentum.*

Why, then, do you walk as if you had swallowed a ramrod?
j.   EPICTETUS—*Discourses.* Ch. XXI.

Wind puffs up empty bladders; opinion, fools.
k.   SOCRATES.

Wine makes all sorts of creatures at table.
l.   HERBERT—*Jacula Prudentum.*

Wisdom provides things necessary, not superfluous.
m.   SOLON.

Wise Men say nothing in dangerous times.
n.   JOHN SELDEN—*Table Talk. Wisdom.*

Within a stone's throw of it.
o.   CERVANTES—*Don Quixote.* Pt. I. Bk. III. Ch. IX.

With tooth and nail.
p.   DU BARTAS—*Divine Weekes and Workes.* First Week. Second Day.

Words and feathers the wind carries away.
q.   HERBERT—*Jacula Prudentum.*

Words are women, deeds are men.
r.   HERBERT—*Jacula Prudentum.*

Words without thoughts never to heaven go.
s.   *Hamlet.* Act III. Sc. 3. L. 99.

Would you know what money is? Go borrow some.
t.   HERBERT—*Jacula Prudentum.*

Yee have many strings to your bowe.
u.   HEYWOOD—*Proverbs.* Pt. I. Ch. XI.

You are in some brown study.
v.   LYLY—*Euphues.* Arber's Reprint. 1579. P. 80.

You cannot know wine by the barrel.
w.   HERBERT—*Jacula Prudentum.*

You cannot put the same shoe on every foot.
x.   PUBLIUS SYRUS—*Maxims.* 596.

You have a wrong sow by the ear.
BUTLER—*Hudibras.* Pt. II. Canto III. L. 580.
y.   GEORGE COLMAN (the Younger)— *Heir-at-Law.* Act I. Sc. 2.

You must lose a fly to catch a trout.
z.   HERBERT—*Jacula Prudentum.*

You must not think, sir, to catch old birds with chaff.
aa.   CERVANTES—*Don Quixote.* Pt. I. Ch. IV.

You must take the will for the deed.
bb.   SWIFT—*Polite Conversation.* Dialogue II.

You shall never want rope enough.
cc.   RABELAIS—*Works. Prologue to the Fifth Book.*

Know thyself.—SOLON.
Consider the end.—CHILO.
Know thy opportunity.—PITTACUS.
Most men are bad.—BIAS.
Nothing is impossible to industry.—PERIANDER.
Avoid excess.—CLEOBULUS.
Suretyship is the precursor of ruin.—THALES.
dd.   *Mottoes of the Seven Wise Men of Greece.* Inscribed in later days in the Delphian Temple.

PROVIDENCE.

And pleas'd th' Almighty's orders to perform,
Rides in the whirlwind and directs the storm.
ee.   ADDISON—*The Campaign.*

Fear not, but trust in Providence,
Wherever thou may'st be.
ff.   THOMAS HAYNES BAYLY—*The Pilot.*

If heaven send no supplies,
The fairest blossom of the garden dies.
gg.   WILLIAM BROWNE—*Visions.* Ch. V.

In some time, his good time, I shall arrive;
He guides me and the bird
    In his good time.
hh.   ROBERT BROWNING—*Paracelsus.* Pt. I.

Behind a frowning providence
He hides a smiling face.
ii.   COWPER—*Light Shining Out of Darkness.*

'Tis Providence alone secures
In every change both mine and yours.
jj.   COWPER—*A Fable. Moral.*

God made bees, and bees made honey,
God made man, and man made money;
Pride made the devil, and the devil made sin;
So God made a cole-pit to put the devil in.
a.   Transcribed by JAMES HENRY DIXON,
            from the fly-sheet of a Bible, belonging
            to a pitman who resided near Hutton-
            Henry, in County of Denham.

Whatever is, is in its causes just.
b.   DRYDEN—*Œdipus.* Act III. Sc. 1.

God tempers the cold to the shorn sheep.
c.   HENRI ESTIENNE—*Le Livre de Proverbs*
                         Epigrammatique.

We sometimes had those little rubs which
Providence sends to enhance the value of its
favours.
d.   GOLDSMITH—*Vicar of Wakefield.* Ch. I.

To a close shorn sheep, God gives wind by
measure.
e.   HERBERT—*Jacula Prudentum.*

              Behind the dim unknown,
Standeth God within the shadow, keeping
      watch above his own.
f.   LOWELL—*The Present Crisis.* St. 8.

* * * his providence
Out of our evil seek to bring forth good.
g.   MILTON—*Paradise Lost.* Bk. I. L. 162.

                  What in me is dark,
Illumine; what is low, raise and support;
That to the height of this great argument
I may assert eternal Providence,
And justify the ways of God to men.
h.   MILTON—*Paradise Lost.* Bk. I. L. 22.

All Nature is but art unknown to thee;
All chance direction, which thou canst not
      see;
All discord, harmony not understood;
All partial evil, universal good;
And spite of pride, in erring reason's spite,
One truth is clear, Whatever is is right.
i.   POPE—*Essay on Man.* Ep. I. L. 289.

But vindicate the ways of God to man.
j.   POPE—*Essay on Man.* Ep. I. L. 16.

Destroy all creatures for thy sport or gust,
Yet cry, if man's unhappy, God's unjust.
k.   POPE—*Essay on Man.* Ep. I. L. 117.

Warms in the sun, refreshes in the breeze.
Glows in the stars, and blossoms in the trees.
l.   POPE—*Essay on Man.* Ep. I. L. 271.

Who finds not Providence all good and wise,
Alike in what it gives, and what denies.
m.   POPE—*Essay on Man.* Ep. I. L. 205.

Who sees with equal eye, as God of all,
A hero perish, or a sparrow fall,
Atoms or systems into ruin hurl'd,
And now a bubble burst, and now a world.
n.   POPE—*Essay on Man.* Ep. I. L. 87.

That very law which moulds a tear,
And bids it trickle from its source,
That law preserves the earth a sphere,
And guides the planets in their course.
o.   SAM'L ROGERS—*On a Tear.* St. 6.

                      Consider
The sparrows of the air of small account:
      Our God doth view
Whether they fall or mount,—
      He guards us too.
p.   CHRISTINA G. ROSSETTI—*Consider.*
                                     St. 2.

But he never would believe that Providence
had sent a few men into the world, ready
booted and spurred to ride, and millions
ready saddled and bridled to be ridden.
q.   RICHARD RUMBOLD—*On the Scaffold.*
            1685. *See* MACAULAY'S *History of*
                  England. Vol. I. Ch. V.

For nought so vile that on the earth doth live
But to the earth some special good doth give.
r.   *Romeo and Juliet.* Act II. Sc. 3.
                                     L. 17.

He that doth the ravens feed,
Yea, providently caters for the sparrow,
Be comfort to my age!
s.   *As You Like It.* Act II. Sc. 3. L. 43.

O God, thy arm was here;
And not to us, but to thy arm alone,
Ascribe we all!
t.   *Henry V.* Act IV. Sc. 8. L. 111.

There is a divinity that shapes our ends,
Rough-hew them how we will.
u.   *Hamlet.* Act V. Sc. 2. L. 10.

We defy augury: there's a special providence in the fall of a sparrow. If it be now,
'tis not to come; if it be not to come, it will
be now; if it be not now, yet it will come;
the readiness is all.
v.   *Hamlet.* Act V. Sc. 2. L. 230.

He maketh kings to sit in soverainty;
He maketh subjects to their powre obey;
He pulleth downe, he setteth up on hy:
He gives to this, from that he takes away;
For all we have is his: what he list doe he
      may.
w.   SPENSER—*Faerie Queene.* Bk. V.
                            Canto II. St. 41.

God tempers the wind to the shorn lamb.
x.   STERNE—*Sentimental Journey.*

And I will trust that He who heeds
      The life that hides in mead and wold,
Who hangs yon alder's crimson beads,
      And stains these mosses green and gold,
Will still, as He hath done, incline
His gracious care to me and mine.
y.   WHITTIER—*Last Walk in Autumn.*
                                     St. 26.

PRUDENCE.

And by a prudent flight and cunning save
A life which valour could not, from the grave.
A better buckler I can soon regain,
But who can get another life again?

   a.   ARCHILOCHUS—*See* PLUTARCH'S *Morals.*
        Vol. I. *Essay on the Laws, etc., of*
               the Lacedemonians.

Put your trust in God, my boys, and keep
your powder dry.

   b.   COL. BLACKER—*Oliver's Advice.*
       See HAYES' *Ballads of Ireland.* 1834.
        Vol. I. P. 191. Attributed to
                  Cromwell.

Beware of desperate steps. The darkest day,
Live till to-morrow, will have pass'd away.

   c.   COWPER—*The Needless Alarm.* L. 132.

According to her cloth she cut her coat.

   d.   DRYDEN—*Fables. Cock and the Fox.*
                     L. 20.

Yes, I had two strings to my bow; both
golden ones, egad! and both cracked.

   e.   FIELDING—*Love in Several Masques.*
                Act V. Sc. 13.

In the embers shining bright
A garden grows for thy delight,
With roses yellow, red, and white.

But, O my child, beware, beware!
Touch not the roses growing there,
For every rose a thorn doth bear.

   f.   R. W. GILDER—*Cradle Song.*

When individuals approach one another
with deep purposes on both sides they seldom
come at once to the matter which they have
most at heart. They dread the electric shock
of a too sudden contact with it.

   g.   NATH. HAWTHORNE—*The Marble Faun.*
                Vol I. Ch. XXII.

But curb thou the high spirit in thy breast,
For gentle ways are best, and keep aloof
From sharp contentions.

   h.   HOMER—*Iliad.* Bk. IX. L. 317.
                   Bryant's trans.

So that every man lawfully ordained must
bring a bow which hath two strings, a title
of present right and another to provide for
future possibility or chance.

   i.   RICHARD HOOKER—*Laws of*
         Ecclesiastical Polity. Bk. V.
         Ch. LXXX. No. 9.

Free livers on a small scale; who are prodigal within the compass of a guinea.

   j.   WASHINGTON IRVING—*The Stout*
                    Gentleman.

The first years of man must make provision
for the last.

   k.   SAM'L JOHNSON—*Rasselas.* Ch. XVII.

Ye diners out from whom we guard our spoons.

   l.   MACAULAY—*Political Georgics.*

In ancient times all things were cheape,
'Tis good to looke before thou leape,
When corne is ripe 'tis time to reape.

   m.   MARTYN PARKER—*The Roxburghe*
          Ballads. An Excellent New Medley.

Be prudent, and if you hear, * * * some
insult or some threat, * * * have the appearance of not hearing it.

   n.   GEORGES SAND—*Handsome Lawrence.*
                     Ch. II.

All these you may avoid but the Lie Direct;
and you may avoid that too, with an If. I
knew when seven justices could not take up
a quarrel, but when the parties were met
themselves, one of them thought but of an If,
as, 'If you said so, then I said so;' and they
shook hands and swore brothers. Your If is
the only peace-maker; much virtue in If.

   o.   *As You Like It.* Act V. Sc. 4. L. 100.

                    Be advis'd;
Heat not a furnace for your foe so hot
That it do singe yourself: we may outrun,
By violent swiftness, that which we run at,
And lose by over-running.

   p.   *Henry VIII.* Act I. Sc. 1. L. 139.

Have more than thou showest,
Speak less than thou knowest,
Lend less than thou owest,
Ride more than thou goest,
Learn more than thou trowest,
Set less than thou throwest.

   q.   *King Lear.* Act I. Sc. 4. L. 131.

In my school days, when I had lost one shaft,
I shot his fellow of the self-same flight
The self-same way with more advised watch,
To find the other forth, and by adventuring
     both
I oft found both.

   r.   *Merchant of Venice.* Act I. Sc. 1. L. 139.

              Love all, trust a few,
Do wrong to none: be able for thine enemy
Rather in power than use, and keep thy friend
Under thy own life's key: be check'd for
     silence,
But never tax'd for speech.

   s.   *All's Well That Ends Well.* Act I.
                  Sc. 1. L. 73.

          Think him as a serpent's egg
Which, hatch'd, would, as his kind, grow
     mischievous,
And kill him in the shell.

   t.   *Julius Cæsar.* Act II. Sc. 1. L. 32.

                  Trust none;
For oaths are straws, men's faiths are wafer-
     cakes,
And hold-fast is the only dog.

   u.   *Henry V.* Act II. Sc. 3. L. 52.

PUBLISHING (*See* OCCUPATIONS).

PUNISHMENT.

See they suffer death,
But in their deaths remember they are men,
Strain not the laws to make their tortures
    grievous.
a.   ADDISON—*Cato.* Act III. Sc. 5.

Some have been beaten till they know
What wood a cudgel's of by th' blow:
Some kick'd until they can feel whether
A shoe be Spanish or neat's leather.
b.   BUTLER—*Hudibras.* Pt. II. Canto I.
                             L. 221.

The twig is so easily bended,
   I have banished the rule and the rod:
I have taught them the goodness of knowl-
    edge,
They have taught me the goodness of God;
My heart is the dungeon of darkness,
   Where I shut them for breaking a rule;
My frown is sufficient correction;
My love is the law of the school.
c.   CHARLES M. DICKINSON—*The Children.*

That is the bitterest of all,—to wear the
yoke of our own wrong-doing.
d.   GEORGE ELIOT—*Daniel Deronda.*
                       Bk. V. Ch. XXXVI.

The object of punishment is, prevention
from evil; it never can be made impulsive to
good.
e.   HORACE MANN—*Lectures and Reports
           on Education.* Lecture VII.

Back to thy punishment,
False fugitive, and to thy speed add wings.
f.   MILTON—*Paradise Lost.* Bk. II.
                           L. 699.
Our torments also may in length of time
Become our elements.
g.   MILTON—*Paradise Lost.* Bk. II. L. 274.

Unrespited, unpitied, unrepriev'd.
h.   MILTON—*Paradise Lost.* Bk. II. L. 185.

Ay—down to the dust with them, slaves as
   they are,
   From this hour, let the blood in their
    dastardly veins,
That shrunk at the first touch of Liberty's
   war,
   Be wasted for tyrants, or stagnant in chains.
i.   MOORE—*Lines on the Entry of the
                Austrians into Naples,* 1821.

Just prophet, let the damn'd one dwell
Full in the sight of Paradise,
Beholding heaven and feeling hell.
j.   MOORE—*Lalla Rookh. Fire
                Worshippers.* L. 1,028.

And still adore the hand that gives the blow.
k.   JOHN POMFRET—*To a Friend Under
                Affliction.* L. 40.

Heaven is not always angry when he strikes,
But most chastises those whom most he likes.
l.   JOHN POMFRET—*To a Friend Under
                Affliction.* L. 89.

But if the first Eve
   Hard doom did receive
When only one apple had she,
   What a punishment new
   Must be found out for you,
Who eating hath robb'd the whole tree.
m.   POPE—*To Lady Montague.*

Some of us will smart for it.
n.   *Much Ado About Nothing.* Act V.
                        Sc. 1. L. 109.

Thou shalt be whipp'd with wire, and stew'd
   in brine,
Smarting in ling'ring pickle.
o.   *Antony and Cleopatra.* Act II. Sc. 5.
                             L. 65.

There is nothynge that more dyspleaseth God
Than from theyr children to spare the rod.
p.   SKELTON—*Magnyfycence.* L. 1,954.

Q.

QUACKERY.

From powerful causes spring the empiric's
   gains,
Man's love of life, his weakness, and his pains;
These first induce him the vile trash to try,
Then lend his name, that other men may buy.
q.   CRABBE—*Borough.* Letter VII. L. 124.

Void of all honor, avaricious, rash,
The daring tribe compound their boasted
   trash—
Tincture of syrup, lotion, drop, or pill;
All tempt the sick to trust the lying bill.
r.   CRABBE—*Borough.* Letter VII. L. 75.

Out, you impostors!
Quack salving, cheating mountebanks! your
   skill
Is to make sound men sick, and sick men kill.
s.   MASSINGER—*Virgin-Martyr.* Act IV.
                            Sc. 1.

I bought an unction of a mountebank,
So mortal that, but dip a knife in it,
Where it draws blood no cataplasm so rare,
Collected from all simples that have virtue
Under the moon, can save the thing from
   death
That is but scratch'd withal.
t.   *Hamlet.* Act IV. Sc. 7. L. 142.

QUALITY.

Things that have a common quality ever quickly seek their kind.
   a.   MARCUS AURELIUS—*Meditations.*
                      Ch. IX. 9.

The rank is but the guinea's stamp,
The man's the gowd for a' that.
   b.   BURNS—*For A' That and A' That.*

Those families, you know, are our upper crust, not upper ten thousand.
   c.   COOPER—*The Ways of the Hour.* Ch. VI.

A demd, damp, moist, unpleasant body!
   d.   DICKENS—*Nicholas Nickelby.*
                      Ch. XXXIV.

Fine by defect, and delicately weak.
   e.   POPE—*Moral Essays.* Ep. II. L. 43.

That air and harmony of shape express,
Fine by degrees, and beautifully less.
   f.   PRIOR—*Henry and Emma.* L. 432.

Come, give us a taste of your quality.
   g.   *Hamlet.* Act II. Sc. 2. L. 451.

Innocence in genius, and candor in power, are both noble qualities.
   h.   MADAME DE STAËL—*Germany.* Pt. II.
                      Ch. VIII.

Nothing endures but personal qualities.
   i.   WALT WHITMAN—*Leaves of Grass.*
           Song of the Broad-Axe. St. 4.

At present there is no distinction among the upper ten thousand of the city.
   j.   N. P. WILLIS—*Necessity for a*
                  Promenade Drive.

QUARRELING.

Those who in quarrels interpose,
Must often wipe a bloody nose.
   k.   GAY—*Fables. The Mastiffs.* L. 1.

But greatly to find quarrel in a straw
When honour's at the stake.
   l.   *Hamlet.* Act IV. Sc. 4. L. 55.

In a false quarrel there is no true valour.
   m.   *Much Ado About Nothing.* Act V.
                  Sc. 1. L. 120.

Thou! why, thou wilt quarrel with a man that hath a hair more, or a hair less, in his beard than thou hast: thou wilt quarrel with a man for cracking nuts, having no other reason but because thou hast hazel eyes.
   n.   *Romeo and Juliet.* Act III. Sc. 1.
                      L. 18.

Thy head is as full of quarrels as an egg is full of meat.
   o.   *Romeo and Juliet.* Act III. Sc. 1.
                      L. 23.

The quarrel is a very pretty quarrel as it stands; we should only spoil it by trying to explain it.
   p.   R. B. SHERIDAN—*The Rivals.* Act IV.
                      Sc. 3.

I won't quarrel with my bread and butter.
   q.   SWIFT—*Polite Conversation.* Dialogue I.

O we fell out, I know not why,
And kiss'd again with tears.
   r.   TENNYSON—*The Princess.* Canto II.
                      Song.

Weakness on both sides is, as we know, the motto of all quarrels.
   s.   VOLTAIRE—*A Philosophical Dictionary.*
                Weakness on Both Sides.

QUOTATION.

There is not less wit nor invention in applying rightly a thought one finds in a book, than in being the first author of that thought.
   t.   BAYLE—*Works.* Vol. II. P. 779.

'Twas not an Age ago since most of our Books were nothing but Collections of Latin Quotations; there was not above a line or two of French in a Page.
   u.   DE LA BRUYÈRE—*The Character or*
          Manners of the Present Age. Ch. XV.
                  Of the Pulpit.

All which he understood by rote,
And, as occasion serv'd, would quote.
   v.   BUTLER—*Hudibras.* Pt. I. Canto I.
                      L. 135.

Perverts the Prophets, and purloins the Psalms.
   w.   BYRON—*English Bards and Scotch*
               Reviewers. L. 326.

With just enough of learning to misquote.
   x.   BYRON—*English Bards and Scotch*
                Reviewers. L. 66.

To copy beauties, forfeits all pretence
To fame—to copy faults, is want of sense.
   y.   CHURCHILL—*The Rosciad.* L. 457.

The greater part of our writers, * * * have become so original, that no one cares to imitate them: and those who never quote in return are seldom quoted.
   z.   ISAAC DISRAELI—*Curiosities of*
              Literature. Quotation.

The wisdom of the wise and the experience of ages may be preserved by QUOTATION.
   aa.   ISAAC DISRAELI—*Curiosities of*
              Literature. Quotation.

A book which hath been culled from the flowers of all books.
   bb.   GEORGE ELIOT—*The Spanish Gypsy.*
                      Bk. II.

A great man quotes bravely, and will not draw on his invention when his memory serves him with a word as good.

   a.   EMERSON—*Letters and Social Aims.*
Quotation and Originality.

By necessity, by proclivity, and by delight, we quote. We quote not only books and proverbs, but arts, sciences, religion, customs, and laws; nay, we quote temples and houses, tables and chairs by imitation.

   b.   EMERSON—*Letters and Social Aims.*
Quotation and Originality.

Next to the originator of a good sentence is the first quoter of it.

   c.   EMERSON—*Letters and Social Aims.*
Quotation and Originality.

We are as much informed of a writer's genius by what he selects as by what he originates.

   d.   EMERSON—*Letters and Social Aims.*
Quotation and Originality.

He that readeth good writers and pickes out their flowres for his own nose, is lyke a foole.

   e.   STEPHEN GOSSON—*In the School of*
Abuse. Loyterers.

Every quotation contributes something to the stability or enlargement of the language.

   f.   SAM'L JOHNSON—*Preface to Dictionary.*

Though old the thought and oft exprest,
'Tis his at last who says it best.

   g.   LOWELL—*For an Autograph.* St. 1.

I have here only made a nosegay of culled flowers, and have brought nothing of my own but the thread that ties them.

   h.   MONTAIGNE—*Essays. Of Physiognomy.*

Nor suffers Horace more in wrong translations
By wits, than critics in as wrong quotations.

   i.   POPE—*Essay on Criticism.* Pt. III.
L. 104.

He ranged his tropes, and preached up patience,
Backed his opinion with quotations.

   j.   PRIOR—*Paulo Purganti and his Wife.*
L. 143.

The devil can cite Scripture for his purpose.

   k.   *Merchant of Venice.* Act I. Sc. 3.
L. 99.

They have been at a great feast of languages, and stolen the scraps.

   l.   *Love's Labour's Lost.* Act V. Sc. 1.
L. 39.

Fine words! I wonder where you stole them.

   m.   SWIFT—*Verses. Occasioned by*
Whitehed's Motto on his Coach.

Some, for *renown*, on scraps of learning dote,
And think they grow immortal as they *quote*.

   n.   YOUNG—*Love of Fame.* Satire 1. L. 89.

R.

RAIN.

We knew it would rain, for the poplars showed
The white of their leaves, the amber grain
Shrunk in the wind,—and the lightning now
Is tangled in tremulous skeins of rain.

   o.   T. B. ALDRICH—*Before the Rain.*

A little rain will fill
The lily's cup which hardly moists the field.

   p.   EDWIN ARNOLD—*The Light of Asia.*
Bk. VI. L. 215.

The rain-drops' showery dance and rhythmic beat,
With tinkling of innumerable feet.

   q.   ABRAHAM COLES—*The Microcosm.*
Hearing. Powers of Sound, etc.

She waits for me, my lady Earth,
  Smiles and waits and sighs;
I'll say her nay, and hide away,
  Then take her by surprise.

   r.   MARY MAPES DODGE—*How the Rain*
Comes. April.

How it pours, pours, pours,
  In a never-ending sheet!
How it drives beneath the doors!
  How it soaks the passer's feet!
How it rattles on the shutter!
  How it rumples up the lawn!
How 'twill sigh, and moan, and mutter,
  From darkness until dawn.

   s.   ROSSITER JOHNSON—*Rhyme of the Rain.*

And the hooded clouds, like friars,
Tell their beads in drops of rain.

   t.   LONGFELLOW—*Midnight Mass for the*
Dying Year. St. 4.

Be still, sad heart, and cease repining;
Behind the clouds the sun is shining;
Thy fate is the common fate of all,
Into each life some rain must fall,
Some days must be dark and dreary.

   u.   LONGFELLOW—*An April Day.*

The ceaseless rain is falling fast,
  And yonder gilded vane,
Immovable for three days past,
  Points to the misty main.

   v.   LONGFELLOW—*Travels by the Fireside.*
St. 1.

The day is cold, and dark, and dreary;
It rains, and the wind is never weary;
The vine still clings to the mouldering wall,
But at every gust the dead leaves fall,
And the day is dark and dreary.
   a.   LONGFELLOW—*The Rainy Day.*

Drip, drip, the rain comes falling,
  Rain in the woods, rain on the sea;
Even the little waves, beaten, come crawling
  As if to find shelter here with me.
   b.   JAMES HERBERT MORSE— *Waiting in the*
                Rain.

For the rain it raineth every day.
   c.   *Twelfth Night.* Act V. Sc. 1. *Song.*
                L. 401.

I bring fresh showers for the thirsting flowers,
  From the seas and the streams;
I bear light shade for the leaves when laid
  In their noonday dreams.
   d.   SHELLEY—*The Cloud.*

I know Sir John will go, though he was
sure it would rain cats and dogs.
   e.   SWIFT—*Polite Conversation.*
               Dialogue II.

The Clouds consign their treasures to the fields;
And, softly shaking on the dimpled pool
Prelusive drops, let all their moisture flow,
In large effusion, o'er the freshen'd world.
   f.   THOMSON—*The Seasons. Spring.* L. 172.

RAINBOW (THE).

God's glowing covenant.
   g.   HOSEA BALLOU—*MS. Sermons.*

And, lo! in the dark east, expanded high,
The rainbow brightens to the setting Sun.
   h.   BEATTIE—*The Minstrel.* Bk. I. St. 30.

'Tis sweet to listen as the night winds creep
From leaf to leaf; 'tis sweet to view on high
The rainbow, based on ocean, span the sky.
   i.   BYRON—*Don Juan.* Canto I. St. 122.

Triumphal arch, that fill'st the sky
When storms prepare to part,
I ask not proud Philosophy
To teach me what thou art.
   j.   CAMPBELL—*To the Rainbow.*

Over her hung a canopy of state,
Not of rich tissue, nor of spangled gold,
But of a substance, though not animate,
Yet of a heavenly and spiritual mould,
That only eyes of spirits might behold.
   k.   GILES FLETCHER—*The Rainbow.* L. 33.

O beautiful rainbow;—all woven of light!
There's not in thy tissue one shadow of night;
Heaven surely is open when thou dost appear,
And, bending above thee, the angels draw
   near,
And sing,—"The rainbow! the rainbow!
The smile of God is here."
   l.   MRS. SARAH J. HALE—*Poems.*

There was an awful rainbow once in heaven;
We know her woof, her texture; she is given
In the dull catalogue of common things.
Philosophy will clip an Angel's wings.
   m.   KEATS—*Lamia.* Pt. II. L. 231.

A rainbow in the morning
Is the Shepherd's warning;
But a rainbow at night
Is the Shepherd's delight.
   n.   *Old Weather Rhyme.*

What skilful limner e'er would choose
To paint the rainbow's varying hues,
Unless to mortal it were given
To dip his brush in dyes of heaven?
   o.   SCOTT—*Marmion.* Canto VI. St. 5.

Mild arch of promise! on the evening sky
Thou shinest fair with many a lovely ray,
Each in the other melting.
   p.   SOUTHEY—*Sonnets. The Evening*
                Rainbow.

Rain, rain, and sun! a rainbow in the sky!
   q.   TENNYSON—*Idylls of the King. The*
            Coming of Arthur. L. 401.

Hung on the shower that fronts the golden
   West,
  The rainbow bursts like magic on mine eyes!
In hues of ancient promise there imprest;
  Frail in its date, eternal in its guise.
   r.   CHARLES TENNYSON TURNER—*Sonnets*
          and Fugitive Pieces. The Rainbow.

Bright pledge of peace and sunshine! the
   sure tie
Of thy Lord's hand, the object of His eye!
When I behold thee, though my light be dim,
Distinct, and low, I can in thine see Him
Who looks upon thee from His glorious
   throne,
And minds the covenant between all and One.
   s.   VAUGHAN—*The Rainbow.*

READING.

Reading is to the mind, what exercise is to
the body. As by the one, health is preserved,
strengthened, and invigorated: by the other,
virtue (which is the health of the mind) is
kept alive, cherished, and confirmed.
   t.   ADDISON—*The Tatler.* No. 147.

Reading maketh a full man.
   u.   BACON—*Of Studies.*

We have not *read* an author till we have
seen his object, whatever it may be, as he
saw it.
   v.   CARLYLE—*Essays. Goethe's Helena.*

The mind, relaxing into needful sport,
Should turn to writers of an abler sort,
Whose wit well managed, and whose classic
   style,
Give truth a lustre, and make wisdom smile.
   w.   COWPER—*Retirement.* L. 715.

Half the gossip of society would perish if the books that are truly worth reading were but read.

a.　Dawson—*Address on Opening the Birmingham Free Library.* Oct. 26, 1866.

The delight of opening a new pursuit, or a new course of reading, imparts the vivacity and novelty of youth even to old age.

b.　Isaac Disraeli—*Literary Character of Men of Genius.* Ch. XXII.

If we encountered a man of rare intellect, we should ask him what books he read.

c.　Emerson—*Letters and Social Aims. Quotation and Originality.*

I like to be beholden to the great metropolitan English speech, the sea which receives tributaries from every region under heaven. I should as soon think of swimming across the Charles river when I wish to go to Boston, as of reading all my books in originals, when I have them rendered for me in my mother tongue.

d.　Emerson—*Essays. Books.*

Our high respect for a well-read man is praise enough of literature.

e.　Emerson—*Letters and Social Aims. Quotation and Originality.*

My early and invincible love of reading, * * * I would not exchange for the treasures of India.

f.　Gibbon—*Memoirs.*

In a polite age almost every person becomes a reader, and receives more instruction from the Press than the Pulpit.

g.　Goldsmith—*The Citizen of the World.* Letter LXXV.

The first time I read an excellent book, it is to me just as if I had gained a new friend. When I read over a book I have perused before, it resembles the meeting with an old one.

h.　Goldsmith—*The Citizen of the World.* Letter LXXXIII.

A man ought to read just as inclination leads him; for what he reads as a task will do him little good.

i.　Sam'l Johnson—*Boswell's Life of Johnson.* 1763.

What is twice read is commonly better remembered than what is transcribed.

j.　Sam'l Johnson—*The Idler.* No. 74.

Many readers judge of the power of a book by the shock it gives their feelings.

k.　Longfellow—*Kavanagh.* Ch. XIII.

In science, read, by preference, the newest works; in literature, the oldest. The classic literature is always modern.

l.　Bulwer-Lytton—*Caxtoniana. Hints on Mental Culture.*

His classical reading is great: he can quote
Horace, Juvenal, Ovid, and Martial by rote.
He has read Metaphysics * * * Spinoza
and Kant;
And Theology too: I have heard him descant
Upon Basil and Jerome. Antiquities, art,
He is fond of. He knows the old masters by
heart,
And his taste is refined.

m.　Owen Meredith (Lord Lytton)— *Lucile.* Canto II. Pt. IV.

　　　　　　　　　Who reads
Incessantly, and to his reading brings not
A spirit and judgment equal or superior,
(And what he brings what need he elsewhere
seek?)
Uncertain and unsettled still remains,
Deep versed in books and shallow in himself,
Crude or intoxicate, collecting toys
And trifles for choice matters, worth a sponge,
As children gathering pebbles on the shore.

n.　Milton—*Paradise Regained.* Bk. IV. L. 322.

He that I am reading seems always to have the most force.

o.　Montaigne—*Apology for Raimond Sebond.*

And better had they ne'er been born,
Who read to doubt, or read to scorn.

p.　Scott—*The Monastery.* Ch. XII.

He hath never fed of the dainties that are bred in a book; he hath not eat paper, as it were; he hath not drunk ink: his intellect is not replenished; he is only an animal, only sensible in the duller parts.

q.　*Love's Labour's Lost.* Act IV. Sc. 2. L. 26.

Read Homer once, and you can read no more,
For all books else appear so mean, so poor,
Verse will seem prose; but still persist to read,
And Homer will be all the books you need.

r.　John Sheffield (Duke of Buckinghamshire)—*An Essay on Poetry.* L. 323.

He that runs may read.

s.　Tennyson—*The Flower.* St. 5.

　　　　　　　　Studious let me sit,
And hold high converse with the mighty
Dead.

t.　Thomson—*Seasons. Winter.* L. 431.

Learn to read slow; all other graces
Will follow in their proper places.

u.　Wm. Walker—*Art of Reading.*

REASON.

Two angels guide
The path of man, both aged and yet young,
As angels are, ripening through endless
  years,
On one he leans : some call her Memory,
And some Tradition ; and her voice is sweet,
With deep mysterious accords : the other,
Floating above, holds down a lamp which
  streams
A light divine and searching on the earth,
Compelling eyes and footsteps. Memory
  yields,
Yet clings with loving check, and shines
  anew,
Reflecting all the rays of that bright lamp
Our angel Reason holds. We had not walked
But for Tradition ; we walk evermore
To higher paths by brightening Reason's
  lamp.
  a.   George Eliot—*Spanish Gypsy.*
                            Bk. II.

You have ravished me away by a Power I
cannot resist ; and yet I could resist till I saw
you ; and even since I have seen you I have
endeavored often " to reason against the
reasons of my Love."
  b.   Keats—*Letters to Fanny Braune.*
                            VIII.

To be rational is so glorious a thing, that
two-legged creatures generally content themselves with the title.
  c.   Locke—*Letter to Antony Collins, Esq.*

But all was false and hollow ; though his
  tongue
Dropt manna, and could make the worse
  appear
The better reason, to perplex and dash
Maturest counsels.
  d.   Milton—*Paradise Lost.* Bk. II.
                            L. 112.

Indu'd
With sanctity of reason.
  e.   Milton—*Paradise Lost.* Bk. VII.
                            L. 507.

Subdue
By force, who reason for their law refuse,
Right reason for their law.
  f.   Milton—*Paradise Lost.* Bk. VI.
                            L. 40.

Yea, marry, now it is somewhat, for now it
is rhyme ; before it was neither rhyme nor
reason.
  g.   Sir Thos. More.

Reason, however able, cool at best,
Cares not for service, or but serves when prest,
Stays till we call, and then not often near.
  h.   Pope—*Essay on Man.* Ep. III. L. 85.

Say first, of God above or man below,
What can we reason but from what we know ?
  i.   Pope—*Essay on Man.* Ep. I. L. 17.

There St. John mingles with my friendly bowl
The Feast of reason and the flow of soul.
  j.   Pope—*Second Book of Horace.*
                        Satire I. L. 128.

Who reasons wisely is not therefore wise ;
His pride in reasoning, not in acting lies.
  k.   Pope—*Moral Essays.* Ep. I. L. 117.

But since the affairs of men rest still incertain,
Let's reason with the worst that may befall.
  l.   *Julius Cæsar.* Act V. Sc. 1. L. 96.

Give you a reason on compulsion ! if reasons
were as plentiful as blackberries, I would
give no man a reason upon compulsion, I.
  m.   *Henry IV.* Pt. I. Act II. Sc. 4.
                            L. 263.

Good reasons must, of force, give place to
  better.
  n.   *Julius Cæsar.* Act IV. Sc. 3. L. 203.

His reasons are two grains of wheat hid in
two bushels of chaff ; you shall seek all day
ere you find them ; and when you have them,
they are not worth the search.
  o.   *Merchant of Venice.* Act I. Sc. 1.
                            L. 16.

I have no other but a woman's reason ;
I think him so because I think him so.
  p.   *Two Gentlemen of Verona.* Act I.
                        Sc. 2. L. 23.

Strong reasons make strong actions.
  q.   *King John.* Act III. Sc. 4. L. 182.

Sure, he that made us with such large dis-
  course,
Looking before and after, gave us not
That capability and god-like reason
To fust in us unus'd.
  r.   *Hamlet.* Act IV. Sc. 4. L. 36.

While Reason drew the plan, the Heart inform'd
The moral page and Fancy lent it grace.
  s.   Thomson—*Liberty.* Pt. IV. L. 262.

And what is reason ? Be she thus defined :
Reason is upright stature in the soul.
  t.   Young—*Night Thoughts.* Night VII.
                            L. 1,526.

Reason progressive, Instinct is complete ;
Swift Instinct leaps ; slow reason feebly
  climbs.
Brutes soon their zenith reach. * * * In
  ages they no more
Could know, do, covet or enjoy.
Were man to live coeval with the sun,
The patriarch pupil would be learning still.
  u.   Young—*Night Thoughts.* Night VII.
                            L. 81.

REBELLION.

The worst of rebels never arm
To do their king or country harm,
But draw their swords to do them good,
As doctors cure by letting blood.
  a.   BUTLER—*Miscellaneous Thoughts.*
                                    L. 181.

Men seldom, or rather never for a length of
time and deliberately, rebel against anything
that does not deserve rebelling against.
  b.   CARLYLE—*Essays. Goethe's Works.*

Rebellion to tyrants is obedience to God.
  c.   *Inscription on a Cannon near which the
         ashes of President John Bradshaw were
         lodged, on the top of hill near
                      Martha Bay in Jamaica.*

Rebellion in this land shall lose his sway,
Meeting the check of such another day.
  d.   *Henry IV.* Pt. I. Act V. Sc. 5. L. 41.

Unthread the rude eye of rebellion.
  e.   *King John.* Act V. Sc. 4. L. 11.

RECKLESSNESS.

I tell thee, be not rash ; a golden bridge
Is for a flying enemy.
  f.   BYRON—*The Deformed Transformed.*
                                    Act II. Sc. 2.

Who falls from all he knows of bliss,
Care little into what abyss.
  g.   BYRON—*The Giaour.* L. 1,091.

                     I am one, my liege,
Whom the vile blows and buffets of the
     world
Have so incens'd that I am reckless what
I do to spite the world.
  h.   *Macbeth.* Act III. Sc. 1. L. 108.

REDEMPTION.

And now without redemption all mankind
Must have been lost, adjudged to death and
     hell
By doom severe.
  i.   MILTON—*Paradise Lost.* Bk. III.
                                    L. 222.

Say, heavenly pow'rs, where shall we find
     such love?
Which of ye will be mortal to redeem
Man's mortal crime, and just th' unjust to
     save?
  j.   MILTON—*Paradise Lost.* Bk. III.
                                    L. 213.

Condemned into everlasting redemption for
this.
  k.   *Much Ado About Nothing.* Act IV.
                                    Sc. 2. L. 58.

Why, all the souls that are were forfeit once ;
And He that might the vantage best have
     took
Found out the remedy.
  l.   *Measure for Measure.* Act II. Sc. 2.
                                    L. 73.

And on his brest a bloodie crosse he bore,
The deare remembrance of his dying Lord,
For whose sweete sake that glorious badge he
     wore.
  m.   SPENSER—*Faerie Queene.* Bk. I.
                                    Canto I. St. 2.

REFLECTION.

The solitary side of our nature demands
leisure for reflection upon subjects on which
the dash and whirl of daily business, so long
as its clouds rise thick about us, forbid the
intellect to fasten itself.
  n.   FROUDE—*Short Studies on Great
                      Subjects. Sea Studies.*

The learn'd reflect on what before they knew.
  o.   POPE—*Essay on Criticism.* Pt. III.
                                    L. 180.

But with the morning cool reflections came.
  p.   SCOTT—*Chronicles of the Canongate.*
                                    Ch. IV.

Think on thy sins.
  q.   *Othello.* Act V. Sc. 2. L. 40.

A soul without reflection, like a pile
Without inhabitant, to ruin runs.
  r.   YOUNG—*Night Thoughts.* Night V.
                                    L. 596.

REFORMATION.

The oyster-women lock'd their fish up,
And trudged away to cry, No Bishop.
  s.   BUTLER—*Hudibras.* Pt. I. Canto II.
                                    L. 537.

All zeal for a reform, that gives offence
To peace and charity, is mere pretence.
  t.   COWPER—*Charity.* L. 533.

But 'tis the talent of our English nation,
Still to be plotting some new reformation.
  u.   DRYDEN—*Prologue to Sophonisba.* L. 9.

He bought a Bible of the new translation,
And in his life he show'd great reformation ;
He walkèd mannerly and talkèd meekly ;
He heard three lectures and two sermons
     weekly ;
He vow'd to shun all companions unruly,
And in his speech he used no oath but "truly ;"
And zealously to keep the Sabbath's rest.
  v.   SIR JOHN HARRINGTON—*Of a Precise
                                    Tailor.*

And like bright metal on a sullen ground,
My reformation, glittering o'er my fault,
Shall show more goodly and attract more eyes
Than that which hath no foil to set it off.
> *a.*   *Henry IV.* Pt. I. Act I. Sc. 2. L. 236.

My desolation does begin to make
A better life.
> *b.*   *Antony and Cleopatra.* Act V. Sc. 2.
> L. 1.

REGRET.

Keen were his pangs, but keener far to feel,
He nursed the pinion, which impell'd the
    steel.
> *c.*   Byron—*English Bards and Scotch
> Reviewers.* L. 823.

Sighing that Nature formed but one such man,
And broke the die—in moulding Sheridan.
> *d.*   Byron—*Monody on the Death of the
> Rt. Hon. R. B. Sheridan.* L. 117.

    Thou wilt lament
Hereafter, when the evil shall be done
And shall admit no cure.
> *e.*   Homer—*Iliad.* Bk. IX. L. 308.
> Bryant's trans.

    No simple word
That shall be uttered at our mirthful board,
Shall make us sad next morning; or affright
The liberty that we'll enjoy to-night.
> *f.*   Ben Jonson—*Epigram CI.*

O lost days of delight, that are wasted in
    doubting and waiting!
O lost hours and days in which we might
    have been happy!
> *g.*   Longfellow—*Tales of a Wayside Inn.*
> Pt. III. *The Theologian's Tale.
> Elizabeth.*

    For who, alas! has lived,
Nor in the watches of the night recalled
Words he has wished unsaid and deeds
    undone.
> *h.*   Sam'l Rogers—*Reflections.* L. 52.

I could have better spar'd a better man.
> *i.*   *Henry IV.* Pt. I. Act V. Sc. 4.
> L. 104.

For of all sad words of tongue or pen,
The saddest are these: " It might have been! "
> *j.*   Whittier—*Maud Muller.* L. 105.

RELIGION.

Children of men! the unseen Power, whose
    eye
Forever doth accompany mankind,
Hath look'd on no religion scornfully
    That men did ever find.
> *k.*   Matthew Arnold—*Progress.* St. 10.

When I am here [Milan] I do not fast on
Saturday. When at Rome I do fast on Saturday.
> *l.*   St. Augustine—*Ep. XXXVI. To
> Casulanus.*

The greatest vicissitude of things amongst
men, is the vicissitude of sects and religions.
> *m.*   Bacon—*Of Vicissitude of Things.*

There was never law, or sect, or opinion
did so much magnify goodness, as the Christian
religion doth.
> *n.*   Bacon—*Essays. Of Goodness, and
> Goodness of Nature.*

It [Calvinism] established a religion without
a prelate, a government without a king.
> *o.*   George Bancroft—*History of the
> United States.* Vol. III. Ch. VI.

Persecution is a bad and indirect way to
plant religion.
> *p.*   Sir Thomas Browne—*Religio Medici.*
> XXV.

Speak low to me, my Saviour, low and sweet
From out the hallelujahs, sweet and low,
Lest I should fear and fall, and miss Thee so
Who art not missed by any that entreat.
> *q.*   E. B. Browning—*Comfort.*

But the religion most prevalent in our
northern colonies is a refinement on the principle of resistance, it is the dissidence of dissent, and the protestantism of the Protestant
religion.
> *r.*   Burke—*Speech on Conciliation with
> America.*

The body of all true religion consists, to be
sure, in obedience to the will of the Sovereign
of the world, in a confidence in His declarations, and in imitation of His perfections.
> *s.*   Burke—*Reflections on the Revolution in
> France.*

The writers against religion, whilst they
oppose every system, are wisely careful never
to set up any of their own.
> *t.*   Burke—*A Vindication of Natural
> Society.* Preface. Vol. 1. P. 7.

People differ in their discourse and profession about these matters, but men of sense are
really but of one religion. * * * "What
religion?" * * * the Earl said, "Men of
sense never tell it."
> Bishop Burnet—*History of his Own
> Times.* Vol. I. Bk. I. Sec. 97.
> Footnote.
> *u.*   See also Benj. Disraeli—*Endymion.*
> Ch. LXXXI.

An Atheist's laugh's a poor exchange
    For Deity offended!
> *v.*   Burns—*Epistle to a Young Friend.*

G— knows I'm no the thing I should be,
Nor am I even the thing I could be,
But twenty times I rather would be
　　An atheist clean,
Than under gospel colours hid be,
　　Just for a screen.
　a.　　Burns—*Epistle to Rev. John M' Math.*
　　　　　　　　　　　　St. 8.

One religion is as true as another.
　b.　　Burton—*Anatomy of Melancholy.*
　　　　　Bk. III.　Sec. IV.　Memb. 2.
　　　　　　　　　　　Subsec. I.

As if Religion were intended
For nothing else but to be mended.
　c.　　Butler—*Hudibras.*　Pt. I.　Canto I.
　　　　　　　　　　　　L. 205.

So, ere the storm of war broke out,
Religion spawn'd a various rout
Of petulant capricious sects,
The maggots of corrupted texts,
That first run all religion down,
And after every swarm its own.
　d.　　Butler—*Hudibras.*　Pt. III.　Canto II.
　　　　　　　　　　　　L. 7.

Synods are mystical Bear-gardens,
Where Elders, Deputies, Church-wardens,
And other Members of the Court,
Manage the Babylonish sport.
　e.　　Butler—*Hudibras.*　Pt. I.　Canto III.
　　　　　　　　　　　L. 1,095.

There's naught, no doubt, so much the
spirit calms as rum and true religion.
　f.　　Byron—*Don Juan.*　Canto II.　St. 34.

His religion at best is an anxious wish,—
like that of Rabelais, a great Perhaps.
　g.　　Carlyle—*Essays. Burns.*

On the whole we must repeat the often repeated saying, that it is unworthy a religious
man to view an irreligious one either with
alarm or aversion; or with any other feeling
than regret, and hope, and brotherly commiseration.
　h.　　Carlyle—*Essays. Voltaire.*

The rigid saint, by whom no mercy's shown
To saints whose lives are better than his own.
　i.　　Churchill—*Epistle to Hogarth.*　L. 25.

Religion, the pious worship of God.
　j.　　Cicero.

Forth from his dark and lonely hiding place,
(Portentous sight!) the owlet atheism,
Sailing on obscene wings athwart the noon,
Drops his blue-fring'd lids, and holds them
　　close,
And hooting at the glorious sun in Heaven,
Cries out, "Where is it?"
　k.　　Coleridge—*Fears in Solitude.*

Men will wrangle for religion; write for it;
fight for it; die for it; anything but—live
for it.
　l.　　C. C. Colton—*Lacon.*　Vol. I.　XXV.

Pity! Religion has so seldom found
A skilful guide into poetic ground!
The flowers would spring where'er she deign'd
　　to stray,
And every muse attend her in her way.
　m.　　Cowper—*Table Talk.*　L. 688.

Religion does not censure or exclude
Unnumbered pleasures, harmlessly pursued.
　n.　　Cowper—*Retirement.*　L. 782.

Religion, if in heavenly truths attired,
Needs only to be seen to be admired.
　o.　　Cowper—*Expostulation.*　L. 492.

　　　　　　　　　The Cross!
There, and there only (though the deist rave,
And atheist, if Earth bears so base a slave);
There and there only, is the power to save.
　p.　　Cowper—*The Progress of Error.*　L. 613.

Sacred religion! Mother of Form and Fear!
　q.　　Sam'l Daniel—*Musophilus.*　St. 47.

I do not find that the age or country makes
the least difference; no, nor the language the
actors spoke, nor the religion which they professed, whether Arab in the desert or Frenchman in the Academy, I see that sensible men
and conscientious men all over the world were
of one religion.
　r.　　Emerson—*Lectures and Biographical
　　　　　　　Sketches. The Preacher.*　P. 215.

Sacrifice is the first element of religion, and
resolves itself in theological language into the
love of God.
　s.　　Froude—*Short Stories on Great
　　　　　　　　　　Subjects. Sea Studies.*

There are at bottom but two possible religions—that which rises in the moral nature
of man, and which takes shape in moral commandments, and that which grows out of the
observation of the material energies which
operate in the external universe.
　t.　　Froude—*Short Studies on Great
　　　　　　　Subjects. Calvinism.*　P. 20.

But our captain counts the image of God,
nevertheless, his image—cut in ebony as if
done in ivory; and in the blackest Moors he
sees the representation of the King of heaven.
　u.　　Fuller—*Holy and Profane States.
　　　　　　　The Good Sea-Captain.*　Maxim 5.

Indeed, a *little skill* in antiquity inclines a
man to Popery; but *depth in that study* brings
him about again to our religion.
　v.　　Fuller—*Holy and Profane States.
　　　　　　　The True Church Antiquary.*
　　　　　　　　　　　　Maxim 1.

We do ourselves wrong, and too meanly
estimate the holiness above us, when we deem
that any act or enjoyment good in itself, is not
good to do religiously.
　w.　　Nath. Hawthorne—*Marble Faun.*
　　　　　　　　　　Bk. II.　Ch. VII.

Dresse and undresse thy soul : mark the decay
And growth of it : if, with thy watch, that too
Be down, then winde up both: since we shall be
Most surely judged, make thy accounts agree.
   a.   HERBERT—*Temple. Church Porch.*
                     St. 76.

Religion stands on tiptoe in our land,
Ready to pass to the American strand.
   b.   HERBERT—*The Church Militant.* L. 235.

My Fathers and Brethren, this is never to be
forgotten that New England is originally a
plantation of religion, not a plantation of
trade.
   c.   JOHN HIGGINSON—*Election Sermon.*
          The Cause of God and His People in
          New England. May 27, 1663.

No solemn, sanctimonious face I pull,
  Nor think I'm pious when I'm only bilious—
  Nor study in my sanctum supercilious
To frame a Sabbath Bill or forge a Bull.
   d.   HOOD—*Ode to Rae Wilson.*

To be of no Church is dangerous.
   e.   SAM'L JOHNSON—*Life of Milton.*

Other hope had she none, nor wish in life, but
    to follow
Meekly, with reverent steps, the sacred feet of
    her Saviour.
   f.   LONGFELLOW—*Evangeline.* Pt. II. V.
                    L. 35.

But he turned up his nose at their murmuring
    and shamming,
And cared (shall I say?) not a d—n for their
    damning;
So they first read him out of their church and
    next minute
Turned round and declared he had never been
    in it.
   g.   LOWELL—*A Fable for Critics.* L. 876.

God is not dumb, that he should speak no
    more;
If thou hast wanderings in the wilderness
And find'st not Sinai, 'tis thy soul is poor.
   h.   LOWELL—*Bibliolatres.*

Puritanism, believing itself quick with the
seed of religious liberty, laid, without knowing
it, the egg of democracy.
   i.   LOWELL—*Among My Books. New*
          England Two Centuries Ago.

Blessed is the man that hath not walked in
the way of the Sacramentarians, nor sat in the
seat of the Zwinglians, nor followed the
Council of the Zurichers.
   j.   MARTIN LUTHER—*Parody of First*
                    Psalm.

The Puritan hated bear-baiting, not because
it gave pain to the bear, but because it gave
pleasure to the spectators.
   k.   MACAULAY—*History of England.*
                 Vol. I. Ch. II.

Life and religion are one, or neither is
anything : I will not say neither is growing to
be anything. Religion is no way of life, no
show of life, no observance of any sort. It is
neither the food nor the medicine of being. It
is life essential.
   l.   GEORGE MACDONALD—*The Marquis of*
                Lossie. Ch. LXI.

The solitary monk who shook the world
From pagan slumber, when the gospel trump
Thunder'd its challenge from his dauntless lips
In peals of truth.
   m.   ROB'T MONTGOMERY—*Luther. Man's*
             Need and God's Supply.

Near, so very near to God,
  Nearer I cannot be;
For in the person of his Son
  I am as near as he.
   n.   CATESBY PAGET—*Hymn.*

Remote from man, with God he passed the
    days,
Prayer all his business, all his pleasure praise.
   o.   PARNELL—*The Hermit.* L. 5.

The Puritan did not stop to think; he recognized God in his soul, and acted.
   p.   WENDELL PHILLIPS—*Speech.* Dec. 18,
                    1859.

We have a Calvinistic creed, a Popish
liturgy, and an Arminian clergy.
   q.   WILLIAM PITT (Earl of Chatham)—See
      Prior's Life of Burke. Ch. X. 1790.

For virtue's self may too much zeal be had;
The worst of madmen is a saint run mad.
   r.   POPE—*To Murray.* Ep. VI. of *Horace.*
                    L. 26.

Religion, blushing, veils her sacred fires,
And unawares Morality expires.
   s.   POPE—*The Dunciad.* Bk. IV. L. 649.

So upright Quakers please both man and God.
   t.   POPE—*The Dunciad.* Bk. IV. L. 208.

I think while zealots fast and frown,
  And fight for two or seven,
That there are fifty roads to town,
  And rather more to Heaven.
   u.   PRAED—*Chant of Brazen Head.* St. 8.

No one is so much alone in the universe as a
denier of God. With an orphaned heart,
which has lost the greatest of fathers, he
stands mourning by the immeasurable corpse
of nature, no longer moved or sustained by the
Spirit of the universe, but growing in its
grave; and he mourns, until he himself
crumbles away from the dead body.
   v.   RICHTER—*Flower, Fruit and Thorn*
          Pieces. First Flower Piece.

Humanity and Immortality consist neither in reason, nor in love; not in the body, nor in the animation of the heart of it, nor in the thoughts and stirrings of the brain of it;—but in the dedication of them all to Him who will raise them up at the last day.

a.   RUSKIN—*Stones of Venice.* Vol. I.
Ch. II.

I always thought
It was both impious and unnatural
That such immanity and bloody strife
Should reign among professors of one faith.

b.   *Henry VI.* Pt. I. Act V. Sc. 1. L. 11.

In religion,
What damned error, but some sober brow
Will bless it and approve it with a text.

c.   *Merchant of Venice.* Act III. Sc. 2.
L. 77.

The moon of Mahomet
Arose, and it shall set:
While, blazoned as on heaven's immortal noon,
The cross leads generations on.

d.   SHELLEY—*Hellas.* L. 237.

A religious life is a struggle and not a hymn.

e.   MADAME DE STAËL—*Corinne.* Bk. X.
Ch. V.

Religion has nothing more to fear than not being sufficiently understood.

f.   STANISLAUS (King of Poland)—
Maxims. No. 36.

The third essential of God's love, to make others happy from itself, is recognized in the gift of eternal life, which is blessedness, satisfaction, and happiness without end.

g.   SWEDENBORG—*True Christian Religion.*
Par. 43.

He made it a part of his religion, never to say grace to his meat.

h.   SWIFT—*Tale of a Tub.* Sec. XI.

We have just enough religion to make us hate, but not enough to make us love one another.

i.   SWIFT—*Thoughts on Various Subjects.*
Moral and Diverting.

What religion is he of?
Why, he is an Anythingarian.

j.   SWIFT—*Polite Conversation.* Dialogue I.

None but God can satisfy the longings of an immortal soul; that as the heart was made for Him, so He only can fill it.

k.   RICHARD CHENEVIX TRENCH—*Notes on the Parables. Prodigal Son.*

Once I journeyed far from home
To the gate of holy Rome;
There the Pope, for my offence,
Bade me straight, in penance, thence
Wandering onward, to attain
The wondrous land that height Cokaigne.

l.   ROBERT WACE—*The Land of Cokaigne.*

See the Gospel Church secure,
And founded on a Rock!
All her promises are sure;
Her bulwarks who can shock?
Count her every precious shrine;
Tell, to after-ages tell,
Fortified by power divine,
The Church can never fail.

m.   CHARLES WESLEY—*Scriptural.*
Psalm XLVIII. St. 9.

Who God doth late and early pray
More of his Grace than Gifts to lend;
And entertains the harmless day
With a Religious Book or Friend.

n.   SIR HENRY WOTTON—*The Character of a Happy Life.* St. 5.

But if man loses all, when life is lost,
He lives a coward, or a fool expires.
A daring infidel (and such there are,
From pride, example, lucre, rage, revenge,
Or pure heroical defect of thought),
Of all earth's madmen, most deserves a chain.

o.   YOUNG—*Night Thoughts.* Night VII.
L. 199.

Religion's all. Descending from the skies
To wretched man, the goddess in her left
Holds out this world, and, in her right, the next.

p.   YOUNG—*Night Thoughts.* Night IV.
L. 550.

REMORSE.

Cruel Remorse! where Youth and Pleasure sport,
And thoughtless Folly keeps her court,—
Crouching 'midst rosy bowers thou lurk'st unseen;
Slumbering the festal hours away,
While Youth disports in that enchanting scene;
Till on some fated day
Thou with a tiger-spring dost leap upon thy prey,
And tear his helpless breast, o'erwhelmed with wild dismay.

q.   ANNA LETITIA BARBAULD—*Ode to Remorse.* St. 6.

Remorse is as the heart in which it grows;
If that be gentle, it drops balmy dews
Of true repentance; but if proud and gloomy,
It is the poison tree, that pierced to the inmost,
Weeps only tears of poison.

r.   COLERIDGE—*Remorse.* Act I. Sc. 1.

Motives, that Judas moved, soon spent their force,
When followed an intolerable remorse,
The dream of avarice was at an end,
He had betrayed his living Lord and Friend.

s.   ABRAHAM COLES—*The Light of the World.* P. 314-315.

Farewell, remorse: all good to me is lost;
Evil, be thou my good.
    a.   MILTON—*Paradise Lost.* Bk. IV.
                         L. 108.

The hell within him.
    b.   MILTON—*Paradise Lost.* Bk. IV. L. 20.

High minds, of native pride and force,
Most deeply feel thy pangs, Remorse!
Fear, for their scourge, mean villains have,
Thou art the torturer of the brave!
    c.   SCOTT—*Marmion.* Canto III. St. 13.

           Abandon all remorse;
On horror's head horrors accumulate.
    d.   *Othello.* Act III. Sc. 3. L. 369.

               Unnatural deeds
Do breed unnatural troubles: infected minds
To their deaf pillows will discharge their
    secrets:
More needs she the divine than the physician.
    e.   *Macbeth.* Act V. Sc. 1. L. 79.

REPENTANCE.

           O ye powers that search
The heart of man, and weigh his inmost
    thoughts,
If I have done amiss, impute it not!
The best may err, but you are good.
    f.   ADDISON—*Cato.* Act V. Sc. 4.

    To sigh, yet not recede; to grieve, yet not
repent!
    g.   CRABBE—*Tales of the Hall.* Bk. III.
                  Boys at School. Last line.

Restore to God his due in tithe and time:
A tithe purloin'd cankers the whole estate.
    h.   HERBERT—*The Temple.* *The Church*
                               Porch.
Who after his transgression doth repent,
Is halfe, or altogether, innocent.
    i.   HERRICK—*Hesperides.* *Penitence.*

           When the scourge
Inexorable, and the torturing hour
Calls us to penance.
    j.   MILTON—*Paradise Lost.* Bk. II. L. 90.

Illusion is brief, but Repentance is long.
    k.   SCHILLER—*The Lay of the Bell.*

But with the morning cool repentance came.
    l.   SCOTT—*Rob Roy.* Ch. XII.

And wet his grave with my repentant tears.
    m.   *Richard III.* Act I. Sc. 2. L. 216.

Under your good correction, I have seen,
When, after execution, judgment hath
Repented o'er his doom.
    n.   *Measure for Measure.* Act II. Sc. 2.
                                  L. 10.

    Well, I'll repent, and that suddenly, while
I am in some liking; I shall be out of heart
shortly, and then I shall have no strength to
repent.
    o.   *Henry IV.* Pt. I. Act III. Sc. 3. L. 5.

          What then? what rests?
Try what repentance can: what can it not?
Yet what can it when one cannot repent?
O wretched state! O bosom black as death!
O limed soul, that struggling to be free
Art more engag'd!
    p.   *Hamlet.* Act III. Sc. 3. L. 64.

Amid the roses, fierce Repentance rears
Her snaky crest; a quick-returning pang
Shoots through the conscious heart.
    q.   THOMSON—*Seasons.* *Spring.* L. 995.

And while the lamp holds out to burn,
The vilest sinner may return.
    r.   ISAAC WATTS—*Hymns and Spiritual*
                        Songs. Bk. I. Hymn 88.

REPOSE.

But quiet to quick bosoms is a hell.
    s.   BYRON—*Childe Harold.* Canto III.
                                St. 42.
What sweet delight a quiet life affords.
    t.   DRUMMOND—*Sonnet.* P. 38.

To husband out life's taper at the close,
And keep the flames from wasting by repose.
    u.   GOLDSMITH—*Deserted Village.* L. 87.

The toils of honour dignify repose.
    v.   HOOLE—*Metastasia.* *Achilles in Lucias.*
                         Act III. Last Scene.

The wind breath'd soft as lover's sigh,
And, oft renew'd, seem'd oft to die,
    With breathless pause between,
O who, with speech of war and woes,
Would wish to break the soft repose
    Of such enchanting scene!
    w.   SCOTT—*Lord of the Isles.* Canto IV.
                                St. 13.
Our foster-nurse of nature is repose,
The which he lacks; that to provoke in him,
Are many simples operative, whose power
Will close the eye of anguish.
    x.   *King Lear.* Act IV. Sc. 4. L. 12.

These should be hours for necessities,
Not for delights; times to repair our nature
With comforting repose, and not for us
To waste these times.
    y.   *Henry VIII.* Act V. Sc. 1. L. 3.

The best of men have ever loved repose:
    They hate to mingle in the filthy fray;
Where the soul sours, and gradual rancour
    grows,
Imbitter'd more from peevish day to day.
    z.   THOMSON—*The Castle of Indolence.*
                           Canto I. St. 17.

REPROOF.

Reproof on her lip, but a smile in her eye.
a.   SAMUEL LOVER—*Rory O' More.*

Fear not the anger of the wise to raise;
Those best can bear reproof who merit praise.
b.   POPE—*Essay on Criticism.* L. 582.

Better a little chiding than a great deal of
heart-break.
c.   *Merry Wives of Windsor.* Act V. Sc. 3.
L. 10.

Chide him for faults, and do it reverently,
When you perceive his blood inclined to
mirth.
d.   *Henry IV.* Pt. II. Act IV. Sc. 4.
L. 37.

I will chide no breather in the world but
myself, against whom I know most faults.
e.   *As You Like It.* Act III. Sc. 2. L. 298.

REPUTATION.

It is a maxim with me that no man was
ever written out of reputation but by himself.
f.   RICHARD BENTLEY—MONK'S *Life of
Bentley.* Vol. I. Ch. VI.

A lost good name is ne'er retriev'd.
g.   GAY—*Fables. The Fox at the Point of
Death.* L. 46.

Reputation is but a synonyme of popularity :
dependent on suffrage, to be increased or
diminished at the will of the voters.
h.   MRS. JAMESON—*Memoirs and Essays.
Washington Allston.*

Reputations, like beavers and cloaks, shall
last some people twice the time of others.
i.   DOUGLAS JERROLD—*Specimens of
Jerrold's Wit. Reputations.*

How many worthy men have we seen survive their own reputation !
j.   MONTAIGNE—*Essays. Of Glory.*

To be pointed out with the finger.
k.   PERSIUS—*Satires.* I. L. 28.

In various talk th' instructive hours they
past,
Who gave the ball, or paid the visit last ;
One speaks the glory of the British queen,
And one describes a charming Indian screen ;
A third interprets motions, looks, and eyes ;
At every word a reputation dies.
l.   POPE—*Rape of the Lock.* Pt. III. L. 11.

But he that filches from me my good name
Robs me of that which not enriches him
And makes me poor indeed.
m.   *Othello.* Act III. Sc. 3. L. 159.

I have offended reputation,
A most unnoble swerving.
n.   *Antony and Cleopatra.* Act III. Sc. 11.
L. 49.

I see my reputation is at stake :
My fame is shrewdly gor'd.
o.   *Troilus and Cressida.* Act III. Sc. 3.
L. 227.

I would to God thou and I knew where a
commodity of good names were to be bought.
p.   *Henry IV.* Pt. I. Act I. Sc. 2. L. 92.

O, I have lost my reputation ! I have lost the
immortal part of myself, and what remains is
bestial.
q.   *Othello.* Act II. Sc. 3. L. 262.

Reputation is an idle and most false impo-
sition ; oft got without merit, and lost without deserving.
r.   *Othello.* Act II. Sc. 3. L. 268.

The purest treasure mortal times afford
Is spotless reputation ; that away,
Men are but gilded loam or painted clay.
s.   *Richard II.* Act I. Sc. 1. L. 177.

Thy death-bed is no lesser than thy land
Wherein thou liest in reputation sick.
t.   *Richard II.* Act II. Sc. 1. L. 95.

Convey a libel in a frown,
And wink a reputation down !
u.   SWIFT—*Journal of a Modern Lady.*
L. 185.

RESIGNATION.

Sustained and soothed
By an unfaltering trust, approach thy grave
Like one that wraps the drapery of his couch
About him, and lies down to pleasant dreams.
v.   BRYANT—*Thanatopsis.* L. 78.

Here's a sigh to those who love me,
And a smile to those who hate ;
And whatever sky's above me,
Here's a heart for every fate.
w.   BYRON—*To Thomas Moore.* St. 2.

To be resign'd when ills betide,
Patient when favours are denied,
And pleased with favours given ;—
Dear Chloe, this is wisdom's part ;
This is that incense of the heart
Whose fragrance smells to heaven.
x.   NATHANIEL COTTON—*The Fireside.*
St. 11.

Give what thou canst, without thee we are
poor ;
And with thee rich, take what thou wilt away.
y.   COWPER—*The Task.* Bk. V. Last lines.

Dare to look up to God and say, Deal with
me in the future as Thou wilt ; I am of the
same mind as Thou art ; I am Thine ; I refuse
nothing that pleases Thee ; lead me where
Thou wilt ; clothe me in any dress Thou
choosest.
z.   EPICTETUS—*Discourses.* Bk. II.
Ch. XVI.

Bends to the grave with unperceived decay,
While resignation gently slopes the way;
And, all his prospects brightening to the last,
His heaven commences ere the world be past.
　　a.　　GOLDSMITH—*Deserted Village.* L. 110.

To-morrow! the mysterious, unknown guest,
　　Who cries to me: "Remember Barmecide,
And tremble to be happy with the rest."
　　And I make answer: "I am satisfied;
I dare not ask; I know not what is best;
　　God hath already said what shall betide."
　　b.　　LONGFELLOW—*To-Morrow.*

To will what God doth will, that is the only
　　　science
　　That gives us any rest.
　　c.　　MALHERBE—*Consolation.* St. 7.
　　　　　　　　　　　　Longfellow's trans.

　　　　　　　　　　　　That's best
Which God sends. 'Twas His will: it is mine.
　　d.　　OWEN MEREDITH (Lord Lytton)—
　　　　　　　　Lucile. Pt. II. Canto VI. St. 29.

The pious farmer, who ne'er misses pray'rs,
　　With patience suffers unexpected rain;
He blesses Heav'n for what its bounty spares,
　　And sees, resign'd, a crop of blighted grain.
But, spite of sermons, farmers would blas-
　　　pheme,
If a star fell to set their thatch on flame.
　　e.　　LADY MARY WORTLEY MONTAGUE—
　　　　　　　　Poem written Oct., 1736.

Man yields to death; and man's sublimest
　　　works
Must yield at length to Time.
　　f.　　THOMAS LOVE PEACOCK—*Time.* L. 65.

Thus ready for the way of life or death,
I wait the sharpest blow.
　　g.　　*Pericles.* Act I. Sc. 1. L. 54.

　　　What's gone and what's past help
Should be past grief.
　　h.　　*Winter's Tale.* Act III. Sc. 2. L. 223.

It seem'd so hard at first, mother, to leave the
　　　blessed sun,
And now it seems as hard to stay—and yet
　　His will be done!
But still I think it can't be long before I find
　　release;
And that good man, the clergyman, has told
　　me words of peace.
　　i.　　TENNYSON—*The May-Queen.*
　　　　　　　　　　　　Conclusion. St. 3.

RESOLUTION.

Fifty-four forty (54° 40′ N.), or fight.
　　j.　　WM. ALLEN—*In the U. S. Senate. On
　　　　the Oregon Boundary Question.* 1844.

If not, resolve, before we go,
That you and I must pull a crow.
Y' 'ad best (quoth Ralpho), as the Ancients
Say wisely, have a care o' the main chance.
　　k.　　BUTLER—*Hudibras.* Pt. II. Canto II.
　　　　　　　　　　　　　　　　L. 499.

　　　　　　　Videlicit,
That each man swore to do his best
To damn and perjure all the rest.
　　l.　　BUTLER—*Hudibras.* Pt. I. Canto II.
　　　　　　　　　　　　　　　　L. 630.

I am in earnest—I will not equivocate—I
will not excuse—I will not retreat a single
inch; AND I WILL BE HEARD.
　　m.　　WILLIAM LLOYD GARRISON—*Salutatory
　　　　　　of the Liberator.* Vol. I. No. 1.
　　　　　　　　　　　　　　　Jan. 1, 1831.

I will be as harsh as truth and as uncom-
promising as justice.
　　n.　　WILLIAM LLOYD GARRISON—*Salutatory
　　　　　　of the Liberator.* Vol. I. No. 1.
　　　　　　　　　　　　　　　Jan. 1, 1831.

Nor cast one longing, ling'ring look behind.
　　o.　　GRAY—*Elegy in a Country Churchyard.*
　　　　　　　　　　　　　　　St. 22.

In truth there is no such thing in man's
nature as a settled and full resolve either for
good or evil, except at the very moment of
execution.
　　p.　　NATH. HAWTHORNE—*Twice-Told Tales.*
　　　　　　　　　　　　Fancy's Show Box.

Hast thou attempted greatnesse?
　　Then go on;
Back-turning slackens resolution.
　　q.　　HERRICK—*Regression Spoils Resolution.*

　　　　　　　For when two
Join in the same adventure, one perceives
Before the other how they ought to act;
While one alone, however prompt, resolves
More tardily and with a weaker will.
　　r.　　HOMER—*Iliad.* Bk. X. L. 257.
　　　　　　　　　　　　Bryant's trans.

Resolve, and thou art free.
　　s.　　LONGFELLOW—*Masque of Pandora.*
　　　　　　　　　　Pt. VI. *In the Garden.*

In life's small things be resolute and great
To keep thy muscle trained: know'st thou
　　　when Fate
Thy measure takes, or when she'll say to thee,
"I find thee worthy; do this deed for me?"
　　t.　　LOWELL—*Epigram.*

Tell your master that if there were as many
devils at Worms as tiles on its roofs, I would
enter.
　　u.　　MARTIN LUTHER—April 16, 1521. See
　　　　　　BUNSEN'S *Life of Luther.* P. 61.

Never tell your resolution beforehand.
　　v.　　JOHN SELDEN—*Table Talk. Wisdom.*

Be stirring as the time; be fire with fire;
Threaten the threat'ner and outface the brow
Of bragging horror: so shall inferior eyes,
That borrow their behaviours from the great,
Grow great by your example and put on
The dauntless spirit of resolution.
  a.   *King John.* Act V. Sc. 1. L. 48.

My resolution's plac'd, and I have nothing
Of woman in me: now from head to foot
I am marble—constant.
  b.   *Antony and Cleopatra.* Act V. Sc. 2.
                   L. 238.

And hearts resolved and hands prepared
The blessings they enjoy to guard.
  c.   Smollett—*Humphry Clinker. Ode to*
                   Leven Water.

REST.

In the rest of Nirvana all sorrows surcease :
Only Buddha can guide to that city of Peace
Whose inhabitants have the eternal release.
  d.   Wm. R. Alger—*Oriental Poetry. A*
                   Leader to Repose.

Silken rest
Tie all thy cares up!
  e.   Beaumont and Fletcher—*Four Plays*
         in One. Sc. 4. *Triumph of Love.*

Absence of occupation is not rest;
A mind quite vacant is a mind distress'd.
  f.   Cowper—*Retirement.* L. 623.

Rest is not quitting the busy career;
Rest is the fitting of self to its sphere.
  g.   John S. Dwight—*True Rest.*

Amidst these restless thoughts this rest I find,
For those that rest not here, there's rest behind.
  h.   Thomas Gataker—*B. D.* Nat. 4.
                   Sep., 1574.

On every mountain height
Is rest.
  i.   Goethe—*Ein Gleiches.*

Calm on the bosom of thy God,
Fair spirit! rest thee now!
  j.   Mrs. Hemans—*Siege of Valencia.*
                   Dirge. Sc. 9.

For too much rest itself becomes a pain.
  k.   Homer—*Odyssey.* Bk. XV. L. 429.
                   Pope's trans.

Oh, some seek bread—no more—life's mere
  subsistence,
And some seek wealth and ease—the common quest;
And some seek fame, that hovers in the distance;
But all are seeking rest.
  l.   Frederick Langbridge—*Seeking Rest.*

Now the hour of rest
Hath come to thee.
  m.   Longfellow—*Delia.*

Rest is sweet after strife.
  n.   Owen Meredith (Lord Lytton)—
              Lucile. Pt. I. Canto VI. St. 25.

               Weariness
Can snore upon the flint, when resty sloth
Finds the down pillow hard.
  o.   *Cymbeline.* Act III. Sc. 6. L. 33.

Who, with a body filled and vacant mind,
Gets him to rest, cramm'd with distressful
  bread.
  p.   *Henry V.* Act IV. Sc. 1. L. 286.

Sleepe after toyle, port after stormie seas,
Ease after warre, death after life, does greatly
  please.
  q.   Spenser—*Faerie Queene.* Bk. I.
                 Canto IX. St. 40.

And rest, that strengthens unto virtuous
  deeds,
Is one with Prayer.
  r.   Bayard Taylor—*Temptation of*
                 Hassan Ben Khaled. St. 4.

Now is done thy long day's work;
Fold thy palms across thy breast,
Fold thine arms, turn to thy rest.
  Let them rave.
  s.   Tennyson—*A Dirge.*

Thou hadst, for weary feet, the gift of rest.
  t.   William Watson—*Wordsworth's*
                 Grave. II. St. 3.

RESULTS.

From hence, let fierce contending nations
  know,
What dire effects from civil discord flow.
  u.   Addison—*Cato.* Act V. Sc. 4.

The thorns which I have reap'd are of the tree
I planted—they have torn me—and I bleed!
I should have known what fruit would spring
  from such a seed.
  v.   Byron—*Childe Harold.* Canto IV.
                 St. 10.

The Present is the living sum-total of the
whole Past.
  w.   Carlyle—*Essays. Characteristics.*

O! lady, we receive but what we give,
And in our life alone doth nature live;
Ours is her wedding-garment, ours her shroud!
  x.   Coleridge—*Dejection. An Ode.* IV.

From little spark may burst a mighty flame.
  y.   Dante—*Paradise.* Canto I. L. 34.

The remedy is worse than the disease.
  z.   Dryden—*Sixteenth Satire of Juvenal.*
                 L. 31.

Consequences are unpitying. Our deeds carry their terrible consequences, quite apart from any fluctuations that went before—consequences that are hardly ever confined to ourselves.

a.   George Eliot—*Adam Bede.* Ch. XVI.

A bad ending follows a bad beginning.

b.   Euripides—*Frag. Melanip.* (*Stob.*)

So comes a reckoning when the banquet's o'er,
The dreadful reckoning, and men smile no more.

c.   Gay—*What D'ye Call't?* Act II. Sc. 9.

That from small fires comes oft no small mishap.

d.   Herbert—*The Temple. Artillerie.*

What dire offence from am'rous causes springs,
What mighty contests rise from trivial things.

e.   Pope—*Rape of the Lock.* Canto I.

The end must justify the means.

f.   Prior—*Hans Carvel.*

   Great floods have flown
From simple sources.

g.   *All's Well That Ends Well.* Act II.
                 Sc. 1. L. 142.

Is not this a lamentable thing, that of the skin of an innocent lamb should be made parchment? that parchment, being scribbled o'er, should undo a man?

h.   *Henry VI.* Pt. II. Act IV. Sc. 2.
                            L. 85.

O most lame and impotent conclusion!

i.   *Othello.* Act II. Sc. 1. L. 162.

Striving to better, oft we mar what's well.

j.   *King Lear.* Act I. Sc. 4. L. 369.

Things bad begun make strong themselves by ill.

k.   *Macbeth.* Act III. Sc. 2. L. 55.

The evening shows the day, and death crowns life.

l.   John Webster—*A Monumental Column.* Last line.

The blood will follow where the knife is driven,
The flesh will quiver where the pincers tear.

m.   Young—*The Revenge.* Act V.

RESURRECTION.

The last loud trumpet's wondrous sound,
Shall thro' the rending tombs rebound,
And wake the nations under ground.

n.   Wentworth Dillon—*On the Day of Judgment.* St. 3.

The trumpet! the trumpet! the dead have all heard:
Lo, the depths of the stone-cover'd charnels are stirr'd:
From the sea, from the land, from the south and the north,
The vast generations of man are come forth.

o.   Milman—*Hymns for Church Service. Second Sunday in Advent.* St. 3.

I see the Judge enthroned; the flaming guard:
The volume open'd!—open'd every heart!

p.   Young—*Night Thoughts.* Night IX.
                           L. 262.

Shall man alone, for whom all else revives,
No resurrection know? Shall man alone,
Imperial man! be sown in barren ground,
Less privileged than grain, on which he feeds?

q.   Young—*Night Thoughts.* Night VI.
                           L. 704.

RETALIATION.

Repudiate the repudiators.

r.   Wm. P. Fessenden—*Pres. Canvass of*
                               1868

And would'st thou evil for his good repay?

s.   Homer—*Odyssey.* Bk. XVI. L. 448.
                          Pope's trans.

She pays him in his own coin.

t.   Swift—*Polite Conversation.*
                          Dialogue III.

RETRIBUTION.

           Remember Milo's end,
Wedged in that timber which he strove to rend.

u.   Wentworth Dillon—*Essays on Translated Verse.* L. 87.

Mine eyes have seen the glory of the coming of the Lord:
He is trampling out the vintage where the grapes of wrath are stored:
He hath loosed the fateful lightning of his terrible swift sword:
      His truth is marching on.

v.   Julia Ward Howe—*Battle Hymn of the Republic.*

Though the mills of God grind slowly, yet they grind exceeding small;
Though with patience He stands waiting, with exactness grinds He all.

w.   Friedrich Von Logau—*Retribution. From the Sinngedichte.* See Longfellow's trans. *Poetic Aphorisms.*

           To be left alone
And face to face with my own crime, had been Just retribution.

x.   Longfellow—*Masque of Pandora.* Pt. VIII. *In the Garden.*

Be ready, gods, with all your thunderbolts;
Dash him to pieces!
a.　　*Julius Cæsar.* Act IV. Sc. 3. L. 81.

But as some muskets so contrive it
As oft to miss the mark they drive at,
And though well aimed at duck or plover
Bear wide, and kick their owners over.
b.　　JOHN TRUMBULL—*McFingal.* Canto I.
L. 95.

REVELATION.

Lochiel, Lochiel! beware of the day;
For, dark and despairing, my sight I may seal
But man cannot cover what God would reveal;
'Tis the sunset of life gives me mystical lore,
And coming events cast their shadows before.
c.　　CAMPBELL—*Lochiel's Warning.*

'Tis Revelation satisfies all doubts,
Explains all mysteries except her own,
And so illuminates the path of life,
That fools discover it, and stray no more.
d.　　COWPER—*The Task.* Bk. II. *The
Time-Piece.* L. 526.

Reason stands aghast at the sight of an "un-
principled, immoral, incorrigible" publick;
And the word of God abounds in such threats
and denunciations, as must strike terror into
the heart of every believer.
e.　　RICHARD HURD—*Works.* Vol. IV.
Sermon 1.

Nature is a revelation of God;
Art a revelation of man.
f.　　LONGFELLOW—*Hyperion.* Bk. III.
Ch. V.

REVENGE.

Revenge is a kind of wild justice; which
the more man's nature runs to, the more
ought law to weed it out.
g.　　BACON—*Of Revenge.*

Sweet is revenge—especially to women.
h.　　BYRON—*Don Juan.* Canto I. St. 124.

Revenge is profitable.
i.　　GIBBON—*Decline and Fall of the Roman
Empire.* Ch. XI.

Behold, on wrong
Swift vengeance waits; and art subdues the
strong.
j.　　HOMER—*Odyssey.* Bk. VIII. L. 367.
Pope's trans.

Revenge, at first though sweet,
Bitter ere long back on itself recoils.
k.　　MILTON—*Paradise Lost.* Bk. IX.
L. 171.

Which, if not victory, is yet revenge.
l.　　MILTON—*Paradise Lost.* Bk. II. L. 105.

One sole desire, one passion now remains
To keep life's fever still within his veins,
Vengeance! dire vengeance on the wretch who
cast
O'er him and all he lov'd that ruinous blast.
m.　　MOORE—*Lalla Rookh. The Veiled
Prophet of Khorassan.*

'Tis an old tale, and often told;
But did my fate and wish agree,
Ne'er had been read, in story old,
Of maiden true betray'd for gold,
That loved, or was avenged, like me!
n.　　SCOTT—*Marmion.* Canto II. St. 27.

Vengeance to God alone belongs;
But, when I think of all my wrongs,
My blood is liquid flame!
o.　　SCOTT—*Marmion.* Canto VI. St. 7.

If a Jew wrong a Christian, what is his humility? Revenge. If a Christian wrong a
Jew, what should his sufferance be by Christian
example? Why, revenge.
p.　　*Merchant of Venice.* Act III. Sc. 1.
L. 71.

If I can catch him once upon the hip,
I will feed fat the ancient grudge I bear him.
q.　　*Merchant of Venice.* Act I. Sc. 3.
L. 47.

If it will feed nothing else, it will feed my
revenge.
r.　　*Merchant of Venice.* Act III. Sc. 1.
L. 55.

Now, infidel, I have you on the hip.
s.　　*Merchant of Venice.* Act IV. Sc. 1.
L. 334.

Vengeance is in my heart, death in my hand,
Blood and revenge are hammering in my
head.
t.　　*Titus Andronicus.* Act II. Sc. 3. L. 38.

Souls made of fire and children of the sun,
With whom Revenge is virtue.
u.　　YOUNG—*The Revenge.* Act V.

REVERENCE.

Henceforth the Majesty of God revere;
Fear him and you have nothing else to fear.
v.　　FORDYCE—*Answer to a Gentleman who
Apologized to the Author for
Swearing.*

What a sweet reverence is that when a
young man deems his mistress a little more
than mortal and almost chides himself for
longing to bring her close to his heart.
w.　　NATH. HAWTHORNE—*The Marble Faun.*
Vol. II. Ch. XV.

When once thy foot enters the church, be
  bare.
God is more there than thou : for thou art
  there
Only by His permission. Then beware,
And make thyself all reverence and fear.
  a.   HERBERT—*The Temple. The Church
                                    Porch.*

RIGHTS.

Among the natural rights of the colonists
are these : First a right to life, secondly to
liberty, thirdly to property ; together with the
right to defend them in the best manner they
can.
  b.   SAM'L ADAMS—*Statement of the Rights
                    of the Colonists, etc. 1772.*

They made and recorded a sort of institute
and digest of anarchy, called the rights of
man.
  c.   BURKE—*On the Army Estimates.*
                              Vol. III. P. 221.

The glittering and sounding generalities of
natural right which make up the Declaration
of Independence.
  d.   RUFUS CHOATE—*Letter to the Maine
                          Whig Committee. 1856.*

Sir, I would rather be right than be President.
  e.   HENRY CLAY—*Speech, 1850. Referring
                    to the Compromise Measure.*

But 'twas a maxim he had often tried,
That right was right, and there he would
  abide.
  f.   CRABBE—*Tales.* Tale XV. *The Squire
                              and the Priest.*

For right is right, since God is God,
  And right the day must win ;
To doubt would be disloyalty,
  To falter would be sin.
  g.   F. W. FABER—*The Right Must Win.*
                                      St. 18.

For the ultimate notion of right is that
which tends to the universal good ; and when
one's acting in a certain manner has this
tendency he has a right thus to act.
  h.   FRANCIS HUTCHESON—*A System of
                  Moral Philosophy. The General
                    Notions of Rights and Laws
                          Explained.* Bk. II.
                                      Ch. III.

We hold these truths to be self-evident,—
that all men are created equal ; that they are
endowed by their Creator with certain in-
alienable rights ; that among these are Life,
Liberty, and the pursuit of happiness.
  i.   THOMAS JEFFERSON—*Declaration of
                              Independence.*

Let us have faith that Right makes Might,
and in that faith let us to the end dare to do
our duty as we understand it.
  j.   ABRAHAM LINCOLN—*Address. New
              York City.* Feb. 21, 1859. See HENRY
                  J. RAYMOND'S *Life and Public
                          Services of Lincoln.*
                                      Ch. III.

Reparation for our rights *at home,* and
security against the like future violations.
  k.   WILLIAM PITT (Earl of Chatham)—
                Letter to the Earl of Shelburne. Sept.
                                      29, 1770.

RIVERS.

And see the rivers how they run
Through woods and meads, in shade and sun,
Sometimes swift, sometimes slow,—
Wave succeeding wave, they go
A various journey to the deep,
Like human life to endless sleep !
  l.   JOHN DYER—*Grongar Hill.* L. 93.

                    Two ways the rivers
Leap down to different seas, and as they roll
Grow deep and still, and their majestic presence
Becomes a benefaction to the towns
They visit, wandering silently among them,
Like patriarchs old among their shining tents.
  m.   LONGFELLOW—*Christus. The Golden
                              Legend.* Pt. V.

By shallow rivers, to whose falls
Melodious birds sing madrigals.
  n.   MARLOWE—*The Passionate Shepherd to
                              His Love.*

Now scantier limits the proud arch confine,
And scarce are seen the prostrate Nile or
    Rhine ;
A small Euphrates thro' the piece is roll'd,
And little eagles wave their wings in gold.
  o.   POPE—*Moral Essays. Ep. to Mr.
                              Addison.* L. 27.

I chatter, chatter as I flow
  To join the brimming river,
For men may come and men may go,
  But I go on forever.
  p.   TENNYSON—*The Brook.*

From Stirling Castle we had seen
  The mazy Forth unravelled ;
Had trod the banks of Clyde and Tay,
  And with the Tweed had travelled ;
And when we came to Clovenford,
  Then said " my winsome marrow,"
" Whate'er betide, we'll turn aside,
  And see the braes of Yarrow."
  q.   WORDSWORTH—*Yarrow Unvisited.*

Afton.

Flow gently, sweet Afton, among thy green
  braes,
Flow gently, I'll sing thee a song in thy
  praise.
a.   Burns—*Flow Gently, Sweet Afton.*

Alph.

In Xanadu did Kubla Khan
  A stately pleasure-dome decree;
Where Alph, the sacred river ran,
Through caverns measureless to man
  Down to a sunless sea.
b.   Coleridge—*Kubla Khan.*

Arno.

At last the Muses rose, * * * And scattered, * * * as they flew,
Their blooming wreaths from fair Valclusa's
  bowers
To Arno's myrtle border.
c.   Akenside—*Pleasures of the
               Imagination.* II.

Avon.

The Avon to the Severn runs,
  The Severn to the sea,
And Wickliff's dust shall spread abroad
  Wide as the waters be.
d.   Daniel Webster—*Quoted in an
          Address before the Sons of New
          Hampshire.* 1849.

Ayr.

Ayr, gurgling, kissed his pebbled shore,
  O'erhung with wild woods, thickening
    green;
The fragrant birch and hawthorn hoar
  Twined amorous round the raptured scene.
e.   Burns—*To Mary in Heaven.*

Farewell, my friends! farewell, my foes!
My peace with these, my love with those.
The bursting tears my heart declare;
Farewell, the bonnie banks of Ayr.
f.   Burns—*The Banks of Ayr.*

Bronx.

Yet I will look upon thy face again,
  My own romantic Bronx, and it will be
A face more pleasant than the face of men.
  Thy waves are old companions, I shall
    see
A well remembered form in each old tree
And hear a voice long loved in thy wild
  minstrelsy.
g.   Joseph Rodman Drake—*Bronx.*

Cam.

Where stray ye, Muses! in what lawn or grove,
  *   *   *   *   *   *
In those fair fields where sacred Isis glides,
Or else where Cam his winding vales divides?
h.   Pope—*Summer.* L. 23.

Chattahoochee.

Out of the hills of Habersham,
  Down the valleys of Hall,
I hurry amain to reach the plain;
  Run the rapid and leap the fall,
Split at the rock, and together again
  Accept my bed, or narrow or wide,
  And flee from folly on every side
With a lover's pain to attain the plain,
    Far from the hills of Habersham,
    Far from the valleys of Hall.
i.   Sidney Lanier—*The Song of the
                  Chattahoochee.*

Clyde.

How sweet to move at summer's eve
  By Clyde's meandering stream,
When Sol in joy is seen to leave
  The earth with crimson beam;
When islands that wandered far
  Above his sea couch lie,
And here and there some gem-like star
  Re-opes its sparkling eye.
j.   Andrew Park—*The Banks of Clyde.*

Dee.

Flow on, lovely Dee, flow on, thou sweet river,
Thy banks' purest stream shall be dear to me
  ever.
k.   John Tait—*The Banks of the Dee.*

"O Mary, go and call the cattle home,
  And call the cattle home,
  And call the cattle home,
  Across the sands o' Dee;"
The western wind was wild and dank wi' foam,
  And all alone went she.
l.   Charles Kingsley—*The Sands o' Dee.*

Doon.

Ye banks and braes o' bonny Doon,
  How can ye bloom sae fresh and fair;
How can ye chant, ye little birds,
  And I sae weary fu' o' care!
m.   Burns—*The Banks o' Doon.*

Dove.

Oh, my beloved nymph, fair Dove,
Princess of rivers, how I love
  Upon thy flowery banks to lie,
And view thy silver stream,
  When gilded by a summer's beam!
  And in it all thy wanton fry,
  Playing at liberty;
And with my angle, upon them
  The all of treachery
I ever learned, industriously to try!
n.   Charles Cotton—*The Retirement.*
                              L. 34.

Isar.

On Linden, when the sun was low,
All bloodless lay the untrodden snow,
And dark as winter was the flow
  Of Isar, rolling rapidly.
o.   Campbell—*Hohenlinden.*

Lee.

On this I ponder
Where'er I wander,
And thus grow fonder,
    Sweet Cork, of thee,—
With thy bells of Shandon,
That sound so grand on
The pleasant waters
    Of the river Lee.
    a.   FATHER PROUT (Francis Mahoney)—
                        The Bells of Shandon.

Leven.

On Leven's banks, while free to rove,
And tune the rural pipe to love,
I envied not the happiest swain
That ever trod the Arcadian plain.
Pure stream ! in whose transparent wave
My youthful limbs I wont to lave ;
No torrents stain thy limpid source,
No rocks impede thy dimpling course,
That sweetly warbles o'er its bed,
With white, round, polish'd pebbles spread.
    b.   SMOLLETT—Ode to Leven Water.

Loire.

How often I have led thy sportive choir,
With tuneless pipe, beside the murmuring
    Loire !
Where shading elms along the margin grew,
And freshen'd from the wave, the zephyr
    flew.
    c.   GOLDSMITH—The Traveller. L. 243.

Merrimack.

Do pilgrims find their way to Indian Ridge,
Or journey onward to the far-off bridge,
And bring to younger ears the story back
Of the broad stream, the mighty Merrimack?
    d.   O. W. HOLMES—The School Boy. L. 247.

Niagara.

"Niagara ! wonder of this western world,
And half the world beside ! hail, beauteous
    queen
Of cataracts !" An angel who had been
O'er heaven and earth, spoke thus, his bright
    wings furled,
And knelt to Nature first, on this wild cliff
    unseen.
    e.   MARIA BROOKS—To Niagara.

Flow on, forever, in thy glorious robe
Of terror and of beauty. Yea, flow on
Unfathomed and resistless. God hath set
His rainbow on thy forehead : and the cloud
Mantled around thy feet. And He doth give
Thy voice of thunder power to speak of Him
Eternally—bidding the lip of man
Keep silence—and upon thine altar pour
Incense of awe-struck praise.
    f.   LYDIA M. SIGOURNEY—Niagara.

Nile.

It flows through old hushed Egypt and its
    sands,
Like some grave mighty thought threading a
    dream.
    g.   LEIGH HUNT—Sonnet. The Nile.

Son of the old moon-mountains African !
    Stream of the Pyramid and Crocodile !
    We call thee fruitful, and that very while
A desert fills our seeing's inward span.
    h.   KEATS—Sonnet. To the Nile.

The Nile, forever new and old,
Among the living and the dead,
Its mighty, mystic stream has rolled.
    i.   LONGFELLOW—Christus. The Golden
                            Legend. Pt. I.

                The higher Nilus swells,
The more it promises ; as it ebbs, the seedsman
Upon the slime and ooze scatters his grain,
And shortly comes to harvest.
    j.   Antony and Cleopatra. Act II. Sc. 7.
                            L. 23.

O'er Egypt's land of memory floods are level,
    And they are thine, O Nile ! and well thou
        knowest
That soul-sustaining airs and blasts of evil,
    And fruits and poisons spring where'er thou
        flowest.
    k.   SHELLEY—Sonnet. To the Nile.
                        (See Keats' Poems.)

Mysterious Flood,—that through the silent
    sands
Hast wandered, century on century,
Watering the length of great Egyptian lands,
    Which were not, but for thee.
    l.   BAYARD TAYLOR—To the Nile.

Nith.

Hail, gentle stream ! forever dear
The rudest murmurs to mine ear !
Torn from thy banks, though far I rove,
The slave of poverty and love,
Ne'er shall thy bard, where'er he be,
Without a sigh remember thee !
    m.   JOHN MAYNE—To the River Nith.

Potomac.

And Potomac flowed calmly, scarce heaving
    her breast,
With her low-lying billows all bright in the
    west,
For a charm as from God lulled the waters to
    rest
    Of the fair rolling river.
    n.   PAUL HAMILTON HAYNE—Beyond the
                            Potomac.

Rhine.

The castled crag of Drachenfels,
  Frowns o'er the wide and winding Rhine,
Whose breast of waters broadly swells
  Between the banks which bear the vine,
And hills all rich with blossom'd trees,
  And fields which promise corn and wine,
And scatter'd cities crowning these,
  Whose far white walls along them shine.
  a.   BYRON—*Childe Harold.* Canto III.
                                    St. 55.

The air grows cool and darkles,
  The Rhine flows calmly on;
The mountain summit sparkles
  In the light of the setting sun.
  b. HEINE—*The Lorelei.*

Beneath me flows the Rhine, and, like the
stream of Time, it flows amid the ruins of the
Past.
  c.   LONGFELLOW—*Hyperion.* Bk. I.
                                    Ch. III.

  The Rhine! the Rhine! a blessing on the
Rhine!
  d.   LONGFELLOW—*Hyperion.* Bk. I. Ch. II.

I've seen the Rhine with younger wave,
O'er every obstacle to rave.
I see the Rhine in his native wild
Is still a mighty mountain child.
  e.   RUSKIN—*A Tour on the Continent. Via
                                    Mala.*

Oh, sweet is thy current by town and by tower,
The green sunny vale and the dark linden
    bower;
Thy waves as they dimple smile back on the
    plain,
And Rhine, ancient river, thou'rt German
    again!
  f.   HORACE WALLACE—*Ode on the Rhine's
            Returning into Germany from France.*

Rhone.

Is it not better, then, to be alone,
  And love Earth only for its earthly sake?
By the blue rushing of the arrowy Rhone
  Or the pure bosom of its nursing lake.
  g.   BYRON—*Childe Harold.* Canto III.
                                    St. 71.

Thou Royal River, born of sun and shower
In chambers purple with the Alpine glow,
Wrapped in the spotless ermine of the snow
And rocked by tempests!
  h.   LONGFELLOW—*To the River Rhone.*

Scheld.

Remote, unfriended, melancholy, slow,
Or by the lazy Scheld or wandering Po!
  i.   GOLDSMITH—*The Traveller.* L. 1.

Schuylkill.

Alone by the Schuylkill a wanderer rov'd,
  And bright were its flowery banks to his
    eye;
But far, very far, were the friends that he
    lov'd,
And he gaz'd on its flowery banks with a
    sigh.
  j.   MOORE—*Lines Written on Leaving
                                Philadelphia.*

St. Lawrence.

The first time I beheld thee, beauteous stream,
  How pure, how smooth, how broad thy
    bosom heav'd!
What feelings rush'd upon my heart!—a
    gleam
  As of another life my kindling soul re-
    ceived.
  k.   MARIA BROOKS—*To the River
                        St. Lawrence.* St. 1.

Tagus.

On, on the vessel flies, the land is gone,
And winds are rude, in Biscay's sleepless
    bay,
Four days are sped, but with the fifth, anon,
New shores descried make every bosom
    gay;
And Cintra's mountain greets them on their
    way,
And Tagus dashing onward to the deep,
His fabled golden tribute bent to pay;
And soon on board the Lusian pilots leap,
And steer 'twixt fertile shores where yet few
    rustics reap.
  l.   BYRON—*Childe Harold.* Canto I.
                                    St. 14.

Teviot.

Sweet Teviot! on thy silver tide
  The glaring bale-fires blaze no more;
No longer steel-clad warriors ride
  Along thy wild and willow'd shore.
  m.   SCOTT—*Lay of the Last Minstrel.*
                            Canto IV. St. 1.

Thames.

There is a hill beside the silver Thames,
  Shady with birch and beech and odorous
    pine;
And brilliant underfoot with thousand gems,
  Steeply the thickets to his floods decline.
  n.   ROB'T BRIDGES—*There is a Hill beside
                            the Silver Thames.*

Slow let us trace the matchless vale of
    Thames;
Fair winding up to where the Muses haunt
In Twit'nham bowers, and for their Pope
    implore.
  o.   THOMSON—*Seasons. Summer.* L. 1,425.

Never did sun more beautifully steep
  In his first splendor, valley, rock, or hill;
Ne'er saw I, never felt, a calm so deep!
  The river glideth at his own sweet will.
Dear God! the very houses seem asleep;
  And all that mighty heart is lying still!
  a.   WORDSWORTH—*Sonnet. Composed*
                    upon Westminster Bridge.

Tiber.

Thou hast fair forms that move
  With queenly tread;
Thou hast proud fanes above
  Thy mighty dead.
Yet wears thy Tiber's shore
  A mournful mien:—
Rome, Rome, thou art no more
  As thou hast been.
  b.   Mrs. HEMANS—*Roman Girl's Song.*

ROMANCE.

Parent of golden dreams, Romance!
  Auspicious queen of childish joys,
Who lead'st along, in airy dance,
  Thy votive train of girls and boys.
  f.   BYRON—*To Romance.*

Romances paint at full length people's woo-
    ings,
  But only give a bust of marriages:
For no one cares for matrimonial cooings.
  There's nothing wrong in a connubial kiss.
Think you, if Laura had been Petrarch's wife,
He would have written sonnets all his life?
  g.   BYRON—*Don Juan.* Canto III. St. 8.

He loved the twilight that surrounds
  The border-land of old romance;
Where glitter hauberk, helm, and lance,
And banner waves, and trumpet sounds,
And ladies ride with hawk on wrist,
  And mighty warriors sweep along,
Magnified by the purple mist,
  The dusk of centuries and of song.
  h.   LONGFELLOW—*Prelude to Tales of a*
                    Wayside Inn. Pt. V. L. 130.

Romance is the poetry of literature.
  i.   MADAME NECKER.

        Lady of the Mere,
Sole-sitting by the shores of old romance.
  j.   WORDSWORTH—*A Narrow Girdle of*
                    Rough Stones and Crags.

ROYALTY.

Ten poor men sleep in peace on one straw
    heap, as Saadi sings,
But the immensest empire is too narrow for
    two kings.
  k.   WM. R. ALGER—*Oriental Poetry.*
                    Elbow Room.

Those graceful groves that shade the plain,
Where Tiber rolls majestic to the main,
And flattens, as he runs, the fair campagne.
  c.   OVID—*Metamorphoses.* Bk. XIV.
                    Æneas Arrives in Italy. L. 8.
                    Sir Sam'l Garth's trans.

Draw them to Tiber banks, and weep your
    tears
Into the channel, till the lowest stream
Do kiss the most exalted shores of all.
  d.   *Julius Cæsar.* Act I. Sc. 1. L. 63.

Yvette.

O lovely river of Yvette!
O darling stream! on balanced wings
The wood-birds sang the chansonnette
That here a wandering poet sings.
  e.   LONGFELLOW—*To the River Yvette.* St. 5.

        Many a crown
Covers bald foreheads.
  l.   E. B. BROWNING—*Aurora Leigh.*
                    Bk. I. L. 754.

God bless the King—I mean the faith's de-
    fender;
God bless (no harm in blessing) the pre-
    tender;
But who the pretender is, or who is King—
God bless us all—that's quite another thing.
  m.   JOHN BYROM—*Miscellaneous Pieces.*

God save our gracious king!
Long live our noble king!
  God save the king!
  n.   HENRY CAREY—*God Save the King.*

Every noble crown is, and on Earth will
forever be, a crown of thorns.
  o.   CARLYLE—*Past and Present.* Bk. III.
                    Ch. VIII.

'Tis a very fine thing to be father-in-law
To a very magnificent three-tailed bashaw.
  p.   GEORGE COLMAN (The Younger)—
                    Blue Beard. Act III. Sc. 4.

Here lies our sovereign lord, the king,
  Whose word no man relies on,
Who never said a foolish thing,
  And never did a wise one.
  q.   *Said by a Courtier of Charles II.*
                    (ROCHESTER?) *To which the King*
                    replied, " That is very true, for
                    my words are my own. My
                    actions are my minister's."

And kind as kings upon their coronation day.
  r.   DRYDEN—*Fables. The Hind and the*
                    Panther. Pt. I. L. 271.

        A man's a man,
But when you see a king, you see the work
Of many thousand men.
  s.   GEORGE ELIOT—*Spanish Gypsy.* Bk. I.

There was a king of Thule,
  Was faithful till the grave,
To whom his mistress dying,
  A golden goblet gave.
  a.   GOETHE—*Faust. The King of Thule.*
                        Bayard Taylor's trans.

As yourselves your empires fall,
And every kingdom hath a grave.
  b.   WILLIAM HABINGTON—*Night.*

                        The rule
Of the many is not well. One must be chief
In war and one the king.
  c.   HOMER—*Iliad.* Bk. II. L. 253.
                        Bryant's trans.

On the king's gate the moss grew gray;
  The king came not. They call'd him dead;
And made his eldest son, one day,
  Slave in his father's stead.
  d.   HELEN HUNT JACKSON—*Coronation.*

God gives not kings the stile of Gods in vaine,
For on his throne his sceptre do they sway;
  And as their subjects ought them to obey,
So kings should feare and serve their God
  againe.
  e.   KING JAMES—*Sonnet Addressed to his
                        son, Prince Henry.*

The trappings of a monarchy would set up
an ordinary commonwealth.
  f.   SAM'L JOHNSON—*Life of Milton.*

A prince without letters is a Pilot without
eyes. All his government is groping.
  g.   BEN JONSON—*Discoveries. Illiteratus
                        Princeps.*

Princes that would their people should do well
Must at themselves begin, as at the head;
For men, by their example, pattern out
Their imitations, and regard of laws:
A virtuous court a world to virtue draws.
  h.   BEN JONSON—*Cynthia's Revels.* Act V.
                        Sc. 3.
They say Princes learn no art truly, but the
art of horsemanship. The reason is, the brave
beast is no flatterer. He will throw a Prince
as soon as his groom.
  i.   BEN JONSON—*Discoveries. Illiteratus
                        Princeps.*

They [Americans] equally detest the pageantry of a king and the supercilious hypocrisy of a bishop.
  j.   JUNIUS—*Letter XXXV.* Dec. 19, 1769.

Ah! vainest of all things
Is the gratitude of kings.
  k.   LONGFELLOW—*Belisarius.* St. 8.

                        A crown,
Golden in show, is but a wreath of thorns,
Brings dangers, troubles, cares, and sleepless
  nights
To him who wears the regal diadem.
  l.   MILTON—*Paradise Regained.* Bk. II.
                        L. 458.

His fair large front and eye sublime declared
Absolute rule; and hyacinthine locks
Round from his parted forelock manly hung
Clustering, but not beneath his shoulders
  broad.
  m.   MILTON—*Paradise Lost.* Bk. IV.
                        L. 300.

'Tis so much to be a king, that he only is so
by being so.
  n.   MONTAIGNE—*Essays. Of the
                        Inconveniences of Greatness.*

          A crown! what is it?
It is to bear the miseries of a people!
To hear their murmurs, feel their discontents,
And sink beneath a load of splendid care!
  o.   HANNAH MORE—*Daniel.* Pt. VI.

The King of France went up the hill,
  With twenty thousand men;
The King of France came down the hill,
  And ne'er went up again.
  p.   DICK TARLTON'S *Song. In a tract called
                        PIGGE'S Corantol; or, News from the
                        North.* Pub. London, 1642.

What is a king? a man condemn'd to bear
The public burthen of the nation's care.
  q.   PRIOR—*Solomon.* Bk. III. L. 275.

A merry monarch, scandalous and poor.
  r.   EARL OF ROCHESTER—*On the King.*

I am called the richest man in all the Christian
  world,
The sun ne'er sets on my dominions.
  s.   SCHILLER—*Don Carlos.* Act I. Sc. 6.

For monarchs seldom sigh in vain.
  t.   SCOTT—*Marmion.* Canto V. St. 9.

O Richard! O my king!
The universe forsakes thee!
  u.   MICHEL JEAN SEDAINE—*Sung at the
                        Dinner given to the French Soldiers in
                        the Opera Salon at Versailles,* Oct.
                        1, 1789.
A substitute shines brightly as a king
Until a king be by, and then his state
Empties itself, as doth an inland brook
Into the main of waters.
  v.   *Merchant of Venice.* Act V. Sc. 1.
                        L. 94.

Ay, every inch a king.
  w.   *King Lear.* Act IV. Sc. 6. L. 109.

Every subject's duty is the king's; but every
  subject's soul is his own.
  x.   *Henry V.* Act IV. Sc. 1. L. 186.

His legs bestrid the ocean; his rear'd arm
Crested the world: his voice was propertied
As all the tuned spheres, and that to friends;
But when he meant to quail and shake the
  orb,
He was as rattling thunder.
  y.   *Antony and Cleopatra.* Act V. Sc. 2.
                        L. 28.

　　　　Let us sit upon the ground
And tell sad stories of the death of kings:
How some have been depos'd, some slain in
　　war,
Some haunted by the ghosts they have depos'd,
Some poison'd by their wives, some sleeping
　　kill'd,
All murder'd.
　　a.　　*Richard II.* Act III. Sc. 2. L. 155.

　　　　　　　　O, how wretched
Is that poor man that hangs on princes'
　　favors!
There is, betwixt that smile we would aspire
　　to,
That sweet aspect of princes, and their ruin,
More pangs and fears than wars and women
　　have;
And when he falls, he falls like Lucifer,
Never to hope again.
　　b.　　*Henry VIII.* Act III. Sc. 2. L. 366.

She had all the royal makings of a queen;
As holy oil, Edward Confessor's crown,
The rod, and bird of peace, and all such em-
　　blems
Laid nobly on her.
　　c.　　*Henry VIII.* Act IV. Sc. 1. L. 87.

　　　　　　The gates of monarchs
Are arch'd so high that giants may jet through
And keep their impious turbans on.
　　d.　　*Cymbeline.* Act III. Sc. 3. L. 4.

　　　　　The king-becoming graces,
As justice, verity, temperance, stableness,
Bounty, perseverance, mercy, lowliness,
Devotion, patience, courage, fortitude,
I have no relish of them.
　　e.　　*Macbeth.* Act IV. Sc. 3. L. 91.

There's such divinity doth hedge a king,
That treason can but peep to what it would.
　　f.　　*Hamlet.* Act IV. Sc. 5. L. 123.

Uneasy lies the head that wears a crown.
　　g.　　*Henry IV.* Pt. II. Act III. Sc. 1.
　　　　　　　　　　　　　　　　　L. 31.
We are enforc'd to farm our royal realm;
The revenue whereof shall furnish us
For our affairs in hand.
　　h.　　*Richard II.* Act I. Sc. 4. L. 45.

Yet looks he like a king; behold, his eye,
As bright as is the eagle's, lightens forth
Controlling majesty.
　　i.　　*Richard II.* Act III. Sc. 3. L. 68.

Kings are like stars—they rise and set, they
　　have
The worship of the world, but no repose.
　　j.　　SHELLEY—*Hellas. Mahmud to Hassan.*
　　　　　　　　　　　　　　　　　L. 195.
Hail, glorious edifice, stupendous work!
God bless the Regent, and the Duke of York!
　　k.　　HORACE AND JAMES SMITH—*Rejected
　　　　　　Addresses. Loyal Effusion.* L. 1.

A prince, the moment he is crown'd,
Inherits every virtue sound,
As emblems of the sovereign power,
Like other baubles in the Tower:
Is generous, valiant, just, and wise,
And so continues till he dies.
　　l.　　SWIFT—*On Poetry.* L. 191.

Hener was the hero-king,
Heaven-born, dear to us,
Showing his shield
A shelter for peace.
　　m.　　ESAIAS TEGNÉR—*Fridthjof's Saga.*
　　　　　　　　　　　　　　Canto XXI. St. 7.

Broad-based upon her people's will,
And compassed by the inviolate sea.
　　n.　　TENNYSON—*To the Queen.* St. 9.

In that fierce light which beats upon a throne.
　　o.　　TENNYSON—*Idylls of the King.*
　　　　　　　　　　　　　　Dedication. L. 26.

And the King with his golden sceptre,
　　The Pope with Saint Peter's key,
Can never unlock the one little heart
　　That is opened only to me.
For I am the Lord of a Realm,
　　And I am Pope of a See;
Indeed I'm supreme in the kingdom
　　That is sitting, just now, on my knee.
　　p.　　C. H. WEBB—*The King and the Pope.*

A partial world will listen to my lays,
While Anna reigns, and sets a female name
Unrival'd in the glorious lists of fame.
　　q.　　YOUNG—*Force of Religion.* Bk. I.
　　　　　　　　　　　　　　　　　L. 6.

RUIN.

Should the whole frame of nature round him
　　break
　　In ruin and confusion hurled,
He, unconcerned, would hear the mighty
　　crack,
　　And stand secure amidst a falling world.
　　r.　　ADDISON—*Horace. Ode III.* Bk. III.

Stern Ruin's ploughshare drives elate,
Full on thy bloom.
　　s.　　BURNS—*To a Mountain Daisy.*

There is a temple in ruin stands,
Fashion'd by long forgotten hands:
Two or three columns, and many a stone,
Marble and granite, with grass o'ergrown!
　　t.　　BYRON—*Siege of Corinth.* St. 18.

The ruins of himself! now worn away
With age, yet still majestic in decay.
　　u.　　HOMER—*Odyssey.* Bk. XXIV.
　　　　　　　　　　　L. 271. Pope's trans.

For, to make deserts, God, who rules man-
　　kind,
Begins with kings, and ends the work by wind.
　　v.　　VICTOR HUGO—*The Vanished City.*

* * * For such a numerous host
Fled not in silence through the frighted
　　deep
With ruin upon ruin, rout on rout,
Confusion worse confounded.
　a.　　MILTON—*Paradise Lost.*　Bk. II.
　　　　　　　　　　　　　　　　L. 993.

Prostrate the beauteous ruin lies; and all
That shared its shelter, perish in its fall.
　b.　　WM. PITT—*The Poetry of the Anti-*
　　　　　　　　　　　　　　　　Jacobin.

　　　　I do love these ancient ruins.
We never tread upon them but we set
Our foot upon some reverend history.
　c.　　JOHN WEBSTER—*The Duchess of Malfi.*
　　　　　　　　　　　　　　Act V.　Sc. 3.

　　　　Final Ruin fiercely drives
Her ploughshare o'er creation.
　d.　　YOUNG—*Night Thoughts.*　Night IX.
　　　　　　　　　　　　　　　　L. 167.

RUMOR.

The flying rumours gather'd as they roll'd,
Scarce any tale was sooner heard than told;
And all who told it added something new,
And all who heard it made enlargements too.
　e.　　POPE—*Temple of Fame.*　L. 468.

I cannot tell how the truth may be;
I say the tale as 'twas said to me.
　f.　　SCOTT—*Lay of the Last Minstrel.*
　　　　　　　　　　　Canto II.　St. 22.

Rumour doth double, like the voice and echo,
The numbers of the fear'd.
　g.　　*Henry IV.*　Pt. II.　Act III.　Sc. 1.
　　　　　　　　　　　　　　　　L. 97.
　　　　　　　　　　Rumour is a pipe
Blown by surmises, jealousies, conjectures,
And of so easy and so plain a stop
That the blunt monster with uncounted heads,
The still-discordant wavering multitude,
Can play upon it.
　h.　　*Henry IV.*　Pt. II.　Act I.　Induction.
　　　　　　　　　　　　　　　　L. 15.

S.

SABBATH.

On Sundays, at the matin-chime,
The Alpine peasants, two and three,
　Climb up here to pray;
Burghers and dames, at summer's prime,
Ride out to church from Chamberry,
　　Dight with mantles gay,
But else it is a lonely time
Round the Church of Brou.
　i.　　MATTHEW ARNOLD—*The Church of*
　　　　　　　　　　Brou.　II.　St. 3.

Thou art my single day, God lends to leaven
What were all earth else, with a feel of heaven.
　j.　　ROBERT BROWNING—*Pippa Passes.*
　　　　　　　　　　　　　　　Sc. 1.

Of all the days that's in the week,
　I dearly love but one day,
And that's the day that comes betwixt
　A Saturday and Monday.
　k.　　HENRY CAREY—*Sally in Our Alley.*

How still the morning of the hallow'd day!
Mute is the voice of rural labour, hush'd
The ploughboy's whistle, and the milkmaid's
　　song.
　l.　　JAMES GRAHAME—*The Sabbath.*　Song.

Gently on tiptoe Sunday creeps,
Cheerfully from the stars he peeps,
Mortals are all asleep below,
None in the village hears him go;
E'en chanticleer keeps very still,
For Sunday whispered, 'twas his will.
　m.　　JOHN PETER HEBEL—*Sunday Morning.*

Sundaies observe: think when the bells do
　　chime,
'Tis angel's musick; therefore come not
　　late.
　n.　　HERBERT—*The Temple.*　*The Church*
　　　　　　　　　　　　　Porch.　St. 65.

The Sundaies of man's life,
Thredded together on time's string,
Make bracelets to adorn the wife
Of the eternal, glorious King.
On Sunday heaven's gates stand ope;
Blessings are plentiful and rife,
　　More plentiful than hope.
　o.　　HERBERT—*The Church.*　*Sunday.*

Now, really, this appears the common case
Of putting too much Sabbath into Sunday—
But what is your opinion, Mrs. Grundy?
　p.　　HOOD—*An Open Question.*　St. 1.

O day of rest! How beautiful, how fair,
How welcome to the weary and the old!
Day of the Lord! and truce to earthly
　　care!
Day of the Lord, as all our days should be!
　q.　　LONGFELLOW—*Christus.*　Pt. III.
　　　　　　　　John Endicott.　Act I.　Sc. 2.

So sang they, and the empyrean rung
With Hallelujahs.　Thus was Sabbath kept.
　r.　　MILTON—*Paradise Lost.*　Bk. VII.
　　　　　　　　　　　　　　　　L. 632.

For, bless the gude mon, gin he had his ain
　　way,
　He'd na let a cat on the Sabbath say
　　" mew ; "
Nae birdie maun whistle, nae lambie maun
　　play,
An' Phœbus himsel' could na travel that day,
　As he'd find a new Joshua in Andie Agnew.
a.　　Moore—*Sunday Ethics.* St. 3.

E'en Sunday shines no Sabbath day to me.
b.　　Pope—*Epistle to Dr. Arbuthnot.*
　　　　　　Prologue to the Satires. L. 12.

See Christians, Jews, one heavy sabbath keep,
And all the western world believe and sleep.
c.　　Pope—*The Dunciad.* Bk. III. L. 99.

The sabbaths of Eternity,
One sabbath deep and wide.
d.　　Tennyson—*St. Agnes' Eve.* St. 3.

SADNESS.

Child of mortality, whence comest thou?
Why is thy countenance sad, and why are
thine eyes red with weeping?
e.　　Anna Letitia Barbauld—*Hymns in
　　　　　　　　　　Prose.* XIII.

Of all tales 'tis the saddest—and more sad,
Because it makes us smile.
f.　　Byron—*Don Juan.* Canto XIII.
　　　　　　　　　　　　　St. 9.

A feeling of sadness and longing,
　That is not akin to pain,
And resembles sorrow only
　As the mist resembles the rain.
g.　　Longfellow—*The Day is Done.* St. 3.

They praise my rustling show, and never see
My heart is breaking for a little love.
h.　　Christina G. Rossetti—*To L. E. L.*

　　　Yet be sad, good brothers,
　　*　　*　　*　　*　　*　　*
Sorrow so royally in you appears,
That I will deeply put the fashion on.
i.　　*Henry IV.* Pt. II. Act V. Sc. 2. L. 49.

We look before and after,
　And sigh for what is not,
Our sincerest laughter
　With some pain is fraught:
Our sweetest songs are those that tell of sad-
　　dest thought.
j.　　Shelley—*To a Skylark.* St. 18.

'Tis impious in a good man to be sad.
k.　　Young—*Night Thoughts.* Night IV.
　　　　　　　　　　　　　L. 676.

SATIRE.

And coxcombs vanquish Berkeley by a grin.
l.　　John Brown—*An Essay on Satire
　　　　　Occasioned by the Death of Mr. Pope.*

Cervantes smiled Spain's chivalry away.
m.　　Byron—*Don Juan.* Canto XIII. St. 11.

Why should we fear; and what? The laws?
They all are armed in virtue's cause ;
And aiming at the self-same end,
Satire is always virtue's friend.
n.　　Churchill—*Ghost.* Bk. III. L. 943.

Unless a love of virtue light the flame,
Satire is, more than those he brands, to blame ;
He hides behind a magisterial air
His own offences, and strips others' bare.
o.　　Cowper—*Charity.* L. 490.

　That fellow would vulgarize the day of judgment.
p.　　Douglas Jerrold—*A Comic Author.*

Men are more satirical from vanity than
from malice.
q.　　La Rochefoucauld—*Maxims.* No. 508.

Damn with faint praise, assent with civil leer,
And without sneering, teach the rest to sneer ;
Willing to wound, and yet afraid to strike,
Just hint a fault, and hesitate dislike ;
Alike reserv'd to blame, or to commend,
A tim'rous foe, and a suspicious friend.
r.　　Pope—*Prologue to Satires.* L. 201.

Satire or sense, alas ! Can Sporus feel?
Who breaks a butterfly upon a wheel?
s.　　Pope—*Prologue to Satires.* L. 307.

Satire's my weapon, but I'm too discreet
To run amuck and tilt at all I meet.
t.　　Pope—*Second Book of Horace.*
　　　　　　Satire I. Bk. II. L. 71.

There are, to whom my satire seems too bold ;
Scarce to wise Peter complaisant enough,
And something said of Chartres much too
　　rough.
u.　　Pope—*Second Book of Horace.* Satire I.
　　　　　　　　　　　　　L. 2.

It is a pretty mocking of the life.
v.　　*Timon of Athens.* Act I. Sc. 1. L. 35.

The empty vessel makes the greatest sound.
w.　　*Henry V.* Act IV. Sc. 4. L. 73.

The tongues of mocking wenches are as keen
　As is the razor's edge invisible,
Cutting a smaller hair than may be seen
　Above the sense of sense; so sensible
Seemeth their conference ; their conceits have
　　wings
Fleeter than arrows, bullets, wind, thought,
　　swifter things.
x.　　*Love's Labour's Lost.* Act V. Sc. 2.
　　　　　　　　　　　　　L. 256.

SCANDAL.

Dead scandals form good subjects for dissec-
　　tion.
y.　　Byron—*Don Juan.* Canto I. St. 31.

Assail'd by scandal and the tongue of strife,
His only answer was a blameless life;
And he that forged, and he that threw the
　　dart,
Had each a brother's interest in his heart.
　　a.　　Cowper—*Hope.*　L. 570.

And though you duck them ne'er so long,
Not one salt drop e'er wets their tongue;
'Tis hence they scandal have at will,
And that this member ne'er lies still.
　　b.　　Gay—*The Mad Dog.*

And there's a lust in man no charm can tame
Of loudly publishing our neighbour's shame;
On eagles' wings immortal scandals fly,
While virtuous actions are but borne to die.
　　c.　　Juvenal—*Satires.*　IX.　Harvey's
　　　　　　　　　　　　　　　　trans.

Praise undeserved is scandal in disguise.
　　d.　　Pope—*Epistles of Horace.*　Ep. I.
　　　　　　　　　　　　　　Bk. II.　L. 413.

The mightier man, the mightier is the thing
What makes him honour'd, or begets him
　　hate;
For greatest scandal waits on greatest state.
　　e.　　*Lucrece.*　L. 1,004.

He rams his quill with scandal and with scoff,
But 'tis so very foul, it won't go off.
　　f.　　Young—*Epistles to Pope.*　Ep. I.
　　　　　　　　　　　　　　　　L. 199.

SCIENCE.

'Twas thus by the glare of false science be-
　　tray'd,
That leads to bewilder, and dazzles to blind.
　　g.　　Beattie—*The Hermit.*

O star-eyed Science, hast thou wander'd there,
To waft us home the message of despair?
　　h.　　Campbell—*Pleasures of Hope.*　Pt. II.
　　　　　　　　　　　　　　　　L. 325.

I value science—none can prize it more,
It gives ten thousand motives to adore:
Be it religious, as it ought to be,
The heart it humbles, and it bows the knee.
　　i.　　Abraham Coles—*The Microcosm.*
　　　　　　　　　　　　　　Christian Science.

While bright-eyed Science watches round.
　　j.　　Gray—*Ode for Music.*　Chorus.　L. 11.

For science is ＊ ＊ ＊ like virtue, its own
exceeding great reward.
　　k.　　Chas. Kingsley—*Health and*
　　　　　　　　　　　　Education.　Science.

One science only will one genius fit,
So vast is art, so narrow human wit.
　　l.　　Pope—*Essay on Criticism.*　Pt. I.　L. 60.

To the natural philosopher, to whom the
whole extent of nature belongs, all the individual branches of science constitute the links
of an endless chain, from which not one can
be detached without destroying the harmony
of the whole.
　　m.　　Friedrich Schoedler—*Treasury of*
　　　　　　　　　　　　Science.　Astronomy.

Science when well digested is nothing but
good sense and reason.
　　n.　　Stanislaus (King of Poland)—*Maxims.*
　　　　　　　　　　　　　　　　No. 43.

SCORN (*See* Contempt).

SCRIPTURE.

His studie was but litel on the Bible.
　　o.　　Chaucer—*Canterbury Tales.*　Prologue.
　　　　　　　　　　　　　　　　L. 4.

A glory gilds the sacred page,
　　Majestic like the sun,
It gives a light to every age,
　　It gives, but borrows none.
　　p.　　Cowper—*Olney Hymns.*　No. 30.

And that the Scriptures, though not every-
　　where
Free from corruption, or entire, or clear,
Are uncorrupt, sufficient, clear, entire
In all things which our needful faith require.
　　q.　　Dryden—*Religio Laici.*　L. 297.

Out from the heart of nature rolled
The burdens of the Bible old.
　　r.　　Emerson—*The Problem.*

The word unto the prophet spoken
Was writ on tablets yet unbroken;
The word by seers or sibyls told,
In groves of oak or fanes of gold,
Still floats upon the morning wind,
Still whispers to the willing mind.
　　s.　　Emerson—*The Problem.*　St. 6.

It was a common saying among the Puritans,
"Brown bread and the Gospel is good fare."
　　t.　　Mathew Henry—*Commentaries.*
　　　　　　　　　　　　　　Isaiah XXX.

Shallows where a lamb could wade and
depths where an elephant would drown.
　　u.　　Mathew Henry—*Of Solomon's Song.*

Bibles laid open, millions of surprises.
　　v.　　Herbert—*The Church.*　Sin.

Starres are poore books, and oftentimes do
　　misse;
This book of starres lights to eternal blisse.
　　w.　　Herbert—*The Church.*　*The Holy*
　　　　　　　　　　　　Scriptures.　Pt. II.

Most wondrous book! bright candle of the
    Lord!
Star of Eternity! The only star
By which the bark of man could navigate
The sea of life, and gain the coast of bliss
Securely.
    a.   Pollok—*Course of Time.* Bk. II.
                       L. 270.

Within that awful volume lies
The mystery of mysteries!
Happiest they of human race,
To whom God has granted grace
To read, to fear, to hope, to pray,
To lift the latch, and force the way:
And better had they ne'er been born,
Who read to doubt, or read to scorn.
    b.   Scott—*Monastery.* Ch. XII.

But Thy good word informs my soul
    How I may climb to heaven.
    c.   Watts—*The Excellency of the Bible.*

How glad the heathens would have been,
That worship idols, wood and stone,
If they the book of God had seen.
    d.   Watts—*Praise for the Gospel.*

The Bible is a book of faith, and a book of
doctrine, and a book of morals, and a book of
religion, of especial revelation from God.
    e.   Daniel Webster—*Completion of
             Bunker Hill Monument,* June 17, 1843.

SCULPTURE (*See* Occupations).

SEASONS (THE).

Our seasons have no fixed returns,
    Without our will they come and go;
At noon our sudden summer burns.
    Ere sunset all is snow.
    f.   Lowell—*To* ——.

Autumn to winter, winter into spring,
Spring into summer, summer into fall,—
So rolls the changing year, and so we change;
Motion so swift, we know not that we move.
    g.   D. M. Mulock—*Immutable.*

January grey is here,
    Like a sexton by her grave;
February bears the bier,
    March with grief doth howl and rave,
And April weeps—but, O ye hours!
Follow with May's fairest flowers.
    h.   Shelley—*Dirge for the Year.* St. 4.

    Ah! well away!
Seasons flower and fade.
    i.   Tennyson—*Every Day hath its Night.*

Spring.

For one swallow does not make spring, nor
    yet one fine day.
    j.   Aristotle—*Ethics.* I. 6.

Fair Spring! whose simplest promise more
    delights
Than all their largest wealth, and through the
    heart
    Each joy and new-born hope
    With softest influence breathes.
    k.   Anna Letitia Barbauld—*Ode to
             Spring.* St. 13.

But when shall spring visit the mouldering
    urn!
Oh, when shall it dawn on the night of the
    grave?
    l.   Beattie—*The Hermit.*

Fled now the sullen murmurs of the North,
The splendid raiment of the Spring peeps
    forth.
His universal green and the clear sky
Delight still more and more the gazing eye.
    m.   Bloomfield—*The Farmer's Boy.
             Spring.* St. 4.

Now Nature hangs her mantle green
    On every blooming tree,
And spreads her sheets o' daisies white
    Out o'er the grassy lea.
    n.   Burns—*Lament of Mary Queen of Scots.*

And the spring comes slowly up this way.
    o.   Coleridge—*Christabel.* Pt. I.

Spring hangs her infant blossoms on the trees,
Rock'd in the cradle of the western breeze.
    p.   Cowper—*Tirocinium.* L. 43.

If there comes a little thaw,
Still the air is chill and raw,
Here and there a patch of snow,
Dirtier than the ground below,
Dribbles down a marshy flood;
Ankle-deep you stick in mud
In the meadows while you sing,
    "This is Spring."
    q.   C. P. Cranch—*A Spring Growl.*

Starred forget-me-nots smile sweetly,
    Ring, blue-bells, ring!
Winning eye and heart completely,
    Sing, robin, sing!
All among the reeds and rushes,
Where the brook its music hushes,
Bright the calopogon blushes,—
    Laugh, O murmuring Spring!
    r.   Sarah F. Davis—*Summer Song.*

Daughter of heaven and earth, coy Spring,
With sudden passion languishing,
Teaching barren moors to smile,
Painting pictures mile on mile,
Holds a cup of cowslip wreaths
Whence a smokeless incense breathes.
　a.　　EMERSON—*May Day.*　St. 1.

Eternal Spring, with smiling Verdure here
Warms the mild Air, and crowns the youth-
　　ful Year.
　　*　　*　　*　　*　　*　　*
The Rose still blushes, and the vi'lets blow.
　b.　　SIR SAM'L GARTH—*The Dispensary.*
　　　　　　　　　Canto IV.　L. 298.

When Spring unlocks the flowers to paint the
　　laughing soil.
　c.　　BISHOP HEBER—*Hymn for Seventh
　　　　　　　　Sunday after Trinity.*

The beauteous eyes of the spring's fair night
With comfort are downward gazing.
　d.　　HEINE—*Book of Songs.　New Spring.
　　　　　　　　　No. 3.*

The spring's already at the gate
　With looks my care beguiling;
The country round appeareth straight
　A flower-garden smiling.
　e.　　HEINE—*Book of Songs.　Catherine.
　　　　　　　　　No. 6.*

I come, I come! ye have called me long,
I come o'er the mountain with light and
　　song:
Ye may trace my step o'er the wakening earth,
By the winds which tell of the violet's birth,
By the primrose-stars in the shadowy grass,
By the green leaves, opening as I pass.
　f.　　MRS. HEMANS—*Voice of Spring.*

Sweet Spring, full of sweet dayes and roses,
　A box where sweets compacted lie,
My musick shows ye have your closes,
　And all must die.
　g.　　HERBERT—*The Church.　Vertue.*　St. 3.

All flowers of Spring are not May's own;
　The crocus cannot often kiss her;
The snow-drop, ere she comes, has flown;—
　The earliest violets always miss her.
　h.　　LUCY LARCOM—*The Sister Months.*

And softly came the fair young queen
　O'er mountain, dale, and dell;
And where her golden light was seen
　An emerald shadow fell.
　　The good-wife oped the window wide,
　　　The good-man spanned his plough;
　'Tis time to run, 'tis time to ride,
　　For Spring is with us now.
　i.　　LELAND—*Spring.*

Came the Spring with all its splendor,
All its birds and all its blossoms,
All its flowers, and leaves, and grasses.
　j.　　LONGFELLOW—*Hiawatha.*　Pt. XXI.
　　　　　　　　　L. 109.

The lovely town was white with apple-blooms,
　And the great elms o'erhead
Dark shadows wove on their ærial looms,
　Shot through with golden thread.
　k.　　LONGFELLOW—*Hawthorne.*　St. 2.

Thus came the lovely spring with a rush of
　　blossoms and music,
Flooding the earth with flowers, and the air
　　with melodies vernal.
　l.　　LONGFELLOW—*Tales of a Wayside Inn.
　　　　　　Pt. III.　The Theologian's Tale.
　　　　　　　　　　Elizabeth.*

The holy spirit of the Spring
　Is working silently.
　m.　　GEORGE MACDONALD—*Songs of the
　　　　　　　　Spring Days.　Pt. II.*

On many a green branch swinging,
Little birdlets singing
Warble sweet notes in the air.
　　　Flowers fair
　　　There I found.
Green spread the meadow all around.
　n.　　NITHART—*Trans. in The Minnesinger
　　　　　　of Germany.　Spring-Song.*

Gentle Spring!—in sunshine clad,
　Well dost thou thy power display!
For Winter maketh the light heart sad,
　And thou,—thou makest the sad heart gay.
　o.　　CHARLES D'ORLÉANS—*Spring.
　　　　　　　　Longfellow's trans.*

Hark! the hours are softly calling
　Bidding Spring arise,
To listen to the rain-drops falling
　From the cloudy skies,
To listen to Earth's weary voices,
　Louder every day,
Bidding her no longer linger
　On her charm'd way;
But hasten to her task of beauty
　Scarcely yet begun.
　p.　　ADELAIDE A. PROCTER—*Spring.*

I wonder if the sap is stirring yet,
If wintry birds are dreaming of a mate,
If frozen snowdrops feel as yet the sun,
And crocus fires are kindling one by one.
　q.　　CHRISTINA G. ROSSETTI—*The First
　　　　　　　　Spring Day.*　St. 1.

There is no time like Spring,
When life's alive in everything,
　Before new nestlings sing,
Before cleft swallows speed their journey back
Along the trackless track.
　r.　　CHRISTINA G. ROSSETTI—*Spring.*　St. 3.

Spring flies, and with it all the train it leads;
And flowers, in fading, leave us but their
　　seeds.
　s.　　SCHILLER—*Farewell to the Reader.*

When daisies pied, and violets blue,
And lady-smocks all silver-white,
And cuckoo-buds of yellow hue
Do paint the meadows with delight.
 a. *Love's Labour's Lost.* Act V. Sc. 2.
          L. 904.

So forth issew'd the Seasons of the yeare:
First, lusty Spring, all dight in leaves of
  flowres
That freshly budded and new bloomes did
  beare,
In which a thousand birds had built their
  bowres
That sweetly sung to call forth paramours;
And in his hand a javelin he did beare,
And on his head (as fit for warlike stoures)
A guilt, engraven morion he did weare:
That, as some did him love, so others did him
  feare.
 b. SPENSER—*Faerie Queene.* Bk. VII.
   Canto VII. *Legend of Constancie.*
            St. 28.

It is the season now to go
About the country high and low,
Among the lilacs hand in hand,
And two by two in fairyland.
 c. ROBT. LOUIS STEVENSON—*Underwoods.*
     It is the Season Now to Go.

O tender time that love thinks long to see,
  Sweet foot of Spring that with her footfall
   sows
  Late snow-like flowery leavings of the
   snows,
Be not too long irresolute to be;
'O mother-month, where have they hidden
  thee?
 d. SWINBURNE—*A Vision of Spring in*
             Winter.

Dip down upon the northern shore,
O sweet new year, delaying long;
Thou doest expectant nature wrong,
Delaying long; delay no more.
 e. TENNYSON—*In Memoriam, 82.*

In the Spring a livelier iris changes on the
  burnish'd dove;
In the Spring a young man's fancy lightly
  turns to thoughts of love.
 f. TENNYSON—*Locksley Hall.* St. 9.

Once more the Heavenly Power
  Makes all things new,
And domes the red-plough'd hills
  With loving blue;
The blackbirds have their wills,
  The throstles too.
 g. TENNYSON—*Early Spring.*

The bee buzz'd up in the heat,
"I am faint for your honey, my sweet."
  The flower said, "Take it, my dear,
  For now is the Spring of the year.
   So come, come!"
    "Hum!"
And the bee buzz'd down from the heat.
 h. TENNYSON—*The Forester.* Act IV. Sc. 1.

The boyhood of the year.
 i. TENNYSON—*Sir Launcelot and Queen*
          Guinevere. St. 3.

Come, gentle Spring; ethereal Mildness, come!
 j. THOMSON—*Seasons. Spring.* L. 1.

Fair-handed Spring unbosoms every grace:
Throws out the snowdrop and the crocus
  first.
 k. THOMSON—*Seasons. Spring.* L. 527.

The Clouds consign their treasures to the
  fields,
And, softly shaking on the dimpled pool,
Prelusive drops, let all their moisture flow
In large effusion, o'er the freshen'd world.
 l. THOMSON—*Seasons. Spring.* L. 173.

'Tis spring-time on the eastern hills!
Like torrents gush the summer rills;
Through winter's moss and dry dead leaves
The bladed grass revives and lives,
Pushes the mouldering waste away,
And glimpses to the April day.
 m. WHITTIER—*Mogg Megone.* Pt. III.

And all the woods are alive with the murmur
   and sound of spring,
  And the rosebud breaks into pink on the
   climbing briar,
  And the crocus bed is a quivering moon of
   fire
Girdled round with the belt of an amethyst
  ring.
 n. OSCAR WILDE—*Magdalen Walks.*

The Spring is here—the delicate footed May,
With its slight fingers full of leaves and
  flowers,
And with it comes a thirst to be away,
In lovelier scenes to pass these sweeter hours.
 o. N. P. WILLIS—*Spring.*

Summer.

In lang, lang days o' simmer,
  When the clear and cloudless sky
Refuses ae wee drap o' rain
  To Nature parched and dry,
The genial night, wi' balmy breath,
  Gars verdure spring anew,
An' ilka blade o' grass
  Keps its ain drap o' dew.
 p. BALLANTINE—*Its Ain Drap o' Dew.*

O thou who passest through our valleys in
Thy strength, curb thy fierce steeds, allay the
  heat
That flames from their large nostrils! Thou,
  O Summer,
Oft pitchest here thy golden tent, and oft
Beneath our oaks hast slept, while we beheld
With joy thy ruddy limbs and flourishing
  hair.
 q. WM. BLAKE—*To Summer.*

But how unlike to April's closing days!
High climbs the sun, and darts his powerful
　　rays;
Whitens the fresh drawn mould and pierces
　　through
The cumbrous clods that tumble round the
　　plough.
　　a.　　Bloomfield—*The Farmer's Boy.*
　　　　　　　　　　　Summer. St. 1.

　　　　　　The sun has drunk
The dew that lay upon the morning grass;
There is no rustling in the lofty elm
That canopies my dwelling, and its shade
Scarce cools me.　All is silent save the faint
And interrupted murmur of the bee,
Settling on the sick flowers, and then again
Instantly on the wing.
　　b.　　Bryant—*Summer Wind.*

Now simmer blinks on flowery braes,
And o'er the crystal streamlet plays.
　　c.　　Burns—*The Birks of Aberfeldy.*

The isles of Greece, the isles of Greece!
　Where burning Sappho loved and sung.
Where grew the arts of war and peace,—
　Where Delos rose, and Phœbus sprung!
Eternal summer gilds them yet,
But all, except their sun, is set.
　　d.　　Byron—*Don Juan.* Canto III. St. 86.

The Indian Summer, the dead Summer's soul.
　　e.　　Mary Clemmer—*Presence.* L. 62.

All green and fair the Summer lies,
　Just budded from the bud of Spring,
With tender blue of wistful skies,
　And winds which softly sing.
　　f.　　Susan Coolidge—*Menace.*

Dust on thy mantle! dust,
　Bright Summer, on thy livery of green!
A tarnish as of rust,
　Dims thy late brilliant sheen;
And thy young glories,—leaf and bud and
　　flower,—
Change cometh over them with every hour.
　　g.　　Wm. D. Gallagher—*August.*

From all the misty morning air, there comes
　　a summer sound,
A murmur as of waters from skies, and trees,
　　and ground.
The birds they sing upon the wing, the pigeons
　　bill and coo.
　　h.　　R. W. Gilder—*A Midsummer Song.*
　　　　　　　　　　　　　St. 2.
Oh, father's gone to market-town, he was up
　　before the day,
And Jamie's after robins, and the man is
　　making hay,
And whistling down the hollow goes the boy
　　that minds the mill,
While mother from the kitchen door is calling
　　with a will,
"Polly!—Polly!—The cows are in the corn!
　　Oh, where's Polly?"
　　i.　　R. W. Gilder—*A Midsummer Song.*

Thou'rt bearing hence thy roses,
　Glad summer, fare thee well!
Thou'rt singing thy last melodies
　In every wood and dell.
　　j.　　Mrs. Hemans—*The Parting of Summer.*

Here is the ghost
Of a summer that lived for us,
Here is a promise
Of summer to be.
　　k.　　Wm. Ernest Henley—*Rhymes and*
　　　　　　　　　　　　　Rhythms.

O for a lodge in a garden of cucumbers!
　O for an iceberg or two at control!
O for a vale that at midday the dew cumbers!
　O for a pleasure trip up to the pole!
　　l.　　Rossiter Johnson—*Ninety-Nine in the*
　　　　　　　　　　　　　Shade.

O summer day beside the joyous sea!
O summer day so wonderful and white,
So full of gladness and so full of pain!
Forever and forever shalt thou be
To some the gravestone of a dead delight,
To some the landmark of a new domain.
　　m.　　Longfellow—*A Summer Day by the*
　　　　　　　　　　　　　Sea. L. 9.

　　　　　　That beautiful season
* * *　the Summer of All-Saints!
Filled was the air with a dreamy and magical
　　light; and the landscape
Lay as if new created in all the freshness of
　　childhood.
　　n.　　Longfellow—*Evangeline.* Pt. I. St. 2.

Very hot and still the air was,
Very smooth the gliding river,
Motionless the sleeping shadows.
　　o.　　Longfellow—*Hiawatha.*　Pt. XVIII.
　　　　　　　　　　　　　L. 54.

But see, the shepherds shun the noonday heat,
The lowing herds to murmuring brooks
　　retreat,
To closer shades the panting flocks remove;
Ye gods! and is there no relief for love?
　　p.　　Pope—*Pastorals.* *Summer.*

Before green apples blush,
　Before green nuts embrown,
Why, one day in the country
　Is worth a month in town.
　　q.　　Christina G. Rossetti—*Summer.*

It's surely summer, for there's a swallow:
Come one swallow, his mate will follow,
The bird race quicken and wheel and thicken.
　　r.　　Christina G. Rossetti—*A Bird Song.*

The summer dawn's reflected hue
To purple changed Loch Katrine blue,
Mildly and soft the western breeze
Just kiss'd the lake, just stirr'd the trees,
And the pleased lake, like maiden coy,
Trembled but dimpled not for joy.
　　s.　　Scott—*Lady of the Lake.* Canto III.
　　　　　　　　　　　　　St. 2.

Summer's parching heat.
   a.   *Henry VI.* Pt. II. Act I. Sc. 1. L. 81.

The middle summer's spring.
   b.   *Midsummer-Night's Dream.* Act II.
                       Sc. 1. L. 82.

Thy eternal summer shall not fade.
   c.   *Sonnet XVIII.*

Heat, ma'am! it was so dreadful here, that
I found there was nothing left for it but to
take off my flesh and sit in my bones.
   d.   SYDNEY SMITH—*Lady Holland's
                 Memoir.* Vol. I. P. 267.

Then came the jolly sommer, being dight
In a thin silken cassock, coloured greene,
That was unlyned all, to be more light.
   e.   SPENSER—*Faerie Queene.* Bk. VII.
                 Canto VII. St. 29.

All-conquering Heat, O, intermit thy wrath!
And on my throbbing temples, potent thus,
Beam not so fierce! incessant still you flow,
And still another fervent flood succeeds,
Pour'd on the head profuse. In vain I sigh,
And restless turn, and look around for night;
Night is far off; and hotter Hours approach.
   f.   THOMSON—*Seasons. Summer.* L. 451.

From brightening fields of ether fair-disclosed,
Child of the Sun, refulgent Summer comes,
In pride of youth, and felt through Nature's
   depth;
He comes, attended by the sultry Hours,
And ever-fanning breezes, on his way.
   g.   THOMSON—*Seasons. Summer.* L. 1.

Patient of thirst and toil,
Son of the desert, e'en the Camel feels,
Shot through his wither'd heart, the fiery blast.
   h.   THOMSON—*Seasons. Summer.* L. 965.

Autumn.

Now Autumn's fire burns slowly along the
   woods,
And day by day the dead leaves fall and melt,
And night by night the monitory blast
Wails in the key-hole, telling how it pass'd
O'er empty fields, or upland solitudes,
Or grim wide wave; and now the power is felt
Of melancholy, tenderer in its moods
Than any joy indulgent Summer dealt.
   i.   WILLIAM ALLINGHAM—*Day and Night
              Songs. Autumnal Sonnet.*

O Autumn, laden with fruit, and stained
With the blood of the grape, pass not, but sit
Beneath my shady roof; there thou mayest
   rest
And tune thy jolly voice to my fresh pipe,
And all the daughters of the year shall dance!
Sing now the lusty song of fruits and flowers.
   j.   WILLIAM BLAKE—*To Autumn.* St. 1.

Autumn wins you best by this, its mute
Appeal to sympathy for its decay.
   k.   ROBERT BROWNING—*Paracelsus.* Sc. 1.

Glorious are the woods in their latest gold and
   crimson,
Yet our full-leaved willows are in their
   freshest green.
Such a kindly autumn, so mercifully dealing
With the growths of summer, I never yet
   have seen.
   l.   BRYANT—*Third of November.*

The melancholy days are come, the saddest of
   the year,
Of wailing winds, and naked woods, and
   meadows brown and sear.
   m.   BRYANT—*The Death of the Flowers.*

All-cheering Plenty, with her flowing horn,
Led yellow Autumn, wreath'd with nodding
   corn.
   n.   BURNS—*Brigs of Ayr.* L. 221.

The mellow autumn came, and with it came
   The promised party, to enjoy its sweets.
The corn is cut, the manor full of game;
   The pointer ranges, and the sportsman beats
In russet jacket;—lynx-like is his aim;
   Full grows his bag, and wonderful his feats.
Ah, nutbrown partridges! Ah, brilliant
   pheasants!
And ah, ye poachers!—'Tis no sport for
   peasants.
   o.   BYRON—*Don Juan.* Canto XIII.
                            St. 75.

Yellow, mellow, ripened days,
   Sheltered in a golden coating;
O'er the dreamy, listless haze,
   White and dainty cloudlets floating;
Winking at the blushing trees,
   And the sombre, furrowed fallow;
Smiling at the airy ease,
   Of the southward flying swallow.
Sweet and smiling are thy ways,
   Beauteous, golden Autumn days.
   p.   WILL CARLETON—*Autumn Days.*

The summer's throbbing chant is done
And mute the choral antiphon;
The birds have left the shivering pines
To flit among the trellised vines,
Or fan the air with scented plumes
Amid the love-sick orange blooms,
And thou art here alone,—alone,—
   Sing, little bird! the rest have flown.
   q.   O. W. HOLMES—*Songs of Many Seasons.
              An Old-Year Song.* St. 4.

I saw old Autumn in the misty morn
Stand shadowless like silence, listening
To silence, for no lonely bird would sing
Into his hollow ear from woods forlorn,
Nor lowly hedge nor solitary thorn;—
Shaking his languid locks all dewy bright
With tangled gossamer that fell by night,
   Pearling his coronet of golden corn.
   r.   HOOD—*Ode. Autumn.*

The Autumn is old;
　　The sere leaves are flying;
He hath gather'd up gold,
　　And now he is dying;—
　　Old age, begin sighing!
　　a.　　Hood—*Autumn.*

The year's in the wane;
　　There is nothing adorning;
The night has no eve,
　　And the day has no morning;
　　Cold winter gives warning!
　　b.　　Hood—*Autumn.*

Season of mists and mellow fruitfulness!
　　Close bosom-friend of the maturing sun;
Conspiring with him how to load and bless
　　With fruit the vines that round the thatch-
　　　　eaves run;
To bend with apples the moss'd cottage trees,
And fill all fruit with ripeness to the core,
　　c.　　Keats—*To Autumn.*

Gone are the birds that were our summer
　　guests,
With the last sheaves return the laboring
　　wains!
　　d.　　Longfellow—*The Harvest Moon.* L. 7.

It was Autumn, and incessant
　　Piped the quails from shocks and sheaves,
And, like living coals, the apples
　　Burned among the withering leaves.
　　e.　　Longfellow—*Pegasus in Pound.*

　　What visionary tints the year puts on,
When falling leaves falter through motion-
　　less air
　　Or numbly cling and shiver to be gone!
How shimmer the low flats and pastures
　　bare,
　　As with her nectar Hebe Autumn fills
The bowl between me and those distant
　　hills,
And smiles and shakes abroad her misty,
　　tremulous hair!
　　f.　　Lowell—*An Indian Summer Reverie.*

Every season hath its pleasures;
　　Spring may boast her flowery prime,
Yet the vineyard's ruby treasures
　　Brighten Autumn's sob'rer time.
　　g.　　Moore—*Spring and Autumn.*

　　　　Autumn
Into earth's lap does throw
Brown apples gay in a game of play,
　　As the equinoctials blow.
　　h.　　D. M. Mulock—*October.*

Sorrow and the scarlet leaf,
　　Sad thoughts and sunny weather;
Ah me! this glory and this grief
　　Agree not well together!
　　i.　　T. W. Parsons—*A Song for September.*

Thus sung the shepherds till th' approach of
　　night,
The skies yet blushing with departing light,
When falling dews with spangles deck'd the
　　glade,
And the low sun had lengthened every shade.
　　j.　　Pope—*Pastorals. Autumn.* Last lines.

Ye flowers that drop, forsaken by the spring,
Ye birds that, left by summer, cease to sing,
Ye trees that fade, when Autumn heats re-
　　move,
Say, is not absence death to those who love?
　　k.　　Pope—*Autumn.* L. 27.

Grieve, O ye Autumn Winds!
　　Summer lies low;
The rose's trembling leaves will soon be shed,
　　For she that loved her so,
　　　　Alas! is dead,
And one by one her loving children go.
　　l.　　Adelaide A. Procter—*Lament for the
　　　　　　　　　　Summer.*

Autumn is a weathercock
　　Blown every way.
　　m.　　Christina G. Rossetti—*Summer.*

This sunlight shames November where he
　　grieves
　　In dead red leaves, and will not let him
　　shun
　　The day, though bough with bough be over-
　　run.
But with a blessing every glade receives
　　High salutation.
　　n.　　Dante Gabriel Rossetti—*Autumn
　　　　　　　　　　　　Idleness.*

The warm sun is failing, the bleak wind is
　　wailing,
The bare boughs are sighing, the pale flowers
　　are dying;
　　And the year
On the earth her deathbed, in a shroud of
　　leaves dead,
　　Is lying.
Come, months, come away,
From November to May,
In your saddest array;
Follow the bier
Of the dead cold year,
And like dim shadows watch by her se-
　　pulchre.
　　o.　　Shelley—*Autumn. A Dirge.*

Divinest Autumn! who may paint thee best,
　　Forever changeful o'er the changeful globe?
Who guess thy certain crown, thy favorite
　　crest,
　　The fashion of thy many-colored robe?
　　p.　　R. H. Stoddard—*Autumn.*

Cold autumn, wan with wrath of wind and
　　rain,
Saw pass a soul sweet as the sovereign tune
That death smote silent when he smote again.
　　q.　　Swinburne—*Autumn and Winter.* I.

Autumn has come;
Storming now heaveth the deep sea with
    foam,
Yet would I gratefully lie there,
Willingly die there.
> *a.*   ESAÍAS TEGNÉR—*Fridthjof's Saga.*
> *Ingeborg's Lament.*

How are the veins of thee, Autumn, laden?
        Umbered juices,
        And pulpèd oozes
Pappy out of the cherry-bruises,
Froth the veins of thee, wild, wild maiden !
        With hair that musters
        In globèd clusters,
In tumbling clusters, like swarthy grapes,
Round thy brow and thine ears o'ershaden ;
With the burning darkness of eyes like pansies,
        Like velvet pansies
        Where through escapes
The splendid might of thy conflagrate fancies ;
With robe gold-tawny not hiding the shapes
        Of the feet whereunto it falleth down,
        Thy naked feet unsandalled ;
With robe gold-tawny that does not veil
        Feet where the red
        Is meshed in the brown,
Like a rubied sun in a Venice-sail.
> *b.*   FRANCIS THOMPSON—*A Corymbus for*
> *Autumn.* St. 2.

Crown'd with the sickle and the wheaten sheaf,
While Autumn, nodding o'er the yellow
    plain,
Comes jovial on.
> *c.*   THOMSON—*Seasons. Autumn.* L. 1.

I love to wander through the woodlands
    hoary
In the soft light of an autumnal day,
When Summer gathers up her robes of glory,
And like a dream of beauty glides away.
> *d.*   SARAH HELEN WHITMAN—*Still Day in*
> *Autumn.*

And Autumn, in his leafless bowers,
    Is waiting for the Winter's snow.
> *e.*   WHITTIER—*Autumn Thoughts.*

Autumn's earliest frost had given
    To the woods below
Hues of beauty, such as heaven
    Lendeth to its bow ;
And the soft breeze from the west
Scarcely broke their dreamy rest.
> *f.*   WHITTIER—*The Fountain.* St. 9.

Winter.

These Winter nights against my window-pane
Nature with busy pencil draws designs
Of ferns and blossoms and fine spray of pines,
Oak-leaf and acorn and fantastic vines,
Which she will make when summer comes
    again—
Quaint arabesques in argent, flat and cold,
Like curious Chinese etchings.
> *g.*   T. B. ALDRICH—*Frost-Work.*

35

O Winter! bar thine adamantine doors :
The north is thine ; there hast thou built thy
    dark,
Deep-founded habitation. Shake not thy
    roofs,
Nor bend thy pillars with thine iron car.
> *h.*   WILLIAM BLAKE—*To Winter.*

When now, unsparing as the scourge of war,
Blasts follow blasts and groves dismantled
    roar ;
Around their home the storm-pinched cattle
    lows,
No nourishment in frozen pasture grows ;
Yet frozen pastures every morn resound
With fair abundance thund'ring to the
    ground.
> *i.*   BLOOMFIELD—*The Farmer's Boy.*
> *Winter.* St. 2.

    Look ! the massy trunks
Are cased in the pure crystal ; each light spray,
Nodding and tinkling in the breath of heaven,
Is studded with its trembling water-drops,
That glimmer with an amethystine light.
> *j.*   BRYANT—*A Winter Piece.* L. 66.

Yet all how beautiful ! Pillars of pearl
Propping the cliffs above, stalactites bright
From the ice roof depending ; and beneath,
Grottoes and temples with their crystal spires
And gleaming columns radiant in the sun.
> *k.*   WM. HENRY BURLEIGH—*Winter.*

The frost performs its secret ministry,
Unhelped by any wind.
> *l.*   COLERIDGE—*Frost at Midnight.* L. 1.

    Every Fern is tucked and set,
'Neath coverlet,
    Downy and soft and warm.
> *m.*   SUSAN COOLIDGE—*Time to Go.*

O Winter! ruler of the inverted year,
  *   *   *   *   *   *
I crown thee king of intimate delights,
Fireside enjoyments, home-born happiness,
And all the comforts that the lowly roof
Of undisturb'd Retirement, and the hours
Of long uninterrupted evening, know.
> *n.*   COWPER—*The Task.* Bk. IV. L. 120.

    There's silence in the harvest field ;
    And blackness in the mountain glen,
And cloud that will not pass away
From the hill-tops for many a day ;
    And stillness round the homes of men.
> *o.*   MARY HOWITT—*Winter.*

'Tis winter, yet there is no sound
    Along the air
Of winds along their battle-ground ;
    But gently there
The snow is falling,—all around
    How fair, how fair !
> *p.*   RALPH HOYT—*Snow. A Winter Sketch.*

On a lone winter evening, when the frost
Has wrought a silence.
　　a.　　KEATS—*On the Grasshopper and Cricket.*

His breath like silver arrows pierced the air,
The naked earth crouched shuddering at his
　　feet,
His finger on all flowing waters sweet
Forbidding lay—motion nor sound was
　　there :—
Nature was frozen dead,—and still and slow,
A winding sheet fell o'er her body fair,
Flaky and soft, from his wide wings of snow.
　　b.　　FRANCES ANNE KEMBLE—*Winter.* L. 9.

　　　　　　　　Every winter,
When the great sun has turned his face away,
The earth goes down into a vale of grief,
And fasts, and weeps, and shrouds herself in
　　sables,
Leaving her wedding-garlands to decay—
Then leaps in spring to his returning kisses.
　　c.　　CHARLES KINGSLEY—*Saint's Tragedy.*
　　　　　　　　　　　　Act III. Sc. 1.

Up rose the wild old winter-king,
　　And shook his beard of snow ;
" I hear the first young hare-bell ring,
　　'Tis time for me to go !
　　　Northward o'er the icy rocks,
　　　Northward o'er the sea,
My daughter comes with sunny locks :
　　This land's too warm for me ! "
　　d.　　LELAND—*Spring.*

Where, twisted round the barren oak,
　　The summer vine in beauty clung,
And summer winds the stillness broke,
　　The crystal icicle is hung.
　　e.　　LONGFELLOW—*Woods in Winter.* St. 3.

But see, Orion sheds unwholesome dews ;
Arise, the pines a noxious shade diffuse ;
Sharp Boreas blows, and nature feels decay,
Time conquers all, and we must time obey.
　　f.　　POPE—*Ode to Winter.* L. 85.

Here feel we but the penalty of Adam,
The seasons' difference, as the icy fang
And churlish chiding of the winter's wind,
Which, when it bites and blows upon my body,
Even till I shrink with cold, I smile and say,
" This is no flattery."
　　g.　　*As You Like It.* Act II. Sc. 1. L. 5.

When icicles hang by the wall,
And Dick, the shepherd, blows his nail,
And Tom bears logs into the hall,
And milk comes frozen home in pail,
When blood is nipp'd and ways be foul,
Then nightly sings the staring owl,
　　　　Tu-whit ;
Tu-who, a merry note,
While greasy Joan doth keel the pot.
　　h.　　*Love's Labour's Lost.* Act V. Sc. 2.
　　　　　　　　　　　　　　　L. 922.

Winter's not gone yet, if the wild-geese fly
　　that way.
　　i.　　*King Lear.* Act II. Sc. 4. L 46.

In winter, when the dismal rain
　　Came down in slanting lines,
And Wind, that grand old harper, smote
　　His thunder-harp of pines.
　　j.　　ALEXANDER SMITH—*A Life Drama.*
　　　　　　　　　　　　　　　Sc. 2.

Green moss shines there with ice encased ;
The long grass bends its spear-like form ;
And lovely is the silvery scene
When faint the sun-beams smile.
　　k.　　SOUTHEY—*Written Dec. 1.* St. 9.

Lastly came Winter cloathed all in frize,
Chattering his teeth for cold that did him
　　chill ;
Whilst on his hoary beard his breath did freese,
And the dull drops, that from his purpled bill
As from a limebeck did adown distill :
In his right hand a tipped staffe he held,
With which his feeble steps he stayed still ;
For he was faint with cold, and weak with
　　eld ;
That scarce his loosed limbes he hable was to
　　weld.
　　l.　　SPENSER—*Faerie Queene.* Canto VII.
　　　　　　　　　Legend of Constancie. St. 31.

Under the snowdrifts the blossoms are sleep-
　　ing,
Dreaming their dreams of sunshine and June,
Down in the hush of their quiet they're
　　keeping
Trills from the throstle's wild summer-sung
　　tune.
　　m.　　HARRIET PRESCOTT SPOFFORD—*Under
　　　　　　　　　　　　the Snowdrifts.*

Dread Winter spreads his latest glooms,
And reigns, tremendous, o'er the conquer'd
　　Year.
How dead the vegetable kingdom lies !
How dumb the tuneful ! Horror wide extends
His desolate domain.
　　n.　　THOMSON—*Seasons. Winter.* L. 1,024.

See, Winter comes, to rule the varied year,
Sullen and sad, with all his rising train ;
Vapors, and Clouds, and Storms.
　　o.　　THOMSON—*Seasons. Winter.* L. 1.

Through the hush'd air the whitening Shower
　　descends,
At first thin wavering ; till at last the Flakes
Fall broad, and wide, and fast, dimming the
　　day
With a continual flow. The cherished Fields
Put on their winter-robe of purest white.
'Tis brightness all ; save where the new Snow
　　melts
Along the mazy current.
　　p.　　THOMSON—*Seasons. Winter.* L. 229.

Make we here our camp of winter;
  And, through sleet and snow,
Pitchy knot and beechen splinter
  On our hearth shall glow.
Here, with mirth to lighten duty,
  We shall lack alone
Woman's smile and girlhood's beauty,
  Childhood's lisping tone.
  a.   WHITTIER—*Lumbermen.* St. 8.

What miracle of weird transforming
Is this wild work of frost and light,
This glimpse of glory infinite?
  b.   WHITTIER—*The Pageant.* St. 8.

Stern Winter loves a dirge-like sound.
  c.   WORDSWORTH—*On the Power of Sound.*
                                      St. 12.

SECRECY.

How can we expect another to keep our
secret if we cannot keep it ourselves.
  d.   LA ROCHEFOUCAULD—*Maxims.* No. 90.

A secret at home is like rocks under tide.
  e.   D. M. MULOCK—*Magnus and Morna.*
                                      Sc. 2.

And whatsoever else shall hap to-night,
Give it an understanding, but no tongue.
  f.   *Hamlet.* Act I. Sc. 2. L. 249.

            But that I am forbid,
To tell the secrets of my prison-house,
I could a tale unfold whose lightest word
Would harrow up thy soul.
  g.   *Hamlet.* Act I. Sc. 5. L. 13.

If you have hitherto conceal'd this sight,
Let it be tenable in your silence still.
  h.   *Hamlet.* Act I. Sc. 2. L. 247.

Two may keep counsel, putting one away.
  i.   *Romeo and Juliet.* Act II. Sc. 4.
                                      L. 209.

Two may keep counsel when the third's away.
  j.   *Titus Andronicus.* Act IV. Sc. 2.
                                      L. 144.

SELF-EXAMINATION.

Summe up at night what thou hast done by
    day ;
And in the morning what thou hast to do.
Dresse and undresse thy soul ; mark the
    decay
And growth of it : if, with thy watch, that too
Be down, then winde up both ; since we
    shall be
Most surely judg'd, make thy accounts
    agree.
  k.   HERBERT—*The Temple.* *The Church
            Porch.* Next to last stanza.

One self-approving hour whole years out-
    weighs
Of stupid starers and of loud huzzas.
  l.   POPE—*Essay on Man.* Ep. IV. L. 249.

            Go to your bosom ;
Knock there, and ask your heart what it doth
    know.
  m.   *Measure for Measure.* Act II. Sc. 2.
                                      L. 136.

            Speak no more :
Thou turn'st mine eyes into my very soul ;
And there I see such black and grained spots
As will not leave their tinct.
  n.   *Hamlet.* Act III. Sc. 4. L. 88.

There is a luxury in self-dispraise ;
And inward self-disparagement affords
To meditative spleen a grateful feast.
  o.   WORDSWORTH—*The Excursion.* Bk. IV.

'Tis greatly wise to talk with our past hours ;
And ask them what report they bore to
    heaven :
And how they might have borne more wel-
    come news.
  p.   YOUNG—*Night Thoughts.* Night II.
                                      L. 376.

SELFISHNESS.

It is difficult to persuade mankind that the
love of virtue is the love of themselves.
  q.   CICERO.

Where all are selfish, the sage is no better
than the fool, and only rather more dangerous.
  r.   FROUDE—*Short Studies on Great
            Subjects. Party Politics.*

Despite those titles, power, and pelf,
The wretch, concentred all in self,
Living, shall forfeit fair renown,
And, doubly dying, shall go down
To the vile dust from whence he sprung,
Unwept, unhonour'd and unsung.
  s.   SCOTT—*Lay of the Last Minstrel.*
                          Canto VI. St. 1.

What need we any spur but our own cause,
To prick us to redress?
  t.   *Julius Cæsar.* Act II. Sc. 1. L. 123.

Love took up the harp of Life, and smote on
    all the chords with might;
Smote the chord of Self, that, trembling,
    pass'd in music out of sight.
  u.   TENNYSON—*Locksley Hall.* L. 33.

SELF-LOVE.

Self-love is a principle of action ; but among
no class of human beings has nature so pro-
fusely distributed this principle of life and
action as through the whole sensitive family
of genius.
  v.   ISAAC DISRAELI—*Literary Character of
            Men of Genius.* Ch. XV.

A gentleman is one who understands and shows every mark of deference to the claims of self-love in others, and exacts it in return from them.

    a.   HAZLITT—*Table Talk. On the Look of a Gentleman.*

Self-love is the greatest of all flatterers.

    b.   LA ROCHEFOUCAULD—*Maxims.* No. 3.

To observations which ourselves we make,
We grow more partial for th' observer's sake.

    c.   POPE—*Moral Essays.* Ep. I. L. 11.

I to myself am dearer than a friend.

    d.   *Two Gentlemen of Verona.* Act II. Sc. 6. L. 23.

O villainous! I have looked upon the world for four times seven years; and since I could distinguish betwixt a benefit and an injury, I never found man that knew how to love himself.

    e.   *Othello.* Act I. Sc. 3. L. 312.

Self-love, my liege, is not so vile a sin
As self-neglecting.

    f.   *Henry V.* Act II. Sc. 4. L. 74.

This self-love is the instrument of our preservation; it resembles the provision for the perpetuity of mankind:—it is necessary, it is dear to us, it gives us pleasure, and we must conceal it.

    g.   VOLTAIRE—*A Philosophical Dictionary. Self-Love.*

SENSE.

If Poverty is the Mother of Crimes, want of Sense is the Father.

    h.   DE LA BRUYÈRE—*The Characters or Manners of the Present Age.* Vol. II. Ch. II,

He had used the word in its Pickwickian sense.

    i.   DICKENS—*Pickwick Papers.* Ch. I.

Him of the western dome, whose weighty sense
Flows in fit words and heavenly eloquence.

    j.   DRYDEN—*Absalom and Achitophel.* Pt. I. L. 868.

Good sense, which only is the gift of Heaven,
And though no science, fairly worth the seven.

    k.   POPE—*Moral Essays.* Ep. IV. L. 43.

'Tis use alone that sanctifies expense
And splendor borrows all her rays from sense.

    l.   POPE—*Moral Essays.* Ep. IV. L. 179.

What thin partitions sense from thought divide.

    m.   POPE—*Essay on Man.* Ep. I. L. 226.

Sense is our helmet, wit is but the plume;
The plume exposes, 'tis our helmet saves.
Sense is the diamond, weighty, solid, sound;
When cut by wit, it casts a brighter beam;
Yet, wit apart, it is a diamond still.

    n.   YOUNG—*Night Thoughts.* Night VIII. L. 1,254.

SENSIBILITY.

Chords that vibrate sweetest pleasure
Thrill the deepest notes of wo.

    o.   BURNS—*Sweet Sensibility.*

Susceptible persons are more affected by a change of tone than by unexpected words.

    p.   GEORGE ELIOT—*Adam Bede.* Ch. XXVII.

Nor peace, nor ease the heart can know
Which, like the needle true,
Turns at the touch of joy or woe,
But turning, trembles too.

    q.   MRS. GREVILLE—*A Prayer for Indifference.*

And the heart that is soonest awake to the flowers
Is always the first to be touch'd by the thorns.

    r.   MOORE—*O Think Not My Spirits.*

It seem'd as if each thought and look
And motion were that minute chain'd
Fast to the spot such root she took,
And—like a sunflower by a brook,
With face upturn'd—so still remain'd!

    s.   MOORE—*Loves of the Angels. First Angel's Story.* L. 33.

Prompt sense of equity! to thee belongs
The swift redress of unexamined wrongs!
Eager to serve, the cause perhaps untried,
But always apt to choose the suffering side!

    t.   HANNAH MORE—*Sensibility.* L. 243.

Since trifles make the sum of human things,
And half our misery from our foibles springs;
Since life's best joys consist in peace and ease,
And though but few can serve, yet all may please;
Oh, let th' ungentle spirit learn from hence,
A small unkindness is a great offence.

    u.   HANNAH MORE—*Sensibility.*

And the touch'd needle trembles to the pole.

    v.   POPE—*Temple of Fame.* L. 431.

SEPTEMBER (See MONTHS).

SERVICE.

                   We are his,
To serve him nobly in the common cause,
True to the death, but not to be his slaves.

    w.   COWPER—*Task.* Bk. V. L. 340.

When I have attempted to join myself to others by services, it proved an intellectual trick,—no more. They eat your service like apples, and leave you out. But love them, and they feel you, and delight in you all the time.

    x.   EMERSON—*Essays. Of Gifts.*

                   Who seeks for aid
Must show how service sought can be repaid.

    y.   OWEN MEREDITH (Lord Lytton)— *Siege of Constantinople.*

Servant of God, well done.

   a.   MILTON—*Paradise Lost.*   Bk. VI.
                                L. 29.

They also serve who only stand and wait.

   b.   MILTON—*Sonnet. On his Blindness.*

A pampered menial drove me from the door.

   c.   THOMAS MOSS—*The Beggar.* (*Altered
                by* GOLDSMITH *from* " *A Liveried
                        Servant,*" *etc.*)

They serve God well,
Who serve his creatures.

   d.   MRS. NORTON—*The Lady of La Garaye.*
                         Conclusion.   L. 9.

Had I but serv'd my God with half the zeal
I serv'd my king, he would not in mine age
Have left me naked to mine enemies.

   e.   *Henry VIII.* Act III. Sc. 2. L. 455.

I am an ass, indeed, you may prove it by
my long ears. I have served him from the
hour of my nativity to this instant, and have
nothing at his hands for my service but blows.
When I am cold, he heats me with beating.

   f.   *Comedy of Errors.* Act IV. Sc. 4.
                                L. 29.

My heart is ever at your service.

   g.   *Timon of Athens.* Act I. Sc. 2. L. 76.

            You know that love
Will creep in service where it cannot go.

   h.   *Two Gentlemen of Verona.* Act IV.
                           Sc. 2. L. 19.

The king [Frederick] has sent me some of
his dirty linen to wash; I will wash yours
another time.

   i.   VOLTAIRE—*Reply to General Manstein.*

Small service is true service while it lasts :
  Of humblest friends, bright Creature ! scorn
     not one ;
The Daisy, by the shadow that it casts,
  Protects the lingering dew drop from the
     Sun.

   j.   WORDSWORTH—*To a Child: Written in
                          Her Album.*

SHADOWS.

What shadows we are, and what shadows
we pursue.

   k.   BURKE—*Speech at Bristol on Declining
                           the Poll.*

Thus shadow owes its birth to light.

   l.   GAY—*The Persian, Sun, and Cloud.*
                                L. 10.

Follow a shadow, it still flies you;
Seem to fly it, it will pursue.

   m.   BEN JONSON—*Song. That Women are
                      but Men's Shadows.*

            Alas ! must it ever be so?
Do we stand in our own light, wherever we go,
And fight our own shadows forever?

   n.   OWEN MEREDITH (Lord Lytton)—
               Lucile. Pt. II. Canto II. St. 5.

Shadows are in reality, when the sun is
shining, the most conspicuous thing in a
landscape, next to the highest lights.

   o.   RUSKIN—*Painting.*

Chequer'd shadow.

   p.   *Titus Andronicus.* Act II. Sc. 3. L. 15.

Come like shadows, so depart !

   q.   *Macbeth.* Act IV. Sc. 1. L. 111.

                   Shadows to-night
Have struck more terror to the soul of Richard
Than can the substance of ten thousand
     soldiers
Armed in proof, and led by shallow Richmond.

   r.   *Richard III.* Act V. Sc. 3. L. 216.

Some there be that shadows kiss ;
Such have but a shadow's bliss.

   s.   *Merchant of Venice.* Act II. Sc. 9. L. 66.

SHAKESPEARE.

    This was Shakespeare's form ;
Who walked in every path of human life,
Felt every passion ; and to all mankind
Doth now, will ever, that experience yield
Which his own genius only could acquire.

   t.   AKENSIDE—*Inscription.* IV.

Others abide our question. Thou art free.
We ask and ask—Thou smilest and art still,
Out-topping knowledge.

   u.   MATTHEW ARNOLD—*Shakespeare.*

There, Shakespeare, on whose forehead climb
The crowns o' the world. Oh, eyes sublime
With tears and laughter for all time.

   v.   E. B. BROWNING—*A Vision of Poets.*

           " With this same key
Shakespeare unlocked his heart," once more !
Did Shakespeare? If so, the less Shakespeare he!

   w.   ROBERT BROWNING—*House.* X.

If I say that Shakespeare is the greatest of
intellects, I have said all concerning him.
But there is more in Shakespeare's intellect
than we have yet seen. It is what I call an
unconscious intellect ; there is more virtue in
it than he himself is aware of.

   x.   CARLYLE—*Essays. Characteristics of
                          Shakespeare.*

Our myriad-minded Shakespeare.

   y.   COLERIDGE—*Biographia Literaria.*
                                Ch. XV.

          When great poets sing,
Into the night new constellations spring,
With music in the air that dulls the craft
Of rhetoric. So when Shakespeare sang or
     laughed
The world with long, sweet Alpine echoes
     thrilled
Voiceless to scholars' tongues no muse had
     filled
With melody divine.

   z.   C. P. CRANCH—*Shakespeare.*

But Shakespeare's magic could not copied be;
Within that circle none durst walk but he.
> *a.*   DRYDEN—*The Tempest. Prologue.*

Nor sequent centuries could hit
Orbit and sum of Shakespeare's wit.
> *b.*   EMERSON—*May Day and Other Pieces.*
>   *Solution.* L. 39.

The passages of Shakespeare that we most
prize were never quoted until within this
century.
> *c.*   EMERSON—*Letters and Social Aims.*
>   *Quotation and Originality.*

What point of morals, of manners, of economy, of philosophy, of religion, of taste, of
the conduct of life, has he not settled? What
mystery has he not signified his knowledge of?
What office, or function, or district of man's
work, has he not remembered? What king
has he not taught state, as Talma taught
Napoleon? What maiden has not found him
finer than her delicacy? What lover has he
not outloved? What sage has he not outseen?
What gentleman has he not instructed in the
rudeness of his behavior?
> *d.*   EMERSON—*Representative Men.*
>   *Shakespeare.*

When Shakespeare is charged with debts to
his authors, Landor replies, "Yet he was more
original than his originals. He breathed upon
dead bodies and brought them into life."
> *e.*   EMERSON—*Letters and Social Aims.*
>   *Quotation and Originality.*

Now you who rhyme, and I who rhyme,
Have not we sworn it, many a time,
That we no more our verse would scrawl,
For Shakespeare he had said it all!
> *f.*   R. W. GILDER—*The Modern Rhymer.*

For a good poet's made, as well as born,
And such wast thou! Look how the father's
     face
Lives in his issue; even so the race
Of Shakespeare's mind and manners brightly
     shine
In his well-turned and true-filèd lines;
In each of which he seems to shake a lance,
As brandished at the eyes of ignorance.
> *g.*   BEN JONSON—*Lines to the Memory of*
>   *Shakespeare.*

He was not of an age, but for all time!
And all the Muses still were in their prime,
When, like Apollo, he came forth to warm
Our ears, or like a Mercury to charm!
> *h.*   BEN JONSON—*Lines to the Memory of*
>   *Shakespeare.*

I remember, the players have often mentioned it as an honour to Shakespeare, that in
his writing (whatsoever he penned) he never
blotted out a line. My answer hath been,
would he had blotted a thousand.
> *i.*   BEN JONSON—*Discoveries. De*
>   *Shakespeare nostrat.*

Nature herself was proud of his designs,
And joyed to wear the dressing of his lines!
Which were so richly spun, and woven so fit,
As since, she will vouchsafe no other wit.
> *j.*   BEN JONSON—*Lines to the Memory of*
>   *Shakespeare.*

           Soul of the Age!
The applause! delight! the wonder of our
     stage!
My Shakespeare rise! I will not lodge thee by
Chaucer, or Spenser, or bid Beaumont lie
A little further off, to make thee room:
Thou art a monument without a tomb,
And art alive still, while thy book doth live
And we have wits to read, and praise to give.
> *k.*   BEN JONSON—*Lines to the Memory of*
>   *Shakespeare.*

Sweet Swan of Avon! What a sight it were
To see thee in our water yet appear.
> *l.*   BEN JONSON—*Lines to the Memory of*
>   *Shakespeare.*

This figure that thou here seest put,
It was for gentle Shakespeare cut,
Wherein the graver had a strife
With Nature, to outdo the life:
Oh, could he but have drawn his wit
As well in brass, as he has hit
His face, the print would then surpass
All that was ever writ in brass;
But since he cannot, reader, look
Not on his picture, but his book.
> *m.*   BEN JONSON—*Lines on a Picture of*
>   *Shakespeare.*

* * * Thou hadst small Latin and less Greek.
> *n.*   BEN JONSON—*Lines to the Memory of*
>   *Shakespeare.*

Shakespeare is not our poet, but the world's,
Therefore on him no speech!
> *o.*   WALTER SAVAGE LANDOR—*To Robert*
>   *Browning.* L. 5.

Then to the well-trod stage anon
If Jonson's learned sock be on,
Or sweetest Shakespeare, Fancy's child,
Warble his native wood-notes wild.
> *p.*   MILTON—*L'Allegro.* L. 131.

What needs my Shakespeare for his honored
     bones
The labors of an age in piled stones?
Or that his hallowed reliques should be hid
Under a star-y-pointing pyramid?
Dear son of Memory, great heir of fame,
What need'st thou such weak witness of thy
     name?
Thou in our wonder and astonishment
Hath built thyself a livelong monument.
> *q.*   MILTON—*An Epitaph.*

Shakspeare (whom you and every playhouse
  bill
Style the divine! the matchless! what you
  will),
For gain, not glory, wing'd his roving flight,
And grew immortal in his own despite.
  a.   POPE—*Imitations of Horace.*   Ep. I.
                        Bk. II.   L. 69.

Few of the university pen plaies well, they
smell too much of that writer *Ovid* and that
writer *Metamorphosis* and talk too much of
Proserpina and Jupiter. Why, here's our fellow Shakespeare puts them all down. Aye,
and Ben Jonson too. O that B. J. is a pesti-
lent fellow, he brought up Horace giving the
poets a pill, but our fellow, Shakespeare, hath
given him a purge that made him beray his
credit.
  b.   *The Return from Parnassus; or, the
            Scourge of Simony.*   Act IV.   Sc. 3.

Shikspur, Shikspur! Who wrote it?
No, I never read Shikspur.
Then you have an immense pleasure to come.
  c.   JAMES TOWNLEY—*High Life Below
                        Stairs.*   Act II.   Sc. 1.

Scorn not the Sonnet.   Critic, you have
  frowned,
Mindless of its just honours; with this key
Shakespeare unlocked his heart.
  d.   WORDSWORTH—*Scorn not the Sonnet.*

SHAME.

  A nightingale dies for shame if another bird
sings better.
  e.   BURTON—*Anatomy of Melancholy.*
                    Pt. I.   Sec. II.   Memb. 3.
                        Subsec. VI.

Love taught him shame, and shame, with love
  at strife,
Soon taught the sweet civilities of life.
  f.   DRYDEN—*Cymon and Iphigenia.*
                        L. 133.

The only art her guilt to cover,
  To hide her shame from every eye,
To give repentance to her lover,
  And wring his bosom, is—to die.
  g.   GOLDSMITH—*Vicar of Wakefield.*
                        Ch. XXIV.

If yet not lost to all the sense of shame.
  h.   HOMER—*Iliad.*   Bk. VI.   L. 350.
                        Pope's trans.

And there's a lust in man no charm can tame
Of loudly publishing our neighbor's shame;
On eagles' wings immortal scandals fly,
While virtuous actions are but born and die.
  i.   JUVENAL—*Satire IX.*   Harvey's trans.

Here shame dissuades him, there his fear prevails,
And each by turns his aching heart assails.
  j.   OVID—*Metamorphoses.*   Bk. III.
            Transformation of Actæon.   L. 73.
                        Addison's trans.

    All is confounded, all!
Reproach and everlasting shame
Sits mocking in our plumes.
  k.   *Henry V.*   Act IV.   Sc. 5.   L. 3.

      He was not born to shame:
Upon his brow shame was asham'd to sit;
For 'tis a throne where honour may be
  crown'd
Sole monarch of the universal earth.
  l.   *Romeo and Juliet.*   Act III.   Sc. 2.
                        L. 91.

O shame! Where is thy blush?
  m.   *Hamlet.*   Act III.   Sc. 4.   L. 82.

  The most curious offspring of shame is
shyness.
  n.   SYDNEY SMITH—*Lecture on the Evil
                        Affections.*

SHIPS.

She bears her down majestically near,
Speed on her prow, and terror in her tier.
  o.   BYRON—*The Corsair.*   Canto III.
                        St. 15.

She walks the waters like a thing of life,
And seems to dare the elements to strife.
  p.   BYRON—*The Corsair.*   Canto I.   St. 3.

The true ship is the ship builder.
  q.   EMERSON—*Essays.   Of History.*

Ships that sailed for sunny isles,
But never came to shore.
  r.   THOS. HERVEY—*The Devil's Progress.*

  Being in a ship is being in a jail, with the
chance of being drowned.
  s.   SAM'L JOHNSON—*Boswell's Life of
                        Johnson.*   An. 1759.

  And the wind plays on those great sonorous
harps, the shrouds and masts of ships.
  t.   LONGFELLOW—*Hyperion.*   Bk. I.
                        Ch. VII.

Build me straight, O worthy Master!
  Staunch and strong, a goodly vessel
That shall laugh at all disaster,
  And with wave and whirlwind wrestle!
  u.   LONGFELLOW—*Building of the Ship.*
                        L. 1.

There's not a ship that sails the ocean,
But every climate, every soil,
Must bring its tribute, great or small,
And help to build the wooden wall!
  v.   LONGFELLOW—*The Building of the Ship.*
                        L. 66.

Like ships that have gone down at sea,
When heaven was all tranquillity.
  w.   MOORE—*Lalla Rookh.   The Light of
                        the Harem.*

And let our barks across the pathless flood
Hold different courses.
    a.   Scott—*Kenilworth.* Ch. XXIX.
                        Introductory verses.

The barge she sat in, like a burnish'd throne,
Burn'd on the water : the poop was beaten
    gold ;
Purple the sails, and so perfumed that
The winds were love-sick with them : the oars
    were silver,
Which to the tune of flutes kept stroke, and
    made
The water which they beat to follow faster,
As amorous of their strokes.
    b.   *Antony and Cleopatra.* Act II. Sc. 2.
                                L . 196.

Ships, dim discover'd, dropping from the
    clouds.
    c.   Thomson—*The Seasons.* *Summer.*
                                L. 946.

SHIPWRECK.

Some hoisted out the boats, and there was one
That begged Pedrillo for an absolution,
Who told him to be damn'd,—in his confusion.
    d.   Byron—*Don Juan.* Canto II. St. 44.

Then rose from sea to sky the wild farewell—
    Then shriek'd the timid, and stood still the
    brave,—
Then some leap'd overboard with fearful yell,
    As eager to anticipate their grave.
    e.   Byron—*Don Juan.* Canto II. St. 52.

Again she plunges ! hark ! a second shock
Bilges the splitting vessel on the rock ;
Down on the vale of death, with dismal cries,
The fated victims shuddering cast their eyes
In wild despair ; while yet another stroke
With strong convulsion rends the solid oak :
Ah Heaven !—behold her crashing ribs divide !
She loosens, parts, and spreads in ruin o'er
    the tide.
    f.   Falconer—*Shipwreck.* Canto III.
                              L. 642.

And fast through the midnight dark and drear,
    Through the whistling sleet and snow,
Like a sheeted ghost, the vessel swept
    Towards the reef of Norman's Woe.
    g.   Longfellow—*The Wreck of the*
                        Hesperus. St. 15.

But hark ! what shriek of death comes in
    the gale,
    And in the distant ray what glimmering sail
Bends to the storm ?—Now sinks the note of
    fear !
Ah ! wretched mariners !—no more shall day
Unclose his cheering eye to light ye on your
    way !
    h.   Mrs. Radcliffe—*Mysteries of*
                        Udolpho. Shipwreck.

A rotten carcass of a boat, not rigged,
Nor tackle, sail, nor mast ; the very rats
Instinctively have quit it.
    i.   *Tempest.* Act I. Sc. 2. L. 146.

                        O, I have suffer'd
With those that I saw suffer : a brave vessel,
Who had, no doubt, some noble creature in
    her,
Dash'd all to pieces. O, the cry did knock
Against my very heart ! Poor souls, they
    perished.
    j.   *Tempest.* Act I. Sc. 2. L. 5.

Or shipwrecked, kindles on the coast
False fires, that others may be lost.
    k.   Wordsworth—*To the Lady Fleming.*

SHOEMAKING (*See* Occupations).

SICKNESS.

The best of remedies is a beefsteak
Against sea-sickness ; try it, sir, before
You sneer, and I assure you this is true,
For I have found it answer—so may you.
    l.   Byron—*Don Juan.* Canto II. St. 13.

                  But when ill indeed,
E'en dismissing the doctor don't *always* suc-
    ceed.
    m.   George Colman (the Younger)—
             Broad Grins. *Lodgings for Single*
                            Gentlemen. St. 7.

Some maladies are rich and precious and
only to be acquired by the right of inheritance
or purchased with gold.
    n.   Nath. Hawthorne—*Mosses from an*
                Old Manse. *The Old Manse.* *The*
                          Procession of Life.

                        A malady
Preys on my heart that med'cine cannot
    reach.
    o.   Maturin—*Bertram.* Act IV. Sc. 2.

He had a fever when he was in Spain,
And when the fit was on him, I did mark
How he did shake ; 'tis true, this god did
    shake :
His coward lips did from their colour fly,
And that same eye whose bend doth awe the
    world
Did lose his lustre.
    p.   *Julius Cæsar.* Act I. Sc. 2. L. 119.

                    My long sickness
Of health and living now begins to mend,
And nothing brings me all things.
    q.   *Timon of Athens.* Act V. Sc. 1. L. 189.

                What, is Brutus sick,
And will he steal out of his wholesome bed,
To dare the vile contagion of the night ?
    r.   *Julius Cæsar.* Act II. Sc. 1. L. 263.

I've known my lady (for she loves a tune)
For *fevers* take an opera in June:
And, though perhaps you'll think the practice
    bold,
A midnight park is sov'reign for a *cold.*
  a.   YOUNG—*Love of Fame.* Satire V.
                         L. 185.

SIGHS.

Sigh'd and look'd, and sigh'd again.
  b.   DRYDEN—*Alexander's Feast.* L. 120.

Implores the passing tribute of a sigh.
  c.   GRAY—*Elegy in a Country Churchyard.*
                         St. 20.

To sigh, yet feel no pain.
  d.   MOORE—*Songs from M. P.; or, The*
                        Blue Stocking.

My soul has rest, sweet sigh! alone in thee.
  e.   PETRARCH—*To Laura in Death.*
                 Sonnet LIV. L. 14.

Yet sighes, deare sighes, indeede true friends
    you are
  That do not leave your left friend at the
    wurst,
But, as you with my breast, I oft have nurst
So, gratefull now, you waite upon my care.
  f.   SIR PHILIP SIDNEY—*Sighes.*

                          Sighs
Which perfect Joy, perplexed for utterance,
Stole from her sister Sorrow.
  g.   TENNYSON—*The Gardener's Daughter.*
                         L. 249.

SIGHT.

And finds with keen, discriminating sight,
Black's not so black;—nor white so very
    white.
  h.   CANNING—*New Morality.*

And for to se, and eek for to be seye.
  i.   CHAUCER—*Canterbury Tales. The Wife*
             of Bath. Preamble. L. 10,594.

The rarer sene, the lesse in mynde,
The lesse in mynde, the lesser payne.
  j.   BARNABY GOOGE—*Sonnettes. Out of*
                 Syght, Out of Mynde.

          And every eye
Gaz'd as before some brother of the sky.
  k.   HOMER—*Odyssey.* Bk. VIII. L. 17.
                     Pope's trans.

For sight is woman-like and shuns the old.
(Ah! he can see enough, when years are told,
Who backwards looks.)
  l.   VICTOR HUGO—*Eviradnus.* IX.

Then purg'd with euphrasy and rue
The visual nerve, for he had much to see.
  m.   MILTON—*Paradise Lost.* Bk. XI.
                         L. 414.

He that had neither beene kithe nor kin,
Might have seene a full fayre sight.
  n.   THOMAS PERCY—*Reliques of Ancient*
          Poetry. Robin Hood and Guy of
                        Gisborne.

There is none so blind as they that won't
see.
  o.   SWIFT—*Polite Conversation.*
                      Dialogue III.

For any man with half an eye,
What stands before him may espy;
But optics sharp it needs I ween,
To see what is not to be seen.
  p.   JOHN TRUMBULL—*McFingal.* Canto I.
                         L. 67.

SILENCE.

But silence never shows itself to so great an
advantage, as when it is made the reply to
calumny and defamation, provided that we
give no just occasion for them.
  q.   ADDISON—*The Tatler.* No. 133.

Deep vengeance is the daughter of deep
    silence.
  r.   ALFIERI—*La Congiura de Pazzi.* I. 1.

There was silence deep as death;
And the boldest held his breath,
For a time.
  s.   CAMPBELL—*Battle of the Baltic.*

Silence is more eloquent than words.
  t.   CARLYLE—*Heroes and Hero Worship.*
                      Lecture II.

Silence is the element in which great things
fashion themselves together; that at length
they may emerge, full-formed and majestic,
into the daylight of Life, which they are
thenceforth to rule.
  u.   CARLYLE—*Sartor Resartus.* Bk. III.
                      Ch. III.

Speech is great; but silence is greater.
  v.   CARLYLE—*Essays. Characteristics of*
                      Shakespeare.

Under all speech that is good for anything
there lies a silence that is better. Silence is
deep as Eternity; speech is shallow as Time.
  w.   CARLYLE—*Essays. Memoir of the Life*
                      of Scott.

And they three passed over the white sands,
between the rocks, silent as the shadows.
  x.   COLERIDGE—*The Wanderings of Cain.*

The silente man still suffers wrong.
  y.   *The Rock of Regard.* J. P. COLLIER'S
                    Reprint. 1576.

Silently as a dream the fabric rose;
No sound of hammer or of saw was there.
  z.   COWPER—*The Task.* Bk. V. L. 144.

Striving to tell his woes, words would not
    come ;
For light cares speak, when mighty griefs are
    dumb.
    a.   SAMUEL DANIEL—*Complaint of*
                Rosamond. St. 114.

Silence is the mother of Truth.
    b.   BENJ. DISRAELI—*Tancred.* Bk. IV.
                                  Ch. IV.

A horrid stillness first invades the ear,
And in that silence we the tempest fear.
    c.   DRYDEN—*Astræa Redux.* L. 7.

Stillborn silence ! thou that art
Flood-gate of the deeper heart !
    d.   RICHARD FLECKNO—*Silence.*

And silence, like a poultice, comes
  To heal the blows of sound.
    e.   O. W. HOLMES—*The Music Grinder.*

Silence that spoke, and eloquence of eyes.
    f.   HOMER—*Iliad.* Bk. XIV. L. 252.
                          Pope's trans.

There is a silence where hath been no sound,
  There is a silence where no sound may be,
In the cold grave—under the deep, deep sea,
Or in wide desert where no life is found,
Which hath been mute, and still must sleep
    profound.
    g.   HOOD—*Sonnets. Silence.*

Not much talk—a great, sweet silence.
    h.   HENRY JAMES, JR.—*A Bundle of Letters.*
                            Letter IV.

Thou foster-child of Silence and slow Time.
    i.   KEATS—*Ode on a Grecian Urn.*

    All was silent as before—
All silent save the dripping rain.
    j.   LONGFELLOW—*A Rainy Day.*

Three Silences there are : the first of speech,
The second of desire, the third of thought.
    k.   LONGFELLOW—*The Three Silences of*
                          Molinos.

What shall I say to you? What can I say
Better than silence is?
    l.   LONGFELLOW—*Morituri Salutamus.*
                          L. 128.

Nothing is more useful than silence.
    m.   MENANDER—*Ex Incert. Comœd.*
                          P. 216.

            You know
There are moments when silence, prolong'd
    and unbroken,
More expressive may be than all words ever
    spoken,
It is when the heart has an instinct of what
In the heart of another is passing.
    n.   OWEN MEREDITH (Lord Lytton)—
             Lucile. Pt. II. Canto I. St. 20.

That silence is one of the great arts of conversation is allowed by Cicero himself, who
says, there is not only an art, but even an
eloquence in it.
    o.   HANNAH MORE—*Essays on Various*
             Subjects. Thoughts on Conversation.

Silence sweeter is than speech.
    p.   D. M. MULOCK—*Magnus and Morna.*
                          Sc. 3.

Be silent and safe—silence never betrays you.
    q.   JOHN BOYLE O'REILLY—*Rules of the*
                        Road. St. 2.

Remember what Simonides said,—that he
never repented that he had held his tongue,
but often that he had spoken.
    r.   PLUTARCH—*Morals.* Vol. I. *Rules for*
                the Preservation of Health.

Said Periander, "Hesiod might as well have
kept his breath to cool his pottage."
    s.   PLUTARCH—*Morals.* Vol. II. *The*
            Banquet of the Seven Wise Men.

Silence in love bewrays more woe
  Than words, though ne'er so witty ;
A beggar that is dumb, you know,
  May challenge double pity.
    t.   SIR WALTER RALEIGH—*The Silent*
                      Lover. St. 9.

Silence more musical than any song.
    u.   CHRISTINA G. ROSSETTI—*Sonnet. Rest.*

Silent in seven languages.
    v.   SCHLEIERMACHER—See *Letter of Zelter*
             to Goethe. March 15, 1830.

        Be check'd for silence,
But never tax'd for speech.
    w.   *All's Well That Ends Well.* Act I.
                      Sc. 1. L. 76.

I'll speak to thee in silence.
    x.   *Cymbeline.* Act V. Sc. 4. L. 29.

        Silence is only commendable
In a neat's tongue dried and a maid not
    vendible.
    y.   *Merchant of Venice.* Act I. Sc. 1. L. 111.

Silence is the perfectest herald of joy :
I were but little happy, if I could say how
    much.
    z.   *Much Ado About Nothing.* Act II.
                    Sc. 1. L. 317.

The rest is silence.
    aa.   *Hamlet.* Act V. Sc. 2. L 368.

        What ; gone without a word?
Ay, so true love should do : it cannot speak ;
For truth hath better deeds than words to
    grace it.
    bb.   *Two Gentlemen of Verona.* Act II.
                  Sc. 2. L. 16.

Silence! Oh, well are Death and Sleep and
   Thou
Three brethren named, the guardians gloomy-
   winged,
Of one abyss, where life and truth and joy
Are swallowed up.
  a.   SHELLEY—*Fragments. Silence.*

Shallow brookes murmur moste, deepe silent
   slide away.
  b.   SIR PHILIP SIDNEY—*The Arcadia.*
            Thirsis and Dorus.

Macaulay is like a book in breeches * * *
He has occasional flashes of silence, that
make his conversation perfectly delightful.
  c.   SYDNEY SMITH—*Lady Holland's*
            Memoir. Vol. I. P. 363.

Silence oppresses with too great a weight.
  d.   SOPHOCLES—*Antig.* 1254.

The deepest rivers make least din,
The silent soule doth most abound in care.
  e.   EARL OF STIRLING—*Aurora.* 1604.
                   Song.

     But let me silent be :
For silence is the speech of love,
The music of the spheres above.
  f.   R. H. STODDARD—*Speech of Love.* St. 4.

Of every noble work the silent part is best,
Of all expression, that which cannot be expressed.
  g.   W. W. STORY—*The Unexpressed.*

Silence, beautiful voice.
  h.   TENNYSON—*Maud.* Pt. V. St. 3.

Come then, expressive Silence.
  i.   THOMSON—*Seasons. A Hymn.* L. 188.

No sound is uttered,—but a deep
And solemn harmony pervades
The hollow vale from steep to steep,
And penetrates the glades.
  j.   WORDSWORTH—*Composed upon an*
        Evening of Extraordinary Splendour
                 and Beauty.
The silence that is in the starry sky.
  k.   WORDSWORTH—*Song at the Feast of*
                Brougham Castle.

SIMPLICITY.

  Nothing is more simple than greatness ; indeed, to be simple is to be great.
  l.   EMERSON—*Literary Ethics.*

  Generally nature hangs out a sign of simplicity in the face of a fool.
  m.   FULLER—*The Holy and Profane States.*
          Of Natural Fools. Maxim I.

To me more dear, congenial to my heart,
One native charm, than all the gloss of art.
  n.   GOLDSMITH—*Deserted Village.* L. 253.

The greatest truths are the simplest : and
so are the greatest men.
  o.   J. C. AND A. W. HARE—*Guesses at*
                    Truth.

     Her head was bare ;
But for her native ornament of hair ;
Which in a simple knot was tied above,
Sweet negligence, unheeded bait of love !
  p.   OVID—*Metamorphoses. Meleager and*
         Atalanta. L. 68. Dryden's trans.

SIN.

I waive the quantum o' the sin,
  The hazard of concealing :
But, och ! it hardens a' within,
  And petrifies the feeling !
  q.   BURNS—*Epistle to a Young Friend.*

Compound for sins they are inclin'd to,
By damning those they have no mind to.
  r.   BUTLER—*Hudibras.* Pt. I. Canto I.
                    L. 215.

But, sad as angels for the good man's sin,
Weep to record, and blush to give it in.
  s.   CAMPBELL—*Pleasures of Hope.* Pt. II.
                    L. 357.

Sin let loose speaks punishment at hand.
  t.   COWPER—*Expostulation.* L. 160.

Come, now again, thy woes impart,
  Tell all thy sorrows, all thy sin ;
We cannot heal the throbbing heart
  Till we discern the wounds within.
  u.   CRABBE—*Hell of Justice.* Pt. II.

I couldn't live in peace if I put the shadow
of a wilful sin between myself and God.
  v.   GEORGE ELIOT—*The Mill on the Floss.*
               Bk. VI. Ch. XIV.

Man-like is it to fall into sin,
Fiend-like is it to dwell therein,
Christ-like is it for sin to grieve,
God-like is it all sin to leave.
  w.   FRIEDRICH VON LOGAU—*Sinngedichte.*
        Sin. See Longfellow's trans.
                Poetic Aphorisms.

Daily with souls that cringe and plot,
We Sinais climb and know it not.
  x.   LOWELL—*The Vision of Sir Launfal.*
                Prelude to Pt. I.

     Her rash hand in evil hour
Forth reaching to the fruit, she pluck'd, she
   eat;
Earth felt the wound, and Nature from her
   seat
Sighing through all her works gave signs of
   woe
That all was lost.
  y.   MILTON—*Paradise Lost.* Bk. IX.
                    L. 780.

Law can discover sin, but not remove,
Save by those shadowy expiations weak.
  a.   Milton—*Paradise Lost.* Bk. XII.
                                L. 290.

So many laws argues so many sins.
  b.   Milton—*Paradise Lost.* Bk. XII.
                                L. 283.

But the trail of the serpent is over them all.
  c.   Moore—*Lalla Rookh. Paradise and*
                         the Peri. L. 206.

In *Adam's* fall—
We sinned all.
  d.   *From the New England Primer.* 1814.

Young Timothy
Learnt sin to fly.
  e.   *From the New England Primer.* 1777.

How shall I lose the sin yet keep the sense,
And love th' offender, yet detest the offence?
  f.   Pope—*Eloise to Abelard.* L. 191.

See sin in state, majestically drunk ;
Proud as a peeress, prouder as a punk.
  g.   Pope—*Moral Essays.* Ep. II. L. 69.

Sin is a state of mind, not an outward act.
  h.   Sewell—*Passing Thoughts on Religion.*
                               Wilful Sin.

                Commit
The oldest sins the newest kind of ways?
  i.   *Henry IV.* Pt. II. Act IV. Sc. 5.
                                L. 126.

Few love to hear the sins they love to act.
  j.   *Pericles.* Act I. Sc. 1. L. 92.

            I am a man
More sinn'd against than sinning.
  k.   *King Lear.* Act III. Sc. 2. L. 58.

It is great sin to swear unto a sin,
But greater sin to keep a sinful oath.
  l.   *Henry VI.* Pt. II. Act V. Sc. 1.
                                L. 182.

          O, fie, fie, fie!
Thy sin's not accidental, but a trade.
  m.   *Measure for Measure.* Act III. Sc. 1.
                                L. 148.

O, what authority and show of truth
Can cunning sin cover itself withal !
  n.   *Much Ado About Nothing.* Act IV.
                            Sc. 1. L. 36.

Robes and furr'd gowns hide all. Plate sin
    with gold,
And the strong lance of justice hurtless
    breaks ;
Arm it in rags, a pigmy's straw doth pierce it.
  o.   *King Lear.* Act IV. Sc. 6. L. 169.

Some rise by sin, and some by virtue fall ;
Some run from breaks of ice, and answer none :
And some condemned for a fault alone.
  p.   *Measure for Measure.* Act II. Sc. 1.
                                L. 38.

Some sins do bear their privilege on earth.
  q.   *King John.* Act I. Sc. 1. L. 261.

Though some of you with Pilate wash your
    hands
Showing an outward pity ; yet you Pilates
Have here deliver'd me to my sour cross,
And water cannot wash away your sin.
  r.   *Richard II.* Act IV. Sc. 1. L. 239.

They say sin touches not a man so near
As shame a woman ; yet he too should be
Part of the penance, being more deep than
    she
Set in the sin.
  s.   Swinburne—*Tristram of Lyonesse.*
               Sailing of the Swallow. L. 360.

SINCERITY.

Loss of sincerity is loss of vital power.
  t.   Bovee—*Summaries of Thought.*
                             Sincerity.

                You know I say
Just what I think, and nothing more nor less,
And, when I pray, my heart is in my prayer.
I cannot say one thing and mean another :
If I can't pray, I will not make believe !
  u.   Longfellow—*Christus.* Pt. III.
              Giles Corey. Act II. Sc. 3.

There is no greater delight than to be conscious of sincerity on self-examination.
  v.   Mencius—*Works.* Bk. VII. Ch. IV.

Bashful sincerity and comely love.
  w.   *Much Ado About Nothing.* Act IV.
                          Sc. 1. L. 55.

But I will wear my heart upon my sleeve
For daws to peck at ; I am not what I am.
  x.   *Othello.* Act I. Sc. 1. L. 64.

He hath a heart as sound as a bell and his
tongue is the clapper, for what his heart
thinks his tongue speaks.
  y.   *Much Ado About Nothing.* Act III.
                          Sc. 2. L. 12.

Men should be what they seem ;
Or those that be not, would they might seem
    none !
  z.   *Othello.* Act III. Sc. 3. L. 126.

O, how much more doth beauty beauteous
    seem
By that sweet ornament which truth doth
    give !
  aa.   *Sonnet LIV.*

SINGERS.

Forever singing, as they shine,
The hand that made us is divine.
  bb.   Addison—*Ode. The Spacious*
                       Firmament on High.

Three merry boys, and three merry boys,
  And three merry boys are we,
As ever did sing in a hempen string
  Under the gallow-tree.
   a.   BEAUMONT AND FLETCHER—*The Bloody
         Brother.* Act III. Sc. 2. *Song.*

The tenor's voice is spoilt by affectation,
  And for the bass, the beast can only bellow ;
In fact, he had no singing education,
  An ignorant, noteless, timeless, tuneless
    fellow.
   b.   BYRON—*Don Juan.* Canto IV. St. 87.

At every close she made, th' attending throng
Replied, and bore the burden of the song :
So just, so small, yet in so sweet a note,
It seemed the music melted in the throat.
   c.   DRYDEN—*Flower and the Leaf.* L. 197.

Olympian bards who sung
  Divine ideas below,
Which always find us young
  And always keep us so.
   d.   EMERSON—*Ode to Beauty.*

So she poured out the liquid music of her
voice to quench the thirst of his spirit.
   e.   NATH. HAWTHORNE—*Mosses from an
          Old Manse. The Birthmark.*

God sent his Singers upon earth
With songs of sadness and of mirth,
That they might touch the hearts of men,
And bring them back to heaven again.
   f.   LONGFELLOW—*The Singers.*

He the sweetest of all singers.
   g.   LONGFELLOW—*Hiawatha.* Pt. VI.
                         L. 21.
Sang in tones of deep emotion,
Songs of love and songs of longing.
   h.   LONGFELLOW—*Hiawatha.* Pt. XI.
                        L. 136.
Or bid the soul of Orpheus sing
Such notes as, warbled to the string,
Drew iron tears down Pluto's cheek.
   i.   MILTON—*Il Penseroso.* L. 105.

Who, as they sung, would take the prison'd
    soul
And lap it in Elysium.
   j.   MILTON—*Comus.* L. 256.

O Carril, raise again thy voice ! let me hear
the song of Selma, which was sung in my
halls of joy, when Fingal, king of shields,
was there, and glowed at the deeds of his
fathers.
   k.   OSSIAN—*Fingal.* Bk. III. St. 1.

Sweetest the strain when in the song
  The singer has been lost.
   l.   ELIZABETH STUART PHELPS—*The Poet
                      and the Poem.*

But would you sing, and rival Orpheus' strain.
The wond'ring forests soon should dance
  again ;
The moving mountains hear the powerful call.
And headlong streams hang listening in their
  fall !
   m.   POPE—*Summer.* L. 81.

Silence, ye wolves ! while Ralph to Cynthía
  howls,
And makes night hideous ;—Answer him, ye
  owls !
   n.   POPE—*The Dunciad.* Bk. 3. L. 165.

But one puritan amongst them, and he sings
psalms to hornpipes.
   o.   *Winter's Tale.* Act IV. Sc. 3. L. 46.

               Every night he comes
With musics of all sorts and songs compos'd
To her unworthiness : it nothing steads us
To chide him from our eaves ; for he persists
As if his life lay on't.
   p.   *All's Well that Ends Well.* Act III.
                        Sc. 7. L. 39.

His tongue is now a stringless instrument.
   q.   *Richard II.* Act II. Sc. 1. L. 149.

                Nay, now you are too flat
And mar the concord with too harsh a descant.
   r.   *Two Gentlemen of Verona.* Act I.
                        Sc. 2. L. 94.

O ! she will sing the savageness out of a bear.
   s.   *Othello.* Act IV. Sc. 1. L. 200.

Thou hast by moonlight at her window sung
With feigning voice verses of feigning love.
   t.   *Midsummer-Night's Dream.* Act I.
                      Sc. 1. L. 30.

Sing again, with your dear voice revealing
    A tone
Of some world far from ours,
  Where music and moonlight and feeling
    Are one.
   u.   SHELLEY—*To Jane. The Keen Stars
                     were Twinkling.*
I do but sing because I must,
And pipe but as the linnets sing.
   v.   TENNYSON—*In Memoriam.* Pt. XXI.

SKY (THE).

And they were canopied by the blue sky,
So cloudless, clear, and purely beautiful,
That God alone was to be seen in Heaven.
   w.   BYRON—*The Dream.* St. 4.

The mountain at a given distance
  In amber lies ;
Approached, the amber flits a little,—
  And that's the skies !
   x.   EMILY DICKINSON—*Poems.* XIX.
               Second Series. Ed. 1891.

How bravely Autumn paints upon the sky
The gorgeous fame of Summer which is fled !
   a.   Hood—*Written in a Volume of*
                             Shakspeare.

          From hyperborean skies,
Embodied dark, what clouds of vandals rise.
   b.   Pope—*Dunciad.* III. L. 85.

Sometimes gentle, sometimes capricious,
sometimes awful, never the same for two
moments together ; almost human in its passions, almost spiritual in its tenderness, almost Divine in its infinity.
   c.   Ruskin—*The True and Beautiful.*
                              The Sky.

  The moon has set
  In a bank of jet
That fringes the Western sky,
  The pleiads seven
  Have sunk from heaven
And the midnight hurries by ;
  My hopes are flown
  And, alas ! alone
On my weary couch I lie.
   d.   Sappho—*Fragment.*
                  J. S. Easby-Smith's trans.

This majestical roof fretted with golden fire.
   e.   *Hamlet.* Act II. Sc. 2. L. 312.

          Heaven's ebon vault,
Studded with stars unutterably bright,
Through which the moon's unclouded grand-
     eur rolls,
Seems like a canopy which love has spread
To curtain her sleeping world.
   f.   Shelley—*Queen Mab.* Pt. IV.

          Of evening tinct,
The purple-streaming Amethyst is thine.
   g.   Thomson—*Seasons. Summer.* L. 150.

Green calm below, blue quietness above.
   h.   Whittier—*The Pennsylvania Pilgrim.*
                           St. 113.
The soft blue sky did never melt
Into his heart ; he never felt
The witching of the soft blue sky !
   i.   Wordsworth—*Peter Bell.* Pt. I.
                           St. 15.

SLANDER.

There are * * * robberies that leave
man or woman forever beggared of peace and
joy, yet kept secret by the sufferer.
   j.   George Eliot—*Felix Holt.*
                      Introduction.
I hate the man who builds his name
On ruins of another's fame.
   k.   Gay—*The Poet and the Rose.*

A generous heart repairs a slanderous tongue.
   l.   Homer—*Odyssey.* Bk. VIII. L. 43.
                         Pope's trans.

If slander be a snake, it is a winged one—
it flies as well as creeps.
   m.   Douglas Jerrold—*Specimens of*
                    Jerrold's Wit. Slander.

              Cut
Men's throats with whisperings.
   n.   Ben Jonson—*Sejanus.* Act I. Sc. 1.

     Where it concerns himself,
Who's angry at a slander, makes it true.
   o.   Ben Jonson—*Catiline.* Act III. Sc. 1.

For enemies carry about slander not in the
form in which it took its rise. * * * The
scandal of men is everlasting ; even then does
it survive when you would suppose it to be
dead.
   p.   Plautus—*Persa.* Act III. Sc. 1.
                        Riley's trans.

'Twas slander filled her mouth with lying
    words ;
Slander, the foulest whelp of Sin.
   q.   Pollok—*Course of Time.* Bk. VIII.
                          L. 725.

Done to death by slanderous tongues
  Was the Hero that here lies.
   r.   *Much Ado About Nothing.* Act V.
                     Sc. 3. L. 3.

For slander lives upon succession,
Forever housed where it gets possession.
   s.   *Comedy of Errors.* Act III. Sc. 1.
                          L. 105.

I am disgrac'd, impeach'd and baffled here,—
Pierc'd to the soul with slander's venom'd
    spear.
   t.   *Richard II.* Act I. Sc. 1. L. 170.

            If I can do it
By aught that I can speak in his dispraise,
She shall not long continue love to him.
   u.   *Two Gentlemen of Verona.* Act III.
                    Sc. 2. L. 46.

I will be hang'd, if some eternal villain,
Some busy and insinuating rogue,
Some cogging, cozening slave, to get some
    office,
Have not devised'd this slander.
   v.   *Othello.* Act IV. Sc. 2. L. 130.

         One doth not know
How much an ill word may empoison liking.
   w.   *Much Ado About Nothing.* Act III.
                    Sc. 1. L. 85.

    Slander'd to death by villains,
That dare as well answer a man indeed
As I dare take a serpent by the tongue :
Boys, apes, braggarts, Jacks, milksops !
   x.   *Much Ado About Nothing.* Act V.
                    Sc. 1. L. 88.

That thou art blamed shall not be thy defect,
For slander's mark was ever yet the fair;

*   *   *   *   *   *

So thou be good, slander doth but approve
Thy worth the greater.
a.   *Sonnet LXX.*

'Tis slander,
Whose edge is sharper than the sword, whose
tongue
Outvenoms all the worms of Nile, whose
breath
Rides on the posting winds and doth belie
All corners of the world; kings, queens and
states,
Maids, matrons, nay, the secrets of the grave
This viperous slander enters.
b.   *Cymbeline.* Act III. Sc. 4. L. 35.

Soft-buzzing Slander; silly moths that eat
An honest name.
c.   THOMSON—*Liberty.* Pt. IV. L. 609.

SLAVERY.

No more slave States and no more slave
territory.
d.   SALMON P. CHASE—*Resolutions Adopted
at the Free-Soil National Convention.*
Aug. 9, 1848.

I would not have a slave to till my ground,
To carry me, to fan me while I sleep,
And tremble when I wake, for all the wealth
That sinews bought and sold have ever earn'd.
e.   COWPER—*The Task.* Bk. II. L. 29.

Slaves cannot breathe in England; if their
lungs
Receive our air, that moment they are free;
They touch our country, and their shackles
fall.
f.   COWPER—*The Task.* Bk. II. L. 40.

Corrupted freemen are the worst of slaves.
g.   DAVID GARRICK—*Prologue to*
ED. MOORE'S *Gamesters.*

Resolved, That the compact which exists between the North and the South is a covenant
with death and an agreement with hell; in-
volving both parties in atrocious criminality,
and should be immediately annulled.
h.   WM. LLOYD GARRISON—*Adopted by the
Mass. Anti-Slavery Society, Fanueil
Hall.* Jan. 27, 1843.

The man who gives me employment, which
I must have or suffer, that man is my master,
let me call him what I will.
i.   HENRY GEORGE—*Social Problems.*
Ch. V.

The very mudsills of society. * * * We
call them slaves. * * * But I will not characterize that class at the North with that term;
but you have it. It is there, it is everywhere,
it is eternal.
j.   JAMES H. HAMMOND—*Speech in the
U. S. Senate.* March, 1858.

Whatever day
Makes man a slave, takes half his worth away.
k.   HOMER—*Odyssey.* Bk. XVII. L. 392.
Pope's trans.

I believe this government cannot endure
permanently half slave and half free.
l.   ABRAHAM LINCOLN—*Speech.* June 17,
1858.

In giving freedom to the slave we assure
freedom to the free,—honorable alike in what
we give and what we preserve.
m.   ABRAHAM LINCOLN—*Annual Message to
Congress.* Dec. 1, 1862.

A soil whose air is deemed too pure for
slaves to breathe in.
n.   LOFFT—*Reports.* P. 2. *Margrave's
Argument.* May 14, 1772.

They are slaves who fear to speak
For the fallen and the weak;

*   *   *   *   *

They are slaves who dare not be
In the right with two or three.
o.   LOWELL—*Stanzas on Freedom.*

O execrable son! so to aspire
Above his brethren, to himself assuming
Authority usurp'd, from God not given.
He gave us only over beast, fish, fowl,
Dominion absolute; that right we hold
By his donation; but man over men
He made not lord; such title to himself
Reserving, human left from human free.
p.   MILTON—*Paradise Lost.* Bk. XII.
L. 64.

Where bastard Freedom waves
Her fustian flag in mockery over slaves.
q.   MOORE—*To the Lord Viscount Forbes,
written from the City of Washington.*

And ne'er shall the sons of Columbia be
slaves,
While the earth bears a plant, or the sea rolls
its waves.
r.   ROBERT PAINE—*Ode. Adams and
Liberty.* 1798.

Base is the slave that pays.
s.   *Henry V.* Act II. Sc. 1. L. 100.

You have among you many a purchas'd
slave,
Which, like your asses and your dogs and
mules,
You use in abject and in slavish parts,
Because you bought them.
t.   *Merchant of Venice.* Act IV. Sc. 1.
L. 90.

Disguise thyself as thou wilt, still,
Slavery! said I—still thou art a bitter draught.
u.   STERNE—*The Sentimental Journey. The
Passport. The Hotel at Paris.*

By the Law of Slavery, man, created in the image of God, is divested of the human character, and declared to be a mere chattel.
a.   CHAS. SUMNER—*The Anti-Slavery Enterprise. Address at New York.* May 9, 1859.

Where Slavery is there Liberty cannot be; and where Liberty is there Slavery cannot be.
b.   CHAS. SUMNER—*Slavery and the Rebellion. Speech before the New York Young Men's Republican Union.* Nov. 5, 1864.

They [the blacks] had no rights which the white man was bound to respect.
c.   ROGER B. TANEY—*The Dred Scott Case.* See HOWARD's *Rep.* Vol. XIX. P. 407.

Slavery is also as ancient as war, and war as human nature.
d.   VOLTAIRE—*A Philosophical Dictionary. Slaves.*

I never mean, unless some particular circumstances should compel me to do it, to possess another slave by purchase, it being among my first wishes to see some plan adopted by which slavery in this country may be abolished by law.
e.   GEORGE WASHINGTON—*Farewell Address.*

That execrable sum of all villanies commonly called the Slave-trade.
f.   JOHN WESLEY—*Journal.* Feb. 12, 1792.

A Christian! going, gone!
Who bids for God's own image?—for his grace,
Which that poor victim of the market-place
    Hath in her suffering won?
g.   WHITTIER—*Voices of Freedom. The Christian Slave.*

Our fellow-countrymen in chains!
    Slaves—in a land of light and law!
Slaves—crouching on the very plains
    Where rolled the storm of Freedom's war!
h.   WHITTIER—*Voices of Freedom. Stanzas.*

What! mothers from their children riven!
    What! God's own image bought and sold!
AMERICANS to market driven,
    And bartered as the brute for gold!
i.   WHITTIER—*Voices of Freedom. Stanzas.*

SLEEP.

What means this heaviness that hangs upon me?
This lethargy that creeps through all my senses?
Nature, oppress'd and harrass'd out with care,
Sinks down to rest.
j.   ADDISON—*Cato.* Act V. Sc. 1.

What probing deep
Has ever solved the mystery of sleep?
k.   T. B. ALDRICH—*Human Ignorance.*

How happy he whose toil
Has o'er his languid pow'rless limbs diffus'd
A pleasing lassitude; he not in vain
Invokes the gentle Deity of dreams.
His pow'rs the most voluptuously dissolve
In soft repose; on him the balmy dews
Of Sleep with double nutriment descend.
l.   ARMSTRONG—*The Art of Preserving Health.* Bk. III. L. 385.

When the sheep are in the fauld, and a' the kye at hame,
And all the weary world to sleep are gane.
m.   LADY ANN BARNARD—*Auld Robin Gray.*

Sleep is a death, O make me try,
By sleeping, what it is to die:
And as gently lay my head
On my grave, as now my bed.
n.   SIR THOMAS BROWNE—*Religio Medici.* Pt. II. Sec. XII.

How he sleepeth! having drunken
    Weary childhood's mandragore,
From his pretty eyes have sunken
    Pleasures to make room for more—
Sleeping near the withered nosegay which
    he pulled the day before.
o.   E. B. BROWNING—*A Child Asleep.*

Of all the thoughts of God that are
Borne inward unto souls afar,
    Along the Psalmist's music deep,
Now tell me if that any is,
For gift or grace, surpassing this—
    "He giveth His beloved sleep."
p.   E. B. BROWNING—*The Sleep.*

Sleep on, Baby, on the floor,
Tired of all the playing,
Sleep with smile the sweeter for
    That you dropped away in!
On your curls' full roundness stand
    Golden lights serenely—
One cheek, pushed out by the hand,
    Folds the dimple inly.
q.   E. B. BROWNING—*Sleeping and Watching.*

Sleep hath its own world,
A boundary between the things misnamed
Death and existence: Sleep hath its own world,
And a wide realm of wild reality,
And dreams in their development have breath,
And tears, and tortures, and the touch of joy.
r.   BYRON—*The Dream.* St. 1.

Now, blessings light on him that first invented this same sleep! it covers a man all over, thoughts and all, like a cloak; it is meat for the hungry, drink for the thirsty, heat for the cold, and cold for the hot. It is the current coin that purchases all the pleasures of the world cheap; and the balance that sets the king and the shepherd, the fool and the wise man, even. There is only one thing, which somebody once put into my head, that I dislike in sleep; it is, that it resembles death; there is very little difference between a man in his first sleep, and a man in his last sleep.
> *a.*   CERVANTES—*Don Quixote.* Pt. II.
>   Ch. LXVIII.

O sleep! it is a gentle thing,
   Beloved from pole to pole!
To Mary Queen the praise be given!
She sent the gentle sleep from Heaven
   That slid into my soul.
> *b.*   COLERIDGE—*Ancient Mariner.* Pt. V.
>   St. 1.

Visit her, gentle Sleep! with wings of healing,
And may this storm be but a mountain-birth,
May all the stars hang bright above her
     dwelling,
Silent as though they watched the sleeping
     Earth!
> *c.*   COLERIDGE—*Dejection. An Ode.* St. 8.

On eyes that watch as well as eyes that weep
Descends the solemn mystery of sleep,
Toiling and climbing to the very close,
The weary Body, longing for repose,
On the gained level of the day's ascent,
Halts for the night and pitches there its tent.
> *d.*   ABRAHAM COLES—*Man, the Microcosm,*
>   *and the Cosmos.*

Care-charmer Sleep, son of the sable Night,
Brother to Death, in silent darkness born;
Relieve my languish, and restore the light.
> *e.*   SAMUEL DANIEL—*Sonnet.* 51. *To*
>   *Delia.*

Awake thee, my Lady-Love!
   Wake thee, and rise!
The sun through the bower peeps
   Into thine eyes.
> *f.*   GEORGE DARLEY— *Waking Song.*

Sister Simplicitie!
Sing, sing a song to me,—
   Sing me to sleep!
Some legend low and long,
Slow as the summer song
   Of the dull Deep.
> *g.*   SIDNEY DOBELL—*A Sleep Song.*

O sleep! in pity thou art made
   A double boon to such as we;
Beneath closed lids and folds of deepest shade
   We think we see.
> *h.*   FROTHINGHAM—*The Sight of the Blind.*

36

Oh! lightly, lightly tread!
   A holy thing is sleep,
On the worn spirit shed,
   And eyes that wake to weep.
> *i.*   MRS. HEMANS—*The Sleeper.*

Then Sleep and Death, two twins of winged
     race,
Of matchless swiftness, but of silent pace.
> *j.*   HOMER—*Iliad.* Bk. XVI. L. 831.
>   Pope's trans.

O sleep, we are beholden to thee, sleep;
Thou bearest angels to us in the night,
Saints out of heaven with palms.
       Seen by thy light
Sorrow is some old tale that goeth not deep;
Love is a pouting child.
> *k.*   JEAN INGELOW—*Sleep.*

I never take a nap after dinner but when I
have had a bad night, and then the nap takes
me.
> *l.*   SAM'L JOHNSON—*Boswell's Life of*
>   *Johnson.* 1775.

O magic sleep! O comfortable bird,
That broodest o'er the troubled sea of the
     mind
Till it is hush'd and smooth! O unconfined
Restraint! imprisoned liberty! great key
To golden palaces.
> *m.*   KEATS—*Endymion.* Bk. I. L. 452.

Breathe thy balm upon the lonely,
     Gentle Sleep!
   As the twilight breezes bless
   With sweet scents the wilderness,
Ah, let warm white dove-wings only
     Round them sweep!
> *n.*   LUCY LARCOM—*Sleep Song.*

Dreams of the summer night!
   Tell her, her lover keeps
Watch! while in slumbers light
     She sleeps!
     My lady sleeps!
       Sleeps!
> *o.*   LONGFELLOW—*Spanish Student.* Act I.
>   Sc. 3. *Serenade.* St. 4.

For I am weary, and am overwrought
With too much toil, with too much care distraught,
And with the iron crown of anguish crowned.
Lay thy soft hand upon my brow and cheek,
   O peaceful Sleep!
> *p.*   LONGFELLOW—*Sleep.*

Thou driftest gently down the tides of sleep.
> *q.*   LONGFELLOW— *To a Child.* L. 115.

                  For his sleep
Was aery light, from pure digestion bred.
> *r.*   MILTON—*Paradise Lost.* Bk. V. L. 3.

           The timely dew of sleep
Now falling with soft slumb'rous weight in-
    clines
Our eyelids.
    a.   MILTON—*Paradise Lost.* Bk. IV.
                        L. 615.

While the bee with honied thigh,
That at her flowery work doth sing,
And the waters murmuring
With such a consort as they keep,
Entice the dewy-feather'd sleep.
    b.   MILTON—*Il Penseroso.* L. 142.

O, we're a' noddin', nid, nid, noddin';
O we're a' noddin' at our house at hame.
    c.   LADY NAIRNE—*We're a' Noddin'.*

Balow, my babe, lye still and sleipe,
It grieves me sair to see thee weipe.
    d.   PERCY—*Reliques. Lady Anne*
                    Bothwell's Lament.

"God bless the man who first invented sleep!"
So Sancho Panza said and so say I;
And bless him, also, that he didn't keep
His great discovery to himself, nor try
To make it,—as the lucky fellow might—
A close monopoly by patent-right.
    e.   J. G. SAXE—*Early Rising.*

Sleep the sleep that knows not breaking,
Morn of toil, nor night of waking.
    f.   SCOTT—*Lady of the Lake.* Canto I.
                        St. 31.

        Bid them come forth and hear me,
Or at their chamber-door I'll beat the drum
Till it cry sleep to death.
    g.   *King Lear.* Act II. Sc. 4. L. 118.

But I pray you, let none of your people stir
me: I have an exposition of sleep come upon
me.
    h.   *Midsummer-Night's Dream.* Act IV.
                     Sc. 1. L. 42.

       Fast asleep? It is no matter;
Enjoy the honey-heavy dew of slumber;
Thou hast no figures nor no fantasies,
Which busy care draws in the brains of men;
Therefore thou sleep'st so sound.
    i.   *Julius Cæsar.* Act II. Sc. 1. L. 229.

          He sleeps by day
More than the wild-cat.
    j.   *Merchant of Venice.* Act II. Sc. 5.
                        L. 47.

He that sleeps feels not the tooth-ache.
    k.   *Cymbeline.* Act V. Sc. 4. L. 177.

I let fall the windows of mine eyes.
    l.   *Richard III.* Act V. Sc. 3. L. 116.

Methought I heard a voice cry, "Sleep no
    more!
Macbeth does murder sleep," the innocent
    sleep.
    m.   *Macbeth.* Act II. Sc. 2. L. 35.

        Not poppy, nor mandragora,
Nor all the drowsy syrups of the world
Shall ever medicine thee to that sweet sleep
Which thou ow'dst yesterday.
    n.   *Othello.* Act III. Sc. 3. L. 330.

On your eyelids crown the god of sleep,
Charming your blood with pleasing heaviness,
Making such difference 'twixt wake and sleep
As is the difference betwixt day and night
The hour before the heavenly-harness'd team
Begins his golden progress in the east.
    o.   *Henry IV.* Pt. I. Act III. Sc. 1.
                     L. 217.

O polish'd perturbation! golden care!
That keep'st the ports of slumber open wide
To many a watchful night! sleep with it now!
Yet not so sound and half so deeply sweet
As he whose brow with homely biggen bound
Snores out the watch of night.
    p.   *Henry IV.* Pt. II. Act IV. Sc. 5.
                     L. 23.

          O sleep, O gentle sleep,
Nature's soft nurse, how have I frighted thee,
That thou no more wilt weigh my eyelids
      down
And steep my senses in forgetfulness?
    q.   *Henry IV.* Pt. II. Act III. Sc. 1.
                     L. 4.

O sleep, thou ape of death, lie dull upon her
And be her sense but as a monument.
    r.   *Cymbeline.* Act II. Sc. 2. L. 31.

Shake off this downy sleep, death's counter-
    feit,
And look on death itself!
    s.   *Macbeth.* Act II. Sc. 3. L. 81.

Sleep shall neither night nor day
Hang upon his pent-house lid.
    t.   *Macbeth.* Act I. Sc. 3. L. 19.

Sleep that knits up the ravell'd sleave of care,
The death of each day's life, sore labour's
    bath,
Balm of hurt minds, great nature's second
    course,
Chief nourisher in life's feast.
    u.   *Macbeth.* Act II. Sc. 2. L. 36.

Sleep, that sometimes shuts up sorrow's eye,
Steal me awhile from mine own company.
    v.   *Midsummer-Night's Dream.* Act III.
                   Sc. 2. L. 435.

This sleep is sound indeed, this is a sleep
That from this golden rigol hath divorc'd
So many English kings.
    w.   *Henry IV.* Pt. II. Act IV. Sc. 5.
                     L. 35.

          Thou lead them thus,
Till o'er their brows death-counterfeiting
    sleep
With leaden legs and batty wings doth creep.
    x.   *Midsummer-Night's Dream.* Act III.
                   Sc. 2. L. 363.

Thy eyes' windows fall,
Like death, when he shuts up the day of life;
Each part, depriv'd of supple government,
Shall, stiff and stark and cold, appear like
    death.
  a.   *Romeo and Juliet.* Act IV. Sc. 1.
                          L. 100.

To sleep, perchance to dream; ay, there's the
    rub;
For in that sleep of death what dreams may
  come
When we have shuffled off this mortal coil,
Must give us pause.
  b.   *Hamlet.* Act III. Sc. 1. L. 65.

Why rather, sleep, liest thou in smoky cribs,
Upon uneasy pallets stretching thee
And hushed with buzzing night-flies to thy
    slumber,
Than in the perfum'd chambers of the great,
Under the canopies of costly state,
And lull'd with sound of sweetest melody?
  c.   *Henry IV.* Pt. II. Act III. Sc. 1. L. 9.

Winding up days with toil and nights with
sleep.
  d.   *Henry V.* Act IV. Sc. 1. L. 296.

And on their lids   *   *   *
The baby Sleep is pillowed.
  e.   SHELLEY—*Queen Mab.* Pt. I.

Sleep, the fresh dew of languid love, the rain
Whose drops quench kisses till they burn
    again.
  f.   SHELLEY—*Epipsychidion.* L. 571.

Come, Sleep: O Sleep! the certain knot of
    peace,
The baiting place of wit, the balm of woe,
The poor man's wealth, the prisoner's release,
Th' indifferent judge between the high and
    low.
  g.   SIR PHILIP SIDNEY—*Astrophel and
                      Stella.* St. 39.

Take thou of me, sweet pillowes, sweetest bed;
A chamber deafe of noise, and blind of light,
A rosie garland and a weary hed.
  h.   SIR PHILIP SIDNEY—*Astrophel and
                      Stella.* St. 39.

Thou hast been called, O Sleep, the friend of
    Woe,
But 'tis the happy who have called thee so.
  i.   SOUTHEY—*The Curse of Kehama.*
                        Canto XV. St. 12.

For next to Death is Sleepe to be compared;
Therefore his house is unto his annext:
Here Sleepe, ther Richesse, and hel-gate them
    both betwext.
  j.   SPENSER—*Faerie Queene.* Bk. II.
                       Canto VII. St. 25.

All gifts but one the jealous God may keep
From our soul's longing, one he cannot—
    sleep.
This, though he grudge all other grace to
    prayer,
This grace his closed hand cannot choose but
    spare.
  k.   SWINBURNE—*Tristram of Lyonesse.
              Prelude to Tristram and Iseult.*
                          L. 205.

She sleeps: her breathings are not heard
  In palace chambers far apart,
The fragrant tresses are not stirr'd
  That lie upon her charmed heart.
She sleeps: on either hand upswells
  The gold fringed pillow lightly prest:
She sleeps, nor dreams, but ever dwells
  A perfect form in perfect rest.
  l.   TENNYSON—*The Day Dream. The
                     Sleeping Beauty.* St. 3.

The mystery
Of folded sleep.
  m.   TENNYSON—*A Dream of Fair Women.*
                          St. 66.

When in the down I sink my head,
Sleep, Death's twin-brother, times my breath.
  n.   TENNYSON—*In Memoriam.*
                        Pt. LXVIII.

For is there aught in Sleep can charm the
    wise?
To lie in dead oblivion, loosing half
The fleeting moments of too short a life—
  *   *   *   *   *   *
Who would in such a gloomy state remain
Longer than Nature craves?
  o.   THOMSON—*Seasons. Summer.* L. 71.

Yet never sleep the sun up. Prayer shou'd
Dawn with the day. There are set, awful
    hours
'Twixt heaven and us. The manna was not
    good
After sun-rising; far day sullies flowres.
Rise to prevent the sun; sleep doth sin glut,
And heaven's gate opens when the world's is
    shut.
  p.   HENRY VAUGHAN—*Rules and Lessons.*
                        St. 2.

Softly, O midnight hours!
  Move softly o'er the bowers
Where lies in happy sleep a girl so fair:
    For ye have power, men say,
    Our hearts in sleep to sway
And cage cold fancies in a moonlight snare.
  q.   AUBREY THOS. DE VERE—*Song.
               Softly, O Midnight Hours.*

Deep rest and sweet, most like indeed to
    death's own quietness.
  r.   VIRGIL—*Æneid.* Bk. VI. L. 522.
                  Wm. Morris' trans.

Hush, my dear, lie still and slumber!
  Holy angels guard thy bed!
  s.   WATTS—*Cradle Hymn.*

'Tis the voice of the sluggard; I hear him complain;
" You've waked me too soon, I must slumber again.

*　　*　　*　　*　　*　　*

A little more sleep and a little more slumber."
a.   WATTS—*Moral Songs. The Sluggard.*

Come, gentle sleep! attend thy votary's prayer,
And, though death's image, to my couch repair;
How sweet, though lifeless, yet with life to lie,
And, without dying, O how sweet to die!
b.   JOHN WOLCOTT (Peter Pindar)—
Epigram on Sleep.

And to tired limbs and over-busy thoughts,
Inviting sleep and soft forgetfulness.
c.   WORDSWORTH—*The Excursion.* Bk. IV.

Creation sleeps. 'Tis as the general pulse
Of life stood still, and nature made a pause.
d.   YOUNG—*Night Thoughts.* Night I.
L. 23.

Tired Nature's sweet restorer, balmy sleep!
He, like the world, his ready visit pays
Where fortune smiles; the wretched he forsakes.
e.   YOUNG—*Night Thoughts.* Night I. L. I.

SMILES.

But owned that smile, if oft observed and near,
Waned in its mirth, and wither'd to a sneer.
f.   BYRON—*Lara.* Canto I. St. 17.

Her very frowns are fairer far
Than smiles of other maidens are.
g.   HARTLEY COLERIDGE—*She is not Fair.*

In came Mrs. Fezziwig, one vast substantial smile.
h.   DICKENS—*Christmas Carol.* Stave 2.

The smile of her I love is like the dawn
Whose touch makes Memnon sing:
O see where wide the golden sunlight flows—
The barren desert blossoms as the rose!
i.   R. W. GILDER—*The Smile of Her I Love.*

Whence that three-cornered smile of bliss?
Three angels gave me at once a kiss.
j.   GEORGE MACDONALD—*Baby.* St. 7.

A smile that glow'd
Celestial rosy red, love's proper hue.
k.   MILTON—*Paradise Lost.* Bk. VIII.
L. 618.

For smiles from reason flow
To brute deny'd, and are of love the food.
l.   MILTON—*Paradise Lost.* Bk. IX.
L. 239.

Eternal smiles his emptiness betray,
As shallow streams run dimpling all the way.
m.   POPE—*Prologue to Satires.* L. 315.

With a smile on her lips, and a tear in her eye.
n.   SCOTT—*Marmion.* Canto V. St. 12.

Nobly he yokes
A smiling with a sigh, as if the sigh
Was that it was, for not being such a smile:
The smile mocking the sigh, that it would fly
From so divine a temple, to commix
With winds that sailors rail at.
o.   *Cymbeline.* Act IV. Sc. 2. L. 51.

One may smile, and smile, and be a villain.
p.   *Hamlet.* Act I. Sc. 5. L. 108.

Seldom he smiles, and smiles in such a sort
As if he mock'd himself, and scorn'd his spirit
That could be mov'd to smile at anything.
q.   *Julius Cæsar.* Act I. Sc. 2. L. 205.

Those happy smilets,
That play'd on her ripe lip, seem'd not to know
What guests were in her eyes; which parted thence,
As pearls from diamonds dropp'd.
r.   *King Lear.* Act IV. Sc. 3. L. 21.

I feel in every smile a chain.
s.   JOHN WOLCOTT (Peter Pindar)—
Pindariana.

A tender smile, our sorrows' only balm.
t.   YOUNG—*Love of Fame.* Satire V.
L. 108.

SNOW.

Lo, sifted through the winds that blow,
Down comes the soft and silent snow,
White petals from the flowers that grow
In the cold atmosphere.
u.   GEORGE W. BUNGAY—*The Artists of the Air.*

Through the sharp air a flaky torrent flies,
Mocks the slow sight, and hides the gloomy skies;
The fleecy clouds their chilly bosoms bare,
And shed their substance on the floating air.
v.   CRABBE—*Inebriety.*

Announced by all the trumpets of the sky,
Arrives the snow, and, driving o'er the fields,
Seems nowhere to alight: the whited air
Hides hills and woods, the river, and the heaven,
And veils the farmhouse at the garden's end.
The sled and traveller stopped, the courier's feet
Delayed, all friends shut out, the housemates sit
Around the radiant fireplace, enclosed
In a tumultuous privacy of storm.
w.   EMERSON—*The Snow-Storm.*

Come, see the north-wind's masonry.
Out of an unseen quarry evermore
Furnished with tile, the fierce artificer
Curves his white bastions with projected roof
Round every windward stake, or tree, or door.
Speeding, the myriad-handed, his wild work
So fanciful, so savage, naught cares he
For number or proportion.
   a.   EMERSON—*The Snow-Storm.*

Out of the bosom of the Air,
  Out of the cloud-folds of her garments
    shaken,
Over the woodlands brown and bare,
  Over the harvest-fields forsaken,
    Silent, and soft, and slow
      Descends the snow.
   b.   LONGFELLOW—*Snow-Flakes.*

The cold winds swept the mountain-height,
  And pathless was the dreary wild,
And, 'mid the cheerless hours of night,
  A mother wandered with her child :
As through the drifting snows she press'd
The babe was sleeping on her breast.
   c.   SEBA SMITH—*The Snow-Storm.*

SOCIETY.

For it is most true that a natural and secret
hatred and aversation towards society in any
man, hath somewhat of the savage beast.
   d.   BACON—*Essays. Civil and Moral. Of
                  Friendship.*

A people is but the attempt of many
To rise to the completer life of one—
And those who live as models for the mass
Are singly of more value than they all.
   e.   ROBERT BROWNING—*Luria.* Act V.
                        L. 334.

Every man is like the company he is wont
to keep.
   f.   EURIPIDES—*Phœmissæ.* Frag. 809.

For every social wrong there must be a
remedy. But the remedy can be nothing less
than the abolition of the wrong.
   g.   HENRY GEORGE—*Social Problems.*
                        Ch. IX.

The noisy and extensive scene of crowds
without company, and dissipation without
pleasure.
   h.   GIBBON—*Memoirs.* Vol. I. P. 116.

I live in the crowds of jollity, not so much
to enjoy company as to shun myself.
   i.   SAM'L JOHNSON—*Rasselas.* Ch. XVI.

He might have proved a useful adjunct, if
not an ornament to society.
   j.   CHARLES LAMB—*Captain Starkey.*

Society is like a large piece of frozen water ;
and skating well is the great art of social life.
   k.   L. E. LANDON.

A system in which the two great commandments were, to hate your neighbour and to love
your neighbour's wife.
   l.   MACAULAY—*Essays. Moore's Life of
                        Lord Byron.*

For solitude sometimes is best society,
And short retirement urges sweet return.
   m.   MILTON—*Paradise Lost.* Bk. IX.
                        L. 249.

Heav'n forming each on other to depend,
A master, or a servant, or a friend,
Bids each on other for assistance call,
Till one man's weakness grows the strength
  of all.
   n.   POPE—*Essay on Man.* Ep. II. L. 249.

           Society is no comfort
To one not sociable.
   o.   *Cymbeline.* Act IV. Sc. 2. L. 12.

                  To make society
The sweeter welcome, we will keep ourself
Till supper-time alone.
   p.   *Macbeth.* Act III. Sc. 1. L. 42.

Whilst I was big in clamour came there in a
  man,
Who, having seen me in my worst estate,
Shunn'd my abhorr'd society.
   q.   *King Lear.* Act V. Sc. 3. L. 208.

Men lived like fishes ; the great ones devoured the small.
   r.   ALGERNON SIDNEY—*Discourses on
              Government.* Ch. II. Sec. XVIII.

Ah, you flavour everything ; you are the
vanille of society.
   s.   SYDNEY SMITH—LADY HOLLAND'S
              Memoir. Vol. I. P. 262.

Society having ordained certain customs,
men are bound to obey the law of society,
and conform to its harmless orders.
   t.   THACKERAY—*The Book of Snobs.* Ch. I.

Society therefore is as ancient as the world.
   u.   VOLTAIRE—*A Philosophical Dictionary.
                        Policy.*

Nor greetings where no kindness is, nor all
The dreary intercourse of daily life.
   v.   WORDSWORTH—*Lines composed a few
            miles above Tintern Abbey.*

Society became my glittering bride,
And airy hopes my children.
   w.   WORDSWORTH—*The Excursion.* Bk. III.

                 There is
One great society alone on earth :
The noble Living and the noble Dead.
   x.   WORDSWORTH—*The Prelude.* Bk. XI.

SOLITUDE.

But little do men perceive what solitude is, and how far it extendeth. For a crowd is not company; and faces are but a gallery of pictures; and talk but a tinkling cymbal, where there is no love.

a.   Bacon—*Essays. Of Friendship.*

Converse with men makes sharp the glittering wit,
But God to man doth speak in solitude.

b.   John Stuart Blackie—*Sonnet.*
              Highland Solitude.

There is no such thing as solitude, nor anything that can be said to be alone and by itself, but God, who is his own circle, and can subsist by himself.

c.   Sir Thomas Browne—*Religio Medici.*
             Pt. II. Sec. X.

Among them, but not of them.

d.   Byron—*Childe Harold.* Canto III.
                 St. 113.

But 'midst the crowd, the hum, the shock of men,
To hear, to see, to feel, and to possess,
And roam along, the world's tired denizen,
With none who bless us, none whom we
   can bless.

e.   Byron—*Childe Harold.* Canto II.
                 St. 26.

He enter'd in his house—his home no more,
For without hearts there is no home;—and felt
The solitude of passing his own door
Without a welcome.

f.   Byron—*Don Juan.* Canto III. St. 52.

He makes a solitude, and calls it—peace!

g.   Byron—*The Bride of Abydos.*
              Canto II. St. 20.

Herself the solitary scion left
Of a time-honour'd race.

h.   Byron—*The Dream.* St. 2.

In solitude, when we are *least* alone.

i.   Byron—*Childe Harold.* Canto III.
                 St. 90.

This is to be alone; this, this is solitude!

j.   Byron—*Childe Harold.* Canto II.
                 St. 26.

'Tis solitude should teach us how to die;
It hath no flatterers; vanity can give
No hollow aid; alone—man with his God
   must strive.

k.   Byron—*Childe Harold.* Canto IV.
                 St. 33.

The world was sad!—the garden was a wild!
And man, the hermit, sigh'd—till woman
   smiled.

l.   Campbell—*Pleasures of Hope.* Pt. II.
                 L. 37.

He is never less at leisure than when at leisure, nor less alone than when he is alone.

m.   Cicero—*De Officiis.* Bk. III. Ch. I.

Alone, alone, all, all alone,
  Alone on a wide, wide sea.

n.   Coleridge—*The Ancient Mariner.*
                 Pt. IV.

So lonely 'twas that God himself
  Scarce seemed there to be.

o.   Coleridge—*The Ancient Mariner.*
                 Pt. VII.

How sweet, how passing sweet is solitude?
But grant me still a friend in my retreat,
Whom I may whisper—solitude is sweet.

p.   Cowper—*Retirement.* L. 740.

I am monarch of all I survey,
  My right there is none to dispute,
From the centre all round to the sea,
  I am lord of the fowl and the brute.

q.   Cowper—*Verses supposed to be written
                by Alexander Selkirk.*

Oh, for a lodge in some vast wilderness,
Some boundless contiguity of shade,
Where rumour of oppression and deceit,
Of unsuccessful or successful war,
Might never reach me more!

r.   Cowper—*The Task.* Bk. II. L. 1.

O solitude, where are the charms
  That sages have seen in thy face?
Better dwell in the midst of alarms,
  Than reign in this horrible place.

s.   Cowper—*Verses supposed to be written
                by Alexander Selkirk.*

Prison'd in a parlour snug and small,
Like bottled wasps upon a southern wall.

t.   Cowper—*Retirement.* L. 493.

Solitude is the nurse of enthusiasm, and enthusiasm is the true parent of genius. In all ages solitude has been called for—has been flown to.

u.   Isaac Disraeli—*Literary Character of
              Men of Genius.* Ch. X.

There is a society in the deepest solitude.

v.   Isaac Disraeli—*Literary Character of
              Men of Genius.* Ch. X.

So vain is the belief
That the sequestered path has fewest flowers.

w.   Thomas Doubleday—*Sonnet. The
                Poet's Solitude.*

Thrice happy he, who by some shady grove,
  Far from the clamorous world, doth live his
    own;
Though solitary, who is not alone,
But doth converse with that eternal love.

x.   Drummond—*Urania; or, Spiritual
                 Poems.*

We enter the world alone, we leave it alone.

y.   Froude—*Short Studies on Great
             Subjects. Sea Studies.*

I was never less alone than when by myself.

z.   Gibbon—*Memoirs.* Vol. I. P. 117.

Nobody with me at sea but myself.
  a.   GOLDSMITH—*The Haunch of Venison.*

Far from the madding crowd's ignoble strife.
  b.   GRAY—*Elegy in a Country Churchyard.*
                                    St. 19.

O Solitude! if I must with thee dwell,
  Let it not be among the jumbled heap
  Of murky buildings: climb with me the
      steep,—
Nature's observatory—whence the dell,
In flowery slopes, its river's crystal swell,
  May seem a span; let me thy vigils keep
  'Mongst boughs pavilion'd, where the deer's
      swift leap
Startles the wild bee from the foxglove bell.
  c.   KEATS—*Sonnet. O Solitude! If I Must
                              With Thee Dwell.*

Why should we faint and fear to live alone,
Since all alone, so Heaven has willed, we die,
Nor even the tenderest heart and next our own
Knows half the reasons why we smile and sigh.
  d.   KEBLE—*The Christian Year.
              Twenty-Fourth Sunday after Trinity.*

Solitude is as needful to the imagination as
society is wholesome for the character.
  e.   LOWELL—*Among my Books. Dryden.*

    Alone!—that worn-out word,
So idly spoken, and so coldly heard;
Yet all that poets sing, and grief hath known,
Of hope laid waste, knells in that word—
    ALONE!
  f.   BULWER-LYTTON—*The New Timon.*
                                    Pt. II.

              And Wisdom's self
Oft seeks to sweet retired solitude,
Where, with her best nurse, Contemplation,
She plumes her feathers, and lets grow her
    wings,
That in the various bustle of resort
Were all too ruffled, and sometimes impaired.
  g.   MILTON—*Comus.* L. 375.

For solitude sometimes is best society,
And short retirement urges sweet return.
  h.   MILTON—*Paradise Lost.* Bk. IX.
                                    L. 249.

Until I truly loved, I was alone.
  i.   MRS. NORTON—*The Lady of La Garaye.*
                              Pt. II. L. 381.

Far in a wild, unknown to public view,
From youth to age a reverend hermit grew;
The moss his bed, the cave his humble cell,
His food the fruits, his drink the crystal well,
Remote from man, with God he pass'd the
    days;
Prayer all his business, all his pleasure praise.
  j.   PARNELL—*The Hermit.*

    Whosoever is delighted in solitude, is either
a wild beast or a god.
  k.   PLATO—*Protag.* I. 337.

Shall I, like an hermit, dwell
On a rock or in a cell?
  l.   SIR WALTER RALEIGH—*Poem.* See
              CAYLEY'S *Life of Raleigh.* Vol. I.

Then never less alone than when alone.
  m.   SAM'L ROGERS—*Human Life.* L. 759.

When, musing on companions gone,
We doubly feel ourselves alone.
  n.   SCOTT—*Marmion.* Canto II.
                                    Introduction.

I love tranquil solitude
And such society
As is quiet, wise, and good.
  o.   SHELLEY—*Rarely, Rarely, Comest Thou.*

Alone each heart must cover up its dead;
Alone, through bitter toil, achieve its rest.
  p.   BAYARD TAYLOR—*The Poet's Journal.
                      First Evening.* Conclusion.

'Tis not for golden eloquence I pray,
  A godlike tongue to move a stony heart—
  Methinks it were full well to be apart
In solitary uplands far away,
Betwixt the blossoms of a rosy spray,
  Dreaming upon the wonderful sweet face
  Of Nature, in a wild and pathless place.
  q.   FREDERICK TENNYSON—*Sonnet.* From
              A Treasury of English Sonnets.
              Edited by David M. Main.

I could live in the woods with thee in sight,
  Where never should human foot intrude:
Or with thee find light in the darkest night,
  And a social crowd in solitude.
  r.   TIBULLUS—*Elegies.* Elegy I.

Often have I sighed to measure
By myself a lonely pleasure,—
Sighed to think I read a book,
Only read, perhaps, by me.
  s.   WORDSWORTH—*To the Small Celandine.*

O! lost to virtue, lost to manly thought,
Lost to the noble sallies of the soul!
Who think it solitude to be alone.
  t.   YOUNG—*Night Thoughts.* Night III.
                                    L. 6.

O sacred solitude! divine retreat!
Choice of the prudent! envy of the great,
By thy pure stream, or in thy waving shade,
We court fair wisdom, that celestial maid.
  u.   YOUNG—*Love of Fame.* Satire V.
                                    L. 254.

This sacred shade and solitude, what is it?
'Tis the felt presence of the Deity,
Few are the faults we flatter when alone.
  v.   YOUNG—*Night Thoughts.* Night V.
                                    L. 172.

SONG.

They sang of love and not of fame;
  Forgot was Britain's glory ;
Each heart recalled a different name,
  But all sang " Annie Laurie."
a.   BAYARD TAYLOR—*A Song of the Camp.*

That music in itself, whose sounds are song,
The poetry of speech.
b.   BYRON—*Childe Harold.* Canto IV.
St. 58.

Unlike my subject now * * * shall be my
    song,
It shall be witty and it sha'n't be long!
c.   EARL OF CHESTERFIELD—*Preface to
Letters.* Vol. I.

And heaven had wanted one immortal song.
d.   DRYDEN—*Absalom and Achitophel.*
Pt. I. L. 197.

The fineness which a hymn or psalm affords
Is when the soul unto the lines accords.
e.   HERBERT—*The Church. A True Hymn.*

He play'd an ancient ditty long since mute,
In Provence call'd, " La belle dame sans
    mercy."
f.   KEATS—*The Eve of St. Agnes.* St. 33.

Listen to that song, and learn it !
Half my kingdom would I give,
        As I live,
If by such songs you would earn it !
g.   LONGFELLOW—*Tales of a Wayside Inn.*
Pt. I. *The Musician's Tale. The
Saga of King Olaf.* Pt. V.

Such songs have power to quiet
  The restless pulse of care,
And come like the benediction
  That follows after prayer.
h.   LONGFELLOW—*The Day is Done.* St. 9.

The song on its mighty pinions
Took every living soul, and lifted it gently to
    heaven.
i.   LONGFELLOW—*The Children of the
Lord's Supper.* L. 44.

Odds life ! must one swear to the truth of a
song?
j.   PRIOR—*A Better Answer.*

Builders, raise the ceiling high,
Raise the dome into the sky,
  Hear the wedding song !
For the happy groom is near,
Tall as Mars, and statelier,
  Hear the wedding song !
k.   SAPPHO—*Fragments.* J. S. Easby
Smith's trans.

Song forbids victorious deeds to die.
l.   SCHILLER—*The Artists.*

The lively Shadow-World of Song.
m.   SCHILLER—*The Artists.*

Now, good Cesario, but that piece of song,
That old and antique song we heard last
    night ;
Methought it did relieve my passion much,
More than light airs and recollected terms
Of these most brisk and giddy-paced times :
Come, but one verse.
n.   *Twelfth Night.* Act II. Sc. 4. L. 2.

Songs consecrate to truth and liberty.
o.   SHELLEY—*To Wordsworth.* L. 12.

Because the gift of Song was chiefly lent,
To give consoling music for the joys
We lack, and not for those which we possess.
p.   BAYARD TAYLOR—*The Poet's Journal.
Third Evening.*

Short swallow-flights of song, that dip
Their wings in tears, and skim away.
q.   TENNYSON—*In Memoriam.*
Pt. XLVIII. St. 4.

Swift, swift, and bring with you
  Song's Indian summer !
r.   FRANCIS THOMPSON—*A Carrier Song.*
St. 2.

Soft words, with nothing in them, make a
song.
s.   EDMUND WALLER—*To Mr. Creech.*
L. 10.

A careless song, with a little nonsense in it
now and then, does not mis-become a monarch.
t.   HORACE WALPOLE—*Letter to Sir
Horace Mann.* 1770.

SORROW.

Ah, nothing comes to us too soon but sorrow.
u.   BAILEY—*Festus.* Sc. *Home.*

Night brings out stars as sorrow shows us
    truths.
v.   BAILEY—*Festus.* Sc. *Water and Wood.
Midnight.*

            Sorrow preys upon
Its solitude and nothing more diverts it
From its sad visions of the other world
Than calling it at moments back to this.
The busy have no time for tears.
w.   BYRON—*The Two Foscari.* Act IV.
Sc. 1.

Men die, but sorrow never dies ;
  The crowding years divide in vain,
And the wide world is knit with ties
  Of common brotherhood in pain.
x.   SUSAN COOLIDGE—*The Cradle Tomb in
Westminster Abbey.*

The path of sorrow, and that path alone,
Leads to the land where sorrow is unknown.
y.   COWPER—*To an Afflicted Protestant
Lady.*

Who never ate his bread in sorrow,
  Who never spent the darksome hours
Weeping, and watching for the morrow,—
  He knows ye not, ye gloomy Powers.
    a.   GOETHE—*Wilhelm Meister.*   Bk. II.
                        Ch. XIII.

Since sorrow never comes too late,
And happiness too swiftly flies.
    b.   GRAY—*Ode on a Distant Prospect of*
                        Eton College.

To each his suff'rings : all are men,
  Condemn'd alike to groan ;
The tender for another's pain,
  Th' unfeeling for his own.
    c.   GRAY—*On a Distant Prospect of Eton*
                    College.   St. 10.

Oh, why should vows so fondly made,
  Be broken ere the morrow,
To one who loves as never maid
  Loved in this world of sorrow ?
    d.   HOGG—*The Broken Heart.*

           A happier lot were mine,
If I must lose thee, to go down to earth,
For I shall have no hope when thou art
    gone,—
Nothing but sorrow.   Father have I none,
And no dear mother.
    e.   HOMER—*Iliad.*   Bk. VI.   L. 530.
                      Bryant's trans.

Sinks my sad soul with sorrow to the grave.
    f.   HOMER—*Iliad.*   Bk. XXII.   L. 543.
                      Pope's trans.

Hang sorrow, care 'll kill a cat.
    g.   BEN JONSON—*Every Man in his Humour.*
         Act I.   Sc. 3.   See also GEO. WITHER
                 —*Poem on Christmas.*

How beautiful, if sorrow had not made
Sorrow more beautiful than Beauty's self.
    h.   KEATS—*Hyperion.*   Bk. I.   L. 36.

          O, Sorrow !
          Why dost borrow
Heart's lightness from the merriment of May ?
    i.   KEATS—*Endymion.*   Bk. IV.

        To Sorrow
     I bade good-morrow,
And thought to leave her far away behind ;
       But cheerly, cheerly,
       She loves me dearly :
She is so constant to me, and so kind.
    j.   KEATS—*Endymion.*   Bk. IV.

      There is no greater sorrow
Than to be mindful of the happy time
In misery.
    k.   LONGFELLOW—*Inferno.*   Canto V.
                        L. 121.

Alas ! by some degree of woe
  We every bliss must gain :
The heart can ne'er a transport know,
  That never feels a pain.
    l.   LORD LYTTLETON—*A Song.*

Weep on ; and, as thy sorrows flow,
I'll taste the luxury of woe.
    m.   MOORE—*Anacreontic.*

Sorrows remembered sweeten present joy.
    n.   POLLOK—*Course of Time.*   Bk. I.
                        L. 464.

Do not cheat thy Heart and tell her,
  " Grief will pass away,
Hope for fairer times in future,
  And forget to-day."
Tell her, if you will, that sorrow
  Need not come in vain ;
Tell her that the lesson taught her
  Far outweighs the pain.
    o.   ADELAIDE A. PROCTER—*Friend Sorrow.*

I was not always a man of woe.
    p.   SCOTT—*Lay of the Last Minstrel.*
                    Canto II.   St. 12.

Down, thou climbing sorrow.
    q.   *King Lear.*   Act II.   Sc. 4.   L. 57.

                Each new morn,
New widows howl, new orphans cry, new
    sorrows
Strike heaven on the face, that it resounds
As if it felt with Scotland and yell'd out
Like syllable of dolour.
    r.   *Macbeth.*   Act IV.   Sc. 3.   L. 4.

Eighty odd years of sorrow have I seen,
And each hour's joy wrecked with a week of
    teen.
    s.   *Richard III.*   Act IV.   Sc. 1.   L. 96.

Forgive me, Valentine : if hearty sorrow
Be a sufficient ransom for offence,
I tender 't here : I do as truly suffer,
As e'er I did commit.
    t.   *Two Gentlemen of Verona.*   Act V.
                     Sc. 4.   L. 74.

Give sorrow words ; the grief that does not
    speak
Whispers the o'er-fraught heart and bids 't
    break.
    u.   *Macbeth.*   Act IV.   Sc. 3.   L. 209.

          Here I and sorrows sit :
Here is my throne, bid kings come bow to it.
    v.   *King John.*   Act III.   Sc. 1.   L. 73.

If sorrow can admit society,
Tell o'er your woes again by viewing mine.
    w.   *Richard III.*   Act IV.   Sc. 4.   L. 38.

I have, as when the sun doth light a storm,
Buried this sigh in wrinkle of a smile :
But sorrow, that is couch'd in seeming glad-
    ness,
Is like that mirth fate turns to sudden sadness.
    x.   *Troilus and Cressida.*   Act I.   Sc. 1.
                        L. 37.

I will instruct my sorrows to be proud.
    y.   *King John.*   Act III.   Sc. 1.   L. 68.

Joy, being altogether wanting,
It doth remember me the more of sorrow.
  a.   *Richard II*. Act III. Sc. 4. L. 13.

One sorrow never comes but brings an heir,
That may succeed as his inheritor.
  b.   *Pericles*. Act I. Sc. 4. L. 63.

Sorrow breaks seasons and reposing hours,
Makes the night morning, and the noon-tide
        night.
  c.   *Richard III*. Act I. Sc. 4. L. 76.

Sorrow ends not when it seemeth done.
  d.   *Richard II*. Act I. Sc. 2. L. 61.

            This sorrow's heavenly;
It strikes where it doth love.
  e.   *Othello*. Act V. Sc. 2. L. 21.

          'Tis better to be lowly born,
And range with humble livers in content,
Than to be perk'd up in a glistering grief,
And wear a golden sorrow.
  f.   *Henry VIII*. Act II. Sc. 3. L. 19.

To weep with them that weep doth ease some
        deal;
But sorrow flouted at is double death.
  g.   *Titus Andronicus*. Act III. Sc. 1.
                                          L. 245.

When sorrows come, they come not single
        spies,
But in battalions.
  h.   *Hamlet*. Act IV. Sc. 5. L. 78.

Wherever sorrow is, relief would be:
If you do sorrow at my grief in love,
By giving love your sorrow and my grief were
        both extermin'd.
  i.   *As You Like It*. Act III. Sc. 5. L. 86.

          Your cause of sorrow
Must not be measur'd by his worth, for then
It hath no end.
  j.   *Macbeth*. Act V. Sc. 8. L. 44.

          Each time we love,
We turn a nearer and a broader mark
To that keen archer, Sorrow, and he strikes.
  k.   ALEXANDER SMITH—*City Poems. A
                                Boy's Dream*.

Prostrate on earth the bleeding warrior lies,
And Isr'el's beauty on the mountains dies.
  How are the mighty fallen!
Hush'd be my sorrow, gently fall my tears,
Lest my sad tale should reach the alien's ears:
Bid Fame be dumb, and tremble to proclaim
In heathen Gath, or Ascalon, our shame
Lest proud Philistia, lest our haughty foe,
With impious scorn insult our solemn woe.
  l.   W. C. SOMERVILLE—*The Lamentation
                of David over Saul and Jonathan*.

Time, thy name is sorrow, says the stricken
  Heart of life, laid waste with wasting flame
Ere the change of things and thoughts re-
      quicken,
  Time, thy name.
  m.   SWINBURNE—*Time and Life*. St. 1.

What shall be done for sorrow
  With love whose race is run?
Where help is none to borrow,
  What shall be done?
  n.   SWINBURNE—*Wasted Love*.

O sorrow, wilt thou rule my blood,
  But sometimes lovely, like a bride,
  And put thy harsher moods aside,
If thou wilt have me wise and good.
  o.   TENNYSON—*In Memoriam*. Pt. LIX.

Smit with exceeding sorrow unto Death.
  p.   TENNYSON—*The Lover's Tale*. L. 597.

That a sorrow's crown of sorrow is remember
      ing happier things.
  q.   TENNYSON—*Locksley Hall*. St. 38.

When I was young, I said to Sorrow,
  "Come and I will play with thee!"
      He is near me now all day,
      And at night returns to say,
"I will come again to-morrow—
  I will come and stay with thee."
  r.   AUBREY THOS. DE VERE—*Song. When
                I was Young I said to Sorrow*.

Past sorrows, let us moderately lament them;
For those to come, seek wisely to prevent
      them.
  s.   JOHN WEBSTER—*Duchess of Malfi*.
                                        Act III. Sc. 2.

Sorrow is held the eldest child of sin.
  t.   JOHN WEBSTER—*Duchess of Malfi*.
                                        Act V. Sc. 5.

Some natural sorrow, loss, or pain,
That has been and may be again.
  u.   WORDSWORTH—*The Solitary Reaper*.

Woes cluster; rare are solitary woes;
They love a train, they tread each other's heel.
  v.   YOUNG—*Night Thoughts*. Night III.
                                          L. 63.

SOUL (THE).

But thou shalt flourish in immortal youth,
Unhurt amidst the wars of elements,
The wrecks of matter, and the crush of worlds.
  w.   ADDISON—*Cato*. Act V. Sc. 1.

A soul as white as Heaven.
  x.   BEAUMONT AND FLETCHER—*The Maid's
                        Tragedy*. Act IV. Sc. 1.

And I have written three books on the soul,
Proving absurd all written hitherto,
And putting us to ignorance again.
  y.   ROBERT BROWNING—*Cleon*.

And he that makes his soul his surety,
I think, does give the best security.

  a.   Butler—*Hudibras.* Pt. III. Canto I.
                             L. 203.

The dome of Thought, the palace of the Soul.

  b.   Byron—*Childe Harold.* Canto II.
                             St. 6.

Everywhere the human soul stands between a hemisphere of light and another of darkness; on the confines of two everlasting hostile empires, Necessity and Freewill.

  c.   Carlyle—*Essays. Goethe's Works.*

No iron chain, or outward force of any kind, could ever compel the soul of man to believe or to disbelieve: it is his own indefeasible light, that judgment of his; he will reign and believe there by the grace of God alone!

  d.   Carlyle—*Heroes and Hero Worship.*
                          Lecture IV.

It is the soul itself which sees and hears, and not those parts which are, as it were, but windows to the soul.

  e.   Cicero.

From the looks—not the lips, is the soul reflected.

  f.   M'Donald Clarke—*The Rejected
                             Lover.*

A corporation has no soul.

  g.   Coke—*Reports.* X. Rep. 32.

The soul of man is larger than the sky,
Deeper than ocean, or the abysmal dark
Of the unfathomed centre.

  h.   Hartley Coleridge—*Poems. To
                          Shakespeare.*

A happy soul, that all the way
To heaven hath a summer's day.

  i.   Richard Crashaw—*In Praise of
       Lessius' Rule of Health.* L. 33.

A fiery soul, which, working out its way,
Fretted the pygmy-body to decay,
And o'er-inform'd the tenement of clay.

  j.   Dryden—*Absalom and Achitophel.*
                        Pt. I. L. 156.

I have a soul that, like an ample shield,
Can take in all, and verge enough for more.

  k.   Dryden—*Sebastian.* Act I. Sc. 1.

The one thing in the world, of value, is the active soul.

  l.   Emerson—*The American Scholar.*

Gravity is the ballast of the soul, which keeps the mind steady.

  m.   Fuller—*The Holy and Profane States.
                           Gravity.*

Build thee more stately mansions, O my soul,
As the swift seasons roll!
Leave thy low-vaulted past!
Let each new temple, nobler than the last,
Shut thee from heaven with a dome more vast,
Till thou at length art free,
Leaving thine outgrown shell by life's unresting sea!

  n.   O. W. Holmes—*The Chambered
                       Nautilus.* St. 5.

And rest at last where souls unbodied dwell,
In ever-flowing meads of Asphodel.

  o.   Homer—*Odyssey.* Bk. XXIV. L. 19.
                        Pope's trans.

The production of souls is the secret of unfathomable depth.

  p.   Victor Hugo—*Shakespeare.* Bk. V.
                             Ch. I.

The limbs will quiver and move after the soul is gone.

  q.   Sam'l Johnson—See Northcote's
                       Johnsoniana. 487.

Ah, the souls of those that die
Are but sunbeams lifted higher.

  r.   Longfellow—*Christus. The Golden
                 Legend.* Pt. IV. *The Cloisters.*

The soul never grows old.

  s.   Longfellow—*Hyperion.* Bk. IV.
                          Ch. VIII.

There was a little man, and he had a little soul;
And he said, "Little Soul, let us try, try, try!"

  t.   Moore—*Little Man and Little Soul.*

Above the vulgar flight of common souls.

  u.   Arthur Murphy—*Zenobia.* Act V.
                         Sc. 1. L. 154.

Or looks on heav'n with more than mortal eyes,
Bids his free soul expatiate in the skies,
Amid her kindred stars familiar roam,
Survey the region, and confess her home.

  v.   Pope—*Windsor Forest.* L. 264.

The soul, uneasy and confin'd from home,
Rests and expatiates in a life to come.

  w.   Pope—*Essay on Man.* Ep. I. L. 97.

Vital spark of heav'nly flame!

  x.   Pope—*Paraphrase of Emperor Hadrian's
          " Ode of the Dying Christian to
                      His Soul."*

My soul, the seas are rough, and thou a stranger
In these false coasts; O keep aloof; there's danger;
Cast forth thy plummet; see, a rock appears;
Thy ships want sea-room; make it with thy tears.

  y.   Quarles—*Emblems.* Bk. III. Ep. XI.

Go, Soul, the Body's guest,
  Upon a thankless errand;
Fear not to touch the best,
  The truth shall be thy warrant.
Go, since I needs must die,
And give them all the lie.
   a.   Sir Walter Raleigh—*The Farewell.*

Yet stab at thee who will,
No stab the soul can kill!
   b.   Sir Walter Raleigh—*The Farewell.*

And her immortal part with angels lives.
   c.   *Romeo and Juliet.* Act V. Sc. 1.
                        L. 19.
Think'st thou I'll endanger my soul gratis?
   d.   *Merry Wives of Windsor.* Act II.
                      Sc. 2. L. 14.

               Thy soul's flight,
If it find heaven, must find it out to-night.
   e.   *Macbeth.* Act III. Sc. 1. L. 141.

       Within this wall of flesh
There is a soul counts thee her creditor.
   f.   *King John.* Act III. Sc. 3. L. 20.

Whate'er of earth is form'd, to earth returns,
       * * * The soul
Of man alone, that particle divine,
Escapes the wreck of worlds, when all things
    fail.
   g.   W. C. Somerville—*The Chase.*
                      Bk. IV. L. 1.

For of the soule the bodie forme doth take;
For soule is forme and doth the bodie make.
   h.   Spenser—*An Hymn in Honour of
                      Beauty.* L. 132.

    The soul is a fire that darts its rays through
all the senses; it is in this fire that existence
consists; all the observations and all the
efforts of philosophers ought to turn towards
this Me, the centre and moving power of our
sentiments and our ideas.
   i.   Madame de Staël—*Germany.* Pt. III.
                      Ch. II.

Her soul from earth to Heaven lies,
  Like the ladder of the vision,
      Whereon go
      To and fro,
  In ascension and demission,
Star-flecked feet of Paradise.
   j.   Francis Thompson—*Scala Jacobi
                Portaque Eburnea.* St. 1.

    What then do you call your soul? What
idea have you of it? You cannot of yourselves, without revelation, admit the existence
within you of anything but a power unknown
to you of feeling and thinking.
   k.   Voltaire—*A Philosophical Dictionary.
                      Soul.*

And keeps that palace of the soul serene.
   l.   Edmund Waller—*Of Tea.* L. 9.

A charge to keep I have,
  A God to glorify:
A never-dying soul to save,
  And fit it for the sky.
   m.   Charles Wesley—*Hymns.* 318.

But who would force the Soul, tilts with a
    straw
Against a Champion cased in adamant.
   n.   Wordsworth—*Ecclesiastical Sonnets.*
        Pt. III. VII. *Persecution of the
                Scottish Covenanters.*

           For the Gods approve
The depth, and not the tumult, of the soul.
   o.   Wordsworth—*Laodamia.*

SOUND.

A thousand trills and quivering sounds
  In airy circles o'er us fly,
Till, wafted by a gentle breeze,
They faint and languish by degrees,
  And at a distance die.
   p.   Addison—*An Ode for St. Cecilia's
                    Day.* VI.

With many a stiff thwack, many a bang,
Hard crab-tree and old iron rang.
   q.   Butler—*Hudibras.* Pt. I. Canto II.
                       L. 831.

To varnish nonsense with the charms of
    sound.
   r.   Churchill—*The Apology.* L. 219.

Conscience avaunt, *Richard's* himself again:
Hark! the shrill trumpet sounds, to horse,
    away,
My soul's in arms, and eager for the fray.
   s.   Colley Cibber—*Richard III. (altered).*
                  Act V. Sc. 3.

A noise like of a hidden brook
  In the leafy month of June,
That to the sleeping woods all night
  Singeth a quiet tune.
   t.   Coleridge—*The Ancient Mariner.*
                Pt. V. St. 18.

By magic numbers and persuasive sound.
   u.   Congreve—*The Mourning Bride.*
                  Act I. Sc. 1.

Small griefs find tongues: full casques are
    ever found
To give, if any, yet but little sound,
Deep waters noyselesse are; and this we
    know,
That chiding streams betray small depth
    below.
   v.   Herrick—*Hesperides. To His Mistresse
        Objecting to Him Neither Toying or
                    Talking.*

I hear a sound so fine there's nothing lives
'Twixt it and silence.
   w.   James Sheridan Knowles—*Virginius.*
                  Act V. Sc. 2.

And filled the air with barbarous dissonance.
    a.   Milton—*Comus.* L. 550.

Sonorous metal blowing martial sounds,
At which the universal host up sent
A shout that tore hell's concave, and beyond
Frighted the reign of Chaos and old Night.
    b.   Milton—*Paradise Lost.* Bk. I. L. 540.

Their rising all at once was as the sound
Of thunder heard remote.
    c.   Milton—*Paradise Lost.* Bk. II. L. 476.

The murmur that springs
From the growing of grass.
    d.   Poe—*Al Aaraaf.* Pt. II. L. 124.

The sound must seem an echo to the sense.
    e.   Pope—*Essay on Criticism.* L. 365.

                 What's the business,
That such a hideous trumpet calls to parley
The sleepers of the house? Speak, speak!
    f.   *Macbeth.* Act II. Sc. 3. L. 86.

Hark! from the tombs a doleful sound.
    g.   Isaac Watts—*Hymns and Spiritual
               Songs.* Bk. II. Hymn 63.

My eyes are dim with childish tears,
  My heart is idly stirred,
For the same sound is in my ears
  Which in those days I heard.
    h.   Wordsworth—*The Fountain.*

SPEECH.

And let him be sure to leave other men their
turns to speak.
    i.   Bacon—*Essays. Civil and Moral.
               Of Discourse.* No. 32.

Discretion of speech is more than eloquence;
and to speak agreeably to him with whom we
deal is more than to speak in good words or
in good order.
    j.   Bacon—*Essays. Of Discourse.*

For brevity is very good,
Where we are, or are not understood.
    k.   Butler—*Hudibras.* Pt. I. Canto I.
                      L. 669.

He who does not make his words rather
serve to conceal than discover the sense of his
heart deserves to have it pulled out like a
traitor's and shown publicly to the rabble.
    l.   Butler—*The Modern Politician.*

His speech was a fine sample, on the whole,
Of rhetoric, which the learn'd call "*rigmarole.*"
    m.   Byron—*Don Juan.* Canto I. St. 174.

Boys flying kites haul in their white winged
  birds;
You can't do that way when you're flying
  words.
"Careful with fire," is good advice we know,
"Careful with words," is ten times doubly so.
Thoughts unexpressed may sometimes fall
  back dead;
But God Himself can't kill them when they're
  said.
    n.   Will Carleton—*The First Settler's
               Story.* St. 21.

Speak not at all, in any wise, till you have
somewhat to speak; care not for the reward
of your speaking, but simply and with undivided mind for the truth of your speaking.
    o.   Carlyle—*Essays. Biography.*

He mouths a sentence as curs mouth a bone.
    p.   Churchill—*The Rosiad.* L. 322.

Think all you speak; but speak not all you
  think:
Thoughts are your own; your words are so
  no more.
Where Wisdom steers, wind cannot make you
  sink:
Lips never err, when she does keep the door.
    q.   Delaune—*Epigram.*

As a vessel is known by the sound, whether
it be cracked or not; so men are proved, by
their speeches, whether they be wise or foolish.
    r.   Demosthenes.

Abstruse and mystic thoughts you must express
With painful care, but seeming easiness;
For truth shines brightest thro' the plainest
  dress.
    s.   Wentworth Dillon—*Essay on
               Translated Verse.* L. 216.

O that grave speech would cumber our quick
  souls
Like bells that waste the moments with their
  loudness.
    t.   George Eliot—*The Spanish Gypsy.*
                      Bk. III.

Speech is but broken light upon the depth
Of the unspoken.
    u.   George Eliot—*The Spanish Gypsy.*
                      Bk. I.

Speech is better than silence; silence is
better than speech.
    v.   Emerson—*Essay on Nominalist and
               Realist.*

The true use of speech is not so much to express our wants as to conceal them.
    w.   Goldsmith—*The Bee.* No. 3.

Know when to speake; for many times it
　　brings
Danger to give the best advice to kings.
　　a.　　HERRICK—*Hesperides. Caution in
　　　　　　　　　　　　　　Councell.*

In man speaks God.
　　b.　　HESIOD—*Works and Days.*

The flowering moments of the mind
Drop half their petals in our speech.
　　c.　　O. W. HOLMES—*To My Readers.*　St. 11.

And endless are the modes of speech, and far
Extends from side to side the field of words.
　　d.　　HOMER—*Iliad.*　Bk. XX.　L. 315.
　　　　　　　　　　　　　　Bryant's trans.

Speak gently! 'tis a little thing
Dropp'd in the heart's deep well:
The good, the joy, that it may bring
　　Eternity shall tell.
　　e.　　G. W. LANGFORD—*Speak Gently.*

It is never so difficult to speak as when we
are ashamed of our silence.
　　f.　　LA ROCHEFOUCAULD—*Maxims.* No. 178.

Speech was made to open man to man, and
not to hide him; to promote commerce, and
not betray it.
　　g.　　DAVID LLOYD—*State Worthies.*

　　　　　　When Adam first of men,
To first of women Eve, thus moving speech,
Turn'd him all ear to hear new utterance flow.
　　h.　　MILTON—*Paradise Lost.*　Bk. IV.
　　　　　　　　　　　　　　　　L. 408.

Speech is like cloth of Arras opened and put
abroad, whereby the imagery doth appear in
figure; whereas in thoughts they lie but as in
packs.
　　i.　　PLUTARCH—*Life of Themistocles.*

Just at the age 'twixt boy and youth,
When thought is speech, and speech is truth.
　　j.　　SCOTT—*Marmion.*　Canto II.
　　　　　　　　　　　　　　Introduction.

　　　　　　I had a thing to say,
But I will fit it with some better time.
　　k.　　*King John.*　Act III.　Sc. 3.　L. 25.

I would be loath to cast away my speech,
for besides that it is excellently well penn'd,
I have taken great pains to con it.
　　l.　　*Twelfth Night.*　Act I.　Sc. 5.　L. 183.

　　　　　　Rude am I in my speech,
And little blessed with the soft phrase of peace;
For since these arms of mine had seven years'
　　pith,
Till now some nine moons wasted, they have
　　us'd
Their dearest action in the tented field,
And little of this great world can I speak,
More than pertains to feats of broil and battle,
And therefore little shall I grace my cause
In speaking for myself.
　　m.　　*Othello.*　Act I.　Sc. 3.　L. 81.

She speaks poniards, and every word stabs.
　　n.　　*Much Ado About Nothing.*　Act II.
　　　　　　　　　　　　　Sc. 1.　L. 255.

Your fair discourse hath been as sugar,
Making the hard way sweet and delectable.
　　o.　　*Richard II.*　Act II.　Sc. 3.　L. 6.

Speech was given to the ordinary sort of
men, whereby to communicate their mind;
but to wise men, whereby to conceal it.
　　p.　　BISHOP SOUTH—*Sermon.* April 30, 1676.

Speech was given to man to disguise his
thoughts.
　　q.　　Attributed to TALLEYRAND by
　　　　　　　　BARRÈRE in *Memoirs.*

Doubtless there are men of great parts that
are guilty of downright bashfulness, that by a
strange hesitation and reluctance to speak
murder the finest and most elegant thoughts
and render the most lively conceptions flat
and heavy.
　　r.　　*The Tatler.*　No. 252.

Oh, but the heavenly grammar did I hold
Of that high speech which angels' tongues turn
　　gold!
So should her deathless beauty take no wrong,
Praised in her own great kindred's fit and
　　cognate tongue.
Or if that language yet with us abode
Which Adam in the garden talked with God!
But our untempered speech descends—poor
　　heirs!
Grimy and rough-cast still from Babel's
　　bricklayers:
Curse on the brutish jargon we inherit,
Strong but to damn, not memorise, a spirit!
A cheek, a lip, a limb, a bosom, they
Move with light ease in speech of working-day;
And women we do use to praise even so.
　　s.　　FRANCIS THOMPSON—*Her Portrait.*

Men use thought only as authority for their
injustice and employ speech only to conceal
their thoughts.
　　t.　　VOLTAIRE—*Dialogue XIV. Le Chapon
　　　　　　　　　　　　　　et la Poularde.*

Choice word and measured phrase, above the
　　reach
Of ordinary men.
　　u.　　WORDSWORTH—*Resolution and
　　　　　　　　　Independence.*　St. 14.

SPIRITS.

Aërial spirits, by great Jove design'd
To be on earth the guardians of mankind:
Invisible to mortal eyes they go,
And mark our actions, good or bad, below:
The immortal spies with watchful care preside,
And thrice ten thousand round their charges
　　glide:
They can reward with glory or with gold,
A power they by Divine permission hold.
　　v.　　HESIOD—*Works and Days.*　L. 164.

All heart they live, all head, all eye, all ear,
All intellect, all sense, and as they please
They limb themselves, and colour, shape, or
size
Assume, as likes them best, condense or rare.
a.   Milton—*Paradise Lost.* Bk. VI.
L. 350.

For spirits when they please
Can either sex assume, or both.
b.   Milton—*Paradise Lost.* Bk. I. L. 423.

Millions of spiritual creatures walk the earth
Unseen, both when we wake, and when we
sleep.
c.   Milton—*Paradise Lost.* Bk. IV.
L. 678.

Of calling shapes, and beck'ning shadows
dire,
And airy tongues that syllable men's names.
d.   Milton—*Comus.* L. 207.

I can call spirits from the vasty deep.
Why, so can I, or so can any man;
But will they come when you do call for
them?
e.   *Henry IV.* Pt. I. Act III. Sc. 1.
L. 52.

Spirits are not finely touched
But to fine issues.
f.   *Measure for Measure.* Act I. Sc. 1.
L. 36.

The air around them
Looks radiant as the air around a star.
g.   Shelley—*Prometheus Unbound.*
Act I. Sc. 1.

SPRING (*See* Seasons).

STAGE (THE) (*See* Occupations—Acting).

STARS.

The spacious firmament on high,
With all the blue ethereal sky,
And spangled heavens, a shining frame,
Their great Original proclaim.
h.   Addison—*Ode. The Spacious
Firmament on High.*

Surely the stars are images of love.
i.   Bailey—*Festus.* Sc. *Garden and
Bower by the Sea.*

The stars,
Which stand as thick as dewdrops on the
fields
Of heaven.
j.   Bailey—*Festus.* Sc. *Heaven.*

What are ye orbs?
The words of God? the Scriptures of the skies?
k.   Bailey—*Festus.* Sc. *Everywhere.*

The sad and solemn night
Hath yet her multitude of cheerful fires;
The glorious host of light
Walk the dark hemisphere till she retires;
All through her silent watches, gliding slow,
Her constellations come, and climb the
heavens, and go.
l.   Bryant—*Hymn to the North Star.*

The number is certainly the cause. The
apparent disorder augments the grandeur,
for the appearance of care is highly contrary
to our ideas of magnificence. Besides, the
stars lie in such apparent confusion, as makes
it impossible on ordinary occasions to reckon
them. This gives them the advantage of a
sort of infinity.
m.   Burke—*On the Sublime and the
Beautiful. Magnificence.*

Cry out upon the stars for doing
Ill offices, to cross their wooing.
n.   Butler—*Hudibras.* Pt. III.
Canto I. L. 17.

And the sentinel stars set their watch in the
sky.
o.   Campbell—*The Soldier's Dream.*

In yonder pensile orb, and every sphere
That gems the starry girdle of the year.
p.   Campbell—*Pleasures of Hope.* Pt. II.
L. 194.

Now twilight lets her curtain down
And pins it with a star.
q.   Lydia Maria Child—*Adapted from
M'Donald Clark.*

While twilight's curtain gathering far,
Is pinned with a single diamond star.
r.   M'Donald Clark—*Death in Disguise.*
L. 227.

Hast thou a charm to stay the morning-star
In his steep course?
s.   Coleridge—*Hymn in the Vale of
Chamouni.*

The stars are golden fruit upon a tree
All out of reach.
t.   George Eliot—*The Spanish Gypsy.*
Bk. II.

The starres, bright sentinels of the skies.
u.   Wm. Habington—*Dialogue between
Night and Araphil.* L. 3.

The starres of the night
Will lend thee their light,
Like tapers cleare without number.
v.   Herrick—*The Night Piece.*

When, like an Emir of tyrannic power,
Sirius appears, and on the horizon black
Bids countless stars pursue their mighty track.
w.   Victor Hugo—*The Vanished City.*

Just above yon sandy bar,
  As the day grows fainter and dimmer,
Lonely and lovely, a single star
  Lights the air with a dusky glimmer.
  a. LONGFELLOW—*Chrysaor.* St. 1.

Silently, one by one, in the infinite meadows
    of heaven,
Blossomed the lovely stars, the forget-me-nots
    of the angels.
  b. LONGFELLOW—*Evangeline.* Pt. I. St. 3.

The night is calm and cloudless,
  And still as still can be,
And the stars come forth to listen
  To the music of the sea.
They gather, and gather, and gather,
  Until they crowd the sky,
And listen, in breathless silence,
  To the solemn litany.
  c. LONGFELLOW—*Christus. The Golden
                    Legend.* Pt. V.

There is no light in earth or heaven
  But the cold light of stars;
And the first watch of night is given
  To the red planet Mars.
  d. LONGFELLOW—*The Light of Stars.* St. 2.

When stars are in the quiet skies,
  Then most I pine for thee;
Bend on me then thy tender eyes,
  As stars look on the sea.
  e. BULWER-LYTTON—*When Stars are in the
                    Quiet Skies.*

A broad and ample road, whose dust is gold,
And pavement stars.
  f. MILTON—*Paradise Lost.* Bk. VII.
                    L. 577.

            And made the stars,
And set them in the firmament of heav'n,
T' illuminate the earth, and rule the day
In their vicissitude, and rule the night.
  g. MILTON—*Paradise Lost.* Bk. VII.
                    L. 348.

      At whose sight all the stars
Hide their diminish'd heads.
  h. MILTON—*Paradise Lost.* Bk. IV. L. 34.

Hither, as to their fountain, other stars
Repairing in their golden urns draw light,
And hence the morning planet gilds her horns.
  i. MILTON—*Paradise Lost.* Bk. VII.
                    L. 364.

Now the bright morning-star, day's harbinger,
Comes dancing from the east.
  j. MILTON—*Song on May Morning.*

So sinks the day-star in the ocean-bed,
And yet anon repairs his drooping head,
And tricks his beams, and with new-spangled
    ore
Flames in the forehead of the morning sky.
  k. MILTON—*Lycidas.* L. 168.

The planets in their station list'ning stood.
  l. MILTON—*Paradise Lost.* Bk. VII.
                    L. 563.

The star that bids the shepherd fold,
Now the top of heaven doth hold.
  m. MILTON—*Comus.* L. 93.

Stars are the Daisies that begem
  The blue fields of the sky,
Beheld by all, and everywhere,
  Bright prototypes on high.
  n. MOIR—*The Daisy.* St. 5.

But soon, the prospect clearing,
  By cloudless starlight on he treads
And thinks no lamp so cheering
  As that light which Heaven sheds.
  o. MOORE—*I'd Mourn the Hopes.*

Led by the light of the Mæonian star.
  p. POPE—*Essay on Criticism.* Pt. III.
                    L. 89.

Ye little stars, hide your diminish'd rays.
  q. POPE—*Moral Essays.* Ep. III. L. 282.

Starry Crowns of Heaven
  Set in azure night!
Linger yet a little
  Ere you hide your light:—
Nay; let Starlight fade away,
Heralding the day!
  r. ADELAIDE A. PROCTER—*Give Place.*

A sky full of silent suns.
  s. RICHTER—*Flower, Fruit, and Thorn
                    Pieces.* Ch. II.

One naked star has waded through
  The purple shallows of the night,
And faltering as falls the dew
  It drips its misty light.
  t. JAMES WHITCOMB RILEY—*The Beetle.*

Thus some who have the Stars survey'd
  Are ignorantly led
To think those glorious Lamps were made
To light *Tom Fool* to bed.
  u. NICHOLAS ROWE—*Song on a Fine
                    Woman Who Had a Dull Husband.*

Her blue eyes sought the west afar,
For lovers love the western star.
  v. SCOTT—*Lay of the Last Minstrel.*
                    Canto III. St. 24.

      Look how the floor of heaven
Is thick inlaid with patines of bright gold:
There's not the smallest orb which thou be-
    hold'st
But in his motion like an angel sings,
Still quiring to the young-ey'd cherubins:
Such harmony is in immortal souls;
But whilst this muddy vesture of decay
Doth grossly close it in, we cannot hear it.
  w. *Merchant of Venice.* Act V. Sc. 1.
                    L. 58.

Our Jovial star reign'd at his birth.
  x. *Cymbeline.* Act V. Sc. 4. L. 105.

These blessed candles of the night.
a. *Merchant of Venice.* Act V. Sc. 1.
                                L. 220.

The skies are painted with unnumber'd
    sparks,
They are all fire and every one doth shine,
But there's but one in all doth hold his place.
b. *Julius Cæsar.* Act III. Sc. 1. L. 63.

The stars above us govern our conditions.
c. *King Lear.* Act IV. Sc. 3. L. 35.

The unfolding star calls up the shepherd.
d. *Measure for Measure.* Act IV. Sc. 2.
                                L. 218.

Two stars keep not their motion in one sphere.
e. *Henry IV.* Pt. I. Act V. Sc. 4. L. 65.

                    Each separate star
Seems nothing, but a myriad scattered stars
Break up the Night, and make it beautiful.
f. BAYARD TAYLOR—*Lars.* Bk. III.
                            Last lines.

Many a night I saw the Pleiads, rising thro'
    the mellow shade,
Glitter like a swarm of fire-flies tangled in a
    silver braid.
g. TENNYSON—*Locksley Hall.* St. 5.

But who can count the stars of Heaven?
Who sing their influence on this lower world?
h. THOMSON—*Seasons. Winter.* L. 528.

For every wave with dimpled face
    That leap'd upon the air,
Had caught a star in its embrace
    And held it trembling there.
i. AMELIA B. WELBY—*Musings.* St. 4.

But He is risen, a later star of dawn.
j. WORDSWORTH—*A Morning Exercise.*

You meaner beauties of the night,
    That poorly satisfy our eyes
More by your number than your light;
    You common people of the skies,—
What are you when the moon shall rise?
k. SIR HENRY WOTTON—*On His Mistress,*
                    the Queen of Bohemia.

Hence Heaven looks down on earth with all
    her eyes.
l. YOUNG—*Night Thoughts.* Night VII.
                            L. 1,103.

One sun by day, by night ten thousand shine;
And light us deep into the Deity;
How boundless in magnificence and might.
m. YOUNG—*Night Thoughts.* Night IX.
                            L. 728.

Who rounded in his palm these spacious orbs
    *   *   *   *   *   *
Numerous as glittering gems of morning dew,
Or sparks from populous cities in a blaze,
And set the bosom of old night on fire.
n. YOUNG—*Night Thoughts.* Night IX.
                            L. 1,260.

STATESMANSHIP (*See* OCCUPATIONS).

STORM.

Hark, hark! Deep sounds, and deeper still,
    Are howling from the mountain's bosom:
There's not a breath of wind upon the hill,
    Yet quivers every leaf, and drops each
        blossom:
Earth groans as if beneath a heavy load.
o. BYRON—*Heaven and Earth.* Pt. I.
                            Sc. 3.

The sky is changed!—and such a change! O
    night,
And storm, and darkness, ye are wondrous
    strong,
Yet lovely in your strength, as is the light
Of a dark eye in woman! Far along,
From peak to peak the rattling crags among
Leaps the live thunder!
p. BYRON—*Childe Harold.* Canto III.
                            St. 92.

Loud roared the dreadful thunder,
The rain a deluge showers.
q. ANDREW CHERRY—*The Bay of Biscay.*

Bursts as a wave that from the clouds impends,
And swell'd with tempests on the ship de-
    scends;
White are the decks with foam; the winds
    aloud
Howl o'er the masts, and sing through every
    shroud:
Pale, trembling, tir'd, the sailors freeze with
    fears;
And instant death on every wave appears.
r. HOMER—*Iliad.* Bk. XV. L. 752.
                        Pope's trans.

Roads are wet where'er one wendeth,
And with rain the thistle bendeth,
    And the brook cries like a child!
Not a rainbow shines to cheer us;
Ah! the sun comes never near us,
    And the heavens look dark and wild.
s. MARY HOWITT—*The Wet Summer.*
                        From the German.

    The winds grow high;
Impending tempests charge the sky;
The lightning flies, the thunder roars;
And big waves lash the frightened shores.
t. PRIOR—*The Lady's Looking-Glass.*

Lightnings, that show the vast and foamy
    deep,
    The rending thunders, as they onward roll,
The loud, loud winds, that o'er the billows
    sweep—
    Shake the firm nerve, appal the bravest
        soul!
u. MRS. RADCLIFFE—*Mysteries of Udolpho.*
                    The Mariner. St. 9.

37

As far as I could ken thy chalky cliffs,
When from thy shore the tempest beat us
    back,
I stood upon the hatches in the storm.
   a.   *Henry VI.* Pt. II. Act III. Sc. 2.
                          L. 101.

Blow, winds, and crack your cheeks! rage!
    blow!
You cataracts and hurricanoes, spout
Till you have drench'd our steeples.
   b.   *King Lear.* Act III. Sc. 2. L. 1.

Blow wind, swell billow, and swim bark!
The storm is up, and all is on the hazard.
   c.   *Julius Cæsar.* Act V. Sc. 1. L. 67.

I have seen tempests, when the scolding
    winds
Have riv'd the knotty oaks, and I have seen
The ambitious ocean swell and rage and foam,
To be exalted with the threat'ning clouds
But never till to-night, never till now,
Did I go through a tempest dropping fire.
   d.   *Julius Cæsar.* Act I. Sc. 3. L. 5.

                 Merciful Heaven,
Thou rather with thy sharp and sulphurous
    bolt
Split'st the unwedgeable and gnarled oak
Than the soft myrtle.
   e.   *Measure for Measure.* Act II. Sc. 2.
                          L. 114.

At first, heard solemn o'er the verge of
    Heaven,
The Tempest growls; but as it nearer comes,
And rolls its awful burden on the wind,
The Lightnings flash a larger curve, and more
The Noise astounds; till overhead a sheet
Of livid flame discloses wide, then shuts,
And opens wider; shuts and opens still
Expansive, wrapping ether in a blaze.
Follows the loosen'd aggravated Roar,
Enlarging, deepening, mingling, peal on peal,
Crush'd, horrible, convulsing Heaven and
    Earth.
   f.   Thomson—*Seasons. Summer.*
                        L. 1,133.

STORY-TELLING.

Dear Ellen, your tales are all plenteously
    stored,
With the joy of some bride and the wealth of
    her lord,
     Of her chariots and dresses,
     And worldly caresses,
And servants that fly when she's waited upon:
But what can she boast if she weds unbeloved?
Can she e'er feel the joy that one morning I
    proved,
When I put on my new gown and waited for
    John?
   g.   Bloomfield—*The Banks of Wye.*
                Gleaner's Song. St. 1.

A schoolboy's tale, the wonder of an hour!
   h.   Byron—*Childe Harold.* Canto II.
                         St. **2.**

A story, in which native humour reigns,
Is often useful, always entertains;
A graver fact, enlisted on your side,
May furnish illustration, well applied;
But sedentary weavers of long tales
Give me the fidgets, and my patience fails.
   i.   Cowper—*Conversation.* L. 203.

In this our spacious isle I think there is not
    one
But he hath heard some talk of Hood and
    Little John,
Of Tuck, the merry friar, which many a ser-
    mon made
In praise of Robin Hood, his outlaws, and
    their trade.
   j.   Drayton—*Polyolbion.*

This story will never go down.
   k.   Henry Fielding—*Tumble-Down Dick.*
                          Air I.

When thou dost tell another's jest, therein
Omit the oaths, which true wit cannot need;
Pick out of tales the mirth, but not the sin.
   l.   Herbert—*Temple. Church Porch.*
                         St. 11.

And what so tedious as a twice-told tale.
   m.   Homer—*Odyssey.* Bk. XII. Last Line.
                      Pope's trans.

                  I hate
To tell again a tale once fully told.
   n.   Homer—*Odyssey.* Bk. XII. L. 566.
                      Bryant's trans.

Soft as some song divine, thy story flows.
   o.   Homer—*Odyssey.* Bk. XI. L. 458.
                      Pope's trans.

An' all us other children, when the supper
    things is done,
We set around the kitchen fire an' has the
    mostest fun
A-list'nin' to the witch tales 'at Annie tells
    about,
An' the gobble-uns 'at gits you
        Ef you
           Don't
              Watch
                Out!
   p.   James Whitcomb Riley—*Little
                    Orphant Annie.*

I cannot tell how the truth may be;
I say the tale as 'twas said to me.
   q.   Scott—*Lay of the Last Minstrel.*
                Canto II. St. 22.

And thereby hangs a tale.
   r.   *Taming of the Shrew.* Act IV. Sc. 1.
                          L. 60.

For seldom shall she hear a tale
So sad, so tender, yet so true.
   s.   Shenstone—*Jemmy Dawson.* St. 20.

He cometh unto you with a tale which holdeth children from play, and old men from the chimney corner.

   a.   SIR PHILIP SIDNEY—*The Defense of Poesy.*

In after-dinner talk,
Across the walnuts and the wine.

   b.   TENNYSON—*The Miller's Daughter.*

A tale in everything.

   c.   WORDSWORTH—*Simon Lee.*

STRATEGY.

There webs were spread of more than common size,
And half-starved spiders prey'd on half-starved flies.

   d.   CHURCHILL—*The Prophecy of Famine.*
                     L. 327.

Those oft are stratagems which errors seem,
Nor is it Homer nods, but we that dream.

   e.   POPE—*Essay on Criticism.* Pt. I.
                     L. 177.

For her own breakfast she'll project a scheme,
Nor take her tea without a stratagem.

   f.   YOUNG—*Love of Fame.* Satire VI.
                     L. 187.

STRENGTH.

Like strength is felt from hope, and from despair.

   g.   HOMER—*Iliad.* Bk. XV. L. 852.
                  Pope's trans.

Strong are her sons, though rocky are her shores.

   h.   HOMER—*Odyssey.* Bk. IX. L. 28.
                  Pope's trans.

And, weaponless himself,
Made arms ridiculous.

   i.   MILTON—*Samson Agonistes.* L. 130.

I would have you call to mind the strength of the ancient giants, that undertook to lay the high mountain Pelion on the top of Ossa, and set among those the shady Olympus.

   j.   RABELAIS—*Works.* Bk. IV.
                  Ch. XXXVIII.

Profan'd the God-given strength, and marr'd the lofty line.

   k.   SCOTT—*Marmion.* *Introduction.*
                  Canto I.

In that day's feats,

*   *   *   *   *   *

He prov'd best man i' the field, and for his meed
Was brow-bound with the oak.

   l.   *Coriolanus.* Act II. Sc. 2. L. 99.

O, it is excellent
To have a giant's strength, but it is tyrannous
To use it like a giant.

   m.   *Measure for Measure.* Act II. Sc. 2.
                     L. 107.

The king's name is a tower of strength,
Which they upon the adverse party want.

   n.   *Richard III.* Act V. Sc. 3. L. 12.

Atlas, we read in ancient song,
Was so exceeding tall and strong,
He bore the skies upon his back,
Just as the pedler does his pack;
But, as the pedler overpress'd
Unloads upon a stall to rest,
Or, when he can no longer stand,
Desires a friend to lend a hand,
So Atlas, lest the ponderous spheres
Should sink, and fall about his ears,
Got Hercules to bear the pile,
That he might sit and rest awhile.

   o.   SWIFT—*Atlas; or, the Minister of State.*

So let it be in God's own might
We gird us for the coming fight,
And, strong in Him whose cause is ours
In conflict with unholy powers,
We grasp the weapons he has given,—
The Light, and Truth, and Love of Heaven.

   p.   WHITTIER—*The Moral Warfare.*

STUDENTS.

Strange to the world, he wore a bashful look,
The fields his study, nature was his book.

   q.   BLOOMFIELD—*Farmer's Boy.* *Spring.*
                     L. 31.

The scholar who cherishes the love of comfort, is not fit to be deemed a scholar.

   r.   CONFUCIUS—*Analects.* Bk. XIV.
                     Ch. III.

Who climbs the grammar-tree, distinctly knows
Where noun, and verb, and participle grows.

   s.   DRYDEN—*Sixth Satire of Juvenal.*
                     L. 583.

The studious class are their own victims; they are thin and pale, their feet are cold, their heads are hot, the night is without sleep, the day a fear of interruption,—pallor, squalor, hunger, and egotism. If you come near them and see what conceits they entertain—they are abstractionists, and spend their days and nights in dreaming some dream; in expecting the homage of society to some precious scheme built on a truth, but destitute of proportion in its presentment, of justness in its application, and of all energy of will in the schemer to embody and vitalize it.

   t.   EMERSON—*Representative Men.*
                    Montaigne.

Ah, pensive scholar, what is fame?
A fitful tongue of leaping flame;
A giddy whirlwind's fickle gust,
That lifts a pinch of mortal dust;
A few swift years, and who can show
Which dust was Bill, and which was Joe?

   u.   O. W. HOLMES—*Poems of the Class of '29. Bill and Joe.* St. 7.

The world's great men have not commonly been great scholars, nor its great scholars great men.

    a.   O. W. HOLMES—*The Autocrat of the Breakfast-Table.* VI.

Deign on the passing world to turn thine eyes,
And pause awhile from Learning to be wise;
There mark what ills the scholar's life assail,
Toil, envy, want, the patron, and the gaol.
See nations, slowly wise and meanly just,
To buried merit raise the tardy bust.

    b.   SAM'L JOHNSON—*The Vanity of Human Wishes.* L. 157.

          Night after night,
He sat and bleared his eyes with books.

    c.   LONGFELLOW—*Christus. The Golden Legend.* Pt. I.

Where should the scholar live? In solitude, or in society? in the green stillness of the country, where he can hear the heart of Nature beat, or in the dark, gray town where he can hear and feel the throbbing heart of man?

    d.   LONGFELLOW—*Hyperion.* Bk. I. Ch. VIII.

And then the whining schoolboy, with his satchel
And shining morning face, creeping like snail
Unwillingly to school.

    e.   *As You Like It.* Act II. Sc. 7. L. 145.

He was a scholar, and a ripe and good one;
Exceeding wise, fair-spoken, and persuading;
Lofty and sour to them that lov'd him not;
But to those men that sought him sweet as summer.

    f.   *Henry VIII.* Act IV. Sc. 2. L. 51.

And with unwearied fingers drawing out
The lines of life, from living knowledge hid.

    g.   SPENSER—*Faerie Queene.* Bk. IV. Canto II. St. 48.

Up! up! my Friend, and quit your books;
Or surely you'll grow double;
Up! up! my Friend, and clear your looks;
Why all this toil and trouble?

    h.   WORDSWORTH—*The Tables Turned.*

STUDY.

Histories make men wise; poets, witty; the mathematics, subtile; natural philosophy, deep; moral, grave; logic and rhetoric, able to contend.

    i.   BACON—*Of Studies.*

When night hath set her silver lamp on high,
Then is the time for study.

    j.   BAILEY—*Festus.* Sc. *A Village Feast.*

          Exhausting thought,
And hiving wisdom with each studious year.

    k.   BYRON—*Childe Harold.* Canto III. St. 107.

Whence is thy learning? hath thy toil
O'er books consumed the midnight oil?

    l.   GAY—*The Shepherd and the Philosopher.*

As turning the logs will make a dull fire burn, so changes of studies a dull brain.

    m.   LONGFELLOW—*Drift-Wood. Table Talk.*

Beholding the bright countenance of truth in the quiet and still air of delightful studies.

    n.   MILTON—*The Reason of Church Government.* Introduction. Bk. II.

Studious of ease, and fond of humble things.

    o.   AMBROSE PHILIPS—*Epistles from Holland, to a Friend in England.* L. 21.

I'll talk a word with this same learned Theban.
What is your study?

    p.   *King Lear.* Act III. Sc. 4. L. 162.

So study evermore is overshot;
While it doth study to have what it would
It doth forget to do the thing it should,
And when it hath the thing it hunteth most,
'Tis won as towns with fire, so won, so lost.

    q.   *Love's Labour's Lost.* Act I. Sc. 1. L. 143.

Study is like the heaven's glorious sun
That will not be deep-searched with saucy looks;
Small have continual plodders ever won,
Save base authority from others' books.

    r.   *Love's Labour's Lost.* Act I. Sc. 1. L. 84.

What is the end of study? Let me know?
Why, that to know, which else we should not know.
Things hid and barr'd, you mean, from common sense?
Ay, that is study's god-like recompense.

    s.   *Love's Labour's Lost.* Act I. Sc. 1. L. 55.

The more we study, we the more discover our ignorance.

    t.   SHELLEY—*Scenes from the Magico Prodigioso of Calderon.* Sc. 1.

One of the best methods of rendering study agreeable is to live with able men, and to suffer all those pangs of inferiority which the want of knowledge always inflicts.

    u.   SYDNEY SMITH—*Second Lecture on the Conduct of the Understanding.*

STUPIDITY.

With various readings stored his empty skull,
Learn'd without sense, and venerably dull.

    v.   CHURCHILL—*The Rosciad.* L. 591.

The fool of nature stood with stupid eyes
And gaping mouth, that testified surprise.

    w.   DRYDEN—*Cymon and Iphigenia.* L. 107.

He is not only dull himself, but the cause of dulness in others.

　　a.　Sam'l Johnson—*Boswell's Life of Johnson.* 1783.

The bookful blockhead, ignorantly read,
With loads of learned lumber in his head.

　　b.　Pope—*Essay on Criticism.* L. 612.

Against stupidity the very gods
Themselves contend in vain.

　　c.　Schiller—*The Maid of Orleans.*
　　　　　　　　　　Act III.　Sc. 6.

Peter was dull; he was at first
　　Dull,—Oh, so dull—so very dull!
Whether he talked, wrote, or rehearsed—
　　Still with this dulness was he cursed—
Dull—beyond all conception—dull.

　　d.　Shelley—*Peter Bell the Third.*
　　　　　　　　　　Pt. VII. XI.

STYLE.

A chaste and lucid style is indicative of the same personal traits in the author.

　　e.　Hosea Ballou—*MS. Sermons.*

Style is the dress of thoughts.

　　f.　Earl of Chesterfield—*Letter to his Son. On Education.* Nov. 24, 1749.

Style! style! why, all writers will tell you that it is the very thing which can least of all be changed. A man's style is nearly as much a part of him as his physiognomy, his figure, the throbbing of his pulse,—in short, as any part of his being which is at least subjected to the action of the will.

　　g.　Fénélon.

One step from the sublime to the ridiculous.
　　Longinus.
　　　Napoleon I. to De Pradt at Warsaw.
　　　　See *Histoire de l'Ambassade dans le Grande Duché de Vasovie* (1812).

　　h.　Thomas Paine—*Age of Reason.* Pt. II.

Expression is the dress of thought, and still
Appears more decent as more suitable;
A vile conceit in pompous words express'd,
Is like a clown in regal purple dress'd.

　　i.　Pope—*Essay on Criticism.* L. 318.

Such labour'd nothings, in so strange a style,
Amaze th' learn'd, and make the learned smile.

　　j.　Pope—*Essay on Criticism.* Pt. II.
　　　　　　　　　　　　　L. 126.

The flowery style is not unsuitable to public speeches or addresses, which amount only to compliment. The lighter beauties are in their place when there is nothing more solid to say; but the flowery style ought to be banished from a pleading, a sermon, or a didactic work.

　　k.　Voltaire—*Philosophical Dictionary.*
　　　　　　　　　　　　　Style.

SUCCESS.

'Tis not in mortals to command success,
But we'll do more, Sempronius,—
We'll deserve it.

　　l.　Addison—*Cato.* Act I. Sc. 2.

Better have failed in the high aim, as I,
Than vulgarly in the low aim succeed
As, God be thanked! I do not.

　　m.　Robert Browning—*The Inn Album.*
　　　　　　　　　　　　　IV.

They never fail who die
In a great cause.

　　n.　Byron—*Marino Faliero.* Act II. Sc. 2.

Now, by St. Paul, the work goes bravely on.

　　o.　Colley Cibber—*Richard III.* Act III.
　　　　　　　　　　　　　Sc. 1.

I came up-stairs into the world; for I was born in a cellar.

　　p.　Congreve—*Love for Love.* Act II.
　　　　　　　　　　　　　Sc. 1.

Hast thou not learn'd what thou art often told,
A truth still sacred, and believed of old,
That no success attends on spears and swords
Unblest, and that the battle is the Lord's?

　　q.　Cowper—*Expostulation.* L. 350.

Th' aspirer, once attain'd unto the top,
Cuts off those means by which himself got up.

　　r.　Sam'l Daniel—*Civil War.* Bk. II.

Success is counted sweetest
　　By those who ne'er succeed.

　　s.　Emily Dickinson—*Success.* Ed. 1891.

Born for success, he seemed
With grace to win, with heart to hold,
With shining gifts that took all eyes.

　　t.　Emerson—*In Memoriam.* L. 60.

One thing is forever good;
That one thing is Success.

　　u.　Emerson—*Fate.*

Peace courts his hand, but spreads her charms in vain;
"Think nothing gain'd," he cries, "till naught remain."

　　v.　Sam'l Johnson—*The Vanity of Human Wishes.* L. 201.

When the shore is won at last,
Who will count the billows past?

　　w.　Keble—*Christian Year. St. John the Evangelist's Day.* St. 5.

I have always believed that success would be the inevitable result if the two services, the army and the navy, had fair play, and if we sent the right man to fill the right place.

　　x.　Austin H. Layard—*Speech in Parliament.* Jan. 15, 1855.

Providence is always on the side of the last reserve.

   a.   *Attributed to* NAPOLEON I.

The race by vigour, not by vaunts, is won.

   b.   POPE—*The Dunciad.* Bk. II. L. 59.

God is generally on the side of the large battalions against the small.

   c.   BUSSY RABUTIN—*Letter IV.* 91.

He that climbs the tall tree has won right to the fruit,
He that leaps the wide gulf should prevail in his suit.

   d.   SCOTT—*The Talisman.* Ch. XXVI.

Fortune is always on the side of the largest battalions.

   e.   MME. DE SÉVIGNÉ—*Letters.* 202.

            Didst thou never hear
That things ill-got had ever bad success?

   f.   *Henry VI.* Pt. III. Act II. Sc. 2.
                         L. 45.

Now is the winter of our discontent
Made glorious summer by this sun of York;
And all the clouds that lour'd upon our house
In the deep bosom of the ocean buried.

   g.   *Richard III.* Act I. Sc. 1. L. 1.

               Such a nature,
Tickled with good success, disdains the shadow
Which he treads on at noon.

   h.   *Coriolanus.* Act I. Sc. 1. L. 263.

           To climb steep hills
Requires slow pace at first.

   i.   *Henry VIII.* Act I. Sc. 1. L. 131.

Have I caught my heav'nly jewel.

       SIR PHILIP SIDNEY—*Astrophel and*
                  Stella. Song II.

   j.   See also *Merry Wives of Windsor.*
                 Act III. Sc. 3. L. 45.

The gods are on the side of the stronger.

   k.   TACITUS—*Hist. IV.* 17.

          There may come a day
Which crowns Desire with gift, and Art with truth,
And Love with bliss, and Life with wiser youth!

   l.   BAYARD TAYLOR—*The Picture of*
              St. John. Bk. IV. St. 86.

It is said that God is always on the side of the heaviest battalions.

   m.   VOLTAIRE—*Letter to M. le Riche.*
                     Feb. 6, 1770.

SUFFERING.

Knowledge by suffering entereth,
And Life is perfected by Death.

   n.   E. B. BROWNING—*A Vision of Poets.*
                     Conclusion.

To each his suff'rings; all are men,
  Condemn'd alike to groan;
The tender for another's pain,
  Th' unfeeling for his own.
Yet ah! why should they know their fate,
Since sorrow never comes too late,
And happiness too swiftly flies?
Thought would destroy their paradise.

   o.   GRAY—*On a Distant Prospect of Eton*
                 College. St. 10.

Ho! why dost thou shiver and shake, Gaffer Grey?
  And why does thy nose look so blue?

   p.   THOMAS HOLCROFT—*Gaffer Grey.*

             And taste
The melancholy joys of evils pass'd,
For he who much has suffer'd, much will know.

   q.   HOMER—*Odyssey.* Bk. XV. L. 434.
                      Pope's trans.

They, the holy ones and weakly,
  Who the cross of suffering bore,
Folded their pale hands so meekly,
  Spake with us on earth no more!

   r.   LONGFELLOW—*Footsteps of Angels.*
                       St. 5

Mirth cannot move a soul in agony.

   s.   *Love's Labour's Lost.* Act V. Sc. 2.
                       L. 867

           For there are deeds
Which have no form, sufferings which have no tongue.

   t.   SHELLEY—*The Cenci.* Act III. Sc. 1.

Those who inflict must suffer, for they see
The work of their own hearts, and that must be
Our chastisement or recompense.

   u.   SHELLEY—*Julian and Maddalo.* L. 494.

SUICIDE.

Who doubting tyranny, and fainting under
Fortune's false lottery, desperately run
To death, for dread of death; that soul's most stout,
That, bearing all mischance, dares last it out.

   v.   BEAUMONT AND FLETCHER—*The Honest*
             Man's Fortune. Act IV. Sc. 1.

         But if there be an hereafter,
And that there is, conscience, uninfluenc'd
And suffer'd to speak out, tells every man,
Then must it be an awful thing to die;
More horrid yet to die by one's *own* hand.

   w.   BLAIR—*The Grave.* L. 398.

Our time is fixed, and all our days are num
  ber'd;
How long, how short, we know not:—this we know,
Duty requires we calmly wait the summons,
Nor dare to stir till Heaven shall give permis.
  sion.

   x.   BLAIR—*The Grave.* L. 417.

Fool! I mean not
That poor-souled piece of heroism, self-
  slaughter;
Oh no! the miserablest day we live
There's many a better thing to do than die!
  a.   DARLEY—*Ethelstan.*

Ah yes, the sea is still and deep,
All things within its bosom sleep!
A single step, and all is o'er,
A plunge, a bubble, and no more.
  b.   LONGFELLOW—*Christus. The Golden
                 Legend.* Pt. V.

                     He
That kills himself to avoid misery, fears it,
And, at the best, shows but a bastard valour.
This life's a fort committed to my trust,
Which I must not yield up till it be forced:
Nor will I. He's not valiant that dares die,
But he that boldly bears calamity.
  c.   MASSINGER—*The Maid of Honour.*
                     Act IV. Sc. 3.

      Against self-slaughter
There is a prohibition so divine
That cravens my weak hand.
  d.   *Cymbeline.* Act III. Sc. 4. L. 78.

                Bravest at the last,
She levell'd at our purposes, and, being royal,
Took her own way.
  e.   *Antony and Cleopatra.* Act V. Sc. 2.
                          L. 338.
He that cuts off twenty years of life
Cuts off so many years of fearing death.
  f.   *Julius Cæsar.* Act III. Sc. 1. L. 101.

The more pity that great folk should have
countenance in this world to drown or hang
themselves, more than their even Christian.
  g.   *Hamlet.* Act V. Sc. 1. L. 29.

You ever-gentle gods, take my breath from me;
Let not my worser spirit tempt me again
To die before you please!
  h.   *King Lear.* Act IV. Sc. 6. L. 221.

There is no refuge from confession but
suicide; and suicide is confession.
  i.   DANIEL WEBSTER—*Argument on the
     Murder of Captain White.* April 6,
     1830.

SUMMER (*See* SEASONS).

SUN (THE).

The sun, which passeth through pollutions
and itself remains as pure as before.
  j.   BACON—*Advancement of Learning.*
                        Bk. II.
See the gold sunshine patching,
  And streaming and streaking across
The gray-green oaks; and catching,
  By its soft brown beard, the moss.
  k.   BAILEY—*Festus.* Sc. *The Surface.*
                        L. 409.

               See the sun!
God's crest upon His azure shield, the Heavens.
  l.   BAILEY—*Festus.* Sc. *A Mountain.*

     The sun, centre and sire of light,
The keystone of the world-built arch of
  heaven.
  m.   BAILEY—*Festus.* Sc. *Heaven.*

Pleasantly, between the pelting showers, the
  sunshine gushes down.
  n.   BRYANT—*The Cloud on the Way.* L. 18.

The sun, too, shines into cesspools, and is
not polluted.
  o.   DIOGENES LAERTIUS—Bk. VI. Sec. 63.

The glorious lamp of heaven, the radiant sun,
Is Nature's eye.
  p.   DRYDEN—*The Story of Acis, Polyphe-
     mus, and Galatea from the Thirteenth
     Book of Ovid's Metamorphoses.*
                          L. 165.

High in his chariot glow'd the lamp of day.
  q.   FALCONER—*The Shipwreck.* Canto I.
                       III. L. 3,
Failing yet gracious,
Slow pacing, soon homing,
A patriarch that strolls
Through the tents of his children,
The sun as he journeys
His round on the lower
Ascents of the blue,
Washes the roofs
And the hillsides with clarity.
  r.   WM. ERNEST HENLEY—*Rhymes and
                          Rhythms.*

  Father of rosy day,
No more thy clouds of incense rise;
    But waking flow'rs,
    At morning hours,
Give out their sweets to meet thee in the skies.
  s.   HOOD—*Hymn to the Sun.* St. 4.

She stood breast-high amid the corn,
Clasp'd by the golden light of morn,
Like the sweetheart of the sun,
Who many a glowing kiss had won.
  t.   HOOD—*Ruth.*

The sun shineth upon the dunghill and is
not corrupted.
  u.   LYLY—*Euphues.* P. 43.

Whence are thy beams, O sun! thy everlasting light? Thou comest forth, in thy
awful beauty; the stars hide themselves in
the sky; the moon, cold and pale, sinks in
the western wave. But thou, thyself, movest
alone.
  v.   MACPHERSON—*The Poems of Ossian.
     Carthon. Ossian's Address to the Sun.*

The gay motes that people the sunbeams.
  w.   MILTON—*Il Penseroso.* L. 8.

The great luminary
Aloof the vulgar constellations thick,
That from his lordly eye keep distance due,
Dispenses light from far.

a.   MILTON—*Paradise Lost.*   Bk. III.
                      L. 576.

Thou sun, of this great world both eye and
    soul.

b.   MILTON—*Paradise Lost.*   Bk. V.
                      L. 171.

And see—the Sun himself!—on wings
Of glory up the East he springs.
Angel of Light! who from the time
Those heavens began their march sublime,
Hath first of all the starry choir
Trod in his Maker's steps of fire!

c.   MOORE—*Lalla Rookh.   The Fire
                      Worshippers.*

As sunshine, broken in the rill,
Though turn'd astray, is sunshine still!

d.   MOORE—*Lalla Rookh.   The Fire
                      Worshippers.*

And the sun had on a crown
Wrought of gilded thistledown,
    And a scarf of velvet vapor
And a raveled rainbow gown;
And his tinsel-tangled hair
Tossed and lost upon the air
    Was glossier and flossier
Than any anywhere.

e.   JAMES WHITCOMB RILEY—*The South
                     Wind and the Sun.*

I 'gin to be aweary of the sun,
And wish the estate o' the world were now
    undone.

f.   *Macbeth.*   Act V.   Sc. 5.   L. 49.

Shine out, fair sun, till I have bought a glass,
That I may see my shadow as I pass.

g.   *Richard III.*   Act I.   Sc. 2.   L. 263.

               That orbed continent the fire
That severs day from night.

h.   *Twelfth Night.*   Act V.   Sc. 1.   L. 278.

The selfsame sun that shines upon his court
Hides not his visage from our cottage, but
Looks on alike.

i.   *Winter's Tale.*   Act IV.   Sc. 4.   L. 455.

When the sun shines let foolish gnats make
    sport,
But creep in crannies when he hides his
    beams.

j.   *Comedy of Errors.*   Act II.   Sc. 2.   L. 30.

In the warm shadow of her loveliness;—
He kissed her with his beams.

k.   SHELLEY—*The Witch of Atlas.*   St. 2.

* * * Because as the sun reflecting upon
the wind of strands and shores is unpolluted
in its beams, so is God not dishonoured when
we suppose him in every of his creatures,
and in every part of every one of them.

l.   JEREMY TAYLOR—*Holy Living.*   Ch. II.
                      Sec. III.

There sinks the nebulous star we call the Sun.

m.   TENNYSON—*The Princess.*   Pt. IV.   L. 1.

The sopped sun—toper as ever drank hard—
         Stares foolish, hazed,
         Rubicund, dazed,
Totty with thine October tankard.

n.   FRANCIS THOMPSON—*A Corymbus for
                      Autumn.* St. 1.

Fairest of all the lights above,
Thou sun, whose beams adorn the spheres,
And with unwearied swiftness move,
To form the circles of our years.

o.   ISAAC WATTS—*Sun, Moon and Stars,
                      Praise Ye the Lord.*

SUNRISE.

The sun had long since in the lap
Of Thetis taken out his nap,
And, like a lobster boil'd, the morn
From black to red began to turn.

p.   BUTLER—*Hudibras.*   Pt. II.   Canto II.
                      L. 29.

    The east is blossoming! Yea, a rose,
Vast as the heavens, soft as a kiss,
Sweet as the presence of woman is,
    Rises and reaches, and widens and grows
Large and luminous up from the sea,
And out of the sea, as a blossoming tree,
    Richer and richer, so higher and higher,
Deeper and deeper it takes its hue;
Brighter and brighter it reaches through
The space of heaven and the place of stars,
Till all is as rich as a rose can be,
    And my rose-leaves fall into billows of fire.

q.   JOAQUIN MILLER—*Sunrise in Venice.*

           The whole east was flecked
With flashing streaks and shafts of amethyst,
While a light crimson mist
Went up before the mounting luminary,
And all the strips of cloud began to vary
Their hues, and all the zenith seemed to ope
As if to show a cope beyond the cope!

r.   EPES SARGENT—*Sunrise at Sea.*

As when the golden sun salutes the morn,
And, having gilt the ocean with his beams,
Gallops the zodiac in his glistering coach,
And overlooks the highest-peering hills.

s.   *Titus Andronicus.*   Act II.   Sc. 1.   L. 5.

He fires the proud tops of the eastern pines
And darts his light through every guilty hole.

t.   *Richard II.*   Act III.   Sc. 2.   L. 42.

    The heavenly-harness'd team
Begins his golden progress in the east.

u.   *Henry IV.*   Pt. I.   Act III.   Sc. 1.
                      L. 221.

See! led by Morn, with dewy feet,
Apollo mounts his golden seat,
   Replete with seven-fold fire;
While, dazzled by his conquering light,
Heaven's glittering host and awful night
   Submissively retire.
   a.   THOMAS TAYLOR—*Ode to the Rising Sun.*

    See how there
      The cowlèd night
Kneels on the Eastern sanctuary-stair.
   b.   FRANCIS THOMPSON—*A Corymbus for*
                       Autumn. St. 5.

But yonder comes the powerful King of Day,
Rejoicing in the East.
   c.   THOMSON—*Seasons. Summer.* L. 81.

The rising sun complies with our weak sight,
First gilds the clouds, then shows his globe of
   light
At such a distance from our eyes, as though
He knew what harm his hasty beams would
   do.
   d.   EDMUND WALLER—*To the King upon*
         His Majesty's Happy Return. L. 1.

SUNSET.

Come watch with me the shaft of fire that
   glows
In yonder West: the fair, frail palaces,
The fading Alps and archipelagoes,
And great cloud-continents of sunset-seas.
   e.   T. B. ALDRICH—*Sonnet. Miracles.*

The death-bed of a day, how beautiful!
   f.   BAILEY—*Festus.* Sc. *A Library and*
                       Balcony.

It was the cooling hour, just when the
   rounded
Red sun sinks down behind the azure hill,
Which then seems as if the whole earth is
   bounded,
   Circling all nature, hush'd, and dim, and
     still,
With the far mountain-crescent half sur-
   rounded
   On one side, and the deep sea calm and chill
Upon the other, and the rosy sky
With one star sparkling through it like an eye.
   g.   BYRON—*Don Juan.* Canto II. St. 183.

                 See! he sinks
Without a word; and his ensanguined bier
Is vacant in the west, while far and near
Behold! each coward shadow eastward
   shrinks,
Thou dost not strive, O sun, nor dost thou cry
Amid thy cloud-built streets.
   h.   FABER—*The Rosary and Other Poems.*
         On the Ramparts at Angoulême.

       The sacred lamp of day
Now dipt in western clouds his parting ray.
   i.   FALCONER—*The Shipwreck.* Canto II.
                           L. 27.

Oft did I wonder why the setting sun
   Should look upon us with a blushing face:
Is't not for shame of what he hath seen done,
   Whilst in our hemisphere he ran his race?
   j.   HEATH—*First Century. On the Setting*
                              Sun.

Purple, violet, gold and white,
   Royal clouds are they;
Catching the spear-like rays in the west—
Lining therewith each downy nest,
   At the close of Summer day.

Forming and breaking in the sky,
   I fancy all shapes are there;
Temple, mountain, monument, spire;
Ships rigged out with sails of fire,
   And blown by the evening air.
   k.   J. K. HOYT—*A Summer Sunset.*

After a day of cloud and wind and rain
Sometimes the setting sun breaks out again,
   And, touching all the darksome woods with
     light,
Smiles on the fields until they laugh and sing,
Then like a ruby from the horizon's ring,
   Drops down into the night.
   l.   LONGFELLOW—*The Hanging of the*
                     Crane. Pt. VII.

Down sank the great red sun, and in golden,
   glimmering vapors
Veiled the light of his face, like the Prophet
   descending from Sinai.
   m.   LONGFELLOW—*Evangeline.* Pt. I.
                            Sec. IV.

Softly the evening came. The sun from the
   western horizon
Like a magician extended his golden wand
   o'er the landscape;
Twinkling vapors arose; and sky and water
   and forest
Seemed all on fire at the touch, and melted
   and mingled together.
   n.   LONGFELLOW—*Evangeline.* Pt. II.
                            Sec. II.

And the gilded car of day,
His glowing axle doth allay
In the steep Atlantic stream.
   o.   MILTON—*Comus.* L. 95.

Now in his Palace of the West,
   Sinking to slumber, the bright Day,
Like a tired monarch fann'd to rest,
   'Mid the cool airs of Evening lay;
While round his couch's golden rim
   The gaudy clouds, like courtiers, crept—
Struggling each other's light to dim,
   And catch his last smile e'er he slept.
   p.   MOORE—*The Summer Fête.* St. 22.

Long on the wave reflected lustres play.
   q.   SAM'L ROGERS—*The Pleasures of*
                   Memory. Pt. I. L. 94.

Methought little space 'tween those hills
  intervened,
But nearer,—more lofty,—more shaggy they
  seemed.
The clouds o'er their summits they calmly did
  rest,
And hung on the ether's invisible breast;
Than the vapours of earth they seemed purer,
  more bright,—
Oh! could they be clouds? 'Twas the necklace
  of night.
  a.   RUSKIN—*The Iteriad. Sunset at*
                                    Low-Wood.

The setting sun, and music at the close,
As the last taste of sweets, is sweetest last.
  b.   *Richard II.* Act II. Sc. 1. L. 12.

When the sun sets, who doth not look for
night?
  c.   *Richard III.* Act II. Sc. 3. L. 34.

                    The sun was down,
And all the west was paved with sullen fire.
I cried, "Behold! the barren beach of hell
At ebb of tide."
  d.   ALEXANDER SMITH—*A Life Drama.*
                                           Sc. 4.

How fine has the day been! how bright was
  the sun,
How lovely and joyful the course that he run!
Though he rose in a mist when his race he
  begun,
  And there followed some droppings of rain:
But now the fair traveller's come to the west,
His rays are all gold, and his beauties are best;
He paints the skies gay as he sinks to his rest,
  And foretells a bright rising again.
  e.   WATTS—*Moral Songs. A Summer*
                                    Evening.

SUPERSTITION.

Foul Superstition! howsoe'er disguised,
  Idol, saint, virgin, prophet, crescent, cross,
For whatsoever symbol thou art prized,
  Thou sacerdotal gain, but general loss!
Who from true worship's gold can separate
  thy dross?
  f.   BYRON—*Childe Harold.*   Canto II.
                                            St. 44.

Superstition is a senseless fear of God.
  g.   CICERO.

My right eye itches, some good luck is near.
  h.   DRYDEN—*Paraphrase of Amaryllis.*
              Third Idyllium of Theocritus. L. 86.

Alas! you know the cause too well;
The salt is spilt, to me it fell.
Then to contribute to my loss,
My knife and fork were laid across;
On Friday, too! the day I dread;
Would I were safe at home, in bed!
Last night (I vow to Heaven 'tis true)
Bounce from the fire a coffin flew.
Next post some fatal news shall tell:
God send my Cornish friends be well!
  i.   GAY—*Fables.* Pt. I.   Fable 37.

Why is it that we entertain the belief that
for every purpose odd numbers are the most
effectual?
  j.   PLINY—*Natural History.*
                            Bk. XXVIII. Ch. 5.

                    Midnight hags,
By force of potent spells, of bloody characters,
And conjurations horrible to hear,
Call fiends and spectres from the yawning
  deep,
And set the ministers of hell at work.
  k.   NICHOLAS ROWE—*Jane Shore.* Act IV.
                                    Sc. 1. L. 240.

Superstition is related to this life, religion
to the next; superstition is allied to fatality,
religion to virtue; it is by the vivacity of
earthly desires that we become superstitious;
it is, on the contrary, by the sacrifice of these
desires that we become religious.
  l.   MADAME DE STAËL—See ABEL STEVENS'
                            Life of Madame de Staël.
                                           Ch. XXXIV.

SUSPICION.

Quoth Sidrophel, If you suppose,
Sir Knight, that I am one of those,
I might suspect, and take th' alarm,
Your bus'ness is but to inform;
But if it be, 'tis ne'er the near,
You have a wrong sow by the ear.
  m.   BUTLER—*Hudibras.* Pt. II. Canto III.
                                            L. 575.

Cæsar's wife should be above suspicion.
  n.   PLUTARCH—*Life of Cæsar.* Ch. X.

All seems infected that the infected spy,
As all looks yellow to the jaundiced eye.
  o.   POPE—*Essay on Criticism.* L. 568.

                    All is not well;
I doubt some foul play.
  p.   *Hamlet.* Act I. Sc. 2. L. 255.

Suspicion always haunts the guilty mind;
The thief doth fear each bush an officer.
  q.   *Henry VI.* Pt. III. Act V. Sc. 6.
                                            L. 11.

Would he were fatter! But I fear him not:
Yet if my name were liable to fear,
I do not know the man I should avoid
So soon as that spare Cassius.
  r.   *Julius Cæsar.* Act I. Sc. 2. L. 198.

SWEETNESS.

Nor waste their sweetness in the desert air.
  s.   CHURCHILL—*Gotham.* Bk. II. L. 20.

And waste its sweetness on the desert air.
  t.   GRAY—*Elegy in a Country Churchyard.*
                                            St. 14.

The two noblest of things, which are sweetness and light.

    a.   SWIFT—*Battle of the Books.*

The sweetest thing that ever grew
  Beside a human door.

    b.   WORDSWORTH—*Lucy Gray.* St. 2.

SYMBOLS.

With crosses, relics, crucifixes,
Beads, pictures, rosaries, and pixes;
The tools of working out salvation
By mere mechanic operation.

    c.   BUTLER—*Hudibras.* Pt. III. Canto I.
    L. 1,495.

Thus in the beginning the world was so made that certain signs come before certain events.

    d.   CICERO—*De Divinations.* I. 118.

Science sees signs; Poetry the thing signified.

    e.   J. C. AND A. W. HARE—*Guesses at
    Truth.*

It [Catholicism] supplies a multitude of external forms in which the spiritual may be clothed and manifested.

    f.   NATH. HAWTHORNE—*The Marble Faun.*
    Vol. II. Ch. XIII.

All things are symbols: the external shows
Of Nature have their image in the mind,
As flowers and fruits and falling of the leaves.

    g.   LONGFELLOW—*The Harvest Moon.*

If he be not in love with some woman, there is no believing old signs: a' brushes his hat o' mornings; what should that bode?

    h.   *Much Ado About Nothing.* Act III.
    Sc. 2. L. 40.

Sometime we see a cloud that's dragonish;
A vapour sometime like a bear or lion,
A tower'd citadel, a pendant rock,
A forked mountain, or blue promontory
With trees upon 't, that nod unto the world,
And mock our eyes with air: thou hast seen
  these signs;
They are black vesper's pageants.

    i.   *Antony and Cleopatra.* Act IV. St. 14.
    L. 2.

Oft on the dappled turf at ease
I sit, and play with similes,
Loose type of things through all degrees.

    j.   WORDSWORTH—*To the Daisy.*

SYMPATHY.

Strengthen me by sympathizing with my strength not my weakness.

    k.   AMOS BRONSON ALCOTT—*Table-Talk.*
    Sympathy.

            Pity and need
Make all flesh kin. There is no caste in blood.

    l.   EDWIN ARNOLD—*Light of Asia.*
    Bk. VI. L. 73.

But there is one thing which we are responsible for, and that is for our sympathies, for the manner in which we regard it, and for the tone in which we discuss it. What shall we say, then, with regard to it? On which side shall we stand?

    m.   JOHN BRIGHT—*Speech on Slavery and
    Secession.* Feb. 3, 1863.

I live not in myself, but I become
Portion of that around me, and to me
High mountains are a feeling, but the hum
Of human cities torture.

    n.   BYRON—*Childe Harold.* Canto III.
    St. 72.

In the desert a fountain is springing,
  In the wide waste there still is a tree,
And a bird in the solitude singing,
  Which speaks to my spirit of *thee.*

    o.   BYRON—*Stanzas to Augusta.*

Striking the electric chain wherewith we are darkly bound.

    p.   BYRON—*Childe Harold.* Canto IV.
    St. 23.

Of a truth, men are mystically united: a mystic bond of brotherhood makes all men one.

    q.   CARLYLE—*Essays. Goethe's Works.*

There is in souls a sympathy with sounds.

    r.   COWPER—*The Task.* Bk. VI. L. 1.

Our souls sit close and silently within,
And their own web from their own entrails
  spin;
And when eyes meet far off, our sense is such,
That, spider like, we feel the tenderest touch.

    s.   DRYDEN—*Mariage à la Mode.* Act II.
    Sc. I.

           The human heart
Finds nowhere shelter but in human kind.

    t.   GEORGE ELIOT—*The Spanish Gypsy.*
    Bk. IV.

The secrets of life are not shown except to sympathy and likeness.

    u.   EMERSON—*Representative Men.*
    Montaigne.

           The man who melts
With social sympathy, though not allied,
Is than a thousand kinsmen of more worth.

    v.   EURIPIDES—*Orestes.* L. 846.

Our sympathy is cold to the relation of distant misery.

    w.   GIBBON—*Decline and Fall of the Roman
    Empire.* Ch. XLIX.

He watch'd and wept, he pray'd and felt for all.

    x.   GOLDSMITH—*The Deserted Village.*
    L. 166.

The craving for sympathy is the common boundary-line between joy and sorrow.
  a.   J. C. AND A. W. HARE—*Guesses at Truth.*

O! ask not, hope thou not too much
Of sympathy below;
Few are the hearts whence one same touch
Bids the sweet fountains flow.
  b.   MRS. HEMANS—*Kindred Hearts.*

We pine for kindred natures
To mingle with our own.
  c.   MRS. HEMANS—*Psyche borne by Zephyrs to the Island of Pleasure.*

Yet, taught by time, my heart has learned to glow
For other's good, and melt at other's woe.
  d.   HOMER—*Odyssey.* Bk. XVIII. L. 269.
          Pope's trans.

A man may be buoyed up by the efflation of his wild desires to brave any imaginable peril; but he cannot calmly see one he loves braving the same peril; simply because he cannot feel within him *that* which prompts another. He sees the danger, and feels not the power that is to overcome it.
  e.   GEORGE HENRY LEWES—*The Spanish Drama.* Ch. II.

World-wide apart, and yet akin,
As showing that the human heart
Beats on forever as of old.
  f.   LONGFELLOW—*Tales of a Wayside Inn.*
          Pt. III. *The Theologian's Tale.*
          Interlude.

But better far it is to speak
  One simple word, which now and then
Shall waken their free nature in the weak
  And friendless sons of men.
  g.   LOWELL—*An Incident in a Railroad Car.* St. 20.

For I no sooner in my heart divin'd,
My heart, which by a secret harmony
Still moves with thine, joined in connection sweet.
  h.   MILTON—*Paradise Lost.* Bk. X.
          L. 357.

Never elated while one man's oppress'd;
Never dejected while another's blessed.
  i.   POPE—*Essay on Man.* Ep. IV.
          L. 323.

Speed the soft intercourse from soul to soul,
And waft a sigh from Indus to the Pole.
  j.   POPE—*Eloise to Abelard.* L. 57.

Somewhere or other there must surely be
  The face not seen, the voice not heard,
The heart that not yet— never yet—ah me!
  Made answer to my word.
  k.   CHRISTINA G. ROSSETTI—*Somewhere or Other.*

If thou art something bring thy soul and interchange with mine.
  l.   SCHILLER—*Votive Tablets. Value and Worth.*

It [true love] is the secret sympathy,
The silver link, the silken tie,
Which heart to heart, and mind to mind
In body and in soul can bind.
  m.   SCOTT—*Lay of the Last Minstrel.*
          Canto V. St. 13.

A sympathy in choice.
  n.   *Midsummer-Night's Dream.* Act I.
          Sc. 1. L. 141.

For thou hast given me in this beauteous face,
A world of earthly blessings to my soul,
If sympathy of love unite our thoughts.
  o.   *Henry VI.* Pt. II. Act I. Sc. 1.
          L. 21.

Sympathy is especially a Christian's duty.
  p.   SPURGEON—*Gleanings Among the Sheaves. Sympathy.*

T.

TAILORING (*See* OCCUPATIONS).

TALENTS.

And sure th' Eternal Master found
His single talent well employ'd.
  q.   SAM'L JOHNSON—*Verses on the Death of Mr. Robert Levet.* St. 7.

Talent is that which is in a man's power!
genius is that in whose power a man is.
  r.   LOWELL—*Among my Books. Rousseau and the Sentimentalists.*

TALK.

It would talk;
Lord, how it talked!
  s.   BEAUMONT AND FLETCHER—*The Scornful Lady.* Act IV. Sc. 1.

But still his tongue ran on, the less
Of weight it bore, with greater ease.
  t.   BUTLER—*Hudibras.* Pt. III.
          Canto II. L. 443

With vollies of eternal babble.
  u.   BUTLER—*Hudibras.* Pt. III. Canto II.
          L. 453.

Words learn'd by rote a parrot may rehearse,
But talking is not always to converse,
Not more distinct from harmony divine
The constant creaking of a country sign.
a.   COWPER—*Conversation.* L. 7.

But far more numerous was the herd of such,
Who think too little, and who talk too much.
b.   DRYDEN—*Absalom and Achitophel.*
          Pt. I. L. 533.

My tongue within my lips I rein;
For who talks much must talk in vain.
c.   GAY—*Introduction to the Fables.* Pt. I.
          L. 57.

Where village statesmen talk'd with looks
   profound.
And news much older than their ale went
   round.
d.   GOLDSMITH—*The Deserted Village.*
          L. 223.

Stop not, unthinking, every friend you meet
To spin your wordy fabric in the street;
While you are emptying your colloquial pack,
The fiend *Lumbago* jumps upon his back.
e.   O. W. HOLMES—*Urania. A Rhymed
          Lesson.* L. 439.

No season now for calm, familiar talk.
f.   HOMER—*Iliad.* Bk. XXII. L. 169.
          Pope's trans.

Then he will talk—good gods, how he will
   talk!
g.   NATHANIEL LEE—*Alexander the Great.*
          Act I. Sc. 1.

In general those who nothing have to say
Contrive to spend the longest time in doing it.
h.   LOWELL—*An Oriental Apologue.* St. 15.

Oft has it been my lot to mark
A proud, conceited, talking spark.
i.   JAMES MERRICK—*The Chameleon.*

His talk was like a stream which runs
   With rapid change from rock to roses;
It slipped from politics to puns;
   It passed from Mahomet to Moses;
Beginning with the laws that keep
   The planets in their radiant courses,
And ending with some precept deep
   For dressing eels or shoeing horses.
j.   PRAED—*The Vicar.*

They never taste who always drink;
They always talk who never think.
k.   PRIOR—*Upon a Passage in the
          Scaligerana.*

   A gentleman, nurse, that loves to hear himself talk, and will speak more in a minute
than he will stand to in a month.
l.   *Romeo and Juliet.* Act II. Sc. 4.
          L. 155.

If I chance to talk a little wild, forgive me;
I had it from my father.
m.   *Henry VIII.* Act I. Sc. 4. L. 26.

   I prythee, take the cork out of thy mouth
that I may drink thy tidings.
n.   *As You Like It.* Act III. Sc. 2. L. 12.

          My lord shall never rest:
I'll watch him, tame and talk him out of
   patience:
His bed shall seem a school, his board a shrift.
o.   *Othello.* Act III. Sc. 3. L. 22.

   No, pray thee, let it serve for table-talk;
Then, howsoe'er thou speak'st, 'mong other
   things
I shall digest it.
p.   *Merchant of Venice.* Act III. Sc. 5.
          L. 93.

Talkers are no good doers; be assur'd
We come to use our hands and not our tongues.
q.   *Richard III.* Act I. Sc. 3. L. 352.

          The red wine first must rise
In their fair cheeks, my lord; then we shall
   have 'em
Talk us to silence.
r.   *Henry VIII.* Act I. Sc. 4. L. 43.

What cracker is this same that deafs our ears
With this abundance of superfluous breath?
s.   *King John.* Act II. Sc. I. L. 147.

She sits tormenting every guest,
Nor gives her tongue one moment's rest,
In phrases batter'd, stale, and trite,
Which modern ladies call polite.
t.   SWIFT—*The Journal of a Modern Lady.*

Good talkers are only found in Paris.
u.   FRANÇOIS VILLON—*Des Femmes de
          Paris.* II.

TEA.

Matrons, who toss the cup, and see
The grounds of *fate* in *grounds of tea.*
v.   CHURCHILL—*The Ghost.* Bk. I. L. 117.

   Tea! thou soft, thou sober, sage, and venerable liquid, * * * thou female tongue-running, smile-smoothing, heart-opening, winktippling cordial, to whose glorious insipidity
I owe the happiest moment of my life, let me
fall prostrate.
w.   COLLEY CIBBER—*Lady's Last Stake.*
          Act I. Sc. 1.

Here, thou, great Anna! whom three realms
   obey,
Dost sometimes counsel take—and sometimes
   tea.
x.   POPE—*Rape of the Lock.* Canto III.
          L. 7.

Thank God for tea! What would the world
do without tea? how did it exist? I am glad
I was not born before tea.
a.   SYDNEY SMITH—*Lady Holland's
         Memoir.*   Vol. I.   P. 383.

         Tea does our fancy aid,
Repress those vapours which the head invade
And keeps that palace of the soul serene.
 b.   EDMUND WALLER—*Of Tea.*

TEARS.

And friends, dear friends,—when it shall be
That this low breath is gone from me,
   And round my bier ye come to weep,
Let One, most loving of you all,
Say, "Not a tear must o'er her fall;
   He giveth His beloved sleep."
 c.   E. B. BROWNING—*The Sleep.*   St. 9.

Thank God for grace,
Ye who weep only! If, as some have done,
Ye grope tear-blinded in a desert place
And touch but tombs,—look up! Those tears
   will run
Soon in long rivers down the lifted face,
And leave the vision clear for stars and sun.
   d.   E. B. BROWNING—*Tears.*

Oh! too convincing—dangerously dear—
In woman's eye the unanswerable tear!
That weapon of her weakness she can wield,
To save, subdue—at once her spear and shield.
   e.   BYRON—*The Corsair.* Canto II. St. 15.

She was a good deal shock'd; not shock'd at
   tears,
   For women shed and use them at their
     liking;
But there is something when man's eye ap-
     pears
Wet, still more disagreeable and striking.
 f.   BYRON—*Don Juan.* Canto V. St. 118.

So bright the tear in Beauty's eye,
Love half regrets to kiss it dry.
   g.   BYRON—*The Bride of Abydos.*
                   Canto I.   St. 8.

There is a tear for all who die,
A mourner o'er the humblest grave.
   h.   BYRON—*Elegiac Stanzas. On the Death
           of Sir Peter Parker,* Bart.

What gem hath dropp'd, and sparkles o'er
   his chain?
The tear most sacred, shed for other's pain,
That starts at once—bright pure—from Pity's
   mine,
Already polish'd by the hand divine!
   i.   BYRON—*The Corsair.* Canto II. St. 15.

A stoic of the woods,—a man without a tear.
   j.   CAMPBELL—*Gertrude of Wyoming.*
                   Pt. I.   St. 23.

For Beauty's tears are lovelier than her smile.
   k.   CAMPBELL—*Pleasures of Hope.* Pt. I.
                       L. 180.

Words that weep and tears that speak.
   l.   ABRAHAM COWLEY—*The Prophet.*
                       St. 2.

And the tear that is wiped with a little address,
May be follow'd perhaps by a smile.
   m.   COWPER—*The Rose.*

No radiant pearl, which crested Fortune
   wears,
No gem, that twinkling hangs from Beauty's
   ears,
Not the bright stars which Night's blue arch
   adorn,
Nor rising suns that gild the vernal morn,
Shine with such lustre as the tear that flows
Down Virtue's manly cheek for others' woes.
   n.   ERASMUS DARWIN—*The Botanic
          Garden.* Pt. II. Canto III. L. 459.

     What precious drops are those,
Which silently each other's track pursue,
Bright as young diamonds in their infant
   dew?
   o.   DRYDEN—*The Conquest of Grenada.*
                Pt. II.   Act III.   Sc. 1.

And weep the more, because I weep in vain.
   p.   GRAY—*Sonnet. On the Death of Mr.
                           West.*

Ope the sacred source of sympathetic tears.
   q.   GRAY—*Progress of Poesy.* III. 1.
                       L. 12.

The tear forgot as soon as shed,
The sunshine of the breast.
   r.   GRAY—*Eton College.* St. 5.

Accept these grateful tears! for thee they flow,
For thee, that ever felt another's woe!
   s.   HOMER—*Iliad.* Bk. XIX. L. 319.
                       Pope's trans.

My tears must stop, for every drop
   Hinders needle and thread.
   t.   HOOD—*Song of the Shirt.*

Oh! would I were dead now,
Or up in my bed now,
To cover my head now
   And have a good cry!
   u.   HOOD—*A Table of Errata.*

E'en like the passage of an angel's tear
That falls through the clear ether silently.
   v.   KEATS—*To One Who Has Been Long in
                       City Pent.*

All kin' o' smily round the lips
An' teary roun' the lashes.
   w.   LOWELL—*The Biglow Papers.* Second
          Series. *The Courtin'.* St. 21.

Thrice he assay'd, and thrice in spite of scorn
Tears, such as angels weep, burst forth.
   a.   Milton—*Paradise Lost.* Bk. I. L. 619.

Without the meed of some melodious tear.
   b.   Milton—*Lycidas.* L. 14.

And the tear that we shed, though in secret
   it rolls,
Shall long keep his memory green in our
   souls.
   c.   Moore—*Oh, Breathe not his Name.*

The glorious Angel, who was keeping
The gates of Light, beheld her weeping;
And, as he nearer drew and listen'd
To her sad song, a tear-drop glisten'd
Within his eyelids, like the spray
   From Eden's fountain, where it lies
On the blue flow'r, which—Bramins say—
Blooms nowhere but in Paradise.
   d.   Moore—*Lalla Rookh. Paradise and
the Peri.*

O dear, dear Jeanie Morrison,
   The thochts o' bygane years
Still fling their shadows ower my path,
   And blind my een wi' tears.
   e.   Wm. Motherwell—*Jeanie Morrison.*

Behold who ever wept, and in his tears
Was happier far than others in their smiles.
   f.   Petrarch—*The Triumph of Eternity!*
L. 95. (*Charlemont.*)

Sweet tears! the awful language, eloquent
Of infinite affection; far too big
For words.
   g.   Pollok—*Course of Time.* Bk. V.
L. 633.

Peter deny'd
His Lord and cry'd.
   h.   *From the New England Primer.* 1777.

But woe awaits a country, when
She sees the tears of bearded men.
   i.   Scott—*Marmion.* Canto V. St. 16.

The tear, down childhood's cheek that flows,
Is like the dewdrop on the rose;
When next the summer breeze comes by
And waves the bush, the flower is dry.
   j.   Scott—*Rokeby.* Canto IV. St. 11.

And he, a marble to her tears, is washed
with them, but relents not.
   k.   *Measure for Measure.* Act III. Sc. 1.
L. 238.

Did he break into tears?
In great measure.
A kind overflow of kindness: there are no
faces truer than those that are so washed.
   l.   *Much Ado About Nothing.* Act I.
Sc. 1. L. 24.

Eye-offending brine.
   m.   *Twelfth Night.* Act I. Sc. 1. L. 30.

He has strangled
His language in his tears.
   n.   *Henry VIII.* Act V. Sc. 1. L. 157.

I am about to weep; but, thinking that
We are a queen, or long have dream'd so,
   certain
The daughter of a king, my drops of tears
I'll turn to sparks of fire.
   o.   *Henry VIII.* Act II. Sc. 4. L. 70.

I cannot weep; for all my body's moisture
Scarce serves to quench my furnace-burning
   heart.
   p.   *Henry VI.* Pt. III. Act II. Sc. 1.
L. 79.

      I did not think to shed a tear
In all my miseries; but thou hast forc'd me,
Out of thy honest truth, to play the woman.
   q.   *Henry VIII.* Act III. Sc. 2. L. 428.

If that the earth could teem with woman's
   tears,
Each drop she falls would prove a crocodile.
   r.   *Othello.* Act IV. Sc. 1. L. 256.

If the boy have not a woman's gift
To rain a shower of commanded tears,
An onion will do well for such a shift.
   s.   *Taming of the Shrew.* Induction.
Sc. 1. L. 124.

If you have tears, prepare to shed them now.
   t.   *Julius Cæsar.* Act III. Sc. 2. L. 173.

I had not so much of man in me,
And all my mother came into mine eyes
And gave me up to tears.
   u.   *Henry V.* Act IV. Sc. 6. L. 30.

      I so lively acted with my tears
That my poor mistress, moved therewithal,
Wept bitterly.
   v.   *Two Gentlemen of Verona.* Act IV.
Sc. 4. L. 174.

Let not women's weapons, water-drops,
Stain my man's cheeks!
   w.   *King Lear.* Act II. Sc. 4. L. 280.

      My plenteous joys,
Wanton in fullness, seek to hide themselves
In drops of sorrow.
   x.   *Macbeth.* Act I. Sc. 4. L. 33.

      No, I'll not weep:
I have full cause of weeping; but this heart
Shall break into a hundred thousand flaws
Or ere I'll weep.
   y.   *King Lear.* Act II. Sc. 4. L. 286.

      One, whose subdu'd eyes,
Albeit unused to the melting mood,
Drop tears as fast as the Arabian trees
Their medicinal gum.
   z.   *Othello.* Act V. Sc. 2. L. 348.

See, see what showers arise,
Blown with the windy tempest of my heart.
a.   *Henry VI.* Pt. III. Act II. Sc. 5.
L. 85.

That instant shut
My woeful self up in a mourning house,
Raining the tears of lamentation.
b.   *Love's Labour's Lost.* Act V. Sc. 2.
L. 817.

The big round tears
Coursed one another down his innocent nose
In piteous chase.
c.   *As You Like It.* Act II. Sc. 1. L. 38.

The liquid drops of tears that you have shed
Shall come again, transform'd to orient pearl,
Advantaging their loan with interest
Of ten times double gain of happiness.
d.   *Richard III.* Act IV. Sc. 4. L. 321.

Then fresh tears
Stood on her cheeks, as doth the honey-dew
Upon a gather'd lily almost wither'd.
e.   *Titus Andronicus.* Act III. Sc. 1.
L. 111.

There she shook
The holy water from her heavenly eyes,
And clamour moisten'd.
f.   *King Lear.* Act IV. Sc. 3. L. 31.

The tears live in an onion that should
water this sorrow.
g.   *Antony and Cleopatra.* Act I. Sc. 2.
L. 176.

Those eyes of thine from mine have drawn
salt tears,
Sham'd their aspect with store of childish
drops.
h.   *Richard III.* Act I. Sc. 2. L. 154.

'Tis the best brine a maiden can season her
praise in.
i.   *All's Well That Ends Well.* Act I.
Sc. 1. L. 55.

What I should say
My tears gainsay ; for every word I speak,
Ye see, I drink the water of mine eyes.
j.   *Henry VI.* Pt. III. Act V. Sc. 4.
L. 73.

Why, man, if the river were dry, I am able
to fill it with my tears : if the wind were
down, I could drive the boat with my sighs.
k.   *Two Gentlemen of Verona.* Act II.
Sc. 3. L. 57.

With sad unhelpful tears, and with dimm'd
eyes
Look after him and cannot do him good.
l.   *Henry VI.* Pt. II. Act III. Sc. 1.
L. 218.

Heaven is not gone, but we are blind with
tears,
Groping our way along the downward slope
of Years !
m.   R. H. STODDARD—*Hymn to the
Beautiful.* L. 33.

Tears, idle tears, I know not what they mean,
Tears from the depths of some divine despair.
n.   TENNYSON—*The Princess.* Canto IV.
L. 21.

Why wilt thou ever scare me with thy tears,
And make me tremble lest a saying learnt,
In days far-off, on that dark earth, be true ?
The gods themselves cannot recall their gifts.
o.   TENNYSON—*Tithonus.* St. 5.

Two aged men, that had been foes for life,
Met by a grave, and wept—and in those
tears
They washed away the memory of their strife ;
Then wept again the loss of all those years.
p.   FREDERICK TENNYSON—*The Golden
City.* Pt. I.

The big round tears run down his dappled
face ;
He groans in anguish.
q.   THOMSON—*Seasons. Autumn.* L. 454.

Tears are the silent language of grief.
r.   VOLTAIRE—*A Philosophical Dictionary.
Tears.*

Yet tears to human suffering are due ;
And mortal hopes defeated and o'erthrown
Are mourned by man, and not by man alone.
s.   WORDSWORTH—*Laodamia.*

Lorenzo ! hast thou ever weigh'd a sigh ?
Or studied the philosophy of tears ?—
*   *   *   *   *   *
Hast thou descended deep into the breast,
And seen their source ? If not, descend with
me,
And trace these briny riv'lets to their springs.
t.   YOUNG—*Night Thoughts.* Night V.
L. 516.

TEMPER.

But certain winds will make men's temper
bad.
u.   GEORGE ELIOT—*Spanish Gypsy.* Bk. I.

O ! bless'd with temper, whose unclouded
ray
Can make to-morrow cheerful as to-day.
v.   POPE—*Moral Essays.* Ep. II. L. 257.

The brain may devise laws for the blood ;
but a hot temper leaps o'er a cold decree :
such a hare is madness the youth, to skip
o'er the meshes of good counsel, the cripple.
w.   *Merchant of Venice.* Act I. Sc. 2.
L. 19.

TEMPERANCE.

Beware the deadly fumes of that insane elation
Which rises from the cup of mad impiety
And go, get drunk with that divine intoxica-
tion
Which is more sober far than all sobriety.
x.   WM. R. ALGER—*Oriental Poetry.
The Sober Drunkenness.*

And he that will to bed go sober,
Falls with the leaf still in October.
　　a.　　Beaumont and Fletcher—*The Bloody
　　　　　Brother. Song.* Act II. Sc. 2.

Of a nature so mild and benign and proportioned to the human constitution as to warm
without heating, to cheer but not inebriate.
　　b.　　Bishop Berkeley—*Siris.* Par. 217.

Call'd to the temple of impure delight
He that abstains, and he alone, does right.
If a wish wander that way, call it home;
He cannot long be safe whose wishes roam.
　　c.　　Cowper—*The Progress of Error.* L. 557.

Temp'rate in every place—abroad, at home,
Thence will applause, and hence will profit
　　come;
And health from either—he in time prepares
For sickness, age, and their attendant cares.
　　d.　　Crabbe—*The Borough.* Letter XVII.
　　　　　　　　　　　　　　　　L. 198.

Abstinence is whereby a man refraineth
from any thyng which he may lawfully take.
　　e.　　Elyot—*Governour.* Bk. III. Ch. XVI.

Drink not the third glass, which thou canst
　　not tame,
When once it is within thee; but before
Mayst rule it, as thou list: and pour the
　　shame,
Which it would pour on thee, upon the floor.
It is most just to throw that on the ground,
Which would throw me there, if I keep the
　　round.
　　f.　　Herbert—*The Temple. The Church
　　　　　Porch. Perirrhanterium.* St. 5.

Abstinence is as easy to me as temperance
would be difficult.
　　g.　　Sam'l Johnson—Hannah More's
　　　　　　　　　　　Johnsoniana. 467.

　　　　　　　　　　Of my merit
On that pint you yourself may jedge:
All is, I never drink no sperit,
Nor I haint never signed no pledge.
　　h.　　Lowell—*The Biglow Papers.* First
　　　　　　　Series. No. VII. St. 9.

　　　　　　　　If all the world
Should in a pet of temp'rance, feed on pulse,
Drink the clear stream, and nothing wear but
　　frieze,
Th' All-giver would be unthank'd, would be
　　unprais'd.
　　i.　　Milton—*Comus.* L. 720.

Impostor; do not charge most innocent
　　Nature,
As if she would her children should be riotous
With her abundance; she, good cateress,
Means her provision only to the good,
That live according to her sober laws,
And holy dictate of spare temperance.
　　j.　　Milton—*Comus.* L. 762.

38

O madness to think use of strongest wines
And strongest drinks our chief support of
　　health,
When God with these forbidden made choice
　　to rear
His mighty champion, strong above compare,
Whose drink was only from the liquid brook.
　　k.　　Milton—*Samson Agonistes.* L. 553.

　　　　　　　　　　Well observe
The rule of Not too much, by temperance
　　taught
In what thou eat'st and drink'st.
　　l.　　Milton—*Paradise Lost.* Bk. XI.
　　　　　　　　　　　　　　　　L. 531.

Ask God for temperance; that's the appliance
　　only
Which your disease requires.
　　m.　　*Henry VIII.* Act I. Sc. 1. L. 124.

Make less thy body hence, and more thy
　　grace;
Leave gormandizing.
　　n.　　*Henry IV.* Pt. II. Act V. Sc. 5.
　　　　　　　　　　　　　　　　L. 56.

TEMPTATION.

Why comes temptation but for man to meet
And master and make crouch beneath his
　　foot,
And so be pedestaled in triumph?
　　o.　　Robert Browning—*The Ring and the
　　　　　　Book. The Pope.* L. 1,185.

I may not here omit those two main plagues,
and common dotages of human kind, wine
and women, which have infatuated and besotted myriads of people: they go commonly
together.
　　p.　　Burton—*Anatomy of Melancholy.*
　　　　　　　　Pt. I. Sec. II. Memb. 3.
　　　　　　　　　　　　　　Subsec. XIII.

The devil tempts us not—'tis we tempt him,
Reckoning his skill with opportunity.
　　q.　　George Eliot—*Felix Holt.*
　　　　　　　　　　　　　　Ch. XLVII.

Many a dangerous temptation comes to us
in fine gay colours, that are but skin-deep.
　　r.　　Mathew Henry—*Commentaries.*
　　　　　　　　　　　　　　Genesis III.

Temptations hurt not, though they have
　　accesse;
Satan o'ercomes none but by willingnesse.
　　s.　　Herrick—*Hesperides. Temptations.*

Honest bread is very well—it's the butter
that makes the temptation.
　　t.　　Douglas Jerrold—*The Catspaw.*

In part she is to blame that has been tried :
He comes too late that comes to be denied.
a.   Lady M. W. Montagu—*The Lady's*
Resolve.

In part to blame is she,
Which hath *without consent* bin only tride ;
He comes *too neere,* that comes to be *denide.*
b.   Sir Thos. Overbury—*A Wife.* St. 36.

But Satan now is wiser than of yore,
And tempts by making rich, not making
poor.
c.   Pope—*Moral Essays.* Ep. III. L. 351.

Bell, book and candle shall not drive me back,
When gold and silver becks me to come on.
d.   *King John.* Act III. Sc. 3. L. 12.

Devils soonest tempt, resembling spirits of
light.
e.   *Love's Labour's Lost.* Act IV. Sc. 3.
L. 257.

How oft the sight of means to do ill deeds
Makes ill deeds done !
f.   *King John.* Act IV. Sc. 2. L. 219.

How quickly nature falls into revolt
When gold becomes her object !
g.   *Henry IV.* Pt. II. Act IV. Sc. 5.
L. 66.

I am that way going to temptation,
Where prayers cross.
h.   *Measure for Measure.* Act II. Sc. 2.
L. 158.

Know'st thou not any whom corrupting gold
Would tempt unto a close exploit of death ?
i.   *Richard III.* Act IV. Sc. 2. L. 34.

Most dangerous
Is that temptation that doth goad us on
To sin in loving virtue.
j.   *Measure for Measure.* Act II. Sc. 2.
L. 181.

Sometimes we are devils to ourselves,
When we will tempt the frailty of our powers,
Presuming on their changeful potency.
k.   *Troilus and Cressida.* Act IV. Sc. 4.
L. 97.

To beguile many and be beguil'd by one.
l.   *Othello.* Act IV. Sc. 1. L. 98.

Let a man be but in earnest in praying
against a temptation as the tempter is in
pressing it, and he needs not proceed by a
surer measure.
m.   Bishop South. Vol. VI. Sermon 10.

Some temptations come to the industrious,
but all temptations attack the idle.
n.   Spurgeon—*Gleanings Among the*
Sheaves. Idleness.

Could'st thou boast, O child of weakness !
O'er the sons of wrong and strife,
Were their strong temptations planted
In thy path of life ?
o.   Whittier—*What the Voice Said.*

THANKFULNESS.

Some hae meat and canna eat,
And some would eat that want it ;
But we hae meat, and we can eat,
Sae let the Lord be thankit.
p.   Burns—*Grace before Meat.*

When I'm not thank'd at all, I'm thank'd
enough,
I've done my duty, and I've done no more.
q.   Henry Fielding—*The Life and Death*
of Tom Thumb the Great. Act I.
Sc. 3.

I am glad that he thanks God for anything.
r.   Sam'l Johnson—*Boswell's Life of*
Johnson. 1775.

To receive honestly is the best thanks for a
good thing.
s.   George MacDonald—*Mary Marston.*
Ch. V.

Your bounty is beyond my speaking ;
But though my mouth be dumb, my heart
shall thank you.
t.   Nicholas Rowe—*Jane Shore.* Act II.
Sc. 1.

I thank you for your voices : thank you :
Your most sweet voices.
u.   *Coriolanus.* Act II. Sc. 3. L. 179.

Let never day nor night unhallow'd pass,
But still remember what the Lord hath done.
v.   *Henry VI.* Pt. II. Act II. Sc. 1. L. 85.

Thou thought'st to help me ; and such thanks
I give
As one near death to those that wish him live.
w.   *All's Well That Ends Well.* Act II.
Sc. 1. L. 133.

THANKSGIVING DAY.

And taught by thee the Church prolongs
Her hymns of high thanksgiving still.
x.   Keble—*The Christian Year. St. Luke*
the Evangelist. St. 18.

Great as the preparations were for the
dinner, everything was so contrived that not
a soul in the house should be kept from the
morning service of Thanksgiving in the
church.
y.   H. B. Stowe—*Oldtown Folks.* P. 345.

Ah! on Thanksgiving day, when from East
　　and from West,
From North and South, come the pilgrim and
　　guest,
When the gray-haired New Englander sees
　　round his board
The old broken links of affection restored,
When the care-wearied man seeks his mother
　　once more,
And the worn matron smiles where the girl
　　smiled before.
What moistens the lips and what brightens
　　the eye?
What calls back the past, like the rich pump-
　　kin pie?
　　a.　　WHITTIER—*The Pumpkin.*

And let these altars, wreathed with flowers
　　And piled with fruits, awake again
Thanksgivings for the golden hours,
　　The early and the latter rain!
　　b.　　WHITTIER—*For an Autumn Festival.*

THIEVING.

No Indian prince has to his palace
More followers than a thief to the gallows.
　　c.　　BUTLER—*Hudibras.* Pt. II. Canto I.
　　　　　　　　　　　　　　　　L. 273.

Kill a man's family, and he may brook it,
But keep your hands out of his breeches'
　　pocket.
　　d.　　BYRON—*Don Juan.* Canto X. St. 79.

Who, to patch up his fame—or fill his purse—
Still pilfers wretched plans, and makes them
　　worse;
Like gypsies, lest the stolen brat be known,
Defacing first, then claiming for his own.
　　e.　　CHURCHILL—*The Apology.* L. 232.

Stolen sweets are best.
　　f.　　COLLEY CIBBER—*The Rival Fools.*
　　　　　　　　　　　　　　　　Act I.
In vain we call old notions fudge
　　And bend our conscience to our dealing.
The Ten Commandments will not budge
　　And stealing will continue stealing.
　　g.　　*Motto of American Copyright League.*
　　　　　　　　　　　Written Nov. 20, 1885.

Stolen sweets are always sweeter:
Stolen kisses much completer:
Stolen looks are nice in chapels:
Stolen, stolen be your apples.
　　h.　　THOMAS RANDOLPH—*Song of Fairies.*

A cutpurse of the empire and the rule,
That from a shelf the precious diadem stole,
And put it in his pocket!
　　i.　　*Hamlet.* Act III. Sc. 4. L. 99.

A plague upon it when thieves cannot be
true one to another!
　　j.　　*Henry IV.* Pt. I. Act II. Sc. 2. L. 29.

He that is robb'd, not wanting what is stol'n,
Let him not know 't, and he's not robb'd at
　　all.
　　k.　　*Othello.* Act III. Sc. 3. L. 342.

In limited professions there's boundless theft.
　　l.　　*Timon of Athens.* Act IV. Sc. 3.
　　　　　　　　　　　　　　　　L. 430.

　　Let me tell you, Cassius, you yourself
Are much condemn'd to have an itching palm.
　　m.　　*Julius Cæsar.* Act IV. Sc. 3. L. 9.

The robb'd that smiles steals something from
　　the thief:
He robs himself that spends a bootless grief.
　　n.　　*Othello.* Act I. Sc. 3. L. 208.

The sun's a thief, and with his great attraction
Robs the vast sea; the moon's an arrant thief,
And her pale fire she snatches from the sun:
The sea's a thief, whose liquid surge resolves
The moon into salt tears: the earth's a thief,
That feeds and breeds by a composture stolen
From general excrement: each thing's a thief;
The laws, your curb and whip, in their rough
　　power
Have uncheck'd theft.
　　o.　　*Timon of Athens.* Act IV. Sc. 3.
　　　　　　　　　　　　　　　　L. 439.

Thieves for their robbery have authority
When judges steal themselves.
　　p.　　*Measure for Measure.* Act II. Sc. 2.
　　　　　　　　　　　　　　　　L. 176.

Thou hast stolen both mine office and my
　　name;
The one ne'er got me credit, the other mickle
　　blame.
　　q.　　*Comedy of Errors.* Act III. Sc. 1.
　　　　　　　　　　　　　　　　L. 44.

Who steals my purse steals trash; 'tis some-
　　thing, nothing;
'Twas mine, 'tis his, and has been slave to
　　thousands;
But he that filches from me my good name
Robs me of that which not enriches him,
And makes me poor indeed.
　　r.　　*Othello.* Act III. Sc. 3. L. 157.

Well, well, be it so, thou strongest thief of all,
For thou hast stolen my will, and made it
　　thine.
　　s.　　TENNYSON—*The Foresters.* Act III.
　　　　　　　　　　　　　　　　Sc. 1.

THOUGHT.

The kings of modern thought are dumb.
　　t.　　MATTHEW ARNOLD—*Stanzas from the
　　　　　　　　　　　　Grande Chartreuse.*

Great thoughts, like great deeds, need
No trumpet.
　　u.　　BAILEY—*Festus.* Sc. *Home.*

　　　　　　　　　　　　　　I stood
Among them, but not of them : in a shroud
Of thoughts which were not their thoughts.
　　a.　　BYRON—*Childe Harold.*　Canto III.
　　　　　　　　　　　　　　　　St. 113.

The power of Thought,—the magic of the
　　Mind !
　　b.　　BYRON—*The Corsair.*　Canto I.　St. 8.

What exile from himself can flee?
　　To zones, though more and more remote,
Still, still pursues, where'er I be,
　　The blight of life—the demon Thought.
　　c.　　BYRON—*Childe Harold.*　To Inez.
　　　　　　　　　　Canto I.　St. 84.　L. 6.

　　　　　　　　　　Whatsoe'er thy birth,
Thou wert a beautiful thought and softly
　　bodied forth.
　　d.　　BYRON—*Childe Harold.*　Canto IV.
　　　　　　　　　　　　　　　　St. 115.

　　Nay, in every epoch of the world, the great
event, parent of all others, is it not the arrival
of a Thinker in the world?
　　e.　　CARLYLE—*Heroes and Hero Worship.*
　　　　　　　　　　　　　　　Lecture I.

Thought once awakened does not again
slumber.
　　f.　　CARLYLE—*Heroes and Hero Worship.*
　　　　　　　　　　　　　　　Lecture I.

With curious art the brain, too finely wrought,
Preys on herself, and is destroyed by thought.
　　g.　　CHURCHILL—*Epistle to Wm. Hogarth.*
　　　　　　　　　　　　　　　　L. 645.

Old things need not be therefore true,
O brother men, nor yet the new ;
Ah ! still awhile the old thought retain,
And yet consider it again !
　　h.　　ARTHUR HUGH CLOUGH—*Ah, yet
　　　　　　　　　　　　Consider it Again.*

Perhaps 'tis pretty to force together
Thoughts so all unlike each other ;
To mutter and mock a broken charm,
To dally with wrong that does no harm.
　　i.　　COLERIDGE—*Christabel.*　Conclusion to
　　　　　　　　　　　　　　　Part II.

In indolent vacuity of thought.
　　j.　　COWPER—*The Task.*　Bk. IV.　The
　　　　　　　　　　　Winter Evening.　L. 297.

Second thoughts, they say, are best.
　　k.　　DRYDEN—*The Spanish Friar.*　Act II.
　　　　　　　　　　　　　　　　Sc. 2.

　　For thoughts are so great—aren't they, sir?
They seem to lie upon us like a deep flood.
　　l.　　GEORGE ELIOT—*Adam Bede.*　Ch. VIII.

　　　　　　Our growing thought
Makes growing revelation.
　　m.　　GEORGE ELIOT—*Spanish Gypsy.*　Bk. II.

Every thought which genius and piety
throw into the world, alters the world.
　　n.　　EMERSON—*Essays.　Of Politics.*

Great men are they who see that spiritual is
stronger than any material force, that thoughts
rule the world.
　　o.　　EMERSON—*Letters and Social Aims.
　　　　　　　　　　　Progress of Culture.*

Not from a vain or shallow thought
His awful Jove young Phidias brought.
　　p.　　EMERSON—*The Problem.*

　　The revelation of thought takes men out of
servitude into freedom.
　　q.　　EMERSON—*Conduct of Life.　Fate.*

Among mortals second thoughts are the
wisest.
　　r.　　EURIPIDES—*Hippolytus.*　438.

Those who think must govern those that toil.
　　s.　　GOLDSMITH—*The Traveller.*　L. 372.

Thoughts that breathe and words that burn.
　　t.　　GRAY—*Progress of Poesy.*　III. 3.　L. 4.

Their own second and sober thoughts.
　　u.　　MATHEW HENRY—*Exposition.*
　　　　　　　　　　　　　　Job VI.　29.

A thought is often original, though you
have uttered it a hundred times.
　　v.　　O. W. HOLMES—*The Autocrat of the
　　　　　　　　　　　　Breakfast Table.*　I.

My thoughts and I were of another world.
　　w.　　BEN JONSON—*Every Man Out of His
　　　　　　　　　　　Humour.*　Act III.　Sc. 3.

Sudden a thought came like a full-blown rose,
Flushing his brow.
　　x.　　KEATS—*The Eve of St. Agnes.*　St. 16.

　　The thoughts that come often unsought,
and, as it were, drop into the mind, are commonly the most valuable of any we have, and
therefore should be secured, because they
seldom return again.
　　y.　　LOCKE—*Letter to Mr. Sam'l Bold.*
　　　　　　　　　　　　　May 16, 1699.

A thought often makes us hotter than a fire.
　　z.　　LONGFELLOW—*Drift-Wood.　Table-Talk.*

　　　　　　My own thoughts
Are my companions.
　　aa.　　LONGFELLOW—*The Masque of Pandora.*
　　　　　　　　Pt. III.　*Tower of Prometheus on
　　　　　　　　　　　　　Mount Caucasus.*

The surest pledge of a deathless name
　　Is the silent homage of thoughts unspoken.
　　bb.　　LONGFELLOW—*The Herons of Elmwood.*
　　　　　　　　　　　　　　　St. 9.

Thoughts so sudden, that they seem
The revelations of a dream.
　　cc.　　LONGFELLOW—*Prelude to Tales of a
　　　　　　　　　　　Wayside Inn.*　Pt. I.　L. 233.

All thoughts that mould the age begin
Deep down within the primitive soul.
　　dd.　　LOWELL—*An Incident in a Railroad Car.*

Thought is valuable in proportion as it is generative.

a. BULWER-LYTTON—*Caxtoniana.*
Essay XIV.

Annihilating all that's made
To a green thought in a green shade.

b. ANDREW MARVELL—*The Garden.*
Translated.

Thought alone is eternal.

c. OWEN MEREDITH (Lord Lytton)—
Lucile. Pt. II. Canto VI. St. 16.

Grand Thoughts that never can be wearied out,
Showing the unreality of Time.

d. RICHARD MONCKTON MILNES (Lord Houghton)—*Sonnet. To Charles Lamb.*

He that has light within his own clear breast,
May sit i' th' centre and enjoy bright day:
But he that hides a dark soul, and foul thoughts,
Benighted walks under the midday sun.

e. MILTON—*Comus.* L. 281.

Thoughts that voluntary move
Harmonious numbers.

f. MILTON—*Paradise Lost.* Bk. III. L. 37.

Man is but a reed, the weakest in nature, but he is a thinking reed.

g. BLAISE PASCAL—*Thoughts.* Ch. II. 10.

Thought can wing its way
Swifter than lightning-flashes or the beam
That hastens on the pinions of the morn.

h. PERCIVAL—*Sonnet.*

Sweetest mother, I can weave no more to-day,
For thoughts of him come thronging,
Him for whom my heart is longing—
For I know not where my weary fingers stray.

i. SAPPHO—*Fragment.* J. S. Easby-Smith's trans.

At Learning's fountain it is sweet to drink,
But 'tis a nobler privilege to think.

j. J. G. SAXE—*The Library.*

Still are the thoughts to memory dear,

k. SCOTT—*Rokeby.* Canto I. St. 33.

A maiden hath no tongue but thought.

l. *Merchant of Venice.* Act III. Sc. 2.
L. 8.

But now behold,
In the quick forge and working-house of thought,
How London doth pour out her citizens!

m. *Henry V.* Act V. Prologue. L. 22.

My thoughts are whirled like a potter's wheel.

n. *Henry VI.* Pt. I. Act I. Sc. 5. L. 19.

The incessant care and labour of his mind
Hath wrought the mure that should confine it in
So thin that life looks through and will break out.

o. *Henry IV.* Pt. II. Act IV. Sc. 4.
L. 118.

A thought by thought is piled, till some great truth
Is loosened, and the nations echo round,
Shaken to their roots, as do the mountains now.

p. SHELLEY—*Prometheus Unbound.*
Act II. Sc. 3.

Come near me! I do weave
A chain I cannot break—I am possest
With thoughts too swift and strong for one lone human breast.

q. SHELLEY—*Revolt of Islam.* Canto IX.
St. 33.

Strange thoughts beget strange deeds.

r. SHELLEY—*The Cenci.* Act IV. Sc. 4.

If I could think how these my thoughts to leave,
Or thinking still, my thoughts might have good end:
If rebel sense would reason's law receive;
Or reason foil'd would not in vain contend:
Then might I think what thoughts were best to think:
Then might I wisely swim, or gladly sink.

s. SIR PHILIP SIDNEY—*Sonnet.*

They are never alone that are accompanied with noble thoughts.

t. SIR PHILIP SIDNEY—*The Arcadia.*
Bk. I.

Oh, the fetterless mind! how it wandereth free
Through the wildering maze of Eternity!

u. HENRY SMITH—*Thought.*

Thinking is but an idle waste of thought,
And naught is everything, and everything is naught.

v. HORACE AND JAMES SMITH—*Rejected Addresses. Cui Bono?*

Thought can never be compared with action, but when it awakens in us the image of truth.

w. MADAME DE STAËL—*Germany.* Pt. I.
Ch. VIII.

What a man *thinks* in his spirit in the world, that he *does* after his departure from the world when he becomes a spirit.

x. SWEDENBORG—*Divine Providence.* 101.

Though man a thinking being is defined,
Few use the grand prerogative of mind.
How few think justly of the thinking few!
How many never think, who think they do.

y. JANE TAYLOR—*Essays in Rhyme.*
On Morals and Manners. Prejudice.
Essay I. St. 45.

And Thought leapt out to wed with **Thought**,
Ere Thought could wed itself with Speech.
   a.   Tennyson—*In Memoriam.* Pt. XXIII.
                               St. 4.

Large elements in order brought,
And tracts of calm from tempest made,
And world-wide fluctuation sway'd,
  In vassal tides that follow'd thought.
   b.   Tennyson—*In Memoriam.* CXII.
                               St. 4.

Yet I doubt not thro' the ages one increasing
    purpose runs,
And the thoughts of men are widened with the
    process of the suns.
   c.   Tennyson—*Locksley Hall.* St. 69.

And yet, as angels in some brighter dreams
  Call to the soul when man doth sleep,
So some strange thoughts transcend our wont-
    ed themes,
  And into glory peep.
   d. | Henry Vaughan—*They are all gone
                into the World of Light.* St. 7.

But hushed be every thought that springs
From out the bitterness of things.
   e.   Wordsworth—*Elegiac Stanzas.
              Addressed to Sir G. H. B.*

Like thoughts whose very sweetness yieldeth
    proof
That they were born for immortality.
   f.   Wordsworth—*Sonnet. On King's
              College Chapel, Cambridge.*

Yet, sometimes, when the secret cup
  Of still and serious thought went round,
It seemed as if he drank it up,
  He felt with spirit so profound.
   g.   Wordsworth—*Matthew.*

Knocks at our hearts, and finds our thoughts
at home.
   h.   Young—*Love of Fame.* Satire I. L. 99.

THUNDER.

                     Far along,
From peak to peak the rattling crags among,
Leaps the live thunder.
   i.   Byron—*Childe Harold.* Canto III.
                             St. 92.

Thy thunder, conscious of the new command,
Rumbles reluctant o'er our fallen house.
   j.   Keats—*Hyperion.* L. 60.

As a storm-cloud lurid with lightning
And a cry of lamentation,
Repeated and again repeated,
Deep and loud
As the reverberation
Of cloud answering unto cloud,
Swells and rolls away in the distance,
As if the sheeted
Lightning retreated,
Baffled and thwarted by the wind's resistance.
   k.   Longfellow—*Christus. The Golden
              Legend.* Epilogue. L. 62.

                    The thunder,
Wing'd with red lightning and impetuous
    rage,
Perhaps hath spent his shafts, and ceases
    now
To bellow through the vast and boundless
    deep.
   l.   Milton—*Paradise Lost.* Bk. I.
                              L. 174.

Are there no stones in heaven
But what serve for the thunder?
   m.   *Othello.* Act V. Sc. 2. L. 234.

                    The thunder,
That deep and dreadful organ-pipe, pro-
    nounc'd
The name of Prosper; it did bass my trespass.
   n.   *Tempest.* Act III. Sc. 3. L. 97.

To stand against the deep, dread-bolted
    thunder?
In the most terrible and nimble stroke
Of quick, cross lightning?
   o.   *King Lear.* Act IV. Sc. 7. L. 33.

TIDES.

All night the thirsty beach has listening lain
      With patience dumb,
Counting the slow, sad moments of her pain;
      Now morn has come,
And with the morn the punctual tide again.
   p.   Susan Coolidge—*Flood-Tide.*

The punctual tide draws up the bay,
With ripple of wave and hiss of spray.
   q.   Susan Coolidge—*On the Shore.*

Love has a tide!
   r.   Helen Hunt Jackson—*Verses. Tides.*

The western tide crept up along the sand,
    And o'er and o'er the sand,
      And round and round the sand,
        As far as eye could see
The rolling mist came down and hid the land:
      And never home came she.
   s.   Charles Kingsley—*The Sands o' Dee.*
                              St. 2.

I saw the long line of the vacant shore,
  The sea-weed and the shells upon the sand,
  And the brown rocks left bare on every hand,
As if the ebbing tide would flow no more.
   t.   Longfellow—*The Tides.*

The tide rises, the tide falls,
The twilight darkens, the curlew calls;
     *   *   *   *   *   *
The little waves, with their soft, white hands,
Efface the footprints in the sands,
  And the tide rises, the tide falls.
   u.   Longfellow—*The Tide Rises, the
                           Tide Falls.*

Tide flowing is feared, for many a thing,
Great danger to such as be sick, it doth bring ;
Sea ebb, by long ebbing, some respite doth
   give,
And sendeth good comfort, to such as shall
   live.
  a.   Tusser—*Five Hundred Points of Good
          Husbandrie.* Ch. XIV. St. 5.

TIME.

Backward, turn backward, O Time in your
   flight!
Make me a child again, just for to-night!
  b.   Elizabeth Akers Allen—*Rock Me to
          Sleep.*

Who well lives, long lives : for this age of ours
Should not be numbered by years, daies, and
   hours.
  c.   Du Bartas—*Divine Weekes and Workes.
          Second Week. Fourth Day.* Bk. II.

Think not thy time short in this world,
since the world itself is not long. The created
world is but a small parenthesis in eternity,
and a short interposition, for a time, between
such a state of duration as was before it and
may be after it.
  d.   Sir Thomas Browne—*Christian
          Morals.* Pt. III. XXIX.

Time, which strengthens Friendship, weakens Love.
  e.   De La Bruyère—*The Characters or
          Manners of the Present Age.* Ch. IV.

Nae man can tether time or tide.
  f.   Burns—*Tam o' Shanter.*

Some wee short hour ayont the twal.
  g.   Burns—*Death and Dr. Hornbook.*

How slowly time creeps till my Phœbe returns!
While amidst the soft zephyr's cool breezes I
   burn.
Methinks if I knew whereabouts he would
   tread
I could breathe on his wings and 'twould melt
   down the lead.
Fly swifter, ye minutes, bring hither my dear,
And rest so much longer for 't when she is
   here.
  h.   John Byrom—*A Pastoral.*

O Time! the beautifier of the dead,
Adorner of the ruin, comforter
And only healer when the heart hath bled—
Time! the corrector where our judgments err,
The test of truth, love,—sole philosopher,
For all besides are sophists, from thy thrift
Which never loses though it doth defer—
Time, the avenger! unto thee I lift
My hands, and eyes, and heart, and crave of
   thee a gift.
  i.   Byron—*Childe Harold.* Canto IV.
                     St. 130.

Out upon Time! it will leave no more
Of the things to come than the things before!
Out upon Time! who forever will leave
But enough of the past for the future to
   grieve.
  j.   Byron—*Siege of Corinth.* St. 18.

Think'st thou existence doth depend on time?
It doth ; but actions are our epochs ; mine
Have made my days and nights imperishable,
Endless, and all alike.
  k.   Byron—*Manfred.* Act II. Sc. 1.

Time writes no wrinkle on thy azure brow—
Such as creation's dawn beheld, thou rollest
   now.
  l.   Byron—*Childe Harold.* Canto IV.
                     St. 182.

   When Youth and Pleasure meet
To chase the glowing Hours with flying feet.
  m.   Byron—*Childe Harold.* Canto III.
                     St. 22.

Yet Time, who changes all, had altered him
In soul and aspect as in age, years steal
Fire from the mind as vigour from the limb :
And life's enchanted cup but sparkles near the
   brim.
  n.   Byron—*Childe Harold.* Canto III.
                     St. 8.

The more we live, more brief appear
  Our life's succeeding stages ;
A day to childhood seems a year,
  And years like passing ages.
  o.   Campbell—*A Thought Suggested by the
          New Year.*

That great mystery of Time, were there no
other ; the illimitable, silent, never-resting
thing called Time, rolling, rushing on, swift,
silent, like an all-embracing ocean tide, on
which we and all the Universe swim like exhalations, like apparitions which *are,* and
then *are not* : this is forever very literally a
miracle ; a thing to strike us dumb,—for we
have no word to speak about it.
  p.   Carlyle—*Heroes and Hero Worship.*
          Lecture I.

Know the true value of time ; snatch, seize,
and enjoy every moment of it. No idleness,
no laziness, no procrastination : never put off
till to-morrow what you can do to-day.
  q.   Earl of Chesterfield—*Letters to his
          Son.* Dec. 26, 1749.

No! no arresting the vast wheel of time,
That round and round still turns with onward
   might,
Stern, dragging thousands to the dreaded
   night
Of an unknown hereafter.
  r.   Charles Cowden Clarke—*Sonnet.
          The Course of Time.*

* * * So often do the spirits
Of great events stride on before the events,
And in to-day already walks to-morrow.
a. COLERIDGE—*The Death of Wallenstein.*
Act V. Sc. 1.

Touch us gently, Time!
Let us glide adown thy stream
Gently,—as we sometimes glide
Through a quiet dream!
b. BARRY CORNWALL—*A Petition to Time.*

His time's forever, everywhere his place.
c. ABRAHAM COWLEY—*Friendship in
Absence.* St. 3.

Nothing is there to come, and nothing past,
But an eternal Now does always last.
d. ABRAHAM COWLEY—*Davideis.* Bk. I.
L. 361.

Time, as he passes us, has a dove's wing,
Unsoil'd, and swift, and of a silken sound.
e. COWPER—*The Task.* Bk. IV. L. 211.

See Time has touched me gently in his race,
And left no odious furrows in my face.
f. CRABBE—*Tales of the Hall.* Bk. XVII.
The Widow. St. 3.

Swift speedy Time, feathered with flying
hours,
Dissolves the beauty of the fairest brow.
g. SAMUEL DANIEL—*Delia.*

But what minutes! Count them by sensation, and not by calendars, and each moment
is a day and the race a life.
h. BENJ. DISRAELI—*Sybil.* Bk. I. Ch. II.

Time, to the nation as to the individual, is
nothing absolute; its duration depends on the
rate of thought and feeling.
i. DRAPER—*History of the Intellectual
Development of Europe.* Vol. I. Ch. I.

Write it on your heart that every day is the
best day in the year. No man has learned
anything rightly, until he knows that every
day is Doomsday.
j. EMERSON—*Society and Solitude. Work
and Days.*

I count my time by times that I meet thee;
These are my yesterdays, my morrows, noons,
And nights, these are my old moons and my
new moons.
Slow fly the hours, fast the hours flee,
If thou art far from or art near to me:
If thou art far, the bird's tunes are no tunes;
If thou art near, the wintry days are Junes.
k. R. W. GILDER—*The New Day.* Pt. IV.
Sonnet VI.

Rich with the spoils of time.
l. GRAY—*Elegy in a Country Churchyard.*
St. 13.

I made a posy while the day ran by;
Here will I smell my remnant out, and tie
My life within this band.
But time did beckon to the flowers, and they
By noon most cunningly did steal away,
And wither'd in my hand.
m. HERBERT—*The Temple. Life.*

Old Time, in whose banks we deposit our
notes,
Is a miser who always wants guineas for
groats;
He keeps all his customers still in arrears
By lending them minutes and charging them
years.
n. O. W. HOLMES—*Poems of the Class of
'29. Our Banker.* 1874.

On me, on me
Time and change can heap no more!
The painful Past with blighting grief
Hath left my heart a wither'd leaf:
Time and change can do no more.
o. RICHARD HENGIST HORNE—*Dirge.*

How short our happy days appear!
How long the sorrowful!
p. JEAN INGELOW—*The Mariner's Cave.*
St. 38.

To the true teacher, time's hour-glass should
still run gold-dust.
q. DOUGLAS JERROLD—*Specimens of
Jerrold's Wit. Time.*

And panting Time toil'd after him in vain.
r. SAM'L JOHNSON—*Prologue on Opening
the Drury Lane Theatre.* L. 6.

Seven hours to law, to soothing slumber
seven,
Ten to the world allot, and all to heaven.
s. SIR WM. JONES—*Ode in Imitation of
Alcæus.*

That old bald cheater, Time.
t. BEN JONSON—*The Poetaster.* Act I.
Sc. 5.

Like wind flies Time 'tween birth and death;
Therefore, as long as thou hast breath,
Of care for two days hold thee free:
The day that was and is to be.
u. OMAR KHAYYÁM—*Bodenstedt's trans.*

A handful of red sand from the hot clime
Of Arab deserts brought,
Within this glass becomes the spy of Time,
The minister of Thought.
v. LONGFELLOW—*Sand of the Desert in an
Hour-Glass.*

Alas! it is not till Time, with reckless hand,
has torn out half the leaves from the Book of
Human Life to light the fires of human passion with, from day to day, that man begins
to see that the leaves which remain are few in
number.
w. LONGFELLOW—*Hyperion.* Bk. IV.
Ch. VIII.

Art is Long, and Time is fleeting.
 a. LONGFELLOW—*A Psalm of Life.* St. 4.

Time has laid his hand
Upon my heart, gently, not smiting it,
But as a harper lays his open palm
Upon his harp, to deaden its vibrations.
 b. LONGFELLOW—*The Golden Legend.*

Time is the Life of the Soul.
 c. LONGFELLOW—*Hyperion.* Bk. II.
                                                Ch. VI.

Time is a feathered thing,
And, whilst I praise
The sparkling of thy looks, and call them
 rays,
Takes wing,
Leaving behind him as he flies
An unperceivèd dimness in thine eyes.
 d. JASPER MAYNE—*Time.*

However we pass Time, he passes still,
 Passing away whatever the pastime,
And, whether we use him well or ill,
 Some day he gives us the slip for the last
 time.
 e. OWEN MEREDITH (Lord Lytton)—*The
                                      Dead Pope.*

When time is flown, how it fled
 It is better neither to ask nor tell,
Leave the dead moments to bury their dead.
 f. OWEN MEREDITH (Lord Lytton)—*The
      Wanderer.* Bk. IV. *Two out of the
                          Crowd.* St. 17.

Time eftsoon will tumble
All of us together like leaves in a gust,
Humbled indeed down into the dust.
 g. JOAQUIN MILLER—*Fallen Leaves Down
                    into the Dust.* St. 5.

                          Day and night,
Seed-time and harvest, heat and hoary frost
Shall hold their course, till fire purge all
 things new.
 h. MILTON—*Paradise Lost.* Bk. XI.
                                                L. 898.

Time will run back and fetch the age of gold.
 i. MILTON—*Hymn on the Nativity.* L. 135.

Time, still as he flies, adds increase to her
 truth,
And gives to her mind what he steals from
 her youth.
 j. EDWARD MOORE—*The Happy Marriage.*

This day was yesterday to-morrow nam'd:
To-morrow shall be yesterday proclaimed:
To-morrow not yet come, not far away,
What shall to-morrow then be call'd? To-day.
 k. OWEN—*To-Day and To-Morrow.*
                                  Bk. III. L. 50.

These are the times that try men's souls.
 l. THOMAS PAINE—*The American Crisis.*
                                                No. 1.

Let time that makes you homely, make you
 sage.
 m. PARNELL—*An Elegy to an Old Beauty.*
                                                L. 35.

The present is our own; but while we speak,
We cease from its possession, and resign
The stage we tread on, to another race,
As vain, and gay, and mortal as ourselves.
 n. THOMAS LOVE PEACOCK—*Time.* L. 9.

                          Time is lord of thee:
Thy wealth, thy glory, and thy name are his.
 o. THOMAS LOVE PEACOCK—*Time.* L. 71.

Time, the foe of man's dominion,
 Wheels around in ceaseless flight,
Scattering from his hoary pinion
 Shades of everlasting night.
 p. THOMAS LOVE PEACOCK—*The Genius of
                    the Thames.* Pt. II. St. 42.

His golden locks Time hath to silver turned,
 O time too swift! O swiftness never ceasing!
His youth 'gainst Time and Age hath ever
 spurned,
 But spurned in vain! Youth waneth by
 increasing.
 q. GEORGE PEELE—*Sonnet. Polyhymnia.*

Time conquers all, and we must time obey.
 r. POPE—*Winter.* L. 88.

Years following years steal something ev'ry
 day,
At last they steal us from ourselves away.
 s. POPE—*Imitations of Horace.* Bk. II.
                                  Ep. 2. L. 72.

Expect, but fear not, Death: Death cannot
 kill,
Till Time (that first must seal his patent) will.
Would'st thou live long? keep Time in high
 esteem:
Whom gone, if thou canst not recall, redeem.
 t. QUARLES—*Hieroglyphics of the Life of
                          Man.* Ep. 6.

He briskly and cheerfully asked him how
a man should kill time.
 u. RABELAIS—*Works.* Bk. IV.
                                                Ch. LXIII.

E'en such is time! which takes in trust
 Our youth, our joys, and all we have;
And pays us naught but age and dust,
 Which, in the dark and silent grave,
When we have wandered all our ways,
Shuts up the story of our days.
And from which grave, and earth, and dust,
The Lord will raise me up, I trust.
 v. SIR WALTER RALEIGH—*Written in his
      Bible.* CAYLEY's *Life of Raleigh.*
                          Vol. II. Ch. IX.

Hour after hour departs,
  Recklessly flying ;
The golden time of our hearts
  Is fast a-dying :
O, how soon it will have faded !
Joy droops, with forehead shaded ;
  And Memory starts.
  a.   John Hamilton Reynolds—*Hour*
                              After Hour.

To vanish in the chinks that Time has made.
  b.   Sam'l Rogers—*Italy. Pæstum.* L. 59.

Like a dart the present glances,
Silent stands the past sublime.
  c.   Schiller—*Proverbs of Confucius.*
                    E. A. Bowring's trans.

Threefold the stride of Time, from first to
  last !
Loitering slow, the Future creepeth.
  d.   Schiller—*Sentence of Confucius.*
                                  Time.
Time flies on restless pinions—constant never.
Be constant—and thou chainest time forever.
  e.   Schiller—*Epigram.*

Time rolls his ceaseless course.
  f.   Scott—*The Lady of the Lake.*
                        Canto III. St. 1.

And, looking on it with lack-lustre eye,
Says very wisely, " It is ten o'clock :
Thus we may see," quoth he, " how the world
    wags."
  g.   *As You Like It.* Act II. Sc. 7. L. 21.

                              Beauty, wit,
High birth, vigour of bone, desert in service,
Love, friendship, charity, are subjects all
To envious and calumniating time.
  h.   *Troilus and Cressida.* Act III. St. 3.
                                    L. 171.
                  Come what come may,
Time and the hour runs through the roughest
    day.
  i.   *Macbeth.* Act I. Sc. 3. L. 146.

          'Gainst the tooth of time
And razure of oblivion.
  j.   *Measure for Measure.* Act V. Sc. 1.
                                    L. 12.

          How many ages hence
Shall this our lofty scene be acted over
In states unborn and accents yet unknown.
  k.   *Julius Cæsar.* Act III. Sc. 1. L. 111.

Let's take the instant by the forward top ;
For we are old, and on our quick'st decrees
The inaudible and noiseless foot of Time
Steals ere we can effect them.
  l.   *All's Well That Ends Well.* Act V.
                          Sc. 3. L. 39.

Make use of time, let not advantage slip ;
Beauty within itself should not be wasted :
Fair flowers that are not gather'd in their
    prime
Rot and consume themselves in little time.
  m.   *Venus and Adonis.* L. 129.

Minutes, hours, days, months, and years,
Pass'd over to the end they were created,
Would bring white hairs unto a quiet grave.
Ah, what a life were this !
  n.   *Henry VI.* Pt. III. Act II. Sc. 5.
                                    L. 38.
O, call back yesterday, bid time return.
  o.   *Richard II.* Act III. Sc. 2. L. 69.

O, how shall summer's honey breath hold out
  Against the wreckful siege of battering days,
When rocks impregnable are not so stout,
  Nor gates of steel so strong, but Time decays ?
O fearful meditation ! where, alack,
  Shall Time's best jewel from Time's chest
    lie hid ?
Or what strong hand can hold his swift foot
    back ?
  Or who his spoil of beauty can forbid ?
  p.   *Sonnet LXV.*

Pleasure and action make the hours seem short.
  q.   *Othello.* Act II. Sc. 3. L. 385.

          See the minutes how they run,
How many make the hour full complete ;
How many hours bring about the day ;
How many days will finish up the year ;
How many years a mortal man may live.
  r.   *Henry VI.* Pt. III. Act II. Sc. 5.
                                    L. 25.
So many hours must I take my rest ;
So many hours must I contemplate.
  s.   *Henry VI.* Pt. III. Act II. Sc. 5.
                                    L. 32.
                  The end crowns all,
And that old common arbitrator, Time,
Will one day end it.
  t.   *Troilus and Cressida.* Act IV. Sc. 5.
                                    L. 224.
The whirligig of time brings in his revenges.
  u.   *Twelfth Night.* Act V. Sc. 1. L. 384.

Time doth transfix the flourish set on youth
And delves the parallels in beauty's brow.
  v.   *Sonnet LX.*

Time goes on crutches till love have all his rites.
  w.   *Much Ado About Nothing.* Act II.
                          Sc. 1. L. 372.

Time hath, my lord, a wallet at his back,
Wherein he puts alms for oblivion,
A great-sized monster of ingratitudes ;
Those scraps are good deeds past ; which are
    devour'd
As fast as they are made, forgot as soon
As done.
  x.   *Troilus and Cressida.* Act III. Sc. 3.
                                    L. 145.

Time is like a fashionable host
That slightly shakes his parting guest by the
　　hand,
And with his arms outstretch'd, as he would fly
Grasps in the comer : welcome ever smiles.
　a.　　*Troilus and Cressida*. Act III. Sc. 3.
　　　　　　　　　　　　　　　L. 165.

Time is the nurse and breeder of all good.
　b.　　*Two Gentlemen of Verona*. Act III.
　　　　　　　　　　　Sc. 1. L. 243.

Time is the old justice that examines all
such offenders, and let Time try.
　c.　　*As You Like It*. Act IV. Sc. 1.
　　　　　　　　　　　　　　　L. 203.

Time shall unfold what plighted cunning
　hides ;
Who cover faults, at last shame them derides.
　d.　　*King Lear*. Act I. Sc. 1. L. 283.

　　　　Time's the king of men,
He's both their parent, and he is their grave,
And gives them what he will, not what they
　　crave.
　e.　　*Pericles*. Act II. Sc. 3. L. 45.

Time, that takes survey of all the world,
Must have a stop.
　f.　　*Henry IV*. Pt. I. Act V. Sc. 4.
　　　　　　　　　　　　　　　L. 82.

Time travels in divers paces with divers
persons.
　g.　　*As You Like It*. Act III. Sc. 2.
　　　　　　　　　　　　　　　L. 326.

We should hold day with the Antipodes,
If you would walk in absence of the sun.
　h.　　*Merchant of Venice*. Act V. Sc. 1.
　　　　　　　　　　　　　　　L. 127.

What is 't o'clock ?
Upon the stroke of four.
　i.　　*Richard III*. Act III. Sc. 2. L. 4.

Yet, do thy worst, old Time ; despite thy
　wrong,
My love shall in my verse ever live young.
　j.　　*Sonnet XIX*.

The flood of time is rolling on ;
We stand upon its brink, whilst *they* are gone
To glide in peace down death's mysterious
　　stream,
Have ye done well ?
　k.　　SHELLEY—*Revolt of Islam*. Canto XII.
　　　　　　　　　　　　　　　St. 27.

Unfathomable Sea ! whose waves are years,
Ocean of Time, whose waters of deep woe
Are brackish with the salt of human tears !
Thou shoreless flood, which in thy ebb and flow
Claspest the limits of mortality !
And sick of prey, yet howling on for more,
Vomitest thy wrecks on its inhospitable
　　shore,
Treacherous in calm, and terrible in storm,
　Who shall put forth on thee,
　　Unfathomable sea ?
　l.　　SHELLEY—*Time*.

For the next inn he spurs amain,
In haste alights, and skuds away,
But time and tide for no man stay.
　m.　　W. C. SOMERVILLE—*The Sweet-Scented
　　　　　　　　　　　　　　Miser*. L. 98.

Time wears all his locks before,
　Take thou hold upon his forehead ;
When he flies he turns no more,
　And behind his scalp is naked.
Works adjourn'd have many stays,
Long demurs breed new delays.
　n.　　ROB'T SOUTHWELL—*Loss in Delay*.

Goe to my Love where she is carelesse layd
　Yet in her winter's bowere not well awake ;
Tell her the joyous time will not be staid
　Unlesse she doe him by the forelock take.
　o.　　SPENSER—*Amoretti*. LXX.

Too late I stayed,—forgive the crime ;
　Unheeded flew the hours,
How noiseless falls the foot of time
　That only treads on flowers !
　p.　　SPENSER—*Lines to Lady A. Hamilton*.

I see that time divided is never long, and
that regularity abridges all things.
　q.　　ABEL STEVENS—*Life of Madame de
　　　　　　　　　　　　Staël*. Ch. XXXVIII.

Ever eating, never cloying,
All-devouring, all-destroying,
Never finding full repast,
Till I eat the world at last.
　r.　　SWIFT—*On Time*.

A wonderful stream is the River Time,
　As it runs through the realms of Tears,
With a faultless rhythm, and a musical
　　rhyme,
And a broader sweep, and a surge sublime
　As it blends with the ocean of Years.
　s.　　BENJAMIN F. TAYLOR—*The Long Ago*.

He that lacks time to mourn, lacks time to
　　mend :
Eternity mourns that. 'Tis an ill cure
For life's worst ills to have no time to feel
　　them.
　t.　　SIR HENRY TAYLOR—*Philip Van
　　　　　　　　　　Artevelde*. Act I. Sc. 5.

Come, Time, and teach me many years,
　I do not suffer in dream ;
　For now so strange do these things seem,
Mine eyes have leisure for their tears.
　u.　　TENNYSON—*In Memoriam*. Pt. XIII.

Six hours in Sleep, in law's grave study six,
Four spend in prayer, the rest on Nature fix.
　v.　　*Translation of lines quoted by* COKE.

Time tries the troth in everything.
　w.　　TUSSER—*Five Hundred Points of Good
　　　　　　Husbandrie*. *The Author's Epistle*.
　　　　　　　　　　　　　　Ch. I.

To wind the mighty secrets of the past,
And turn the key of time.
    a.   HENRY KIRK WHITE—*Time.* L. 249.

In records that defy the tooth of time.
    b.   YOUNG—*The Statesman's Creed.*

Nought treads so silent as the foot of Time;
Hence we mistake our autumn for our prime.
    c.   YOUNG—*Love of Fame.* Satire V.
                        L. 497.

Procrastination is the thief of time:
Year after year it steals, till all are fled,
And to the mercies of a moment leaves
The vast concerns of an eternal scene.
    d.   YOUNG—*Night Thoughts.* Night I.
                        L. 390.

The bell strikes one. We take no note of time
But from its loss: to give it then a tongue
Is wise in man.
    e.   YOUNG—*Night Thoughts.* Night I.
                        L. 55.
        Time is eternity;
Pregnant with all eternity can give;
Pregnant with all that makes archangels smile.
Who murders Time, he crushes in the birth
A power ethereal, only not adorn'd.
    f.   YOUNG—*Night Thoughts.* Night II.
                        L. 107.

Time wasted is existence, used is life.
    g.   YOUNG—*Night Thoughts.* Night II.
                        L. 149.

We push time from us, and we wish him back;
    *   *   *   *   *   *
Life we think long and short; death seek and shun.
    h.   YOUNG—*Night Thoughts.* Night II.
                        L. 174.

We see time's furrows on another's brow,
    *   *   *   *   *   *
How few themselves in that just mirror see!
    i.   YOUNG—*Night Thoughts.* Night V.
                        L. 627.

While man is growing, life is in decrease,
And cradles rock us nearer to the tomb;
Our birth is nothing but our death begun.
    j.   YOUNG—*Night Thoughts.* Night V.
                        L. 717.

TOASTS.

My boat is on the shore,
  And my bark is on the sea:
But, before I go, Tom Moore,
  Here's a double health to thee!
    k.   BYRON—*To Thomas Moore.*

Were 't the last drop in the well,
  As I gasp'd upon the brink,
Ere my fainting spirit fell,
  'Tis to thee that I would drink.
    l.   BYRON—*To Thomas Moore.* St. 4.

Ho! stand to your glasses steady!
  'Tis all we have left to prize.
A cup to the dead already,—
  Hurrah for the next that dies.
    m.   BARTHOLOMEW DOWLING—*Revelry in India.*

And he that will this health deny,
Down among the dead men let him lie.
    n.   DYER—*Published in the early part of the reign of George I.*

Drink to me only with thine eyes,
  And I will pledge with mine;
    o.   BEN JONSON—*The Forest. To Celia. Drink to Me Only with Thine Eyes.*

To the old, long life and treasure;
To the young, all health and pleasure.
    p.   BEN JONSON—*Metamorphosed Gipsies. Third Song.*

The cannons to the heavens, the heavens to earth,
"Now the king drinks to Hamlet."
    q.   *Hamlet.* Act V. Sc. 2. L. 288.

Here's to the maiden of bashful fifteen:
Here's to the widow of fifty;
Here's to the flaunting, extravagant quean;
  And here's to the housewife that's thrifty.
    Chorus: Let the toast pass,—
           Drink to the lass,
I'll warrant she'll prove an excuse for the glass.
    r.   R. B. SHERIDAN—*School for Scandal.* Act III. Sc. 3. *Song.*

First pledge our Queen this solemn night,
  Then drink to England, every guest;
That man's the best Cosmopolite
  Who loves his native country best.
    s.   TENNYSON—*Hands All Round.*

Here's a health to the lass with the merry black eyes!
Here's a health to the lad with the blue ones!
    t.   WM. WINTER—*Blue and Black.*

TOBACCONISTS (*See* OCCUPATIONS).

TO-DAY.

Out of Eternity
The new Day is born;
  Into Eternity
At night will return.
    u.   CARLYLE—*To-Day.*

To-day is ours; what do we fear?
To-day is ours; we have it here.
Let's treat it kindly, that it may
Wish, at least, with us to stay.
Let's banish business, banish sorrow;
To the gods belongs to-morrow.
    v.   ABRAHAM COWLEY—*Anacreontique. The Epicure.* L. 7.

Days that need borrow
No part of their good morrow,
From a fore-spent night of sorrow.
> a.   RICHARD CRASHAW— *Wishes to his*
>   *(Supposed) Mistress.* St. 27.

What dost thou bring to me, O fair To-day,
That comest o'er the mountains with swift
        feet?
> b.   JULIA C. R. DORR— *To-Day.*

Happy the man, and happy he alone,
He, who can call to-day his own :
He who, secure within, can say,
To-morrow, do thy worst, for I have liv'd
        to-day.
> c.   DRYDEN— *Imitation of Horace.* Bk. III.
>   Ode XXIX. L. 65.

Nothing that is can pause or stay ;
The moon will wax, the moon will wane,
The mist and cloud will turn to rain,
The rain to mist and cloud again,
To-morrow be to-day.
> d.   LONGFELLOW— *Kéramos.* L. 34.

TO-MORROW.

Dreaming of a to-morrow, which to-morrow
Will be as distant then as 'tis to-day.
> e.   TOME BURGUILLOS— *To-Morrow, and*
>   *To-Morrow.* John Bowring's
>   trans.

How oft my guardian angel gently cried,
  "Soul, from thy casement look, and thou
        shalt see
  How he persists to knock and wait for thee !"
And, O ! how often to that voice of sorrow,
  "To-morrow we will open," I replied,
And when the morrow came I answered still,
  "To-morrow."
> f.   TOME BURGUILLOS— *To-Morrow.*
>   Longfellow's trans. L. 9.

A shining isle in a stormy sea,
  We seek it ever with smiles and sighs ;
To-day is sad. In the bland To-be,
  Serene and lovely To-morrow lies.
> g.   MARY CLEMMER— *To-Morrow.*

Defer not till to-morrow to be wise,
To-morrow's Sun to thee may never rise ;
Or should to-morrow chance to cheer thy
        sight
With her enlivening and unlook'd for light
How grateful will appear her dawning rays !
As favours unexpected doubly please.
> h.   CONGREVE— *Letter to Cobham.* L. 61.

To-morrow's fate, though thou be wise,
Thou canst not tell nor yet surmise ;
Pass, therefore, not to-day in vain,
For it will never come again.
> i.   OMAR KHAYYÁM. Bodenstedt's trans.

Far off I hear the crowing of the cocks,
And through the opening door that time
        unlocks
Feel the fresh breathing of To-morrow creep.
> j.   LONGFELLOW— *To-Morrow.*

To-morrow you will live, you always cry ;
In what fair country does this morrow lie,
That 'tis so mighty long ere it arrive ?
Beyond the Indies does this morrow live?
'Tis so far-fetched, this morrow, that I fear
'Twill be both very old and very dear.
"To-morrow I will live," the fool does say :
To-day itself's too late ;—the wise lived yes-
        terday.
> k.   MARTIAL— *Epigrams.* Bk. V.
>   Ep. LVIII.

To-morrow the dreams and flowers will fade.
> l.   MOORE— *Lalla Rookh. The Light of*
>   *the Harem. Song.*

To-morrow is, ah, whose?
> m.   D. M. MULOCK— *Between Two Worlds.*

To-morrow, what delight is in to-morrow !
What laughter and what music, breathing joy,
Float from the woods and pastures, wavering
        down,
Dropping like echoes through the long to-day,
Where childhood waits with weary expec-
        tation.
> n.   T. B. READ— *The New Pastoral.*
>   Bk. VI. L. 163.

To-morrow, and to-morrow, and to-morrow,
Creeps in this petty pace from day to day
To the last syllable of recorded time,
And all our yesterdays have lighted fools
The way to dusty death.
> o.   *Macbeth.* Act V. Sc. 5. L. 19.

Where art thou, beloved To-morrow?
When young and old, and strong and weak,
Rich and poor, through joy and sorrow,
Thy sweet smiles we ever seek,—
In thy place—ah ! well-a-day !
We find the thing we fled—To-day !
> p.   SHELLEY— *To-Morrow.*

To-morrow yet would reap to-day,
  As we bear blossoms of the dead ;
  Earn well the thrifty months, nor wed
Raw Haste, half-sister to Delay.
> q.   TENNYSON— *Love Thou the Land.* St. 24.

In human hearts what bolder thoughts can
        rise,
Than man's presumption on to-morrow's
        dawn !
Where is to-morrow?
> r.   YOUNG— *Night Thoughts.* Night I.
>   L. 374.

To-morrow is a satire on to-day,
And shows its weakness.
> s.   YOUNG— *The Old Man's Relapse.* L. 6.

Some say "to-morrow" never comes,
　A saying oft thought right;
But if to-morrow never came,
　No end were of "to-night."
The fact is this, time flies so fast,
　That e'er we've time to say
"To-morrow's come," presto! behold!
　"To-morrow" proves "To-day."
　　a.　　*Author Unknown.* From *Notes and*
　　　　　Queries. Fourth Series. Vol. XII.

TONGUES.

The firste vertue, sone, if thou wilt lerne,
Is to restreyne and kepen wel thy tonge.
　　b.　　CHAUCER—*Canterbury Tales. The*
　　　　　Manciple's Tale. L. 18,213.

The windy satisfaction of the tongue.
　　c.　　HOMER—*Odyssey.* Bk. IV. L. 1,092.
　　　　　　　　　　　Pope's trans.

I should think your tongue had broken its
　chain!
　　d.　　LONGFELLOW—*Christus. The Golden*
　　　　　　　　　Legend. Pt. IV.

Many a man's tongue shakes out his master's undoing.
　　e.　　*All's Well That Ends Well.* Act II.
　　　　　　　　　　Sc. 4. L. 23.

My tongue's use is to me no more
Than an unstringed viol or a harp.
　　f.　　*Richard II.* Act I. Sc. 3. L. 161.

　My tongue, though not my heart, shall have
his will.
　　g.　　*Comedy of Errors.* Act IV. Sc. 2.
　　　　　　　　　　　　L. 18.

So on the tip of his subduing tongue
All kind of arguments and question deep,
　All replication prompt, and reason strong,
For his advantage still did wake and sleep;
To make the weeper laugh, the laugher weep,
He had the dialect and different skill,
Catching all passions in his craft of will.
　　h.　　*Lover's Complaint.* L. 120.

　　　　The heart hath treble wrong
When it is barr'd the aidance of the tongue.
　　i.　　*Venus and Adonis.* L. 329.

Tongues I'll hang on every tree,
That shall civil sayings show.
　　j.　　*As You Like It.* Act III. Sc. 2. L. 135.

　　　　　You play the spaniel,
And think with wagging of your tongue to
　win me.
　　k.　　*Henry VIII.* Act V. Sc. 3. L. 126.

Is there a tongue like Delia's o'er her cup,
That runs for ages without winding up?
　　l.　　YOUNG—*Love of Fame.* Satire 1.
　　　　　　　　　　　　L. 281.

TONSORIAL (*See* OCCUPATIONS).

TRAVELLING.

The travelled mind is the catholic mind
educated from exclusiveness and egotism.
　　m.　　AMOS BRONSON ALCOTT—*Table-Talk.*
　　　　　　　　　　Travelling.

Travelling is no fool's errand to him who
carries his eyes and itinerary along with him.
　　n.　　AMOS BRONSON ALCOTT—*Table-Talk.*
　　　　　　　　　　Travelling.

Travel, in the younger sort, is a part of
education; in the elder, a part of experience.
He that travelleth into a country before he
hath some entrance into the language, goeth
to school, and not to travel.
　　o.　　BACON—*Of Travel.*

Go far—too far you cannot, still the farther
The more experience finds you: And go
　sparing;—
One meal a week will serve you, and one suit,
Through all your travels; for you'll find it
　certain,
The poorer and the baser you appear,
The more you look through still.
　　p.　　BEAUMONT AND FLETCHER—*The*
　　　　　Woman's Prize. Act IV. Sc. 5.
　　　　　　　　　　L. 199.

　　　　　I depart,
Whither I know not; but the hour's gone by
When Albion's lessening shores could grieve
　or glad mine eye.
　　q.　　BYRON—*Childe Harold.* Canto III.
　　　　　　　　　　　St. 1.

Yon sun that sets upon the sea
　We follow in his flight;
Farewell awhile to him and thee,
　My native Land—Good-night!
　　r.　　BYRON—*Childe Harold.* Canto I.
　　　　　　　　St. 13. *Song.*

He travels safest in the dark night who
travels lightest.
　　s.　　FERNANDO CORTEZ—See PRESCOTT'S
　　　　　Conquest of Mexico. Bk. V. Ch. III.

　　　　In travelling
I shape myself betimes to idleness
And take fools' pleasure.
　　t.　　GEORGE ELIOT—*The Spanish Gypsy.*
　　　　　　　　　　Bk. I.

Know most of the rooms of thy native
country before thou goest over the threshold
thereof.
　　u.　　FULLER—*The Holy and Profane States.*
　　　　　Of Travelling. Maxim IV.

　　　　One who journeying
Along a way he knows not, having crossed
A place of drear extent, before him sees
A river rushing swiftly toward the deep,
And all its tossing current white with foam,
And stops and turns, and measures back his
　way.
　　v.　　HOMER—*Iliad.* Bk. V. L. 749.
　　　　　　　　　Bryant's trans.

As the Spanish proverb says, "He who would bring home the wealth of the Indies must carry the wealth of the Indies with him." So it is in travelling: a man must carry knowledge with him, if he would bring home knowledge.

    a.   Sam'l Johnson—*Boswell's Life of Johnson.* 1778.

Let him go abroad to a distant country; let him go to some place where he is not known. Don't let him go to the devil where he is known.

    b.   Sam'l Johnson--*Boswell's Life of Johnson.* 1773.

The use of travelling is to regulate imagination by reality, and, instead of thinking how things may be, to see them as they are.

    c.   Sam'l Johnson—Piozzi's *Johnsoniana.* 154.

Much have I travell'd in the realms of gold,
  And many goodly states and kingdoms seen;
  Round many western islands have I been,
Which bards in fealty to Apollo hold.

    d.   Keats—*On First Looking into Chapman's Homer.*

The marquise has a disagreeable day for her journey.

    e.   Louis XV.—*While Looking at Mme. de Pompadour's Funeral.*

Better sit still where born, I say,
  Wed one sweet woman and love her well,
Love and be loved in the old East way,
  Drink sweet waters, and dream in a spell,
Than to wander in search of the Blessed Isles,
And to sail the thousands of watery miles
In search of love, and find you at last
On the edge of the world, and a curs'd out-
  cast.

    f.   Joaquin Miller—*Pace Implora.*

Does the road wind up-hill all the way?
  Yes, to the very end.
Will the day's journey take the whole long
  day?
  From morn to night, my friend.

    g.   Christina Rossetti—*Up-Hill.*

Farewell, Monsieur Traveller: look you lisp and wear strange suits, disable all the benefits of your own country.

    h.   *As You Like It.* Act IV. Sc. 1. L. 33.

I'll put a girdle round about the earth
In forty minutes.

    i.   *Midsummer-Night's Dream.* Act II. Sc. 1. L. 175.

I spake of most disastr'us chances,
*   *   *   *   *   *
Of being taken by the insolent foe
And sold to slavery, of my redemption thence
And portance in my travels' history:
Wherein of antres vast and deserts idle,
Rough quarries, rocks and hills whose heads
  touch heaven,
It was my hint to speak—such was the pro-
  cess;
And of the cannibals that each other eat.

    j.   *Othello.* Act I. Sc. 3. L. 134.

* * * the sundry contemplation of my travels, in which my often rumination wraps me in a most humorous sadness.

    k.   *As You Like It.* Act IV. Sc. 1. L. 17.

              Travell'd gallants,
That fill the court with quarrels, talk, and
  tailors.

    l.   *Henry VIII.* Act I. Sc. 3. L. 19.

When I was at home, I was in a better place;
but travellers must be content.

    m.   *As You Like It.* Act II. Sc. 4. L. 17.

I pity the man who can travel from Dan to Beersheba and cry, " 'Tis all barren!"

    n.   Sterne—*Sentimental Journey. In the Street. Calais.*

I always love to begin a journey on Sundays, because I shall have the prayers of the church to preserve all that travel by land or by water.

    o.   Swift—*Polite Conversation.* Dialogue II.

'Tis a mad world (my masters) and in sadnes
I travail'd madly in these dayes of madnes.

    p.   John Taylor—*Wandering to see the Wonders of the West.*

We are two travellers, Roger and I.
  Roger's my dog.

    q.   J. T. Trowbridge—*The Vagabonds.*

TREASON.

        Is there not some chosen curse,
Some hidden thunder in the stores of heaven,
Red with uncommon wrath, to blast the man
Who owes his greatness to his country's ruin?

    r.   Addison—*Cato.* Act I. Sc. 1.

This principle is old, but true as fate,
Kings may love treason, but the traitor hate.

    s.   Thomas Dekker—*The Honest Whore.* Pt. I. Act IV. Sc. 4.

Treason is not own'd when 'tis descried;
Successful crimes alone are justified.

    t.   Dryden—*Medals.* L. 207.

O that a soldier so glorious, ever victorious in
    fight,
Passed from a daylight of honor into the
    terrible night;
Fell as the mighty archangel, ere the earth
    glowed in space, fell—
Fell from the patriot's heaven down to the
    loyalist's hell!
  a.   Thos. Dunn English—*Arnold at
                                        Stillwater.*

With evil omens from the harbour sails
    The ill-fated ship that worthless Arnold
    bears;
God of the southern winds, call up thy gales,
And whistle in rude fury round his ears.
  b.   Philip Freneau—*Arnold's Departure.*

Rebellion must be managed with many
swords; treason to his prince's person may
be with one knife.
  c.   Fuller—*The Holy and Profane States.
                                        The Traitor.*

Treason doth never prosper: what's the
    reason?
Why if it prosper, none dare call it treason.
  d.   Sir John Harrington—*Epigrams.*
                                        Bk. IV. Ep. V.

The man who pauses on the paths of treason,
Halts on a quicksand, the first step engulfs
    him.
  e.   Aaron Hill—*Henry V.* Act I. Sc. 1.

For while the treason I detest,
The traitor still I love.
  f.   Hoole—*Metastatio. Romulus and
                                        Hersilia.* Act I. Sc. 5.

The traitor to Humanity is the traitor most
    accursed;
Man is more than Constitutions; better rot
    beneath the sod,
Than be true to Church and State while we
    are doubly false to God.
  g.   Lowell—*On the Capture of Certain
                                        Fugitive Slaves near Washington.*

Hast thou betrayed my credulous innocence
With vizor'd falsehood and base forgery?
  h.   Milton—*Comus.* L. 697.

Oh, colder than the wind that freezes
    Founts, that but now in sunshine play'd,
Is that congealing pang which seizes
    The trusting bosom, when betray'd.
  i.   Moore—*Lalla Rookh. The Fire
                                        Worshippers.*
Oh, for a tongue to curse the slave
    Whose treason, like a deadly blight,
Comes o'er the councils of the brave,
    And blasts them in their hour of might!
  j.   Moore—*Lalla Rookh. The
                                        Fire-Worshippers.*

He [Cæsar] loved the treason, but hated the
traitor.
  k.   Plutarch—*Life of Romulus.*

Et tu Brute! Then fall, Cæsar!
  l.   *Julius Cæsar.* Act III. Sc. I. L. 77.

I am sorry I must never trust thee more,
But count the world a stranger for thy sake:
The private wound is deepest.
  m.   *Two Gentlemen of Verona.* Act V.
                                        Sc. 4. L. 69.

I did pluck allegiance from men's hearts,
Loud shouts and salutations from their
    mouths,
Even in the presence of the crowned king.
  n.   *Henry IV.* Pt. I. Act III. Sc. 2.
                                        L. 52.

          Know, my name is lost;
By treason's tooth bare-gnawn and canker-
    bit.
  o.   *King Lear.* Act V. Sc. 3. L. 121.

Smooth runs the water where the brook is
    deep;
And in his simple show he harbours treason.
  p.   *Henry VI.* Pt. II. Act III. Sc. 1.
                                        L. 53.
Some guard these traitors to the block of
    death;
Treason's true bed and yielder up of breath.
  q.   *Henry IV.* Pt. II. Act IV. Sc. 2.
                                        L. 122.

Tellest thou me of "ifs"? Thou art a traitor:
Off with his head!
  r.   *Richard III.* Act III. Sc. 4. L. 77

          The man was noble,
But with his last attempt he wiped it out:
Destroy'd his country, and his name remains
To the ensuing age abhorr'd.
  s.   *Coriolanus.* Act V. Sc. 3. L. 145.

          Though those that are betray'd
Do feel the treason sharply, yet the traitor
Stands in worse case of woe.
  t.   *Cymbeline.* Act III. Sc. 4. L. 87.

To say the truth, so Judas kiss'd his master,
And cried "all hail!" whereas he meant all
    harm.
  u.   *Henry VI.* Pt. III. Act V. Sc. 7.
                                        L. 33.

Treason and murder ever kept together,
As two yoke-devils sworn to either's purpose,
Working so grossly in a natural cause,
That admiration did not hoop at them.
  v.   *Henry V.* Act II. Sc. 2. L. 105.

Treason is but trusted like the fox
Who, ne'er so tame, so cherish'd and locked
    up,
Will have a wild trick of his ancestors.
  w.   *Henry IV.* Pt. I. Act V. Sc. 2.
                                        L. 9.

TREES AND PLANTS.

Part I.—Unclassified Arbora.

The place is all awave with trees,
　Limes, myrtles, purple-beaded,
Acacias having drunk the lees
　Of the night-dew, faint headed,
And wan, grey olive-woods, which seem
The fittest foliage for a dream.
　　a.　　E. B. Browning—*An Island.*

Stranger, if thou hast learned a truth which
　　needs
No school of long experience, that the world
Is full of guilt and misery, and hast seen
Enough of all its sorrows, crimes and cares,
To tire thee of it, enter this wild wood
And view the haunts of Nature.　The calm
　　shade
Shall bring a kindred calm, and the sweet
　　breeze
That makes the green leaves dance, shall waft
　　a balm
To thy sick heart.
　　b.　　Bryant—*Inscription for the Entrance to
　　　　　　　　　　　　　　　a Wood.*

The groves were God's first temples.　Ere man
　　learned
To hew the shaft, and lay the architrave,
And spread the roof above them,—ere he
　　framed
The lofty vault, to gather and roll back
The sound of anthems; in the darkling wood,
Amidst the cool and silence, he knelt down
And offered to the Mightiest solemn thanks
And supplication.
　　c.　　Bryant—*A Forest Hymn.*

　　　　The shad-bush, white with flowers,
Brightened the glens; the new leaved butter-
　　nut
And quivering poplar to the roving breeze
Gave a balsamic fragrance.
　　d.　　Bryant—*The Old Man's Counsel.* L. 28.

No tree in all the grove but has its charms,
Though each its hue peculiar.
　　e.　　Cowper—*The Task.* Bk. I.　L. 307.

Where is the pride of Summer,—the green
　　prime,—
　The many, many leaves all twinkling?—three
On the mossed elm; three on the naked
　　lime
　Trembling.—and one upon the old oak tree!
　Where is the Dryad's immortality?
　f.　　Hood—*Ode. Autumn.*
39

　　　　　　　　It was the noise
Of ancient trees falling while all was still
Before the storm, in the long interval
Between the gathering clouds and that light
　　breeze
Which Germans call the Wind's bride.
　　g.　　Leland—*The Fall of the Trees.*

This is the forest primeval.
　　h.　　Longfellow—*Evangeline.*
　　　　　　　　　　　　　　　Introduction.
Oh! proudly then the forest kings
　Their banners lift o'er vale and mount;
And cool and fresh the wild grass springs,
　By lonely path, by sylvan fount;
There, o'er the fair leaf-laden rill,
　The laurel sheds her cluster'd bloom,
And throned upon the rock-wreathed hill
　The rowan waves his scarlet plume.
　　i.　　Edith May—*A Forest Scene.*

And all amid them stood the Tree of Life,
High eminent, blooming ambrosial fruit
Of vegetable gold.
　　j.　　Milton—*Paradise Lost.* Bk. IV.
　　　　　　　　　　　　　　　　　L. 218.
Cedar, and pine, and fir, and branching palm,
A sylvan scene, and as the ranks ascend
Shade above shade, a woody theatre
Of stateliest view.
　　k.　　Milton—*Paradise Lost.* Bk. IV.
　　　　　　　　　　　　　　　　　L. 139.
Woodman, spare that tree!
　Touch not a single bough!
In youth it sheltered me,
　And I'll protect it now.
　　l.　　George P. Morris—*Woodman, Spare
　　　　　　　　　　　　　　　That Tree.*
　　　　　　　When the sappy boughs
Attire themselves with blooms, sweet rudi-
　　ments
Of future harvest.
　　m.　　John Phillips—*Cider.* Bk. II. L. 437.

Grove nods at grove.
　　n.　　Pope—*Moral Essays.* Ep. IV. L. 117.

The highest and most lofty trees have the
most reason to dread the thunder.
　　o.　　Rollin—*Ancient History.* Bk. VI.
　　　　　　　　　　　　　　　Ch. II. Sec. I.
So bright in death I used to say,
　So beautiful through frost and cold!
A lovelier thing I know to-day,
　The leaf is growing old,
And wears in grace of duty done,
The gold and scarlet of the sun.
　　p.　　Margaret E. Sangster—*A Maple
　　　　　　　　　　　　　　　Leaf.*

A barren detested vale, you see it is;
The trees, though summer, yet forlorn and
    lean,
O'ercome with moss and baleful mistletoe.
  a.   *Titus Andronicus.* Act II. Sc. 3. L. 93.

But, poor old man, thou prunest a rotten tree,
That cannot so much as a blossom yield
In lieu of all thy pains and husbandry.
  b.   *As You Like It.* Act II. Sc. 3. L. 63.

Hath not old custom made this life more
    sweet
Than that of painted pomp? Are not these
    woods
More free from peril than the envious court?
  c.   *As You Like It.* Act II. Sc. 1. L. 2.

Under the greenwood tree
Who loves to lie with me,
And tune his merry note
Unto the sweet bird's throat,
Come hither, come hither, come hither:
No enemy here shall he see,
But winter and rough weather.
  d.   *As You Like It.* Act II. Sc. 5. L. 1.

Who am no more but as the tops of trees,
Which fence the roots they grow by and de-
    fend them.
  e.   *Pericles.* Act I. Sc. 2. L. 29.

Now all the tree-tops lay asleep,
    Like green waves on the sea,
As still as in the silent deep
    The ocean-woods may be.
  f.   SHELLEY—*The Recollection.* II.

The trees were gazing up into the sky,
Their bare arms stretched in prayer for the
    snows.
  g.   ALEX. SMITH—*A Life-Drama.* Sc. 2.

The laurell, meed of mightie conquerours
    And poets sage; the firre that weepeth still;
The willow, worne of forlorne paramours;
    The eugh, obedient to the bender's will;
    The birch, for shafts; the sallow for the
        mill;
    The mirrhe sweete-bleeding in the bitter
        wound;
    The warlike beech; the ash for nothing ill;
The fruitfull olive; and the platane round;
    The carver holme; the maple seldom inward
        sound.
  h.   SPENSER—*Faerie Queene.* Bk. I.
                              Canto I. St. 8.

                     The woods appear
With crimson blotches deeply dashed and
    crossed,—
Sign of the fatal pestilence of Frost.
  i.   BAYARD TAYLOR—*Mon-Da-Min.* St. 38.

Now rings the woodland loud and long,
    The distance takes a lovelier hue,
    And drowned in yonder living blue
The lark becomes a sightless song.
  j.   TENNYSON—*In Memoriam.* Pt. CXV.

O Love, what hours were thine and mine,
In lands of palm and southern pine;
    In lands of palm, of orange-blossom,
Of olive, aloe, and maize, and vine.
  k.   TENNYSON—*The Daisy.* St. 1.

The linden broke her ranks and rent
    The woodbine wreaths that bind her,
And down the middle buzz! she went
    With all her bees behind her!
The poplars, in long order due,
    With cypress promenaded,
The shock-head willows two and two
    By rivers gallopaded.
  l.   TENNYSON—*Amphion.* St. 5.

The woods are hush'd, their music is no
        more;
    The leaf is dead, the yearning past away;
New leaf, new life—the days of frost are o'er;
    New life, new love, to suit the newer day:
New loves are sweet as those that went be-
    fore:
    Free love—free field—we love but while we
        may.
  m.   TENNYSON—*Idylls of the King. The
                              Last Tournament.* L. 276.

But see the fading many-coloured Woods,
Shade deep'ning over shade, the country
    round
Imbrown; crowded umbrage, dusk and dun,
Of every hue from wan declining green
To sooty dark.
  n.   THOMSON—*Seasons. Autumn.* L. 950.

                     Some to the holly hedge
Nestling repair; and to the thicket some;
Some to the rude protection of the thorn.
  o.   THOMSON—*Seasons. Spring.* L. 634.

Welcome, ye shades! ye bowery Thickets
    hail!
Ye lofty Pines! ye venerable Oaks!
Ye Ashes wild, resounding o'er the steep!
Delicious is your shelter to the soul.
  p.   THOMSON—*Seasons. Summer.* L. 469.

Sure thou did'st flourish once! and many
    springs,
Many bright mornings, much dew, many
    showers,
Passed o'er thy head; many light hearts and
    wings,
Which now are dead, lodg'd in thy living
    bowers.
And still a new succession sings and flies;
Fresh groves grow up, and their green
    branches shoot
Towards the old and still-enduring skies;
While the low violet thrives at their root.
  q.   VAUGHAN—*The Timber.*

A brotherhood of venerable Trees.
  r.   WORDSWORTH—*Sonnet composed at
                              Castle ——.*

Part II.—Classified Arbora.

Acacia.
Acacia.

A great acacia, with its slender trunk
And overpoise of multitudinous leaves,
(In which a hundred fields might spill their
    dew
And intense verdure, yet find room enough)
Stood reconciling all the place with green.
  a.   E. B. Browning—*Aurora Leigh.*
                       Bk. VI.

                     The lawn,
Which, after sweeping broadly round the
    house,
Went trickling through the shrubberies in a
    stream
Of tender turf, and wore and lost itself
Among the acacias, over which you saw
The irregular line of elms by the deep lane
Which stopped the grounds and dammed the
    overflow
Of arbutus and laurel.
  b.   E. B. Browning—*Aurora Leigh.* Bk. I.

Pluck the acacia's golden balls,
And mark where the red pomegranate falls.
  c.   Julia C. R. Dorr—*Under the*
                         Palm-Trees.

Light-leaved acacias, by the door,
  Stood up in balmy air,
Clusters of blossomed moonlight bore,
  And breathed a perfume rare.
  d.   George MacDonald—*Song of the*
                  Spring Nights. Pt. I.

Our rocks are rough, but smiling there
Th' acacia waves her yellow hair,
Lonely and sweet, nor loved the less
For flow'ring in a wilderness.
  e.   Moore—*Lalla Rookh. Light of the*
                  Harem. Song.

The slender acacia would not shake
  One long milk-bloom on the tree;
The white lake-blossom fell into the lake
  As the pimpernel dozed on the lea;
But the rose was awake all night for your
    sake,
  Knowing your promise to me;
The lilies and roses were all awake,
  They sighed for the dawn and thee.
  f.   Tennyson—*Maud.* Pt. XXII. St. 8.

Almond.
Amygdalus communis.

Almond blossom, sent to teach us
That the spring days soon will reach us.
  g.   Edwin Arnold—*Almond Blossoms.*

Blossom of the almond trees,
April's gift to April's bees.
  h.   Edwin Arnold—*Almond Blossoms.*

With a bee in every bell,
Almond bloom, we greet thee well.
  i.   Edwin Arnold—*Almond Blossoms.*

White as the blossoms which the almond tree,
Above its bald and leafless branches bears.
  j.   Margaret J. Preston—*The Royal*
                        Preacher. St. 5.

Like to an almond tree ymounted hye
  On top of greene Selinis all alone,
With blossoms brave bedecked daintily;
  Whose tender locks do tremble every one,
  At everie little breath, that under heaven is
    blowne.
  k.   Spenser—*Faerie Queen.* Bk. I.
                     Canto VII. St. 32.

Apple.
Pyrus Malus.

What plant we in this apple tree?
Sweets for a hundred flowery springs
To load the May-wind's restless wings,
When, from the orchard-row, he pours
Its fragrance through our open doors;
  A world of blossoms for the bee,
Flowers for the sick girl's silent room,
For the glad infant sprigs of bloom,
  We plant with the apple tree.
  l.   Bryant—*The Planting of the Apple*
                          Tree.

    And what is more melancholy than the old
apple-trees that linger about the spot where
once stood a homestead, but where there is
now only a ruined chimney rising out of a
grassy and weed-grown cellar? They offer
their fruit to every wayfarer—apples that are
bitter-sweet with the moral of time's vicissitude.
  m.   Nath. Hawthorne—*Mosses from an*
                  Old Manse. The Old Manse.

The blossoms and leaves in plenty
  From the apple tree fall each day;
The merry breezes approach them,
  And with them merrily play.
  n.   Heine—*Book of Songs. Lyrical*
                  Interlude. No. 63.

Fragrant blossoms fringe the apple boughs.
  o.   Amelia B. Welby—*Hopeless Love.*

Ash.

Fraxinus.

The ash her purple drops forgivingly
And sadly, breaking not the general hush ;
  The maple swamps glow like a sunset sea,
Each leaf a ripple with its separate flush ;
  All round the wood's edge creeps the skirt-
    ing blaze,
  Of bushes low, as when, on cloudy days,
Ere the rain falls, the cautious farmer burns
    his brush.
  a.   LOWELL—*An Indian-Summer Reverie.*
                            St. 11.

Aspen.

Populus Tremuloides.

What whispers so strange at the hour of mid-
    night,
  From the aspen leaves trembling so wildly?
Why in the lone wood sings it sad, when the
    bright
  Full moon beams upon it so mildly?
  b.   INGEMANN—*The Aspen.*

At that awful hour of the Passion, when
the Saviour of the world felt deserted in His
agony, when—
  "The sympathizing sun his light withdrew,
  And wonder'd how the stars their dying Lord
    could view "—
when earth, shaking with horror, rung the
passing bell for Deity, and universal nature
groaned, then from the loftiest tree to the
lowliest flower all felt a sudden thrill, and
trembling, bowed their heads, all save the
proud and obdurate *aspen*, which said, " Why
should *we* weep and tremble ? we trees, and
plants, and flowers are pure and never sinned!"
Ere it ceased to speak, an involuntary trembling seized its every leaf, and the word went
forth that it should never rest, but tremble on
until the day of judgment.
  c.   *Legend.* From *Notes and Queries.*
            First Series. Vol. VI. No. 161.

Beneath a shivering canopy reclined,
Of aspen leaves that wave without a wind,
I love to lie, when lulling breezes stir
The spiry cones that tremble on the fir.
  d.   JOHN LEYDEN—*Noontide.*

And the wind, full of wantonness, wooes like a
    lover
The young aspen-trees till they tremble all
    over.
  e.   MOORE—*Lalla Rookh. Light of the
                            Harem.*

Beech.

Fagus.

Oh, leave this barren spot to me !
Spare, woodman, spare the beechen tree !
  f.   CAMPBELL—*The Beech-Tree's Petition.*

Birch.

Betula.

Rippling through thy branches goes the sun-
    shine,
  Among thy leaves that palpitate forever,
And in thee, a pining nymph had prisoned
  The soul, once of some tremulous inland
    river,
Quivering to tell her woe, but ah! dumb,
    dumb forever.
  g.   LOWELL—*The Birch Tree.*

Cedar.

Cedrus.

O'er yon bare knoll the pointed cedar shadows
Drowse on the crisp, gray moss.
  h.   LOWELL—*An Indian-Summer Reverie.*

Thus yields the cedar to the axe's edge,
Whose arms gave shelter to the princely eagle.
  i.   *Henry VI.* Pt. III. Act V. Sc. 2.
                            L. 11.
High on a hill a goodly Cedar grewe,
Of wond'rous length and streight proportion,
That farre abroad her daintie odours threwe ;
'Mongst all the daughters of proud Libanon,
Her match in beautie was not anie one.
  j.   SPENSER—*Visions of the World's Vanitie.*
                            St. 7.

Cherry.

Cerasus.

Sweet is the air with the budding haws, and
    the valley stretching for miles below
Is white with blossoming cherry-trees, as if
    just covered with lightest snow.
  k.   LONGFELLOW—*Christus. Golden
                            Legend.* Pt. IV.

And in the warm hedge grew lush eglantine,
Green cowbind and the moonlight-colored
    May,
And cherry blossoms, and white cups whose
    wine
Was the bright dew yet drained not by the
    day.
  l.   SHELLEY—*The Question.* St. 3.

Chestnut.

Castanea Vesca.

        When I see the chestnut letting
All her lovely blossoms falter down, I think,
    " Alas the day !"
  m.   JEAN INGELOW—*The Warbling of
                            Blackbirds.*

The chestnuts, lavish of their long-hid gold,
  To the faint Summer, beggared now and
    old,
Pour back the sunshine hoarded 'neath her
    favoring eye.
  n.   LOWELL—*An Indian-Summer Reverie.*
                            St. 10.

Citron.

Citrus Medica.

Awake! the morning shines, and the fresh
    field
Calls us; we lose the prime, to mark how
    spring
Our tended plants, how blows the citron
    grove,
What drops the myrrh, and what the balmy
    reed.
How nature paints her colours, how the bee
Sits on the bloom, extracting liquid sweet.
    a.   MILTON—*Paradise Lost.* Bk. V.
                                  L. 20.

Cocoanut.

Cocos Nucifera.

Oh, the green and the graceful—the cocoanut
    tree!
The lone and the lofty—it loves like me
The flash, the foam of the heaving sea,
And the sound of the surging waves
In the shore's unfathomed caves.
With its stately shaft and its verdant crown,
And its fruit in clusters drooping down.
    b.   FRANCES S. OSGOOD—*The Cocoanut Tree.*

Cypress.

Cupressus.

Dark tree! still sad when other's grief is fled,
The only constant mourner o'er the dead.
    c.   BYRON—*Giaour.* L. 286.

Elder.

Sambucus.

O leave the elder-bloom, fair maids!
    And listen to my lay.
    d.   COLERIDGE—*Introduction to the Tale of
                       the Dark Ladie.*

Elm.

Ulmus.

Under the cooling shadow of a stately Elm,
    Close sate I by a goodly River's side,
Where gliding streams the rocks did over-
    whelm;
A lonely place, with pleasure dignified.
I once that loved the shady woods so well,
Now thought the rivers did the trees excel,
And if the sun would ever shine, there would
    I dwell.
    e.   ANNE BRADSTREET—*Contemplations.*
                                St. 21.

         And the great elms o'erhead
Dark shadows wove on their aërial looms,
Shot through with golden thread.
    f.   LONGFELLOW—*Hawthorne.* St. 2.

In crystal vapour everywhere
Blue isles of heaven laughed between,
And far, in forest-deeps unseen,
The topmost elm-tree gather'd green
    From draughts of balmy air.
    g.   TENNYSON—*Sir Launcelot and Queen
                          Guinevere.*

Fig.

Ficus.

Close by a rock, of less enormous height,
Breaks the wild waves, and forms a danger-
    ous strait;
Full on its crown, a fig's green branches rise,
And shoot a leafy forest to the skies.
    h.   HOMER—*Odyssey.* Bk. XII. L. 125.
                                  Pope's trans.

So counsel'd he, and both together went
Into the thickest wood; there soon they chose
The fig-tree, not that kind for fruit renowned,
But such as at this day to Indians known
In Malabar or Decan spreads her arms,
Branching so broad and long, that in the
    ground
The bended twigs take root, and daughters
    grow
About the mother tree, a pillar'd shade
High overarch'd, and echoing walks between.
    i.   MILTON—*Paradise Lost.* Bk. IX.
                                L. 1,099.

Fir.

Abies.

A lonely fir-tree is standing
    On a northern barren height;
It sleeps, and the ice and snow-drift
    Cast round it a garment of white.
    j.   HEINE—*Book of Songs. Lyrical
                           Interlude.* No. 34.

I remember, I remember
    The fir-trees dark and high;
I used to think their slender tops
    Were close against the sky.
    k.   HOOD—*I Remember, I Remember.*

In a drear-nighted December,
    Too happy, happy tree,
Thy branches ne'er remember
    Their green felicity.
    l.   KEATS—*Stanzas.*

Kindles the gummy bark of fir or pine,
And sends a comfortable heat from far,
Which might supply the sun.
    m.   MILTON—*Paradise Lost.* Bk. X.
                                L. 1,076.

Hawthorn.

Cratægus Oxyacanthus.

The hawthorn I will pu' wi' its lock o' siller
    gray,
Where, like an aged man, it stands at break
    o' day.
    n.   BURNS—*O Luve Will Venture In.*

The hawthorn-trees blow in the dew of the
morning.
    o.   BURNS—*The Chevalier's Lament.*

Yet, all beneath the unrivall'd rose,
The lowly daisy sweetly blows;
Tho' large the forest's monarch throws
      His army shade,
Yet green the juicy hawthorn grows,
      Adown the glade.
a.   Burns—*The Vision.*   Duan II.   St. 21.

Yet walk with me where hawthorns hide
  The wonders of the lane.
b.   Ebenezer Elliott—*The Wonders of*
                      the Lane.   L. 3.

The hawthorn-bush, with seats beneath the
    shade
For talking age and whispering lovers made!
c.   Goldsmith—*The Deserted Village.*
                             L. 13.

And every shepherd tells his tale
Under the hawthorn in the dale.
d.   Milton—*L'Allegro.* L. 67.

Then sing by turns, by turns the Muses sing;
Now hawthorns blossom.
e.   Pope—*Spring.* L. 41.

Gives not the hawthorn-bush a sweeter shade
To shepherds looking on their silly sheep
Than doth a rich embroider'd canopy
To kings that fear their subjects' treachery?
f.   *Henry VI.* Pt. III.   Act II.   Sc. 5.
                             L. 42.

The Hawthorn whitens; and the juicy Groves
Put forth their buds, unfolding by degrees,
Till the whole leafy Forest stands displayed,
In full luxuriance, to the sighing gales.
g.   Thomson—*Seasons.   Spring.*   L. 90.

Hemlock.
Tsuga Canadensis.

O hemlock-tree! O hemlock-tree! how faith-
    ful are thy branches!
Green not alone in summer time,
  But in the winter's frost and rime!
O hemlock-tree! O hemlock-tree! how faith-
    ful are thy branches!
h.   Longfellow—*The Hemlock-Tree.*

Hickory.
Carya.

Under the hickory-tree, Ben Bolt,
  Which stood at the foot of the hill,
Together we've lain in the noonday shade,
  And listened to Appleton's mill.
The mill-wheel has fallen to pieces, Ben Bolt,
  The rafters have tumbled in,
And a quiet which crawls round the walls as
    you gaze
Has followed the olden din.
i.   Thos. Dunn English—*Ben Bolt.*

Holly.
Ilex.

Green, slender, leaf-clad holly-boughs
Were twisted gracefu' round her brows,
I took her for some Scottish Muse,
    By that same token,
An' come to stop those reckless vows,
    Would soon be broken.
j.   Burns—*The Vision.*   Duan I.   St. 9.

Those hollies of themselves a shape
  As of an arbor took.
k.   Coleridge—*The Three Graves.*   Pt. IV.
                             St. 24.

All green was vanished save of pine and yew,
That still displayed their melancholy hue;
Save the green holly with its berries red,
And the green moss that o'er the gravel spread.
l.   Crabbe—*Tales of the Hall.*

And as, when all the summer trees are seen
      So bright and green,
The Holly leaves a sober hue display
      Less bright than they,
But when the bare and wintry woods we see,
What then so cheerful as the Holly-tree?
m.   Southey—*The Holly-Tree.*

O Reader! hast thou ever stood to see
    The Holly-tree?
The eye that contemplates it well perceives
    Its glossy leaves
Ordered by an Intelligence so wise
As might confound the Atheist's sophistries.
n.   Southey—*The Holly-Tree.*   St. 1.

Larch.
Larix.

I have look'd o'er the hills of the stormy north,
And the larch has hung all his tassels forth.
o.   Mrs. Hemans—*The Voice of Spring.*

Laurel.
Laurus Nobilis.

The laurel-tree grew large and strong,
  Its roots went searching deeply down;
It split the marble walls of Wrong,
  And blossomed o'er the Despot's crown.
p.   Richard Hengist Horne—*The Laurel*
                                Seed.

Lilac.
Syringa Vulgaris.

    The lilac spread
Odorous essence.
q.   Jean Ingelow—*Laurance.*   Pt. III.

I am thinking of the lilac-trees,
  That shook their purple plumes,
And when the sash was open,
  Shed fragrance through the room.
r.   Mrs. Anna S. Stephens—*The Old*
                                Apple-Tree.
The purple clusters load the lilac-bushes.
s.   Amelia B. Welby—*Hopeless Love.*

Linden.

Tilia.

The linden in the fervors of July
Hums with a louder concert.
  a.   Bryant—*Among the Trees.*

If thou lookest on the lime-leaf,
  Thou a heart's form will discover;
Therefore are the lindens ever
  Chosen seats of each fond lover.
  b.   Heine—*Book of Songs. New Spring.*
               No. 31. St. 3.

Lotus.

Zizyphus Lotus.

Where drooping lotos-flowers, distilling balm,
Dream by the drowsy streamlets sleep hath
  crown'd,
While Care forgets to sigh, and Peace hath
  balsamed Pain.
  c.   Paul H. Hayne—*Sonnet. Pent in*
              this Common Sphere.

Oh! what are the brightest that e'er have
  blown
To the lote-tree, springing by Alla's throne,
Whose flowers have a soul in every leaf.
  d.   Moore—*Lalla Rookh. Paradise and*
              the Peri.

They wove the lotus band to deck
And fan with pensile wreath their neck.
  e.   Moore—*Odes of Anacreon. Ode LXX.*

A spring there is, whose silver waters show
Clear as a glass the shining sands below:
A flowering lotos spreads its arms above,
Shades all the banks, and seems itself a grove.
  f.   Pope—*Sappho to Phaon.* L. 177.

The lotos bowed above the tide and dreamed.
  g.   Margaret J. Preston—*Rhodope's*
              Sandal.

Magnolia.

Magnolia.

Fragrant o'er all the western groves
The tall magnolia towers unshaded.
  h.   Maria Brooks— *Written on Seeing*
              Pharamond.

A languid magnolia showers
  From its shivering leaflets the dew;
'Tis lonely and bare of its flowers,
  That decked once its branches with blue.
  i.   Theudobach—*The Transplanted*
              Magnolia.

Mahogany.

Swietenia Mahogoni.

Christmas is here:
Winds whistle shrill,
Icy and chill,
Little care we:
Little we fear
Weather without,
Sheltered about
The Mahogany-Tree.
  j.   Thackeray—*The Mahogany-Tree.*

Maple.

Acer.

That was a day of delight and wonder.
While lying the shade of the maple trees
  under—
He felt the soft breeze at its frolicksome
  play;
He smelled the sweet odor of newly mown
  hay.
  k.   Thos. Dunn English—*Under the Trees.*

Mulberry

Morus.

O, the mulberry-tree is of trees the queen!
Bare long after the rest are green;
But as time steals onwards, while none per-
  ceives
Slowly she clothes herself with leaves—
Hides her fruit under them, hard to find.
    *　 *　 *　 *　 *　 *

But by and by, when the flowers grow few
And the fruits are dwindling and small to
  view—
Out she comes in her matron grace
With the purple myriads of her race;
Full of plenty from root to crown,
Showering plenty her feet adown,
While far over head hang gorgeously
Large luscious berries of sanguine dye,
  For the best grows highest, always
    highest,
  Upon the mulberry-tree.
  l.   D. M. Mulock—*The Mulberry-Tree.*

Oak.

Quercus.

Young Oak! when I planted thee deep in the
  ground,
  I hoped that thy days would be longer than
    mine;
That thy dark-waving branches would flourish around,
  And ivy thy trunk with its mantle entwine.
  m.   Byron—*To an Oak at Newstead.*

A song to the oak, the brave old oak,
  Who hath ruled in the greenwood long;
Here's health and renown to his broad green
    crown,
  And his fifty arms so strong.
There's fear in his frown when the Sun goes
  down,
  And the fire in the West fades out;
And he showeth his might on a wild midnight,
  When the storms through his branches
    shout.
  n.   H. F. Chorley—*The Brave Old Oak.*

The oak, when living, monarch of the wood;
The English oak, which, dead, commands
  the flood.
  o.   Churchill—*Gotham.* I. 303.

Old noted oak! I saw thee in a mood
Of vague indifference; and yet with me
Thy memory, like thy fate, hath lingering
    stood
For years, thou hermit, in the lonely sea
Of grass that waves around thee!
  a.   JOHN CLARE—*The Rural Muse.*
                        Burthorp Oak.

The monarch oak, the patriarch of the trees,
Shoots rising up, and spreads by slow degrees.
Three centuries he grows, and three he stays
Supreme in state; and in three more decays.
  b.   DRYDEN—*Palamon and Arcite.*
                    Bk. III. L. 1,058.

The oaks with solemnity shook their heads;
  The twigs of the birch-trees, in token
Of warning, nodded,—and I exclaim'd:
  " Dear Monarch, forgive what I've spoken!"
  c.   HEINE—*Songs. Germany.*
                        Caput XVII.

Those green-robed senators of mighty woods,
Tall oaks, branch-charmed by the earnest
    stars,
Dream, and so dream all night without a stir.
  d.   KEATS—*Hyperion.* Bk. I. L. 73.

The proud tree low bendeth its vigorous form,
Whose freshness and strength have braved
    many a storm;
And the sturdy oak shakes that ne'er trem-
    bled before
Though the years of its glory outnumber
    three-score.
  e.   ELIZABETH C. KINNEY—*The Woodman.*

The tall Oak, towering to the skies,
The fury of the wind defies,
From age to age, in virtue strong.
Inured to stand, and suffer wrong.
  f.   MONTGOMERY—*The Oak.*

Hail, hidden to the knees in fern,
  Broad Oak of Sumner-chace,
Whose topmost branches can discern
  The roofs of Sumner-place!
  g.   TENNYSON—*The Talking Oak.* St. 8.

There grewe an aged tree on the greene;
A goodly Oake sometime had it bene,
With armes full strong and largely displayd,
But of their leaves they were disarayde:
The bodie bigge, and mightely pight,
Thoroughly rooted, and of wond'rous hight;
Whilome had bene the king of the field,
And mochell mast to the husband did yielde,
And with his nuts larded many swine:
But now the gray mosse marred his rine;
His bared boughes were beaten with stormes,
His toppe was bald, and wasted with wormes,
His honour decayed, his braunches sere.
  h.   SPENSER—*Shepheard's Callender.*
                        Februarie.

Olive.

Olea Europæa.

See there the olive grove of Academe,
Plato's retirement, where the Attic bird
Trills her thick-warbled notes the summer
    long.
  i.   MILTON—*Paradise Regained.* Bk. IV.
                        L. 244.

Orange.

Citrus Aurantium.

Yes, sing the song of the orange-tree,
  With its leaves of velvet green;
With its luscious fruit of sunset hue,
  The fairest that ever were seen;
The grape may have its bacchanal verse,
  To praise the fig we are free;
But homage I pay to the queen of all,
  The glorious orange-tree.
  j.   J. K. HOYT—*The Orange-Tree.*

The orange with the lime-tree vies
In shedding rich perfume.
  k.   MARIA JAMES—*Ode for the Fourth of*
                        July.

          Beneath some orange-trees,
Whose fruit and blossoms in the breeze
Were wantoning together free,
Like age at play with infancy.
  l.   MOORE—*Lalla Rookh. Paradise and*
                      the Peri.

If I were yonder orange-tree
  And thou the blossom blooming there,
I would not yield a breath of thee
  To scent the most imploring air!
  m.   MOORE—*If I Were Yonder Wave, My*
                      Dear.

'Twas noon; and every orange bud
Hung languid o'er the crystal flood,
Faint as the lids of maiden eyes
Beneath a lover's burning sighs!
  n.   MOORE—*I Stole Along the Flowery*
                      Bank.

Palm.

Phœnix Dactylifera.

As the palm-tree standeth so straight and so
    tall,
The more the hail beats, and the more the
    rains fall.
  o.   LONGFELLOW—*Annie of Tharaw.*
               Trans. from the German of
                  Simon Dach. L. 11.

First the high palme-trees, with braunches
    faire,
Out of the lowly vallies did arise,
And high shoote up their heads into the skyes.
  p.   SPENSER—*Virgils Gnat.* L. 191.

Next to thee, O fair gazelle,
O Beddowee girl, beloved so well;

Next to the fearless Nedjidee,
Whose fleetness shall bear me again to thee;

Next to ye both I love the Palm,
With his leaves of beauty, his fruit of balm;

Next to ye both I love the Tree
Whose fluttering shadow wraps us three
With love, and silence, and mystery!
    a.   BAYARD TAYLOR—*The Arab to the Palm.*

Of threads of palm was the carpet spun
Whereon he kneels when the day is done,
And the foreheads of Islam are bowed as one!

To him the palm is a gift divine,
Wherein all uses of man combine,—
House and raiment and food and wine!

And, in the hour of his great release,
His need of the palm shall only cease
With the shroud wherein he lieth in peace.

"Allah il Allah!" he sings his psalm,
On the Indian Sea, by the isles of balm;
"Thanks to Allah, who gives the palm!"
    b.   WHITTIER—*The Palm-Tree.*

Pear.

Pyrus Communis.

            I ask in vain
Who planted on the slope this lofty group
Of ancient pear-trees that with spring-time burst
Into such breadth of bloom.
    c.   BRYANT—*Among the Trees.*

The great white pear-tree dropped with dew from leaves
And blossom, under heavens of happy blue.
    d.   JEAN INGELOW—*Songs with Preludes.*
                         Wedlock.

        A pear-tree planted nigh:
'Twas charg'd with fruit that made a goodly show,
And hung with dangling pears was every bough.
    e.   POPE—*January and May.* L. 602.

Pine.

Pinus.

             Shaggy shade
Of desert-loving pine, whose emerald scalp
Nods to the storm.
    f.   BYRON—*The Prophecy of Dante.*
                     Canto II. L. 63.
Risest from forth thy silent sea of pines.
    g.   COLERIDGE—*Hymn Before Sunrise in
                       the Vale of Chamouni.*

'Twas on the inner bark, stripped from the pine,
   Our father pencilled this epistle rare;
Two blazing pine knots did his torches shine,
   Two braided pallets formed his desk and chair.
    h.   DURFEE—*What-Cheer.* Canto II.

As sunbeams stream through liberal space
And nothing jostle or displace,
So waved the pine-tree through my thought
And fanned the dreams it never brought.
    i.   EMERSON—*Woodnotes.* II.

'Tis night upon the lake. Our bed of boughs
Is built where—high above—the pine-tree soughs.
'Tis still,—and yet what woody noises loom
Against the background of the silent gloom!
One well might hear the opening of a flower
If day were hushed as this.
    j.   R. W. GILDER—*The Voice of the Pine.*

                The pines grow gray
A little, in the biting wind.
    k.   HELEN HUNT JACKSON—*March.*

Like two cathedral towers these stately pines
   Uplift their fretted summits tipped with cones;
   The arch beneath them is not built with stones,
Not Art but Nature traced these lovely lines,
   And carved this graceful arabesque of vines;
   No organ but the wind here sighs and moans,
   No sepulchre conceals a martyr's bones,
No marble bishop on his tomb reclines.
Enter! the pavement, carpeted with leaves,
   Gives back a softened echo to thy tread!
Listen! the choir is singing; all the birds,
In leafy galleries beneath the eaves,
   Are singing! listen, ere the sound be fled,
And learn there may be worship without words.
    l.   LONGFELLOW—*Sonnets. My Cathedral.*

The pine is the mother of legends.
    m.   LOWELL—*The Growth of a Legend.*

Under the yaller pines I house,
   When sunshine makes 'em all sweet-scented,
An' hear among their furry boughs
   The baskin' west-wind purr contented.
    n.   LOWELL—*The Biglow Papers.* Second
                           Series. No. 10.

To archèd walks of twilight groves,
And shadows brown that Sylvan loves,
Of pine.
    o.   MILTON—*Il Penseroso.* L. 133.

Here also grew the rougher rinded pine,
The great Argoan ship's brave ornament.
    p.   SPENSER—*Virgils Gnat.* L. 209.

                Ancient Pines,
Ye bear no record of the years of man.
Spring is your sole historian.
    q.   BAYARD TAYLOR—*The Pine Forest of
                           Monterey.*

Stately Pines,
But few more years around the promontory
Your chant will meet the thunders of the sea.

   a.   BAYARD TAYLOR—*The Pine Forest of*
      Monterey.

Poplar.
Populus Fastigiata.

Trees that, like the poplar, lift upward all
their boughs, give no shade and no shelter,
whatever their height. Trees the most lovingly shelter and shade us, when, like the
willow, the higher soar their summits, the
lowlier droop their boughs.

   b.   BULWER-LYTTON—*What Will He Do*
      With It? Bk. XI. Ch. X.
      Introductory lines.

Sloe.
Prunus Spinosa.

From the white-blossomed sloe, my dear
   Chloe requested,
A sprig her fair breast to adorn.
No! by Heav'n, I exclaim'd, may I perish,
If ever I plant in that bosom a thorn.

   c.   JOHN O'KEEFE—*The Thorn.*

In the hedge the frosted berries glow,
The scarlet holly and the purple sloe.

   d.   SARAH HELEN WHITMAN—*A Day of*
      the Indian Summer.

Spice.
Umbellularia Californica.

The Spice-Tree lives in the garden green,
   Beside it the fountain flows;
And a fair Bird sits the boughs between,
   And sings his melodious woes.

   *   *   *   *   *   *

That out-bound stem has branches three;
   On each a thousand blossoms grow;
And old as aught of time can be,
   The root stands fast in the rocks below.

   e.   JOHN STERLING—*The Spice-Tree.*
      Sts. 1 and 3.

Sycamore.
Acer Pseudo-Platanus.

Yon night moths that hover where honey
   brims over
From sycamore blossoms.

   f.   JEAN INGELOW—*Songs of Seven. Seven*
      Times Three.

Thorn.
Cratægus.

Beneath the milk-white thorn that scents the
   evening gale.

   g.   BURNS—*The Cotter's Saturday Night.*
      St. 9.

Tulip-Tree.
Liriodendron Tulipifera.

Heed not the night; a summer lodge amid
   the wild is mine—
'Tis shadowed by the tulip-tree, 'tis mantled
   by the vine.

   h.   BRYANT—*A Strange Lady.* St. 6.

The tulip-tree, high up,
Opened, in airs of June, her multitude
Of golden chalices to humming birds
And silken-winged insects of the sky.

   i.   BRYANT—*The Fountain.* St. 3.

Willow.
Salix.

Willow, in thy breezy moan,
   I can hear a deeper tone;
Through thy leaves come whispering low,
   Faint sweet sounds of long ago—
      Willow, sighing willow!

   j.   MRS. HEMANS—*Willow Song.*

All a green willow, willow,
All a green willow is my garland.

   k.   JOHN HEYWOOD—*The Green Willow.*

      A subtle red
Of life is kindling every twig and stalk
Of lowly meadow growths; the willows wrap
Their stems in furry white.

   l.   HELEN HUNT JACKSON—*March.*

The willow hangs with sheltering grace
   And benediction o'er their sod,
And Nature, hushed, assures the soul
   They rest in God.

   m.   CRAMMOND KENNEDY—*Greenwood*
      Cemetery.

Near the lake where drooped the willow,
Long time ago.

   n.   GEORGE P. MORRIS—*Near the Lake.*

Know ye the willow-tree,
   Whose grey leaves quiver,
Whispering gloomily
   To yon pale river?

Lady, at even-tide
   Wander not near it:
They say its branches hide
   A sad, lost spirit!

   o.   THACKERAY—*The Willow-Tree.*

Yew.
Taxus.

Careless, unsocial plant! that loves to dwell
'Midst skulls and coffins, epitaphs and
   worms:
Where light-heel'd ghosts and visionary
   shades,
Beneath the wan, cold Moon (as Fame re-
   ports)
Embodied, thick, perform their mystic
   rounds.
No other merriment, dull tree! is thine.

   p.   BLAIR—*The Grave.* L. 22.

For there no yew nor cypress spread their
   gloom
But roses blossom'd by each rustic tomb.

   q.   CAMPBELL—*Theodric.* L. 22.

Slips of yew
Sliver'd in the moon's eclipse.
   a.   *Macbeth.*   Act IV.   Sc. 1.   L. 27.

Of vast circumference and gloom profound,
This solitary Tree! A living thing
Produced too slowly ever to decay;
Of form and aspect too magnificent
To be destroyed.
   b.   WORDSWORTH—*Yew-Trees.*

There is a Yew-tree, pride of Lorton Vale,
Which to this day stands single, in the midst
Of its own darkness, as it stood of yore.
   c.   WORDSWORTH—*Yew-Trees.*

This lonely Yew-tree stands
Far from all human dwelling.
   d.   WORDSWORTH—*Lines left upon a Seat*
                            in a Yew-tree.

TRIALS.

Pray, pray, thou who also weepest,—
    And the drops will slacken so;
Weep, weep—and the watch thou keepest,
    With a quicker count will go.
Think,—the shadow on the dial
    For the nature most undone,
Marks the passing of the trial,
    Proves the presence of the sun.
   e.   E. B. BROWNING—*Fourfold Aspect.*

The child of trial, to mortality
    And all its changeful influences given;
On the green earth decreed to move and die,
    And yet by such a fate prepared for heaven.
   f.   SIR HUMPHREY DAVY—*Written after*
               Recovery from a Dangerous Illness.

But noble souls, through dust and heat,
Rise from disaster and defeat
    The stronger.
   g.   LONGFELLOW—*The Sifting of Peter.*
                               St. 7.

Our dearest hopes in pangs are born,
The kingliest Kings are crown'd with thorn.
   h.   GERALD MASSEY—*The Kingliest Kings.*

Rocks whereon greatest men have oftest
    wreck'd.
   i.   MILTON—*Paradise Regained.*   Bk. 2.
                              L. 228.

A grievous burthen was thy birth to me;
Tetchy and wayward was thy infancy.
   j.   *Richard III.*   Act IV.   Sc. 4.   L. 167.

As sure as ever God puts His children in the
furnace, He will be in the furnace with them.
   k.   SPURGEON—*Gleanings among the*
              Sheaves. Privileges of Trial.

There are no crown-wearers in heaven who
were not cross-bearers here below.
   l.   SPURGEON—*Gleanings among the*
                 Sheaves. Cross-Bearers.

Trials teach us what we are; they dig up
the soil, and let us see what we are made of;
they just turn up some of the ill weeds on to
the surface.
   m.   SPURGEON—*Gleanings among the*
               Sheaves. The Use of Trial.

TRIFLES.

Seeks painted trifles and fantastic toys,
And eagerly pursues imaginary joys.
   n.   AKENSIDE—*The Virtuoso.* St. 10.

These little things are great to little man.
   o.   GOLDSMITH—*The Traveller.* L. 42.

The soft droppes of raine perce the hard
Marble, many strokes overthrow the tallest
Oke.
   p.   LYLY—*Euphues.* ARBER's reprint.
                           1579.   P. 81.

At every trifle scorn to take offence;
That always shows great pride or little sense.
   q.   POPE—*Essay on Criticism.* L. 386.

A snapper-up of unconsidered trifles.
   r.   *A Winter's Tale.*   Act IV.   Sc. 3.
                               L. 26.

Come, gentlemen, we sit too long on trifles,
And waste the time, which looks for other
    revels.
   s.   *Pericles.*   Act II.   Sc. 3.   L. 92.

Trifles, light as air.
   t.   *Othello.*   Act III.   Sc. 3.   L. 322.

A trifle makes a dream, a trifle breaks.
   u.   TENNYSON—*Sea Dreams.* L. 140.

Think nought a trifle, though it small appear;
Small sands the mountain, moments make
    the year.
   v.   YOUNG—*Love of Fame.* Satire VI.
                              L. 205.

TRUST.

The greatest trust between man and man is
the trust of giving counsel.
   w.   BACON—*Essays. Of Counsel.*

                          Dear, I trusted you
As holy men trust God. You could do naught
That was not pure and loving,—though the
    deed
Might pierce me unto death.
   x.   GEORGE ELIOT—*The Spanish Gypsy.*
                               Bk. III.

Youth, health, and hope may fade, but there
    is left
A soul that trusts in Heaven, though thus of
    all bereft.
  a.   Emma Catherine Embury—*Sonnet.*
                  Confidence in Heaven.

Trust men, and they will be true to you;
treat them greatly, and they will show themselves great.
  b.   Emerson—*Essays. On Prudence.*

                       I too
Will cast the spear and leave the rest to Jove.
  c.   Homer—*Iliad.* Bk. XVII. L. 622.
                      Bryant's trans.

                 If he were
To be made honest by an act of parliament
I should not alter in my faith of him.
  d.   Ben Jonson—*The Devil Is an Ass.*
                     Act IV. Sc. 1.

Better trust all and be deceived,
  And weep that trust and that deceiving,
Than doubt one heart, that, if believed,
  Had blessed one's life with true believing.
  e.   Frances Anne Kemble—*Faith.*

O holy trust! O endless sense of rest!
  Like the beloved John
To lay his head upon the Saviour's breast,
  And thus to journey on!
  f.   Longfellow—*Hymn.* St. 5.

To be trusted is a greater compliment than
to be loved.
  g.   George Macdonald—*The Marquis of
                Lossie.* Ch. IV.

That, in tracing the shade, I shall find out
    the sun,
Trust to me!
  h.   Owen Meredith (Lord Lytton)—
          Lucile. Pt. II. Canto VI. St. 15.

        "Eyes to the blind"
Thou art, O God! Earth I no longer see,
Yet trustfully my spirit looks to thee.
  i.   Alice Bradley Neal—*Blind.* Pt. II.

You may trust him in the dark.
  j.   *Roman Proverb Cited by Cicero.*

               I well believe
Thou wilt not utter what thou dost not know;
And so far will I trust thee.
  k.   *Henry IV.* Pt. I. Act II. Sc. 3.
                     L. 114.

Let every eye negotiate for itself,
And trust no agent.
  l.   *Much Ado About Nothing.* Act II.
                 Sc. 1. L. 185.
My life upon her faith!
  m.   *Othello.* Act I. Sc. 3. L. 295.

TRUST (PUBLIC).

All persons possessing any portion of power
ought to be strongly and awfully impressed
with an idea that they act in trust, and that
they are to account for their conduct in that
trust to the one great Master, Author, and
Founder of society.
  n.   Burke—*Reflections on the Revolution in
                      France.*

To execute laws is a royal office; to execute
orders is not to be a king. However, a political executive magistracy, though merely
such, is a great trust.
  o.   Burke—*Reflections on the Revolution in
                      France.*

Public officers are the servants and agents
of the people, to execute laws which the
people have made and within the limits of a
constitution which they have established.
  p.   Grover Cleveland—*Letter of
          Acceptance as Candidate for
          Governor.* Oct. 7, 1882.
          See W. O. Stoddard's
          Life of Cleveland.
          Ch. IX.

I repeat, * * * that all power is a trust—
that we are accountable for its exercise.
  q.   Benj. Disraeli—*Vivian Grey.*
                Bk. VI. Ch. VII.

Public office is a public trust, the authority
and opportunities of which must be used as
absolutely as the public moneys for the public
benefit, and not for the purposes of any individual or party.
  r.   Dorman B. Eaton—*The "Spoils"
         System and Civil-Service Reform.*
         Ch. III. *The Merit System.*

It is not fit the public trusts should be
lodged in the hands of any till they are first
proved and found fit for the business they
are to be entrusted with.
  s.   Mathew Henry—*Commentaries.*

When a man assumes a public trust, he
should consider himself as public property.
  t.   Thos. Jefferson—See Rayner's *Life
         of Jefferson.* P. 356.

Public office is a public trust.
  u.   Dan. S. Lamont—*Motto of a Campaign
         Pamphlet.* 1884.

The appointing power of the Pope is treated
as a public trust, and not as a personal per-
quisite.
  v.   Chas. Sumner—*Speech in the United
         States Senate.* May 31, 1872.

TRUTH.

Yet the deepest truths are best read between the lines, and, for the most part, refuse to be written.

   a.   Amos Bronson Alcott—*Concord Days.*
                June. Goethe.

But no pleasure is comparable to the standing upon the vantage ground of Truth.

   b.   Bacon—*Essays. Of Truth.*

Who never doubted, never half believed,
Where doubt, there truth is,—'tis her shadow.

   c.   Bailey—*Festus.* Sc. *A Country
        Town. Market-Place. Noon.* L. 29.

How sweet the words of Truth, breath'd from the lips of Love.

   d.   Beattie—*The Minstrel.* Bk. II.
                    St. 53.

Whoever lives true life will love true love.

   e.   E. B. Browning—*Aurora Leigh.*
              Bk. I. L. 1,096.

Truth crushed to earth shall rise again:
  Th' eternal years of God are hers;
But Error, wounded, writhes in pain,
  And dies among his worshippers.

   f.   Bryant—*The Battle Field.* St. 9.

For truth is precious and divine;
Too rich a pearl for carnal swine.

   g.   Butler—*Hudibras.* Pt. II. Canto II.
                    L. 257.

More proselytes and converts use t' accrue
To false persuasions than the right and true;
For error and mistake are infinite,
But truth has but one way to be i' th' right.

   h.   Butler—*Miscellaneous Thoughts.*
                    L. 113.

True as the dial to the sun,
Although it be not shin'd upon.

   i.   Butler—*Hudibras.* Pt. III.
             Canto II. L. 175.

But now being lifted into high society,
  And having pick'd up several odds and
    ends
Of free thoughts in his travels for variety,
  He deem'd, being in a lone isle, among
    friends,
That without any danger of a riot, he
  Might for long lying make himself amends;
And singing as he sung in his warm youth,
Agree to a short armistice with truth.

   j.   Byron—*Don Juan.* Canto III.
                    St. 83.

No words suffice the secret soul to show,
For Truth denies all eloquence to Woe.

   k.   Byron—*The Corsair.* Canto III.
                    St. 22.

'Tis strange—but true; for truth is always
  strange,
Stranger than fiction.

   l.   Byron—*Don Juan.* Canto XIV.
                  St. 101.

A man protesting against error is on the way towards uniting himself with all men that believe in truth.

   m.   Carlyle—*Heroes and Hero Worship.*
                    Lecture IV.

We have oftener than once endeavoured to attach some meaning to that aphorism, vulgarly imputed to Shaftesbury, which however we can find nowhere in his works, that "ridicule is the test of truth."

   n.   Carlyle—*Essays. Voltaire.*

When fiction rises pleasing to the eye,
Men will believe, because they love the lie;
But truth herself, if clouded with a frown,
Must have some solemn proof to pass her
    down.

   o.   Churchill—*Epistle to Hogarth.*
                    L. 291.

O, Truth is easy, and the light shines clear
In hearts kept open, honest and sincere.

   p.   Abraham Coles—*The Evangel.* P. 183.

The power to bind and loose to Truth is
  given:
The mouth that speaks it is the mouth of
  Heaven.
The power, which in a sense belongs to none,
Thus understood belongs to every one.

   q.   Abraham Coles—*The Evangel.* P. 181.

But truths on which depends our main con-
  cern,
That 'tis our shame and misery not to learn,
Shine by the side of every path we tread
With such a lustre he that runs may read.

   r.   Cowper—*Tirocinium.* L. 77.

But what is truth? 'Twas Pilate's question
  put
To Truth itself, that deign'd him no reply.

   s.   Cowper—*The Task.* Bk. III. L. 270.

For truth is unwelcome, however divine.

   t.   Cowper—*The Flatting Mill.* St. 6.

Jane borrow'd maxims from a doubting
  school,
And took for truth the test of ridicule;
Lucy saw no such virtue in a jest,
Truth was with her of ridicule the test.

   u.   Crabbe—*Tales of the Hall.* Bk. VIII.
                    L. 126.

Nature * * * has buried truth deep in the bottom of the sea.

   v.   Democritus—*Quoted by Cicero.*
        Academic Questions. Bk. II. Ch. X.
                C. D. Yonge's trans.

For truth has such a face and such a mien,
As to be lov'd needs only to be seen.

   w.   Dryden—*The Hind and the Panther.*
                  Pt. I. L. 33.

Truth has rough flavours if we bite it through.
a.   GEORGE ELIOT—*Armgart.* Sc. 2.

The nobler the truth or sentiment, the less
imports the question of authorship.
b.   EMERSON—*Letters and Social Aims.*
                    Quotation and Originality.

Though love repine and reason chafe,
  There came a voice without reply,
" Tis man's perdition to be safe,
  When for the truth he ought to die."
c.   EMERSON—*Quatrains. Sacrifice.*

Truth only smells sweet forever, and illusions, however innocent, are deadly as the
canker worm.
d.   FROUDE—*Short Studies on Great
                    Subjects. Calvinsim.*

Lest men suspect your tale untrue,
Keep probability in view.
e.   GAY—*The Painter who Pleased Nobody
                    and Everybody.*

One truth discovered is immortal, and en-
titles its author to be so : for, like a new substance in nature, it cannot be destroyed.
f.   HAZLITT—*The Spirit of the Age.
                    Jeremy Bentham.*

Dare to be true, nothing can need a lie ;
A fault which needs it most, grows two
  thereby.
g.   HERBERT—*The Temple. The Church
                    Porch.*

Truth is tough. It will not break, like a
bubble, at a touch ; nay, you may kick it
about all day, like a foot-ball, and it will be
round and full at evening.
h.   O. W. HOLMES—*The Professor at the
                    Breakfast Table.* V.

The best way to come to truth being to ex-
amine things as really they are, and not to
conclude they are, as we fancy of ourselves,
or have been taught by others to imagine.
i.   LOCKE—*Human Understanding.*
                    Bk. II. Ch. XII.

To love truth for truth's sake is the principal part of human perfection in this world,
and the seed-plot of all other virtues.
j.   LOCKE—*Letter to Anthony Collins, Esq.*
                    Oct. 29, 1703.

When by night the frogs are croaking, kindle
  but a torch's fire ;
Ha! how soon they all are silent! Thus
  Truth silences the liar.
k.   FRIEDRICH VON LOGAU—See
                    Longfellow's trans. *Poetic
                    Aphorisms. Truth.*

Get but the truth once uttered, and 'tis like
A star new-born that drops into its place
And which, once circling in its placid round,
Not all the tumult of the earth can shake.
l.   LOWELL—*A Glance Behind the Curtain.*
                    L. 173.

Put golden padlocks on Truth's lips, be callous as ye will,
From soul to soul, o'er all the world, leaps
  one electric thrill.
m.   LOWELL—*On the Capture of Certain
                    Fugitive Slaves near Washington.*

Then to side with Truth is noble when we
  share her wretched crust,
Ere her cause bring fame and profit, and 'tis
  prosperous to be just ;
Then it is the brave man chooses, while the
  coward stands aside,
Doubting in his abject spirit, till his Lord is
  crucified.
n.   LOWELL—*The Present Crisis.*

Truth forever on the scaffold. Wrong forever
  on the throne.
o.   LOWELL—*The Present Crisis.*

Arm thyself for the truth !
p.   BULWER-LYTTON—*The Lady of Lyons.*
                    Act V. Sc. 1.

Truth makes on the ocean of nature no one
track of light—every eye looking on finds its
own.
q.   BULWER-LYTTON—*Caxtoniana.*
                    Essay XIV.

But there is no veil like light—no adamantine armor against hurt like the truth.
r.   GEORGE MACDONALD—*The Marquis of
                    Lossie.* Ch. LXXI.

Truth, when not sought after, sometimes
  comes to light.
s.   MENANDER—*Ex Verberatá.* P. 160.

Not a truth has to art or to science been
  given,
But brows have ached for it, and souls toil'd
  and striven ;
And many have striven, and many have
  fail'd,
And many died, slain by the truth they
  assail'd.
t.   OWEN MEREDITH (Lord Lytton)—
                    Lucile. Pt. II. Canto VI. St. 1.

Ev'n them who kept thy truth so pure of
  old,
When all our fathers worshipp'd stocks and
  stones,
Forget not.
u.   MILTON—*Sonnet. Massacre in
                    Piedmont.*

Truth is as impossible to be soiled by any
outward touch as the sunbeam.
v.   MILTON—*The Doctrine and Discipline
                    of Divorce.*

Who ever knew truth put to the worse in
a free and open encounter?
w.   MILTON—*Areopagitica.*

I speak truth, not so much as I would, but as much as I dare; and I dare a little the more as I grow older.

a.   MONTAIGNE—*Essays. Of Repentance.*

This world is all a fleeting show,
  For man's illusion given;
The smiles of joy, the tears of woe,
Deceitful shine, deceitful flow,—
  There's nothing true but Heaven.

b.   MOORE—*This World is all a Fleeting Show.*

Farewell then, verse, and love, and ev'ry toy,
The rhymes and rattles of the man or boy;
What right, what true, what fit we justly call,
Let this be all my care—for this is all.

c.   POPE—*First Book of Horace.* Ep. I. L. 17.

'Tis not enough your counsel still be true;
Blunt truths more mischief than nice falsehoods do.

d.   POPE—*Essay on Criticism.* Pt. III. L. 13.

When truth or virtue an affront endures,
Th' affront is mine, my friend, and should be yours.

e.   POPE—*Epilogue to Satires.* Dialogue II. L. 207.

And simple truth miscall'd simplicity,
And captive good attending captain ill.

f.   *Sonnet LXVI.*

                    But 'tis strange:
And oftentimes, to win us to our harm,
The instruments of darkness tell us truths,
Win us with honest trifles, to betray 's
In deepest consequence.

g.   *Macbeth.* Act I. Sc. 3. L. 122.

But wonder on, till truth make all things plain.

h.   *Midsummer-Night's Dream.* Act. V. Sc. 1. L. 129.

If circumstances lead me, I will find
Where truth is hid, though it were hid indeed
Within the centre.

i.   *Hamlet.* Act II. Sc. 2. L. 157.

Mark now, how a plain tale shall put you down.

j.   *Henry IV.* Pt. I. Act II. Sc. 4. L. 281.

Methinks the truth should live from age to age,
As 'twere retail'd to all posterity,
Even to the general all-ending day.

k.   *Richard III.* Act III. Sc. 1. L. 76.

            Tell truth and shame the devil.
If thou have power to raise him, bring him hither,
And I'll be sworn I have power to shame him hence.

l.   *Henry IV.* Pt. I. Act III. Sc. 1. L. 59.

That truth should be silent I had almost forgot.

m.   *Antony and Cleopatra.* Act II. Sc. 2. L. 110.

They breathe truth that breathe their words in pain.

n.   *Richard II.* Act II. Sc. 1. L. 8.

            To thine own self be true,
And it must follow, as the night the day,
Thou canst not then be false to any man.

o.   *Hamlet.* Act I. Sc. 3. L. 78.

            Truth is truth
To the end of reckoning.

p.   *Measure for Measure.* Act V. Sc. 1. L. 45.

Truth needs no colour, with his colour fix'd;
Beauty no pencil, beauty's truth to lay;
But best is best, if never intermix'd.

q.   *Sonnet CI.*

What, can the devil speak true?

r.   *Macbeth.* Act I. Sc. 3. L. 107.

The truth is always right.

s.   SOPHOCLES—*Antigone.* 1195. Oxford trans. (Revised by Buckley.)

Truth and, by consequence, liberty, will always be the chief power of honest men.

t.   MADAME DE STAËL—*Coppet et Weimar. Letter to Gen. Moreau*

Truth is the work of God; lies are the works of man.

u.   MADAME DE STAËL—*Germany.* Pt. IV. Ch. II

Tell truth, and shame the devil.

v.   SWIFT—*Mary, the Cookmaid's Letter.*

And friendly free discussion calling forth
From the fair jewel Truth its latent ray.

w.   THOMSON—*Liberty.* Pt. II. L. 220.

There are truths which are not for all men, nor for all times.

x.   VOLTAIRE—*Letter to Cardinal de Bernis.* April 23, 1761.

There is nothing so powerful as truth; and often nothing so strange.

y.   DANIEL WEBSTER—*Argument on the Murder of Captain White.* Vol. VI. P. 68.

The sages say, Dame Truth delights to dwell
(Strange Mansion!) in the bottom of a well:
Questions are then the Windlass and the rope
That pull the grave old Gentlewoman up.

z.   JOHN WOLCOTT (Peter Pindar)— *Birthday Ode.*

Truths that wake
To perish never.
   a.   WORDSWORTH—*Ode. Intimations of
                              Immortality.* St. 9.

Truth never was indebted to a lie.
   b.   YOUNG—*Night Thoughts.* Night VIII.
                              L. 587.

TWILIGHT.

          The sunbeams dropped
Their gold, and, passing in porch and niche,
Softened to shadows, silvery, pale, and dim,
As if the very Day paused and grew Eve.
   c.   EDWIN ARNOLD—*Light of Asia.*
                              Bk. II. L. 466.

          Fair Venus shines
Even in the eye of day; with sweetest beam
Propitious shines, and   shakes a trembling
   flood
Of softened radiance from her dewy locks.
   d.   ANNA LETITIA BARBAULD—*A Summer
                   Evening's Meditation.* L. 10.

When the sun's last rays are fading
   Into twilight soft and dim.
   e.   THEODORE L. BARKER—*Thou Wilt Think
                          of Me Again.*

The summer day is closed, the sun is set:
Well they have done their office, those bright
   hours,
The latest of whose train goes softly out
In the red west.
   f.   BRYANT—*An Evening Reverie.*

                 Parting day
Dies like the dolphin, whom each pang im-
   bues
With a new colour as it gasps away,
The last still loveliest, till—'tis gone—and all
   is gray.
   g.   BYRON—*Childe Harold.* Canto IV.
                              St. 29.
'Twas twilight, and the sunless day went
   down
   Over the waste of waters; like a veil,
Which, if withdrawn, would but disclose the
   frown
Of one whose hate is mask'd but to assail.
   h.   BYRON—*Don Juan.* Canto II. St. 49.

How lovely are the portals of the night,
   When stars come out to watch the daylight
   die.
   i.   · THOMAS COLE—*Twilight.* See
           LOUIS L. NOBLE's *Life and Works of
                           Cole.* Ch. XXXV.

Now the last red ray is gone;
   Now the twilight shadows hie.
   j.   SUSAN COOLIDGE—*Angelus.*

          Beauteous Night lay dead
Under the pall of twilight, and the love-star
   sickened and shrank.
   k.   GEORGE ELIOT—*Spanish Gypsy.*
                              Bk. II.

Along the west the golden bars
   Still to a deeper glory grew;
Above our heads the faint few stars
   Looked out from the unfathomed blue;
And the fair city's clamorous jars
   Seemed melted in the evening hue.
   l.   W. B. GLAZIER—*Cape-Cottage at
                              Sunset.*

In the twilight of morning to climb to the top
   of the mountain,—
Thee to salute, kindly star, earliest herald of
   day,—
And to await, with impatience, the gaze of
   the ruler of heaven.—
Youthful delight, oh, how oft lur'st thou me
   out in the night.
   m.   GOETHE—*Venetian Epigrams.*

Sweet shadows of twilight! how calm their
   repose,
While the dewdrops fall soft in the breast of
   the rose!
How blest to the toiler his hour of release
When the vesper is heard with its whisper of
   peace!
   n.   O. W. HOLMES—*Poems of the Class of
                   '29. Our Banker.* St. 12.

          The lengthening shadows wait
The first pale stars of twilight.
   o.   O. W. HOLMES—*Poems of the Class of
                   '29. Even Song.* St. 6.

Like our dawn, merely a sob of light.
   p.   VICTOR HUGO—*La Legende des Siècles.*

The gloaming comes, the day is spent,
   The sun goes out of sight,
And painted is the occident
   With purple sanguine bright.
   q.   ALEXANDER HUME—*The Story of a
                          Summer Day.*

The sun is set; and in his latest beams
Yon little cloud of ashen gray and gold,
Slowly upon the amber air unrolled,
The falling mantle of the Prophet seems.
   r.   LONGFELLOW—*A Summer Day by the
                              Sea.*

The twilight is sad and cloudy,
   The wind blows wild and free,
And like the wings of sea-birds
   Flash the white caps of the sea.
   s.   LONGFELLOW—*Twilight.*

The west is broken into bars
   Of orange, gold, and gray;
Gone is the sun, come are the stars,
   And night infolds the day.
   t.   GEORGE MACDONALD—*Songs of the
                          Summer Nights.*

Dim eclipse, disastrous twilight.
   u.   MILTON—*Paradise Lost.* Bk. I. L. 597.

From that high mount of God whence light
   and shade
Spring both, the face of brightest heaven
   had changed
To grateful twilight.
  a.   Milton—*Paradise Lost.* Bk. V.
                            L. 643.

O, the sweet, sweet twilight just before the
   time of rest,
When the black clouds are driven away, and
   the stormy winds suppressed.
  b.   D. M. Mulock—*Thirty Years.*
                    Twilight in the North.

O, Twilight! Spirit that does render birth
To dim enchantments, melting heaven with
   earth,
Leaving on craggy hills and running streams
A softness like atmosphere of dreams.
  c.   Mrs. Norton—*Picture of Twilight.*

      * * * th' approach of night
The skies yet blushing with departing light,
When falling dews with spangles deck'd the
   glade,
And the low sun had lengthen'd ev'ry shade.
  d.   Pope—*Pastorals. Autumn.* L. 98.

     In the vale beneath the hill
The evening's growing purple strengthens.
  e.   Margaret J. Preston—*Old Songs and*
                    New. Afternoon.

Night was drawing and closing her curtain
up above the world, and down beneath it.
  f.   Richter—*Flower, Fruit, and Thorn*
                    Pieces. Ch. II.

Twilight's soft dews steal o'er the village-
   green,
With magic tints to harmonize the scene.
Stilled is the hum that through the hamlet
   broke
When round the ruins of their ancient oak
The peasants flocked to hear the minstrel
   play,
And games and carols closed the busy day.
  g.   Sam'l Rogers—*Pleasures of Memory.*
                         Pt. I. L. 1.

Ah, County Guy, the hour is nigh,
   The sun has left the lea,
The orange flower perfumes the bower,
   The breeze is on the sea.
  h.   Scott—*Quentin Durward.* Ch. IV.

Gilding pale streams with heavenly alchemy.
  i.   *Sonnet XXXIII.*

        Look, the gentle day
Before the wheels of Phœbus, round about
Dapples the drowsy east with spots of grey.
  j.   *Much Ado About Nothing.* Act V.
                      Sc. 3. L. 25.

The glow-worm shows the matin to be near,
And 'gins to pale his uneffectual fire.
  k.   *Hamlet.* Act I. Sc. 5. L. 89.
   40

The hour before the heavenly-harness'd team
Begins his golden progress in the east.
  l.   *Henry IV.* Pt. I. Act III. Sc. 1.
                          L. 221.

The weary sun hath made a golden set,
And, by the bright track of his fiery car,
Gives signal of a goodly day to-morrow.
  m.   *Richard III.* Act V. Sc. 3. L. 19.

The west yet glimmers with some streaks of
   day :
Now spurs the lated traveller apace,
To gain the timely inn.
  n.   *Macbeth.* Act III. Sc. 3. L. 5.

Twilight, ascending slowly from the east,
Entwined in duskier wreaths her braided
   locks
O'er the fair front and radiant eyes of day ;
Night followed, clad with stars.
  o.   Shelley—*Alastor.*

            Now the soft hour
Of walking comes ; for him who lonely loves
To seek the distant hills, and there converse
With Nature, there to harmonize his heart,
And in pathetic Song to breathe around
The harmony to others.
  p.   Thomson—*Seasons. Summer.* L. 1,378.

TYRANNY.

  A king ruleth as he ought, a tyrant as he
lists, a king to the profit of all, a tyrant only
to please a few.
  q.   Aristotle.

             The tyrant now
Trusts not to men : nightly within his chamber
The watch-dog guards his couch, the only
   friend
He now dare trust.
  r.   Joanna Baillie—*Ethwald.* Pt. II.
                         Act V. Sc. 3.

Th' oppressive, sturdy, man-destroying villains,
Who ravag'd kingdoms, and laid empires
   waste,
And in a cruel wantonness of power,
Thinn'd states of half their people, and gave
   up
To want the rest.
  s.   Blair—*The Grave.* L. 9.

                  Tyranny
Absolves all faith ; and who invades our
   rights,
Howe'er his own commence, can never be
But an usurper.
  t.   Henry Brooke—*Gustavus Vasa.*
                       Act IV. Sc. 1.

Think'st thou there is no tyranny but that
Of blood and chains? The despotism of
    vice—
The weakness and the wickedness of luxury—
The negligence—the apathy—the evils
Of sensual sloth—produce ten thousand
    tyrants,
Whose delegated cruelty surpasses
The worst acts of one energetic master,
However harsh and hard in his own bearing.
  a.   Byron—*Sardanapalus.* Act I. Sc. 2.

                       Tyranny
Is far the worst of treasons. Dost thou deem
None rebels except subjects? The prince
    who
Neglects or violates his trust is more
A brigand than the robber-chief.
  b.   Byron—*The Two Foscari.* Act II.
                            Sc. 1.

There is nothing more hostile to a city than
a tyrant, under whom in the first and chiefest place, there are not laws in common, but
one man, keeping the law himself to himself,
has the sway, and this is no longer equal.
  c.   Euripides—*Suppliants.* 429. Oxford
            trans. (Revised by Buckley.)

'Twixt kings and tyrants there's this differ-
    ence known :
Kings seek their subjects' good, tyrants their
    owne.
  d.   Herrick—*Kings and Tyrants.*

Men are still men. The despot's wickedness
Comes of ill teaching, and of power's excess,—
Comes of the purple he from childhood wears,
Slaves would be tyrants if the chance were
    theirs.
  e.   Victor Hugo—*The Vanished City.*

      Bleed, bleed, poor country !
Great Tyranny ! lay thou thy basis sure,
For goodness dares not check thee !
  f.   *Macbeth.* Act IV. Sc. 3. L. 31.

For how can tyrants safely govern home,
Unless abroad they purchase great alliance?
  g.   *Henry VI.* Pt. III. Act III. Sc. 3.
                            L. 69.

For what is he they follow? truly, gentlemen,
A bloody tyrant, and a homicide :
One rais'd in blood, and one in blood estab-
    lish'd ;
One that made means to come by what he
    hath,
And slaughter'd those that were the means to
    help him ;
A base foul stone, made precious by the foil
Of England's chair, where he is falsely set;
One that hath ever been God's enemy.
  h.   *Richard III.* Act V. Sc. 3. L. 245.

I knew him tyrannous, and tyrants' fears
Decrease not, but grow faster than the years.
  i.   *Pericles.* Act I. Sc. 2. L. 84.

            O nation miserable,
With an untitled tyrant bloody-scepter'd
When shalt thou see thy wholesome days
    again?
  j.   *Macbeth.* Act IV. Sc. 3. L. 103.

This tyrant, whose sole name blisters our
    tongues,
Was once thought honest.
  k.   *Macbeth.* Act IV. Sc. 3. L. 12.

A company of tyrants is inaccessible to all
    seductions.
  l.   Voltaire—*A Philosophical Dictionary.*
                            Tyranny.

The sovereign is called a tyrant who knows
no laws but his caprice.
  m.   Voltaire—*A Philosophical Dictionary.*
                            Tyranny.

U.

UMBRELLA-MAKING

(*See* Occupations).

UNBELIEF.

The fearful Unbelief is unbelief in yourself.
  n.   Carlyle—*Sartor Resartus. The
           Everlasting No.* Bk. II. Ch. VII.

There is no strength in unbelief. Even the
unbelief of what is false is no source of might.
It is the truth shining from behind that gives
the strength to disbelieve.
  o.   George Macdonald—*The Marquis of
           Lossie.* Ch. XLII.

Unbelief is blind.
  p.   Milton—*Comus.* L. 519.

More strange than true. I never may believe
These antique fables, nor these fairy toys.
  q.   *Midsummer-Night's Dream.* Act V.
                          Sc. 1. L. 2.

UNDERTAKERS (*See* Occupations).

UNITY.

Two Souls in one, two Hearts into one Heart !
  r.   Du Bartas—*Divine Weekes and Workes.*
           First week, sixth day. L. 1,057.

Two souls with but a single thought,
Two hearts that beat as one.

   a.   Von Munch Bellinghausen—
         Ingomar, the Barbarian. Act II.
         Sc. 1. Maria Lovell's trans.

When bad men combine, the good must associate; else they will fall, one by one, an unpitied sacrifice in a contemptible struggle.

   b.   Burke—*Thoughts on the Cause of the
         Present Discontent.*

I never use the word "nation" in speaking of the United States. I always use the word "Union" or "Confederacy." We are not a nation but a *union*, a confederacy of equal and sovereign States.

   c.   J. C. Calhoun—*To Oliver Dyer.*
         Jan. 1, 1849.

The Constitution in all its provisions looks to an indestructible union composed of indestructible States.

   d.   Salmon P. Chase—*Decision in Texas
         vs. White.* See Werden's *Private
         Life and Public Services of
         Salmon P. Chase.* P. 664.

Like two single gentlemen rolled into one.

   e.   Geo. Colman (the Younger)—*Broad
         Grins. Lodgings for Single Gentlemen.*

By uniting we stand, by dividing we fall.

   f.   John Dickinson—*The Liberty Song.*

When our two lives grew like two buds that kiss
At lightest thrill from the bee's swinging chime,
Because the one so near the other is.

   g.   George Eliot—*Brother and Sister.*
         Pt. I. St. 1.

We must all hang together or assuredly we shall all hang separately.

   h.   Benj. Franklin—*At Signing of the
         Declaration of Independence.*
         July 4, 1776.

Our Union is river, lake, ocean, and sky:
Man breaks not the medal, when God cuts the die!
Though darkened with sulphur, though cloven with steel,
The blue arch will brighten, the waters will heal!

   i.   O. W. Holmes—*Brother Jonathan's
         Lament for Sister Caroline.* St. 7.

There with commutual zeal we both had strove
In acts of dear benevolence and love;
Brothers in peace, not rivals in command.

   j.   Homer—*Odyssey.* Bk. IV. L. 241.
         Pope's trans.

Then none was for a party;
  Then all were for the state;
Then the great man helped the poor,
  And the poor man loved the great:
Then lands were fairly portioned;
  Then spoils were fairly sold:
The Romans were like brothers
  In the brave days of old.

   k.   Macaulay—*Lays of Ancient Rome.
         Horatius.* St. 32.

Oh, shame to men! devil with devil damn'd
Firm concord holds, men only disagree
Of creatures rational.

   l.   Milton—*Paradise Lost.* Bk. II.
         L. 496.

The union of lakes—the union of lands—
  The union of States none can sever—
The union of hearts—the union of hands—
  And the flag of our Union for ever!

   m.   George P. Morris—*The Flag of Our
         Union.*

        So we grew together,
Like to a double cherry, seeming parted,
But yet a union in partition;
Two lovely berries moulded on one stem:
So, with two seeming bodies, but one heart;
Two of the first, like coats in heraldry,
Due but to one and crowned with one crest.

   n.   *Midsummer-Night's Dream.* Act III.
         Sc. 2. L. 208.

They're as like each other as are peas.

   o.   Swift—*Horace.* Bk. I. Ep. V.
         L. 138.

Their meetings made December June.
  Their every parting was to die.

   p.   Tennyson—*In Memoriam.* XCVII.

Liberty and Union, now and forever, one and inseparable.

   q.   Daniel Webster—*Second Speech on
         Foot's Resolution.* Jan. 26, 1830.

One Country, one Constitution, one Destiny.

   r.   Daniel Webster—*Speech.* March 15,
         1837.

UNKINDNESS.

As "unkindness has no remedy at law," let its avoidance be with you a point of honor.

   s.   Hosea Ballou—*MS. Sermons.*

Hard Unkindness' alter'd eye,
  That mocks the tear it forced to flow.

   t.   Gray—*Eton College.* St. 8.

In nature there's no blemish but the mind;
None can be call'd deform'd but the unkind.

   u.   *Twelfth Night.* Act III. Sc. 4.
         L. 401.

        She hath tied
Sharp-tooth'd unkindness, like a vulture here.

   v.   *King Lear.* Act II. Sc. 4. L. 136.

        Unkindness may do much;
And his unkindness may defeat my life,
But never taint my love.

   w.   *Othello.* Act IV. Sec. 2. L. 158.

V.

VALENTINE'S DAY.

On paper curiously shaped
  Scribblers to-day of every sort,
In verses Valentines yclep'd,
  To Venus chime their annual court.
I too will swell the motley throng,
  And greet the all auspicious day,
Whose privilege permits my song
  My love thus secret to convey.
  a.   HENRY G. BOHN—*MS. Dictionary of*
         Poetical Quotations. Valentines.

Oft have I heard both youths and virgins say,
Birds chuse their mates and couple too this
    day:
But by their flight I never can devine
When I shall couple with my valentine.
  b.   HERRICK—*To his Valentine, on St.*
             Valentine's Day.

No popular respect will I omit
To do the honour on this happy day,
When every loyal lover tasks his wit
His simple truth in studious rhymes to
    pay,
And to his mistress dear his hopes convey.
Rather thou knowest I would still outrun
All calendars with Love's whose date alway
Thy bright eyes govern better than the
    Sun,—
For with thy favour was my life begun,
And still I reckon on from smiles to smiles,
And not by summers, for I thrive on none
But those thy cheerful countenance compiles;
Oh! if it be to choose and call thee mine,
Love, thou art every day my Valentine!
  c.   HOOD—*Sonnet. For the 14th of*
                  February.

Oh, cruel heart! ere these posthumous papers
  Have met thine eyes, I shall be out of
  breath;
Those cruel eyes, like two funereal tapers,
  Have only lighted me the way to death.
Perchance thou wilt extinguish them in
  vapours,
When I am gone, and green grass covereth
Thy lover, lost; but it will be in vain—
It will not bring the vital spark again.
  d.   HOOD—*A Valentine.*

Hail to thy returning festival, old Bishop
Valentine! Great is thy name in the rubric,
Thou venerable arch flamen of Hymen. * * *
Like unto thee, assuredly, there is no other
mitred father in the calendar.
  e.   CHARLES LAMB—*Essays. Valentine's*
                      Day.

Apollo has peeped through the shutter,
  And awaken'd the witty and fair;
The boarding-school belle's in a flutter,
  The twopenny post's in despair;
The breath of the morning is flinging
  A magic on blossom and spray,
And cockneys and sparrows are singing
  In chorus on Valentine's day.
  f.   PRAED—*Song for 14th of February.*

         Saint Valentine is past;
Begin these wood-birds but to couple now?
  g.   *Midsummer-Night's Dream.* Act IV.
                    Sc. 1. L. 144.

To-morrow is Saint Valentine's day,
  All in the morning betime,
And I a maid at your window,
  To be your Valentine.
  h.   *Hamlet.* Act IV. Sc. 5. L. 48.

VALOR.

But where life is more terrible than death, it
is then the truest valour to dare to live.
  i.   SIR THOMAS BROWNE—*Religio Medici.*
                      Pt. XLIV.

There is always safety in valor.
  j.   EMERSON—*English Traits. The Times.*

Valor consists in the power of self-recovery.
  k.   EMERSON—*Essays. Circles.*

         A valiant man
Ought not to undergo, or tempt a danger,
But worthily, and by selected ways.
He undertakes with reason, not by chance.
His valor is the salt t' his other virtues,
They're all unseason'd without it.
  l.   BEN JONSON—*New Inn.* Act IV.
                        Sc. 3.

      In vain doth valour bleed,
While Avarice and Rapine share the land.
  m.   MILTON—*Sonnet. To the Lord General*
                        Fairfax.

He's truly valiant that can wisely suffer
The worst that man can breathe and make
  his wrongs
His outsides, to wear them like his raiment,
  carelessly;
And ne'er prefer his injuries to his heart.
To bring it into danger.
  n.   *Timon of Athens.* Act III. Sc. 5.
                        L. 31.

       'Tis much he dares;
And, to that dauntless temper of his mind,
He hath a wisdom that doth guide his valour
To act in safety.
  o.   *Macbeth.* Act III. Sc. 1. L. 51.

What valour were it, when a cur doth grin,
For one to thrust his hand between his teeth,
When he might spurn him with his foot,
     away?
a.   *Henry VI.* Pt. III. Act I. Sc. 4.
                                    L. 56.

     When valour preys on reason,
It eats the sword it fights with.
b.   *Antony and Cleopatra.* Act III.
                             Sc. 3. L. 199.

But dream not helm and harness
     The sign of valor true;
Peace hath higher tests of manhood
     Than battle ever knew.
c.   WHITTIER—*Poems. The Hero.* St. 19.

VANITY.

     It beareth the name of Vanity Fair, because
the town where it is kept is "lighter than
vanity."
d.   BUNYAN—*Pilgrim's Progress.* Pt. I.

Ecclesiastes said that "all is vanity,"
     Most modern preachers say the same, or
         show it
By their examples of true Christianity :
     In short, all know, or very soon may know it.
e.   BYRON—*Don Juan.* Canto VII. St. 6.

Sooth'd with the sound, the king grew vain :
Fought all his battles o'er again ;
And thrice he routed all his foes, and thrice
     he slew the slain.
f.   DRYDEN—*Alexander's Feast.* L. 66.

     Vanity is as ill at ease under indifference
as tenderness is under a love which it cannot
return.
g.   GEORGE ELIOT—*Daniel Deronda.*
                             Bk. I. Ch. X.

     Those who live on vanity must not unrea-
sonably expect to die of mortification.
h.   MRS. ELLIS—*Pictures of Private Life.*
                 Second Series. The Pains of
                         Pleasing. Ch. III.

How many saucy airs we meet,
From Temple Bar to Aldgate street !
i.   GAY—*The Barley-Mow and Dunghill.*
                                    L. 1.

Vain? Let it be so! Nature was her teacher,
What if a lovely and unsistered creature
Loved her own harmless gift of pleasing
     feature.
j.   O. W. HOLMES—*Iris, Her Book.*
         The Professor at the Breakfast-Table.
                                    X.

What is your sex's earliest, latest care,
Your heart's supreme ambition? To be fair.
k.   LORD LYTTLETON—*Advice to a Lady.*
                                    L. 17.

And not a vanity is given in vain.
l.   POPE—*Essay on Man.* Ep. II. L. 290.

Here files of pins extend their shining rows,
Puffs, powders, patches, bibles, billet-doux.
m.   POPE—*Rape of the Lock.* Canto I.
                                    L. 137.

Hoy-day, what a sweep of vanity comes this
     way !
n.   *Timon of Athens.* Act I. Sc. 2.
                                    L. 137.

Light vanity, insatiate cormorant,
Consuming means, soon preys upon itself.
o.   *Richard II.* Act II. Sc. 1. L. 38.

Where doth the world thrust forth a vanity—
     *   *   *   *   *   *
That is not quickly buzz'd into his ears?
p.   *Richard II.* Act II. Sc. 1. L. 24.

Maud Muller looked and sighed : "Ah me!
That I the Judge's bride might be !
He would dress me up in silks so fine,
And praise and toast me at his wine."
q.   WHITTIER—*Maud Muller.* L. 35.

Meek Nature's evening comment on the
     shows
That for oblivion take their daily birth
From all the fuming vanities of earth.
r.   WORDSWORTH—*Sonnet. Sky. Prospect*
                 from the Plain of France.

VARIETY.

Amidst the soft variety I'm lost.
s.   ADDISON—*Letter from Italy.* L. 100.

The earth was made so various, that the
     mind
Of desultory man, studious of change
And pleased with novelty, might be indulged.
t.   COWPER—*The Task.* Bk. 1. L. 506.

Variety's the very spice of life,
That gives it all its flavour.
u.   COWPER—*The Task.* Bk. II. L. 606.

Variety's the source of joy below,
From whence still fresh-revolving pleasures
     flow,
In books and love the mind one end pursues,
And only change the expiring flame renews.
v.   GAY—*Epistles. To Bernard Lintot, on*
                     a Miscellany of Poems.

Countless the various species of mankind,
Countless the shades which sep'rate mind
     from mind ;
No general object of desire is known,
Each has his will, and each pursues his own.
w.   WM. GIFFORD—*Perseus.*

     How widely its agencies vary,—
To save, to ruin, to curse, to bless,—
As even its minted coins express,
Now stamp'd with the image of good **Queen**
     Bess,
     And now of a Bloody Mary.
x.   HOOD—*Miss Kilmansegg. Her Moral.*

Wherefore did Nature pour her bounties forth
With such a full and unwithdrawing hand,
Covering the earth with odours, fruits, and flocks,
Thronging the seas with spawn innumerable,
But all to please and sate the curious taste?
   a.   MILTON—*Comus.* L. 710.

Not chaos-like together crush'd and bruis'd,
But, as the world, harmoniously confused ;
Where order in variety we see,
And where, though all things differ, all agree.
   b.   POPE—*Windsor Forest.* L. 13.

Variety alone gives joy :
The sweetest meats the soonest cloy.
   c.   PRIOR—*The Turtle and the Sparrow.*
L. 234.

When our old Pleasures die,
Some new One still is nigh ;
Oh ! fair Variety !
   d.   NICHOLAS ROWE—*Ode for the New Year.*
1717.

Age cannot wither her, nor custom stale
Her infinite variety.
   e.   *Antony and Cleopatra.* Act II. Sc. 2.
L. 240.

VICE.

Vice gets more in this vicious world
Than piety.
   f.   BEAUMONT AND FLETCHER—*Love's Cure.*
Act III. Sc. 1.

Vice itself lost half its evil, by losing all its grossness.
   g.   BURKE—*Reflections on the Revolution in France.*

      But all have prices,
From crowns to kicks, according to their vices.
   h.   BYRON—*Don Juan.* Canto V. St. 27.

To sanction Vice, and hunt Decorum down.
   i.   BYRON—*English Bards and Scotch Reviewers.* L. 621.

And lash the Vice and Follies of the Age.
   j.   SUSANNAH CENTLIVRE—*Prologue to The Man's Bewitched.*

Ne'er blush'd, unless, in spreading vice's snares,
She blunder'd on some virtue unawares,
   k.   CHURCHILL—*The Rosciad.* L. 137.

Vice stings us, even in our pleasures, but virtue consoles us, even in our pains.
   l.   C. C. COLTON—*Lacon.* CCXCVI.

We do not despise all those who have vices, but we despise all those who have not a single virtue.
   m.   LA ROCHEFOUCAULD—*Maxims.* No. 195.

Saint Augustine ! well hast thou said,
   That of our vices we can frame
A ladder, if we will but tread
   Beneath our feet each deed of shame.
   n.   LONGFELLOW—*The Ladder of St. Augustine.* St. 1.

The heart resolves this matter in a trice,
" Men only feel the smart, but not the vice."
   o.   POPE—*Horace.* Bk. II. Ep. II.
L. 216.

Vice is a monster of so frightful mien,
As to be hated needs but to be seen ;
Yet seen too oft, familiar with her face,
We first endure, then pity, then embrace.
   p.   POPE—*Essay on Man.* Ep. II. L. 217.

      O dishonest wretch !
Wilt thou be made a man out of my vice ?
   q.   *Measure for Measure.* Act III. Sc. 1.
L. 137.

O, what a mansion have those vices got
   Which for their habitation chose out thee,
Where beauty's veil doth cover every blot,
   And all things turn to fair that eyes can see !
   r.   *Sonnet XCV.*

There is no vice so simple but assumes
Some mark of virtue on his outward parts.
   s.   *Merchant of Venice.* Act III. Sc. 2.
L. 81.

Vice repeated is like the wand'ring wind,
Blows dust in others' eyes, to spread itself.
   t.   *Pericles.* Act I. Sc. 1. L. 97.

VICTORY.

The victory of endurance born.
   u.   BRYANT—*The Battle-Field.* St. 8.

Kings may be blest, but Tam was glorious,
O'er a' the ills o' life victorious.
   v.   BURNS—*Tam o' Shanter.*

Who thought he 'ad won
The field as certain as a gun.
   w.   BUTLER—*Hudibras.* Pt. I. Canto III.
L. 11.

Out spoke the victor then,
   As he hail'd them o'er the wave,
Ye are brothers ! ye are men !
   And we conquer but to save ;
So peace instead of death let us bring ;
   But yield, proud foe, thy fleet,
   With the crews, at England's feet,
   And make submission meet
      To our King.
   x.   CAMPBELL—*The Battle of the Baltic.*

Not one of all the purple host
   Who took the flag to-day
Can tell the definition
   So clear of victory,

As he, defeated, dying,
   On whose forbidden ear
The distant strains of triumph
   Break agonized and clear.
   y.   EMILY DICKINSON—*Poems. Success.*
Ed. 1891.

They see nothing wrong in the rule, that to the victors belong the spoils of the enemy.

   a.   W. L. MARCY—*Speech in the United States Senate.* 1832.

Who overcomes
By force, hath overcome but half his foe.

   b.   MILTON— *Paradise Lost.* Bk. I.
L. 648.

Then should some cloud pass over
The brow of sire or lover,
     Think 'tis the shade
     By Victory made
Whose wings right o'er us hover!

   c.   MOORE—*Battle Song.*

We have met the enemy and they are ours.

   d.   OLIVER HAZARD PERRY—*Letter to Gen. Harrison after the Victory on Lake Erie.* Sept. 10, 1813.

But if
We have such another victory, we are undone.

   e.   Attributed to PYRRHUS by BACON— *Apothegms.* No. 193.

We conquered France, but felt our captive's charms,
Her arts victorious triumph'd o'er our arms.

   f.   POPE—*Horace.* Bk. II. Ep. I. L. 263.

Hail to the Chief who in triumph advances.

   g.   SCOTT—*Lady of the Lake.* Canto II.
St. 19.

With dying hand, above his head,
He shook the fragment of his blade,
   And shouted " Victory!—
Charge, Chester, charge! on, Stanley, on ! "
Were the last words of Marmion.

   h.   SCOTT—*Marmion.* Canto VI. St. 32.

A victory is twice itself when the achiever brings home full numbers.

   i.   *Much Ado About Nothing.* Act I.
Sc. 1. L. 8.

I came, saw, and overcame.

   j.   *Henry IV.* Pt. II. Act IV. Sc. 3.
L. 45.

Then with the losers let it sympathize;
For nothing can seem foul to those that win.

   k.   *Henry IV.* Pt. I. Act V. Sc. 1. L. 8.

Thus far our fortune keeps an upward course,
And we are grac'd with wreaths of victory.

   l.   *Henry VI.* Pt. III. Act V. Sc. 3.
L. 1.

To whom God will, there be the victory!

   m.   *Henry VI.* Pt. III. Act II. Sc. 5.
L. 15.

" But what good came of it at last?"
   Quoth little Peterkin.
" Why, that I cannot tell," said he;
" But 'twas a famous victory."

   n.   SOUTHEY—*Battle of Blenheim.*

VILLAINY.

Calm, thinking villains, whom no faith could fix,
Of crooked counsels and dark politics,

   o.   POPE—*Temple of Fame.* L. 410.

And thus I clothe my naked villainy
With old odd ends, stol'n out of holy writ,
And seem a saint, when most I play the devil.

   p.   *Richard III.* Act I. Sc. 3. L. 336.

O villainy! Ho! let the door be lock'd;
Treachery! seek it out.

   q.   *Hamlet.* Act V. Sc. 2. L. 322.

The learned pate
Ducks to the golden fool : all is oblique;
There's nothing level in our cursed natures,
But direct villainy.

   r.   *Timon of Athens.* Act IV. Sc. 3.
L. 17.

Villain and he be many miles asunder.

   s.   *Romeo and Juliet.* Act III. Sc. 5.
L. 82.

VIRTUE.

Curse on his virtues! they've undone his country.

   t.   ADDISON—*Cato.* Act IV. Sc. 4.

Sweet are the slumbers of the virtuous man!

   u.   ADDISON—*Cato.* Act V. Sc. 4.

One's outlook is a part of his virtue.

   v.   AMOS BRONSON ALCOTT—*Concord Days. April Outlook.*

Virtue and sense are one; and, trust me, still
A faithless heart betrays the head unsound.

   w.   ARMSTRONG—*Art of Preserving Health.* Bk. IV. L. 265.

Virtue, the strength and beauty of the soul,
Is the best gift of Heaven : a happiness
That even above the smiles and frowns of fate
Exalts great Nature's favourites : a wealth
That ne'er encumbers, nor can be transferr'd.

   x.   ARMSTRONG—*Art of Preserving Health.* Bk. IV. L. 284.

Certainly virtue is like precious odours, most fragrant when they are incensed or crushed.

   y.   BACON—*Essays. Of Adversity.*

Virtue is like a rich stone, best plain set.

   z.   BACON—*Essays. Of Beauty.*

Whilst shame keeps its watch, virtue is not wholly extinguished in the heart.

   aa.   BURKE—*Reflections on the Revolution in France.*

Virtue is not malicious; wrong done her
Is righted even when men grant they err.

   bb.   GEORGE CHAPMAN—*Monsieur D'Olive.* Act I. Sc. 1. L. 127.

The firste vertu, sone, if thou wolt lerne,
Is to restreyne, and kepe wel thy tonge.
    a.   Chaucer—*Canterbury Tales. The
Manciple's Tale.* L. 18,213.

Virtue is a habit of the mind, consistent
with nature and moderation and reason.
    b.   Cicero—*Rhetorical Invention.* Bk. II.
Sc. LIII.

Well may your heart believe the truths I tell;
'Tis virtue makes the bliss, where'er we dwell.
    c.   Collins—*Eclogue I.* L. 5. *Selim.*

Is virtue a thing remote? I wish to be
virtuous, and lo! virtue is at hand.
    d.   Confucius—*Analects.* Bk. I. Ch. IV.

Virtue is not left to stand alone. *He who
practices it* will have neighbors.
    e.   Confucius—*Analects.* Bk. IV.
Ch. XXV.

And he by no uncommon lot
Was famed for virtues he had not.
    f.   Cowper—*To the Rev. William Bull.*
L. 19.

The only amaranthine flower on earth
Is virtue.
    g.   Cowper—*The Task.* Bk. III. L. 268.

Virtue alone is happiness below.
    h.   Crabbe—*The Borough.* Letter XVI.

And virtue, though in rags, will keep me
warm.
    i.   Dryden—*Imitation of Horace.* Bk. I.
Ode XXIX. L. 87.

The only reward of virtue is virtue.
    j.   Emerson—*Essays. Friendship.*

The virtue in most request is conformity.
Self-reliance is its aversion. It loves not real-
ities and creators, but names and customs.
    k.   Emerson—*Essays. First Series.
Self-Reliance.*

Shall ignorance of good and ill
Dare to direct the eternal will?
Seek virtue, and, of that possest,
To Providence resign the rest.
    l.   Gay—*The Father and Jupiter.*

Yet why should learning hope success at
court?
Why should our patriots' virtues cause sup-
port?
Why to true merit should they have regard?
They know that virtue is its own reward.
    m.   Gay—*Epistle to Methuen.* L. 39.

And even his failings leaned to virtue's side.
    n.   Goldsmith—*Deserted Village.* L. 164.

The virtuous nothing fear but life with
shame,
And death's a pleasant road that leads to
fame.
    o.   Geo. Granville (Lord Lansdowne)—
Verses written 1690. L. 47.

Only a sweet and virtuous soul,
Like seasoned timber, never gives.
    p.   Herbert—*The Church. Virtue.*

Virtue, dear friend, needs no defence,
The surest guard is innocence:
None knew, till guilt created fear,
What darts or poison'd arrows were.
    q.   Horace—*Odes.* Bk. I. Ode XII.
St. 1. Wentworth Dillon's trans.

Some of 'em [virtues] like extinct volcanoes,
with a strong memory of fire and brimstone.
    r.   Douglas Jerrold—*The Catspaw.*
Act III. Sc. 1.

To be discontented with the divine discontent, and to be ashamed with the noble shame,
is the very germ of the first upgrowth of all
virtue.
    s.   Chas. Kingsley—*Health and Educa-
tion. The Science of Health.*

Virtue is an angel, but she is a blind one,
and must ask of Knowledge to show her the
pathway that leads to her goal.
    t.   Horace Mann—*A Few Thoughts for a
Young Man.*

God sure esteems the growth and complet-
ing of one virtuous person, more than the
restraint of ten vicious.
    u.   Milton—*Areopagitica. A Speech for
the Liberty of Unlicensed Printing.*

Or, if Virtue feeble were,
Heaven itself would stoop to her.
    v.   Milton—*Comus.* L. 1,022.

Virtue could see to do what Virtue would
By her own radiant light, though sun and
moon
Were in the flat sea sunk.
    w.   Milton—*Comus.* L. 373.

Virtue may be assailed, but never hurt,
Surprised by unjust force, but not inthralled;
Yea, even that which mischief meant most
harm
Shall in the happy trial prove most glory.
    x.   Milton—*Comus.* L. 589.

I find that the best virtue I have has in it
some tincture of vice.
    y.   Montaigne—*Essays. That we Taste
Nothing Pure.*

For virtue only finds eternal Fame.
    z.   Petrarch—*The Triumph of Fame.*
Pt. I. L. 183.

But sometimes virtue starves while vice is
fed.
What then? Is the reward of virtue bread?
    aa.   Pope—*Essay on Man.* Ep. IV. L. 149.

Court-virtues bear, like gems, the highest
rate,
Born where Heav'n's influence scarce can
penetrate.
In life's low vale, the soil the virtues like,
They please as beauties, here as wonders
strike.
> a.   POPE—*Moral Essays.* Ep. I. L. 141.

Know then this truth (enough for man to
know)
"Virtue alone is happiness below."
> b.   POPE—*Essay on Man.* Ep. IV. L. 309.

O let us still the secret joy partake,
To follow virtue even for virtue's sake.
> c.   POPE—*Temple of Fame.* L. 364.

There is nothing that is meritorious but
virtue and friendship; and indeed friendship
itself is only a part of virtue.
> d.   POPE—*On his Death-Bed.* JOHNSON'S
> *Life of Pope.*

The soul's calm sunshine and the heartfelt
joy,
Is virtue's prize.
> e.   POPE—*Essay on Man.* Ep. IV. L. 168.

Virtue may choose the high or low degree,
'Tis just alike to virtue, and to me;
Dwell in a monk, or light upon a king,
She's still the same belov'd, contented thing.
> f.   POPE—*Epilogue to Satires.* Dialogue I.
> L. 137.

Virtue she finds too painful an endeavour,
Content to dwell in decencies forever.
> g.   POPE—*Moral Essays.* Ep. II. L. 163.

Sweet drop of pure and pearly light;
   In thee the rays of Virtue shine;
More calmly clear, more mildly bright,
   Than any gem that gilds the mine.
> h.   SAM'L ROGERS—*On a Tear.*

According to his virtue let us use him,
With all respect and rites of burial.
> i.   *Julius Cæsar.* Act V. Sc. 5. L. 76.

Assume a virtue, if you have it not.
> j.   *Hamlet.* Act III. Sc. 4. L. 160.

For in the fatness of these pursy times
Virtue itself of vice must pardon beg.
> k.   *Hamlet.* Act III. Sc. 4. L. 153.

                His virtues
Will plead like angels, trumpet-tongued,
against
The deep damnation of his taking-off.
> l.   *Macbeth.* Act I. Sc. 7. L. 18.

             I hold it ever,
Virtue and cunning were endowments greater
Than nobleness and riches: careless heirs
May the two latter darken and expend;
But immortality attends the former,
Making a man a god.
> m.   *Pericles.* Act III. Sc. 2. L. 27.

My heart laments that virtue cannot live
Out of the teeth of emulation.
> n.   *Julius Cæsar.* Act II. Sc. 3. L. 13.

The trumpet of his own virtues.
> o.   *Much Ado About Nothing.* Act V.
> Sc. 2. L. 87.

To show virtue her own feature, scorn her
own image, and the very age and body of the
time his form and pressure.
> p.   *Hamlet.* Act III. Sc. 2. L. 25.

Virtue is bold, and goodness never fearful.
> q.   *Measure for Measure.* Act III. Sc. 1.
> L. 215.

Virtue is chok'd with foul ambition.
> r.   *Henry VI.* Pt. II. Act III. Sc. 1.
> L. 143.

Virtue itself turns vice, being misapplied;
And vice sometimes by action dignified.
> s.   *Romeo and Juliet.* Act II. Sc. 3.
> L. 21.

Virtue that transgresses is but patched with
sin; and sin that amends is but patched with
virtue.
> t.   *Twelfth Night.* Act I. Sc. 5. L. 52.

Virtue often trips and falls on the sharp-
edged rock of poverty.
> u.   EUGÈNE SUE.

Virtue, the greatest of all monarchies.
> v.   SWIFT—*Ode.* To the Hon. Sir William
> Temple.

What, what is virtue, but repose of mind,
   A pure ethereal calm, that knows no storm;
Above the reach of wild ambition's wind,
   Above those passions that this world deform
And torture man.
> w.   THOMSON—*Castle of Indolence.*
> Canto I. St. 16.

Virtue's a stronger guard than brass.
> x.   EDMUND WALLER—*Epigram Upon the
> Golden Medal.* L. 14.

Good company and good discourse are the
very sinews of virtue.
> y.   IZAAK WALTON—*Compleat Angler.*
> Pt. I. Ch. II. (Continued.)

Few men have virtue to withstand the
highest bidder.
> z.   GEORGE WASHINGTON—*Moral Maxims.*
> *Virtue and Vice. The Trial of Virtue.*

             I have ever thought,
Nature doth nothing so great for great men,
As when she's pleas'd to make them lords of
truth.
Integrity of life is fame's best friend,
Which nobly, beyond death, shall crown the
end.
> aa.   JOHN WEBSTER—*The Duchess of Malfi.*
> Act V. Sc. 5.

To Virtue's humblest son let none prefer
Vice, though descended from the conqueror.
   a.   Young—*Love of Fame.* Satire I.
                                     L. 141.

Virtue alone outbuilds the pyramids :
Her monuments shall last, when Egypt's
   fall.
   b.   Young—*Night Thoughts.* Night VI.
                                     L. 314.

VISIONS.

And like a passing thought, she fled
In light away.
   c.   Burns—*The Vision.* Last lines.

The people's prayer, the glad diviner's theme!
The young men's vision, and the old men's
   dream !
   d.   Dryden—*Absalom and Achitophel.*
                          Pt. I.　L. 238.

Visions of glory, spare my aching sight!
Ye unborn ages, crowd not on my soul.
   e.   Gray—*The Bard.* III. 1. L. 11.

Abou Ben Adhem (may his tribe increase !)
Awoke one night from a deep dream of peace,
And saw, within the moonlight in his room,
Making it rich, and like a lily in bloom,
An angel, writing in a book of gold ;
Exceeding peace had made Ben Adhem bold,
And to the presence in the room he said—
"What writest thou ?" The Vision raised its
   head,
And, with a look made all of sweet accord,
Answered, " The names of those who love the
   Lord."
   f.   Leigh Hunt—*Abou Ben Adhem and*
                             the Angel.

It is a dream, sweet child ! a waking dream,
A blissful certainty, a vision bright,
Of that rare happiness, which even on earth
Heaven gives to those it loves.
   g.   Longfellow—*The Spanish Student.*
                          Act III.　Sc. 5.

An angel stood and met my gaze,
   Through the low doorway of my tent ;
The tent is struck, the vision stays ;
   I only know she came and went.
   h.   Lowell—*She Came and Went.*

Gorgons, and Hydras, and Chimæras dire.
   i.   Milton—*Paradise Lost.* Bk. II.
                                L. 628.

O visions ill foreseen ! Better had I
Liv'd ignorant of future, so had borne
My part of evil only.
   j.   Milton—*Paradise Lost.* Bk. XI.
                                L. 763.

My thoughts by night are often filled
   With visions false as fair :
For in the past alone, I build
   My castles in the air.
   k.   Thos. Love Peacock—*Castles in the*
                             Air. St. 1.

Hence the fool's paradise, the statesman's
   scheme,
The air-built castle, and the golden dream,
The maid's romantic wish, the chemist's
   flame,
And poet's vision of eternal fame.
   l.   Pope—*Dunciad.* Bk. III. L. 9.

Our revels now are ended. These, our actors,
As I foretold you, were all spirits, and
Are melted into air, into thin air ;
And, like the baseless fabric of this vision,
The cloud-capped towers, the gorgeous palaces,
The solemn temples, the great globe itself,
Yea, all which it inherit, shall dissolve,
And, like this insubstantial pageant faded,
Leave not a rack behind.
   m.   *Tempest.* Act IV. Sc. 1. L. 148.

But shapes that come not at an earthly call,
Will not depart when mortal voices bid.
   n.   Wordsworth—*Dion.* V.

Fond man ! the vision of a moment made !
Dream of a dream ! and shadow of a shade !
   o.   Young—*Paraphrase on Part of the*
                        Book of Job. L. 187.

VOICE.

Her voice changed like a bird's :
There grew more of the music, and less of the
   words.
   p.   Robert Browning—*Flight of the*
                         Duchess. St. 15.

The devil hath not, in all his quiver's choice,
An arrow for the heart like a sweet voice.
   q.   Byron—*Don Juan.* Canto XV. St. 13.

His voice no touch of harmony admits,
Irregularly deep, and shrill by fits.
The two extremes appear like man and wife
Coupled together for the sake of strife.
   r.   Churchill—*Rosciad.* L. 1,003.

The voice of the people is the voice of God.
   s.   Hesiod—*Works and Days.* 763.

The voice so sweet, the words so fair,
As some soft chime had stroked the air ;
And though the sound had parted thence,
Still left an echo in the sense.
   t.   Ben Jonson—*Eupheme.* IV.

          Her silver voice
Is the rich music of a summer bird,
Heard in the still night, with its passionate
   cadence.
   u.   Longfellow—*The Spirit of Poetry.*
                                L. 55.

Oh, there is something in that voice that
   reaches
The innermost recesses of my spirit !
   v.   Longfellow—*Christus.* Pt. I. *The*
                      Divine Tragedy. The First
                      Passover. Pt. VI.

Thy voice
Is a celestial melody.
> a.   LONGFELLOW—*Masque of Pandora.*
>   Pt. V.

How sweetly sounds the voice of a good
    woman!
It is so seldom heard that, when it speaks,
It ravishes all senses.
> b.   MASSINGER—*The Old Law.* Act IV.
>   Sc. 2. L. 34.

The Angel ended, and in Adam's ear
So charming left his voice, that he awhile
Thought him still speaking, still stood fix'd
    to hear.
> c.   MILTON—*Paradise Lost.* Bk. VIII.
>   L. 1.

The people's voice is odd,
It is, and it is not, the voice of God.
> d.   POPE—*To Augustus.* Bk. II. Ep. I.
>   L. 89.

Her voice was like the voice the stars
    Had when they sang together.
> e.   DANTE GABRIEL ROSSETTI—*The*
>   *Blessed Damozel.* St. 10.

A sweet voice, a little indistinct and muffled,
which caresses and does not thrill; an utterance which glides on without emphasis, and
lays stress only on what is deeply felt.
> f.   GEORGES SAND—*Handsome Lawrence.*
>   Ch. III.

Her voice was ever soft,
Gentle and low, an excellent thing in woman.
> g.   *King Lear.* Act V. Sc. 3. L. 272.

Two voices are there; one is of the sea,
One of the mountains: each a mighty Voice.
> h.   WORDSWORTH—*Thought of a Briton on*
>   *the Subjugation of Switzerland.*

W.

WAR.

A thousand glorious actions that might
    claim
Triumphant laurels, and immortal fame,
Confus'd in crowds of glorious actions lie,
And troops of heroes undistinguished die.
> i.   ADDISON—*Campaign.* L. 304.

From hence, let fierce contending nations
    know
What dire effects from civil discord flow.
> j.   ADDISON—*Cato.* Act V. Sc. 4.

My voice is still for war.
> k.   ADDISON—*Cato.* Act II. Sc. 1.

O great corrector of enormous times,
Shaker of o'er-rank states, thou grand decider
Of dusty and old titles, that healest with
    blood
The earth when it is sick, and curest the
    world
O' the pleurisy of people.
> l.   BEAUMONT AND FLETCHER—*The Two*
>   *Noble Kinsmen.* Act V. Sc. 1.

Gaily! gaily! close our ranks!
    Arm! Advance!
    Hope of France!
Gaily! gaily! close our ranks!
Onward! Onward! Gauls and Franks!
> m.   BÉRANGER—*Les Gaulois et François.*
>   C. L. Betts' trans.

It is magnificent, but it is not war.
> n.   GENERAL PIERRE BOSQUET—*On the*
>   *Charge of the Light Brigade.*

He who did well in war, just earns the right
To begin doing well in peace.
> o.   ROBERT BROWNING—*Luria.* Act II.
>   L. 354.

Lay down the axe; fling by the spade;
    Leave in its track the toiling plough;
The rifle and the bayonet-blade
    For arms like yours were fitter now;
And let the hands that ply the pen
    Quit the light task, and learn to wield
The horseman's crooked brand, and rein
    The charger on the battle-field.
> p.   BRYANT—*Our Country's Call.*

Scots, wha hae wi' Wallace bled;
Scots, wham Bruce has aften led,
Welcome to your gory bed,
    Or to victory!
> q.   BURNS—*Bruce to his Men at*
>   *Bannockburn.*

Bloody wars at first began,
The artificial plague of man,
That from his own invention rise,
To scourge his own iniquities.
> r.   BUTLER—*Satire. Upon the Weakness*
>   *and Misery of Man.* L. 105.

For those that fly may fight again,
Which he can never do that's slain.
> s.   BUTLER—*Hudibras.* Pt. III. Canto III.
>   L. 243.

For those that run away, and fly,
Take place at least o' th' enemy.
> t.   BUTLER—*Hudibras.* Pt. I. Canto III.
>   L. 609.

In all the trade of war, no feat
Is nobler than a brave retreat.
> u.   BUTLER—*Hudibras.* Pt. I. Canto III.
>   L. 607.

And there was mounting in hot haste : the
    steed,
  The mustering squadron, and the clattering
    car,
Went pouring forward with impetuous speed,
  And swiftly forming in the ranks of war ;
  And the deep thunder peal on peal, afar
And near ; the beat of the alarming drum
  Roused up the soldier ere the morning star ;
While throng'd the citizens with terror dumb,
Or whispering with white lips—"The foe !
    they come ! they come ! "
  a.   BYRON—*Childe Harold.* Canto III.
                  St. 25.

Battle's magnificently stern array !
  b.   BYRON—*Childe Harold.* Canto III.
                  St. 28.

Hand to hand, and foot to foot :
Nothing there, save death, was mute ;
Stroke, and thrust, and flash, and cry
For quarter or for victory,
Mingle there with the volleying thunder.
  c.   BYRON—*Siege of Corinth.* St. 24.

Like the leaves of the for⸍   when summer is
    green,
That host with their b⸍ ⸍ers at sunset were
    seen ;
Like the leaves of the forest when autumn
    hath blown,
That host on the morrow lay wither'd and
    strown !
  d.   BYRON—*The Destruction of Sennacherib.*

The Assyrian came down like the wolf on the
    fold,
And his cohorts were gleaming in purple and
    gold.
  e.   BYRON—*The Destruction of Sennacherib.*

War, war is still the cry, " War even to the
    knife ! "
  f.   BYRON—*Childe Harold.* Canto I.
                  St. 86.
The combat deepens. On, ye brave,
Who rush to glory, or the grave !
Wave, Munich ! all thy banners wave,
  And charge with all thy chivalry.
  g.   CAMPBELL—*Hohenlinden.*

When the battle rages loud and long,
  And the stormy winds do blow.
  h.   CAMPBELL—*Ye Mariners of England.*

War will never yield but to the principles of
universal justice and love, and these have no
sure root but in the religion of Jesus Christ.
  i.   WM. ELLERY CHANNING—*Lecture on
                  War.* Sec. II.

But war's a game, which, were their subjects
    wise,
Kings would not play at.
  j.   COWPER—*The Task.* Bk. V. L. 187.

Hence jarring sectaries may learn
Their real interest to discern ;
That brother should not war with brother,
And worry and devour each other.
  k.   COWPER—*The Nightingale and
                        Glow-Worm.*
Carry his body hence !
  Kings must have slaves :
Kings climb to eminence
  Over men's graves :
So this man's eye is dim ;
Throw the earth over him !
  l.   HENRY AUSTIN DOBSON—*Before Sedan.*

They now to fight are gone ;
Armor on armor shone ;
Drum now to drum did groan,
  To hear was wonder ;
That with the cries they make,
The very earth did shake ;
Trumpet to trumpet spake,
  Thunder to thunder.
  m.   DRAYTON—*Ballad of Agincourt.* St. 8.

War, he sung, is toil and trouble ;
Honour but an empty bubble.
  n.   DRYDEN—*Alexander's Feast.* L. 99.

By the rude bridge that arched the flood,
  Their flag to April's breeze unfurl'd ;
Here once the embattl'd farmers stood,
  And fired the shot heard round the world.
  o.   EMERSON—*Hymn sung at the completion
              of the Concord Monument.*

Under the sod and the dew,
  Waiting the Judgment Day ;
Love and tears for the Blue,
  Tears and love for the Gray.
  p.   FRANCIS M. FINCH—*The Blue and the
                        Gray.*
There never was a good war or a bad peace.
  q.   BENJ. FRANKLIN—*Letter to Quincy.*
                        Sept. 11, 1773.

For he who fights and runs away
May live to fight another day ;
But he who is in battle slain
Can never rise and fight again.
  r.   GOLDSMITH—*The Art of Poetry on a
        New Plan.* Vol. II. P. 147. See
        also RAY—*History of the Rebellion.*
        P. 48. (1752).

I * * * purpose to fight it out on this
line if it takes all summer.
  s.   U. S. GRANT—*Despatch from
            Spottsylvania Court House.*
                   May 11, 1864.

No terms except an unconditional and immediate surrender can be accepted. I propose to move immediately upon your works.
  t.   U. S. GRANT—*To Gen. S. B. Buckner.
        Fort Donelson.* Feb. 16, 1862.

Let the only walls the foe shall scale
  Be ramparts of the dead !
  a.   PAUL H. HAYNE—*Vicksburg.*

I war not with the dead.
  b.   HOMER—*Iliad.* Bk. VII. L. 485.
                                Pope's trans.

Our business in the field of fight
Is not to question, but to prove our might.
  c.   HOMER—*Iliad.* Bk. XX. L. 304.
                                Pope's trans,

So ends the bloody business of the day.
  d.   HOMER—*Odyssey.* Bk. XXII. L. 516.
                                Pope's trans.

          The chance of war
Is equal, and the slayer oft is slain.
  e.   HOMER—*Iliad.* Bk. XVIII. L. 388.
                                Bryant's trans.

Earth was the meadow, he the mower strong.
  f.   VICTOR HUGO—*La Légende des Siècles.*

Oh, East is East, and West is West, and never
    the twain shall meet
Till earth and sky stand presently at God's
    great judgment seat ;
But there is neither East nor West, border
    nor breed nor birth
When two strong men stand face to face, tho'
    they come from the ends of the earth !
  g.   RUDYARD KIPLING—*Barrack-Room
          Ballads. Ballad of East and West.*

When Greeks joined Greeks, then was the
tug of war !
  h.   NATHANIEL LEE—*The Rival Queens ; or,
          Alexander the Great.* Act IV. Sc. 2.

To arms ! to arms ! ye brave !
  Th' avenging sword unsheathe,
March on ! march on ! all hearts resolved
  On victory or death !
  i.   JOSEPH ROUGET DE LISLE—*The
                          Marseilles Hymn.*

Is it, O man, with such discordant noises,
  With such accursed instruments as these,
Thou drownest Nature's sweet and kindly
    voices,
  And jarrest the celestial harmonies?
  j.   LONGFELLOW—*Arsenal at Springfield.*
                                      St. 8.

Ez fer war, I call it murder,—
  Ther you hev it plain and flat ;
I don't want to go no furder
  Than my Testyment fer that.
  k.   LOWELL—*The Biglow Papers.* No. 1.

It don't seem hardly right, John,
  When both my hands was full,
To stump me to a fight, John,
  Your cousin, too, John Bull !
    Ole Uncle S. sez he, " I guess
      We know it now," sez he,
    " The lion's paw is all the law,
      According to J. B.,
      That's fit for you an me."
  l.   LOWELL—*The Biglow Papers.
          Jonathan to John.* St. 1.

We kind o' thought Christ went agin war an'
    pillage.
  m.   LOWELL—*The Biglow Papers.* No. 3.

Oh ! wherefore come ye forth in triumph
    from the North,
  With your hands and your feet, and your
    raiment all red ?
And wherefore doth your rout send forth a
    joyous shout ?
  And whence be the grapes of the wine-press
    which ye tread ?
  n.   MACAULAY—*The Battle of Naseby.*

War in men's eyes shall be
A monster of iniquity
  In the good time coming.
Nations shall not quarrel then,
  To prove which is the stronger ;
Nor slaughter men for glory's sake ;—
  Wait a little longer.
  o.   CHARLES MACKAY—*The Good Time
                          Coming.* St. 3.

Some undone widow sits upon mine arm,
And takes away the use of it ; and my sword,
Glued to my scabbard with wronged orphan's
    tears,
Will not be drawn.
  p.   MASSINGER—*A New Way to Pay Old
                          Debts.* Act V. Sc. 1.

March to the battle-field,
  The foe is now before us ;
Each heart is Freedom's shield,
  And heaven is shining o'er us,
  q.   B. E. O'MEARA—*March to the Battle-
                                      Field.*

And high above the fight the lonely bugle
    grieves.
  r.   GRENVILLE MELLIN—*Bunker Hill.*

There is war in the skies !
  s.   OWEN MEREDITH (Lord Lytton)—
          Lucile. Pt. I. Canto IV. St. 12.

        Arms on armour clashing bray'd
Horrible discord, and the madding wheels
Of brazen chariots ray'd ; dire was the noise
Of conflict.
  t.   MILTON—*Paradise Lost.* Bk. VI.
                                      L. 209.

          Black it stood as night,
Fierce as ten furies, terrible as hell,
And shook a dreadful dart.
  u.   MILTON—*Paradise Lost.* Bk. II.
                                      L. 670.

My sentence is for open war.
  v.   MILTON—*Paradise Lost.* Bk. II. L. 51.

        Others more mild,
Retreated in a silent valley, sing
With notes angelical to many a harp
Their own heroic deeds and hapless fall
By doom of battle.
  w.   MILTON—*Paradise Lost.* Bk. II.
                                      L. 546.

So frown'd the mighty combatants, that hell
Grew darker at their frown.
　　a.　　Milton—*Paradise Lost.* Bk. II.
　　　　　　　　　　　　　　L. 719.
The brazen throat of war.
　　b.　　Milton—*Paradise Lost.* Bk. XI.
　　　　　　　　　　　　　　L. 713.
Th' imperial ensign, which, full high advanc'd,
Shone like a meteor, streaming to the wind.
　　c.　　Milton—*Paradise Lost.* Bk. I.
　　　　　　　　　　　　　　L. 536.
To overcome in battle, and subdue
Nations, and bring home spoils with infinite
Man-slaughter, shall be held the highest pitch
Of human glory.
　　d.　　Milton—*Paradise Lost.* Bk. XI.
　　　　　　　　　　　　　　L. 691.
What boots it at one gate to make defence,
And at another to let in the foe?
　　e.　　Milton—*Samson Agonistes.* L. 560.

　　　What though the field be lost?
All is not lost; the unconquerable will,
And study of revenge, immortal hate
And courage never to submit or yield,
And what is else not to be overcome.
　　f.　　Milton—*Paradise Lost.* Bk. I. L. 105.

In the wars of the European powers in
matters relating to themselves we have never
taken any part, nor does it comport with our
policy so to do. It is only when our rights
are invaded or seriously menaced that we
resent injuries or make preparation for our
defence.
　　g.　　James Monroe—*Annual Message.*
　　　　　　　　　　　　　　Dec. 2, 1823.

'Tis a principle of war that when you can
use the lightning, 'tis better than cannon.
　　h.　　Napoleon I.

"Go, with a song of peace," said Fingal;
"go, Ullin, to the king of swords. Tell him
that we are mighty in war; that the ghosts of
our foes are many."
　　i.　　Ossian—*Carthon.* L. 269.

She saw her sons with purple death expire,
Her sacred domes involved in rolling fire,
A dreadful series of intestine wars,
Inglorious triumphs and dishonest scars.
　　j.　　Pope—*Windsor Forest.* L. 323.

War its thousands slays,
Peace its ten thousands.
　　k.　　Porteus—*Death.* L. 178.

　　　　　The waves
Of the mysterious death-river moaned;
The tramp, the shout, the fearful thunder-roar
Of red-breathed cannon, and the wailing cry
Of myriad victims, filled the air.
　　l.　　Prentice—*Lookout Mountain.* L. 16.

The morning came, there stood the foe;
　Stark eyed them as they stood;
Few words he spoke—'twas not a time
　For moralizing mood:
"See there the enemy, my boys!
　Now, strong in valor's might,
Beat them or Betty Stark will sleep
　In widowhood to-night."
　　m.　　J. P. Rodman—*Battle of Bennington.*

The guard dies but never surrenders.
　　n.　　Rougemont—*Invented days after the
　　　　　Battle of Waterloo.* Attributed to
　　　　　　Cambronne. See Fournier—
　　　　　　　　L' Esprit dans L' Histoire.

　　　　　　　　Righteous Heaven,
In thy great day of vengeance! Blast the
　　traitor
And his pernicious counsels, who, for wealth,
For pow'r, the pride of greatness, or revenge,
Would plunge his native land in civil wars.
　　o.　　Nicholas Rowe—*Jane Shore.* Act III.
　　　　　　　　　　　　Sc. 1. L. 198.

"Charge, Chester, charge! On, Stanley, on!"
Were the last words of Marmion.
　　p.　　Scott—*Marmion.* Canto VI. St. 32.

In the lost battle,
　Borne down by the flying.
Where mingles war's rattle
　With groans of the dying.
　　q.　　Scott—*Marmion.* Canto III. St. 11.

One blast upon his bugle horn
　Were worth a thousand men.
　　r.　　Scott—*Lady of the Lake.* Canto VI.
　　　　　　　　　　　　　　　St. 18.
Still from the sire the son shall hear
Of the stern strife, and carnage drear,
　Of Flodden's fatal field,
When shiver'd was fair Scotland's spear,
　And broken was her shield!
　　s.　　Scott—*Marmion.* Canto VI. St. 34.

　　　　　　　All was lost,
But that the heavens fought.
　　t.　　*Cymbeline.* Act V. Sc. 3. L. 3.

And all the gods go with you! upon your
　　sword
Sit laurel victory! and smooth success
Be strew'd before your feet!
　　u.　　*Antony and Cleopatra.* Act I. Sc. 3.
　　　　　　　　　　　　　　L. 99.

　　　　Blow, wind! come, wrack!
At least we'll die with harness on our back.
　　v.　　*Macbeth.* Act V. Sc. 5. L. 51.

Cæsar's spirit, ranging for revenge,
With Até by his side come hot from hell,
Shall in these confines with a monarch's voice
Cry "Havoc," and let slip the dogs of war.
　　w.　　*Julius Cæsar.* Act III. Sc. 1. L. 270.

Fight, gentlemen of England! fight, bold
    yeomen!
Draw, archers, draw your arrows to the head!
Spur your proud horses hard, and ride in
    blood;
Amaze the welkin with your broken staves!
  a.   *Richard III.* Act V. Sc. 3. L. 338.

          Follow thy drum;
With man's blood paint the ground, gules,
    gules;
Religious canons, civil laws are cruel;
Then what should war be?
  b.   *Timon of Athens.* Act IV. Sc. 3.
                    L. 58.

From camp to camp through the foul womb
    of night
The hum of either army stilly sounds.
  c.   *Henry V.* Act IV. Chorus. L. 4.

          Give me the cups;
And let the kettle to the trumpet speak,
The trumpet to the cannoneer without,
The cannons to the heavens, the heavens to
    earth.
  d.   *Hamlet.* Act V. Sc. 2. L. 285.

Grim-visag'd war hath smoothed his wrinkled
    front.
  e.   *Richard III.* Act I. Sc. 1. L. 9.

          He is come to open
The purple testament of bleeding war.
  f.   *Richard II.* Act III. Sc. 3. L. 93.

He which hath no stomach to this fight,
Let him depart; his passport shall be made.
  g.   *Henry V.* Act IV. Sc. 3. L. 35.

I drew this gallant head of war,
And cull'd these fiery spirits from the world,
To outlook conquest and to win renown
Even in the jaws of danger and of death.
  h.   *King John.* Act V. Sc. 2. L. 113.

          Lay on, Macduff,
And damn'd be him that first cries "Hold,
    enough!"
  i.   *Macbeth.* Act V. Sc. 8. L. 33.

Let's march without the noise of threat'ning
    drum.
  j.   *Richard II.* Act III. Sc. 3. L. 51.

Now for the bare-pick'd bone of majesty
Doth dogged war bristle his angry crest
And snarleth in the gentle eyes of peace.
  k.   *King John.* Act IV. Sc. 3. L. 148.

Once more unto the breach, dear friends,
    once more;
Or close the wall up with our English dead.
  l.   *Henry V.* Act III. Sc. 1. L. 1.

Our battle is more full of names than yours,
Our men more perfect in the use of arms,
Our armour all as strong, our cause the best;
Then reason will our hearts should be as
    good.
  m.   *Henry IV.* Pt. II. Act IV. Sc. 1.
                  L. 154.

        O war! thou son of hell.
Whom angry heavens do make their minister,
Throw in the frozen bosoms of our part
Hot coals of vengeance! Let no soldier fly.
He that is truly dedicate to war
Hath no self-love, nor he that loves himself
Hath not essentially but by circumstance
The name of valour.
  n.   *Henry VI.* Pt. II. Act V. Sc. 2.
                  L. 33.

Put in their hands thy bruising irons of
    wrath,
That they may crush down with heavy fall
The usurping helmets of our adversaries.
  o.   *Richard III.* Act V. Sc. 3. L. 110.

Sound trumpets! let our bloody colours wave!
And either victory, or else a grave.
  p.   *Henry VI.* Pt. III. Act II. Sc. 2.
                  L. 173

The armourers, accomplishing the knights,
With busy hammers closing rivets up,
Give dreadful note of preparation.
  q.   *Henry V.* Act IV. Chorus. L. 12.

          The arms are fair,
When the intent of bearing them is just.
  r.   *Henry IV.* Pt. I. Act V. Sc. 2.
                  L. 88.

The bay-trees in our country all are wither'd
And meteors fright the fixed stars of heaven;
The pale-fac'd moon looks bloody on the
    earth
And lean-look'd prophets whisper fearful
    change;
Rich men look sad and ruffians dance and
    leap,
The one in fear to lose what they enjoy,
The other to enjoy by rage and war.
  s.   *Richard II.* Act II. Sc. 4. L. 8.

The cannons have their bowels full of wrath,
And ready mounted are they to spit forth
Their iron indignation 'gainst your walls.
  t.   *King John.* Act II. Sc. 1. L. 210.

     The fire-eyed maid of smoky war
All hot and bleeding will we offer them.
  u.   *Henry IV.* Pt. I. Act IV. Sc. 1.
                  L. 114.

          The nimble gunner
With linstock now the devilish cannon
    touches,
And down goes all before them.
  v.   *Henry V.* Act III. Chorus. L. 32.

There are few die well that die in a battle.
a.   *Henry V.* Act IV. Sc. 1. L. 148.

They shall have wars and pay for their presumption.
b.   *Henry VI.* Pt. III. Act IV. Sc. 1.
L. 114.

Thou know'st, great son,
The end of war's uncertain.
c.   *Coriolanus.* Act V. Sc. 3. L. 140.

Thus far into the bowels of the land
Have we march'd without impediment.
d.   *Richard III.* Act V. Sc. 2. L. 3.

Tut, tut; good enough to toss; food for powder, food for powder; they'll fill a pit as well as better.
e.   *Henry IV.* Pt. I. Act IV. Sc. 2.
L. 71.

We must have bloody noses and crack'd crowns,
And pass them current too. God's me, my horse!
f.   *Henry IV.* Pt. I. Act II. Sc. 3.
L. 96.

Your breath first kindled the dead coal of wars
And brought in matter that should feed this fire;
And now 'tis far too huge to be blown out
With that same weak wind which enkindled it.
g.   *King John.* Act V. Sc. 2. L. 83.

                    Then more fierce
The conflict grew; the din of arms, the yell
Of savage rage, the shriek of agony,
The groan of death, commingled in one sound
Of undistinguish'd horrors.
h.   Southey—*Madoc.* Pt. II. XV.

But, Virginians, don't do it, for I tell you that the flagon,
Filled with blood of Old Brown's offspring, was first poured by Southern hands;
And each drop from Old Brown's life-veins, like the red gore of the Dragon,
May spring up a vengeful Fury, hissing through your slave-worn lands:
            And Old Brown,
            Osawatomie Brown,
May trouble you worse than ever, when you've nailed his coffin down.
i.   E. C. Stedman—*How Old Brown Took Harper's Ferry. Written during Brown's Trial.* Nov., 1859.

The crystal-pointed tents from hill to hill.
j.   E. C. Stedman—*Alice of Monmouth.*
XI.

War! war! war!
      Heaven aid the right!
God move the hero's arm in the fearful fight!
God send the women sleep in the long, long night,
When the breasts on whose strength they leaned shall heave no more.
k.   E. C. Stedman—*Alice of Monmouth.*
VII.

Hobbes clearly proves that every creature
Lives in a state of war by nature.
l.   Swift—*Poetry. A Rhapsody.*

War, that mad game the world so loves to play.
m.   Swift—*Ode to Sir Wm. Temple.*

Cannon to right of them,
Cannon to left of them,
Cannon in front of them,
      Volley'd and thunder'd.
n.   Tennyson—*Charge of the Light Brigade.*

A great and lasting war can never be supported on this principle [patriotism] alone. It must be aided by a prospect of interest, or some reward.
o.   George Washington—*Letter to John Banister. Valley Forge,* April 21, 1778.

To be prepared for war is one of the most effectual means of preserving peace.
p.   George Washington—*Speech to Both Houses of Congress.* Jan. 8, 1790.

Nothing except a battle lost can be half so melancholy as a battle won.
q.   Duke of Wellington—*Despatch.* 1815.

Oh, a strange hand writes for our dear son—
      O, stricken mother's soul!
All swims before her eyes—flashes with black—
      she catches the main words only;
Sentences broken—*gun-shot wound in the breast, cavalry skirmish, taken to hospital;
At present low, but will soon be better.*
r   Walt Whitman—*Drum-Taps. Come up from the Fields, Father.*

They came with banner, spear, and shield;
And it was proved in Bosworth field,
Not long the Avenger was withstood—
Earth help'd him with the cry of blood.
s.   Wordsworth—*Song at the Feast of Brougham Castle.* St. 3'

WATER.

A cup of cold Adam from the next purling stream.
t.   Tom Brown—*Works.* Vol. IV. P. 11.

Till taught by pain,
Men really know not what good water's
  worth;
If you had been in Turkey or in Spain,
Or with a famish'd boat's-crew had your
  berth,
Or in the desert heard the camel's bell,
You'd wish yourself where Truth is—in a well.
  a.   Byron—*Don Juan.* Canto II. St. 84.

Water, water, everywhere,
  And all the boards did shrink;
Water, water, everywhere,
  Nor any drop to drink.
  b.   Coleridge—*Ancient Mariner.* Pt. II.
             St. 9.

Water its living strength first shows,
When obstacles its course oppose.
  c.   Goethe—*God, Soul, and World.*
             Rhymed Distichs.

The thirst that from the soul doth rise,
  Doth ask a drink divine;
But might I of Jove's nectar sup,
  I would not change for thine.
  d.   Ben Jonson—*The Forest. Song.*
        To Celia. Drink to Me Only With
             Thine Eyes.

Water is the mother of the vine,
The nurse and fountain of fecundity,
The adorner and refresher of the world.
  e.   Chas. Mackay—*The Dionysia.*

The rising world of waters dark and deep.
  f.   Milton—*Paradise Lost.* Bk. III.
             L. 11.

A Rechabite poor Will must live,
  And drink of Adam's ale.
  g.   Prior—*The Wandering Pilgrim.*

Honest water, which ne'er left man in the
  mire.
  h.   *Timon of Athens.* Act I. Sc. 2. L. 59.

More water glideth by the mill
Than wots the miller of.
  i.   *Titus Andronicus.* Act II. Sc. 1. L. 85.

'Tis rushing now adown the spout,
  And gushing out below,
Half frantic in its joyousness,
  And wild in eager flow.
The earth is dried and parched with heat,
  And it hath long'd to be
Released from out the selfish cloud,
  To cool the thirsty tree.
  j.   Elizabeth Oakes Smith—*Water.*

And so never ending,
But always descending.
  k.   Southey—*The Cataract of Lodore.*

"How does the Water
Come down at Lodore?"
  l.   Southey—*The Cataract of Lodore.*
  41

'Tis a little thing
To give a cup of water: yet its draught
Of cool refreshment, drain'd by feverish lips,
May give a thrill of pleasure to the frame
More exquisite than when nectarian juice
Renews the life of joy in happiest hours.
  m.   Thos. Noon Talfourd—*Sonnet III.*

How sweet from the green mossy brim to
  receive it,
As, poised on the curb, it inclined to my
  lips!
Not a full blushing goblet could tempt me to
  leave it,
The brightest that beauty or revelry sips.
  n.   Samuel Woodworth—*The Old Oaken*
             Bucket.

WEAKNESS.

But the concessions of the weak are the
concessions of fear.
  o.   Burke—*Speech on the Conciliation of*
             America.
Amiable weakness.
  p.   Henry Fielding—*Tom Jones.* Bk. X.
             Ch. VIII.
Amiable weakness of human nature.
  q.   Gibbon—*Decline and Fall of the*
          Roman Empire. Ch. XIV.

And the weak soul, within itself unbless'd,
Leans for all pleasure on another's breast.
  r.   Goldsmith—*The Traveller.* L. 271.

A mass enormous! which, in modern days
No two of earth's degenerate sons could raise.
  s.   Homer—*The Iliad.* Bk. XX. L. 387.
             Pope's trans.

Soft-heartedness, in times like these,
  Shows sof'ness in the upper story!
  t.   Lowell—*The Biglow Papers.* Second
            Series. No. 7.

Eye me, blest Providence, and square my trial
To my proportion'd strength.
  u.   Milton—*Comus.* L. 329.

If weakness may excuse,
What murderer, what traitor, parricide,
Incestuous, sacrilegious, but may plead it?
All wickedness is weakness; that plea, there-
  fore,
With God or man will gain thee no remission.
  v.   Milton—*Samson Agonistes.* L. 831.

To be weak is miserable,
Doing or suffering.
  w.   Milton—*Paradise Lost.* Bk. I. L. 157.

I know and love the good, yet ah! the worst
  pursue.
  x.   Petrarch—*To Laura in Life.*
            Canzone XXI.

Heaven forming each on other to depend,
A master, or a servant, or a friend,
Bids each on other for assistance call,
Till one man's weakness grows the strength
    of all.
a.   POPE—*Essay on Man.* Ep. II. L. 249.

Weakness to be wroth with weakness!
    woman's pleasure, woman's pain—
Nature made them blinder motions bounded
    in a shallower brain.
b.   TENNYSON—*Locksley Hall.* St. 75.

WEALTH.

There are, while human miseries abound,
A thousand ways to waste superfluous wealth,
Without one fool or flatterer at your board,
Without one hour of sickness or disgust.
c.   ARMSTRONG—*Art of Preserving Health.*
                            Bk. II. L. 195.

I have mental joys and mental health,
Mental friends and mental wealth,
I've a wife that I love and that loves me;
I've all but riches bodily.
d.   WM. BLAKE—*Mammon.*

Since all the riches of this world
    May be gifts from the devil and earthly
        kings,
I should suspect that I worshipped the devil
    If I thanked my God for worldly things.
e.   WM. BLAKE—*Riches.*

Who hath not heard the rich complain
Of surfeits, and corporeal pain?
He barr'd from every use of wealth,
Envies the ploughman's strength and health.
f.   GAY—*Fables. The Cookmaid, Turnspit,
                            and Ox.*

The ideal social state is not that in which
each gets an equal amount of wealth, but in
which each gets in proportion to his contri-
bution to the general stock.
g.   HENRY GEORGE—*Social Problems.*
                            Ch. VI.

And to hie him home, at evening's close,
To sweet repast, and calm repose.
    *   *   *   *   *   *
From toil he wins his spirits light,
From busy day the peaceful night;
Rich, from the very want of wealth,
In heaven's best treasures, peace and health.
h.   GRAY—*Ode on the Pleasure Arising
                            from Vicissitude.* L. 87.

For wealth, without contentment, climbs a
    hill,
To feel those tempests which fly over ditches.
i.   HERBERT—*The Church Porch.* St. 19.

Base wealth preferring to eternal praise.
j.   HOMER—*Iliad.* Bk. XXIII. L. 368.
                            Pope's trans.

Know from the bounteous heavens all riches
    flow;
And what man gives, the gods by man bestow.
k.   HOMER—*Odyssey.* Bk. XVIII. L. 26.
                            Pope's trans.

These riches are possess'd, but not enjoy'd!
l.   HOMER—*Odyssey.* Bk. IV. L. 118.
                            Pope's trans.

Poor worms, they hiss at me, whilst I at
    home
Can be contented to applaud myself, * * *
    with joy
To see how plump my bags are and my barns.
m.   BEN JONSON—*Every Man Out of His
                            Humour.* Act I. Sc. 1.

The rich man's son inherits cares;
    The bank may break, the factory burn,
A breath may burst his bubble shares,
    And soft, white hands could hardly earn
    A living that would serve his turn.
n.   LOWELL—*The Heritage.*

Infinite riches in a little room.
o.   MARLOWE—*The Jew of Malta.* Act I.
                            Sc. 1.

But wealth is a great means of refinement;
and it is a security for gentleness, since it
removes disturbing anxieties.
p.   IK. MARVEL—*Reveries of a Bachelor.
                            Over his Cigar.* III.

                    Let none admire
That riches grow in hell; that soil may best
Deserve the precious bane.
q.   MILTON—*Paradise Lost.* Bk. I. L. 690.

Get place and wealth, if possible, with grace;
If not, by any means get wealth and place.
r.   POPE—*Epistles of Horace.* Ep. I.
                            Bk. I. L. 103.

What riches give us let us then inquire:
Meat, fire, and clothes. What more? Meat,
    clothes, and fire.
Is this too little?
s.   POPE—*Moral Essays.* Ep. III. L. 79.

Lack of desire is the greatest riches.
t.   SENECA.

All gold and silver rather turn to dirt!
As 'tis no better reckon'd, but of those
Who worship dirty gods.
u.   *Cymbeline.* Act III. Sc. 6. L. 54.

            If thou art rich, thou art poor;
For, like an ass whose back with ingots bows,
Thou bear'st thy heavy riches but a journey,
And death unloads thee.
v.   *Measure for Measure.* Act III. Sc. 1.
                            L. 25.

O what a world of vile ill-favour'd faults
Looks handsome in three hundred pounds a
    year !
 a. *Merry Wives of Windsor.* Act III.
          Sc. 4. L. 32.

Through life's dark road his sordid way he
    wends,
An incarnation of fat dividends.
 b. Sprague—*Curiosity.* St. 25.

No, he was no such charlatan—
Count de Hoboken Flash-in-the-Pan—
 Full of gasconade and bravado,
But a regular, rich Don Rataplane,
 Santa Claus de la Muscavado,
 Senor Grandissimo Bastinado !
His was the rental of half Havana
And all Matanzas ; and Santa Ana,
Rich as he was, could hardly hold
A candle to light the mines of gold
Our Cuban owned.
 c. E. C. Stedman—*The Diamond Wedding.*
            St. 7.

If Heaven had looked upon riches to be a
valuable thing, it would not have given them
to such a scoundrel.
 d. Swift—*Letter to Miss Vanhomrigh.*
          Aug. 12, 1720.

He that is proud of riches is a fool. For if
he be exalted above his neighbors because he
hath more gold, how much inferior is he to a
gold mine !
 e. Jeremy Taylor—*Holy Living.* *Of*
     Humility. Ch. II. Sc. IV.

Can wealth give happiness? look round and
    see
What gay distress ! what splendid misery !
Whatever fortunes lavishly can pour,
The mind annihilates, and calls for more.
 f. Young—*Love of Fame.* Satire V.
            L. 394.

Much learning shows how little mortals
    know ;
Much wealth, how little worldlings can enjoy.
 g. Young—*Night Thoughts.* Night VI.
            L. 519.

WEEDS.

Call us not weeds, we are flowers of the sea.
 h. E. L. Aveline—*The Mother's Fables.*

In the deep shadow of the porch
 A slender bind-weed springs,
And climbs, like airy acrobat,
 The trellises, and swings
And dances in the golden sun
 In fairy loops and rings.
 i. Susan Coolidge—*Bind-Weed.*

The wolfsbane I should dread.
 j. Hood—*Flowers.*

To win the secret of a weed's plain heart.
 k. Lowell—*Sonnet XXV.*

         I will go root away
The noisome weeds which without profit suck
The soil's fertility from wholesome flowers.
 l. *Richard II.* Act III. Sc. 4. L. 37.

          Nothing teems
But hateful docks, rough thistles, kecksies,
    burs,
Losing both beauty and utility.
 m. *Henry V.* Act V. Sc. 2. L. 51.

Now 'tis the spring, and weeds are shallow-
    rooted ;
Suffer them now, and they'll o'ergrow the
    garden
And choke the herbs for want of husbandry.
 n. *Henry VI.* Act III. Sc. 1. L. 31.

The summer's flower is to the summer sweet,
 Though to itself it only live and die,
But if that flower with base infection meet,
 The basest weed outbraves his dignity ;
For sweetest things turn sourest by their
    deeds ;
Lilies that fester smell far worse than weeds.
 o. *Sonnet XCIV.*

WELCOME.

'Tis sweet to hear the watch-dog's honest bark
 Bay deep-mouth'd welcome as we draw near
  home ;
'Tis sweet to know there is an eye will mark
 Our coming, and look brighter when we
  come.
 p. Byron—*Don Juan.* Canto I. St. 123.

Come in the evening, or come in the morning,
Come when you're looked for, or come with-
    out warning,
Kisses and welcome you'll find here before
    you,
And the oftener you come here the more I'll
    adore you.
 q. Thomas O. Davis—*The Welcome.*

         The atmosphere
Breathes rest and comfort and the many
    chambers
Seem full of welcomes.
 r. Longfellow—*The Masque of Pandora.*
           Pt. V. L. 33.

Welcome, my old friend,
Welcome to a foreign fireside.
 s. Longfellow—*To an Old Danish*
           Song-Book.

Shall I meet other wayfarers at night ?
 Those who have gone before.
Then must I knock, or call when just in sight ?
 They will not keep you standing at that door.
 t. Christina G. Rossetti—*Up Hill.*

A table full of welcome makes scarce one
    dainty dish.
  a.   *Comedy of Errors.* Act III. Sc. 1.
                            L. 23.
                Bid that welcome
Which comes to punish us, and we punish it
Seeming to bear it lightly.
  b.   *Antony and Cleopatra.* Act IV. Sc. 14.
                            L. 136.
His worth is warrant for his welcome.
  c.   *Two Gentlemen of Verona.* Act II.
                      Sc. 4. L. 102.
 I hold your dainties cheap, sir, and your
    welcome dear.
  d.   *Comedy of Errors.* Act III. Sc. 1.
                            L. 21.
    I reckon this always, that a man is never
undone till he be hanged, nor never welcome
to a place till some certain shot be paid and
the hostess say " Welcome !"
  e.   *Two Gentlemen of Verona.* Act II.
                    Sc. 5. L. 3.
Sir, you are very welcome to our house:
It must appear in other ways than words,
Therefore I scant this breathing courtesy.
  f.   *Merchant of Venice.* Act V. Sc. 1.
                            L. 139.
    Small cheer and great welcome makes a
merry feast.
  g.   *Comedy of Errors.* Act III. Sc. 1.
                            L. 26.
                Trust me, sweet,
Out of this silence yet I pick'd a welcome.
  h.   *Midsummer-Night's Dream.* Act V.
                    Sc. 1. L. 99.
          Welcome ever smiles,
And farewell goes out sighing.
  i.   *Troilus and Cressida.* Act III. Sc. 3.
                            L. 168.

WICKEDNESS.

There is a method in man's wickedness,
    It grows up by degrees.
  j.   BEAUMONT AND FLETCHER—*A King
        and No King.* Act V. Sc. 4.

The majority is wicked.
  k.   BIAS.

The world loves a spice of wickedness.
  l.   LONGFELLOW—*Hyperion.* Ch. VII.
                            Bk. I.
Destroy his fib, or sophistry—in vain !
The creature's at his dirty work again.
  m.   POPE—*Prologue to the Satires.* L. 91.

Are you call'd forth from out a world of men,
To slay the innocent?
  n.   *Richard III.* Act 1. Sc. 4. L. 186.

'Cause I's wicked,—I is. I's mighty wicked,
anyhow, I can't help it.
  o.   HARRIET BEECHER STOWE—*Uncle Tom's
                        Cabin.* Ch. XX.

WIFE.

    Wives are young men's mistresses; com-
panions for middle age ; and old men's nurses.
  p.   BACON—*Of Marriage and Single Life.*

And while the wicket falls behind
Her steps, I thought if I could find
A wife I need not blush to show
I've little further now to go.
  q.   WILLIAM BARNES—*Not Far to Go.*

She is a winsome wee thing,
She is a handsome wee thing,
She is a bonny wee thing,
    This sweet wee wife o' mine.
  r.   BURNS—*My Wife's a Winsome Wee
                                Thing.*

Be thou the rainbow to the storms of life !
The evening beam that smiles the clouds
    away
And tints to-morrow with prophetic ray !
  s.   BYRON—*The Bride of Abydos.*
                    Canto II. St. 20.

    Thy wife is a constellation of virtues; she's
the moon, and thou art the man in the moon.
  t.   CONGREVE—*Love for Love.* Act II.
                            Sc. 1.
What is there in the vale of life
Half so delightful as a wife,
When friendship, love, and peace combine
To stamp the marriage-bond divine?
  u.   COWPER—*Love Abused.*

Oh! 'tis a precious thing, when wives are
    dead,
To find such numbers who will serve instead :
And in whatever state a man be thrown,
'Tis that precisely they would wish their own.
  v.   CRABBE—*Tales. The Learned Boy.*

The wife was pretty, trifling, childish, weak;
She could not think, but would not cease to
    speak.
  w.   CRABBE—*Tales. Struggles of Conscience.*

                You know I met you,
Kist you, and prest you close within my arms,
With all the tenderness of wifely love.
  x.   DRYDEN—*Amphitryon.* Act III. Sc. 1.

She commandeth her husband, in any equal
matter, by constant obeying him.
  y.   FULLER—*The Holy and Profane States.
        The Good Wife.* Bk. I. Maxim I.
                            Ch. I.
A wife, domestic, good, and pure,
Like snail, should keep within her door ;
But not, like snail, with silver track,
Place all her wealth upon her back.
  z.   W. W. HOW—*Good Wives.*

He knew whose gentle hand was at the latch,
Before the door had given her to his eyes.
  aa.   KEATS—*Isabella.* St. 3.

But thou **dost make** the very night itself
Brighter than day.

   a.   Longfellow—*Christus. The Divin*
                Tragedy. The First Passover.
                      Pt. III. L. 133.

Sail forth into the sea of life,
O gentle, loving, trusting wife,
And safe from all adversity
Upon the bosom of that sea
Thy comings and thy goings be!
For gentleness and love and trust
Prevail o'er angry wave and gust;
And in the wreck of noble lives
Something immortal still survives.

   b.   Longfellow—*The Building of the Ship.*
                        L. 368.

How much the wife is dearer than the bride.

   c.   Lord Lyttleton—*An Irregular Ode.*

O wretched is the dame, to whom the sound,
"Your lord will soon return," no pleasure
    brings.

   d.   Maturin—*Bertram.* Act II. Sc. 5.

In the election of a wife, as in
A project of war, to err but once is
To be undone forever.

   e.   Thos. Middleton—*Anything for a Quiet*
                 Life. Act I. Sc. 1.

                     Awake,
My fairest, my espous'd, my latest found,
Heaven's last best gift, my ever new delight!

   f.   Milton—*Paradise Lost.* Bk. V. L. 17.

For nothing lovelier can be found
In woman, than to study household good,
And good works in her husband to promote.

   g.   Milton—*Paradise Lost.* Bk. IX.
                        L. 232.

            What thou bidd'st
Unargu'd I obey, so God ordains;
God is thy law, thou mine; to know no more
Is woman's happiest knowledge and her
    praise.

   h.   Milton—*Paradise Lost.* Bk. IV.
                        L. 635.

All other goods by fortune's hand are given,
A wife is the peculiar gift of heaven.

   i.   Pope—*January and May. From*
                 Chaucer. L. 51.

But what so pure, which envious tongues will
    spare?
Some wicked wits have libell'd all the fair.
With matchless impudence they style a wife
The dear-bought curse, and lawful plague of
    life;
A bosom-serpent, a domestic evil,
A night-invasion and a mid-day-devil.
Let not the wife these sland'rous words re-
    gard.
But curse the bones of ev'ry living bard.

   j.   Pope—*January and May.* L. 43.

She who ne'er answers till a husband cools,
Or, if she rules him, never shews she rules;
Charms by accepting, by submitting sways,
Yet has her humour most when she obeys.

   k.   Pope—*Moral Essays.* Ep. II. L. 261.

A light wife doth make a heavy husband.

   l.   *Merchant of Venice.* Act V. Sc. 1.
                        L. 130.

                    As for my wife,
I would you had her spirit in such another;
The third o' the world is yours; which with a
    snaffle
You may pace easy, but not such a wife.

   m.   *Antony and Cleopatra.* Act II. Sc. 2.
                        L. 61.

Happy in this, she is not yet so old
But she may learn; happier than this,
She is not bred so dull but she can learn;
Happiest of all is, that her gentle spirit
Commits itself to yours to be directed.

   n.   *Merchant of Venice.* Act III. Sc. 2.
                        L. 162.

I will be master of what is mine own;
She is my goods, my chattels; she is my
    house,
My household stuff, my field, my barn,
My horse, my ox, my ass, my anything;
And here she stands, touch her whoever dare.

   o.   *Taming of the Shrew.* Act III. Sc. 2.
                        L. 231.

                  Should all despair
That have revolted wives, the tenth of man-
    kind
Would hang themselves.

   p.   *Winter's Tale.* Act I. Sc. 2. L. 198.

          Why, man, she is mine own,
And I as rich in having such a jewel
As twenty seas, if all their sand were pearl,
The water nectar and the rocks pure gold.

   q.   *Two Gentlemen of Verona.* Act II.
                    Sc. 4. L. 168.

My dear, my better half.

   r.   Sir Philip Sidney—*Arcadia.* Bk. III.

Of earthly goods, the best is a good wife;
A bad, the bitterest curse of human life.

   s.   Simonides.

Light household duties, ever more inwrought
    With placid fancies of one trusting heart
That lives but in her smile, and turns
    From life's cold seeming and the busy mart,
With tenderness, that heavenward ever
    yearns
To be refreshed where one pure altar burns.
Shut out from hence the mockery of life;
Thus liveth she content, the meek, fond,
    trusting wife.

   t.   Elizabeth Oakes Smith—*The Wife.*

A love still burning upward, giving light
To read those laws, an accent very low
In blandishment, but a most silver flow
Of subtle-paced counsel in distress,
Right to the heart and brain, tho' undescried,
Winning its way with extreme gentleness
Thro' all the outworks of suspicious pride;
A courage to endure and to obey:
A hate of gossip parlance and of sway,
Crown'd Isabel, thro' all her placid life,
The queen of marriage, a most perfect wife.
> a.   TENNYSON—*Isabel.*

The world well tried—the sweetest thing in life
Is the unclouded welcome of a wife.
> b.   N. P. WILLIS—*Lady Jane.*   Canto II.
> St. XI.

WILL.

A willing heart adds feather to the heel,
And makes the clown a winged Mercury.
> c.   JOANNA BAILLIE—*De Montfort.*
> Act III.   Sc. 2.

He that complies against his will,
Is of his own opinion still,
Which he may adhere to, yet disown,
For reasons to himself best known.
> d.   BUTLER—*Hudibras.*   Pt. III.
> Canto III.   L. 547.

The commander of the forces of a large
State may be carried off, but the will of even
a common man cannot be taken from him.
> e.   CONFUCIUS—*Analects.*   Bk. IX.
> Ch. XXV.

There is nothing good or evil save in the
will.
> f.   EPICTETUS.

To deny the freedom of the will is to make
morality impossible.
> g.   FROUDE—*Short Studies on Great*
> *Subjects. Calvinism.*

The only way of setting the will free is to
deliver it from wilfulness.
> h.   J. C. AND A. W. HARE—*Guesses at*
> *Truth.*

The readinesse of doing doth expresse
No other but the doer's willingnesse.
> i.   HERRICK—*Hesperides. Readinesse.*

A boy's will is the wind's will.
> j.   LONGFELLOW—*My Lost Youth.*

The star of the unconquered will,
He rises in my breast,
Serene, and resolute, and still,
And calm, and self-possessed.
> k.   LONGFELLOW—*The Light of Stars.* St. 7.

And binding nature fast in fate,
Left free the human will.
> l.   POPE—*The Universal Prayer.*   St. 3.

We sought therefore to amend our will, and
not to suffer it through despite to languish
long time in error.
> m.   SENECA—*Of Benefits.*   Bk. 5.
> Ch. XXV.   Ep. 67.

My will enkindled by mine eyes and ears,
Two traded pilots 'twixt the dangerous shores
Of will and judgment.
> n.   *Troilus and Cressida.*   Act II.   Sc. 2.
> L. 63.

That what he will he does, and does so much
That proof is call'd impossibility.
> o.   *Troilus and Cressida.*   Act V.   Sc. 5.
> L. 28.

            All
Life needs for life is possible to will.
> p.   TENNYSON—*Love and Duty.*   L. 82.

Our wills are ours, we know not how;
Our wills are ours, to make them thine.
> q.   TENNYSON—*In Memoriam.*
> Introduction.   St. 4.

WIND.

Blow, Boreas, foe to human kind!
Blow, blustering, freezing, piercing wind!
Blow, that thy force I may rehearse,
While all my thoughts congeal to verse!
> r.   JOHN BANCKS—*To Boreas.*

There is strange music in the stirring wind!
> s.   REV. WM. L. BOWLES—*Sonnets and*
> *Other Poems. November.*

A breeze came wandering from the sky,
   Light as the whispers of a dream;
He put the o'erhanging grasses by,
   And softly stooped to kiss the stream,
The pretty stream, the flattered stream,
   The shy, yet unreluctant stream.
> t.   BRYANT—*The Wind and Stream.*

The faint old man shall lean his silver head
   To feel thee; thou shalt kiss the child
       asleep,
And dry the moistened curls that overspread
   His temples, while his breathing grows more
       deep.
> u.   BRYANT—*The Evening Wind.* St. 4.

Where hast thou wandered, gentle gale, to
   find
The perfumes thou dost bring?
> v.   BRYANT—*May Evening.* St. 2.

Wind of the sunny south! oh, still delay
  In the gay woods and in the golden air,
  Like to a good old age released from care,
Journeying, in long serenity, away.
In such a bright, late quiet, would that I
  Might wear out life like thee, mid bowers
      and brooks,
And, dearer yet, the sunshine of kind
    looks,
And music of kind voices ever nigh ;
And when my last sand twinkled in the glass,
Pass silently from men as thou dost pass.
  a.   BRYANT—*October.* L. 5.

As winds come whispering lightly from the
    West,
Kissing, not ruffling, the blue deep's serene.
  b.   BYRON—*Childe Harold.* Canto II.
                          St. 70.

  When the stormy winds do blow ;
When the battle rages loud and long,
  And the stormy winds do blow.
  c.   CAMPBELL—*Ye Mariners of England.*

Soft blows the wind that breathes from that
    blue sky !
  d.   COLERIDGE—*From the German.*

The winds of winter wailing through the
    woods ;
The mighty laughter of the vernal floods.
  e.   ABRAHAM COLES—*The Microcosm.*
                        Music of Nature.

How silent are the winds !
  f.   BARRY CORNWALL— *English Songs and*
        Other Small Poems. The Sea in
                          Calm.

The moaning winds of Autumn sang their
    song.
  g.   BARRY CORNWALL—*A Sicilian Story.*
                        St. XX.

The winds that never moderation knew,
Afraid to blow too much, too faintly blew ;
Or out of breath with joy, could not enlarge
Their straighten'd lungs or conscious of their
    charge.
  h.   DRYDEN—*Astræa Redux.* L. 242.

          Perhaps the wind
Wails so in winter for the summer's dead,
And all sad sounds are nature's funeral cries
For what has been and is not.
  i.   GEORGE ELIOT—*The Spanish Gypsy.*
                        Bk. I.

  The wind moans, like a long wail from some
despairing soul shut out in the awful storm !
  j.   W. H. GIBSON—*Pastoral Days. Winter.*

The wind, the wandering wind
  Of the golden summer eves—
Whence is the thrilling magic
  Of its tunes amongst the leaves?
Oh, is it from the waters,
  Or from the long, tall grass?
Or is it from the hollow rocks
  Through which its breathings pass?
  k.   MRS. HEMANS—*The Wandering Wind.*

An ill wind that bloweth no man good—
The blower of which blast is she.
  l.   JOHN HEYWOOD—*Idleness.* St. 5.

Madame, bear in mind
That princes govern all things—save the
    wind.
  m.   VICTOR HUGO—*The Infanta's Rose.*

Chill airs and wintry winds ! my ear
  Has grown familiar with your song;
I hear it in the opening year,
  I listen, and it cheers me long.
  n.   LONGFELLOW—*Woods in Winter.* St. 7.

I hear the wind among the trees
Playing celestial symphonies ;
I see the branches downward bent,
Like keys of some great instrument.
  o.   LONGFELLOW—*A Day of Sunshine.*
                        St. 3.

The winds with wonder whist,
Smoothly the waters kisst.
  p.   MILTON—*Hymn on the Nativity.* St. 5.

When the gust hath blown his fill,
Ending on the rustling leaves,
With minute drops from off the eaves.
  q.   MILTON—*Il Penseroso.* L. 128.

While rocking winds are piping loud.
  r.   MILTON—*Il Penseroso.* L. 126.

Never does a wilder song
Steal the breezy lyre along,
When the wind in odors dying,
Wooes it with enamor'd sighing.
  s.   MOORE—*To Rosa.*

Loud wind, strong wind, sweeping o'er the
    mountains,
  Fresh wind, free wind, blowing from the
    sea,
Pour forth thy vials like streams from airy
    mountains,
  Draughts of life to me.
  t.   D. M. MULOCK—*North Wind.*

And the South Wind—he was dressed
With a ribbon round his breast
That floated, flapped, and fluttered
    In a riotous unrest
    And a drapery of mist
    From the shoulder to the wrist
Floating backward with the motion
    Of the waving hand he kissed.
  u.   JAMES WHITCOMB RILEY—*The South*
                      Wind and the Sun.

  Take a straw and throw it up into the
air, you may see by that which way the wind
is.
  v.   JOHN SELDEN—*Table Talk. Libels.*

What wind blew you hither, Pistol?
Not the ill wind which blows no man to good.
  w.   *Henry IV.* Pt. II. Act V. Sc. 3.
                          L. 89.

O wild West Wind, thou breath of Autumn's
　　being,
Thou, from whose unseen presence the leaves
　　dead
Are driven, like ghosts from an enchanter
　　fleeing,
Yellow, and black, and pale, and hectic red,
Pestilence-stricken multitudes.
　a.　　SHELLEY—*Ode to the West Wind.* Pt. I.

　　　　　　　　　O wind,
If Winter comes, can Spring be far behind?
　b.　　SHELLEY—*Ode to the West Wind.* Pt. V.

Through the gaunt woods the winds are
　　shrilling cold,
Down from the rifted rock the sunbeam pours
Over the cold gray slopes, and stony moors.
　c.　　FREDERICK TENNYSON—*First of March.*

　　　　　　　A fresher Gale
Begins to wave the wood, and stir the stream,
Sweeping with shadowy gust the fields of
　　corn;
While the Quail clamors for his running
　　mate.
　d.　　THOMSON—*Seasons. Summer.*
　　　　　　　　　　　　　L. 1,655.

Except wind stands as never it stood,
It is an ill wind turns none to good.
　e.　　TUSSER—*Five Hundred Points of Good
　　　　　Husbandrie. Description of the
　　　　　Properties of Winds.* Ch. XII.

I dropped my pen; and listened to the wind
　That sang of trees uptorn and vessels tost;
A midnight harmony and wholly lost
To the general sense of men by chains con-
　　fined
Of business, care, or pleasure,—or resigned
　　To timely sleep.
　f.　　WORDSWORTH—*Sonnet* (*Composed while
　　　　　the Author was engaged in writing a
　　　　　tract occasioned by the Convention
　　　　　　　　　　　　　of Cintra*).

WINE AND SPIRITS.

I hang no ivie out to sell my wine;
The nectar of good wits will sell itself.
　g.　　ALLOT—*England's Parnassus. Sonnet
　　　　　　　　　　　　　to the Reader.*

Old Simon the cellarer keeps a rare store
　Of Malmsey and Malvoisie.
　h.　　G. W. BELLAMY—*Simon the Cellarer.*

John Barleycorn was a hero bold,
　Of noble enterprise,
For if you do but taste his blood,
　'Twill make your courage rise,
'Twill make a man forget his wo;
　'Twill heighten all his joy.
　i.　　BURNS—*John Barleycorn.* St. 13

So Noah, when he anchor'd safe on
The mountain's top, his lofty haven,
And all the passengers he bore
Were on the new world set ashore,
He made it next his chief design
To plant and propagate a vine,
Which since has overwhelm'd and drown'd
Far greater numbers, on dry ground,
Of wretched mankind, one by one,
Than all the flood before had done.
　j.　　BUTLER—*Satire upon Drunkenness.*
　　　　　　　　　　　　　L. 105.

Few things surpass old wine; and they may
　　preach
Who please, the more because they preach in
　　vain,—
Let us have wine and women, mirth and
　　laughter,
Sermons and soda-water the day after.
　k.　　BYRON—*Don Juan.* Canto II. St. 178.

Sweet is old wine in bottles, ale in barrels.
　l.　　BYRON—*Sweet Things.* St. 5.

Which cheers the sad, revives the old, inspires
The young, makes Weariness forget his toil,
And Fear her danger; opens a new world
When this, the present, palls.
　m.　　BYRON—*Sardanapalus.* Act I. Sc. 1.

Alcohol is not wine but an atrocious usurper
of its name and rights. The wine of the
cluster is the pure blood of the grape. Death
follows life, and corruption death, and there
results a deadly something, which men call
wine, but wrongly for it is no longer vinous.
The **vine** disowns it. It is a corpse, not a
living thing.
　n.　　ABRAHAM COLES—*The Evangel.* P. 230.

Taking our stand on the immovable rock of
Christ's character we risk nothing in saying,
that the wine of *miracle* answered to the wine
of *nature*, and was not intoxicating. No
counter proof can equal the force of that
drawn from His attributes. It is an indecency
and a calumny to impute to Christ conduct
which requires apology.
　o.　　ABRAHAM COLES—*The Evangel.* Note.
　　　　　　　　　　　　　P. 209.

The modest water saw its God and blushed.
　p.　　ABRAHAM COLES—*Translation of
　　　　　CRASHAW'S Epigram, Nympha pudica
　　　　　　　　　　　Deum vidit et erubuit.*

Sing! Who sings
To her who weareth a hundred rings?
　　Ah, who is this lady fine?
　　The Vine, boys, the Vine!
　　The mother of the mighty Wine,
　　A roamer is she
　　O'er wall and tree
And sometimes very good company.
　q.　　BARRY CORNWALL—*A Bacchanalian
　　　　　　　　　　　　　Song.*

Ten thousand casks,
Forever dribbling out their base contents,
Touch'd by the Midas finger of the state,
Bleed gold for ministers to sport away.
Drink, and be mad then; 'tis your country
　　bids!
a.　　COWPER—*The Task.*　Bk. IV.　L. 504.

The conscious water saw its God and blushed.
b.　　CRASHAW—*Translation of His Own
　　　　　　Epigram on the Miracle of Cana.
　　　　　　St. John's Gospel.*　Ch. II.

When Christ, at Cana's feast by power divine,
Inspir'd cold water with the warmth of wine,
See! cried they, while in red'ning tide it
　　gush'd,
The bashful stream hath seen its God and
　　blush'd.
c.　　CRASHAW—*Poëmata et Epigrammata.*
　　　　　　　　　　Aaron Hill's trans.

When asked what wines he liked to drink
he replied, "That which belongs to another."
d.　　DIOGENES LAERTIUS—*Lives and
　　　　　　Opinions of Eminent Philosophers.
　　　　　　Diogenes.*　VI.　Yonge's trans.

Bring me wine, but wine which never grew
　　In the belly of the grape,
Or grew on vine whose tap-roots, reaching
　　through
　　Under the Andes to the Cape,
Suffered no savor of the earth to escape.
e.　　EMERSON—*Bacchus.*　St. 1.

From wine what sudden friendship springs?
f.　　GAY—*Fables.*　Pt. II.　Fable 6.

Let schoolmasters puzzle their brain,
　　With grammar, and nonsense, and learning;
Good liquor, I stoutly maintain,
　　Gives genius a better discerning.
g.　　GOLDSMITH—*She Stoops to Conquer.*
　　　　　　　　　Act I.　Sc. 1.　*Song.*

Call things by their right names * * *
Glass of brandy and water! That is the current, but not the appropriate name; ask for
a glass of liquid fire and distilled damnation.
h.　　ROBERT HALL—GREGORY'S *Life of
　　　　　　Hall.*　Vol. I.　P. 59.

Sparkling and bright, in liquid light,
　　Does the wine our goblets gleam in;
With hue as red as the rosy bed
　　Which a bee would choose to dream in.
i.　　CHARLES FENNO HOFFMAN—*Sparkling
　　　　　　　　　　　　and Bright.*

And wine can of their wits the wise beguile,
Make the sage frolic, and the serious smile.
j.　　HOMER—*Odyssey.*　Bk. XIV.　L. 520.
　　　　　　　　　　Pope's trans.

As for the brandy, "nothing extenuate";
and the water, put nought in in malice.
k.　　DOUGLAS JERROLD—*Jerrold's Wit.*
　　　　　　　　　　Shakespeare Grog.

Claret is the liquor for boys; port for men;
but he who aspires to be a hero must drink
brandy.
l.　　SAM'L JOHNSON—*Boswell's Life of
　　　　　　　　　Johnson.*　1779.

But that which most doth take my muse and
　　me,
Is a pure cup of rich Canary wine,
Which is the mermaid's now, but shall be
　　mine.
m.　　BEN JONSON—*Epigram CI.*

Dance and Provençal song and sunburnt
　　mirth!
Oh for a beaker full of the warm South,
Full of the true, the blushful Hippocrene!
With beaded bubbles winking at the brim,
And purple-stained mouth.
n.　　KEATS—*Ode to a Nightingale.*

There is a devil in every berry of the grape.
o.　　*The Koran.*

　　Filled with the wine
　　Of the vine
　　Benign
That flames so red in Sansavine.
p.　　LONGFELLOW—(Quoted) *Hyperion.*
　　　　　　　　　　　　Ch. VIII.

Things of greatest profit are set forth with
least price. Where the wine is neat there
needeth no ivie bush.
q.　　LYLY—*Euphues.*　A. 3.

Bacchus, that first from out the purple
　　grape,
Crushed the sweet poison of misused wine.
r.　　MILTON—*Comus.*　L. 46.

O Roman punch! O potent Curaçoa!
O Maraschino! Maraschino O!
Delicious drams! Why have you not the art
To kill this gnawing Book-worm in my heart?
s.　　MOORE—*Twopenny Post Bag.*　See
　　　　　　　　　Appendix, Letter VII.

It has become quite a common proverb that
in wine there is truth.
t.　　PLINY—*Natural History.*　Bk. XIV.
　　　　　　　　　　　Sec. 14.

We care not for money, riches, nor wealth;
Old sack is our money, old sack is our wealth.
u.　　THOMAS RANDOLPH—*The Praise of
　　　　　　　　　　Old Sack.*

Come, come, good wine is a good familiar
creature, if it be well used; exclaim no more
against it.
v.　　*Othello.*　Act II.　Sc. 3.　L. 313.

　　Give me a bowl of wine:
I have not that alacrity of spirit,
Nor cheer of mind, that I was wont to have.
w.　　*Richard III.*　Act V.　Sc. 3.　L. 72.

Give me a bowl of wine;
In this I bury all unkindness.
a.   *Julius Cæsar.* Act IV. Sc. 3. L. 158.

He calls for wine : "A health," quoth he, as if
He had been abroad, carousing to his mates
After a storm.
b.   *Taming of the Shrew.* Act III. Sc. 2.
L. 172.

O thou invisible spirit of wine, if thou hast
no name to be known by, let us call thee devil!
c.   *Othello.* Act II. Sc. 3. L 283.

Day and night my thoughts incline
To the blandishments of wine,
Jars were made to drain, I think ;
Wine, I know, was made to drink.
d.   R. H. STODDARD—*A Jar of Wine.*

The hop for his profit I thus do exalt,
It strengtheneth drink, and it favoureth malt:
And being well brewed, long kept it will last,
And drawing abide—if you draw not too fast.
e.   TUSSER—*Five Hundred Points of Good
Husbandrie. A Lesson When and
Where to Plant a Good Hop-Yard.*
Ch. XLIII.

WINTER (*See* SEASONS).

WISDOM.

Wisdom of our ancestors.
f.   BURKE—*Thoughts on the Cause of the
Present Discontent.*

But these are foolish things to all the wise,
And I love wisdom more than she loves me ;
My tendency is to philosophise
On most things, from a tyrant to a tree ;
But still the spouseless virgin *Knowledge* flies,
What are we ? and whence come we? what
shall be
Our *ultimate* existence? What's our present?
Are questions answerless, and yet incessant.
g.   BYRON—*Don Juan.* Canto VI. St. 63.

But they whom truth and wisdom lead
Can gather honey from a weed.
h.   COWPER—*The Pine-Apple and Bee.*
L. 35.

It seems the part of wisdom.
i.   COWPER—*The Task.* Bk. IV. L. 336.

Knowledge is proud that he has learn'd so
much ;
Wisdom is humble that he knows no more.
j.   COWPER—*The Task.* Bk. VI. L. 96.

Wisdom and goodness are twin-born, one
heart
Must hold both sisters, never seen apart.
k.   COWPER—*Expostulation.* L. 634.

The bearings of this observation lays in the
application on it.
l.   DICKENS—*Dombey and Son.*
Ch. XXIII.

Who are a little wise the best fools be.
m.   DONNE—*The Triple Fool.*

Man thinks
Brutes have no wisdom, since they know not
his :
Can we divine their world ?
n.   GEORGE ELIOT—*The Spanish Gypsy.*
Bk. II.

Wisdom makes but a slow defence against
trouble, though at last a sure one.
o.   GOLDSMITH—*Vicar of Wakefield.*
Ch. XXI.

I'll tell the names and sayings and the places
of their birth,
Of the seven great ancient sages so renowned
on Grecian earth,
The Lindian Cleobulus said, "The mean was
still the best" ;
The Spartan Chilo, "Know thyself," a heaven-
born phrase confessed.
Corinthian Periander taught "Our anger to
command, "
"Too much of nothing," Pittacus, from Mity-
lenes' strand ;
Athenian Solon this advised, "Look to the
end of life,"
And Bias from Priene showed, "Bad men are
the most rife";
Milesian Thales urged that "None should e'er
a surety be" ;
Few were their words, but if you look, you'll
much in little see.
p.   *From the Greek.* Author unknown.

The heart is wiser than the intellect.
q.   J. G. HOLLAND—*Kathrina.* Pt. II.
St. 9.

Chiefs who no more in bloody fights engage,
But, wise through time, and narrative with
age,
In summer-days like grasshoppers rejoice,
A bloodless race, that send a feeble voice.
r.   HOMER—*Iliad.* Bk. III. L. 199.
Pope's trans.

For never, never, wicked man was wise.
s.   HOMER—*Odyssey.* Bk. II. L. 320.
Pope's trans.

How prone to doubt, how cautious are the
wise!
t.   HOMER—*Odyssey.* Bk. XIII. L. 375.
Pope's trans.

In youth and beauty wisdom is but rare !
u.   HOMER—*Odyssey.* Bk. VII. L. 379.
Pope's trans.

Nothing can be truer than fairy wisdom.
It is as true as sunbeams.
v.   DOUGLAS JERROLD—*Specimens of
Jerrold's Wit. Fairy Tales.*

Ripe in wisdom was he, but patient, and
simple, and childlike.
  a.   Longfellow—*Evangeline.* Pt. I. III.
                                      L. 11.

            Be wise;
Soar not too high to fall; but stoop to rise.
  b.   Massinger—*Duke of Milan.* Act I.
                                   Sc. 2. L. 45.

            But to know
That which before us lies in daily life,
Is the prime wisdom.
  c.   Milton—*Paradise Lost.* Bk. VIII.
                                      L. 192.

  Socrates * * *
Whom, well inspir'd, the oracle pronounc'd
Wisest of men.
  d.   Milton—*Paradise Regained.* Bk. IV.
                                      L. 274.

Though wisdom wake, suspicion sleeps
At wisdom's gate, and to simplicity
Resigns her charge, while goodness thinks no
    ill
Where no ill seems.
  e.   Milton—*Paradise Lost.* Bk. III.
                                      L. 686.

  The most manifest sign of wisdom is a continual cheerfulness: her state is like that of
things in the regions above the moon, always
clear and serene.
  f.   Montaigne—*Essays.* Bk. I.
                                   Ch. XXV.

When swelling buds their od'rous foliage shed,
And gently harden into fruit, the wise
Spare not the little offsprings, if they grow
Redundant.
  g.   John Philips—*Cider.* Bk. I.

Tell (for you can) what is it to be wise?
'Tis but to know how little can be known,
To see all other's faults, and feel our own.
  h.   Pope—*Essay on Man.* Ep. IV. L. 260.

Wouldst thou wisely, and with pleasure,
Pass the days of life's short measure,
From the slow one counsel take,
But a tool of him ne'er make;
Ne'er as friend the swift one know,
Nor the constant one as foe.
  i.   Schiller—*Proverbs of Confucius.*
                        E. A. Bowring's trans.

  Wisdom does not show itself so much in
precept as in life—in a firmness of mind and
mastery of appetite. It teaches us to do, as
well as to talk; and to make our actions and
words all of a color.
  j.   Seneca—*Epistle XX.*

            Full oft we see
Cold wisdom waiting on superfluous folly.
  k.   *All's Well That Ends Well.* Act I.
                                   Sc. 1. L. 115.

  Thou shouldst not have been old till thou
hadst been wise.
  l.   *King Lear.* Act I. Sc. 5. L. 48.

To that dauntless temper of his mind,
He hath a wisdom that doth guide his valour
To act in safety.
  m.   *Macbeth.* Act III. Sc. 1. L. 52.

  Well, God give them wisdom that have it;
and those that are fools, let them use their
talents.
  n.   *Twelfth Night.* Act I. Sc. 5. L. 14.

Wisdom and fortune combating together,
If that the former dare but what it can,
No chance may shake it.
  o.   *Antony and Cleopatra.* Act III. Sc. 13.
                                      L. 79.

As for me, all I know is that I know nothing.
  p.   Socrates—*Plato. Phædrus.* Sec. 235.

  The doorstep to the temple of wisdom is a
knowledge of our own ignorance.
  q.   Spurgeon—*Gleanings among the
                        Sheaves. The First Lesson.*

        By Wisdom wealth is won;
But riches purchased wisdom yet for none.
  r.   Bayard Taylor—*The Wisdom of Ali.*

" The Prophet's words were true;
The mouth of Ali is the golden door
Of Wisdom."
            When his friends to Ali bore
These words, he smiled and said: "And
      should they ask
The same until my dying day, the task
Were easy; for the stream from Wisdom's
      well,
Which God supplies, is inexhaustible."
  s.   Bayard Taylor—*The Wisdom of Ali.*

Nor is he the wisest man who never proved
      himself a fool.
  t.   Tennyson—*Locksley Hall Sixty Years
                        After.* St. 124.

'Tis held that sorrow makes us wise.
  u.   Tennyson—*In Memoriam.* Pt. CVIII.

            Wisdom sits alone,
Topmost in heaven:—she is its light—its God;
And in the heart of man she sits as high—
Though grovelling eyes forget her oftentimes,
Seeing but this world's idols. The pure mind
Sees her forever: and in youth we come
Fill'd with her sainted ravishment, and kneel,
Worshipping God through her sweet altar
      fires,
And then is knowledge " good."
  v.   N. P. Willis—*The Scholar of Thibet.
                        Ben Khorat.* Pt. II. L. 93.

And he is oft the wisest man
Who is not wise at all.
  w.   Wordsworth—*The Oak and the Broom.*

Wisdom is ofttimes nearer when we stoop
Than when we soar.
  x.   Wordsworth—*The Excursion.* Bk. III.
                                      L. 232.

Be wise with speed;
A fool at forty is a fool indeed.
   a.   Young—*Love of Fame.* Satire II.
            L. 281.

But wisdom, awful wisdom! which inspects,
Discerns, compares, weighs, separates, infers,
Seizes the right, and holds it to the last.
   b.   Young—*Night Thoughts.* Night VIII.
            L. 1,253.

On every thorn, delightful wisdom grows,
In every rill a sweet instruction flows.
   c.   Young—*Love of Fame.* Satire I.
            L. 249.

Teach me my days to number, and apply
My trembling heart to wisdom.
   d.   Young—*Night Thoughts.* Night IX.
            L. 1,312.

Wisdom, though richer than Peruvian mines,
And sweeter than the sweet ambrosial hive,
What is she, but the means of *happiness?*
That unobtain'd, than folly more a fool.
   e.   Young—*Night Thoughts.* Night II.
            L. 496.

WISHES.

" Man wants but little here below
   Nor wants that little long,"
'Tis not with me exactly so;
   But 'tis so in the song.
My wants are many, and, if told,
   Would muster many a score;
And were each wish a mint of gold,
   I still should long for more.
   f.   John Quincy Adams—*The Wants of
        Man.* The quoted lines from
        Goldsmith—*Hermit.* St. 8.

Every wish
Is like a prayer—with God.
   g.   E. B. Browning—*Aurora Leigh.*
            Bk. II.

Little I ask; my wants are few;
   I only wish a hut of stone
(A *very plain* brown stone will do),
   That I may call my own;
And close at hand is such a one
In yonder street that fronts the sun.
   h.   O. W. Holmes—*Contentment.*

Wert thou all that I wish thee, great, glorious
   and free,
First flower of the earth, and first gem of
   the sea.
   i.   Moore—*Remember Thee.*

Thy wish was father, Harry, to that thought:
I stay too long by thee, I weary thee.
   j.   *Henry IV.* Pt. II. Act IV. Sc. 5.
            L. 93.

Where nothing wants that want 'itself doth
   seek.
   k.   *Love's Labour's Lost.* Act IV. Sc. 3.
            L. 237.

I've often wished that I had clear,
For life, six hundred pounds a year,
A handsome house to lodge a friend,
A river at my garden's end,
A terrace walk, and half a rood
Of land, set out to plant a wood.
   l.   Swift—*Imitation of Horace.* Bk. II.
            Satire 6.

Like our shadows,
Our wishes lengthen as our sun declines.
   m.   Young—*Night Thoughts.* Night V.
            L. 661.

WIT.

He must be a dull Fellow indeed, whom
neither Love, Malice, nor Necessity, can inspire with Wit.
   n.   De La Bruyère—*The Characters or
            Manners of the Present Age.*
            Ch. IV.

Aristotle said * * * melancholy men of
all others are most witty.
   o.   Burton—*Anatomy of Melancholy.*
        Pt. I. Sec. 3. Memb. 1.
            Subsect. 3.

Great wits and valours, like great states,
Do sometimes sink with their own weights.
   p.   Butler—*Hudibras.* Pt. II. Canto I.
            L. 269.

We grant, although he had much wit,
H' was very shy of using it,
As being loth to wear it out,
And therefore bore it not about;
Unless on holy days or so,
As men their best apparel do.
   q.   Butler—*Hudibras.* Pt. I. Canto I.
            L. 45.

Good wits will jump.
       Buckingham—*The Chances.* Act IV.
            Sc. 1.
       John Byrom—*The Winners.* L. 39.
       Cervantes—*Don Quixote.* Pt. II.
            Ch. XXXVIII.
   r.   Laurence Sterne—*Tristram Shandy.*

Don't put too fine a point to your wit for
fear it should get blunted.
   s.   Cervantes—*The Little Gypsy.*

I am a fool, I know it; and yet, Heaven
help me, I'm poor enough to be a wit.
   t.   Congreve—*Love for Love.* Act I.
            Sc. 1.

His wit invites you by his looks to come,
But when you knock, it never is at home.
   u.   Cowper—*Conversation.* L. 303.

Wit, now and then, struck smartly, shows
a spark.
   v.   Cowper—*Table Talk.* L. 665.

Ev'n wit's a burthen, when it talks too long.
   w.   Dryden—*Sixth Satire of Juvenal.*
            L. 573.

Great wits are sure to madness near allied,
And thin partitions do their bounds divide.
a.   DRYDEN—*Absalom and Achitophel.*
                              Pt. I. L. 163.

Wit will shine
Through the harsh cadence of a rugged line.
b.   DRYDEN—*To the Memory of Mr. Oldham.*
                                   L. 15.

Their heads sometimes so little that there is
no room for wit; sometimes so long, that
there is no wit for so much room.
c.   FULLER—*The Holy and Profane States.*
         Bk. IV. Ch. XII. *Of Natural Fools.*
                              Maxim I.

As a wit, if not first, in the very first line.
d.   GOLDSMITH—*Retaliation.* L. 96.

Wit is the salt of conversation, not the food.
e.   HAZLITT—*Lectures on the English
                    Comic Writers.* Lecture I.

Wit's an unruly engine, wildly striking
   Sometimes a friend, sometimes the engineer :
Hast thou the knack? pamper it not with
   liking ;
But if thou want it, buy it not too deare.
Many affecting wit beyond their power,
Have got to be a deare fool for an houre.
f.   HERBERT—*The Temple. The Church
                              Porch.* St. 41.

Wit, like money, bears an extra value when
rung down immediately it is wanted. Men
pay severely who require credit.
g.   DOUGLAS JERROLD—*Specimens of
                              Jerrold's Wit. Wit.*

This man [Chesterfield] I thought had been
a lord among wits ; but I find he is only a
wit among lords.
h.   SAM'L JOHNSON—*Boswell's Life of
                              Johnson.* 1754.
A man does not please long when he has
only one species of wit.
i.   LA ROCHEFOUCAULD—*Maxims.* No. 438.

A small degree of wit, accompanied by good
sense, is less tiresome in the long run than a
great amount of wit without it.
j.   LA ROCHEFOUCAULD—*Maxims.* No. 529.

And one may say that his wit shines at the
expense of his memory.
k.   ALAIN RENÉ LE SAGE—*Gil Blas.*
                              Bk. III. Ch. XI.

Wit is the flower of the imagination.
l.   LIVY.

Whose wit, in the combat, as gentle as bright,
Ne'er carried a heart-stain away on its blade.
m.   MOORE—*Lines on the Death of
                              Sheridan.* St. 11.

Wit is the most rascally, contemptible,
beggarly thing on the face of the earth.
n.   MURPHY—*The Apprentice.*

A wit with dunces, and a dunce with wits.
o.   POPE—*Dunciad.* Bk. IV. L. 92.

For wit and judgment often are at strife,
Though meant each other's aid, like man and
   wife.
p.   POPE—*Essay on Criticism.* L. 82.

How the wit brightens ! how the style refines !
q.   POPE—*Essay on Criticism.* L. 421.

If faith itself has different dresses worn,
What wonder modes in wit should take their
   turn ?
r.   POPE—*Essay on Criticism.* L. 446.

So modest plainness sets off sprightly wit,
For works may have more wit than does 'em
   good,
As bodies perish through excess of blood.
s.   POPE—*Essay on Criticism.* L. 302.

True wit is nature to advantage dress'd,
What oft was thought, but ne'er so well expressed.
t.   POPE—*Essay on Criticism.* Pt. II. L. 97.

You beat your pate, and fancy wit will come ;
Knock as you please, there's nobody at home.
u.   POPE—*Epigram.*

Fine wits destroy themselves with their own
plots, in meddling with great affairs of state.
v.   JOHN SELDEN—*Table Talk. Wit.*

A good old man, sir : he will be talking, as
they say, When the age is in, the wit is out.
w.   *Much Ado About Nothing.* Act III.
                              Sc. 5. L. 36.

Great men may jest with saints ; 'tis wit in
   them ;
But, in the less, foul profanation.
x.   *Measure for Measure.* Act II. Sc. 2.
                              L. 127.

He doth, indeed, show some sparks that are
like wit.
y.   *Much Ado About Nothing.* Act II.
                              Sc. 3. L. 193.

His eye begets occasion for his wit ;
For every object that the one doth catch,
The other turns to a mirth-moving jest.
z.   *Love's Labour's Lost.* Act II. Sc. 1.
                              L. 69.

I am not only witty in myself, but the
cause that wit is in other men.
aa.   *Henry IV.* Pt. II. Act I. Sc. 2. L. 11.

Look, he's winding up the watch of his wit ;
by and by it will strike.
bb.   *Tempest.* Act II. Sc. 1. L. 12.

Make the doors upon a woman's wit and it
will out at the casement ; shut that and 'twill
out at the key-hole ; stop that, 'twill fly with
the smoke out at the chimney.
cc.   *As You Like It.* Act IV. Sc. 1. L. 162.

Rudeness is a sauce to his good wit,
Which gives men stomach to digest his words,
With better appetite.
> *a.*　*Julius Cæsar.*　Act I.　Sc. 2.　L. 304.

Since brevity is the soul of wit,
And tediousness the limbs and outward flourishes,
I will be brief.
> *b.*　*Hamlet.*　Act II.　Sc. 2.　L. 90.

Sir, your wit ambles well; it goes easily.
> *c.*　*Much Ado About Nothing.*　Act V.
> Sc. 1.　L. 159.

They have a plentiful lack of wit.
> *d.*　*Hamlet.*　Act II.　Sc. 2.　L. 201.

Those wits that think they have thee, do very oft prove fools; and I, that am sure I lack thee, may pass for a wise man; for what says Quinapalus? "Better a witty fool than a foolish wit."
> *e.*　*Twelfth Night.*　Act I.　Sc. 5.　L. 37.

Thy wit is as quick as the greyhound's mouth; it catches.
> *f.*　*Much Ado About Nothing.*　Act V.
> Sc. 2.　L. 11.

To leave this keen encounter of our wits,
And fall somewhat into a slower method.
> *g.*　*Richard III.*　Act I.　Sc. 2.　L. 115.

Man could direct his ways by plain reason, and support his life by tasteless food; but God has given us wit, and flavour, and brightness, and laughter, and perfumers, to enliven the days of man's pilgrimage, and to "charm his pained steps over the burning marle."
> *h.*　Sydney Smith—*Dangers and*
> *Advantages of Wit.*

One wit, like a knuckle of ham in soup, gives a zest and flavour to the dish, but more than one serves only to spoil the pottage.
> *i.*　Smollett—*Humphrey Clinker.*

Wit consists in knowing the resemblance of things which differ, and the difference of things which are alike.
> *j.*　Madame de Staël—*Germany.*　Pt. III.
> Ch. VIII.

It is having in some measure a sort of wit to know how to use the wit of others.
> *k.*　Stanislaus (King of Poland)—*Maxims*
> *and Moral Sentences.*

Though I am young, I scorn to flit
On the wings of borrowed wit.
> *l.*　George Wither—*The Shepherd's*
> *Hunting.*

Against their wills what numbers ruin shun,
Purely through want of wit to be undone!
Nature has shown by making it so rare,
That wit's a jewel which we need not wear.
> *m.*　Young—*Epistle to Mr. Pope.*　Ep. II.
> L. 80.

WOMAN.

Loveliest of women! heaven is in thy soul,
Beauty and virtue shine forever round thee,
Bright'ning each other! thou art all divine!
> *n.*　Addison—*Cato.*　Act III.　Sc. 2.

Divination seems heightened and raised to its highest power in woman.
> *o.*　Amos Bronson Alcott—*Concord Days.*
> *August. Woman.*

On one she smiled, and he was blest;
She smiles elsewhere—we make a din!
But 'twas not love which heaved her breast,
Fair child!—it was the bliss within.
> *p.*　Matthew Arnold—*Euphrosyne.*

But woman's grief is like a summer storm,
Short as it violent is.
> *q.*　Joanna Baillie—*Basil.*　Act V.
> Sc. 3.

Not she with trait'rous kiss her Saviour stung,
Not she denied him with unholy tongue;
She, while apostles shrank, could danger brave,
Last at his cross, and earliest at his grave.
> *r.*　Eaton S. Barrett—*Woman.*　Pt. I.
> L. 141.

Oh, woman, perfect woman! what distraction
Was meant to mankind when thou wast made a devil!
What an inviting hell invented.
> *s.*　Beaumont and Fletcher—*Comedy of*
> *Monsieur Thomas.*　Act III.　Sc. 1.

Then, my good girls, be more than women, wise:
At least be more than I was; and be sure
You credit anything the light gives life to
Before a man.
> *t.*　Beaumont and Fletcher—*The Maid's*
> *Tragedy.*　Act II.　Sc. 2.

A worthless woman! mere cold clay
As all false things are! but so fair,
She takes the breath of men away
Who gaze upon her unaware:
I would not play her larcenous tricks
To have her looks!
> *u.*　E. B. Browning—*Bianca among the*
> *Nightingales.*　St. 12.

You forget too much
That every creature, female as the male,
Stands single in responsible act and thought,
As also in birth and death.
> *v.*　E. B. Browning—*Aurora Leigh.*
> Bk. II.　L. 472.

Auld Nature swears, the lovely dears
Her noblest work she classes, O:
Her 'prentice hand she tried on man,
An' then she made the lasses, O.
> *w.*　Burns—*Green Grow the Rashes.*

Thy daughters bright thy walks adorn,
Gay as the gilded summer sky,
Sweet as the dewy milk-white thorn,
Dear as the raptured thrill of joy.
   a.   Burns—*Address to Edinburgh.*

To see her is to love her,
And love but her forever;
For nature made her what she is,
And never made anither!
   b.   Burns—*Bonny Lesley.*

The souls of women are so small,
That some believe they've none at all;
Or if they have, like cripples, still
They've but one faculty, the will.
   c.   Butler—*Miscellaneous Thoughts.*

A lady with her daughters or her nieces
Shine like a guinea and seven-shilling pieces.
   d.   Byron—*Don Juan.* Canto III. St. 60.

And whether coldness, pride, or virtue dignify
A woman, so she's good, what does it signify?
   e.   Byron—*Don Juan.* Canto XIV.
                         St. 57.

And whispering, "I will ne'er consent"—
consented.
   f.   Byron—*Don Juan.* Canto I. St. 117.

But O ye lords of ladies intellectual,
Inform us truly, have they not henpecked
   you all?
   g.   Byron—*Don Juan.* Canto I. St. 22.

But she was a soft landscape of mild earth,
Where all was harmony, and calm, and quiet,
   Luxuriant, budding; cheerful without
   mirth.
   h.   Byron—*Don Juan.* Canto VI. St. 53.

Heart on her lips, and soul within her eyes,
Soft as her clime, and sunny as her skies.
   i.   Byron—*Beppo.* St. 45.

Her stature tall—I hate a dumpy woman.
   j.   Byron—*Don Juan.* Canto I. St. 61.

I love the sex, and sometimes would reverse
   The tyrant's wish, " that mankind only had
One neck, which he with one fell stroke might
   pierce;"
My wish is quite as wide, but not so bad,
And much more tender on the whole than
   fierce;
   It being (not *now,* but only while a lad)
That womankind had but one rosy mouth,
To kiss them all at once, from North to South.
   k.   Byron—*Don Juan.* Canto VI. St. 27.

I've seen your stormy seas and stormy women,
And pity lovers rather more than seamen.
   l.   Byron—*Don Juan.* Canto VI. St. 53.

       She was his life,
The ocean to the river of his thoughts,
Which terminated all.
   m.   Byron—*The Dream.* St. 2.

Soft as the memory of buried love,
Pure as the prayer which childhood wafts
   above.
   n.   Byron—*The Bride of Abydos.* Canto I.
                         St. 6.

What a strange thing is man! and what a
   stranger
Is woman! What a whirlwind is her head,
And what a whirlpool full of depth and danger
Is all the rest about her.
   o.   Byron—*Don Juan.* Canto IX. St. 64.

The world was sad; the garden was a wild;
And man, the hermit, sigh'd—till woman
   smiled.
   p.   Campbell—*Pleasures of Hope.* Pt. II.
                         L. 37.

Of all the girls that are so smart,
   There's none like pretty Sally.
   q.   Henry Carey—*Sally in our Alley.*

Heaven has no rage like love to hatred turned,
Nor hell a fury like a woman scorned.
   r.   Congreve—*The Mourning Bride.*
                    Act III. Sc. 2.

The sweetest noise on earth, a woman's
   tongue;
A string which hath no discord.
   s.   Barry Cornwall—*Rafaelle and
                   Fornarina.* Sc. 2.

Her air, her manners, all who saw admired;
Courteous though coy, and gentle, though
   retired:
The joy of youth and health her eyes display'd,
And ease of heart her every look convey'd.
   t.   Crabbe—*Parish Register.* Pt. II.

Whoe'er she be,
That not impossible she,
That shall command my heart and me.
   u.   Crashaw—*Wishes to his (Supposed)
                      Mistress.*

Man was made when Nature was
But an apprentice, but woman when she
Was a skilful mistress of her art.
   v.   *Cupid's Whirligig.* 1607.

And, like another Helen, fir'd another Troy.
   w.   Dryden—*Alexander's Feast.* L. 154.

And that one hunting, which the devil design'd
For one fair female, lost him half the kind.
   x.   Dryden—*Theodore and Honoria.*
                      L. 427.

A woman's counsel brought us first to woe,
And made her man his paradise forego,
Where at heart's ease he liv'd; and might
   have been
As free from sorrow as he was from sin.
   y.   Dryden—*Cock and the Fox.* L. 557.

I am resolved to grow fat and look young till forty, and then slip out of the world with the first wrinkle and the reputation of five and twenty.

> *a.*　　Dryden—*The Maiden Queen.*
> Act III.　Sc. 1.

She hugg'd the offender, and forgave the offence;
Sex to the last.

> *b.*　　Dryden—*Cymon and Iphigenia.* L. 367.

For the beauty of a lovely woman is like music.

> *c.*　　George Eliot—*Adam Bede.*
> Ch. XXXIII.

Her lot is made for her by the love she accepts.

> *d.*　　George Eliot—*Felix Holt.*
> Ch. XLIII.

When greater perils men environ,
Then women show a front of iron;
And, gentle in their manner, they
Do bold things in a quiet way.

> *e.*　　Thomas Dunn English—*Betty Zane.*

For silence and chaste reserve is woman's genuine praise, and to remain quiet within the house.

> *f.*　　Euripides.

Are women books? says Hodge, then would mine were
An Almanack, to change her every year.

> *g.*　　Benj. Franklin—*Poor Richard,* Dec.,
> 1737.

Where is the man who has the power and skill
To stem the torrent of a woman's will?
For if she will, she will, you may depend on't;
And if she won't, she won't; so there's an end on't.

> *h.*　　*From the Pillar Erected on the Mount in the Dane John Field, Canterbury.*
> *Examiner,* May 31, 1829.

A cat has nine lives and a woman has nine cats' lives.

> *i.*　　Fuller—*Gnomologia.*

And when a lady's in the case,
You know all other things give place.

> *j.*　　Gay—*Fables. The Hare and Many Friends.* L. 41.

How happy could I be with either,
Were t'other dear charmer away!
But, while ye thus tease me together,
To neither a word will I say.

> *k.*　　Gay—*The Beggar's Opera.* Act II.
> Sc. 2.

If the heart of a man is depressed with cares,
The mist is dispell'd when a woman appears.

> *l.*　　Gay—*The Beggar's Opera.* Act II.

'Tis a woman that seduces all mankind;
By her we first were taught the wheedling arts.

> *m.*　　Gay—*The Beggar's Opera.* Act I.
> Sc. 1.

I am a woman—therefore I may not
　Call to him, cry to him,
　Fly to him,
Bid him delay not!

> *n.*　　R. W. Gilder—*A Woman's Thought.*

When lovely woman stoops to folly,
　And finds too late that men betray,
What charm can soothe her melancholy?
　What art can wash her guilt away?

> *o.*　　Goldsmith—*Vicar of Wakefield.*
> Ch. XXIV.

Mankind, from Adam, have been women's fools;
Women, from Eve, have been the devil's tools:
Heaven might have spar'd one torment when we fell;
Not left us women, or not threatened hell.

> *p.*　　Geo. Granville (Lord Lansdowne)—
> *She-Gallants.*

First, then, a woman will, or won't,—depend on't;
If she will do't, she will; and there's an end on't.
But, if she won't, since safe and sound your trust is,
Fear is affront: and jealousy injustice.

> *q.*　　Aaron Hill—*Epilogue to Zara.*

O woman, woman, when to ill thy mind
Is bent, all hell contains no fouler fiend.

> *r.*　　Homer—*Odyssey.* Bk. XI. L. 531.
> Pope's trans.

She moves a goddess, and she looks a queen.

> *s.*　　Homer—*Iliad.* Bk. III. L. 208.
> Pope's trans.

　　　　What mighty woes
To thy imperial race from woman rose.

> *t.*　　Homer—*Odyssey.* Bk. XI. L. 541.
> Pope's trans.

But, alas! alas! for the woman's fate,
Who has from a mob to choose a mate!
'Tis a strange and painful mystery!
But the more the eggs the worse the hatch;
The more the fish, the worse the catch;
The more the sparks the worse the match;
　Is a fact in woman's history.

> *u.*　　Hood—*Miss Kilmansegg. Her Courtship.* St. 7.

God in his harmony has equal ends
For cedar that resists and reed that bends;
For good it is a woman sometimes rules,
Holds in her hand the power, and manners, schools,
And laws, and mind; succeeding master proud,
With gentle voice and smiles she leads the crowd,
The somber human troop.

> *v.*　　Victor Hugo—*Eviradnus.* V.

O woman! thou wert fashioned to beguile :
So have all sages said, all poets sung.
a.   JEAN INGELOW—*The Four Bridges.*
St. 68.

I am very fond of the company of ladies.
I like their beauty, I like their delicacy, I like
their vivacity, and I like their *silence.*
b.   SAM'L JOHNSON—SEWARD'S
Johnsoniana. 617.

Ladies, stock and tend your hive,
Trifle not at thirty-five;
For, howe'er we boast and strive,
Life declines from thirty-five;
He that ever hopes to thrive
Must begin by thirty-five.
c.   SAM'L JOHNSON—*To Mrs. Thrale, when
Thirty-five.* L. 11.

Wretched, un-idea'd girls.
d.   SAM'L JOHNSON—*Boswell's Life of
Johnson.* 1752.

And where she went, the flowers took thickest root,
As she had sow'd them with her odorous
foot.
e.   BEN JONSON—*The Sad Shepherd.*
Act I. Sc. 1.

Maids must be wives and mothers, to fulfil
Th' entire and holiest end of woman's being.
f.   FRANCES ANNE KEMBLE—*Woman's
Heart.*

A Lady with a lamp shall stand
In the great history of the land,
    A noble type of good,
      Heroic womanhood.
g.   LONGFELLOW—*Santa Filomena.* St. 10.

The life of woman is full of woe,
Toiling on and on and on,
With breaking heart, and tearful eyes,
The secret longings that arise,
Which this world never satisfies!
Some more, some less, but of the whole
Not one quite happy, no, not one!
h.   LONGFELLOW—*Christus.   The Golden
Legend.* Pt. II.

Earth's noblest thing, a Woman perfected.
i.   LOWELL—*Irene.* L. 62.

'Twas kin' o' kingdom-come to look
On sech a blessed cretur.
j.   LOWELL—*The Biglow Papers.
Introduction to Second Series.
The Courtin'.* St. 7.

A cunning woman is a knavish fool.
k.   LORD LYTTLETON—*Advice to a Lady.*

The most beautiful object in the world, it
will be allowed, is a beautiful woman.
l.   MACAULAY—*Essays.   Criticisms on
the Principal Italian Writers.*
No. 1.

Of all wild beasts on earth or in sea, the greatest is a woman.
m.   MENANDER—*E Supposititio.* P. 182.

O woman, born first to believe us;
   Yea, also born first to forget;
Born first to betray and deceive us,
   Yet first to repent and regret.
n.   JOAQUIN MILLER—*Charity.*

A bevy of fair women.
o.   MILTON—*Paradise Lost.* Bk. XI.
L. 582.

    For nothing lovelier can be found
In woman, than to study household good.
p.   MILTON—*Paradise Lost.* Bk. IX.
L. 232.

Grace was in all her steps, heaven in her eye,
In every gesture dignity and love.
q.   MILTON—*Paradise Lost.* Bk. VIII.
L. 488.

         My latest found,
Heaven's last best gift, my ever new delight!
r.   MILTON—*Paradise Lost.* Bk. V. L. 18.

Oh! why did God, * * * create at last
  *   *   *   *   *   *
This novelty on earth, this fair defect
Of nature, and not fill the world at once
With men as angels without feminine.
s.   MILTON—*Paradise Lost.* Bk. X.
L. 888.

Disguise our bondage as we will,
'Tis woman, woman rules us still.
t.   MOORE—*Sovereign Woman.* St. 4.

    My only books
    Were woman's looks,
And folly's all they've taught me.
u.   MOORE—*The Time I've Lost in Wooing.*

    For if a young lady has that discretion and
modesty, without which all knowledge is
little worth, she will never make an ostenta-
tious parade of it, because she will rather be
intent on acquiring more, than on displaying
what she has.
v.   HANNAH MORE—*Essays on Various
Subjects.   Thoughts on Conversation.*

A penniless lass wi' a lang pedigree.
w.   LADY NAIRNE—*The Laird o' Cockpen.*

Who trusts himself to women, or to waves,
Should never hazard what he fears to lose.
x.   OLDMIXON—*Governor of Cyprus.*

O woman! lovely woman! Nature made
    thee
To temper man : we had been brutes without
    you ;
Angels are painted fair, to look like you :
There's in you all that we believe of Heaven,
Amazing brightness, purity, and truth,
Eternal joy, and everlasting love.
y.   THOMAS OTWAY—*Venice Preserved.*
Act I. Sc. 1.

42

What mighty ills have not been done by
        woman!
Who was't betray'd the Capitol?   A woman;
Who lost Mark Antony the world? A woman;
Who was the cause of a long ten years' war,
And laid at last old Troy in ashes? Woman;
Destructive, damnable, deceitful woman!
a.   THOMAS OTWAY—*The Orphan*.   Act III.
                                            Sc. 1.

            Who can describe
Women's hypocrisies! their subtle wiles,
Betraying smiles, feign'd tears, inconstancies!
Their painted outsides, and corrupted minds,
The sum of all their follies, and their false-
        hoods.
b.   THOMAS OTWAY—*Orpheus*.

Still an angel appear to each lover beside,
But still be a woman to you.
c.   PARNELL—*When thy Beauty Appears*.

To chase the clouds of life's tempestuous
        hours,
To strew its short but weary way with flow'rs,
New hopes to raise, new feelings to impart,
And pour celestial balsam on the heart;
For this to man was lovely woman giv'n,
The last, best work, the noblest gift of
        Heav'n.
d.   THOMAS LOVE PEACOCK—*The Visions of
                                            Love*.
And mistress of herself, though china fall.
e.   POPE—*Moral Essays*.   Ep. II.   L. 268.

Fine by defect, and delicately weak.
f.   POPE—*Moral Essays*.   Ep. II.   L. 43.

Ladies, like variegated tulips, show
'Tis to their changes half their charms we
        owe.
g.   POPE—*Moral Essays*.   Ep. II.   L. 41.

Men some to business, some to pleasure take;
But every woman is at heart a rake;
Men some to quiet, some to public strife;
But every lady would be queen for life.
h.   POPE—*Moral Essays*.   Ep. II.   L. 215.

Most women have no characters at all.
i.   POPE—*Moral Essays*.   Ep. II.   L. 2.

O! bless'd with temper, whose unclouded ray
Can make to-morrow cheerful as to-day;
She who can own a sister's charms, or hear
Sighs for a daughter with unwounded ear;
She who ne'er answers till a husband cools,
Or, if she rules him, never shows she rules.
j.   POPE—*Moral Essays*.   Ep. II.   L. 257.

Offend her, and she knows not to forgive;
Oblige her, and she'll hate you while you
        live.
k.   POPE—*Moral Essays*.   Ep. II.   L. 137.

Our grandsire, Adam, ere of Eve possesst,
Alone, and e'en in Paradise unblest,
With mournful looks the blissful scenes sur-
        vey'd,
And wander'd in the solitary shade.
The Maker saw, took pity, and bestow'd
Woman, the last, the best reserv'd of God.
l.   POPE—*January and May*.   L. 63.

Woman's at best a contradiction still.
m.   POPE—*Moral Essays*.   Ep. II.   L. 270.

Be to her virtues very kind;
Be to her faults a little blind.
n.   PRIOR—*An English Padlock*.

That if weak women went astray,
Their stars were more in fault than they.
o.   PRIOR—*Hans Carvel*.

A woman is the most inconsistent compound of obstinacy and self-sacrifice that I
am acquainted with.
p.   RICHTER—*Flower, Fruit, and Thorn
                                        Pieces*.   Ch. V.
Angels listen when she speaks;
        She's my delight, all mankind's wonder;
But my jealous heart would break
        Should we live one day asunder.
q.   EARL OF ROCHESTER—*Song.   My Dear
                                Mistress has a Heart*.   St. 2.

O Woman! in our hours of ease,
Uncertain, coy, and hard to please,
And variable as the shade
By the light quivering aspen made;
When pain and anguish wring the brow,
A ministering angel thou!
r.   SCOTT—*Marmion*.   Canto VI.   St. 30.

Widowed wife and wedded maid.
s.   SCOTT—*The Betrothed*.   Last chapter.

Woman's faith, and woman's trust,
Write the characters in dust.
t.   SCOTT—*The Betrothed*.   Ch. XX.

A child of our grandmother Eve, a female;
or, for thy more sweet understanding, a
woman.
u.   *Love's Labour's Lost*.   Act I.   Sc. 1.
                                            L. 266.
Age cannot wither her, nor custom stale
Her infinite variety.
v.   *Antony and Cleopatra*.   Act II.   Sc. 2.
                                            L. 240.
            Ah me, how weak a thing
The heart of woman is!
w.   *Julius Cæsar*.   Act II.   Sc. 4.   L. 39.

            A maid
That paragons description and wild fame;
One that excels the quirks of blazoning pens,
And in the essential vesture of creation
Does tire the ingener.
x.   *Othello*.   Act II.   Sc. 1.   L. 61.

And is not my hostess of the tavern a most
sweet wench?
As the honey of Hybla, my old lad of the
castle.
a.   *Henry IV.* Pt. I. Act I. Sc. 2. L. 45.

A woman mov'd is like a fountain troubled,
Muddy, ill-seeming, thick, bereft of beauty.
b.   *Taming of the Shrew.* Act V. Sc. 2.
L. 142.

Fair ladies mask'd are roses in their bud :
Dismask'd, their damask sweet commixture
shown,
Are angels veiling clouds, or roses blown.
c.   *Love's Labour's Lost.* Act V. Sc. 2.
L. 295.

Frailty, thy name is woman !—
A little month, or ere those shoes were old
With which she follow'd my poor father's
body,
Like Niobe, all tears ;—why she, even she,
* * * married with my uncle.
d.   *Hamlet.* Act I. Sc. 2. L. 146.

Have I not in a pitched battle heard
Loud 'larums, neighing steeds, and trumpets'
clang?
And do you tell me of a woman's tongue?
e.   *Taming of the Shrew.* Act I. Sc. 2.
L. 206.

Have you not heard it said full oft,
A woman's nay doth stand for nought?
f.   *Passionate Pilgrim.* L. 339.

Her sighs will make a battery in his breast;
Her tears will pierce into a marble heart;
The tiger will be mild whiles she doth mourn;
And Nero will be tainted with remorse,
To hear and see her plaints.
g.   *Henry VI.* Pt. III. Act III. Sc. 1.
L. 37.

If ladies be but young and fair,
They have the gift to know it.
h.   *As You Like It.* Act II. Sc. 7. L. 37.

If, one by one, you wedded all the world,
Or from the all that are took something good,
To make a perfect woman, she you kill'd
Would be unparallel'd.
i.   *Winter's Tale.* Act V. Sc. 1. L. 13.

I grant I am a woman, but withal,
A woman that Lord Brutus took to wife :
I grant I am a woman ; but withal
A woman well-reputed ; Cato's daughter.
j.   *Julius Cæsar.* Act II. Sc. 1. L. 292.

I thank God I am not a woman, to be
touched with so many giddy offences as
He hath generally taxed their whole sex
withal.
k.   *As You Like It.* Act III. Sc. 2.
L. 366.

Muse not that I thus suddenly proceed ;
For what I will, I will, and there an end.
l.   *Two Gentlemen of Verona.* Act I.
Sc. 3. L. 64.

Never give her o'er ;
For scorn at first makes after-love the more.
If she do frown, 'tis not in hate of you,
But rather to beget more love in you ;
If she do chide, 'tis not to have you gone,
For why, the fools are mad if left alone.
m.   *Two Gentlemen of Verona.* Act III.
Sc. 1. L. 94.

O most delicate fiend !
Who is't can read a woman?
n.   *Cymbeline.* Act V. Sc. 5. L. 47.

One woman is fair, yet I am well ; another
is wise, yet I am well : another virtuous, yet
I am well ; but till all graces be in one woman,
one woman shall not come in my grace.
o.   *Much Ado About Nothing.* Act II.
Sc. 3. L. 27.

Run, run, Orlando : carve on every tree
The fair, the chaste, and unexpressive she.
p.   *As You Like It.* Act III. Sc. 2. L. 9.

Say that she rail, why then I'll tell her plain
She sings as sweetly as a nightingale ;
Say that she frown ; I'll say she looks as clear
As morning roses newly wash'd with dew ;
Say she be mute and will not speak a word ;
Then I'll commend her volubility,
And say she uttereth piercing eloquence.
q.   *Taming of the Shrew.* Act II. Sc. 1.
L. 171.

She is a woman, therefore may be woo'd ;
She is a woman, therefore may be won.
r.   *Titus Andronicus.* Act II. Sc. 1.
L. 82.

She's beautiful and therefore to be woo'd :
She is a woman, therefore to be won.
s.   *Henry VI.* Pt. I. Act V. Sc. 3.
L. 78.

She speaks poniards, and every word stabs :
if her breath were as terrible as her terminations, there were no living near her ; she
would infect to the north star.
t.   *Much Ado About Nothing.* Act II.
Sc. 1. L. 255.

Then let thy love be younger than thyself,
Or thy affection cannot hold the bent :
For women are as roses, whose fair flower
Being once display'd, doth fall that very
hour.
u.   *Twelfth Night.* Act II. Sc. 4. L. 37.

There was never yet fair woman but she
made mouths in a glass.
v.   *King Lear.* Act III. Sc. 2. L. 35.

'Tis beauty that doth oft make women proud ;
But, God he knows, thy share thereof is
small :
'Tis virtue that doth make them most ad-
mired ;
The contrary doth make thee wondered at :
'Tis government that makes them seem divine.
w.   *Henry VI.* Pt. III. Act. I. Sc. 4.
L. 128.

To be slow in words is a woman's only virtue.
  a.   *Two Gentlemen of Verona.*   Act III.
                                Sc. 1. L. 338.

Two women plac'd together makes cold
  weather.
  b.   *Henry VIII.* Act I. Sc. 4. L. 22.

Why are our bodies soft and weak and smooth,
Unapt to toil and trouble in the world,
But that our soft conditions and our hearts
Should well agree with our external parts?
  c.   *Taming of the Shrew.* Act V. Sc. 2.
                                        L. 165.

Why, then thou canst not break her to the
  lute?
Why, no; for she hath broke the lute to me.
  d.   *Taming of the Shrew.* Act II. Sc. 1.
                                        L. 148.

Women will love her that she is a woman
More worth than any man; men, that she is
The rarest of all women.
  e.   *Winter's Tale.* Act V. Sc. 1. L. 110.

Would it not grieve a woman to be over-
master'd with a piece of valiant dust? to
make an account of her life to a cloud of wayward marl?
  f.   *Much Ado About Nothing.* Act II.
                                Sc. 1. L. 63.

        You are pictures out of doors,
Bells in your parlours, wild-cats in your
  kitchens,
Saints in your injuries, devils being offended,
Players in your housewifery, and housewives
  in your beds.
  g.   *Othello.* Act II. Sc. 1. L. 110.

A lovely lady garmented in light.
  h.   SHELLEY—*The Witch of Atlas.* St. 5.

One moral's plain, * * * without more
  fuss;
Man's social happiness all rests on us:
Through all the drama—whether damn'd or
  not—
Love gilds the scene, and women guide the
  plot.
  i.   R. B. SHERIDAN—*The Rivals.* Epilogue.

She is her selfe of best things the collection.
  j.   SIR PHILIP SIDNEY—*The Arcadia.*
                                Thirsis and Dorus.

What will not woman, gentle woman, dare
When strong affection stirs her spirit up?
  k.   SOUTHEY—*Madoc.* Pt. II. II.

She is pretty to walk with,
And witty to talk with,
And pleasant too, to think on.
  l.   SIR JOHN SUCKLING—*Brennoralt.*
                                Act II. Sc. 1.

Of all the girls that e'er was seen,
  There's none so fine as Nelly.
  m.   SWIFT—*Ballad on Miss Nelly Bennet.*

Prince, give praise to our French ladies
  For the sweet sound their speaking carries;
'Twixt Rome and Cadiz many a maid is,
  But no good girl's lip out of Paris.
  n.   SWINBURNE—*Translation from Villon.*
                    Ballad of the Women of Paris.

A woman's honor rests on manly love.
  o.   ESAIAS TEGNÈR—*Fridthjof's Saga.*
                                        Canto VIII.

Airy, fairy Lilian.
  p.   TENNYSON—*Lilian.*

A rosebud set with little wilful thorns,
And sweet as English air could make her, she.
  q.   TENNYSON—*The Princess.* Prologue.
                                        L. 153.

For woman is not undeveloped man
But diverse; could we make her as the man
Sweet love were slain; his dearest bond is this
Not like to like but like in difference.
  r.   TENNYSON—*The Princess.* VII.

Queen rose of the rosebud garden of girls.
  s.   TENNYSON—*Maud.* Pt. I. XXII.
                                        St. 9.

With prudes for proctors, dowagers for deans,
And sweet girl-graduates in their golden hair.
  t.   TENNYSON—*The Princess.* Prologue.
                                        L. 141.

Woman is the lesser man.
  u.   TENNYSON—*Locksley Hall.* St. 76.

She wears that body but as one indues
A robe, half careless, for it is the use.
  v.   FRANCIS THOMPSON—*Her Portrait.*
                                        St. 7.

He is a fool who thinks by force or skill
To turn the current of a woman's will.
  w.   SIR SAM'L TUKE—*Adventures of Five
                    Hours.* Act V. Sc. 3. L. 483.

"Woman" must ever be a woman's highest
  name,
And honors more than "Lady," if I know
  right.
  x.   WALTER VON DER VOGELWEIDE—
                *Translated in the Minnesinger of
                Germany. Woman and Lady.*

  All the reasonings of men are not worth one
sentiment of women.
  y.   VOLTAIRE.

  Very learned women are to be found, in the
same manner as female warriors; but they are
seldom or ever inventors.
  z.   VOLTAIRE—*A Philosophical Dictionary.
                                        Women.*

  My wife is one of the best wimin on this
Continent, altho' she isn't always gentle as a
lamb, with mint sauce.
  aa.   ARTEMUS WARD—*A War Meeting.*

Not from his head was woman took,
As made her husband to o'erlook;
Not from his feet, as one designed
The footstool of the stronger kind;
But fashioned for himself, a bride;
An equal, taken from his side.
> a.   CHARLES WESLEY—*Short Hymns on
> Select Passages of the Holy Scriptures.*

Shall I, wasting in despaire,
Dye because a woman's faire?
Or make pale my cheeks with care
Cause another's rosie are?
Be shee fairer than the day,
Or the flow'ry meads in May;
   If she be not so to me,
   What care I how faire shee be?
> b.   GEORGE WITHER—*Mistresse of
> Philarete. Percy's Reliques.*

A Creature not too bright or good
For human nature's daily food;
For transient sorrows, simple wiles,
Praise, blame, love, kisses, tears and smiles.
> c.   WORDSWORTH—*She was a Phantom
> of Delight.*

And now I see with eye serene,
The very pulse of the machine;
A Being breathing thoughtful breath,
A Traveller betwixt life and death;
The reason firm, the temperate will,
Endurance, foresight, strength, and skill.
> d.   WORDSWORTH—*She was a Phantom
> of Delight.*

A perfect Woman, nobly planned
To warn, to comfort, and command.
> e.   WORDSWORTH—*She was a Phantom
> of Delight.*

Shalt show us how divine a thing
   A Woman may be made.
> f.   WORDSWORTH—*To a Young Lady.
> Dear Child of Nature.*

She was a Phantom of delight
When first she gleamed upon my sight;
A lovely Apparition, sent
To be a moment's ornament.
> g.   WORDSWORTH—*She was a Phantom
> of Delight.*

   And beautiful as sweet!
And young as beautiful! and soft as young!
And gay as soft! and innocent as gay.
> h.   YOUNG—*Night Thoughts.* Night III.
> L. 81.

WONDERS.

A schoolboy's tale, the wonder of an hour!
> i.   BYRON—*Childe Harold.* Canto II.
> St. 2.

Long stood the noble youth oppress'd with
   awe,
And stupid at the wondrous things he saw,
Surpassing common faith, transgressing nature's law.
> j.   DRYDEN—*Theodore and Honoria.*
> L. 217.

I saw a flie within a beade
Of amber cleanly buried.
> k.   HERRICK—*The Amber Bead.*

The bee enclosed, and through the amber
   shown
Seems buried in the juice which was his own.
> l.   MARTIAL—*Epigrams.* Bk. IV.
> Sec. XXXII.

Pretty! in amber to observe the forms
Of hairs, or straws, or dirt, or grubs, or
   worms!
The things, we know, are neither rich nor
   rare,
But wonder how the devil they got there.
> m.   POPE—*Prologue to the Satires.* L. 169.

   Can such things be,
And overcome us like a summer's cloud,
Without our special wonder?
> n.   *Macbeth.* Act III. Sc. 4. L. 110.

O day and night, but this is wondrous strange.
> o.   *Hamlet.* Act I. Sc. 5. L. 164.

Stones have been known to move and trees to
   speak.
> p.   *Macbeth.* Act III. Sc. 4. L. 123.

'Twas strange, 'twas passing strange;
'Twas pitiful, 'twas wondrous pitiful.
> q.   *Othello.* Act I. Sc. 3. L. 160.

There's something in a flying horse,
There's something in a huge balloon.
> r.   WORDSWORTH—*Peter Bell.* Prologue.
> St. 1.

WOOING.

Why don't the men propose, mamma?
   Why don't the men propose?
> s.   THOMAS HAYNES BAYLY—*Songs and
> Ballads. Why Don't the Men Propose?*

Alas! to seize the moment
   When heart inclines to heart,
And press a suit with passion,
   Is not a woman's part.

If man come not to gather
   The roses where they stand,
They fade among their foliage,
   They cannot seek his hand.
> t.   BRYANT—*Song.* Trans. from the
> Spanish of IGLESIAS.

Woo the fair one when around
   Early birds are singing;
When o'er all the fragrant ground
   Early herbs are springing:
When the brookside, bank, and grove
   All with blossoms laden,
Shine with beauty, breathe of love,
   Woo the timid maiden.
> u.   BRYANT—*Love's Lessons.*

And let us mind, faint heart ne'er wan
A lady fair.

> BURNS—*To Dr. Blacklock.*
> WM. ELLERTON—*George a-Greene*
> (*ballad written about* 1569).

a.   PHINEAS FLETCHER—*Brittain's Ida.*
Canto V. St. I.

Duncan Gray cam here to woo,
  Ha, ha, the wooing o't!
On blithe Yulenight when we were fou,
  Ha, ha, the wooing o't!
Maggie coost her head fu' high,
Looked asklent and unco skeigh,
Gart poor Duncan stand abeigh:
  Ha, ha! the wooing o't!

b.   BURNS—*Duncan Gray.*

He that will win his dame must do
As love does when he draws his bow;
With one hand thrust the lady from,
And with the other pull her home.

c.   BUTLER—*Hudibras.* Pt. II. Canto I.
L. 449.

She that with poetry is won,
Is but a desk to write upon;
And what men say of her they mean
No more than on the thing they lean.

d.   BUTLER—*Hudibras.* Pt. II. Canto I.
L. 591.

Do proper homage to thine idol's eyes;
But not too humbly, or she will despise
Thee and thy suit, though told in moving
  tropes:
Disguise even tenderness, if thou art wise.

e.   BYRON—*Childe Harold.* Canto II.
St. 34.

Not much he kens, I ween, of woman's breast,
Who thinks that wanton thing is won by
  sighs.

f.   BYRON—*Childe Harold.* Canto II.
St. 34.

Some are soon bagg'd but some reject three
  dozen.
'Tis fine to see them scattering refusals
And wild dismay, o'er every angry cousin
(Friends of the party) who begin accusals,
Such as—" Unless Miss (Blank) meant to have
  chosen
Poor Frederick, why did she accord perusals
To his billets? *Why* waltz with him? Why,
  I pray,
Look *yes* last night, and yet say *No* to-day?"

g.   BYRON—*Don Juan.* Canto XII. St. 34.

'Tis an old lesson; time approves it true,
  And those who know it best, deplore it
  most;
When all is won that all desire to woo,
  The paltry prize is hardly worth the cost.

h.   BYRON—*Childe Harold.* Canto II.
St. 35.

      'Tis enough—
Who listens once will listen twice;
Her heart be sure is not of ice,
And one refusal no rebuff.

i.   BYRON—*Mazeppa.* St. 6.

Never wedding, ever wooing,
Still a lovelorn heart pursuing,
Read you not the wrong you're doing
  In my cheek's pale hue?
All my life with sorrow strewing;
  Wed or cease to woo.

j.   CAMPBELL—*The Maid's Remonstrance.*

So mourn'd the dame of Ephesus her Love,
And thus the Soldier arm'd with Resolution
Told his soft Tale, and was a thriving Wooer.

k.   COLLEY CIBBER—*Richard III.* (altered).
Act II. Sc. 1.

Faint heart hath been a common phrase, faire
  ladie never wives.

l.   J. P. COLLIER'S *Reprint of The Rocke of*
Regard (1576). P. 122.

I'll woo her as the lion woos his brides.

m.   JOHN HOME—*Douglas.* Act I. Sc. 1.

The surest way to hit a woman's heart is to
take aim kneeling.

n.   DOUGLAS JERROLD—*Douglas Jerrold's*
Wit. The Way to a Woman's Heart.

Follow a shadow, it still flies you,
  Seem to fly it, it will pursue:
So court a mistress, she denies you;
  Let her alone, she will court you.
Say are not women truly, then,
Styled but the shadows of us men?

o.   BEN JONSON—*The Forest. Song. That*
Women are but Men's Shadows.

If I am not worth the wooing, I surely am not
  worth the winning.

p.   LONGFELLOW—*Courtship of Miles*
Standish. Pt. III. L. 111.

The nightingales among the sheltering boughs
Of populous and many-nested trees
Shall teach me how to woo thee, and shall
  tell me
By what resistless charms or incantations
They won their mates.

q.   LONGFELLOW—*The Masque of Pandora.*
Pt. V. L. 62.

His heart kep' goin' pity-pat,
  But hern went pity-Zekle.

r.   LOWELL—*Introduction to The Biglow*
Papers. Second series. *The Courtin'.*
St. 15.

And every shepherd tells his tale
Under the hawthorn in the dale.

s.   MILTON—*L'Allegro.* L. 67.

Her virtue and the conscience of her worth,
That would be woo'd, and not unsought be
  won.

t.   MILTON—*Paradise Lost.* Bk. VIII.
L. 502.

If I speak to thee in friendship's name,
  Thou think'st I speak too coldly;
If I mention Love's devoted flame,
  Thou say'st I speak too boldly.

u.   MOORE—*How Shall I Woo?*

'Tis sweet to think that where'er we rove
  We are sure to find something blissful and
    dear;
And that when we're far from the lips we
    love,
  We've but to make love to the lips we are
    near.
  a.   Moore—*'Tis Sweet to Think.*

Happy Mary Anerly, looking O so fair!
There's a ring upon your hand, and there's
    myrtle in your hair.
Somebody is with you now: Somebody I see,
Looks into your trusting face very tenderly.
  b.   Arthur Jas. Munby—*Mary Anerly.*

Ah, whither shall a maiden flee,
  When a bold youth so swift pursues,
And siege of tenderest courtesy,
  With hope perseverent, still renews!
  c.   Coventry Patmore—*The Chase.*

They dream in courtship, but in wedlock
    wake.
  d.   Pope—*Wife of Bath.* L. 103.

It was a happy age when a man might have
wooed his wench with a pair of kid leather
gloves, a silver thimble, or with a tawdry lace;
but now a velvet gown, a chain of pearl, or a
coach with four horses will scarcely serve the
turn.
  e.   Rich—*My Lady's Looking Glass.*

Lightly from fair to fair he flew,
  And loved to plead, lament, and sue,—
Suit lightly won, and short-lived pain,
  For monarchs seldom sigh in vain.
  f.   Scott—*Marmion.* Canto V. St. 9.

A heaven on earth I have won by wooing
    thee.
  g.   *All's Well That Ends Well.* Act IV.
                 Sc. 2. L. 66.

Be merry, and employ your chiefest thoughts
To courtship and such fair ostents of love
As shall conveniently become you there.
  h.   *Merchant of Venice.* Act II. Sc. 8.
                       L. 43.

I was not born under a rhyming planet, nor
I cannot woo in festival terms.
  i.   *Much Ado About Nothing.* Act V.
                 Sc. 2. L. 40.

           Most fair,
Will you vouchsafe to teach a soldier terms
Such as will enter at a lady's ear
And plead his love-suit to her gentle heart?
  j.   *Henry V.* Act V. Sc. 2. L. 98.

         O gentle Romeo,
If thou dost love, pronounce it faithfully.
Or if thou think'st I am too quickly won,
I'll frown and be perverse and say thee nay,
So thou wilt woo: but else, not for the world.
  k.   *Romeo and Juliet.* Act II. Sc. 2.
                      L. 93.

Say that upon the altar of her beauty
You sacrifice your tears, your sighs, your
    heart:
Write till your ink be dry and with your tears
Moist it again, and frame some feeling line,
That may discover such integrity.
  l.   *Two Gentlemen of Verona.* Act III.
                 Sc. 2. L. 73.

She wish'd she had not heard it, yet she
    wish'd
That heaven had made her such a man: She
    thank'd me,
And bade me, if I had a friend that lov'd her,
I should but teach him how to tell my story
And that would woo her.
  m.   *Othello.* Act I. Sc. 3. L. 162.

That man that hath a tongue, I say, is no
    man,
If with his tongue he cannot win a woman.
  n.   *Two Gentlemen of Verona.* Act III.
                 Sc. 1. L. 104.

Was ever woman in this humour woo'd?
Was ever woman in this humour won?
  o.   *Richard III.* Act I. Sc. 2. L. 228.

We cannot fight for love, as men may do;
We should be woo'd and were not made to
    woo.
  p.   *Midsummer-Night's Dream.* Act II.
                 Sc. 1. L. 241.

Win her with gifts, if she respect not words;
Dumb jewels often in their silent kind
More than quick words do move a woman's
    mind.
  q.   *Two Gentlemen of Verona.* Act III.
                 Sc. 1. L. 89.

       Women are angels, wooing:
Things won are done, joy's soul lies in the
    doing:
That she belov'd knows nought that knows
    not this:
Men prize the thing ungain'd more than it is.
  r.   *Troilus and Cressida.* Act I. Sc. 2.
                      L. 312.

Wooing thee, I found thee of more value
Than stamps in gold or sums in sealed bags;
And 'tis the very riches of thyself
That now I aim at.
  s.   *Merry Wives of Windsor.* Act III.
                 Sc. 4. L. 15.

Bring therefore all the forces that ye may,
And lay incessant battery to her heart;
Playnts, prayers, vowes, truth, sorrow, and
    dismay;
Those engins can the proudest love convert:
  And, if those fayle, fall down and dy before
    her;
So dying live, and living do adore her.
  t.   Spenser—*Amoretti and Epithalamion.*
                 Sonnet XIV.

He sat by her side and her soft hand he
　　pressed ;
He felt, in the pressure returned him thrice
　　blessed,
Enraptured gazing
On her whom he honored beyond all prais-
　　ing.
　　a.　　ESAIAS TEGNÈR—*Fridthjof's Saga.*
　　　　　　　　　　Canto IV.　St. 4.

Quiet, Robin, quiet!
You lovers are such clumsy summer-flies,
Forever buzzing at your lady's face.
　　b.　　TENNYSON—*The Foresters.* Act IV.
　　　　　　　　　　　　　　Sc. 1.

WORDS.

Words of affection, howsoe'er express'd,
The latest spoken still are deem'd the best.
　　c.　　JOANNA BAILLIE—*Address to Miss
　　　　　　Agnes Baillie on her Birthday.*
　　　　　　　　　　　　　　L. 126.

'Tis a word that's quickly spoken,
Which being restrained, a heart is broken.
　　d.　　BEAUMONT AND FLETCHER—*The
　　　　　　Spanish Curate.* Act II.
　　　　　　　　　　Sc. 5.　*Song.*

When we desire to confine our words, we
commonly say they are spoken under the rose.
　　e.　　SIR THOMAS BROWNE—*Vulgar Errors.
　　　　　　Of Speaking Under the Rose.*

High Air-castles are cunningly built of
Words, the Words well bedded also in good
Logic-mortar; wherein, however, no Knowl-
edge will come to lodge.
　　f.　　CARLYLE—*Sartor Resartus.* Bk. I.
　　　　　　　　　　　　　　Ch. VIII.

Words writ in waters.
　　g.　　GEORGE CHAPMAN—*Revenge for
　　　　　　Honour.* Act V.　Sc. 2.

Words are but empty thanks.
　　h.　　COLLEY CIBBER—*Woman's Wit.* Act V.

Without knowing *the force* of words, it is
impossible to know men.
　　i.　　CONFUCIUS—*Analects.* Bk. XX.
　　　　　　　　　　　　　　Ch. III.

Words that weep, and tears that speak.
　　j.　　COWLEY—*The Prophet.* St. 2.　L. 8.

But words once spoke can never be recall'd.
　　k.　　WENTWORTH DILLON—*Art of Poetry.*
　　　　　　　　　　　　　　L. 442.

It used to be a common saying of Myson's
that men ought not to seek for things in
words, but for words in things; for that
things are not made on account of words but
that words are put together for the sake of
things.
　　l.　　DIOGENES LAERTIUS—*Lives of the
　　　　　　Philosophers.* Bk. I.　*Myson.* Ch. 3.

And torture one poor word ten thousand
ways.
　　m.　　DRYDEN—*Mac Flecknoe.* L. 208.

Our words have wings, but fly not where we
　　would.
　　n.　　GEORGE ELIOT—*The Spanish Gypsy.*
　　　　　　　　　　　　　　Bk. III.

What if my words
Were meant for deeds.
　　o.　　GEORGE ELIOT—*The Spanish Gypsy.*
　　　　　　　　　　　　　　Bk. III.

'Twas he that ranged the words at random
　　flung,
Pierced the fair pearls and them together
　　strung.
　　p.　　FIRDOUSI—*Auvari Suhaili.* Eastwick's
　　　　　　　　　　　　　　trans.

For words are wise men's counters—they do
but reckon by them—but they are the money
of fools.
　　q.　　THOMAS HOBBES—*The Leviathan.*
　　　　　　　　　　Pt. I.　Ch. IV.　Sc. 15.

There is no point where art so nearly
touches nature as when it appears in the form
of words.
　　r.　　J. G. HOLLAND—*Plain Talks on
　　　　　　Familiar Subjects.　Art and Life.*

Words sweet as honey from his lips distill'd.
　　s.　　HOMER—*Iliad.* Bk. I.　L. 332.
　　　　　　　　　　　　　Pope's trans.

I am not yet so lost in lexicography, as to
forget that words are the daughters of earth,
and that things are the sons of heaven.
　　t.　　SAM'L JOHNSON—*Preface to his
　　　　　　　　　　　　Dictionary.*

Fair words gladden so many a heart.
　　u.　　LONGFELLOW—*Tales of a Wayside Inn.
　　　　　　The Musician's Tale.*

Speaking words of endearment where words
of comfort availed not.
　　v.　　LONGFELLOW—*Evangeline.* Pt. I.　V.
　　　　　　　　　　　　　　L. 43.

There comes Emerson first, whose rich words,
　　every one,
Are like gold nails in temples to hang trophies
　　on.
　　w.　　LOWELL—*A Fable for Critics.*

Words are men's daughters, but God's sons
are things.
　　x.　　SAMUEL MADDEN—*Boulter's Monument.*
　　　　　　(*Said to have been inserted by Dr.
　　　　　　Johnson.*)

It is as easy to draw back a stone thrown
with force from the hand, as to recall a word
once spoken.
　　y.　　MENANDER—*Ex Incert. Comœd.*
　　　　　　　　　　　　　　P. 216.

Words, however, are things; and the man
who accords
To his language the license to outrage his
soul,
Is controll'd by the words he disdains to control.
   a.   Owen Meredith (Lord Lytton)—
            Lucile. Pt. I. Canto II. St. VI.

How many honest words have suffered corruption since Chaucer's days!
   b.   Thomas Middleton—*No Wit, No Help,*
             Like a Woman's. Act II. Sc. 1.

His words, * * * like so many nimble
and airy servitors, trip about him at command.
   c.   Milton—*Apology for Smectymnuus.*

And to bring in a new word by the head
and shoulders, they leave out the old one.
   d.   Montaigne—*Essays. Upon some Verses*
                 of Virgil.

Words are like leaves; and where they most
abound,
Much fruit of sense beneath is rarely found.
   e.   Pope—*Essay on Criticism.* L. 309.

        They say * * *
That, putting all his words together,
'Tis three blue beans in one blue bladder.
   f.   Prior—*Alma.* Canto I. L. 26.

O! many a shaft, at random sent,
Finds mark the archer little meant!
And many a word, at random spoken,
May soothe or wound a heart that's broken!
   g.   Scott—*Lord of the Isles.* Canto V.
                      St. 18.
Syllables govern the world.
   h.   John Selden—*Table Talk. Power.*

A fine volley of words, gentlemen, and
quickly shot off.
   i.   *Two Gentlemen of Verona.* Act II.
                  Sc. 4. L. 33.

But words are words; I never yet did hear
That the bruis'd heart was pierced through
the ear.
   j.   *Othello.* Act I. Sc. 3. L. 218.

But yesterday the word of Cæsar might
Have stood against the world; now lies he
there,
And none so poor to do him reverence.
   k.   *Julius Cæsar.* Act III. Sc. 2. L. 123.

Familiar in his mouth as household words.
   l.   *Henry V.* Act IV. Sc. 3. L. 52.

Good words are better than bad strokes.
   m.   *Julius Cæsar.* Act V. Sc. 1. L. 29.

He draweth out the thread of his verbosity
finer than the staple of his argument.
   n.   *Love's Labour's Lost.* Act V. Sc. 1.
                        L. 18.

Here are a few of the unpleasant'st words
That ever blotted paper!
   o.   *Merchant of Venice.* Act III. Sc. 2.
                        L. 254.

How long a time lies in one little word!
Four lagging winters and four wanton springs
End in a word: such is the breath of kings.
   p.   *Richard II.* Act I. Sc. 3. L. 213.

I know thou'rt full of love and honesty,
And weigh'st thy words before thou givest
them breath.
   q.   *Othello.* Act III. Sc. 3. L. 118.

Madam, you have bereft me of all words,
Only my blood speaks to you in my veins.
   r.   *Merchant of Venice.* Act III. Sc. 2.
                        L. 177.

My words fly up, my thoughts remain below:
Words without thoughts never to heaven go.
   s.   *Hamlet.* Act III. Sc. 3. L. 97.

These words are razors to my wounded heart.
   t.   *Titus Andronicus.* Act I. Sc. 1.
                        L. 314.

        'Tis well said again;
And 'tis a kind of good deed to say well:
And yet words are no deeds.
   u.   *Henry VIII.* Act III. Sc. 2. L. 152.

        Unpack my heart with words,
And fall a-cursing, like a very drab.
   v.   *Hamlet.* Act II. Sc. 2. L. 614.

What do you read, my lord?
  Words, words, words.
   w.   *Hamlet.* Act II. Sc. 2. L. 193.

Words are grown so false, I am loath to
prove reason with them.
   x.   *Twelfth Night.* Act III. Sc. 1. L. 28.

Words pay no debts, give her deeds.
   y.   *Troilus and Cressida.* Act III. Sc. 2.
                        L. 58.
Words, words, mere words, no matter from
the heart.
   z.   *Troilus and Cressida.* Act V. Sc. 3.
                        L. 108.

Zounds! I was never so bethump'd with words
Since I first call'd my brother's father dad.
   aa.   *King John.* Act II. Sc. 1. L. 466.

      We know not what we do
When we speak words.
   bb.   Shelley—*Rosalind and Helen.*
                        L. 1,108.

Words are but holy as the deeds they cover.
   cc.   Shelley—*The Cenci.* Act II. Sc. 2.

The artillery of words.
   dd.   Swift—*Ode to Sancroft.* L. 13.

Deep in my heart subsides the infrequent
　　word,
And there dies slowly throbbing like a
　　wounded bird.
a.　　Francis Thompson—*Her Portrait.*
　　　　　　　　　　　　　　　St. 3.

WORK.

When Adam dolve, and Eve span,
　Who was then the gentleman?
b.　　*Lines used by* John Ball *in Wat*
　　　　　　　　　　Tyler's Rebellion.

　　　　　　By the way,
The works of women are symbolical.
We sew, sew, prick our fingers, dull our sight,
Producing what? A pair of slippers, sir,
To put on when you're weary—or a stool
To tumble over and vex you * * * curse
　　that stool!
Or else at best, a cushion where you lean
And sleep, and dream of something we are
　　not,
But would be for your sake. Alas, alas!
This hurts most, this * * * that, after all,
　　we are paid
The worth of our work, perhaps.
c.　　E. B. Browning—*Aurora Leigh.*
　　　　　　　　　　Bk. I. L. 465.

　　　Free men freely work:
Whoever fears God, fears to sit at ease.
d.　　E. B. Browning—*Aurora Leigh.*
　　　　　　　　　　Bk. VIII. L. 784.

　　　　　　Get leave to work
In this world,—'tis the best you get at all.
e.　　E. B. Browning—*Aurora Leigh.*
　　　　　　　　　　Bk. III. L. 164.

　　　　Let no one till his death
Be called unhappy. Measure not the work
Until the day's out and the labour done.
f.　　E. B. Browning—*Aurora Leigh.*
　　　　　　　　　　Bk. V. L. 78.
And still be doing, never done.
g.　　Butler—*Hudibras.* Pt. I. Canto I.
　　　　　　　　　　　　　　L. 204.

All work, even cotton-spinning, is noble;
work is alone noble.
h.　　Carlyle—*Past and Present.* Bk. III.
　　　　　　　　　　　　　　Ch. IV.

Genuine Work alone, what thou workest
faithfully, that is eternal, as the Almighty
Founder and World-Builder himself.
i.　　Carlyle—*Past and Present.* Bk. II.
　　　　　　　　　　　　　　Ch. XVII.

With hand on the spade and heart in the sky
　Dress the ground and till it;
Turn in the little seed, brown and dry,
　Turn out the golden millet.
Work, and your house shall be duly fed:
　Work, and rest shall be won;
I hold that a man had better be dead
　Than alive when his work is done.
j.　　Alice Cary—*Work.*

Each natural agent works but to this end,—
To render that it works on like itself.
k.　　George Chapman—*Bussy D'Ambois.*
　　　　　　　　　　　Act III. Sc. 1.

Nowher so besy a man as he ther was,
And yet he semed bisier than he was.
l.　　Chaucer—*Canterbury Tales. Prologue.*
　　　　　　　　　　　　　　L. 321.

All Nature seems at work, slugs leave their
　　lair—
The bees are stirring—birds are on the wing—
And Winter, slumbering in the open air,
Wears on his smiling face a dream of Spring!
And I the while, the sole unbusy thing,
Nor honey make, nor pair, nor build, nor
　　sing.
m.　　Coleridge—*Work without Hope.* St. 1.

Too busy with the crowded hour to fear to live
　　or die.
n.　　Emerson—*Quatrains. Nature.*

How bething the, gentliman,
　How Adam dalf, and Eve span.
o.　　*MS. of the Fifteenth Century. British
　　　　　　　　　　　　　　Museum.*

Plough deep while sluggards sleep.
p.　　Benj. Franklin—*Poor Richard.*
　　　　　　　　　　Preface to 1758.

In every rank, or great or small,
'Tis industry supports us all.
q.　　Gay—*Man, Cat, Dog, and Fly.* L. 63.

He that well his warke beginneth
　The rather a good ende he winneth.
r.　　Gower—*Confessio Amantis.*

Joy to the Toiler!—him that tills
　The fields with Plenty crowned;
Him with the woodman's axe that thrills
　The wilderness profound.
s.　　Benjamin Hathaway—*Songs of the
　　　　　　　　　　　　　　Toiler.*

Chase brave employments with a naked sword
Throughout the world.
t.　　Herbert—*The Church Porch.* St. 15.

The fiction pleased; our generous train com-
　　plies,
Nor fraud mistrusts in virtue's fair disguise.
The work she plyed, but, studious of delay,
Each following night reversed the toils of day.
u.　　Homer—*Odyssey.* Bk. XXIV.
　　　　　　　　　　L. 164. Pope's trans.

For men must work and women must weep,
And the sooner it's over the sooner to sleep,
　And good-bye to the bar and its moaning.
v.　　Chas. Kingsley—*Three Fishers.*

Who first invented work, and bound the free
And holyday-rejoicing spirit down * * *
To that dry drudgery at the desk's dead
　　wood? * * *
Sabbathless Satan!
w.　　Charles Lamb—*Work.*

Never idle a moment, but thrifty and thoughtful of others.
 a.　Longfellow—*Courtship of Miles Standish*. Pt. VIII. L. 46.

No man is born into the world whose work
Is not born with him; there is always work,
And tools to work withal, for those who will;
And blessed are the horny hands of toil!
 b.　Lowell—*A Glance Behind the Curtain*. L. 202.

God be thank'd that the dead have left still
 Good undone for the living to do—
Still some aim for the heart and the will
 And the soul of a man to pursue.
 c.　Owen Meredith (Lord Lytton)—*Epilogue*.

Man hath his daily work of body or mind
Appointed.
 d.　Milton—*Paradise Lost*. Bk. IV. L. 618.

　The work under our labour grows
Luxurious by restraint.
 e.　Milton—*Paradise Lost*. Bk. IX. L. 208.

Nothing is impossible to industry.
 f.　Periander of Corinth.

Ease and speed in doing a thing do not give the work lasting solidity or exactness of beauty.
 g.　Plutarch—*Life of Pericles*.

Work first, and then rest.
 h.　Ruskin—*Seven Lamps of Architecture*. The Lamp of Beauty.

Hard toil can roughen form and face,
And want can quench the eye's bright grace.
 i.　Scott—*Marmion*. Canto I. St. 28.

What work's, my countrymen, in hand?
 where go you
With bats and clubs? The matter? speak, I
 pray you.
 j.　*Coriolanus*. Act I. Sc. 1. L. 55.

Why, universal plodding poisons up
The nimble spirits in the arteries,
As motion and long-during action tires
The sinewy vigour of the traveller.
 k.　*Love's Labour's Lost*. Act IV. Sc. 3. L. 305.

How many a rustic Milton has passed by,
Stifling the speechless longings of his heart,
In unremitting drudgery and care!
How many a vulgar Cato has compelled
His energies, no longer tameless then,
To mould a pin, or fabricate a nail!
 l.　Shelley—*Queen Mab*. Pt. V. St. 9.

In books, or work, or healthful play.
 m.　Isaac Watts—*Divine Songs*. XX.

Thine to work as well as pray,
Clearing thorny wrongs away;
Plucking up the weeds of sin,
Letting heaven's warm sunshine in.
 n.　Whittier—*The Curse of the Charter-Breakers*. St. 21.

WORLD (THE).

The wrecks of matter, and the crush of worlds.
 o.　Addison—*Cato*. Act V. Sc. 1.

　　　This restless world
Is full of chances, which by habit's power
To learn to bear is easier than to shun.
 p.　John Armstrong—*Art of Preserving Health*. Bk. II. L. 453.

Wandering between two worlds, one dead,
 The other powerless to be born,
With nowhere yet to rest my head,
 Like these, on earth I wait forlorn.
 q.　Matthew Arnold—*Stanzas from the Grande Chartreuse*.

Earth took her shining station as a star,
In Heaven's dark hall, high up the crowd of worlds.
 r.　Bailey—*Festus*. Sc. *The Centre*.

I take the world to be but as a stage,
Where net-maskt men doo play their personage.
 s.　Du Bartas—*Divine Weekes and Workes*. Dialogue Between Heraclitus and Democritus.

He sees that this great roundabout,
The world, with all its motley rout,
 Church, army, physic, law,
Its customs and its businesses,
Is no concern at all of his,
 And says—what says he?—Caw.
 t.　Vincent Bourne—*The Jackdaw*. Cowper's trans.

In this bad, twisted, topsy-turvy world,
Where all the heaviest wrongs get uppermost.
 u.　E. B. Browning—*Aurora Leigh*. Bk. V. L. 981.

The wide world is all before us—
 But a world without a friend.
 v.　Burns—*Strathallan's Lament*.

Well, well, the world must turn upon its axis,
 And all mankind turn with it, heads or tails,
And live and die, make love and pay our taxes,
 And as the veering winds shift, shift our sails.
 w.　Byron—*Don Juan*. Canto II. St. 4.

Such is the world. Understand it, despise it, love it; cheerfully hold on thy way through it, with thy eye on highest loadstars!
 x.　Carlyle—*Essays*. Count Cagliostro. Last lines.

The true Sovereign of the world, who moulds the world like soft wax, according to his pleasure, is he who lovingly sees into the world.
a.   CARLYLE—*Essays. Death of Goethe.*

It is a shining glass, which a breath may destroy, and which a breath has produced.
b.   DE CAUX—*Comparing the world to his hour-glass.*

Such stuff the world is made of.
c.   COWPER—*Hope.* L. 211.

And for the few that only lend their ear, That few is all the world.
d.   SAMUEL DANIEL—*Musophilus.* St. 97.

I am a citizen of the world.
e.   DIOGENES LAERTIUS.

The world is a wheel, and it will all come round right.
f.   BENJ. DISRAELI—*Endymion.* Ch. LXX.

The world's an inn, and death the journey's end.
g.   DRYDEN—*Palamon and Arcite.* Bk. III. L. 887.

Creation's heir, the world, the world is mine!
h.   GOLDSMITH—*The Traveller.* L. 50.

Earth is but the frozen echo of the silent voice of God.
i.   HAGEMAN—*Silence.*

The world's a theatre, the earth a stage, Which God and nature do with actors fill.
j.   HEYWOOD—*Dramatic Works.* Vol. I. *The Author to His Book. Prefix to Apology for Actors.*

There are two worlds; the world that we can measure with line and rule, and the world that we feel with our hearts and imaginations.
k.   LEIGH HUNT—*Men, Women, and Books. Fiction and Matter of Fact.*

The Earth goes on the Earth glittering with gold;
The Earth goes on the Earth sooner than it wold;
The Earth builds on the Earth castles and towers;
The Earth says to the Earth, all this is ours.
l.   *Inscription on the Ruined Gate at Melrose Abbey.*

It is an ugly world. Offend
Good people, how they wrangle,
The manners that they never mend,
The characters they mangle.
They eat, and drink, and scheme, and plod,
And go to church on Sunday—
And many are afraid of God—
And more of Mrs. Grundy.
m.   FREDERICK LOCKER—*The Jester's Plea.*

This world, where much is to be done and little to be known.
n.   SAM'L JOHNSON—*Prayers and Meditations. Against Inquisitive and Perplexing Thoughts.*

Upon the battle ground of heaven and hell I palsied stand.
o.   MARIE JOSEPHINE—*Rosa Mystica.* P. 231.

The world goes up and the world goes down,
And the sunshine follows the rain;
And yesterday's sneer and yesterday's frown
Can never come over again,
Sweet wife.
No, never come over again.
p.   CHARLES KINGSLEY—*Dolcino to Margaret.*

If all the world must see the world
As the world the world hath seen,
Then it were better for the world
That the world had never been.
q.   LELAND—*The World and the World.*

One day with life and heart,
Is more than time enough to find a world.
r.   LOWELL—*Columbus.* Last lines.

The world in all doth but two nations bear, The good, the bad, and these mixed everywhere.
s.   MARVELL—*The Loyal Scot.*

The world's a stage on which all parts are played.
t.   THOS. MIDDLETON—*A Game of Chess.* Act V. Sc. II.

Above the smoke and stir of this dim spot Which men call Earth.
u.   MILTON—*Comus.* L. 5.

                A boundless continent,
Dark, waste, and wild, under the frown of night
Starless expos'd.
v.   MILTON—*Paradise Lost.* Bk. III. L. 423.

                Brightest seraph, tell
In which of all these shining orbs hath man
His fixed seat, or fixed seat hath none,
But all these shining orbs his choice to dwell.
w.   MILTON—*Paradise Lost.* Bk. III. L. 667.

Hanging in a golden chain
This pendent world.
x.   MILTON—*Paradise Lost.* Bk. II. L. 1,051.

The world was all before them, where to choose
Their place of rest, and Providence their guide.
y.   MILTON—*Paradise Lost.* Bk. XII. L. 646.

It is a very good world to live in,
To lend, or to spend, or to give in ;
But to beg, or to borrow, or to get a man's own,
It's the very worst world that ever was
    known.
  a.   *Attributed to* Earl of Rochester.

          All the world's a stage,
And all the men and women merely players.
  b.   *As You Like It.* Act II. Sc. 7. L. 139.

How weary, stale, flat and unprofitable
Seem to me all the uses of this world !
  c.   *Hamlet.* Act I. Sc. 2. L. 133.

I hold the world but as the world, Gratiano :
A stage where every man must play a part.
  d.   *Merchant of Venice.* Act I. Sc. 1.
                        L. 76.

The earth hath bubbles, as the water has,
And these are of them.
  e.   *Macbeth.* Act I. Sc. 4. L. 79.

          The world is grown so bad,
That wrens **make prey** where eagles dare not
    perch.
  f.   *Richard III.* Act I. Sc. 3. L. 70.

This wide and universal theatre
Presents more woful pageants than the scene
Wherein we play in.
  g.   *As You Like It.* Act II. Sc. 7. L. 137.

Why, then, the world's mine oyster,
Which I with sword will open.
  h.   *Merry Wives of Windsor.* Act II.
                     Sc. 2. L. 2.

The world's great age begins anew,
  The golden years return,
The earth doth like a snake renew
  Her winter weeds outworn.
  i.   Shelley—*Hellas.* Last chorus.

O Earth ! all bathed with blood and tears, yet
  never
Hast thou ceased putting forth thy fruit and
  flowers.
  j.   Madame de Staël—*Corinne.*
        Bk. XIII. Ch. IV. L. E. L.'s
                        trans.

This world surely is wide enough to hold both
  thee and me.
  k.   Sterne—*Tristram Shandy.* Bk. II.
                       Ch. XII.

There was all the world and his wife.
  l.   Swift—*Polite Conversation.*
                     Dialogue III.

So many worlds, so much to do,
So little done, such things to be.
  m.   Tennyson—*In Memoriam.*
                     Pt. LXXIII.

Anchorite, who didst dwell
With all the world for cell !
  n.   Francis Thompson—*To the Dead
        Cardinal of Westminster.* St. 5.

Even the linked fantasies, in whose blossomy
  twist
I swung the earth a trinket at my wrist.
  o.   Francis Thompson—*The Hound of
                      Heaven.* L. 126.

The world is a comedy to those who think,
a tragedy to those who feel.
  p.   Horace Walpole—*Letter to Sir Horace
                     Mann.* 1770.

Feast, and your halls are crowded ;
  Fast, and the world goes by.
  q.   Ella Wheeler Wilcox—*Solitude.*

Laugh and the world laughs with you,
  Weep and you weep alone ;
For the sad old earth must borrow its mirth,
  But has trouble enough of its own.
  r.   Ella Wheeler Wilcox—*Solitude.*

I have my beauty,—you your Art—
Nay, do not start :
One world was not enough for two
Like me and you.
  s.   Oscar Wilde—*Her Voice.*

The world is too much with us ; late and
  soon,
Getting and spending we lay waste our powers ;
Little we see in Nature that is ours.
  t.   Wordsworth—*Miscellaneous Sonnets.*
                     Pt. I. XXXIII.

          When the fretful stir
Unprofitable, and the fever of the world
Have hung upon the beatings of my heart.
  u.   Wordsworth—*Lines composed a few
            miles above Tintern Abbey.*

Let not the cooings of the world allure thee ;
Which of her lovers ever found her true ?
  v.   Young—*Night Thoughts.* Night VIII.
                     L. 1,279.

WORSHIP.

                  Ah, why
Should we, in the world's riper years, neglect
God's ancient sanctuaries, and adore
Only among the crowd and under roofs
That our frail hands have raised ?
  w.   Bryant—*A Forest Hymn.* L. 16.

He wales a portion with judicious care ;
And "Let us worship God !" he says, with
  solemn air.
  x.   Burns—*The Cotter's Saturday Night.*
                     St. 12.

Isocrates adviseth Demonicus, when he
came to a strange city, to worship by all
means the gods of the place.
  y.   Burton—*Anatomy of Melancholy.*
        Pt. III. Sec. IV. Memb. I.
                    Subsec. V.

The heart ran o'er
With silent worship of the great of old!—
The dead, but sceptred sovereigns, who still
    rule
Our spirits from their urns.
  a.   Byron—*Manfred.* Act III. Sc. 4.

Man always worships something; always
he sees the Infinite shadowed forth in something finite; and indeed can and must so see
it in any finite thing, once tempt him well to
fix his eyes thereon.
  b.   Carlyle—*Essays. Goethe's Works.*

Praise him each savage furious beast
That on his stores do daily feast;
And you tame slaves, of the laborious plough,
Your weary knees to your Creator bow.
  c.   Wentworth Dillon—*A Paraphrase
        on Psalm CXLVIII.* L. 53.

And what greater calamity can fall upon a
nation than the loss of worship.
  d.   Emerson—*An Address.* July 15, 1838.

I don't like your way of conditioning and
contracting with the saints. Do this and I'll
do that! Here's one for t'other. Save me and
I'll give you a taper or go on a pilgrimage.
  e.   Erasmus—*The Shipwreck.*

Ay, call it holy ground,
The soil where first they trod.
They have left unstained, what there they
    found—
Freedom to worship God.
  f.   Mrs. Hemans—*The Landing of the
                Pilgrim Fathers.*

Resort to sermons, but to prayers most:
Praying's the end of preaching.
  g.   Herbert—*The Temple. The Church
                    Porch.* St. 69.

All labourers draw hame at even,
  And can to others say,
"Thanks to the gracious God of heaven,
  Whilk sent this summer day."
  h.   Alexander Hume—*Evening.* St. 2.

Ev'n them who kept thy truth so pure of old,
When all our fathers worshipp'd stocks and
    stones.
  i.   Milton—*On the Late Massacre in
                        Piedmont.*

      How often from the steep
Of echoing hill or thicket have we heard
Celestial voices to the midnight air,
Sole, or responsive each to other's note,
Singing their great Creator?
  j.   Milton—*Paradise Lost.* Bk. IV.
                            L. 680.

Every one's true worship was that which he
found in use in the place where he chanced to
be.
  k.   Montaigne (Quoting Apollo)—
                Apology for Raimond Sebond.

Pompey bade Sylla recollect that more
worshipped the rising than the setting sun.
  l.   Plutarch—*Life of Pompey.*

    Get a prayer-book in your hand,
And stand betwixt two churchmen.
  m.   *Richard III.* Act III. Sc. 7. L. 47.

          Stoop, boys: this gate
Instructs you how to adore the heavens and
    bows you
To morning's holy office.
  n.   *Cymbeline.* Act III. Sc. 3. L. 2.

To compel man to Divine Worship by
threats and punishments is injurious. Forced
worship shuts evils in; which then lie hidden
like fires in wood beneath the ashes, that
continually foment and spread until they
burst forth into a flame.
  o.   Swedenborg—*Divine Providence.*
                            No. 136,137.

WORTH.

'Tis virtue, wit, and worth, and all
That men divine and sacred call;
For what is worth, in anything,
But so much money as 't will bring?
  p.   Butler—*Hudibras.* Pt. II. Canto I.
                            L. 463.

      'Tis fortune gives us birth,
But Jove alone endues the soul with worth.
  q.   Homer—*Iliad.* Bk. XX. L. 290.
                            Pope's trans.

This mournful truth is everywhere confess'd,
Slow rises worth by poverty depress'd.
  r.   Sam'l Johnson—*London.* L. 175.

What can ennoble sots, or slaves, or cowards?
Alas! not all the blood of all the Howards.
  s.   Pope—*Essay on Man.* Ep. IV. L. 215.

Worth makes the man, and want of it the
    fellow.
The rest is all but leather or prunello.
  t.   Pope—*Essay on Man.* Ep. IV. L. 203.

I would that I were low laid in my grave;
I am not worth this coil that's made for me.
  u.   *King John.* Act II. Sc. 1. L. 164.

O, how thy worth with manners may I sing,
  When thou art all the better part of me?
What can mine own praise to mine own self
    bring?
  And what is't but mine own when I praise
    thee?
  v.   *Sonnet XXXIX.*

A pilot's part in calms cannot be spy'd,
In dangerous times true worth is only tri'd.
  w.   Stirling—*Doomes-day. The Fifth
                            Houre.*

It is a maxim, that those to whom everybody allows the second place have an undoubted title to the first.

   a.   SWIFT—*Tale of a Tub. Dedication.*

All human things
Of dearest value hang on slender strings.

   b.   EDMUND WALLER—*Miscellanies.* I.
            L. 163.

But though that place I never gain,
Herein lies comfort for my pain :
   I will be worthy of it.

   c.   ELLA WHEELER WILCOX—*I Will be
           Worthy of It.*

WOUNDS.

           H' had got a hurt
O' th' inside of a deadlier sort.

   d.   BUTLER—*Hudibras.* Pt. I. Canto III.
            L. 309.

What deep wounds ever closed without a
   scar?
The heart's bleed longest, and but heal to
   wear
That which disfigures it.

   e.   BYRON—*Childe Harold.* Canto III.
            St. 84.

Thou hast wounded the spirit that loved thee
   And cherish'd thine image for years ;
Thou hast taught me at last to forget thee,
   In secret, in silence, and tears.

   f.   MRS. DAVID PORTER—*Thou Hast
           Wounded the Spirit.*

He in peace is wounded, not in war.

   g.   *The Rape of Lucrece.* L. 831.

No, 'tis not so deep as a well, nor so wide as
a church door; but 'tis enough, 'twill serve.

   h.   *Romeo and Juliet.* Act III. Sc. 1.
            L. 99.

Show you sweet Cæsar's wounds, poor, poor
   dumb mouths,
And bid them speak for me.

   i.   *Julius Cæsar.* Act III. Sc. 2. L. 229.

The private wound is deepest : O time most
   accurs'd
'Mongst all foes that a friend should be the
   worst.

   j.   *Two Gentlemen of Verona.* Act V.
           Sc. 4. L. 71.

The wound of peace is surety,
Surety secure.

   k.   *Troilus and Cressida.* Act II. Sc. 2.
            L. 14.

What wound did ever heal but by degrees?

   l.   *Othello.* Act II. Sc. 3. L. 377.

WRONGS.

The multitude is always in the wrong.

   m.   WENTWORTH DILLON—*Essay on
           Translated Verse.* L. 184.

Higher than the perfect song
   For which love longeth,
Is the tender fear of wrong,
   That never wrongeth.

   n.   BAYARD TAYLOR—*Improvisations.*
           Pt. 5.

Wrongs unredressed, or insults unavenged.
      WORDSWORTH—*The Excursion.*
           Bk. III. L. 377.

Y.

YOUTH.

Young men soon give and soon forget affronts ;
Old age is slow in both.

   p.   ADDISON—*Cato.* Act II. Sc. 5.

Youth dreams a bliss on this side death.
It dreams a rest, if not more deep,
More grateful than this marble sleep ;
It hears a voice within it tell :
Calm's not life's crown, though calm is
   well.
'Tis all perhaps which man acquires,
But 'tis not what our youth desires.

   q.   MATTHEW ARNOLD—*Youth and Calm.*
           L. 19.

Young men are fitter to invent than to judge ;
fitter for execution than for counsel ; and
fitter for new projects than for settled business.

   r.   BACON—*Of Youth and Age.*

Our youth we can have but to-day ;
We may always find time to grow old.

   s.   BISHOP BERKELEY—*Can Love be
           Controlled by Advice?*

Young fellows will be young fellows.

   t.   BICKERSTAFF—*Love in a Village.*
           Act II. Sc. 2.

Ah! happy years! once more who would not
   be a boy!

   u.   BYRON—*Childe Harold.* Canto II.
           St. 23.

And both were young, and one was beautiful.

   v.   BYRON—*The Dream.* St. 2.

           Her years
Were ripe, they might make six-and-twenty
   springs ;
But there are forms which Time to touch
   forbears,
And turns aside his scythe to vulgar things.

   w.   BYRON—*Don Juan.* Canto V. St. 98.

Youth is to all the glad season of life; but often only by what it hopes, not by what it attains, or what it escapes.

    a.   Carlyle—*Essays. Schiller.*

As I approve of a youth that has something of the old man in him, so I am no less pleased with an old man that has something of the youth. He that follows this rule may be old in body, but can never be so in mind.

    b.   Cicero—*Cato; or, An Essay on Old Age.*

Life went a-Maying
With Nature, Hope, and Poesy;
    When I was young!
When I was young?—Ah, woful when!

    c.   Coleridge—*Youth and Age.*

Be it a weakness, it deserves some praise,
We love the play-place of our early days;
The scene is touching, and the heart is stone,
That feels not at that sight, and feels at none.

    d.   Cowper—*Tirocinium.* L. 296.

Youth, what man's age is like to be, doth show;
We may our ends by our beginnings know.

    e.   Sir John Denham—*Of Prudence.*
                                  L. 225.

Youth should watch joys and shoot them as they fly.

    f.   Dryden—*Aureng-Zebe.* Act III.
                                   Sc. 1.

Olympian bards who sung
    Divine ideas below,
Which always find us young,
    And always keep us so.

    g.   Emerson—*Essays. The Poet.*
                             Introduction.

Youth holds no society with grief.

    h.   Euripides. L. 73.

O happy unown'd youths! your limbs can bear
The scorching dog-star and the winter's air,
While the rich infant, nurs'd with care and pain,
Thirsts with each heat and coughs with every rain!

    i.   Gay—*Trivia.* Bk. II. L. 145.

Fair laughs the morn, and soft the zephyr blows,
While proudly rising o'er the azure realm
In gallant trim the gilded vessel goes,
Youth on the prow, and Pleasure at the helm.

    j.   Gray—*The Bard.* Pt. II. St. 2.

The insect-youth are on the wing,
Eager to taste the honied spring,
And float amid the liquid noon!

    k.   Gray—*Ode on the Spring.* St. 3. L. 5.

There is a feeling of Eternity in youth which makes us amends for everything. To be young is to be as one of the Immortals.

    l.   Hazlitt—*Table Talk. The Feeling of*
                               Immortality in Youth.

Ah, youth! forever dear, forever kind.

    m.   Homer—*Iliad.* Bk. XIX. L. 303.
                                Pope's trans.

Youth! youth! how buoyant are thy hopes! they turn,
Like marigolds, toward the sunny side.

    n.   Jean Ingelow—*The Four Bridges.*
                                  St. 56.

Towering in confidence of twenty-one.

    o.   Sam'l Johnson—*Letter to Bennet*
                             Langton. Jan., 1758.

How beautiful is youth! how bright it gleams
With its illusions, aspirations, dreams!
Book of Beginnings, Story without End,
Each maid a heroine, and each man a friend!

    p.   Longfellow—*Morituri Salutamus.*
                                 L. 66.

In its sublime audacity of faith,
"Be thou removed!" it to the mountain saith,
And with ambitious feet, secure and proud,
Ascends the ladder leaning on the cloud!

    q.   Longfellow—*Morituri Salutamus.*

Standing with reluctant feet,
Where the brook and river meet,
Womanhood and childhood fleet!

    r.   Longfellow—*Maidenhood.*

Youth comes but once in a lifetime.

    s.   Longfellow—*Hyperion.* Bk. II.
                                 Ch. X.

Every street has two sides, the shady side and the sunny. When two men shake hands and part, mark which of the two takes the sunny side; he will be the younger man of the two.

    t.   Bulwer-Lytton—*What Will He Do*
                  With It? Bk. II. Heading of
                               Ch. XV.

Youth, that pursuest with such eager pace
    Thy even way,
Thou pantest on to win a mournful race:
    Then stay! oh, stay!
Pause and luxuriate in thy sunny plain;
    Loiter,—enjoy:
Once past, Thou never wilt come back again,
    A second Boy.

    u.   Richard Monckton Milnes—*Carpe*
                                  Diem.

'Tis now the summer of your youth : time
has not cropped the roses from your cheek,
though sorrow long has washed them.
  a.   EDWARD MOORE—*The Gamester.*
                         Act III. Sc. 4.

The smiles, the tears
Of boyhood's years,
The words of love then spoken.
  b.   MOORE—*Oft in the Stilly Night.*

We think our fathers fools, so wise we grow ;
Our wiser sons, no doubt, will think us so.
  c.   POPE—*Essay on Criticism.* Pt. II.
                            L. 238.

When the brisk minor pants for twenty-one.
  d.   POPE—*Epistle I.* Bk. I. L. 38.

Crabbed age and youth cannot live together ;
  Youth is full of pleasance, age is full of care ;
Youth like summer morn, age like winter
    weather ;
  Youth like summer brave, age like winter
    bare.
Youth is full of sport, age's breath is short ;
  Youth is nimble, age is lame ;
Youth is hot and bold, age is weak and cold ;
  Youth is wild, and age is tame.
Age, I do abhor thee ; youth I do adore thee.
  e.   *The Passionate Pilgrim.* St. 12.

       For youth no less becomes
The light and careless livery that it wears,
Than settled age his sables, and his weeds
Importing health and graveness.
  f.   *Hamlet.* Act IV. Sc. 7. L. 79.

Is in the very May-morn of his youth,
Ripe for exploits and mighty enterprises.
  g.   *Henry V.* Act I. Sc. 2. L. 120.

       My salad days ;
When I was green in judgment.
  h.   *Antony and Cleopatra.* Act I. Sc. 5.
                            L. 73.

      The spirit of a youth
That means to be of note, begins betimes.
  i.   *Antony and Cleopatra.* Act IV. Sc. 4.
                            L. 26.

Thou art thy mother's glass, and she in thee
Calls back the lovely April of her prime :
So thou through windows of thine age shall
  see.
Despite of wrinkles this thy golden time.
  j.   *Sonnet III.*

Hail, blooming Youth !
May all your virtues with your years im-
  prove,
Till in consummate worth you shine the pride
Of these our days, and succeeding times
A bright example,
  k.   WM. SOMERVILLE—*The Chase.* Bk. III.
                            L. 389.

Youth should be a savings-bank.
  l.   MADAME SWETCHINE.

What is that to him that reaps not harvest of
  his youthful joys,
Though the deep heart of existence beat forever like a boy's ?
  m.   TENNYSON—*Locksley Hall.* St. 70.

What unjust judges fathers are, when in regard to us they hold
That even in our boyish days we ought in
  conduct to be old,
Nor taste at all the very things that youth and
  only youth requires ;
They rule us by their present wants not by
  their past long-lost desires.
  n.   TERENCE—*The Self-Tormentor.* Act I.
           Sc. 3. F. W. Ricord's trans.

A youth to whom was given
So much of earth, so much of heaven.
  o.   WORDSWORTH—*Ruth.*

To be young was very heaven !
  p.   WORDSWORTH—*The Prelude.* Bk. XI.

Youth is not rich in time ; it may be poor ;
Part with it as with money, sparing ; pay
No moment but in purchase of its worth,
And what it's worth, ask death-beds ; they
  can tell.
  q.   YOUNG—*Night Thoughts.* Night II.
                            L. 47.

Z.

ZEAL.

There is no greater sign of a general decay
of virtue in a nation, than a want of zeal in
its inhabitants for the good of their country.
  r.   ADDISON—*Freeholder.* No. 5.

Zealous, yet modest.
  s.   BEATTIE—*The Minstrel.* Bk. I. St. 11.
43

Through zeal knowledge is gotten, through
lack of zeal knowledge is lost ; let a man who
knows this double path of gain and loss thus
place himself that knowledge may grow.
  t.   BUDDHA.

For zeal's a dreadful termagant,
That teaches saints to tear and cant.
  u.   BUTLER—*Hudibras.* Pt. III. Canto II.
                            L. 673.

Awake, my soul! stretch every nerve,
  And press with vigour on;
A heavenly race demands thy zeal,
  And an immortal crown.
  a.   PHILIP DODDRIDGE—*Zeal and Vigour
                    in the Christian Race.*

I remember a passage in Goldsmith's "Vicar
of Wakefield," which he was afterwards fool
enough to expunge: "I do not love a man
who is zealous for nothing."
  b.   SAM'L JOHNSON—*Boswell's Life of
                    Johnson.* 1779.

A Spirit, zealous, as he seemed, to know
More of the Almighty's works, and chiefly
    Man,
God's latest image.
  c.   MILTON—*Paradise Lost.* Bk. IV.
                            L. 565.

                But his zeal
None seconded, as out of season judged,
Or singular and rash.
  d.   MILTON—*Paradise Lost.* Bk. V.
                            L. 849.

                But zeal moved thee;
To please thy gods thou didst it!
  e.   MILTON—*Samson Agonistes.* L. 895.

So shall they build me altars in their zeal,
Where knaves shall minister, and fools shall
    kneel:
Where faith may mutter o'er her mystic spell,
Written in blood—and Bigotry may swell
The sail he spreads for Heav'n with blasts
    from hell!
  f.   MOORE—*Lalla Rookh. Veiled Prophet
                    of Khorassan.*

Zeal is very blind, or badly regulated, when
it encroaches upon the rights of others.
  g.   PASQUIER QUESNEL.

For virtue's self may too much zeal be had:
The worst of madmen is a saint run mad.
  h.   POPE—*Horace.* Bk. I. Ep. VI. L. 26.

I have more zeal than wit.
  i.   POPE—*Imitations of Horace.* Bk. II.
                    Satire VI. L. 56.

Poets heap virtues, painters gems, at will,
And show their zeal, and hide their want of
    skill.
  j.   POPE—*Moral Essays.* Ep. II. L. 185.

Zeal then, not charity, became the guide.
  k.   POPE—*Essay on Man.* Ep. III. L. 261.

We do that in our zeal our calmer moment
would be afraid to answer.
  l.   SCOTT—*Woodstock.* Heading of
                            Ch. XVII.

Terms ill defined, and forms misunderstood,
And customs, when their reasons are un-
    known,
Have stirred up many zealous souls
To fight against imaginary giants.
  m.   TUPPER—*Proverbial Philosophy. Of
                            Tolerance.*

Press bravely onward!—not in vain
  Your generous trust in human kind;
The good which bloodshed could not gain
  Your peaceful zeal shall find.
  n.   WHITTIER—*To the Reformers of
                            England.*

ZEPHYRS.

Let Zephyr only breathe
  And with her tresses play.
  o.   DRUMMOND—*Song. Phœbus, Arise.*

Fair laughs the morn, and soft the zephyr
    blows.
  p.   GRAY—*The Bard.* I. 2. L. 9.

                And soon
Their hushing dances languished to a stand,
Like midnight leaves when, as the Zephyrs
    swoon,
All on their drooping stems they sink un-
    fanned.
  q.   HOOD—*The Plea of the Midsummer
                            Fairies.*

What joy have I in June's return?
My feet are parched—my eyeballs burn,
  I scent no flowery gust;
But faint the flagging Zephyr springs,
With dry Macadam on its wings,
  And turns me "dust to dust."
  r.   HOOD—*Town and Country. Ode
                    Imitated from Horace.*

And on the balmy zephyrs tranquil rest
The silver clouds.
  s.   KEATS—*Posthumous Poems. Sonnets.
                Oh! How I Love on a Fair
                            Summer's Eve.*

And soften'd sounds along the waters die:
Smooth flow the waves, the zephyrs gently
    play.
  t.   POPE—*Rape of the Lock.* Canto II.
                            L. 50.

Lull'd by soft zephyrs thro' the broken pane.
  u.   POPE—*Prologue to Satires.* L. 42.

Soft is the strain when zephyr gently blows.
  v.   POPE—*Essay on Criticism.* Pt. II.
                            L. 366.

Soft o'er the shrouds aerial whispers breathe,
That seemed but zephyrs to the train beneath.
  w.   POPE—*Rape of the Lock.* Canto II.
                            L. 58.

The balmy zephyrs, silent since her death,
Lament the ceasing of a sweeter breath.
  x.   POPE—*Winter.* L. 45.

Quotations from Latin Authors

AND

Latin Law Maxims.

A.

ACTION.

Quod est, eo decet uti : et quicquid agas, agere pro viribus.

What one has, one ought to use: and whatever he does he should do with all his might.

a. Cicero—*De Senectute.* IX.

Est modus in rebus, sunt certi denique fines Quos ultra citraque nequit consistere rectum.

There is a mean in all things ; and, moreover, certain limits on either side of which right cannot be found.

b. Horace—*Satiræ.* I. 1. 106.

In medias res.

Into the midst of things.

c. Horace—*Ars Poetica.* CXLVIII.

Quid tam dextro pede concipis ut te conatus non pœniteat votique peracti ?

What is there that you enter upon so favorably as not to repent of the undertaking and the accomplishment of your wish ?

d. Juvenal—*Satiræ.* X. 5.

Actus dei nemini facit injuriam.

The act of God injures no one.

e. *Law Maxim.*

Factum a judice quod ad ejus officium non spectat, non ratum est.

An act of a judge which does not relate to his office, is of no force.

f. *Law Maxim.*

Nunquam ædepol temere tinniit tintinnabulum ;
Nisi quis illud tractat aut movet, mutum est, tacet.

The bell never rings of itself; unless some one handles or moves it it is dumb.

g. Plautus—*Trinummus.* IV. 2. 162.

Actum ne agas.

Do not do what is already done.

h. Terence—*Phormio.* II. 3. 72.

Non omnia possumus omnes.

We cannot all do all things.

i. Virgil—*Eclogæ.* VIII. 63.

ADMIRATION.

Nil admirari prope est res una, Numici,
Solaque, quæ possit facere et servare beatum.

Not to be lost in idle admiration is the only sure means of making and of preserving happiness.

j. Horace—*Epistolæ.* I. 6. I.

Omitte mirari beatæ
Fumum et opes strepitumque Romæ.

Cease to admire the smoke, wealth, and noise of prosperous Rome.

k. Horace—*Carmina.* III. 29. 11.

ADVERSITY.

Æquam memento rebus in arduis
Servare mentem.

Remember to be calm in adversity.

l. Horace—*Carmina.* II. 3. 1.

Adversæ res admonent religionum.

Adversity reminds men of religion.

m. Livy—*Annales.* V. 51.

Gaudent magni viri rebus adversis non aliter, quam fortes milites bellis.

Great men rejoice in adversity just as brave soldiers triumph in war.

n. Seneca—*De Providentia.* IV.

Adversis etenim frangi non esse virorum.

Brave men ought not to be cast down by adversity.

o. Silius Italicus—*Punica.* X. 618.

Magnum, atque in magnis positum populisque virisque adversam ostentare fidem.

It is noble and so regarded both among nations and individuals to keep faith in adversity.

p. Silius Italicus—*Punica.* XI. 163.

ADVICE.

Omne supervacuum pleno de pectore manat.
> Superfluous advice is not retained by the full mind.
a.   Horace—*Ars Poetica.*   CCCXXXVII.

Quidquid præcipies esto brevis.
> Whatever advice you give, be short.
b.   Horace—*Ars Poetica.*   CCCXXXV.

Consilia qui dant prava cautis hominibus,
Et perdunt operam et deridentur turpiter.
> Those who give bad advice to the prudent, both lose their pains and are laughed to scorn.
c.   Phædrus—*Fabulæ.*   I. 25.

Facile omnes, quum valemus, recta consilia ægrotis damus.
> We all, when we are well, give good advice to the sick.
d.   Terence—*Andria.*   II. 1. 9.

AFFLICTION.

Damna minus consueta movent.
> The afflictions to which we are accustomed, do not disturb us.
e.   Claudianus—*In Eutropium.*   II. 149.

Crede mihi, miseris cœlestia numina parcunt;
Nec semper læsos, et sine fine, premunt.
> Believe me, the gods spare the afflicted, and do not always oppress those who are unfortunate.
f.   Ovid—*Epistolæ Ex Ponto.*   III. 6. 21.

Dubiam salutem qui dat adflictis negat.
> He who tenders doubtful safety to those in trouble refuses it.
g.   Seneca—*Œdipus.*   CCXIII.

Quæ regio in terris nostri non plena laboris.
> What region of the earth is not full of our calamities?
h.   Virgil—*Æneid.*   I. 460.

AGE (OLD).

Senex cum extemplo est, jam nec sentit, nec sapit;
Ajunt solere eum rursum repuerascere.
> When man reaches the last stage of life,—
> "Sans sense, sans taste, sans eyes, sans everything,"—they say that he has grown a child again.
i.   Plautus—*Mercator.*   II. 2. 24.

Senectus insanabilis morbus est.
> Old age is an incurable disease.
j.   Seneca—*Epistolæ Ad Lucilium.*   CVIII. 29.

Turpis et ridicula res est elementarius senex: juveni parandum, seni utendum est.
> An old man in his rudiments is a disgraceful object.   It is for youth to acquire, and for age to apply.
k.   Seneca—*Epistolæ Ad Lucilium.*
                                    XXXVI. 4.

Vetera extollimus recentium incuriosi.
> We extol ancient things, regardless of our own times.
l.   Tacitus—*Annales.*   II. 88.

Vitium commune omnium est,
Quod nimium ad rem in senectâ attenti sumus.
> It is a vice common to all, that in old age we are too much attached to worldly interests.
m.   Terence—*Adelphi.*   V. 8. 30.

Annus enim octogesimus admonet me, ut sarcinas colligam, antequam proficiscar e vita.
> For my eightieth year warns me to pack up my baggage before I leave life.
n.   Varro—*De Re Rustica.*   I. 1.

AGREEMENT.

Nunquam aliud Natura aliud Sapientia dicit.
> Nature never says one thing, Wisdom another.
o.   Juvenal—*Satiræ.*   XIV. 321.

Rara est adeo concordia formæ
Atque pudicitiæ.
> Rare is the union of beauty and purity.
p.   Juvenal—*Satiræ.*   X. 297.

Mansit concordia discors.
> Agreement exists in disagreement.
q.   Lucan—*Pharsalia.*   I. 98.

Discors concordia.
> Agreeing to differ.
r.   Ovid—*Metamorphoses.*   I. 433.

AGRICULTURE.

Cujus est solum, ejus est usque ad cœlum.
> He who owns the soil, owns up to the sky.
s.   *Law Maxim.*

Continuâ messe senescit ager.
> A field becomes exhausted by constant tillage.
t.   Ovid—*Ars Amatoria.*   III. 82.

Tempus in agrorum cultu consumere dulce est.
> Time spent in the cultivation of the fields passes very pleasantly.
u.   Ovid—*Epistolæ Ex Ponto.*   II. 7. 69.

Laudato ingentia rura,
Exiguum colito.
> Praise a large domain, cultivate a small state.
v.   Virgil—*Georgica.*   II. 412.

AMBITION.

Prima enim sequentem, honestum est in secundis, tertiisque consistere.

When you are aspiring to the highest place, it is honorable to reach the second or even the third rank.

a.   CICERO—*De Oratore.*   I.

Nil mortalibus arduum est :
Cœlum ipsum petimus stultitiâ.

Nothing is too high for the daring of mortals : we would storm heaven itself in our folly.

b.   HORACE—*Carmina.*   I.   3.   37.

Vestigia nulla retrorsum.

No steps backward.

c.   HORACE—*Epistolæ.*   I.   1.   74.

Velle parum est ; cupias ut re potiaris oportet ;
Et faciat somnos hæc tibi cura breves.

To wish is of little account ; to succeed you must earnestly desire ; and this desire must shorten thy sleep.

d.   OVID—*Epistolæ Ex Ponto.*   III. 1.   35.

An erit, qui velle recuset
Os populi meruisse ? et cedro digna locutus
Linquere, nec scombros metuentia carmina
nec thus.

Lives there the man with soul so dead as to disown the wish to merit the people's applause, and having uttered words worthy to be kept in cedar oil to latest times, to leave behind him rhymes that dread neither herrings nor frankincense.

e.   PERSIUS—*Satiræ.*   I.   41.

Licet ipsa vitium sit ambitio, frequenter tamen causa virtutum est.

Though ambition in itself is a vice, yet it is often the parent of virtues.

f.   QUINTILIAN—*De Institutione Oratoria.*   II.   22.

Si vis ad summum progredi, ab infimo ordire.

If you wish to reach the highest, begin at the lowest.

g.   SYRUS—*Maxims.*

ANCESTRY.

Stemmata quid faciunt, quid prodest, Pontice, longo,
Sanguine censeri pictosque ostendere vultus.

Of what use are pedigrees, or to be thought of noble blood, or the display of family portraits, O Ponticus ?

h.   JUVENAL—*Satiræ.*   VIII. 1.

Nam genus et proavos et quæ non fecimus ipsi
Vix ea nostra voco.

Birth and ancestry, and that which we have not ourselves achieved, we can scarcely call our own.

i.   OVID—*Metamorphoses.* XIII. 140.

Majorum gloria posteris lumen est, neque bona neque mala in occulto patitur.

The glory of ancestors sheds a light around posterity ; it allows neither their good nor bad qualities to remain in obscurity.

j.   SALLUST—*Jugurtha.*   LXXXV.

Qui genus **jactat suum**
Aliena laudat.

He who boasts of his descent, praises the deeds of another.

k.   SENECA—*Hercules Furens.*   CCCXL.

ANGER.

Ira est libido puniendi ejus, qui videatur læsisse injuriâ.

Anger is the desire of punishing the man who seems to have injured you.

l.   CICERO—*Tusculanarum Disputationum.*   IV.   9.

Fœnum habet in cornu.

He has hay on his horns.

m.   HORACE—*Satiræ.*   I.   4.   34.

Ira furor brevis est : animum rege : qui nisi paret imperat.

Anger is momentary madness, so control your passion or it will control you.

n.   HORACE—*Epistolæ.*   I.   2.   62.

Trahit ipse furoris
Impetus, et visum est lenti quæsisse nocentem.

They are borne along by the violence of their rage, and think it is a waste of time to ask who are guilty.

o.   LUCAN—*Pharsalia.*   II.   109.

Quamlibet infirmas adjuvat ira manus.

Anger assists hands however weak.

p.   OVID—*Amorum.*   I.   7.   66.

Ut fragilis glacies **interit ira morâ.**

Like fragile ice anger passes away in time.

q.   OVID—*Ars Amatoria.*   I.   374.

Quamvis tegatur proditur vultu furor.

Anger, though concealed, is betrayed by the countenance.

r.   SENECA—*Hippolytus.*   CCCLXIII.

Ne frena animo permitte calenti ;
Da spatium, tenuemque moram ; male cuncta ministrat
Impetus.

Give not reins to your inflamed passions ; take time and a little delay ; impetuosity manages all things badly.

s.   STATIUS—*Thebais.*   X.   703.

Furor arma ministrat.

Their rage supplies them with weapons.

t.   VIRGIL—*Æneid.*   I.   150.

Tantæne animis cœlestibus iræ.

Can heavenly minds such anger entertain ?

u.   VIRGIL—*Æneid.*   I.   11.

ART.

Oculi picturis tenentur, aures cantibus.

The eyes are charmed by paintings, the ears by music.

a.   CICERO—*Academici.* IV. 7.

Pictoribus atque poetis
Quidlibet audendi semper fuit æqua potestas.

Painters and poets have equal license in regard to everything.

b.   HORACE—*Ars Poetica.* 9.

Nequeo monstrare et sentio tantum.

I only feel, but want the power to paint.

c.   JUVENAL—*Satiræ.* VII. 56.

Arte citæ veloque rates remoque moventur;
Arte levis currus, arte regendus Amor.

By science, sails, and oars, ships are rapidly moved; science moves the light chariot, and it establishes love.

d.   OVID—*Ars Amatoria.* I. 3.

AVARICE.

Avaritiam si tollere vultis, mater ejus est tollenda, luxuries.

If you wish to remove avarice you must remove its mother, luxury.

e.   CICERO—*De Oratore.* II. 40.

Ac primam scelerum matrem, quæ semper habendo
Plus sitiens patulis rimatur faucibus aurum,
Trudis Avaritiam.

Expel avarice, the mother of all wickedness, who, always thirsty for more, opens wide her jaws for gold.

f.   CLAUDIANUS—*De Laudibus Stilichonis.* II. 111.

Crescit amor nummi quantum ipsa pecunia crescit.

The love of pelf increases with the pelf.

g.   JUVENAL—*Satiræ.* XIV. 139.

Non propter vitam faciunt patrimonia quidam,
Sed vitio cæci propter patrimonia vivunt.

Some men make fortunes, but not to enjoy them; for, blinded by avarice, they live to make fortunes.

h.   JUVENAL—*Satiræ.* XII. 50.

Desunt inopiæ multa, avaritiæ omnia.

Poverty wants much; but avarice, everything.

i.   SYRUS—*Maxims.*

B.

BEAUTY.

O matre pulchra filia pulchrior.

O daughter, more beautiful than thy lovely mother. .

j.   HORACE—*Carmina.* I. 16. 1.

Nihil est ab omni
Parte beatum.

Nothing is beautiful from every point of view.

k.   HORACE—*Carmina.* II. 16. 27.

Auxilium non leve vultus habet.

A pleasing countenance is no slight advantage.

l.   OVID—*Epistolæ Ex Ponto.* II. 8. 54.

Raram facit misturam cum sapientiâ forma.

Beauty and wisdom are rarely conjoined.

m.   PETRONIUS ARBITER—*Satyricon.* XCIV.

Nimia est miseria nimis pulchrum esse hominem.

It is a great plague to be too handsome a man.

n.   PLAUTUS—*Miles Gloriosus.* I. 1. 68.

Fortuna facies muta commendatio est.

A pleasing countenance is a silent commendation.

o.   SYRUS—*Maxims.*

Gratior ac pulchro veniens in corpore virtus.

Even virtue is fairer when it appears in a beautiful person.

p.   VIRGIL—*Æneid.* V. 344.

Nimium ne crede colori.

Trust not too much to beauty.

q.   VIRGIL—*Eclogæ.* II. 17.

BEGGARY.

Qui timide rogat,
Docet negare.

He who begs timidly courts a refusal.

r.   SENECA—*Hippolytus.* 593.

BEGINNINGS.

Incipe; dimidium facti est cœpisse. Supersit
Dimidium : rursum hoc incipe, et efficies.

Begin; to begin is half the work. Let half still remain; again begin this, and thou wilt have finished.

s.   AUSONIUS—*Epigrammata.* LXXXI. L.

Incipe quidquid agas : pro toto est prima
operis pars.

Begin whatever you have to do : the beginning of a work stands for the whole.

a.   AUSONIUS—*Idyllia.* XII. *Inconnexa.*
5.

Omnium rerum principia parva sunt.

The beginnings of all things are small.

b.   CICERO—*De Finibus Bonorum et
Malorum.* V. 21.

Dimidium facti qui cœpit habet.

What's well begun, is half done.

c.   HORACE—*Epistolæ.* I. 2. 40.

Cujusque rei potissima pars principium est.

The principal part of everything is the beginning.

d.   *Law Maxim.*

Victuros agimus semper, nec vivimus unquam.

We are always beginning to live, but are
never living.

e.   MANILIUS—*Astronomica.* IV. 899.

Cœpisti melius quam desinis. Ultima primis cedunt.

Thou beginnest better than thou endest.
The last is inferior to the first.

f.   OVID—*Heroides.* IX. 23.

Principiis obsta : sero medicina paratur,
Cum mala per longas convaluere moras.

Resist beginnings : it is too late to employ
medicine when the evil has grown strong by
inveterate habit.

g.   OVID—*Remedia Amoris.* XCI.

Deficit omne quod nascitur.

Everything that has a beginning comes to
an end.

h.   QUINTILIAN—*De Institutione Oratoria.*
V. 10.

Quidquid cœpit, et desinit.

Whatever begins, also ends.

i.   SENECA—*De Consolatione ad Polybium.* I.

BELIEF.

Fere libenter homines id, quod volunt, credunt.

Men willingly believe what they wish.

j.   CÆSAR—*Bellum Gallicum.* III. 18.

Tarde quæ credita lædunt credimus.

We are slow to believe what if believed
would hurt our feelings.

k.   OVID—*Heroides.* II. 9.

BENEFITS.

Sociis atque amicis auxilia portabant Ro-
mani, magisque dandis quam accipiundis
beneficiis amicitias parabant.

The Romans assisted their allies and
friends, and acquired friendships by giving
rather than receiving kindness.

l.   SALLUST—*Catilina.* VI.

Beneficium non in eo quod fit aut datur
consistit sed in ipso dantis aut facientis animo.

A benefit consists not in what is done or
given, but in the intention of the giver or
doer.

m.   SENECA—*De Beneficiis.* I. 6.

Eodem animo beneficium debetur, quo datur.

A benefit is estimated according to the
mind of the giver.

n.   SENECA—*De Beneficiis.* I. 1.

Qui dedit beneficium taceat ; narret, qui accepit.

Let him that hath done the good office
conceal it ; let him that hath received it
disclose it.

o.   SENECA—*De Beneficiis.* II. 11.

BENEVOLENCE.

Nec sibi sed toti genitum se credere mundo.

He believed that he was born, not for himself, but for the whole world.

p.   LUCAN—*Pharsalia.* II. 383.

Misero datur quodcunque, fortunæ datur.

Whatever we give to the wretched, we
lend to fortune.

q.   SENECA—*Troades.* 697.

Non ignara mali miseris succurrere disco.

Being myself no stranger to suffering, I
have learned to relieve the sufferings of
others.

r.   VIRGIL—*Æneid.* I. 630.

BOOKS.

Quicquid agunt homines, votum, timor, ira,
voluptas, gaudia, discursus, nostri est farrago
libelli.

The doings of men, their prayers, fear,
wrath, pleasure, delights, and recreations,
are the subject of this book.

s.   JUVENAL—*Satiræ.* I. I. 85.

Seria cum possim, quod delectantia malim
Scribere, tu causa es lector.

Thou art the cause, O reader, of my dwelling on lighter topics, when I would rather
handle serious ones.

t.   MARTIAL—*Epigrammata.* V. 16. 1.

Distrahit animum librorum multitudo.
A multitude of books distracts the mind.
a.   Seneca—*Epistolæ Ad Lucilium.* II. 3.

BRAVERY.

Fortis vero, dolorem summum malum
judicans; aut temperans, voluptatem summum bonum statuens, esse certe nullo modo
potest.
No man can be brave who thinks pain the
greatest evil; nor temperate, who considers
pleasure the highest good.
b.   Cicero—*De Officiis.* I. 2.

Rebus in angustis facile est contemnere vitam;
Fortiter ille facit qui miser esse potest.
In adversity it is easy to despise life; he
is truly brave who can endure a wretched
life.
c.   Martial—*Epigrammata.* XI. 56. 15.

Audentes deus ipse juvat.
God himself favors the brave.
d.   Ovid—*Metamorphoses.* X. 586.

Omne solum forti patria est.
The brave find a home in every land.
e.   Ovid—*Fasti.* I. 493.

Fortes et strenuos etiam contra fortunam
insistere, timidos et ignaros ad desperationem
formidine properare.
The brave and bold persist even against
fortune; the timid and cowardly rush to
despair through fear alone.
f.   Tacitus—*Annales.* II. 46.

Fortes fortuna adjuvat.
Fortune favors the brave.
g.   Terence—*Phormio.* I. 4. 26.

BUSINESS.

Quam quisque novit artem, in hac se exerceat.
Let a man practise the profession which
he best knows.
h.   Cicero—*Tusculanarum Disputationum.*
I. 18.

Caput est in omni negotio, nôsse quid
agendum sit.
The most important part of every business
is to know what ought to be done.
i.   Columella—*De Re Rustica.* I. 1.

Aliena negotia curo,
Excussus propriis.
I attend to the business of other people,
having lost my own.
j.   Horace—*Satiræ.* II. 3. 19.

Quod medicorum est
Promittunt medici, tractant fabrilia fabri.
Physicians attend to the business of physicians, and workmen handle the tools of
workmen.
k.   Horace—*Epistolæ.* II. 1. 115.

Sed tamen amoto quæramus seria ludo.
Setting raillery aside, let us attend to serious matters.
l.   Horace—*Satiræ.* I. 1. 27.

Consilia callida et audacia primâ specie læta,
tractatu dura, eventu tristia sunt.
Hasty and adventurous schemes are at
first view flattering, in execution difficult,
and in the issue disastrous.
m.   Livy—*Annales.* XXXV. 32.

Dominum videre plurimum in rebus suis.
The master looks sharpest to his own
business.
n.   Phædrus—*Fabulæ.* II. 8. 28.

Non enim potest quæstus consistere, si eum
sumptus superat.
There can be no profit, if the outlay exceeds it.
o.   Plautus—*Pœnulus.* I. 2. 74.

Ne sutor ultra crepidam.
Shoemaker, stick to your last.
p.   *Proverb quoted by* Pliny the Elder—
Historia Naturalis. XXXV. 10. 36.

Quâ pote quisque in eâ conterat arte diem.
Let every one engage in the business with
which he is best acquainted.
q.   Propertius—*Elegiæ.* II. 1. 46.

Prius quam incipias consulito, et ubi con-
sulueris mature facto opus est.
Advise well before you begin: and when
you have decided, act promptly.
r.   Sallust—*Catilina.* I.

Omnia inconsulti impetus cœpta, initiis
valida, spatio languescunt.
All inconsiderate enterprises are impetuous at first, but soon languish.
s.   Tacitus—*Annales.* III. 58.

Par negotiis neque supra.
Neither above nor below his business.
t.   Tacitus—*Annales.* VI. 39.

Cujuslibet tu fidem in pecuniâ perspiceres,
Verere ei verba credere?
Do you fear to trust the word of a man,
whose honesty you have seen in business?
u.   Terence—*Phormio.* I. 2. 10.

Omnibus nobis ut res dant sese, ita magni
atque humiles sumus.
We all, according as our business prospers
or fails, are elated or cast down.
v.   Terence—*Hecyra.* III. 2. 20.

C.

CALUMNY.

Nihil est autem tam volucre, quam male-
dictum; nihil facilius emittitur; nihil citius
excipitur, latius dissipatur.

Nothing is so swift as calumny; nothing is
more easily uttered; nothing more readily
received; nothing more widely dispersed.

a. Cicero—*Oratio Pro Cnaeo Plancio.*
XXIII.

Conscia mens recti famæ mendacia risit:
Sed nos in vitium credula turba sumus.

The mind conscious of innocence despises
false reports: but we are a set always ready
to believe a scandal.

b. Ovid—*Fasti.* IV. 311.

Non soles respicere te, cum dicas injuste
alteri?

Do you never look at yourself when you
abuse another person?

c. Plautus—*Pseudolus.* II. 2. 18.

CAPACITY.

Illud tamen in primis testandum est, nihil
præcepta atque artes valere nisi adjuvante natura.

One thing, however, I must premise, that
without the assistance of natural capacity,
rules and precepts are of no efficacy.

d. Quintilian—*Proœmium.* I. 4.

CARE.

Majores fertilissium in agro oculum domini
esse dixerunt.

Our fathers used to say that the master's
eye was the best fertilizer.

e. Pliny the Elder—*Historia Naturalis*
XVIII. 84.

Nimis in veritate, et similitudinis quam
pulchritudinis amantior.

Too exact, and studious of similitude
rather than of beauty.

f. Quintilian—*De Institutione Oratoria.*
XII. 10. 9.

Boni pastoris est tondere pecus non deglu-
bere.

A good shepherd shears his flock, not
flays them.

g. Suetonius—*Vitæ Duodecim Cæsarum.*

Non quam multis placeas, sed qualibus
stude.

Do not care how many, but whom, you
please.

h. Syrus—*Maxims.*

CAUSE.

In bello parvis momentis magni casus inter-
cedunt.

In war events of importance are the result
of trivial causes.

i. Cæsar—*Bellum Gallicum.* I. 21.

Causa latet: vis est notissima.

The cause is hidden, but the result is
known.

j. Ovid—*Metamorphoses.* IV. 287.

Felix qui potuit rerum cognoscere causas.

Happy the man who has been able to
learn the causes of things.

k. Virgil—*Georgica.* II. 490.

CHANCE.

Quam sæpè fortè temerè eveniunt, quæ non
audeas optare!

How often things occur by mere chance,
which we dared not even to hope for.

l. Terence—*Phormio.* V. 1. 31.

CHANGE.

An id exploratum cuiquam potest esse, quomodo sese habiturum sit corpus, non dico ad
annum sed ad vesperam?

Can any one find out in what condition
his body will be, I do not say a year hence,
but this evening?

m. Cicero—*De Finibus Bonorum et*
Malorum. II. 228.

Nihil est aptius ad delectationem lectoris
quam temporum varietates fortunæque vicis-
situdines.

There is nothing better fitted to delight
the reader than change of circumstances and
varieties of fortune.

n. Cicero—*Epistolæ.* V. 12.

Asperius nihil est humili cum surgit in altum.

Nothing is more annoying than a low man
raised to a high position.

o. Claudianus—*In Eutropium.* I. 181.

Mobile mutatur semper cum principe vulgus.

The fickle populace always change with
the prince.

p. Claudianus—*De Quarto Consulatu*
Honorii Augusti Panegyris. CCCII.

Amphora cœpit
Institui; currente rotâ cur urceus exit?

A vase is begun; why, as the wheel goes
round, does it turn out a pitcher?

a.   Horace—*Ars Poetica.* XXI.

Diruit, ædificat, mutat quadrata rotundis.

He pulls down, he builds up, he changes
squares into circles.

b.   Horace—*Epistolæ.* I. 1. 100.

Non si male nunc et olim
Sic erit.

If matters go badly now, they will not always be so.

c.   Horace—*Carmina.* II. 10. 17.

Non sum qualis eram.

I am not what I once was.

d.   Horace—*Carmina.* IV. I. 3.

Optat ephippia bos piger, optat arare ca-
ballus.

The lazy ox wishes for horse-trappings,
and the steed wishes to plough.

e.   Horace—*Epistolæ.* I. 14. 43.

Plerumque gratæ divitibus vices.

Change generally pleases the rich.

f.   Horace—*Carmina.* III. 29. 13.

Quod petiit spernit, repetit quod nuper om-
isit.

He despises what he sought; and he seeks
that which he lately threw away.

g.   Horace—*Epistolæ.* I. 1. 98.

Quo teneam vultus mutantem Protea nodo?

With what knot shall I hold this Proteus,
who so often changes his countenance?

h.   Horace—*Epistolæ.* I. 1. 90.

Jus publicum privatorum pactis mutari non
potest.

A public right cannot be changed by private agreement.

i.   *Law Maxim.*

Omnia mortali mutantur lege creata,
Nec se cognoscunt terræ vertentibus annis,
Et mutant variam faciem per sæcula gentes.

Everything that is created is changed by
the laws of man; the earth does not know
itself in the revolution of years; even the
races of man assume various forms in the
course of ages.

j.   Manilius—*Astronomica.* 515.

Mens mutatione recreabitur; sicut in cibis,
quorum diversitate reficitur stomachus, et
pluribus minore fastidio alitur.

Our minds are like our stomachs; they
are whetted by the change of their food, and
variety supplies both with fresh appetite.

k.   Quintilian—*De Institutione Oratoria.*
             I. 11. 1.

Nihil est periculosius in hominibus mutatâ
subito fortunâ.

Nothing is more dangerous to men than a
sudden change of fortune.

l.   Quintilian—*De Institutione Oratoria.*
             CCLX.

Corporis et fortunæ bonorum ut initium
finis est. Omnia orta occidunt, et orta senes-
cunt.

As the blessings of health and fortune
have a beginning, so they must also find an
end. Everything rises but to fall, and increases but to decay.

m.   Sallust—*Jugurtha.* II.

Corpora lente augescent, cito extinguuntur.

Bodies are slow of growth, but are rapid
in their dissolution.

n.   Tacitus—*Agricola.* II.

CHARACTER.

Suus quoque attributus est error:
Sed non videmus, manticæ quid in tergo est.

Every one has his faults: but we do not see
the wallet on our own backs.

o.   Catullus—*Carmina.* XXII. 20.

Importunitas autem, et inhumanitas omni
ætati molesta est.

But a perverse temper and fretful disposition make any state of life unhappy.

p.   Cicero—*De Senectute.* III.

Minime sibi quisque notus est, et difficillime de se quisque sentit.

Every one is least known to himself, and it
is very difficult for a man to know himself.

q.   Cicero—*De Oratore.* III. 9.

Ut ignis in aquam conjectus, continuo
restinguitur et refrigeratur, sic refervens fal-
sum crimen in purissimam et castissimam
vitam collatum, statim concidit et extinguitur.

As fire when thrown into water is cooled
down and put out, so also a false accusation
when brought against a man of the purest
and holiest character, boils over and is at
once dissipated, and vanishes.

r.   Cicero—*Oratio Pro Quinto Roscio*
             Comœdo. VI.

Argillâ quidvis imitaberis udâ.

Thou canst mould him into any shape
like soft clay.

s.   Horace—*Epistolæ.* II. 2. 8.

Falsus honor juvat et mendax infamia terret,
Quem nisi mendosum et mendacem?

Whom does false honor aid, and calumny
deter, but the vicious and the liar?

t.   Horace—*Epistolæ.* I. 16. 39.

Integer vitæ scelerisque purus
Non eget Mauri jaculis neque arcu.

The man who is pure in life and free from guilt, needs not the aid of Moorish bows and darts.
a. Horace—*Carmina.* I. 22. 1.

Paullum sepultæ distat inertiæ
Celata virtus.

Excellence when concealed, differs but little from buried worthlessness.
b. Horace—*Carmina.* IV. 9. 29.

Servetur ad imum
Qualis ab incepto processerit, et sibi constet.

Let the character as it began be preserved to the last; and let it be consistent with itself.
c. Horace—*Ars Poetica.* CXXVI.

Famæ ac fidei damna majora sunt quam quæ æstimari possunt.

The injury done to character is greater than can be estimated.
d. Livy—*Annales.* III. 72.

Video meliora proboque,
Deteriora sequor.

I see and approve better things, I follow the worse.
e. Ovid—*Metamorphoses.* VII. 20.

Dixi omnia, quum hominem nominavi.

After I have named the man, I need say no more.
f. Pliny the Younger—*Epistolæ.* IV. 22.

Optimum et emendatissimum existimo, qui ceteris ita ignoscit, tanquam ipse quotidie peccet; ita peccatis abstinet, tanquam memini ignoscat.

The highest of characters, in my estimation, is his, who is as ready to pardon the moral errors of mankind, as if he were every day guilty of some himself; and at the same time as cautious of committing a fault as if he never forgave one.
g. Pliny the Younger—*Epistolæ.* VIII. 22.

Tecum habita, et nôris quam sit tibi curta supellex.

Retire within thyself, and thou will discover how small a stock is there.
h. Persius. *Satiræ.* IV. 52.

Udum et molle lutum es: nunc, nunc properandus et acri
Fingendus sine fine rotâ.

Thou art moist and soft clay; thou must instantly be shaped by the glowing wheel.
i. Persius—*Satiræ.* III. 23.

Inerat tamen simplicitas ac liberalitas, quæ, nisi adsit modus in exitium vertuntur.

He possessed simplicity and liberality, qualities which beyond a certain limit lead to ruin.
j. Tacitus—*Annales.* III. 86.

In turbas et discordias pessimo cuique plurima vis: pax et quies bonis artibus indigent.

In seasons of tumult and discord bad men have most power; mental and moral excellence require peace and quietness.
k. Tacitus—*Annales.* IV. 1.

Re ipsâ reperi,
Facilitate nihil esse homini melius neque clementiâ.

I have found by experience that there is nothing better for a man than mildness and clemency.
l. Terence—*Adelphi.* V. 4. 6.

Accipe nunc Danaûm insidias, et crimine ab uno
Disce omnes.

Learn now of the treachery of the Greeks, and from one example the character of the nation may be known.
m. Virgil—*Æneid.* II. 65.

CHEERFULNESS.

Leve fit quod bene fertur onus.

That load becomes light which is cheerfully borne.
n. Ovid—*Amorum.* I. 2. 10.

CHILDHOOD.

Pietas fundamentum est omnium virtutum.

The dutifulness of children is the foundation of all virtues.
o. Cicero—*Oratio Pro Cnæo Plancio.* XII.

Nil dictu fœdum visuque hæc limina tangat
Intra quæ puer est.

Let nothing foul to either eye or ear reach those doors within which dwells a boy.
p. Juvenal—*Satiræ.* XIV. 44.

Parentes objurgatione digni sunt, qui nolunt liberos suos severâ lege proficere.

Parents deserve reproof when they refuse to benefit their children by severe discipline.
q. Petronius Arbiter—*Satyricon.* IV.

Pudore et liberalitate liberos
Retinere, satius esse credo, quam metu.

It is better to keep children to their duty by a sense of honor and by kindness than by fear.
r. Terence—*Adelphi.* I. 1. 32.

Ut quisque suum vult esse, ita est.

As each one wishes his children to be, so they are.

a. TERENCE—*Adelphi.* III. 3. 46.

COMPANIONSHIP.

Nati sumus ad congregationem hominum et ad societatem communitatemque generis humani.

We have been born to associate with our fellow-men, and to join in community with the human race.

b. CICERO—*De Finibus Bonorum et Malorum.* IV. 2.

Nullius boni sine sociis jucunda possessio est.

No possession is gratifying without a companion.

c. SENECA—*Epistolæ Ad Lucilium.* VI.

Comes jucundus in viâ pro vehiculo est.

A pleasant companion on a journey is as good as a carriage.

d. SYRUS—*Maxims.*

COMPARISONS.

Hoc ego, tuque sumus : sed quod sum, non potes esse:
Tu quod es, e populo quilibet esse potest.

Such are thou and I: but what I am thou canst not be; what thou art any one of the multitude may be.

e. MARTIAL—*Epigrammata.* V. 13. 9.

Sunt bona, sunt quædam mediocria, sunt mala plura.

Some are good, some are middling, the most are bad.

f. MARTIAL—*Epigrammata.* I. 17. 1.

Multos qui conflictari adversis videantur beatos ; ac plerosque quamquam magnos per opes, miserrimos ; si illi gravem fortunam constanter tolerant, hi prosperâ inconsulte utantur.

Many who seem to be struggling with adversity are happy, whilst some in the midst of riches are miserable ; this is the case when the former bear the pressure with constancy, and the latter employ their wealth thoughtlessly.

g. TACITUS—*Annales.* VI. 22.

Duo quum idem faciunt, sæpe ut possis dicere,
Hoc licet impune facere huic, illi non licet :
Non quod dissimilis res sit, sed quod is sit.

When two persons do the self-same thing, it oftentimes falls out that in the one it is criminal, in the other it is not so ; not that the thing itself is different, but he who does it.

h. TERENCE—*Adelphi.* V. III. 37.

Sic canibus catulos similes, sic matribus hædos
Nôram ; sic parvis componere magna solebam.

Thus I knew that pups are like dogs, and kids like goats ; so I used to compare great things with small.

i. VIRGIL—*Eclogæ.* I. 23.

COMPENSATION.

Multa ferunt anni venientes commoda secum :
Multa recedentes adimunt.

The coming years bring many advantages with them : retiring they take away many.

j. HORACE—*Ars Poetica.* CLXXV.

Sæpe creat molles aspera spina rosas.

The prickly thorn often bears soft roses.

k. OVID—*Epistolæ Ex Ponto.* II. 2. 34.

Primo avulso, non deficit alter.

When the first is plucked, a second will not be wanting.

l. VIRGIL—*Æneid.* VI. 143.

CONFIDENCE.

Ultima talis erit quæ mea prima fides.

My last confidence will be like my first.

m. PROPERTIUS—*Elegiæ.* II. 20. 34.

Nusquam tuta fides.

Confidence is nowhere safe.

n. VIRGIL—*Æneid.* IV. 373.

CONQUEST.

Jus belli, ut qui vicissent, iis quos vicissent, quemadmodum vellent, imperarent.

It is the right of war for conquerors to treat those whom they have conquered according to their pleasure.

o. CÆSAR—*Bellum Gallicum.* I. 36.

Veni, vidi, vici.

I came, I saw, I conquered.

p. JULIUS CÆSAR—See SUETONIUS— *Cæsar.* XXXVII.

Cede repugnanti ; cedendo victor abibis.

Yield to him who opposes you ; by yielding you conquer.

q. OVID—*Ars Amatoria.* II. 197.

Male vincetis, sed vincite.

You will hardly conquer, but conquer you must.

r. OVID—*Metamorphoses.* IX. 509.

Bis vincit qui se vincit in victoriâ.

He conquers twice who conquers himself in victory.

s. SYRUS—*Maxims.*

CONSCIENCE.

Hic murus aëneus esto,
Nil conscire sibi, nullâ pallescere culpâ.

Be this thy brazen bulwark, to keep a clear conscience, and never turn pale with guilt.

a.   Horace—*Epistolæ.* I. 1. 60.

Conscia mens ut cuique sua est, ita concipit intra
Pectora pro facto spemque metumque suo.

According to the state of a man's conscience, so do hope and fear on account of his deeds arise in his mind.

b.   Ovid—*Fasti.* I. 485.

Nihil est miserius quam animus hominis conscius.

Nothing is more wretched than a guilty conscience.

c.   Plautus—*Mostellaria.* III. 1. 13.

Sic vive cum hominibus, tanquam deus videat; sic loquere cum deo, tanquam homines audiant.

Live with men as if God saw you; converse with God as if men heard you.

d.   Seneca—*Epistolæ Ad Lucilium.* X.

CONSEQUENCES.

Ut sementem feceris, ita metes.

As thou sowest, so shalt thou reap.

e.   Cicero—*De Oratore.* II. 65.

CONTENT.

Ille potens sui
Lætusque deget, cui licet in diem
Dixisse Vixi; cras vel atrâ
  Nube polum pater occupato,
Vel sole puro, non tamen irritum
Quodcunque retro est efficiet.

That man lives happy and in command of himself, who from day to day can say I have lived. Whether clouds obscure, or the sun illumines the following day, that which is past is beyond recall.

f.   Horace—*Carmina.* III. 29. 41.

          Multa petentibus
Desunt multa; bene est cui deus obtulit
Parca quod satis est manu.

Those who want much, are alway much in need; happy the man to whom God gives with a sparing hand what is sufficient for his wants.

g.   Horace—*Carmina.* III. 16. 42.

Nec vixit malê qui natus moriensque fefellit.

Nor has he spent his life badly who has passed it in privacy.

h.   Horace—*Epistolæ.* I. 17. 10.

Quanto quisque sibi plura negaverit,
A dis plura feret. Nil cupientium
Nudus castra peto.

The more a man denies himself, the more he shall receive from heaven. Naked, I seek the camp of those who covet nothing.

i.   Horace—*Carmina.* III. 16. 21.

Quod satis est cui contigit, nihil amplius optet.

Let him who has enough ask for nothing more.

j.   Horace—*Epistolæ.* I. 2. 46.

          Sit mihi mensa tripes et
Coucha salis puri et toga quæ defendere frigus
  Quamvis crassa queat.

Let me have a three-legged table, a dish of salt, and a cloak which, altho' coarse, will keep off the cold.

k.   Horace—*Satiræ.* I. 3. 13.

Sit mihi quod nunc est, etiam minus et mihi vivam
Quod superest ævi—si quid superesse volunt di.

Let me possess what I now have, or even less, so that I may enjoy my remaining days, if Heaven grant any to remain.

l.   Horace—*Epistolæ.* I. 18. 107.

Qua positus fueris in statione, mane.

Stay in that station in which you have been placed.

m.   Ovid—*Fasti.* II. 674.

Habeas ut nactus: nota mala res optima est.

Keep what you have got; the known evil is best.

n.   Plautus—*Trinummus.* I. 2. 25.

Si animus est æquus tibi satis habes, qui bene vitam colas.

If you are content, you have enough to live comfortably.

o.   Plautus—*Aulularia.* II. 2. 10.

Aliena nobis, nostra plus aliis placent.

The circumstances of others seem good to us, while ours seem good to others.

p.   Syrus—*Maxims.*

Vivite felices, quibus est fortuna peracta
Jam sua.

Be happy ye, whose fortunes are already completed.

q.   Virgil—*Æneid.* III. 493.

CONTENTION.

Ex magno certamine magnas excitari ferme iras.

Great contests generally excite great animosities.

r.   Livy—*Annales.* III. 40.

Ducibus tantum de funere pugna est.
> The chiefs contend only for their place of
> burial.
> *a.*   LUCAN—*Pharsalia.* VI. 811.

Cadit statim simultas, ab altera parte deserta ; nisi pariter, non pugnant.
> A quarrel is quickly settled when deserted
> by one party : there is no battle unless there
> be two.
> *b.*   SENECA—*De Ira.* II. 34.

Nimium altercando veritas amittitur.
> In excessive altercation, truth is lost.
> *c.*   SYRUS—*Maxims.*

CONTEST.

Stimulos dedit æmula virtus.
> He was spurred on by rival valor.
> *d.*   LUCAN—*Pharsalia.* I. 120.

Acer et ad palmæ per se cursurus honores,
Si tamen horteris fortius ibit equus.
> The spirited horse, which will of itself
> strive to beat in the race, will run still more
> swiftly if encouraged.
> *e.*   OVID—*Epistolæ Ex Ponto.* II. 11. 21.

CORRUPTION.

Male verum examinat omnis
Corruptus judex.
> A corrupt judge does not carefully search
> for the truth.
> *f.*   HORACE—*Satiræ.* II. 2. 8.

Corruptissimâ republicâ, plurimæ leges.
> The more corrupt the state, the more laws.
> *g.*   TACITUS—*Annales.* III. 27.

COURAGE.

Animus tamen omnia vincit.
Ille etiam vires corpus habere facit.
> Courage conquers all things : it even gives
> strength to the body.
> *h.*   OVID—*Epistolæ Ex Ponto.* II. 7. 75.

Audentem forsque Venusque juvant.
> Fortune and Love befriend the bold.
> *i.*   OVID—*Ars Amatoria.* I. 608.

Saucius ejurat pugnam gladiator, et idem
Immemor antiqui vulneris arma capit.
> The wounded gladiator forswears all fight-
> ing, but soon forgetting his former wound
> resumes his arms.
> *j.*   OVID—*Epistolæ Ex Ponto.* I. 5. 37.

Teloque animus præstantior omni.
> A spirit superior to every weapon.
> *k.*   OVID—*Metamorphoses.* III. 54.

Bonus animus in malâ re, dimidium est mali.
> Courage in danger is half the battle.
> *l.*   PLAUTUS—*Pseudolus.* I. 5. 37.

Pluma haud interest, patronus an cliens pro-
> bior sit
Homini, cui nulla in pectore est audacia.
> It does not matter a feather whether a man
> be supported by patron or client, if he him-
> self wants courage.
> *m.*   PLAUTUS—*Mostellaria.* II. 1. 64.

Non solum taurus ferit uncis cornibus hostem,
Verum etiam instanti læsa repugnat ovis.
> Not only does the bull attack its foe with
> its crooked horns, but the injured sheep
> will fight its assailant.
> *n.*   PROPERTIUS—*Elegiæ.* II. 5. 19.

Fortuna opes auferre, non animum potest.
> Fortune can take away riches, but not
> courage.
> *o.*   SENECA—*Medea.* CLXXVI.

Virtus in astra tendit, in mortem timor.
> Courage leads to heaven ; fear, to death.
> *p.*   SENECA—*Hercules Œtæus.* LXXI.

Ave, Cæsar, morituri te salutant.
> Hail, Cæsar, those who are about to die
> salute thee.
> *q.*   SUETONIUS—*Claudius.* XXI.

Exigui numero, sed bello vivida virtus.
> Small in number, but their valor tried
> in war, and glowing.
> *r.*   VIRGIL—*Æneid.* V. 754.

Macte novâ virtute, puer ; sic itur ad astra.
> Go on and increase in valor, O boy ! this
> is the path to immortality.
> *s.*   VIRGIL—*Æneid.* IX. 641.

COVETOUSNESS.

Semper avarus eget.
> The covetous man is ever in want.
> *t.*   HORACE—*Epistolæ.* I. 2. 56.

Quicquid servatur, cupimus magis : ipsaque
> furem
Cura vocat. Pauci, quod sinit alter, amant.
> We covet what is guarded ; the very care
> invokes the thief. Few love what they
> may have.
> *u.*   OVID—*Amorum.* III. 4. 25.

Amittit merito proprium qui alienum appetit.
> He deservedly loses his own property, who
> covets that of another.
> *v.*   PHÆDRUS—*Fabulæ.* I. 4. 1.

Verum est aviditas dives, et pauper pudor.
> True it is that covetousness is rich, mod-
> esty starves.
> *w.*   PHÆDRUS—*Fabulæ.* II. 1. 12.

Alieni appetens sui profusus.

Covetous of the property of others and prodigal of his own.

a.   Sallust—*Catilina.* V.

COWARDS.

Nec tibi quid liceat, sed quid fecisse decebit Occurrat, mentemque domet respectus ho-
nesti.

Do not consider what you may do, but what it will become you to have done, and let the sense of honor subdue your mind.

b.   Claudianus—*De Quarto Consulatu Honorii Augusti Panegyris.* CCLXVII.

Timidi est optare necem.

To wish for death is a coward's part.

c.   Ovid—*Metamorphoses.* IV. 115.

Virtutis expers verbis jactans gloriam Ignotos fallit, notis est derisui.

A coward boasting of his courage may de-
ceive strangers, but he is a laughing-stock to those who know him.

d.   Phædrus—*Fabulæ.* I. 11. 1.

Canis timidus vehementius latrat quam mordet.

A cowardly cur barks more fiercely than it bites.

e.   Quintus Curtius Rufus—*De Rebus Gestis Alexandri Magni.* VII. 4. 13.

Ignavissimus quisque, et ut res docuit, in periculo non ausurus, nimis verbis et linguâ feroces.

Every recreant who proved his timidity in the hour of danger, was afterwards boldest in words and tongue.

f.   Tacitus—*Annales.* IV. 62.

CREDULITY.

Credat Judæus Apella non ego.

The Jew Apella may believe this, not I.

g.   Horace—*Satiræ.* I. 5. 100.

CRIME.

Exemplo quodcumque malo committitur, ipsi Displicet auctori.

Every crime will bring remorse to the man who committed it.

h.   Juvenal—*Satiræ.* XIII. 1.

Multi committunt eadem diverso crimina fato ;
Ille crucem sceleris pretium tulit, hic diadema.

Many commit the same crimes with a very different result. One bears a cross for his crime ; another a crown.

i.   Juvenal—*Satiræ.* XIII. 103.

Nam scelus intra se tacitum qui cogitat ullum, Facti crimen habet.

For whoever meditates a crime is guilty of the deed.

j.   Juvenal—*Satiræ.* XIII. 209.

Se judice, nemo nocens absolvitur.

By his own verdict no guilty man was ever acquitted.

k.   Juvenal—*Satiræ.* XIII. 2.

Nemo repente venit turpissimus.

No one ever became very wicked all at once.

l.   Juvenal—*Satiræ.* II. 83.

Non faciat malum, ut inde veniat bonum.

You are not to do evil that good may come of it.

m.   *Law Maxim.*

Plus peccat auctor quam actor.

The instigator of a crime is worse than he who perpetrates it.

n.   *Law Maxim.*

Solent occupationis spe vel impune quædam scelesta committi.

Wicked deeds are generally done, even with impunity, for the mere desire of occupation.

o.   Ammianus Marcellinus—*Annales.* XXX. 9.

Ars fit ubi a teneris crimen condiscitur annis.

Where crime is taught from early years, it becomes a part of nature.

p.   Ovid—*Heroides.* IV. 25.

Pœna potest demi, culpa perennis **erit.**

The punishment can be remitted ; the crime is everlasting.

q.   Ovid—*Epistolæ Ex Ponto.* I. 1. 64.

Ad auctores redit
Sceleris coacti culpa.

The guilt of enforced crimes lies on those who impose them.

r.   Seneca—*Troades.* 870.

Cui prodest scelus,
Is fecit.

He who profits by crime is guilty of it.

s.   Seneca—*Medea.* 500.

Dumque punitur scelus,
Crescit.

While crime is punished it yet increases.

t.   Seneca—*Thyestes.* XXXI.

Nefas nocere vel malo fratri puta.

Consider it a crime to injure a brother even if he be wicked.

u.   Seneca—*Thyestes.* CCXIX.

Nullum caruit exemplo nefas.

No crime has been without a precedent.

v.   Seneca—*Hippolytus.* 554.

Prosperum ac felix scelus
Virtus vocatur; sontibus parent boni;
Jus est in armis, opprimit leges timor.

Successful crime is dignified with the name of virtue; the good become the slaves of the impious; might makes right; fear silences the power of the law.
a.   SENECA—*Hercules Furens.* CCLI.

Qui non vetat peccare, cum possit, jubet.

He who does not prevent a crime when he can, encourages it.
b.   SENECA—*Troades.* CCXCI.

Scelere velandum est scelus.

One crime has to be concealed by another.
c.   SENECA.—*Hippolytus.* 721.

Amici vitium si feras, facis tuum.

If you share the crime of your friend, you make it your own.
d.   SYRUS—*Maxims.*

Neque femina amissâ pudicitiâ alia abnuerit.

When a woman has lost her chastity, she will shrink from no crime.
e.   TACITUS—*Annales.* IV. 3.

CURE.

Vulnera nisi tacta tractataque sanari non possunt.

Wounds cannot be cured unless they are probed.
f.   LIVY—*Annales.* XXVIII. 27.

Tempore ducetur longo fortasse cicatrix,
Horrent admotas vulnera cruda manus.

The wound will perhaps be cured in the process of time, but it shrinks from the touch while it is fresh.
g.   OVID—*Epistolæ Ex Ponto.* I. 3. 15.

Pars sanitatis velle sanari fuit.

It is part of the cure to wish to be cured.
h.   SENECA—*Hippolytus.* CCXLIX.

CUSTOM.

Consuetudo manerii et loci est observanda.

The custom of the manor and the place must be observed.
i.   *Law Maxim.*

Consuetudo pro lege servatur.

Custom is held to be as a law.
j.   *Law Maxim.*

Optimus legum interpres consuetudo.

Custom is the best interpreter of laws.
k.   *Law Maxim.*

Vetustas pro lege semper habetur.

Ancient custom is always held or regarded as law.
l.   *Law Maxim.*

D.

DANGER.

In summo periculo timor misericordiam non recipit.

In extreme danger, fear turns a deaf ear to every feeling of pity.
m.   CÆSAR—*Bellum Gallicum.* VII. 26.

Quid quisque vitet nunquam homini satis
Cautum est in horas.

Man is never watchful enough against dangers that threaten him every hour.
n.   HORACE—*Carmina.* II. 13. 13.

Nunquam est fidelis cum potente societas.

A partnership with men in power is never safe.
o.   PHÆDRUS—*Fabulæ.* I. 5. 1.

Nihil tam firmum est cui periculum non sit etiam ab invalido.

Nothing is strong that may not be endangered even by the weak.
p.   QUINTUS CURTIUS RUFUS—*De Rebus Gestis Alexandri Magni.* VII. 8. 25.

Contemptum periculorum assiduitas periclitandi dabit.

Constant exposure to dangers will breed contempt for them.
q.   SENECA—*De Providentia.* IV.

Scit eum sine gloria vinci, qui sine periculo vincitur.

He knows that the man is overcome ingloriously, who is overcome without danger.
r.   SENECA—*De Providentia.* III.

Caret periculo qui etiam tutus cavet.

He is safe from danger who is on his guard even when safe.
s.   SYRUS—*Maxims.*

Citius venit periculum, cum contemnitur.

Danger comes the sooner when it is despised.
t.   SYRUS—*Maxims.*

Si cadere necesse est, occurendum discrimini.

If we must fall, we should boldly meet the danger.
u.   TACITUS—*Annales.* II. 1. 33.

Latet anguis in herba.
  A snake is lurking in the grass.
  a.   VIRGIL—*Eclogæ.* III. 93.

DARING.

In rebus asperis et tenui spe fortissima
quæque consilia tutissima sunt.
  In great straits and when hope is small,
  the boldest counsels are the safest.
  b.   LIVY—*Annales.* XXV. 38.

Audendo magnus tegitur timor.
  By daring, great fears are concealed.
  c.   LUCAN—*Pharsalia.* IV. 702.

Nemo timendo ad summum pervenit locum.
  No one reaches a high position without
  daring.
  d.   SYRUS—*Maxims.*

Audendum est; fortes adjuvat ipsa Venus.
  Dare to act! Even Venus aids the bold.
  e.   TIBULLUS—*Carmina.* I. 2. 16.

Audentes fortuna juvat.
  Fortune helps the bold.
  f.   VIRGIL—*Æneid.* X. 284.

DEATH.

Qui nunc it per iter tenebricosum
Illuc unde negant redire quemquam,
  Who now travels that dark path to the
  bourne from which they say no one returns.
  g.   CATULLUS—*Carmina.* III. 11.

Soles occidere et redire possunt;
Nobis cum semel occidit brevis lux,
Nox est perpetua una dormienda.
  Suns may set and rise; we, when our short
  day has closed, must sleep on during one
  never-ending night.
  h.   CATULLUS—*Carmina.* V. 4.

Emori nolo: sed me esse mortuum nihil
æstimo.
  I do not wish to die: but I care not if I
  were dead.
  i.   CICERO—*Tusculanarum Disputationum.*
                                I. 8.

Supremus ille dies non nostri extinctionem
sed commutationem affert loci.
  That last day does not bring extinction to
  us, but change of place.
  j.   CICERO—*Tusculanarum Disputationum.*
                                I. 49.

Undique enim ad inferos tantundem viæ
est.
  There are countless roads on all sides to
  the grave.
  k.   CICERO—*Tusculanarum Disputationum.*
                                I. 43.

44

Vetat dominans ille in nobis deus, injussu
hinc nos suo demigrare.
  The divinity who rules within us, forbids
  us to leave this world without his command.
  l.   CICERO—*Tusculanarum Disputationum.*
                                I. 30.

Omnia mors æquat.
  Death levels all things.
  m.   CLAUDIANUS—*De Raptu Proserpinæ.*
                                II. 302.

Mors ultima linea rerum est.
  Death is the last limit of all things.
  n.   HORACE—*Epistolæ.* I. 16. 79.

Omne capax movet urna nomen.
  In the capacious urn of death, every name
  is shaken.
  o.   HORACE—*Carmina.* III. 1. 16.

Omnes eodem cogimur; omnium
Versatur urnâ serius, ocius
Sors exitura.
  We are all compelled to take the same
  road; from the urn of death, shaken for all,
  sooner or later the lot must come forth.
  p.   HORACE—*Carmina.* II. 3. 25.

Pallida mors æquo pulsat pede pauperum
    tabernas
Regumque turres.
  Pale death, with impartial step, knocks at
  the hut of the poor and the palaces of kings.
  q.   HORACE—*Carmina.* I. 4. 13.

              Mors sola fatetur
Quantula sint hominum corpuscula.
  Death alone discloses how insignificant
  are the puny bodies of men.
  r.   JUVENAL—*Satiræ.* X. 172.

Pavido fortique cadendum est.
  The coward and the courageous alike
  must die.
  s.   LUCAN—*Pharsalia.* IX. 582.

Victorosque dei celant, ut vivere durent,
Felix esse mori.
  The gods conceal from those destined to
  live how sweet it is to die, that they may
  continue living.
  t.   LUCAN—*Pharsalia.* IV. 519.

Adde repertores doctrinarum atque leporum;
Adde Heliconiadum comites; quorum unus
    Homerus
Sceptra potitus, eadem aliis sopitu quiete est.
  Nay, the greatest wits and poets, too, cease
    to live;
  Homer, their prince, sleeps now in the
    same forgotten sleep as do the others.
  u.   LUCRETIUS—*De Rerum Natura.*
                                III. 1,049.

Nascentes morimur, finisque ab origine pendet.

> We begin to die as soon as we are born, and the end is linked to the beginning.

a.   MANILIUS—*Astronomica.* IV. 16.

Hic rogo non furor est ne moriare mori?

> This I ask, is it not madness to kill thyself in order to escape death?

b.   MARTIAL—*Epigrammata.* II. 80. 2.

Nec mihi mors gravis est posituro morte dolores.

> Death is not grievous to me, for I shall lay aside my pains by death.

c.   OVID—*Metamorphoses.* III. 471.

Quocunque adspicias, nihil est nisi mortis imago.

> Wherever you look there is nothing but the image of death.

d.   OVID—*Tristium.* I. 2. 23.

Stulte, quid est somnus, gelidæ nisi mortis imago?
Longa quiescendi tempora fata dabunt.

> Thou fool, what is sleep but the image of death? Fate will give an eternal rest.

e.   OVID—*Amorum.* II. 9. 41.

          Ultima semper
Expectanda dies homini est, dicique beatus
Ante obitum nemo et suprema funera debet.

> Man should ever look to his last day, and no one should be called happy before his funeral.

f.   OVID—*Metamorphoses.* III. 135.

Quem di diligunt adolescens moritur dum valet, sentit, sapit.

> He whom the gods love dies young, while he is in health, has his senses and his judgment sound.

g.   PLAUTUS—*Bacchides.* IV. 7. 18.

Omnibus a supremâ die eadem, quæ ante primum; nec magis a morte sensus ullus aut corpori aut animæ quam ante natalem.

> His last day places man in the same state as he was before he was born; nor after death has the body or soul any more feeling than they had before birth.

h.   PLINY the Elder—*Historia Naturalis.* LVI. 1.

Nec forma æternum, aut cuiquam est fortuna perennis.
Longius, aut propius, mors sua quemque manet.

> Beauty is fading, nor is fortune stable; sooner or later death comes to all.

i.   PROPERTIUS—*Elegiæ.* II. 28. 57.

Optima mors parca quæ venit apta die.

> That death is best which comes appropriately at a ripe age.

j.   PROPERTIUS—*Elegiæ.* III. 5. 18.

Dies iste, quem tamquam extremum reformidas, æterni natalis est.

> This day, which thou fearest as thy last, is the birthday of eternity.

k.   SENECA—*Epistolæ Ad Lucilium.* CII.

Eripere vitam nemo non homini potest;
At nemo mortem; mille ad hanc aditus patent.

> Any one may take life from man, but no one death; a thousand gates stand open to it.

l.   SENECA—*Phœnissæ.* CLII.

Incertum est quo te loco mors expectet: itaque tu illam omni loco expecta.

> It is uncertain in what place death may await thee; therefore expect it in any place.

m.   SENECA—*Epistolæ Ad Lucilium.* XXVI.

          Interim pœna est mori,
Sed sæpe donum; pluribus veniæ fuit.

> Sometimes death is a punishment; often a gift; it has been a favor to many.

n.   SENECA—*Hercules Oetæus.* 930.

Bis emori est alterius arbitrio mori.

> To die at the command of another, is to die twice.

o.   SYRUS—*Maxims.*

Honesta mors turpi vitâ potior.

> An honorable death is better than a dishonorable life.

p.   TACITUS—*Agricola.* XXXIII.

Usque adeone mori miserum est?

> Is it then so sad a thing to die?

q.   VIRGIL—*Æneid.* XII. 646.

DECEIT.

Improbi hominis est mendacio fallere.

> It is the act of a bad man to deceive by falsehood.

r.   CICERO—*Oratio Pro Murena.* XXX.

Irrepit in hominum mentes dissimulatio.

> Dissimulation creeps gradually into the minds of men.

s.   CICERO—*De Oratore.* III. 53.

Pia fraus.

> A pious fraud.

t.   OVID—*Metamorphoses.* IX. 711.

Incedis per ignes
Suppositos cineri doloso.

> You tread on smoldering fires covered by deceitful ashes.

u.   HORACE—*Carmina.* II. 1. 7.

Fronti nulla fides.

> Trust not to outward show.

v.   JUVENAL—*Satiræ.* II. 8.

Calvo turpius est nihil **comato.**

There is nothing more contemptible than a bald man who pretends to have hair.

a.　　Martial—*Epigrammata.* X. 83. 12.

Cætera fortunæ, non mea, turba fuit.

The rest of the crowd were friends of my fortune, not of me.

b.　　Ovid—*Tristium.* I. 5. 34.

　　　　　Furtum ingeniosus ad omne,
Qui facere assueret, patriæ non degener artis,
Candida de nigris, et de candentibus atra.

Skilled in every trick, a worthy heir of his paternal craft, he would make black look white, and white look black.

c.　　Ovid—*Metamorphoses.* XI. 313.

Impia sub dulci melle venena latent.

Deadly poisons are concealed under sweet honey.

d.　　Ovid—*Amorum.* I. 8. 104.

　　　　　Fronte politus
Astutam vapido servas sub pectore vulp**em**

Though thy face is glossed with specious art, thou retainest the cunning fox beneath thy vapid breast.

e.　　Persius—*Satiræ.* V. 116.

Habent insidias hominis blanditiæ mali.

The smooth speeches of the wicked are full of treachery.

f.　　Phædrus—*Fabulæ.* I. 19. 1.

Non semper ea sunt quæ videntur ; decipit Frons prima multos.

Things are not always what they seem ; first appearances deceive many.

g.　　Phædrus—*Fabulæ.* IV. 2. 16.

Alterâ manu fert lapidem, alterâ panem ostendat.

He carries a stone in one hand, and offers bread with the other.

h.　　Plautus—*Aulularia.* II. 2. 18.

Erras, me decipere haud potes.

No, you can't deceive me.

i.　　Plautus—*Mercator.* V. 2. 90.

Nemo omnes, neminem omnes fefellerunt.

No one has deceived the whole world, nor has the whole world ever deceived any one.

j.　　Pliny the Younger—*Panegyricus.*
　　　　　　　　　　　　　　LXII.

Turpe est aliud loqui, aliud sentire : quanto turpius aliud scribere, aliud sentire.

It is dishonorable to say one thing and think another ; how much more dishonorable to write one thing and think another.

k.　　Seneca—*Epistolæ Ad Lucilium.* XXIV.

Non aliter vives in solitudine, aliter in foro.

You should not live one way in private, another in public.

l.　　Syrus—*Maxims.*

Nulli jactantius mœrent quam qui maxime lætantur.

None grieve so ostentatiously as those who rejoice most in heart.

m.　　Tacitus—*Annales.* II. 77.

Hinc nunc præmium est, qui recta prava faciunt.

There is a demand in these days for men who can make wrong conduct appear right.

n.　　Terence—*Phormio.* VIII. 2. 6.

Nam qui mentiri, aut fallere insuêrit patrem,
　　aut
Audebit : tanto magis audebit cæteros.
Pudore et liberalitate liberos
Retinere satius esse credo, quam metu.

For he who has acquired the habit of lying or deceiving his father, will do the same with less remorse to others. I believe that it is better to bind your children to you by a feeling of respect, and by gentleness, than by fear.

o.　　Terence—*Adelphi.* I. 1. 30.

DEEDS.

Acta deos nunquam mortalia fallunt.

The deeds of men never escape the gods.

p.　　Ovid—*Tristium.* I. 2. 97.

Di pia facta vident.

The gods see the deeds of the righteous.

q.　　Ovid—*Fasti.* II. 117.

Ipse decor, recti facti si præmia desint,
Non movet.

Men do not value a good deed unless it brings a reward.

r.　　Ovid—*Epistolæ Ex Ponto.* II. 3. 13.

Respue quod non es.

Do not attempt to do what you cannot.

s.　　Persius—*Satiræ.* IV. 51.

Nequam illud verbum **est,** Bene vult, nisi qui benefacit.

"He wishes well" is worthless, unless the deed go with it.

t.　　Plautus—*Trinummus.* II. 4. 38.

Nemo beneficia in calendario scribit.

Nobody makes an entry of his good deeds in his day-book.

u.　　Seneca—*De Beneficiis.* I. 2.

DELAY.

Unus homo nobis cunctando restituit rem,
Non ponebat enim rumores ante salutem.

One man by delay restored the state, for he preferred the public safety to idle report.

v.　　Ennius—*Quoted in* Cicero.

Nulla unquam de morte cunctatio longa est.

When a man's life is at stake no delay is too long.

a.   JUVENAL—*Satiræ.* VI. 221.

De morte hominis nulla est cunctatio longa.

When the death of a human being may be the consequence, no delay that is afforded is long.

b.   *Law Maxim.*

Tolle moras—semper nocuit differre paratis.

Away with delay— it always injures those who are prepared.

c.   LUCAN—*Pharsalia.* I. 281.

Longa mora est nobis omnis, quæ gaudia differt.

Every delay that postpones our joys, is long.

d.   OVID—*Heroides.* XIX. 3.

Tardo amico nihil est quidquam iniquius.

Nothing is more annoying than a tardy friend.

e.   PLAUTUS—*Pœnulus.* III. 1. 1.

Omnis nimium longa properanti mora est.

Every delay is too long to one who is in a hurry.

f.   SENECA—*Agamemnon.* CCCCXXVI.

Quod ratio nequiit, sæpe sanavit mora.

What reason could not avoid, has often been cured by delay.

g.   SENECA—*Agamemnon.* CXXX.

Pelle moras; brevis est magni fortuna favoris.

Away with delay; the chance of great fortune is short-lived.

h.   SILIUS ITALICUS—*Punica.* IV. 734.

Deliberando sæpe perit occasio.

The opportunity is often lost by deliberating.

i.   SYRUS—*Maxims.*

DESIRE.

Nitimur in vetitum semper, cupimusque negata.

We are always striving for things forbidden, and coveting those denied us.

j.   OVID—*Amorum.* III. 4. 17.

Velle suum cuique est, nec voto vivitur uno.

Each man has his own desires; all do not possess the same inclinations.

k.   PERSIUS—*Satiræ.* V. 53.

DESPAIR.

Nil desperandum Teucro duce et auspice Teucro.

Never despair while under the guidance and auspices of Teucer.

l.   HORACE—*Carmina.* I. 7. 27.

Desperatio magnum ad honeste moriendum incitamentum.

Despair is a great incentive to honorable death.

m.   QUINTUS CURTIUS RUFUS—*De Rebus Gestis Alexandri Magni.* IX. 5. 6.

DIFFICULTIES.

Nil agit exemplum, litem quod lite resolvit.

The illustration which solves one difficulty by raising another, settles nothing.

n.   HORACE—*Satiræ.* II. 3. 103.

Nulla est tam facilis res, quin difficilis siet, Quum invitus facias.

There is nothing so easy in itself but grows difficult when it is performed against one's will.

o.   TERENCE—*Heauton-Timoroumenos.*
                     IV. 6. 1.

DIGNITY.

Otium cum dignitate.

Ease with dignity.

p.   CICERO—*Oratio Pro Publio Sextio.* XLV.

Facilius crescit dignitas quam incipit.

Dignity increases more easily than it begins.

q.   SENECA—*Epistolæ Ad Lucilium.* CI.

DISCONTENT.

Curtæ nescio quid semper abest rei.

Something is always wanting to incomplete fortune.

r.   HORACE—*Carmina.* III. 24. 64.

Qui fit, Mæcenas, ut nemo quam sibi sortem, Seu ratio dederit, seu fors objecerit, illâ Contentus vivat? laudet diversa sequentes.

How does it happen, Mæcenas, that no one is content with that lot in life which he has chosen, or which chance has thrown in his way, but praises those who follow a different course?

s.   HORACE—*Satiræ.* I. 1. 1.

Æstuat infelix angusto limite mundi.

Unhappy man! He frets at the narrow limits of the world.

t.   JUVENAL—*Satiræ.* X. 168.

DISCORD.

Discordia est ira acrior odio, intimo corde concepta.

Discord is anger more bitter than hatred, conceived in the inmost breast.

u.   CICERO—*Tusculanarum Disputationum.*
                     IV. 9.

DISEASE.

Aëre non certo corpora languor habet.
Sickness seizes the body from bad ventilation.
a.   OVID—*Ars Amatoria.* II. 310.

Vitiant artus ægræ contagia mentis.
Diseases of the mind impair the bodily powers.
b.   OVID—*Tristium.* III. 8. 25.

DISGRACE.

Odiosum est enim, cum a prætereuntibus dicatur:—O domus antiqua, heu, quam dispari dominare domino.
It is disgraceful when the passers-by exclaim, "O ancient house! alas, how unlike is thy present master to thy former one."
c.   CICERO—*De Officiis.* CXXXIX.

Abiturus illuc priores abierunt,
Quid mente cæca torques spiritum?
Tibi dico, avare.
Since you go where all have gone before, why do you torment your disgraceful life with such mean ambitions, O miser?
d.   PHÆDRUS—*Fabulæ.* IV. 19. 16.

Id demum est homini turpe, quod meruit pati.
That only is a disgrace to a man which he has deserved to suffer.
e.   PHÆDRUS—*Fabulæ.* III. 11. 7.

Hominum immortalis est infamia;
Etiam tum vivit, cum esse credas mortuam.
Disgrace is immortal, and living even when one thinks it dead.
f.   PLAUTUS—*Persa.* III. 1. 27.

E.

EATING.

Esse oportet ut vivas, non vivere ut edas.
Thou shouldst eat to live; not live to eat.
g.   CICERO—*Rhetoricorum Ad C. Herennium.*
IV. 7.

Jejunus raro stomachus vulgaria temnit.
A stomach that is seldom empty despises common food.
h.   HORACE—*Satiræ.* II. 2. 38.

Festo die si quid prodegeris,
Profesto egere liceat nisi peperceris.
Feast to-day makes fast to-morrow.
i.   PLAUTUS—*Aulularia.* II. 8. 10.

ECONOMY.

Magnum vectigal est parsimonia.
Economy is a great revenue.
j.   CICERO—*Paradoxa.* VI. 3. 49.

ELOQUENCE.

In causâ facili cuivis licet esse diserto.
In an easy cause any man may be eloquent.
k.   OVID—*Tristium.* III. 11. 21.

Magna eloquentia, sicut flamma, materiâ alitur, et motibus excitatur et urendo clarescit.
It is the eloquence as of a flame; it requires matter to feed it, motion to excite it, and it brightens as it burns.
l.   TACITUS—*De Oratoribus.* XXXVI.

ENEMY.

Pereant amici, dum unà inimici intercidant.
Let our friends perish, provided that our enemies fall at the same time.
m.   CICERO—*Oratio Pro Rege Deitaro.* IX.

ENJOYMENT.

Carpe diem, quam minime credula postero.
Enjoy the present day, trusting very little to the morrow.
n.   HORACE—*Carmina.* I. 11. 8.

Ride si sapis.
Be merry if you are wise.
o.   MARTIAL—*Epigrammata.* II. 41. 1.

Quam vellem longas tecum requiescere noctes,
Et tecum longos pervigilare dies.
How could I, blest with thee, long nights employ;
And how with thee the longest day enjoy!
p.   TIBULLUS—*Carmina.* III. 6. 53.

ENVY.

Rabiem livoris acerbi
Nulla potest placare quies.
Nothing can allay the rage of biting envy.
q.   CLAUDIANUS—*De Raptu Proserpinæ.*
III. 290.

Ego si risi quod ineptus
Pastillos Rufillus olet, Gargonius hircum, lividus et mordax videar?
If I smile at the strong perfumes of the silly Rufillus must I be regarded as envious and ill-natured?
r.   HORACE—*Satiræ.* I. 4. 91.

Invidus alterius marescit rebus opimis;
Invidia Siculi non invenere tyranni
Majus tormentum.
The envious pine at others' success; no greater punishment than envy was devised by Sicilian tyrants.
s.   HORACE—*Epistolæ.* I. 2. 57.

A proximis quisque minime anteiri vult.
> No man likes to be surpassed by those of his own level.

a.   Livy—*Annales.* XXXVIII. 49.

Invidiam, tamquam ignem, summa petere.
> Envy, like fire, soars upward.

b.   Livy—*Annales.* VIII. 31.

Ingenium magni detractat livor Homeri.
> Envy depreciates the genius of the great Homer.

c.   Ovid—*Remedia Amoris.* CCCLXV.

Pascitur in vivis livor ; post fata quiescit.
> Envy feeds on the living. It ceases when they are dead.

d.   Ovid—*Amorum.* I. 15. 39.

Summa petit livor : perflant altissima venti.
> Envy assails the noblest : the winds howl around the highest peaks.

e.   Ovid—*Remedia Amoris.* CCCLXIX.

EQUALITY.

Par in parem imperium non habet.
> An equal has no power over an equal.

f.   Law Maxim.

Quod ad jus naturale attinet, omnes homines æquales sunt.
> All men are equal before the natural law.

g.   Law Maxim.

Et sceleratis sol oritur.
> The sun shines even on the wicked.

h.   Seneca—*De Beneficiis.* III. 25.

EQUITY.

Bonus judex bonum judicat et equitatem strictæ legi præfert.
> A good judge decides fairly, preferring equity to strict law.

i.   Law Maxim.

In omnibus quidem, maxime tamen in jure, æquitas est.
> In all things, but particularly in the law, there is equity.

j.   Law Maxim.

ERROR.

Cujusvis hominis est errare ; nullius, nisi insipientis, in errore perseverare. Posteriores enim cogitationes (ut aiunt) sapientiores solent esse.
> Any man may make a mistake ; none but a fool will stick to it. Second thoughts are best as the proverb says.

k.   Cicero—*Philippicæ.* XII. 2.

Culpa enim illa, bis ad eundem, vulgari reprehensa proverbio est.
> To stumble twice against the same stone, is a proverbial disgrace.

l.   Cicero—*Epistolæ.* X. 20.

Errare mehercule malo cum Platone, quem tu quanti facias, scio quam cum istis vera sentire.
> By Hercules ! I prefer to err with Plato, whom I know how much you value, than to be right in the company of such men.

m.   Cicero—*Tusculanarum Disputationum.* I. 17.

Ille sinistrorsum hic dexrorsum abit, unus utrique
Error, sed variis illudit partibus.
> One goes to the right, the other to the left ; both are wrong, but in different directions.

n.   Horace—*Satiræ.* II. 3. 50.

EVENTS.

Certis rebus certa signa præcurrunt.
> Certain signs precede certain events.

o.   Cicero—*De Divinatione.* I. 52.

Ex parvis sæpe magnarum momenta rerum pendent.
> Events of great consequence often spring from trifling circumstances.

p.   Livy—*Annales.* XXVII. 9.

In tantâ inconstantiâ turbâque rerum nihil nisi quod preteriit certum est.
> In the great inconstancy and crowd of events, nothing is certain except the past.

q.   Seneca—*De Consolatione ad Marciam.* XXII.

EVIL.

Solent occupationis spe vel impune quædam scelesta committi.
> Wicked acts are accustomed to be done with impunity for the mere desire of occupation.

r.   Ammianus Marcellinus—*Historia.* XXX. 9.

Omne malum nascens facile opprimitur ; inveteratum fit plerumque robustius.
> Every evil in the bud is easily crushed ; as it grows older, it becomes stronger.

s.   Cicero—*Philippicæ.* V. 11.

Quid nos dura refugimus
Ætas, quid intactum nefasti
Liquimus?
> What has this unfeeling age of ours left untried, what wickedness has it shunned ?

t.   Horace—*Carmina.* I. 35. 34.

Magna inter molles concordia.

There is great unanimity among the dissolute.

a.   JUVENAL—*Satiræ.* II. 47.

Fere fit malum malo **aptissimum.**

Evil is fittest to consort with evil.

b.   LIVY—*Annales.* I. 46.

Notissimum quodque malum maxime tolerabile.

The best known evil is the most tolerable.

c.   LIVY—*Annales.* XXIII. 3.

Genus est mortis male vivere.

An evil life is a kind of death.

d.   OVID—*Epistolæ Ex Ponto.* III. 4. 75.

Mille mali species, mille salutis erunt.

There are a thousand forms of evil ; there will be a thousand remedies.

e   OVID—*Remedia Amoris.* V. 26.

Omnia perversas possunt corrumpere mentes.

All things can corrupt perverse minds.

f.   OVID—*Tristium.* II. 301.

Male partum male disperit.

Ill gotten is ill spent.

g.   PLAUTUS—*Pœnalus.* IV. 2. 22.

Pulchrum ornatum turpes mores pejus cœno collinunt.

Bad conduct soils the finest ornament more than filth.

h.   PLAUTUS—*Mostellaria.* I. 3. 133.

Maledicus a malefico non distat nisi occasione.

An evil-speaker differs from an evil-doer only in the want of opportunity.

i.   QUINTILIAN—*De Institutione Oratoria.*
                       XII. 9. 9.

Per scelera semper sceleribus certum est iter.

The way to wickedness is always through wickedness.

j.   SENECA—*Agamemnon.* CXV.

Serum est cavendi tempus in mediis malis.

It is too late to be on our guard when we are in the midst of evils.

k.   SENECA—*Thyestes.* CCCCLXXXVII.

Si velis vitiis exui, longe a vitiorum exemplis recedendum est.

If thou wishest to get rid of thy evil propensities, thou must keep far from evil companions.

l.   SENECA—*Epis'olæ Ad Lucilium.* CIV.

Solent suprema facere securos mala.

Desperate evils generally make men safe.

m.   SENECA—*Œdipus.* CCCLXXXVI.

O cæca nocentum consilia !
O semper timidum scelus !

Oh, the blind counsels of the guilty !
Oh, how cowardly is wickedness always !

n.   STATIUS—*Thebais.* II. 489.

Malorum facinorum ministri quasi exprobrantes aspiciuntur.

Partakers of evil deeds are regarded as reproaching them.

o.   TACITUS—*Annales.* XIV. 62.

Mala mens, malus animus.

A bad heart, bad designs.

p.   TERENCE—*Andria.* I. 1. 137.

Nimia illæc licentia
Profecto evadet in aliquod magnum malum.

Excessive licentiousness will most certainly terminate in some great mischief.

q.   TERENCE—*Adelphi.* III. 4. 63.

EXAMPLE.

Componitur orbis
Regis ad exemplum ; nec sic inflectere sensus
Humanos edicta valent, quam vita regentis.

The people are fashioned according to the example of their kings ; and edicts are of less power than the life of the ruler.

r.   CLAUDIANUS—*De Quarto Consulatu*
        Honorii Augustii Panegyris. CCXCIX.

Avidos vicinum funus ut ægros
Exanimat, mortisque metu sibi parcere cogit ;
Sic teneros animos aliena opprobria sæpe
Absterrent vitiis.

As a neighboring funeral terrifies sick misers, and fear obliges them to have some regard for themselves ; so, the disgrace of others will often deter tender minds from vice.

s.   HORACE—*Satiræ.* I. 4. 126.

Unde tibi frontem libertatemque parentis,
Cum facias pejora senex ?

Whence do you derive the power and privilege of a parent, when you, though an old man, do worse things (than your child) ?

t.   JUVENAL—*Satiræ.* XIV. 56.

Inspicere tamquam in speculum in vitas omnium
Jubeo atque ex aliis sumere exemplum sibi.

We should look at the lives of all as at a mirror, and take from others an example for ourselves.

u.   TERENCE—*Adelphi.* III. 3. 62.

Felix quicumque dolore alterius disces posse cavere tuo.

Happy thou that learnest from another's griefs, not to subject thyself to the same.

v.   TIBULLUS—*Carmina.* III. 6. 43.

Bonum est fugienda aspicere in alieno malo.

It is well to learn from the misfortunes of others what should be avoided.

a.   Syrus—*Maxims.*

Sequiturque patrem non passibus æquis.

He follows his father with unequal steps.

b.   Virgil—*Æneid.* II. 724.

EXCESS.

Ne mente quidem recte uti possumus, multo cibo et potione completi.

We can not use the mind aright, when we are filled with excessive food and drink.

c.   Cicero—*Tusculanarum Disputationum.*
                    V. 35.

          Quin corpus onustum
Hesternis vitiis, animum quoque prægravat unâ
Atque affigit humo divinæ particulam auræ.

The body loaded by the excess of yesterday, depresses the mind also, and fixes to the ground this particle of divine breath.

d.   Horace—*Satiræ.* II. 2. 77.

EXCITABILITY.

Excitabat enim fluctus in simpulo.

He used to raise a storm in a teapot.

e.   Cicero—*De Legibus.* III. 16.

EXCUSE.

Quod exemplo fit, id etiam jure fieri putant.

Men think they may justly do that for which they have a precedent.

f.   Cicero.—*Epistolæ.* IV. 3.

EXPERIENCE.

Stultorum eventus magister est.

Experience is the teacher of fools.

g.   Livy—*Annales.* XXII. 39.

Semper enim ex aliis alia proseminat usus.

Experience is always sowing the seed of one thing after another.

h.   Manilius—*Astronomica.* I. 90.

Nam in omnibus fere minus valent præcepta quam experimenta.

In almost everything, experience is more valuable than precept.

i.   Quintilian—*De Institutione Oratoria.*
                    II. 5. 5.

Experto credite.

Believe one who has tried it.

j.   Virgil—*Æneid.* XI. 283.

F.

FAILURE.

Stat magni nominis umbra.

He stands the shadow of a mighty name.

k.   Lucan—*Pharsalia.* I. 135.

Vertentem sese, frustra sectabere cantum
Cum rota posterior curras et in axe secundo.

Thou, like the hindmost chariot wheels, art curst
Still to be near but never to be first.

l.   Persius—*Satiræ.* V. 71. Dryden's
                       trans.

Quod si deficiant vires, audacia certe
Laus erit: in magnis et voluisse sat est.

Although strength should fail, the effort will deserve praise. In great enterprises the attempt is enough.

m.   Propertius—*Elegiæ.* II. 10. 5.

Fuimus Troes; fuit Ilium.

We have been Trojans; Troy was.

n.   Virgil—*Æneid.* II. 324.

FALSITY.

Splendide mendax.

Splendidly mendacious.

o.   Horace—*Carmina.* III. 11. 35.

Falsus in uno, falsus in omnibus.

False in one thing, false in everything.

p.   *Law Maxim.*

FAME.

Miserum est aliorum incumbere famæ.

It is a wretched thing to live on the fame of others.

q.   Juvenal—*Satiræ.* VIII. 76.

Clarum et venerabile nomen.

An illustrious and ancient name.

r.   Lucan—*Pharsalia.* IX. 203.

Nolo virum facili redimit qui sanguine famam;
Hunc volo laudari qui sine morte potest.

I do not like the man who squanders life for fame; give me the man who living makes a name.

s.   Martial—*Epigrammata.* I. 9. 5.

Si post fata venit gloria non propero.

If fame comes after death, I am in no hurry for it.

t.   Martial—*Epigrammata.* V. 10. 12.

Immensum gloria calcar habet.

The love of fame gives an immense stimulus.

a. Ovid—*Epistolæ Ex Ponto.* IV. 2. 36.

Ingenio stimulos subdere fama solet.

The love of fame usually spurs on the mind.

b. Ovid—*Tristium.* V. 1. 76.

At pulchrum est digito monstrari et dicier hic est.

It is pleasing to be pointed at with the finger and to have it said, " There goes the man."

c. Persius—*Satiræ.* I. 28.

Omnia post obitum fingit majora vetustas :
Majus ab exsequiis nomen in ora venit.

Time magnifies everything after death ; a man's fame is increased as it passes from mouth to mouth after his burial.

d. Propertius—*Elegiæ.* III. 1. 23.

Etiam sapientibus cupido gloriæ novissima exuitur.

The love of fame is the last weakness which even the wise resign.

e. Tacitus—*Annales.* IV. 5.

Modestiæ fama neque summis mortalibus spernenda est.

Modest fame is not to be despised by the highest characters.

f. Tacitus—*Annales.* XV. 2.

In tenui labor, at tenuis non gloria.

The object of the labor was small, but not the fame.

g. Virgil—*Georgica.* IV. 6.

FAMILIARITY.

Quod crebro videt non miratur, etiamsi cur fiat nescit. Quod ante non vidit, id si evenerit, ostentum esse censet.

A man does not wonder at what he sees frequently, even though he be ignorant of the reason. If anything happens which he has not seen before, he calls it a prodigy.

h. Cicero—*De Divinatione.* II. 22.

FATE.

Nulla vis humana vel virtus meruisse unquam potuit, ut, quod præscripsit fatalis ordo, non fiat.

No power or virtue of man could ever have deserved that what has been fated should not have taken place.

i. Ammianus Marcellinus—*Historia.*
XXIII. 5.

Quidquid delirant reges, plectuntur Achivi.

Whenever monarchs err, the people are punished.

j. Horace—*Epistolæ.* I. 2. 14.

Sæpius ventis agitatur ingens
Pinus, et celsae graviore casu
Decidunt turres feriuntque summos
Fulgura montes.

The lofty pine is oftenest shaken by the winds ; high towers fall with a heavier crash ; and the lightning strikes the highest mountains.

k. Horace—*Carmina.* II. 10. 9.

In se magna ruunt : lætis hunc numina
rebus
Crescendi posuere modum.

Mighty things haste to destruction : this limit have the gods assigned to human prosperity.

l. Lucan—*Pharsalia.* I. 81.

Sed quo fata trahunt, virtus secura sequetur.

Whither the fates lead virtue will follow without fear.

m. Lucan—*Pharsalia.* II. 287.

Nullo fata loco possis excludere.

From no place can you exclude the fates.

n. Martial—*Epigrammata.* IV. 60. 5.

Geminos, horoscope, varo
Producis genio.

O natal star, thou producest twins of widely different character.

o. Persius—*Satiræ.* VI. 18.

Sæpe calamitas solatium est nosse sortem suam.

It is often a comfort in misfortune to know our own fate.

p. Quintus Curtius Rufus—*De Rebus Gestis Alexandri Magni.* IV. 10. 27.

Fata volentem ducunt, nolentem trahunt.

The fates lead the willing, and drag the unwilling.

q. Seneca—*Epistolæ Ad Lucilium.* CVII.

Multi ad fatum
Venere suum dum fata timent.

Many have reached their fate while dreading fate.

r. Seneca—*Œdipus.* 993.

Nemo fit fato nocens.

No one becomes guilty by fate.

s. Seneca—*Œdipus.* 1,019.

Alea jacta est.

The die is cast.

t. The exclamation of Cæsar as he crossed the Rubicon. Suetonius—*Cæsar.*
XXXII.

Ad restim mihi quidem res rediit planissume.
  Nothing indeed remains for me but that I
should hang myself.
a.   TERENCE—*Phormio.* IV. 4. 5.

Perge ; decet. Forsan miseros meliora se-
quentur.
  Persevere : It is fitting, for a better fate
awaits the afflicted.
b.   VIRGIL—*Æneid.* XII. 153.

Quisque suos patimur manes.
  We bear each one our own destiny.
c.   VIRGIL—*Æneid.* VI. 743.

Quo fata trahunt retrahuntque sequamur.
  Wherever the fates lead us let us follow.
d.   VIRGIL—*Æneid.* V. 709.

FAULTS.

Ea molestissime ferre homines debent quæ
ipsorum culpâ ferenda sunt.
  Men ought to be most annoyed by the
sufferings which come from their own faults.
e.   CICERO—*Epistolæ Ad Fratrem.* I. 1.

Nam vitiis nemo sine nascitur, optimus ille
  est
Qui minimis urgetur.
  No man is born without faults, he is best
who has the fewest.
f.   HORACE—*Satiræ.* I. 3. 68.

Culpa tenet suos auctores.
  A fault finds its own authors.
g.   *Law Maxim.*

Quia, qui alterum incusat probi, eum ipsum se intueri oportet.
  Because those, who twit others with their
faults, should look at home.
h.   PLAUTUS—*Truculentus.* I. 2. 58.

Amici vitium ni feras, prodis tuum.
  Unless you bear with the faults of a friend,
you betray your own.
i.   SYRUS—*Maxims.*

Invitat culpam qui delictum præterit.
  He who overlooks a fault, invites the commission of another.
j.   SYRUS—*Maxims.*

FAVOR.

Gratia, quæ tarda est, ingrata est: gratia
  namque
Cum fieri properat, gratia grata magis.
  A favor tardily bestowed is no favor ; for
a favor quickly granted is a more agreeable
favor.
k.   AUSONIUS—*Epigrammata.*
                                    LXXXII. 1.

Nam improbus est homo qui beneficium
scit sumere et reddere nescit.
  That man is worthless who knows how to
receive a favor, but not how to return one.
l.   PLAUTUS—*Persa.* V. 1. 10.

Nam quamlibet sæpe obligati, si quid unum
neges, hoc solum meminerunt, quod negatum
est.
  For however often a man may receive an
obligation from you, if you refuse a request,
all former favors are effaced by this one
denial.
m.   PLINY the Younger—*Epistolæ.* III. 4.

Beneficium accipere, libertatem est vendere.
  To accept a favor is to sell one's freedom.
n.   SYRUS—*Maxims.*

Neutiquam officium liberi esse hominis puto
Cum is nihil promereat, postulare id gratiæ
  apponi sibi.
  No free man will ask as favor, what he
can not claim as reward.
o.   TERENCE—*Andria.* II. 1. 32.

FEAR.

Crux est si metuas quod vincere nequeas.
  It is tormenting to fear what you cannot
overcome.
p.   AUSONIUS—*Septem Sapientum Sententiæ
            Septenis Versibus Explicatæ.* VII. 4.

In summo periculo timor misericordiam
non recipit.
  In extreme danger fear feels no pity.
q.   CÆSAR—*Bellum Gallicum.* VII. 26.

Timor non est diuturnus magister officii.
  Fear is not a lasting teacher of duty.
r.   CICERO—*Philippicæ.* II. 36.

Quærit, et inventis miser abstinet, ac timet
uti.
  The miser acquires, yet fears to use his
gains.
s.   HORACE—*Ars Poetica.* 170.

                        Quia me vestigia terrent
Omnia te adversum spectantia, nulla retrorsum.
  I am frightened at seeing all the footprints
directed towards thy den, and none returning.
t.   HORACE—*Epistolæ.* I. 1. 74.

Major ignotarum rerum est terror.
  Apprehensions are greater in proportion
as things are unknown.
u.   LIVY—*Annales.* XXVIII. 44.

Monstrum horrendum, informe, ingens, cui
lumen ademptum.

An immense, misshapen, marvelous **monster** whose eye is out.

a.　　Virgil—*Æneid.* III. 658.

Multos in summa pericula misit
Venturi timor ipse mali.

The mere apprehension of a coming evil
has put many into a situation of the utmost
danger.

b.　　Lucan—*Pharsalia.* VII. 104.

Et metus ille foras præceps Acheruntis agun-
dus,
Funditus humanam qui vitam turbat ab imo,
Omnia suffuscans mortis nigrore, neque ullam
Esse voluptatem liquidam puramque relin-
quit.

The dreadful fear of hell is to be driven
out, which disturbs the life of man and
renders it miserable, overcasting all things
with the blackness of darkness, and leaving no pure, unalloyed pleasure.

c.　　Lucretius—*De Rerum Natura.*
　　　　　　　　　　　　III. 37.

Membra reformidant mollem quoque saucia
tactum :
Vanaque sollicitis incutit umbra metum.

The wounded limb shrinks from the
slightest touch ; and a slight shadow alarms
the nervous.

d.　　Ovid—*Epistolæ Ex Ponto.* II. 7. 13.

Quem metuit quisque, **perisse cupit.**

Every one wishes that the man whom he
fears would perish.

e.　　Ovid—*Amorum.* II. 2. 10.

Terretur minimo pennæ stridore columba
Unguibus, accipiter, saucia facta tuis.

The dove, O hawk, that has once been
wounded by thy talons, is frightened by
the least movement of a wing.

f.　　Ovid—*Tristium.* I. 1. 75.

Ad deteriora credenda proni metu.

Fear makes men believe the worst.

g.　　Quintus Curtius Rufus—*De Rebus
　　　　Gestis Alexandri Magni.* IV. 3. 22.

Ubi explorari vera non possunt, falsa per
metum augentur.

When the truth cannot be clearly made
out, what is false is increased through fear.

h.　　Quintus Curtius Rufus—*De Rebus
　　　　Gestis Alexandri Magni.* IV. 10. 10.

Ubi intravit animos pavor, id solum
metuunt, quod primum formidare cœperunt.

When fear has seized upon the mind,
man fears that only which he first began to
fear.

i.　　Quintus Curtius Rufus—*De Rebus
　　　　Gestis Alexandri Magni.* IV. 16. 17.

Quem neque gloria neque pericula excitant,
nequidquam hortere : timor animi auribus
officit.

The man who is roused neither by glory
nor by danger it is in vain to exhort;
terror closes the ears of the mind.

j.　　Sallust—*Catilina.* LVIII.

Necesse est multos timeat, quem multi
timent.

He must necessarily fear many, whom
many fear.

k.　　Seneca—*De Ira.* II. 11.

Optanda mors est, sine metu mortis mori.

To die without fear of death is to be desired.

l.　　Seneca—*Troades.* 869.

Si vultis nihil timere, cogitate omnia esse
timenda.

If you wish to fear nothing, consider that
everything is to be feared.

m.　　Seneca.—*Quæstionum Naturalium.*
　　　　　　　　　　　　VI. 2.

Primus in orbe deos fecit timor.

Fear in the world first created the gods.

n.　　Statius—*Thebais.* III. 661.

　　　　　Tunc plurima versat
Pessimus in dubiis augur timor.

Then fear, the very worst prophet in misfortunes, anticipates many evils.

o.　　Statius—*Thebais.* III. 5.

Minor est quam servus dominus qui servos
timet.

The master who fears his slaves is inferior to his slaves.

p.　　Syrus—*Maxims.*

Stultum est timere quod vitare non potes.

It is foolish to fear what you cannot
avoid.

q.　　Syrus—*Maxims.*

Timidus se vocat cautum, parcum sordidus.

The coward calls himself cautious, the
miser thrifty.

r.　　Syrus—*Maxims.*

Etiam fortes viros subitis terreri.

Even the bravest men are frightened by
sudden terrors.

s.　　Tacitus—*Annales.* XV. 59.

Degeneres animos timor arguit.

Fear is the proof of a degenerate mind.

t.　　Virgil—*Æneid.* IV. 13.

Timeo Danaos et dona ferentes.

I fear the Greeks, even when they bring
gifts.

u.　　Virgil—*Æneid.* II. 49.

FICKLENESS.

Formosis levitas semper amica fuit.

Fickleness has always befriended the beautiful.

a.   PROPERTIUS—*Elegiæ.* II. 16. 26.

FIDELITY.

Barbaris ex fortunâ pendet fides.

The fidelity of barbarians depends on fortune.

b.   LIVY—*Annales.* XXVIII. 17.

Poscunt fidem secunda, at adversa exigunt.

Prosperity asks for fidelity; adversity exacts it.

c.   SENECA—*Agamemnon.* 934.

Pretio parata vincitur pretio fides.

Fidelity bought with money is overcome by money.

d.   SENECA—*Agamemnon.* CCLXXXVII.

FIRE.

Tua res agitur, paries cum proximus ardet.

Your own property is concerned when your neighbor's house is on fire.

e.   HORACE—*Epistolæ.* I. 18. 84.

Igne quid utilius? si quis tamen urere tecta
Comparet audaces instruit igne manus.

What is more useful than fire? Yet if any one prepares to burn a house, it is with fire that he arms his daring hands.

f.   OVID—*Tristium.* II. 267.

Parva sæpe scintilla contempta magnum excitavit incendium.

A spark neglected has often raised a conflagration.

g.   QUINTUS CURTIUS RUFUS—*De Rebus Gestis Alexandri Magni.* VI. 3. 11.

FLATTERY.

Assentatio, vitiorum adjutrix, procul amoveatur.

Let flattery, the handmaid of the vices, be far removed (from friendship).

h.   CICERO—*De Amicitia.* XXIV.

Adulandi gens prudentissima laudat
Sermonem indocti, faciem deformis amici.

The skilful class of flatterers praise the discourse of an ignorant friend and the face of a deformed one.

i.   JUVENAL—*Satiræ.* III. 86.

Qui se laudari gaudent verbis subdolis,
Serâ dant pœnas turpes pœnitentiâ.

They who delight to be flattered, pay for their folly by a late repentance.

j.   PHÆDRUS—*Fabulæ.* I. 13. 1.

Si vir es, suspice, etiam si decidunt, magna conantes.

If thou art a man, admire those who attempt great things, even though they fail.

k.   SENECA—*De Brevitate.* XX.

Vitium fuit, nunc mos est, adsentatio.

Flattery was formerly a vice; it has now become the fashion.

l.   SYRUS—*Maxims.*

Pessimum genus inimicorum laudantes.

Flatterers are the worst kind of enemies.

m.   TACITUS—*Agricola.* XLI.

FOLLY.

Est proprium stultitiæ aliorum vitia cernere, oblivisci suorum.

It is the peculiar quality of a fool to perceive the faults of others, and to forget his own.

n.   CICERO—*Tusculanarum Disputationum.* III. 30.

Stultorum plena sunt omnia.

All places are filled with fools.

o.   CICERO—*Epistolæ.* IX. 22.

Adde cruorem
Stultitiæ, atque ignem gladio scrutare.

To your folly add bloodshed, and stir the fire with the sword.

p.   HORACE—*Satiræ.* II. 3. 275.

Misce stultitiam consiliis brevem:
Dulce est desipere in loco.

Mingle a little folly with your wisdom; a little nonsense now and then is pleasant.

q.   HORACE—*Carmina.* IV. 12. 27.

Stultorum incurata malus pudor ulcera celat.

The shame of fools conceals their open wounds.

r.   HORACE—*Epistolæ.* I. 16. 24.

Quantum est in rebus inane!

How much folly there is in human affairs.

s.   PERSIUS—*Satiræ.* I. 1.

In pertusum ingerimus dicta dolium, operam ludimus.

We are pouring our words into a sieve, and lose our labor.

t.   PLAUTUS—*Pseudolus.* I. 3. 135.

Si stimulos pugnis cædis manibus plus dolet.

If you strike the goads with your fists, your hands suffer most.

u.   PLAUTUS—*Truculentus.* IV. 2. 54.

Stultus est qui fructus magnarum arborum spectat, altitudinem non metitur.

He is a fool who looks at the fruit of lofty trees, but does not measure their height.

v.   QUINTUS CURTIUS RUFUS—*De Rebus Gestis Alexandri Magni.* VII. 8.

Inter cætera mala hoc quoque habet
Stultitia semper incipit vivere.

Among other evils folly has also this, that
it is always beginning to live.

a.   SENECA—*Epistolæ Ad Lucilium.*   13.

Quid est dementius quam bilem in homines
collectam in res effundere.

What is more insane than to vent on
senseless things the anger that is felt towards
men?

b.   SENECA—*De Ira.*   II.   26.

Absentem lædit cum ebrio qui litigat.

He hurts the absent who quarrels with a
drunken man.

c.   SYRUS—*Maxims.*

Improbe Neptunum accusat qui iterum
naufragium facit.

He is foolish to blame the sea, who is
shipwrecked twice.

d.   SYRUS—*Maxims.*

FORCE.

Quod ab initio non valet, tractu temporis
convalescere non potest.

That which had no force in the beginning
can gain no strength from the lapse of time.

e.   *Law Maxim.*

Quod alias bonum et justum est, si per vim
aut fraudem petatur, malum et injustum est.

What otherwise is good and just, if it be
aimed at by fraud or violence, becomes evil
and unjust.

f.   *Law Maxim.*

Cogi qui potest, nescit mori.

He who can be forced (to act against his
will), does not know how to die.

g.   SENECA—*Hercules Furens.* CCCCXXVI.

FORESIGHT.

Commodius esse opinor duplici spe utier.

I think it better to have two strings to
my bow.

h.   TERENCE—*Phormio.* IV. 2. 13.

Istuc est sapere, non quod ante pedes modo est
Videre, sed etiam illa, quæ futura sunt
Prospicere.

That is to be wise to see not merely that
which lies before your feet, but to foresee
even those things which are in the womb of
futurity.

i.   TERENCE—*Adelphi.* III. 3. 32.

FORGETFULNESS.

Etiam oblivisci quod scis interdum expedit.

It is sometimes expedient to forget what
you know.

j.   SYRUS—*Maxims.*

FORGIVENESS.

Æquum est
Peccatis veniam poscentem reddere rursus.

It is right for him who asks forgiveness
for his offenses to grant it to others.

k.   HORACE—*Satiræ.* I. 3. 74.

Ignoscito sæpe alteri nunquam tibi.

Forgive others often, yourself never.

l.   SYRUS—*Maxims.*

FORTITUDE.

Suum cuique incommodum ferendum est,
potius quam de alterius commodis detra-
hendum.

Every man should bear his own grievances
rather than detract from the comforts of
another.

m.   CICERO—*De Officiis.* III. 6.

Justum et tenacem propositi virum
Non civium ardor prava jubentium,
Non vultus instantis tyranni,
Mente quatit solidâ.

The man who is just and resolute will not
be moved from his settled purpose, either
by the misdirected rage of his fellow citizens,
or by the threats of an imperious tyrant.

n.   HORACE—*Carmina.* III. 3. 1.

Ducimus autem
Hos quoque felices, qui ferre incommoda vitæ,
Nec jactare jugum vitâ didicere magistrâ.

We deem those happy who, from the experience of life, have learned to bear its ills,
without being overcome by them.

o.   JUVENAL—*Satiræ.* XIII. 20.

Qui sua metitur pondera ferre potest.

He who weighs his burdens, can bear them.

p.   MARTIAL—*Epigrammata.* XII. 99. 8.

Leve fit quod bene fertur onus.

The burden which is well borne becomes
light.

q.   OVID—*Amorum.* I. 2. 10.

In re malâ animo si bono utare, adjuvat.

Fortitude is a great help in distress.

r.   PLAUTUS—*Captivi.* II. 1. 8.

Quod sors feret feremus æquo animo.

Whatever chance shall bring, we will bear
with equanimity.

s.   TERENCE—*Phormio.* I. 2. 88.

FORTUNE.

Quivis beatus, versâ rotâ fortunæ, ante
vesperum potest esse miserrimus.

Any one who is prosperous may by the
turn of fortune's wheel become most
wretched before evening.

t.   AMMIANUS MARCELLINUS—*Historia.*
                     XXVI. 8.

Si fortuna juvat, caveto tolli ;
Si fortuna tonat, caveto mergi.

If fortune favors you do not be elated ; if
she frowns do not despond.

a.　　AUSONIUS—*Septem Sapientium
Sententiæ Septenis Versibus
Explicatæ.* IV. 6.

Suæ quemque fortunæ maxime pœnitet.

Every one is dissatisfied with his own fortune.

b.　　CICERO—*Epistolæ.* VI. 1.

Vitam regit fortuna, non sapientia.

It is fortune, not wisdom, that rules
man's life.

c.　　CICERO—*Tusculanarum Disputationum.*
LIX.

Eheu ! quam brevibus pereunt ingentia fatis.

Alas ! by what slight means are great affairs brought to destruction.

d.　　CLAUDIANUS—*In Rufinum.* II. 49.

Fors juvat audentes.

Fortune favors the brave.

e.　　CLAUDIANUS—*Epistolæ.* IV. 9.

Cui non conveniet sua res, ut calceus olim,
Si pede major erit subvertet ; si minor, uret.

If a man's fortune does not fit him, it is
like the shoe in the story ; if too large it
trips him up, if too small it pinches him.

f.　　HORACE—*Epistolæ.* I. 10. 42.

Horæ
Momento cita mors venit aut victoria læta.

In a moment comes either death or joyful
victory.

g.　　HORACE—*Satiræ.* I. 1. 7.

Maximæ cuique fortunæ minime credendum est.

The least reliance can be placed even on
the most exalted fortune.

h.　　LIVY—*Annales.* XXX. 35.

Non temere incerta casuum reputat, quem
fortuna numquam decepit.

He whom fortune has never deceived,
rarely considers the uncertainty of human
events.

i.　　LIVY—*Annales.* XXX. 30.

Raro simul hominibus bonam fortunam
bonamque mentem dari.

Men are seldom blessed with good fortune
and good sense at the same time.

j.　　LIVY—*Annales.* XXX. 42.

Posteraque in dubio est fortunam quam vehat
ætas.

It is doubtful what fortune to-morrow
will bring.

k.　　LUCRETIUS—*De Rerum Natura.*
III. 10. 98.

Fortuna multis dat nimis, satis nulli.

Fortune gives too much to many, enough
to none.

l.　　MARTIAL—*Epigrammata.* XII. 10. 2.

Casus ubique valet : semper tibi pendeat
hamus,
Quo minime credas gurgite, piscis erit.

Luck affects everything ; let your hook
always be cast ; in the stream where you
least expect it, there will be a fish.

m.　　OVID—*Ars Amatoria.* III. 425.

Donec eris felix, multos numerabis amicos ;
Tempora si fuerint nubila solus eris.

As long as you are fortunate you will
have many friends, but if the times become
cloudy you will be alone.

n.　　OVID—*Tristium.* I. 9. 5.

Fortuna miserrima tuta est :
Nam timor eventus deterioris abest.

The most wretched fortune is safe ; for
there is no fear of anything worse.

o.　　OVID—*Epistolæ Ex Ponto.* II. 2. 31.

Intra fortunam quisque debet manere suam.

Every man should stay within his own
fortune.

p.　　OVID—*Tristium.* III. 4. 26.

Actutum fortunæ solent mutarier ; varia
vita est.

Man's fortune is usually changed at once ;
life is changeable.

q.　　PLAUTUS—*Truculentus.* II. 1. 9.

Fortuna humana fingit artatque ut lubet.

Fortune moulds and circumscribes human
affairs as she pleases.

r.　　PLAUTUS—*Captivi.* II. 2. 54.

Nam multa præter spem scio multis bona
evenisse,
At ego etiam qui speraverint, spem decepisse
multos.

For I know that many good things have
happened to many, when least expected ;
and that many hopes have been disappointed.

s.　　PLAUTUS—*Rudens.* II. 3. 69.

Nulli est homini perpetuum bonum.

No man has perpetual good fortune.

t.　　PLAUTUS—*Curculis.* I. 3. 32.

Præsente fortunâ pejor est futuri metus.

Fear of the future is worse than one's
present fortune.

u.　　QUINTILIAN—*De Institutione Oratoria.*
XII. 5.

Breves et mutabiles vices rerum sunt, et
fortuna nunquam simpliciter indulget.

The fashions of human affairs are brief
and changeable, and fortune never remains
long indulgent.
a. QUINTUS CURTIUS RUFUS—*De Rebus
Gestis Alexandri Magni.* IV. 14. 20.

Sed profecto Fortuna in omni re domina-
tur; ea res cunctas ex lubidine magis, quam
ex vero, celebrat, obscuratque.

But assuredly Fortune rules in all things;
she raises to eminence or buries in oblivion
everything from caprice rather than from
well-regulated principle.
b. SALLUST—*Catilina.* VIII.

Aurea rumpunt tecta quietem,
Vigilesque trahit purpura noctes.
O si pateant pectora ditum,
Quantos intus sublimis agit
Fortuna metus.

Golden palaces break man's rest, and purple
robes cause watchful nights.
Oh, if the breasts of the rich could be seen into,
what terrors high fortune places within!
c. SENECA—*Hercules Œtæus.* 646.

Felix, quisquis novit famulum
Rogemque pati,
Vultusque potest variare suos!
Rapuit vires pondusque malis,
Casus animo qui tulit æquo.

Happy the man who can endure the
highest and the lowest fortune. He, who
has endured such vicissitudes with equanimity, has deprived misfortune of its power.
d. SENECA—*Hercules Œtæus.* CCXXVIII.

Iniqua raro maximis virtutibus
Fortuna parcit. Nemo se tuto diu
Periculis offerre tam crebris potest,
Quem sæpe transit casus, aliquando invenit.

Adverse fortune seldom spares men of the
noblest virtues. No one can with safety
expose himself often to dangers. The man
who has often escaped is at last caught.
e. SENECA—*Hercules Furens.* CCCXXV.

Minor in parvis Fortuna furit,
Leviusque ferit leviora deus.

Fortune is gentle to the lowly, and heaven
strikes the humble with a light hand.
f. SENECA—*Hippolytus.* 1,124.

O Fortuna, viris invida fortibus,
Quam non æque bonis præmia dividis!

O Fortune, that enviest the brave, what
unequal rewards thou bestowest on the
righteous!
g. SENECA—*Hercules Furens.* 524.

Præcipites regum casus
Fortuna rotat.

Fortune turns on her wheel the fate of
kings.
h. SENECA.—*Agamemnon.* LXXI.

Quidquid in altum, fortuna tulit, ruitura
levat.

Whatever fortune has raised to a height,
she has raised only to cast it down.
i. SENECA—*Agamemnon.* C.

Quid non dedit fortuna non eripit.

Fortune cannot take away what she did
not give.
j. SENECA—*Epistolæ Ad Lucilium.* LIX.

Fors æqua merentes
Respicit.

A just fortune awaits the deserving.
k. STATIUS—*Thebais.* I. 661.

Fortuna nimium quem favet, stultum facit.

When fortune favors a man too much, she
makes him a fool.
l. SYRUS—*Maxims.*

Fortuna vitrea est, tum cum splendet fran-
gitur.

Fortune is like glass; when she shines,
she is broken.
m. SYRUS—*Maxims.*

Miserrima est fortuna quæ inimico caret.

That is a very wretched fortune which has
no enemy.
n. SYRUS—*Maxims.*

Non equidem invideo; miror magis.

Indeed, I do not envy your fortune; I
rather am surprised at it.
o. VIRGIL.—*Eclogæ.* I. 11.

FREEDOM.

Nulla enim minantis auctoritas apud liberos
est.

To freemen, threats are impotent.
p. CICERO.—*Epistolæ.* XI. 3.

Fallitur egregio quisquis sub principe credet
Servitutem. Nunquam libertas gratior extat
Quam sub rege pio.

That man is deceived who thinks it slavery to live under an excellent prince. Never
does liberty appear in a more gracious form
than under a pious king.
q. CLAUDIANUS—*De Laudibus Stilichonis.*
III. 113.

Ea libertas est quæ pectus purum et firmum
gestitat.

That is true liberty which bears a pure and
firm breast.
r. ENNIUS.

Libertas ultima mundi
Quo steterit ferienda loco.

The remaining liberty of the world was to
be destroyed in the place where it stood.
a.   Lucan—*Pharsalia.* VII. 580.

Quicquid multis peccatur, inultum est.

All go free when multitudes offend.
b.   Lucan—*Pharsalia.* V. 260.

Non bene, crede mihi, servo servitur amico ;
Sit liber, dominus qui volet esse meus.

Service cannot be expected from a friend
in service ; let him be a freeman who wishes
to be my master.
c.   Martial—*Epigrammata.* II. 32. 7.

An quisquam est alius liber, nisi ducere
vitam
Cui licet, ut voluit ?

Is any man free except the one who can
pass his life as he pleases?
d.   Persius—*Satiræ.* V. 83.

Libertatem naturâ etiam mutis animalibus
datam.

Liberty is given by nature even to mute
animals.
e.   Tacitus—*Annales.* IV. 17.

Rarâ temporum felicitate, ubi sentire quæ
velis, et quæ sentias dicere licet.

Such being the happiness of the times,
that you may think as you wish, and speak
as you think.
f.   Tacitus—*Annales.* I. 1.

FRIENDSHIP.

Secundas res splendidiores facit amicitia, et
adversas partiens communicansque leviores.

Friendship makes prosperity brighter,
while it lightens adversity by sharing its
griefs and anxieties.
g.   Cicero—*De Amicitia.* VI.

Vulgo dicitur multos modios salis semel
edendos esse, ut amicitia munus expletum sit.

It is a common saying that many pecks of
salt must be eaten before the duties of
friendship can be discharged.
h.   Cicero—*De Amicitia.* XIX.

Dulcis inexpertis cultura potentis amici ;
Expertus metuit.

To have a great man for an intimate friend
seems pleasant to those who have never
tried it ; those who have, fear it.
i.   Horace—*Epistolæ.* I. 18. 86.

Nil ego contulerim jucundo sanus amico.

While I keep my senses I shall prefer
nothing to a pleasant friend.
j.   Horace—*Satiræ.* I. 5. 44.

Nulla fides regni sociis omnisque potestas
Impatiens consortis erit.

There is no friendship between those associated in power ; he who rules will always
be impatient of an associate.
k.   Lucan—*Pharsalia.* I. 92.

Scilicet ut fulvum spectatur in ignibus aurum
Tempore in duro est inspicienda fides.

As the yellow gold is tried in fire, so the
faith of friendship must be seen in adversity.
l.   Ovid—*Tristium.* I. 5. 25.

Vulgus amicitias utilitate probat.

The vulgar herd estimate friendship by its
advantages.
m.   Ovid—*Epistolæ Ex Ponto.* II. 3. 8.

Hospes nullus tam in amici hospitium diverti
potest,
Quin ubi triduum continuum fuerit jam odi-
osus siet.

No one can be so welcome a guest that he
will not become an annoyance when he
has stayed three continuous days in a friend's
house.
n.   Plautus—*Miles Gloriosus.* III. 3. 12.

Nihil homini amico est opportuno amicius.

There is nothing more friendly than a
friend in need.
o.   Plautus—*Epidicus.* III. 3. 43.

Quod tuum'st meum'st ; omne meum est
autem tuum.

What is thine is mine, and all mine is
thine.
p.   Plautus—*Trinummus.* II. 2. 47.

Idem velle et idem nolle ea demum firma
amicitia est.

To desire the same things and to reject the
same things, constitutes true friendship.
q.   Sallust—*Catilina.* XX.

Amicitia semper prodest, amor etiam aliquando nocet.

Friendship always benefits ; love sometimes injures.
r.   Seneca.—*Epistolæ Ad Lucilium.*
XXXV.

Amici vitium ni feras, prodis tuum.

Unless you bear with the faults of a friend
you betray your own.
s.   Syrus—*Maxims.*

Amicum lædere ne joco quidem licet.

A friend must not be injured, even in jest.
t.   Syrus—*Maxims.*

Amicum perdere est damnorum maximum.
> To lose a friend is the greatest of all losses.
> *a.*   Syrus—*Maxims.*

Secrete amicos admone, lauda palam.
> Reprove your friends in secret, praise them openly.
> *b.*   Syrus—*Maxims.*

FRUGALITY.

Serviet eternum qui parvo nesciet uti.
> He will always be a slave, who does not know how to live upon a little.
> *c.*   Horace—*Epistolæ.* I. 10. 41.

Sera parsimonia in fundo est.
> Frugality, when all is spent, comes too late.
> *d.*   Seneca—*Epistolæ Ad Lucilium.* I.

FUTURITY.

Aliquod crastinus dies ad cogitandum dabit.
> To-morrow will give some food for thought.
> *e.*   Cicero—*Epistolæ Ad Atticum.* XV. 8.

Quod est ante pedes nemo spectat: cœli scrutantur plagas.
> No one sees what is before his feet: we all gaze at the stars.
> *f.*   Cicero—*De Divinatione.* II. 13.

Prudens futuri temporis exitum
Caliginosa nocte premit deus.
> A wise God shrouds the future in obscure darkness.
> *g.*   Horace—*Carmina.* III. 29. 29.

Quid sit futurum cras, fuge quærere: et
Quem Fors dierum cunque dabit, lucro
Appone.
> Cease to inquire what the future has in store, and to take as a gift whatever the day brings forth.
> *h.*   Horace—*Carmina.* I. 9. 13.

Vive sine invidiâ, mollesque inglorius annos
Exige; amicitias et tibi junge pares.
> May you live unenvied, and pass many pleasant years unknown to fame; and also have congenial friends.
> *i.*   Ovid—*Tristium.* III. 4. 43.

>   Cum altera lux venit
Jam cras hesternum consumpsimus; ecce aliud cras
Egerit hos annos, et semper paulum erit ultrâ.
> When another day has arrived, we will find that we have consumed our yesterday's to-morrow; another morrow will urge on our years, and still be a little beyond us.
> *j.*   Persius—*Satiræ.* V. 67.

Sunt aliquid Manes; letum non omnia finit.
Luridaque evictos effugit umbra rogos.
> There is something beyond the grave; death does not put an end to everything, the dark shade escapes from the consumed pile.
> *k.*   Propertius—*Elegiæ.* IV. 7. 1.

Calamitosus est animus futuri anxius.
> The mind that is anxious about the future is miserable.
> *l.*   Seneca—*Epistolæ Ad Lucilium.*
>   XCVIII.

Dabit deus his quoque finem.
> God will put an end to these also.
> *m.*   Virgil—*Æneid.* I. 199.

G.

GAIN.

Necesse est facere sumptum, qui quærit lucrum.
> He who seeks for gain, must be at some expense.
> *n.*   Plautus—*Asinaria.* I. 3. 65.

Lucrum malum æquale dispendio.
> An evil gain equals a loss.
> *o.*   Syrus—*Maxims.*

Hoc scitum'st periculum ex aliis facere tibi
quid ex usu sit.
> From others' slips some profit from one's self to gain.
> *p.*   Terence—*Heautontimorumenos.*
>   I. 2.

GAMBLING.

Aleator quantum in arte melior tanto est nequior.
> The gambler is more wicked as he is a greater proficient in his art.
> *q.*   Syrus—*Maxims.*

GENEROSITY.

Conveniens homini est hominem servare voluptas.
Et melius nullâ quæritur arte favor.
> It is a pleasure appropriate to man, for him to save a fellow-man, and gratitude is acquired in no better way.
> *r.*   Ovid—*Epistolæ Ex Ponto.* II. 9. 39.

45

Repente liberalis stultis gratus est,
Verum peritis irritos tendit dolos.

A man that suddenly becomes generous may please fools, but he vainly lays snares for the wise.

a. PHÆDRUS—*Fabulæ.* I. 23. 21.

GENIUS.

Ducis ingenium res
Adversæ nudare solent, celare secundæ.

Adversity usually reveals the genius of the general, while good fortune conceals it.

b. HORACE—*Satiræ.* II. 8. 73.

Ubi jam valideis quassatum est viribus ævi
Corpus, et obtuseis ceciderunt viribus artus,
Claudicat ingenium delirat linguaque mensque.

When the body is assailed by the strong force of time and the limbs weaken from exhausted force, genius breaks down, and mind and speech fail.

c. LUCRETIUS—*De Rerum Natura.*
III. 452.

Ingenio stat sine morte decus.

The honors of genius are eternal.

d. PROPERTIUS—*Elegiæ.* III. 2. 24.

Illud ingeniorum velut præcox genus, non temere unquam pervenit ad frugem.

It seldom happens that a premature shoot of genius ever arrives at maturity.

e. QUINTILIAN—*De Institutione Oratoria.*
I. 3. 1.

Nullum magnum ingenium sine mixturâ dementiæ fuit.

There has never been any great genius without a spice of madness.

f. SENECA—*De Animi Tranquillitate.*
XVII. 10.

Nullum sæculum magnis ingeniis clausum est.

No age is shut against great genius.

g. SENECA—*Epistolæ Ad Lucilium.* CII.

GENTLENESS.

Suaviter in modo, fortiter in re.

Gentle in manner, firm in reality.

h. AQUAVIVA—*Industriæ ad Curandos
Animæ Morbos.*

Peragit tranquilla potestas
Quod violenta nequit; mandataque fortius urget
Imperiosa quies.

Power can do by gentleness that which violence fails to accomplish ; and calmness best enforces the imperial mandate.

i. CLAUDIANUS—*De Consulatu Mallii Theo-
dori Panegyris.* CCXXXIX.

At caret insidiis hominum, quia mitis, hirundo.

The swallow is not ensnared by men because of its gentle nature.

j. OVID—*Ars Amatoria.* II. 149.

GIFTS.

Parvis mobilis rebus animus muliebris.

A woman's mind is affected by the meanest gifts.

k. LIVY—*Annales.* VI. 34.

Quisquis magna dedit, voluit sibi magna remitti.

Whoever makes great presents, expects great presents in return.

l. MARTIAL—*Epigrammata.* V. 59. 3.

Acceptissima semper munera sunt auctor quæ pretiosa facit.

Those gifts are ever the most acceptable which the giver makes precious.

m. OVID—*Heriodes.* XVII. 71.

Majestatem res data dantis habet.

The gift derives its value from the rank of the giver.

n. OVID—*Epistolæ Ex Ponto.* IV. 9. 68.

Res est ingeniosa dare.

Giving requires good sense.

o. OVID—*Amorum.* I. 8. 62.

Cum quod datur spectabis, et dantem adspice !

While you look at what is given, look also at the giver.

p. SENECA—*Thyestes.* CCCCXVI.

Bis dat qui cito dat.

He gives twice who gives quickly.

q. SYRUS—*Maxims.*

GLORY.

Gloria virtutem tanquam umbra sequitur.

Glory follows virtue as if it were its shadow.

r. CICERO—*Tusculanarum Disputationum.*
I. 45.

Fulgente trahit constrictos Gloria curru
Non minus ignotos generosis.

Glory drags all men along, low as well as high, bound captive at the wheels of her glittering car.

s. HORACE—*Satiræ.* I. 6. 23.

Cineri gloria sera est.

Glory paid to our ashes comes too late.

t. MARTIAL—*Epigrammata.* I. 26. 8.

Nisi utile est quod facimus, stulta est gloria.

Unless what we do is useful, our glory is vain.

u. PHÆDRUS—*Fabulæ.* III. 17. 12.

Magnum iter adscendo; sed dat mihi gloria
    vires.
    I am climbing a difficult road; but the
glory gives me strength.
a.   Propertius—*Elegiæ.* IV. 10. 3.

Heu, quam difficilis gloriæ custodia est.
    Alas! how difficult it is to retain glory!
b.   Syrus—*Maxims.*

Et ipse quidem, quamquam medio in spatio
integræ ætatis ereptus, quantum ad gloriam,
longissimum ævum peregit.
    As he, though carried off in the prime of
life, had lived long enough for glory.
c.   Tacitus—*Agricola.* XLIV.

GOD.

Nihil est quod deus efficere non possit.
    There is nothing which God cannot do.
d.   Cicero—*De Divinatione.* II. 41.

       Valet ima summis
Mutare, et insignem attenuat deus,
Obscura promens.
    God can change the lowest to the highest,
abase the proud, and raise the humble.
e.   Horace—*Carmina.* I. 34. 12.

Estne dei sedes nisi terra et pontus et aër
Et cœlum et virtus? Superos quid quærimus
    ultra?
Jupiter est quodcumque vides, quodcumque
    moveris.
    Is there any other seat of the Divinity
than the earth, sea, air, the heavens, and
virtuous minds? why do we seek God elsewhere? He is whatever you see; he is
wherever you move.
f.   Lucan—*Pharsalia.* IX. 578.

Exemplumque dei quisque est in imagine
    parvâ.
    Every one is in a small way the image of
God.
g.   Manilius—*Astronomica.* IV. 895.

Quis cœlum possit nisi cœli munera nosse?
Et reperire deum nisi qui pars ipse deorum
    est?
    Who can know heaven except by its gifts?
and who can find out God, unless the man
who is himself an emanation from God?
h.   Manilius—*Astronomica.* II. 115.

Est deus in nobis.
    There is a God within us.
i.   Ovid—*Fasti.* VI. 5.

Nihil ita sublime est, supraque pericula tendit
Non sit ut inferius suppositumque deo.
    Nothing is so high and above all danger
that is not below and in the power of God.
j.   Ovid—*Tristium.* IV. 8. 47.

Sed tamen ut fuso taurorum sanguine centum,
Sic capitur minimo thuris honore deus.
    As God is propitiated by the blood of a
hundred bulls, so also is he by the smallest
offering of incense.
k.   Ovid—*Tristium.* II. 75.

Est profecto deus, qui, quæ nos gerimus,
auditque et videt.
    There is indeed a God that hears and sees
whate'er we do.
l.   Plautus—*Captivi.* II. 2. 63.

Deum non immolationibus et sanguine
multo colendum: quæ enim ex trucidatione
immerentium voluptas est? sed mente pura,
bono honestoque proposito. Non templa illi,
congestis in altitudinem saxis, struenda sunt;
in suo cuique consecrandus est pectore.
    God is not to be worshiped with sacri-
fices and blood; for what pleasure can He
have in the slaughter of the innocent? but
with a pure mind, a good and honest purpose. Temples are not to be built for Him
with stones piled on high; God is to be
consecrated in the breast of each.
m.   Seneca—*Fragment.* V. 204.

GODS (THE).

Omnia fanda, nefanda, malo permista furore,
Justificam nobis mentem avertere deorum.
    The confounding of all right and wrong,
in wild fury, has averted from us the gracious favor of the gods.
n.   Catullus—*Carmina.* LXIV. 406.

Quid datur â divis felici optatius horâ?
    What is there given by the gods more de-
sirable than a happy hour?
o.   Catullus—*Carmina.* LXII. 30.

O dii immortales! ubinam gentium sumus?
    Ye immortal gods! where in the world
are we?
p.   Cicero—*In Catilinam.* I. 4.

Di me tuentur.
    The gods my protectors.
q.   Horace—*Carmina.* I. 17. 13.

Nec deus intersit nisi dignus vindice nodus.
    Nor let a god come in, unless the difficulty
be worthy of such an intervention.
r.   Horace—*Ars Poetica.* CXCI.

Quanto quisque sibi plura negaverit,
A dis plura feret.
    The more we deny ourselves, the more the
gods supply our wants.
s.   Horace—*Carmina.* III. 16. 21

Scire, deos quoniam propius contingis, oportet.
    Thou oughtest to know, since thou livest
near the gods.
t.   Horace—*Satiræ.* XXI. 6. 52.

Nam pro jucundis aptissima quæque dabunt
    di,
Carior est illis homo quam sibi.

    For the gods, instead of what is most
pleasing, will give what is most proper.
Man is dearer to them than he is to himself.
    a.   JUVENAL—*Satiræ.* X. 349.

Apparet divom numen, sedesque quietæ;
Quas neque concutiunt ventei, nec nubila
    nimbeis.
Aspergunt, neque nix acri concreta pruina
Cana cadens violat; semper sine nubibus
    æther
Integer, et large diffuso lumine ridet.

    The gods and their tranquil abodes appear,
which no winds disturb, nor clouds bedew
with showers, nor does the white snow,
hardened by frost, annoy them; the heaven,
always pure, is without clouds, and smiles
with pleasant light diffused.
    b.   LUCRETIUS—*De Rerum Natura.* III. 18.

Cui homini dii propitii sunt aliquid objiciunt
    lucri.

    The gods give that man some profit to
whom they are propitious.
    c.   PLAUTUS—*Persa.* IV. 3. 1.

Di nos quasi pilas homines habent.
    The gods play games with men as balls.
    d.   PLAUTUS—*Captivi Prologue.* XXII.

Dum homo est infirmus, tunc deos, tunc
hominem esse se meminit: invidet nemini,
neminem miratur, neminem despicit, ac ne
sermonibus quidem malignis aut attendit,
aut alitur.

    When a man is laboring under the pain
of any distemper, it is then that he recol-
lects there are gods, and that he himself is
but a man; no mortal is then the object of
his envy, his admiration, or his contempt,
and having no malice to gratify, the tales
of slander excite not his attention.
    e.   PLINY the Younger—*Epistolæ.* VII.
                        26.

Mundus est ingens deorum omnium templum.
    The world is the mighty temple of the gods.
    f.   SENECA—*Epistolæ Ad Lucilium.* X.

Desine fata deum flecti sperare precando.
    Cease to think that the decrees of the gods
can be changed by prayers.
    g.   VIRGIL—*Æneid.* VI. 376.

Jamque dies, ni fallor adest quem semper
    acerbum
Semper honoratum (sic dii voluistis) habeo.

    That day I shall always recollect with
grief; with reverence also, for the gods so
willed it.
    h.   VIRGIL—*Æneid.* V. **49.**

GOLD.

Aurum per medios ire satellites
Et perrumpere amat saxa potentius
Ictu fulmineo.

    Gold loves to make its way through
guards, and breaks through barriers of stone
more easily than the lightning's bolt.
    i.   HORACE—*Carmina.* III. 16. 9.

Auro pulsa fides, auro venalia jura,
Aurum lex sequitur, mox sine lege pudor.

    By gold all good faith has been banished;
by gold our rights are abused; the law
itself is influenced by gold, and soon there
will be an end of every modest restraint.
    j.   PROPERTIUS—*Elegiæ.* III. 13. 48.

Quid non mortalia pectora cogis,
Auri sacra fames?

    Accursed thirst for gold! what dost thou
not compel mortals to do?
    k.   VIRGIL—*Æneid.* III. 56.

GOODNESS.

Cui bono?
    What's the good of it? for whose advantage?
    l.   CICERO—*Oratio Pro Sextio Roscio
                      Amerino.* XXX.

Ergo hoc proprium est animi bene consti-
tuti, et lætari bonis rebus, et dolere contrariis.

    This is a proof of a well-trained mind, to
rejoice in what is good and to grieve at the
opposite.
    m.   CICERO—*De Amicitia.* XIII.

Homines ad deos nullâ re propius acce-
dunt, quam salutem hominibus dando.

    Men in no way approach so nearly to the
gods as in doing good to men.
    n.   CICERO—*Oratio Pro Quinto Ligario.* XII.

                    Vir bonus est quis?
Qui consulta patrum, qui leges juraque servat.

    Who is a good man? He who keeps the
decrees of the fathers, and both human and
divine laws.
    o.   HORACE—*Epistolæ.* I. 16. 40.

Rari quippe boni: numero vix sunt totidem
    quot
Thebarum portæ, vel divitis ostia Nili.

    The good, alas! are few: they are scarcely
as many as the gates of Thebes or the mouths
of the Nile.
    p.   JUVENAL—*Satiræ.* XIII. 26.

Bonum necessarium extra terminos necessi-
    tatis non est bonum.

    Necessary good is not good beyond the
bonds of necessity.
    q.   *Law Maxim.*

Segnius homines bona quam mala sentiunt.

    Men have less lively perception of good than of evil.

a.   Livy—*Annales.* XXX. 21.

        Si veris magna paratur
Fama bonis, et si successu nuda remoto
Inspicitur virtus, quicquid laudamus in ullo
Majorum, fortuna fuit.

    If honest fame awaits the truly good ; if setting aside the ultimate success excellence alone is to be considered, then was his fortune as proud as any to be found in the records of our ancestry.

b.   Lucan—*Pharsalia.* IX. 593.

Bono ingenio me esse ornatam, quam auro multo mavolo.
Aurum fortuna invenitur, natura ingenium bonum.
Bonam ego, quam beatam me esse nimio dici mavolo.

    A good disposition I far prefer to gold ; for gold is the gift of fortune; goodness of disposition is the gift of nature. I prefer much rather to be called good than fortunate.

c.   Plautus—*Pœnulus.* I. 2. 90.

Itidemque ut sæpe jam in multis locis,
Plus insciens quis fecit quam prudens boni.

    And so it happens oft in many instances ; more good is done without our knowledge than by us intended.

d.   Plautus—*Captivi Prologue.* XLIV.

Esse quam videri bonus malebat.

    He preferred to be good, rather than to seem so.

e.   Sallust—*Catilina.* LIV.

Bonitas non est pessimis esse meliorem.

    It is not goodness to be better than the very worst.

f.   Seneca—*Epistolæ Ad Lucilium.*

GOVERNMENT.

In principatu commutando civium
Nil præter domini nomen mutant pauperes.

    In a change of government, the poor seldom change anything except the name of their master.

g.   Phædrus—*Fabulæ.* I. 15.

Invisa nunquam imperia retinentur diu.

    A hated government does not last long.

h.   Seneca—*Phœnissæ.* VI. 60.

Omnium consensu capax imperii, nisi imperâsset.

    In the opinion of all men he would have been regarded as capable of governing, if he had never governed.

i.   Tacitus—*Annales.* I. 49.

Et errat longé meâ quidem sententiâ
Qui imperium credit gravius esse aut stabilius,
Vi quod fit, quam illud quod amicitiâ adjungitur.

    It is a great error, in my opinion, to believe that a government is more firm or assured when it is supported by force, than when founded on affection.

j.   Terence—*Adelphi.* I. 1. 40.

Hæ tibi erunt artes, pacisque imponere morem
Parcere subjectis et debellare superbos.

    This shall be thy work : to impose conditions of peace, to spare the lowly, and to overthrow the proud.

k.   Virgil—*Æneid.* VI. 852.

GRATITUDE.

Gratus animus est una virtus non solum maxima, sed etiam mater virtutum omnium reliquarum.

    A thankful heart is not only the greatest virtue, but the parent of all the other virtues.

l.   Cicero—*Oratio Pro Cnæo Plancio.*
                        XXXIII.

Non est diuturna possessio in quam gladio ducimus ; beneficiorum gratia sempiterna est.

    That possession which we gain by the sword is not lasting ; gratitude for benefits is eternal.

m.   Quintus Curtius Rufus—*De Rebus Gestis Alexandri Magni.* VIII. 8. 11.

Gratia pro rebus merito debetur inemtis.

    Thanks are justly due for things got without purchase.

n.   Ovid—*Amorum.* I. 10. 43.

Qui gratus futurus est statim dum accipit de reddendo cogitet.

    Let the man, who would be grateful, think of repaying a kindness, even while receiving it.

o.   Seneca—*De Beneficiis.* II. 25.

GREATNESS.

Nemo vir magnus aliquo afflatu divino unquam fuit.

    No man was ever great without divine inspiration.

p.   Cicero—*De Natura Deorum.* II. 66.

Urit enim fulgore suo qui prægravat artes
Intra se positas ; extinctus amabitur idem.

    That man scorches with his brightness, who overpowers inferior capacities, yet he shall be revered when dead.

q.   Horace—*Epistolæ.* II. 1. 13.

Magnam fortunam magnus animus decet.
A great mind becomes a great fortune.
a.   SENECA—*De Clementia*. I. 5.

GRIEF.

Nullus dolor est quem non longinquitas
temporis minuat ac molliat.
   There is no grief which time does not
lessen and soften.
b.   CICERO—*Epistolæ*. IV. 5.

Quis desiderio sit pudor aut modus
Tam cari capitis?
   What impropriety or limit can there be in
our grief for a man so beloved?
c.   HORACE—*Carmina*. I. 24. 1.

Ponamus nimios gemitûs: flagrantior æquo
Non debet dolor esse viri, nec vulnere major.
   Let us moderate our sorrows. The grief
of a man should not exceed proper bounds,
but be in proportion to the blow he has received.
d.   JUVENAL—*Satiræ*. XIII. 11.

Illa dolet vere qui sine teste dolet.
   She grieves sincerely who grieves unseen.
e.   MARTIAL—*Epigrammata*. I. 34. 4.

Strangulat inclusus dolor, atque exæstuat
        intus,
Cogitur et vires multiplicare suas.
   Suppressed grief suffocates, it rages within
the breast, and is forced to multiply its
strength.
f.   OVID—*Tristium*. V. 1. 63.

Curæ leves loquuntur, ingentes stupent.
   Light griefs are communicative, great
ones stupefy.
g.   SENECA—*Hippolytus*. 607.

Levis est dolor qui capere consilium potest.
   That grief is light which can take counsel.
h.   SENECA—*Medea*. I. 55.

Magnus sibi ipse non facit finem dolor.
   Great grief does not of itself put an end to
itself.
i.   SENECA—*Troades*. 786.

GROWTH.

Post id, frumenti quum alibi messis maxi-
        ma'st
Tribus tantis illi minus reddit, quam obse-
        veris.
Heu! istic oportet obseri mores malos,
Si in obserendo possint interfieri.
   Besides that, when elsewhere the harvest
of wheat is most abundant, there it comes up
less by one-fourth than what you have
sowed. There, methinks, it were a proper
place for men to sow their wild oats, where
they would not spring up.
j.   PLAUTUS—*Trinummus*. IV. 4. 128.

GUILT.

In ipsa dubitatione facinus inest, etiamsi ad
id non pervenerint.
   Guilt is present in the very hesitation,
even though the deed be not committed.
k.   CICERO—*De Officiis*. III. 8.

Omne animi vitium tanto conspectius in se
Crimen habet, quanto major qui peccat ha-
        betur.
   Every vice makes its guilt the more conspicuous in proportion to the rank of the
offender.
l.   JUVENAL—*Satiræ*. VIII. 140.

Ingenia humana sunt ad suam cuique le-
vandam culpam nimio plus facunda.
   Men's minds are too ingenious in pallia-
ting guilt in themselves.
m.   LIVY—*Annales*. XXVIII. 25.

Facinus quos inquinat æquat.
   Those whom guilt stains it equals.
n.   LUCAN—*Pharsalia*. V. 290.

Nulla manus belli, mutato judice, pura est.
   Neither side is guiltless if its adversary is
appointed judge.
o.   LUCAN—*Pharsalia*. VII. 263.

Heu! quam difficile est crimen non prodere
vultu.
   Alas! how difficult it is to prevent the
countenance from betraying guilt.
p.   OVID—*Metamorphoses*. II. 447.

Dum ne ob male facta peream, parvi æstimo.
   I esteem death a trifle, if not caused by
guilt.
q.   PLAUTUS—*Captivi*. III. 5. 24.

Omnes bonos bonasque accurare addecet,
Suspicionem et culpam ut ab se segregent.
   All good men and women should be on
their guard to avoid guilt, and even the
suspicion of it.
r.   PLAUTUS—*Trinummus*. I. 2. 41.

Haud est nocens, quicumque non sponte
est nocens.
   He is not guilty who is not guilty of his
own free will.
s.   SENECA—*Hercules Œtæus*. 886.

           Multa trepidus solet
Detegere vultus.
   The fearful face usually betrays great
guilt.
t.   SENECA—*Thyestes*. CCCXXX.

Fatetur facinus is qui judicium fugit.
   He who flees from trial confesses his guilt.
u.   SYRUS—*Maxims*.

H.

HABIT.

Consuetudo quasi altera natura.
> Habit is, as it were, a second nature.
> a.   Cicero—*De Finibus Bonorum et Malorum.* V. 25.

Consuetudo naturâ potentior est.
> Habit is stronger than nature.
> b.   Quintus Curtius Rufus—*De Rebus Gestis Alexandri Magni.* V. 5. 21.

Abeunt studia in mores.
> Pursuits become habits.
> c.   Ovid—*Heroides.* XV. 83.

Morem fecerat usus.
> Habit had made the custom.
> d.   Ovid—*Metamorphoses.* II. 345.

Nil consuetudine majus.
> Nothing is stronger than habit.
> e.   Ovid—*Ars Amatoria.* II. 345.

Inter pocula.
> Over their cups.
> f.   Persius—*Satiræ.* I. 30.

Frangas enim citius quam corrigas quæ in pravum induerunt.
> Where evil habits are once settled, they are more easily broken than mended.
> g.   Quintilian—*De Institutione Oratoria.* I. 3. 3.

Gravissimum est imperium consuetudinis.
> The power of habit is very strong.
> h.   Syrus—*Maxims.*

Inepta hæc esse, nos quæ facimus sentio;
Verum quid facias? ut homo est, ita morem geras.
> I perceive that the things that we do are silly; but what can one do? According to men's habits and dispositions, so one must yield to them.
> i.   Terence—*Adelphi.* III. 3. 76.

Quam multa injusta ac prava fiunt moribus!
> How many unjust and wicked things are done from mere habit.
> j.   Terence—*Heauton-Timoroumenos.* IV. 7. 11.

HAIR.

Cui flavam religas comam
Simplex munditiis?
> For whom do you bind your hair, plain in your neatness?
> k.   Horace—*Carmina.* I. 5. 4.
> Milton's trans.

Munditiis capimur: non sine lege capillis.
> We are charmed by neatness of person; let not thy hair be out of order.
> l.   Ovid—*Ars Amatoria.* III. 133.

HAPPINESS.

Non potest quisquam beate degere, qui se tantùm intuetur, qui omnia ad utilitates suas convertit; alteri vivas oportet, si vis tibi vivere.
> No man can live happily who regards himself alone, who turns everything to his own advantage. Thou must live for another, if thou wishest to live for thyself.
> m.   Seneca—*Epistolæ Ad Lucilium.* XLVIII.

O terque quaterque beati.
> O thrice, four times happy they!
> n.   Virgil—*Æneid.* I. 94.

HATRED.

Odi et amo. Quare id faciam, fortasse requiris.
Nescio, sed fieri sentio et excrucior.
> I hate and I love. Perchance you ask why I do that. I know not, but I feel that I do and I am tortured.
> o.   Catullus—*Carmina.* LXXXV. 1.

Odi profanum vulgus et arceo.
> I hate the profane and vulgar herd and shun it.
> p.   Horace—*Carmina.* III. 1. 1.

> Magna pars vulgi levis
Odit scelus spectatque.
> Most of the giddy rabble hate the evil deed they come to see.
> q.   Seneca—*Troades.* XI. 28.

Id agas tuo te merito ne quis oderit.
> Take care that no one hates you justly.
> r.   Syrus—*Maxims.*

Accerima proximorum odia.
> The hatred of relatives is the most violent.
> s.   Tacitus—*Annales.* IV. 70.

Proprium humani ingenii, odisse quem læseris.
> It is human nature to hate those whom we have injured.
> t.   Tacitus—*Agricola.* XLII.

Procul O procul este profani.
> Hence, far hence, ye vulgar herd!
> u.   Virgil—*Æneid.* VI. 258.

HEALTH.

Qui salubrem locum negligit, mente est captus atque ad agnatos et gentiles deducendus.

    He who overlooks a healthy spot for the site of his house is mad and ought to be handed over to the care of his relations and friends.

a.   Varro—*De Re Rustica.* I. 2.

HEAVEN.

Cedit item retro, de terra quod fuit ante,
In terras; et, quod missum est ex ætheris oreis,
Id rursum cæli relatum templa receptant.

    What came from the earth returns back to the earth, and the spirit that was sent from heaven, again carried back, is received into the temple of heaven.

b.   Lucretius—*De Rerum Natura.*
                           II. 999.

Non est ad astra mollis e terris via.

    The ascent from earth to heaven is not easy.

c.   Seneca—*Hercules Furens.*
                         CCCCXXXVII.

HISTORY.

Præcipium munus annalium reor, ne virtutes sileantur, utque pravis dictis, factisque ex posteritate et infamiâ metus sit.

    The principal office of history I take to be this : to prevent virtuous actions from being forgotten, and that evil words and deeds should fear an infamous reputation with posterity.

d.   Tacitus—*Annales.* III. 65.

HOME.

Nullus est locus domesticâ sede jucundior.

    There is no place more delightful than one's own fireside.

e.   Cicero—*Epistolæ.* IV. 8.

Domus sua cuique est tutissimum refugium.

    Every man's house is his safest refuge.

f.   *Law Maxim.*

HONESTY.

Omnia quæ vindicaris in altero, tibi ipsi vehementer fugienda sunt.

    Everything that thou reprovest in another, thou must most carefully avoid in thyself.

g.   Cicero—*In Verrem.* II. 3. 2.

Semper bonus homo tiro est.

    An honest man is always a child.

h.   Martial—*Epigrammata.* XII. 51. 2.

Mens regnum bona possidet.

    An honest heart possesses a kingdom.

i.   Seneca—*Thyestes.* CCCLXXX.

HONOR.

Turpe quid ausurus, te sine teste time.

    When about to commit a base deed, respect thyself, though there is no witness.

j.   Ausonius—*Septem Sapientum Sententiæ*
                 Septenis Veribus Explicatæ.
                           III. 7.

Nulla est laus ibi esse integrum, ubi nemo est, qui aut possit aut conetur rumpere.

    There is no praise in being upright, where no one can, or tries to corrupt you.

k.   Cicero—*In Verrem.* II. 1. 16.

Semper in fide quid senseris, non quid dixeris, cogitandum.

    In honorable dealing you should consider what you intended, not what you said or thought.

l.   Cicero—*De Officiis.* I. 13.

Summum crede nefas, animum præferre pudori,
Et propter vitam vivendi perdere causas.

    Believe it to be the greatest of all infamies, to prefer your existence to your honor, and for the sake of life to lose every inducement to live.

m.   Juvenal—*Satiræ.* VIII. 83.

Quod pulcherrimum idem tutissimum est.

    What is honorable is also safest.

n.   Livy—*Annales.* XXXIV. 14.

Et ille quidem plenus annis abiit, plenus honoribus, illis etiam quos recusavit.

    He died full of years and of honors, equally illustrious by those he refused as by those he accepted.

o.   Pliny the Younger—*Epistolæ.* II. 1.

Suum cuique decus posteritas rependit.

    Posterity gives to every man his true honor.

p.   Tacitus—*Annales.* IV. 35.

HOPE.

Ægroto dum anima est, spes est.

    To the sick, while there is life there is hope.

q.   Cicero—*Epistolæ Ad Atticum.* IX. 10.

Maxima illecebra est peccandi impunitatis spes.

    The hope of impunity is the greatest inducement to do wrong.

r.   Cicero—*Oratio Pro Animo Milone.*
                           XVI.

Et res non semper, spes mihi semper adest.
> My hopes are not always realized, but I always hope.
>
> *a.*   Ovid—*Heroides.* XVIII. 178.

Ego spem pretio non emo.
> I do not buy hope with money.
>
> *b.*   Terence—*Adelphi.* II. 2. 12.

Spes fovet, et fore cras semper ait melius.
> Hope ever urges on, and tells us to-morrow will be better.
>
> *c.*   Tibullus—*Carmina.* II. 6. 20.

>   Speravimus ista
> Dum fortuna fuit.
> Such hopes I had while fortune was kind.
>
> *d.*   Virgil—*Æneid.* X. 42.

HUMILITY.

Parvum parva decent.
> Humble things become the humble.
>
> *e.*   Horace—*Epistolæ.* I. 7. 44.

Da locum melioribus.
> Give place to your betters.
>
> *f.*   Terence—*Phormio.* III. 2. 37.

HUNGER.

Socratem audio dicentem, cibi condimentum esse famem, potionis sitim.
> I hear Socrates saying that the best seasoning for food is hunger; for drink, thirst.
>
> *g.*   Cicero—*De Finibus Bonorum et Malorum.* II. 28.

Bona summa putes, aliena vivere quadra.
> To eat at another's table is your ambition's height.
>
> *h.*   Juvenal—*Satiræ.* V. 2.

Græculus esuriens in cœlum, jusseris, ibit.
> Bid the hungry Greek go to heaven, he will go.
>
> *i.*   Juvenal—*Satiræ.* III. 78.

Magister artis ingenique largitor venter.
> Hunger is the teacher of the arts, and the bestower of invention.
>
> *j.*   Persius—*Satiræ. Prologue.* X.

Nec rationem patitur, nec æquitate mitigatur nec ulla prece flectitur, populus esuriens.
> A hungry people listens not to reason, nor cares for justice, nor is bent by any prayers.
>
> *k.*   Seneca—*De Brevitate Vitæ.* XVIII.

I.

IGNORANCE.

Causarum ignoratio in re novâ mirationem facit.
> In extraordinary events ignorance of their causes produces astonishment.
>
> *l.*   Cicero—*De Divinatione.* II. 22.

Ignoratione rerum bonarum et malarum maxime hominum vita vexatur.
> Through ignorance of what is good and what is bad, the life of men is greatly perplexed.
>
> *m.*   Cicero—*De Finibus Bonorum et Malorum.* I. 13.

Qui ex errore imperitæ multitudinis pendet, hic in magnis viris non est habendus.
> He who hangs on the errors of the ignorant multitude, must not be counted among great men.
>
> *n.*   Cicero—*De Officiis.* I. 19.

Lex succurit ignoranti.
> The law succors the ignorant.
>
> *o.*   *Law Maxim.*

O miseras hominum menteis! oh, pectora cæca!
> How wretched are the minds of men, and how blind their understandings.
>
> *p.*   Lucretius—*De Rerum Natura.* II. 14.

Pro superi! quantum mortalia pectora cæcæ, Noctis habent.
> Heavens! what thick darkness pervades the minds of men.
>
> *q.*   Ovid—*Metamorphoses.* VI. 472.

Quantum animis erroris inest!
> What ignorance there is in human minds.
>
> *r.*   Ovid—*Fasti.* II. 789.

Quod latet ignotum est; ignoti nulla cupido.
> What is hid is unknown: for what is unknown there is no desire.
>
> *s.*   Ovid—*Ars Amatoria.* III. 397.

>   Etiam illud quod scies nesciveris;
> Ne videris quod videris.
> Know not what you know, and see not what you see.
>
> *t.*   Plautus—*Miles Gloriosus.* II. 6. 89.

Illi mors gravis incubat qui notus nimis omnibus ignotus moritur sibi.
> Death presses heavily on that man, who, being but too well known to others, dies in ignorance of himself.
>
> *u.*   Seneca—*Thyestes.* CCCCI.

Quid crastina volveret ætas,
Scire nefas homini.

    Man is not allowed to know what will happen to-morrow.
    a.   STATIUS—*Thebais.* III. 562.

Omne ignotum pro magnifico.
    Everything unknown is magnified.
    b.   TACITUS—*Agricola.* XXX.

Homine imperito nunquam quidquid injustius,
Qui nisi quod ipse facit nihil rectum putat.

    Nothing can be more unjust than the ignorant man, who thinks that nothing is well done by himself.
    c.   TERENCE—*Adelphi.* I. 2. 18.

Ita me dii ament, ast ubi sim nescio.
    As God loves me, I know not where I am.
    d.   TERENCE—*Heauton-Timoroumenos.*
                             II. 3. 67.

    Namque inscitia est,
Adversum stimulum calces.

    It is consummate ignorance to kick against the pricks.
    e.   TERENCE—*Phormio.* I. 2. 27.

IMAGINATION.

Delphinum appingit sylvis, in fluctibus aprum.

    He paints a dolphin in the woods, and a boar in the waves.
    f.   HORACE—*Ars Poetica.* XXX.

IMITATION.

Pindarum quisquis studet æmulari,
Iule ceratis ope Dædaleâ
Nititur pennis, vitreo daturus
Nomina ponto.

    He who studies to imitate the poet Pindar, O Julius, relies on artificial wings fastened on with wax, and is sure to give his name to a glassy sea.
    g.   HORACE—*Carmina.* IV. 2. 1.

Respicere exemplar vitæ morumque jubebo
Doctum imitatorem, et veras hinc ducere voces.

    I would advise him who wishes to imitate well, to look closely into life and manners, and thereby to learn to express them with truth.
    h.   HORACE—*Ars Poetica.* CCCXVII.

          Dociles imitandis
Turpibus ac pravis omnes sumus.

    We are all easily taught to imitate what is base and depraved.
    i.   JUVENAL—*Satiræ.* XIV. 40.

IMMORTALITY.

Nemo unquam sine magnâ spe immortalitatis se pro patriâ offerret ad mortem.

    No one could ever meet death for his country without the hope of immortality.
    j.   CICERO—*Tusculanarum Disputationum.*
                               I. 15.

Dignum laude virum Musa vetat mori;
Cœlo Musa beat.

    The muse does not allow the praise-deserving hero to die: she enthrones him in the heavens.
    k.   HORACE—*Carmina.* IV. 8. 28.

Exegi monumentum aere perennius
Regalique situ pyramidum altius,
Quod non imber edax, non Aquilo impotens
Possit diruere aut innumerabilis
Annorum series et fuga temporum.
Non omnis moriar, multaque pars mei
Vitabit Libitinam.

    I have reared a memorial more enduring than brass, and loftier than the regal structure of the pyramids, which neither the corroding shower nor the powerless north wind can destroy; no, not even unending years nor the flight of time itself. I shall not entirely die. The greater part of me shall escape oblivion.
    l.   HORACE—*Carmina.* III. 30. 1.

Tamque opus exegi quod nec Jovis ira nec ignes
Nec poterit ferrum, nec edax abolere vetustas.
Cum volet illa dies quæ nil nisi corporis hujus
Jus habet, incerti spatium mihi siniat ævi;
Parte tamen meliore mei super alta perennis
Astra ferar, nomenque erit indelebile nostrum.

    And now have I finished a work which neither the wrath of Jove, nor fire, nor steel, nor all-consuming time can destroy. Welcome the day which can destroy only my physical man in ending my uncertain life. In my better part I shall be raised to immortality above the lofty stars, and my name shall never die.
    m.   OVID—*Metamorphoses.* XV. 871.

De nihilo nihil, in nihilum nil posse resciti.
    Out of nothing nothing can come, and nothing can become nothing.
    n.   PERSIUS—*Satiræ.* III. 84.

Postquam est mortem aptus Plautus: comœdia luget
Scena deserta, dein risus ludus jocusque
Et numeri innumeri simul omnes collacrumarunt.

    Plautus has prepared himself for a life beyond the grave; the comic stage deserted weeps; laughter also and jest and joke; and poetic and prosaic will bewail his loss together.
    o.   *Epitaph of* PLAUTUS, *written by himself.*

IMPOSSIBILITY.

Non cuivis homini contingit adire Corinthum.
Every man cannot go to Corinth.
a.　Horace—*Epistolæ.* I. 17. 36.

Nec tecum possum vivere, nec sine te.
I can neither live with you nor without
you.
b.　Martial—*Epigrammata.* XII. 47. 2.

INCLINATION.

Tu si animum vicisti potius quam animus te
est quod gaudias.
If you have overcome your inclination
and not been overcome by it, you have
reason to rejoice.
c.　Plautus—*Trinummus.* II. 29.

Naturæ sequitur semina quisque suæ.
Every one follows the inclinations of his
own nature.
d.　Propertius—*Elegiæ.* III. 9. 20.

INDOLENCE.

Vitanda est improba syren—desidia.
That destructive siren, sloth, is ever to be
avoided.
e.　Horace—*Satiræ.* II. 3. 14.

Variam semper dant otia mentem.
An idle life always produces varied inclinations.
f.　Lucan—*Pharsalia.* IV. 704.

Cernis ut ignavum corrumpant otia corpus
Ut capiant vitium ni moveantur aquæ.
Thou seest how sloth wastes the sluggish
body, as water is corrupted unless it moves.
g.　Ovid—*Epistolæ Ex Ponto.* I. 5. 5.

Difficultas patrocinia præteximus segnitiæ.
We excuse our sloth under the pretext of
difficulty.
h.　Quintilian—*De Institutione Oratoria.*
I. 12.

Blandoque veneno
Desidiæ virtus paullatim evicta senescit.
Valor, gradually overpowered by the delicious poison of sloth, grows torpid.
i.　Silius Italicus—*Punica.* III. 580.

Utque alios industria, ita hunc ignavia ad
famam protulerat.
Other men have acquired fame by industry, but this man by indolence.
j.　Tacitus—*Annales.* XVI. 18.

INFLUENCE.

Si possem sanior essem.
Sed trahit invitam nova vis ; aliudque Cupido,
Mens aliud.
If it were in my power, I would be wiser ;
but a newly felt power carries me off in
spite of myself ; love leads me one way, my
understanding another.
k.　Ovid—*Metamorphoses.* VII. 18.

Casta ad virum matrona parendo imperat.
A virtuous wife when she obeys her husband obtains the command over him.
l.　Syrus—*Maxims.*

INGRATITUDE.

Nil homine terra pejus ingrato creat.
Earth produces nothing worse than an ungrateful man.
m.　Ausonius—*Epigrammata.* CXL. 1.

Nihil amas, cum ingratum amas.
You love a nothing when you love an ingrate.
n.　Plautus—*Persa.* II. 2. 46.

Ut acerbum est, pro benefactis cum mali
messem metas.
How bitter it is to reap a harvest of evil
for good that you have done.
o.　Plautus—*Epidicus.* V. 2. 53.

Ingratus est, qui beneficium accepisse se
negat, quod accepit : ingratus est, qui dissimu-
lat : ingratus, qui non reddit ; ingratissimus
omnium, qui oblitus est.
He is ungrateful who denies that he has
received a kindness which has been bestowed upon him ; he is ungrateful who
conceals it ; he is ungrateful who makes no
return for it ; most ungrateful of all is he
who forgets it.
p.　Seneca—*De Beneficiis.* III. 1.

Ingratus unus miseris omnibus nocet.
One ungrateful man does an injury to all
who are in suffering.
q.　Syrus—*Maxims.*

Beneficia usque eo læta sunt dum videntur
exsolvi posse ; ubi multum antevenere pro
gratiâ odium redditur.
Benefits are acceptable, while the receiver
thinks he may return them ; but once exceeding that, hatred is given instead of
thanks.
r.　Tacitus—*Annales.* IV. 18.

INJURY.

Prohibetur ne quis faciat in suo, quod nocere possit in alieno.
It is forbidden that any man should do
that on his own property which may injure
the property of another.
s.　*Law Maxim.*

Volenti non fit injuria.

    To one who willingly embarks in any cause, no injury is done.

a.   *Law Maxim.*

Plerumque dolor etiam venustos facit.

    A strong sense of injury often gives point to the expression of our feelings.

b.   PLINY the Younger—*Epistolæ.* III. 9.

Aut potentior te, aut imbecillior læsit: si imbecillior, parce illi; si potentior, tibi.

    He who has injured thee was either stronger or weaker. If weaker, spare him; if stronger, spare thyself.

c.   SENECA—*De Ira.* III. 5.

INJUSTICE.

Dat veniam corvis, vexat censura columbas.

    The verdict acquits the raven, but condemns the dove.

d.   JUVENAL—*Satiræ.* II. 63.

INNOCENCE.

Quam angusta innocentia est, ad legem bonum esse.

    What narrow innocence it is for one to be good only according to the law.

e.   SENECA—*De Ira.* II. 27.

INQUISITIVENESS.

Percunctatorem fugito, nam garrulus idem est.

    Shun the inquisitive person, for he is also a talker.

f   HORACE—*Epistolæ.* I. 18. 69.

Incitantur enim homines ad agnoscenda quæ differuntur.

    Our inquisitive disposition is excited by having its gratification deferred.

g.   PLINY the Younger—*Epistolæ.* IX. 27.

INSANITY.

Nimirum insanus paucis videatur, eo quod Maxima pars hominum morbo jactatur eodem.

    He appears mad indeed but to a few, because the majority is infected with the same disease.

h.   HORACE—*Satiræ.* II. 3. 120.

O major tandem parcas, insane, minori.

    Oh! thou who art greatly mad, deign to spare me who am less mad.

i.   HORACE—*Satiræ.* II. 3. 326.

Quisnam igitur sanus? Qui non stultus.

    Who then is sane? He who is not a fool.

j.   HORACE—*Satiræ.* II. 3. 158.

I demens! et sævas curre per Alpes,
Ut pueris placeas et declamatio fias.

    Go, madman! rush over the wildest Alps, that you may please children and be made the subject of declamation.

k.   JUVENAL—*Satiræ.* X. 166.

Hei mihi, insanire me ajunt, ultro cum ipsi insaniunt.

    They call me mad, while they are all mad themselves.

l.   PLAUTUS—*Menæchmi.* V. 2. 90.

Insanus omnis furere credit ceteros.

    Every madman thinks all other men mad.

m.   SYRUS—*Maxims.*

INSTRUCTION.

Quod enim munus reipublicæ afferre majus, meliusve possumus, quam si docemus atque erudimus juventutem?

    What greater or better gift can we offer the republic than to teach and instruct our youth?

n.   CICERO—*De Divinatione.* II. 2.

Doctrina sed vim promovet insitam.

    Instruction enlarges the natural powers of the mind.

o.   HORACE—*Carmina.* IV. 4. 33.

Adde, quod ingenuas didicisse fideliter artes
Emollit mores, nec sinit esse fervos.

    To be instructed in the arts, softens the manners and makes men gentle.

p.   OVID—*Epistolæ Ex Ponto.* II. 9. 47.

Fas est ab hoste doceri.

    It is lawful to be taught by an enemy.

q.   OVID—*Metamorphoses.* IV. 428.

Domi habuit unde disceret.

    He need not go away from home for instruction.

r.   TERENCE—*Adelphi.* III. 3. 60.

Ab uno disce omnes.

    From one learn all.

s.   VIRGIL—*Æneid.* II. 65.

Disce, puer, virtutem ex me, verumque laborem;
Fortunam ex aliis.

    Learn, O youth, virtue from me and true labor; fortune from others.

t.   VIRGIL—*Æneid.* XII. 435.

INSULT.

        Quid facies tibi,
Injuriæ qui addideris contumeliam?

    What will thou do to thyself, who hast added insult to injury?

u.   PHÆDRUS—*Fabulæ.* V. 3. 4.

Sæpe satius fuit dissimulare quam ulcisci.

It is often better not to see an insult than to avenge it.

a.   SENECA—*De Ira.*   II. 32.

INTEMPERANCE.

Libidinosa etenim et intemperans adolescentia effœtum corpus tradit senectuti.

A sensual and intemperate youth hands over a worn-out body to old age.

b.   CICERO—*De Senectute.*   IX.

Quid non ebrietas designat? Operta recludit; Spes jubet esse ratas; in prælia trudit inermem.

What does drunkenness not accomplish? It discloses secrets, it ratifies hopes, and urges even the unarmed to battle.

c.   HORACE—*Epistolæ.*   I. 5. 16.

Nihil aliud est ebrietas quam voluntaria insania.

Drunkenness is nothing but voluntary madness.

d.   SENECA—*Epistolæ Ad Lucilium.*
                                            LXXXIII.

J.

JESTING.

Nec lusisse pudet, sed non incidere ludum.

The shame is not in having sported, but in not having broken off the sport.

e.   HORACE—*Epistolæ.*   I. 14. 36.

          Si quid dictum est per jocum,
Non æquum est id te serio prævortier.

If anything is spoken in jest, it is not fair to turn it to earnest.

f.   PLAUTUS—*Amphitruo.*   III. 2. 39.

Asperæ facetiæ, ubi nimis ex vero traxere, Acram sui memoriam relinquunt.

A bitter jest, when it comes too near the truth, leaves a sharp sting behind it.

g.   TACITUS—*Annales.*   XV. 68.

JUDGMENT.

Fundamenta justitiæ sunt, ut ne cui noceatur, deinde ut communi utilitati serviatur.

The foundations of justice are that no one shall suffer wrong; then, that the public good be promoted.

h.   CICERO—*De Officiis.*   I. 10.

Justitia suum cuique distribuit.

Justice renders to every one his due.

i.   CICERO—*De Legibus.*   I. 15.

Meminerimus etiam adversus infimos justitiam esse servandam.

Let us remember that justice must be observed even to the lowest.

j.   CICERO—*De Natura Deorum.*   III. 15.

Summum jus, summa injuria.

Extreme justice is extreme injustice.

k.   CICERO—*De Officiis.*   I. 10.

              Diis proximus ille est
Quem ratio non ira movet: qui factor rependens
Consilio punire potest.

He is next to the gods whom reason, and not passion, impels; and who, after weighing the facts, can measure the punishment with discretion.

l.   CLAUDIANUS—*De Consulatu Malii
              Theodori Panegyris.*   CCXXVII.

              Observantior æqui
Fit populus, nec ferre negat, cum viderit ipsum
Auctorem parere sibi.

The people become more observant of justice, and do not refuse to submit to the laws when they see them obeyed by their enactor.

m.   CLAUDIANUS—*De Quarto Consulatu
              Honorii Augusti Panegyris.*   CCXCVII.

Raro antecedentem scelestum
Deseruit pede pœna claudo.

Justice, though moving with tardy pace, has seldom failed to overtake the wicked in their flight.

n.   HORACE—*Carmina.*   III. 2. 31.

Ad quæstionem juris respondeant judices ad quæstionem facti respondeant juratores.

Let the judges answer to the question of law, and the jurors to the matter of fact.

o.   *Law Maxim.*

Aliquis non debet esse judex in propria causa.

No man should be judge in his own case.

p.   *Law Maxim.*

Hominem improbum non accusari tutius est quam absolvi.

It is safer that a bad man should not be accused, than that he should be acquitted.

q.   LIVY—*Annales.*   XXXIV. 4.

Judicis officium est ut res ita tempora rerum
Quærere.

> The judge's duty is to inquire about the
> time, as well as the facts.

a.   OVID—*Tristium.* I. 1. 37.

Paucite paucarum diffundere crimen in
ɔmnes.

> Do not lay on the multitude the blame
> that is due to a few.

b.   OVID—*Ars Amatoria.* III. 9.

Nam mala emptio semper ingrata est, eo
naxime, quod exprobrare stultitiam domino
·idetur.

> For a dear bargain is always annoying,
> particularly on this account, that it is a re-
> flection on the judgment of the buyer.

c.   PLINY the Younger—*Epistolæ.* I. 24.

Qui statuit aliquid, parte inauditâ alterâ,
Æquum licet statuerit, haud æquus fuerit.

> He who decides a case without hearing
> the other side, though he decide justly,
> cannot be considered just.

d.   SENECA—*Medea.* CXCIX.

Si judicas, cognosce; si regnas, jube.

> If you judge, investigate; if you reign,
> command.

e.   SENECA—*Medea.* CXCIV.

Bonis nocet quisquis pepercerit malis.

> He hurts the good who spares the bad.

f.   SYRUS—*Maxims.*

Judex damnatur cum nocens absolvitur.

> The judge is condemned when the guilty
> is acquitted.

g.   SYRUS—*Maxims.*

Initia magistratuum nostrorum meliora,
ferme finis inclinat.

> Our magistrates discharge their duties
> best at the beginning; and fall off toward
> the end.

h.   TACITUS—*Annales.* XV. 31.

Ita comparatam esse naturam omnium,
aliena ut melius videant et dijudicent, quam
sua.

> The nature of all men is so formed that
> they see and discriminate in the affairs of
> others, much better than in their own.

i.   TERENCE—*Heauton-Timoroumenos.*
III. 1. 94.

Suo sibi gladio hunc jugulo.

> With his own sword do I stab this man.

j.   TERENCE—*Adelphi.* V. 8. 35.

Discite justitiam moniti et non temnere
divos.

> Being admonished, learn justice and de-
> spise not the gods.

k.   VIRGIL—*Æneid.* VI. 620.

JUSTICE.

Etiam illud adjungo, sæpius ad laudem
atque virtutem naturam sine doctrinâ, quam
sine naturâ valuisse doctrinam.

> I add this also, that natural ability with-
> out education has oftener raised man to
> glory and virtue, than education without
> natural ability.

l.   CICERO—*Oratio Pro Licinio Archia.* VII.

Fiat justitia ruat cœlum.

> Let justice be done, though the heavens
> should fall.

m.   *Motto of Emperor Ferdinand I.*

Arma tenenti
Omnia dat qui justa negat.

> He who refuses what is just, gives up
> everything to him who is armed.

n.   LUCAN—*Pharsalia.* I. 348.

Neque enim lex est æquior ulla,
Quam necis artifices arte perire sua.

> Nor is there any law more just, than that
> he who has plotted death shall perish by
> his own plot.

o.   OVID—*Ars Amatoria.* I. 655.

K.

KINDNESS.

Sed tamen difficile dictu est, quantopere
·conciliat animos hominum comitas affabili-
·tasque sermonis.

> It is difficult to tell how much men's
> minds are conciliated by a kind manner
> and gentle speech.

p.   CICERO—*De Officiis.* II. 14.

Nemini credo, qui large blandus est dives
pauperi.

> I trust no rich man who is officiously
> kind to a poor man.

q.   PLAUTUS—*Aulularia.* II. 2. 30.

Ubicumque homo est, ibi beneficio locus est.

> Wherever there is a human being there
> is an opportunity for a kindness.

r.   SENECA—*Thyestes.* CCXIV.

Bis gratum est, quod dato opus est, ultro si
offeras.

> If what must be given is given willingly
> the kindness is doubled.

s.   SYRUS—*Maxims.*

Inopi beneficium bis dat, qui dat celeriter.

> He confers a double kindness on a poor
> man who gives quickly.

t.   SYRUS—*Maxims.*

Pars beneficii est, quod petitur, si cito neges.

It is kindness to immediately refuse what you intend to deny.

   a.   Syrus—*Maxims.*

KNAVERY.

His nunc præmium est qui recta prava faciunt.

Knavery's now its own reward.

   b.   Terence—*Phormio.* V. 1. 6.

KNOWLEDGE.

Animi cultus quasi quidam humanitatis cibus.

The cultivation of the mind is a kind of food supplied for the soul of man.

   c.   Cicero—*De Finibus Bonorum et Malorum.* V. 19.

Nam non solum scire aliquid, artis est, sed quædam ars etiam docendi.

Not only is there an art in knowing a thing, but also a certain art in teaching it.

   d.   Cicero—*De Legibus.* II. 19.

Nec enim ignorare deus potest, quâ mente quisque sit.

God cannot be ignorant of a man's character.

   e.   Cicero—*De Divinatione.* II. 60.

Nescire autem quid ante quam natus sis acciderit, id est semper esse puerum.

Not to know what happened before one was born is always to be a child.

   f.   Cicero—*De Oratore.* XXXIV.

Nec scire fas est omnia.

One cannot know everything.

   g.   Horace—*Carmina.* IV. 4. 22.

Si quid novisti rectius istis
Candidus imperti, si non, his utere mecum.

If you know anything better than this candidly impart it ; if not, use this with me.

   h.   Horace—*Epistolæ.* I. 6. 67.

E cœlo descendit nosce te ipsum.

This precept descended from Heaven: know thyself.

   i.   Juvenal—*Satiræ.* XI. 27.

Et teneo melius ista quam meum nomen.

I know all that better than my own name.

   j.   Martial—*Epigrammata.* IV. 37. 7.

Ego te intus et in cute novi.

I know the man within and without.

   k.   Persius—*Satiræ.* III. 30.

Scire tuum nihil est, nisi te scire hoc sciat alter?

Is then thy knowledge of no value, unless another know that thou possessest that knowledge?

   l.   Persius—*Satiræ.* I. 27.

O quanta species cerebrum non habet!

O that such beauty should be so devoid of understanding!

   m.   Phædrus—*Fabulæ.* I. 7. 2.

Plus scire satius est, quam loqui.

It is well for one to know more than he says.

   n.   Plautus—*Epidecus.* I. 1. 60.

Faciunt næ intelligendo, ut nihil intelligant.

Faith! by too much knowledge they bring it about that they know nothing.

   o.   Terence—*Andria. Prologue.* XVII.

L.

LABOR.

Arbores serit diligens agricola, quarum adspiciet baccam ipse numquam.

The diligent farmer plants trees, of which he himself will never see the fruit.

   p.   Cicero—*Tusculanarum Disputationum.* I. 14.

Vulgo enim dicitur, *Jucundi acti labores :* nec male Euripides : concludam, si potero, Latine : Græcum enim hunc versum nôstis omnes : *Suavis laborum est præteritorum memoria.*

It is generally said, "Past labors are pleasant," Euripides says, for you all know the Greek verse, "The recollection of past labors is pleasant."

   q.   Cicero—*De Finibus Bonorum et Malorum.* II. 32.

Quod tantis Romana manus contexuit annis
Proditor unus iners angusto tempore vertit.

What Roman power slowly built, an unarmed traitor instantly overthrew.

   r.   Claudianus—*In Rufinum.* II. 52.

O laborum
Dulce lenimen.

O sweet solace of labors.

   s.   Horace—*Carmina.* I. 32. 14.

Qui studet optatam cursu contingere metam
Multa tulit fecitque puer, sudavit et alsit.

He who would reach the desired goal must, while a boy, suffer and labor much and bear both heat and cold.

   t.   Horace—*Ars Poetica.* CCCCXII.

Nil actum credens dum quid superesset agendum.

Thinking that nothing was done, if anything remained to do.

   u.   Lucan—*Pharsalia.* II. 657.

Labor est etiam ipsa voluptas.

Labor is itself a pleasure.

   v.   Manilius—*Astronomica.* IV. 155.

Stultus labor est ineptiarum.
    Labor bestowed on trifles is silly.
    a.   MARTIAL—*Epigrammata.* II. 86. 10.

Ardua molimur ; sed nulla nisi ardua virtus.
    I attempt a difficult work ; but there is
no excellence without difficulty.
    b.   OVID—*Ars Amatoria.* II. 537.

Dum vires annigue sinunt. tolerate labores.
Jam veniet tacito curva senecta pede.
    While strength and years permit, endure
labor ; soon bent old age will come with silent foot.
    c.   OVID—*Ars Amatoria.* II. 669.

Facilis descensus Averno, * * *
Sed revocare gradum, superasque evadere ad
    auras
Hic labor, hoc opus est.
    The descent into hell is easy, but to recall
your steps, and re-ascend to the upper air,
this is labor, this is work.
    d.   VIRGIL—*Æneid.* VI. 126.

Labor omnia vincit improbus.
    Stubborn labor conquers everything.
    e.   VIRGIL—*Georgica.* I. 145.

LANGUAGE.

Falsa orthographia, sive falsa grammatica,
non vitiat concessionem.
    False spelling or false grammar does not
vitiate a grant.
    f.   *Law Maxim.*

Negatas artifex sequi voces.
    He attempts to use language which he
does not know.
    g.   PERSIUS—*Satiræ. Prologue.* XI.

LAUGHTER.

Nam risu inepto res ineptior nulla est.
    Nothing is more silly than silly laughter.
    h.   CATULLUS—*Carmina.* XXXIX. 16.

Quid rides?
Mutato nomine de te fabula narratur.
    Why do you laugh? Change but the
name, and the story is told of yourself.
    i.   HORACE—*Satiræ.* I. 1. 69.

Nimium risus pretium est, si probitatis im-
pendio constat.
    A laugh costs too much when bought at
the expense of virtue.
    j.   QUINTILIAN—*De Institutione Oratoria.*
                          VI. 3. 5.

LAW.

Quid leges sine moribus
Vanæ proficiunt?
    Of what use are laws, inoperative through
public immorality?
    k.   HORACE—*Carmina.* III. 24. 35.

Dormiunt aliquando leges, nunquam mori-
untur.
    The laws sometimes sleep, but never die.
    l.   *Law Maxim.*

Certis * * * legibus omnia parent.
    All things obey fixed laws.
    m.   MANILIUS—*Astronomica.* I. 479.

Sunt superis sua jura.
    The gods have their own laws.
    n,   OVID—*Metamorphoses.* IX. 499.

Nescis tu quam meticurosa res sit ire ad
judicem.
    You little know what a ticklish thing it is
to go to law.
    o.   PLAUTUS—*Mostellaria.* V. 1. 52.

Inertis est nescire, quid liceat sibi.
Id facere, laus est, quod decet; non, quod
    licet.
    It is the act of the indolent not to know
what he may lawfully do. It is praiseworthy to do what is becoming, and not
merely what is lawful.
    p.   SENECA—*Octavia.* CCCCLIII.

Jus summum sæpe summa est malitia.
    The strictest law sometimes becomes the
severest injustice.
    q.   TERENCE—*Heauton-Timoroumenos.*
                          IV. 5. 48.

Quod vos jus cogit, id voluntate impetret.
    What the law insists upon, let it have of
your own free will.
    r.   TERENCE—*Adelphi.* III. 4. 44.

LEARNING.

Nosse velint omnes, mercedem solvere
    nemo.
    All wish to be learned, but no one is will-
ing to pay the price.
    s.   JUVENAL—*Satiræ.* VII. 157.

Homines, dum docent, discunt.
    Men learn while they teach.
    t.   SENECA—*Epistolæ Ad Lucilium.* VII.

Discipulus est priori posterior dies.
    Each day is the scholar of yesterday.
    u.   SYRUS—*Maxims.*

LIFE.

Brevis a naturâ nobis vita data est; at memoria bene reditæ vitæ sempiterna.

The life given us by nature is short; but the memory of a well-spent life is eternal.

a.   CICERO—*Philippicæ.* XIV. 12.

Natura dedit usuram vitæ tanquam pecuniæ, nullâ præstitutâ die.

Nature has lent us life at interest, like money, and has fixed no day for its payment.

b.   CICERO—*Tusculanarum Disputationum.* I. 39.

Nemo parum diu vixit, qui virtutis perfectæ perfecto functus est munere.

No one has lived a short life who has performed its duties with unblemished character.

c.   CICERO—*Tusculanarum Disputationum.* I. 45.

Animula, vagula, blandula
Hospes comesque corporis!
Quæ nunc abibis in loca,
Pallidula, frigida nudula
Nec ut soles dabis joca?

O fleeting soul of mine, my body's friend and guest, whither goest thou, pale, fearful, and pensive one? Why laugh not as of old?

d.   HADRIAN—*Ad Animam.* See POPE'S paraphrase, *A Dying Christian to His Soul.*

Ars longa, vita brevis est.

Art is long, but life is fleeting.

e.   HIPPOCRATES—*Aphorismi.* I. Translated from the Greek.

Exacto contentus tempore vita cedat uti conviva satur.

Content with his past life, let him take leave of life like a satiated guest.

f.   HORACE—*Satiræ.* I. 1. 118.

Vitæ summa brevis spem nos vetat inchoare longam.

The short space of life forbids us to lay plans requiring a long time for their accomplishment.

g.   HORACE—*Carmina.* I. 4. 15.

Vivendi recte qui prorogat horam
Rusticus expectat dum defluat amnis; at ille
Labitur et labetur in omne volubilis ævum.

He who postpones the hour of living as he ought, is like the rustic who waits for the river to pass along (before he crosses); but it glides on and will glide on forever.

h.   HORACE—*Epistolæ.* I. 2. 41.

Natio comœda est.

All the world's a stage.

i.   JUVENAL—*Satiræ.* III. 100.

46

Festinat enim decurrere velox
Flosculus angustæ miseræque brevissima vitæ
Portio; dum bibimus dum serta unguenta puellas
Poscimus obrepit non intellectâ senectus.

The short bloom of our brief and narrow life flies fast away. While we are calling for flowers and wine and women, old age is upon us.

j.   JUVENAL—*Satiræ.* IX. 127.

Ampliat ætatis spatium sibi vir bonus: hoc est vivere bis, vitâ posse priore frui.

A good man doubles the length of his existence; to have lived so as to look back with pleasure on our past existence is to live twice.

k.   MARTIAL—*Epigrammata.* X. 23. 7.

Non est, crede mihi sapientis dicere "vivam."
Sera nimis vita est crastina, vive hodie.

It is not, believe me, the act of a wise man to say, "I will live." To-morrow's life is too late; live to-day.

l.   MARTIAL—*Epigrammata.* I. 16. 11.

Non est vivere, sed valere vita.

Life is not mere living, but the enjoyment of health.

m.   MARTIAL—*Epigrammata.* VI. 70. 15.

Id quoque, quod vivam, munus habere dei.

This also, that I live, I consider a gift of God.

n.   OVID—*Tristium.* I. 1. 20.

Natura vero nihil hominibus brevitate vitæ præstitit melius.

Nature has given to man nothing of more value than shortness of life.

o.   PLINY the Elder—*Historia Naturalis.* VII. 5. 1. 3.

Ignaviâ nemo immortalis factus: neque quisquam parens liberis, uti æterni forent, optavit; magis, uti boni honestique vitam exigerent.

No one has become immortal by sloth; nor has any parent prayed that his children should live forever; but rather that they should lead an honorable and upright life.

p.   SALLUST—*Jugurtha.* LXXXV.

Vita ipsa quâ fruimur brevis est.

The very life which we enjoy is short.

q.   SALLUST—*Catilina.* I.

Ante senectutem curavi ut bene viverem, in senectute (curo) ut bene moriar; bene autem mori est libenter mori.

Before old age I took care to live well; in old age I take care to die well; but to die well is to die willingly.

r.   SENECA—*Epistolæ Ad Lucilium.* LXI.

Atqui vivere, militare est.

> But life is a warfare.
>
> a.   Seneca—*Epistolæ Ad Lucilium*. XCVI.

Exigua pars est vitæ quam nos vivimus.

> The part of life which we really live is short.
>
> b.   Seneca—*De Brevitate Vitæ*. II.

Molestum est, semper vitam inchoare; male vivunt qui semper vivere incipiunt.

> It is a tedious thing to be always beginning life; they live badly who always begin to live.
>
> c.   Seneca—*Epistolæ Ad Lucilium*. XXIII.

Non domus hoc corpus sed hospitium et quidem breve.

> This body is not a home, but an inn; and that only for a short time.
>
> d.   Seneca—*Epistolæ Ad Lucilium*. CXX.

Non vivere bonum est, sed bene vivere.

> To live is not a blessing, but to live well.
>
> e.   Seneca—*Epistolæ Ad Lucilium*. LXX.

Prima quæ vitam dedit hora, carpit.

> The hour which gives us life begins to take it away.
>
> f.   Seneca—*Hercules Furens*. VIII. 74.

Propera vivere et singulos dies singulas vitas puta.

> Make haste to live, and consider each day a life.
>
> g.   Seneca—*Epistolæ Ad Lucilium*. CI.

Rebus parvis alta præstatur quies.

> In humble life there is great repose.
>
> h.   Seneca—*Hercules Furens*. CCCCLXIX.

Si ad naturam vivas, nunquam eris pauper; si ad opinionem, numquam dives.

> If you live according to nature, you never will be poor; if according to the world's caprice, you will never be rich.
>
> i.   Seneca—*Epistolæ Ad Lucilium*. XVI.

Vita, si scias uti, longa est.

> Life, if thou knowest how to use it, is long enough.
>
> j.   Seneca—*De Brevitate Vitæ*. II.

O vita, misero longa! felici brevis!

> O life! long to the wretched, short to the happy.
>
> k.   Syrus—*Maxims*.

LOSS.

Si quis mutuum quid dederit, sit pro proprio perditum;
Cum repetas, inimicum amicum beneficio invenis tuo.
Si mage exigere cupias, duarum rerum exoritur optio;
Vel illud, quod credideris perdas, vel illum amicum amiseris.

> What you lend is lost; when you ask for it back, you may find a friend made an enemy by your kindness. If you begin to press him further, you have the choice of two things—either to lose your loan or lose your friend.
>
> l.   Plautus—*Trinummus*. IV. 3. 43.

Periere mores, jus, decus, pietas, fides,
Et qui redire nescit, cum perit, pudor.

> We have lost morals, justice, honor, piety and faith, and that sense of shame which, once lost, can never be restored.
>
> m.   Seneca—*Agamemnon*. CXII.

Diem perdidi.

> I have lost a day.
>
> n.   Titus—See *Suetonius*. *Titus*. VIII.

LOVE.

Difficile est longum subito deponere amorem.

> It is difficult at once to relinquish a long-cherished love.
>
> o.   Catullus—*Carmina*. LXXVI. 13.

Mulier cupido quod dicit amanti,
In vento et rapidâ scribere oportet aquâ.

> What woman says to fond lover should be written on air or the swift water.
>
> p.   Catullus—*Carmina*. LXX. 3.

Vivamus, mea Lesbia atque amemus.

> My Lesbia, let us live and love.
>
> q.   Catullus—*Carmina*. V. 1.

Vivunt in venerem frondes omnisque vicissim
Felix arbor amat; mutant ad mutua palmæ
Fœdera.

> The leaves live but to love, and in all the lofty grove the happy trees love each his neighbor.
>
> r.   Claudianus—*De Nuptiis Honorii et Mariæ*. LXV.

Si sine amore, jocisque
Nil est jucundum, vivas in amore jocisque.

> If nothing is delightful without love and jokes, then live in love and jokes.
>
> s.   Horace—*Epistolæ*. I. 6. 65.

Non amo te, Sabidi, nec possum dicere quare;
Hoc tantum posse dicere: non amo te.

> I do not love thee, Sabidius, nor can I
> say why; I can only say this, "I do not
> love thee."
>
> MARTIAL—*Epigrammata.* I. 33. 1.

I do not love you, Dr. Fell.
The reason why I cannot tell;
But only this I know full well,
I do not love you, Dr. Fell.

a.   TOM BROWN'S *Paraphrase.*

Credula res amor est.

> Love is a credulous thing.
>
> *b.*   OVID—*Metamorphoses.* VII. 826.
>   *Heroides.* VI. 21.

Hei mihi! quod nullis amor est medicabilis
herbis.

> Ah me! love can not be cured by herbs.
>
> *c.*   OVID—*Metamorphoses.* I. 523.

Militat omnis amans.

> Every lover is a soldier.
>
> *d.*   OVID—*Amorum.* I. 9. 1.

Moribus et formâ conciliandus amor.

> Love must be attracted by beauty of mind
> and body.
>
> *e.*   OVID—*Heroides.* VI. 94.

Non bene conveniunt, nec in unâ sede
morantur,
Majestas et amor.

> Majesty and love do not well agree, nor
> do they live together.
>
> *f.*   OVID—*Metamorphoses.* II. 846.

Otia si tollas, periere cupidinis arcus.

> If you give up your quiet life, the bow of
> Cupid will lose its power.
>
> *g.*   OVID—*Remedia Amoris.* CXXXIX.

Quicquid Amor jussit non est contemnere
tutum.
Regnat, et in dominos jus habet ille deos.

> It is not safe to despise what Love com-
> mands. He reigns supreme, and rules the
> mighty gods.
>
> *h.*   OVID—*Heroides.* IV. 11.

> Qui finem quæris amoris,
(Cedit amor rebus) res age; tutus eris.

> If thou wishest to put an end to love, at-
> tend to business (love yields to employ-
> ment); then thou wilt be safe.
>
> *i.*   OVID—*Remedia Amoris.* CXLIII.

Qui non vult fieri desidiosus, amet.

> Let the man who does not wish to be idle,
> fall in love.
>
> *j.*   OVID—*Amorum.* I. 9. 46.

Res est soliciti plena timoris amor.

> Love is a thing full of anxious fears.
>
> *k.*   OVID—*Heroides.* I. 12.

Ut ameris, amabilis esto.

> To be loved, be lovable.
>
> *l.*   OVID—*Ars Amatoria.* II. 107.

Amor et melle et felle est fœcundissimus:
Gustu dat dulce, amarum ad satietatem usque
aggerit.

> Love has both its gall and honey in abun-
> dance: it has sweetness to the taste, but it
> presents bitterness also to satiety.
>
> *m.*   PLAUTUS—*Cistellaria.* I. 1. 71.

Auro contra cedo modestum amatorem.

> Find me a reasonable lover against his
> weight in gold.
>
> *n.*   PLAUTUS—*Curculio.* I. 3. 45.

Qui amat, tamen hercle si esurit, nullum
esurit.

> He that is in love, faith, if he be hungry,
> is not hungry at all.
>
> *o.*   PLAUTUS—*Casina.* IV. 2. 16.

Qui in amore præcipitavit pejus perit, quam
si saxo saliat.

> He who falls in love meets a worse fate
> than he who leaps from a rock.
>
> *p.*   PLAUTUS—*Trinummus.* II. 1. 30.

Scilicet insano nemo in amore videt.

> Everybody in love is blind.
>
> *q.*   PROPERTIUS—*Elegiæ.* II. 14. 18.

Amor timere neminem verus potest.

> True love can fear no one.
>
> *r.*   SENECA—*Medea.* XLI. 6.

Non potest amor cum timore misceri.

> Love cannot be mixed with fear.
>
> *s.*   SENECA—*Epistolæ Ad Lucilium.* XLVII.

Nulla vis major pietate verâ est.

> No power is greater than true affection
> (for parents).
>
> *t.*   SENECA—*Thyestes.* 549.

Odit verus amor nec patitur moras.

> True love hates and will not bear delay.
>
> *u.*   SENECA—*Hercules Furens.* 588.

Qui blandiendo dulce nutrivit malum,
Sero recusat ferre, quod subiit, jugum.

> He who has fostered the sweet poison of
> love by fondling it, finds it too late to refuse
> the yoke which he has of his own accord
> assumed.
>
> *v.*   SENECA—*Hippolytus.* CXXXIV.

Si vis amari, ama.

> If you wish to be loved, love.
>
> *w.*   SENECA—*Epistolæ Ad Lucilium.* IX.

Amor animi arbitrio sumitur, non ponitur.

> Love is in our power, but not to lay it aside.
>
> *x.*   SYRUS—*Maxims.*

Cogas amantem irasci, amare si velis.

You must make a lover angry if you wish him to love.

a.   SYRUS—*Maxims.*

Tum, ut adsolet in amore et ira, jurgia, preces, exprobratio, satisfactio.

Then there is the usual scene when lovers are excited with each other, quarrels, entreaties, reproaches, and then fondling reconcilement.

b.   TACITUS—*Annales.* XIII. 44.

Amantium iræ amoris integratio est.

Quarrels of lovers renew their love.

c.   TERENCE—*Andria.* III. 3. 23.

Omnia vincit amor, et nos cedamus amori.

Love conquers all things; let us yield to love.

d.   VIRGIL—*Eclogæ.* X. 69.

Quis fallere possit amantem?

Who can deceive a lover?

e.   VIRGIL—*Æneid.* IV. 296.

LYING.

Ita enim finitima sunt falsa veris ut in præcipitem locum non debeat se sapiens committere.

So near is falsehood to truth that a wise man would do well not to trust himself on the narrow edge.

f.   CICERO—*Academici.* IV. 21.

Hercle audivi esse optimum mendacium.
Quicquid dei dicunt, id rectum est dicere.

By Hercules! I have often heard that your piping-hot lie is the best of lies: what the gods dictate, that is right.

g.   PLAUTUS—*Mostellaria.* III. 1. 134.

M.

MALICE.

Hoccin est credibile, aut memorabile,
Tanta vecordia innata cuiquam ut siet,
Ut malis gaudeant alienis, atque ex incommodis
Alterius, sua ut comparent commoda?

It is to be believed or told that there is such malice in men as to rejoice in misfortunes, and from another's woes to draw delight.

h.   TERENCE—*Andria.* IV. 1. 1.

MAN.

Homo ad duas res, ad intelligendum et ad agendum, est natus.

Man was born for two things—thinking and acting.

i.   CICERO—*De Finibus Bonorum et Malorum.* II. 13.

Ad unguem factus homo.

A man polished to the nail.

j.   HORACE—*Satiræ.* I. 5. 32.

Metiri se quemque suo modulo ac pede verum est.

Every man should measure himself by his own standard.

k.   HORACE—*Epistolæ.* I. 7. 98.

Consilia res magis dant hominibus quam homines rebus.

Men's plans should be regulated by the circumstances, not circumstances by the plans.

l.   LIVY—*Annales.* XXII. 39.

Suave mari magno, turbantibus æquora ventis
E terrâ magnum alterius spectare laborum.

It is pleasant, when the sea runs high, to view from land the great distress of another.

m.   LUCRETIUS—*De Rerum Natura.* II. 1.

Os homini sublime dedit cœlumque tueri
Jussit; et erectos **ad sidera** tollere vultus.

God gave man an upright countenance to survey the heavens, and to look upward to the stars.

n.   OVID—*Metamorphoses.* I. 85.

Mille hominum species et rerum discolor usus;
Velle suum cuique est nec voto vivitur uno.

There are a thousand kinds of men, and their sense of things is various: each has his own inclination, nor do all live for the same object.

o.   PERSIUS—*Satiræ.* V. 52.

Piper, non homo.

He is pepper, not a man.

p.   PETRONIUS ARBITER.

Homo homini lupus.

Man is a wolf to man.

q.   PLAUTUS—*Asinaria.* II. 4. 88.

Homo vitæ commodatus, non donatus est.

Man has been lent, not given, to life.

r.   SYRUS—*Maxims.*

Homo sum, humani nihil a me alienum puto.

I am a man; what concerns man must concern me.

s.   TERENCE—*Heauton-Timoroumenos.*
                            I. 1. 25.

MANNERS.

Quæ fuerant vitia mores sunt.

What once were vices, are now the manners of the day.
a.   Seneca—*Epistolæ Ad Lucilium.*
                     XXXIX.

Obsequium amicos, veritas odium parit.

Obsequiousness begets friends; truth, hatred.
b.   Terence—*Andria.* I. 1. 41.

MATRIMONY.

Prima societas in ipso conjugio est: proxima in liberis; deinde una domus, communia omnia.

The first bond of society is marriage; the next, our children; then the whole family and all things in common.
c.   Cicero—*De Officiis.* I. 17.

Felices ter et amplius
Quos irrupta tenet copula, nec malis
Divulsus querimoniis
Supremâ citius solvet amor die.

Happy and thrice happy are they who enjoy an uninterrupted union, and whose love, unbroken by any complaints, shall not dissolve until the last day.
d.   Horace—*Carmina.* I. 13. 17.

Hac quoque de causâ, si te proverbia tangunt,
Mense malos Maio nubere vulgus ait.

For this reason, if you believe proverbs, let me tell you the common one: "It is unlucky to marry in May."
e.   Ovid—*Fasti.* V. 489.

Si qua voles apte nubere, nube pari.

If thou wouldst marry wisely, marry thine equal.
f.   Ovid—*Heroides.* IX. 32.

MEDICINE.

Ægri quia non omnes convalescunt, idcirco ars nulla medicina est.

Because all the sick do not recover, therefore medicine is not an art.
g.   Cicero—*De Natura Deorum.* II. 4.

Dulcia non ferimus; succo renovamus amaro.

We do not bear sweets; we are recruited by a bitter potion.
h.   Ovid—*Ars Amatoria.* III. 583.

Graviora quædam sunt remedia periculis.

Some remedies are worse than the disease.
i.   Syrus—*Maxims.*

Ægrescitque medendo.

The medicine increases the disease.
j.   Virgil—*Æneid.* XII. 46.

MEMORY.

Memoria est thesaurus omnium rerum et custos.

Memory is the treasury and guardian of all things.
k.   Cicero—*De Oratore.* I. 5.

Vita enim mortuorum in memoriâ vivorum est posita.

The life of the dead is placed in the memory of the living.
l.   Cicero—*Philippicæ.* IX. 5.

Patriæ quis exul se quoque fugit.

What exile from his country is able to escape from himself?
m.   Horace—*Carmina.* II. 16. 19.

At cum longa dies sedavit vulnera mentis,
Intempestive qui fovet illa novat.

When time has assuaged the wounds of the mind, he who unseasonably reminds us of them, opens them afresh.
n.   Ovid—*Epistolæ Ex Ponto.* IV. 11. 19.

Impensa monumenti supervacua est: memoria nostra durabit, si vitâ meruimus.

The erection of a monument is superfluous; the memory of us will last, if we have deserved it in our lives.
o.   Pliny the Younger—*Epistolæ.* IX. 19.

Facetiarum apud præpotentes in longum memoria est.

The powerful hold in deep remembrance an ill-timed pleasantry.
p.   Tacitus—*Annales.* V. 2.

Forsan et hæc olim meminisse juvabit.

Perhaps the remembrance of these things will prove a source of future pleasure.
q.   Virgil—*Æneid.* I. 203.

Quique sui memores alios fecêre merendo.

These who have ensured their remembrance by their deserts.
r.   Virgil—*Æneid.* VI. 664.

Si genus humanum et mortalia temnitis arma,
At sperate deos memores fandi atque nefandi.

If ye despise the human race, and mortal arms, yet remember that there is a God who is mindful of right and wrong.
s.   Virgil—*Æneid.* I. 542.

MERCY.

Mortem misericors sæpe pro vitâ dabit.

Mercy often inflicts death.
t.   Seneca—*Troades.* 329.

Pulchrum est vitam donare minori.

It is noble to grant life to the vanquished.
u.   Statius—*Thebais.* VI. 816.

MERIT.

Virtute ambire oportet, non favitoribus.
Sat habet favitorum semper, qui recte facit.

We should try to succeed by merit, not by favor. He who does well will always have patrons enough.

a.   PLAUTUS—*Amphitruo. Prologue.*
                                LXXVIII.

MIND.

Frons est animi janua.

The forehead is the gate of the mind.

b.   CICERO—*Oratio De Provinciis
                        Consularibus.* XI.

In animo perturbato, sicut in corpore, sanitas esse non potest.

In a disturbed mind, as in a body in the same state, health can not exist.

c.   CICERO—*Tusculanarum Disputationum.*
                                III. 4.

Morbi perniciores pluresque animi quam corporis.

The diseases of the mind are more and more destructive than those of the body.

d.   CICERO—*Tusculanarum Disputationum.*
                                III. 3.

Acclinis falsis animus meliora recusat.

A mind that is charmed by false appearances refuses better things.

e.   HORACE—*Satiræ.* II. 2. 6.

Quæ lædunt oculum festinas demere; si quid
Est animum, differs curandi tempus in annum.

If anything affects your eye, you hasten to have it removed; if anything affects your mind, you postpone the cure for a year.

f.   HORACE—*Epistolæ.* I. 238.

            Cum corpore ut una
Crescere sentimus pariterque senescere mentem.

We plainly perceive that the mind strengthens and decays with the body.

g.   LUCRETIUS—*De Rerum Natura.* III.
                                446.

            Rationi nulla resistunt.
Claustra nec immensæ moles, ceduntque recessus:
Omnia succumbunt, ipsum est penetrabile cœlum.

No barriers, no masses of matter, however enormous, can withstand the powers of the mind; the remotest corners yield to them; all things succumb, the very heaven itself is laid open.

h.   MANILIUS—*Astronomica.* I. 541.

Corpore sed mens est ægro magis ægra; malique
In circumspectu stat sine fine sui.

The mind is sicker than the sick body; in contemplation of its sufferings it becomes hopeless.

i.   OVID—*Tristium.* IV. 6. 43.

Horrea formicæ tendunt ad inania nunquam,
Nullus ad amissas ibit amicus opes.

Ants do not bend their ways to empty barns, so no friend will visit the place of departed wealth.

j.   OVID—*Tristium.* I. 9. 9.

Mensque pati durum sustinet ægra nihil.

The sick mind can not bear anything harsh.

k.   OVID—*Epistolæ Ex Ponto.* I. 5. 18.

Mens sola loco non exulat.

The mind alone can not be exiled.

l.   OVID—*Epistolæ Ex Ponto.* IV. 9. 41.

            Animus quod perdidit optat,
Atque in præteritâ se totus imagine versat.

The mind wishes for what it has missed, and occupies itself with retrospective contemplation.

m.   PETRONIUS ARBITER—*Satyricon.*

Animus æquus optimum est ærumnæ condimentum.

A well-balanced mind is the best remedy against affliction.

n.   PLAUTUS—*Rudens.* II. 3.

Habet cerebrum sensus arcem; hic mentis est regimen.

The brain is the citadel of the senses: this guides the principle of thought.

o.   PLINY the Elder—*Historia Naturalis.*
                                XI. 49. 2.

Valentior omni fortuna animus est: in utramque partem ipse res suas ducit, beatæque miseræ vitæ sibi causa est.

The mind is the master over every kind of fortune: itself acts in both ways, being the cause of its own happiness and misery.

p.   SENECA—*Epistolæ Ad Lucilium.*
                                XCVIII.

Mens agitat molem.

Mind moves matter.

q.   VIRGIL—*Æneid.* VI. 727.

Nescia mens hominum fati sortisque futuræ,
Et servare modum, rebus sublata secundis.

The mind of man is ignorant of fate and future destiny, and can not keep within due bounds when elated by prosperity.

r.   VIRGIL—*Æneid.* X. 501.

MISAPPROPRIATION.

Mutos enim nasci, et egere omni ratione satius fuisset, quam providentiæ munera in mutuam perniciem convertere.

For it would have been better that man should have been born dumb, nay, void of all reason, rather than that he should employ the gifts of Providence to the destruction of his neighbor.

s.   QUINTILIAN—*De Institutione Oratoria.*
                                XII. 1. 1.

MISFORTUNE.

Levis est consolatio ex miseriâ aliorum.
> The comfort derived from the misery of others is slight.

a.   CICERO—*Epistolæ.* VI. 3.

Medio de fonte leporum
Surgit amari aliquid, quod in ipsis floribus angat.
> Full from the fount of joy's delicious springs
> Some bitter o'er the flowers its bubbling venom flings.

b.   LUCRETIUS—*De Rerum Natura.* IV. 1,129. Byron's trans. in *Childe Harold.* I. 82.

Quicumque amisit dignitatem pristinam
Ignavis etiam jocus est in casu gravi.
> Whoever has fallen from his former high estate is in his calamity the scorn even of the base.

c.   PHÆDRUS—*Fabulæ.* I. 21. 1.

Calamitas virtutis occasio est.
> Calamity is virtue's opportunity.

d.   SENECA—*De Providentia.* IV.

Ignis aurum probat, misera fortes viros.
> Fire tries gold, misery tries brave men.

e.   SENECA—*De Providentia.* V.

Nihil infelicius eo, cui nihil unquam evenit adversi, non licuit enim illi se experiri.
> There is no one more unfortunate than the man who has never been unfortunate, for it has never been in his power to try himself.

f.   SENECA—*De Providentia.* III.

Nil est nec miserius nec stultius quam prætimere. Quæ ista dementia est, malum suum antecedere !
> There is nothing so wretched or foolish as to anticipate misfortunes. What madness it is in your expecting evil before it arrives !

g.   SENECA—*Epistolæ Ad Lucilium.* XCVIII.

Quemcumque miserum videris, hominem scias.
> When you see a man in distress, recognize him as a fellow man.

h.   SENECA—*Hercules Furens.* 463.

Bonum est fugienda adspicere in alieno malo.
> It is good to see in the misfortunes of others what we should avoid.

i.   SYRUS—*Maxims.*

Tu ne cede malis, sed contra audentior ito.
> Yield not to misfortunes, but advance all the more boldly against them.

j.   VIRGIL—*Æneid.* VI. 95.

MODERATION.

Auream quisquis mediocritatem deligit tutus caret obsoleti sordibus tecti, caret invidenda sobrius aula.
> Who loves the golden mean is safe from the poverty of a tenement, is free from the envy of a palace.

k.   HORACE—*Carmina.* II. 10. 5.

Modus omnibus in rebus, soror, optimum est habitu ;
Nimia omnia nimium exhibent negotium hominibus ex se.
> In everything the middle course is best: all things in excess bring trouble to men.

l.   PLAUTUS—*Pœnulus.* I. 2. 29.

Modica voluptas laxat animos et temperat.
> Moderate pleasure relaxes the spirit, and moderates it.

m.   SENECA—*De Ira.* II. 20.

Bonarum rerum consuetudo pessima est.
> The too constant use even of good things is hurtful.

n.   SYRUS—*Maxims.*

MODESTY.

Maximum ornamentum amicitiæ tollit, qui ex eâ tollit verecundiam.
> He takes the greatest ornament from friendship, who takes modesty from it.

o.   CICERO—*De Amicitia.* XX.

Cui pudor et justitiæ soror incorrupta fides nudaque veritas quando ullum inveniet parem?
> What can be found equal to modesty, uncorrupt faith, the sister of justice, and undisguised truth?

p.   HORACE—*Carmina.* I. 24. 6.

Adolescentem verecundum esse decet.
> Modesty becomes a young man.

q.   PLAUTUS—*Asinaria.* V. 1. 8.

MONEY.

Et genus et formam regina pecunia donat.
> All powerful money gives birth and beauty.

r.   HORACE—*Epistolæ.* I. 6. 37.

Licet superbus ambules pecuniæ,
Fortuna non mutat genus.
> Though you strut proud of your money, yet fortune has not changed your birth.

s.   HORACE—*Epodi.* IV. 5.

Populus me sibilat, at mihi plaudo
Ipse domi, simul ac nummos contemplor in arcâ.
> The people hiss me, but I applaud myself at home, when I contemplate the money in my chest.

t.   HORACE—*Satiræ.* I. 1. 66.

Quærenda pecunia primum est; virtus post nummos.

Money is to be sought for first of all; virtue after wealth.

a.   HORACE—*Epistolæ.* I. 1. 53.

Quo mihi fortunam, si non conceditur uti?

Of what use is a fortune to me, if I can not use it?

b.   HORACE—*Epistolæ.* I. 5. 12.

Rem facias rem,
Recte si possis, si non, quocumque modo rem.

A fortune—make a fortune; by honest means if you can; if not, by any means make a fortune.

c.   HORACE—*Epistolæ.* I. 1. 65.

Ploratur lacrimis amissa pecunia veris.

Money lost is bewailed with unfeigned tears.

d.   JUVENAL—*Satiræ.* XIII. 134.

Quantum quisque suâ nummorum condit in arcâ,
Tantum habet et fidei.

Every man's credit is proportioned to the money which he has in his chest.

e.   JUVENAL—*Satiræ.* III. 143.

Luat in corpore, qui non habet in ære.

Who can not pay with money, must pay with his body.

f.   *Law Maxim.*

Nec quicquam acrius quam pecuniæ damnum stimulat.

Nothing stings more deeply than the loss of money.

g.   LIVY—*Annales.* XXX. 44.

In pretio pretium nunc est; dat census honores,
Census amicitias; pauper ubique jacet.

Money nowadays is money; money brings office; money gains friends; everywhere the poor man is down.

h.   OVID—*Fasti.* I. 217.

Pecuniam in loco negligere maximum est lucrum.

To despise money on some occasions is a very great gain.

i.   TERENCE—*Adelphi.* II. 2. 8.

MOURNING.

Si vis me flere, dolendum est
Primum ipsi tibi.

If you wish me to weep, you must mourn first yourself.

j.   HORACE—*Ars Poetica.* CII.

MUSIC.

Citharœdus
Ridetur chordâ qui semper oberrat eâdem.

The musician who always plays on the same string, is laughed at.

k.   HORACE—*Ars Poetica.* 355.

Vixere fortes ante Agamemnona
Multi: sed omnes illacrimabiles
Urgentur, ignotique longâ
Nocte, carent quia vate sacro.

Many heroes lived before Agamemnon, but they are all unmourned, and consigned to oblivion, because they had no bard to sing their praises.

l.   HORACE—*Carmina.* IV. 9. 25.

Etiam singulorum fatigatio quamlibet se rudi modulatione solatur.

Men, even when alone, lighten their labors by song, however rude it may be.

m.   QUINTILIAN—*De Institutione Oratoria.*
I. 81.

Cantabitis, Arcades montibus
Hæc vestris: soli cantare periti Arcades.
O mihi tum quam molliter ossa quiescant,
Vestra meos olim si fistula dicat amores.

Arcadians skilled in song will sing my woes upon the hills. Softly shall my bones repose, if you in future sing my loves upon your pipe.

n.   VIRGIL—*Eclogæ.* X. 31.

N.

NATURE.

Meliora sunt ea quæ naturâ quam illa quæ arte perfecta sunt.

Things perfected by nature are better than those finished by art.

o.   CICERO—*De Natura Deorum.* II. 34.

Naturam expellas furcâ, tamen usque recurrit.

You may turn nature out of doors with violence, but she will still return.

p.   HORACE—*Epistolæ.* I. 10. 24.

Regia, crede, mihi res est succurrere lapsis.

Believe me it is noble to aid the afflicted.

q.   OVID—*Epistolæ Ex Ponto.* II. 9. 11.

Natura vero nihil hominibus brevitate vitæ præstitit melius.

Nature has given man no better thing than shortness of life.

r.   PLINY the Elder—*Historia Naturalis.*
VII. 51. 3.

Ut natura dedit, sic omnis recta figura.

Every form as nature made it is correct.

s.   PROPERTIUS—*Elegiæ.* II. 18. 25.

Natura semina scientiæ nobis dedit, scientiam non dedit.

　Nature has given us the seeds of knowledge, not knowledge itself.
a.　　Seneca—*Epistolæ Ad Lucilium.* CXX.

Nunc omnis ager, nunc omnis parturit
　　arbos,
Nunc frondent sylvæ, nunc formosissimus
　　annus.

　Now every field and every tree is in bloom. The woods are in full leaf, and the year in its highest beauty.
b.　　Virgil—*Eclogæ.* III. 56.

NECESSITY.

　Æqua lege necessitas
Sortitur insignes et imos.

　Necessity takes impartially the highest and the lowest.
c.　　Horace—*Carmina.* III. 1. 14.

Necessitas ultimum et maximum telum est.

　Necessity is the last and strongest weapon.
d.　　Livy—*Annales.* IV. 28.

Discite quam parvo liceat producere vitam,
Et quantum natura petat.

　Learn on how little man may live, and how small a portion nature requires.
e.　　Lucan—*Pharsalia.* IV. 377.

Magister artis ingeniique largitor venter.

　The belly is the teacher of art and the bestower of genius.
f.　　Persius—*Satiræ. Prologue.* X.

Qui e nuce nucleum esse vult, frangat nucem.

　He who would eat the kernel, must crack the shell.
g.　　Plautus—*Curculio.* I. 1. 55.

Efficacior omni arte imminens necessitas.

　Necessity when threatening is more powerful than device of man.
h.　　Quintus Curtius Rufus—*De Rebus*
　　　　　　　　　Gestis Alexandri Magni.
　　　　　　　　　　　　IV. 3. 23.

NOBILITY.

Inquinat egregios adjuncta superbia mores.

　The noblest character is stained by the addition of pride.
i.　　Claudianus—*De Quarto Consulatu*
　　　　　　　Honorii Augustii Panegyris. 305

Par nobile fratrum.

　A noble pair of brothers.
j.　　Horace—*Satiræ.* II. 3. 243.

NOVELTY.

Est natura hominum novitatis avida.

　Human nature is fond of novelty.
k.　　Pliny the Elder—*Historia Naturalis.*
　　　　　　　　　　　　XII. 5. 3.

O.

OBEDIENCE.

Qui modeste paret, videtur qui aliquando imperet dignus esse.

　He who obeys with modesty appears worthy of being some day a commander.
l.　　Cicero—*De Legibus.* III. 2.

Ibit eo quo vis qui zonam perdidit.

　The man who has lost his purse will go wherever you wish.
m.　　Horace—*Epistolæ.* II. 2. 40.

OBSCURITY.

Bene qui latuit, bene vixit.

　He who has lived obscurely and quietly has lived well.
n.　　Ovid—*Tristium.* III. 4. 25.

Eo magis præfulgebat quod non videbatur.

　He shone with the greater splendor, because he was not seen.
o.　　Tacitus—*Annales.* III. 76.

OPINION.

Denique non omnes eadem mirantur amantque.

　All men do not, in fine, admire or love the same thing.
p.　　Horace—*Epistolæ.* II. 2. 58.

Nequam hominis ego parvi pendo gratiam.

　I set little value on the esteem of a worthless man.
q.　　Plautus—*Bacchides.* III. 6. 29.

Quot homines, tot sententiæ.

　As many men, so many opinions.
r.　　Terence—*Phormio.* II. 4. 14.

Scinditur incertum studia in contraria vulgus.

　The uncertain multitude is divided by opposite opinions.
s.　　Virgil—*Æneid.* II. 39.

OPPORTUNITY.

Nostra sine auxilio fugiunt bona. Carpite florem.

Our advantages fly away without aid. Pluck the flower.
a.   OVID—*Ars Amatoria.* III. 79.

Occasio ægre offertur, facile amittitur.

A good opportunity is seldom presented, and is easily lost.
b.   SYRUS—*Maxims.*

ORATORY.

Is enim est eloquens, qui et humilia subtiliter, et magna graviter, et mediocria temperate potest dicere.

He is an eloquent man who can treat humble subjects with delicacy, lofty things impressively, and moderate things temperately.
c.   CICERO—*De Oratore.* XXIX.

Intererit multum Davusne loquatur an heros.

It makes a great difference whether Davus or a hero speaks.
d.   HORACE—*Ars Poetica.* CXIV.

Præterea multo magis, ut vulgo dicitur viva vox afficit: nam licet acriora sint, quæ legas, ultius tamen in ammo sedent, quæ pronuntiatio, vultus, habitus, gestus dicentis adfigit.

Besides, as is usually the case, we are much more affected by the words which we hear, for though what you read in books may be more pointed, yet there is something in the voice, the look, the carriage, and even the gesture of the speaker, that makes a deeper impression upon the mind.
e.   PLINY the Younger—*Epistolæ.* II. 3.

P.

PATIENCE.

Durum! sed levius fit patientiâ
Quicquid corrigere est nefas.

It is hard! But what can not be removed, becomes lighter through patience.
f.   HORACE—*Carmina.* I. 24. 19.

Æquo animo pœnam, qui meruere, ferant.

Let those who have deserved their punishment, bear it patiently.
g.   OVID—*Amorum.* II. 7. 12.

Sua quisque exempla debet æquo animo pati.

Every one ought to bear patiently the results of his own conduct.
h.   PHÆDRUS—*Fabulæ.* I. 26. 12.

Nihil tam acerbum est in quo non æquus animus solatium inveniat.

There is nothing so disagreeable, that a patient mind can not find some solace for it.
i.   SENECA—*De Animi Tranquilitate.* X.

Furor fit læsa sæpius patientia.

Patience, when too often outraged, is converted into madness.
j.   SYRUS—*Maxims.*

Durate, et vosmet rebus servate secundis.

Persevere and preserve yourselves for better circumstances.
k.   VIRGIL—*Æneid.* I. 207.

Superanda omnis fortuna ferendo est.

Every misfortune is to be subdued by patience.
l   VIRGIL—*Æneid.* V. 710.

PATRIOTISM.

Nihil ex omnibus rebus humanis est præclarius aut præstantius quam de republicâ bene mereri.

Of all human things nothing is more honorable or more excellent than to deserve well of one's country.
m.   CICERO—*Epistolæ.* X. 5.

O fortunata mors quæ, naturæ debita, pro patriâ potissimum redita!

O happy death, which though due to nature is most nobly given for our country.
n.   CICERO—*Philippicæ.* XIV. 12.

Patria est communis omnium parens.

Our country is the common parent of all.
o.   CICERO—*Orationes in Catilinam.* I. 7

Dulce et decorum est pro patriâ mori.

It is sweet and glorious to die for one's country.
p.   HORACE—*Carmina.* III. 2. 13.

Non ille pro caris amicis
Aut patriâ timidus perire.

He dares to die for his country or his friends.
q.   HORACE—*Carmina.* IV. 9. 51.

Amor patriæ ratione valentior.

The love of country is more powerful than reason itself.
r.   OVID—*Epistolæ Ex Ponto.* I. 3. 29.

Nescio quâ natale solum dulcedine captos
Ducit, et immemores non sinit esse sui.

Our native land charms us with inexpressible sweetness, and never allows us to forget that we belong to it.

a.　　Ovid—*Epistolæ Ex Ponto.* I. 3. 35.

Patria est ubicumque vir fortis sedem elegerit.

A brave man's country is wherever he chooses his abode.

b.　　Quintus Curtius Rufus—*De Rebus Gestis Alexandri Magni.* VI. 4. 13.

Præferre patriam liberis regem decet.

A king should prefer his country to his children.

c.　　Seneca—*Troades.* 332.

Servare cives, major est virtus patriæ patri.

To preserve the life of citizens, is the greatest virtue in the father of his country.

d.　　Seneca—*Octavia.* 444.

PEACE.

Cedant arma togæ.

War leads to peace.

e.　　Cicero—*De Officiis.* I. 22.

Mars gravior sub pace latet.

A severe war lurks under the show of peace.

f.　　Claudianus—*De Sexto Consulatu Honorii Augusti Panegyris.* 307

Nec sidera pacem
Semper habent.

Nor is heaven always at peace.

g.　　Claudianus—*De Bello Getico.* LXII.

Sævis inter se convenit ursis.

Savage bears keep at peace with one another.

h.　　Juvenal—*Satiræ.* XV. 164.

Candida pax homines, trux decet ira feras.

Fair peace becomes men; ferocious anger belongs to beasts.

i.　　Ovid—*Ars Amatoria.* III. 502.

Auferre, trucidare, rapere, falsis nominibus imperium, atque, ubi solitudinem faciunt, pacem appellant.

To rob, to ravage, to murder, in their imposing language, are the arts of civil policy. When they have made the world a solitude, they call it peace.

j.　　Tacitus—*Agricola.* XXX.

Miseram pacem vel bello bene mutari.

A peace may be so wretched as not to be ill exchanged for war.

k.　　Tacitus—*Annales.* III. 44.

PERJURY.

Nec jurare time; Veneris perjuria venti
Irrita per terras et freta summa ferunt,
Gratia magna Jovi; vetuit pater ipse valere,
Jurâsset cupide quicquid ineptus amor.

Fear not to swear; the winds carry the perjuries of lovers without effect over land and sea, thanks to Jupiter. The father of the gods himself has denied effect to what foolish lovers in their eagerness have sworn.

l.　　Tibullus—*Carmina.* I. 4. 21.

Perjuria ridet amantium Jupiter et ventos irrita ferre jubet.

At lovers' perjuries Jove laughs and throws them idly to the winds.

m.　　Tibullus—*Carmina.* III. 6. 49.

PHILOSOPHY.

Fuge magna, licet sub paupere tecto
Reges et regum vitâ procurrere amicos.

Avoid greatness; in a cottage there may be more real happiness than kings or their favorites enjoy.

n.　　Horace—*Epistolæ.* I. 10. 32.

Quo me cumque rapit tempestas deferor hospes.

Wherever the storm carries me, I go a willing guest.

o.　　Horace—*Epistolæ.* I. 1. 15.

Injuriarum remedium est oblivio.

The remedy for wrongs is to forget them.

p.　　Syrus—*Maxims.*

Etiam quæ sibi quisque timebat
Unius in miseri exitium conversa tulere.

What each man feared would happen to himself, did not trouble him when he saw that it would ruin another.

q.　　Virgil—*Æneid.* II. 130.

PHYSICIAN.

Medicus nihil aliud est quam animi consolatio.

A physician is nothing but a consoler of the mind.

r.　　Petronius Arbiter—*Satyricon.*

Crudelem medicum intemperans æger facit.

A disorderly patient makes the physician cruel.

s.　　Syrus—*Maxims.*

PLACE.

Mitius exilium faciunt loca.

The place makes the banishment more bearable.

t.　　Ovid—*Epistolæ Ex Ponto.* II. 7. 63.

PLEASURE.

Ludendi etiam est quidam modus retinendus, ut ne nimis omnia profundamus, elatique voluptate in aliquam turpitudinem delabamur.

In our amusements a certain limit is to be placed that we may not devote ourselves to a life of pleasure and thence fall into immorality.

a.   Cicero—*De Officiis.* I. 29.

Voluptas mentis (ut ita dicam) præstringit oculos, nec habet ullum cum virtute commercium.

Pleasure blinds (so to speak) the eyes of the mind, and has no fellowship with virtue.

b.   Cicero—*De Senectute.* XII.

Ficta voluptatis causâ sint proxima veris.

Let the fictitious sources of pleasure be as near as possible to the true.

c.   Horace—*Ars Poetica.* 338.

Sperne voluptates; nocet empta dolore voluptas.

Despise pleasures; pleasure bought by pain is injurious.

d.   Horace—*Epistolæ.* I. 2. 55.

Vivo et regno, simul ista reliqui
Quæ vos ad cœlum effertis rumore secundo.

I live and reign since I have abandoned those pleasures which you by your praises extol to the skies.

e.   Horace—*Epistolæ.* I. 10. 8.

Quantas ipse deus lætos generavit in usûs
Res homini plenâque dedit bona gaudia dextrâ.

How many things God has formed for joyous purposes, and has distributed pleasures with a full right hand.

f.   Silius Italius—*Punica.* XV. 55.

Voluptates commendat rarior usus.

Rare indulgence produces greater pleasure.

g.   Juvenal—*Satiræ.* XI. 208.

Quod licet est ingratum quod non licet acrius urit.

What is lawful is undesirable; what is unlawful is very attractive.

h.   Ovid—*Amorum.* II. 19. 3.

Usque adeo nulli sincera voluptas,
Solicitique aliquid lætis intervenit.

No one possesses unalloyed pleasure; there is some anxiety mingled with the joy.

i.   Ovid—*Metamorphoses.* VII. 453.

Dum licet inter nos igitur lætemur amantes;
Non satis est ullo tempore longus amor.

Let us enjoy pleasure while we can; pleasure is never long enough.

j.   Propertius—*Elegiæ.* I. 19. 25.

Diliguntur immodice sola quæ non licent;
* * * non nutrit ardorem concupiscendi, ubi frui licet.

Forbidden pleasures alone are loved immoderately; when lawful, they do not excite desire.

k.   Quintilian—*Declamationes.*
              XIV. 18.

Prævalent illicita.

Things forbidden have a secret charm.

l.   Tacitus—*Annales.* XIII. 1.

Trahit sua quemque voluptas.

His own especial pleasure attracts each one.

m.   Virgil—*Eclogæ.* II. 65.

POETRY.

Non satis est pulchra esse poemata, dulcia sunto.

It is not enough that poetry is agreeable, it should also be interesting.

n.   Horace—*Ars Poetica.* 99.

Nonumque prematur in annum.

Let your poem be kept nine years.

o.   Horace—*Ars Poetica.* 388.

Versus inopes rerum, nugæque canoræ.

Verses devoid of substance, melodious trifles.

p.   Horace—*Ars Poetica.* CCCXXII.

Facit indignatio versum.

Indignation produces the verse.

q.   Juvenal—*Satiræ.* I. 79.

Musæo contigens cuncta lepore.

Gently touching with the charm of poetry.

r.   Lucretius—*De Rerum Natura.*
              IV. 9.

Verba togæ sequeris, junctura callidus acri,
Ore teres modico, pallentes radere mores
Doctus, et ingenuo culpam defigere ludo.

Confined to common life thy numbers flow,
And neither soar too high nor sink too low;
There strength and ease in graceful union meet,
Though polished, subtle, and though poignant, sweet;
Yet powerful to abash the front of crime
And crimson error's cheek with sportive rhyme.

s.   Persius—*Satiræ.* V. 14. Gifford's
              trans.

Tale tuum carmen nobis, divine poeta,
Quale sopor fessis in gramine.

Thy verses are as pleasing to me, O divine poet, as sleep is to the wearied on the soft turf.

t.   Virgil—*Eclogæ.* V. 45.

POETS.

Adhuc neminem cognovi poetam, qui sibi non optimus videretur.
  I have never yet known a poet who did not think himself super-excellent.
  a.   Cicero—*Tusculanarum Disputationum.*
                                    V. 22.

Aut insanit homo, aut versus facit.
  The man is either mad or he is making verses.
  b.   Horace—*Satiræ.* II. 7. 117.

Disjecti membra poetæ.
  The scattered remnants of the poet.
  c. , Horace—*Satiræ.* I. 4. 62.

Genus irritabile vatum.
  The irritable tribe of poets.
  d.   Horace—*Epistolæ.* II. 2. 102.

                        Mediocribus esse poetis
Non homines, non di, non concessere columnæ.
  Neither men, nor gods, nor booksellers' shelves permit ordinary poets to exist.
  e.   Horace—*Ars Poetica.* 372.

Quod si me lyricis vatibus inseris,
Sublimi feriam sidera vertice.
  If you rank me with the lyric poets, my exalted head shall strike the stars.
  f.   Horace—*Carmina.* I. 1. 35.

Non scribit, cujus carmina nemo legit.
  He does not write whose verses no one reads.
  g.   Martial—*Epigrammata.* III. 9. 2.

                        Carmina lætum
Sunt opus et pacem mentis habere volunt.
  The poet's labors are a work of joy, and require peace of mind.
  h.   Ovid—*Tristium.* V. 12. 4.

POSSESSION.

Non tibi illud apparere si sumas potest.
  If you spend a thing you can not have it.
  i.   Plautus—*Trinummus.* II. 4. 12.

Nihil enim æque gratum est adeptis, quam concupiscentibus.
  An object in possession seldom retains the same charms which it had when it was longed for.
  j.   Pliny the Younger—*Epistolæ.* II. 15.

POVERTY.

Meo sum pauper in ære.
  Tho' poor, I live on my own income.
  k.   Horace—*Epistolæ.* II. 2. 12.

Pauper enim non est cui rerum suppetet usus.
  He is not poor who has the use of necessary things.
  l.   Horace—*Epistolæ.* I. 12. 4.

Cantabit vacuus coram latrone viator.
  The traveler without money will sing before the robber.
  m.   Juvenal—*Satiræ.* X. 22.

Cum furor haud dubius, cum sit manifesta phrenesis
Ut locuples moriaris, egentis vivere fato.
  It is unmistakable madness to live in poverty only to die rich.
  n.   Juvenal—*Satiræ.* XIV. 136.

Haud facile emergunt quorum virtutibus obstat
Res angusta domi.
  They do not easily rise whose abilities are repressed by poverty at home.
  o.   Juvenal—*Satiræ.* III. 164.

Nil habet infelix paupertas durius in se
Quam quod ridiculos homines facit.
  Cheerless poverty has no harder trial than this, that it makes men the subject of ridicule.
  p.   Juvenal—*Satiræ.* III. 152.

Paupertas fugitur, totoque arcessitur orbe.
  Poverty is shunned and persecuted all over the globe.
  q.   Lucan—*Pharsalia.* I. 166.

Non est paupertas, Nestor, habere nihil.
  To have nothing is not poverty.
  r.   Martial—*Epigrammata.* XI. 32. 8.

Inops, potentem dum vult imitari, perit.
  The poor trying to imitate the powerful, perish.
  s.   Phædrus—*Fabulæ.* I. 24. 1.

In principatu commutando civium
Nil præter domini nomen mutant pauperes.
  In a change of government the poor change nothing but the name of their masters.
  t.   Phædrus—*Fabulæ.* I. 15. 1.

Non qui parum habet, sed qui plus cupit, pauper est.
  Not he who has little, but he who wishes for more, is poor.
  u.   Seneca—*Epistolæ Ad Lucilium.* II.

POWER.

Fit in dominatu servitus, in servitute dominatus.
  He is sometimes slave who should be master; and sometimes master who should be slave.
  v.   Cicero—*Oratio Pro Rege Deiotaro.* XI.

Et qui nolunt occidere quemquam
Posse volunt.
  Those who do not wish to kill any one, wish they had the power.
  w.   Juvenal—*Satiræ.* X. 96.

A cane non magno sæpe tenetur aper.

 The wild boar is often held by a small dog.

a. Ovid—*Remedia Amoris.* 422.

Ut desint vires tamen est laudanda voluntas.

 Though the power be wanting, yet the wish is praiseworthy.

b. Ovid—*Epistolæ Ex Ponto.* III. 4. 79.

Minimum decet liberè cui multum licet.

 He who has great power should use it lightly.

c. Seneca—*Troades.* 336.

Quod non potest vult posse, qui nimium potest.

 He who is too powerful, is still aiming at that degree of power which is unattainable.

d. Seneca—*Hippolytus.* 215.

Malè imperando summum imperium amittitur.

 The highest power may be lost by misrule.

e. Syrus—*Maxims.*

Cupido dominandi cunctis affectibus flagrantior est.

 Lust of power is the most flagrant of all the passions.

f. Tacitus—*Annales.* XV. 53.

Imperium cupientibus nihil medium inter summa et præcipitia.

 In the struggle between those seeking power there is no middle course.

g. Tacitus—*Annales.* II. 74.

Imperium flagitio acquisitum nemo unquam bonis artibus exercuit.

 Power acquired by guilt was never used for a good purpose.

h. Tacitus—*Annales.* I. 30.

Potentiam cautis quam acribus consiliis tutius haberi.

 Power is more safely retained by cautious than by severe councils.

i. Tacitus—*Annales.* XI. 29.

Suspectum semper invisumque dominantibus qui proximus destinaretur.

 Rulers always hate and suspect the next in succession.

j. Tacitus—*Annales.* I. 21.

Flectere si nequeo superos, Acheronta movebo.

 If I can not influence the gods, I shall move all hell.

k. Virgil—*Æneid.* VII. 312.

Possunt quia posse videntur.

 They are able because they think they are able.

l. Virgil—*Æneid.* V. 231.

PRAISE.

Trahimur omnes laudis studio, et optimus quisque maxime gloriâ ducitur.

 We are all excited by the love of praise, and the noblest are most influenced by glory.

m. Cicero—*Oratio Pro Licinio Archia.* XI.

Laudator temporis acti.

 A eulogist of past times.

n. Horace—*Ars Poetica.* 173.

Principibus placuisse viris non ultima laus est.

 To please great men is not the last degree of praise.

o. Horace—*Epistolæ.* I. 17. 35.

Id facere laus est quod decet, non quod licet.

 He deserves praise who does not what he may, but what he ought.

p. Seneca—*Octavia.* 454.

PRAYER.

Orandum est ut sit mens sana in corpore sano.

 Our prayers should be for a sound mind in a healthy body.

q. Juvenal—*Satiræ.* X. 356.

In vota miseros ultimus cogit timor.

 Fear of death drives the wretched to prayer.

r. Seneca—*Agamemnon.* 560.

Nulla res carius constat quam quæ precibus empta est.

 Nothing costs so much as what is bought by prayers.

s. Seneca—*De Beneficiis.* II. 1.

PREJUDICE.

Vulgus ex veritate pauca, ex opinione multa æstimat.

 The rabble estimate few things according to their real value, most things according to their prejudices.

t. Cicero—*Oratio Pro Quinto Roscio Comœdo.* X.

PREPARATION.

In omnibus negotiis prius quam aggrediare, adhibenda est præparatio diligens.

 In all matters, before beginning, a diligent preparation should be made.

u. Cicero—*De Officiis.* I. 21.

In pace ut sapiens aptarit idonea bello.

 Like as a wise man in time of peace prepares for war.

v. Horace—*Satiræ.* II. 2. 111.

Sperat infestis, metuit secundis
Alteram sortem, bene preparatum
Pectus.

A well-prepared mind hopes in adversity
and fears in prosperity.

a. HORACE—*Carmina.* II. 10. 13.

PROGRESSION.

Equidem æternâ constitutione crediderim
nexuque causarum latentium et multo ante
destinatarum suum quemque ordinem immu-
tabili lege percurrere.

For my own part I am persuaded that
everything advances by an unchangeable
law through the eternal constitution and
association of latent causes, which have been
long before predestinated.

b. QUINTUS CURTIUS RUFUS—*De Rebus
Gestis Alexandri Magni.* V. 11. 10.

PROOF.

Pluris est oculatus testis unus, quam auriti
decem.
Qui audiunt, audita dicunt; qui vident, plane
sciunt.

One eye-witness is of more weight than
ten hearsays. Those who hear, speak of
what they have heard; those who see, know
beyond mistake.

c. PLAUTUS—*Truculentus.* II. 6. 8.

PROPHECY.

Bene qui conjiciet, vatem hunc perhibebo
optimum.

I shall always consider the best guesser
the best prophet.

d. CICERO—*De Divinatione.* II. 5.

PROSPERITY.

In rebus prosperis, superbiam, fastidium
arrogantiamque magno opere fugiamus.

In prosperity let us most carefully avoid
pride, disdain, and arrogance.

e. CICERO—*De Officiis.* I. 26.

Ut adversas res, secundas immoderate ferre,
levitatis est.

It shows a weak mind not to bear prosperity as well as adversity with moderation.

f. CICERO—*De Officiis.* I. 26.

Res secundæ valent commutare naturam, et
raro quisquam erga bona sua satis cautus est.

Prosperity can change man's nature; and
seldom is any one cautious enough to resist
the effects of good fortune.

g. QUINTUS CURTIUS RUFUS—*De Rebus
Gestis Alexandri Magni.* X. 1. 40.

Felix se nescit amari.

The prosperous man does not know
whether he is loved.

h. LUCAN—*Pharsalia.* VII. 727.

Si numeres anno soles et nubila toto,
Invenies nitidum sæpius isse diem.

If you count the sunny and the cloudy
days of the whole year, you will find that
the sunshine predominates.

i. OVID—*Tristium.* V. 8. 31.

Est felicibus difficilis miseriarum vera
æstimatio.

The prosperous can not easily form a right
idea of misery.

j. QUINTILIAN—*De Institutione Oratoria.*
IX. 6.

Quantum caliginis mentibus nostris objicit
magna felicitas!

How much does great prosperity overspread the mind with darkness.

k. SENECA—*De Brevitate Vitæ.* XIII.

Semel profecto premere felices deus
Cum cœpit, urget; hos habent magna exitus.

When God has once begun to throw down
the prosperous, He overthrows them altogether: such is the end of the mighty.

l. SENECA—*Hercules Œtæus.* 713.

PROVIDENCE.

Deus haec fortasse benignâ
Reducet in sedem vice.

Perhaps Providence by some happy
change will restore these things to their
proper places.

m. HORACE—*Epodi.* XIII. 7.

Deus quædam munera universo humano
generi dedit, a quibus excluditur nemo.

God has given some gifts to the whole
human race, from which no one is excluded.

n. SENECA—*De Beneficiis.* IV. 28.

Nec mirum quod divina natura dedit agros,
ars humana ædificavit urbes.

Now is it surprising, because it is Providence that has given us the country and
the art of man that has built the cities.

o. VARRO—*De Re Rustica.* III. 1.

PRUDENCE.

Multis terribilis, caveto multos.

If thou art terrible to many, then beware
of many.

p. AUSONIUS—*Septem Sapientum Sententiæ
Septenis Versibus Explicatæ.* IV. 5.

Malo indisertam prudentiam, quam loqua-
cem stultitiam.

I prefer silent prudence to loquacious folly.

q. CICERO—*De Oratore.* III. 35.

Non est ab homine nunquam sobrio postulanda prudentia.

Prudence must not be expected from a man who is never sober.

a.   CICERO—*Philippicæ.* II. 32.

Parvi enim sunt foris arma, nisi est consilium domi.

An army abroad is of little use unless there are prudent counsels at home.

b.   CICERO—*De Officiis.* I. 22.

Prudentia est rerum expectandarum fugiendarumque scientia.

Prudence is the knowledge of things to be sought, and those to be shunned.

c.   CICERO—*De Officiis.* I. 43.

Nullum numen habes si sit prudentia.

One has no protecting power save prudence.

d.   JUVENAL—*Satiræ.* X. 365. Also *Satiræ.* XIV. 315.

Crede mihi; miseros prudentia prima relinquit.

Believe me; it is prudence that first forsakes the wretched.

e.   OVID—*Epistolæ Ex Ponto.* IV. 12. 47.

Extrema primo nemo tentavit loco.

No one tries extreme remedies at first.

f.   SENECA—*Agamemnon.* 153.

Consilio melius vinces quam iracundiâ.

You will conquer more surely by prudence than by passion.

g.   SYRUS—*Maxims.*

Deliberandum est diu, quod statuendum semel.

That should be considered long which can be decided but once.

h.   SYRUS—*Maxims.*

Difficilem oportet aurem habere crimina.

One should not lend a ready ear to criminal charges.

i.   SYRUS—*Maxims.*

Plura consilio quam vi perficimus.

We accomplish more by prudence than by force.

j.   TACITUS—*Annales.* II. 26.

Ratio et consilium, propriæ ducis artes.

Forethought and prudence are the proper qualities of a leader.

k.   TACITUS—*Annales.* XIII. 20.

Omnia prius experiri verbis quam armis sapientem decet.

It becomes a wise man to try negotiation before arms.

l.   TERENCE—*Eunuchus.* V. 1. 19.

Ut quimus, aiunt, quando ut volumus, non licet.

As we can, according to the old saying, when we can not, as we would.

m.   TERENCE—*Andria.* IV. 5. 10.

Litus ama: * * * altum alii teneant.

Keep close to the shore: let others venture on the deep.

n.   VIRGIL—*Æneid.* V. 163.

PUNISHMENT.

Cavendum est ne major pœna quam culpa sit; et ne iisdem de causis alii plectantur, alii ne appellentur quidem.

Care should be taken that the punishment does not exceed the guilt; and also that some men do not suffer for offenses for which others are not even indicted.

o.   CICERO—*De Officiis.* I. 23.

Culpam pœna premit comes.

Punishment follows close on crime.

p.   HORACE—*Carmina.* IV. 5. 24.

Ne scuticâ dignum horribili sectere flagello.

Do not pursue with the terrible scourge him who deserves a slight whip.

q.   HORACE—*Satiræ.* I. 3. 119.

Quidquid multis peccatur inultum est.

The sins committed by many pass unpunished.

r.   LUCAN—*Pharsalia.* V. 260.

Estque pati pœnas quam meruisse minus.

It is less to suffer punishment than to deserve it.

s.   OVID—*Epistolæ Ex Ponto.* I. 1. 62.

Si quoties homines peccant sua fulmina mittat
Jupiter, exiguo tempore inermis erit.

If Jupiter hurled his thunderbolt as often as men sinned, he would soon be out of thunderbolts.

t.   OVID—*Tristium.* II. 33.

Deos agere curam rerum humanarum credi, ex usu vitæ est: pœnasque maleficiis, aliquando seras, nunquam autem irritas esse.

It is advantageous that the gods should be believed to attend to the affairs of man; and the punishment for evil deeds, though sometimes late, is never fruitless.

u.   PLINY the Elder—*Historia Naturalis.* II. 5. 10.

Corrigendus est, qui peccet, et admonitione et vi, et molliter et aspere, meliorque tam sibi quam alii faciendus, non sine castigatione, sed sine ira.

He, who has committed a fault, is to be corrected both by advice and by force, kindly and harshly, and to be made better for himself as well as for another, not without chastisement, but without passion.

a. SENECA—*De Ira.* I. 14.

Maxima est factæ injuriæ pæna, fecisse: nec quisquam gravius adficitur, quam qui ad supplicium pœnitentiæ traditur.

The severest punishment a man can receive who has injured another, is to have committed the injury; and no man is more severely punished than he who is subject to the whip of his own repentance.

b. SENECA—*De Ira.* III. 26.

Nec ulla major pœna nequitiæ est, quam quod sibi et suis displicet.

There is no greater punishment of wickedness than that it is dissatisfied with itself and its deeds.

c. SENECA—*Epistolæ Ad Lucilium.* XLII.

Quod antecedit tempus, maxima venturi supplicii pars est.

The time that precedes punishment is the severest part of it.

d. SENECA—*De Beneficiis.* II. 5.

Sequitur superbos ultor a tergo deus.

An avenging God closely follows the haughty.

e. SENECA—*Hercules Furens.* 385.

Habet aliquid ex iniquo omne magnum exemplum, quod contra singulos, utilitate publicâ rependitus.

Every great example of punishment has in it some injustice, but the suffering individual is compensated by the public good.

f. TACITUS—*Annales.* XIV. 44.

Punitis ingeniis, gliscit auctoritas.

When, men of talents are punished, authority is strengthened.

g. TACITUS—*Annales.* IV. 35.

Ah, miser! et si quis primo perjuria celat,
Sera tamen tacitis Pœna venit pedibus.

Ah, wretch! even though one may be able at first to conceal his perjuries, yet punishment creeps on, though late, with noiseless step.

h. TIBULLUS—*Carmina.* I. 9. 3.

R.

RARITY.

Felix ille tamen corvo quoque rarior albo.

A lucky man is rarer than a white crow.

i. JUVENAL—*Satiræ.* VII. 202.

Rara avis in terris.

A rare bird on earth.

j. JUVENAL—*Satiræ.* VI. 165.

RASHNESS.

Audax omnia perpeti
Gens humana ruit per vetitum nefas.

The human race afraid of nothing, rushes on through every crime.

k. HORACE—*Carmina.* I. 3. 25.

Non semper temeritas est felix.

Rashness is not always fortunate.

l. LIVY—*Annales.* XXVIII. 42.

Paucis temeritas est bono, multis malo.

Rashness brings success to few, misfortune to many.

m. PHÆDRUS—*Fabulæ.* V. 4. 12.

47

REASON.

Domina omnium et regina ratio.

Reason is the mistress and queen of all things.

n. CICERO—*Tusculanarum Disputationum.*
II. 21.

Nihil potest esse diuturnum cui non subest ratio.

Nothing can be lasting when reason does not rule.

o. QUINTUS CURTIUS RUFUS—*De Rebus
Gestis Alexandri Magni.*
IV. 14. 19.

Hoc volo, sic jubeo, sit pro ratione voluntas.

I will it, I so order, let my will stand for a reason.

p. JUVENAL—*Satiræ.* VI. 223.

Quid nobis certius ipsis
Sensibus esse potest? quî vera ac falso notemus.

What can give us more sure knowledge than our senses? How else can we distinguish between the true and the false?

q. LUCRETIUS—*De Rerum Natura.*
I. 700.

Nam et Socrati objiciunt comici, docere eum quomodo pejorem causam meliorem faciat.

For comic writers charge Socrates with making the worse appear the better reason.

a.   Quintilian—*De Institutione Oratoria.*
II. 17. 1.

REBELLION.

Seditiosissimus quisque ignavus.

The most seditious is the most cowardly.

b.   Tacitus—*Annales.* IV. 34.

      Sævitque animis ignobile vulgus,
Jamque faces et saxa volant.

The rude rabble are enraged; now fire-brands and stones fly.

c.   Virgil—*Æneid.* I. 149.

RELIGION.

Deos placatos pietas efficiet et sanctitas.

Piety and holiness of life will propitiate the gods.

d.   Cicero—*De Officiis.* II. 3.

Res sacros non modo manibus attingi, sed ne cogitatione quidem violari fas fuit.

Things sacred should not only not be touched with the hands, but not violated in thought.

e.   Cicero—*Orationes in Verrem.* II.
4. 45.

Nihil enim in speciem fallacius est quam prava religio.

Nothing is more deceitful in appearance than false religion.

f.   Livy—*Annales.* XXXIX. 16.

Tantum religio potuit suadere malorum!

How many evils has religion caused!

g.   Lucretius—*De Rerum Natura.* I. 102.

Scilicet adversis probitas exercita rebus
Tristi materiam tempore laudis habet.

Righteousness tried by adversity has good grounds for glorying in its sorrow.

h.   Ovid—*Tristium.* V. 5. 49.

Animus hoc habet argumentum divinitatis suæ, quod illum divina delectant.

The soul has this proof of its divinity: that divine things delight it.

i.   Seneca—*Quæstionum Naturalium.*
Præfet ad 1 lib.

REPENTANCE.

Nam sera nunquam est ad bonos mores via.
Quem pœnitet peccasse, pæne est innocens.

It is never too late to turn from the errors of our ways:
He who repents of his sins is almost innocent.

j.   Seneca—*Agamemnon.* 242.

Nec unquam primi consilii deos pœnitet.

God never repents of what He has first resolved upon.

k.   Seneca—*De Beneficiis.* VI. 23.

Cave ne quidquam incipias, quod post pœniteat.

Take care not to begin anything of which you may repent.

l.   Syrus—*Maxims.*

Velox consilium sequitur pœnitentiâ.

Repentance follows hasty counsels.

m.   Syrus—*Maxims.*

RESIGNATION.

Omnem crede diem tibi diluxisse supremum.

Believe that each day which shines upon you is the last.

n.   Horace—*Epistolæ.* I. 4. 13.

Summam nec metuas diem, nec optes.

You should neither fear nor wish for your last day.

o.   Martial—*Epigrammata.* X. 47. 13.

Placato possum non miser esse deo.

If God be appeased, I can not be wretched.

p.   Ovid—*Tristium.* III. 40.

Placeat homini quidquid deo placuit.

Let that please man which has pleased God.

q.   Seneca—*Epistolæ Ad Lucilium.*
LXXIV.

Unum est levamentum malorum pati et necessitatibus suis obsequi.

One alleviation in misfortune is to endure and submit to necessity.

r.   Seneca—*De Ira.* III. 16.

Vitæ est avidus quisquis non vult
Mundo secum pereunte mori.

He is greedy of life who is not willing to die when the world is perishing around him.

s.   Seneca—*Thyestes.* 882.

Quoniam id fieri quod vis non potest
Id velis quod possis.

As you can not do what you wish, you should wish what you can do.

t.   Terence—*Andria.* II. 1. 6.

RESISTANCE.

Cum tempus necessitasque postulat, decertandum manu est, et mors servituti turpidinique antiponenda.

When time and need require, we should resist with all our might, and prefer death to slavery and disgrace.

u.   Cicero—*De Officiis.* I. 23.

RESPONSIBILITY.

Culpam majorum posteri luunt.

Posterity pays for the sins of their fathers.
a. Quintus Curtius Rufus—*De Rebus
Gestis Alexandri Magni*. VII. 5.

REST.

O! quid solutis est beatius curis!
Cum mens onus reponit, ac peregrino
Labore fessi venimus larem ad nostrum
Desideratoque acquiescimus lecto.
Hoc est, quod unum est pro laboribus tantis.

O, what is more sweet than when the
mind, set free from care, lays its burden
down; and, when spent with distant travel,
we come back to our home, and rest our
limbs on the wished-for bed? This, this
alone, repays such toils as these!
b. Catullus—*Carmina*. 31. 7.

Homines quamvis in turbidis rebus sint,
tamen, si modo homines sunt, interdum
animis relaxantur.

Men, in whatever anxiety they may be,
if they are men, sometimes indulge in
relaxation.
c. Cicero—*Philippicæ*. II. 15.

Da requiem; requietus ager bene credita
reddit.

Take rest; a field that has rested gives a
bountiful crop.
d Ovid—*Ars Amatoria*. II. 351.

Detur aliquando otium
Quiesque fessis.

Let the weary at length possess quiet rest.
e. Seneca—*Hercules Furens*. 927.

Arcum intensio frangit, animum remissio.

Straining breaks the bow, and relaxation
relieves the mind.
f. Syrus—*Maxims*.

Et "Bene," discedens dicet, "placideque
quiescas;
Terraque securæ sit super ossa levis."

And at departure he will say, "Mayest
thou rest soundly and quietly, and may
the light turf lie easy on thy bones."
g. Tibullus—*Carmina*. II. 4. 49.

Deus nobis hæc otia fecit.

God has given us this repose.
h. Virgil—*Eclogæ*. 1. 6.

REVENGE.

At vindicta bonum vita jucundius ipsa
nempe hoc indocti.

Revenge is sweeter than life itself. So
think fools.
i. Juvenal—*Satiræ*. XIII. 180.

Minuti
Semper et infirmi est animi exiguique voluptas
Ultio.

Revenge is always the weak pleasure of
a little and narrow mind.
j. Juvenal—*Satiræ*. XIII. 189.

Sæpe intereunt aliis meditantes necem.

Those who plot the destruction of others
often fall themselves.
k. Phædrus—*Fabulæ*. Appendix.
VI. 11.

Inhumanum verbum est ultio.

Revenge is an inhuman word.
l. Seneca—*De Ira*. II. 31.

Malevolus animus abditos dentes habet.

The malevolent have hidden teeth.
m. Syrus—*Maxims*.

Odia in longum jaciens, quæ reconderet,
auctaque promeret.

Laying aside his resentment, he stores it
up to bring it forward with increased bitterness.
n. Tacitus—*Annales*. I. 69.

RICHES.

Crescentem sequitur cura pecuniam
Majorumque fames.

Increasing wealth is attended by care and
by the desire of greater increase.
o. Horace—*Carmina*. III. 16. 17.

Et genus et virtus, nisi cum re, vilior algâ est.

Noble descent and worth, unless united
with wealth, are esteemed no more than
seaweed.
p. Horace—*Satiræ*. II. 5. 8.

Imperat aut servit collecta pecunia cuique.

Riches either serve or govern the possessor.
q. Horace—*Epistolæ*. I. 10. 47.

Omnis enim res,
Virtus, fama, decus, divina, humanaque
pulchris
Divitiis parent.

For everything divine and human, virtue,
fame, and honor, now obey the alluring influence of riches.
r. Horace—*Satiræ*. II. 3. 94.

Dives fieri qui vult
Et cito vult fieri.

He who wishes to become rich wishes to
become so immediately.
s. Juvenal—*Satiræ*. XIV. 176.

Misera est magni custodia census.

The care of a large estate is an unpleasant
thing.
t. Juvenal—*Satiræ*. XIV. 304.

Rarus enim ferme sensus communis in illâ
Fortunâ.

Common sense among men of fortune is rare.

a. Juvenal—*Satiræ.* VIII. 73.

Facile est momento quo quis velit, cedere
possessione magnæ fortunæ; facere et parare
eam, difficile atque arduum est.

It is easy at any moment to resign the
possession of a great fortune; to acquire it
is difficult and arduous.

b. Livy—*Annales.* XXIV. 22.

Opum furiata cupido.

The ungovernable passion for wealth.

c. Ovid—*Fasti.* I. 211.

Opes invisæ merito sunt forti viro,
Quia dives arca veram laudem intercipit.

Riches are deservedly despised by a man
of honor, because a well-stored chest intercepts the truth.

d. Phædrus—*Fabulæ.* IV. 12. 1.

Repente dives nemo factus est bonus.

No good man ever became suddenly rich.

e. Syrus—*Maxims.*

RIDICULE.

Ridiculum acri
Fortius et melius magnas plerumque secat res.

Ridicule often cuts the Gordian knot
more effectively than the severity of satire.

f. Horace—*Satiræ.* I. 10. 14.

RIGHT.

Mensuraque juris
Vis erat.

Might was the measure of right.

g. Lucan—*Pharsalia.* I. 175.

RIVER.

Viam qui nescit quâ deveniat ad mare
Eum oportet amnem quærere comitem sibi.

He who does not know his way to the
sea should take a river for his guide.

h. Plautus—*Pœnulus.* III. 3. 14.

ROYALTY.

An nescis longos regibus esse manus?

Knowest thou not that kings have long
hands?

i. Ovid—*Heroides.* XVII. 166.

Est aliquid validâ sceptra tenere manu.

It is something to hold the scepter with a
firm hand.

j. Ovid—*Remedia Amoris.* 480.

Ars prima regni posse te invidiam pati.

The first art to be learned by a ruler is to
endure envy.

k. Seneca—*Hercules Furens.* 353.

Omne sub regno graviore regnum est.

Every monarch is subject to a mightier
one.

l. Seneca—*Hercules Furens.* 614.

RUMOR.

Vana quoque ad veros accessit fama timores.

Idle rumors were also added to well-
founded apprehensions.

m. Lucan—*Pharsalia.* I. 469.

Hi narrata ferunt alio; mensuraque ficti
Crescit et auditus aliquid novus adjicit auctor.

Some report elsewhere whatever is told
them; the measure of fiction always increases, and each fresh narrator adds something to what he has heard.

n. Ovid—*Metamorphoses.* XII. 57.

Nam inimici famam non ita ut nata est ferunt.

Enemies carry a report in form different
from the original.

o. Plautus—*Persa.* III. 1. 23.

Ad calamitatem quilibet rumor valet.

Every rumor is believed against the unfortunate.

p. Syrus—*Maxims.*

Haud semper erret fama; aliquando et
elegit.

Rumor does not always err; it sometimes
even elects a man.

q. Tacitus—*Agricola.* IX.

Extemplo Libyæ magnas it Fama per urbes:
Fama malum quo non velocius ullum;
Mobilitate viget, viresque acquirit eundo;
Parva metu primo; mox sese attollit in auras,
Ingrediturque solo, et caput inter nubilia
    condit.

*   *   *   *   *   *

Monstrum, horrendum ingens; cui quot sunt
    corpore plumæ
Tot vigiles oculi subter, mirabile dictu,
Tot linguæ, totidem ora sonant, tot subrigit
    aures.

Straightway throughout the Libyan cities
flies rumor;—the report of evil things than
which nothing is swifter; it flourishes by
its very activity and gains new strength by
its movements; small at first through fear,
it soon raises itself aloft and sweeps onward
along the earth. Yet its head reaches the
clouds. * * * A huge and horrid monster
covered with many feathers: and for every
plume a sharp eye, for every pinion a biting
tongue. Everywhere its voices sound, to
everything its ears are open.

r. Virgil—*Æneid.* IV. 173.

S.

SAFETY.

Salus populi suprema lex.
 The safety of the State is the highest law.
 a. JUSTINIAN—*Twelve Tables.*

Erubuit: salva res est.
 He blushes: all is safe.
 b. TERENCE—*Adelphi.* IV. 5. 9.

SATIETY.

Omnibus in rebus voluptatibus maximis
fastidium finitimum est.
 In everything satiety closely follows the
greatest pleasures.
 c. CICERO—*De Oratore.* III. 25.

Continuis voluptatibus vicina satietas.
 Satiety is a neighbor to continued pleasures.
 d. QUINTILIAN—*Declamationes.*
          XXX. 6.

     Nam id arbitror
Adprime in vitâ esse utile ut ne quid nimis.
 I hold this to be the rule of life, "Too
much of anything is bad."
 e. TERENCE—*Andria.* I. 1. 33.

SATIRE.

Difficile est satiram non scribere.
 It is difficult not to write satire.
 f. JUVENAL—*Satiræ.* I. 29.

SATISFACTION.

Ohe! jam satis est.
 Now, that's enough.
  HORACE—*Epistolæ.* I. 5. 12.
 g. Also MARTIAL—*Epigrammata.* IV.
          91. 1.
Sed tacitus pasci si posset corvus, haberet
Plus dapis, et rixæ multo minus invidiæque.
 If the crow had been satisfied to eat his
prey in silence, he would have had more
meat and less quarreling and envy.
 h. HORACE—*Epistolæ.* I. 17. 50.

Nullius boni sine sociis jucunda possessio est.
 There is no satisfaction in any good without a companion.
 i. SENECA—*Epistolæ Ad Lucilium.* VI.

SEA (THE).

Mare quidem commune certe est omnibus.
 The sea is certainly common to all.
 j. PLAUTUS—*Rudens.* IV. 3. 36.

Rari nantes in gurgite vasto.
 A few swimming in the vast deep.
 k. VIRGIL—*Æneid.* I. 118.

SECRECY.

Occultæ inimicitiæ magis timendæ sunt
quam aperatæ.
 Secret enmities are more to be feared than
open ones.
 l. CICERO—*Orationes in Verrem.* II. 5.
          71.

Arcanum neque tu scrutaveris ullius unquam, commissumve teges et vino tortus et irâ.
 Never inquire into another man's secret;
but conceal that which is intrusted to you,
though pressed both by wine and anger to
reveal it.
 m. HORACE—*Epistolæ.* I. 18. 37.

Vitæ postscenia celant.
 Men conceal the past scenes of their lives.
 n. LUCRETIUS—*De Rerum Natura.* IV.
          1,182.
Alium silere quod voles, primus sile.
 If you wish another to keep your secret,
first keep it yourself.
 o. SENECA—*Hippolytus.* 876.

Latere semper patere, quod latuit diu.
 Leave in concealment what has long been
concealed.
 p. SENECA—*Œdipus.* 826.

Miserum est tacere cogi, quod cupias loqui.
 You are in a pitiable condition when you
have to conceal what you wish to tell.
 q. SYRUS—*Maxims.*

Tacitum vivit sub pectore vulnus.
 The secret wound still lives within the
breast.
 r. VIRGIL—*Æneid.* IV. 67.

SELFISHNESS.

Esto, ut nunc multi, dives tibi pauper
amicis.
 Be, as many now are, luxurious to yourself, parsimonious to your friends.
 s. JUVENAL—*Satiræ.* V. 113.

Hac re videre nostra mala non possumus;
Alii simul delinquunt, censores sumus.
 Hence we can not see our own faults; when
others transgress, we become censors.
 t. PHÆDRUS—*Fabulæ.* IV. 10. 4.

Omnes sibi malle melius esse quam alteri.

    Each one wishes for his own advantage, rather than that of others.

a.   TERENCE—*Andria.* II. 5. 16.

SERENITY.

In animi securitate vitam beatam ponimus.

    We think a happy life consists in tranquility of mind.

b.   CICERO—*De Natura Deorum.* I. 20.

Cur in theatrum, Cato, severe, venisti?

    Why, Cato, do you enter the theater with such a look of severity?

c.   MARTIAL—*Epigrammata.* I. 1. 3.

Altissima quæque flumina minimo sono labuntur.

    Still waters run deep.

d.   QUINTUS CURTIUS RUFUS—*De Rebus Gestis Alexandri Magni.* VII. 4. 13.

SHAME.

Male parta, male dilabuntur.

    What is dishonorably got, is dishonorably squandered.

e.   CICERO—*Philippicæ.* II. 27.

Negligere quid de se quisque sentiat, non solum arrogantis est, sed etiam omnino dissoluti.

    To disregard what the world thinks of us is not only arrogant but utterly shameless.

f.   CICERO—*De Officiis.* I. 28.

                 Omnia Græcè !
Cum sit turpe magis nostris nescire Latinè.

    Everything is Greek, when it is more shameful to be ignorant of Latin.

g.   JUVENAL—*Satiræ.* VI. 187.

Næ simul pudere quod non oportet cœperit; quod oportet non pudebit.

    As soon as she (woman) begins to be ashamed of what she ought not, she will not be ashamed of what she ought.

h.   LIVY—*Annales.* XXXIV. 4.

Pessimus quidem pudor vel est parsimoniæ vel frugalitatis.

    The worst kind of shame is being ashamed of frugality or poverty.

i.   LIVY—*Annales.* XXXIV. 4.

             Pudet hæc opprobria nobis
Et dici potuisse et non potuisse repelli.

    I am not ashamed that these reproaches can be cast upon us, and that they can not be repelled.

j.   OVID—*Metamorphoses.* I. 758.

Nam ego illum periisse duco, cui quidem periit pudor.

    I count him lost, who is lost to shame.

k.   PLAUTUS—*Bacchides.* III. 3. 80.

Domini pudet non servitutis.

    I am ashamed of my master and not of my servitude.

l.   SENECA—*Troades.* 989.

SILENCE.

Est et fideli tuta silentio merces.

    There is likewise a reward for faithful silence.

m.   HORACE—*Carmina.* III. 2. 25.

Rarus sermo illis et magna libido tacendi.

    Their conversation was brief, and their desire was to be silent.

n.   JUVENAL—*Satiræ.* II. 14.

Exigua est virtus, præstare silentia rebus ;
Et contra gravis est culpa, tacenda loqui.

    To be silent is but a small virtue; but it is a serious fault to reveal secrets.

o.   OVID—*Ars Amatoria.* II. 603.

Tacere multis discitur vitæ malis.

    Silence is learned by the many misfortunes of life.

p.   SENECA—*Thyestes.* 319.

SIN.

Cui peccare licet peccat minus. Ipsa potestas Semina nequitiæ languidiora facit.

    He who has it in his power to commit sin, is less inclined to do so. The very idea of being able, weakens the desire.

q.   OVID—*Amorum.* III. 4. 9.

Palam mutire plebeio piaculum est.

    It is a sin for a plebeian to grumble in public.

r.   PHÆDRUS—*Fabulæ.* III. *Epilogue.* 34.

Homines qui gestant, quique auscultant crimina,
Si meo arbitratu liceat, omnes pendeant,
Gestores linguis, auditores auribus.

    Your tittle-tattlers, and those who listen to slander, by my good will should all be hanged—the former by their tongues, the latter by the ears.

s.   PLAUTUS—*Pseudolus.* I. 5. 12.

Aliena vitia in oculis habemus; a tergo nostra sunt.

    Other men's sins are before our eyes; our own behind our backs.

t.   SENECA—*De Ira.* II. 28.

Magna pars hominum est, quæ non peccatis irascitur sed peccantibus.

The greater part of mankind are angry with the sinner and not with the sin.

a.   SENECA—*De Ira.* II. 28.

Omnes mali sumus. Quidquid itaque in alio reprehenditur, id unusquisque in suo sinu inveniet.

We are all sinful. Therefore whatever we blame in another we shall find in our own bosoms.

b.   SENECA—*De Ira.* III. 26.

Nec tibi celandi spes sit peccare paranti;
Est deus, occultos spes qui vetat esse dolos.

When thou art preparing to commit a sin, think not that thou wilt conceal it; there is a God that forbids crimes to be hidden.

c.   TIBULLUS—*Carmina.* I. 9. 23.

SLAVERY.

Nimia libertas et populis et privatis in nimiam servitutem cadit.

Excessive liberty leads both nations and individuals into excessive slavery.

d.   CICERO—*De Republica.* I. 44.

Nemo liber est, qui corpóri servit.

No man is free who is a slave to the flesh.

e.   SENECA—*Epistolæ Ad Lucilium.* XCII.

SLEEP.

Et idem
Indignor quandoque bonus dormitat Homerus;
Verum opere longo fas est obrepere somnum.

I, too, am indignant when the worthy Homer nods; yet in a long work it is allowable for sleep to creep over the writer.

f.   HORACE—*Ars Poetica.* 358.

Alliciunt somnos tempus motusque merumque.

Time, motion and wine cause sleep.

g.   OVID—*Fasti.* VI. 681.

SORROW.

Stultum est in luctu capillum sibi evellere, quasi calvitio mæror levaretur.

It is foolish to pluck out one's hair for sorrow, as if grief could be assuaged by baldness.

h.   CICERO—*Tusculanarum Disputationum.*
III. 26.

Oderunt hilarem tristes tristemque jocosi.

The sorrowful dislike the gay, and the gay the sorrowful.

i.   HORACE—*Epistolæ.* I. 18. 89.

Nulla dies mærore caret.

There is no day without sorrow.

j.   SENECA—*Troades.* 77.

SOUL (THE).

Imago animi vultus est, indices oculi.

The countenance is the portrait of the soul, and the eyes mark its intentions.

k.   CICERO—*De Oratore.* III. 59.

Ignoratur enim, quæ sit natura animai;
Nata sit, an contra nascentibus insinuetur;
Et simul intereat nobiscum, morte diremta,
An tenebras Orci visat, vastasque lacunas:
An pecudes alias divinitus insinuet se.

For it is unknown what is the real nature of the soul, whether it be born with the bodily frame or be infused at the moment of birth, whether it perishes along with us, when death separates the soul and body, or whether it visits the shades of Pluto and bottomless pits, or enters by divine appointment into other animals.

l.   LUCRETIUS—*De Rerum Natura.* I. 113.

Deus est in pectore nostro.

There is a divinity within our breast.

m.   OVID—*Epistolæ Ex Ponto.* III. 4. 93.

Est deus in nobis, et sunt commercia cœli.
Sedibus ætheriis spiritus ille venit.

There is a god within us, and we have intercourse with heaven. That spirit comes from abodes on high.

n.   OVID—*Ars Amatoria.* III. 549.

SPEECH.

Brevis esse laboro, obscurus fio.

In laboring to be concise, I become obscure.

o.   HORACE—*Ars Poetica.* XXV.

Lingua mali pars pessima servi.

The tongue is the vile slave's vilest part.

p.   JUVENAL—*Satiræ.* IX. 120.

Sæpe tacens vocem verbaque vultus habet.

The silent countenance often speaks.

q.   OVID—*Ars Amatoria.* I. 574.

Odiosa est oratio, cum rem agas, longinquum loqui.

It is a tiresome way of speaking, when you should despatch the business, to beat about the bush.

r.   PLAUTUS—*Mercator.* III. 4. 23.

Sermoni huic obsonas.

You drown him by your talk.

s.   PLAUTUS—*Pseudolus.* I. 2. 74.

De mortuis nil nisi bonum.

Concerning the dead nothing but good shall be spoken.

t.   *Translated from* PLUTARCH—*Life of Solon.*

Absenti nemo ne nocuisse velit.

Let no one be willing to speak ill of the absent.

u.   PROPERTIUS—*Elegiæ.* II. 19. 32.

Deus ille princeps, parens rerum fabrica-
torque mundi, nullo magis hominem separavit
a ceteris, quæ quidem mortalia sunt, animalibus, quam dicendi facultate.

God, that all-powerful Creator of nature
and Architect of the world, has impressed
man with no character so proper to dis-
guish him from other animals, as by the
faculty of speech.

a. QUINTILIAN—*De Institutione Oratoria.*
II. 17. 2.

Talis hominibus est oratio qualis vita.

Men's conversation is like their life.

b. SENECA—*Epistolæ Ad Lucilium.* 114.

Sæpius locutum, nunquam me tacuisse
pœnitet.

I have often regretted having spoken,
never having kept silent.

c. SYRUS—*Maxims.*

Sermo animi est imago; qualis vir, talis et
oratio est.

Conversation is the image of the mind; as
the man, so is his speech.

d. SYRUS—*Maxims.*

Nullum est jam dictum quod non dictum sit
prius.

Nothing is said nowadays that has not
been said before.

e. TERENCE—*Eunuchus. Prologue.* XLI.

Vox faucibus hæsit.

My voice stuck in my throat.

f. VIRGIL—*Æneid.* II. 774. III. 48.
IV. 280.

STUDY.

Hæc studia adolescentiam alunt, senectutem oblectant, secundas res ornant, adversis
solatium et perfugium præbent, delectant
domi, non impediunt foris, pernoctant nobiscum, peregrinantur, rusticantur.

These (literary) studies are the food of
youth, and consolation of age; they adorn
prosperity, and are the comfort and refuge
of adversity; they are pleasant at home,
and are no incumbrance abroad; they accompany us at night, in our travels, and in
our rural retreats.

g. CICERO—*Oratio Pro Licinio Archia.*
VII.

SUCCESS.

Tametsi prosperitas simul utilitasque con-
sultorum non obique concordent, quoniam
captorum eventus superæ sibi vindicant
potestates.

Yet the success of plans and the advantage to be derived from them do not at all
times agree, seeing the gods claim to themselves the right to decide as to the final result.

h. AMMIANUS MARCELLINUS—*Annales.*
XXV. 3.

Omne tulit punctum qui miscuit utile dulci.

He has carried every point, who has mingled the useful with the agreeable.

i. HORACE—*Ars Poetica.* 343.

Quid te exempta juvat spinis è pluribus una.

What does it avail you, if of many thorns
only one be removed ?

j. HORACE—*Epistolæ.* II. 2. 212.

Successus improborum plures allicit.

The success of the wicked entices many
more.

k. PHÆDRUS—*Fabulæ.* II. 3. 7.

Plus potest qui plus valet.

The stronger always succeeds. (The weakest goes to the wall.)

l. PLAUTUS—*Truculentus.* IV. 3. 30.

Sperat quidem animus: quo eveniat, diis in
manu est.

The mind is hopeful; success is in God's
hands. (Man proposes, God disposes.)

m. PLAUTUS—*Bacchides.* I. 2. 36,

Honesta quædam scelera successus facit.

Success makes some crimes honorable.

n. SENECA—*Hippolytus.* 598.

Deos fortioribus adesse.

The gods are on the side of the stronger.

o. TACITUS—*Annales.* IV. 17.

SUFFERING.

Leniter ex merito quidquid patiare ferendum
est,
Quæ venit indigne pœna dolenda venit.

What is deservedly suffered must be
borne with calmness, but when the pain is
unmerited, the grief is resistless.

p. OVID—*Heriodes.* V. 7.

Levia perpessi sumus
Si flenda patimur.

We have suffered lightly, if we have suffered what we should weep for.

q. SENECA—*Agamemnon.* 665.

SUFFRAGE.

Nam ego in istâ sum sententiâ, quâ te fuisse
semper scio, nihil ut fuerit in suffragiis voce
melius.

I am of the opinion which you have always held, that "viva voce" voting at elections is the best method.

r. CICERO—*De Legibus.* III. 15.

Non ego ventosæ plebis suffragia venor.

I court not the votes of the fickle mob.

s. HORACE—*Epistolæ.* I. 19. 37.

SUPERFLUITY.

Omne supervacuum pleno de pectore manat.
  Everything that is superfluous overflows
  from the full bosom.
a.   HORACE—*Ars Poetica.* 337.

SUPERSTITION.

Accedit etiam mors, quæ quasi saxum
Tantalo semper impendit : tum superstitio,
quâ qui est imbutus quietus esse numquam
potest.
  Death approaches, which is always impending like the stone over Tantalus : then
  comes superstition with which he who is
  imbued can never have peace of mind.
b.   CICERO—*De Finibus Bonorum et*
Malorum. I. 8.

Superstitio, in quâ inest inanis timor
Dei ; religio, quæ dei pio cultu continetur.
  There is in superstition a senseless fear of
  God ; religion consists in the pious worship
  of Him.
c.   CICERO—*De Natura Deorum.* I. 42.

Superstitione tollendâ religio non tollitur.
  Religion is not removed by removing
  superstition.
d.   CICERO—*De Divinatione.* II. 72.

Minimis etiam rebus prava religio inserit
deos.
  A foolish superstition introduces the influences of the gods even in the smallest
  matters.
e.   LIVY—*Annales.* XXVII. 23.

SUSPICION.

Cautus enim metuit foveam lupus, accipiter-
que
Suspectos laqueos, et opertum milvius hamum.
  The wolf dreads the pitfall, the hawk suspects the snare, and the kite the covered
  hook.
f.   HORACE—*Epistolæ.* I. 16. 50.

Ad tristem partem strenua est suspicio.
  The losing side is full of suspicion.
g.   SYRUS—*Maxims.*

Omnes quibus res sunt minus secundæ magis
  sunt, nescio quomodo,
Suspiciosi ; ad contumeliam omnia accipiunt
  magis ;
Propter suam impotentiam se credunt negligi.
  All persons as they become less prosperous, are the more suspicious. They take
  everything as an affront; and from their
  conscious weakness, presume that they are
  neglected.
h.   TERENCE—*Adelphi.* IV. 3. 14.

SWEARING.

Juravi linguâ, mentem injuratam gero.
  I have sworn with my tongue, but my
  mind is unsworn.
i.   CICERO—*De Officiis.* III. 29.

In totum jurare, nisi ubi necesse est, gravi
viro parum convenit.
  To swear, except when necessary, is unbe-
  coming to an honorable man.
j.   QUINTILIAN—*De Institutione Oratoria.*
IX. 2.

T.

TALENTS.

Magni est ingenii revocare mentem a sensibus, et cogitationem a consuetudine abdu-
cere.
  It is a proof of great talents to recall the
  mind from the senses, and to separate
  thought from habit.
k.   CICERO—*Tusculanarum Disputationum.*
I. 16.

TEARS.

Hinc illæ lacrymæ.
  Hence these tears.
     HORACE—*Epistolæ.* I. 19. 41.
l.   TERENCE—*Andria.* I. 1. 99.

Est quædam flere voluptas ;
Expletur lacrymis egeriturque dolor.
  It is some relief to weep; grief is satisfied
  and carried off by tears.
m.   OVID—*Tristium.* IV. 3. 37.

Interdum lacrymæ pondera vocis habent.
  Tears are sometimes as weighty as words.
n.   OVID—*Epistolæ Ex Ponto.* III. 1. 158.

Sunt lacrymæ rerum et mentem mortalia
tangunt.
  Tears are due to human misery, and human sufferings touch the mind.
o.   VIRGIL—*Æneid.* I. 462.

THIRST.

Est in aquâ dulci non invidiosa voluptas.
  There is no small pleasure in pure water.
p.   OVID—*Epistolæ Ex Ponto.* II. 7. 73.
Miserum est opus,
Igitur demum fodere puteum, ubi sitis fauces
tedet.
  It is wretched business to be digging a
  well just as thirst is mastering you.
q.   PLAUTUS—*Mostellaria.* 11. 1. 32.

TIME.

Opinionum enim commenta delet dies; naturæ judicia confirmat.

   Time destroys the groundless conceits of men; it confirms decisions founded on reality.
a.   Cicero—*De Natura Deorum.* II. 2.

O tempora! O mores!

   O what times are these! what morals!
b.   Cicero—*Orationes In Catilinam.* I. 2.

Damnosa quid non imminuit dies?

   What does not destructive time destroy?
c.   Horace—*Carmina.* III. 6. 45.

Eheu! fugaces labuntur anni.

   Alas! the fleeting years are passing away.
d.   Horace—*Carmina.* II. 14. 1.

Quidquid sub terrâ est, in apricum proferet
       ætas;
Defodiet condetque nitentia.

   Time will bring to light whatever is hidden; it will cover up and conceal what is now shining in splendor.
e.   Horace—*Epistolæ.* I. 6. 24.

Singula de nobis anni prædantur euntes.

   Each passing year robs us of some possession.
f.   Horace—*Epistolæ.* II. 2. 55.

Truditur dies die.

   One day is pressed on by another.
g.   Horace—*Carmina.* II. 18. 15.

Æquo stat fœdare tempus.

   Time stands with impartial law.
h.   Manilius—*Astronomica.* III. 360.

Volat hora per orbem.

   The hours fly along in a circle.
i.   Manilius—*Astronomica.* 1. 641.

                   Caducis
Percussu crebro saxa cavantur aquis.

   Stones are hollowed out by the constant dropping of water.
j.   Ovid—*Epistolæ Ex Ponto.* II. 7. 39.

Labitur occulte, fallitque volubilis ætas,
Ut celer admissis labitur amnis aquis.

   Time steals on and escapes us, like the swift river that glides on with rapid stream.
k.   Ovid—*Amorum.* I. 8. 49.

Temporis ars medicina fere est.

   Time is generally the best medicine.
l.   Ovid—*Remedia Amoris.* 131.

Tempus edax rerum.

   Time that devours all things.
m.   Ovid—*Metamorphoses.* XV. 234.

Utendum est ætate; cito pede labitur ætas.

   We must improve our time; time goes with rapid foot.
n.   Ovid—*Ars Amatoria.* III. 65.

Longissimus dies cito conditur.

   The longest day soon comes to an end.
o.   Pliny the Younger—*Epistolæ.* IX.
                                  36.

Tanto brevius omne, quanto felicius tempus.

   The happier the time, the quicker it passes.
p.   Pliny the Younger—*Epistolæ.*
                                VII. 14.

Infinita est velocitas temporis quæ magis apparet respicientibus.

   The swiftness of time is infinite, which is still more evident to those who look back upon the past.
q.   Seneca—*Epistolæ Ad Lucilium.* XLIX.

Maximum remedium iræ mora est.

   Time is the greatest remedy for anger.
r.   Seneca—*De Ira.* II. 29.

Nemo tam divos habuit faventes,
Crastinum ut possit sibi polliceri.

   Nobody has ever found the gods so much his friends that he can promise himself another day.
s.   Seneca—*Thyestes.* 619.

Nullum ad nocendum tempus angustum est malis.

   No time is too short for the wicked to injure their neighbors.
t.   Seneca—*Medea.* 292.

Volat ambiguis
Mobilis alis hora.

   The swift hour flies on double wings.
u.   Seneca—*Hippolytus.* 1141.

Per varios præceps casus rota volvitur ævi.

   The wheel of time rolls downward through various changes.
v.   Silius Italicus—*Punica.* VI. 121.

Fugit irreparabile tempus.

   The irreclaimable time flies.
w.   Virgil—*Georgica.* III. 284.

TRAVELLING.

Cœlum, non animum mutant, qui trans mare
      currunt.
Strenua nos exercet inertia, navibus atque
Quadrigis petimus bene vivere; quod petis
      hic est.

   They change their sky not their mind who cross the sea. A busy idleness possesses us: we seek a happy life, with ships and carriages: the object of our search is present with us.
x.   Horace—*Epistolæ.* I. 11. 27.

TREASON.

Nemo unquam sapiens proditori credendum putavit.

    No wise man ever thought that a traitor should be trusted.

a.   Cicero—*Orationes In Verrem.* II. 1. 15.

Ipsa se fraus, etiamsi initio cautior fuerit, detegit.

    Treachery, though at first very cautious, in the end betrays itself.

b.   Livy—*Annales.* XLIV. 15.

TRIFLES.

Levitatis est inanem aucupari rumorem.

    His is a trifling character who seeks for fame through silly reports.

c.   Cicero—*Oratio In Lucium Pisonem.* XXIV.

Hæ nugæ seria ducent
In mala.

    These trifles will lead to serious mischief.

d.   Horace—*Ars Poetica.* 451.

Quid dignum tanto feret hic promissor hiatu?
Parturiunt montes; nascetur ridiculus mus.

    What will this boaster produce worthy of this mouthing? The mountains are in labor; a ridiculous mouse will be born.

e.   Horace—*Ars Poetica.* 138.

Atque utinam his potius nugis tota illa dedisset
Tempora sævitiæ.

    Would to heaven he had given up to trifles like these all the time which he devoted to cruelty.

f.   Juvenal—*Satiræ.* IV. 150.

Dare pondus idonea fumo.

    Fit to give weight to smoke.

g.   Persius—*Satiræ.* V. 20.

Magno iam conatu magnas nugas.

    By great efforts obtain great trifles.

h.   Terence—*Heautontimorumenos.* IV. 1. 8.

TROUBLE.

           Hoc scito nimio celerius
Venire quod molestum est, quam id quod cupide petas.

    Know this, that troubles come swifter than the things we desire.

i.   Plautus—*Mostellaria.* I. 1. 70.

TRUTH.

Pericula veritati sæpe contigua.

    Truth is often attended with danger.

j.   Ammianus Marcellinus—*Annales.* XXVI. 1.

Veritatis absolutus sermo ac semper est simplex.

    The language of truth is unadorned and always simple.

k.   Ammianus Marcellinus—*Annales.* XIV. 10.

Judicis est semper in causis verum sequi.

    It is a judge's duty in all trials to follow truth.

l.   Cicero—*De Officiis.* II. 14.

Naturâ inest mentibus nostris insatiabilis quædam cupiditas veri videndi.

    Our minds possess by nature an insatiable desire to know the truth.

m.   Cicero—*Tusculanarum Disputationum.* I. 18.

Nihil est veritatis luce dulcius.

    Nothing is more delightful than the light of truth.

n.   Cicero—*Academici.* IV. 10.

O magna vis veritas!

    O mighty power of truth!

o.   Cicero—*Oratio Pro Cælio Rufo.* XXVI.

Qui semel a veritate deflexit, hic non majore religione ad perjurium quam ad mendacium perduci consuevit.

    He who has once deviated from the truth, usually commits perjury with as little scruple as he would tell a lie.

p.   Cicero—*Oratio Pro Quinto Roscio Comœdo.* XX.

Magna est veritas et prævalebit.

    Truth is mighty and it will prevail.

q.   *Translated from* Esdras. IV. 41.

Nuda veritas.

    The naked truth.

r.   Horace—*Carmina.* I. 24. 7.

Quid verum atque decens curo et rogo, et omnis in hoc sum.

    My cares and my inquiries are for decency and truth, and in this I am wholly occupied.

s.   Horace—*Epistolæ.* I. 1. 11.

Ridentem dicere verum,
Quid vetat?

    What forbids a man to speak the truth in a laughing way?

t.   Horace—*Satiræ.* I. 24.

Veritatem laborare nimis sæpe, aiunt, extingui nunquam.

    It is said that truth is often eclipsed but never extinguished.

u.   Livy—*Annales.* XXII. 39.

Non opus est verbis, credite rebus.

    There is no need of words; believe facts.

v.   Ovid—*Fasti.* II. 734.

Ego verum amo, verum volo mihi dici; men-
　dacem odi.
　　I love truth and wish to have it always
　spoken to me: I hate a liar.
　a.　　PLAUTUS—*Mostellaria.* I. 3. 26.

Dum omnia quærimus, aliquando ad verum,
ubi minime expectavimus, **pervenimus.**
　　While we are examining into everything
　we sometimes find truth where we least ex-
　pected it.
　b.　　QUINTILIAN—*De Institutione Oratoria.*
　　　　　　　　　　　　　　XII. 8. 3.

Involuta veritas in alto latet.
　　Truth lies wrapped up and hidden in the
　depths.
　c.　　SENECA—*De Beneficiis.* VII. 1.

Veritas odit moras.
　　Truth hates delays.
　d.　　SENECA—*Œdipus.* **850.**

Veritatem dies aperit.
　　Time discovers truth.
　e.　　SENECA—*De Ira.* II. 22.

Veritatis simplex oratio est.
　　The language of truth is simple.
　f.　　SENECA—*Epistolæ Ad Lucilium.* XLIX.

Veritas visû et morâ, falsa festinatione et
incertis valescunt.
　　Truth is confirmed by inspection and
　delay: falsehood by haste and uncertainty.
　g.　　TACITUS—*Annales.* II. 39.

TYRANNY.

Quid violentius aure tyranni?
　　What is more cruel than a tyrant's ear?
　h.　　JUVENAL—*Satiræ.* IV. 86.

Gaudensque viam fecisse ruinâ.
　　He rejoices to have made his way by ruin.
　i.　　LUCAN—*Pharsalia.* I. 150.

U.

UBIQUITY.

Nusquam est, qui ubique est.
　　He who is everywhere is nowhere.
　j.　　SENECA—*Epistolæ Ad Lucilium.* II.

UNCERTAINTY.

Quis scit, an adjiciant hodiernæ crastina
　summæ
Tempora di superi?
　　Who knows whether the gods will add
　to-morrow to the present hour?
　k.　　HORACE—*Carmina.* IV. 7. 17.

Ludit in humanis divina potentia rebus,
Et certam præsens vix habet hora fidem.
　　Heaven makes sport of human affairs,
　and the present hour gives no sure promise
　of the next.
　l.　　OVID—*Epistolæ Ex Ponto.* IV. 3. 49.

Omnia sunt hominum tenui pendentia filo:
Et subito casu, quæ valuere, ruunt.
　　All human things hang on a slender
　thread: the strongest fall with a sudden
　crash.
　m.　　OVID—*Epistolæ Ex Ponto.* IV. 3. 35.

Dum in dubio est animus, paulo momento
huc illuc impellitur.
　　When the mind is in a state of uncertainty
　the smallest impulse directs it to either side.
　n.　　TERENCE—*Andria.* I. 5. 32.

UNHAPPINESS.

Graviora quæ patiantur videntur jam hominibus quam quæ metuant.
　　Present sufferings seem far greater to men
　than those they merely dread.
　o.　　LIVY—*Annales.* III. 39.

Ego esse miserum credo, cui placet nemo.
　　I believe that man to be wretched whom
　none can please.
　p.　　MARTIAL—*Epigrammata.* V. 28. 9.

Perfer et obdura; dolor hic tibi proderit olim.
　　Have patience and endure; this unhappi-
　ness will one day be beneficial.
　q.　　OVID—*Amorum.* III. 11. 7.

　　　　Miserias properant suas
Audire miseri.
　　The wretched hasten to hear of their own
　miseries.
　r.　　SENECA—*Hercules Œtæus.* 754.

UNIFORMITY.

　　　　　　　　Servetur ad imum,
Qualis ab incepto processerit, et sibi constet.
　　From first to last work should maintain
　its character and in all things be consistent.
　s.　　HORACE—*Ars Poetica.* 126.

Cantilenam eandem canis.
　　You are harping on the same string.
　t.　　TERENCE—*Phormio.* III. 2. 10.

UNITY.

Etenim omnes artes, quæ ad humanitatem pertinent, habent quoddam commune vinculum, et quasi cognatione quâdam inter se continentur.

All the arts which belong to polished life have some common tie, and are connected as it were by some relationship.

a.   CICERO—*Oratio Pro Licinio Archia.* I.

Neque est ullum certius amicitiæ vinculum, quam consensus et societas consiliorum et voluntatum.

There is no more sure tie between friends than when they are united in their objects and wishes.

b.   CICERO—*Oratio Pro Cnæo Plancio.* II.

Concordiâ res parvæ crescunt, discordiâ maximæ dilabantur.

By union the smallest states thrive, by discord the greatest are destroyed.

c.   SALLUST—*Jugurtha.* X.

Auxilia humilia firma consensus facit.

Union gives strength to the humble.

d.   SYRUS—*Maxims.*

Quo res cunque cadant, unum et commune
    periculum,
Una salus ambobus erit.

Whatever may be the issue we shall share one common danger, one safety.

e.   VIRGIL—*Æneid.* II. 709.

V.

VICE.

Alitur vitium vivitque tegendo.

Vice thrives and lives by concealment.

f.   VIRGIL—*Georgica.* III. 454.

VIRTUE.

Accipere quam facere injuriam præstat.

It is better to receive than to do a wrong.

g.   CICERO—*Tusculanarum Disputationum.*
    V. 19.

Est haec sæculi labes quædam et macula virtuti invidere, velle ipsum florem dignitatis infringere.

It is the stain and disgrace of the age to envy virtue, and to be anxious to crush the very flower of dignity.

h.   CICERO—*Oratio Pro Lucio Cornelio
    Balbo.* VI.

Honor est præmium virtutis.

Honor is the reward of virtue.

i.   CICERO—*Brutus.* LXXXI.

In virtute sunt multi adscensus.

In the approach to virtue there are many steps.

j.   CICERO—*Oratio Pro Cnæo Plancio.*
    XXV.

Nam quæ voluptate, quasi mercede aliquâ, ad officium impellitur, ea non est virtus sed fallax imitatio simulatioque virtutis.

That which leads us to the performance of duty by offering pleasure as its reward, is not virtue, but a deceptive copy and imitation of virtue.

k.   CICERO—*Academici.* IV. 46.

Nam ut quisque est vir optimus, ita difficillime esse alios improbos suspicatur.

The more virtuous any man is, the less easily does he suspect others to be vicious.

l.   CICERO—*Epistolæ Ad Fratrem.* I. 1.

Nec vero habere virtutem satis est, quasi artem aliquam, nisi utare.

It is not enough merely to possess virtue, as if it were an art; it should practised.

m.   CICERO—*De Republica.* I. 2.

Virtute enim ipsâ non tam multi præditi esse, quam videri volunt.

Fewer possess virtue, than those who wish us to believe that they possess it.

n.   CICERO—*De Amicitia.* XXVI.

Ipsa quidem virtus præmium sibi.

Virtue is indeed its own reward.

o.   CLAUDIANUS—*De Consulatu Malli
    Theodorii Panegyris.* I.

Vile latens virtus.

Virtue when concealed is a worthless thing.

p.   CLAUDIANUS—*De Quarto Consulatu
    Honorii Augusti Panegyris.* 222.

Nihil tam alte natura constituit quo virtus non possit eniti.

Nature has placed nothing so high that virtue can not reach it.

q.   QUINTUS CURTIUS RUFUS—*De Rebus
    Gestis Alexandri Magni.* VII.
    11. 10.

Mea virtute me involvo.

I wrap myself up in my virtue.

r.   HORACE—*Carmina.* III. 29. 55.

Oderunt peccare boni virtutis amore.

The good hate sin because they love virtue.

s.   HORACE—*Epistolæ.* I. 16. 52.

Vilius argentum est auro virtutibus aurum.
> Silver is less valuable than gold, gold than virtue.
> *a.*   Horace—*Epistolæ.* I. 1. 52.

Virtus est vitium fugere, et sapientia prima.
> Virtue consists in avoiding vice, and is the highest wisdom.
> *b.*   Horace—*Epistolæ.* I. 1. 41.

> Virtutem incolumem odimus,
Sublatam ex oculis quærimus.
> We hate virtue when it is safe; when removed from our sight we diligently seek it.
> *c.*   Horace—*Carmina.* III. 24. 31.

Nobilitas sola est atque unica virtus.
> Virtue is the only and true nobility.
> *d.*   Juvenal—*Satiræ.* VIII. 20.

Probitas laudatur et alget.
> Virtue is praised and freezes.
> *e.*   Juvenal—*Satiræ.* I. 74.

> Semita certe
Tranquillæ per virtutem patet unica vitæ.
> The only path to a tranquil life is through virtue.
> *f.*   Juvenal—*Satiræ.* X. 363.

Tanto major famæ sitis est quam
Virtutis: quis enim virtutem amplectitur ipsam
Præmia si tollas.
> The thirst for fame is much greater than that for virtue; for who would embrace virtue itself if you take away its rewards?
> *g.*   Juvenal—*Satiræ.* X. 140.

Virtutem videant, intabescantque relictâ.
> Let them (the wicked) see the beauty of virtue, and pine at having forsaken her.
> *h.*   Persius—*Satiræ.* III. 38.

Qui per virtutem peritat, non interit.
> He who dies for virtue, does not perish.
> *i.*   Plautus—*Captivi.* III. 5. 32.

Virtus, etiamsi quosdam impetus a naturâ sumit, tamen perficienda doctrinâ est.
> Although virtue receives some of its excellencies from nature, yet it is perfected by education.
> *j.*   Quintilian—*De Institutione Oratoria.*
> XII. 2. 1.

Divitiarum et formæ gloria fluxa atque fragilis; virtus clara æternaque habetur.
> The glory of riches and of beauty is frail and transitory; virtue remains bright and eternal.
> *k.*   Sallust—*Catilina.* I.

Marcet sine adversario virtus.
> Virtue withers away if it has no opposition.
> *l.*   Seneca—*De Providentia.* II.

Explorant adversa viros. Perque aspera dura Nititur ad laudem virtus interrita clivo.
> Adversity tries men; but virtue struggles after fame regardless of the adverse heights.
> *m.*   Silius Italicus—*Punica.* IV. 605.

Puras deus non plenas adspicit manus.
> God looks at pure, not full, hands.
> *n.*   Syrus—*Maxims.*

Mens sibi conscia recti.
> A soul conscious of its own rectitude.
> *o.*   Virgil—*Æneid.* I. 604.

Stat sua cuique dies; breve et irreparabile tempus
Omnibus est vitæ; set famam extendere factis
Hoc virtutis opus.
> Every man has his appointed day; life is brief and irrevocable; but it is the work of virtue to extend our fame by our deeds.
> *p.*   Virgil—*Æneid.* X. 467.

W.

WANT.

Tam deest avaro quod habet, quam quod non habet.
> The miser is as much in want of what he has, as of what he has not.
> *q.*   Syrus—*Maxims.*

WAR.

Bellum autem ita suscipiatur, ut nihil aliud, nisi pax, quæsita videatur.
> Let war be so carried on that no other object may seem to be sought but the acquisition of peace.
> *r.*   Cicero—*De Officiis.* I. 23.

Silent leges inter arma.
> The law is silent during war.
> *s.*   Cicero —*Oratio Pro Annio Milone.* IV.

Postquam Discordia tetra
Belli ferratos postes portasque refregit.
> When discord dreadful bursts her brazen bars,
> And shatters locks to thunder forth her wars.
> *t.*   Horace—*Satiræ.* I. 4. 60. (*Quoted.*
> *Original not known, thought to be*
> *from* Ennius.)

Alta sedent civilis vulnera dextræ.
> The wounds of civil war are deeply felt.
> *u.*   Lucan—*Pharsalia.* I. 32.

Non tam portas intrare patentes
Quam fregisse juvat; nec tam patiente colono
Arva premi, quam si ferro populetur et igni;
Concessâ pudet ire viâ.

> The conqueror is not so much pleased by entering into open gates, as by forcing his way. He desires not the fields to be cultivated by the patient husbandman; he would have them laid waste by fire and sword. It would be his shame to go by a way already opened.
> a. LUCAN—*Pharsalia.* II. 443.

Nulla fides pietasque viris qui castra sequuntur.

> Good faith and probity are rarely found among the followers of the camp.
> b. LUCAN—*Pharsalia.* X. 407.

    Omnibus hostes
Reddite nos populis—civile avertite bellum.

> Make us enemies of every people on earth, but prevent a civil war.
> c. LUCAN—*Pharsalia.* II. 52.

Adjuvat in bello pacatæ ramus olivæ.

> In war the olive branch of peace is of use.
> d. OVID—*Epistolæ Ex Ponto.* I. 1. 31.

Fortuna belli semper ancipiti in loco est.

> The fortune of war is always doubtful.
> e. SENECA—*Phœnissæ.* VI. 9.

Miseram pacem vel bello bene mutari.

> Even war is better than a wretched peace.
> f. TACITUS—*Annales.* III. 44.

Ratio et consilium propriæ ducis artes.

> The proper qualities of a general are judgment and deliberation.
> g. TACITUS—*Annales.* III. 20.

Dolus an virtus quis in hoste requirat?

> Who asks whether the enemy were defeated by strategy or valor?
> h. VIRGIL—*Æneid.* II. 390.

Sævit amor ferri et scelerata insania belli.

> The love of arms and the mad wickedness of war are raging.
> i. VIRGIL—*Æneid.* VII. 461.

Una salus victis nullam sperare salutem.

> The only safety for the conquered is to expect no safety.
> j. VIRGIL—*Æneid.* II. 354.

WATCHFULNESS.

Multorum te etiam oculi et aures non sentientem, sicuti adhuc fecerunt, speculabuntur atque custodient.

> Without your knowledge, the eyes and ears of many will see and watch you, as they have done already.
> k. CICERO—*Orationes In Catilinam.* I. 2.

Oculos et vestigia domini, res agro saluberrimas, facilius admittit.

> He allows very readily, that the eyes and footsteps of the master are things most salutary to the land.
> l. COLUMELLA—*De Re Rustica.* IV. 18.

Caret periculo, qui etiam tutus cavet.

> He is free from danger, who, even when safe, is on his guard.
> m. SYRUS—*Maxims.*

WEAKNESS.

    Alieno in loco
Haud stabile regnum est.

> The throne of another is not stable for thee.
> n. SENECA—*Hercules Furens.* 344.

WICKEDNESS.

Animi labes nec diuturnitate vanescere nec omnibus ullis elui potest.

> Mental stains can not be removed by time, nor washed away by any waters.
> o. CICERO—*De Legibus.* II. 10.

Nullum scelus rationem habet.

> No wickedness has any ground of reason.
> p. LIVY—*Annales.* XXVIII. 28.

WINE.

Fœcundi calices quem non fecere disertum.

> Whom has not the inspiring bowl made eloquent?
> q. HORACE—*Epistolæ.* I. 5. 19.

Nunc vino pellite curas.

> Now drown care in wine.
> r. HORACE—*Carmina.* I. 7. 32.

Quis post vina gravem militiam aut pauperiem crepat?

> Who prates of war or want after his wine?
> s. HORACE—*Carmina.* I. 18. 5.

Spes donare novas largus, amaraque
Curarum eluere efficax.

> Mighty to inspire new hopes, and able to drown the bitterness of cares.
> t. HORACE—*Carmina.* IV. 12. 19.

In proverbium cessit, sapientiam vino adumbrari.

> It has passed into a proverb, that wisdom is overshadowed by wine.
> u. PLINY the Elder—*Historia Naturalis.* XXIII. 23. 1.

WISDOM.

Quis nam igitur liber? Sapiens qui sibi imperiosus.

Who then is free? The wise man who can govern himself.

a.   HORACE—*Satiræ.* II. 7. 83.

Sapere aude.

Dare to be wise.

b.   HORACE—*Epistolæ.* I. 2. 40.

Utiliumque sagax rerum et divina futuri.

Sagacious in making useful discoveries.

c.   HORACE—*Ars Poetica.* 218.

Victrix fortunæ sapientia.

Wisdom is the conqueror of fortune.

d.   JUVENAL—*Satiræ.* XIII. 20.

Quisquis plus justo non sapit, ille sapit.

Whoever is not too wise is wise.

e.   MARTIAL—*Epigrammata.* XIV. 10. 2.

Feliciter sapit qui alieno periculo sapit.

He gains wisdom in a happy way, who gains it by another's experience.

f.   PLAUTUS—*Mercator.* IV. 7. 40.

Nemo solus satis sapit.

No man is wise enough by himself.

g.   PLAUTUS—*Miles Gloriosus.* III. 3. 12.

Nemo mortalium omnibus horis sapit.

No one is wise at all times.

h.   PLINY the Elder—*Historia Naturalis.* VII. 41. 2.

Melius in malis sapimus, secunda rectum auferunt.

We become wiser by adversity; prosperity destroys our appreciation of the right.

i.   SENECA—*Epistolæ Ad Lucilium.* XCIV.

Nulli sapere casu obtigit.

No man was ever wise by chance.

j.   SENECA—*Epistolæ Ad Lucilium.* LXXVI.

Dictum sapienti sat est.

A word to the wise is sufficient.

k.   TERENCE—*Phormio.* III. 3. 8.

Isthuc est sapere non quod ante pedes modo est

Videre sed etiam illa, quæ futura sunt Prospicere.

True wisdom consists not in seeing what is immediately before our eyes, but in foreseeing what is to come.

l.   TERENCE—*Adelphi.* III. 3. 32.

WOMAN.

Nulla fere causa est, in quâ non fœmina litem.

There are few disputes in life, which do not originate with a woman.

m.   JUVENAL—*Satiræ.* VI. 242.

Parvula, pumilio, chariton mia tota merum sal.

A little, tiny, pretty, witty, charming darling she.

n.   LUCRETIUS—*De Rerum Natura.* IV. 1158.

Uxori nubere nolo meæ.

My wife shall not rule me.

o.   MARTIAL—*Epigrammata.* VIII. 12. 2.

Mulieri nimio male facere melius est onus, quam bene.

A woman finds it much easier to do ill than well.

p.   PLAUTUS—*Truculentus.* II. 5. 17.

Multa sunt mulierum vitia, sed hoc e multis maximum,

Cum sibi nimis placent, nimisque operam dant ut placeant viris.

Women have many faults, but of the many this is the greatest, that they please themselves too much, and give too little attention to pleasing the men.

q.   PLAUTUS—*Pœnulus.* V. 4. 33.

Nam multum loquaces merito omnes habemus,

Nec mutam profecto repertam ullam esse Hodie dicunt mulierem ullo in seculo.

I know that we women are all justly accounted praters; they say in the present day that there never was in any age such a wonder to be found as a dumb woman.

r.   PLAUTUS—*Aulularia.* II. 1. 5.

Aut amat aut odit mulier, nihil est tertium.

A woman either loves or hates: she knows no medium.

s.   SYRUS—*Maxims.*

Novi ingenium mulierum;

Nolunt ubi velis, ubi nolis cupiunt ultro.

I know the nature of women. When you will, they will not; when you will not, they come of their own accord.

t.   TERENCE—*Eunuchus.* IV. 7. 42.

Dux femina facti.

A woman was leader in the deed.

u.   VIRGIL—*Æneid.* I. 364.

Varium et mutabile semper, Fœmina.

A woman is always changeable and capricious.

v.   VIRGIL—*Æneid.* IV. 569.

WORDS.

Nescit vox missa reverti.
　A word once escaped can never be recalled.
　a.　HORACE—*Ars Poetica.* 390.

　　　　　　　　　　　Tristia mæstum
Vultum verba decent; iratum, plena mina-
　rum;
Ludentem, lasciva; severum, seria dictu.
　Sorrowful words become the sorrowful;
angry words suit the passionate; light words
a playful expression; serious words suit the
grave.
　b.　HORACE—*Ars Poetica.* 105.

Fere totus mundus exerceat histrionem.
　Almost the whole world are players.
　c.　PETRONIUS ARBITER—*Satyricon.* Frag.

Satis eloquentiæ sapientiæ parum.
　Enough words little wisdom.
　d.　SALLUST—*Catilina.* V.

WRITING.

Piger scribendi ferre laborem;
Scribendi recte, nam ut multum nil moror.
　Too indolent to bear the toil of writing;
I mean of writing well; I say nothing
about quantity.
　e.　HORACE—*Satiræ.* I. 4. 12.

Sæpe stilum vertas, iterum quæ digna legi
　sint
Scripturus.
　Often turn the stile [correct with care], if
you expect to write anything worthy of
being read twice.
　f.　HORACE—*Satiræ.* I. 10. 72.

Scribendi recte sapere est et principium et
fons.
　Knowledge is the foundation and source
of good writing.
　g.　HORACE—*Ars Poetica.* 309.

Sumite materiam vestris, qui scribitis, æquam
　Viribus.
　Ye who write, choose a subject suited to
your abilities.
　h.　HORACE—*Ars Poetica.* XXXVIII.

Tantum series juncturaque pollet.
　Of so much force are system and connection.
　i.　HORACE—*Ars Poetica.* 242.

ubi plura nitent in carmine, non ego paucis
Offendar maculis, quas aut incuria fudit,
Aut humana parum cavit natura.
　Where there are many beauties in a poem
I shall not cavil at a few faults proceeding
either from negligence or from the imper-
fection of our nature.
　j.　HORACE—*Ars Poetica.* 351.

　　　　　　　　　Tenet insanabile multo
Scribendi cacoëthes, et ægro in corde senescit.
　An incurable itch for scribbling takes
possession of many, and grows inveterate in
their insane breasts.
　k.　JUVENAL—*Satiræ.* VII. 51.

　　　　　Præbet mihi littera linguam:
Et, si non liceat scribere, mutus ero.
　This letter gives me a tongue; and were I
not allowed to write, I should be dumb.
　l.　OVID—*Epistolæ Ex Ponto.* II. 6. 3.

Scripta ferunt annos; scriptis Agamemnona
　nosti,
Et quisquis contra vel simul arma tulit.
　Writings survive the years; it is by writings that you know Agamemnon, and those
who fought for or against him.
　m.　OVID—*Epistolæ Ex Ponto.* IV. 8. 51.

Non est aliena res, quæ fere ab honestis
negligi solet, cura bene ac velociter scribendi.
　Men of quality are in the wrong to undervalue, as they often do, the practise of a fair
and quick hand in writing; for it is no
immaterial accomplishment.
　n.　QUINTILIAN—*De Institutione Oratoria.*
　　　　　　　　　　　　　　　　I. 5.

Y.

YOUTH.

Prima commendatio proficiscitur a modes-
tiâ, tum pietate in parentes, tum in suos
benevolentiâ.
　The chief recommendation [in a young
man] is modesty, then dutiful conduct
toward parents, then affection for kindred.
　o.　CICERO—*De Officiis.* II. 13.

Teneris, heu, lubrica moribus ætas!
　Alas! the slippery nature of tender youth.
　p.　CLAUDIANUS—*De Raptu Proserpinæ.*
　　　　　　　　　　　　　　　III. 227.

Dissimiles hic vir, et ille puer.
　How different from the present man was
the youth of earlier days!
　q.　OVID—*Heroides.* IX. 24.

QUOTATIONS

FROM

MODERN FOREIGN LANGUAGES.

A.

ABILITY.

Les méchants sont toujours surpris de trouver de l'habileté dans les bons.

The wicked are always surprised to find ability in the good.

a. VAUVENARGUES—*Réflexions.* CIII.

Die Menschen gehen wie Schiesskugeln weiter, wenn sie abgeglättet sind.

Men, like bullets, go farthest when they are smoothest.

b. JEAN PAUL RICHTER—*Titan.* Zykel 26.

ACCIDENT.

Nichts unter der Sonne ist Zufall—am wenigsten das wovon die Absicht so klar in die Augen leuchtet.

Nothing under the sun is accidental, least of all that of which the intention is so clearly evident.

c. LESSING—*Emilia Galotti.* IV. 3.

Was der Ameise Vernunft mühsam zu Haufen schleppt, jagt in einem Hui der Wind des Zufalls zusammen.

What the reason of the ant laboriously drags into a heap, the wind of accident will collect in one breath.

d. SCHILLER—*Fiesco.* Act II. Sc. 4.

ADVICE.

Un fat quelquefois ouvre un avis important.

A fop sometimes gives important advice.

e. BOILEAU—*L'Art Poétique.* IV. 50.

Vom sichern Port lässt sich's gemächlich rathen.

One can advise comfortably from a safe port.

f. SCHILLER—*Wilhelm Tell.* I. 1. 146.

No adventures mucho tu riqueza
Por consejo de ome que ha pobreza.

Hazard not your wealth on a poor man's advice.

g. MANUEL CONDE LUCANOR.

AGE (OLD).

En vieillissant, on devient plus fou et plus sage.

When men grow old, they become more foolish and more wise.

h. LA ROCHEFOUCAULD—*Maximes.*

La vieillesse est un tyran qui défend, sur peine de la vie, tous les plaisirs de la jeunesse.

Old age is a tyrant who forbids, upon pain of death, all the pleasures of youth.

i. LA ROCHEFOUCAULD—*Maximes.* 461.

L'on craint la vieillesse, que l'on n'est pas sûr de pouvoir atteindre.

We dread old age, which we are not sure of being able to attain.

j. LA BRUYÈRE—*Les Caractères.* XI.

L'on espère de vieillir, et l'on craint la vieillesse; c'est-à-dire, l'on aime la vie et l'on fuit la mort.

We hope to grow old and we dread old age; that is to say, we love life and we flee from death.

k. LA BRUYÈRE—*Les Caractères.* XI.

Peu de gens savent être vieux.

Few persons know how to be old.

l. LA ROCHEFOUCAULD—*Maximes.* 448.

Das Alter ist nicht trübe weil darin unsere Freuden, sondern weil unsere Hoffnungen aufhören.

What makes old age so sad is, not that our joys but that our hopes cease.

m. JEAN PAUL RICHTER—*Titan.* Zykel 34.

Das Alter macht nicht kindisch, wie man spricht,
Es findet uns nur noch als wahre Kinder.

Age childish makes, they say, but 'tis not true;
We're only genuine children still in Age's season.

n. GOETHE—*Faust. Vorspiel auf dem Theater.* L. 180.

Wenn man alt ist, muss man mehr thun als
da man jung war.

When we are old, we must do more than
when we were young.

a. GOETHE—*Sprüche in Prosa.* III.

ALLEGORY.

L'allégorie habite un palais diaphane.

Allegory dwells in a transparent palace.

b. LEMIERRE—*Peinture.* III.

APPEARANCE.

Garde-toi, tant que tu vivras,
De juger des gens sur la mine.

Beware so long as you live, of judging
people by appearances.

c. LA FONTAINE—*Fables.* VI. 5.

Même quand l'oiseau marche on sent qu'il a
des ailes.

Even when the bird walks one feels that
it has wings.

d. LEMIERRE—*Fastes.* Chant. I.

Das Betragen ist ein Spiegel in welchem
jeder sein Bild zeigt.

Behavior is a mirror in which every one
shows his image.

e. GOETHE—*Die Wahlverwandtschaften.*
II. 5. *Aus Ottiliens Tagebuche.*

ART.

Die Kunst ist zwar nicht das Brod, aber der
Wein des Lebens.

Art is indeed not the bread but the wine
of life.

f. JEAN PAUL RICHTER.

Kunst ist die rechte Hand der Natur. Diese
hat nur Geschöpfe, jene hat Menschen ge-
macht.

Art is the right hand of Nature. The
latter has only given us being, the former
has made us men.

g. SCHILLER—*Fiesco.* II. 17.

Schwer ist die Kunst, vergänglich ist ihr
Preis.

Art is difficult, transient is her reward.

h. SCHILLER—*Wallenstein. Prolog.* L. 40.

Von der Freiheit gesäugt wachsen die
Künste der Lust.

All the arts of pleasure grow when suckled by freedom.

i. SCHILLER—*Der Spaziergang.* L. 122.

L'arte vostra quella, quanto puote,
Seque, come il maestro fa il discente;
Si che vostr'arte a Dio quasi è nipote.

Art, as far as it is able, follows nature, as
a pupil imitates his master; thus your art
must be, as it were, God's grandchild.

j. DANTE—*Inferno.* XI. 103.

AUDACITY.

De l'audace, encore de l'audace, toujours de
l'audace.

Audacity, more audacity, always audacity.

k. DANTON *during the French Revolution.*

La crainte fit les dieux; l'audace a fait les rois.

Fear made the gods; audacity has made
kings.

l. CRÉBILLON *during the French
Revolution.*

Und setzet ihr nicht das Leben ein,
Nie wird euch das Leben gewonnen sein.

If you do not dare to die you will never
win life.

m. SCHILLER—*Wallenstein's Lager.*
XI. Chorus.

Wo das Herz reden darf braucht es keiner
Vorbereitung.

When the heart dares to speak, it needs
no preparation.

n. LESSING—*Minna von Barnhelm.* V. 4.

Questa lor tracotanza non è nuova.

This audacity of theirs is not new.

o. DANTE—*Inferno.* VIII. 124.

B.

BEAUTY.

L'air spirituel est dans les hommes ce que la
régularité des traits est dans les femmes : c'est
le genre de beauté où les plus vains puissent
aspirer.

A look of intelligence in men is what regularity of features is in women: it is a style
of beauty to which the most vain may
aspire.

p. LA BRUYÈRE—*Les Caractères.* XII.

Damals war nichts heilig, als das Schöne.

In days of yore [in ancient Greece] nothing was sacred but the beautiful.

q. SCHILLER—*Die Götter Griechenlands.*
St. 6.

Das ist das Loos des Schönen auf der Erde!

That is the lot of the beautiful on earth.

r. SCHILLER—*Wallenstein's Tod.* IV.
12. 26.

Die Wahrheit ist vorhanden für den Weisen.
Die Schönheit für ein fühlend Herz.

Truth exists for the wise, beauty for the
feeling heart.
a.   Schiller—*Don Carlos.* IV. 21. 186.

Schön war ich auch, und das war mein
Verderben.

I too was fair, and that was my undoing.
b.   Goethe—*Faust.* I. 25. 30.

No todas hermosuras enamoran, que algunas
alegran la vista, y no rinden la voluntad.

All kinds of beauty do not inspire love;
there is a kind which only pleases the sight,
but does not captivate the affections.
c.   Cervantes—*Don Quixote.* II. 6.

BEGGARY.

Mieux vaut goujat debout qu'empereur en-
terré.

Better a living beggar than a buried
emperor.
d.   La Fontaine—*La Matrone d' Ephèse.*

Borgen ist nicht viel besser als betteln.

Borrowing is not much better than begging.
e.   Lessing—*Nathan der Weise.* II. 9.

Der wahre Bettler ist
Doch einzig und allein der wahre König.

The real beggar is indeed the true and
only king.
f.   Lessing—*Nathan der Weise.* II. 9.

BEGINNINGS.

C'est le commencement de la fin.

It is the beginning of the end.
     Ascribed to Talleyrand *in the*
                Hundred Days.
g.   *Also to* Gen. Augereau. 1814.

La distance n'y fait rien; il n'y a que le
premier pas qui coûte.

The distance is nothing; it is only the
first step that costs.
h.   Mme. du Deffand—*Letter to Horace*
                Walpole, June 6, 1767.

Doch wisst ihr, in der Hitze des Verfolgens,
Verliert man bald den Anfang aus den
     Augen.

Still thou knowest that in the ardor of
pursuit men lose sight of the goal from
which they start.
i.   Schiller—*Piccolomini.* III. 1. 62.

BITTERNESS.

Aucun fiel n'a jamais empoisonné ma plume.

No gall has ever poisoned my pen.
j.   Crébillon—*Discours de Réception.*

Tant de fiel entre-t-il dans l'âme des dévots?

Can such bitterness enter into the heart of
the devout?
k.   Boileau—*Lutrin.* I. 12.

BLOOD.

Le sang qui coule est-il donc si pur?

Is the blood shed then so pure?
l.   Barnave *on hearing of the massacre of*
              the colonists of San Domingo.

Blut ist ein ganz besondrer Saft.

Blood is a juice of rarest quality.
m.   Goethe—*Faust.* I. 4. 214.

BLUSHES.

Les hommes rougissent moins de leurs
crimes que de leurs faiblesses et de leur vanité.

Men blush less for their crimes than for
their weaknesses and vanity.
n.   La Bruyère—*Les Caractères.* II.

L'innocence à rougir n'est point accoutumée.

Innocence is not accustomed to blush.
o.   Molière—*Don Garcie de Navarre.*
                         II. 5.

Bello è il rossore, ma è incommodo qualche
volta.

The blush is beautiful, but it is sometimes
inconvenient.
p.   Goldoni—*Pamela.* I. 3.

BRAVERY.

Les hommes valeureux le sont au premier
coup.

Brave men are brave from the very first.
q.   Corneille—*Le Cid.* II. 3.

Dem Muthigen hilft Gott.

God helps the brave.
r.   Schiller—*Wilhelm Tell.* I. 2. 132.

Hoch klingt das Lied vom braven Mann,
Wie Orgelton und Glockenklang;
Wer hohes Muths sich rühmen kann
Den lohnt nicht Gold, den lohnt Gesang.

Song of the brave, how thrills thy tone
     As when the Organ's music rolls;
No gold rewards, but song alone,
     The deeds of great and noble souls.
s.   Bürger—*Lied vom Braven Mann.*

Zwar der Tapfere nennt sich Herr der Länder
Durch sein Eisen, durch sein Blut.

The brave man, indeed, calls himself lord
of the land, through his iron, through his
blood.
t.   Arndt—*Lehre an den Menschen.* 5.

C.

CARE.

Qui veut voyager loin ménage sa monture.

He who will travel far spares his steed.
a. RACINE—*Plaideurs.* I. 1.

Wer gar zu viel bedenkt, wird wenig leisten.

He that is overcautious will accomplish little.
b. SCHILLER—*Wilhelm Tell.* III. 1. 72.

CHANGE.

Heureux qui, dans ses vers, sait d'une voix
    légère
Passer du grave au doux, du plaisant au sévère.

Happy the poet who with ease can steer
From grave to gay, from lively to severe.
c. BOILEAU—*L'Art Poetique.* I. 75.

Il n'y a rien de changé en France; il n'y a
qu'un Français de plus.

Nothing has changed in France, there is
only a Frenchman the more.
d.   *Reported by* M. BUGNOT *in the Moniteur
    as the words of* COMTE D'ARTOIS, *on
    his entrance into Paris.* See M. DE
    VAULABELLE—*Hist. des Deux
    Restaurations.* 3d Édit. II.
    Pp. 30, 31.

J'avais vu les grands, mais je n'avais pas vu
les petits.

I had seen the great, but I had not seen the
small.
e. ALFIERI—*Reason for Changing his
    Democratic Opinions.*

Nous avons changé tout cela.

We have changed all that.
f. MOLIÈRE—*Le Médecin Malgré lui.*
    II. 6.

On commence par être dupe,
On finit par être fripon.

We begin by being dupe, and end by being rogue.
g. DESCHAMPS—*Reflexion sur le Jeu.*

Meno erra chi si promette variazione nelle
cose del mondo, che chi se le persuade ferme
e stabili.

He is less likely to be mistaken who looks
forward to a change in the affairs of the
world, than he who regards them as firm
and stable.
h. GUICCIARDINI—*Storia d'Italia.*

Nè spegner può per star nell'acqua il foco;
Nè può stato mutar per mutar loco.

Such fire was not by water to be drown'd,
Nor he his nature changed by changing
    ground.
i. ARIOSTO—*Orlando Furioso.* XXVIII.
    89.

CHARACTER.

Au demeurant, le meilleur fils du monde.

In other respects the best fellow in the
world.
j. CLEMENT MAROT—*Letter to Francis I.*

Cet animal est tres méchant;
Quand on l'attaque il se défend.

This animal is very malicious; when attacked it defends itself.
k. *From a song,* La Ménagerie.

Chevalier sans peur et sans reproche.

Knight without fear and without reproach.
l. *Applied to* CHEVALIER BAYARD.

Coups de fourches ni d'étrivières,
Ne lui font changer de manières.

Neither blows from pitchfork, nor from
the lash, can make him change his ways.
m. LA FONTAINE—*Fables.* II. 18.

Il embellit tout ce qu'il touche,

He adorns all that he touches.
n. FÉNÉLON—*Lettre sur les Occupations
    de l'Académie Française.* Sect. 4.

Je ne puis rien nommer si ce n'est par son
    nom;
J'appelle un chat un chat, et Rollet un fripon.

I can call nothing by name if that is not
his name. I call a cat a cat, and Rollet a
rogue.
o. BOILEAU—*Satires.* I. 51.

La physionomie n'est pas une règle qui nous
soit donnée pour juger des hommes: elle nous
peut servir de conjecture.

Physiognomy is not a guide that has been
given us by which to judge of the character
of men: it may only serve us for conjecture.
p. LA BRUYÈRE—*Les Caractères.* XII.

Le moi est haïssable.

Egoism is hateful.
q. PASCAL—*Pensées Diverses.*

Les hommes, fripons en détail, sont en gros
de très-honnêtes gens.

Men, who are rogues individually, are in
the mass very honorable people.
r. MONTESQUIEU—*De l'Esprit.* XXV.

Les maximes des hommes décèlent leur cœur.

The maxims of men reveal their characters.

a.   Vauvenargues—*Réflexions.* CVII.

Messieurs, nous avons un maître, ce jeune homme fait tout, peut tout, et veut tout.

Gentlemen, we have a master; this young man does everything, can do everything and will do everything.

b.   *Attributed to* Sieyès, *who speaks of* Bonaparte.

On n'est jamais si ridicule par les qualités que l'on a que par celles que l'on affecte d'avoir.

The qualities we have do not make us so ridiculous as those which we affect to have.

c.   La Rochefoucauld—*Maximes.* 134.

Peu d'hommes ont esté admirez par leurs domestiques.

Few men have been admired by their servants.

d.   Montaigne—*Essais.* III. 2.

Auch ich war in Arkadien geboren.

I, too, was born in Arcadia.

      Bartholomew Schidoni. *Motto of* Goethe's *Travels in Italy.*

e.   See also Schiller—*Resignation.* I.

Aufrichtig zu sein kann ich versprechen; unparteiisch zu sein aber nicht.

I can promise to be upright, but not to be without bias.

f.   Goethe—*Sprüche in Prosa.* III.

Da krabbeln sie nun, wie die Ratten auf der Keule des Hercules.

They [the present generation] are like rats crawling about the club of Hercules.

g.   Schiller—*Die Räuber.* I. 2.

Der Feige droht nur, wo er sicher ist.

The coward only threatens when he is safe.

h.   Goethe—*Torquato Tasso.* II. 3. 207.

Es bildet ein Talent sich in der Stille,
Sich ein Charakter in dem Strom der Welt.

Talent is nurtured in solitude; character is formed in the stormy billows of the world.

i.   Goethe—*Torquato Tasso.* I. 2. 66.

           Gemeine Naturen
Zahlen mit dem, was sie thun, edle mit dem, was sie sind.

Common natures pay with what they do, noble ones with what they are.

j.   Schiller—*Unterschied der Stände.*

Individualität ist überall zu schonen und zu ehren als Wurzel jedes Guten.

Individuality is everywhere to be guarded and honored as the root of all good.

k.   Jean Paul Richter—*Titan.* Zykel 111.

Kein Talent, doch ein Charakter.

No talent, but yet a character.

l.   Heine—*Atta Troll.* Caput 24.

Nie zeichnet der Mensch den eignen Charakter schärfer als in seiner Manier, einen Fremden zu zeichnen.

A man never shows his own character so plainly as by his manner of portraying another's.

m.   Jean Paul Richter—*Titan.* Zykel 110.

Welch' hoher Geist in einer engen Brust.

What a mighty spirit in a narrow bosom.

n.   Goethe—*Torquato Tasso.* II. 3. 199.

Brama assai, poco spera e nulla chiede.

He, full of bashfulness and truth, loved much, hoped little, and desired naught.

o.   Tasso—*Gerusalemme.* II. 16.

Cada uno es come Dios le hijo, y aun peor muchas vezes.

Every one is as God made him, and often a great deal worse.

p.   Cervantes—*Don Quixote.* XI. 5.

CHILDHOOD.

Ah, il n'y a plus d'enfant.

Ah, there are no children nowadays.

q.   Molière—*Le Malade Imaginaire.*
                      II. 2.

L'enfance est le sommeil de la raison.

Childhood is the sleep of reason.

r.   Rousseau—*Émile.* Bk. II.

Les enfants n'ont ni passé ni avenir; et, ce qui ne nous arrive guère, ils jouissent du présent.

Children have neither past nor future; and that which seldom happens to us, they rejoice in the present.

s.   La Bruyère—*Les Caractères.* XI.

Mais un fripon d'enfant (cet âge est sans pitié).

But a rascal of a child (that age is without pity).

t.   La Fontaine—*Fables.* IX. 2.

Glücklicher Säugling! dir ist ein unendlicher Raum noch die Wiege,
Werde Mann, und dir wird eng die unendliche Welt.

Happy child! the cradle is still to thee a vast space; but when thou art a man the boundless world will be too small for thee.

u.   Schiller—*Das Kind in der Wiege.*

Wage du zu irren und zu träumen.
Hoher Sinn liegt oft im kind'schen Spiel.

Dare to err and to dream. Deep meaning often lies in childish plays.

v.   Schiller—*Theklo.* St. 6.

CHOICE.

Devine, si tu peux, et choisis, si tu l'oses.
Guess, if you can, and choose, if you dare.
a.   CORNEILLE—*Héraclius.* IV. 4.

Se soumettre ou se démettre.
Submit or resign.
b.   GAMBETTA.

CHURCHES.

Pour soutenir tes droits, que le ciel autorise,
Abîme tout plutôt ; c'est l'esprit de l'Église.
To support those of your rights authorized
by Heaven, destroy everything rather than
yield ; that is the spirit of the Church.
c.   BOILEAU—*Lutrin.* Chant I. 185.

Die Kirch' allein, meine lieben Frauen,
Kann ungerechtes Gut verdauen.
The church alone beyond all question
Has for ill-gotten goods the right digestion.
d.   GOETHE—*Faust.* I. 9. 35.

CLEVERNESS.

C'est une grande habileté que de savoir
cacher son habileté.
To know how to hide one's ability is great
skill.
e.   LA ROCHEFOUCAULD—*Maximes.* 245.

Il n'est rien d'inutile aux personnes de sens.
Sensible people find nothing useless.
f.   LA FONTAINE—*Fables.* V. 19.

On peut être plus fin qu'un autre, mais non
pas plus fin que tous les autres.
We can be more clever than one, but not
more clever than all.
g.   LA ROCHEFOUCAULD—*Maximes.* 394.

COMPARISONS.

Du même fonds dont on néglige un homme
de mérite l'on sait encore admirer un sot.
The same principle leads us to neglect a
man of merit that induces us to admire a
fool.
h.   LA BRUYÈRE—*Les Caractères.* XII.

Il y a fagots et fagots.
There are fagots and fagots.
i.   MOLIÈRE—*Le Médecin Malgré lui.*
I. 6.

Qui n'est que juste est dur, qui n'est que
sage est triste.
He who is not just is severe, he who is not
wise is sad.
j.   VOLTAIRE—*Epître au Roi de Prusse.*
1740.

Tant la plume a eu sous le roi d'avantage
sur l'épée.
So far had the pen, under the king, the
superiority over the sword.
k.   SAINT SIMON—*Mémoires.* Vol. III.
P. 517 (1702). Ed. 1856.

Tel maître, tel valet.
As the master so the valet.
Like master, like man.
l.   *Attributed to* CHEVALIER BAYARD
by M. Ciniber.

Einem ist sie die hohe, die himmlische Göttin,
dem andern
Eine tüchtige Kuh, die ihn mit Butter versorgt.
To one it is a mighty heavenly goddess,
to the other an excellent cow that furnishes
him with butter.
m.   SCHILLER—*Wissenschaft.*

Was glänzt ist für den Augenblick geboren;
Das Aechte bleibt der Nachwelt unverloren.
What dazzles, for the moment spends its
spirit ;
What's genuine, shall posterity inherit.
n.   GOETHE—*Faust. Vorspiel auf dem
Theater.* L. 41.

L'ape e la serpe spesso
Suggon l'istesso umore ;
The bee and the serpent often sip from the
selfsame flower.
o.   METASTASIO—*Morte d'Abele.* I.

CONQUEST.

À vaincre sans péril on triomphe sans gloire.
We triumph without glory when we conquer without danger.
p.   CORNEILLE—*Le Cid.* II. 2.

Sai, che piegar si vede
Il docile arboscello,
Che vince allor che cede
Dei turbini al furor.
Know that the slender shrub which is
seen to bend, conquers when it yields to the
storm.
q.   METASTASIO—*Il Trionfo di Clelia.*
I. 8.

CONSCIENCE.

La conscience des mourants calomnie leur vie.
The conscience of the dying belies their
life.
r.   VAUVENARGUES—*Réflexions.*
CXXXVI.

Zwei Seelen wohnen, ach ! in meiner Brust,
Die eine will sich von der andern trennen.
Two souls, alas! reside within my breast,
and each withdraws from and repels its
brother.
s.   GOETHE—*Faust.* I. 2. 307.

O dignitosa coscienza e netta,
Come t' è picciol fallo amaro morso.

O faithful conscience, delicately pure, how doth a little failing wound thee sore!
a.   DANTE—*Purgatorio.* III. 8.

Se tosto grazia risolva le schiume
Di vostra conscienza, si che chiaro
Per essa scenda della mente il fiume.

So may heaven's grace clear away the foam from the conscience, that the river of thy thoughts may roll limpid thenceforth.
b.   DANTE—*Purgatorio.* XIII. 88.

COUNSEL.

C'est une importune garde, du secret des princes, à qui n'en à que faire.

The secret counsels of princes are a troublesome burden to such as have only to execute them.
c.   MONTAIGNE—*Essais.* III. 1.

Che spesso avvien che ne' maggior perigli
Son più audaci gli ottimi consigli.

For when last need to desperation driveth,
Who dareth most he wisest counsel giveth.
d.   TASSO—*Gerusalemme.* VI. 6.

Dicen, que el primer consejo
Ha de ser de la muger.

They say that the best counsel is that of woman.
e.   CALDERON—*El Médico de su Honra.*
                        I. 2.

COURAGE.

C'est dans les grands dangers qu'on voit les grands courages.

It is in great dangers that we see great courage.
f.   REGNARD—*Le Légataire.*

On ne peut répondre de son courage quand on n'a jamais été dans le péril.

We can never be certain of our courage until we have faced danger.
g.   LA ROCHEFOUCAULD—*Premier*
                    Supplément. 42.

Ei di virilità grave e maturo,
Mostra in fresco vigor chiome canute.

Grave was the man in years, in looks, in word,
His locks were gray, yet was his courage green.
h.   TASSO—*Gerusalemme.* I. 53.

CREATION.

Wie aus Duft und Glanz gemischt
Du mich schufst, dir dank ich's heut.

As thou hast created me out of mingled air and glitter, I thank thee for it.
i.   RÜCKERT—*Die Sterbende Blume.* St. 8.

CREDULITY.

Incrédules les plus crédules. Ils croient les miracles de Vespasien, pour ne pas croire ceux de Moïse.

The incredulous are the most credulous. They believe the miracles of Vespasian that they may not believe those of Moses.
j.   PASCAL—*Pensées.* II. XVII. 120.

Nicht die Kinder bloss speist man mit Märchen ab.

It is not children only that one feeds with fairy tales.
k.   LESSING—*Nathan der Weise.* III. 6.

CRIME.

C'est plus qu'un crime, c'est une faute.

It is more than a crime, it is a mistake.
l.   *Attributed to* TALLEYRAND, *also to*
                    FOUCHÉ.

Du repos dans le crime! ah! qui peut s'en flatter.

To be at peace in crime! ah, who can thus flatter himself.
m.   VOLTAIRE—*Oreste.* I. 5.

La crainte suit le crime, et c'est son châtiment.

Fear follows crime and is its punishment.
n.   VOLTAIRE—*Semiramis.* V. 1.

Le crime d'une mère est un pesant fardeau.

The crime of a mother is a heavy burden.
o.   RACINE—*Phèdre.* III. 3.

Le crime fait la honte et non pas l'échafaud.

The crime and not the scaffold makes the shame.
p.   THOS. CORNEILLE—*Essex.* IV. 3.
          Quoted by CHARLOTTE CORDAY.

Denn alle Schuld rächt sich auf Erden.

For all guilt is avenged on earth.
q.   GOETHE—*Wilhelm Meister.*

                    Il reo
D'un delitto è chi'l pensa: a chi l' ordisce
La pena spetta.

The guilty is he who meditates a crime; the punishment is his who lays the plot.
r.   ALFIERI—*Antigone.* II. 2.

    Non nella pena,
Nel delitto è la infamia.

Disgrace does not consist in the punishment, but in the crime.
s.   ALFIERI—*Antigone.* I. 3.

    Oh! ben provvide il cielo,
Ch' uom per delitto mai lieto non sia.

Heaven takes care that no man secures happiness by crime.
t.   ALFIERI—*Oreste.* I. 2.

CRITICISM.

La critique est aisée, et l'art est difficile
Criticism is easy, and art is difficult.
a.   Destouches—*Glorieux.* II. 5.

Die Kritik nimmt oft dem Baume
Raupen und Blüthen mit einander.
Criticism often takes from the tree
Caterpillars and blossoms together.
b.   Jean Paul Richter—*Titan.* Zykel
105.

CRUELTY.

Contre les rebelles c'est cruauté que d'estre
humain, et humanité d'estre cruel.
It is cruelty to be humane to rebels, and
humanity is cruelty.
c.   *Attributed to* Charles IX.—*According
to* M. Fournier, *an expression taken
from a sermon of* Corneille Muis,
Bishop of Bitoute. *Used by*
Catherine de Medicis.

Je voudrais bien voir la grimace qu'il fait à
cette heure sur cet échafaud.
I would love to see the grimace he [Mar-
quis de Cinq-Mars] is now making on the
scaffold.
d.   Louis XIII.—See *Histoire de Louis
XIII.* IV. P. 416.

CUSTOM.

Ein tiefer Sinn wohnt in den alten Bräuchen.
A deep meaning often lies in old customs.
e.   Schiller—*Marie Stuart.* I. 7. 131.

Nicht fremder Brauch gedeiht in einem Lande.
Strange customs do not thrive in foreign
soil.
f.   Schiller—*Demetrius.* I. 1.

Che l' uso dei mortali è come fronda.
In ramo, che sen va, ed altra viene.
The customs and fashions of men change
like leaves on the bough, some of which go
and others come.
g.   Dante—*Paradiso.* XXVI. 137.

D.

DANGER.

Gardez-vous bien de lui les jours qu'il com-
munie.
Beware of him the days that he takes
Communion.
h.   Du Lorens—*Satires.* I.

Il n'y a personne qui ne soit dangereux pour
quelqu'un.
There is no person who is not dangerous
for some one.
i.   Mme de Sévigné—*Lettres.*

DEATH.

La mort sans phrase.
Death without phrases.
j.   *Alluding to the long addresses made by*
Robespierre *and his men when
voting.*

Le lâche fuit en vain ; la mort vole à sa suite ;
C'est en la défiant que le brave l'évite.
It is vain for the coward to flee ; death
follows close behind ; it is only by defying
it that the brave escape.
k.   Voltaire—*Le Triumvirat.* IV. 7.

Nous sommes tous mortels, et chacun est
pour soi.
We are all mortal, and each one is for
himself.
l.   Molière—*L'École des Femmes.* II. 6.

On n'a point pour la mort de dispense de
Rome.
Rome can give no dispensation from death.
m.   Molière—*L'Étourdi.* II. 4.

Qui ne craint point la mort ne craint point
les menaces.
He who does not fear death cares naught
for threats.
n.   Corneille—*Le Cid.* II. 1.

Der lange Schlaf des Todes schliesst unsere
Narben zu, und der kurze des Lebens unsere
Wunden.
The long sleep of death closes our scars,
and the short sleep of life our wounds.
o.   Jean Paul Richter—*Hesperus.* XX.

Die Todten reiten schnell.
The dead ride swiftly.
p.   Bürger—*Leonore.*

Gut' Nacht, Gordon.
Ich denke einen langen Schlaf zu thun.
Good night, Gordon. I am thinking of
taking a long sleep.
q.   Schiller—*Wallenstein's Tod.* V. 5.
85.

Muore per metà chi lascia un' immagine di
se stesso nei fígli.
He only half dies who leaves an image of
himself in his sons.
r.   Goldoni—*Pamela.* II. z.

DECEIT.

Car c'est double plaisir de tromper le trompeur.

It is double pleasure to deceive the deceiver.
a.   La Fontaine—*Fables.* II. 15.

Il faut distinguer entre parler pour tromper et se taire pour être impénétrable.

We must distinguish between speaking to deceive and being silent to be reserved.
b.   Voltaire—*Essai sur les Mœurs.*
Ch. CLXIII.

Le bruit est pour le fat, la plainte pour le sot;
L'honnête homme trompé s'éloigne et ne dit mot.

The silly when deceived exclaim loudly; the fool complains; the honest man walks away and is silent.
c.   La Noue—*La Coquette Corrigée.* I. 3.

L'hypocrisie est un hommage que le vice rend à la vertu.

Hypocrisy is the homage which vice renders to virtue.
d.   La Rochefoucauld—*Maximes.* 218.

On est aisément dupé par ce qu'on aime.

We are easily fooled by that which we love.
e.   Molière—*Le Tartuffe.* IV. 3.

On ne trompe point en bien; la fourberie ajoute la malice au mensonge.

We never deceive for a good purpose; knavery adds malice to falsehood.
f.   La Bruyère—*Les Caractères.* XI.

Pour tromper un rival l'artifice est permis;
On peut tout employer contre ses ennemis.

Artifice is allowable in deceiving a rival; we may employ everything against our enemies.
g.   Richelieu—*Les Tuileries.*

Savoir dissimuler est le savoir des rois.

To know how to dissemble is the knowledge of kings.
h.   Richelieu—*Miranne.*

Vous le croyez votre dupe: s'il feint de l'être, qui est plus dupe, de lui ou de vous?

You think him to be your dupe; if he feigns tŏ be so who is the greater dupe, he or you?
i.   La Bruyère—*Les Caractères.* V.

Man wird nie betrogen, man betrügt sich selbst.

We are never deceived; we deceive ourselves.
j.   Goethe—*Sprüche in Prosa.* III.

Wir betrügen und schmeicheln niemanden durch so feine Kunstgriffe als uns selbst.

We deceive and flatter no one by such delicate artifices as we do our own selves.
k.   Schopenhauer—*Die Welt als Wille.*
I. 350.

Non mancano pretesti quando si vuole.

Pretexts are not wanting when one wishes to use them.
l.   Goldoni—*La Villeggiatura.* I. 12.

DEEDS.

Les belles actions cachées sont les plus estimables.

Noble deeds that are concealed are most esteemed.
m.   Pascal—*Pensées.* I. IX. 21.

Quelque éclatante que soit une action, elle ne doit pas passer pour grande, lorsqu'elle n'est pas l'effet d'un grand dessein.

However resplendent an action may be, it should not be accounted great unless it is the result of a great design.
n.   La Rochefoucauld—*Maximes.* 160.

Und künftige Thaten drangen wie die Sterne
Rings um uns her unzählig aus der Nacht.

And future deeds crowded round us as the countless stars in the night.
o.   Goethe—*Iphigenia auf Tauris.* II.
1. 121.

Wer gar zu viel bedenkt wird wenig leisten.

He who considers too much will perform little.
p.   Schiller—*Wilhelm Tell.* III. 1.

DENIAL.

Ich bin der Geist der stets verneint.

I am the Spirit that denies.
q.   Goethe—*Faust.* I. 3. 163.

DEVIL (THE).

Tout faiseur de jôurnaux doit tribut au Malin.

Every newspaper editor owes tribute to the devil.
r.   La Fontaine—*Lettre à Simon de Troyes.* 1686.

Auch die Kultur, die alle Welt beleckt,
Hat auf den Teufel sich erstreckt.

Culture which smooth the whole world licks,
Also unto the devil sticks.
s.   Goethe—*Faust.* I. 6. 160.

Nein, nein! Der Teufel ist ein Egoist
Und thut nicht leicht um Gottes Willen,
Was einem Andern nützlich ist.

No, no! The devil is an egotist,
And is not apt, without why or wherefore,
"For God's sake," others to assist.
t.   Goethe—*Faust.* I. 4. 124.

Verflucht wer mit dem Teufel spielt.
Accursed be he who plays with the devil.
a.　Schiller—*Wallenstein's Tod.* I. 3.
64.

DIFFICULTIES.

Die grössten Schwierigkeiten liegen da, wo
wir sie nicht suchen.
The greatest difficulties lie where we are
not looking for them.
b.　Goethe—*Sprüche in Prosa.* P. 236.

DISCERNMENT.

Après l'esprit de discernement, ce qu'il y a
au monde de plus rare, ce sont les diamants et
les perles.
The rarest things in the world, next to a
spirit of discernment, are diamonds and
pearls.
c.　La Bruyère—*Les Caractères.* XII.

Lynx envers nos pareils, et taupes envers nous.
Lynx-eyed toward our equals, and moles
to ourselves.
d.　La Fontaine—*Fables.* I. 7.

Qu'on me donne six lignes écrites de la
main du plus honnête homme, j'y trouverai
de quoi le faire pendre.
If you give me six lines written by the
hand of the most honest of men, I will find
something in them which will hang him.
e.　*Attributed to* Richelieu.

Gute Menschen können sich leichter in
schlimme hineindenken als diese in jene.
Good men can more easily see through
bad men than the latter can the former.
f.　Jean Paul Richter—*Hesperus.* IV.

DISEASE.

Doch ein gekränktes Herz erholt sich schwer.
A wounded heart can with difficulty be
cured.
g.　Goethe—*Torquato Tasso.* IV. 4. 24.

D'ogni pianta palesa l'aspetto
Il difetto, che il tronco nasconde
Per le fronde, dal frutto, o dal fior.
The canker which the trunk conceals is
revealed by the leaves, the fruit, or the
flower.
h.　Metastasio—*Giuseppe Riconosciuto.* I.

DISSATISFACTION.

La bouche obéit mal lorsque le cœur mur-
mure.
The mouth obeys poorly when the heart
murmurs.
i.　Voltaire—*Tancrède.* I. 4.

Les délicats sont malheureux,
Rien ne saurait les satisfaire.
The fastidious are unfortunate: nothing
can satisfy them.
j.　La Fontaine—*Fables.* II. 1.

DISTRUST.

Usurpator diffida
Di tutti sempre.
A usurper always distrusts the whole world.
k.　Alfieri—*Polinice.* III. 2.

DOUBT.

Vous ne prouvez que trop que chercher à
connaître
N'est souvent qu' apprendre à douter.
You prove but too clearly that seeking to
know
Is too frequently learning to doubt.
l.　Mme Deshoulières.

Non menno che saper, dubbiar m'aggrata.
Doubting charms me not less than knowledge.
m.　Dante—*Inferno.* XI. 93.

DRESS.

En fait de parure il faut toujours rester au
dessous de ce qu'on peut.
In the matter of dress it is well always to
keep within one's means.
n.　Montesquieu—*Pensées Diverses.*

L'habit ne fait le moine.
The dress does not make the monk.
o.　Rabelais—*Prologue.* I.

Che quant' era più ornata, era più brutta.
Who seems most hideous when adorned
the most.
p.　Ariosto—*Orlando Furioso.* XX. 116.

La ropa no da ciencia.
Dress does not give knowledge.
q.　Yriarte—*Fables.* XXVII.

DUTY.

Le devoir des juges est de rendre justice, leur
métier est de la différer ; quelques uns savent
leur devoir, et font leur métier.
A judge's duty is to grant justice, but his
practice is to delay it : even those judges
who know their duty adhere to the general
practice.
r.　La Bruyère—*Les Caractères.*

Was aber ist deine Pflicht? Die Forderung
des Tages.
But what is your duty? What the day demands.
s.　Goethe—*Sprüche in Prosa.* III. 151.

E.

EATING.

Dis moi ce que tu manges, je te dirai ce que tu es.

Tell me what you eat, and I will tell you what you are.

a.   BRILLAT SAVARIN—*Physiologie du Gout.*

Je veux que le dimanche chaque paysan ait sa poule au pot.

I want every peasant to have a chicken in his pot on Sundays.

b.   HENRY IV. of France.

L'appétit vient en mangeant.

Appetite comes with eating.

c.   RABELAIS—*Gargantua.* I. 5.

Le véritable Amphitryon
Est l'Amphitryon où l'on dine.

The genuine Amphitryon is the Amphitryon with whom we dine.

d.   MOLIÈRE—*Amphitryon.* III. 5.

L'abstenir pour jouir, c'est l'épicurisme de la raison.

To abstain that we may enjoy is the epicurianism of reason.

e.   ROUSSEAU.

Un dîner réchauffé ne valut jamais rien.

A warmed-up dinner was never worth much.

f.   BOILEAU—*Lutrin.* I. 104.

L'anima mia gustava di quel cibo,
Che saziando di sè, di sè s'asseta.

My soul tasted that heavenly food, which gives new appetite while it satiates.

g.   DANTE—*Purgatorio.* XXXI. 128.

END (THE).

En toute chose il faut considérer la fin.

We ought to consider the end in everything.

h.   LA FONTAINE—*Fables.* III. 5.

Et le chemin est long du projet à la chose.

The road is long from the project to its completion.

i.   MOLIÈRE—*Le Tartuffe.* III. 1.

Par les mêmes voies on ne va pas toujours aux mêmes fins.

By the same means we do not always arrive at the same ends.

j.   ST. REAL.

Die schönen Tage in Aranjuez
Sind nun zu Ende.

The lovely days in Aranjuez are now at an end.

k.   SCHILLER—*Don Carlos.* I. 1. 1.

Ich bin der Letzte meines Stamms; mein Name
Endet mit mir.

I am the last of my race. My name ends with me.

l.   SCHILLER—*Wilhelm Tell.* II. 1. 100.

ENEMY.

Le corps d'un ennemi mort sent toujours bon.

The body of a dead enemy always smells sweet.

m.   *Attributed to* VESPASIAN *and* CHARLES IX. of France.

Les dons d'un ennemi leur semblaient trop à craindre.

To them it seemed that the gifts of an enemy were to be dreaded.

n.   VOLTAIRE—*La Henriade.* Ch. II.

ENNUI.

L'ennui naquit un jour de l'uniformité.

One day ennui was born from uniformity.

o.   MOTTE.

Le secret d'ennuyer est celui de tout dire.

The secret of being tiresome is in telling everything.

p.   VOLTAIRE—*Discours Préliminaire.*

Tous les genres sont bons, hors le genre ennuyeux.

All styles are good except the tiresome kind.

q.   VOLTAIRE—*L'Enfant Prodigue.*
         Préface.

Ein Gelehrter hat keine Langeweile.

A scholar knows no ennui.

r.   JEAN PAUL RICHTER—*Hesperus.* 8.

ENTHUSIASM.

Sonderbarer Schwärmer!

Enthusiast most strange.

s.   SCHILLER—*Don Carlos.* III. 10. 277.

Zwang erbittert die Schwärmer immer, aber bekehrt sie nie.

Opposition embitters the enthusiast but never converts him.

t.   SCHILLER—*Cabale und Liebe.* III. 1.

ENVY.

Les envieux mourront, mais non jamais
l'envie.
    The envious will die, but envy never.
a.   MOLIÈRE—*Le Tartuffe.* V. 3.

L'invidia, figliuol mio, se stessa macera,
E si dilegua come agnel per fascino.
    Envy, my son, wears herself away, and
droops like a lamb under the influence of
the evil eye.
b.   SANNAZARO—*Ecloga Sesta.*

EQUALITY.

Siempre acostumbra hacer el vulgo necio.
De le bueno y lo malo igual aprecio.
    The foolish and vulgar are always accus-
tomed to value equally the good and the
bad.
c.   YRIARTE—*Fables.* XXVIII.

ERROR.

Les plus courtes erreurs sont toujours les
meilleures.
    The smallest errors are always the best.
d.   MOLIÈRE—*L'Etourdi.* IV. 4.

Quand tout le monde a tort, tout le monde
a raison.
    When every one is in the wrong, every
one is in the right.
e.   LA CHAUSSÉE—*La Gouvernante.* I. 3.

Est giebt Menschen die gar nicht irren, weil
sie sich nichts Vernünftiges vorsetzen.
    There are men who never err, because
they never propose anything rational.
f.   GOETHE—*Sprüche in Prosa.* III.

Es irrt der Mensch so lang er strebt.
    While man's desires and aspirations stir,
He can not choose but err.
g.   GOETHE—*Faust.*   Prolog im Himmel.
                            Der Herr. L. 77.

EVIL.

Et tous maux sont pareils alors qu'ils sont
extrêmes.
    All evils are equal when they are extreme.
h.   CORNEILLE—*Horace.* III. 4.

Souvent la peur d'un mal nous conduit dans
un pire.
    Often the fear of one evil leads us into a
worse.
i.   BOILEAU—*L'Art Poétique.* I. 64.

Das eben ist der Fluch der bösen That,
Das sie fortzeugend immer Böses muss gebären.
    The very curse of an evil deed is that it
must always continue to engender evil.
j.   SCHILLER—*Piccolomini.* V. 1.

Das Leben ist der Güter höchstes nicht
Der Uebel grösstes aber ist die Schuld.
    Life is not the supreme good, but the su-
preme evil is to realize one's guilt.
k.   SCHILLER—*Die Braut von Messina.*

Den Bösen sind sie los, die Bösen sind ge-
blieben.
    The Evil One has left, the evil ones remain.
l.   GOETHE—*Faust.* I. 6. 174.

Al mondo mal non è senza rimedio.
    There is no evil in the world without a
remedy.
m.   SANNAZARO—*Ecloga Octava.*

Non è male alcuno nelle cose umane che
non abbia congiunto seco qualche bene.
    There is no evil in human affairs that has
not some good mingled with it.
n.   GUICCIARDINI—*Storia d'Italia.*

Superbia, invidia ed avarizia sono
Le tre faville che hanno i cori accesi.
    Three sparks—pride, envy, and avarice—
have been kindled in all hearts.
o.   DANTE—*Inferno.* VI. 74.

Como el hacer mal viene de natural cosecha,
fácilmente se aprende el hacerle.
    Inasmuch as ill-deeds spring up as a
spontaneous crop, they are easy to learn.
p.   CERVANTES—*Coloquio de los Perros.*

EXAMPLE.

L'exemple est un dangereux leurre;
Où la guêpe a passé, le moucheron demeure.
    Example is a dangerous lure: where the
wasp got through the gnat sticks fast.
q.   LA FONTAINE—*Fables.* II. XVI.

EXPERIENCE.

Da dacht ich oft: schwatzt noch so hoch
gelehrt,
Man weiss doch nichts, als was man selbst
erfährt.
    I have often thought that however learned
you may talk about it, one knows nothing
but what he learns from his own experience.
r.   WIELAND—*Oberon.* II. 24.

Tu proverai sì come sa di sale
Lo pane altrui, e com' è duro calle
Lo scendere e'l salir per l'altrui scale.
    Thou shalt know by experience how salt
the savor is of other's bread, and how sad
a path it is to climb and descend another's
stairs.
s.   DANTE—*Paradiso.* XVII. 58.

EYES.

Si vous les voulez aimer, ce sera, ma foi,
pour leurs beaux yeux.

If you wish to love, it shall be, by my
faith, for their beautiful eyes.
a.   Molière—*Les Précieuses Ridicules.*
                                                    XVI.

Der Blick des Forschers fand
Nicht selten mehr, als er zu finden wünschte.

The eye of Paul Pry often finds more than
he wished to find.
b.   Lessing—*Nathan der Weise.* II. 8.

Die blauen Veilchen der Aeugelein.
Those blue violets, her eyes.
c.   Heine—*Lyrisches Intermezzo.* XXXI.

Wenn ich in deine Augen seh'
So schwindet all' mein Leid und Weh.
Whene'er into thine eyes I see,
All pain and sorrow fly from me.
d.   Heine—*Lyrisches Intermezzo.* IV.

Parean l' occhiaje anella senza gemme.
Their eyes seem'd rings from whence the
gems were gone.
e.   Dante—*Purgatorio.* XXIII. 31

F.

FAITH.

Die Botschaft hör' ich wohl, allein mir fehlt
      der Glaube ;
Das Wunder ist des Glaubens liebstes Kind.
Your messages I hear, but faith has not been
      given ;
The dearest child of Faith is Miracle.
f.   Goethe—*Faust.* I. 1. 413.

FAME.

C'est un poids bien pesant qu'un nom trop
tôt fameux.
What a heavy burden is a name that has
become too famous.
g.   Voltaire—*La Henriade.* Ch. III.

Je ne dois qu'à moi seul toute ma renommée.
To myself alone do I owe my fame.
h.   Cornéille—*L' Excuse à Ariste.*

Tel brille au second rang, qui s'eclipse au
premier.
He shines in the second rank, who is
eclipsed in the first.
i.   Voltaire—*La Henriade.* I.

Der rasche Kampf verewigt einen Mann,
Er falle gleich, so preiset ihn das Lied.
Rash combat oft immortalizes man.
If he should fall, he is renowned in song.
j.   Goethe—*Iphigenia auf Tauris.* V. 6.
                                                    43.

La vostra nominanza é color d'erba,
Che viene e va ; e quei la discolora
Per cui ell' esce della terra acerba.
All your renown is like the summer
flower that blooms and dies ; because the
sunny glow which brings it forth, soon
slays with parching power.
k.   Dante—*Purgatoria.* XI. 115.

Non é il mondan romore altro che un fiato
Di vento, che or vien quinci ed or vien quindi,
E muta nome, perchè muta lato.
The splendors that belong unto the fame
of earth are but a wind, that in the same
direction lasts not long.
l.   Dante—*Purgatoria.* XI. 100.

FATE.

On est, quand on veut, maître de son sort.
We are, when we will it, masters of our
own fate.
m.   Ferrier—*Adraste.*

Tes destins sont d'un homme, et tes vœux
sont d'un dieu.
Your destiny is that of a man, and your
vows those of a god.
n.   Voltaire—*La Liberté.*

Blindlings that er blos den Willen des Ge-
      schickes.
Man blindly works the will of fate.
o.   Wieland—*Oberon.* IV. 59.

Der Mensch erfährt, er sei auch wer er mag,
Ein letztes Glück und einen letzten Tag.
Man, be he who he may, experiences a last
piece of good fortune and a last day.
p.   Goethe—*Sprüche in Reimen.* III.

Der Zug des Herzens ist des Schicksals Stimme.
The heart's impulse is the voice of fate.
q.   Schiller—*Piccolomini.* III. 8. 82.

Des Schicksals Zwang ist bitter.
The compulsion of fate is bitter.
r.   Wieland—*Oberon.* V. 60.

Du musst (herrschen und gewinnen
Oder dienen und verlieren
Leiden oder triumphiren)
Amboss oder Hammer sein.
Thou must (in commanding and winning,
or serving and losing, suffering or triumph-
ing) be either anvil or hammer.
s.   Goethe—*Grosscophta.* II.

Mach deine Rechnung mit dem Himmel,
Vogt!
Fort musst du, deine Uhr ist abgelaufen.
  Make thine account with Heaven, governor,
  Thou must away, thy sand is run.
a. | Schiller—*Wilhelm Tell.* IV. 3. 7.

          Sperre dich, so viel du willst!
Des Himmels Wege sind des Himmels Wege.
  Struggle against it as thou wilt, yet Heaven's ways are Heaven's ways.
b.   Lessing—*Nathan der Weise.* III. 1.

Che l'uomo il suo destin fugge di raro.
  For rarely man escapes his destiny.
c.   Ariosto—*Orlando Furioso.* XVIII.
                                        58.

FEAR.

De loin, c'est quelque chose; et de près, ce
n'est rien.
  From a distance it is something; and
  nearby it is nothing.
d.   La Fontaine—*Fables.* IV. 10.

Il faut tout attendre et tout craindre du
temps et des hommes.
  We must expect everything and fear
  everything from time and from men.
e.   Vauvenargues—*Réflexions.* CII.

Ich weiss, dass man vor leeren Schrecken
    zittert;
Doch wahres Unglück bringt der falsche
    Wahn.
  I know that oft we tremble at an empty
  terror, but the false phantasm brings a real
  misery.
f.   Schiller—*Piccolomini.* V. 1. 105.

Wenn ich einmal zu fürchten angefangen
Hab' ich zu fürchten aufgehört.
  As soon as I have begun to fear I have
  ceased to fear.
g.   Schiller—*Don Carlos.* I. 6. 68.

Wer nichts fürchtet ist nicht weniger mäch-
tig, als der, den Alles fürchtet.
  The man who fears nothing is not less
  powerful than he who is feared by every
  one.
h.   Schiller—*Die Räuber.* I. 1.

Wir Deutschen fürchten Gott, sonst aber
Nichts in der Welt.
  We Germans fear God, but nothing else
  in the world.
i.   Prince Bismarck—*In the Reichstag.*
                                        1887.

Bello in si bella vistà anco è l'orrore,
E di mezzo la tema esce il diletto.
  Horror itself in that fair scene looks gay,
  And joy springs up e'en in the midst of fear.
j.   Tasso—*Gerusalemme.* XX. 30.

El miedo tiene muchos ojos.
  Fear has many eyes.
k.   Cervantes—*Don Quixote.* III. 6.

FIRMNESS.

J'y suis, j'y reste.
  I am here, here I remain.
l.   Marshal MacMahon.

Aber wer fest auf dem Sinne beharrt, der
bildet die Welt sich.
  He who is firm in will molds the world
  to himself.
m.   Goethe—*Hermann und Dorothea.*
                                        IX. 303.
Sta come torre ferma, che non crolla
Giammai la cima per soffiar de' venti.
  Be steadfast as a tower, that doth not bend
  its stately summit to the tempest's shock.
n.   Dante—*Purgatorio.* V. 14

FLATTERY.

On croit quelquefois haïr la flatterie; mais
on ne hait que la manière de flatter.
  We sometimes think that we hate flattery,
  but we only hate the manner in which it is
  done.
o.   La Rochefoucauld—*Maximes.* 329.

Es ist dem Menschen leichter und geläufiger,
zu schmeicheln als zu loben.
  It is easier and handier for men to flatter
  than to praise.
p.   Jean Paul Richter—*Titan.* Zykel 34.

FOLLY.

Ce livre n'est pas long, on le voit en une heure;
La plus courte folie est toujours la meilleure.
  This book is not long, one may run over
  it in an hour; the shortest folly is always
  the best.
q.   La Girandière—*Le Recueil des Voyeux
                                        Epigrammes.*
Hélas! on voit que de tout temps
Les petits ont pâti des sottises des grands.
  Alas! we see that the small have always
  suffered for the follies of the great.
r.   La Fontaine—*Fables.* II. 4.

Le sot est comme le peuple, qui se croit riche
de peu.
  The fool is like those people who think
  themselves rich with little.
s.   Vauvenargues—*Réflexions.* CCLX.

L'exactitude est le sublime des sots.
  Exactness is the sublimity of fools.
t.   Attributed to Fontenelle, *who
                                        disclaimed it.*

Qui se croit sage, ô ciel! est un grand fou.

He who thinks himself wise, O heavens! is a great fool.

a.   VOLTAIRE—*Le Droit du Seigneur.*
IV. 1.

Qui vit sans folie n'est pas si sage qu'il croit.

He who lives without committing any folly is not so wise as he thinks.

b.   LA ROCHEFOUCAULD—*Maximes.* 209.

Un fat est celui que les sots croient un homme de mérite.

A coxcomb is one whom simpletons believe to be a man of merit.

c.   LA BRUYÈRE—*Les Caractères.* XII.

Un sot n'a pas assez d'étoffe pour être bon.

A fool has not material enough to be good.

d.   LA ROCHEFOUCAULD—*Maximes.* 387.

Un sot trouve toujours un plus sot qui l'admire.

A fool always finds one still more foolish to admire him.

e.   BOILEAU—*L'Art Poétique.* I. 232.

Da macht wieder jemand einmal einen dummen Streich.

Somebody is again doing a stupid thing.

f.   GOETHE—*Clavigo.* Act III.

Noth und Jammer sind die Gaben
So die Thorheit ernten kann.

Want and sorrow are the gifts that folly may earn.

g.   SCHUBART—*Der Bettler.*

Wer nicht liebt Wein, Weib, und Gesang,
Der bleibt ein Narr sein Leben lang.

He who loves not wine, woman, and song,
Remains a fool his whole life long.

h.   Attributed to LUTHER, *probably a saying of J. H. Voss.*

Chi conta i colpi e la dovuta offesa,
Mentr' arde la tenzon, misura e pesa?

A fool is he that comes to preach or prate,
When men with swords their right and wrong debate.

i.   TASSO—*Gerusalemme.* V. 57.

FORCE.

La force est la reine du monde, et non pas l'opinion; mais l'opinion est celle qui use de la force.

Force and not opinion is the queen of the world; but it is opinion that uses the force.

j.   PASCAL—*Pensées.* Art. XXIV. 92.

L'aimable siècle où l'homme dit à l'homme,
Soyons frères, ou je t'assomme.

Those glorious days, when man said to man, Let us be brothers, or I will knock you down.

k.   LE BRUN.

Plus fait douceur que violence.

Gentleness succeeds better than violence.

l.   LA FONTAINE—*Fables.* VI. 3.

Est ist hier wie in den alten Zeiten
Wo die Klinge noch alles that bedeuten.

It is now as in the days of yore when the sword ruled all things.

m.   SCHILLER—*Wallenstein's Lager.* VI. 140.

Di qui nacque che tutti li profeti armati vinsero, e li disarmati rovinarono.

Hence it happened that all the armed prophets conquered, all the unarmed perished.

n.   MACHIAVELLI—*Il Principe.* C. 6.

FORGIVENESS.

Qui pardonne aisément invite à l'offenser.

He who forgives readily only invites offense.

o.   CORNEILLE—*Cinna.* IV. 4.

FORTUNE.

C'est la fortune de France.

It is the fortune of France.

p.   PHILIP the Fortunate.

Fortune aveugle suit aveugle hardiesse.

Blind fortune pursues inconsiderate rashness.

q.   LA FONTAINE—*Fables.* X. 14.

Il lit au front de ceux qu'un vain luxe environne,
Que la fortune vend ce qu'on croit qu'elle donne.

We read on the forehead of those who are surrounded by a foolish luxury, that Fortune sells what she is thought to give.

r.   LA FONTAINE—*Philémon et Baucis.*

La fortune ne paraît jamais si aveugle qu' à ceux à qui elle ne fait pas de bien.

Fortune never seems so blind as to those upon whom she confers no favors.

s.   LA ROCHEFOUCAULD—*Maximes.* 391.

Das Glück erhebe billig der Beglückte.

It is the fortunate who should extol fortune.

t.   GOETHE—*Torquato Tasso.* II. 3. 115.

Ein Tag der Gunst ist wie ein Tag der Ernte,
Man muss geschäftig sein sobald sie reift.

The day of fortune is like a harvest day,
We must be busy when the corn is ripe.

u.   GOETHE—*Torquato Tasso.* IV. 4. 62.

Che sovente addivien che'l saggio è'l forte.
Fabro a se stesso è di beata sorte.

They make their fortune who are stout and wise,
Wit rules the heavens, discretion guides the skies.

v.   TASSO—*Gerusalemme.* X. 20.

FREEDOM.

Der Mensch ist frei geschaffen, ist frei
Und würd' er in Ketten geboren.

Man is created free, and is free, even
though born in chains.
a.   SCHILLER—*Die Worte des Glaubens.*
St. 2.

Frei athmen macht das Leben nicht allein.

Merely to breathe freely does not mean to live.
b.   GOETHE—*Iphigenia auf Tauris.* I.
2. 54.

Freiheit ist nur in dem Reich der Träume
Und das Schöne blüht nur im Gesang.

Freedom is only in the land of dreams,
and the beautiful only blooms in song.
c.   SCHILLER—*The Beginning of the New
Century.* St. 9.

O, nur eine freie Seele wird nicht alt.

Oh, only a free soul will never grow old !
d.   JEAN PAUL RICHTER—*Titan.* Zykel
140.

FRIENDSHIP.

La blessure est pour vous, la douleur est
pour moi.

The wound is for you, but the pain is
for me.
e.   CHARLES IX. *to* COLIGNY *who was
fatally wounded in the massacre of St.
Bartholomew's Day.*

Les amis—ces parents que l'on se fait soi-même.

Friends, those relations that one makes
for one's self.
f.   DESCHAMPS—*L'Ami.*

Le sort fait les parents, le choix fait les amis.

Chance makes our parents, but choice
makes our friends.
g.   DELILLE—*Pitié.*

Soyons amis, Cinna, c'est moi qui t'en
convie.

Let us be friends, Cinna, it is I who invite
you to be so.
h.   CORNEILLE—*Cinna.* V. 3.

Un livre est un ami qui ne trompe jamais.

A book is a friend that never deceives.
i.   GUILBERT DE PIXÉRÉCOURT.

Wer nicht die Welt in seinen Freunden sieht
Verdient nicht, dass die Welt von ihm erfahre.

He who does not see the whole world in
his friends, does not deserve that the world
should hear of him.
j.   GOETHE—*Torquato Tasso.* I. 3. 68.

Quien te conseja encobria de tus amigos.
Engañar te quiere assaz, y sin testigos.

He who advises you to be reserved to your
friends wishes to betray you without witnesses.
k.   MANUEL CONDE LUCANOR.

FUTURITY.

Après nous le déluge.

After us the deluge.
l.   MME. POMPADOUR—Attributed also to
Louis XV.

Je m'en vay chercher un grand peut-estre.

I am going to seek a great perhaps.
m.   RABELAIS—*His last words, according to*
MOTTEUX.

Le présent est gros de l'avenir.

The present is great with the future.
n.   LEIBNITZ.

Etwas fürchten und hoffen und sorgen,
Muss der Mensch für den kommenden Morgen.

Man must have some fears, hopes, and
cares, for the coming morrow.
o.   SCHILLER—*Die Braut von Messina.*

G.

GENIUS.

Entre esprit et talent il y a la proportion
du tout à sa partié.

Between genius and talent there is the
proportion of the whole to its parts.
p.   LA BRUYÈRE—*Les Caractères.* XII.

Das erste und letzte, was vom Genie gefor-
dert wird, ist Wahrheits-Liebe.

The first and last thing required of genius
is the love of truth.
q.   GOETHE—*Sprüche in Prosa.* III.

Das Licht des Genie's bekam weniger
Fett, als das Licht des Lebens.

The lamp of genius burns quicker than
the lamp of life.
r.   SCHILLER—*Fiesco.* II. 17.

GIFTS.

Denn der Wille
Und nicht die Gabe macht den Geber.

For the will and not the gift makes the
giver.
s.   LESSING—*Nathan der Weise.* I. 5.

Denn Geben ist Sache des Reichen.
For to give is the business of the rich.
a.   GOETHE—*Hermann und Dorothea.*
I. 15.

Denn was ein Mensch auch hat, so sind's
am Ende Gaben.
For whatever a man has, is in reality
only a gift.
b.   WIELAND—*Oberon.* II. 19.

Die Gaben
Kommen von oben herab, in ihren eignen
Gestalten.
Gifts come from above in their own pecu-
liar forms.
c.   GOETHE—*Hermann und Dorothea.*
Canto V. L. 69.

Gleich schenken? das ist brav. Da wird er
reüssiren.
Presents at once? That's good. He is sure
to succeed.
d.   GOETHE—*Faust.* I. 7. 73.

GLORY.

Aucun chemin de fleurs ne conduit à la gloire.
No flowery road leads to glory.
e.   LA FONTAINE—*Fables.* X. 14.

La gloire n'est jamais où la vertu n'est pas.
Glory is never where virtue is not.
f.   LE FRANC—*Didon.*

GOD.

L'impossibilité où je suis de prouver que
Dieu n'est pas, me decouvre son existence.
The very impossibility in which I find
myself to prove that God is not, discloses
to me his existence.
g.   LA BRUYÈRE—*Les Caractères.* XVI.

Si Dieu n'existait pas, il faudrait l'inventer.
If God did not exist, it would be necessary to invent him.
h.   VOLTAIRE—*Epitre à l'Auteur des Trois
Imposteurs.*

Es lebt ein Gott zu strafen und zu rächen.
There is a God to punish and avenge.
i.   SCHILLER—*Wilhelm Tell.* IV. 3. 37.

Wie einer ist, so ist sein Gott,
Darum ward Gott so oft zu Spott.
As a man is, so is his God; therefore God
was so often an object of mockery.
j.   GOETHE—*Gedichte.*

Ha sotto i piedi il Fato e la Natura.
Ministri umili; e'l moto e chi'l misura.
Under whose feet (subjected to His grace),
Sit nature, fortune, motion, time, and place.
k.   TASSO—*Gerusalemme.* IX. 56.

GOODNESS.

Das Uebel macht eine Geschichte und das
Gute keine.
Sin writes histories, goodness is silent.
l.   GOETHE—*See* RIEMER, *Mittheilungen
über Goethe.* II. 9. 1810.

Denn Gott lohnt Gutes, hier gethan, auch
hier noch.
For God rewards good deeds done here
below—rewards them here.
m.   LESSING—*Nathan der Weise.* I. 2.

Weiss
Dass alle Länder gute Menschen tragen.
Know this, that every country can produce good men.
n.   LESSING—*Nathan der Weise.* II. 5.

GOVERNMENT.

La corruption de chaque gouvernement
commence presque toujours par celle des
principes.
The deterioration of a government begins
almost always by the decay of its principles.
o.   MONTESQUIEU—*De l' Esprit.* VIII.
Ch. I.

Les républiques finissent par le luxe; les
monarchies, par la pauvreté.
Republics end through luxury; monarchies through poverty.
p.   MONTESQUIEU—*De l' Esprit.* VII.
Ch. IV.

L'état c'est moi.
I am the state.
q.   *Attributed to* LOUIS XIV.

Welche Regierung die beste sei? Diejenige
die uns lehrt uns selbst zu regieren.
What government is the best? That
which teaches us to govern ourselves.
r.   GOETHE—*Sprüche in Prosa.* III.

Gli ambasciadori sono l'occhio e l'orecchio
degli stati.
Ambassadors are the eye and ear of states.
s.   GUICCIARDINI—*Storia d' Italia.*

GRATITUDE.

La reconnaissance est la mémoire du cœur.
Gratitude is the memory of the heart.
t.   MASSIEU *to the* ABBÉ SICARD.

L'ingratitude attire les reproches comme la
reconnaissance attire de nouveaux bienfaits.
Ingratitude calls forth reproaches as gratitude brings renewed kindnesses.
u.   MME. DE SÉVIGNÉ—*Lettres.*

GREATNESS.

Il n'appartient qu'aux grands hommes
d'avoir de grands défauts.

It is the prerogative of great men only to
have great defects.

a.   LA ROCHEFOUCAULD—*Maximes.*

Les grands ne sont grands que parceque
nous les portons sur nos épaules ; nous n'avons
qu'à les secouer pour en joncher la terre.

The great are only great because we carry
them on our shoulders ; when we throw
them off they sprawl on the ground.

b.   MONTANDRÉ—*Point de l' Ovale.*

Les grands ne sont grands que parceque
nous sommes à genoux : relevons nous.

The great are only great because we are
on our knees. Let us rise up.

c.   PRUD'HOMME—*Révolutions de Paris.*
           Motto.

Es ist der Fluch der Hohen, dass die Niedern
Sich ihres offnen Ohrs bemächtigen.

The curse of greatness :
Ears ever open to the babbler's tale.

d.   SCHILLER—*Die Braut von Messina.* I.

GRIEF.

Le ciel me prive d'une épouse qui ne m'a jamais donné d'autre chagrin que celui de sa mort.

Heaven deprives me of a wife who never
caused me any other grief than that of her
death.

e.   LOUIS XIV.

Wer sich entschliessen kann, besiegt den
Schmerz.

He who is resolute conquers grief.

f.   GOETHE—*Torquato Tasso.* III. 2. 84.

Se a ciascun l'interno affanno
Si leggesse in fronte scritto,
Quanti mai, che invidia fanno,
Ci farebbero pietà !

If our inward griefs were seen written on
our brow, how many would be pitied who
are now envied !

g.   METASTASIO—*Giuseppe Riconosiuto.* I.

GROWTH.

Im engen Kreis verengert sich der Sinn.
Es wächst der Mensch mit seinen grössern
     Zwecken.

In a narrow circle the mind contracts.
Man grows with his expanded needs.

h.   SCHILLER—*Prolog.* I. 59.

H.

HAPPINESS.

Le bonheur des méchants comme un torrent
s'écoule.

The happiness of the wicked flows away
as a torrent.

i.   RACINE—*Athalie.* II. 7.

Le bonheur semble fait pour être partagé.

Happiness seems made to be shared.

j.   CORNEILLE—*Notes par Rochefoucauld.*

On n'est jamais si heureux, ni si malheureux, qu'on se l'imagine.

We are never so happy, nor so unhappy,
as we suppose ourselves to be.

k.   LA ROCHEFOUCAULD—*Maximes.*

Où peut-on être mieux qu'au sein de sa
famille ?

Where can we better be than in the
bosom of our family ?

l.   DU LORENS—*Lucile.*

Das beste Glück, des Lebens schönste Kraft
Ermattet endlich.

The highest happiness, the purest joys of
life, wear out at last.

m.   GOETHE—*Iphigenia auf Tauris.* IV. 5. 9.

Des Menschen Wille, das ist sein Glück.

The will of a man is his happiness.

n.   SCHILLER—*Wallenstein's Lager.* VII.
           25.

Ich habe genossen das irdische Glück,
Ich habe gelebt und geliebet.

I have enjoyed earthly happiness,
I have lived and loved.

o.   SCHILLER—*Piccolomini.* III. 7. 9.

HASTE.

Le trop de promptitude à l'erreur nous expose.

Too great haste leads us to error.

p.   MOLIÈRE—*Sganarelle.* I. 12.

HATRED.

Qui vit haï de tous ne saurait longtemps vivre.

He who is hated by all can not expect to
live long.

q.   CORNEILLE—*Cinna.* I. 2.

Der grösste Hass ist, wie die grösste Tugend
und die schlimmsten Hunde, still.

The greatest hatred, like the greatest virtue and the worst dogs, is silent.

r.   JEAN PAUL RICHTER—*Hesperus.* XII.

HEART.

L'oreille est le chemin du cœur.

The ear is the avenue to the heart.
a. VOLTAIRE—*Réponse au Roi de Prusse.*

HEROES.

Il faut être bien héros pour l'être aux yeux de son valet-de-chambre.

A man must indeed be a hero to appear such in the eyes of his valet.
b. MARSHAL CATINAT.

Il n'y a pas de grand homme pour son valet-de-chambre.

No man is a hero to his valet.
c. MME. DE CORNUEL. *See* MLLE AÏSSÉ—
        Lettres. 161.

Es gibt für den Kammerdiener keinen Helden.

To a valet no man is a hero.
d. GOETHE—*Wahlverwandtschaften.* II. 5.
      Aus Ottilien's Tagebüche.

HISTORY.

L'histoire n'est que le tableau des crimes et des malheurs.

History is only the register of crimes and misfortunes.
e. VOLTAIRE—*L'Ingénu.* X.

Der Historiker ist ein rückwärts gekehrter Prophet.

The historian is a prophet looking backwards.
f. SCHLEGEL—*Athenæum. Berlin.*
        I. 2. 20.

Die Weltgeschichte ist das Weltgericht.

The world's history is the world's judgment.
g. SCHILLER—*Resignation.* 17.

HONOR.

Faisons ce que l'honneur exige.

Let us do what honor demands.
h. RACINE—*Bérénice.* IV. 4.

Ici l'honneur m'oblige, et j'y veux satisfaire.

Here honor binds me, and I wish to satisfy it.
i. CORNEILLE—*Polyeucte.* IV. 3.

L'honneur est comme une île escarpée et sans bords;
On n'y peut plus rentrer dès qu'on en est dehors.

Honor is like an island, rugged and without shores; we can never re-enter it once we are on the outside.
j. BOILEAU—*Satires.* X. 167.

Mais sans argent l'honneur n'est qu'une maladie.

But without money honor is nothing but a malady.
k. RACINE—*Plaideurs.* I. 1.

Tout est perdu, fors l'honneur.

All is lost save honor.
l. FRANCIS I.—*Letter to his mother after the*
   battle of Pavia. See CHATEAUBRIAND
   —*Études Historiques.* I. P. 128.

Das Herz und nicht die Meinung ehrt den Mann.

What he feels and not what he does honors a man.
m. SCHILLER—*Wallenstein's Tod.* IV. 8. 70.

Nichtswürdig ist die Nation, die nicht
Ihr alles freudig setzt an ihre Ehre.

That nation is worthless which does not joyfully stake everything on her honor.
n. SCHILLER—*Die Jungfrau von Orleans.*
        I. 5. 81.

Perchè non i titoli illustrano gli uomini, ma gli uomini i titoli.

For titles do not reflect honor on men, but rather men on their titles.
o. MACHIAVELLI—*Dei Discorsi.* III. 38.

HOPE.

L' espérance, toute trompeuse qu'elle est, sert au moins à nous mener à la fin de la vie par un chemin agréable.

Hope, deceitful as it is, serves at least to lead us to the end of life along an agreeable road.
p. LA ROCHEFOUCAULD—*Maximes.* 168.

Bei so grosser Gefahr kommt die leichteste Hoffnung in Anschlag.

In so great a danger the faintest hope should be considered.
q. GOETHE—*Egmont.* II.

Verzweifle keiner je, dem in der trübsten Nacht
Der Hoffnung letzte Sterne schwinden.

Let no one despair, even though in the darkest night the last star of hope may disappear.
r. SCHILLER—*Oberon.* I. 27.

Wir hoffen immer, und in allen Dingen
Ist besser hoffen als verzweifeln.

We always hope, and in all things it is better to hope than to despair.
s. GOETHE—*Torquato Tasso.* III. 4. 197.

Lasciate ogni speranza voi ch'entrate.

Abandon hope, all ye who enter here.
t. DANTE—*Inferno.* III. 1. 9.

Senza speme vivemo in desio.

Still desiring, we live without hope.
u. DANTE—*Inferno.* IV. 42.

I.

IGNORANCE.

Rien n'est si dangereux qu'un ignorant ami:
Mieux vaudrait un sage ennemi.
> Nothing is so dangerous as an ignorant
> friend ; a wise enemy is worth more.
a.   LA FONTAINE—*Fables*. VIII. 10.

Es ist nichts Schrecklicher als eine thätige
Unwissenheit.
> There is nothing more frightful than an
> active ignorance.
b.   GOETHE—*Sprüche in Prosa*.   III.

IMAGINATION.

Celui qui a de l'imagination sans érudition
a des ailes, et n'a pas de pieds.
> He who has imagination without learning
> has wings but no feet.
c.   JOUBERT.

C'est l'imagination qui gouverne le genre
humain.
> The human race is governed by its imagi-
> nation.
d.   NAPOLEON I.

Es ist nichts fürchterlicher als Einbild-
ungskraft ohne Geschmack.
> There is nothing more fearful than imag-
> ination without taste.
e.   GOETHE—*Sprüche in Prosa*.   III.

IMITATION.

C'est un bétail servile et sot à mon avis
Que les imitateurs.
> Imitators are a slavish herd and fools in
> my opinion.
f.   LA FONTAINE—*Clymène*. V. 54.

Der Mensch ist ein nachahmendes Geschöpf.
Und wer der Vorderste ist, führt die Heerde.
> An imitative creature is man; whoever is
> foremost, leads the herd.
g.   SCHILLER—*Wallenstein's Tod*. III.
                                       4.   9.

L'imitazione del male supera sempre l'e-
sempio ; come per il contrario, l'imitazione
del bene è sempre inferiore.
> He who imitates what is evil always goes
> beyond the example that is set; on the
> contrary, he who imitates what is good
> always falls short.
h.   GUICCIARDINI—*Storia d' Italia*.

INDOLENCE.

L'indolence est le sommeil des esprits.
> Indolence is the sleep of the mind.
i.   VAUVENARGUES—*Reflexions*.   390.

INJUSTICE.

L'injustice à la fin produit l'indépendance.
> Injustice in the end produces indepen-
> dence.
j.   VOLTAIRE—*Trancrède*. III. 2.

INNOCENCE.

Mais l'innocence enfin n'a rien à redouter.
> But innocence has nothing to dread.
k.   RACINE—*Phèdre*. III. 6.

On devient innocent quand on est malheureux.
> We become innocent when we are un-
> fortunate.
l.   LA FONTAINE—*Nymphes de Vaux*.

O mon Dieu, conserve-moi innocente, donne
la grandeur aux autres !
> O God, keep me innocent; make others
> great !
m.   CAROLINE MATILDA—*Scratched on a
>   window of the Castle Fredericksborg.*

INSOLENCE.

Qui se laisse outrager, mérite qu'on l'outrage;
Et l'audace impunie enfle trop un courage.
> He who allows himself to be insulted de-
> serves to be so ; and insolence, if unpunish-
> ed, increases !
n.   CORNEILLE—*Heraclius*. I. 2.

Kein Heiligthum heisst uns den Schimpf
ertragen.
> No sacred fane requires us to submit to
> insult.
o.   GOETHE—*Torquato Tasso*. II. 3. 191.

INSTINCT.

Nous n'écoutons d'instincts que ceux qui
                    sont les nôtres.
Et ne croyons le mal que quand il est venu.
> 'Tis thus we heed no instincts but our own,
> Believe no evil, till the evil's done.
p.   LA FONTAINE—*Fables*. I. 8,

Ein guter Mensch in seinem dunkeln Drange
Ist sich des rechten Weges wohl bewusst.
> A good man, through obscurest aspirations,
> Has still an instinct of the one true way.
q.   GOETHE—*Faust. Prolog im Himmel.
>   Der Herr.* L. 88.

J.

JEALOUSY.

Les hommes sont la cause que les femmes ne s'aiment point.

Men are the cause of women not loving one another.
a.   La Bruyère.

O, der alles vergrössernden Eifersucht.

O jealousy! thou magnifier of trifles.
b.   Schiller—*Fiesco.* I. 1.

JESTING.

Diseur de bon mots, mauvais caractère.

A jester, a bad character.
c.   Pascal—*Pensées.* Art. VI. 22.

La moquerie est souvent une indigence d'esprit.

Jesting, often, only proves a want of intellect.
d.   La Bruyère.

Der Spass verliert Alles, wenn der Spassmacher selber lacht.

A jest loses its point when the jester laughs himself.
e.   Schiller—*Fiesco.* I. 7.

JOY.

Die Freude macht drehend, wirblicht.

Joy makes us giddy, dizzy.
f.   Lessing—*Minna von Barnhelm.* II. 3.

JUDGMENT.

On est quelquefois un sot avec de l'esprit; mais on ne l'est jamais avec du jugement.

We sometimes see a fool possessed of talent, but never of judgment.
g.   La Rochefoucauld—*Maximes.* 456.

Denn aller Ausgang ist ein Gottesurtheil.

For every event is a judgment of God.
h.   Schiller—*Wallenstein's Tod.* I. 7. 32.

Bisogna che i giudici siano assai, perchè pochi sempre fanno a modo de' pochi.

There should be many judges, for few will always do the will of few.
i.   Machiavelli—*Dei Discorsi.* I. 7.

JUSTICE.

L'amour de la justice n'est, en la plupart des hommes, que la crainte de souffrir l'injustice.

The love of justice is, in most men, nothing more than the fear of suffering injustice.
j.   La Rochefoucauld—*Maximes.*

On ne peut être juste si on n'est pas humain.

One can not be just if one is not humane.
k.   Vauvenargues—*Réflexions.* XXVIII.

Nicht Stimmenmehrheit ist des Rechtes Probe.

The proof of justice lies not in the voice of the majority.
l.   Schiller—*Marie Stuart.* II. 3.

Cima di giudizio non s'avvalla.

Justice does not descend from its pinnacle.
m.   Dante—*Purgatorio.* VI. 37.

K.

KNOWLEDGE.

Faites comme si je ne le savais pas.

Act as though I knew nothing.
n.   Molière—*Le Bourgeois Gentilhomme.*
                                  II. 6.

Il connoît l'univers, et ne se connoît pas.

He knoweth the universe, and himself he knoweth not.
o.   La Fontaine—*Fables.* VIII. 26.

Laissez dire les sots : le savoir a son prix.

Let fools the studious despise,
There's nothing lost by being wise.
p.   La Fontaine—*Fables.* VIII. 19.

Vous parlez devant un homme à qui tout Naples est connu.

You speak before a man to whom all Naples is known.
q.   Molière—*L'Avarc.* V. 5.

Eigentlich weiss man nur wenn man wenig weiss; mit dem Wissen wächst der Zweifel.

We know accurately only when we know little; with knowledge doubt increases.
r.   Goethe—*Sprüche in Prosa.*

Wer viel weiss
Hat viel zu sorgen.

He who knows much has many cares.
s.   Lessing—*Nathan der Weise.* IV. 2.

Willst du dich selber erkennen, so sieh' wie die andern es treiben ;
Willst du die andern versteh'n, blick in dein eigenes Herz.

If you wish to know yourself observe how others act.
If you wish to understand others look into your own heart.
t.   Schiller—*Xenien.*

L.

LABOR.

Der Mohr hat seine Arbeit gethan, der Mohr kann gehen.

> The Moor has done his work, the Moor may go.
> *a.*   SCHILLER—*Fiesco.* III. 4.

LANGUAGE.

L'accent du pays où l'on est né demeure dans l'esprit et dans le cœur comme dans le langage.

> The accent of one's country dwells in the mind and in the heart as much as in the language.
> *b.*   LA ROCHEFOUCAULD—*Maximes.* 342.

L'accent est l'âme du discours, il lui donne le sentiment et la vérité.

> Accent is the soul of a language; it gives the feeling and truth to it.
> *c.*   ROUSSEAU—*Émile.* I.

La grammaire, qui sait régenter jusqu'aux rois,
Et les fait, la main haute, obéir à ses lois.

> Grammar, which knows how to lord it over kings, and with high hands makes them obey its laws.
> *d.*   MOLIÈRE—*Les Femmes Savantes.* II. 6.

LAUGHTER.

Ce n'est pas être bien aisé que de rire.

> He is not always at ease who laughs.
> *e.*   ST. EVREMOND.

La plus perdue de toutes les journées est celle où l'on n'a pas rit.

> The most completely lost of all days is that on which one has not laughed.
> *f.*   CHAMFORT.

Tel qui rit vendredi, dimanche pleurera.

> He who laughs on Friday will weep on Sunday.
> *g.*   RACINE—*Plaideurs.* I. 1.

Niemand wird tiefer traurig als wer zu viel lächelt.

> No one will be more profoundly sad than he who laughs too much.
> *h.*   JEAN PAUL RICHTER—*Hesperus.* XIX.

Cio ch'io vedeva mi sembrava un riso
Dell' universo.

> What I saw was equal ecstasy :
> One universal smile it seemed of all things.
> *i.*   DANTE—*Paradiso.* XXVII. 5.

LAW.

La charte sera désormais une vérité.

> The charter will henceforth be a reality.
> *j.*   LOUIS PHILIPPE.

La loi permet souvent ce que défend l'honneur.

> The law often allows what honor forbids.
> *k.*   SAURIN—*Spartacus.* III. 3.

Le bruit des armes l'empeschoit d'entendre **la voix** des lois.

> The clatter of arms drowns the voice of the law.
> *l.*   MONTAIGNE—*Essais.* III. I.

Es erben sich Gesetz und Rechte
Wie eine ew'ge Krankheit fort.

> All rights and laws are still transmitted,
> Like an eternal sickness to the race.
> *m.*   GOETHE—*Faust.* I. 4. 449.

Ove son leggi,
Tremar non dee chi leggi non infranse.

> Where there are laws, he who has not broken them need not tremble.
> *n.*   ALFIERI—*Virginia.* II. 1.

Perchè, così come i buoni costumi, per mantenersi, hanno bisogno delli leggi; così le leggi per osservarsi, hanno bisogno de' buoni costumi.

> For as laws are necessary that good manners may be preserved, so there is need of good manners that laws may be maintained.
> *o.*   MACHIAVELLI—*Dei Discorsi.* I. 18.

LEARNING.

Ils n'ont rien appris, ni rien oublie.

> They have learned nothing, and they have forgotten nothing.
> *p.*   Attributed to TALLEYRAND.

Pardieu! les plus grands clercs ne sont pas les plus finis.

> Indeed the greatest scholars are not the wisest men.
> *q.*   REGNIER.

Que nuist savoir tousjours et tousjours apprendre, fust ce
D'un sot, d'une pot, d'une que—doufle
D'un mouffe, d'un pantoufle.

> What harm in learning and getting knowledge even from a sot, a pot, a fool, a mitten, or a slipper.
> *r.*   RABELAIS—*Pantagruel.* III. 16.

LIBERTY.

L'arbre de la liberté ne croit qu'arrosé par
le sang des tyrans.

> The tree of liberty grows only when
> watered by the blood of tyrants.

a.　　BARÉRE—*Speech in the Convention
Nationale.* 1792.

Le Césarisme, c'est la démocratie sans la
liberté.

> Cæsarism is democracy without liberty.

b.　　TAXILE DELORD—*L'Histoire du
Second Empire.*

Rendre l'homme infâme, et le laisser libre,
est une absurdité qui peuple nos forêts d'as-
sassins.

> To brand man with infamy, and let him
> free, is an absurdity that peoples our forests
> with assassins.

c.　　DIDEROT.

LIFE.

Chaque instant de la vie est un pas vers la
mort.

> Every moment of life is a step toward the
> grave.

d.　　CRÉBILLON—*Tite et Bérénice.* I. 5.

Condition de l'homme, inconstance, ennui,
inquietude.

> The state of man is inconstancy, ennui,
> anxiety.

e.　　PASCAL—*Pensées.* Art. VI. 46.

Dieu est le poëte, les hommes ne sont que les
acteurs. Ces grandes pièces qui se jouent sur
la terre ont été composées dans le ciel.

> God is the author, men are only the play-
> ers. These grand pieces which are played
> upon earth have been composed in heaven.

f.　　BALZAC—*Socrate Chrétien.*

J'ai vécu.

> I have survived.

g.　　*Said by* SIÈYES *after the Reign of Terror,
when asked what he had done.*

La plupart des hommes emploient la pre-
mière partie de leur vie à rendre l'autre mis-
érable.

> Most men employ the first part of life
> to make the other part miserable.

h.　　LA BRUYÈRE—*Les Caractères.* XI.

Ma vie est un combat.

> My life is a struggle.

i.　　VOLTAIRE—*Le Fanatisme.* II. 4.

Das Spiel des Lebens sieht sich heiter an,
Wenn man den sichern Schatz im Herzen
trägt.

> The game of life looks cheerful when one
> carries a treasure safe in his heart.

j.　　SCHILLER—*Piccolomini.* III. 4. 50.

Der Mensch hat hier dritthalb Minuten, eine
zu lächeln—eine zu seufzen—und eine halbe
zu lieben : denn mitten in dieser Minute stirbt
er.

> Man has here two and a half minutes—one
> to smile, one to sigh, and a half to love : for
> in the midst of this minute he dies.

k.　　JEAN PAUL RICHTER—*Hesperus.* IV.

Des Lebens Mai blüht einmal und nicht
wieder.

> The May of life blooms once and never
> again.

l.　　SCHILLER—*Resignation.* St. 2.

Die Parzen und Furien ziehen auch mit ver-
bundnen Händen um das Leben, wie die Gra-
zien und die Sirenen.

> The Fates and Furies, as well as the
> Graces and Sirens, glide with linked hands
> over life.

m.　　JEAN PAUL RICHTER—*Titan.* Zykel 140.

Die Rose blüht nicht ohne Dornen. Ja:
wenn nur aber nicht die Dornen die Rose
überlebten.

> The rose does not bloom without thorns.
> True : but would that the thorns did not
> outlive the rose.

n.　　JEAN PAUL RICHTER—*Titan.*
Zykel 105.

Die uns das Leben gaben, herrliche Gefühle
Erstarren in dem irdischen Gewühle.

> The fine emotions whence our lives we mold
> Lie in the earthly tumult dumb and cold.

o.　　GOETHE—*Faust.* I. 1. 286.

Ein unnütz Leben ist ein früher Tod.

> A useless life is an early death.

p.　　GOETHE—*Iphigenia auf Tauris.* I.
2. 63.

Grau, theurer Freund, ist alle Theorie
Und grün des Lebens goldner Baum.

> My worthy friend, gray are all theories
> And green alone Life's golden tree.

q.　　GOETHE—*Faust.* I. 4. 515.

Im Ganzen—haltet euch an Worte.

> On words let your attention center.

r.　　GOETHE—*Faust.* I. 4. 467.

Jeder Mensch hat eine Regen-Ecke seines
Lebens aus der ihm das schlimme Wetter
nachzieht.

> Every man has a rainy corner of his life
> out of which foul weather proceeds and
> follows after him.

s.　　JEAN PAUL RICHTER—*Titan.*
Zykel 123.

Nicht der Tummelplatz des Lebens — sein
Gehalt bestimmt seinen Werth.

> Tis not the mere stage of life but the **part**
> we play thereon that gives the value.

t.　　SCHILLER—*Fiesco.* III. 2.

Nicht seine Freudenseite kehrte dir
Das Leben zu.

Life did not present its sunny side to thee.
a. SCHILLER—*Marie Stuart.* II. 3. 136.

Nur Thaten geben dem Leben Stärke, nur
Mass ihm Reiz.

Only deeds give strength to life, only
moderation gives it charm.
b. JEAN PAUL RICHTER—*Titan.* Zykel 145.

O Gott, das Leben ist doch schön!

O God, how beautiful is life!
c. SCHILLER—*Don Carlos.* IV. 21. 233.

Sein Spruch war: leben und leben lassen.

His saying was: live and let live.
d. SCHILLER—*Wallenstein's Lager.* VI.
106. 110.

Wir, wir leben! Unser sind die Stunden
Und der Lebende hat Recht.

We, we live! ours are the hours, and the
living have their claims.
e. SCHILLER—*An die Freude.* St. 1.

Il torre altrui la vita
È facoltà comune
Al più vil della terra; il darla è solo
De' Numi, e de' Regnanti.

To take away life is a power which the
vilest of the earth have in common; to give
it belongs to gods and kings alone.
f. METASTASIO—*La Clemenza di Tito.*
III. 7.

Nel mezzo del cammin di nostra vita
Mi ritrovai per una selva oscura,
Che la diritta via era smarrita.

In the midway of this our mortal life,
I found me in a gloomy wood, astray,
Gone from the path direct.
g. DANTE—*Inferno.* I.

Questo misero modo
Tengon l' anime triste di coloro
Che visser senza infamia e senza lodo.

This sorrow weighs upon the melancholy
souls of those who lived without infamy or
praise.
h. DANTE—*Inferno.* III. 36.

Spesso è da forte,
Più che il morire, il vivere.

Ofttimes the test of courage becomes
rather to live than to die.
i. ALFIERI—*Oreste.* IV. 2.

Bien predica quien bien vive.

He who lives well is the best preacher.
j. CERVANTES—*Don Quixote.* VI. 19.

LIGHT.

Nur der Gewissenswurm schwärmt mit der
Eule. Sünder und böse Geister scheun das
Licht.

Only the worm of conscience consorts
with the owl. Sinners and evil spirits
shun the light.
k. SCHILLER—*Liebe und Cabale.* V. I.

Wo viel Licht ist, ist starker Schatten.

Where there is much light, the shadows
are deepest.
l. GOETHE—*Götz von Berlichingen.* I. 24.

Fra l' ombre un lampo solo
Basta al nocchier fugace,
Che già ritrova il polo,
Già riconosce il mar.

In the dark a glimmering light is often
sufficient for the pilot to find the polar star,
and to fix his course.
m. METASTASIO—*Achille.* I. 6.

LOVE.

Amour! amour! quand tu nous tiens
On peut bien dire, Adieu, prudence.

O tyrant love, when held by you,
We may to prudence bid adieu.
n. LA FONTAINE—*Fables.* IV. 1.

Ce qui fait que les amants et les maitresses
ne s'ennuient point d'être ensemble; c'est
qu'ils parlent toujours d'eux mêmes.

The reason why lovers and their mistress-
es never tire of being together is that they
are always talking of themselves.
o. LA ROCHEFOUCAULD—*Maximes.* 312.

Et l'on revient toujours à ses premiers amours.

One always returns to his first love.
p. ST. JUST.

Il faut cognoistre avant qu'aimer.

We should know [a person] before we love.
q. MARTIAL D'AUVERGNE—*L'Amant
rendu Cordelier à l'Observance
d'Amour.*

L'amour est un égoïsme à deux.

Love is an egotism of two.
r. ANTOINE DE SALLE.

L'amour est souvent un fruit de mariage.

Love is often a fruit of marriage.
s. MOLIÈRE—*Sganarelle.* I. 1.

Le commencement et le déclin de l'amour
se font sentir par l'embarras où l'on est de se
trouver seuls.

The beginning and the end of love are
both marked by embarrassment when the
two find themselves alone.
t. LA BRUYÈRE—*Les Caractères.* IV.

Ach die Zeiten der Liebe rollen nicht zurück, sondern ewig weiter hinab.
> Ah! The seasons of love roll not back-
> ward but onward, downward forever.
a.   Jean Paul Richter—*Hesperus.* IX.

Arm in Arm mit dir,
So fordr' ich mein Jahrhundert in die
     Schranken.
> Thus Arm in Arm with thee I dare defy my
> century into the lists.
b.   Schiller—*Don Carlos.* I. 9. 97.

Die Liebe vermindert die weibliche
Feinheit und verstärkt die männliche.
> Love lessens woman's delicacy and in-
> creases man's.
c.   Jean Paul Richter—*Titan.* Zykel 34.

       Die Liebe wintert nicht
Nein, nein! Ist und bleibt Frühlings-Schein.
> Love knows no winter; no, no! It is, and
> remains the sign of spring.
d.   Ludwig Tieck—*Herbstlied.*

Ein liebendes Mädchen wird unbewusst
kühner.
> A loving maiden grows unconsciously
> more bold.
e.   Jean Paul Richter—*Titan.* Zykel 71.

Es ist eine alte Geschichte,
Doch bleibt sie immer neu.
> It is an ancient story
> Yet is it ever new.
f.   Heine—*Lyrisches Intermezzo.* 39.

Es ist eine der grössten Himmelsgaben,
So ein lieb' Ding im Arm zu haben.
> It is one of Heaven's best gifts to hold
> such a dear creature in one's arms.
g.   Goethe—*Faust.*

In einem Augenblick gewährt die Liebe
Was Mühe kaum in langer Zeit erreicht.
> Love grants in a moment
> What toil can hardly achieve in an age.
h.   Goethe—*Torquato Tasso.* II. 3. 76.

Man liebt an dem Mädchen was es ist,
Und an dem Jüngling was er ankündigt.
> Girls we love for what they are;
> Young men for what they promise to be.
i.   Goethe—*Die Wahrheit und Dichtung.*
                III. 14.

Nicht Fleisch und Blut; das Herz macht
uns zu Vätern und Söhnen.
> It is not flesh and blood but the heart
> which makes us fathers and sons.
j.   Schiller—*Die Räuber.* I. 1.

O dass sie ewig grünen bliebe,
Die schöne Zeit der jungen Liebe.
> O that it might remain eternally green,
> The beautiful time of youthful love.
k.   Schiller—*Lied von der Glocke.*

Raum ist in der kleinsten Hütte
Für ein glücklich liebend Paar.
> In the smallest cot there is room enough
> for a loving pair.
l.   Schiller—*Der Jüngling am Bache.*
                 St. 4.

Und Lust und Liebe sind die Fittige zu gros-
sen Thaten.
> Love and desire are the spirit's wings to
> great deeds.
m.   Goethe—*Iphigenia auf Tauris.* II.
                1. 107.

Was ist das Leben ohne Liebesglanz!
> What is life without the light of Love!
n.   Schiller—*Wallenstein's Tod.* IV. 12.

Wenn ich dich lieb habe, was geht's dich an?
> If I love you, what business is that of yours?
o.   Goethe—*Wilhelm Meister.* IV. 9.

Zwei Seelen und ein Gedanke,
Zwei Herzen und ein Schlag!
> Two souls with but a single thought,
> Two hearts that beat as one.
p.   Von Münch Bellinghausen—*Der
> Sohn der Wildnis.* II. 1.

Amor, ch'al cor gentil ratto s'apprende.
> Love, that all gentle hearts so quickly know.
q.   Dante—*Inferno.* V. 100.

Amor ch' a nullo amato amar perdona.
> Love, which insists that love shall mutual be.
r.   Dante—*Inferno.* V. 103.

Che amar chi t'odia, ell'è impossibil cosa.
> For 'tis impossible
> Hate to return with love.
s.   Alfieri—*Polinice.* II. 4.

LYING.

Il faut bonne mémoire après qu'on a menti.
> A good memory is needed once we have lied.
t.   Corneille—*Le Menteur.* IV. 5.

La satire ment sur les gens de lettres pendant leur vie, et l'éloge ment après leur mort.
> Satire lies about literary men while they
> live and eulogy lies about them when they
> die.
u.   Voltaire—*Lettre à Bordes.*
               Jan. 10, 1769.

Un menteur est toujours prodigue de ser-
ments.

A liar is always lavish of oaths.
a. CORNEILLE—*Le Menteur.* III. 5.

Wenn ich irre kann es jeder bemerken ;
wenn ich lüge, nicht.

When I err every one can see it, but not
when I lie.
b. GOETHE—*Sprüche in Prosa.* III.

A giurar presti i mentitor son sempre.

Liars are always most disposed to swear.
c. ALFIERI—*Virginia.* II. 3.

Se non volea pulir sua scusa tanto,
Che la facesse di menzogna rea.

But that he wrought so high the specious
tale,
As manifested plainly 'twas a lie.
d. ARIOSTO—*Orlando Furioso.* XVIII. 84.

M.

MAN.

Ah! pour être devot, je n'en suis pas moins
homme.

Ah! to be devout, I am none the less
human.
e. MOLIÈRE—*Le Tartuffe.* III. 3.

Il est plus aisé de connaître l'homme en
général que de connaître un homme en par-
ticulier.

It is easier to know mankind in general
than man individually.
f. LA ROCHEFOUCAULD—*Maximes.* 436.

Le style c'est de l'homme.

The style is the man himself.
g. BUFFON—*Œuvres Choisies.* Liv. I.
P. 25.

Der edle Mensch ist nur ein Bild von Gott.

The noble man is only God's image.
h. LUDWIG TIECK—*Genoveva.*

Der Mensch ist, der lebendig fühlende,
Der leichte Raub des mächt'gen Augenblicks.

Man, living, feeling man is the easy prey
of the powerful present.
i. SCHILLER—*Die Jungfrau von Orleans.*
III. 4. 54.

Die Menschen fürchtet nur, wer sie nicht
kennt
Und wer sie meidet, wird sie bald verkennen.

He only fears men who does not know
them, and he who avoids them will soon
misjudge them.
j. GOETHE—*Torquato Tasso.* I. 2. 72.

Lass uns, geliebter Bruder, nicht vergessen,
Dass von sich selbst der Mensch nicht schei-
den kann.

Beloved brother, let us not forget that
man can never get away from himself.
k. GOETHE—*Torquato Tasso.* I. 2. 85.

O insensata cura dei mortali,
Quanto son difettivi sillogismi
Quei che ti fanno in basso batter l'ali !

O mortal cares insensate, what small worth,
In sooth, doth all those syllogisms fill,
Which make you stoop your pinions to the
earth !
l. DANTE—*Paradiso.* XI. 1.

MATRIMONY.

Le mariage est comme une forteresse assi-
égée ; ceux qui sont dehors veulent y entrer
et ceux qui sont dedans en sortir.

Marriage is like a beleaguered fortress ;
those who are without want to get in, and
those within want to get out.
m. QUITARD—*Études sur les Proverbes
Français.* P. 102.

Par un prompt désespoir souvent on se marie.
Qu'on s'en repent après tout le temps de sa vie.

Men often marry in hasty recklessness
and repent afterward all their lives.
n. MOLIÈRE—*Les Femmes Savantes.*
V. 5.

Denn ein wackerer Mann verdient ein be-
gütertes Mädchen.

For a brave man deserves a well-endowed
girl.
o. GOETHE—*Hermann und Dorothea.*
III. 19.

MEMORY.

Il se veoid par expérience, que les mémoires
excellentes se joignent volontiers aux juge-
ments débiles.

Experience teaches that a good memory
is generally joined to a weak judgment.
p. MONTAIGNE—*Essais.* I. 9.

Les souvenirs embellissent la vie, l'oubli
seul la rend possible.

Remembrances embellish life but forgetfulness alone makes it possible.
q. GEN'L CIALDINI—*Written in an album.*

Nessun maggior dolore
Che ricordarsi del tempo felice
Nella miseria.　　　　No greater wo
Can be than to remember happy days
In misery.
a.　　Dante—*Inferno.* V. 121.

MERIT.

Il y a du mérite sans élévation mais il n'y a
point d'élévation sans quelque mérite.
There is merit without elevation, but
there is no elevation without some merit.
b.　　La Rochefoucauld—*Maximes.* 401.

La faveur des princes n'exclut pas le
mérite, et ne le suppose pas aussi.
The favor of princes does not preclude
the existence of merit, and yet does not
prove that it exists.
c.　　La Bruyère—*Les Caractères.* XII.

Le mérite des hommes a sa saison aussi
bien que les fruits.
There is a season for man's merit as well
as for fruit.
d.　　La Rochefoucauld—*Maximes.* 291.

Le monde récompense plus souvent les apparences de mérite que le mérite même.
The world rewards the appearance of
merit oftener than merit itself.
e.　　La Rochefoucauld—*Maximes.* 166.

MIND.

La gravité est un mystère du corps inventé
pour cacher les défauts de l'esprit.
Gravity is a mystery of the body invented
to conceal the defects of the mind.
f.　　La Rochefoucauld—*Maximes.* 257.

Un corps débile affoiblit l'âme.
A feeble body weakens the mind.
g.　　Rousseau—*Émile.* I.

Wer fertig ist, dem ist nichts recht zu machen,
Ein Werdender wird immer dankbar sein.
A mind, once formed, is never suited after,
One yet in growth will ever grateful be.
h.　　Goethe—*Faust. Vorspiel auf dem
Theater.* L. 150

La pluma es lengua del alma.
The pen is the tongue of the mind.
i.　　Cervantes—*Don Quixote.* V. 16.

MISERY.

Il ne se faut jamais moquer des misérables,
Car qui peut s'assurer d'être toujours heureux?
We ought never to scoff at the wretched,
for who can be sure of continued happiness?
j.　　La Fontaine—*Fables.* V. 17.

Frei geht das Unglück durch die ganze Erde!
Misery travels free through the whole world!
k.　　Schiller—*Wallenstein's Tod.* IV.
11. 31.

Tanto è miser l'uom quant' ei si riputa.
Man is only miserable so far as he thinks
himself so.
l.　　Sannazaro—*Ecloga Octava.*

MODERATION.

Juste milieu.
The just medium.
m.　　Louis Philippe.

Aus Mässigkeit entspringt ein reines Glück.
True happiness springs from moderation.
n.　　Goethe—*Die Natürliche Tochter.* II.
5. 79.

MODESTY.

Wenn jemand bescheiden bleibt, nicht beim
Lobe, sondern beim Tadel, dann ist er's.
When one remains modest not after praise
but after blame, then is he really so.
o.　　Jean Paul Richter—*Hesperus.* 12.

MONEY.

Les beaux yeux de ma cassette!
Il parle d'elle comme un amant d'une mai-
tresse.
The beautiful eyes of my money-box!
He speaks of it as a lover of his mistress.
p.　　Molière—*L'Avare.* V. 3.

Point d'argent, point de suisse.
No money, no service.
q.　　Racine—*Plaideurs.* I. 1.

MORTALITY.

Hier ist die Stelle wo ich sterblich bin.
This is the spot where I am mortal.
r.　　Schiller—*Don Carlos.* I. 6. 67.

MUSIC.

Blasen ist nicht flöten, ihr müsst die Finger
bewegen.
To blow is not to play on the flute; you
must move the fingers.
s.　　Goethe—*Sprüche in Prosa.* III.

Die Baukunst ist eine erstarrte Musik.
Architecture is frozen music.
t.　　Goethe—*Conversation with Eckermann.*
March 23, 1829.

Musik ist Poesie der Luft.
Music is the poetry of the air.
u.　　Jean Paul Richter.

Sie zog tief in sein Herz, wie die Melodie eines Liedes, die aus der Kindheit heraufklingt.
It sank deep into his heart, like the
melody of a song sounding from out of
childhood's days.
v.　　Jean Paul Richter—*Hesperus.* XII.

N.

NATURE.

Chassez le naturel, il revient au galop.
Drive the natural away, it returns at a gallop.
a.   Destouches—*Glorieux.* V. 3.

Blumen, Blätter, Früchte sind also aus Luft gewebte
Kinder des Lichts.
Flowers, leaves, fruit are therefore air-woven children of light.
b.   Moleschott—*Licht und Leben.* P. 29.

Der Schein soll nie die Wirklichkeit erreichen
Und siegt Natur, so muss die Kunst entweichen.
The ideal should never touch the real;
When nature conquers, Art must then give way.
c.   Schiller—*To* Goethe *when he put* Voltaire's *Mahomet on the Stage.* St. 6.

Warum wird mir auf einmal lieblich helle,
Als wenn im nächt'gen Wald uns Mondenglanz umweht?
Whence all around me glows the air so brightly,
As when in woods at night the mellow moonbeam lies?
d.   Goethe—*Faust.* I. 1. 336.

NECESSITY.

Il faisoit de nécessité vertu.
He made a virtue of necessity.
e.   Rabelais—*Gargantua.* I. 11.

Le superflu, chose très nécessaire.
The superfluous, a very necessary thing.
f.   Voltaire—*Le Mondain.*

Ernst ist der Anblick der Nothwendigkeit.
Stern is the visage of necessity.
g.   Schiller—*Wallenstein's Tod.* I. 4. 45.

Denn nur vom Nutzen wird die Welt regiert.
For the world is ruled by interest alone.
h.   Schiller—*Wallenstein's Tod.* I. 6. 37.

Necessità c'induce, e non diletto.
It is necessity and not pleasure that compels us.
i.   Dante—*Inferno.* XII. 87.

NOBILITY.

Ein edler Mensch zieht edle Menschen an,
Und weiss sie fest zu halten, wie ihr thut.
A noble soul alone can noble souls attract;
And knows alone, as ye, to hold them.
j.   Goethe—*Torquato Tasso.* I. 1. 59.

Il sangue nobile è un accidente della fortuna; le azioni nobili caratterizzano il grande.
Noble blood is an accident of fortune; noble actions characterize the great.
k.   Goldoni—*Pamela.* I. 6.

NOVELTY.

Sehen Sie, die beste Neuigkeit verliert, sobald sie Stadtmärchen wird.
Observe, the best of novelties palls when it becomes town talk.
l.   Schiller—*Fiesco.* III. 10.

Wie machen wir's, dass alles frisch und neu
Und mit Bedeutung auch gefällig sei?
How shall we plan, that all be fresh and new—
Important matter yet attractive too?
m.   Goethe—*Faust. Vorspiel auf dem Theater.* L. 15.

O.

OPINION.

Ils ont les textes pour eux; disait-il, j'en suis faché pour les textes.
They have the texts in their favor; said he, so much the worse for the texts.
n.   Royer-Collard—*Words of disapproval of the Fathers of Port Royal on their doctrine of grace.*

Je connais quelqu'un qui a plus d'esprit que Napoléon, que Voltaire, que tous les ministres présents et futurs: c'est l'opinion.
I know where there is more wisdom than is found in Napoleon, Voltaire, or all the ministers present and to come—in public opinion.
o.   Talleyrand—*In the Chamber of Peers.* 1821.

OPPORTUNITY.

L'occasion de faire du mal se trouve cent fois par jour, et celle de faire du bien une fois dans l'année.

> The opportunity for doing mischief is found a hundred times a day, and of doing good once in a year.

a.   Voltaire—*Zadig.*

Mes jours s'en sont allez errant.

> My days are gone a-wandering.

b.   Villon—*Grand Testament.*

Der den Augenblick ergreift,
Das ist der rechte Mann.

> Yet he who grasps the moment's gift,
> He is the proper man.

c.   Goethe—*Faust.* I. 4. 494.

Pflücke Rosen, weil sie blühn,
Morgen ist nicht heut!
Keine Stunde lass entfliehn,
Morgen ist nicht heut.

> Gather roses while they bloom,
> To-morrow is yet far away.
> Moments lost have no room
> In to-morrow or to-day.

d.   Gleim—*Benutzung der Zeit.*

ORATORY.

Ce que l'on conçoit bien s'énonce clairement,
Et les mots pour le dire arrivent aisément.

> Whatever we conceive well we express clearly, and words flow with ease.

e.   Boileau—*L'Art Poètique.* I. 153.

L'éloquence est au sublime ce que le tout est à sa partie.

> Eloquence is to the sublime what the whole is to its part.

f.   La Bruyère—*Les Caractères.* I.

L'éloquence est une peinture de la pensée.

> Eloquence is a painting of the thoughts.

g.   Pascal—*Pensées.* XXIV. 88.

Allein der Vortrag macht des Redners Glück.
Ich fühl es wohl noch bin ich weit zurück.

> Yet through delivery orators succeed,
> I feel that I am far behind indeed.

h.   Goethe—*Faust.* I. 1. 194.

Es trägt Verstand und rechter Sinn,
Mit wenig Kunst sich selber vor.

> With little art, clear wit and sense
> Suggest their own delivery.

i.   Goethe—*Faust.* I. 1. 198.

P.

PASSION.

L'absence diminue les médiocres passions et augmente les grandes, comme le vent éteint les bougies et allume le feu.

> Absence diminishes little passions and increases great ones, as the wind extinguishes candles and fans a fire.

j.   La Rochefoucauld—*Maximes.* 276.

Toutes les passions ne sont autre chose que les divers degrés de la chaleur et de la froideur du sang.

> All the passions are nothing else than different degrees of heat and cold of the blood.

k.   La Rochefoucauld—*Premier Supplemént.* VIII.

Entbehren sollst du! sollst entbehren.

> Thou shalt abstain,
> Renounce, refrain,

J.   Goethe—*Faust.* I. 4.

PAST (THE).

Ils sont passés ces jours de fête.

> The days of rejoicing are gone forever.

m.   Du Lorens—*Le Tableau Parlant.*

Mais où sont les neiges d'antan?

> But where are the snows of yester year?

n.   Villon—*Ballade des Dames du Temps Jadis.*

Du sprichst von Zeiten die vergangen sind.

> Thou speakest of times that long have passed away.

o.   Schiller—*Don Carlos.* I. 2. 48.

Wer kann was Dummes, wer was Kluges denken,
Das nicht die Vorwelt schon gedacht.

> Who can think wise or stupid things at all that were not thought already in the past.

p.   Goethe—*Faust.* II. 2. 1.

PATIENCE.

La patience est amère, mais son fruit est doux.

> Patience is bitter, but its fruit is sweet.

q.   Rousseau.

La patience est l'art d'espérer.

> Patience is the art of hoping.

r.   Vauvenargues—*Réflexions.* CCLI.

Patience et longueur de temps.
Font plus que force ni que rage.

> By time and toil we sever
> What strength and rage could never.

s.   La Fontaine—*Fables.* II. 11.

PATRIOTISM.

À tous les cœurs bien nés que la patrie est chère !

How dear is the fatherland to all noble hearts !
a.   Voltaire—*Tancrède.* III. 1.

Je meurs content, je meurs pour la liberté de mon pays.

I die content, I die for the liberty of my country.
b.   *Attributed to* Le Pelletier, *also to*
De Lannes.

La patrie est aux lieux où l'âme est enchaî-née.

Our country is that spot to which our heart is bound.
c.   Voltaire—*Le Fanatisme.* I. 2.

Un enfant en ouvrant ses yeux doit voir la patrie, et jusqu'à la mort ne voir qu'elle.

The infant, on first opening his eyes, ought to see his country, and to the hour of his death never lose sight of it.
d.   Rousseau.

PEACE.

L'empire, c'est la paix.

The empire is peace.
e.   Napoleon III.—*At Bordeaux.*   Oct. 9,
1852.

Die Ruhe eines Kirchhofs !

The churchyard's peace.
f.   Schiller—*Don Carlos.* III. 10. 220.

Es kann der Frömmste nicht im Frieden bleiben,
Wenn es dem bösen Nachbar nicht gefällt.

The most pious may not live in peace, if it does not please his wicked neighbor.
g.   Schiller—*Wilhelm Tell.* IV. 3. 124.

PECULIARITY.

Eigenthümlichkeit ruft Eigenthümlichkeit hervor.

One peculiarity calls out another.
h.   Goethe—*Sprüche in Prosa.* III.

PHILOSOPHY.

Se moquer de la philosophie c'est vraiment philosophe.

To ridicule philosophy is truly philo-sophical.
i.   Pascal—*Pensées.* Art. VII. 35.

PLEASURE.

Je l'ai toujours dit et senti, la véritable jouissance ne se décrit point.

I have always said and felt that true en-joyment can not be described.
j.   Rousseau—*Confessions.* VIII.

Zu oft ist kurze Lust die Quelle langer Schmerzen !

Too oft is transient pleasure the source of long woes.
k.   Wieland—*Oberon.* II. 52.

POETS.

Neuere Poeten thun viel Wasser in die Tinte.

Modern poets mix too much water with their ink.
l.   Goethe—*Sprüche in Prosa.* III.

Wer den Dichter will verstehen
Muss in Dichters Lande gehen.

Whoever would understand the poet
Must go into the poet's country.
m.   Goethe—*Noten auf West-O. Divans.*

POISON.

Es ist Arznei, nicht Gift, was ich dir reiche.

It is medicine, not poison, I offer you.
n.   Lessing—*Nathan der Weise.* I. 2.

In gährend Drachengift hast du
Die Milch der frommen Denkart mir verwan-delt.

To rankling poison hast thou turned in me the milk of human kindness.
o.   Schiller—*Wilhelm Tell.* IV. 3. 3.

POLICY.

Tenez bonne table et soignez les femmes.

Keep a good table and don't forget the ladies.
p.   Napoleon I.—*Instructions to* Abbé de
Pradt.

Der Mutter schenk' ich,
Die Tochter denk' ich.

I make presents to the mother, but think of the daughter.
q.   Goethe—*Sprüche in Reimen.* III.

POSSESSION.

Quand on n'a pas ce que l'on aime,
Il faut aimer ce que l'on a.

When we have not what we love, we must love what we have.
r.   Bussy-Rabutin—*Lettre à Mme. de
Sevigne,* 1667.

Un tiens vaut, ce dit-on, mieux que deux tu l'auras.
L'un est sûr, l'autre ne l'est pas.

It is said, that the thing you possess is worth more than two you may have in the future. The one is sure and the other is not. (*A bird in the hand is worth two in the bush.*)
s.   La Fontaine—*Fables.* V. 3.

Denn was man schwarz auf weiss besitzt
Kann man getrost nach Hause tragen.
> For what one has in black and white,
> One can carry home in comfort.
a.   GOETHE—*Faust.* I. 4. 42.

POVERTY.

La pauvreté des biens est aysee à guerir; la
pauvreté de l'âme, impossible.
> The lack of wealth is easily repaired; but
> the poverty of the soul is irreparable.
b.   MONTAIGNE—*Essais.* III. 10.

L'or même à la laideur donne un teint de
beauté:
Mais tout devient affreux avec la pauvreté.
> Gold gives an appearance of beauty even
> to ugliness: but with poverty everything
> becomes frightful.
c.   BOILEAU—*Satires.* VIII. 209.

POWER.

Le seigneur Jupiter sait dorer la pilule.
> My lord Jupiter knows how to gild the
> pill.
d.   MOLIÈRE—*Amphitryon.* III. 11.

Le trident de Neptune est le sceptre du monde.
> The trident of Neptune is the sceptre of
> the world.
e.   LEMIERRE.

Qui peut ce qui lui plaît, commande alors
qu'il prie.
> Whoever can do as he pleases, commands
> when he entreats.
f.   CORNEILLE—*Sertorius.* IV. 2.

Der Mensch kann was er soll; und wenn er
sagt, er kann nicht so will er nicht.
> A man can do what he ought to do; and
> when he says he cannot, it is because he
> will not.
g.   FICHTE—*Letter.* 1791.

Du bist noch nicht der Mann den Teufel
festzuhalten.
> Neither art thou the man to catch the
> fiend and hold him!
h.   GOETHE—*Faust.* I. 3. 336.

Ich fühle eine Armee in meiner Faust.
> I feel an army in my fist.
i.   SCHILLER—*Die Räuber.* II. 3.

Kann ich Armeen aus der Erde stampfen?
Wächst mir ein Kornfeld in der flachen
Hand?
> Can I summon armies from the earth?
> Or grow a cornfield on my open palm?
j.   SCHILLER—*Die Jungfrau von Orleans.*
                                    I. 3.

PRAISE.

Cela est beau, et je vous louerais davantage
si vous m'aviez loué moins.
> That is fine, and I would have praised you
> more had you praised me less.
k.   *Attributed to* LOUIS XIV.

PRAYER.

Die Gabe zu beten ist nicht immer in un-
serer Gewalt.
> The gift of prayer is not always at our
> command.
l.   LESSING—*Emilia Galotti.* II. 6.

PREJUDICE.

Les préjugés, ami, sont les rois du vulgaire.
> Prejudices, friend, govern the vulgar crowd
m.   VOLTAIRE—*Le Fanatisme.* II. 4.

Chi non esce dal suo paese, vive pieno di
pregiudizj.
> He who never leaves his country is full of
> prejudices.
n.   GOLDONI—*Pamela.* I. 14.

PRESENT (THE).

Die Gegenwart ist eine mächtige Göttin.
> The present is a powerful deity.
o.   GOETHE—*Torquato Tasso.* IV. 4. 67.

PROCRASTINATION.

Morgen, Morgen, nur nicht heute;
Sprechen immer träge Leute.
> To-morrow, to-morrow, not to-day,
> Hear the lazy people say.
p.   WEISSE—*Der Aufschub.*

PROGRESSION.

Il est un terme de la vie au-delà duquel en
rétrograde en avançant.
> There is a period of life when we go back
> as we advance.
q.   ROUSSEAU—*Émile.* II.

Qui n'a pas l'esprit de son âge,
De son âge a tout le malheur.
> He who has not the spirit of his age, has
> all the misery of it.
r.   VOLTAIRE—*Lettre à Cideville.*

Vogue la galère.
> Row on whatever happens.
s.   RABELAIS—*Gargantua.* I. 3.

PROMISES.

Promettre c'est donner, espérer c'est jouir.
> To promise is to give, to hope is to enjoy.
t.   DELILLE—*Jardins.* I.

PROPERTY.

Je prends mon bien où je le trouve.
I take my property wherever I find it.
a.　　MOLIÈRE.

La propriété c'est le vol.
Property is theft.
b.　　PROUDHON—*Qu'est ce que c'est que la
　　　　　　　Propriété.* Pub. in 1840.

La propriété exclusive est un vol dans la
nature.
Exclusive property is a theft in nature.
c.　　BRISSOT.

PROSPERITY.

C'est un faible roseau que la prospérité.
Prosperity is a feeble reed.
d.　　DANIEL D'ANCHÈRES—*Tyr et Sidon.*

La prospérité fait peu d'amis.
Prosperity makes few friends.
e.　　VAUVENARGUES—*Réflexions.* XVII.

Le remords s'endort durant un destin pros-
père et s'aigrit dans l'adversité.
Remorse goes to sleep during a prosperous
period and wakes up in adversity.
f.　　ROUSSEAU—*Confessions.* I. II.

Alles in der Welt lässt sich ertragen,
Nur nicht eine Reihe von schönen Tagen.
Everything in the world may be endured,
except only a succession of prosperous days.
g.　　GOETHE—*Sprüche in Reimen.* III.

PROVIDENCE.

Dieu mesure le froid à la brebis tondue.
God measures the cold to the shorn lamb.
h.　　HENRI ESTIENNE—*Prémices, etc.* P. 47.

Le hasard est un sobriquet de la Providence.
Chance is a nickname for Providence.
i.　　CHAMFORT.

Es ist dafür gesorgt, dass die Bäume nicht
in den Himmel wachsen.
Care is taken that trees do not grow into
the sky.
j.　　GOETHE—*Wahrheit und Dichtung.*
　　　　　　　　　　　Motto to Pt. III.

PRUDENCE.

Glissez, mortels, n'appuyez pas.
Glide gently, mortals, weigh not too hard.
k.　　ROY—*On a picture of a winter scene
　　　　　　　　　　with skaters.*

Le trop d'expédients peut gâter une affaire.
Too many expedients may spoil an affair.
l　　LA FONTAINE—*Fables.* IX. 14.

50

Wer sich nicht nach der Decke streckt,
Dem bleiben die Füsse unbedeckt.
He who does not stretch himself according to the coverlet finds his feet uncovered.
m.　　GOETHE—*Sprüche in Reimen.* III.

PUBLIC (THE).

Le public! le public! combien faut-il de
sots pour faire un public?
The public! the public! how many fools
does it require to make the public?
n.　　CHAMFORT.

Ich wünschte sehr, der Menge zu behagen,
Besonders weil sie lebt und leben lässt.
I wish the crowd to feel itself well treated,
Especially since it lives and lets me live.
o.　　GOETHE—*Faust Vorspiel auf dem
　　　　　　　　　　　Theater.* L. 5.

Wer dem Publicum dient, ist ein armes Thier;
Er quält sich ab, niemand bedankt sich dafür.
He who serves the public is a poor
animal; he worries himself to death and no
one thanks him for it.
p.　　GOETHE—*Sprüche in Reimen.* III.

PUNISHMENT.

Du spottest noch? Erzittre! Immer schlafen
Des Rächers Blitze nicht.
Thou mockest? Tremble! the avenger's
lightning bolts do not forever dormant lie.
q.　　WIELAND—*Oberon.* I. 50.

PURITY.

Les choses valent toujours mieux dans leur
source.
The stream is always purer at its source.
r.　　PASCAL—*Lettres Provinciales.* IV.

Ganz unbefleckt geniesst sich nur das Herz.
Only the heart without a stain knows
perfect ease.
s.　　GOETHE—*Iphigenia auf Tauris.* IV.
　　　　　　　　　　　　　4. 123.

Qual diverrà quel fiume,
Nel lungo suo cammino,
Se al fonte ancor vicino
È torbido così?
What will the stream become in its length-
ened course, if it be so turbid at its source?
t.　　METASTASIO—*Morte d' Abele.* I.

Quell' onda, che ruina
Dalla pendice alpina,
Balza, si frange, e mormora
Ma limpida si fa.
That water which falls from some Alpine
height is dashed, broken, and will murmur
loudly, but grows limpid by its fall.
u.　　METASTASIO—*Alcide al Bivio.*

Q.

QUESTIONS.

Denn wenn sich Jemand versteckt erklärt,
so ist Nichts unhöflicher als eine nene Frage.

For when any one explains himself
guardedly, nothing is more uncivil than to
put a new question.

a.   JEAN PAUL RICHTER—*Hesperus.* II.

QUOTATION.

C'est souvent hasarder un bon mot et vouloir le perdre que de le donner pour sien.

A good saying often runs the risk of being
thrown away when quoted as the speaker's
own.

b.   LA BRUYÈRE—*Les Caractères.* II.

R.

RAGE.

Dem tauben Grimm, der keinen Führer hört.
Deaf rage that hears no leader.

c.   SCHILLER—*Wallenstein's Tod.* III.
20. 16.

READINESS.

Rien ne sert de courir : il faut partir à point.

To win a race, the swiftness of a dart
Availeth not without a timely start.

d.   LA FONTAINE—*Fables.* VI. 10.

READING.

Zwar sind sie an das Beste nicht gewöhnt,
Allein sie haben schrecklich viel gelesen.

What they're accustomed to is no great
matter,
But then, alas! they've read an awful deal.

e.   GOETHE—*Faust. Vorspiel auf dem
Theater.* L. 13.

REASON.

La parfaite raison fuit toute extremité,
Et veut que l'on soit sage avec sobriété.

All extremes does perfect reason flee,
And wishes to be wise quite soberly.

f.   MOLIÈRE—*Le Misanthrope.* I. 1.

La raison du plus fort est toujours la meilleure.

The reasoning of the strongest is always
the best.

g.   LA FONTAINE—*Fables.* I. 10.

Mais la raison n'est pas ce qui règle l'amour.
But it is not reason that governs love.

h.   MOLIÈRE—*Le Misanthrope.* I. 1.

On aime sans raison, et sans raison l'on hait.

We love without reason. and without reason we hate.

i.   REGNARD—*Les Folies Amoureuses.*

RELIGION.

L' institut des Jesuites est une épée dont la
poignée est à Rome et la pointe partout.

The Order of Jesuits is a sword whose
handle is at Rome and whose point is every
whére.

j.   M. DUPIN—*Proces de tendance.* 1825.

REPENTANCE.

Chacun s'égare, et le moins imprudent,
Est celui-là qui plus tôt se repent.

Every one goes astray, but the least imprudent are they who repent the soonest.

k.   VOLTAIRE—*Nanine.* II. 10.

Der Wahn ist kurz, die Reu ist lang.
The dream is short, repentance long.

l.   SCHILLER—*Lied von der Glocke.*

D'uomo è il fallir, ma dal malvagio il buono
Scerne il dolor del fallo.

To err is human ; but contrition felt for
the crime distinguishes the virtuous from
the wicked.

m.   ALFIERI—*Rosmunda.* III. 1.

REPUTATION.

Das Aergste weiss die Welt von mir, und ich
Kann sagen, ich bin besser als mein Ruf.

The worst of me is known, and I can
say that I am better than the fame I bear.

n.   SCHILLER—*Marie Stuart.* III. 4. 208.

Denn ein wanderndes Mädchen ist immer
von schwankendem Rufe.

For a strolling damsel a doubtful reputation bears.

o.   GOETHE—*Hermann und Dorothea.*
VII. 93.

Ich halte nichts von dem, der von sich denkt
Wie ihn das Volk vielleicht erheben möchte.

I consider him of no account who esteems
himself just as the popular breath may
chance to raise him.

a.   GOETHE—*Iphigenia auf Tauris.* II. 1.
140.

RESULTS.

Guter Wille ist höher als aller Erfolg.

Good-will is of more value than the result
that follows.

b.   GOETHE—*Stella.* V.

REVENGE.

Je ne te quitterai point que je ne t'aie vu
pendu.

I will not leave you until I have seen you
hanged.

c.   MOLIÈRE—*Le Medicin Malgré Lui.*
III. 9.

REVOLUTION.

Je suis le signet qui marque la page où la
révolution s'est arrêtée; mais quand je serai
mort, elle tournera le feuillet et reprendra sa
marche.

I am the signet which marks the page
where the revolution has been stopped; but
when I die it will turn the page and resume
its course.

d.   NAPOLEON I. *to* COUNT MOLÉ.

RICHES.

Ich heisse
Der reichste Mann in der getauften Welt;
Die Sonne geht in meinem Staat nicht unter.

I am called the richest man in Christendom. The sun never sets on my dominions.

e.   SCHILLER—*Don Carlos.* I. 6. 60.

RIVERS.

Les rivières sont des chemins qui marchent
et qui portent où l'on veut aller.

Rivers are roads that move and carry us
whither we wish to go.

f.   PASCAL—*Pensées.* VII. 38.

ROYALTY.

La clémence est la plus belle marque
Qui fasse à l'univers connaître un vrai mon-
arque.

Clemency is the surest proof of a true
monarch.

g.   CORNEILLE—*Cinna.* IV. 4.

La cour est comme un édifice bâti de mar-
bre; je veux dire qu'elle est composée d'hommes fort durs mais fort polis.

The court is like a palace built of marble;
I mean that it is made up of very hard but
very polished people.

h.   LA BRUYÈRE—*Les Caractères.* VIII.

Le premier qui fut roi, fut un soldat heureux;
Qui sert bien son pays, n'a pas besoin d'aïeux.

The first king was a successful soldier;
He who serves well his country has no need
of ancestors.

i.   VOLTAIRE—*Mérope.* I. 3.

Le roi règne et ne gouverne pas.

The king reigns but does not govern.

j.   THIERS, *in the National Newspaper,*
July 1st, 1830.

L'état!—c'est moi!

The state!—it is I!

k.   *Attributed to* LOUIS XIV. *of France.*

Malheureuse France! Malheureux roi!

Unhappy France! Unhappy king!

l.   ÉTIENNE BÉQUET—*Heading in the*
Journal des Débats, when CHARLES X.
was driven from the throne.

Tout citoyen est roi sous un roi citoyen.

Every citizen is king under a citizen king.

m.   FAVART—*Les Trois Sultanes.* II. 3.

Veuve d'un peuple-roi, mais reine encore du
monde.

[Rome] Widow of an imperial people,
but still queen of the world.

n.   GILBERT.

Wenn die Könige bau'n, haben die Kärrner
zu thun.

When kings are building, draymen have
something to do.

o.   SCHILLER—*Kant und Seine Ausleger.*

S.

SATISFACTION.

Est bien fou du cerveau
Qui prétend contenter tout le monde et son
père.

He is very foolish who aims at satisfying
all the world and his father.

p.   LA FONTAINE—*Fables.* III. 1.

Il plaît à tout le monde et ne saurait se plaire.

He [Moliére] pleases every one but can not
please himself.

q.   BOILEAU—*Satires.* II.

Mach' es Wenigen recht; vielen gefallen ist
schlimm.

Satisfy a few; to please many is bad.

r.   SCHILLER—*Votivtafeln.*

Nul n'est content de sa fortune ;
Ni mécontent de son esprit.

No one is satisfied with his fortune, nor dissatisfied with his intellect.

a.   DESHOULIÈRES.

SECRECY.

C'est toujours un mauvais moyen de lire dans le cœur des autres que d'affecter de cacher le sien.

It is always a poor way of reading the hearts of others to try to conceal our own.

b.   ROUSSEAU—*Confessions.* II.

Il faut laver son linge sale en famille.

One should wash his soiled linen in private.

c.   NAPOLEON I.

L'on confie son secret dans l'amitié, mais il échappe dans l'amour.

We trust our secrets to our friends, but they escape from us in love.

d.   LA BRUYÈRE—*Les Caractères.* IV.

Rien ne pèse tant qu'un secret :
Le porter loin est difficile aux dames ;
Et je sais même sur ce fait
Bon nombre d'hommes qui sont femmes.

Nothing is so oppressive as a secret : women find it difficult to keep one long ; and I know a goodly number of men who are women in this regard.

e.   LA FONTAINE—*Fables.* VIII. 6.

Toute révélation d'un secret est la faute de celui qui l'a confié.

When a secret is revealed, it is the fault of the man who confided it.

f.   LA BRUYÈRE—*Les Caractères.* V.

Wer den kleinsten Theil eines Geheimnisses hingibt, hat den andern nicht mehr in der Gewalt.

He who gives up the smallest part of a secret has the rest no longer in his power.

g.   JEAN PAUL RICHTER—*Titan.* Zykel 123.

SELF-ESTEEM.

Wer sich nicht zu viel dünkt ist viel mehr als er glaubt.

He who does not think too much of himself is much more esteemed than he imagines.

h.   GOETHE—*Sprüche in Prosa.* III.

SELFISHNESS.

Chacun chez soi, chacun pour soi.

Every one for his home, every one for himself.

i.   M. DUPIN.

L'amour-propre offensé ne pardonne jamais.

Offended self-love never forgives.

j.   VIZÉE—*Les Aveux Difficiles.* VII.

Voyez le beau rendez-vous qu'il me donne :
cet homme là n'a jamais aimé que lui-même.

Behold the fine appointment he makes with me ; that man never did love any one but himself.

k.   MME. DE MAINTENON, *when* LOUIS XIV.
in dying said, "*Nous nous renverrons
bientôt*" (*We shall meet again*).

SENSE.

Entre le bon sens et le bon goût il y a la différence de la cause à son effet.

Between good sense and good taste there is the difference between cause and effect.

l.   LA BRUYÈRE—*Les Caractères.* XII.

SEVERITY.

La violence est juste où la douceur est vaine.

Severity is allowable where gentleness has no effect.

m.   CORNEILLE—*Héraclius.* I. 1.

Zu strenge Ford'rung ist verborgner Stolz.

Too rigid scruples are concealed pride.

n.   GOETHE—*Iphigenia auf Tauris.* IV.
4. 120.

SHAME.

Maggior difetto men vergogna lava.

Less shame a greater fault would palliate.

o.   DANTE—*Inferno.* XXX. 142.

SILENCE.

Il ne voit que la nuit, n'entend que le silence.

He sees only night, and hears only silence.

p.   DELILLE—*Imagination.* IV.

La douleur qui se tait n'en est que plus funeste.

Silent anguish is the more dangerous.

q.   RACINE—*Andromaque.* III. 3.

Les gens sans bruit sont dangereux ;
Il n'en est pas ainsi des autres.

Silent people are dangerous ; others are not so.

r.   LA FONTAINE—*Fables.* VIII. 23.

Le silence du peuple est la leçon des rois.

The silence of the people is a lesson for kings.

s.   SOANEN, *Bishop of Senax ; also* ABBÉ
DE BEAUVAIS.—*Funeral oration over
Louis XV.*

Le silence est l'esprit des sots,
Et l'une des vertus du sage.
> Silence is the genius of fools and one of
> the virtues of the wise.
> *a.*   BONNARD.

Doch grosse Seelen dulden still.
> Great souls suffer in silence.
> *b.*   SCHILLER—*Don Carlos.* I. 4. 52.

> Alta vendetta
D'alto silenzio è figlia.
> Deep vengeance is the daughter of deep
> silence.
> *c.*   ALFIERI—*La Congiura de' Pazzi.* I. 1.

SINGING.

Ce qui ne vaut pas la peine d'être dit, on le
chante.
> That which is not worth speaking they
> sing.
> *d.*   BEAUMARCHAIS—*Barbier de Séville.*
> I. 1

Tout finit par des chansons.
> Everything ends with songs.
> *e.*   BEAUMARCHAIS—*Mariage de Figaro.*
> End.

SLEEP.

Tu dors, Brutus, et Rome est dans les fers.
> Thou sleepest, Brutus, and yet Rome is
> in chains.
> *f.*   VOLTAIRE—*La Mort de César.* II. 2.

SOCIETY.

La Société est l'union des hommes, et non
pas les hommes.
> Society is the union of men and not the
> men themselves.
> *g.*   MONTESQUIEU—*De l'Esprit.* X. 3.

La société est partagée en deux classes : les
tondeurs et les tondus. Il faut toujours être
avec les premiers contre les seconds.
> Society is divided into two classes: the
> shearers and the shorn. We should always
> be with the former against the latter.
> *h.*   TALLEYRAND.

Le sage quelquefois évite le monde de peur
d'être ennuyé.
> The wise man sometimes flees from society
> from fear of being bored.
> *i.*   LA BRUYÈRE—*Les Caractères.* V.

SOLITUDE.

Wer sich der Einsamkeit ergiebt,
Ach ! der ist bald allein.
> Whoever gives himself up to solitude,
> Ah ! he is soon alone.
> *j.*   GOETHE—*Wilhelm Meister.* II. 13.

SORROW.

Car il n'est si beau jour qui n'amène sa nuit.
> For there is no day however beautiful
> that is not followed by night.
> *k.*   *On the tombstone of* JEAN D' ORBESAN
> *at Padua.*

Ach ! aus dem Glück entwickelt oft sich
Schmerz.
> Alas ! sorrow from happiness is oft evolved.
> *l.*   GOETHE—*Die Natürliche Tochter.* II.
> 3. 17.

Die Leiden sind wie die Gewitterwolken ;
in der Ferne sehen sie schwarz aus, über uns
kaum grau.
> Sorrows are like thunderclouds—in the
> distance they look black, over our heads
> scarcely gray.
> *m.*   JEAN PAUL RICHTER—*Hesperus.* XIV.

Kurz ist der Schmerz, und ewig ist die Freude!
> Brief is sorrow, and endless is joy.
> *n.*   SCHILLER—*Die Jungfrau von Orleans.*
> V. 14. 44.

Meine Ruh ist hin,
Mein Herz ist schwer.
> My peace is gone, my heart is heavy.
> *o.*   GOETHE—*Faust.* I. 15.

SPEECH.

A raconter ses maux souvent on les soulage.
> By speaking of our misfortunes we often
> relieve them.
> *p.*   CORNEILLE—*Polyeucte.* I. 3.

Faire de la prose sans le savoir.
> To speak prose without knowing it.
> *q.*   MOLIÈRE—*Bourgeois Gentilhomme.*
> II. 6.

Ils n'emploient les paroles que pour déguiser leurs pensées.
> They only employ words to disguise their
> thoughts.
> *r.*   VOLTAIRE—*Dialogues.* XIV.
> *Le Chapon et la Poularde.*

Je vous ferai un impromptu à loisir.
> I shall make you an impromptu at my
> leisure.
> *s.*   MOLIÈRE—*Les Précieuses Ridicules.* I.
> 12.

La parole a été donnée à l'homme pour
déguiser sa pensée.
> Speech was given to man to disguise his
> thoughts.
> *t.*   TALLEYRAND—*See* BARÈRE'S *Mémoires.*

Le cœur sent rarement ce que la bouche ex-
prime.
> The heart seldom feels what the mouth
> expresses.
> *u.*   CAMPISTRON—*Pompeia.* XI. 5.

Quand on se fait entendre, on parle toujours bien,
Et tous vos beaux dictons ne servent de rien.

> When we are understood, we always speak well, and then all your fine diction serves no purpose.

a. MOLIÈRE—*Les Femmes Savantes.* II. 6.

Revenons à nos moutons.

> To return to the subject.

b. PIERRE BLANCHET—*L'Avocat Pathelin.*

Tout ce qu'on dit de trop est fade et rebutant.

> That which is repeated too often becomes insipid and tedious.

c. BOILEAU—*L'Art Poétique.* I. 61.

Voulez-vous qu'on croie du bien de vous? N'en dites point.

> Do you wish people to speak well of you? Then do not speak at all yourself.

d. PASCAL—*Pensées.* VI. 59.

Du sprichst ein grosses Wort gelassen aus.

> Thou speakest a word of great moment calmly.

e. GOETHE—*Iphigenia auf Tauris.* I. 3. 88. 1.

Er spricht Unsinn; für den Vernünftigen Menschen giebt es gar keinen Zufall.

> He talks nonsense; to a sensible man there is no such thing as chance.

f. LUDWIG TIECK—*Fortunat.*

Man lernt Verschwiegenheit am meisten unter Menschen, die Keine haben—und Plauderhaftigkeit unter Verschwiegenen.

> One learns taciturnity best among people who have none, and loquacity among the taciturn.

g. JEAN PAUL RICHTER—*Hesperus.* XII.

Was ist der langen Rede kurzer Sinn?

> What is the short meaning of this long harangue?

h. SCHILLER—*Piccolomini.* I. 2. 160.

Chi parla troppo non può parlar sempre bene.

> He who talks much cannot always talk well.

i. GOLDONI—*Pamela.* I. 6.

Lo tuo ver dir m'incuora
Buona umiltà e gran tumor m'appiani.

> The truth thy speech doth show, within my heart reproves the swelling pride.

j. DANTE—*Purgatorio.* XI. 118.

STORM.

C'est l'éclair qui paraît, la foudre va partir.

> It is the flash which appears, the thunderbolt will follow.

k. VOLTAIRE—*Oreste.* II. **7.**

C'est une tempête dans un verre d'eau.

> It is a tempest in a tumbler of water.

l. PAUL, GRAND-DUC DE RUSSIE—*Of the insurrection in Geneva.*

Der Sturm ist Meister; Wind und Welle spielen Ball mit dem Menschen.

> The storm is master. Man, as a ball, is tossed twixt winds and billows.

m. SCHILLER—*Wilhelm Tell.* IV. 1. 59.

STUPIDITY.

La faute en est aux dieux, qui la firent si bête.

> The fault rests with the gods, who have made her so stupid.

n. GRESSET—*Méchant.* II. 7.

Schad' um die Leut'! Sind sonst wackre Brüder. Aber das denkt, wie ein Seifensieder.

> A pity about the people! they are brave enough comrades, but they have heads like a soapboiler's.

o. SCHILLER—*Wallenstein's Lager.* XI. 347.

SUCCESS.

Il n'y a au monde que deux manières de s'élever, ou par sa propre industrie, ou par l'imbécilité des autres.

> There are but two ways of rising in the world : either by one's own industry or profiting by the foolishness of others.

p. LA BRUYÈRE—*Les Caractères.* VI.

J'ai toujours vu que, pour réussir dans le monde, il fallait avoir l'air fou et être sage.

> I have always observed that to succeed in the world one should appear like a fool but be wise.

q. MONTESQUIEU—*Pensées Diverses.*

Le succès de la plupart des choses dépend de savoir combien il faut de temps pour réussir.

> The success of most things depends upon knowing how long it will take to succeed.

r. MONTESQUIEU—*Pensées Diverses.*

Médiocre et rampant, et l'on arrive à tout.

> Be commonplace and creeping, and you attain all things.

s. BEAUMARCHAIS—*Barbier de Séville.* III. 7.

Qui bien chante et bien danse fait un métier qui peu avance.

> Singing and dancing alone will not advance one in the world.

t. ROUSSEAU—*Confessions.* V.

Ja, meine Liebe, wer lebt, verliert * * * aber er gewinnt auch.

> Yes, my love, whosoever lives, loses, * * * but he also wins.

u. GOETHE—*Stella.* I.

Wenn ihr's nicht fühlt ihr werdet's nicht erjagen.

You'll never attain it unless you know the feeling.

a.   GOETHE—*Faust.* I. 1. 182.

Ha sempre dimostrato l'esperienza, e lo dimostra la ragione, che mai succedono bene le cose che dipendono da molti.

Experience has always shown, and reason also, that affairs which depend on many seldom succeed.

b.   GUICCIARDINI—*Storia d' Italia.*

SUSPICION.

Les soupçons importuns
Sont d'un second hymen les fruits les plus communs.

Disagreeable suspicions are usually the fruits of a second marriage.

c.   RACINE—*Phèdre.* II. 5.

Argwohnen folgt auf Misstrauen.
Suspicion follows close on mistrust.

d.   LESSING—*Nathan der Weise.* V. 8.

T.

TALENTS.

Ne forçons point notre talent;
Nous ne ferions rien avec grâce:
Jamais un lourdaud, quoi qu'il fasse,
Ne saurait passer pour galant.

Let us not overstrain our talents, lest we do nothing gracefully: a clown, whatever he may do, will never pass for a gentleman.

e.   LA FONTAINE—*Fables.* IV. 5.

Nul n'aura de l'esprit, hors nous et nos amis.

No one shall have wit save we and our friends.

f.   MOLIÈRE—*Les Femmes Savantes.* III. 2.

TARDINESS.

Spät kommt ihr—doch ihr kommt!
You come late, yet you come!
(*Better late than never.*)

g.   SCHILLER—*Piccolomini.* I. 1. 1.

Il fornito
Sempre con danno l'attender sofferse.

It is always those who are ready who suffer in delays.

h.   DANTE—*Inferno.* XXVIII. 98.

TASTE.

Racine passera comme le café.
Racine will pass away as the taste for coffee.

i.   *Attributed to* MME. DE SÉVIGNÉ.

THEOLOGY.

Die Theologie ist die Anthropologie.
Theology is Anthropology.

j.   FEUERBACH—*Wesen des Christenthums.*

THOUGHT.

Ah! comme vous dites, il faut glisser sur bien des pensées, et ne pas faire semblant de les voir.

Ah! as you say, we should slip over many thoughts and act as though we did not perceive them.

k.   MME. DE SÉVIGNÉ—*Lettres.* 70.

La clarté orna les pensées profondes.
Clearness is the ornament of profound thought.

l.   VAUVENARGUES—*Réflexions.* IV.

Les grandes pensées viennent du cœur.
Great thoughts come from the heart.

m.   VAUVENARGUES—*Réflexions.* CXXVII.

Lorsqu'une pensée est trop faible pour porter une expression simple, c'est la marque pour la rejeter.

When a thought is too weak to be expressed simply, it is a proof that it should be rejected.

n.   VAUVENARGUES—*Réflexions.* III.

Es lebt ein anders denkendes Geschlecht!
There lives a race which otherwise does think.

o.   SCHILLER—*Wilhelm Tell.* II. 1. 206.

Sempre il miglior non è il parer primiero.
First thoughts are not always the best.

p.   ALFIERI—*Don Garzia.* III. 1.

TIME.

Le temps fuit, et nous traîne avec soi:
Le moment où je parle est déjà loin de moi.

Time flies and draws us with it. The moment in which I am speaking is already far from me.

q.   BOILEAU—*Épîtres.* III. 47.

Que pour les malheureux l'heure lentement
fuit!

How slowly the hours pass to the unhappy.
a.   SAURIN—*Blanche et Guiscard.* V. 5.

Qu'une nuit paraît longue à la douleur qui
veille!

How long the night seems to one kept
awake by pain.
b.   SAURIN—*Blanche et Guiscard.* V. 5.

Vingt siècles descendus dans l'éternelle nuit.
Y sont sans mouvement, sans lumière et sans
bruit.

Twenty ages sunk in eternal night. They
are without movement, without light, and
without noise.
c.   LEMOINE—*Œuvres Poétiques.* Saint
Louis.

Die Zeit ist selbst ein Element.

Time is itself an element.
d.   GOETHE—*Sprüche in Prosa.* III.

Doch zittre vor der langsamen,
Der stillen Macht der Zeit.

Yet tremble at the slow, silent power of
time.
e.   SCHILLER—*Wallenstein's Tod.* I. 3. 32.

Ein stiller Geist ist Jahre lang geschäftig;
Die Zeit nur macht die feine Gährung kräftig.

Long is the calm brain active in creation;
Time only strengthens the fine fermentation.
f.   GOETHE—*Faust.* I. 6. 36.

So schaff' ich am sausenden Webstuhl der
Zeit.

Thus at Time's humming loom I ply.
g.   GOETHE—*Faust.* I. 1. 156.

Tag wird es auf die dickste Nacht, und, kommt
Die Zeit, so reifen auch die spät'sten Früchte.

Day follows on the murkiest night, and,
when the time comes, the latest fruits will
ripen.
h.   SCHILLER—*Die Jungfrau von Orleans.*
III. 2. 60.

O, wer weiss
Was in der Zeiten Hintergrunde schlummert.

Who knows what may be slumbering in
the background of time!
i.   SCHILLER—*Don Carlos.* I. 1. 44.

Was man von der Minute ausgeschlagen
Gibt keine Ewigkeit zurück.

Eternity gives nothing back of what one
leaves out of the minutes.
j.   SCHILLER—*Resignation.* St. 18.

Che'l perder tempo a chi più sa più spiace.

The wisest are the most annoyed at the
loss of time.
k.   DANTE—*Purgatorio.* III. 78.

No ay memoria à quien el tiempo no acabe,
ni dolor que nuerte no le consuma.

There is no remembrance which time
does not obliterate, nor pain which death
does not put an end to.
l.   CERVANTES—*Don Quixote.* III. 1.

TRADE.

Une nation boutiquière.

A nation [England] of shopkeepers.
m.   NAPOLEON—*First used by* BARÈRE,
*before the National Convention, June
11, 1794.*

TRAVELLING.

Zählt der Pilger Meilen,
Wenn er zum fernen Gnadenbilde wallt?

Does the pilgrim count the miles
When he travels to some distant shrine?
n.   SCHILLER—*Wallenstein's Tod.* IV. 11.
33.

Un viaggiatore prudente non disprezza mai
il suo paese.

A wise traveler never despises his own
country.
o.   GOLDONI—*Pamela.* I. 16.

TRIFLES.

Peu de chose nous console, parceque peu de
chose nous afflige.

A little thing comforts us because a little
thing afflicts us.
p.   PASCAL—*Pensées.* VI. 25.

Das kleinste Haar wirft seinen Schatten.

The smallest hair throws its shadow.
q.   GOETHE—*Sprüche in Prosa.* III.

TROUBLE.

Le chagrin monte en croupe et galope
avec lui.

Trouble rides behind and gallops with
him.
r.   BOILEAU—*Epître.* V. 44.

Die Müh' ist klein, der Spass ist gross.

The trouble is small, the fun is great.
s.   GOETHE—*Faust.* I. 21. 218.

TRUST.

La confiance que l'on a en soi fait naître la
plus grande partie de celle que l'on a aux autres.

The confidence which we have in ourselves gives birth to much of that which
we have in others.
t.   LA ROCHEFOUCAULD—*Premier
Supplément.* 49.

TRUTH.

La vérité n'a point cet air impétueux.
  Truth has not such an urgent air.
  a.   BOILEAU—*L'Art Poétique.* I. 198.

La vérité ne fait pas tant de bien dans le
monde, que ses apparences y font de mal.
  Truth does not do so much good in the
  world, as the appearance of it does evil.
  b.   LA ROCHEFOUCAULD—*Maximes.* 59.

Le contraire des bruits qui courent des af-
faires ou des personnes est souvent la vérité.
  The opposite of what is noised about
  concerning men and things is often the truth.
  c.   LA BRUYÈRE—*Les Caractères.* XII.

Le vrai peut quelquefois n'être pas vraisem-
blable.
  At times truth may not seem probable.
  d.   BOILEAU—*L'Art Poétique.* III. 48.

Si je tenais toutes les vérités dans ma main,
je me donnerais bien de garde de l'ouvrir aux
hommes.
  If I held all of truth in my hand I would
  beware of opening it to men.
  e.   FONTENELLE.

Si la bonne foi était bannie du reste du
monde, il faudrait qu'on la trouvât dans la
bouche des rois.
  Though good faith should be banished
  from the rest of the world, it should be
  found in the mouths of kings.
  f.   JEAN II. See *Biographie Universelle.*

Die Treue warnt vor drohenden Verbrechen,
Die Rachgier spricht von den begangenen.
  Truth warns of threatening crimes,
  Malice speaks of those which were com-
  mitted.
  g.   SCHILLER—*Don Carlos.* III. 4. 124.

Ein guter Mensch, in seinem dunkeln Drange,
Ist sich des rechten Weges wohl bewusst.
  A good man, through obscurest aspirations
  Has still an instinct of the one true way.
  h.   GOETHE—*Faust. Prolog im Himmel.*

TYRANNY.

Il n'appartient, qu' aux tyrans d'être toujours en crainte.
  None but tyrants have any business to be
  afraid.
  i.   HARDOUIN DE PÉRÉFIXE—*Attributed to*
                                  HENRY IV.

Les habiles tyrans ne sont jamais punis.
  Clever tyrants are never punished.
  j.   VOLTAIRE—*Mérope.* V. 5.

N'est-on jamais tyran qu'avec un diadème?
  Is there no tyrant but the crowned one?
  k.   CHÉNIER—*Caius Gracchus.*

Tremblez, tyrans, vous êtes immortels.
  Tremble, ye tyrants, for ye can not die.
  l.   DELILLE—*L'Immortalité de l'Âme.*

Tyran, descends du trône et fais place à ton
maître.
  Tyrant, step from the throne, and give
  place to thy master.
  m.   CORNEILLE—*Héraclius.* I. 2.

U.

UGLINESS.

L'or donne aux plus laids certain charme
    pour plaire,
Et que sans lui le reste est une triste affaire.
  Gold gives to the ugliest thing a certain
    charming air,
  For that without it were else a miserable
    affair.
  n.   MOLIÈRE—*Sganarelle.* I.

UNDERSTANDING.

Il n'est pas nécessaire de tenir les choses
pour en raisonner.
  It is not necessary to retain facts that we
  may reason concerning them.
  o.   BEAUMARCHAIS—*Barbier de Séville.*
                                    V. 4.

Quand celui à qui l'on parle ne comprend
pas et celui qui parle ne se comprend pas,
c'est de la métaphysique.
  When he to whom one speaks does not
  understand, and he who speaks himself does
  not understand, this is Metaphysics.
  p.   VOLTAIRE.

Was man nicht versteht, besitzt man nicht.
  What we do not understand we do not
  possess.
  q.   GOETHE—*Sprüche in Prosa.* III.

UNITY.

Il opine du bonnet comme un moine en
Sorbonne.
  He adopts the opinion of others like a
  monk in the Sorbonne.
  r.   PASCAL—*Lettres Provinciales.* II.

Entzwei und gebiete! Tüchtig Wort,
Verein und leite! Bessrer Hort.

> Divide and command, a wise maxim ;
> Unite and guide, a better.
> *a.*   GOETHE—*Sprüche in Reimen.* III.

Seid einig—einig—einig.

> Be united—united—united.
> *b.*   SCHILLER—*Wilhelm Tell.* IV. 2. 158.

Was uns alle bändigt, das Gemeine.

> The universal subjugator, the common-
> place.
> *c.*   GOETHE—*Taschenbuch für Damen auf
> das Jahr* 1806.

Wir sind ein Volk, und einig wollen wir
handeln.

> We are one people and will act as one.
> *d.*   SCHILLER—*Wilhelm Tell.* II. 2. 258.

V.

VANITY.

Ce qui nous rend la vanité des autres in-
supportable, c'est qu'elle blesse la nôtre.

> That which makes the vanity of others
> unbearable to us is that which wounds our
> own.
> *e.*   LA ROCHEFOUCAULD—*Maximes.* 389.

Il est difficile d'estimer quelqu'un comme il
veut l'être.

> It is difficult to esteem a man as highly as
> he would wish.
> *f.*   VAUVENARGUES—*Réflexions.* LXVII.

On parle peu quand la vanité ne fait pas
parler.

> We say little if not egged on by vanity.
> *g.*   LA ROCHEFOUCAULD—*Maximes.* 137.

VARIETY.

Diversité, c'est ma devise.

> Diversity, that is my motto.
> *h.*   LA FONTAINE—*Paté d'Anguille.*

Weil Verschiedenheit des Nichts mehr
ergötzt, als Einerleiheit des Etwas.

> For variety of mere nothings gives more
> pleasure than uniformity of something.
> *i.*   JEAN PAUL RICHTER—*Levana.*
> *Fragment V.* I. 100.

VICTORY.

La victoire me suit, et tout suit la victoire.

> Victory follows me, and all things follow
> victory.
> *j.*   SCUDÉRI—*L'Amour Tyrannique.*

VIRTUE.

Faut d'la vertu, pas trop n'en faut,
L'excès en tout est un défaut.

> Some virtue is needed, but not too much.
> Excess in anything is a defect.
> *k.*   MONVEL—*From a comic opera, Erreur
> d'un Moment. Quoted by* DESAUGIERS.
> See FOURNIER, *L'Esprit des Autres.*
> Chap. XXXV.

J'aime mieux un vice commode
Qu'une fatigante vertu.

> I prefer an accommodating vice to an ob-
> stinate virtue.
> *l.*   MOLIÈRE—*Amphitryon.* I. 4.

La naissance n'est rien où la vertu n'est **pas.**

> Birth is nothing where virtue is not.
> *m.*   MOLIÈRE—*Don Juan.* IV. 6.

La vertu d'un cœur noble est la marque
certaine.

> Virtue alone is the unerring sign of a
> noble soul.
> *n.*   BOILEAU—*Satires.* V. 42.

Où la vertu va-t-elle se nicher?

> Where does virtue go to lodge?
> *o.*   *Exclamation of* MOLIÈRE.

Toutes grandes vertus conviennent aux
grands hommes.

> All great virtues become great men.
> *p.*   CORNEILLE—*Notes de Corneille par
> La Rochefoucauld.*

W.

WAR.

Ein Schlachten war's, nicht eine Schlacht, zu
nennen!

> It was a slaughter rather than a battle.
> *q.*   SCHILLER—*Die Jungfrau von Orleans.*
> I. 9. 50.

Con disavvantaggio grande si fa la guerra
con chi non ha che perdere.

> We fight to great disadvantage when
> we fight with those who have nothing to
> lose.
> *r.*   GUICCIARDINI—*Storia d'Italia.*

WEAKNESS.

On affaiblit toujours tout ce qu'on exagère.
 We always weaken whatever we exaggerate.
 a. La Harpe—*Mélanie.* I. 1.

Das sterbliche Geschlecht ist viel zu schwach
In ungewohnter Höhe nicht zu schwindeln.
 The mortal race is far too weak not to grow dizzy on unwonted heights.
 b. Goethe—*Iphigenia auf Tauris.* I. 3. 98.

Die Limonade ist matt wie deine Seele—
versuche!
 This lemonade is weak like your soul—
try it!
 c. Schiller—*Cabale und Liebe.* V. 7.

WINE.

Am Rhein, am Rhein, da wachsen uns're
 Reben.
 On the Rhine, on the Rhine, there grow our vines.
 d. Claudius—*Rheinweinlied.*

Der Wein erfindet nichts, er schwatzt's nur
aus.
 Wine tells nothing, it only tattles.
 e. Schiller—*Piccolomini.* IV. 7. 42.

WISDOM.

Ce n'est pas être sage
D'être plus sage qu'il ne le faut.
 It is not wise to be wiser than is necessary.
 f. Quinault—*Armide.*

Il est bon de frotter et limer notre cervelle
contre celle d'autrui.
 It is good to rub and polish our brain against that of others.
 g. Montaigne—*Essais.* I. 24.

Il est plus aisé d'être sage pour les autres,
que pour soi-même.
 It is easier to be wise for others than for ourselves.
 h. La Rochefoucauld—*Maximes.*

Qui aura esté une fois bien fol ne sera nulle
aultre fois bien sage.
 He who has once been very foolish will at no other time be very wise.
 i. Montaigne—*Essais.* III. 6.

Die Weisheit ist nur in der Wahrheit.
 Wisdom is only found in truth.
 j. Goethe—*Sprüche in Prosa.* III.

WISHES.

On ne peut désirer ce qu'on ne connaît pas.
 We cannot wish for that we know not.
 k. Voltaire—*Zaïre.* I. 1.

Kennst du das Land wo die Citronen blühen,
Im dunkeln Laub die Gold-Orangen glühn,
Ein sanfter Wind vom blauen Himmel weht
Die Myrte still und hoch der Lorbeer steht?
Kennst du es wohl?
 Dahin! Dahin,
Möcht' ich mit dir, O mein Geliebter, ziehn.
 Knowest thou the land where the lemon-trees flourish, where amid the shadowed leaves the golden oranges glisten,—a gentle zephyr breathes from the blue heavens, the myrtle is motionless, and the laurel rises high? Dost thou know it well? Thither, thither, fain would I fly with thee, O my beloved!
 l. Goethe—*Wilhelm Meister.* *Mignon's Lied.*

Was man in der Jugend wünscht, hat man
im Alter die Fülle.
 What one has wished for in youth, in old age one has in abundance.
 m. Goethe—*Wahrheit und Dichtung.*
      Motto to Part II.

WIT.

La raillerie est un discours en faveur de son
esprit contre son bon naturel.
 Raillery is a mode of speaking in favor of one's wit at the expense of one's better nature.
 n. Montesquieu—*Pensées Diverses.*

L'impromptu est justement la pierre de
touche de l'esprit.
 Repartee is precisely the touchstone of the man of wit.
 o. Molière—*Les Précieuses Ridicules.* X.

On peut dire que son esprit brille aux
dépens de sa mémoire.
 One may say that his wit shines at the expense of his memory.
 p. Le Sage—*Gil Blas.* III. XI.

Que les gens d'esprit sont bêtes.
 What silly people wits are!
 q. Beaumarchais—*Barbier de Séville.*
      I. 1.

Mit wenig Witz und viel Behagen
Dreht jeder sich im engen Zirkeltanz
Wie junge Katzen mit dem Schwanz.
 With little wit and ease to suit them,
 They whirl in narrow circling trails,
 Like kittens playing with their tails.
 r. Goethe—*Faust.* I. 5. 94.

WOMAN.

Les femmes ont toujours quelque arrière-
pensée.
 Women always have some mental reservation.
 s. Destouches—*Dissipateur.* V. 9.

Souvent femme varie
Bien fol est qui s'y fie.

    Woman is often fickle—foolish is he who trusts her.

a.   François I.—*Scratched with his ring on a window of Chambord Castle. See* Brantôme—*Discours. Vies des Dames galantes.* IV.

Toute fille lettrée restera fille toute sa vie, quand il n'y aura que des hommes sensés sur la terre.

    Every blue-stocking will remain a spinster as long as there are sensible men on the earth.

b.   Rousseau—*Émile.* I. 5.

Une femme bel-esprit est le fléau de son mari, de ses enfants, de ses amis, de ses valets, de tout le monde.

    A blue-stocking is the scourge of her husband, children, friends, servants, and every one.

c.   Rousseau—*Émile.* I. 5.

Das Ewig-Weibliche zieht uns hinan.

    The eternal feminine doth draw us on.

d.   Goethe—*Faust.* II. 5.

Denn das Naturell der Frauen
Ist so nah mit Kunst verwandt.

    For the nature of women is closely allied to art.

e.   Goethe—*Faust.* II. I.

Denn geht es zu des Bösen Haus
Das Weib hat tausend Schritt voraus.

    When toward the Devil's House we tread,
Woman's a thousand steps ahead.

f.   Goethe—*Faust.* I. 21. 147.

Der Umgang mit Frauen ist das Element guter Sitten.

    The society of women is the foundation of good manners.

g.   Goethe—*Die Wahlverwandtschaften.*
II. 5.

Ehret die Frauen! sie flechten und weben
Himmlische Rosen in's irdische Leben.

    Honor women! they entwine and weave heavenly roses in our earthly life.

h.   Schiller—*Würde der Frauen.*

Ein edler Mann wird durch ein gutes Wort
Der Frauen weit geführt.

    A noble man is led by woman's gentle words.

i.   Goethe—*Iphigenia auf Tauris.* I. 2.
162.

Es ist doch den Mädchen wie angeboren,
dass sie allem gefallen wollen, was nur Augen hat.

    The desire to please everything having eyes seems inborn in maidens.

j.   Salomon Gessner—*Evander und Alcima.* III. 1.

Ich hab' es immer gesagt: das Weib wollte die Natur zu ihrem Meisterstücke machen.

    I have always said it—Nature meant woman to be her masterpiece.

k.   Lessing—*Emilia Galotti.* V. 7.

Was hätt' ein Weiberkopf erdacht, das er
Nicht zu beschönen wüsste?

    What could a woman's head contrive
Which it would not know how to excuse?

l.   Lessing—*Nathan der Weise.* III.

Femmina è cosa garrula e fallace:
Vuole e disvuole, è folle uom chi sen fida,
Sì tra se volge.

    Women have tongues of craft, and hearts of guile,
They will, they will not; fools that on them trust;
For in their speech is death, hell in their smile.

m.   Tasso—*Gerusalemme.* XIX. 84.

Ne l'onde solca, e ne l'arena semina,
E'l vago vento spera in rete accogliere
Chi sue speranze fonda in cor di femina.

    He ploughs the waves, sows the sand, and hopes to gather the wind in a net, who places his hopes on the heart of woman.

n.   Sannazaro—*Ecloga Octava.*

La muger que se determina á ser honrada, entre un ejército de soldados lo puede ser.

    The woman who is resolved to be respected can make herself so even amidst an army of soldiers.

o.   Cervantes—*La Gitanilla.*

Una muger no tiene.
Valor para el consejo, y la conviene Casarse.

    A woman needs a stronger head than her own for counsel—she should marry.

p.   Calderon—*El Purgatorio de Sans Patricio.* III. 4.

WORDS.

Le monde se paye de paroles; peu approfondissent les choses.

    The world is satisfied with words. Few appreciate the things beneath.

q.   Pascal—*Lettres Provinciales.* II.

Souvent d'un grand dessein un mot nous fait juger.

    A single word often betrays a great design.

r.   Racine—*Athalie.* II. 6.

Der Worte sind genug gewechselt,
Lasst mich auch endlich Thaten sehn.

    The words you've bandied are sufficient;
'Tis deeds that I prefer to see.

s.   Goethe—*Faust. Vorspiel auf dem Theater.* L. 182.

Ein Wörtlein kann ihn fällen.
A single little word can strike him dead.
a. LUTHER, *of the Pope.*

Es macht das Volk sich auch mit Worten Lust.
The rabble also vent their rage in words.
b. GOETHE—*Torquato Tasso.* II. 2. 201.

Gewöhnlich glaubt der Mensch, wenn er nur Worte hört,
Es müsse sich dabei doch auch was denken lassen.
Man usually believes, if only words he hears,
That also with them goes material for thinking.
c. GOETHE—*Faust.* I. 6. 230.

Schnell fertig ist die Jugend mit dem Wort.
Youth is too hasty with words.
d. SCHILLER—*Wallenstein's Tod.* II. 2. 99.

WORK.

Chacun son métier;
Les vaches seront bien gardées.
Each one to his own trade; then would the cows be well cared for.
e. FLORIAN—*Le Vacher et le Garde-chasse.*

Hâtez-vous lentement; et, sans perdre courage,
Vingt fois sur le métier remettez votre ouvrage.
Hasten slowly, and without losing heart, put your work twenty times upon the anvil.
f. BOILEAU—*L'Art Poétique.* I. 171.

Le fruit du travail est le plus doux des plaisirs.
The fruit derived from labor is the sweetest of pleasures.
g. VAUVENARGUES—*Réflexions.* 200.

Quanto mas que cada uno es hijo de sus obras.
The rather since every man is the son of his own works.
h. CERVANTES—*Don Quixote.* I. 4.

WORLD (THE).

Le monde est le livre des femmes.
The world is woman's book.
i. ROUSSEAU.

Tout est pour le mieux dans le meilleur des mondes.
Everything is for the best in this best of possible worlds.
j. VOLTAIRE—*Candide.* I.

Was ist ihm nun die Welt? ein weiter leerer Raum,
Fortunen's Spielraum, frei ihr Rad herum zu rollen.
What is the world to him now? a vast and vacant space, for fortune's wheel to roll about at will.
k. WIELAND—*Oberon.* VIII. 20.

Eppur si muove.
But it does move.
l. GALILEO—*Before the Inquisition.* 1632.

Il mondo è un bel libro, ma poco serve a chi non lo sa leggere.
The world is a beautiful book, but of little use to him who cannot read it.
m. GOLDONI—*Pamela.* I. 14.

Vien dietro a me, e lascia dir le genti.
Come, follow me, and leave the world to its babblings.
n. DANTE—*Purgatorio.* V. 13.

WORTH.

Il est plus facile de paraître digne des emplois qu'on n'a pas que de ceux que l'on exerce.
It is easier to appear worthy of a position one does not hold, than of the office which one fills.
o. LA ROCHEFOUCAULD—*Maximes.* 164.

La couronne vaut bien une messe ou Paris vaut bien une messe.
The crown, or Paris, is well worth a mass.
p. *Attributed to* HENRY IV.

Le jeu ne vaut pas la chandelle.
The game is not worth the candle.
q. *French Proverb Quoted by* LORD CHESTERFIELD.

Z.

ZEAL.

Blinder Eifer schadet nur.
Blind zeal can only do harm.
r. LICHTWER—*Die Katzen und der Hausherr.*

Der Freunde Eifer ist's, der mich
Zu Grunde richtet, nicht der Hass der Feinde.
The zeal of friends it is that razes me,
And not the hate of enemies.
s. SCHILLER—*Wallenstein's Tod.* III.
18   Last Lines.

MOTTOES

FROM

THE LATIN AND FRENCH.

LATIN.

A.

A cruce salus.
  Salvation (by means of the cross).
  a.   Motto of the Irish Earl of Mayo.

A cuspide corona.
  By my spear, a crown.
  b.   Motto of the Irish Viscount Middleton.

Ad astra per aspera.
  To the stars through difficulties.
  c.   Motto of Kansas.

A Deo et rege.
  By God and the king.
  *d.   Motto of Earl Harrington, and Earl
                                    Stanhope.*

Ad majorem Dei gloriam.
  For the greater glory of God.
  e.   Motto of the Society of Jesus.

Æquam æquanimiter.
  With equanimity.
  f.   Motto of Lord Sheffield.

Æquam servare mentem.
  To be unmoved.
  g.   Motto of Lord Rivers.

Afflavit Deus et dissipantur.
    The breath of God has gone forth, and
  they are dispersed.
  *h.   Inscription on a medal struck in the
            reign of Queen Elizabeth, on the de-
            struction of the Spanish Armada.*

Animis opibusque parati.
    Prepared in mind and resources; (ready to
  give life and property).
  i.   Motto of South Carolina.

Animo et fide.
  By courage and faith.
  j.   Motto of the Earl of Guildford.

Animus et prudentia.
  Courage and prudence.
  k.   Motto of General Sir David Ochterlony.

Appetitus rationi pareat.
  Let the appetite be obedient to reason.
  l.   Motto of the Irish Earl Fitz William.

At spes non fracta.
  But my hope is not broken.
  m.   Motto of the second Earl Hopetoun.

Auctor pretiosa facit.
  The giver makes the gift more precious.
  n.   Motto of the Earl of Buckingham.

Audaciter et sincere.
  Boldly and sincerely.
  o.   Motto of Lords Clare and Clive.

Aut disce, aut discede; manet sors tertia,
    cædi.
    Either learn, or depart; a third course
  is open to you, and that is, submit to be
  flogged.
  *p.   Motto of the Schoolroom of Winchester
                                    College.*

Aut nunquam tentes aut perfice.
  Either never attempt or else accomplish.
  q.   Motto of the Duke of Dorset.

Avi memorantur avorum.
    I count grandfathers' grandfathers. (I
  follow a long train of ancestors.)
  r.   Motto of Lord Grantley.

B.

Basis virtutum constantia.
  Constancy is the foundation of all virtues.
  s.   Motto of Viscount Hereford.

Benigno numino.
  Under a favoring providence.
  t.   Motto of Pitt, Earl of Chatham.

C.

Candide et constanter.
  Candidly and constantly.
  u.   Motto of the Earl of Coventry.

Candor dat viribus alas.
Truth gives wings to strength.
a.   Motto of the Irish Earl of Belvedere.

Cavendo tutus.
Safe by caution.
b.   Motto of the House of Cavendish.

Civilitas successit barbarum.
Civilization succeeds barbarism.
c.   Territorial Motto of Minnesota.

Clarior e tenebris.
More bright from obscurity.
d.   Motto of the Irish Earl of Miltown.

Cogito, ergo sum.
I think, therefore I exist.
e.   Maxim of Descartes.

Confido, conquiesco.
I trust, and am content.
f.   Motto of the Second Earl of Dysart.

Consequitur quodcunque petit.
He attains whatever he pursues.
g.   Motto of the Irish Earl Bective.

Consilio et animis.
By wisdom and courage.
h.   Motto of the Second Earl of Lauderdale.

Constantia et virtute.
By constancy and virtue.
i.   Motto of Lord Amherst.

Cor unum, via una.
One heart, one way.
j.   Motto of the Earl of Exeter.

Crescite, et multiplicamini.
Increase, and multiply.
k.   Motto of Maryland.

Crescit sub pondere virtus.
Virtue grows under an imposed weight.
l.   Motto of the Earl of Dunbigh.

Cruce, dum spiro, fido.
While I breathe I trust in the cross.
m.   Motto of the Irish Viscount Netterville.

D.

Data fata secutus.
Following his declared fate.
n.   Motto of Lord St. John.

Decori decus addit avito.
He adds honor to his ancestral honors.
o.   Motto of the Second Earl of Kellie.

Decrevi.
I have decreed.
p.   Motto of the Irish Earl of Westmeath.

De monte alto.
From a high mountain.
q.   Motto of the Irish Baron De Montalt.

Deo adjuvante non timendum.
By God's aid there is nothing to be feared.
r.   Motto of the Irish Viscount Fitz William.

Deo date.
Give to God.
s.   Motto of Lord Arundel.

Deo duce, ferro comitante.
My God my guide, and my sword my companion.
t.   Motto of the Irish Earl of Charlemont.

Deo, non fortunâ.
From God, not fortune.
u.   Motto of Lord Digby.

Deo, Patriæ, Amicis.
For God, my country, and my friends.
v.   Motto of Baron Colchester.

Dirigo.
I lead.
w.   Motto of Maine.

Divide et impera.
Divide and govern.
x.   Motto of Louis XI.

Dominus providebit.
God will provide.
y.   Motto of the Second Earl of Glasgow.

Ducit amor patriæ.
The love of my country leads me.
z.   Motto of the Irish Baron Milford.

Dum spiro, spero.
Whilst I breathe, I hope.
aa.   Motto of the Irish Viscount Dillon.

E.

Ense petit placidam sub libertate quietem.
By the sword she seeks a quiet peace with liberty.
bb.   Motto of Massachusetts.

Esse quam videri malim.
I would rather be than seem to be.
cc.   Motto of the Earl of Winterton.

Et decus et pretium recti.
Both the ornament and the reward of virtue.
dd.   Motto of the Duke of Grafton and Lord
Southampton.

Etiam quod esse videris.
Be what you seem to be.
ee.   Motto of Lord Sondes.

Et nos quoque tela sparsimus.
We, too, have hurled weapons.
  a.   *Motto of Lord Rawdon.*

Excelsior.
Still higher.
  b.   *Motto of New York.*

Excitari non hebescere.
Spirited, not inactive.
  c.   *Motto of Lord Walsingham.*

Exitus acta probat.
The result justifies the deed.
  d.   *Motto of Washington.*

F.

Factum est.
It has been done.
  e.   *Motto of the Plasterers' Company of*
                       London.

Fare—fac.
Speak—act.
  f.   *Motto of the Second Baron Fairfax.*

Fari quæ sentiat.
To speak what he thinks.
  g.   *Motto of the Earl of Oxford, and of*
                    Lord Walpole.

Fax mentis honestæ gloria.
Glory is the torch of a noble mind.
  h.   *Motto of the Nova Scotia Baronetage.*

Fax mentis, incendium gloriæ.
The torch of the mind is the flame of glory.
  i.   *Motto of the Irish Earl of Granard.*

Festina lente.
Hasten slowly.
  j.   *Motto of Baron Plunket.*

Fiat justitia, ruat cœlum.
Let justice be done, though the heavens fall.
  k.   *Motto of Ferdinand I.*

Fide et amore.
By faith and love.
  l.   *Motto of the Earl of Hertford.*

Fide et fiduciâ.
By faith and courage.
  m.   *Motto of the Second Earl of Roseberry.*

Fide et fortitudine.
By faith and fortitude.
  n.   *Motto of the Earl of Essex.*

Fidei coticula crux.
The cross is the touchstone of faith.
  o.   *Motto of Earl Clarendon, Earl Jersey,*
           and of the Irish Earl Grandison.

Fideli certi merces.
The faithful are certain of their reward.
  p.   *Motto of Earl Boringdon.*

Fidelis ad urnam.
Faithful to the ashes.
  q.   *Motto of the Irish Baron Sunderlin.*

Fideliter.
Faithfully.
  r.   *Motto of the Scotch Baron Banff.*

Fides probata coronat.
Approved faith wears a crown.
  s.   *Motto of the Scotch Earl of Marchmont.*

Fidus et audax.
Faithful and intrepid.
  t.   *Motto of the Irish Baron Lismore.*

Finem respice.
Look to the end.
  u.   *Motto of Lord Clifton.*

Flecti non frangi.
To bend, not to break.
  v.   *Motto of the Irish Viscount Palmerson.*

Fortem posce animum.
Ask for a brave soul.
  w.   *Motto of Lord Say and Sele.*

Forte scutum, salus ducum.
A strong shield is the safety of leaders.
  x.   *Motto of the Irish Earl Clermont.*

Fortes fortuna juvat.
Fortune favors the brave.
  y.   *Motto of Baron Bloomfield.*

Forti et fideli nil difficile.
Nothing is difficult to the brave and faithful.
  z.   *Motto of the Irish Baron Muskerry.*

Fortis cadere, cedere non potest.
The brave man may fall, but cannot yield.
  aa.   *Motto of the Irish Earl of Drogheda.*

Fortis sub forti fatiscet.
A brave man will yield to a braver man.
  bb.   *Motto of the Irish Earl of Upper Ossory.*

Fortiter et recte.
Courageously and honorably.
  cc.   *Motto of Lord Heathfield.*

Fortiter geret crucem.
He will bravely support the cross.
  dd.   *Motto of the Irish Baron Donaghmore.*

Fortitudine et prudentiâ.
By fortitude and prudence.
  ee.   *Motto of Earl Powis.*

Fortuna sequatur.
Let fortune follow.
  ff.   *Motto of the Earl of Aberdeen.*

Frangas non flectas.
You may break, but not bend me.
a. *Motto of the Marquis of Stafford.*

Fuimus.
We have been.
b. *Motto of the Earl of Aylesbury and of the Scotch Earl Elgin.*

G.

Gaudet tentamine virtus.
Virtue rejoices in temptation.
c. *Motto of Earl Dartmouth.*

Gloria virtutis umbra.
Glory is the shadow (*i. e.* the companion) of virtue.
d. *Motto of the Irish Baron Longford.*

H.

Hæc generi incrementa fides.
This faith will furnish new increase to our race.
e. *Motto of Marquis Townshend.*

Honesta quam splendide.
Honestly rather than brilliantly.
f. *Motto of Viscount Barrington.*

Honor virtutis præmium.
Honor is the reward of virtue.
g. *Motto of Lord Boston and Earl Ferrers.*

Hora est semper.
It is always time.
h. *Motto of Earl Pomfret.*

Humani nihil alienum.
Nothing human is foreign to me.
i. *Motto of Earl Talbot.*

I.

Illæso lumine solem.
With sight unhurt to view the sun; (the quality ascribed to the eagle.)
j. *Motto of Lord Loughborough.*

Indignante invidiâ florebit justus.
The just man will flourish in spite of envy.
k. *Motto of the Irish Earl Glendore.*

In ferrum pro libertate ruebant.
For freedom they rushed upon the sword.
l. *Motto of Earl Leicester.*

In hoc signo spes mea.
In this sign (or standard) is my hope.
m. *Motto of the Irish Viscount Taaffe.*

51

In hoc signo vinces.
Under this sign (standard) thou shalt conquer.
n. *Motto of the Emperor Constantine I.*

In te, Domine, speravi.
In thee, O Lord, have I trusted.
o. *Motto of the Scotch Earl of Strathmore.*

Integra mens augustissima possessio.
A pure mind is the most august possession.
p. *Motto of the Irish Lord Blayney.*

In utroque fidelis.
Faithful in both.
q. *Motto of the Scotch Viscount Falkland.*

Invitum sequitur honor.
Honor follows him against his inclination.
r. *Motto of Irish Marquis Donegal.*

J.

Justitia tenax.
Tenacious of justice.
s. *Motto of Baron Hastings.*

Justitiæ soror fides.
Faith the sister of justice.
t. *Motto of Lord Thurlow.*

L.

Labor ipse voluptas.
Labor is itself a pleasure.
u. *Motto of Lord King.*

Laus Deo.
Praise be to God.
v. *Motto of Viscount Arbuthnot.*

Libertas.
Liberty.
w. *Motto of the Irish Baron Carbery.*

Libertas sub rege pio.
Liberty under an upright king.
x. *Motto of Viscount Sidmouth.*

M.

Magistratus indicat virum.
The office shows the man.
y. *Motto of Earl Lonsdale.*

Malo mori quam fœdari.
I had rather die than be debased.
z. *Motto of the Irish Earl of Athlone and of Viscount Kingsland.*

Manu forte.
With brave hand.
aa. *Motto of the Scotch Baron Reay.*

Manus hæc inimica tyrannis.
This hand is an enemy to tyrants.
bb. *Motto of Lord Carysfort.*

Mediocra firma.
The middle station is the safest.
a.   *Motto of the Earl of Verulam.*

Memoriâ in æternâ.
In eternal remembrance.
b.   *Motto of the Irish Viscount Tracey.*

Mens conscia recti.
A mind conscious of rectitude.
c.   *Motto of the Irish Viscount Ashbrook*
        and of Lord Macartney.

Montani semper liberi.
Moutaineers are always freemen.
d.   *Motto of West Virginia.*

Moveo et propitior.
I rise and am appeased.
e.   *Motto of the Irish Baron Welles.*

Mutare vel timere sperno.
I scorn to change or fear.
f.   *Motto of the Duke of Beaufort.*

N.

Nec cupias nec metuas.
Neither desire nor fear.
g.   *Motto of Lord Dover, and of the Earl*
        of Hardwicke.

Ne cede malis.
Do not yield to misfortune.
h.   *Motto of Earl Albermarle.*

Nec male notus eques.
A well-known knight.
i.   *Motto of the Irish Viscount Southwell.*

Nec placidâ contentus quiete est.
Nor is he content with soft repose.
j.   *Motto of Earl Peterborough.*

Nec pluribus impar.
Not unequal to many.
k.   *Motto of Louis XIV.*

Nec prece nec pretio.
Neither by bribe nor by entreaty.
l.   *Motto of the Irish Viscount Bateman.*

Nec quærere nec spernere honorem.
Neither to seek nor to despise honors.
m.   *Motto of Viscount Bolingbroke.*

Nec temere nec timide.
Neither rashly nor timidly.
n.   *Motto of the Duke of Cleveland and of*
        the Earls of Bradford and Munster.

Nec timeo nec sperno.
I neither fear nor despise.
o.   *Motto of the Irish Viscount Boyne.*

Nemo me impune lacessit.
No man provokes me with impunity.
p.   *Motto of the Order of the Thistle.*

Ne obliviscaris.
Do not forget.
q.   *Motto of the Duke of Argyll.*

Ne tentes, aut perfice.
Attempt not, or accomplish.
r.   *Motto of the Irish Marquis of Downshire.*

Ne vile fano.
Bring nothing base to the temple.
s.   *Motto of the Earl of Westmoreland.*

Ne vile velis.
Incline to nothing base.
t.   *Motto of Lord Abergavenny.*

Nobilitatis virtus non stemma character.
Virtue not pedigree should characterize
nobility.
u.   *Motto of Earl Grosvenor.*

Nil desperandum.
Never despair.
v.   *Motto of the Earl of Lichfield.*

Nil nisi cruce.
Nothing unless through suffering.
w.   *Motto of the Marquis of Waterford.*

Nisi Dominus, frustra.
Unless the Lord is with you all is in vain.
x.   *Motto of the City of Edinburgh.*

Non conscire sibi.
To be conscious of no fault.
y.   *Motto of Earl Winchelsea.*

Non inferiora secutus.
Not having followed mean pursuits.
z.   *Motto of Lord Montford.*

Non nobis solum sed toti mundi nati.
Born not for ourselves alone but for the
whole world.
aa.   *Motto of the Irish Baron Rokeby.*

Non quo, sed quomodo.
Not by whom, but in what manner, the
business is done.
bb.   *Motto of the Earl of Suffolk.*

Non revertar inuitus.
I will not return unavenged.
cc.   *Motto of the Irish Earl Lisburne.*

Non sibi sed patriæ.
Not for self but for country.
dd.   *Motto of Earl Romney.*

Numini et patriæ asto.
I stand for God and my country.
ee.   *Motto of the Scotch Lord Aston.*

Nunc aut nunquam.
Now or never.
a.   Motto of the Irish Viscount Kilmorey.

Nunquam non paratus.
Never unprepared.
b.   Motto of Marquis Annandale.

O.

Omne solum forti patria.
The brave make every clime their country.
c.   Motto of Lord Balfour.

Omnia bona bonis.
All things are good to the good.
d.   Motto of the Irish Viscount Wenman.

Opera illius mea sunt.
His works are mine.
e.   Motto of Lord Brownlow.

Ora et labora.
Pray and labor.
f.   Motto of the Scotch Earl Dalhousie.

P.

Palmam qui meruit ferat.
Let him who has won it bear the palm.
g.   Motto of Lord Nelson.

Patria cara, carior libertas.
Country is dear, but liberty dearer.
h.   Motto of Earl Radnor.

Patriæ infelici fidelis.
Faithful to my unhappy country.
i.   Motto of the Irish Earl of Courtown.

Patriis virtutibus.
By ancestral virtues.
j.   Motto of the Irish Baron Leitrim.

Peraget angusta ad augusta.
Through difficulties to grandeur.
k.   Motto of the Irish Earl of Massareene.

Periculum fortitudine evasi.
Bravely avoid peril.
l.   Motto of Baron Hartland.

Periissem ni periissem.
I had perished unless I had perished.
m.   Motto of the Scotch Baron Newark.

Perseverando.
By perseverance.
n.   Motto of Lord Ducie and Viscount
Halifax.

Per vias rectas.
Through straight paths.
o.   Motto of Baron Dufferin.

Post nubila Phœbus.
After clouds, sunshine.
p.   Motto of the Irish Baron Shuldham.

Præsto et persto.
I perform and I persevere.
q.   Motto of the Scotch Earl of Haddington.

Probitas verus honor.
Probity is true honor.
r.   Motto of the Irish Viscount Chetwynd.

Probum non pœnitet.
The honest man does not repent.
s.   Motto of Lord Sandys.

Pro Christo et patriâ.
For Christ and my country.
t.   Motto of the Earl of Kerr.

Prodesse quam conspici.
To be rather than to seem.
u.   Motto of Lord Somers.

Pro libertate patriæ.
For my country's liberty.
v.   Motto of the Irish Baron Massey.

Pro magnâ chartâ.
For the great charter.
w.   Motto of Lord Le Despencer.

Pro rege et patriâ.
For my king and country.
x.   Motto of the Second Earl of Leven.

Pro rege, lege, et grege.
For the king, the law, and the people.
y.   Motto of Lord Brougham.

Q.

Quæ amissa, salva.
What has been lost is safe.
z.   Motto of the Scotch Lord of Kintore.

Qualis ab incepto.
The same from the beginning.
aa.   Motto of the Irish Lord Clanbrassil.

Quem te deus esse jussit.
What God commanded you to be.
bb.   Motto of the Irish Baron Sheffield.

Quid verum atque decens.
What is just and honorable.
cc.   Motto of the Irish Viscount Dungannon.

Qui invidet minor est.
He who envies, admits his inferiority.
dd.   Motto of Lord Cadogan.

Quæ sursum volo videre.
I desire to see those things which are above.
ee.   Motto of Lord Dunraven.

Qui uti scit, ei bona.
That man should be possessed of wealth,
who knows its proper use.
ff.   Motto of Lord Berwick.

R.

Recte et suaviter.
  Justly and mildly.
  a.   Motto of Lord Scarsdale.

Regnant populi.
  The people rule.
  b.   Motto of Arkansas.

Renovato nomine.
  By a revived name.
  c.   Motto of the Irish Baron Westcote.

S.

Salus per Christum Redemptorem.
  Salvation through Christ the Redeemer.
  d.   Motto of the Scotch Earl of Moray.

Salus populi suprema est lex.
  The welfare of the people is the highest law.
  e.   Motto of Missouri.

Semper fidelis.
  Always faithful.
  f.   Motto of Lord Onslow.

Semper paratus.
  Always ready.
  g.   Motto of Lord Clifford.

Sero sed serio.
  Late, but seriously.
  *h.   Motto of the Scotch Marquis of Lothian,
            and of the Marquis of Salisbury.*

Servabo fidem.
  I will keep faith.
  i.   Motto of Lord Sherborne.

Servata fides cineri.
  Faithful to the memory of my ancestors.
  j.   Motto of Lord Harrowby.

Sic semper tyrannis.
  So be it always to tyrants.
  k.   Motto of Virginia.

Si Deus nobiscum, quis contra nos?
  If God be with us, who shall be against us?
  l.   Motto of the Irish Viscount Mountmorris.

Si quæris peninsulam amœnam, circumspice.
  If thou seekest a beautiful peninsula, behold it here.
  m.   Motto of Michigan.

Si sit prudentia.
  If there be prudence.
  n.   Motto of Lord Auckland.

Sola juvat virtus.
  Virtue alone assists me.
  o.   Motto of the Scotch Baron Blantyre.

Sola nobilitas virtus.
  Virtue alone is true nobility.
  p.   Motto of the Marquis of Abercorn.

Sola salus servire Deo.
  Our only safety is in serving God.
  q.   Motto of the Irish Earl of Ross.

Sola virtus invicta.
  Virtue alone is invincible.
  r.   Motto of the Duke of Norfolk.

Spectemur agendo.
  Let us be seen by our deeds.
  *s.   Motto of Earl Beaulieu, and of the Irish
                        Viscount Cliefden.*

Spero meliora.
  I hope for better things.
  *t.   Motto of Scotch Viscount Stormont, and
              the Scotch Baron Torphichen.*

Spes durat avorum.
  The hope of my ancestors endures.
  u.   Motto of Earl Rochford.

Spes mea Christus.
  Christ is my hope.
  v.   Motto of the Irish Baron Lucan.

Spes mea in Deo.
  My hope is in God.
  w.   Motto of Teynham.

Spes tutissima cœlis.
  The safest hope is in Heaven.
  x.   Motto of the Irish Earl of Kingston.

Stant cetera tigno.
  The rest stand on a beam.
  y.   Motto of Earl Aboyne.

Stat promissa fides.
  The promised faith remains.
  z.   Motto of the Scotch Baron Lindores.

Studiis et rebus honestis.
  By honest pursuits and studies.
  aa.   Motto of Lord Ashburton.

Sub cruce candidâ.
  Under the fair cross.
  bb.   Motto of Lord Lovell.

Sub hoc signo vinces.
  Under this sign thou shalt conquer.
  cc.   Motto of the Irish Viscount De Vesci.

T.

Tandem fit surculus arbor.
  The shoot at length becomes a tree.
  dd.   Motto of the Marquis of Waterford.

Templa quam dilecta!
  Temples how beloved!
  ee.   Motto of the Marquis of Buckingham.

Timet pudorem.
He fears shame.
a.   Motto of the Irish Viscount Downe.

Triumpho morte tam vitâ.
I triumph in death, as in life.
b.   Motto of the Irish Viscount Allen.

Tuebor.
I will defend.
c.   The Motto of Viscount Torrington.

Tu ne cede malis.
Yield not to misfortunes.
d.   Motto of the Irish Baron Milton.

Tuum est?
Is it yours?
e.   Motto of Earl Cowper.

U.

Ubi lapsus?—Quid feci?
Where am I fallen?—What have I done?
f.   Motto of Viscount Courtenay.

Ubique patriam reminisci.
Everywhere to remember our country.
g.   Motto of Earl Malmesbury.

Uni æquus virtuti.
Friendly to virtue alone.
h.   Motto of the Earl of Mansfield.

Unica virtus necessaria.
Virtue is the only thing necessary.
i.   Motto of the Irish Earl Mornington.

Ut apes geometriam.
As bees (practise) geometry.
j.   Motto of the Marquis of Lansdown.

Utcumque placuerit Deo.
As it shall please God.
k.   Motto of Earl Howe.

Ut prosim.
That I may do good.
l.   Motto of Lord Foley.

Ut quocunque paratus.
Prepared on every side.
m.   Motto of the Irish Earl of Cavan.

V.

Ventis secundis.
With prosperous winds.
n.   Motto of Lord Hood.

Veritas vincit.
Truth conquers.
o.   Motto of the Scotch Earl Marishall.

Ver non semper viret.
It is not always spring.
p.   Motto of Lord Vernon.

Victoria concordia crescit.
Victory grows out of concord.
q.   Motto of Lord Amherst.

Vigilantibus.
To the watchful.
r.   Motto of the Irish Viscount Gosford.

Vincit amor patriæ.
The love of my country conquers.
*s.   Motto of the Irish Viscount Molesworth
                    and Lord Muncaster.*

Vincit qui se vincit.
He conquers who conquers himself.
t.   Motto of Lord Howard of Walden.

Vincit veritas.
Truth conquers.
*u.   Motto of the Irish Earls of Ballamont
                    and Montrath.*

Virescit vulnere virtus.
Virtue flourishes from a wound.
v.   Motto of the Scotch Earl of Galloway.

Virtus ariete fortior.
Virtue is stronger than a battering ram.
w.   Motto of the Earl of Abingdon.

Virtus in actione consistit.
Virtue consists in action.
x.   Motto of Lord Craven.

Virtus in arduis.
Virtue in difficulties.
y.   Motto of the Irish Viscount Cullen.

Virtus incendit vires.
Virtue kindles strength.
z.   Motto of the Irish Viscount Strangford.

Virtus mille scuta.
Virtue is a thousand shields.
aa.   Motto of the Earl of Effingham.

Virtus probata florebit.
Virtue when encouraged will flourish.
bb.   Motto of the Earl of Brandon.

Virtus requiei nescia sordidæ.
Valor which knows not mean repose.
cc.   Motto of the Irish Viscount Desart.

Virtus semper viridis.
Virtue is always flourishing.
dd.   Motto of the Irish Viscount Belmore.

Virtus sola nobilitat.
Virtue alone can ennoble.
ee.   Motto of Baron Wallscourt.

Virtus vincit invidiam.
Virtue conquers envy.
ff.   Motto of the Marquis of Cornwallis.

Virtute ac fide.
　By virtue and faith.
　　a.　Motto of the Earl of Oxford, and the Irish
　　　　　　　　　　　　　　Viscount Melbourne.

Virtute ac labore.
　By virtue and toil.
　　b.　Motto of the Scotch Earl Dundonald.

Virtute et operâ.
　By virtue and industry.
　　c.　Motto of the Irish Earl of Fife.

Virtute fideque.
　By virtue and faith.
　　d.　Motto of the Scotch Baron Ellbank.

Virtute non astutia.
　By virtue, not by craft.
　　e.　Motto of the Irish Viscount Perry.

Virtute non viris.
　By virtue, not by men.
　　f.　Motto of the Irish Earl of Kerry.

Virtute quies.
　Content in virtue.
　　g.　Motto of Baron Mulgrave.

Virtuti nihil obstat et armis.
　Nothing can resist valor and arms.
　　h.　Motto of the Earl of Aldborough.

Virtuti non armis fido.
　I trust to virtue and not to arms.
　　i.　Motto of Lord Gray de Wilton.

Virtutis amor.
　The love of virtue.
　　j.　Motto of the Irish Earl Annesley.

Virtutis avorum præmium.
　The reward of the virtue of my ancestors.
　　k.　Motto of the Irish Baron Templetown.

Virtutis fortuna comes.
　Fortune is the comrade of virtue.
　　l.　Motto of the Duke of Wellington and of
　　　　　　the Irish Barons Newhaven and
　　　　　　　　　　　　　　　　　Haberton.

Vis unita fortior.
　In union there is strength.
　　m.　Motto of the Irish Earl Mount Cashel.

Vitæ via virtus.
　Virtue is the way of life.
　　n.　Motto of the Irish Earl of Portarlington.

Vivere sat vincere.
　To conquer is to live enough.
　　o.　Motto of the Irish Earl of Sefton.

Vive ut vivas.
　Live so that you may live.
　　p.　Motto of Baron Abercromby.

Vivit post funera virtus.
　Virtue survives the grave.
　　q.　Motto of the Irish Earl of Shannon.

Vix ea nostra voco.
　I can scarcely call these things our own.
　　r.　Motto of the Duke of Argyll and the Earl
　　　　　　　　　　　　　　　of Warwick.

Volens et potens.
　Willing and able.
　　s.　Motto of Nevada.

Volo non valeo.
　I am willing but unable.
　　t.　Motto of the Earl of Carlisle.

Vota vita mea.
　My life is devoted.
　　u.　Motto of the Irish Earl of Meath.

FRENCH.

A.

Au bon droit.
　To the just right.
　　v.　Motto of the Earl of Egremont.

Avise la fin.
　Consider the end.
　　w.　Motto of the Second Earl of Cassilis.

Aymez loyauté.
　Love loyalty.
　　x.　Motto of the Duke of Bolton.

B.

Bonne et belle assez.
　Good and handsome enough.
　　y.　Motto of the Earl of Fauconberg.

Boutez en avant.
　Push forward.
　　z.　Motto of the Irish Earl of Barrymore.

C.

Courage sans peur.
　Courage without fear.
　　aa.　Motto of Viscount Gage.

Craignez honte.
　Fear shame.
　　bb.　Motto of the Duke of Portland.

Crains Dieu tant que tu viveras.
　Fear God as long as you live.
　　cc.　Motto of Lord Athlumney.

D.

De bon vouloir servir le roy.
  To serve the king with good will.
  a.   *Motto of the Earl of Tankerville.*

Droit et avant.
  Right and forward.
  b.   *Motto of Viscount Sydney.*

E.

En Dieu est ma fiance.
  In God is my trust.
  c.   *Motto of the Irish Earl of Carhampton.*

En Dieu est tout.
  In God is everything.
  d.   *Motto of the Earl of Strafford.*

En la rose je fleuris.
  I flourish in the rose.
  e.   *Motto of the Duke of Richmond.*

En parole je vis.
  I live in the word.
  f.   *Motto of Lord Stowell.*

En suivant la vérité.
  In following truth.
  g.   *Motto of the Earl of Portsmouth.*

Espérance en Dieu.
  Hope in God.
  h.   *Motto of the Duke of Northumberland.*

Espérance et Dieu.
  Hope and God.
  i.   *Motto of Lord Lovaine.*

F.

Fidélité est de Dieu.
  Fidelity is of God.
  j.   *Motto of the Irish Viscount Powerscourt.*

Foy en tout.
  Faith is everything.
  k.   *Motto of the Earl of Sussex.*

Foy pour devoir.
  Faith for duty.
  l.   *Motto of the Duke of Somerset.*

G.

Gardez bien.
  Take care.
  m.   *Motto of the Scotch Earl of Eglinton.*

Gardez la foi.
  Guard the faith.
  n.   *Motto of the Irish Baron Kensington.*

H.

Haut et bon.
  Great and good.
  o.   *Motto of the Irish Viscount Doneraile.*

Honi soit qui mal y pense.
  Evil to him who evil thinks.
  p.   *Motto of the Order of the Garter and of
                    Great Britain.*

J.

Jamais arrière.
  Never behind.
  q.   *Motto of the Scotch Earl of Selkirk.*

J'ay bonne cause.
  I have good reason.
  r.   *Motto of the Marquess of Bath.*

Je n'oublierai jamais.
  I shall never forget.
  s.   *Motto of the Earl of Bristol.*

Je suis prêt.
  I am ready.
  t.   *Motto of the Irish Earl of Farnham.*

L.

Le bon temps viendra.
  The good time will come.
  u.   *Motto of Earl Harcourt.*

Le roi et l'état.
  The king and the State.
  v.   *Motto of the Earl Ashburnham.*

Le roi le veut.
  The king wills it.
  w.   *Motto of Lord Clifford.*

Liberté toute entière.
  Liberty complete.
  x.   *Motto of the Irish Earl of Lanesborough.*

Loyal je serai durant ma vie.
  I shall be loyal during my life.
  y.   *Motto of Lord Stourton and Lord
                    Mowbray.*

Loyauté m'oblige.
  Loyalty binds me.
  z.   *Motto of the Duke of Ancaster.*

Loyauté n'a honte.
  Loyalty has no shame.
  aa.   *Motto of the Duke of Newcastle.*

M.

Maintien le droit.
  Maintain the right.
  bb.   *Motto of Lord Chandos.*

N.

N'oubliez.
 Do not forget.
 a.   Motto of the Duke of Montrose.

Nous maintiendrons.
 We will maintain.
 b.   Motto of the Earl of Suffolk.

O.

Oublier je ne puis.
 I cannot forget.
 c.   Motto of Lord Colville.

P.

Patience passe science.
 Patience surpasses knowledge.
 d.   Motto of Viscount Falmouth.

Pensez à bien.
 Think for the best.
 *e.   Motto of the Earl of Lovelace and Lord
                                    Wentworth.*

Pour bien désirer.
 To desire good.
 f.   Motto of Lord Dacre.

Pour y parvenir.
 To attain the object.
 g.   Motto of the Duke of Rutland.

Prend moi tel que je suis.
 Take me just as I am.
 h.   Motto of the Irish Viscount Loftus.

Prêt d'accomplir.
 Ready to perform.
 i.   Motto of the Earl of Shrewsbury.

Prêt pour mon pays.
 Ready for my country.
 j.   Motto of Lord Monson.

Q.

Qui pense?
 Who thinks?
 k.   Motto of the Irish Earl of Howth.

S.

Sans changer.
 Without changing.
 *l.   Motto of the Earl of Derby, the Viscount
            Eversley, and Lord Stanley of Alderey.*

Sans Dieu rien.
 Without God, nothing.
 m.   Motto of Lord Petre.

Si je puis.
 If I can.
 n.   Motto of the Earl of Newburgh.

Soyez ferme.
 Be firm.
 o.   Motto of the Irish Earl of Carrick.

Suivez raison.
 Follow reason.
 *p.   Motto of the Marquess of Sligo and
                                    Lord Kilmaine.*

Sur espérance.
 In hope.
 q.   Motto of Lord Moncrieff.

T.

Tâche sans tache.
 A work without a stain.
 r.   Motto of the Scotch Earl of Northesk.

Tiens à la vérité.
 Stick to the truth.
 s.   Motto of Lord de Blaquiere.

Tiens à ta foy.
 Keep thy faith.
 t.   Motto of Earl Bathurst.

Toujours en vedette.
 Always on guard.
 u.   Motto of Frederick the Great.

Toujours prêt.
 Always ready.
 *v.   Motto of the Irish Marquis of Antrim
                        and Earl Clanwilliam.*

Toujours propice.
 Always propitious.
 w.   Motto of the Irish Viscount Cremorne.

Tout bien ou rien.
 All good or none.
 x.   Motto of the Earl of Gainsborough.

Tout d'en haut.
 All from above.
 y.   Motto of Lord Bellew.

Tout vient de Dieu.
 All things come from God.
 z.   Motto of Lord Clinton and Lord Leigh.

U.

Un je servirai.
 One I will serve.
 *aa.   Motto of the Earls of Carnavon,
                            Pembroke, and Powis.*

Un Roy, une foy, une loy.
 One King, one faith, one law.
 *bb.   Motto of the Irish Marquis of
                                    Clanricarde.*

V.

Verité sans peur.
 Truth without fear.
 cc.   Motto of Lord Middleton.

QUOTED AUTHORS.

Nativity, Dates of Birth and Death, and Further Characterization.

NOTE.—The first line of figures gives year of birth, the second death. The letter L signifies living. The figures underneath the name refer to pages upon which the author is quoted.

A.

ABD-EL-KADER, Arab chief..ALGERIA, 1807–1883
131
ADAM OF COBSHAM.
432
ADAMS, JOHN, statesman, 2nd Pres. U. S.
    UNITED STATES, 1735–1826
281 302
ADAMS, JOHN QUINCY, 6th Pres. U. S.,
    UNITED STATES, 1767–1848
86 131 470 484 652
ADAMS, SAMUEL, patriot and orator,
    UNITED STATES, 1722–1803
91 529
ADAMS, MRS SARAH FLOWER, poet,
    ENGLAND, 1805–1848
487
ADDISON, JOSEPH, writer..ENGLAND, 1672–1719
24   26   33   54   63   77   86   88
105 107 109 113 118 124 149 150
163 169 180 185 186 200 205 259
263 277 287 295 296 305 315 330
332 336 343 354 355 368 382 383
388 397 404 409 420 426 435 446
452 468 487 509 512 515 523 526
535 551 553 556 560 570 572 575
581 607 629 631 635 654 667 671
673
ADY, THOMAS, writer on witchcraft,
    ENGLAND, 1656(61)–
38
ÆSCHYLUS, tragic poet....GREECE, B.C. 525–456
46 143 205 413 459 490
AGESILAUS, "The Great," king of
    Sparta.............GREECE, B.C. 445–361
253
AIKEN, JOHN, miscellaneous writer,
    ENGLAND, 1747–1822
48
AKENSIDE, MARK, poet...ENGLAND, 1721–1770
312 341 369 530 549 619
ALCÆUS, lyric poet,
    GREECE, flourished about B.C. 600
281
ALCOTT, AMOS BRONSON, teacher and
    philosopher...UNITED STATES, 1799–1888
63 271 344 587 606 621 631 654
ALDRICH, JAMES, poet and journalist,
    UNITED STATES, 1810–1856
131 463
ALDRICH, THOMAS BAILEY, poet and
    prose writer.....UNITED STATES, 1836–L.
114 130 159 166 171 191 233 392
394 396 415 464 483 514 545 560
585
ALDRIDGE, IRA, negro tragedian,
    UNITED STATES, 1810–1867
205

ALEXANDER, WM., Earl of Stirling,
    poet, statesman, and courtier,
    SCOTLAND, about 1567–1640
338 555 670
ALFIERI, VITTORIO, poet and drama-
    tist..................ITALY, 1749–1803
553 757 760 763 775 777 778 779
786 789 791
ALGER, WM. R., minister and writer,
    UNITED STATES, 1823–1905
62 109 154 161 191 378 397 463
466 498 526 533 592
ALI BEN ABU TALEB, see TALEB.
ALISON, RICHARD, writer....16th or 17th Cent.
194 432
ALLEN, ELIZABETH AKERS, "Florence
    Percy," poet.....UNITED STATES, 1832–L.
8 189 333 599
ALLEN, WILLIAM, lawyer and politi-
    cian..........UNITED STATES, 1806–1879
525
ALLINGHAM, WILLIAM, poet,
    IRELAND, about 1828–1889
196 239 543
ALLOT, ROBERT, compiler of England's
    Parnassus. ENGLAND, 15th and 16th Cent.
648
ALPHONSO X., "The Wise," king of
    Castile.................SPAIN, 1226–1284
122
AMBROSE, ST., Latin father and writer,
    GAUL, 340–397
481
AMES, FISHER, orator and statesman,
    UNITED STATES, 1758–1808
482
AMMIANUS MARCELLINUS, Roman his-
    torian..........ANTIOCH, died about 395
687 694 697 701 744 747
ANCHÈRES, DANIEL, poet....FRANCE, 1586–
785
ANDERSEN, HANS CHRISTIAN, author,
    DENMARK, 1805–1875
345
ANGELO BUONAROTTI, MICHAEL, paint-
    er, sculptor, and architect,
    ITALY, 1474–1563
297 325 452
ANTISTHENES, cynic and philosopher,
    GREECE, flourished about B.C. 400 or 375
324
ANTONINUS, MARCUS AURELIUS, emperor
    and philosopher.........ITALY, 121–180
154 188 279 326 513
APPLETON, THOMAS GOLD, wit, essay-
    ist, and poet..UNITED STATES, 1812–1884
98

BARNFIELD, RICHARD, poet,
ENGLAND, about 1574-1605
50 392
BARON, MARIE LE.
59
BARR, MARY A., writer...SCOTLAND, 1852-
238
BARRETT, EATON S., satirist.IRELAND, 1785-1820
654
BARRINGTON, GEORGE, transported
convict who wrote on Australian
topics...............ENGLAND, 1755-1835
468
BARRY, MICHAEL J..........About 1815-
132
BARTAS, GUILLAUME DE SALLUSTE DU,
poet and diplomat....FRANCE, 1544-1590
74 88 112 127 156 191 205 281
324 369 410 415 439 501 507 509
599 626 667
BARTOL, CYRUS AUGUSTUS, clergyman
and writer..............U. S., 1813-1900
270 431
BARTON, BERNARD, poet...ENGLAND, 1784-1849
226
BASTARD, THOS., epigrammatist,
ENGLAND, 1598-1618
494
BATES, LEWIS J., poet...............1832-
267 329 330 368
BAXTER, RICHARD, theologian,
ENGLAND, 1615-1691
149 449
BAYARD, PIERRE DU TERRAIL, "Chevalier sans peur et sans reproche,"
national hero...FRANCE, about 1475-1524
757 759
BAYLE, PIERRE, philosopher and
critic................FRANCE, 1647-1706
513
BAYLY, THOMAS HAYNES, poet,
ENGLAND, 1797-1839
2 32 94 127 240 322 374 378
379 404 408 444 509 661
BEATTIE, JAMES, poet.....SCOTLAND, 1735-1803
8 47 48 77 91 109 161 199
200 205 210 284 313 315 374 410
487 515 538 539 621 673
BEAUMARCHAIS, dramatist and writer,
FRANCE, 1732-1799
789 790 793 795
BEAUMONT, FRANCIS, dramatic poet,
ENGLAND, 1585-1615
154
BEAUMONT AND FLETCHER. See BEAU-
MONT, FRANCIS; AND FLETCHER, .
JOHN.
3 22 33 38 64 88 104 114
132 146 155 161 187 200 205 256
259 284 286 290 292 311 333 343
344 345 370 387 410 454 461 465
473 485 495 496 498 499 500 501
502 504 505 506 508 509 526 557
570 582 588 593 606 630 635 644
654 664
BEAUVAIS, JEAN B. C. M. de, Bishop of
Senez................FRANCE, 1731-1790
788
BECCARIA, CASARE DI BONESANA, Philosophical and political writer
ITALY, 1738-1793
292
BEDDOES, THOMAS LOVELL, poet,
ENGLAND, 1803-1849
355

BEDE, "The Venerable," monk and
ecclesiastical writer,
ENGLAND, about 673-735
502
BEE, BERNARD E., general...U. S., 1845-1861
77
BEECHER, CATHERINE E., author,
UNITED STATES, 1800-1878
231
BEECHER, HENRY WARD, clergyman
and writer.....UNITED STATES, 1813-1887
77 163 216 228 344 345 426 492
BEERS, ETHEL LYNN, poet,
UNITED STATES, 1827-1879
442 471 495
BELLAMY, G. W.,
648
BELLINGHAUSEN, VON MÜNCH, See
MÜNCH-BELLINGHAUSEN.
BENJAMIN, PARK, poet and journalist,
UNITED STATES, 1809-1864.
216 458
BENNETT, HENRY,
95
BENNETT, WM. C., poet,
ENGLAND, about 1820-189t
30
BENSERADE, ISAAC DE, poet, FRANCE, 1612-1691
38
BENTHAM, JEREMY, jurist and philos-
opher...............ENGLAND, 1748-1832
292
BENTLEY, RICHARD, critic and classical
scholar.............ENGLAND, 1662-1742
96 281 524
BENTZEL-STERNAU, C. E., statesman
and writer.........GERMANY, 1767-1850
71
BEQUET, ETIENNE, journalist and critic,
FRANCE, about 1800-1838
787
BÉRANGER, PIERRE JEAN DE, poet,
FRANCE, 1780-1857
8 33 110 635
BERKELEY, BISHOP GEORGE, metaphysician and writer...ENGLAND, 1684-1753
492 593 671
BERNARD OF CLAIRVAUX (ST.), ecclesi-
astic.................FRANCE, 1091-1153
92
BERRY, DOROTHY
471
BERTIN, MADEMOISELLE, milliner to
Marie Antoinette.
FRANCE. Latter part of 18th Cent.
254 414
BETTS, CRAVEN L., poet and translator, -L.
8 33 635.
BEVIS OF HAMPTOUN, SIR, a hero of
medieval romance.
425
BIAS OF PRIENE, one of the seven sages,
GREECE, about B.C. 566
172 276 509 644
BICKERSTAFF, ISAAC, dramatist,
IRELAND, about 1735-after 1787
110 307 318 490 671
BIRD, ROBERT MONTGOMERY, author,
UNITED STATES, 1805-1854.
159
BISMARCK VON SCHONHAUSEN, KARL
OTTO, statesman.......GERM.. 1813-1898
767
BLACKBURN, THOMAS,
164
BLACKER, COLONEL, British officer, 1780-1826
511

BLACKIE, JOHN STUART, classical scholar and writer......SCOTLAND, 1809–1895
566

BLACKLOCK, THOS., poet and divine,
161 SCOTLAND, 1721–1791

BLACKSTONE, SIR WILLIAM, jurist,
444 ENGLAND, 1723–1780

BLAIR, ROBERT, poet and clergyman,
SCOTLAND, 1699–1746
16 24 118 132 200 225 263 279
284 396 415 458 582 618 625

BLAKE, WILLIAM, artist and poet,
ENGLAND, 1757–1828
17 22 30 170 245 284 355 369
541 543 545 642

BLAMIRE, SUSANNA, poet..ENGLAND, 1747–1794
70

BLANCHARD, LAMAN, journalist and
littérateur,.........ENGLAND, 1803–1845
101 257 475

BLANCHET, PIERRE, dramatic poet,
FRANCE, about 1459–1519
790

BLEECKER, ANNE E., poet,
UNITED STATES, 1752–1783
216 225

BLOOMFIELD, ROBERT, poet,
ENGLAND,1766–1823
284 320 333 355 539 542 545 578
579

BOBART, JACOB, botanist, GERMANY, –1719
3

BODENSTEDT, FRIEDRICH M. VON,
writer, journalist, and translator,
GERMANY, 1819–1892
135 240 258 270 449 600 605

BOHN, HENRY G., publisher,
ENGLAND, 1796–1884
628

BOILEAU–DESPREAUX, NICHOLAS, poet
and satirist.........FRANCE, 1636–1711
475 754 756 757 759 764 765 768
772 782 784 790 791 792 793 794
797

BOISTE, PIERRE CLAUDE VICTOIRE, lexicographer,...........FRANCE, 1765–1824
104.

BOKER, GEORGE H., poet,
UNITED STATES, 1823–1890
330 355

BOLINGBROKE (Viscount), HENRY ST.
JOHN, Author......ENGLAND, 1678–1751
301

BONAR, HORATIUS, D.D., clergyman,
poet, and writer.....SCOTLAND, 1808–1890
164

BONNARD, BERNARD DE, poet,
FRANCE, 1744–1784.
789

BONSTETTEN, CHARLES VICTOR DE, philosopher and writer,
9 SWITZERLAND, 1745–1832

BOOTH, BARTON, actor,....ENGLAND, 1681–1733
212

BORBONIUS, MATTHIAS.
507

BOSQUET, PIERRE, general and marshal.................FRANCE, 1810–1861
635

BOSWELL, JAMES, lawyer and biographer (see pages where Samuel
Johnson is quoted)..SCOTLAND, 1740–1795

BOTTA, ANNE C. LYNCH, poet,
321 UNITED STATES, about 1820–1891

BOURNE, VINCENT, scholar and
writer.............ENGLAND, 1698–1747
667

BOVEE, CHRISTIAN NESTELL, author
and editor.....UNITED STATES, 1820–1904
157 187 427 556

BOWLES, REV. WM. LISLE, poet,
ENGLAND, 1762–1850
39 45 55 225 239 646

BOWRING, EDGAR ALFRED, writer and
translator..........ENGLAND, 1826–
40 52 337 362 420 602 651

BOWRING, LL.D., SIR JOHN, statesman and linguist...ENGLAND, 1792–1872
243

BOYESEN, HJALMAR HJORTH, novelist,
NORWAY, 1848–1895
153 333 355

BOYLE, ROBERT, chemist and philosopher................IRELAND, 1626–1691
374

BRADLEY, MARY E., writer,
UNITED STATES, 1835–
236

BRADSTREET, ANNE, poet..ENGLAND, 1613–1672
613

BRADY, NICHOLAS, author and divine,
(See TATE AND BRADY),
IRELAND, 1659–1726

BRAINARD, JOHN G. C., poet,
UNITED STATES, 1796–1828
99 404

BRAMSTON, REV. JAMES, satirical poet,
ENGLAND, –1744
432

BRANTÔME, PIERRE DE BOURDEILLES,
historian.............FRANCE, 1540–1614
796

BRERETON, JANE, poet.....ENGLAND, 1685–1740
251

BRETON, NICHOLAS, poet..ENGLAND, 1555–1624
38 355 507

BRIDGES, ROBERT S., author and poet,
ENGLAND, 1844–
238 532

BRIGHT, JOHN, statesman..ENGLAND, 1811–1889
281 370 587

BRILLAT–SAVARIN, AUTHELME, littérateur.................FRANCE, 1755–1826
764

BRISSOT DE WARVILLE, JEAN PIERRE,
Girondist leader and political
writer...........FRANCE, 1754–1793
785

BROMLEY, ISAAC H., editor....U. S., 1833–1898
482

BRONTÉ, CHARLOTTE, "Currer Bell,"
novelist.............ENGLAND, 1816–1855
345

BROOKE, HENRY, political and miscellaneous writer.......IRELAND, 1706–1783
625

BROOKE, LORD (SIR FULKE GREVILLE),
poet and writer.....ENGLAND, 1554–1628
503

BROOKS, MARIA, poet.UNITED STATES, 1795–1845
216 233 240 531 532 615

BROOKS, PHILLIPS, D.D., bishop,
scholar, and pulpit orator,
UNITED STATES, 1835–1893
164 273

(BROUGHAM, LORD) HENRY, orator,
statesman, and author,
SCOTLAND, 1779–1868
154 170 336

GARRISON, WILLIAM LLOYD, editor and
philanthropist. UNITED STATES, 1805–1879
468 525 559

GARTH, SIR SAMUEL, physician and
poet...........ENGLAND, 1670–1718 (19)
133 155 157 319 411 533 540

GASCOIGNE, GEORGE, poet..ENGLAND, 1535–1577
170 501

GATAKER, THOMAS, divine and critic,
526 ENGLAND, 1574–1654

GAUTIER, THÉOPHILE, littérateur and
critic..........FRANCE, about 1811–1872
57 192

GAY, JOHN, poet.........ENGLAND, 1688–1732
9 27 34 42 44 53 54 62
69 87 94 110 113 114 121 133
134 144 170 173 182 185 201 204
206 213 217 232 235 251 254 260
264 269 295 306 307 312 321 322
323 330 331 341 347 353 358 368
375 411 428 432 437 440 442 445
453 458 464 470 486 507 513 524
527 538 549 558 580 586 589 622
629 632 642 649 656 666 672

GEORGE, HENRY, political economist,
UNITED STATES, 1839–1897
184 332 338 492 559 565 642

GESSNER or GESNER, SALOMON, poet and
artist...........SWITZERLAND, 1730–1787
796

GIBBON, EDWARD, historian,
ENGLAND, 1737–1794
79 256 283 358 437 445 516 528
565 566 587 641

GIBBONS, THOMAS, clergyman and
author.............ENGLAND, 1720–1785
79 319

GIBSON, WM. HAMILTON, artist and
author.......UNITED STATES, 1850–1896
99 392 647

GIFFORD, WILLIAM, critic and author,
ENGLAND, 1756–1826
105 418 476 629

GIL VICENTE, See VICENTE.

GILBERT, NICHOLAS JOSEPH L., satirical
poet ....FRANCE, 1751–1780
787

GILDER, RICHARD WATSON, poet, journalist and writer.UNITED STATES, 1844–L.
79 94 134 197 241 309 352 358
409 476 479 511 542 550 564 600
617 656

GILLERT, C. F.
165

GILMAN, CAROLINE, author,
244 246 UNITED STATES, 1794–1888

GIUSTI, GIUSEPPE, satiric poet..ITALY, 1809–1850
453

GLADSTONE, RT. HON.WILLIAM EWART,
statesman, orator, and author,
79 251 ENGLAND, 1809–1898

GLAZIER, WILLIAM BELCHER, poet,
624 UNITED STATES, 1827–

GLEIM, JOHANN W. L., poet,
782 GERMANY, 1719–1803

GOETHE, JOHANN WOLFGANG VON, poet,
GERMANY, 1749–1832
4 9 150 192 206 238 248 258
291 293 314 318 342 369 370 428
459 499 502 508 526 534 569 624
641 754 755 756 758 759 760 762
763 765 766 767 768 769 770 771
772 773 774 775 776 777 778 779
780 781 782 783 784 785 786 787
788 789 790 791 792 793 794 795
796 797

GOLDONI, comic author......ITALY, 1707–1793
756 761 762 781 784 790 792 797

GOLDSMITH, OLIVER, poet and prose
writer...............IRELAND, 1728–1774
2 3 6 7 9 13 14 19
20 23 27 28 38 41 42 48
61 65 66 79 88 89 96 102
105 109 110 111 113 115 118 121
124 126 128 143 156 172 188 190
194 208 211 212 215 229 239 260
264 266 267 270 280 282 287 289
293 297 300 303 307 312 313 314
329 337 338 340 342 347 358 368
369 371 375 379 387 389 392 402
411 415 422 428 437 443 446 450
455 468 472 473 479 481 482 484
486 488 490 498 500 503 506 510
516 523 525 531 532 551 555 567
573 587 589 596 614 619 632 636
641 649 650 653 656 668

GOOD, JOHN MASON, physician and
author..............ENGLAND, 1764–1827
28 293

GOODALE, DORA READ, poet,
UNITED STATES, 1866–L.
222 224 225 228 230 235 245 247
248

GOODALE, ELAINE, poet,
UNITED STATES, 1863–L.
221 222 223 225 229 231 235 236
250

GOOGE, BARNABY, poet and translator,
ENGLAND, about 1538–1594
503 553

GORDON, THOS., writer and translator,
SCOTLAND, 1685–1750
439

GOSSON, STEPHEN, divine and dramatist.................ENGLAND, 1554–1623
514

GOULD, HANNAH FLAGG, poet,
UNITED STATES, 1789–1865
459

GOWER, JOHN, "The Moral Gower,"
poet..........ENGLAND, about 1325–1408
666

GRAFTON, RICHARD, printer and historian.....ENGLAND, died about 1572
390

GRAHAME, JAMES, poet and divine,
SCOTLAND, 1765–1811
536

GRAHAME, JAMES, See MONTROSE, MAR-
QUIS OF.

GRAINGER, JAMES, poet and physician,
SCOTLAND, about 1723–1767
266 295

GRANT, MRS. ANNE, author,
SCOTLAND, 1755–1838
144

GRANT, ULYSSES S., general and 18th
Pres. U. S.....UNITED STATES, 1822–1885
163 437 470 636

GRANVILLE, GEORGE (Lord Lands-
downe), statesman and poet,
ENGLAND, 1667–1735
34 111 135 173 188 206 334 378
632 656

GRAVES, RICHARD, divine and writer,
ENGLAND, 1715–1804
206

GRAY, DAVID, poet,.......SCOTLAND, 1838–1861
99 394

Home, John, dramatist...Scotland, 1724–1808
104 409 507 662

Homer, poet,
Smyrna or Chios (Scio), about b.c. 1000
2 10 15 16 25 28 29 34
41 60 61 69 70 74 80 89
97 113 117 119 122 130 135 144
146 150 155 160 162 188 197 199
201 206 211 234 251 256 260 264
271 272 274 276 277 286 287 289
295 297 300 301 302 303 309 313
314 316 317 318 320 333 339 340
347 353 354 359 371 373 375 385
387 388 400 402 403 415 420 443
470 472 477 486 493 504 508 511
519 525 526 527 528 534 535 551
553 554 558 559 561 569 571 574
577 578 579 582 588 589 590 606
613 620 627 637 641 642 649 650
656 664 666 670 672 674

Hood, Edwin Paxton, clergyman and
author,.............England, 1820–1885
192

Hood, Thomas, author and humorist,
England, 1798–1845
4 10 23 38 39 48 52 62
70 86 87 89 126 135 160 166
187 199 218 225 227 232 233 238
241 244 247 248 278 293 303 304
314 339 342 380 383 388 395 397
400 422 430 432 443 446 456 459
473 484 521 536 543 544 554 558
583 590 609 613 628 629 643 656
674

Hood, Thomas, Jr., writer,
England, 1835–1874
323

Hooker, Richard, divine and author,
England, 1553–1600
387 502 511

Hoole, John, dramatist and translator..................England, 1727–1803
108 523 608

Hooper, Ellen Sturgis
163

Hooper, Lucy, poet, United States, 1816–1841
231

Hopkinson, Joseph, jurist and author,
301 United States, 1770–1842

Horace, Quintus Horatius Flaccus,
poet.....................Italy, b.c. 65–8
10 12 162 167 206 260 278 396
422 428 431 479 632 649 675 676
677 678 679 680 682 683 684 685
686 687 688 689 690 692 693 694
695 696 697 698 700 701 702 704
705 706 707 708 709 710 711 713
714 715 716 717 719 720 721 722
724 725 726 727 728 729 730 731
732 733 734 735 736 737 738 739
740 741 742 743 744 745 to 753

Horne, Richard Hengist, poet and
dramatist...........England, 1807–1884
102 287 322 424 600 614

Horne, Thomas Hartwell, bishop
and author........England, 1780–1862
500

Hoskyns, Abrahall, writer.......pres. cent.
55

How, William Walsham, English
clergyman and writer.........1823–1897
644

Howarth, Ellen C., ("Clementine")
poet, United States,.........1827–1899
7 8 380

Howe, Julia Ward, poet,
United States, 1819–L.
258 527

Howells, William Dean, author,
United States, 1837–L.
43 291 394

Howitt, Mary, author and moralist.
England, about 1804–1888
111 196 237 246 324 468 545 577

Howitt, William, author.
England, 1795–1879
230

Hoyt, J. K., journalist and writer,
compiler of "The Cyclopedia of
Practical Quotations,"
United States, 1820–1895
396 585 616

Hoyt, Ralph, clergyman and poet,
United States, 1810–1878
400 545

Hudson, ballad writer and singer,
England, first part of 19th cent.
495

Hugo, Victor Marie, lyric poet and
novelist. ....France, 1802–1885
34 42 46 91 99 160 185 267
270 280 334 359 397 535 553 571
575 624 626 637 647 656

Hume, Alexander, poet and minister,
Scotland, about 1560–1609
624 670

Hunt, Helen, see Jackson, Helen
Hunt

Hunt, James Henry Leigh, poet and
littérateur..........England, 1784–1859
80 160 213 233 238 241 244 248
323 359 409 448 452 470 485 531
634 668

Hunter, John,
80

Hurd, Richard, D.D., writer and
critic..............England, 1720–1808
528

Hurdis, Rev. James, poet,
England, 1763–1801
48 503

Hutcheson, Francis, metaphysician,
Ireland, 1694–1747
4 498 529

Hutchinson, Ellen M., (Mrs. Cortis-
soz), author and journalist,
237 United States, pres. cent.

I.

Ingelow, Jean, poet......England, 1830–1897
39 60 89 157 186 195 201 218
223 224 225 226 228 229 230 233
234 236 241 245 317 348 359 371
386 394 397 402 459 488 561 600
612 614 617 618 657 672

Ingemann, Bernhard S., poet and
novelist...........Denmark, 1789–1862
612

Ingram, John K., author, Ireland. 1823–
468

Insulus, Alanus de, author,
England, 12th cent.
495

Iphicrates, see Hippocrates,

Iriarte, or Yriarte, Tomas de, writer
and translator,
Teneriffe, about 1750–1790
763 765

Irving, Washington. author and
humorist......United States. 1783–1859
59 143 301 371 389 511

MORE, SIR THOMAS, wit, philosopher,
and statesman......ENGLAND, 1480–1535
517
MORELL, THOMAS, D.D., scholar and
critic,..............ENGLAND, 1703–1784
301
MORRIS, GEORGE P., lyric poet and
journalist......UNITED STATES, 1802–1864
214 609 618 627
MORRIS, LEWIS, British poet..WALES, 1835–L.
164
MORRIS, WILLIAM, poet....ENGLAND, 1834–1896
59 100 391 563
MORSE, JAMES HERBERT, author,
UNITED STATES, 1841–
515
MORTON, THOMAS, dramatist,
ENGLAND, 1764–1838
5 50 461 503 508
MOSCHUS, pastoral poet,
GREECE, lived about 200 B.C.
235
MOSS, THOMAS, clergyman and poet,
ENGLAND, 1740–1808
473 549
MOTHERWELL, WILLIAM, poet,
SCOTLAND, 1798–1835
58 380 411 591
MOTTE, ANTOINE HOUDART DE LA, critic
and dramatist........FRANCE, 1672–1731
764
MUHLENBERG, WILLIAM AUGUSTUS,
clergyman and poet,
UNITED STATES, 1796–1877
349
MÜLLER, NICLAS, printer and poet,
GERMANY, 1809–1875
228
MULOCK, DINAH MARIA, See MRS.
CRAIK.
MUNBY, ARTHUR JAMES, poet,
ENGLAND, 1829–
663
MÜNCH-BELLINGHAUSEN, E. F. J.,
"Friedrich Halm," poet and
dramatist..........GERMANY, 1806–1871
627 778
MURPHY, ARTHUR, dramatic and mis-
cellaneous writer,
IRELAND, about 1727–1805
445 571 653

N.

NADAUD, GUSTAVE, French writer,
musician, and singer.........1820–1893
97
NAIRNE, LADY CAROLINE OLIPHANT,
poet...............SCOTLAND, 1766–1845
204 268 562 657
NAPIER, SIR W. F. P., general and
historian...........IRELAND, 1785–1860
354
NAPOLEON BONAPARTE (I.), Emperor
of France........CORSICA, 1769(8)–1821
38 71 144 315 374 436 506 582
638 783 787 788 792
NAPOLEON III., CHARLES LOUIS, Emperor of France......FRANCE, 1808–1873
470 783
NEAL, ALICE BRADLEY, See HAVEN,
ALICE.
NEALE, JOHN MASON, hymnologist
and ecclesiastical historian,
165   ENGLAND, 1818–1866
NEAVES, CHARLES LORD, author,
371   ENGLAND, 1800–1876

NECKER, MADAME SUSANNE CURCHOD,
leader in literary circles,
SWITZERLAND, 1739–1794
157 533
NEIDHART VON NEUENTHAL, "Nithen"
or "Nithart," minnesinger and
lyric poet.......GERMANY, 13th Century
540
NELSON, HORATIO, naval hero and
admiral............ENGLAND, 1758–1805
164
NEWELL, ROBERT H., "Orpheus C.
Kerr," author and editor,
UNITED STATES, 1836–1901
249 255
NEWMAN, JOHN HENRY, Roman Cath-
olic prelate and writer,
ENGLAND, 1801–1890
298
NICOLL, ROBERT, poet.....SCOTLAND, 1814–1837
35 285
NILES, NATHANIEL, divine, inventor,
and author....UNITED STATES, 1741–1828
469
"NITHART," See NEIDHART VON NEUEN-
THAL
NOEL, THOMAS, poet...ENGLAND, 19th Century
63 484
NORRIS, JOHN,
329
"NORTH, CHRISTOPHER" See WILSON,
JOHN.
NORTON, CAROLINE E. S., writer,
ENGLAND, 1808–1877
67 261 475 549 567 625
NORTON, DELLE W., poet,   1840–
55

O.

O'HARA, KANE, dramatist..IRELAND, 1722–1782
490
O'HARA, THEODORE, poet,
UNITED STATES, 1820–1867
272
O'KEEFE, JOHN, dramatist..IRELAND, 1747–1833
167 280 618
OLDMIXON, JOHN, historical and political writer........ENGLAND, 1673–1742
657
OLDYS, WILLIAM, biographer and bib-
liographer....ENGLAND, about 1690–1791
323
OMAR KHAYYAM "The Tentmaker,"
author and mathematician,
PERSIA, 1025–1123
135 258 270 297 348 352 449 600
605
O'MEARA, BARRY EDWARD, Napoleon's
physician at St. Helena,
IRELAND, 1780–1836
637
OPIE, MRS. AMELIA, author,
261   ENGLAND, 1769–1853
O'REILLY, JOHN BOYLE, LL.D., poet
and journalist......IRELAND, 1844–1890
108 158 172 190 272 306 470 554
"O'REILLY, MILES," See CHARLES G.
HALPINE.
ORLEANS, CHARLES D', See CHARLES
ORRERY, ROGER BOYLE, EARL OF,
statesman, soldier, and dramatist................IRELAND, 1621–1679
480
OSGOOD, FRANCES S., poet,
UNITED STATES, 1811–1850
210 249 339 406 613

PROPERTIUS, Roman elegiac poet,
UMBRIA, about B.C. 50
680 684 686 690 696 697 700 705
706 707 708 715 723 728 732 743

"PROUT, FATHER," See MAHONY, FRANCIS
PRUD'HOMME (SULLY), poet, FRANCE, 1839-L
771

PRUDHON, CHAS. F. J., comedian,
FRANCE, 1845-L
785

PSEUDO-SALLUST, name given to the
spurious Sallust.
256 497

PULTENEY, WILLIAM, statesman and
orator.............. ENGLAND, 1684-1764
331

PYCHOWSKA, L. D.
230

PYPER, MARY
183

PYTHAGORAS, philosopher and mathematician...... GREECE, about B.C. 582-500
91 489 494

Q.

QUARLES, FRANCIS, poet...ENGLAND, 1592-1644
13 61 131 137 143 209 234 235
297 369 382 383 440 496 500 501
505 571 601

QUESNEL, PASQUIER, Roman Catholic
theologian............FRANCE, 1634-1719
674

QUINAULT, PHILIPPE, dramatist,
FRANCE, 1635-1688
795

QUINCEY, THOMAS DE, author,
ENGLAND, 1785-1859
354

QUINCY, JOSIAH, lawyer and patriot,
UNITED STATES, 1744-1775
259

QUINTILIAN, MARCUS FABIUS, Roman
rhetorician and critic,
SPAIN, about A.D. 35-95
29 677 679 681 682 695 696 702
706 711 715 720 726 728 732 735
738 741 744 745 748 750 753

QUINTUS, CURTIUS RUFUS, Roman historian, supposed to have lived
after Augustan Age.
687 688 692 697 699 700 703 709
711 729 731 735 737 739 742 749

R.

RABELAIS, FRANÇOIS, humorist and
satirist........FRANCE, about 1495-1553
26 39 93 153 162 252 337 340
386 390 398 407 494 498 499 501
503 504 506 508 509 579 601 763
764 769 775 781 784

RABUTIN, See BUSSY-RABUTIN.

RACINE, JEAN BAPTISTE, tragic poet,
FRANCE, 1639-1699
757 760 771 772 773 775 780 788
791 796

RADCLIFFE, MRS. ANN WARD, novelist,
ENGLAND, 1764-1823
206 552 577

RALEIGH, SIR WALTER, officer, historian, poet, colonizer and
courtier............ENGLAND, 1552-1618
38 88 103 119 137 158 209 302
361 442 464 465 554 567 572 601

53

RAMSAY, ALLAN, poet.....SCOTLAND, 1685-1758
204

RANDOLPH, THOMAS, poet and dramatist..... ....ENGLAND, 1605-1634
595 649

RANSFORD, EDWIN, singer, song writer,
and composer of music,
475   ENGLAND,1805-1876

RAPIN, RENÉ SIEUR DE, Jesuit and
writer of prose and Latin
poetry...............FRANCE, 1621-1687
235

RAUPACH, ERNST B.S., dramatic poet,
SILESIA, 1784-1852
146

RAVENSCROFT, JOHN STARK, Bishop of
North Carolina.UNITED STATES, 1772-1830
195

RAY, WILLIAM, poet.UNITED STATES, 1771-1827
121

READ, THOMAS BUCHANAN, poet and
painter........UNITED STATES, 1822-1872
243 249 417 605

REGNARD, JEAN FRANÇOIS, writer of
comedy.............FRANCE, 1655-1709
760 786

REGNIER, MATHURIN, satiric poet,
775   FRANCE, 1573-1613

REYNOLDS, JOHN HAMILTON, poet,
ENGLAND, 1795-1852
193 602

RHODES, HUGH, author...ENGLAND, 16th Cent.
83

RHODES, WILLIAM B., dramatist and
translator.......Last half of 18th Cent.
130

RICH, RICHE, OR RYCHE, CAPTAIN
BARNABY, author and poet,
ENGLAND, 16th and 17th Cent.
663

RICHARD ROLLE DE HAMPOLE,
491

RICHELIEU, ARMAND JEAN DU PLESSIS,
DUC DE, cardinal and states-
man..................FRANCE, 1585-1642
762 763

RICHTER, JEAN PAUL FRIEDRICH, novelist and writer.....GERMANY, 1763-1825
17 173 209 252 521 576 625 658
754 755 758 761 763 764 767 769
771 775 776 777 778 780 786 788
789 790 794

RICORD, FREDERICK WM., American
poet, translator, and scholar,
WEST INDIES, 1819-1897
24 240 248 373 453 673

RILEY, HENRY THOMAS, translator
and scholar...................1819-1878
58 105 507 508

RILEY, JAMES WHITCOMB, poet and
dialect writer..UNITED STATES, 1852-L
47 266 304 322 576 578 584 647

RIVERS, ANTHONY WOODVILLE, EARL
OF, poet and translator,
503   ENGLAND, 1442-1483

ROBESPIERRE, MAXIMILIEN, chief of
the Jacobins.........FRANCE, 1758-1794
761

ROCHE, JAMES JEFFREY,poet.IRELAND, 1847-
164

ROCHEFOUCAULD, see LA ROCHEFOUCAULD.

ROCHESTER, JOHN WILMOT, EARL OF,
a profligate courtier, wit, writer
of songs, satires, etc.,
ENGLAND, 1647-1680
534 658 669

RODMAN, J. P.,
638

ROGERS, JOHN, clergyman and martyr,
ENGLAND, 1505–1555
374

ROGERS, SAMUEL, poet.....ENGLAND, 1763–1855
6   16   40   69   83   90   98   117
137 210 304 361 379 381 398 407
429 510 519 567 585 602 625 633

ROLAND, MADAME MANON JEANNE
PHILIPON DE LA PLATIÈRE, highly gifted woman, sympathizer
with the Republicans and Gi-
rondists.............FRANCE, 1754–1793
344

ROLLIN, CHARLES, historian.FRANCE, 1661–1741
609

ROSCOE, THOS., author and translator,
ENGLAND, 1790–1871
452

ROSCOE, WILLIAM, historian and poet,
ENGLAND, 1753–1831
67 398 400

ROSENBERG, CHARLES GEORGE,
275

ROSS, JOHN, Bishop of Exeter, writer,
ENGLAND,   –1792
101

ROSSETTI, CHRISTINA G., poet,
ENGLAND, 1830–1894
11   49   51   54   57   59   100 138
151 165 187 219 238 243 249 280
308 349 362 381 394 401 451 460
463 472 510 537 540 542 544 554
588 607 643

ROSSETTI, DANTE GABRIEL, painter
and poet...........ENGLAND, 1828–1882
144 231 298 398 544 635

ROUGEMONT, maker of *bons mots*, con-
temporary with Napoleon I.
638

ROUGET, CLAUDE JOSEPH ROUGET DE
LISLE, soldier and song writer,
FRANCE, 1760–1836
272 637

ROUSSEAU, JEAN JACQUES, philosopher
and writer......SWITZERLAND, 1712–1778
3 758 764 775 780 782 783 784
785 788 790 796 797

ROUX, LE, See LE ROUX DE LINCY.

ROWE, NICHOLAS, dramatist and poet,
ENGLAND, 1673–1718
36   62 138 305 312 318 362 382
388 491 576 586 594 630 638

ROY, JEAN BAPTISTE DE, landscape
and cattle painter...BELGIUM, 1759–1839
785

ROYDON, MATTHEW,
25   83

ROYER-COLLARD, PIERRE PAUL, philosopher and statesman,
781   FRANCE, 1763–1845

RÜCKERT, FRIEDRICH, poet, GERMANY,1788–1866
760

RUMBOLD, COL. RICHARD, Republican
implicated in Rye-House Plot,
510   ENGLAND, d. about 1685

RUSBY, HENRY H.,
225

RUSKIN, JOHN, writer and art critic,
ENGLAND, 1819–1900
1   20   29   36   98 103 118 129
164 173 187 395 403 425 426 447
452 471 491 522 532 549 558 586
667

RUSSELL, LORD JOHN, author, orator,
and statesman......ENGLAND, 1792–1878
3 83 493

RYSWICK or RYSWYK, JAN VAN, poet,
NETHERLANDS, 1811–
453

S.

SAADI or SADI, SHAIKH MUSLIH AL
DIN, poet...... .PERSIA, about 1190–1291
101

SAGE, LE, See LE SAGE.

ST. JOHN, HENRY, See BOLINGBROKE.

SAINTINE, JOSEPH XAVIER BONIFACE,
miscellaneous writer,
FRANCE, 1798–1865
73

SAINT-REAL, ABBÉ, historical writer,
FRANCE, 1639–1692
764

SALES, FRANCIS DE, bishop and writer,
FRANCE, 1567–1622
299

SALIS, J. G. VON,
308

SALLUST, CAIUS SALLUSTIUS CRISPUS,
Roman historian,
ITALY, B.C. 86–34
677 679 680 682 687 699 703 704
709 721 749 750 753

SALVANDY, NARCISSE ACHILLE, COMTE
DE, publicist, politician, and
historian............FRANCE, 1795–1856
129

"SAND, GEORGES," See MME. DUDE-
VANT,

SANDYS, GEORGE, poet,
ENGLAND, 1577–about 1644
451

SANGSTER, MARGARET E., author,
UNITED STATES, 1838–L.
95 222 609

SANNAZARO, JACOPO, poet.....ITALY, 1458–1530
765 780 796

SAPPHO, lyric poet.GREECE, lived about B.C. 600
51 280 558 568 597

SARGENT, EPES, journalist and writer,
UNITED STATES, 1812–1880
460 584

SAURIN, BERNARD JOSEPH, dramatist,
FRANCE, 1706–1781
775 792

SAVAGE, RICHARD, poet,
ENGLAND, about 1698–1743
320 409

SAWYER, MRS. CAROLINE M., author
and translator.UNITED STATES, 1812–1894
219

SAXE, J. G., humorous poet, journalist, and lecturer,
UNITED STATES, 1816–1887
11   36   69   72 103 169 291 311
335 345 349 422 434 448 562 597

SCARRON, PAUL, dramatist and bur-
lesque poet.........FRANCE, 1610–1660
184

SCHELLING, FRIEDRICH WILHELM JO-
SEPH VON, philosopher,
GERMANY, 1775–1854
426

SCHIDONI, BARTHOLOMEO, painter,
ITALY, 1560–1615
758

STAËL, MADAME DE STAËL-HOLSTEIN,
ANNE LOUISE GERMAINE NECKER
DE, writer...........FRANCE, 1766–1817
152 170 255 271 294 365 388 408
480 489 494 513 522 572 586 597
623 654 669
STANHOPE, GEORGE, pulpit orator and
translator..........ENGLAND, 1660–1728
370
STANIFORD,
3
STANISLAUS LESZCZYNSKI,
King of Poland, 1677–1766
159 501 522 538 654
STATIUS, PUBLIUS PAPINIUS, Roman
poet............ITALY, about 60–100
677 695 699 703 714 725
STEDMAN, EDMUND C., poet and critic,
UNITED STATES, 1833–L
37 43 44 56 84 185 207 223
230 335 377 395 640 643
STEELE, SIR RICHARD, essayist, dramatist, and politician,
84 185 472   IRELAND, 1672–1729
STEERS, FANNY,
259
STEPHENS, MRS. ANNA S., novelist,
UNITED STATES, 1813–1886
614
STERLING, JOHN, poet and writer,
ISLAND OF BUTE, 1806–1844
173 618
STERNE, LAURENCE, humorist and
novelist............IRELAND, 1713–1768
76 106 125 289 372 419 510 559
607 652 669
STEVENS, ABEL, clergyman, editor,
and historical writer,
UNITED STATES, about 1815–1897
103 155 271 603
STEVENS. GEORGE A., dramatist and
actor...............ENGLAND, 1720–1784
446
STEVENSON, ROBERT LOUIS, poet,
essayist, and novelist.
SCOTLAND, 1850–1895
90 262 408 541
STEWART, MRS. DUGALD..SCOTLAND, 1765–1838
381
STILL, JOHN, learned prelate and
writer............. ENGLAND, 1543–1607
162 163
STIRLING, EARL OF, See ALEXANDER, WM.
ST. JUST,
777
STODDARD, RICHARD HENRY, poet,
UNITED STATES, 1825–1903
17 37 90 91 131 147 148 155
287 395 412 460 480 544 555 592
650
STODDART, THOMAS TOD, author,
59   SCOTLAND, 1810–1880
STONE, DAVID M., editor,
UNITED STATES, 1817–1895
502
STORY, JOSEPH, jurist,
UNITED STATES, 1779–1845
436
STORY, WILLIAM WETMORE, lawyer,
sculptor, and author,
UNITED STATES, 1819–1895
249 480 555
STOWE, HARRIET ELIZABETH BEECHER,
novelist and writer,
UNITED STATES, 1812–1896
17 594 644

SUCKLING, SIR JOHN, poet,
ENGLAND, about 1608–1642
84 108 129 153 189 196 253 331
365 502 660
SUE, MARIE JOSEPH EUGENE, novelist,
FRANCE, 1804–1857
633
SUETONIUS, CAIUS TRANQUILLUS, Latin
historian............born about 70 A.D.
681 684 686 697 722
SUMNER, CHARLES, statesman,
UNITED STATES, 1811–1874
84 202 471 560 620
SWEDENBORG, EMANUEL, naturalist,
mathematician, scientist, and
theologian..........SWEDEN, 1688–1772
76 85 87 141 187 275 299 316
351 365 486 522 597 670
SWETCHINE, MADAME ANNE SOPHIE,
author...............RUSSIA, 1782–1857
673
SWIFT, JONATHAN, satirist and man of
letters......... ....IRELAND, 1667–1745
12 15 18 24 25 48 61 68
88 96 103 126 143 161 168 169
199 202 213 215 220 253 265 280
287 296 323 326 328 336 351 365
372 377 399 409 418 455 458 480
494 495 496 497 498 499 500 503
505 506 507 509 513 514 515 522
524 527 535 553 579 587 589 603
607 623 627 633 640 643 652 660
665 669 671
SWINBURNE, ALGERNON CHARLES, poet,
ENGLAND, 1837–L.
32 57 76 91 141 161 207 233
235 236 237 243 292 299 327 366
391 447 480 541 544 556 563 570
660
SYRUS, PUBLIUS, (*Publilius*), mimo-
grapher,....................SYRIA, B. C. 42
7 30 85 257 494 495 497 500
502 504 505 509 677 678 681 684
685 686 688 689 690 691 692 696
698 699 700 701 703 704 705 706
707 710 711 715 716 718 719 720
722 723 724 725 727 730 731 734
736 738 739 740 741 744 745 749
750 751 752

T.

TACITUS, CAIUS CORNELIUS, historian,
ITALY, about 54, died after 117
439 497 582 676 680 682 683 684
686 687 688 690 691 693 695 697
699 700 704 707 709 711 712 714
715 717 718 724 725 729 731 732
734 736 737 738 739 740 744 748
751
TAGGART, CYNTHIA, poet,
UNITED STATES, 1801–1849
238
TAIT, JOHN
530
TALEB, ALI BEN ABU, caliph,
ARABIA, about 602–661
262
TALFOURD, SIR THOMAS NOON, dramatist, poet, and jurist.ENGLAND, 1795–1854
87 351 641
TALLEY, SUSAN ARCHER, poet,
250   UNITED STATES, 19th Cent.
TALLEYRAND-PÉRIGORD, CHARLES
MAURICE DE, diplomatist, statesman, and wit........FRANCE, 1754–1838
574 756 760 775 781 789

VOLTAIRE, FRANÇOIS MARIE AROUET, historian, dramatist, critic, satirist, writer, and poet, FRANCE, 1694–1778
21   68   73   102   185   275   302   313
429   441   452   474   478   482   513   548
549   560   565   572   574   581   582   592
623   626   660   759   760   761   762   763
764   766   768   770   772   773   776   778
781   782   783   784   786   787   789   790
793   795   797

W.

WACE or EUSTACE, ROBERT, Anglo-Norman poet,
ISLE OF JERSEY, about 1124–1174
522

WALKER, K. K. C.,
506

WALKER, WILLIAM,
516

WALLACE, HORACE BINNEY, lawyer and writer....UNITED STATES, 1817–1852
484 532

WALLACE, JOHN AIKMAN,
490

WALLACE, WILLIAM ROSS, poet,
UNITED STATES, about 1819–1881
402 490

WALLER, EDMUND, poet...ENGLAND, 1605–1687
37   49   93   96   123   207   243   298
367   378   413   423   429   466   481   568
572   585   590   633   671

WALPOLE, HORACE, author,
ENGLAND, 1717–1797
70   268   302   447   568   669

WALPOLE, SIR ROBERT, statesman,
ENGLAND, 1676–1745
70   189   447   486

WALTON, IZAAK, author..ENGLAND, 1593–1683
18   19   141   168   184   295   354   442
478   498   504   633

WARBURTON, WILLIAM, prelate, theologian, and critic...ENGLAND, 1698–1779
173

WARD, ARTEMUS, See BROWNE, CHARLES FARRAR.

WARD, ELIZABETH STUART PHELPS, author........UNITED STATES, 1844–L.
557

WARD, MRS. HUMPHRY (Mary Augusta Arnold), English novelist,
TASMANIA, 1851–L.
190

WARD, NATHANIEL, preacher and author.......ENGLAND, about 1578–1652
454

WARD, THOMAS, poet......ENGLAND, 1652–1708
92

WARNER, ANNA B., "Amy Lothrop," poet.........UNITED STATES, pres. cent.
226

WARNER, CHARLES DUDLEY, author,
UNITED STATES, 1829–1900
424

WARNER, WILLIAM, poet,
ENGLAND, about 1558–1609
62 196

WARTON, THOMAS, poet and critic,
ENGLAND, 1728–1790
22 48 56 294 475

WASHINGTON, GEORGE, soldier, statesman, and 1st Pres. U. S.,
UNITED STATES, 1732–1799
85   106   263   265   269   402   560   633
640

WATSON, WILLIAM,
85 275 526

WATTS, ALARIC ALEXANDER, journalist and littérateur......ENGLAND, 1799–1864
292

WATTS, ISAAC, sacred poet, ENGLAND, 1674–1748
32   113   141   156   157   185   200   243
286   298   322   351   373   386   466   497
523   539   563   564   573   584   586   667

WAYLAND, FRANCIS, D.D., clergyman, educator, and author,
UNITED STATES, 1796–1865
29 481

WEBB, CHARLES HENRY, author,
UNITED STATES, 1834–1905
535

WEBSTER, DANIEL, statesman, orator, and lawyer....UNITED STATES, 1782–1852
12   93   97   115   116   123   214   283
318   319   325   333   338   339   344   424
439   469   508   530   539   583   623   627

WEBSTER, JOHN, dramatist,
ENGLAND, 17th Cent.
12   56   141   207   273   287   290   295
299   305   378   493   498   527   536   570
633

WEBSTER, NOAH, philologist and lexicographer.....UNITED STATES, 1758–1843
340

WEISSE, CHRISTIAN FELIX, miscellaneous writer........GERMANY, 1726–1804
784

WELBY, AMELIA B., poet,
UNITED STATES, 1821–1852
244 381 577 611 614

WELLINGTON, ARTHUR WELLESLEY, DUKE OF, statesman and general,
IRELAND, 1769–1852
97 146 319 433 640

WELLS, ANNA MARIA, poet,
UNITED STATES, 1797–
56

WESLEY, CHARLES, clergyman and hymn writer........ENGLAND, 1708–1788
166 522 572 661

WESLEY, JOHN, clergyman, founder of Methodism.......ENGLAND, 1703–1791
99 560

WEST, BENJAMIN, painter,
UNITED STATES, 1738–1820
336

WESTMACOTT, CHARLES M., author,
1788–1868
457

WHATELY, RICHARD, prelate and theologian..............ENGLAND, 1787–1863
16 305

WHITE, HENRY KIRKE, poet,
ENGLAND, 1785–1806
72 112 239 268 604

WHITEHEAD, PAUL, satiric poet,
ENGLAND, 1710–1774
47 114

WHITELOCKE, BULSTRODE, statesman,
ENGLAND, 1605–1676
68

WHITMAN, SARAH HELEN POWER, poet and critic, UNITED STATES, 1803–1878
220 222 223 229 237 249 545 618

WHITMAN, WALT. poet,
UNITED STATES, 1819–1892
85   115   159   287   323   430   431   439
452   472   513   640

MISCELLANEOUS AUTHORITIES CITED.

A HEALTH TO THE GENTLEMANLY PRO-
    FESSION OF SERVING-MEN........   1598
    494 507

AN OFFERING TO LANCASHIRE.
    102

A PROPER NEW BALLAD IN PRAISE OF
    MY LADY MARQUES.
    497

A VETERAN OF SMOKEDOM.
    456

CUPID'S WHIRLIGIG..................   1607
    655

GESTA ROMANORUM. A collection of one
    hundred and eighty-one stories,
    first printed about 1473. The
    first English version appeared
    in 1824, translated by the Rev.
    C. Swan (Bohn's Standard
    Library).
    44

HARLEIAN LIBRARY OR MISCELLANY
    A collection of rare pamphlets
    from the Library of Robert
    Harley, first Earl of Oxford,
    and now in the British Museum.
    120 211

JOHAN THE HUSBANDE, TYB HIS WYFE,
    AND SYR JHAN THE PRIEST.
    499

JOLLY ROBYN ROUGHHEAD (author
    unknown).
    107

KORAN (AL KORAN; ARABIC). The
    sacred book of the Mohamme-
    dans. It was composed chiefly,
    if not wholly, by Mohammed,
    though claimed by believers to
    have been revealed by the Angel
    Gabriel.
    80 275 294 649

LAW MAXIMS.
    675 676 679 682 687 688 692 694
    696 698 701 708 712 713 715 716
    717 720 728

MERIE TALES OF THE MADMEN OF
    GOTTAM.
    494

NEW ENGLAND PRIMER. The oldest
    known copy extant is 1737. The
    second impression was adver-
    tised in press by Benj. Harris, of
    Boston, as early as 1691.
    126 133 349 464 488 556 591

NOTES AND QUERIES.
    606 612

DICK TARLTON or TARLETON was the
    most popular comic actor and
    jester of his day, d. 1588.
    534

PIERS PLOUGHMAN. Allegorical and
    satirical poem by Wm. Lang-
    lan. It was begun in 1362.
    Printed first in 1550.
    499

POOR ROBIN'S ALMANAC. This first
    appeared in 1663. Discontinued
    in 1828.
    392

REGIMEN SANITATIS SALERNITANUM. Ed. 1607
    440

RETURN FROM PARNASSUS. Supposed
    by Sir John Hawkins to have
    been written by some of the
    wits and scholars of Cambridge.
    390 551

ROXBURGHE BALLADS. A collection of
    old English ballads commenced
    by Harley, Earl of Oxford, and
    augmented by West and Pearson
    and especially the Duke of Rox-
    burghe. It is now in the British
    Museum.
    138 262 349

SPECTATOR. English periodical printed
    daily from March 1st, 1711, to
    Dec. 6th, 1712. Addison and
    Steele were the principal con-
    tributors.
    22 499

STRATFORD JUBILEE, II. I..............   1779
    504

TATLER. English periodical founded
    by Steele in 1709. Discontinued
    in 1711.
    59 574

THE BRITISH PRINCES.
    24

THE COOKS AND CONFECTIONERS' DIC-
    TIONARY. London.............   1724
    431

THE SMOKER'S GUIDE.
    456

THE ROCK OF REGARD. J. P. Collier's
    Reprint........................   1576
    553 662

Concordance to Quotations.

INDEXES.

I certainly think that the best book in the world would owe the most to a good index, and the worst book, if it had but a single good thought in it, might be kept alive by it.

 a. HORACE BINNEY—*To S. Austin*

Allibone.

An index is a necessary implement. * * * Without this, a large author is but a labyrinth without a clue to direct the readers within.

 b. FULLER—*Worthies of England.*

How index-learning turns no student pale, Yet holds the eel of science by the tail.

 c. POPE—*The Dunciad.* Bk. I. L. 279.

Those authors, whose subjects require them to be voluminous, would do well, if they would be remembered as long as possible, not to omit a duty which authors, in general, but especially modern authors are too apt to neglect—that of appending to their works a good index.

 d. HENRY ROGERS—*The Vanity and*

Glory of Literature.

Concordance to Quotations.

NOTE.—In this concordance are included quotations from English authors and the English translations of quotations from foreign languages. The italic letter refers to the place on the page where the quotation may be found. The eight authors quoted most frequently are indicated in the concordance by signs: Shakespeare *; Milton **; Wordsworth ¶; Byron ‖; Tennyson †; Lowell ††; Pope ‡; Longfellow §.

since all a., so Heaven has.567 *d*
solitary, who is not alone..566 *x*
the fools are mad if left a.*659*m*
they are never a. that are..597 *t*
think it solitude to be alone.567 *t*
this is to be alone; this‖....566 *j*
thou art here alone,—alone.543 *q*
though not quite alone‖ ... 9 *d*
till supper-time alone*....565 *p*
to be left a. and face to§...527 *x*
top of green Selinis all a ...611 *k*
until I truly loved I was a..567 *i*
we enter the world alone..566 *y*
when we are least alone‖...566 *i*
world in which I moved a..150 *d*
Alonso–A. of Aragon was.... 10 *q*
Alonzo–A. the Brave was the.359 *s*
Alph–A.,the sacred river ran.530 *b*
Alps and A. on A. arise‡.....402 *u*
fading A.and archipelagoes585 *e*
frozen ridges of the Alps*.172 *q*
the eagle of the Alps...... 46 *d*
Alpine–A. peasants, two or...536 *i*
on the Alpine rose..........242 *l*
Altar–a. was one agate stone.278 *i*
before the same a.with me.158 *f*
bow before thine a., love...365 *l*
by his horns to the a.......278 *n*
her sweet altar fires........651 *v*
refreshed where one pure.545 *t*
upon the a. of her beauty*.663 *l*
upon thine a. pour incense.531 *f*
Altars–build me a. in their..674 *f*
flame that burns upon its a.201 *f*
let these a. wreathed with.595 *b*
lonely altars sprinkle... ..220 *h*
rear altars to freedom......258 *e*
strike for your a. and your.468 *p*
Altar-stairs–world's a.†.....268 *l*
Alter–a. decree established*.438 *q*
alter in my faith of him..620 *d*
circumstances alter cases... 96 *r*
Alteration–alters when it a*..317 *o*
time makes no alteration... 22 *g*
Altercation–excessive a.... 686 *c*
Altered–changes all, had a.‖..599 *n*
Altering–a. it for some new...474 *q*
Alternative–a. must women.. 92 *f*
Always–let those who a......361 *i*
Am–I am not what I am*.....556 *x*
I am not what I once was..682 *d*
I am the state.............770 *q*
speak of me as I am*.......332 *r*
Amaranth–immortal a.**....221 *j*
the amaranth bright........219 *l*
Amaranthine–a. flower on...632 *g*
pluck the a. flower¶.......198 *u*
Amaranths–a. such as.......221 *k*
breaking a, he looks........221 *h*
Amaranthus–a. all his**.....221 *i*
Amaryllis–milky-bell'd a.†...221 *l*
A-maying-met her once a**.. 29*m*
Amaze–a. the welkin with*..639 *a*
a. the learn'd, and make‡..581 *j*
Amazed–a. and curious......383*m*
a. the gazing rustics rang'd.342 *c*
Amazement–exclamation of.460 *b*
Ambassador–a. is an honest*.305 *p*
an ambassador of love*... 365 *f*
as God's ambassador, the..450 *b*
footman with an a..........435 *e*
Ambassadors–a. are the eye.770 *s*
Amber–a. enveloped the tiny.176 *s*
a. sweet of love is turn'd...327 *q*
a. sweets the smothered....479 *j*
a. the musk and civet......205 *b*
bedropped with amber.... 59 *q*
In amber lies........ ..... 557 *x*
in a. to observe the forms‡.661*m*
liquid a. drop from‡........242 *u*
of amber cleanly buried....661 *k*
preserved forever in a......324 *g*
sepulchre in amber........323 *c*
the amber flits a little......557 *x*
through the amber shown..661 *l*
when tipp'd with a.mellow‖.456 *f*
Ambition–a. and revenge**.. 13 *j*

a. has but one reward for·· 14 *i*
ambition has no rest....... 13 *g*
ambition is no cure........ 13 *t*
a. is our idol on whose..... 14 *f*
ambition of a private man.486 *g*
a.'s aims are crossed‡...... 13 *o*
ambition's debt is paid*.... 13 *v*
a. to commend my deeds**.146 *q*
a. to fill up my heart‖......356 *q*
and ambition of man......137 *u*
bids a. rise to nobler ......367 *d*
built with divine ambition.417 *v*
by low ambition and the... 12 *t*
capable of this ambition*..461 *q*
choked with foul ambition*.633 *r*
fling away ambition* ....14 *a*
high ambition, lowly laid.. 13 *u*
ill-weaved a., how much*.. 13 *x*
in false ambition's hand.... 14 *j*
in heaven ambition cannot.365 *n*
instruments of ambition...435 *e*
mad ambition trumpeteth.. 14 *g*
make ambition virtue*.....204 *t*
my soul's ambition........276 *g*
pours fierce ambition in a‡. 13 *r*
reach of wild ambition's....633*w*
reign is worth a. though**.. 13 *k*
rules the unreined ambition 14 *h*
soldier without a. is to..... 12 *o*
such joy ambition finds..** 13*m*
though ambition in itself...677 *f*
vaulting ambition, which*. 13*w*
was utterly without a...... 1 *a*
who, like a., lures men.....445 *t*
wild ambition loves to slide 13 *a*
young ambition's ladder*.. 14 *d*
your heart's supreme a....629 *k*
Ambitions–with great a.§... 13 *f*
Ambitious–born without a.. 12 *p*
Cæsar was ambitious*..... 14 *b*
substance of the a. is*..... 14 *c*
with a. feet secure.§. ....672 *q*
Ambles–your wit a. well; it*.654 *c*
Ambrosia–A. for Apicius....166 *n*
Ambrosial–blooming a.**....609 *j*
than the sweet a. hive......652 *e*
Amen–"a."stuck in my*.....489 *f*
let me say 'a.' betimes*....153 *l*
Amend–a. our will, and not.646*m*
Amended–done cannot be*...152 *j*
Amends–husband that will‡..311 *r*
long lying make himself a.‖621 *j*
sin that a. is but patched*..633 *t*
America–A. half brother of..115 *a*
America has furnished to...115 *h*
America is to have no......281 *j*
America lie folded already.370 *y*
A. shall hold her place.....188*m*
history of America........302 *n*
young man there is A......115 *c*
American–A.institutions had.115 *h*
goes to an American play..115 *q*
if I were an A., as I am....469 *i*
I also am an American.....469 *s*
I was born an American...469 *p*
looks at an A. picture......115 *q*
pass to the A. strand ......521 *b*
reads an American book...115 *g*
Virginian but an American.468 *q*
what I call the A. idea......282 *s*
Americans–A. to market....560 *x*
good A. when they die go.. 98 *g*
Amethyst–purple-streaming.558 *g*
streaks and shafts of a.....584 *r*
Amethystine–with an a. light.545 *j*
Amiable–amiable weakness..641 *p*
a. weakness of human.....641 *q*
Amiss–if I have done amiss..523 *f*
Amity–a. is ty'd with band..263 *u*
a. that wisdom knits not*..265 *k*
two commands, hold a.**..282 *y*
Among–a. them, but not of‖..596 *a*
Amorous–As a. of their*.....552 *b*
from a. causes springs‡....527 *x*
still amorous and fond......389 *k*
twined amorous round the.530 *e*
Amour–enforce a desperate..485*m*

Amphitryon–the genuine a...764 *d*
the true amphitryon is the.506 *n*
Amuck–to run a. and tilt‡....537 ,
Amuse–little more than to a..115 *c*
sent to a. not to enslave.... 14 *q*
Amusement–a. of the........ 87 *n*
mercy to the next a........ 15 *d*
next a. mortgages........ 15 *d*
Amusements–friend to public 14 *u*
in our a. a certain limit....732 *a*
Amusers–recreators and a... 66*m*
Anacreon's–A. morals are a‖..478 *l*
Analytic–skilled in analytic..124 *e*
Anarch–thy hand, great A.‡.. 77 *d*
Anarchist–maxim of the A...281 *g*
Anarchy and digest of a.....529 *c*
eternal anarchy amidst**... 77 *c*
Anatomical–a. construction‖.166 *i*
Anatomies–as so many a.....156 *f*
Anatomist–work for the a....452 *q*
Ancestor–I am my own a..... 15 *l*
Ancestors–backward to their. 15 *f*
but his illustrious a. is like. 15*m*
chaos ancestors of nature** 416 *k*
down from many a.*....... 88 *f*
glorious ancestors enlarge. 16 *c*
glory of ancestors sheds ...677 *j*
has no need of ancestors...787 *i*
hope of my a. endures......804 *u*
our ancestors are very good 15 *o*
our rural a., with little‡ ..424 *f*
the virtue of my ancestors.806 *k*
wild trick of his a.*........608*w*
wisdom of our ancestors...650 *f*
Ancestral–ancestral voices...493 *c*
Ancestry–birth and ancestry 677 *i*
records of our ancestry....709 *b*
Anchor–see the dolphin's a...430 *e*
the anchor is hidden§.......210 *r*
Anchorage–soul to its a...... 89 *n*
Anchored–a. to the bottom*..250 *j*
Noah, when he a. safe on...648 *j*
Anchorite–a. who didst.......669 *n*
saint-ship of an anchorite‖..303 *a*
tempt the dying a. to eat..168 *t*
Anchors–bark with two a ...500*ff*
Ancient–a. of days august‖... 97*m*
as ancient as the world.....565 *u*
his a., trusty, drouthy.....100 *o*
in ancient times all things..511*m*
O a. house! alas, how......693 *c*
reverence what is ancient..127 *g*
slavery is also as a. as war.560 *d*
spokes as ye a. of ye parish.493 *r*
they that marry a. people..375 *i*
we extol ancient things......676 *l*
Ancients–a. dreaded death...134 *l*
Anderson–John A. my jo.....466 *q*
Andes–under the A. to the...649 *e*
Andie–new Joshua in A......537 *a*
Andrew–how A.slyly sent....478 *j*
Anemone–A. in snowy hood..217 *g*
O white anemone..........221 *i*
Anemones–a. and seas......221 *p*
brink the anemones.......221 *q*
circles of anemones.......221*m*
Anerly–happy Mary Anerly..663 *b*
Angel–action how like an a.*372 *u*
a guardian a. o'er his life... 16 *u*
a ministering angel thou...658 *r*
an angel shook his wings... 16 *i*
an a. stood and met my††..634 *h*
an angel who had been o'er.531 *e*
a. answered, nay sad soul ..144*m*
a. appear to each lover ....658 *c*
a. comfortings can hear....268 *p*
a. for the woman in a kiss..334*m*
angel hands to valor.......214 *e*
a. of light! who from the...584 *c*
a. on the outward side*....312 *v*
a.'s visits short and bright.329 *t*
angel with a trumpet said§.126 *h*
a.,writing in a book of gold.634 *f*
as far as angel's ken**...... 16 *p*
clip an angel's wings.......515*m*
consideration like an a.*...107 *b*
custom, is angel yet*.......127 *o*

denouncing angel's pen....331 *f*
drew an angel down........ 16 *k*
dropped from an a.'s wing¶.471 *v*
e'en a.'s wings are fictions.. 16 *j*
glorious a., who was........591 *d*
God's angel cries, forbear..404 *d*
have mercy mighty angel..382 *g*
He asks no angel's wing‡...349 *p*
high speech which angel's..574 *s*
his motion like an a. sings*.576*w*
hold the fleet a. fast until he 16 *h*
in the angel's keeping......316 *d*
lark that singest like an a...159 *r*
like a. visits few and far... 16 *g*
man nor a. can discern**...312 *l*
more angel she, and you*..102 *e*
must be an angel..... .. 207 *x*
my angel,—his name ....258 *j*
my guardian angel gently..605 *f*
neither can angel or man... 86 *d*
painted angel could we see.351 *u*
passage of an angel's tear..590 *v*
pluckt from an a.'s wing...471 *o*
quill from an angel's wing.471 *q*
recording a. as he wrote it..419 *v*
sentinel a. sitting high in...382 *g*
she drew an angel down....318 *p*
she is an angel*. .... 36 *v*
singest like an angel.......159 *r*
soar of angel's wings......274 *t*
solemn a. of eternal peace..479 *i*
sweep of an angel's wings..165 *k*
talents a. bright if......... 14 *j*
the angel did with Jacob...141 *s*
the angel ended, and in**...635 *c*
the angel says : " write "§..479 *t*
the angel who bends over.. 80 *s*
though an a. should write..452 *a*
thou hovering angel**.....198 *a*
'tis a.'s musick ; therefore..536 *n*
virtue is an a., but she is...632 *t*
who wrote like an angel...182 *s*

Angelic–marked the mild a.‖..132*w*
   to the angelic symphony**.406 *v*
Angelical–notes a. to many**.637*w*
Angels–agree as a. do above. 367 *s*
   and angels entertained.... 413 *g*
   and flights of a. sing thee*.. 16 *v*
   angels, all pallid and wan..137 *j*
   a. are bright still though*.. 16*w*
   a. are painted fair, to look..657 *y*
   angels are praising the Son.165 *o*
   a. are whispering with thee 31*m*
   angels come and go, the.... 17 *b*
   angels could do no more.... 2 *k*
   angels draw near.......... 515 *l*
   angels fear to tread‡.......251 *z*
   a. gave me at once a kiss...564 *j*
   a. held their residence**....425 *r*
   a. in some brighter dreams.598 *d*
   a. laugh, too, at the good...340 *q*
   a. listen when she speaks...658 *q*
   angels must love Ann*.....203*w*
   angels of our hearth.......111 *o*
   angels of our Heaven.......111 *o*
   angels that side by side ... 67 *i*
   a. tremble while they gaze.415 *o*
   a. uncertain'd that repose.136 *g*
   are angels veiling clouds*..659 *c*
   as a. are, ripening through.517 *a*
   ascend like a. beautiful....378 *h*
   as make the angels weep*..491 *g*
   as the blessed angels turn..351 *t*
   bearest a.to us in the night.561 *k*
   benediction God's a. come.. 8 *l*
   be the speech of angels....404 *s*
   bloom where angels tread.230 *p*
   bright with beckoning a...473 *q*
   but sad as a. for the good.. 16 *f*
   by that sin fell the a. how* 14 *a*
   by the better angels of our.469 *a*
   caused the angels to fall... 86 *d*
   descending angels sung.... 94 *d*
   does well,acts nobly,angels. 97 *c*
   drag angels down........319 *h*
   forget-me-nots of the a.§...576 *b*
   glorious fault of angels‡.. 208 *e*

God's angels come to us††.. 16 *n*
holy angels guard thy bed.563 *s*
I have no angels left now... 17 *d*
I heard the angels call†.....391 *k*
immortal part with a. lives.572 *c*
language spoken by a§.....405*w*
like good a. to my end*.....489 *h*
like those of angels........279*m*
liveried angels lackey her** 87 *u*
lives as angels do...........207 *x*
men as angels without**...657 *s*
men would be a., a. would‡.. 13 *p*
ne'er like a. till our passion465 *l*
our acts our a. are, or good 4*m*
pourtraict of bright a. hew. 37 *i*
pure in thought as a. are...361 *u*
sad as a. for the good man's555 *s*
sceptred a. held their**....298 *g*
tears such as a. weep**....591 *a*
that the angels began.... 95 *j*
the a. with us unawares... 16 *o*
the shining angels climb... 94 *o*
they are angels of God in... 89 *q*
those of a. short and far... 16 *d*
to men and angels only....264 *u*
two angels guide the path..517 *a*
two a.issued where but one§135 *o*
will plead like angels*.....633 *l*
with angels shared by‖....357 *q*
women are angels, wooing*663 *r*
Anger–a. and jealousy can...327 *o*
   a. assists hands however...677 *p*
   anger belongs to beasts....731 *i*
   a. is like a full-hot horse*.. 17 *o*
   a. is momentary madness..677 *m*
   anger is one of the sinews.. 17 *l*
   a. is the desire of punishing.677 *l*
   a.seeks its prey—something 17 *k*
   anger's my meat; I sup*... 17 *p*
   anger storms at large...... 18 *d*
   anger, though concealed...677 *r*
   a. wishes that all mankind. 17*m*
   can heavenly minds such a.677 *u*
   choler, planteth anger*.... 17 *t*
   discord is a. more bitter....692 *u*
   fear not the a. of the wise‡.524 *v*
   like fragile ice a. passes....677 *q*
   modest a. of a satiric spirit.125 *c*
   never anger made good*... 17 *u*
   our anger to command....650 *p*
   pain to feel much anger... 17 *j*
   pale in her a. washes all*...156 *o*
   that carries a.as the flint*.. 18 *b*
   touch me with noble a.!*... 17 *v*
   what sudden a's. this,*..... 18 *a*
   wine and anger to reveal...741*m*
Angle–a brother of the angle. 18 *s*
   and with my a. upon them. 580 *v*
   give me my mine a., we'll*. 18 *i*
   his angle trembling in his‡. 18 *t*
Angler–an excellent a. and... 18 *n*
   if he be an honest angler... 19 *a*
   is born an angler.......... 18 *q*
   on the a's. trysting-tree.... 59 *d*
Anglers–good for any but a..168 *y*
Angling–angling deserves.... 19 *b*
   a. is somewhat like poetry. 18 *o*
   a. may be said to be so like. 18 *p*
   angling will prove to be.... 18 *r*
   be quiet and go a-angling.. 18*m*
   for a.-rod he took a sturdy. 18 *f*
   innocent recreation than.... 19 *g*
   say of a. as Dr. Boteler did 19 *g*
   the pleasant'st a. is‡to see*. 18 *j*
Angry–allays an angry mind. 33*m*
   angry but with thy tailor..454 *q*
   angry with my friend...... 17 *e*
   Heaven is not always a....512 *l*
   I was angry with my foe... 17 *e*
   make a lover angry........724 *a*
   such angry passions rise...466 *c*
   who's angry at a slander...558 *o*
Anguish–a. pierces to the....149 *c*
   drops of a. falling fast and§479 *v*
   ease the a. of a torturing*423 *h*
   he groans in anguish......592 *q*
   hopeless a. pour'd his groan 41 *q*

iron crown of a. crowned§..561 *p*
pain and a. wring the brow658 *r*
silent anguish is the more..788 *q*
will close the eye of a.*.....523 *x*
Animal–an a. without......495 *l*
   frame the little animal.... 53 *l*
   honest, guileless animal... 21 *o*
   man is a noble a., splendid.370 *b*
   this a. is very malicious....757 *k*
Animals–all a. that breathe§.452 *l*
   animals are such agreeable.260 *h*
   paragon of animals*.......372 *r*
   souls of animals infuse*...198 *i*
Animate–though not a........515 *k*
Animated–thou a.torrid zone.321 *p*
Animation–a. of the heart of.522 *a*
Animosities–excite great a...685 *r*
Ankle-deep–a. you stick in...539 *q*
Ankle–or ankle sprain.......453 *b*
Ankles-against her ankles....223 *p*
   ankles sunken in asphodel.222 *j*
Ann–be heaven A.hath a way*203*w*
Anna–here, thou, great A.!‡..589 *u*
   while A. reigns, and sets a..535 *o*
Annie–all sang "A. Laurie"..568 *a*
Annihilate-ye gods a.‡......293 *u*
Annihilates–mind a. and......643 *f*
Annihilating–a. all that's....597 *b*
   but by annihilating die**...316 *k*
Anniversaries–a. of the§..... 302 *g*
Announced–a. by all the......564*w*
Annoys–whose scent the fair.456 *g*
Anodynes–those little a......296 *s*
Another–a. and the same.... 188 *c*
   another yet the same‡......101*w*
   arms ye forge a. bears......152 *l*
   robes ye weave a. wears....152 *l*
   wealth ye find a. keeps......152 *l*
Answer–answer echoes‡.....169 *q*
   answer him, ye owls‡......557 *m*
   a. pealed from that high†...275 *u*
   a. such high things*.......467 *s*
   a. was a blameless life......538 *a*
   answer Who and What.....446 *p*
   answer with some rhyme...493 *r*
   answer would stop them*..326 *k*
   as well a. a man indeed*....558 *z*
   for I have found it answer‖.552 *l*
   hill to hill a. each other in† 95 *f*
   made answer to my word..588 *k*
   shortest answer is doing...506 *f*
   to answer wisely...........380 *p*
Answerable–a. to the people.283 *d*
Answered–every tear is a. by.391 *q*
   jealous souls will not be a.*328 *c*
   morrow came I a. still......605 *f*
Answering–of a. thy sweet... 52 *h*
Answers–a. life's great end...352 *c*
   a. till a husband cools‡.....658 *j*
   Echo answers "where"‖....149 *e*
   God a. sharp and sudden...487 *h*
   ne'er a.till a husband cools‡.645 *k*
Ant–reason of the ant........754 *d*
   set thee to school to an ant*.455 *p*
Ants–ants do not bend their..726 *j*
   ants never sleep...........321 *k*
   spiders,flies,or a.entombed.324 *g*
Antagonist–a. is our helper..300 *b*
   critic is not the antagonist.124 *r*
Antecedents–party whose a..482 *h*
Antedate–both a.our mission.240 *i*
Anthem–an anthem for the..187 *i*
   the pealing anthem swells..405 *k*
   thy plaintive anthem fades. 51 *f*
Anthems–and a. clear**......406 *g*
   back the sound of anthems.609 *c*
Anthropology–theology is a..791 *j*
Antic–old father a. the law*..438 *i*
   there the antic sits*........140 *s*
Anticipate–a. the relish of... 22 *d*
   eager to a. their grave‖.....552 *e*
Antidote–antidote should be.. 65 *r*
   my bane and antidote. ... 150 *i*
   sweet oblivious antidote*..441 *c*
   the antidote to fear........337 *e*
Antidotes–his a. are poison*..441*m*

unlike to A.'s closing days..542 a
well apparelled A. on the*..392 l
when A. winds grew soft...391 o
Apron-where is thy leather*..431 i
Apt-apt to blame the fates‖.. 6 o
Aquilegia-a. sprinkled on the 222 d
Arab-an Arab, by his earnest. 62 e
Arab with a stranger for a‖ 329 l
Jas in the Arab language...232 n
whether Arab in the desert.520 r
Arabia-A. breathes from‡....447 s
perfumes of A. will not*. 292 k
Arabie-of Arabie the blest**..447 f
Arabs-fold their tents like§..415 r
Araby-under A.'s soft sun .. 53 f
Arabesque-a. of vines§......617 l
Arabesques-quaint a. in....545 g
Aranjuez-lovely days in A...764 k
Arbiter-next him high a. **.. 73 o
Arbitrator—old common a.*.602 t
Arbor-as of an arbor took....614 k
Arbutus-a. in the wood .... 217 g
overflow of a. and laurel...611 b
perfect, sweet arbutus.....222 h
tender, sweet arbutus.....222 g
Arcadia-I, too, was born in A.758 e
Arcadian-ever trod the A ..531 b
Arcadians-A. skilled in song..728 n
Arcady-hopes to see fair A...356 d
lead Love in. To Arcady..356 d
Arch-a low, dim-lighted arch.226 p
an arch of azure. .... 98 e
arch of London bridge......267 n
beneath this starry arch...492 k
black arch the keystane....384 s
broken a. of London bridge. 95 f
limits the proud a. confine‡ 529 o
mild arch of promise......515 p
stars which night's blue a..590 n
the a. beneath them is not§.617 l
the blue a. will brighten...627 i
this gorgeous a. with golden 417 v
triumphal a. that fill'st the.515 j
under the sky's gray arch..391 l
world-built a. of heaven....583m
Arched-arched so high that*..535 d
Arches-columns..,pyramids143 l
with nodding a., broken‡... 98 n
Archangel-fell as the mighty.608 a
less than a. ruined**........153 d
Archangels-makes a. smile...604 f
summoning a.to proclaim**331 e
Archer-both the a. and the...312 g
Cupid archer of archers... 87 l
fiery archer making pain...277 n
insatiate a., could not one..142 l
mark the a. little meant ... 665 g
than a common archer..... 87 l
to that keen archer sorrow.570 k
Archers-a. ever have two... 87 l
draw, a., draw your arrows*639 a
Archipelagoes-fading Alps...585 e
Architect-and some the a.**.425 t
architect built his great§..425 n
a. of his own fortunes.....497 l
can be an architect........426 b
some the architect**........208 g
Architects-architects of fate§206 q
its merry a. so small had... 59m
Architectural-a. plan upon...303 h
Architecture-a. is frozen.....780 t
a. is the work of nations...425 t
value of a. depended.......425 v
Architrave-lay the a., and a.,.609 c
Arcs-earth the broken arcs..279 n
Arctic-flow into the arctic§... 10 j
Arcturi-arcturi of the earth..220 g
Are-a. what these twain were.141 h
everything but what they a.312 l
noble ones with what they..758 j
nor are, nor e'er will be.... 84 x
tell you what you are ....764 a
they were, they a., they yet 61 s
to be what we are...... 96 t
to see them as they are....607 c.
we are for onc†‡..........148 a
we know what we are, but*338 e

Argoan-A. ship's brave.......617 p
Argosy-from gilded argosy...224 k
heaps like a wrecked a...... 68 i
Argue-argue not against**...198 c
vanquished he could a. still. 27 f
Arguing-arguing with the††.. 27 j
be calm in a. for fierceness. 27 f
in a. too the parson owned.. 27 f
Argument-a knock-down a..494aa
for lack of argument*...... 27 q
found you an argument.... 27 h
hand with an argument.... 27 i
height of this great a.**....510 h
in a. similes are like songs.. 27 n
in a. with men a woman**.. 27 l
knock-down a. 'tis but a. .. 27 c
knowest thou what a.......318 s
meter-making argument...476 q
the only a. available with†† 27 j
prove by force of argument 26 t
the argument of tyrants....414 f
the staple of his argument*665 n
want of argument supplied 27 d
with his argument wrong.. 27 e
Argumentation-delight in.... 27 w
Arguments-a. and question*.606 h
ear-kissing arguments*. ... 27 r
say, fools for arguments.... 26 u
Arise-a. or be forever fallen** 5 f
Aristocracy-be an a.........283 f
Jews are among the a.......329 a
to him is aristocracy......321 o
Ark-and into Noah's Ark...389 t
lay their hand upon the a...490 l
mouldy rolls of Noah's Ark.118 c
straight out of the Ark.... 25 r
to the long-labouring ark. 45 k
Arm-arm! advance! hope of.635m
a. it in rags, a pigmy's*....556 o
a. should conquer twenty..133 j
a. thyself for the truth....622 p
but to thy arm alone*......510 t
have not I an arm as big*.. 70 j
my arm is sore; best*...... 15 b
O God, thy arm was here*..510 t
on her lover's a. she leant†.366 h
on its own right arm.......477 f
or a. th' obdured breast**..467 m
rear'd a. crested the world*.534 y
shaken by thy naval arm...327m
take his fortune by the a*..388m
the auld moon in hir arme..398 l
thus arm in arm with thee.778 b
widow sits upon mine arm..637 p
worst of rebels never arm..518 a
Armed-a. at all points to ...269 j
a. at point exactly*........495 r
a. in virtue's cause. ....537 n
a. prophets conquered....768 n
a. so strong in honesty*....305 l
a.to suffer with a quietness*467 r
he's armed without that's‡.106 d
soldier a. with resolution..662 k
soldiers armed in proof*.. .549 r
thrice is he arm'd that*....333 a
when doubly armed to bear.346 z
Armies-raises a. in a nation's‡390 b
summon a. from the earth.784 j
Armor-adamantine armor...622 r
a. all as strong our cause*..639m
a. is his honest thought....305 q
armor on armor shone.....636m
arms on a. clashing bray'd**637 t
no armour against fate.....141 b
to put his a. off and rest....142 a
Armourers-a. acc'mplishing*639 q
Arms-against a world in a... 81 q
all in arms all plumed*.... 46 p
a man at a. must now serve.470 w
and his fifty a. so strong...615 n
a. full strong and largely..616 h
a. nor the gown, priests‖..421 p
a. on armour clashing**....637 t
a. outstretched as he*......603 a
a., take your last embrace*139 f
a. ye forge,another bears..152 l
bare arms stretched in.....610 g

bones out of their arms....484 j
broken under arms........444 t
close in my a. thou art.....377 q
cross their a. and hang*... 62 w
dear creature in one's a.....778 g
desert in arms be crowned. 69 p
exercise and proof of arms* 73 k
faith; invincible in arms... 77 k
fit arms against a war‡....256 n
fold thine a., turn to thy†.526 s
for a. like yours were fitter.635 p
he laid down his arms......443 i
hug it in mine arms*.......139 s
hundred arms the cypress'258 o
in one another's arms**....300 t
lay down my arms, never..469 i
lotos spreads its a.‡.......615 f
love's arms were wreathed*366 n
made arms ridiculous**....579 l
mine arms about that body*363 p
muscles of his brawny a..§.430 h
my soul's in a., and eager..572 s
negotiation before arms...736 l
overpowered with arms.... 69 o
patient arms will fold......229m
perfect in the use of arms*.639m
Proteus to wreath your a.*. 56 b
resist valor and arms......806 h
since these a. of mine had*.574m
spreads its fragrant arms..244 r
strong than traitor's a.*....320 a
sweet faces, rounded arms*383 k
take arms against a*.......159 f
take thou thy a. and come.443 g
the arms are fair when the*639 r
the clatter of a. drowns....775 l
the din of arms, the yell....640 h
their clean arms bared‖....431 o
the nurse of arms..........115 n
the white arms‖...........211 b
to arms! to arms! ye brave.637 l
triumphed o'er our arms‡..631 f
virtue and not to arms.....806 i
white a. wreathed lightly..129 k
white arms that encircle.. 89 h
whose a. gave shelter to*...612 l
why do strong a. fatigue...181 o
with fire that he arms......700 f
with soft white arms......147 x
you close within my arms..644 x
yourself into my arms.....333 r
Army-a. and the navy had..581 x
a. of the world's desires*..104 w
a. is a school in which the..442 y
army's stir and wave......229 p
Austrian a.awfully arrayed442 t
church, army, physic, law.667 t
hum of either a. stilly*....639 c
I feel an army in my fist...784 i
like a golden-shielded army400 q
like an army defeated¶....391m
Arminian-and an A. clergy..521 q
Armistice-a short a. with‖..621 j
Arno-to A.'s myrtle border..530 c
Arnold-worthless A. bears...608 b
Aromatic-in aromatic pain‡..242 t
Arose-third morning He a...165 l
Arras-speech is like cloth of.574 l
Array-cheapens his array....240 c
in your saddest array......544 o
linnet in thy green array¶.. 50 f
magnificently stern array‖.636 b
sorrow's dark array....... 3 c
Arrayed-a., the lilies cry....234 h
Austrian army awfully a..442 t
in glory are arrayed.......233 s
Arrears-pay glad life's a....346 b
Arresting-a. the vast wheel..599 r
Arrive-so mighty long ere it.605 k
Arrival-a. of a thinker in....596 e
at the arrival of an hour*..350 g
Arrogance-knees feed a.....491m
Arrow-a. for the heart like‖..634 q
shot mine a. o'er the house* 3 p
swifter than arrow*........294 u
the arrow flies............205 p
Arrow-heads-like a. of gold..394 l

Arrows-Cupid kills with a.*.364 p
darts or poisoned a. were..632 q
fleeter than a., bullets*....537 x
fly his scattered golden a...401 e
his breath like silver a.....546 b
'mid the thick arrows......206 d
nymph with arrows keen** 88 a
over whose heads those a..378 c
shot their arrows round....227 b
slings and arrows of*......159 f
swift-winged a. of light ...385 k
your arrows to the head*...639 a
Arrowy-the a. Rhone‖........532 g
Arsenal-shook the a. and**..462 g
Art-all nature is but art‡...510 l
all the adulteries of art....414 o
a master of the art§...... 90 c
a masterpiece of art has...452 k
and art a nature...........478 w
and art is difficult.........761 a
antiquities, a., he is fond of.516m
art and author craft are... 64 l
art and power will go on as.150 q
art a revelation of man§....528 f
art, as far as it is able, ...755 j
a. can wash her guilt away.656 o
art could not feign.........247 j
art imitates nature, and....414 c
art in fact, is the effort.... 28 q
art in knowing a thing.....719 d
art is difficult........... 755 h
art is indeed not the bread.755 f
art is long, and time is§....601 a
art is long but............721 e
art is power§............ 28m
art is the child of Nature§.. 28 n
a.is the perfection of nature410 d
a.is the right hand of natnre755 g
a. may err, but nature.....495 t
art must be to moderate...388w
art of artisans make a......281 d
art of man that has built...735 o
art of reading as well as.... 28 a
art remains the one way... 27 y
art's and friendship's......302 v
a. so nearly touches nature.664 r
art subdues the strong.‡.. 528 j
art that nature makes*... 412m
art—the art to blot‡.......429 g
art to find the mind's*....195 x
art with truth.. ....582 l
as a subject of fine art....426 c
a skilful mistress of her a..655 v
belly is the teacher of art..729 f
better than those finished..728 o
beyond the reach of art‡...283 l
but a. O man, is thine alone 29 d
chiefs of elder art!......... 67 t
comes from a., not chance‡.429 j
cookery is become an art..431m
either upon an a. or upon.. 29 r
elder days of art§..........277 k
every note with art........169 b
every walk of art.........428 i
for art is nature made by.. 29 a
framing an artist a. hath*.. 29 f
giveth grace unto every a.§.296 u
glory and good of art...... 27 y
hath prosperous art when*. 27 t
he tried each art, reprov'd.450 l
his art with nature's*...... 29 e
history of the a.of printing.451 t
howe'er concealed by art..487 a
howe'er disguised by art..475aa
human art built the cities..413 e
if art assist her not.........257 g
in sweet music is such art*.407 f
in the elder days of art§....431 f
is the great a. of social life.565 k
it is an art worthy the.... 19 b
it's clever. but is it art..... 28 l
knows the high art of what.345 a
life is short, art long.... 347 v
made rare by art's refining.192 e
marks the progress of art.. 29 c
more by art than force of‡. 28 j
music is the prophet's art§.406 a

nature is the art of God....410 d
nature reproduced in art§.. 28 p
Nature's handmaid, art....410 q
next to nature, art........473 f
no art to find the mind's*..386 l
no chymic art can ....112 l
nor art with nature........410 d
not Art but Nature traced§.617 l
not a truth has to art or to.622 i
not without art, but yet to.410m
of my tuneful art........ .260 s
only art her guilt to cover.551 g
ornaments their want of a.‡480 q
perfection of an a. consists. 28 f
perfection of a.is to conceal 29 b
piety in art, poetry in art.. 28 k
ply your finest art......... 18 l
poetry a mere mechanic a.476 l
princes learn no art truly..534 i
principles of decorative a.. 28 s
professor of our art........ 32 q
rapidly. a. most cherishes...472 a
seeks popularity in art. ...446 q
so vast is art, so narrow‡..538 l
strength, but art, obtains‡. 28 j
stronger far than art.......413 u
swear I use no art at all*...321 f
temperament and not of a.‖ 77 u
temple of art is built.......28 h
than all the gloss of art....555 n
the art of horsemanship...534 i
the last and greatest art‡..429 g
the poet in his art must....480 s
these mixed with a. and to‡.386 l
tender strokes of art‡......422 n
'tis all thou art and all‡....137 k
to a's. strict limits bounds.369 o
unmatched by art..........194 r
variance with art nor art... 27 x
war's glorious a., and gives.404 e
was almost lost in art......124m
when art is too precise..... 23 j
when Nature conquers, art.781 c
with curious a. the brain...596 c
with little a., clear wit and.782 i
world and art another...... 27 x
you your art..............669 s
Artful-artful to no end‡....349 n
Arts-all arts are vain......257 g
a. and sciences are not cast.289m
a. and sciences the benefits 63 t
a. at least all such as could‖.341 s
arts, in most cruel wise....430 d
a. in which the wise excel..429 s
a. of pleasure grow when..755 i
a. which belong to polished.749 a
fashion's brightest a. decoy.329 p
Greece mother of arts **... 97 n
grew the arts of war and‖..542 d
her arts victorious‡.......631 f
import yet nobler a. from‡.129 b
instructed in the arts......716 p
learn'd in nobler arts......269 k
love and reverence all a....421 q
no a., no letters, no society.347 w
of all the arts great music.405 r
peace, dear nurse of arts*..471 f
silence is one of the great a.554 o
sweet a. of thy reign. ....386 q
taught the wheedling a....656m
the a.of pleasure in despotic 1 g
the inglorious a. of peace..470 q
their sons with arts*......279 c
tillage begins, other a......424 p
well versed in the arts......182 l
with lenient arts extend a‡. 11 a
Artaxerxes–A.'s throne**...462 q
Arteries–spirits in the a.*...667 k
Artery–makes each petty a.*.207 h
Article–a. at highest rate is‖.. 7 f
be snuffed out by an a.‖.*..385 h
deny each a. with oath*....103 v
Articulate–he should be a....447 j
Artifice–a. is allowable in...762 q
sense can artifice disdain... 25 t
Artificer–fierce a. curves his.565 a
Artifices–delicate a. as we do.762 k

Artificial–all things are a.....410 d
a. strife lives in these*.....447 d
a. wings fastened on with..714 g
things are a. for nature is.. 27 x
Artillery–by infallible a......157 o
Heaven's a. thunder*......119 s
the artillery of words......665dd
Artisans–a. on canvas or in... 28 i
Artist–born an a. so no man.. 18 q
essence of an a. is that he..447 j
gave laws to the artist..... 29 h
in framing an a. art hath*.. 29 f
marks the true artist...... 28 t
the artist envies what......173w
the artist never dies§....... 28 o
things the knowing a. may.423 p
Artists–a. may produce...... 28 r
two kinds of artists in..... 28 g
Ascalon–heathen Gath, or A.570 i
Ascend–a. I follow thee**...420 f
by which he did ascend*... 14 d
dignity of being we ascend‖351 w
our proper motion we a.**.492 l
Ascent–a. from earth to......712 c
should be nobility of ascent 15 n
Ascension–in ascension and..572 j
Ash–against my grained a.*..363 p
ash her purple drops††.....612 a
from yon tall ash 'mid . 42m
the ash for nothing ill......610 h
Ashamed–are a. of our silence.574 f
ashamed of my master......742 l
a. of what she ought.......742 h
a. that these reproaches....742 j
ashamed to meet the eyes.. 69 s
a. with the noble shame....632 s
begins to be ashamed......742 h
hell might be ashamed of..387 j
Ashes–above their ashes pale.141 k
as flames from ashes§......302 g
a., little brook! will bear¶..158 k
ashes of my chance*...... 73 v
ashes to the taste§.........265w
beauty for ashes, and oil...330 d
but now to silent ashes‡....143 o
but turns to ashes ....266 i
cinders, ashes, dust........359 o
e'en in our ashes live their.411 d
faithful to the ashes........800 q
from his ashes may be†....249m
from the ashes of dead men.201 f
glory paid to our ashes.....706 t
in itself to ashes burn§.....296 v
laid at last old Troy in...658 a
lie lightly on my ashes.....284 e
not riches adorn men's a...396 l
over a few poor ashes I sit.. 10 p
splendid in ashes...........370 b
the ashes of his fathers....136 e
thy ashes, thy one brief....324 f
to the ashes of the just is‡.333 i
ye a. wild, resounding o'er.610 p
Ashore–on the new world set.648 j
Ask–all we a. is to be let....317 u
and ask till ye receive....472 n
a. not, hope thou not too...588 b
ask not of me, love.........355 c
ask of the great sun........355 c
ask of thyself what beauty.355 c
ask sin of what may be....355 c
a. the same until my dying.651 s
ask what is darkness.......355 c
ask what is good..........355 c
ask what is fashion.........355 c
ask what is folly of the....355 c
ask what is happiness of...355 c
ask what is sweetness.... 355 c
better neither to a. nor tell.601 f
cease to ask of me........181 a
doth ask a drink divine....641 d
I dare not ask§........525 b
I know not, I ask not......361 d
little I ask, my wants.....652 h
never thought to ask......240 c
to ask who are guilty......677 o
who feares to aske, doth... 38m
Asking–had for the asking††.102 u

B.

every stag hound b........451 s
Bayes–drunk o' th' b. to-day.176 t
Bay-leaves–with eating b-l...176 i
Bayonet-blade-rifle and the..635 p
Bayonets-chains are worse..470m
  feared than a thousand b..436 d
Bay-trees-b-t. in our*........639 s
Be-better not to be at all†....418 n
  cared not to be at all**..... 91 t
  cease to do and be....... 10 r
  had as lief not be as live to*.350 j
  it was a luxury to be......368 v
  I would rather be than.....799cc
  nor are, nor e'er will be.... 84 x
  such as be the same as be.. 62 a
  such to be as be we would.. 62 a
  to be, contents his natural‡349 p
  to be is more of wonderful.386 r
  to be or not to be*.........159 f
  to be rather than to seem..803 u
  to be we know not what, we.133 l
  what things to be are††... 81 h
  ye still shall be...........226 j
Be-all-b-a. and the end-all*...350 u
Beach-across the narrow b... 56 n
  all night the thirsty b. has.598 p
  a stroll upon the beach.... 351 o
  b. a poor Exile of Erin....117 q
  behold! the barren b. of...586 d
  bordering the beach........238 d
  dote upon it—from the b...459 u
  down the beach we flit.... 56 n
Beaches-on sandy beaches†...221 l
Beacon-b. kindling from afar 31 q
  beacon of the wise*........159 b
Beade-I saw a flie within a b.661 k
Beadroll-on fame's eternal b.480 p
Beads-amber bracelets, b.*... 24 i
  Ave-Maries on his beads*..489 e
  beads of morning strung¶.309 e
  beads, pictures, rosaries...587 c
  beads they told.............173 x
  b. while she numbered..... 31m
  how many beads there are.355 i
  jewels for a set of beads*..434 p
  men are at their beads*....109 d
  telling his b. in penance.... 55 a
  tell their beads in drops§..514 l
  yon alder's crimson b......510 y
Beak-bird of the amber beak 44 b
  good morrow to thy sable b. 44 c
  thy tiny b. the gory points. 55 n
  toil of b. and added claw... 43 p
Beaks-their grasping b....... 54 b
Beaker-b. full of the warm..649 n
Beam-b. not so fierce.........543 f
  beam propitious shines.....624 d
  doubtful b. long nods from‡158 p
  evening b. that smiles the‖.492 v
  fancy's beam enlarges‡.....203 t
  fretful at the obtrusive b..369 d
  kiss the beam he sends to..401 c
  no one beame of comfort..299 a
  not a b., nor air, nor leaf‖.346 q
  of th' eternal coeternal b.**352 n
  rest stand on a beam.....804 y
Beams-and in his latest b.§...624 r
  b. do soonest captivate.....192 e
  candle throws his beams*..147 d
  gay b. of lightsome day....398 r
  gilt the ocean with his b.*..584 s
  his hasty beams would do..585 d
  hurls his glistring beams... 29 q
  keeps his golden beams.....235 l
  kissed her with his beams.584 k
  scattered with all its b.....338 l
  sun, whose b. adorn the....584 o
  the hoist-up of beams......431 k
  tricks his b., and with**....576 k
  whence are thy b., O sun..583 v
Bean-fields-scent of b-f......223 d
Beans-abstain from beans... 494 f
  blue b. in one blue bladder.665 f
  'tis three blue beans........665 f
Bear-authority be a stubborn*29 t
  bear another's misfortunes‡388 i
  bear his own grievances....701m

bear like the Turk‡........328 b
bear the brunt in a minute.346 b
b. the miseries of a people.534 o
bear those ills we have*....467 o
bear up and steer**........198 c
bear what is ordained......466 u
bear what man has borne§.416 b
  borne, and yet must bear.. 72 o
  bush suppos'd a bear*......209 w
  bush we see's a bear........209 i
  flesh and blood can't b. it..311 b
  friend should bear his*.....262 c
  gave pain to the bear.......126 i
  it gave pain to the bear...521 k
  look on it, lift it, bear it...348 h
  monarch, warm'd a bear‡.. 19 i
  savageness out of a bear*..557 s
  seeming to bear it lightly*.644 b
  still b. up and steer right** 61 f
  the rugged Russian bear*..130 j
  to bear is to conquer.......205 v
  to b. is to conquer our fate.467 a
  to learn to b. is easier than.667 p
  what happens let us bear..110 n
  when doubly arm'd to bear.346 z
Bearable-hell is more b .....298 v
Bearbaiting-Puritan hated b.126 i
Bearing-b. boughs may live*.266 p
  the b. and the training†....402 h
Bear-gardens-mystical b-g...520 e
Bear-like-b-l., I must fight*.149 u
Bears-bears her down‖.......551 o
  b. keep at peace with one.731 h
  bears leisurely lick their...289m
  let bears and lions growl...157 i
Beard-another b. springs up.177 p
  b. be shook with danger*...120 a
  b. is white, Olus, your hair.176 e
  by its soft brown beard....583 k
  chin the springing b. began458 f
  dye your b., though you....176 e
  long chin with beard.......157 j
  loose his b., and hoary hair.291 e
  own beard full grown......178 o
  shook his beard of snow...546 d
  what a b. hast thou got*....458 g
  when the mind (like a b.)..476 n
  whilst on his hoary b. his..546 f
  whiskers and a forky b.‡..458 a
  whose b. descending swept. 38 l
  whose b. they have sing'd*.458 h
Bearded-b. like the pard*....444 k
  the tears of b. men.........591 i
Beards-b. of Hercules and*..121 s
Beast-a black sheep is a .....494 d
  a wild beast or a god......567 k
  and presently a beast*......326 k
  bird, beast, and flower....410 t
  both man and bird and b...487 q
  brave beast is no flatterer..534 i
  each savage furious beast..670 c
  little better than a beast*.. 84 o
  while the beast lived was*.. 21 j
Beasts-a mixture of wild b.‖. 69 k
  fled to brutish beasts......331 t
  kin to the beasts by........ 38 u
  learn from the beasts the‡.440 o
  not God's, and not the b.'s..492 d
  of all wild b. on earth or in.657m
  transform ourselves into*..326m
  wild b. came forth the**....416 l
Beat-b. them or Betty Stark..638m
  beat with fist instead of a..449 u
  beat upon mine little heart† 32 j
  b. your pate, and fancy wit‡653 u
  hast beat me out*..........161 e
  quickly found to b. a dog*.461m
  two hearts that b. as one...627 a
Beaten-he that is b. may be..305 u
  have been b. till they know.512 b
Beatific-enjoyed in vision**..369 k
Beating-b. of my own heart..296 y
  he heats me with beating*.549 f
Beatings-b. at the heart.... 402 a
  upon the b. of my heart¶...669 u
Beats-b. on forever as of old§588 f
  b. with his blood and trust†402 g

it beats in the heart........348 t
light which beats upon a†..535 o
Beau-beau is one who. .....254 l
  here comes Monsieur le B.*414 t
Beaumont-as witty as B.††...411 l
  bid Beaumont lie a little...550 k
Beauties-admire by far thy‖.456 f
  all his b. could survey...... 74 o
  and his beauties are best...586 e
  bathing their beauties......250 f
  beauties in vain their‡..... 36 c
  beauties of exulting Greece452 r
  b. of your mind adore..... 60 c
  beauties that appear.......245 f
  flowers unfold their b......401 c
  guard their b. from the....458 k
  like birds whose b.languish 60 w
  many beauties in a poem...753 j
  meaner b. of the night....577 k
  modestly conceals her b.... 35 s
  they please as b., here‡....638 a
  to copy beauties forfeits...513 y
Beautifier-the b. of the‖ ... 599 i
Beautiful-and b. as sweet....661 h
  and young as beautiful.....661 h
  appears in a b. person.....678 p
  b. all round thee lying.... 36 m
  beautiful are never desolate 33 l
  b. as God meant you......300 i
  b. as is the rose in June...459m
  beautiful as woman's blush.222 b
  beautiful, but none alike...247 x
  b. in form and feature§.... 35 c
  b. object in the world......657 l
  b. only blooms in song.....769 c
  beautifulseems right....... 33 o
  b. through frost and cold..609 p
  become b. in the inner man 37 g
  befriended the beautiful...700 a
  calm, how b. comes on.....479 s
  clear, and purely beautiful‡657 w
  death is b. as feet of†‡.....186 c
  feathers are more b.*......102 g
  God's prophet. of the b....478 h
  how b. if sorrow had not...569 h
  how calm, how beautiful... 71 g
  is a beautiful woman......657 l
  is beautiful is good........280 n
  most beautiful things in the 36 h
  name of which was b....... 33 q
  nothing is b. from every...678 k
  O daughter more beautiful.678 j
  she's b. and therefore to*..659 s
  she was beautiful*........215 l
  soon also be beautiful..... 280 n
  the beautiful rests on the.. 34m
  true, the wise, the beautiful.260 v
  was sacred, but the b.......755 g
  yet all how beautiful .....545 k
  young, and one was b.‖....671 v
Beautifuller-far b. than its..186 n
Beautifully-blue, darkly,....460m
Beauty-all beauty void......417 t
  all His glory and beauty... 92 n
  all kinds of b.do not inspire.756 c
  all the beauty of the sun*..364 k
  all the b. of the world 'tis... 37 r
  all things of beauty are not 36 j
  amaranthus all his b.**.....221 i
  and beauty of the soul.....631 x
  and b.should be kind as well 34 p
  a thing of b. is a joy forever 34 w
  autumn beauty stood......246 b
  beautiful than B's. self....569 h
  Beauty and her chivalry‖..211 c
  beauty and sadness always. 35 h
  beauty and the silent note.355 p
  b. and virtue shine forever.654 n
  b. and wisdom are rarely...678m
  beauty apprehended from.. 33 p
  beauty as the first of May*.393 g
  beauty beauteous seem*...556aa
  b. born of murmuring¶....413m
  beauty but skin deep.......329 h
  beauty but skin·deep...... 36 b
  b. comes, we scarce know.. 36 n
  beauty cost her nothing.... 34 d

---

b. dead, black chaos comes*139 _g_
beauty doth varnish age*... 36 _o_
b. draws more than oxen..495_gg_
beauty draws us with a‡...291 _l_
beauty's ensign yet is*......36 _t_
b. fires the blood how love. 34 _k_
beauty for ashes, and oil...380 _d_
b. for confiding youth¶.....466 _d_
beauty for the feeling heart756 _o_
b. immortal awakes from..315 _o_
b. indemnifies the want of..175 _r_
beauty is a witch*.........36 _p_
beauty is bought by*..... 36 _q_
beauty is but a vain*..... 36 _r_
beauty is fading............690 _i_
beauty is its own excuse...240 _c_
beauty is nature's brag**.. 35_m_
beauty is nature's coin**... 35 _n_
b. is the index of a larger.. 34 _t_
beauty is truth,............ 35 _a_
b. like wit, to judges should 35 _f_
beauty makes this vault*.. 36_w_
beauty more than queenly.227 _f_
b. no pencil, b.'s truth*....623 _q_
b. of a lovely woman is like.656 _c_
beauty of the lilies.........258 _n_
beauty of thy mind*.......147 _j_
beauty passeth praise.......225 _g_
b. provoketh thieves*...... 36 _s_
beauty richly fraught......117 _a_
Beauty's midnight hair...244 _o_
beauty soon grows familiar 33 _j_
beauty's secret nearer..... 247 _l_
beauty stands in the**..... 35 _o_
B's. tears are lovelier than.590 _k_
b's veil doth cover every*..630 _r_
b. that accompanies what is   7 _s_
beauty that addresses itself 36 _i_
beauty that has awakened.. 28 _g_
beauty that shocks you‡... 82 _p_
B. to forego her wreath....   8 _p_
b.too rich for use for earth* 37 _a_
b. was lent to nature as the 34 _r_
Beauty watched to imitate‖ 74 _h_
b., wit, high birth, vigor of*602 _h_
b. within itself should not*.602_m_
bright the tear in B's. eye‖.590 _g_
brightest that b. or revelry.641 _n_
brilliant beauty glows..... 247 _g_
come to behold thy beauty. 36 _a_
conscious stone to beauty.. 28 _c_
daily beauty in his life*.... 83_m_
deathless b. take no wrong.574 _s_
dissolves the b. of the......600 _g_
does its beauty refine......292 _i_
dreamed that life was b....163 _t_
dream of beauty glides.....545 _d_
dust swept from their b....267 _f_
Elysian b. melancholy¶... 37 _w_
enamour'd and beheld b.**. 35 _p_
essence of all beauty...... 33 _p_
expression is action, b. is...101 _k_
fatal gift of beauty‖........116 _t_
flower of glorious beauty.. 34 _j_
for beauty being poor and.375 _u_
forth in thy awful beauty..583 _v_
from partial beauty won...370 _k_
gypsy beauty full..........225 _e_
hangs from Beauty's ears..590 _n_
hasten to her task of b.....540 _p_
her match in b. was not....612 _j_
her pensive beauty¶........234 _s_
holiday time of my beauty*449 _g_
hour with beauty's chain..155 _n_
hues of b. such as Heaven..545 _f_
I have my b.—you your art.669 _s_
I like their beauty.........657 _b_
in b. faults conspicuous.... 34 _o_
in matchless beauty........229 _f_
in matchless b. shining....192 _e_
in youth and b. wisdom is‡.650 _u_
Isr'el's b. on the mountains.570 _l_
just as one beauty‡........254_m_
light from her own beauty. 37 _f_
lines where beauty lingers‖.132_w_
losing both b. and utility*..643_m_
love beauty at first sight... 34 _e_

make beauty attractive,....88 _l_
make his beauty disappear.367 _v_
marble grows to beauty....452 _j_
meek beauty dost lean.....234 _n_
much beauty as could die..183 _g_
music even in the beauty..404_m_
naked b. more adorn'd**... 35 _q_
Nature thought beauty too 35 _h_
of March with beauty*.....226 _n_
on beauty's breast was seen434 _t_
or eye, we beauty call‡......36 _d_
our serious beauty show...288_m_
perspective of vegetable b.425 _t_
power yet upon thy b.* .. 139 _e_
preserves her beauty 'mid¶235 _d_
queen devoid of b. is not .. 34 _v_
rail against her beauty*....388 _k_
rare is the union of b. and..676 _p_
rather than of beauty......681 _f_
robe of terror and of beauty531 _f_
royalty of beauty's mien....34 _v_
see the beauty of virtue....750 _h_
she in beauty, education*...185 _b_
she was Beauty's self........37 _q_
shine with beauty, breathe.661 _u_
shrines of beauty...........382 _a_
solidity or exactness of b..667 _g_
soon as a sweet beauty.... 33_m_
spirit of all beauty.........163 _r_
spring up into beauty......270 _s_
strength and radiant b..... 79 _t_
style of beauty to which...755 _p_
such beauty should be.....719_m_
summer vine in b. clung§..546 _e_
teaches such beauty as*....193 _n_
the beauty of the world*...372 _t_
then b. is its own excuse for 34 _l_
there's b. all around our... 34 _s_
the parallels in b's. brow*..602 _v_
the power of b. I remember 34 _t_
they have lost their beauty.475 _p_
thick, bereft of beauty*....659 _b_
thou art all beauty or all...472 _b_
thou a type of beauty......237 _r_
thy marvelous beauty......212 _t_
thyself what beauty is......355 _c_
'tis beauty calls, and glory. 35 _b_
'tis b. that doth oft make*.659_w_
'tis b.truly blent whose red* 37 _e_
to die for b. than live for...133 _s_
to draw true b. shows a....446 _k_
true beauty dwells in¶..... 38 _a_
truest truth, the fairest b..478 _t_
trust not to too much b....678 _q_
upon the altar of her b.*...663 _t_
walking in beauty to her...397_m_
walks in b. like the night‖.. 33 _t_
what beauty is her dole.... 37_m_
what's female beauty, but. 38 _b_
who gave thee O B. the keys 34 _n_
who his spoil of b. can*....602 _z_
wife can see her beauty.... 24 _p_
will lose his beauty*........484 _q_
with b. we can virtue join.. 36 _e_
with him is beauty slain*.. 77 _f_
with storied beauty........220 _t_
withers the b.'s transient...156 _g_
year in its highest beauty..729 _b_
yet beauty, tho' injurious** 35 _r_
youth and beauty's pride.. 69 _p_
youth, talents,b. thus decay 11 _h_
Beaux—where none are b. 'tis. 35 _g_
while punctual b. reward‖..454 _t_
Beaver—dear the b. is to him.492_w_
Beavers—reputations, like b..524 _t_
Becalmed—lie b. by the shores 89 _n_
Because—because it was he...361 _b_
Beck—far too slight a beck...240_m_
Beckons—and b. us away....137 _f_
which beckons me away....141 _q_
Becks—nods, and becks, and**383 _r_
Beclouding—b. here leads to.. 78 _n_
b. here leads to dissipation.341 _v_
Become—conveniently b. you*663 _t_
humble things become......713 _e_
ill white hairs b. a fool*....328 _s_
what is become of him.....336 _t_

Becomes—nothing so b.a man*471 _e_
well b. her when she speaks478 _v_
Becoming—do what is b......720 _p_
Bed—a bed by night, a chest..303 _r_
accept my b., or narrow or.530 _i_
and hastes to bed...... ....217 _k_
angels guard thy bed.......32 _o_
approach a bed may show. 38 _d_
are the weans in their b. for 32 _b_
as my tears fill her bed.....366 _b_
back on his chintz bed.....283 _b_
becomest thy b. fresh lily*.234 _e_
bed he dreams upon........243 _b_
bed of thy repose.......... 36 _a_
born in bed in bed......... 38 _d_
brimstone bed at break of..153 _r_
brooding in their liquid b.‖. 47 _d_
buried in beds of moss. ...249 _s_
but sups and goes to bed...183 _c_
couched in a curious bed*..112 _e_
delicious banquet by his b.*369 _f_
down a rocky bed..........224 _l_
driven bed of down*....... 127 _p_
earth in an earthy bed‡....366 _q_
fashionable owls to bed.....53 _e_
goes to bed wi' the sun*....235 _n_
goes to bed thirsty rises....499 _j_
go to bed by day.......... 90 _t_
go to bed with the lamb.... 38 _e_
grave's a quiet bed.........286 _g_
his bed shall seem a school*.589 _o_
holy angels guard thy bed.563 _s_
hues as red as the rosy bed.649 _t_
in bed we laugh in......... 38 _d_
I were safe at home, in bed.586 _i_
kissed and put to bed.......90 _u_
lamp and gone to bed§......464 _o_
lies in his bed*.............288 _k_
limbs on the wished for....789 _b_
lovers to bed 'tis almost*.. 384 _z_
maker of the dead man's...458 _p_
near on her lowly bed his...94 _g_
O bed ! O bed ! delicious bed.38 _g_
on a thorny rose bed.......366 _a_
on my grave, as now my...560 _n_
on our own delightful bed.416 _q_
or up in my bed now.......590 _u_
our bed of boughs is.......617 _j_
our own delightful bed.....38 _h_
pendent bed and procreant* 50 _h_
smooth the bed of death‡.. 11 _a_
steal out of his wholesome*552 _r_
sweet pillowes, sweetest...563 _h_
sweetly warbles o'er its bed.531 _b_
that glistereth in bed......494 _jj_
that will to bed go sober...593 _q_
the bed be blest........... 88 _c_
the bed has become a....... 38 _t_
the bed of honour lain.....305 _u_
the moss his bed, the cave.567 _j_
to light Tom Fool to bed...576 _u_
treason's true bed and*....608 _q_
welcome and bed of love be 48 _o_
welcome to your gory bed.635 _q_
where our bed arranged....52 _j_
who goes to bed and doth..488 _h_
without the bed her other*.292 _n_
with the lark to bed.......503 _w_
yet one hour in his bed*....160 _s_
Bed-fellows—with strange*...387 _t_
Beds—beds of the Eumenides.299 _u_
housewives in your beds*..660 _g_
lies not on beds of down....61 _v_
make thee beds of roses....218 _t_
Beddowee—O Beddowee girl..617 _a_
Bedlam—in durance, exile B.‡.429 _k_
Bee—a hunting with the bee..393 _r_
as brisk as a bee in.........113 _t_
as busie as a bee...........495 _u_
b. hive's hum shall soothe.117 _j_
b. itself would have desired.322 _d_
bee reels from bough to...322 _g_
bee returns with evening's.322 _e_
bee sits on the bloom**....613 _a_
bee sucks, there suck I*....197 _h_
bee to the blossom........465_m_
bee whose buzzing........322 _d_

Shakespeare *; Milton **; Wordsworth ¶; Byron ‖; Tennyson †; Lowell ††; Pope ‡; Longfellow §.

till no man believe him..... 83 *f*
to believe or to disbelieve...571 *d*
to love is to believe.........367 *h*
western world b. and sleep‡537 *c*
wish we soon believe .... . 39 *o*
woman, born first to b. us.657 *n*
Believed–doubted, never half.158 *l*
if believed, had blessed.....620 *e*
juggling fiends no more b*492 *r*
nothing is so firmly believed 39 *f*
they b. faith I'm puzzled††. 39 *d*
wise man that believed. .... 32 *r*
Believer–b. is God's miracle.386 *p*
the great believer makes...352 *h*
the heart of every believer.528 *e*
Believes–b. 'tis always left...208 *q*
each believes his own‡.....331 *q*
Belinda–inscribe B's. name‡..291 *m*
Bell–a heavy tolling funeral..476 *v*
and the Sabbath bell that.. 40*m*
b., book, and candle shall*.594 *d*
b. of Atri famous for all§.. 40 *f*
b. set in the rushing shoals. 41 *i*
b. thou soundest merrily§.. 40 *c*
b. thou soundest solemnly§ 40 *c*
chimes the passing bell.... 41 *b*
clear green bell. ....225 *f*
convent b. suddenly in the§. 40 *e*
desert heard the camel's b‖.641 *a*
ever after as a sullen bell*.415 *b*
heard the convent bell§.... 40 *e*
heart as sound as a bell*...556 *y*
its great red bell...........247 *f*
merry as a marriage bell‖..404 *o*
music but our passing bell.140 *w*
name the bell with joy..... 40 *o*
passing bell for Deity......612 *c*
setting a jacinth b. a-swing322 *y*
sleep sound till the b. brings135 *i*
than the bell rings*........381*m*
the bell never rings of itself.675 *g*
the b. strikes one. We take.604 *e*
the church going bell...... 39 *s*
the dinner bell‖........... 39 *q*
twilight and evening bell†.465 *d*
under the Old South bell... 54 *l*
was but moral of this bell.. 41 *b*
will bear away the bell.....451 *s*
with a bee in every bell.....611 *i*
Bell-man–fatal b-m. which*.. 52 *q*
Bells–and streaky bells of....222 *d*
bells are the voice of the§.. 40 *d*
bells call others, but......495 *jj*
b. have been anointed and§. 40 *i*
bells in your parlours*......660 *q*
bells of clearest blue .. ..230 *h*
b. of Rylstone seemed to¶..490 *d*
b. on Christmas Day§...... 94 *i*
b.that rang without a hand† 25 *l*
b. that waste the moments.573 *t*
b. themselves are the best§ 40 *h*
bid the merry bells ring*.... 41 *a*
blue bells at whose birth.. 220 *f*
cheerful Sabbath b.... 40 *b*
Christmas b. from hill to†.. 95 *f*
church b. ringing clear.... 40 *p*
Easter bells be ringing....165 *j*
flung from its b. a sweet..231 *k*
for a cap and b. our lives††102 *u*
glows with purple bells....219 *q*
hang porcelain b. that§....449*m*
hark! the loud-voiced bells. 41 *g*
instruments to melancholy* 75 *x*
its stately bells..........219 *f*
light of its tremulous bells.234 *p*
loud vociferous b. and§.... 40 *q*
mellow wedding b. golden. 40 *k*
merry bells below were....135 *i*
of our leader's bells......127 *h*
of those Shandon bells..... 40 *d*
of those village bells...... 39 *r*
ring, happy bells, across†.. 41 *e*
ring out wild bells, to the†. 41 *f*
ring snow-white b. your...165 *n*
sweet b. jangled out of*.... 40 *q*
sweet the tuneful bells..... 39 *p*

those evening bells, those.. 40 *j*
tune of the b. ring-a-ding.. 39 *u*
uppe, O Boston bells....... 39 *v*
we ring the b. and we raise. 94 *e*
when the bells do chime....536 *n*
with a tower and bells...... 95 *n*
with thy bells of Shandon..531 *a*
Bell-wether–sad b-w. to the....141 *a*
Belle–boarding-school b. in a.628 *f*
'tis vain to be a belle....... 35 *g*
Belles–ye b. and ye flirts, and.114 *o*
Bellies–the shining bellies... 53 *l*
Bellow–b. through the vast**598 *l*
deigned to hiccup or to b.‖.483 *d*
the beast can only bellow‖..557 *b*
Bellowed–so strutted and b.*.423 *f*
Bellows–b. blows up sin*.....215 *o*
Belly–b. is the commanding...504*cc*
belly is the teacher of art..729 *f*
but belly, God send thee...162 *v*
does not mind his b. will...167 *c*
in the belly of the grape...649 *e*
spent under his belly......508 *j*
Belongs–that which b. to....649 *d*
to each other belongs......375 *r*
understood b. to every one.621 *q*
Beloved–and 'tis b. by many. 19 *d*
creature that is beloved*...108 *o*
die for their beloved ......361 *l*
grief for a man so beloved.710 *c*
He giveth His b. sleep.....590 *c*
knew she was by him b.‖...356 *t*
same, b. contented thing‡..683 *f*
Beloveds–behind living b....107*m*
Below–like a little heaven b...298 *u*
Belshazzar–B. had a letter...448 *a*
Belt–b. of an amethyst ring..541 *n*
drawn for belt about......227 *b*
let go belt and all........... 20*m*
Belted–mak a belted knight..370 *d*
Ben Adhem–B. A's. name led.409 *v*
Ben Battle–B. B. was a soldier443 *i*
Ben Bolt–fallen to pieces, B.B.614 *l*
remember sweet Alice, B.B.379 *s*
Bench–b. of heedless bishops.455 *r*
Bend–b. and take my being...243 *l*
Bend brightly o'er my......217 *g*
bend its stately summit...767 *n*
break, but not bend me....801 *a*
to bend, not to break......800 *v*
Bender–obedient to the b's..610 *h*
Bendeth–b. its vigorous form.616 *e*
Bending–bending like a bow.213 *q*
bending like Moses'.......223 *h*
bending with our fulness...241 *q*
so bending tries to veil the.452 *r*
Bends–and reed that bends...656 *v*
bends not as I tread**......226 *a*
she b. him, she obeys him§.375 *q*
Benediction–b. God's angels.. 8 *l*
benediction o'er their sod..618*m*
b. of these covering*....... 60 *u*
come like the benediction§.568 *h*
face like a benediction....194 *q*
Benefaction–b. to the towns§.529*m*
Benefit–a b. consists not in...679*m*
benefit and an injury*.....548 *e*
b. is estimated according...679 *r*
benefit of the public......437*m*
can he ever quite lose the b.455 *h*
for the b. of the people.... 281 *q*
Benefits–b. are acceptable...715 *r*
benefits are mightily*.....272 *h*
b. are there in common....263 *u*
born to do benefits*....... 87 *b*
disable all the benefits of*..607 *h*
for benefits designed...... 14 *q*
remember the b. we have..508 *f*
Benevolence–grafts b. even.. 15 *h*
prince of a state love b.... 282 *r*
Benighted–b. walks under**. 82 *c*
Benison–like a celestial b.§.. 31 *k*
Benizon–our love, our b.*.... 90 *q*
Bent-affection cannot hold*..364 *r*
the top of my bent*...... 145 *i*
Benumbed–feel b., and wish‖.420 *n*
Bequeath–can we bequeath*.139 *t*

Bequeathed–b. by bleeding‖..257 *w*
bequeathed you nothing...179 *a*
Bereft–b. me of all words*....665 *r*
Berkeley–coxcombs vanquish537 *t*
Berries–b. of the brier rose...217 *e*
green holly with its b. red..614 *t*
in the hedge the frosted b..618 *d*
lovely berries moulded*....262 *k*
luscious b. of sanguine dye.615 *t*
seeks cedar b. blue, his††... 55 *l*
shading its Ethiop berries..218 *h*
two lovely b. moulded on*.627 *n*
wholesome berries thrive*.266 *r*
Berry–devil in every b. of the.649 *o*
have made a better berry. 19 *g*
Berth–b. was of the wombe..197 *t*
supplied with a berth††....285 *g*
Beseech–I do b. you chiefly*.409 *p*
Besotted–alas! how b. Rome.179 *t*
infatuated and besotted....593 *p*
Bespake–was a man b. a..... 458 *r*
Best–a man's best things are. 60 *r*
best from worst............247 *e*
best in me comes from. ....232 *n*
best in this kind are but*..315 *g*
b. is best, if never*........623 *q*
best known evil is the most.695 *c*
b. of men have ever loved..523 *z*
best things are the truest..358 *n*
cried up for our best act*..331 *w*
desires of the b. and wisest.385*w*
each man do his best*...... 5 *q*
each man swore to do his b.525 *t*
everything is for the b. in..797 *j*
fear not to touch the best..572 *a*
for the best grows highest.615 *t*
fortunate if the best fall... 63 *s*
give house-room to the b... 91 *q*
he does the best he can.... 69 *o*
his b. things are done in††..411 *t*
I know not what is best§...525 *b*
of best things the collection.660 *j*
or friends with the best....387 *a*
prov'd b. man i' the field*.579 *t*
shows its best face at first..279 *o*
stand among our best†....184 *j*
than the best of men*..... 811 *v*
that's best which God sends525 *d*
the best die first.. ....206 *e*
the best fellow in the world.757 *j*
the b. may err, but you are.523 *f*
the best of men............271 *h*
the best of things...........155 *l*
this is the best of all.......357 *o*
thou best-humor'd man.....479 *f*
to the best things of life...480 *v*
way that seems the best... 91 *v*
what we oft do best*......331*w*
when he is best, he is*..... 84 *o*
Bestial–what remains is b.*..524 *q*
Bestow–the gods by man b†..642 *k*
Bestride–when I b.him I soar* 47 *q*
Bethlehem–king of B.§...... **226** *g*
the king of Bethlehem§.... 94 *h*
Betide–said what shall b.§...525 *b*
that may bityde............265 *x*
Bethumped–so b. with*......665*aa*
Betray–b. the heart that¶....413 *k*
betray us in deepest*...... 145 *q*
b. you without witnesses..769 *k*
born first to betray........657 *n*
finds too late that men b...156 *r*
man should betray, and lye482 *b*
of tender happiness b.¶.... 85 *v*
to betray's in deepest*.....623 *q*
trusted may betray........360*m*
Betrayed–betrayed by the...677 *r*
b. his living Lord and......522 *s*
betrayed my credulous**..608 *h*
b. the capitol? a woman...658 *a*
maiden true b. for gold... 528 *n*
the land's betray'd‡.........390 *b*
though those that are b.*..608 *t*
thou hast betray'd me....312 *o*
trusting bosom, when b....608 *i*
yet Britain not betray'd‡....454 *f*
Betrays–betrays great guilt..710 *t*

assisted at the birth........215 *t*
at their first birth..........22 *g*
at the moment of birth ...743 *i*
at thy birth*................287 *d*
at thy b. the fairy ladies**.368*m*
because of its birth........249 *a*
birth and ancestry.........677 *i*
b. is nothing but our death.604 *j*
b. is nothing where virtue..794*m*
b. of plots and their last....105 *a*
blue bells at whose birth...220 *f*
borrow thy auspicious b...407*w*
crushes in the b. a power..486 *e*
day of thy birth............258 *e*
death borders upon our b..134 *h*
fortieth day from his birth.340 *u*
fresh from b. a little soul.. 32 *i*
glory in their birth*........273 *f*
grace which on my b. have. 93 *v*
grievous burthen was thy*619 *j*
happy fragrant birth........218 *p*
have a new b. of freedom..469 *b*
he crushes in the birth.....604 *f*
high b. was a thing which.. 16 *a*
I do not remember my birth.59 *r*
ignorant of his birth and*..489 *o*
indemnifies the want of b..175 *r*
jovial star reigned at his b.*576 *x*
money gives b. and beauty.727 *x*
near the birth of Christ†... 95 *f*
noble by birth yet nobler§..418 *g*
no lack before our birth...135 *h*
not on his humble birth....379 *c*
oblivion take their daily b.¶629 *v*
our b. is nothing but our...351 *x*
owe their birth.............226 *f*
places of their birth........650 *p*
repeats the story of her b..397 *d*
the pangs of a poetic birth.478 *t*
time 'tween b. and death...600 *u*
'tis fortune gives us birth..670 *q*
whatsoe'er thy b. thou∥...596 *d*
ye bid us hail our birth..... 67 *f*
Birthday–a b.; and now a day. 60 *a*
is that a b. 'tis alas‡........ 60 *g*
laburnum on his b.........218 *e*
my birthday, and a§....... 60 *d*
my b. how many years ago. 59 *r*
my b.! what a different.... 60 *f*
the birthday of eternity...690 *k*
your birthday as my own to 60 *e*
Birthdays–on all my b.......240 *n*
Birthplace–and color of its b. 80 *e*
great Homer's b............202 *g*
Birthright–sustenance and b. 84 *v*
Births–plenties and joyful b.*471 *f*
Biscay–in Biscay's sleepless∥.532 *l*
Biscuit–dry as the*..........421 *j*
the (hard) biscuit which...181 *q*
Bishop–a bishop what you‡.. 82*w*
bishop and abbot and..... 48 *a*
bishop Love will be........359 *k*
church without a bishop...281 *o*
hypocrisy of a bishop......534 *j*
no marble b. on his tomb§..617 *l*
old Bishop Valentine.......628 *e*
trudged away to cry........518 *s*
when Bishop Berkeley∥....385 *t*
Bishops–bench of heedless...455 *r*
Bit–champ'd the golden bit... 20 *p*
hair of the dog that bit....291 *h*
reptile concealed bit his...481 *j*
Bite–bark is worse than his...499 *x*
bite the hand that fed them.281 *i*
dare bite the best*.........372 *p*
flavours if we bite it.......622 *a*
lest it should bite its*.....381 *n*
man recover'd of the bite.. 20 *a*
scorpion died of the bite...481 *j*
smaller still to bite 'em....323 *b*
ten times her old bite††....208 *d*
you can't see to bite........322 *s*
Bites–but gapes and bites...213 *i*
make three bites of a......501*dd*
with angry teeth he bites..113 *a*
Bitter–bitter ere long.......528 *k*
bitter is his pill...........220*m*

bitter it is to reap..........715 *o*
bitter o'er the flowers......727 *b*
compulsion of fate is b....766 *r*
how bitter a thing it is*....293 *x*
find bitter to taste.........351 *q*
my own less bitter†........354 *s*
physic that's bitter to*....125 *u*
Bitterer–bitterer now than I.391 *e*
bitterer than a thousand....144*m*
Bitterest–that is the b. of all.512 *d*
Bittern–b. booming in the...268 *o*
Bitterness–bitterness enter...756 *b*
bitterness of death, is.....308*aa*
drown the bitterness of....751 *t*
out the bitterness of¶......598 *e*
temper life's worst b...... 8 *d*
Bitter-sweet–apples that are.611*m*
Bivouac–b. of the dead......272*w*
dog would break thy b......443 *e*
Black–a white man black, a..456 *i*
black as the damning.......331 *f*
black is a pearl in a........434 *b*
black it stood as night**...153 *b*
b. look white, and white...691 *c*
black, red and white........113 *e*
black's not so black........553 *h*
devil wear black*..........153*m*
lass with the merry black..604 *t*
morn from black to red....584 *p*
O bosom black as death*...523 *p*
one has in black and white.784 *a*
see such b. and grained*...547 *n*
though ne'er so black*......215 *n*
white will have its blacke..101 *v*
Blackberries–plentiful as b..517*m*
Blackbird–all save the b...... 42*m*
a slender young b. built,... 43 *a*
O blackbird sing me†......43 *b*
the b. sings along the...... 43 *c*
to a b. 'tis to whistle......353 *d*
while the blackbird sings.. 43 *c*
Blackbirds–again the b. sing.392 *p*
b. have their wills†........541 *g*
blackbirds southward fly...394 *j*
Blackbrowed–loving b*.....417 *f*
Blackguards–id est b. both∥...157 *a*
Blackness–b. of that§.......130 *n*
to sooty b. from the........ 54 *q*
Blacks–b. had no rights.....560 *c*
Blacksmith–beside the b.'s§..430 *g*
Black-walnut– fruit of the...395 *d*
Blade–an' ilka b. o' grass....541 *p*
b. of grass is always a......300 *r*
first b. blown to.............243 *n*
heart-stain away on its b....653*m*
not alone for the b. was....430 *i*
repose the vengeful b.......470 *a*
the fragment of his b......681 *h*
the notches on the b.......443 *b*
trenchant b. Toledo trusty.470 *c*
Blades–on slender b. of¶.....309 *e*
we give our shining b......469 *e*
Bladder–a slit and a b...... 18 *e*
blue beans in one blue b...665 *f*
Bladders–boys that swim on*491 *k*
green earther pots, b.*.....441 *e*
swim on bladders*.........273 *d*
wind puffs up empty b......509 *k*
Blaize–lament for Madame..486 *j*
Blame–alike reserv'd to‡.....537 *r*
blame it too much.........270*m*
b. that is due to a few......718 *b*
blame the mote that dims.330 *y*
blame where you must....124 *t*
free from blame†..........249 *o*
in part to blame is she......594 *b*
nor blame me, for thou.....486 *l*
praise nor the b. is our..... 96 *n*
praise or justly blame......126 *a*
she is to b. that has been...594 *a*
the other mickle blame*...595 *q*
they blame at night‡.......461 *d*
those he brands, to blame..537 *o*
to order without blame.....26 *h*
we blame the drunkard....325 *q*
Blamed–b. shall not be thy*..559 *a*
Blanc–Mont Blanc is the∥....402 *o*

Blanch–b. without the¶.....466 *d*
Blanched–b. with fear*.....210 *h*
Blandishment–low in b.†.....646 *a*
Blandishments–b. of life.....121 *n*
blandishments will not.....259 *c*
the blandishments of wine.650 *d*
Blank–b. of nature's works**.149*m*
creation's blot, creation's b.319 *n*
leaves a blank behind......385 *j*
Blaspheme–farmers would b.525 *e*
Blasphemer–each b. quite‡... 60 *h*
Blasphemy–b. 'twill pass for∥.124 *f*
soldier is flat blasphemy*.. 60 *i*
Blast–all he lov'd that.......528*m*
battles of wave and blast..359 *d*
b. proclaims most deeds**..202 *b*
b. upon his bugle horn......638 *r*
bleak blows the blast.......484 *k*
blower of which b. is she...647 *i*
hard, steel b. is blowing...391 *e*
night the monitory b........543 *i*
or the midnight blast∥......493 *a*
rushing of the blast........391 *c*
the blast is chill, yet....... 43 *f*
to b. the man who owes....607 *r*
trances of the blast.........110 *h*
Blasted–b. with excess of....415 *o*
blown but blasted**........136 *r*
Blasting–b. all love's........328 *j*
Blasts–blasts follow b. and...545 *i*
b. them in their hour of....608 *j*
many blasts to shake*......287 *g*
Blaze–bathe them in the b.... 43 *o*
brighten at the blaze.......303 *j*
burst out into sudden b..**202 *d*
in Liberty's unclouded b....344 *h*
knee-deep blaze.............277 *i*
skirting b. of bushes low††.612 *a*
the sapphire blaze..........134 *f*
wrapping ether in a blaze..578 *f*
Blazon–give thee five-fold b*..271 *l*
Bleach–leave them to b......255 *a*
Bleak–b. as where ye grow...230 *b*
virtue's steely bones look*. 83 *u*
Bleared–bleared his eyes§....580 *c*
Bleat–bleat the one at the*...320 *o*
the bleat of flocks..........230 *i*
Bled–b. in Freedom's cause..301 *j*
Scots, wha hae wi' Wallace.635 *q*
that my heart has bled.... 60 *v*
Bleed–b., bleed poor country*626 *f*
bleed for man, to teach.... 92 *q*
b. gold for ministers to....649 *a*
carcasses b. at the sight....403 *l*
others bleed for, bleed for..357 *q*
the heart's blood longest∥..671 *e*
we bleed, we tremble.......253 *k*
Bleeding–all hot and b. will*.639 *u*
and b. at his feet........... 309 *o*
dead and bleeding fresh*...430 *n*
hail, O bleeding head and... 92 *i*
my love lies bleeding.......357 *e*
Bleeds–heart that b. and.....344 *a*
which b. away even as a*...139 *k*
Blemish–in nature there's no*627 *u*
little speck and b. find......330 *y*
outward view of b. or of**. 61 *f*
Blenheim–dog of B. birth.... 20 *d*
Bless–b. him, also, that he...562 *e*
bless the gude mon, gin he.537 *a*
b. the hand that gave......60 *p*
b. the while the bright-eye.454 *b*
fast until he bless thee.... 16 *h*
God b. the man who first...562 *e*
God bless the king.........533*m*
God bless the regent........535 *k*
God. b. us all that's quite..533*m*
heaven bless thee ! thou*... 36 *v*
Jove bless thee, master*... 60 *t*
none whom we can bless∥..566 *e*
old man, God bless you....457 *i*
once b. our human ears**... 94 *k*
pain can't b. heaven quits..150 *h*
sober brow will bless it*....522 *c*
to bless him, if he can......276 *f*
to bless the thing it loves..360 *k*
to gaze in his eyes, and bless483 *e*

with none who bless us‖....566 *e*
Blessed-aiming at the b.‡....491 *a*
alone is b. who ne'er was...349 *s*
and I bless'd them unaware 60 *n*
blessed again to hold.......224 *i*
b. are the horny hands of††.667 *b*
b. be agriculture! if one....424 *o*
b. dwell in th' Paradises....463*m*
b. is the man that hath not.521 *j*
blessed with temper whose‡592 *v*
chief among the "b. three" 86 *i*
dejected while another's b.‡588 *i*
had blessed one's life with.620 *e*
half part of a blessed man*376 *t*
is a blessed place........... 57 *g*
nor what God blessed once.101 *b*
O! b. with temper whose‡..658 *j*
on sech a blessed cretur††.657 *j*
or bless'd with little‡.......256 *n*
virtuous have already been.474 *b*
what the blessed do above.298 *t*
what may, I have been b.‖.483 *j*
when b. none but such as.. 62 *a*
Blessedness-b. dwells in the..463*m*
blessedness of being little*. 6*w*
dies in single blessedness*.293*w*
Blesses-b. his stars, and.....368 *t*
heaven b. humble earth....111 *o*
he b. heav'n for what its...525 *e*
which love most blesses....219 *l*
Blesseth-it b. him that gives*382 *p*
Blessing-a b. on the Rhine§..532 *d*
adversity is the blessing... 60 *k*
as a blessing or a curse§....318 *v*
blessing that money cannot.295 *t*
blessing undesired by.......271 *b*
debt being a public blessing142 *v*
doth boast thy blessing**..393 *e*
every blessing known in life368 *i*
expectation makes a b......189 *o*
God bless (no harm in b.)..533*m*
health is the second b......295 *t*
heaven's blessing thinks... 91 *h*
in b. others bless'd‡....... 60 *q*
life, like every other b.....348 *f*
prosperity is the b. of the.. 60 *k*
pull a blessing on thee....382 *k*
steal immortal blessing*....335 *e*
to us a national blessing....142 *u*
with a blessing every glade.544 *n*
Blessings-amid my list of b.. 60 *v*
a world of earthly b. to*....588 *o*
b. are plentiful and rife.....536 *o*
b. be with them and¶.....481 *g*
blessings for curses*....... 86 *x*
blessings light on him that.561 *a*
blessings star forth forever 60 *l*
b. they enjoy to guard.....526 *c*
b. which a government.....482 *s*
for blessings ever wait on.. 60 *o*
heavenly b.without number 32 *o*
how b. brighten as they.... 60*w*
such b. Nature pours.......413 *s*
Blest-always to be blest‡....308 *l*
blest be y-e man...........183 *t*
blest is he who crowns in..338*w*
blest with thee, long nights.693 *p*
it is twice blest*.... .. ..382 *p*
kings may be blest, but Tam630 *v*
mortals always to be blest. 60 *j*
seeming blest, they grow... 13 *b*
smiled, and he was blest...654 *p*
spot of earth supremely b..304 *f*
the blest to-day is as‡...... 60 *s*
views supremely blest‡....425 *a*
Blew-blew soul-animating¶.. 61 *j*
cared not how it blew.....182*m*
Blight-b. of life—the demon‖.596 *c*
ere sin threw a b. o'er the..136 *v*
treason, like a deadly blight608 *j*
Blighted-they are oft b......307 *q*
Blind-a blind bargain........494 *e*
a b. man killed the parson's.451 *s*
always represented as blind332 *a*
and blind of light..........563 *h*
and dazzles, to blind......538 *g*
be to her faults a little blind658 *n*

b.among enemies O worse** 61 *e*
b. councils of the guilty....695 *n*
blind fortune pursues......768 *q*
blind my een wi' tears......591 *e*
b. his soul with clay†.......402 *g*
blind their understandings.713 *p*
blind to former as to‡......206 *x*
blind to hear him speak*...483 *q*
blind zeal can only do harm.797 *r*
but love is b. and lovers*....362 *q*
Cupid blind did rise‡.......360 *h*
everybody in love is blind..723 *v*
eyes to the blind...........620 *i*
fortune never seems so b...768 *s*
gaze an eagle blind*........362 *j*
hour of blind old Dandolo‖. 9 *f*
Hylas should become blind.178 *d*
love must needs be blind...357 *o*
make their children blind*.107 *c*
more believe old Homer b..478 *u*
none so b.as they that won't553 *o*
none so b. as those that will 61 *b*
one horse was blind¶...... 20 *r*
owl more blind than a lover376 *g*
owl that with eye is blind.. 52 *k*
own stronger errors blind..230 *y*
tell your poor blind boy.... 61 *a*
that is strucken b. cannot*. 61 *h*
the learn'd are blind‡......342 *j*
there's none so b. as they.. 61 *i*
though she be blind........255*w*
thou wast blind before....274 *c*
unbelief is blind**.........626 *p*
we are blind with tears....592*m*
winged Cupid painted b*...363 *v*
Blinded-b. by avarice, they..678 *h*
Blinder-nature made them b.†642 *t*
Blindfold-walk through b....151 *j*
Blindly-man b.works the will.766 *o*
Blindness-beauty or all b. I..472 *b*
b. to the future! kindly‡...151 *n*
only in our blindness......333 *k*
our b. is a dark profound.. 8 *t*
Blinds-it blinds the eyes....456 *i*
prejudice blinds us.........490 *j*
Bliss-all he knows of bliss‖...518 *g*
and love with bliss........582 *l*
beyond the b. of dreams**.162 *o*
b. in possession will not last 61 *s*
b. is the same in subject or‡ 61 *t*
bliss of men below. ....276 *l*
bliss through eternity......276 *g*
bliss was it in that dawn¶.. 62 *b*
bowers of bliss conveyed....85 *l*
but not bliss, create.......287 *q*
certainty of waking b. I**...61 *r*
cuckold lives in bliss*......328 *e*
excells all other bliss......385 *f*
find that bliss which only.. 61 *n*
gain the coast of bliss......539 *a*
happiness thou only bliss.. 61*m*
hath every bliss in store...358 *k*
have but a shadow's bliss*.549 *s*
how exquisite the bliss..... 8 *f*
hues of bliss more brightly 61 *o*
human bliss to human woe. 38 *d*
in mutual and partaken b.** 35 *n*
island of bliss! amid.......327*m*
is the bliss of solitude¶..... 62 *c*
it was the bliss within.....654 *p*
lights to eternal blisse.....538*w*
makes the sum of bliss... 34 *r*
no greater b. then such to be 62 *a*
only bliss of Paradise. .....293 *b*
own selves our bliss must..293 *a*
place the b. in action some‡ 61 *u*
plays a flame of bliss.......334*m*
relations mingle into bliss..304 *r*
second bliss in joy.........261 *r*
simplest b. the millions of. 61*w*
some place the b. in action‡.342 *j*
substantial never-fading b.148*m*
tears of bliss among it......219 *j*
tender tie on earthly bliss.. 62 *d*
there is such real bliss....131 *e*
there's a b. beyond all that.376 *f*
the sum of earthly bliss**..506 *k*

the way to b. lies not on beds 61 *v*
thou art a soul in b. but I*.. 8 *i*
thou source of all my bliss.484 *n*
three-cornered smile of b..564 *j*
throned in highest bliss**..173 *b*
'tis a bliss to die‡......... 61 *p*
'tis virtue makes the bliss.632 *c*
unending is this bliss the.. 61 *l*
virtue only makes our bliss‡337 *u*
vital principle of bliss......295 *s*
we every bliss must gain... 61 *q*
where ignorance is bliss....314 *h*
which attained the higher b.483 *t*
whose eccho is heaven's b..489*w*
winged hours of bliss have.307 *j*
with Socrates for bliss..... 93 *h*
youth dreams a bliss on this671 *q*
Blissful-sure to find..........663 *a*
Blisters-b. on the tongue.....457 *b*
name blisters our tongues*626 *k*
Blithe-no lark so blithe as he.110 *b*
Block-changes with the next*433 *b*
chip of the old block...... 77 *r*
chippe of the same block.. 89 *a*
stoop to the b. than these*.489 *l*
Blockhead-b. bit by fleas.....322 *s*
blockhead rubs his‡......251*aa*
b.'s insult points the.......328 *q*
b. with melodious voice....455 *s*
bookful b., ignorantly read‡581 *b*
no man but a blockhead....428 *p*
why blockhead! he goes....426 *o*
Blocks-b. are better cleft....251 *b*
Blood-all the b. within me§..359 *t*
and ride in blood*.........689 *a*
and welt'ring in his blood..388 *d*
are cold in blood‖..........356 *u*
beats with his b. and trust‡402 *g*
beauty fires the b.......... 34 *k*
b. and revenge are*......528 *t*
b. hath been shed ere now*.403 *q*
blood hath bought blood*..184 *t*
b. in their dastardly veins.512 *u*
b. is a juice of rarest......756*m*
b. is nipp'd and ways be*..546 *h*
blood is the base of all......132 *d*
blood is thicker than water.496*m*
b.more stirs to rouse a lion* 5 *t*
blood of all the Howards‡...670 *s*
b. of Old Brown's offspring.640 *i*
blood of the sun as he......239 *b*
blood shed then so pure....756 *i*
blood speaks to you in my*665 *r*
b. stuffed in skins is British 368*w*
b., though it sleep a time...403*m*
blood to the rose...........216 *i*
blood was thin and old....329 *c*
blood which was shed......216 *i*
b. will follow where the....527*m*
charming your blood with*562 *v*
cleanse the tainted blood...275 *g*
clear bubble of blood.......247 *f*
cold b. each mean detail....146 *o*
conduits of my blood froze* 12 *b*
curdled the blood..........231 *o*
descended of a gentler b.*..387 *t*
devise laws for the blood*..592*w*
doctors cure by letting b...518 *a*
drink my blood as I drink..142 *b*
drop of manly blood........358 *e*
eloquent blood spoke in her 25 *n*
felt in the blood¶..........210*w*
flesh and b. can't bear it...311 *b*
flesh and blood so cheap...484 *q*
flutters in b., and panting‡. 54 *g*
freeze thy young blood*....209 *q*
frenzy's fever'd blood......212 *d*
glories of our blood........207 *n*
guiltless of his country's b.201 *d*
had sown in your blood....374 *a*
him with the cry of blood¶.640 *s*
his blood inclined to mirth*524 *d*
His blood, 'tis said, down... 55 *k*
his country's blood........284 *s*
in fraternal blood.........283 *e*
in his sacred blood*.......284 *a*
I'll not shed her blood*..... 36 *x*

violet's beautiful blue......217 c
why does thy nose look so..582 p
wi' its unchanging blue.....231 g
Bluebell-bluebell to the rose.245 f
frail bluebell peereth over†.233 a
hang-head bluebell.........223 h
wild bluebell is the.........223 i
Bluebells-large b. tented....218 n
ring, bluebells, ring........228 h
ring bluebells, ring.........539 r
Bluebird-b's. warble know....248 c
meadows piped the b.§.... 43 e
whither away, b. wither.... 43 f
Bluebirds-have contracted 43 d
Blueness-breath and b. is....248 p
Bluer-Psyche, b. far are.....194 f
Blue-stocking-a b-s. is the...796 c
every b-s. will remain......796 b
sagacious blue-stocking... 81 q
Blunder-frae monie a b. free.421 h
in men this blunder.........103 m
youth is a b., manhood a... 9 l
Blundered-have b. into......463 u
she b. on some virtue.......630 k
Blunt-with the b. whetstone.505 d
Blunted-fear it should get...652 s
Blush-a blush in the midst of. 62 q
a b. is no language.........62 n
and b. to give it in.........555 s
a wife I need not b. to show.644 q
before green apples b.......542 q
b. and cry 'guilty'*........106 n
b. and gently smile.........218 a
blush, as much to stoop....422 h
blush, as thinking their*....335 e
beautiful as woman's b.....222 b
blush, happy maiden........333 o
blush of bashfulness‖...... 62 i
blush to find it fame‡ ......202 l
blush to give it in......... 16 f
b. to see you so attir'd*.....211 p
cheek the blush alone‖.... 62 j
do not b. to wish it so.....464 f
every b. that kindles...... 62 s
false accusation blush*....320 m
flower is born to b. unseen.420 w
friendship's well-feigned b.‖ 62 h
girls b. sometimes, because. 62 f
I had to blush for you......178 g
men b. less for their crimes.756 n
not accustomed to b.......756 o
perceive whether I b. or*... 63 a
ready with a blush*........ 62 t
shame ! where is thy b.*...551 m
the b. is beautiful ....756 p
the blush of Even¶........221 e
the sudden b. devours.... 62 f
yet will she b. here*....... 63 d
Blushed-b. as he gave it in...419 v
b. like the waves of hell‖.... 62 q
have b. yourself to death..464 f
he b. and blushing with*... 63 c
Miss frown'd and blush'd...375 k
ne'er b.unless, in spreading.630 k
saw its God and blushed...648 p
seen its God and blushed...649 c
water saw its God and b.....649 b
Blushes-beat away those b.*. 62 u
blushes : all is safe.........741 b
blushes mock the crimson. 56 c
come, quench your b. and* 62 v
lovely maid with blushes.. 62 e
nicety and prolixious b.*... 63 b
outblushes all the bloom... 35 t
reflect back her blushes....242 h
suffused with blushes......250 o
the man that blushes is not 63 f
the rising b., which her.... 62 o
who blushes at the name...468 t
Blushing-blushing in pride..243 r
b. is the color of virtue.... 62 p
blushing kiss the beam he..401 c
blushing like the morn**...376 d
blushing with him wistly*. 63 c
marks upon a b. face..... 62 l
pretty her b. was and†..... 63 e
religion, blushing veils her‡521 s

saw a youth blushing...... 62 m
skies yet b. with departing‡544 j
Blusterer-b. to the fight......239 p
Blustering-a blustering band.443 c
Boar-a boar which my friend.177 k
boar, being badly fed. .....179 h
wild boar is often held.....734 a
Board-a school,his b. a shrift*589 o
fool or flatterer at your b. .642 v
sees round his board.... ..595 a
turkey smokes on every b.. 94 f
uttered at our mirthful b..519 f
Boards-all the b. did shrink..641 b
each day his b. were fild....309 i
turbots dignify my boards‡213 m
Boarding-school-b-s. belle's...628 f
Boarding-schools-in b-s. may.455 s
Boast-and make no b. of it*..342 p
any one make a boast of it. 16 a
apter to despond than b....427 s
b. if she weds unbeloved....578 g
b. themselves most of their..95 q
can boast sincere felicity...110 n
couldst thou b., O child of..594 o
he lives to build, not boast..320 e
howe'er we b. and strive...657 c
is an empty boast‡.........154 q
man can b. that he has trod.396 o
my boast through time....276 g
not anything to boast of.... 15 m
of thee I b. great empire...117 r
O vain boast*..............207 a
such is the patriot's boast..468 n
veil the matchless boast....452 r
with lilies boast and*...... 36 y
Boaster-will this b. produce.747 e
Boastful-b. of her hoard ....303 q
Boasting-where b. ends......273 m
Boasts-boasts of his descent.677 k
pouring b. from his little... 43 g
Boat-a rotten carcass of a b.*552 t
b. seems sharpening its keel 63 j
drive the b. with my sighs*592 k
leaky b. on a sea of wisdom 66 d
my boat is on the shore‖...604 k
one b. hard rescued from...350 b
swiftly glides the bonny b. 63 g
Boatman-b., come, thy fare..141 r
Boats-brings in some boats*.256 r
little boats must keep near.498 r
some hoisted out the boats‖552 d
Boat's-crew-a famish'd b-c.‖.641 a
Boatwise-and b. dropped o'..405 p
Bob-stood to bob for whale.. 18 f
Bobolink-b.! that in the..... 43 l
the crack-brained bobolink. 43 m
Bobolinkon-there blew a b... 43 k
Bobolinks-five b. laughing... 43 j
the b. are singing out of.....43 n
the b. from silence rouse... 43 n
Bodes-croak b. me no good....54 s
Bodice-the bodice aptly laced 36 f
Bodied-and softly b. forth‖...596 d
Bodies-and exercise their b.. 14 m
as b.perish through excess‡653 s
ask not bodies (doomed....267 i
bodies soft and weak and*.660 c
cover the friendless b. of... 56 e
deposed b. to the ground*..139 t
in their bodies, force*......273 f
puny bodies of men....... 689 r
save our deposed bodies*...285 r
two bodies with one‡......260 w
two seeming b. but one*....262 k
with two seeming b. but*...627 n
Bodily-I've all but riches b..642 d
Boding-infected house b to*. 55 d
Bodleians-labours to these B.344 v
Body-a faultless body and‡..385 q
a feeble body weakens the.780 g
age and body of the time*..633 p
a man's body and his mind.372 x
as was her sweet bodie... 35 v
away from the dead b......521 v
be absent from the body... 2 t
bear from hence his body*.285 o
beasts by his body......... 38 u

beauty of mind and body..723 e
bites and blows upon my b.*546 g
b. and material substance.. 64 n
body and soul like peevish.378 f
b. did contain a spirit*..... 13 x
b. is assailed by the strong.706 c
b., the mind and the heart. 9 a
body to the earth*.........139 u
body to their lasting rest*.. 45 f
carry his body hence. .....636 l
cleanness of body was ever. 99 e
commanding part of the b.504 cc
daily work of b. or mind**.667 d
even from the body's purity 88 k
exercise is to the body.... 515 t
follow'd my poor father's*.659 d
for all my body's moisture*591 p
go, soul, the body's guest...572 a
gravity is a mystery of the.780 f
has in his whole body.......280 t
his body couched in a*.....112 e
his body to that pleasant*..138 n
I know not of her b. till I... 37 m
in body and in soul can bind362 h
indisposition of body.......879 a
in the body of his mistress.495 t
joint and motive of her b.*339 z
leaving his body as*........107 b
less than mind and body... 19 c
like little body with*.......116 a
little b. lodged a mighty‡..385 t
make less thy body hence*.593 n
make the charmed body††.384 w
man is of soul and body...372 u
may be old in body but can.672 b
means to make the body*..496 t
mind in a sound body......293 i
mind that makes the body*386 g
mind to suffer with the b.*.321 t
mine arms about that b.*..363 p
moist unpleasant body.....513 d
my body's friend.........721 d
not b. enough to cover his..386 k
of the soule the b. forme...572 h
or hoop his body more*....126 f
patch up thine old b. for*.. 11 n
presence of b. came to be.. 2 t
say her body thought..... 25 n
she wears that b. but as one660 v
short of His can and body.326 a
sickness broken body...... 22 b
soule do from his b. sever..316 s
supports the body too.....307 c
the b. bigge, and mightely.616 h
the body charms, because.. 38 b
the body of a dead enemy..764 m
the body's delicate*........259 f
the Egyptian's body.......221 a
they act in a body.. ....427 e
this b. is not a home.......722 d
thy husband commits his*..377 p
till heart and body and life.144 w
to adorn my body*........205 h
weary b., longing for repose561 d
what hides the b. oft the... 23 n
whose body nature is and‡.411 v
whose b. other ladies well. 37 n
winna let a poor body......359 p
with a b. filled and vacant*.526 p
Boggle-mind begins to b. at..464 c
Boggles-diversified with b...213 t
Bohea-'twixt reading and b‡.849 o
Boil-the vulgar boil, the‡....431 t
Boiling-to a b. pot flies come.507 o
Boils-b. and plagues plaster* 1 i
b. pure gold o'er the.......130 v
Bold-a bold bad man........ 84 u
a warrior so b. and a virgin.359 s
be bold! first gate ....119 c
bold in the practice of‡.....440 p
bold man that first eat an..168 v
bold of your worthiness*...438 g
bold, quick, ingenious*.... 90 p
do b. things in a quiet way.656 e
in that freedom bold¶......259 i
fortune befriends the bold.497 dd
fortune helps the bold......689 f

lowlier droop their boughs.618 *b*
'mongst b. pavilion'd ......567 *c*
on lofty boughs to build... 49 *r*
our bed of b. is built.......617 *j*
stooping boughs above me.239 *d*
the bare b. are sighing ....544 *o*
the sheltering boughs§....662 *q*
when the sappy boughs ...609*m*
Bought–because you b. them*559 *t*
b. it with an hundred* ....279 *f*
b. with nothing but with...361 *s*
but is not bought§.........359 *y*
fidelity b. with money.....700 *d*
God's own image b. and...560 *i*
is b. endlesse renowne..... 351 *e*
life is not to be b. with‡....347 *y*
names were to be b.*......524 *p*
never to be bought‡........293 *q*
Bounce–comes our master B.422 *g*
Bound–b. in earth, in sea, in*.344 *f*
bound me to thee...... ...259 *g*
mark, without a bound....459 *k*
shall Death be bound‡......268 *b*
too small a bound*.........13 *x*
wherewith we are darkly‖..587 *p*
Boundaries–had b. in old time 78 *t*
Boundary–a b. between the‖..560 *r*
Boundary–line–b–l. between...588 *a*
Bounded–b. o'er the swelling.445 *s*
b. by the St. John's.........469 *u*
Boundless–b. as the sea* ....364 *h*
b. in magnificence and.....577*m*
sources of wealth be b.....389 *b*
Bounds–b. his narrow'd reign.369 *o*
b. of freedom wider yet†....454 *i*
from vulgar b. with‡........283 *l*
He fills, He bounds‡........275 *p*
partitions do their b........653 *a*
pass'd the flaming b. of....415 *o*
stepping o'er the b. of*....389 *i*
to due b. confined‡.........386 *b*
Bounties–nature pour her**.630 *a*
Bountiful–b. blind woman*...272 *h*
Bounty–b. had not eyes*.....343 *g*
b. is beyond my speaking..594 *t*
daily owe the b. of thy.....382 *k*
fed by the b. of earth.......424 *c*
for his b. there was no*..... 41 *s*
for what its b. spares......525 *e*
his former bounty fed......319 *l*
kindest b. of the skies...... 60 *e*
largest b. may extend*.....365 *e*
large was his bounty and.. 41 *l*
my b. is as boundless as*..364 *h*
open hand scatters its b..... 95 *a*
those his former b. fed.....388 *d*
Bourbon–Bourbon or Nassau.183 *q*
Bourn–bourne from which...689 *q*
bourne of time and place†..268 *j*
from whose bourn*........268 *h*
Bow–accompanied by his b..103 *e*
better is to b. than breake.496 *f*
bid kings come b. to it*.....569 *v*
b. of cupid will lose.......723 *g*
b. our heads before thee¶..486 *z*
b. that guards the tartar....399 *g*
b. to any save to the God*..489 *l*
b. too tensely strung is....504*ff*
b. which hath two strings.511 *i*
every dew-drop paints a b.†154 *h*
from the Tartar's bow*....294 *u*
had two strings to my b....511 *e*
has two strings t' his bow.485*m*
have two strings unto our..507 *i*
huntress of the silver bow.397 *o*
like the aërial bow‖......... 33 *s*
many strings to your b.....509 *u*
radiant b. of pillared fires.. 29 *n*
rather to bowe than breke.503 *u*
straining breaks the bow...739 *f*
the bow is bent.............205 *p*
two strings to a bow....... 87 *i*
two strings to my bow.....701 *h*
two strings to one b.......305 *x*
unto the b. the cord is§....375 *q*
when he draws his bow....662 *c*
Bow-bell–sound of B-b.......499 *p*

Bowed–bow'd to its idolatries‖317 *s*
Bows–aid of Moorish b. and..683 *a*
b. you to morning's holy*..670 *n*
penning b. and making.... 422 *b*
Bowels–b. of the harmless*...121 *v*
b. of ungrateful Rome*.... 33 *g*
far into the b. of the land*.640 *d*
gnaws the bowels*........157 *f*
their b. full of wrath*.....639 *t*
Bower–born in a bower......322 *k*
bower of roses by.........242 *n*
cliff a narrow bower...... 219 *q*
into the pleached bower*..231 *e*
jasmine b., all bestrown...232*m*
rising from thy b. of green.235 *e*
Rose sat in her bower.....243 *o*
rosy b. beside a brook..... 355 *l*
shadowy woodland bower.. 71 *h*
sun through the b. peeps...561 *f*
thy bower is ever green.... 44 *r*
will keep a b. quiet for us.. 34*w*
Bowers–amidst these humble.307 *t*
autumn in his leafless b....545 *e*
b. a flood of light ....390 *o*
crouching 'midst rosy b....522 *q*
fills the air and leafy b.... 51 *e*
fragrant spirits of the b....232 *n*
from fair Valchusa's bower.530 *c*
heaven's happy bowers....241 *k*
in scented bowers.........216 *n*
in Twit'nham bowers, and.532 *o*
lodg'd in thy living bowers.610 *q*
softly o'er the bowers......563 *q*
they their silver b. leave... 17 *a*
to the bowers of bliss...... 85 *l*
woven its wavy bowers†...231 *f*
Bowl–fill up the b. then, fill..162 *f*
give me a bowl of wine*...649*w*
give me a bowl of wine*...650 *a*
his b. that sparkled........138 *b*
in a b. to sea went wise....251*w*
inspiring b. made eloquent.751 *q*
the b. between me and††...544 *f*
to drain the bowl‡.........211 *h*
trusted that the flowing b.326 *e*
what ask you for the b.....457 *i*
with my friendly bowl†....517 *j*
Box–Arabia breathes from‡..447 *s*
b. where sweets compacted.540 *q*
in a wrong boxe...........499 *y*
Boxes–account of empty b.*.441 *e*
Boy–age 'twixt boy and .....574 *j*
a second boy...............672 *u*
beat forever like a b.'s.†... 673*m*
b. have not a woman's*....551 *s*
b. of five years old serene..277*m*
b. stood on the burning....301 *h*
b.'s will is the wind's will§.646 *j*
give to your boy, your.....357*w*
I call myself a boy......... 91 *b*
increase in valor, O boy....686 *s*
lad of mettle a good boy*... 83 *r*
lines of my boy's face*.....381 *n*
lovely living b. my hope....88 *t*
love is a b, by poets styl'd..356 *j*
my b. has done his duty....163 *g*
O lord! my b., my Arthur*..90 *o*
see my boy again*.........268 *e*
some dreamy b., untaughts§.90 *c*
than when I was a boy......314 *j*
the b. that minds the mill..542 *i*
'tis a parlous boy*......... 90 *p*
when I was a tiny boy .....89 *r*
who would not be a boy‖...671 *u*
within which dwells a b....683 *p*
would I were a b. again.... 90 *a*
you hear that b. laughing..340 *q*
Boyhood–b.'s friend hath....260 *v*
for b.'s time of June....... 91 *d*
fruit loved of boyhood....267 *a*
of boyhood's years........673 *b*
the b. of the year†.........541 *i*
Boyish–even in our b. days...673 *n*
Boys–as flies to wanton b.*..277 *u*
boys, apes, braggarts*.....558 *x*
b. flying kites haul in their.573 *n*
boys must not have the.... 10 *e*

b. who being mature in*....475*w*
claret is the liquor for b....649 *l*
like little wanton boys*.....273 *d*
three merry boys are we...557 *a*
votive train of girls and b.‖.533 *f*
wanton b. that put coppers.328 *p*
wooing in my boys......... 90 *j*
Bracelet–b. of the truest*....485 *a*
Bracelets–b. to adorn the....536 *o*
braids and bracelets‖......211 *b*
with amber b., beads*...... 24 *i*
Brackish–b. with the salt of..603 *l*
Bradshaw–b. bullied in a.....432 *r*
Brae–primrose down the b....216 *o*
Braes–among thy green b.....530 *a*
b. o' Balquhither...........117 *k*
run about the braes........100 *p*
see the braes of Yarrow¶..529 *q*
simmer blinks on flowery.542 *c*
the braes of Balloch........144 *j*
ye banks and b. o' bonny..530*m*
Brag–beauty is nature's b.**. 35*m*
brave Spanish soldiers b....484 *b*
left this vault to brag of*...350 *g*
Braggart–b. shall be found*..122 *h*
knows himself a braggart*.122 *h*
Braggarts–b. and prince of... 43 *g*
Braggeth–ill-husbandry b....424 *l*
Brags–b. of his impudence..428 *l*
brags of his substance*....103 *r*
Brahmin–the B. talks of..... 15 *a*
Braid–tangled in a silver b†..577 *g*
Braided–once b. for me......292 *c*
'twas a thing to be braided.291 *f*
Brain–and burning brain....335 *x*
blind life within the brain†.489 *u*
books the children of the.. 68 *j*
bounded in a shallower b.†.642 *b*
b. gets as dry as an empty.476 *n*
b. is the citadel of the......726 *o*
b. may devise laws for*....592*w*
brain of this foolish*.......341 *c*
brain too finely wrought...596 *g*
children of an idle brain*..160 *v*
each busy brain creates its.160*m*
fire enough in my brain††..315 *a*
fumes of it invade the b... 29 *s*
heat-oppressed brain*...... 25 *g*
his b. which is as dry as*...421 *j*
it turns the brain like cat..456 *i*
long is the calm b. active..792 *f*
madness in the brain...... 17 *g*
out of the carver's brain...430 *q*
poet's heart than brain ...296*w*
polish our brain............795 *g*
press the brain a little.....205 *n*
productions of the brain...161 *h*
schoolmasters puzzle their.649 *g*
should possess a poet's b...479 *a*
stirrings of the brain of it.522 *a*
the warder of the brain*...381 *p*
very coinage of your b.*...315 *j*
visions of a busy brain.....159 *k*
whatever comes from the.. 80 *e*
written troubles of the b.*.441 *c*
Brains–and excise our b.....454 *d*
blew out his b. down in.... 20 *q*
brains were out the man*..124 *a*
brains with care*..........279 *c*
busy care draws in the b.*.562 *i*
empires in their brains††...385 *x*
if rack his brains he can...129 *f*
in the brains of men.......129 *f*
steal away their brains*...326*m*
strains from hard-bound b.‡480 *h*
unhappy b. for drinking*..326 *i*
when the brains were out*.403 *q*
Brake–b. them to our faces..267 *f*
bread and brake it......... 92 *j*
from the b. the whirring‡.. 54 *g*
scurvy face in it, brake....112 *r*
Bramble–b. of the brake....223 *l*
Brambles–sleeps on b.......163 *f*
Bramins–flow'r, which B. say.591 *d*
Branch–a green b. swinging.540 *n*
Branches–bald and leafless...611 *j*
branches are of an. .....114 *p*

close, uncrowded branches .236 *j*
decked once its b. with ...615 *i*
faithful are thy branches§.614 *h*
it braunches rough.........220*m*
naked b. make a fitful......394 *j*
rippling through thy b.††..612 *q*
storm through his b...... .615 *n*
that thy dark-waving b.‖..615*m*
the b. downward bent§.....647 *o*
their b. spread a city...... 54 *h*
their giant branches toss'd.459 *q*
their green branches shoot.610 *q*
they say its branches hide.618 *o*
thy b. ne'er remember.....613 *l*
topmost b. can discern†... 616 *q*
Branching–b. so broad and**.613 *i*
Branchless–b. were the‖......325 *o*
than yours so branchless*..306 *s*
Brand–distaff—not the b.‖....109 *e*
parts us shall bring a b.*..108*m*
the horseman's crooked b..635 *p*
Brands–those he brands to..537 *o*
Brandy–are fou o' brandy....101 *d*
b. nothing "extenuate".649 *k*
glass of brandy and water.649 *h*
hero must drink brandy...649 *l*
sipped brandy and water...162 *e*
to taste a little brandy.....482 *a*
Brass–as well in b. as he has.550*m*
clods of iron and brass**..430 *j*
durable than b. or stone.... 12 *r*
evil manners live in brass*. 84 *c*
more lasting than brass....396 *q*
stronger guard than brass.633 *x*
the summoning brass... . 323 *n*
this thy wall of brass‡......106 *d*
walls of beaten brass*.....350 *o*
was ever writ in brass......550*m*
Brat–the stolen b. be known.595 *e*
Bravado–gasconade and b....643 *c*
Brave–a b. man's country...731 *b*
a b. man will yield to a ...800*bb*
a brave soul is a thing..... 70 *l*
Alonzo the brave was the..359 *s*
ask for a brave soul.......800*w*
behold the b. oppressed‖... 69 *k*
b. any imaginable peril....588 *e*
brave deserve the fair.......69 *y*
b. find a home in every....680 *e*
b. love mercy, and delight.121 *g*
bravely is not therefore b.‡ 70 *q*
brave man is he who can... 70 *e*
brave man is not he who....208 *n*
brave man seeks not....... 69 *o*
brave man struggling‡.....206*w*
b. men are brave from the.756 *q*
b. men ought not to be. ..675 *o*
brave men were living‖.... 69 *j*
brave men would act.......208 *h*
b. to camp 'midst rock.....165 *d*
bridge in the brave days... 70 *d*
but be gentle as brave......116 *j*
combat even with the b.....443 *g*
coward and the brave......135 *k*
defying it that the brave...761 *k*
difficult to the brave and...800 *r*
fears of the b. and follies..348 *d*
fortune favors the brave...680 *q*
fortune favors the brave...702 *y*
fortune favors the brave...800 *e*
God helps the brave.......756 *r*
God Himself favors the b..680 *d*
home of the brave........214 *a*
hopes of living to be b.**..170 *q*
how sleep the brave........468 *i*
in the brave days of old...627 *k*
intimidates the brave......290 *g*
misery tries brave men....727 *e*
no man can be brave who..680 *b*
o'er the councils of the b...608 *j*
song of the brave..........756 *s*
so that my life be brave*...347 *u*
strong, the b. the virtuous.355 *b*
sword the b. man draws.... 70 *a*
that enviest the brave....703 *q*
the b. and bold persist.....680 *f*
the brave live on..........121 *n*

the brave love mercy and.. 69 *r*
the b. make every clime....803 *c*
the brave man chooses††...622 *n*
the b. man indeed calls....756 *t*
the brave man may fall....800*aa*
the combat deepens........636 *g*
there's a brave fellow§.... 70 *c*
those who b. its dangers§..460 *d*
'tis more b. to live than... 70 *f*
to arms! to arms! ye brave.637 *i*
toll for the brave....... ... 69*m*
torturer of the brave.......523 *c*
truly brave, when they‖.... 69 *k*
truly b. who can endure....680 *c*
what's b. what's noble*.... 70 *k*
whoever is b. should be a.. 70*m*
Bravely–press b. onward... .674 *n*
the work goes bravely on..581 *o*
Braver–a b. soldier never*...444 *b*
Bravery–double change of b.* 24 *i*
true bravery is shown by... 70 *b*
upon malicious bravery*...326 *f*
Bravest–appal the b. soul...577 *u*
b. are the tenderest.. 444 *p*
b. at the last she levell'd*..583 *p*
was discipled of the b.*.... 70 *i*
with the bravest mind.‡.. 373 *q*
Bray–he'll bray you in a..... 27 *i*
Brazen–be this thy brazen...685 *a*
Brazier–be a b. by his face*..195*w*
Breach–clos'd the breach....208 *s*
more honor'd in the b.*....127 *l*
once more into the breach*.639 *l*
Bread–a crust of b. and‡....167 *p*
art is indeed not the bread.755 *f*
ate his bread in sorrow....569 *a*
beg bitter b. thro' realms..444 *t*
bitter b. of banishment*.....33 *h*
bread and beefe kept in....309 *i*
b. in independent state....339 *k*
bread is the staff of life....496 *n*
bread which strengthens...431 *r*
brown b. and the gospel is.538 *t*
children ask for bread we..281 *j*
Christ, the living bread....449 *q*
cramm'd with distressful*.526 *p*
crust of b. and liberty‡....344 *b*
crust of brown b. and a pot.166 *d*
cut the b. another sows‡...279 *b*
cutting bread and butter...366 *u*
far to seek thy bread..... 44 *b*
government for bread......281 *i*
grossly, full of bread*.....403 *s*
halfe a loafe than no b.....496 *e*
half-penny worth of b.*....326 *l*
He took the bread and. ... 92 *j*
honest bread is very well..593 *t*
I have eaten his bread.....357 *h*
is daily bread to thousands.440 *t*
is the reward of virtue b.‡.632*aa*
leaven, the b. of heaven....166 *a*
loaf of b., the walrus .....166 *k*
met with home-made b......304 *a*
no b. and butter of mine...317 *t*
not give the b. of life......450 *k*
offers b. with the other....691 *h*
quarrel with my bread and.513 *q*
savor is of other's bread...765 *s*
smell of bread and butter‖. 89 *e*
some seek b.—no more ....526 *l*
that b. should be so dear...484 *q*
touch of holy bread*.......335 *d*
unsavory b. and herbs.....304 *b*
you pine for bread........476*m*
Breadth–for length and b... 427 *d*
the breadth of man†..... 85 *h*
Break–and b. it to our hope*.492 *r*
bending staff I would not..198 *q*
better is to bow than b.....496 *f*
bowe than breke is........503 *u*
b. an oath he never made..418 *u*
break, but not bend me....801 *a*
break but one of a........152 *p*
break, falter and are still.. 39 *t*
break her to the lute*......660 *d*
break, like a bubble, at a...622 *h*
break, you may shatter....242 *g*

but some heart did break†.354 *s*
crystal break for fear......181 *t*
heart and bids it break*...569 *u*
I'd b. her spirit or I'd b....874 *j*
it stands at break o' day....613 *n*
or I'd break her heart,....374 *j*
nothing b. our band but....375 *s*
partings break the heart‖..464 *t*
study to break it and not*..419 *r*
then be not poor, but b. it..485 *f*
to bend, not to break.......800 *v*
who shuns not to b. one*....419 *p*
Breakers–more dangerous b.‖459 *h*
wanton'd with thy b.‖......459 *d*
Breakfast–for her own b.....579 *f*
then to breakfast with*.... 26 *e*
Breakfasts–dresses for b..... 22 *s*
Breaking–day is near the b...138 *g*
heart is b. for a little love.537 *h*
that knows not breaking...562 *f*
while my heart's breaking.464 *q*
Breaks–b. a butterfly upon‡..537 *s*
breaks on the soul and by..343 *o*
b. there, and buries its.....459 *b*
heart that bleeds and b....344 *q*
man breaks not the medal.627 *i*
Breast–and in my breast†...249 *n*
and tear his helpless b....522 *q*
a sprig her fair breast to...618 *c*
breast-high, amid the corn.583 *t*
b. ne'er learn'd to glow‡....491 *b*
breast the wave of life.....135 *e*
breast this jewel lies......293 *z*
breast with wounds‖.......442 *x*
broad breast, full eye*... 21 *d*
bird with the scarlet b.¶... 56 *g*
crimson of thy breast..... 56 *c*
descended deep into the b..592 *t*
divinity within our breast.743*m*
drags a laboring breast†...100 *g*
drains the breast‖.........329 *l*
dwells in the b. of man.... 6 *e*
dwells in the human b....463*m*
eternal in the human b.‡...308 *l*
gather round an aching b..416 *q*
golden b. bedropped with.. 59 *q*
her fair young breast......232 *o*
her glowing breast........243 *k*
he rises in my breast§.....646 *k*
her open breast...........235 *o*
his true maiden's breast...362 *i*
idle wing and smirched b... 47 *j*
kindly breast will hold me.229*m*
lay upon her breast........243*m*
light within his own**..... 82 *c*
lives within the breast.....741 *r*
love which heaved her b...654 *p*
make a battery in his b.*..659 *q*
mood of a much troubled*.193*w*
nature's learned breast....410 *a*
of her snowy breast........ 37 *s*
on beauty's b. was seen...434 *l*
one lone human breast....597 *q*
one sucking on her breast..374 *c*
on her white breast a‡.....434 *k*
on his b. a bloodie crosse..518*m*
on the ether's invisible b...586 *a*
on thy b. to be borne‖.....459 *d*
or arm the' obdured b.**...467*m*
our breast the living fires..868 *a*
pity warm'd the master's..474 *a*
place me on that breast .. 241 *g*
pleasure on another's b....641 *r*
pure and firm breast......703 *r*
purpose in the glowing b..456 *a*
render back from out thy‖.442*w*
reside within my breast....759 *s*
ribbon round his breast....647 *u*
round its b. the rolling....102 *q*
scarce heaving her b......581 *n*
sober brownness of thy b... 55 *n*
sunshine of the breast....307 *v*
swells at my b. and turns..379 *u*
the bird of ruddy breast.... 55 *k*
the sunshine of the breast..590 *r*
thou tamer of the human.. 6 *r*
thy head upon my breast‖..334 *d*

to and fro in his breast§....359 *z*
to Chloe's b. young Cupid.355 *j*
to sooth a savage breast....405 *a*
trembles in the breast......488 *q*
with dauntless breast....201 *d*
within his own clear b.**..105 *r*
wonder of the breast......296 *q*
wrapt a breast‖.............. 23 *b*
Breast-plate–b-p. made of....227 *b*
Breasts–breasts of the rich...703 *c*
b. on whose strength they.640 *k*
in their celestial b..........420*m*
Breath–a b. may destroy.....668 *b*
a breath revives him‡.....272 *x*
age's breath is short*......673 *g*
although thy b. be rude*...319 *q*
and yielder up of breath*..608 *q*
ardent breath perfume....245 *f*
as long as thou hast b......600 *u*
at a b. and the flowers§....135 *p*
at everie little breath that.611 *k*
beard his breath did freese.546 *l*
be discharg'd of breath*....149 *q*
borne away with every b.‖. 96 *l*
breath and blueness is....248 *p*
b. can make them as a.....143 *g*
breathing thoughtful b.¶...661 *d*
b. may burst his bubble††..642 *z*
breath of a maiden's yes...359 *d*
b. of an unfee'd lawyer*....438 *w*
b. of Autumn's breeze.....246 *p*
breath of flowers........230 *i*
breath of flowers is far....216 *b*
b. of Heaven must swell.... 63 *i*
b. of life his nostrils drew‡.457 *f*
b. of some to no caress¶....221 *e*
b. of wind upon the hill‖....577 *o*
b. rides on the posting*....559 *b*
b. sanctifies the air.... ...233 *n*
breath which frames my...187 *a*
burns with its blistering b.394 *o*
call the fleeting breath.....134 *e*
ceasing of a sweeter b.‡...674 *x*
Cobham! to the latest b.‡..465 *q*
created by his breath.....370 *v*
deep, mouth-honor breath* 11 *r*
down and out of breath*..199 *p*
dulcet and harmonious b.*.383 *j*
every breath of eve that....100 *h*
fancy'd life in other's b.‡...202 *o*
fly away, fly away breath*.138 *p*
for the dying breath......134 *a*
genial night, wi' balmy b...541 *p*
good man yields his b......316 *n*
had borne my b. away....380 *b*
heaven's breath smells*.... 50 *h*
her breath in sudden sighs.394 *o*
his breath like cauler air... 81 *t*
his b. like silver arrows....546 *b*
his life a breath of God... 369 *q*
honey of thy breath*......139 *e*
hope's perpetual b.¶......272 *l*
if her b. were as terrible*..659 *t*
it taints the breath........456 *i*
keep my breath to cool... 153 *h*
kept his breath to cool his..554 *s*
lightly draws its breath¶... 91 *e*
low breath is gone from me.590 *c*
not flattered its rank b.‖....317 *s*
not yield a breath of thee..616*m*
or Cytherea's breath*......219 *s*
or out of b. with joy......647 *h*
shall be out of breath......628 *d*
sighed my English b.*.....319 *h*
spare your b. to cool your.504 *i*
such is the b. of kings*....665 *p*
suck my last b. and catch‡.187 *o*
summer's honey b. hold*..602 *p*
superfluous breath*.......589 *s*
sweet climate by my b.....459*m*
sweet is the b. of morn**...400*m*
take my breath from me*..583 *h*
takes the breath of men...654 *u*
the boldest held his b......553 *s*
the heaven's breath*..... 364 *g*
their departing breath.....248 *u*
the north wind's breath...134 *p*

the vital breath and die‡... 75 *s*
this life of mortal breath§.135 *r*
'tis b. thou lack'st, and*.... 7 *n*
twin-brother times my b.†.563 *n*
unfortunate, weary of b....135 *d*
voiceless, fragrant breath..165 *n*
waits for b. to reinspire him 57 *b*
which a b. has produced....668 *b*
whisper above thy breath§.135 *q*
with breath all incense‖....399 *q*
with his prophet breath ...233 *h*
with mine own b. release*.. 1 *c*
without a breath.........136 *u*
word had b., and wrought† 92 *s*
your b. first kindled the*...640 *g*
you the doors of breath*...139 *f*
Breathe–b. a little longer...136 *w*
b. freely does not mean....769 *b*
b. such divine enchanting*‡406 *c*
b. their words in pain*.....623 *n*
b. truth that breathe their*340 *b*
I breathe Heaven's airt... 318 *d*
I could b. on his wings.....599 *h*
slaves cannot b. in England.559 *f*
they b. truth that breathe*623 *n*
thoughts that b. and words.596 *t*
while I b. I trust in the.....799*m*
whilst I breathe I hope....799*aa*
worst that man can b.*....628 *n*
Breathed–and b. a perfume..611 *d*
b. with joy as they wander.391 *n*
hardly breathed for fear†.. 88 *j*
this day I breathed first*...350 *x*
Breather–chide no b. in the* 524 *e*
Breathes–b.rest and comfort§643 *r*
breathes scanty life........387 *n*
b. upon a bank of violets*..407 *k*
no life that breathes with†.141 *p*
who breathes must suffer..349 *s*
Breathing–b. grows more....646 *u*
b. of to-morrow creep§.....605 *j*
breathing soft and low.....135 *e*
for breathing in their faces*326 *j*
like the tyrannous b.*.....335 *n*
point of mortal breathing*, 73 *l*
through which its b.'s pass.647 *k*
watched her b. thro' the... 135 *e*
Breathings–her b. are not†...563 *l*
Breathless–hanging b.on thy¶469 *c*
Breaths–in thoughts not b....345*m*
Bred–are bred in a book*....516 *q*
power that bred it*........231 *e*
she is not bred so dull but*645 *n*
Breeches–b. cost him but a...454 *t*
Macaulay is like a book in..555 *c*
out of his breeches' pocket‖595 *d*
so have your breeches......484 *k*
the breeches and all that...432 *u*
the length of breeches....205 *e*
women wear the breeches..374 *k*
Breed–bear them, breed and. 15 *t*
breed for barren metal*....265 *l*
breed in the cat's eare.....500 *x*
hopes the scaly breed‡...... 18 *h*
breed and haunt I have*... 50 *h*
of a noble breed............ 20 *n*
this happy breed of men*..116 *b*
Breeder–and b. of all good*..603 *b*
Breeding–to show your b.....471 *u*
Breeze–battle and the breeze.214 *b*
b. came wandering from...646 *t*
breeze can find a tongue...394 *b*
breeze floats o'er thee.....235 *e*
b. from the northward free.445 *r*
breeze her sweets¶........234 *s*
breeze most softly lulling...238 *p*
b. of Nature stirring in his¶413 *i*
can flowery breeze........242*m*
chance sends the breeze... 73 *s*
come at by the breeze¶.... 46 *a*
cradle of the western b.....539 *p*
dancing in the breeze¶....226 *s*
far as the breeze can bear‖.444 *x*
flag to April's b. unfurl'd..636 *o*
he felt the soft b. at its.... 615 *k*
in the breeze nods lonely...229 *d*
it breaks at every breeze... 62 *d*

loved to breast the breeze..399 *p*
nod in the breeze..........232 *s*
on every passing breeze....134 *n*
refreshes in the breeze‡....411 *v*
ripple with the ruffling b...446 *a*
soft breeze from the west..545 *f*
soft the western breeze....542 *s*
sweet b. that makes the...609 *b*
the breeze is on the sea....625 *h*
the summer b. comes by...591 *j*
wafted by a gentle breeze..572 *p*
when the breeze was gone..405 *i*
Breezes–apple-blooms upon..391 *q*
as the twilight b. bless.... 561 *n*
ever-fanning b. on his way.543 *q*
March breezes blew keen...226 *q*
merry b. approach them....611 *n*
no fragrance in April b....391 *n*
thy first breezes bring....394 *q*
wandering b. touch them..404 *l*
when lulling breezes stir...612 *d*
wing of vernal breezes....221 *r*
zephyr's cool b. I burn.....599 *h*
Breezy–the b. call of incense.400 *a*
Breidablick–glimpse of B ...278 *i*
Brembul–sweete as is the b...223 *k*
Brere–grows upon a brere....220*m*
Brethren–amongst my b.*...412 *f*
father, mother, b., all in‡..375 *n*
men that they are brethren.403 *p*
three brethren named, the.555 *a*
Brevity–b. is the soul of wit*654 *b*
for brevity is very good....573 *k*
to please by brevity........178 *j*
Brewed–being well b., long...650 *e*
Brews–as he b. so shall he...162*m*
Briar–on the climbing briar.541 *n*
Bribe–b. the poor possession‡347 *y*
by b. nor by entreaty......802 *l*
the small discredit of a b.‡.437 *u*
too poor for a bribe......256 *h*
Bribed–brib'd the rage of‡... 95 *s*
Bribes–b. a senate and the‡..390 *b*
fingers with base bribes*... 70 *s*
Brick–and every man a b. ... 506 *a*
mass of brick, and smoke‖. 98 *c*
Brick-dust–b-d. man with....113 *e*
Bricklayer–became a b.when*439 *o*
Bricks–b. are a. at this day*..439 *n*
bricks, one after another...439 *p*
Bridal–b.of the earth and sky.131 *a*
is brightening to his bridal†161 *l*
our bridal flowers serve*... 75 *x*
when the b. party to the§.. 40 *c*
Bridal-chamber–come to the.134 *i*
Bride–became my glittering¶565*w*
blooming eastern bride.... 69 *p*
consent to be his bride.... 70 *n*
darkness as a bride*........139 *s*
fashioned for himself, a b..661 *a*
gain a soft and gentle bride.356 *k*
Germans call the wind's b..609 *g*
joy of some b. and the......578 *g*
so, like a bride............247 *c*
sometimes lovely, like a b.†570 *o*
the judge's bride might be.629 *q*
the wife is dearer than the.645 *c*
through the b.'s fair locks. 40 *p*
took the b. about the neck*385 *s*
who'll be my bride........228 *f*
Bridegroom–b.'s ear*.........376 *n*
Phoebus fresh as b. to his.. 29 *q*
Brides–brides of summer sun.233 *l*
lion woos his brides........662*m*
play uppe the b. of Enderby 39 *v*
rivals opium and his brides‖456 *f*
Bridge–arch of London B....267 *n*
b. that arched the flood....636 *o*
b. there was not to convey.362 *c*
broken arch of London B.. 95 *r*
cross the b. till you come§.497 *b*
Faith builds a bridge......198 *v*
February makes a b.... .. 390 *q*
golden b. is for a flying‖...518 *f*
looking for over the bridge.367 *c*
Peschiera when thy b.I.... 91*m*
praise the b. that carried..503*m*

How calm, how beautiful.. 71 *g*
in calm it glassed the......460 *o*
never felt a calm so deep¶.533 *a*
night is c. and cloudless§..416 *c*
no soothing calm is blest.. 31 *g*
now meekly calm, now.....449 *t*
remember to be calm in....675 *l*
seas are made c. and still..445 *o*
shall bring a kindred c....609 *b*
slumbrous calm are fled....470 *n*
so c. are we when passions.466 *b*
tracts of c. from tempest†..598 *b*
treacherous in calm and....603 *l*
where all was harmony‖....655 *h*
Calmer-c. moment would....674 *l*
Calmly-c. he looked on‡... 183 *l*
Calmness-c. best enforces...706 *i*
Calms-a pilot's part in c ...670 *w*
much the spirit calms as‖..520 *f*
powers by deepest c. are...485 *q*
Calopogon-bright the c......539 *r*
Calumniating-envious and*.602 *h*
Calumnies-c. against which.. 71 *m*
Calumnious-'scapes not c.*.. 71 *q*
Calumny-back-wounding c.*. 71 *p*
c. is only the noise of...... 71 *k*
calumny will sear virtue..* 71 *o*
honor aid, and c. deter....682 *t*
nothing is so swift as c.....681 *a*
reply to calumny and.....553 *q*
shalt not escape calumny*. 71 *n*
system of c., pursued...... 71 *l*
Calvary-Christ toiled up..... 55 *n*
Calves-quarters—and his c...430 *m*
Calvinistic-have a C. creed..521 *q*
Cam-Cam his winding vales‡530 *h*
Camadera-C.'s quiver.......221 *p*
Cambyses-new C.thundering‖115 *j*
Came-I came from God and..316 *j*
I came, I saw, I conquered.684 *p*
I c., saw, and overcame*...631 *j*
know she came and went††.634 *h*
the first who came away‖..311 *k*
Camel-Death is a black c....181 *s*
desert heard the c.'s bell‖..641 *a*
e'en the camel feels.......543 *h*
hard to come as for a c.*...154 *l*
Camomile-though the c.*... 224 *a*
wreaths of camomile......440 *l*
Camp-followers of the camp.751 *b*
from c. to c. through the*..639 *c*
here our camp of winter...547 *a*
Campagne-runs, the fair c...593 *c*
Camping-ground-eternal c-g.272 *w*
Can-if I can.............808 *w*
short of His can and body..326 *a*
the youth replies, I can....163 *n*
we can not, as we would...736 *m*
you can and you can't......158 *c*
Cana-when Christ at C's....649 *c*
Canary-cup of rich C. wine.649 *m*
Cancatenation-of...... 97 *a*
Cancel-c. and tear to pieces*.417 *c*
power to c. his captivity*..344 *e*
Candid-be c. where we can‡..873 *t*
be candid where you can....124 *t*
from the candid friend..... 72 *b*
Candidly-c. and constantly..798 *u*
Candle-bell, book, and c.*...594 *d*
candle of the Lord........539 *a*
did not see the candle*.....273 *g*
farthing candle to the sun.. 68 *q*
fit to hold a candle........112 *s*
game is not worth the c....797 *u*
here burns my c. out; ay*..151 *u*
hold a c. to light the mines.643 *c*
how far that little candle*.147 *d*
light a candle to the sun...352 *u*
light my candle from their.352 *e*
lights a candle to the sun. 251 *l*
light such a candle........212 *t*
modesty's a c. to thy merit.389 *f*
not worth the candle...... 14 *t*
out, out brief candle*......350 *r*
that is not worth the c......500 *z*
with a candle within...... 267 *d*
Candle-light-by yellow c-l.... 90 *t*

Candles-blessed c. of the*....577 *a*
heaven's pale c. stored......186 *t*
night's c. are burnt out*...400 *w*
their candles are all out*...298 *q*
when the c. are out all.....508 *z*
Candor-and candor in power.513 *h*
candor is the seal of a noble 71 *r*
Cane-lofty cane, a sword.....254 *n*
nice conduct of a clouded‡. 457 *k*
Canker-deadly as the c......622 *d*
eaten by the canker ere it*.362 *m*
loathsome canker lives in* 208 *l*
the canker which the trunk 763 *h*
the eating canker dwells*...143 *l*
the worm, the c., and the‖.. 9 *e*
Cankered-c. not the whole...230 *b*
Cankers-c. the whole estate..274 *o*
Cannibal-the name of c. flea.323 *a*
Cannibals-each other eat*....607 *j*
Cannikin-why clink the c....161 *u*
Cannon-c. to left of them†...640 *h*
even in the c.'s mouth* ... 444 *k*
fatal cannon's womb*......149 *q*
from roaring cannon .....134 *d*
of red-breathed cannon....638 *l*
the devlish c. touches*.....639 *v*
'tis better than cannon.....638 *h*
Cannon-ball-c-b. took off his.448 *t*
Cannon-balls-hard as c-b.....107 *j*
cannon-balls may aid ......267 *o*
Cannoneer-trumpet to the c.*639 *d*
Cannons-c. have their*..... 639 *d*
the c. to the heavens*... 639 *d*
Canons-religious c., civil*....639 *b*
Canopied-c. by the blue sky‖.557 *w*
thou art c. and clothed.... 44 *b*
with ivy canopied**........231 *b*
Canopies-the c. of costly*...563 *c*
Canopy-a rich embroider'd*..614 *f*
beneath a shivering c.....612 *d*
c. which love has spread...417 *p*
c. which love has spread...558 *f*
hung a canopy of state.....515 *k*
my canopy the skies*......412 *a*
string of her lawn canopie.324 *h*
Canst-what I am thou c. not.684 *e*
Cant-builds on heavenly c.... 93 *h*
can and you can't........158 *c*
c. of criticism is the most..125 *w*
c. of hypocrites may be the.125 *w*
of this stamp is the cant of.481 *o*
supplied with c. the lack... 85 *q*
Cants-c. which are canted in 125 *w*
Canvas-artisans on c. or in.. 28 *i*
canvas rot entirely away..446 *o*
Lely on animated canvas‡..447 *a*
the canvas glow'd beyond.. 28 *e*
Cap-a c. by night a stocking.. 23 *e*
cap of black neats' leather.180 *l*
cap of velvet could not§....291 *j*
fethers in his cappe........301 *g*
for a c. and bells our lives††102 *u*
green jacket, red cap......196 *p*
her cap, far whiter than... 24 *j*
Capable-c.of believing in God.316 *t*
feel capable of doing§......331 *d*
ingenious, forward, c.*..... 90 *p*
was capable of knowing....314 *l*
Capability-c. and god-like*..517 *r*
Capacities-c. of every kind..170 *m*
Capacity-assistance of.......681 *d*
capacity for joy admits....329 *k*
more capacity for love than‖ 78 *a*
thy c. receiveth as the sea*364 *l*
to my capacity*............364 *e*
Cap-à-pie-arm'd at point*....495 *r*
Cape-Andes to the cape.....649 *e*
Caper-provokes the c. which.129 *i*
Capers-c. nimbly in a lady's*252 *n*
Capital-a creation of active c.142 *v*
ask the patronage of c......339 *p*
c. of the orator is in the....462 *h*
c. solicits the aid of labor..339 *p*
Capitol-betray'd the C.....658 *a*
guardian of the capitol.... 54 *q*
Capitols-stood her c., and....268 *o*
Capon-and is equal to c. in... 54 *e*

the capon burns, the pig*..432 *d*
Caprice-knows no laws but...626 *m*
Capricious-c. than a reigning 236 *i*
gentle, sometimes c........558 *c*
petulant c. sects.........520 *d*
Caps-silken coats, and c.,and*24 *i*
the white c. of the sea§.....624 *s*
they threw their c. as they* 26 *p*
with their c. and shouts*..483 *p*
Captain-c. counts the image.520 *u*
good attending c. ill*......623 *f*
hear of Captain Wattle..... 78 *v*
honourable c. there drops*. 6 *v*
in the c.'s but a choleric*... 60 *i*
lost a good c., to make of..443 *m*
your captain calls to you...134 *d*
Captains-some of our city c..211 *a*
Captivate-c. her favorite fly.323 *j*
while they captivate.......325 *a*
Captive-c. good attending*...623 *f*
felt our captive's charms‡..631 *f*
Captivity-power to cancel*...344 *e*
sink in the soft c. together.355 *b*
Captures-till swoln with c... 54 *b*
Capulets-tombs of the C.....284 *k*
Car-and the gilded c. of day**585 *o*
seated in thy silver car....398 *a*
some hang upon his car....483 *e*
the bright track of his fiery*625 *m*
Carcass-a rotten c. of a boat*.552 *i*
Carcasses-c. bleed at the.....403 *l*
Carcassonne-see fair C....... 97 *r*
Card-conscience is a sure c..494 *j*
he's a sure card..........499 *h*
reason the c., but passion‡.349 *m*
Card-players-c-p. wait till††..285 *g*
Cards-an old age of cards‡...349 *n*
at cards for kisses.........360 *h*
c. were at first for benefits. 14 *q*
patience and shuffle the c..467 *b*
those of cards and dice.....269 *k*
yet neither spinnes, nor c..412 *r*
Cardinal-and, father C.,.I*...268 *e*
C. Lord Archbishop of.... 48 *a*
Care-a fig for c.,a fig for woe.111 *f*
age is full of care*........673 *e*
a load of splendid care....534 *o*
and every care resign .....358 *q*
and harass'd out with c....560 *j*
and still care not a pin‡....318 *i*
and with a care*..........210 *b*
appearance of c. is highly..575 *m*
begone, old care, and I..... 72 *f*
beneath the level of all c...378 *c*
beyond his love and care...276 *a*
brains with care*.........279 *c*
burthen of the nation's c...534 *q*
busy c. draws in the brains*563 *i*
care is no cure, but*....... 72 *i*
care keeps his watch in..*.. 72 *j*
care, mistrust, and treason*112 *e*
care of a large estate......739 *t*
care of the pence..........169 *t*
care that is entered once... 72 *d*
c. to our coffin adds a nail..341 *f*
care's an enemy to life*.... 72 *l*
care, whom not the gayest. 72 *q*
chief and constant care....312 *i*
death came with friendly c.182 *j*
did not care a button for it.498 *ff*
don't care most for those.. 80 *d*
doth most abound in care..555 *e*
doth the general care*......288 *r*
drudgery and care........667 *l*
finger on the lips of care§..416 *b*
from c. and from cash he is.110 *a*
from care I'm free........109 *x*
full of trouble and full of§.304 *c*
God's ever watchful care...233 *t*
good old age released from.647 *a*
half my care and duty*....311 *w*
hang sorrow, c.'ll kill a cat.569 *g*
happiness, and all our c....359 *q*
have a c. o'the main chance.525 *k*
His gracious c. to me and..510 *y*
His useful c. was ever nigh. 41 *d*
I c. for nobody, not I, if no.110 *b*

I'll care for nae body.......110 *e*
incessant care and labour*. 72*m*
I sae weary, fu' o' care...530*m*
killing c.and grief of heart*407 *f*
let this be all my care‡.....623 *c*
life devoid of c. a shadow... 57 *d*
little c. we; little we fear..615 *j*
looks my care beguiling....540 *e*
man's first care should be. 296 *k*
men of books assume the.. 68 *r*
mind set free from care...739 *b*
nature all her care she letts.412 *r*
neither cauld nor care ....268 *a*
nor care beyond to-day..... 89*m*
now drown care in wine....751 *r*
O earliest singer! O care... 49 *e*
of business, c., or pleasure¶648 *f*
old c. has a mortgage on... 72 *h*
old care, thee and I shall... 72 *f*
one for you shall care .....227 *f*
one is past, another care....72 *c*
pale my cheeks with care..661 *b*
past or coming void of care 51 *b*
perturbation! golden care*. 72 *n*
perturbation! golden care*.562 *p*
portion of the weight of c.§488 *k*
portion with judicious c....669 *x*
poverty, no smiling care....112 *o*
retreats from c., that never. 9 *t*
ride over c.'s coming billow339 *j*
sat and public care**.....153 *j*
so to me what care I...... 37 *t*
Sport, that wrinkled C.**..340 *t*
take care...............807*m*
take care of themselves... 281 *d*
take no care who chafes*..108 *d*
tells o' never-ending care... 48 *l*
the ambitious c. of men.... 10 *e*
their care and must be.....277 *g*
the ravell'd sleave of c.*...562 *u*
the restless pulse of c.§...568 *h*
too much c. distraught§...561 *p*
truce to earthly care§.....536 *q*
weedye crop of care........294 *i*
weep away the life of care. 72 *o*
we fond of toil and care...351 *r*
well and with a care* ..... 5 *u*
what care I how chaste..... 88 *c*
what c. I how faire shee be.661 *b*
where c. lodges, sleep will*. 72 *j*
while care forgets to sigh..615 *c*
whose preventing care‡....256 *n*
with me past care*........506 *z*
world is trouble and care. 347 *j*
your sex's earliest, latest c.629 *k*
you waite upon my care*..553 *f*
Care-charmer–c-c. sleep,.....561 *e*
Cared–lies one who ne'er c.‡..183 *p*
Careful–c. ere ye enter in....218 *o*
careful with fire............573 *n*
careful with words........ 573 *n*
Careless–c. and careful hands181 *t*
careless in the mossy.... 248 *p*
c. of the damning sin.......419 *a*
where she is carlesse lay'd.603 *o*
Cares–against eating c. lap** 72 *e*
all the cares of gain........ 9 *p*
all their cares beguil'd.... 14 *s*
and humble cares¶........272 *k*
and their attendant cares ..593 *d*
brought up to years with c.345 *j*
c. must still be double to...306 *c*
cares not a pin‡...........183 *p*
constant cares were to......409 *f*
earth where cares abound¶ 49 *s*
for light c. speak, when....554 *a*
he c. for nothing! a king....142 *b*
his cares dividing............ 16 *u*
if no one cares for me......318 *q*
is depressed with cares.....656 *l*
life's little c. and little pains346 *z*
light c. speak, great ones ..501 *i*
loves, and nobler cares¶....481 *q*
miser should his c.employ‡387 *k*
ne cares nor fretts.........412 *r*
no carking cares are there.433 *d*
not subdued by mortal c...370 *v*

O mortal c.insensate, what.779 *l*
one that cares for thee*... 311 *x*
prints of worrying cares....455 *j*
rich man's son inherits c.††.642 *n*
silken rest, tie all thy c. up.526 *e*
small c. of daughter, wife..304 *h*
the c., that infest the day§.415 *r*
their loves and cares......219*m*
waste them with vexatious 72 *g*
with no more cares to think 43 *k*
world of clouding cares.... 16 *o*
Care-wearied–c-w. man......595 *a*
Career–not quitting the busy.526 *g*
Caress–no caress invited¶...221 *e*
wooing the caress‖.........456 *f*
Caressed–critic, hated yet c.‖.124 *f*
titter'd, caress'd, kiss'd so.358*w*
Caresses–and worldly c...... 578 *g*
caresses and does not thrill.635 *f*
Cargo–groaning c. of despair.446 *f*
Carnage–c.and his conquests‖470 *d*
strife, and c.drear.........638 *s*
Carnal–rich a pearl for carnal621 *g*
Carnation–c. purple, azure**.224 *c*
carnation vine with lupin....219 *f*
Carnations–are our c.*......229 *f*
rhetoric of carnations ....448 *g*
Carnegie–Johnny C. lies here183 *s*
Carnivorous–man is a c.‖.....166 *i*
Caroling–thou should'st be c. 43 *p*
thy dower is thy caroling... 44 *b*
Carols–carols as he goes...... 88 *n*
carols right joyously and... 59 *f*
Christmas c. until morn§.. 94 *j*
familiar carols play§...... 94 *i*
games and c. closed the....625 *q*
Carousing–abroad,c. to his*..650 *b*
Carp–c. in scales bedropp'd‡.213 *l*
Carpenter–c.dresses his plank431 *j*
c. puts forth his hands.....431 *g*
c.'s known by his chips.....494 *g*
i‡ is some carpenter*.......431 *h*
why, sir, a carpenter*......431 *i*
Carpentry–c. within himself.431 *e*
Carpet–c. knights will make. 211 *a*
palm was the carpet spun..617 *b*
Carpets–c. every stitch of‖...368 *a*
Carriages–carriages he hath*439 *k*
Carried–has c. every point....744 *i*
Carrier–c.'s not commission'd448 *b*
Carrotty–Philænis you are c.175 *j*
Carry–carry all he knew.....342 *b*
Cart–drawn by the cart..... 28 *l*
now travers'd the cart......464 *t*
set the c. before the horse..508*hh*
Carts–set c. before the horses503 *b*
Carve–how c. way i' the life..466 *f*
run Orlando; carve on*.....659 *p*
Carved–c. for many a year...134 *q*
carved out of his domain.. 314*m*
c. this graceful arabesque§.617 *l*
c. with figures strange.....430 *q*
precious jewel carved most.476 *v*
Carver–out of the c.'s brain..430 *q*
Carvers–the carvers we; the..422 *a*
Casca–rent the enviousCasca*126*m*
Case–as the case stands.....495*aa*
the reasons of the case ....438 *d*
when a lady's in the case..656 *j*
wrapped up in his case††...285 *g*
your case can be no worse.439 *t*
Casement–at my c. sing¶..... 56 *i*
soul, from thy c. look......605 *f*
will out at the casement*...653*cc*
Cases–circumstances alter c.. 96 *r*
piled high with cases in my 64 *f*
Cash–from care and from c..110 *a*
the most by ready cash‖.. .70 *o*
Casket–when the rich casket 90 *l*
Casks–ten thousand c. forever649 *a*
Casques–full casques are ever572 *v*
Cassias–while c. blossom.....224 *d*
Cassius–soon as that spare C.*586 *r*
Cassock–in a thin silken c...543 *e*
Cast–elated or cast down....680 *v*
not cast aside so soon*.....461 *e*
Caste–stamps the caste of† ..373*w*

there is no caste in blood...587 *l*
Castle–from Sterling Castle.¶529 *q*
hung in the castle hall..... 94 *a*
man's house is his castle... .303 *l*
old lad of the castle*........659 *a*
the air-built c., and the‡...634 *l*
to him as his castle.........303*m*
Castles–beautiful castles in††315 *a*
build castles in Spain......496 *p*
build castles in the air......496 *q*
building c. in the ayre......499 *y*
earth castles and towers...668 *l*
my castles in the air........634 *k*
Casualty-force and road of c.*. 50 *g*
Casuist–Cupid is a casuist...276 *n*
Casuists-soundest c. doubt‡. 145 *u*
Cat–a cat has nine lives....656 *i*
a cat may look at a king...494 *h*
brain like cat in pan........456 *i*
breed in the cat's eare......500 *x*
c. in gloves catches no mice504*hh*
cat's averse to fish........278 *s*
cat will mew and dog*......152 *c*
cat would eat fish, and......504*ii*
cat would watch a mouse..503*kk*
far from mouse, or cat, or. 21 *l*
for my cat and dog 19*m*
hang sorrow, care'll kill a c.569 *q*
he'd na let a cat on the.... 537 *a*
I call a cat a cat............757 *o*
I never do swing a cat..... 19 *k*
monstrous tail our cat has. 19 *j*
never shunn'd the cat*..... 21 *n*
play with my cat who...... 14*w*
poor cat i' the adage*......122 *i*
room to swing a cat there.. 19 *k*
thou art a cat and rat...... 78 *i*
weasel nor wild cat will her 55 *k*
woman has nine cat's lives.656 *i*
Cats–c. of all colours black.. 19 *l*
confound the cats......... 19 *l*
when cats run home and‡.. 53 *d*
would rain cats and dogs..515 *e*
your courtly civet c. can‡..447 *t*
Catalogue–c. of common....515*m*
figure in the catalogue.....446 *p*
Catalpa's–c.'s blossoms flew.¶224 *e*
Cataplasm–no c. so rare*....441 *j*
Cataracts–beauteous queen..531 *e*
c. and hurricanoes spout*..578 *b*
Catch–c., ere she change‡....100 *a*
c. him once upon the hip*..528 *q*
c. me just at dinner-time†..480 *t*
catch old birds with chaff .509*aa*
fish, the worse the catch...656 *u*
object that the one doth c.*653 *z*
trying to catch me, Rufus...179 *h*
Catched–'ere they're catch'd.251 *d*
Catches–sang out of tune,....453 *e*
Catechism–so ends my c.*....306 *y*
Cateress-she,good cateress,**593 *f*
Caterpillars–c. and blossoms. 761 *b*
Caters-c. for the sparrow*...510 *s*
Cates-feed on cates,and have* 69 *d*
Cathay–a cycle of Cathay†...496 *d*
Cathedral–Gothic c. is a.....425 *i*
like two c. towers these§..617 *l*
span of some c. roof........425*m*
Cathedrals–men build as c... 77 *n*
Catholic–Roman Catholic.... 95 *r*
traveled mind is the c......606*m*
Cato–a vulgar Cato has......667 *l*
Cato, give his little senate‡ 26*m*
heroic, stoic Cato,‖......... 77 *t*
reputed; Cato's daughter*.659 *j*
Cattle–go and call the cattle. 530 *l*
mortal c. in a penfold......418 *t*
storm-pinched cattle lows..545 *i*
the cattle are grazing¶.....424 *s*
Catullus–C. scarcely has a‖..478 *l*
Caught–are ever c. by glare.‖369 *i*
I c. my heavenly jewel.....582 *j*
small flies were caught.....436 *o*
Cause–arms deserts his cause 69 *o*
as our cause is just*...... 72 *v*
breaks in her cause........344 *a*
c. and not the death that..374 *b*

SHAKESPEARE *; MILTON **; WORDSWORTH ¶; BYRON ‖; TENNYSON †; LOWELL ††; POPE ‡; LONGFELLOW §.

women have no c. at all‡...658 *i*
write the c. in dust........658 *t*
Charge-a c. to keep I have..572*m*
c., Chester, charge!........631 *h*
c. most innocent nature**..593 *j*
c. with all thy chivalry....636 *g*
conscious of his awful c. ...450 *g*
conscious of their charge..647 *h*
mothers what a holy c......402 *e*
to simplicity resigns her**.651 *e*
true is the charge, nor by..116 *p*
Charger-c. on the battle-field635 *p*
Charges-c. for a looking*....205 *h*
die to save charges........387 *f*
round their charges glide..574 *v*
Charging-and c. them years.600 *n*
Chariot-a fiery chariot borne   4 *n*
a golden c. in the midst.... 45 *e*
chariot wheels art curst....696 *l*
high in his c. glow'd the...583 *q*
off our chariot wheels......343 *a*
science moves the light c.. 678 *d*
Chariots-of brazen c. ray'd**637 *t*
of her c. and dresses .....578 *g*
our c. and our horsemen*..439 *l*
Charities-c. that soothe and¶.164 *v*
Charity-act a c. sometimes.. 86 *l*
a little earth for charity*... 86 *u*
charity and personal force. 85 *p*
charity buildeth up........336 *l*
charity is a virtue of the.. 86 *b*
charity itself consists in.... 87 *d*
c. itself fulfils the law**... 86 *w*
charity to all mankind..... 86 *a*
c., which renders good*.... 86 *x*
day for melting charity*... 86 *v*
did c. prevail, the press....435 *q*
hath a great charity....... 86 *k*
in charity there is no...... 86 *d*
mankind's concern is c.‡... 86 *s*
pity gave ere c. began......473 *u*
rarity of Christian charity. 86 *h*
sever love from charity*... 86 *w*
soft-handed charity........ 86 *j*
sweet Saint Charity††...... 86 *p*
sweet sake and charity††... 38 *n*
true charity, a plant....... 86 *f*
undo a Jew is charity .. ...329 *d*
voice of Christian charity.. 86 *e*
with charity for all........ 86 *n*
zeal then, not charity‡....674 *k*
Charlatan-he was no such c..643 *c*
Charles-empire of Charles V.483 *r*
navy of C. the Second......445 *j*
Charlotte-a love for C........366 *u*
Charm-a c. for every woe,..307 *i*
blest with that charm......304 *n*
charm but for a day........241 *j*
charm dissolves apace*....130 *s*
c. his pained steps over the.654 *h*
charm is strangely given...221 *n*
charm of earliest birds**...400*m*
charm that has bound......216 *c*
charm that lulls to sleep...264*m*
c. the interval that lowers.. 2 *r*
c. to stay the morning-star.575 *s*
for a c. as from God lulled..531 *n*
forbidden have a secret c.. 732 *l*
in man no charm can tame.538 *c*
kind as well as charm...... 34 *p*
life can charm no more.....403 *e*
like a mercury to charm...550 *h*
lust in man no c. can tame.551 *i*
mock a broken charm......596 *v*
musick! soft c. of heav'n..407*w*
music oft has such a c.*....407 *u*
music that would charm*l.408*n*
one native charm than all..411 *c*
poppy hath a charm for....238 *i*
power to c. down insanity..320 *v*
shall we charm the hours..393 *n*
sleep can charm the wise.. 563 *o*
soothing charm o'er all the. 51 *q*
such a c. in melancholy....379 *f*
sweetest charm of woman.. 71 *r*
the charm of woman†...... 85 *h*
this is the charm, by sages.112 *k*

what charm can sooth her.656 *o*
wondrous, witching c .....191 *s*
Charmed-charmed with the.409 *v*
from all that c. before..... 42 *i*
I bear a charmed life*......350 *i*
make the charmed body††..384*w*
Charmer-charmer sinner it‡.252 *f*
t'other dear charmer away.656 *k*
Charmers-like other c.‖..... 456 *f*
Charming-c. is divine*......473 *h*
charming your blood with*562 *o*
ever charming, ever new....410 *s*
he saw her c. but he.......389 *j*
so c. left his voice**......635 *c*
Charms-against whose c.*... 36 *p*
a heaven of charms divine‡ 34 *u*
April's c. are swept away .391 *p*
changes half their c. we‡...658 *g*
charms by accepting,‡.....645 *k*
c. her downcast modesty..389 *j*
c. strike the sight, but‡.... 82 *q*
doubting c. me not less....763*m*
fading charms of face...... 34 *h*
felt our captive's charms‡.631 *f*
gave its simple charms....244 *j*
grove but has its charms..609 *e*
image c. he must behold‡... 3 *b*
in charms that fix th'......117 *a*
music has charms to sooth.405 *a*
only teaches c. to last‡.... 82 *t*
own a sister's c., or hear‡..658 *j*
proof against thy sweet.... 26 *j*
resistless charms or§......662 *q*
rivers wove their charms..147 *x*
solitude, where are the c...566 *s*
spreads her c. in vain.....581 *v*
sweets I know, the c. I feel.166 *f*
the charms of sound.......572 *r*
thousand charms to show..258 *g*
thy charms improved......224 *j*
to rate her charms*......203 *w*
unite their charms to......294 *g*
will half your c. impair.... 60 *c*
Charnels-stone cover'd c... 527 *o*
Chart-c. of true patriotism.469 *v*
laid down in any chart§ ... 90 *c*
Charter-c. will henceforth...775 *j*
for the great charter...... 803*w*
large a c. as the wind*....344 *d*
Chartres-of C. much too‡...537 *u*
Charybdis-I fall into C.*...152 *k*
seek to avoid C. you fall..508*hh*
Chase-c. brave employments.666 *t*
c. the glowing hours with‖.599*m*
fame's glorious chase.....203 *e*
first the bloody c. began‡.. 87 *o*
long c. o'er hills, dales‖.... 87 *h*
made me seek the chase... 87 *l*
nose in piteous chase......592 *c*
race in shifting chase......460 *g*
roused them to the chase.. 54 *b*
youth beguiled the chase..155 *d*
Chasm-an horrid chasm..... 24 *a*
hands across the bloody c..482 *p*
Chaste-be thou as c. as ice*.. 71 *n*
chaste as the icicle*.... ...398 *v*
chaste as unsunn'd snow*.. 88 *d*
if she seem not c. to me.... 88 *c*
the fair, the chaste, and*..659 *p*
they who call'd her c.‖.... 397 *j*
what care I how c. she be.. 88 *c*
Chastened-c. down the‖.....191 *q*
c. from evil to good........374 *a*
Chastens-c. whom he loves.. 8 *j*
Chastisement-our c. or......582 *u*
Chastises-c. those whom.....512 *l*
Chastity-of honor which.. 87 *s*
clothed on with chastity†.. 88 *j*
Heaven is saintly c.**...... 87 *u*
ice of chastity is in them*.. 88 *g*
my chastity's the jewel*...88 *f*
sacred rays of chastity** .. 88 *a*
'tis chastity, my brother**. 88 *a*
woman has lost her c......688 *e*
Chat-I choose to c. where'er.113 *h*
Chatham-C.'s language was.486 *g*
Chatted-others to be c. with..66 *n*

Chattel-declared to be a......560 *a*
Chattels-my goods, my c.*..645 *o*
Chatter-c., c., as I flow‡.... 71 *e*
Chatterton-I thought of C.¶.481 *h*
Chaucer-corruption since C..665 *b*
Dan C., well of English....480 *p*
Chauntress-thee, c., oft the** 51*m*
Cheap-c. sitting as standing.507 *g*
flesh and blood so cheap..484 *q*
I hold your dainties cheap*644 *d*
ill ware is never cheap....500*m*
Cheaper-fool but at the c....142 *s*
Cheat-and but c. our ear... 41 *b*
being cheated as to cheat..497 *c*
c. thy Heart and tell her...569 *o*
consider life 'tis all a cheat.347 *h*
to cheat one's self........ 257 *q*
Cheated-let's not be cheated.251 *o*
likely to be cheated in....506*nn*
of being c. as to cheat.....475 *e*
Ravenna lately cheated....176 *b*
show let's not be cheated..144 *i*
wat ye how she cheated....144 *j*
Cheater-old bald c., Time....600 *t*
Cheating-knaves in c. fools..436 *s*
Check-as 'tis c. they prove.. 87*m*
check of such another day*.518 *d*
check to loose behaviour... 84 *w*
goodness dares not c. thee*626 *f*
yet clings with loving c....517 *a*
Checked-be c. for silence*...511 *s*
Checker-board-c-b. of nights.348 *i*
Checks-and c., and slays.... 348 *i*
thy friendly checks forego.105 *n*
Cheek-as hang on Hebe's **.383 *r*
bashful maiden's cheek....486 *u*
bear'st a cheek for blows*.122 *k*
before the cheek is dry....253 *k*
cheek all bloom‖...........399 *q*
cheek all purple with‖..... 33 *s*
cheek the map of days*...195 *z*
cloistered cheek as pale....234 *n*
down Virtue's manly c.....590 *n*
feed on her damask c.*....467 *u*
heaven in your cheek*....107 *e*
His changing cheek his‖... 34 *c*
hue of my fresh cheek.....327 *t*
in each c. appears a pretty*154 *v*
in my cheek's pale hue.....662 *j*
kemb'st the tuzzes on thy.457 *o*
language in her eye, her*..339 *z*
leans her c. upon her head*.364 *n*
mantling on the maiden's.. 62 *r*
might touch that cheek*...364 *n*
o'er her warm cheek and..358 *s*
one cheek, pushed out by..560 *q*
ornament of his c. hath*..458 *f*
pink with cheek of red.....217 *f*
rose growing on's cheek...360 *h*
rose on her c. is my joy....355 *k*
shows in her c. the roses‡.. 7 *t*
smiling c. proves more....874 *g*
tears down Pluto's c.**....557 *i*
that loves a rosy cheek....143 *e*
the roses from your cheek.673 *a*
upon the cheek of night*.. 37 *a*
upon thy cheek lay I this*.335 *t*
whiteness in thy cheek*....210 *d*
Cheeks-and in thy cheeks**.. 36 *t*
blood spoke in her cheeks.. 25 *n*
c. as fresh as rose in June.464 *u*
cheeks of the meadow......228 *c*
c. so rare a white was on...196 *e*
c. within his bending*......108 *t*
crack your cheeks! rage*..578 *b*
fresh tears stood on her c.*592 *e*
her cheeks like the dawn§.. 35 *d*
his little c. in their pure‖.. 30 *t*
his rawbone c. through....485 *q*
lean, sallow c., long chin..157 *j*
pale my cheeks with care..661 *b*
puffing his cheeks out.....462 *a*
rise in their fair cheeks*...589 *r*
ruby of your cheeks*......210 *h*
stain my man's cheeks*...591*w*
wet my c. with artificial*..145 *l*
Cheer-and make good c...... 95 *h*

chance to cheer thy sight..605 *h*
c. our dreams invaded.....228 *d*
cheer the hours away.....294 *g*
c. the poor man's heart.... 95 *c*
fling out with cheer.......214 *c*
go in and cheer the town*.147 *b*
let us be of good cheer††..388 *g*
nor cheer of mind*.... ....649 *w*
small cheer and great*.....644 *g*
that c. but not inebriate..186 *q*
to cheer but not inebriate..593 *b*
what man ! be o' good c.*..138 *l*
with festal cheer† .... 211 *s*
Cheered–c. up the heavy*....333 *l*
c. me as a lovely beam.....160 *o*
cheered up himself with... 88*m*
c. with thoughts of Christ.449 *q*
Cheerful–a c. word for me...493 *e*
c. and hopeful than to be.. 10 *b*
cheerful as the holly-tree.614*m*
c. at morn he wakes........ 88 *n*
c. look makes a dish a.....494 *i*
cheerful without mirth‖....655 *h*
heart a cheerful hour......295 *l*
he did with cheerful will.. 85 *q*
make to-morrow c. as‡.....592 *v*
of cheerful yesterdays¶....112*m*
to-morrow c. as to-day‡....658 *j*
whatever c. and serene....307 *c*
Cheerfully–look c. upon me*. 88 *s*
Cheerfulness–continual c...651 *f*
health and cheerfulness....295 *j*
no warmth no c...........395 *i*
Cheering–thinks no lamp so.576 *o*
Cheerless–c. over hills of...396 *j*
Cheerly–c. she loves me.....569 *j*
Cheers–cheers each part*....223 *g*
c. the sad, revives the old‖.648*m*
listen, and it c. me long§..647 *n*
Cheese–c. cakes dripping....176 *k*
digestive cheese and fruit.167 *d*
made of green cheese......251 *c*
moon was made of green...398*m*
not made of green cheese*.397 *h*
pippins and c. to come*....168 *g*
rather live with c. and*... 69 *d*
thick-walled c., the best... 21 *l*
Chemist–the chemist of love.358 *u*
the chemist's flame‡..... ..634 *l*
the starving c. in his‡.....425 *a*
Chequered–c. shadow*......549 *p*
Chequering–c. the eastern*..401 *b*
Cherish–heart must have to§.296 *v*
life let us c., while yet.....351 *r*
Cherished–c. by her child-like*164 *k*
c. in all our hearts.........469 *u*
cherished in slimy waters..114 *n*
c. still the nearer death*...138 *o*
c. thine image for years....671 *f*
ne'er so tame, so cherish'd*608*w*
Cherries–c. fairly do enclose.432 *l*
cherries grow that none....194 *l*
like to a double cherry*....627 *h*
make three bites of a c....501*dd*
Cherry-bloom–with c-b.......228 *o*
Cherry-blooms–c-b. will be...165 *j*
Cherry-blossoms–and c-b.....612 *l*
rain on cherry-blossoms....72 *a*
Cherry-bruises–pappy out of.545 *b*
Cherry-trees–blossoming c-t.§612 *k*
Cherub–c. contemplation**..109 *a*
c. who had lost his way††... 31 *n*
musical c. soar singing.... 48 *o*
Cherubs–c. well might envy‖. 31 *a*
Cherubim–the helmed c.**.... 16 *s*
was hatch'd a cherubim...182 *h*
Cherubin–young-eyed c.*.....576*w*
Chess-tables and some to c...211 *l*
you wish to play at chess..180 *k*
Chest–c. contriv'd a double..303 *r*
c. intercepts the truth.......740 *d*
c. or house is more than he.431 *e*
from time's chest lie hid*..602 *p*
has a whole chest full...... 48 *b*
Chester–charge, C., charge.631 *h*
Chests–c. containing ingots‖..389 *l*

Chestnut–a spreading c. tree§430 *h*
as will a chestnut in*......119 *s*
chestnut was ever the only*291 *t*
I see the chestnut letting..612*m*
Chestnuts–c. lavish of their††612 *n*
gathering tawny chestnuts.395 *d*
Cheveril–c. consciences that...105 *b*
Chew–noble friend, c. upon*.467 *s*
politicians c. on wisdom‡..482 *u*
Chewed–some few to be c.... 64 *c*
Chewing–c. the food of*......204 *b*
Chicken–I swear she's no c... 12 *g*
peasant to have a c. in....764 *b*
Chickens–count their c.......251 *d*
curses are like young c....496*cc*
would eat c. i' the shell*...168 *q*
Chid–c. their wanderings but 38 *l*
Chide–c. him for faults, and*524 *d*
c. no breather in the*......524 *e*
chide me not, laborious....222 *l*
if she do c., 'tis not to have*659*m*
to c. him from our eaves*..557 *p*
which he seems to chide...129 *l*
with sorrow chide us not*.. **ſ** *r*
Chides–c. himself for longing.528*w*
Chiding–better a little c.*....524 *c*
c. of the winter's wind*....546 *g*
c. streams betray small....572 *v*
Chief–brilliant c. irregularly. 27 *k*
c. among the "blessed...... 86 *i*
chief from the war........165 *o*
chief of a thousand........283 *j*
hail to the c. who in.......681 *g*
of bard and chief.........245 *z*
one must be chief in war...534 *c*
returns like a chief from...165 *o*
vain was the chief's‡.......480 *j*
Chief-justice–c-j. was rich.... 81 *p*
Chiefs–c. contend only for...686 *a*
c. contend 'till all the prize‡ 13 *o*
c. who no more in bloody‡.650 *r*
Chieftains–so many high c... 74*m*
Chiel–c.'s amang you taking.435 *k*
Child–c. of our grandmother*658 *u*
a happy Christian child.... 93 *v*
always to be a child.......719 *f*
a mighty mountain child..532 *e*
and a wine-bred child.....495 *k*
and scared eye, like a child. 55*m*
art the fondest child.......242 *k*
as yet a child, nor yet a‡...429 *l*
a two years child¶.........246 *q*
behold the c. by nature's‡.. 90 *k*
been any Christian child*..188 *l*
bidding her earliest c. arise.391 *j*
boast, O c. of weakness....594 *o*
but a rascal of a child......758 *t*
calm as a cradled child in..460 *l*
change of joy–not a child.. 91 *b*
child is father of the man¶. 91 *g*
c. of misery, baptized in...387 *r*
child of mortality, whence.537 *e*
c. of suffering, thou may'st 484 *p*
child of the sun, refulgent.543 *g*
child of trial, to mortality..619 *f*
child the moment when it‖..329 *l*
child to hold his tongue.....89 *j*
child will not rest till it.....327 *r*
fancy's fondness for the c..427 *n*
happy c.! the cradle is still.758 *u*
has grown a child again....676 *i*
he the new world's child...340 *h*
honest man is always a c...712 *h*
hover o'er my happy child. 30 *r*
impatient child that hath*. 24 *f*
it is a dream, sweet child§..634 *c*
kingdom of God to a child.. 89 *q*
kiss the child asleep.......646 *u*
laugh like a child as they..239 *h*
let thy lowly child.........488 *a*
lie down like a tired child.. 72 *o*
like a three years' child...353 *p*
lose his child's heart ....286 *y*
love is a pouting child.....561 *k*
make me a c. again, just for599 *j*
mother may forget the c...379 *o*
not a child: I call..........91 *b*

O c.! O new-born denizen§. 31 *k*
old man is twice a child*... 11 *k*
seen a curious child¶......353 *u*
show'st thee in a child*....319 *v*
simple c. that lightly¶..... 91 *e*
simplicity, a child‡........183 *n*
smiles on her slumbering c. 31 *b*
soothed its child of air.....203 *r*
spare the rod and spoil the.356 *j*
spirit of a child that....... 91 *c*
spirit of a little child...... 91 *a*
that knows his own child*.500*aa*
the burnt c. dreads the.....504*gg*
the child of the skies. ....115 *d*
the eldest child of sin......570 *t*
the training of a child‡.....402 *h*
to have a thankless child*..319 *s*
to strangle the child.......327 *r*
weeps like a tired c. who...392 *d*
whilst that the c. is.........455 *k*
Childhood–about a holy c. as. 16 *e*
a day to c. seems a year...599 *o*
a place in childhood that...402 *b*
bring childhood's flower*..227 *l*
c. has no forebodings...... 89 *l*
c. is the sleep of reason....758 *r*
childhood shows the man** 90 *h*
childhood's lisping tone....547 *a*
childhood's lovely face.... 90 *s*
c. waits with weary.......605 *n*
freshness of childhood§....542 *n*
from childhood's hour.....155 *f*
give me my childhood again 8 *n*
how my c. fleeted by.......380 *s*
in the days of childhood.... 40 *l*
out of childhood's days....780 *v*
piece of childhood thrown. 88 *u*
prayer which c. wafts‖.....655 *n*
purple he from c. wears....626 *e*
tear, down c.'s cheek......591 *j*
time of my childhood......242 *n*
weary c.'s mandragore.....560 *o*
womanhood and c. fleet§...672 *r*
Childish–age c. makes, they..754 *n*
attract my childish view...230 *h*
dim with childish tears¶...573 *h*
store of childish drops*....592 *h*
sweet childish days¶. ... 91 *f*
was a childish ignorance...314 *j*
Childless–c. and crownless‖..387*m*
c. cherubs well might‖..... 31 *a*
Childlike–cherished by her*..164 *k*
patient and simple and c-l.§651 *a*
Childly–it is the c. heart: we..17 *b*
Childness–varying c. cures*.. 88 *r*
Children–about her own c....427 *l*
air-woven c. of light.... ...781 *b*
airy hopes my children¶....565*w*
an' all us other children....578 *p*
benefit their c. by severe...683 *q*
better to keep children....683 *r*
bind your children to you..691 *o*
but, c., you should never...466 *c*
children are the keys of.... 90 *v*
children ask for bread we...281 *j*
c. fill the groves with......395 *d*
c. follow'd with endearing. 7 *v*
c. gath'ring pebbles**..... 90 *g*
c. have neither past nor....758 *s*
children kind and natural*.116 *a*
children know, instinctive.. 90*m*
children laugh loud as they 89 *o*
children of an idle brain*..160 *v*
c. of men! the unseen.....519 *k*
children of night...........159 *d*
children of one mother....308 *x*
children of Summer‖.......221 *b*
children pluck, and††......228 *e*
children's arms round the..304 *i*
children should know*.....155 *y*
children to pick and sell....247 *f*
children we of smiles...... 76 *q*
children were no more§.... 90 *b*
children with their play....346 *t*
c. with the streamlets sing.392 *e*
dutifulness of children.....683 *o*
each one wishes his children684 *a*

is all that I claim..... ....379 w
Claimed–that may be c...... 69 g
Claiming–then claiming......595 e
Claims–smile at the c. of†...418 o
Clamour–and c. moistened*..592 f
  an hour in clamour*......381 m
  a quick and merry c..... ...454 b
  big in c. came there in.... 565 q
  c. keep her still awake*....377 m
  c. of the crowded street.§.. 81 o
  with the c. keep her*......377 m
Clapper–me the purple c.....225 f
  tongue is the clapper*.....556 y
Clapper-clawing–one another 156 w
Claps–still with after claps..386 w
Claret–c. is the liquor for.... 649 l
  swim in good claret......213 p
Clarion–pen became a c. §....471 r
  sound the c. fill the fife ...350 c
Clarity–the hillsides with c..583 r
Clashed–they never clash‖d..374 n
Clasp–eager to c. hands......482 p
Clasps–gold c., lock in the*.. 68 e
Classic–classic literature is..516 l
  of a few classic tragedies..329 a
Classical–his c. reading is...516 m
Claw–beak and added claw... 43 p
  sharp-edged tooth and c.... 17 k
Clay–all are made of clay§...449 o
  a mortal made of clay*....203 w
  any shape like soft clay....682 s
  blind his soul with clay†....402 g
  Cæsar dead and turned to*.152 b
  c. and clay differs*........154 s
  clay at thy feet............241 h
  clay will be remoulded....182 c
  foolish-compounded clay*.341 c
  formed of common clay§... 35 c
  from our dull clay these...129 f
  gilded loam or painted c.*.524 s
  he took the clay for the....449 l
  mere clay wherein the††...151 b
  o'er-inform'd the tenement.571 j
  of such quicksilver clay‖..317 n
  porcelain c. of human kind.418 b
  porcelain of human clay‖..370 h
  temper'd clay was made...182 h
  this c., well mixed with§..449 o
  thou art moist and soft c..683 i
  though all are made of c. §.184 q
  was moulded out of clay§..452 l
  woman! mere cold clay....654 u
  yet, thy moist c. is pliant..449 k
Clean–as clean as you can†..188 h
  c. your finger before you..496 x
  grew more c. and white.....333 t
  keep clean be as fruit...... 99 h
  keep clean, bear fruit......289 t
  wash her clean again*.....290 m
Cleanliness–c. is indeed next 99 i
Cleanly–leave sack and live*. 99 g
Cleanness–c. of body was.... 99 e
Cleanse–c. the stuff'd bosom*441 c
  cleanse the tainted blood..275 q
Cleansed–occasionally c.....492 b
Clear–always c. and serene..651 f
  as clear and as manifest as.495 v
  as clear as a whistle......495 w
  c., more mildly bright......633 h
  the coast was clear......504 jj
Clearness–c. is the ornament.791 l
Clematis–the wild c. comes..224 l
Clemency–c. is the surest....787 q
  mildness and clemency....683 l
Cleobulus–the Lindian C.....650 p
Cleon–Cleon dwelleth in a...483 q
  C. hath ten thousand acres.483 q
Cleopatra–if the nose of C... 75 m
  with less than Cleopatra...357 w
Clergy–and an Arminian c...521 q
  their c. with lustrations.. 52 l
Clergyman–and that good†...525 l
  God preaches, a noted c....450 i
Clerical–arms of the clerical. 63 u
Clerk–goes the clerk........450 d
Clethra-flower–white-spiked..250 ♭
Clever–c. men are good but... 78 ¢

its clever, but is it art..... 28 l
let who will be clever......280 h
we can be more c. than....759 q
Click–click of the trowels....439 p
Clients–c.s' causes hereafter.436 q
  to make clients lay........460 u
Cliff–as some tall cliff that..102 q
  cliff a narrow bower......219 q
  grow I from the c., sweet..367 a
  high cliff's ragged edge....229 s
  on this wild cliff unseen...531 e
Cliffs–could ken thy chalky*.578 a
  hoar c. the loud sea-waves.327 m
  laughs inly behind her c...327 l
  there on the cragged cliffs. 54 b
Climate–but every c., every§.551 v
  sweet c. by my breath.....459 m
  writ in the c. of heaven§...405 w
Climb–c. upward to what*...152 f
  fain would I climb........209 j
  fearless minds c. soonest*..119 j
  hard it is to c. the steep...200 d
  he knows how to climb... 190 p
  how I may climb to heaven.539 c
  shall not climb to heaven..297 k
  Sinais c. and know it not††.555 x
  the shining angels climb... 94 o
  to c. steep hills requires*..582 i
  'twas strong to climb......231 r
Climber–the c. upward*..... 14 d
Climbing–and c. shakes his.. 48 n
  down, thou c. sorrow*.....569 q
  weariness of c. heaven......399 b
Climbs–c., like airy acrobat.643 l
  climbs the upland lawn....246 f
  climb'st the skies..........399 e
  climbs up the desolate blue.398 k
  devil c. into the belfry§....450 r
  he climbs, he pants, he.... 12 u
  he that c. the tall tree has..582 d
Clime–cold in clime are cold‖.356 u
  in every clime ador'd‡.....489 a
  in every age and c. we see..442 a
  in some brighter clime.....345 n
  our tongue is known in ....468 s
  poet in a golden c. was born†481 z
  soft as her c., and sunny‖..655 t
  sweet golden clime.........245 n
  thou art is clime for me....321 p
  welcome in every clime....120 f
Climes–humours turn with‡. 75 r
  to traverse c. beyond the.. 172 e
Cling–c. closer, closer, life...375 s
  c. closer heart to heart.....375 s
  closest cling to earth......218 p
Clings–man c. because the...358 c
Clink–clink the cannakin....161 u
  tinsel c. of compliment†....103 i
Cloak–a c., which altho'coarse685 k
  better than a cloak§........360 a
  face be like a wet cloak,*...341 b
  in his sad-colored cloak....396 a
  martial cloak, around him..444 s
  thine old cloak about thee. 23 s
  thoughts and all, like a c ...561 a
  with his martial c. around..142 c
Cloaks–reputations, like......524 i
  wise men put on their c.*..189 n
Clock–clock does strike by...341 q
  c. hath strucken twelve*...432 d
  clock upbraids me with*....434 r
  c. worn out with eating time 9 m
  count the slow clock‡......349 o
  finger of a clock............203 n
  hour by Shrewsbury c.*....199 p
  varnish'd clock that.......303 r
Clocks–fairy c. strike their...217 k
  like c., they must be.......492 b
Clock-work–goings of this...372 c
Clod–has earth a clod.......284 n
  lifeless c. outstretched lie. 87 f
Clods–cumbrous clods that ..542 a
  not one of nature's c.......311 s
Clog–c. the last sands of life‖.464 h
Cloister–chanted from his c.. 49 e
Cloistered–flown his c. flight* 42 j
Cloisters–peculiar walks, c... 14 m

walk the studious c. pale**352 l
Close–at every c. she made,..557 c
  souls sit c. and silently.....587 s
  still at every close........227 j
Close-buttoned–c-b. to the...370 r
Closet–closet and his church.273 r
  do very well in a closet... .373 l
  one by one back in the c..348 i
Cloth–according to her c....511 d
  O' the cloth of gold........223 q
  speech is like c. of Arras...574 i
Clothe-I c. my naked villainy*631 p
Clothed–c. on with chastity†. 88 j
  spiritual may be c. and....587 f
Clothes–brushers of ....126 c
  butcher in his killing c.....430 p
  c. are all the soul thou hast 22 l
  c. are after such a*........205 k
  c. but winding-sheets for..140 w
  c. herself with leaves......615 l
  clothes ought to be our.... 23 d
  coarse clothes are best.....107 h
  cold according to clothes...498 k
  dead friends' clothes......255 a
  he made those clothes*....455 c
  kindles in cloathes........ 23 t
  know'st me not by my c.*..455 c
  meat, fire, and clothes‡....642 s
  she wears her clothes as.... 24 k
  shows his c.! alas! he shows. 23 n
  this man is his clothes*.... 24 g
  tombs are the clothes of...396 p
  when he put on his c....... 41 j
Clothing–c. the palpable and.400 s
  proud of new c. springeth.. 52 f
  whose c. is humility......310 p
Cloud–a c., and a rainbow's.. 392 n
  a cloud lay cradled near....100 h
  a cloud takes all away*.....364 k
  and the flying cloud.......351 c
  angry night c. swells with..395 l
  an houri had rolled a c.....463 p
  a rainy c. possess'd the†.... 95 g
  a sable cloud turn forth**.. 99 s
  behind the c. the starlight..309 d
  choose a firm cloud before‡100 a
  c. answering unto cloud§.. 598 k
  c. mantled around thy feet§531 f
  c. nor speck nor stain......417 r
  c. of ashen gray and gold§.624 r
  cloud of wayward marl*....660 f
  cloud that near us hangs§..380 l
  cloud that rises upward†...100 g
  c. that will not pass away..545 o
  a curse is like a cloud...... 60 l
  dispel this cloud the light‡. 61 c
  fast flying cloud...........490 w
  from every stormy cloud,..395 n
  from out the selfish cloud..641 j
  gone and a c. in my heart†.148 v
  in mist or cloud on mast... 42 f
  in such a c. dost bind us...457 c
  ladder leaning on the c.§...672 q
  like a summer's cloud*....661 n
  Mercy stood in the c. with..382 i
  mist and cloud will turn§.. 605 d
  oft the cloud which wraps. 8 e
  see a c. that's dragonish*..587 i
  see yonder little cloud§.... 99 q
  should some c. pass over...631 c
  spher'd in a radiant c.**...352 k
  strips of c. began to vary..584 r
  swan pause in her cloud†.. 58 n
  the August c. suddenly....394 d
  the flying c.,the frosty†.... 41 f
  thickest cloud earth ever..101 b
  weary the cloud falleth.... 75 f
  wounded the thick cloud..396 k
  yonder solitary c. floats§... 99 p
Cloud-built–amid thy c-b....585 h
Cloud-capped–c-c. towers*..634 m
Cloud-continents–c-c. of.....585 e
Cloud-cup–gold o'er the c-c.'s130 v
Cloud-folds–c-f. of her§......565 b
Cloudlets–and dainty c......543 p
  c. are lazily sailing........ 99 n
Clouds–after c., sunshine....803 p

SHAKESPEARE *; MILTON **; WORDSWORTH ¶; BYRON ‖; TENNYSON †; LOWELL ††; POPE ‡; LONGFELLOW §.

all its clouds incumbent....367 a
and clouds are low........186 r
are angels veiling clouds*..659 c
behind the clouds the sun§.514 u
between the gathering c. ...609 g
black c. are driven away....625 b
blown c. hover, Sark .....327 l
chequering the eastern c.*..401 b
c. all other clouds dispel...457m
clouds and eclipses stain*..208 l
clouds appear like rocks... 99 u
clouds as dark as sciences.457 n
clouds, beneath the....... 71 g
c. come o'er the sunset‖.... 9 d
c. consign their treasures...515 f
clouds o'er their summits..586 a
a clouds of morn...............165 d
c. on clouds in volumes... 99 v
c. on the western side grow.100 b
c. perish'd darkness had‖..130 l
c. rise thick about us .....518 n
clouds that gather round¶. 100 i
c. that lour'd upon our*...582 g
clouds the only birds that.. 99 o
dark and many-folded c.§..392 f
dim gray c. are drifting....394 p
dipt in western clouds......585 i
dragons cut the c. full fast* 29 o
dropping from the clouds..552 c
edges eastern clouds with . 87 k
first gilds the clouds, then.585 d
fleecy c. their chilly bosoms564 v
for beyond the clouds......297 t
gaudy c., like courtiers....585 p
heavily in c. brings on......205 n
hooded c., like friars§ ....514 t
idle as clouds that rove ...322 n
in a robe of clouds‖........402 o
it plays with the clouds....459 k
its head reaches the c......740 r
laughing the c.away with‖.399 q
looks in the c. scorning*... 14 d
make the shifting c. be.... 99 k
no c. are in the morning....395 b
no pity sitting in the c.*...474 e
Oh! could they be clouds...586 a
opening curtains of the c..397 m
praise the evening c.......100 c
rest the silver clouds......674 s
rolling clouds are spread...102 q
rolling clouds to soar‖......205 u
royal clouds are they......585 k
saw two clouds at morning. 99 l
seas and lowering clouds...416 t
sees God in clouds‡ ....275 n
sings amid the dawning c.. 49 p
sit in the clouds*............253 a
small clouds are sailing¶..391m
smiles the clouds away‖....492 v
strewn with colored clouds. 99m
tempest clouds are driven. 46 f
that from the c. impends‡ .577 r
the clouds dispell'd......208 t
though when clouds arise†† 81 j
through rolling c. to soar‖. 46 b
through the darkest c.*....306 j
thy clouds of incense rise..583 s
to chase the clouds of life's.658 d
tops do buss the clouds*...100 d
vapors, and c., and storms..546 o
very clouds move on......392 u
what clouds of vandals rise‡558 b
when clouds appear, wise*.189 n
who tinged these c. with...100 c
with rolling fleecy c....... 99 i
with the threat'ning c.*...578 d
Cloudy—sunny and the c. ..735 i
Cloven—though c. with steel..627 i
Clovenford—we came to C.¶..529 q
Clover—a c. any time to him..321 o
and green clover*....... .. 226 c
clover I discover...........224 n
clover is too sweet.........225 a
of the purple clover‡......233 a
sweet with clover..........245 l
Clover-bloom—c-b. and sweet.225 c
c-b. falleth around.........224m

Clovers—of c. and of noon....321 n
Clown—a c., whatever he may.791 e
ancient days by emperor... 51 g
clown a winged Mercury...646 c
c. in regal purple dress'd‡..581 i
Grovendraad, an honest c..453m
mated with a clown†.......377 t
was no cobbling clown.....453 c
Cloy—beyond their measure‡ .155 l
most delightful pleasures c.505 u
sweetest meats the soonest.630 c
Cloying—ever eating, never c.603 r
Cloys—that which cloys......174 t
Club—about the c. of Hercules 758 g
his club to make the fire*..377 c
Clubs—c. typical of strife..... 14 p
go you with bats and c.*...667 j
Cluster—cluster from the vine 266 x
woes c.; rare are solitary...570 v
Clusters—c. imitate the grape 266 t
c. of blossomed moonlight.611 d
fruit in c. drooping down..613 b
in drowsy clusters cling.... 42 i
purple c. load the lilac.....614 s
smoky clusters rise.........224 l
Clutch—lives to c. the golden†454 h
Clyde—C.'s meandering......530 j
the banks of Clyde and Tay¶529 q
Cnidos—Paphian Queen to C...452 o
Coach—c. with four horses...663 e
go, call a coach, and let a...439 i
in his glistering coach*....400 u
my c.! good-night, ladies*..439 j
O for a coach, ye gods....439 i
when I am in my coach*...439m
Coach'd—c. it round the town.215 u
Coach-house—cottage with a..310 h
Coal—black and burning as a‖.191 r
c. that must be cool'd*..... 8 c
if by fire of sooty coal th'*424 t
it is a fire it is a coal.......361 k
the dead coal of wars*.....640 q
Coal-pit—God made a c-p. to..510 a
Coals—hot c. of vengeance*..639 n
like living c. the apples§....544 e
perfect woman over the c..499 v
rasher on the c. for money* 93 u
swallowed the blazing coals 174 q
Coarsest—to the lives of c.††...477 j
Coast—c. of fertile Phthia....160 n
coast thy sluggish crare*..379 j
gain the coast of bliss......539 a
stern and rock-bound c. ..459 q
the coast was clear........504jj
Coasts—round thy rocky c....327m
stranger in these false c....571 y
Coat—an old drab c. all..... 23 o
don his coat of gold.......232 r
furry c.and his gauzy wing.322 g
her cloth she cut her coat..511 d
I cast loose my buff c., each 20m
in my green velvet coat*...381 n
long brown c. that buttoned 23 h
painted c. which Joseph... 6 l
spoil his c. with scanting*..172 r
stick in his coat...........256 b
wear a long black coat..... 23 g
Coats—dawn, their yellow c...228 d
gold coats spots you*......226 b
like coats in heraldry*.....627 n
when they pay for coats‖...454 t
with silken c., and caps*... 24 i
Coaxing—resist her c.manner 373 n
Cobbled—as he c. and.........453 e
Cobbler—a c., produced......452 t
art a cobbler, art thou*....453 n
as you would say, a c.*....453 o
the cobbler apron'd‡.......256m
Cobblers—c. must thrust their 454 a
emperors and c. are cast...101 s
kings to c. 'tis the same....201 c
ye tuneful c.! still your‖...452 u
Cobbling—c. in his native....453m
was no cobbling clown.....453 c
Cobham—and you brave C‡..465 q
Cobwebs—c. out of my eyes... 78 h
laws were like cobwebs....436 o

rushes strewed, cobwebs*..432 i
Cock—at crowing of the cock. 24 s
cry cock-a-diddle-dow* .... 44 e
c. of the heath so wildly.... 44 c
c. with lively din scatters** 44 d
I hear the crowing cock§....117 h
the cock of their hats .....433 a
the c. that is the trumpet*. 44 f
the early village c. hath*... 44 g
the jolly cock's crowing....416 p
the morning cock crew*.... 44 h
the thistle cock's crying...416 p
Cocking—c. of a pistol‖.......163 e
Cock-loft—c-l. is empty, in...314 e
cock-loft is unfurnished....386 d
Cockneys—c. and sparrows...628 f
Cocks—crowing of the cocks§.605 j
the fate of fighting cocks..436m
Cocoa-nut—c-n. with its stony.267 b
graceful—the c-n. tree.....613 b
Code—lead the civil code ....479 d
Coeval—man to live c. with...517 u
Coffee—or o'er cold c. trifle‡..349 o
the taste for coffee.........791 i
Coffin—care to our c. adds a... 72 p
from the fire a coffin flew ..586 i
no useless coffin enclosed..444 s
you've nailed his c. down...640 i
Coffin'd—rake from c. clay‖...123 k
Coffins—'midst skulls and c...618 p
Cohesive—c. power of the vast 281m
Cohorts—his c. were gleaming‖636 e
Coigne—buttress nor c. of*... 50 h
Coil—I am not worth this c.*..670 u
shuffled off this mortal c.*.563 b
Coiling—c., climbing, turning.228 h
Coin—among men like coin†..103 i
c. must not be hoarded**... 35 n
current c. that purchases..561 a
pays him in his own coin...527 t
Coinage—very c. of your*....315 j
Coined—c. an epithet for a...409 t
Coiner—some c. with his tools*145 j
Coins—authors, like c., grow‡429 f
c. are harden'd by th' allay. 38 v
c. between a dying miser's.394 i
even its minted c. express..629 x
Cokaigne—land that height C.522 l
Cold—are cold in blood‖......356 u
as cold as cucumbers......495 x
beautiful through frost and.609 p
both foot and hand go cold.162 v
brow never cold............376 f
came up in the cold........226 q
cold as the snow ....330 r
c.in clime are cold in blood‖356 u
cold that did him chill......546 l
could not sleep for cold††..315 u
even till I shrink with cold*546 g
extremes of hot and cold*..191 h
falls c. and ceaseless, wore. 3 a
for he was faint with cold..546 l
God measures the cold to..785 h
God sends c. according to..498 k
God tempers the c. to the..510 c
grows c. even in the summer 34 j
heat for the cold...........561 a
his feathers, was a-cold... 52 o
in one cold place in the.... 74 a
it made me cold............232 p
love keeps the cold out§...360 q
makes cold weather*......660 b
neither cauld nor care....268 a
of pain, darkness and cold..346 b
park is sov'reign for a c....553 a
round him ere he scarce†..480 x
straight is cold again*......18 b
sympathy is c. to the......587 w
the day is cold, and dark§.515 a
think how cold the dress...23 p
'tis bitter cold, and I am*.. 86 y
when I am c. he heats me*.549 f
yellows with his cold......395 a
Colder—c. than the wind that..608 i
Coldly—she c. said, her......460 b
think'st I speak too coldly.662 u
Coldness—c., pride, or virtue‖.655 e

strong c. that I do*........103 v
Conceptions-lively c.flat and.574 r
Concern-is no c. at all of his.667 t
matter they had no c. in...296 i
Concerns-and its vast c......346 w
concerns of an eternal scene604 d
c. man must concern me...724 s
mild c. of ordinary life¶....319 k
where it concerns himself..558 o
Concert-hums with a louder.615 a
Concessions-c. of fear.......641 o
concessions of the weak are.641 o
Conciliated-minds are c......718 p
Concise-laboring to be c.....743 o
Conclusion-Christian-like c.* 93 k
lame and impotent c.*......527 i
Concord-all c.'s born of.....494gg
c. of sweet sounds*.........407 s
concord with humanity¶...227 r
firm c. holds, men only**...627 l
mar the concord with too*.557 r
milk of concord into hell*... 77 g
soul's quiet sinews of c... 375 h
victory grows out of c.....805 q
Concordia-c. is the word.... 40 o
Concourse-c. of atoms..... 96 k
Concurrence-sweet c. of the.488 i
Condemn-c. the fault*.....208 g
Condemned-a man c. to bear.534 q
condemn'd alike to groan..582 o
c. for a fault alone*........556 p
c. into everlasting........518 k
condemn'd upon surmises*.328 l
c. whole years in absence‡.. 3 b
fault's condemn'd ere it*..208 g
justice on the self c.||.......105 h
much c. to have an*......595m
Condemns-acquits the raven.716 d
condemns itself in youth to387 b
Condescend-c. to take a bit..215 r
Condition-a condition which.482 j
at the top of his condition..428 d
c. circumstance is not the‡.. 61 t
c. upon which God hath....343 r
condition which high......264 f
on this c. that you received133 v
shame from no c. rise‡....306 i
what c. his body will be....681m
Conditioning-your way of c..670 e
Conditions-govern our c.*...577 c
regardeth no conditions...360 g
soft c. and our hearts*.....660 c
Conduct-account for their c..620 n
conduct toward parents...753 o
do not inspire conduct..... 7 k
genteel in personage, c.,and 78 b
his c. still right with his... 27 e
impute to Christ c. which..648 o
in conduct to be old........673 n
nice c. of a clouded cane‡..457 k
our c. are our own..... 79 j
the conduct true‡... ......125 p
to extravagant conduct.... 78 n
would be his future c......181 b
Conducting-c. them to peace399 r
Conductors-which serve as..477m
Conduits-c. of my blood*.... 12 b
Cones-spiry c. that tremble.612 d
Coney-coney is not to be....167 e
Confections-for my c.*......447w
Confederacies-c. in vice.....263 k
Confederacy-c. of equal and.627 c
Confederates-c. against my*.108 a
Confer-c. with kings and.... 64 e
minds that have nothing¶.471 z
nothing to confer¶ ......386 o
Conference-c. a ready man..341 n
meaning in love's c.*......320 n
seemeth their c.*..........537 x
to hear our conference.... 48 j
Confess-and c. her home‡...571 v
c. thee freely of thy sin*...103 v
c. yourself to heaven*.....103w
everlasting yawn c.‡......313m
Confess'd-truth is every.....670 r
Confession-and suicide is c...583 i
confession of his true*.....103 x

no refuge from confession.583 i
Confessor-c. like unto§ .....135 q
ghostly c., a sin-absolver*. 33 f
physician c., nor lawyer...496ff
Confidence-c. is a plant of...104 j
c. is conqueror of men....104 p
c. is nowhere safe........684 n
c. is that feeling by which..104 c
c. of reason give¶..........148 n
c. of twenty-one ....672 o
c. was a plant of slow.....104 d
c. will be like my first.....684m
c. with you that discerns*..104m
filial confidence inspired...274 d
in the c. of pray'r..........487 d
I renounce all c.*..........104 l
not respect confidence.....104 a
the c. which we have......792 t
the growth of confidence.. 104 d
who has lost c. can lose....104 b
wisdom is consum'd in c..* 104 o
Confident-advised than c...330 g
as I am c. and kind*.......104 k
confident to-morrows¶....112m
Confine-desire to c. our....664 e
mure that should c. it in*..597 o
very verge of her confine*. 12 d
Confin'd-soul, uneasy and c.‡571w
Confines-circle grazes the c..355m
in these confines with a*...638w
on the confines of earth...297 q
Confirmations-c. strong as*..328 h
Confirm'd-long c. by age‡....265 d
Conflagration-raised a c....700 g
Conflict-c. with unholy....579 p
irrepressible conflict......113 d
more fierce the c. grew....640 h
the noise of conflict**.....637 t
the rueful c., the heart¶...383 a
through the heat of c.¶.... 85 r
Conflicts-fighting its terrible.148 q
Conformity-virtue in most ..632 k
Confound-c. the Atheist's...614 n
c. the cats! All cats—... 19 l
one thing can confound me.169 n
Confounded-all is c., all*....551 k
order confounded lies......417 t
Confronts-a condition which.482 j
Confusion-all in sweet c.....415 n
and by confusion stand**.. 77 c
author of c. and lies.......152 r
c. heard his voice**........462 s
c. worse confounded**....536 a
hail, blest c.! here. .... 15 a
in ruin and c. hurl'd..... 535 r
live on thy confusion*.....300w
stars lie in such apparent c.575m
Congeal-cool and c. again*..461 q
Congenial-c. to my heart...411 c
dear, c. to my heart.......555 n
Conger-wife may feed of a c.494 t
Congratulate-c. each other§.394 t
Congreeing-c. in a full and*..282 x
Congregation-c. in every...269m
the largest congregation.. 95 o
Congress-c. of Vienna does..282 t
Conjectures-c. on the public.435 t
Conjoined-c. to God by faith.316 t
Conjugial-c. love is celestial.365 s
Conjurations-c. horrible to .586 k
Conjure-c. thee by all the*..130 r
in vain she did c. him.....464 u
scholar would c. her*......377 c
Conjuring-it beats Pinetti's c.169 a
Connection-joined in c.**....588 h
system and connection....753 i
Connections-you'd no c......489 v
Connubial-wrong in a c.kiss||.533 g
Conquer-c. love that run....357 f
conquer we must when....214 i
conquer willing hearts**..472 v
hardly c., but c. you.......684 r
like Douglas c., or like.....104 u
no law except to c..........502 i
should c. twenty worlds...104 i
sign thou shalt conquer....804cc
strong enough to conquer..282 q

to bear is to c. our fate.....467 a
to c. is to live enough.....806 o
to conquer our fate.......205 v
we conquer but to save....630 x
we c. without danger......759 p
yielding you conquer......684 q
Conquered-for he c. me....287 p
French we c. once.........205 e
I came, I saw, I c.........684 p
misfortune had c. her.....388 q
safety for the conquered...751 j
we c. France, but felt‡.....631 f
Conqueror-confidence is c...104 p
c. is not so much pleased..751 a
descended from the c......634 a
grand c., enriching........338 s
hero the c. worm.........137 j
Conquerors-beates all c......133 j
brave c.! for so you*.......104w
meed of mightie c.........610 h
outlaws c. should||.........301 s
right of war for c ....684 o
Conquers-and c. its desire..368 g
c. twice who c. himself....684 s
c. when it yields to the...759 g
courage c. all things......686 h
daily conquers them......258 l
He c. who conquers ....805 t
justice c. evermore.......332 i
labor c. everything.......720 e
love conquers all things...724 d
their country c. with their||491 t
time c. all, and we must‡.. 601 t
truth conquers.............805 u
truth conquers ....805 o
Conquest-after the c. of....266 u
c. of this conqueror**.....202 s
conquest to my foe*.......139 u
hardest c. of the mind‡....385 r
nature of a conquest*......471 d
the c. but One could foil..466 o
the rage of conquest.......278 v
'tis a firmer conquest......255 g
Conquests-Carnage and his||.470 d
still makes new c. and‡.... 82 t
to outlook c. and to*......639 h
Conscience-a still and quiet*106 k
bend our c. to our dealing..595 g
catch the c. of the king*...423 l
chancellor's conscience ...253 r
cleere c. is a sure carde...494 j
confuted by his conscience.305 c
c. avaunt, Richard's......572 s
c. hath a thousand*.......106m
c. have vacation...........105 c
conscience in everything...106 t
conscience is a coward.....105 p
conscience is but a word*..106 l
c. is harder than..........105 o
conscience! man's most....105 n
conscience ne'er asleep....105 v
conscience of a life well‡...106 a
c. they're straitlac'd.......436 r
c. wakens who can..... 105 l
c. wakes despair**........105 t
c. with injustice is*.......333 a
fire called conscience......106 u
foam from the c...........760 b
free from conscience......200 t
guilt of c. take*..........106 j
is for a good conscience....489 d
keep a clear conscience....685 a
let his tormentor c.**......105 s
man's c. is the oracle of||..105 i
O c., into what abyss**....105 u
O coward conscience, how*106 o
O faithful c., delicately....760 u
peace of conscience**......198 b
policy sits above c.*.......474 c
quiet c. makes one||.......105 d
sixteen the c. rarely||......105 e
state of a man's c ....685 b
than a guilty conscience...685 c
theatre for virtue is c......105 j
the c. of her worth**......662 t
the c. of the dying........759 r
the conscience of us all....448 a

by faith and courage...... 800m
by wisdom and courage....799 h
carried new strength and...318 u
c. and courage beauty and.101 h
c. and his mercy strive.... 83 e
courage and prudence.....798 k
courage—an independent..118 s
c. as roused with rage*....119 r
c. conquers all things.....686 h
c. in danger is half the...686 l
courage, is on all hands...118 t
courage leads to heaven...686 p
c. mounteth with occasion*119 k
c. never to submit or**....638 f
courage, the highest gift..118 s
courage, the mighty......118 s
c. to the sticking*.........119 t
courage without fear......806aa
coward boasting of his c...687 d
direst foe of courage......209 e
fear to die but courage....119 h
few persons have courage.118 u
have courage to declare...121 d
he himself wants courage..686m
if our courage could refuse.118 q
immortal c. in the human.165 d
is want of courage........121 b
lack courage to tell truth..121 k
motto, "c. and strength...391 a
never be certain of our c...760 g
ofttimes the test of c......777 t
riches, but not courage....686 o
the man had c. was a‡....311 q
to bear his courage up....118 n
truth is courage.........199 a
'twill make your c. rise...648 i
was his courage green....760 h
we see great courage......760 f
why courage then what*...119 u
worth, c., honor, these... 84 v
Courageously-c. and........800cc
Courages-charm of the best.118 r
Courier-the c.'s feet delayed.564w
Course-c. of Nature is the....413 t
c. of true love never did*..362 o
determine on some course*145w
in his steep course.....575 s
lovely and joyful the c....586 e
our course is chosen.......445 t
runs a headlong course...358 j
that whose course is run... 6 f
thou what c. thou wilt*...387 c
time rolls his ceaseless c..602 f
Westward the c. of empire.492 c
Courser-c. paw'd the ground 20 p
Coursers-c. of themselves...388w
Courses-hold different c....552 a
honorable c. with a sure...104 c
Court-and c. the flower.....240 c
a virtuous c. a world to...534 h
c. a mistress she denies...662 o
court of appeal against....330 v
court where hourly........ 64 e
farewell the hopes of c.*...308 t
fill the c. with quarrels*...607 l
glorious c. where hourly...344 n
good manners at the court*102 f
into a royal court with....232 q
it cometh into court and§... 40 f
keeps death his court*....140 s
let her alone, she will c....662 o
love rules the court.......362 g
man may range the court‖.356 q
mockable at the court*....102 f
never saw the court.......287 n
never sway in court*......444 b
other Members of the c....520 e
peril than the envious c*...610 c
sun that shines upon his c.*584 i
the court is like a palace..787 h
to court the sky.........246 g
Venus chime their annual.628 a
Courted-are obsequiously c..177 d
girls again be courted.... 90 j
Courteous-all such is c......120 i
courteous and well-bred...120 g
courteous, though coy, and655 t

old age is c.—no one more. 9 q
the Retort Courteous*.....120 n
Courteously-to hear c......330 p
Courtesy-but none for c*.... 20 j
c. grows in court; news in.120 i
c. was in him more........120 h
c. would invent some*.....326 i
dissembling c.! How fine*.120 k
honest offer'd courtesy**..120 j
in a heart of courtesy.....120 q
mirror of all courtesy*....120m
scant this breathing c.*....644 f
siege of tenderest courtesy.663 c
time enough for courtesy..120 e
very pink of courtesy*.....120 l
which men call courtesy...120 f
Courtier-whose c.'s face....235 g
Courtiers-gaudy clouds like.585 p
Courtly-cream of c. sense‡..451 e
Courts-and c. of princes**..120 j
as other c. o' the nation...105 c
born for courts or great‡...310 s
courts to be closed........129 n
pleasure in despotic c...... 1 g
sang they in your courts...165 a
shown in c., at feasts**.... 35m
who courts the flattery....215 e
Courtship-a c. flowing here.117 e
they dream in courtship‡..663 d
to c. and such fair ostents*663 h
Court-virtue-c-v. bear, like‡.633 a
Cousin-o'er every angry c.‖..662 g
your c., too, John Bull††..637 l
Covenant-c. with death....559 h
God's glowing covenant..515 g
minds the c. between all..515 s
Cover-c. his mind decently..386 k
cover of an old book......182 q
c. up the embers that§....464 o
man cannot c. what God..528 c
to cover my head now.....590 u
who cover faults, at least*.603 d
Covered-c. it all over with..137 u
Covering-a c. overhead.....244 h
Coverings-old moth-scented.344 v
Coverlet-according to his...497m
grassy coverlet of God....141 k
neath c., downy and soft..545m
on the green coverlet*.....292 n
Covers-night's black mantle.415 f
oft covers a good man....290 p
Covert-and from its covert. 87 f
what the covert yield‡.... 87 p
Covet-sin to covet honor*...120 v
we covet what is guarded..686 u
Covetous-am not c. for gold*120 v
courts you is a covetous...177 d
c. man is ever in want....686 t
c. of the property of others687 a
Covetousness-cause of c....120 w
confound their skill in c.*.120w
covetousness is rich.......686w
much c. constant..........111 i
Covets-c. less than misery*..147 c
covets that of another.....686 v
who c. more is evermore...111 d
Cow-c. is a very good animal. 19 o
curst c. hath short horns..494 n
excellent c. that furnishes.759m
killed the parson's cow....451 s
stomachs like a cow......166 p
Cowbind-green c. and the...612 l
Cows-kiss till the c. come...333 q
the c. are in the corn.....542 i
the c. be well cared for....797 e
Coward-a c., a most devout*.121 o
a slanderous coward*......172 q
conscience is a coward....105 p
c. boasting of his courage.687 d
c. never on himself relies..121 c
c. sneaks to death, the....121 n
c. that would not dare....121m
each c. shadow eastward...585 h
flattery to name a c.......122 n
fool solely a coward*... ... 83 u
he lives a c., or a fool.....522 o
I was a c. on instinct*....324 p

live a c. in thine own*......122 i
O c. conscience, how*......106 o
rat and a coward to boot... 78 i
the base, the coward......135 k
the c. calls himself cautious699 r
the c. only threatens when.758 h
the c. stands aside††......622 n
thou wretch, thou c.*.....122 f
vain for the c. to flee......761 k
wish for death is a c.'s...687 c
Cowardice-c. in noble *.....122 e
c. to rest mistrustful*....121 t
distrust is c. and prudence. 4 u
falsehood is cowardice....199 a
is pale, cold c. in noble*...467 x
twit with c. a man*....... 109 n
Cowardize-can c. his breath..118 p
Cowardly-c. cur barks......687 e
timid and c. rush to......680 f
Cowards-c. are cruel, but...121 j
c. die many times before*..121 q
c. fight when they can fly*.122 d
c. may fear to die........119 h
c. mock the patriot's fate..468 t
c., whose hearts are all as*.121 s
does make c. of us all*.....106 q
hide your heads like c.*....119 o
tell truth—the cowards...121 k
word that cowards use*...106 i
would be c. if they dare...121 d
Cowled-there the c. night...585 b
Cowslip-c. is a country......225 q
cowslip's velvet head**....226 a
even in cowslip time......225 r
first wan cowslip, wet.....225 s
freckled cowslip, burnet*..226 c
holds a cup of c. wreaths..540 a
ilk cowslip cup shall.......225 o
in a cowslip's bell I lie*....197 h
May, with c.-braided locks.393 k
nesh yonge coweslipe......225 p
pearl in every c.'s ear*.....154 g
the cowslip springs....... 220 o
yellow c., and the pale**...393 e
Cowslip-garland-c-g. on her.393 k
Cowslips-c. bedeck the......225 n
c. deck the plain.........225m
c. gild the level green......225 l
cowslips on the hill†.......226 e
c. paint the smiling.......217 t
c. tall her pensioners*.....226 b
knot of cowslips...........225 k
talk of to-morrow's c...... 70 u
tall cowslips nodding......225 t
Coxcomb-a c. is one whom..768 c
c. claims distinction......254 k
O murderous c.*..........252 s
Coxcombs-c. vanquish......537 l
some made coxcombs‡....252 c
Coy-and one too coy.......174 t
courteous though coy, and.655 t
he would be coy..........327 q
lips are coy to tell.........218 s
uncertain, coy, and hard to.658 r
Coz-my pretty little coz*....364 j
Crab-tree-hard c-t. and old..572 q
Crack-eat the kernel must c.729 g
hear the mighty crack....535 r
will sure crack both*......419 p
without crack or flaw§.... 40 h
Cracked-c. and never well..498 e
it be cracked or not.......573 r
Cracker-what c. is this*....589 s
Crackling-c. of the gorse...230 c
Cradle-baby in his c. in the..135 i
bed and procreant c.*...... 50 h
bending by the c. of her†... 25 l
between the c. and the....347 i
c. first he fostered was....123 e
c. of the western breeze...539 p
c. stands in our grave.....134 h
cradle where it lies*.......204 d
curst from his cradle......345 j
fling round my c. their.... 40 l
hand that rocks the cradle.402 i
happy child! the c. is still..758 u
not changed in my cradle.. 74 l

rocked in the c. of the deep.460 r
rock the c. of reposing age‡ 11 a
the cradle and the tomb...349 r
Cradled-a cloud lay c. near..100 h
cradled in the winds........239 p
c. into poetry by wrong....480 o
like a c. creature lies.....459 k
peerless as e'er was c.††.... 46 r
Cradles-c. rock us nearer to..604 j
Craft-passions in his c. of*..606 h
the trade of the gentle c... 453 d
Crag-castledc.of Drachenfels‖582 a
eagle's on the crag.........111 o
he clasps the crag with†... 46 m
up the low c. and ruin'd... 231 d
Crags-peak the rattling c.‖..598 i
the rattling c. among‖......577 p
weather-beaten c. retain...219 q
Crankiness-from all risk of††442 f
Cranks-quips and c. and**. .383 r
Crannies-creep in c. when*..584 j
Cranny-every c. but the right354 j
Crape-a saint in c. is twice‡.. 82 w
Crare-coast thy sluggish c.*.379 j
Crave-my mind forbids to c.385 f
will, not what they c.*.....603 e
Cravens-that c. my weak*...583 d
Craving-c. for sympathy is..588 a
Crawl-c. offensive to mine...324 i
Crawlin-whare ye gaun, ye c.324 a
Crawls-quiet which c. round.614 i
Crazy-to a c. ship all winds..507 q
Creaking-c. of a country....589 a
Cream-all the well-whip'd c.‡451 e
Create-c. a soul under the**.296 d
c. phantoms that seem to§..452m
kindle and c. the whole....417 t
morning, new c. thee......454 q
'tis God-like to create....345 b
why did God c. at last**...657 s
Created-all is c. and goes. ...206 g
created by his breath......370 v
created in the image......560 q
c. me out of mingled air...760 l
e'er c. solely for itself....413 r
joint-stools were then c....431 a
man is so c. that as to his.. 316 t
that all men are c. equal...529 i
to the end they were c.*...602 n
when thou wast created..460 p
Creates-c. from its own....308 z
c. preserves destroys......352 d
what it fears creates......209 g
Creating-of Nature's own c..418 q
Creation-amid its gay c.hues.412w
at the creation I would ....122 o
behold the world's c........123 e
bodiless c. ecstasy*.......315 j
come so near creation*....447 q
c. is great, and............122 p
c. of a thousand forests....370 y
c.'s blot, creation's blank.. 79m
c.'s heir, the world, the....668 h
c. sleeps. 'Tis as the......418 a
essential vesture of the c.*....658 x
every scene of the c........428 i
fairest creation can bring..239 k
her delicate creation¶....315 k
her ploughshare o'er c.....536 d
in his rich creation.......406 p
ник dissolved, the whole c.123 g
mars C.'s plan.........369 o
mind a false creation*..... 25 g
new c. of my tailor's.......454 n
new c. rises to my sight‖..446 h
of the king's c. you may be372 v
shut up from all the fair c. 87 f
such as c.'s dawn beheld‖..599 l
the lords o' the creation... 26 s
the sole author of c....... 73 q
the whole creation moves‡.123 j
Creations-acts his own c....273 t
Creator-C. drew his spirit...182 n
depends on his Creator....356 h
endowed by their Creator..529 i
great C. from his work**...122 v
his great Creator drew....133m

moved the C. in his**......123 b
singing their great C.**....670 j
weary knees to your C.....670 c
worships his Creator. ... .370 o
Creators-they have new c....454 s
Creature-c., female as the...654 v
c. not too bright or good¶..661 c
c. of circumstances ... 96 o
c. of habits and infirmities.326 u
c.'s at his dirty work‡......644m
c. shall be purified.........267 p
drink, pretty c., drink¶... 163 c
every c. is annexed........356 h
every c. lives in a state of..640 l
gay c. as thou art¶.........322 o
impulse every c. stirs .....409 x
lovely, lordly creature‡....254 g
noble c. in her*............552 j
no creature loves me*......148 u
not a creature but myself*.491 w
not a c. was stirring........ 94m
of their c. comforts........100 j
on sech a blessed cretur††..657 j
so fair a creature formed§.. 85 c
there is no c. loves me*....474 d
Creatures-c. dumb and§.... 40 f
creatures you dissect‡.....349 l
destroy all c. for thy‡......510 k
good c. may be living‡.....311 r
heaven from all c.‡........206 y
human creatures' lives....126 q
life which all c. love.......345 h
meaner creatures kings*..308w
millions of spiritual c.**...575 c
of creatures rational**......627 l
the creatures of men.... 96 o
who serve his creatures....549 d
Credence-I feyth and ful c... 65 a
Credit-blest paper c.‖ last‡..114 u
corpse of Public Credit...123 j
c. requires still more time.104 d
man's c. is proportioned. ..728 e
pay severely who .. ....653 q
private credit is wealth....123 h
than to fill with credit.....260 l
the one ne'er got me c.*....595 q
you c. anything the light ..654 t
Creditor-soul counts thee*...572 f
Credulities-those old c. to¶..302m
Credulity-folly of c.........251 p
Credulous-incredulous are...760 j
love is a c. thing..........723 b
Creed-Athanasian C. is the..158 b
code or creed confined.... 285 a
deed, and not the creed§...451 a
hands the creed of creeds‡.. 92 s
have a Calvinistic creed....521 q
life to thy neighbor's c.....318 s
Pagan suckled in a c.¶.... 92 e
put your c. into your deed.146 l
sapping a solemn c. with‖..157 q
was the creed of slaves... 414 f
whatever c. be taught‖.....105 i
Creeds-c. but men's actions..146 p
if our creeds agree.........158 f
than in half the creeds†....159 h
Creek-every winding c.† ....235 a
Creeks-among flowery c.¶... 71 f
Creep-c. in crannies when*..584 j
c. in service where it*..... 549 h
it made me creep..........232 p
how some men creep*......256 v
teach him to creep till.....190 p
thro' the moss the ivies c.†.412 t
Creeping-c. where no life...232 c
Creeps-c. in this petty*.....605 o
it flies as well as creeps...558m
Creole-C. of Cuba laughs...266 w
Crept-c. in at Myra's pocket.355 j
Crescent-eastern hanging c...400 r
thin clear c. lustrous.......397 q
Cresses-c. from the rill.....234 o
Crest-and crowned with one*.627 n
beneath its snowy crest ...223 a
dogged war bristle his*....639 k
gentle curve of its lowly c. 54m
God's c. upon his azure...583 l

high c., short ears*......... 21 d
joy brightens his crest**...308 g
rears her snaky crest.....523 q
shoulders and white his c.. 43 h
with silver crest...........227 p
Crew-his undaunted crew ...182m
mirth, admit me of thy c.**383 s
Crews-the c., at England's...630 x
Cribs-sleep, liest thou in*... 563 c
Cricket-c. on the hearth**...304 c
the cricket's chirr.........304m
Cried-c. him up and down...358 h
c. out God, God, God three*138 l
Crier-a crier of green sauce..494 l
Cries-and hear their cries....272 t
c. of pain are music for his.183 q
echoes with unvaried c.... 48 i
first c. "Hold, enough "*...639 l
laughs and c., and eats.... 31 e
the brook c. like a child....577 s
with my assiduous c.**....488 n
with the c. they make.....636m
Crime-abash the front of c...732 s
a life of injury and crime..338 h
bethink yourself of any c.*489 j
consecrate a crime‖........123 k
c. deemed innocent on....123 l
c. destroys more Edens....123 n
crime has been without....687 v
c. has to be concealed.....688 c
crime is everlasting........687 q
crime is not punished......123m
c. is punished it yet........687 t
c. is taught from early.....687 p
c. to injure a brother......687 u
crime to love too well‡.....361 n
face to face with my own§..527 x
fear follows c. and is its...760 n
follows close on crime.....736 p
every c. will bring remorse.687 h
excuse for c. is indeed.....123 p
imputed to them as a c ....402 n
instigator of a c. is worse..687 n
it is more than a crime....760 l
man's mortal c., and**....518 j
now madden to crime‖.....336 v
numbers sanctified the c...403 p
one bears a cross for his c..687 i
on through every crime....737 k
or consecrate a crime‖.....476 f
punishment, but in the c..760 s
secures happiness by c.....760 t
share the c. of your friend.688 d
she will shrink from no c...688 e
stayed,—forgive the c......603 p
successful c. is dignified...688 s
that persuades to crime....299 u
the c. makes the shame....760 p
the c.of a mother is a heavy.760 o
to be at peace in crime....760m
want exasperated into c... 41 t
who does not prevent a c..688 b
whoever meditates a c.....687 j
who profits by c. is guilty..687 s
will o'ertake the crime....403 n
without the owner's c.¶....466 d
Crimes-all his c.broad blown*403 s
as crimes do grow.........277 g
c. chew'd swallow'd*.......123 t
c. sospeedily can venge*...332 x
c. that 'scape or triumph‡..437 v
guilt of enforced c. lies....687 r
justice while she winks at.332 g
liberty! how many c. .....344 q
many commit the same c..687 i
men blush less for their c..756 n
other c. may pass for .....320 c
picture of human crimes..302 k
poverty is the mother of c..548 h
reach the dignity of c.....290 s
register of crimes and.....772 e
successful c. alone are.... 607 t
success makes some c......744 n
these have c. accounted...123 o
truth warns of threatening.793 q
undivulged c., unwhipp'd*.124 b
vice atone for c. by prayer‖487m

keeps nor crust nor crumb*499 n
live merely on the c. or....347 q
our upper crust...........513 c
share her wretched c.††....622 n
underneath this crust......182 l
Crutch-shoulder'd his c......443 d
Crutches–lean on c. made of..290 n
time goes on c. till love*...602 w
Cry–all cry and no wool......502 jj
and have a good cry.......590 u
and the wailing cry.......638 l
begins the scandal and the†480 x
call to him, cry to him....656 n
choice to cry or laugh‖.....182 f
cry did knock against*.....552 j
cry not to be born........132 c
cry not when his father...210 q
dismal cry rose slowly.....276 i
him with the cry of blood¶.640 s
ill-boding cry, portends.... 52 p
it do cry out itself enough* 8 h
language but a cry†........ 32 k
laugh or cry or take more.. 80 d
moche crye and no Wull...502 a
mock the cry that she had. 52 n
shall cry to Heaven....... 382 k
she never will c. till she's††.479 w
take up the cry and send...396 e
war, war is still the cry‖...636 f
when we are born we cry*.350 z
when we hear it cry*....... 6 u
with no language but a c.†.372 z
with that boding c. along.. 42 l
Cry'd–Peter deny'd his Lord.591 h
Crying–an infant c. in the†...372 z
infant crying for the light†. 32 k
Crystal–cased in the pure c..545 j
crystal break for fear......181 t
crystal by the fancy††.....203 p
crystal of the azure seas...230 i
in c. vapor everywhere†....613 g
into transparent crystal§...270 t
languid o'er the c. flood....616 n
shallop of crystal†.........278 j
the crystal on his brow....360 h
Crystal-pointed–c-p. tents....640 j
Cubs–lick their c. into shape.289m
Cuckold–c. lives in bliss*....328 e
Cuckoo–before the shallow**. 51 n
c. builds not for himself*... 44 t
fed the cuckoo so long*.... 57 h
he sings cuckoo, cuckoo,*.. 44 u
list!—'twas the cuckoo¶.... 45 b
note the hollow c. sings.... 45 a
responsive to the c.'s note.. 44 o
the c.'s bird useth the*..... 44 s
the cuckoo sings unseen.... 45 h
the c. then on every tree**. 44 u
the merry c. messenger.... 44 v
Cuckoo-buds–c-b. of yellow*.541 a
Cuckoo-flowers–sweet c-f.†..226 d
Cuckoopint–O c., toll me......225 f
Cucumbers–as cold as c......495 x
in a garden of cucumbers..542 l
sunbeams out of c.........253 f
Cud–as with the cud an......166 p
Cuddles–on c. low behind... 53 h
Cudgel's-wood a c.'s of by..512 b
Cue–motive and the c. for*...423m
Cuff–this cuff was but to*....353 t
Cuffs–c. and farthingales*.... 24 i
Cull–c. me from the bower...241 q
Cullambine–and purple c....229 k
Culled–c. from the flowers...513bb
Culminate–and c. above.....284 p
Culmination–union and c. of.421 q
Cultivate–c. a small state....676 v
c. literature on a little......354 h
Cultivation–c. of the mind...719 c
time spent in the c. of.... 676 u
Culture–blame the c. not‡...424 f
c. which smooth the whole.762 s
what culture will entice....266 d
without culture they......115m
Cunning–c. in fence, I'ld*....122 b
cunning in music and the*.455 n
c. sin cover itself withal*..556 n

c. woman is a knavish fool.657 k
hence, bashful cunning*....320 l
plighted cunning hides*....603 d
prudent flight and c. save..511 a
the cunning known‡.......465 s
to c. men I will be very*....455 o
very c. of the scene*...... 423 f
virtue and cunning were*..316 q
Cup–a charmed cup, O Fame.201 g
a cup of cold Adam from..640 t
between the c. and the lip.502aa
bursts her twin cup in....238 j
cup of curious dyes.......238 r
cup of rich canary wine....649m
cup that shall be death.... 31 h
cup to the dead already....604m
dipped its cup in the.......239 b
dregs of fortune's cup.‡....256 j
filched a cup belonging....179 i
fill its little cup twice......226 r
freely welcome to my cup.323 e
from the cup of mad. ....592 x
give a cup of water....... 87 e
inordinate c. is unblessed*.326 h
leave a kiss but in the cup.334 o
life's enchanted cup but‖..599 n
matrons, who toss the cup.589 v
moonlight-colored cup.....234 g
round as to a golden cup...397 r
shade-blossoming cup.....238 a
sparkling in a golden cup*.112 e
though the c. that I drain..142 b
thy verdant cup does fill...323m
to give a cup of water.....641m
tongue like Delia's o'er her.606 l
when the secret cup¶......598 g
whose charmed cup**......277 p
Cupid–bolt of Cupid fell*....237m
bow of Cupid will lose.....723 g
Cupid and my Campaspe..360 h
Cupid archer of archers.. 87 i
Cupid blind did rise...... 360 h
Cupid is a casuist........ 276 n
Cupid is a knavish lad*....278 b
Cupid is a murderous boy..277 n
Cupid kills with arrows*...364 p
C. 't has long stood void....297 e
giant-dwarf Dan Cupid*...278 f
note which Cupid strikes..355 p
silent note which C. strikes.404m
wind-swift Cupid wings*...364 a
winged C. painted blind*...363 v
with Cupid's curse....... 75 n
young Cupid slyly stole... 355 j
Cupids–c. every one dear....359 k
Cupola–a huge dun c., like a‖. 98 c
Cups–be in their flowing c.*...409 q
c. make any guilty men....162 l
c. that cheer but not......186 q
c. with tears**.......... 221 i
give me the c.; and let *...639 d
over their cups..........711 f
turns wooden c. to gold...112 l
white cups whose wine....612 l
Cur–'bout the ears of the old..500 j
cowardly c. barks more....687 e
when a cur doth grin*.....629 a
Curaçoa–punch! O potent c.649 s
Curb–as poised on the c. it...641 n
c. thou the high spirit in...511 h
rusty c. of old father antic*438 i
your c. and whip in their*..595 o
Curded–c. by the frost from*.398 v
Curdled–curdled the blood...231 o
Curds–shepherd's homely c.*112 e
Cure–ambition is no c. for.... 13 t
and shall admit no cure. ..519 e
care is no c. but*......... 72 i
cheap and universal cure..307 o
condition for a c. might be.440 f
cure is bitterer still‡.......357 a
doctors c. by letting blood..518 a
he wounds to cure........ 83 e
ill c. for life's worst ills...603 t
ills demand a speedy cure.. 4 u
king can cause or cure....172 w
postpone the c. for a year..726 f

the c. to wish to be cured...688 h
'tis an ill cure for life's.....403 i
to cure, it easy*...........156 n
we for cure apply........127 i
wise for cure on exercise...440 b
Cured–c. yesterday of my...440 q
difficulty be cured........763 g
in time, had cur'd me*.....100 n
madman is not cured......324 r
the cure to wish to be c....688 h
wound will perhaps be c...688 g
Cures–crown c. not the......506 c
c. in me thoughts that*.... 88 r
Curfew–c. must not ring....417 u
Curfew tolls the knell......186 s
Curing–c. of a strong disease*441 a
Curiosity–always excite c...436 a
by way of curiosity......873 l
for too much curiosity*....127 b
heed of a gluttonous c.....379 t
mine own jealous c.*......126 x
stirs my c. nor spleen......281 p
that low vice—curiosity‖...126 q
Curious–amazed and curious.383m
and curious are to hear**..126 w
Curl–I barter curl for curl†..441 q
in a golden curl†.........383 l
on your curls' full...... 560 g
Curled–more c. state unfold..234 k
Curlew–the curlew calls§....598 u
Curlier–his hair became c...370 p
Curls–ambrosial curls upon..276 t
auburn locks, ye golden c...479 l
dry the moistened c.'s that.646 u
golden curls, and quiver...358 h
'mid thy clustering curls..292 e
shakes his ambrosial curls.277 c
Curly-headed–c.-headed‖.... 89 d
Currant–c. must escape.....266 t
Current–along the mazy c...546 p
and pass them current too*.640 j
but must be current**..... 35 n
genial current of the soul..484 o
sweet is thy c. by town.....532 f
tossing c. white with foam..606 v
Currents-corrupted c. of*....438 p
Curs–as curs mouth a bone...573 p
curs of low degree..... ... 19 q
like to village curs*.......172 u
Curse–blest leisure is our c...343 a
cancelled that curse.......237 r
concludes with Cupid's c... 75 n
but a c. is like a cloud.... 60 l
c. of an evil deed is that...765 j
c. on all laws but those‡....438 a
c. on his ill-betiding croak. 54 s
curse on his virtues.......631 v
c. the bones of every‡......645 j
curse the hopeless world...206 e
c. upon thy venom'd stang.432m
ignorance is the c. of God*.337 y
I know how to curse*......340 f
open foe may prove a c....312 h
record with a c. annexed..123 l
the bitterest c. of human..645 s
the dear-bought c., and‡...645 j
the curse of greatness.....771 d
there not some chosen c...607 r
tongue to curse the slave...608 j
Cursed–c. be that wretch*...430 d
c. be the man the poorest..374 j
each curs'd his fate........206 h
this dullness was he cursed.581 a
Curses–blessings for curses*. 86 x
c. are like young chickens..496 cc
c. not loud, but deep*..... 11 r
curses not unfrequently....432 k
Curst–chariot wheels are c...696 j
curst be he yt moves......183 t
c. be the verse, how well‡..477 q
curst by Heaven's decree..368 z
curst from his cradle......345 j
is intolerable curst*.......208 k
the spot is curst¶........ 76 r
Curtain–Anarch! lets the c‡.. 77 d
breast the c. of repose.... 38 h
closing her c. up above.....625 f

SHAKESPEARE*; MILTON**; WORDSWORTH¶; BYRON‖; TENNYSON†; LOWELL††; POPE‡; LONGFELLOW§.

D.

d. along the dingy days.... 65 *i*
danced, I say, right well‖..127 *r*
danced without theatrical‖.127 *r*
late they danc'd before....445 *h*
when she d.—oh, heaven...129 *d*
Dancer-he, perfect d. climbs.129 *e*
Dancers-d. whirl round......128 *j*
Dances-d. about the sun.....100 *e*
d. ended all the fairy‡......196 *t*
dances in the golden sun...643 *i*
d. here and she dances......322 *p*
dances with the hours......242 *s*
in hamlets d. on the green..362 *g*
not walk, but it dances.....282 *i*
of the dizzying dances§...128 *l*
she dances such a way......253 *v*
their hushing d. languished674 *q*
to midnight dances and‡...387 *l*
to their dances more than..277 *f*
Dancing-comes d. from**....576 *j*
dancing has begun now......128 *j*
dancing in the breeze¶....226 *s*
d. in the chequer'd shade**128 *q*
dancing in yonder green...324 *b*
ever d. round the pole.....399 *q*
can't go on dancing........127 *q*
master of dancing so slow.127 *q*
men and women dancing...128 *g*
merry, dancing, drinking..383 *p*
singing and d. alone will...790 *t*
twelve dancers are dancing.128 *k*
we are d. on a volcano.....129 *o*
Dandelion-said young D.....228 *f*
Dandelions-queerly called d. 228 *c*
star-disked dandelions......218 *d*
the dandelions shine.......220 *s*
Danger-and fear her danger‖.648*m*
bravely dares the danger..208 *n*
companions in their d......208 *v*
could danger brave....   ...654 *r*
courage in danger is half...686 *l*
danger comes the sooner...688 *t*
d. of our former tooth*....129 *u*
danger of violent death...347 *w*
d. to give the best advice..574 *a*
danger will wink on**......461 *j*
delay always heeds d......496 *ii*
even in the jaws of d.*.....639 *h*
extreme d., fear turns a....688*m*
extreme to equal d. tends..191 *b*
great d. to such as be sick.599 *a*
he sees the d., and feels....588 *e*
in so great a danger the...772 *q*
keep aloof; there's d......571 *y*
last of danger and distress‖132*w*
man come in danger by it.. 86 *d*
neither by glory or by d....699 *j*
nettle, danger, we pluck*..129 *q*
no form of danger shakes..118 *p*
of the utmost danger......699 *b*
overcome without danger..688 *r*
pleas'd with the d., when..129*m*
quailed to danger's brow‖..129 *l*
safe from d. who is on his..688 *s*
shape of d. can dismay¶.... 85 *v*
share one common danger.749 *e*
should boldly meet the d..688 *w*
strength in times of danger.391 *a*
there's d. on the deep.....444 *u*
to a blank of danger*......185 *v*
to bring it into danger*....628 *n*
undergo, or tempt a d......628 *l*
until we have faced d ....760 *g*
we conquer without d......759 *p*
worthy d. and deserved*... 76 *e*
your danger is in discord§.282 *l*
Dangerous-are they very d.*174 *g*
delays are d. in war........147 *k*
delays have d. ends*.... .. 496 *j*
d. is that temptation*......594 *j*
d. to be touched*.........266 *n*
forms a dangerous strait.‡.613 *h*
in d. times true worth.....670*w*
insincerity is the most d..144 *h*
learning is a d. thing‡......342 *i*
not d. for some one.......761 *i*
nothing in d. times.......509 *n*

nothing is so d. as an.......773 *a*
of no church is dangerous..521 *e*
silent people are d.. ......788 *r*
something in me d.*.......129 *p*
turns up more d. breakers‖.459 *h*
you're straightway d......320 *s*
Dangerously-d. dear‖........590 *e*
Dangers-brings dangers,**...534 *l*
constant exposure to d. ...688 *q*
d. that threaten him every.688 *n*
d. thou canst make us......325 *n*
himself often to dangers...703 *e*
it is in great d. that we.....760 *f*
lov'd me for the dangers*..365 *a*
sing the dangers of the sea. 446 *b*
the dangers of the seas... 304 *j*
those who brave its d.§.....460 *d*
Daniel-D. come to judgment*331 *l*
well languag'd Danyel.....339 *q*
Danny-they're hangin' D....443 *k*
Dante-and D. nodded his.....409 *e*
Dante sleeps afar‖......... 98 *b*
on Dante's track...........299 *t*
purple lilies D. blew...... .233 *h*
Dapples-d. the drowsy east*.625 *j*
Dare-are slaves who d. not‡‡.559 *o*
cowards if they dare. .....121 *d*
coward that would not d...469 *k*
dare, and yet I may not...158 *q*
dare the elements to strife‖551 *p*
dare to act! Even.........689 *e*
d. to be true, nothing can..622 *g*
dare to do our duty as we..529 *j*
dare to malign him........276 *n*
d. to write as funny as I....310 *y*
fain would I but I d. not....158 *q*
former d. but what it can*.651 *o*
I dare a little the more....623 *a*
I dare do all that may*.....119 *n*
"I dare not" wait upon, "I*122 *l*
if you do not d. to die you.755*m*
no, no, I dare not........464 *r*
that dare as well answer*..558 *x*
the hearts that dare are... 85 *d*
truest valour to d. to live..628 *i*
what man dare I dare*.....130 *l*
what they d. to dream of‡‡130 *e*
will to do, the soul to dare.383 *t*
woman, gentle woman, d...660 *k*
you must not dare for*....382 *s*
Dared-and dared the sturdy.239 *p*
none hath d., thou hast...137 *u*
thought he nobly dared.†..130 *d*
we dared not even to hope.681 *l*
Dares-bearing all mischance.582 *v*
bravely dares the danger..208 *n*
dares not put it to..........130 *f*
dares this pair of boots. .. 130 *q*
that dares love attempt*..363 *a*
'Tis much he d. ; and to*..628 *o*
who dares do more is none*119 *n*
Dareth-d. most, he wisest...760 *d*
Daring-d. great fears are...689 *c*
high for the d. of mortals..677 *b*
high position without d....689 *d*
loving are the daring......444 *p*
more dazzlingly when d.‖.456 *f*
Dar'st-d. thou then to beard.130 *h*
Dark-and after that the d.†..465 *d*
best of dark and bright‖.... 33 *t*
betwixt the d. and light†... 25 *l*
d. and doubtful love to run.427 *p*
dark as pitch..............496*ee*
d. as winter was the flow..530 *o*
d. green and gemm'd......236 *j*
d. the night with breath all.415 *l*
d. with excessive bright**.352*m*
days must be dark and§....514 *u*
ever-during d. surrounds**.149*m*
going to leap into the dark.499*kk*
green to sooty dark.......610 *n*
he travels safest in the d...606 *s*
hunt it in the dark.........339 *t*
in the dark a glimmering..777*m*
irrecoverably d.‖ total**... 61 *d*
is a dark profound......... 8 *t*
leave us d., forlorn and gray 11 *h*

may trust him in the dark.620 *j*
mournful rustling in the§..380 *j*
no rest—no dark.........398 *k*
now travels that d. path....689 *q*
O, d., d., d., amid the**... 61 *d*
o'er the d. her silver**......416*m*
O radiant dark ! O darkly..415*m*
or the abysmal dark.......571 *h*
so dark as sages say.......345 *q*
softly d. and darkly pure‖..186 *p*
stronger than the dark....164 *u*
that for ways that are d....144 *l*
the dark was over all†......391 *k*
the day is cold, and dark§..515 *a*
the enchanted dark.......159 *j*
through the dark..........323 *k*
what dark days seen*...... 3 *f*
what in me is d., illumine**510 *h*
wide o'er the d., by....... 399 *h*
worse than the d. before§.. 90 *b*
your light grows dark by*.352 *t*
Darken-natures double d.††.. 81 *j*
Darkened-d. room to muse†..429 *k*
darken'd with her shadow‖.356 *t*
hushed and d. room§......135 *o*
though d. with sulphur....627 *i*
Darker-d. than the darkest.†.237 *p*
long for one d. than night..175 *f*
Darkest-the d. day live till...511 *c*
Darkly-blue, d. deeply......460*m*
Darkness-against the d......352 *h*
ask what is darkness......355 *c*
canopied in darkness*.....193 *p*
come d., moonrise..........51 *r*
cried out in the d.........488 *j*
d. again and a silence§.....150 *v*
d. bends down like.........130 *o*
d. came the hands†........207 *r*
darkness from light........132 *o*
darkness had no need‖.....130 *l*
darkness how profound....418 *a*
darkness is fled. Now.....401 *c*
darkness itself appear.....352 *v*
d. now rose as daylight**..418 *j*
darkness of slumber and§..130*m*
darkness rooted there.....246 *i*
day is ended d. shrouds...416 *t*
death has made his d.†.....141*m*
defining night by d., death.100 *s*
distant voice in the§......150 *v*
encounter d. as a bride*....139 *s*
falter in the darkness..... 39 *t*
from d. until dawn........514 *s*
in darkness there is no.... 92 *k*
in my darkness and tears.. 10 *p*
in silent darkness born....561 *c*
instruments of d. tells us*..145 *g*
jaws of d. do devour*.....130 *q*
let us weep in our d........403 *j*
melting the darkness......130 *s*
midst of its own darkness¶.619 *c*
no d., but ignorance*.....314 *r*
no light but rather d.**....299 *e*
of pain, darkness and cold.346 *b*
of the primitive darkness..338 *i*
passed the door of d.......135 *g*
pray in the d. if there ...487 *n*
prince of d. is a gentleman*153 *o*
rather darkness visible**...338 *i*
raven down of darkness**.. 16 *r*
ring out the darkness of†... 41 *c*
scatters the rear of d**..... 44 *d*
second bidding d. fled**....462 *s*
slope thro' d. up to God†...268 *l*
the dungeon of darkness...512 *c*
the jaws of d. do devour*...171 *h*
to darkness and to me.....186 *s*
to thy state of darkness*..130 *r*
universal d. buries all‡..... 77 *d*
war with the lines of d....415 *e*
what thick d. pervades....713 *q*
where light in darkness*...352 *t*
Darling-Spring's last born d.392 *s*
the poet's darling¶.........227 *s*
this darling of the gods.... 90 *e*
Darlings-darlings of June...233 *l*
darlings of the early.....248 *f*

breathed upon dead........550 e
but they are dead¶........198 s
Cæsar d. and turned to*...152 b
can believe her dead......134 b
care not if I were dead....689 i
concerning the d. nothing..743 t
constant mourner o'er the‖613 c
cup to the dead already....604 m
d. and bleeding fresh*.....430 n
dead, but gone before......137 v
dead have all heard........527 o
d. he is not, but departed§.183 k
d. know it not, nor profit..458 t
d. on the field of honour...306 d
dead, that good old man.... 23 o
dead past bury its dead§.. 5 a
d. scandals form good‖.....537 y
dead the debt is due.......140 q
d. the sweet musician§.....405 s
d. the vegetable kingdom..546 n
dead who do not return ...132 g
dead within an hour*...... 36 r
doubly d. in that she died..137 i
English oak, which d......615 o
ever died dropped dead....359 h
for he being d. with him is* 77 f
for the queenliest dead ....137 i
from the ashes of d. men...201 f
great Pan is dead..........276 i
happier to be dead........133 s
heart must cover up its d..567 p
he being d., with him is*..139 g
he is dead and gone.......137 g
he mourns the d. who lives.403 k
home of the great dead.... 60 m
honours of the dead....... 13 u
hopeless lays his dead away150 f
immortal d. who live again.318 r
I mourn the dead........ 40 a
I shall be dead............226 l
I war not with the dead‡...637 b
John Lee is d., that good... 23 o
kept it since, by being d....200 v
lain for a century dead†...366 q
leave the d. moments to...601 f
lives whom we call dead§..316 i
living and the noble dead¶.565 x
maker of the d. man's bed.458 p
man though dead retains.‡816 o
many friends alive as d....142 n
Mary being dead ....137 e
my love is dead...........408 d
noble letters of the dead†..449 i
no past is dead for us.....316 d
not dead but gone before..361 v
not that I dead dead*...... 41 a
Oh! would I were d. now...590 v
Old Grimes is d., that good 23 g
our Patriarch Poet, dead...479 i
O ye d.poets, who are§....479 v
profane the service of the*.140 n
raise the d. to life than to§.452 w
remnant of our Spartan d..‖442 w
sleeping but never dead††. 418 h
taker may fall dead*......149 q
the beautifier of the dead‖.599 l
the dead be dead.........292 o
the dead have left still....667 c
the dead ride swiftly .....761 p
the dormitory of their d... 54 c
the King is d.! long live....505 l
the life of the dead. ......725 l
the living and the dead¶... 25 m
the sheeted d. did squeak*.140 d
they call'd him dead .....534 d
those two are dead¶.......198 s
till Pity's self be dead....403 e
tombs are the clothes of...396 p
tongues unto the silent d.§. 66 r
two months d.; nay, not*...149 r
two of them are dead... 506 mm
up with our English death*.639 l
vanish'd like their dead‡... 98 n
weary d. on their way up...136 k
we bear blossoms of the d.†605 q
what is the old king d.*....140 n
when I am d. my dearest...138 c

---

when I am d., no pageant..403 f
when one thinks it dead...693 f
who hath bent him o'er the‖132 w
whom we thought d. is.....138 j
with the mighty dead......516 t
would I were d. if God's...150 a
ye say "Abdallah's d."....131 v
Deadlier-th' inside of a d.sort671 d
Deadly-d.as the canker worm622 d
d. poisons are concealed...691 d
Dead Sea-D. S. fruit that...266 i
Deaf-a chamber d. of noise..563 h
d. as he that will not hear..509 h
d. rage that hears no .....786 c
d. to counsel it runs a......358 j
have ears more d. than*...146 a
none so d. as those.......295 x
to counsel deaf*..........215 m
turn the deaf ear.........296 i
Deafness-d. each one laughs. 8 t
Deafs-this same that d. our*.589 s
Deal-and to d. plainly I*. ... 11 v
d. with me in the future...524 z
Dealing-conscience to our d..595 g
man of upright dealing....454 o
Dealings-whose own hard d.* 93 f
Deals-d. on his own soul‖...105 h
Dean-cushion and soft d.‡...299 n
Deans-dowagers for d.†.....660 t
Dear-Ah youth! forever d.‡..672 m
all my soul held dear ... 312 o
art more dear to me††.....228 e
ask not a life for the d. ones.487 t
be a d. fool for an houre...653 f
both very old and very d...605 k
convincing—dangerously‖..590 e
cost you d. before he's.....427 s
d. as the light that visits...358 r
d. as the raptured thrill....655 a
d. as the ruddy drops that.358 r
d. as they grow old‡.......429 f
d., congenial to my heart..555 n
d., for his whistle.........251 m
d. to a man than his life...351 g
d. to me as light and life...356 g
emblem o' my dear.......238 f
forever sad! forever dear‡..409 l
makes the remembrance*..486 x
more d. is meadow breath.. 91 r
my d., my better half......645 r
my d. that love of.........357 g
oh how fondly dear.......380 c
resting-places for the dear.136 k
so dear I love him that**..361 a
so desolate but something‖.148 p
stream shall be d. to me...530 k
tales that to me were so d..379 n
that bread should be so d..484 q
the thoughts to memory d..597 k
to me more d. congenial to.411 c
what thy soul holds dear*..315 f
wonderful d. and pleasant.345 h
your welcome dear*.......644 d
Dearer-am d. than a friend*.548 d
dearer than his horse†.....466 a
dearer than self possesses‖.148 p
leather was not dearer than.453 f
man is dearer to them.....708 a
own as d. far than they....333 o
the land is d. for the sea....460 c
Dearest-d. and the best made117 r
things of dearest value....671 b
Dearie-o'er me and my d . 356 g
Dears-swears, the lovely d..654 w
Dearth-men expect a d.*.....189 n
Death-absence d. to those‡..544 k
accelerates my death.......137 a
a close exploit of death*...594 i
adjudged to d. and hell**..518 i
a doleful hymn to his own* 45 f
after death has the body...690 h
after his patient's death*..441 i
a lump of death—a chaos‖.. 76 v
amiable lovely death*......139 c
ancients dreaded death....134 l
and cried out Death**......136 q
and death unloads thee*...642 v

---

and if in death still lovely.142 m
and look on d. itself*......562 s
and my life in death.......276 g
an honorable d. is better...690 p
are but monuments of d....140 w
as, also in birth and death.654 v
at the point of death*......139 q
a useless life is an early d..776 p
base the fear of death.....210 l
be absolute for d.; either*..145 v
became precious by death..176 s
before the voice of death...134 k
behind her Death close**...136 n
beyond d. shall crown the.633 aa
beyond the reach of d. He..164 s
big with death.............105 a
birth is nothing but our d..604 j
bitterness of d, is hope...308 aa
blaze forth the d. of*......140 p
breaker d. that soldereth..375 s
bridge across the gulf of d.198 v
brother to Death, in silent.561 e
but a death more slow......324 f
but our death begun........351 x
call our own but death*....139 v
can this be death‡.........137 p
cause and not the d. that...374 b
certain but d. and taxes....502 t
cherish'd still the nearer*..138 o
cold, appear like death*...563 a
come away, come away, d.*138 p
come, D., and snatch me...156 u
confessor like unto D.§....135 g
count it death to falter.....141 d
covenant with death.......559 h
coward sneaks to d., the...121 n
cruel as death and hungry.311 j
cruel d. is always near.....349 g
danger and deserved d.*.... 76 e
danger of violent death ...347 w
death after life............526 g
d. aims with fouler spite...137 i
D., all eloquent! you only‡.137 n
d. alone discloses who.....689 r
death and his brother sleep.140 v
death and sleep and thou...555 a
death a necessary end*.....121 g
d. approaches, which is....745 b
d., as the Psalmist saith*..139 b
D. be merciful and pass... 32 c
D. be not proud though....133 k
d. betimes is comfort not...137 h
death borders upon our....134 h
D. broke at once the vital..135 f
death by dust.............100 s
D. calls you to the crowd of140 x
D. came with friendly care.182 j
death cannot be denied. ...174 q
Death cannot kill ....601 t
D. comes to all. His cold..137 f
d. cometh soon or late.....136 e
death confounds 'em all...133 v
d.-counterfeiting sleep.....562 x
death crowns life..........527 l
d. denyed ev'n fools would.142 i
d. denyed poor man would.142 i
d. does not put an end.....705 k
d. follows close behind....761 b
death follows life and.....648 n
death grinned horrible**...136 o
Death had the majority....132 m
D. has made his darkness‡.141 m
D. has so many doors to let.132 i
D. hath a thousand doors to.136 h
death hath ten thousand...141 u
death his fopperies........254 p
d. his soule do from his...316 s
D., if thou wilt, fain would 141 i
Death in a whiteness......231 o
death in itself is nothing...133 l
death in my hand*.........528 t
death in the wood.........231 o
d. is a black camel which..131 s
death is a guest divine.....142 b
death is another life.......132 e
d. is beautiful as feet of††.136 c
d. is delightful. D. isdawn136 j

SHAKESPEARE *; MILTON **; WORDSWORTH ¶; BYRON ‖; TENNYSON †; LOWELL ††; POPE ‡; LONGFELLOW §.

their right and wrong d....768 i
well skill'd in debate......152 u
Debauch–sick of the night's..369 d
Debauchee–and d. of dew....162 i
Debility–of weakness and d.* 12 a
Debonair–easy debonair and. 78 s
Debt–ambitions d. is paid*... 13 v
are in debt you hate....263 g
by physic some by debt....430 b
cancel my debt (too great).255 i
dead the debt is due........140 u
d. being a public blessing..142 v
d. if it is not excessive.....142 u
double debt to pay........308 r
funding our national d....142 v
I'm still in debt............334 i
in prison for debt........424m
not such a word as debt....263 u
pay every debt as if God...142 t
payment for so great a d.*.377 p
produce their d. instead of. 16 c
slender d. to Nature's......143 a
three-quarters of his d.... 178 d
two ways of paying debt...169 s
Debtor–am I your debtor†...188 h
every man a d. to his......421 k
Debts–d. to his authors....550 e
dies pays all debts*......139 p
I pay my debts, believe‡...310 s
other debts than those. 269 k
we call our old debts‖....105 c
words pay no d., give her*.665 y
Decalogue–hear the D. and¶.106 v
Decay–accumulates, and men143 g
age is not all d. it is the.... 10 n
are subject to decay....206 b
before d.'s effacing‖......132w
cold gradations of d......135 f
d. and growth of it........521 a
d., nor fading knows......219 l
d. of all our ideas....... 143 j
d. of its principles........770 o
fares it still in our decay¶. 12 n
grave with unperceived d..525 a
growth to meet decay....226 k
halo hovering round d.‖....143 c
hastes to swift decay ......442 e
is growing to decay.......289 l
mark the d. and growth...547 k
open only to decay§......218 q
sign of a general d. of virtue673 r
so my hopes decay‡........376 r
sympathy for its decay....543 k
talents, beauty, thus d...... 11 h
this muddy vesture of d.*.576w
time makes these decay....143 e
to decorate decay........231 q
too slowly ever to decay¶.619 b
with unperceived decay...143 i
with its swift decay††....187 s
yet still majestic in d.‡....535 u
Decays–age unconscious of‡.. 10 c
and in three more d........616 b
and now decays...... 349 r
from life by slow decays.‡.470 k
Deceased–he first d. she for..142 f
Deceit–d. should dwell*....145 f
d. should steal such gentle*145 e
God is not averse to d......143 p
men favour the deceit....347 h
quicksand of deceit*....... 145 c
rumor of oppression and d.566 r
show means most d.*......145 k
w. hug the dear deceit....144 d
Deceitful–d. shine, d. flow....623 b
false deceitful sudden*... 83 t
fires covered by d. ashes...690 u
Deceive–at length d. 'em... 39 h
bad man to d. by falsehood690 r
between speaking to d.....762 b
can deceive a lover........724 e
d. not thy physician......496ff
d. the deceiver............762 a
d. us, seeming to be......410 t
first appearances d. many. 691 g
first we practice to d. ....144 x
her sweet tongue could d..144w

nothing is more easy than.144 g
thyself no more d. thy...... 10 u
we d. and flatter no one by.762 k
we d. ourselves............762 j
we never d. for a good.....762 f
you can't deceive me.....691 i
Deceived–d. in your true......144m
d. the mother of mankind**153 i
d. the whole world........691 j
d. with ornament*......145 h
fortune has never d.......702 i
men find pleasure to be d..144 r
the silly when d. exclaim..762 c
trust all and be deceived...620 e
we are never deceived....762 j
Deceivers–men were d.*......212 e
Deceives–friend that never d.769 i
love d. the best of women‡359 y
the daisy but deceives......227 o
Deceiving–allowable in d. a..762 g
habit of lying or d. his.....691 o
hope but deceiving......167 l
roof in words d.**........461 t
those arts of deceiving....144 r
trust and that d............620 e
December–a drear-nighted...396 f
D. drops no weak relenting.396 d
D. fragrant chaplets blow‡.396 h
D.'s bareness everywhere*. 3 f
D. seem sweet May........189 h
D. when they wed*........377 f
depths of drear D.........391 e
hail to D.! say they all.... 396 e
in D. ring every day§......396 g
meetings and D. June†....627 p
mirth of its December....380 s
soon seek roses in D.‖......124 q
sun that brief D. day......396 j
wind beat dark D.*......... 12 c
Decencies–dwell in d.‡......633 g
those thousand d.**....... 5 h
Decency–and die with d....137 c
emblem right meet of d.... 24 j
for decency and truth......747 s
want of d. is want of sense.389 e
Decent–appears more d. as‡.581 i
came of decent people..... 95 k
Decide–and to d. impartially.330 p
come the moment to d.††..145 y
d. not rashly§...............145 p
d. when doctors disagree‡..145 u
Decided–d. on what they will.145 s
twelve honest men have d.331 h
Decider–thou grand d. of... 635 l
Decides–joking d. great**....145 t
Decipher–we d. the whole man340m
Decision–d. made can never§.145 p
voice of any true d.*......146 a
Deck–on d. beneath the......446 e
stood on the burning d....301 h
wove the lotus band to d...615 e
Decks–white are the d.‡.....577 r
Declaration–of independence.529 d
support of this d., we......419 d
Declarations–in his d........519 s
passionate declarations... 448 g
Declare–have heard her d.... 22 r
Decline–usually its decline... 29 c
Declines–life d. from thirty..657 c
Decorate–d. the fading year..219 f
Decorations–the solemn d....459 c
Decorum–hunt D. down......630 i
with d. all things carry'd.. 375 k
Decrease–heaven may d. it*..377 b
Decree–alter a d. established*438 z
curst by Heaven's d........368 x
leaps o'er a cold decree*..592w
your Majesty's humane d... 92 c
Decreed–I have decreed .....799 p
what is d. must be*......207 d
Decrees–d. of the Gods can...708 q
mould a mighty state's d.†.454 h
on our quick'st d.*...... 11 o
the d. of the fathers........708 o
Decrepitude–judging by your179 o
Dedicate–that is truly d. to*.639 n
Dee–across the sands o' D....530 l

flow on, lovely D., flow on.530 k
Deed–a good d. unless it.....691 r
and in every deed§........418 f
as a good d. accomplished§. 4 x
better not do the deed......187 v
burning d. and thought§..348 p
creed into your deed......158 c
deed go with it*............147 i
deed I intend is great ....146 v
d. is chronicled in hell*....123 u
d. is like the Heaven's. 146w
d. of death art thou*......123 r
deed of dreadful note*....123 v
deed without a name*....146 y
devours the d. in the*......491 i
dignified by the doer's d.*. 147 a
first will do some valiant d.146 n
I find thee worthy: do††... 525 t
in every deed of mischief.. 79 l
make an ugly d. look fair*.464 d
no great deed is done ......286 o
one good deed dying*......147 h
our feet each d. of shame§.630 n
praises itself but in the d.*491 i
put your creed into your d.146 l
some honourable deed be.. 306 e
somewhat the d., much....486 h
so shines a good deed in*...147 d
take the good-will for the d.508 d
take the will for the d......509bb
tells of a nameless deed....206 z
the better day the better d.504dd
the better day, the worse d.504ee
the deed might pierce......619 x
the result justifies the d....800 d
the will for the deed......506 r
thinking the deed, and not§451 a
thought and deed, not..... 15 p
Thy Will, for deed I do...507 d
'tis a kind of good d. to*...665 u
worthless unless the d. go.691 t
would the d. were good*...123 u
Deeds–ambition to**........146 q
asks what good d. he has.. 80 s
as the deeds they cover....665cc
be nameless in worthy d....310 e
be seen by our deeds......804 s
black deeds do lean on.... 290 n
blast proclaims most d.**..202 b
days fruitful of golden d.**146 s
d. inimitable like the sea...146 g
deeds are known in words..146 x
deeds are males, words....496gg
deeds are our doomsmen...146 p
d. are sometimes better.... 7 c
deeds carry their terrible..527 a
deeds find me the words**.146 t
deeds, not words.... ....496hh
deeds of high resolve......372 u
deeds of men never escape.691 p
d. shall be in water writ....146 d
deeds themselves though**146 q
deeds undone............519 h
deeds which are harvest...146 k
deeds which have no form.582 t
deeds worth praise and*....147 b
doeth ill deeds vile.........146 c
doing d. of hospitality*... 309 n
doth right d. is twice born.146 c
easy to beget great deeds..146 o
emblems of deeds that are‖.336 v
excused his devilish d.**...414 d
fame is the perfume of 497 s
fear on account of his d....685 b
foul deeds will rise*........123 s
future d. crowded round...762 o
gloss on faint deeds*......265 f
gods see the deeds of the...691 q
good deeds in his day-book.691 u
great thoughts, like great..595 u
heaven are plac'd by their.146m
heroic d. and hapless fall**637w
in d., not years, piercing‖.. 9 c
inspires immortal deeds....367 d
little deeds of kindness....146 u
loveliness of perfect d.†.... 92 s
makes ill deeds done*......594 f

man of mighty deeds.......135 a
massive deeds and great§..206 q
matter for virtuous deedes.146 h
measure by thy deeds*.....147 j
noble d. that are concealed.762m
nobler by great deeds§.....418 g
no man's good deeds.......83 d
only d. give strength to life777 b
our deeds determine us....146 j
praises the d. of another...677 k
precious deeds in one that*147 g
proof of deeds not words..146 f
purchased by the deeds we.306 e
render the d. of mercy*....382 q
rewards his deeds with*....147 c
set a gloss on faint deeds.* 73 b
sourest by their deeds*....643 o
strengthens unto virtuous.526 r
the deeds of his fathers....557 k
the gentle deeds of mercy..382 k
these unlucky d. relate*...332 r
those scraps are good d.*..602 x
thoughts beget strange d..597 r
'tis d. that I prefer to see..796 s
to awe whom yet with d.**146 r
truth hath better d. than*.554bb
unnatural deeds do breed*.523 e
vaunting vile deeds........206 e
victorious deeds to die.....568 l
wait on virtuous deeds.... 60 o
we live in deeds not years.345m
with deeds requite thy*....147 f
words are women d. are....509 r
words pay no debts, give*.665 y
words were meant for d....664 o
worse d. worse sufferings**105 t
yet words are no deeds*....665 u
you do the d. and your**.146 t
Deep-always-wind-obeying*..460 j
blue deep in yon sky....... 31 j
blue waves of the deep.... 71 h
but the deep are dumb.....465 v
call spirits from the vasty*575 e
deep and bright within....257 k
deep in my heart subsides.666 a
d. into the generous mind.484 t
d. waters noyselesse are.. .572 v
hearts! let's seek the deep. 48 f
home on the rolling deep..460 i
I find no way from deep**.105 u
in the lowest d. a lower**..101 q
irregularly deep and shrill.634 r
lie too deep for tears¶.....221 f
monsters of the deep are‖..459 g
not so deep as a well*......112 g
others venture on the deep.736 n
rocked in the cradle of the.460 r
still waters run deep.......742 d
swimming in the vast deep.741 k
the blue deep's serene‖....647 b
there's danger on the d....444 u
thou art deep and bright..101 a
though deep yet clear...... 78 u
'tis not so d. as a well, nor*671 h
various journey to the d...529 l
vast and boundless deep**.598 l
where the brook is deep*..504 b
Deep-blue-d-b. tinged with..230 j
Deepest-is deepest in him.... 64 o
smoothest, the water is d. 508 ff
Deeply-blue, darkly, deeply.460m
Deeps-all the deeps below...274 p
come blue deeps.......... 99 m
Deep-searched-d-s. with*...580 r
Deer-a-chasing the deer......296 n
stricken deer that left the..388 c
where the deer's swift leap.567 c
yield up their deer to*......279 g
Deface-d. their ill-placed... 344 n
Defacing-d. first, then.......595 e
Defamed-defamed by every.†271 r
Defeat-are triumph and d.§.. 81 c
but wailings of defeat......351 d
rise from disaster and d§...619 g
unkindness may d. my life*627 w
Defeated-as he, d. dying.....608 y
mortal hopes d. and¶.......592 s

Defect-blamed shall not be*·559 a
but some defect in her*... 283m
cause of this defect*........ 72 u
excess than the defect§.....119 d
fine by d. and delicately‡...658 f
glory from defect arise....272m
let a d. which is possibly...175 v
pure heroical defect of.....522 o
repair a defect of character 79 f
this fair defect of nature**.657 s
Defects-conceal the d. of the.780 f
exhibit the defects of bad..446 r
no man's defects sought... 83 d
reckon up our d. than to... 78 e
to have great defects......771 a
your defects to know‡......261 u
Defence-admit of no defence.389 e
as well for his defence......303m
awake endeavour for d*....119 k
cheap defence of nations...143 b
dear friend, needs no d.....632 q
gate to make defence**....172 l
greatest d. and ornament..444 v
in cases of d. 'tis best to*..172 r
knavery is the best defence.336 f
millions for d., but not.....469 h
one gate to make defence**638 e
preparation for our d ......638 q
proportions of d. are fill'd*.172 r
stand in your own defence*119 o
stand up in Wit's defence..341 h
wisdom makes but a slow..650 o
Defend-defend against your..260 e
defend me from my friends263 d
defend myself from my.....263 d
ease, relieve, defend........105 n
God defend the right.......498 z
I will defend................805 c
preserve, protect, and d....419 h
ready to guard and d. it....344 i
right to d. them in the best.529 b
Defendant-d. and plaintiff††.285 g
plaintiff, d., gentlemen.....437 d
Defended-d. by all our hands.469 u
fireside howsoe'er d.§ 136 a
Defender-mean the faith's d.533m
Defends-when attacked it d..757 k
Defer-d. not till to-morrow..605 h
'tis madness to defer.......147 q
Deferred-sickening pang of..308 s
Defiance-defiance in their...490 v
hearts bid the tyrants d...468 f
in his cottage bid defiance.304 l
Defies-and defies its point....118m
Defiled-touch pitch will be d.*506 x
Definition-can tell the d.....630 y
definition of life is false....348 v
Deform-d. and torture man..633w
Deformed-d. but the*.......627 u
d., crooked, old and, seer*.. 83 n
deformed in their rooms.... 89 c
how d. dost thou look*.....314 s
senseless and d. convulsive. 18 d
Deformity-d. of which the... 25 p
Defy-defy the devil*........153 q
I do it, him and I spit*......172 v
records that d. the tooth of.604 b
Defying-d. it that the brave..761 k
Degenerate-d. mind.........699 t
earth's d. sons could raise‡.641 s
of degenerate man.........278 v
stupidity of the most d....385w
Degrades-d. the great......290 g
Degree-author, in some d....428 f
but all in the degree‡......372 a
but a squire of low degree.421 d
but of a low degree....... 23 s
but place, d., and form*... 73 c
by some degree of woe.....569 l
choose the high or low d‡..633 f
many more of lesser d...... 48 a
observe d., priority, and*.. 462 x
speech and degree.........398 q
take but d. away, untune*.407 q
Degrees-ever heal but by d.*.467 q
fine, by degrees. .. .. 36 f
it grows up by degrees.....644 j

scoring the base d. by*..... 14 d
spreads by slow degrees....616 b
that estates, d. and offices*.383 h
Deist-d. sighed with saving..451 f
though the deist rave.....520 p
Deity-Deity adored, is joy...276 b
Deity believed, is joy.......276 b
Deity beloved, is joy.......276 b
fits it to bespeak the Deity.404 f
for Deity offended..........519 v
gentle Deity of dreams.....560 l
light us deep into the Deity.577m
passing bell for Deity.......612 c
the felt presence of the D..567 v
the present is a powerful...784 o
Dejected-d. while another's‡.588 i
not easily dejected.........290 r
Dejection-in our d. do we¶... 76 s
Delay-away with delay.....692 c
away with delay...........692 h
but studious of delay‡......666 u
chides his infamous delay..401 p
d. always heeds danger....496ii
d. is too long to one who is.692 f
delay leads impotent*......147 n
d. that postpones our joys.692 d
die needs no delay.........137 h
do not d.; the golden§......147m
fly to him, bid him d. not...656 n
has often been cured by d..692 g
haste, half-sister to delay†.605 g
life is at stake no d. is too..692 a
man by d. restored the.....691 v
no d. that is afforded is.....692 b
persuade d. what boots to..464 u
practice is to delay it... ...763 r
reprov'd each dull delay....450 l
saddens at the long delay..147 p
take time and a little d.....677 s
unseen hands d. the coming 151 g
weak or sick with long d...487 n
will not bear delay.........723 u
Delaying-sweet new year d.†.541 e
Delays-abatements and d.*.. 76 d
d. are dangerous in war....147 k
d. have dangerous ends*...496jj
life for delays and doubts. .346 s
long demurs breed new d...603 n
truth hates delays.........748 d
who suffer in delays.......791 h
Delft-D. with all its wares§.. 97 t
Delia-tongue like D.'s o'er...606 l
Deliberates-woman that d....355 a
Deliberating-often lost by d..692 i
Deliberation-d. sat and**....153 j
Delicacies-disdaining little d.424 k
less costly delicacies........177 k
Delicacy-finer than her d....550 d
greatest d. among birds....181 g
I like their delicacy........657 b
love lessens woman's d.... 778 c
refinement is false d........101m
true delicacy is solid. 101m
Delicate-the body's delicate*259 f
Delicately-and d. weak‡.....658 f
Delicious-not good is not**...280 j
Deliciousness-d. was spell'd..241 u
loathsome his own d.*...... 26 f
Delight-account than mere d.173 g
and home-felt delight*..... 61 r
and lap me in delight.......457m
a vision of delight¶........ 57 i
day of delight and wonder.615 k
degree of d. and that no....147 r
d. hath a joy in it either...341 f
delight of mankind††.......270 u
d. of opening a new pursuit516 b
d. still more and more......539m
dimness with its own d‖.... 34 c
drooping spirits in d.**... 162 o
enjoy delight with libertie.412 q
feel more exquisite delight.426 t
give delight and hurt not*.327 i
go to it with delight*. .....442 n
gravestone of a dead d.§...131 c
guilt exalts the keen d.‡....290 j
harmony or true delight**.184 r

SHAKESPEARE *; MILTON **; WORDSWORTH ¶; BYRON ‖; TENNYSON †; LOWELL ††; POPE ‡; LONGFELLOW §.

d. too much of a good thing496 w
d. what God would have us488 c
dread more than we d.......365 q
general object of d.is known629 w
has no more to desire......281 n
help thy d. in killing a Pike 18 e
I d. to see those things....803ee
I do d. we may be*.......148 e
lack of d. is the greatest...642 t
like flowers and bear d....148 k
lift from earth our low d.‖.357 c
love and d. are the spirit's..778m
moth with vain desire‖.....103 c
neither desire nor fear.....802 g
nurse of young desire......307 j
one sole d., one passion...528m
or kindle soft desire .... 2 e
pined away with desire....245 n
Priam checked his son's d.*148 d
pureness to desire, a mount359 l
satisfy the sharp desire**..266 g
the second of desire§......554 k
the soul's sincere desire...488 v
this fond desire............315 l
to pray is to desire........488 c
to succeed you must.. ....677 d
unknown there is no d.....713 s
vision of fulfill'd desire...297 w
which crowns d. with gift .582 l
which was not desire‖......191 v
who lives as they desire...403 k
your true heart's desire...144m
Desired–begs to be d. to give*343 f
no more to be desired......110 g
Desires–ambitious worldly d. 12 p
army of the world's d.*....104 w
d. not from the bottom of. 488 c
desires to live long........ 12 f
d. what it has not..........245 c
dwell not in my desires*...120 v
each man has his own d....692 k
efflation of his wild d......588 e
infinite in his desires......371 k
man's d. and aspirations..765 g
mind from vain d. is.......111 b
of my young desires........261 r
sacrifice of these desires...586 l
she lingers my desires*.... 398 s
soft d. I can trace.......... 30 q
swift desires that dart§....302 q
their past long-lost d.......673 n
'tis not what our youth d..671 q
vivacity of earthly d.......586 l
wings it with sublime d....404 f
Desireth–d. great matters...297 d
Desiring–still d., we live......772 u
Desk–formed his d. and chair.617 h
is but a d. to write upon...662 d
the desk's dead wood......666 w
Desks–d. Apollo's sons repair408 a
Desolate–beautiful are..... 33 l
d.—Life is so dreary......148 q
none are so d. but some‖..148 p
no one so utterly desolate§.148 s
no soul is d. as long.......148 r
so utterly desolate§........206 r
Desolation–Babylon in all its.385m
d. does begin to make*....148 t
Despair–and d. most fits*....189 k
and sorrow hates d.........507gg
better to hope than to d....772 s
birds that are within d.....378 d
brother devil to Despair...158 r
changed for Despair.......257 f
conscience wakes d.**......105 t
crushes into dumb d.§......488 k
d. is a great incentive......692m
d. of ever being saved......149 b
depths of some divine d.†..592 n
d. the shadow of a starless.150 d
despair to get in...........155m
d. through fear alone ......680 f
fiercer by despair**........149 k
final hope is flat d.**......149 l
greater mischief than d.....158 n
grief and dark despair..... 48 l
groaning cargo of d........446 f

heaven quits us in d......150 h
hope, and from despair‡..579 g
I shall d. There is no*.....474 d
I, wasting in despaire.....661 b
let no one d., even though..772 r
never despair....... ......802 v
never d. while under the...692 l
nothing but despair*......149 v
of nothing but despair*....149 n
Old Age is not Despair ... 9 k
on its head despair........232 p
pangs and fury of d... .. 149 a
question of Despair‖.......149 e
reason would despair......360 i
recklessness and d.........149 h
resolution from despair**.308 h
should all d. that have*....645 p
the message of despair....538 h
there breathes despair‖....204 j
this kind of d. is one of the.149 b
thou the accents of d.‖.....487m
was in utter despair........ 23 a
where seraphs might d.‖...369 i
worse than despair........308aa
Despaireth–idleness ever d..339 l
Despatch–D. is the soul of...441 s
Desperate–beware of d.......149 g
marriage is a d. thing.....376m
though d. of success**......472m
thoughts of d. men*........387 d
try one d. med'cine........439 t
Desperation–need to d.......760 d
Desperat'st–d. is the wisest...439 t
Despise–d. all those who....630m
d. me, I'm the prouder for.490 r
d. money on some.........728 i
d. thee and thy suit‖......662 e
despise the human race ..725 s
I neither fear nor despise..802 o
learn justice and d. not....718 k
more manly to despise....507 k
understand it, d. it, love it.667 x
Despised–and most lov'd d.*. 84 k
dull, hated, d. in the....... 52m
world and despised........137 u
Despises–he d. what he.....682 g
he who despises one......353 c
Despoiled–d. the gardens... 233 l
Despond–apter to d. than...427 s
slough was Despond......149 d
Despotism–d. of vice‖.......626 a
Despots–blossomed o'er the..614 p
the despot's wickedness...626 e
Dessert–this same d. is not so‡167 p
Destinies–d.are fraught with§102 s
great men's destinies††.....151 b
portals of our earthly d....151 j
Destiny–Constitution, one D.627 c
day we fashion Destiny....207 u
each one our own destiny..698 c
how glorious man's d.§....151 a
I bear the shears of d.* ...152 g
inevitable as destiny§......201 u
new chances of coming d..152 n
not design, but destiny....151 h
or brave can shun his d....150 u
rarely man escapes his d...767 c
task which d. has set...... 150 s
the destiny of to-morrow..150 r
wiving goes by destiny*...498 x
your d. is that of a man....766 n
Destroy–a breath may d. ....668 b
consuming time can d......714m
d. all creatures for thy‡...510 k
d. everything rather than..759 c
d. his fib or sophistry‡.....644m
d. their paradise...........582 o
destructive time d.........746 c
fine wits d. themselves with653 v
one to d. is murder........404 e
powerless north wind can..714 l
safer to be that which we*..507 n
Destroyed–and cannot be d.¶382 b
Destroy'd his country*.....608 s
is d. by thought..........596 g
when once d. can never....143 g
Destroyer–time the great d..354 b

Destroys–Creates, preserves,.352 d
Destroys the mighty-......274 g
first d. their mind........320 t
Destruction–by d. dwell in*..507 n
hath driven destruction...165 o
plot the d. of others......739 k
startles at destruction......315 l
that usher to destruction...481 s
things haste to d..........697 l
Desuetude–innocuous d......436 x
Desultory–mind of d. man...629 l
Detail–cold blood each mean.146 o
Detect–d. the subtlest fold of.327 p
lose it in the moment you‡..349 l
we scarcely detect it.......348 l
Detectives–while medical d..321 l
Detector–death-bed's a d. of.142 g
Deter–d. a man from so vain.200 c
Determination–has a good d.145 e
Determine–loss how to d.....154m
though men d., the gods...506ii
we d. our deeds...........146 j
Detest–equally d. the.......534 j
for while the treason I d...608 j
they detest at leisure‖.....294 x
yet detest the offence‡.....556 f
Detests–my heart d. him.‡...199 g
Detraction–d. will not suffer*306 y
Deuce–the d. was to pay....302 p
Development–dreams in‖....560 r
Device–and no d.—Press on!..492 n
interpret your device......276 n
I smell a device*...........500 w
'tis plate of rare device*...434 s
Devices–d. still are*.........207 j
fine devices in his head....372 c
from all d. human††. .....251 t
scorns to bend to mean d..118 s
Devil–abashed the d. stood**.354 l
a devil at everything....... 2 c
also unto the d. sticks....762 s
and a devil at home.......312 c
and a mid-day devil‡.. 645 j
and the devil made sin....510 a
as I hate the devil.........295 d
a synonyme for the d......409 i
a-walking the d. is gone...153 r
balance with the devil‖....105 e
been the devil's tools......656 p
brave the de'il ....246 o
but the devil to pay ..... 82 t
but the devil whoops, as... 28 l
call'd the d. and he came..152 u
can the devil speak true*..623 r
cole-pit to put the d. in...510 a
defy the devil*...........153 q
devil, and no monster*....153 p
d. always builds a chapel.. 95 c
devil can cite Scripture*..514 k
d. climbs into the belfry§..450 r
devil cross my prayer*....153 t
devil design'd for one fair..655 x
d. did grin for his darling.310 h
d. have all the good tunes.405 f
devil himself which is.....152 r
d. in every berry of the....649 o
devil in his sneer‖.........109 g
d. is a woman just now....153 a
devil lead the measure*...207 c
devil sends us cooks.......431 q
d.'s in the moon for‖.......397 j
devil take the hin'most....152 s
deil tak the hindmost......294 t
d. that told me I did well*..123 n
devil this melancholy is...379 b
devil understands Welsh*..310 z
devil was sick, the devil a..153 k
d. wear black*............153m
devil will have a chapel...508bb
devil will not have me*.. .299 r
d. with devil damn'd**.....627 l
devil would also build a....497 ff
don't let him go to the d...607 b
doubt is brother devil.....158 r
give the devil his due......498 d
go that the d. dryveth......499 a
got over the devil's back...508 j

Diver-the d. Omar plucked††477 k
Divers-d.under the water doe445 o
Diversified-d. with boggles ..213 i
Diversity-D., that is my....794 h
  universal quality is d........461 b
Divert-D. her eyes with‡....213 a
Divide-distance shall no§....189 f
  Divide and command......794 a
  divide and govern.........799 x
  how can we divide........324 o
  loving hearts divide......172m
  they do divide our being‖..159 n
  years could us divide.....261m
  Divided-d.by opposite.......729 s
  divided we fall............214m
  house d. against itself......282 j
  time d. is never long......603 q
  united yet d., twain at.....430 r
Dividends-incarnation of fat.643 b
  man with dividends§.......97 q
Divides-d. one thing entire*. 288 g
Dividing-stand, by d. we fall.627 f
Divination-d. seems........654 o
Divine-are fou' o' love d....101 d
  being a d., a ghostly*...... 33 f
  divine in its infinity........558 o
  divine is love and scorneth.361 s
  divine than all divinities...260 j
  divine things delight it.....738 i
  doth ask a drink divine....641 d
  fortified by power divine..522m
  good d. that follows his*....451 l
  hand that made us is d....556bb
  lovely she's divine.......203 s
  makes them seem d.*......659 w
  may kill a sound divine....450 a
  men d. and sacred call....670 p
  more needs she the d.*....523 e
  particle of divine breath...696 d
  save the spirit of man is d.‖370 j
  sculpture is more divine§..452 l
  show us how d. a thing¶...661 f
  shrewd and sound divine..451 f
  style the divine! the‡......551 a
  than aught d. or holy else**369 k
  the fear of some d. and.... 420 a
  thou art all divine.........654 n
  to compel man to D.......670 o
  to forgive, divine‡.......255 p
  truth is unwelcome, how.. 621 t
  wait for and divine... ....208 i
Divin'd-sooner in my heart**588 h
Divinely-d. bent to*.........378 i
  hoary crest d. led........397 o
Diviner-the glad d.'s theme..634 d
Diviners-truest d. of nature.480 b
Divining-d. rods of Magi...216 f
Divinity-d. doth hedge a*...535 f
  D. had catch'd the itch.... 2 b
  d. in odd numbers*.........152 d
  d. that shapes our ends*...510 u
  d. that stirs within us......315 l
  d. who rules within us,...689 l
  d. within our breast.. ...743m
  proof of its divinity........738 i
  seat of the Divinity........707 f
Division-equal d. of unequal.482 l
  write d., and draw.......448 e
Divisions-heal d., to relieve‡. 60 g
Divorce-d. of steel falls on*..489 h
Divorc'd-this golden rigol*..562w
Dizziness-love is like a d....359 c
Dizzy-d. on unwonted.......795 b
Do-all may d. what has by... 6 d
  attempt to d. what you...691 s
  believe you can d. as...... 2 i
  but to d. what lies clearly.. 4 e
  but what we do.........268 q
  cannot all do all things ...675 i
  cease to do and be....... 10 r
  confident I can do very....428 r
  damn'd if you do.........158 c
  die is all we have to do....346aa
  do anything but die........457 a
  d. noble things not dream..280 h
  do this and I'll do that.....670 e
  do well and right and let... 4 o

do what is already done....675 h
  do with might and main... 4 l
  ever do nothing but that*..129 h
  first words are "How do...175 l
  gave man a thing to do.... 92 o
  guilty to what we wildly d.* 73 u
  Hercules himself d. what*.152 c
  how not to do it........ ...282 b
  if we do well here we shall.347 j
  it teaches us to do.........651 j
  let us do or die..... .....343m
  man do but be merry*....384 n
  much one man can do..... 5 e
  nothing I suppose to do....175 l
  pay with what they do....758 j
  right and not to do it .....121 b
  say "How d. you do"......178 r
  should do with all his.....675 a
  so much to do, so little‡....669m
  theirs but to do and die†... 6 a
  to-morrow let us do or die. 4 d
  we know not what we do...665bb
  what you can do to-day...599 q
  when two persons do the.. 684 h
  which you can do to-day...502 l
  will to do, the soul to dare.383 t
  wish what you can do......738 t
Doat-neither to d. too much.375 t
Dobbin-D. my fill horse*....458 g
Docks-nothing teems but*...643m
Doctor-and Dr. Dyet......440 t
  banished the d., and‡ .....440 n
  by d.'s bills to play the d.'s‡440 p
  Diaulus, lately a doctor....174 r
  dismissing the d. don't...552m
  d.'s brow should smile.....440 l
  drink you with no d........177 h
  fee the d. for a nauseous..440 b
  generally the best doctor..440m
  I do not love you Dr. Fell..723 a
  must women have a d. or.. 92 f
  next Dr. Merryman.......440 t
  silent d. shook his head....440 e
  still first Dr. Quiet........440 t
  seize the doctor too*......441 b
  tell your d. that y' are ill..440 r
  used to do also as a d......174 r
Doctors-decide when d.‡.....145 u
  d. cure by letting blood....518 a
  ere d. learn'd to kill.......440 c
  in learned doctors' spite...457m
  like d. thus when much‡... 27m
  the d. and the sages.......399 o
Doctrine-a book of d.........589 e
  explain thy d. by thy life...158 j
  in d. uncorrupt ....450 g
  not for the d., but‡.........406 s
  prove their d. orthodox...157 o
  saving d. preach'd to all‡ .158 g
  teacher's d. sanctified¶...158 k
  the doctrine of ill-doing*...320 o
  whose d. and whose life....450 c
Doctrinal-faith in d. matters197m
Doctrines-d. which they....450 j
  what makes all d. plain...157 p
Document-d. written in.....399 l
Documents-different d......435m
Dodder-yellow d. gliding...228 h
Doeg-doeg, though without..476 o
Doer-other but the doer's...646 i
  mute spoke loud the d.**..146 g
Doers-talkers are no good d.*589 q
Does-d. after his departure..597 x
  handsome is that handsome498w
  man d. which exalts him...146 e
  sees and does it............ 4 a
  that what he will he does*.646 o
Dog-a dog's obey'd in office*. 30 b
  dog him still with after....386w
  dog is drowning, every one.508 u
  dog it was that died....... 20 a
  dog of Blenheim birth...... 20 d
  dog salutes the smiling.... 19 p
  d. shall bear him company‡.349 p
  dog smarts for what that..113 n
  d.'s walking on his hind...450 p
  dog would break thy......443 e

farmer's dog bark at a*.... 30 b
  fire with the dog's foot.....507 x
  for my cat and dog...... 19m
  hair of the dog that bit...291 h
  held by a small dog...... 734 a
  Highness' dog at Kew‡.... 20 c
  hold-fast is the only dog*...511 u
  I had rather be a dog and*.109 r
  in that town a d. was found. 19 q
  mew and d. will have his*..152 c
  ope my lips let no d. bark*.461 u
  quickly found to beat a d.*.461m
  Roger's my d.—come here. 20 g
  scalded d. fears cold water.506 d
  something better than hist.466 a
  tail must wag the dog...... 28 l
  third dog one of the two....113 a
  whose dog are you‡...... 20 c
Dog-days-to shake in d-d., in.120 s
Doggedly-he set himself d...428 n
Dog'rel-in dog'rel verse of... 87 m
Dogs-as dogs upon their*...382 s
  contempt for the dogs......181 k
  d. and all, Tray, Blanche*.. 20 e
  fierceness English dogs*...122 c
  her slow dogs of war......365 h
  knew that pups are like d..684 i
  let d. delight to bark and..157 i
  let slip the dogs of war*...638w
  like your asses and your*..559 t
  little d. do at strangers....174 c
  many dogs there be, both.. 19 q
  summons the d. and greets. 87 k
  that dogs must eat*.......311 h
  the worst dogs is silent.... 771 r
  throw physic to the dogs*..441 c
  what dogs are these*......432 e
  when two d. are fighting...113 a
  would rain cats and dogs..515 e
Dog-star-the scorching d-s...672 i
Doing-be up and doing§..... 4w
  capable of d. before all the. 70 b
  doing of the will of God....420 d
  doing or suffering**.......641 w
  doing what I pleased......110 g
  ease and speed in d. a thing.667 g
  joy's soul lies in the doing*.663 r
  pleasing in doing it.......164 g
  readiness of doing doth....646 i
  shortest answer is doing...506 f
  still be doing, never done..666 g
  whatever is worth d. at all.508 i
Doings-the doings of men...679 s
Doit-the beggarly last doit...484 l
Dole-ask their humble dole..294 j
  weighing delight and dole*.145m
Dollar-the almighty d. that..389 s
Dollars-bags of d. coins‖.....389 l
  cost five hundred dollars... 22 r
  twelve hundred d. won't... 20 q
Dolorous-a voice of d. pitch..484 r
Dolour-like syllable of d.*...569 r
Dolphin-dies like the d.‖.....624 g
  ere the d. dies its..........134 k
  mermaid on a d.'s back*...383 j
  paints a d. in the woods....714 f
  see the D.'s anchor forged..480 e
Dolphin-like-delights were*.. 41 s
Dolphins-pleas'd to see the...445 f
Domain-extends his desolate.546 n
  landmark of a new d.§.....131 c
  of nature's wide domain...369 o
  praise a large domain......676 v
  reach her broad domain....236 d
Dome-d. its vast immensity..413 f
  d. of many-colored glass...351 b
  high d. re-echoes to his‡...457 j
  him of the western dome...548 j
  raise the d. into the sky....568 k
  the d. of Thought, the‖....571 b
  well-proportioned dome‡...425 s
  with a dome more vast.....571 n
Domes-her sacred domes‡...688 j
Domestic-a bosom-serpent,‡.645 j
  color of domestic life......304 h
  domestic happiness, thou..293 b
  equality of two d. powers*.184 s

expense of my domestic....269 f
smooth current of d. joy...172 w
wife, d., good and pure...644 z
Dominion–and this is thy d.¶..50 f
d. absolute ; that right**...559 p
grace is founded in d.......460 t
supreme d. through the.... 46 c
time, the foe of man's d....601 p
Dominions–d. of earth.. .....258 e
ether's high, unknown d... 4 n
sets upon their d........483 n
sun ne'er sets on my d....534 s
Donation–by his donation**..559 p
Done–and a' is d. in vain.....196 l
and wish 'twere done .....345 i
apostles would have d. as‖.. 93 b
but to have d. and to have. 10 r
d. and cannot be undone§...359 v
d. cannot be now amended*..152 j
done, thought, gained or... 64 k
done without example*....210 b
done with so much ease....410 r
has poster'ty done for us..484 h
have ye done well ....603 k
it has been done..........800 e
I've d. my duty, and I've..594 q
know what ought to be d..680 i
not have d. to yourselves..508 s
now a' is done that men....196 l
something must be d. for..446 p
surprised to find it d. at...450 p
things done well*........210 b
things won are d., joy's*...663 r
thou hast done for me.....379 o
we have already done§....331 d
well it were done quickly*. 5 o
were done, when 'tis done*. 5 o
whatever he did was done..283 i
what hath it done, that in*.131 m
what have I done.........805 f
what's done cannot be*....508 p
what's done we partly.... 4 b
what you have done......428 s
world where much is to be.668 n
Donkeys–Janet! Donkeys....20 h
Doom–an equal d. clipp'd ..471 a
battered with the shocks†.351 m
by doom of battle**.......637 w
deplore their doom........205 s
even to the edge of doom*.108 t
hard doom did receive‡...512 m
hell by doom severe**....518 i
he meets his doom..... 114 s
regardless of their d. the.. 89 m
repented o'er his doom*...523 n
shall be thy doom.......227 d
to the crack of doom*.....127 c
Doom'd–d. that path to‡....150 t
Doomsday–d. is near ; die*..119 l
every day is doomsday....600 j
last till doomsday*........458 v
then is doomsday near*...305 m
Doomsmen–deeds are our d..146 p
Doon–braes o' Bonny Doon..530 m
Door–a hatch before the d...500 cc
beside a human door¶.....587 b
brought him to your door..473 w
click'd behind the door....303 r
door had given her to his..644 aa
door on his own genius....446 g
door that time unlocks§....400 i
enters in at a door§......135 m
God enters by a private d..274 l
golden door of Wisdom...651 s
he knocks at the door..... 9 g
he's rapping at the door... 69 b
just above my chamber d.. 55 b
keep you standing at that..643 l
king dead? as nail in door*.140 n
let the door be lock'd*....631 q
luck knocks at his door...368 g
obedience is the key to.....420 e
o'erhead an open door.....394 m
old landlord's hospitable‡.. 484 w
opening door that time§...605 j
passed the d. of darkness..135 q
pity me, open the door*.... 38 r

she does keep the door.....573 q
should keep within her d..644 z
shut the door, good John‡..144 v
slow creaking turns the d..474 a
solitude of passing his‖....566 f
so wide as a church door*..671 h
sweep the dust behind*....462 w
Yet turns he not from the. 9 q
Door-handles–d-h. turned†... 25 l
Doors–and bolted d. that†.... 25 l
bar thine adamantine d...545 h
death hath so many d. to..132 i
death hath a thousand d...136 h
doors all were of brass.....425 e
doors be shut upon him*..252 q
d. upon a woman's wit*.. .658 cc
drives beneath the doors...514 s
from its force, nor d., nor. 482 t
heavens, your living d. **..122 v
hostess clap to the doors*..384 i
men shut their d. against*. 11 q
noiseless d. close after us..151 j
ten thousand several d.....141 u
th' infernal doors**.......299 l
thousand d. that lead to...132 n
through our open doors....611 l
write on your d. the§......119 q
Doorside–our d. queen......226 i
Doorstep–d. into a world§...115 e
d. to the temple of wisdom.651 q
Doorway–the low d. of my††.634 h
Dormitory–the d. of their... 54 c
Dose–he had administer'd a..456 e
scrawl, the d. the better...440 r
Dotage–streams of d. flow...348 g
Dotages–common d. of.....593 p
Dotard–fly dotard, fly‡.....160 a
Dote–d. on his very absence,* 3 g
love the sea? I d. upon it.459 u
Nature they say, doth d.††.122 u
on scraps of learning d....514 n
what dust we d. on when*..187 n
Dotes–who dotes yet doubts*328 e
Double–confers a d. kindness718 t
double his troubles........500 b
require a d. maintenance..375 g
surely you'll grow d.¶.....580 h
Doubled–d. fac'd is d.**....202 b
the kindness is doubled....718 s
Doubt–affirmance breeds a d.419 b
all the gods but Doubt. ....158 r
becomes d. realized........158 o
clouded with d. and.......143 h
d. a greater mischief than.158 n
D. and Discord step 'twixt‖.156 x
d. and exultation.........210 p
d. is brother devil to......158 r
d. would be disloyalty.....529 g
faith in honest doubt†......198 n
fill thy soul with doubt§....135 q
frequently learning to d....763 l
has left us in doubt........208 a
hinge nor loop to hang a d.*159 c
how prone to d. how.‡....650 t
in doubt my oracles........261 r
keeps a d. in reserve......473 d
modest d. is call'd the*.....159 b
more faith in honest d.†....159 h
never stand to doubt...... 4 q
nor doubt a wife..........375 t
once in d. is once to be*....159 e
soundest casuists d., like‡..145 u
terrible d. of appearances.159 i
than d. one heart, that, if..620 e
the mists of d. prevail.... 89 n
the shafts of doubt........198 q
where d., there truth is...621 c
who read, to d., or read....516 p
with knowledge doubt.....774 r
yet I d. not thro' the ages†.598 c
Doubted–I d. of this saw, till. 95 p
who never d., never half...621 c
Doubter–from the mighty d.352 h
Doubtful–dark and d. love..427 p
d. beam long nods from‡..158 p
slow process of the d. years480 w
Doubting–begin with d......159 g

d. charms me not less......763 m
d. in his abject spirit††....622 n
from a doubting school....621 u
love her d. and anguish....358 m
wasted in d. and waiting§..519 g
who d. tyranny and..... .582 v
Doubts–bound in to saucy d.*158 s
d. are traitors and make us*159 d
in D., Counsellors in...... 68 o
life for delays and d. no....346 s
littlest d. are fear*........365 d
revelation satisfies all d....528 d
who dotes yet doubts*....328 e
Dough–my cake is dough*. .211 v
Douglas–D. in his hall......130 h
D. in red herrings. .. ..442 c
for D. spoke, and Malcom. 486 u
O D, O Douglas, tender .... 80 c
Dove–snowy d.trooping with* 45 s
a stock d. sing or say¶..... 46 a
as when the d. returning.. 45 k
beloved nymph, fair Dove. 530 n
beside the springs of D.¶ .421 f
cooing of an unseen dove .. 37 o
dove's in our green tree ...111 o
dove's low nest for me.....111 o
gently as any sucking d.*.. 45 r
has a dove's wing..........600 e
hear the murmuring dove. 45 h
in shooting at the dove.... 451 s
on the burnish'd dove†....541 f
patient as the female d.*... 45 q
plumage spare the dove‡.. 46 s
pronounce but "love"*....148 i
serpent than the dove.....336 e
snow-white D. of heaven...130 t
sweet Dove, unto my song. 45 m
the d. and very blessed*.... 45 t
the dove, O hawk.......699 f
the d. on silver pinions..... 45 o
the d. sit there together ... 46 q
the serpent than the d..... 81 r
the tender dove in firry†... 45 u
the wode d. upon the..... 45 j
white d.'s feet are wet.....392 d
whitest d.'s unsullied .... 54 q
wings of the dove‖.........334 e
Doves–d. do peck the*......122 d
d. will peck in safeguard*.119 q
doves with noisome stench*122 c
drives the trembling d.‡... 45 p
his mother's doves.........360 h
like d., that the exalted.... 45 l
nimble-pinioned d. draw*..364 a
stock doves nestled there.. 54 h
swift the trembling d.‡.... 45 p
that pair of billing d....... 45 m
the moan of d. in†........412 u
there my little d. did sit... 45 i
Dove-wings–let warm white.561 n
Dowagers–d. for deans†......660 t
Dower–funeral d. of present‖116 z
little children's dower....223 n
odour are not its dower ...245 c
our mortal dower........237 r
thy d. is thy carolling..... 44 b
Dower'd–d. with the hate†..481 a
Down–and the world goes d.. 74 w
come down at Lodore......641 l
I'm up and d. and round... 96 g
in the d. I sink my head†...563 n
is d. can fall no lower......499 l
is d. needs fear no fall .....499 m
raven of darkness**..... 16 r
some go down... ....257 j
tell who should down*.... 17 s
this story will never go d..578 k
to spread a doubtful d.....458 b
up and d. 'twixt heaven... 94 o
up and d. ! up and down....57 d
who aspires must d. as**... 13 j
Downs–all in the D. the fleet.445 d
in the dewy downs†........226 o
round the spicy downs†....235 a
Downstairs–you kick me d...144 p
Downward–d.bent admiring**369 k
Doxy–orthodoxy is my d....158 i

Drenched-d. on the other side355 *l*
  you have d. our steeples*..578 *b*
Dresden-at D. on the Elbe... 98 *a*
Dress-be plain in d. and sober 23 *r*
  beyond the pomp of dress.. 24 *n*
  clothe me in any d. thou....524 *z*
  come up to their Easter d..165*m*
  disorder in the d. kindles in 23 *i*
  dress all day‡........ ....129 *a*
  d., and reticent demureness 24*m*
  d. and undresse thy soul...547 *k*
  d. by yellow candle-light....90 *t*
  d. does not give knowledge763 *q*
  d. does not make the monk.763 *o*
  d. me up in silks so fine....629 *q*
  expression is the dress of‡..581 *l*
  growing careless of my d.. 11 *e*
  how cold the d. they wore. 23 *p*
  in the matter of dress it is.763 *n*
  noble youth did dress*.....188 *u*
  O fair undress, best dress.. 24 *o*
  she had on a dress.......... 22 *r*
  step and d. alike express...128 *g*
  style is the d. of thoughts..581 *f*
  though in another dress§... 10 *i*
  thro' the plainest dress...573 *s*
  worth while to dress and...150 *r*
Dressed-April d. in all his*...392 *k*
  clown in regal purple d.‡..581 *i*
  in purple dressed...........225 *d*
  nature to advantage d.‡....653 *t*
  proud man d. in a little*....491 *g*
  Robert of Lincoln is gayly. 43 *h*
  South wind-he was d......647 *u*
  still to be drest............. 23*m*
Dresser-bring it from the d.*.432 *c*
Dresses-d. for breakfasts..... 22 *s*
  d. for Winter, Spring...... 22 *s*
  d. to dance in, and flirt in... 22 *s*
  faith itself has different‡....653 *r*
  neat-handed Phillis d.**....431 *s*
  of her chariots and d......578 *g*
Dressing-d. eels or shoeing..589 *j*
  groves are of thy d.**.....393 *e*
  wear the d. of his lines.....550 *j*
Drew-she d. an angel down...318 *p*
  that drew th' essential.....183 *f*
  that Shakespeare drew‡....329 *f*
Dribbling-d. out their base..649 *a*
Drift-know I cannot drift....276 *a*
  white with the drift.........228 *b*
Drifted-met and then d......378 *k*
Driftest-d. gently down the§.561 *q*
Drifting-quick d. to and fro.. 57 *d*
Drift-wood-the scattered..... 56 *n*
Drink-affection and use of d.326 *p*
  and drink of Adam's ale....641 *g*
  anon we'll d. a measure*....384 *q*
  come on, old fellow, and d.142 *b*
  drink and be mad then.....649 *a*
  d. and be merry, lads.......376 *g*
  d. deep draughts of its.....230 *o*
  d. deep, or taste not the‡..342 *i*
  d. down all unkindness*....162 *t*
  drink five bottles, bilk the. 78 *q*
  drink life to the lees†......351 *l*
  d., my jolly lads, drink.....376 *g*
  d. no more than a sponge..162 *s*
  drink not the third glass..593 *f*
  drink out of his glass.......177 *a*
  d., pretty creature, drink¶.163 *c*
  d. sweet waters, and dream.607 *f*
  d. the clear stream and**..593 *i*
  d. the water of mine eyes*.592 *j*
  d. the winds as drinking....334 *t*
  d. to-day and drown all....161 *s*
  d. to England, every guest†.604 *s*
  d. to me only with thine....604 *o*
  drink to the lass............604 *r*
  drink when I have occasion.162 *b*
  drink with discerning......376 *g*
  drink with him that wears.163 *v*
  drink with me and drink...323 *e*
  drink you with no doctor...177 *h*
  eat little flesh, and drink...168 *r*
  eat they drink and it**....316*m*
  every creature drink but I.162 *f*

every one offers him drink.508 *u*
excessive food and drink...696 *c*
fountain, it is sweet to d...597 *j*
given us the use of drink..326 *p*
he brews, so shall he d.... 162*m*
his cold thin drink out of*.112 *e*
his drink the crystal well..567 *j*
if it be death so to drink...141 *h*
I never drink no sperit††...593 *h*
invited to d. at any man's..162 *d*
is another's meat or d......508 *q*
it strengtheneth d. and it..650 *e*
kill a constable and drink.. 78 *q*
let them heartily drink....340 *s*
more than food and drink..485 *r*
need have you of drink.....179 *l*
never taste who always d..162 *r*
nor any drop to drink.....641 *b*
old wine to drink.......... 8 *r*
old wine to drink. .... 10 *q*
such drink deserves to be..181 *l*
that I may d. thy tidings*.589 *n*
they eat, and drink, and...668*m*
they eat, they drink**......211 *i*
to thee that I would drink‖.604 *l*
'twas meat, and d. and....457 *n*
where the d. goes in, there.508*dd*
whose d. was only from**..593 *k*
will drink to him†..........211 *s*
wine, I know, was made to.650 *a*
wines he liked to drink.... 649 *d*
with you I will drink to....142 *b*
Drinking-d. hot punch......162 *h*
  d. largely sobers us again‡.342 *i*
  d. makes wise but dry......161 *p*
  harm in d. can there be....161 *t*
  red-hot with drinking*.....326 *j*
  merry, dancing, drinking..383 *p*
  that d. thirsteth still......460 *h*
  unhappy brains for d.*....326 *i*
  with constant d. fresh..... 162 *g*
Drinks-and d. and stares....213 *i*
  drinks and gapes for drink.162 *g*
  drinks it only with a trio.. 181*m*
  drinks my spirit up.......327 *t*
  drinks till morning........174*m*
  now the king d. to Hamlet*.604 *a*
  strongest d. our chief**....593 *k*
  yet only eats and drinks....427 *v*
Drink'st-eat'st and d.**......593 *l*
  what drink'st thou oft*....215 *p*
Drip-drip in my hand.......239 *h*
  drops the light d. of the‖... 63 *h*
Drips-it d. its misty light....576 *t*
Drive-doth d. out another...465 *j*
Driveller-swift expires a d...348 *d*
Driven-better to be d. out... 89 *f*
Driveth-go that the dyvell d.499 *a*
Drives-by strength d. out*...317 *p*
  drives him to and fro.‡....287 *x*
  who d. fat oxen should.....509 *g*
Driving-and driving out......129 *f*
Drooping-d. for thy sighe...231 *h*
  drooping heavy eyed.......217 *e*
  snowdrops drooping early..219 *g*
Drop-a drop of patience*....467 *p*
  all will drop out of it.......379 *t*
  d. from old Brown's life....640 *i*
  drop of manly blood........358 *e*
  d. of pure and pearly light.633 *h*
  drop overfills it††........ 293 *l*
  dropp to quenche a thirst..334 *q*
  each drop she falls would*.591 *r*
  every drop hinders needle.590 *t*
  first swete dropp of our...334 *q*
  keep "a drop serene".......238 *i*
  keps its ain drap o' dew....541 *p*
  memory, like a drop that.. 3 *a*
  men drop so fast ere life's..142 *n*
  nor any drop to drink.....641 *b*
  single drop of sweetness....321*m*
  take a drop in water........440 *a*
  the last drop in the well‖...604 *l*
Drops-damning d. that fall..331 *f*
  dear as the ruddy d. that.. 7 *w*
  d. earliest to the ground*..149 *p*
  d. of anguish falling fast§..479 *v*

d. that from his purpled...546 *l*
  in drops of sorrow*........329 *x*
  liquid d. of tears that you*.592 *d*
  million drops of gold.......223 *g*
  minute d. from off the**...647 *g*
  my d. of tears I'll turn*....591 *o*
  prelusive d., let all their...515 *f*
  red drops fell like blood‖...223 *e*
  store of childish drops*....592 *h*
  the drops will slacken so...619 *e*
  what precious d. are those.590 *o*
Dropsied-a d. honour*.......147 *a*
Dropt-d. on the world a.....493 *b*
Dross-each ounce of dross††.102 *u*
  gold can separate thy d.‖...586 *f*
  it is dross, usurping ivy*..300*w*
Drovier-spoken like an*......430 *o*
Drown-an elephant would d.538 *u*
  drown all sorrow...........161 *s*
  drown him by your talk...743 *s*
  d. me in thy sister's flood*.383 *i*
  drown me on my return...174 *k*
  d. or hang themselves*.....583 *g*
  feather or to drown a fly..460 *s*
  I'll drown my book*....... 67 *v*
Drowned-chance of being d..551 *s*
  d. far greater numbers.....648 *j*
  like a d. man, a fool*.......326 *o*
  ships have been drowned...445 *h*
Drownest-d. nature's sweet§.637 *j*
Drowning-dog is d. every....508 *u*
Drowns-a third d. him*......326 *o*
Drowse-d. on the crisp††....612 *h*
Drowsy-dull ear of a d.*.....350 *n*
  makes heaven d. with*....362 *l*
Drudge-condemn'd to d.‖....435 *l*
Drudgery-dry d. at the..... 666*w*
  unremitting d. and care....667 *l*
Drudging-is always d........427 *v*
Drug-no Lethean drug for...446 *f*
Druid-yonder grave a D. lies.284 *q*
Druids-D. did the savages....254 *o*
Drum-beat of the alarming‖.636 *a*
  chamber-door I'll beat the*562 *g*
  d. now to drum did groan..636*m*
  follow thy d. with man's*..639 *b*
  melancholy as an unbraced.378 *u*
  muffled d.'s sad roll........272*w*
  noise of threat'ning drum*.639 *j*
  not a d. was heard, not a...444 *r*
  pulpit, drum ecclesiastic...449 *u*
  spirit-stirring drum*. .... 204 *t*
  stormy music in the drum.404 *r*
Drum-beat-morning d-b......116 *e*
Drummer-d., strike up, and*.444 *c*
Drums-as if old d. worn out.157 *j*
  like muffled drums are§....348 *k*
  the drums and bugles......134 *d*
Drunk-Acacias having d......609 *a*
  all learned and all drunk...325 *r*
  drunk with choler*......... 17*w*
  d. with that sweet food.... 53 *f*
  get d. with that divine.....592 *x*
  get very drunk; and when‖.325 *o*
  gloriously d. obey the......325 *s*
  he hath not drunk ink*....516 *q*
  little makes you both d....162 *d*
  pleasure to be drunk.......325 *v*
  queen shall be as d. as we..325 *v*
  reasonable must get d.‖....325 *o*
  state, majestically drunk‡.556 *g*
  then hasten to be drunk....325 *u*
  though he never was d......162 *c*
Drunkard-d. clasp his teeth..326 *q*
  d. reeling from a feast ....163 *f*
  I am a drunkard*..........326 *k*
  one d. loves another*......326 *n*
  we blame the drunkard....325 *g*
Drunkards-d. most devoutly.180 *n*
Drunken-d. deep of joy..... 330 *b*
  e'en drunken Andrew felt..330 *h*
  he that is drunken.. ....325*w*
  quarrels with a d. man....701 *c*
  what's a d. man like*......326 *o*
Drunkenness-d. an expression325 *t*
  d. is an immoderate........326 *p*
  drunkenness is nothing....717 *d*

d. not accomplish..........717 c
Drury-old D.'s pride and.....422 p
Dry-brain gets as dry as an..476 n
dry as the remainder*......421 j
I being dry sit idly sipping.161 q
if the river were d., I am*..592 k
I would fain die a d. death*.140 f
keep your powder dry.... 511 b
love half regrets to kiss it‖.590 g
my very roof was dry*.....362 k
they whose hearts are d.¶..142 w
waves the bush, the flower.591 j
Dryad's-where is the D......609 f
Dryden-e'en copious D.‡. ...429 g
Drying-d. up a single tear‖..107 n
Ducats-daughter! O my d.*.. 93 q
O my Christian ducats*.... 93 q
Duck-the duck decoys you...181 d
well aimed at d. or plover..528 b
with a goose or a duck.... 18 e
you d. them ne'er so long..538 b
ducks and drakes with.....501cc
ducks to the golden fool*..631 r
Due-due in tithe and time...274 o
give the devil his due......498 d
restore to God His due in..523 h
that to us alle is due......413 v
will give the devil his d.*..499 t
Duke-a marquis, d., and a'.370 c
and the Duke of York.....535 k
bears a d.'s revenues on*..491 o
D. of Norfolk deals in malt.442 c
Dukedom-prize above my*..345 d
Dukedoms-grant no d......258 k
Dulcet-d. sounds in break*..376 n
uttering such dulcet and*..383 j
Dull-beyond all conception.581 d
changes of studies a dull§..580m
he is not only dull himself.581 a
he must be a dull fellow...652 n
Jack a dull boy in the end..495m
more dull and negligent....281 k
Peter was dull; he was at..581 d
see two dull lines with.....386 u
sense and venerably dull...580 v
she is not bred so dull but*.645 n
stuff so fat and dull*......120 a
Dulness-cause of dulness ..581 a
this dullness was he cursed.581 d
d.! whose good old cause‡.480 f
Dumb-a beggar that is d.....554 t
a thing to strike us dumb..599 p
but ah! d., dumb forever††.612 g
but, alas, she is d., and††...479 w
but the deep are dumb.....465 v
d. jewels often in their*....663 q
dumb men throng to see*..483 g
God is not dumb, that he††521 h
handles or moves it it is d..675 g
how dumb the tuneful.....546 n
mighty griefs are dumb....554 a
modern thought are dumb.595 t
modest men are dumb.....383 e
no such thing as a d. poet..447 j
poor, poor d. mouths*.....671 i
should have been born d....726 s
the oracles are dumb**....461 t
though my mouth be d....594 t
to write I should be dumb.753 l
voice of the desert never...411 e
Dumb-bells-with frivolous..181 o
Dumbness-speech in their*..340 d
Dumpling-I should never of.169 a
Dumps-joke to cure the d...328 w
Dumpy-I hate a d. woman‖..655 j
Dun-dreaming darkly of a d.374 o
Duncan-D. Gray cam here..662 b
Dunce-d. awakens dunce...251 h
d. that has been kept at....170 g
d. that has been sent to....170 g
how like a very dunce......473 o
like a well-meaning d.††...402m
the puff of a dunce........215 c
Dunces-a wit with d. and‡...653 o
Dung-fly that feeds on dung.328 o
Dungeon-d. grate he shakes.321 a
dungeon horrible, on all**..299 e

d. oped its hungry door††..373 z
d. that I'm rotting in.......491 u
heart is the d. of darkness.512 c
himself is his own d.**.... 82 c
nor airless d. nor strong*..350 o
worse than chains d. or**.. 61 e
Dungeons-brightest in d. ‖..491 t
the hue of dungeons*......299 p
Dung-hill-sun shineth upon.583 u
Dung-hills-tulips upon d-h..247 e
Dupe-greater d., he or you..762 i
head is always the d. of.....505 j
we begin by being dupe....757 g
woe to the dupe that.......206 j
you think him to be your..762 i
Dupes-d. are men to custom.127 g
Durance-in d. exile, Bedlam‡.429 k
Duration-d. depends on the.600 i
duration we cannot hope...396m
state of duration as was...599 d
Dusk-bumps along the dusk.322 h
but at dusk-he's abroad.. 52m
d. of centuries and of§.....533 h
rich dusk through.........223 j
through the pale dusk§....285 e
Dust-and kissed the dust... 92 c
and much learned dust....112 t
a piece of valiant dust*....660 f
be crumbled into dust.....401m
blended in dust together...284 r
blossom in the dust....... 5w
blows dust in others' eyes*630 t
but noble souls through d.§619 g
cinders, ashes, dust........359 o
come to dust*.............139 h
condemned thee to dust...165 e
death by dust.............100 s
down to the dust and as‖..132 u
down to the d. with them..512 i
d. and painted fragments‡.209 h
dust claims dust-and we..140 u
d. of servile opportunity¶..461 s
dust on thy mantle! dust..542 g
d. swept from their beauty.267 f
dust to its narrow house...134 o
d. we tread upon was once‖346 j
dust would hear her and†..366 q
eyes are full of dust.......490 j
fashioned of the self-same§.382 h
father's d. is left alone†....286 e
faults were thick as dust*..265 r
flourish when he sleeps in..381 u
frail as dust it meet thine..323 t
grains of titillating dust‡..457 j
heap of d. alone remains‡..137 k
he resign his very dust.....401 g
hid in the d. from sight....241 d
holds the dust............401m
hour may lay it in the d.‖..281 l
indeed down into the dust.601 g
in the dust, be equal made.141 b
in the d. they raise the.....113 e
is this quintessence of d.*..372 r
lifts a pinch of mortal d....579 u
nigh is grandeur to our d..163 n
or but writes in dust.......345 j
pays us naught but age....601 v
plume is trailing in the d..443 e
precious d. is laid.........182 h
provoke the silent dust....134 e
road, whose dust is gold**.576 f
sleep in dust through......217 u
sleeping in the dust.......260 v
sweep the d. behind the*..462w
the dust is old upon my...382 a
the dust on antique time*.127m
the mouldering dust.......182 l
to digg HE dvst...........183 t
together have one dust*...185 a
to the vile d. from whence.547 s
turns me "dust to dust"..674 r
we turn to d. and all our...150 o
what d. we dote on, when‡.137 n
when we are dust.........226 j
which dust was Bill and... 579 u
whose dust is both dark*..154 s
Wickliff's d. shall spread..530 d

write the characters in d...658 t
wrote them in the dust....420 x
Dusty-dirty and d., but as‖... 98 c
Duties-light household d.ever645 t
new occasions teach new††163 v
on duties well performed§..411 i
property has its d. as well.483m
Dutifulness-d. of children....683 o
Dutifully-d. trod until now..453 h
Duty-a duty not a sin. ..... 99 j
a judge's duty is to........763 r
and found that life was d..163 t
aw'd to d. by superior sway163 k
but what is your duty......763 s
constitutes a pledge of d..163 x
dare to do our duty as we..529 j
doing their practical duty.164 g
duty as we understand it..163 u
d. becomes a part of his...490 t
d. grows thy law enjoyment164 h
d. is the path that all may.164 c
d. requires we calmly wait.582 x
d's a slave that keeps the..361 h
d. hath no place for fear...164 n
d. whispers low, thou must163 n
endeavor to do thy duty...164 f
especially a Christian's d...588 p
faith for duty............807 l
false to present duty......163 i
God helps us do our duty..164 a
half my care and duty*...311w
her child-like duty*.......164 k
hold, in high poetic duty..478 l
import from all duty free‖.128 d
in his d. prompt at every..450 n
itself another form of d....164 g
I've done my d. and I've...594 q
kissed you in the path of d.163 r
legislate each duty........ 72 r
man will do his duty......164 d
my boy has done his duty..163 g
perceive here a divided d.*164 j
performance of duty.......749 k
performing a public duty..163 q
rank for her meant duty...163 l
reward of one duty is the..163m
simple duty hath no place..164 n
subject's duty is the king's*534 x
such d. as the subject owes*164 l
the form of positive duty..163 p
the path of d. was the way†164m
thy sum of duty let two...164 e
toil and heavenward duty.. 79 t
wears in grace of d. done..609 p
where d. leads, my course..163 s
with mirth to lighten d.....547 a
zeal and duty are not slow**164 b
Dwarf-a dwarf on a giant's..494 g
d. sees farther than the.... 2 d
feeble dwarf, dauntlessly..104 p
stirring d. we do allowance*107 a
Dwell-anchorite, who didst d.669 n
at ease for aye to dwell†...475 y
content to d. in decencies‡.633 g
Dame Truth delights to d..623 z
d. in such a gorgeous*.... .145 f
d. in the midst of alarms...566 s
d. with me to heighten¶...382 c
dwell with you there......374 a
fiend-like is it to d. therein.555w
let the damn'd one dwell...512 j
nothing ill can d. in such*.. 37 d
rest can never dwell**....308 i
shining orbs his choice**..668w
there he delights to dwell.. 92 n
there would I dwell.......613 e
will strive to d. with 't*.... 37 d
ye who dwell at home......460 n
Dwelling-far from all¶......619 d
here a goodly dwelling*....426 f
that canopies my dwelling.542 b
Dwelling-houses-d-h. built to426 a
Dwelling-place-blest is thy.. 48 o
desert were my d-p.‖......356 s
Dwellings-among the d.¶.... 59 p
visit oft the dwellings**.... 16 q
Dwells-hell d. within myself.296m

SHAKESPEARE *; MILTON **; WORDSWORTH ¶; BYRON ‖; TENNYSON †; LOWELL ††; POPE ‡; LONGFELLOW §.

joy forever dwells**........204 n
man d. apart, though not..371 g
Dwelt–dwelt among the¶....421 f
dwelt from eternity**..... 352 n
Dwindled–d. one by one§....264 w
Dye–berries of sanguine....615 l
pass'd the Tyrian dye..... 24 b
tinged in transport's dye..381 t
d. your beard, though you.176 e
Dyed–covered with d. locks..177 c
d. her tender bosom red.... 55 k
nature dyed this colour....181 u
Dyes–brush in d. of heaven..515 o
burn with roseate dyes....242 o
cup of curious dyes........238 r
displays her purple d.‡....230 l
in dull terrestrial dyes.....446 t
of unnumbered dyes........220 t
suffusion of celestial dyes.. 62 k
ten thousand dyes‡........203 t
Dyet–and Dr. Dyet........440 t
Dying–and now he is dying..544 a
as he, defeated, dying.....630 y
but who, living and d.‡....183 p
Christian can only fear d..134 l
doubly d., shall go down...547 s
d., bless the hand that gave133 n
dying for their love of.....247 n
dying for twenty years....315 q
d. he could wish to blot... 479 q
d. man to dying men.......449 r
d. mention it within*......284 n
faith beholds the d. here..298 j
not in music dying........250 k
so dying live, and living do.663 t
the conscience of the d.....759 r
thought her d. when she...135 e
to whom his mistress d. ...534 a
with groans of the d.......638 q
yet is never dying........360 s
Dynasty–d. of dead gods....240 b

E.

Eager–and wild in e. flow....641 j
Eagerness–life, what glorious483 i
Eagle–as bright as is the e.'s*535 i
as high as the eagle...... 59 o
at that close tread the e.... 46 d
but he not less the eagle†.. 46 n
e. nestles near the sun.....111 o
eagle of flowers...........246 i
e.'s fate and mine are..... 207 s
eagle's on the crag........111 o
e. stricken with a dart.....205 o
e. suffers little birds*...... 46 k
fierce e. cleaves the liquid‡. 45 p
flies an eagle flight bold*.. 46 i
gaze an eagle blind*........362 j
imbibes with eagle eye.....246 f
in the eagle's down†........278 l
Jove's bird the Roman e.*.. 46 j
like a young e. who has....114 s
like the eagle free........445 b
like thine own e. that soars316 b
lover's eyes will gaze an e.*362 t
pinion that the Theban e... 46 c
shelter to the princely e.*..612 t
struck eagle stretched‖.....205 u
swiftly the fierce e. moves‡ 45 p
that once an e. stricken... 46 g
that the exalted eagle spy.. 45 t
the e. sailed incessantly... 46 t
the wonder of the eagle†... 46 n
to the princely eagle*......139 u
Eagles–baited like e. having* 46 p
eagles dare not perch*....669 f
e. wave their wings in gold‡529 o
on e.s' wings immortal ...538 c
owls pass for eagles........180 e
shall e. not be eagles†..... 46 n
Ear–a flea in one's ear........494 u
a lover's e. will hear the*..362 j
and in Adam's ear**........635 c
and she shall lean her ear¶.413m
applying to his ear the¶....127 d

behind her dainty ear......291 i
breed in the cat's eare.....500 x
daughter with unwounded‡658 j
did you get that pearly e.. 296 b
dreaming bridegroom's e.*.376 n
dull e. of a drowsy man*...350 n
e. a stranger to thy*.......108 e
eare did heare that tong... 83 h
ear has grown familiar§....647 n
ear hath not heard its......297 t
ear is ever open**..........255 o
ear is the avenue to the....772 a
ear of him that hears it*...328 r
fearful hollow of thine e.*. 52 b
few that only lend their e..668 d
flea which I have in my e..506cc
for my e. thou art singing.377 q
give every man thy ear*....331 n
have a wrong sow by the e.586m
healthful e. to hear of it*..296 h
hearing e. is always found.104 f
he whose inward ear.......268 p
hope to please a Cinna's e.. 47 q
it came o'er my e. like the*407 k
I was all e., and took in**..296 d
I will enchant thine e.*.....462 k
jar upon the ear‖...........163 e
let the ear glean after.....426 r
lost on poet's ear...........215 q
never turn away thine e...487 g
nor e. can hear nor‖........105 g
nor eye nor list'ning ear...418 a
not to the sensual ear but. 405m
open ear for tattlers .. ..280 v
pierced through the e.*.....665 j
ravish'd ear to greet.......192 d
ready e. to criminal........736 i
Romeo sticks in his e. a....476 n
rudest murmurs to mine e.581m
softly her warm e. lays††..393 q
stillness first invades the e.554 c
than meets the ear**.......296 e
that Marius' ear smells....175 q
the eye and e. of states....770 s
the tip is jewel of the e....435 b
to knock at your ear*... ..353 t
to the inward e. devout.... 51 i
turn'd him all e. to hear**.574 h
turn the deaf ear..........296 i
wake with a bug in your e.367 k
went away with a flea in...499 q
went in at the one eare....508 e
will enter at a lady's ear*..663 j
word of promise to our e.*.492 r
Eardrops–ladies' e. deck the.222 n
Ear–kissing–e-k. arguments*. 27 r
Ear–witnesses–than ten e-w...192 h
Ears–and wode hath e.......504 x
'bout the e. of the old cur..500 j
creep in our ears*.........407 t
e. ever open to the babbler's771 d
e. with sounds seraphic‡...137 q
eies and eares and.......... 83 h
eyes and ears of many .....751 k
fine long e. and full of.... 20 d
glean the broken ears*....294 h
hang's from Beauty's e.....590 n
have ears more deaf than*..146 a
if men had ears‖...........404 q
in pitiless ears full many...324 d
its ears are open..........740 r
learned than the ears*..... 5 p
lend me your ears*.........296 f
little pitchers have wide e..501 l
men's ears should be*....215m
mentions hell to e. polite‡..299 n
mine ears that heard*......215 l
music to attending ears*...363 n
nail'd by the ears..........126 p
once bless our human e.**.406 e
prove it by my long ears*..549 f
quickly buzz'd into his e.*. 629 p
reason why asses had e.... 19 h
same sound is in my e.¶....573 h
she gave me ears...........272 k
short e.. straight legs, and* 21 d
that aged e. play truant*..172 a

the ears by music......... 678 a
thine ears o'ershaden...../.545 b
this same that deafs our e.*589 s
tongues, and hedges ears..507ff
to younger e. the story.....531 d
to warm our ears...........550 h
which have two ears..... 54 f
with ravish'd ears..........276m
Earldom–insignificancy.... 78 k
Earliest–oft, the e. of the... 55 j
Early–e., bright, transient...142 k
gut to git up airly††.......275 c
play-place of our e. days...672 d
so early o' mornings....... .236 g
Earn–by such songs you§...568 g
e. well the thrifty months†.605 q
I earn that I eat*..........111 t
white hands could††.......642 n
Earnest–better oft than e.**.145 t
I am in e.–I will not......525m
in e. in praying against....594m
to turn it to earnest.......717 f
Earnings–division of........482 l
Earns–e. the right to begin..635 o
Earth–a heaven on earth*...298 d
a heaven on e. I have won*663 g
all earth forgot and all.....111 n
all earth's little pain......316 d
all guilt is avenged on e....760 q
all the earth relieveth*....193 q
all the fuming vanities¶....629 r
alone on e. as I am now‖... 9 g
and be e. insensible**......149 i
and chill the solemn e......141 j
and earth reply...........166 b
and the old e. was young...412 s
as heaven from earth*.....257 u
ashes, gentle earth........284 e
a soft landscape of mild e.‖655 h
atheist, if e. bears so......520 p
Autumn into e.'s lap.......544 h
awake thou wintry e.....164 r
axis of the e. sticks out... 97 g
bare e. exposed he lies..... 319 l
bare e., proud of new..... 52 f
body to the earth*.........189 u
bound in e., in sea, in sky*.344 f
bridal of the e. and sky....131 a
circles the e. with one......116 e
closest cling to earth......218 p
clothe the general e. with..110 h
comes more nearer e.*.....398 u
come to the e. by and by... 75 f
convulsing Heaven and....578 f
could frame in earth......412 p
covering the e. with**.....630 a
delver in earth's clod††..... 31 n
despise the e. where cares¶ 49 s
dew-bead gem of e. and....154 c
down from heaven to e....356 h
e. and sky are then ....222 b
e. bears no balsams for....489 o
e. changes but thy soul.... 74 c
earth contained no tomb‖.. 399 c
e. does not know itself .. .682 j
e. doth like a snake renew.669 i
e. felt the wound, and**...555 y
e. flits fast and time.......138 g
earth from heaven away...253 c
e. gets its price for what††.102 u
e. glittering with gold......668 l
earth glowed in space......608 a
e. goes down into a vale....546 c
e. goes on the Earth.......668 l
e. groans as if beneath a‖..577 o
E. help'd him with the¶....640 s
earth in an earthy bed†....366 q
earth I no longer see.......620 u
e. is but an echo of the‖....404 q
e. is but the frozen echo...668 i
e. is dried, and parched....641 g
e. is here so kind, that just424 b
e. lies laughing where.... .235 c
e. lies shadowy dark below358 n
earth o'erwhelm them*....123 s
e. proudly wears the.......425 h
e. returns back to the e....712 b

e.'s a thief, that feeds*.....595 o
earth's at play.............165 l
e's base built on stubble**.196 o
e..'s biggest country'st†...115 f
earth's bosom bare.........239 b
e.'s degenerate sons could‡.641 s
e.'s firmament do shine§...218 r
e.'s foundations crack......299 t
e.'s full rivers cannot fill..460 h
earth's garden-close......216 i
earth's greatest nation††...115 f
earth's grief is sorest....222 e
e., shaking with horror....612 c
e. shall glisten in the ray..267 o
e. smiles with flowers....276 l
e.'s noblest thing, a††....657 i
e.'s prolific lap.........237 o
e.'s silence lives, and....405 g
e.'s wide regions round...459 k
earth teem'd around me...217 d
e. that lightly covers her...183 d
earth the broken arcs......279 n
e. the very noon of night..384 u
e. took her shining station.667 r
e. was beautiful as if§....394 h
e. was the meadow.......637 f
e. which kept the world*...152 b
earth whirls and††........248 i
e. will live by her's.......409 x
earth with crimson beam..530 j
e., with her thousand......486 f
face of the earth would....75 m
feeble worm of the earth...371 r
feeds the green earth††....187 s
find a harbour in the earth*368 d
first flower of the earth....652 i
fix him to the earth.......123 h
flooding the e. with§.....540 l
floor the e. so green and..413 f
for me, my lady Earth....514 r
for the sad old e. must....669 r
from the ends of the e....637 g
Fuller's earth.............182 r
girdle round about the e.*.607 i
give him a little e. for*.... 11 t
glance from heaven to e.*.480 n
go forth upon the earth.... 35 h
gold once out of the e. is...396 l
great in the earth as in‡...411 v
great society alone on e.¶..565 x
haunting the cold earth....415 e
Heaven looks down on e...577 l
Heaven tries e. if it be in††393 q
He on earth did taste.... 19 e
his back to earth‖........442 x
if that the e. could teem*..591 r
in days far off on that dark†592 o
inhabitants o' the earth*... 25 k
in this broad e. of ours....472 n
is the last of e.! I am.....131 t
is there evil but on e.†.....188 f
I swung the e. a trinket at.669 o
law of heaven and e. is life‖436 t
law preserves the earth a..510 o
lay her i' the earth*.......285 q
less of earth in them......210 v
lift from e. our low desire‖.357 c
listen to E.'s weary voices.540 p
lot of the beautiful on e....755 r
love e. only for its earthly‖532 g
make our e. an Eden like. 146 u
making earth a hell‖.......297 l
man marks the e. with‖...459 f
mantle overveil'd the e.*..417 e
man upon this earth......136 e
meager, cloddy e. to*......425 b
melting heaven with e ....625 c
memory of e.'s bitter¶....883 a
model of the barren e.*....139 v
monarch of the universal*.551 l
more things in heaven*....473 l
mortal mixture of e.'s**..406 c
my footstool E., my‡......412 a
naked e. crouched.........546 b
nightly to the listening e..397 d
no light in e. or heaven§..576 d
none on e. above her......361 u

no savor of the e. to escape.649 e
nought beyond, O earth...358 x
O E.! all bathed with .... 669 j
o'er the wakening earth.. .540 f
of all earth's madmen....522 o
of the harmless earth......121 v
of peace on e., good-will§.. 94 i
O happy earth.............253 u
on e. I wait forlorn........667 q
on e. will forever be.......533 o
one to earth reveals.......187 a
on the bare. e. expos'd he‡.388 c
on the confines of earth....297 q
on the earth doth live*....510 r
on the e. her deathbed.....544 o
on the green e. decreed....619 f
poetry of e. is never dead..477 z
pomp rule reign but e.*....140 r
prostrate on e. the bleeding.570 l
purger of earth, and.......459m
regions under earth*.......300 n
renounces e. to forfeit....269 h
rich e.'s ample round††....228 e
roses of earth which fell...222 j
round this opacous e.**...352 p
seemed to walk the earth§.302 g
shall be the e.'s last man.. 479 g
she sits young while the e..144 w
shot my being through e...343 n
slumbering on the earth...473 g
so much of e., so much¶...673 o
Son of Heav'n and E.,**...420 g
sons of e.! attempt ye still‡ 13 q
soul from e. to heaven lies.572 j
spake with us on e. no§....582 r
spot which men call e.**..668 u
summon armies from the e.784 j
sweeps the wide earth‡...320 f
sweetest heaven on earth*.203 w
swept from the e. and.....420 x
that earth is foul, that....451 g
the daughters of earth....664 t
the dying e.'s last poet....479 g
the earth a stage.........422 f
the e. builds on the e......668 l
the earth covereth.........440 s
the e. hath bubbles, as the*669 e
the earth is rocking........171 d
the earth is yours.........447 b
the e. says to the earth....668 l
the earth's refreshed..... 99 u
the e. was made so various.629 t
the e. when it is sick......635 l
the e. with Orient pearl**.400 l
the heaven on earth.......375 h
the heavens to earth......639 d
the rival of the earth‖.....211 d
the whole e. is bounded‖..585 g
thing on the face of the e..653 n
things learned on e. we....472 a
thirsty e. soaks up the.....162 g
this ancient e. was young.. 51 q
this earth of majesty*.....116 b
this novelty on earth**....657 s
this vast ball, the E.§......452 l
thou bleeding piece of e.*.404 a
though fix'd on earth.... 246 i
throw the e. over him......636 l
till e. and sky stand.......637 g
t' illuminate the e., and**..576 g
to that pleasant country's*138 n
to the e. some special*....510 r
truth crushed to e. shall ..621 f
tumult of the e. can shake††622 l
turn when we are earth ...135 h
two paces of the vilest e.*. 13 x
unto e. give back that glow.229 p
unto the fame of earth ...766 l
upon the lap of earth .....379 c
vapours of e. they seem...586 a
very earth did shake 636m
vile e. to earth resign*.....149 r
wander earth around..... 343 a
watched the sleeping e... 561 c
whate'er of e. is form'd,...572 g
what region of the earth...676 h
what were all earth else...536 j

when the e. grows pale..... 51 o
while the e. bears a plant..559 r
whole e. rings with...... ..488 t
whom on e. alone we love.. 45 h
whose table earth‖.........269 g
Earthbound–lost spirit e..... 59 g
Earthen–treasures from an e.450 o
Earthenware–served up in†.360 f
Earthlier–e. happy is the*..376 p
Earthly–be, on this e. sphere.344 a
e. could surpass her‖......447m
e. power doth then show*..382 p
flagg'd not in the e. strife..315 n
heavenly cant its e. sway.. 93 h
naught earthly may abide.. 75 a
of e. goods, the best is.....645 s
the sum of e. bliss**.......506 k
throw aside these e. bands.148 b
Earthquake–gloom of e. and.447 i
Earth-scenes–pictures all e-c.298 l
Earthward–e. where they....221 h
Ease–at e. for aye to dwell†..475 y
at ease who laughs.........775 e
bliss in action, some in e.‡.342 j
consistent with your ease.. 98 h
done with so much ease....410 r
e. after warre, death......526 q
e. and alternate labor......112 j
e. and speed in doing a....667 g
e. in his possessions......132 k
e. of heart her every look..655 t
e. the heart can know......548 q
e. the pain that he must... 55 n
ease with dignity..........692 p
ease with safe disgrace††..101 o
e. would recant vows**....419 i
elegance of ease........... 30 o
fears to sit at ease.........666 d
Greek and Latin speaks....353 f
heart's ease must kings*... 73 f
heightens e. with grace ... 24 o
he rests at ease beneath....323 o
it bore with greater ease...588 t
joy or e. let affluence or‡..106 a
live at home at ease........304 j
never at heart's ease*......174 g
nights devoid of ease......405 v
on the dappled turf at e.¶..587 j
poet's dignity and ease‡...259 b
poet who with e. can steer.757 c
point with modesty and e.171m
smiling at the airy ease....543 p
Solomon, he lived at e.**..173 a
some seek wealth and e.... 526 l
studious of ease, and fond.580 o
take mine e. in mine inn*..433 j
to hours of ease..........304 n
to live at e., and not be....485 r
true e. in writing comes‡..429 j
vanity is as ill at e. under. 629 g
where at heart's e. he liv'd.655 y
with an age of ease...... .. 9 t
with little wit and e. to... 795 r
with greater e. than made. 143 a
without labour there were. 338 r
with so much ease........283 i
woman! in our hours of e..658 r
yet prodigal of ease.......347 e
you write with e., to show.471 u
Easier–e. to be critical than.124 p
Easily–e. things go wrong...151 d
Easiness–a property of e.*...458 u
care, but seeming ....573 s
East–and from her native**.. 352 k
available with an e. wind††. 27 j
dancing from the e., and**.393 e
dapples the drowsy east*..625 j
day glimmer'd in the e.... 398 n
E. is E., and West is West.637 g
e. unseen is brightening†...161 l
E., west, north. and south. 95 j
Father touch the east†......401 h
from e. and from west ....595 a
from e. to west his course..426 e
from the e. glad message..415 c
golden progress in the e.*..625 l
hard E. blows over their... 76 n

his golden progress in the*.562 o
in the dark e., expanded ..515 h
in the e. doth rise.........253 e
I've wandered e., I've......380 r
rejoicing in the East.......585 c
the e. and western bars.....492 f
the east is blossoming.... .584 q
the golden window of the*.400 t
the whole e. was flecked...584 r
up the e. he springs.......584 c
west explains the east.... .100 t
your window for the e.... 48 n
Easter-before the E. morn...165 k
Christ will rise on E......164 u
come up to their E. dress..165m
E. devotions would in......165m
E.-Sunday the full§........165 g
glorify this Easter day... 165 n
no sun upon an E. day....129 j
peal soon that E. morn††... 86 p
risen Christ! O E. flower..164 t
sun upon an E. day.......253 v
the Jews spend at Easter.. 329 b
Eastern-e. conduits ran... 239 b
eastern lands they talk....2.9m
the e. sanctuary-stair.....585 b
Eastward-e. and westward..404 h
Easy-abstinence is as e. to..593 g
comes easy to him†........402 g
custom will render it e.... 91 v
dislike one too easy......174 t
e., in itself but grows......692 o
easy to performance........154 j
in an e. cause any man.....698 k
nothing is more e. than to.144 g
thinks, good easy man*....151 r
'tis as easy as lying*.......199 s
'tis easy to be true.........75 w
Eat-and some wad e. that...594 p
bad men live that they may 168 u
cannot e. but little meat...163 a
e. a bushel of salt with him.495 ii
eat an honest name........559 c
e. in dreams the custard‡..160 p
e. like wolves and fight*....444 e
e. of the fish that hath fed* 151 p
eat some and pocket up‡...167 s
eat, speak, and move*......207 c
e. they drink and in**......316m
e. thy cake and have it.... 496 bb
e. to live; not live to eat..693 g
eat up the little ones*......213 o
hae meat and canna eat....594 p
he hath not eat paper*......516 g
I earn that I eat*...........111 t
now eat up her own*.......284 b
shal ete with a feend.......505 cc
she pluck'd, she eat**.....555 y
some hae meat and canna..594 p
strive mightily, but e. and*168 l
tell me what you eat.......764 a
tempt the dying anchorite.168 t
that dogs must eat*........311 h
that must e. with the devil*.498 jj
they eat and drink and....668m
they eat, they drink**......211 i
they e. your service like...548 x
think that I could e. one...166 p
though we e. little flesh...168 r
till I eat the world at last..603 r
to e. at another's table is...713 h
to eat no fish*.............88 s
wise men eat them......497 aa
Eaten-e. me out of house*..319 r
e. on the insane root*......321 j
I have eaten his bread.....357 h
worms have e. them but*..372 o
Eater-e. of broken meats*...336 g
Eating-appetite comes to...502 e
appetite comes with e......764 c
e. hath robb'd the whole‡..512m
e. the bitter bread of*.... 33 h
ever e., never cloying......603 r
pleasure in eating ....167 a
sneer as they like about e..389 n
Eats-daily his own heart he.301 e
eats neither partridge......166 d

e. the sword it fights with*.629 b
never begs, and seldom e...339 k
that is proud eats up*......491 i
the fool that e. till he is sick 451 s
yet only e. and drinks......427 v
Eat'st-what thou e. and**...593 l
Eaves-e. were dripping yet..416 h
leafy galleries beneath§....617 l
minute drops from off the**647 q
to chide him from our e.*..557 p
Ebb-mathematic e. and flow.459m
sea-e., by long ebbing.... .599 a
which in thy e. and flow...603 l
Ebbs-as it e. the seedsman*.531 j
Ebony-image—cut in e. as if.520 u
Eccentric-takes the most e..397 p
Ecclesiastic-pulpit, drum e..449 u
Ecclesiastical-e. lyric ......158 b
Echo-all the church did e.*..335 s
applaud thee to the very*..441 f
a softened e. to thy tread§..617 l
earth is but the frozen e....668 i
echo answers—"Where"‖.149 e
e. caught faintly the.......297 q
e. mocks the hounds*......169 l
echo of the spheres‖.......404 q
e. repeats only the last part201 b
e.'s answering sounds..... 87 m
e. sits amid the voiceless.. 169m
e. waits with art and care..169 f
even e. speaks not on these.169 d
holy groan, a loud echo.... 41 b
how sweet the answer echo169 t
I heard the great e. flap†...169 p
invisible as E.'s self¶..... 45 b
left an e. in the sense......634 t
let e., too, perform her part169 b
like the voice and echo*....536 g
living e., bird of eve...... 50 j
render back an echo¶.......413 h
seem an e. to the sense‡....573 e
sink while there's an e.‖...468 e
sweetest e., sweetest**....169 h
whose e. is heaven's blisse..489 w
Echoes-and more than e. talk‡169 j
answer, e., answer dying†..169 g
bugle, blow, set the wild†..169 g
cruelly sweet are the e.....379 q
dropping like e. through...605 n
e. be choked with snows.... 97 o
help the echoes tell. 204m
long, sweet Alpine e......549 z
million horrible bellowing†69 o
multitudinous e. awoke§...169 g
mysterious haunts of e. old169 r
our e. roll from soul to†...169 g
pursuing e. calling 'mong.169 c
so e. answered when her... 51 g
the e. of their glee.........395 d
the echoes that remain....466m
tires their e. with unvaried. 48 i
voice in sullen echoes......206 z
when the e. had ceased§....169 g
Echoing-e. walks between**.613 i
Eclipse-dark! total e.**..... 61 d
e. disastrous twilight**....624 u
gardens e. you 'tis........217 d
In dim e., disastrous**.... 75 g
silver'd in the moon's e.*..619 a
soft and sweet eclipse......335 w
Eclipsed-his death e. the.... 403 h
is e. in the first...........766 i
truth is often eclipsed......747 u
Eclipses-clouds and e. stain*208 l
Economy-e. is a great.......693 j
e., the poor man's mint....170 b
join with e. magnificence‡..170 a
riches spring from e ......102 n
Ecstacies-dissolve me into**406 g
Ecstacy-and warm as e...... 78 p
bodiless creation e.*.......315 j
great poet's hidden e......476 v
lie in restless ecstacy*.....106 h
or waked to ecstacy the.... 79 s
very ecstacy of love*.......364 v
Eddy-swift the feather'd e... 58 c
Eden-E., where delicious**..463 r

make our earth an E. like..146 u
of E. stood disconsolate....463 s
other E., demi paradise*...116 b
through E. took their**.... 38 e
Edens-crime destroys more..123 n
Edge-e. is sharper than the*.559 b
e. of tempestuous years....325 p
even to the e. of doom*....108 t
finest e. is made with the..505 d
no jesting with e. tools....500 dd
no jesting with e. tools....505 ee
on the e. of the world, and.607 f
river's trembling edge......228 j
the razor's edge invisible*.537 x
Edges-sharp or subtle e.....251 b
Edict-spurn at his e. and*...404 b
Edicts-e. are of less power...695 r
Edifice-hail, glorious .....535 k
Edified-whoe'er was e.......155 k
Edinburgh-I westward.....95 p
Edition-Christians of the... 93 j
more elegant edition......182 q
Editions-e. of Balbec and...268 n
Editor-e. sat in his sanctum.435m
every newspaper e. owes...762 r
Educated-e. beyond his.....482 v
e. from exclusiveness and..606m
Education-ability without e.718 l
a liberal education........342 e
a part of education........606 o
are left without e...........170 w
by e. must have been......170 i
e. alone can conduct.......170 p
e. commences at the.......170 d
e. is the only interest......170 r
e. is to cherish and.......170m
he had no singing e.‖......557 b
is a liberal education....... 84 w
just e. forms the man......170 k
making e. not only††.......170 o
or a refined education......305 s
she in beauty, e.*.........185 b
'tis education forms the‡..170 s
Eel-adder better than the e.*102 g
eel, in shining volumes‡...213 l
e. of science by the tail‡...844 c
Eels-dressing e. or shoeing..589 j
Effect-cause of this effect*.. 72 u
e. has its cause and I..... 72 s
e. of plate and lacquey's..180 n
e. with a thousand years..484 g
for this e. defective*....... 72 u
gentleness has no effect....788m
ill e. because they shock...102 i
steals ere we can e. them*.602 l
thy worst e. is banishing..456 g
Effects-again in its effects..105 k
dire e. from civil discord..526 u
effects are in their cause.. 72 r
e. that seem to flow forth.. 28 f
Efflation-e. of his wild......588 e
Effluence-bright e. of**....352 n
Effort-by vigorous e. and an. 85 x
e. of a valiant mind......190 c
e. will deserve praise......696m
Effulgence-e. of the noontide446 v
Effusion-flow in large e......541 l
in large e., o'er the.......515 f
Egg-as an e. is full of meat*.513 o
dropped into the yoke of...447 k
full as an egg of wisdom..484 t
learned roast an egg‡......431 t
the egg of democracy††....521 i
think him as a serpent's e.*511 t
trifling with a plover's e...374 o
yelk of an addled egg..... 28 l
Eggs-flat sands hoard your e. 42 a
full of eggs..............167 e
going as if he trod upon e..498 n
like nest e., to make clients460 u
the more the e. the worse..656 u
those bright blue eggs¶.... 57 i
who sat hatching her e.... 43 a
Eglantine-and with e.*.....220 b
dew-sweet eglantine......244 l
e. embalm'd the air........219 q
e. exhaled a breath ....244 t

SHAKESPEARE*; MILTON**; WORDSWORTH¶; BYRON‖; TENNYSON†; LOWELL††; POPE‡; LONGFELLOW§.

a gray eye is a sly eye......191 *l*
and a tear in her eye..... .564 *n*
and downcast eye.......... 36 *l*
and golden eye...........227 *p*
and more the gazing eye...539*m*
and woo the public eye....446 *p*
an eye discerning*.........122 *a*
any man with half an eye..553 *p*
anything affects your eye.726 *f*
as far as eye could see.....598 *s*
a thunderbolt in mine eye*. 17 *s*
basilisk unto mine eye*....209 *u*
bear welcome in your eye*..482 *c*
beauteous eye of heaven*...252 *y*
beauty as a woman's eye*. 193 *n*
because they shock the e...102 *i*
blind mine een wi' tears...591 *e*
blue eye of the violet ......249 *t*
boldest eye goes down.....455 *j*
bright the tear in Beauty's‖590 *f*
but a smile in her eye....524 *a*
changing, like a joyless e..399 *b*
close the eye of day**.... 51 *n*
coloring from an eye¶......100 *i*
defiance in their eye.......490 *v*
dislike an eye that§.... .192 *n*
distinguish by the eye.....331 *j*
distinguish them by the e..386 *e*
elles the eye of day........227 *h*
entered at an eye..........294 *f*
even in the eye of day......624 *d*
evening closes Nature's e..323 *j*
every eye gaz'd as before‡.553 *k*
every e. negotiate for itself*363 *z*
every plume a sharp eye...740 *r*
explain the asking eye‡.... 11 *a*
e. along the sheet has run..436*m*
e. begets occasion for his*.653 *z*
eye can distinguish ......192 *s*
e. can threaten like a......191 *x*
eie did see that face...... 83 *h*
eye has danced to see......214 *g*
eye hath not seen it........297 *t*
e. in neaven would through*193 *o*
e. is the first circle; the.... 96 *e*
eye lights eye in good.... .263 *n*
e. like Mars to threaten*..193 *j*
e. me, blest Providence**..641 *u*
eye of a yellow star........355 *i*
eye of the body is not..... 36 *i*
e. of the intellect sees in all.471 *x*
e. shall be instructed ......274 *c*
e. that wept essential love.382 *t*
e. the answerable tear‖....590 *e*
eye was dim and cold .....329 *c*
e. was in itself a soul..... 34 *a*
eye where feeling plays¶.. 37 *u*
e. would emulate the*.....193 *t*
face illumin'd with her e.193 *q*
fades in his eye and........ 33 *j*
fault lives in his eye*.....193 *w*
fer from e., fer from herte.497 *w*
fiction rises pleasing to the621 *o*
fire in each eye‡..........251 *y*
friendship closes its eye...264 *o*
fringed curtains of thine*..193 *v*
from day's garish eye**....131 *q*
full eye, small head, and*.. 21 *d*
gifted with an e. and a soul301 *u*
grieve or glad mine eye‖...606 *q*
hard unkindness alter'd e..627 *t*
harmonie in her bright e.. 35 *e*
heaven in her eye**.........657 *q*
her eye was bright..........34 *f*
her timid blue eye.........249 *d*
hidden from the eye¶.......249 *u*
his eye, as bright as is*.....535 *i*
his eye did heal it up*......193*m*
his eye gracious*........ 255 *o*
his fair large front and e.**534*m*
his lordly e. keep distance**584 *a*
I have a good e., uncle*...193 *s*
I have my eye on...........228 *f*
imbibes with eagle eye....246 *f*
immortal hand or e. could. 22 *a*
in an e. thou art alive...192 *k*
in every old man's eye*.... 72 *j*

in her eye a thought........191 *k*
in my mind's e. Horatio*..315 *e*
in the eye of day§..........218 *q*
in the e. of nature he has¶.413 *j*
inward e. which is the¶... 62 *c*
is a power behind the e... 320 *v*
is murder in mine eye*...193 *x*
its eye of blue.............231 *h*
its soft black eye.........155 *f*
I saw her eye was bright... 34 *f*
just opened eye............250 *n*
lack-lustre e. and idle wing 47 *j*
language in her e., her*....339 *z*
light of a pleasant eye......294 *d*
looked upon by a loving e..391 *n*
lost one eye he offers......178 *d*
lustre in your eye*........107 *e*
man a microscopic eye‡....193 *f*
master's eye was the best..681 *e*
meek confiding eye.........250 *p*
mercy show her better e...382 *j*
mind your eye.... ..... 20 *g*
moon and azure eye........ 44 *c*
more peril in thine eye....193 *h*
mote that dims their eye...330 *y*
murders of your eye‡......291 *m*
my right e. itches, some...586 *h*
neath her favoring eye††...612 *n*
no bird had ever eye††.... 46 *r*
nor eye to watch and......111 *n*
no eye nor list'ning ear....418 *a*
nothing situate under*....344 *f*
not 'scape the Almighty e.420 *x*
now I see with e. serene¶..661 *d*
of a dark eye in woman‖...577 *p*
one eye doth please........192 *h*
one eye on death..........198 *w*
on it with lack-lustre e.*..602 *g*
opening the violet eye......237 *q*
penetrated the eye... ...192 *s*
pity dwells not in this e*..474 *i*
places that the e. of heaven*298 *n*
postern of a small needle's*154 *l*
power this e. shoots forth*. 83 *q*
primrose opes its eye ......239 *j*
quickest e. for in others....208 *b*
radiant sun, is nature's e..583 *p*
re-opes its sparkling e......530 *j*
rude eye of rebellion*......518 *e*
same e. whose bend doth*..552 *p*
sees with equal e., as God‡.151 *n*
set honour in one e. and*..318 *k*
show to his e. an image of¶413 *h*
shuts the eye of day.......132 *f*
since last her speaking e.‖. 74 *h*
skarf up the tender e. of*..417 *g*
skin contents the eye*.....102 *g*
sky on which you closed. 344 *k*
some chip falleth in his e...505 *n*
sorrow's eye, glazed with*.288 *g*
so this man's e. is dim.....636 *l*
splendour of his precious*.425 *b*
stretch our e. when capital*123 *t*
sweet to know there is an.‖643 *p*
the error of our e. directs*.185 *x*
the e. and ear of states.....770 *s*
the eye of God because it.. 91 *a*
the e. of Paul Pry often....766 *b*
the e. that contemplates it.614 *n*
the great e. of heaven......196 *d*
the harvest of a quiet e. ¶.194 *i*
the lustre of the eye..... . 8 *p*
the object of His eye......515 *s*
the poet's e., in a fine.*.....480 *n*
the power in his eye‡...... 30 *e*
the sleepy e. that spoke‡...447 *a*
thine e. be not a flatterer*..474 *f*
thine e. was on the censer.192 *i*
thy e. on highest loadstars.667 *x*
'tis not a lip, or eye.‡......36 *d*
to a discerning eye........320 *s*
to catch the reader's eye...435 *g*
to the ground escapes the e154 *s*
to view with hollow eye....485 *b*
turn full upon me thy e....191 *l*
unclose his cheering e. to..552 *h*
under a cruel eye......... .170 *e*

unforgiving eye and a.....196 *c*
unpresumptuous eye. . 274 *d*
unseen by any human e.¶..250 *a*
view me with a critic's e...462 *d*
violet lifts its tender e......217 *p*
want can quench the eye's.667 *i*
what brightens the eye.....595 *a*
when man's eye appears‖..590 *f*
which is its eye‡............234 *g*
whose certain e. foresees..274 *r*
who sees with equal e.,‡...510 *n*
will close the e. of anguish*523 *x*
winning eye and heart.....539 *r*
wish to her dewy blue e.†..449 *h*
with a threatening eye*....257 *c*
with eye like his ....246 *i*
with his glittering eye.....353 *p*
within her tender eye§.....192 *g*
world both eye and soul**..584 *b*
yellow to the jaundiced e.‡586 *o*
Eyeballs-my e. burn.......674 *r*
  my eyeballs roll‡..........137 *o*
Eyebrow-her e.'s shape was‖. 33 *s*
Eyed-Stark eyed them as...638*m*
Eyelash-the e. dark, and.....36 *l*
Eyelids-e. heavy and red....339 *c*
  inclines our eyelids**. .....562 *a*
  love's dropp'd eyelids .....248 *p*
  on your e. crown the god*..562 *o*
  opening e. of the morn**...400 *o*
  smile within his e. plays.... 62 *e*
  tir'd e. upon tir'd eyes†....408 *h*
  weigh my eyelids down*....562 *q*
Eyebright-trembling e.¶....221 *e*
Eye-offending-e-f. brine*...591*m*
Eyes-addresses itself to the e. 36 *r*
  all swims before her e......640 *r*
  a lover's eyes will gaze an*.362 *j*
  and eloquence of eyes.‡....472 *t*
  and glittering e. that....... 45 *i*
  and soul within her e.‖.....655 *i*
  and tearful eyes§..........657 *h*
  and those wild eyes that†... 92 *s*
  and with dimm'd eyes*.....592 *l*
  another man's eyes*........293 *x*
  appears a hero in our e.....455 *s*
  are eyes half defiant.......191 *s*
  ashamed to meet the e. of. 69 *s*
  as in a theatre, the e. of*...423 *a*
  as well as e. that weep.....561 *d*
  at such a distance from our585 *d*
  at the eyes of ignorance....550 *c*
  bandaged e. he never errs..358 *g*
  because thou hast hazel e.*513 *n*
  been violets, her eyes......766 *c*
  before mine eyes in**......136*m*
  betray itself in the eyes...191 *w*
  black e. and lemonade.....298 *k*
  black e., with a wondrous..191 *s*
  bleared his e. with books§..580 *c*
  blows dust in others' eyes*630 *t*
  blue eyes are pale..........194 *h*
  blue eyes shimmer with....194 *g*
  blue were Ariadne's eyes..194 *f*
  blue were her e. as the§... 35 *d*
  bounty had not e. behind*.343 *g*
  bright eyes and faces‖......162 *a*
  bright eyes, light eyes......196 *g*
  bright e. of the dear one‖..200 *j*
  bright e. rain influence**..192 *w*
  brings the tears into her e..394 *o*
  brown eyes are the for..194 *h*
  by female lips and e., that‖455 *f*
  by human eyes unseen.....413 *q*
  carries his e. and itinerary.606 *n*
  cheats the e. of gallery....144 *f*
  child with pensive eyes.... 31 *b*
  closed his e. in endless....134 *f*
  coldly eyes the youthful*. 62 *t*
  compelling e. and footsteps517 *a*
  dark by losing of your e.*.352 *t*
  dark eyes are dearer far...193 *g*
  darkness of e. like pansies.545 *b*
  deep brown e. running.....194 *h*
  deep e. amid the gloom§...192*m*
  did bestow two eyes.......192 *e*
  dimness in thine eyes......601 *d*

mark his favourite flies*...257 a
prodigal's f—then worse¶..152 q
Favorites–f. made proud by*.231 b
favourites of heaven¶......221 e
great Nature's favorites...631 x
heaven gives its f.‖　......132 v
prime f. were the Pelicans. 54 a
Favors–f. unexpected doubly605 h
forget the f. received .....508 f
for her favors call‡......202m
former f. are effaced......698m
hangs on princes' f.*.....535 b
if fortune favors.........702 a
lively sense of future f....189 q
my hospitable f. you*.....309 l
oft favors, oft rejects ....236 i
patient when f. are denied.524 x
pleased with f. given ....524 x
rubies, fairy favours*.....226 b
wi' f. secret sweet.........271aa
your f. nor your hate*.....318 b
Fawning–thrift may follow*.215 q
Fay–daughter of a Fay......196 q
Fealty–bards in fealty to...607 d
Fear–all f., none aid you‡...300 k
all fear of an end.........365 p
and Fear her danger‖......648m
as hope and fear alternate. 75 u
as this term of fear*........209 y
balances your f. and hope. 129 e
banish that f.; my flame...357 k
base the fear of death ....210 l
beg nor f. your favours*...318 b
best safety lies in fear*...495kk
blanch'd with fear*........210 h
but we f. to be we know...133 l
concessions of fear.......641 q
continual f. and danger of..347 w
courage without fear......806aa
creating awe and fear*..... 73 c
despair through f. alone...680 f
desponding f. of feeble.....210 j
die without f. of death ...699 l
dread and fear of kings*...382 p
duty hath no place for f...164 n
eat our meal in fear*...... 209 n
e'en in the midst of fear...767 j
exempt themselves from f.* 5 u
expect, fear not, death.601 t
extreme danger, f. turns a.688m
faint and f. to live alone...567 d
faint cold fear thrills*.....209 s
fear always springs from..208 w
fear each bush we see's...209 i
fear embalmed before he..141 a
f. everything from time....767 e
fear feels no pity.... ...698 g
f. follows crime, and is its..760 n
fear, for their scourge....523 c
f. God as long as you......806cc
fear has many eyes.......767 k
f. has seized upon the mind699 i
f. in children is increased..132 b
f. in the world first........699 n
f. is affront; and jealousy..656 q
fear is an ague.........208 p
f. is cruel and mean......208 x
f. is not a lasting teacher..698 r
fear is the parent of ....209 a
f. is the proof of a........699 t
f. itself not the object......209 e
f. made the gods, audacity.755 l
f. makes men believe .....699 g
f. many, whom many f.....699 k
fear not, but trust in......509 ff
fear not in a world§........209 c
f. not the anger of the‡... 524 b
fear of death drives.......734 r
fear o' hell's the.........208 o
f. of Him who is a¶.......378 e
f. on account of his deeds..685 b
f. oppresseth strength*....210 f
f. or hope may be inspired.152 n
f. stared in her eyes†. .....210 i
fear, the last of ills..........208 t
f., the very worst prophet.699 o
f. this, for it will come*...122 h

fear though fleeter than...208 q
f. to cope malicious*...... 5 v
fear, to death..............686 p
fear was greater than.....208 q
f. we die before we laugh..340 j
foolish to fear ....699 q
have nothing else to fear..528 v
he who does not f. death...761 n
he who feels no fear.....208 n
his breast hope or fear....105 w
I f.I am not in my perfect* 11 v
I f. the Greeks, even......699 u
imagining some fear*......209 w
increased through fear ... 699 h
I neither f. nor despise....802 o
in f. to lose what they*... 639 s
innocence a fear‡.........477 q
I scorn to change or f......802 f
is the tender f. of wrong...671 n
it is tormenting to fear....698 p
knight without fear and....757 l
last of all our evils, f......307 d
lest I should f. and fall....519 q
little care we, little we f... 615 j
littlest doubts are fear*...365 d
love can fear no one......723 r
madness—to die for f ...175m
men converts to fear*..... 76 e
mixed with fear...........723 s
mother of Form and F... 520 q
my name were liable to f.*.586 r
neither desire nor fear....802 g
neither f. nor wish for.....738 o
no more may fear to die...134 o
O word of f. unpleasing to* 44 u
often the f.of one evil leads765 i
others did him feare...... 541 b
paradise shall cast out f...463 t
part of men to fear*.......209 v
persuasion do the work**..472 v
pierce through pride and††477 j
poise of hope and f.**..... 82 h
regret, or there to fear‡... 183 l
shrink away with fear... 36 a
sinks the note of fear.....552 h
small at first through f....740 r
so kings should f. and....534 e
soon as I have begun to f..767 g
sordid birth from fear....118 s
stop with the f. I feel..... 54m
sudden hope and fear.....247 b
superstition is a senseless f.586 g
than fear of life...........210 l
then f. to hate and hate*... 76 e
that men should fear*.....121 q
the antidote to fear.......337 e
the f. of some divine and...420 a
the fear that kills*.........150 g
there his fear prevails....551 j
there is no f. of anything..702 o
there's f. in his frown when615 n
the virtuous nothing fear..632 o
thief doth f. each bush an*586 g
those who f. not guilt, yet..370 n
those who have no fear ...448 c
thyself all reverence and f.529 a
till guilt created fear......632 q
time to f. when tyrants*...335 f
to-day is ours; what do we.604 v
to f. the birds of prey*.....439 b
to fear the foe*...........210 f
to f. to live or die.........666 n
to hope rather than f.**... 82 h
'twas a fear which oft*....209 r
trembl'd with f. at your...379 s
truth without fear.........808cc
you wish to f. nothing.....699m
we fear nae evil...........325 n
we Germans f. God, but...767 t
what should be the fear*...351 a
which we often fear*......295 g
who can f. too many stars.355 u
who have, fear it ....704 t
whose being I do fear*....271 a
why should we f.; and what537 n
with anxious fear I wait...330 q
with hope farewell fear**..149 j

Feared–everything is to be f.699m
feared than a thousand....436 d
is feared by every one......767 h
issue are to be feared*.....210 b
man feared would happen.731 q
the numbers of the fear'd*.536 q
times was Peter feared¶...210 k
Fearful–and goodness never*.633 q
it is a fearful thing‖......133 a
lovely and a fearful thing‖.356 n
makes it fearful*..........288 s
pale, f., and pensive one....721 d
Fearing–by f. to attempt*...159 d
f. what thine eyes behold..402 a
in fearing to be spilt*.....328 f
thousand deaths in f. one..142 h
Fearless–apt to fear for the..208 v
fearless and first, and§.... 90 c
Fears–all my fears are laid§.. 16m
allow his fears to rise.....209 k
and delicate fears¶........272 k
base, fears nothing known. 81 s
daring, great fears are.....689 c
dawns from fears.........243 e
fears he shall be poor*....485 d
fears do make us traitors*.209 p
f. of the brave, and follies..348 d
fears our hopes belied....135 e
f. that only which he first..699 i
fears to sit at ease.........666 d
feels nor fears ideal pains..467 e
full of anxious fears.......723 k
full of fears*.............209 o
heated hot with burning f.†351m
he only f. men who does...779 j
hopes and then our fears..140 u
hopes belied our fears.....135 e
hopes in adversity and f....735 a
humanity with all its f.§...469 e
into what abyss of fears**.105 u
it dawns from fears.......219 r
loves the man whom he f..208m
man must have some fears.769 o
man who f. nothing is not..767 h
master who f. his slaves....699 p
miser acquires, yet fears..698 s
more pangs and f. than*...535 b
naturally born to fears*...209 o
nor fears torment.........111 b
not without many fears...107 l
perform according to our..492 q
present fears are less*....209 x
sailors freeze with fears‡..577 r
saucy doubts and fears*...158 s
scalded dog f. cold water..506 d
sick and capable of fears*..209 o
to avoid misery, fears it...583 c
tyrant's f. decrease not*...626 i
without our fears.........370 k
what it fears creates......209 g
when it dawns from fears..308 r
when little f. grow great*..365 d
whoever f. God, fears to...666 d
who fears not to do ill.....200 t
who fears to speak of.....468 t
whom he f. would perish..699 e
Feast–a great feast of*......514 l
and f. and frolic—and then. 94 e
and protracted feast......326 e
an old accustom'd feast*...211 q
cheerful look makes a dish.494 t
chief nourisher in life's f.*.562 u
city feast of it*.............211 l
enough is as good as a f....497 f
enough's a feast‡.........167 s
feast and your halls are....669 q
f. of reason and the flow‡..517 j
feast to-day makes fast....693 i
flutters from feast to feast.254 l
gap in our great feast*.....290 a
going to a feast......... .. 23m
his rest and makes up his..166 d
let them freely f., sing and 14 n
lights are out his feast.....138 b
men are born to feast......210 x
my share of the feast*......211 o
Nature's temperate f. rose‡183 l

SHAKESPEARE *; MILTON **; WORDSWORTH ¶; BYRON ‖; TENNYSON †; LOWELL ††; POPE ‡; LONGFELLOW §.

f. and trees are not ......371 s
f. are sweet with clover....245 l
fields deserted lie§........ 40 c
fields have lost their......225 a
f. might spill their dew .. 611 a
f. where sacred Isis glides‡530 k
f. which promise corn‖....532 a
f. with green were clad....183 r
f. with Plenty crowned....666 s
floods the calm f. with....397 f
for oute of olde f., as men. 9 i
from brightening f. of....543 g
hunt in f. for health....440 b
in joyless f. and thorny... 56 d
in those holy fields*....... 92 r
'midst the desert fruitful‡.230 l
mortgages our fields....... 15 d
o'er your flowing fields....294 j
on the f. of heaven........575 j
pass'd o'er empty fields....543 i
show'd how f. were won....443 d
smiles on the f. until they§.585 l
stern in the joyless fields.. 396 a
the cherished f. put on....546 p
the f. his study, nature... 579 q
their treasures to the f.... 515 f
through the azure f. of air.417 b
what more happy fields‡...219 n
yonder argent f. above‡.... 277 t
Fiend—and defy the foul f.*.. 67 x
f. lumbago jumps upon....589 e
hell contains no fouler f.‡..656 r
knows a frightful fiend....208 r
man to catch the fiend... 784 h
no fiend in hell can........109 i
O most delicate fiend*....659 n
shal ete with a feend. 505cc
cince the f. pass'd **......299m
thou marble-hearted f.*...319 v
ugliest fiend of hell........327 t
Fiend-like—f-l. is it to dwell..555w
Fiends—call f. and spectres..586 k
from the f. that plague... 42 f
juggling f. no more........492 r
Fierce—beam not so f........543 f
f. as frenzy's fever'd......212 d
f. as ten furies, terrible**..153 b
lion is not so f. as they....505m
safer being meek than f....101 b
Fierceness—call'd us for our*122 c
for fierceness makes....... 27 g
Fiercer—f. by despair**.....149 k
Fiercest—f. agonies hath. ....470 b
Fiery—no f. throbbing pain. 135 f
Fife—fill the fife............273 b
sound the clarion, fill the f.350 c
the ear-piercing fife*......204 t
Fifteen—to the maiden of....604 r
Fifth—the fifth did whirl*....426m
Fifty—at fifty chides his......401 p
forty or fifty how can I tell. 59 r
here's to the widow of f....604 r
Fifty-four-f-f., forty or fight.525 f
Fig—a fig for care. ....318 h
a fig for the vicar...........335 c
a fig for woe...............318 h
full on its crown, a fig's‡...613 h
praise the f. we are free....616 j
that you want a fig........266 b
Figs—love long life better*....350 p
name of the prophet, figs..500 s
Fig-tree-leaf of a young f-t...447 k
they chose the fig-tree**....613 i
Fig-trees—f-t. knowing no... 63 u
Fight—business in the field‡..637 c
chide and fight............113 f
cowards f. when they can*.122 d
dare to f. for such a land...121m
dark and desperate fight§..130 n
feast and not to fight......210 x
fifty-four, forty or fight....525 j
f. against imaginary giants.674m
fight, an other daie........121 f
f. begins within himself.... 77 o
fight, bold yeomen*........639 u
fight for two or seven......521 u
f. gentlemen of England*..639 a

f. it out on this line.........636 s
fight like devils*...........444 e
f. our own shadows forever.549 n
f. thou with shafts of......389 r
fight virtue's cause........341 h
fought the better fight**... 93 f
f. when I cannot choose*... 83 s
gird us for the coming f....579 p
good at a fight but better.. 82 i
harder matter to fight†'...199bb
hath no stomach to this f.*639 g
high above the f. the lonely.637 z
I give the f. up; let there...420 t
let graceless zealots fight‡.349 i
live to fight another day....636 r
lures thee from that fight..367 f
must fight the course*.....149 u
never rise and fight again..636 r
never rise to fight again....121 l
ready for the fight..........226 h
rise to fight again..........121 h
say it was in fight*.........122 g
stump me to a f. John††....637 l
they now to f. are gone....636m
those that fly may f. again.635 s
to fight for such a land....469 k
to spirit up the others to f..482 e
turn and fight another day.121 l
warrior famoused for f.*....444 l
warrior in the heat of f.....119 b
we cannot f. for love, as*...663 p
we f. to great disadvantage.794 r
we'll forth and fight*......147 b
will f. her young ones in*.. 59 n
Fighting—dream of f. fields...443 r
for want of f. was grown...470 c
fyghtynge for Kynge......442 z
in feasting as in fighting....211 a
slain f. for his country.....135 b
two dogs are fighting ......113 a
Fights—eats the sword it f.*..629 b
fights and runs away......121 l
fights and runs away......121 h
fights in love's name......367 f
gain'd a hundred f.†.......444 q
more in bloody f. engage‡..650 r
whoever f. whoever falls...332 i
who fights by my side ... 158 f
Figure—a fixed f. for the*....109 o
f. that thou here seest put.550m
new f. to dance with my...127 q
primary figure is repeated. 96 e
resolveth from its figure*..139 k
see the f. of the house*....426 h
sky, thy figure floats along. 56 p
want of f. and a small‡....484 v
Figures—carved with figures..430 q
feelings not in f. on a dial..345m
f. that almost move§.......449 n
heav'nly f. from his pencil‖.446 h
'midst all the gorgeous f....458 q
no figures nor no fantasies*.562 i
pencill'd figures are ev'n*..447 f
Filbert-hedge—f-h. with.....250 r
Filches—f. from me my good*.524m
Files—files of pins extend‡...629m
said Files-on-Parade......443 k
Filial—untie the filial band...118 k
Fill—f. a pit as well as better*.640 e
fill up the bowl............162 f
he only can fill it..........522 k
the gust hath blown his f.**.647 q
to fill it with my tears*....592 k
world can never fill.......379 r
Filled—f. with fury, rapt.....465 k
Fills—he fills he bounds‡....275 p
thrills as it f. every animate.348 t
Filthy—but a f. piece of work*.447 h
Find-fast bind, fast find*....497 u
find out, if you can........326 t
f. the thing we fled to-day..605 p
if I could f. a wife I need...644 q
if it f. heaven, must f. it*...572 e
I shall find one............136 h
safe bind, safe find......503aa
search will f. it out........326 s
shall never find it more*...461 r

stay a little, and news will.504m
sure to find something.....663 a
time enough to f. a world††.668 r
to f. the other forth*......511 r
to help you f. them**..... 298 f
when you find him out*....490 n
which always f. us young..672 g
who can find out God.....707 h
world can't find me out.... 96 g
Finding—f. a fellow-creature.210 p
of finding an idea.........210 p
Finds—f. too late that men...656 o
the eye of Paul Pry often f.766 b
Fine—fine by defect, and‡...513 e
fine by degrees and...... 36 f
fine stands in record*......208 g
there's none so f. as Nelly..660m
things were as f. as could..356m
to fine the faults*........208 g
touch, how exquisitely f.‡..324 l
Fineness—f. which a hymn...568 e
Finest—wish them finest....247 e
Fingal—F. king of shields....557 k
Finger—by the Midas f. of the.649 a
clean your f. before you...496 x
finger of a clock...........203 n
f. on all flowing waters....546 b
f. wet the letters fair...... 68 g
God's finger touched him†.141 n
in her little finger.........280 t
layest thy f. on the lips§...416 b
point as with silent f. to the 95 l
pointed at with the finger..697 c
point his slow unmoving*..109 o
pointed out with the f......524 k
spires whose silent f. points† 96 b
Fingers—a dying miser's f....394 l
business at their f.s' ends..454 p
fingers burn with roseate...242 o
fingers down, to feel in.....247 d
fingers weary and worn....339 c
f. were made before forks..497 x
God laid his f. on the......401 o
how her f. went when they.408 q
kiss'd the fingers of this...333 t
must move the fingers.....780 s
on his fingers sardonyxes...176 j
rings put upon his fingers*.369 f
sew, prick our f. dull our...666 c
slight f. full of leaves.....541 o
smile upon his fingers' end*.138 t
taper f. catching at all.....238 c
touch me with thy golden..459 s
unwearied f. drawing out..580 g
where my weary f. stray...597 i
whose gentle f. bound it....454 b
with trembling f. did wet†.. 95 g
written by f. ghostly§......318 v
written by God's fingers...345 g
Finished—begun, and finished.160 c
finished by such as she*....376 t
thou wilt have finished....678 s
Finisher—of greatest works*.331 o
Finite—bury under the finite..286 k
Fins—perch with f. of Tyrian‡.213 t
Fir—cedar, and pine, and f.**.609 k
cones that tremble on the f.612 d
fir and branching palm**..609 k
ground of sombre fir......222 p
kindles the gummy bark**.613m
the firre that weepeth.....610 h
Firbloome-sweet is the f — 220m
Fir-tree—lonely f-t. is standing613 j
Fir-trees—f-t. dark and high..613 k
Fire—a clear f. a clean hearth. 14 v
a glass of liquid fire and....649 h
a little fire is quickly*......465 x
all the fatt's in the fire.....495 f
as fire is of light..........336 w
asshen olde is fyr yreke...212 s
a tempest dropping fire*...578 d
a thousand years of fire....144m
autumn's f. burns slowly...543 i
be fire with fire*...........526 a
beheld a huge f. shine‖....431 o
being purg'd a f. sparkling*363 r
blew the fire that burns*...174 e

Fling-fling out with cheer...214 c
Flint-as the f. bears fire*.... 18 b
can snore upon the flint*...526 o
rough hearts of flint*......442m
the everlasting flint*.......253 t
the fire i' the flint*.........213 d
Flip-eager round the.........163 b
Flippant-wife grows f. in...375 j
Flirt-f. that coach'd it round.215 u
f. with Juliet the Brahmin. 15 a
Flirtation-f. depraves it......114 n
f. is like the slime on water.114 n
word flirtation................215 t
Flirting-now f. at their length446 a
Flirts-ye belles and ye f.....114 o
Flitted-gone—flitted away†...148 v
Flitting-raven, never f....... 55 b
Float-float upon the waves¶.250 l
float amid the liquid noon..672 k
Floated-f. down the glassy...405 p
floated like the stream§....291 j
seemed and floated slow...100 h
they floated on and........ 99 j
Floating-f. backward with...647 u
Floats-floats, tho' unseen...485 z
Flock-shepherd shears his f..681 g
taught you, my dear f......451 l
tree a dull despondent f.... 50 e
there is no f. however§...136 a
wether of the flock*.........149 p
Flocks-avails it me the f.‡...361m
closer shades the panting f.‡542 p
flocks thick-nibbling........225 b
or f. or herds, or human**.149m
the beat of flocks..........230 i
white flocks sleeping...... 94 n
Flodden-of F.'s fatal field...638 s
Flog-flog them upon all‖.....455 e
Flood-accidents by f. and*... 3 g
all the f. before had done..648 j
another fervent f. succeeds.543 f
barks across the pathless f..552 o
bridge that arched the f....636 o
dead, commands the f.*....615 o
eyes in flood with laughter*341 e
flood may bear me far†....268 j
f. of time is rolling on......603 k
gifts in gracious flood......280 e
languid o'er the crystal f..616 n
lave them hourly in the f.*. 58 l
lie upon us like a deep f....596 l
like a bold f. o'erbear*..... 33 g
like a general flood‡.......114 t
methought the melancholy*140 q
mysterious f. that through.531 l
past into the level flood†... 96 h
taken at the f., leads on*...461 o
thou shoreless f. which in..603 l
Flood-gate-f-g. of the deeper.554 d
is of so flood-gate and*.....288 r
Floods-f. the calm fields with.397 f
great f. have flown from*..386 s
laughter of the vernal f....647 e
likened best to floods and..465 v
moon, the governess of f*..399 a
of memory f. are level......531 k
thickets to his f. decline...532 n
Floor-f. the earth so green..413 f
how the floor of heaven*...576 w
nicely sanded floor.........303 r
pour on thee, upon the f...593 f
sleep on, baby, on the f....560 q
warm from f. to ceilin'††...319 b
Flora-Flora's brilliant race...247 j
head of Flora's dance......245 f
Florence-ungrateful F.‖.... 98 b
Florins-manuscripts better..353 x
Flossier-was glossier and f..584 e
Flounders-gudgeons, f.‡....213m
Flourish-f. in immortal.....570w
princes and lords may f.... 143 g
sure thou did'st f. once....610 q
the just man will f. in.......801 k
time doth transfix the f.*..602 v
Flout-gild, but to f. the ruins.398 r
Flow-and the flow of soul‡..517 j
chatter as I flow†..........529 p

could I flow like thee......188 l
f. as hugely as the sea*.....491 p
flow gently, sweet Afton...530 a
flow in large effusion......541 l
f. on, forever, in thy......531 f
f. on, lovely Dee, flow on...530 k
mathematic ebb and flow..459m
O could I flow like thee.... 78 u
should flow like waters....113 j
which in thy ebb and flow..603 l
Flows-forth f. beneath a low.226 p
Flower-a broad magnolia f... 71 h
a faded f., a broken ring... 8 a
a flower that dies*..... 36 r
a flower, the gods.........223 b
amaranthine f. on earth..632 g
and not a flower adorns....148 o
April flower of sun.........248 j
art the sweetest flower....242 k
beauty's transient flower...156 g
bird, beast, and flower....410 t
bloom a wintry flower....241 g
blue f. which—Bramins...591 d
both the f. doth stay and...321 s
bright consummate f.**...219 e
bring childhood's flower...227 l
bruise their master's f.....321 s
call that brilliant flower...236 o
dear common f. that††....228 e
each punctual flower......217 k
fair f. dishevell'd in the....133 h
fateful f. beside the rill....226m
find a mystic flower......247 b
finest flower of all........244 f
first flower of the earth....652 i
f. being once display'd*...659 u
f. enjoys the air¶..........173 h
f. is born to blush unseen..420w
flower is only a weed§.....160 g
flower not unlike to this...225 i
floure of floures alle........227 h
flower of her kindred......242 h
flower of mercy...........238 i
flower of song bloom on§..228 l
f. of sweetest smell is shy¶.408m
flower of the golden horn..225 g
flower of virgin light......233 g
flour of wyfly pacience.....467 c
f. said, " Take it, my dear†.541 h
flower, she touched on†....197 j
flower so strangely bright..224 b
f. that blooms and dies.....766 k
flower that cheapens his...240 c
f. that first appeared¶......235 d
flower that one would be..244 f
flower that shall be mine¶..224 f
flower that's like thy face*.230 k
flower that smells of honey.233 c
flower that smiles to-day...241 n
flower that sweetly shows..359 g
flower the dews have‖.....186 p
flower whence came thy...229 g
f. with base infection*....643 o
from every opening flower.322 f
gave us a soulless flower...231 o
gives scent to every f......410 n
glory in the flower¶........466 r
God's own home to f. on... 31 r
hast thou the f. there*....221 g
hear the opening of a f....617 j
humble flower long time...249 p
just like the f. that buds... 74 o
keep my faded flower...... 7 y
latest flower of Spring....224 n
let it flower first, then....266 b
liberty alone that gives....343 p
like a sun-f. by a brook...548 s
like the midnight flower...187 f
little western flower*.....237m
lone flower hemmed¶.....245 i
look like the innocent f.*..482 c
lovely little flower is free¶.259 i
lurks in every flower......134 n
majestic flower! how.....235 e
man a flower...........348 b
meanest f. that blows¶.... 221 f
nipt my flower sae early....132 p

no other flower I see¶.....227 r
nor prest a flower.........254 b
not a flower but shows...217 l
O fairest f.; no sooner**...136 r
orange f. perfumes the....625 h
pale, mournful flower....231 l
pitying the lonely flower..249 p
pluck the flower..........730 a
pure large flower.........223 f
purest flower that blows..219 l
richer flower than daisies..227 f
rind of this small flower*..223 g
same flower that smiles.... 74 q
seasons flower and fade†...539 l
see the perfect flower.....243 c
seize the f. its bloom is...475 c
simple flower deceives¶...239 s
sip from the selfsame f.....759 o
spring the fairest flower...242 s
summer's flower is to the*.643 o
sweeter flower did Nature.240 h
sweetest f. of all the field*.139 d
sweetest f. wild nature....244 c
the constellated flower.....220 g
there is a flower, a........227 p
the sculptured flower.....240 q
the story f. like closes....132 e
'tis but a little faded f....380 c
very flower of dignity.....749 h
waves the bush the f. is...591 j
what a beautiful flower....243 t
white f. of a blameless†....351 n
wit is the flower of the....653 l
Flower-apples-about her....240m
Flower-cups-white f-c. hung.235 e
Flower-garden-a f-g. smiling.540 e
Flower-girl-f-g.'s prayer....216 j
Flowering-f. in a wilderness.611 v
many flowering islands lie.327 k
Flower-de-luce-f. being one*.228m
flower-de luce bloom on§..228 l
Floweret-f. of the brook....228 n
fresh f. pluck ere it close..351 r
meanest f. of the vale....463 o
like a gem the flow'ret.... 242 l
Flowerets-f. in the sunlight§.218 q
sweetest of all the f......230 p
sweet flowerets that unfold.221 p
Flower-pot-a ruddy f-p....457 i
Flowers-above all the f......243 t
all f. of Spring are not....540 h
and fulfilling flowers......393 n
another May new buds and.393 j
are human flowers......234 h
at a breath and the f.§....135 p
at shut of evening f.**....187 d
awake to the flowers.....349 e
blossom two flowers.....241 k
breath of flowers..........230 l
brilliant f. are pale and...395m
broken f. and crushed.... 52 j
buds into ripe flowers....240 a
but weary way with f......658 d
do bring May flowers.....392 o
dreams and f. will fade...605 l
eagle of flowers...........246 i
either flowers or veil......264 p
even in the simplest f......233 t
fair vernal f. laugh forth..164 r
fairest f. o' the season*....220 c
far day sullies flowers.....563 p
flooding the earth with f.§.540 l
flow'rs aloft shading**.....221 j
flowers alone can say......219 k
f. and fruits of love are‖.... 9 e
flowers, and leaves and§...540 j
flowers are honey-dew....186 r
flowers are intermingled¶..238 h
f. are like the pleasures*..220 d
flowers are Love's..........216 f
flowers are words.........217 n
f. before the blast! what...197 q
flowers, bright flowers....217 u
flowers fair there I found..540 n
f. for the sick girl's silent..611 l
flowers grow in the vale...248 r
f. gynnen for to sprynge... 65 a

foolish as to anticipate. ...727 g	and noiseless f. of time*....602 l	Forbids–God that f. crimes..743 c
f. ofttimes teach the wise. ..299 w	and the prettiest foot......253 n	Force–fate show thy force*..207 d
f. things to all the wise‖...650 q	another a short foot.......253 r	f. and not opinion is the....768 j
foolish to admire him......768 e	aside with unreluctant f...483 i	force else can get the .....389 r
foolish to blame the sea....701 d	both foot and hand go cold.162 v	force from f. must ever.... 76 j
foolish to fear.............699 q	far be trodden by his foot..355 t	f. his soul so to his own*...423 g
more f. and more wise......754 h	fire with the dog's foot.....507 x	force is of brutes, but...... 69 o
never said a foolish thing..533 v	foot already in the grave...253 q	force of nature could no....479 b
no God. the foolish saith...410 g	foot has music in 't... .... 81 t	force their way to me¶..... 25m
once been very foolish...... 795 i	foot more light............254 e	force them, though it was.427 q
penny wise, pound foolish.503 e	foot on the golden stair... 32 c	f. whole regions, in despite.476 e
the f. and vulgar are.......765 c	gauger walked with........408 d	from its f. nor doors, nor..482 t
very f., fond old man*...... 11 v	halting for the wearied f...348 a	have spent its novel force†.466 a
whether they be wise or f..573 r	hand to hand, and foot to‖..636 c	more than your f. move*...271 x
Foolishly–love f. is better...366 t	head with f. hath private..371 b	no force in the beginning..701 e
Fools–and fools call Nature..273 v	hold his swift foot back*...602 p	no iron chain or outward f.571 d
are fools who roam.......298 a	measure we call a foot.....253 r	prove by f. of argument....26 t
are the money of fools.....664 q	my foot is on my native....409 g	prudence than by force.....736 j
as dull fools suppose**.....473 h	nay, her foot speaks*......339 z	subdue by force**..........517 f
call their masters fools‡...440 p	needlessly sets foot.......260 a	supported by force.........709 j
do very oft prove fools*....654 e	noiseless falls the foot of...603 p	surprised by unjust f.**....632 x
empty bladders, opinion, f.509 k	noiseless foot of time*.. ... 11 o	than equivalent to force....337 k
fair words make fools......493 p	now from head to f. I am*.526 b	that thy f. I may rehearse.646 r
farce; if people f. will be.. 16 b	one foot in sea*............212 e	'tis pretty to f. together...596 t
fools are my theme‖........251 f	one foot in the grave......502 ff	to have the most force......516 o
fools are not mad folks*....252m	O, so light a foot*........253 t	who could f. the soul¶......572 n
fools are stubborn as...... 88 v	shoe for a little foot......253m	who overcomes by force**.631 b
fools as we wet, so fools....493 p	should human f. intrude...567 r	who thinks by f. or skill....660 w
f. consult interpreters in..161 h	so silent as the f. of Time..604 c	without knowing the f. of..664 i
f. discover it and stray no..528 d	spurn him with his foot*..629 a	Forced–f. me out of thy*....591 q
f. laugh i' the alehouse*....464 c	steps with a tender foot‡..254 g	f. worship shuts evils in...670 o
f. make feasts and wise....497aa	sting the luckless foot.....143 q	till it be forced............121 j
fools may our scorn.......173 t	sweet foot of spring that...541 d	who can be forced..........701 g
fools mis-define thee......273 n	swift of foot misfortune is.388 e	Forces–bring therefore all...663 t
f. rush in where angels‡...251 z	the better foot before*....294 s	opposing and enduring f...113 d
fools shall kneel.........674 f	the same shoe on every f..509 x	Forcibly–f. if we must......470 e
fools that on them trust....796m	time goes with rapid foot..746 n	Fordoes–makes me or f.*....417 n
fools that pride can boast..254 k	to the sole of our foot......498 a	Fords–sing at the fords of... 58 j
fools that stand in better*..252w	we set our f. upon some...536 c	Forebodings–childhood has.. 89 i
fools they cannot die. ...253 j	with her odorous foot.....657 e	Foredates–f. its hundred....236 n
fools thy power despise....365w	Foot-ball–all day like a f-b...622 h	Forefather–on his f.'s feet...203 d
fools to disport ourselves*..174 i	Foote–ever-laughing F's‖....421 p	Forefathers–f. had no other*.452 c
fools who came to scoff....450m	laugh must sigh for F.‖....421 p	think of your forefathers...484 e
fools who flock'd to swell‖..284 l	Foot-fall–eve's silent f-f....187 a	Forefinger–f. of an*........197 c
for f. admire, but men of‡.. 6 j	hark to the foot-fall.. ....492 k	stretch'd f. of all time†....435 c
government let f. contest‡.349 i	with her foot-fall sows....541 d	Forego–f. me now, come to..464 u
have been women's fools...656 p	Footing–a thing in footing‖..127 r	Forehead–bend thy f.¶ .....245 i
how many fools does it....785 n	'twixt his stretch'd f.*....422 t	f., nay the valley*........ 90 n
knaves in cheating fools...436 s	Footman–footman with an...435 e	f. of our faults*...........438 p
let f. the studious despise..774 p	of the footman's hand.....134 a	f. of the morning sky**....576 k
little wise, the best f. be...509 c	Foot-path–jog on the f-p.*..384 l	his f. wears thick rows....455 j
may please fools; but he..706 a	Footprints–efface the f. in§.598 u	His God-like f. by the..... 55 k
men may live fools........253 j	f. directed towards thy....698 t	joy droops, with f.........602 a
mock sad fools withal*.....161 d	f. of departed men.........141 e	Shakespeare, on whose f .549 v
most wise are greatest f....338 n	f. of their age are ††........151 b	take thou hold upon his f..603 n
Nature meant but fools‡...252 c	footprints on the sands§....188 s	unbashful forehead woo*.. 12 a
never-failing vice of fools‡.491 c	Footstep–a footstep a low†.. 25 t	well the forehead high..... 36 l
none but f. would keep*....350 s	Footsteps–and light f. lightly. 55 j	we read on the f. of those...768 r
of f. who value Nature not. 43 p	as home his footsteps he...118 j	your forehead louers.......328 a
old men are fools. ....251 g	coming footsteps cheats...254 a	Foreheads–covers bald f.....533 l
paradise of fools to few**..463 q	compelling eyes and f......517 a	f. of Islam are bowed ....617 b
places are filled with fools.700 o	echo of its f. through......201 q	Foreign–a f. nation is a kind.484 i
play the fool with*........253 a	eyes and f. of the master...751 t	breath in f. clouds*...... 33 h
print it, and shame the f.‡.452 b	footsteps may be found....274 j	f. hands thy decent limbs‡.137m
serve like other fools‡.....252 v	footsteps of a throne¶......254 h	f. troop was landed in my..469 t
shame of f. conceals their..700 r	like footsteps upon wool†..417 s	intercourse with f. nations.468 j
silence is the genius of f....789 a	plants his footsteps in.....274 e	journey to some f. court‖..427 h
slavish herd and fools.....773 f	the f. of Truth and the.. ..338 i	thrive in foreign soil.......761 f
sleep did mock sad fools*..161 d	tread in the f. of my........500 v	wandering on a f. strand.. 118 j
teacher of fools.............696 g	Footstool–f. of the stronger..661 a	welcome to a f. fireside§...643 s
the food of fools...........215 r	my f. earth, my canopy‡...412 a	Foreigners–all f. excel‖.... 127 r
the f. are mad if left alone*.659m	the footstool of humility...310 q	Foreknowledge–f. absolute**109 b
the gaze of f. and pageant‡.491 b	Fop–a fop? in this brave....254 o	Forelock–doe him by the f..603 o
the sublimity of fools......767 t	a fop sometimes gives......754 e	on occasion's f. watchful**.461 k
think old men fools.......251 v	a fop their passion‡.........349 n	round from his parted f.**.534m
this great stage of fools*...350 z	fiery fop with new..........163 f	seize time by the forelock..503ee
those that are f., let them*.651 n	fop to plague his brother‡.254m	take Time by the forelock..504 r
thrive at Westminster on‡.438 b	the solemn fop............251 j	Foreman–f. takes out his ...437 d
to please the fools.........199 d	Fopperies–death his f.......254 p	Forenoon-a good,wholesome*439 d
we think our fathers f.‡...673 c	Fopplings–f. grin to show....254 i	Fore-plane–tongue of his f-p.431 j
what f. these mortals be*...501 u	Fops–persisting f. we know‡.185 r	Foresaw–sees what he f.¶... 85 r
what gift to fools avails‡...272 v	Forage–pain scant f. earns... 43 p	Foresee–f. and to control...150 r
word which knaves and f..205 f	Forbear–God's angel cries f..404 d	f. even those things which.701 i
yesterdays have lighted f.*.605 o	Forbearance–f. ceases to be..466 x	Foreseeing–f. what is to come752 l
young men are fools........251 g	Forbidden–f. have a secret...732 l	Fore-spurrer–f-s. comes*...365 f
Foolscap–like a f. crown‖.... 98 c	God with these forbidden**593 k	Forest–at the forest edge...225 e
Foot–a f. the deformity of.... 25 p	striving for things f.......692 j	broad f. in its summer....394 a

SHAKESPEARE *; MILTON **; WORDSWORTH ¶; BYRON ‖; TENNYSON †; LOWELL ††; POPE ‡; LONGFELLOW §.

Garrick-our G.'s a salad..... 79 q
Garrulous-g. recounts the.. 12 i
Gars-gentle dames! it g. me. 7 d
Garter-familiar as his g.*..482 d
 star or g. does in England.458m
Gartered-cross g. a fashion*. 24 e
Garth-G. did not write his‡..429m
Gas-telegraphs, printing g..327 c
Gasconade-full of g. and.....643 c
Gashes-twenty trenched g.*.140 b
Gasp-follow thee, to the last*368 b
 g. thy gasp and groan. ....138 g
Gasped-as I gasp'd upon the‖604 l
Gasping-g. from out the.....387 n
Gate-and near the sacred g..189 p
 be bold, first gate..........119 c
 beckoning at the gate...... 32 c
 before the g. of Paradise...154 w
 behold this gate of pearl...284 g
 boots it at one g. to make**638 c
 glory's morning gate .....131 u
 golden orientall g. of....... 29 q
 heaven's g. opens when the563 p
 Heaven's golden gate ... 284 g
 one morn a Peri at the g...463 s
 on the king's g. the moss. 534 d
 openest the mysterious g.§ 31 k
 open thy gate of mercy*..382 n
 passion-flower at the g.†...366 r
 rear'd its everlasting gate..122 s
 sleeps at wisdom's gate**..651 e
 spring's already at the g...540 e
 stoop, boys: this g.*........670 n
 the gate of the mind.....726?b
 the golden gate is fled.....134°C
 too bold, third gate........119 c
 to the g. of holy Rome.....522 l
 western gate of heaven§...187 b
 writ on Paradise's gate...206 j
Gates-battering the g. oft..489 l
 charge of the g. of heaven.390m
 gates of golden-rod.......229m
 g. that now stood open**.. 299m
 g. that open still toward... 57 b
 hateful to me are the g....144 o
 her ever-during gates**...298 e
 his gates were ope........309 i
 keeping the g. of light.....591 b
 kneels at the g. of all......131 s
 morning opes her golden*..400 x
 nor g. of steel so strong*...602 p
 on Sunday, heaven's g....536 o
 shut the g. of mercy on...382 f
 storms at fortune's gates. 368 g
 the g. of monarch's*.....585 d
 the g. of the grave shall...141 l
 their coward g. on*.......193 x
 through the g. of death....488 j
 to the g. of heaven¶........383 a
 unbarr'd the g. of light**..400 k
Gath-in heathen G., or.....570 l
Gather-stoop and gather me.249 p
 they g. and g. and gather§.416 c
Gathered-be g. together§....210 s
 with ease g., not harshly**. 10 s
Gatherer-g. and disposer of..474 u
Gathering-the rose.......505dd
Gathers-g. port-cannons....205 e
Gaudy-fancy, rich, not g.*... 24 c
 neat, not gaudy...........502 h
Gauger-g. played the flute..408 d
 g. walked with willing foot.408 d
Gauls-onward! G. and.....635m
Gauntlet-a g. with a gift in..487 h
Gauze-owre g. an' lace......324 a
Gave-g. enough to any ......256 i
 what we gave, we have....102 o
Gay-all will be gay when....223 n
 and gay as soft and........661 h
 face that's anything but g..423 o
 far from the g. cities and‡117 f
 from grave to gay........757 c
 furze unprofitably gay....229 c
 gay and festive scenes....211 t
 g. as the gilded summer....655 a
 gayest of the g. through a. 44 a
 gay little man in gray......110 a

not, if I could, be gay.....379 f
 sorrowful dislike the gay..743 i
 thou makest the sad heart.540 o
Gayety-the g. of nations...408 h
 the muse of g. brings ill... 175 i
Gayly-g. the troubadour...404 j
Gaze-Arab by his earnest g... 62 e
 gaze on the stars high ...248m
 gaze with all the town.....126 u
 gone from my g. like a... 2 v
 him sit for other's gaze ...456 i
 scans with poetic g. the....414 e
 stood and met my gaze††..634 h
 the g. of fools and pageant‡491 b
 to g. in his eyes, and bless.483 c
 to gratify the gloating g... 48 p
 who g. upon her unaware. 654 u
Gazed-g. each on other*....210 a
 g. on each other with.....359 s
 still they g., and still the. 342 b
 while I stood and gazed....343 n
 wistly on him gazed* .... 63 c
Gazelle-nurs'd a dear g., to..155 f
 to thee, O fair gazelle......617 a
Gazelles-g. so gentle and... 20 k
Gazer-g. wipe his eye 241m
Gazes-infant when it g. on a‖329 i
Gayest-g. ever true and....246 c
Gazette-big enough for the..435 e
Gazing-comfort are. .....540 d
 enraptured g. on her whom664 a
 g. up 'mid the dim........186 b
 with gazing fed*..........204 d
Geese-all our g. are swans. 494kk
 as wild g. that the creeping* 47 i
 or rob Rome's ancient g.‡.. 47 h
 souls of g., that bear*......122 k
Gelliflowers-with gelliflowers229 k
Gem-any g. that gilds the...683 h
 as a g. of the old rock......500 o
 best gem upon her zone...425 h
 bright g. instinct with¶....408 l
 cast not the clouded g.....404 d
 first gem of the sea........652 i
 full many a g. of purest...484 e
 gem of his authority§.....226 g
 glow-worm lights his gem..323 k
 hope's gentle gem.........228 n
 like a g. the flow'ret......242 l
 night itself does the rich..484 c
 no g. that twinkling hangs.590 n
 what g. hath dropp'd and‖.590 l
Gems-break into a thousand. 63 n
 court-virtues bear, like g.‡683 a
 feet like sunny g. on an†..253w
 gems of morning dew......577 n
 g. on his fingers, there are.176 j
 gems pave thy radiant....401 d
 g. the starry girdle of the..575 p
 no gems of any kind....... 24 l
 painters gems‡..........674 j
 rich and rare were the g..434 j
 these g. have life in them..434 d
 whence the g. were gone..766 e
 winter's crystal g. be......396 d
Genealogical-account of ... 15 p
General-G. C. is a dreffle††..107 k
 make him an ill general... 75 i
 of him a bad general......443m
 pledge the health of our g.443 j
 qualities of a general.....751 g
Generalities-sounding g.....529 d
 that the glittering g.......462 b
Generation-from a former g. 12 j
 from generation to g...... 63 q
 serve thy g., this thy fate.435 p
Generations-do g. press on¶.309 f
 no hungry g. tread........ 51 g
 the cross leads g. on......522 d
 vast g. of man are come...527 o
Generative-as it is g ....597 a
Generosity-pulses stirred to.318 v
Generous-a g. heart repairs‡.558 l
 deep into the g. mind......484 t
 generous in its bloom......236 e
 our g. train complies‡.....666 u
 suddenly becomes g........706 a

the generous prodigal.....442 y
Genial-g. as the light.....120 f
Genius-between g. and......769 p
 check young G.' proud....125 i
 companion of genius......270 g
 divisions of men of g......270 j
 door on his own genius....446 g
 envy depreciates the g....694 c
 every thought which g....596 n
 every work of genius......270 f
 flashes of genius.........118 r
 genius and its rewards....270 l
 genius appears deepest...270 n
 g. breaks d., and mind....706 c
 genius brightly shine .....270 r
 g. can never despise......271 d
 genius commands thee....115 d
 genius, grandeur, worth.. 85 o
 genius has been slow......270 s
 g. inspires this thirst .....271 b
 g. is essentially creative..271 c
 g. is that in whose power††588 r
 g. is the master of nature..270 p
 genius, like humanity.....270 o
 genius must be born......270 k
 g., the highest example..200 q
 genius was such.........270m
 g., wit, and spirit of a....493 q
 gives a better discerning649 q
 great g. without a spice...706 f
 honors of g. are eternal...706 d
 innocence in genius, and...513 h
 intelligence is to genius...270 e
 legacies that a great g.... 63 q
 man of g. returns to......326 u
 many men of g. must ....270 h
 my genius is rebuk'd*....271 a
 necessary ingredient of g..467 f
 no g. can long or often....104 f
 no great genius was ever.. 77 i
 no more men of genius....270 g
 no word of genius††......270 u
 no work of genius††......270 u
 obedience, bane of all g...485 y
 of a writer's genius......514 d
 own g. only could acquire.549 t
 particular man of genius...270 h
 perfection of poetic g.....310 x
 piety is not inferior to...175 e
 premature shoot of genius.706 e
 reveals the genius of......706 b
 science only will one g. fit‡588 l
 sensitive family of genius..547 v
 shut against great genius..706 g
 splendid proof of genius...477 n
 that fire is genius§........270 t
 the lamp of genius burns..769 r
 the substitute for genius..427 o
 the true parent of genius..566 u
 thing required of genius...769 q
 three-fifths of him g. and††.871 o
 to raise the g. and to‡.....422 n
 with genius from the gods.311 s
Geniuses-greatest g. and...315 u
Genteel-g. in personage.... 78 b
Gentian-lonely g. blossoms..229 i
 the gentian nods in dewy..229 h
 the gentian reigned......229 f
Gentian-flower-blue g-f.....229 d
Gentility-a cottage of g.....310 h
Gentianellas-eyes of g......191 o
Gentle-as gentle as bright..653m
 because of its g. nature...706 g
 g. and low, an excellent*..635 g
 g. as a lamb with mint....660aa
 gentle in manner. ......706 h
 g. in their manner, they...656 e
 g. means and easy tasks*..271w
 g. minde by gentle deeds..271 q
 g. person made a Jack*....271 c
 g., sometimes capricious..558 c
 gentle, though retired.....655 t
 g. ways are best and......511 h
 gentle yet not dull.........188 l
 he is gentil that doth......271 s
 his life was g. and the*....372 k
 I am meek and gentle*.....404 a

the trade of the g. craft....453 d
they are as gentle*.........271 v
though g. yet not dull...... 78 u
Gentleman–affable and*......271 k
a fine puss g. that's........447 o
a gentleman born master*.271 j
a gentleman is one who....548 a
a g. nurse that loves to*...589 l
but like a gentleman‖.....127 r
darkness is a gentleman*..153 o
gentleman and scholar......22 p
g. has he not instructed. ..550 d
g. is disposed to swear*....419 u
God Almighty's g. .... 93 d
honourable gentleman*....271 n
how bething the g..........666 o
I am a gentleman*.........271 l
I was a gentleman*........271m
Jack became a gentleman*.271 o
makes a Jack a gentleman.456 i
old name of gentleman*....271 r
since I was a gentleman....271 g
St. Patrick was a gentleman271 i
the first true gentleman....271 h
who was then the g........666 b
will never pass for a g......791 e
written–"gentleman"‖.. 271 f
Gentlemen–amusement of... 87 n
conversation among g.... 113 s
cooks are gentlemen......431m
fight, g. of England*.......639 a
gentlemen use books as.... 67 c
God Almighty's gentlemen.271 i
mob of g. who wrote‡.......436 w
seamen were not g........445 j
three gentlemen at once....271 p
two single g. rolled into....627 e
which gentlemen have*..271 n
ye gentlemen of England..445m
Gentleness–deeds require*....147 f
g. and love and trust§......645 b
gentleness has no effect....788m
gentleness shall force*......271 x
g. succeeds better than....768 l
let gentleness my strong*..271 u
patience and g. is power...485 t
power can do by g..........706 i
security for gentleness....642 p
way with extreme g.†......646 a
Gentler–a g. heart did*......444 b
Gentlest–in things that g....485 q
Gentlewoman–grave old g....623 z
Gentlewomen–g. handle...... 67 c
Gently–as g. lay my head....560 n
but use all gently*.........423 k
gently steal upon the ear‡.406 u
move but gently on........388w
so gently o'er me stealing..381 f
speak gently! 'tis a little...574 r
Gentry–the g. of Shropshire. 18 e
Genuine–genuine and easy... 7 s
what's g. shall posterity...759 n
Geography–in despite o' g....476 e
Geometric–for he by g......341 r
Geometry–bees (practise) g..805 i
which leads to geometry....341 ;
Geraldine–to G.'s were..... 453 h
German–river, thou'rt G.....532 f
Germans–breeze which G....609 g
G. call the wind's bride....609 g
the G. that of—the air.....483 k
we G. fear God, but........767 u
Gestic–skill'd in gestic lore... 89 k
Gesture–and natural in g....450 g
dumbness of the gesture*.. 83 q
every g. dignity, and **....657 q
language in their very g...340 d
with an invincible g........466 u
Gestures–eyes and g., eager..120 q
words and extravagant g...176 t
Get–thing I cannot get*......111 s
Gets–it gets thee nothing....419 c
Getting–g. and spending we¶.669 t
getting up seems not so....199 h
Ghastly–g. in the glare of...398 j
Ghost–and Scipio's g. walks.. 24 r
especially the ghost.......422 p

g. of a summer that lived..542 k
like an ill-used ghost.......279m
like a sheeted g. the§......552 g
moon, pale g. of night..... 415 e
O solemn ghost†...........265 s
there needs no ghost my*... 25 j
what beck'ning g. along‡... 25 f
Ghosts–at whose approach*. 29 o
despairing g. complain....236 i
driven like g. from an.....648 a
g. and forms of fright§.... 25 d
g. of defunct bodies....... 25 a
g. of our foes are many....638 i
look for g. but none will¶.. 25m
shoals of visionary ghosts‡. 25 c
some haunted by the g.*...535 a
where light-heel'd g. and..618 p
Giant–a dwarf on a giant's..494 q
a stone the giant dies......134 g
as when a giant dies*......322 j
before a sleeping giant*....107 a
excellent to have a giant's*.579m
g. shoulders to mount on.. 2 d
g.'s unchained strength....257 v
great as when a g. dies*....138 r
sees farther than the giant. 2 d
tyrannous to use it like a*.579m
Giants–against imaginary g..674m
giants that had fled.......104 p
shoulders of g. see more....503 g
startled giants by Nile's‖..115 j
strength of the ancient g..579 j
that g. may jet through*..535 d
Gibbets–g. keep the lifted....404 e
Giddy–and make men g...... 29 s
fancies are more g. and*...377 e
Gift–a gauntlet with a gift..487 h
a gift unsought............237 f
April's g. to April's bees..611 h
a sacred g. to man........493 b
bosom-weight, your¶......473m
boy have not a woman's g*.591 s
courage, the highest g.....118 s
crave of thee a gift‖.......599 i
dost thou accept the gift§..145 p
fatal gift of beauty‖........116 l
for g. or grace, surpassing.560 p
for weary feet, the g. of...526 t
g. derives its value from...706 n
g. doth stretch itself as*...269 e
gift has autumn poured....424 r
gift of eternal life.........522 g
gift of friendship..........224 j
gift of noble origin¶.......272 l
g. of song was chiefly lent..568 p
gift of which fortune......256 b
gift without the giver††....272 e
heaven's last best g., my**.645 f
heaven's next best gift....318 e
I live, I consider a gift.....721 n
in reality only a gift........770 b
is the best g. of heaven....631 x
life itself the inferior of.343 s
loved her own harmless g..629 j
nature's noblest gift my‖..471 p
noblest gift of heav'n.....658 d
only is the g. of heaven‡...548 k
than one great gift........207 p
the gift, to be true........272 b
the giver makes the gift...798 n
the palm is a gift divine...617 b
the will and not the gift...769 s
they have the g. to know*.659 h
this is a gift that I have*...315 i
true love's the gift which..362 h
what g. to fools avails‡....272 c
which crowns desire with g.582 t
wife is the peculiar g. of‡..645 i
Gifted–g. with little of the..319 h
Gift-horse–gift-horse in the..272 a
Giftie–wad some power the..310 f
Gifts–all gifts but one the..563 k
bring our precious g. to.... 94 c
cannot recall their gifts‡..592 o
gifts and alms are the...... 86 c
gifts appertinent to man*..266m
gifts are ever the most....706m

gifts come from above in..770 c
gifts in gracious flood......280 e
g. of an enemy were to be..764 n
g. that cost them nothing..272 a
g. that folly may earn.....768 g
gifts that God hath sent§..406 a
heaven except by its gifts..707 h
heaven's best gifts to hold.778 g
here Ceres' g. in waving‡..424 g
his grace than g. to lend..522 n
largest gifts of heaven....205 s
may be g. from the devil..642 e
mistake in her gifts*......272 h
of g. there seems none....271 z
rich gifts wax poor*.......272 i
shining g. that took all...581 t
take gifts with a sigh. ....272 g
tempering her gifts that... 86 j
that her gifts may*.......272 h
the heavenly gifts........260 t
the meanest gifts. ...... 706 k
when they bring gifts.....699 u
win her with gifts*.......272 j
Gild–g. but to flout, the....398 r
gild it with the happiest*..199m
gild the brown horror.....399 t
how to gild the pill........784 d
to gild refined gold*...... 252 y
Gilded–gay with gilded wings 50 c
gilded by a summer's beam.530 n
men are but gilded loam*..524 s
Gilding–g. pale streams*....625 i
Gilds–first gilds the clouds..585 d
love gilds the scene......660 i
Gillian–whoop, Jack! kiss G..335 c
Gills–and out at his gills... 19 f
Gillyvors–and streak'd g.*..229 j
garden rich in gillyvors*...229 j
Gilt–gilt the ocean with his*.400 u
Ginger–sinament and ginger.195 n
Girdle–gems the starry g. of.575 p
g. round about the earth*.607 i
g. round about the world..445 a
Girdled–g. round with the..541 n
Girl–each girl when pleased..455 s
flowers for the sick girl's..611 l
girl that loves him not*....252 p
heretic girl of my soul....158 f
lies in happy sleep a girl..563 q
no good g.'s lip out of.....660 n
O Beddowee g. beloved so..617 a
the girl smiled before......595 a
unlesson'd g., unschool'd*.338 c
while the bright-eyed girl..454 b
young g. over her hoary...400 r
Girl-graduates–sweet g-g.†..660 t
Girls–all the g. that e'er was.660m
girls blush sometimes...... 62 f
girls we love for what they.778 i
in your girls again........ 90 j
lads and girls all must*....139 h
the girls all cried........ 254 j
the girls that are so smart.655 q
the rosebud garden of g.†..660 s
votive train of g. and boys‖.533 f
would to dance with girls..422 h
wretched un-idea'd girls..657 d
Give–begs to be desired to*. 343 f
counsel, give me mine*.... 7 g
give and eke receive it‖.... 7 f
g. place to your betters....713 f
give me liberty or give me.343 v
give to God each moment.. 347 b
give to the wretched......679 q
g. us their most precious... 64 r
give what thou canst......524 y
give, you gods, give to....357 w
he can give little to his...498dd
if you shall marry, you*...376 v
more I give to thee*........364 h
never give her o'er*.......659m
not what we give††........272 e
she did not give..........703 j
to-day I would give§.......261 e
to g. is the business of the. 770 a
we give and what we.....559m
we receive but what we....526 x

willing to g. all that he has.337 *j*
Given-be given away by a...375 *o*
given them to such a. ...643 *d*
heaven alone that is g.††...102 *u*
look at what is given......706 *p*
looked a g. horse in the....498*cc*
that is given away††......275 *d*
Giver-flowing of the g. unto.272 *b*
gift without the giver††...272 *e*
look also at the giver......706 *p*
most acceptable which the.706*m*
the g. makes the gift more.798 *n*
the g.'s loving thought§...380 *i*
the mind of the giver......679 *n*
Givers-givers prove unkind*.272 *i*
Gives-alike in what it gives‡.510*m*
fortune gives too much....702 *l*
g. twice who gives quickly.706 *q*
g. up everything to him....718 *n*
God g. with a sparing hand.685 *g*
he that g. us in these days.439 *h*
hour which g. us life......722 *f*
it blesseth him that gives*.382 *p*
receives, but nothing g.... 79*m*
seasoned timber, never g..632 *p*
what man g., the gods by‡.642 *k*
Giving-g. requires good....706 *o*
godlike in giving but the....82 *i*
in giving, a man receives...272 *f*
Givings-his g. rare, save‡....312 *n*
Glacier-king of the peak and. 46 *d*
Glad-and to be g. or sad I... 10 *r*
g. I was not born before....590 *a*
g. of other men's good*....111 *t*
g. the heathens would have.539 *d*
g. your errand to fulfil§...479 *v*
grieve or g. mine eye‖......606 *q*
have been glad of yore¶....330 *e*
how I can be glad........225 *r*
makest glad and radiant§...228 *k*
often, glad no more¶......330 *e*
thoughts that shall g. the††.428 *x*
to g. me with its soft black.155 *f*
youth is to all the g. season.672 *a*
Gladden-words g. so many§..664 *u*
Gladdening-g. every one.....225 *e*
Gladness-couch'd in seeming*569 *x*
face with g. overspread¶...196 *k*
glanc'd gladness round the‖. 74 *h*
hospitality sitting with g.§.309 *j*
laugh forth your ancient g.164 *r*
so full of g. and so full§...542*m*
sun insists on gladness....153*w*
Glade-and murky glade.....231 *l*
furrowed glade and dell....237 *g*
points to yonder glade‡.... 25 *f*
Glades-and penetrates the¶..555 *j*
Gladiator-wounded gladiator 686 *j*
Glance-fleet is a g. of the...385 *k*
of the smooth g. beware....367 *k*
sunshine of glance........129 *k*
Glances-g. of hatred that....294*aa*
shimmer with angel g......194 *g*
Glare-are ever caught by‖....369 *i*
by the g. of false science....538 *g*
Glass-a glass is good........280 *l*
a glass of liquid fire and...649 *h*
brittle g. that's broken*... 36 *r*
clear as a g. the shining‡...615 *f*
dome of many-coloured g..351 *b*
drink not the third glass...593 *f*
drink out of his glass......177 *a*
flesh is but the glasse....401*m*
fortune is like glass......703*m*
get thee glass eyes; and*...482*w*
g. antique twixt thee and..101 *a*
g., China and reputation...498 *e*
glass wherein the noble*...188 *u*
it is a shining g. which a...668 *b*
its pure still g. pictures...298 *l*
last sand twinkled in the..647 *a*
made mouths in a glass*...659 *v*
nature's a glass of††......411 *l*
Praxiteles did by his glass..112 *r*
pride hath no other g.*....491*m*
pride is his own glass*....491 *i*
prove an excuse for the g..604 *r*

rising sudden to the g......313 *o*
the glass of fashion*.......205 *j*
till I have bought a glass*..584 *g*
thou art thy mother's g.*...673 *j*
whose house is of g. must..509 *i*
within this g. becomes§....600 *v*
Glasses-and the musical g....113 *o*
fill all the glasses there.....162 *f*
mother puts her glasses on.436*m*
read without its glasses....448 *a*
stand to your g. steady....604*m*
Glassy-his name to a g. sea..714 *q*
Gleam-casts a g. over this**.. 99 *s*
gleam as of another life....532 *k*
g. on the years that shall be.464 *p*
Gleamed-she g. upon my¶...661 *q*
Gleams-visible in the g.†† .. 81 *h*
Glean-g. the broken ears*...294 *h*
Glebe-stubborn g. has broke.423 *s*
Glee-faith and inward glee¶...46 *a*
forward and frolic g. was..195 *o*
running over with glee....194 *h*
the echoes of their glee....395 *d*
with counterfeited glee....455 *i*
Gleemen-loud the g. sing§...396 *g*
Glen-down the rushy glen....196 *p*
Glencairn-remember thee G.379 *o*
Glens-treads the sequestered258 *d*
Glide-g. adown thy stream...600 *b*
g. gently, mortals, weigh..785 *k*
to g. in peace down death's.603 *k*
wish you could g. o'er‖....368 *u*
Glides-g. on and will glide...721 *h*
Glimmer-g. the rich dusk....223 *j*
to glimmer in my mind....307 *j*
Glimmering-gone-g.‖......466 *h*
Glimmers-g. on the forest§..398 *e*
Glimpse-give but a g. and... 35 *s*
Glimpses-give it some faint††384*w*
g. of forgotten dreams†...161 *j*
g. that would make¶.......92 *e*
shadowy g. disconnect....132 *e*
Glisten-all silence an' all g.††416 *f*
Glistens-nor all that g. gold..144 *k*
Glistereth-not gold that g...494*jj*
Glisters-all that g. is not gold.495 *e*
Glitter-brighter the glitter...257 *h*
g. toward the light........226 *h*
Glittering-g. with the......228 *p*
that the g. generalities....462 *b*
Glitters-which g. is not gold..369*m*
Gloaming-g. comes, the day.624 *q*
g. treads the heels of day..366 *c*
g. o' the wood, the throssil. 58 *p*
then when the g. comes... 48 *o*
Gloating-g. upon a sheep's..430*m*
Globe-all that tread the g....132 *v*
annual visit o'er the globe. 44 *q*
changeful o'er the........544 *p*
four quarters of the globe..115 *g*
globe is a vast head a......171 *g*
of the whole globe........116 *e*
passport round the globe..120 *f*
rattle of a g. to play.. .....357 *w*
shows his globe of light... 585 *d*
skill'd in the g. and sphere.445 *c*
the great globe itself*......634*m*
turns the spotty globe to..115 *o*
we the globe can compass*.197 *b*
Gloom-background of the...617 *j*
but a nest of gloom........ 43 *n*
g. of earthquake and......447 *i*
g. of my bachelor days is..456*m*
house a sudden gloom§....135 *o*
iron dug from central g.†..351*m*
journey through the aery**352 *k*
mingled with the gloom...103 *d*
not chase my gloom away..379 *f*
sunk in the quenching g...417 *t*
to counterfeit a gloom**...352 *q*
vault's dayless gloom‖....491 *t*
who see in twilight's g....479 *k*
Glooms-in shadowy glooms..225 *e*
winter spreads his latest g. 546 *n*
Gloomy-but if proud and g..522 *r*
g. as night he stands‡....... 25 *o*
g. calm of idle vacancy....313 *l*

in such a g. state remain..563 *o*
Glories-and thy young g.....542 *g*
field October's g. fade......394 *j*
glories like glow-worms....273 *k*
glories of our blood... ... 207 *n*
hour his glories faded......125 *t*
the glories of our blood....141 *b*
Glorify-a God to glorify....572*m*
glorify what else is........273 *a*
Glorious-a g. life or grave..437 *l*
all that's good and g.‖.....496 *u*
great, glorious and free....652 *i*
how g. man's destiny§...151 *a*
make thee g. by my pen...202 *e*
may be g. to write††......428 *x*
sweet and glorious to die..730 *p*
Glory-adds new glory to the‡291*m*
all His g. and beauty...... 92 *n*
all its glory fades........133 *h*
and into glory peep........598 *d*
are warm'd by glory......285 *b*
awake him to g. again....134*m*
awake to glory............272 *t*
break forth in glory......217 *u*
by the love of glory...... 12 *q*
chief g. of every people....428 *q*
Columbia to glory arise....115 *d*
difficult it is to retain g....707 *b*
discerning souls was g....163 *l*
do not seek glory.........273 *i*
dying glory smiles‖....... 99 *a*
excess of g. obscured**... 153 *d*
for gain, not g., wing'd‡...551 *a*
forgot was Britain's g.....568 *a*
glimpse of g. infinite......547 *b*
g., and thy name are his...601 *o*
glory built on selfish......272 *p*
g. doth this world put on§.411 *i*
g. drags all men along.....706 *s*
glory follows virtue.......706 *r*
glory from defect arise....272*m*
g. from his gray hairs gone388 *r*
g. gilds the sacred page....538 *p*
g. gives me strength......707 *a*
g. guards with solemn....272*w*
glory in his bosom........258 *n*
glory in the flower¶......466 *v*
glory in their birth*......273 *f*
glory is like a circle*......273 *c*
g. is never where virtue is.770 *f*
g. is the shadow of virtue..801 *d*
glory is the torch.........800 *h*
g. jest and riddle of the....371 *v*
g. nor reprieve from death.119 *b*
g. now to be a man........273 *j*
g. of a firm capacious‡....385 *a*
glory of an April day*......364 *k*
g. of April and May......243 *t*
g. of riches and of beauty..750 *k*
g. of the British queen‡....524 *l*
glory of this life*.........273 *e*
g. paid to our ashes......706 *t*
glory's full array.........241 *g*
glory shows the way...... 35 *b*
glory's morning gate......131 *u*
glory then for me.........240 *k*
go where g. waits thee....202 *f*
greater g. dim the less*...273 *g*
great is the glory¶........273 *t*
happy trial prove most g.**632 *x*
have their glory¶........224 *g*
him who walked in g. and¶.481 *h*
his glory still gleams..... 89 *g*
in all thy glory..........234 *h*
in a sea of glory*.........273 *d*
influenced by glory.......734*m*
in glory are arrayed.......233 *s*
into glory peep...........161 *n*
kindle g. from the stone...146 *x*
literature is an avenue to g.354 *a*
lived long enough for g....707 *c*
lose the glory of the form.. 8 *p*
meridian of my glory*....152 *a*
mightier g. than when†...214 *q*
mine eyes have seen the g.527 *v*
mock'd with glory*.......273 *h*
neither by g. nor by......699 *j*

no flowery roads leads to g.770 e
no g. in star or blossom....391 n
o'er Glory's din‖............105 i
one g. an' one shame††....309 v
on wings of g. up the. ... 584 c
our glory is vain............706 u
paradise islands of g.......308 y
paths of g. lead but.....272 q
pitch of human glory**...638 d
race that led to glory's‖.... 97 m
radiant with the g. and††.. 16 n
scamp for the g. of God††.437 p
set the stars of glory. .....258 h
sing of g. to God and of.... 95 j
slaughter men for g.'s......637 o
so expensive as glory......273 i
still to a deeper g. grew....624 l
summers in a sea of glory*.491 k
the first in glory‡.......272 s
the glory dies not..........272 n
the g. of ancestors sheds...677 j
the glory of Him who§......272 u
the greater glory of God..798 e
the way to glory†..........164 m
thirst of glory boast‡.....125 j
this g. and this grief.......544 l
this goin where g. waits††.272 v
this, like thy g. Titan......472 q
through g.'s morning-gate.463 l
'tis thy glory alone.......406 k
track the steps of Glory‖...272 o
trust you with their glory. 65 j
'twas glory once to be......273 j
visions of glory spare my..634 e
we rise in glory.... ......273 m
we triumph without g......759 p
who pants for glory‡......272 x
who rush to g., or the......636 g
years of its g. outnumber..616 e
Gloss-in their newest gloss*..461 k
gloss on faint deeds*.......265 f
nor aught of burrowed g.... 24 l
read every text and g. over.473 a
shining g. that vadeth*.. 36 r
to set a g. on faint deeds*.. 73 b
Glossier-was g. and flossier..584 e
Glove-a g. upon that hand*..364 n
were hand and glove......312 f
Gloves-cat in g. catches no..504 hh
g., I'll wear them for*...... 24 d
matrons flung gloves*......483 g
of him a pair of gloves.....335 b
pair of kid leather gloves..663 e
Glow-breast ne'er learned‡..491 b
glow for other's good‡....588 d
glow of lofty thought......117 a
in a solid glow...... ......246 a
more brightly g. chastis'd.. 61 o
one with fiery glow .....241 k
to a transparent glow‖.... 33 s
touch of Nature's genial g.412 e
Glows-g. in ev'ry heart......487 a
Glow-worm-fiery g-w.'s eyes*197 e
g-w. lights her little spark.323 j
g-w. lights his gem.........323 k
g-w. shows the matin*....625 k
health to the glow-worm..323 i
her eyes the glow-worme..192 g
Glow-worms-do upon g-w. 50 m
glories like g-w............273 k
g-w. on the ground.... ....323 g
Glue-g. themselves in*......291 q
sure sweet sement, g., and.334 l
Glum-among the g. I hold....113 h
fasting makes glum......161 p
Glutton-g., at another's cost.431 q
independent and a g......179 b
of praise a mere glutton...215 c
Gluttony-addicted to g......178 h
g. kills more than the......498 f
Gnat-he form'd this g. who..323 l
the gnat sticks fast.....765 q
Gnats-g. around a vapour.... 16 e
like g. and flare up bodily. 62 f
sun shines let foolish g.*..584 j
Gnaw-g. you so your nether*465 w
Gnomes-g. direct, to every‡.457 j

Go-and g. along with him*..388 m
and go at last............218 a
before I go, Tom Moore‖...604 k
but I go on forever†....... 71 e
but one to bid him go......464 u
come and men may go†.... 71 e
do not go forth*...........104 o
don't let him go to the....607 b
"go not yet"...........230 n
go we know not where*...268 f
go where all have gone.....693 d
he must needes go that the499 a
I've little further now to go644 q
knowing if we wish to go§.411 j
let him go where no man .. 83 f
man cannot go to Corinth..715 a
not to go along with him..452 e
shall I bid her goe ....464 r
'tis time for me to go.....546 d
whereon go to and fro.....572 j
Goad-temptation that doth*.594 j
Goads-g. with your fists.....700 u
Goal-lose sight of the g. from756 i
or verges to some goal‡....371 y
pathway that leads to her..682 t
reach the desired goal.....719 t
upward, till the g. ye win..348 h
Goat-mountain g. hangs......181 k
Goats-g., which I complain..176 t
Gobble-uns-the g-u. 'at gits..578 p
Goblet-a golden g. gave......534 a
fill up the g. and reach.....161 p
not a full blushing g.could.641 n
touch the g. no more§.... 326 b
Goblets-g. constantly refilled177 h
g. of which thy lips......180 f
wine our g. gleam in.......649 i
Goblins-talk with g., owls*..197 g
God-abandons, G. himself... 33 l
acquaint thyself with G....274 c
a foe to G. was ne'er true...263 h
a g. out of a machine.... 494 v
a God to glorify...........572 m
all but G. is changing......274 u
all things come from G......808 z
alone even G. is deprived..466 e
among G.'s suffering poor††373 z
and as God he taught...... 93 a
and God the stuff‖.....123 c
and many are afraid of G..668 m
and more of God........273 o
angler, and now with G..... 18 n
an offense against God....123 m
apprehension how like a g.*372 r
are but the varied God....275 v
are farthest from God.... 95 q
as a man is, so is his God..770 j
as a sort of god‖.......... 53 k
ascends with it to God§.... 4 x
as God loves me...........714 d
as G.'s ambassador, the....450 b
as holy men trust God.....619 x
a' should not think of G.*..138 l
as it shall please God...... 805 k
as it were, G.'s grandchild.755 j
ask G. for temperance*...593 m
as offerings unto God§.....425 n
assumes the god...........276 m
attribute to G. himself*...382 p
awful mystery of God ....296 q
a wild beast or a god.......567 k
bashful stream hath seen..649 c
be forgotten even by G....420 t
be in God's own might.....579 p
believer is God's miracle...386 p
bids for God's own image...560 q
builds a church to G. and‡. 96 a
bugles sound the truce of..471 i
bush with God may meet..103 k
but G.'s sons are things...664 x
by God and the king.......798 d
by G.'s aid there is nothing799 t
by the grace of God........428 a
calm on the bosom of thy..526 j
capable of believing in G..316 t
captain counts the image..520 u
caught at God's skirts....487 j

cold marble leapt to life a..452 n
conjoined to G. by faith...316 t
conscience is the oracle of‖.105 t
conscious water saw its G..649 t
consider a gift of God......721 n
cried out G., G., G., three*.138 l
crown the god of sleep*....562 o
dare to look up to God.....524 z
debt as if God wrote.......142 t
deny a God destroy man's. 38 u
desire what G. would have488 c
devote ourselves to G. is...273 w
did not G. sometimes......488 s
doing of the will of God....420 d
echo of the silent voice of..668 i
equal eye, as God of all‡...510 n
especial revelation from G.539 e
event is a judgment of G...774 h
ever pass to God ....187 d
every one is as God made..758 p
faith in God.................197 t
fall shall thunder, God....274 b
fat, oily man of God.......451 r
fear G. as long as you.....806 cc
fidelity is of God...........807 j
finger of G. has planted§..225 h
for a charm as from G.....531 n
for God and my country...802 ee
for G., my country, and...799 v
"for G.'s sake," others to..762 t
for G. will deign to visit** 16 q
freedom to worship God....670 f
friends given by God.......261 r
from G. he could not free..425 j
from God, not fortune.....799 u
from that good G. who... 8 j
from that high mount of**.625 a
gifts that God hath sent§..406 a
gift which God has given..362 h
give God thanks,and make*342 p
give to God................799 s
give to G. each moment as.347 b
give us a G.—a living......275 q
G. all mercy is a God..... 276 c
G. Almighty first planted. 269 r
G. Almighty's gentlemen..271 i
G. alone can comprehend..276 d
God alone is life.... .....351 f
G. alone was to be seen in‖.557 w
G. and nature do with......668 j
G. and Nature met in†.....353 a
God—and your native land.468 p
G. answers sharp and......487 h
G. befriend us, as our*.... 72 v
G. be thank'd that the dead667 c
G. blessed once prove......101 b
G. bless (no harm in ....533 m
G. bless the man who......562 e
God bless the Regent......535 k
G. bless us all—that's quite533 m
G. buildeth up His living..303 b
G. calleth preaching folly..450 o
G. can change the lowest..707 e
G. cannot be ignorant.....719 e
G.can satisfy the longings.522 k
God closely follows........737 e
G. commanded you to be..803 bb
G. could have made a..... 19 g
God defend the right*.....498 g
G. doth late and early pray522 n
G. enters by a private door325 f
G. erects a house of prayer 95 o
God from a beautiful......275 x
G. gives not kings the stile.534 e
G. gives, since all effects... 72 r
G. gives wind by measure..507 p
G. gives with a sparing....685 g
G. give them wisdom that*651 n
G. grants liberty only to..344 i
God had sifted three§.... 275 b
G. has a father's pity......133 f
G. has commanded time....107 o
G. has formed for joyous..782 f
G. has given some gifts....735 n
God has given us...........739 h
G. has given us wit and....654 h
G. has given you one face*.312 r

G. hath already sai.l what§525 b
G. hath given liberty to....343 r
G. hath given us the use of326 p
G. hath giv'n me a.........326 a
God hath joined let.......198 e
G. hath set His rainbow....531 f
G. hath sworn to lift on...310 l
God helps the brave........756 r
G. helps those who help....300 p
God helps us do our duty..164 a
God he passed the days....521 o
G. Himself can't kill them.573 n
G. himself, favors the.....680 d
G. in his harmony has......656 w
God? inspiring God 275w
God is abroad and.........274 j
G. is always on the side of.582m
G. is at work on man......276 f
G. is generally on the side.582 c
G. is its author, and not.. 404 k
God is marching on........258 n
G. is not averse to deceit.143 p
G. is not dumb, that he††..521 h
G. is not to be worshipped.707m
G. I sought for was not....274 p
God is our fortress*......275 r
God is propitiated.......707 k
G. is the author, men are..776 f
G. is the One Miracle to....386 r
G. is the perfect poet.....273 t
G. is, they are, man......492 d
G. is thy law, thou mine**..645 h
God is truth and light. ...275 k
God keeps a niche.........267 f
G. laid his fingers on the...401 o
God lends to leaven ......536 j
G. looks at pure, not full...750 n
G. loves, do not live long..506gg
G. made a cole-pit to put...510 a
God made all pleasures....475 q
G. made bees, and bees....510 a
G. made him and therefore*372 i
G. made himself an awful† 275 u
G. made man, and man.....510 a
G. made the country, and..498 h
G. made two great lights**.426 j
G. makes sech nights all††..416 f
G. mark thee to his grace*. 32 g
G. may be had for the††....102 u
G. measures the cold to....785 h
God moves in a.............274 e
G. move the hero's arm in.640 k
G. never did make a more. 19 p
G. never gave man a....... 92 o
G. never made his work....440 b
God never meant that......274 f
God never repents of.......738 k
G. never sendeth mouth....498 i
G. not dishonoured when...584 l
g. of avenues and gates§...277 l
G. offers to every mind.... 91 p
god of love, with roses....242 s
God of their fathers.......254 t
God only excepted......... 22 g
God only, who made us....233 i
G. or Nature hath..........385 f
G. preaches, a noted ......450 i
G. rewards good deeds done770m
G. said "Let Newton be "‡183m
G.'s ancient sanctuaries...669w
G. save our gracious king..367 p
God save the king.........533 n
God save the mark*........498 j
God's best attribute......255 t
G.'s crest upon His azure..583 l
G. sends cold according to.498 k
God sends good meat......432 k
God sends us meat, yet....431 l
G. send the women sleep...640 k
G. sent his singers upon§..557 f
G.'s ever-watchful care....233 t
G.'s finger touched him*...141 n
God's glowing covenant....515 g
G.'s great judgment seat...637 g
God shall be my hope*.....275 s
God shall pardon me*......255 q
God shrouds the future....705 g

God's in His Heaven.......273 u
G.'s knowledge, and are....298 l
G.'s light his likeness takes352 h
G.'s mill grinds slow but...498 l
G.'s own image bought and560 i
God's own time is best.....198 r
G.'s side is a majority....275 j
God's soldier be he*.......444 f
G. spoke and it came......296 b
G. suffers him to be§.... 152w
God's universal law**.....376 c
G. supplies is inexhaustible651 s
G. sure esteems the**......632 u
G.'s will and ours.........158 a
G.'s wisdom and God's.... 273 n
g. tailor and god mercer...454 s
G. takes a text, and.......467 g
G. tempers the cold to the.510 c
G. tempers the wind to....510 x
G., that all powerful.......744 a
G. that forbids crimes ....743 c
God that is within us .....351 u
G., the best maker of all*..376 r
G. the first garden made...269 s
God! there is no God.... 275 a
God thought about me.... 31 o
G. to man doth speak in...566 b
G. to punish and avenge...770 i
G. to ruin has designed ....320 t
G. was so intensely real....273 g
G. was so often an object..770 j
g. we now behold with.....277 r
G., who is able to prevail..141 s
G., who is his own circle...566 c
G., who loveth all his works309 d
G.! who rules mankind....535 v
God, whose puppets. .....273 s
God will provide............799 y
God will put an end 705m
God wills it††.............293 l
God within us............707 i
gone the god to see.........276 o
good luck a g. count all...368 b
good of God above.......355 c
grand thief into G.'s**.....451 c
grassy coverlet of God....141 k
great God of 'heaven‖.....487m
groves were G.'s first.....609 c
has pleased God...........738 g
hath ever been G.'s enemy*626 h
hear, O G., hear Him......488 j
heart within and God§.... 5 a
he died fearing God*....... 39 l
hell is the wrath of God...298w
he shall not die, by God....419 v
he thanks G. for anything.594 r
he, too, is G.'s minister§...152w
himself, an act of God.....369 q
himself and G. for us all...317 t
himself from G. he could.. 28 c
him was God or devil.... 79 b
his Father and his God.... 86 g
his life a breath of God. ..369 q
his tomb the imprisoned G.165 a
hope and God..............807 i
hope, he called, belief in G.487 t
hope in God...............807 h
I came from God and......316 j
if God be appeased.........738 p
if G. be with us, who shall.804 t
if God did not exist...... 770 h
if there were no God.....275 y
ignorance is the curse of*. 337 y
image of his God...........284 n
in God is everything......807 d
in God is my trust.........807 c
in God is our trust.......214 c
in God's eternal day.......351 k
in man speaks God... .....574 b
into the love of God.......520 s
is like a prayer with God .652 g
is no god but God.........490 b
is obedience to God.......518 c
is the voice of God ......634 s
it is the attribute of God..333 d
I trust in G.—the right.....410 h
just are the ways of G.**..332 o

justify the ways of G. to**.510 h
kills the image of God**.... 67 n
kin to God by his spirit...., 38 u
know my God commands...274 n
learn to seek God....... ...190 v
"let us worship God".....669 x
light (G.'s eldest daughter)352 g
lightning does the will of G.482 t
like G. in love and power.. 476 c
lo! God is great‖..........274 a
loves God and his law......274 k
loves them—God or man.. 33 l
love which is the essence.. 358 f
making a man a god*......633m
man, G.'s latest image**....674 c
man is a fallen god who....371 k
man is unjust, but G. is§...332m
man proposes, but God . 501ee
man proposes, G. disposes.744m
man was made like God....274 i
many are afraid of God.... 80 v
meet my God awake.......136 f
mind of G. high-bless'd**..488 o
modest water saw its G....648 p
my G., my Father, and....274 h
my God, my guide.........799 t
my God to know...........274 p
my hope is in God 804w
nature is and G. the soul‡..411 v
nature is a revelation of§.. 528 f
nature is the art of God....410 d
nature is the art of God....413 t
nature's good and God's...410 h
nature up to nature's God.411 s
naught but God can.......273 p
nearer, my God, to thee...487 c
negotiates between G. and.450 b
neither God nor man†.....255 u
noblest work of God‡... 371 u
no god but God‖...........274 a
no God there were... .....273w
nor let a god come in.... 707 r
not G.'s, and not the.... 492 d
not the voice of God‡.....635 d
nothing which G. cannot.707 d
nothing with G. can be§.... 19 s
not on man, but God†..... 60 h
of G. above or man below‡.517 i
of the universe to God.... 92 g
of what I call god.........273 v
one God, one law, one†....123 f
one sole God..............275 f
one the jealous G. may....563 k
on G.'s and Satan's brood..358 g
only safety is in serving G.804 q
omnipotence of G. shines. .486 a
our God doth view.. ......510 p
own integrity and God.... 85m
pack and label men for G..463 u
pass into the rest of God...229m
pious worship of God ......520 j
poetry is itself a thing of..476 c
praise be to God...........801 v
praised G. and his works**486 o
pray G. to guard them from487 t
pray to G. to cast that wish487 o
presume not G. to scan‡...371 x
put your trust in G., my...511 b
Quakers please both man‡.521 t
rampart of God's house....298m
recognized God in his soul..521 p
remember that there is a...725 s
restore to God his due....274 o
reverence to God, to society 99 e
right since God is God. ...529 g
sanction of the God‡......277 c
scamp for the glory of God.437 p
seeing G. without holiness.149 b
seek God elsewhere.......707 f
sees God in clouds‡.......275 n
seldom think upon our G...100 c
send up our thanks to God.424 q
servant of G., well done**..549 a
served my God with half*..549 e
serve their God againe....534 e
she is its light—its God....651 v
show likest God's*........382 p

SHAKESPEARE *; MILTON **; WORDSWORTH ¶; BYRON ‖; TENNYSON †; LOWELL ††; POPE ‡; LONGFELLOW §

leave us leisure to be good.342 u
life is not the supreme g...765 k
love my country's good*...469m
luxury of doing good.......279 r
luxury of doing good......280 b
made impulsive to good....512 e
make good things from....247 e
man is conscious of good..105 w
material enough to be g...768 d
meant, " My son, be g."... 7 h
mingled yarn g. and ill*...350 w
my religion is to do good.469 g
nature equal g. produce‡...191 f
nature's good and God's...410 h
necessary g. is not good....708 q
never be one lost good.....279 n
no g. comes of those that..317 h
nor suddenly good 501kk
nothing g. or evil save in..646 f
nothing is fair or g. alone.318 s
of good than of evil.......709 a
of moral evil and of good¶.413 l
one, and one of good‡.....122 t
one thing is forever good..581 u
O, rank is good, and......367 j
order of good things for..326 p
our greatest g. and what..307 d
out of good still to find**..187 u
pleasure of doing good to..387 q
pleasure the highest good..680 b
poetry, but choicely good.478 b
provision only to the g.**..593 j
public good be promoted..717 h
pursue some fleeting good.280 c
put himself upon his g.‖..503 b
read the g. with smiles...351 t
rejoice in what is good....708m
renders good for bad*..... 86 x
seeming evil still educing.198 p
she was g. as she was fair..361 u
sight of you is g. for sore..506 g
since good the more**.....280 k
so far he does speak....187aa
some g. mingled with it...765 n
some of g., some of evil**. 67 q
some said, it might do g... 64 h
some things are good......684 f
so thou be g. slander doth*.559 a
strong antipathy of good‡. 72 t
such as are good men**....280 j
tends to the universal g....529 h
than to study household*.657 p
that bloweth no man good.647 l
that I may do good........805 l
that makes true good......357 z
the dead nothing but good.743 t
the evil and the good......358 g
the good, alas! are few....708 p
the g. and bad together*...436 l
the good die first¶.........142 e
the good hate sin.........749 s
the good he scorned.......279m
the good love heaven§.....359 w
the good man never dies...316 n
the good must associate...627 b
the g., the bad, and these..668 s
the g. thereof consists**.... 35 n
then is knowledge "good".651 v
there is no man so good....437 s
the worst speak something.467 q
think not the good........382 k
thou evil for his g. repay‡.527 s
Thou good Supreme.......148m
thou through g. and evil...360m
'tis only noble to be good‡.418 p
to be noble we'll be good..418 j
to be obscurely good......109 u
to bring us g. or to work..191 s
to desire good...........808 j
to do good sometime*......147 e
to make bad g., and good*.407 u
to make some good but*... 29 f
took something good*......659 i
too much of a good thing.484 c
to see his good qualities... 78 f
to the earth some special*.510 r
traced the lives of these¶..471 v

truly great who are truly ..506 w
truth does not do so much.793 b
trust that good shall fall†..309 b
'twas for the g. of my......468 k
vain and doubtful good*... 36 r
value equally,the g. and the765 c
was good shall be good.....279 n
what g. came of it at last..631 n
what good I see.........279 k
what he finds good of .....439 q
what otherwise is good....701 j
what's the good of it?......708 l
what's to me the good.....280m
while good news baits**....436 b
who imitates what is good.773 h
who is a good man?.......708 o
wilt have me wise and g.†..570 o
wiser being good than bad.101 b
wish to be good.........280 a
with good or ill, with false.351 t
woman, so she's g., what‖..655 e
works parent of good**....275 h
worst speaks something g.450 o
would the deed were g.*..123 u
yet not too g. to be true...414 r
you good men and true*...372 f
you're good for Madge....280m
you're not good for me....280m
Good-bye-g.b., my paper's..448 k
g.b. to the bar and its .....666 v
so I'll say, " good-by "....178 r
Good-for-nothing-curly‖..... 89 d
Good-humour-g.h. can‡..... 83 a
g.h. only teaches‡.......... 82 t
keep good-humour still‡... 83 a
Good-luck-g.l. a god count..368 h
Goodly-it is a g. sight to see‖117 o
Goodman-g. Robin.......107 h
g. spanned his plough.....540 v
Good-morning-bid me g.m..345 n
Good-morrow-part of their..130 w
to sorrow I bade g-m......509 j
Good-nature-g.n. and good‡.255 p
Good-natured-the g.n. man..124 t
Goodness-and God's g.....273 n
and g. never fearful*.....633 q
a piece of simple g.......448 h
at a like goodness still*....280 q
celestial grace of g. that... 34 h
did so magnify goodness..519 n
from men two kinds of g..164 g
g. dares not check thee*...626 f
goodness is silent........770 l
g. leade him not.........280 d
goodness of knowledge...512 c
goodness thinks no ill**...104 h
goodness to be better.....709 f
greatness, on goodness....286 v
how awful goodness is**...354 l
imperceptibly advance in.. 66 g
I thank the g. and the..... 93 v
recanting goodness, sorry* 73 b
she has more goodness....280 t
some soul of goodness*....280 p
taught me the g. of God..512 c
to laugh were want of g.‡..340 x
wisdom and g. are twin...650 k
wisdom and g. they are...273 n
your great goodness*.....280 r
Good-night-a fair g-n.....204 q
and say good-night....... 111 l
g-n.! as we so oft have§....464 o
good-night, Gordon.......761 q
g.n.! parting is such sweet*464 v
gude nicht, and joy.......204 o
have to say, g-n. again....464 f
my coach! G-n. ladies*...439 j
my native land, g-n.‖.......606 r
our good-night kiss.......136 g
say g-n. till it be*........464 v
say not good-night.......345 n
till then, good-night.....464 f
to bid me good-night..... 89 h
to each, a fair g-n.......417 d
Goods-all other g. by‡......645 i
are stuffed with goods...... 77m
evils rather than of g......91 n

half his g. on the counter..482 a
keep what g. the gods.....500jj
of earthly g., the best is...645 s
she is my g., my chattels*.645 o
Good-sense-g.s. must ever‡..255 p
Good-wife-g.w. oped the.....540 i
Good-will-g.w. and peace..... 94 d
g.w. is of more value than.787 b
g.w. makes intelligence....325 g
good-will to men§......... 94 i
liberal professions of g.w.. 6 b
of good-will to man....... 95 j
professions of g.w.........263 e
take the g.w. for the deed.508 d
Goose-a goose, a justice.... 26 t
but every goose can........ 2 i
had a g. in his sleeve.....505 f
larger than a fat goose.....181 f
snap with a g. or a duck... 18 e
so screams a g.where swans 47 g
there swims no g. so gray‡.376 j
the royal game of goose... 14 r
to see a g. and a belt the... 18 e
what is sauce for the g ....508 t
when every g. is cackling*. 52 a
Gooseberry-the g. pye.....266 c
worth a gooseberry*......266m
Goose-pen-write with a g-p..471 t
Gordian-G. knot of it he will*482 d
Gore-shedding seas of g...107 n
the red g. of the dragon....640 i
Gorged-she must not be full* 47 b
Gorging-g. their hapless... 54 b
Gorgons-G., and Hydras**..634 i
Gormandizing-leave g.*.....593 n
Gorse-gay g. bushes in their.230 v
Gorse-flower-crackling of...230 c
Gorses-mountain g., do ye..230 a
mountain g. ever-golden...230 b
Gospel-brown bread and the.538 t
emanation from the g......333 d
g. of the Golden Rule§.....451 a
gospel trump thunder'd...521m
lineaments of g. bookes.... 25 q
support of Christ's G......374 c
the G. church secure......522m
under G. colours hid be ...520 a
Gossamer-g. stirs with less..359 d
with tangled g. that fell...543 r
Gossip-a hate of g. parlance†646 a
if my gossip Report*......281 a
gossip is a sort of smoke...280 w
half the gossip of society..516 a
Gothic-G. cathedral is a....425 i
Goths-now to the G. as swift* 57 o
Gout-belaboured by the .... 8 t
good company—the g. or‖. 9 d
pretend that he had the g..177 l
Govern-divide and govern..799 x
g. my passions with.......465 u
govern those that toil......282 f
princes g. all things—save..647m
riches either serve or g....739 q
stars above us, g. our*.....577 c
syllables g. the world......665 h
teaches us to g. ourselves.770 r
those who think must g....596 s
to govern wrong‡.........282 v
tyrants safely g. home*....626 g
Governed-g. by grave......281 q
g. by its imagination......773 d
if he had never g.........709 i
Governess-moon, the g. of*..399 a
Governing-regarded as.....709 i
Government-a change of g..709 g
a hated government......709 h
all his g. is groping......534 q
an old, lazy government...281 k
bees for government......281 f
blessings which a g.......482 s
Conservative G. is an.....282 c
depriv'd of supple g.*.....563 a
deterioration of a g.......770 o
dissension hinder g.*......157 h
do in my government......281 n
for forms of government‡..349 i
G. at Washington.........281 h

SHAKESPEARE *; MILTON **; WORDSWORTH ¶; BYRON ||; TENNYSON †; LOWELL ††; POPE ‡; LONGFELLOW §.

Grim-visaged-g.v. war hath*639 e
Grin-devil did g. for his.....310 h
every g., so merry, draws.. 72 p
for me to sit and grin.....432 u
g. on me, and I will think*.139 c
vanquish Berkeley by a g.537 l
wear one universal grin....410 v
when a cur doth grin*.....629 a
Grins-g. of his own invention452 i
Grinned-death g. horrible**.136 o
Grind-but they grind woe. ..498m
g. the bones out of their...484 j
life is one demd horrid g..347 a
mill will never g. with the.505 q
that man has an axe to g..482 a
they g. exceeding small...527 w
though the mills of God g..527 w
Grinding-must needs tarry*.431 u
Grinds-God's mill g. slow....498 l
Grindstone-noses to the g...499bb
their noses to the g.....499cc
Gristle-it were but in the g..115 b
Groan-conception that I do*.103 v
condemn'd alike to groan..569 c
gasp thy gasp and groan..138 g
give him grace to groan*..283 n
g., the knell, the pall.....134 j
rescued by our holy g.... 41 b
the groan of death........640 h
Groaned-universal nature g.612 c
Groaning-g. ever for the past466 f
lay g. fretful at the......369 d
Groans-cool with mortifying*384 p
earth g. as if beneath a‖..577 o
he groans in anguish......592 q
with g. of the dying...... 638 q
Groat-where I gave a g.‡....106 c
Groats-want guineas for g..600 n
Grog-shop-wild-blazing g-s..325 p
Groom-prince as soon as his.534 i
the happy g. is near......568 k
Grooves-ringing g.of change‡ 76 o
Grope-g. tear-blinded in a...590 d
Groping-g. our way along...592m
Gross-g. as a mountain*.....199 r
Grossly-so g. in a natural*..608 v
Grossness-g. of his nature†..377 t
hiding the g. with fair*....145 h
losing all its grossness....630 g
measureless g. and the ....472 h
Grotesques-no g. in nature..410 f
Groton-flowed over G.Height397 k
Grotto-teach my g. green to.357 d
Grottoes-g. and temples with545 k
homes amidst green leaves. 42 a
my g. are shaded with.....412 n
Ground-all take your ground 40 o
ay, call it holy ground..... 670 f
battle g. of heaven and hell668 o
beat the g. for kissing*....326 j
bodies to the ground*......139 t
bright metal on a sullen g.*519 a
committed to the ground..396 l
dress the g. and till it......666 j
g. beneath them trembles..128 j
g. to presume ability....... 2 a
have a slave to till my g...559 e
having waste g. enough*..389 h
idle burden to the g.‡.....313 k
is scattered on the g......351 v
just to throw that on the g.593 f
lark left his g. nest**...... 48 r
let us sit upon the g.*......535 a
loves the ground¶.........234 s
man's blood paint the g.*..639 b
on the g. her lowly......... 49 b
part nearest the ground.... 77 n
plats of fruitful g.†...... 43 b
secretly making the g.....318 n
stirrup and the ground.....330 u
strowe me the ground......220 l
the faded ground..........229 h
the ground is bright. ....216 m
the vantage g. of truth....621 b
thou scorner of the g..... 49 n
'tis haunted, holy ground‖.303 b
to deck the g. where....... 55 i

to him is under ground.... 15m
touches the ground........128 q
tract of inland g.¶.........127 d
trodden to the ground.... 6 q
willing still to quit the g..351 p
Ground-birds-g-b. hidden....225 d
Grounds-g. of fate in g. of...589 v
proceed upon just g.*......332 t
stopped the g. and damned611 b
Grouped-g. their dark......219 q
Groups-clustering into g....249 e
Grove-a g. hushed with the. 37 o
and seems itself a grove‡..615 f
arching portals of the g. ..390 o
could field or g.,could any¶413 h
from the grove of roses....243 r
gleam over this tufted**... 99 s
grove nods at grove‡......269 w
g. of myrtles made ......392 r
in what lawn or grove‡....530 h
song in the grove........410 b
the olive g. of Academe**..616 i
who by some shady grove..566 x
Groves-all the western.....615 h
and g. a joyous sound......393 o
by frequenting sacred g...413 g
cloisters, terraces, g..... 14m
fountain-heads and.......465 g
fresh g. grow up........610 q
gloom from the groves....219 f
groves a joyous sound......284 j
groves dismantled roar... 545 i
g. of oak or fanes of gold..538 s
g. were God's first temples609 c
hear, O you groves........277 f
juicy g. put forth their....614 q
o'er shady g. they hover... 56 e
those graceful g. that shade533 x
through g. deep and high..362 i
valleys g. or hills or fields..360 n
Grovel-souls that grovel....101 q
Grovelling-g. eyes forget....651 v
Grovels-hope still g. in this..205 s
Grow-grain will g. and*.....398 a
g. faster than the years*...626 i
g. for happy lovers†.......229 a
g. on like the foxglove and.317 e
g. not as this face grows... 76 h
lilies how thy grow........233 t
ne'er make grow againe....466 l
out of which all things g... 75 f
resolved to g. fat and look..656 a
seeming blest, they g. to... 13 b
surely you'll g. double¶....580 h
they grow redundant .....651 g
trees do not g. into the sky.785 j
where soil is, men grow....371 j
Growing-every happy g......392 e
from the growing of grass.573 d
g. careless of my dress... 11 e
growing deeper in my sighs. 11 e
growing dimmer in the eyes. 11 e
g. fainter in my laugh...... 11 e
growing fonder of my staff. 11 e
growing frugal of my gold. 11 e
g. Jock,when ye're sleeping289 y
growing like a tree........289 j
growing near earth........249 a
g. one's own choice words..448 g
growing straight out of....233 t
I'm g. wise; I'm g.—yes... 11 e
man is g., life is in decrease.604 j
music is in all g. things....405 q
Grows-faster it grows*..... 224 a
grows? where g. it not‡....424 j
it grows up by degrees.....644 j
man g. with his expanded..771 h
not born where 't grows*..377 g
three centuries he grows...616 b
verb, and participle grows.579 s
Grow'st-g. beside the way††.228 e
Growth-as quick a growth...226 k
bless thy secret growth.... 99 h
children of a larger growth.501jj
decay and growth of it.....521 a
genuine growth of night...426 p
grown his growth lasts.....289 f

grows with his growth‡....156 j
growth of human will‖....357 b
g. of the intellect.........325 f
growth that dwindles......289 l
growth that is not towards 289 l
idle weeds are fast in g.*..289 s
in vigorous g. and turned..307 q
man is the nobler g. our...369 r
mark the decay and g.....547 k
one yet in growth will ever.780 h
plant of slow growth. ....265 t
slow of growth...........270 s
slow of g. but are rapid....682 n
strongest principle of g.... 91 o
the growth of confidence..104 d
yet in g. will ever grateful.780 h
Grudge-feed fat the ancient*528 q
g. all other grace to prayer.563 k
the ancient g. I bear him*..528 q
Grumble-g. a little now and..358 o
Grundy-and more of Mrs. G..668m
what will Mrs. Grundy say.508 r
your opinion, Mrs. Grundy.536 p
Grunt-g. and sweat under*..268 h
Guard-always on guard......808 u
anger made good g. for*... 17 u
blessings they enjoy to g...526 c
from whom we g. our.....511 l
g. dies but never surrenders638 n
guard our native seas......214 b
g. their beauties from the..458 k
holy angels guard thy bed.563 s
pray God to g. them from..487 t
ready to g. and defend it...344 i
some guard these traitors*.608 q
surest guard is innocence..632 q
sword and lance to guard.. 68m
that guard our native seas.444 y
the flaming guard.........527 p
too late to be on our g.....695 k
virtue's a stronger g. than.633 x
when safe, is on his guard..751m
Guarded-is kept and g. as a..127 c
Guardian-g. Naiad of the....353 s
my g. angel gently cried...605 f
Guardians-eunuchs are the g. 68 r
guardian for a thousand...246 o
guardians gloomy-winged..555 a
guardians still we'll be.....246 o
the g. of mankind...... ...574 v
Guards-g. its passage make..278 u
he guards us too..........510 p
who guards her, or with**.311 o
Gudgeons-g., flounders‡....213m
swallow g. 'ere they're.....251 d
Guerdon-fair g. when we**..202 d
rosebud for a guerdon.....240 j
Guess-am vicious in my g.*..328 g
Guess, if you can and......759 a
Guesse I may............226 l
square our g. by shows*..490 p
Guesser-guesser the best...735 d
Guest-and be my guest......290 e
an unintruding g., I watch'd 58 s
constantly, Matho, a g. ....176 h
death is a guest divine.....142 b
dog salutes the smiling g... 19 p
drink to England, every g.†604 s
go Soul, the Body's guest..572 a
guest that best becomes*..290 b
here's our chief guest*.....290 a
historian and thy guest§... 99 c
I go a willing guest........731 o
invited many a guest*......211 q
life like a satiated guest...721 f
like an unbidden guest¶....245 i
mysterious, unknown g.§...525 b
received a welcome guest..474 j
she sits tormenting every g.589 t
slightly shakes his parting* 608 a
so welcome a guest that....704 n
speed the going guest‡.....289 v
speed the parting guest‡...264 s
stranger for a guest¶......329 l
the guest betray'd. ....182 h
the pilgrim and guest......595 a
thou hast been our guest.. 56 c

shaking his dewie hayre... 29 q
smallest hair throws its....792 q
strung with his hair*.......278 a
that hath a hair more*....513 n
the most resplendent hair¶.466 d
there's myrtle in your hair.663 b
thy dusk hair deck. ......249 g
to her with a single hair...485 s
too her dusky hair¶.... 37 x
too much hair there*....195 s
to quench the hair*. .. ..458 h
tresses of her hair of gold§.291 j
waved her golden hair....307 m
wear in your shining hair.227 f
with a single hair‡.........291 l
women with such hair....290 v
your h. is white, your face.356 d
Hairs–bring white h. unto a*602 n
collect your straggling h...180 b
comes sooner by white h..* 11 x
going over the same h....178 o
glory from his gray h....388 r
h. on his brow were silver..329 c
ill white h. becomes a fool*328 s
many sons as I have h.*....444 f
multitude of those her h.*291 g
no more than two hairs....461 b
of h., or straws, or dirt‡...661 m
Hairy–marvellous h. about*.458 d
Halcyon–telling of h. days..230 i
the celebrated h. of the.... 48 e
Hale–you are h., Father..... 12 e
Half–h., and then the whole.399 g
h. part of a blessed man*...376 l
h. the world knows not how498 v
he hears but h. who hears..490 h
how the other h. liveth .. 337 v
keep this whole h. entirely.175 g
man could h. his wishes....500 b
my dear, my better half....645 r
nothing h. so sweet in life..361 c
one h. in day, the other...351 c
what's well begun is h.done679 c
Half–deity–half-dust, h.d.‖..370 f
Half–dust–h-d. half-deity‖...370 f
Half–free–half-slave and h.*.282 j
Half–knowing-h-k.everything337 n
Half–moon–h-m. made with*.195 s
Half–penny-worth–h-p-w of*.326 l
Half–sister–haste, h-s. to†....605 q
Half–slave–h-s. and.........282 j
Half–starved–h-s. spiders...579 d
prey'd on h-s. flies........579 d
Hall–Douglas in his hall.....180 h
down the valleys of Hall...530 i
finished their wee hall.... 59 m
he moves in the hall.......283 j
holly dress the festive h.... 95 e
in Heaven's dark h., high..667 r
ivy climbs the crumbling..231 g
station in the hall§........117 i
sweet in that old hall .....129 d
through the h. there....... 26 h
walls of Cumnor Hall......398 f
Halls–and in marble halls.... 23 p
bedeck your h. and round..418 e
halls of dazzling light......211 t
in h., in gay attire is seen..362 g
once through Tara's h. ....406 m
sung in my halls of joy ....557 k
than in tap'stry halls**....120 j
through her marble h.§....416 a
to your dreary marble h...101 g
Hallelujah–and applauding..165 i
cheerful voice, hallelujah..165 h
Hallelujahs–from out the h..519 q
rung with hallelujahs**....526 r
Hallow'd–not words duly h.*.489 k
so h. and so gracious*.... 49 l
what's hallow'd ground....284 n
Halo–h. hovering round‖....143 c
sheds a halo of repose......250 c
Halos–smiles that are h. of .. 89 h
Halter–come and cut the h..189 e
each halter let fall ..... 20 m
e'er felt the halter draw...439 f
fitted the halter, now......464 t

threats of a "halter".....259 c
will come, and cut the h....375 i
Halting–h. for the wearied...348 a
Halts–h. on a quicksand, the.608 e
Halves–he admires his h.....430 m
Ham–wit like a knuckle of h.654 i
Hamlet–king drinks to H.*..604 g
sure as Lear or H. lives....422 g
the tragedy of Hamlet.....422 g
through the h. broke ......625 g
when the hamlet is still... 410 b
Hamlets–in h., palaces, and..358 h
in h., dances on the green..362 g
Hammer–be either anvil or..766 s
either be anvil or h.§...... 81 b
falls the polished hammer. 454 b
no sound of h. or of saw....553 z
stand with his hammer*...430 k
yet I'll hammer it out*.....491 w
Hammered–as he cobbled and453 z
h. to the anvil's chime§....430 f
Hammering–h. in my head*...528 t
Hammers–and hearing the§..430 g
h. closing rivets up*.......689 q
Hampden–village H. that...201 d
Hamstring–conceit lies in his*422 t
Hand–adore the h. that.....512 k
a feather in h. is better ...494 s
a firm, bold hand......... 28 i
a friend to lend a hand....579 o
a glove upon that hand*...364 n
a hand open as day*........ 86 v
a hand to execute .... 78 l
a hand to execute........ 79 l
and filled her hand........228 o
and wither'd in my hand...600 m
Aprile! hand-in-hand .....259 o
a strange h. writes for our.640 r
better one byrde in h. than496 h
bird in the hand for a....498 gg
bird in the hand is worth..494 c
bird in the hand is........783 s
bite the h. that fed them...281 i
bless the h. that gave the..133 n
bloody and invisible hand*.417 g
bondman in his own h.*....344 e
by the h. leads us to rest§..411 j
close at hand is such.......111 g
cunning hand laid on*.... 37 e
death in my hand*........528 t
Death lays his icy hand....141 b
delicacy of their hand‖....292 g
dying h., above his head...631 h
exploit have I in hand*....296 h
feel the pressure of a h§...448 j
fierce h. hath with king's*.139 j
firstlings of my hand*..... 5 m
frame of h., nail, finger*... 90 n
friendly h. has brushed....324 i
from one hand drooped*...278 m
full and unwithdrawing**.630 a
gentle h. was at the latch..644 aa
get a prayer-book in your*670 m
grace his closed h. cannot..563 k
hand and heart......198 e
h. and heart to this vote...469 r
h. beckoning at the gate... 32 c
hand grasps at hand.......263 n
hand in hand with**...... 33 e
h. is an enemy to tyrants..801 bb
h., lie in your own.........259 o
h. must take my plight*...311 w
h. of an old friend§........261 d
h. of a woman is often......292 i
hand of heav'n submit**...420 f
h. of him here torpid lies..183 f
h. of little employment*...421 n
h. shall burn in never*.....239 j
h. strikes blows worthy....179 f
h. that follows intellect§..325 e
h. that made us is divine...556 bb
hand that opes the year's..151 j
h. that rocks the cradle....402 i
h. that rounded Peter's... 425 j
h. that rules the world..... 402 i
hand the lightning forms‡.. 13 r
h. to h., and foot to foot‡...636 c

h. upheaves the billows....274 g
h. upholding his head......435 m
h. without a heart........360 k
hath pawn'd an open h. in*121 t
heart, the kindlier hand†... 41 e
he laid his h. upon "the...460 g
held all of truth in my h...793 e
here's my hand*...........204 u
her other fair h. was*......292 n
her rash h. in evil hour**..555 y
her soft hand he pressed...664 a
his cold and sapless h.....137 f
his hand is so decorated...176 j
his h. unstained, his‡......454 f
his h. was known in**......425 r
his red right hand** ....292 j
hold mortality's strong h.*.140 k
holds h. with any princess*185 s
hollow of her hand........221 a
icy hand on kings.........207 n
if this cursed hand*.......255 v
immortal h. or eye could... 22 a
in his h. a javelin he did...541 b
in his h. the thing became¶ 61 j
keeps his heart and hand..375 t
laying his hand upon§......135 l
lays his h. on woman......122 n
lay their h. upon the ark.. 490 l
lay thy soft h. upon my§...561 p
leans her cheek upon her*.364 n
less than woman's hand‖...109 e
let my hand, this hand.....259 o
licks the h. just rais'd‡....475 r
lies clearly at hand....... 4 e
little h. thou openest§.... 31 k
living from h. to mouth....501 o
mortal hand can e'er......116 q
my h. alone my work can.. 19 c
not the h. that bore it......192 i
offence's gilded h. may*....438 p
of the waving h. he kissed .647 u
open h. scatters its bounty 95 a
papers in each hand‡.....251 y
parting guest by the h.*...603 a
place my hand in thine...376 k
polished by the h. divine‖..590 i
prayer moves the h. which490 v
prentice hand she tried on.654 w
rather chop this hand*....109 s
right h. carry gentle peace*471 g
see a hand you cannot see..141 g
sweeten this little hand*...292 k
swifter h. doth the swift..182 a
take you in h. sir with an.. 27 i
that cravens my weak h*..583 d
the firstlings of my hand*.297 g
the hand and head that....451 g
the hand hath done........ 182 a
the hand to execute .... 80 q
the lifted hand in awe.....404 e
the motion of my hand§....449 o
there's a ring upon your h..663 b
they cannot seek his hand..661 t
this hand will protect.....181 s
this my hand will rather*..404 c
thrust his h. between his*..629 a
thy careless hand.........227 n
tie of thy Lord's hand.....515 s
time has laid his hand§... 601 b
to die by one's own hand..582 w
to lend a hand............492 h
touch of a vanish'd hand‡..148 l
turn your hand to......... 2 c
'twas a h., white, delicate..292 i
unbless'd thy h. if in this.. 16 l
unseen the hand which....281 p
views from thy h. no noble. 3 v
warm in his mother's h....380 a
waved her lily hand........204 l
we met, hand to hand......151 o
were hand and glove......312 f
what strong h. can hold*..602 p
with brave hand..........801 aa
with h. on the spade and..666 j
with my h. at midnight*...333 l
with one hand he put......144 u
with one hand thrust the...662 c

with rosy hand unbarr'd**.400 k
woe to the h. that shed*....404 a
wonder of dear Juliet's h*.292m
worse than a bloody leaves..297 h
you give away this hand*...376 v
Hands–aching hands and....345 i
affection hateth nicer h....328 i
and not of the hands...... 86 b
backward-hidden h. that...392 h
blessed are the horny h.††.667 b
both my hands was full††..637 l
both these snowy hands...464 f
built without hands........413 f
by foreign h. thy dying‡..137m
by long-forgotten hands‖..535 t
by unseen h. uplifted§..... 99 p
clapped my h., laughed.... 20m
clasped h. close and fast..151 o
come, knit hands and**... 128 o
darkness came the hands†..207 r
dirt was trumps what h.... 99 f
eager to clasp h. across...482 p
folded their pale h. so§..582 r
fold your h., Baby Louise.. 31 c
for idle hands to do........497cc
forks and h. before knives.497 x
h. across and down the....129 d
hands before knives.......168 x
h. divine have wrought....274 c
hands in rapture seize...... 65 j
hands like a fairy's........ 31 c
hands of invisible spirits§..360 c
h. promiscuously applied‖.128 c
h. that the rod of empire... 79 s
h. that wist not though....141 h
h. together are press'd....128 k
h. upraised as with one .. 396 e
hath not a Jew hands*. ....329 g
hearts resolved and hands.526 c
her hands unto his chin....154 u
her ivory h. on the ivory..408 j
I warm'd both h. against..473 f
keep your h. out of his‖....595 d
kings have long hands.....740 i
kiss the lady's hands‖ .....292 h
large and sinewy hands§...430 h
lavish of her hands‖.......128 b
letters unto trembling h.†.449 j
lift their right hands.....259 h
little h. were never made..466 c
mouths without hands.....443 c
Nature with folded hands§.411 g
never but by British hands.468 d
not by other's hands.......205 o
our frail h. have raised....669 w
pale and trembling hands.241 k
pleasures are ever in our‡.475 s
pulled by smutty hands....233 f
put in their hands thy*....639 o
rounded under female h†.. 96 i
seem'd washing his hands.314w
the hands that ply the pen.635 p
the h. that wound are soft. 85 d
their broad h. only bare....430 e
their little glowing hands.227m
the palms of my hands....122 l
they lift not h. of prayer†.489 u
two h. upon the breast and.137 b
unseen h. delay the coming.151 g
watch that wants both h...313 g
we come to use our h. and*.589 o
whatsome'er their hands*.195 r
when hands clasped h..... 62 k
when two men shake h.....672 t
while their h. were still... 85 q
white hands could hardly††642 n
whose hands are pure......450 c
with mine own h I give*... 1 c
with their soft white h.§...598 u
wrought with human h.†-.. 92 s
your hands and your feet.637 n
Hande₁–Mynheer H.'s but a..112 s
Handful–a h. of red sand§...600 v
handful to the tribes. .... 132 r
Hand-in-glove–he were....265 n
Handiwork–fair your h.‖...452 u
hurra for my handiwork!..430 i

Handkerchers–scarfs and*...483 g
Handkerchief–knit my h*...333 l
Handle–h.'s at the bottom.... 68m
h. to profane the leaves....344 v
handle toward my hand*... 25 h
handle which fits them all.199 e
that can handle them...... 2 h
Handled–h. with a chain....320 s
Handmaid–nature's h., art..410 q
truth is its [justice's] h....333 d
Handsaw–know a hawk*....338 b
Handsome–Fabulla, you...178 p
good and h. enough........806 y
h. is that handsome does..498 w
looks h. in three hundred*.643 a
plague to be too h. a man..678 n
she is a h. wee thing......644 r
whisper how h. she is...... 37 j
Hang–drown or hang*........583 g
h. no ivie out to sell my....648 g
h. sorrow, care'll kill a cat.569 p
hang them on the horns*.. 26 p
hang themselves in hope..189 e
I'll h. my head and perish*.234 f
in them which will h. him.763 o
lilies hang their heads‡....234 a
shall all hang separately..627 h
some hang upon his car....483 e
that I should h. myself....698 a
tenth of mankind would h*.645 p
thieves at home must h....114 q
we must all h. together or.627 h
wretches h. that jurymen‡.330 i
Hanged–be hanged forthwith387 f
h. if some eternal villain*.558 v
never undone till he be h*.644 e
seen you hanged...........787 c
should all be hanged......742 s
Hanging–deserve h.ten times437 s
h. and wiving goes by*.....498 x
h. in a golden chain**......668 x
h. was the worst use a man.498 y
left him hanging there.... 47 s
they're h. Danny Deever..443 k
Hangman–or even a h........421 l
the hangman's axe§........174 f
the hangman's whip......208 o
Hangs–and thereby h. a*....350 w
h. both thief and true man*279 g
that h. on the bough*......384m
Hans–H. Grovendraad an...453m
Hap–else shall h. to-night*.. 547 f
Happen–h. more frequently..308 k
Happened–but have h. once..461 h
things have h. to many ...702 s
Happens–what h. new fame**126w
Happier–a h. lot were mine..569 e
h. far than others in their..591 f
happier for having been...294 b
happier in the passion....359 q
happier than I know**......293m
h. than this, she is not*... 645 n
long days are no h. than...130 w
remembering h. things†...570 q
should be happier now.....355 d
Happiest–h. moment of my..589w
h. of all, is, that her*......645 n
happiest of Spring's.......218 p
who is the happiest of men.293 d
Happily–man can live h......711m
Happiness–a glimpse of h....133 t
and h. without end........522 g
and of preserving h........675 f
ask what is happiness of...355 c
be sure of continued h.....780 j
but for my happiness......329 e
but the means of happiness.652 e
can wealth give happiness.643 f
conducive to the h.......... 4 s
domestic h. thou only..... 61m
double gain of happiness*..592 d
emblem of h. blest.......... 48 o
ev'n a happiness...........293 h
fix'd to no spot is h.‡......293 q
greatest happiness of the..292 r
greatest h. of the greatest.498 s
h., and all our care........359 g

h. compared to thee.......323m
happiness consists in......293 f
happiness consists not in..261 a
h. for man,—the hungry‖..166 p
happiness in his path......104 a
h. is cheap enough........292 p
happiness is produced.....433 f
happiness lies in the.......293 v
h. no second Spring.......393 j
happiness of existence.....265m
happiness of the times.....704 f
h.! our being's end‡.......293 s
h. resides in things........294 f
h. seems made to be.......771 j
happiness so short a day...292 u
happiness springs from....780 n
happiness that even above.631 x
happiness the rural maid..110 q
happiness to lie in these..293 p
h. too swiftly flies........582 o
h. was born a twin‖........292 s
happiness we prize........293 a
knowledge is not h.‖......336 u
look into happiness*.......293 x
man's social h. all rests on.660 f
more real h. than kings...731 n
of human happiness.......294 a
of that rare happiness§....634 g
other men's happiness.... 354 b
our pastime and our h.¶... 68 p
overthrow heap'd h. upon*. 6 w
rays of happiness§........293 j
relish of any happiness.... 22 d
secures h. by crime.......760 t
sorrow from h. is oft.......789 l
the happiness of mankind..202w
the h. of the wicked.. ....771 i
the highest happiness......771m
the pursuit of happiness...529 r
thought of tender h.¶..... 85 v
thus happiness depends...293 c
to fireside h., to hours....304 n
to make his happiness, if..461 g
too familiar happiness¶....204 g
true happiness ne'er.......294 f
views of happiness....... 294 e
virtue alone is h. below‡...663 b
virtue alone is h. below....632 h
what we deem our h.‖.....150m
will of a man is his h.......771 n
world of h. their harmony. 40 k
ye seek for happiness.... 293 y
Happy–a happy accident....494 y
ah! h. years! once more‖...671 u
at all happy without you..359 n
be happy but be...........294 c
but h. they the happiest...378 b
destined to be h. with you.316 f
earthlier happy is the*.....293w
faces happy as fair‖........162 a
for happy hours the rose..238 i
four times happy they.....711 n
happy am I; from care....109 x
happy and thrice happy...725 d
happy are the apples......266 f
happy are they who die in..443 n
h. art thou as if every day§.368 k
h. could I be with either...656 k
happy, happy, happy pair. 69 p
h. he with such a mother†.402 g
h. in this she is not yet*....645 n
h. is he born and taught...305 q
h. is that humble pair......378 c
h. is the blameless vestal's‡.421 b
h. the man who has been...681 k
h. Mary Anerly, looking O.663 b
happy, nor so unhappy.....771 k
happy now because God††..293 l
h. soul, that all the way... 571 i
h. state in this world......293 i
h. the heart that keeps its.378 h
h. the man and happy he..605 c
h. the man to whom God...685 g
happy the man, of mortals.111 b
happy the people whose...301 t
happy through piety.......294 c
h. twenty years hence.....294 b

Hatched–'ere they're h......251 d
was hatched a cherubin...182 h
which, h., would, as his*...511 t
Hatches–upon the h. in the*.578 a
Hatchet–buried was the§.....470 o
Hatchets–and his h. lead‡....431 g
Hatching– h. my tender...... 45 m
Hate–a smile to those who‖..524 w
begets in brethren hate....278 r
but the traitor hate.. .....607 s
dower'd with the hate of†..481 a
feel it and h. it in silence...201 p
for I h. yet love thee, so....456 n
frown, 'tis not in h. of*....659 m
giddy rabble hate the evil..711 q
hate him as I hate the.....295 d
hate in the like extreme‡...359 f
h. is mask'd but to assail‖..624 h
hate the engendering of*..491 j
hate the foes of God......274 k
hate the man that‡.........264 c
h. the profane and vulgar..711 p
hate to return with love....778 s
hate upon no better a*.....215 j
hearts that hate thee*......364 f
his hate of sin..............298 w
I do hate him as I do*......295 h
I hate a dumpy woman‖...655 j
I hate and I love...........711 o
I hate him for he is a*......295 f
I hate inconstancy‖........317 n
in time we hate that*......295 g
it is human nature to h....711 t
love is sunshine, h. is§....348 m
not hate but glory made‡...113 b
no h. lost between us.......505 jj
nor love thy life, nor h.**..349 b
not the h. of enemies......797 s
no well-bred hate, or......112 o
oblige her, and she'll h.‡..658 k
or begets him hate*........538 e
owe no man hate*.........111 t
power to love or hate.....206 s
religion to make us hate...522 i
revenge immortal h.**....103 a
skill in a true hate*......295 'i
study of revenge**. ......638 f
that fear to h. and hate*... 76 e
the h. of those below‖....104 r
think that we h. flattery...767 o
to h. your neighbour and..565 l
we h. virtue when it is safe 750 c
without reason we hate....786 i
wounds of deadly hate**...295 e
your favours nor your h.* .318 b
Hated–and h. iniquity.......332 l
dull, h., despised in the... 52 m
h. needs but to be seen‡...630 p
hated the traitor.........608 k
hated with a hate‖.........294 y
he who is h. by all can not.771 q
I, a Jew, be h. thus........329 e
whom I hated so‖..........207 v
Hater–like a good hater.....295 c
very good hater............295 b
Hates–h. the smell of roses..241 p
no one h. you justly......711 r
woman either loves or h...752 s
Hateth–who h. me but for...329 e
nearer we are to h. her....359 p
Hath–nothing, yet h. all....112 n
that h. it doth not know...458 r
whose heart h. never......118 j
Hatred–glances of h. that...294 aa
h. is by far the longest‖...294 x
h. is given instead of....715 r
h. is self-punishment .....294 w
hatred without end ......295 a
love to hatred turned......357 p
natural and secret h......565 d
rage like love to h. turned .655 r
the greatest h., like the...771 r
the h. of relatives..........711 s
while h.'s fagots burn......268 p
Hauberk–where glitter h.§..533 h
Haughtiness–h. of humility..310 k

Haughty–follows the h......737 e
frank, h., rash,—the...... 27 k
h., gallant, gay Lothario...491 e
Haul–attempts to h. down ..214 d
Haunt–from his dark h ..... 18 l
h. him by night§..........479 t
Haunted–some h. by the*...535 a
Haunting–h. the cold earth..415 e
Haunts–afar from h. of men 21 h
busy haunts of men........ 97 f
h. of meadow rue......... 236 b
haunts the guilty mind*...586 q
view the h. of nature .....609 b
Haut-boy–murmurs the h-b..408 a
Havana–the rental of half H.643 c
Have–but what we h. been..331 k
for all we have is his......510 w
go to those who have it....485 p
h.more than thou showest*511 q
house of H. and the house.492 g
what we h. we prize not*. .483 s
you can not have it........733 i
Haven–their h. under the hill†446 c
Having-content is our best*.112 c
h. nothing, yet hath all ...484 d
none h., or a very few......129 f
Havoc–cry " H.," and let slip*638 w
make h., scot free........162 k
Hawk–know a h. from a*..... 47 o
I soar, I am a hawk*...... 47 q
ladies ride with h. on§....533 h
or hears the h. when‡...... 46 s
the dove, O hawk..........699 f
the sharpe h. which her.... 53 j
wild h. stood with the† .... 47 r
Hawk'd–mousing owl h. at*.. 47 a
Hawks–between two h.*..... 47 m
h. do tower so well*....... 47 p
love hawking? thou hast*. 47 n
their h. and hounds*.......273 f
Haws–air with the budding§.612 b
Hawthorn–birch and h. hoar.530 e
fragrant h. brambles......393 d
green the juicy h. grows...614 a
h. buds, that ope§........ 35 d
h. I will pu' wi' its lock...613 n
h.'s budding in.. . ... 216 o
h. whitens, and the . .614 q
under the h. in the dale**..662 s
Hawthorn-bush–h-b. a*......614 f
h-b., with seats beneath....614 c
spreading h-b........... 58 s
Hawthorns–now h. blossom‡614 e
walk with me where h. ..614 b
Hawthorn-trees–h-t. blow in.613 o
Hay–desire to a bottle of h.*148 g
harvest of the new-mown h.447 n
hay on his horns..........677 m
needle in a bottle of hay...502 k
odor of newly mown h.....615 k
reposing himself in the h. .481 j
rich breath of h. fields..... 43 c
sweet h. hath no fellow*..148 q
the man is making hay ...542 i
the tedded hay.............294 k
Hazard–all is on the h.*......578 c
h. not your wealth on a...754 g
h. what he fears to lose...657 x
men that hazard all*......269 c
Hazards–greatest h. are......104 q
hazards we can run......263 l
Haze–o'er the dreamy......543 p
soft h., like a fairy dream.. 71 h
Hazel-blooms–the h-b., in...391 d
Hazel-eyes–because thou*...513 n
He–because it was he........361 b
Head–a head for wrongs*...122 a
all heart they live all h.**..575 o
and lay the head......... 38 h
and their h. the prow....410 q
an obedient head........217 k
as gently lay my head.....560 n
as take lodgings in a h. ..385 e
at his h. a green grass...137 g
banish'd from the frosty*..368 d
betrays the h. unsound....631 w
bore up his branching h.** 21 s

cornfields bow the head....394 e
cut off my head...........213 k
dangle on his head........277 r
dint of head-combing....473 o
disdains to hide his h......385 o
draw on its head...........232 n
drew this gallant h. of*....639 h
dying hand, above his h...631 h
fine devices in his head....372 c
flowers, with starry h......223 j
from h. to foot I am*......108 q
from his h. was woman....661 a
from the crown of our h.to.498 a
gently falling on thy h..... 32 o
glorious church, the.......164 s
hail, O bleeding H., and.... 92 i
hammering in my head*...528 t
hanging down his head....226 l
hangs his h. for shame ....468 t
hang thy ghastly head....231 l
h. is always the dupe of..505 j
h. is as full of quarrels*..513 o
h., not yet by time........291 a
h. that lies in calm content112 i
head to contrive, and a. ...79 l
head to contrive a tongue. 78 l
h. was silver'd o'er with.. ..9 p
h. were as full of kinks.... 31 e
h. which statuaries loved.. 25 p
h. with foot hath private...371 b
heart, not on my head*....112 a
held your head*...........333 l
he lifts his head at......... 46 d
her head was bare.........555 p
her head was bowed........ 31 f
here rests his h. upon the..379 c
his comprehensive head‡..454 f
hit the nail on the head....499 aa
house to put's h. in has a*.426 q
I'll hang my h. and perish*234 j
in the down I sink my h.†..563 n
I shall decline my head....226 l
it burns the h., it blinds....456 i
its h. reaches the clouds...740 r
John A. Logan is the h....482 g
largeness of his head......246 e
lay the head down on......416 q
let my head stoop to the*..489 l
lifts the head and lies‡.....397 a
Maggie coost her head fu..562 b
must, this old gray head...469 t
my head is a map.........110 o
my imperfections on my*..138 q
nodded his imperial h......409 e
now from h. to foot I am*..526 b
nowhere yet to rest my h..667 q
off with his head*.........608 r
O good gray head which†.. 12 h
one small h. should carry..342 b
one's immortal head.......276 t
on his h. (as fit for warlike 541 b
on horror's head horrors*..523 d
overthrow the head.......255 g
pillow that fair head......137 e
pour'd on the h. profuse...543 f
precious jewel in his head*. 7 a
raven cried h.-off! head-off. 87 l
roofe to shroud his head...201 i
rosie garland and a weary.563 h
scan him from h. to feet†..126 b
scarlet head appear.......238 r
shall lean his silver head..646 u
show thy h. by day nor*...106 j
slippers on your head .....180 l
small h. and nostril wide*.. 21 d
some tired h. for comfort..112 i
sunken head and sadly.....234 t
sunshine settles on his h...402 s
sunshine settles on its h...102 q
tall, the wise, the reverend.185 e
that it had it h. bit off by*. 57 h
the hand and head that...451 g
the head of the table.....508 cc
thy head thy sovereign*...311 x
thy head upon my breast‖.334 d
to cover my head now.....590 u
to lay his head upon the§..620 f

Shakespeare *; Milton **; Wordsworth ¶; Byron ‖; Tennyson †; Lowell ††; Pope ‡; Longfellow §.

drops that warm my h.....358 *r*
each h. is freedom's shield.637 *q*
each heart is whispering...303 *v*
ear is'the avenue to the h..772 *a*
ease of h. her every look..655 *t*
ease the heart can know....548 *q*
eat not thy heart :......... 72 *g*
enrich not tne h. of another§ 8 *b*
evening twilight of the h...296 *t*
every human h. is human§.309 *u*
every pang that rends the h.307 *u*
eyes, but not my heart.....414 *o*
faint h. faire lady ne'er....122*m*
faint heart hath been a.....662 *l*
faint heart ne'er wan.......662 *a*
faint h ne'er won fair lady.497 *r*
faithless h. betrays the.....631*w*
false heart doth know*..... 3 2 *q*
fear his heart rebounds**..196 *s*
feelings rush'd ipon my h.532 *k*
fer from eye, fer fron h...497 *w*
fervent heart goes forth§..1 1 *j*
felt along the heart¶......210 *w*
first burst frae this heart...380 *r*
firstlings of my heart*.... 5*m*
flag of the free h.'s hope...214 *e*
flood-gate of the deeper h..554 *d*
fountains in the human h..406 *v*
from the h. of nature rolled.538 *r*
furnace-burning heart*....591 *p*
gall in her heart and a.....369 *e*
give me back my heart‖....296 *p*
glow in thy heart, and‡....106 *a*
glows, in ev'ry heart......487 *a*
good heart is a letter.....195 *g*
grief tears his heart‡......287 *x*
guiltless heart, to range...112 *o*
guilt's in that heart........361 *d*
had a heart to resolve.... 79 *l*
hand and h. to this vote....469 *r*
hand upon my h., gently‖..601 *b*
hand without a heart......360 *k*
happy the h. that keeps its.378 *h*
hard was the heart........196 *i*
hatching my tender h. so.. 45*m*
healer when the h. hath‖..599 *i*
heart a cheerful hour......295 *l*
h., and mind, and thoughts.286 *b*
h. another heart divines§...359 *u*
h. as far from fraud*......257 *u*
h. asks pleasure first......296 *s*
h. as sound as a bell*..... 556 *y*
heart a withered leaf......287 *y*
h. believe the truths I tell..632 *c*
h. can ne'er a transport...569 *l*
heart dance with joy.... .191 *x*
h. distrusting asks if......329 *p*
heart embracing heart....261 *r*
h. for falsehood framed....199 *x*
heart giveth grace unto§...296 *u*
h. has an instinct of what..554 *n*
h. has learned to glow‡.....588 *d*
heart hath its own memory§380 *i*
heart inclines to heart.....661 *t*
heart in love with night§..398 *e*
h. is a free and a fetterless.297 *b*
heart is a small thing......297 *d*
h. is breaking for a little...537 *h*
h. is ever at your service*.549 *g*
heart is its own fate........205 *r*
h. is like an instrument....296 *x*
heart is not here..........296 *n*
h. is so full of emotion§....210 *s*
heart is so full that a††....293 *l*
heart is the dungeon of...512 *c*
h. is the home of the great. 60*m*
heart is true as steel*......212 *p*
heart is turn'd to stone*.. 297 *f*
h. is wiser than the intellect650 *v*
heart knock at my ribs**..209*m*
h. laments that virtue*....633 *n*
heart made pure shall......274 *c*
h. may give a useful lesson.341 *w*
h. must cover up its dead...567 *p*
heart must have to cherish‡296 *v*
heart must needs advise...69 *g*
h. new-fir'd I follow you*..198 *h*

heart of a maiden is stolen.297 *a*
h. of a man is depressed...656 *l*
h of another is passing....554 *n*
h. of life, laid waste with...570*m*
heart of man is the place...296*m*
heart of man knoweth......283 *s*
heart of man suffice to**...123 *a*
heart of nature beat§..... .580 *d*
heart of the devout........756 *k*
h. of the world I leap......115 *k*
h. on her lips, and soul‖....655 *i*
h. recalled a different name.568 *v*
h. resolves this matter in‡.630 *o*
h. rocked its babe of bliss..203 *r*
heart's ease! one could.....237 *t*
heart's ease or pansy .....237 *n*
heart's ease that the poets.237 *f*
heart's form will discover..615 *b*
heart shall thanl you......594 *t*
h ' impulse is the voice of.766 *q*
heart' in the High.ands....296 *n*
hea t's lightness from the..569 *i*
heart susceptible of pity...117 *d*
h that bleeds and breaks..344 *a*
heart that doth not keep...380 *d*
heart that has truly loved..361 *f*
h. that is soonest awake...349 *e*
heart then, knew of pain... 90 *a*
heart though unknown§....206 *r*
heart to conceive the....... 80 *q*
h. to h., and mind to mind.588*m*
heart was as great as......255 *l*
heart was full of feeling....266 *e*
heart was in his work§.....296 *u*
heart was made for Him...522 *k*
heart was one of those‖....296 *o*
heart which love of thee‖..491 *t*
h. which makes us fathers.778 *j*
heart whose softness‖..... 34 *a*
h. with h. in concord beats¶ 38 *a*
heart within and God§..... 5 *a*
heart within thee burned...186 *o*
h. with kindliest motion†...265 *s*
h. without a stain knows...785 *s*
h. with room for every joy.296 *l*
heart with strings of steel*.489 *g*
heart with such memories.242 *g*
h. would hear her and†.....366 *g*
he has a very large heart.. 81 *o*
her bounding heart........229 *n*
here's a h. for every fate‖..524*w*
her heart, be sure, is not‖..353 *o*
hiding one thing in his h....144 *o*
his h. as far from fraud*... 83 *p*
his heart doth ache........203*m*
his h. kep' goin' pity-pat††.662 *r*
his heart was darken'd‖....356 *t*
his sinking heart confess‖.. 34 *c*
his uncorrupted heart‡....454 *f*
hold thee to my heart......358 *q*
home is where the heart is.499*dd*
hope my heart can cheer...308 *c*
hope to my heart comes...165 *j*
how hast thou the heart*.. 33 *f*
how oft with merry heart..458 *s*
human h. finds nowhere...587 *t*
I am sick at heart*......... 86 *y*
incapable of winning her h.103 *h*
incense of the h. may rise...297 *c*
incessant battery to her h..663 *t*
in her crimson heart.......243 *o*
in her h. did mercy come*.382 *o*
in my heart of heart*......372 *h*
in my inmost h. I keep my. 7 *y*
in the h. of man she sits...651 *v*
in the heart's deep well ...574 *e*
into every h. his words.....318 *u*
into thine heart and write§.428 *u*
in whose heart one passion§.300 *y*
I shall be out of h. shortly*523 *o*
is that incense of the h....524 *x*
it beats in the heart.......348 *t*
it had only one heart...... 17*m*
it is the childly heart; we... 17 *b*
it sank deep into his h......780 *v*
it will make thy h. sore§...326 *b*
jot of heart or hope**..... 61 *f*

keeps his heart and hand..375 *l*
left my h. a wither'd leaf..600 *o*
lie upon her charmed h.†..563 *l*
life treads on life and h....150 *j*
light heart lives long*...... 88 *q*
living h. and hearthstone..469 *a*
look in thy h. and write....429 *t*
love gushed from my h.... 60 *n*
love-suit to her gentle h.*..663 *j*
love which lifts the heart..367 *f*
make room, my heart......296 *q*
man's h., at once inspirits..309 *h*
man whose h. is warm.....450 *c*
melt into his heart¶........558 *i*
memory of the heart.......770 *t*
merry heart goes all*......384 *l*
mine with my h. in 't*......204 *u*
most constant heart*......385 *g*
mother's heart is weak‡‡..402 *c*
music in my heart I bore¶..408 *t*
my book and heart........464 *s*
my h. hath one poor*......414 *x*
my heart is harmless as my.366 *b*
my h. is idly stirred¶......573 *h*
my h. is in my prayer§.....556 *u*
my h. is weary waiting....393 *d*
my h. untravell'd fondly...379 *v*
my jealous h. would break.658 *q*
my peace is gone, my h. is.789 *o*
my poor heart is broken... 48 *l*
my tongue, though not my*606 *g*
my trembling h. to wisdom.652 *d*
my true love hath my h....365 *j*
naked human heart........297 *i*
noble h. hath pawn'd an*..121 *t*
no matter from the heart*.665 *z*
of its own frail heart††.... 81 *h*
old tune on the heart......379 *q*
on and up where Nature's h.411*m*
one day with life and h.††..668 *r*
one flag, one land, one h...468 *r*
one h. must hold both.....650 *k*
one heart, one way........799 *q*
on his h. the torrent......367 *b*
open'd every heart........527 *p*
open my h. and you will...116 *k*
opens in each heart........ 86 *t*
or I'd break her heart.....374 *j*
or too firm a heart‖........361 *n*
O serpent h. hid with a*...312 *u*
O teach my heart‡.........489 *b*
over my heart the while...192 *f*
partings break the h. they‖.464 *z*
pierce into a marble heart*659 *q*
place in my heart's love*...215 *i*
poet's heart than brain....296*w*
poor h. would fain deny*... 11 *r*
preaching down a†........451 *q*
prefer his injuries to his*..628 *n*
quiver'd in his heart‖......205 *u*
rain-drop upon his heart..209 *k*
razors to my wounded h.*..665 *r*
remorse is as the h. in....522 *r*
restrained, a h. is broken..664 *d*
sae true his heart......... 81 *t*
safe within its central h...472 *h*
search the heart of man...523 *f*
secret of a weed's plain h.††643 *k*
sees your h. wreck'd with‖.114 *g*
set the heart on fire*...... 8 *c*
sever my fond heart......204 *k*
Shakespeare unlocked his h549 *w*
Shakespeare unlocked his*.551 *d*
shall command my h. and..655 *u*
shoots through the.......523 *q*
showing that the human h.588 *f*
sick h. shows, that I must*.139 *u*
silken chains about the h..369 *c*
sleeps on his own heart¶...194 *i*
solemn image to my heart¶322 *o*
some have not a heart.....296 *r*
some heart did break†.....289 *d*
some h. though unknown§.148 *s*
song through many a h.§...479 *u*
sooner in my h. divin'd.**.588 *h*
sought heart's ease........237 *n*
speaks what's in his heart* 17 *q*

speechless longings of his..667 l
stay at home, my heart§...304 c
steals o'er the heart........304 g
still some aim for the h.....667 c
stop the heart a minute....295 n
stout heart and resolute....339 j
subtlest fold of the heart...327 p
surest way to hit a woman's662 n
sweet concurrence of the h.488 i
take for want of heart‖..... 77 u
tale to many a feeling h....346 q
temple is an humble heart.487 e
tender heart; a will§........ 81 a
tenderest h. and next our..567 d
than doubt one h., that, if..620 e
than my heart cool with*..384 p
that mighty h. is lying¶....533 u
that my heart has bled.... 60 v
that warm my heart......260 s
the angel heart of man††... 81 g
the dupe of the heart.....505 j
the fragrant h. of bloom... 43 n
the gentlest heart‡........271 t
the h. hath treble wrong*..606 i
the heart inform'd........517 s
the h. it humbles, and it...538 i
the h. of every believer....528 e
the heart of woman is*....658 w
the h. ran o'er with silent‖.670 a
the h. riven with vain¶....383 a
the heart's bleed longest‖..671 e
the h. seldom feels what...789 u
the h. that not yet—never..588 k
the heart, which others....357 q
the hiccups from the h.....110 f
the larger h., the kindlier†. 41 c
the o'er fraught heart*....288 w
there to harmonize his h...625 p
the roving h. gathers no....74 u
the simple heart of all...†† 81 g
this h. shall break into a*..591 y
thoughts come from the h..791 m
though we sever, my fond h.334 j
thou makest the sad h. gay.540 u
throbbing heart of man§...580 d
through his wither'd h.....543 h
through the heart.........539 k
thy habitation is the h.‖...491 t
till h. and body and life....144 w
tired heart shall cease to...147 l
to hide the feeling heart...312 a
to move a stony heart....567 q
touched his strong heart...479 l
touch the heart be thine‡..261 s
two hearts into one heart..626 r
unlock the one little heart..535 p
unpack my h. with words*.665 v
upon many a heart§.......135 l
upon the beatings of my.¶.669 u
vengeance is in my heart*.528 t
virtue of the heart .... 86 b
waft a balm to thy sick h...609 p
warm the heart............159 k
wear him in my h.'s core*..372 h
wear his cross upon the h..312 y
wear my h. upon my*......556 x
weighs upon the heart*....441 c
whatever comes from the h. 80 e
what h. can think.........313 i
what heart of man....... 26 j
what his heart thinks*.....556 y
when the h. dares to speak.755 n
when the h. murmurs.....763 i
where at h.'s ease he liv'd..655 y
which heart to heart......362 h
while his heart doth ache...110 c
while my h.'s breaking.....464 q
who holds her heart.......254 a
who lost my heart while‡..361 m
whom my h. is longing....597 i
whose heart hath tried‖...189 t
wild as the heart when....460 o
windy tempest of my h.*..592 a
winning eye and heart.....539 r
winter maketh the light h..540 o
win the h. than overthrow.255 q
with a fervent h. goes forth§411 i

with a heart at ease........ 99 k
with an orphaned heart....521 v
with beating h. that no love. 55 m
with breaking heart§.......657 h
with h. never changing....376 f
within a brother's heart....297 j
witnin a mother's heart....401 s
within thine own heart....337 x
with nature's h. in tune....411 u
with outspread heart.......239 o
woman is at heart a rake‡..658 h
words gladden so many a§.664 u
wound a h. that's broken...665 g
write to the mind and h....426 r
yet her h. is ever near††....360 e
you know my heart........464 m
you need a heart. ....479 e
young heart's grace....... 90 s
your heart's supreme......629 k
Heart-ache-h-a. and the*....140 j
Heart-break-great deal of*..524 c
Heartless-in my h. breast...335 x
Heart-opening-h-o. wink....589 w
Hearts-admission to our h...355 a
allegiance from men's h.*..608 n
and hearts of guile........796 m
and h. of oak our men.....468 b
between hearts that love...157 e
cherish those hearts that*..364 f
combine your h. in one*...376 r
conquer willing hearts**...472 v
ensanguined h. clubs...... 14 p
enthroned in the h. of*...382 p
faint h. faire ladies never.497 q
feeling h. touch them.....210 u
few are the h. whence one..588 b
first in the hearts of his... 80 t
first in the hearts of his... 80 u
gentle-humored hearts....113 h
give your hearts to*........262 m
golden time of our hearts..602 a
great h. expand..........263 n
heard of hearts unkind¶....284 c
hearts all in tune.........267 a
hearts are all as false*.....121 s
h. are dry as summer dust¶142 f
h. bid the tyrants defiance.468 f
h. in love use their own*...363 d
h. of men are their books..371 p
h. of oak are our ships.... 79 k
hearts resolved and hands.526 c
hearts should be as good*..639 m
hearts that beat like thine..111 o
h. that scorn'd to serve*.. 472 f
h., though stout and brave§348 k
h. would lose future.......118 q
heedless h. is lawful prize..144 k
home-keeping hearts are§..304 c
home to our h. the truth‖..446 h
in all the people's hearts*.. 84 g
in h. kept open, honest....621 p
in human h. what bolder...605 r
in one fate their hearts....378 b
keep two h. together that¶.378 e
kind h. are more than†....418 p
knocks at our h., and finds.598 h
let your hearts be strong...119 b
lie safe in our hearts....... 90 f
live in h. we leave behind...379 p
many light h. and wings...610 q
march on ! all h. resolved..637 i
no hearts like English h.†..116 c
of finite hearts that yearn.465 h
our hearts are warm......400 q
our h. in sleep to sway.....563 q
our h., our hopes, are all§..118 f
O weary h. ! O slumbering§102 s
passion of great hearts††..467 l
reading the h. of others...788 b
rough hearts of flint*......442 m
soft conditions and our h*..660 c
some hearts are hidden....296 r
strengthened our hearts§..450 q
such h. of oak as they be.†.116 c
that human hearts endure.172 w
the hearts that dare are.... 85 d
their hearts were set.......251 w

the work of their own h....582 u
thousand h. beat happily‖..128 a
to steal away your hearts*.462 m
touch and search the h.§....40 d
touch the hearts of men§...557 f
two h. that beat as one....778 p
two h. in life were single...184 h
two loving hearts divide...172 m
union of h.—the union of..627 m
without h. there is no home‖566 f
young hearts romancing...129 a
your hearts have sold......293 y
Heartsome-h. wi' thee I hae.204 p
Heart-stain-ne'er carried a..653 m
Heartstrings-h. are about...328 n
Heart-throbs-count time by..345 m
Hearth-angels of our hearth.111 o
clear fire, a clean h. and the 14 v
cricket on the hearth**.....304 d
danced upon the hearth**..368 m
embers on the h. are dead..415 k
on our hearth shall glow...547 a
yield thee a hearth and....304 b
Hearths-fires light up the h.§277 t
Hearth-stone-heart and h-s..469 a
Heat-a comfortable h.**.... 613 m
allay the h. that flames....541 q
all conquering h. O intermit543 f
and parched with heat.....641 j
at a white heat now.......430 e
degrees of heat and cold...782 k
force of fervent heat......430 l
for one h., all know, doth..465 j
freezes up the heat of life*.209 s
heat and hoary frost*......601 h
heat for the cold.........561 a
heat, ma' am! it was so....543 d
heat of the long day.......345 i
liver rather h. with wine*..384 p
music religious h. inspires..404 f
neither heat nor light......273 k
one draught above h.*.....326 o
promises of youthful heat. 9 j
scorched with barren h....245 k
shun the noonday h.‡......542 p
summer's parching heat*..543 a
the bee buzz'd up in the h.†541 h
thirsts with each h. and...672 i
Heated-h. hot with burning†.351 m
Heating-to warm without h.593 p
Heats-far-off h. through....321 p
unscattered by heats......224 j
Heath-dare the purple heath.230 m
e'en wild heath displays‡..230 l
heath thy blossoms grew..230 h
land of brown heath......116 q
modest heath, that glows..219 l
my foot is on my native h..409 n
on my native heath.......118 l
range on thy h. covered...118 i
the purple heath.........219 h
Heather-bonny heather bell..246 o
low in the heather blooms.. 48 o
world of heather..........229 b
Heath-flower-ne'er from the.254 e
Heaths-unharbour'd h.***... 88 a
Heathens-glad the h. would.539 d
Heaven-a fate prepared for..619 f
a flash from Heaven......343 o
against h.'s hand or will**.. 61 f
a h. of charms, divine‡.... 34 u
a heaven on earth*........298 a
a h. on earth I have won*..663 g
a heaven unto a hell*......283 q
a high hope for a low h*...467 n
all heaven around us......111 n
all that we believe of h....657 y
all this, and heaven too....297 u
and all to heaven. ....600 s
and approving Heaven....112 j
and Gods in heaven......485 j
and h. is shining o'er us...637 q
and love of heaven.......579 p
angels of our heaven......111 o
are friends in heaven......261 q
argue not against h.'s**...119 f
ascent from earth to h.....712 c

SHAKESPEARE *; MILTON **; WORDSWORTH ¶; BYRON ‖; TENNYSON †; LOWELL ††; POPE ‡; LONGFELLOW §.

as heaven from earth*.....257 u
as high as heaven, as deep.495 y
a soul as white as heaven..570 x
a soul that trusts in heaven.620 a
awful rainbow once in h..515m
battering the gates of h.†..489 t
battleground of h. and hell..668 o
beauteous eye of heaven*..252 y
beholding h. and feeling...512 j
bestowed on heaven alone‖. 23 b
beteem the winds of h.*....364 o
blue, boundless heaven....194 a
blue isles of heaven†....613 q
born where h.'s influence‡.633 a
bread of heaven............166 a
breaks the serene of h......417 r
brightest h. of invention*..477 t
brush in dyes of heaven...515 o
by tracing Heaven his....274 q
by which we fly to heaven*314 q
can lift to Heaven an......274 d
can make a heaven of hell**386 a
charge of the gates of H...390m
circle mark'd by heaven‡..151 n
convulsing h. and earth...578 f
courage leads to heaven...686 p
crystal urns of heaven.....171 d
curst by heaven's decree..368 x
dance upon a jig to H.‡...406w
dare the plants look up to*.490 o
dear to Heaven is saintly**. 87 u
deed is like the Heaven's..146w
descended from Heaven....719 i
distant from heaven alike..495 a
down from h. to earth......356 h
each heart a little heaven.. 86 t
each in heaven shall roll...355 u
earth in them than heaven.210 v
earth is registered in H.....123 l
e'en to the h.'s blue vault.. 40 n
endures what H. ordains...467 e
eye in h. would through*...193 o
face of brightest h. had**..625 a
face of heaven so fine*.....363 e
fair and open face of h.....117 g
fairest love from h. above..357 y
far from fraud as heaven*. 83 p
fell from the patriot's h....608 a
finger points to heaven¶... 96 b
flew up to h.'s chancery....419 v
for Love is h. and claims its. 95 a
for love is heaven.........362 g
fought in heaven**........149 k
fragrance smells to heaven.524 x
from H. proceed the woes‡.297 v
from H. ('twas all he wish'd) 41 l
from home and from H..... 89 g
full fix'd on heaven........198w
full of h. to me, as when††.477 j
further off from heaven...314 j
gate of greatest heaven.... 29 q
gaze of the ruler of h.....624m
gentle rain from heaven*..382 p
gentle sleep from Heaven..561 b
get peace in heaven........471 b
getting to heaven at last...450 i
glance from h. to earth*...480 n
glimmering verge of h.....186 b
gloomy was Heaven........327 q
God keeps a niche in H....267 f
God's in His Heaven.......273 u
go then merrily to Heaven.383 n
grace could fly to heaven*.298 s
great God of Heaven‖....487m
hand of heaven submit!**..420 f
happiness of heaven.......355 c
has conjunction with h.... 85 a
he blesses H. for what its..525 e
hear My Son in heaven††...86 p
heard no more in h.**.. ..153 g
H. allots thee for thy board.304 b
h. alone that is given††.....102 u
H. alone the genuine seeds†477 b
heaven always at peace ...731 q
h., always pure, is without.708 b
heaven a perfect round....279 n
heaven around us.........293 n

heaven before mine eyes**.406 g
H. blesses humble earth....111 o
Heav'n but the vision......297w
H. but tries our virtue by.. 8 e
heaven commences ere the.297 r
H. doom'd the Greeks‡.....297 v
h. except by its gifts.......707 h
H. first taught letters for‡.448 l
Heaven forbids, it is true...173 d
h. forming each on other‡..642 a
H. from all creatures‡......206 y
H. gave him all at once..... 74 o
H. gives our years of......346 k
H. gives to those it loves§.634 c
H. grant any to remain... 685 l
H. had looked upon riches.643 d
h. had made her such a*...663m
heaven had wanted one....568 d
Heaven has bounteously... 12 j
H. has joined great issues¶. 85 s
Heaven has no rage like....357 p
Heaven hath done for this‖.117 o
H. hath my empty words*.489 n
heaven in her eye**.......657 q
Heaven is above all yet*....330 j
heaven is in thy soul......654 n
Heaven is not always angry 512 l
H. is not gone, but we are..592m
heaven itself is laid open...726 h
h. itself upon the past has.496 q
H. itself would stoop to**..632 v
H. looks down on earth....577 l
Heaven looks down on me†.318 d
Heaven makes sport of....748 l
Heaven means to be one...297m
H. might have spar'd one..656 p
H. ne'er helps the men who 5 x
heaven not so large as......297 n
Heaven open'd wide**.....298 e
H. opens on my eyes; my‡.187 q
Heaven best gifts to hold..778 g
heaven's distant lamps§....298 c
Heaven's ebon vault.......417 p
Heaven sends us good meat.431 q
h.'s eternal year is thine...297 p
Heaven's face doth glow*..298 p
h.'s gate opens when the...563 p
H.'s glittering host and....585 a
H. shall give permission...582 x
Heaven's happy bowers....241 k
H.'s help is better than....300 a
heaven's high cope. . .....257 f
heaven's immortal noon...522 d
Heaven's last best gift**...645 f
heaven's next best gift.....318 e
H. still with laughter the‡.. 13 q
heaven strikes the humble.703 f
H. surely is open when.....515 l
heaven's warm sunshine in.667 n
H.'s ways are H.'s ways....767 b
Heaven takes care to grant.487 u
heaven that clear obscure‖.186 p
Heaven, that every virtue‡.333 i
H., that made me honest...305 h
H. to mankind impartial‡.293 r
H. tries earth if it be in††.393 q
heaven was all tranquillity 551 w
Heaven was her help.......190 b
Heaven were not Heaven...189 o
hell I suffer seems a h.**..101 q
hell that are not Heaven...267 p
his blessed part to H., and*.139m
his face to heaven‖........442 x
his h. commences ere the.525 a
holds the h.'s tent-hangings397 e
home is high in heaven..... 46 f
hopes in heaven do dwell*.308 t
hope to go to heaven......251 k
hope to merit Heaven‖.....297 l
how I may climb to h......539 c
how the floor of heaven*..576w
hues were born in heaven..214 e
hungry Greek go to h......713 i
I'd call them heaven*.....203w
if h. send no supplies.......509gg
if h. would make me such*.363 j
if it find h., must find it*...572 e

I have an oath in heaven*..419 l
infinite meadows of h.§....576 b
in Heaven ambition cannot.365 n
in H. his looks and**......369 k
in heaven's best treasures.642 h
in H.'s dark hall, high up..667 r
instrument of Heaven......151 h
intercourse with heaven...743 n
in the court of heaven*....378 q
in the firmament of h.**..576 g
is it in heav'n a crime‡....361 n
is light from heaven‖......357 c
is the best gift of Heaven.631 x
is the mouth of Heaven...621 q
journey like the path to..**298 f
just are the ways of h.‡...297 v
kind of H. to be deluded...419 f
knells call, Heaven invites.130 b
languages in earth or H.... 92 g
largest gifts of Heaven....295 s
law of h. and earth is life‖.436 t
led down from Heaven..... 92 q
led the way to heaven..... 85 k
life itself the inferior gift..343 s
life, quite in the verge of h.142 o
lifted it gently to heaven§..568 i
lift my soul to heaven*....489 h
lit in the heaven of dear...233 c
livery of the court of H....312m
looks on h. with more‡....571 v
makes h. drowsy with*....278 a
make thine account with..767 a
marriage-robes for h......296 x
marriages are made in H.†.378 a
matches are made in h.....501 ii
may h.'s grace clear away..760 b
melting heaven with earth.625 c
merciful H. thou rather*..578 e
more he shall receive......685 i
more than H. pursue‡.....106 e
more things in h. and*....473 l
mountains kiss high h......403 b
noblest gift of Heav'n.....658 d
no! by H., I exclaim'd.....618 c
no light in earth or h.§....576 d
not comprehend the h.‡...193 f
not h. itself upon the past.150 p
nothing situate under h.'s*.344 f
nothing true but Heaven...623 b
now at h.'s gate she....... 48 q
offering H. holds dear.....344 a
offspring of h. first born**.352 n
of the King of heaven......520 u
one minute of H. is worth.475 o
only is the gift of H.‡.....548 k
on the fields of heaven....575 j
order is H.'s first law‡.....462 v
out of heaven from God...123 d
Persian's h. is eas'ly made.298 k
places that the eye of h.*..298 n
points of H. and home¶... 50 a
prayer ardent opens h......490 g
prayers are heard in h.....489 q
rage of ill-requited h.‡.... 95 s
rain-drop had a whole h.§..154 d
rather more to Heaven....521 u
receives what H. has sent..110 q
righteous H. in thy great..638 o
reign with Him in Heaven.165 c
report they bore to h......547 p
requires no other heaven...190 u
riches of H.'s pavement**..369 k
rose! the joy of heaven....242 s
round the vault of heaven. 99 v
safest hope is in Heaven...804 x
same port—heaven........261 m
self-same h. that frowns*..298 o
shall cry to Heaven.......382 k
shall not climb to Heaven.297 k
shall practise in heaven....472 a
she, in the vault of heaven.397 n
should ascend to heav'n**.488 o
should H. refuse to hear...487 q
shrieks to pitying Heaven‡.209 h
shut out from h. it makes..460 h
shut thee from h. with a...571 n
snatch me to Heaven......413 b

soars toward heaven........ 77 *n*
so is heaven................ 89 *s*
so much of heaven¶........673 *o*
son of heaven and earth**.420 *g*
Son of H.'s eternal King**. 94 *l*
so souls in heaven are.....146*m*
soul from earth to h. lies..572 *j*
spirits are in heaven¶......198 *s*
spirit that was sent from...712 *b*
starry cope of heaven**....298 *h*
starry crowns of Heaven...576 *r*
state, Heaven is pitched.... 17 *d*
steals the key of heaven....338 *o*
still the starry heaven......165 *k*
storm h. itself in our folly.677 *b*
strike heaven on the face*.569 *r*
succour dawns from H.... 300 *l*
sweetest heaven on earth*.203*w*
sword of h. will bear*......303 *f*
taken quick to heaven....315 *t*
takes wing with h. again... 32 *i*
taste of Heaven below.....367 *h*
thank'd Heaven that he‡...183 *l*
than serve in heaven**.... 13 *i*
that ever points to H....... 80 *k*
that Heaven is gracious....451 *g*
that light which H. sheds..576 *o*
that nature hung in h.**...416 *n*
the ears and eyes of H.....488 *e*
the glorious lamp of h.....583 *p*
the good love heaven§......359 *w*
the heaven on earth.......375 *h*
the heaven's glorious sun*.580 *r*
the help of h. we count*....490 *p*
their way up to heaven....136 *k*
them back to h. again§....557 *f*
the purple walls of H.....384 *x*
there no heaven nor fall....305 *n*
there no stones in heaven*.598*m*
there's husbandry in h.*...298 *q*
the sword of h. will bear*.451 *k*
the top of h. doth hold**...576*m*
the type of heaven's....... 34 *r*
the verge of heaven........578 *f*
the years of H. with all...316 *d*
they have struck H.'s tent. 17 *d*
thine old body for h.*..... 11 *n*
things are the sons of h....664 *t*
thorny way to heaven*....451 *j*
thoughts never to h. go*...665 *s*
thou to heaven hast gone..276 *o*
through the bars of h.....397 *q*
thunder in the stores of h..607 *r*
thy blue course in heaven.. 36 *a*
thy prospect heaven........246 *i*
'tis heaven alone that††....275 *d*
'tis heaven itself that....315 *l*
'tis like a little h. below... 298 *u*
to be seen in Heaven‖.....557*w*
to be young was very h.¶..673 *p*
to find the way to heaven*.309 *n*
to h. hath a summer's day.571 *i*
to heav'n remov'd**........221 *j*
to the gates of Heaven¶...383 *a*
toward the topmost h......409 *e*
'twas whispered in Heaven.297 *q*
under heaven expands......227*m*
under heaven is blowne....611 *k*
unfolds both h. and earth*.130 *q*
unstained from heaven..... 32 *d*
wafted up to heaven§...... 99 *p*
waking dawn'd in heaven.136 *q*
walk ye, in H.'s sweet air..374 *a*
war! H. aid the right..... 640 *k*
was light from Heaven.....465 *i*
was register'd in H. ere....150 *o*
watch the changeless h.....108 *j*
we in heaven shall one....138 *e*
wherewith we fly to h.*....337 *y*
wife is the peculiar gift of‡.645 *i*
wish to heaven is sent......116 *o*
with a feel of heaven......536 *j*
with heav'n between.......448 *e*
workmanship of heaven....418 *b*
world-built arch of h......583*m*
writ in the climate of h.§..405*w*
you give away h.'s vows*..376 *v*

young was very Heaven¶.. 62 *b*
Heaven-born-h-b. dear to us.535*m*
Heaven-gate-singing up**... .486 *p*
Heavenly-builds on h. cant.. 93 *h*
can heavenly minds such...677 *u*
more the Heavenly power†.541 *g*
say h. pow'rs where**......518 *j*
when Music, h. maid......404 *v*
Heavens-and spangled h....575 *h*
angry h. do make their*....639 *n*
before the hollow heavens.460 *p*
bounteous h. all riches‡....642 *k*
climb the heavens, and go..575 *l*
gracious h.! he cries out...427 *q*
heaven of h. up-caught....409 *e*
h. began their march......584 *c*
h. look dark and wild.....577 *s*
heavens should fall........252 *q*
h. their holiest hue........417 *b*
heavens the little can......287 *j*
h. themselves blaze forth*.140 *p*
Heavens! what thick.......713 *q*
his azure shield the H......583 *l*
how to adore the heavens*.670 *n*
in the sweet heavens*......255 *r*
nine h. are eight paradises.463*m*
of these covering heavens*. 60 *u*
O, h., if you do love old*... 11 *u*
open, ye heavens, your**...122 *v*
patient till the h. look*....467 *q*
remembers the heavens....371 *k*
so smile the h. upon this*.. 5 *r*
that the heavens fought*..638 *t*
the cannons to the h.*.... 639 *d*
the h. themselves, the*....462 *x*
the heavens to earth*.....639 *d*
then the heavens are bluest.358 *n*
though the heavens fall....800 *k*
through the blue h. above.392 *u*
under h. of happy dew.....617 *d*
wit rules the heavens.....768 *v*
yon blue heavens above†... 15 *r*
Heavenward-h. ever yearns.645 *t*
Heaviest-h. wrongs get......667 *u*
Heaviness-but h. foreruns*.. 73 *t*
what means this h.........560 *j*
Heaving-kept h. to and fro..135 *e*
Heavy-pursed-your h-p.... 162 *k*
Hebe-hang on H.'s cheek**..383 *r*
Hebe's here, May is here...392 *q*
there ever-youthful Hebe..277 *i*
with her nectar Hebe††....544 *f*
Hebrew-H. knelt in the.....329 *c*
H. will turn Christian*..... 93 *t*
Hector-better like H. in the§.119 *v*
my Hector still survives....375 *n*
Hecuba-what's H. to him*..423*m*
Hedge-along the flowery h...366 *c*
divinity doth h. a king*....535 *f*
hedge about the sides......244 *h*
hedge on high is quick.... .231 *c*
in the hedge the frosted....618 *d*
nor lowly h. nor solitary...543 *r*
pull not down your hedge..501 *x*
some to the holly hedge... 610 *o*
warm hedge grew lush.....612 *l*
Hedges-of sweet briar h.....244 *n*
tongues, and hedges ears...507 *ff*
when hedges sprout........225 *r*
Hedge-side-on a hedge-side..228 *f*
Hedge-sparrow-h-s. fed*.... 57 *h*
Heed-for himself will take¶..313 *q*
take h. and ponder well§...428*w*
Heedeth-counsel, a wise son.494 *o*
Heeds-delay always heeds...496 *ii*
heeds not, he hears not....134*m*
trust that he who heeds....510 *y*
Heel-feather to the heel.,... 646 *c*
from heel to toe...........128 *g*
heel of limping winter*....392 *l*
off-heel insidiously aside...129 *i*
tread each other's heel.....388 *t*
Heels-an income at its heels.441 *v*
at his heels a stone........137 *g*
at his heels, close at his.... 12 *u*
gloaming treads the h. of..366 *c*
good to the h. the well..... 74 *s*

grow out at heels*........ 256 *p*
heels of pleasure........ ...375 *b*
strawe them at their h..... 67 *c*
Heifer-who finds the h.*....430 *n*
Height-although his h. be*..317 *o*
bold to leap a height. .....231 *r*
from her mountain height.258 *h*
h. that lies forever in the§. 13 *e*
on every mountain height..526 *n*
worth's unknown,*........108 *t*
years, to loftier height¶.... 12*m*
Heights-h. by great men§...339 *g*
vapours linger round the¶.382 *c*
Heir-born the free heir of...369 *o*
comes but brings an heir*..570 *b*
creation's h., the world the.668 *h*
great heir of fame**....... 550 *g*
heir of joy and sorrow¶....227 *r*
heir to the rich Midas.....177 *h*
Numa made me his heir....180 *d*
perfumes or wine to your..181 *n*
shocks that flesh is h. to*..140 *j*
th' impatient heir‖........189 *c*
whatever an heir, or a‡....183 *p*
Heirs-careless h. may the*..633*m*
on earth have made us h.¶.481 *g*
Helen-like another H. fir'd..655*w*
Helicon-eternal dews of H...414 *e*
from H.'s harmonious.... 70 *v*
taste the stream of H......478 *v*
Heliotrope-change it to a h..238 *c*
faint, fair heliotrope......217 *f*
from heliotrope was shed..230 *p*
Heliotropes-h. with meekly..220 *n*
Hell-a heaven unto a hell*..283 *q*
all hell broke loose**. ...299 *f*
all places shall be hell.....267 *p*
an agreement with hell....559 *h*
and feeling hell............512 *j*
another room in hell*......139 *j*
are the gates of hell...... 144 *o*
a shout that tore hell's**..573 *b*
as I do hell pains*.........295 *h*
avarice in the vaults of h..365 *n*
barren beach of hell.......586 *d*
battleground of heaven.....668 *o*
bearing souls to hell.......299 *d*
beneath all depth in hell*..332 *t*
bid him go to h. to hell.....209 *b*
black is the badge of hell*.299 *p*
break loose from hell**.... 91 *u*
can make a heaven of h.**.386 *a*
Christ our God. h.'s empire.165 *b*
come hot from hell*.......638*w*
deed is chronicled in hell*..123 *u*
detests him as the gates‡...199 *g*
evil spirits with hell...... 85 *a*
fear o' hell's the...........208 *o*
from h. one step no more**.299 *k*
furies, terrible as hell**....153 *b*
h. contains no fouler fiend‡656 *r*
h. dwells within myself....296*m*
hell for horses..............497 *e*
hell for women.............497 *e*
hell grew darker at their**.638 *a*
hell is empty and all*......299 *a*
h. is full of good intentions.299 *o*
h. is full of good meanings.298 *z*
hell is more bearable.......208 *v*
hell is no other but a......299 *a*
hell is paved with good....299 *c*
hell is the wrath of God....298*w*
hell I suffer seems a**......299 *j*
h. it is in suing long to bide.155 *i*
h.'s grim tyrant feel th'‡...268 *b*
hell the shadow from......297*w*
hell trembled at the**.....136 *q*
hell itself breathes out*....417 *o*
hell might be ashamed of...387 *j*
in h. a place stone-built....298 *x*
in hell that they must live..299 *v*
in the throat of hell....... .299 *u*
invites, hell threatens......130 *b*
I shall move all hell.......734 *k*
lead apes in hell forever...375 *e*
lead apes in hell*..........377 *l*
light-house of hell.........325 *p*

---

like the waves of hell‖...... 62 g
making earth a hell‖.......297 l
man may live as quiet in*..377 c
mentions h. to ears polite‡.299 n
milk of concord into hell*.. 77 g
more than hell to shun‡....106 e
mounted for hell on the††..128m
myself am hell**...........299 j
no fiend in hell can........109 i
no hell for authors in hell..427 a
nor h. a fury like a woman..655 r
or not threatened hell......656 p
out of hell leads up to**...299 i
O war! thou son of hell*...639 m
play all my tricks in hell...298 y
quiet to quick bosoms is‖..523 s
reign in h. than serve in**. 13 i
secrets of the sepulchres...299 t
set the ministers of h. at..586 k
should set hell on fire*.....299 r
some of them, in hell......436 q
terrible as hell**...........637 u
that reigns in hell.........153 a
that riches grow in hell**..642 q
the descent into hell... ...720 d
the dreadful fear of hell...699 c
the hell within him** .....523 b
the injur'd lover's hell**...327 v
there no heaven nor hell...305 n
the smoke of hell—that....463 i
this is the news from hell.414 s
though in hell**............ 13 k
thou profoundest hell**....299 g
to heaven or to hell*.......151 s
tortures of that inward h.‖.105 g
torture souls feel in hell...299 v
to the loyalist's hell.......608 a
'twas muttered in hell.....297 q
ugliest fiend of hell........327 t
use that word in hell*...... 33 f
vast hell can hold*.........153 n
what an inviting hell.......654 s
with blasts from hell......674 f
Hel-gate-h-g. them both.....563 f
Helm-dream not helm and...629 c
helm of daffodillies........226 h
look to the h., good master.445 t
make a skillet of my h.*....432 b
where glitter hauberk, h.§.533 h
Helmet-his h. now shall..‥.470w
sense is our h., wit is but..548 n
'tis our helmet saves.....548 n
Helmets-usurping h. of our*.639 c
Helmsman-the h. answered§.460 d
Help-encumbers him with h.300 g
God helps those who help..300 p
gone and what's past h.**..525 h
Heaven's h. is better than..300 a
h. and ornament thereto...421 k
help by so much reading.. 64 g
help! help! he's gone......321 a
help is none to borrow.....570 n
h. me, Cassius, or I sink*..300m
help me this once*.........300 n
help others out of a fellow.300 c
help the feeble up*.........300 o
h. us in our utmost need§..451 a
help your mother to make.266 c
help you to grow as........300 i
Lord h. 'em, how I pities...445 n
ran to help me when I fell.402 f
since there's no help.......334 g
such h, as man must have..299 w
the help of heaven we*....490 p
the means to help him*....626 h
the name of help grew*....147 u
they cannot h. themselves.149 h
thou thought'st to h. me*..594 w
trade it may help, society‡.390 b
won't let God help us.....317 v
Helper-antagonist is our h..300 b
Helpful-more h. than all...473 t
Helpings-with gentle h..... 17 c
Helps-God helps the brave...756 f
Heaven ne'er h. the men... 5 x
Hem-dead on the h. of May..392m
Hemisphere-between a h. of.571 c

our h. he ran his race.....585 j
walk the dark h. till.......575 t
Hemlock-h.'s fragrant......230 e
Hemlock-tree-O h-t.! how§..614 h
Hemp-or hemp departed....356 k
Hempen-sing in a h. string..557 z
Hen-short-legged hen if we..167 e
Hens-the fesant hens of.... 54 f
Hence-far h. ye vulgar......711 u
Henpecked-they not h. you‖.655 g
Hepatica-blue hepatica.....230 q
Hepe-bereth the rede hepe..223 k
Herald-lark, the h. of the*.. 49 j
the h. of a noisy world.....435 r
the perfectest h. of joy*...554 z
Heralding-heralding the day.576 r
Heraldry-by h., proved.....203 d
like coats in heraldry*.....627 n
Heralds-h. from off our*....184 t
heralds rake from‖.........123 k
heralds to astonish us*.....209 v
love's heralds should be*..364 a
Herb-herb named in Latine..225 i
mark this curious herb....246 n
tend, plant, h., and flower**424 e
Herbaceous-oh h. treat......168 t
Herbarium-press best in the. 80 d
Herbless-seasonless, h.‖.....76 w
Herbs-choke the h. for want*643 n
early herbs are springing..661 u
gather'd the enchanted h.*441 l
herbs that scatter'd grow..304 b
lashes are the h. that look..191 p
love cannot be cured by h..723 c
more than h. and flowers...111 h
no doubt is a dinner of h...167 j
of h., and other country**..431 s
small herbs have grace*...289 q
sweet h. that searching eye.234 o
wholesome h. should grow.269 u
Hercules-about the club of..758 g
beards of H. and frowning*121 s
father, than I to Hercules*..102 d
Hercules have turned spit*.377 c
Hercules himself do what* 152 c
Hercules to bear the pile...579 o
love a Hercules*...........364 d
Herd-deer that left the h....388 c
herd would wish to reign...212 d
more numerous was the h..589 b
the lowing herd winds.....186 s
Herds-lowing herds to‡.....542 p
or flocks, or h., or human**149m
Here-I am h. here I remain..767 l
I am h.; I shall remain h...145 r
neither here nor there*....507 l
now h. now there, now.... 57 d
Hereafter-but if there be an.582w
of an unknown hereafter...599 r
points out an hereafter....315 l
the good hereafter........268 p
yet in the word "h."*..... 431 u
Hereditary-attends h........ 15 h
hereditary bondsmen‖.... 257 x
Heresy-holds becomes his**. 39 e
Heretic-h. girl of my soul...158 f
heretic in the truth**..... 39 e
Heritage-h. of old age is not. 9 k
noble by h. generous...... 78 b
part of earth's eternal h.... 79 n
that heritage of woe‖......370 g
Heritages-heirs to amplest§.. 66 r
Hermes-that moly that H**.277 o
Hermetic-with strange h....439 s
Hermit-a reverend h. grew..567 j
a sceptred hermit.......... 82 o
gentle hermit of the dale...300 e
I like an hermit, dwell.....567 l
man, the hermit, sigh'd...566 l
thou hermit, in the lonely..616 a
Hermitage-that for an h.....111 k
Hero-a h. perish, or a‡.....151 n
a man must indeed be a h..772 b
appears a h. in our eyes....455 s
aspires to be a h. must....649 l
Davus or a hero speaks....730 d
each man is a hero and....301 d

embarrassed—never h.‖....418 v
every one of us be a hero...301 a
God move the h.'s arm....640 k
h. always should be tall....301 c
h. is as much as one§.......301m
h. is not fed on sweets.....301 e
hero is the world-man.....300 y
hero lies still while the....134m
hero mean sincere man...301 a
a hero weeps; he is grown..309 o
hero, when his sword......301 f
in death a hero as in‡...... 80 h
is a hero and more.........209 e
it aids the hero, bids.......367 d
John Barleycorn was a h...648 i
know what a hero is§ 301m
millions a hero...........403 p
no man is a h. to his......502 r
orator who is not a hero....462 c
pushes the h. of yesterday.301 k
see the conquering hero...301 o
that proves the hero born‡. 10 c
the god-like hero sate...... 69 p
the Hero that here lies*...558 r
to a valet no man is a h....772 d
want a h.; an uncommon‖..300 z
worship of a hero.......301 b
Heroes-actors were also the.329 a
easy to be h. as to sit††....301 n
heroes as great have died‡.301 i
heroes! heaven-born band.301 j
h. in evil as well as in good.301 l
many heroes lived before...728 l
the heroes of old...........346 b
the heroes of your line.... .418 e
troops of h. undistinguished635 i
Heroic-good, heroic§........657 g
heroic deeds and hapless**.637w
heroic, stoic Cato‖........ 77 t
Heroically-heroically mad...476 o
Heroine-each maid a h.§....672 p
Heroism-poor-souled piece of583 a
the essence of heroism....104 e
Hero-king-Hener was the...535m
Hero-worship-h-w. exists...300aa
Herrings-Douglas in red h...442 c
neither h. nor frankincense.677 c
Herself-she'll close and be*..129 u
Hesitate-and h. dislike‡....537 r
Hesitation-in the very h.....710 k
Hesperides-in the H.*......364 d
ladies of the Hesperides**.. 35 l
this fair Hesperides*.......266 n
Hesperus-H. entreats thy...398 a
Hesperus that led the**....416m
Heterodoxy-h. is another...158 i
Hew-hew down and fell the*.389 l
of somebody to h. and.....470 c
Heweth-man that h. over...505 n
Hexameter-in the h. rises...476 i
Hexameters-epigrams in h...177 e
Hey-day-h-d. in the blood*... 11m
Hiccup-deign'd to h. or to‖..483 d
Hiccups-h. from the heart...110 f
Hickory-tree-under the h-t...614 l
Hid-cough, cannot be hid...501w
find where truth is hid*....623 i
h. himself among women..143 r
things h. and barr'd, you*..580 s
what is hid is unknown....713 s
Hidden-hidden in the green†.249 o
Hide-broad buttock, tender*. 21 d
cannot hide from view....248 k
disdains to hide his head...385 o
hide in cooling trees......323 o
h. their diminished heads**.499 u
h. their want of skill‡ ......674 j
h. themselves in drops*....591 x
h. with ornaments their‡...480 g
h. your diminish'd rays‡...576 p
how to hide one's ability...759 e
lies to h. it, makes it two..200 a
may man within him h.*...312 v
nay, and hide away...... 514 r
parchment hide...........157 j
seek to hide themselves*...329 x
to hide the fault I see‡.....343 e

Hideous–and makes night h.‡557 n
  making night hideous*.....417 k
  more h. when thou show'st*319 v
  most h. when adorned......763 p
  trembled at the h. name**.136 q
Hides–crannies when he*.....584 j
  he that h. a dark soul**....597 e
  h. a dark soul and foul**..352 o
  h. from himself its state..348 c
  hides the book of fate‡.....206 y
  h. the ruin that it feeds....232 b
  plighted cunning hides*....603 d
Hidest–that hidest in shade.231 l
Hiding–hiding of the fault*..208 f
Hiding-place–dark and lonely157 r
Hiding-places–their h-p.....236 l
High-arch'd so h. that giants*535 d
  as h. as heaven, as deep.....495 y
  as h. as the eagle by...... 59 o
  failed in the h. aim, as I...581 m
  h. as metaphysic wit..... 336 s
  judge between the h. and..563 j
  low as high he soared**.....13 j
  nothing is so high........707 j
  not proudly high...........236 j
  so high, that looking......298 m
  stand h. have many blasts*.152 e
  they that stand high*......287 g
  to Him no high no low‡.....275 p
  when h. and happy-need I‖.129 l
High-birth–h-b., vigour of*..602 h
High-born–where h-b. men‖...74 h
High-day–h-d. wit in........486 y
Higher–h. a man is in grace*310 w
  h. and onward drags a†....100 g
  higher than a two years¶..246 q
  h. than the perfect song....671 n
  lower to the higher next††.492 j
  one h. than himself dwells. 6 e
  sad soul go higher.........144 m
  see nothing h. than himself. 82 l
  selves to higher things†....373 c
  still higher................800 b
  sunbeams lifted higher§....571 r
Highest–aspiring to the h....677 a
  for the best grows highest.615 l
  highest and the lowest.....729 c
  if you wish to reach the h..677 g
  lowest to the highest......707 e
High-fed–h-f., long-lived..... 54 a
Highland–my sweet H. Mary.356 g
  spare his Highland Mary..203 a
Highlands–heart's in the H..296 n
High-life–nothing but h-l....113 o
Highly–what thou wouldst*. 84 n
High-road–h-r. that leads....115 p
Hill–a cot beside the hill.....117 j
  apart sat on a hill retir'd**.109 b
  April's coming up the hill..392 a
  by the wind-beaten hill ..117 q
  contentment climbs a h....642 i
  down behind the azure h.‖.585 g
  each h.; joyous the birds**.376 d
  heard on the hill...........410 b
  high on a h. a goodly cedar.612 j
  h. beside the silver Thames.532 n
  if the hill will not come to..481 m
  in the vale beneath the h...625 e
  king of France went up....534 p
  knowledge is the h. which.164 c
  liken it to climbing up a‖..200 k
  Mahomet will go to the h...481 m
  mine be the breezy hill.... 284 d
  noonday quiet holds the‡.. 71 i
  o'er every h. that under...227 m
  o'er h. and field October's..394 j
  oozes from the rocky hill.. 21 h
  over hill and plain.........507 b
  search the hill, the dale....245 h
  steep of echoing hill or**..670 j
  stood at the foot of the h..614 i
  surprised the hill..........228 d
  tents from hill to hill......640 j
  their haven under the hill†.446 c
  the top of the bare hill¶...391 m
  upon the rock-wreathed h.609 i
Hillock–pipe on her pastoral†.471 k

Hills–across the hills they†..366 h
  along the h. of Galilee the.. 94 n
  and my h. are white over..412 n
  beats strong amid the hills.411 m
  buffet round the hills†.....169 p
  cheerless over h. of gray...396 j
  daisies on the aguish hills..218 k
  digs h. because they do*...509 e
  domes the red-plough'd h.†541 g
  down between the hills..... 71 a
  everlasting h., changeless..108 j
  face of the high hills.......275 e
  fancy's rays the hills. .....346 e
  from the far-off hills..... 40 b
  from the inmost hills†.....417 s
  frosty summits of the h....400 r
  h. all rich with blossom'd‖.532 a
  h. peep o'er hills and Alps‡.402 u
  h. resound his worth.......277 f
  hills whose heads touch*...607 j
  infamous hills and**...... 88 a
  leaving on craggy h. and..625 c
  little space 'tween those h.586 a
  o'er the h. of the stormy...614 o
  on low hills outspread..... 394 e
  on thy seven h. of yore.... 98 m
  overlooks the highest*.....584 s
  over the h. and far away...367 s
  over the h. and far away...408 d
  over the h. and far away...411 b
  scatterings of the hills¶....238 h
  smite the hills with day....401 e
  spanning the h. like dawn.. 29 n
  the hills of Habersham....530 i
  the h. our fathers trod....424 q
  the hills were glad to bear¶.490 d
  to climb steep h. requires*.582 i
  to seek the distant hills....625 p
  walks on the windy hills...247 m
  whited air hides hills and..564 w
Hillside–h. of this life.......230 b
  up the hillside; and now... 51 f
Hillsides–the h. with.. .....583 r
Hill-tops–far h-t. towering..131 f
Hillyho-ho ! h. ! heigh O....395 b
Himself–each one is for h....761 l
  ennobled by himself by‡....454 g
  every man for h., and.....317 t
  every man for himself......497 j
  every one for himself......788 l
  God H. can't kill them.....573 n
  he but save himself........354 m
  h. can be his parallel...... 85 l
  himself he knoweth not....774 o
  h. is his own dungeon**....105 r
  how to love himself*......548 e
  lord of h.;—that heritage‖.370 g
  lord of h., though not.....484 d
  man sprung from himself. 15 s
  never to h. hath said.......118 j
  ruins of h. ! now worst†....535 u
  think too much of h.......788 h
  unless above h. he can.....370 u
Hind-pard to the hind*......101 y
Hinders–every drop hinders.590 l
Hindmost–Deil tak the h.....294 l
  devil take the hin'most....152 s
Hinge–no hinge nor loop*....159 c
Hinges–hinges of the knee*..215 q
  off the hinges.............. 407 c
  on golden hinges moving**.298 e
  on their hinges grate**.....299 l
Hint–it was my h. to speak*.607 j
  just hint a fault, and‡.....537 r
  lucky hint at truths........270 n
  upon this hint I spake*....365 a
Hints–hints for the better...122 o
Hip–catch him once upon*...528 q
  have yee him on the hip..498 aa
  I have you on the hip*.....500 g
  infidel, I have you on the*..528 s
Hippocreme–blushful H......649 n
Hire–h. me twenty cunning*.432 a
Hired–oblivion is not to be h.420 l
Hirelings–church lewd h.**..451 c
His–'tis h. at last who says††.514 g
Hiss–dismal universal hiss**.109 k

hiss of spray................598 q
  poor worms, they hiss at...642 m
Historian–h. and thy guest§. 99 c
  h. is a prophet looking.....772 f
  historian is wise.......... 301 u
  h. of my country's woes‡..302 e
  historian of my infancy¶...322 o
  Spring is your sole h.......617 q
Historians–all men are h.....302 b
Histories–h. are as perfect...301 u
  histories make men wise...170 c
  sin writes histories........770 l
  which supersede all h...... 65 n
History–anything but h. for.302 l
  a product of history.......336 x
  below the dignity of h..... 302 h
  changed the history of the.302 c
  exceeds an infamous h.. .310 e
  fact in woman's history....656 u
  gather out of history a....302 j
  great history of the land‡..657 g
  h., as it lies at the root.... 301 v
  h. casts its shadow far§...302 f
  history fades into fable....143 h
  [History] hath triumphed.302 i
  h. in all men's lives*.......493 i
  h. is as a tale that is told..371 h
  history is little else than a.302 k
  history is philosophy......301 p
  history is the essence......302 a
  h. is only the register of...772 e
  history must be false......302 l
  history of America........302 n
  history of pin-heads......344 t
  h. shall with full mouth*..184 d
  H.'s purchased page to‖...301 s
  h. with all her volumes‖...301 r
  love's history, as life's.....366 g
  principal office of history..712 d
  read their h. in a nation's..302 d
  single event of past h......190 v
  stock of history¶..........302 m
  the dignity of history......301 q
  the history of the world...428 b
  the world's history is the..772 g
  they who live in history§...302 g
  thy history fully unfold*... 84 h
  unwritten h. unfathomed.. 31 e
  upon some reverend h......536 c
History-books–blank in h-b. 301 t
Hit–but just to hit‡.........324 m
  hand can always hit.......205 t
  hard is to say harder to**..360 u
  hit, a very palpable hit*...422 s
  h. hard unless it rebounds. 4 t
  hit the nail on the head....499 aa
  lie, 'twill seem a lucky hit‖.124 f
  surest way to h. a woman's.662 n
Hither–come h. come*.......610 d
Hive–comrades in the..... ...322 e
  shall make a h. for bees...470 w
  stock and tend your hive...657 c
  than the sweet ambrosial..652 e
Hives–from their h. and*....122 c
Hiving–h. wisdom with‖.....580 k
Hoard–farmer's wintry h....424 r
  why he would h. up those. 48 b
Hoarded–his most h. chest‖..329 l
Hoards–hoards his rising.....387 h
  still he sighs, for hoards...387 h
Hobbes–H. clearly proves...640 l
Hobby-horses–puppet plays. 14 n
Hobgoblin–of little minds....107 i
Hoboken–count de H........643 c
Hobson–'tis H.'s choice;.... 92 d
Hock–hock itself be less‖....128 d
Hocus-pocus-law is a sort of.437 q
Hoeder–H. the blind old§....277 j
Hog–hog in Epicurus' sty.... 21 t
  steal the hog, and give the.504 n
  the hog that ploughs not‡. 21 v
Hogs–raise the price of h.*... 93 u
  than hogs eat acorns.......353 f
Hoist–h. me up and show*...104 x
Hold–her roomy h. within...446 f
  first cries "h., enough"*..639 i
  h. so fast as love can do ...356 i

in a general honest thought*418 *l*
in hearts keep open, h., and.621 *p*
I should be honest..........305 *n*
love him that is honest*.... 83 *s*
made h. by an act of........620 *d*
of an "honest man".......... 85 *n*
party h. is party expediency482 *k*
that byrd ys not honest....504*w*
though it be honest, it is*..415 *a*
tis well to be honest........ 75 *d*
titles are marks of h. men..418 *r*
twelve h. men have decided331 *h*
was once thought honest*.626 *k*
whip me such h. knaves*..336 *i*
win us with honest trifles*...623 *g*
world's grown honest*.....305*m*
Honestly–h. rather than......801 *f*
to receive h. is the best.....594 *s*
Honesty–arm'd so strong in.*305 *l*
departs with his own h......305 *d*
found them in mine h.*....305 *j*
full of love and honesty*...665 *q*
honesty is the best policy..305 *b*
neither honesty, manhood*. 84 *i*
not length, but honestie....305 *e*
whose honesty the devil*...174 *e*
you'll show a little h.*....106 *n*
Honey–and bees made h.....510 *a*
as the honey of Hybla*......659 *a*
Attic h. thickens the nectar.181 *l*
both its gall and honey......723*m*
doth stay and honey run..321 *s*
drain those honey wells.....321 *t*
faint for your h., my sweet†541 *t*
flower that smells of honey.233 *c*
gather h. all the day........322 *f*
gather h. from a weed.....650 *h*
hoarding golden honey.....392 *q*
h. in her mouth, gall in .. 369 *e*
h. of delicious memories†..381 *v*
hover where h. brims over.618 *f*
Hyblæn or Hymethian h...180 *h*
moon—so called—of honey.397 *p*
nor h. make, nor pair......666*m*
shaking out honey.........229 *b*
sweetest h. is loathsome in*. 26 *f*
the pedigree of honey......321 *o*
words sweet as h. from‡....664 *s*
Honey–bags–h–b. steal from*.197 *e*
Honey–bee–h–b. that wanders321*m*
Honey–bees–work the h–b.*...322 *b*
Honeycomb–milk and h...... 17 *k*
their mighty honeycomb....322 *e*
Honey–cups–h–c. bending low.220 *u*
Honey–dew–doth the h–d*....592 *z*
he on honey–dew hath fed..166*m*
Honeyed–kisses h. by oblivion334 *h*
Honeysuckle–h. link'd........231 *a*
honeysuckle loved to crawl.231 *d*
h. round the porch†.........231 *f*
plucked a honeysuckle.....231 *c*
tilted honeysuckle horns... 47 *s*
with flaunting h.*........231 *b*
Honeysuckles–h. ripen'd by*.231 *e*
Honey–throated–O h–t. warbler52 *h*
Honor–a good livery of h.*...306*m*
all is lost save honor.......772 *l*
and in honour clear‡........454 *g*
an honour to Shakespeare.550 *i*
a roll of honour............281 *r*
be with you a point of h....627 *s*
book of h. razed quite*....444 *l*
but honor is of man....... 69 *o*
can honour set a leg*......306 *y*
chastity of h. which felt.... 87 *s*
dead on the field of honour.306 *d*
died full of h. and years....403 *j*
discerning thine h. from*..122 *a*
every man his true honor....712 *p*
feel your honor grip.......208 *o*
fortunes, and our sacred h.419 *d*
from top of honour*.......156 *v*
helps the hurt that h. feels†390 *h*
here h. binds me, and I.....772 *i*
his honour decayed, his....616 *h*
his h. rooted in dishonor†. 85 *q*
honour and shame from no‡306 *i*

h., but an empty bubble....473 *s*
h. comes to you be ready to.306 *f*
h. follows him against his..801 *r*
h. hath no skill in surgery*.306 *y*
h. is a mere scutcheon*... 306 *y*
honor is like an island......772 *j*
honour is not won..........306 *e*
honour is purchas'd by the.306 *e*
h. is the reward of virtue..749 *i*
h. is the reward of virtue..801 *q*
h. is to feel no sin†. ......106 *d*
honor lies in honest toil....305*w*
h., love, obedience, troops* 11 *r*
h. on this happy day.......628 *c*
honour peereth in the......306 *j*
honour pricks me on*......306 *y*
honour's at the stake*......513 *l*
h. sinks where commerce..111 *a*
honour sits smiling at the..307 *a*
h. that but tedious**.......103 *f*
h., the spur that pricks....306 *g*
h. to his ancestral honors..799 *o*
h. travels in a strait so*....306 *q*
h. were purchased by the*.483 *a*
honor without deserving...256 *c*
h. women ! they entwine..796 *h*
hurts h. than deep wounds.305 *t*
if I lose mine honour*......306 *s*
in fair honor's field.........210 *x*
it is a dropsied honour*....147 *a*
jealous in honour*........444 *k*
let h. in one eye and death*318 *k*
let us do what h. demands.772 *h*
lie in h.'s truckle–bed.....305 *u*
loved I not honor more.....360 *d*
mine honour let me try*...306 *v*
money brings h., friends**390 *a*
new–made h. doth forget*. ·306 *k*
passed from a daylight of..608 *a*
perseverance keeps h.*....472 *p*
place where h.'s lodged....305 *t*
pluck bright honour from*.306 *u*
pluck up downed h. by*...306 *l*
post of h. is a private......109 *u*
post of h. shall be mine....110 *p*
power to honour you......290 *e*
probity is true honor.......803 *r*
public honor is security....123 *h*
sense of h. is of so fine.....305 *s*
sense of h. subdue your....687 *b*
sin to covet honor*.......120 *v*
smatch of honour in it*....306 *x*
staff of h. for mine age*... 11 *p*
stake everything on her h..772 *n*
than wound my honor....305 *r*
that clear honour*.........306 *t*
that honour would thee do*116 *a*
the bed of honour lain....305 *u*
the law often allows what.775 *k*
there all the honour lies‡...306 *i*
those of honour pay.......269 *k*
'tis a throne where honour*.551 *l*
titles do not reflect honor...772 *o*
titles of honour add not....305 *y*
to defend your honour.....305 *x*
toils of h. dignify repose...523 *v*
virtue, fame, and honor...739 *r*
void of all h., avaricious...512 *r*
welcome maids of honor...248 *n*
what is honour ? a word*..306 *y*
when h. dies, the man......373 *f*
while the h. thou hast.....305 *v*
whom does false honor aid.682 *t*
without money honor is....772 *k*
woman's h. rests on manly.660 *o*
woo h., but to wed it*.....306*w*
your existence to your h....712*m*
Honorable–all h men*........306 *o*
Brutus is an h. man*.......306 *o*
for he's honourable*.......306 *p*
h. and upright life.........721 *p*
honorable is also safest...712 *n*
in h. dealing you should...712 *l*
it is h. to reach the second.677 *a*
more honorable than age....10 *o*
what is just and honorable..803*cc*
Honorably–courageously and800*cc*

Honored–by strangers h. and‡137*m*
forever h., and forever‡....403 *g*
h. beyond all praising......664 *a*
more h. in the breach*....127 *l*
the law ; it has honored us.439 *g*
what makes him h.*........538 *e*
who is honored now but....329 *e*
Honors–add greater h. to*... 39 *l*
and h. more than "lady".660 *x*
bears his blushing h.*...... 76 *f*
birth–day of medical h..... 98 *i*
deprived of h. or of wealth..354 *a*
fading h. of the dead...... 13 *u*
full of years and of h.......712 *o*
he does honors a man......772*m*
he gave his h. to the*......139*m*
h. and employments rise...114 *r*
h. are great burdens.......306 *c*
honors come by diligence..102 *n*
h. of genius are eternal....706 *d*
h. thrive, when rather*....306 *r*
in more substantial h......418 *j*
mindless of its just h. ¶....551 *d*
of any height of honors... 80 *r*
seek nor to despise h.......802*m*
shine in more substantial..306 *h*
white honours wed........218 *h*
Hood–anemone in snowy h..217 *g*
a page of Hood may do a.. 74 *s*
talk of H. and Little John.578 *j*
with him that wears a h...163 *a*
Hoods–all hoods make not.*.494 *ii*
Hoodwinked–judgment h....409 *c*
Hoof–basest horn of his h.*.278 *d*
Hoof'd–round–hoof'd.*...... 21 *d*
Hoofs–hoofs of a swinish... 341 *o*
Hook–arming wire of your... 19 *f*
attaine by hooke or crooke.309 *a*
by hooke or crooke*.......496 *v*
by hook or crook has......508*gg*
flung his golden h. down...397 *q*
his h. was such as heads.... 18 *f*
kite the covered hook.....745 *f*
let your h. always be cast..702*m*
my bended h. shall pierce*. 18 *i*
they are a baited hook.....177 *d*
two–inched h. is better I... 18 *e*
Hookas–divine in h. glorious‖456 *f*
Hoop–about a hoop of gold*.434 *n*
admiration did not h. at*..608 *v*
the h.'s bewitching round.453 *k*
without a hoop, without....128 *g*
Hooting–h. at the glorious..520 *k*
Hoots–that nightly h. and*.. 53 *b*
Hop–hop a little from her*..364 *x*
hop for his profit I thus....650 *e*
Hopped–that h. from side... 47 *f*
Hope–abandon h. all ye who.772 *t*
about the neck of hope†...366 *n*
a chastened hope that ever. 80 *k*
a high h. for a low heaven*.467 *n*
alive with sudden hope....230 *q*
all hope abandon, ye who..307 *p*
a mother's secret hope.....307 *x*
and break it to our hope*..492 *r*
arm ! advance ! h. of France635*m*
as forlorn hope.............156 *v*
as h. and fear alternate... 75 *u*
ask not, h. thou not too....588 *b*
auspicious hope! in thy....307 *i*
bear H.'s tender blossoms..308 *q*
better to h. than to despair.772 *s*
bitterness of death, is h...308*aa*
blessed leisure for love or..342 *v*
boy, my hope, my hap..... 88 *t*
but I always hope.........713 *a*
can innocence hope for....320 *i*
Christ is my hope....... 804 *v*
each joy and new–born h...539 *k*
earthly h., how bright so..307*w*
exchanges h. for certainty..365 *q*
Faith and H. triumphant..164 *u*
fear or h. may be inspired.152 *n*
feed on hope, to pine with.155 *i*
final hope is flat despair**.149 *l*
fooled with h. men favour.347 *h*
for peace do not hope......470 *v*

SHAKESPEARE *; MILTON **; WORDSWORTH ¶; BYRON ‖; TENNYSON †; LOWELL ††; POPE ‡; LONGFELLOW §.

fresh h. the lover's heart**. 51 *l*
God shall be my hope*.....275 *s*
hang themselves in hope...375 *i*
having naught else but h. §.308 *d*
heavenly h. is all serene...307 *w*
hits where h. is coldest*....189 *k*
h. against hope and ask....308 *j*
hope and God............ .807 *i*
h. and youth are children. 308 *x*
hope beyond the shadow...316 *g*
hope dead lives nevermore. 308 *p*
h., deceitful as it is, serves.772 *p*
hope ebbs and flows like... 74 *a*
hope elevates, and joy**...308 *g*
hope enchanted smiled......307 *m*
hope ever urges on.........713 *c*
hope for a season. ....258 *c*
hope for fairer times in...569 *o*
hope hath happy place.....307 *k*
h., he called, belief in God.487 *i*
hope in God ... .807 *h*
hope is a lover's staff*.... 308 *u*
hope is brightest when it..243 *c*
hope is but the dream of. 308 *n*
hope is theirs by fancy fed.307 *v*
h. is the sweetest of the....307 *y*
h. kiss'd love, and love†...366 *n*
h., like a cordial innocent.309 *h*
hope like the gleaming ...307 *s*
hope may vanish but can.. 76 *i*
hope my heart can cheer...308 *c*
hope never comes**........299 *e*
h. not for impossibilities...317 *j*
hope! of all ills that........307 *o*
hope of impunity is the....712 *r*
h. of my ancestors endures.804 *n*
hope persevereth, still.....663 *c*
hope's gentle gem..........228 *n*
hope smiled when your¶...221 *b*
h. springs eternal in the‡..308 *l*
hope's perpetual breath¶..272 *l*
hope springs exulting on..307 *g*
hope starves without. .....267 *e*
hope still grovels in this...205 *s*
h. tells a flattering tale ...309 *q*
h. that is unwilling to be¶.150 *g*
h. the balm and life-blood.307 *c*
h. though hope were lost..307 *e*
h.! thou nurse of young....307 *f*
hope to meet shortly again. 2 *p*
hope to my heart.......... 165 *j*
h. travels through, nor.‡...308 *m*
h. will make thee young...308 *x*
hope withering fled—and¶.149 *f*
hope, with eyes so fair.... 307 *n*
hope with hope exulting...261 *r*
hope with meaning rife.... 60 *a*
hope without an object....307 *t*
I do not buy hope ....713 *b*
I hope for better things....804 *t*
in a patient hope I rest.....198 *r*
I incline to hope rather**.. 82 *h*
in Faith and H. the world‡. 86 *s*
in hope.....................808 *q*
in this sign is my hope....801 *m*
in trembling hope repose.. 86 *g*
is man a child of hope¶....309 *f*
is there any hope?‡........275 *u*
is there no hope? the sick.440 *c*
jot of heart or hope**....... 61 *f*
last star of hope may......772 *r*
least can spare is hope....307 *d*
leave the light of hope...307 *j*
left his Hope with all .....309 *d*
let not hope prevail........309 *g*
life there is hope............712 *q*
life was all men's hope....299 *w*
like strength is felt from‡..579 *g*
love can h. where reason..360 *i*
love would die when hope†.366 *n*
mercie ever h. to have.....382 *t*
might hope for it here......470 *t*
more plentiful than hope.536 *o*
my hope is in God..........804 *w*
my hope is not broken....798 *m*
my own hope is, a sun...101 *b*
never to hope again*......535 *b*

no change, no pause, no h...150 *c*
no h. when thou art gone...569 *e*
none without h. e'er lov'd..360 *i*
of hope laid waste.........567 *f*
other hope had she none§...521 *f*
other medicine but only*..308 *v*
out of hope of all*..........211 *o*
poise of hope and fear**... 82 *h*
pray, if thou canst, with h.487 *n*
promise—hope—believe‖...204 *j*
safest hope is in Heaven...804 *x*
setting of a great hope is§.308 *e*
sickening pang of hope... 308 *s*
so farewell h. and with**..149 *j*
so is hope changed.........257 *f*
sorrow'd after hope†.......366 *n*
speak of hope to the.......217 *u*
still on hope relies....... 307 *u*
sudden hope and fear......247 *b*
sweet Hope! celestial......308 *b*
the faintest h. should be...772 *q*
the hope of immortality...714 *j*
there clung one hope like‖.307 *h*
there is life there's hope...307 *r*
the tender leaves of hope*. 76 *f*
things which you don't h..308 *k*
though h. be weak or sick.487 *n*
through the sunset of hope.308 *y*
thrown from his hope**....257 *r*
to hope is to enjoy.........784 *t*
to hope till hope creates... 308 *z*
to hope, to know...........367 *h*
true h. is swift and flies*... 57 *q*
vain is the h. by colouring.446 *t*
walk with banish'd hope†..366 *m*
we h. to grow old and we..754 *k*
we hope to live.............293 *o*
we live by Admiration, H.¶.351 *w*
we live without hope.......772 *u*
we may gain from hope**..308 *h*
what hope of harmony*·...407 *h*
what is h. but deceiving....167 *l*
whence this pleasing hope.315 *l*
when hope was born†......401 *h*
when hope was high..... ..155 *d*
when h. was young and.... 56 *f*
where my own did h. to sip484 *a*
where there is no hope.....308 *a*
whilst I breathe, I hope. ..799 *aa*
white-handed hope**.......198 *a*
who bids me hope, and....308 *f*
with a sure h. and trust....104 *c*
within his breast hope......105 *w*
with Nature, H., and Poesy672 *c*
work without h. draws......307 *l*
worth, so also has Hope.... 74 *k*
you never bade me h., 'tis..492 *p*
youth, health, and h., may.620 *a*
Hoped-loved much, h. little..758 *o*
Hopeful-cheerful and h. than 10 *b*
the mind is hopeful......744 *m*
Hopeless-h. lays his dead....150 *f*
thieves, all h. of their lives*122 *d*
Hopes-airy h. my children¶..565 *w*
and long hopes joy.........501 *p*
between me and my hopes.312 *o*
dearest h. in pangs are born619 *h*
farewell the h. of court*...308 *t*
high hopes of living**......170 *q*
his hopes became a part.... 79 *n*
h. are not always realized..713 *a*
hopes belied our fears......135 *e*
h. have been disappointed..702 *s*
h. have precarious life......307 *q*
h. I had while fortune......713 *d*
h. in adversity and fears...735 *a*
h. in heaven do dwell*..... 308 *t*
h., like tow'ring falcons...308 *o*
hopes of honest men.......300 *j*
h. on the heart of woman..796 *n*
h. that fall like flowers....197 *q*
h. that make us men†......309 *c*
hopes, what are they¶......309 *e*
joys but that our h. cease..754 *m*
late on hopes depended*...508 *x*
mighty to inspire new h....751 *t*
mistress dear his h. convey.628 *c*

mortal h. defeated and¶....592 *s*
my fondest hopes decay....155 *f*
my hopes are flown........558 *d*
new hopes to raise.........658 *d*
of all our h. have built.....141 *i*
often only by what it h....672 *a*
our hearts, our h., are all§..118 *f*
our hopes and then our....140 *u*
pays our h. with something347 *g*
promise according to our h.492 *q*
ratifies hopes, and urges...717 *c*
reaps from the h. which... 13 *h*
so my hopes decay‡........376 *i*
the hopes of all men‖......325 *o*
the h. of future years§......469 *c*
though varying wishes, h..381 *c*
upon my startled hopes....324 *i*
wholly hopes to be.........492 *d*
without our h., without....370 *k*
youth! how buoyant are...672 *n*
Hoping-patience is the art of782 *r*
Horace-H. giving the poets..551 *b*
nor suffers H. more in‡ ...514 *i*
quote H., Juvenal..........516 *m*
then farewell Horace‖......207 *v*
Horatio-in my mind's eye H.*315 *e*
Horizon-and on the h. black.575 *w*
h. which it forms is the.... 96 *e*
ruby from the h.'s ring§.....585 *l*
Horn-basest h. of his hoof is*278 *d*
blow his wreathed horn¶... 92 *e*
h. before from age to age... 68 *m*
fed her exhausted horn....399 *d*
flower of the golden h......225 *g*
from out her lavish horn...424 *r*
his h. full of good news*....449 *e*
huntsman winds his horn.. 87 *j*
huntsman with the cheerful 87 *k*
Moses lends his Pagan h.‡.. 75 *t*
of horn and morn and...... 87 *m*
Plenty with her flowing h..543 *n*
pour'd through the mellow.378 *v*
then h. for h. they stretch..294 *l*
wind the merry horn....... 87 *f*
with pellucid h. secured are 68 *g*
Hornpipes-sings psalms to*..557 *o*
Horns-curst cow hath short.494 *n*
hang them on the h. o'*.... 26 *p*
he has hay on his horns....677 *m*
shrilly to the well-tun'd h.*169 *l*
Horny-blessed are the h.††..667 *b*
Horrid-except that h. one‖...478 *l*
Horror-after dreams of h....470 *b*
brow of bragging h.*........526 *a*
earth shaking with horror.612 *c*
filled up with horror .....105 *a*
gild the brown horror......399 *t*
h. heavy sat on every......208 *t*
h. itself in that fair scene..767 *j*
horror wide extends his....546 *n*
inward h. of falling into....315 *l*
offence inspires less h......437 *i*
swings the scaly h. of his**153 *h*
Horrors-abyss of fears and**105 *u*
hail, horrors, hail**........299 *g*
on horror's head horrors*..523 *d*
sound of undistinguish'd h.640 *h*
Horse-a dark h., which had.. 20 *o*
a h., a horse, my kingdom* 21 *b*
a h. should have*.......... 21 *d*
a h. to fly, to swim the.... 21 *a*
argument, a man's no h.... 26 *t*
dearer than his horse†......466 *a*
give me another horse*... 21 *c*
God's me, my horse*.......640 *f*
h. doth with the horseman.389 *o*
h. is drawn by the cart.... 28 *l*
like a full-hot horse*....... 17 *o*
looked a given h. in the....498 *cc*
my h., my ox, my ass*......645 *o*
my h. without peer........ 20 *m*
one horse was blind¶.. .... 20 *r*
philosophy is a good h. in..473 *e*
prove the better horse......505 *i*
run their horse to death* .. 38 *s*
set the cart before the h...503 *hh*
some in their horse*........273 *f*

SHAKESPEARE *; MILTON **; WORDSWORTH ¶; BYRON ‖; TENNYSON †; LOWELL ††; POPE ‡; LONGFELLOW §.

SHAKESPEARE *; MILTON **; WORDSWORTH ¶; BYRON ‖; TENNYSON †; LOWELL ††; POPE ‡; LONGFELLOW §.

while the rich infant nurs'd 672 *i*
Infatuated–i. and besotted...593 *p*
Infect–sickness doth infect*..156 *q*
  would i. to the north star*.659 *t*
Infected–i. some chairs and..114 *p*
  i. that the infected spy ‡...586 *o*
  i. with the same disease....716 *h*
  raven o'er the i. house*.... 55 *d*
  saws off th' infected part..439 *r*
Infection–against i. and the* 116 *b*
  flower with base i. meet*...643 *o*
Infects–oft i. the wisest*.....209 *r*
Inferior–i. is he to a gold mine 643 *e*
  the last is i. to the first....679 *f*
Inferiority–admits his i......803*dd*
  those pangs of inferiority..580 *u*
Infidel–a daring i. (and such..522 *o*
  i., I have you on the hip*...528 *s*
Infidels–Jews might kiss and‡434 *k*
Infinite–binds us to the i......198 *h*
  for both are infinite*......364 *h*
  how infinite in faculty* ...372 *r*
  is an Infinite in him......286 *k*
  sees the I. shadowed forth..670 *b*
  things seemed infinite¶.... 39 *n*
Infinitude–stood vast i.**....462 *s*
Infinity–divine in its infinity.558 *c*
  of a sort of infinity.......575*m*
Infirm–infirm and weary§... 10 *l*
Infirmities–bear his friend's*.262 *c*
  creature of habits and i....326 *u*
Infirmity–infirmity doth*....295 *q*
  last i. of noble mind.......385 *b*
  last i. of noble mind*....202 *d*
Inflict–those who inflict.....582 *u*
Influence–bereaves of their¶.319 *j*
  born where Heav'n's i.‡...633 *a*
  bright eyes rain influence** 192 *w*
  celestial i. round me shed..308 *b*
  circle of its influence...... 15 *n*
  constant i. a peculiar grace¶319 *q*
  influence if now I court*...256 *w*
  influence of one true loving.318 *q*
  i. of the most received*....207 *c*
  i. on the public mind.......427 *e*
  shed their selectest i.** ...376 *d*
  sing their i. on this lower ..577 *h*
  unawed by influence and.. 436 *n*
  vivifying i. in man's life... 6 *e*
  with softest i. breathes.....539 *k*
Influenced–i. even by the....125 *h*
Influences–ideas, atoms, i....336 *q*
  its changeful i. given......619 *f*
  potent in their own i......151 *e*
Inform–bus'ness is but to i..586*m*
  inform the mind...........325 *a*
Information–find i. upon it...337 *l*
Informations–i. against this* 174 *e*
Informed–where we desire to 26 *r*
Informing–judges without i..331 *c*
Infortune–worste kynde of i. 387 *y*
Infraction–prize th. i. of..... 43 *p*
Ingener–does tire the i.*.....658 *x*
Ingenious–bold, quick, i.*.... 90 *p*
  for those ingenious men ..354 *a*
Inglorious–mute i. Milton....284 *s*
Ingloriously–is overcome i....688 *r*
  not i. or passively..........146 *n*
Ingots–ass whose back with* 642 *v*
  chests containing ingots‖..389 *l*
Ingrateful–multitude to be*..319 *u*
Ingratitude–as man's i.*......319 *u*
  hate i. more in a*..........319 *t*
  i. calls forth reproaches....770 *u*
  ingratitude is monstrous*..319 *u*
  i. more strong*............320 *a*
  ingratitude of those who...319 *o*
  i's. a weed of every clime...319*m*
  i. thou marble-hearted*....319 *v*
Ingratitudes–monster of i.*..602 *x*
Ingredient–i. is a devil*.....326 *h*
  necessary i. of genius......467 *f*
Ingredients–i. of our*........332 *w*
Ingress–a man's i. into the...347 *j*
Inhabitant–pile without i....518 *r*
Inhabitants–i. have the......526 *d*
  inhabitants o' the earth*....25 *k*

Inherit–doth inherit pain*....463 *h*
  inherit in the grave........286 *b*
  i. righteousnesse then......342 *h*
  tho' he i. nor the pride..... 46 *c*
Inheritance–by the right of..552 *n*
  i. of free descent*.........438 *n*
  inheritance of it*..........252 *u*
  your i. in luxuries........179 *q*
Inheritor–succeed as his i.*..570 *b*
  thou little young i. of a‖ ... 30 *s*
Inherits–i. every virtue ......535 *l*
  rich man's son i. carest†...642 *n*
Inhuman–ev'ythin' thet's††..309 *v*
Inhumanity–i. is caught......126 *o*
  man's i. to man ....870 *e*
Iniquities–scourge his own i..635 *r*
Iniquity–and hated iniquity..332 *l*
  brother of iniquity........269 *q*
  monster of iniquity........ 687 *o*
Injure–I ne'er could i. you...199 *x*
  i. the property of another..715 *s*
Injured–forgiveness to the i..255 *j*
  friend must not be injured.704 *t*
  he who has injured thee....716 *c*
  the man who seems to have 677 *l*
  those whom we have i......711 *t*
Ingers–i. all on 'em the††....309 *v*
Injures–hate the man that i.‡.264 *r*
  the act of God i. no one....675 *e*
Injuries–neck under your i.*. 33 *h*
  prefer his i. to his heart*...628 *n*
  resent injuries or make....638 *g*
  saints in your injuries*....660 *g*
Injury–a life of i. and crime..388 *h*
  benefit and an injury*......548 *e*
  hast added insult to injury 716 *u*
  injury done to character....683 *d*
  no injury is done.... ....716 *a*
  strong sense of i. often ....716 *b*
  than to revenge an injury..507 *k*
  ungrateful man does an i...715 *q*
Injustice–and jealousy i.....656 *q*
  authority for their i.......574 *t*
  i. in the end produces......773 *j*
  justice is extreme i........717 *k*
  i. swift, erect and.........320 *f*
  mortgage his injustice.....212 *h*
  the fear of suffering i......774 *j*
  the severest injustice......720 *q*
  with i. is corrupted*.......333 *a*
Ink–all whites are ink*......292 *l*
  a small drop of ink‖.......427 *i*
  be gall enough in thy ink*..471 *t*
  dipt me in i. my parents‡..429 *l*
  fallen into a pit of ink*....290*m*
  kept from paper, pen, and.429 *n*
  he hath not drunk ink*....516 *q*
  much water with their ink.783 *l*
  the i. of the scholar is more.429 *d*
  to drown in ink...........471 *n*
  until his i. were temper'd*.480*m*
  worse for ink and thee.....471 *n*
  write till your ink be dry*..663 *l*
Inlaid–i. with patines of*....576 *w*
Inland–though i. far we be¶..317 *b*
  tract of inland ground¶....353 *u*
Inlaying–i. their intricate....394 *f*
Inmate–some i. of the skies‡. 16 *l*
Inn–by a good tavern or inn..433 *j*
  dark inn, the grave........285 *n*
  for the next inn he spurs..603*m*
  harbour'd in one inn.......493 *p*
  not a home, but an inn.....722 *d*
  reached a village inn¶......433 *l*
  take mine ease in mine inn*.433 *j*
  the world's an i., and death 668 *q*
  the worst i.'s worst room‡.433 *h*
  to gain the timely inn*.....625 *n*
  warmest welcome, at an i...433 *k*
  world's an i., and death....110 *n*
Inn-keeper–a crafty i-k. at...176 *b*
Inns–from i. of molten blue..162 *i*
  should not go to inns......260 *k*
Innocence–betrayed my**....608 *h*
  blow that i. can give......320 *h*
  but innocence shall make*.320*m*
  can innocence hope for.....320 *i*

even i. loses courage........71*m*
glides in modest innocence.143 *i*
her innocence a child....... 78 *z*
innocence a fear ‡..........477 *q*
i. has nothing to dread.....773 *k*
innocence has record made. 90 *s*
innocence in genius, and...513 *h*
i. is not accustomed to.....756 *o*
mind conscious of i........681 *b*
Mirth and Innocence ‖......292 *t*
narrow innocence it is.....716 *e*
O, white i., that thou......320 *p*
plain and holy innocence*..320 *l*
sense, sweet, of my i.*.....320 *n*
stumbles on i. sometimes..332 *g*
surest guard is i..........632 *q*
temper joined with i....... 88 *l*
was innocence for i.*......320 *o*
where glad i. reigns........117 *k*
Innocency–of our lost i...... 23 *d*
Innocent–and innocent as gay 661 *h*
  both are cheering and i.... 30 *s*
  crime deemed i. on earth.. 123 *l*
  halfe, or altogether i......523 *i*
  illusions, however innocent 622 *d*
  innocent, though free..... 77 *k*
  God made all pleasures i...475 *q*
  minds i. and quiet take....491 *v*
  noble and innocent girl... 87 *t*
  O God, keep me innocent..773*m*
  oh, keep me innocent......320 *j*
  that's innocent within ‡ ...106 *d*
  to slay the innocent*......644 *n*
  we become i. when we .....773 *l*
Innocuous–i. desuetude these436 *x*
Inordinate–every i. cup is*...326 *h*
Inquisitive–not so i., nor so.. 93 *g*
  shun the inquisitive person 716 *f*
Inquisitor–will of its i.......296 *s*
Insane–eaten on the i. root*..321 *j*
  fumes of that i. elation....592 *x*
  more insane than to vent..701 *b*
  one vast insane asylum....321 *b*
Insanity–power to charm... 320 *v*
Inscription–emigrant is the§.183 *k*
  i. moulders from the.......143 *h*
  let there be no i. upon my.182 *p*
  th' i. value but the rust‡... 22 *i*
Inscriptions–in lapidary i. a..419 *e*
Insect–amber enveloped the.176 *s*
  fair insect ! that, with....324 *d*
  happy insect! what can be.323*m*
  i. midst his works I view...321 *r*
  the i.'s gilded wings‡..... 46 *s*
  winged i., or the chrysalis.483 *i*
Insects–i. of each tiny size...394 *b*
  insects there is stirred....405 *q*
  plants, pursuing insects... 45 *d*
  silken-wing'd i. of the sky.391 *o*
Insect-tribes–compared your.424 *k*
Insect-youth–the i-y. are on..672 *k*
Insensible–'tis i., then*......306 *y*
Inseparable–one and i........627 *q*
Inside-hurt o' th' i. of a.....671 *d*
Insignificancy–i. and an.... 78 *k*
Insincerity–i. is the most....144 *h*
Insinuate–but i. what is true.480 *u*
Insipidity–to whose glorious.589*w*
Insnare–imperial race i.‡....291 *l*
Insolence-flown with i. and**416 *i*
  insolence if unpunished....773 *n*
Inspects–wisdom! which i....652 *b*
Inspiration–boldest lyric i...479 *d*
  i. expounds experience.....100 *t*
  my theme, my i...........276 *g*
  the sibyl without the i.....101 *c*
  without the inspiration... 314 *y*
Inspirations–inventions. i....118 *r*
Inspire–can inspire with wit.652 *n*
  i. it most are fortunate... .365 *i*
  inspire mirth and youth**.393 *e*
Inspired-eyes upraised as...378 *v*
  Homer who i. the poet.....481 *d*
  inspired by loftier views...346 *z*
  fury, rapt, inspired....... 17 *h*
  Socrates, whom, well i.**..651 *d*
  with fury, rapt, inspir'd....465 *k*

SHAKESPEARE *; MILTON **; WORDSWORTH ¶; BYRON ‖; TENNYSON †; LOWELL ††; POPE ‡; LONGFELLOW §.

or out of breath with joy..647 h
our joy is dead and only....329 o
pain for promised joy....154 x
perfect joy therein I find..385 f
promise of exceeding joy..394 g
quaff immortality and j.**316m
remember days of joy.....287 u
renews the life of joy in...641m
rose on her cheek is my j..355 k
second bliss in joy........261 r
short is his joy ; he feels‡.. 54 g
sighs which perfect joy†....553 g
smiles of joy, the tears....623 b
snatch a fearful joy........329 q
Sol in joy is seen to leave..530 j
song of great joy that the.. 95 j
source of every joy........109 y
stars weep, sweet with joy.153 x
stern joy which warriors...443 p
still the secret j. partake‡..633 c
such joy ambition finds**.. 13m
sung in my halls of joy....557 k
sweeten present joy.......569 n
sweetest joy, the wildest...355 g
sweet joy which comes. ...330 c
sweet Robin is all my joy*.329 v
tell me not of joy......... 57 e
their pleasure takes joy...293 d
the j. of youth and health..655 t
the joy is mutual, and I'm.334 i
the joy, that it may bring..574 e
the perfectest herald of*...554 z
the power of imparting joy.190 u
the raptured thrill of joy..655 a
there's j. in the mountains¶391 m
the touch of joy‖.........560 r
this is alone life, joy......472 q
till joy shall overtake.....138 a
to joy and play............346 e
treasury of everlasting j.*..298 s
true joy are reaping‖.......329 l
turns at the touch of joy...548 q
'twill heighten all his joy..648 i
variety alone gives joy....630 c
variety's the source of joy.629 v
wear a face of j., because¶.330 e
what music, breathing joy.605 n
will give joy to me... ...290 e
wish you all the joy that*..330 w
with all that joy can give‡.463 f
with careless j. we thread..236 d
with joy and love**.......146 s
work of joy and require....733 h
world no joy but this......131 e
writhed not at passed joy..329 r
Joyful–j. let the poet be....478 n
Joyous–God has formed for..732 f
Joyousness–half frantic in..641 j
Joys–and half our j. renew...380 q
a spirit-voyce, and vocall j.489 w
but breathes, like perfect j. 41 h
chief of all love's joys.....358 a
consoling music for the j...568 p
Deity believed, is joy......276 b
delay that postpones our j.692 d
fading are the j. we dote...329 t
hide our joys no longer*....400 y
if you'd dip in such joys...162 k
in youth to petty joys.....387 n
joys are bubble-like........329 i
joys, but that our hopes...754m
joys delicious springs......727 b
j. of benevolent friendship.387 q
joys of marriage are the...375 h
joys seasoned high and....330 f
joys that out of darkness§.302 q
joys too exquisite to last...329 s
joys with age diminish.....345 u
life's best joys consist in..548 u
mental joys and mental....642 d
morning wake us to no....150 r
my joys to this are folly...378 t
my plenteous j. wanton*..329 x
of his youthful joys‡......673m
other j. are but toys; only. 19 d
our youth, our j., and all...601 v
pay his wisdom for his j...309 h

pleasure all the j. of sense‡475 t
pursues imaginary joys....619 n
pursue their unpolluted j.. 45 n
queen of childish joys‖....533 f
remember'd j. are never.. 61 s
rob us of our joys......... 90 j
sacred j. of home depend..304 h
secret j. and secret smiles. 30 q
still be double to his joys..306 c
taste the melancholy joys‡.582 q
that clutch the joys.......392 h
the purest joys of life......771 m
these are joys like beauty..329 h
youth should watch j. and.672 f
Judas–J. had given them the.144 n
motives, that J. moved.....522 s
so J. kiss'd his Master*.....608 u
Judge–adversary is.........710 o
a judge is just‡........... 82 w
a judge's duty is to.......763 r
an act of a j. which does...675 f
a perfect j. will read each‡.125 l
corrupt judge does not....686 f
crushed by an angry j.'s... 55 n
fitter to invent than to j...671 r
forbear to judge for we*...331 m
four things belong to a j...330 p
good judge decides fairly..694 i
half as sober as a judge...498 u
I see the judge enthroned..527 p
j. better than the people...423 p
judge human character... 81 o
judge in his own case......717 p
judge is condemned when..718 g
judge not the preacher....450 o
judge of all things.........371 r
judge of the man..........331 j
judge others according to..330 x
j. ourselves by what we§...331 d
j.'s duty in all trials.......747 l
j.'s duty is to inquire......718 a
judge us by what we§......331 d
j. whose dictate fix'd the...133 v
judge you as you are*......331 p
mind which is the proper..386 e
my friend, judge not me...330 u
neutrality of an impartial..330 h
powers to speak and judge.103 t
refuse you for my judge*..330m
seest I judge not thee......330 u
shall not be my judge*.....172 p
sole judge of truth‡.......371 v
the j.'s bride might be......629 q
th' indifferent j. between...563 g
there sits a judge*.........330 j
to judge of the character..757 p
to offend and judge are*...330 n
unto the frowning judge*..330 o
wary how ye judge........158 a
who is a righteous judge¶.378 e
you are a worthy judge*...330 l
you yourself may judge††.593 h
Judged–j. by the motive. ...330 r
j. not by what we might...331 k
shall be most surely j .... 547 k
Judges–a fool with judges...251 j
her judges are corrupted..320 i
hungry judges soon the‡...330 i
j. alike of the facts and...331 h
j. and senates have been‡..279 a
judges have been babes*...331 o
j. ought to be more learned.330 g
j. shall be obliged to go....129 n
judges steal themselves*..189 a
judges without informing..331 c
there should be many j....774 i
what unjust j. fathers are..673 n
when j. steal themselves*..595 p
Judging–acquit himself of j.331 c
j. people by appearances...755 c
judging the future but.....331 b
writing or in judging ill‡...429 i
Judgment–after execution*..523 n
against the world's j.......330 v
better of the judgment....173 a
but never of judgment.....774 g
cold is the j. of man.......330 r

criterion of j. touching. ...197m
critics to their j. too‡......429 e
Daniel come to judgment*.331 l
defend against your j......330 w
event is a j. of God........774 h
fear judgment; to fight*... 83 s
form our j. of the true.....385 w
from your j. must expect..330 q
God's great j. seat.........637 q
He, which is the top of j*..331 p
his judgment sound...... 151 l
in babes hath j. shown*....331 o
I stand for judgment*.....331 s
I was green in judgment*..673 h
j. and deliberation.........751 g
j. equal or superior**......516 n
j. falls upon a man........331 i
judgment of any man or... 78 f
judgment of the buyer....718 c
j.! thou art fled to*........331 t
joined to a weak judgment.779 p
leaves of the J. Book...... 366 e
leaves the judgment free..475 h
light, that j. of his........571 d
mistake of our judgment..185 o
never out of judgment....343 b
next to sound judgment...330 t
of judgment and of mercy.450 b
of the want of judgment..380 e
proceed to judgment*.....331 q
reserve thy judgment*....331 n
shores of will and j.*......646 n
surrender j. hoodwinked..409 c
their judgment's right.....126 a
through thorns of j........103 d
thy j. to do aught**.......465 p
until the day of judgment.612 c
urging of that word, j.*....331 v
vulgarize the day of j......537 p
waiting the Judgment Day.636 p
waits upon the judgment*.. 11m
when the judgment's weak.490 k
wit and j. often are at‡....653 p
with critic judgment scan..383 c
Judgments–argue with j.... 26 r
delivers brawling j.†...... 314 u
j. as our watches‡.........331 g
men's judgments are a*....331 r
where our judgments err‖.599 i
Juggles–priestcraft never....451 o
Juggling–j. fiends no more*..492 r
Juice–blood is a j. of rarest..756m
buried in the j. which was.661 l
divine, nectareous juice‡...234 u
juice of subtile virtue lies..228 r
than when nectarian juice.641m
Juices–umbered j. and.....545 b
Juliet–lancers flirt with J.... 15 a
July–linden, in the fervors..394 a
the flashing bars of July...394 c
the second day of July,1776.302 u
the warmth of its July....380 s
trickling rainbow of July..459m
Jump–good wits will jump..652 r
j. for the gentleman. ...... 20 g
j. with common spirits*... 91 x
Jumping–quickly j. up again. 20 d
stampin', an' he's j........449 t
June–April, June, and.......390 j
at the feel of June.... ......323 n
dreams of sunshine and...546m
for boyhood's time of J... 91 d
ice in J. hope, constancy‖..124 g
in the leafy month of J....572 t
it is the month of June....393 s
joy have I in J.'s return....674 r
J. falls asleep upon her....393 p
J. may be had by the††....102 u
J. may pour her warm red.393 a
meetings made December†.627 p
newly sprung in June......356 f
not the twenty-first of J.‖..397 j
opened in airs of June.....391 o
paths of J. more beautiful.393 a
so rare as a day in June††..393 q
that in flowery June.......393 o
Junes–the wintry days are J.600 k

SHAKESPEARE *; MILTON **; WORDSWORTH ¶; BYRON ‖; TENNYSON †; LOWELL ††; POPE ‡; LONGFELLOW §.

K.

kindle to love or wrath....352 *i*
Kindly-let's treat it kindly..604 *v*
rough, he was kindly§......333 *j*
use 'em kindly they rebel.. 80 *b*
Kindness-a kind overflow of*591 *l*
and think it k. to his......118 *e*
beams of kindness.........191 *x*
confers a double kindness.718 *t*
have received a kindness ..263 *n*
how to return a kindness .262 *p*
human kindness bred¶.....196 *k*
kill a wife with kindness*..377*m*
kindness is wisdom.......333 *g*
kindness to immediately...719 *a*
little deeds of k. little words146 *u*
milk of human kindness*..333*m*
no dearth of kindness......333 *k*
nor greetings where no k.¶565 *v*
of kindness and of love¶....333 *n*
opportunity for a kindness718 *r*
rather than receiving k....679 *l*
save in the way of kindness.122 *n*
the kindness is doubled....718 *s*
trust your kindness†......265 *r*
who does a kindness is not‡ 5 *k*
Kindnesses-k. which make ..263 *b*
Kindred-flower of her k.....242 *h*
k. points of heaven and¶... 50 *a*
like kindred drops been....402 *r*
pine for kindred natures...588 *c*
that k. feelings might......309 *t*
King-a cat may look at a k..494 *h*
a king ruleth as he ought..625 *q*
a king to the profit of all...625 *q*
am I king of those*........288 *y*
and is a king indeed.......436 *u*
a scavenger and k. 's the.. 16 *b*
authority forgets a dying†. 30 *c*
Ay, every inch a king*....534*w*
bene the king of the field..616 *h*
body of any king.........323 *c*
but when you see a king ...583 *s*
by God and the king.......798 *d*
catch the conscience of the*423 *l*
damned for never a king's*419 *o*
divinity doth hedge a k.*..535 *f*
do abuse the king that*....215 *o*
elm-tree for our king......289 *d*
eternal, glorious King......536 *o*
every citizen is k. under a..787*m*
Fingal, king of shields....557 *k*
for my king and country...803 *x*
God bless the king........533*m*
God save our gracious king533 *n*
God save the king.........533 *n*
good king near his end....187 *g*
government without a king519 *o*
great k. himself doth woo* 447*w*
hail to the K. of Bethlehem§ 94 *h*
hath eat of a king*........151 *p*
he cares for nothing a king 142 *b*
her governor, her king*....376 *s*
in war and one the king....534 *c*
is the King of Kings....... 94 *g*
king and officers of sorts*..322 *b*
k. has he not taught state..550 *d*
king hath so graciously....453 *d*
k. himself has followed her 6 *g*
King James us'd to call.... 11 *i*
King of England cannot ..304 *l*
K. of France went up the..534 *p*
k. of intimate delights.....545 *n*
"k. of spears! " he said....443 *h*
king of the cold white..... 46 *d*
king of the peak and....... 46 *d*
k. reigns but does not.....787 *j*
king should prefer his.....731 *c*
k's. name is a tower of*....579 *n*
k's. stamp can make the....373 *g*
K. Stephen was a worthy...454 *t*
k., the law, and the people.803 *y*
king was a successful.....787 *t*
king was horsed thore......120 *h*
king with crown and......134 *c*
k. with his golden sceptre..535 *v*
liberty under an upright k.801 *x*
long live our noble king...533 *n*

long live the king.........505 *l*
minister, but if a king‡... 82*w*
more than ever king did...305 *h*
now the king drinks to*....604 *q*
of the King of heaven......520 *u*
of the k's. creation you....372 *v*
on the k's. gate the moss...534 *d*
one king, one faith, one...808*bb*
or light upon a king‡......683 *f*
orders is not to be a king ..620 *o*
O Richard ! O my king.....534 *u*
our sovereign lord, the k...583 *q*
pageantry of a king........534 *j*
presence of the crowned*..608 *n*
rounds the mortal temples* 140 *s*
says my k. with accent.... 91 *b*
shake hands with a king...118 *e*
sing, long live the king.....367 *q*
subject or in king‡........ 61 *t*
subject's duty is the k's.*..534 *x*
substitute shines brightly* 534 *v*
that no king can corrupt*..330 *j*
the daughter of a king*.. 591 *o*
The Hub, the King Pin.....482 *g*
their k. or country harm...518 *a*
the king and the state...... 807 *v*
the king came not.........534 *d*
the king grew vain.........490 *u*
the k. is dead ! Long live..505 *l*
the king wills it...........807*w*
the powerful King of day...585 *c*
there was a king of Thule...534 *a*
the true and only king. ...756 *f*
Time's the king of men*...603 *e*
'tis so much to be a king...534 *n*
to be your king...........258 *j*
to serve the king with good 807 *a*
to the king of swords.......638 *i*
unhappy France! unhappy787 *l*
until a king be by*.........534 *v*
was K. Bradmond's palace.425 *e*
what is a king? a man......534 *q*
what, is the old k. dead*....140 *n*
wish to be thy king........212 *d*
yet looks he like a king*....535 *i*
you have drank with the k.453 *d*
zeal I serv'd my king*......549 *e*
Kingdom-a k. for it was too*. 13 *x*
every k. hath a grave.......534 *b*
half my k. would I give§...568 *g*
his mind his k. and his..... 78 *r*
I'm supreme in the k.......535 *p*
k. of perpetual night*......140 *q*
liken the k. of God to..... 89 *g*
mind to me a kingdom is...385 *f*
my kingdom for a horse*.. 21 *b*
whose kingdom is a school.455 *j*
Kingdoms-and of dead k. I...382 *a*
goodly states and k. seen...607 *d*
kiss'd away kingdoms and* 335 *u*
sifted three kingdoms§.....275 *b*
who ravag'd k., and laid...625 *s*
Kingdom-come-kin' o' k-c.††.657 *j*
Kingly-longest kingly line...444 *a*
the pride of kingly sway*.. 1 *c*
Kings-a lesson for kings....788 *s*
and fall of many kings*....326 *g*
a noble farce wherein kings422 *k*
ape the swoln dialogue||....421 *p*
audacity has made kings...755 *l*
begins with k., and ends...535 *v*
bid kings come bow to it*..569 *v*
cocks, or fighting kings....436*m*
confer with kings and......344 *n*
divorc'd so many English*.562*w*
dread and fear of kings*...382 *p*
ease must kings neglect*... 73 *f*
example of their kings.....695 *r*
falsehood is worse in k.*....199 *t*
feet and heads of kings....449 *l*
found in the mouths of k...798 *f*
give the best advice to k... 7 *j*
God gives not kings the ...534 *e*
green palaces the first k...413 *q*
have kings that privates*.. 73 *f*
icy hand on kings........ 207 *n*
is the gratitude of kings§..534 *k*

king as k. upon their......533 *r*
kingliest k. are crown'd....619 *h*
kings are like stars—they..535 *j*
kings climb to eminence....636 *l*
k. forget that they are men 403 *p*
k. for such a tomb would** 285 *h*
kings have long hands......740 *t*
kings have no such couch†.286 *d*
kings it makes gods, and*..308*w*
k. may be blest, but Tam..630 *v*
kings may love treason ....607 *s*
kings must have slaves.....636 *l*
k. of modern thought are..595 *t*
k. seek their subject's good 626 *d*
k. that fear their subject's* 614 *f*
k. to cobblers 'tis the same 201 *c*
kings to sit in soverainty...510*w*
kings will be tyrants from..481 *n*
kings would not play at... .636 *j*
knowledge of kings.........762 *h*
laws, and priests and k.....369 *o*
meaner creatures kings*...308*w*
more real happiness than..731 *n*
patience gazing on kings*..467 *t*
proudly then the forest k...609 *i*
sad stories of the death of* 535 *a*
so kings should feare and..534 *e*
state without kings or......281 *o*
such is the breath of kings* 665 *p*
teach kings to fiddle‡......129 *b*
that seldom kings enjoy*...112 *a*
the best advice to kings....574 *a*
the great King of kings*...404 *b*
the palaces of kings......689 *q*
the right divine of kings‡..282 *v*
too narrow for two k.......533 *k*
'twixt k. and tyrants......626 *d*
what are k. and crowns....232 *e*
when kings are building....787 *o*
with kings and emperors.. 64 *e*
King-cup-fair is the k-c..... 232 *t*
royal king-cup bold........232 *d*
King-cups-gold-eyed k-c.† ...233 *a*
king-cups and daisies......232 *s*
king-cups fill the meadow..400 *q*
King-fisher-a k-f. the........ 48 *e*
Kinks-kinks and curious... 31 *e*
Kinsmen-thousand k. of.....587 *v*
Kirk-frae Maiden Kirk to....116 *n*
Kiss-a k. from my mother..336 *j*
all humbled kiss the rod*..363 *h*
a more orthodox kiss......158 *f*
angel for the woman in a k.334*m*
angels gave me at once a...564 *j*
as they kiss consume*..... 147 *v*
but as a kiss may live......335 *x*
crocus cannot often k. her .540 *h*
Dian's kiss, unask'd §......359 *y*
do sunder and not kiss*...335 *o*
drew with one long kiss†...336 *c*
for every kiss I owe........335 *a*
for winds to kiss...........218 *j*
give him that parting kiss* 335 *n*
give me a kisse, and to.....334 *k*
hyacinthe wooes thy kisse.231 *h*
I do not wish to kiss you...179*m*
I kiss close................334 *b*
I kiss my hand.... .....111 *l*
I kiss thee with a most*....335 *g*
I kiss your hair...........111 *l*
immortal with a kiss....... 35 *j*
in short my deary k. me... 23 *t*
in that close k. and drank†.366 *n*
I rest content I kiss.........111 *l*
I will kiss thee into rest||...334 *d*
kind kiss before we part....334 *f*
kiss a sleeping man........335 *b*
k. before they are married* 335 *j*
kiss before we part.........204 *b*
k. dead Cæsar's wounds*...284 *a*
k. him, at least not now, he|| 30 *t*
k. I carried from thee*......335*m*
k. in which he half forgets.334 *s*
kiss, long as my exile*......335*m*
kiss me, so long but as a...335 *x*
kiss me, then every........335 *a*
kiss of mother and of .....325 *y*

it is not safe to know......267 *i*
know all that better.......719 *j*
know anything better......719 *h*
know a subject ourselves...337 *l*
k. her was to love her.....361 *u*
k. his step and touch......237 *d*
k. how little can be known‡.651 *h*
k. more than my betters... 19 *h*
know naught but fame*....338 *d*
know not what's resisted...336 *p*
know not what we may be*.338 *e*
know not what you know.713 *t*
know not where I am......714 *d*
know our friends in*......268 *e*
know the man within......719 *k*
k. then this truth, enough‡.633 *b*
k. then thyself, presume‡..371 *x*
know thy opportunity.....509*dd*
know thyself...............719 *i*
know what happened......719 *f*
learn the world to know....337 *w*
let him not k. 't, and he's*.595 *k*
more I know I know.......337 *s*
much we know but more... 76 *q*
no more could know. .....517 *u*
not allowed to know......7.4 *a*
not to k. me argues**.....314 *n*
only so much do I know....190 *e*
or very soon may know it‖..629 *e*
pattern in himself to k.*....451 *k*
pity those I do not know*..332 *s*
reason but from what we‡.517 *i*
shalt know ere long§.......209 *c*
shows how little mortals k.342 *s*
so well to know her own**...111*m*
suffer'd, much will know‡..582 *q*
that hath it doth not k.....458 *r*
that seeking to know......763 *l*
that to k., which else we*..580 *s*
the indolent not to know...720 *p*
the more we know.......255 *s*
they have the gift to k. it*.659 *h*
those who k. thee know... 82 *j*
thou oughtest to k., since..707 *t*
to k. no more is woman's**.645 *k*
to k. that which before us**651 *c*
to k., to esteem, to love...346 *q*
to hope, to know........367 *h*
those who know it best‖....662 *h*
to be we k. not what, we...133 *l*
to them we k. not, and we..127 *i*
too much to k. is to know*.338 *d*
transcends the what we k.§.411 *j*
unless another know that...719 *l*
we k. accurately only......774 *r*
we know not anything†.....309 *b*
we know not what we do...665*bb*
we know what we are, but*.338 *e*
well for one to k. more.....719 *n*
we should k. before we love.777 *q*
what thou dost not know*..620 *k*
when all pretend to know..337 *h*
when I would k. thee my... 66 *i*
when you k. a thing, to....336 *y*
world to know it‖..........327 *n*
wouldst thou other men k..337 *x*
would'st thou k. thyself...337 *x*
you do not know a thing...336 *y*
Knowest–full little k. thou...155 *i*
k. me not by my clothes*...455 *c*
k. thou the land where the.795 *l*
speak less than thou k.*....511 *q*
thou know'st great son*....640 *c*
Knoweth–no man k. him... 83 *f*
Knowing–art in k. a thing...719 *d*
love of k. without the......341 *v*
not knowing what they do. 86 *a*
who k. nothing knows but†.420 *k*
will grow more knowing... 66 *g*
Knowledge–adding of k. to... 65 *n*
addition to true knowledge.337 *p*
all knowledge and wonder..336 *k*
attain to any kind of k.....337 *i*
ask of knowledge to show...632 *t*
being mature in knowledge*475*w*
binds his soul to knowledge.338 *o*
carry knowledge with him.607 *a*

desire of k. in excess....... 86 *d*
desire of k. is the natural...837 *j*
diffused k. immortalizes....337 *o*
domain of universal k....314*m*
done without our k...... .709 *d*
dress does not give k.......763 *q*
fault of our knowledge.....185 *o*
from knowledge ignorance.132 *o*
from living knowledge hid..580 *g*
God's knowledge, and are..298 *l*
goodness of knowledge.....512 *c*
great step to knowledge.....337 *d*
half our k. we must‡.......337 *t*
is woman's happiest k.**..645 *k*
k. alone is the being of....338 *i*
k. and wisdom far from....336 *z*
k. being to be had only.....185 *o*
k. bloweth up, but charity.336 *l*
k. by suffering entereth...582 *n*
k. comes, but wisdom†.....338 *j*
k. comes of learning.......337 *b*
k. conscious peace and....148*m*
k. dwells in heads replete..336 *z*
knowledge delightful....... 88 *l*
k., in truth, is the great....338 *l*
k. is but sorrow's spy......267 *i*
k. is indeed, that which....336 *j*
knowledge is little worth...657 *v*
knowledge is more than....337 *k*
k. is not happiness‖........336 *u*
knowledge of two kinds..337 *l*
k. is ourselves to know‡....337 *u*
knowledge is power........336*m*
k. is proud that he..........337 *a*
k. is the amassed thought .337 *f*
knowledge is the antidote..337 *e*
k. is the foundation.. . ...753 *g*
k. is the hill which few....164 *c*
k. is the only fountain.....338*m*
knowledge leads to woe....313 *r*
knowledge of kings......762 *h*
knowledge of myself*.....252 *r*
k. of that which is not....337 *g*
knowledge of thy works....413 *b*
k. of our own ignorance....651 *i*
k. that is not power......337 *g*
knowledge the sail....... 79 *v*
k. the wing wherewith*...337 *y*
knowledge, use and reason.337 *e*
knowledge we behold the..123 *e*
k. will come to lodge......664 *f*
less than knowledge.......763*m*
life of k. is not often......338 *h*
literature of knowledge....354 *g*
make out that k. to others.337*m*
manners must adorn k....373 *l*
might improve my k.**....337 *r*
nor knowledge to the wise.185 *f*
out-topping knowledge....549 *u*
own increase of knowledge.337*m*
passion, knowledge, fame‡.111 *p*
patience surpasses k......808 *d*
pursuit of k.under........336 *n*
quickly comes such k.‖....356 *t*
reader the most knowledge.427 *l*
scantiness of k. our delight.158 *a*
seeds of knowledge........729 *a*
share with thee knowledge. 29 *d*
spouseless virgin K.‖......650 *g*
sweetly uttered k.........338 *g*
the beginning of k........ 336 *w*
the book of k. fair**......149*m*
then is knowledge "good"..651 *v*
the price for knowledge....189 *b*
through zeal k. is gotten...673 *t*
thy knowledge of no value.719 *l*
too much knowledge.......719 *o*
tree of diabolical k........345 *e*
true k. leads to love¶......338 *p*
vaults into knowledge.....313 *t*
want of k. always inflicts..580 *u*
what is all knowledge too..336 *x*
what is k. but grieving.....167 *l*
where k. leads to woe..... 91 *j*
which is the seed of k......336 *k*
who loves not knowledge†..338 *k*
with k. doubt increases....774 *r*

without your knowledge...751 *k*
worthy the k. and practice. 19 *b*
Knowledges–men's wits and.. 64 *b*
Known–all things needful to.448 *b*
are things to be known....314*m*
devil where he is known...607 *b*
done and little to be known.668 *n*
do to be forever known.....200 *s*
he woulde be known......429 *a*
k. you love you better still.360 *r*
place where he is not k.....607 *b*
the known evil is best......685 *n*
the result is known.........681 *j*
whats'ever's to be known..336 *r*
when they are known......103 *t*
Knows–all he knows of bliss‖.518 *g*
he who k. much has many.774 *s*
k. better than he practices. 79 *h*
k. little, who will tell his...104 *g*
knows more accuses with..105 *o*
one k. nothing but what....765 *r*
she k. her man, and when..485 /*s*
that he knows no more.....650 *j*
who knows but he will sit..268*m*
who knows nothing base... 81 *s*
with Him that all things k.*490 *p*
Köln–Köln a town of monks.. 97 *s*
Kubla-Khan–Xanadu did K-K.530 *b*
Kye-a' the kye at hame......560*m*

L.

Label–pack and l. men for...463 *u*
Labor–a boy, suffer and l....719 *t*
Adam, well may we l.**...424 *e*
alternate l. useful life...... 112 *j*
and the labour done........666 *f*
capital solicits the aid of l..339 *p*
care and l. of his mind*...597 *o*
cheerful l. while each day.110 *q*
cheers the tars' l. or the‖...456 *f*
difficulty and l. hard*.....154 *k*
earth's life, earth's labor... 40 *n*
end to end with l. keen....342 *a*
every labour sped..........303 *g*
exempted from secular l...428 *d*
had my l. for my travail*..339*m*
his labor is a chant........321 *n*
honest l. bears a lovely... 338 *t*
is labor, this is work......720 *d*
joy that springs from l.§..339 *f*
l. and digest things most..427 *s*
l. bestowed on trifles......720 *a*
l. cannot produce without..338 *v*
l. conquers everything... 720 *e*
labor health, from health..109 *y*
labor in this country is....339 *p*
l. is discovered to be the...338 *s*
l. is for future hours......424 *a*
labor is in itself............719 *v*
labor is itself a pleasure...801 *u*
labor is life! 'tis the still...339 *i*
labour is light where love.493 *p*
l. is rest—from the sorrows.339 *j*
l. is the lot of man below‡..339 *b*
l. itself is but a sorrowful..338 *u*
labor of Omnipotence.....323 *l*
l. there shall come forth§..339 *e*
l. was to kill the time......313 *o*
l. we delight in, physics*..339 *n*
l. without any play, boys..495*m*
l., you know, is prayer.....489 *s*
learn to l. and to wait§..... 4*w*
little labor, little are our...338 *x*
lose our labor.............700 *t*
man who by his l. gets.....339 *k*
many still most l. for the‖.338 *q*
mute is the voice of rural..536 *l*
never despise labour......271 *d*
painful l., both by sea and*377 *p*
patient of l. when the end‡.424 *h*
pray and labor.............803 *f*
right of labor to its own...338 *v*
sore labour's bath*.......562 *u*
the fruit derived from l....797 *q*
through long days of l.§....405 *v*

SHAKESPEARE *; MILTON **; WORDSWORTH ¶; BYRON ‖; TENNYSON †; LOWELL ††; POPE ‡; LONGFELLOW §.

as seas do l., show white...493 *n*
atheist's l.'s a poor........519 *v*
children l. loud as they...340 *q*
choice to cry or laugh!....182 *f*
fear we die before we l. at.340 *j*
fools laugh i' the alehouse*464 *c*
growing fainter in my l..... 11 *e*
I laugh at the world, and...110 *a*
I l. for hope hath happy...307 *k*
in bed we laugh, in........ 38 *d*
landlord's l. was ready....340 *k*
laugh and be fat..........500*kk*
l., and be fat, sir, your....340 *s*
l. and the world laughs....669 *r*
laugh as I pass in thunder..100 *e*
laugh at any mortal thing!.340 *l*
laugh at the jests or......211 *e*
l. at the world," says he...110 *a*
l. at your friends, and if‡.. 340 *v*
laugh before we are happy..340 *j*
laugh costs too much.....720 *j*
l., if but for an instant only.340 *u*
laugh like a child as they..239 *h*
laugh, like parrots at*.... 84 *d*
l. not too much ; the......340 *j*
l., O murmuring Spring...228 *h*
l., O murmuring Spring...231 *m*
l., O murmuring Spring...236 *j*
l., O murmuring Spring...539 *r*
laugh where we must‡....373 *t*
lesse at thine own things l.340 *p*
loud l. that spoke the.....415 *h*
people that do not laugh... 80 *d*
see him l. till his face be*..341 *h*
shall laugh at all disaster§..551 *u*
they laugh that win*......341 *d*
to l. is proper to the man..340 *y*
to l. were want of goodness‡340 *x*
to make the weeper laugh*606 *h*
whoever loves a l. must!....421 *p*
why do you laugh.........720 *i*
why laugh not as of old....721 *d*
wilt not laugh at poets..... 360 *l*
you may laugh the more‡..340 *v*
Laughable–swear the jest be* 84 *d*
Laughed–clapped my hands.. 20*m*
full well they laughed......455 *i*
laughed to scorn.........676 *c*
one has not laughed.......775 *f*
when he's l. and said his say423 *v*
Laugher–laugh, the l. weep*.606 *w*
Laughing–ever–l. Foote's!....421 *p*
laughing, quaffing.........383 *p*
l. the clouds away with!....399 *q*
truth in a laughing way....747 *t*
you hear that boy l........340 *q*
Laughing-stock–a l-s. to those 687 *d*
Laughs–always at ease who...775 *e*
and Jove but laughs at.....357 *v*
each one laughs about..... 8 *t*
fair laughs the morn......672 *j*
he laughs and cries, and... 31 *e*
he who laughs too much...775 *h*
he who laughs on Friday...775 *g*
jester laughs himself......774 *e*
laughs and stretches out!.. 31 *a*
l. inly behind her cliffs....327 *l*
l. like a babe just roused...392 *e*
laughs loudest of all...... 89 *o*
laughs out to behold.......266 *w*
laughs the sense of mis'ry.. 78 *s*
man that loves and l.‡....340 *w*
poor man that knows him .340 *q*
she laughs with a harvest..424 *b*
they say, Jove laughs*....362 *n*
witty man laughs least....340 *p*
Laughter–am stabb'd with*..341 *a*
career of laughter* ....335 *l*
contempt and laughter of..484 *t*
eyes in flood with l.*......341 *e*
Heav'n still with l. the‡.... 13 *q*
house of l. makes a house..341 *k*
how much lies in laughter.340*m*
invent anything that* .....341 *c*
l. almost ever cometh of...341 *f*
laughter hath only a ....341 *f*
L. holding both his sides**.383 *r*

l. of the vernal floods.......647 *e*
low gurgling l., as sweet...340 *o*
mirth and l., sermons !.....648 *k*
our sincerest laughter.....537 *j*
silly than silly laughter....720 *h*
tears and l. for all time ...549 *v*
the rabble's laughter.......268 *p*
the squirrel's laughter.....394 *g*
to shake with l. ere the....120 *s*
unextinguish'd l. shakes‡..340 *r*
what large laughter........409 *e*
what l. and what music....605 *n*
when her lovely laughter..432 *l*
with mirth and l. let*......384 *p*
with songs and l. blent.....391 *q*
with whispered l. slipped .. 47 *s*
worldly tears and laughter 21 *l*
Launcelot–L. lookys he upon 120 *h*
Laura–Laura had been......533 *g*
Laureate–strew the l.**.... .221 *i*
Laurel–ivy climbs the l......232 *a*
laurel bursts its buds .... 233 *b*
l. for the perfect prime ... 11 *d*
laurell, meed of mightie ...610 *h*
l. sheds her cluster'd bloom 609 *l*
laurell to grow............. 66 *c*
overflow of arbutus and l..611 *b*
sword sit laurel victory*...638 *u*
the laurel rises high.......795 *l*
Laurels–claim triumphant .l.635 *i*
Laurel-tree–the l-t. grew....614 *p*
Laurustine–white l. seems...233 *c*
Lave–although she l. them*.. 58 *l*
Lavender–hot l., mints,*... 235 *n*
lupin and with lavender...219 *f*
Lavished–l. on those shining .217 *j*
Law–and his will his law.... 78 *r*
and I challenge law*......438 *n*
as adversaries do in law*...438 *k*
a scarecrow of the law*....439 *b*
base of all things–law and.132 *d*
be convict by course of l.*.438 *f*
been a truant in the law*..438 *l*
but is this law ? ay, marry* 438 *j*
buys out the law*.........438 *p*
by the L. of Slavery, man..560 *a*
charge you by the law*....331 *q*
charity itself fulfils the l.*. 86 *w*
church, army, physic, law.667 *t*
common l. itself is nothing.437 *b*
crowner's quest law*......438 *j*
custom is held to be as a l..688 *j*
dictate fix'd the law.......133 *v*
drowns the voice of the l...775 *l*
eleven points in the law....436 *v*
frame the law unto my*....438 *l*
God is thy law, thou**.....645 *h*
God's universal law**......376 *c*
good opinion of the law....439 *f*
hath in the table of his l.*..404 *b*
he hath resisted law*......438*m*
higher law than the........106 *f*
if rebel sense would reason's597 *s*
in a thousand pounds of l..451 *s*
in l's. grave study six......603 *v*
in l., what plea so tainted*..145 *h*
in the law, there is equity..694 *j*
interpreter of that law....275 *f*
is murder by the law......404 *e*
is the life of the law........437 *b*
it is to go to law...........720 *o*
just l. will interfere with ..437 *f*
king the l., and the people.803 *y*
law can discover sin, but**.556 *a*
law ends, there tyranny....437 *t*
lawful that law bar no*....439 *c*
l. in calmness made and¶.. 85 *r*
l. is a sort of hocus-pocus..437 *q*
l. is set over the magistrate 436 *w*
law is silent during war....750 *s*
law is the last result of....437*m*
l. itself is influenced by....708 *j*
law of all men's minds....409 *x*
l. of heaven and earth is !..436 *t*
law of sacrifice............163 *p*
l., or sect or opinion did....519 *n*
l. preserves the earth a ....510 *o*

l. shall scorn him further*.438*m*
law succors the ignorant....713 *o*
l. than the Constitution... 488 *e*
law which he happens not..281 *g*
law which is perfection....437 *b*
law which moulds a tear...510 *o*
live obedient to the law....279 *k*
love has never known a l..367 *j*
love is the l. of the school..512 *c*
loves God and his law......274 *k*
magistrate is a speaking l..436 *w*
nature's great law, and....409 *x*
necessity knows no law....502 *i*
nede hath no lawe ....502 *j*
nice sharp quillets of the*..438 *h*
no remedy at law..........627 *s*
no rigid law forbids........ 8 *o*
nothing is law that is not..438 *d*
obey the law of society....565 *t*
offends no law and is a....436 *u*
old father antic the law*..438 *i*
one God, one law, one†....123 *f*
one King, one faith, one l..808*bb*
one man, keeping the l....626 *c*
One sole ruler—his Law ....275 *f*
order is Heaven's first law‡462 *v*
or triumph o'er the law‡...437 *v*
o' the windy side of the l.*.438 *s*
ought law to weed it out...528 *g*
people is the highest law....804 *e*
pity is the virtue of the l..*474 *h*
preferring equity to strict.694 *i*
prize the infraction of her.. 43 *p*
progress is the law of life..492 *e*
reason for their l. refuse**.517 *f*
recognizes a better law ... 79 *h*
rich men rule the law......437 *j*
seven hours to law, to......600 *s*
State is the highest law....741 *a*
strictest law sometimes ....720 *q*
the bloody book of law*....438 *t*
the Giver of the Law. .....455 *j*
the Law ! It has honored us 439 *g*
the law often allows what..775 *k*
the lion's paw is all the ††..637 *l*
the question of law.........717 *o*
there any law more just....718 *o*
there was never l., or sect..279 *l*
the rigour of penal law....437 *i*
the teachers of our law**.. .337 *r*
the world affords no l.*....485 *f*
'tis rigour and not law*....328 *d*
transgressing nature's l....661 *j*
trumpets under the Law§...40 *h*
unchanging law of God....282 *s*
we are for law, he dies*....438 *y*
wedded love, mysterious** 376 *b*
what the law insists upon..720 *r*
when law can do no right*.439 *c*
who to himself is law .....436 *u*
you know the law* ......330 *l*
Lawful–l. to be taught by....716 *q*
merely what is lawful .....720 *p*
only this, lawful is....... 19 *d*
Law-givers–Poets should be..479 *d*
Laws–according to her**.....593 *j*
all rights and laws are still.775*m*
all thy lawes forever ....367 *n*
and most biting laws*..... 439 *a*
and regard of laws........534 *h*
are not laws in common....626 *c*
as love knoweth no lawes...360 *q*
base laws of servitude.....258 *j*
beginning with the l. that..589 *j*
best interpreter of laws... 688 *k*
brain may devise laws for*.592 *w*
break all reason's laws‡....125 *o*
civil laws are cruel*........639 *b*
commonwealth abounded ..439 *e*
comprehensive system of... 28 *f*
curse on all laws but those‡ 438 *a*
each thing's a thief ; the*..595 *o*
equal laws which it had....281 *o*
eternal laws so far as we...437 *g*
Father ! no prophet's l. l!..487 *f*
for the stable laws........410 *h*
gods have their own laws..720 *n*

SHAKESPEARE *; MILTON **; WORDSWORTH ¶; BYRON ‖; TENNYSON †; LOWELL ††; POPE ‡; LONGFELLOW §.

there he came to lie*.......154 v
to give the lie, pull noses...120 g
was indebted to a lie..... ..624 b
who loves to lie with me*..610 d
would I gratefully l. there.545 a
you lie—under a mistake ..199w
your piping-hot lie.........724 g
Lied—once we have lied.......778 t
Lies—author of confusion...152 r
  books are lies frae end to.. 64 i
  compliments and lies**....103 f
  dash'd and brew'd with l..199 d
  eulogy lies about them....778 u
  expect to find lies in...... 33 a
  for wisdom never lies‡... .199 f
  here lies our sovereign lord.533 q
  here lies what once was....183 h
  how the other half lies....498 v
  lies are like the father*....199 r
  lies are the works of man..623 u
  lies to hide it makes it two.200 a
  nor honied lies of rhyme‖..476 f
  satire lies about literary. .778 u
  the blackest of lies†...... .199bb
  this member ne'er l. still..538 b
  though I know she lies*.... 39m
  though in rags he lies.... .369 u
  throng and stress of lies....100 k
  who speaks not truly lies*..199 u
Liest—thou l. in thy throat*.. 73 j
Lieth—he that lieth till no.... 83 f
Life—achieve it before life be. 13 h
  above earth's life earth's.. 40 n
  a fool his whole life long...509 f
  a glorious life, or grave....437 l
  ah, what a life were this*..602 n
  a life beyond the grave.....714 o
  a life of injury and crime..338 h
  a l. which valour could not.511 a
  all life needs for life is†.. 646 p
  all life not be purer and....319 d
  all life this truth declares..488 t
  all that life is love..........267 r
  all their life changed in....141 h
  all the voyage of their l.*..461 o
  all, when life is lost.......522 o
  always beginning life.......722 c
  amid l.'s pains, abasements 317 c
  an account of her life to a*.660 f
  and lengthens life*.........384 b
  and life itself were new.... 56 f
  and my life in death.......276 g
  and so make life, death....280 h
  and the race a life..........600 h
  answers life's great end....352 c
  answer was a blameless l..588 z
  anything the light gives l..654 t
  a single life's no burthen...375 g
  as in life a friend‡........ 80 h
  ask not a life for the dear..487 t
  a strange volume of real l..448 i
  a subtle red of life is.......618 l
  as we advance in life we... 2 f
  as yet not come to life*....493 i
  at the flaming forge of l.§..348 p
  a useless life is an early...776 p
  a well-written life is almost346 l
  bankrupt of life yet........347 e
  be as fruit, earn life ..... 99 b
  before us lies in daily life**651 c
  begin to make a better life.148 t
  blandishments of life are..121 n
  blight of life—the demon‖..596 c
  blind life within the brain†.489 u
  book of human l. to light§..600w
  bread is the staff of life....496 n
  breathed life in them......309 t
  breathes scanty life........387 n
  breath of life his nostrils†..457 j
  breeds life to feed him. ...133 q
  brightness of our life is§...308 e
  bring us to enjoy life...... 65 s
  but a map of busy life......346w
  but a quantity of life*......139 k
  but life is fleeting... ....721 e
  but life with shame........632 o
  by life's unresting sea......571 n

by medicine life may be*...441 b
by rules severe his life he..450 j
by the Tree of Life**.......221 j
called the staff of life......481 r
calm's not life's crown.....671 q
can get another life again..511 a
care's an enemy to life*.... 72 l
cast away one's own life....262 o
certain in man's life.........136 i
change of many-colour'd l.428 o
chief nourisher in life's*...562 u
cling closer, closer l. to life.375 s
cold marble leapt to life a..452 n
common walk of virtuous l.142 o
concentred in a l. intense‖. 346 g
confederates against my*..108 a
conscience of a life well‡...106 a
consider life 'tis all a cheat.347 h
conversation is like their l.744 b
convert this life into its..... 76m
cool sequestered vale of l..347 t
corals to cut life upon.... 88w
corne, which is the staffe of496aa
count life but little worth..395m
course of my long l. hath§. 10 k
creeping where no life..... 232 c
crowded hour of glorious l.350 c
cuts off twenty years of l.*.583 f
daily beauty in his life*.... 83m
days of life's short measure651 l
death crowns life...........527 l
death is strong but life.....164 u
death is the crown of life..142 i
death or life shall thereby*145 v
definition of life is false....348 r
denizen of life's great city§ 31 k
desert where no l. is found.554 g
dishonorable life............690 p
doctrine by thy life........158 j
doors to let out life, I shall.136 h
dost thou love life? then...347 p
draughts of life to me......647 t
dreamed that l. was beauty163 t
dreary intercourse of¶......565 v
drink life to the lees†......351 l
earth is life for life‖..... ..436 t
employ the first part of l..776 h
enlarge my life with.......348 v
envied, were our life........ 94 f
espoused at the expense of.461 a
every man's life is a fairy..345 g
every moment of life is a..776 d
expatiates in a l. to come‡.571 w
faith as temper l.'s worst.. 8 d
fatigued with life, he.......133 d
feels its life in every limb¶. 91 e
first a right to life..........529 b
flowers to the daily life.... 96 s
fool his whole life long... 768 h
forget that life had pain or. 56 f
for life's worst ills..........403 i
for life to come is... ......212 j
found that life was duty...163 t
found your life distasteful.345 u
frame life so that...........267 k
freight, a vanish'd life†....446 d
friend to life's decline. .... 9 t
from l.'s cold seeming and.645 t
from Life's many frets......296 x
from life's tumults fly......284 h
gave life a zest..............457 n
general pulse of l. stood....564 d
gift of eternal life..........522 g
give us the luxuries of life.464 b
gleam as of another life....532 k
glorious thing human l. is§.151 a
glory of this life*...........273 e
God alone is life............351 f
greatest love of l. appears.351 p
green alone l.'s golden tree.776 q
had blessed one's life with..620 e
had he life, or had..... ... 92 l
hands against the fire of l..473 f
happiest moment of my l..589w
has lent us life, as we do a.133 e
has lived a short life.......721 c
heart of l. laid waste with..570m

heavenly roses in our......796 h
hence the mockery of life..645 t
here my life must end*.. .350 v
he shuts up the day of l*...563 a
hillside of this life..........280 b
Him whose life was love.... 92 h
his life a breath of God....369 o
his life as he pleases........704 d
his l.. I'm sure was in the..346 r
his life is Christ, his death. 93 e
his l. may make thee gold..165 ·
his life to eternity.........351 g
his life to meet the..... . .141 a
his life was gentle and the*372 k
honorable and upright l...721 p
hopes have precarious l....307 q
hour in each man's life....461 q
hour of glorious life........273 b
hour which gives us life...722 f
how beautiful is life........777 c
how carve way i' the life..466 f
how short is l. how frail...347 r
how short is the longest l..316 f
human l. to endless sleep.529 l
I bear a charmed life*.... 350 i
I count life just a stuff....346 a
if l. be all past praying for.488 j
if life did ride upon a*.....350 q
I have but one life to lose..468 o
ill care for life's worst ills..603 t
illuminates the path of l....528 d
in every path of human l..549 t
in heaven the trees of l.**.298 i
in life did harbor give.....183 g
in life's last scene what....348 d
in life's low vale, the soil‡..633 a
in life's small things be††..525 t
in life there are meetings..378 o
inundation of life..........192 a
in our l. alone doth nature.526 x
integrity of life is fame's..633aa
in midst of life we be......136 d
in thy path of life...... ...594 o
into an angelic life...... ... 76m
into each life some rain§...514 u
is better than l. with love..164 f
is existence, used is life....604 g
is life too short. 260m
is the great art of social l..565 k
is there in the vale of life..644 u
is the stuff life is made of..347 p
it is easy to despise life... 70 e
it is life essential..........521 l
keep l.'s fever still within..528m
labor is life! 'tis the still....339 i
lag-end of my life*.........111 q
lamp of a man's life......295 n
lawful plague of life‡.....645 j
learnt life from the poets..480 q
lent us life at interest.....721 b
let l. be short; else shame*350 l
life all other passions fly..365 n
life and an immortal soul.318 e
life and love for Greece....212 l
l. and power are scattered.338 l
life and religion are one....521 l
life being weary of these*..350 o
life believe is not a dream.345 q
life blood of the soul......307 c
life by the spirit comes....281 o
life can charm no more....403 e
life can little more supply‡371 w
life consists not in living..177 f
life contains a thousand....351 s
l. declines from thirty-five.657 c
life did not present its.... .777 a
life dissolving vegetate‡.... 75 s
life exempt from public*..350 f
life for delays and doubts..346 s
l., for my country and the.469 f
life from youth to age...... 44 o
life given us by nature.....721 o
life has pass'd with me but.346 u
life hath had some smatch*306 x
life hath more awe than....345 l
life hath quicksands§......347 d
life hath set no landmarks.348 s

sweet delight a quiet l......523 *t*
take l. too seriously and....150 *r*
take not away the life you..347 *f*
taught the sweet civilities..551 *f*
tell how human l. began**.349 *a*
than fear of life.........210 *l*
than shortness of life......721 *o*
than the lamp of life......769 *r*
that bears the name of life*140 *o*
that life and love can die...395 *b*
that l. is long which answers352 *c*
that l. looks through*......350 *j*
that make up my life*.....350 *v*
that we life pursue. ......347 *g*
the best of life is but‖......325 *o*
the death of each day's life*562 *u*
the energy of life may be...315 *n*
the fount of life**.........221 *j*
the game of l. looks cheerful 776 *j*
the God who gave us life...343 *w*
the l. of the husbandman..424 *c*
the luve o' l.'s young day...380 *v*
the May of l. blooms once..776 *l*
then marble, soften'd into‡.452 *p*
there is a life above.......267 *r*
there is life there's hope...307 *r*
there my life centres......381 *b*
there's l. in the fountains¶.391 *m*
the scourge of life and....463 *i*
the short sleep of l. our...761 *o*
the Sundaies of man's life..536 *o*
the sweetest thing in life..646 *b*
the time of life is short*...350 *q*
the wheels of weary l. at... 9*m*
the wind is, so is mortal l..401 *k*
the wine of life......755 *f*
the wine of life is drawn*..350 *g*
think of this life*........350 *j*
third of l. is pass'd in sleep‖132 *t*
this is alone life, joy.......472 *q*
this life's a fort committed.583 *c*
this string of life........299 *w*
thought is the measure of l.348 *j*
thread of life with pain‡...347 *x*
thro all her placid life†....646 *a*
through l.'s uncertain race. 75 *u*
thy favour was my life.....628 *c*
thy life's a miracle*........350 *y*
thy own life's key*.......262 *h*
tie my l. within this band..600*m*
time is short, life is short..362 *a*
time is the life of the soul§.601 *c*
'tis from high life high‡.... 82*w*
'tis not a l., 'tis but a piece. 88 *u*
'tis not the mere stage of l.776 *t*
'tis the soldier's life*......444*m*
'tis the sunset of l. gives me.528 *c*
to a life beyond life**...... 67*m*
to all the glad season of l...672 *a*
to husband out l.'s taper...523 *u*
took a man's life with him. 78 *d*
too near the fire of life.... 62 *f*
to outdo the life.........550*m*
torment your disgraceful..693 *d*
to take away l. is a power...777 *f*
travel'd life's dull round...433 *k*
trunk of life's strange tree‖.325 *o*
unbought grace of life......156 *s*
under thy own life's key*..511 *s*
unkindness may defeat my*627 *w*
vanities of life forego..... 11 *g*
voice of a deep life within..198 *k*
walk on through life.......242 *d*
walk through life serenely.227 *f*
wastes his life and blood...427 *v*
wast so full of l., or death§.135 *v*
waters like a thing of life‖..551 *u*
way of l. is fallen into*.... 11 *r*
web of our life is of a......350 *w*
we drag the load of life....343 *a*
we'ld jump the l. to come*.350 *u*
we love l. and we flee from.754 *k*
were death denyed, to live.142 *i*
we seek a happy life.......746 *x*
what life is in thy ray......131 *e*
what makes life dreary is..402 *k*
when Jove gave us l. he‡...339 *b*

when life is rather new‖....117 *n*
when life seemed formed... 90 *a*
while the life of the master.175 *o*
while there is life there is..712 *q*
white flower of a blameless†351 *n*
whoever lives true life......356 *a*
who is pure in life, and free.683 *a*
whose life is a bubble......345 *s*
whose life is the to come... 67 *f*
whose life is in the right‡..198 *f*
whoso lives the holiest life.303 *d*
with her own blood to life. 53 *s*
with his past life.........721 *f*
wretch condemn'd with life.307 *u*
yes, this is life..........351 *d*
Life-blood–l-b. of a master**. 67*m*
very life-blood of*........156 *q*
Lifeless–sweet, though l. yet.564 *b*
Lifelike–l. that the silver...175 *u*
Life-veins–drop from old.....640 *i*
Lift–God hath sworn to lift..310 *l*
look on it, lift it, bear it....348 *h*
Lifted–l. it gently to heaven§.568 *i*
Light–air-woven children of..781 *b*
A jax was for light§........130 *n*
a light for after times .....381 *s*
a l. wife doth make a heavy*645 *l*
all that light attended§.....264*w*
and all was light‡.........352 *s*
and blind of light..........563 *h*
and restore the light.... .561 *e*
and unlook'd for light.....605 *h*
and women in a better l.‖..415 *h*
angel of l.! who from the..584 *c*
anything the l. gives life to.654 *t*
are sweetness and light.....418*m*
April, with its changing l.§.192 *q*
as fire is of light..........336*w*
a spring of light...... .... 34 *f*
a steady, lambent light§....192 *n*
babe, to greet the light.....349*w*
bereft of l. their seeing**... 61 *f*
be, too, for l.—for strength§488 *k*
blasted with excess of light.415 *o*
bowers a flood of light......390 *o*
but in the evening, light....398 *j*
but in unapproached l.**...352 *n*
but the cold light of stars§.416 *d*
by her own radiant light**.632*w*
by his conquering light....585 *a*
by this good l., this is a*....121 *p*
by whose dear light.......323 *h*
by your number than your.577 *k*
casting a dim religious l.**.352 *l*
Christ that gives us light... 92 *k*
clouds with rosy light......87 *k*
clouds with streaks of l.*...401 *b*
collected light compact.....435 *d*
commands all light........370 *z*
common as light is love....365 *i*
corn shall seem as light*...152 *h*
corruption springs from l..352 *d*
dark and light had seen†... 25 *l*
darkness from light from..132 *o*
darkness, if there be no l..487 *n*
dawn, merely a sob of light.624 *y*
day with all its light.......460 *o*
dead flush of light........224 *b*
dear as the l. that visits....260 *s*
dear to me as light and life.356 *g*
dispenses light from far**..584 *a*
dotted with specks of light.397 *k*
drainless shower of light...477 *f*
dreamy and magical l.§....542 *n*
drop of pure and pearly l..633 *h*
due light to the misled**...416 *n*
each other's light to dim...585 *p*
ere you hide your light.....576 *r*
faith beholds a feeble light.198 *r*
Father of light and life.....148*m*
Father of L.! great God of‖487*m*
find l. in the darkest night..567 *r*
flecked with the cherry l...456*m*
fled in light away..........634 *c*
flowers made of light.......218 *e*
flying cloud, the frosty l.†.. 41 *f*
fond memory brings the l...380 *n*

for his sleep was aery l.**..561 *r*
from grave to l, from......476 *p*
from the outer light........153 *y*
from those flames no l.**..130 *p*
gave King Henry light*....151 *u*
gives a l. to every age.....538 *p*
God and Nature met in l.†..353 *a*
God's l. his likeness takes...352 *h*
golden light of morn......583 *t*
glorious host of light......575 *l*
glorious light is thine¶.... 50 *a*
great sun what is light.....355 *c*
hail holy light! offspring**.352 *n*
halls of dazzling light......211 *t*
hell leads up to light** .... .299 *i*
Hesperus entreats thy l....398 *a*
he that has light within**...82 *c*
his blinding light ....358 *g*
his own indefeasible light..571 *d*
home and light is come†... 53 *d*
horns hung out her l.......397 *i*
implore your light he sings. 48 *n*
infant crying for the light†.372 *s*
in light ineffable.........275 *v*
in little rivulets of light§...398 *e*
in ocean sunk the lamp of l.415 *p*
intense light will not make.352 *f*
in the dark a glimmering l.777*m*
in the fairest point of light.383 *b*
in their golden urns draw**.576 *i*
into the light of things¶.... 58 *r*
it drips its misty light......576 *t*
it is light that enables us... 92 *b*
its l. shall linger round us..443 *l*
keeping the gates of L.....591 *d*
knelt in the dying light.....329 *c*
lakes goes answering light.169 *i*
leave the l. of Hope behind.307 *j*
lies forever in the light§.... 13 *e*
light a candle to the sun....352 *u*
l. and shade spring both**..625 *a*
l. burdens, long borne.....501 *h*
light cares speak, great....501 *t*
light dies before thy†...... 77 *d*
l. divine and searching....517 *a*
l. (God's eldest daughter)..352 *g*
light heart lives long*...... 88 *p*
l. he leaves behind him lies§.319 *a*
light his shadow........275 *k*
light inscrutable burned...278 *i*
light is mingled with. .....103 *d*
l. is the first of painters....352 *f*
light is the task when......300 *f*
light is thy element.......246 *a*
l. my candle from their....352 *e*
light of a pleasant eye.....294 *d*
light of Fashion's room....244 *o*
light of heaven restore.... 61 *c*
light of jurisprudence......437 *c*
light of somewhat yet to...195 *a*
l. of the Mæonian star‡....576 *p*
l. of truth thence derived...365 *v*
l. seeking light doth light*..352 *t*
l. shone, and order from**..462 *s*
light such a candle........212 *t*
light that made darkness...352 *v*
l. that shone when Hope†..401 *h*
light them at the fiery*.....197 *e*
l. the touches are that kiss.406 *q*
l. thickens, and the crow*..417 *j*
l. through every guilty*....584 *t*
l. thro' holes yourselves‡...125 *k*
light to gods and men.....276 *s*
l. translateth night; 'tis...100 *t*
light upon her face§........195 *d*
l. us deep into the Deity...577*m*
l. which beats upon a†....535 *o*
l. will repay the wrongs of..131 *i*
l. within his own clear**...105 *r*
live by thy l., and earth...409 *x*
load becomes l. which is...683 *n*
long pains are light.......103 *b*
lost! the l. withdrawn....388 *r*
love indeed is light from‖..357 *c*
lovely lady garmented in l.660 *h*
love's holiest, rarest light..219 *l*
memory lends her light no. 11 *g*

loss how to determine......154m
loss might leave the soul ..198 q
loss of dirt.. ....293 p
l. of sincerity is l. of vital..556 t
removeth is suer of loss.... 76 p
saw and pined his loss**...354 l
sit and wail their loss*.... 354 q
some natural sorrow, l., or¶570 u
that loss is common would†384 s
the loss of all those years..592 p
the loss of money..........728 g
time but from its loss......604 e
to contribute to my loss.. .586 i
Losses–l., that have of late so*442m
Lost–air, nor leaf is lost‖.... 346 q
all is lost save honor...... 772 t
all is not lost; th'**........103 a
all lost things are in the...316 d
all was lost, but that the*. 638 t
a lost good name is ne'er...524 g
amidst the soft variety, I'm629 s
better to have loved and l.†366 s
but being lack'd and lost.*483 s
cause was l. through you ..178 g
character is lost all is lost.354 n
common mass of matter l.‡354 e
have fought and lost....... 91m
I am not lost, for we.......138 e
I have lost a day ....722 n
I have lost my reputation*.524 q
I'm lost, in wonder, love ..382 d
in the Temple lost outright352 i
I've lost a day............354 u
know, my name is lost*....608 o
"life is not lost," said she..351 e
lost, except a little life‖....420 n
lost him half the kind......655 x
lost in a convent's solitary‡448m
lost morals, justice, honor.722m
lost the immortal part*....524 q
lost to all the sense of‡.....551 h
lost to manly thought .....567 t
lost to the noble sallies.....567 t
lost to virtue, lost to manly567 t
love's too precious to be l.†366 o
made but to be lost ....143 l
neither won nor lost.......206 h
never lost an English gun†.444 q
no hate lost between us....505jj
no indication of what's lost 354 k
no love lost between us ....357 h
not at all, are never lost...506bb
nothing except a battle l ...640 q
not lost, but gone before...502 v
one lost to nature ....269 n
praising what is lost*......486 x
quick read, quick lost......435 o
quiet sense of something l.†354 r
shall be no love lost.......505hh
shame which once lost.....722m
so fallen! so lost! the light.388 r
so lost in lexicography.....664 t
sooner lost and worn*......377 e
that all was lost**.........555 y
the main lost, cast the by..493 p
tho' lost to sight to mem'ry380 f
though the field be lost**..103 a
to be lost when sweetest... 75 j
we missed it, lost it forever461 h
what has been lost is safe..803 z
whatsoever thing is lost....354 j
what though the field be l.**688 f
what we left we lost.......102 o
what you lend is lost......722 r
when faith is l., when honor373 f
when health is l. something354 n
when wealth is l. nothing ..354 n
who lost Mark Antony the..658 a
who lost my heart while‡..361m
with fire, so won, so lost*..580 q
woman that deliberates is l.355 a
Lot–a happier l. were mine..569 e
await our future lot........ 7 x
fixed thy lowly lot.... ....226 f
hard their lot who neither.206 h
has it been my lot to mark.589 i
he by no uncommon lot....632 f

her lot is made for her by..656 d
I've bourne a weary lot....380 r
I wish thy lot now bad....256 l
labor is the lot of man‡ ....339 b
lot of the beautiful on earth755 r
loving lot was cast........241 o
the lot must come forth ...689 p
though bleak our lot.......400 g
want, if sickness be thy lot 261 o
Lote-tree–to the l-t.,springing615 d
Loth–thus aged men full loth 11 g
Lothario– gallant gay l.... .491 e
Lotion–tincture of syrup, l.. 512 r
Lotos–flowering l. spreads‡..615 f
l. blooms below the barren†235 a
lotos blooms by every†.....235 a
l. bowed above the tide and615 g
lotos the name‡ ....234 u
lotos flower is troubled....234 t
stone lotos cups, with.....234 v
within the lotos flower.....235 b
wove the lotos band to deck615 e
Lotos-dust–yellow l-d. is†....235 a
Lotos-flowers–where droop'g 615 c
Lottery–fortune's false l.....582 v
Loud–l. withal, that would ..487 n
the world so loud, and they 67 e
Louers–your forehead louers 328 a
Lour–smile she or lour*.....376 c
Louvre–been to the L. and... 98 h
Lovable–to be loved, be l....723 l
Love–a brother's l. exceeds..356 b
absence conquers love ..... 3 h
absence death to those who‡544 k
afar our light of love..... 31 q
a kingly power their love..402 e
all beauty, I call love...... 33 p
all for love we paired......223 s
all hearts in love use*......265 g
all she loves is love‖........356 p
all that life is love.........267 r
all their quantity of love*..363 c
a l. still burning upward†..646 a
always returns to his first l.777 p
amber sweet of l. is turn'd.327 q
a mighty pain to love it is..357 r
an ambassador of love*....365 f
and a half to love....... ...776 k
and are of love the food**..154 t
and be thy love......'.....361 t
and everlasting love.......657 y
and love but her forever...655 b
and l. me, it was sure to...155 f
and Love of Heaven.......579 p
and love the night ....329 n
and Love with bliss ....582 t
and the love of sway‡......465 r
and very few to love¶......421 f
angels must love Ann*.....203 w
a poet not in l. is out at sea.478 f
a poet without love were...317 g
are but ministers of love...357m
are fou' o' love divine......101 d
as honor, l., obedience*.... 11 r
as is the voice of love......415 l
ask not of me, love........355 c
as l. and I late harbour'd..493 p
as l. does when he draws..662 c
as l. knoweth no lawes......360 l
as love's young dream......361 c
aspiring youth beware of l.367 b
as some did him l., so others541 b
at all but love to pay......434 l
at his call love him¶......313 q
attracted by the love of... 12 q
a well of l., a spring of .... 34 f
a whole eternity of love....298 j
a woman's love is mighty†402 c
ay, as true l. should do*....554bb
beautiful time of youthful.778 k
because they love the lie...621 o
because, you see, I l. you..367 i
beggared L. may go all bare356 d
beginning and the end of l.777 t
be good that love me......261 a
be in love with night*......363 e
best to l. wisely no doubt..366 t

beyond His love and care...276 a
bishop Love will be........359 k
blasting all Love's paradise328 j
blessed leisure for L. or.....342 v
bow before thine altar, L..365 l
breaking for a little love....537 h
brightly o'er my love.......217 g
brings my love to me in...415 d
bring their own love....... 89 s
burns with one love‡.......264 r
burns for l. and money too.485m
but I do love thee*....... ..364m
but I love you, sir.........355 r
but is it what we love..... 357 z
but love from l. toward*...363 q
but l. is blind, and lovers*.362 q
but love–strong love.....216 f
but never taint my love*...627 w
butterfly's deep in love.....322 l
by faith and love ....800 l
by heaven I do love*.......362 s
by the love she accepts.....656 d
can be wise and love......359 a
cannot hold love out*......363 a
cannot l. as I have loved...355 e
canopy which l. has spread.417 p
can tell love's feeling......219 k
can't live upon l. deserves..499 i
carry half my l. with him*.311 w
cause was–all for love.....365m
change old love for new.....75 n
character of his love....... 76m
chief of all love's joys......358 a
command, nothing in l.*.... 30 a
common as light is love....365 i
conduct to mutual love....309 t
conjugial l. is celestial.....365 s
conquer l. that run away..104 s
constrained to love thee...118 a
converse with that eternal.566 x
could I l. less. I should....355 d
course of true l. never did *362 o
crime to love too well‡.....361 n
dame of Ephesus her love..662 k
dear love of old...........212 j
difference in his love*.....291 s
dispute, and practice love.367 q
divine is love and scorneth.361 s
do it with a sort of love....250 q
do not l. that do not show..506 v
do not l. thee, Sabidius...723 a
do sorrow at my grief in l.*570 i
dost thou l. life ? then do..347 p
doves draw love*..........364 a
each time we love we turn..570 k
eaten them, but not for l.*..372 o
engines can the proudest l..663 t
enough to make us love....522 t
envy I with love.... .....206 f
esteem and love were‡.... ..279 a
eternal love and instant....448 i
even so by love the young*.362m
everlasting l., restrain thy.485 l
everybody in love is blind..723 q
every gesture dignity and*657 q
exercise, study and love... 9 a
express no kinder sign of*.335 h
eye that wept essential love382 i
fairest l. from heaven above357 g
fall the tears of love........216m
fancy, when they love... ..36 g
farewell, l., and all thy....367 n
farewell then verse, and l.‡ 623 c
far from the lips we love...663 a
fathom deep I am in love*.364 j
faults, I love thee still.....118 a
few love what they may....686 u
fights in Love's name......367 f
first consciousness of l.§....360 b
fooled by that which we l..762 e
forgotten, and love forlorn†141 o
for I hate, yet l. thee, so...456 n
for I love thee.............355 q
for ladies' love unfit....... 34 i
for l., if thou art all........358 x
for love is heaven.........362 q
for l. is heaven and claims. 95 a

SHAKESPEARE *; MILTON **; WORDSWORTH ¶; BYRON ‖; TENNYSON †; LOWELL ††; POPE ‡; LONGFELLOW §.

for love's humility is love's.366 *d*
for to be wise and love*....363 *b*
fortune ripens with thy l.*.381 *l*
for which love longeth.....671 *n*
free love—free field—wet..610*m*
fresh dew of languid love..563 *f*
friendship is love...........264 *p*
friendship, l., and peace...644 *u*
friendship, weakens Love..599 *e*
from love so sweet, O......304 *i*
from the lips of Love......621 *d*
from without I still call l.. 33 *p*
fruits of love are gone‖.... 9 *e*
gather the rose of l. whilest.365 *o*
genial power of love......276 *l*
gentleness and l. and trust§.645 *b*
girls we l. for what they...778 *i*
giving l. your sorrow and*.570 *i*
glue and lime of love......334 *l*
god of love, with roses.....242 *s*
gods love die young‖.......150 *n*
gods love dies young.......151 *l*
goe to my L. where she is..603 *o*
go off hungry, leaving love..17 *k*
graces in my love do dwell*283 *q*
greatest l. of life appears..351 *p*
greatest miracle of l. is the.114 *l*
great in war, are great in l. 118 *s*
great love grows there*....365 *d*
grief shows much of love*..288 *u*
hail, wedded love**........376 *b*
hand in sign of love*......121 *t*
happy trees love each his..722 *r*
harder still are those of l...355 *n*
hate to return with love....778 *s*
hating no one love but‖...356 *s*
have not what we love.....783 *r*
have your love*...........262 *g*
heart in love with night§....398 *e*
hearts in l. use their own*.363 *d*
heart that no l. understands 55*m*
heart which l. of thee alone‖491 *t*
her I love so dearly†.......220 *r*
her l. voe the jay o' my....374 *f*
herself complimented by l.103 *h*
he sang of love with¶...... 46 *a*
he was all for love and.... 78 *v*
he woold l. and she woold..355 *o*
Him whose life was Love... 92 *h*
his l. at once and dread.... 93 *a*
his l. sincere his thoughts* 83 *p*
hold so fast as love can do.356 *t*
holy love's illusive dreams.367 *e*
honor rests on manly love..660 *o*
hope kiss'd l., and love†...366 *n*
how many times do I love..355 *i*
how to love himself*.......548 *e*
I do not love a man.........674 *b*
I do not love thee, Sabidius.174 *v*
I do not l. you, Dr. Fell.....723 *a*
if ever thou shalt l. in*.....108 *o*
if I l. you, what business is.778 *o*
if music be the food of l.*..407 *k*
if there's delight in love. ..357 *q*
if thy l. be deep as mine...360 *l*
if you wish to love.........766 *a*
if you would be loved, l....500 *e*
I hate and I love...........711 *o*
I have been servant of Love456*m*
I know and l. the good, fer.641 *x*
I love him well, and.......357 *h*
I l. thee, as the good love§..359*w*
I love thee, I love but thee.366 *e*
I love thee most........ ...117 *r*
I love thee so, Dear, that I..355 *s*
I l. the sex, and sometimes‖.655 *k*
I'm lost in wonder, love....382 *d*
in books and l. the mind...629 *v*
indenture of my love*.......335 *t*
in l. as your rhymes speak*.362 *p*
in l., faith, if he be hungry.723 *o*
In l. there is no lack.......493 *p*
in l. with some woman*....587 *h*
in love with your Juno....180 *c*
in peace, L. tunes the......362 *g*
in reason, nor in love.......522 *a*
in search of l., and find you.607 *f*

into the l. of God...........520 *s*
is better than life with love.164 *f*
is human love the growth‖.357 *b*
is love's true pride.........366 *d*
is pervious to love.........358 *g*
is the love of truth.........769 *q*
is there no relief for love‡..542 *p*
I tell thee love is Nature's..357 *i*
it establishes love..........678 *d*
it sings of love that........ 44 *p*
it strikes where it doth l.*..570 *e*
jealousy their dawn of l....374 *h*
Jove, for your l., would*...365 *q*
kill the best of passions, l..367 *d*
kindle to Love or Wrath...352 *i*
kings may love treason....607 *s*
know her was to love her..361 *u*
know how to love with men 27 *w*
knowing that we love each 358 *s*
known you love you better 360 *r*
know that I love thee......361 *d*
know the inly touch of l.* .362 *t*
labor is light where love...493 *p*
lack of love from love......132 *o*
last, not least in love*......364*w*
leaves live but to love......722 *r*
let those l. now who never.361 *i*
let thy l. be younger than* 364 *r*
let us live and love.........722 *q*
life and love for Greece....212 *l*
life is love and love is death457 *h*
life which all creatures love345 *h*
life without the light of l.. 778 *n*
light of love the purity of‖. 34 *a*
like God in love and power 476 *c*
like love is but a name.... 264 *j*
live in love and jokes.......722 *s*
lives true life will love true 621 *e*
live with me and be my l...360 *n*
long-cherished love........722 *o*
long love doth so*..........364 *s*
love a Hercules*...........364 *d*
love all, trust a few*.......511 *s*
l. alters not with his brief* 108 *l*
love, and a cough, cannot..501*w*
love and be loved in the old 607 *f*
l. and desire are the spirit's778*m*
l. and friendship exclude...263 *p*
l., and silence, and mystery617 *c*
love and tears for the Blue.636 *p*
love and the smiling face...304*m*
love an ingrate.............715 *n*
love any one but himself...788 *k*
love befriend the bold......686 *i*
love begins with love ......356 *c*
love better is than fame ...366 *f*
love but her and l. forever.356 *e*
love buys not with the.....360 *k*
love came first to earth.... 241 *o*
love can fear no one........723 *r*
L. can hope where Reason..360 *i*
love cannot be cured.......723 *c*
love cannot be mixed......723 *s*
l. can scarce deserve the‖..356 *u*
love conquers all things...724 *q*
l. contending with....... §359 *z*
l. could walk with banish'd†366*m*
love deceives the best of‡..359 *e*
l. did make thee run into*..363 *k*
love does doat in liking....360 *s*
l. dwells not in lip-depths‖.366 *l*
l. earth only for its earthly‖532 *q*
l. encinctured with reserve 24*m*
love exalts the mind........ 34 *k*
love, fair looks, and true*..377 *p*
l. foolishly is better than... 366 *t*
love free as air at sight of‡361 *o*
love gilds the scene........660 *i*
love gives itself, but is not§359 *y*
l. goes in with Folly's dress 356 *q*
love goes toward love as*..363 *g*
love grants in a moment...778 *h*
l. had ripened into speech .266 *e*
l. half regrets to kiss it dry‖590 *g*
love has a tide.............359 *i*
love has been received a ...474 *j*
love has both its gall.......723*m*

l. has never known a law.. 367 *j*
love has no thought of self.360 *k*
l. he bore to learning was...342 *d*
‎ľ. her doubting and anguish358*m*
love him that is honest* ... 83 *s*
love illumes the realms of. 362 *d*
love in a cottage is hungry 367 *k*
love in a hut with water ...359 *o*
l. in a shower safe shelter..355 *l*
love indeed is anything....360 *s*
love indeed is light from ‖..357 *c*
l. in its essence is spiritual.365 *t*
l. in others what we lack...155 *t*
l. inspires with strength...102 *p*
love in time is healed again 359 *r*
l. is a boy by poets styl'd ..356 *j*
love is a credulous thing...723 *b*
love is all in fire and yet is.360 *s*
l. is a lock that linketh .....358 *t*
love is an egotism of two ..777 *r*
love is a pouting child.....561 *k*
l. is a smoke raised with*..363 *r*
love is a thing full..........723 *k*
l. is blind and lovers cannot* 61 *g*
love is compatible with....101 *j*
love is ever sick and yet is.360 *s*
l. is ever the beginning of..336*w*
love is ever true and yet is.360 *s*
l. is hurt with jar and fret†366 *k*
love is in our power........723 *x*
love is like a dizziness......359 *c*
love is like fire.............355 *n*
love is loveliest when......243 *e*
l. is made a vague regret†..366 *k*
love is much in winning....360 *s*
l. is not love which alters*.317 *o*
l. is often a fruit of ....777 *s*
l. is principle, and has its ..357 *s*
love is something awful....236 *g*
love is soon sated..........176 *f*
love is sunshine, hate is§..348*m*
life is sweet, love is sweet..362 *a*
love is that orbit of the ...355*m*
l. is the emblem of eternity365 *p*
love is the law of the school512 *c*
love is the life of man......365 *u*
l. is the secret sympathy...588*m*
love is the sweetest thing ..164 *g*
l. is the tyrant of the heart 358 *j*
love is your master*........363 *s*
love it for his sake.........223 *l*
l. keeps his revels where*..363 *t*
love keeps the cold out§....360 *a*
love knows no winter ......778 *d*
love laid his sleepless head.366 *a*
love leads me one way......715 *k*
l. leads to present rapture.359 *r*
l. lends life a little grace... 74 *a*
love lent me wings.........207 *k*
l. lessens woman's delicacy778 *c*
love lies bleeding in the....285 *c*
l. lieth deep; love dwells†.366 *l*
love like a shadow flies*...363 *u*
l. long life better than*....350 *p*
l. looks not with the eyes*.363 *v*
love, love, my love........358 *n*
love made those hollows*..154 *v*
love may lead love in ......356 *d*
love may transform me*...363 *o*
love me and reward me*...145 *d*
love me for myself alone...360*m*
love me, it was sure to die.. 20 *l*
love me little, love me long360 *o*
l. me, myself, and not my..259 *u*
l. me with exceeding love..360*m*
love mourn'd long and†....366 *n*
love must be attracted.....723 *e*
l. must kiss that mortal's..356 *d*
love must needs be blind...357 *o*
l. my love that loveth her..358*m*
l. my neighbor as myself...356 *l*
love of yours was mine....357 *g*
l. night the most because..415 *d*
l. of all your native land...118 *c*
love of country is more....790 *r*
l. of knowing without the.. 78 *h*
love of greatness.... ......286 *l*

SHAKESPEARE *; MILTON **; WORDSWORTH ¶; BYRON ‖; TENNYSON †; LOWELL ††; POPE ‡; LONGFELLOW §.

there is love too long for...359 *l*
there L. lived, and there he*154 *v*
the seasons of l. roll not...778 *a*
the smiles of love adorn...370 *e*
the sweet poison of love...723 *v*
the test of truth, love‖.....599 *i*
the traitor still I love.....608 *f*
the wee little whimpering l.456*m*
they escape from us in l....788 *d*
they that l. mirth, let them.340 *s*
things with intensest love..343 *n*
third essential of God's l...522 *g*
this is L. as wise men say..361 *g*
though he l. her not........355 *r*
though youth gave l. and .. 10 *t*
thou'rt full of love and*...665 *q*
thrift, but none of love*...377 *o*
thy l. be younger than*.....659 *u*
thy true l.'s recompense*...381 *l*
till l. have all his rites*....602*w*
'tis for my love—'tis for...264 *c*
'tis not a fault to love.....355 *b*
to beget more l. in you*....659*m*
to be idle, fall in love.......723 *j*
to business that we l. we*..442 *n*
to know, to esteem, to l....346 *q*
to l. again and be again‖...356 *q*
to l., and to be loved......265*m*
to love, but love in vain....357 *r*
to l. her is a liberal 84*w*
to love is to believe........367 *h*
to l. me also in silence.....355 *u*
too divine to love.......... 35 *k*
to see her is to love her....655 *b*
true knowledge leads to l.¶.338 *p*
true l. has been my death†.366 *j*
true l. is but a humble ††...360 *f*
true love hates ....723 *u*
true love's the gift which ..362 *h*
true love there can be......327 *u*
truth of truths is love.....355 *h*
tune the rural pipe to l.....531 *b*
turns to thoughts of love†..541 *f*
understand it, despise it,...667 *x*
unheeded bait of love.......555 *p*
unrelenting foe to love.. .257 *i*
us that trade in love*......407 *q*
verses of feigning love*....557 *l*
very bond of love* ....493 *l*
very ecstasy of love*.......364 *v*
very flame of love*........280 *q*
virtue is the love of........547 *q*
want of love tormenteth*..365 *c*
watch o'er what they love‖.329 *l*
wayward is this foolish l*..363 *h*
we always l. those who..... 6 *h*
we are all born for love....357 *u*
we bury love.................255 *c*
we cannot fight for love*...663 *p*
we love but while we may†610*m*
we love life and we flee....754 *k*
we love peace as we abhor.470*m*
we love without reason ....786 *i*
Werther had a love for.....366 *u*
we should know before.....777 *q*
what I love determines......358 *b*
what love can do that*....363 *a*
what l. can ever cure this....149 *c*
what Love commands.......723 *h*
what love I note*......... 291 *q*
what love! this midnight ..417 *v*
what moment l. begins§....359 *x*
what thing is love..........361 *b*
what 'tis to love*..........363 *f*
what 'tis to love ? how*...365 *c*
when I l. thee not Chaos*..364*m*
when l begins to sicken*... 73 *g*
when love is at its best.....359 *j*
when L. speaks, the voice*.278 *a*
when love's well-timed 'tis.355 *b*
when my dear l. and I...... 59 *a*
where Death like Love .....457 *h*
where love is great, the*...365 *d*
where there is no love......566 *a*
which love has made‡......438 *a*
which Love most blesses...219 *l*

who falls in love...........723 *p*
who in the l. of Nature.....410 *j*
who love the Lord..........634 *f*
who l. too much, hate‡.....359 *f*
whom none can l., whom...79*m*
whom on earth alone we l.. 45 *h*
whom the gods l. dies......690 *g*
whose love is bold.... ....367 *l*
why did she love him‖ ....357 *b*
why I love this youth*......363 *l*
wife that I l. and that.....642 *d*
wildest woe is love.‖........355 *g*
will love true love..........356 *a*
with joy and love**.......146 *s*
with love's sorrow.........250 *e*
with oaths of love* ......362 *k*
without the l. of learning..341 *v*
with unearthly love........261 *r*
woman's love can win**...360 *u*
women know no perfect l. .358 *c*
women will l. her that*.....660 *e*
words of l. then spoken ...673 *b*
world and l. were young...361 *t*
world's love is vain........463 *a*
would not love at all ......327 *q*
wroth with one we love ... 17 *g*
ye both I love the Palm....617 *a*
yet all love is sweet.......365 *i*
you know that love will*...549 *h*
Younker prancing to his*..400 *x*
your love can labour*.....184 *q*
your scenes of l., so flowing 422 *a*
youth fades; love droops. 307 *x*
youth, hope and love§......189 *g*
you wished to be loved, l...723*w*
Love-chant-utter forth his .. 51 *a*
Love-ditty-soul of his latest . 99 *d*
Loved-and lov'd his country‡311 *q*
at first sight they love*....357 *j*
better to have l. and lost†..366 *s*
compliment than to be l....620 *q*
for she that loved her so... 544 *l*
has loved knows not ......218 *s*
heart that has truly loved..361 *f*
He [Cæsar] l. the treason..608 *k*
her father l. me oft invited* 350 *h*
him that loved the rose....243 *q*
I had a friend that l. her*..663*m*
I have lived and loved......771 *o*
I have not l. the world‖... .317 *s*
I l her, that she did pity*..365 *a*
I l. you ere I knew you....360 *r*
I saw and loved ....358 *l*
I've lived and loved.......350 *a*
let those who always loved 361 *i*
loved a tree or flower.....155 *f*
loved but they sighed*....364 *i*
loved by those who are too. 67 *k*
loved her own harmless....629 *j*
loved I not honor more....360 *d*
l. in this world of sorrow..569 *d*
loved justice and hated.....332 *l*
l. me for the dangers*.....365 *a*
loved much, hoped little...758 *o*
loved my friends as I do...259*m*
lov'd needs only to be seen.621*w*
lov'd not at first sight......360 *p*
l., or was avenged, like me.528 *n*
l. so slight a thing†........366 *p*
lov'd the brightest fair....360 *i*
l. the less for flow'ring.....611 *e*
loved three whole days.....108 *u*
loved ye long and well......216 *c*
none ever loved, but at....357 *j*
not that I l. Cæsar less*...368 *c*
reason why I loved him....361 *b*
sooner looked but they l.*..364 *i*
that I loved Rome more*. .368 *c*
the heart that loved her¶..413 *k*
them that had l. it best..... 1 *r*
the souls we loved†........317 *a*
the spirit that loved thee ,.671 *f*
those that he l. so long.....361 *v*
thou hast not loved*.......363 *k*
to be l., be lovable ....723 *l*
until I truly l., I was alone.567 *l*
use him as though you l.... 19 *f*

who ever l. that lov'd......360 *p*
who ne'er loved them* ....215 *j*
ye shall be loved again§....102 *s*
you've play'd, and l., and‡.349 *j*
Love-in-idleness-call it*....237*m*
Love-letter-prove a true l-l...448 *q*
Love-letters-have I 'scaped*.449 *q*
Lovelier-crown'd 'twould l. . 35 *u*
l. thing I know to-day......609 *p*
nothing l. can be found**...657 *p*
Loveliest- l. of lovely........240 *q*
l. of women ! heaven......654 *n*
the last still l., till—'tis‖... 624 *q*
Love-light-pure and holy l-l..334*m*
Loveliness-dim and solitary‖.415 *j*
her l. I never knew until... 34 *f*
its l. increases, it will never 34*w*
lay down in her loveliness.. 34 *q*
loveliness needs not the.... 24 *n*
majesty of loveliness‖..... 34 *c*
my loveliness is born......243 *d*
rare capricious loveliness .395 *h*
thy pure loveliness........224 *j*
warm shadow of her l......584 *k*
Lovelorn-a l. heart pursuing.662 *j*
Lovely-and built to be l......426 *a*
and if in death still l........142*m*
beautiful than thy lovely...678 *j*
her own shape how l.**....354 *j*
husband's eye looks lovely. 24 *p*
how l. he appears........ ‖ 30 *t*
l. and a fearful thing‖......356 *n*
l. and unsistered creature..629 *j*
lovely as the day§.......... 35 *c*
lovely as these wings of...328 *f*
lovely being, scarcely‖..... 83 *r*
lovely in their lives........259 *s*
l. lady garmented in light..660 *h*
lovely, she's divine .. ....203 *s*
lovely woman stoops to....656 *o*
more l. than Pandora**... 35 *q*
sometimes l., like a bride†.570 *o*
yet lovely in your strength‖ 577 *p*
Lover-abide and every lover.349 *u*
affliction taught a lover ‡..361 *p*
a hapless lover courts thy. 48 *l*
all mankind love a lover...358 *d*
a lover's ear will hear*....302 *j*
a lover's eyes will gaze an*362 *j*
a l.'s soul lives in the body.495 *x*
angel appear to each lover.658 *c*
as a lover of his mistress...780 *p*
beneath a l.'s burning sighs616 *n*
can deceive a lover.......724 *e*
chosen seats of each fond l.615 *b*
dreamer turned to lover...233 *g*
every lover is a soldier.....723 *d*
every loyal l. tasks his wit.628 *c*
find me a reasonable lover.723 *n*
for lover's thoughts........237 *e*
friend and l. of the pipe...457 *n*
give repentance to her l.....551 *g*
hope is a lover's staff*....308 *u*
hope the l.'s heart does**.. 51 *l*
in a lover's eyes*.........363 *r*
is happy as a lover¶........ 85 *s*
I was always a lover of soft 42 *c*
lover has he not outlived...550 *d*
l. in the husband may be...311 *j*
l. of letters loves power too 428 *c*
lover or crown to thee.....241 *h*
lover, sick to death*......364 *q*
l.'s pain to attain the plain 530 *i*
l.'s sonnets turned to holy.470*w*
maiden and her lover.......222 *a*
make a lover angry........724 *a*
man that true l. of mine..398 *q*
no lover has that pow'r....485*m*
on her l.'s arm she leant†..366 *h*
owl more blind than a l.....376 *g*
pale and wan, fond lover...365 *r*
pressing l. seldom wants...362 *b*
propositions of a lover*....363*m*
rejects a lover's prayer....236 *i*
shall the lover rest ....362 *i*
some banish'd lover‡.......448 *l*
soul meets soul on l's. lips.335 *u*

SHAKESPEARE *; MILTON **; WORDSWORTH ¶; BYRON ‖; TENNYSON †; LOWELL ††; POPE ‡; LONGFELLOW §.

Majestic-m. like the sun ....538 p
m., though in ruin**........153 j
m. with her swelling sails..446 a
yet still m. in decay‡.....535 u
Majestical-m. in life or††.... 81 g
Majestically-bears her down‖.551 o
Majesty-Arthur struts in‖...421 p
attribute to awe and m.*..382 p
bare-pick'd bone of m....639 k
controlling majesty*......535 i
in rayless m. now stretches 418 a
kindness to his majesty...118 e
m. and love do not ....723 f
rise in m. to meet thine††. 418 h
rising in clouded majesty**398 h
the Majesty of God revere.528 v
the next, in majesty. ......479 b
to see her abdicate this m.. 1 b
Majority-death had the m...132m
on God's side is a majority.275 j
the majority is wicked.....644 k
the voice of the majority...774 l
'tis the majority in this....320 s
Make-could we make her†....660 r
make haste to live..........722 g
which, as it seems, m. thee*455 c
Maker-image of his M. hope* 14 a
in his Maker's steps of fire.584 c
m. of the dead man's bed ..458 p
praise their M. as they move 40 n
the M. saw, took pity‡.....658 l
they would thank their m..454 s
vocal with the M.'s praise‡. 95 s
Makes-because he makes...453 a
he m., destroys, remakes...132 e
makes great presents......706 l
m. me or fordoes me quite*417 n
makes them bursts them ..329 i
tongue of him that m. it*..328 r
Making-stigmatical in m.*... 83 n
to the making up of a man.454 g
Makings-the royal m. of a*..535 c
Maladies-m. are rich and....552 n
Malady-a m. preys on my...552 o
a wearisome malady.......295 o
cough is not your malady..180 i
malady most incident*....219 s
medicine worse than the m.500 c
Malcolm-and Malcolm heard.486 u
Male-creature, female as the.654 v
Malebolge-called M. of an...298 x
Malecontent-arms like a m.*. 56 b
Malefactions-proclaimed*....423 f
Malefactor-monstrous m.*...158 t
Males-deeds are m., words .496gg
Malevolent-m. have hidden..739m
Malice-bearing no m. or ill.. 86 a
crooked m. nourishment*..372 p
knavery adds malice to ... 762 f
malice denies that it.......264 o
m. in men as to rejoice...724 h
m. of this age shapes*.....266m
m. remains in danger of*..129 u
m. speaks of those which...793 g
malice toward none........ 86 n
neither Love, M. nor........652 n
poison, malice domestic*...138 k
set down aught in malice*.332 r
water, put nought in in m..649 k
Malicious-this animal is very 757 k
virtue is not malicious.....631bb
Malign-dare to malign him..276 n
Malignity-motiveless m......402 j
Mallets-the blows of the m..431 k
Mallows-m., crisp dill, or...235 f
Malmsey-of M. and Malvoisie.648 h
Malt-and it favoureth malt..650 e
Duke of Norfolk deals in..442 c
Malvoisie-of Malmsey and M.648 h
Mammon-cursed M. be when 369 j
M. led them on**..........369 k
M. pine amidst his store‡..369 l
M. the least erected**......369 k
M. wins his way where‖....369 i
the throne of M. grey.....369 h
treasures here do M.'s sons 369m
Man-a bold bad man .... 84 u

actions show the man‡..... 5 k
a good man, through.......773 q
a hearty old man.......... 12 e
aid, like man and wife‡....653 p
a little worse than a man*.. 84 o
all that may become a m.*.119 n
all the breadth of man†.... 85 h
a man had better be dead..666 j
a man he seems of¶..........112m
a man is not a wall........325 k
a man not perfect, but... 79 n
a man of mark§............371m
a man's a man, but when ..533 s
a man's a man for a' that..370 c
a man so various...........212 a
a man's worth something.. 77 o
a man that's fond........... 4 r
and each man a friend§.....672 p
and man made money......510 a
and resume the man‡......371 d
and well-bred man........120 d
an imitative creature is m..773 g
a noble m. is led by........796 i
an old m., broken with the*. 11 t
an old man in his ....676 k
any m. with half an eye....553 p
appear like man and wife..634 r
a proper man as one shall*.372 e
are great to little man......619 o
are misery and man‡......347 x
argument a man's no horse 26 t
artificial plague of man....635 r
art is a revelation of man§.528 f
art the m. in the moon §...644 t
a sacred gift to man........493 b
as a man is, so is his God*.770 j
a self-made man? Yes.....370 o
as man; false man........371 l
as man's ingratitude*......319 q
a tailor make a man*......455 b
at thirty man suspects.....401 p
a very man—not one........311 s
a very unclubable man.... 80 n
bark of man could.........539 a
be a m. before thy mother.506kk
bees work for m. and yet..321 s
before a man..............654 t
before man made us††.....371 n
be trod by man...........284 n
bidding the lip of m. keep .531 f
bird whom m. loves best¶.. 56 g
both m. and bird and beast.487 q
both m. and womankind... 77 j
blessed is the m. that hath 521 s
but art, O man, is thine..... 29 d
but honor is of man........ 69 o
but m., curs'd man, on.... 94 f
but man over men**.......559 p
cannot make a man††......122 u
childhood shows the man** 90 h
child is father of the man¶. 91 g
chimera, then, is man......371 r
closing full in man ....122 r
cold is the judgment of m..330 r
conference a ready man....341 n
confess yourself an old m..180 b
could we make her as the†.660 r
critic let the man be lost‡..125 j
cursed be the man the....374 j
dear to a man than his ....351 g
did m. compute existence‖.346 h
doubtful down and promise 458 b
drops, stain my man's*.... 17 v
each man do his best*..... 5 q
each m. is a hero and.....301 d
each man unknowing.....267 k
education forms the man..170 k
ere man learned to hew....609 c
every man desires to live... 12 f
every man feels††.......... 5 c
every man for himself......497 j
every man for himself and.317 t
every man has at times in . 82 l
every man is like the......565 f
every man is odd*.........497 k
every m. is or should be an 327 a
every man is the son of....797 h

every man will do his duty .164 d
every man upon this earth. 136 e
every man with him was... 79 b
faint old man shall lean....646 u
fat, oily man of God.......451 r
fine day a fine young man..380 g
fine man hath your tailor..454 r
fond man! the vision of a..634 o
fond m. though all the......418 e
foremost m. of all this*... 70 s
for man's offence**.......221 j
for one man who can.... 6 p
foolish-compounded clay*.341 c
from the present man......753 q
gently scan your brother..343 c
give me that man that is*..465 y
glorious goodly frame of..369 s
glory now to be a man .....273 j
God made man, and man..510 a
God to man doth speak in..566 b
goings of this clock-work ..372 c
go West, young man! go..498 q
guilt like man's be e'er‖...487m
habit by the inward man*..461 f
handsome and charming...152 u
happy man's without......293 g
happy the man, and happy.605 c
hath man his fixed seat**..668 w
heart of a m. is depressed..656 l
heaven had made her such*663m
he felt as a man...........210m
he is pepper, not a man...724 p
he is the proper man......782 c
here comes a man of*...... 7 o
he was a m. and a Positivist370 p
he was a m. take him for*..372 j
highest style of man...... 93 x
his m. with scissors nicks*.458 h
hold the faithful mirror up.422 j
honest and a perfect man..370 z
honest man's the noblest‡..371 u
how beautiful it is for a m..142 a
how can man die better....469 d
how can man then*........ 14 a
how much less the man...318m
how poor a thing is man . 370 u
how poor a thing is man ..372 d
I am a man; what concerns724 s
I do not love a man.......674 b
if a man do not erect in this*381m
if man abandons, God.... 33 l
if man come not to gather.661 t
if m.'s unhappy, God's‡...510 k
I have named the man.....683 j
inhumanity to man........ 126 e
in man speaks God.......574 b
interest of man on earth...333 f
in the heart of m. she sits..651 v
intimates eternity to man..315 l
in Wit a man‡............183 n
is a well-made m. who has.145 o
is caught from man........126 o
is man a child of hope¶....309 f
is the tragedy, "Man"....137 j
it mars a man, it mars a...456 l
I venerate the man whose..450 c
judge of the man.........331 j
judgment falls upon a man.331 t
laborin' m. an' laborin'††..309 v
labour is the lot of man‡...330 b
less than man, I am not*...159 a
let each man think himself.369 g
let him pass for a man*...372 i
lies are the works of man..623 u
like an aged man, it stands.613 n
like peevish man and wife..378 f
life of man less than a span.345 j
life of man solitary, poor..847 w
little man all in gray......110 a
lost to manly thought.....567 t
lot of man but once to die..500ee
love is the life of man.....365 u
lustre gives to man........ 8m
made a m. out of my vice*.630 q
made by Man to Man the.. 29 a
made thee to temper man..657 y
make man better be.......289 j

place and m. for every*....461 p
sight of m. to do ill deeds*.594 f
take the m. whereby I*.....150 b
the means he raises........486 h
the m. to help him**......626 h
Meant–more is m. than **....296 c
Measure–could find my m... 96 g
days of life's short m......651 i
delightful m. or a dance*..315 f
fate thy measure takes ††..525 t
God hath giv'n me a m.....326 a
man should m. himself....724 k
measure not the work.....666 f
m. your mind's height....385 c
often have I sighed to m.¶.567 c
taking the measure*,......285 s
that knows no measure....370 l
they m. by thy deeds*....147 j
thought is the m. of life...348 j
to tread a m. with you*...129 g
was thy delighted m......307 n
world that we can m.....668 k
Measured–be m. by his*....570 l
life is not so, by the.....346 y
measur'd by my soul......386 m
m. on a three-year-old's....101 l
Measurements–m. more or..469 u
Measures–better than all m.. 49 n
measures all our time....401 m
measures back his way....606 v
m., not men, have always..481 r
measures seas and lands...445 c
not men, but measures....481 o
sweet in Lydian m. ....473 s
through m. fine as she....408 e
Meat–a butcher gazing at..430 m
anger's my meat; I sup*... 17 p
are butcher's meat.......422 a
as an egg is full of meat* ..513 o
best seasoning for meat....311 e
both guestes and meate... 26 h
burnt; and so is all the m.*432 g
but he sendeth meat......498 i
cannot eat but little meat..163 a
dish of meat is too good...168 y
God sends good meat......432 k
God sends us meat, yet....431 l
Heaven sends us good m.. 431 q
is another's m. or drink...508 q
it is too choleric a meat*..168 e
let the meat cool ere*.....211 l
little meat and a great§....167 i
meat, fire and clothes‡ ....642 s
m. was made for mouths*..311 h
mock the m. it feeds on*..328 e
out did the meate.........211 q
say grace to his meat ....522 h
some hae m. and canna ...166 g
the fallacious meat.......213 h
'twas m. and drink and....457 n
yet roast m., beheld‖431 o
Meats–eater of broken m.*..336 g
for books are as meats**... 67 q
hudling of many meats....167 m
sweetest m. the soonest....630 c
Mecca–M. saddens at the....147 p
Meccas–the M. of the mind..285 a
Mechanic–by mere m........587 c
poetry a mere m. art......476 l
Medal–man breaks not the...627 i
Medals–living m. see her‡..115 q
Meddles–m. with cold iron‖ ..442 v
that m. with cold iron....472 i
Meddling–m. with great....653 v
Medea–in such a night M.*....441 h
Medica–whole materia m....440 h
Medical–birth-day of m...... 98 l
while medical detectives...321 l
Medicinable–griefs are m.*...288 v
Medicinal–learned he was in..439 s
trees their medicinal gum*.591 z
Medicine–and jurisprudence..342 a
and medicine of men ......459 m
and medicine power*......223 g
by medicine life may be*...441 b
food nor the m. of being...521 l
med'cine cannot reach....552 o

m. for a troubled mind.....410 c
medicine for the soul.......66 e
medicine increases the....725 j
medicine is not an art......725 g
m., not poison, I offer you .783 n
m. thee to that sweet sleep*562 n
medicine the less*........288 j
m. worse than the malady .500 c
miserable have no other* ..308 v
pouring his medicine......283 b
preceptial m. to rage*.....288 o
the best medicine........746 l
too late to employ m......679 g
try one desp'rate med'cine.439 t
Mediocrity–a m. of success... 8 q
Meditates–whoever m. a......687 j
Meditating–m. that she*.....140 l
Meditation–Divinely bent to*.378 t
maiden meditation fancy*..378 j
mind for m.'s meant.... 91 r
O fearful m! where, alack*602 p
Meditations–thoughts to....378 g
Meditative–to m. spleen a¶..547 o
Medium–no cold m. knows‡..264 r
the just medium..........780 m
Meed–for his m. was crow* :579 l
m. of some melodious**...591 b
that now merres his m....491 d
Meek–and suns grow m. and.394 k
I am meek and gentle*.....404 a
meek and lowly, pure.... 86 i
safer being m. than fierce..101 b
Meet–an instant meet.......207 o
as two floating planks m...378 k
bold I can m.—perhaps.... 72 b
did not meet again........268 i
everywhere we meet.......351 d
extremes meet ....191 c
eyes m. far off, our sense..587 s
hope to m. shortly again... 2 p
if we do m. again, we'll*...464 w
I need never meet or .....264 q
in heaven shall one day m..138 e
I will go meet them*...... 5 n
leap to meet thee§........359 t
live again if not to meet... 212 j
m. and either do or die.... 3 t
meet him everywhere ....262 s
meet him in the court of*..378 q
m. him were I tied to*.....172 q
m. if not to meet in love ...212 j
meet me at the road........ 71 a
m. my ain dear somebody..366 c
m. other wayfarers at.....643 t
meet with such an one.....259 p
ne'er to m., or ne'er to....471 m
never the twain shall meet.637 q
only part to meet again....464 n
run half-way to meet it....368 j
run to m. what he would**288 b
shall we three meet again*.378 r
the hope to meet again.....308 c
this it is not meet*.........125 v
till we meet shall pant....204 k
times that I meet thee....600 k
to meet no more........262 n
to meet their Dad.......303 i
we meet thee like a¶.....228 q
where they m. they ......232 n
Meeting–joy of m. not§......378 n
meeting of gentle lights....196 f
meeting overhead.........224 l
m. were bare without it*...73 d
our meeting spots.......261 r
the meeting of an old one...516 h
Meetings–in life there are m..378 o
m. made December, June‡.627 p
merry m. to solace.......383 o
Meets–m. his Waterloo at....151 k
Melancholy–a green and*....467 u
and to be melancholy*....362 s
can soothe her melancholy.656 o
damn'd as melancholy.....378 s
devil this melancholy is....379 b
displayed their m. hue....614 l
hardships, prevent m.....379 d
has its chord in melancholy.383 q

homes, a melancholy train.172 e
melancholy as a battle won.640 q
m. as an unbraced drum....378 u
m. god protect thee*....... 76 c
m. is not, as you conceive..379 a
m. is the nurse of frenzy*..379 h
m. madness of poetry......477 e
m. marked him for his......379 c
m. men of all others........652 o
melancholy, slow.........532 i
moping m., and moon**....379 e
most musical most m......40 m
most musical most m...... 50 p
most musical, most m.**... 51 m
note of it is his m.*......379 k
of spirit's melancholy......276 i
O m.! who ever yet.*......379 j
pale M. sate retired........378 v
power is felt of m.........543 i
so sweet as melancholy....378 t
such a charm in m........379 f
suck m. out of a song*......379 i
the m. days are come......543 m
there is nothing m......... 50 p
what is more m. than......611 m
Mellow–speeches when half‖.483 d
too mellow for me....266 h
whether grave or mellow..259 k
Mellowed–fruit that m. long..133 o
m. to that tender light‖.... 33 t
Mellowness–age a mature m.. 9 j
Melodies–air with m. vernal§.540 l
heard m. are sweet......405 m
melodies gush from the....220 u
of wonderful melodies§.. .405 v
singing thy last melodies...542 j
sweetest m. are those¶......408 n
teasing with their m........394 b
the holy m. of love arise§..470 p
thousand m. unheard......210 u
where melodies alone are§.. 42 d
Melodious–along m. ways.... 43 o
move in melodious time**..406 e
need of some m. tear**....591 b
Melody–and a ringing sweet.. 58 e
as her melody she sang.... 51 d
aye falling in m. back. ....476 i
blundering kind of m......476 o
could you view the m......195 f
filled with melody divine...540 z
is a celestial melody§.......685 a
luve's like the melodie....356 f
mazy-running soul of m.... 52 g
m. loud and sweet that†.... 58 n
senses with charmed m.....408 k
sound of sweetest melody*.563 c
the hungry dark with m.... 52 d
unwearying words of m....398 p
view the melodie of ev'ry.. 35 e
Melon–m. to perfume each....266 d
Melons–friends are like m....261 l
Melrose–view fair M. aright..398 r
Melt–melt and soon must¶....382 c
melt at others' woe‡.......491 b
melt at other's woe‡.......588 d
melt itself into the sea*....207 i
melt off and leave the..... 71 g
now m. into sorrow, now‖...336 v
soft blue sky did never m.¶.558 i
solid flesh would melt*....149 s
'twould m. down the lead...599 h
Melted–melted in her depth..248 j
Melting–each in the other m.515 p
unused to the m. mood*....591 z
Melts–man who m. with....587 v
m. like kisses from a‖.....353 e
minutes melts away......217 r
Member–on the vicious m....439 r
this m. ne'er lies still......538 b
Members–ivories of her pure.401 o
Memnon–soft as M.'s harp... 51 i
touch makes M. sing......564 i
Memnons–new M. singing in..267 f
Memorial–I have reared a....714 l
sweetest m. the first kiss‖.334 e
Memorials–themselves m.....396 n
Memories–heart with such m.242 f

honey of delicious m.†.....381 v
liars ought to have good...199 y
m. of sweet summer eves..381 y
m. which survive us here..323 f
our m. by monuments.......396m
pyramids set off his m......200 e
soothed by no m. of....... 89 i
those memories to me..... 381 x
Memorize–not m. a spirit....574 s
Memory–a good m. is.......779 p
a good m. is needed once...778 t
a land of memory†........381 v
and Memory starts....... 602 a
appetite of thy memory...379 t
as the memory of a dream.381 q
at last she sought out M.†..366 n
badness of m. every one...380 e
but a majestic memory§...380 h
by the memory of it.......294 b
cells where M. slept........ 39 r
dear son of Memory**......550 v
expense of his memory.....795 p
fond m. brings the light....380 n
food of saddest m. kept....335 x
from the table of my m.*..381 o
good acts in memory....... 4 f
hail, m., hail ! in thy.......381 a
heart hath its own m.§.... 380 t
hope a great man's m.*...381 i
in every man's m., with.... 65 m
in his own page his m......479 j
in vain does M. renew.... .381 t
I wept for memory........381 c
keep his m. green in our...591 c
leaves of m. seemed to§....380 j
left his awful memory......381 s
m. brightens o'er the past§.380 l
m. fed the soul of Love†...366 n
m. have its force and...... 74 k
memory [is] like a purse...379 t
memory is the treasury.....725 k
m. lends her light no more. 11 g
memory of a beginning....365 p
m. of a well-spent life......721 a
memory of a wrong.......255 l
memory of buried love‖....655 n
m. of earth's bitter leaven¶.383 a
m. of fire and brimstone...632 r
memory of the heart.......770 t
memory of the living.......725 l
m. of the past will stay....380 q
memory of us will last.....725 o
m. plays an old tune on the.379 q
m. serves him with a word.514 a
memory's wards to let......249 l
memory takes them........379 t
m., the warder of the*.....381 p
mem'ry will bring back....381 f
memory yields, yet clings..517 a
night of life some m.*...... 12 b
not a good memory........199 k
oblivion and m. are wise....420 o
o'er Egypt's land of m......531 k
O, it comes o'er my m.*.... 55 d
place in thy m. Dearest....379w
planted in his memory*....252w
pleasing m. of all he stole‡.474 r
pluck from the memory*....441 c
silent shore of memory¶....382 b
sitt'st for aye like m........398 j
so let their memory be.....184 h
some call her Memory......517 a
speck upon your m., alack.420 r
sweet their memory still....379 r
sweet the m. is to me§......118 g
the mystic chords of m. ...469 a
there sits a blessed m.......381 b
the thoughts to m. dear....597 k
tho' lost to sight to m.....380 f
thoughts to m. dear......381 d
thy m., like thy fate......616 a
to his memory for his jests.381 r
ventricle of memory*......315 i
wakes the bitter m.**......105 t
washed away the m. of....592 p
white star made of m........233 c
Men–afar from haunts of m.. 21 h

aged men., that had been...592 p
all men are historians.. ...302 b
all men have their price.... 70 t
all men make faults*.......208 l
all m., nor for all times.....623 x
all m. think all men mortal..401 p
all the reasonings of m. are.660 y
ambitious care of men..... 10 e
amongst the sons of m. how332 h
among the dead m. let him.604 n
and friendless sons of m.††.588 g
and justifiable to men**...332 o
and makes men mad*.....398 u
and men to soar†..........131 o
as men do a-land*..........213 o
a thousand kinds of men...724 o
bear the shapes of men*....122 k
been many great men*.....215 j
be m. and let your hearts..119 b
busy haunts of men.... 97 f
but not without m.'s hands.405 f
but the shadows of us m...662 o
by virtue, not by m........806 f
cities and the ways of m.‡..97 h
contest with men above .... 26 r
dear to gods and m. is‡.... 477 b
diverse m. have diverse.... 14 l
drawing days out that m.*.140 c
fair women and brave m.‖.211 c
fate of gods and men**....206 t
fear of little men.........196 p
finds too late that m. .... .656 o
for m. like butterflies*....372 g
for m. may come and men† 71 e
for most m. (till by losing‖.460 v
forth from out a world of*.644 n
free m. freely work.......666 d
free soil, free men........259 d
great Nature made us††...371 n
great scholars great men...580 a
great virtues become.......794 p
guilty men escape not.....277 g
he only fears m. who does .779 j
hopes that make us men†...309 c
hum, the shock of men‖....566 e
if kiss'd by other men.....334 p
if you do love old men* .... 11 u
impossible to know men....664 i
in m. we various ruling‡... 82 v
intelligence in m. is what ..755 p
into the trunks of men*...198 i
its men's lives..............213 n
journeymen had made*....423 j
justify the ways of God to**510 h
Literary M. are a perpetual 353 v
Lord over m. on earth, and 485 j
made m. and not made *...372 l
makes m. good Christians.. 93w
makes slaves of m., and of .485 y
married m. be this a........375 t
measures, not m., have....481 r
m. and women merely*.....669 b
men are April when they* .377 f
men are but children of....501jj
men are but gilded loam*..524 s
men are made by nature...184 n
men are mere warehouses . 77m
m. are only the players....776 f
m. are merriest when*....384 f
m. are still men. The .....626 e
m. are the cause of women 774 a
men are the sport of‖...... 96 m
men are we, and must¶.....289 e
men as angels without**...657 s
m. below, and saints above.362 g
men, by their example. ....534 h
m. dare trust themselves*..372m
men deal with life as ......346 t
m. die, but sorrow never...568 x
men fear Death as children 132 b
men have all these ‖.......356 q
m. have died from time*...372 o
m. have lost their reason*..331 t
men have oftest wreck'd*†.619 i
m., like bullets, go farthest.754 b
men like children move....206 p
m. may rise on stepping† ..373 c

m must be taught as if‡....325 c
m. must reap the things.... 76 j
m. must work and women .666 v
m. of polite learning and a.342 e
m. of sense never tell it....519 u
m. only disagree of** ..... 627 l
m. only feel the smart‡,...630 o
m. prize the thing* ..... 663 r
m. residing in the city.. ...371 s
m.'s faiths are wafer-cakes*511 u
m. should be what they*...556 z
m. should put an enemy*..326m
men smile no more.........351 u
m. some to business, some‡ 658 h
m. some to quiet, some to‡.658 h
m.'s plans should be .. ....724 l
men still had faults........207 x
m.'s vows are women's*....377 g
men that keep a¶.........224 f
m. that make envy and*...372 p
m. that they are brethren..403 p
m. their best apparel do...652 g
m. the most infamous are..370 n
m. the weak anxieties of... 10 e
men were deceivers*......212 e
m. were developed from. .371 q
m. who grasp at praise....552 a
men who undertake..... 2 a
men willingly believe what 679 j
m. would be angels‡.......491 a
most men are bad........509dd
no m. like Englishmen†....116 c
not m. but measures......481 o
O friends, be men; so act.. 69 s
oh, shame to men! devil**.627 l
part of men to fear*.......209 v
period men in common....135 k
port for men.. ....649 l
remember they are men...512 a
roll of common men*......103 s
schemes o' mice an' men...154 x
silent brutes to singing m..342 g
society is the union of m...789 g
takes the breath of men....644 u
tears of bearded men......591 i
than the best of men*.....311 v
that all men are created ...529 t
the doings of men........679 s
the hopes of all men‖......325 o
the race of men obey......358 i
think less of men.........273 o
this happy breed of men*..116 b
though m. determine, the..506 ti
thy men of might‖..........97 m
tide in the affairs of men†‡.348 q
tide in the affairs of men*..461 o
Time's the king of men* ..603 e
to men and angels only....264 u
tongues of dying men*....340 b
to the general sense of m.¶.648 f
touch the hearts of men§...557 f
transform men into ....379 b
upon the paths of men§....319 a
venerable m! you have ... 12 j
ways of God to men**.....275 g
we count the act of men*..490 p
were God Almighty's m...376w
were worth a thousand m..638 r
when m. are rul'd by*......282 z
where m. are who know...281 d
which show what m. are... 96 p
why don't the m. propose..661 s
wise men say nothing in....509 n
with m. as if God saw you..685 d
with twenty thousand men 584 p
women and m. in the......348 q
women as well as men.....361 l
words are men's daughters 664 x
words are women, deeds...509 r
worst m. often give the.... 7 c
wouldst thou other men....337 x
young m. soon give and....671 p
Mend–and scorns to mend....428 l
foot gear to mend on his... 453 e
lacks time to mend........403 i
living now begins to mend*552 q
mend when thou canst; be*342 x

mourn lacks time to mend .603 _t_
nearer they are to mend§.. 75 _c_
physicians m. or end us∥..489 _u_
they may mend mankind..325 _a_
things always mend......256 _i_
to mend or be rid on't*....350 _t_
work for man to mend.....440 _b_
Mendacious-splendidly m ....696 _o_
Mendacity-tempted into m... 41 _t_
Mended-crack'd and never ..498 _e_
　little said is soonest m......501_m_
　m. from that tongue‡.......451 _d_
　mended that were worse §.. 75 _c_
　nothing else but to be m...520 _c_
　old houses mended......425 _f_
Mender-a m. of bad soles*....453 _p_
Mendicity-m. shall not be.... 41 _t_
Mends-it m. their morals∥....455 _e_
Menial-pampered m. drove ..549 _c_
Mental-imperfect m. vision.. 28 _i_
　m. friends and mental ......642 _d_
　m. joys and mental health. 642 _d_
　mental stains cannot be ....751 _o_
　our mental constitution.. 79 _o_
Mention-we never m. her....408 _q_
Mentioned-m. not at all......203 _b_
Mercer-god tailor and god m.454 _s_
Merchandise-m. went on..... 23 _a_
　no merchandise of sin......446 _f_
　privilege for his m.........452 _h_
　Rialto hath its merchandise 441 _q_
　scentless merchandise......224 _k_
　where looks are m......... 70 _q_
Merchant-m. of great traffic*442 _j_
　m. over-polite to his........482 _a_
　m., to secure his treasure..442 _h_
　press a royal m. down*.....442_m_
Merchants-m. venture trade*322 _b_
Mercies-get very great m.....489 _q_
　m. bloom in sweet relief...103 _d_
　m. of a moment leaves.....604 _d_
　when all thy m. O my God.382 _d_
Merciful-be m. as well as§....382 _h_
　be merciful to me, a fool...489 _o_
　then in being merciful*....278 _g_
Mercury-clown a winged M...646 _c_
　like a Mercury to charm....550 _h_
　mercury of man is fix'd‡...289 _o_
Mercy-and his mercy strive.. 83 _e_
　angel voices sung the m. ... 16 _t_
　boundless reach of mercy*.123 _r_
　brave love m., and delight..121 _q_
　flower of Mercy...........238 _l_
　God all m, is a God........276 _c_
　good unask'd, in m. grant..488_m_
　have m., mighty angel:.....382 _g_
　in her heart did m. come*.. 382 _o_
　m. but murders pardoning*382 _l_
　m. ever hope to have.......382 _t_
　m. I askt, mercy I found...330 _u_
　m. is above this sceptered*.382 _p_
　m. is not itself that oft*...382_m_
　mercy I to others show‡....343 _e_
　m. often inflicts death......725 _t_
　m. show her better eye.....382 _j_
　mercy sighed farewell∥.....149 _j_
　m. stood in the cloud with..382 _i_
　m. to him that shows it....382 _e_
　m. weeps them out again...331 _f_
　not m. unto others show...382 _t_
　of judgment and of m....450 _b_
　open thy gate of mercy*...382 _n_
　quality of m. is not*......382 _p_
　render the deeds of m.*...382 _q_
　shut the gates of m. on... 382 _f_
　sweet m. is nobility's*......278 _g_
　sweet Mercy! to the gates¶.383 _l_
　temper so justice with m.**332 _p_
　that mercy show to me‡....343 _e_
　the gentle deeds of m......382 _k_
　thy mercy set me free......487 _d_
　to talk of mercy*..........382 _s_
　trust His m. humbly for....164 _a_
　we cry for mercy to the.... 15 _d_
　we do pray for mercy*....382 _q_
　when m. seasons justice*...382 _p_
　where his mercy shines....274 _f_

whereto serves mercy*.....382 _r_
whom no mercy's shown...520 _i_
withhold in m. what we ask.488 _s_
Mere-lady of the M., sole¶....533 _j_
Meridian-m. of my glory*....152 _a_
Merit-appearance of m......780 _e_
　but merit wins the soul‡... 82 _q_
　by merit, not by favor......726 _a_
　by m. raised to that bad**.153 _f_
　dare be just to m. not their.332 _h_
　deny him m. if you can....383 _c_
　displays distinguished m....418 _q_
　envy will merit as‡.........174 _b_
　fault, all merit place.......124 _h_
　her m. lessen'd yours......328 _a_
　hope to merit Heaven∥......297 _l_
　merit wins the soul‡...... 86 _c_
　modesty is to m. what......389 _c_
　modesty's a candle to thy..389 _f_
　nature doth with merit*...365 _e_
　of my m. on that pint you††.593 _h_
　oft got without merit*.....524 _r_
　of your great merit.......260 _c_
　one m. of poetry few......478 _a_
　or amplest merit**....... 360 _u_
　purchas'd by the m. of the*306 _t_
　rest on outside merit‡......252 _e_
　season for man's merit.....780 _d_
　silence that accepts m...... 26 _k_
　sufficiency of m. is to know.383 _g_
　test of merit.............200_m_
　the existence of merit.....780 _c_
　the merit of poetry, in its..477_m_
　there is merit without......780 _b_
　thy father's m. sets thee...382 _b_
　to be a man of merit......768 _c_
　to buried m. raise the......580 _b_
　to neglect a man of merit..759 _h_
　to true m. should they have632_m_
　wish to m. the people's....677 _e_
Meritorious-m. but virtue‡..265 _c_
Merits-careless their m. or...473 _u_
　causes, noblest merits......205 _t_
　his merits to disclose..... 86 _g_
　lost on hearers that our m‡.486 _k_
　merits all his own.........383 _c_
　obtain that which he m.....383 _d_
　on their own m. modest....383 _e_
　values the merits of others.293 _d_
Mermaid-m. on a dolphin's*..383 _j_
　than the M. Tavern........433 _g_
　train me not, sweet m.*....383 _i_
　which is the m.'s now......649_m_
　would be a mermaid fair†..383 _l_
Merrier-but a merrier man*..384 _h_
　m. than the nightingale§...353 _r_
　the more the merrier......505 _r_
Merriest-men are m. when*..384 _f_
Merrily-and each m. goes....128 _k_
　go then merrily to heaven..383 _n_
　matter, m. set down*...... 33 _c_
　merrily hent the stile-a*... 384 _l_
　merrily shall I live now*..384_m_
Merrimack-stream the M.....531 _d_
Merriment-in harmless m.....295 _u_
　no other m. dull tree..... .618 _p_
　the merriment of May......569 _i_
Merry-a merry monarch....534 _r_
　be m. all, with holly dress.. 95 _e_
　be m. and employ your*....663 _h_
　drink and be merry, lads...376 _g_
　England was m. England... 95 _c_
　fool to make me merry*....252 _o_
　guid to be m. and wise....367 _o_
　have they been merry*.....139 _q_
　he was nor sad nor merry*.191 _h_
　how oft, with m. heart.....458 _s_
　I am not m. but I do*......384 _j_
　if you can be merry then*..384 _c_
　I'll be merry and free......110 _e_
　man do but be merry*......384 _n_
　m. as a marriage bell∥......128 _a_
　m. as the day is long*......384 _e_
　merry both night and day..110 _a_
　merry, dancing, drinking...383 _p_
　m. heart goes all the day*..384 _l_
　merry if you are wise......693 _o_

merry lark was up.........135 _i_
m., nimble, stirring spirit*. 88 _q_
simple, m., tender knack... 88 _w_
this priest he merry is.. ...450 _f_
three m. boys are we......557 _a_
'tis good to be merry.......268 _r_
'tis well to be m. and wise.. 75 _d_
welcome makes a m. feast*.644 _q_
what, shall we be merry?*..384 _i_
Merry-man-next Dr. M-m....440 _t_
Meshes-m. of good counsel*..592_w_
Mesmerized-they m. and.... 47 _s_
Mess-favorite of full many∥..483 _d_
Message-bearer of the m..... 45 _k_
　carrying a m. that is......405 _e_
　from the East glad m.......415 _c_
　give to a gracious m.*......415 _a_
　message to him every wave190 _p_
　my m. will go kissingly to. 448 _q_
　the message of despair.....538 _h_
Messages-fair speechless m.*.193 _u_
　m., that pass from land§...448 _j_
　your m. I hear but faith....766 _f_
Messenger-loud, the m. of... 49 _p_
　m. of grace to guilty men...450 _g_
　music sweeps by me as a...405 _e_
Messengers-send his winged** 16 _q_
　the messengers of God..... 17 _b_
Messes-other country m.**..431 _s_
Messmates-m., hear a........446 _b_
Met-as when we innocently..162 _l_
　fools as we m., so fools.....493 _p_
　hail fellow, well met.......498 _t_
　if we had never met... ....374 _g_
　know how first he m. her...366 _u_
　many friends I've met......379_m_
　m. and then drifted from..378 _k_
　night that first we met.....24C _d_
　no sooner m., but they*....364 _'_
　part of all that I have met†.319 _s_
　twain have m. like the ships262 _n_
　we have m. the enemy and.631 _d_
　we met, hand to hand......151 _o_
　we m.—'twas in a crowd...378 _l_
　when they m. in the way...157 _c_
　you know I m. you, kist...644 _x_
Metal-bright m. on a sullen*.519 _a_
　here's m. more attractive*.499 _d_
　metal better or heavier.....373 _q_
　metal of a man is tested††.. 81 _l_
　metal of his friend*........265 _l_
　no metal can, no*..........174 _f_
　sonorous m. blowing**.....573 _b_
Metals-m. of drossiest ore**..424 _t_
Metamorphosis-writer m. and551 _b_
Metaphysic-dark as sciences.457 _n_
　m. wit can fly.............336 _s_
Metaphysical-physical and...478_m_
Metaphysics-he has read m...516_m_
　this is metaphysics........793 _p_
Meteor-flaming m. shone for.290 _x_
　like a swift-fleeting m......490_w_
　meteor flag of England.....214 _a_
　shone like a m. streaming**638 _c_
　stream'd, like a meteor.....291 _e_
Meteor-ray-misled by Fancy's465 _i_
Meteors-m. fright the fixed*.639 _s_
Meter-making-m-m...........476 _y_
Method-he had not the m.... 70 _p_
　into a slower method*..... 27 _s_
　m. in man's wickedness....644 _j_
　m. is not less requisite....113 _g_
　mind has its own method..385 _n_
　the m. of drawing up......436 _p_
　there is method in't*.......321 _q_
Methods-graces which no‡...407 _a_
Metre-lives redress in m......254 _o_
Metres-for it is not m., but...476 _v_
Mettle-Corinthian, a lad of*.. 83 _r_
　I see there's m. in thee*... 84 _p_
　like a man of mettle.......119 _a_
Mew-cat will mew and dog*..152 _c_
　on the Sabbath say "mew".537 _a_
Mice-all the mice desert it...508 _i_
　cat in gloves catches no m.504_hh_
　like little mice...........253 _v_
　schemes o' m. an' men....154 _x_

mind of each man is........105 w
mind of man is ignorant....726 r
m. quite vacant is a mind..526 f
mind receives a secret...... 88 k
m., relaxing into needful...515 w
mind's all-gentle graces.... 38 b
m.'s construction in the*...195 x
m. serene for contemplation110 p
mind, set free from care....739 b
mind's evil lusts and deadly299 u
mind steady on its keel††..442 f
m.'s the standard of the...386 m
m. strengthens and decays.726 g
mind that builds for aye¶..413 o
mind that can embrace.....385 u
m. that makes the body*....386 g
m., that very fiery particle‖385 a
m. the music breathing ‖... 34 a
m. to me a kingdom is.....385 f
m. to suffer with the body*321 i
mind which is the proper...386 e
m. wishes for what it has..726 m
mind would be disposed....117 l
minister to a m. diseas'd*...441 c
monarch of his mind.......356 l
move a woman's mind*....272 j
my mind forbids to crave ..385 f
narrow circle the mind.....771 h
narrow'd his mind........270 m
nature of the human mind.385 w
next for health of mind...489 d
noble mind is here*........386 h
noble mind's delight......264 u
no blemish but the mind*. 627 u
nor cheer of mind*. ......649 w
not his haughty mind*.....155 o
not in my perfect mind*... 11 v
not less than m. and body. 19 c
not mind his belly........167 c
not to enslave the mind.... 14 q
offers to every m. its choice 91 p
of the new-born mind......402 e
oft the mind discovers...... 23 n
oh the fetterless m.! how it597 u
our mind had sketched.....160 c
out of m. as soon as out....503 c
out of syght, out of mynd..503 d
pen is the tongue of the m..780 i
permit the m. to look out ..385 l
poppies for a weary mind..239 c
power to broaden the m. ...326 r
prevalent as to concern**..488 o
pure mind sees her forever.651 v
put us still in mind........ 41 b
quiet mind is richer than...111 c
rarer sene, the lesse in m..553 j
reading is to the mind... ..515 t
reason rules the mind......470 f
recall the mind from the ..745 k
refresh the mind of man*..407 p
ruled—mind, body and.... 127 i
same m. as Thou art.......524 z
seal of a noble mind....... 71 r
shades which sep'rate m. ..629 w
she had a frugal mind......475 i
sick mind cannot bear....726 k
sin is a state of m., not an..556 h
sound mind in a healthy...734 q
sound mind in a sound......293 v
speech beneficent of mind‡ 80 g
spirit of the chainless m.‖..491 t
spoke the vacant mind....340 n
strength of m. is exercise‡.386 c
sufferings touch the mind.745 o
summer m. snowhid in††... 81 k
supports the mind........307 c
talk only to conceal the m..340 i
teach the m. its proper....422 j
the balance of the mind‡...386 b
the beauty of thy mind*...147 j
the gate of the mind.......726 b
the health of the mind.....515 t
the heaven of her mind.... 37 m
the human mind in ruins..385 m
the immortal mind of man.370 v
the largeness of his mind... 80 j
the Meccas of the mind....285 a

the mind is hopeful.........744 m
the mind is in a state of....748 n
the mind is its own place**.386 a
the m. one end pursues ....629 v
the mind that grows........325 f
the mind turns fool........253 k
the powers of the mind....726 h
the torch of the m. is the...800 i
they have no mind to. .....555 r
thy mind is a very opal*... 76 c
to change the mind ....108 i
to communicate their m....574 p
to dissipation of mind......341 v
torture of the m. to lie*....106 h
travelled m. is the catholic .606 m
troubled sea of the mind...561 m
true poem is the poet's m...476 t
true, strong, and sound m..385 u
use the mind aright.... ..696 c
virtue, but repose of mind..633 w
virtue is a habit of the m...632 b
weakness of mind is the....507 hh
wears the active mind......385 j
well-balanced mind is the ..726 n
well-prepared mind hopes..735 a
what is matter? never m...385 v
what is mind? no matter...385 v
when the m. is quicken'd*..386 f
when the m. (like a beard)..476 n
when the mind's free*......259 f
whispers to the willing m...538 s
whose untutored mind‡....275 n
wiser mind mourns less.¶... 12 n
with a body filled and *....526 p
with equal mind, what.....110 n
with mind serene...........112 o
with the bravest mind‡....373 q
woman, when to ill thy m.‡656 r
wounds of the mind.......725 n
wretched for his mind*.... 343 q
write to the m. and heart...426 r
years steal fire from the‖ ..599 n
your absence of m. we..... 2 t
Mindful—m. of the happy§...569 k
Minds—and corrupted minds..658 b
balm of hurt m., great*....562 u
by music m. an equal‡....406 t
can corrupt perverse m....695 f
can heavenly m. such......677 u
experience of innumerable.337 f
fearless minds climb*......119 j
high m., of native pride ...523 c
infected m. to their deaf*..523 e
in m. the most retentive...143 j
law of all men's minds ....409 x
linketh noble minds ......358 t
men's m. are as variant as..402 n
m. are not ever craving.... 65 f
m. could then meet minds..448 e
m. innocent and quiet......111 k
m. made better by their....318 r
m. that have nothing to¶..386 o
m. which are naturally....305 s
monument of vanished m.. 65 g
myself in other men's m.... 66 k
on whose wings great m.... 14 f
spur of noble m., the end.. 26 i
sweet content such minds..111 c
there is in human minds...713 r
the richest minds need not.344 l
to exhilarate their m. and.. 14 m
whose sluggish minds......210 x
wisdom in m. attentive to..336 z
Mine—all m. from your pretty* 32 j
beat upon m. you are mine† 32 j
inferior is he to a gold m....643 e
in thy exhaustless mine....381 a
it was mine—it is not I....131 v
I will pledge with mine.....604 o
may be mine no longer.....174 n
pure—from Pity's mine‖...590 t
she is m. own, and I as*...377 k
thou art m., thou hast....377 q
wed her for a m. of gold*..208 k
what is thine is mine.......704 p
what is yours is mine......508 n
what thou art is mine**...376 a

while in the mine..........270 r
why, man, she is mine own* 645 q
Minerva-owle the wise M.'s.. 53 c
Mines—candle to light the m..643 c
Lord Stafford mines for ..442 c
mountains big with mines..413 c
richer than Peruvian m...652 e
Mingle—sorrow all m. into ..101 x
to mingle with our own...588 c
Mingled—m. and yet separate‖374 n
mingled into one .... 99 j
Mingles—where mingles war's.638 q
Minister—by the weakest m.*.331 o
heavens do make their m. *.639 n
he too is God's minister§...152 w
minister, but still a man‡..371 t
m. to a mind diseas'd*.....441 c
minister to himself*..... .441 c
spirit for my minister‖....356 8
statue of a celebrated m....104 d
the minister of Thought§...600 v
Ministering-a m. angel thou..658 r
Ministers-are but m. of Love.357 m
are ministers of Fate*......207 m
bleed gold for m. to sport..649 a
m. present and to come....781 o
set the m. of hell at work..586 k
so long by watchful m.‡....114 t
Ministry-frost performs its..545 l
Minnows-m. sporting in the..230 i
this Triton of the minnows* 29 u
Minor-when the brisk minor‡673 d
Minster-silent in our m. of.†.184 j
Minstrel-hear the m. play....625 g
m.! pilgrim of the sky¶.... 49 s
no minstrel needs...... ..409 j
that the minstrel has told...376 f
this M. lead, his sins¶......383 a
Minstrelsy-brayed with m.*..384 o
loved in thy wild m........530 g
Mint-from the m. walks forth†480 i
lamb, with mint sauce....660 aa
savory latter-mint.........218 o
that hath a m. of phrases*.171 s
the poor man's mint.......170 b
were each wish a m. of ....652 f
Mints-hot lavender, mints*.. 235 n
Minuet-inconsolable to the..150 e
Minute-bear the brunt in a..346 b
one m. of Heaven is worth.475 o
show the minute hand..... 113 r
still work for the m. and ..470 v
Minutes-but what m.! count 600 h
damned m. tells he o'er*...328 e
earth in forty minutes*....607 i
fly swifter, ye m., bring....599 h
here two and a half m..... 776 k
lending them m. and......600 n
m., hours, days, months*..602 n
see the m. how they run*..602 r
watchful m. to the hour*..333 l
Miracle-accept a m. instead..386 u
believer is God's miracle..386 p
dearest child of Faith is....766 f
God is the One M. to man..386 r
greatest m. of love is the...114 l
literally a miracle...... .. 599 p
man is the m. in nature...386 r
marriage is the life-long...375 p
m. of weird transforming..547 f
this is a m. and that no....352 b
thy life's a miracle*.......350 y
what is a m? 'tis a reproach386 v
wine of m. answered to....648 o
Miracles-believe the m. of...760 j
for miracles are ceased*...386 t
m. have by the greatest*...386 s
m. of power whose fame... 29 i
Miraculous-m., because of..433 d
with most m. organ*.... ..423 f
Mire-cast into the mire.....341 q
great pails of puddled m.*.458 h
ne'er left man in the m.*...641 h
were it made out of mire..358 u
Mirrhe-the m. sweete.......610 h
Mirror-behaviour is a m. in..755 e
consulting the mirror.....178 o

Mock-achievements m. me*.. 5 n
all m. him outright by day. 52m
cowards m. the patriot's...468 t
makes sport to m. itself*...387w
mock a broken charm.. ...596 i
mock our eyes with air*...587 i
m. thee for thy faint blue.391 g
mock the good housewife*.272 h
mock the meat it feeds on*.328 e
m. the time with fairest*...312 q
pray do not mock me*..... 11 v
Mockable-country is most*..102 f
Mocked-as if he mock'd*....564 q
mocked her as they fell....227 o
m. himself and scorned his*155 r
m. thee for too much*......127 b
m. with a crown of thorns.. 55 n
mock'd with glory*........273 h
Mocker-arch-m. and mad.... 50 k
Mockery-bear about the m..‡387 t
delusion, a m., and a.......494 p
flag in m. over slaves......559 q
hence the mockery of life..645 t
in monumental mockery*..472 p
mockery over slaves.......214 l
often an object of m.......770 j
Mockest-thou m.? Tremble.785 q
Mocking-m. the sunset.....237 k
pretty m. of the life* .....537 v
sits, m. in our plumes*....551 k
thicket the mocking bird§. 50 i
Mocks-comforts while it m..464 a
it mocks the skies......... 459 k
mocks me with the view...280 c
m. the tear it forced to....627 t
Mode-established mode......127 h
Model-England I m. to thy *..116 a
m. of the barren earth*....139 v
then draw the model*......426 h
Modell'd-and m. it within.. 58 s
Models-live as m. for the....565 e
models of nations... ......287 a
on modern m. to be wrought 22 j
Moderate-be moderate, be m.*389 a
m. pleasure relaxes the....727m
to moderate their haste....388w
Moderately-therefore love*..364 s
Moderation-happiness......780 n
moderation gives it charm.777 b
m. is the silken string.... 388 u
m. of fortunate people.....388 v
reformed by their m.......318 o
tell you me of moderation*.389 a
the ring of moderation....389 b
winds that hear m. knew..647 h
Modern-in m. days no two‡..641 s
Modes-endless are the m....574 d
for m. of faith let graceless‡349 i
what wonder m. in wit‡...653 r
Modest-her m. looks the.....389 g
looks so m. all the while‖..397 j
modest and shy as a nun... 43 g
m. as morning when she*.. 62 t
modest fame is not to be...697 f
modest looks the cottage..239m
modest men are dumb......383 e
m. water saw its God and..648 p
remains m. not after praise.780 o
so m. plainness sets off‡....653 s
the Quip modest* .... 27 v
tho' modest on his‖.......⁰71 f
was a modest flower........248 i
zealous, yet modest........ 77 k
Modesty-charms her.........389 j
discretion and m., without.657 v
m. becomes a young man..727 q
m. is that feeling by which.389 d
m. is to merit what shade..389 c
m. may more betray our*..389 h
m.'s a candle to thy merit. 389 f
modesty starves...........686w
modesty, uncorrupt faith.727 p
obeys with m. appears.....420 b
press your point with m...171m
pure and vestal modesty*...335 e
stepping o'er the bounds*..389 i
the modesty of nature*..... 5 s

who obeys with modesty...729 l
who takes m. from it.......727 o
Modification-m. of my oft...258 p
Mogul-m., and mugwump..482 g
Moiety-robb'st me of a m*..288 n
Moist-thou art m. and soft..683 i
Moistens-what m. the lips..595 a
Moists-hardly m. the field..514 p
Moisture-dry up the m......235 j
for all my body's m.*.....591 p
let all their moisture flow..515 f
Mold-flower of simple mold..223 f
Mole-for a wart or a mole‡..126 b
learn of the mole to‡......342 k
Mole-catcher-was a m-c......421 o
Mole-hill-make a mountain..507 t
overhung a mole-hill large. 58 s
Mole-hills-faculties throw....473 o
Moles-and m. to ourselves..763 d
Moly-and sweet is moly......220m
Moment-can a m. show¶... 37 u
each moment is a day......600 h
enjoy every moment of it..599 q
face some awful moment¶.. 85 s
for one transcendent m.††.148 a
give to God each m. as. ...347 b
grasps the moment's gift..782 c
improve each m. as it flies.348 b
in the flash of the m.††....411 l
lucky m. when it is...... 66 g
mercies of a m. leaves......604 d
moment in which I am....791 q
moment sped too soon....131 b
moment watched for by all. 16 t
m. when we say "'twill..151 g
never idle a m. but§.......667 a
pay no m. but in purchase.673 q
strange m. must it be.....132 l
swallow at the same m.....507 s
to be a m.'s ornament¶... 661 g
to seize the moment.......661 t
vision of a moment made.634 o
what m. love begins§......359 x
years shall as a m. be..... 61 l
Moments-are m. in life§.....210 s
bells that waste the m......573 r
counting the slow, sad m..598 p
fleeting m. of too short a...563 o
flowering m. of the mind..574 c
golden moments fly§......147m
last moments to assuage... 92 c
leave the dead m. to bury..601 f
love shall my m. employ...355 k
make an eternity of m.‖....464 h
m. lost have no room......782 d
moments make the year...619 o
moments when silence.....554 n
our m. or our years........351 q
what, anxious m. pass.....105 a
while golden moments flit..161 q
Monarch-a merry m........534 r
becomes the throned m.*.382 p
Britain's m. once ....432 r
dear m. forgive what I've..616 c
does not misbecome a m....568 t
every m. is subject........740 l
flutters in the pageant of‖..120 r
fur that warms a m.‡...... 19 i
large the forest's m.......614 a
man the m. of his mind...356 l
monarch of all I survey....566 q
m. of the universal earth*.551 t
monarch of the wood......615 o
monarch's bags and coffers.279 i
monster but monarch there.231 n
proof of a true monarch....787 q
proud daughter of that m..483 o
the monarch crown'd‡.....256m
the monarch hears........276m
the m. oak, the patriarch..616 b
the monarch of a shed....303 q
tired m. fann'd to rest.....585 p
with a monarch's voice*...638w
Monarchies-greatest of all m..633 v
m. through poverty.......770 p
weight of mightiest m.**...154 p
Monarchs-eastern m. show..458 k

fate of mighty monarchs...73 x
fear of change perplexes ** 75 g
m. are too poor to buy.....379 g
monarchs must obey.......206 b
m. seldom sigh in vain.....663 f
the gates of monarchs*....535 d
Monarchy-trappings of a m.282 h
Monday-a Saturday and M..536 k
Monday in the mall........258 k
Money-and man made m. ..510 a
blessing that money cannot.295 t
books and m. plac'd for....460 u
burns for love and m. too.485m
cannot pay with m. must..728 f
contemplate the m. in my.727 t
despise m. on some........728 i
get money, money still‡....158 g
glad you have the money*.390 d
if m. go before, all ways.390 e
lay out money on a rope.387 f
lends out money gratis*....295 f
m. brings honor, friends**.390 a
m. gives birth and beauty.727 r
m. is a good soldier, sir*...390 f
m. is to be sought..........728 a
money lost is bewailed.....728 d
m. not a contemptible.....389 q
m. now-a-days is money....728 h
m. was made not to........389 o
m. which he has in his.....728 e
no money, no service. .....780 q
nothing comes amiss, so*...390 q
old sack is our m. old sack.649 u
part with it as with m......673 q
pleasant it is to have m....389 n
ready m. is Aladdin's lamp‖.389 l
so much m. as 't will bring.670 p
still get money, boy.......389 t
strut proud of your m......727 s
the loss of money.........728 g
the money of fools........664 q
they called lack of money..390 c
thy pursse full of mony...342 h
time is money..............507 e
traveler without money....733m
we care not for m. riches...649 u
without m. honor is........772 k
wit like m. bears an extra..653 g
would you know what m...509 t
wrote except for money...428 p
Money-bags-dream of m-b.*..161 c
Money-box-eyes of my m....780 p
Moneys-public m. for the...620 r
Monitor-m. of fleeting¶....245 j
the monitor expressed¶... 353 u
Monk-a m. in the Sorbonne..793 l
devil a monk would be.....153 k
dress does not make the m.763 o
dwell in a m. or light upon‡.633 f
many a monk and many... 48 a
m. scarce known beyond††..119 e
the solitary m. who shook.521m
Monkey-mischief-making m.‖89 d
Monkeys-men were........371 q
Monks-all hoods make not*..494ii
I envy them, those monks.173 x
Köln, a town of monks..... 97 s
Monopoly-m. by patent-right562 e
such m. of fame...........202 q
Monotone-I hear thy m. deep.59 b
Monster-a m. of iniquity.....637 o
a very weak monster*.....121 p
devil, and no monster*....153 p
green-eyed m. which doth*.328 e
many-headed m. of the‡....422m
many-headed m. thing.....212 d
marvelous m. whose eyes..699 a
m., but monarch there.....231 n
m. dwelt whom I came.....323 a
m. of ingratitudes*........602 x
m. of the multitude*......319 u
m. with uncounted heads*.536 h
poor, credulous monster*..121 p
that m. called Paine........463 i
the monster of Aetolia....177 k
this many-headed m........506dd
thou m., Ignorance*.......314 s

better the more than less§ .119 d
hurries back for more......269 a
I still should long for more 652 f
it says more and in fewer..478 a
it was nothing more¶ ......239 q
makes my number more*..211 q
my more-having would *...112 b
no m. of that Hal an thou*.148 h
of days that are no more...380 d
the more the merrier......505 r
the m. we live, more brief .599 o
Moriou–a guilt, engraven m..541 b
Morn–always m. somewhere§102 t
and greets the dappled m.. 87 k
another morn risen on......344 k
approach of even or morn**149 m
as the modest morne......239 n
blessed m. has come again.400 d
blushing like the morn**...376 d
came peeping in at morn..380 b
changeless m. succeeds to..108 j
descry the m.'s approach** 48 r
dew-drops in the breeze of.154 z
do mislead the morn*......335 p
each new m., new widows.*569 r
fair laughs the m., and soft672 z
floures so fresh at morne..372 w
fresh as the roseate morn..238 u
from m. to night, my friend 607 g
from m. to noon he fell*...153 c
glory of the morn is shed§.. 31 k
golden sun salutes the m..*400 u
grey-ey'd m. smiles on the*401 b
he cheers the morn*........193 q
her last dewy morn ....391 p
I came at morn.............183 r
in the dewy morn.........243 d
led by M., with dewy feet..585 a
love-song to the morn......400 e
meek-eyed Morn appears ..401 i
m. and cold indifference....318 j
m. foretold a cloudy noon.349 w
morn from black to red ...584 p
m. her earliest tears bestow†285 l
m., in russet mantle clad*..400 v
m. in the white wake of†..401 g
m. is up again, the dewy‖ .399 q
morn leaves for the........243 l
morn of toil, nor night of..443 r
Morn! she is the source of.400 c
morn the cherry-blooms...165 j
m., wak'd by the circling**400 k
night that had no morn....416 s
no morn shall break.......138 a
now m., her rosy steps in**400 l
of horn and m. and hark... 87 m
of incense-breathing morn.400 a
on the pinions of the morn.597 h
opening eyelids of the m.** 400 o
rise, happy morn, rise†.....401 h
rivers on that sacred morn. 94 b
salutation to the morn*.... 44 g
summer m. is bright and...399 p
suns that gild the vernal m.590 n
sweet is the breath of m.**400 m
that knows not morn†......141 o
the golden light of morn ..583 t
the morn not waking till... 48 q
the rich unfolding morn...400 f
this the happy morn**..... 94 l
ushers in the morn .... 87 j
wet o' the morn...........217 a
Morning–a fine m., nothing's400 h
all in the m. betime* .....628 n
a m. sun, and a wine-bred..495 k
and the day has no morning544 b
and wakes the m., from*... 49 k
April day in the morning ..392 n
awake! the m. shines**....613 a
beads of morning strung¶..309 e
bows you to m.'s holy*....670 n
breath of the m. is flinging.628 f
brightly breaks the m......400 g
burns up the m.'s chill.....395 j
dewdrops are the gems of.154 b
dewy m.'s gentle wine.....323 m
each morning ope..........220 p

each m., when my waking . 56 f
every m. she displays...... 235 o
hailed the morning ray.....242 f
happy May morning§ ......393 c
high-domed of morning ... 57 b
how beautiful is morning..400 q
in life's happy m. hath hid.136 v
in morning's beam........246 h
in the m. stick them in... 67 c
in the m. what thou hast..547 k
laughed in the m.'s eyes...187 k
light of the morning ......214 r
makes the night morning*.570 c
modest as m. when she* ... 62 t
morning blossoms out of...141 c
morning climbs to find.....131 b
m., faintly touched with...400 r
m. fair came forth with**..400 n
morning left behind.......131 b
m. of the hallowed day ....536 l
m. opes her golden gates*..400 x
m. paints the Orient. ......242 o
morning shows the day**.. 90 h
m. somewhere in the world102 r
m. steals upon the night*..130 s
morning to bring light.....276 s
m. wake us to no new joys.150 r
never m. wore to evening†.354 s
oft a little morning rain....345 q
oft as the morning ray .... 98 o
or come in the morning....643 q
pleasant is thy morning....346 e
rainbow in the morning....515 n
saw two clouds at morning 99 j
some praise at m. what‡...461 d
stars of m. dew-drops** ...154 e
the clear October morning.395 b
the dew of the morning....613 o
the m. came, there stood...638 m
the morning gray..........131 g
the morning lowers........205 n
the morning sky the lark ..445 r
'tis almost morning*.......364 x
welcome m. with its rays of 470 b
when did m. ever break....400 p
with the m. cool reflections 518 p
with the m. cool repentance 523 l
Morning-gate–glory's m-g...463 l
Morning-glory–blossoming...236 f
sturdy morning-glory......236 e
Mornings–brushes his hat o'*587 h
many bright mornings.....610 q
to give her music o' m.* ...407 j
Morning-star–charm to stay.575 s
m-s., day's harbinger**....576 j
Morrison–dear Jeanie M....591 e
Morrow–broken ere the m... 569 d
country does this m. lie...605 k
for the coming morrow....769 o
he rose the morrow morn..388 a
Indies does this m. live...605 k
m. came I answered still...605 f
m. was a bright September§394 h
of the night for the m......148 j
part of their good morrow.605 a
say good-night till it be m.*464 v
'tis so far-fetched, this m..605 k
trusting very little to the.693 n
watching for the morrow .569 a
Morrows–my morrows, noons600 k
Morsel–his tongue as a sweet 499 e
Mortal–abjure the m. made‖.317 n
all men think all men m...401 p
amongst my brethren m.*.412 j
a mortal made of clay*....203 w
bestows on most of mortal‖ 78 a
depart when m. voices bid¶634 n
fates of mortal men‡......206 m
gay, and m. as ourselves...601 n
informs our mortal part‡..411 v
know the m. through a ...369 n
laugh at any mortal thing‖.340 l
little more than mortal....528 w
man's m. crime, and just**518 j
may say of the mortal‡ ....183 p
more than mortal eyes‡....571 v
mortal cattle in a penfold..418 t

m. mixture of earth's** ....406 c
m. part suggests its every.401 o
mortal right-lined circle./... 96 d
m. to cut it off; to cure it*.156 n
mortal vision is a grievous.330 s
no mortal can see ....488 r
no mortal hath won.......316 b
no m. thing can bear so....442 i
purest treasure m. times*..524 s
raised a mortal to the skies 16 k
shuffled off this m. coil*....563 b
so mortal that, but dip*...512 t
spot where I am mortal ...780 r
stirs this mortal frame....357 m
teach this m. how to die...316 o
that thou couldst mortal be 142 d
the m. race is far too weak.795 b
to mortal it were given ....515 o
what mortal knows his‡....206 x
why should the spirit of m.490 w
will be mortal to redeem **518 j
with mortal thing it may be 442 i
years a m. man may live*..602 r
Mortality–child of trial, to m.619 f
child of m. whence comest.537 e
claspest the limits of m.... 603 l
frame above mortality.....201 g
hold m.'s strong hand*.....140 k
I've shook off old mortality454 n
m.'s too weak to bear......329 t
nothing serious in m.*.....350 g
thoughts of m. cordial .....401 l
to frail m. shall trust ... . 345 j
watch o'er man's m.¶......100 t
would I meet mortality**..149 i
Mortals–and m. the sweets of 410 b
are m. urged through‡......486 t
are to mortals given.......210 v
compel mortals to do .....708 k
ere m. all his beauties......74 o
happy the man of mortals.111 b
high for the daring of m...677 b
how little mortals know...643 g
in m. to command success.581 l
mortals always to be blest. 60 j
m. are all asleep below....536 m
mortals bend their will‡....387 b
mortals call the moon.....399 c
raise mortals to the skies.319 h
shows how little m. know.342 s
to mortals is a providence.190 j
vital movement m. feel....307 c
we are all m., and each one761 l
what fools these m. be*....501 u
where wretched m. sigh...148 b
Mortar–bray you in a m..... 27 i
Mortgage-m. his injustice ..212 h
old care has a m. on every. 72 h
Mortgages–amusement m.... 15 d
Mortification–die of m. ......629 h
Mortified–seeming m. men...312 j
Mortify–remains to m. a wit†422 m
Mosaics–dead leaves their....395 k
ye bright Mosaics........220 i
Moses–Moses' sister over M..223 h
not believe those of M......760 j
Pan to Moses lends his‡.... 75 t
passed from Mahomet to..589 j
Moslem–M's. ottoman‖......456 f
Moss–bind the m. in leafy...248 q
brown beard, the moss.....583 k
drowse on the crisp, gray††612 h
fern and moss to creep ....239 d
gray m. marred his rine....616 h
green m. that o'er the......614 l
how true she warp'd the... 58 s
'mid creeping moss and....239 g
moss shines there with ice..546 k
o'ercome with m. and*.....610 a
on the king's gate the m....534 d
rolling, can gather no m.... 76 p
rolling stone gathers no m. 74 u
rolling stone gathers no m. 495 s
the m. his bed, the cave...567 j
thro' the m. the iviest......412 t
through winter's m. and...541 m
with golden moss..........232 m

with hoary moss, and...... 55 *i*
with moss and mould ......231 *l*
Moss-beds–purpled the m-b...217 *v*
Mosses–here are cool m.†.....412 *i*
  m. creep to her dancing....217 *p*
  stains these m. green and..510 *y*
  the pines and mosses of... 71 *i*
Moss-rose–for the moss-rose..240 *k*
Mote-blame the m. that......330 *y*
Motes–m. that people the**..324 *e*
Moth–desire of moth for....148 *j*
  moth to the flame..........465*m*
  moth with vain desire†....103 *c*
  so man, the moth is not...370 *t*
  what gained we, little m...324 *f*
  young moth flutters by ....239 *j*
Moths–as the m. around a.... 16 *e*
  maidens like m. are ever‖..369 *i*
  silly moths that eat ......559 *c*
  yon night m. that hover....618 *f*
Mother–a kiss from my m....336 *d*
  a m. is a mother still......401 *r*
  a m.'s secret hope outlives.307 *x*
  and no dear mother.......569 *e*
  baby smiled m. wailed.... 32 *l*
  beautiful than thy lovely..678 *j*
  bed his happy m. lies.... 94 *g*
  care-wearied man seeks....595 *a*
  children of one mother....308 *x*
  come home to my mother*.4 *d*
  drop into thy m.'s lap**....349 *c*
  earth, a fatal mother ......141 *j*
  education commences at...170 *d*
  Eve, our credulous m.**... 257 *s*
  every m's heart forlorn...309 *q*
  extend a mother's breath‡. 11 *a*
  father m. brethren all in‡..375 *n*
  features of the m.'s face§.. 28 *n*
  happy he with such a m.†..402 *g*
  he's all the mother's from* 90 *p*
  ignorance is the mother....314 *t*
  I make presents to the m...783 *q*
  its mother was weeping.... 31 *l*
  kiss of m. and of sister....335 *y*
  make it well ? My mother .402 *f*
  man before thy mother....370 *a*
  man before your mother..370 *s*
  m. from the kitchen door..542 *i*
  m. may forget the child....379 *o*
  m. of all wickedness........678 *f*
  mother of Dews............401 *i*
  m. of light! how fairly dost397 *o*
  m. of the mighty Wine....648 *q*
  m. puts her glasses on....436*m*
  m. said to her daughter....401 *t*
  mother's heart is weak††..402 *c*
  m.'s love grows by giving.. 31 *h*
  m. smiled, baby wailed.... 32 *l*
  mother's when she feels...134 *i*
  mother wandered with her.565 *c*
  m. who talks about her ....427 *t*
  my mother came into my*.591 *u*
  necessity is the m. of ......414 *c*
  necessity, thou mother of..414 *l*
  O, stricken m.'s soul ......640 *r*
  pine is the m. of legends††.617*m*
  Poverty is the m. of ......548 *h*
  Poverty is the m. of health 503 *l*
  remove its m. luxury......678 *e*
  rest on their m.'s breast...100 *e*
  sacred religion ! Mother of 520 *q*
  silence is the m. of Truth..554 *b*
  sit down, every m.'s son* ..423 *b*
  so loving to my mother*...364 *o*
  the crime of a mother is a..760 *o*
  their Dacian mother‖......302 *o*
  the mother made no sound. 31 *f*
  the mother of invention....414*m*
  thou art thy m.'s glass*...673 *j*
  watch the mournful m..... 31 *b*
  water is the mother of the.641 *e*
  within a mother's heart....401 *s*
Mother-month–O m-m.......541 *d*
Mothers–heads against their. 88 *v*
  m. from their children.....560 *i*
  m. what a holy charge....402 *e*
  suck as mortal m. can......196 *q*

wives and m. to fulfil... ..657 *f*
Mother-tongue–was his m-t.. 486 *g*
Mother-wit–Nature by her...412 *p*
Motion–cooks in m. with‖....431 *o*
  devoid of sense and m.**...316 *l*
  end motion here*..........149 *r*
  his motion like an angel *..576*w*
  magic of m. and sunshine..129 *k*
  m. all the interim is*......123 *q*
  m. and long-during*.......667 *k*
  m. nor sound was there....546 *b*
  m. so swift, we know not ..539 *g*
  motion there was rest .. 100 *h*
  m. were that minute......548 *s*
  our proper m. we ascend**.492 *l*
  the m. of a muscle this¶... 6 *c*
  the motion of my hand§.. .449 *o*
  two stars keep not their*..577 *e*
Motions–blinder m. bounded†642 *b*
  interprets m., looks‡......524 *l*
  m. of the forming wheel...449 *k*
Motive–judged by the m......330 *r*
  m. and the cue for passion*423*m*
  path, m., guide, original...274 *s*
  want of motive...........402 *k*
Motive-hunting–m-h. of a....402 *j*
Motives–m. of their action...402 *n*
  m., that Judas moved .... 522 *s*
  sinister and interested m...259 *v*
  ten thousand m. to adore..538 *i*
Motley–m.'s the only wear*..252 *t*
  world with all its m. rout..667 *t*
Motto–m., "Courage and...391 *a*
  motto of all quarrels......513 *s*
  principle is ever my m.....491 *q*
  this be our motto.... ......214 *i*
Mould–becomes a living m... 452 *i*
  be of vulgar mould........429 *w*
  cast in the same mould ....101 *s*
  heavenly and spiritual m...515 *k*
  m. of a man's fortune .....255 *v*
  now take the mould.......449 *k*
  shaft of Orient mould ....217 *v*
  the mould of form*...... 205 *j*
  through the brown mould .226 *q*
  to m. a pin, or fabricate a..667 *l*
  very m. and frame of*..... 90 *n*
  whitens the fresh-drawn...542 *a*
  will this perishing mould..358 *u*
  with moss and mould.....231 *l*
Moulder–m. piecemeal on‖... 91 *l*
Moulding–moulding men†.....207 *r*
Moulds–cast into these ...... 418 *b*
Mount–high m. of God**....625 *a*
  I mount ! I fly! O Grave‡..137 *q*
  mount of consecration.....359 *l*
  whether they fall or m.....510 *p*
Mountain–along the m. side¶.481 *h*
  a mighty mountain child...532 *e*
  anon becomes a m.*.......494*dd*
  blackness in the m. glen....545 *o*
  by mountain gorge........221 *i*
  Cintra's m. greets them‖...532 *l*
  come o'er the m. with......540 *f*
  dew on the mountain......138 *h*
  forked mountain or blue*..587 *i*
  Freedom from her m......214 *f*
  from a high mountain.. ..799 *q*
  from every mountain side..469 *n*
  from the m.'s bosom‖.....577 *o*
  into that m. mystery.......447 *l*
  make a m. of a mole-hill...507 *t*
  m. at a given distance......557 *x*
  mountain peaks attest.....165 *d*
  m. sheep are sweeter, but.. 21 *r*
  m. summit sparkles........532 *b*
  one m., one sea, one river..410 *k*
  on every mountain height .526 *i*
  robes the mountain in its..402 *p*
  set a huge m. 'tween my*...108 *r*
  small sands the mountain..619 *v*
  storm be but a m-birth.....561 *c*
  the dew on the mountain..354 *p*
  the mountayne dyghte... 227 *g*
  throws down one m.*......509 *e*
  to the mountain saith§.....672 *q*
  trod the mountain height..414 *e*

up the airy mountain .....196 *p*
wood and wild and m. dell.. 40*m*
Mountain-crescent–far m-c.‖..585 *p*
Mountaineer-shod like a m...367 *k*
Mountaineers–m. are always.802 *d*
Mountains–amid the voiceless169*m*
  blue Franconian m.§........ 98 *f*
  comest o'er the m. with....605 *b*
  do the mountains now ....597 *p*
  fit for the mountains and*.373 *v*
  green mountains round ....284 *j*
  high m. are a feeling‖.... 97 *e*
  his native mountains more.118 *d*
  make mountains level *....207 *i*
  mountains are in labor.....747 *e*
  m. are the beginning......403 *a*
  mountains big with mines..413 *c*
  mountains catch the gale..219 *h*
  mountains interposed make402 *r*
  m. kiss high heaven........460 *k*
  mountains look on‖...... 116 *i*
  mountains of Switzerland..258 *d*
  m. piled on m. to the skies‡ 13 *q*
  moving m. hear the‡......557*m*
  one of the mountains¶.....635 *h*
  rivulets from the m.§......162 *n*
  steepy mountains yield....360 *n*
  the broad blue m. lift...... 43 *o*
  the monarch of mountains‖402 *o*
  there's joy in the m.¶......391*m*
  waves and mountains§.....118 *g*
Mountain-tops–m.t. that*....407 *o*
Mountebank–unction of a m.*512 *t*
Mountebanks–cheating m.....512 *s*
Mounted–high as we have m.¶ 76 *s*
  m. are they to spit forth*..639 *t*
  mounted on his back......254 *r*
  not mounted yet on his**..136 *n*
Mounting–there was m. in‖..636 *a*
Mounts–m. no higher than a*386 *j*
Mourn–countless thousands..370 *e*
  he that lacks time to m....603 *t*
  m. a mischief that is past*.387 *e*
  mourn little harebells......216 *n*
  m. thy ravish'd hair‡......291*m*
  mourn you for him*.......285 *o*
  that lacks time to mourn...403 *i*
  whiles she doth mourn*...659 *g*
  who thinks must mourn ...349 *s*
  wonder how they mourn...205 *s*
  you must m. first yourself.728 *j*
Mourned–and forever m‡. ..403 *g*
  are m. by man, and not by¶592 *s*
  m. the dame of Ephesus...662 *k*
  m. till Pity's self be dead...403 *e*
Mourner–constant m. o'er‖...613 *c*
  I know–is all the mourner 345 *t*
  m. o'er the humblest grave¶590 *h*
Mourners–like fond weeping.134*m*
Mournful–m. looks the‡......658 *l*
Mourning–m. her ravished... 51 *p*
  often left me mourning¶...284 *c*
  up in a mourning house* ..592 *b*
Mourns–always m. the dead. 244 *s*
  Eternity mourns that......403 *i*
  he m. the dead who lives...408 *k*
  mourns less for what age¶. 12 *n*
  Nature m. her worshipper.480 *l*
  nothing dies but something‖132 *s*
Mournst–m. the daisy's fate..227 *d*
Mouse–a mouse of any soul‡. 21*m*
  a wylie m. that should.....500 *x*
  cat would watch a mouse..503*kk*
  entered, far from m., or cat 21 *l*
  m. never shunn'd the cat*. 21 *n*
  m.'s herte nat worth a leek 21 *k*
  mouse that always trusts‡. 21*m*
  m. that hath but one hole..505 *v*
  nimble m. between the ribs 64 *f*
  not a mouse shall disturb*.462*w*
  quiet as a mouse.......... 43 *d*
  ridiculous m. will be born. 747 *e*
  stirring–not even a mouse. 94*m*
  there was a mouse.... .... 21 *l*
Mouser-grave thinking m.....215 *u*
Mouth–a cool m., and warm..494 *k*
  and gaping mouth, that....580*w*

SHAKESPEARE *; MILTON **; WORDSWORTH ¶; BYRON ‖; TENNYSON †; LOWELL ††; POPE ‡; LONGFELLOW §.

glory, and thy n. are his...601 o
good name in man and*.... 83 l
good or evil name depends.260 p
good without a name*......147 a
habitation and a name*....480 n
had their name thence**...304 e
he left a Corsair's n. to‖....408 r
he left the name...........201 r
her name is never heard....408 q
I can call nothing by name.757 o
if his n. be George I'll call*.306 k
illustrious and ancient n...696 r
in friendship's name......662 u
inquire his name elsewhere184 k
into an empty name. 268m
king's n. is a tower of*....579 n
know, my name is lost*....608 o
late, redeem thy name......409m
lend his n., that other men.512 q
like love, is but a name....264 j
living makes a name.......696 s
loves another of the name*326 n
magnify Thy name¶.......486 z
man who builds his name..558 k
marble with his name‡..... 96 a
meet in my name...........232 n
my name ends with me....764 l
my name is MacGregor....409 n
my n. is Norval; on the....409 f
my name shall never die...714m
my n. were liable to fear*..586 r
n. awakens all my woes‡...448 n
name but cannot know....275 z
name in Latine......266 k
name of friendship......264 e
name of Robert Burns.....285 j
name of the Prophet—figs..500 s
n. ourselves its sovereigns‖370 f
name perishes from record.371 h
n. remains to the ensuing*.608 s
name the bigger light*....426 l
name through Europe ring286 n
name to every fixed star*.426 n
name upon the strand......255 d
name was writ in water....409 e
n. which before thee no...316 b
no name to be known by*..650 c
of every friendless name.. 80 p
office and my name*.......595 q
O n. forever sad! forever‡..409 l
one Name above all....... 92m
out of his Christian name.409 i
passion for the n. of‖......408 s
Phœbus! what a name‖....409 a
pledge of a deathless n.§...596bb
poems read without a name126 a
recalled a different name..568 a
Roland his pet n., my horse 20m
Sancho Panza by n. is my.. 74 l
scarce deserve the name*..356 u
see one's name in print‖.... 64 j
shadow of a mighty name..696 k
sigh and soften out the n...409 h
speaks but Romeo's n......171 t
stamps God's own n. upon.144 e
swiftly fades thy name.....435 p
take not His n., who made.419 c
takes a specious name.....404 e
than my own name.......719 j
that bears the name of life*140 o
the gentle n. of Spring.....391 b
the grand old name†.......271 r
the magic of a name......200 l
the name of Prosper*......200 l
the n. that dwells on every.409 j
the sound of my name.....379w
thing with dreary name....133 g
thrice-glorious name .....468 l
thy name in the rubric .. 628 e
Time thy name is sorrow..570m
'tis a venerable name .... 429 y
to the fascination of a name409 c
to win a lasting name......409 d
what is thy n., faire maid..409 k
what is your name*........409 p
what i' devil's name*......455 d
what n. Achilles assumed..143 r

what's in a name? that*....409 s
what's in a name...........465m
what the dickens his n. is*.409 o
what thy lordly n. is on the.417 a
whistling of a name‡......202 k
whistling of a name.......409 v
who blushes at the name..468 t
whose conquering name*..275 r
whose n. was writ in water.183 h
with a good name*. ......170 t
with a terrible name.......409 t
woman's highest name....660 x
worth an age without a n..350 c
yet fears the name........200 t
your name is great*.......287 i
Named—I have n. the man...683 f
named of the wind.........221 o
n. thee but to praise....... 79 u
Nameless—be nameless in...310 h
Names—battle is more full*..639m
but names and customs....632 k
commodity of good n.*....524 p
distinguish'd but by n.*....409 r
doth forget men's names*..306 k
fairest of names..........282 u
few the immortal names...201 e
happy we had other n.*.... 76 h
names are mine...........244 k
n. he loved to hear.........134 q
n. in his wild aëry flight*..202 b
names of their founders....254 s
n. of those who love the....634 f
R in their names..........213 e
saved other's n. but left...310 t
syllable men's names**....575 d
then shall our n. familiar*..409 q
things by their right n......649 h
winne ourselves good n....146 h
Nankin—and yonder by N.§..449m
Nap—afternoon nap in his..463 p
nap he snatched............154w
never take a n. after.......561 l
of Thetis taken out his nap.584 p
then the nap takes me......561 l
to nap by daylight..........246 e
Napkins—dip their napkins*..284 a
Naples—man to whom all N..774 q
N. sitteth by the sea.,..... 98 e
Napoleon—[N.] had a kind of. 2 h
N.'s presence in the field...319 i
Talma taught Napoleon....550 d
Narcissus—N. is the glory....203 f
Narrative—n. with age‡......650 r
Narrow—n. and pedantic to..332 e
too n. for two kings.......533 k
Nassau—Bourbon or N. claim.183 q
Nasty—a man of n. ideas.... 88 i
Natal—n. star, thou.........697 o
Nation—a foreign nation is a..484 i
and spirit of a nation... .. 493 q
calamity can fall upon a n.670 d
corner-stone of a nation§...115 e
earth's greatest nation††...1.5 f
hath made our n. free......368 a
history in a nation's eyes..302 d
language of the nation.....339w
nation of shopkeepers......792m
nation of shopkeepers......442 q
n. should have a correct... 83 t
never use the word "n.".".627 c
not a nation but a union...627 c
of a shopkeeping nation...442 r
of virtue in a nation.......673 r
O n. miserable, with an*...626 r
one nation evermore......468 r
preserved us a nation......214 i
preserves us a nation......214m
raises armies in a n.'s aid‡.390 b
talent of our English n.....518 u
that n. is worthless which..772 n
this nation under God......282 k
time, to the n., as to the....600 i
National—be to us a n. blessing142 u
n. tragedy lasting for......329 a
not what is n. in them§.....479 r
our N. Independence......302 p
were funding our n. debt...142 v

Nations—and building up n...338 s
calls up the tuneful n....... 49 p
cheap defence of nations...143 b
chieftains, so many brave.. 74m
defence of nations.........156 s
fierce contending nations...635 j
greatness of n. is in........ 84 y
ingenious youth of nations‖.455 e
intercourse with foreign n.468 j
make enemies of nations..402 r
nations heard, entranced..406 r
nations lift their right.....259 h
n. shall not quarrel then...637 o
news from all n. lumbering.435 r
of distant nations..........327m
on half the n., and**...... 75 g
peace among the nations§..470 o
place in the family of n....188m
see n., slowly wise and....580 b
subdue n., and bring**....638 d
the gayety of nations......403 h
the nations echo round.....597 p
the Niobe of nations‖.......387m
the work of nations.......425 t
wake the n. underground..527 n
world in all doth but two..668 s
Native—bind him to his n.... 118 d
cobbling in his native town.453m
dear, my native soil........116 o
God—and your native land.468 p
I am native here and to*...127 l
loves his n. country best‡..604 s
my n. Land—Good-night‖..606 r
my Native Land...........117 r
my own, my native land....118 j
one native charm, than all.555 n
one's native land receding‖.117 x
our n. land charms us......781 a
own dear native scenes...117 k
resigns his n. rights for....369 o
think there thy n. soil**...311 p
to their proper n. use......479m
violet of his native land*...249m
Nativity—hour of my n. to*...549 f
n., chance, or death*.......368 q
your nativity was cast¶.....221 b
Natural—accompanies what.. 7 s
do it more natural*........283 p
drive the natural away.....781 a
natural selection or the....186 d
on the stage he was n......422 d
painting is almost the n.*..447 f
the n. alone is permanent§.411 s
term of natural selection...410 p
'twas natural to please.....283 t
Naturalists—n. observe, a flea.323 b
Naturally—n. noble.........305 s
Nature—accuse not N. she **.411 n
all nature cries aloud......409w
all N. is but art unknown‡.510 i
all nature's difference......293 r
all Nature seems at work..666m
all Nature under tribute...428 i
all N. worships there.......413 f
all thy nature's weakness..343 h
a n. wise with finding††.... 81 h
and art a nature..........478w
and fools call Nature......273 v
and knelt to Nature first...531 e
and Nature does require*...412 f
a noble of Nature's own... 85 j
a portion nature requires..729 e
are n.'s funeral cries......647 i
art imitates n., and........414 c
Art is N. made by man.... 29 a
Art is the child of Nature§. 28 n
Art is the right hand of N..755 g
art may err, but n. cannot..495 t
art so nearly touches n.....664 r
art that nature makes*.....412m
auld n. swears, the lovely..654w
a woman, it is of nature...357 s
better angels of our nature.469 a
binding n. fast in fate‡.....646 l
blank of Nature's works**..149m
bore in nature's quire, the. 49 q
breeze of N. stirring in his¶.413 t

the top, is Nature's text†..492 *j*
the womb of Nature and**.411 *q*
things are of that nature...203*m*
things perfected by n.......728 *o*
through n. to eternity*... .140 *g*
throughout n. this primary 96 *c*
thy laws in N.'s works‖.....487 *l*
till pitying N. signs the.... 10 *f*
times to repair our n.* ....523 *y*
tired N.'s sweet restorer....564 *e*
'tis Nature's fault alone....383 *c*
to her mothe. N all her....412 *r*
toils of n. true, wreath..... 56*m*
to N. parched and dry......541 *p*
tone of languid Nature....117 *c*
to the solid ground of N.¶. 413 *o*
touch of N.'s genial glow ..412 *e*
trace the naked nature‡ ..480 *g*
traffics with man's n.*.....447 *f*
transgressing n.'s law......661 *j*
truest diviners of nature..480 *b*
true to the poles of n......347 *n*
true wit is n. to advantage‡653 *t*
turn nature out of doors..728 *p*
universal nature groaned..612 *c*
unjust to n. and himself...373 *h*
up to Nature's God‡.......412 *c*
view the haunts of Nature.609 *b*
voice of nature cries.......411 *d*
waken their free n. in the††588 *q*
weakness of human n......641 *q*
were one in N.'s plan...... 79 *t*
we see in N. that is ours¶..669 *t*
what he is from Nature....286 *p*
what nature wants‖........279 *b*
when n. conquers, art......781 *c*
which frugal n. lent him...401 *q*
who can paint like N.......412*w*
who in the love of N. holds.410 *j*
whole extent of n. belongs.538*m*
whole frame of n. round...535 *r*
whose body Nature is and‡ 411 *o*
who value N. not a straw .. 43 *p*
wild nature yields.........244 *c*
wise nature did never put..369 *p*
with his nature mixed‡....289 *o*
with N., Hope, and Poesy..672 *c*
with N.'s heart in tune....411 *u*
work of nature.............402 *n*
yet do I fear thy nature*...333*m*
Natures–and of opposed n.*..438 *x*
level in our cursed n.*......631 *r*
n. double-darken gloomy†† 81 *j*
of opposed natures*........330 *n*
pine for kindred natures..588 *c*
same with common n...... 80 *b*
spirits have just such n...298 *y*
whose n. never vary††... 81 *k*
Naught–n. is everything....597 *v*
Nauseous–fee the doctor for.440 *b*
Nautilus–the little n. to‡..... 63 *o*
Naval–shaken by thy n. arm.327*m*
Navigate–n. the sea of life...539 *a*
Navigators–side of the ablest 445 *e*
Navy–army and the n. had...581 *x*
n. of Charles the Second...445 *j*
the royal n. of England....444 *v*
Nay–a woman's n. doth*.....659 *f*
be perverse and say thee*..663 *k*
he will he shall have nay...461 *i*
I'll say her n., and hide....514 *r*
will he shall have nay..... 91 *k*
Nazareth–Christ, the Child of. 94 *n*
Near–he comes too n., that...594 *b*
if it be, 'tis ne'er the near..586*m*
if thou art n., the wintry..600 *k*
look'd to n. have neither...273 *k*
n. but never to be first.....696 *l*
near me now all day.......570 *r*
rose cries, "She is near‡..366 *r*
so very near to God........521 *n*
the one so n. the other is...627 *g*
there were no living n.*....659 *t*
yet forever near‡..........324 *n*
Nearby–n., it is nothing.....767 *d*
Nearer–and n. as they came‖.431 *n*
but n.—more lofty,—more..586 *a*

nearer, my God, to Thee...487 *c*
Nearest–acted on by what is‖. 77 *u*
best things are n' him ..... 60 *r*
Neat–in a neat's tongue*.....554 *y*
neat, not gaudy...........502 *h*
still to be n., still to be.....462 *r*
Neatness–neatness of person.711 *l*
plain in your neatness......711 *k*
Necessaries–dispense with...464 *b*
Necessary–foundations of.... 34*m*
inability in n. things.......473 *c*
not in those necessary......293 *p*
omission to do what is n.*.185 *v*
the superfluous, a very n...781 *f*
use of necessary things....733 *l*
wisdom provides things n..509*m*
Necessities–call in question*.414 *j*
should be hours for n*.....523 *y*
Necessity–by n., by proclivity514 *b*
empires, N. and Freewill..571 *c*
from a beautiful n........275 *x*
he made a virtue of n......781 *e*
is no virtue like n*........414 *k*
it is n. and not pleasure...781 *i*
it was her stern necessity..410 *t*
legs for n., not for flexure*. 20 *j*
make a virtue of n........501*bb*
make a virtue of n*.......507 *u*
make a virtue of n........414 *a*
maken vertu of necessité..413 *v*
nature means necessity....409 *y*
necessity and chance**.....206 *v*
n. doth front the universe..466 *u*
necessity invented stools...431 *b*
n. is stronger far than art..413 *u*
n. is the last and strongest.729 *d*
n. is the mother of ....414 *c*
n. knows no law except....502 *i*
necessity's sharp pinch*...414 *i*
n. takes impartially........729 *c*
necessity the mother of....414*m*
n., the tyrant's plea**.....414 *d*
necessity—thou best of ...414 *h*
n., thou mother of the.....414 *l*
n. was the argument of....414 *f*
n. when threatening.......729 *h*
stern is the visage of n.....781 *g*
stronger than necessity....414 *b*
teach thy n. to reason*....414 *k*
thine, severe necessity....414 *e*
Neck–about the n. of hope†..366 *n*
arching proud his n., with.. 58 *o*
face, and your neck.......176 *a*
mankind had only one n... 17*m*
mankind only had one n.‖..655 *k*
masses down her neck§.....291 *y*
round a young man's neck.291 *d*
stooped my n. under your*. 33 *h*
swan, with arched n.**... 58 *i*
took the bride about the*..335 *s*
Necklace–n., an India in‖......211 *b*
the necklace of night.......586 *a*
Necks–trust our necks to.... 15 *t*
Nectar–draughts of its nectar.230 *o*
draws nectar in a sieve.....307 *l*
enshrined in its own n......322 *a*
might I of Jove's n. sup....641 *d*
n. of good wits will sell....648 *g*
ne'er saw nectar on a lip...484 *a*
sap that turns to nectar....266 *e*
the water nectar and the*..377 *k*
vines yield nectar**.......298 *i*
with frugal n. smooth and. 8 *o*
with her n. Hebe††........544 *f*
Nectarean–when n. juice.... 87 *e*
Nectareous–divine, n. juice‡.234 *u*
Nedjidee–to the fearless N...617 *a*
Need–but in times of n., at...443 *c*
deserted at his utmost n...388 *d*
do me many if I need.......263 *b*
for human need...........238 *i*
help us in our utmost n.§..451 *a*
his need of the palm shall..617 *b*
in bitter n. will borrow....410 *g*
is no need of such vanity*..342 *p*
Nede hath no lawe.........502 *j*
n. to desperation driveth...760 *d*

pity and n. make all flesh..587 *l*
that my need is most......299*w*
want a friend in need .....260 *d*
when did I not need her....480 *r*
when he must need me*....262 *f*
when time and n. require..738 *u*
yield them to thy bitter n..324 *d*
you need a heart..........479 *e*
Needed–are n. by each one..318 *s*
sought me when I n. her...480 *r*
Needful–all things to be.....448 *b*
Needs–more n. she the*......523 *e*
who not n. shall never*....262 *e*
Needle–daughter throws her.436*m*
fine needle and silk........ 19 *f*
hinders n. and thread......590 *t*
needle in a bottle of hay...502 *k*
needle to the pole.........212 *g*
plying her n. and thread...339 *c*
postern of a small n.'s*....154 *l*
touch'd n. trembles to‡....548 *v*
which like the n. true .. 548 *q*
Needles–the Lydian, filed n..421 *o*
Needy–n. knife-grinder !.....484 *k*
Negatives–than n. a score.... 27 *o*
Neglect–a most faint*......126 *x*
and all neglect, perforce... 67 *r*
living, if neglect can kill§..479 *v*
neglect God's ancient......669*w*
still neglect all office*.....295 *q*
sweet n. more taketh me...414 *o*
to neglect a man of merit..759 *h*
wise and salutary n........414 *n*
Neglected–presume that.....745 *h*
Neglecting–sin as self n*.....548 *f*
Negligence–sweet n. .... 555 *p*
to whom labour is n........478*w*
Negligences–his noble n......414 *p*
Negligent–more dull and n...281 *k*
than by the negligent*.....294 *g*
Negotiate–every eye n. for*..265 *g*
Negotiates–n. between God...450 *b*
Negotiation–n. before arms..736 *l*
Neighbor–her next door n... 1 *b*
its n. to embrace‡........412 *b*
life to thy n.'s creed........318 *s*
love my n. as myself.......356 *l*
love your n.'s wife.........565 *k*
love your n., yet pull not..501 *x*
n.'s house is on fire........700 *k*
please his wicked n........788 *g*
publishing our n.'s.........551 *t*
to hate your n. and to.....565 *t*
will change his n‡........111 *p*
wrangle with a n. causes..101 *s*
Neighbour'd–n. by fruit*.....266 *r*
Neighborhood–plant n. and*. 98 *s*
Neighborhoods–aërial n. of§.398 *d*
Neighbors–exalted above his.642 *e*
near n. that they touch....101 *u*
neighbors to ourselves....101 *t*
practices it will have n....632 *e*
souls of your neighbors....319 *c*
their next-door n..........208 *b*
th' invited neighbors to....294 *g*
Neighs–n. piercing the*...... 21 *e*
Neither–n. live with you nor.715 *b*
to n. a word will I say .... 114 *i*
Nelly–there's none so fine as.660*m*
Nemesis–inappeas'ble N......105 *l*
Neptune–N.'s deep invisible..445 *a*
N.'s sullen month appears.395 *l*
stands as Neptune's park*.327 *j*
the trident of N. is the....784 *e*
will all great N.'s ocean*...404 *c*
would not flatter N.*.. ....418 *k*
Nero–N. went up and down..421 *o*
N. will be tainted with*....659 *q*
Nerve–Numean lion's nerve*.207 *h*
n. vibrating thousands of..171 *g*
shake the firm n., appal...577 *u*
than strength of n. or¶....367*m*
visual n. for he had**......853*m*
Nerves–n. shall never*......130 *j*
strengthens our nerves....300 *b*
tearing my n. wi' bitter. .432*m*
Nest–a n. is under way for... 43 *d*

SHAKESPEARE *; MILTON **; WORDSWORTH ¶; BYRON ||; TENNYSON †; LOWELL ††; POPE ‡; LONGFELLOW §.

n. by distance made more..378 *v*
notes in cadence ....128 *h*
n. well tuned to her sad.... 51 *p*
reward the grateful notes‖.454 *l*
still your notes prolong‖. .452 *u*
the molten golden n. and .. 40 *k*
thrill the deepest n. of wo..548 *o*
thy liquid n. that close**... 51 *n*
through thy piercing n.....323 *p*
trills her thick warbled n.*.616 *i*
wake the grove to n. of.... 50 *j*
warble his delicious notes.. 51 *a*
where n. of liquid utterance 43 *p*
Noteless-an ignorant, n.‖....557 *b*
Nothing-and n. long..........212 *a*
believing in n. at all††.... 39 *d*
brought n. of my own......514 *h*
die of n. but a rage to live‡.468 *f*
everything by starts and... 78 *x*
gives to airy nothing*......480 *n*
good voyage of nothing*...108 *p*
great or to be nothing...... 14 *f*
having n., yet hath all......484 *d*
he cares for n.! a king.....142 *b*
in hevin' n. o' the sort††...491 *r*
near by it is nothing.......767 *d*
n. brings me all things*....552 *q*
nothing but with self.....361 *s*
n. can become nothing.....714 *n*
n., if not critical*..........125 *t*
n. is beautiful from every..678 *k*
nothing is delightful.......722 *s*
nothing is so high.........707 *j*
n. is so swift as calumny...681 *a*
n. is strong that may not.. 688 *p*
n., situate under heaven's*.344 *f*
nothing whatever to wear . 23 *a*
n. when you are used to it.507*m*
out of nothing nothing.....714 *n*
soft words with n. in them.568 *s*
soon have n. to refuse.....181 *a*
starve with nothing*......168 *m*
thank you for nothing ....504 *v*
that nothing was done ....719 *u*
time you take to say n.....178 *c*
'tis not for n. that we life..347 *y*
'tis something, nothing*...595 *r*
trust that man in n., who ..106 *i*
Too much of nothing,......650 *p*
where n. wants that*......652 *k*
who does nothing ....203 *f*
who has enough ask for n..685 *j*
who is zealous for n........674 *b*
yet indeed is nothing......360 *s*
you gave me n. for 't*.....438 *w*
Nothingness-bearable than...298 *v*
first dark day of n.‖........132 *w*
my nothingness, my wants.489 *p*
never pass into nothingness 34 *w*
n. the whole substantial....409 *z*
Nothings-labour'd n., in so‡.581 *j*
variety of mere n. gives....794 *l*
Notion-and foolish notion...310 *f*
n. very speedily of his......344 *u*
Notions-soon their crude n... 27 *p*
we call old notions fudge...595 *g*
Nought-doth stand for n...659 *f*
n. venter nought have.....502 *x*
of falling into nought......315 *l*
Noun-knows where n. and ..579 *s*
Nourished-n. in the womb*..315 *i*
Nourisher-chief n. in life's*..562 *u*
the nourisher of kinds.....459*m*
Nourishment-fed with n......323*m*
found light and n........... 64 *o*
malice nourishment*.......372 *p*
n. in frozen pasture.......545 *i*
n. which is called*..........167 *t*
supply the same n........ 65 *d*
they have their n.*.........490 *o*
Novel-given away by a Novel 375 *o*
read in many a novel.......101 *g*
Novelties-best of n. palls....781 *l*
nature is fond of novelty ..729 *k*
pleased with n., might be..629 *t*
this novelty on earth**.....657 *s*
vivacity and n. of youth....516 *b*

what a novelty.............371 *r*
November-April, June, and..390 *j*
fie upon thee, November...395 *h*
no birds, November ....395 *i*
N. days are clear and .....395 *j*
N. thundering from the...396 *d*
N. woods are bare and still.395 *j*
the bleak N. winds.........395 *e*
these dark November days.395*m*
thirty dayes hath N. ......390 *k*
this sunlight shames N....544 *n*
wild N. come at last.......395 *o*
Now-an eternal N. does.....600 *d*
as we are n. so must you...183 *c*
at last the fleeting now....267*m*
eternal n. shall ever last...186 *b*
I am not now that which‖.. 74 *i*
now or never...............803 *a*
Nowhere-ah me! he's n......168 *s*
'tis nowhere to be found‡..293 *u*
who is everywhere is n.....748 *j*
Nuisance-by night a n. and.. 19 *l*
Number-by your n. than.....577 *k*
happiness of the greatest..292 *r*
happiness of the greatest..498 *s*
naught cares he for n.....565 *a*
number all your graces*...193 *r*
n. is certainly the cause...575*m*
n. of his slaine enemys.....301 *g*
teach me thy days to n.....652 *d*
Numbered-all our days are..582 *x*
be n. by years, daies .....599 *c*
sands are n. that make up*.350 *v*
Numbers-add to golden n....507 *r*
brings home full numbers*.631 *i*
by magic n. and persuasive.572 *u*
deep, his numbers flowed..406 *r*
divinity in odd numbers*..368 *q*
for every purpose odd n...586 *j*
I lisp'd in n., for the‡......429 *l*
inform'd by magic n.......405 *a*
in mournful numbers§....348 *n*
in numbers warmly pure.. 78*m*
life thy numbers flow......732 *s*
move harmonious n.**.....597 *f*
n. sanctified the crime.....403 *p*
n. who will serve instead. .644 *v*
round n. are always false..199 *i*
the n. of the fear'd*.......536 *g*
the n. soft and clear‡......406 *u*
there's luck in odd n.......368 *l*
what numbers claim.......429 *y*
Numbs-it n. the soul, it......456 *i*
Numerous-more n. was the..589 *b*
n. as glittering gems.......577 *n*
Nun-holy time is quiet as a¶.187 *l*
nun's, demure and meek...185 *c*
shy as a nun is she....... 43 *g*
violet is a nun..............248 *o*
you become a nun.........359 *k*
Nuptial-n. of his son a*......290 *b*
to the n. bower I led her**..376 *d*
Nuremburg-N. the ancient§.. 98 *f*
Nurse-babe will scratch the* 82 *f*
bear them, breed and n..... 15 *t*
be his n., diet his sickness*.311 *u*
being put to nurse*.........439 *o*
best n., Contemplation**..567 *g*
meet nurse for a poetic.....116 *q*
melancholy is the n. of*...379 *h*
n. and fountain of fecundity641 *e*
nurse of frenzy* ....379 *h*
n. of manly sentiment and.143 *b*
nurse of young desire.....307 *s*
peace, dear n. of arts*....471 *f*
recollect a n. called Ann...380 *q*
sleep, nature's soft nurse*.562 *q*
solitude is the nurse of....566 *u*
the nurse of second woe*..382*m*
Time is the n. and breeder*.603 *b*
will scratch the nurse*....363 *h*
Nursed-n. in whirling storms 239 *p*
n. my little one a month...196 *q*
n. with care and pain.....672 *i*
Nursery-the n. of brooding.. 54 *c*
Nurses-and old men's n.....644 *p*
some make pretty nurses..102 *l*

Nursing-n. her wrath to keep 17 *f*
Nurst-must be slowly n.‖....311 *d*
my breast, I oft have n.....553 *f*
Nut-brain gets as dry as an..476 *n*
sweet is the nut............220*m*
Nut-brown-n-b. maid........161 *r*
quaff the nut-brown ale....161 *r*
spicy nut-brown ale**......162 *p*
Nutmeg-be rough as n.......420 *c*
Nutmegs-n. and cloves......195 *n*
Nuts-a man for cracking n.*.513 *n*
before green n. embrown...542 *g*
his n. larded many swine..616 *h*
n. from brown October's...395 *c*
nuts were falling...........267 *a*
take the n. from the fire...507 *z*
Nutriment-with double n....560 *l*
Nutrition-draw n.‡.........349 *h*
Nymph-a n. more white than.175 *f*
beloved n. fair Dove........530 *n*
Grecian chisel trace a n... 36 *k*
haste thee, N., and bring**383 *r*
like a quiver'd nymph**... 88 *a*
nymph to the bath.........243 *k*
a pining n. had prisoned††.612 *g*
Nymphs-but tell me, nymphs 97 *s*
fresh n. encounter every*..302 *u*
of his drill'd n., but like‖...127 *r*
ye nymphs that reign...... 97 *s*

O.

Oak-a goodly O. sometime. .616 *h*
and hearts of oak our men.468 *b*
and one upon the old oak..609 *f*
a song to the o., the brave .615 *n*
bend a knotted oak.........405 *a*
close as oak and ivy stand. 151 *o*
convulsion rends the solid o.552 *f*
English oak, which dead...615 *o*
fell the hardest-timber'd o.*339 *l*
fruit of many an oak......177 *k*
hearts of oak are our ships 79 *k*
many an oak that grew.....398 *f*
o. from a small acorn grows289 *g*
oak of Sumner-chace†.....616 *g*
o., when living, monarch of 615 *o*
old noted oak! I saw thee.616 *a*
our ships were British oak.468 *b*
overthrow the tallest Oke. .619 *p*
raven on yon left-hand oak. 54 *s*
standing long an oak.......289 *j*
sturdy o. shakes that ne'er 616 *e*
such hearts of o. as they †.116 *c*
tall oak, towering to the...616 *f*
the monarch oak, the......616 *b*
the ruins of their ancient o.625 *g*
took a sturdy oak......... 18 *f*
twisted round the barren§.546 *e*
unwedgeable and gnarled*.578 *e*
was brow-bound with the**.579 *l*
young O.! when I planted‖.615*m*
Oak-leaf-the purple o-l. falls.394 *l*
Oaks-across the gray-green..583 *k*
beneath our o. hast slept...541 *q*
have riv'd the knotty o.*...578 *d*
knotted oaks adorn‡.......242 *u*
oaks that flourish for a....270 *s*
o. with solemnity shook....616 *c*
tall o., branch-charmed....616 *d*
tall o. from little acorns....462 *d*
widely waving o. enclose... 56*m*
ye venerable Oaks ....610 *p*
Oar-drip of the suspended o.‖ 63 *h*
ply every oar and cheerly.. 48 *f*
second an oar or a sail.....354 *g*
soft moves the dipping oar. 63 *g*
spread the thin oar and‡... 63 *o*
Oars-but o. alone can ne'er.. 63 *i*
by science, sails and oars ..678 *d*
cut with her golden o. the* 18 *j*
like a pair of oars ....440 *d*
oars were silver which*....552 *b*
our oars keep time.........63*m*
with falling oars they kept. 63 *k*
Oath-break an o. he never...418 *u*

or odor's breath............242 m
radiance and odour.......245 c
stealing and giving odour*.407 k
sweet and wholesome o....447 n
thine odor like a key......249 l
while the odour flew.....249 j
with odour wooing me.....242 a
Odorous–the lilac spread o...614 q
Odors–as o. crushed are...... 6 i
covering the earth with**630 a
drowsed with o. strange... 47 s
her daintie odours threwe. 612 j
o. crushed are sweeter.... 83 g
o. from the spicy shrub**.376 d
o. sweet proclaim the spot.238 t
odours were of power.... 244 i
rise o. of ploughed field§...117 h
Sabean o. from the spicy** 447 r
shed their nightly odours..415 k
spread rich o. through....221 a
the amorous odors of......220 q
tne wind in odors dying....647 s
virtue is like precious o....631 y
O'er–a single step, and all is§583 b
O'ercomes–Satan o. none.....593 s
O'ergrow–they'll o. the*...648 n
O'erjoyed–o. that they††.....228 e
O'erleaps–ambition which o.* 13 w
O'erlook–her husband to o....661 a
O'er–shoot–sure never to o–s.‡324 m
O'erstep–o. not the modesty*. 5 s
O'erthrown–noble mind is*...386 h
O'erthrows–a breath o.‡.....272 x
O'ertook–purpose never is*..147 i
Of–among them but not of‖..566 d
Off–off the hinges.........407 c
off with his head*.........608 r
well to be off with the old.360 q
Offence–all's not o. that*.....495 c
an offense against God....123 m
appear offence in us*...... 84 g
confront the visage of o.*..382 r
dire o. from am'rous‡......527 e
dismissed o. would after*...332 s
every nice o. should bear*.125 v
forgave the offence........656 b
for man's offence**.......221 j
for our offence was slain...165 h
gives offence to peace.....518 t
less dang'rous is tn' o.‡....429 i
neither give o. to others....481 l
offence inspires less horror 437 i
O.'s gilded hand may*......438 p
readily only invites offence 768 o
sufficient ransom for o.*...569 t
that hir was doon offence..467 c
there the Pope, for my o...522 l
tongue did make offence*..193 m
trifle scorn to take offence‡619 q
turns a sour offence*......362 r
unkindness is a great o.....548 u
what is my offence*.......330 o
yet detest the offence‡.....556 f
Offences–forgiveness for his. 701 k
his own o., and strips......537 o
so many giddy offences*...609 k
Offend–fearful to offend¶...245 i
o. good people, how they.. 668 m
o. her, and she knows not‡.698 k
to o., and judge, are*......438 x
Offended–devils being o.* .. 660 g
I have o. reputation*...... 524 n
in what has he o.? he whose 21 o
Offender–hugged the o......255 k
love th' o., yet detest‡.....556 f
offender never pardons.....255 m
Offenders–examines all such*603 c
Offending–most o. soul*....120 v
Offends–o. no law and is a....436 u
Offensive–crawl to o. mine...324 i
Offer'd–take when once 'tis*.461 r
Offering–o. Heaven holds....344 a
Offerings–as o. unto God§....425 n
Offers–you are liberal in o.*.. 38 q
Office–a dog's obeyed in o.*.. 30 b
Circumlocution Office......282 b
does not relate to his o.... 675 f

hast stolen both mine o.*...595 q
hath but a losing office*....415 b
in whatever o., business ... 87 d
let the tender o. long‡...... 11 a
men's o. to speak patience*467 z
o. and affairs of love*......363 p
office which one fills........797 o
public o. is a public trust..620 r
public o. is a public trust..620 u
seals of office glitter in..... 12 u
seekers of o. are sure of†† .285 q
the office shows the man...801 y
they have done their office.624 f
to execute laws is a royal..620 o
to get some office*........558 v
to morning's holy office*...670 n
turn from their office to*.. 75 x
Officer–fear each bush an o. *586 c
Officers–invectives 'gainst* ..122 d
king and o. of sorts*......322 b
o. of the government......281 q
public o. are the servants..620 p
Offices–distinct o. and of*...438 x
estates, degrees, and o.*.. 306 i
imperfect o. of prayer¶....490 e
stars for doing ill offices...575 n
that estates, degrees and *.383 h
Official–I take the o. oath....419 g
Officious–o. innocent sincere. 80 p
Offspring–night her **.....416 j
offspring of a dark and....239 p
o. of heaven first born**...352 n
o. of shame is shyness....551 n
peace the o. is of power....471 j
source of human o.**....376 b
the offspring of Love......327 r
Time's noblest offspring is.492 c
to tempt its new-fledg'd o..450 l
Offsprings–spare not the....651 g
Oftener–o. you come here...643 q
Ogle–to patch, nay ogle‡...129 a
Ohio–Ohio's shores and....115 i
Oil–ashes, and oil of joy....330 d
as holy oil, Edward*......535 c
calme and still with oile....445 o
consumed the midnight oil.580 l
incomparable oil.‖.......447 m
lamps with everlasting o.**.416 n
midnight oil ....501 ll
oil on troubled waters......502 ee
o. that's in me should set*.299 r
o., vinegar, sugar, and.... 79 q
our wasted o. unprofitably.346 v
pouring o. on the sea make.445 p
winds slipping the smooth.445 p
with odorous oil they head.457 o
without the oil and ...... 87 c
Oily–fat, oily man of God...451 r
Old–a good o. man, sir: he*..653 w
always find time to grow...671 s
and old men's nurses......644 p
an old man, broken with.*..86 u
an old man's heart........294 d
as you are o. and reverend.* 11 l
awhile the o. thought......596 h
because they're old....... 22 j
blessing of tne Old........ 60 k
both get so o. and withered.375 l
both very o. and very dear.605 k
confess yourself an o. man.180 b
dear as they grow old‡.....429 f
die, but the old§............136 b
draws into port the old....350 b
faint o. man shall lean his.646 u
for we are o., and on our*..602 l
free soul will never grow...769 d
friends are either o. or ugly178 p
growing a little old....... 20 g
grown old before my time.. 11 d
he is, old Jack Falstaff*.... 33 i
how o. I am! I'm eighty... 97 r
if you yourselves are old*.. 11 u
in conduct to be old.......673 n
in the brave days of old....627 k
is not o. wine wholesomest. 12 k
know how to be old........ 10 g
last to lay the old aside‡...212 n

love everything that's old.. 9 s
may be o. in body, but can.672 b
Nature abhors the old...... 1 f
new is older than the old..260 y
no man would be old...... 12 f
off with the old love...... 75 d
of the o. man in him.......672 b
o. age is slow in both......671 p
o. as aught of time can be..618 e
o. as I am for ladies love... 34 i
old folk and young§ ....128 l
o., long life and treasure...604 p
old lovers are soundest.... 12 k
old man, God bless you....457 i
old men are fools..........251 g
o. men from the chimney...579 a
o. men know young men...231 v
old men sleep longest......346 c
old soldiers, sweetheart... 12 k
old things need not be.....596 k
old, unhappy, far-off¶ ....466 q
old wood burn brightest... 12 k
one is never too old, Thais.176 g
persons know how to be o..754 l
pleased with an old man...672 b
ring out the old, ring†...‖ 41 e
sad, revives the o. inspires 648 m
said he in times of old¶... 76 r
she is not yet so old*......645 n
sorrows of a poor old man..473 u
speak of when we are old*. 12 e
subject we old men are to*.190 o
the old men's dream......634 d
the soul never grows o.§...571 s
think old men fools.......251 v
though an old man, do....695 t
though I look old, yet I*... 12 a
though old the thought††..514 q
thou hadst grown old§.....185 n
thou shouldst not have*...651 l
thyself as old as Fate......407 v
to be forty years old...... 10 b
very foolish, fond, o. man. 11 v
we call o. notions fudge....595 g
we hope to grow o. and we.754 k
what is it to grow old..... 8 p
when men grow old.......754 h
when we are o., we must...755 a
when young and o., and....605 p
woman-like and shuns the..553 l
yes, I'm growing old....... 11 e
you are o., Father........... 12 e
you are old; Nature*....... 12 d
Old age–sad old age and fear.299 u
Oldest–commit the o. sins*..556 t
Old-fashioned–o-f. poetry...473 b
sake of o-f. folks........216 d
Olive–in war the o. branch..751 d
of o., aloe, and maize†.....610 k
the fruitful olive.........610 h
the o. grove of Académe**.616 i
vine and o. lovely Spain...117 a
Olives–fruitful o. vines of... 63 u
Olive-woods–wan, grey o-w..609 a
Olympain–O. bards who sung.557 d
Olympus–mighty mount O...276 t
on O. tottering Ossa‡......402 t
Omar–the diver O. pluckedt†.477 k
Omen–o. but his country's‡... 70 a
Omens–evil o. from the......608 b
Omission–o. to do what is*...185 v
Omnipotence–labor of o......323 l
o. of God shines forth......486 a
to span omnipotence and...370 t
Omniscience–short of an o....327 p
On–keeps you on and off-ing‡.114 g
on, Stanley, on...........638 p
you are on with the new...360 y
Once–I am not what I once..682 d
once in each man's life....368 g
once to every man and††...145 g
Ondines–sylphs and o. and... 99 d
One–a flea in one's ear......494 u
grow one in the sense......263 n
how many lives we live....346 o
I owe you one.............500 u
just between twelve and o.*138 l

we are p. the worth of our.666 c
Pails-great p. of puddled*..:458 h
Pain-after a great deal of p.. 44 j
all earth's little pain......316 d
a mighty pain to love it is..357 r
and short-lived pain........663 f
and so full of pain§........542m
and to smile in pain......476 b
and with a secret pain....408 i
breathe their words in pain*340 b
but grief and pain.........154 x
common brotherhood in p.568 x
die of a rose in aromatic‡..447 u
error wounded, writhes in..621 f
eternal passion! eternal p.. 50 l
excuse from pain ....296 s
extremity of his p. and....463 d
far outweighs the pain....569 o
find a pain in that........326 a
gave p. to the bear........ 126 i
grief the family of pain‡...386 b
heart then knew of pain... 90 a
heedless of your pain......419 b
her face is full of pain ....395 o
he's free from all pain....134m
in p., in sickness, we for...127 i
leisure is p.; take off our...343 a
lesse in mynde, the lesser..553 j
lesson of your own pain....190 v
lies comfort for my pain...671 c
long ailments wear out p..501 p
lover's p. to attain the....530 i
making pain his joy........277 n
may feel too much pain... 17 j
moon look'd forth as tho'..416 h
more of pain or pleasure...354 v
neither love nor sense of p.188 o
never mind the pain‖.......455 e
no fiery, throbbing pain....135 f
not unmixed with pain§....378 n
of surfeits and corporeal p.642 f
of p., darkness and cold...346 b
opine they feel the pain...208 p
p. and anguish wring the..658 r
p. can't bless heaven quits.150 h
p. in every peopled sphere†.188 f
p. is no longer pain when...463 g
p. is not the fruit of pain...463 c
p. is unmerited, the grief..744 p
p. of finite hearts that....465 h
peace hath balsamed p....615 c
place but keep the pain...156 r
place farthest from pain**. 91 u
pleasure bought by pain..732 p
pleasures to another's p...126 f
pleasure which is born of p.475 n
pulse of pain to calm....242 p
recant vows made in pain**.419 i
reliev'd their pain........ 38 l
rest itself becomes a pain‡.526 k
sacred, shed for other's p.‖.590 i
sad moments of her pain..598 p
sense of pain was§.........169 g
sigh, yet feel no pain.....155 n
sleep that no p. shall.....138 a
softens every pain.........404 g
so full of pain§............131 c
studies or his usual pain*..407 p
sweet is pleasure after p..463 b
sweet is pleasure after p..475 j
tender for another's pain...582 o
that is not akin to pain§ ..537 g
that monster called Paine..463 i
that never feels a pain.....569 l
the pain is for me..........769 e
the p. of any distemper...708 e
the pain that he must bear. 55 n
there is purpose in pain...463 e
thinks p. the greatest evil..680 b
this vale of pain..........475 v
till taught by p., men‖......641 a
till thought grew pain..... 3 a
though full of pain**......316 l
thread of life with pain‡...347 x
'tis a p. that pain to miss..357 r
to sigh, yet feel no pain....553 d
triumph! hark! what pain.. 50 l

turns the past to pain......379 u
turnes to pleasing paine....475 x
turns with ceaseless pain..379 v
vain which with pain*.....147 w
wail, as of souls in pain§...348 o
we are born in others' p....463 j
we delight in, physics p.*..339 n
when pain grows sharp...351 p
with ceaseless pain......... 2 n
with like weight of pain*.. 6 u
with p. purchas'd doth.....463 h
with some p. is fraught....537 j
woman's pain,†............642 b
wrought him endless pain..202 g
years of rankling pain....157 d
you purchase p. with all‡..463 f
Painful-the one is as p.....132 a
virtue she finds too p. an‡..633 g
Pains-all thy pains and*....610 b
amid life's p., abasements..317 c
are according to his paines.338 x
cares and little p. refuse...346 z
doth in sharp p. abound.... 8 t
feels nor fears ideal pains..467 e
find it worth his pains....454 d
little pains in a due hour...269 b
long pains are light........103 b
my paynes his prey.......255 d
of all pains, the greatest...357 r
p. and penalties of idleness‡313m
p. of love be sweeter far...357 x
p. of power, are real......485 p
pleasure in poetic pains....478 s
pleasure is a man of p....463 k
such p. such pleasures....128 g
taken great pains to con it*574 l
to know the p. of power...485 p
virtue consoles us, even...630 l
Paint-Autumn! who may p...544 p
he best can p. them who‡..446 u
I must invent and paint...446 p
man's blood p. the ground*639 b
no words can p............ 82 j
or p. the full-orb'd ruler...446 t
p. 'em truest praise 'em....446 g
paint for other minds......446 q
paint the laughing soil....540 c
p. the meadows with*.....541 a
p. the rainbow's varying...515 o
Romances p. at full length‖ 533 q
so fierce as they paint him.505m
such a sin to paint‡.......129 a
to paint the lily*..........252 y
want the power to paint...678 c
who can paint like Nature.412w
Painted-all my fancy p. her..203 s
angels are p. fair, to look...657 y
darkly p. on the crimson... 56 p
flower the Painted Cup...236 o
gilded loam or p. clay*....524 s
skies are painted with*....577 b
their painted outsides.....658 b
well that painted it*..... .447 h
Painter-a flattering p., who..446m
a stone-cutter or a p. could*455 b
being a landscape painter..447 b
being a figure painter.....447 b
better that made the p.**..447 h
curious p. doth pursue¶....71 f
flower or animal painter...447 b
I would I were a p..........447 l
mother made me a p.......336 d
or a handless painter......447 j
some great painter dips....447 i
the painter's art to me.....382 a
works of any great p......480 v
Painters-light is the first of..352 f
p. and poets have equal...678 b
poets heap virtues p. gems†674 f
poets like p., thus unskill'd†480 f
Painting-and that was P...421 q
contrast with the great....102 i
not more than p. can...... 36 g
p. and sculpture and...... 28 h
p. in unchanged strength..347 k
p. is almost the natural*...447 f
p. with all its technicalities447 c

sculpture is more than p.§.452m
Paintings-are statues, and§..452 l
eyes are charmed by p....678 a
Paints-he paints the skies...586 e
p. a dolphin in the woods..714 f
Pair-happy is that humble p.378 e
nor honey make, nor pair..666m
Pairs-fitly them in p. thou**. 21 g
Palace-a very stately p...... 33 q
Cleon dwelleth in a palace..483 q
every p., every city almost. 14m
in a transparent palace....755 b
in his palace of the West...585 p
in p. chambers far apart†..563 l
in the palace of the Sun...334 g
key that opes the palace**..136 t
knocks at the palace......206 n
palace and a prison on‖.... 99 a
prince has to his palace....595 c
such a gorgeous palace*...145 f
that p. of the soul serene...590 b
the lofty p. then his........ 48 g
then tower'd the palace....122 s
the palace of the soul‖....571 b
was King Bradmond's p....425 c
Palace-door-near the p-d....355 i
Palace-gates-thirty p-g.....166 c
Palaces-fair, frail p., the....585 c
green p. the first kings....413 q
in hamlets, p., and parks.. 358 h
key to golden palaces......561m
'mid pleasures and palaces304 k
p. are crumbling to the‖... 98 p
palaces break man's rest...708 c
the gorgeous palaces*.....634m
the heavenly palaces......186 b
Palate-have to rectify your..167 e
titillate the p. of Silenus..166 n
Palates-p. both for sweet*...377 d
Pale-bond which keeps me*..417 q
'gins to p. his ineffectual*.625 k
in my cheek's pale hue....662 j
it lies I know p. and white..181 c
look'd deadly pale*........210 a
pale and brief 233m
p. and silent settles into... 18 d
pale and wan, fond lover...365 r
pale as moonlight snow....234 n
p. death with impartial....689 q
p. his lips as the dead....366 a
pale in her anger*.........399 a
p. my cheeks with care....661 b
p., trembling, tir'd, the‡...577 r
so silent, sweet, and pale... 51 r
they are thin and p., their..579 g
thou pale for weariness....399 b
Pale-eyed-p-e. priest.......**.493 f
Pall-the pall of twilight....624 k
which pierc'd the pall‖.....234 l
Palls-when this, the present‡.648m
Pallas-comes to-day Pallas†..278 k
commune held by P. and...276 g
the pallid bust of Pallas... 55 b
Pallets-braided p. formed....617 h
uneasy p. stretching thee*.563 c
Palliating-ingenious in p....710m
Pallor-turned to deathly p.... 92 i
Palm-Allah, who gives the...617 b
as a harper lays his open§..601 b
bear the palm alone*......257 e
do not dull thy palm*......262 c
has won it bear the palm..808 g
his need of the palm shall..617 b
I love the Palm.... ....617 a
in lands of p. and southern†610 k
life line in the palm........292 t
like some tall palm the....122 s
palm of ploughman*.......292 l
the p. is a gift divine......617 b
to have an itching palm*...595m
threads of p. was the......617 b
who rounded in his p......577 n
Palms-fold thy p. across thy†526 s
fronded palms in air......276 a
the palms of Paradise.....141 c
Palm-tree-as the p-t.§......616 o
of the palm-tree bower....236 n

p. of their good morrow....605 a
p. with it as with money...673 q
perform her part...........169 b
seems the part of wisdom..650 i
sexton's dreary part.......458 s
shall never, never part....358 q
shall never part...........464 s
she hath done her part**...411 n
then part forever..........207 o
'tis but a part we see‡ ....371 y
two lives that once part...464 p
what passes in good part...110 f
yet are loth to part.......378 f
you and I must part........375 s
Partakers–p. of evil deeds...695 o
Parted–never to be p. with...262 t
parted for ever............362 i
they say he parted well*...465 n
we two parted in silence‖ ..464 j
Parting–at our p., we will be.162 l
at the p., all the church*...335 s
good-night! parting is*....464 v
in every p. there is an......464 l
their every parting was to†627 p
this our parting spring¶...56 i
this parting was well made*464 w
where parting is unknown .298 j
Partings–and p. yet to be....465 e
p. break the heart they‖....464 i
pang of all the p. gone......465 e
Parts–agree with our*......660 c
all parts are played........668 t
if parts allure thee‡.......202 k
many ages played their p..422 k
p. of one stupendous‡......411 v
p. remaining as they**....326 d
p. us shall bring a brand*..108 m
rehearse your parts*.......422 b
the light and spritely p.....422 p
Parthenon–proudly wears ..425 h
Parthian–nor, like the P.....466 s
Partial–authors are p. to‡....429 e
p, for th' observer's sake‡..548 c
Participle–verb and p. grows 579 s
Particle–particle of divine....696 d
that very fiery p‖.........385 h
Partisanship–plot by which..482 g
Partition–yet a union in p.*..627 n
Partitions–p. do their bounds 653 a
thin p. sense from thought‡548 m
Partner–p. in the trade......264 l
while his lov'd partner.....303 q
Partners–unhappy p. of.....294 j
Partnership–p. with men in..688 o
Partridge–eats neither p....166 d
like as a fearful p.........53 q
mark'd a partridge quake . 53 h
partridge is dearer.........181 g
the partridge whirs........395 b
who finds the p. in the*....53 i
Partridges–ah, nut-brown p.‖543 o
Party–any individual or p....620 r
he serves his party best....482 q
honesty is p. expediency...482 k
justice discards party......332 a
none was for a party.......627 k
p. whose antecedents have .482 h
the promised p., to enjoy‖..543 o
to party gave up what was.270 m
true to one party††........107 k
we join ourselves to no p...468 q
who hears one party only..490 h
Pass–and p. them current too*640 f
blaze and pass away‡.......202 j
but pass and die...........254 a
never comes to pass ....317 i
owls pass for eagles.......180 e
p. and speak one another§..378 m
pass away nor leave a rack.186 i
p. silently from men as.....647 a
ships that p. in the night§..378 m
straight and treacherous¶ .309 e
the narrow pass...........245 k
they p. unheeded by.......161 q
to see great Pompey pass*.189 m
turning for them who p.¶..461 s
we pass and speak one§....150 v

Passage–each dark p. shun... 68 q
p. of an angel's tear ....590 v
repeats the passage of the.. 92 g
that p. is what I call the...476 k
unseen, can passage find*..364 g
Passages–p. that lead to.....425 k
Passed–p. methought the*....140 q
when she had p. it seemed§.405 u
Passenger–sea the p. e'er‖...459 h
Passengers–all the p. he bore.648 j
Passers–the p. in the city§...394 h
Passes–man passes away....371 h
nod as she passes by......217 p
take what p. in good part..110 f
through rocky passes¶.....71 f
Passing–"p. away" is written 74 p
passing away..............241 l
speak each other in p.§....150 v
Passion–a fop their passion‡.349 n
angels till our passion dies.465 l
awful hour of the Passion..612 c
by passion driven..........465 i
chastisement but without..737 a
control your p. or it will...677 n
counsel turns to passion*..288 c
dark with passion.........224 b
did relieve my p. much*...568 n
each to his passion ....465 m
eternal p. eternal pain....50 l
felt every passion ....549 t
fires of human p. with§....600 w
his p. shall have spent†....466 a
I discern infinite passion...465 h
in a dream of passion*....423 g
in her first passion woman‖356 p
Jove in a passion..........171 q
less than Action and P.....336 x
no p. gratified except‡....82 s
one p. doth expel another..465 j
one passion now remains...528 m
one passion stands for all..300 y
passion, all confused‡......371 v
passion fears revealing....219 k
passion for wealth‡........740 c
passion is the gale‡........349 m
p., knowledge, fame‡......111 p
passion so pale...........234 p
passion we feel than in....359 q
patience all the p. of††....467 t
places which pale p. loves..465 g
press a suit with passion...661 t
put yourselves into a p.....175 t
reason, and not p., impels..717 t
red wine of life and passion.393 a
ruling p. conquers reason‡.465 t
ruling p. strong in death‡..465 q
search then the ruling p.‡..465 t
shocks of p. can prepare*‖.466 d
simplest man with passion.462 e
some bloody p. shakes*....465 w
something with p. clasp§...296 v
sudden p. languishing.....540 a
take heed lest p. sway**...465 p
that is not passion's slave*.372 t
that passion alone in the...209 f
the cue for passion*.......423 m
the p. ending, doth the*...465 aa
the p. of great hearts†† ....81 t
the passion to proceed....456 n
the whirlwind of passion*.423 k
to ourselves in p. we*.....465 aa
vows with so much passion.419 f
what is passion but pining.167 l
where passion leads or....91 s
with a p. would I shake*...465 z
Passionate–its p. cadence§...634 u
Passion-flower–p-f. at the†...366 r
Passionless–that p. bright...398 k
Passions–absence diminishes.782 j
all thoughts, all passions...357 m
but the noblest p. to inspire.479 q
catching all p. in his craft*606 h
consider their p. and are‖..70 c
govern my p. with absolute.465 u
human in its passions......558 c
if we resist our passions it is 465 n
kill the best of p., love.....367 d

licentious p. and vices of...318 o
life all other passions fly...365 n
p. are likened best to floods.465 v
p. are nothing else than....782 k
p. are the only orators.....462 e
p. jostle and displace......194 r
p. oft, to hear her shell....404 v
p. that this world deform..633 w
reins to your inflamed p...677 s
strength of the passions...80 m
such angry passions rise..466 c
through our p. shown‡....203 ℓ
various ruling p. find‡....465 r
when passions are no more.466 b
Passion-waves–p-w. are lulled 296 t
Passover–Christ is our P.....166 a
Passport–his p.shall be made*639 g
passport round the globe...120 f
Passports–not pedigree, are.. 15 p
Past–actions of the past§.... 10 h
amid the ruins of the p.§...532 c
and maintains the past‡... 82 t
and nothing past..........186 h
as the Past is given........ 67 f
audible voice of the Past....64 n
be able to enjoy our p. life.179 n
be thankful for the past...110 j
but it is p.: come day, come.151 o
children have neither p.nor.758 s
comes to me out of the P..§380 k
dead past bury its dead§.... 5 a
deem the irrevocable Past§.190 l
drink to the solemn past...142 b
enough of the past for the‖.599 j
eternal landscape of the p.†466 p
false to the past sweet......212 j
fifty years are past........ 8 t
from the luminous past††.. 81 h
future but by the past......331 b
giant fossils of my past.... 64 f
gone and what's past help*.525 h
groaning ever for the past.466 f
hallowed quiet of the p.††.466 k
I know the past and thence.190 u
Iliad as memorial of the P..420 o
in eternity no past†.........186 k
in the past alone, I build...634 k
leave thy low-vaulted past.571 n
memory brightens o'er the§380 l
mem'ry of the p. will stay..380 q
mighty secrets of the past 604 a
mischiefs that are past.....251 q
more exquisite when past..329 s
no past is dead for us.......316 d
not heaven itself upon the..150 p
o'er the p. oblivion‡.......420 p
of the future is the past‖..:466 i
pain'd by the past.........186 r
painful past with blighting 287 y
pain when it is past........463 g
p. and to come seems best*.155 g
past lives o'er again........105 k
p. the future two eternities186 g
plan the future by the p....267 g
remedies are p., the griefs*508 x
silent stands the p. sublime602 c
soul of the whole P. Time.. 64 n
spins the future and the p .186 i
sum total of the whole P...526 w
the past Hours weak and...466 o
there are Voices of the P...466 m
there is no P., so long as.... 67 h
things that are p. never to.466 e
time be past, present, or to 22 g
to come and nothing p......186 e
triumphs in the past.......466 s
turns the past to agony....381 t
turns the past to pain......379 u
upon the p. has power......466 j
we read the p. by the light.190 h
what calls back the past...595 a
what's past, and what's to*420 q
what's p. is prologue*......466 v
which is p. is beyond recall 685 f
Pasts–futures fruits of all...189 s
Paste–p. made from beans...175 v
which serves as p. and*....139 v

Pict–from a naked P. his..... 22 m
Picture–a p. is a poem.......446 i
is the best picture§.......446 s
it is a little p. painted well.476 v
look here, upon this p.*....447 e
look not on his picture*....550m
looks at an American p....115 g
man who did this p. draw..446 j
one p. in ten thousand.....446 o
picture give us of these ...237 n
picture of human crimes...302 k
picture placed the busts...251 a
p. that approaches§.......446 s
sake of a sweet picture....447 l
shade is to figures in a p..389 c
song, p., form, space......410 l
Pictures–feeble p. and the... 28 i
fine p. suit in frames......107 h
my eyes make pictures....159 s
painting p. mile on mile...540 a
p. all earth scenes........298 l
pictures in the fire‡.......213 a
p. must not be too........446 l
p. placed for ornament and 14 r
p., taste, Shakespeare.....113 o
you are p. out of doors*....660 g
Picturesque–not be too p...446 l
Pie–and make a dirt pie....182 l
the rich pumpkin pie......595 a
Pies–as many mince p. as... 95 b
of p. custards and tarts...182 l
simplicity talks of pies...367 k
Piece–a small Euphrates‡...529 o
p. of a churchyard fits.....495 q
thou blessing of earth*...404 a
Piecemeal–p. they win this‡..488 c
Pieces–dash themselves to...152 e
helpless p. of the game He.348 l
thunderbolts; dash him to*.528 a
Pierce–might p. me unto...619 x
p. through pride and fear††.477 j
to pierce another.........206 d
Pierced–p. the fair pearls and.664 z
pierc'd to the soul with*...558 l
Pierian–taste not the P.‡...342 i
Piety–happy through piety..294 c
p. and holiness of life.....738 d
piety delight inspires......276 b
p. in art--poetry in art..... 28 k
p. is not inferior to your...175 e
p. throw into the world....596 n
plain roofs as p. could‡... 95 s
vicious world than piety...630 f
whose p. would not grow...468 w
Pig–he snored like a pig....462 a
pig falls from the spit*....432 d
the capon burns, the pig*..432 d
weke! so cries a pig*......432 f
Pigs–naturally as p. squeak..353 d
Pigeon–the nest of a p. is.... 54 l
Pigeon-egg–thou p-e. of*.. 54 j
Pigeons–and tame p. peas...353 f
pecks up wit as pigeons*... 54 i
pigeons feed their young*.414 t
the pigeons bill and coo....542 h
wood-p. cooed there, stock. 54 h
Pigmies–p. placed on the....503 g
Pigmy–a p.'s straw doth*....556 o
fretted the p.-body to decay 571 j
Pike–desire in killing a p..... 18 e
when a P. suns himselfe and 18 e
when the P. is at home.... 18 e
Pikes–p. the tyrants of the‡..213 l
Pikestaff–point is plain as a..505 v
Pilate–P. wash your hands*..556 r
'twas P.'s question put....621 s
Pile–p. without inhabitant...518 r
pile with servile toil.......396 o
Pilfered–bard whom p.‡.....480 h
Pilfers–still p. wretched.....595 e
Pilgrim–and still I am a p...382 a
day like a weary pilgrim§..187 n
does the p. count the miles.792 n
fill up my p.'s script††...... 38 n
forth with p. steps**.....400 n
land of the P.'s pride.....469 n
minstrel ! p. of the sky¶.... 49 s

our pilgrim stock wuz†††.... 81 m
the pilgrim and guest......595 a
the Pilgrim of Eternity....186 j
Pilgrimage-taper or go on a.670 e
the days of man's p.......654 h
Pilgrims–do p. find their way.531 d
pilgrims, to th' appointed...110 n
rests for weary pilgrims...285 i
Pill-bitter is his pill.......220m
Horace giving the poets a. 551 b
how to gild the pill.......784 d
lotion, drop, or pill.......512 r
p. that at the present......440 i
Pills–you gave me bitter p.*..441 n
Pillage–agin war an' p.††....637m
p. they with merry march*.322 b
Pillar–a well deserving p.*...331 q
pillar of my trust........260 v
seem'd a pillar of state**...153 j
Pillar'd–p. shade high over**.613 i
Pillars–antique p. massy**...352 l
around the pillars of the...236 n
bend thy p. with thine.....545 h
'mid the dim pillars high..186 b
pillars of pearl propping...545 k
who shall fix her pillars‡...338 k
Pill'ry–window like a pill'ry..126 p
Pillow–finds the down p.*...526 o
felt it beat under my p..... 64 f
gold fringed p. lightly†....563 l
pillow that fair head......137 e
that on his pillow lies......141 a
Pillowed–baby Sleep is p....563 e
winds are pillow'd on the... 47 l
Pillows–around our p. golden. 17 b
deaf p. will discharge*.....106 s
he lays for us the p.......369 j
minds to their deaf p.*....124 c
take thou of me sweet p....563 h
Pilot–a p.'s part in calms...670 w
but if the pilot slumber.... 73 s
daring pilot in extremity..129m
here's to the pilot that....444 z
hope to see my Pilot face†..268 j
is a pilot without eyes....534 g
pilot of my proper woe‖...300 d
pilot of the Galilean Lake*. 92 p
pilot! 'tis a fearful night....444 u
p. to find the polar star....777m
Pilots–on board the Lusian‖.532 l
p. have need of mariners...445 i
two traded p. 'twixt the*...646 n
Pimpernel–blossoms of the p.238 d
p. dozed on the leaf.......611 f
Pin–a sacred pin............. 6 l
and still care not a pin‡....318 i
cares not a pin‡..........183 p
my life at a pin's fee*......139 r
pin a day's a groat.........169 u
pricked him like a pin††....334 r
set my life at a pin's fee*...351 a
the Hub, the King pin.....482 g
to mould a p., or fabricate.667 l
Pinned–p. with a single......575 r
Pin-head-moon is a silver....397 e
Pin-heads–history of p-h....344 t
Pins–and p. it with a star...575 q
files of p. extend their‡....629m
Pincers–quiver where the p..527m
Pinch–necessity's sharp p.*...414 t
Pinches–my own shoe p......500 a
tell where it p. me........453 l
Pindar–imitate the poet P...714 g
Pindaric–weavers boast P.‖...454 l
Pine–and towering pine....230 s
apple from the pine......266 x
cedar, and p., and fir, and**609 k
grew the rougher rinded p.617 p
gummy bark of fir or p.**..613m
lofty p. is oftenest shaken..697 k
Mammon p. amidst his‡...369 l
palm and southern pine†...610 k
p. for kindred natures.....588 c
p. is the mother of††......617m
pine with feare............155 i
shade of desert-loving p.‖..617 f
stripped from the pine....617 h

Sylvan loves, of pine**.....617 o
then most I pine for thee...576 e
through penurie and p...485 g
two blazing p. knots did...617 h
vanished save of p. and....614 l
you pine for bread........476m
Pined–saw and p. his loss**...354 l
she pin'd in thought*......467 u
Pine-groves–one sound to....410 t
pine-groves, with your....274 b
Pines–among the p. and.... 71 a
ancient pines, ye bear no...617 a
balm and golden pines....218 o
fine spray of pines........545 g
forth thy silent sea of p...617 g
his thunder-harp of p......546 j
p. a noxious shade diffuse‡.546 f
stately p., but few more...618 a
the p. grow gray a little...617 k
tops of the eastern pines**.584 l
towers these stately p.§...617 l
under the yaller p. I†† ... 617 n
ye lofty p.! ye venerable...610 p
Pine-tree–high above the....617 j
waved the p-t. through my.617 l
Pinion–he nursed the p.‖...519 c
joy of voice and pinion¶.... 50 f
joy that moves the pinion..329 u
scattering from his hoary p.601 p
Pinions–and spread those p... 42 g
borne on buoyant p....... 4 n
on the pinions of the morn.597 h
soaring p. hovered o'er.... 48 g
song on its mighty p.§.....568 l
stoop your pinions to the...779 l
the dove on silver p........ 45 o
time flies on restless p......602 e
waving thy silver p. o'er...308 b
Pink–bring hether the p.....229 k
in clouded pink or........245 k
I will pu' the pink.........238 f
p. I would not slight......238 g
pink with cheek of red....317 f
she's the p. o' womankind..238 f
very pink of perfection....472 c
very pink of courtesy*....120 l
wild pink crowns the¶....238 h
you take a pink...........238 e
Pinks–in clever daffodils and.448 f
buy roses and pinks.......216 j
Pious–p. action we do sugar*.313 b
p. may not live in peace...783 g
p. when I'm only bilious...521 d
the p. farmer, who ne'er...525 e
Pipe–and in a p. delighteth..456 j
does your p. taste sweetly.457 i
glorious in a pipe‖.........456 j
Jack shall pipe, and Jill....500 ii
p. but as the linnets sing†..557 v
pipe for fortune's finger*. 257 b
pipe of Hermes*.........278 d
p. on her pastoral hillock†.471 k
pipe to smoke in cold .....280 l
p. to the spirit ditties of no.405m
p. whose fragments are....325 k
rhyme the p., and time....462 p
rumour is a p. blown*.....536 h
the p., with solemn.......456 h
the while his red-tipt p.....433 e
tune the rural p. to love...531 b
wilt thou have p. and reed..393 n
with tuneless p., beside the.531 c
Pipes–and rarely p. the†...... 59 e
chill p. the stormy wind...233 l
pipes and whistles in his*.. 11 j
to many a row of pipes**...406 b
ye soft pipes play on......405m
Piping–rocking winds are**..647 r
Piping-hot–your p-h. lie....724 g
Pippins–old p. toothsomest.. 12 k
pippins and cheese*......168 g
Pirate–lures the P., and‡...390 b
Pistol–cocking of a p., when‖.163 e
wind blew you hither, p.*..647 w
Pit–but a soundlesse pit....299 a
fallen into a pit of ink*....290m
fill a p. as well as better*...640 e

SHAKESPEARE *; MILTON **; WORDSWORTH ¶; BYRON ‖; TENNYSON †; LOWELL ††; POPE ‡; LONGFELLOW §.

many-headed monster of‡..422m
on the burnin' pit††........163w
Pitch-above the p., out of....407 c
 dark as pitch.............496ee
 p. of human glory**........638 d
 touch p. will be defiled*....506 x
 what validity and pitch*....364 l
Pitcher-does it turn out a p..682 a
Pitchers-little p. have wide...501 l
Pitches-p. there its tent......561 d
Pitchfork-blows from p......757m
 on her with a p............. 24 k
Pitchy-p. knot and beechen..547 a
Pitfall-wolf dreads the p......745 f
Pith-had seven years' p.*....574m
Pitied-p. in a Christian......329 e
 p. who are now envied......771 g
Pities-Lord help 'em, how....445 n
 that Power that p. me.....473 v
 what beggar pities not*....474 f
Pitiful-p., 'twas wondrous p.*661 q
 see fair hair be pitiful......291 c
 who should be p., if you*...451 n
Pittacus-P., from Mitylene's.650 p
Pittance-live with that small.111 d
Pity-age is without pity......758 t
 and p. 'tis 'tis true*........321 f
 capricious p. which would.309 o
 challenge double pity.....554 t
 die, no soul shall pity me*..474 d
 e'en pity scarce can wish it‖. 62 i
 fear feels no pity.........698 q
 for pity makes the world...345 h
 God has a father's pity.....133 f
 heart susceptible of pity...117 d
 I learn to pity them........473 v
 I lov'd her that she did p.*365 a
 in myself no p. to myself*.474 d
 I spy some p. in thy looks*.474 f
 love will have a sense of p.§359 v
 "my ladye fayre" for p....102 l
 my p. hath been balm to*..474 g
 no p. sitting in the clouds*.474 e
 now moved with pity‖...... 69 k
 now with pity to dispense..474 c
 of simple human pity ....473 t
 or sigh with pity*..........211 e
 out of holy pity*...........280 r
 petitions, pity and*........461 q
 p. and need make all flesh.587 l
 p. distress is but human... 86 q
 p. gave ere charity began..473 u
 pity is it that we can die...468 a
 p. is the virtue of the law*.474 h
 pity lovers, rather more‖...655 l
 p. melts the mind to love..473 s
 p. never leaves the gentle..474 j
 p.'s akin to love; and every.474 k
 pity speaks to grief........473 r
 pity's the straightest.......473 p
 p. swells the tide of love..142m
 p. the sorrows of a poor....473w
 p. those I do not know*....332 s
 pity warm'd the master's..474 a
 pure-from Pity's mine‖....590 f
 showing an outward pity*.556 r
 sleep ! in p. thou art made.561 h
 soft-eyed Pity once led..... 92 q
 speak with me, pity me*... 38 r
 tear-falling p. dwells not*..474 i
 tear for pity and a hand*.. 86 v
 that she did pity them*....129 t
 the Maker saw, took pity‡.658 l
 the sweet moan of pity....430 r
 till Pity's self be dead......403 e
 'tis true, 'tis pity*.........321 f
 we first endure, then p.‡...630 p
Pity-pat-his heart kep'goin'††662 r
Pity-Zekle-but hen went††..662 r
Pixies-that p. were the wags.453 j
Place-agree upon the first p.*211 l
 a jolly place, said he¶...... 76 r
 all other things give place.656 j
 allows the second place....671 a
 and in every place......... 95m
 any means get wealth and‡.642 r
 a p. in childhood that....402 b

art thou aught else but p.*. 73 c
ask him for my p. again*..326 k
ask no place.............. 114 r
crossed a p. of drear extent606 v
degree, priority and place* 462 x
everywhere his place.....499 z
fill the right place.........581 x
fixed p.in the chain of being 452 k
flaming bounds of place....415 o
fly by change of place**... 299 k
found in some p. of my*...467 p
found in use in the p. where.670 k
from place to place††....... 86 o
get place and wealth, if‡...642 r
gratitude of p. expectants. 189 q
had you seen the place......237 d
home, I was in a better p.*607m
in such a place as this......479 p
in thy p.—ah! well-a-day...605 p
kick in that place more....305 t
kiss the p. to make it well. 402 f
lowest p. when virtuous*...147 a
no p. each way is happy.. 117 e
no place like Home........304 k
one in all doth hold his p.*577 b
On sic a place............ 324 a
p. and means for every*....461 p
p. and time are subject to.381 a
p. at least o' th' enemy.....635 t
place farthest from pain**. 91 u
p. in thy memory, Dearest.379w
p. makes the banishment..731 t
p. where he is not known...607 b
p. where honour's lodged..305 t
p. where human harvests§.285 f
place would daze and......249 q
reconciling all the p. with.611 a
reign in this horrible place.566 s
some by a place—as tend‖... 70 o
temp'rate in every place...593 d
that p. that does contain...344 n
the first in place‡..........272 s
the place is dignified by*...147 a
to place no sanctity**......303 c
the mind is its own p.**....386 a
though that p. I never gain.671 c
to th' appointed place we..110 n
usurp a place they well. ..483 e
Places-about the rugged p..247 b
 all places are distant from.495 a
 follow in their proper p.....516 u
 p. that the eye of heaven*.298 b
 p. which pale passion loves.465 g
 sides thet give places††......107 k
 their proper places‖........283 g
Placid-Bacchus, why so p...276 q
Plagiarism-p. of orators is...474 n
Plagiarists-dealers than p.....474 t
Plagiary-accounted p**......474 p
Plague-a p. upon it when*...595 j
 artificial plague of man....635 r
 falls the plague............216 l
 false, fair woman, and p...366 b
 fop to plague his brother‡.254m
 it is my nature's plague*. 328 g
 lawful plague of life‡.......645 j
 p. to be too handsome a....678 n
 red plague rid you*........340 f
Plagues-boils and p. plaster*. 1 i
 omit these two main p.....593 p
 p., good Heaven, thy wrath 72 b
Plain-amain to reach the p...530 i
 cold upon the plain......248 h
 make all things plain*... 623 h
 over hill and plain........507 b
 pain to attain the plain...530 i
 p. as a nose in a man's face.503 i
 plain in your neatness....711 k
 p. tale shall put you down*623 j
 plain without pomp, and.. 79 a
 point is plain as a pikestaff..505 y
 running o'er the plain.... 20 d
 so plain a man am I........ 33 n
 the solitary plain.........249 p
 trod the Arcadian plain....531 b
 wide extended p. is billowy.423 q
Plainly-best being p. told*...305 i

Plainness-plainness sets off‡.653 s
Plains-o'er the conquered p..131 f
 on the plains descend¶.....245 i
 plains are everlasting as...286 i
 whiten the green p. under 100 e
Plaint-and plaint of Woe.....487 g
Plaints-to hear and see her p.*659 g
Plaintiff-defendant and p.**.285 g
 p., defendant, gentlemen..437 d
 the plaintiff's the man......437 d
Plaintive-full many a p.thing.324 d
Plan-but not without a p.‡..349 g
 excels at a plan............428 h
 for a plausible plan........129 f
 mars Creation's plan......369 o
 on the good old plan........ 85 q
 not without a plan‡........371 w
 some worn-out plan††......122 u
 while Reason drew the p...517 s
 will the deed and the plan.330 r
 you can never plan........267 g
Planned-penned and p. them.451 g
 woman, nobly planned¶....661 s
Plans-disputing about His p.420 d
 still pilfers wretched plans.595 e
Planet-a rhyming p.*........663 i
 morning planet gilds her**.576 i
 now the fleeting moon no*.108 g
 there's some ill p. reigns*.467 y
 to the red planet Mars§....576 d
Planets-guides the p. in their.510 o
 planets and this centre*....462 x
 p. in their radiant courses.589 f
 p.in their station list'ning**576 l
 then no planets strike*.... 49 l
 tune to which the p. roll...406 p
 we p. that are not able.....162 u
Plank-carpenter dresses his.431 j
 plank of the ivory floor....408 e
Planks-as two floating p. ....378 k
Plant-careless, unsocial p....618 p
 confidence was a p. of slow.104 d
 dainty plant is the.........232 c
 fame is no p. that grows**.202 c
 fix'd like a plant on his‡...349 h
 its sides I'll plant with.....244 l
 leaves of that shy plant¶..234 s
 plant divinely nurs'd....... 86 f
 p. divine, of rarest virtue..457 b
 plant of slow growth......265 t
 p. of slow growth in an....104 j
 plant sprung up to wither.. 66 c
 plant we in this apple-tree.611 l
 rare old plant is the ivy....232 c
 tend, p., herb, and flower**.424 e
 vigorous plant that lifts§....225 h
 while the earth bears a p...559 r
Plantation-p. of religion....521 c
 plantation of trade........521 c
Planted-when I p. thee deep‖615m
 who p. on the slope this...617 c
Plants-aromatic p. bestow no 6 q
 dare the p. look up to*.....490 o
 plants suck in the earth....162 g
 plants thou graft'st may*.289 r
 spring our tended plants**.613 a
Plaster-plaster on my chin...179m
 should bring the plaster*...441 o
Plastering-p. and bandaging.177 l
Platane-and the p. round....610 h
Plate-effect of plate and.....180 n
 melted down my plate..... 22 j
 plate sin with gold*........556 o
 'tis p. of rare device* .....434 s
Plates-and plates fly about...177m
Plato-I prefer to err with P..694m
 P.'s retirement, where**...616 n
 Plato, thou reasonest well..315 l
Platter-cleanly p. on the.....303 q
 Plausible-reverend than p...380 g
Plautus-P. has prepared.....714 o
Play-age with infancy..616 l
 and I will p. with thee.....570 r
 and with them merrily p...611 n
 a p. there is, my lord, some*422 u
 at Christmas p., and make. 95 h
 beheld thee p. the Sexton's.458 s

brief as I have known a p..*422 *u*
but better at a play........ 82 *i*
cannot play alone.... ......287 *w*
children with their p.....346 *t*
doo play their personage.. 667 *s*
earth's at play............165 *l*
every man must p. a part*.669 *d*
fret me you cannot play*..109 *p*
goes to an American play..115 *g*
good p. needs no epilogue*.423 *e*
guilty creatures sitting*...423 *f*
have me sing and play.....406 *l*
holdeth children from p....579 *a*
I doubt some foul play*....586 *p*
I fearless play............213 *k*
I sit, and p. with similes*..587 *j*
is there no p. to ease the*..423 *h*
it is a sunny hour of play..361 *q*
kings would not p. at......636 *j*
labor without any p., boys.495*m*
ladies yede to play........211 *f*
man sing or p. the better..405 *d*
multitude, can p. upon it*.536 *h*
not p. her larcenous tricks.654 *u*
our whole life is like a p...348 *q*
p. all my tricks in hell....298 *y*
play all the comfort.....,,..169 *b*
play at precedence with... 1 *b*
p. false, and yet wouldst*.. 84 *n*
play is the tragedy, "Man"137 *j*
p., made for delight, and...423 *p*
play to ease the anguish*.. 15 *c*
p. uppe, play uppe, O Boston 39 *v*
p. uppe The Brides of...... 39 *v*
rattle of a globe to p.......357 *w*
scene wherein we p. in*...669 *g*
she kissed me once in p.,..334 *g*
than arts of play.........269 *k*
that heard him play*.......407 *f*
the little victims play....89*m*
the p. is done ; the curtain.423 *o*
the play's the thing*......423 *l*
the sunny garden play.... 90 *u*
this may be play to you....506*jj*
to joy and play............346 *e*
truth to play the woman*..591 *q*
watch your play..........321 *l*
we have a play extempore*.384 *i*
wheels of life gliblier to p.. 8 *o*
when I play not............158 *q*
when I p. with my cat who. 14 *w*
when most I p. the devil*..631 *p*
will not let my play run....421 *r*
work, or healthful play....667*m*
world so loves to play.....640*m*
wrecks of play behold.....269 *l*
you p. the spaniel, and*....606 *k*
Playbill–p. which is said to..422 *q*
Played–and my Campaspe p.360 *h*
p. familiar with his hoary..460 *q*
sweetly played in tune....356 *f*
you've p. and loved and‡... 10 *v*
Player–like a strutting p.*...422 *t*
p. here, but in a fiction*...423 *g*
when the tired p. shuffles...74 *s*
Players–men and women*...669 *b*
p. have often mentioned...550 *l*
p., in your housewifery*...660 *g*
there be p. that I have seen* 423 *j*
whole world are players...753 *c*
will you see the p. well*...423 *c*
Playhouse–every p. bill‡....551 *a*
Playing–ever amid our p.... 459 *i*
tired of all the playing....560 *q*
Playmates–p. of the rose... 218 *o*
Play-place–p-p. of our early..672 *d*
Plays–meaning often lies in..758 *v*
plays are like suppers......422 *a*
the university pen plaies...551 *b*
who plays with the devil...763 *a*
Playthings–takes away our§.411 *j*
Plea–necessity the tyrant's**.414 *d*
that p. therefore, with**...641 *v*
that with tender plea......241 *u*
what p. so tainted and*....145 *h*
Plead–fain would I plead.....141 *i*
golden fee for which I p.*..462 *l*

loved to p., lament, and....663 *f*
p. **his** love-suit to her*....663 *j*
plead that cause wherein..305 *c*
precedent will plead.......147 *q*
their cause I plead—plead..333 *h*
who p. for love and look*.. 68 *b*
will plead like angels*.....633 *l*
Pleasance–youth is full of p.*673 *e*
Pleasant–a face more p. than.530 *g*
all that was p. in man.... 79 *p*
from pleasant to severe....476 *p*
in company a very p.‖.....483 *d*
intimate friend seems p...704 *i*
past labors are pleasant...719 *q*
p. it is to have money......389 *n*
pleasant too, to think on...660 *l*
p., when the sea runs.....724*m*
p. with a heart at ease.. 99 *k*
prove to be so pleasant.... 18 *r*
thousand p. things......... 69 *c*
Pleasantries–p. upon all....177 *a*
Pleasantry–an ill-timed ....725 *p*
Please–all the year please....232 *s*
a man does not p. long....653 *i*
as it shall please God......805 *k*
at once both p. and preach‡.422 *l*
but cannot p. himself......787 *q*
coy, and hard to please.....658 *r*
desire to please everything.796 *j*
distant prospects p. us.....411 *a*
if thou desire to please....120 *i*
it was natural to please....410 *r*
just as he please..........361 *h*
learn to please............268 *s*
let that please man........738 *q*
lives not to p. himself......427 *v*
live to p. must please to...508 *h*
may p. fools, but he vainly.706 *u*
must always please........475 *z*
other requisites to please.. 30 *v*
p. another wine-sprung....326 *a*
p. children and be made...716 *k*
pleasure has ceased to p...475 *k*
p. myself with, while my..464 *q*
seasons and their change**.114 *b*
sight should ever please...277 *s*
studious to please, yet not..13 *d*
the certainty to please....304 *n*
they p., are pleas'd they....13 *b*
they p. as beauties, here‡..633 *a*
to die before you please*...583 *h*
to please by brevity........178 *j*
to please many is bad .....787 *r*
to p. thy gods thou didst**.674 *e*
'twas natural to please.....283 *i*
unexpected doubly please..605 *h*
was surest to please.......215 *c*
we that live to p., must.....422 *i*
whom, you please..........681 *h*
yet all may please........548 *u*
your sonnets sure shall‖...452 *u*
Pleased–do what I p., and....110 *q*
inclining to be pleased.....124 *n*
p. too little or too much‡...191 *e*
p. to the last he crops the‡.475 *r*
p. with favours given......524 *x*
thou hast pleased thyself.. 13 *s*
who are pleased themselves.475 *z*
Pleases–he p. every one.....787 *q*
his life as he pleases......704 *d*
p. one against his will......124 *n*
whoever can do as he p.....784 *f*
Pleasing–a p. countenance...678 *l*
a pleasing countenance....678 *o*
gift of pleasing feature.....629 *j*
left so p. on their ear‡......353 *q*
most p. of all sounds that..487 *b*
pleasing most when........169 *n*
pleasing to be pointed at...697 *c*
pleasing ware is half sold...503 *j*
they be graceful and p.....164 *g*
turnes to pleasing paine....475 *x*
Pleasure–all his p. praise....567 *j*
and take fool's pleasure...606 *t*
an immense p. to come.....551 *c*
arts of pleasure grow when 755 *i*
a well-spring of pleasure... 32 *n*

behold what p. is pursuit..483 *i*
blend our p. or our pride§..310 *b*
but content and pleasure... 19 *d*
by myself a lonely p.¶......567 *s*
can take his pleasure........281 *n*
care not for p. when I play.158 *q*
death treads in P.'s........476 *a*
dissipation without p.......565 *h*
doubtless the p. is as great.475 *e*
enjoy p. while we can......732 *j*
fair p.'s smiling train‡.....386 *b*
fictitious sources of p......732 *c*
follow p., and then will.....497 *z*
for his own pleasure all....132 *e*
full of p., void of strife..... 19 *d*
gardens takes his p**.......269 *c*
give a shock of pleasure... 87 *e*
heart asks pleasure first...296 *s*
heels of pleasure.........375 *b*
his adjunct pleasure*.... 273 *f*
I fly from pleasure, because 475 *k*
impression of p. in itself...336 *k*
it is a double p. to deceive..762 *a*
itself a pleasure...........719 *v*
knew the pensive pleasure.379 *q*
labor is itself a pleasure...801 *u*
leagues of pleasure........263 *k*
leans for all p. on another's.641 *r*
limb in pleasure drowns.... 24 *o*
little pleasure of the game.308 *o*
little p. in the house when.. 2*w*
live in p. when I live to Thee347 *b*
look back with pleasure....721 *k*
luxury is an enticing p......369 *e*
make business a pleasure..475 *d*
man of p. is a man of pains.463 *k*
men find p. to be deceived..144 *r*
moderate p. relaxes the....727*m*
more of pain or pleasure...354 *v*
necessity and not pleasure.781 *i*
no pleasure is comparable..621 *b*
no pleasure ta'en*.........269 *d*
no pure unalloyed pleasure.699 *c*
nor to his pleasure power..356 *l*
Ods me I marle what p.....456 *l*
owe every pleasure and.... 96 *g*
painefull p. turnes to......475 *x*
p. admitted in undue degree‡475 *s*
p. and action make the*....602 *q*
p. and revenge have ears*..146 *a*
pleasure at the helm.......672 *j*
p. attracts each one........732*m*
p. appropriate to man......705 *r*
p. blinds (so to speak).....732 *b*
pleasure bought by pain...732 *d*
pleasure, howe'er disguis'd475*aa*
pleasure in poetic pains....478 *s*
pleasure in pure water.....745 *g*
p. in the pathless woods‖...475 *f*
pleasure is in darts and...276 *q*
pleasure, like the midnight.187 *f*
pleasure never is at home..475*m*
p. of doing good to others..387 *g*
p. of love is in loving......359 *g*
p. of the fleeting year*.... 3 *f*
pleasure quite debarred...266 *j*
pleasure, sure, in being mad320 *u*
pleasure the highest good...680 *b*
pleasure the servant, virtue.475 *i*
pleasure to be drunk.......325 *v*
p. to live on that bright§...393 *c*
pleasure to the spectators.126 *i*
pleasure trip up to the pole.542 *l*
p. which is born of pain....475 *n*
possesses unalloyed p......732 *i*
produces greater pleasure.732 *g*
profit and the most p....... 66 *b*
reason's whole p., all the‡..475 *t*
reason with pleasure‖......208 *a*
return, no pleasure brings..645 *q*
roses of p. seldom last long.475 *p*
some to pleasure take‡.... 658 *h*
source of future pleasure..725 *q*
stock of harmless pleasure.403 *h*
sweet is p. after pain.......463 *b*
taste of pleasure flies......295 *l*
that pleasure miss'd her‡.. 82 *s*

the arts of p. in despotic... 1 _g_
their moments of pleasure.421 _t_
the longest pleasure........294 _x_
their pleasure takes joy....293 _d_
the love of p., and the‡....465 _r_
the pleasure is as great....497 _c_
those call it pleasure and‡.. 61 _u_
though on p. she was bent.475 _i_
those call it Pleasure, and‡.342 _j_
thrill of p. to the frame...641 _m_
through affections of p......354 _g_
'tis impious p. to delight in. 34 _p_
to frown at pleasure, and to.476 _b_
to their present pleasure*..475 _w_
transient p. the source of..783 _k_
trim gardens takes his p.**.342 _w_
virtue and p. both to dwell. 91 _q_
vibrate sweetest pleasure..548 _o_
weak pleasure of a little...739 _j_
we'll have our p. o'er......159 _k_
when P. treads the paths...476 _a_
wherein he finds a p........326 _a_
whispered promised p.......307 _n_
wisely, and with pleasure..651 _i_
with pleasure dignified.....613 _e_
with p. own your errors‡...125 _n_
woman's p., woman's pain†.642 _b_
years of pleasure here......132 _k_
young, all health and p.....604 _p_
youth and pleasure meet‖..599 _m_
youth and pleasure sport..522 _q_
youth of pleasure wasteful.345 _u_
Pleasure-dome-stately p-d..530 _b_
Pleasure-house-soul, a lordly†475 _y_
Pleasures-abandoned those p.732 _e_
a life of p. and thence......732 _a_
all other pleasures are.....357 _x_
all the pleasures of youth..754 _i_
choicest p.of life lie, within.389 _b_
delicate p. that spring......170 _v_
doubling his p. and his..... 16 _u_
eternity of pleasures......375 _h_
every age has its p., its....475 _b_
forbidden pleasures alone..732 _k_
fresh-revolving p. flow.....629 _v_
God made all p. innocent...475 _q_
is the sweetest of pleasures.797 _g_
its pleasures imaginary....485 _p_
know its p., we must go....485 _p_
'mid p. and palaces.......304 _k_
most delightful p. cloy.....505 _u_
not the hope of new p......150 _r_
objects of delicious p....... 65 _j_
our lawful p. to fulfill.....389 _o_
our pleasures are past‖....334 _e_
our pleasures die and then.140 _u_
owes its p. to another's.....126 _f_
p. and our discontents§.....289 _k_
p. are ever in our hands‡...475 _s_
p. are like poppies spread..475 _c_
p. in this vale of pain......475 _v_
p. lie thickest where no....475 _a_
pleasures might me move..361 _t_
pleasures newly found¶....224 _h_
pleasures now alike are o'er.128 _q_
p. of all the spheres.......475 _o_
p. of the present day......347 _b_
p. of the world cheap......561 _a_
pleasures of the world*....131 _l_
pleasures of the world**...220 _d_
p. to make room for more..560 _o_
p. with a full right hand...732 _f_
season hath its pleasures..544 _g_
shalt steal our p. too......380 _q_
sooth'd his soul to p.......473 _s_
stings us, even in our p....630 _t_
thus p. fade away; youth.. 11 _h_
unless our p. are mixed.....176 _f_
unnumbered pleasures......520 _n_
unreprov'd pleasures free**383 _s_
we will all the p. prove.....360 _n_
when our old Pleasures die.630 _d_
Plebeian-sin for a plebeian..742 _r_
Pledge-and solemn pledge¶..378 _f_
bright pledge of peace.....515 _s_
haint never signed no p.††.593 _h_
I will pledge with mine....604 _u_

mutually p. to each other,..419 _d_
p. of blithesome May††....228 _e_
p. our Queen this solemn†..604 _s_
surest p. of a deathless§...596_bb_
Pledged-king hath so........453 _d_
Pledges-p. of a fruitful tree.218 _a_
Pleiads-I saw the Pleiads†...577 _p_
the pleiads seven..........558 _d_
Plenipotentiary-with a p....435 _e_
Plenties-arts, p. and joyful*.471 _f_
Plentiful-more p. than hope..536 _o_
Plenty-all-cheering P., with..543 _n_
fields with Plenty crowned.666 _s_
full of plenty from root to.615 _l_
plenty as well as want.....191 _b_
plenty makes us poor.......484 _m_
scatter p. o'er a smiling.... 41 _m_
showering plenty her feet..615 _l_
simple plenty crowned.....211 _a_
whose p. made him pore....485 _h_
with smiling plenty and*...268 _g_
Pleurisy-growing to a p*.... 280 _q_
O' the pleurisy of people....635 _l_
Plight-hand must take my p*.311 _w_
p. me the full assurance*...377 _i_
sit in silver plight ....218 _i_
Plighted-we p. our troth... 358_w_
Plod-drink, and scheme, and p.668_m_
Plodders-continual plodders*580 _r_
Plodding-universal plodding**667 _k_
Plot-first survey the plot*... 426 _h_
plot by which partisanship.482 _g_
poor plot, with vegetables.304 _b_
was a great plot of state...282 _p_
with souls that cringe and††555 _x_
women guide the plot......660 _i_
Plots-birth of p. and their...105 _a_
whoever plots the sin*......461 _n_
with their own plots.......653 _v_
Plotted-p. death shall perish.718 _o_
Plotting-bent still plotting... 4 _p_
p. some new reformation...518 _u_
Plough-avail the plough or...258 _k_
following his plough along¶481 _h_
good man spanned his p... 540 _i_
learn of the mole to plough‡342 _k_
p. deep and straight with...424 _a_
p. deep while sluggards....666 _p_
seized the Plough, and.....424 _k_
slaves, of the laborious p....670 _c_
the sacred Plough.........424 _k_
the steed wishes to plough.682 _e_
track the toiling plough....635 _p_
tumble round the plough..542 _a_
Ploughboy-hushed the p.'s...536 _l_
the P. is whooping¶........391 _m_
Ploughman-envies the p's...642 _r_
p. homeward plods........186 _s_
the heavy p. snores*......417 _l_
Ploughmen-ye rigid P.! bear.424 _a_
Ploughs-he p. the waves....796 _n_
the hog that p. not nor‡.... 21 _v_
Ploughshare-fashioned the .430 _i_
her p. o'er creation ....536 _d_
ruin's p. drives.............227 _d_
the p. and the rake.........430 _d_
Pluck-hand may p. them ...241 _s_
pluck the flower............730 _d_
there's a man of pluck§.... 70 _c_
Plucked-first is p. a second...684 _l_
gather'd not harshly p.**.. 10 _s_
pluck'd them as we pass'd..241 _o_
she pluck'd, she eat**......555 _y_
Plumage-beak and glossy p.. 44 _c_
gives out his snowy p. to... 58 _o_
p. of birds in some tropical129 _k_
strip him of his plumage..123 _h_
varying p. spare the dove‡..46 _s_
Plume-dowle that's in my p.*207_m_
every plume a sharp eye....740 _r_
graceful tossing plume of..229 _s_
nodding plume of ostrich..458 _t_
p. exposes, 'tis our helmet.548 _v_
p. is trailing in the dust....443 _e_
two birds of gayest p.**.... 46 _s_
who has lent his plume....114 _s_
wit is but the plume......548 _n_

Plumelets-when rosy p. tuft† 59 _e_
Plumes-fan the air with.....543 _q_
her plumes fall flat**...... 35 _o_
his advanced plumes*......109 _c_
his plumes to cool.........240 _c_
in p. like estridges were.... 46 _o_
myriad glimmering plumes229 _p_
of painted p., that hopped...47 _f_
on the wing, their glossy p..60_w_
shook their purple p.......614 _r_
sits mocking in our p*.....551 _k_
Plummet-cast forth thy p...571 _y_
did ever plummet sound*.. 67 _v_
Plump-he look'd p. and fair.313 _d_
p. my bags are and my.....642_m_
Plums-sweetest of the p....307 _y_
Plunder-jangle and plunder. 56 _j_
never plunder seeks........258 _o_
Plundered-there he p. snug‡.474 _r_
Plunge-a p., a bubble, and§..583 _b_
Plunges-again she p.! hark...552 _f_
p. and bears me........... 87 _g_
Plunging-and p. shows us... 48 _f_
Plural-plural I appear......213 _k_
Pluto-visits the shades of P..743 _l_
Plutonian-night's P. shore...417 _a_
Plymouth-P. Rock that had§.115 _e_
Po-lazy Scheld or wandering 532 _i_
Poachers-ye poachers!—'Tis‖543 _o_
Pocket-and put it in his p.*..595 _l_
eat some and pocket up‡....167 _s_
ounce of poison in one p.....81 _q_
out of his breeches' p.‖.....595 _d_
scruple to pick a pocket...328 _k_
while it picks yeer pocket..437 _q_
Pocket-hole-Myra's p-h......355 _j_
Poem-a poem should be long.476 _r_
argument that makes a p..476 _q_
but is a heroic p. of its sort.346 _n_
every word was once a p....476 _r_
great poem produced in a..477 _n_
heroic poem of its sort.....476 _h_
if I publish this p. for......452 _q_
is no heroic p. in the world.476 _h_
like to be married to a P...375 _o_
many beauties in a poem...753 _j_
p. round and perfect as a...477_w_
poem without words......446 _i_
scarcely has a decent poem‖478 _t_
true p. is the poet's mind..476 _t_
your p. be kept nine years.732 _o_
Poems-pay for p.—when‖....454 _l_
p. read without a name....126 _a_
Poesy-and golden cadence of*477 _u_
genuine seeds of p. are‡....477 _b_
in Poesy a decent pride.... 478 _e_
more we feel of poesie......476 _c_
Nature, Hope, and Poesy..672 _c_
never did Poesy appear††..477 _j_
shoot of climbing poesy...367 _a_
shower of light is poesy....477 _f_
the flowers of poesy bloom§.430 _f_
Poet-a p.? God forbid.......478 _j_
a p. not in love is out at...478 _f_
a P. without Love were a..478_m_
be so sublime a poet......454 _e_
can judge a poet's worth...478 _t_
critic fann'd the P.'s fire‡...125 _r_
divine poet, as sleep......732 _t_
ever p. so trusted before...479 _n_
flattery lost on poet's......215 _g_
for a good poet's made.....550 _q_
"give me a theme," the.....479 _e_
God is the perfect poet....273 _t_
great poet's hidden ecstacy.476 _v_
had no p., and they died‡...480 _j_
happy the p. who with ease.757 _c_
here a wandering p. sings§.533 _e_
Homer who inspired the p.481 _d_
in autumn the poet is sad..481 _n_
in his own verse the p. still.479 _j_
in Spring the Poet is glad..481 _e_
in Summer the Poet is gay.481 _e_
joyful let the Poet be......478 _n_
lies the p.'s native land§...325 _j_
lunatic, The lover and the..315 _h_
maintain a poet's.‡.........259 _b_

serves only to spoil the p...654 *i*
Potter-centre of the p.'s§.... 97 *l*
  easy to the p.'s hand.....449 *k*
  p. near his modest cot.....449 *l*
  whirled like a p.'s wheel*...597 *n*
Pouch-by his side a p. he.....439 *s*
Poulterer-scape the p.'s knife 94 *f*
Poultice-silence, like a p....554 *e*
Pound-claim a p. of flesh*...332 *v*
  penny wise, pound foolish..503 *e*
Pounds-in a thousand p. of..451 *s*
  pounds will take care of....169 *t*
  six hundred pounds a year.652 *l*
  three hundred p. a year*....643 *q*
  we prefer books to pounds..353 *x*
Pour-p. the shame, which it..593 *f*
  they pour they overflow.... 58 *t*
Pours-how it pours, pours....514 *s*
Pouter-p., tumbler, and.....371 *q*
Poverty-all p. was scorn'd*..147 *u*
  an age of poverty*.........485 *b*
  contented even p. is joy....111 *i*
  content with p., my soul....110 *l*
  equal poverty of mind.....209 *l*
  excludes but one evil,—p...484 *s*
  great is Poverty...........287 *o*
  I pay thy p., and not thy*.485 *f*
  madness to live in poverty.733 *n*
  monarchies through p.....770 *p*
  my p., but not my will*....485 *f*
  no splendid poverty, no....112 *o*
  nothing is not poverty.....733 *v*
  penny in the urn of p......144 *u*
  pitied in a Christian p.....329 *e*
  poverty and death††........16 *n*
  p. has no harder trial......733 *p*
  poverty, hunger, and dirt..484 *r*
  p. is in want of much but.. 30 *m*
  poverty is no sin..........503 *k*
  poverty is shunned........733 *q*
  p. is the mother of crimes.548 *h*
  p. is the mother of health..503 *l*
  poverty or chains .... 369 *b*
  p. of the soul is irreparable.784 *f*
  p. stood smiling in my‡..... 41 *o*
  poverty, thy thousand ills.484 *t*
  poverty wants much........678 *i*
  repressed by p. at home....733 *o*
  rich in greatest poverty....112 *l*
  rich in poverty, enjoys.....110 *q*
  sharp-edged rock of p......633 *u*
  she scorns our poverty*....491 *o*
  slave of poverty and love..531 *m*
  slow rises worth by p......670 *r*
  steep'd me in p. to the*.....485 *e*
  with p. everything becomes 784 *c*
Powder-food for p., food for*640 *e*
  keep your powder dry......511 *b*
  violently as hasty p. fir'd*..149 *q*
  where's the p. for the hair*.128 *q*
  with strange hermetic p....439 *s*
Powdered-p. th' inside of his.456 *e*
  still to be p. still perfum'd. 23 *m*
Powders-puffs, p., patches‡..629 *m*
Power-addition to human p..337 *p*
  aim beyond our pow'r......110 *i*
  and candor in power.......513 *h*
  and of power's excess......626 *e*
  a kingly power their love..402 *e*
  a little p. a little transient.. 14 *i*
  all-enslaving power........279 *h*
  a p. ethereal, only not......604 *f*
  a p. they by Divine........574 *v*
  appointing p. of the Pope..620 *v*
  art and p. will go on as... 150 *q*
  art is power§.............. 28 *m*
  birth a power ethereal.....486 *e*
  blessed power deliver us...144 *y*
  but well our p. to use‡..... 83 *a*
  chief p. of honest men.....623 *t*
  clothes itself with sudden..402 *l*
  desire of power in excess... 86 *d*
  despite those titles, power..547 *s*
  dost thou thy p. display....540 *o*
  earthly p. doth then show*.382 *p*
  emblems of the sovereign p.535 *l*
  enjoy that p. which suits‡..173 *e*

equal has no p. over an.....694 *f*
exercise of a new power.....485 *o*
exerting an unwearied p....410 *v*
fools thy power despise....365 *w*
for a forty-parson p. to‖....312 *v*
fortified by power divine..522 *m*
for wealth, for pow'r.......638 *o*
gray-flits the shade of p.‖..485 *n*
hath strange power**...... 35 *r*
he hath no p., that hath not.485 *k*
he who has great power....734 *c*
highest p. may be lost by..734 *e*
holds in her hand the p....656 *v*
holy with power He on the. 92 *h*
how p. could condescend‖.. 53 *k*
I found no power to vie....414 *e*
if there's a p. above us....409 *w*
in a cruel wantonness of p.625 *s*
inexplicable and fated p...361 *j*
in whose power a man is††.588 *r*
is a p. behind the eye......320 *v*
is loss of vital power......556 *t*
its highest p. in woman....654 *o*
its power to prove.......... 3 *h*
knowledge is power........336 *m*
knowledge that is not p.... 337 *g*
lies not in our power.....206 *s*
life and p. are scattered....338 *l*
like God in love and p.....476 *c*
loosens every power.......210 *j*
lover of letters loves p. too.428 *c*
lust of p. is the most.......734 *f*
man who has the p. and....656 *h*
more the heavenly power†.541 *g*
mutters of dissevering p.**.485 *u*
no lover has that pow'r....485 *m*
nymphs! what p. divine .. 97 *s*
ocean hath no tone of p....233 *o*
pains of power are real.....485 *p*
patience and gentleness is.485 *t*
peace the offspring is of p..471 *j*
power above with ease‡....274 *q*
power acquired by guilt....734 *h*
p. and privilege of a parent.695 *t*
p. be wanting, yet the wish.734 *v*
p. be within the recesses... 28 *q*
p. can do by gentleness....706 *t*
power confronted power*..184 *t*
power give more than food.485 *r*
power has arisen up in the.281 *m*
p. in his eye that bow'd the† 30 *e*
power is felt of melancholy.543 *i*
p. is more safely retained..734 *t*
p., like a desolating........485 *y*
power no power resists....274 *n*
p. of thought—the magic‖..596 *b*
power that bred it*........231 *e*
power that brought me....240 *c*
power that grinds them....279 *h*
p. that is to overcome it...588 *e*
p. to bind and loose to.... .621 *q*
power to broaden the mind.326 *r*
p. to cancel his captivity*..344 *r*
p. to charm down insanity.320 *v*
power to dismiss itself*....350 *o*
p. to shame him hence*....623 *l*
p. unknown to you of......572 *k*
power which has dotted....116 *e*
p., which in a sense belongs.621 *q*
p. which the vilest of the...777 *f*
praise the Power that......214 *i*
princes and p. so splendid.. 74 *m*
rather in power than use*..511 *s*
ravished me away by a p...517 *b*
Roman p. slowly built......719 *r*
secret of its power........ 7 *y*
severity of the public p.*..438 *m*
shadow of some unseen p..485 *z*
subjects to their p. obey...510 *w*
sun's and her power is....235 *h*
supreme in power........ 231 *o*
take who have the power¶.486 *c*
that all power is a trust....620 *q*
that hath not p. to use....485 *k*
that P. that pities me......473 *v*
that p. which erring men**. 73 *p*
the balance of power......486 *b*

the devil hath power*......485 *x*
the force of temporal p.*.. .382 *p*
the literature of power....354 *g*
the miracles of p. whose... 29 *t*
the pomp of power it was‖. 53 *k*
the power of habit.........711 *h*
the p. of self-recovery....628 *k*
there is no p. in Venice*....438 *q*
th'' eternal p. convinc'd.... 8 *e*
the unseen Power........ 519 *k*
the will and the p. are... .151 *t*
the wreck of power to rest.396 *o*
those seeking power ....734 *q*
'tis god-like to have p.....485 *l*
'tis one same p. creates....352 *d*
'tis the supreme of power..477 *f*
to know the pains of p....485 *p*
to the man despotic p.**...376 *c*
upon the past has power....466 *j*
wad some p. the giftie gie.310 *f*
want the power to paint....678 *c*
were in my power........715 *k*
what a mental p. this eye*. 83 *q*
which is in a man's p.††....588 *r*
which means almost p......466 *v*
wish they had the power...733 *w*
wrought in power..........247 *b*
ye have power, men say...563 *q*
Powerful-he who is too p...734 *d*
imitate the powerful.......733 *s*
nothing so p. as truth......623 *y*
Powers-blots out our p......385 *j*
conflict with unholy p.....579 *p*
divine and supreme p......420 *a*
lay waste our powers¶.....669 *t*
mere mechanic powers....113 *j*
mightiest p. by deepest....485 *q*
o'er lesser powers that be..402 *i*
of all p. the mightiest far..485 *j*
O ye powers that search...523 *f*
p. of eloquence ample.... 200 *q*
p. shed round him in the¶..319 *k*
resigns his powers.........284 *r*
say heavenly p. where**...518 *j*
tempt the frailty of our p.*594 *k*
Utica contracts your p.....485 *w*
ye not, ye gloomy powers.569 *a*
Practicable-in a nation....281 *c*
Practice-I saw a p. growing..440 *f*
first we practice to deceive.144 *x*
loudly vaunt not p.‖.......312 *e*
more his p. wrought.......450 *j*
practice is to delay it.......763 *r*
practice of mistaken rules‡ 440 *p*
p. the profession which....680 *h*
reduce it to practice.......197 *m*
shall practice in heaven...472 *a*
think the practice bold....553 *a*
worthy the knowledge and. 19 *b*
Practices-knows better than. 79 *h*
p. it will have neighbors...632 *e*
Practised-p. what he preach'd107 *q*
Practising-of never p. it....114 *k*
Prague-o'er P.'s proud arch..258 *c*
Prairie-wanderers of the p....236 *o*
Prairies-p. covered with....115 *i*
Praise-all his pleasure p....521 *o*
all the praise that I can...477 *a*
a refusal of p. is a desire...486 *m*
a seller's praise belongs*...442 *o*
bear reproof who merit p.‡.524 *b*
beauty passeth praise......225 *g*
but my best praise is.......262 *q*
chant thy p., Hypocrisy‖...312 *e*
conjunction with praise....201 *p*
damn with faint p., assent‡.537 *r*
deeds worth praise and*....147 *b*
delightful p.!—like summer 486 *u*
demands your praise‖.....427 *h*
deserves p. who does not...734 *p*
devours the deed in the p.*.491 *i*
disprais'd were no small**.486 *q*
effort will deserve praise...696 *m*
envy is a kind of praise....173 *t*
excited by the love of p....734 *m*
few sons attain the praise‡. 89 *p*
flatter and praise*.........215 *n*

SHAKESPEARE *; MILTON **; WORDSWORTH ¶; BYRON ‖; TENNYSON †; LOWELL ††; POPE ‡; LONGFELLOW §.

flatter than to praise......767 p
for vulgar praise..........305 d
he praise their wisdom.....437 h
however we do p. ourselves*377 e
incense of awe-struck p....531 f
in peals of praise.........165 b
in praise of Robin Hood....578 j
in praise of thee..........391 b
in your notes his praise**.486 p
is vain who writes for p...486aa
is woman's genuine p.......656 f
it deserves some praise....672 d
knowledge and her praise** 645 h
maiden can season her p.*..592 i
men who grasp at praise....352 a
mine own when I p. thee*...670 r
much, that gathers praise..429 o
muse His praise............275 v
named thee but to praise... 79 u
neither praise nor pelf....287 b
no praise in being upright..712 k
offices of prayer and p.¶..490 e
of praise a mere glutton...215 c
ought we deserve no p......163 h
paint 'em truest p. 'em....446 g
pay not thy praise to......286 i
poets lose half the p. they..481 c
praise a large domain......676 v
praise and toast me at his.629 q
p. enough of literature....516 e
p. enough to fill the......486 g
p. from a friend, or‡......486 k
praise him each savage.....670 c
p. him still in the songs..278 n
p. in three hundred verses.179 d
p. is only praise when well.486 i
p. it so hath he good cause.166 d
praise me and make an*.....252 r
praise me not too much.....486 l
p. no man e'er deserved....486aa
p. nor the blame is our own. 96 n
praise of which I¶.........224 h
praise of wit to write.....254 i
p. Patricio's high desert‡..454 f
p. the bridge that carried.503m
p. the discourse of an.....700 i
p. the fig we are free.....616 j
praise the ones that grow..237 d
praise the power that......214 i
p. the sea, but keep on land 503 n
p. the sparkling of thy....601 d
praise they that will times.111 e
p. to our French ladies....660 v
p. undeserved is scandal‡...538 d
p. yourself extravagantly..174 u
pudding against empty p.‡.486 s
rehearse his worthy p......316 s
remains modest not after p.780 o
sacred lust of praise‡.....486 t
scarcely can praise it.....270m
short to speak thy praise..276 g
sick alive of Envy and of P.‡ 11 b
some p. at morning what‡..461 d
song in thy praise.........530 a
sound of woman's praise....486 n
swells the note of praise..405 h
that of your own praise....487 b
the last degree of praise..734 o
the love of praise, howe'er.487 a
there were none to praise¶..421 f
the thirst of praise....... 12 t
the work some praise**. ..298 q
they p. my rustling show...537 h
those who spoke her p......486 j
to Mary Queen the p. be....561 b
to pay for your praise.....178 n
to their right p. and true*. 52 a
uplift in praise...........227m
vocal with the Maker's p.‡.. 95 s
wealth preferring to‡......642 j
we justly p. or justly blame,126 a
what can mine own p. to*...670 v
whose noble p. praises a...471 o
women we do use to p. even.574 s
Praised-and p., unenvy'd‡...454 g
desire to be praised twice..486m
hymning p. God and**.....486 o

I would have praised you..784 k
Jove, and my stars be p.*..449 c
praised by others..........259 v
praised in her own great...574 s
Praise-deserving-p-d. hero to.714 k
Praises-bees, humming p....227 b
burning words and praises.217 j
delight in thy praises‖......200 j
faintly then he praises....486 h
live upon their praises¶...221 c
not praises of the crowd..118 s
our p. are our wages*......486w
p. itself but in the deed*...491 i
p. the deeds of another....677 k
p. those who follow a......692 s
speak your praises.........227 f
swells with the p. which...428 l
thousand voices, p. God....486 f
Praising-angels are p. the..165 o
high-day wit in p. him*....486 y
honored beyond all p......664 a
praising most, dispraises..486 h
praising what is lost*.....486 x
rose that all are praising..240 e
Pranks-p. that never fail....211 e
Prankt-prankt with white..228 j
Prate-p. and preach about..312 f
Praters-justly accounted p..752 r
Prattle-his p. to be tedious*..423 a
joyous as my children's p.. 43 l
sage or cynic p. as he will‖..356 r
Praxiteles-P. did by his glass.112 r
when did P. see me thus...452 o
Pray-any wish thou darest..487 o
bed, and doth not pray.....488 h
be not afraid to p.........487 n
climb up here to pray......536 i
could p. to move, prayers*.108 n
down to the chapel and p.§. 25 d
for golden eloquence I p...567 q
God doth late and early p..522 n
he that will learn to pray..488 g
if I can't p., I will not§.....556 u
I p. thee, Lord, my soul...488 v
left now, Sweet, to p. to... 17 d
pray and labor.............803 f
p. God to guard them......487 t
p., if thou canst, with hope.487 n
p. in the darkness, if there.487 n
p., thou who also weepest..619 e
p. to be perfect, though...487 o
p. together, in whatever...489 r
p. to God to cast that wish.487 o
pray to-morrow*...........384 i
scoff remain'd to pray.....450m
seraph may p. for a sinner.487 t
sinner must p. for himself..487 t
therefore let us pray......487 i
thine to work as well as p..667 n
to p. for them that have*... 93 k
to p. is to desire...........488 c
to scoff, remain'd to pray..488 f
we do pray for mercy*....382 q
when I would p. and think*.489 n
when I p., my heart is in§..556 u
will I p., for thou wilt hear‖487 l
with what words to pray**.488 p
Prayed-he p. and felt for all.450 n
he pray'd by quantity......488w
prayed ! so, I was afraid...487 j
thrusts the thing we have..487 h
upon this wise I prayed...297 n
watch'd and wept, he p....587 x
yet God, when prayed......488 b
Prayer-and now a prayer§.... 40 h
arms stretched in p. for...610 g
attend thy votary's p......564 b
breathe a prayer full in....117 g
devil cross my prayer*.....153 l
erects a house of prayer... 95 o
every wish is like a prayer..652 g
eyes are homes of silent p.†.194 c
flower-girl's prayer.......216 j
four spend in p., the rest..603 v
from the prayer of Want...487 g
heav'n to raise a prayer...489 v
he is given to prayer*.....489 i

if by p. incessant I could**.488 n
imperfect offices of p. and¶.490 f
in p. the lips ne'er act the..488 i
in the confidence of p......487 d
is one with Prayer.........526 r
kneeling at her evening p.§.411 g
labor, you know, is prayer.489 s
let one unceasing, earnest§.488 k
like one in prayer I stood§..488 l
making their lives a prayer.490 c
my heart is in my prayer§..556 u
my p. would bound back to.487 t
offers a deceitful prayer...488 c
other grace to prayer......563 k
pale in prayer ....233 n
part in this effectual p.¶....490 d
prayer all his business.....567 j
p. ardent opens heaven.....490 q
p. is the soul's sincere.....488 q
p. is the spirit speaking...487 f
prayer is the world in tune.489w
p. moves the Hand which...490 a
p. of Ajax was for light§...130 n
prayer shou'd dawn with...563 p
p. which childhood wafts‖..655 n
prayer will be answered§...197 u
p. you learned above Baby. 31 c
rejects a lover's prayer....236 i
so a good p., though often..488 e
still prayer of devotion....488 f
swears a prayer or two*....209 l
that follows after prayer...568 h
that same p. doth teach*...382 q
the gift of p., is not always.784 l
the people's p., the glad..634 d
the prayer of Noah.........488 j
the wretched to prayer....734 r
they lift not hands of p.†...489 u
things are wrought by p.† 489 u
to prayer—lo‖...............274 a
very lives are prayer..... 90 v
vice atone for crimes by p.‖487m
we can conclude the p......487 u
when P. is of no avail†.....490 f
with storms of prayer†.....489 i
yet this will prayer**......488 o
Prayer-book-get a p-b. in*..670m
Prayers-believe and say my‡310 s
but to prayers most........670 g
changed by prayers........708 g
comforts here, but p*......100 n
earth rings with prayers..488 t
ejaculations are short p....488 d
enough to say my p.* 489m
feed on p., which are his...470w
first let thy prayers ascend.489 c
grant folly's p. that hinder.487 v
have the p. of the church..607 o
hearts, our hopes, our p.§..118 f
into our p., with gentle... 17 c
make of your prayers one*.489 h
morning walks, and p.‡....349 o
my p. are not words duly*.489 k
playnts, p., vowes, truth..663 r
p. are heard in heaven very489 q
p. do afterwards redress...398 e
prayers should be for a....734 q
set it in my prayers*......409 p
sudden on some prayers....487 h
to my holy prayers*.......130 r
what is bought by prayers.734 s
where prayers cross*......594 h
who ne'er misses pray'rs.. 525 e
whose very looks are p.....488 u
yet prayers and wishes*....489 k
your sighs and prayers....131 v
Prayeth-he p. best, who....487 p
he p. well, who loveth.....487 q
Praying-if life be all past p..488 j
in earnest in p. against....594m
p.'s the end of preaching..670 g
Prays-thus the suppliant p..348 c
Pray'st-p. thou for riches...369 h
Preach-because they p. in‖..648 k
both please and preach‡....422 l
comes to preach or prate...768 l
flowers preach to us........219 o

value at a little price....... 7 g
vigilance is the p. of.....343 q
Prices-all have p., from‖..... 70 o
Prick-it is a p. it is a sting..361 k
  sew, p. our fingers, dull....666 c
Pricked-pricked and holden..230 b
Prickly-p. thorn often bears..684 k
Pricks-honour pricks me on*306 y
  kick against the p ....714 e
Pride-advance their pride*..231 e
  and pride so great*........147 u
  as we sink in pride.....273m
  be humble out of pride.....310 o
  blend our pleasure or our¶.310 b
  by the pride within..... 20 n
  coldness, p., or virtue‖.....655 e
  eternal soul of pride.......192 l
  fly p., says the*......... 53 n
  fools that pride can boast..254 k
  full of pride, uphold††....228 e
  high minds, of native p.....523 c
  his pride in reasoning‡...517 k
  hues that wait on female p. 53 l
  in poesy a decent pride.....478 e
  in pride, in reas'ning p.‡..491 u
  I saw with gawdy pride.... 47 f
  is love's true pride.........366 d
  itt's p. that putts the.... 23 s
  let p. go afore, shame will.501 a
  lost their rounded pride....217 o
  modest unaffected pride.....239 g
  my high-blown pride*.....491 k
  nodded with conscious p...355 l
  nor the p. nor ample pinion. 46 c
  outworks of suspicious p.†.646 a
  peacock in his p. before†... 53 g
  pierce through p. and fear††477 j
  p., cruelty and ambition of.137 u
  p., disdain, and arrogance.735 e
  pride hath no other glass*. 491m
  p. in their port, defiance in.490 v
  p. is at the bottom of all...491 f
  p. is his own glass*.........491 i
  p. made the devil, and.....510 a
  p. of all others the most...490 t
  p. of greatness, or revenge.638 o
  pride of the gardener's.....238 g
  p. still is aiming at the‡...491 a
  pride that apes humility...310 h
  pride that licks the dust‡... 82 p
  pride the market-place§.... 97 t
  p. the never-failing vice‡..491 c
  pride, two bent knees 17m
  p. was never made for man.322 r
  reproves the swelling p....790 j
  rich in their pride.........230 g
  rose with all her pride.....242 r
  scruples are concealed p...788 n
  show itself but p., for*....491m
  shows great p. or little‡...619 q
  sparks, pride, envy, and....765 o
  spite of pride, in erring‡...510 i
  that perished in his pride¶.481 h
  the pedant's pride.........324 o
  the pride of kingly sway*.. 1 c
  tow'ring in her p. of place* 47 a
  vanity, and pride, and.....313 s
  was then the pride of man.491 d
  where is the p. of summer.609 f
  who cries out on pride*....491 p
  worth you shine the pride.673 k
  wretched was his pride..... 41 k
Priest-been priest of Portagas456m
  inspires the pale-eyed p.**.493 f
  perhaps thou wert a priest†451 o
  p. hath his fee who comes††102 u
  than p. e'er chanted from.. 49 e
  this priest he merry is......450 f
  writer, like a p., must be...428 d
Priestcraft-p. never owns...451 o
Priesthood-a perpetual p....353 v
Priests-arms nor the gown‖..421 p
  laws and priests and kings.369 o
  p., tapers, temples, swim‡..361 r
Prig-dear friend Orator P...462 a
Primal-p. duties shine aloft¶164 p
Prime-even in the prime*...362m

gather'd in their prime*...602m
green p. the many, many..609 f
in the prime of life.......707 c
laurel for the perfect p..... 11 d
lovely April of her prime*.673 j
of the joyous prime. ....197 i
our autumn for our prime.604 c
past their prime..........206 e
quickly past the prime.... 217 r
we lose the p., to mark**..613 a
Primer-armed with his p ....170 f
Primeval-this is the forest p.§609 h
Primitive-manner of p. man.457 q
  within the p. soul††.....596dd
Primrose-and the pale p.**..393 e
  bright yellow primrose.....239 d
  greets the p.'s birth......239 i
  pale p., nor the azur'd.....230 k
  p. banks how fair.........239 f
  p. by a river's brim¶......239 q
  primrose down the brae....216 o
  primrose for a veil had¶...239 s
  primrose opes its eye......239 j
  p. path of dalliance treads 451 j
  primrose was to him¶.......239 q
  soft, silken primrose**....136 r
  soft star-like primrose....218 p
  sweet as the primrose.. ..239m
  sweet as the p. peeps......389 g
  the primrose pale.........219 q
  'tis the first primrose.....239 e
  welcome pale primrose ....239 g
  when the p. makes a¶..... 56 h
  wish I were a primrose....239 d
Primrose-eyes-p-e. each....220 p
Primroses-bountiful p.......239 o
  pale primroses, that die*...219 s
  primroses are waken'd....218 i
  p. burst where I stand.....239 h
  primroses by shelter'd rills.218 k
  primroses make a capital..239 l
  primroses the spring¶......239 r
  primroses will have¶ .....224 g
  tuft of evening primroses..240 a
Primrose-stars-p-s. in the...540 f
Prince-a p., the moment he..535 l
  a p. without letters is a....534 g
  begging p. what beggar*...474 f
  beyond a prince's delicates*112 e
  character of the P. of......422 q
  no Indian p. has to his.....595 c
  painted vest P. Voltiger had 22m
  p. can mak a belted knight.304 u
  P. Edward all in gold as he. 46 o
  prince of a State love......282 r
  p. of darkness is a*.........153 o
  Prince of Peace was born.. 94 b
  p. who neglects or violates‖.626 b
  throw a prince as soon as..534 i
  treason to his p.'s person..608 c
Princely-pricks the p. mind.306 g
Princes-and sat as princes**.298 g
  beggars enjoy when p.......111 c
  favor of p. does not.......780 q
  hangs on princes' favor*...535 b
  made proud by princes*...231 e
  p. and lords may flourish..143 g
  p. govern all things—save..647m
  princes learn no art truly..534 i
  p. that would their people..534 h
  p. were priviledg'd to kill..403 p
  so many proud p. and......74m
  that sweet aspect of p.*....535 b
  that thou so many p. at*...140 a
  the secret counsels of p. are 760 c
  women, like princes, find...261 i
Princess-bracelet of the*....435 a
  princess of the world*......185 b
  princess wrought it me*...333 l
Principal-man, who here‡...371 y
  the p. part of everything...679 d
Principle-acts on that p.....305 o
  don't believe in p.††........491 s
  free trade is not a p........282 d
  health is the vital p.......295 s
  living rock of principle.... 79 g
  love is p., and has its.... ..357 s

p., by which each slight....410 p
p. has taken full effect..... 71 l
principle is ever my motto..491 q
p. [patriotism] alone......640 o
subjects are rebels from p..481 n
'tis a p. of war that when..638 h
why is this p. conceal'd...458 q
Principles-and P. with Times‡ 75 r
  but the triumph of p......470 h
  decay of its principles.... 770 o
  deeply skilled in all the p..481 s
  ez to my princerples, I..††.491 r
  oftener chang'd their p.... 24 q
  on selfish principles........272 p
  p. of decorative art...... 28 s
  principles of eternal justice 282 s
  principles of human liberty 338m
  p. of universal justice......636 i
Print-although the p. be*.....90 n
  commeth in p. because he..429 a
  faith, he'll prent it........435 k
  I will rhyme and print‡....429 k
  p. it, and shame the fools‡.452 b
  print wears out, and at last.143 j
  print would then surpass..550m
  quarrel in p. by the book*. 68 c
  see one's name in print‡.... 64 j
  some said, John p. it, others 64 k
  'tis devils must print......452 a
  transforms old p. to zigzag 144 f
  what's this? Print.........427 q
Printing-artisans in p........435 k
  caused printing to be used* 452 c
  history of the art of p......451 t
  telegraphs, printing, gas...327 c
Printer-the jour p. with gray 452 d
Printers-which the p. have.. 65 p
Prints-p. of worrying cares.455 f
Prior-abbot and p. were..... 48 a
  once was Matthew Prior...183 q
Priority-observe degree, p.*.462 x
Prism-poultry, prunes, and.. 73 a
Prison-a palace and a prison‖ 99 a
  a prison of larger room....303 n
  in prison for debt.........424m
  p. where I live unto the*...491 w
  stone walls do not a prison.491 v
Prisoned-nymph had p.††....612 q
  p. in a parlour snug and...566 t
Prisoner-on the p.'s life*... 331 u
  poor the pris'ner and the..138 d
  p. in his twisted gyves*....364 x
  takes the reason prisoner*.321 j
  the poor, the prisoner......382 k
  the prisoner's release......563 g
Prison-house-secrets of my*.547 g
Prisoners-lived happy p..... 47 e
Privacy-of a sainted p....... 21 l
  p., an obscure nook for me.420 t
  tumultuous p. of storm.... 564 w
Private-ambition of a p. man 486 g
  give me a private station...110 p
  is his private property.....428 j
  one way in p., another in..691 t
  post of honor is a private..109 u
  private credit is wealth...128 h
  serv'd no private end‡.....454 g
  that private men enjoy*... 78 f
  the p. wound is deepest*...608m
  therein tax any p. party*..491 p
  wash his soiled linen in p..788 c
Privates-kings that p. have*. 73 f
Privilege-a nobler p. to.....597 j
  death is the p. of human...138 d
  p. for his merchandize.....452 h
  privilege of putting him...283 b
  privilege permits my song..628 a
  sins do bear their p. on*...556 q
Privileged-is p. beyond the..142 o
  less privileged than grain..527 q
  princes were p. to kill.....403 p
Prize-all the prize is lost‡... 13 o
  all we have left to prize...604m
  art, obtains the prize*.... 28 j
  but their Prize a Sot‡.....349 n
  climbing for the prize......231 c
  excels in what we prize....455 s

the r. also vent their rage..797 b
Rabelais–R. or the Fathers...452 h
Race–a bloodless r., that‡...650 r
a heavenly race demands...674 a
and the race a life.........600 h
another r. the following‡...371 e
a race of other days........344 h
a simple race.............215 g
beauteous race the last....229 d
beheld when the r. begun..460 q
bird r. quicken and wheel..542 r
follow and r. in shifting...460 q
forget the human race‖...356 s
girt to run a race........ 98 o
glory of his race......203 f
I am the last of my race...764 l
imperial r. from woman‡...656 t
life's uncertain race........ 75 u
lord of human race........354 u
love whose race is run. ...570 n
not boast a generous race..320 e
noteless as the r. from....310 t
of a time-honour'd race‖...566 h
one half the human race§..488 k
our hemisphere he ran his.585 j
race of man is found‡......371 e
r. of Shakespeare's mind..550 g
r. that led to glory's goal‖.. 97 m
rose in a mist when his race586 e
so lose the race...........203 e
the latest of her race .....395 o
the one selected race.... 95 m
the r. by vigour, not by‡...582 b
the race is won............137 b
the r. of ev'ry virtue join'd 60 c
there lives a race which....791 o
thou runn'st thy race....276 l
to another r., as vain, and..601 n
twins of winged race....561 j
various race supply‡.......213 l
win a mournful race ......672 u
Racer–r., and hack may be..371 j
Races–Brahmin talks of r.... 15 a
preservation of favoured r.188 d
races better than we§.......308 d
Racing–fragrant sweet-fern..228 h
Racine–R. will pass away as.791 l
Rack–leave not a r. behind*..634m
nor leave a rack behind....186 i
then we rack the value*....483 s
Radiance–flood of softened r.624 d
glowing radiance rare.....238 u
moving radiance twinkles..323 k
radiance and odour.......245 c
stains the white radiance..351 b
Radiant–all r., as others have.487 t
r. as the air around a star..575 g
Rafters–r. have tumbled in..614 i
with smoky rafters**.......120 j
Rage–and impetuous rage**..598 l
brib'd the r. of ill requited‡ 95 s
crack your cheeks! rage*..578 b
deaf r. that hears no leader.786 c
die here in a rage like a.... 18 c
emotions both of rage‖....109 q
gratified except her rage‡.. 82 s
heaven has not r. like love..655 r
heroic rage that even his... 79 n
nothing but a r. to live‡...463 f
preceptial medicine to r.*..288 o
rage of his fellow citizens.701 n
repress'd their noble rage..484 o
storm or woman's rage‖.... 6 o
strength and rage could....782 s
strong without r. without.. 78 u
subdues the rage of poison.404 g
swell the soul to rage...... 2 e
their r. supplies them with.677 t
the violence of their rage..677 o
to enjoy by rage and war*..639 s
vent their rage in words...797 b
very tyranny and r. of his*.467 r
what ill-starr'd rage‡......265 d
where the r. of the vulture‖336 v
with r. doth sympathize*..119 r
with your own native rage‡422 o
yell of savage rage.........640 h

Raged–hot colts being r.*....497gg
Rags–arm it in r., a pigmy's*556 o
fathers that wear rags*....107 c
in unwomanly rags........339 c
one flaunts in rags‡......256m
r. and hags and hideous.... 97 s
though in rags he lies......369 n
virtue, though in r., will...110 l
Rail–chance to nod I'll r.and*377m
drunkards most devoutly r.180 v
rail against her beauty‡...338 k
say that she r., why then*..659 q
they r. reviled; as often.... 27 d
Railed–r.on Lady Fortune*..256 q
Raillery–r. is a mode of ....795 n
setting raillery aside.....680 l
Railroad–coppers on the r....328 p
Raiment–house and r. and...617 b
in homelye r. drest........107 h
raiment blood-dyed and....165 o
serves for food and r.§....360 a
splendid r. of the spring...539m
wear them like his raiment*628 n
woman in white r. graceful160 v
your raiment all red........637 n
Rain–a little rain will fill...514 p
and a weeping rain........151 d
and cloud will turn to rain§605 d
a scarlet rain.............222 d
beads in drops of rain§....514 t
before the bitter rain......249 p
beneath a veil of rain.....395 o
black night and driving r..445 q
by shining ranks of rain....392 a
ceaseless r. is falling fast§.514 v
coughs with every rain....672 l
dancing with the rain.....244 f
dark November's rain.....395 n
drip, the r. comes falling...515 b
early and the latter rain...595 b
ere the rain falls, the††...612 a
feet are wet with rain.....392 d
frank as rain on cherry.... 72 a
garden after the rain.......165 j
gentle rain from heaven*..382 p
gusty rain had ceased.... 416 h
I dissolve it in rain ....100 o
into each life some r. must§514 u
in tremulous skeins of r....514 o
like the r. shall fill them§.. 8 b
melts into streams of rain..394 d
never will rain roses.......241 i
no rain be sure disturbs... 99 t
of evening rain...........355 i
oft a little morning rain...345 q
patience suffers unexpected525 e
rain and sun! a rainbow†..515 q
r. a shower of commanded*591 s
rain enough in the*..... ...255 r
rain in the woods, rain....515 b
rain it raineth every day*..515 c
rain whose drops quench...563 f
refuses ae wee drap o' rain.541 p
silent save the dripping r.§554 j
some droppings of rain....586 e
sunshine and rain at once*.193 y
sunshine follows the r...... 74 w
sunshine shall follow the r.102 v
the mist resembles the r.§..537 g
the rain a deluge showers..577 q
the rain and wind beat*.... 12 c
the rain is over and past‖..391m
the soft droppes of r. perce.619 p
thirsty earth soaks up the..162 q
the trickling rain doth fall.185 c
thunder lightning or in r.*.378 r
weary rain falls ceaseless..394 n
we knew it would rain.. .514 o
when we shall hear the r.*.396 i
winter when the dismal r..546 j
with r. the thistle bendeth.577 s
would rain cats and dogs...515 e
Rainbow–and sing,—"The r"515 l
a rainbow in the sky†......515 q
a rainbow's warning.... ..392 n
a raveled rainbow gown....584 e
awful r, once in heaven....515m

but a rainbow at night.....515 n
God hath set His rainbow..531 f
hue unto the rainbow*......29 q
O, beautiful r. ; all woven..515 l
paint the rainbow's varying515 o
passing rainbow dreams...160 k
rainbow brightens to the...515 h
r. bursts like magic on.....515 r
rainbow galaxies of earth's220 h
rainbow in the morning....515 n
rainbow shines to cheer us.577 s
rainbow to the storms of‖..492 v
the r. based on ocean‖......515 i
trickling rainbow of July..459m
unto the rainbow*.........252 y
Rainbowed–r. out in tears....296 x
Rain-drop–down comes r-d... 57 j
every dewdrop and r-d.§....154 d
rain-drop upon his heart...209 k
Rain-drops–like diamonds all 393 b
the r-d.s' showery dance....514 q
listen to the r-d. falling....540 p
Raining–raining the tears of*592 b
Rains–come when the rains..390 o
it rains, and the wind is§..515 o
more the rains fall§.......616 o
rains fall, suns rise††......248 t
rains have been productive.179 j
rains might rust or ... ...263 l
soft April rains...........237 o
Rain-storms–driven in by r-s. 55m
Rain-wet–on the rain-wet....395 k
Rainy–rainy corner of his life776 s
Raise–Lord will r. me up, I..601 v
may chance to raise him...787 a
raise the soul above all....405 r
thou have power to r. him*623 l
Raised–behold them raised...267 f
one r. in blood, and one*...626 h
Raises–r. one man above....336 j
Raiseth–that raiseth me.....487 c
Rake–Ovid's a r., as half his‖478 l
woman is at heart a rake‡..658 h
Rally–and bid you rally here. 69 s
Ram–r. thou thy fruitful*...436 j
Rambles–for the pleasant r. .398 d
r. in valleys and forests...169 k
Rampart–corse to the r. we..444 r
rampart of God's house....298m
Ramparts–be r. of the dead..637 a
Ramrod–had swallowed a r..509 h
Ran–r. to help me when I fell.402 f
Rancour–gradual r. grows...523 z
season'd by love which no.167 j
Random–many a word at r...665 g
Rang–child's laugh r. through135 i
Rank–from the r. of the giver.706 n
in every rank, or great or..666 q
leave of age or rank........192 a
no matter what his rank... 66 o
O, rank is good, and ......367 j
rank for her meant duty...163 l
r. is a farce if people fools. 16 b
r. is but the guinea's stamp.513 b
starts from his rank..... ..369 o
Ranks–adown their shining r. 17 b
are seen in glittering r.**.. 16 s
barriers between different.170 v
gaily ! close our ranks.....635m
Ransom–sufficient r. for*....569 t
Rant–when you r. and swear.485 s
Rap–r.! upon the well-worn..454 b
Raphaels–talk'd of their R... 109 j
Rapid–run the r. and leap....530 l
Rapidly–works done least r...472 a
Rapids–the r. are near and... 63m
Rapine–avarice and r.**.....628m
Rapt–with fury, r., inspir'd..465 k
Rapture–a r. on the lonely‖..475 f
feel rapture; but not such‖.329 l
love leads to present r......359 r
r. the imprisoned soul*....263 w
r. warms the mind‡........125 l
with rapture behold.......115 d
Raptured–round the r. scene.530 e
Raptures–all in r. their own.478 o
hoards his rising r. fill.....387 h

late redeem thy name......409 m
not to redeem his time but.142 s
upon the cross suffer to r..166 c
will be mortal to redeem**.518 j
Redeemer–to soothe the dear 55 k
Redemption–everlasting r.*..518 k
glorious King of R.........165 o
our great r. from above**.. 94 l
without r. all mankind**....518 i
Redress–prayers do.........388 l
r. of unexamined wrongs...548 i
seek how to r. their*.......354 c
things past r. are now*....506 z
to prick us to redress*.....547 t
Redundant–they grow r.....651 g
Reed–and reed that bends...656 v
cork and bending reed‡.... 18 h
drank this with a reed out.163 d
he is a thinking reed...... 597 l
katydid works her........323 q
man is but a reed, the.....597 g
music in the sighing of a r.‖404 q
smote with r. by striking.. 92 i
vernal-scented reed........222 d
what the balmy reed**.... 613 a
wilt thou have pipe and r...393 n
Reeds–a fringe of reeds.....233 r
all among the r. and rushes.539 l
built among the reeds§.... 99 c
house is built with reeds... 55 a
tall flowering-r. which.....240 b
Reef–round the coral reef†... 92 s
the r. of Norman's Woe§...552 g
Reeling–r. through endless...162 i
Reels–Scotch r. avaunt! and‖.128 b
Refined–above their peers r..429 y
and his taste is refined....516 m
Refinement–r. a science.. ..478 w
refinement on the principle.519 r
too great r. is false.........101 m
wealth is a great means of.642 q
Refines–how the style r.‡....407 b
love sincere refines upon...357 k
Reflect–learn'd r. on what‡..518 o
Reflection–a soul without r...518 r
at the age of reflection.....451 t
leisure for r. upon subjects.518 n
reflection of thy nature....418 c
r. on those kinds of objects143 j
Reflections–bear all r........257 k
cool reflections came......518 p
in vain sedate reflections‡..337 t
to bear all reflections......101 a
Reflects–just r. the other‡...269 w
love r. the thing beloved†..366 i
Reform–all zeal for a reform.518 t
Reformation–my r.glittering*519 a
plotting some new r........518 u
show'd great reformation..518 v
Reformed–r. by their.......318 o
Reforms–and r. his plan.....401 p
Refrain–hear the wild r......408 l
Refraineth–man r. from.....593 e
Refresh–invented to r. men's 14 o
refresh the mind of man*..407 p
refresh them with new..... 4 f
Refreshed–r. where one pure.645 t
Refresher–adorner and r. of..641 e
Refreshing–r. that they......221 q
Refreshment–draught of cool 87 e
fill them full of r.§........ 8 b
without r. on the road.....451 g
Refuge–no r. from confession583 i
patriotism is the last r.... 468 v
Refusal–and one r. no rebuff‖662 i
a r. of praise is a desire to.486 m
begs timidly courts a r.....678 r
Refusals–scattering r.‖. ... 662 q
Refuse–could r. the present..118 q
he that made it did r. it....458 r
one, and one refuse.......241 k
r. nothing that pleases....524 z
refuse you for my judge*..330 m
soon have nothing to r. ....181 a
Refuses–He who r. nothing..181 a
Befute–who can r. a sneer ..109 l
Regal–wears the r. diadem**534 l

Regard–and regard of laws..534 h
manner in which we r. it..587 m
popular regard pursue.....261 a
Regardless–r. of our own....676 l
Regards–virtue alone has....468 l
Regent–God bless the Regent.535 k
moon (sweet r. of the sky) 398 f
Regerminate–another year r.235 f
Regime–days of the old r....327 c
Regimen–too strict a r......295 o
Regiment–r.'s in 'ollow......443 k
Regiments–Both R. or none.. 91 i
Region–soul in some region..377 g
survey the r., and confess‡.571 v
through what r. enchanted.374 a
what region of the earth...676 h
Regions–force whole r. in....476 e
frozen regions of the north.344 g
regions under earth*.......300 n
the regions above the moon651 f
those spacious r. where....186 i
unknown r. dare descry.... 6 m
Registered–is r. in Heaven ..123 l
r. in heav'n ere time. ......150 o
Regret–first to repent and r..657 n
love is made a vaguer r.†...366 k
old age a regret........... 9 l
saw nothing to regret‡.....183 l
then judge of my regret...374 g
Regrets–a harvest of barren. 13 h
Regularity–r. abridges all....603 q
Rehearse–r. his worthy praise316 s
rehearse your parts*.......423 b
rote a parrot may rehearse.589 a
their own works rehearse..478 p
Rehearsed–he talked, wrote..581 d
or suddaine is rehearsed...349 v
Reign–bounds his narrow'd r.369 o
herd would wish to reign...212 d
here may we r. secure**.... 13 k
live and reign since I. .....732 e
r. in hell than serve in**... 13 i
r. in this horrible place....566 s
r. is worth ambition**..... 13 k
sweet arts of Thy reign....386 q
their ancient reign......... 98 l
Reigned–to have wrought or.386 r
Reignest–r.in thy golden hall.398 o
Reigns–chaos that r. here**.. 77 a
r. more or less, and glows..487 a
r., tremendous, o'er the....546 n
Rein–keep a stiff r., and move388 w
Reined–cannot be r. again*.. 17 q
Reins–reason's hand the r....203 v
r. to your inflamed passions677 s
Reinforcement–r. of forty ...319 i
r. we may gain from**.....308 h
Reinspire–r. him from the... 57 b
Reject–some r. three dozen‖.662 g
Rejected–r. several suitors‖..114 f
Rejoice–great men rejoice in.675 n
like grasshoppers rejoice‡.650 r
malice in men as to rejoice.724 h
r. at friends but newly*....262 j
rejoice in the present.......758 s
rejoice in what is good.....708 m
Rejoices–r. to have made his.748 i
Rejoicing–r. in the East......585 c
singing and rejoicing......479 g
Relate–these unlucky deeds*.332 r
Relation–r. of distant misery.587 w
Relations–friends, those r....769 f
relations mingle into bliss.304 r
Relatives–the hatred of r.....711 s
Relaxation–indulge in r......739 c
r. relieves the mind ....739 f
Relaxing–mind, relaxing into 515 w
Release–before I find r.†.....525 i
hour of his great release...617 b
inhabitants have the.......526 d
signs the last release....... 10 f
the prisoner's release......563 g
Relents–but relents not*.....591 k
Reliance–r. and hope are....159 i
Relic–fair Greece! sad r. of‖..116 g
Relics–crosses, r., crucifixes..587 c
pure r. of a blameless life..323 f

relics of the ancient saints.344 m
Relief-bloom in sweet relief..103 d
fly for relief and lay.......138 d
find relief in music........405 d
for this r. much thanks*... 86 y
give her Lord relief........ 57 k
her works in high relief§...452 l
is there no relief for love‡..542 p
'tis a poor relief we gain...156 r
wherever sorrow is, relief*.570 i
Relies–whose word no man r..533 g
Relieve–and relieve us, poor.309 s
thus to r. the wretched.... 41 k
to relieve the oppress'd‡... 60 q
Religion–a book of religion..539 e
about again to our r........520 v
adversity reminds men of..675 m
Christian religion doth....519 n
established a r. without....519 o
first element of religion. ...520 s
first run all religion down..520 d
his religion at best is an...520 g
in r. what damned error*...145 h
life and religion are one....521 l
look'd on no r. scornfully..519 k
many evils has religion....738 g
men's minds about to r....472 x
men will wrangle for r.....520 l
morality without r. is only§399 m
my religion is to do good...469 g
nature and religion are....265 p
one r. is as true as another.520 b
part of his religion........522 h
plantation of religion......521 c
pledged to R., Liberty......436 n
really but of one religion...519 u
religion, blushing, veils her‡521 s
r. consists in the pious.....745 c
r. does not censure or......520 n
r. has nothing more to.....522 f
r. has so seldom found. .520 m
r., if in heavenly truths....520 o
religion is no way of life...521 l
religion it was fit..........157 o
religion leads the way......113 j
r. most prevalent in our...519 r
religion's all. Descending.522 p
r. spawn'd a various rout..520 d
religion stands on tiptoe...521 b
religion, the pious worship.520 j
religion to make us hate...522 l
religion to virtue..........586 l
religion were intended....520 e
r. which they professed....520 r
rum and true religion‖.....520 f
Sacred r.! Mother of Form.520 c
sure root but in the r.......636 i
the body of all true r.......519 s
than false religion.........738 f
way to plant religion.......519 p
were of one religion.......520 r
what religion is he of?.....522 j
writers against religion....519 t
Religions–of sects and r......519 m
two possible religions.....520 t
Religious–be it r., as it ought.538 i
casting a dim r. light**....352 l
coward, religious in it*....121 o
if not religious he will be...82 m
I know thou art religious*.106 l
religious book or friend....522 n
r. canons, civil laws*.......639 b
religious life is a struggle..522 e
religious men are at*.......109 d
that we become religious...586 l
unworthy a religious man..520 h
when r. sects ran mad he... 39 g
Religiously-good to do r.....520 w
Reliques–that his hallowed**.550 q
Relish–I do not relish well*... 26 n
I have no relish of them*..535 e
imaginary r. is so sweet*...189 i
relish grown callous.......215 o
relish of their creature....100 j
r. of the saltness of time*.. 11 w
relish with content........110 l
relish with divine delight..274 c

with a relish that inviteth..456 *j*
Relished-r. by the wisest....310*aa*
Reluctant-stalked off r 279*m*
  standing with r. feet§......672 *r*
Rely-r. on him as on myself..264 *g*
Remain-I am here, here I r ..767 *l*
  till naught remain..........581 *v*
Remained-anything r. to do.719 *u*
Remains-be kind to my r....330*w*
  dust alone remains of thee‡137 *k*
  remains nothing to be seen.143 *l*
  this is all remains of thee‖..182 *g*
Remedied-are not to be r.*... 72 *i*
Remedies-extreme r. are....440 *g*
  r. are past, the griefs are*..508 *x*
  remedies are worse ....725 *i*
  remedies is a beef-steak‖...552 *l*
  remedies which will benefit441 *p*
  r. worse than the disease....505 *z*
Remedy-best r. against......726 *n*
  found out the remedy*......518 *l*
  r. can be nothing less than.565 *g*
  remedy for time misspent..313 *p*
  r. for wrongs is to forget....731 *p*
  r. is worse than the disease.505*ff*
  time is the greatest r......746 *r*
  unkindness has no r. at....627 *s*
  without a remedy..........765*m*
Remember-briefly thyself r.*381 *h*
  bubblings ne'er remember..396 *f*
  don't you r. sweet Alice....379 *s*
  I'll r. thee, Glencairn....379 *o*
  I remember, I remember...380 *b*
  I remember, I remember...613 *k*
  I remember the roses......218 *e*
  it r. what it passed is ....387 *y*
  Oh ! still remember me....202 *f*
  pray, love, remember*.....237 *l*
  remember Barmecide§......525 *b*
  r. happy days in misery....780 *a*
  r. me the more of sorrow*.570 *a*
  r. my birth you see....... 59 *r*
  r. only such as these§..... 16*m*
  r. such things were*......381 *k*
  r. that there is a God......725 *s*
  r. the benefits we have....508 *f*
  remember thee ! yea*.....381 *o*
  r. what the Lord hath*....594 *v*
  remember you handsomely 180 *k*
  some I remember.........261 *p*
  sweet pangs of it r. me*....108 *o*
  than to remember thee....380 *o*
  thy branches ne'er r......613 *l*
  when I remember all......380 *p*
  without a sigh r. thee... .531*m*
Remembered-cups freshly*..409 *q*
  mistakes remember'd....255 *b*
  r. joys are never past..... 61 *s*
  r. tolling a departed*......415 *b*
  sorrows r. sweeten........569 *n*
Remembering-r. happier†...570 *q*
  soul r. my good friends*...381 *l*
Remembers-r. the heavens...371 *k*
  Remember'st-r. not the* ...363 *k*
Remembrance-dearest r. ‖. .334 *e*
  ensured their remembrance725 *r*
  flowers of remembrance..237 *f*
  fond r. hidden deep.......380 *d*
  hold in deep remembrance.725 *p*
  in eternal remembrance...802 *b*
  makes the r. dear*.......486 *x*
  no remembrance possible..420 *o*
  no r. which time............792 *l*
  perishes from r...........508*w*
  point of this r. is*.......381 *j*
  r. of his dying Lord.......518*m*
  r. of my former love*......317 *p*
  r. of these things.........725 *q*
  r. wakes with all her......379 *u*
  sweet r. of the just.......381 *u*
  that's for remembrance*..244 *u*
  tokens of remembrance....264 *q*
Remembrancers-our r. of our 23 *d*
Remembrances-r. embellish 779 *q*
Reminds-r. us of others....286 *p*
Remission-gain thee no r.**.641 *v*
Remnant-r. of uneasy light¶.353 *b*

smell my remnant out.....600*m*
  the remnant of mine age*..164 *k*
Remorse-abandon all r.*.....523 *d*
  a strong remorse within....105 *q*
  bred a kind of r. in me*....331 *v*
  cruel r. ! where youth.....522 *q*
  every crime will bring r....687 *h*
  farewell r. ; all good to**..149 *j*
  feel thy pangs, Remorse...523 *c*
  followed an intolerable r...522 *s*
  Nero will be tainted with r.*659 *g*
  r. goes to sleep during a...785 *f*
  r. is as the heart in which..522 *r*
  sit Remorse and Grief......299 *u*
Remote-r. from man, with...567 *j*
  r., unfriended, melancholy.532 *i*
Removal-r. of that which is.133 *f*
Remove-drags at each r. a... 2 *n*
  if you wish to r. avarice...678 *e*
Removed-be thou removed§.672 *l*
  cause of strife remov'd so‡.438 *b*
Remover-bends with the r.*.317 *o*
Removeth-who often r. is.... 76 *p*
Renewed-oft r., seem'd oft..523*w*
  r. by repeated exercises...143 *j*
Renounce-renounce, refrain.782 *l*
Renovation-capable of....... 64 *b*
Renown-and to win r.*.....639 *h*
  but deathless my renown‡.201 *l*
  gained so much renown...276 *p*
  give infamy renown..... 14 *j*
  here's health and r. to his..615 *n*
  is bought endlesse r.......351 *e*
  renown and grace is dead*.350 *g*
  r. is like the summer......766 *k*
  shall forfeit fair renown..547 *s*
  some, for r., on scraps.....514 *n*
  when their renown is heard.443 *n*
  wight of high renowne.... 23 *s*
Renowned-no less r. than**..470 *r*
Rent-her rent is sorrow....297 *e*
  r. the envious Casca made*126*m*
Rental-the rental of half...643 *c*
Rents-anticipated rents and.142 *s*
Repaid-can be repaid.......548 *y*
Repair-in constant repair...264 *t*
  instant of r. and health*..441 *a*
  times to r. our nature*....523 *y*
Repairs-r. his drooping**....576 *k*
Reparation-r. for our rights.529 *k*
Repartee-r. is precisely the..795 *o*
Repast-never finding full r...603 *r*
  to sweet r., and calm.....642 *h*
Repay-tenfold all that love..360*m*
Repeal-r. of bad or obnoxious437 *j*
Repeated-repeated and§.....598 *k*
  repeated too often becomes.790 *c*
Repeating-in the last r.*.....281 *b*
  repeating us by rote††....122 *u*
  r. your ultimate word......169 *k*
Repent-adventure too little.. 8 *q*
  do not repent these things*.149 *v*
  first to repent and regret...657 *n*
  grieve, yet not repent......523 *q*
  honest man does not r..... 803 *s*
  I'll r., and that suddenly*..523 *o*
  may repent at leisure......375 *b*
  my prayers, I would r.*....489*m*
  no strength to repent*.....523 *o*
  r. afterward all their lives.779 *n*
  repent of the undertaking..675 *d*
  r. what's past; avoid*......103*w*
  that we may repent§....... 4 *x*
  they who r. the soonest...786 *k*
  transgression doth repent..523 *i*
  which you may repent......738 *l*
Repentance-amid the roses..523 *q*
  but Repentance is long....523 *k*
  dews of true repentance...522 *r*
  folly by a late repentance..700 *j*
  give r. to her lover........551 *g*
  morning cool r. came......523 *l*
  repentance dear doth pay..361 *g*
  repentance follows hasty...738*m*
  repentance long..........786 *l*
  try what repentance can*..523 *p*
  whip of his own repentance737 *b*

Repentant-grave with my r.*523*m*
Repented-never r. that he...554 *r*
  repented o'er his doom*....523 *n*
Repents-God never r. of....738 *k*
  who repents of his sins is...738 *j*
Repetitions-with his r., long.488*w*
Repining-heart and cease r.§.514 *u*
Replication-all r. prompt*...606 *h*
Replies-frame his fair r‡....199 *f*
Reply-had what to reply**..257 *r*
  hear his faint reply 225*m*
  our sole reply shall be.....469 *j*
  reply to calumny and.....553 *q*
  that deign'd him no reply..621 *s*
  the R. Churlish ; the*.... 27 *v*
  theirs not to make r., theirs‡. 6 *a*
Replying-r. shrilly to the*...169 *l*
Report-enemies carry a r....740 *o*
  epitaph than their ill r.*...423 *c*
  he report thy words**.....280 *x*
  how he may report**......436 *c*
  if my gossip Report*......281 *a*
  ill report while you live*..184 *b*
  killed with r. that old man**171 *n*
  men but by report.........287 *n*
  own report a linguist*.....353 *j*
  r. elsewhere whatever is...740 *n*
  r. me and my cause aright*.436 *k*
  report they bore to heaven.547 *p*
  rumor-the report of evil..740 *r*
  sell me your good report*.279 *d*
Reports-bring me no more r.*436 *f*
  innocence despises false r..681 *b*
Repose-action; beauty is r...101 *k*
  ah! can I e'er know repose.42 *b*
  as if drinking its repose... 16 *e*
  between truth and repose.. 91 *p*
  breast the curtain of r. .. 38 *h*
  calm their repose..........624 *n*
  dissolve in soft repose.....560 *l*
  finds but short repose‡....272 *x*
  foster-nurse of nature is r.*523 *x*
  from wasting by repose....523 *u*
  given us this repose.......739 *h*
  gives the world repose....118 *b*
  he content with soft repose.802 *j*
  manners had not that r.*..373*w*
  men have ever loved r.....523 *z*
  provide more heart's r.....304 *b*
  repast, and calm repose...642 *h*
  sheathes in calm r. the....470 *a*
  sheds a halo of repose.....250 *c*
  the curtain of repose......416 *q*
  the rapture of r. that's‖...132*w*
  there is great repose......722 *h*
  to break r. till dawn of day.136 *u*
  toils of honour dignify r...523 *v*
  uncertain'd that repose....136 *g*
  virtue, but repose of mind.633*w*
  wakes from short repose... 88 *n*
  weary body, longing for r..561 *d*
  wish to break the soft r....523*w*
  with comforting repose*...523 *y*
  worship of the world, but..535 *j*
Reposing-r. himself in the...481 *j*
Representative-no r. at......281 *j*
Representatives-r. of certain 260 *n*
Represented-are not r.......281 *j*
Reprisal-hear this rich r.*...317 *f*
Reproach-fear and without r.757 *l*
  miracle ? 'Tis a reproach..386 *v*
  r. and everlasting shame*..551 *k*
  r. of having descended....302 *h*
  writing their own r.*......292 *l*
Reproaches-avoid the r......296 *k*
  ingratitude calls forth r...770 *u*
  quarrels, entreaties, r.....724 *b*
Reproof-parents deserve r..683 *q*
  reproof on her lip, but a...524 *a*
  the Reproof Valiant*.... 27 *v*
  those best can bear r.‡....524 *b*
Reprove-r. your friends.....705 *b*
  tender may reprove........360*m*
Reproved-r. each dull delay..450 *l*
Reprovest-thou r. in another712 *q*
Reptile-r. concealed bit his..481 *j*
Reptiles-I askt the reptiles..274 *p*

SHAKESPEARE *; MILTON **; WORDSWORTH ¶; BYRON ‖; TENNYSON †; LOWELL ††; POPE ‡; LONGFELLOW §.

of undisturb'd retirement..545 n
Plato's r., where the**......616 i
r. rural quiet, friendship..112 j
r. urges sweet return**....565 m
Retort–the Retort Courteous* 27 v
Retreat–nobler than a brave.635 q
one would not retreat, nor‖ 26 w
retreat a single inch ......525 m
sacred solitude! divine r...567 u
still a friend in my r......566 p
the loopholes of retreat...110 k
'tis sweet, in some retreat. 45 h
Retreats–dwells in deep r.¶. 38 a
green retreats of Academus 341 l
r. from care that never..... 9 t
sunless r. of the ocean.....488 r
Retribution–been just r.§...527 x
Return–appearance and r....105 c
at night will return.......604 u
dead who do not return....132 g
little tasks make large r...342 g
my love had no return†....366 j
own them, welcome its r.. 60 c
passed return no more§....145 p
retirement urges sweet r.**565 m
return to his former fall...388 p
r. to Lochaber no more....204 p
she bade me return.......205 a
swift return diurnal**....352 y
they seldom return again..596 y
thought that she bade me..465 b
to return to the subject....790 b
wishes are all I can r.*.....489 k
your lord will soon return.645 d
Returning–year after year r..392 h
Returns–always r. to his first 777 p
earth r. back to the earth..712 b
returns at a gallop........781 a
returns to tell us of......135 g
seasons have no fixed r.††..539 f
Reunites–r. whom it separates 133 j
Reveal–cover what God would 528 c
reveal its central fold.....402 a
sweet thefts to reveal.....123 o
Revealing–passion fears r....219 k
Reveals–while she hides r... 35 s
Revel–know the revel's ripe..231 n
the revel of the earth.‖.... 99 b
to the late revel.........326 e
Revellers–you moonshine r.*.197 a
Revelry–brightest that......641 n
sound of revelry by night‖.211 c
Revels–lead the r.of the May¶ 50 f
looks for other revels*....619 s
love keeps his r. where*...363 t
our revels now are ended*.634 m
the winds their revels keep 460 i
what revels are in hand*... 15 c
whose midnight revels**...196 s
Revelation–at a r. of man§..528 f
especial r. from God......539 e
makes growing revelation..596 m
nature is a r. of God§.....528 f
on revelation's wall ......448 a
r. of thought takes men....596 q
r. satisfies all doubts......528 d
Revelations–r. of a dream§..596 cc
Revenge–ambition and r.**.. 13 j
blood and revenge are*.....528 l
doth bellow for revenge*.. 55 e
example? why, revenge*...528 p
forgiveness is better than..497 bb
his humility? Revenge*....528 p
if not victory, is yet r.**...528 l
pride of greatness, or r.....638 o
r., at first though sweet**..528 k
r. have ears more deaf*....146 a
revenge, immortal hate**..103 a
r. is a kind of wild justice..523 g
revenge is always the weak 739 j
r. is an inhuman word......739 l
revenge is profitable .....528 i
r. is sweeter than life.....739 i
scorning to revenge an....255 g
settles into fell revenge.... 18 d
spirit, ranging for revenge*638 w
study of r., immortal**....638 f

sweet as my revenge*......385 m
sweet is r.—especially to‖. 528 h
than to revenge an injury..507 k
will feed my revenge*.....528 r
with whom R. is virtue.....528 u
Revengeful–fix r. eyes......403 m
Revenges–brings in his r.*...602 u
Revenue–economy is a great 693 j
out a young man's r.*......398 s
r. whereof shall furnish*...535 h
streams of r. gushed.......123 j
Revenues–bears a duke's r.*.491 o
Reverberation–as the r.§......598 k
faint and far reverberation 406 p
Reverberations–r. of the....273 r
Revere–the Majesty of God r.528 v
Revered–shall be r. when....709 q
Reverence–by r. and obedience 93 g
due reverence to God ...... 99 e
feel trust and reverence....148 r
in myn herte have hem in r. 65 a
meet is the reverence......278 n
none so poor to do him r.*..665 k
reverence for antiquity.... 22 g
reverence the power.......279 h
r. to yond peeping moon..398 g
r. what is ancient.........127 g
sweet r. is that when.....528 w
thyself all r. and fear......529 a
with reverence and sorrow†† 81 h
Reverend–as you are old and*11 l
reverend than plausible... 330 g
Reverential–with r. tread...447 l
Reveries–reveries so airy.... 155 b
Reverse–sad r. soon starts to.381 t
Reversion–bright r. in the‡..361 n
reversion ever dragging†...188 e
Review–can surely review††..125 f
come to his last review ....134 d
Reviewers–r. are forever....125 a
reviewers are usually......124 l
what the reviewers say....124 k
Reviled–they rail, r.; as often 27 d
Revised–revised and corrected 182 l
Revives–for whom all else r..527 q
sad, r. the old, inspires‖....648 m
Revolt–by thy revolt, O*... 377 q
nature falls into revolt*....279 c
Revolted–that have r. wives*.645 p
Revolution–the r. has been..787 d
Revolutions–r. are not made. 75 o
revolutions of the times*..207 i
r. never go backward...... 75 p
Reward–ambition has but.... 14 i
a sure reward succeeds.... 60 o
can not claim as reward....698 o
interest or some reward....640 o
is the r. of virtue bread?‡..632 aa
its own reward.............749 o
like virtue a r. to itself.... 18 r
now its own reward........719 b
only r. of virtue is virtue..632 j
ornament and the r. of....799 dd
r. for faithful silence.......742 m
reward of your speaking..573 o
reward for its great toils...322 a
r. of one duty is the power.163 m
reward the grateful notes‖..454 l
r. with glory or with gold..574 v
that virtue is its own r....632 m
transient is her reward....755 h
unless it brings a reward..691 r
virtue is her own reward..507 cc
virtue is its own reward...507 dd
virtue is to herself the....507 ee
worth r., vice punishment. 3 u
worthy r. for its great toils 176 g
Rewards–due r. can man....468 l
genius and its rewards....270 l
God r. good deeds done....770 m
no gold rewards, but song.756 s
rewards his deeds with*...147 c
the world r. the appearance 780 e
what unequal rewards.....703 q
Rhetoric–dulls the craft of r.549 z
for rhetoric he could not..461 v
in odorous rhetoric of.....448 g

logic and r. able to contend.580 i
r. which the learn'd call‖..573 m
sweet smoke of rhetoric*..340 c
Rhetorician–r. can prove that 461 w
the r. Sabinæus to bathe...175 p
Rheum–and a quarter in r.*..381 m
Rheumatic–r. diseases do*...399 a
Rhine–a blessing on the R.§..532 d
beneath me flows the R.§..532 c
by the castled Rhine§......218 r
imported from the R.‖....128 d
on the R. there grow our..795 d
prostrate Nile or Rhine‡..529 o
R., ancient river, thou'rt...532 f
Rhine flows calmly on......532 b
Rhine in his native wild...532 e
R. with younger wave......532 e
river Rhine it is well...... 97 s
the wide and winding R.‖..532 a
wash the river Rhine...... 97 s
Rhinoceros–the arm'd r. or*.130 j
Rhodora–found the fresh R..240 c
Rhodora! if the sages......240 c
Rhone–like the R. by‖......374 n
rushing of the arrowy R.‖..532 g
Rhyme–and a musical rhyme 603 s
and one for rhyme........476 c
barren flattery of a rhyme 476 m
epic's stately rhyme.......203 a
have reason for my rhyme.477 x
honied lies of rhyme‖......123 k
I will rhyme and print‡....429 k
making legs in rhyme......422 b
may reason war with r....477 d
neither rhyme nor reason..517 g
nor honied lies of rhyme‖..476 f
now you who rhyme......550 f
ornaments of rhyme§..... 206 q
received nor r. nor reason..477 x
rhime us to reason.......254 o
r. nor reason can express*.362 p
rhyme the pipe, and Time..462 p
r. the rudder is of verses..476 d
speak but one r. and I*....148 i
taught me to rhyme*......362 s
that write in r. still make..476 e
the ripple of laughing r....476 n
turn o'er some idle rhyme 313 o
walks forth the man of r.‡.480 i
with some r., rotten.......493 r
Rhymed–its sort, r. or......346 n
Rhymes–in love as your r.*..362 p
r. and rattles of the man‡..623 c
r. that dread neither......677 e
streets their merry r.§....396 g
truth in studious r. to......628 c
Rhyming–born and a r.*....663 i
Rhythm–r. that love's aching 415 l
with a faultless rhythm...603 s
Rhythmic–dance and r. beat.514 q
Rialto–fathom under the R.‖.404 p
soul's Rialto hath its...... 441 q
Ribbed–ribbed and paled in*.327 j
Ribs–behold her crashing r..552 j
heart knock at my ribs*...209 m
make rich the ribs*.......211 m
under the ribs of death**..296 d
Ribbon–r. round his breast...647 u
ribbon to stick in.........256 b
Ribbons–streaming blue r...367 c
Rice–best not stir the rice...481 q
Rich–all alike are rich......134 c
all is as r. as a rose can be..584 q
am just as rich as you..... 335 a
and being r., my virtue*... 38 t
and die rich...............320 r
and rich without a show... 79 a
and with thee r. take what.524 y
as rich in having such a*...645 q
became suddenly rich......740 e
become suddenly rich.....181 b
chief-justice was r., quiet.. 81 p
conceit more rich in r*......103 r
corn for her. men only*...311 h
coveteousness is her rich...686 w
fancy; rich, not gaudy*.... 24 c
faults that are r. are fair*..208 i

ring in the valiant man†... 41 c
ring out old shapes of†..... 41 d
ring out the darkness of†.. 41 c
ring out their delight...... 40 k
r. out the narrowing lust†. 41 d
ring out the old, ring†.... 41 e
r. out the thousand wars†.. 41 d
ring out, wild bells to†... 41 f
r. out, ye crystal spheres**406 c
r. under the load of sorrow*467 z
r. with a soft, melodious§..449m
ruby from the horizon's r.§.585 l
there's a r. upon your hand.663 b
the ring of moderation.....389 b
your ring first, and here*..435 a
Ring-dove–soft r-d.'s cooing.415 l
Ringers–good r., pull your... 39 v
r. ran by two, by three.... 39 v
Ringing–merry bells below...135 i
Ringlets–wanton r. loop......291 i
Rings–about with tiny rings.238 c
caps, and golden rings*.... 24 i
clasps her r. on every hand.238 b
green and silky rings......236 e
more wide the floating r.‡..171 a
rich rings which on his....205 b
r. put upon his fingers*....369 f
the bell never r. of itself...675 g
their eyes seem'd r. from..766 e
weareth a hundred rings...648 q
Ring-ting–r-t ! I wish I were..239 d
Riot–blaze of r. cannot last*..173 o
without any danger of a r.‖.621 j
Riotous–in a riotous unrest..647 u
r. with her abundance**...593 j
when riotous guilty living. 31 h
Ripe-busy when the corn is..768 u
her years were ripe‖.......671 w
r. for exploits and mighty*.673 g
r. in wisdom was he, but§..651 a
we ripe and ripe*........350 e
will first be ripe*........266 o
Ripened–souls are r. in our...369 r
Ripeness–fill all fruit with r..544 c
Ripening–a r., nips his root*.. 76 f
r. through endless years...517 a
the r. the swelling of the... 10 n
Ripens–fortune r. with thy*..381 l
Ripest–r. fruit first falls*...266 g
Ripple–r. of wave and hiss..598 q
r. with the ruffling breeze..446 a
the r. of laughing rhyme...476 n
Rippling–r. through thy††...612 g
Rise–and employments rise..114 r
and successive rise‡........371 e
attempt ye still to rise‡... 13 g
but stoop to rise..........651 b
created half to rise‡.......371 v
Greentrees r. above them...183 b
I rise and am appeased... 802 e
let it rise till it meet......214 r
let us rise up... ....771 c
likewise with Him may r.....165 w
love of God shall r. a star...373 y
make your courage rise....648 x
rise again, with twenty*....124 a
rise and shine ....232 n
rise, happy morn, rise†....401 h
rise in low estate..........276 g
rise in majesty to meet ††...418 h
rise more fresh and bright..250 f
rise to fight again....... ...121 h
rise to prevent the sun....563 p
rise up, rise up, Xarifa......126 u
rise with the lark, and with 48 g
scarce seen, they rise......157 b
sets to rise, ascend........284 p
some rise by sin, and some*.556 p
that r. and fall, that swell..352 a
they rise, they break‡......190 r
to r. with the lark, and go. 507 w
we rise betime*............442 n
whence or why they rise...361 j
Risen–Christ is risen........164 r
Christ the Lord is risen.....166 b
he is risen, a later star of ¶.577 j
Jesus Christ is risen to-day.166 c

Lord has risen to-day ......165 f
Lord is risen to-day ....165 h
risen far above him........319 o
risen three fingers well.....247 f
ris'n who is the First and...164 s
Rises–everything r. but to ..682m
he rises early to do wrong .416 g
with him rises weeping* ...235 n
who riseth from a feast*...211 r
Rising–and so he'll die and r.*378 q
better than early rising....300 a
foretells a bright r. again..586 e
her r. sweet, with charm**.400m
in his r. seem'd a pillar...**153 j
more worshipped the r.... 670 l
r. all at once was as the** .573 c
rising o'er the eastern hill§.398 e
rising with Aurora's light..480 t
ways of rising in the world.790 p
Rite–burial rite be read ......137 i
observe the rite of May*..393 h
Rites–all respect and r. of*..633 i
till love have all his rites*..602w
Ritual–whatever tongue or r.489 r
Rival–allowable in deceiving.762 r
and rival Orpheus' strain‡..557m
as the rival of the author..124 r
jealous lookout as a rival..208 b
O rival of the rose... ......240 c
rival in the light of day¶...315 k
the bard, the rival bard's..173w
the rival of the earth ‖......211 d
without rival to shine...... 79 p
Rivals–not r. in command‡...627 j
r. opium and his brides ‖....456 f
witlings sneer and rivals... 13 d
River–Alph, the sacred r. ran.580 b
a r. at my garden's end...652 l
a river for his guide........740 h
a r. rushing swiftly toward.606 v
a rushing river............213 k
by a goodly river's side...613 e
gloomily to yon pale river..618 o
his mane is like a river.... 20 n
if the r. were dry, I am* ...592 k
join the brimming river†...529 p
let him drink of the river ..190 p
like a running river be.....403 d
like the foam on the river..354 p
like the r., swift and clear§.479 u
like the swift r. that glides.746 k
lived on the River Dee.....110 b
never seen a river.........191 d
of the fair rolling river.....531 n
of the river Lee ....531 a
O lovely river of Yvette§...583 e
one sea, one r., and see all..410 k
primrose by a river's brim¶239 q
Rhine, ancient r., thou'rt...532 f
r. glideth at his own sweet ¶.533 a
river linger to kiss§ ....228 l
river of feeling overflows§..302 q
r. of thy thoughts may roll.760 b
river of unfailing source....406 r
river onward glide.........250 h
river's summer walk.......222 p
river's trembling edge......228 j
smooth the gliding river§..542 o
stream is the River Time ..603 s
swim the river, villain ..... 21 a
the brook and river meet§..672 r
the foam on the river......138 h
the river from the lake ‖....374 n
the r. of his thoughts‖.....655m
the river to pass along....721 h
thou royal r., born of sun§.532 h
tremulous inland river††...612 g
we'll to the river* .... 18 l
River-buds–and starry r.-b...228 j
starry river-buds..........250 g
River-child–lull its r.-c. to‖...374 n
Rivers–as brooks make r.....290 t
being suffer'd, r. cannot* ..465 x
by rivers gallopaded†......610 l
deepest r. make least din...555 c
earth's full rivers cannot..460 h
friendship is like rivers....265 o

long r. down the lifted face.590 d
princess of r., how I love ..530 n
r. are roads that move and.787 f
rivers cannot quench* .....213 b
rivers to the ocean ....185 z
rivers wove their charms ..147 z
see the r., how they run...529 l
shallow r. to whose falls ..529 n
stained earth's silver rivers. 94 b
the r. did the trees excel...613 e
through the rivers wade... 453 c
two ways the rivers leap§..529m
River-ways–freighted are.. 394 g
Rivets–hammers closing r.* .639 q
oaths like r. forced into....419 b
Rivulet–met above the......395 e
r. of text shall meander... 68 h
waves of the r. glancing...322 p
Rivulets–myriads of r.† .....,.412 u
r. dance their wayward ¶ ..413m
r. from the mountains§....162 n
trace these briny r. to.....592 t
Road–a broad and ample r.**.576 f
along an agreeable road...772 p
any r. you can't go amiss..321 b
climbing a difficult road...707 a
death's a pleasant r. that...632 o
fringing the dusty road††..228 e
is no expeditious road.....463 u
life's dark r. his sordid way.643 b
no flowery road leads to...770 e
on a lonesome road ....208 r
r. wind up-hill all the way..607 g
rough, a weary road......346 f
rough is the road, your....484 k
take the same road ......689 p
the end of my road.......374 f
the r. is long from the.....764 i
the unfrequented road....245 k
this quiet wood road......229 f
upon the desert road......107 p
we keep the road.........127 h
who takes no private road‡.412 c
Roads–block the roads and§..277 l
rivers are r. that move and.787 f
r. are wet where'er one....577 s
r. on all sides to the grave.689 k
there are fifty r. to town ..521 u
Roadside–golden-rod of the..229 l
roadside thicket hiding ...228 h
waft from the r. bank......244 r
Roam–love to roam o'er the..445 k
o'er sea or land we roam...304 g
O who would roam.......304 i
r. along, the world's tired‖.566 e
though we may roam ... 304 k
where'er I roam, whatever.379 v
where'er we roam, his first.468 n
Roamed–have r. o'er many...379m
I roam'd apace .... 87 l
Roamer–r. is she o'er wall ..648 g
Roar–and music in its roar‡..475 f
and she says roar.........463 o
don't ye hear it roar now...445 n
he did not only sigh but r..463 d
in my time heard lions r.*..119 s
in the song of its roar .....459 t
I will roar you as gently*.. 45 r
loosen'd aggravated roar...578 f
Roared–roared the dreadful..577 q
Roarings–waves in r. round†. 92 s
Roast–her that ruled the rost499 f
he ruleth all the roste.....499 g
learned roast an egg‡......431 t
Rob–not r. me of a treasure..379 g
r. me of free nature's ......413 a
robbe Peter and pay Paule§.503 z
slays more than you rob*..441m
Robbed–he 's not r. at all*....595 k
he that is r., not wanting*..595 k
r. that smiles, steals*.....595 n
Robber–sing before the r....733m
Robber-chief–brigand than‖..626 b
Robberies–r. that leave man .558 j
Robbers–but for supporting* 70 s
with robbers' hands my*. .309 l
Robbery–thieves for their r.*595 p

SHAKESPEARE *; MILTON **; WORDSWORTH ¶; BYRON ‖; TENNYSON †; LOWELL ††; POPE ‡; LONGFELLOW §.

SHAKESPEARE *; MILTON **; WORDSWORTH ¶; BYRON ‖; TENNYSON †; LOWELL ††; POPE ‡; LONGFELLOW §.

ray what glimmering sail...552 h
s. for Porta Rique.........321 p
s. forth into the sea of life§.645 b
sail he spreads for Heav'n..674 f
sail on even keel ....445 g
s. on, O Union, strong and§.469 c
s. the thousands of watery.607 f
sail through life towards...261 m
s. where'er the surge may‖.150 l
second an oar or a sail.....354 g
so low a sail to strike*......109 s
spread the sail..........445 t
the little nautilus to sail‡.. 63 o
the whirring sail goes†..... 53 d
Sailed–sailed with me before.209 b
slow sail'd the weary†......383 k
Sailest–s. wide to other lands 42 g
Sailing–lazily s. o'er the blue 99 n
Sailor–before Noah was a s.*.438 v
bringest the s. to his wife†.446 d
hear a brother sailor.......446 b
mind is a good sailor....... 4 k
s. when the prize has‖.....329 l
Sailors–s. freeze with fears‡.577 r
winds that s. rail at*.....564 o
Sails–behold the threaden s.* 445 u
by science, s., and oars.....678 a
head-winds right for royal.301 e
majestic with her swelling.446 a
purple the sails, and so*...552 b
s. forth the stripling bold..350 b
ships rigged out with s. of.585 k
the white and rustling s....445 b
winds shift, shift our sails‖ 667 w
Saint–as. in crape is twice‡.. 82 w
by s., by savage, and by‡...489 a
Edinburgh's Saint Giles.... 95 p
idol, s., virgin, prophet‖....586 f
in white, like a saint......233 p
is a saint run mad‡ ....674 h
low St. James' up to‡ .....158 g
might become a saint‡.....129 a
patron saint in armor shines68 m
saint abroad and a devil....312 c
St. John mingles with my‡.517 j
see Christ's chosen saint... 93 e
seem a s., when most I play*631 p
sinner it or saint it‡.......252 f
therefore no true s. allows.374 l
the rigid saint, by whom no520 i
the ruins of St. Paul's......267 n
the ruins of St. Paul's......268 n
thou be saint or sinner.....134 c
to catch a s., with saints*..172 l
up to high St. Paul‡........158 g
weakest s. upon his knees..487 s
whither saint or sinner.....311 s
Saintlike–innocent, s. air..... 31 c
Saints–bait to draw s. from††128 m
conjure thee by all the s.*..130 r
contracting with the saints.670 c
crew of errant saints.......157 o
great men may jest with s.*653 x
images of canonized saints*303 e
men below, and s. above...362 g
no silver s., by dying misers‡95 s
relics of the ancient saints.344 m
saints in your injuries*.....660 g
saints only have such faces§195 d
s. out of heaven with palms561 k
saints themselves will......272 e
saints who taught and led.. 85 k
s. will aid if men will call..487 r
teaches s. to tear and cant.673 u
to s. whose lives are better.520 i
Saintship–s. of an anchorite‖.303 a
Sake–but would be for your..666 c
dear child Jesus' sake...... 94 c
for Christ's sweet sake††....86 o
" for God's s.," others to...762 l
for thy sake, tobacco, I....457 a
for whose sweete sake that.518 m
sake of the friendship§.....265 a
Salaam–hat that bows to no.432 w
Salad–better s. ushering the.167 e
his fingers in the s. bowl...168 t
make a capital salad.......239 l

my salad days; when I*....673 h
our Garrick's a salad....... 79 q
Sale–s. of chapmen's tongues*36 q
to things of sale a seller's*.442 o
Sallies–noble s. of the soul...567 t
Sallow–the s. for the mill...610 h
Sallowness–to haggard s. ...327 t
Sally–there's none like pretty655 q
Sally Lunn–with a grace the.374 o
Salmon–and the first salmon§ 97 q
the salmon vaut........ 213 g
Salt–abundance of Attic salt.177 a
call it Attic salt‖..........124 f
death is the universal salt..132 d
eat a bushel of s. with him.495 ii
how salt the savor is ....765 s
its beauty and s. of truth... 64 g
many pecks of salt.........704 h
ne'er knew salt, or heard‡..314 i
not one salt drop e'er wets.538 b
salt is spilt, to me it fell...586 i
salt of most unrighteous* .376 q
table, a dish of salt ....685 k
the salt of human tears....603 l
valor is the s. t' his other. .628 l
wit is the s. of conversation653 e
Saltness–relish of the s. of*.. 11 w
Saltpetre–s. should be digg'd*121 v
Salutation–receives high s....544 n
salutation to the morn*.... 44 g
Salutations–loud shouts and*608 n
Salute–about to die s. thee...686 q
I often s. you, you never....176 n
s. thee with our early*....393 e
salute you with an eternal.176 n
Salutes–dog s. the smiling... .19 p
golden sun s. the morn*....584 s
Salvation–errand of s. sent... 94 d
fee-simple of his s.*........252 u
Salvation by means of.......798 a
s. through Christ the.. .804 d
tools of working out s......587 c
Salve–lips covered with s....179 m
patience is sorrow's salve..467 d
" salve " is writ beneath...394 m
Samaritan–acts like a s......457 f
do the Samaritan without.. 87 c
Same–always and never the..410 a
another and the same......188 c
another yet the same‡.....101 w
by the s. means we do not..764 j
leave us and find us the s.. 75 e
s. with common natures...420 c
things are still the s. they.. 22 g
Sample–his speech was a fine‖573 m
Sancho Panza–S. P. by name. 74 l
so S. P. said and so........562 e
Sanctified–numbers the....403 p
Sanctifies–breath s. the air...233 d
Sanctimonious–s. face I pull.521 d
Sanction–received the s......215 t
sanction of the god‡.......277 c
to sanction vice and hunt‖.630 l
Sanctities–day's dead s......187 k
Sanctity–Indu'd with s. of*..517 e
kissing is as full of s.*......335 d
to place no sanctity**......303 c
Sanctuaries–God's ancient s.669 w
Sanctuarize–should murder*.403 u
Sanctuary–desire to raze the*389 h
quiet in hell as in a s.*......377 c
taking s. in the crowd.....428 l
the eastern sanctuary stair.585 b
Sanctum–editor sat in his s..435 m
study in my s. supercilious521 d
Sand–a handful of red sand§.600 v
and wrote upon the sand...459 o
but heaps of sand ....143 h
crept up along the sand.....598 s
if all their s. were pearl*...377 k
last s. twinkled in the glass.647 a
like foam or sand..........391 i
o'er and o'er the sand......598 s
petals dipped in sand......234 v
shells upon the sand§......598 t
sows the sand..............796 n
wrote on in the sand........ 86 r

Sandal-shoon–upon my "s-s."382 a
Sandals–with winged s. shod. 17 b
Sand-piper–one little s-p. and 56 n
Sands–across the s. o' Dee....530 l
books are drenched sands.. 68 i
clog the last sands of life‖..464 h
footprints in the sands§.....598 u
life's latest sands are.......279 s
on the flat sands hoard..... 42 a
passed over the white sands553 x
s. are number'd that make*350 v
small sands the mountain..619 v
the shining sands below‡...615 f
through the silent sands...531 l
Sandy–just above yons. bar§.576 a
Sane–assent, and you are s...320 s
fitter being sane than mad.101 b
who then is sane ?....... .716 j
Sang–all s. "Annie Laurie"..568 a
he worked and sang from...110 b
how s. they in your courts.165 a
laughed and s., any noise . 20 m
sang every night as he......292 o
s. in tones of deep emotion§557 h
s. of love and not of fame..568 a
sang out of tune, ancient...453 e
sang with many a change§. 94 j
she s. ful loude and cleere.. 45 j
so sang they, and the**.....536 r
what song the Syrens sang.143 r
when they sang together...635 e
Sanguinaria–s. from whose...223 e
Sans–s. sense, sans taste, sans676 i
Sansavine–flames so red in§..649 p
Santa Claus–S-C. de la......643 c
Sap–if the sap is stirring yet.540 i
infect thy sap and live on*.300 w
milky sap of its inner cell..267 b
sap is stagnant.............313 e
sap that turns to nectar....266 e
stalks with honeyed sap....237 o
without their sap how‖.....325 o
Sapless–those sapless scales..234 l
Sapling–like to a wind-blown.367 a
Sapphire–like s., pearl*......220 a
Sapphires–firmament with**.416 m
the sapphire blaze.........415 o
Sappho–burning S. loved and‖542 d
S.'s ode a good example‖....478 l
tenth is S. maid divine.....276 r
Sark–Sark, fairer than aught327 l
Sash–when the s. was open...614 r
Sashes–knack of tying sashes 88 w
Sat–as when he sat down.....167 j
he sat by her side and her..664 a
she sat like Patience on a*. 397 b
where we sat side by side..357 y
Satan–indignation S. stood**.153 e
on God's and S.'s brood....358 g
Sabbathless Satan.........666 w
Satan exalted sat by merit*153 f
S. finds some mischief still.497 cc
S. hous'd within this man*.130 r
S. now is wiser than of yore‡594 c
S. o'ercomes none but by...593 s
S., so call him now, his**...153 g
S. trembles when he sees...487 s
Satan was now at hand**...153 b
so S., whom repulse upon**472 m
to Paradise the Arabs say.. 53 m
Satanic–the Satanic school...153 s
Satchel-schoolboy with his s.*580 c
Satellites–Jove's s. are less‡..277 t
Satiate–s. the hungry dark.. 52 d
Satiated–life like a s. guest..721 f
Satiates–new appetite while..764 g
Satiety–s. closely follows the.741 c
satiety is a neighbor..... .741 d
Satire–implicit s. on mankind386 v
let satire be my song‡..... 251 f
my s. seems too bold‡......537 u
not to write satire.........741 f
satire does not look pretty.183 j
s. is always virtue's friend.537 n
s. is more than those he....537 o
s. lies about literary men..778 u
satire. or sense, alas‡......537 s

to-morrow is a s. on to-day.605 t
s.'s my weapon, but I'm‡ ..537 t
s.'s the sauce, high-season'd422 a
Satirical—more s. from vanity 537 q
Satirist-a would-be satirist‖..435 l
satirist of nature's school.. 50 k
Satisfaction—no s. in any good 741 i
satisfaction in themselves .100 j
windy s. of the tongue‡....606 c
Satisfied-answer: "I am s.,"§525 b
crow had been s. to eat.....741 h
jealousy is never satisfied..327 p
others, not so s., unhorse ..483 e
paid that is well satisfied*.111 r
satisfied with his fortune..788 a
them fully satisfied** ....332 p
Satisfies-no great object, s...155 s
this world never satisfies§..657 h
while it s. it censures......386 v
Satisfy-can satisfy the soul..273 p
nothing can satisfy them..763 j
satisfy a few ....787 r
that poorly satisfy our eyes577 k
Satisfying-s. all the world....787 p
Saturday-a S. and Monday ..536 k
Saturn-son of Saturn gave...276 t
Satyr-Hyperion to a satyr* :102 b
Sauce-a crier of green sauce.494 l
for sauce by sweating.....167 a
lamb, with mint sauce.....660aa
limons and wine for sauce.167 e
nor seeks for sauce where.. 25 v
rudeness is a sauce to his*.654 a
satire's the sauce, high.....422 a
sauce for a gander... ......508 l
sauce to make me hunger*.112 b
sauce to meat is ceremony. 73 d
to the mysterious sauce....177 k
what is sauce for the goose.508 l
with cloyless sauce his*.... 26 c
Sauces-sundrie s. are more ..167m
Saucy-deep searched with s.*580 r
how many s. airs we meet..629 i
Savage-along the s. mind‖... 69 k
by saint, by s., and by‡.....489 a
feel our savage kin ....236 d
music on the savage race..413 q
no savage fierce, bandit**.. 88 a
savage sits upon the stone. 268 o
somewhat of the s. beast...565 d
stories of savage men......115 c
the noble savage ran........258 i
to soothe a savage breast..405 a
Savageness-sing the s. out*..557 s
Savages-Druids did the s.....254 o
the labour of the savages.. 87 n
Save-and delight to save... 69 r
God s. our gracious king..533 n
God save the king.........533 n
God save the mark* ....498 j
he but save himself 354m
is the power to save........520 p
just th' unjust to save**...518 j
may be meant to save‖.....284m
never-dying soul to save...572m
save a sinking land‡........300 k
s. each object of his love‡..274 q
save me and I'll give you a.670 e
s. them by the barrel-load .463 u
save, to ruin, to curse, to ..629 x
save your own soul first....319 c
still be ready to save........116 j
to save the whole sawes off.439 r
we conquer but to save... 630 x
Saved-mine I saved and hold 345 u
of ever being saved.........149 b
penny saved is two pence ..169 u
saved some trifling thing... 8 a
saved you six thousand....179 a
souls must be saved*.......298 r
what's saved affords no....354 k
Saves-saves all beings but....297 i
Savings-bank-youth should..673 l
Saviour-crimsoned with thy. 55 n
men that our S. dear did... 19 e
sacred feet of her Saviour§.521 f
S.'s birth is celebrated*.... 49 l

s. of the silver-coasted isle†469 o
S. of the world felt deserted612 c
scorns the Saviour's yoke..312 p
speak low to me my S......519 q
the Saviour bent down..... 86 r
trait'rous kiss her S. stung.654 r
trust our S. every day ....165 n
'twas thus the Saviour said 233 t
upon the Saviour's breast§.620 f
Savor-no s. of the earth to...649 e
rob of half its savor.......243m
s. of certain stews‖........431 n
Savors-freckles live their s.*.226 b
Savoury-what's homely s.*..311 g
Saw-for that one he saw....112 r
that no one saw...........248 i
Saws-his saws are toothless‡.431 g
s. off th' infected part......439 r
Say-and yet say no to-day‖..662 g
I had a thing to say*......574 k
I s. the tale as 'twas said to.536 f
knew not what to say he‖..418 v
learned of myself to say ...181 r
never say " Fail " again...502 n
say better than silence is§..554 l
say his s. though a whole§. 70 c
s. I will with patience hear*107 f
say just what I think§......556 u
say nothing but what hath.474m
say one thing and mean§...556 u
so long as we can s. " This*388 n
that no more must say is* .340 b
those who nothing have ††.589 h
time to s. to-morrow's come606 a
'tis a kind of good deed to..665 u
we s. little if not egged on .794 g
what men say of her they..662 d
what should I s. my tears*.592 j
what will Mrs. Grundy say.461 c
you could s. Jack Robinson495hh
Sayest-in that thou s. all ....386 r
say't that should not say't.506hh
Saying-a good s. often runs..786 b
a saying oft thought right.606 a
deed of saying is quite out* 189 l
s. all one feels and thinks..448 f
tremble lest a s. learnt†....592 o
what are the wild waves s..459 i
where that s. was born*....493 t
write on your doors the s.§.119 d
Sayings-s. of philosophers... 88m
that shall civil s. show*....606 j
Says-s.—what says he ? caw.667 t
'tis his at last who says it††514 g
when a woman s. she loves. 355 r
Scab-prove the s. of churches 96 c
scab of the church........184 k
Scabbard-sword glued to my637 p
Scaffold-and not the scaffold.760 p
making on the scaffold. ..761 d
on the scaffold high........132 h
truth forever on the s.††...622 o
Scaffoldage-footing and the*.422 t
Scalded-s. dog fears cold....506 d
Scale-for he by geometric s. 341 r
free livers on a small scale.511 j
held the scale of empire....424 k
s. in hand Dame Justice‡...438 b
woman, in this s., the weed.457 g
would not sink i' the scale..464 a
Scales-earth in dubious s.‡..277 b
scales bedropp'd with gold‡ 213 l
Scalp-behind his s. is naked..603 n
pine, whose emerald scalp‖ 617 f
Scalps-king of the cold white 46 d
Scaly-hopes the scaly breed‡ 18 h
scaly, slippery, wet, swift..213 i
Scamp-come here, you scamp 20 g
to choke a poor s. for††....437 p

Scan-gently s. your brother .343 c
learn thyself to scan .. ....322 r
merits or their faults to s..473 u
mind its proper face to s...422 j
more plentifull to scan.....369 s
presume not God to scan‡..371 x
s. him from head to feet‡..126 b
Scandal-act though s. would.203 h
and the scandal hit‡........ 82 s
assail'd by scandal and the.538 a
begins the s. and the cry†..480 x
give virtue s., innocence‡..477 q
greatest scandal waits on*.538 e
he rams his quill with s....538 f
is scandal in disguise‖.....538 d
ready to believe a scandal.681 b
s. of men is everlasting....558 p
they scandal have at will...538 b
Scandalous-monarch, s. and.534 r
Scandals-dead s. form good‖.537 y
wings immortal s. fly.....538 c
Scant-scant this breathing*..644 f
Scanting-s. a little cloth*... 172 r
'Scape-crimes that 'scape or†437 v
Scar-closed without a scar‖..671 e
s. nobly got or a noble scar*306m
Scarred-s. the moon with*...363 p
Scars-and dishonest scars‡...638 j
death closes our scars......761 o
he jests at s. that never*...498hh
Scarce-makes s. one dainty*.644 a
Scarcity-s. they will turn...281 i
Scare-ever s. me with thy†..592 o
Scarecrow-a s. of the law*...439 b
Scared-s. out of his seven....503bb
scared with eerie sounds†.. 25 l
Scarf-and a scarf of velvet...584 e
Scarfs-maids their scarfs*...483 g
with scarfs, and fans, and*. 24 i
Scarlet-gold and s. of the sun609 p
in frightful scarlet........241 t
Scarlet-s. berries tell where..222 p
Scathe-have done s. to us*.... 93 k
Scattered-all summer she s..227 o
is scattered on the ground.351 v
scattered as they flew.....530 c
Scatterings-s. of the hills¶...238 h
Scatters-scatters on the air..237 q
Scavenger-a s. and king's the 16 b
Scene-a sylvan s., and as**...609 k
concerns of an eternal s....604 d
each lonely s. shall thee....403 e
each s. a different dish.....422 a
every s. some moral let it‡.422 t
good man's shining scene. 8m
horror itself in that fair s..767 j
how fare you in this scene..449 q
in life's last scene what.....348 g
live o'er each s., and be†...422 n
love gilds the scene........660 i
lovely is the silvery scene..546 k
o'er all this scene of man‡..371 w
o'er this changing scene...307 w
of such enchanting scene..523 w
one fair s. or kindly smile..379m
our lofty s. be acted over*..602 k
range the sylvan scene....112 o
round the raptured scene..530 e
s. precariously subsists too‡422 o
scene wherein we play in*..669 g
silent, solemn scene......284 r
that enchanting scene.....522 q
that memorable scene...... 5 d
the s. is touching, and the..672 d
very cunning of the scene*.423 f
view the whole scene, with.383 c
wraps this moveless scene.417 p
Scenery-end of all natural s..403 a
Scenes-blissful s. survey'd‡..658 l
conceal the past scenes.....741 n
gay and festive scenes .... 211 t
in lovlier s. to pass these...541 o
lovely s. at distance hail...307 n
new s. and changes must..185aa
when histrionic scenes‖....421 p
your s. of love, so flowing..422 a
your surly s., where rant...422 a

Scent-amber s. of odorous**.447 c
as the scent to the rose.....381 x
gives scent to every flower.410 n
nature gave one scent to...410 t
quicken'd at the scent**...266 g
rose's scent is bitterness...243 q
scent in every leaf.........244 k
scent of bean-fields........223 d
s. of the roses will hang...242 q
scent—oh that's divine......244 k
scent survives their close...243 q
scent that steals from the..232 p
scent the desert and.......244 t
scent the dewy way.........393 d
scent the evening sky......249 k
s. the most imploring air..616m
whose s. hath lur'd them... 53 f
whose s. the fair annoys...456 q
you'll make a scent........246 n
Scented—scented and bright..247 c
Scents-pleasant s. the noses..393 s
sweet scents the wilderness561 n
that s. the evening gale...618 g
Sceptic-s. could inquire for.. 26 v
Scepticism-s. is the first††..125 e
Sceptre-her leaden s. o'er a..418 a
his sceptre do they sway...534 e
king with his golden s.....535 p
sceptre and crown must...141 b
sceptre shows the force of*382 p
s. to control the world*... 11 p
sceptre with a firm hand..740 j
unwieldy s. from my hand* 1 c
wields a mighty sceptre....402 i
Sceptred-above this s. sway*.382 p
a sceptred hermit.......... 82 o
Sceptres-sheaf of s. left......240 b
s. have no charms for thee.468 t
Scheld-lazy S. or wandering..532 i
Scheme-achieve his scheme..160 c
drink, and s., and plod....668m
scheme built on a truth...579 t
she'll project a scheme....579 f
the statesman's scheme‡...634 l
Schemer-will in the s. to....579 t
Schemes-best laid s. o' mice .154 x
hasty and adventurous s..680m
our most romantic schemes160 s
schemes men lay for fame.200 f
Scholar-a s. knows no ennui.764 r
each day is the scholar.....720 u
gentleman and scholar..... 22 p
he was a scholar,and a ripe*580 f
ills the scholar's life assail.580 b
Madame Rose is a scholar...114 h
mark what ills the s.'s life.342 f
pensive s., what is fame....579 u
s. who cherishes the love of579 r
s. would conjure her*.......377 c
soldier than in the scholar*444 o
the ink of the s. is more....429 d
where should the s. go§...580 d
Scholars-greatest s. are not..775 q
great scholars great men ..580 a
the land of scholars.......115 n
School-and the s. for the day 89 h
army is a s. in which the...442 y
erecting a grammar s.*....452 c
from a doubting school.....621 u
go to s. in a summer morn.170 e
his bed shall seem a s.*.....589 o
love is the law of the s.....512 c
no s. of long experience...609 b
school with heavy looks*..363 q
set thee to s. to an ant*...455 p
tell tales out of schoole....504 u
the Satanic school.........153 s
the school of coquettes....114 h
the school of mankind.....188 i
to s., and not to travel.....606 o
unwillingly to school*.....580 e
whose kingdom is a school.455 j
School-boy-a s-b.'s tale, the‖..578 h
every s. boy and school....451 t
frights the school-boy..... 52 p
school-boy whips his taxed.283 b
school-boy, with his satchel118 n

the school-boy knows......223 l
whining s-b. with his*......580 e
School-boys-like s-b., at the..346 e
s-b. from their books*......363 q
Schooled-s. in a strange‖ ....455 f
Schoolmaster-s. over the.....127 q
the schoolmaster is abroad.170 f
Schoolmasters-s. puzzle their649 q
s. will I keep within*.......455 o
Schoolmates-s.'s marriage...436m
Schools-all jargon of the s...455m
and in famous schooles....338 n
and manners, schools......656 v
in s., some graduate§...... 90 c
maxim in the schools......215 r
noisy jargon of the schools.455 l
pay to ancient schools....124 h
schools have yet so much..273 n
sounding jargon of the s..455 g
the maze of schools‡.......252 c
Schuylkill-alone by the S. a..532 j
Science-branches of science..538m
bright-eyed S. watches.....538 j
by s., sails, and oars, ships.678 d
by the glare of false s......538 g
comyth al this newe s.that. 9 i
eel of science by the tail‡..844 c
fair S. frowned not on his..379 c
for science is like virtue...538 k
hardest science to forget‡..361 p
how s. dwindles and how.. 68 q
in s., read, by preference..516 j
instrument of science......339 x
I value s.—none can prize..538 i
law is a sort of hocus-pocus437 q
moral and political science.477 v
no s.fairly worth the seven‡548 k
O star-eyed S., hast thou..538 h
phrenology—a s. that by...473 o
refinement a science.......478w
root of all science.........301 v
science. but an exchange‖..336 u
science imagination.......270 i
s. moves the light chariot..678 d
s. only will one genius fit‡..538 l
s. ranks as monstrous..... 16 j
science sees signs; poetry..587 e
s. that gives us any rest....525 c
s. when well digested is....538 n
the proper S. and subject..370m
where S., young and bright414 e
Sciences-arts and s. are not..289m
arts and s. the benefit..... 63 t
books must follow s. and.. 64 a
dark as s. metaphysic......457 n
fully in those sciences*....455 n
keys of Sciences...........353 z
s. and most of all the‖.....341 s
Scion-herself the solitary s.‖.566 h
Scipio-like S., buried by the‖. 98 b
Scissors-his man with s.*....458 h
Scoff-fools who came to s.....450m
never to scoff at the.......780 j
with hollow s. the raven... 87 l
with scandal and with scoff538 f
Scoffer-product of a s.'s pen¶429 x
Scoffing-palm of scoffing we. 50 k
s. his state and grinning*..140 s
wreck'd with an inward s.‖.114 q
Scolding-s. from Carlyle or.. 74 s
screams and scolding fail‡. 83 a
Score-and paid his score*....465 a
books but the s. and the*..452 c
drink five bottles bilk the s. 78 q
would muster many a s....652 f
Scorn-canst make us scorn..325 n
deal of scorn looks*.......109 t
disdain and scorn ride*....193 l
firm philosopher can s.....341 q
fools may our scorn........173 t
for the time of scorn*......109 o
I am held in scorn..........238 r
law shall s. him further*...438m
meanest wretch they scorn. 61 w
on the pedestal of scorn‖..109 f
or read to scorn...........539 b
pain of fancied scorn and.. 62 l

s. at first makes after-love* 659m
scorn for miserable aims...318 r
scorn her own image*......412 l
scorn not one¶.............549 j
s. to me to harp on such a†.366 p
sound of public scorn**....109 k
teach not thy lips such s.*.335 q
the scorn of scorn†........481 a
thrice in spite of scorn**..591 a
we scorn her most*........256 t
with impious scorn insult..570 t
Scorned-fury like a woman s.655 r
he s. his own who felt.....473 q
s. his spirit that could*....564 q
scorn'd! slighted! dismiss'd109 t
Scorner-thou s. of the ground 49 n
Scornful-shook it with a s....456 e
Scornfully-on no religion s...519 k
Scorning-s. the base degrees* 14 d
Scorns-s. the Saviour's yoke,312 p
she scorns our poverty*....491 o
Scorpion-s. died of the bite..481 j
Scotch-a S. understanding..328 v
Scotched-s. the snake, not*..129 u
Scotchman-noblest prospect.115 p
Scotchman if he be caught..170 n
Scotia-O S.! my dear, my....116 o
Scotland-as if it felt with S.*569 r
flowers o' Scotland....... 246 o
one hour of Scotland......116m
shiver'd was fair S.'s spear.638 s
the flowers of Scotland.....218 c
Scots-cakes and brither Scots116 n
S., wham Bruce has....... 685 q
S., wha hae wi' Wallace....685 q
the Scots are poor, cries....116 p
Scottish-for some S. muse...614 j
Scoundrel-given them to....643 d
last refuge of a scoundrel..468 v
scoundrel maxim..........503cc
Scourge-a blue-stocking is...796 c
and scourge the tool.......489 o
fear, for their scourge..... 523 c
scourge his own iniquities.635 r
that was "the s. of God"..396 o
the s. of life and death's...463 l
when the s. inexorable**...523 j
whose iron s. and tort'ring. 6 r
with the terrible scourge..736 q
Scraps-and stolen the scraps*514 l
on scraps of learning dote..514 n
those s. are good deeds*....602 x
Scratch-graves an arrowed. s 63 j
will scratch the nurse*.....363 h
Scratched-purpose to be s.... 2 b
that is but s. withal*......512 t
Scrawl-the worse the s., the..440 r
Screamed-again the women.451 s
Screams-s. of horror rend‡...209 h
such screams to hear.......321 a
Screen-describes a charming‡524 l
I behold the screen......... 25 t
just for a screen...........520 a
this thy screen, and this‡..106 d
Scribbler-every little busy s. 428 l
s. of some low lampoon‖...435 l
Scribblers-s. to-day of every.628 a
Scribbling-itch for s........753 k
Scribe-but undoes the s.‡...437 u
Scrip-fill up my pilgrim's††. 86 o
requital-ope his leathern**440 k
Scripture-devil can cite S.*..514 k
piece of Scripture*........187 x
rammin' S. in our gun††...300 h
that was Scripture........421 q
Scriptures-s. of the skies....575 k
s., though not everywhere..538 q
Scruple-some s. rose, but‡...106 c
Scruples-s. are concealed....788 n
scruples dark and nice..... 2 b
Sculler-like a sculler plies...440 d
Sculptor-a s. wields the chisel452 j
person who is not a great s.426 b
s. does not work for the....452 q
the far-fam'd sculptor.....200 f
Sculpture-and that is s. §....452 l
frieze with bossy s.**..... 425 z

hath man his fixed seat**...668 w
he held his seat ; a friend‡.309 r
her wild, sequester'd seat..378 v
made the throne her seat..388 k
seat in some poetic nook...470 l
seat is up on high*.........139 j
seat of the Divinity ... .. 707 f
seat of the Zwinglians.....521 j
sit on a prophet's seat‡.....126 b
up to our native seat**....492 l
Seats-hawthorn-bush with s.614 c
lindens ever chosen seats of615 b
Seceded-say to the s. States..282 w
Second-allows the s. place...671 a
he shines in the s. rank ...766 i
it is honorable to reach the.677 a
s. thoughts are the wisest..596 r
s. thoughts, they say, are..596 k
second and sober thoughts.596 u
Second-hand-s-h. dealers ...474 t
Secrecy-infinite book of s.*..493 g
queen of s., the violet......192 k
Secret-a mother's s. hope...307 x
another man's secret.......741 m
another to keep our secret.547 d
another to keep your s.....741 o
a s. at home is like rocks...547 e
a secret that thou dar'st ...223 h
beauty's secret nearer .....247 d
confiding the secret to.....286 g
heart's secret was at once.. 62 k
his dear friend's secret tell.374 t
in many a secret place¶....413 m
keeps the secret it betrays§.359 u
kept secret by the sufferer.558 t
learn the s. of the sea§....460 d
love thus secret to convey..628 a
s. enmities are more to be..741 l
secret in the grave, he bade.420 x
s. of a weed's plain heart††.643 k
secret of being tiresome ...764 p
secret of its power .... 7 y
s. of the sounding wire§....430 q
s. of unfathomable depth..571 p
secret scarcely lisping of... 71 l
secret wound still lives.....741 t
smallest part of a secret...788 g
so oppressive as a secret ...788 e
still the secret joy partake‡633 c
suffice thes. soul to show‖.621 k
the s. counsels of princes ..760 c
though in secret it rolls....591 c
though secret she retire‡...190 o
three may keep a s. if....506 mm
when a secret is revealed. 788 f
when the secret cup¶.......598 g
will hold a secret.........251 u
with s. course, which no...172 w
Secrets-discharge their s.*...523 e
fault to reveal secrets.....742 o
hear her s. so bewrayed* .. 63 d
her open secrets wrung.....412 s
pillows will discharge their*124 c
mighty secrets of the past..604 a
nay, the s. of the grave*....559 b
s. of life are not shown ...587 u
secrets of my prison-house*547 p
s. of state no more I wish..281 p
s. of the sepulchers of hell.299 t
the secrets of the soul......194 r
trust him not with your s..144 q
trust our s. to our friends..788 d
weighty s., and we must... 43 d
Sect-adverse sect denied....27 p
law, or sect, or opinion did.519 n
slave to no s., who takes no‡158 h
Sectaries-jarring s. may learn636 k
Sects-petulant capricious s..520 d
vicissitudes of sects and...519 m
when religious s. ran mad.. 39 j
Secure-s. amidst a falling...535 r
secure within, can say......605 c
Secures-'tis Providence alone 509 jj
Securities-are the natural s... 15 h
Security-does give the best s.571 a
public honor is security...123 h
s. against the like future...529 k

security for any one........179 l
security for gentleness....642 p
sense of security in an old†† 67 b
Sedge-bird-a s-b. built its little57 c
Seditious-the most s. is......738 b
Seduces-woman that s. all...656 m
Seductions-to all seductions.626 l
See-always what you see‖...312 d
calmly see one he loves....588 e
can see what is invisible....180 j
days are nights to s. till I*. 3 e
dumb men throng to see*..483 g
ere I see thy face......... 2 r
for gentlemen who see ....197 o
for he had much to see**...553 m
for one short hour to see†..317 a
full oft we s. cold wisdom*.651 k
give me to s. and Ajax‡.... 61 c
gods see everywhere§......277 k
hope to see my Pilot face†..268 j
I am Pope of a See.........535 p
I desire to see those things.803 ee
in that just mirror......604 i
I shall ne'er s. your graces. 19 h
may s. my shadow as I pass*584 g
ne'er shall see him more... 23 g
ne'er shall see him more... 23 o
never see him more......... 23 h
see a church by daylight* .193 s
see and approve better.....683 e
see and to be seen.........503 dd
see, but cannot reach, the§. 13 e
see but dimly through the§ 298 c
see enough, when years are553 l
see her was to love her... .356 e
see in a summer's day*.. .372 e
see it ere I die..... ....116 m
see only with their eyes....314 x
see oursel's as ithers see us310 f
see that face of her's*...... 90 q
see thee now though late..409 m
s. the things thou dost not*482 w
see, too, in the world..... 96 s
see what is not to be seen..553 p
shoulders of giants s. more 503 g
still I see thee, still I hear.. 2 q
taught the world to see.....478 u
the gods see everywhere§..431 f
they that won't see ....553 o
those that will not see.... 61 b
through him that all men s.478 n
thus we may s., quoth he*.602 g
'tis but a part we see‡..... 371 y
to hear, to s., to feel, and‖..566 e
to se, and eek for to be seye553 i
to see all other's faults‡...651 h
to see her is to love her.....655 b
we s. thee like the patriarch473 g
we shall see and know*....268 e
we think we see...........561 h
which thou canst not see‡..411 w
you can't see to bite........322 s
you see is none of mine....399 g
Seed-all have got the seed... 2 j
flowers and bears no seed††187 s
her disk of seed†.........246 l
nestles the seed perfection.472 h
robs not one light s. from..411 f
seed of religious liberty††..521 t
seed, which sown in.....221 a
spring from such a seed‖...526 v
the seed that's cast........197 q
turn in the little seed......666 j
who soweth good seed......279 s
Seed-plot-the s-p. of all other.622 j
Seeds-genuine s. of poesy‡...477 b
leave us but their seeds....540 s
look into the seeds of time*338 a
seeds of knowledge........729 a
which in their seeds*......493 i
Seedsman-as it ebbs, the s.*.531 j
Seed-time-s-t. and harvest**.601 h
Seeing-desert fills our s.'s...,531 h
optics seeing as the†.......203 t
seeing have forgot**..... 61 f
s. I saw not, hearing not†..161 k
Seek-death seek and shun...604 h

seek him rather where.....274 f
seek it ere it come to light..354 j
seek thee in vain by the..... 2 v
they cannot seek his hand..485 p
thy sweet smiles we ever s.605 p
to seek a great perhaps....769 m
unto all who seek ....280 e
want itself doth seek*.....652 k
we seek it ever with smiles.605 g
world was not to seek me.. 201 s
Seeking-go to those who are.485 p
s. the bubble reputation*..444 k
those seeking power.......734 g
Seeks-but he who s. all things 13 h
man who seeks one thing... 13 h
who s., and will not take*..461 r
who seeks for aid must.....548 y
Seem-are they what they s.. 76 q
be good rather than to s. so709 e
be not what you seem‖.....312 d
be what you seem to be...799 ee
grow to what they seem... 13 b
I would rather be than s. ..799 cc
men should be what they*.556 z
not always what they seem691 g
no less than I seem*........ 83 s
s. a saint,when most I play*631 p
s. everything but what they312 i
so things s. right no matter144 c
to be rather than to seem..803 u
Seeming-all good s., by thy*.377 g
by seeming otherwise*.....384 j
from life's cold s. and .....645 t
like her seeming*..........215 l
Seems-better than he seems.280 u
Seen-all the girls that e'er...660 m
because he was not seen...729 o
because thou art not seen*.319 q
eye hath not seen it........297 t
goodly states and kingdoms607 d
hated needs but to be seen‡30 p
he woulde be seen........ 429 a
I had s. the great but I had757 e
lov'd needs only to be seen.621 w
rarer s., the lesse in mynde.553 j
scarce are s. the prostrate‡.529 o
that I spake as having s.†..161 k
the book of God had seen...539 d
to be seen in Heaven‖......557 w
to be seen to be admired...520 o
to be taken, to be seen.....123 o
we have seen better days*.388 o
Seers-word by s. or sibyls... 538 s
Sees-little thing to do s. and. 4 a
reason no one sees him......426 o
sees what is before his feet.705 f
s. with equal eye, as God‡..151 n
soul itself which sees and..571 e
Seize-eternal shall we seize..267 m
happiness, if then he s. it..461 g
reach not to seize it before..306 f
s. the flow'r its bloom is....238 k
Seizes-s. the right, and holds.652 b
Seizure-to whose soft s.*....292 l
Select-very wise and s. in the485 o
Selection-natural s. or the...188 d
term of Natural Selection..410 p
Selects-what he s. as by what514 d
Self-aims that end with self..318 r
dearer than self, possesses‖148 p
fitting of self to its sphere.526 g
love has no thought of self.360 k
mistress of mine own self†.318 d
nature's s.'s thy Ganymede323 m
not for s. but for country..802 dd
nothing but with self.......361 s
self with each generous§...359 z
she is her s. of best things..660 j
smote the chord of Self†....547 u
swear by thy gracious self*419 m
to thine own self be true*..623 o
wretch, concentred all in s.547 s
Self-approving-one s-a. hour†547 l
Self-begetting-s-b. wonder...375 p
Self-conquest-s-c. is the..... 104 v
Self-denial-there lies the s-d..146 o
Self-disparagement-inward¶.547 o

Self-dispraise–a luxury in¶...547 *o*
Self-distrust–s-d. is the cause157 *k*
  self-knowledge is s-d. .....337 *i*
Self-educated–s-e. are marked170 *h*
Self-embalmed–lies s-e........479 *j*
Self-esteem–s-e. grounded**.. 82 *d*
Self-improvement–time for ..484 *j*
Selfish–where all are s., the..547 *r*
Selfishness–mark of s........279 *h*
Self-knowledge–first step to..337 *i*
Self-love–claims of s-l. in ...548 *a*
  hath no s-l. nor he that*....639 *n*
  more self-love than love....327 *s*
  offended s-l. never forgives 788 *j*
  s-l. and the love of the......299 *s*
  s-l. is a principle of action..547 *v*
  s-l. is the greatest of all....548 *b*
  s-l. is the instrument of our548 *g*
  s-l., my liege, is not so*....548 *f*
Self-lovers–these overdrest... 23 *n*
Self-made–a s-m. man? Yes...370 *o*
  respects self-made men....170 *l*
Self-mettle–s-m. tires him*... 17 *o*
Self-offences–by s-o.*........303 *f*
Self-possessed–calm and s-p.§646 *k*
Self-punishment–hatred is....294*w*
Self-recovery–the power of...628 *k*
Self-reliance–s-r. is its ......632 *k*
Self-reproach–feel no s-r.¶....106 *v*
Self-sacrifice–obstinacy and..658 *p*
Self-slaughter–against s-s.*...583 *d*
  heroism, self-slaughter....583 *a*
Self-subsisting–the s-s......275 *a*
Self-taught–s-t., I sing; by ‡.477 *b*
Self-transmutative–s-t. form.352 *d*
Self-trust–s-t. is the essence .104 *e*
Selves–own s. our bliss must.293 *a*
  stepping-stones of their†...373 *c*
Selinis–top of greene S. all...611 *k*
Sell-ivie out to sell my wine.648 *g*
  nectar of good wits will s ..648 *g*
  sell, not to read, them ....177 *n*
  sell the fee-simple*........252 *u*
Seller–a s.'s praise belongs*..442 *o*
Selma–hear the song of S.....557 *k*
Semblance–outward s. of the. 90 *s*
  we paint the semblance of. 36 *e*
Sement–sure sweet s., glue..334 *l*
Semi-Solomon–kind of s-S....337 *n*
Semptress–the tucked-up s.. 458 *n*
Senate–bribes a s., and the‡..390 *b*
  give his little senate laws‡. 26*m*
  the Roman s. when within. 52 *l*
Senates–and make s. dance‡. 129 *b*
  judges and s. have been‡...279 *a*
  listening s. hang upon ....172 *d*
Senators–custom,most grave*127 *p*
  green-robed s. of mighty...616 *d*
Sender–to the great sender* .362 *r*
Sensation–count them by....600 *h*
Sensations–s. sweet felt¶....210*w*
Sense–above the s. of sense*.537 *x*
  after your own sense*......438 *t*
  all her rays from sense‡...548 *l*
  all intellect, all sense**...575 *a*
  also with good sense‖......127 *r*
  a man of sense can artifice. 25 *t*
  and is of sense forlorn......388 *a*
  and laugh us into sense....341 *h*
  and spirit of sense*........292 *l*
  avarice is that of sense‡.... 7 *l*
  but good sense and reason.538 *n*
  chance is a word void of s.. 73 *y*
  clear wit and sense........782 *i*
  conceal than discover the s.573 *l*
  cook should double one s...182 *b*
  copy faults, is want of s....513 *y*
  cream of courtly sense‡....451 *e*
  dare to have s. yourselves‡422 *o*
  devoid of s. and motion**..316 *l*
  eyes meet far off, our s. is.587 *s*
  for one for s., and one for..476 *e*
  fortune and sense ......702 *j*
  fruit of s. beneath is rarely‡665 *e*
  giving requires good sense.706 *o*
  good sense and good taste..788 *l*
  good sense defac'd‡........252 *c*

good s., which only is the‡ .548 *k*
great pride or little sense‡ .619 *q*
hath the daintier sense*....421 *n*
her s. but as a monument*.562 *r*
if all want sense............467 *g*
if rebel s. would reason's..597 *s*
is that fine s. which men ...120 *f*
is want of sense ....389 *e*
it enchants my sense*......189 *i*
kissing full s. into empty... 88*w*
learn'd without sense ......580 *v*
left an echo in the sense....634 *t*
lose the sin yet keep the s‡.556 *f*
lost to all the s. of shame‡.551 *h*
madness is divinest sense..320 *s*
men of sense approve‡..... 6 *j*
men of sense are really ....519 *u*
men of sense never tell it ..519 *u*
more betray our sense* ....389 *h*
my sense with their........241 *u*
mystic Sense is found.....205*w*
odour within the sense....231 *k*
palls upon the sense....... 33 *j*
palter with us in a double*.492 *r*
pleasure, all the joys of s.‡.475 *t*
proceeds from want of s....490 *t*
prompt sense of equity .....548 *t*
quiet s of something lost† 354 *r*
sans s. sans taste, sans eyes. 676 *i*
satire or sense, alas‡......537 *s*
seem an echo to the sense‡.573 *e*
sense in Lethe steep*......204 *a*
s. is our helmet, wit is but..548 *n*
s. is the diamond, weighty.548 *n*
sense of justice is a noble..333 *c*
s. of pain was the silence§..169 *g*
s., these thoughts, these...129 *f*
sense the starkest madness.320 *s*
strike pleasant on the sense 40 *b*
take the sense, sweet, of* ..320 *n*
than mislead our sense‡....429 *i*
the want of sense ....251 *r*
thin partitions sense from‡.548*m*
through s. and nonsense....476 *o*
to the general s. of men¶...648 *f*
to the inward sense........ 33 *p*
unbless'd with sense above429 *y*
violenteth in a s. as strong*339 *a*
virtue and sense are one ...631*w*
want of Sense is the Father548 *l*
whose weighty sense........548 *j*
wit, accompanied by good .653 *j*
wives have sense like them*377 *d*
word in its Pickwickian s..548 *i*
words that make no sense. 88*w*
work of skill, surpassing s.323 *l*
Senseless–s. and deformed ... 18 *d*
the most s. and fit man*.... 84 *q*
vent on senseless things....701 *b*
Senses–bless my s. with the ..238 *s*
entrancing our senses with.408 *k*
huzzaed out of my seven s.499*hh*
I keep my senses............704 *j*
it ravishes all senses........635 *b*
knowledge than our senses 737 *q*
on his senses burst.......... 1 *q*
out of my seven senses.....499 *ii*
perspective of the senses...314 *x*
power to touch our s. so**..406 *e*
scared out of his seven s...503*bb*
senses gradually wrapt ....159 *r*
slays all senses with*......223 *g*
so their rising senses*......130 *s*
steep in y s.in forgetfulness*562 *q*
Sensible–s. in the duller* ....516 *q*
sensible of in himself ......472 *q*
sensible men on the earth..796 *b*
sensible people find nothing759 *f*
s. seemeth their conference*537 *x*
to be now a sensible man*..326 *k*
Sensibility–wanting s........260 *a*
want of sensibility........251 *r*
Sensitive–s. of their faults...260 *u*
sensitive, swift to resent§.. 81 *d*
Sensitive-plant–s-p. has no...245 *c*
sensitive-plant in a garden.245 *b*
Sensual–not to the s. ear, but405*m*

Sent–she s. for me in haste to440 *f*
Sentence–half a s. at a time..456 *h*
he mouths a s. as curs......573 *p*
my s. is for open war**.....637 *v*
originator of a good s.......514 *c*
soon the sentence sign‡ ...330 *l*
with some rhyme, rotten s.493 *r*
Sentences–and honeyed s.*...172 *c*
Sententious–Cato, the s.‖....259 *r*
Sentiment–nurse of manly s..156 *s*
s. is intellectualized††.....208 *p*
the nobler the truth or s ..622 *b*
worth one s. of women....660 *y*
Sentimentalities–the highest.462 *h*
Sentimentally–s. I am........405 *o*
Sentiments–all the beautiful†† 5 *c*
Sentinel–s. angel sitting high.382 *g*
s. stars set their watch in..575 *o*
watch-worn and weary s....142 *v*
Sentinels-critics are s. in the§125 *d*
starres, bright s. of the....575 *u*
Sentry-sun shall be sentry...234 *j*
Separate–forever s., yet‡.....324 *n*
mingled and yet separate‖..374 *n*
Separately–shall all hang s...627 *h*
Separates–reunites whom it..133 *f*
September–a bright S. morn§.394 *h*
September thy first ....394 *g*
thirty days hath S..........390 *j*
Sepulchre–myself my s. a**..387 *s*
no s. conceals a martyr's§..617 *l*
Rome her own sad s.‡......98 *n*
sepulchre in amber.........323 *c*
the sepulchre, wherein*....285 *t*
watch by her sepulchre....544 *o*
Sepulchred–s. in such**......285 *h*
Sequestered–s. path has.....566*w*
Seraph–behold the s.'s face††. 16 *n*
brightest s. tell, in which**668*w*
no seraph's fire‡............349 *g*
s. may pray for a sinner....487 *t*
spake the seraph Abdiel**.212*m*
Seraphim–and sworded s.**.. 16 *s*
for the seraphim high veil..165 *o*
s. her to hymn, might...... 3 *i*
Seraphs–s. share with thee.. 29 *d*
where s. might despair‖....369 *i*
Serene–always clear and s...651 *f*
breaks the s. of heaven ....417 *r*
conscience makes one so s.‖105 *d*
serene amidst alarms...... 77 *k*
s., and resolute, and still§..646 *k*
serene, still, and free‡......183 *p*
stoop'd down s., and wrote.420 *x*
Serenities–s. unthawed, and.234 *k*
Serenity–journeying in long..647 *a*
Serious–attend to serious ....680 *l*
nothing s. in mortality*....350 *q*
serious words suit the ...753 *b*
the serious smile‡..........649 *j*
trifles will lead to serious..747 *d*
very serious things to jest‖.421 *p*
would rather handle s. ones679 *t*
Seriously–late, but seriously .804 *h*
take life too seriously and..150 *r*
Sermon–a living s. of the....450 *j*
a sermon on a hat..........433 *a*
fool so wise a sermon made.451 *s*
him who a sermon flies.....476*w*
in thy own s. thou that the 57 *g*
many a s. made in praise...578 *j*
now a s. and now a prayer§ 40 *h*
perhaps turn out a sermon. 73 *n*
s. never said or showed.....451 *g*
the sermon is never long...450 *i*
Sermons–resort to s., but to..670 *g*
s. and soda-water the day‖..648 *k*
sermons in stones and good*350 *f*
spite of s., farmers would..525 *e*
two sermons weekly.......518 *v*
Serpent–but be the s. under*.482 *c*
more of the serpent than...336 *e*
O serpent heart,hid with a*312 *u*
poison'd by the s.'s sting... 53 *s*
s. grasped that through....202 *q*
serpent sting thee twice*...320 *b*
sharper than a s.'s tooth*..319 *s*

spit on a s., and his vigor... 21 p
take a s. by the tongue*....558 x
the bee and the s. often sip.759 o
the infernal s.; he it was**.153 i
think him as a s.'s egg*....511 t
trail of the s. is over them..556 c
Serpents–no s. in the world...143 q
which is poyson to serpents481 k
Servant–a master, or a s., or‡642 a
he can give little to his s..498dd
I have been servant of love.456m
pleasure the s. virtue......475 l
s. of God well done, well**. 93 f
Servants–admired by their s.758 d
bad servants wound their...201 c
my silent servants wait....344 q
public officers are the s....620 p
s. of his providence........413 d
s. that fly when she's......578 g
Serve–a thing which all things 70 l
but 'tis enough, 'twill s.*...671 h
eager to serve, the cause...548 t
hearts that scorn'd to s.*...472 f
him we serve's away*......202 r
must now s. on his knees...470 w
numbers who will s.instead644 v
one I will serve............808aa
serve him truly that will*.. 83 s
s. his time to every trade‖..124 f
s. it thus to me that love it*432 c
serve their God againe. ..534 e
s. thy generation, this thy..435 p
s. who only stand and*....549 b
than serve in heaven**..... 13 i
they serve God well, who...549 d
they serve him best**......275 i
this bids to s., and that to‡.342 j
though but few can serve..548 u
to serve the Devil in.......312m
we are his, to serve him...548w
what serve for the thunder*598m
who serve his creatures....549 d
Served–s. him from the hour*549 f
s. my God with half the*...549 e
zeal I serv'd my king*......549 e
Serves–but s. when prest‡...517 h
he serves his party best....482 q
who s. the country best....482 q
Serveth–s. not another's will.305 q
Service–bone, desert in s.*...602 h
cares not for service‡.....517 h
command was service......163 l
creep in s. where it cannot*549 h
done the state some s.*.....332 r
for my service but blows*..549 f
from a friend in service... 704 c
heart is ever at your s.*....549 g
in s. high, and anthems**..406 g
made of faith and service*.363 f
morning s. of Thanksgiving594 y
no money, no service......780 q
service is the same with....273 s
service was of great array.211 f
show how s. sought can be.548 y
small service is true s.¶....549 j
strong for service still......291 a
the service of the time*.... 70 i
they eat your s. like apples.548 x
what was the s. for which I 34 n
Servile–a s. race who in mere.124 h
Serving–or s. and losing....766 s
s. man's wife may starve..494 t
to die for her is s. Thee.....368 a
Servitors–nimble and airy s.**665 c
Servitude–base laws of s.....258 i
of servitude into freedom..596 q
servitude, the worst of ills..127 g
Set–all, except their sun is s.‖542 d
a rich stone, best plain set.631 z
just as they're set, too fast318 l
s. less than thou throwest*.511 q
sun hath made a golden s.*.625m
they're set, too fast or slow436 v
Settee–devised the soft s......430 r
Setting–haste now to my s.*..152 u
Sets–flower that never sets...220 g
my sun sets to rise again...345 u

sun ne'er sets on my......534 s
sunne never sets in the.....484 b
sun never sets on the......483 r
sun never sets upon their..483 n
sun that sets upon the sea‖.606 r
the sun never sets.........483 o
when the sun s., who doth*586 c
Seven–nay, we are seven¶....198 s
seven times one to-day..... 60 b
set all at six and seven....503gg
Sever–half broken-hearted to‖464 j
though we sever, my fond..464 k
Severe–be as holy as severe*.330 k
from lively to severe......757 c
from pleasant to severe...476 p
or, if severe in aught......342 d
then be severe.............437 l
who is not just is severe...759 j
Severed–I s. from thy side‖..259 q
our state cannot be s.**....376 a
Severity–s. is allowable....788m
s. of the public power*.....438m
with such a look of severity742 c
Severn–Avon to the S. runs..530 d
Severn to the narrow¶......158 k
Sew–apple dumplings sew...169 a
s., prick our fingers, dull...666 c
Sewer–common s. of Paris and 98 d
Sewers–reign o'er s. and sinks 97 s
Sex–either sex assume, or**..575 b
I love the s., and sometimes‖655 k
poorest of the sex have....126 r
sex is ever to a soldier‡....443 h
sex to the last.............656 b
s. whose presence civilizes..456 c
taxed their whole s. withal*659 k
your s.'s earliest, latest care629 k
Sexes–the sexes at once to....114 o
Sexton–beheld thee play the.458 s
leaned a sexton old on his..458 o
like a sexton by her grave. 539 h
our honest sexton tells.... 95 n
s., hoary-headed chronicle.458 p
sexton's hand, my grave...284 j
the s.'s hand, my grave to..398 o
Shackles–shake off the s.....269 k
their shackles fall.........559 f
Shad–the s-bush, white with.609 d
Shade–a blacker depth of s...399 f
above s., a woody theatre**609 k
a shade immense............417 t
as soon dislodge a shade....344 o
beneath the quivering s.‡.. 18 h
boundless contiguity of s ..470 g
by the shade it casts.......385 c
checkered s. and sunshine.348m
Cinthia, mistress of the s.. 53 e
dark shade escapes from...705 k
folds of deepest shade......561 h
fragrance to the shade....233 s
give no shade and no shelter618 b
gray flits the s. of power‖..485 n
green thought in a green s.597 b
grieve when even the s.¶...289 e
half in shade and half......243 o
hawthorne bush a sweeter*614 f
her lustre and the shade...397 i
I bear light shade for the.. 515 d
in her starry s. of dim and‖.415 j
in the chequer'd shade**...128 p
in the chequer'd shade‡....125 k
its shade scarce cools me..542 b
lain in the noonday shade..614 i
lengthen'd ev'ry shade‡....625 d
light and s. spring both**..625 a
no shade, no shine, no.....395 i
or in thy waving shade....567 u
or more welcome shade.... 85 l
pillar'd s.high over-arch'd**613 i
pines a noxious s. diffuse‡.546 f
pleasant s. which agrove... 50 n
Pompey's shade complains. 24 r
rising thro' the mellow s.†.577 g
scarce cast a shade........221m
seats beneath the shade...614 a
shade deep'ning over shade610 n
s. is to figures in a picture. 389 c

s. for the leaves when laid.100 e
s. of the maple-trees under.615 k
shade that follows wealth..264m
shining youth into the s....142 s
silence and its shade........117 d
sings in the shade when.... 49 b
sitting in a pleasant shade..392 r
strength of s. and light‖....446 h
sun had lengthened every‡.544 j
sunshine and in shade......261 n
that, in tracing the shade.. 620 h
the calm s. shall bring a...609 b
this sacred s. and solitude..567 v
thrown a little shade.......56 o
throws his army shade......614 a
'tis the shade by Victory...631 c
under whose shade the*....139 u
variable as the shade......658 r
wander'd in the solitary s.‡.658 l
Shades–and visionary shades.618 p
closer s. the panting flocks‡.542 p
crowns, in shades like these 9 t
doleful s. where peace**...299 e
ere the s. of evening close..351 v
false flitting s. our minds..161 h
hov'ring shades of night...160m
of darkness and of shades** 77 a
send me to the s. before....150 u
s. all the banks, and seems‡.615 f
shades of everlasting night.601 p
shades of forty ages stood‖.115 j
s. that met above the merry 395 s
s. which sep'rate mind....629 w
soon as the evening shades.397 d
welcome, ye s.! ye bowery..610 p
Zamara's shades............221 k
Shadow–a dream, a s., bubble451 s
and shadow of a shade.... 634 o
an emerald shadow fell....540 i
a shadow on the snow..... 57 d
beneath their palmy s.....229 h
brow a shadow fling..... 255 e
chequer'd shadow*........549 p
cooling s. of a stately elm..613 e
daisy, by the s. that it¶....549 j
darken'd with her shadow‖.356 t
disdains the s. which*.....582 h
each coward s. eastward...585 h
find e'en in the shadow.... 52 j
fluttering s. wraps us......617 a
follow a s., it still flies you.662 o
glory is the s. of virtue....801 d
have but a s.'s bliss*......549 s
have just enough shadow..487 t
hemlock's fragrant shadow 230 e
history casts its s. far§.... 302 f
in itself a shadow..........203 c
life's but a walking s.*....350 r
light such shadow fling:... 32 a
love is sunshine, hate is s.§.348m
love like a shadow flies*...363 u
may see my s. as I pass*...584 g
one shadow of night...... 515 t
shadow from a soul on fire.297 w
shadow of a dream........316 g
shadow of a leafy bough...201 o
shadow of a mighty name. 696 k
shadow of a starless night..150 d
s. of a wilful sin......555 v
s. of some unseen power...485 z
s. on those features fair§...185 o
s. owes its birth to light....549 l
s. proves the substance‡...174 b
s., that lies floating on..... 55 b
slight shadow alarms......699 d
smallest hair throws its s..792 q
standeth God within the†‡. 510 f
swift as a s., short as*......171 h
takes no shadow from them 351 t
the deep s. of the porch....643 i
the shadow of a dream*.... 14 c
the shadow on the dial.....619 e
throws his s. on the floor.. 55 b
truth is—'tis her shadow...621 c
warm s. of her loveliness...584 k
where in the s. of a great... 8 l
Shadowed–sees the Infinite s.670 b

Shearers-the s. and the shorn789 h
Shears-bears the shears of*..152 g
　hold the vital shears**....206 t
　shepherd shears his flock..681 g
Sheaves-quail among the s.§. 54 o
　with the last s. return.§....544 d
Shed-for women s. and use‖..590 f
　meanest shed yield thee....304 b
　myrtle round your ruin'd..476m
　prepare to shed them now*.591 t
　rais'd to shed his blood‡....475 r
　roofs the ruined shed......244 p
　tear forgot as soon as shed.307 v
　the monarch of a shed......303 q
Sheds-found in lowly sheds**120 j
Sheen-dims thy late brilliant542 g
　their matchless sheen......223 q
Sheep-a black s. is a biting..494 d
　are white over with sheep..412 n
　ensample to his s. he gaf..188 k
　injured s. will fight its ....686 n
　like a sheep, his life.......141 a
　looking on their silly s.*...614 f
　men better than sheep or†.489 u
　mountain s. are sweeter... 21 r
　never a good sheep year.... 21 q
　preserv'd my sheep‡......,361m
　s.'s or bullock's personals..430m
　the cold to the shorn s.....510 c
　the sheep are in the fauld..560m
　to a close shorn sheep, God.507 p
　valley sheep are fatter..... 21 r
Sheet-eye along the s. has ...436m
　from the crumbling sheet..232 p
　in a never-ending sheet....514 s
　in its winding sheet.......247 o
　not in s. nor in shroud we..444 s
　sterling pounds per sheet‖.124 f
　wet s. and a flowing sea....445 b
Sheets-saw him fumble with*138 l
　spreads her s. o' daisies....539 n
Shelf-from a s. the precious*595 i
　laid upon the shelf ....257 f
Shell-and kill him in the s.*..511 t
　a rose-lipped shell that....405 k
　a smooth-lipped shell¶.....353 u
　eat chickens i' the shell*....168 q
　leaving thine outgrown s...571 n
　outward shell of sinne ....182 h
　passions oft, to hear her s.404 v
　pearly s. was in my hand...459 o
　shaved with a s. when he..457 q
　slumbers in the shell......210 u
　sonnet? 'Tis the pearly s..476 v
　take ye each a shell‡.......438 b
Shell-fish-keep your s-f. to..181 e
　s-f. just come from being..181 i
Shells-s. lie on the shore....459 l
　shells upon the sand§..... 598 t
Shelter-all that shared its s..536 b
　and shelter for thy head...304 b
　a shelter for peace... ....535m
　delicious is your s. to the.610 p
　find shelter here with me..515 b
　give no shade and no s....618 b
　love in a shower safe s....355 l
　shelter but in human kind.587 t
　shelter is in sight ....107 p
　shelter o'er thee throw.....225 g
　shelter where our spirits ..141 t
　whose arms gave s. to the*.139 u
Sheltered-in youth it s. me..609 l
　s. in a golden coating.....543 p
Sheltering-s. while it clings..236 e
Shelved-s. around us lie.....345 f
Shelves-may dash us on the.. 73 s
Shepherd-Dick, the s., blows*546 h
　every shepherd's tongue...361 t
　every s. tells his tale**.....662 s
　is the shepherd's delight..515 n
　shepherd shears his flock..681 g
　shepherd's homely curds*..112 e
　shepherd to his fold ......226 r
　star calls up the shepherd*577 d
　star that bids the s. fold**..576m
　the shepherd's warning....515 n
　tunes the shepherd's reed..362 g

Shepherdess-from s. up to... 23 p
　shepherdess of England's..284 g
　shepherdess pass'd by.....248 t
Shepherds-s. at the grange§. 94 j
　s. looking on their silly...*.614 f
　s. shun the noonday heat‡.542 p
　sung the shepherds till th'‡544 j
Sheridan-in moulding S.‖...519 d
Sheriff's-dines to-day at the.434 h
Shield-a s. against the shafts.198 q
　a strong shield is the safety800 x
　at once her spear and s.‖...590 e
　broken was her shield ....638 s
　desire to shield, and save‖.. 69 k
　His azure s. the Heavens..583 f
　like an ample shield. .....256 c
　set up his lilied shield......223 q
　shield you in all sorts of...458 j
　showing his shield.........535m
　spear, but left the shield...69 q
　that like an ample shield..571 k
Shields-Fingal, king of shields557 k
　virtue is a thousand s. 805aa
Shift-do well for such a s.*...591 s
　winds shift, s. our sails‖....667w
Shilling-guinea and seven-s.‖.655 d
　Philip and Mary on a s....389 k
　positively cost a shilling...456 c
　with the other took a s.....144 u
Shillings-drakes with s. 501cc
　rather than forty s. I had*. 67w
Shine-and then they shine...104 q
　fire and every one doth s.*.577 b
　s. by the side of every path.621 t
　shine in more substantial..306 h
　shine like a guinea and‖...655 d
　shine now thou art gone...323 f
　shine with azure, green and 60w
　s. with beauty, breathe....661 u
　singing, as they shine......556bb
　they shine on all alike‡... .193 e
　who dare shine, if not......429 y
　without his help to shine...162 u
Shined-although it be not s..621 i
Shines-beam propitious s.....624 d
　each day which s. upon you738 n
　his wit s. at the expense....653 k
　it threatens while it shines.493 o
　shines on a distant field§..380 l
　shines preserved in a tear..322 a
　substitute s. brightly as a*.534 v
　sun s. let foolish gnats*....584 j
　sun, too, s. into cesspools..583 o
　virtues where he shines....357 i
Shinest-s. fair with many a..515 p
Shineth-s. on one part or....484 b
　sun s. upon the dunghill..583 u
Shining-that was s. on him‖..356 o
Ship-a great ship asks deep..494w
　Argoan s.'s brave ornament617 p
　as in a foundering ship§....359 z
　away the good ship flies....445 b
　every day brings a ship....448 c
　every ship brings a word...448 c
　gallant ship so lustily......445 s
　good ship bear so well......267 b
　ill-fated s. that worthless..608 b
　in a ship is being in a jail...551 s
　not a s. that sails the ocean551 v
　sail on, O Ship of State§...469 c
　scuttled s. or cut a throat‡.373 k
　s. is struggling, all in vain.445 q
　speed on the ship;—but let.446 f
　swell'd with tempest's on‡.577 r
　the gallant ship; along her.446 a
　the home traveller's s. or... 68 o
　to a crazy s. all winds are..507 q
　true ship is the ship,builder551 f
Shipping-and smoke, and s.‖. 98 c
　fishes first to s. did impart.410 q
Ships-and the stately s.go on†446 c
　are as ships that divide.....464 p
　by science, sails,and oars, s.678 d
　hearts of oak are our ships. 79 k
　hurrying tides and the s....115 i
　in tall ships richly built....445 a
　launch'd a thousand ships. 35 j

like s. at sea an instant.....207 a
　like ships, they steer their..476 d'
　our ships were British oak.468 b
　s., dim discover'd, dropping552 c
　ships have been drown'd....445 h
　s. rigged out with sails of..585 k
　s. that have gone down at..551w
　ships that pass in the night§378m
　s. that sailed for sunny isles551 r
　twain have met like the s..262 n
Shipwrecked-or s-w.,kindles¶552 k
Shirt-has never a shirt...... 22 n
　pale martyr in his s. of fire.874 d
　ruffles when wanting a s... 23 f
　song of the shirt !..........484 r
　their principles than shirt.. 24 q
　when wanting a shirt ....369 a
　without a shirt...........293 g
Shiver-cling and s. to be††...544 f
　shiver when thou'rt named.284 f
　why dost thou s. and shake582 p
Shivered-s.was fair Scotland's638 s
Shivering-welcomes in the s.474 a
Shoal-many a s. marks this...445 t
Shoals-s. of visionary ghosts‡ 25 c
Shock-bulwarks who can s..522m
　give a shock of pleasure to. 87 e
　hum, the shock of men‖....566 v
　s. blind nature cannot shun198 v
　s. it gives their feelings§....516 k
　sink beneath the shock‖... 91 l
Shocked-not s. at tears‖.....590 f
　she was a good deal s.‖....590 f
Shocks-s. of passion can't....466 d
　the thousand natural s.*...140 f
Shod-shod like a mountaineer367 k
　the damsel, deftly shod....453 h
Shoe-dooty like a worn-out.††163w
　fling her old shoe after†...368 s
　for good lucke, cast an old.502 y
　holding out his shoe, asked.453 l
　last extend the s. too wide.453 b
　like the shoe in the story...702 f
　makes a great shoe........253m
　my own shoe pinches me...500 a
　shoe has power to wound..453 k
　the same s. on every foot. .509 x
　want of a nail the s. is lost.497ee
　wearer knows where the s..506 q'
Shoeing-dressing eels or s....589 f
Shoemaker-s. a good..... ...253m
　s. makes a good shoe......453 a
　shoemaker, stick to your...680 p
Shoemakers-more be called s.453 d
　shoemakers quietly stick††.285 g
Shoes-bootes and s. are torn454 a
　ere those shoes were old*..659 d
　little blue unused shoes.... 30 p
　makes shoes go barefoot....499w
　more than over s. in love*.362 v
　old s., they were easiest for 11 i
　perhaps your shoes‖........452 u
　shoes were on their feet... 20 r
　surgeon to old shoes*......453 n
　that those shoes would buy 30 p
　those little blue shoes.... . 30 p
　those s. that no little feet.. 30 p
　too short the modish shoes.453 b
　to wear out their shoes*....453 q
Shoestring-a carelesse s. in.. 23 f
Shone-being purely s. upon.. 88 b
　diminish'd lustre shone....101 i
　far off his coming shone**.. 22 c
　she s. upon the hills and...399 f
　she shone upon the lake....399 f
　s.like a meteor, streaming**628 c
　s.with the greater splendor.729 o
　soon as e're she s. straight..397 h
　while she lived she shone...201 o
Shook-and s. a dreadful**...637 u
　I've s. off old mortality....454 n
　not to be shook thyself.....327 m
　s. it with a scornful look...456 e
　shook the tree too rough...240 n
Shoon-latchets of his sandal§187 b
Shoot-neighbors shoot thee.† 43 b
　shoot folly as it flies‡.......373 t

s. my abhorr'd society*....565 q
Shuns–any one shuns evils..187aa
Shut–full that it cannot shut.379 t
  instant s.my woeful self up*592 b
  it oped and s. Ah! was he.154w
  shut against great genius..706 g
  shut of evening flowers**. 187 d
  's. that and 'twill out at*....653cc
  shut up in measureless*.....112 d
Shutter–it rattles on the s....514 s
  peeped through the s.......628 f
Shutters–close the s. fast......186 q
Shuttle–life is a shuttle*.....350m
Shy–blossom enchantingly s.249 d
  flower of sweetest smell is¶408m
  h' was very shy of using it.652 q
Shyness–offspring of shame is551 n
Sibyl–contortions of the sibyl 101 c
  this sibyl, sweet and......295w
Sick–all tempt the s. to trust.512 r
  being sick, have in some*..441 g
  devil was sick, the devil a..153 k
  fall one day extremely s...454 o
  flowers for the sick girl's..611 l
  give good advice to the s.676 d
  great danger to such as be. 599 a
  have made me sick*.......441 g
  he felt deadly sick and..... 44 j
  I am sick at heart*........ 86 y
  is to make sound men sick.512 s
  love is ever sick and yet is.360 s
  lover, sick to death*......364 q
  makes you both drunk and.162 d
  mind is sicker than the s...726 i
  not so sick, my lord*......441 d
  perhaps was sick, in love‡.. 75 q
  sick and capable of fears*..209 o
  sick alike of envy and of‡.. 11 b
  sick do not recover........725 g
  s. of prey, yet howling on..603 l
  s. of the night's debauch...369 d
  sick that surfeit with too*.168m
  sick mind cannot bear......726 k
  the earth when it is sick....635 l
  the fool that eats till he is.451 s
  thou liest in reputation s.*524 t
  tie up the knocker, say I'm‡144 v
  troubles from a sick soul..105 l
  what, is Brutus sick*......552 r
  when I was sick you gave*.441 n
Sicken–love begins to sicken* 73 g
Sicklied–s. o'er with the pale*106 q
Sickly–indispos'd and s. fit*..156m
Sickness–diet his s., for it*..311 u
  eternal sickness to the race775m
  in health, in s., thus the...348 c
  my long sickness of health*552 q
  one hour of s. or disgust...642 c
  prepares for sickness, age..593 d
  s. doth infect the very*.....156 q
  sickness broken body......133 t
  sickness seizes the body...693 a
  sorrow and s. poverty and.††16 n
Sickle–cheeks within his*... 108 t
  crown'd with the s. and the545 c
  harvest to their s. yield....423 s
  in others' corn his sickle...112 p
  s. from the lightening skies399 j
  with his sickle keen§......135 p
Sicklemen–you sunburnt s.*.302 u
Side–aspiration sees only††..483 p
  be strong upon my side*...108 r
  come thou on my side*.....474 f
  doing on the other side....132 l
  equal taken from his side..661 a
  failings leaned to virtue's..632 n
  fortune is always on the s..582 e
  gods are on the side of the.582 k
  God is always on the side..582m
  God is generally on the s...582 c
  he sat by her side and her..664 a
  neither leans on this s. nor‡388 x
  or down the glowing side‖..128 c
  o' the windy s. of the law*.438 s
  side of the last reserve.....582 a
  ten to one that side is cast..436 r
  to choose the suffering s...548 t

to side with Truth is noble††622 n
  the wrong side of thirty... 12 g
  with Atè by his s. come hot*638w
  where we sat side by side..357 y
  which side shall we stand..587m
Sides–be said on both sides.. 26 q
  every street has two sides..672 t
  laughter holding both his**383 r
  on all s. that give places††.107 k
  spur to prick the s. of my*. 13w
  weakness on both sides is..513 s
Siege–siege of Lucknow†.....214 q
  siege of tenderest courtesy.663 c
  wastes a ten years's. before362 b
  wreckful s. of battering*...602 p
Sieges–battles, s. fortunes*.. 350 h
Sieve–draws nectar in a sieve307 l
  umbrella proved a sieve....458 l
  water in a sieve*.......... 7 p
  words into a sieve..........700 t
Sigh–a moan, a sigh, a sob....401 k
  as if the sigh was that*....564 o
  a s. too deep, or a kiss too..151 d
  balmiest s. which vernal...417 p
  banks with a sigh.........532 j
  buried this s. in wrinkle*..569 x
  every sigh with songs and.391 q
  fills my bosom when I sigh.379 g
  give sigh for sigh.........242 h
  hast thou ever weigh'd a s..592 t
  he did not only s. but roar..463 d
  he gave a deep sigh........289 c
  how 'twill sigh, and moan.514 s
  monarchs seldom s. in vain663 f
  my soul has rest, sweet s...553 e
  of laughter with a sigh*....335 l
  one to smile, one to sigh...776 k
  or sigh with pity..........211 e
  reasons why we smile and.567 d
  sigh a contrite suppliant...274 t
  s. and soften out the name.409 h
  sigh for what is not........537 j
  sigh for the toothache*....432 p
  sigh to those who love me‖.524w
  s. that filters through the..404 l
  sigh that hurts by easing*.. 76 d
  sigh no more, ladies*......212 e
  some sigh for this and that.456 k
  stream with a perpetual s..148 o
  take gifts with a sigh......272 g
  that I sometimes sigh...... 89 r
  the passing tribute of a s...553 e
  the smile mocking the s.*..564 o
  th' eternal sigh‡..........293 s
  thy sighe of dewe..........231 h
  to sigh, yet feel no pain...155 n
  to sigh, yet not recede.....523 g
  'twill cost a sigh a tear ...345 n
  waft a s. from Indus to the‡588 j
  where wretched mortals s..148 b
  while Care forgets to sigh..615 c
  wind breath'd soft as.....523w
  without a sigh remember..531m
  yokes a smiling with a s.*.564 o
Sighed–for his country he s...117 q
  loved but they sighed*.....364 i
  man the hermit, sigh'd till.655 p
  often have I s. to measure‖567 s
  sigh'd and look'd, and.....553 b
  sighed but they asked*.....364 i
  sigh'd from all her caves**.136 q
  s. for the dawn and thee†..611 j
  s. to think I read a book¶..567 s
  sighed with saving sorrow.451 f
  when I beheld this I sighed372 y
Sighing–around me sighing..233 e
  cease vowing and sighing.416 p
  farewell goes out sighing*.644 i
  friends go sighing round...149 c
  music in the s. of a reed‖..404 q
  old age, begin sighing.....544 a
  s. that Nature formed‖.....519 d
  s. through all her works**.555 y
  thus forever sighing..... 36m
  sweetly mournful sighing..214 c
  wooes it with enamor'd s...647 s
Sighs–and more persuasive‡..472 t

beneath a lover's burning s.616 n
drive the boat with my s.*..592 k
ever with smiles and sighs.605 g
growing deeper in my s.... 11 e
hear his sighs though**....488 p
  her breath in sudden sighs.394 o
  her s. will make a battery*.659 g
  I can hear your sighs and..131 v
  made of sighs and tears*...363 f
  morn! she is the source of..400 c
  one's sighs and passionate.448 g
  on the Bridge of Sighs‖.... 99 a
  painful noise of sighs......100 k
  pale with her sighs........241 f
  sighs for a daughter with‡.658 j
  sighs for sables which‖....189 c
  sighs which perfect joy†...553 g
  smiles and waits and sighs.514 r
  sovereign of s. and groans*.278 f
  still breath'd in sighs‡.....409 l
  still he s., for hoards are...387 h
  temper'd with love's sighs*480m
  wanton thing is won by s.‖.662 f
  with the fume of sighs*....363 r
  yet s., deare sighs, indeede.553 f
Sight–allure the captive s....238 t
  and vanish'd from our s.*. 44 h
  a sight not so awful as that385m
  as soon as out of sight. ....503 c
  at this sight my heart*.. ..297 j
  at first sight they loved....357 j
  at whose s. all the stars**..310 n
  at whose sight like the sun.101 i
  beauty at first sight...... 34 e
  blessings of the sight...... 61 a
  chance to cheer thy sight..605 h
  charms strike the sight but‡82 q
  come in sight once in a††.. 428 x
  complies with our weak s..585 d
  could not want sight who..478 u
  despairing, my s. I may....528 c
  dull our s. producing what.666 c
  feels not at that sight, and.672 d
  for s. is woman-like and...553 l
  full, to glad the sight*.....147 u
  gladden'd my sight.... ...217 d
  half so fine a sight.......253 v
  have seene a full fayre s...553 n
  hideous sight, a naked.....297 i
  hitherto conceal'd this s.*.547 h
  it is a goodly sight to see‖..117 o
  it is an awkward sight‖....117 n
  is half so fine a sight.......129 j
  knock, or call when just in.643 t
  know by sight very well...409 t
  lose sight of their objects..327 o
  lov'd not at first sight......360 p
  mocks the slow sight.......564 v
  O loss of s. of thee I most** 61 e
  once removed from sight..508w
  one dearest sight I have.... 97 r
  orbs doth sight appear*.... 61 f
  out of s., art nursing April's391 f
  out of syght, out of mynd..503 d
  pass'd in music out of s.†..547 u
  she gleamed upon my s.¶..661 g
  sight of her I love..........238 s
  s. of means to do ill deeds*.594 f
  s. of that immortal sea¶...317 b
  sight of thee was glad¶....224 h
  s. of you is good for sore...506 g
  skipping in s. then lost‖... 98 c
  spare my aching sight......272 r
  sun goes out of sight.......624 q
  swim before my sight‡.....361 r
  tho' lost to s. to mem'ry...380 f
  tis a shameful sight........113 f
  until his failing sight‖. ... 34 c
  understood her by her s.... 25 n
  we credit most our sight...192 h
  what a sight it were........550 l
  which only pleases the s...756 c
  with keen, discriminating.553 h
  with sharpen'd sight pale‡. 22 r
  woods with thee in sight...567 r
Sighted–s. in intelligences...336 q
Sights–a mirror is of heavenly386 l

SHAKESPEARE *; MILTON **; WORDSWORTH ¶; BYRON ‖; TENNYSON †; LOWELL ††; POPE ‡; LONGFELLOW §.

s. is a death, O make me...560 n
sleep! it is a gentle thing..561 b
sleep, liest thou in smoky*563 c
sleep, little baby, sleep.... 32 m
sleep no more*..............562 m
Sleep on, Baby, on the floor560 q
s. shall neither night nor*..562 t
sleeps his last sleep...... 134 m
s. that knits up the ravell'd*562 u
sleep that no pain shall...138 a
s. that sometime shuts up*..562 v
s., the fresh dew of languid563 f
sleepe, ther Richesse, and..563 j
s. the sleep that knows not.443 v
sleep those eyes may close.184 a
s. to creep over the writer.743 j
s., we are beholden to thee.561 k
sleep will never lie*........ 72 j
sleep with it now*..........562 p
s. with smile the sweeter for560 q
solved the mystery of sleep560 k
sooner it's over the sooner.666 v
soul when man doth sleep..598 d
still let me sleep*..........204 a
still must sleep profound..554 g
streamlets s. hath crown'd.615 c
sweet restorer, balmy s.....564 e
sweet s. angel mild hover.. 30 r
sweet sleep be with us one.159 k
sweet sleep with soft down. 30 r
take a pleasant sleep.......240 a
ten poor men sleep in peace533 k
the dewy-feathered sleep**562 b
the forest depths, that s. .. 47 l
the innocent sleep*.........562 m
the lonely gentle Sleep.....561 n
the long s. of death closes..761 o
the night is without sleep..579 t
then to go to sleep.........296 s
the poppy hangs in sleep†..412 v
the short sleep of life our..761 o
the solemn mystery of s...561 d
the timely dew of sleep**..562 a
things lie "down to sleep"395 j
things within its bosom s.§.583 b
thinking of taking a long s..761 q
third of life is pass'd in s.║.132 l
this sleep is sound indeed*.562 w
till it cry sleep to death*...562 g
to die:—to sleep: no more*..140 j
to fan me while I sleep.....559 e
to fill thy sleep............303 p
to give their readers sleep‡.480 k
to s., perchance to dream*.563 b
to weep, to sleep, and weep349 w
visit her, gentle Sleep! with561 l
watch, while some must s.*151 t
weary world to s. are gane.560 m
western world believe and‡.537 c
we wake, and when we s.**575 c
when to soft Sleep we give.159 j
while sluggards sleep......666 p
who first invented sleep....562 e
wrapt in a half sleep.......159 r
yet never sleep the sun up..563 p
yet 'twill only be a sleep...141 c
Sleepers—the s. of the house*.573 f
Sleepest—s. soft in the song of459 l
thou s., Brutus, and yet....789 f
thou sleep'st so sound*....562 i
Sleepeth—how he s.! having..560 o
Sleeping-babe was s. on her.565 c
before a sleeping giant*....107 a
by sleeping, what it is to...560 n
sleeping but never dead††..418 h
sleeping in our crowns.....238 m
s. in the blood, a whoreson*156 p
sleeping in the dust........260 v
sleeping near the withered.560 o
sleeping when she died.....135 e
they love while sleeping║..329 l
where she lies sleeping....133 i
Sleepless—love laid his s. head366 a
s. soul that perished in¶...481 h
s. themselves to give their‡480 k
Sleeps—and sleeps again*....209 l
creation sleeps. 'Tis as the.564 d

flourish when he s. in dust.381 u
he sleeps by day more than*562 j
he smiles and s., sleep on║.. 30 s
Homer, their prince, sleeps689 u
it sleeps, and the ice and...613 j
moonlight sleeps upon this*407 i
she sleeps; her breathings†562 l
she sleeps! my lady sleeps§561 o
she s., nor dreams, but†....563 l
she sleeps; on either hand†.563 l
s., feels not the toothache*.562 k
sleeps on brambles till he..163 f
sleeps on his own heart¶...194 i
s. sound till the bell brings 135 l
till tired, he s., and life's‡.137 r
wisdom wake, suspicion*.651 e
Sleepy-head—little Indian s-h. 90 u
Sleet—and soaking sleet.....453 b
sleet or come snow........212 i
the whistling s. and snow§.552 g
through sleet and snow ...547 a
when showers of driving.. 55 g
Sleeve—a sleeve? 'tis like a*..455 d
fasten on this s. of thine*..377 a
had a goose in his sleeve...505 f
the ravell'd sleave of care*562 u
wear my heart upon my**.556 x
Slender—hang on s. strings...671 b
Slept—and slept in peace*....139 m
catch his last smile e'er he.585 p
dying when she slept.......135 e
he slept an iron sleep. .....443 f
side by side, they slept..... 54 b
slept in their shades........413 g
s. out-doors when nights... 20 g
still have slept together*...262 l
touched him, and he slept† 141 n
'twas winter,—and I slept..183 r
while their companions s.§.339 g
Slid—his hand slid smoothly..202 g
Slide—ambition loves to slide. 13 a
goodness loves to slide.....286 v
let the world slide.........501 c
let the world slide.........318 h
who s. along the grassy....143 g
Slight—pink I would not s... 238 g
s. means are great affairs..702 d
Slighting—s. quite abash'd**. 35 o
Slights—slights the other.....353 c
Slime—even from out thy s.║.459 g
seedsman upon the slime*.531 j
Slimy—cherished in s. waters.114 h
Slings—s. and arrows of*... ...159 f
Slip—feet s. than the tongue.496 i
fool who lets s. a bird in..498 gg
Judas had given them the..144 n
let slip the dogs of war*...638 w
let the world slip*..........501 d
some day he gives us the s.601 v
Slipper—a mitten, or a slipper775 r
compose at once a s. and║..452 u
the well-worn slipper feels. 74 s
Slippers—a pair of s., sir .... 666 c
slippers on your head......180 l
Slippery-scaly, s., wet, swift213 i
slippery nature of tender . 753 p
stands upon a s. place*.....495 n
Slips—from others' slips.....705 p
slips of yew silver'd in*....619 a
Slipt—would have s. like him*151 v
Slit—forked stick with a slit... 18 e
Sloe—holly and the purple sloe618 d
the white-blossomed sloe..618 c
Slope—low and sunny slope...230 q
s. thro' darkness up to†....268 l
the dappled slope.........294 k
the downward s. of years..592 m
Slopes—green s. paraded.....228 d
over the cold gray slopes...648 c
resignation gently s. the...525 a
s. are drowned in song ....236 b
Sloth—become immortal by s.721 b
delicious poison of sloth....715 i
destructive siren, sloth....715 e
evils of sensual sloth║.....626 a
excuse our sloth under the 715 h
prosperity engenders s.....503 o

resty s. finds the down*....526 o
sloth views the towers......202 v
s. wastes the sluggish.....715 g
Slouch-s. becomes a walk....443 a
Slough—casted s. and fresh*..386 f
slough was Despond..... 149 d
Slow-aged men, full loth... 11 g
as tardy as too slow*.......364 s
complains that we are slow 24 r
from the s. one counsel....651 i
melancholy, slow..........582 z
old age is slow in both.....671 p
requires slow pace at first*.582 i
s. of growth, but are rapid.682 n
slow this old moon wanes*.398 s
slow to believe what if.....679 k
they're set, too fast or s....436 r
to be slow in words is a*...660 a
"too forward as too slow" 493 p
wisely and slow*...........294 v
Slower—into a s. method*.... 27 s
Slowly—how s. the hours pass792 a
spring comes s. up this....539 o
Slug—on the slug and snail§... 44 k
Sluggard—'tis the voice of the564 a
Sluggardized—dully s. at*....313 n
Sluggards—while s. sleep......666 p
Slugs—slugs leave their lair.666 m
Slumber—a little more s......564 a
but if the pilot slumber.... 73 s
darkness of slumber and§..130 m
does not again slumber....596 f
down to your shady s......367 k
e'er s.'s chain has bound...380 n
honey-heavy dew of s.*...562 i
I must slumber again......564 a
in dreamless s. bound.....460 l
keep'st the ports of s.*....562 p
lie still and slumber....... 32 o
night-flies to thy slumber*.563 c
nights in careless s. spent.111 c
patient in a senseless s....439 r
roll in trance or s., round..160 k
sinking to s., the bright....585 p
slumberre sweete its eye...231 h
soothing slumber seven....600 s
tideless expansion of s....394 f
wert not sent for slumber║.415 i
world from pagan slumber.521 m
Slumberer-s's window pane..400 d
Slumberers—nation's s......146 w
Slumberest-s. at a foeman's. 443 e
Slumbering—s. in the........792 i
slumbering on the earth...473 g
s. the festal hours.........522 q
'tis might half s. on.......477 f
wakens the s. ages.........319 f
Slumbers—all our s. soft and§450 q
and slumbers light.........204 q
balmy s. wak'd with*......444 m
dreams, and s. light.......417 d
in dewy slumbers bound. ..229 h
sweet are the s. of the.....631 u
watch! while in s. light§...561 o
work—and pure s. shall....339 j
Slumb'rous—soft s. weight**.562 a
Sly—tough and devilish sly... 78 w
Smack—such a clamorous s.*.335 s
Small—and small dishearten..127 f
battalions against the......582 c
beginnings of all things....679 b
compare great things with.684 i
devoured the small........565 r
each thing both in s. and...150 s
house, though thou art s...303 t
in life's small things be††..525 i
many a s. maketh a grate..501 ff
not seen the small.........757 c
one so s. who knowing†....420 k
reach the small ....283 c
s. at first through fear....740 r
s. have always suffered....767 r
s. have continual plodders*580 r
small in number, but .....686 p
s. service is true service¶..549 q
succeed in small things§... 13 f
the great, the small......133 v

SHAKESPEARE *; MILTON **; WORDSWORTH ¶; BYRON ║; TENNYSON †; LOWELL ††; POPE ‡; LONGFELLOW §.

things, both great and s.....487 *p*
think so small a thing...... 32 *q*
trifle, though it s. appears .619 *o*
Smallest–say the s. part......480 *s*
Small-pox–charm'd the s-p.‡.129 *a*
Smart–for every bitter smart 238 *i*
  Gineral C is a dreffle s.††...107 *k*
  men only feel the s., but‡..630 *o*
  some of us will s. for it*.....512 *n*
  the girls that are so smart..655 *q*
Smarting–s. in ling'ring*.....512 *o*
Smeared–with spittle vilely s. 92 *i*
Smell–after by the smell.....247 *m*
  chill the wintry smell.....141 *j*
  faint, sweet smell of that...232 *o*
  flower of sweetest smell¶..221 *d*
  hates the smell of roses....241 *p*
  he s. fire, whose gown.....508 *c*
  I smell a device*..........500 *w*
  lilies that fester s. far*....643 *o*
  quoth Hudibras, I s. a rat..143 *t*
  smell a rat..................504 *a*
  smell a rose through a. ...240 *o*
  s. my remnant out ......347 *u*
  s. of bread and butter¶..... 89 *e*
  smell so sweetly always....175 *h*
  s. sweet and blossom in the 5 *w*
  s. to a turf of fresh earth ..401 *l*
  s. too much of that writer .551 *b*
  taste the smell of dairy ... 244 *n*
  two should smell it.........240 *o*
  would smell as sweet*......409 *s*
  with whose sweet smell*...243 *h*
  yeeldeth no smell..........225 *i*
Smells–breath s. wooingly*.. 50 *h*
  enemy always s. sweet.....764 *m*
  flower that s. of honey......233 *c*
  fragrance s. to heaven. ....524 *x*
  often smells of wine.......176 *i*
  smells of balm.............254 *l*
  that Acerra smells.........174 *m*
  truth only s. sweet forever. 622 *d*
Smelt–for this, being smelt*.223 *g*
  it smelt so faint .... 232 *p*
  it smelt so sweet..........232 *p*
  Papilus smelt it...........178 *b*
  yet s. roast meat, beheld¶..481 *o*
Smile–and the serious smile‡.649 *j*
  and to smile in pain.......476 *b*
  are lovlier than her smile..590 *k*
  a s. that glow'd celestial** .564 *k*
  a smile to those who hate¶.524 *w*
  a smile within his eyelids. . 62 *e*
  a tender s., our sorrows'..564 *t*
  because it makes us s.¶.....537 *f*
  betwixt a smile and tear*..370 *i*
  blush and gently smile.....218 *a*
  brightly smile and sweetly..255 *e*
  brightness of their smile...216 *l*
  but a smile in her eye......524 *a*
  but owned that s., if oft¶...564 *f*
  can smile at Fate..........205 *s*
  catch his last s. e'er he....585 *p*
  could be moved to s. at*...155 *r*
  doctor's brow should s......440 *l*
  feel in every s. a chain.....564 *s*
  follow'd perhaps by a s....590 *m*
  Heaven is your s. but your.32 *m*
  he saw me smile.......... 57 *e*
  lives but in her smile, and.645 *t*
  look backward with a s.....466 *s*
  makes archangels smile.....542 *k*
  make the learned smile‡....581 *j*
  meet again, we'll s. indeed*464 *w*
  men smile no more.........527 *c*
  mov'd to s. at any thing*...564 *q*
  no s. till thou appearest....459 *s*
  one may smile, and smile*..564 *p*
  one fair scene or kindly s..379 *m*
  one to smile, one to sigh....776 *k*
  one universal s. it seemed..775 *i*
  one vast substantial smile..564 *h*
  reasons why we s. and sigh.567 *d*
  share the good man's smile. 7 *v*
  Shropshire do merrily s..... 18 *e*
  sigh in wrinkle of a smile*..569 *x*
  sleep with s. the sweeter...560 *q*

smile, and be a villain*.....312 *t*
s., and murder whiles I....145 *l*
smile and tears were like*..190 *x*
smile and whisper this......131 *v*
s. at the claims of long†....418 *o*
smile of April's face........250 *p*
s. of her I love is like the...564 *i*
s. of the blue firmament....117 *g*
smile she or lour**.........376 *c*
s., sweet baby, smile for you 32 *m*
s. the Heavens upon this*.. 5 *r*
smile–though I shall not...255 *e*
smile to see me pass.......147 *x*
s. upon his fingers' ends*...138 *l*
smile we would aspire to*..535 *b*
some seem to smile.........216 *e*
stir beneath his smile.......237 *d*
summer news, s. to't*......414 *w*
teeth in way of smile*..... 84 *d*
the infant's waking smile.. 31 *g*
the s. mocking the sigh*...564 *o*
the smile of God is here.....515 *l*
they s. so when one's right¶.455 *f*
thou shouldst s. no more...142 *d*
three-cornered s. of bliss...564 *j*
vain tribute of a smile.... 215 *g*
we smile, perforce, when¶..421 *p*
when one's wrong they s.¶..455 *f*
when you gave her a smile.379 *s*
who lived upon a smile....313 *d*
why do they not smile......217 *c*
witching s. of May to grace.395 *h*
with a s. on her lips, and a.564 *n*
with her faint smile........222 *o*
without the s. from partial.370 *k*
woman's s. and girlhood's..547 *a*
Smiled–and s. in her face... 31 *m*
  Cervantes smiled Spain's¶..537 *m*
  hope enchanted smiled.....307 *m*
  of darkness till it smiled**. 16 *r*
  on my birth have smiled... 93 *v*
  on one she s., and he was..654 *p*
  sigh'd–till woman smiled..566 *l*
  smiled like yon knot.......225 *k*
  the girl smiled before.....595 *a*
  'twas spring, I smiled......183 *r*
  until she smiled on me..... 34 *f*
Smiles–and wreathed smiles**383 *r*
  betraying s., feign'd tears..658 *b*
  children we of smiles and.. 76 *q*
  eternal s. his emptiness‡....564 *m*
  ever with smiles and sighs.605 *g*
  fair but faithless s. each....120 *t*
  father's welcome smiles....303 *o*
  flower that smiles to-day...241 *n*
  for smiles from reason**...564 *l*
  grace, a few sad smiles.... 74 *a*
  grey-ey'd morn s. on the*..401 *b*
  he s., and sleeps !–sleep on. 30 *s*
  joys and secret smiles little. 30 *q*
  merchandise and s. are sold 70 *q*
  only smiles on us...........329 *o*
  read the good with smiles..351 *t*
  reckon on from s. to smiles.628 *c*
  seldom he s. and smiles in*.155 *r*
  she s. elsewhere–we make.654 *p*
  soft s. by human-kindness¶ 196 *k*
  s. and roses are blending...315 *o*
  smiles and tones more dear.381 *y*
  smiles and waits and sighs.514 *r*
  s. at my best meanings†....318 *d*
  smiles at the drawn dagger.118 *m*
  smiles from reason flow*...564 *l*
  smiles in such a sort*.......564 *q*
  s. in yeer face while it picks.437 *q*
  smiles of joy, the tears......623 *b*
  smiles of other maidens are.564 *q*
  s. on her slumbering child.. 31 *b*
  s. on the fields until they§..585 *l*
  s. sae sweetly on her knee..379 *o*
  smiles that are halos.......'89 *h*
  smiles that make wrinkles.387 *o*
  s. that seem akin to tears...408 *i*
  smiles the clouds away¶....492 *v*
  smiles with pleasant light..708 *b*
  than others in their smiles.591 *f*
  the robb'd that smiles*.....595 *n*

the s. and frowns of fate...631 *x*
the smiles, the tears........673 *b*
the smiles of love adorn...370 *e*
thy sweet s. we ever seek...605 *p*
welcome ever smiles*......644 *t*
with gentle voice and s.....656 *v*
with sunny smiles between.349 *w*
wreath your crisped smiles.459 *a*
worn matron s. where the..595 *a*
year s. as it draws near its. 394 *k*
Smile-smoothing–s.-s., heart..589 *w*
Smilest–thou s. and art still..549 *u*
  will think thou smilest*....139 *c*
Smilets–s. that play'd on her.193 *y*
Smiling–by your s. you seem*372 *r*
  caught from man from.....126 *o*
  fair pleasure's s. train‡....386 *b*
  he hides a smiling face.....509 *ii*
  smiling at grief*...........467 *w*
  s. at the sale of truth......307 *a*
  still smiling though the....360 *m*
  we cannot help smiling at..387 *o*
  with a smiling cheek*.....145 *b*
  with smiling plenty and*...268 *g*
  yokes a smiling with a sigh*564 *o*
Smily-kin' o' s. round the††..590 *w*
Smit–smit with exceeding†...570 *p*
Smith–I saw a s. stand with*.430 *k*
  s. and his penny both are..506 *i*
  the payneful smith, with...430 *l*
  the smith a mighty man§..430 *h*
  the s. his iron measures§...430 *f*
Smithfield–he went towards.374 *c*
Smiths–grim smiths ranking.430 *e*
  taught smiths who before..430 *d*
Smithy–village s. stands§....430 *h*
Smitten–are we now smitten.205 *o*
Smoke–above s. and stir of**.668 *u*
  cease to admire the smoke..675 *k*
  fill him full of s. and embers456 *l*
  give weight to smoke.......747 *g*
  glimpses through the s... 268 *p*
  gossip is a sort of smoke...280 *w*
  held out in the smoke......216 *j*
  he who doth not s. hath....457 *e*
  I knew by the smoke that so 470 *t*
  love is a smoke rais'd with*.363 *r*
  no great s. arise, but there.505 *bb*
  smoke a cigar through a...456 *d*
  s. the monstrous rubbish..456 *c*
  sweet smoke of rhetoric*...340 *c*
  the s. of hell–that monster.463 *i*
  the s. out at the chimney*.653 *cc*
Smoked-puddings s. upon‡...167 *q*
Smoker–a s. and a brother...456 *b*
Smokes–the man who smokes 457 *f*
Smoking–cigar I am s........456 *c*
Smoky–worse than a s. house* 69 *d*
Smooth–how pure, how s....532 *k*
  love never did run smooth*. 362 *o*
  s. as those that mutually...120 *t*
  s. runs the water where*...608 *p*
  s. speeches of the wicked...691 *f*
  so smooth he daub'd*... .313 *a*
Smoothest–streame runneth..509 *ff*
  when they are smoothest...754 *b*
Smoothing–s. the raven**... 16 *r*
Snaffle–with a s. you may*...645 *m*
Snail–creeping like snail*....580 *o*
  like s., should keep within.644 *z*
  like snail, with silver track 644 *z*
  on the slug and snail§..... 44 *k*
  whiting to a snail.........213 *f*
Snails–like snails did creep...253 *o*
Snake–bright skin yearly like¶ 74 *f*
  earth doth like a s. renew..669 *l*
  glistered the dire snake**..257 *s*
  if slander be a snake.......558 *m*
  like a wounded s., drags‡..477 *p*
  scotch'd the s., not killed*.129 *u*
  s. is lurking in the grass...689 *a*
Snakes–ere the s. her sweet..144 *w*
Snap–which our artists call s. 18 *e*
Snapper-up–of unconsidered*619 *r*
Snare–careless of the snare†..270 *c*
  delusion, a mockery, and a.494 *p*
  springe to snare them all...114 *e*

Shakespeare *; **Milton** **; **Wordsworth** ¶; **Byron** ‖; **Tennyson** †; **Lowell** ††; **Pope** ‡; **Longfellow** §.

therewith a youth to snare.318 t
Snares–life hath snares§.....348 l
  spreading vice's snares.....630 k
  s. of death surround us....136 d
Snaring–the ord'nary s. .... 18 e
Snarleth–s. in the gentle eyes*639 k
Snatch–snatch a fearful joy..329 q
  we must snatch, not take‡.337 t
Snatched–all at once ; then s. 74 o
  I am snatched to a far .....118 i
Sneaking–it is s. off:—I feel it 122 l
Sneer–and wither'd to a s.¶...564 f
  creed with a solemn sneer‖.157 q
  devil in his sneer‖ ....109 g
  s. as they like about eating 389 n
  teach the rest to sneer‡....537 r
  though Witlings sneer and. 13 d
  we sneer in health‖ ....439 u
  who can refute a sneer......509 d
  yesterday's sneer and......668 p
Sneering–without s., teach‡..537 r
Sneers–escaped his public s.‖.421 p
Snore–can s. upon the flint*..526 o
Snored–he snored like a pig..462 a
Snores–s. out the watch of*..562 p
  the heavy ploughman s.*..417 l
Snoring–heard the cabin s....446 e
  was s. serenely near the....463 p
Snorting–s. foam'd, and...... 20 p
Snow–a little s. tumbled*....494dd
  and there a patch of snow..539 q
  arrives the s., and, driving.564w
  as pure as snow *........... 71 n
  as snow in harvest *........ 84 f
  betwixt the tufts of snow..110 h
  bloodless lay the untrodden530 o
  chaste as unsunn'd snow*.. 88 d
  cold as the snow...........330 r
  comes the soft and silent s.564 u
  drift the fields with snow§.277 l
  ere sunset all is snow††.....539 f
  from his wide wings of s....546 b
  frost from purest snow*.... 88 e
  glazed the s. and clothed...390 o
  harvests nod beneath the‡..396 h
  just covered with lightest§.612 k
  kindle fire with snow*......362 t
  morning's s. is gone by....395 j
  O excellent snow ....177 h
  peaks of perpetual snow...322 n
  rosebuds fill'd with snow..432 l
  shook his beard of snow....546 d
  singer with the crown of††.480 a
  skin of hers than snow*.... 36 x
  sleet or come snow........212 i
  slow descends the snow§...565 b
  snow in its purity..........223 b
  snow in minutes melts.....217 r
  snow lay in many a place..226 q
  speck is seen on snow...... 34 o
  spotless ermine of the s.§...532 h
  than whiteness to snow, or.101 t
  the new snow melts........546 p
  the snow hath retreated¶. 391 m
  the s. is falling–all around545 p
  the whistling sleet and s.§..552 g
  through sleet and snow ....547 a
  tinged its braided snow ....100 h
  waiting for the winter's s...545 e
  whiter than the driven snow24 j
  whiter than new snow*..... 88 h
  winter's drizzle snow*..... 12 b
  wish a snow in May's*...... 95 d
  with a diadem of snow‖....402 o
  yon piles of snow..........274 b
Snow-drift–last s-d. melts....222 e
Snow-drifts–under the s-d....546m
Snow-drop–behold the s-d....245 h
  chaste Snow-drop¶.........245 j
  simple snow-drop..........245 f
  the s-d. ere she comes ....540 h
  throws out the s-d. and....541 k
Snow-drops–frozen s-d. feel..540 q
  snow-drops drooping early.219 q
  s-d. that plead for pardon.. 76 n
Snow-flake–s-f. white and....247 o
Snow-flakes–s-f. fall upon the482 t

Snowhid–summer mind s.††.. 81 k
Snows–as through the........565 c
  bloom not in the snows.....237 b
  echoes be choked with s.... 97 o
  leavings of the snows......541 d
  prayer for the snows. ......610 g
  silent under other snows‡..286 e
  snows and white as they¶..245 i
  the snows of yester year...782 n
  through freezing s., and....453 b
Showyard–dead beside the s..135 i
Snuff–a charge of s. the wily‡457 j
  only took snuff.............109 j
  rather than live in snuff....119 h
  s. mundungus to his nose..456 e
  snuff that will abate it*....280 q
Snuff-box–a snuff-box gilt ...254 n
  fill his snuff-box........... 22 n
  of amber s-b. justly vain‡..457 k
Snuffed–be s. out by an‖.....385 h
Snuffing–s. with a wrythed..205 b
Snug–s. as a bug in a rug.....504 c
  snug little island...........327 g
Snugness–little wren's in s.¶. 59 p
Soaks–it s. the passer's feet..514 s
Soap-hands with invisible s..314w
Soap-boiler–heads like a s-b's.790 o
Soar–alike unfit to sink or s.‖370 f
  and men to soar†.... ......131 o
  rolling clouds to soar‖.....205 u
  soar not too high to fall... 651 b
  than when we soar¶........651 x
  though not to soar. ....315 b
  wise who s, but never roam¶ 50 a
  wont to soar so high ....207 s
Soared–low as high he s.**.... 13 j
Soars–shall he who s., inspir'd846 z
  that yon s.on golden wing**109 a
Sob–a sob, a storm, a strife ..401 k
  dawn, merely a sob of light624 p
Sobs–April s. while these are.392 d
Sober–half as s. as a judge...498 u
  more s. far than all sobriety592 x
  nothing in Nature's sober..162 f
  second and sober thoughts.596 u
  sober brow will bless it*... 145 h
  tavern ne'er goes s. home..180 n
  that will to bed go sober...593 a
  walk sober off, before a‡...349 j
Soberest–was the s. man .....180 n
Sobers–drinking largely s. us‡342 i
Sobriety–sober far than all s.592 x
Sociability–rarest virtue of s. 71 r
Sociable–long lived, and s. and 54 a
  to one not sociable*........565 o
Social–a s. crowd in solitude.567 r
  capacity in social life.......260 l
  for every s. wrong there....565 g
  man's s. happiness all rests660 i
  path of social life...........143 q
  social friend, I love thee. ..457m
  the ideal s. state is not that642 q
Society–author and founder..620 n
  aversation toward society..565 d
  being lifted into high s.‖....621 j
  below the rest of the s......185 d
  brook! whose s. the poet¶.. 71 f
  great s. alone on earth¶....565 x
  half the gossip of society...516 a
  homage of society to some.579 t
  if sorrow can admit s.*.....569w
  in proportion as society.... 66 a
  in solitude, or in society §...580 d
  make society the sweeter*.565 g
  no arts, no letters, no s. .. 347w
  not an ornament to society.565 j
  obey the law of society.....565 t
  prejudicial to society.......123m
  reverence to God, to society 99 e
  shunn'd my abhorr'd s.* ...565 y
  standing policy of civil s....332 f
  s. as is quiet, wise, and....567 o
  s. became my glittering¶...565w
  society extend‡.............390 b
  s. having ordained certain..565 t
  s. in the deepest solitude...566 v
  s. is divided into two classes789 h

s. is like a large piece of ...565 k
s. is no comfort to one*.....565 o
s. is now one polished ‖..... 68 s
society is the union of men789 g
s. is wholesome for the††...567 e
s. therefore is as ancient as.565 u
s. where none intrudes‖ ...475 f
solder of society.............263m
solitude sometimes is best**565m
sometimes flees from s. .... 789 i
the perpetuation of s. itself 15 h
the s. of women is the .....796 g
the vanille of society.......565 s
the very mudsills of society 559 j
unfriendly to s.'s chief joys456 g
what society can sort**.....184 r
youth holds no s. with grief 672 h
Sock-Jonson's learned s. be**550 p
Socrates–chance with S. for.. 93 h
  see one promontory (said S.)410 k
  S., whom, well inspir'd** ..651 d
  writers charge S. with.....738 q
Sod–as snow-flakes fall upon.482 t
  benediction o'er their sod..618m
  better rot beneath the s.††.608 g
  feel the grassy sod 229m
  idols tumble to the sod.....490 b
  slide along the grassy sod..143 g
  the sod scarce heaved......220 f
  under the sod and the dew.636 p
Soda-water–sermons and s-w.‖648 k
Sofa–luxury the accomplish'd431 b
  s. 'twas half a sin to sit‖...368 u
  wheel the sofa round...... 186 q
Soft–and soft as young......661 h
  be soft as sinews of the*...489 g
  own the s. impeachment...103 y
  soft as a kiss...............584 q
  s. as her clime, and sunny‖.655 i
  soft as silk remains.........119 a
  s. ,as some song divine,‡... 578 o
  s. as the memory of buried‖655 n
  s. is the strain when zephyr‡674 v
  s. o'er the shrouds aërial‡..674w
  s. to the weak and noble...345 h
  where the virgins are s. as‖370 j
Soften–sigh and s. out the....409 h
Softened–then marble, s.into‡452 p
Softens–even s. brutes and...367 d
Soft-eyed–from the soft-eyed‡477 q
Soft-heartedness-s-h., in††.. :641 t
Softness–for s. she and sweet**82 d
  s. in the upper story††......641 t
  softness like atmosphere of625 c
Soil–blame the culture, not‡.424 j
  but every climate, every s.§551 v
  cultured soil and genial....244 o
  free soil, free men..........259 d
  grows on mortal soil**.....202 c
  He who owns the soil.......676 s
  if that soil grow sterile ....367 a
  nor soil it much............233 g
  paint the laughing soil.....540 c
  s. out of which such men‡††.280 i
  soil where first they trod...258m
  s. whose air is deemed too..559 n
  suck the soil's fertility*.....643 l
  that soil may best deserve**642 q
  the soil the virtues like‡....633 a
  the s. where first they trod.670 f
  they dig up the soil, and let619m
  where soil is, men grow....371 j
  within the common soil....396 o
Soiled–s.with all ignoble use‡271 r
  truth is as impossible to**.622 v
  wash his soiled linen in.....788 c
Soils–bad conduct s. the finest695 h
Sol–Sol in joy is seen to leave.530 j
Solace–been their mutual s.. 47 e
  find some solace for it ...730 i
  merry meetings to solace..383 o
  sweet solace of labors.....719 s
Sold–all are to be sold if‖.... 70 o
  all virtue now is sold.......389 u
  merely sold you what was.176 h
  not have sold her for it*....363 j
  pleasing ware is half sold..503 j

were never to be sold‡.... .279 a
your hearts have sold.....293 s
Solder-point-blank would s..439 s
    solder of society.......263 m
Soldereth-breaker Death that375 s
Soldier-a braver s. never*....444 b
    ask the brave s., who fights158 f
    a soldier, and afear'd*......444 d
    back to a successful s.....444 a
    Ben Battle was a s. bold....443 i
    driveth o'er a s.'s neck*....161 b
    every lover is a soldier....723 d
    God's soldier be he*.......444 f
    have been a soldier*......121 v
    I am a soldier and unapt to*444 h
    if soldier, chase brave......437 l
    I said an elder soldier,not*..444 i
    king was a successful s.....787 i
    let no soldier fly*..........639 w
    let the s. be abroad if he...170 f
    money is a good soldier, sir*390 f
    O that a soldier so glorious.608 a
    relish him more in the s.*..444 o
    roused up the s. ere the‖...636 a
    sex is ever to a soldier‡....443 h
    s. a mere recreant prove*..444 j
    soldier among sovereigns..443 o
    s. arm'd with resolution...662 k
    s. fit to stand by Cæsar*...444 g
    s., full of strange oaths*....444 k
    s. in full military array....170 f
    soldier is flat blasphemy*.. 60 i
    soldier, rest! thy warfare..443 r
    s.'s honour was compos'd...201 h
    soldier's last tattoo......272 w
    soldier wake, thy war-horse443 e
    soldier without ambition... 12 o
    the broken soldier, kindly..443 d
    'tis the soldier's life*......444 m
    vouchsafe to teach a s.*....663 j
Soldiers-amidst an army of s.796 o
    brave s. triumph in war...675 n
    brave Spanish soldiers brag484 b
    miserly s. are like monsters442 v
    old soldiers, are surest...... 12 k
    sleep, s.! still in honoured..444 p
    soldiers armed in proof*....549 r
    s. armed in their stings*...322 b
    s. out of the highlands of.. 8 k
    ye living soldiers of the....134 d
Sole-jack-boot with double s.453 c
    now shape the sole..........454 b
    to the sole of our foot......498 a
Soles-a mender of bad soles*.453 p
    let firm, well hammer'd s..453 b
    pegging on soles as he sang453 e
Solemn-heard s. o'er the.....578 f
    the s. decorations all.......459 c
Solemnity-oaks with s. shook616 c
Solemnized-s. with pomp and302 n
Solicit-s. for it straight*......489 j
Solicitor-best-moving fair s.*.438 g
Solid-nothing more s. to say.581 k
    s. pudding against empty‡.486 s
    to the s. ground of nature¶ 413 o
Solidity-give the work lasting667 g
Soliloquy-Iago's s.—the.....402 j
Solitary-herself the s. scion‖.566 h
    life of man s., poor, nasty. 347 w
    rare are solitary woes.....388 t
    solitary side of our nature.518 n
    solitary, who is not alone..566 x
    wander'd in the s. shade‡...658 l
Solitude-a social crowd in s..567 r
    bird in the solitude singing‖587 o
    enforcing his own solitude. 41 i
    gives himself up to solitude789 j
    how passing sweet is s.....566 p
    I love tranquil solitude.....567 o
    in solitude, or in society§..580 d
    in s., when we are least‖.....566 i
    is the bliss of solitude¶... 62 c
    makes a s. and calls it peace‖470 d
    man doth speak in solitude566 b
    men perceive what s. is.....566 a
    midst of a vast s., take his.267 n
    no such thing as solitude...566 c

sacred s.! divine retreat...567 u
    society in the deepest s.....566 v
    solitude! if I must with thee567 c
    s. is as needful to the††.....567 e
    s.is the nurse of enthusiasm566 u
    s. of passing his own door‖.566 f
    s. sometimes is best**......565 m
    solitude, they call it peace.731 j
    s., where are the charms...566 s
    sorrow preys upon its s.‖..568 w
    talent is nurtured in s......758 i
    the dismaying solitude.....268 o
    think it solitude to be alone567 t
    this sacred shade and s....567 v
    this, this is solitude‖......566 j
    'tis s. should teach us how‖566 k
    to sweet retired solitude*.567 g
    whosoever is delighted in s.567 k
    wrapped in the solitude of. 82 o
Solomon-S.,he lived at ease***173 a
    thou wert not, Solomon....234 h
Solon-Athenian Solon, this...650 p
Solution-solution sweet......218 m
Solve-solve 'em in a trice..... 2 b
Solved-s.the mystery of sleep560 k
Somber-the s. human troop..656 v
Sombred-moon looks s...... 47 l
Some-some things are good..684 f
Somebody-meet my ain dear.366 c
    somebody is with you now.663 b
Something-if thou art s.......588 l
    something given that way..504 f
    s. must be done for May...446 p
    steals trash; tis s., nothing* 83 l
    that something still‡.......293 s
    'tis something, nothing*....595 r
    when health is lost s.......354 n
Somewhat-s. which we name.275 z
Somewhere-always morn s..§102 f
    dream that s. there......... 91 c
    s. or other there must.....588 k
Son-and keep his only son....409 f
    beheld the duteous son, the172 e
    every one is the son of.... 78 g
    execrable s.! so to aspire**559 p
    from the sire the son shall..638 s
    hear My Son in heaven††... 86 p
    my Arthur, my fair son*... 90 o
    I her frail s., amongst my*.412 f
    in the person of his Son....521 n
    is England's greatest son†..444 q
    made his eldest s., one day.534 d
    me, that never had a son*...109 q
    my s. has not fallen without443 n
    ne'er entail'd from son to s.341 y
    rich man's son inherits††...642 n
    sit down, every mother's*..423 b
    son of heav'n and earth**..420 g
    Son of Heaven's eternal**.. 94 l
    son of his own works.......797 h
    son of the desert, e'en the..543 h
    s. of the old moon-mount...531 h
    that son, who on the quiet** 1 h
    the son most dear‡.........183 o
    unfeather'd two-legged ... 320 d
    when her son was lost.....358 h
Sons-amidst the s. of reason.418 q
    amongst the s. of men how.332 h
    and friendless s. of men††..588 g
    but God's sons are things..664 x
    desks Apollo's sons repair..408 a
    earth's degenerate sons‡...641 s
    few s. attain the praise of‡. 15 j
    forth the sons of Belial**..416 i
    had I a dozen sons—each*..469 l
    his sons, the fairest**...... 81 v
    image of himself in his sons761 r
    many sons as I have hairs*.444 f
    our wiser sons, no doubt‡..673 c
    sons of Columbia be slaves.559 r
    s. of earth! attempt ye still‡ 13 q
    sons of wrong and strife...594 o
    s. with purple death expire‡638 j
    s. to fetters are consign'd‖.491 t
    strong are her sons‡.......579 h
    things are the s. of heaven.664 t
Song-Alexandrine ends the‡.477 p

all my song shall be........487 c
    all this for a song..........495 g
    and her s. is the sweetest .. 55 h
    and the vision of song .. 338 i
    and will the faults of song.169 f
    Arcadians skilled in song..728 n
    a slipper and a song‖.......452 u
    a s. to the oak, the brave..615 n
    Atlas we read in ancient s..579 o
    beautiful only blooms in s..769 c
    bore the burden of the s....557 e
    burden of the song........227 j
    but 'tis so in the song......652 f
    careless s., with a little....568 t
    dance and Provençal song.649 n
    dost sparkle into song..... 71 a
    dusk of centuries and of s.§533 h
    familiar with your song§...647 n
    far into the land of song§..302 j
    feeling than song..........296 w
    flower of song, bloom on§..228 l
    flows his s. through many§479 u
    formed the magic of his s. .479 h
    funeral song be sung......137 i
    gift of s. was chiefly lent ..568 p
    gods and men is sacred s.‡..477 b
    go, with a s. of peace.......638 i
    greet her with his song**.. 48 r
    gypsy children of s. born§. 32 t
    hear but their low, lone s.. 459 i
    hear the song of Selma.....557 k
    hear the wedding song.....568 k
    he is renowned in song.....766 j
    her s.,told when this ancient 51 q
    her song was sung in..... 51 q
    higher than the perfect s..671 n
    I'll sing thee a song in.....530 a
    in pathetic song to breathe.625 p
    in the song the singer.....557 l
    is but a sorrowful song.....338 u
    lark becomes a sightless†..610 j
    lend me your song, ye..... 52 g
    let satire be my song‖......251 f
    lies the Land of Song§.....325 j
    listen to that s., and learn§.568 g
    lively shadow-world of s...568 m
    loud is the summer's busy..394 b
    love wine, woman, and s....509 f
    may turn out a sang.... . 73 n
    melody of a s. sounding....780 v
    musical than any song.....554 u
    never a s. that you have.. 59 a
    never does a wilder song...647 s
    nightingale sings his song. 52 i
    no gold rewards, but song..756 s
    nothing in them, make a...568 s
    old and antique song we*..568 n
    one glad choral song.......239 i
    one grand sweet song .....280 h
    prepare the song, the feast. 95 e
    privilege permits my song .628 a
    rapt in her song†..........270 c
    repeat her song of "May"...392 s
    richer strain to the song...347 m
    roll through us in song.....347 n
    salute thee with our early*‡393 e
    shall be my song...........568 c
    sing a song to me.........561 g
    singing a s. almost divine§.380 k
    sleep'st soft in the s. of its.459 f
    slopes are drowned in song.236 b
    soft, as some s. divine‡.... .578 o
    slow as the summer song...561 g
    song charms the sense**...109 b
    s. forbids victorious deeds .568 l
    song for our banner......214 m
    s., however rude it may be.728 m
    song of a secret bird........161 i
    s. of great joy that the..... 95 j
    s. of leaves, and summer... 43 c
    song of the brave..........756 s
    Song of the Shirt !........484 r
    s. on its mighty pinions§...568 i
    song., picture, form, space.410 l
    song's Indian summer......568 r
    s. which no stranger hath..377 q
    sound in the song of love§..360 c

suck melancholy out of a*.379 *i*
sunshine and from song....229 *m*
swallow-flights of s., that†.568 *q*
swear to the truth of a s....568 *j*
that mighty orb of song¶ ..481 *i*
the burden of his song......110 *b*
the nightingale's song......410 *b*
the song for me¶............ 46 *a*
the song of the orange-tree 616 *j*
thrush your s. is passing... 59 *a*
thy blithesome song was....55 *n*
to her sad s., a tear-drop...591 *d*
twixt a song and kiss.......203 *r*
wanted one immortal song.568 *d*
what s. the Syrens sang.....143 *r*
what they teach in song....480 *o*
whose song first told us.... 43 *f*
whose sprightly song....... 47 *e*
whose sounds are song‖ ...568 *b*
wine, woman, and song ....768 *h*
woods are glad with song..245 *l*
worthy song from earnest..478 *i*
Songs–and songs of longing§.557 *h*
as pleasant s.. at morning§.450 *q*
beautiful as songs of the§..470 *p*
but Virgil's songs are pure‖478 *l*
by such s. you would earn§568 *g*
echoing angelic songs.... .. 92 *m*
everything ends with songs789 *e*
have ceased their songs. .. 42 *m*
hums the songs of the.. ...254 *l*
I had my Book of S. and.... 67 *w*
its deep songs of joy......297 *t*
ladies now make pretty s....102 *l*
matchless songs does......323 *h*
my s. have followed you... 3 *i*
notes of joy, to s. of love.... 50 *j*
our sweetest s. are those...537 *j*
Phœbus, sang those songs.276 *p*
sing no sad songs...........138 *c*
sing the songs he loved†....211 *s*
songs and sonnets here*.... 67 *w*
songs compos'd to her* ... 557 *p*
s. consecrate to truth and..568 *o*
s. have power to quiet§ ....568 *h*
songs in love : they must ... 27 *n*
s. make and wel endite.....478 *o*
s. of love and songs of§....557 *h*
s. of sadness and of mirth§.557 *f*
strange bird singing the s..405 *k*
whose household words are 42 *d*
with s. and laughter blent. 391 *q*
Sonnet–scorn not the sonnet¶551 *l*
S.? 'tis the tear that fell....476 *v*
thought that the sonnet††..477 *h*
what is a s.? 'tis the pearly 476 *v*
Sonnets–lover's s. turn'd to. 470 *w*
written s. all his life‖.......533 *g*
your s. sure shall please‖...452 *u*
Sonnetteer–starv'd hackney‡.407 *b*
Soon–death cometh soon or..136 *e*
nothing comes to us too s..568 *u*
soon that I am done for.....182 *i*
you've waked me too s., I..564 *a*
Sooner–make an end the s...294 *n*
s. it's over the sooner to....666 *v*
Soonest–soonest pass away...240 *q*
Sooth–an overcome sooth...262 *r*
Soothe–can poets soothe you.476*m*
can s. her melancholy......656 *o*
content can s.,where'er....112 *k*
s. or wound a heart that's .665 *g*
to soothe the savage breast.405 *a*
Soothed–sooth'd his soul to..473 *s*
s. with the sound, the king.629 *f*
Soothers–the tongues of s.*..215 *i*
Sophist–wit, s., songster... 50 *k*
Sophistries–the atheist's s..614 *n*
Sophistry–destroy his fib, or‡644*m*
sort of lively sophistry....114 *a*
Sophists–combat with the s.. 27 *w*
for all besides are sophists‖599 *i*
Soprano–s., basso, even the‖..404 *p*
Sorbonne–a monk in the S....793 *r*
Sore–if your friends are sore‡340 *v*
you rub the sore*..........441 *o*

Sorrow–after-hours with s.*.. 5 *r*
and my sorrow's cure*. ... 90 *o*
and so beguile thy sorrow*.345 *c*
and sorrow hates despair...507*gg*
and wear a golden sorrow*.570 *f*
a sorrow's crown of s. is†...570 *j*
ate his bread in sorrow....569 *a*
blight or sorrow fade.. ...182 *j*
brief is s. and endless is....789 *n*
business, banish sorrow....604 *v*
cheer my mind in sorrow¶.382 *c*
comes to us through s......330 *c*
do s. at my grief in love*...570 *l*
down, thou climbing s.*....569 *q*
drink to-day and drown all.161 *s*
eighty odd years of sorrow*569 *s*
fail not for sorrow........348 *h*
fold me from sorrow.......229*m*
fore-spent night of sorrow..605 *a*
free from s. as he was from.655 *y*
giving love your s. and my*570 *l*
give s. words ; the grief*...569 *u*
hang s., care'll kill a cat....569 *g*
hearty s. be a sufficient*...569 *l*
here sorrow cannot reach‖..162 *a*
her rent is sorrow........297 *e*
how beautiful, if s. had not.569 *h*
hush'd be my s., gently... 570 *l*
if s. can admit society*.....569 *w*
in drops of sorrow*.........591 *x*
in sorrow than in anger*...195 *q*
is but sorrow's spy........337 *c*
joy and sorrow all mingle...101 *x*
knowledge is but s.'s spy...267 *i*
lands where s. is unknown.568 *y*
leave with signs of sorrow..440 *e*
life with sorrow strewing..662 *j*
lightnings of his song in s..186 *j*
loved in this world of s.....569 *d*
memories of outlived s..... 89 *i*
memory a rooted sorrow*...441 *c*
men die, but sorrow never..568 *x*
must play fool to sorrow*..442 *k*
my life is full of sorrow....349 *l*
night of sorrow.............130*w*
no day without sorrow.....743 *j*
none, " there is no sorrow ".410 *q*
no sorrow in thy song..... 44 *r*
nothing but sorrow ....569 *e*
now melt into sorrow, now‖.336 *v*
often to that voice of sorrow605 *f*
one s. never comes but*...570 *b*
or tales of sorrow done......443 *d*
patience and sorrow strove*190 *x*
patience is sorrow's salve...467 *d*
parting is such sweet s.*...464 *v*
pluck out one's hair for s...743 *h*
receipt to make s. sink....340 *s*
regions of sorrow**........299 *e*
remember me the more of*.570 *a*
resembles sorrow only§.....537 *g*
ring under the load of s.*...467 *z*
shall be done for sorrow...570 *n*
shuts up sorrow's eye*.....562 *v*
sighed with saving sorrow..451 *f*
smit with exceeding s.†....570 *p*
some natural s., loss, or¶...570 *u*
s. and sickness, poverty††.. 16 *n*
sorrow and the scarlet leaf.544 *i*
sorrow breaks seasons and*.570 *c*
s. but more closely tied....157 *e*
sorrow comes with years... 88 *v*
sorrow's dark array........ 3 *c*
s. ends not when it seemeth*570 *d*
s. flouted at is double*.....570 *g*
s. from happiness is oft.....789 *l*
sorrow has crossed the life.292 *i*
s. is held the eldest child...570 *t*
sorrow is some old tale that.561 *k*
sorrow's keenest wind¶. ..198 *u*
s. long has washed them....673 *a*
s. more beautiful than.....569 *h*
s. need not come in vain....569 *o*
s. never comes too late....582 *o*
s. of the meanest thing§....310 *b*
sorrow plough'd by shame‖.116 *l*
s. preys upon its solitude‖..568*w*

sorrow shows us truths....568 *v*
sorrow so royally in you*..537 *i*
sorrow, that is couch'd in*.569 *x*
sorrow ! why dost borrow..569 *i*
sorrow, wilt thou rule my.†570 *o*
stole from her sister s.†....553 *g*
strength to meet sorrow....210 *t*
sphere of our sorrow......148 *j*
tales of love and sorrow....237 *h*
that should water this s....592 *g*
that sorrow makes us wise†.651 *u*
the path of s., and that....568 *j*
there is no greater sorrow§.569 *k*
there's nae sorrow there...268 *a*
this sorrow's heavenly*....570 *e*
this s. weighs upon the....777 *h*
thought of sorrow free....249 *l*
thy sorrowe is in vaine....466 *l*
time, thy name is sorrow...570*m*
to S. I bade good-morrow...569 *j*
to that keen archer, Sorrow570 *k*
to us too soon but sorrow...568 *u*
want and s. are the gifts....768 *g*
wear a golden sorrow* ... 112 *f*
whatever crazy s saith†....141 *p*
wherever s. is, relief would*570 *i*
with sorrow sighing.......261 *r*
with sorrow to the grave‡..569 *j*
would banish sorrow.......326 *e*
young, I said to Sorrow....570 *r*
your cause of s. must not*.570 *j*
your hearts of s. and your*.155 *p*
Sorrowful–how long the s....600 *p*
s. dislike the gay..........743 *i*
Sorrowing–goeth a sorrowing 69 *h*
Sorrows–engross his sorrows.259 *n*
enough of all its sorrows...609 *b*
few were my sorrows too...277*m*
for transient sorrows¶.....661 *c*
here I and sorrows sit*.....569 *v*
instruct my s. to be proud*.569 *y*
in the rest of Nirvana all s..526 *d*
moderate our sorrows .....710 *d*
our sorrows' only balm....564 *t*
past s., let us moderately...570 *s*
pierced by our sorrows and 55 *n*
pity the sorrows of a poor..473*w*
s. are like thunderclouds...789*m*
s. remembered sweeten.....569 *n*
s. strike heaven on the*....569 *r*
s. woven with delights......151 *e*
swallows other sorrows*....288 *r*
tell all thy sorrows, all.....555 *u*
the sorrows that greet us...359 *j*
waste their s. at my bier...423 *f*
weep on ; and, as thy s. ...569*m*
when s. come, they come*.570 *h*
will indulge my s., and.....149 *a*
Sorry–sorry ere 'tis shown*..265 *f*
s. that I spell'd the word...367 *i*
Sorts–wine makes all s. of...509 *l*
Sot–but their prize a son‡...349 *n*
even from a sot, a pot.....775 *r*
Sots–what can ennoble s. or‡.670 *s*
Sought–love s. is good, but*.364 *c*
men that s. him sweet*....580 *f*
miss one thing we sought...260 *y*
s. in vain that sought the..487 *k*
s. me when I needed her....480 *r*
sought they thus afar......197 *r*
truth when not s. after......622 *s*
unknowing what he s.......110*m*
who sought no more......486c*a*
Soul–a corporation has no s..571 *g*
active as that soul was**... 67 *o*
adds his soul to every other.269 *h*
affirmations of the soul††.. 38 *w*
a fiery s., which, working..571 *j*
a great soul will be strong.. 79 *e*
a little s. scarce fledged.... 32 *i*
a lover's s. lives in the body495 *i*
always that of the soul... 36 *i*
among your s.'s forlornest.420 *r*
and beauty of the soul.....631 *x*
and enlarge the soul.......326 *e*
and his soul sincere...... 41 *l*
and soul within her eyes‖...655 *i*

SHAKESPEARE *; MILTON **; WORDSWORTH ¶; BYRON ‖; TENNYSON †; LOWELL ††; POPE ‡; LONGFELLOW §.

speech in their dumbness*.340 d
s. is better than silence ....573 v
s. is but broken light upon.573 u
s. is great; but silence is...553 v
s. is like cloth of Arras....574 i
speech is shallow as Time..553 w
s. is silver, silence is golden.504 k
speech was given to man to.789 t
s. was given to the ordinary.574 p
s. was made to open man..574 t
the first of speech§........554 k
the poetry of speech‖.......568 b
the truth thy s. doth show.790 j
thought, by s. or action.... 28 b
true use of s is not so much.573 w
wed itself with speech†....598 a
when thought is speech...574 j
with s. of war and woes....523 w
under all s. that is good...553 w
Speeches–proved, by their s..573 r
speeches when half mellow‖483 d
Speechless–stifing the s......667 l
Speed–doth spare to speed...493 p
ease and s. in doing a thing.667 v
more haste, ever the worst.505 s
speed on her prow, and‖....551 o
speed the going guest‡.....289 v
speed the parting guest‡...264 s
then away they speed......262 n
the speed that spins the...186 i
to thy speed add wings**..512 f
with the speed of its flight.385 k
Spell–and dream in a spell...607 f
by the master's spell......210 u
daisy's mocking spell......227 o
find some secret spell....216 c
no one can spell...........409 t
so potent is the spell....128 f
spell of the moment........ 36 i
subtlest spell by far.....129 d
trance, or breathed spell**.493 f
Spelled–sorry that I s. the...367 l
Spelling–false s. or false...720 f
Spells–force of potent s., of..586 k
I'll weave my spells........245 d
Spend–s. a thing you can not..733 i
spend them at my pleasure*419 a
to lend, or to spend, or to...669 a
Spending–getting and s. we¶.669 t
Spends–s. a bootless grief*..595 n
Spent–nor has he s. his life...685 h
spent it frank and freely...272 a
spent under his belly......508 j
what we spent, we had.....102 o
Sphere–acts second to some‡.371 y
all quit their s. and rush‡..491 a
be, on this earthly sphere..344 a
fitting of self to its sphere.526 g
law preserves the earth a s.510 o
orb, and every sphere......575 p
pain in every people s.+....188 f
skill'd in the globe and s....445 c
sphere of our sorrow......148 j
their motion in one sphere*.577 e
to that happier sphere.....298 j
whose sphere is the largest. 2 g
Spher'd–s. in a radiant**....352 k
Spheres–all the s. may sink.. 61 l
as all the tuned spheres*...534 y
beams adorn the spheres...584 o
echo of the spheres|.......404 q
lest the ponderous spheres.579 o
madly from their spheres*.383 j
music of the spheres above.555 f
pleasures of all the spheres.475 o
ring out, ye crystal s.**.... 94 k
stars united in their s.‖....374 n
start from their spheres*.209 q
the music of the spheres...404 m
to reach new s. of pure..... 4 n
to shake the spheres.......276 m
Sphinx–riddles as any sphinx. 31 e
Spice–doth spice the day.... 95 l
variety's the very s. of life.629 u
with summer spice†........246 l
world loves a spice of§.... 644 l
Spices–woodbine s. are†....250 s

Spice-time–birds that in the.. 53 f
Spice-tree–the s-t. lives in the618 e
Spick–is spick and span new.305 v
spick and span new........504 l
Spicy-citron-tree or s. grove.233 k
Spider–much like a subtle s..324 j
or a s.'s web adorning¶.....309 e
said a spider to a fly.......324 k
s. like we feel the tenderest.587 s
s.'s most attenuated thread 62 d
spider, who confin'd. .....324 h
the spider's touch, how‡...324 l
Spiders–flies, and s., and the.323 c
half-starved s prey'd on...579 d
lately had two spiders....324 i
s., flies, or ants entombed..324 g
Spies–come not single spies*.570 h
immortal s. with watchful..574 v
Spike–long as the spike end.218 i
Spikes–s. of purple flame....222 d
Spills–s. itself in fearing to*..328 f
Spilt-grain shall not be s.+..366 o
in fearing to be spilt*.....328 f
spilt on the ground like§...210 s
Spin–dost not toil nor spin§..228 k
spin, daughter Mary.......292 d
s. forever down the ringing† 76 o
s. your wordy fabric in the.589 e
their own entrails spin....587 s
web of Fate we spin.......207 u
Spindle–adamantine s.**....206 t
Spinoza–Spinoza and Kant...516 m
Spins–s. the flying world§....449 o
Spinster–knot of s. kadydids.323 p
Spires–Manhattan with s.....115 i
spires of closely clustered..245 k
s. whose "silent finger¶.... 96 b
Spirit-accusing s. which flew.419 v
a fairer s. or more welcome 85 l
affection stirs her spirit up.660 k
almost like spirit be††......384 w
and the fiercest spirit**....149 k
and there his s. shaped her¶ 39 n
anger of a satiric spirit....125 c
an unaccustom'd spirit*....160 t
a sad, lost spirit...........618 o
as full of s. as the month*..393 f
a s., zealous as he seemed**.674 c
being spirit truest proof... 37 n
body did contain a spirit*.. 13 x
boundless spirit all........275 w
breathe the enlivening s....456 a
by his spirit.... .... 38 u
Cæsar's s., ranging for*....638 w
clear spirit doth raise**....202 d
Creator drew his spirit....182 n
curb thou the high s. in thy.511 h
destroy the spirit utterly.. 76 m
drew his s., as the sun the..133 m
drinks my spirit up .....327 t
ere my fainting spirit fell‖.604 l
eternal s. of the chainless‖.491 t
exhilarate the spirit, and...410 o
fair spirit! rest thee now..526 j
felt with s. so profound*‖..598 g
foolish extravagant spirit*.315 i
for thy spirit did devise.... 24 m
free spirit of mankind. .. 257 v
friends in Spirit Land.....263 f
genius, wit, and s. of a.....493 q
gentler on the s. lies†.....408 h
gentle s. commits itself to*.376 s
gentle voice my s. can cheer 160 e
gifted with little of the s...319 h
Great Spirit, give to me... 297 n
Great Spirit governs all....284 h
has not the s. of his age....784 r
her spirit's harmonies......401 o
her wing'd s. is feather'd... 7 g
his fiery spirit rose flaming.409 e
his spirit grew robust...... 65 i
holyday–rejoicing s. down. 666 w
holy s. of the spring......540 m
humble tranquil spirit.... 271 h
I am the spirit that denies..762 q
I'd break her s. or I'd break.374 j
I never drink no sperit†+...593 h

is the spirit of the church..759 c
I would you had her s. in*.645 m
least erected s. that fell**..369 k
leaves the spirit free......367 f
liberty a loosened s. brings. 65 v
life by the spirit comes.....231 o
like a lost s. earth bound-.. 59 g
mighty s. in a narrow bosom758 n
moment spends its spirit...759 n
much the spirit calms as‖..520 f
my boding spirit shroud...308 b
nimble, stirring spirit*..... 88 q
noblest spirit is most...... 12 q
no spirit dare stir abroad*. 49 l
not memorise a spirit.....574 s
not that alacrity of spirit*.649 w
of the spirit one††........203 q
on the worn spirit shed.....561 i
O thou invisible s. of wine*.650 c
pipe to the s. ditties of no..405 m
prayer is the s. speaking...487 f
presiding s. here to-day¶... 50 f
quench the thirst of his s...557 e
quintessence of public s...163 b
recesses of my spirit§ ... .634 v
restless spirit never could..316 g
retentive to the strength*..350 o
same s. that its author‡....125 l
save the s. of man is divine‖.370 j
scorn'd his s. that could*...564 q
send my spirit o'er the deep‖ 203 p
speaks to my spirit of thee‖ 587 o
spirit comes from abodes...743 n
spirit felt thee there......343 n
spirit for my minister‖.... 356 s
spirit from head to foot is.. 76 m
spirit immortal, the tomb..316 b
spirit of a little child...... 91 a
spirit of criticism......... 319 c
s. of man has found light... 64 o
spirit of my dream*......159 m
s. of nature! all sufficing...414 l
spirit of night...........417 q
spirit of self-sacrifice¶.....148 n
spirit of the universe.......521 v
s. of youth in everything*..392 k
spirit so on earth to be.....487 o
s. superior to every weapon.686 k
s. took its everlasting flight134 b
spirit who must choose....241 k
that her gentle s. commits*.645 u
the dauntless spirit of*....526 a
the spirit is upon you.....447 b
the s. of a child that waits.. 91 c
the spirit of a youth*..... 673 i
thinks in his s. in the world.597 x
thou hast wounded the s...671 f
to s. up the others to fight.482 e
to the spirit of liberty.....343 k
tranquil its s. seemed and..100 h
trustfully my s. looks to...620 i
twilight! spirit that does..625 c
when he becomes a spirit...597 a
why should the s. of mortal 490 w
with a quietness of spirit*..467 r
worser s. tempt me again*.583 h
Spirited–spirited, not inactive 800 c
Spiritless–a dreamer, yet‖....473 n
Spirits-aerials., by great Jove574 v
all spirits, and are melted*.684 m
bathe the drooping s.**....162 o
by evil spirits with hell . 85 a
by good spirits man has... 85 a
call s. from the vasty deep*.575 e
choice s. get finally laid†+..285 q
contain celestial spirits*...107 b
cull'd these fiery s from*..639 h
eyes of s. might behold....515 k
familiar spirits, that are*..300 n
fragrant s. of the bowers..232 n
good spirits and evil spirits 85 a
hands of invisible spirits§..360 c
health and spirits go amiss.295 s
he wins his s. light........ 642 h
join blest s. in celestial...148 b
nimble s in the arteries*..667 k
of all the evil spirits..... 144 h

than an unobserved star ...398 b
the most received star*....207 c
the nebulous s. we call the†584m
the silver evening star††....360 e
the twinkle of a star ....351 k
thy dark up like a star..... 31 q
tongue in every star that..384 r
twinkles like a star§........192 n
twinkling of a star ....101 f
wake of the morning star‡.401 g
westward the s. of empire .492 a
while he gazes on a star....426 i
white star made of memory233 c
with a single diamond star.575 r
would infect to the north*. 659 t
Star-chamber—make a s-c. *..472w
Star-eyed–s-e. intelligence....435 o
O s-e. Science, hast thou...538 h
Starless-night s. expos'd**....668 v
Starlight–behind the cloud...309 d
cloudless s. on he treads...576 o
let starlight fade away....576 r
Starry–beneath this s. arch..492 k
first of all the starry choir.584 c
round of starry folds.......235 j
starry cope of heaven**....298 h
Stars–above the lofty stars...714m
all the stars of heaven ....413 f
amid her kindred stars‡....571 v
and made the s., and set**..576 g
and pavement stars**....576 f
and the stars are old.......366 e
as night, the life-inclining..420 u
as night to s. woe lustre... 8m
as stars look on the sea ...576 e
at whose sight all the**....576 h
beauty of a thousand stars. 35 i
bids countless stars pursue 575w
blesses his stars, and thinks368 t
blossomed the lovely stars§576 b
Brutus is not in our stars* .372 n
build beneath the stars..... 14 k
but a myriad scattered s...577 f
but the cold light of stars§.416 d
by the luckiest stars*......368 p
certain s. shot madly from*383 j
changeless march the stars108 j
cheerfully from the s. he...536m
come are the stars.........624 l
count the stars of Heaven. 577 h
cry out upon the stars for .575 n
cut him out in little stars*.363 o
day stars! that ope........220 h
duties shine aloft like s. ¶..164 p
ere the stars were visible¶..433 l
glows in the stars and‡.....411 v
head shall strike the stars*.733 f
high souls, like those far††.428 x
him who never sees the s...150 f
in yonder stars............287m
Jove and my s. be praised*.449 c
kings are like s.—they rise.535 j
lantern thus close up the**416 n
like stars by day..........216 j
like the voice the stars.....635 e
like yonder s. so bright and 40 n
'midst the stars inscribe‡..291m
moon and the s. by night ..234 j
night and all her stars.....492 j
night brings out stars as...568 v
night followed, clad with s.625 o
night shows s. and women‖.415 h
night, with all her stars....417w
of nature and their stars...427 g
of stars and flowers........381 y
on the field of stars........397 q
other stars repairing**.....576 i
our heads the faint few s..624 l
pierce the night like stars.318 r
sentinel s. set their watch.575 o
set the stars of glory.......258 h
shooting s. attend thee....192 g
silence and the wakeful s..351 i
sky is filled with s. invisible§10 i
sky the stars are met‖ .....186 p
s. are poore books, and.... 538 w
stars above us, govern our*577 c

stars are forth, the moon‖..415 j
s. are golden fruit upon a..575 t
s. are in the quiet skies.....576 e
stars are the daisies that...576 n
stars arise and the night is§416 e
s., bright sentinels of the ..575 u
stars come forth to listen§.416 c
s. come out to watch the...624 l
stars fade one by one ......416 p
s. hang bright above her...561 c
stars have lit the welkin...214 e
s. hide their diminish'd**..310 n
s. hide themselves in the...583 v
stars lie in such apparent..575m
s. of midnight shall be¶....413m
starsof morning**.........154 e
stars of the jasmine glow..232 k
stars shall fade away......315m
stars that beam on high....264 q
stars that have a different .399 b
stars that in the earth's§...218 r
s. their dying Lord could...612 c
stars through difficulties...798 c
stars to set—but all.......134 p
s. united in their spheres‖.374 n
stars were glittering in the.397 q
s. were more in fault than..658 o
s. which Night's blue arch. 590 n
stars will blossom..........248 e
studded with stars Odin's..278 i
studded with stars.........417 p
taken the s. from the night††148 v
tears which stars weep......153 x
thanks his stars he was‡..251aa
the countless stars in the ..762 o
the first pale s. of twilight.624 o
the fixed stars of heaven*..639 s
the frosty stars are gone...401 f
the s. of the night will lend.575 v
the s. are images of love...575 i
the s. come forth to listen§.576 c
the s. rush forth in myriads415 e
the s. they glisten, glisten..415 q
the s., which stand as thick575 j
this book of s. lights to....538 w
till the blue stars twinkle.. 18 k
two eyes like stars*........209 q
two stars keep not their*..577 e
upward to the stars....... 724 n
vision clear for s. and sun .590 d
when stars illume the sky.. 2 u
who can fear too many s...355 u
who have the s. survey'd...576 t
whom gentler stars unite..378 b
with golden stars above†...481 a
ye little stars hide your‡...576 q
Star-spangled–s-s. banner....224 i
Stared-and s. with his foot‡.. 47 r
Starers–of stupid s. and of‡..547 l
Stares–and drinks, and stares213 i
s. foolish, hazed, rubicund.584 n
Stark-shall, stiff and s. and*.563 a
Start–start at wagging of a*.423 d
start at shame.............370 n
without a timely start.....786 d
Started–s. and threw yourself333 r
s. like a guilty thing*.....290 l
Startled–startled by the leap.240 a
Startles-s. at destruction.....315 l
Starve–serving man's wife...494 t
starve us all, or near it.....311 b
starve with feeding*....... 17 p
starve with nothing*...... 168m
Starved–drank and starved.. 20 g
Starves–hope s. without.....267 e
modesty starves 686w
sometimes virtue starves‡..388 j
Starving–the s. chemist in‡..425 a
State–all were for the state .627 k
artisans make a state......281 d
asked what State he hails..469 j
broken with the storms of* 11 t
by the Midas finger of the.649 a
commiseration of his s.*....442m
confession of his true s.*..103 x
cultivate a small state. ....676 v
deny my sacred state*..... 1 c

done the s. some service*..332 r
eastern monarchs show....458 k
her s. is like that of things.651 f
hides from himself its s....348 c
his pre-existent state‡.....206 x
his state empties itself*....534 v
his state is kingly**.......275 i
hung a canopy of state.... 515 k
I am the state.............770 q
in such a gloomy s. remain.563 o
is the state of man*.........151 r
keep a stable changeless s.. 74 d
knows no interest of state..281 k
laws preserve each state‡..462 t
man by delay restored the.691 v
man's wretched state that..372w
meddling with great affairs653 v
might our state improve...309 t
mould a mighty s's decrees†454 h
nor church nor s. escaped‖.421 p
of each corrupted state.... 98 d
on the quiet state of men** 1 h
our s. cannot be sever'd**..376 a
O wretched s.! O bosom*..523 p
palace, then in awful state.122 s
rotten in the s. of Denmark*483 b
ruin or to rule the state....282 e
safety of the state.........741 a
sail on, O Ship of State§...469 c
scandal waits on greatest. *538 e
scoffing his s. and grinning†140 s
secrets of s. no more I wish281 p
seem'd a pillar of state**..153 j
see sin in s., majestically‡..556 g
serve to form a state‖......281 l
sin is a s. of mind, not an.. 556 h
so vanishes our state.......349 r
star for every state.. ...214 r
s. beneath the firmament..281 f
state far worser than it is*.208 k
s. in wonted manner keep..398 a
s. is one vast insane asylum321 b
state of duration as was...599 d
s. without kings or nobles..281 o
stays supreme in state.....616 b
than be true to church††..608 g
the canopies of costly s.*..563 c
the king and the state.....807 v
the more corrupt the state.686 g
the state!—it is I..........787 k
the s. of man is inconstancy 776 e
this is the state of man*.... 76 f
was a great plot of state..282 p
whatever state a man be...644 v
when the sun in all his s....463 l
will rush into the state*...488 q
wounds the body of a state.125 c
you keep your s., Heaven is 17 d
State-house–s-h. is the hub of 97 p
States–equal and sovereign s.627 c
goodly s. and kingdoms....607 d
in s. unborn and accents*..602 k
no more slave S. and no....559 d
of indestructible States.... 627 d
on States dissevered.......283 e
say to the seceded States..282w
shaker of o'er-rank states..635 l
states are great engines....281 e
the eye and ear of states..770 s
thinn'd states of half their.625 s
union of S. none can sever.627m
valours, like great states...652 p
Statesman–chymist, fiddler, s .78 x
no s. e'er will find it worth.454 d
so great a statesman should 454 e
standard of a statesman ...454 c
statesman and buffoon....212 a
s., yet friend to truth ‡ ...454 g
the statesman's scheme‡...634 l
too nice for a statesman.... 79 r
you show us a s. who.......454 j
Statesmen–adored by little s.107 i
s. at her council met†.....454 i
village s. talk'd with looks.589 d
Station–any other station or.260 l
give me, a private station..110 p
her shining station as a star667 r

SHAKESPEARE*; MILTON**; WORDSWORTH ¶; BYRON ‖; TENNYSON †; LOWELL ††; POPE ‡; LONGFELLOW §.

planets in their s. list'ning**576 *l*
republic her station........214*m*
stay in that s. in which 685*m*
Stations-high s., tumult......287 *q*
Statuaries-s. loved to copy... 25 *p*
Statue-base of Pompey's s.*.320 *a*
ere humane statue purg'd..403 *d*
fix'd statue on the pedestal||109 *f*
nobles bended, as to Jove's*483 *g*
stands the s. that enchants.452 *r*
s. falls from the pedestal..143 *h*
s. of a celebrated minister..104 *d*
the more the statue grows.45⁑ *i*
Statues-are statues, and not§452 *l*
deface their ill-placed s....344 *n*
dumb statues or breathing**210 *a*
the lumpy statues.......... 28 *i*
trees cut in statues‡........269 *w*
Stature-a s. undepressed in¶. 12*m*
her s. tall—I hate a dumpy||655 *j*
reason is upright stature..517 *t*
stature somewhat low......301 *c*
their books of stature small 68 *g*
to reach full stature††....492 *j*
Statutes-we have strict s.*...439 *a*
Stay-and I'll still s., to have..304 *o*
come and stay with thee...570 *r*
I asked not to stay.......349 *q*
I s. a little longer, as one§..464 *o*
I stay too long by thee*...652 *j*
must I stay and here*......350 *v*
my stay, my guide and*...275 *s*
nor would she s. nor dares. 53 *h*
nothing that is can pause§ .605 *d*
no vile hold to stay him up*495 *n*
now it seems as hard to s.†.525 *i*
says I must not stay.......141 *q*
so his stay with us*†....... 31 *n*
s. a little, and news will find 504*m*
stay awhile that we may...294 *n*
s. him no longer than to.... 19 *a*
s. in that station in which..685*m*
stay the cooling too*......431 *u*
stay yet here awhile........218 *a*
to wish her stay**........283 *k*
time and tide for no man s.603*m*
wear it but only stay......434 *l*
wish at least, with us to s..604 *v*
Stayed-s.,—forgive the crime 603 *p*
Stays-adjourn'd have many s.603 *n*
s. for us at the park gate*..439*m*
stays till we call‡..........517 *h*
the lover rooted stays......358 *e*
yet He stays His car......274 *t*
Steadfast-be s. as a tower...767 *n*
Steady-keeps the mind steady571*m*
Steaks-greasy steaks from...180 *n*
Steal-and bid her steal*....231 *e*
as silently steal away §... 415 *r*
cunningly did steal away..347 *u*
glad if I can steal one......474 *q*
I will not steal them....... 60 *b*
judges steal themselves*...189 *a*
maiden herself will steal...297 *a*
most authors s. their works‡429*m*
steal a few hours from the..416 *r*
s. away give little warning.345 *n*
s. from the world, and not‡421 *c*
steal from the writings of..474 *o*
steal himself into a man's*.490 *n*
s. pieces of money and hide 48 *b*
s. the hog, and give the feet.504 *n*
steal! to be sure they may.474 *s*
s. us from ourselves away‡601 *s*
steal young children out of 89 *c*
they steal in and out......253 *n*
they steal my thunder.....421 *v*
to steal away your hearts*.462*m*
when judges s. themselves*595 *p*
years following years s.‡....601 *s*
Stealer-the stand o' the s.*...279 *g*
Steals-robb'd that smiles s.*.595 *n*
s. ere we can effect them*..602 *l*
steals from her youth......601 *j*
s. my purse steals trash*...595 *r*
time who s. our years away 380 *q*
year after year it s., till all.604 *d*

Stealing-friar preached......505 *f*
honest but for stealing.....454 *o*
so gently o'er me stealing..381 *f*
stealing and giving*........249 *g*
s. will continue stealing....595 *q*
Stealth-do good by stealth‡..202 *l*
Steam-balloons and steam...327 *c*
steam of the golden-rods...229 *r*
thy height'ning steam......457 *c*
travelled like steam........267 *a*
Steam-engine-s-e. in trousers 84 *t*
Steamy-throws up a steamy.186 *q*
Steed-Gamaun is a dainty s.. 20 *n*
he mounts the warrior's s..362 *q*
my steed obeys............. 87 *g*
s. and mustering squadron||636 *a*
steed that knows his rider||.459 *e*
steed threatens steed in*... 21 *e*
the neighing steed*........204 *t*
travel far spares his steed..757 *a*
Steeds-curb thy fierce steeds 541 *f*
his steeds to water*...... 49 *h*
loud 'larums, neighing s.*..659 *e*
turning loose his steeds....483 *e*
Steel-blade was the bright s..430 *l*
clad in complete steel**.... 88 *a*
divorce of steel falls on me*489 *h*
foeman worthy of their s...443 *p*
heart with strings of steel*.489 *g*
impell'd the steel||........519 *c*
lock'd up in steel*.........333 *a*
my man's as true as steel*.502 *f*
nor gates of s. so strong*...602 *p*
no workman steel, no......425 *l*
patience as with triple s.**.467 *m*
though cloven with steel...627 *i*
with hoops of steel*.......262 *i*
Steep-climb with me the s...567 *c*
how often from the s.**....670 *j*
resounding o'er the steep..610 *p*
vaulting up the terraced s..229 *f*
Steep'd-s. me in poverty to..485 *e*
Steeple-church and no steeple494 *b*
on it put a steeple......... 95 *k*
Steeples-s. are loud in their.. 39 *u*
wilderness of s. peeping on|| 98 *c*
with spire steeples......... 95 *l*
you have drench'd our s.*..578 *b*
Steer-in his verse can gently.476 *p*
I steer my bark, and sail...445 *g*
like ships, they steer their .476 *d*
steer from grave to gay‡...114 *c*
steer right onward**....... 61 *f*
steer 'twixt fertile shores||..532 *l*
up and down doth he steer. 58 *f*
Steer'd-we're s. by fate......205 *t*
Steering-s. with his fleet§.... 90 *c*
Steers-where Wisdom steers.573 *q*
Steersman's-s.'s part is...... 73 *s*
Stem-hangs from thy laden s.229 *q*
moulded on one stem*......262 *k*
s. the torrent of a woman's656 *h*
that out-bound stem has...618 *e*
whose brittle stem........223 *e*
Stems-all on their drooping s.674 *q*
poppies nod upon their s...216 *g*
their stems in furry white..618 *l*
Stenches-two and seventy s.. 97 *s*
Step-a single s., and all is§...583 *b*
a step more true...........254 *e*
by him one step below *...174 *h*
fetter the step of freedom..258 *d*
first step engulfs him......608 *e*
first step that costs. ......756 *h*
first step to self-knowledge 337 *i*
from hell on s. no more**.299 *k*
I hear that creaking step... 69 *b*
keep s. to the music of the.468 *g*
know his step and touch...237 *d*
one s. above the ridiculous. 75 *l*
one s. from the sublime to.581 *h*
so every step, exampled*..174 *h*
step, a blow¶............. 6 *c*
step and dress alike........128 *g*
take a single step..........260 *n*
trace my step o'er the. .. 540 *f*
to step aside is human......343 *c*

walks with level step the...401 *f*
with majestic step goes....118 *p*
with zealous step he......246 *f*
wrench the unwary step...453 *b*
your step be light........184 *a*
Stepdame-like to a s. or a*...398 *s*
stepdame to her son*......101 *y*
Stepped-stepped to the sky..403 *j*
Stepping-s. o'er the bounds*.389 *i*
Stepping-stones-rise on s-s.†.373 *c*
Steps-ask the number of s...126 *t*
beware of desperate steps..149 *g*
charm his pained s. over...654 *h*
each day my s. grow slow..395 *j*
ferns bend her s. to greet..217 *p*
forth with pilgrim steps**.400 *n*
grace was in all her steps**657 *q*
grief thy steps attend....261 *o*
he steps right onward......443 *a*
his feeble s. he stayed still. 546 *l*
impell'd with steps... ...280 *c*
in his Maker's steps of fire.584 *c*
invites my s. and points to‡ 25 *f*
meekly with reverent s.§...521 *f*
no steps backward........677 *c*
now morn, her rosy s. in**.400 *l*
sad s. by which it hath¶....413 *h*
steps are of light that......128 *g*
steps of the sun...........261 *o*
thy steps I follow with my.318 *c*
thy steps no more than a*..315 *f*
tottering steps and slow...313 *o*
wandering steps and slow** 33 *g*
with how sad steps, Omoon399 *e*
Sterling-modern reigning s.||.389 *l*
Stern-magnificently s. array||636 *b*
stern in the joyless fields..396 *a*
s. men with empires in††...385 *x*
Steward-backward s. for the‡369 *l*
hereditary bore, the s..... 69 *a*
Stew'd-and stew'd in brine*..512 *o*
Stews-savour of certain-s.||..431 *n*
Stick-beat with fist instead..449 *u*
but the forked s. with a.... 18 *e*
twirled my stick..........254 *j*
Sticketh-but sticketh nere...220 *m*
Sticking-place-courage to*...119 *t*
Sticks-though it s. to the pot481 *c*
Stiff-shall, s. and stark and*.563 *a*
Stifling-s. the speechless....667 *l*
Stigmatical-s. in making*.... 83 *n*
Stile-merrily hent the s.-a*..384 *l*
often turn the stile........753 *f*
sitting on the stile, Mary...357 *y*
the stile of Gods in vaine..534 *e*
Still-and still as still can be§.416 *c*
be s. sad heart and cease§..514 *u*
better sit s. where born, I..607 *f*
hot and still the air was§...542 *o*
still as in the silent deep...610 *f*
s. as night or summer's**..154 *p*
still small voice is wanted..105*m*
take heed of still waters....504 *q*
'tis the still water faileth..339 *i*
Stillness-great s. dropped... 241 *r*
modest s. and humility*...471 *e*
soft s., and the night*......407 *i*
s. first invades the ear .... 554 *c*
stillness of the country§...580 *d*
s. round the homes of men.545 *o*
summer winds the s. broke§546 *e*
Stilly-oft in the stilly night..380 *n*
Stimulus-gives an immense..697 *a*
Sting-and a sting in her tail..369 *e*
death! where is thy sting ‡.137 *q*
he draws the sting of life.. 85 *x*
it is a prick, it is a sting...361 *k*
leave a sting within......297 *j*
left a sting behind........202 *g*
serpent sting thee twice*...320 *b*
sharp sting behind it..... 717 *q*
sting the luckless foot......143 *q*
sun, and sting the soul.....143 *q*
Stinger-'tis a stinger.......507 *h*
Stings-soldiers armed in*...322 *b*
stings you for your pains..119 *a*
Stink-thou'dst stink and be..454 *q*

we raise the strain......... 94 e
Strains–blew soul-animating¶481 f
strains that might create**.296 d
Strait–as serves a present s...281 k
such a s. the wisest may....155 j
travels in a strait so*.......306 q
Strait-laced-conscience......318 l
Straits–in great straits.....689 b
Strand-knits me to thy......116 q
on a foreign strand.........118 j
pass to the American s.....521 b
to that far distant strand..362 c
to thy rugged strand.......118 k
Wapping or the Strand‖......456 f
Strange–a s. hand writes for..640 r
but this is wondrous s.*....661 o
hath s. places cramm'd*.....421 j
more strange than true*...626 a
new, to something strange§ 75 b
often nothing so strange...623 y
so s. do these things seem†.603 u
s.—is it not ?—that of the..135 c
s. that thou shouldst live...352 b
s. to the world, he wore....579 q
strange, 'twas passing s.*..661 q
thoughts beget s. deeds.....597 r
'tis s.—but true ; for truth‖.621 l
what a s. thing is man‖.....655 o
Stranger–a s. is woman‖.....655 o
no stranger to suffering....679 r
s. and the poor are sent‡... 41 n
stranger for a guest*.......329 l
s. in these false coasts.....571 y
strange, s. than fiction‖....621 l
world a s. for thy sake*....608 m
Strangers–by s. honour'd and†137 m
little dogs do at strangers..174 c
s. and foes do sunder*.....335 o
we may be better s.*.......148 e
Strangle–to s. the child......227 r
Strangled–s. his language in*.591 n
Stratagem–her tea without a 579 f
Stratagems–s. and spoils*....407 s
s. which errors seem‡......579 e
Straw–a pigmy's s. doth*.....556 o
as the light s. and rapid...424 n
in peace on one s. heap.....533 k
start at wagging of a s.*...423 d
take a s. and throw it up...647 v
tickled with a straw‡....... 90 k
tilts with a s. against a¶...572 n
to find quarrel in a straw*..513 l
Straws–errors, like s., upon..185 k
for oaths are straws*.......511 u
of hairs, or straws, or dirt‡.661 m
Strawberries–Dr. Boteler said 19 g
great strawberries at the...265 v
Strawberry–bloomed the s.¶..221 e
dainty strawberry flower..245 l
like strawberry wives......265 v
spare the strawberry¶......245 m
s. grows underneath*......266 r
s. there was so ripe.........333 r
Stray–fools discover it, and..528 d
Streaks–s. and shafts of......584 r
Stream–a running stream....293 f
a wonderful s. is the river..603 s
bashful s. hath seen its....649 c
by a slow broad stream†....270 b
by Bendemeer's stream.....242 n
by thy pure s., or in thy...567 u
cloudy stream is flowing...391 e
Clyde's meandering s......530 j
come over the s. to me.....355 l
death's mysterious stream.603 k
drink the clear s., and**...593 i
drops of a s. that issue.... 72 r
far-off stream is dumb†.... 53 d
glide adown thy stream....600 b
grass floweth like a s.††...300 s
hail, gentle s.! forever.....531 m
his talk was like a s. which.589 j
his sacred stream..........235 b
in the steep Atlantic s.**..585 o
in the s. the long-leaved†..412 t
its mighty, mystic stream§.531 i
like the stream of Time§....532 c

oars the silver stream*..... 18 j
O darling s.! on balanced§..533 e
of the broad s., the mighty.531 d
pure stream! in whose....531 b
rapid stream of time.......352 a
shy, yet unreluctant stream646 t
softly stooped to kiss the s.646 t
soft stream did glide......250 g
stir the s., sweeping with...648 d
stream auriferous plays....413 c
stream from Wisdom's well 651 s
stream has overflowed§.... 71 b
s. is always purer at its...785 r
stream my great example..188 l
stream of rich distill'd**..447 o
stream of the Pyramid and.531 h
stream which overflowed¶.382 b
s. with a perpetual sigh....148 o
the lapsing stream, is heard 47 l
the meadow and stream... 2 v
the next purling stream....640 t
the pretty s., the flattered..646 t
the s. runneth smoothest...508 ff
the stream runs fast....... 63 m
thy banks' purest s. shall..530 k
thy s. my great example... 78 u
till the lowest stream*.....533 d
urn a sacred stream.......351 i
vapors hug the stream.....395 b
view thy silver stream....530 n
what will the s. become in.785 t
wreaths into her stream**..219 a
yon rocks the stream inurn229 t
Streamers–length the s. play.446 a
Streamlet–o'er the crystal s. 542 c
Streamlets–children with the392 e
dream by the drowsy s....615 c
o'er flowing streamlets‖...264 w
woodland streamlets flow..224 l
Streams–broad are these s... 87 g
chiding s.betray small....572 v
gilding pale streams with* .625 i
headlong s. hang listening¶ 557 m
hundred s. ere the same as.159 p
in purling s. or hemp.......356 k
liquid lapse of**...........411 o
large streams from little...462 d
likened best to floods and s.465 v
like small streams.........157 b
our plenteous streams‡....213 l
shallow s. run dimpling‡...564 m
s. from airy mountains.....647 t
streams of dotage flow... 348 d
s. of revenue burst forth...123 j
streams of truth will roll..347 n
s. rejoiced that winter's.... 70 u
streams run down her oil'd.458 n
streams that ever flow‡....222 k
s. that keep a summer††... 81 k
s. with softest sound are¶..413 n
streams with vernal-scented222 d
the seas and the streams..'515 d
the streams wake, laughing392 p
where gliding s., the rocks.613 e
Street–across the noisy s. I... 58 t
back from the village s.§...117 i
clamor of the crowded s.§.. 81 c
every street has two sides..672 t
street that fronts the sun..652 h
the passers in the city s.§..394 h
threading the s. with idle..378 p
wordy fabric in the street..589 e
Streets–amid thy cloud-built.585 h
gibber in the Roman s.*...140 d
men about the streets*... .453 q
walls and unpaved streets.123 d
when night darkens the s.**416 i
Strength–all below is s., and.. 79 c
and spend her s. with*.... 58 k
as my strength wears away465 u
assurance of s. there is.....157 k
breasts on whose s. they....640 k
buries its tumultuous s.....459 b
can gain no strength from.701 e
carried new s. and courage.318 u
excellent to have a giant's*579 m
fear oppresseth strength*..210 f

freshness and s. have......616 e
from strength to strength..315 n
gives strength to the body.686 h
glory gives me strength....707 a
grows the strength of all‡..642 a
in unchanged strength.....347 k
in union there is strength..806 m
is no strength in unbelief..626 o
light—for strength to bear§488 k
like s. is felt from hope‡....579 g
my proportion'd strength**641 u
my strength in age.........276 g
my strength is waned now..299 w
name is a tower of strength*579 n
one nail by strength drives*317 p
Phœbus in his strength*...219 s
ploughman's s. and health.642 f
profan'd the God-given s...579 k
retentive to the s. of*......350 o
rugged strength and radiant 79 t
s. and rage could never....782 s
strengthens with his s.‡....156 j
strength in times of danger391 a
strength is in your union§.282 t
s. match'd with strength*..184 t
s. of feeble arms combined.443 g
s. of mind is exercise‡......386 c
s. of the ancient giants.....579 j
strength thus tested ......224 j
s. to await our future lot... 7 x
strength to meet sorrow... 210 h
strength unto your foe*....210 f
sympathizing with my s...587 k
than s. of nerve'or sinew¶..387 n
the strength to disbelieve¶.626 o
the tranquil s. of men...... 74 a
thro' sense of strength.....236 d
topics to your strength‖....427 j
to spend their s. in furthest 4 j
try the soul's strength on..346 a
virtue kindles strength ...805 z
water its living s. first......641 c
weakness grows the s. of‡.. 82 u
weakness than from our s..465 n
with strength and patience.466 t
years of fading strength...346 k
yet lovely in your strength‖577 p
Strengthen–strengthen me by587 k
Strengthens–bread which s..431 r
mind s. and decays.......726 g
strengthens our nerves.....112 q
s. with his strength‡......289 n
Stretch–s. himself according.785 m
s. our eye when capital*....123 t
Stretcheth–s. his legs.......497 m
Strewings–give her strewings188 d
Stricken–s. deer that left the.388 c
Stride–like a peacock—a s.*.. 53 p
threefold the s. of Time....602 d
Strife–and the tongue of s....538 a
artificial s. lives in these*..447 d
clubs typical of strife..... 14 p
crowd's ignoble strife......567 b
dare the elements to strife‖551 p
flagg'd not in the earthly s.315 n
for the sake of strife.......634 r
for the strife is hard¶......273 l
I hold such strife*.........471 c
immanity and bloody s.*...522 b
in the common strife¶......319 k
of the stern strife, and.....638 s
ortolans eaten in strife.....167 j
rally to a nobler strife the.104 p
rest is sweet after strife....526 n
shall end this strife*........ 98 m
some to public strife‡......658 h
staunch of strife..........264 n
storm nor in the strife‖.....420 n
s. and the discouragement§472 l
strong in its strife. ... ...319 d
the memory of their strife.592 p
the petty strife, which.... 304 h
together for the sake of s..374 p
void of strife................. 19 d
wak'd with strife.........444 m
wedded days with strife...374 h
Strike–and yet afraid to s.‡...537 r

SHAKESPEARE *; MILTON **; WORDSWORTH ¶; BYRON ||; TENNYSON †; LOWELL ††; POPE ‡; LONGFELLOW §.

fine dishes on your table. . .180 a
from the t. of my memory*381 o
hath in the t. of his law*. . .404 b
his eyes on his dusty old t. .435m
keep a good t. and don't. . . .783 p
over the t.,—look out for. . . 20 g
put fine dishes on your t. . .180 a
servants for every table. . . .177m
the head of the table. 508cc
the table is this place.'. . . . .422 a
three-legg'd t., O ye fates. .431 c
to eat at another's t. is your713 h
whose table earth‖. . . . . .269 g
Table-cloth–great deal of§. . .167 i
Tables-my t.,—meet it is I*. .312 t
near a thousand t. pined¶. . .102 k
their t. were stor'd full*. . . .147 u
Tablet-moulders from the. . .143 h
Tablets-writ on tablets yet. . .538 s
Table-talk-let it serve for t-t.*589 p
Tabors-hobby-horses, tabors. 14 n
Taciturnity-one learns t. best790 g
Tackle-though thy t.'s torn.*195 y
Taffeta-thy doublet of*. . . . . . 76 c
Tags-tipped these funny t. . .453 j
Tagus-T. dashing onward‖. . .532 l
Tail-and a sting in her tail . . .369 e
cut off my tail. . . . . .213 k
Dobbin my fill horse has*. .458 g
eel of science by the tail‡. . .844 c
fox, when he had lost his . .481 p
horror of his folded tail**. .153 h
monstrous t. our cat has. . . 19 j
peacock sweep along his t.* 53 o
proud t. of a splendid bird .181 p
so long was his tail and so. . 43 a
tail must wag the dog. . . . . 28 l
tail takes in his teeth. . . . . .213 g
their tail the rudder, and. . .410 q
thin mane, thick tail*. . . . . 21 d
treading on my tail. . . . . . . .213 f
whose tail's a diadem‖. . . . . . 53 k
with a dragon's tail. . . . . . . 18 f
Tails-kittens playing with. . .795 v
tails of both hung down¶. . . 20 r
Tailor-angry but with thy t. .454 q
a tailor make a man*. . . . . .455 b
a tailor though a man of. . .454 o
come, tailor, let us see't*. . .455 d
commending a t. for his. . . .454 p
fine man hath your tailor. .454 r
god tailor and god mercer. .454 s
great is the tailor, but not .454m
he call'd the taylor lowne. .454 t
new creation of my tailor's.454 n
no, nor thy tailor, rascal*. . .455 c
tailor and the cook forsake.126 r
tailor make thy doublet*. . 76 c
t.'s lays be longer than‖. . . .454 l
unpaid t. snatch'd away‡. . .455 a
Tailors-quarrels, talk and t.*607 l
some score or two of t.*. . . .205 h
t. had their business at. . . . .454 p
Taint-but never t. my love*. .627 w
or any taint of vice*. . . . . . .319 t
Tainted-Nero will be t. with* 659 d
what plea so t. and corrupt*438 o
Take-believe and take it. . . . . 92 j
can take in all, and verge. .571 k
doe him by the forelock t. . .603 o
knew but what you take. . . .440 r
take away those things. . . . .432 n
take me just as I am. . . . . . .808 h
t. my house when you do*. .150 b
take not away the life you.347 f
take the instant by the*. . . .602 l
t. what thou wilt away. . . . .524 y
take when once 'tis offer'd*461 r
they should t. who have¶ . .486 c
we must snatch not take‡. . .337 t
which he may lawfully t. . .593 e
which of them shall I t. ?*. . 92 b
Taken-all are not taken. 107m
some are taken from me. . . .195 b
when t. to be well shaken. .439 v
Takes-and him that takes*. . .382 p
death never t. one alone§. . .135m

from that he takes away. . .510w
like that it takes away‖. 329m
Taking-off-damnation of his*633 l
Tale-ancient tale new told*. .281 b
and thereby hangs a tale*. .350 e
and wonder at the tale. . . . . 24 s
as a tale that is told. . . . . . .371 h
a schoolboy's tale, the‖. . . .578 h
a tale in everything¶. . . . . . .579 c
at some mournful tale. . . . .211 e
brings in a several tale*. . . .106m
cease from thy enamoured. 52 e
dark words begins my t ¶. . .490 f
every shepherd tells his**. .614 d
every tale condemns me*. . .106m
hear by tale or history*. . . 362 o
his homely tale this very¶. 46 a
honest t. speeds best being*305 i
hope tells a flattering tale. .309 g
I could a t. unfold whose*. .547 g
I hate to tell again a tale*. .578 n
I say the t. as 'twas said to.536 f
knows not the tender tale. .218 s
lest my sad t. should reach.570 l
life's but a span, or a t., or.349 v
makes up life's t. to many. 346 q
many a t. their music tells. 40 j
men suspect your t. untrue622 e
moon takes up the. . . . . . . .397 d
moral or adorn a tale. . . . .201 r
plain t. shall put you down*623 j
seldom shall she hear a t. . .578 s
so high the specious tale. . .779 d
so like an old t., that the*. .414 u
sorrow is some old t. that. .561 k
tale that's merrier than§. . .353 r
t. enfold whose lightest*. . .209 q
tale was sooner heard than‡536 e
t. which holdeth children. .579 a
tedious as a twice-told tale*350 n
tedious as a twice-told tale‡578m
the tale that I relate. . . . . . .375 c
'tis an old t., and often told528 n
told his soft tale and. . . . . .662 k
told the merriest tale . . . . . 95 c
turns a Persian t. for half‡.480 h
were some tale of a tub . . . 39 i
Tales-a-list'nin' to the witch.578 p
Dear Ellen, your t. are all. .578 q
different tales of love. . . . .237 h
drank her whisper'd tales‡.366 n
ears play truant at his t.*. .172 a
is increased with tales. . . . .132 b
of all t. 'tis the saddest‖. . 537 f
pick out of tales the mirth.578 f
so many tales are told. . . . . 48 e
t. that to me were so dear. .379 n
telling tales of the fairy. . .267 a
tell tales out of schoole. . . .504 u
weavers of long tales. . . . . .578 i
Talent-between genius and . .769 p
is a man of talent. . . . . . . .177 t
master of talent. . . . . .270 p
murder, like talent, seems.403 o
no t. but yet a character. . .758 l
single talent well employ'd.421m
t. is nurtured in solitude. . .758 i
t. is that which is in a†. . . .588 r
t. of our English nation. . .518 u
Talents-impartially their t. .170 k
let them use their talents*.651 n
not overstrain our talents.791 c
proof of great talents. . . . .745 k
t. angel-bright if wanting. 14 j
talents that attract people.319 c
tried their talents at one. .124 l
youth, t., beauty, thus. . . . 11 h
Talk-always talk who never.589 k
and more than echoes talk‡169 j
and who talk too much. . . .589 b
and witty to talk with. . . . .660 l
as well as to talk. . . . . .651 j
drown him by your talk. . . .743 s
have 'em t. us to silence*. . .589 r
his talk was like a stream. .589 j
however learned you may. .765 r
I cannot t. with civet in the447 o

if I chance to talk a little*. .589m
I'll talk a word with this*. .580 p
in after-dinner t. across†. . .579 b
in various t. th' instructive‡524 l
it becomes town talk. . . . . .781 l
it needs no talk. . . . . .358 v
it would talk; Lord, how it 588 s
let's talk of graves* . . . . .184 e
loves to hear himself talk*.589 l
man would talk to make. . .113 g
not much talk—a great. . . .554 h
now for calm, familiar t.‡. .589 f
quarrels, talk and tailors *.607 l
spent an hour's t. withal*. .384 h
talk but a tinkling cymbal .566 q
talk him out of patience*. .589 o
talk of nothing but high. . . .113 o
t. only to conceal the mind.340 i
t. six times with the same‖.374m
talk together still†. . . . . . . .226 e
t. to me, in any summer*. . 69 d
t. too much of Proserpina.551 b
then he will t.—good gods. .589 g
they talk in flowers 219m
when I can t. I'll tell Mama380 g
Talked-Adam in the garden. .574 s
and talk'd meekly. . . . . . . .518 v
he t., wrote, or rehearsed. .581 d
talked like poor Poll. . . . . . .182 s
talked the night away. . . . . .443 d
village statesmen t. with. .589 d
what others talked of while 85 q
Talker-he is also a talker. . . .716 f
Talkers-good t. are only. . . . .589 u
talkers are no good doers*.589 q
Talking-always talking of. .777 o
for t. age and whispering. .614 c
he will be t., as they say*. .653 w
I profess not t.; only this*. 5 q
proud, conceited, t. spark. .589 t
Talks-for who t. much must.113m
he t. of wood; it is some*. .431 h
he talks to me that never*. .109 q
he who talks much cannot.790 t
t. quite glibly of church. . .1 2 u
tongue when'er he talks. . . .472 r
when it talks too long. . . . . .652 w
who t. much must talk in. .589 c
Tall-divinely t. and most†. . . 37 l
exceeding t. and strong. . . .579 o
hero always should be tall.301 c
her stature tall—I hate a‖. .655 j
so t. and bold as they be†. . .116 c
so tall to reach the pole. . . .386m
tall as Mars, and statelier. .568 k
t. men had ever very empty369 p
tall, the wise, the reverend 141 t
Tally-books but the score*. . .452 c
Talmud-the Talmud and the.385 a
Tam-but Tam was glorious. .630 v
Tame-I'll watch him, t. and* 589 o
is t., it's humble, and waits* 11m
lust in man no charm can. .551 l
ne'er so t., so cherish'd*. . .608 w
which thou canst not tame.593 f
Tameless-no longer t. then. . .667 l
Tamer-thou t. of the human. 6 r
Taming-out a monster t. . . . 269 j
Tammie-as T. glow'red. 383m
Tampering-guilt lie in the t. .325 q
tampering with the causes.325 q
Tandaradi-T.! sweetly sang. . 52 j
Tangled-richly t. overhead. . .222 q
Tankard-totty with thine. . . .584 n
Tantalus-like the stone over.745 b
Taper-call their "midnight‖.200 k
curl round his midnight t. .457 x
I'll give you a t. or go on. . .670 e
moths around a taper. . . . . . 16 e
the gleaming t.'s light. . . . .307 s
to husband out life's taper.523 u
yet the taper glows. . . . . . . .351 r
yon taper cheers the vale. .300 e
Taper-light-or with t.-l.*. . . .252 y
Tapers-answer, ye evening t.479 l
bid the tapers twinkle fair. 94 e
but sad, funereal tapers§. . .298 c

you'd drop a teare.......... 35 _e_
Tear-drop–a t-d. glisten'd...591 _d_
  dash the t-d. from my eye.. 89 _r_
Tear-glands–grief two t-g.... 17 _m_
Tears–accept these grateful‡.590 _k_
  and gave me up to tears*...591 _u_
  and he, a marble to her t.*.591 _k_
  and tears, and tortures‖....560 _r_
  and tears that speak........664 _j_
  and weep your tears*......533 _d_
  a night of t.! for the gusty.416 _h_
  as my tears fill her bed.....366 _b_
  away in transient tears..... 90 _a_
  baptized in tears...........387 _r_
  bathed with blood and tears 669 _j_
  Beauty's t. are lovelier than 590 _k_
  behold their tears......... 272 _t_
  betraying smiles, feign'd t.658 _b_
  beyond this vale of tears...267 _c_
  big round t. run down his..592 _q_
  blind my een wi' tears.....591 _e_
  blot the ill with tears......351 _l_
  brings the t. into her eyes..394 _o_
  bursting tears my heart....530 _f_
  busy have no time for tears‖568 _w_
  cannot stop their tears..... 88 _v_
  can tears speak griefe......239 _n_
  carried off by tears........745 _m_
  cease your t. and let it lie..131 _v_
  clean with tears........... 255 _a_
  cloud swells with tears... 395 _l_
  cups with tears**...........221 _i_
  did he break into tears*...591 _l_
  dim with childish tears¶...573 _h_
  dip their wings in tears†...568 _q_
  dipt in baths of hissing t.†.351 _m_
  drop tears as fast as the*...591 _z_
  drown'd these news in t.*..414 _v_
  drown the stage with t.*....423 _m_
  embalm'd in tears.........243 _e_
  ever scare me with thy t.†.592 _o_
  ever wept, and in his tears.591 _f_
  eyes have leisure for their†.603 _u_
  eyes with tears were red...366 _a_
  fall the tears of love........216 _m_
  flattered to t. this aged man 405 _l_
  fountain of sweet tears¶...272 _k_
  fresh t. stood on her cheeks*592 _e_
  friendship's tears.........216 _m_
  gave me up to tears*. .....402 _d_
  gently fall my tears........570 _l_
  grave with my repentant t. *523 _m_
  hence these tears. ....745 _l_
  her death-bed steeps in t...391 _p_
  her income tears............297 _e_
  her tears will pierce into a*.659 _j_
  his language in his tears..591 _n_
  hopes, your prayers, our t.§.118 _j_
  if you have t., prepare to*..591 _t_
  in silence and tears‖........464 _j_
  in those tears they washed.592 _p_
  in thy sister's flood of t.*...383 _i_
  iron t. down Pluto's cheek**557 _i_
  kiss'd again with tears†....513 _r_
  leaves millions in tears....403 _j_
  lie too deep for tears¶......221 _f_
  like Niobe, all tears*......659 _d_
  lips which kiss the t. away.333 _o_
  liquid drops of t. that you*.592 _d_
  lively acted with my tears*591 _v_
  love and tears for the blue.636 _p_
  made of sighs and tears*..363 _f_
  make it with thy tears.....571 _y_
  mine have draw salt tears*592 _h_
  mine own t. do scald like*.. 8 _i_
  morn her earliest t. bestow‡285 _l_
  my darkness and tears..... 10 _p_
  my drops of t. I'll turn*....591 _o_
  my t. must stop, for every.590 _t_
  not shock'd at tears‖..... ...590 _f_
  net. dim the sweet look§...411 _h_
  of toil and of tears......... 8 _n_
  rainbow'd out in tears......296 _x_
  raining the tears of*.......592 _b_
  runs through the realms of.603 _s_
  sacred source of...........590 _q_
  salt of most unrighteous t.*376 _q_

sands of life with tears‖....464 _h_
see your falling tears.......131 _v_
she sees the t. of bearded...591 _i_
shower of commanded t.*..591 _s_
sick of worldly tears and... 21 _l_
smiles that seem akin to t..408 _i_
soul of love with tears†....366 _n_
starting tears each eye‡....457 _j_
stanch thy bootlesse teares.138 _e_
strangled his language in*.340 _a_
studied the philosophy of t.592 _t_
sweet April's tears........392 _m_
sweet tears! the awful.....591 _g_
tears all in vain........... 8 _n_
t. and laughter for all time.549 _v_
t. are due to human misery.745 _o_
tears are sometimes........745 _n_
t. are the silent language..592 _r_
t. from the depths of some†.592 _n_
t., idle tears, I know not†..592 _n_
tears of bliss among it......219 _j_
tears of the first morn......225 _s_
tears of the sky for the loss.154 _a_
tears of wrath and strife...386 _a_
t. such as angels weep**...591 _a_
tears that you may shed....286 _g_
t. to human suffering are¶..592 _s_
tears to the wind-flower....216 _l_
tears which stars weep.....153 _x_
teem with woman's tears*..591 _r_
the big round t. coursed*. 592 _c_
the moon into salt tears....595 _o_
the salt of human tears.....603 _l_
the smiles, the tears.......673 _b_
the tears live in an onion*..592 _g_
the tears of mournful eve..154 _b_
the tears of woe...........623 _b_
those t. will run soon in...590 _d_
through the crystal tears*..193 _k_
to fill it with my tears*.....592 _k_
we are blind with tears....592 _m_
weep and tears that speak.590 _l_
weeps only tears of poison.522 _r_
wet with tears of the.......225 _s_
what should I say my t.*..592 _j_
when embalm'd in tears....243 _e_
with artificial tears*........145 _l_
with blinding tears*........288 _g_
with lovers' tears*.........363 _r_
with mine own t. I wash*... 1 _c_
with sad unhelpful t., and*.592 _l_
with your t. moist it again*.663 _l_
worse than tears drown*...288 _d_
wronged orphan's tears....637 _p_
you sacrifice your tears*...663 _l_
Teary–an' teary roun' the†.590 _w_
Tease–thus tease me together 114 _i_
Teasing–half t. and half.....392 _s_
  teasing with their melodies.394 _b_
Te Deum–together sung*....407 _r_
Tedious–his prattle to be t.*..423 _a_
  life is as t. as a twice-told*.350 _n_
  O, he's as t. as is a tir'd*... 69 _d_
  so tedious is this day*...... 24 _f_
  tedious as a twice-told‡....578 _m_
  tedious than the dial eight*.365 _b_
  which makes it tedious*...422 _u_
Tediousness–t. the limbs and*654 _b_
Teeth–black, Læcania white..176 _l_
  chattering his t. for cold...546 _l_
  drunkard clasp his teeth...326 _q_
  even to the and forehead*.438 _p_
  lips might freeze to my t.*.432 _q_
  out of the t. of emulation*.633 _n_
  show their teeth are white.254 _i_
  show their teeth in way of*. 84 _d_
  smash his teeth with.......181 _q_
  spyght of his tethe........500 _t_
  tail takes in his teeth.....213 _g_
  teeth of time.............203 _a_
  thrust his hand between*...629 _a_
  waves show their t. in the..408 _j_
  with angry teeth he bites..113 _a_
  you had four teeth........174 _l_
Telegraphs–electric t.........327 _c_
Tell–better neither to ask nor601 _f_
  canst not t. nor yet surmise.605 _i_

I can talk I'll tell mama....380 _g_
I hate to tell again a tale...578 _n_
let ill tidings t. themselves*415 _a_
men of sense never tell it...519 _u_
striving to tell his woes....554 _a_
tell her that wastes........243 _s_
tell his wife all he knows...104 _a_
tell how the truth may be..536 _f_
tell me not in mournful§..348 _n_
tell thee where that saying*493 _t_
t. what's doing on the other*132 _l_
t. you no more if I preach..347 _j_
tell your resolution.........525 _v_
tell you what you are......764 _a_
why, that I cannot tell.... .631 _n_
Tell-tales–t-t. of their ....220 _p_
Temper–a cheerful t. joined... 88 _l_
  bless'd with t., whose‡.....658 _j_
  dauntless t. of his mind*...628 _o_
  feeble temple should*......257 _e_
  her fickle t. has oft been....397 _p_
  hot t. leaps o'er a cold*...592 _w_
  made thee to temper man..657 _y_
  minds an equal t. know‡...406 _r_
  take his t. from his dinner.311 _s_
  t. and fretful disposition...682 _p_
  temper the glare of the sun.487 _t_
  touch of celestial temper**.199 _j_
  winds will make men's t...592 _u_
Temperament–t. and not of‖.. 77 _u_
Temperance–ask God for t.*.593 _m_
  beget a t. that may give*..423 _k_
  by temperance taught**...593 _l_
  dictate of spare t.**........593 _j_
  in a pet of temp'rance**...593 _l_
  justice, verity, t.*.........535 _e_
  rein'd again to temperance* 17 _q_
  t. would be difficult.......593 _g_
  with temperance alone‡....295 _p_
Temperate–t. in every place..593 _d_
  temperate who considers...680 _b_
  the temperate will¶.......661 _d_
Tempers–fortune gives to....388 _v_
  God tempers the cold to the.510 _c_
Tempest–a t. dropping fire*..578 _d_
  born of tempest............247 _b_
  from thy shore the t. beat*.578 _a_
  ocean into tempest wrought460 _s_
  silence we the tempest fear.554 _c_
  surge may sweep the t.'s‖.150 _l_
  t. in a tumbler of water....790 _l_
  tempest itself lags behind..385 _k_
  the t. growls ; but as it....578 _f_
  tracts of calm from t.†.....598 _b_
  very torrent, t., and, as I*..423 _k_
  windy tempest of my heart*592 _a_
Tempests–and the loud t.....134 _m_
  break nor tempests roar....133 _u_
  I have seen tempests, when*578 _d_
  looks on t. and is never*...317 _o_
  rocked by tempests§.......532 _h_
  swell'd with t. on the ship‡577 _r_
  tempests charge the sky...577 _t_
  to feel those t., which fly..642 _i_
Tempestuous–life's t. hours..658 _d_
Temple–and the t. of his gods.469 _d_
  a temple in ruin stands‖....535 _t_
  burnt the temple of Diana.200 _g_
  call'd to the t. of impure...593 _c_
  chiefest temple I'll erect*..286 _a_
  doorstep to the t. of wisdom651 _q_
  dwell in such a temple*... . 37 _d_
  fame's proud temple shines 200 _d_
  favored t. is an humble....310 _d_
  floor of nature's temple....220 _i_
  fly from so divine a temple* 564 _o_
  in Fame's great temple§...201 _t_
  in the temple lost outright.352 _i_
  into the temple of heaven..712 _b_
  let each new t. nobler than..571 _n_
  nothing base to the temple.802 _s_
  only of the temple's uses... 28 _h_
  t. and tower went down‖... 76 _t_
  t. bar to Aldgate street....629 _i_
  temple is an humble heart..487 _e_
  temple of fame stands upon 201 _f_
  temple of their hireling....279 _h_

Shakespeare *; Milton **; Wordsworth ¶; Byron ‖; Tennyson †; Lowell ††; Pope ‡; Longfellow §.

temple to fame in rubble...429 b
the temple rear'd its. .....122 s
went into the t., there to**.337 r
where God hath a temple..508bb
world is the mighty temple.708 f
Temples-broken t. spread‡... 98 n
grottoes and t. with their..545 k
groves were God's first t....609 c
hang on her temples*......291 p
like gold nails in temples††.664 w
mortal temples of a king*..140 s
my temples bare..........343 n
on my throbbing t., potent.543 f
talk not of t., there is one..413 f
temples are not to be built.707 m
temples how beloved......804ee
the temples of his gods....136 e
the solemn t., the great*..634m
they are temples at once.... 67 d
we quote t. and houses.....514 b
Temporal-the force of t.*...382 p
Tempt-all t. the sick to trust.512 r
devils soonest tempt*.....594 e
must tempt the dark abyss.337 w
once t, him well to fix his...670 b
t. unto a close exploit of*..594 i
t. the frailty of our powers*.594 k
t. the rover through the....323 j
t. you to eternity of kissing 334 n
to tempt its new-fledg'd...450 l
undergo, or tempt a danger.628 l
worser spirit t. me again*..583 h
Temptation-admits t........329 k
against a temptation as....594m
dangerous is that t.*......594 j
many a dangerous t........593 r
safe from temptation, safe§316 q
temptation to transgress**.119 q
that makes the temptation.593 t
that way going to t.*......594 h
virtue rejoices in t........801 c
why comes t. but for......593 o
Temptations-some t. come to 594 n
strong temptations planted.594 o
temptations attack the idle.594 n
t. hurt not, though........593 s
Tempted-t. me to accept....269 f
Tempter-t. is in pressing it..594m
the tempter stood**......257 r
Tempts-t. by making rich‡..594 c
t. your wandering eyes.....144 k
that tempts the eye.......266 i
the devil t. us not—'tis we..593 q
Ten-t. to one that side is cast.436 r
ten to the world allot......600 s
upper ten thousand.......513 c
upper ten thousand of the..513 j
Tenth-t. of mankind would *.645 p
Ten-to-oners-the t-t-o, were in 20 o
Tenanted-t. by taste and love 77 m
Tenantless-graves stood t.*...140 d
Tendance-by her fair t.**....219 b
must give my tendance to*.412 f
Tended-watched and tended§.136 a
Tendency-my tendency is to‖650 q
Tender-all tender like gold...322 l
and tender in address... ..450 g
grow tender at his ditty....102 l
half teasing and half tender 392 s
much more t. on the whole‖ 655 k
O Douglas t. and trewe.... 80 c
so sad, so t., yet so true....578 s
tender for another's pain...582 o
t. handed stroke a nettle...119 a
tender may reprove.......360m
thou art tender to 't*......126 j
to bear too tender or too‡..361 n
Tenderest-bravest are the t...444 p
Tender-hearted-for a lady...356 k
Tenderly-looks t. down ....250 e
Tenderness-disguise even t.‖.662 e
spiritual in its tenderness...558 c
t. is under a love which it..629 g
tenderness of wifely love..644 x
t. that heavenward.......645 l
Tendrils-all tendrils green..218 h
red tendrils and pink......231 a

round these with t. strong¶ 68 p
Tenement-o'er-inform'd the..571 j
of the ruined tenement....304 l
Tenets-in some nice t. might.346 r
nice tenets might be wrong197 n
our t. just the same at last‡ 27 m
tenets with books, and‡....373 u
Tennis-balls-already stuffed*458 f
Tennis-court-in that vast t-c.*151 g
Tenor-held the t. of his way.. 11 c
noiseless t. of their way....347 t
tenor's voice is spoilt by‖..557 b
Tent-and pitches there its t..561 d
have struck heaven's tent.. 17 d
pitchest here thy golden t..541 q
the low d..orway of my t.††634 h
the t. is struck, the vision††634 h
Tent-hangings-heaven's t-h..397 e
Tents-crystal-pointed tents..640 j
fold their t.,like the Arabs§.415 r
little tents of odour........243 b
old among their shining t.§.529m
silent tents are spread.....272w
the tents of his children....583 r
Termagant-zeal's a dreadful.673 u
Terminations-terrible as her*659 t
Terms-airs and recollected t.*568 n
cannot woo in festival t.*..663 i
happiest terms I have*... .199m
no terms except an.......636 t
t. ill defined, and forms....674m
to teach a soldier terms*...663 j
Terrace-a terrace walk, and..652 l
Terraces-walks, cloisters, t... 14m
Terrestrial-to all t. things he 21 c
Terrible-approach is seen so*106 g
a terrible man with a......409 t
a t. thing to be pestered††..479w
nothing terrible in death...136 u
t. as her terminations*.....659 t
terrible he rode alone.......443 b
thou art terrible—the tear..134 j
Terrifies-neighboring funeral695 s
Territory-no more slave t....559 d
Terror-and terror in her tier‖.551 o
armed with a new terror....133 c
dissent the mortal terror...451 f
frown was full of terror....208 s
overcome his own terror.. .209 e
perch and not their terror*.439 b
robe of terror and beauty 531 f
spake the grisly Terror**...136 s
terror and delight.........327m
t., Cassius, in your threats*.305 l
terror closes the ears.......699 j
t. to the soul of Richard*...549 r
the citizens with t. dumb‖..636 a
the gap in heats of terror.. 64 f
we tremble at an empty t..767 f
Terrors-know the t. of the ...460 n
terrors and troubles from a105 l
terrors of that horrid shore 42 i
Tesselate-temple tesselate...220 l
Test-belief is the real test.... 39 a
ridicule is the t. of truth....621 n
the test of truth, love‖ .....599 i
took for truth the test of...621 u
with her of ridicule the test621 u
Testament-hear but this t.*..284 a
purple t. of bleeding war*.639 f
than my t. fer that††.......637 k
Tested-metal of a man is t.†† 81 l
Tests-peace hath higher t. of.629 c
Testy-touchy, t., pleasant....259 k
Tetchy-t. and wayward*.....619 j
Tether-man can t. time or...599 f
Teucer-auspices of Teucer...692 l
Teviot-sweet T.! on thy......532m
Text-approve it with a text*.145 h
a square of text that looks† 68 l
critics should pervert the t. 68m
God takes a t. and preacheth467 g
holy text around she strews183 a
holy text of pike and gun..157 o
pronounce a text..........450 e
read ev'ry t. and gloss over473 x
rivulet of text shall....... 68 h

the top, is nature's text††..492 j
Texts-have the t. in their....781 n
maggots of corrupted t.....520 d
Texture-her t.; she is given..515m
Thais-lovely Thais by his side 69 p
Thales-Milesian T. urged that650 p
Thames-hill beside the silver.532 n
matchless vale of Thames..532 o
my Thames affords‡........213m
the bosom of Father Thames 63 n
Thank-heart shall thank you.594 t
I thank you for your voices*594 u
Moor t. me, love me and*...145 d
now let us t. th' eternal ... 8 e
t. God for tea! What would590 a
t. God I am not a woman*..659 k
t. Him for the golden-rod...229 p
thank you for nothing......504 v
they would t. their maker. 454 s
whom none can thank.....319 n
Thanked-God be t. that the..667 c
nobody thanked him for it..873.r
not t. at all, I'm thank'd...163 o
she t. me, and bade me*....663m
t. my God for worldly .....642 e
when I'm not thank'd at all594 q
Thankful-t. heart is not only.709 l
Thanking-t. God, whose§....430 f
Thankit-Lord be thankit....166 g
Thankless-t., inconsistent....373 h
to have a thankless child*..319 s
Thanks-best t. for a good....594 s
for this relief, much thanks*86 y
give God t., and make no*..342 p
he t. God for anything......594 r
I am even poor in thanks*. 38 p
I give thee thanks in part*.147 f
more of thanks and less....110 f
no one thanks him for it....785 p
send up our thanks to God.424 q
small t. are still the market‖ 77 f
such thanks I give*........594w
solemn t. and supplication.609 c
thanks are justly due......709 n
thanks of millions yet to be301 f
"t. to Allah, who gives.....617 b
thanks to Ceres yield‡......424 i
t. to the gracious God of...670 h
words are but empty thanks664 h
Thanksgiving-hymns of high594 x
morning service of T.......594 y
on T. day, when from......595 a
Thanksgivings-for the golden595 b
Thatch-gold or roof of t.§....135m
set their thatch on flame...525 e
t. smokes in the sun thaw..110 h
Thatch-eaves-round the t-e...544 c
Thaw-t. and resolve itself*...149 s
there comes a little thaw...539 f
Theatre-above shade, a**... 609 k
as in a t., the eyes of men*.423 a
Cato, do you enter the t....742 c
everybody has his own t...422 e
theatre for virtue.........105 j
the world's a t., the earth..668 j
this wide and universal t.*669 g
vast universe serves for a t.422 k
Theatres-t., pageants, games 14m
Theban-this same learned T.*580 p
Thebes-gates of Thebes .....708 p
Thee-are all with t.,—are all§118 f
rises silent to Thee.........488 r
to live with thee and be....361 t
Theft-exclusive property is a785 c
power have uncheck'd t.*..595 o
property is theft..........785 b
there's boundless theft*....595 l
Thefts-sweet thefts to reveal123 o
Theme-choose what t. we....113 j
example as it is my theme. 78 u
fools are my theme‖........251 f
"give me a t.," the little...479 e
no t. more plentiful to scan.369 s
the glad diviner's theme...634 d
thou, my all! my theme...276 g
'tis not a theme you need..479 e
Themes-transcend our ..... .598 d

Themselves–t. are they.......263 f
  t. in that just mirror see....604 i
  virtue is the love of t.......547 q
Theologians–t. call—and......197 t
Theological–in t. language....520 s
Theology–and even, alas, T.. 342 a
  and t. too; I have heard...516m
  theology is anthropology...791 j
Theories–gray are all theories776 q
Theory–confronts us—not a..482 j
There–neither here nor t.*....507 l
Thermopylæ–make a new T.‖442w
Thespis–T. the first professor 32 q
Thetis–of T.taken out his nap584 f
Thick–dash'd through t. and.476 o
  muddy, ill-seeming, thick*.659 b
  through thick and thin....309 a
  through thick and thin she.108 f
Thicker–blood is t. than......496m
  thicker than itself with*...255 r
Thicket–and to the t. some...610 o
  roadside thicket hiding.....228 h
  steep of echoing hill or t.**670 j
  from the neighboring t. the§ 50 i
Thickets–food the t. yield‡...342 k
  t. to his floods decline.....532 n
  thorny thickets leaves.... 56 d
  ye bowery thickets hail....610 p
Thief–each thing's a t.; the*..595 o
  earth's a thief, that feeds*.595 o
  followers than a t. to the...595 c
  I will show thee a thief....503ll
  procrastination is the t. of..604 d
  robe upon a dwarfish thief* 30 a
  saves the thief*...........279 g
  so clomb the first grand**..451 c
  sworn twelve have a t. or*.331 u
  the moon's an errant thief.595 o
  the sea's a t., whose*......595 o
  the sun's a t. and with his*.595 o
  t. doth fear each bush an*..586 q
  thou strongest thief of all†.595 s
Thieves–beauty provoketh t.* 36 s
  desperate t., all hopeless*..122 d
  thieves at home must hang.114 q
  t. cannot be true one to.*...595 j
  t. for their robbery have*..595 p
Thigh–rosy thigh half buried†278 l
  the bee with honied thigh**562 b
Thighs–crop their waxen t.*..197 e
  load his little thighs.. .....321 r
Thimble–silver t., or with a...663 e
Thin–dash'd through thick...476 o
  so t. that life looks through*597 o
  they are t. and pale, their..579 t
  through thick and thin ....309 a
  through thick and t. she...108 f
Thine–what is thine is mine...704 p
Thing–each t. both in small..150 s
  each t.'s a thief ; the laws*.595 o
  how poor a thing is man...370 u
  no the thing I should be....520 a
  not the thing you kiss....131 v
  saved some trifling thing... 8 a
  speak gently! 'tis a little t.574 e
  the play's the thing*.......423 l
  t. that I was born to do..,..146 i
  too much of a good thing..484 c
Things–all other t. give place.656 j
  all t. have an equal right...347 f
  as things are unknown.....698 u
  a time for all things*......505gg
  brought all t. to their......479m
  but God's sons are things..664 x
  but words are things, and‖.427 i
  can such things be*........661 n
  clay for the earthen things.449 l
  in the midst of things .....675 c
  more t. in heaven and earth*473 l
  of the main chance of t.*...493 i
  sad vicissitude of things.... 76 l
  sad vicissitudes of things..476 u
  seek for things in words....664 l
  seeming to be many things.410 t
  the eternal fitness of things 462 q
  the sake of things......... 664 l
  these little t. are great to..619 o

things are of that nature...203m
  t. are the sons of heaven...664 t
  t. at the worst will cease*..152 f
  t. bad begun make strong*.527 k
  t done well, and with a care* 5 u
  things ill-got had ever bad* 582 f
  things of to-day......... ..146 k
  t. sweet to taste prove*....506aa
  things that are not at all...506bb
  t. to come than the things‖.599 j
  things unknown propos'd‡.325 c
  t. were as fine as could....356m
  t. which must be must be..164 a
  though words and things¶..486 d
  to t. of sale a seller's praise*442 o
  vainest of all things§.......534 k
  when all things I heard.... 91 d
  words, however, are things665 a
Think–always talk who never.589 k
  and learn to think.........429 n
  a nobler privilege to think..597 j
  be his bride nor think o'.... 70 n
  comedy to those that t.....669 p
  dares think one thing‡.....199 g
  greatly t. or bravely die‡...361 n
  how many never t., who...597 y
  I cannot sit and think.... .. 66 k
  I t. him so because I think*.517 p
  I think, therefore I exist...799 e
  let each man think himself.369 q
  little do you think upon...445m
  live and think............501 n
  made me think the most... 66 b
  not be bound to think.....485 r
  otherwise does think......791 o
  perhaps millions think‖....427 i
  pleasant too, to think on...660 l
  Puritan did not stop to t...521 p
  say just what I think§......556 u
  she could not t., but would.644w
  space to think and feel.....484 j
  t. all you speak ; but speak573 q
  think for the best.........808 e
  t. justly of the thinking....597 y
  t. less of himself than he...310 v
  think of this life*.........350 j
  think on thy sins*.........518 q
  think too much of himself.788 h
  those who t. must govern..190 i
  'tis sweet to t. that where'er 663 x
  to live, as well as to think.. 79 e
  to think and to feel.......270 j
  to think their slender tops..613 k
  what heart can think......313 j
  when I would pray and t.*.489 n
  who can t. wise or stupid...782 p
  who t. themselves most wise338 v
  who t. too little, and who..589 b
Thinker–arrival of a t. in the.596 e
Thinking–art of thinking..... 28 a
  goes material for thinking.797 c
  he is a thinking reed.......597 g
  I everywhere am thinking..192 f
  little one thinking about... 31 e
  man a thinking being is...597 y
  thinking and acting........724 i
  t. is but an idle waste of...597 v
  thinking of thee, still thee.. 3 a
  t. still, my thoughts might.597 s
  too much thinking to have‡ 83 c
  without thinking on asses.. 19 h
Thinks–evil to him who evil..807 p
  goodness thinks no ill**....651 e
  he most lives who t. most...345m
  he who t. himself wise.....768 a
  seldom thinks with more...167 b
  smokes, thinks like a sage..457 f
  so far as he t. himself so....780 l
  t. good easy man, full*.....151 r
  thinks greatly of himself...286m
  thinks himself immortal...401 p
  t. in his spirit in the world..597 x
  t. what ne'er was, nor is‡...472 d
  to speak what he thinks...800 q
  what his heart thinks*.....556 y
  who thinks............808 k
  who thinks must mourn...349 s

Third–a third course is open..798 p
  the t. o' the world is yours*645m
  to make a t., she join'd the.479 b
Thirst–accursed t. for gold...708 k
  a thirst of glory boast‡.....125 j
  bottle does not quench t....506 s
  comes a thirst to be away..541 o
  dropp to quenche a thirst..334 q
  for drink, thirst...........713 g
  help the t. that dominates..325 q
  patient of thirst and toil....543 h
  pines with thirst amidst‡...162 j
  quench the t. of his spirit..557 e
  thirst for noble pickle......181 i
  thirst is mastering you....745 q
  thirst for fame is much....750 q
  t. that from the soul doth..641 d
  with eager t., by folly or by. 98 d
Thirsteth–drinking t. still....460 h
Thirsts–t. with each heat and 672 i
Thirsty–drink for the thirsty.561 a
  goes to bed t. rises healthy.499 j
Thirty–at thirty man.........401 p
  thirty days hath September.390 j
  thirty days to each affix....390 i
  wrong side of thirty....... 12 g
Thirty-one–all the rest have..390 j
  every other thirty-one......390 i
Thirty-five–must begin by...657 c
  life declines from t-f......657 c
  trifle not at thirty-five.....657 c
Thistle–the thistle springs‡..219 n
  thistle's purple bonnet.....218 c
  with rain the t. bendeth....577 s
Thistle-breed–not of t-b......240 f
Thistle-down–white t-d.......246 p
  wrought of gilded t-d......584 e
Thistles–rough t., kecksies*..643m
Thorn–are crown'd with t....619 h
  a t. her song book making.. 52 f
  beneath the milk-white t...618 g
  coquetry is the thorn that..114 n
  dewy milk-white thorn.....655 a
  drop from every thorn‡....242 u
  erect this aged thorn¶......246 g
  every rose a t. doth bear...511 f
  God is more there than thou529 a
  hedge nor solitary thorn...543 r
  he only asks a thorn.......466 t
  I have a thorn.............243 l
  linger'd on the thorn......242 e
  ne'er the rose without the t.496 s
  on every t., delightful......652 c
  peeps beneath the thorn....239m
  plant in that bosom a t.*...618 c
  prickly t. often bears soft..684 k
  quick with thorn..........231 c
  rude protection of the t....610 o
  sparkling on the thorn..▪..154 f
  the rankling thorn to wear.351 r
  there is a thorn¶.... .... 246 q
  the rose and t. the treasure.101 x
  upon a thorn......... ....243 d
  without thorn the rose**...219 d
Thorn-tree–blackbird bright in. 43 a
Thorns–by the thorns and by.231 c
  crown, didst tear the thorns 55 n
  forever be a crown of t.....533 o
  gather thorns for flowers...333 k
  is but a wreath of thorns**.534 l
  its thorns outgrown.... ....241 t
  mocked with a crown of t.. 55 n
  pricked by the thorns.....505dd
  rose does not bloom without776 n
  roses have thorns*........208 l
  set with little wilful thorns†660 q
  sharp crown of t. upon§....479 v
  thorns which I have reap'd‖526 v
  to be touch'd by the thorns.548 r
  touch'd by the thorns......349 e
  with a crown of thorns.... 92 i
Thorny–clearing t. wrongs...667 n
  life is t., and youth is vain. 17 q
  thorny blooms and so......230 b
  thorny point of bare*......120 o
Thou–for thou must die......131 a
Thought–a cast of thought... 36 l

adds to the thought........251 *a*
amassed t. and experience..337 *f*
and lands t. smoothly......198 *v*
and less of thought.......110 *f*
a penny for your thought..495 *p*
a t. by thought is piled.....597 *p*
a thought disloyal.........237 *a*
a thought is often original..596 *v*
a t. often makes us hotter§.596 *z*
author of that thought.....513 *t*
a well of lofty thought ... 80 *k*
awhile the old t. retain....596 *h*
be it thought and done*.... 5*m*
be noble in every thought§.418 *f*
burning deed and thought§.348 *p*
but a single thought.......778 *p*
but thought and no longer.171 *g*
by want of thought........187 *r*
calm ev'ry t., inspirit‡...106 *a*
capable of sober thought...117 *d*
chaos of thought and‡.....371 *v*
corroding every thought...328 *j*
deeper than all thought....210 *o*
delicate t., that cannot....237 *g*
destroyed by thought......596 *q*
done, t., gained or been.. 64 *k*
eares and ev'ry thought .. 83 *h*
easily be thought than said.289 *b*
ere T. could wed itself†....598 *a*
ever having had a t. of it...427 *c*
every t. of that soft kind..474 *k*
every thought that genius§598 *s*
every thought which genius596 *n*
exhausting t., and hiving‖..580 *k*
explore the t., explain the‡. 11 *a*
father, to that thought*....652 *j*
first in loftiness of thought.479 *b*
fly that tyrant, thought.....343 *a*
for thought is tired of.....204 *e*
for want of thought........314 *b*
general honest thought*...418 *l*
glow of lofty thought......117 *a*
God thought about me..... 31 *o*
green t. in a green shade...597 *b*
heroical defect of thought..522 *o*
he thought at heart like‖... 87 *h*
high seas of thought§...... 90 *c*
his mind a thought, his life 369 *q*
human t. is the process....325*m*
if each thought and look...548 *s*
incertain thought imagine*.140 *i*
indolent vacuity of thought 596 *j*
I thought so once but......182 *l*
I thought you and he.......265 *n*
kings of modern t. are dumb595 *t*
knew an evil thought......279 *u*
learning without t. is labor.341 *u*
life is but thought..........346 *p*
life—the demon Thought‖..596 *c*
like an idle thought......246 *p*
like a passing t., she fled..634 *c*
like a pleasant thought¶...228 *a*
like dew, upon a thought‖..427 *i*
loaded with a thought......222 *l*
lost to manly thought.... 567 *t*
lowly rustic thought......249 *q*
lurking thought surprise...276 *n*
magnanimity of thought...401 *p*
men use t. only as authority574 *u*
no great thought..........155 *s*
no tongue but thought*....597 *l*
ocean of thought...........260 *n*
of still and serious t.¶.....598 *g*
oh idle thought in nature.. 50 *p*
one corrupted thought.....479 *q*
one t. of thee puts all‡....361 *r*
one wandering t. pollutes...152*m*
ornament of profound t....791 *l*
our growing thought makes596*m*
pale cast of thought*.......106 *q*
pebbles of our puddly t.... 74 *b*
pleasing dreadful thought.185*aa*
possessed a t. and claims‖..148 *p*
power of t.—the magic‖.....596 *b*
pure in t. as angels are.....361 *u*
raise the t. and touch‡.....325 *d*
rate of thought and feeling.600 *i*

rear the tender thought....456 *a*
revelation of t. takes men..596 *q*
roses kindled into thought. 62 *r*
send me back a thought.....237 *f*
sense from thought divide‡.548*m*
sepulchres of thought§..... 66 *q*
she knew an evil thought...182 *o*
she pin'd in thought*......467 *u*
sober, second t. of the.....482 *f*
some grave mighty thought531 *y*
strange seas of t. alone¶....452 *s*
sudden thought strikes me.264 *t*
tell of saddest thought.....537 *j*
than all poetic thought†.... 92 *s*
the dome of thought, the‖..571 *b*
the dress of thought‡......581 *i*
the giver's loving thought§.380 *i*
the interpreters of thought§ 42 *d*
the minister of thought§....600 *v*
the noon of thought........384 *r*
the principle of thought....726 *o*
these pearls of t. in††. ...477 *k*
the teacher in her thought.455 *s*
the third of thought§......554 *k*
the vehicle of thought......447 *c*
the whitest thought........233 *g*
though old the thought††..514 *g*
thought alone is eternal....597 *c*
thought and deed, not...... 15 *p*
t. and her shadowy brood..381 *a*
thought as a sage..........210*m*
t. been shared by thee.....374 *g*
t. came like a full-blown...596 *x*
t. can never be compared..597 *w*
thought can wing its way..597 *h*
thought grew sweeter and.191 *k*
thought her like her*......215 *l*
thought himself so.........286 *s*
thought is deeper than....210 *o*
thought is discharged......192 *a*
t. is the measure of life.. .348 *j*
thought is the wind....... 79 *v*
thought is too weak to be..791 *n*
t. is valuable in proportion.597 *a*
t. is wedded unto thee§...392 *g*
t. leapt out to wed with†..598 *a*
t. may grace them more...386 *l*
thought of other years††..248 *s*
thought of sorrow free.....249 *l*
thought of thinking souls..353*w*
t. once awakened does.....596 *f*
thought or act accountable.111 *b*
t.'s a weapon stronger......267 *o*
thought's hushed hour.....233 *o*
t. would destroy their......582 *o*
throbb'd not there a t.‖....284 *l*
thus he eas'd his thought‡..106 *c*
tides that follow'd thought†598 *b*
till thought grew pain..... 3 *a*
to each a tender thought§..285 *e*
to raise the thought†......261 *s*
to this thought I hold.....258 *l*
united to a jealous thought.327 *q*
utterance of t. by speech... 28 *b*
wafts embodied thought...448 *e*
want of thought ....490 *t*
weigh the thought that.....253 *e*
wert a beautiful thought‖..596 *d*
what can be called thought.301 *v*
what he greatly t. he‡......130 *d*
what oft was t., but ne'er‡.653 *t*
when he thought of you...300 *i*
when thought is speech....574 *j*
who thought he 'ad won...630*w*
wide as human thought... 29 *i*
with but a single thought..627 *a*
working house of thought*.597*m*
Thoughtful—the t. and the...396 *c*
thrifty and t. of others§....667 *a*
Thoughtless—t., thankless...320 *q*
warning for a t. man¶......413 *h*
Thoughts—abstrse and ....573 *s*
against despairing t.*.......308 *u*
all thoughts, all passions...357*m*
amidst these restless t. this.526 *h*
and foul thoughts**........105 *r*
and over-busy thoughts¶...564 *c*

a sea of blue thoughts......192 *f*
bears his thoughts above*.. 47 *p*
best of t. which he hath....371 *g*
best t. of the greatest sages§ 66 *r*
better than our thoughts... 7 *c*
bolder thoughts can rise...605 *r*
chasing all thoughts unholy 40*m*
childish t., like flowers.....195 *a*
commune with t. of tender.378 *h*
commune with thy t..... .303 *p*
crown my thoughts with*.. 5*m*
cures in me thoughts that*. 88 *r*
dark soul and foul t.**.....352 *o*
dark t. my boding spirit....308 *b*
day and night my t.incline.650 *d*
dead, and their great t......60 *m*
disguise his thoughts.......789 *t*
disguise their thoughts.....789 *v*
employ your chiefest t.*...663 *h*
ends of free thoughts‖......621 *j*
first t. are not always......791 *p*
for lover's thoughts........237 *e*
for t. are so great—aren't..596 *l*
grand t. that never can....597 *d*
great thoughts, great..... 81 *u*
great t., like great deeds...595 *u*
heads replete with t. of....336 *z*
high erected t. seated in a..120 *q*
himself with any such t.*..138 *l*
his looks and thoughts**...369 *k*
his thoughts immaculate*. 83 *p*
hospitable t. intent**......309 *k*
images and precious t.¶....382 *b*
immortality to the thoughts426 *s*
interpreters of their t...... 4 *v*
in thoughts more elevate**.109 *b*
in thoughts not breaths....345*m*
in t. they lie but as in packs574 *i*
kind thoughts contentment111 *h*
link his written thoughts‖..426 *s*
most precious thoughts.... 64 *r*
my own thoughts are my§.596*aa*
my thoughts and I were of.596 *w*
my t. are whirled like a*...597 *n*
my t. by night are often....634 *k*
my t. congeal to verse .....646 *r*
my thoughts I did recoil*..381 *v*
my thoughts of white.......233 *q*
my t. remain below*.......665 *s*
not whiter than the t.††... 480 *a*
of love unite our thoughts*588 *o*
of thoughts unspoken§....596*bb*
our t. and our conduct.... 79 *j*
our thoughts are ours*.....207 *j*
our t. as boundless‖.........444 *x*
our thoughts at home... 598 *h*
painting of the thoughts...782 *q*
pious t. as harbingers to... 22 *b*
river of thy t. may roll....760 *b*
second and sober thoughts.596 *u*
second thoughts are best...694 *k*
second t. are the wisest.....596 *r*
second t.,they say, are best596 *k*
serve your best t.as gypsies474 *s*
should be thoughts*.......364 *a*
shroud of t.which were not‖596 *a*
side; into our thoughts... 17 *c*
slave of my t., obedient‖...471 *p*
slip over many thoughts...791 *k*
something like t. assembled129 *f*
soul, and foul thoughts**..597 *e*
stranger to thy thoughts*..108 *e*
strange t. transcend our...161 *n*
style is the dress of t.......581 *f*
submit all his thoughts....437 *s*
such thoughts resigne......107 *h*
suspect the t. of others*... 93 *r*
sweet are the thoughts that111 *c*
that's for thoughts*.......237 *l*
their t., their very lives... 90 *v*
the river of his thoughts‖..655*m*
these my thoughts to leave597 *s*
these t., these speculative..129 *f*
t. and stirrings of the......522 *a*
t. and sunny weather......544 *i*
t. are winged to summer...395*m*
thoughts are your own....573 *q*

nothing but Corsican thyme 180 *h*
pun-provoking thyme......300 *x*
the thyme her purple¶.....221 *e*
vervain, and flexile thyme..219 *l*
wild mountain thyme......117 *k*
wild t., and valley-lilies...234 *o*
wild thyme blows*.......247 *a*
Thyrsus–twist about a t......231 *r*
Thyself–ask of t. what beauty355 *c*
continuest such, owe to t.**.420 *g*
know thyself..............509*dd*
retire within thyself........683 *h*
shall thyself be learned....337 *g*
Sire to t., thyself as old as..407 *w*
Tiber–draw then to T.*......533 *d*
T. rolls majestic to the main533 *c*
yet wears thy T.'s shore...533 *b*
Tickle–tickle and entertain us.427*m*
tickle her with a hoe and...424 *b*
tickle where she wounds*..120 *k*
Tickled–t. with a straw‡.... 90 *k*
Tickling–a scornful tickling..341 *f*
Ticklish–know what a t......720 *o*
Tide–across the t. to see her..452 *o*
at full of tide, and*....... 58*m*
bears me through the tide. 87 *g*
came the tyde and........ 255 *b*
ebbing tide would flow no§.598 *i*
e'en at the turning o' th'*..138 *l*
in red'ning tide it gush'd..,649 *c*
in a scarlet tide...............239 *a*
is like rocks under tide....547 *e*
it runs as runs the tide..... 75 *a*
lotos bowed above the t.....615 *g*
love has a tide...............598 *r*
man can tether time or t...599 *f*
of hell at ebb of tide.......586 *d*
O tide of the years......... 8 *n*
punctual t. draws up the..598 *q*
resist both wind and tide...207 *k*
restless fields of tide......116 *f*
swim against the tide*..... 58 *k*
Teviot ! on thy silver tide..532*m*
the t. rises, the tide falls§..598 *u*
tide-flowing is feared, for...599 *a*
t. in the affairs of men††..348 *q*
tide in the affairs of men*..461 *o*
time and t. for no man stay 603*m*
western t. crept up along..598 *s*
wind raves, the t. runs high 56 *n*
with the morn the punctual 598 *p*
Tides–both with moons and...371 *b*
gently down the t. of sleep§ 561 *q*
high t. in the calendar*... 131*m*
hurrying t. and the ships..115 *i*
t. that follow'd thought†...598 *b*
tides were in their grave‖..130 *l*
Tidings–convey'd the dismal..455 *i*
let ill t. tell themselves*...415 *a*
proclaims t. of good to Zion 40 *b*
ram thou thy fruitful t.*....436 *j*
sweet tidings of the sun's*. 55 *c*
that I may drink thy t.*...589 *n*
Tie–a tie and obligation... 15 *t*
careless shoe-string in......453 *g*
have some common tie.....749 *a*
itself a holy tie.............264 *a*
link'd in one heavenly tie..376 *f*
silver link, the silken tie...362 *h*
sure tie between friends....749 *b*
tender tie on earthly bliss.. 62 *d*
that love endures no tie....357 *v*
the silver link, the silken t. 588*m*
t. my life within this band.600*m*
tie of thy Lord's hand......515 *s*
Ties–sight of human ties‡....361 *o*
the thread that ties them...514 *h*
wide world is knit with ties 568 *x*
Tier–and terror in her tier‖...551 *o*
Tiger–like the shark and t.‖..311 *c*
or the Hyrcan tiger*. .....130 *j*
tiger, burning bright in the 22 *a*
t. will be mild whiles she*..659 *g*
Tiger-lilies–gorgeous t-l......233 *d*
Tiger-spring–thou with a t-s..522 *q*
Tight–tight little island......327 *g*
Tiles–at Worms as tiles on its.525 *u*

Tillage–by constant tillage...676 *t*
when t. begins, other arts..424 *p*
Tilt–and tilt at all I meet‡....537 *t*
Tilts–t. with a straw against¶.572 *n*
Tilt-yard–his study is his t-y.*303 *e*
Timber-like season'd t. never 80 *a*
wedged in that t. which....527 *u*
Time–age and body of the t..412 *l*
age, but for all time........550 *h*
all notion of time...........365 *p*
always find t. to grow old..671 *s*
and noiseless foot of Time*.602 *t*
and Time the warder........462 *p*
and turn the key of time...604 *a*
and unthinking time........383 *p*
and we must time obey‡....546 *f*
arresting the vast wheel of.599 *r*
art is long, and time is§....348 *k*
as aye since time began....479 *g*
at a certain time...........279 *r*
a time for all things*.......505*gg*
at the loss of time..........792 *k*
at T.'s humming loom I ply792 *l*
because the time was ripe.. 64 *f*
becomes the spy of Time§...600 *v*
beguile the time look like*..196 *b*
be stirring as the time*....526 *a*
between this t. and that ... 2 *r*
bounds of place and time...415 *o*
bourne of Time and Place‡..268 *j*
brief chronicles of the t.*..423 *c*
busy have no t. for tears‖..568*w*
but as time steals onwards.615 *l*
but fades in time...........319*m*
but only time for grief......342 *v*
but proper time to marry...375 *c*
by the time we live..........346 *y*
by time and place ...... 86 *j*
by time and toil we sever...782 *s*
by time subdued (what will 24 *a*
cheer'd up the heavy time*333 *l*
chime move in melodious** 94 *k*
choose thine own time......345 *n*
circumstances of time...... 22 *g*
come Time, and teach me†.603 *u*
consuming t. can destroy..714*m*
count time by heart-throbs.345*m*
day is the child of Time....131 *n*
day out of night, t. out of..150 *q*
days of time begun.........261 *g*
destructive time destroy...746 *c*
do not squander time.......347 *p*
door that time unlocks§....400 *i*
doubts no time does give...346 *s*
dreadful interval of time...105 *a*
dust on antique time*......127*m*
each time she was there.... 23 *a*
earth flits fast and time...138 *g*
e'en such is time ! which...601 *v*
enrich the time to come*...268 *g*
envious and calumniating*.602 *h*
envy Time transported.....90 *j*
error in the round of time†.185 *y*
existence doth depend on t.‖599 *k*
eye of t. beholds no name‡.201 *j*
fear everything from time..767 *e*
fit it with some better t.*..574 *k*
flood of time is rolling on..603 *k*
fools with the time*........253 *a*
forms which T. to touch‖..671*w*
for the time of scorn*......109 *o*
foster-child of Silence and..554 *i*
from Time's chest lie hid*..602 *j*
'gainst the tooth of time*..602 *j*
God's own time is best .....198 *r*
God's time is our harvest...267 *e*
golden time of our hearts..602 *a*
grief which time does not..710 *b*
grown old before my time.. 11 *d*
hath triumphed over Time.302 *t*
he that lacks time to mourn603 *t*
his bosom the record of t...190 *p*
his due in tithe and time...523 *h*
his golden locks T. hath to.601 *q*
his time is forever.........499 *z*
his time is spent*..........143*m*
his t.'s forever, everywhere600 *c*

his youth 'gainst Time and.601 *q*
how a man should kill time601 *u*
however we pass Time, he..601 *e*
I count my t. by times that 600 *k*
I forget all time**..........114 *b*
if time is precious, no book. 64*m*
I had liv'd a blessed time*..350 *g*
illustrious of the days of t.. 94 *d*
improve our time..........746 *n*
in some t., his good time..509*hh*
interposition, for a time...599 *d*
in that sweet time..........219 *l*
into time's infinite sea.... 10 *r*
in time's great wilderness..186 *g*
in time there is no present†186 *k*
irreclaimable time flies....746*w*
is no time like spring......540 *r*
is the thief of time.........604 *d*
it is always time...........801 *h*
joyous t. will not be staid..603 *o*
keep Time in high esteem..601 *t*
know the time to go........217 *k*
know the true value of t...599 *q*
labor was to kill the time..313 *o*
lacks time to mourn........603 *t*
last syllable of recorded t.*605 *o*
leaves have their t. to fall..134 *p*
let time that makes you....601*m*
life is short and t. is swift..347 *l*
like the stream of Time§...532 *c*
like wind flies Time 'tween.600 *u*
long time ago..... ....618 *n*
long time you take.........178 *c*
look into the seeds of time*338 *j*
look like the time*.........482 *o*
love's not T's. fool though*108 *t*
make the time to do so too.434 *l*
make use of time, let not*.602*m*
man can tether t. or tide...599 *f*
may in length of time**....512 *g*
may syllables jar with t....477 *d*
measures all our time......401*m*
mock the time with fairest*312 *y*
moral of time's vicissitude. 611*m*
more time than poor.......264 *d*
move in melodious time**..406 *e*
mourn, lacks time to mend.603 *t*
must yield at length to T...525 *f*
my boast through time.....276 *g*
near to witching t. of night 415 *g*
never-resting thing called..599 *p*
Nick of Time...............502 *o*
noiseless falls the foot of t. 603 *p*
noiseless foot of time*..... 11 *o*
no remembrance which t...792 *l*
no time is too short for... 746 *t*
no time to break jests......328 *n*
no time to feel them........403 *i*
ocean of T., whose waters..603 *l*
old bald cheater, Time......600 *t*
old common arbitrator, T.*602 *t*
old T., in whose banks we..600 *n*
old Time is still a........... 74 *q*
on all important time......354 *u*
one life ;—a little gleam of.346*m*
on the sands of time*.......188 *s*
opening door that time§....605 *j*
O tender t. that love thinks541 *d*
O Time in your flight......599 *b*
O time most accurs'd* .... 671 *j*
O T. the beautifier of the‖..599 *i*
O t. too swift ! O swiftness.601 *q*
Our t. is fixed, and all our..582 *x*
out of time and harsh*..... 40 *g*
out upon T ! it will leave‖..599 *j*
panting T. toil'd after him.428 *o*
place and T. are subject to.381 *a*
prevent waste of time......325 *b*
provident of his t. that is...100 *r*
rapid stream of time.......352 *a*
record the flight of time.... 40 *n*
relish of the saltness of t.*. 11*w*
remedy for time misspent..313 *p*
requiring a long time.......721 *g*
rich with the spoils of time600 *l*
seize time by the forelock..503*ee*
set to true time..........492 *b*

shall T.'s best jewel from*.602 p
short time to stay as you....226 k
showing the unreality of T.597 d
silent power of time........792 e
slowly time creeps till my. 599 h
so silent as the foot of Time604 c
so strong, but Time decays*602 p
speech is shallow as Time..553 w
spend the longest time in††589 h
spend the time to end it*...147 c
stern fate and time........206 e
stream is the River Time...603 s
stretch'd forefinger of all† .435 c
strong force of time........706 c
such a t. as this it is not*...125 v
sunflower, weary of time....245 n
swiftness of time is infinite.746 q
swift speedy T., feathered.600 g
take time and a little delay.677 s
take Time by the forelock...504 r
take time enough‖..........283 g
taught by t., my heart‡.....588 d
tedious waste of time** ....103 f
teeth of Time..............203 a
that defy the tooth of Time.604 b
that great mystery of Time.599 p
that lacks time to mourn...403 i
that time would e'er be o'er142 d
the background of time.....792 i
the dim verge of the time†† 81 h
the good time will come....807 u
the happier the time.......746 p
then is the time for study..580 j
there's a good time coming 267 q
there's a gude time coming 268 d
these walls of Time§........206 q
the time of roses...........241 o
the time is out of joint*....506 l
the t. will come my own....375 s
the wrecks of time.........250 c
this bank and shoal of time 350 u
thou chainest time forever.602 e
threefold the stride of Time.602 d
till T. (that first must seal .601 i
time and chance combine...357 g
t. and change can heap no..600 o
time and the hour runs*. .602 i
t. and tide for no man stay.603 m
time approves it true‖......662 h
time as he passes us has a..600 e
time be past, present, or to 22 g
time both meet to hear*....107 f
t. cannot make them more. 22 g
time completely silver'd...291 g
a time conquers all, and we‡.546 f
t. destroys the groundless..746 a
t. did beckon to the flowers.347 u
time discovers truth........748 e
time divided is never long..603 q
time doth not breathe.....297 t
time doth no present to ....267 m
t. doth transfix the flourish*602 v
t., eft-soon will tumble.....601 g
t. enough to find a world††.668 r
time fleeth on, youth...... 75 a
t. flies and draws us with it791 o
time flies, death urges.....130 b
time flies on restless pinions602 e
time flies so fast, that e'er.606 a
time for moralizing mood..638 m
time for self-improvement.484 j
time for work,—yet take...302 v
t. goes on crutches till love*602 v
time goes with rapid foot..746 n
time has assuaged..........725 n
time has criticized for us††. 67 b
time has laid his hand§....601 b
t. has not cropped the roses673 a
a time has touched it in his§.291 k
t. has touched me gently in600 f
time hath made them pure. 67 j
t. hath, my lord, a wallet*..602 x
time hath nothing blur'd.. 84 a
time is a feathered thing..601 d
time is come round*........350 x
time is eternity ; pregnant. 604 f
time is generally the best..746 l

time is itself an element....792 d
time is like a fashionable*..603 a
time is lord of thee ; thy... 601 o
time is money.............507 e
time is short, life is short ..362 a
time is still a flying........241 n
time is the greatest remedy746 e
time is the life of the soul§.601 c
t. is the nurse and breeder* 603 b
t. is the old justice that*...603 c
time makes these decay....143 e
time only strengthens the..792 f
t. rolls his ceaseless course.602 f
time's blest wings of peace.471 x
time's deform'd hand*.....288 t
time shall not see‖..........259 g
time shall unfold what*....603 d
t.'s hoar wings grow young.161 m
time short in this world....599 d
time's iron feet can print no.460 f
time's noblest offspring is..492 c
t. spent in the cultivation..676 u
t.'s perspective the home... 68 o
time's revolving wheels ....186 i
time stands with impartial.746 h
time steals on and escapes..746 k
time's the king of men*....603 e
time, still as he flies, adds..601 j
time that devours all ......746 m
t., that takes survey of all* 603 f
t. the avenger ! unto thee‖ .599 l
t. the corrector where our‖.599 i
time, the foe of man's ....601 p
time the great destroyer of 354 b
time, thy name is sorrow...570 m
time to console the afflicted107 v
t., to the nation, as to the.. 600 i
t. travels in divers paces*..603 g
time tries the troth in......603 w
time unfolds eternity ... 100 t
t. wasted is existence, used.604 g
t. wears all his locks before603 n
time which strengthens....599 e
time who steals our years..380 q
time will bring to light....746 e
time will come when every. 186 h
time will come, sweet§.....189 f
t. will run back and fetch**601 i
time with reckless hand§...600 w
t. writes no wrinkle on ‖....599 l
'tis but the t. and drawing*140 c
'tis time for me to go.......546 d
'tis time to run, 'tis time to540 t
to beguile the t., look like*.482 c
together on time's string...536 o
to part her time 'twixt‡....349 o
to speak before your time*.185 u
to the shades before my t...150 u
to the true teacher, time's .600 c
touch us gently, Time...... 600 b
true value of time.........599 q
type of time or care........202 e
urged at a t. unseasonable*281 b
vanish in the chinks that T.602 b
verge of time e'en now.....186 d
very witching t. of night*..417 o
wastes her time and me....243 s
waste the t., which looks*..619 s
we push time from us, and.604 h
we see time's furrows on...604 i
we take no note of time....604 e
what time hath blurr'd.....487 l
wheel of time goes round..329 u
wheel of t. rolls downward.746 v
when the time comes.......792 h
when t. and need require...738 u
when time is broke and no*407 m
when t. is flown, how it fled601 f
whirligig of t. brings in his*602 u
who murders t. he crushes.604 f
wise through time, and....650 r
with the waste of time*... 434 r
worn out with eating time . 9 m
yesterday, bid time return*602 o
yet, do thy worst, old T.*..603 j
yet time who changes all‖..599 n
youth is not rich in time...673 q

you wish the t. were now...464 f
Time-honor'd-of a t-h. race‖..566 h
Timeless-t. tuneless fellow‖..557 b
Time-piece-ancient t-p. says§117 i
Times- a light for after times381 s
all men, nor for all times...623 x
all tongues, and times...... 15 a
and principles with times‡. 75 r
bear me back to times .....466 m
brisk and giddy-paced t.*..568 n
corrector of enormous t....635 l
dead times revive in thee¶.322 o
dear times dead to me......233 c
events of times.............270 f
fatness of these pursy t.*.. 633 k
full twenty times was¶.....210 k
hopes better t., and sips....433 g
how many times do I love..355 i
lived in the tide of times*..404 a
many times do I love again.355 i
nature of the t. deceas'd* ..493 i
old times, old manners, old 9 s
praise they that will times.111 e
principles with times‡......373 u
regardless of our own t.....676 l
seven times one to-day..... 60 b
soft-heartedness, in t. like††641 t
talk six times with the‖....374 m
there are t. when patience .466 w
thousand times ere one can324 c
thou speakest of times that782 o
t. are these ! what morals..746 b
t. change and we change...507 f
times do shift ; each thing.. 74 r
times that try men's souls.601 l
times when I remember'd†.249 o
Timotheus-T. yield the prize. 16 k
Timid-shriek'd the t., and‖...552 e
t. and cowardly rush to ...680 f
woo the timid maiden......661 u
Timidity-proved his t........687 f
Timidly-neither rashly nor t.802 n
steals timidly away........249 b
Timothy-T. learnt sin to fly.556 e
Tinct-will not leave their t.*.547 n
Tincture-manners take a t.‡..203 t
perfumed tincture of the*.447 aa
some tincture of vice.......632 y
tincture of syrup, lotion...512 r
Tinkling-t. of innumerable..514 c
Tint-tint, Prince Jesus, a....194 d
Tinted-t. and shadowed by...100 f
Tintings-mystical t. that....230 j
Tints-magic t. to harmonize.625 g
tints, as when there glows..195 k
tints of rainbow hue.......237 k
tints so gay and bold.......100 c
tints to-morrow with‖......492 v
varied t., all fused in one§..449 m
visionary t., the year puts††544 f
warm tints along the way..230 q
Tiny-tiny, pretty, witty..... 752 n
Tip-the tip is jewel of the ear.435 t
t. of his subduing tongue*.606 h
Tipped-t. these funny tags..453 j
Tippenny-wi' t. we fear nae. 325 n
Tipple-tipple in the deepe...213 j
Tipsy-tipsy with his weight...43 m
Tiptoe-jocund day stands*..400 w
on tiptoe Sunday creeps....536 m
religion stands on tiptoe....521 b
sweet peas, on tiptoe for a.238 c
Tire-does tire the ingener*..658 x
tire of all creation........ 97 p
tire our patience than‡.....429 i
Tired-till t., he sleeps, and‡..137 r
tired of all the playing.....560 q
tired out with fun ....323 o
to t. limbs and over-busy¶..564 c
Tires-he tires betimes that*..204 q
sad tires in a mile-a*....... 88 p
your sad tires in a mile-a*..384 f
Tiresome-except the t. kind.764 q
secret of being tiresome....764 p
Tissue-not of rich tissue, nor.515 k
there's not in thy tissue....515 l
Tissues-shining t. in the sun.217 o

t-m. shall be yesterday.....601 *k*
to-morrow's life is too late.721 *l*
to-morrow speak what......107 *j*
t-m.'s sun to thee may. ...605 *h*
to-morrow the dreams and.605 *l*
t-m.! the mysterious§......525 *b*
t-m. we will open, I replied 605 *f*
t-m., what delight is in ...605 *n*
t-m. will be as distant then.605 *e*
to-morrow will be better....713 *c*
to-morrow will be dying....241 *n*
to-morrow will give........705 *e*
t-m. yet would reap to-day†605 *q*
t-m. you will live, you......605 *k*
what will happen t-m.......714 *a*
a where is to-morrow........605 *r*
yesterday t-m. nam'd......601 *k*
To-morrows–confident t-m.¶..112*m*
Tone-affected by a change of 548 *p*
a tone of some world. .....557 *u*
down upon that pool of t...405 *p*
I can hear a deeper tone....618 *j*
its t. could reach the rich..484 *r*
the tone of languid Nature.410 *o*
tone in which we discuss it.587*m*
Tones–in its hollow t. are.....493 *d*
perfect joys, tender tones... 41 *h*
singing in soothing tones... 70 *w*
smiles and tones more dear 381 *y*
stole from the varying t.§..430 *q*
t. that touch and search§... 40 *d*
whose tones are sweet and§380 *k*
Tongs–sure the shovel and t..375 *r*
Tongue–and the dawning, t...300 *j*
a maiden hath no t. but*...597 *l*
and kepe wel thy tonge ... 632 *a*
and the tongue of strife....538 *a*
apter than thy tongue. ....210 *d*
as if a living tongue spake§ 66 *r*
a tongue to persuade....... 78 *l*
attend thy tongue.........271 *y*
a woman's tongue ....655 *s*
barr'd the aidence of the t.*606 *i*
bears not a humble tongue*494 *z*
before the t. hath spoke...182 *a*
be not thy tongue thy own*462 *j*
blisters on the t. would.....457 *b*
breeze can find a tongue ..394 *b*
child to hold his tongue.... 89 *j*
close to the speaking t......104 *f*
denied him with unholy t...654 *r*
discomfort guides my t.*...149 *n*
drop e'er wets their tongue538 *z*
dwells on every tongue....409 *j*
eare did heare that t....... 83 *h*
ere music's golden tongue .405 *l*
every pinion a biting t......740 *r*
every shepherd's tongue...361 *t*
every tongue brings in a*..106*m*
every t. that speaks but*...171 *t*
faster than his tongue*.....193*m*
feet slip than the tongue...496 *i*
from his sweet tongue§.....450 *q*
glum I hold my tongue.....113 *h*
godlike t. to move a stony..567 *q*
he rolls it under his tongue499 *e*
her t. one moment's rest...589 *t*
his prating t. had changed. 54 *c*
his t. is now a stringless*..557 *q*
his t. sounds ever after as*.415 *b*
if with his t. he cannot win*663 *n*
in a neat's tongue dried*...554 *y*
in the slanderous tongue*.. 71 *p*
in a tongue no man could†.275 *u*
iron t. of midnight hath*...384 *z*
I speak without a tongue ..169 *n*
kindred's fit and cognate t..574 *s*
letter gives me a tongue...753 *l*
let the candied tongue* ... 215 *q*
Lord of the golden tongue.. 85 *o*
love's t. proves dainty*.....364 *d*
man that hath a tongue*...215 *n*
many a man's t. shakes*...606 *e*
mended from that tongue‡.451 *d*
mountain 'tween my heart*108 *r*
murder, though it have no*423 *f*
music of his own vain t.*...407 *n*

my tongue and soul in this*312 *s*
my t.'s use is to me no*.... 606 *f*
my t., though not my*......606 *g*
my tongue within my lips..113*m*
nor ear can hear nor t.‖.....105 *g*
no tongue to wound us.....293 *n*
no tongue will speak*.......403 *r*
of a woman's tongue* .....119 *s*
of so perplex'd a tongue ...427 *n*
or tongue express.........313 *j*
our t. is known in every .. 468 *s*
pen is the t. of the mind....780 *i*
persuasion tips his tongue.472 *r*
pray together, in whatever.489 *r*
put your t. in your purse..503 *t*
repairs a slanderous t.‡....558 *l*
restreyne and kepen wel...606 *b*
school'd in a strange t.‖....455 *f*
skillful alike with tongue§.451 *a*
speak the tongue¶.........259 *j*
speak with double tongue. .146 *l*
still his t. ran on, the less...588 *l*
sufferings which have no t..582 *t*
take a serpent by the t.*...558 *x*
tell me of a woman's t.*....659 *e*
that he had held his tongue.554 *r*
that man that hath a t.*...663 *n*
that my t. were in the*.....465 *z*
that t. that more hath*... 68 *b*
the angel tongue. ....216 *c*
thinks his tongue speaks*..556 *y*
though his t. dropped**....312 *k*
tip of his subduing tongue*606 *h*
to give it then a tongue....604 *r*
tongue dropt manna**......517 *d*
t. had broken its chain§....606 *d*
t. in every star that talks...384 *r*
tongue is the clapper*......556 *y*
tongue is the vile slave's...743 *p*
t. like Delia's o'er her cup..606 *l*
tongue must be confuted...305 *c*
t. of him that makes it*....328 *r*
tongue of his fore-plane...431 *j*
tongue of leaping flame....579 *u*
tongue outvenoms all the*.559 *b*
tongue soe'er speaks false* 199 *u*
tongue to curse the slave..608 *j*
t. victorious as her eyes‡...361 *q*
t. within my lips I rein......589 *c*
trippingly on the tongue*..423 *k*
understanding, but no t.*..547 *f*
vibrant on every iron t.§...430 *g*
wagging of your t. to win*.606 *k*
what words of t. or seraph*123 *a*
windy satisfaction of the t.‡606 *c*
with a faltering tongue..... 58 *h*
with his tongue he cannot*.215 *n*
with mine own t. deny*.... 1 *c*
words of tongue or pen....519 *j*
Tongueless–a t. mouth*......184 *d*
deed dying t. slaughters*...147 *h*
Tongue-running–thou female589 *w*
Tongues–all t. speak of him*.486 *v*
an host of tongues*. ......415 *a*
by slanderous tongues*.....558 *r*
by their t., the latter by...742 *s*
envious t. will spare‡......645 *j*
finds tongues in trees*.....350 *f*
from innumerable t.**...... 109 *k*
hands and not our tongues*589 *q*
here are met all tongues... 15 *a*
lovers' tongues by night*..363 *n*
name blisters our tongues*.626 *k*
sale of chapmen's tongues* 36 *q*
small griefs find tongues...572 *v*
ten thousand tongues...... 92*m*
ten well-developed tongues.258 *o*
there are t. are hands*.... 76 *d*
their own tongues*........265 *g*
the tongues of soothers*...215 *i*
thousand several tongues*.106*m*
thousand t. t' allure him...464 *u*
t. I'll hang on every tree*..606 *j*
tongues of dying men*......340 *b*
t. of mocking wenches*....537 *x*
t. that syllable men's**....575 *d*
t. unto the silent dead§.... 66 *r*

to silence envious tongues* 471 *g*
use their own tongues*.....363 *d*
voiceless to scholars' t. no..549 *z*
walls have t., and hedges...507*ff*
whispering t. can poison... 17 *g*
women have t. of craft.....796*m*
Tongue-tied–t-t. simplicity*..364 *e*
To-night–child again, just for 599 *b*
curfew must not ring t-n...417 *u*
else shall hap to-night*....547 *f*
end were of "to-night".....606 *a*
must find it out to-night*..572 *e*
never till t-n., never till*...578 *d*
watch t-n. pray to-morrow*.384 *i*
Tool–and scourge the tool. .489 *o*
a tool of him ne'er make...651 *i*
Tools–and t. to work withal††.667 *b*
are the t. without, which...431 *e*
been the devil's tools ......656 *p*
coiner with his t. made*....145 *j*
great use out of evil tools.187 *t*
no jesting with edge tools.500*dd*
no jesting with edge tools..505*ee*
sin has many tools.........199 *e*
tools of sharp or subtle....251 *b*
t. of working out salvation.587 *c*
t. to him that can handle... 2 *h*
Tooth–Adonis hath a sweete t.499*jj*
against the tooth of time*..602 *j*
a tooth drawer was a kind.432 *n*
by treason's tooth* ....608 *o*
old trot with ne'er a t.*....390 *g*
records that defy the t. of..604 *b*
sharp-edged t. and claw... 17 *k*
sharper than a serpent's t.*319 *s*
thy tooth is not so keen*...319 *q*
with tooth and nail........509 *p*
Toothache–endure the t.*...432 *o*
sigh for the toothache*....432 *p*
sleeps feels not the t.*.....562 *k*
Toothless–his saws are t.‡...431 *g*
Toothpicks–supply of t......251 *s*
Top–above the streamful top.213 *g*
his t. was bald, and wasted.616 *h*
instant by the forward top*602 *l*
I shall die at the top........143 *n*
mother's from the t. to toe*. 90 *p*
once attain'd unto the top..581 *r*
on her ungrateful top*.....319 *p*
round at the top he has.....403 *j*
spiky t. has wounded the..396 *k*
the t. of heaven doth hold**576*m*
Tops–fires the proud t. of the*584 *t*
more but as the t. of trees*.610 *e*
to think their slender tops..613 *k*
Toper–the sopped sun-t. as...584 *n*
Topic–'tis a rich topic.......269*m*
Topics–authors! suit your t.‖.427 *j*
fashionable topics such as..113 *o*
Torch–his t. of purple fire....393 *k*
quenched my torch's ray...160 *q*
the torch of the mind is....800 *i*
Torch-dance–in the t-d.......323 *g*
Torches–candles from their..352 *e*
kindle but a torch's fire§...622 *k*
knots did his torches shine.617 *h*
teach the t. to burn bright* 37 *a*
Tories–save the monarchy of‡ 47 *h*
Torment–hopes deceive nor..111 *b*
live when to live is torment*350 *k*
spar'd one t. when we fell..656 *p*
t. your disgraceful life.....693 *d*
Tormenting–it is t. to fear...698 *p*
she sits t. every guest......589 *t*
Tormentor–let his t.**......105 *s*
Torments–our t. also may**..512 *q*
torments dwell about thee.354 *v*
t. lie in the small circle....375 *a*
Torn–t. out half the leaves§..600*w*
torn, trampled under feet..435 *o*
Torpedo–than it becomes a t. 113 *t*
Torrent–hark what a t. gush!..58 *t*
nought but the t. is heard..410 *b*
on his heart the t. softness.367 *b*
sharp air a flaky t. flies....564 *v*
so the loud torrent and the.118 *d*
stemm'd the torrent of a...120 *c*

SHAKESPEARE *; MILTON **; WORDSWORTH ¶; BYRON ∥; TENNYSON †; LOWELL ††; POPE ‡; LONGFELLOW §.

truant by his marks ......358 h
t. husband should return ‖.311 k
Truants–those t. from home. 89 g
Truce–bugles sound the t. of*471 i
for a flag of truce*........214 p
truce to earthly care§.....536 q
Truckle-bed–lie in honour's..305 u
Trudg'd–t. along unknowing.314 b
True–and pity 'tis 'tis true*..321 f
and thy friend be true.....212 r
be honest and true.........367 o
be t. to your soul, dearest..367 a
be true to your word and..108 k
Briton still to Briton true..468 d
can the devil speak true*..623 r
course of t. love never did* 362 o
dare to be t., nothing can..622 g
Douglas tendir and trewe.. 80 c
heart is true as steel*......212 p
insinuate what is true.....480 u
it is as true as sunbeams...650 v
kept him falsely true†......307 b
life in all that's true.......192 l
life will love true love......621 e
love is ever true and yet is 360 s
lovers ever found her true.669 v
makes the true man kill'd* 279 g
may to yourself be true.....367 r
more strange than true*....626 g
my man's as true as steel*.502 f
my t.-love hath my heart .365 j
never man was trewe.......355 o
not be therefore true.......596 h
nothing true but Heaven...623 b
one religion is as t. as.....520 b
prov'd true before.........157 p
say that she was true......33 k
tender, yet so true.........578 s
than be t. to Church and††.608 g
the other one is true.......349 i
the true Amphithyron......506 n
the true and the false......737 o
the warrior for the true... 367 f
thieves cannot be t. one to*595 j
time approves it true‖ .... 662 h
'tis easy to be true.........212 o
'tis strange—but t.; for ‖...621 l
to be honest and true....... 75 d
to thine own self be true*..623 o
t. and brave and downright 85 q
true as the dial to the sun..621 i
true as the needle..........212 g
true but for lying,—honest 454 o
true fix'd and resting*......108 n
true Jack Falstaff*........ 33 i
t., the wise, the beautiful..260 v
true to each other†........212 q
true to one party††........107 k
true to the death, but not..548 w
were they t.?—time cannot. 22 g
what right, what t., what‡.623 c
which is too true and§..... 265 a
whoever lives true life......356 a
will love true love..........356 a
yet not too good to be true.414 r
you good men and true*...372 f
your counsel still be true‡..623 d
Truer–no faces truer than*..591 l
truer than fairy wisdom...650 v
Truest–best things are the t..358 n
t. valour to dare to live... 628 i
Truly–used no oath but " t ".518 v
Trump–gospel t. thunder'd..521 m
last trump be played††.....285 g
the shrill trump*..........204 i
Trumps–if dirt was t. what.. 99 f
Trumpet–angel with a t.§...126 h
and trumpet sounds§.......533 h
brays the loud trumpet...408 a
deeds, need no trumpet...595 u
hark! the shrill t. sounds..572 s
he blew no trumpet in...... 85 q
he shifted his trumpet.....109 j
hideous t. calls to parley*..573 f
his own trumpet*.........491 v
his t. shrill hath thrice...... 44 v
kettle to the t. speak*......639 d

loud t.'s wondrous sound...527 n
no t.-blast profaned the.... 94 b
the t.! the dead have all...527 o
thing became a trumpet¶.. 61 j
trumpet of his own virtues*633 o
trumpet to trumpet spake.636 m
Trumpeteth–mad ambition t. 14 g
Trumpets–all the t. of the....564 w
and trumpets' clang*..... .659 e
silver snarling t. 'gan......405 n
sound t.! let our bloody*...639 p
Trumpet-tongued–against*..633 l
Trunk-ivy thy t. with its‖...615 m
t. may be discharg'd of*...149 g
Trunks–look! the massy t...545 j
Trust–and love and trust§...645 b
and trust no agent* ....363 d
and woman's trust ....658 t
as holy men trust God.....619 x
a wise man will not trust...157 n
before you trust in critics ‖.124 j
but trust in Providence....509 ff
by an unfaltering trust.....524 v
chant—we trust in thee....359 k
feel trust and reverence...148 r
frail mortality shall trust...345 j
friend he now dare trust...625 r
generous t. in human kind.674 n
government is a trust.......281 q
half on t., and half to try .197 p
how frail is human trust...347 r
I must never t. thee more*.608 m
in God is my trust.........807 c
in God is our trust.........214 i
I trust, and am content ...799 f
I trust my fate to thee.....376 k
love all, trust a few*.......511 s
man assumes a public t....620 t
may trust him in the dark..620 j
neglects or violates his t.‖..626 b
O holy trust ! O endless§...620 f
old friends to trust and old. 8 r
old friends to t.! old authors 10 q
parts that none will trust‡.. 82 p
pillar of my trust..........260 v
public office is a public t...620 r
public office is a public t...620 u
put his trust in Providence182 m
put your t. in God, my boys511 b
safe and sound your t. is...656 q
so far will I trust thee*....620 k
till no man trust him...... 83 f
that all power is a trust....620 q
that will put me in trust.. 83 s
the greatest t. between man619 w
the trust of giving counsel.619 w
they act in trust..... ......620 n
treated as a public trust...620 v
trust all and be deceived...620 e
trust and the trustees are..281 q
trust him not with your....144 q
trust in all things high†...402 q
t. men, and they will be....620 b
trust no future, howe'er §.. 5 a
t. none ; for oaths are*....511 u
trust not him that hath*...104 n
trust not the physician*...441 m
t. not too much to beauty..678 q
trust not to outward show.690 v
trust not yourself‡.........261 u
trust our necks to gripe of.484 h
trust our Savior...........165 n
trust that good shall fall†..309 b
t. that man in nothing, who106 t
trust themselves with men*372 m
trust the word of a man...680 u
trust to me.................620 h
trust your kindness†......265 r
truth, and love and trust... 90 s
weep that trust and that...620 e
which takes in trust........601 v
you may trust me, linnet.. 60 b
Trusted–dear I trusted you..619 x
ever poet so trusted before 479 n
my open-nature t. in.......312 o
O Lord, have I trusted.....801 o
to be trusted is a greater...620 g

treason is but t. like the*...608 w
trusted may betray........360 m
Trustees–committee-men or.. 26 t
trust and the t. are created.281 q
Trustfully–t. my spirit looks.620 i
Trusting–fancies of one t.....645 t
t. bosom, when betray'd...608 i
Trusts–a soul that trusts in..620 a
it is not fit the public t....620 s
of nature t. the mind that¶.413 o
the tyrant now t. not to... 625 r
t. himself to women, or to .657 x
trusts in God that as well‡.183 p
Truth–all life this t. declares.488 t
all the test of truth...... .290 q
alone has found the truth§.490 m
and speech is truth........574 j
armistice with truth‖......621 j
arm thyself for the truth..622 p
art with truth............582 t
as harsh as truth..........525 n
ask if truth be there... ... 33 k
at all a friend to truth*.. . 330 m
authority and show of t.*..556 n
beauty, and salt of truth... 64 g
beauty is truth, truth..... 35 a
being so near the t. as I*... 96 x
best way to come to truth. 622 i
bind and loose to t. is...... 621 q
breathe t. that breathe*....340 f
buried deep truth e'er lies. 337 w
but divine melodious truth. 51 h
but what is truth ? 'twas...621 s
charming for their truth....448 f
chest intercepts the truth..740 d
choice between truth and.. 91 p
consecrate to t. and liberty 568 o
countenance of truth**.... 580 n
Dame T. delights to dwell..623 z
depository of the truth.....371 r
desire to know the truth...747 m
deviated from the truth....747 p
dignity of truth is lost.....154 o
each claiming truth........112 t
error and truth alike.......185 f
error which some truth....198 q
excessive altercation, t. is .686 c
fair jewel t. its latent ray..623 w
fault and truth discourtesy 27 g
fiction lags after truth... .441 r
find where truth is hid*...623 t
first path to truth‖......... 6 o
for decency and truth......747 s
for the t. he ought to die...622 c
for the t. of things time.... 22 g
for the t. of your speaking.573 o
give them t. to build on.... 450 h
give the t. one martyr††....373 z
give t. a lustre, and make..515 w
God is truth and light......275 k
get but the truth once††. ..622 l
gravestones tell truth......284 i
great truth is loosened.....597 p
heap't for t. to o'erpeer*...127 m
held all of truth in my hand793 e
heretic in the truth**...... 39 e
he 'stablished t., or startled451 f
his truth is marching on...527 v
how sweet the words of t...621 d
hurt like the truth.........622 r
I love truth and wish......748 a
increase to her truth......601 z
in following truth..........807 g
in peals of truth...........521 m
in respect of t. and error is. 22 g
in the light of truth thy ¶..148 n
in the strife of truth with††145 q
in wine there is truth......649 t
is often the truth..........793 c
I speak t., not so much as..623 a
is the love of truth.........769 q
justice, and undisguised t..727 p
kept thy t. so pure of old**622 u
knew t. put to the worse**.622 w
know then this t. (enough‡.633 b
language of truth is.......747 k
language of truth is simple748 f

U

Unloads–and death u. thee*..642 v
　unloads upon a stall to rest579 o
Unlock–u. the one little heart535 v
Unlocked–Shakespeare u.¶...551 d
Unlucky–count all u. men...368 h
Unman–it unman's one quite‖117 n
　let's not unman each other‖464 h
Unmanageable–prove an u....495 o
Unmapped–a great deal of u. 79 d
Unmarked–u. they bud......241 s
Unmarried–die u. ere they*..219 s
Unmeasured–u. by the flight 267 r
Unmoved–bear u. the‡......385 r
　to be unmoved...........798 g
Unnatural–breed u. troubles*523 e
　foul, strange and u.*......403 t
　impious and unnatural*....522 b
　neither u., nor unjust... 15 q
　nothing is u., that is......317 l
　unnatural deeds do breed*.523 e
Unobserved–may pass over u.435 g
Unobtained–that u., than... 652 e
Unpack–u. my heart with*...665 o
Unparallel'd–would be u.*...659 i
Unpitied–unrespited u.** .... 82 q
Uupleasant'st–few of the u.*.665 o
Unpolluted–is u. in its beams584 l
Unpopular–every country u..482 s
Unprejudiced–u. you scan...372 c
Unprepared–an u. season.....240 t
　men are unprepared* ......140 h
　never unprepared........803 b
Unprofitable–weary, stale*...669 c
Unprofitably–wasted oil u....420 v
Unpunished–murder may....408 n
　many pass unpunished....736 r
Unpurchased–with u. hand ..482 r
Unquiet–u. meals make ill*..507bb
Unreality–showing the u. of..597 d
Unreconciled–u. as yet to*...489 j
Unredressed–wrongs u., or¶..388 s
Unremembering–went her u.465 e
Unreprieved–unpitied, u.*...512 h
Unrespited–u., unpitied*.....512 h
Unrest–in a riotous unrest...647 u
Unrivaled–u. in the glorious.535 q
Unsafest–uncertain ways u..158 h
Unsaid–words he has wished.519 h
Unsatisfied–to the u.*.......436 k
Unschooled–unlesson'd girl*.338 c
Unseasonable–urged at a*...281 b
Unseasoned–all u. without it.628 l
Unseen–floats, tho' unseen...485 z
　in things unseen.........294 f
　may lie unseen by day....434 c
　sincerely who grieves u.....710 e
　thus let me live unseen‡...421 c
　unknown, unseen by thee..141 t
　unseen by any human eye¶250 a
　walk the earth unseen**...575 c
Unsettled–and u. still**......516 n
Unshamed–u., though foil'd. 69 o
Unsistered–u. creature......629 j
Unskilled–thus u. to trace‡...480 g
Unsought–given u. is better*.364 c
　not unsought be won**... 662 t
Unspoken–depth of the u....573 n
Unstaid–u. and skittish in*...108 o
Unstained–they have left u..258m
Unstringed–an u. viol or a* ..606 f
Unsuitable–use of words u. ..339 s
Unsung–but left his own u...310 t
Unsworn–my mind is u......745 o
Untaught–better unborn than170 l
　some dreamy boy u.§..... 90 c
　unborn than untaught....314 o
Unthanked–All-giver would**593 i
Unthinking–and u. time.....388 p
Untie–folly may easily u.*...265 k
　mortal hand can e'er u....116 q
Untrained–u. and wildly free.244 o
Untravelled–my heart u......379 v
Untrodden–dwelt among the¶421 f
Untrue–men suspect your ...622 e
Untune–untune that string*. 407 q
Unveiled–u. her peerless**...416m
Unutterable–looked u. things501 r

Unwatched–must not u. go*..321 e
Unwelcome–truth is u........621 t
Unwept–u., unhonour'd and. 547 s
Unworldliness–loves in its u..356 b
Unworthiness–compos'd to*..557 p
Unworthy–u. to love her‖....200 j
Unwrinkled–u. by the wind..460 o
Unwritten–u. only still§......428 w
Up–and some go up and.....257 j
　the world goes up and the.. 74 w
　up and down and round... 96 g
　up and down 'twixt heaven 94 o
　up and down, up and down. 57 a
Upbraids–clock u. me with*..434 r
Up–hill–road wind u–h. all....607 g
　we shall escape the u–h. by.472 o
Upland–that upland height...248 f
Uplands–in solitary u. far....567 q
　marching to the u. fair.....400 q
Upper–sof'ness in the u.††...641 t
　upper ten thousand.......513 c
　u. ten thousand of the city.513 j
Upright–I can promise to be.758 f
　look! it stands upright*....291 r
　man of upright dealing.....454 o
　no praise in being u........712 k
Uproar–wild u. stood ruled** 462 s
Upspringing–u. from the.....236 f
Up–stairs–came u–s. into the..581 p
Upward–fortune keeps an*..631 l
Urge–u. them while their*...461 q
Urged–the wise have urged..354 u
　u. at a time unseasonable*.281 b
Urges–hope ever urges on....713 c
Urn–bubbling and loud.......186 q
　can storied urn or........134 e
　follow to his urn*..... ...285 o
　from its mysterious urn...351 i
　has filled his urn where.... 16 i
　in the capacious u. of death.689 o
　shaping many an u. and pot.449 l
　u. of death shaken for all...689 p
Urns–in their golden urns..**576 i
　is breaking the crystal urns171 d
　lamps in old sepulchral u. .346 v
　spirits from their urns‖....670 c
　two urns by Jove's high‡...122 t
Usage–pleads your fair u.*...107 e
　shrunk by usage†.........203 k
Usance–the rate of u. here*..295 f
Use–and as fit to use..... ...321 s
　and takes away the u. of it.637 p
　barr'd from every use of...642 f
　brought it would not u. it..458 r
　concur to general use‡.....191 f
　derives its value from its u.348 f
　equal right to the u. of land 338 v
　eyes of a man are of no use 192 j
　few use the grand.........597 y
　for woman shed and u.‖....590 f
　found in use in the place...670 k
　get to live; then live and u.389 q
　great use out of evil tools..187 t
　hanging was the worst use.498 y
　how these rascals use me..421 r
　it is still her use to let the*.485 b
　knowledge, use and reason.337 e
　makes no more u. of them. 48 b
　make use of ev'ry friend‡..261 u
　make use of time, let not*..602m
　my tongue's u. is to me no* 606 f
　not for show planted, but u.269 u
　rather in power than use*..511 s
　ripe and fit for use........ 9 j
　rusts for want of use......270 o
　soiled with all ignoble use†.271 r
　that hath not power to u...485 k
　'tis u. alone that sanctifies‡.548 l
　to their proper native use..479m
　true u. of speech is not so..573 w
　tyrannous to u. it like a*...579m
　unless he use them wisely..345 a
　u. alone makes money not..389 c
　use be preferred before....425 d
　use doth breed a habit*....290 u
　use every man after his*...333 c
　u. him as though you loved 19 f

　u. in abject and in slavish*.559 t
　use of strongest**.........593 k
　use the mind aright......696 c
　we come to u. our hands*..589 q
　what one has, one ought to.675 a
　whether we u. him well or.601 e
　who knows its proper use..803ff
　world's u. is cold, world's. .463 a
Used–is existence, used is life 604 g
　let them be well used*.....423 c
　nothing when you are u. to.507m
Useful–more u. than silence..554m
　useful with the agreeable..744 i
　what we do is useful.......706 u
Usefully–let him live u.......488 a
Usefulness–excellence and u.265 p
　u. comes by labour, wit by 120 i
Useless–sensible people find..759 f
　u. each without the other§.375 q
　u. if it goes as when it......313 g
　world are the most useless. 36 h
Uses–all the u. of this world* 669 c
　all uses of man combine...617 b
　sweetest uses given to..... 36 j
　the uses of adversity*..... 7 a
Usher–that u. to destruction..481 s
Using–H' was very shy of u..652 q
Usquebae–wi' u. we'll face...325 n
Usurer–ruthless u.'s gold....360 k
Usurp–u. a place they well...483 e
Usurper–a u. always distrusts763 k
　be but an usurper.........625 t
Utica–no pent-up U. contracts485 w
Utility–losing both beauty*..643m
　ornament interferes with u. 28 s
　subordinate to that of u.... 28 s
Utter–long or often utter.....104 f
　thou wilt not u. what thou*.620 k
Utterance–hear new u. flow**574 h
　large u. of the early gods...277 h
　make thy utterance divine.. 14 b
　perplexed for utterance†...553 g
　throw one warning u....... 58 t
　utterance clear to all men†† 86 g
　utterance which glides.....685 f
　whose utterance I cannot...275 e
Uttered–utter'd all the soul..261 r
　uttered it a hundred times.596 v
Uttereth–uttereth piercing*..659 q
Utters–one thing in his heart.144 o

V.

Vacancy–gloomy calm of idle313 l
Vacant–has one v. chair§....136 a
　mind quite v. is a mind ....526 f
　spoke the vacant mind ....415 n
Vacation–conscience have v..105 c
Vacuity–indolent vacuity of.596 j
Vagrant–all the v. train......38 l
Vain–all delights are vain*...463 h
　all delights are vain*......147 w
　and a' is done in vain......196 l
　and youth is vain........... 17 g
　call it not v.—they do not..480 l
　dazzle let the vain design‡..325 d
　I grant the man is v. who. 486aa
　in vain doth valour bleed**628m
　less vain than to suppose... 35 u
　more, because I weep in v...590 p
　of amber snuff-box justly‡.457 k
　serves to prove the living v.458 t
　sought in vain that sought.487 k
　the king grew vain........490 u
　therefore, not to-day in v...605 i
　to another race, as v., and..601 n
　to love, but love in vain....357 r
　tricks that are vain........144 l
　vain as the leaf upon......212 d
　v.? Let it be so ! Nature ..629 j
　vain or shallow thought....596 p
　vain was the chief's‡......480 j
Vainest–vainest of all things§534 k
　vainest of the worst........206 e
Valclusa–from fair V.'s......530 c
Vale–barren detested vale*...300 u
　behind the cloudy vale of‡.415 p

beyond this vale of tears...267 *r*
cool sequestered v. of life..347 *t*
green sunny vale and the ..532 *f*
in life's low v., the soil the‡633 *a*
in the first wooded vale.... 51 *q*
in the v. beneath the hill....625 *e*
is therein the vale of life.. 644 *u*
Naiad-like lily of the vale..234 *p*
o'er woody vale and .... 87 *g*
pride of Lorton Vale¶......619 *c*
sequester'd v. of rural life. 11 *c*
sprinkle the vale below ....248 *d*
swells from the vale and...102 *q*
the clovered vale...........225 *b*
vale from steep to steep¶...555 *j*
v. that at midday the dew..542 *l*
violet-embroidered vale**..169 *h*
violet in the vale..........219 *h*
will I go to the rosy vale.. 52 *i*
Vales-Cam his winding v.‡..530 *h*
the Delphian vales........285 *a*
Valentine-art every day my .628 *c*
couple with my valentine..628 *b*
in chorus on V.'s day......628 *f*
old Bishop Valentine......628 *e*
Saint Valentine is past*....628 *g*
to be your Valentine**.....628 *h*
to-morrow is Saint V.'s*...628 *h*
Valentines-verses V. yclep'd. 628 *a*
Valet-as the master so the v. 759 *l*
in the eyes of his valet....772 *b*
to a valet no man is a hero.772 *d*
Valet-de-chambre-hero to ...502 *r*
Valiant-a piece of v. dust*..660 *f*
a valiant man ought not to.628 *l*
effort of a valiant mind....190 *c*
he's not v. that dares die..583 *c*
he's truly valiant that can*628 *n*
not valiant that dares die..121 *j*
proved valiant or discreet‡..203 *d*
ring in the valiant man†.... 41 *c*
thought he had been a v.*.... 73 *i*
thou little valiant, great* ..122 *f*
true Jack Falstaff, valiant* 33 *i*
valiant, being as he is*..... 33 *i*
v. never taste of death but*121 *q*
Validity-v. and pitch soe'er*.364 *l*
v. of those attainments....483 *f*
Valley-in round v. depths....394 *e*
light in the valley below†....449 *h*
retreated in a silent v.**..637 *w*
through the snowy v. flies.391 *c*
v. of the Pegnitz where§... 98 *f*
valley sheep are fatter..... 21 *r*
valley stretching for miles§ 612 *k*
valley under the hill........247 *o*
world a valley so sweet....411 *t*
Valleys-down the v. of Hall..530 *i*
out of the lowly v. did....616 *p*
passest through our v. in ..541 *q*
v., groves or hills or fields .360 *n*
Valor-a life which v. could..511 *a*
angel hands to valour......214 *e*
best part of valor ....155 *w*
better part of valor is*.....156 *d*
but a bastard valor ......121 *j*
but their valor tried in war686 *r*
by strategy or valor........751 *h*
contemplation he and v.**. 82 *a*
for valour, is not Love a*..364 *d*
for valour to assail**.......457 *r*
in vain doth valour bleed**628 *m*
increase in valor, O boy....686 *s*
my v. is certainly going!...122 *l*
realms their valour saved..444 *t*
resist valor and arms.......806 *h*
shows but a bastard valor..583 *c*
so full of valour that they*.326 *j*
spurred on by rival valor ..686 *d*
strong in valor's might.....638 *m*
that doth guide his valour*651 *m*
the name of valour* ......639 *n*
there is always safety in v..628 *j*
there is no true valour*... 513 *m*
the sign of valor true.......629 *c*
the sons of reason, valor... 85 *j*
truest valour to dare to live628 *i*

truth and valor wearing. ..444 *p*
v. consists in the power of .628 *k*
valor is the salt t' his other628 *l*
valour is to be found in....211 *a*
valor plucks dead lions*....122 *j*
v. which knows not mean..805 *cc*
what v. were it, when a*...629 *a*
when v. preys on reason* ..629 *b*
while virtue, v., wisdom**. 13 *l*
wisdom that doth guide*...628 *o*
Valours-great wits and v....652 *p*
Valuable-thought is v. in...597 *a*
valuable of any we have...596 *y*
what is valuable is not new.508 *m*
Value-according to their real734 *t*
derives its v. from its use..348 *f*
enhance the value of its....510 *d*
essential value is the adding 65 *n*
for its intrinsic value......373 *l*
has an enhanced value.....301 *d*
I found thee of more value*663 *s*
I value science—none can..538 *i*
I wash away my value*.... 1 *c*
know the true v. of time...599 *q*
money, bears an extra v...653 *q*
of v., is the active soul.....571 *l*
singly of more v. than they565 *r*
their value's great* ....434 *s*
then we rack the value*....483 *s*
things of dearest value....671 *b*
value at a little price........ 7 *g*
v. equally the good and the765 *c*
v. from the stamp and..... 68 *k*
Valued-most are v. where.... 35 *f*
Vamp-curl the glassy v.....454 *b*
Vandals-what clouds of v.‡..558 *b*
Vane-and yonder gilded v.§..514 *v*
Vanes-vanes and roofs of§...398 *d*
Vanille-the vanille of society565 *s*
Vanish-melt and soon must¶ 382 *c*
vanish in the chinks that...602 *b*
vanish like lightning.......319 *j*
Vanities-all the fuming v.¶...629 *r*
the vanities of life forego... 11 *g*
worth than empty vanities*489 *k*
Vanity-beareth the name of.629 *d*
egged on by vanity.........794 *p*
is no need of such vanity*..342 *p*
lighter than vanity.........629 *d*
light vanity, insatiate*.....629 *o*
loathe the expense, the v ..117 *e*
makes the vanity of others.794 *e*
more satirical from vanity.537 *q*
not a v. is given in vain‡...629 *l*
others are but vanity.......365 *n*
said that "all is vanity"∥..629 *e*
save me from folly, vanity.148 *m*
the world thrust forth a*..629 *p*
those who live on v. must..629 *h*
vanity, and pride, and......313 *s*
vanity can give no hollow∥.566 *k*
v. is as ill at ease under....629 *g*
v. to persuade the world...344 *s*
what a sweep of vanity*...629 *n*
Vanquished-quite v. him*...320 *a*
shall never vanquish'd be* .108 *d*
though v. he could argue... 27 *f*
Vantage-coigne of v.*........ 50 *h*
he that might the vantage*518 *l*
the v. ground of Truth.....621 *b*
Vapor-and a scarf of velvet..584 *e*
a vapour at the best ....451 *s*
gnats around a vapour.... 16 *e*
hills, is lost in vapour∥....200 *k*
in crystal v. everywhere†...613 *g*
moon hung like a v. in the.398 *n*
to see the friendly vapor...457 *n*
v. sometime like a bear or*587 *i*
Vapors-extinguish them in..628 *d*
golden, glimmering v.§.....585 *m*
twinkling v. arose; and§....585 *n*
v., and clouds, and storms.546 *o*
vapors hug the stream......395 *b*
vapours linger round the¶.382 *c*
v. of earth they seemed....586 *a*
v. which the head invade...590 *b*
where cooling v. breathe‡.. 18 *h*

Variable-love prove*........317 *q*
variable as the shade......658 *r*
Variance-v. upon many..... 348 *r*
Varies-how instinct v. in the‡324 *n*
Variety-amidst the soft v...629 *s*
cloy without variety.......505 *u*
gay v. one universal blot..417 *t*
her infinite variety*.......630 *e*
in his travels for variety∥..621 *j*
led thro' a sad v. of woe‡...448 *m*
oh! fair variety...........630 *d*
order in variety we see‡....462 *u*
stale her infinite variety*..658 *v*
variety alone gives joy ....639 *c*
v. of mere nothings gives...794 *i*
v.'s the source of joy below629 *v*
v.'s the very spice of life...629 *u*
variety of untried being...185 *aa*
where order in v. we see‡..630 *b*
with sweet variety.........222 *b*
Various-a man so various...212 *a*
Varletry-shouting v. of*....104 *x*
Varlets-pot-boiling v. stay at.210 *x*
Varnish-this the blue v.‡..... 22 *i*
v. nonsense with the charms572 *r*
Vary-vary your vile days...213 *i*
Vase-a vase is begun........682 *a*
shatter the vase if........242 *q*
to a vase of gold..........234 *k*
vase, in which roses.......242 *g*
Vassal-v. to the tyrant wife..374 *j*
Vast-so v. is art, so narrow‡.588 *l*
Vault-aisle and fretted vault405 *h*
deep damp v. the darkness.142 *p*
fetters and the damp v.'s∥..491 *t*
framed the lofty vault......609 *c*
Heaven's ebon vault.......417 *p*
left this vault to brag of*..350 *g*
this vault a feasting* ...... 36 *w*
v. high-domed of morning. 57 *b*
Vaulter-green little v., in the323 *n*
Vaulting-v. up the terraced..229 *f*
Vaunt-and grow to vaunt... 3 *m*
Vaunting-v. vile deeds ....206 *e*
Vaunts-not by vaunts is won‡582 *b*
Vegetable-dead the vegetable546 *n*
fruit of vegetable gold...**609 *j*
Vegetables-bears v. in a∥...166 *i*
dying vegetables life‡...... 75 *s*
poor plot, with vegetables.304 *b*
Vegetate-life dissolving v.‡... 75 *s*
Vehicle-v. of virtue, truth...435 *q*
Veil-beauty's veil doth cover*630 *r*
either flowers or veil......264 *p*
in a veil of yellow gauze...399 *j*
mysterious v. of brightness397 *i*
pull'd off her v. of light....397 *i*
pluck off thy veil..........256 *a*
primrose for a veil had¶....239 *s*
retreats whose veil is¶..... 38 *a*
there is no veil like light...622 *r*
veil spun from the cobweb.312 *a*
veil the matchless boast... 452 *r*
veil, which, if withdrawn∥.624 *h*
whom the veil...........136 *v*
Veiled-v.the light of his face*585 *m*
Veiling-are angels v. clouds*659 *c*
Veils-ye veils that deck my.. 33 *n*
Vein-stretch the swelling v..453 *b*
through every vein........313 *d*
Veins-blood in their dastardly512 *i*
blood speaks to you in my*665 *r*
froth the veins of thee, wild545 *b*
harebell, like thy veins*.. .230 *k*
her veins ran lightning∥.... 33 *s*
large veins would bleed....324 *d*
life leaps in the veins......348 *t*
ran in my veins*..........271 *m*
slide into his veins........325 *w*
through all the veins*......149 *q*
v. of thee, autumn, laden.545 *b*
Vendible-a maid not v.*.....554 *y*
Venerable-of v. trees¶......610 *r*
v. men! you have come... 12 *j*
Venerate-I v. the man whose.450 *c*
Venge-crimes so speedily*...332 *x*
Vengeance-hot coals of v...*.639 *n*

either v., or else a grave*..639 p
for quarter or for victory‖ .636 c
God will, there be the v.*..631 m
grac'd with wreaths of v.*.631 l
if not v., is yet revenge*..528 l
mark his victory. .. ... 239 p
on victory or death........637 i
or to victory.... ....635 q
so clear of victory........630 y
sword sit laurel victory*..638 u
'tis the shade by victory..631 c
to rise in open victory¶.... 12m
victory follows in its train.333 d
victory follows me........794 j
v. grows out of concord...805 q
victory of endurance born.630 u
victory's in believing††.... 39 c
we have such another v....631 e
where is thy victory‡....137 g
Vienna–congress of V. does...282 i
View–attract my childish v..230 h
death within my view*....139 k
enchantment to the view...402 p
fair to outward view...... 34 f
from afar to the flight...308 o
mocks me with the view... 280 c
keep probability in view...622 e
landscape tire the view....410 s
observation with extensive.421 i
peeped so fair to view¶....221 e
sad reverse soon starts to..381 t
theatre of stateliest view**.609 k
'tis sweet to view on high‖.515 i
transported with the view. 382 d
v. each loved one blotted‖.. 9 g
view fair Melrose aright ...398 k
v. me with a critic's eye....462 d
v. some well-proportion'd‡.425 s
wild, unknown to public v...567 j
Views–chemist in his golden‡425 u
critics have no partial v...126 a
in my v. let both united be.347 b
views of happiness ......294 e
Vigilance–eternal v. is the....343 q
the steersman's part is v... 73 s
Vigils–let me thy v. keep.....567 c
pensive poets painful v.‡...480 k
Vigor–and press with v. on...674 a
as vigour from the limb‖...599 n
exist in undiminished vigor 95 r
health and vigor spring....394 g
high birth, vigour of bone*602 h
keep these in parallel v..... 9 a
my v. relents I pardon ....343 k
serpent, and his v. flies ... 21 p
sinewy v. of the traveller* .667 k
the race by v., not by‡....582 b
undiminished vigour.......267 n
Vile–makes nice of no vile*...495 n
nought so v. that on the*....510 r
'tis a vile thing to die*....140 h
Vilest–the v. sinner may....523 r
Village–at her work the v....476 u
back from the v. street§....117 i
in the village hears him go.536m
v. all declar'd how much ..342 g
Villages–in these peculiar v..389 s
Villain–condemns me for a*..106m
hang'd if some eternal v.*..558 v
here's a villain ....170 u
it calls me villain .... .. 269 n
needy v.'s general home.... 98 d
one murder made a villain.403 p
smile and be a villain*..... 312 t
thou villain base know'st*.455 c
v., a horse—villain, I say... 21 a
v. and he be many miles* ..631 s
v. dwelling in all Denmark*336 h
v. with a smiling cheek*....145 b
Villanies–execrable sum of...560 f
Villainous–there's v. news*....414 y
v.—licentious—abominable 436 l
Villains–calm, thinking v.‡...631 o
man-destroying villains.. ..625 s
scourge,mean villains have523 c
slander'd to death by v.*...558 x
Villany–but direct villany*.. 631 r

I clothe my naked villany*.631 p
O villany! Ho! let the door*631 q
put on for villany*........ 377 g
valiant, great in villainy*..122 f
Vindicate–v. the ways of‡...373 t
Vindication–v. of the worth..448 h
Vine–banks which bear the‖..532 a
cluster from the vine.... 266 x
grew on v whose tap-roots.649 e
my husband, I. a vine*....377 a
of the vine benign§.........649 p
plant and propagate a vine.648 j
summer v. in beauty clung§546 e
the drunken vine‡.........232 f
the gadding vine**........300 t
the mother of the vine....641 e
the vine, boys, the vine....648 q
the v. still clings to the§...515 a
'tis mantled by the vine....618 h
vine is a nest for flies......367 k
vine of glossy sprout.......218 h
Vines–blossom-clustered v...222 g
bosom'd deep in vines‡...293 t
down thro' the vines..... 59 h
flit among the trellised v....543 v
fruitful olives,v. of Engaddi 63 u
graceful arabesque of v.§..617 l
there grow our vines.......795 d
vines yield nectar**........298 i
with fruit the v. that round.544 c
Vinegar–oil, vinegar, sugar... 79 q
Vineyard–dig a v. is a.......181 o
the v.'s ruby treasures....544 g
Vintage–he is trampling out.527 v
the vintage flow............294 k
Vintners–the true poets, like.422 a
Viol–an unstringed v. or a*..606 f
Viola–spin a tress for Viola..292 d
Violated–goddess v. brought.344 g
Violence–better than violence768 l
blown with restless v.*.....140 i
borne along by the violence 677 o
by fraud or violence........701 f
reign of violence is o'er§...126 h
Violent–over violent, or over 79 b
short as it violent is........654 q
these violent delights have*147 v
v. property foredoes itself*.364 v
Violenteth–v. in a sense as*..389 a
Violently–v. as hasty*.......149 q
Violet–and violet flower... 219 q
a poor little violet††........248 t
a vi'let on the meadow....248 i
becomes an April violet†..249 n
blue eye of the violet......249 t
deep-blue violet............248 r
delicious spring-time violet249 l
distinguish the tints of a v.192 s
from the violet's beak....220 u
here and there a violet.....284 d
low v. thrives at their root.610 q
modest lowly violet........248 k
perfume on the violet*.....29 q
queen of secrecy, the violet 192 k
tell of the violet's birth....540 f
tender violet bent in......249 k
the deep-blue violet........248 r
the humble violet ....216 g
the violet-embroidered vale169 h
the violet's lips............321 m
the violet sweet. ....217 r
the yellow violet sat......222 d
timid, bashful violet.......217 f
violet by a mossy stone¶....248 g
violet darkly blue ....220 t
violet in the vale...........219 h
violet in the wood.........220 n
violet is a nun.............248 o
violet lay dead while......249 j
violet less brightness......249 a
violet lifts its tender eye...217 p
violet of his native land†..152 o
violet of our early days....248 g
violet's beautiful blue.....217 c
violet ! sweet violet††......248 s
violet thinks, with her....249 d
violet would thy dusk......249 q

we sought the violet.......249 s
wrapping the violet.......247 o
yellow violet's modest bell. 248 e
young May violet grows....247 q
Violets–a bank of violets*...249 g
and hooded violets........221 q
and the vi'lets blow.......540 b
and the violets white.....218 i
April violets glow. . .....249 e
are showers of v. found .... 55 j
are the darling violets.....248 l
call its violets forth......247 r
deep violets, you liken.....247 p
earliest v. always miss her.540 h
Europe's violets, faintly...217 v
for v. pluckt, the sweetest.466 l
fresh violets open every day398 b
grass and violets sprang ... 51 d
languid violets love to lie..249 r
May violets spring*........285 q
not like to mix violets......239 q
nursing April's violets....391 f
roses red and violets......220 k
shade the violets..........248 q
shrinking as violets.......249 b
spring violets over the lea..194 g
spring violets under the...249 c
the purple violets*........220 e
there are violets¶..........224 g
the smell of violets†.... ...249 o
the violets golden.........248 d
timid, blue-eyed violets....233 s
upon a bank of violets*...407 k
violets bathe in the wet....217 a
violets blue and white......247 n
violets bloom beneath......248 e
violets come again.........248 h
v. dim, but sweeter than*..219 s
violets to adorn...........218 l
violets for the mouth......226 h
violets heavenly blue......216m
violets make the air.......220 p
violets of five seasons¶.....250 a
violets ope their purple ...220 o
violets prattle and titter...248m
violets spring in the.......248 b
violets that first appear...250 b
violets transform'd to eyes.193 b
violets—were blossoming..248 f
violets were past their.....248 u
violets whisper from the... 249 f
violets you liken to........237 g
we are violets blue........248 p
when daisies pied and v.*..541 a
when violets lean..........248 a
where early violets die.....362 i
who are the violets*.......249 i
Violins–Antonio Stradivari's.405 f
comes of making violins...200w
Viper–remember the viper...333 r
Viper-locks–Discord wild her.299 u
Virgil–V.'s songs are pure‖...478 l
Virgin–a virgin so bright....359 s
bashful v.'s sidelong looks.358 p
flower of virgin light.......242 g
from the soft-eyed v. steal‡ 477 q
or veiled v.'s holier word... 49 e
soil her virgin purity**.... 88 a
spouseless v. Knowledge‖...650 g
virgin's-bower..............250 k
virgin mother born**...... 94 l
virgin shrouded in snow...245 n
with'ring on the v. thorn*..376 p
Virgins–proud virgins of the.250 b
where the virgins are soft‖.370 j
youths and virgins say....628 b
Virginian–I am not a V. but..468 q
Virginians–V., don't do it for 640 i
Virginia-reel–V-r. a bait††...128m
Virtue–according to his v.*..633 i
adds a grace to virtue.....367 d
all virtue now is sold ....389 u
a man whose v. genius.... 85 o
and lo! virtue is at hand..632 d
and without virtue........343 j
are lovers of virtue....... 18m
armed in virtue's cause...537 n

SHAKESPEARE*; MILTON **; WORDSWORTH ¶; BYRON ‖; TENNYSON †; LOWELL ††; POPE ‡; LONGFELLOW §.

great v. become great men.794 *p*
her virtues were so rare......34 *d*
his v. will plead like angels*633 *l*
men of the noblest virtues.703 *e*
only see their virtues......260 *u*
pass for virtues in him....320 *c*
patriots' v. cause support..632*m*
poets heap v., painters‡....674 *j*
thee and thy virtues here*. 84 *k*
the pearl-chain of all v....388 *u*
the salt t' his other virtues.628 *l*
the seed-plot of all other v.622 *j*
the soil the virtues like‡....633 *a*
to her virtues be a friend ..328 *a*
to make thy virtues........383 *b*
trumpet of his own virtues*633 *o*
vertues dying never........316 *s*
v. formed the magic of his.479 *h*
[v.] like extinct volcanoes. 632 *r*
v. thou dost loudly vaunt‖.312 *e*
virtues we write in water*...84 *c*
virtues where he shines....357 *i*
v. with your years improve.673 *k*
wear your virtues as a.....227 *f*
wife is a constellation of v..644 *t*
Virtuous-another v., yet I*..659 *o*
a sweet and virtuous soul..632 *p*
hour of virtuous liberty....343 *l*
I wish to be virtuous.......632 *d*
of daily virtuous living....324 *s*
of one virtuous person**...632 *u*
prevent v. actions from....712 *d*
slumbers of the v. man....631 *u*
strong, the brave, the v....355 *b*
sweet and virtuous soul.... 80 *a*
the more virtuous any man 749 *l*
the virtuous nothing fear..632 *o*
v. actions are but born and.551 *i*
v. and vicious every man‡..372 *a*
v. have already been blessed474 *t*
virtuous things proceed*...147 *a*
weakness of a v. mind......309 *o*
Virtuousest-seems wisest**..111*m*
Visage-all his v. wann'd*....423 *g*
bold visage middle age.... .195 *o*
confront the v. of offence*.382 *r*
hides not his v. from our*..584 *i*
hail, whose v. sweet and.... 92 *i*
stern is the v. of necessity..781 *g*
with devotion's visage*....313 *b*
Visible-communion with her.410 *j*
Vision-a most rare vision*....160 *u*
a vision of delight¶......... 57 *i*
baseless fabric of this v.*..634*m*
blissful certainty, a vision§.634 *d*
dazzle the vision feminine..352*m*
enjoyed in v. beatific**......369 *k*
mortal vision is a grievous.330 *s*
poet's v. of eternal fame‡...634 *l*
the ladder of the vision....572 *j*
the point of vision alters...190 *h*
the tent is struck, the v.††.634 *h*
the young men's v., and....634 *d*
v. and the faculty divine¶..478 *c*
v. clear for stars and sun..590 *d*
vision of a moment made..634 *o*
vision of fulfill'd desire....297 *w*
vision raised its head......634 *f*
was it a vision or a......... 51 *f*
Visions-O v. ill foreseen**....634 *j*
visions of a busy brain....159 *k*
visions of glory, spare.....272 *r*
visions of the other world‖.568*w*
with visions false as fair...634 *k*
Visit-or paid the visit last‡...524 *l*
to trusted man his annual v. 56 *d*
to v. oft the dwellings of**. 16 *q*
v. her face too roughly*....364 *o*
v. it by the pale moonlight.398 *r*
world, his ready v. pays....564 *b*
Visitations-souls whose..... 85 *e*
visitations daze the world..319 *f*
Visiting-a v. acquaintance... 15 *o*
Visits-angel's v. short and...329 *t*
his v. there are frequent... 92 *n*
like angel v. few and far... 16 *g*
visits like those of.........279*m*

visits these sad eyes........260 *s*
Visual-v. nerve for he had**.553*m*
Vital-bring the vital spark...628 *d*
v. in every part not as**...316 *k*
v. spark of heav'nly flame‡571 *x*
Vitals-out of my own vitals.. 53 *r*
preys on my vitals..........327 *t*
Vivacity-I like their vivacity.657 *b*
v. and novelty of youth....516 *b*
where the vivacity of the.. 80*m*
Vizard-with a virtuous v.*...145 *e*
Vizier-criticism his prime v. .125 *i*
Vizor-between a v. and a....312 *b*
Vizored-v. falsehood and**...608 *h*
Vocal-v. with the Maker's‡.. 95 *s*
with music, vocal spark¶....408 *l*
Vocation-be the vocation fit.. 40 *n*
Hal, 'tis my vocation*......339 *o*
to labor in his vocation*...339 *o*
Voice-aggravate my v. so*... 45 *r*
and her voice is sweet......517 *a*
as is the voice of love.... 415 *l*
a sweet v., a little indistinct635 *f*
a thrilling voice replies.... 98 *o*
audible voice of the Past... 64 *n*
a voice of dolorous pitch..484 *r*
a v. whose tones are sweet §380 *k*
blockhead with melodious. 455 *s*
but few thy voice*..........331 *n*
came a v. without reply...622 *c*
confusion heard his voice**462 *s*
can honour's v. provoke ...134 *e*
Carril, raise again thy v....557 *k*
delight heard I that voice¶. 45 *b*
distant v. in the darkness§.150 *v*
drowns the v. of the law...775 *l*
each a mighty voice¶......635 *h*
echo of the silent v. of God.668 *i*
face not seen, the v. not....588 *k*
familiar v. wearies not ever365 *i*
healing voice of Christian.. 86 *e*
hear a voice in every wind.329 *q*
hear a v. long loved in.....580 *g*
hear a v. you cannot hear..141 *q*
heart like a sweet voice‖...634 *q*
her silver voice is the§......634 *u*
her voice was ever soft*....635 *g*
his big manly v. turning*.. 11 *j*
his voice no longer heard...301 *h*
his v. no touch of harmony 634 *r*
his voice shook the.........208 *s*
his voice was buried¶...... 46 *a*
his voice was propertied*..534 *y*
I hear its voice again....... 44 *p*
in joy of voice and pinion¶. 50 *f*
is not, the voice of God‡.. .635 *d*
is the voice of fate........766 *q*
is the voice of God........634 *s*
it hears a v. within it tell ..671 *q*
kind the voice and glad.... 87 *g*
leave behind a v. that in.... 85 *e*
like the voice and echo*....536 *g*
like the v. of one who from. 40 *b*
like the voice the stars......635 *e*
liquid music of her voice..557 *e*
look and a voice then§......150 *v*
methought I heard a v. cry*562*m*
mute is the voice of rural..536 *l*
my voice is still for war...635 *k*
nature's own voice......... 47 *l*
no voice or hideous hum**.461 *t*
often to that v. of sorrow..605 *f*
of the voice of God¶........164 *o*
one v. of comfort seems to.100 *k*
only a look and a voice§....378*m*
on their ear his voice‡.....353 *q*
or but a wandering voice¶.. 45 *c*
or hear a voice§ ....261 *e*
shall have a voice and give§411 *i*
silence, beautiful voice†....555 *h*
small voice of gratitude....283 *u*
so charming left his v.**...635 *c*
something in that voice§...634 *v*
sound of a v. that is still†..148 *l*
still small voice is wanted..105*m*
tender broken v. that fills..415 *l*
tenor's voice is spoilt by‖..557 *b*

that send a feeble voice‡...650 *r*
the book is a living voice...429 *u*
the people's voice is odd‡...635 *d*
the voice divine of human..169 *e*
the v. I hear this passing... 51 *g*
the voice prophetic§........360 *c*
they too have a voice......274 *b*
thou its melancholy voice.. 42 *l*
thrill of a happy voice .....294 *d*
thy gentle v. my spirit can..160 *e*
thy voice is a celestial§.....635 *a*
'tis the v. of the sluggard..564 *a*
to be a v. as from above lİke 40 *n*
tune thy jolly voice to my..543 *j*
voice changed like a bird's.634 *p*
voice, in sullen echoes......206 *z*
voice is in the wind........275 *e*
v. is still living immortal..169 *k*
voice of a good woman.....635 *b*
voice of all the gods*.......278 *a*
v. of the desert never dumb411 *e*
v. of England in the east‡..184 *j*
voice of faithful friend....261 *p*
voice of nature cries ......411 *d*
v. of one who goes before..393 *a*
voice of promise............217 *a*
v. rise like a fountain†.....489 *u*
v. of the people is the......634 *s*
v. sounds like a prophet's..493 *d*
v. of sweetest tone bright..402 *b*
v. so sweet, the words so...634 *t*
v. sounds like a prophet's..301 *f*
voice stuck in my throat...744 *f*
voice that in the distance.. 319 *f*
voice, the look, the carriage730 *e*
voice upon the slope†......275 *u*
voice which from the skies.404 *d*
voice will run from hedge..323 *o*
what voice did on my spirit 91*m*
whispers the small voice‖..105 *i*
with a gracious voice*.....145 *h*
with a monarch's voice*....638*w*
with feigning v. verses*....557 *t*
with gentle v. and smiles..656 *v*
your dear voice revealing..557 *u*
Voiced-shrill-v., and loud, the 49 *p*
Voiceless-in her v. woe‖......387*m*
v. to scholars' tongues.....549 *z*
Voices-ancestral voices......493 *c*
angel v. sung the mercy of. 16 *t*
celestial voices to the**....670 *j*
depart when mortal v. bid¶ 634 *n*
earth, with her thousand v.486 *f*
follow where airy v. lead...316 *e*
join v., all ye living souls** 486 *p*
I thank you for your v.*....594 *u*
listen to Earth's weary v...540 *p*
many v. joining round me..169 *n*
moans round with many v.†187 *j*
music of kind v. ever nigh..647 *a*
nature's sweet and kindly§.637 *j*
soft voices had they. ......241 *u*
stranger's voices, hard and..31 *f*
sweet voices mysteriously.. 58 *c*
tender v. to make soft the..107*m*
there are voices of the past 466*m*
two v. are there, one is of¶.413 *p*
v. keep tune and our oars.. 63*m*
voices pursue him by day§.479 *t*
your v. break and falter.... 39 *t*
Void-they have left an aching379 *r*
Volcano-cold upon the dead†143 *o*
dancing on a volcano......129 *o*
Volcanoes-[virtues] like.....632 *r*
Volley-a fine v. of words*....665 *i*
Volley'd-v. and thunder'd†..640 *n*
Vollies-v. of eternal babble..588 *u*
Voltiger-a vest as admired V. 24 *b*
Volubility-I'll commend her* 659 *q*
Volume-a strange v. of real..448 *l*
closes his v. and ascends§.. 4 *x*
the small, rare v., black.... 22 *e*
the volume open'd! open'd.527 *p*
within that awful v. lies....539 *b*
Volumes-dear v.! you have.. 65 *j*
golden volumes! richest..... 65 *j*
history with all her v.‖. ...301 *r*

how volumes swell......... 68 *q*
volumes that I prize above* 68 *a*
whole volumes in folio*....429 *q*
Voluntary–thoughts that v.**597 *f*
Volunteer–instinct comes a‡..324*m*
Voluptuous–with its v. swell‖ 404 *o*
Voluptuously–v. dissolve.....560 *l*
Vomitest–v. thy wrecks on..,603 *l*
Vortex–fly in a v. of the sky. 54 *d*
Votaries–v. drenched on the.355 *l*
Votary–attend thy v.'s prayer564 *b*
Vote–hand and heart to this..469 *r*
 he shall v. for Gineral C.††.107 *k*
 vote for nothing but.......251 *s*
 vote that autumn's gone... 57 *j*
 v. that shakes the turrets..482 *r*
Voters–the will of the voters.524 *h*
Votes–as long as I count the.483 *c*
 questions but the price of.. 70 *r*
 votes in their hands are left.170 *w*
 votes of the fickle mob.....744 *s*
Vow–single v. that is vow'd*.419 *s*
 the patron of his vow some 50 *c*
 vow an eternal misery......419 *j*
Vowing–cease v. and sighing.416 *p*
Vows–baggage? Only vows...359 *q*
 hour when lover's vows‖...186 *p*
 men's vows are women's*..377 *g*
 our v. are heard betimes...487 *u*
 over their maiden vows.... 76 *n*
 playnts, prayers, v. truth..663 *t*
 recant vows made in pain** 419 *i*
 should v. so fondly made...569 *d*
 to stop those reckless vows.614 *j*
 vows are worn away‡.......376 *i*
 vows with so much passion.419 *f*
 when lovers' v. seem sweet‖ 50 *o*
 you give away heaven's v.*376 *v*
 your vows those of a god ...766 *n*
Voyage–all the v. of their life*461 *o*
 good voyage of nothing*...108 *p*
Voyaging–v. through¶.......452 *s*
Vulcan–is Vulcan's wife.....277 *n*
Vulgar–a vulgar Cato has....667 *l*
 bow the vulgar great.. ...279 *h*
 but by no means vulgar*... 83 *j*
 far hence, ye vulgar herd..711 *u*
 govern the vulgar crowd...784*m*
 take with the vulgar......429*w*
 the foolish and vulgar are..765 *c*
 the v. boil, the learned‡...431 *t*
 turns aside his scythe to‖..671 *w*
 v. flight of common souls..571 *u*
Vulgarity–Jeffersonian v. ...154 *r*
Vulgarize–v. the day of.....537 *p*
Vulture–unkindness like a*..627 *v*
 where the rage of the v.‖..336 *v*

W.

Waded–one naked star has w.576 *t*
Wading–two among them w..229 *b*
Wafer–cakes–men's faiths*..511 *u*
Waft–seas roll to waft me‡ .412 *a*
 to w. us home the message.538 *h*
 w. a feather, or to drown a.460 *s*
Wag–mad w.! who pardon'd‖.421 *p*
 that would not wag nor....437 *n*
 world may wag at will.....456 *k*
Wager–own opinions by a w.‖.460 *v*
Wagers–arguments use w.... 26 *u*
Wages–our praises are our*..147 *h*
Wagging–w. of your tongue*.606 *q*
Wags–how the world wags*..602 *g*
 that Pixies were the wags..453 *j*
Wail–like a long wail from...647 *j*
 runs a loud perpetual w.§..348 *o*
 sit and wail their loss*.....354 *q*
 to wail friends lost*.......262 *j*
 w. ring out from Purgatory 382 *g*
 with a sharp w., as if the...349*w*
Wailing–bundle of w., and... 31 *i*
 hush thy w., cease to....... 50 *j*
Wailings–but w. of defeat....351 *d*
Wains–return the laboring w§544 *d*
Wainscot–sing in comely w.... 68*m*
Wainscot–mouse–only the....396 *b*

Waist–bosom to thy slender.. 36 *f*
 round her w. she felt it‡....366 *h*
 round the slight w. or‖.....128 *c*
 strapp'd w., and frozen.....435 *r*
Waistcoat–upheaved his w...166 *p*
Wait–all things wait for and..276 *n*
 choose to w. upon Him here 19 *e*
 forelock watchful wait**..461 *k*
 "for if I wait " said she .. 240 *k*
 him who will but wait§....467 *i*
 if a man will only wait.....189 *d*
 learn to labor and to wait§.. 4 *w*
 lily whispers, "I wait "†...366 *r*
 persists to knock and w....605 *f*
 proud to w. where Beauty‖. 74 *h*
 serve who only stand and**.549 *b*
 some things are ill to wait.317 *e*
 told in a single word: W.§..428 *v*
 wait a little longer........267 *o*
 wait a little longer........637 *o*
 wait upon her..............248 *n*
 with anxious fear I wait...330 *q*
Waited–new gown and w. for.578 *g*
Waiting–my heart is weary...393 *d*
 waiting for the May.......393 *d*
 waiting him, we longest....260 *y*
 waiting on the shingle..... 213 *j*
 wasted in doubting and w.§519 *g*
 what are you w. for here...367 *c*
 with patience He stands w.527*w*
Waits–she w. for me, my lady.514 *v*
 waits for the night........234 *t*
 waits the fulfilment.......207 *q*
 w. with weary expectation.605 *n*
 which waits and grieves....227 *o*
Wake–and tremble when I w.559 *e*
 but in wedlock wake‡......663 *d*
 difference 'twixt w. and*..562 *o*
 do not wake me yet§.......160 *f*
 dream of those that wake..308 *n*
 he will wake soon‖........ 30 *t*
 nor begin to wake. ... .346 *c*
 should die before I wake...488 *v*
 through the foamy wake... 45 *d*
 though wisdom wake**.....651 *e*
 truths that w. to perish¶..624 *a*
 wake at the self-same......160 *c*
 wake the nations under....527 *n*
 wake the sleeping soul.....275 *q*
 we w., and when we sleep**.575 *c*
 we wake eternally.........316 *a*
Waked–I wak'd, she fled**...155 *e*
 morn, w. by the circling**.400 *k*
 waked and kindled by the..407 *d*
 waked by bugle notes......228 *d*
 when w. with note of fire...443 *s*
 you've w. me too soon, I....564 *a*
Waken–truth you w. then you 85 *c*
 w. their free nature in the††.588 *g*
Wakens–conscience wakens..105 *l*
 w. the slumbering ages.....319 *f*
Wakes–at country w. sung... 32 *q*
 it w. the soul, and lifts it...404 *f*
 near him when he wakes*..369 *f*
 the dreamer wakes.........159 *p*
 w. the nation's slumberers.146 *w*
Waking–her rested sense a... 52 *f*
 nor night of waking.......562 *f*
 shall ne'er know waking...138 *i*
 waking dawn'd in heaven...136 *g*
Wales–w. a portion with.....669 *x*
Walk–and ye sall w. in silk... 70 *n*
 a terrace walk, and half....652 *l*
 a walk divided it‡.. ......270 *a*
 common w. of virtuous life.142 *o*
 but nobody says "w. in.... 9 *q*
 I pursue my walk..........244 *n*
 joy to walk at will. ....246 *p*
 may do but only walk......333 *p*
 not walk, but it dances.....282 *i*
 river's summer walk.......222 *p*
 round it ran a walk†.......270 *a*
 she is pretty to walk with...660 *l*
 slouch becomes a walk.....443 *a*
 than those that walk*......426 *n*
 upon our way, walk with... 67 *i*
 walk a little faster........213 *f*

w. as if you had swallowed 509 *j*
walk beneath it steadfastly.348 *h*
walk evermore to higher....517 *a*
walk hence with that*..... 308 *u*
walk in absence of the sun* 603 *h*
walk in fear and dread.....208 *r*
w. in the thick foot-prints..141 *e*
walk into my parlour.......324 *k*
walk sober off before a‡... 10 *v*
w. the studious cloisters** 352 *l*
walk through blindfold.....151 *j*
walk through life serenely..227 *f*
walk with hand in hand††..360 *f*
walk with me where. ......614 *b*
w. ye in Heaven's sweet air.374 *a*
we walk as heretofore...... 17 *b*
Walked–and w. in Paradise..463 *l*
 he w. mannerly and talk'd.518 *v*
 she has walk'd before...... 6 *g*
 walked abroad at noon... . 183 *r*
 w. straight out of the Ark.. 25 *r*
Walking–a–w. the devil is....153 *r*
 dog's w. on his hind legs...450 *p*
 not walking I am reading.. 66 *k*
 soft hour of walking comes.625 *p*
 walking across the floor§...254 *d*
Walks–already w. to–morrow.600 *a*
 and echoing w. between**..425 *p*
 arched w. of twilight**....617 *o*
 a supper that walks.......177*m*
 awfully he w. the round....274 *j*
 benighted w. under the** .697 *e*
 daughters bright thy w....655 *a*
 echoing walks between**...613 *i*
 even when the bird w. one..755 *d*
 eye nature's w., shoot folly‡373 *t*
 peculiar walks, cloisters... 14*m*
 poor man's barren walks...229 *p*
 spirit walks of every day...131 *r*
 that w. at dead of night.... 24 *s*
 to morning w. and prayers‡ 349 *o*
 w. among his peers unread.371 *g*
 walks on the windy hills...247*m*
 w. over the western wave.417 *q*
 w. the waters like a thing‖.551 *p*
 walks up and down*.......288 *k*
 walks upon the wind‡ .....275 *l*
 walks with hasty strides....458 *n*
 who fastest w., but walks..185 *s*
Wall–a man is not a wall....325 *k*
 be a rose upon the wall...355 *t*
 clings to the mouldering§.515 *a*
 close the w. up with our*..639 *l*
 crag and ruin'd wall......231 *d*
 dry leaves upon the wall...395 *g*
 feather-bed betwixt a wall...88 *f*
 icicles hang by the wall*...546 *h*
 on revelation's wall........448 *a*
 patch a wall to expel the*..152 *b*
 roamer is she o'er w. and...648 *g*
 scale thy wall by night§....189 *f*
 shone on the old oak wall.. 94 *a*
 standing like a stone wall... 77 *l*
 the whitewash'd wall......303 *r*
 this thy wall of brass‡......106 *d*
 to build the wooden wall§..551 *v*
 wall that circles it about...298 *x*
 wasps upon a southern w..566 *t*
 weakest goes to the wall...744 *l*
 weather on the outward*... 50 *g*
 whiten'd w. provoke the‡...429 *k*
 within this wall of flesh*...572 *f*
Wall-flower–w-f., how.. ....250 *c*
 wall-flower is sublime.....250 *c*
 wall-flower on each rifted..219 *f*
Walls–as that the w.worn thin385 *l*
 crawls round the w. as you.614 *i*
 far white w. along them‖...532 *a*
 hunger broke stone walls*..311 *h*
 indignation 'gainst your*..639 *t*
 solid walls to break.......278 *u*
 split the marble walls of...614 *p*
 stone walls do not a prison.491 *v*
 talk along the walls‡.......169 *j*
 the purple w. of Heaven...384 *x*
 the windows and the walls.425 *e*
 these are cities and walls...281 *d*

water-lily starts and†.......250 *j*
wild water-lily restore......250 *d*
Waterloo–meets his W. at last 151 *k*
Water-men–w-m. who advance 63 *l*
Water-plants–slime on w-p.. 114 *n*
Waters–a murmur as of w...542 *h*
and roaring waters*........327 *j*
and the w. murmuring**..562 *b*
breast of w. broadly swells‖532 *a*
by me upon the waters*....407 *t*
deep waters noyselesse are.572 *v*
drink sweet w., and dream.607 *f*
dusky w. shudder as they..395 *f*
fearing the waters of Lethe.179 *t*
finger on all flowing w.....546 *b*
fish in troubled waters..... 18 *g*
gentle winds and waters‖..186 *p*
great ship asks deep waters 494 *w*
its w. returning back to§... 8 *b*
o'er the waters blue........249 *j*
oh, is it from the waters..647 *k*
oil on troubled waters......502 *ee*
once more upon the waters‖459 *e*
over the waste of water..624 *h*
rising world of w. dark**...641 *f*
silent waters heaven is seen.191 *p*
smoothly the w. kisst**.....647 *p*
still waters run deep.......742 *d*
take heed of still waters....504 *q*
the bright waters meet.....411 *t*
the pleasant waters........531 *a*
the still-closing waters*....207 *m*
the waters and the wind...151 *q*
the waters will heal.......627 *i*
turbid waters shining......237 *g*
walks the w. like a thing‖..551 *p*
waters of wide Agony....327 *k*
waters run too slow........394 *q*
where the rushing w. gleam 230 *f*
where the scattered w. rave 460 *t*
where these pure w. rise... 16 *i*
whose silver waters show‡.615 *f*
whose waters of deep woe.603 *l*
wide as the waters be......530 *d*
words writ in waters........664 *g*
Water-side–over the w-s.......322 *n*
Watery–leaves his watery nest 48 *n*
Wave–a break of the wave...490 *w*
a wave of the ocean........297 *b*
base of the w. to the billow's 57 *a*
battles of wave and blast...359 *d*
breast the wave of life.....135 *e*
bursts as a w., that from‡..577 *r*
dies a wave along the shore 132 *j*
every wave in every brook.. 51 *i*
every w. with dimpled face.577 *t*
freshen'd from the wave....531 *c*
furious as the sweeping w.‖ 69 *k*
hail'd them o'er the wave..630 *x*
instant death on every w‡..577 *r*
I saw from out the wave‖.. 99 *a*
life on the ocean wave......460 *i*
message to him every wave 190 *p*
of aspen leaves that wave..612 *d*
of moonlit w. and willowy..381 *y*
on the w. reflected lustres..585 *v*
Rhine with younger wave..532 *e*
ripple of w. and hiss of....598 *q*
spangling the w. with lights 475 *v*
succeeds a woe as wave a w. 72 *c*
the foam itself, the wave... 47 *j*
the wave is deeper blue‖...186 *p*
triumph shall wave........214 *i*
walk over the western w....417 *q*
w. and whirlwind wrestle§.551 *u*
w. came rolling high and...459 *o*
w. in the tempestucus...... 23 *j*
w., Munich! all thy........636 *q*
wave o' th' sea, that you*..129 *h*
w. succeeding wave they go.529 *l*
Waved–it waved on high.....214 *g*
waved her lily hand........204 *t*
Wavelets–her bows the w..... 63 *n*
how its wavelets drown one 191 *l*
Waves–along the w. dost thou 42 *l*
breaking w. dashed high...459 *q*
breaks the wave and‡....613 *h*

Britannia, rule the waves..116 *d*
but came the waves........255 *d*
dubious w. of error toss'd..185 *j*
even the little w., beaten...515 *b*
eyes that watch the waves† 92 *s*
foam-crested waves........223 *b*
green waves on the sea.....610 *f*
he ploughs the waves......796 *n*
listen to the hissing waves . 63 *j*
o'er the w. on their stormy. 57 *a*
on the waves built a city... 99 *d*
sea! whose waves are years603 *t*
smooth flow the waves‡....674 *t*
sound of the surging waves 613 *b*
the little w., with their soft§598 *u*
the raging waves of ocean .397 *h*
the sea rolls its waves......559 *r*
the waves of the mysterious638 *l*
the wild waves reach their. 56 *n*
the woods and the waves§.. 50 *i*
though waves are changing 347 *k*
thy w. are old companions.530 *g*
thy waves as they dimple ..532 *f*
to women, or to waves.....657 *x*
washed by the waves ......258 *e*
waves and mountains§.... 118 *g*
waves are brightly glowing 459 *t*
waves were dead; the tides‖130 *l*
w. bound beneath me as a‖.459 *e*
waves clasp one another...460 *k*
waves come to behold...... 36 *a*
w. lash the frightened shores 577 *t*
waves of emerald and gold.423 *q*
w. show their teeth in the..408 *j*
what are the wild w. saying 459 *i*
when the w. went high he..129 *m*
when waves were rough....157 *e*
whilst breezy w. toss up....459 *r*
white waves break tether..391 *i*
winds and waves are always 445 *e*
with over-matching waves* 58 *k*
ye waves in silence sleep...470 *i*
ye waves that o'er th'.....459 *a*
Wax–even as a form of wax*.139 *k*
moulds the world like soft .668 *a*
the moon will w., the moon 605 *d*
wax to receive‖ ....296 *o*
why he's a man of wax*....372 *t*
Waxing–w. so fast from night 397 *v*
Way–a dim and perilous w.¶.486 *d*
adorns and cheers our way.307 *s*
along a way he knows not..606 *v*
and led the way..........450 *l*
Ann hath a way*.........203 *w*
ask of the Learn'd the way‡342 *j*
a way so to control*........203 *w*
bad and indirect way......519 *p*
bent their way............ 227 *k*
cheerfully hold on thy way.667 *x*
conversing I forget the way 113 *n*
do bold things in a quiet w.656 *e*
find that better way‡.......489 *b*
flowers, lost its way........392 *d*
follow when we lead the w.‡188 *q*
furthest from his way......185 *s*
groping our way along the 592 *m*
guide my lonely way.......300 *e*
had his ain way...........537 *a*
have her w. or have her fits 375 *j*
he his w. tugs she t'other..375 *j*
he hit upon a way.........129 *f*
held the tenor of his way... 11 *c*
his sordid way he wends...643 *b*
how carve way i' the life...466 *f*
I find no way, from deep**.105 *u*
I knew there was but one*.138 *l*
imagine it to lie that way*.315 *f*
instinct of the one true w...793 *h*
led the way to heaven...... 85 *k*
long is the way and hard**299 *i*
love soon found the way...362 *c*
making the hard w. sweet*574 *o*
measures back his way.....606 *v*
mind my compass and my.445 *f*
multitude a way to peace...488 *j*
next w. home's the farthest 505 *w*
noiseless tenour of their w.347 *t*

one heart, one way........799 *j*
on her charm'd way.......540 *p*
only pretty Fanny's way...373 *s*
only w. of setting the will..646 *h*
our headlong way.........242 *l*
plods his weary way.......186 *s*
point us out the way....... 57 *n*
prudence points the way...465 *o*
ready for the w. of life or*.525 *g*
rises dark o'er the way.....349 *f*
royal, took her own way*...583 *e*
self-same w. with more*...511 *v*
something given that way.504 *f*
surest w. to hit a woman's.662 *n*
that starts i' the w. before*.145 *w*
that way going to*.........594 *h*
that way she came.........248 *i*
the better way is hidden...348 *a*
the way to wickedness.....695 *j*
the w. until the peacock led 53 *m*
thorny way to heaven*....451 *j*
though lone the w. as that. 85 *m*
to find the w. to heaven*...309 *n*
to strew its short but weary.658 *d*
way already opened........751 *a*
way himself will choose*... 7 *n*
way of all flesh ....207 *t*
w. of the Sacramentarians..521 *j*
way that seems the best.... 91 *v*
way through the world.....373 *l*
way to kill a wife with*... 377 *m*
way to seem the shorter....498 *p*
went her unremembering w.465 *e*
were like a better way*.....190 *x*
which way the wind is.....647 *v*
which, working out its w...571 *j*
who would not, finding w.** 91 *u*
worlds, and led the way....188 *n*
Way-farers–meet other w-f ..643 *t*
Ways–all w. do lie open.....390 *e*
and by what abject ways‡..486 *t*
and smiling are thy ways..543 *p*
and ways be foul*..........546 *h*
appear in other ways than*.644 *f*
are the winding ways..... 22 *k*
best of all w. to lengthen...416 *r*
cheerful w. of men cut.**..149 *m*
direct his ways by plain....654 *h*
Heaven's w. are Heaven's..767 *b*
he of their wicked ways**..451 *b*
just are the w. of God**....332 *o*
justify the w. of God to**..510 *h*
ranged its silvan ways......229 *f*
sins the newest kind of w.*556 *i*
that for w. that are dark...144 *l*
the many thousand ways§..359 *u*
the rugged ways ....245 *k*
vindicate the ways of God‡.373 *t*
ways and means of........173 *d*
w. are offered to our will††.101 *o*
ways of God to man‡.......510 *j*
ways to waste superfluous.642 *c*
we have wandered all our..601 *v*
word ten thousand ways....664 *m*
Waysides–w. scorched with ..245 *k*
Wayward–tetchy and w. was*619 *j*
w. is this foolish love*......363 *h*
w. sisters, depart in peace.282 *w*
Weak–admiration only of**... 35 *o*
and delicately weak†.......658 *f*
concessions of the w. are...641 *o*
defect and delicately w.‡... 82 *r*
fallen and the weak††......209 *d*
for the fallen and the w.††.559 *o*
how w. a thing the heart*.658 *w*
lest thou shouldst be w.....212 *l*
mortality's too w. to bear..329 *t*
not weak of soul . ...212 *l*
one so w. to venture his....479 *p*
person's weak points......208 *b*
protest of the w. against...338 *u*
soft to the w. and noble....345 *h*
so w. thou art, that fools...365 *w*
the mortal race is far too w.795 *b*
though I am w., yet God...488 *b*
to be weak is miserable **..641 *w*
waken their free nature††..588 *g*

---

weak head with strongest‡.491 c
weak is man, so ignorant...488 s
weak soul, within itself....641 r
we must have a weak spot. 80 d
whom he loves is w. and...358 c
Weaken-w. whatever we ....795 a
Weakens-being able, w. the..742 q
friendship weakens love ...599 e
Weaker-either stronger or w.716 c
Weakest-by the w. minister*331 o
conceit in weakest bodies* .103 q
reed, the weakest in nature597 g
weakest goes to the wall....744 l
w., however strong, who...157 k
w. saint upon his knees....487 s
Weakness-all thy nature's w.343 h
all wickedness is w.** .....641 v
amiable weakness ....641 p
amiable w. of human.....641 q
and shows its weakness....605 t
be it a weakness, it descrves672 d
be wroth with weakness†...642 b
boast, O child of weakness .594 o
by its w. overcomes††......402 c
fame is the last weakness..697 e
gives in your weakness* ...210 f
if weakness may excuse** .641 v
in the greater weakness§...318 v
man's love of life, his w....512 q
means of weakness and*. .. 12 a
of your own weakness......473 c
thy very w. hath brought§ .359 v
till one man's w. grows the‡642 a
w. of a virtuous mind.....309 o
w. of mind is the only......507hh
weakness on both sides is..513 s
w. subservient to our....... 15 h
w. than from our strength.465 n
weakness to be wroth with†642 b
weakness to lament* .....119 u
weapon of her w. she can‖..590 e
wrong because of weakness 33 o
Weal-plunge for the‡........ 47 h
publick w. requires that a..482 b
purg'd the gentle weal*....403 q
Wealth-all her w. upon her..644 z
all the wealth I had*......271m
all this [w.] excludes but...484 s
any means get wealth and‡.642 r
as men of w. may venture. 25 t
barr'd from every use of w.642 f
be possessed of wealth....803ff
but for his wealth.........329 e
by wisdom wealth is won...651 r
can w. give happiness.....643 f
deprived of honours or of..354 a
discontented even wealth is111 i
dropped, her wealth.......241 r
employ their wealth.......684 g
excess of wealth is cause of120 u
for wealth, for pow'r......638 o
for w.,without contentment642 i
get place and wealth, if‡...642 r
get riches first, get w.**.... 13 l
gets an equal amount of w.642 g
great is Wealth...........287 o
hazard not your w. on a....754 g
home the w. of the Indies..607 a
if we our wealth obey... ..389 o
lack of w. is easily repaired784 b
let w. and commerce, laws.418 i
little wealth to lose*....... 7 b
long as all the increased w.492 g
loss of wealth is loss......293 g
may match in wealth††... 228 e
mental friends and mental.642 d
much wealth, how little...643 g
old sack is our wealth.....649 u
passion for wealth.........740 c
pay for the w. that you get 72 h
place of departed wealth...726 j
possession of family w. and 15 h
private credit is wealth....123 h
riches, ignorance of w.....314 g
sake of accumulating w....387 q
seal and guerdon of wealth235 q
shade that follows wealth..264m

some in their wealth* .....273 f
some seek wealth and ease.526 l
some wit, some wealth.....256 c
sources of w. be boundless.389 b
than all their largest w....539 k
the poor man's w., the....563 g
the very want of wealth....642 h
the wealth of seas.........197 r
thrive in wealth amain**.. 13 l
time is lord of thee: thy w.601 o
'twixt a miser and his w.*.471 c
type of all the wealth.....229 n
using all their wealth.....445 a
virtue after wealth........728 a
ways to waste superfluous.642 c
wealth and freedom reign..111 a
w. is a great means of.....642 p
w. is attended by care.....739 o
wealth lies buried ....216 f
wealth of her lord.........578 g
w. of Indian provinces.....114 q
wealth of the Czar......... 22 q
w. preferring to eternal‡...642 j
w. that ne'er encumbers...631 x
wealth that sinews bought.559 e
wealth when there's such..375 u
w. ye find another keeps...152 l
when w. is lost nothing.....354 n
where w. accumulates and.143 g
worldly wealth consumeth.262 a
worth, unless united with..739 p
wretched man outlive his*.485 b
Wealthy-w. in my friends*..262 d
Weapon-satire's my w., but‡537 t
thought's a w. stronger....267 o
w. of her weakness she can‖590 e
weapon of the lord.........182 e
w. that comes down as still.482 t
Weaponless-w. himself**....579 i
Weapons-buried were all§...470 o
hurt with the same w*.....329 q
supplies them with w......677 t
too, have hurled weapons..800 a
w.holy saws of sacred writ*303 e
we grasp the weapons he...579 p
women's w. water-drops*..591 w
Wear-being loth to w. it out.652 q
better to w. out than to rust 4 h
get that I wear*...........111 t
I'll w. them for your sake*. 24 d
in the wide world to wear.. 22 r
may not wear them*....... 24 f
might w. out life like thee..647 a
nature seems to wear one. .410 v
nothing wear but frieze**..593 i
the rankling thorn to wear.351 r
the worse for wear........432 s
used to w. a long brown coat 23 h
used to wear an old drab... 23 o
w. him in my heart's core*372 h
wear in your shining hair..227 f
wear out than to rust out...500bb
w. them like his raiment*..628 n
which we need not wear....654m
with nothing to wear...... 22 q
women wear the breeches..374 k
Wearer-merit of the wearer*.383 h
w. knows where the shoe..506 q
Wearers-there are no crown.619 l
Wearing-not linen you're w.126 g
Wears-fashion w. out more*.205 i
he w. his faith but as the*..433 b
him who wears the regal**.534 l
she w. that body but as one660 v
so wears she to wear*.... ..377 e
Wearied-can be wearied out.597 d
lie not down w. 'neath.....339 j
Weariness-art thou pale for..399 b
makes weariness forget‖...648m
opiate of idle w. the mindes 68 o
weariness can snore upon*.526 o
wearinesse may tosse him..280 d
wisdom won with w ....356 d
Weary-all knees were weary 488 w
by thee, I weary thee*.....6.52 j
days of absence, I am w.... 3 c
fingers weary and worn... 339 c

for w. feet, the gift of rest.526 t
from a weary night.........136 j
heaven upon earth to the w. 88 g
I am so w. of toil and of... 8 n
I am weary, and am§.......561 p
I'm weary aften whiles....303 o
infirm and weary§......... 10 l
I sae weary, fu' o' care....530m
through many a w. year...380 c
to put on when you're w...666 c
w. grows the unclouded....236 b
weary Him with my**......488 n
weary of a golden.........223 t
w. of all, shall want some* 499 n
weary of breath...........388 f
weary of solid firmness*...207 i
weary, stale, flat and*.....669 c
w. with disasters tugg'd*..350 t
welcome to the w. and the§536 c
Weasel-w. nor wildcat will.. 55 k
Weather-bald pate from the.180 l
bright or cloudy weather..236 p
come the wild weather.....212 i
endure wind and weather*.507 j
fate's serenest weather....207 q
foul weather proceeds and.776 s
get the weather stain......231 s
in fierce March weather...391 i
makes cold weather*......660 b
prove fair weather. .. ..108 u
'scaped the wind and w....456 j
through cloudy weather...345 n
thoughts and sunny w....544 i
through wind and weather. 20 g
w. without, sheltered about615 j
window in stormy weather.377 s
winter and rough weather*610 d
Weather-cock-Autumn is a..544m
Weathered-pilot that w. the.444 z
Weathers-color in all w.††...197 v
shield you in all sorts of w.458 j
weathers every sky..... ...227 p
Weather-wise-some are w-w.504 d
Weave-I can weave no more.597 i
what a tangled web we w...144 x
Weaved-ill-w. ambition*.... 13 x
Weaver-here the weaver sat.237 d
Weavers-w.of long tales....578 i
Moorland w.boast Pindaric‖454 l
Weaving-pattern which was.345 p
Web-in her web's centre....324 h
or a spider's w. adorning¶..309 e
pluck one thread and the..152 p
stain'd w. that whitens.... 88 b
'tis a thin web which......201 h
w. from their own entrails.587 s
web of Fate we spin ....207 u
web of our life is of a*. . .350 w
web which spreadeth wide.324 j
what a tangled w.we weave144 x
Webs-w. were spread of more579 d
Wed-December when they*..377 f
if she deny to wed, I'll*....376 u
must love, and wed.......392 v
thought leapt out to wed†.598 a
'tis best to wed...........223 s
too much haste to wed.....238 b
wed her for a mine of gold*208 k
wed itself with speech†....598 a
wed nothing short of......375 l
wed one sweet woman and.607 f
wed or cease to woo.......662 j
wed raw Haste, half sister†605 q
woo honour, but to wed it*806 w
Wedded-blasted were their..374 h
hail, w. love, mysterious*.376 b
our ring of wedded love...375 s
soul is wedded unto mine..333 s
wedded to calamity*...... 8 g
widowed wife and w. maid.376 l
you wedded all the world*.659 i
Wedding-in all the w. cake .307 y
never wedding, ever wooing662 j
our w. cheer to a sad*.... 75 x
Wedding-coat-a bright black. 43 h
Wedding-day-barefoot on*...377 l
weep upon his w-d.*........384 c

Wedding-dresses–w-d. ready‖.374m
Wedding-garlands–to decay..546 c
Wedding-garment–ours is her526 x
Wedding-gown–about a w-g. . 23 l
Wedding-ring–circle of a w-r.375 a
Wedding-song–hear the w-s..568 k
  like a w-s. all-melting .... 51 c
Wede–are a' wede away......217 s
Wedges–cleft with wedges...251 b
Wedlock–but in w. wake‡....663 d
  honest w. is a glorious‡....376 h
  wedlock indeed hath oft....375 d
  w.'s a lane where there is..376 g
Weds–boast if she weds....578 g
Wednesday–he that died o'*..306 y
Wee–baloo, baloo my w., wee 31 d
  she is a winsome w. thing..644 r
  this sweet w. wife o' mine..644 r
  th' expectant wee things...303 i
Weed–basest w. out-braves*..643 o
  beneath some pleasant w...323 o
  flower is only a weed§.....160 g
  frail snowy weed........238 i
  from a mistress than a w...456 n
  gather honey from a weed.650 h
  O Jupiter, try the weed....457 g
  ought law to weed it out...528 g
  pernicious weed: whose...456 g
  secret of a w.'s plain heart††643 k
  tobacco, an outlandish w...456 i
  weed flung from the rock‖.150 l
  weed of every clime.......319m
  woman, in this scale, the...457 g
Weeds–bittern booming in....268 o
  call us not weeds, we are.. 643 h
  her winter weeds outworn. 669 i
  idle w. are fast in growth*.289 s
  ill weeds on to the surface .619m
  I noted in tattered weeds* .441 e
  like weeds uplifted........391 i
  memory, in widow's weeds381 w
  noxious weeds he sips......321m
  plucking up the w. of sin...667 n
  root away the noisome w.*.643 l
  smell far worse than w.*...643 o
  we are weeds without it....343 p
  weeds are shallow-rooted*.643 n
  weeds do grow apace*......289 q
  weeds make haste*........289 q
  weeds of glorious feature..412 q
  whether to weeds or flowers371 j
Week–and the week is gone. .507 c
  days that's in the week.....536 k
  for a week escape a great*.490 n
  keep a week away*........365 b
  one meal a week will serve.606 p
  wrecked with a w. of teen*.569 s
Week-day–his w-d. meal‡....167 r
Weeks–been fou for weeks....100 o
  spent six consecutive w..... 23 a
Weep–a man may w. upon*..384 c
  and unapt to weep*........444 h
  and women must weep.....666 v
  as make the angels weep*..491 g
  as well as eyes that weep..561 q
  calm for those who weep...285 i
  cannot weep for them......288 z
  deed, than weep it done....187 v
  doe ye weep, sweet babes...239 n
  eyes that wake to weep....561 i
  fair daffadills, we weep....226 k
  foolish ones shall weep....141 c
  I am about to weep; but*..591 o
  I cannot w.; for all my*....591 p
  if you wish me to weep.....728 j
  I might not weep for thee..142 d
  it is some relief to weep....745m
  laugh, the laugher weep*..606 h
  leaves the wretch to weep..264m
  let us weep in our darkness403 j
  long-leaved flowers weep†..412 t
  men weep over may be‖....284m
  more, because I weep in....590 p
  my bier ye come to weep...590 c
  nature loves to weep.......153 w
  no, I'll not weep*..........591 y
  old women weep for joy....483 e

tears which stars weep.....153 x
  that he should w. for her*..423m
  thing to weep for..........255 c
  'tis that I may not weep‖...340 l
  to w., to sleep, and weep....349 w
  to weep, yet scarce know...155 n
  weep and you weep alone..669 r
  w. no more, lady, weep no.466 l
  weep not for him...........403 j
  w. not for those whom the.136 v
  w. on; and, as thy sorrows.569m
  weep that trust and that...620 e
  weep to record, and blush..555 s
  weep, weep–and the watch619 e
  w. with them that weep*...570 g
  were cause indeed to weep. 74 d
  what we should weep for..744 g
  will weep on Sunday.......775 g
  words that w. and tears....590 l
  ye who weep only ! If, as...590 d
  you desire him to weep ....177 d
Weeper–to make the weeper*606 h
Weeping–April stops at last..392 g
  for you will have weeping . 32m
  hear the children weeping. 88 v
  I have full cause of w.*. .591 y
  let us go weeping...........133 t
  long years of weeping.....374 a
  smile, but your weeping... 32m
  thine eyes red with w......537 e
  thy weeping is in vaine....138 e
  w. at the feet and head....131 v
Weeps–and the widow w.*...381m
  April w. while these are so.392 d
  comic stage deserted w.....714 o
  hero weeps, he is grown....309 o
  mercy w. them out again...331 f
  w. like a tired child who ...392 d
  white rose w. "She is late†366 r
Weigh–bar to w. true worth..330 s
  weigh less than a single††. 5 c
  w. not the thin ore where‖..389 l
  weigh the man, not his title373 g
Weigh'd–hast thou ever w. a.592 t
Weigh'st–w. thy words*......665 q
Weighing–in equal scale w.*.145m
Weighs–Jove w. affairs of‡...277 b
  weighs upon the heart*....441 c
  who duly weighs an hour...354 u
  who weighs his burdens...701 p
Weight–falling with soft**...562 a
  for our offense by weight*. 30 c
  less of weight it bore......588 t
  the w. of seventy years¶... 12m
  thrice their weight in gold. 22 f
  too great weight and.......246 e
  unendurable its weight....268 i
  weight from off my head*.. 1 c
  w. of any misery, before it. 22 d
  what w. your shoulders ‖...427 j
  with too great a weight....555 d
Weights–a noise of falling†... 25 l
  sink with their own w......652 p
Weke–w.! so cries a pig*.....432 f
Welcome–a table full of w.*..644 a
  bay deep-mouth'd w. as‖...643 p
  bear welcome in your eye*.482 c
  bid that w. which comes*...644 b
  coming with w. at our††....136 c
  freely welcome to my cup..323 e
  hail with welcome sweet... 16 t
  is w. to my soul..........474 k
  kisses and w. you'll find....643 q
  one more, most welcome*..211 q
  say, "Welcome friend"... 73 h
  small cheer and great w.*..644 g
  society the sweeter w.*....565 p
  so welcome a guest that....704 n
  sweet will thy welcome and 48 o
  the hostess say ''W."*.....644 e
  unclouded w. of a wife....646 b
  very w. to our house*......644 f
  warmest w., at an inn.....433 k
  welcome as a friend¶. . ....245 i
  welcome ever smiles*.....644 i
  w. in every clime as breath.120 f
  welcome make the rest.....289 u

welcome merry Christmas. 95 c
  welcome, my old friend§...643 s
  w. my return at night.... 87 g
  w. peaceful evening in .. .186 g
  welcome the coming‡ .. . 289 v
  w. thee, and wish thee**...393 e
  welcome thy entering......390 o
  w. to a foreign fireside§....643 s
  welcome to our table......168 k
  welcome to the north again 43 l
  w. to the weary and the§...536 q
  welcome to your gory bed. 635 q
  without a welcome‖.......566 f
  worth is warrant for his*...644 c
  yet art thou welcome¶.....245 i
  yet I pick'd a welcome*....644 h
  your welcome dear*.......644 d
Welcomes–deeds, hollow w.*. 73 b
  seem full of welcomes§.... 643 r
  w. and farewells been said.394m
  welcomes every changing..227 p
  w. in the shivering pair....474 a
Welcomest–w. when they are*290 d
Well–all is not well; I doubt*586 p
  all's well that ends well*..495 d
  another is wise, yet I am*..659 o
  another virtuous, yet I am*659 o
  be digging a well.........745 q
  but to live well...........722 e
  have ye done well.... ....603 k
  his drink the crystal well..567 j
  if we do w. here we shall do347 j
  in the bottom of a well.....623 z
  in the heart's deep well....574 e
  it is not done well; but you450 p
  looking w. can't move her..365 r
  may be he is not well*.....295 q
  must fast till he is well.....451 s
  my Cornish friends be well.586 i
  not so deep as a well, nor*.112 g
  oft we mar what's well*...527 j
  one woman is fair, yet I am*659 o
  speak sometimes merely w.179 q
  stream from wisdom's well651 s
  the burden which is w......701 q
  the devil was w., the devil.153 k
  the last drop in the well‖...604 l
  'tis not so deep as a w.,nor*671 h
  walnut-tree over the well..323 q
  we all, when we are well...676 d
  well of English undefyled.480 p
  w. to be off with the old love360 q
  what's well begun, is half..679 c
  where truth is–in a well‖..641 a
  who well lives, long lives..599 c
Well-bred–and well-bred man120 d
  courteous and well-bred... 126 g
  sensible, and w-b. man....373m
Well-done–servant of God**.549 a
Well-endowed–a w-e. girl ...779 o
Well-filled–a little house w-f.494bb
Well-made–is a w-m. man....145 o
Well-meaning–w-m. dunce.††402m
Well-read–respect for a w-r..516 e
Well-reputed–a woman w-r.*659 j
Wells–into empty wells .....155 b
  purest wells of English....340 h
Well-spent–as rare as a w-s..346 l
Well-spring–a well-spring of. 32 n
  friend, my well-spring....260 i
Well-timed–when love's w-t..355 b
Welkin–amaze the w. with*..639 a
  stars have lit the welkin...214 e
Welsh-devil understands W.*310 z
Wench–a most sweet wench*.659 a
  wooed his w. with a pair...663 e
Wenches–tongues of*... ....537 x
Wener–of W. or of Wetter...440 a
Went–know she came and††..684 h
  made a finer end and w.*...136 l
  where she w., the flowers..657 e
Wept–behold who ever wept.591 f
  eye that w. essential love..382 i
  he watch'd and wept, he...450 n
  I wept for memory........381 c
  I w. thy absence–o'er and. 3 a
  men o'er him wept‖.......403 c

SHAKESPEARE *; MILTON **; WORDSWORTH ¶; BYRON ‖; TENNYSON †; LOWELL ††; POPE ‡; LONGFELLOW §.

met by a grave, and wept..592 p
therewithal, wept bitterly*591 v
watch'd and w., he pray'd..587 x
wept again the loss of all..592 p
wept for the roses of earth.222 j
w. o'er his wounds, or tales443 d
who w. with delight when..379 s
Were-dream of things that||..97m
  remember such things*....381 k
  they were—they are—they.. 61 s
  things that ne'er were..... 84 x
  upward to what they were*152 f
Werther-W. had a love for...366 u
West-along the w. the golden524 l
  deserted the west........ 59 h
  east is east, and w. is west.637 g
  eyes sought the west afar..362 f
  fair traveller's come to the.586 e
  fire in the west fades out...615 n
  from east and from west...595 a
  from east to w. his course.426 o
  fronts the golden west.....515 r
  glows in yonder west......585 e
  go West, young man! go....498 q
  her blue eyes sought the w.576 v
  in his palace of the west...585 p
  softly out in the red west..624 f
  spear-like rays in the west.585 k
  the east and western bars. .492 f
  the w. was paved with sullen586 d
  topples round the dreary†.100 q
  to the beauteous west......100 h
  west explains the east.....100 t
  west has opened its gates.. 36 a
  west is broken into bars....624 t
  w. yet glimmers with some*625 n
Western-Him of the w.dome.548 j
  lovers love the w. star......576 v
  western giant smiles.......115 o
  w. world believe and sleep‡537 c
Westminster-thrive at W.‡...428 b
  try Westminster and view|.182 f
Westward-eastward and w...404 h
  then westward-ho*........204 w
  w. the course of empire.....492 c
  w. the star of empire......492 a
West-wind-baskin' w-w....††617 u
Wet-all dirty and wet.....326 t
  are they wet even yet††....248 s
  roads are wet where'er one577 s
  some because 'tis wet.....430 b
Wether-tainted w. of the*....149 p
Wetter-of Wener or of W....440 a
Whale-stood to bob for w... 18 f
  who says a whale's a bird..168 s
Wharfs-of the adjacent w.*..447 v
What-he knew what is what.498 ii
  he knew what's what.......336 s
  tell us w. and where they†.317 a
  w. I am thou canst not be..684 e
Wheat-chaff and take the w..321 q
  harvest of w. is most......710 j
  have a cake out of the w.*.431 u
  reasons are two grains of*..517 o
  short emerald wheat.......247 j
  wheat for this planting§....275 b
Wheat-ear-out from the w-e.238 l
Wheedling-taught the w. arts656m
Wheel-arresting the vast w..599 r
  bound upon a wheel of fire* 8 i.
  butterfly upon a wheel‡....537 s
  fortune's w. to roll about..797 k
  motions of the forming w..449 k
  shaped by the glowing w...683 i
  shoulder to the wheel..... 4 c
  so close to the rapid wheel. 54m
  the noisy wheel was still... 71 d
  the world is a w., and it will668 f
  this quick revolving wheel.186 h
  touches some wheel‡......371 j
  turn, turn my wheel§.....449 o
  twirl your wheel with......292 d
  wheel of time goes round.329 u
  w. of time rolls downward..746 v
  while she turns the giddy..476 u
  whirled like a potter's w.*..597 n
  your wheel is out of order.484 k

Wheeled-fiery-w. throne**...109 a
Wheels-and the madding**. 637 t
  before the w. of Phœbus**..625 j
  hesitating w. of life gliblier 8 o
  off our chariot wheels......843 a
  Time's revolving wheels....186 l
  w. around in ceaseless flight601 v
  wheels her pale course**...196 s
  wheels of the dizzying§....128 l
  w.of weary life at last stood 9m
Wheel-work-was man made..289 f
Wheeze-wit began to wheeze 440 q
Whelp-puppy, w. and hound. 19 q
  the foulest whelp of sin....558 q
Whelps-like w., we crying*. .122 c
Where-echo answers—"W."||149 e
  tell us what and w.they be†317 o
  where in the world are we.707 p
Wherefore-every why hath*.497 o
  for every why he had a..... 26 v
  Romeo!wherefore art thou*127 a
Whetstone-with the blunt w.505 d
Whim-though by w., envy..124 j
Whip-deserves a slight whip.736 q
  w. me such honest knaves*.336 i
  your curb and w. in their*.595 o
Whipp'd-shalt be w. with*....512 o
  w. the offending Adam*....107 b
Whipping-should 'scape w.*.333 i
Whip-poor-will-moan of the. 59 i
  mysterious whip-poor-will 59 g
  w-p-w. wails on the moor.. 59 h
Whirl-w. in narrow circling.795 r
Whirled-w. together at.....391 i
Whirligig-w. of time brings*602 u
Whirlpool-w. full of depth||..655 o
Whirlwind-Odin, thou w....485 j
  rides in the whirlwind.....509ee
  the whirlwind of passion*..423 k
  wave and w. wrestle§......551 u
  what a w. is her head||......655 o
  whirlwind's fickle gust.....579 u
Whirlwinds-in dark'ning w.424 n
  w. of tempestuous**......212 u
Whisper-full well the busy..455 i
  Nestor you whisper into it,175 y
  secrets, and we must w..... 43 d
  shape the w. of the throne†454 h
  smile and whisper this.....131 v
  the trees began to w.†......391 k
  whisper above thy breath§.185 q
  w. softness in chambers**..406 i
  whisper—solitude is sweet .566 p
  with a well-bred w. close...450 e
  with its whisper of peace...624 n
Whispered-Sunday w., 'twas.536m
  sweet in every w. word||....384 t
  'twas whispered in Heaven.297 q
  whisper'd it to the woods**376 d
  whisper'd of peace........241 u
  w. promised pleasure......307 n
  whose dirge is whisper'd by405 c
Whispering-and w. lovers....614 c
  angels are w. with thee..... 31 m
  as winds come w. lightly|| .647 b
  each heart is whispering...303 v
  or w. with white lips||.......636 a
  whispering gloomily to yon618 o
  whispering into some one's254 l
  w., "I will ne'er consent"||655 f
  w. to each other half†......383 k
  world goes w. to its own...149 c
Whisperings-foul w. are*....280 y
  throats with whisperings...558 n
  w., wooings, liquid ripples.415 l
Whispers-aerial w. breathe‡.674 w
  light as the w. of a dream.646 t
  weird w., bells that rang†.. 25 l
  what w. so strange at the..612 b
  w. the o'er-fraught heart*..569 u
  whispers the small voice|| .105 i
  w. to the willing mind......538 s
Whist-winds with wonder**..647 p
Whistle-as clear as a whistle.495 w
  blackbird 't is to whistle...353 d
  could whistle them back....212 b
  dear, for his whistle.......251 m

hir jolly w. wel y-wette....504 h
homely whistle to sweet...112 l
hush'd the ploughboy's w..536 l
pay too much for your w...387 g
nae birdie maun whistle....537 a
w., and I'll come to you, my509 a
w., and she'll come to you.509 b
w. in rude fury round his..608 b
whistle them back.........260 g
Whistled-w. as he went, for..314 b
Whistles-pipes and w. in his* 11 j
Whistling-quail is w. free....395 b
  whistling aloud to bear....118 n
  w. down the hollow goes.. 542 i
  whistling of a name‡.......202 k
  whistling to keep myself...208 u
Whitbread-W.'s best entire..162 q
White-are white over with...412 n
  a soul as white as Heaven..570 x
  as seas do laugh show w...493 n
  a white so perfect........234 d
  black look w., and white...691 c
  black, red and white......113 e
  everye white will have its..101 v
  grew more clean and white 333 t
  in white and gold.........228 b
  less and less w. its mark... 60 f
  livers white as milk*......121 s
  makes you look so white...443 k
  my thoughts of white.....233 q
  nor white so very white....553 h
  one as white as snow......241 k
  one has in black and white.784 a
  pale and white and cold...131 v
  red or white as snow... ..233 d
  round it a garment of w....613 j
  shroud of white, stuck*....138 p
  their stems in furry white.618 l
  w. as the blossoms which..611 q
  white as the foam.........223 b
  w. as the whitest dove's .. 54 q
  white doth hide the green..391 e
  white man was bound to...560 c
  white rose in red rose..... 76 n
  white with blossoming§...612 k
  white with the drift.......228 b
  winter-robe of purest white546 p
Whiteness-death in a w......231 o
  in angel w. beat away*.... 62 u
  pearl less whiteness.......249 a
  the whiteness of his soul||..403 c
  whiteness in thy cheek*....210 d
White-thorn-ere yet a w-t..391 d
  fixed in a w-t. bush its. .... 57 c
White-throat-happy w-t. on. 59 j
White-wash'd-the w-w. wall .303 r
Whither-w. away, Robin..... 56 c
Whiting-whiting to a snail..213 f
Whittle-to w. the Eden Tree. 28 l
Whoe'er-w. she be, that not..655 u
Whole-half, and then the w..399 g
  is this the whole||......... 97 m
  one stupendous whole‡....123 c
  parts of one stupendous‡...411 v
  proportion of the w. to its.769 p
  survey the w., nor seek‡....125 l
  to save the whole sawes off.439 r
  whole in himself.........287 b
  whole is in proportion.....270 e
  whole is to its part........782 f
Wholesome-see thy w. days*626 j
  society is w. for the†......567 e
  w. as air and genial as the .120 f
Whom-not by whom, but in. 802bb
Whoops-but the devil w., as. 28 l
Why-causes why and*....... 27 u
  every w. hath a wherefore*497 o
  for every why he had a..... 26 v
  we know not why.........127 j
Wick-a kind of wick*.......280 q
Wicks-there are three wicks.295 n
Wicked-became very w. all..687 l
  cause I'se wicked,—I is ....644 o
  he of their wicked ways**..451 b
  I's mighty wicked, anyhow 644 o
  never, w. man was wise‡....650 s.
  show compassion on the w..474 t

SHAKESPEARE *; MILTON **; WORDSWORTH ¶; BYRON ||; TENNYSON †; LOWELL ††; POPE ‡; LONGFELLOW §.

smooth speeches of the w..691 *f*
success of the wicked......744 *k*
sun shines even on the w..694 *h*
the happiness of the w....771 *i*
the majority is wicked....644 *k*
the wicked prize itself*.....438 *p*
veriest wicked rest in peace 67 *j*
w. acts are accustomed ...694 *r*
w. are always surprised....754 *a*
w. deeds are generally done687 *o*
wicked in their flight.......717 *n*
wicked things are done....711 *j*
w. to injure their neighbors746 *r*
Wickedness—all w. is**......641 *v*
how cowardly is w..........695 *n*
method in man's w..........644 *j*
mother of all wickedness..678 *f*
no w. has any ground......751 *p*
punishment of wickedness.737 *c*
the way to wickedness......695 *j*
wickedness has it shunned.694 *t*
world loves a spice of w.§..644 *t*
Wicket—while the w. falls......644 *q*
Wickliff—W.'s dust shall.....530 *d*
Wide-so w. as a church door*671 *h*
wide and universal theatre*669 *g*
wide or short in human wit‡324*m*
Widened—thoughts of men†...598 *c*
Widening—w. slowly silence†.408 *f*
Widow—and the w. weeps*....381*m*
here's to the w. of fifty....604 *r*
memory in widow's weeds. 381 *w*
undone w. sits upon mine..637 *p*
w., husbandless, subject*..209 *o*
w. of an imperial people ...787 *n*
Widow-comfort—my w-c.*.... 90 *o*
Widowed—w. wife and wedded376 *l*
Widowhood–in w. to-night....638*m*
Widows–new widows howl*...569 *r*
Wife–Adam's first w. is she..318 *t*
a fishmonger's wife may....494 *t*
aid, like man and wife‡....653 *p*
a light wife doth make a*..645 *l*
and the faithful wife......374 *h*
appear like man and wife..634 *r*
as for my w., I would you*.645*m*
as the husband is the w. is†377 *t*
a w. I need not blush to....644 *q*
bracelets to adorn the wife.536 *o*
bringest the sailor to his†..446 *d*
Cæsar's wife should be.....586 *n*
Christian and thy loving*.. 199 *m*
half so delightful as a w. ..644 *u*
Heaven deprives me of a...771 *e*
he that hath a wife and ...374 *e*
his children and his wife.. 69 *s*
his w. and children being ..374 *c*
husband frae the wife...... 7 *d*
impudence they style a w.‡645 *j*
in the election of a w., as in 645 *e*
knowe yf my wyfe be badde432 *q*
Laura had been Petrarch's‖533 *g*
like peevish man and wife. 378 *f*
little wife well will'd are...494*bb*
Lord Brutus took to wife*..659 *j*
love your neighbor's wife..565 *l*
loving, trusting wife§......645 *b*
man and wife coupled... ..374 *p*
married w. a twelvemonth..196 *q*
my wife is one of the best.660*aa*
my wife shall not rule......752 *o*
nor doubt a wife..........375 *t*
of Adam's first w. Lilith ..144*w*
our author in the wife‡.....311 *r*
pace easy, but not such a*.645*m*
prove an unmanageable w..495 *o*
Roy's wife of Aldivalloch. 144 *j*
serving-man's wife may....494 *t*
such the w. had fallen to..374 *j*
sweet w. No, never come..668 *p*
tell his wife all he knows...104 *g*
the best is a good wife.....645 *s*
the friend of my wife.......176 *c*
the meek, fond, trusting w.645 *t*
the w. is dearer than the,..645 *c*
this sweet wee w. o' mine..644 *r*
tir'd horse, a railing wife*.. 69 *d*

unclouded welcome of a w.646 *b*
vassal to the tyrant wife...374 *j*
was all the world and his..669 *t*
way to kill a wife with*....377*m*
weeping w. and children...102 *j*
well choosing of his wife..375 *u*
widowed w. and wedded....376 *l*
w. brighten'd vire at the...374 *f*
wife can see her beauty in.. 24 *p*
w., domestic, good and pure644 *z*
w. grows flippant in reply..375 *j*
w. is a constellation of......644 *t*
w. is the peculiar gift of‡...645 *i*
w. Joan and goodman......107 *h*
w. that I love and that.....642 *d*
w. these sland'rous words‡.645 *j*
wife was pretty, trifling....644*w*
wife when she obeys her...715 *l*
wife, where danger or**....311 *o*
worthy of this noble wife*.377 *j*
wyfe me wrong wyth alle...432 *q*
Wifely-flour of w. pacience..467 *c*
tenderness of w. love..... 644 *x*
Wig–a great wig..........462 *a*
Wight–w. of high renowne... 23 *s*
Wights-swift, staring wights.213 *i*
Wild-dwell this wild**.......126 *w*
If I chance to talk a little*..589*m*
in the houseless wild§......225 *h*
of all w. beasts on earth or.657*m*
Rhine in his native wild...532 *e*
the garden was a wild......566 *l*
the wild are constant‡......465 *s*
western wind was w. and...530 *l*
when wild in woods......258 *i*
wild as the heart when...460 *o*
wild, unknown to public...567 *j*
wither'd and so wild*...... 25 *k*
Wild-briar-w-b. overtwined...250 *r*
Wild-cat–more than the w-c.* 562 *j*
Wild-cats-w-c. in your*......660 *g*
Wilderness-flow'ring in a w. 611 *e*
hast wanderings in the††...521 *h*
in the lonely wilderness... 66*m*
lodge in some vast w......566 *r*
of a steep wilderness**......463 *r*
sweet scents the wilderness.561 *n*
this bleak wilderness below.487 *q*
thrills the w. profound.....666 *s*
wilderness of sweets**......216 *a*
Wild-flower-w-f. wreath....219 *l*
Wild-flowers-spring the w-f..217 *i*
Wild-fowl–chase the w-f.....§277 *l*
Wild-geese-w-g. fly that way*546 *i*
Wildings-wildings of nature..217 *d*
Wildness-w. of the place......245 *k*
Wild-rose-bloomed the sweet.222 *p*
petal from a w-r. blown....405 *p*
the wild-rose dreams......220 *n*
wild-rose roofs the ruined..244 *p*
Wilds-in distant w. by human 413 *q*
sandy perilous wilds** ..... 88 *a*
Wild-swan–the w-s. pause†... 58 *n*
Wile-by no fond wile, no..... 31 *g*
with endearing wile........ 7 *v*
Wiles-little pretty infant w...30 *q*
quips, and cranks, and**...383 *r*
reconciles by mystic wiles. 358 *g*
sorrows, simple wiles¶......661 *c*
their subtle wiles..........658 *b*
Wilfulness-deliver it from w.646 *h*
Will-amend our w., and not..646*m*
and his will his law........ 78 *r*
arranging to make your w..176 *k*
as if by one great will......492 *k*
based on the w., and the...281 *h*
because he will not........784 *g*
beyond its own sweet will..367 *j*
boy's w. is the wind's will§.646 *j*
but executes a freeman's w.482 *t*
but one faculty, the will...655 *c*
by his permissive will**....312 *l*
complies against his will...646 *d*
could frame my w. to it*...438 *l*
current of a woman's will..660*w*
diminished at the w. of the.524 *h*
doing of the will of God....420 *d*

each has his w., and each...629 *w*
enslaves the w., nor leaves..475 *k*
everlasting love, restrain...485 *l*
evil save in the will.........646 *f*
eye that bow'd the will†... 30 *e*
fairly make your will‡.....349 *j*
firm in w. molds the world..767*m*
first, then, a woman w., or..656 *q*
for if she will, she will.....656 *h*
for life is possible to will†..646 *p*
for the heart and the will...667 *c*
for what I w. I will, and*...659 *l*
gives them what he w., not*.603 *e*
growth of human will‖......357 *b*
guilty of his own free will..710 *s*
having my will, I should....110 *g*
heart; a will inflexible§.... 81 *a*
heart shall have his will*...606 *g*
he that w. not when he may 91 *k*
he will, he shall have nay..461 *i*
hope to change the will**...488 *n*
if she will do't, she will....656 *q*
if they had their will.......480 *c*
if Thy will be so*..........268 *g*
impresses his will in the...274*m*
iron w. of one stout heart...104 *p*
I will it, I so order........737 *p*
leads the will to desperate*.364 *v*
left free the human will‡....646 *l*
lightning does the w. of God.482 *t*
make your w. less often.....176 *k*
man blindly works the w. of.766 *o*
mortals bend their will‡....387 *b*
my more headier will*......156*m*
my poverty, but not my w.*485 *f*
my w. enkindled by mine*..646 *n*
not to command our will....389 *o*
obedient to my will‖.......471 *p*
or to incline his will**......488 *o*
passions in his craft of will*.606 *h*
pleases one against his will.124 *n*
pray they have their will*...295 *i*
puzzles the will*...........268 *h*
Rechabite poor W. must live 641 *g*
serveth not another's will...305 *q*
shores of w. and judgment*.646 *n*
star of the unconquered w.§.646 *k*
stout heart and resolute w..339 *j*
take the will for the deed..509*bb*
tardily and with a weaker...525 *r*
that to live by one man's w..387 *q*
that what he w. he does*...646 *o*
the temperate will¶.......661 *d*
the unconquerable will**...638 *f*
the will and not the gift.....769 *s*
the will and the power are..151 *i*
the will for the deed.......506 *r*
the will to do, the soul.......195 *o*
they will, they will not.....796*m*
thou hast stolen my will†...595 *s*
thy royal will be done....... 92 *c*
thy will, for deed I do......507 *d*
to deny the freedom of the..646 *g*
to direct the eternal will....632 *l*
torrent of a woman's will...656 *h*
to thy husband's will**......311*m*
t. w. what God doth will....525 *c*
'twas His will: it is mine....525 *d*
unconquerable will**........103 *a*
upon her people's will†.....535 *n*
ways are offered to our w...††101 *o*
we are, when we will it.....766*m*
what I will is fate**........206 *v*
when he will he shall have.. 91 *k*
who has no w. but by her...374 *j*
wide as his will‡ ....274 *q*
will in us is over-rul'd......206 *s*
will not when he may......461 *i*
w. of a man is his happiness.771 *n*
w. of even a common man...646 *c*
will of God is all in all.....132 *c*
will to do, the soul to dare..383 *t*
without our w. they come††..539 *f*
wit that wants resolved w.*. 83 *o*
yet His will be done†........525 *i*
your own free will...........720 *r*
you will and you won't .....158 *c*

Shakespeare *; Milton **; Wordsworth ¶; Byron ‖; Tennyson †; Lowell ††; Pope ‡; Longfellow §.

many light hearts and w....610 q
mid-air suspend their w.‡.. 49 d
my w. are shaken the dews.100 e
night with her sullen w.**.416 l
on balanced wings§........533 e
on the w. of borrowed wit..654 l
on whose w. great minds... 14 f
on wings of flame..........188 c
on wings of glory up the...584 c
on wings of wind came‡....294 o
our words have w., but fly.664 n
prisoner underneath her*.. 45 g
ranks with w. display'd**.. 16 s
sailing on obscene wings..157 r
see white w. lessening up... 16 o
shakes his dewy wings..... 48 n
she hides her wings........ 37 j
show not their mealy w.*..372 y
spirit's w. to great deeds..778m
spreads his light wings‡....361 o
spread thy golden w. in.... 45 m
sweep of an angel's wings.165 k
their conceits have wings*.537 x
those quivering wings¶.... 49 s
time's blest w. of peace....471 a
time's hoar wings..........161m
to the eyes in his black w.415 c
to thy speed add wings**..512 f
trim their bustling wings... 43 c
truth gives w. to strength.799 a
underneath the silky w....405 q
upper limbs, so wings...... 16 j
wave their wings in gold‡... 46 h
while the wings aspire, are¶ 49 s
white and heavenly wings.. 94 g
whose w. right o'er us hover631 c
wind-swift cupid wings*...364 a
wings!—are fictions....... 16 j
wings are in growing....... 90 f
wings in high pursuit......261 r
wings of an ostrich........315 b
wings of gentle flush o'er..238 c
wings of the dove‖.........334 e
w., one black, the other**..202 b
w. that can bear me back...466m
with clangs of wings and... 46 l
with her dusky w. and her§ 57 l
with plain brown wings.... 43 i
with wings of healing......561 c
Wink—danger will wink on**.461 j
I'll wink and couch*........197 f
never came a wink too soon 380 b
Wink'd—shall not be w. at*...123 t
winked and nodded with...355 l
Winkie-Wee Willie W. rins... 32 b
Winks—justice while she w. at332 q
Winktippling—w. cordial......589 w
Winnipissiogie—Lake of W....440 a
Winnow'd—w. with so rough* 152 h
Winter—age is as a lusty w.*.. 12 a
age like winter weather*...673 e
autumn to w., winter.......589 g
chiding of the w.'s wind*...546 g
cold winds of winter blown. 55 g
cold winter gives warning..544 b
cruel as winter............330 r
dark and stubborn W. dies.391 j
dark as w. was the flow....550 o
dog-star and the w.'s air...672 i
early hours, of w.'s past or. 51 b
every w. when the great sun 546 c
from w.'s powerful wind*..139 u
heel of limping w. treads*..392 l
here our camp of winter...547 a
her winter weeds outworn..669 i
hid in sap-consuming w.'s*. 12 b
his fragrant winter store...321m
housewives all the w.'s rage458 k
in the w.'s frost and rime§..614 h
in winter I get up at night.. 90 t
is as poor as winter*.......485 d
lark beside the dreary w...135 i
like a w. hath my absence* 3 f
long withstood the w.'s..... 24 a
love knows no winter......778 d
no labouring i' the winter*.455 p
nor winter freeze..........186 h

not in the winter..........241 o
no winter in thy year...... 44 r
on a lone winter evening...546 a
O, wind, if winter comes...648 b
O w.! bar thine adamantine.545 h
slayer of the w. art thou...391 b
streams, rejoiced that w.'s. 70 u
then winter is at hand*.....189 n
there was no winter in't.... 41 s
'twas winter—and I slept...183 r
unto a winter's day ....183 c
warn'd of approaching w... 58 c
winds of w. wailing through647 e
w. and rough weather*.....610 d
winter change to spring‡...309 b
winter clothed all in frize..546 l
w. comes, to rule the varied.546 o
w. for the summer's dead...647 i
winter from your lips**.....335 l
winter is come and gone...289 a
w. lingering chills the lap..392 t
w. loves a dirge-like sound¶ 547 c
w. maketh the light heart..540 o
winter nights against my...545 g
winter of our discontent*...582 g
w.! ruler of the inverted...545 n
w.'s crystal gems be spared.396 d
winter's leisure to regale...433 e
w. slumbering in the open..666m
winter's not gone yet, if*...546 i
w. spreads his latest glooms546 n
winter stands uncertain by.250 p
w. when the dismal rain...546 j
w., yet there is no sound...545 p
yet in her w.'s bowere not..603 o
Winter-king—the wild old w-k.546 d
Winterly—if w. thou need'st*.414w
Winter-robe-w-r. of purest..546 p
Winters—four lagging w.*....665 p
ran he on ten winters more. 9m
whether his w. be eighteen‖ 6 o
winter's gloomy night......245 h
Wintry—ere to their wintry. 58 c
leaves in w. weather ..... 380 p
the wintry days are June..600 k
through the wintry hours..217 u
wintry blasts unmoved.....224 j
Wipe—wipe away all trivial*..381 o
Wire—and a ring of wire...... 18 e
arming wire through his... 19 f
guides the master wire.....281 p
secret of the sounding w.§.430 z
shalt be whipp'd with wire*512 o
wire, a hidden path for a...171 e
Wires—puppets led about by. 30 o
Wisdom—amity that w. knits*265 k
and all men's wisdom.....493 s
and make wisdom smile...515w
beauty and w. are rarely...678m
be truer than fairy wisdom.650 v
brutes have no wisdom....650 n
but wisdom, awful wisdom.652 b
but wisdom lingers‡.......388 j
by wisdom and courage...799 h
by wisdom wealth is won..651 r
Chloe, this is wisdom's part524 x
cold wisdom waiting on*...651 k
doorstep to the temple of.651 q
earth sounds my wisdom‡..201 k
fires of w. and knowledge.. 98 i
folly with your wisdom....700 q
fortune, not w., that rules..702 c
for wisdom never lies‡....199 f
full as an egg of wisdom...484 c
gains wisdom in a happy...752 f
God give them w. that*....651 n
God's wisdom and God's...273 n
God, whose boundless w.§..430 f
golden door of wisdom....651 s
golden wisdom's power....235 b
He praise their wisdom....437 h
hiving wisdom with each‖..580 k
in youth and beauty w. is‡.650 u
is the prime wisdom**.....651 c
is woman's wisdom†.......402 h
justice without wisdom is..332 j
kindness is wisdom. . .....333 g

knowledge and w. far from.336 z
larger fact than wisdom.... 34 t
last result of human w.....437m
last result of wisdom......258 l
liberty without wisdom....343 j
love w. more than she‖....650 g
manifest sign of wisdom is.651 f
man of w. is the man of...373 j
more helpful than all w....473 t
more w. than is found......781 o
my trembling heart to w...652 d
on every thorn delightful..652 c
pay his w. for his joys.....309 h
politicians chew w. past‡482 u
riches purchased w. yet for.651 r
ripe in w. was he but§.... 651 a
seems the part of wisdom..650 l
serve the ends of wisdom..487 v
sleeps at wisdom's gate**..104 k
stream from Wisdom's well 651 s
strides of human wisdom..274 f
thanne is it w. as thynketh.413 v
thence derived is wisdom..365 v
then Wisdom prostrate lies 367 b
though w. wake, suspicion**104 h
thou open'st w.'s way**....190 o
to wisdom he's a fool*......252 z
virtue, w., valour, wit**...360 u
we court fair wisdom. that.567 u
what wisdom shines.......417 v
where wisdom steers, wind.573 q
whom truth and w. lead...650 h
w. and fortune combating*.651 o
wisdom and goodness are..650 k
w. and goodness they w....273 n
wisdom and wit are........251 a
wisdom another ....676 o
w. at one entrance quite**..149m
w. consists not in seeing...752 l
w. does not show itself so..651 j
w. in minds attentive to...336 z
w. is humble that he knows650 j
w. is ofttimes nearer¶......651 x
w. is only found in truth...795 j
w. is push'd out of life....147 q
wisdom is the conqueror...752 d
wisdom makes but a slow...650 o
w. married to immortal¶...478 d
wisdom mounts her zenith.384 r
wisdom of our ancestors... 15 e
wisdom picks friends......201 h
w., piety, delight or use... 65 h
w. provides things necessary509m
wisdom sit in want........ 13 l
w. sits alone, topmost in...651 v
wisdom's self oft seeks to**567 g
w. that doth guide his**...628 o
wisdom, though richer.....652 e
wisdom will get in anyhow. 66 d
wisdom with mirth.........208 a
w. won with weariness.....356 d
wit and w. are born with a..342m
wit and w. of New England340 h
with universal wisdom.....101 j
words little wisdom ......753 d
your w. is consum'd in*.... 104 o
Wise—ah! was he wise...... 154w
a little too wise they say do494ee
and follies of the wise.....348 d
and never did a wise one...533 q
and puzzle all the wise.....199 d
another is w., yet I am well*659 o
arts in which the wise excel429 s
be merry and wise.........268 r
be more than women, wise..654 t
be timely wise.............295 t
be wise; soar not too high..651 b
be wise to-day; 'tis madness147 q
be wise with speed.........652 a
both polite and wise.......114 d
call'd the beacon of the w.*.159 b
can be wise and love.......359 a
cautious are the wise‡.....650 t
competition worthy a wise. 371 i
converse with him that is w.*83 s
counsel a wise son heedeth.494 o
dare to be wise.............752 b

drinking makes wise ......161 p
easier to be wise for others.795 h
ever wise by chance......752 j
exceeding w., fair spoken*.580 f
fate, though thou be wise..605 i
fathers fools so w. we grow‡103 n
fear not the anger of the w.‡524 b
fellow is wise enough* .....252 x
first be wise and good**....343 x
fool and a wise man......251 n
foolish things to all the w.‖.650 g
for to be wise and love*....363 b
from learning to be wise....580 b
fullness makes us wise.....337 w
give unto me made lowly¶.148 n
gray but never wise........128 f
guid to be merry and wise .367 o
he is no wise man that. ....74 v
he is wise who can instruct.324 s
he who thinks himself wise 768 a
histories make men wise....580 i
I'm growing wise; I'm... 11 e
is not so wise as he thinks..768 b
it is not wise to be wiser...795 f
laws wise as nature‡.......462 t
less than to be wise‡ .... 28 j
little wise, the best fools be.509 c
marry you and he is wise...178 q
may pass for a wise man*...654 f
men are never very wise...485 o
merry if you are wise.....693 o
more foolish and more w....754 h
more w. more learn'd, more‡82 w
most who are themselves w. 65 o
nature is always w.in every 413 d
never, wicked man was w.‡650 s
no other time be very wise.795 i
nor knowledge to the wise..185 f
not be chronicled for wise*.363 s
nothing lost by being wise..774 p
not too wise is wise........752 e
oblivion and memory are w.420 o
old till thou hadst been w.*651 l
only the wise profit by it.... 7 r
only wretched are the wise.314 q
penny wise, pound foolish..503 e
people are more nice than w.504 e
poets utter great and wise..480 d
reverend, you should be w.* 11 l
sacred groves grew wise....413 g
season and untimely wise... 85 o
sleep can charm the wise...563 o
slowly wise and meanly just580 b
society as is quiet, wise,and567 o
so wise, so grave, of so.....437 n
spirits of the wise sit*......253 a
that sorrow makes us wise‡651 u
the table with a wise man§.113 u
the virtues of the wise.....789 a
the wisdom of the wise....513aa
the wise lived yesterday....605 k
the w. (minstrel or sage)... 67 i
this is Love as wise men say.361 q
till to-morrow to be wise....605 h
'tis folly to be wise.......314 h
'tis well to be merry and w. 75 d
'tis wise to learn ....345 b
to a wise man ports and*...298 n
tongue is wise in man......604 e
truth exists for the wise...756 a
type of the wise who soar¶. 50 a
went wise men three......251 w
what fool is not so wise*....419 t
what is it to be wise‡.... ..651 h
what man would be wise ...190 p
when a wise man gives*.... 7 q
whether they be wise or....573 r
who can think w. or stupid.782 p
who is not wise at all¶......651 w
who is not wise is sad......759 j
who think themselves most 338 n
wilt have me w. and good†.570 o
wine can of their wits the‡.649 j
wise at all times.........752 h
wise enough by himself....752 g
w. father that knows his*. 500aa
wise for cure on exercise...440 b

wise if a minister; but‡ .... 82 w
wise if we be made content 197 t
wise man in time of peace..734 v
wise man knows himself*...252 v
wise man loses nothing.....354m
wise man who can govern..752 a
wise men eat them.......497aa
w. men ne'er sit and wail*..354 q
wise men say nothing in....509 n
w. men, whereby to conceal574 p
wise through time and‡....650 r
wise to talk with our past..547 p
wise with the history of††.. 81 h
wishes to be wise quite.....786 f
wooes him to be wise......384 r
words are w. men's counters664 q
word to the wise.........752 k
Wisely—best to love w., no....366 t
be wisely worldly, but not..496 k
then might I wisely swim..597 s
who reasons wisely is not‡.517 k
wisely and slow*.........294 v
wisely, and with pleasure..651 i
Wiser—a sadder and a w. man 388 a
become wiser by adversity.752 i
grow w. and better as my..465 u
heart is wiser than the.....650 q
I am no wiser than a daw*.438 h
I would be wiser ....715 k
man is the wiser for his....342m
our wiser sons, no doubt‡..672 c
Satan now is wiser than of‡594 c
stand no wiser than before.342 a
Wisest—desires of the best....385 w
desp'rat'st is the w. course.439 t
he is oft the wisest man¶...651 w
nor is he the w. man who†..651 t
oft infects the wisest*....‥.209 r
oracle pronounc'd w. of**. 651 d
relished by the w. men....310aa
seems wisest, virtuousest**111m
the w. are the most annoyed792 k
wisest, brightest, meanest‡.202 k
Wish—accomplishment of....675 d
any wish thou darest not..487 o
and wish to be no more‖....420 n
at best is an anxious wish..520 g
believe what they wish.....679 j
cannot w. for that we know795 k
did my fate and w. agree...528 n
each other every w. they...358 k
each silent wish conveys...448 e
each wish is like a prayer..652 g
if you wish to reach the....677 g
if a wish wander that way..593 c
my w. is quite as wide but‖ 655 k
not what we wish, but what488m
oft-expressed wish ....258 p
pray to God to cast that....487 o
reverse the tyrant's wish‖..655 k
such as are out wish to get.375 f
tell my wish to her dewy‡..449 h
that hinder folly's wish....487 v
the maid's romantic wish‡..634 l
they would wish their own.644 v
thy w. was father, Harry*. 652 j
to wish is of little account.677 d
warmest wish to heaven is.116 o
were each wish a mint of..652 f
wert thou all that I w. thee.652 i
we wish him back.........604 h
what ardently we wish we . 39 o
w., at least, with us to stay 604 v
wish for death is a coward's687 c
wish in life, but to follow§.521 f
w. that if he be an honest.. 19 a
wish that the spring would.317 e
wish that thou wert by..... 2 u
wish them a fair departure* 3 g
wish to be thy king.........212 d
wish what you can do......738 t
wish you all the joy that*..329 w
wish yourself where Truth‖641 a
you do not wish, I do......176 r
Wished—devoutly to be w.*..140 j
one has wished for in youth795m
she w. she had not heard*..663m

wished that I had clear.....652 i
Wishes—be safe whose wishes.593 c
"He w. well " is worthless.691 t
man could half his wishes .500 b
my wishes don't go far.....456 k
my w. more worth than*....480 k
their country's wishes, blest468 i
their wishes all confin'd....110 s
though varying w., hopes..381 e
w. for his own advantage ..742 a
wishes lengthen as our sun.652m
wishes to become rich......739 s
yet prayers and wishes*....489 k
Wishart—pipe of W.'s best...467 n
Whiskers—hoary w. and a‡...458 a
Wit—a bastard by his wit....430 b
accept a miracle instead of.386 u
affecting wit beyond their .653 f
age is in, the wit is out*....508 q
although he had much wit.652 q
and wit good natured ...... 88 l
and wit that knows no gall.384 q
a proverb is one man's wit.493 s
as a wit, if not first in the .. 79 p
a small degree of wit......653 j
a sort of w. to know how to654 k
authors are partial to their‡429 e
a wit with dunces, and a‡..653 o
beauty like wit, to judges.. 35 f
beauty, wit, high birth*....602 h
between wit and wit........101 h
blasphemy, 'twill pass for‖.124 f
brevity is the soul of wit*..496 o
but oh my wit is not.......446 p
can inspire with wit........652 n
cause that wit is in other*.653aa
craves a kind of wit*.......252 x
devise, wit ; write, pen*....429 q
doors upon a woman's wit*653cc
ev'n w.'s a burthen when it 652 w
every loyal lover tasks his.628 c
eye begets occasion for his*653 z
fame that wit could ever...356 d
fancy wit will come‡.......653 u
fool than a foolish wit*.....654 e
fury still outran the wit‡ .. 82 s
genius, wit, and spirit of a.493 q
God has given us wit and...654 h
hast so much wit..........180m
have a plentiful lack of w.*654 d
have more zeal than wit‡..674 i
he but have drawn his wit .550m
he wants wit that wants*... 83 o
high-day wit in praising*..486 y
his wit invites you by his..652 u
his w. shines at the expense795 p
how the wit brightens‡.....477 s
I embrace the wit.........117 e
I'm poor enough to be a w..652 t
in favor of one's w. at the..795 n
in wit a man‡ ....183 n
is a sauce to his good wit*.654 a
is no room for wit..........653 c
its style of wit, and its own475 b
learning and his wit.......157 o
mark no mortal wit. ....205 t
metaphysic wit can fly.....336 v
no more wit than a*....... 93 p
no one shall have wit save .791 f
no wit for so much room...653 c
of wit will condescend.....215 r
only a wit among lords....653 h
only one species of wit....653 i
on the wings of borrowed...654 l
past the wit of man*........160 u
pecks up wit as pigeons*... 54 i
plainness sets off sprightly‡653 s
poets' wit hath ever writt... 87m
praise of wit to write......254 i
read each work of wit‡....125 l
remains to mortify a wit‡..422m
sharp the glittering wit ...566 b
since brevity is the soul of*654 b
some wit, some wealth. .. 256 c
so narrow human wit‡.....538 t
sparks that are like wit*...653 y
stand up in Wit's defence..341 h

still inspires my wit........ 34 i
still some want of wit*.....288 u
sum of Shakespeare's wit...550 b
the age is in, the wit is out*653 w
the baiting place of wit.... 563 g
there the wit goes out.....508dd
the wit began to wheeze....440 q
the young and tender wit*..362m
thy w. is as quick as the*..654 f
'tis virtue, w., and worth...670 p
'tis w. in them, but, in the*.653 x
too fine a point to your w..652 s
too much w. makes the†...130 a
too proud for a wit........ 79 r
true wit is nature to‡.....653 t
use the wit of others.......654 k
want of wit to be undone..654m
what wonder modes in w.‡.653 r
when cut by wit, it casts...548 n
which true wit cannot need.578 l
whose w., in the combat, as 653m
whose wit well managed...515w
wide or short in human w.‡324m
will vouchsafe no other w..550 j
winding up the watch of*..653bb
wisdom and wit are........251 a
w. and judgment often are‡653 p
wit and wisdom are born..342m
wit and wisdom of New....340 h
wit apart, it is a diamond..548 n
wit brightens! how the‡...407 b
wit by ease................120 i
wit consists in knowing the.654 j
with little w. and ease to...795 r
wit is but the plume......548 n
w. is news only to ignorance 340 p
wit is the flower of the......653 l
wit is the most rascally...653 n
w. is the salt of conversation653 e
wit is the wine; but 'tis so..422 a
w. like a knuckle of ham...654 i
w. like money, bears an....653 g
w. nor invention in applying513 v
wit, now and then, struck...652 v
wit of poets triumphs......478 q
wit rules the heavens......798 v
w.'s a jewel which we need.654m
wit's an unruly engine......653 f
w., sophist, songster Yorick 50 k
w. that can creep and pride‡ 82 p
w. to seize the flitting guest368 g
witty fool than a foolish w.*496 c
wit was more than man.... 78 z
w. will shine through the...653 b
works may have more w.‡.653 s
your w. ambles well; it*....654 c
Wits-and we have w. to read.550 k
at our wittes end.........495cc
bankrupt quite the wits*...211m
brilliant wits and musing... 65 j
by w., than critics in as‡...514 i
ever homely wits* ....304 p
fine w. destroy themselves..653 v
good wits will jump........652 r
great wits and valours....652 p
great wits are sure to......653 a
keen encounter of our w.*. 27 s
men's w. and knowledges...64 b
muster your wits: stand in*119 o
nectar of good w. will sell..648 g
some wicked wits have‡....645 j
the greatest w. and poets..689 u
this keen encounter of our*.654 q
warming his five wits†.... 53 d
what silly people wits are..795 q
wine can of their wits the‡.649 j
wits are gamecocks to one..428 e
wits from wool-gathering..498bb
w. that think they have*...654 e
Witty-and witty to talk with.660 l
as witty as Beaumont††....411 l
awaken'd the w. and fair...628 f
better a witty fool than a*.654 e
desired by two witty peers. 19 h
jesting is witty...........177 a
more learned than witty...330 g
not only witty in myself*..653aa

of all others are most witty652 o
tiny, pretty, w., charming..752 n
useful, new, or wittie..... 120 i
w. and it shan't be long....568 c
witty man laughs least.....240 p
words, though ne'er so w...554 t
Witch-a-list'nin' to the w....578 p
beauty is a witch, against*. 36 p
nor witch hath power to*.. 49 l
pea is but a wanton witch..238 b
the witch he loved before..144 w
Witchcraft-w. I have us'd*..365 a
Witching-near to w. time of.415 q
very w. time of night*......417 o
witching hour of night.....415 q
w. of the soft blue sky¶....558 t
with witching power.......216 c
With-better with them or...345 a
no one to blush with me*.. 62 w
with thee, or without thee..180m
Wither-age cannot w. her*..630 e
content to wither..........233m
wither and die in a day....243 t
Wither'd-and w. in my hand.600m
both get so old and w.......375 l
gather'd lily almost w.*....592 e
lay wither'd and strown||..636 d
when he's forsaken w. and. 10 d
wither'd and so wild*...... 25 k
withered tufts of asters....222 p
With'ring -w. in my bloom‡..448m
withering on the ground‡..371 e
w. on the virgin thorn*.....376 p
Withers-life within that w....10 n
Withheld- been w. one thing..485 j
Withhold-w. in mercy what..488 s
Within-birds that are w.....378 d
from within outwards..... 79 i
God that is within us......351 u
know the man within.... .719 k
they that are w. would fain 375 d
Without-better with them or.345 a
birds w. despair to get in...376 e
could do w. you, Chloe....176 a
they that are w. would fain.375 d
without him live no life**..361 a
with thee, or without thee..180m
Witlings-though W. sneer and 13 d
Witness-need'st thou such**.550 j
performing without witness 70 b
producing holy witness*...145 b
there is no witness........712 j
witness still of excellency*.310 u
Witnesses-betray you.......769 k
for w., like watches, go.....436 r
the winding up witness....436 r
Wives-Fabius buries his w...178 l
faire ladie never wives. ..662 l
maids must be wives and...657 f
some poison'd by their w.*.535 c
that have revolted wives*..645 p
when they are wives*......377 f
when wives are dead......644 v
wives are young men's....644 p
wives have sense like them*377 d
wives in their husband's|... 2m
Wiving-hanging and w. goes*498 x
Woe-a charm for every woe*.307 i
aged in this world of woe||.. 9 c
a hasty man ne'er wanted..493 p
and a fig for woe.........318 h
and melt at other's woe‡...588 d
and plaint of woe..........487 q
and the suits of woe*...... 83 k
bear about the mockery of‡.387 t
bitter w. that love or reason 76 j
bitter woe the fate........206 k
but they grind woe........498m
by sabler tints of woe..... 61 o
by some degree of woe.....569 l
deep devotedness of woe... 3 a
degree of w. we every bliss 61 q
discover sights of woe*....299 e
gave signs of woe**.........555 y
gave us life, he gave us w.‡339 b
headstrong liberty is*.....344 f
horrid hideous notes of w.||.493 a

human bliss to human woe. 38 d
hunger frost and woe...... 23 c
in her voiceless woe||.......387m
knowledge leads to woe....313 r
laughter makes a house of.341 k
led thro' a sad variety of‡..448m
life of woman is full of w.§.657 h
life protracted is protracted348 q
lose future years of woe...118 q
make a man forget his wo..648 i
my bliss and all my woe....484 n
'neath W.'s weeping willow329 j
not always a man of woe...569 p
of wit, the balm of woe.....563 g
one great woe of life.......355 e
or melt at others' woe‡....491 b
pilot of my proper woe||....300 d
quivering to tell her woe††.612 g
raging impotence of woe‡..287 x
root of all our woe**.......257 s
scorn insult our solemn w..570 l
share of mortal woe.......346 z
sing woe, and alas is me... 55 a
sleep, the friend of woe...563 i
stands in worse case of w.*.608 t
taste the luxury of woe....569m
that ever felt another's w.‡590 s
that heritage of woe||.......370 g
the black the woe||.........284 l
the nurse of second woe*..382m
the suits of woe*...........288 e
the tears of woe...........623 b
thrill the deepest notes of..548 o
thus woe succeeds a woe... 72 c
till not a woe the bleak..... 86 j
truth denies all eloquence||.621 k
waste brings woe, and....507gg
where knowledge leads to w. 91 i
who felt another's woe.....473 q
whose waters of deep woe..603 l
wildest woe is love.........355 g
w. awaits a country, when.591 i
woe, destruction, ruin and*140 z
woe to the dupe that.......206 j
Woeful-instant shut my w.*.592 b
Woes-again thy w. impart..555 u
and sings his melodious w..618 e
from Heaven proceed the‡..297 v
historian of my country's‡.302 e
manly cheek for other's w..590 n
name awakens all my w.‡.. 448 n
rare are solitary woes .....388 t
sing my woes.............728 n
sings out her woes, a thorn. 52 f
source of long woes........783 k
still her w. at midnight rise 51 k
striving to tell his woes.....554 a
tell o'er your w. again by*.569 w
than all thy woes can stir*..149 v
what mighty woes to thy‡..656 t
with speech of war and w..523 w
w. cluster; rare are solitary570 v
woes of hopeless lovers....405 c
woes that wait on age||..... 9 q
woes to draw delight.......724 h
Wolf-man is a wolf to man..724 q
set'st the w. where he the**461 n
the w. behowls the moon*..417 l
the wolf on the fold|| .....636 e
wolf dreads the pitfall.....745 f
w. must die in his own skin506 t
Wolfsbane-the w. I should..643 j
Wolves-eat like w. and fight*444 e
moon from the wolves.....252 g
silence ye w.! while Ralph‡557 n
the w. have prey'd: and*... 29 p
Woman-alas! for the w's....656 u
all the charm of woman†... 85 h
angel for the w. in a kiss..334m
and woman's trust........658 t
Antony the world? a w.....658 a
a perfect w., nobly planned¶661 e
as a woman's mood........212 d
as shame a woman........556 s
a stranger is woman||......655 o
assuage a woman's envy..173 u
a woman may be made¶...661 f

a w. mov'd is like a*.......659 b
a w. needs a stronger head.796 p
a woman perfected††......657 i
a w.'s counsel brought us..655 y
a woman's head contrive...796 l
a w.'s love is mighty††.... 402 c
a w.'s nay doth stand for*..659 f
a woman sometimes rules..656 v
a woman's tongue..........655 s
a w. that Lord Brutus*...659 j
a woman well-reputed* ...659 j
a worthless w.! mere cold..654 u
beauty of a lovely w. is....656 c
been done by woman......658 a
believe a w. or an epitaph‖.124 q
best counsel is that of w....760 e
bestow'd w., the last‡......658 l
betray'd the capitol? a w.658 a
books were w.'s looks.....657 u
boy have not a w.'s gift*...591 s
can be found in woman**..657 p
cannot win a woman*......215 n
cunning w. is a knavish fool657 k
current of a woman's will..660 w
damnable, deceitful w......658 a
dearth of words, a w. need.114 d
do move a woman's mind*.663 q
doors upon a w.'s wit*.....653cc
dye because a w.'s faire....661 b
excellent thing in woman*.635 g
fact in woman's history....656 u
false fair w., and plague...366 b
favourite be feeble w.'s¶...367 m
fetch a perfect woman over.499 v
first, then, a w. will, or.....656 q
frailty, thy name is w*.....659 d
from his head was w. took..661 a
fury like a w. scorned......655 r
fury of a disappointed w....109 i
greatest is a woman ......657 m
hand of a woman is often...292 i
he cannot win a woman*....663 n
he who loves not wine, w....768 h
holiest end of w.'s being...657 f
honest w. of her word*.....281 a
hopes on the heart of w....796 n
I am a w.—therefore I may.656 n
I grant I am a w., but*......659 j
I hate a dumpy woman‖....655 j
imperial race from w. rose‡.656 t
in love with some woman.*.587 h
in w., than to study**......645 g
in woman's eye the‖........590 e
is a beautiful woman......657 l
is a woman just now......153 s
is a woman's only virtue*..660 a
is not a woman's part......661 t
is w.'s genuine praise......656 f
is woman's happiest**......645 h
is woman's wisdom†......402 h
its highest power in w......654 o
I ween, of w.s' breast‖.... 662 f
kind in woman's breast¶...378 e
Latin-bred w. seldom end..495 k
lays his hand on woman....122 n
less than woman's hand‖...109 e
life of w. is full of woe§...657 h
lovely w. stoops to folly...656 o
man of woman born.......150 u
man's mind, but a w.'s*....108 r
marry this man and w......377 s
move a woman's mind*....272 j
nature meant w. to be......796 k
no nor woman neither*...147 t
nothing of woman in me*..526 n
of a dark eye in woman‖...577 p
oh, woman, perfect w......654 s
one w. is fair, yet I am*....659 o
on woman Nature did......192 e
originate with a woman....752 m
other but a w.'s reason*...517 p
O woman! lovely woman...657 y
paths that lead to a w.'s love473 p
pearl in a woman's eye.....434 b
preference to woman......457 g
she is a w., therefore may*659 r
sigh'd—till w. smiled.......566 l

sound of woman's praise...486 n
still be a woman to you. ...658 c
still gentler sister woman..343 c
such is woman's lot ......242 j
surest way to hit a w.'s...662 n
sweet as the presence of w.584 q
sweetest charm of woman. 71 r
teem with w.'s tears*.....591 r
tell me of a w.'s tongue*...119 s
thank God I am not a w.*...659 k
than woman's lightness*..389 h
the heart of woman is*.....658 w
there was never yet fair w.*659 v
the world is woman's book.797 i
thus should woman be ....242 i
thy name is woman*......257 o
till all graces be in one w.*.659 o
'tis w.'s whole existence‖...356 g
tolerable w. will accept....375 l
to make a perfect woman*.659 i
to man was lovely w. giv'n.658 d
to me—a woman—bring....201 g
torrent of woman's will... 656 h
Troy in ashes? Woman...658 a
truth to play the woman*..591 d
understanding, a w.*......658 u
unto the man is woman§...375 q
virtue dignify a woman*...655 e
voice of a good woman.....635 b
wed one sweet w. and love..607 f
when a man loves a woman.357 t
when a woman appears....656 l
when a w. says she loves a..355 r
who is't can read a woman*659 n
with so good a woman*... 252 s
w. always feels herself.....103 h
w., born first to believe us..657 n
w. either loves or hates....752 s
w. ever goes by the worse**27 l
w. finds it much easier....752 p
w. has lost her chastity....688 e
w. has nine cat's lives......656 i
w. he forgets to kiss ....334 v
w., gentle woman, dare....660 k
w.! in our hours of ease....658 r
w. in this humour woo'd*..663 o
w., in this scale, the weed..457 g
woman in white raiment...160 n
w. is always changeable...,752 v
w. is at heart a rake‡.......658 h
w. is not undeveloped man†660 r
woman is often fickle......796 a
woman is the lesser man†..660 u
w. is the most inconsistent.658 p
woman like a dew-drop... 87 r
woman loves a woman.....357 t
woman loves her lover‖.....356 p
"w." must ever be a w.'s..660 x
woman, naturally born to*.209 o
w. preaching is like a dog's.450 p
woman rules us still.......657 t
w.'s at best a contradiction‡658m
w. sat in unwomanly rags..339 c
w.'s a thousand steps ahead796 f
w. says to fond lover......722 p
w.'s faith, and woman's...658 t
woman's gentle words. ..796 i
w.'s grief is like a summer.654 q
w.'s honor rests on manly..660 o
woman's love can win**....360 u
woman's mind is affected..706 k
w.'s pleasure, woman's†...642 b
woman's plighted faith....157 n
w.'s smile and girlhood's..547 a
woman take an elder than*377 e
w. that deliberates is lost..355 a
woman that reigns in Hell.153 a
w. that seduces all mankind656 m
w.! thou wert fashioned...657 a
w. was leader in the deed..752 u
w. when she was a skilful.655 v
w., when to ill thy mind‡..656 r
w. with nothing to wear... 22 q
would it not grieve a w.*...660 f
Womanhood-good, heroic§..657 g
she grew to womanhood‖..114 f
w. and childhood fleet§....672 r

Womanish-a w. complaint....133 e
Womankind-best of w.‡.....359 e
both man and womankind. 77 j
faith in womankind†......402 g
she's the pink o' womankind238 f
the wale o' womankind.... 35 z
w. had but one rosy mouth‖655 k
Woman-like-for sight is w-l..553 l
Women-a bevy of fair w.**...657 o
again the women screamed.451 s
and women must weep.....666 v
are w. books? says Hodge..656 g
as all other women are††...360 e
be more than women, wise.654 t
candles are out all w. are..508 z
dear dead women all......290 v
describe w.'s hypocrisies...658 b
doth oft make w. proud*...659 w
England is a paradise for...497 e
fair women and brave men‖211 c
fears than war or women*.129 s
for women are as roses*... 659 u
for w. shed and use them‖..590 f
from us fairest of women.. 3 i
gifts to women*...........272 h
God send the w. sleep in...640 k
good men and women.....710 r
have been women's fools...656 p
have I lik'd several women*283m
hell for women ....497 e
hid himself among women.143 r
honor women! they entwine796 h
if weak w. went astray.....658 o
I have met with w. whom..375 o
I know the nature of w.....752 t
in w. two almost divide‡...465 r
let not women's weapons*. 17 v
let us have wine and w.‖...648 k
loveliest of women! heaven654 n
love of w.! it is known‖.....356 n
manners of women are.....281 c
men and women merely*...669 b
must women have a doctor. 92 f
my wife is one of the best.660aa
nature of women is closely.796 e
night shows stars and w. in‖415 h
not left us women, or not..656 p
old women weep for joy...483 e
prevalent humor of women114 j
revenge—especially to w‖...528 h
say are not w. truly, then..662 o
she excels all women......291 d
souls of w. are so small....655 c
stormy seas and stormy w.‖655 l
than wars and w. have*....535 b
the rarest of all women*...660 e
the society of women is the.796 g
trusts himself to w., or to..657 x
two w. plac'd together*....660 b
very learned w. are to be..660 z
vows are women's traitors*377 g
when men are rul'd by w.*.282 l
wine and women, old age..721 j
wine and w., which have..593 p
women always have some..795 s
w. and men in the crowd...148 q
w. and music should never. 9 u
w. are all justly accounted.752 r
women are angels, wooing*663 r
women as well as men......361 l
w. find it difficult to keep. 788 e
w., from Eve, have been...656 p
women guide the plot.... 660 i
women have many faults..752 q
w. have no characters at‡..658 i
w. have tongues of craft..796 m
w. know no perfect love...358 c
w. know not the whole of..114 m
women know the way to... 88 w
wine, like princes, find...261 i
w. not loving one another..774 a
w. pardoned all, except‖...194 o
w. show a front of iron....656 e
w.'s weapons, water-drops*591 w
women wear the breeches..374 k
w. we do use to praise even574 s
w. will love her that she*...660 e

w. with a mischief to their.   7 *i*
words are w., deeds are....509 *r*
works of w. are symbolical.666 *c*
worn than women's are*...377 *e*
worth one sentiment of w.. .660 *y*
Womb–the foul w. of night* .639 *c*
   the womb of Nature and**.411 *d*
   wide womb of uncreated**.316 *l*
   womb of pia mater*.......315 *i*
   womb so to the tomb......345 *j*
Won–all is won that all desire‖662 *h*
   and so fairly won*..........131 *k*
   faint heart ne'er won fair..497 *r*
   leave what with his toil he .320 *d*
   melancholy as a battle won640 *q*
   neither won nor lost........206 *h*
   not by vaunts is won‡......582 *b*
   not unsought be won**......662 *t*
   she that with poetry is w...662 *d*
   therefore may be won*.... 659 *r*
   the shore is won at last....581 *w*
   they won and pass'd away‖ .97 *m*
   they won their mates§.....662 *q*
   things won are done, joy's*663 *r*
   think'st I am too quickly*.663 *k*
   'tis won as towns with fire*580 *q*
   wanton thing is won by‖....662 *f*
   who thought he 'ad won....630 *w*
   who w. it—now what think.457 *i*
   with fire, so won, so lost*. .580 *q*
   woman in this humour w.*.663 *o*
Wonder–all mankind's w.....658 *q*
   a man does not wonder at..697 *h*
   at once the wonder........327 *m*
   day of delight and wonder.615 *k*
   how passing wonder He....373 *i*
   I'm lost in wonder, love...382 *d*
   on the white wonder*......292 *m*
   our w. and astonishment**.550 *q*
   self-begetting w. daily.....375 *p*
   still the wonder grew .....342 *b*
   that no wonder waits him‖.   9 *c*
   the mute wonder lurketh*.172 *c*
   the wonder of an hour‖....578 *h*
   the w. of the eagle were†.. 46 *n*
   to hear was wonder........636 *m*
   winds with wonder whist**647 *p*
   without our special w.*....661 *n*
   with wonder his form did I 152 *u*
   wonder by her was formed.231 *o*
   wonder how you fill us.... 321 *l*
   wonder of our stage.......550 *k*
   wonder of the world........396 *k*
   w. of this western world...531 *e*
   wonder on, till truth make*623 *h*
   w. why the setting sun....585 *j*
Wondered–doth make thee*..659 *w*
Wonderful–very w. things no 31 *e*
   w. dear and pleasant.......345 *h*
   wonderful is man..........373 *i*
Wonders–here as w. strike‡..633 *a*
   the land strange w. breed..456 *i*
   the wonders of the lane....614 *b*
   w. of the world abroad.....313 *n*
   w. that I yet have heard*..121 *q*
   wonders to perform .... ..274 *e*
Wondrous–stupid at the w...661 *j*
   think what w. beings these. 42 *d*
   wondrous in his ways......274 *j*
Won't–a woman will, or w...656 *q*
   if she won't, she won't.....656 *h*
   if she won't, since safe and 656 *q*
   will and you won't........158 *c*
Woo–and that would w. her*.663 *m*
   Duncan Gray came here to.662 *b*
   great king himself doth*...447 *w*
   I cannot woo in festival*...663 *z*
   men are April when they*..377 *f*
   so thou wilt woo* ....663 *k*
   teach me how to woo thee§ 662 *q*
   wed or cease to woo........662 *j*
   were not made to woo*....663 *p*
   won that all desire to woo‖.662 *h*
   w. her as the lion wooes his662 *m*
   woo honour, but to wed it*.306 *w*
   woo on, with odour........242 *a*
   woo the fair one when......661 *u*

woo the timid maiden......661 *u*
   would toy and woo......... 57 *e*
Wooed–pensively he wooed¶. 46 *a*
   that would be wooed and ** 82 *b*
   therefore may be woo'd*...659 *r*
   we should be w. and were*.663 *p*
   woman in this humour w.*.663 *o*
   woo'd by the gale......... .248 *r*
   w. his wench with a pair...663 *e*
Wooer–the w. who can flatter451 *s*
   was a thriving wooer......662 *k*
Wooes–lion wooes his brides .662 *m*
   wooes him to be wise......384 *r*
   w. it with enamor'd sighing647 *s*
   wooes like a lover.........612 *e*
Wooing–go w. in my boys... 90 *j*
   Ha, ha, the wooing o'......662 *b*
   if I am not worth the w.§...662 *p*
   never wedding, ever w....662 *j*
   to cross their wooing......575 *n*
   women are angels, wooing*663 *r*
   won by wooing thee*.......663 *g*
   wooing the caress‖.........456 *f*
   w. thee I found thee of*....663 *s*
Wooings–full-length people's‖533 *g*
   whisperings, w., liquid.... .415 *l*
Wood–all round the wood's†† 612 *a*
   and wode hath eres........504 *x*
   aster in the wood........ 216 *l*
   begins to wave the wood†..648 *g*
   brown October's wood......395 *c*
   death in the wood..........231 *o*
   enter this wild wood....... 609 *b*
   found me in a gloomy w....777 *g*
   he talks of w.; it is some*..431 *h*
   hollow behind the wood†...169 *o*
   impulse from a vernal w.¶.413 *l*
   in every wood and dell.....542 *j*
   in the darkling w., amidst..609 *c*
   into the thickest wood **...613 *i*
   I was born in a w. to be ....497 *d*
   monarch of the wood.......615 *o*
   mountain of felled wood*..177 *k*
   not stones nor wood, nor...281 *d*
   old w. best to burn, old wine 8 *r*
   old wood burn brightest... 12 *k*
   old w. to burn! Old wine to 10 *q*
   over wood and stream...... 71 *h*
   set out to plant a wood.....652 *l*
   stately children of the w....230 *s*
   ten in the wood.............496 *h*
   the dull gray wood........249 *t*
   through the w.'s full strains 59 *b*
   till she's out of the wood††.479 *w*
   why in the lone w. sings it..612 *b*
   wing to the rooky wood†... 44 *l*
   w. a cudgel's of by th' blow512 *b*
   wood's warm side ....239 *g*
Woodbine–climb the w. leaves 58 *a*
   clumps of woodbine........250 *r*
   folds of dark woodbine.... 230 *s*
   with luscious woodbine*....220 *b*
   with the w. alternating.....393 *d*
   w. through the windows....250 *q*
   w. wreaths that bind her†..610 *l*
Woodbines–w. hanging...... 216 *n*
Wood-birds–w-b. but to*..... 628 *g*
   w-b. sang the chansonnette§533 *e*
Woodcocks–like w. upon‖....311 *c*
   live like woodcocks.........166 *i*
Wood-grapes–w-g. were......267 *a*
Woodland–glooming w. art so 52 *h*
   music of the w. depths......394 *a*
   rings the w. loud and long†610 *j*
   to her woodland home......222 *i*
   tremulous w. things........221 *q*
   woodland hollows thickly..394 *p*
Woodlands–in firry w.†...... 45 *u*
   our woodlands adorn......217 *a*
   over the w. brown and bare§565 *b*
   wander through the w......545 *d*
Woodlark–sweet warbling w.. 48 *l*
Woodman–the w.'s axe that..666 *s*
   woodman, spare that tree..609 *l*
   w., spare that beechen tree.612 *f*
Wood-notes–warble his**.....550 *p*
Wood-nymph–the w-n. wild..242 *k*

Wood-robin–the w-r. sings at..55 *h*
Wood Street–at the corner ¶.. 59 *f*
Woods–all the w. are alive...541 *n*
   all the woods are still**.... 51 *l*
   and smote the woods.......395 *e*
   a stoic of the woods,—a man 590 *j*
   bare and wintry woods.....614 *m*
   bending above the spicy w.394 *q*
   delay in the gay woods.....647 *q*
   fading many-colored w.....610 *n*
   feet to trace the w. and ....413 *a*
   fill the woods with light.... 71 *a*
   float from the woods and...605 *n*
   gaunt w., in ragged scant .395 *f*
   glorious are the w. in their.543 *l*
   Greta woods are green......412 *d*
   how bow'd the w. beneath..423 *s*
   I could live in the w. with..567 *r*
   in the woods a fragrance...222 *q*
   loved the shady w. so well .613 *e*
   matted woods where birds. 42 *i*
   November w. are bare and.395 *j*
   o'erhung with wild woods..530 *e*
   out in the lonely woods ....232 *q*
   pleasure in the pathless w.‖475 *f*
   rain in the woods, rain.... 515 *b*
   senators of mighty woods..616 *d*
   soon as the woods on shore. 63 *m*
   thee the wild woods await.. 43 *p*
   the woods and the waves§.. 50 *l*
   the w. appear with crimson 610 *i*
   the w. are hush'd, their†...610 *m*
   the woods are in full leaf...729 *b*
   the w. grow still and dim... 52 *m*
   through the gaunt w. the..648 *c*
   through the w. I reverent..395 *i*
   to-morrow to fresh woods** 75 *h*
   to roam the woods.........453 *c*
   to the sleeping w. all night.572 *t*
   to the woods below........545 *f*
   touching all the darksome§.585 *l*
   unfrequented woods.......290 *u*
   wailing winds, and naked w.543 *m*
   when wild in woods........258 *i*
   whisper'd it to the woods**.376 *d*
   wide are these woods....... 87 *g*
   woods against a stormy sky 459 *q*
   woods are glad with song...245 *l*
   w. more free from peril*...610 *c*
   woods of autumn burn......224 *l*
   woods the bluebird's.......248 *c*
Woof–we know her woof.....515 *m*
Wool-like footsteps upon w.†.417 *s*
   many go out for w., and...501 *gg*
   moche crye and no wull....502 *q*
   shear swine, all cry and no.502 *jj*
Wool-gathering–ran a w-g....254 *r*
   thoughts ran a w-g........ .502 *q*
   wits from wool-gathering..498 *bb*
Woolly–w. fleeces spread..... 99 *q*
Word–a cheerful w. for me...493 *e*
   a honest man's word.......305 *a*
   and every word stabs*.....659 *t*
   alone!—that worn-out word 567 *f*
   a single little w. can strike.797 *a*
   a single word often betrays 796 *r*
   as to recall a word once....664 *y*
   at every w. a reputation‡..524 *l*
   audience for a word*.......107 *d*
   before thy uncreating w.‡.. 77 *d*
   be true to your w. and your 108 *k*
   bring in a new w. by the...665 *d*
   choice word and measured¶574 *u*
   Christ—the one great word. 92 *q*
   drops some careless word§.210 *s*
   end in a w.; such is the*...665 *p*
   every ship brings a word...448 *c*
   every w. was once a poem..476 *r*
   for a tricksy word*.........252 *w*
   for every word I speak*....592 *j*
   give me but one kind w. to.464 *q*
   good w. informs my soul...539 *c*
   he sinks without a word....585 *h*
   He was the word that...... 92 *j*
   I live in the word..........807 *f*
   I'll talk a w. with this same*580 *p*
   ill w. may empoison liking* 558 *w*

it is not a lucky word......317 h
keep the w. of promise to*.492 r
knells in that word—alone.567 f
last w. pricked him like a††.334 r
lies in one little word*.....665 p
lightest w. would harrow*..547 g
made answer to my word...588 h
many a word at random....665 g
neither my good word*....106 j
never wanted a good word.486 j
no simple word that shall..519 f
no such word as—fail......196 n
not such a word spoke*....209 y
one word be chang'd but‡.. 74 t
repeating your ultimate w.169 k
sharp's the word with her.503ii
she spoke no evil word.....182 o
sorry that I spell'd the w...367 i
speakest a word of great...790 e
speak one simple word††..588 g
spoke no evil word... ....279 u
subsides the infrequent w..666 c
suit the action to the word*. 5 s
sweet in every whisper'd w.||384 t
sword of God's word......328m
take thy word for faith*...419 p
task me to my word*.......215 i
that charming word. ......308 f
that once familiar word...408 d
that word did make it...... 92 j
that word—that fatal word||.204 j
that word, that kiss shall..335 x
their word's sufficient.....124 k
the Word had breath†...... 92 s
they spake not a word*....210 a
thou has given thy word...377 h
to neither a w. will I say...656 k
torture one poor word ten..664m
to the hearing of the Word.319 c
unfold whose lightest w.*..209 q
urging of that word*.......331 v
voice sounds like a........493 d
wait on his word..........274 t
what; gone without a w.*..554bb
what is honour? A word*.306 y
what is in that w. honour*.306 y
when that w. was brought.409 e
whose w. no man relies on.533 q
will not speak a word*.....171 u
wisest word man reaches...280 x
with that word—banished*. 33 f
w. by seers or sybils told...538 s
w. for word without a book*353 l
w. impossible is not in my..506 u
w. in its Pickwickian sense.548 i
word is as good as the bank306 b
w. of God abounds in such.528 c
w. once escaped can never.753 a
word that floats on the§....210 r
word that must be||........204 i
word that's quickly spoken664 d
word the vessel brings.....448 c
word they wish to hear....448 c
word to the wise.........752 k
w. unto the prophet spoken538 s
w. which knaves and fools.205 f
yesterday the w. of Cæsar*665 k
Words-affected by the words730 e
a fine volley of words*.....665 i
agony with words*... .....288 o
all very good words.......73 a
all words ever spoken.....554 n
and words that burn.......596 t
appear in other ways than*644 f
appears in the form of w...664 r
army of good words*.......252w
art is built of words........ 28 h
betwixt two charming w.*.335 n
boldest in w. and tongue...687 f
breathe their w. in pain*..340 b
burning words and praises.217 j
but words are things, and||.427 t
but words are words*......665 j
by hir wordes ne hir face...467 c
by ten w., my lord, it is*...422 u
by the w. which we hear...730 e
by winning w. to conquer**472 v

"careful with w." is ten....573 n
catches the main w. only...640 r
controll'd by the words he.665 a
cunningly built of words...664 f
dark w. begins my tale¶... 490 f
dearth of w. a woman need 114 g
deeds are males, w. females496gg
deeds find me the words** .146 t
deeds, not words..........496hh
deeds than w. to grace it* .554bb
desire to confine our w.....664 e
drank the precious words.. 65 i
Emerson first, whose rich††664w
employ w. to disguise their789 r
fair words make fools......493 g
far too big for words.......591 g
few of the unpleasant'st*..448 r
few were their w. but if....650 p
few words he spoke.......638m
fine w.! I wonder where...514m
fire of love with words*...362 t
flowers are words.........217 n
flow from all her words**.. 5 h
flows in fit words and.....548 j
foolish words and empty...285 b
for of all sad w. of tongue. 519 j
frames my w., accelerates.137 a
give sorrow w.; the grief*.569 u
good words are better than*665m
growing one's own choice..448 g
hard words again.........107 j
heaven hath my empty w.*489 n
he that ranged the words. .664 p
his w. are bonds, his oaths* 83 p
his words like so many**...665 c
honest words have suffered665 b
how sweet the w. of truth..621 d
if only words he hears.....797 c
if she respect not words*..663 q
immodest w. admit of no..389 e
into every heart his words.318 u
into w. his longing gushes.. 62 e
in words that kindle glory.146 x
it says more and in fewer w.478 a
jewels five-words-long†....435 c
know all words are faint... 82 j
know thee not no w. can... 82 j
labor'd words could speak..374 g
lie in three words, health‡..475 t
little words of love.......146 u
long-tailed w. in osity and..339 w
make his w. rather serve...573 l
make our actions and w...651 j
mouth as household words*665 l
more eloquent than words.553 t
more than quick w. do*....663 q
my w. fly up, my thoughts*665 s
not in the words—but in...427 o
not words duly hallow'd*..489 k
not words, for they.......219 k
no w. suffice the secret soul||621 k
on w. let your attention....776 r
our burning words........261 r
our w. have wings, but fly.664 n
poem without words.......446 i
poetry—the best w. in their476 j
preach without words of...451 h
proof of deeds not words..146 f
prose—words in their best..476 j
putting all his w. together.665 f
repeats his words*........288 k
roof in words deceiving**..461 t
say nine words in ten hours.178 c
say what words fail of......434 d
seek for things in words....664 l
serious words suit the.....753 b
she respect not words*.....272 j
so bethump'd with words*.665aa
soft w. with nothing in them568 s
some ten words long*......422 u
sorrowful words become.. 753 b
speak in good w. or in good573 j
stomach to digest his w.*...654 a
stringing pretty words that 88 w
sweet the words repeat§.... 94 i
swift words outrun.........182 a
that actions no words..... 6 b

the artillery of words.....665dd
the last words of Marmion.631 h
there is no need of words...747 v
these words are razors to*.665 t
the silent-speaking words†.449 i
the words of God..........575 k
the words move slow‡.....125 s
the world is satisfied with..796 o
though words and things¶.486 d
thy w. I grant are bigger*.. 70 j
to be slow in words is a*...660 a
told me words of peace†....525 i
to side the field of words...574 d
two narrow w., Hic jacet..137 u
two words to that bargain..505ll
unpack my heart with w.*.665 v
use of words unsuitable to.339 s
vent their rage in words. .797 b
voice so sweet, the w. so..634 t
weigh'st thy w. before*....665 j
weighty as words.........745 n
what words of tongue or**.123 a
when we speak words......665bb
when you're flying words. 573 n
where words are scarce*...340 b
while w. of learned length.342 c
whose household w. are§.. 42 d
why do not words and kiss¶378 e
with heavenly words....... 7 g
without knowing the force.664 i
with what words to pray*.488 p
woman's gentle words......796 i
w. and feathers the wind..509 o
w. are but empty thanks...664 h
words are but holy as the..665cc
w. are but the signs of ideas339 x
w. are grown so false, I*...665 x
words are like leaves‡......665 e
words are men's daughters664 x
w. are put together for the 664 l
words are so no more .....573 q
words are the daughters of664 t
w. are wise men's counters.664 q
w. are women, deeds are...509 r
w. as hard as cannon balls.107 j
words could e're have......219 k
words could never utter ..366 u
words flow with ease.......782 e
words gladden so many a§.664 u
words he has wished unsaid519 h
words, however, are things 665 a
words into a sieve........700 t
w. learn'd by rote a parrot.589 a
words little wisdom.......753 d
w., mere words, no matter*665 z
w. of affection, howsoe'er..665 x
w. of comfort availed not§.664 v
w. of endearment where§..664 v
w. of love then spoken....673 b
w. once spoke can never be664 k
w. pay no debts, give her*. 665 y
w. sweet as honey from his‡664 o
w. that dropped from his§..450 q
w. that weep and tears that590 l
w., though ne'er so witty ..554 t
words thou hast spoken....259 g
words were meant for deeds664 o
w. without thoughts never*665 s
words, words, words*......665w
w. worthy to be kept by...677 e
words would not come.....554 a
words writ in waters.......664 q
words you've bandied are..796 s
worship without words§...617 l
write her fair words still*..257 d
yet words are no deeds*...665 u
you have bereft me of all*. 665 r
youth is too hasty with w..797 r
Wordy-spin your w. fabric...589 e
Wore-she wore a wreath....240 d
wore earth about him.....271 h
Work-alive when his w. is...666 j
all nature seems at work...666m
all w., even cotton-spinning666 h
and tools to work withal††.667 b
architecture is the w. of...425 t
as tedious as to work*....302 t

SHAKESPEARE *; MILTON **; WORDSWORTH ¶; BYRON ||; TENNYSON †; LOWELL ††; POPE ‡; LONGFELLOW §.

at her flowery w. doth** ...562 *b*
at her work the village.....476 *u*
attempt a different work...720 *b*
a work too great for fame .435 *p*
a work without a stain.....808 *r*
bees work for man and yet.321 *s*
but a filthy piece of work*.447 *h*
code and the day's work...479 *d*
creature's at his dirty w.‡..644*m*
day's work hath ceased†....184 *j*
done thy long day's work†.526 *s*
edifice, stupendous work...535 *k*
finished a w. which neither.714*m*
free men freely work......666 *d*
frivolous work of polished.505 *g*
genuine work alone, what. 666 *i*
get leave to work in this...666 *e*
get myself into more w.*...453 *q*
give the w. lasting solidity.667 *g*
God is at work on man.....276 *f*
God never made His w. for 440 *b*
heart was in his work§.....296 *u*
her noblest w. she classes..654*w*
his six days' w. a world**..122 *v*
his w. needs a frolic health.428 *d*
his w. was strong and clean453*m*
in books or w.; or healthful667*m*
is labor, this is work......720 *d*
judge of a great work.....427 *u*
let her work prevail†.......338 *k*
love of that which your w..447 *b*
man hath his daily w. of**.667 *d*
measure not the w. until...666 *f*
men must w. and women..666 *v*
my hand alone my w. can... 19 *c*
myriad-handed, his wild w.565 *a*
noblest work of God‡......371 *u*
our work is not design, but..151 *h*
people I could w. for with a 421 *l*
put your w. twenty times...797 *f*
still w. for the minute and.470 *v*
that well his w. beginneth..666 *r*
the grave there is no work..492 *n*
the last best work, the.....658 *d*
the Moor has done his w....775 *a*
there is always w.. and††...667 *b*
the work goes bravely on...581 *o*
the work of Chloe..........179 *c*
the w. of their own hearts..582 *u*
the work she plyed, but‡...666 *u*
the work some praise**.....425 *r*
thine to w. as well as pray.667 *n*
this shall be thy work... ..709 *k*
time for work—yet take....302 *v*
to begin is half the work...678 *s*
truth is the work of God...623 *u*
what a piece of work is a*. 372 *l*
what w.'s, my countrymen*667 *j*
when his w. is ended dares.416 *g*
where work and mirth... .294 *g*
who first invented work....666*w*
whose work is done........466 *s*
whose w. is not born with††667 *b*
work—and pure slumbers.339 *j*
w., and rest shall be won...666 *j*
w., and your house shall be666 *j*
w. an unknown good man..318 *n*
work because the spirit is. 28 *g*
work begun how soon**... 123 *b*
work first, and then rest...667 *h*
work is alone noble........666 *h*
work like madness in the...357 *n*
w. of many thousand men..533 *s*
w. of skill, surpassing sense323 *l*
work shall not be lost......182 *q*
work the honey-bees*......322 *b*
w.—thou shalt ride over...339 *j*
work under our labour**...667 *e*
w. with a stout heart and...339 *j*
work without hope draws.307 *l*
w., worship therefore let us487 *i*
worth of our w. perhaps....666 *c*
Worked—he w. and sang, from110 *b*
I w. with patience which...466 *v*
worked both hard and long 97 *i*
Working—from her w. all his*423 *j*
is working silently.........540*m*

working in these walls§.....206 *q*
Working-house-w-h. of*.....597*m*
Workings—of mighty w.......296 *a*
Workman—in respect of a*...453 *o*
no w. steel, no pond'rous...425 *l*
w. was no cobbling clown...453 *c*
Workmanship—wonder at**... 35*m*
workmanship of heaven....418 *b*
of workmanship so rare‖...368 *u*
Workmen—w. crowded......123 *d*
w. handle the tools of. ....680 *k*
w. strive to do better*..... 120*w*
Works—agent w. but to this ..666 *k*
are thy glorious works**...275 *h*
faith produce no works....198 *e*
fashions all her w. in high§452 *l*
God, who loveth all His w.309 *d*
good w. in her husband**..645 *g*
himself in his w. even be...428 *f*
his works are mine. ......803 *e*
immediately upon your w..636 *t*
insect midst his w. I view..321 *r*
it still visibly works.......318*m*
knowledge of thy works....413 *b*
lies are the works of man..623 *u*
lord of all the w. of nature.412 *q*
make copies of their works 426 *q*
men's sublimest works.....525 *f*
man their works must eye*.197 *f*
more of the Almighty's w.**674 *c*
nature's works to me**....149*m*
of greatest w. is finisher*..331 *o*
our mightiest works die....150 *o*
read the greatest w. of any480 *v*
recount almighty works**.123 *a*
sighing through all her**..555 *y*
son of his own works ......797 *h*
taste His works..........274 *c*
that it works on like itself .666 *k*
the fat of others' works....474 *l*
the man from his works....429 *v*
through all her w. he must 409*w*
where lurks it? how w. it..348 *t*
works adjourn'd have many603 *n*
w. and thoughts if they ....74 *k*
w. may have more wit than‖653 *s*
w. of any great painter.....480 *v*
w. of the intellect are great325 *h*
w. of women are symbolical666 *c*
works, though wondrous ..274 *f*
Workshop—laboratory and w.113 *l*
World—a budding world......218 *g*
acquaintance with the w... 6 *b*
adorner and refresher of...641 *e*
affairs of the world...... .757 *h*
against the w.'s judgment.330 *v*
aged in this world of woe‖.. 9 *c*
all corners of the world*...559 *b*
all the Christian world.....534 *s*
all the riches of this world.642 *e*
all the sensual w. proclaim.550 *c*
all the uses of this world*..669 *c*
all the world contains..... 74 *p*
all the w. must see the.....668 *q*
all the w. will be in love*...363 *e*
all the world's loves in its..356 *b*
all this cold and hollow w..401 *s*
all to all the w. besides....371 *b*
a man's ingress into the w..347 *j*
and the fever of the world¶.669 *u*
and the world goes down...668 *p*
and world to world........ 92 *g*
another and a better world.298 *a*
around the habitable w.....279 *t*
a partial w. will listen to my535 *q*
as ancient as the world.....565 *u*
as the w., harmoniously‡..462 *u*
a world to virtue draws....534 *h*
a world without a friend...667 *v*
bad, twisted, topsy-turvy..667 *u*
banish all the world*....... 33 *i*
because the w. is populous*491 *w*
be found in the world......470 *t*
bestride the narrow w.*....287 *h*
burst, and now a world‡...510 *n*
busy world an idler too....313 *h*
but for the whole world...679 *p*

but the world is small, when172*m*
buy a w. of happy days*...161 *a*
came up stairs into the w. .581 *p*
commences ere the w. be...525 *a*
cannot live all to this w..... 82*m*
can we divine their world..650 *n*
cooings of the w. allure...669 *v*
contagion to this world*...417 *o*
creation's heir, the w, the.668 *h*
curest the world...........635 *l*
curtain her sleeping world.417 *p*
deceived the whole world..691 *j*
deed in a naughty world*..147 *d*
deign on the passing w. to .580 *b*
dim world of clouding cares 16 *o*
do to spite the world*.....518 *h*
dropt on the w.—a sacred..493 *b*
egress out of the world....347 *j*
envy of the world ....115 *c*
ere the world be past......297 *r*
fabric of our world depends123 *d*
far from the clamorous w..566 *x*
fast and the w. goes by.....669 *q*
fear not in a world§........209 *c*
few men into the world.....510 *q*
forth from out a w. of men*644 *n*
foremost man of all this*..372 *q*
for in the world above.....375 *s*
for pity makes the world..345 *h*
for still the world prevail'd341 *g*
for that world to come. ...132 *j*
from the w.'s rose-bed he.. 466 *t*
girdle round about the w...507 *v*
give the world a proof.....146 *f*
glory doth this w. put on§. 411 *i*
good be out of the world...205 *g*
good-bye, proud w.! I'm...133 *r*
governs the whole world...252 *j*
great as the world.........255 *l*
great world spin forever†.. 76 *o*
half the w. knows not how.498 *v*
half the world was his.....287*m*
hand that rules the world..402 *i*
hand which moves the w...490 *a*
heart of the world I leap...115 *k*
his six days work, a w.**...122 *v*
holds out this world.......522 *p*
honours to the w. again*...139*m*
how the world wags*......602 *g*
I am a citizen of the world.668 *e*
I am in this earthly world*..147 *e*
idly busy rolls their world..313 *i*
if all the world should in**.593 *i*
if the world will be gulled..148 *s*
I have not loved the w.‖....317 *s*
I hold the w. but as the w.*669 *d*
I laugh at the w. and the...110 *a*
imagination rules the w....315 *c*
in every epoch of the w. .. 596 *e*
infernal world! and thou**299 *g*
inheritor of a w. scarce less‖30 *s*
intercourse with the world.478*w*
in the wide world, a valley.411 *t*
in the w. may be endured..785 *g*
in the world's riper years..669 *w*
in this earthly world*...... 5 *l*
in this world a man must§.. 81 *b*
is like the rolling world....351 *c*
is written on the world.... 74 *p*
I take the w. to be but as a.667 *s*
it has mantled a world.....130 *o*
it is an ugly w. Offend....668*m*
it were better for the world668 *q*
I were of another world....596*w*
kept the world in awe*.....152 *b*
kept the world in awe.....133 *v*
killed the world above.....212 *j*
king of this world.........133 *q*
language of another world‖415 *j*
laugh and the w. laughs...669 *r*
laugh at the w.," says he...110 *a*
learn the world to know...337 *w*
leave the world no copy*...126 *n*
leaves the w. to darkness..186 *s*
leave this world without...689 *l*
lend me to the world....... 60 *e*
let the world go...........318 *h*

w. where much is to be ...668 n
world will be too small for. 758 u
w. will turn when we are.. 135 h
w. with long, sweet Alpine.549 z
w. without a native home..303 n
w.-without-end bargain*....376 o
would I shake the world*..465 z
would the world be to us§...90 b
yours to the world's end....453 d
you wedded all the world*.659 i
World-builder-Founder and.666 i
World-jewelled-Night comes.415 e
Worldlings-little w. can.....643 g
Worldly-ambitious w.desires 12 p
attached to w. interest.....676 m
be wisely worldly, but not.496 k
most loathed worldly life*.140 e
scorneth worldly pelf......361 s
thanked my God for w.....642 e
weary of these w. bars*....350 o
w. suits would he be*......378 i
worldly thought o'ertakes. 48 m
World-man-hero is the w-m..300 y
Worlds-allur'd to brighter w.450 l
and the crush of worlds....570 w
best of possible worlds....797 j
conquer twenty worlds.....133 j
dreams of better worlds...159 r
escapes the wreck of w.....572 g
exhausted worlds and then 428 o
feet the worlds divide.....116 f
flesh that mad'st all w..... 94 d
high up the crowd of w....667 r
if the w. in worlds enclosed 1 q
search of foreign worlds**. 6 n
so many w., so much to do†669 m
the crush of worlds........315 m
there are two worlds.......668 k
wandering between two w..667 q
with golden worlds inlaid..417 v
worlds had gone to war....286 i
World-sirens-rest from w-s..339 j
World-wide-w-w. apart, and§588 f
Worm-feeble w. of the earth.371 r
fish with the w. that hath*.151 p
foot upon a worm..........260 a
hero the conqueror worm..137 j
like a worm i' the bud*....467 u
the darkness and the worm142 p
the worm she preferred.... 43 a
the w., the canker, and the‖ 9 e
the worm to weave‡.......342 k
trifle for a w. to part with*.469 f
worm is in the bud of youth143 f
worm of conscience still*..106 p
w. will turn being trodden*119 q
Worms-as many devils at W.525 u
dainty fattings for the w...140 w
damp, the w. and the rats.. 69 e
even w. shall perish on‖ ...132 u
food alike for worms.......135 k
gilded tombs do worms*...285 p
lies here food for worms..182 q
of worms and epitaphs*...184 e
or grubs, or worms‡.......661 m
out-venoms all the w. of*...559 b
poor w., they hiss at me...642 m
slackness breeds w. but the 4 p
w.have eaten them but not*372 o
Wormwood-hyssop and w...148 o
Worn-never be w., nor shine.373 l
sooner lost and worn*......377 e
worn away with age‡.......535 u
w. now in their newest*....461 e
worn out Christendom*....205 k
w. some twenty years ago..205 c
Worry-w. and devour each..636 k
Worse-goes by the worse**... 27 l
I have seen worse§........400 h
make the worse appear**..517 d
often a great deal worse...758 p
remedy is w. than the......526 z
the worse for the fishes....440 h
the worse for the texts.....781 n
the worse for wear.........432 s
the w., the nearer they§.... 75 c
the w. the scrawl, the dose.440 r

the worst are no worse*....315 g
things, I follow the worse..683 e
though an old man, do w..695 t
to be worse than worst.....140 i
what must be worse**......380 m
w. unto that is worst of....388 p
your case can be no worse..439 t
Worse-bodied-ill-faced, w-b.*. 83 n
Worship-every one's true w..670 k
forced w. shuts evils in.....670 o
freedom to worship God...258 m
less a worship than before§.359 v
let us worship God.........669 x
pious worship of God......520 j
silent w. of the great of‖..670 a
than the loss of worship....670 d
the worship of the world...535 j
to compel man to Divine W.670 o
too fair to worship......... 35 k
we that w. him, ignoble....183 h
who from true w.'s gold‖..586 f
who worship dirty gods*...642 u
work, w. therefore let us...487 i
w. by all means the gods...669 y
w. idols, wood and stone...539 d
worship not the true God... 82 m
worship of a hero..........301 b
w. to the garish sun*......363 e
worship without words§....617 l
your pragmatical w........101 h
Worshipped-fathers w.**...622 u
more w., the rising than....670 l
that I worshipped the devil.642 e
w. at innumerable shrines..382 a
worshipp'd while blooming.242 j
w. with a waxen epitaph*..184 d
worshipped with sacrifices.707 m
Worshipper-nature mourns..480 l
Worshippers-dies among his.621 f
than do thy worshippers*.. 73 e
Worshipping-w. God through 651 v
Worships-all nature w. there 413 f
man always w. something..670 b
worships his creator........370 o
Worst-better than the very..709 f
by seeing the w., which*...508 x
for when at worst..........256 l
men believe the worst......699 g
the w. is not so long as we*.388 n
the worst of me is known...786 n
the worst pursue...........641 x
the w. speak something....467 g
things at the w. will cease*.152 f
to-morrow, do thy worst...605 c
when he is worst, he is*... 84 o
worst come to the worst...501 e
worst of rebels never arm..518 a
w. speaks something good..450 o
w. that man can breathe*..628 n
worst that may befall*.....517 l
Worst-humour'd-with the...479 f
Worth-bar to weigh true w..330 s
be measur'd by his worth*.570 j
bids afflicted w. retire to.... 10 f
buds the promise of........492 u
can count their worth*.... 103 r
can judge a poet's worth...478 t
endues the soul with w.‡...670 q
gold which is worth gold...504 y
how thy w. with manners*.670 v
I am not w. this coil that*..670 u
if I am not w. the wooing§.662 p
if wanting worth.......... 14 j
inborn worth his acts‡..... 80 f
in dangerous times true w.670 w
in purchase of its worth....673 q
is worth an age............273 b
it's worth, ask death-beds..673 q
more worth than any man*.660 e
none was worth my strife..473 f
raise my worth too high....322 r
slow rises w. by poverty....670 r
stones of small w. may lie..434 c
takes half his w. away‡.....559 k
the conscience of her w.**.. 82 b
the thought of worth.......274 q
the worth and choice.......261 a

they are not w. the search* 517 o
thousand kinsmen of more.587 v
thy worth the greater*.....559 a
till in consummate w. you..673 k
'tis virtue, wit, and worth..670 p
total worth of man........358 f
various yet equal in its w...163 l
were it w. one's while a....870 aa
were w. a thousand men....638 r
whatever is w. doing at all.508 i
what is w., in anything.....670 p
whose worth's unknown*..317 o
worth a gooseberry*.......266 m
w., courage, honor, these.. 84 v
worth is warrant for his*...644 c
w. makes the man, and‡...670 t
w. of our work perhaps....666 c
worth of the treasures.....452 f
worth two in the bush......494 c
worth, unless united with..739 p
Worthier-many a w. son‖....310 q
Worthiness-bold of your w.*.438 g
virtue and to worthiness*.. 84 g
Worthless-a w. woman! mere 654 u
man is w. who knows......698 l
Worthy-I find thee w.; do†† .525 f
it is easier to appear w.... 797 o
I will be worthy of it.......671 c
worthy of this noble wife*.377 j
worthy of thy loving.......355 q
write anything worthy.....753 f
Wot-wot not what they are*.426 n
Would-but what man w. do..146 e
"I dare not" wait upon "I*.122 i
not what we would be.... .151 i
shall not when he wold-a...104 i
should do when we would*. 76 d
wold not when he might....104 i
"would" changes and hath* 76 d
would not when he might..461 l
Would'st-what thou would'st* 84 n
Wound-a little failing w. 760 o
cleansed, and wound up....492 b
earth felt the w., and**... .555 y
ever cure this wound...... 149 c
feel th' eternal wound‡....268 b
felt a stain like a wound.... 87 s
forgetting his former w....686 j
grief of a wound*..........306 y
gun-shot w. in the breast...640 r
he feels the fiery wound‡... 54 q
limb, each w. and scar.....134 d
no tongue to wound us.....293 n
of the w. he made light....481 j
shoe has power to wound..453 k
soothe or w. a heart that's..665 q
straight wound up anew....289 f
than wound my honour....305 r
that never felt a wound*..498 hh
the hands that wound are.. 85 d
the private w. is deepest*..671 j
the wound is for you but...769 e
the w. of peace is surety*..671 k
virtue flourishes from a w..805 v
willing to w., and yet‡.....537 r
w. did ever heal but by*....467 q
wound him as they fly.....466 s
wound the loud winds*.....207 m
w. will perhaps be cured....688 q
Wounded-a man deep-w. may 17 j
error w., writhes in pain...621 f
he in peace is w., not in*...671 q
like a w. snake, drags‡.....477 p
thou hast w. the spirit.....671 f
w. limb shrinks from......699 d
Wounds-balm to heal their*.474 q
bind up my wounds*....... 21 c
conceals their open w.......700 r
discern the w. within.......555 u
fate never w. more deep....328 q
flies through these w. to*...382 n
he wounds to cure......... 83 e
his breast with wounds‖....442 x
kiss dead Cæsar's wounds*.284 a
over thy wounds now do I*404 a
show you sweet Cæsar's*..671 i
than deep wounds before...305 t

the bleeding lover's w.‡....406 t
the short sleep of life our..761 o
wept o'er his w., or tales...443 d
what deep w. ever closed‖..671 e
with wounds in His side....165 o
wounds cannot be cured...688 f
w. nine miles point-blank..439 s
wounds of civil war.......750 u
wounds of deadly hate**...295 e
wounds of fire are hard to .355 n
wounds of the mind ....725 n
wounds the body of a state.125 c
w. with incessant strokes..105 v
Wrack-blow, wind! come, w*.638 v
Wrangle-and w. and jangle...56 j
men will w. for religion...520 l
people, how they wrangle..668m
that makes us wrangle.....101 s
Wrap-wrap myself up in my.749 r
Wrapped-w. away from life..220 n
w. in the spotless ermine§..532 h
Wrapper-your folded w.....225 f
Wrath-bruising irons of w.*..639 c
dews his wrath allay.....17 n
grapes of wrath are stored.527 v
heat, O intermit thy wrath.543 f
I told it not, my w. did grow 17 e
I told my w., my w. did end 17 e
measure of my wrath*.....17 r
now wild in wrath........449 t
nursing her w. to keep it...17 f
red with uncommon wrath.607 r
their bowels full of wrath*.639 l
wan with w. of wind and..544 q
wrath consume me quite..352 i
Wreath-beauty to forego her 8 p
fan with pensile w. their...615 e
is but a wreath of thorns**.534 l
rosy-tinted wreath........222 h
Sir Proteus to w. your*....56 b
thinking of a wreath......231 r
wild-flower wreath......219 l
wreath of Harmodius.....236 k
wreath of roses . ...240 d
w.'s of brightest myrtle...219 j
Wreaths-blooming w. from..530 c
entwined in duskier w.....625 o
grac'd with w. of victory*.631 l
our w. of parsley spread...395 l
sweet garland wreaths**...219 a
woodbine w. that bind her†610 l
wreaths for each toil.....307 l
wreaths of camomile.....440 l
wreaths that endure¶.....198 u
Wreck-creates from its own.308 z
escapes the w. of worlds...572 g
in the w. of noble lives§...645 b
own wreck the thing it....308 z
the wreck of power to rest. 396 o
till o'er the wreck.......188 c
Wrecked-men have oftest**..388 h
w. with a week of teen*...569 s
Wrecks-rising on its w. at§..190 l
the w. of matter, and the..570w
the wrecks of time........250 c
vomitest thy wrecks on its.603 l
Wren-a musician than the*...52 z
and then the wren gan.....59 l
I took the w.'s nest, Heaven 59m
poor wren the most.*......59 n
robin-redbreast and the w...56 e
the wren with little quill*..58 q
with the little wren's¶....59 p
w. mounted as high as the...59 o
Wrens-as little w. but newly. 59 k
wrens be wrens†.........46 n
wrens make prey where*...187 z
Wrestled-w. with him as the.141 s
Wrestles-he that w. with us..112 q
Wretch-curs'd be that wretch430 d
is a wretch whom it were..122 n
live like a wretch ....320 r
meanest wretch they scorn. 61 w
miser; base, ignoble w.*...387 l
O dishonest wretch*......630 q
the poorest wretch in life..374 j
vengeance on the w. who...528m

w., concentred all in self...547 s
wretch condemn'd with life307 u
Wretched-can not be w......738 p
forsakes the wretched.....736 e
give to the wretched......679 q
in his conception wretched.345 j
it is a wretched thing to....696 q
life! long to the wretched.722 k
most w. men are cradled ..480 o
never to scoff at the w.....780 j
only wretched are the wise.314 p
peace may be so wretched.731 k
the wretched he forsakes..564 e
very wretched fortune. ....703 n
was wretched ev'n as we..182 e
w. are the minds of men...713 p
wretched before evening..701 t
wretched for his mind*....343 q
wretched fortune is safe..702 o
wretched hasten to hear of.748 r
wretched is that poor man*535 b
w. love to think of thee....141 f
wretched thing forlorn¶...246 q
wretched, un-idea'd girls.. 657 d
w. whom none can please..748 p
Wretchedness-estate of.....488 s
waves of w. swell.........325 p
Wretches-feel what w. feel*.441 k
to wretches such as I......346 f
w. hang that jurymen‡....330 i
Wrinkle-sigh in w. of a smile*569 x
time writes no w. on thy ‖..599 l
what stamps the w. deeper‖..9 g
with the first wrinkle.....656 a
w. on fair Venus' brow....327 q
Wrinkled-are w. like my§....10 h
smoothed his w. front*....639 e
Wrinkles-and w., the d--d‖..215 a
despite of w. this thy*....673 j
let old wrinkles come*....384 p
make w. and not dimples..387 o
thick rows of wrinkles....455 j
try to conceal your w......175 v
Wrist-earth a trinket at my..669 o
falling down to your wrist.291 f
gave a thumb to his wrist..370 p
ladies ride with hawk on§..533 h
the shoulder to the wrist...647 u
Writ-holy saws of sacred w.*303 e
one writ with me in sour*..388 l
proofs of holy writ*.......328 h
so holy writ in babes*.....331 o
stol'n out of holy writ*....631 p
was ever writ in brass.....550m
whose name was writ in...183 h
words writ in waters.......664 g
Write-a man may w. at any..428 n
and write mine epitaph*...184 g
as though I lived to write..429 p
but to w. and read comes*.170 t
certain he could write and.342 d
could souls to bodies, write448 e
dare to write as funny as I..310 y
devise, wit ; write, pen*...429 q
for this men write, speak‖..200 k
hand wherewith I write....333 t
he can write and read and*170 u
he who would write and††..125 f
he will write a book......427 c
into thine heart and write§.428 u
is but a desk to write upon 662 d
look in thy heart and w....429 j
masters of the things they.342 l
may be glorious to write††.428 x
no man can write anything 428 b
provoke the skew'r to w.‡..429 k
sit down to write.........480 t
so may he cease to write...429 n
some w. confin'd by physic 430 b
speak or write to him......264 q
that w. in rhyme still make476 e
the Angel says "write"§...479 t
their stars, to write.......427 q
though an angel should w..452 a
to write I should be dumb. 753 l
virtues we write in water*..84 c
why did I write? what sin‡429 l

write anything worthy.....753 f
write his own Dispensary‡.429m
write much, and to write...428 s
w. so fast as men run mad.430 a
w. the characters in dust...658 t
write till your ink be dry*.663 l
write to the mind and heart426 r
write with a goose-pen*....471 t
yourself w. nothing, your..175 d
ye who write, choose a....753 h
you w. with ease, to show.471 u
Writer-of a writer's genius..514 d
one w. for instance, excels.428 h
regard the writer's end‡...125 p
smell too much of that w...551 b
so must the writer, whose..429w
that writer does the most..427 l
work regard the w.'s end‡.429 h
w., like a priest, must be...428 d
Writers-in ink what w. think.471 n
most popular writers......435 s
souls of all the writers that344 v
style ! why, all w. will tell. 581 g
that readeth good writers..514 e
the greater part of our w...513 z
turn to w. of an abler sort..515w
writers against religion....519 l
writers cannot them digest125 b
w., especially when they...427 e
Writes-a strange hand writes640 r
but he writes nothing who. 175 n
but writes in dust.........345 j
for one who writes amiss‡..125 q
is vain who w. for praise..486aa
thinks he writes divinely..427 b
thinks he w. reasonably...427 b
think that what he w. is....428 b
w. because his father writ..430 b
w. himself "Armigero"*...271 j
writes them in return......254 l
w. to make his barrenness‡.480 h
Writest-what w. thou?.....634 f
Writing-an art of writing...28 a
angel, w. in a book of gold.634 f
appear in writing or in‡....429 f
art of writing billet-doux..448 f
bear the toil of writing....753 e
conversation than in w....113 g
easy w.'s curst hard.......471 u
for your w. and reading*..342 p
masterpiece is w. well.....429 s
no talent at writing.......427 c
quick hand in writing.....753m
source of good writing....753 g
true ease in w. comes from‡429 j
writing an exact man......341 n
w. comes by the grace of..428 a
w. well; I say nothing......753 e
Writings-comprehension of§.428 t
publishing of his own w....452 e
steal from the writings....474 o
writings survive the years.753m
w. that convict you of theft180 e
Written-a well-written life is346 l
erased nor w. o'er again§...428w
refuse to be written.......621 a
should be written on air...722 p
whatever hath been w.§....428w
"w. in water," swiftly.....485 p
Writhed-w. not at passed joy329 r
Wrong-all right and wrong..707 n
almost seems a wrong......97 r
always in the wrong.......212 a
and other than the wrong..410 h
answering one foul wrong*332 s
both are w. but in different694 n
by going wrong all things††75 c
condemn the w. and yet....82 k
cradled into poetry by w....480 o
dally with w. that does no..596 i
day of w. through the little*156 a
despite thy w., my love*...603 j
do wrong to none*.........511 s
easily things go wrong.....151 q
every one is in the wrong..765 e
find herein a wrong ......69 g
flight to do thee wrong.....56 p

for every social w. there...565 g
have a wrong sow by the...586 m
have done the wrong......255 j
he rises early to do wrong.416 g
his can't be w. whose life‡..349 i
if I am w., O teach my‡....489 b
in a wrong Boxe..........499 y
inflicts no sense of wrong..448 d
is the tender fear of wrong.671 r
lawful that law bar no w.*.439 c
make w. conduct appear...691 n
may gang a kennin' wrang.343 c
memory of a wrong......255 j
multitude is always in the.671 m
of right and w. he taught..449 p
on w. swift vengeance‡....528 j
opposing wrong affords....79 o
our country, right or wrong468 j
people once are in the w...185 s
read you not the w. you're.662 j
receive than to do a wrong.749 g
right of an excessive w,...500 r
silente man still suffers w..553 y
sons of wrong and strife..594 o
sorrow and from wrong...229 m
split the marble walls of w.614 g
stronger than the wrong..164 u
than the abolition of the w.565 g
the heart hath treble w.*...606 i
the year goes wrong......267 e
to stand and suffer wrong..616 f
we are both in the wrong...185 m
we wrong with mournful...133 g
when one's w. they smile‖..455 f
who if once wrong‡........185 r
wrong because of weakness 33 o
wrong done her is righted.631 bb
w. forever on the throne††.622 o
w. in a connubial kiss‖.....533 g
Wrong-doing-yoke of our...512 d
Wronged-but think'st him*..108 i
Wronger-loves not his w.*...328 e
Wrongs-clearing thorny w...667 n
good for righting wrongs..102 l
heaviest w. get uppermost.667 u
oppress'd with wrongs*....209 o
redress of unexamined w...548 i
when I think of all my w...528 o
write their w. in marble...420 x
w. his outsides, to wear*...628 n
wrongs of base mankind‡..385 r
w. unredressed, or insults¶388 s
Wrote-agayne I wrote it.....255 d
and wrote upon the sand...459 o
he talked, w., or rehearsed.581 d
I wrote her name..........255 d
reading what they never w.450 e
Shikspur! who wrote it.....551 c
who wrote like an angel...182 s
who wrote with ease‡......436 e
wrote except for money....428 p
wrote on in the sand......86 r
wrote them in the dust.....420 x
Wroth-weakness to be w.†...642 b
wroth with one we love....17 g
Wrought-brain too finely w..596 g
fortunes must be wrought‡348 p
that firste he wroughte.....188 k
to have w. or reigned......386 r
w. with attributes divine...417 v

X.

Xanadu-X. did Kubla Khan..530 b
Xarifa-rise up, X.! lay your..126 u
Xerxes-or X. the splendid....200 q
X. the great did die, and so 133 p

Y.

Yarn-mingled y. good and*..350 w
Yarrow-see the braes of Y.¶.529 c
thy genuine image Y.¶.....382 c
Yawn-churchyards y. and*...417 o
everlasting yawn confess‡.313 m
like a yawn of fire.........239 b
Yawning-I dozing lay and y..446 e

y. make another yawn.....188 j
Year-all the daughters of the.543 j
almanacs of the last year..4 i
and the year on the earth..544 o
a y. hence, but this evening 681 m
bier of the dead cold year..544 o
birds of this y. in the nests.502 m
comes but once a year......95 h
crowns the youthful year..540 b
days will finish up the y.*...602 r
decorate the fading year...219 f
each shall crown the year..355 u
every y. and month sends‖.300 z
first roses of the y. shall‡...285 l
funeral of the former year‡ 60 g
gems the starry girdle of...575 p
hear it in the opening y.§..647 n
heaven's eternal y. is thine.297 p
in the circling year........40 n
in the year of our Lord.....98 i
leap year is never a good...21 q
long year through the¶.....227 r
many a year ago..........323 a
months that fill the year...222 b
moments make the year...619 v
newe corn from y. to yere..9 i
nc winter in thy year......44 r
of that glad y. that once‡..449 i
opens all the year........276 l
opes the y.'s fair gate.....151 j
passing year robs us of....746 f
pleasure of the fleeting y.*..3 f
preach a whole year.......347 j
rolling year is full of Thee.275 v
ruler of the inverted year..545 n
six hundred pounds a year.652 i
so Life's year begins and...10 t
so rolls the changing year..539 g
sweet new year, delaying‡.541 e
the boyhood of the year‡..541 i
the perfect circle of the year396 d
the saddest of the year.....543 m
the snows of yester year...782 n
the year goes wrong.......267 e
the year's in the wane......544 b
time o' the year between*..191 h
to childhood seems a year..599 o
to rule the varied year.....546 o
visionary tints the y. puts††544 f
while the year is young.....237 f
with the revolving year....289 a
with the y. seasons return**149 m
y. after year it steals, till...604 d
year by year we lose......261 b
y. draws to the "golden...476 n
year grows rich as it.......279 s
year of the age of gold....327 c
y. smiles as it draws near..394 k
y. were playing holidays*..302 i
Years-ah! happy y.! once‖..671 u
a hundred years of the....327 c
along the waste of years...107 p
and charging them years..600 n
a thousand y. a poor man..154 w
a thousand y. shall as a....61 l
a thousand years their‖....99 a
began a thousand y. ago‡..60 s
be numbered by y., daies..599 c
blends with the ocean of y.603 s
braved a thousand years...214 b
brought up to y. with cares345 j
Cascellius numbers sixty y.177 i
count a man's years, until..9 o
crime is taught from early.687 p
crowding y. divide in vain..568 x
crowding years in one brief 91 d
cuts off so many years of*.139 o
cuts off twenty y. of life*..583 f
debts in at sixty years‖.....105 e
dim with the mist of years‖485 n
edge of tempestuous years.325 p
effect with a thousand y...484 g
eighty odd y. of sorrow*...569 s
else years are in vain......190 n
equality of years, of birth.375 u
fifty years are past........8 t
fifty y. of Europe than†....496 d

flag has braved a thousand.444 y
fleeting years are passing..746 d'
flight of years.............267 r
form the circles of our y...584 o
for years beyond our ken§.319 a
fourteen hundred y. ago*..92 r
full of years and of honors.712 o
gleam on the y. that shall..464 p
grave was the man in years760 h
grow faster than the y.*...162 i
her years were ripe.‖......671 w
how many y. ago? Twenty.59 r
I'm eighty years.........97 r
in deeds not y., piercing the‖ 9 c
in the world's riper years..669 w
justice, judgment with y..190 n
many y. of fearing death*.583 f
monitor of fleeting years¶..245 j
nature sink in years.......315 m
nine y. have brought him..91 b
no great disparity of years‖374 n
of boyhood's years......673 b
O tide of the years........8 n
our moments or our years.351 q
record of the years of man.617 q
redeem Life's years of ill‖..356 r
see enough, when y. are..553 l
set is the sun of my years..10 p
slow process of the......480 w
slow years darklier roll....333 o
strength of y. when it is...341 m
such difference in years....375 u
such hours 'gainst y. of‖..346 h
the downward slope of y...592 m
the first years of man must511 k
the golden years return....669 i
the long lapse of years....61 l
the loss of all those years..592 p
the pages of our years....351 t
th' eternal y. of God are...621 f
the weight of seventy y.¶..12 m
the y. of heaven with all...316 d
the y. we wish, the better..60 c
thought of other years††..248 s
thousand y. scarce serve‖..281 l
time who steals our years..380 q
to be seventy y. young is..10 b
twice ten hundred years‡..22 i
unending y. nor the flight..714 l
up for fourscore years.....9 m
virtues with your years....673 k
waste of all devouring y.‡..98 n
we let the years go........255 a
we live in deeds not years..345 m
whole years outweighs‡....106 b
whose waves are years....603 l
wisdom is the man of y...373 j
worn some twenty y. ago..205 c
writings survive the years.753 m
y. a mortal man may live*.602 r
y. bring many advantages.684 f
years fleet away with the‖.334 e
y. follow'ng years steal ‡..601 s
years have not seen‖......259 q
years leave us and find us..75 e
years like passing ages....599 o
years of fading strength...346 k
y. of its glory outnumber..616 e
years of rankling pain.....157 d
years permit, endure labor 720 c
y. steal fire from the mind‖599 n
years that bring the¶......386 n
y. that through my portals§277 l
Yearn-of finite hearts that y.465 h
Yearned-yearned in silence..222 a
Yearning-the leaf is dead†..610 m
Yearnings-y. for equal......482 l
Yell-yell of savage rage.....640 h
Yell'd-y. out like syllable of*569 r
Yells-mean those yells and..321 a
Yellow-bright and y., hard..278 t
bright with yellow glow...246 g
mine is perfect yellow*...291 s
yellow as sunshine........237 f
y. to the jaundiced eye‡..586 o
Yellow-bird-y-b. where did..59 q
Yeoman-a jolly y., marshall..26 h

fed a rout of y. with his....309 *i*
Yeomen–fight, bold yeomen*639 *a*
Yes–breath of a maiden's yes 359 *d*
her yes, once said to you ..145 *n*
look yes last night and yet‖662 *g*
shall be yes forever more ..145 *n*
won't say "Y.," and keeps‖ 114 *g*
Yesterday–call back y., bid*..602 *o*
great families of y. we.... 15 *i*
I may reflect on yesterday.150 *r*
our yesterday's to-morrow.705 *j*
pushes the hero of y. .....301 *k*
since y. I have been§......189 *f*
sneer, and y.'s frown......668 *p*
the wise lived yesterday ..605 *k*
this day was y. to-morrow.601 *k*
to-day is not yesterday.... 74 *k*
yesterday's frown can never 74 *w*
y. the word of Cæsar might*665 *k*
Yesterdays–of cheerful y.¶..112*m*
these are my y., my ......600 *k*
whose y. look backward....466 *s*
y. have lighted fools*.....605 *o*
Yet–"but yet" is as a gaoler*158 *t*
I do not like "but yet," it*.158 *t*
Yew–eugh, obedient to the ..610 *e*
for there no y. nor cypress.618 *q*
shroud of white stuck all*.138 *p*
slips of yew silver'd in*....619 *a*
vanished save of pine and..614 *l*
Yew-tree–there is a y-t.¶....619 *c*
this lonely yew-tree stands¶619 *d*
yew-tree, and all round†....270 *a*
y-t. pride of Lorton Vale¶..619 *c*
Yield–must y. at length to...525 *f*
never to submit or yield**.103 *a*
not y. up till it be forced...121 *j*
y., proud foe, thy fleet......630 *x*
y. them to thy bitter need..324 *d*
yield to him who opposes..684 *q*
Yielded–y. with no discontent 69 *q*
Yielder–and y. up of breath*.608 *q*
Yields–conquers when it y. to759 *q*
Yoke–best bear his mild y.**275 *t*
bow beneath the same y....388 *q*
forgets even such a y. as...334 *s*
must make the y. uneasy..375 *u*
y. of our own wrong-doing.512 *d*
Yoked–is so yoked by a fool* 363 *s*
you are y. with a lamb*.... 18 *b*
Yoke-devils–as two y-d.*.....608 *v*
Yokes–y. a smiling with a*...564 *o*
to draw in y. is chargeable.375 *g*
Yorick–Alas, poor Yorick!‖ ..421 *p*
songster, Y. of thy tribe.... 50 *k*
York–and the Duke of York.535 *k*
summer by this sun of Y.*.582 *g*
Younker–Y. prancing to his*400 *x*
Young–always find us young.557 *d*
and soft as young.........661 *h*
and the old Earth was y.... 412 *s*
and young as beautiful.....661 *h*
antiquity was young when.460 *p*
bit off by it young*........ 57 *h*
both were y. and one was‖.671 *v*
ever died so young.........137 *i*
ever have been young¶.....246 *q*
fight her young ones in*... 59 *n*
for young hot colts being*.497*gg*
gods love dies young.......151 *l*
gods love die young‖.......150 *n*
hearts of young and old§... 40 *d*
her young on yonder tree .. 48 *f*
hope will make thee young308 *x*
I am young–so is she......355 *k*
if he be caught young.....170 *n*
in a young man is modesty.753 *o*
in my verse ever live y.* ...603 *j*
inspires the young, makes‖648*m*
isle protective of his young 58 *o*
ladies be but y. and fair*..659 *h*
look young till forty ....656 *a*
love and I were young.... 59 *a*
mourning her ravish'd y. or 51 *p*
old folk and young§........128 *l*
she died so young.........137 *i*
she sits, y. while the earth.144 *w*

teacher and the taught are‖455 *f*
that dies married young*..377 *n*
the luve o' life's y. day....380 *r*
the y. men's vision, and....634 *d*
these young things lie ..... 90 *f*
though I am young, I scorn 654 *l*
thus you seem young......178 *p*
to be seventy years y. is.... 10 *b*
to be young is to be as .....672 *l*
to be y. was very heaven¶.. 62 *b*
to warm her y. and to teach 57 *a*
when I was young.........672 *c*
when we were young..... 755 *a*
when young and old, and ..605 *k*
which always find us y.....672 *q*
whilest that the childe is y.455 *k*
whom the gods love dies y.690 *g*
wives are young men's.....644 *p*
world and love were young 361 *t*
y., all health and pleasure.604 *p*
young are just on trial.....262 *r*
y. fellows will be young....671 *t*
young, I said to sorrow....570 *r*
y. men are fitter to invent .671 *r*
young men are fools.......251 *g*
young men for what they..778 *i*
y. men soon give and soon.. 77 *h*
young men think old.......251 *g*
young without lovers‡.....349 *n*
Younger–thy love be y. than*659 *u*
You–as we are now so must..183 *c*
as you and you as he* .....151 *v*
Yours–better I were not y.*..306 *s*
if your riches are yours....500 *d*
is it yours..................805 *e*
it begins to be yours......174 *p*
room for, Yours sincerely..448 *k*
what is yours is mine......508 *n*
Yourself–may to y. be true..367 *r*
unbelief in yourself.......626 *n*
you never look at yourself.681 *c*
Yourselves–not have done to.508 *s*
Youth–a bold y. so swift.....663 *c*
age 'twixt boy and youth..574 *j*
ah youth! forever dear‡....672*m*
all the pleasures of youth..754 *i*
and youth is vain.......... 17 *g*
as I approve of a youth that672 *b*
aspiring. beware of love..367 *b*
aspiring youth that fired...200 *p*
a youth of frolics‡ ... .349 *n*
a y. to whom was given¶...673 *o*
beardless youth manages...283 *b*
beauty, for confiding y.¶ ..466 *d*
bounds of freakish youth..291 *a*
come best in youth‖........ 6 *o*
condemns itself in youth*.387 *n*
crabbed age and y. cannot*673 *e*
done it from my youth....290 *q*
ere youth had sped.........223 *s*
feeling of Eternity in youth672 *i*
fit to instruct her youth*...455 *o*
flourish in immortal youth.315*m*
follow'd baffled youth‖.... 78 *a*
for youth no less becomes* 673 *f*
great is youth.............287 *o*
gulf-stream of our y. may§. 10 *j*
hail, blooming Youth......673 *k*
hare is madness the youth*.592*w*
heart is gone, ere youth‖... 62 *j*
his y. 'gainst time and....601 *q*
home-keeping y. have*.....304 *p*
Hope and Y. are children..308 *x*
how beautiful is youth§....672 *p*
in flower of youth and.... 69 *p*
ingenious youth of nations‖ 455 *e*
in my y. I never did apply*.‡12 *a*
in pride of y., and felt.....543 *q*
in the lexicon of youth....196 *n*
in y. and beauty wisdom‡..650 *u*
in youth it sheltered me.... 609 *l*
in y. we come fill'd with...651 *v*
it is for youth to acquire...676 *k*
it the prime of youth*... 400 *x*
life with wiser youth......582 *l*
long kiss, a kiss of youth‖..334 *c*
long stood the noble youth.661 *j*

loveless y. to unrespected‡. 82 *s*
loves the meat in his youth* 26 *b*
May-morn of his youth*...673 *q*
more perilous to youth....369 *b*
more than a youth is not*..159 *a*
nature of tender youth.....753 *p*
no less than youth itself§.. 10 *i*
now green in youth, now‡..371 *e*
one has wished for in youth795*m*
our youth, our joys, and all601 *v*
passionate youth expires...460 *o*
recounts the feats of youth 12 *i*
retention of the spirit of y.. 80 *j*
roses for the flush of youth 11 *d*
shining y. into the shade...142 *s*
something of the youth....672 *b*
spirit of y. in everything*..392 *k*
spring, like youth, fresh... 9 *j*
steals from her youth......601 *j*
summer of your youth......673 *a*
the flourish set on youth*..602 *v*
the joy of y. and health her 655 *t*
therewith a youth to snare.318 *t*
the spirit of a youth*......673 *t*
those of youth a seeming ..346 *k*
'tis not on youth's smooth‖. 62 *j*
'tis not what our y. desires.671 *q*
'tis youth's frenzy—but‖...357 *a*
to the delusion of Youth... 9 *k*
thy youth hath fled .... 10 *u*
vehemence of youth.......195 *o*
vivacity and novelty of y...516 *b*
warm'd with youth's blood. 87 *f*
wear out thy youth*.......313 *n*
where unbruised youth*... 72 *j*
who die in youth...........443 *n*
who would not be that y...468 *a*
why I love this youth*.....363 *l*
woe to the youth...........203 *v*
worm is in the bud of y...143 *f*
years of his youth.........252 *h*
y. and only youth requires.673 *n*
youth and pleasure meet‖..128 *e*
youth and pleasure sport..522 *q*
youth beguiled the chase...155 *d*
youth comes but once§.....672 *s*
youth disports in that......522 *q*
y. dreams a bliss on this...671 *q*
youth fades; love droops...307 *x*
youth gave love and roses.. 10 *t*
y., health, and hope may...620 *a*
y. holds no society with....672 *h*
youth, hope and love§.....189 *g*
y.! how buoyant are thy...672 *n*
youth I do adore thee*.....673 *e*
Y. is a blunder; Manhood a 9 *l*
youth is full of pleasance*.673 *e*
youth is full of sport*......673 *e*
youth is hot and bold*.....673 *e*
y. is nimble, age is lame*..673 *e*
youth is not rich in time...673 *q*
y. is to all the glad season.672 *a*
y. is too hasty with words..797 *d*
y. is wild, and age is tame* 673 *e*
youth like summer morn*..673 *e*
y. makes so fair and passion234 *p*
youth of earlier days......753 *q*
y. of labour with an age.... 9 *l*
youth of pleasure wasteful.345 *u*
Y. on the prow, and. .... 672 *j*
youth perpetual dwells in§.162 *n*
youth pined away with....245 *n*
youth replies I can.........163 *n*
y. should be a savings-bank673 *l*
y. should watch joys and ..672 *f*
youth soon is gone .... 75 *a*
youth, talents, beauty, thus 11 *h*
y., that pursuest with such 672 *u*
y. to age a reverend hermit567 *j*
y. to fortune and to fame...379 *c*
y. waneth by increasing....601 *q*
y. we can have but to-day..671 *s*
y. what man's age is like to 672 *e*
youth when it is luxuriant.341*m*
Youthful–word had in my y.. 60 *f*
Youths–heard both y. and . .628 *b*
O happy unown'd youths..672 *i*

Yron-hardest y. soone doth..430 *l*
Yulenight-on blithe Y. when.662 *b*
Yvette-O lovely river of Y.§.533 *e*

Z.

Zaccheus-Z. he did climb the..126 *v*
Zeal-all zeal for a reform....518 *t*
  a righteous zeal inspired...451 *g*
  blind z. can only do harm..797 *r*
  build me altars in their z....674 *f*
  but zeal moved thee**......674 *e*
  desperate in my zeal‡...... 47 *h*
  have more zeal than wit‡..674 *i*
  his zeal, none seconded**..674 *d*
  lest z., now melted by the*.461 *q*
  race demands thy zeal.....674 *a*
  serv'd my God with half*...549 *e*
  show their zeal, and hide‡..674 *j*
  the zeal of friends it is.....797 *s*
  through z. knowledge is....673 *t*
  too much zeal be had‡......674 *h*
  virtue's self may too much‡521 *r*
  want of z. in its inhabitants 673 *r*
  we do that in our z. our....674 *l*

with commutal z. we both‡.627 *j*
  your peaceful z. shall find..674 *n*
  zeal and duty are not slow**461 *k*
  z. is very blind, or badly....674 *g*
  zeal outruns his promise¶..245 *i*
  z.'s a dreadful termagant...673 *u*
  zeal then, not charity‡....674 *k*
Zealots-graceless z. fight‡....349 *i*
  while z. fast and frown.....521 *u*
Zealous-a spirit, z. as he**...674 *c*
  zealous, yet modest........673 *s*
  stirred up many z. souls...,674*m*
  sweet is z. contemplation*.109 *d*
  who is zealous for nothing..674 *b*
  zealous, yet modest........ 77 *k*
Zed-z.! thou unnecessary*...340 *e*
Zenith-all the z. seemed to...584 *r*
  brutes soon their z. reach..517 *u*
  dropt from the z. like a**..153 *c*
  z., doth depend upon*......256 *w*
  wisdom mounts her zenith.384 *r*
Zephyr-faint the flagging Z..674 *r*
  let Zephyr only breathe....674 *o*
  soft the zephyr blows......672 *j*

the zephyr flew...... .....531 *o*
  when zephyr gently blows‡.674 *v*
  z.'s cool breezes I burn.....599 *h*
  Z. with Aurora playing**.. 29*m*
Zephyrs-as the z. swoon.....674 *q*
  blow, zephyrs, blow........214 *c*
  but z. to the train beneath‡ 674*w*
  lull'd by soft zephyrs thro'‡ 674 *u*
  on the balmy z. tranquil...674 *s*
  the balmy z., silent since‡..674 *x*
  vernal zephyrs breathe in..417 *p*
  z. bland breathe'd o'er...... 71 *j*
  zephyrs blowing below*...271 *v*
  zephyrs gently play‡.......674 *t*
Zest-gave life a zest.........457 *n*
  z. and flavour to the dish...654 *i*
Zeus-Zeus came to earth to..276 *o*
Zion-die upon the walls of Z.142 *a*
Zodiac-gallops the z. in his*..584 *s*
Zone-each zone obeys thee‖..459 *g*
  the zone of calms..........224 *d*
Zones-to z., though more‖....596 *c*
Zurichers-council of the Z...521 *j*
Zwinglians-seat of the Z.....521 *j*

SHAKESPEARE *; **MILTON** **; **WORDSWORTH** ¶; **BYRON** ‖; **TENNYSON** †; **LOWELL** ††; **POPE** ‡; **LONGFELLOW** §

CONCORDANCE

TO

LATIN AND MODERN

FOREIGN QUOTATIONS.